International Directory of

COMPANY

HISTORIES

International Directory of

COMPANY HISTORIES

VOLUME 11

Editor
Paula Kepos

St. James Press

An International Thomson Publishing Company

NEW YORK • LONDON • BONN • BOSTON • DETROIT • MADRID
MELBOURNE • MEXICO CITY • PARIS • SINGAPORE • TOKYO
TORONTO • WASHINGTON • ALBANY NY • BELMONT CA • CINCINNATI OH

The paper used in this publication meets the minimum requirements of American National Standard for Information Sciences— Permanence Paper for Printed Library Materials, ANSI Z39.48-1984.

This book is printed on recycled paper that meets Environmental Protection Agency Standards.

Library of Congress Catalog Number: 89-190943

British Library Cataloguing in Publication Data

International directory of company histories. Vol. 11
I. Paula Kepos
338.7409

ISBN 1-55862-326-4

Printed in the United States of America
Published simultaneously in the United Kingdom

The trademark **ITP** is used under license.

Cover photograph of the World Financial Center and Winter Garden courtesy of Timothy Hursley.

10 9 8 7 6 5 4 3 2 1

CONTENTS _____

Preface . . . . page ix
List of Abbreviations xi

Company Histories

A.O. Smith Corporation 3
Abbott Laboratories 7
AirTouch Communications 10
American Crystal Sugar Company 13
American General Finance Corp. 16
American Management Systems, Inc. 18
Archer-Daniels-Midland Company 21
Associated Milk Producers, Inc. 24
Associated Natural Gas Corporation 27
BarclaysAmerican Mortgage Corporation 29
Bayerische Motoren Werke AG 31
Becton, Dickinson & Company 34
Big Rivers Electric Corporation 37
The Body Shop International PLC 40
C.H. Robinson, Inc. 43
Cadence Design Systems, Inc. 45
Chiat/Day Inc. Advertising 49
Chrysler Corporation 53
Cirrus Logic, Incorporated 56
Cisco Systems, Inc. 58
CompuAdd Computer Corporation 61
CTG, Inc. 64
Datapoint Corporation 67
The Davey Tree Expert Company 71
Dillard Paper Company 74
Dun & Bradstreet Software Services Inc. 77
Duty Free International, Inc. 80
Echlin Inc. 83
El Camino Resources International, Inc. 86
Eli Lilly & Company 89
Emge Packing Co., Inc. 92
Enesco Corporation 94
Enterprise Oil plc 97
Esselte Pendaflex Corporation 100
Fiat S.p.A. 102

First Commerce Corporation 105
First Empire State Corporation 108
First Financial Management Corporation . . . 111
First Hawaiian, Inc. 114
First Security Corporation 117
First Tennessee National Corporation 120
First USA, Inc. 122
First Virginia Banks, Inc. 125
Firstar Corporation 127
Fiserv Inc. 130
FMC Corporation 133
Ford Motor Company 136
Forest Laboratories, Inc. 141
Fourth Financial Corporation 144
Franklin Quest Co. 147
Fujitsu-ICL Systems Inc. 150
Gaylord Entertainment Company 152
General Nutrition Companies, Inc. 155
The Geon Company 158
Green Tree Financial Corporation 162
Grumman Corporation 164
Guardian Royal Exchange Plc 168
H.J. Heinz Company 171
Health Systems International, Inc. 174
Hospitality Franchise Systems, Inc. 177
Huntington Bancshares Inc. 180
IDB Communications Group, Inc. 183
Illinois Central Corporation 186
Infinity Broadcasting Corporation 190
Ingram Industries, Inc. 193
International Telephone & Telegraph
    Corporation 196
Invacare Corporation 200
Istituto per la Ricostruzione Industriale
    S.p.A. 203

IVAX Corporation 207
The J.M. Smucker Company 210
Jefferson-Pilot Corporation 213
Jones Apparel Group, Inc. 216
Kendall International, Inc. 219
Kenetech Corporation 222
Keystone International, Inc. 225
Kimco Realty Corporation 228
KLA Instruments Corporation 231
Komag, Inc. 234
KU Energy Corporation 236
Kwik Save Group plc 239
La Quinta Inns, Inc. 242
Lam Research Corporation 245
Lechters, Inc. 248
Lee Enterprises, Incorporated 251
Leggett & Platt, Incorporated 254
Lennar Corporation 257
Leucadia National Corporation 260
Litton Industries, Inc. 263
Lockheed Corporation 266
Magma Power Company 270
MAI Systems Corporation 273
McDonnell Douglas Corporation 277
Meditrust 281
Mentor Graphics Corporation 284
Mercantile Bankshares Corp. 287
Merck & Co., Inc. 289
Meredith Corporation 292
Meridian Bancorp, Inc. 295
Mesa Airlines, Inc. 298
MFS Communications Company, Inc. 301
Michigan National Corporation 304
Micron Technology, Inc. 307
Minerals Technologies Inc. 310
Minnesota Power & Light Company 313
Molex Incorporated 317
Montana Power Company 320
Morrison Restaurants Inc. 323
Motorola, Inc. 326
Multimedia, Inc. 330
National Health Laboratories Incorporated . . 333
National Service Industries, Inc. 336
NBD Bancorp, Inc. 339
Nevada Power Company 342
New Plan Realty Trust 345
Nine West Group Inc. 348
Nissan Motor Company, Ltd. 350

Noble Affiliates, Inc. 353
Nordson Corporation 356
North West Water Group plc 359
Northrop Corporation 363
NovaCare, Inc. 366
Ohio Casualty Corp. 369
Old Kent Financial Corp. 371
Old Republic International Corp. 373
Overseas Shipholding Group, Inc. 376
PacifiCare Health Systems, Inc. 378
Paging Network Inc. 381
Payless Cashways, Inc. 384
PECO Energy Company 387
The Pep Boys—Manny, Moe & Jack 391
Policy Management Systems Corporation . . . 394
Potter & Brumfield Inc. 396
PowerGen PLC 399
Praxair, Inc. 402
Progressive Corporation 405
Racal-Datacom Inc. 408
Raytheon Company 411
Republic New York Corporation 415
Riverwood International Corporation 420
Roche Biomedical Laboratories, Inc. 424
Rockwell International Corporation 427
Rollins, Inc. 431
Rust International Inc. 435
Saab-Scania AB 437
St. Jude Medical, Inc. 458
Seagull Energy Corporation 440
Sensormatic Electronics Corp. 443
Signet Banking Corporation 446
Snapple Beverage Corporation 449
Sotheby's Holdings, Inc. 452
Southtrust Corporation 455
Standard Microsystems Corporation 462
Star Banc Corporation 465
Sterling Software, Inc. 468
Stewart & Stevenson Services Inc. 471
Stryker Corporation 474
Sumitomo Corporation 477
SunAmerica Inc. 481
SunGard Data Systems Inc. 484
Sunrise Medical Inc. 486
Synopsis, Inc. 489
T. Rowe Price Associates, Inc. 493
The Talbots, Inc. 497
Tellabs, Inc. 500

Teradyne, Inc. 502
Texas Instruments Inc. 505
Thames Water plc 509
Thermo Instrument Systems Inc. 512
Thomas & Betts Corp. 515
3Com Corp. 518
Tidewater Inc. 522
Tomkins plc 525
Toyota Motor Corporation 528

Transatlantic Holdings, Inc. 532
TriMas Corp. 534
Triton Energy Corporation 537
TRW Inc. 540
Vail Associates, Inc. 543
Vodafone Group plc 547
Volkswagen A.G. 549
West One Bancorp 552
Wherehouse Entertainment Incorporated 556

Index to Companies and Persons 559
Index to Industries 737
Notes on Contributors 751

PREFACE

International Directory of Company Histories provides detailed information on the development of the world's largest and most influential companies. To date, *Company Histories* has covered more than 2000 companies in eleven volumes.

Inclusion Criteria

Most companies chosen for inclusion in *Company Histories* have achieved a minimum of US$200 million in annual sales and are leading influences in their industries or geographical locations. State-owned companies that are important in their industries and that may operate much like public or private companies also are included. Wholly owned subsidiaries are presented if they meet the requirements for inclusion.

St. James Press does not endorse any of the companies or products mentioned in this book. Companies that appear in *Company Histories* were selected without reference to their wishes and have in no way endorsed their entries. The companies were given the opportunity to participate in the compilation of the articles by providing information or reading their entries for factual accuracy, and we are indebted to many of them for their comments and corrections. We also thank them for allowing the use of their logos for identification purposes.

Entry Format

Each entry in this volume begins with a company's legal name, the address of its headquarters, its telephone number and fax number, and a statement of public, private, state, or parent ownership. A company with a legal name in both English and the language of its headquarters country is listed by the English name, with the native-language name in parentheses.

Also provided are the company's earliest incorporation date, the number of employees, and the most recent sales figures available. Sales figures are given in local currencies with equivalents in U.S. dollars. For some private companies, sales figures are estimates. The entry lists the exchanges on which a company's stock is traded, as well as the company's principal Standard Industrial Classification codes. American spelling is used, and the word ''billion'' is used in its American sense of one thousand million.

Sources

The histories were compiled from publicly accessible sources such as general and academic periodicals, books, annual reports, and material supplied by the companies themselves. *Company Histories* is intended for reference use by students, business people, librarians, historians, economists, investors, job candidates, and others who want to learn more about the historical development of the world's most important companies.

Cumulative Indexes

An Index to Companies and Persons provides access to companies and individuals discussed in the text. Beginning with Volume 7, an Index to Industries allows researchers to locate companies by their principal industry.

ABBREVIATIONS FOR FORMS OF COMPANY INCORPORATION

A.B.	Aktiebolaget (Sweden)
A.G.	Aktiengesellschaft (Germany, Switzerland)
A.S.	Atieselskab (Denmark)
A.S.	Aksjeselskap (Denmark, Norway)
A.Ş.	Anomin Şirket (Turkey)
B.V.	Besloten Vennootschap met beperkte, Aansprakelijkheid (The Netherlands)
Co.	Company (United Kingdom, United States)
Corp.	Corporation (United States)
G.I.E.	Groupement d'Intérêt Economique (France)
GmbH	Gesellschaft mit beschränkter Haftung (Germany)
H.B.	Handelsbolaget (Sweden)
Inc.	Incorporated (United States)
KGaA	Kommanditgesellschaft auf Aktien (Germany)
K.K.	Kabushiki Kaisha (Japan)
LLC	Limited Liability Company (Middle East)
Ltd.	Limited (Canada, Japan, United Kingdom, United States)
N.V.	Naamloze Vennootschap (The Netherlands)
OY	Osakeyhtiöt (Finland)
PLC	Public Limited Company (United Kingdom)
PTY.	Proprietary (Australia, Hong Kong, South Africa)
S.A.	Société Anonyme (Belgium, France, Switzerland)
SpA	Società per Azioni (Italy)

ABBREVIATIONS FOR CURRENCY

DA	Algerian dinar	Dfl	Netherlands florin
A$	Australian dollar	NZ$	New Zealand dollar
Sch	Austrian schilling	N	Nigerian naira
BFr	Belgian franc	NKr	Norwegian krone
Cr	Brazilian cruzado	RO	Omani rial
C$	Canadian dollar	P	Philippine peso
DKr	Danish krone	Esc	Portuguese escudo
E£	Egyptian pound	SRls	Saudi Arabian riyal
Fmk	Finnish markka	S$	Singapore dollar
FFr	French franc	R	South African rand
DM	German mark	W	South Korean won
HK$	Hong Kong dollar	Pta	Spanish peseta
Rs	Indian rupee	SKr	Swedish krona
Rp	Indonesian rupiah	SFr	Swiss franc
IR£	Irish pound	NT$	Taiwanese dollar
L	Italian lira	B	Thai baht
¥	Japanese yen	£	United Kingdom pound
W	Korean won	$	United States dollar
KD	Kuwaiti dinar	B	Venezuelan bolivar
LuxFr	Luxembourgian franc	K	Zambian kwacha
M$	Malaysian ringgit		

International Directory of

COMPANY

HISTORIES

A. O. Smith Corporation

11270 West Park Place
P.O. Box 23972
Milwaukee, Wisconsin 53223-0972
U.S.A.
(414) 359-4000
Fax: (414) 359-4180

Public Company
Incorporated: 1904 as A. O. Smith Company
Employees: 10,800
Sales: $1.19 billion
Stock Exchanges: American
SICs: 3713 Truck and Bus Bodies; 3714 Motor Vehicle Parts and Accessories; 3621 Motors and Generators; 3639 Household Appliances, Nec; 3594 Fluid Power Pumps and Motors

A. O. Smith Corporation is a diversified manufacturer of automotive structural components, electric motors, residential and commercial water heaters, fiberglass piping systems, livestock feed storage systems, and storage tanks. The company ranks among the United States' 500 largest publicly held industrial concerns, having grown from a turn-of-the-century bicycle parts factory to a modern manufacturer.

Although A. O. Smith was founded in 1904, the company traces its history back to the mid-19th century, when Charles Jeremiah (C. J.) Smith emigrated to the United States from England. The journeyman metal tradesman ventured all the way to Milwaukee, Wisconsin, and, after being self-employed for a decade, went to work for the Milwaukee Railroad Shop. As a highly skilled workman, he made a good living, but went back into business for himself in 1874, when he opened a machine shop and began manufacturing baby carriage parts. Two of Smith's four sons, Charles S. and George H., joined the family firm in the mid-1880s.

As bicycles became popular in the last decade of the century, C. J. Smith and Sons branched out. By 1895, it was the largest manufacturer of steel bicycle parts in the United States. The patriarch called in his eldest son, Arthur (A. O.), an architectural engineer specializing in large buildings, to help build a five-story factory for the growing family business. After two years of close work with his father, A. O. decided to join the company permanently as treasurer. By then, C. J. Smith and Sons had declared itself the largest manufacturer of component bicycle parts in the world.

Increasing overcapacity in that industry and the advent of the automobile brought another change to C. J. Smith and Sons. In 1899 the family sold its business to the Federal Bicycle Corporation of America, a then-legal monopoly known as the "Bicycle Trust." A. O. retained management of the Milwaukee (or "Smith Parts") Branch of the Trust. Arthur Smith indulged his personal interest in the composition and manufacture of automobile frames with two years of "tinkering" that culminated in the sale of his first automotive frame to the Peerless Motor Car Co. in 1902. Word of his frame, which was lighter, stronger, more flexible, and cheaper than conventional ones, spread quickly: by the following year, Smith had contracts with six major automobile manufacturers.

A. O. Smith quit Federal in 1903, bought the Smith Parts Co. from his former employer, and incorporated it as A. O. Smith Company in 1904. The company's sales totaled $375,733 and profits topped $100,000 that first year. Unfortunately, patriarch C. J. Smith also passed away in 1904.

In April 1906, Henry Ford contracted with A. O. Smith for frames. At the time, the company was only producing ten pressed steel frames a day. Ford needed 10,000 frames in four months, a ten-fold increase in the prevailing production rate. Realizing that adding workers and space would only consume valuable time in training and construction, Smith looked for ways to increase efficiency through technological improvements. He and his team of engineers retooled existing presses to produce two corresponding halves of an auto frame simultaneously and arranged the presses to form a continuous assembly line. The delivery of 10,000 A. O. Smith frames that August helped Ford introduce his popularly priced Model N late in 1906 and attracted ever more automobile manufacturers to the supplier. Because A. O. Smith soon found itself turning away business, it soon built a new, larger headquarters on 135 acres on the outskirts of Milwaukee to accommodate demand. By the end of the decade, A. O. Smith was manufacturing 110,000 frames per year, over 60 percent of the auto industry's requirements.

Three years later, when A. O. Smith died, his son Lloyd Raymond (Ray) was made president. Ray's was not just a dynastic leadership, however. Both A. O. and L. R. Smith were later inducted into the Automotive Hall of Fame and the Wisconsin Business Hall of Fame. The 23-year-old former company secretary had previously proposed manufacturing improvements that multiplied A. O. Smith's production rate seven times: by 1916, the company was manufacturing 800,000 frames per year—half the auto industry's needs. Called "decisive, restless and a profound thinker" by corporate historians, Ray Smith also propelled the family company into new ventures. Smith bought a license to manufacture "The Motor Wheel," a small gas engine that could be attached to a bicycle's rear wheel to make a "motorbike." The company sold 25,000 of the vehicles nationwide from 1914 to 1919, and even applied the technology to a small wooden "sports car" called the Smith Flyer.

L. R. Smith's reluctance to pay for the marketing support necessary to maintain such products' popularity, combined with the fact that the United States was thoroughly embroiled in the First World War, brought diversification to a halt in 1919. A. O. Smith manufactured hollow-steel artillery vehicle poles and bomb casings for the war effort. By war's end, the company was producing 6,500 bomb casings per day, thanks to a welding breakthrough that produced stronger bonds in less time.

Throughout the war years, a team of Smith's best engineers formulated a revolutionary plan to automate the company's frame production process. Although expensive—construction consumed $6 million by 1920—the "Mechanical Marvel" they created produced 7,200 frames on two 180-man shifts per day. The machines performed 552 separate functions, including forming, trimming, and riveting. It took A. O. Smith 15 years to recoup its investment in the Mechanical Marvel (which was designated a National Historic Mechanical Engineering Landmark in 1979), but the plant ran practically without stop until 1958.

The Mechanical Marvel only marked the beginning of an enterprising decade, during which the company's 500-person engineering department developed new applications for the welding process formulated during World War I. A welded coupling designed to link seamless steel casings for oil drilling rigs soon became a petroleum industry standard. High pressure tanks for gasoline refineries developed by A. O. Smith could withstand three times the pressure of customary tanks. Engineers also modified those tanks for use in the paper, chemical refining, and other industries by adding an anticorrosive, stainless steel liner to the tanks. During the 1920s, A. O. Smith also originated the large-diameter, high-pressure pipe that launched the natural gas transmission industry and made natural gas a viable alternative to coal and oil. The company captured every order for large diameter pipe in the country. As the authority in this industry, Smith had to send its own employees out to weld pipeline installations around the world.

A. O. Smith was thus well positioned when the stock market crash of October 1929 ushered in the Great Depression. It had a two-year backlog of pipe orders and a dominant position in its other markets. However, as auto sales fell from 4.4 million in 1929 to less than 2 million in 1931, the company was forced to cut employment by 10 percent at its main plant. In 1930, sales plummeted from $57 million to $9 million and the company suffered an operating loss of $5 million the following year. L. R. brought in an outsider, William C. Heath, to play "bad cop." Heath cut executive salaries by 50 percent and reduced the operating staff by one-fourth, but even these measures did not bring the company into the black. In May 1932, 3,000 employees—almost half the total company's payroll—were laid off. Corporate historians noted that "Demand for frames was so low, supervisors painted them by hand to save the expense of starting the automatic equipment."

A. O. Smith's "savior" came from a highly unlikely source—the December 1933 repeal of Prohibition. The end of that "noble experiment" brought America's brewing capital, Milwaukee, back to life, and A. O. Smith utilized its technical creativity to profit from the rebirth. The company quickly introduced a steel beer barrel with a special liner that protected the beer from metallic migration. The new keg's quick acceptance enabled A. O. Smith to recall 450 laid-off workers. The company also developed an innovative process to fuse glass to the interior of 35,000 gallon tanks that resulted in the superior cleanliness demanded by the brewing industry.

Ray Smith left day-to-day management of the company to Heath after suffering a heart attack in 1934. Heath lead the company to apply its glass-and-steel fusing process in A. O. Smith's first mass consumer product, the water heater. Before the product's introduction, most homeowners had to replace their all-steel water heaters often due to corrosion, or spend prohibitive amounts on stainless-steel ones. Although A. O. Smith developed its affordable, durable, glass-lined model in 1936 and was able to mass-produce it by 1939, world war interrupted the company's plans a second time.

Smith began to expand through acquisitions before World War II, purchasing Smith Meter Co., a Los Angeles firm that produced petroleum line measuring devices in 1937. The company diversified into electric motors with the 1940 acquisition of Los Angeles-based Sawyer Electrical Manufacturing Company and Whirl-A-Way Motors in Dayton, Ohio. By the end of the 1950s, electric motors, especially hermetically sealed ones, were A. O. Smith's best-selling product.

By the time the United States entered the Second World War in 1941, A. O. Smith had already submitted proposals for aerial bombs made of welded pipe, won the government contracts, and built a factory to produce them. The company's engineers developed better, cheaper propeller blades and manufactured landing gears for B-17 "Flying Fortress" and B-29 "Super Fortress" fighter bombers. The company was such a vital wartime supplier that Adolf Hitler targeted it in an unexecuted invasion of America.

The investment of over $50 million in new plants and equipment before 1950 propelled A. O. Smith to unprecedented success in the booming postwar American economy. As new housing starts jumped to 4,000 per day and auto production soared to one million a month, the company was poised to prosper. Volume at the centrally located Kankakee waterheater plant built in 1947 doubled twice before 1950, with the help of retail giant Sears, Roebuck & Co., which sold A. O. Smith waterheaters under a private label. Monthly production grew from 15,000 to 48,000 within less than ten years after the war's end. In addition, A. O. Smith supplied all of Chevrolet's automotive frames during the 1950s, when that make was the most popular in America. The contract helped establish A. O. Smith as the largest independent supplier of chassis frames to the auto industry in the postwar era. Petroleum pipeline sales also recovered quickly and Smith formed a joint venture with steelmaker ARMCO to create a pipe factory in Texas close to customers.

Diversification continued under Heath in the postwar era, with the development of Harvestore glass-lined silos that were filled from the top, emptied from the bottom, and were dark-colored to prevent wintertime freezing of the feed stored inside. After a slow start, the silos were well accepted by U.S. farmers, and the company offered them overseas in Germany and the United Kingdom beginning in the 1960s. A. O. Smith started investigating the fiberglass industry in 1953 in cooperation with Dow, forming a Reinforced Plastics Division in 1957. The company soon developed fiberglass pipe and fittings for special niche applications in oil fields, and later made fiberglass Corvette Sting Ray bodies.

Diversification was accompanied by rationalization. When A. O. Smith's patent on the glass-lined water heater expired in 1955 and competition was opened, Smith eased out of the private-label segment, and scaled back efforts in the residential market to concentrate on the commercial segment with its leading Burkay brand. The company also phased out pressure containers like beer and petroleum tanks in the late 1950s. A. O. Smith's own success thwarted some of its business interests. The completion of the U.S. Transcontinental Pipeline System significantly reduced the demand for pipe, eventually forcing the company to sell its steel pipe business in Texas to its partner, ARMCO. Despite these withdrawals from certain markets, sales at A. O. Smith increased from $190 million in 1946 to $280 million by 1960.

A. O. Smith's automotive division endured several upheavals throughout the 1960s, 1970s, and 1980s that threatened its existence. The proliferation of car models in the 1960s challenged Smith's adaptive ability and compelled it to retool from riveted frames to more adaptable welded frames. At the same time, 45 percent of U.S. auto production converted to unitized frame construction, effectively eliminating the need for a conventional frame. General Motors' decision to stick with the tried-and-true isolated frame construction kept the automotive division afloat for the time being.

L. B. "Ted" Smith was elected chairman and chief executive officer and Urban Kuechle became president in 1967. The team sought out new businesses to replace the ones that had been eliminated. In 1969 alone, A. O. Smith acquired Layne & Bowler Pump company in Los Angeles, Bull Motors of the United Kingdom, and a majority interest in Armor Elevator, the sixth-largest elevator manufacturer in the United States. The company also pushed its international growth, forming a Mexican affiliate to manufacture auto frames, Canadian and Netherlands water heater subsidiaries, and a consumer products division in Japan. Successive earnings records in 1968 and 1969 seemed to affirm the acquisition spree, as sales rose to $355 million in 1969 and soared to $600 million in 1973.

Unfortunately, the ensuing decade ushered in a myriad of problems that impaired A. O. Smith. The government wage and price freeze mandated in 1971 squeezed profit margins, and the Arab oil embargo that started in 1973 forever harmed sales of full-size, gas-consuming cars, which constituted the majority of Smith's remaining frame market. Labor unrest also plagued many Smith divisions. A ten-month strike at Armor Elevator, which had just completed two years of acquisitions, crippled that subsidiary in 1972. The following year saw strikes at plants in Pennsylvania and Kentucky and the first labor halt at the Milwaukee factory in its 100-year history.

L. B. Smith and President Jack Parker divested Armor Elevator, Bull Motors, and Meter Systems in 1975. After the strikes were settled and the government lifted the wage and price freeze, inflation set in. Still, A. O. Smith began to recover in the last half of the decade, winning a new contract with General Motors

and expanding the Harvestore and Electrical Products divisions. Sales increased $100 million from 1976 to 1977 and profits were also on the rise.

However, General Motors' 1980 announcement that it would convert all of its production to front-wheel drive, unitized body autos threatened the survival of the $270 million automotive segment of A. O. Smith's $836 million business. Luckily, the massive automaker took over eight years to phase out full-framed vehicles (A. O. Smith delivered its last Cadillac frame in 1990), and A. O. Smith used that time to transform its automotive division. Automotive, which had made truck frames since 1905, shifted its primary focus to the expanding market for trucks, vans, and sport utility vehicles, winning contracts with Ford, Chrysler, and General Motors in 1980 alone. By 1985, light truck frames were the corporation's single largest product line. Smith also won a contract to produce components for the critically acclaimed and top-selling Ford Taurus in the early 1980s.

The company would meet other challenges under the leadership of Tom Dolan, who became president in 1982 and advanced to chairman and chief executive officer upon the retirement of L. B. Smith. Pressures from auto manufacturers, who were themselves influenced by intense foreign competition, spurred A. O. Smith to simultaneously reduce costs and increase quality. It was no simple task for the automotive division, which was then characterized by hostility between labor and management and 20 percent defect rates. Management embarked on a three-stage strategy to increase employee involvement through quality circles, labor-management task forces, and cooperative work teams. Although the plan initially met resistance from union leaders, six years of gradual change effected impressive results: the productivity growth rate doubled in 1988 and defects were reduced to 3 percent. The work teams also enabled A. O. Smith to save money by drastically reducing the ratio of foremen to workers from 1-to-10 in 1987 to 1-to-34 in 1988.

During this period of cultural revolution, A. O. Smith was hit hard by recessions in 1980 and 1982. Hundreds of workers were laid off as auto sales fell to their lowest levels in twenty years. The company slashed capital spending and expenses, cut officer salaries by 10 percent, and let one-fourth of the corporate staff go. Even more layoffs were necessary later in the decade, as the company reduced net employment from a high of 12,300 in 1986 to 9,400 in 1990.

The farming crisis that occurred at this same time reduced the Harvestore subsidiary's sales from $140 million in 1979 to $21 million by 1984. The division shuttered two plants and consolidated all operations at the main DeKalb, Illinois, plant. A. O. Smith eventually shifted the subsidiary's focus to municipal water storage tanks and sold Harvestore's U.K. subsidiary. Although its revenues remained small, Harvestore did eventually return to profitability.

A. O. Smith's problems compounded in the early 1980s, as competition in the water heater industry exposed internal problems. Inefficient plants cost the Water Products Division $10 million in 1981 alone. The subsidiary closed one factory and opened a more efficient one, and other cost-cutting measures helped it achieve profitability in 1983 after four successive years of losses. Continuing efforts helped the division become one of A. O. Smith's most consistently profitable divisions, setting profit records in 1986, 1988, and 1990.

A. O. Smith's electric motors division was one of the corporation's few consistently bright spots in the 1980s. Despite fairly intense competition, the subsidiary was able to establish operations in Mexico and Texas and even acquire a primary competitor's small motor business. The unit set a profit record of $45 million in 1985. Smith's fiberglass business had also recovered from the shocks of the previous decade to set four successive years of record profits beginning in 1987.

Despite an inconsistent earnings record in the 1980s—the company only achieved two successive profitable years during the decade—A. O. Smith did manage to pay cash dividends on its common stock every year since 1940. Having endured a grueling six years at the company's helm and achieving several of his goals, Tom Dolan retired from the chief executive office in 1988. Robert J. O'Toole assumed that office, adding the chair in 1991. He directed the company's implementation of "just-in-time" delivery of automotive products through the construction of five regional assembly plants in close proximity to customers. Although the firm recorded a net loss in 1992, its return to profitability the following year coincided with a general economic recovery in the United States. O'Toole hoped that the combination of internal efficiency and a beneficial economic environment would result in continued profitability.

Principal Subsidiaries: Smith Fiberglass Products Inc.; A. O. Smith Enterprises Ltd. (Canada); A. O. Smith Electric Motors (Ireland) Ltd.; A. O. Smith Water Products Company B.V. (Netherlands); A. O. Smith Harvestore Products, Inc.; AgriStor Credit Corporation.

Further Reading:

Hoerr, John, "The Cultural Revolution at A. O. Smith," *Business Week,* May 29, 1989, pp. 66, 68.

Wright, Charles S. and Roger S. Smith, "*A Better Way": The History of A. O. Smith Corporation,* Milwaukee: A. O. Smith Corporation, 1992.

—April Dougal Gasbarre

Abbott Laboratories

Abbott Laboratories

One Abbott Park Road
Abbott Park, Illinois 60064-3500
U.S.A.
(708) 937-6100
Fax: (708) 937-1511

Public Company
Incorporated: 1900 as Abbott Alkaloidal Company
Employees: 49,659
Sales: $8.41 billion
Stock Exchanges: New York London Zurich Basle Geneva
    Boston Cincinnati NASDAQ Philadelphia Pacific
    Lausanne
SICs: 2834 Pharmaceutical Preparations; 2833 Medicinals
    and Botanicals; 2835 Diagnostic Substances; 2844 Toilet
    Preparations; 2879 Agricultural Chemicals, Not Elsewhere
    Classified; 3841 Surgical and Medical Instruments; 3845
    Electromedical Equipment; 3826 Laboratory Analytical
    Instruments

Abbott Laboratories is one of the oldest and most successful of
America's pharmaceutical companies. While ethical drugs only
accounted for one-fourth of its annual sales in the early 1990s,
Abbott ranked as a top manufacturer of medical diagnostic
equipment, with an emphasis on blood analyzers, and was also a
leading producer of infant formulas under the Similac and
Isomil brands, which commanded over half of the $3 billion
American market. Abbott's consumer brands also included
Clear Eyes and Murine eye care products; Selsun Blue
shampoo; and Ensure nutritional supplement. Moreover, the
company held the patent on the "truth serum" sodium
pentothal and continued to lead sales of the antibiotic erythromycin, which it introduced in 1952.

Abbott Laboratories has its origin in the late nineteenth century
in a small pharmaceutical operation run from the kitchen of a
Chicago physician named Wallace Calvin Abbott. As did other
physicians of the time, Dr. Abbott commonly prescribed mor-
phine, quinine, strychnine, and codeine—all of which were
liquid alkaloid extracts—for his patients. Because they existed
only in a liquid form, these drugs were prone to spoilage over
time, mitigating their effectiveness as treatments. In 1888, Dr.
Abbott heard that a Belgian surgeon had developed alkaloids in
solid form. Alkaloid pills soon became available in Chicago,

but Dr. Abbott was dissatisfied with their quality, and he decided to manufacture his own.

Dr. Abbott began to advertise his products to other doctors in
1891. So successful was his business that he eventually sold
shares to other doctors and incorporated his operation in 1900 as
the Abbott Alkaloidal Company. By 1905, annual sales had
grown to $200,000. During World War I, Abbott's company
was essential to the medical community, as several important
drugs, manufactured exclusively by German companies, were
no longer available in the United States. Abbott developed
procaine, a substitute for the German novocaine, and barbital, a
replacement for veneral.

After the war, Abbott continued to concentrate on the research
and development of new drugs. In 1921, the company established a laboratory in Rocky Mount, North Carolina, which
developed a number of new drugs, including sedatives, tranquil-
izers, and vitamins. Even after Dr. Abbott's death that year, the
company continued to invest heavily in new product development and aggressive marketing campaigns.

DeWitt Clough was named president of the company in 1933,
ending a period of somewhat stale communal leadership. A
more dynamic character than any since Dr. Abbott, Clough is
best remembered for the inauguration of the company magazine, *What's New?*. The publication had such a positive impact
on worker morale and public opinion that several of Abbott's
competitors started similar publications.

During World War II, Abbott once again played an important
role in battlefield and hospital health care. By this time, American pharmaceutical companies such as Abbott were much less
dependent on Germany's companies, particularly the IG
Farben—a conglomeration of the world's most advanced drug
manufacturers. After the war, much of the IG Farben's research
was turned over to American manufacturers. Abbott, however,
had little to gain from this information; it was already a worthy
competitor on its own.

After the departure of DeWitt Clough in 1945, Abbott shifted its
attention to the development of antibiotics. The company developed erythromycin, which, under the brand names Erythrocin
and E.E.S., constituted a significant portion of Abbott's prescription drug sales for several decades—even after the expiration of its 17-year patent. Sales of the drug increased dramatically when it was found to be an effective treatment for
Legionnaire's disease.

Abbott stumbled onto a lucrative new product when one of its
researchers accidentally discovered that a chemical with which
he had been working had a sweet taste. The chemical, a cyclamate, could be used as an artificial sweetener. Initially, from
1950, it was marketed to diabetics, but in the 1960s, as Americans became more health and diet conscious, it was increasingly
used as a sugar substitute in a wide variety of foods.

By the mid-1960s, Abbott had gone several years without a
major breakthrough in research, and none was projected at any
time in the immediate future. Then, in 1967, Edward J. Ledder
was named president of the company. He advocated a reduction
in Abbott's emphasis on pharmaceuticals by diversifying into
other fields. In the years that followed, Abbott introduced an

array of consumer products, including Pream non-dairy creamer, Glad Hands rubber gloves, Faultless golf balls, and Sucaryl, the cyclamate sugar substitute. In an effort to ensure the success of Abbott's consumer product line, Ledder placed Melvin Birnbaum, a highly experienced and able manager he had hired away from Revlon, in charge of the division. Ledder's policy of diversification laid the groundwork for more flexible corporate strategies. No longer exposed exclusively within the pharmaceuticals market, Abbott was able to cross-subsidize failing operations until they could be rehabilitated.

Despite this flexibility, Abbott soon realized new obstacles to its growth. The company's hospital products competed in a limited, institutional market. New drugs had greater profit margins but were subject to government approval procedures that kept companies waiting for several years before they could market their discoveries. Consumer products, on the other hand, involved more expensive marketing and generated less profit than pharmaceuticals. Unable to increase profits without substantial risk, Abbott's management decided to maintain the strategies that were in place.

Cyclamate sales had grown so dramatically that by 1969 they accounted for one-third of Abbott's consumer product revenues—or about $50 million. The increasing popularity of cyclamates as an ingredient in diet foods, however, led the FDA to conduct an investigation of possible side effects from their overuse. The FDA's research was widely criticized as "fragmentary" and "fatally flawed," but it was nonetheless used as evidence that cyclamates were carcinogenic. The market collapsed in August 1970 when the FDA banned domestic sales of cyclamates. Abbott, which overnight had suffered the loss of one of its most profitable operations, protested the ban, but was unable to reverse the decision. Although the company continued to petition the FDA, subsequent studies have confirmed that metabolization of cyclamates can lead to chromosome breakage and bladder cancer.

Less than a year after cyclamates were banned, Abbott was forced to recall 3.4 million bottles of intravenous solution. The bottles were sealed with a varnished paper called Gilsonite, which, it was discovered, harbored bacteria. The contamination was discovered only when health care workers noticed and then investigated the high incidence of infection in patients who had been administered Abbott's intravenous solutions. The Center for Disease Control linked the contaminated solutions to at least 434 infections and 49 deaths. With sales down from $17.9 million to $3 million, Abbott's share price began to fall. Abbott moved quickly to replace its Gilsonite seals with synthetic rubber, but the company was unable to regain its leadership of the intravenous market. Litigation resulted in the company eventually pleading no contest to a charge of conspiracy and paying a $1,000 fine.

The crises of the early 1970s left the company's upper echelon of management weakened and vulnerable to criticism. Although Edward Ledder was recognized for the success of his diversification program (and largely excused for his inability to prevent either the cyclamate ban or the intravenous solution crisis), conditions were obviously ripe for the expression of talent by a new manager. Robert Schoellhorn, a veteran of the chemical industry, was just such a manager. His efforts as a vice-presi-

dent in the hospital products division at Abbott resulted in a revenue increase of 139 percent for that division between 1974 and 1979. He correctly predicted that the next most profitable trend in health care would be toward cost-effective analysis and treatment. Schoellhorn was later promoted to president and chief operating officer of the company.

Abbott Laboratories registered an annual sales growth rate of 15.5 percent and an earnings growth rate of 16.5 percent by 1979. This expansion was attributed by financial analysts to the company's increased productivity, reduced costs, expansion into foreign markets, and greater involvement in hospital nutritionals and diagnostic testing equipment. The company also introduced three new drugs in 1979: Depakene, an anticonvulsant, Tranxene, a mild tranquilizer, and Abbokinase, a treatment for blood clots in the lungs. All three products were the direct result of the company's increased investment in research and development in the mid-1970s.

Utilizing its knowledge of intravenous solution production, vitamin therapy, and infant formula, Abbott developed a comprehensive nutritional therapy program to speed the recovery of hospital patients and thereby reduce medical care costs. In the 1980s, as many as 65 percent of all hospital patients suffered from some form of malnutrition, so Abbott was highly successful in marketing their program. Another advantage of adult nutritional products was that they had a place in the growing home care market.

Abbott had similar success marketing its lines of diagnostic equipment. Electronic testing devices developed by Abbott proved more accurate than manual procedures. In order to strengthen the technical end of its diagnostic equipment research, Abbott hired two top executives away from Texas Instruments to head the division.

Robert Schoellhorn, who advanced to chairperson and chief executive officer in 1979, continued to emphasize investment in pharmaceutical research and development in the 1980s. Seven new drugs introduced in 1982 accounted for 17 percent of sales in 1985. Foreign operations also remained extremely important to Abbott, and the company had over 75 foreign subsidiaries and manufacturing facilities in more than 30 countries. Schoellhorn continued to support Ledder's original diversification policy. The introduction of Murine eye-care products and Selsun Blue dandruff shampoo served to expand the domestic consumer product line and promised to provide earning stability in the event of a downturn in any of the company's other markets.

Schoellhorn was also credited with promoting Abbott's emphasis on diagnostic equipment, especially blood analyzers. These devices were increasingly used to detect legal and illegal substances in the bloodstream. Abbott led the trend, developing the first diagnostic tests for Acquired Immune Deficiency Syndrome (AIDS) and hepatitis. The company's "Vision" blood analyzer fit on a desktop and performed 90 percent of typical blood tests within eight minutes. By the end of the 1980s, sales of blood analysis devices were a billion dollar business, and medical diagnostic products (at $2.3 million per year) constituted nearly half of Abbott's annual sales.

Schoellhorn was widely praised as the driving force behind Abbott's phenomenal growth during the 1980s—sales nearly tripled, profits doubled, and the pharmaceutical company rose to 90th from 197th on *Fortune*'s list of the world's top 500 companies. The leader's aggressive management style, however, often led to conflict. Over the course of the 1980s, three presidents—James L. Vincent (1981); Kirk Raab (1985); and Jack W. Schuler (1989)—quit. In December 1989, Abbott's board of directors unseated Schoellhorn, who in turn sued the company for his job. Abbott accused Schoellhorn of misappropriation of company assets and "fraudulent conduct," adding that the former CEO exercised stock options worth $9.3 million within days of his release. Schoellhorn was succeeded by vice-chairperson Duane L. Burnham.

Unlike many of its competitors (including Merck & Co., Smith-Kline Beecham plc, and Eli Lilly & Co.), Abbott had not acquired a drug distribution manager in the early 1990s. Instead, the company plowed funds into research and development. R & D outlays rose from 5.2 percent of sales in 1982 to over ten percent of sales by 1994. That year marked the company's 23rd consecutive earnings lift and helped Abbott's stock hold its value better than most competitors in the uncertain health care environment of the early 1990s.

Principal Subsidiaries: Abbott Biotech, Inc.; Abbott Chemicals, Inc.; Abbott Health Products, Inc.; Abbott Home Infusion Services of New York, Inc.; Abbott International Ltd.; Abbott Ltd. of Puerto Rico; Abbott Laboratories International Co.; Abbott Laboratories Pacific Ltd.; Abbott Laboratories (Puerto Rico) Inc.; Abbott Laboratories Residential Development Fund, Inc.; Abbott Laboratories Services Corp.; Abbott Manufacturing, Inc.; Abbott Trading Company, Inc.; Abbott Universal Ltd.; CMM Transportation, Inc.; Corporate Alliance, Inc.; Exact Science, Inc.; Fuller Research Corporation; Laser Surgery Partnership; Medlase Holding Corporation; North Shore Properties, Inc.; Oximetrix de Puerto Rico, Inc.; Oximetrix, Inc.; Sequoia Turner Corporation; Sequoia Turner Export Corp.; Solartek Products, Inc.; Sorenson Research Co., Inc.; Swan-Myers, Inc.; TAP Pharmaceuticals Inc. (50%); Tobal Products Inc. The company also owns subsidiaries in the following countries: Argentina, Australia, Austria, Bahamas, Belgium, Bermuda, Brazil, Canada, Chile, China, Colombia, Ecuador, El Salvador, England, France, Germany, Greece, Grenada, Guatemala, Hong Kong, India, Indonesia, Ireland, Italy, Jamaica, Japan, Korea, Lebanon, Malaysia, Mexico, Mozambique, the Netherlands, New Zealand, Nigeria, Pakistan, Panama, Peru, Philippines, Portugal, Singapore, South Africa, Spain, Sweden, Switzerland, Taiwan, Thailand, Turkey, Uruguay, and Venezuela.

Further Reading:

Berss, Marcia, "Aloof But Not Asleep," *Forbes,* August 29, 1994, pp. 43–44.
Kogan, Herman, *The Long White Line: The Story of Abbott Laboratories,* New York: Random House, 1963.

—updated by April Dougal Gasbarre

Communications

AirTouch Communications

One California Street
San Francisco, California 94108
U.S.A.
(415) 658-2000
Fax: (415) 658-2034

Public Company
Incorporated: 1984
Employees: 5,000
Sales: $988 million
Stock Exchanges: New York Pacific
SICs: 4812 Radiotelephone Communications; 6719 Holding
    Companies, Not Elsewhere Classified

AirTouch Communications, one of the world's leading wireless telecommunications organizations, serves the needs of over three million cellular phone and paging customers in the United States, Europe, and Asia. AirTouch operates through four entities: AirTouch International, AirTouch Cellular, AirTouch Paging, and AirTouch Teletrac. AirTouch Cellular is the fifth largest cellular provider in the United States, while AirTouch Paging, the nation's third largest provider of paging services, operates in more than 100 metropolitan areas in 15 states. In 1994 PacTel Corporation was spun off into an entirely independent company, and renamed AirTouch Communications.

AirTouch Communications, formerly PacTel Corporation, was originally established in 1984 as a subsidiary of Pacific Telesis Group. Following the mandated breakup of the American Telephone and Telegraph Company, Pacific Telesis, like many other regional Bell companies, established two divisions. The first focused on regulated local telephone service. The second, its PacTel Corporation, focused on developing cellular, paging, and other less stringently regulated telecommunications services.

AirTouch's largest operating segment, AirTouch Cellular (formerly PacTel Cellular), was launched to facilitate communications for the 1984 Olympic Games in Los Angeles. By the year's end, the organization provided cellular service to approximately 15,000 subscribers in California. In subsequent years, AirTouch Cellular experienced significant growth in the number of cellular phone subscribers. According to a report in *Communication News,* by early 1987 the company boasted more than 60,000 subscribers in the Los Angeles area. To meet

the needs of its subscribers, the company operated more than 55 cell sites, each carefully chosen to maximize signal transmission. A typical cell site housed sensitive communications equipment within a 484-square-foot structure built with factory-made panels. Special ventilating and air conditioning equipment helped maintain the climate control.

AirTouch Paging was established in 1986 when Pacific Telesis Group acquired Communications Industries. The company, originally known as PacTel Paging, provides paging services to nearly 1.5 million customers. Paging units are small, portable units that are carried by the subscriber. When activated, a paging unit alerts its owner to incoming telephone calls by beeping or vibrating. Most early paging units were capable of displaying a numeric message. Some sophisticated units developed later also offer a menu of pre-programmed messages and the ability to receive alphanumeric messages up to 240 characters in length. In 1987, PacTel's international subsidiary began offering regional paging service in Bangkok, Thailand.

Throughout the late 1980s, AirTouch saw rapid growth in the popularity of wireless telecommunications service, and, by the decade's end, the company was serving 339,000 subscribers. AirTouch continued to grow through acquisitions, partnerships, and increased market penetration during the early 1990s. In 1991, the company introduced a retail marketing strategy for pagers. By establishing retail outlets, the company was able to reach nontraditional customers such as family users. In 1994, AirTouch's retail distribution channel network consisted of more than 2,500 locations.

Evolving technology also played a role in the company's growth. In 1991, AirTouch began participating in a Japanese consortium to provide long-distance telephone service between Japan and other nations. The company's 5,200-mile-long undersea fiber optic cable was the first of its kind to provide a direct communications link between the United States and Japan.

Technological innovations also led to the formation of AirTouch Teletrac (formerly PacTel Teletrac) in 1991. Teletrac began operation in Los Angeles to provide tracking service for stolen vehicles and corporate fleets. Teletrac systems operates through a network of antennae, which carries radio signals to aid in mapping a vehicle's position on a computer screen. According to a company statement, "In an area as large as 4,500 square miles, a vehicle's location can be pinpointed within approximately 100 feet." Corporate fleet tracking systems achieved popularity with courier services, law enforcement agencies, transit systems, and ambulance services because they improved dispatcher efficiency, reduced operating expenses, and enhanced customer service.

AirTouch also pioneered Code Division Multiple Access (CDMA) digital cellular technology. CDMA works by assigning an electronic code to a call signal, which permits more calls to occupy the same space and be dispersed across a radio frequency band. The technology, said to increase call-handling capacity by as much as 20 times the rate handled by conventional analog technology, was also touted as offering clearer service and more transparent handoffs from cell to cell. In early 1992, AirTouch was the first of the nation's cellular carriers to announce a commitment to the CDMA format, and, in January

1994, the company pledged to invest almost $250 million to install CDMA technology in California and Georgia. The Los Angeles system was expected to be operational in mid-1995.

In another bid to improve its technological offerings, AirTouch formed the Data Group to participate in the advancement of data transmission services. Data transmission capabilities enables cellular customers to access databases and on-line services. As a result of its efforts, a new technology for data transmission, cellular digital packet data (CDPD), was introduced in 1994. CDPD enabled data to be transmitted more quickly and efficiently than previous technologies by breaking the data into segments, called "packets," that could be sent using intervals between voice traffic on multiple channels instead of requiring a dedicated channel. The data packets were then reassembled and routed to the receiver. CDPD is expected to assist in integrating cellular telephones with laptop computers, mobile field service terminals, automated teller machines, credit verifiers, and even vending machines.

In September 1992, AirTouch introduced a patented microcell transceiver to improve cellular service in certain environments. In areas where radio signals were obstructed, such as canyons, tunnels, and congested urban locations, cellular callers sometimes encountered interrupted service. Microcell transceivers are small, low-power devices which can be deployed in strategic locations to provide better service to difficult areas.

Other new technologies in which AirTouch played a developmental role included the Global Standard for Mobile Communications (GSM), which was adopted by more than 70 countries, and the European Radio Message System (ERMES), a digital paging standard developed through a joint venture in France. AirTouch also participated in devising a cellular data service for United Parcel Service (UPS) that permitted the development of a nationwide package tracking system.

During 1992, Pacific Telesis decided to spin off AirTouch as an independent company. Several reasons were given for the split. First, it was felt that a focus exclusively on wireless services would enable the company to operate more efficiently in its specialized niche. In addition, becoming independent would free the subsidiary from regulatory restrictions placed on "Baby Bells" following the break-up of the nation's telephone industry. Some industry analysts also pointed out that the division would better serve the needs of the company's diverse stockholders. While traditional telephone utility shareholders tended to be conservative investors seeking regular dividends and low risk, many investors in innovative wireless telecommunication companies were willing to forgo dividends in favor of long-term growth. By separating the two companies, Pacific Telesis retained its traditional focus on line-based communications in California and Nevada, including local and toll telecommunications, data and video services, and access to long-distance providers as well as directory advertising. AirTouch focused on wireless communications including cellular, paging, wireless data services, and vehicle location.

An initial public offering (IPO) in December 1993 raised $1.38 billion to capitalize AirTouch. The IPO was the largest involving a technological corporation and the third largest IPO of any kind in U.S. history. Sixty million shares were offered at $23

per share, 42 million in the United States and Canada, 13.5 million in Europe, and 4.5 million in Asia. Capital raised was slated for debt retirement, investment in cellular licenses around the world, and the development of new technologies. At the time of the IPO, Pacific Telesis continued to hold 88 percent of AirTouch's stock. The following April, Pacific Telesis shareholders were given stock in the new company and the spin off was completed. In conjunction with the final separation, the name AirTouch was adopted.

In the third quarter of 1994, AirTouch reported that it served more than 3.1 million customers around the world, including 1.3 million U.S. cellular customers, 275,000 international cellular customers, and 1.4 million U.S. paging customers. AirTouch's largest domestic cellular market was located in southern California, covering the Los Angeles and San Diego areas.

The company's international cellular activities are focused in Germany, Portugal, Sweden, Belgium, Japan, Italy, and South Korea. In Germany, AirTouch was the second largest partner in a cellular company, Mannesmann Mobilfunk GmbH (MMO), providing service to nearly 800,000 and, according to one estimate, processing more than ten million calls per week. In Portugal, AirTouch held a 23 percent ownership interest in Telecel, a cellular provider with 70,000 subscribers as of September 1994. In Sweden, AirTouch held a 51 percent interest in NordicTel Holdings, Sweden's digital cellular consortium. In Japan, AirTouch participated in five joint ventures serving customers in Tokyo, Osaka, Nagoya, the Kyushu/Okinawa region, and Chugo ku. In Italy, a consortium in which AirTouch International held a 10.2 percent ownership interest, Omnitel-Pronto Italia, was awarded a cellular license and expected to begin servicing the Italian population by early 1996. In South Korea, AirTouch served as the lead foreign partner and operator, holding a 11.3 percent ownership interest in a consortium that was awarded a cellular license and expected to begin servicing Seoul, Pusan, and Taegu by early 1996. In May 1994, AirTouch announced that it had come to an agreement with the state-owned Belgian telecommunications company, Belgacom, to form a joint venture to provide mobile communications. In December of 1994, AirTouch was the lead partner in a consortium awarded a digital cellular license in Spain.

AirTouch's international paging services were provided in Portugal, Spain, France, and Thailand. In Spain, AirTouch's paging service was launched in 1993 through Sistelcom-Telemensje, an organization in which AirTouch held a 17.5 percent indirect ownership interest. In Portugal, AirTouch owned 23 percent of Telechamada which provided paging service in a geographic area covering more than 90 percent of the nation's population. In France, AirTouch owned an 18.5 percent interest in the paging company, Infomobile. In Thailand, AirTouch operated paging services through two companies, a joint venture and a subsidiary.

In the United States, AirTouch offered paging services in 100 different markets including Atlanta, Dallas/Fort Worth, Detroit, Houston, Los Angeles, Phoenix, St. Louis, San Diego, San Francisco, Seattle, and Tampa/St. Petersburg. Other wireless services available in the United States included vehicle location services offered in Chicago, Dallas/Fort Worth, Houston, Los

Angeles, Detroit, and Miami. Mobile data services were offered within the company's domestic cellular markets.

In July 1994, AirTouch announced an agreement with U S West to combine domestic cellular properties. The agreement gave the joint venture, Wireless Management Company, cellular licenses in 16 of the nation's top 30 markets and more than 1.8 million customers. Wireless Management Company was initially expected to be approximately 70 percent owned by AirTouch. According to a statement from AirTouch Cellular, the move created the third largest cellular company in the United States in terms of "POPs," an industry term quantifying potential customers by multiplying the population of a region by the telecommunication carrier's percent interest in the area. AirTouch Cellular held licenses to serve 53.4 million POPs. In October, AirTouch formed a partnership with US West, Bell Atlantic, and NYNEX to provide nationwide wireless services. The companies also formed a partnership for the purpose of participating in the FCC's December broadband auctions for Personal Communications Services (PCS) licenses.

Also in July 1994, AirTouch Paging won a two-way nationwide radio-frequency paging license at an FCC auction. The ability afforded by the frequency was expected to enable the company to offer new paging services scheduled to debut in 1996. These included acknowledgement paging, telemetry, data transmission, and limited two-way messaging.

AirTouch introduced two new customer services during the summer of 1994. AirTouch Cellular unveiled AirTouch One Number service, which consolidated multiple numbers such as home, office, cellular, and pager numbers under a single gateway number. Customers using the service were able to screen calls and choose whether to respond with a recorded reply message, route the call to a voice mail system, or be immediately connected. The second new service, Display Messaging, received and stored pages, short messages, and voice mail messages even when the cellular phone was already in use or turned off. Callers were able to send three types of messages to Display Messaging subscribers: a telephone number, a short message selected from a pre-programmed list of messages, or voice mail.

In the mid-1990s, AirTouch executives planned to continue their strategy of growth through expansion into new U.S. markets, increased penetration in existing markets, and participation in international joint ventures. The company also planned to remain at the forefront of new technology. It entered into domestic partnerships to bid on personal communications services (PCS), the next generation of wireless services with anywhere/anytime communications capabilities. According to *The Wall Street Journal,* industry analysts anticipated that some PCS frequencies, scheduled to be auctioned by the FCC in top markets such as New York City, would cost as much as $3 billion. In addition, AirTouch planned to invest $275 million in Globalstar, a global access, satellite-based mobile telephone system slated to begin service in 1998. Under an announced agreement, AirTouch Communications would provide exclusive service for the United States, Japan, Indonesia, Australia, Switzerland, the Netherlands, Belgium, Portugal, and the Caribbean.

Principal Subsidiaries: AirTouch Cellular; AirTouch Paging; AirTouch International; AirTouch Teletrac (51%).

Further Reading:

Carlsen, Clifford, "PacTel Unit Moves Into New Golden Age of the Wireless," *San Francisco Business Times,* June 11, 1993.

Cauley, Leslie, "AirTouch Begins Independent Life with Hefty Assets and High Hopes," *The Wall Street Journal,* April 4, 1994.

"Cellular System Uses Pre-Engineered Structures for Flexibility in Housing Its Cell-Site Equipment," *Communication News,* April 1987.

Cochran, Thomas N., "A Baby Bell Tolls: Does PacTel's $1.3 Billion Offer Bode Ill for Cellular?," *Barron's,* November 22, 1993.

"Pacific Telesis Group Plans Digital Network," *The Wall Street Journal,* January 13, 1994.

Ramirez, Anthony, "Pacific Telesis Plans to Split in Two," *The New York Times,* December 12, 1992.

Titch, Steven, "PacTel Chooses CDMA Format; TIA to Develop Standard," *Telephony,* February 17, 1992.

—Karen Bellenir

American Crystal Sugar Company

101 N. 3rd Street
Moorhead, Minnesota 56560
U.S.A.
(218) 236-4400
Fax: (218) 236-4422

Farm Cooperative
Incorporated: 1973
Employees: 3,427
Sales: $542.87 million
SICs: 2063 Beet Sugar

American Crystal Sugar Company is a 2,145-member agricultural cooperative based in the Red River Valley region of northwestern Minnesota and northeastern North Dakota, a region sometimes referred to in the sugarbeet industry as the nation's "sugar bowl." American Crystal is the largest U.S. processor of beet sugar, and its position as a top competitor in sugar production was strengthened in 1993 through the formation of United Sugars Corporation. A marketing company formed in partnership with Southern Minnesota Beet Sugar Cooperative of Renville, Minnesota, and Minn-Dak Farmers Cooperative of Wahpeton, North Dakota (the upper Midwest's two other major sugarbeet growing co-ops), United Sugars ranks among the nation's top three sugar suppliers, contributing some 15 to 17 percent of the entire domestic sugar supply. American Crystal's history goes back to 1899, and the company has been a pioneering force in the industry, particularly since 1973, when a group of growers assumed both ownership and management of the originally family-controlled concern. American Crystal is also a partner with Minn-Dak and Southern Minnesota in Midwest Agri-Commodities, which markets some 35 percent of all sugarbeet molasses and 38 percent of all sugarbeet pulp produced in the United States.

During the late nineteenth century, sugarbeets were still little more than an experimental crop in the Red River Valley. However, by then beet sugar was a major commodity in Europe, outpacing in tonnage that of imported cane sugar. A German chemist named Andreas Marggraf had experimented with sugar extraction from the *Beta vulgaris* as early as 1747, and, in 1802, the first German sugarbeet factory was built. Another stimulus to the industry came in 1811, when Napoleon sought to outflank a British blockade of France's chief raw sugar source, the West

Indies. Under Napoleon, some 40 sugarbeet processing factories were soon established in France. For countries and regions with colder climates, sugarbeets offered the possibility of a huge new source of income, a crop that could directly compete in quality with sugarcane, which is limited to tropical and subtropical growing areas.

According to Walter Ebeling in *The Fruited Plain,* "the first successful beet-sugar factory in the United States was established in California in 1879." California, in fact, would prove a key growing region for sugarbeets for roughly the next hundred years; Ebeling noted that as late as 1975 the state led the country in production, followed by Idaho, Colorado, and Washington. The American Beet Sugar Company, was owned by the Oxnard family and based in Denver, was one of the first sugarbeet producers. Through the early decades of the twentieth century, American Beet developed into a six-plant operation over three states: Colorado, California, and Nebraska.

At the same time, a beet-processing plant owned by the Minnesota Sugar Company had sprung up in Chaska, southwest of Minneapolis and St. Paul. By 1919, Red River Valley farmers were experiencing success with sugarbeet growing and had begun shipping their harvest to the Chaska plant. Minnesota Sugar, in turn, commenced "large scale experiments in the Valley," according to *50 Years in the Valley,* an American Crystal retrospective. Closely affiliated with Minnesota Sugar was the Northern Sugar Company of Mason City, Iowa, which also figured largely in the early development of the Red River Valley.

In 1922, a crisis was at hand for Colorado's American Beet Sugar Company, which was fast becoming a neglected and vulnerable family business. Following a board meeting convened in April of that year, a special committee was formed to investigate and redirect the company. Then, in June, three successive events—the resignation of second American Beet president Robert Oxnard; the death of original company president Henry Oxnard; and the resignation of chairperson and appointed president H. Rieman Duval—threw the already beleaguered company into a tailspin. Although Duval's resignation was at first rejected, he was eventually replaced by R. Walter Leigh.

By 1924, with Leigh at the helm, the Colorado company was facing the possibility of dissolution. Only three of its six plants were still operating, and only one of these three, the Oxnard, California, plant, was considered sufficient to handle present operations without costly renovation. Leigh recommended that American Beet, if it intended to survive, should seek out new territories and either acquire or form a coalition with other successful beet operations. Both American Beet's chief chemist and vice-president ventured to Minnesota that year to explore the Red River territory and the possibility of an alignment, if not merger, with Northern Sugar and Minnesota Sugar.

During this time, the Commercial Clubs of Grand Forks, North Dakota, and East Grand Forks, Minnesota, had been negotiating with Minnesota Sugar over the construction of what would be the Valley's first sugarbeet processing plant. H. A. Douglas, president of both Minnesota and Northern Sugar, had announced the prior year that his Chaska-based company would commit $1 million toward the construction of the proposed plant, provided the area's farmers and business leaders raised an additional $500,000. The completion of the deal appeared a foregone conclusion—considering the high interest of all parties involved—until a conference with Douglas at the behest of American Beet was held in Chicago in September 1924. During that meeting, American Beet representatives indicated the company's interest in entering new locations while possibly relocating its idle factories or acquiring existing factories. Following another conference in October, during which a purchase price for both Northern and Minnesota Sugar was discussed, American Beet completed negotiations in November, acquiring Minnesota Sugar for $1.97 million and Northern for $2.45 million. The deal included the property involved in the East Grand Forks development but did not obligate American Beet to build a factory there.

Rumors and speculation abounded among Valley growers and civic leaders through the spring of 1925, when the acquisition was finalized. Shortly thereafter, American Beet officials cleared the air. The construction of a plant would be postponed and a local in-progress sale of stock in the East Grand Forks development, named the Red River Sugar Company, would need to be rescinded. Fortunately for the beet farmers, the wait for a new plant was not long. In 1926, American Beet erected a 2,000-tons-per-day capacity plant. Early that same year, the farmers established the Red River Valley Beet Growers Association, which would work in cooperation with American Beet on a number of matters, including acreage allotment. An early indication of the venture's success was the negotiated expansion from 10,500 acres planted in 1926 to 20,000 acres in 1927.

By 1934, American Beet had changed its name to American Crystal Sugar Company and had come to depend heavily on the Red River Valley for its prosperity. That year was a particularly devastating one for the sugarbeet industry, however, due not only to the nation's crippled economy but also to an outbreak of "curly top," an insect-transmitted virus that ruined over 85 percent of the sugarbeet crop across the country. The East Grand Forks operation was the only American Crystal unit to post a profit. All told, the company lost $1.3 million in 1934. However, both it and the sugarbeet industry as a whole rebounded over the next several years, thanks to the work of plant breeders who developed superior beet hybrids that were more resistant to "curly top" and other viruses.

According to *50 Years in the Valley:* "East Grand Forks and the Valley beet industry flourished during World War II, just as it had during the Great Depression and other times of economic strife. It made consistent profits while many of the Company's other plants faltered. The consistent high quality of Valley sugarbeets contrasted with those produced in other parts of the country because of the Valley's fertile soils, productive farmers and comparatively better moisture conditions. Certainly there were bad years in the Valley, but its overall consistency made it a sugarbeet mecca."

Following the war, American Crystal readied for expansion, purchasing land for two additional plants in 1946. Two years later, the company completed construction of what was essentially the first new factory in the industry in almost two decades. This plant was located in Moorhead, Minnesota, about 70 miles

south of East Grand Forks. Completion of the other plant, in Crookston, Minnesota, followed in 1954. In 1965, a fourth American Crystal plant was brought into operation, this time in Drayton, North Dakota.

By then the American sugar industry was beginning to undergo changes, prompted by Fidel Castro's coup in Cuba. Cuba, a historically large supplier of sugar to the United States, was penalized by an amendment to the Sugar Act that redistributed the country's quota and ultimately benefited U.S. sugar producers. Although Congressional support for the U.S. sugar industry would become increasingly important in later years, the Cuban situation had only a limited effect on domestic sugar production. With the early 1970s came cutbacks in planted acres for American Crystal. In 1973, amidst depressed conditions in the industry, Red River Valley acreage was at 150,000 and trending downward. The company was then operating only six of its 11 plants (four of which had become mainstays of the Red River Valley economy) and had curtailed any plans for future development. As Steve Brandt wrote in *Corporate Report Minnesota:* "American Crystal Sugar was a moribund Denver-based company, held by a trust that was content to reap company profits for philanthropic activities that had been laid down by the firm's founding family. Management seemed bent on restricting operations."

Members of the Beet Growers Association had for some time recognized the gravity of the situation, and—hoping to capitalize on possibilities for the future, if plant improvements and other actions were undertaken—had already made plans in late 1971 to acquire a nine percent interest in American Crystal that was up for sale. The Association was headed by executive secretary Aldrich Bloomquist, who in a letter to Crystal executives proposed at the same time an ambitious alternative plan: the sale of the entire company to the growers. By February 1973, the $66 million deal was sealed, with approximately one-third of the money to come from area farmers (through $100 per acre equity stakes) and the remaining two-thirds through long-term financing from the Bank for Cooperatives in St. Paul.

In 1974, its first full year as a farmer-owned cooperative, American Crystal announced plans for a new $40 million plant, to be built adjacent to the original East Grand Forks factory, which would be renovated at the same time. Together, the improvements would allow the company to expand acreage by up to 14 percent, a growth-oriented move the Growers Association had fought for repeatedly, and increasingly unsuccessfully, during the latter years of outside ownership. The company also grew during the 1970s by absorbing the Red River Valley Cooperative, which was proceeding with the construction of a factory in Hillsboro, North Dakota, at about the same time as the East Grand Forks expansion. Meanwhile, two additional Midwestern sugarbeet co-ops were chartered, both in 1972. One was a North Dakota group called Minn-Dak Farmers Cooperative (Minn-Dak), which formed in the Wahpeton area and proceeded to dedicate a plant there before the 1974 harvest. The other was Southern Minnesota Beet Growers Cooperative (SMBGC), which was established after that area's Growers Association received word in 1971 that the Chaska plant was due to close forever at the end of the season. SMBGC began construction of their $60 million plant, located east of Renville in southern Minnesota, in early 1973. In an early sign of partnership, American Crystal managed the plant until 1978, when SMBGC took control.

The timing of all of this heady growth in the "sugar bowl" could hardly have been more fortunate, for sugar prices were just about to skyrocket. Although U.S. farmers were typically prevented from suffering, or benefiting, from volatility in sugar prices, a new farm bill completed in 1973 contained no such stipulation. Egerstrom summarized the unusual situation: "American farmers produce about half the sugar consumed annually in the United States. The rest is surplus from other sugar countries that sell most of their exports under contracts at fixed prices. There weren't surpluses of anything during the early 1970s. Sugar crops around the world that were spared drought were raked by hurricanes and other natural problems. American Crystal and the Red River Valley beet growers were in for a windfall. World sugar prices shot up from about 15 cents a pound to as high as 70 cents." As Bloomquist remarked, "We had farmers who recovered their entire investment in the co-op that first year." Of course, sooner or later the opposite scenario would occur, as in 1977 when a worldwide sugar surplus developed. American Crystal and its fellow co-ops have since successfully lobbied for a strong national sugar support program, despite occasional opposition from consumer groups and food processors.

In 1984, American Crystal joined Minn-Dak and SMBGC as a partner in Midwest Agri-Commodities. Headquartered in Corte Madera, California, near San Francisco, Midwest was established to market beet byproducts, namely molasses and pelletized pulp, which was used principally as feed for dairy cattle. In 1993, Japanese buyers represented Midwest's largest customer base, purchasing some 63 percent of the pulp produced by Midwest, a figure that in turn represented more than 60 percent of all beet pulp imported by Japan. European markets were also a key destination for the three co-ops' byproducts.

In June 1991, American Crystal announced plans to construct a $31 million molasses desugarization plant at its East Grand Forks site in order to increase the co-op's production capacity. Desugarization involves extracting approximately 86 percent of the sugar contained in the molasses produced as a byproduct during sugar production. The facility was expected to produce some 130 million more pounds of sugar from the same tonnage of beets then being processed. Due to delays involving the Minnesota Pollution Control Agency, the plant was not completed until just prior to the 1993–94 processing campaign.

By 1993, as a cooperative American Crystal had invested over $200 million in plants, equipment, improvements, and research designed to enhance efficiency and increase profitability for its members. By almost all accounts the money has been well spent. Not only does the cooperative generate an estimated $1 billion annually to the economy of the Red River Valley, but it also continues to set high industry standards for quality while simultaneously setting new records for sugar production (1.9 billion pounds of sugar in 1993), total net beet payment ($284 million), and sugar sales (1.8 billion pounds). In addition, while more than 80 percent of the co-op's sugar was purchased by food processors, including General Mills, Sara Lee, Nestlé, Hershey's, and Kraft, the company's namesake brand of packaged sugar ranked number one among retailers in the upper Midwest.

Regarding the co-ops future, CEO Joseph P. Famalette was optimistic. A former executive with Minnesota-based processor International Multifoods, Famalette was hired in 1991 to replace retiring CEO Al Bloomquist. He told Forbes in July 1994 that within two years American Crystal—due to its ongoing push for higher efficiency—could sustain its profitability even if the current import quota system favoring U.S. sugar producers were eliminated. He also added that co-ops, through prudent cross-investment, could steadily advance toward the goal of evolving into major food companies themselves. Forbes writer Norm Alster commented that American Crystal and another sugar beet co-op "will invest $51 million in Northern Corn Processors. This will give the two beet producers 51% of NCP's equity, with farmers individually owning the other 49%," Famalette observed. "If I have flour, sugar and high-fructose corn syrup, there aren't a lot of food products I can't make. . . . This is a revolution, and you're just beginning to see the pieces of it coming together."

Affiliated Companies: Midwest Agri-Commodities; ProGold; United Sugars Corporation.

Further Reading:

Alster, Norm, "Getting the Middleman's Share," *Forbes,* July 4, 1994, pp. 108–09.

Brandt, Steve, "Poor Prices Put Crystal on Spot with Beet Farmers," *Minneapolis Tribune,* March 29, 1982, pp. B3–B4.

Brandt, Steve, "Sweet Deal," *Corporate Report Minnesota,* January 1986, pp. 91–6.

"Cereal Investigation Doesn't Concern Beet Fiber Producer," *Star Tribune* (Minneapolis), July 9, 1989, p. 4B.

"Company News," *Star Tribune* (Minneapolis), June 26, 1991, p. 2D.

"Cooperatives Pool Beet Production," *Star Tribune* (Minneapolis), December 27, 1984.

Ebeling, Walter, *The Fruited Plain: The Story of American Agriculture,* Berkeley: University of California Press, 1979.

Egerstrom, Lee, "Sweet Profits: Red River Valley's Sugar Beet Goes on with Savory Sales for American Crystal," *Pioneer Press* (St. Paul), December 10, 1984, pp. 1, 9–10.

50 Years in the Valley, Moorhead, Minnesota: American Crystal Sugar Company, 1976.

Johnson, Rona K., "Red River Valley Beet Harvest Set to Start," *Agweek,* August 29, 1994, p. 29.

Jones, Jim, "Growers Soured by Sugar Bill Loss," *Minneapolis Star,* October 25, 1978.

Kennedy, Tony, "Crystal Sugar's New CEO Happy to Run Own Show," *Star Tribune* (Minneapolis), February 10, 1992, p. 2D; "3 Sugar Beet Co-ops Sign Merger Deal," *Star Tribune* (Minneapolis), November 3, 1993, p. 3D; "Three Sugar Co-ops Are Planning to Join Forces," *Star Tribune* (Minneapolis), March 15, 1993, p. 1B.

Phelps, David, "Organized, Well-Financed Lobby Effort Helps Make Life Sweet for Sugar Growers," *Star Tribune* (Minneapolis), March 19, 1987, p. 10A.

"President of Crystal Sugar Co. Beats Ouster Bid, Then Resigns," *Star Tribune* (Minneapolis), January 21, 1986, p. 11B.

Schmickle, Sharon, "Red River's Beet Boom Means a Bust for Belize," *Star Tribune* (Minneapolis), April 16, 1989, p. 25A.

Struck, Myron, "American Crystal is Top State PAC," *Star Tribune* (Minneapolis), July 11, 1988, p. 4D.

"Sugar Glut May Lead to Sales Quotas," *Star Tribune* (Minneapolis), April 7, 1993, p. 3D.

—Jay P. Pederson

American General Finance Corp.

P. O. Box 59
601 N. W. Second Street
Evansville, Indiana 47701-0059
U.S.A.
(812) 424-8031
Fax: (812) 469-5682

Wholly Owned Subsidiary of American General Corp.
Incorporated: 1967 as CrediThrift Financial
Employees: 7,300
Total Assets: $7.6 billion
SICs: 6141 Personal Credit Institutions

Among the largest consumer-credit companies in the United States, American General Finance Corp. (AGF) issues and services loans, insurance policies, and credit card accounts to individuals and families through over 1,200 branches in 39 states. Enjoying tremendous growth and steadily increasing assets, AGF is regarded as unique in the industry for its focus on extending its services to individuals and families with total incomes of less than $50,000, many of whom have credit lines considered "imperfect." AGF is a subsidiary of the American General Corp., an insurance and financial services conglomerate based in Houston, Texas.

AGF traces its history to 1921, when a small company known as Interstate Finance Corp. was established in the southwestern Indiana city of Evansville for the purpose of underwriting sales for the Inland Motor Truck Company, also based in Evansville. Interstate began issuing consumer loans in 1928, and, by the following year, the rapidly growing company was writing credit-related insurance policies.

By 1942, Interstate Finance had established three branch offices and, according to one advertisement, offered "friendly financing" in the form of personal loans ranging from $10 to $300, business loans, and a wide range of insurance coverage. The following year, Interstate purchased a local loan company known as the Evansville Morris Plan Co., representing the first in a series of acquisitions that would continue into the 1980s and would prove integral to the company's growth strategy. During this time, Evansville's economy and population were booming, bolstered by the emergence of several local shipyards during World War II, and the insurance and lending businesses in the area also enjoyed steady growth.

By the mid 1950s, Interstate had established five branch offices in Evansville, as well as executive offices downtown. During the postwar period of heightened consumerism, Interstate advertisements began emphasizing the financing they made available for automobiles, appliances, televisions, radios, and furniture. The company also strengthened its insurance division, purchasing the Merit Life Insurance Company in 1957. In 1967, Interstate Finance was incorporated as CrediThrift Financial, and, over the next ten years, the company steadily increased its presence, purchasing the assets of Morlan Pacific and establishing branch offices throughout the country.

By the early 1980s, CrediThrift oversaw operations at 537 branch offices, and its growth and success had attracted the attention of industry leaders, including Houston-based American General Corp., one of the largest providers of retirement annuities, life-insurance products, and loans in the United States. In 1982, American General acquired CrediThrift for $150 million, as part of its plan to embark on one of the most aggressive acquisitions programs in the insurance industry. Unlike many of American General's acquisitions, CrediThrift was accorded considerable autonomy and was allowed to retain many of its top executives, including CEO and chairperson Wendell L. Dixon, who had been with the company since 1973 and had helped define the terms of the company's sale.

With greater financial resources, CrediThrift began diversifying its offerings. In 1984, the company launched a Visa/MasterCard program through which it offered a credit card called the More Card. Acquisitions also continued under the parentage of American General. In 1983, CrediThrift purchased the assets of General Finance, and, five years later, it acquired CommoLoCo Operations, a loan company based in Puerto Rico, as well as Manufacturers Hanover Consumer Credit Division ("Manny Hanny"), for which it paid $750 million.

In 1988, CrediThrift reported profits of $85 million on sales of $930 million. The Manny Hanny purchase had effectively doubled the size of CrediThrift's operations. As the company was becoming an increasingly important subsidiary of American General, it proved slow to incorporate and consolidate the operations of its recent acquisitions, which resulted in lower earnings figures for its parent and prompted criticism from Wall Street analysts.

Furthermore, CEO and chairperson Dixon, then aged 65, retired from CrediThrift in 1988. American General Corp. assumed a greater interest in its subsidiary's day-to-day operations, and dramatic changes in CrediThrift's corporate culture began to take place. First, a management development program, Model-Netics, was installed at CrediThrift, and, in a process referred to as "enculturation," the company gradually adopted its parent's management techniques and policies. Then, American General executives were gradually placed in leadership positions within the Evansville company.

To oversee operations during this transition period, American General sent two of its Houston executives to Evansville: CFO Edwin G. Pickett and Michael G. Atnip, a personal assistant of American General CEO Harold S. Hook. Primary among their concerns for the future of CrediThrift was the standardization of operations among its finance holdings. Toward that end, the company's chief consumer finance companies—CrediThrift, General Finance, and Manufacturers Hanover—were consolidated and the company was renamed American General Finance Corp. (AGF).

In 1989, after one year at AGF, Pickett left the company. Also that year, Atnip was named senior vice-president of administration, and John J. Bolger, who had assumed leadership upon Dixon's retirement, was replaced by American General executive Roy W. Haley. Several other AGF officials resigned from the company during this time, and two of the company's board members were replaced by American General Corp. executives.

Despite the high turnover rate among its top officials, AGF reported record profits in 1990. Under Haley, AGF became the sixth largest consumer finance company in the United States in 1990. According to *Credit Magazine,* AGF attributed much of its success to the high quality of its customer service. Relying heavily on feedback from customers, AGF found that its services were generally regarded as superior to those of banks, which were cited as impersonal and, often, uncooperative. In addition to emphasizing personal service, AGF worked to decrease the amount of time involved in processing loan applications.

Employing the services of the telemarketing agency Telenational Marketing, AGF established a one-hour loan service in such test locations as Fresno, California; Orlando, Florida; and Shreveport, Louisiana. Under the program, customers called a toll-free phone number and provided Telenational operators with background information and authorization for the transmittal of credit reports. Telenational operators received the credit reports by facsimile machine and then faxed the completed application to AGF, where loan officers evaluated the information and returned the customers call within an hour, either granting or declining the loan. Another program initiated during this time involved a new line of credit cards, referred to as Private Label cards, which AGF serviced for retailers across the country. Successful in its own right, the Private Label credit card program also afforded AGF access to a wider clientele to which it could market insurance and other financing services.

In April of 1990, American General Corp. became the subject of a takeover bid by the Torchmark Corporation, an insurance company based in Birmingham, Alabama, which offered $6.4 billion to acquire the company. When the bid was refused, Torchmark undertook a proxy battle to win seats on the American General board and announced that, if successful, it would sell off AGF. Although American General won its battle with Torchmark, CEO Hook announced in May of 1990 that American General would be put up for sale, stating that "we recognized that . . . we were in play. We wanted to be in control of the

process." Hook's decision to sell American General was reportedly prompted by his desire to retain the assets of AGF, reflecting the importance and economic potential of AGF as part of the American General package. Moreover, as a subsidiary, AGF was prepared to be sold off separately if a buyer was ultimately not found.

Hook took American General off the auction block later that year, and, while several other subsidiaries were then divested, AGF remained under the auspices of American General. Over the next year, operations at AGF were successfully consolidated, and, in the Evansville *Courier and Press,* Atnip stated: "I think we can honestly say that to a large extent it (management shakeup) is behind us now. . . . I think we're out of the valley of despair." By 1992, AGF had extended loans to 2.3 million American families. Acquisitions that year included Provident Financial Corp. of South Carolina and Credit Centers Inc. of Mississippi.

Under the leadership of Haley's successor, president and CEO Daniel Leitch III, AGF experienced record setting highs in several areas, including earnings, lending volume, and insurance sales. Investment gains for 1993 were reported at $4.6 million, up from $1.3 million the previous year, while the company's customer base increased by nearly 400,000. Furthermore, the company's credit card division experienced profit increases of 30 percent, due to continued sales of the More Card as well as rapidly increasing sales of its Private Label credit cards. Card servicing growth prompted AGF to begin construction on a new, 25,000 square foot facility in Evansville. Through a new computer automation program known as CLASS (Customer Lending and Solicitation System), implemented in 1993, AGF hoped to streamline operations and provide faster service to customers at all of its branches. Espousing what Leitch referred to as a "high-tech, high touch" approach, AGF thus sought to incorporate the benefits of technology while maintaining its reputation for personal service. As it entered the mid-1990s, the company was committed to becoming the national leader in each of the markets it served.

Further Reading:

Derk, James S., "American General Finance: One of the Country's Largest Consumer-Credit Companies," *Indiana Business Magazine,* June 1993, pp. 39–41.

Sword, Doug, "American General Put on Auction Block," *Courier and Press* (Evansville, Indiana), May 3, 1990.

——, "Dixon's Retirement Launched Quiet Revolution at American General," *Courier and Press* (Evansville, Indiana), May 13, 1990.

Thomas, Gregory E., "Customers Say Service Is Our Competitive Edge," *Credit Magazine,* March/April 1990, pp. 16–20, 39.

—Tina Grant

American Management Systems, Inc.

4050 Legato Road
Fairfax, Virginia 22033
U.S.A.
(703) 267-8000
Fax: (703) 267-5111

Public Company
Incorporated: 1970
Employees: 3,200
Sales: $364 million
Stock Exchanges: NASDAQ
SICs: 8741 Management Services; 7373 Computer Integrated
    Systems Design; 7374 Data Processing and Preparation;
    8243 Data Processing Schools

American Management Systems, Inc. (AMS) specializes in assisting large organizations with their use of information technology. AMS provides technological consulting services, customized software, and systems integration services for its customers, a large percentage of which are either large corporations or government agencies. The company focuses its efforts on the needs of several specific industries. Along with federal and local government agencies, the following types of companies make up the bulk of AMS's customers: telecommunications companies, financial institutions, educational institutions, insurance companies, and pharmaceutical companies. Billing and collections, credit management, and organization-wide financial management are among the business functions AMS products serve within these target industries. AMS maintains offices in 35 North American and European cities. Since the company was founded in 1970, it recorded an impressive string of 24 straight years of growth through 1993.

AMS was founded in 1970 by five former Defense Department "Whiz Kids." Each of these Pentagon alumni were experts in systems analysis and management. Two of the co-founders were Charles O. Rossotti, who became chairman and president of AMS, and Patrick W. Gross, who also became a long-time member of upper management. Rossotti and company set up shop in the Washington, D.C., suburb of Arlington, Virginia. From early in its history, a substantial share of AMS's revenue was derived from contracts with federal agencies. The company grew quickly during the 1970s. During its first decade of operation, AMS prospered by concentrating primarily on its consult-

ing business and selling customized software to large organizations, both government and corporate.

Around 1980, things took a turn for the worse at AMS. According to Rossotti, the company's strategy became unfocused. Rather than emphasizing the areas in which it was already successful, the company moved into too many other business segments. One particular move that failed to pay off was the company's attempt to mass market software packages for minicomputers. AMS also tried to expand through acquisitions in the early 1980s. In 1981 the company purchased Executive Systems, Inc., which was sold off again just four years later.

After hitting bottom in 1981, AMS staged an impressive comeback over the next few years. In 1982 the company reorganized in order to shift focus back to its areas of expertise. All of its minicomputer-related businesses were eliminated, as were its time-sharing operations. The company also dumped all of its products aimed at small businesses. At that point, AMS began to focus on specific vertical markets and to concentrate on combining professional services, such as consulting with packaged software, for users in the largest size bracket. By targeting mainly the markets it had already penetrated, the company was able to avoid mass marketing, which had caused AMS headaches in the past. With its strategy revamped, AMS was able to once again boast a growth rate approaching 20 percent a year.

AMS's decision to base its business on the combination of packaged software with professional services proved to be ahead of its time. Although this approach was virtually unheard of when AMS adopted it around 1982, it was becoming fairly common by the middle of the decade. By that time, AMS had forged strong partnerships with a number of major companies, for whom it was providing such products as credit management and automated credit application software for banking industry customers; financial management systems for government installations; and administrative systems for academic institutions. Typically, AMS would provide a generic software package that it had adapted to meet the specific needs of the customer. Support services were then added to the mix.

In the mid-1980s, AMS carefully expanded its focus to include joint marketing agreements with hardware and software companies. In 1985, AMS entered an agreement with Tandem Computers Inc. to jointly market a credit collection software package designed by AMS to run on Tandem mainframe computers. Another joint marketing agreement was reached later in the year with Software AG. That agreement covered versions of AMS software for government, educational, and oil and gas finance systems to be used with Software AG's Adabas database management system.

AMS's business expanded in several directions in 1986. In one important development, the company began making inroads into the lucrative telecommunications market. Around that time, the company unveiled a new package of administrative software for order processing and billing tailored specifically for that industry. MCI Communications Corporation, then emerging as an industry powerhouse, was among the company's new customers in the telecommunications field. In July 1986, AMS announced that 12 state, county, and municipal governments had begun using financial management systems produced by the company. Software license fees and revenue from support services for these government deals amounted to $6 million for the year. Several acquisitions also took place in 1986. During that year, AMS purchased Anacomp, Inc.'s BANKSERV product line for $800,000. Data Base Management Inc. and The Courseware Developers were also acquired for a total of $5.25 million. For 1986, AMS earned net income of $5.2 million on $136 million in revenue. Government contracts were making up about a third of that business.

AMS achieved record highs in both net income and revenues in 1987, earning $7.6 million on $174 million in sales. Although revenue continued to climb, the company's net income slumped somewhat during the next two years. Company officials cited a number of reasons for this slip. Foremost was a 17 percent decrease in business from the federal government, largely the result of slowdowns at the Defense Department. The company's rapid early growth also led to higher overhead, interest, and software development expenses. In addition, a suspended contract led to an earnings write-off, and in 1989 the company's new preferred stock began paying dividends, which are calculated against net income per share. During 1989, AMS suffered its first quarterly loss in seven years, and, for the year, profit slipped to $6.2 million.

An even greater drop in profits in 1989 was prevented by a strengthening of ties between AMS and IBM. In July, IBM purchased 10 percent interest in AMS, acquiring $18 million in AMS stock. The two companies also entered a long-term arrangement under which AMS would develop software, starting with financial services applications, to run on IBM machines. This infusion of cash from IBM helped to offset the tightening of Defense Department purse strings.

AMS quickly recovered from the setbacks of 1989, despite continued military cutbacks. By 1990, the company saw sharp increases in its business from civilian federal agencies and from financial services institutions. Business from state and local governments, universities, and other corporate customers were all on the rise as well. The telecommunications industry was a particularly fertile area for AMS around this time. Companies in that field increased their business with AMS by around 75 percent in 1990. By that time, federal business was generating about one-fourth of the company's business. Military agencies, however, accounted for only about 15 percent of revenues, compared with a peak of 26 percent as recently as 1988. Nevertheless, AMS's earnings were back on track, reaching nearly $11 million in 1990 on revenue of $260 million.

In 1991, AMS managed to perform well in the face of adversity. Due to a generally sickly economy, the company's core business, namely systems integration for telecommunications and financial services firms, all but vanished as a source of new growth. This time, government consulting contracts helped fill the gaps left by disappearing private sector funds. The company's partnership with IBM also continued to flourish. In 1991 the two firms teamed up to develop the Image and Record Management system, AMS's first foray into the imaging business. AMS also reached a new deal with NYNEX Mobile Communications to design a billing and customer management system tailored for the cellular phone industry. During the year, AMS beefed up its international operations considerably. After

a 43 percent increase in 1991, international business accounted for over 10 percent of the company's total revenue. In the dismal business climate of that time, AMS managed to increase its revenue to $284 million and its net income to $12.6 million.

Rossotti announced he was stepping down as president of AMS in 1992 in order to concentrate on broader strategic issues rather than day-to-day company decisions. He remained chairman and chief executive. Two longtime AMS executives were named to take over the company's operations: Philip M. Giuntini, with AMS almost since the beginning, was named president, and Paul A. Brands, who had worked for the Environmental Protection Agency and the Defense Department before joining AMS in 1977, was named vice-chairman. Because Giuntini and Brands had already been overseeing about 60 percent of the company's operations prior to the move, the shift in titles did not represent a significant change in leadership at AMS.

By the end of 1992, AMS was clearly one of the best-performing high-tech firms around. Over five years, the company had doubled its sales and tripled its net income, which had jumped to over $19 million for 1992. Nearly half the company's revenue was coming from some level of government, and the rest of its customers were large, loyal corporations and institutions. AMS's ten-year compound growth rate was a healthy 19 percent. In 1993 Brands picked up the additional role of chief executive officer, while Rossotti remained chairman. Brands became the first nonfounder to hold that position at AMS. In April 1993, AMS opened its Center for Advanced Technologies in Fairfax, Virginia, and increased its emphasis on research operations. The company also boosted its European presence by opening offices in Munich and Lisbon during the year.

Toward the end of 1993, AMS acquired Vista Concepts, Inc., from NYNEX. Vista is a leading provider of software for the global securities market. In late 1993 and into 1994, AMS joined an industry trend by adapting its software for client/server systems; previously, most of its software had been engineered for IBM mainframes. Client/server revenue was expected to account for over one-third of the company's total by 1994. In July 1994, AMS announced that it was awarded a $20 million contract by Swedish cellular phone company Telia Mobitel for a billing and customer management system. Telia Mobitel was the fifth major European cellular carrier to sign a contract with AMS in two years.

For 1993, AMS recorded revenue of $364 million, its 24th consecutive annual increase. Net income dipped slightly, due in part to a dramatic decrease in revenue from IBM, whose mainframes it was abandoning. AMS also began buying back blocks of its own stock from IBM. As it faced the rest of the 1990s, AMS planned to continue investing heavily in research in order to stay at the forefront of its industry.

Principal Subsidiaries: Data Base Management, Inc.; AMS Courseware Developers; AMS Management Systems Canada Inc.; AMS Operations Corporation; AMS Technical Systems, Inc.; AMS Management Systems Deutschland GmbH (Germany); AMS Management Systems Europe, S.A./N.V. (Belgium); AMS Management Systems U.K. Ltd.

Further Reading:

"American Management Systems: Despite Government Cutbacks, It's Staging a Comeback," *Barron's,* October 29, 1990, pp. 43–44.

Betts, Mitch, "American Management Systems Rebounds, Plays on Strength," *Computerworld,* July 28, 1986, p. 80; "IBM Continues Sugar Daddy Role, Buying Into AMS Future," *Computerworld,* July 24, 1989, p. 73.

Dubashi, Jagannath, "American Management Systems: Wiring for Profit," *Financial World,* April 27, 1993, pp. 16–18.

Ricciuti, Mike, "American Management Systems Inc. (The Datamation 100)," *Datamation,* June 15, 1992, p. 149.

Sugawara, Sandra, "AMS Names New President, Vice Chairman," *Washington Post,* October 20, 1992, p. C1.

—Robert R. Jacobson

Archer-Daniels-Midland Company

4666 E. Faries Parkway
P.O. Box 1470
Decatur, Illinois 62526-5666
U.S.A.
(217) 424-5200
Fax: (217) 424-5839

Public Company
Incorporated: 1923
Employees: 14,000
Sales: $11.37 billion
Stock Exchanges: New York Boston NASDAQ Philadelphia
   Pacific
SICs: 2075 Soybean Oil Mills; 2076 Vegetable Oil Mills,
   Not Elsewhere Classified; 2074 Cottonseed Oil Mills; 279
   Edible Fats and Oils, Not Elsewhere Classified; 2046 Wet
   Corn Milling; 2041 Flour and Other Grain Mill Products;
   2062 Cane Sugar Refining; 2083 Malt; 5153 Grain and
   Beans

The Archer-Daniels-Midland Company, a consistently successful firm with a quiet and conservative profile, ranks as America's largest processor of agricultural commodities, with leading positions in oilseed processing, flour milling, corn refining,
and corn wet milling. Other interests in the mid-1990s included
granaries, peanut shelling, rice milling, and sugar refining. With
129 plants in the United States and 50 overseas, Archer-Daniels-Midland (ADM), calls itself the ''Supermarket to the
World.'' The company's attitude is direct and optimistic:
''Food is a growth business. Globally there are 85 million more
mouths to feed each year; the equivalent of the current population of Mexico, or more than one-third of the U.S. population.
ADM plans to participate in this growth.''

Archer-Daniels-Midland has always been clearly focused and
has expressed no intentions to diversify outside of food-related
businesses. Since its early years, the company's methods have
been consistent—strong research and development which emphasizes new production methods and uses for agricultural
products, coupled with a bottom-line mandate for high performance and cost efficiency.

John W. Daniels began crushing flaxseed in Ohio in 1878, and
in 1902 he moved to Minneapolis, Minnesota, to organize the
Daniels Linseed Company. The entire company consisted of

one flax crushing plant which made three products, including
raw linseed oil, boiled linseed oil, and linseed cake or meal. In
1903, George A. Archer joined the firm, and in a few years it
became the Archer-Daniels Linseed Company. Archer also
brought experience to the firm, as his family had been in the
business of crushing flaxseed since the 1830s. Archer and Daniels then hired a young bookkeeper by the name of Samuel
Mairs. Mairs would later become the company's chairperson
when the business was much larger and significantly more
affluent.

These three men had a common goal of ''year round production
at low margins,'' a goal which continued to direct the company
in the 1990s. Archer and Daniels used hydraulic presses to
process flaxseed, and their linseed oil was essentially the same
as that used by the ancient Egyptians. In the early years, profits
were low, but Archer-Daniels Linseed never finished a year in
debt. They also grew slowly, buying the stock of the Toledo
Seed & Oil Company as well as the Dellwood Elevator Company, a grain elevator firm.

In 1923, the company purchased the Midland Linseed Products
Company and then incorporated as the Archer-Daniels-Midland
Company. The 1920s also brought other significant changes.
Archer, Daniels, and Mairs began the scientific exploration of
ways to alter the chemical structure of linseed oil. This project
initiated the company's successful research and development
program. Research and development allocations were not commonplace for companies at that time, and the market was
startled by the company's slogan: ''Creating New Values From
America's Harvests.''

Throughout the 1920s the company made steady purchases of
oil processing companies in the midwest. At the same time, it
was also engaged in other agricultural activities. It built eleva-
tors on Minneapolis loading docks to store grain awaiting shipment down the Mississippi to other ports. Then, in 1930,
Archer-Daniels-Midland purchased the Commander-Larabee
Company, a major flour miller with plants in Minnesota, Kansas, and Missouri. Commander-Larabee was capable of producing 32,000 barrels per day. The purchase of Commander-
Larabee had two additional advantages; it allowed ADM to
coordinate its oil by-product business with Commander-
Larabee's feed-stuff by-product business, and the mutual sales
effort lowered overhead. During this time, the company also
discovered how to extract lecithin from soybean oil, reducing
the price of lecithin from ten dollars to one dollar per pound.
(Lecithin was widely used as an emulsifier in the food and
confectionery industries.) As a result of Archer-Daniels-Midland's growth maneuvers and research, the company had
$22.5 million in assets by 1938.

As a linseed oil manufacturer, Archer-Daniels-Midland interacted with more than just the food market. The paint product
industry used drying oils in the manufacture of various products, and the three major oils used were linseed, tung, and
perilla. These oils added critical gloss and hardness properties
to paint finishes. The demand for drying oil in the paint industry
fluctuated widely because it depended heavily on construction.
Demand for domestic drying oil was also affected by the availability and price of foreign oils, since most oils were imported
from the Far East and South America. Added to these two

variables was the quality and size of each year's harvest. Even during the Depression and coping with all these variations in a struggling economy, the company made a profit. This was because Archer-Daniels-Midland had been working on ways to adapt oils to sell to new markets, including soaps, drugs, brake fluids, lubricants, petroleum, and chemicals.

Since Archer-Daniels-Midland knew the value of its research department, it appropriated 70 percent of its earnings (one to two million dollars annually) back into the business for development and expansion. One result was a process whereby the usable fibers (the tow) of flax straw (a waste product up to then) could be used in the manufacture of flax papers. World War II made it impossible to increase the company's facilities as much as it wished; nevertheless, the company's capacities grew significantly from 1930 to 1945. From a 1929 processing capacity of 20 million bushels of flaxseed per day, the company could process 36.6 million bushels per day by 1945. Wheat flour capacity went from zero to 30 million bushels per day. Grain storage capacity increased from 7.5 million to 50.4 million bushels per day.

The immediate postwar years from 1946 through 1949 showed dramatic growth; sales increased 287 percent, and net income increased 346 percent. In 1949, sales were $277 million, with a $12 million net profit. Archer-Daniels-Midland was well positioned in several market areas because it supplied basic ingredients to a wide range of industries. The company was the leading U.S. processor of linseed oil, the fourth largest flour miller, and it had become the largest soybean processor. It also served the paint, leather, printing, gasoline, paper, cosmetics, pharmaceuticals, rubber, ceramics, munitions, and insecticides industries.

The conservative management style had consistently safeguarded the company's success. For instance, whenever possible, Archer-Daniels-Midland hedged its purchases of raw products by sales in the futures markets or by forward sales of the completed products. By the end of fiscal year 1949, the company had no bank debt, and it had paid a dividend every year from 1927 onward. All plants were kept at a high state of operating efficiency, using modern, streamlined methods. There had also been a change in the processing level. The company began to put its products through advanced physical processing instead of selling them in a raw or semi-finished state. This increased profit margins. Overall, management estimated that 40 percent of its increase in sales from 1939 to 1949 was due to new products and methods developed within the company.

Because the company supplied core oils used in foundry industries, the outbreak of the Korean War increased demands on production through the early 1950s. The company was also increasing its outlay for whale oil procurement, which it had begun in the 1930s, and began increasing its production of protein concentrates, marketing them extensively for stock-feeding purposes.

When company president Thomas L. Daniels (son of the founder) and chairperson Samuel Mairs celebrated Archer-Daniels-Midland's fiftieth anniversary in 1952, the company was manufacturing over 700 standard products and had extended its operations overseas. More foreign expansion followed in Peru, Mexico, the Netherlands, and Belgium. In these ventures, the company specialized in partnerships with local interests. President Daniels expressed the company's attitude toward foreign involvement in the late 1950s when he said: "ADM looks with particular favor on Western Europe as an area of great chemical producers. . . . All industry there is expanding rapidly, both for local consumption and for export to other parts of the world."

Archer-Daniels-Midland had weathered the Depression and World War II, but ran into trouble during the 1960s. Although it made several grain production and storage purchases in the early 1960s, unstable commodities prices and the company's chemicals operations were causing losses. Net earnings were $75 million in 1963 and then declined to about $60 million in 1964, dropping even further to $50 million the following year. By 1965, the company could not cover its dividend. At this time, John Daniels, president and grandson of one of the founders, and Shreve M. Archer, Jr., one of the directors, asked a new man to join their leadership team with the purchase of a block of the Archer family stock. His name was Dwayne O. Andreas, and he effectively took control and revolutionized Archer-Daniels-Midland.

Andreas' low profile appealed to the company management and so did his background. He came from a long-term farm products background, first with his father, and then on his own. One of the first things Andreas did was eliminate a 27-person public relations department. Eschewing the advice of analysts and often declining to talk to reporters, Andreas was a unique executive. His political views often contradicted those of the business world in general; for example, he advocated increases in the corporate income tax rate.

Andreas believed that one specific product could do a great deal to turn the company around, namely soybeans. Andreas recalled, "I knew that ADM was a dozen years ahead of everyone else in textured vegetable protein research, and I believed that was where important action was going to be." Whereas scientists advocated an almost pure protein product derived from the soybean, Andreas encouraged the development of textured vegetable protein, a 50 percent protein soy product which was far more economical to produce. His increasing power in the company (by 1968 he was chair of the executive committee) made his plans a reality. Andreas described his actions thus: "One of the first things I did was to take the edible soy out of the lab and construct a plant in Decatur (Illinois) to make all the grades of edible soy protein in 1969." He expected to exceed the plant's capacity by 1976. However, by 1973, with doubled production, the plant was already short of demand. Textured vegetable protein (TVP) was widely used in foodstuffs, and soybean oil later became the number one food and cooking oil in use.

The company also sold its troublesome chemical properties to Ashland Oil & Refining Company for $35 million in 1967. That year, it acquired the Fleischmann Malting Company, which would become a very profitable producer of malts for the food and beverage industry. Andreas proved expert at maintaining a good profit margin on soybeans too. Two or three cents shaved off costs made large differences in this slender profit margin item. In this area, Andreas's management rules of efficiency and profitability echoed the founders' practices.

With unprofitable operations sold, profitable ones newly acquired, and the increasing success of the soybean, the company entered another major area of operations. In 1971, it purchased Corn Sweetners, Inc., producer of high fructose syrups, glutens, oil, and caramel color. Corn Sweetners brought good returns for Archer-Daniels-Midland and increased the company's finished-food capabilities.

Throughout the 1970s, the company built textured vegetable protein plants in Europe and South America. In addition, Dwayne Andreas brought several other members of his family into Archer-Daniels-Midland as the company expanded. (In fact, a 1988 treatment in *Financial World* characterized ADM as the Andreas "family dynasty.") Three Andreas family members became heads of various divisions, although the company continued to retain one Archer and one Daniels in high-ranking positions into the 1990s.

From the net low of $50 million in earnings in 1965, net earnings were near $117 million in 1973. This increase paralleled the upward swing in U.S. soybean production and exports from 700 million bushels per day in 1965 to 1.3 billion in 1973.

That growth continued through the 1970s and into the 1980s. During this time, Archer-Daniels-Midland had several major subdivisions, the largest of which was the Oilseed Processing Division. In this division, soy products soon outstripped linseed and all others, earning Andreas the nickname "Soybean King." The next largest, Corn Sweetners Division, produced ethanol in addition to high-fructose products. In fact, the Decatur, Illinois, plant was the single largest source of ethanol in the United States. Archer-Daniels-Midland Milling Company processed the company's grains, and in 1986 the milling division became even larger when ADM absorbed Growmark, a large midwestern grain merchandising and river terminal cooperative. The new wholly-owned subsidiary was called ADM/Growmark.

Another division, the Columbian Peanut Company acquired in 1981, produced oil and peanut products, and Archer-Daniels-Midland was the leading domestic peanut sheller. Gooch Foods, Inc. was the company's market name for a line of pasta products, which increased in demand since the advent of microwave pasta dishes. Other divisions of Archer-Daniels-Midland included Southern Cotton Oil Company, Fleischmann Malting Company, Inc., American River Transportation Company, Supreme Sugar Company, and the British Arkady Co., Ltd., which was a supplier of specialty products to the bakery industry.

ADM made its first-ever foray into consumer food products with the characteristically low-profile launch of its Harvest Burger brand soy-based meat substitute in the early 1990s. The product's reduced fat, calories, and cholesterol attracted American consumers, many of whom sought out the product even before it had advertising support. In 1993, the Pillsbury Company assumed responsibility for supermarket retailing of Harvest Burgers. For the hungry of the world, the soy product was an inexpensive source of protein with a longer shelf life than traditional sources like meat and milk. And as CEO Andreas pointed out in a 1993 interview with *Direct Marketing* magazine, "You can feed 20 times as many people off of an acre of land by raising soy alone, than growing soy and feeding it to an animal and then eating that animal." Andreas called the development of the meat-like soy product "the most important food development of this century."

Feeding the hungry of the world was just one of Andreas' business/humanitarian interests. The corporate leader also used his influence to promote no-till farming (a method that reduced soil erosion), environmentalism in general, and the use of ethanol as a fuel additive. Of course, ADM had a vital interest in ethanol, which was one of the company's most important products in the era of the Clean Air Act.

As the twenty-first century approached, ADM faced a momentous change: although the company's septuagenarian CEO did not appear ready to yield his leadership position, that eventuality loomed large. Upon his retirement, Dwayne Andreas would take with him three decades of personal and political relationships that ranged from presidents to popes. Direction of the company would likely fall to president and second-in-command James R. Randall, or to son and senior vice-president Michael Andreas.

In the early 1990s, ADM's over $1 billion in capital spending focused on European operations and biochemicals. As trade barriers in Eastern Europe and the Americas fell, and ratification of the General Agreement on Tarriffs and Trade appeared certain, Andreas hoped bring further geographic diversification to ADM. The foray into biochemistry focused on advanced techniques for the creation of evermore efficient animal feeds. These investments echoed ADM's heritage of endeavoring to be the low-cost, high-tech producer.

Principal Subsidiaries: ADM Milling Co.; ADM Arkady; ADM/Growmark; Tabor Grain Co.; Smoot Grain Co.; Collingwood Grain Co.; Fleischmann-Kurth Malting Co., Inc.; Gooch Foods, Inc.; Supreme Sugar Co., Inc.; Southern Cotton Oil Co.; ADM Investor Services, Inc.; American River Transportation Co.; Hickory Point Bank & Trust; Archer Daniels Midland Shipping Co.; Dominion Malting Ltd.; The British Arkady Co. Ltd.; Agrinational Insurance Co.; ADM FAR East Ltd.; ADM Mexico, Inc.; ADM International Ltd.; ADM Ingredients Ltd.; ADM Europort B.V. (Netherlands); ADM Agri Industries; ADM Australia (Pty) Ltd.

Further Reading:

Neal, Mollie, "Reaping the Rewards of Skillful Marketing While Helping Humanity," *Direct Marketing,* September 1993, pp. 24–26.
Sachar, Laura, "Top Seed," *Financial World,* May 3, 1988, pp. 2–28.

—updated by April Dougal Gasbarre

Associated Milk Producers, Inc.

6609 Blanco Road
San Antonio, Texas 78279-0287
U.S.A.
(210) 340-9100
Fax: (210) 340-9158

Private Company
Incorporated: 1969
Employees: 4,500
Sales: $2.69 billion
SICs: 5143 Dairy Products, Except Dried or Canned

Associated Milk Producers, Inc. (AMPI) is the largest dairy cooperative in the United States. AMPI's 13,400 member farms delivered 15.7 billion pounds of milk in 1993, about 11 percent of the nation's total supply. The company also supplies similar shares of the country's cheese (649 million pounds) and butter (138 million pounds), as well as 21 percent of its dried whey and 18 percent of its nonfat dry milk.

AMPI's operations are divided geographically into three semi-autonomous divisions. The Morning Glory Farms Region is comprised of member farms located in eastern Wisconsin, Illinois, Indiana, Ohio, and Michigan. This region's most important milk market is the Chicago area. Cheese, sour cream, and frozen yogurt are also produced by Morning Glory Farms. The North Central Region, which includes western Wisconsin, Minnesota, Missouri, Iowa, Nebraska, and South Dakota, processes most of its milk into cheese and other products that are marketed under the name State Brand and numerous other private labels. AMPI's Southern Region supplies mainly Grade A drinking milk. Farms in Arkansas, New Mexico, Oklahoma, Texas, and several other states are part of this region.

AMPI's political action committee, C-TAPE (Committee for Thorough Agricultural Political Education), is one of the largest of its kind in the United States. C-TAPE spends hundreds of thousands of dollars annually lobbying for dairy price supports and other dairy and agricultural policy issues. Owned by its membership, AMPI provides its members marketing and related services, as well as such benefits as credit, insurance, and retirement programs.

Agricultural cooperatives emerged in the United States after the 1922 enactment of the Capper-Volstead Act, which gave small farmers the right to join forces, thereby obtaining greater control over the supply and price of their products. But with the decline of both milk consumption and dairy farm income in the late 1960s, dairy co-ops began to band together into larger and larger entities. Six dairy cooperatives in Kansas, Texas, Arkansas, and Oklahoma merged in 1967 to form Milk Producers, Inc. (MPI). MPI acquired eight more southwestern co-ops in its first year. By 1969, MPI had expanded north, with member farms located in South Dakota and Minnesota. That year, MPI merged with 14 smaller co-ops in the Chicago area to form AMPI.

Harold Nelson had organized the consolidation. Nelson had been manager of the Texas Milk Producers Federation and the general manager of MPI before he became AMPI's first general manager. John Butterbrodt, a member from a Wisconsin cooperative, was elected president. AMPI set up headquarters in San Antonio, Texas. Two other large dairy cooperatives, Mid-American Dairymen, Inc. and Dairymen, Inc., were formed around the same time as AMPI through similar consolidation processes.

Because of economic pressures, smaller dairy cooperatives throughout the central part of the United States were eager to join the growing AMPI. Before it was two years old, AMPI was the biggest dairy cooperative in the country. By 1971, AMPI had 45,000 members, thanks in part to a merger that year with Pure Milk Products Cooperative, a fairly large Wisconsin organization. Many of the largest markets in the central United States, including Chicago, Madison, Indianapolis, Houston, Dallas, San Antonio, and Memphis, were getting at least three-fourths of their raw milk supply from AMPI by the middle of 1972.

Despite its economic success, AMPI spent much of the next few years embroiled in a series of legal controversies. Shortly after AMPI was formed, the company established a political trust called TAPE, an acronym for Trust for Agricultural Political Education, which later became C-TAPE. In 1972, consumer advocate Ralph Nader began to argue that recent increases in federal price supports for dairy products (a reversal of a previous decision) were the result of illegal contributions by TAPE and the political arms of the other large diary co-ops to President Nixon's re-election campaign. Suits were filed against the Commodity Credit Corp. and Agriculture Secretary Earl Butz, asking for a rollback of the increases on the grounds that they were illegal because they were made on the basis of political rather than economic considerations. A month later, a civil antitrust suit was filed in federal court charging AMPI with a number of monopolistic practices. The suit alleged that AMPI had, among other things, manipulated the milk supply to control prices, and conspired with milk haulers and processors against independent competitors.

AMPI's situation got much worse; its political operations were soon tied in with the Watergate investigation. In 1974, two high-ranking AMPI officials pleaded guilty to a range of charges concerning campaign contributions. First, David Parr, special counsel to AMPI, admitted that he had authorized illegal contributions to Hubert Humphrey's unsuccessful 1968 presidential campaign. Parr also admitted authorizing payments to several other lesser campaigns, as well as allowing co-op employees to work on these campaigns while on the AMPI payroll. Nelson pleaded guilty to a series of campaign-fund violations shortly thereafter. While the company's legal entanglements were unfolding, Nelson was succeeded as general manager of AMPI in 1972 by George L. Mehren, a former assistant secretary of agriculture under President Lyndon Johnson.

The most widely publicized episode of this period was the charge that representatives of AMPI, specifically attorney Jake Jacobsen, had bribed Treasury Secretary John Connally. The charges against Connally and Jacobsen alleged that AMPI had paid Connally in return for special consideration in dairy price support issues. Litigation involving AMPI eventually forced the co-op's top managers to spend as much as a quarter of their time in hearings and depositions. By 1975, Connally was acquitted of the bribery charges. Ironically, Jacobsen, the chief witness against him, was convicted by a different jury of paying the bribe. As a result of the scandal, AMPI owed over $16 million in unpaid taxes and fraud penalties from 1972 and 1973.

AMPI was damaged by the scandal's negative publicity as well as an industry slump, but remained a leading force in the American economy. Between 1971 and 1974, AMPI lost about 12 percent of its members, some leaving in response to the company's political complications. Eighteen percent of all dairy farms folded over the same period, victims of a periodic slump in the industry. Nevertheless, by 1974 AMPI ranked 155th on *Fortune* magazine's list of America's largest industrial corporations. The company was supplying 12.5 percent of the nation's wholesale raw milk, and was running the largest cheese-processing plant in the country. C-TAPE, despite a drop in contributions in the wake of Watergate, was the second richest special interest lobbying group in the United States, just behind an American Medical Association-headed coalition.

During the late 1970s, AMPI worked to revive its image. The company reorganized its corporate structure, establishing a system of semi-autonomous regional groups under separate management teams. In spite of all the scandals and convictions, C-TAPE continued to operate successfully, and was instrumental in winning further price supports for milk as soon after the turmoil as 1976.

By the early 1980s, AMPI appeared to be back on track. The co-op had about 32,000 members in 20 states and Canada by 1981, and its annual sales had reached $2.4 billion. In 1982, the suit for monopolistic practices originally filed in 1971 finally made it into the federal courts. The case, which had been initiated by the National Farmers' Organization, was decided in favor of AMPI and two fellow cooperatives. But within months, an appeals court ruled that AMPI and the others had conspired to eliminate competition, and the decision was reversed. The U.S. Supreme Court later upheld the appeals court ruling in 1989. The case did not harm AMPI's ability to sway the industry, however. In 1983, C-TAPE helped in the defeat of a bill in Congress that would have cut price supports for dairy farms.

AMPI dropped in membership by 1985, but its revenues remained about the same. AMPI's 23,300 member farms were delivering about 15.7 billion pounds of milk by 1985, and the company's revenue remained around $2.4 billion. Growth for the co-op came through mergers and acquisitions. In 1986,

AMPI strengthened its position in the Great Lakes area by merging its Mid-States Region with the Morning Glory Farms Cooperative, a 2,200-member group based in Shawano, Wisconsin. The combined unit was dubbed the Morning Glory Farms Region. In September of 1986, AMPI's North Central region acquired the largest cheese plant in the country, Falls Dairy in Jim Falls, Wisconsin. The plant had an annual cheese output of 84 million pounds (mainly for Kraft), processed from about a billion pounds of milk. Together, AMPI's plants in all three regions produced 126 million pounds of butter (10 percent of the U.S. output); 218 million pounds of nonfat dry milk (17 percent); 334 million pounds of American cheese (12 percent); and 160 million pounds of dry whey (16 percent) in 1986. By 1988, the co-op marketed well over 17 billion pounds of milk, compared with 7.5 billion pounds for its closest rival, Mid-America Dairymen.

Under general manager Ira Rutherford, the co-op earned over $12 million in 1989, triple the previous year's figure, on sales of just under $3 billion. A total of $42 million was invested in new property, facilities, and equipment during the year, much of it at the new Stephenville, Texas, plant, a 96,000 square-foot facility capable of making cheese and whey from 1.4 million pounds of milk a day.

As the 1990s began, things took a turn for the worse at AMPI. In 1990 farm milk prices took a 25 percent plunge. AMPI lost $27 million for the year, its first net loss. Attrition of dairy farms continued to erode AMPI's membership numbers, and this decline accelerated during the early 1990s. Furthermore, AMPI's total milk deliveries began to shrink year by year. Although the company managed to record sales of $3.06 billion for 1990, the outlook was bleak. In 1991 Ira Rutherford resigned as general manager, a post he had held for 12 years. He was replaced by Noble Anderson, head of the company's Southern Region. That year AMPI managed to turn a modest profit ($698,000), although membership and deliveries continued to decline.

In 1992, AMPI recorded its second largest loss in three years. Most of the damage resulted from the bankruptcy of Hawthorn-Mellody, a major customer to whom AMPI had extended a great deal of credit over the years. For the year, the company posted a loss of $12.6 million, absorbed mostly by the Morning Glory Farms Region. In spite of the problems, AMPI managed to devote $31 million to the purchase of new property and equipment. In the summer of 1992, the company opened a new cheese plant south of Roswell, New Mexico. The plant, able to produce 190,000 pounds of cheese a day, was to become the largest in the AMPI system.

By 1993, the finances of AMPI had improved but membership had dropped. AMPI member farms numbered 13,400, nearly a 50 percent decrease over ten years. But the company had improved its results dramatically over the previous year, posting a net margin of $10.8 million on sales of $2.7 billion. In an effort to keep costs in check, a number of plants were closed, sold, or leased, as the company concentrated on cash management policies.

Into the mid-1990s, the trend toward fewer and larger dairy farms continued, and was reflected in AMPI's membership figures. Nevertheless, AMPI's dominant position among dairy suppliers remained intact. And the co-op will probably retain its leading position as long as dairy farms continue to exist in sufficient numbers for cooperation to make sense.

Principal Subsidiaries: AMPI Investment Corporation; Northland Foods Cooperative, Inc.

Further Reading:

"Associated Milk Charged with Monopoly in 14-State Area by Justice Department," *Wall Street Journal,* February 2, 1972, p. 6.

"Associated Milk Offers to Settle U.S. Antitrust Suit," *Wall Street Journal,* June 21, 1974, p. 2.

Blair, Jess F., "New Mexico Dairy Plant to Open Soon," *Feedstuffs,* June 29, 1992, p. 11.

Clark, Edward, "AMPI Shows $12 Million Loss in 1992," *Feedstuffs,* April 12, 1993, p. 7.

"Ex-Dairy Co Op Aide Admits Conspiracy to Bribe Connally in Milk-Price Matter," *Wall Street Journal,* August 1, 1974, p. 3.

Falk, Carol H., "Connally Is Acquitted of Bribery Charge and Indicates He May Return to Politics," *Wall Street Journal,* April 18, 1975, p. 5.

"Large Milk Co Op Assessed by I.R.S.," *New York Times,* April 14, 1976, p. 59.

McMenamin, Michael, and Walter McNamara, *Milking the Public,* Chicago: Nelson-Hall, 1980.

"Milk Co Op Aide Pleads Guilty to Clearing Campaign Gifts to Humphrey and Others," *Wall Street Journal,* July 24, 1974, p. 8.

Naughton, James M., "Connally Acquitted of Bribery Charge; Hints He May Resume Political Career," *New York Times,* April 18, 1975, p. 1.

Otto, Alison, and Jerry Dryer, "Movers and Shakers," *Dairy Foods,* April 1987, p. 41.

Shaffer, Richard A., "How a Big Dairy Co Op Helps Farmers Despite Legal Woes and Industry Slump," *Wall Street Journal,* November 5, 1974, p. 32.

—Robert R. Jacobson

Associated Natural Gas Corporation

370 17th Street, Suite 900
Denver, Colorado 80202
U.S.A.
(303) 595-3331
Fax: (303) 595-0480

Public Company
Incorporated: 1983 as Natural Gas Associates
Employees: 708
Sales: $1.47 billion
Stock Exchanges: New York
SICs: 4923 Gas Transmission and Distribution

Associated Natural Gas Corporation (ANG) is one of the largest independent natural gas companies in the United States. ANG is involved in virtually every phase of the natural gas business, including purchasing, gathering, processing, transportation, and marketing. The company purchases gas from a number of major and independent producers, then gathers and processes it using company-owned pipelines and processing plants. The gas is then sold to industrial end-users, local distribution companies, or wholesalers. ANG also handles natural gas liquids (NGLs) and crude oil. In 1993, the company owned about 8,000 miles of pipeline, and had gathering, processing, or transmission facilities in nine southern and southwestern states: Alabama, Arkansas, Colorado, Kansas, Louisiana, Mississippi, New Mexico, Oklahoma, and Texas. These facilities included 32 natural gas gathering systems, 13 natural gas processing plants, five fractionation facilities for NGLs (where NGLs are separated into component products such as ethane, propane, or butane), and two NGL transmission pipelines. Well over 7,000 producing wells are connected to the ANG system. The company processed, marketed, or gathered 1.21 billion cubic feet of natural gas daily in 1993. In addition, ANG transported 24,400 barrels of NGLs and transported and traded more than 61,000 barrels of crude oil each day during that year.

ANG began as a partnership under the name Natural Gas Associates (NGA) in 1983. Cortlandt S. Dietler, who had started the Western Crude oil company in the mid-1960s and successfully ran it until 1980 when he sold it to Getty Oil, recognized in the early 1980s that the role of natural gas as an energy source in the United States would increase dramatically in the coming years. He established NGA to take advantage of the changes that were occurring in the oil and gas industry, both in regulation and in the market. Changes in regulations for the natural gas industry made it easier for companies to gain access to interstate pipelines for transporting natural gas owned by others. Dietler noted that gathering, processing, and marketing were functions essential to both producers and end-users of natural gas. He hoped that the new company would prosper through its ability to react more quickly than its larger, plodding rivals to the industry's shifting demands.

Natural Gas Associates' first natural gas processing and gathering system went into operation in March 1983. The company processed its first cubic foot of natural gas at a plant near Kersey, Colorado. The plant, with a daily capacity of 10 million cubic feet, was part of a system 18 miles long connected to 22 natural gas wells. Continuous drilling and the construction of hundreds of miles of additional pipeline expanded the company's Colorado system greatly over the next few years.

The company's survival, however, was tied to the aggressive marketing employed by Dietler and his associates. When the system's natural gas volume began to exceed the needs of the local utility companies, NGA mounted its first serious marketing effort, initially using the yellow pages as its source for potential customers. As most companies struggled to stay afloat while demand for fuel decreased and supply grew in the industry, NGA was able to sustain its early growth through the mid-1980s. Largely thanks to Dietler's reputation and marketing savvy, NGA managed to expand through several acquisitions. In 1986, the company purchased the Colorado Gathering & Processing Corporation, a subsidiary of Wichita Industries. The Colorado Gathering system was adjacent to NGA's own Colorado operation, and was therefore easily assimilated into its existing system. NGA was also active in the mid-continent region in 1986, purchasing two parallel pipelines in Oklahoma at a Federal Bankruptcy Court auction. The lines, which ran between the towns of Cyril and Duncan, were then connected to several other pipeline systems, enabling the company to offer gas redelivery service to producers in the gas- and oil-rich Anadarko Basin. One result of this acquisition was the formation of the company's ATTCO Pipeline Company subsidiary. ATTCO (from Associated Transport and Trading Company) Pipeline was created to operate the crude oil gathering system that arose from one half of that purchase. Adjacent crude oil gathering systems were later bought from Phillips, Shell, Sun, and Mobil, transforming the system into a sprawling 900-mile chain of facilities covering a good chunk of southern Oklahoma and north Texas.

By 1987, NGA had annual sales of $85.3 million and net income of $1.1 million. More acquisitions came during that year. In February, NGA acquired the Minden gas gathering and processing plant in northern Louisiana, giving the company more of a presence in the Gulf Coast area. The Pantera gathering system, adjacent to the company's existing Colorado operations, was purchased in October from Pantera Energy Corporation.

In 1988, the company more than doubled its revenue to $189 million, and it went public with an initial stock offering. Around the same time, the company's name was changed to Associated Natural Gas Corporation (ANG). As ANG, the company's program of expansion through acquisitions continued at a brisk pace. Among the year's purchases were the Wilcox gas processing plant in Lavaca County, Texas, and an associated natural gas liquids pipeline. The Wilcox plant, with a capacity of 235 million cubic feet per day, processed gas gathered by the Texas Eastern Transmission Company's system. The following year, ANG bought the Milfay gathering and processing system in Creek County, Oklahoma, giving the company a solid presence in the eastern part of that state. This foothold was bolstered over the next few years by the acquisitions of several neighboring systems, including those of ARCO, Silver City, Patriot, Texaco, Blue Bell, Sand Springs, Conoco, and Triok. The addition of those systems enabled ANG to quadruple the amount of gas put through the Milfay plant.

Further acquisitions followed as ANG entered the 1990s. In 1990, the company purchased natural gas gathering systems from Galaxy Energies Inc. and AD-AM Gas Company. Both systems were located in Alabama's Black Warrior Basin, covering Pickens, Fayette, and Lamar Counties. ANG's revenue took another leap for the year, reaching $292 million, and the company recorded a $3.3 million profit, compared to a small deficit the previous year. ANG prospered in 1991. The company's Mid Continent Division took a giant leap forward by merging 940 miles of gas gathering pipelines from MEGA Natural Gas Company into its own operations in the Anadarko Basin and eastern Oklahoma. Major strides were made in Colorado as well. ANG bought Panhandle Eastern Corporation's Wattenberg System, consisting of over 1,200 miles of pipeline and eight compressor stations in the Denver-Julesberg basin, for $48 million. From Apache Corporation, ANG purchased the Spindle field pipeline gathering and gas processing facilities in Adams and Weld Counties, Colorado for $34 million. The producing part of this purchase was then sold off to other companies. With these purchases, ANG's pipeline system in Colorado was stretched to 1,350 miles, helping boost the company's net income to over $10 million, on sales of $636 million, for 1991.

During 1992, the company expanded operations in all of its major areas of activity. In Colorado, the company added 200 miles of gas gathering lines and two processing plants near its existing Wattenberg operations by purchasing all of the gas processing and gathering properties of Gerrity Oil & Gas Corporation. But most of ANG's activity in 1992 was concentrated in Oklahoma, where the company consolidated its system in the eastern part of the state with gathering and processing facilities acquired from Triumph, Finlay, and Philips Petroleum. The Philips purchase alone added 1,900 miles of natural gas pipeline. In addition, purchases of competing systems from ARCO and Exxon boosted the company's operations in the Arkoma Basin, initially acquired in the MEGA merger.

ANG sustained its momentum through 1993. In June, the company acquired a gas gathering system in the final stages of construction from Evergreen Resources, Inc. The system, initially 37 miles long, connected Evergreen production sites to pipeline owned by El Paso Natural Gas Company. Around the same time, ANG announced the joint formation, with Evergreen, of ANGI Ltd., a gas marketing company to operate in the United Kingdom. A few months later, ANG beefed up its Gulf Coast operations with the $32.5 million purchase of four natural gas pipeline systems, plus certain contractual gas storage rights, from Endevco Inc. Among the properties involved were the Ada gathering system in Louisiana and the Chalybeate Springs pipeline system in Louisiana and Arkansas. Those two systems together gather 70,000 million cubic feet of gas per day. The purchase also included the Leaf River pipeline system and other properties in Mississippi, totaling 547 miles of pipeline.

The company continued to expand through acquisitions in 1994. In July, the company merged with Grand Valley Gas Company. Grand Valley, based in Salt Lake City, Utah, had facilities for gathering and processing in New Mexico, Kansas, Texas, Oklahoma, Wyoming, and Utah. A new wholly-owned subsidiary, Associated Gas Services, Inc., was formed at the same time to combine the existing marketing activities of Grand Valley and ANG.

If ANG's influence in the oil and gas industry is tied to its record of growth, the company appears poised to assume an important role in whatever new form the industry ends up taking. As the U.S. oil and gas industry has reshaped itself, ANG's consistent program of expansion through acquisitions and new construction has strengthened the company's industry position.

Principal Subsidiaries: Associated Natural Gas, Inc.; Associated Transport and Trading Company; Associated Interstate Pipeline Company; Associated Intrastate Pipeline Company; Associated Louisiana Intrastate Pipeline Company; ATTCO LA Company; ATTCO NGL Pipeline Company; ATTCO Pipeline Company; AIM Pipeline Company; ANGI Ltd.; Associated Natural Gas (U.K.) Ltd.; Associated Gas Services, Inc.

Further Reading:

"Associated Acquires System," *Oil Daily,* June 4, 1993, p. 5.
"Firms File Merger Statement," *Oil Daily,* April 19, 1994, p. 2.
"Panhandle Eastern Pipeline," *Wall Street Journal,* July 12, 1991, p. C13.
"Pipeline Systems Sold," *Oil Daily,* September 15, 1993, p. 5.

—Robert R. Jacobson

BarclaysAmerican Mortgage Corporation

5032 Parkway Plaza Boulevard
Charlotte, North Carolina 28217-1962
U.S.A.
(704) 357-7600
Fax: (704) 357-7625

Wholly Owned Subsidiary of BarclaysAmerican Corporation
Incorporated: 1984
Employees: 700
Total Assets: $500 million
SICs: 6162 Mortgage Bankers

BarclaysAmerican Mortgage Corporation is one of the largest home loan servicers in the United States. The company is a unit of BarclaysAmerican Corporation, which is in turn a subsidiary of the giant British banking empire Barclays PLC. Mortgage servicers act as middlemen between borrowers and investors. They generally receive fees for collecting monthly loan payments and then passing them along to investors as securities. They often perform other administrative services such as insurance payments and tax management. In the mid-1990s, BarclaysAmerican serviced somewhere in the range of $30 billion in mortgages.

BarclaysAmerican Mortgage Corporation was formed in 1984 as a way for BarclaysAmerican Corporation to break into mortgage lending, an area into which it had sought to expand. The new firm was based in Charlotte, North Carolina, where the headquarters of its parent company were also located. Lee Shelton was named company president. Barclays' move to create a U.S. mortgage company came at a time when a number of large companies, including General Motors Acceptance Corporation (GMAC) and American Can Co., were moving into the once sparsely populated field. BarclaysAmerican hoped to take advantage of its high name recognition among home buyers, to whom it would market itself directly and more aggressively than traditional mortgage brokers.

By 1985, BarclaysAmerican Mortgage had five offices, all located in the South (Virginia, South Carolina, Tennessee, and North Carolina). That number was tripled later in the year with the acquisition of Northwestern Mortgage Co., a subsidiary of Northwestern Financial Corporation, also based in the Charlotte area. Northwestern Mortgage brought with it a mortgage servicing portfolio worth approximately $600 million.

Besides the South, six other regional "hubs" across the United States were identified as targets for the company's expansion. BarclaysAmerican Mortgage continued to grow both in size and geographical scope through the second half of the 1980s, primarily by acquiring smaller mortgage servicers. The company ranked 98th in size among mortgage companies in the United States by the end of 1987 according to a survey by *American Banker.* Over the next year, BarclaysAmerican's mortgage servicing portfolio grew to $2.8 billion, and it moved up in rank to 77th by the same annual survey.

By the middle of 1989, BarclaysAmerican Mortgage had doubled its number of offices to 20, including branches in Florida, Kentucky, and Ohio in addition to its initial core states. During the one year period ending in June 1989, the company nearly tripled the size of its servicing portfolio with several acquisitions. The most significant of these was the $28 million purchase of Merrill Lynch Realty Inc.'s mortgage servicing portfolio, which represented the rights to manage about $989 million in mortgage loans. That acquisition lifted the value of Barclays-American's portfolio to about $6 billion.

As the 1990s began, BarclaysAmerican Mortgage continued gain ground on its larger competitors. Interestingly, this ongoing expansion was taking place at a time when its ultimate parent company, Barclays PLC, was more or less withdrawing from the consumer banking business in the United States. This withdrawal included the sale of BarclaysAmerican Financial, its consumer finance unit, to Primerica Corporation. Nevertheless, BarclaysAmerican broke into the top 20 among U.S. mortgage servicers in 1990, after ending 1989 ranked 54th according to *American Banker,* with a portfolio totaling $6.7 billion. Several more purchases contributed to this ascent. One such deal was the acquisition of $1 billion in servicing rights from ComFed Bancorp, a company with headquarters in Lowell, Massachusetts.

However, the relationship forged around 1990 with Norwest Mortgage Inc. of Des Moines, Iowa, proved most vital to establishing BarclaysAmerican as a major powerhouse in the mortgage industry. That year, BarclaysAmerican signed a three-year contract that brought the company most of the servicing rights on new loans made by Norwest. The arrangement benefited both companies immensely. Norwest could concentrate on lending, its major strength, while leaving the servicing to BarclaysAmerican, a specialist in that area. The Norwest deal represented a coup for BarclaysAmerican, in that the company essentially stole a major customer from GMAC, the former servicer for much of Norwest's new loan business.

With a steady inflow of servicing business from the rapidly growing Norwest, BarclaysAmerican's own growth accelerated even more. In the second half of 1990 alone, the dollar value of the company's servicing portfolio grew by 56 percent, to $17 billion. The new rush of growth also enabled BarclaysAmerican to become the second largest issuer of Government National Mortgage Association (Ginnie Mae) securities, after finishing 1989 ranked 31st. The Ginnie Mae securities were often issued as part of a transaction begun by a government-insured loan originated by Norwest. The loans would then serve as collateral for the securities, and BarclaysAmerican would retain the servicing rights on the loans after issuing the securities.

In 1991, Shelton resigned from BarclaysAmerican in order to take part in a newly-formed mortgage firm in Columbia, South Carolina. Michael Prior, an executive vice-president at the parent company's New York office, was selected to take over as chief executive officer of the mortgage subsidiary. By the middle of that year, the company's mortgage servicing portfolio had grown to about $20 billion. In addition, a shift had begun to take place in the balance between government and conventional mortgage servicing. As much as 95 percent of BarclaysAmerican's business had been government servicing in 1987. By 1991, government servicing accounted for only 40 percent of the company's total.

BarclaysAmerican's rank among U.S. home loan servicers rose to 12th by the end of 1992. The value of the company's portfolio by that time was about $28 billion. In early 1993, Prior left the CEO spot at BarclaysAmerican Mortgage to take a position at the New York office as managing director of global services. He was replaced by David Beal, who had served as president of Norwest in the early 1980s, when that company was the nation's number two mortgage servicer. The change in corporate leadership at BarclaysAmerican was accompanied by further strategic moves, as the company began preparing to work more closely with Barclays de Zoete Wedd (BZW), another arm of the sprawling Barclays empire. The plans called for BarclaysAmerican to step up its production of high-balance mortgages. BZW would then pass the loans on to investors in the form of securities.

BarclaysAmerican unveiled a new product in late 1993—a home loan that could be transferred to a subsequent buyer of the home. Under the new program's terms, a new buyer could assume the mortgage as long as he or she met the same financial conditions as the original homeowner. The main advantage of this type of assumable mortgage was that a buyer could lock in at a particular interest rate, a major benefit in the event of a hike in lending rates. The company's initial assumable mortgage deal was a 30-year fixed-rate assumable mortgage. Its interest rate was slightly higher than that of conventional home loans. This sort of arrangement also benefitted the servicing company. Since an assumable mortgage tended to have a longer life, greater servicing fees were generated over time. The value of the servicing rights for these loans was therefore increased. Consistent with earlier announced plans, the program was to be securitized through BZW.

Further Reading:

Adams, Jerry, ''Barclays Takes Aim at Mortgage Market with Web of Regional Lending Offices,'' *American Banker,* September 24, 1985, p. 6.
''Boardroom View,'' *Mortgage Banking,* March 1991, p. 9.
Cline, Kenneth, ''Barclays Unit Charts Steady Growth in Mortgage Servicing,'' *American Banker,* May 25, 1990, p. 10.
Roosevelt, Phil, ''Barclays American Buys Merrill's Mortgage Rights,'' *American Banker,* June 28, 1989, p. 2; ''With Norwest Deal, Barclays Unit Surging,'' *American Banker,* January 30, 1991, p. 6; ''A Top Banker Returns to Lead Barclays Unit,'' *American Banker,* January 29, 1993, p. 9.
Saft, James H., ''Barclays Offers Assumable Loan,'' *American Banker,* November 12, 1993, p. 11.

—Robert R. Jacobson

Bayerische Motoren Werke AG

Petuelring 130, BMW Haus, D-8000
Munich 40
Germany
(089) 3895-0
Fax: 38 95.8858

Public Company
Incorporated: 1917
Employees: 71,034
Sales: DM29.01 billion
Stock Exchanges: Vienna Berlin Stuttgart Bremen Düsseldorf
    Frankfurt Hamburg Hanover Munich
SICs: 3711 Motor Vehicles & Car Bodies; 5012 Automobiles
    & Other Motor Vehicles; 3751 Motorcycles, Bicycles &
    Parts

Bayerische Motoren Werke AG, popularly known as BMW, is a
global manufacturer and marketer of luxury automobiles. However, the company was not always known as a car maker. It was
originally an aircraft engine manufacturer and was also a major
producer of motorcycles. Competing in the luxury car and
motorcycle market, BMW enjoyed vigorous sales during the
1980s, but faced a host of problems during the 1990s, as
conditions in the European automobile industry and manufacturing problems peculiar to Germany threatened to diminish the
company's once-stalwart position. In 1994, BMW purchased
Rover Group Ltd., a British manufacturer of luxury sport-utility
vehicles, which substantially improved the company's chances
for a return to the profitable 1980s and the likelihood of a robust
twenty-first century.

Although not officially established until 1917, BMW can trace
its heritage back to 1913 when Karl Rapp started to build
aircraft engines for Austria in anticipation of World War I.
Rapp-Motorenwerke's top customer was Franz Josef Popp,
general inspector of Emperor Franz Josef's army. Popp hired
Max Friz, an aircraft engine designer from Austro-Daimler;
together in Munich they established Bayerische Werke based on
the engineering ideas of Rapp.

Popp, an engineer, took charge of administration while Friz
served as senior designer. A third associate, Camillo Castiglioni
from Vienna, looked after the accounts. The trio began their
enterprise at the old Rapp factory, then moved to the Moosacher

Strasse factory, also in Munich, in 1918. There, Friz designed
and built the company's first aircraft engine.

At the end of the war, Bayerische Motoren turned to the
production of train brakes, and when in 1922 the Moosacher
Strasse factory was sold to Knorr-Bremse, BMW employees
moved to another Munich location, the former Ottowerke plant
on the Lerchenauer Strasse. (Ottowerke had been founded by
Gustav Otto, son of Nikolaus August Otto, inventor of the four-
stroke internal combustion engine.)

Despite the 1923 Treaty of Versailles' ban on aircraft production in Germany, Bayerische Motoren continued to operate and
thrive. Their 12-cylinder engines were used on international
flights by ace pilots such as Lpuschow, Gronau, and Mittelholzer, and more than a thousand BMW VI engines were sold to
the Soviet Union. Production continued to rise steadily through
the 1930s.

The company's interests in motorcycle manufacture developed
rapidly in the early 1920s. The first model, the R32, consisted of
a flat twin engine and drive shaft housed in a double-tube frame,
with valves in an inverted arrangement to keep the oil clean.
Ernst Henne, riding an R32, broke the world motorcycle speed
record at 279.5 kph (173.35 mph) in 1929; his record held until
1937.

In 1928, Bayerische Motoren acquired the ailing Fahrzeugwerke Eisenach, and a year later the Dixi, BMW's first luxury
car, was produced at the Eisenach site. The Dixi won the 1929
International Alpine Rally, covering the mountain route in five
days. But despite its success, the Dixi created major financial
problems for BMW, and a merger with Daimler-Benz was
discussed in detail. Meanwhile, a partnership contract was
agreed; Dr. Wilhelm Kissel, Daimler-Benz's chairperson, and
Popp, at Bayerische Motoren, joined each other's supervisory
boards. However, a smaller 6-cylinder model of the Dixi proved
to be a most effective competitor in the Daimler-Benz market,
and Popp dropped the merger plans.

Another Dixi, the DA2, based on the 6-cylinder model, was
introduced in Berlin in July 1929. It featured improved handling, better brakes, and a more attractive interior. Despite the
stock market crash in October 1929 and the subsequent depression (17,000 German firms were forced into bankruptcy, including one of Bayerische Motoren's shareholders, the Danat-Bank)
the company avoided financial disaster. 5,390 DA2s, the "mini
car at a mini price," were sold in 1929; this was increased the
following year to 6,792 cars.

When Hitler assumed power in 1933, Bayerische Motoren,
along with other German automotive companies, was required
to manufacture airplane engines for the new air force, the
Luftwaffe. In the same year, BMW acquired licenses to produce
the 525 bhp Hornet engine and to develop small radial engines
for sports planes. The company also launched its 300 automobile series with the 303, the first car to feature the long-familiar
"kidney" shape. Lighter than comparable models, the 303 was
50 percent more powerful. Its success encouraged BMW to
introduce two popular compact sports models, the 315 and the
319. Early in 1936, the 326 model was launched in both sedan
and convertible versions. The all-steel bodied 327 was also
introduced that year, and in September Popp unveiled the stan-

dard-production 328, which proved to be the fastest sports car of its time; it won the Italian Mille Miglia race in 1938.

The company's rising production of aircraft engines and armored motorcycles resulted in an expansion of facilities at the Milbertshofen plant on the Lerchenauer Strasse, which had previously been devoted to motorcycle manufacturing. A 1939 edict of the German Ministry of Aviation required Brandenburgische Motorenwerke to merge with Bayerische Motoren, and a new factory, Allach, was constructed with government money. The Allach buildings, tucked away in woods near Munich, were constructed at a distance from one another to minimize damage in the event of an air raid.

BMW played an important role in the German war effort and at the height of Nazi domination the company operated plants as far afield as Vienna and Paris. In two crucial areas of military technology, BMW was in the vanguard: with the guidance of Dr. Hermann Oestrich of the German aviation test center, the company developed the 003, the first jet engine to enter standard production; and under conditions of intense secrecy, it opened a rocket testing and production plant at Zuhlsdorf.

Intent on maintaining a plentiful supply of military aircraft, the Nazi government instructed Bayerische Motoren in 1941 to halt all motor car production. Popp, who had been at the company helm for 25 years, refused. He was forced to resign and narrowly avoided internment in a concentration camp. It was left to his successor, Fritz Hille, to institute Bayerische Motoren's automatic system of monitoring production—a mechanical forerunner of the computer.

After the defeat of the Nazis, Allied Command ordered the dismantling of many BMW facilities; at the same time, reconstruction of the now-divided Germany got underway. In the immediate postwar years, few West Germans were in a position to buy cars, but by 1948, the year of German currency reform, there was a substantial need for motorcycles. BMW produced a new model out of spare parts provided by dealers. Known as the R24, this motorcycle was put into production and in 1949 almost 10,000 machines came off the assembly line. 1950's production increased to 17,000, 18 percent of which were exported.

Bayerische Motoren's return to car manufacturing in 1951 proved to be a disappointment. The 501 model, a 6-cylinder conservatively styled car with few technical innovations, was not well received; neither was its successor, the 502, which featured a V8 engine. The company pinned its hopes on the 503 and 507 models, highlights of the 1955 Frankfurt Motor Show. Both cars were designed by Albrecht Graf Goertz and were powered by Alex von Falkenhausen engines. However, they proved to be too expensive for the majority of West German motorists. To add to BMW's woes, their motorcycle sales dropped drastically, and the Allach factory had to be sold.

The company's fortunes revived a little in the late 1950s during the era of the "bubble car." Their Isetta mini-car, a mere 2.29 meters (7.51 feet) in length and fitted with motorcycle engines, reached a speed of 53 mph. Customer interest in the machine was short-lived, but it enabled BMW to recoup some of its recent losses.

To capitalize on the increasing market for cars—albeit inexpensive ones—Bayerische Motoren introduced the rear-engined 700 LS model in August 1959. Available as a coupé or convertible, and powered by motorcycle engines, the 700 LS was initially unprofitable. By 1965, however, when annual sales reached 18,000 units, the car had become the company's first long-term success of the postwar years.

BMW's fortunes further improved with the launching of their 1500 model. Indeed, this first ''sports sedan'' secured the company's prominence in the automotive market for the foreseeable future. The balance sheet showed a profit of DM 3.82 million in 1963 and a 6 percent dividend was paid. By the end of the decade, the company's long-suffering shareholders were much happier. Nine more models had been introduced, sales for 1969 set a new record of 144,788 cars, and turnover was up to DM 1.4 billion.

The 1970s, a period of dramatic growth in Western Europe, proved to be a time of significant reorganization and development at BMW. All motorcycle production was moved to West Berlin, a new plant was opened, the popular 520 sports sedan was launched (1972), the Dingolfing plant in Lower Bavaria was further expanded (providing jobs for 15,000 farmworkers), and following the establishment of the European Economic Community, BMW subsidiaries were set up in member countries. Halfway through the decade, a U.S. importing, marketing, distribution, and support subsidiary was formed in Montvale, New Jersey, and later in the 1970s the company built a car plant at Steyr in Austria.

Early in the 1970s, it appeared that Bayerische Motoren's interests in motor racing, operated by BMW Motorsport GmbH, might be curtailed; in fact, however, the company was able to expand its racing activities. For some years, BMW had been the leading producer of racing car engines in the classification known as Formula 2; the company now decided to compete in the Formula 1 market as well. Success was swift. In 1975, Nelson Piquet won the Formula 1 World Championship in a BMW-powered Brabham. This was the first turbo-charged engine to win in the 34-year history of Formula 1 racing.

The Steyr plant in Austria commenced operation in the early 1980s as a producer of turbo-charged diesel engines. By the mid-1980s, the factory was a major petrol engine manufacturer and at full capacity could turn out 150,000 engines a year. Another factory, at Spandau in West Berlin, opened in the spring of 1984 to make BMW's new four-cylinder, watercooled K series of motorcycles. This machine won the January 1985 Paris-Dakar Rally, the world's toughest and longest off-road race. The company's motorcycles won this rally four times in its first six years.

BMW's car sales during the 1970s and 1980s increased along with the demand for higher-priced models, and healthy domestic sales were enhanced by the successes of foreign subsidiaries. In 1984, for example, BMW of North America sold 71,000 cars. On the other hand, motorcycle sales suffered. High unemployment, high interest rates, and loan restrictions decreased the purchasing power of a crucial motorcycle market—young Europeans; and competition from Japan became fierce.

As the company entered the 1990s, competition from Japanese car manufacturers represented perhaps the greatest threat to BMW's future growth, although high German labor costs continued to be a perennial problem. Adopting design characteristics from European luxury models, the Japanese produced cars of similar quality, yet sold the cars at substantially lower prices than those offered by European manufacturers, including BMW. Exacerbating BMW's woes, economic conditions in Europe soured during the early 1990s, portending dismal financial results for the coming years. However, despite these ominous developments, BMW entered the decade in sound shape. BMW exhibited a vitality few other European car manufacturers could muster, thanks to robust sales during the 1980s and comparatively small debt. In this regard, BMW was the exception rather than the norm in a troubled European automobile industry. However, the 1990s promised to be a much different decade than the 1980s, when luxury items and luxury cars sold extremely well, and as the company charted its future it braced itself for less profitable times.

As the recession increased its intensity, BMW's financial performance suffered, but not to the extent that other European manufacturers exhibited. The most glaring decline in the company's growth took place at its U.S. operations, where the Japanese struck their first blow in the luxury car market, and the German mark's strength against the dollar slowed sales and squeezed profit margins. By 1992, BMW of North America was recording a 50 percent decline in sales from the subsidiary's peak years in the mid-1980s. BMW management regarded the American situation as boding ill for its European operations. To strengthen its position in the United States, the company announced plans that year to construct an approximately $300 million assembly plant near Spartanburg, South Carolina, which, through the plant's state-of-the-art equipment, was designed to produce 72,000 cars a year. Half of this annual production volume the company planned to export overseas, which lessened BMW's dependence on its domestic production facilities and the associated high labor costs of German workers.

In 1993, von Kuenheim ended his 23-year reign at BMW and was replaced by Bernd Pischetsrieder, who had spent his entire career at BMW. Under Pischetsrieder's stewardship, BMW concluded a momentous acquisition that promised to dramatically change the company's future and bolster its position worldwide. In January 1994, less than a year after gaining control of BMW, Pischetsrieder announced the acquisition by BMW of Rover Group Ltd., the esteemed British manufacturer of sport-utility vehicles. The purchase, a $1.2 billion deal, immediately doubled BMW's share of the European market to 6.4 percent and gave the company a prestigious presence in the sport-utility market, which was growing exponentially during the early 1990s. The purchase of Rover Group stunned the industry, particularly Honda Motor Company, which held the remaining 20 percent interest in the British car manufacturer and did not learn of BMW's purchase until three days before Pischetsrieder's announcement.

BMW's prospects after the acquisition of Rover Group were exceedingly and justifiably brighter. The merger brought together two of the few car manufacturers to generate profit in 1993 and gave BMW a much more diverse product line to match against the company's mounting competition. The most pressing task for BMW during the mid-1990s involved the consolidation of Rover Group into the company's existing corporate and manufacturing structure, the successful completion of which augured a more profitable future.

Principal Subsidiaries: BMW Ingenieur-Zentrum GmbH; BMW Rolls-Royce GmbH (50.5%); BMW Bank GmbH; BMW Maschinenfabrik Spandau GmbH; KONTRON GmbH; BMW Leasing GmbH; BMW Motorrad GmbH; BMW Fahrzeugtechnik GmbH; BMW INTEC Beteiligungs GmbH; BMW M GmbH; KONTRON Elektronik GmbH; BMW Motoren Gesellschaft m.b.H. (Austria); BMW Coordination Center N.V. (Belgium); BMW France S.A.; BMW (South Africa) (Pty) Ltd.; BMW Finance N.V. (Netherlands); BMW Austria Gesellschaft m.b.H.; BMW Overseas Enterprises N.V. (Curacao); BMW Holding AG (Switzerland); BMW (Schweiz) AG (Switzerland); BMW Holding AG (Switzerland); BMW Japan Corp.; BMW Holding Corporation (USA); BMW Ltd. (Great Britain); BMW Italia S.p.A.; BMW Iberica S.A. (Spain); BMW Australia Ltd.; BMW Belgium S.A.; BMW Canada Inc.; BMW Nederland B.V.; BMW Sverige AB (Sweden); BMW New Zealand Ltd.

Further Reading:

Flynn, Julia, "How BMW Zipped In—And Called Rover Right Over," *Business Week,* February 14, 1994, p. 44.
Kurylko, Diana T., "Profit Fell, BMW Discloses," *Automotive News,* January 31, 1994, p. 2.
Kurylko, Diana T., "10 Years of BMW Growth Stalling Now," *Automotive News,* March 29, 1993, p. 4.
Loeffelholz, Suzanne, "Kuenheim's Complaint; the BMW CEO Spurns the Japanese and Berates Washington, Wall Street and Detroit," *FW,* January 9, 1990, p. 26.
Marquardt, Stephan, "BMW's Bold Gamble: Buying Rover Makes BMW Twice as Big as Mercedes," *Automotive Industries,* April 1994, p. 44.
McElroy, John, "Why Can't Germany Compete?," *Automotive Industries,* August 1992, p. 22.
"Then There Were Seven," *The Economist,* February 5, 1994, p. 19.

—updated by Jeffrey L. Covell

**BECTON
DICKINSON**

Becton, Dickinson & Company

One Becton Road
Franklin Lakes, New Jersey 07417
U.S.A.
(201) 848-6800
Fax: (201) 847-6475

Public Company
Incorporated: 1906
Employees: 17,600
Sales: $1.39 billion
Stock Exchanges: New York
SICs: 3841 Surgical and Medical Instruments; 3069
   Fabricated Rubber Products, nec; 3842 Surgical
   Appliances and Supplies; 3845 Electromedical Equipment;
   2835 Diagnostic Substances

Becton, Dickinson & Company manufactures and markets medical supplies and devices and diagnostic systems for use by health care professionals, medical research institutions, and the general public. Products include infectious disease diagnostic kits and tests, needles and syringes, blades and scalpels, and gloves and blood collection products. The company's Bard Parker branded general surgery products and Beaver specialty surgery items dominated their respective markets in the early 1990s. With operations in the United States and 27 countries around the world, international business contributed 44 percent of Becton, Dickinson's 1993 sales and 32 percent of its operating income. Although the firm's stock performance has been characterized as ''boring,'' its emphasis on many of the basics of health care helped it face the vacillations of that industry in the early 1990s.

The company was founded in 1898 by two salesmen, Maxwell W. Becton and Fairleigh S. Dickinson, as a venture to manufacture medical thermometers. The enterprise remained a conservatively managed, family-run business throughout its first 50 years. Becton, Dickinson entered the affluent postwar years with a solid market share in medical supplies and was well prepared for a major expansion. The company recognized that its traditional approach to business would not be appropriate for the future. Therefore, in 1948, the sons of the founders, Henry P. Becton and Fairleigh Dickinson, Jr.—both astute businessmen—assumed managerial control of the company.

With Dickinson as chief executive officer and Becton serving in a variety of other capacities during the 1950s, Becton, Dickinson gradually expanded its product line. By 1964, over 8,000 products were being manufactured by Becton, Dickinson, including a broad line of medical supplies of superior diagnostic accuracy. The company divided its business into four operating divisions—medical health, laboratory, animal research and testing, and overseas sales. In the course of an acquisition program, Becton, Dickinson purchased Carworth Inc., the leading producer of laboratory mice, and several specialized research laboratories. Increasingly, however, Becton, Dickinson's strongest growth was experienced in the market for disposable items. In 1964, such products as disposable syringes and needles accounted for 60 percent of the company's $70 million in sales.

During the 1970s, Becton, Dickinson continued to make gains in the medical supplies business, despite increasingly difficult market conditions. The world oil crisis of 1973–74 caused a reduction in petrochemical feedstocks, which, in turn, made medical raw materials difficult to obtain. In addition, the Food and Drug Administration planned to adopt the same strict certification standards for diagnostic equipment as it had applied to pharmaceuticals. This would delay the commercial introduction of new products and, with technological advances, expose them to higher rates of obsolescence. Although these conditions lessened Wall Street's interest in companies in the medical industry, Becton, Dickinson remained highly optimistic. With sales figures doubling every five years and with 19 percent of all sales derived from overseas, Dickinson declared to shareholders that the company did not fear the impending device regulation, but instead was helping the FDA to formulate its new regulations.

When the FDA's Medical Device Act was enacted, Becton, Dickinson found, to some dismay, that 85 percent of its products were subject to the new regulation. Wesley J. Howe, who succeeded Dickinson as president and chief executive officer in 1974, was confident that the company's products would be able to meet all the new FDA requirements; to be sure, he hired a team of legal and technical experts to guarantee standardization.

Despite growing regulation, the early years of Howe's direction were marked by a continuity of policies; Howe was hand-picked by Dickinson and dedicated to the same conservative style of management. To increase efficiency, Howe automated and integrated more of the company's facilities and reduced his staff by 13 percent. In order to increase his influence, he also replaced 14 of the company's 17 division presidents.

Howe's leadership was proving highly effective. In one area, Becton, Dickinson's marketing approach was particularly effective: targeting insulin users through doctors, diabetes associations, camps, pharmacies, and pharmacy schools. With control of almost 100 percent of the insulin syringe market, Becton, Dickinson's sales increased to $456 million in 1975.

This success, however, was greatly compromised in the boardroom by Fairleigh Dickinson, who, despite having relinquished his posts voluntarily, continued to demand managerial control. At the heart of the matter was a conflict between family members determined to maintain control and board members who favored control by a more professional corporate elite. Although Howe remained above this conflict, several other important managers did not; ultimately, Dickinson would order Howe to fire them. In 1977, four board members resigned. With morale an increasingly serious problem, Howe asserted his position. Four new, "unprejudiced" board members were named to the board and Dickinson was relegated to the ceremonial post of chairman. But the power struggle was not over.

Dickinson was asked to approach the Salomon Brothers investment banking firm and initiate a study on a company Howe wanted Becton, Dickinson to acquire. When completed, the study warned of numerous problems with the takeover. Howe maintained that Dickinson had sabotaged the study and, when the situation proved unresolvable, ordered Dickinson removed from the payroll.

Dickinson then resorted to another strategy. With 4.5 percent of the company's stock, Dickinson authorized Salomon Brothers to line up additional investors to lead a takeover of Becton, Dickinson. A Salomon agent named Kenneth Lipper approached several companies, including Avon, American Home Products, Monsanto, and Squibb, in an effort to set up a takeover. Becton, Dickinson's attorneys warned Lipper that his action was illegal. Rather than call off the search for buyers, Lipper challenged the attorneys to stop him in court—cognizant that a well-publicized court battle would only gain more attention for his cause.

On January 16, 1978, before Lipper could be stopped, Becton, Dickinson learned that the Philadelphia-based Sun Oil Company, had acquired 34 percent of its stock. The transaction lasted only 15 minutes and involved 6.5 million shares at a purchase price of $45 each—well above the trading price of $33. Sun created a special subsidiary called LHIW (for "Let's Hope It Works") to manage the shares until a controlling majority of shares could be acquired.

The takeover had severe consequences. Like Becton, Dickinson, Sun had just emerged from an important battle against founding family interests. H. Robert Sharbaugh, chief executive officer of Sun, came into strong disagreement over the takeover with the founding Pew family and was eventually forced out of the company. Becton, Dickinson, in the meantime, learned that Sun's purchase had been conducted off the trading floor, in violation of numerous laws. Finally, three Becton, Dickinson shareholders sued Fairleigh Dickinson, complaining that they had been excluded from Sun's tender offer.

The New York Stock Exchange refused to file charges against Salomon and instead turned the matter over to the Securities and Exchange Commission. At this point, Sun decided to dispose of its interest in Becton, Dickinson and offered to indemnify Salomon against any liabilities resulting from court action. The legality of the takeover was no longer in question. Instead, the question concerned the manner in which Sun should dispose of its Becton, Dickinson shares. With Sun no longer in pursuit of Becton, Dickinson, the only clear beneficiaries of the takeover were the lawyers left to pick up the pieces.

Ironically, Sun and Becton, Dickinson had a common interest in the divestiture. If the 34 percent share were placed on the market in one parcel, share prices would plummet and Sun would lose millions. Becton, Dickinson, on the other hand, opposed summary disposal because large blocks of its shares could fall under the control of still other hostile acquisitors. An agreement was finally reached in December 1979, under which Sun would distribute a 25-year debenture convertible into Becton, Dickinson shares. The unprecedented agreement ensured both a gradual spin-off of Becton, Dickinson shares and the maintenance of stable share prices. Although the agreement was said to have cost Sun extremely large sums of money, it was satisfied with the arrangement.

Fairleigh Dickinson continued to seek injunctive relief from the SEC and remained under attack from Becton, Dickinson shareholders demanding the return of the $15 million profit from the original Sun tender offer. Sun's board at this time was nervously awaiting the response of its shareholders to the costly defense of Salomon Brothers. Around this time, American Home Products made a brief and uncharacteristic hostile bid for 2.5 percent of Becton, Dickinson—by comparison with Sun, a minor incident. Ironically, Sun's debenture scheme prevented any company from gaining greater control of Becton, Dickinson.

The first order of business after this debacle, according to Wesley Howe, was to position Becton, Dickinson for future growth. With company profits rising, Howe arranged to reinvest cash on hand into new projects. He reorganized the company into 42 units so that each division's performance could be more accurately scrutinized. Unprofitable operations, such as a computer parts manufacturer, were either sold or closed down. Older products were reassessed, and in some cases improved; for instance, insulin syringes were redesigned for more accurate dosages. Foreign sales were stepped up, and, despite a negative effect on earnings, an expansion of the product line was carried out. Whereas some new products were added by takeovers, others, such as the balloon catheter, were developed internally.

The expansion had been justified to ensure future viability, but by 1983 bad investments had cost the company $75 million—$23 million alone from a failed immuno-assay instrument division. Bad planning caused production stoppages and cost overruns. Howe then came under criticism for failing to invest heavily enough in research and development. With remedial measures in place, the company's financial condition had improved greatly by 1985. That year the company declared an $88 million profit on sales of $1.44 billion. Much of this turnaround, however, came from nonoperating profits resulting from the sale of unprofitable divisions and a reduction in overhead. Howe instituted a new strategy involving slower growth rates and raised productivity. To balance this more modest business plan, Howe allocated a 5.1 percent share of revenue to research and development, particularly for more cost-effective new products, and purchased a 12 percent share of a company that manufactured equipment for synthesizing DNA.

In the late 1980s, Becton faced increased competition on the domestic front, but continued to maintain its estimated 70 percent to 80 percent share of the needle and syringe market. Sales increased from $1.71 billion in 1988 to $2.47 billion in 1993 as Becton, Dickinson moved into many new global markets and accelerated new proprietary product introductions. The firm focused expansion efforts on Latin America, Asia-Pacific, and Europe. International sales rose 29 percent in 1988 alone, and by 1993, that segment contributed 44 percent of annual sales. Wesley Howe, who was credited by Robert Teitelman of *Financial World* with re-energizing Becton, Dickinson, retired that year and was supplanted by Raymond V. Gilmartin.

Becton, Dickinson introduced new drug delivery and blood handling products in the 1990s that helped reduce health care workers' exposure to acquired immune deficiency syndrome (AIDS) and hepatitis. Some of the company's newest diagnostic tests helped researchers and physicians determine when to begin drug therapy for cancer and AIDS patients. In 1993, the firm moved its PRECISE brand pregnancy test from the professional to the over-the-counter market. Becton, Dickinson's investment of 5.6 percent of its 1993 revenues represented a continuing accent on new product introductions.

As criticism of high health care costs accelerated in the early 1990s, the wisdom of Howe's shift to more cost-effective new product introductions became evident. Becton, Dickinson positioned its diagnostic tests as accurate, fast ways to reduce health care costs by speeding diagnosis and treatment. The firm also emphasized that its products were not discretionary, and expressed confidence in the security of its markets, despite uncertainty among health care companies generally. In fact, Gary Cohen, vice-president of marketing and development, noted in 1993's annual report, "Since volume, not price, drives our growth, expanded access to health care for the nation's uninsured . . . will further expand our business."

Principal Subsidiaries: Avandave Limited (Ireland); Bauer & Black, Inc.; BD Avac-medische Artikelen (Netherlands); Becton, Dickinson AcuteCare Holdings, Inc.; Becton, Dickinson Alaska, Inc.; Becton, Dickinson and Company, Ltd. (Ireland); Becton, Dickinson B.V. (Netherlands); Becton, Dickinson Diagnostics Inc.; Becton, Dickinson Distribution Center N.V. (Belgium); Becton, Dickinson Electronic Co.; Becton, Dickinson Fabersanitas S.A. (Spain); Becton, Dickinson - France, S.A.; Becton, Dickinson Hellas S.A. (Greece); Becton, Dickinson Overseas Services, Ltd.; Becton, Dickinson O.Y. (Finland); Becton, Dickinson Pty, Ltd. (Australia); Becton, Dickinson Research Corporation; Becton, Dickinson Vascular Access Inc.; Becton, Dickinson Worldwide, Inc.; Benex, Ltd. (Ireland); Cell Analysis Systems, Inc.; Collaborative Biomedical Products, Inc.; DWS, Inc.; JLI Leasing, Inc.; Johnston Laboratories, Inc.; MICROPETTE, Inc.; Valdeoliva, S.A. (Spain). The company also lists subsidiaries in the United Kingdom, Switzerland, Sweden, Germany, Panama, Canada, Columbia, Mexico, Singapore, Turkey, Brazil, British West Indies, Italy, Korea, Philippines, Malaysia, Thailand, Venezuela, Bermuda, and Japan.

Further Reading:

Teitelman, Robert, "The Devil and the Deep Blue Sea," *Financial World,* June 14, 1988, pp. 30–31.

—updated by April Dougal Gasbarre

Big Rivers Electric Corporation

P. O. Box 24
Henderson, Kentucky 42420
U.S.A.
(502) 827-2561
Fax: (502) 827-2561

Private Company
Incorporated: 1961 as Big Rivers Rural Electric Cooperative
  Corporation
Employees: 860
Total Assets: $1.18 billion
SICs: 4911 Electric Services

Big Rivers Electric Corporation is a cooperative engaged in providing electric power to over 80,000 customers in western Kentucky. Consisting of four member systems (Henderson-Union Electric Cooperative, Meade County Rural Electric Cooperative Corporation, Jackson Purchase Electric Cooperative Corporation, and Green River Electric Corporation), Big Rivers serves portions of 27 Kentucky counties and ranks third among all American power cooperatives in sales of kilowatt hours. Moreover, Big Rivers maintains over 11,000 miles of transmissions lines, through which electricity is channeled to local households and industrial facilities, including coal mines, paper mills, and aluminum smelters.

The origins of Big Rivers Electric may be traced to the mid-1930s, when Kentucky's first rural electric cooperative was founded. Although electric power had become available in most U.S. cities by this time, the country's farming communities were largely without the service. Only about ten percent of America's nearly 6.8 million farms had access to electric power by 1935. Lacking the convenience of electricity—which was used increasingly to power such new appliances as the washing machine and the radio—farm families also experienced severe losses of property and lives, due to the flammability of the kerosene on which they relied to fuel lamps.

Supplying the country's rural areas with electricity became a focus of relief projects in the aftermath of the Great Depression. On May 11, 1935, by order of President Franklin D. Roosevelt, the Rural Electrification Administration (REA) was formed as a division of the U.S. Department of Agriculture. The REA was a nonprofit agency dedicated to providing rural areas with inexpensive electric service. Through an initial investment of

$75,000 from the Emergency Relief Appropriation Act of 1935, as well as other subsequent government loans, the REA, according to Roosevelt's official executive order, sought ''to initiate, formulate, administer, and supervise a program of approved projects with respect to the generation, transmission, and distribution of electric energy in rural areas.''

The first company to provide electric power to rural Kentucky was the Henderson Electric Cooperative, founded in the northwestern county of Henderson on May 30, 1936. In October of that year, Henderson Electric began providing service to its first customer, Frank T. Street, who owned and operated the Cardinal Farms outside the city of Henderson. In June of 1937, the Rural Electric Cooperative Corporation (RECC) system in western Kentucky was expanded to include Meade County RECC, Union County RECC, and Green River RECC. The Union County co-op was later merged with Henderson Electric to form Henderson-Union RECC.

For more than 20 years, the western Kentucky co-ops obtained their electrical power from previously established utility companies that served cities and towns. Entering into agreements with these utilities for purchasing wholesale power, the co-ops retained responsibility for overseeing the transmission of electrical power to farming communities. During this time, much of rural Kentucky received electric power services, helping area farmers compete on a national level and helping residents realize a higher standard of living. However, the co-ops soon recognized that economies of scale could be achieved by constructing their own power plants and transmission lines, which would improve their services and decrease their service rates.

Toward that end, in 1961, representatives from the Henderson-Union, Green River, and Meade County RECCs held a meeting at which they agreed to establish a cooperative that would maintain its own electrical generation facility. The new organization was incorporated in November of that year under the name Big Rivers Electric Corporation, reflecting the fact that several large rivers ran through its service area.

After briefly considering a move to continue the practice of contracting for electricity through a new power plant near Owensboro, the founders of Big Rivers opted to proceed with their original plan of establishing an independent facility. Their proposal included the construction of a coal-fired power plant with a net capacity of 65 megawatts, as well as nearly 266 miles of transmission lines. Funding for the project was readily granted by the REA, which approved an $18 million loan to Big Rivers in July of 1962.

However, in seeking to obtain the required certificate of convenience and necessity from Kentucky's Public Service Commission (PSC), Big Rivers encountered resistance. Strong objections to the Big Rivers plan from existing utility companies compelled the PSC to schedule hearings on the matter. Specifically, utility companies—including Owensboro Municipal Utilities and Kentucky Utilities—argued that Big Rivers was proposing to serve an area already adequately supplied with power and that their plans for a new facility had been not been properly disclosed to the public.

Nevertheless, Big Rivers contracted with manufacturers for the boilers, turbines, and other machinery necessary for the power plant; since the company had yet to achieve PSC approval, these contracts all carried cancellation clauses. Moreover, Big Rivers designated a site for the plant in a location that would straddle the border of Henderson and Webster counties.

In September of 1962, the first in a series of PSC hearings was held. Subsequent hearings during the next six months resulted in PSC approval of the required certificate on April 5, 1963. Big Rivers had successfully argued that although adequate power was available in the area, the quality of service among existing utilities was unsatisfactory and the rates charged were exorbitant. Moreover, Big Rivers had procured several previously published articles on their plans as proof that they had not operated in secrecy. Although the opposing utilities filed an appeal, the PSC approval was eventually upheld in February 1965. The new Big Rivers power plant, which had been under construction for two years and had incurred costs of $11 million, was completed in October of 1965. Named the Robert A. Reid generating plant, after one of the Big Rivers founders, the facility became operational on January 1, 1966.

During this time, demand for electricity in western Kentucky was steadily increasing. Big Rivers' rural and small business market averaged an annual growth rate of more than ten percent. Furthermore, demand for electricity was augmented by the region's emerging aluminum industries, which maintained smelters and other facilities requiring large amounts of electricity. Such companies as Anaconda Aluminum and National Southwire were attracted to the competitive rates offered by Big Rivers. To service the power needs of National Southwire's aluminum smelter operations, as well as the mills of the National Aluminum Company, Big Rivers began construction on another facility, the Kenneth C. Coleman plant, situated in Hancock County on the banks of the Ohio River. Consisting of three separate units with a total net capacity of 455 megawatts, the Coleman plant became fully operational in 1972. Big Rivers also entered into an agreement to operate a new power plant constructed by the city of Henderson, Kentucky. The Henderson Municipal Power and Light Station Two was erected adjacent to Big Rivers' Robert A. Reid plant and consisted of two units, generating 315 megawatts, which became operational in 1973 and 1974.

Studies indicated that dramatic increases in the need for electric power in western Kentucky would continue well into the 1980s. According to a 1977 forecast, electricity usage among residences, farms, and small businesses in the Big Rivers service area was expected to realize a nearly ten percent annual growth rate into the late 1980s. In order to meet the projected demand, Big Rivers devised an aggressive plan for expansion that included building another major two-unit power plant. Located in Ohio County, Kentucky, and named after D. B. Wilson, who had served on the board of the Meade County RECC since 1966, the facility would increase the company's total capacity to 1,235 megawatts. Receiving loans from the REA, Big Rivers began construction on the Wilson plant in 1980, designating a completion date in 1984.

However, unexpected declines in the demand for electricity soon proved problematic. New studies indicated that demand had been overestimated by as much as seven percent. Moreover, economic recession in 1982 and 1983 led to severe slumps in

the American aluminum industry, a major Big Rivers customer. In 1981, Big Rivers was forced to terminate its plans for the second unit of the Wilson plant. Nevertheless, encouraged by Anaconda Aluminum's plans to purchase 100 megawatts of power for a new smelting operation, Big Rivers continued construction on the first unit of the Wilson plant. In addition, in 1984, the Jackson Purchase Electric Cooperative—a member of the Big Rivers co-op since 1977 serving the far western part of Kentucky around the city of Paducah—began purchasing its power from Big Rivers, as its purchase contract with another supplier expired.

However, as cooperatives marked the fiftieth anniversary of rural electrification in 1985, many such operations, including Big Rivers, encountered severe financial problems. Economic recession and slumps in the power industry had devastated many co-ops, which had much smaller client bases than did the urban utility companies; according to the REA, co-ops at that time averaged five customers per mile of transmission line, while public utilities reported nearly 50 customers per mile of line. Moreover, during this time, as part of an attempt to cut federal spending and the national deficit, the Reagan administration introduced a proposal to terminate the REA and discontinue its low-interest loan program for co-ops. Although the REA survived these efforts, the financial condition of the country's power co-ops remained weak. At Big Rivers, sales of the electricity generated by the Wilson plant were slow, creating an excess supply. Moreover, although construction of the Wilson plant had been completed in 1984 for under the budgeted amount, the company carried a heavy debt load, totaling $1.1 billion, with no apparent means of repayment. In January of 1985, Big Rivers defaulted on a $19 million payment on an REA loan, and a foreclosure suit against the company was filed by the U.S. Justice Department, an unprecedented move in the industry.

Later that year, Big Rivers was granted a reprieve from the foreclosure suit, which was suspended while the company strove to find a means of recovery. During this time, Big Rivers considered filing for bankruptcy or selling off its operations. The company also sought to implement rate increases, a plan that was ultimately rejected by the Kentucky PSC, which found that such increases would not be in the best interest of Big Rivers' largest customers, the struggling aluminum industries.

Denied the rate increases, Big Rivers encountered further problems when National Southwire petitioned the government for a decrease in the rates it was then paying to Big Rivers. The aluminum smelter argued that Big Rivers' rates were higher than those charged to any other aluminum producer and that, given the industry's heavy reliance on electric power during a period of strong foreign competition and weak domestic markets, these higher rates could eventually force National Southwire to close down. National Southwire was joined by Alcan Aluminum in its petition.

The aluminum companies' hearings continued for much of 1986–87, which proved particularly difficult years for Big Rivers, despite government audits determining that the co-op's rates were fair, given the economic distress in the industry, and that charges that Big Rivers general manager William Thorpe received an unreasonably high salary were unfounded. Still, Big

Rivers remained engulfed in heated negotiations over its proposed means of recovery. In March of 1987, the company's plans for rate increases and debt restructuring were again rejected by the PSC, which suggested that Big Rivers continue negotiations with the REA, its other creditors, and the aluminum companies. In response, the REA temporarily halted any further financing to all electric and telephone co-ops in Kentucky, a widely criticized move prompted by the agency's concern over the potential for similar default situations in the future.

By August of 1987, some resolutions were reached regarding the future of Big Rivers. First, the PSC finally approved a rate increase that would affect all Big Rivers customers, including the aluminum companies, which would be charged on a flexible rate basis reflecting fluctuations in the price of aluminum. Second, after making some revisions ordered by the PSC, Big Rivers arrived at an acceptable debt restructuring program, expected to save the company $1.2 billion in interest charges and other debt service fees. In September, Big Rivers implemented its first rate increase since 1981. That month, the company also completed its first debt refinancing of $250 million, which reportedly would result in annual savings of $900,000 for Big Rivers. Another refinancing, of a $319 million REA loan, was completed in February of 1988.

The following year, Big Rivers was granted a second rate increase, and although the aluminum companies again protested, negotiations resulted in a settlement. Having found a solution to its economic problems and having reached an agreement with National Southwire and Alcan, Big Rivers looked forward to more stable, prosperous years. A rate increase totaling $6.9 million, or about two percent per customer, was granted Big Rivers in 1990.

By 1991, the thirtieth anniversary of the company's incorporation, Big Rivers plants were generating over 1,700 megawatts of power and using nearly 5 million tons of coal annually in the process, bolstering sales among the mining companies of western Kentucky. Moreover, Big Rivers anticipated further rate increases to offset the costs involved in rehabilitating its facilities to comply with the Clean Air Act of 1990. Just as the company's economic condition appeared to be improving, however, a scandal began to emerge that would again prove challenging to the future of Big Rivers.

Prompted by a lawsuit involving bribery charges filed in 1991 by a Kentucky coal company against its top officials, a federal investigation of several individuals in western Kentucky and southern Indiana business communities was undertaken by the FBI and IRS. The following year, evidence surfaced targeting William Thorpe for accepting bribes from a mining company that had sought contracts to supply coal to Big Rivers. Although Thorpe denied the allegations, he was replaced as general manager at Big Rivers by Paul A. Schmitz, who had served the company for 15 years.

Criminal investigations and indictments involving Thorpe and several other local businessmen were ongoing in 1994. Moreover, a 1992–93 audit of Big Rivers performed by the PSC alleged that the co-op had overcharged its customers for electric service by a total of $13 million over the previous two years. Thus, Big Rivers faced the possibility of having to refund large amounts to its ratepayers, including area aluminum companies. Under the leadership of Schmitz, however, Big Rivers contested the allegations of overcharging and strove to keep the co-op afloat in order to continue providing electric power to rural western Kentucky.

Further Reading:

Chitlik, Alan, "The Politics of Power: Players Take Sides in Coming BREC Battle," *Messenger-Inquirer* (Owensboro, Kentucky), November 20, 1986.

Hayden, Maureen, "Big Rivers Fights $13 Million Refund," *The Evansville Courier,* August 6, 1994.

——, "Former Big Rivers Chief Indicted," *The Evansville Courier,* June 29 1994, pp. A1, A3.

Hershberg, Ben Z., "Big Rivers Granted Request for $6.9 Million Rate Hike," *Courier-Journal* (Louisville, Kentucky), December 22, 1990.

——, "Head of Big Rivers Electric Has Hopes for a Brighter Future," *Courier-Journal* (Louisville, Kentucky), March 31, 1986.

Koenig, Bill, "Anniversary Outlook for REMC Not So Golden," *Indianapolis Star,* June 14, 1985.

Matyi, Bob, "Big Rivers," *Courier and Press* (Evansville, Indiana), August 1, 1986.

The Progress of Power, Henderson, Kentucky: Big Rivers Electric Corporation, 1991.

—Tina Grant

The Body Shop International PLC

Watersmead Business Park
Littlehampton, W. Sussex BN17 6LF
England
903 717107
Fax: 903 726250

Public Company
Incorporated: 1976
Employees: 1,926
Sales: $666 million
Stock Exchanges: London
SICs: 5999 Retail Stores, Not Elsewhere Classified

The Body Shop International PLC is one of England's most successful retailers of cosmetics and personal care products, with over 1,100 stores in 45 countries. The company is best known for pioneering the natural-ingredient cosmetics market and establishing social responsibility as an integral part of company operations. In fact, The Body Shop has received more attention for its ethical stances, such as its refusal to use ingredients that are tested on animals, its monetary donations to the communities in which it operates, and its business partnerships with developing countries, than for its products. The company manufactures over 400 products; its most popular include its Colourings cosmetics, the Mother & Baby product line, and its Mostly Men products. Anita Roddick, founder of the company, has built this phenomenal success by flouting industry conventions. In 1991, *Business Week* quoted this cosmetic industry leader as saying: "We loathe the cosmetic industry with a passion. It's run by men who create needs that don't exist."

Roddick entered the industry in 1976 when she used £4,000 to open a small stand-alone shop of natural-ingredient cosmetics and personal care products. Her goal was to support herself and her two daughters while her husband, Gordon, spent two years riding horseback from Buenos Aires to New York. Her store design, product packaging, and marketing approach all originated from her need to economize. Roddick painted the walls dark green to hide cracks, rather than to suggest respect for the environment, and the award-winning clear plastic bottles were actually urine sample containers purchased from a local hospital. When Roddick's original supply of bottles ran out, and she did not have enough money to buy more, the Body Shop's famous refill policy was born.

Other hallmarks of the company were born during this frugal period. Handwritten labels, packed with product information, established the Body Shop's candid approach to customer relations. For example, one of the first products, a henna hair treatment, sported a label explaining that the product smelled like manure but was great for the hair. Also during this time, Roddick developed an aversion to advertising; not wanting to spend the time or money on advertising, she instead relied on press coverage to spread the word about the fledgling company.

Success came quickly; the first store thrived, and Roddick opened another before the company's first year was over. Returning home in 1977, Gordon Roddick joined his wife in the enterprise. They decided to franchise the operation during the company's second year, and by 1984 The Body Shop boasted 138 stores, 87 of which were located outside of the United Kingdom. Franchising outpaced the opening of company-owned stores over the years, until franchises accounted for 89 percent of Body Shop stores in 1994. The company's fast-paced development continued when it went public in April 1984. The Roddicks kept 27.6 percent of the company's stock, Gordon Roddick became company chairperson and the finances as well, and Anita Roddick continued as managing director, essentially determining the course the company would take.

During this time, Roddick decided to encourage and contribute to social and environmental change through her company. Although she first allied The Body Shop with established groups, such as Greenpeace, Amnesty International, and Friends of the Earth, she soon began her own campaigns, particularly ones that focused on recycling and ending animal testing in the cosmetics industry. Body Shops displayed posters and made petition sheets available to customers. By the mid-1990s, franchises were asked to support two to three campaigns a year, on such topics as AIDS education, voter registration, and animal testing in the cosmetics industry.

In 1987, Roddick began The Body Shop's Trade Not Aid program. Combining the company's need for exotic natural ingredients with its mission of social responsibility, the program established business partnerships with struggling communities. By purchasing such ingredients as blue corn from the Pueblo Indians in New Mexico and Brazil nut oil from the Kayapo Indians of the Amazon River Basin, the Trade Not Aid program avoided exploiting native peoples and helped developing countries earn money selling renewable resources rather than destroying their habitat. The Body Shop's ethical practices also included aiding communities close to home. For example, the soapmaking factory the company founded in Glasgow returned 25 percent of after-tax profits to the economically depressed city. The retail store in New York's Harlem established a policy of giving 50 percent of store profits to local community groups. Other charitable activities included donating £230,000 in 1991 to start a weekly newspaper to be sold by the homeless in London.

The Body Shop fared just as well publicly as it had privately. In its first eight years on the London Stock Exchange, its stock price rose 10,944 percent. Between November 1986 and November 1991, investors realized a 97.2 percent annual return. In 1991, sales were up 46 percent from the year before to $238.4 million; net profits were $26.2 million, up 71 percent from the previous year. The company's notoriety also increased dramatically. Profiles of Roddick appeared in numerous magazines, from *People* to *Forbes*. The company was cited in *Business Week* as a pioneer in marketing. The magazine explained The Body Shop's appeal as follows: "Typical Body Shoppers are at the back of the baby boom, a skeptical group. They distrust advertising and sales hype, demand more product information than their elders, and are loyal to companies they consider responsible corporate citizens."

The Body Shop opened its first stores in the United States in 1988; all were owned directly by the company. Deciding that the company needed to first adjust to the new market, particularly to selling in shopping malls, Roddick postponed franchising any stores until 1990. The first franchise opportunity prompted 2,000 applicants, whom Roddick screened through a written questionnaire, asking such unconventional questions as what books and movies the applicants liked and how they would want to die. "I want people who are politically aware and want a livelihood which is values-led," Roddick explained in *Working Woman.*

In the autumn of 1993, The Body Shop opened new headquarters in Raleigh, North Carolina, to help manufacture and distribute its U.S. product lines. The new facility was needed to reach and support the company's goal of 500 stores in the United States by the year 2000. Sales figures in 1994 supported that vision of aggressive growth. U.S. sales had grown by 47 percent in the first half of fiscal 1994 to $44.6 million, with profits up 63 percent to $1.9 million. However, Allan Mottus, a U.S. cosmetics industry consultant, warned in *Working Woman* that The Body Shop would have difficulty in the coming years: "Opening new doors is one thing. Sustaining business is another. Americans are not as brand-loyal as Europeans. They will look at products and price."

Such competition was already challenging The Body Shop by the mid-1990s, both in the United States and elsewhere. H2O Plus, Goodebodies, Bath & Body Works, Origins, and Garden Botanika were also offering natural products in simple packaging, but usually for a lower price. The company's two first major competitors appeared in 1990. That year, Estée Lauder Inc. introduced Origins, a product line with natural ingredients packaged in recycled containers. Leslie Wexner, owner of the Limited, opened Bath & Body Works in the United States in the fall of 1990; 18 months later he had 100 stores grossing $45 million. Although Roddick brushed off many of the U.S. lookalikes as too small to be a threat, she sued Wexner for copying her stores too closely. "It was becoming confusing between the two businesses," Gordon Roddick explained in *Working Woman,* noting that Body Shop customers "were bringing in Wexner's containers to be refilled." Roddick reports having settled with Wexner out of court. However, Bath & Body Works continued to pose a threat to The Body Shop in both the United States and England, where it opened its first shop in the fall of 1994.

In 1994, L'Oréal entered the natural-style product market with its Planet Ushuaia line of deodorants, shampoos, and other personal care products. Like Bath & Body Works, L'Oréal copied the bright coloring of The Body Shop packaging and emphasized exotic ingredients. The same year, Procter & Gam-

ble, with its vast resources, also entered the fray with their purchase of Ellen Betrix, a German company that had introduced Essentials natural cosmetics early in 1994.

The Body Shop's phenomenal growth slowed somewhat in 1992. Fiscal 1993 profits (the company's year ends February 28) were down 15 percent from the previous year, from £25.2 million to £21.5 million. Roddick criticized dissatisfied investors in *Working Woman* as "speculators who make their money off buying and selling. That is where the greed factor comes in. They expected us to make £23 million. Tough—we made £21 million." However, the company seemed to recover some of its momentum the following year: pretax profits for the first half of fiscal 1994 were £10 million, a 20 percent increase over the same period in 1993.

The Body Shop faced other problems in the first half of the 1990s, as its reputation as a socially responsible company was repeatedly challenged. The first attack came from a British television program entitled "Body Search," which accused The Body Shop of misleading customers with its "Against Animal Testing" product label. The Body Shop's policy, designed as an incentive for companies to eliminate their animal testing, rejected ingredients that had been tested on animals in the previous five years. The television program, however, charged the company with using ingredients that had been tested on animals. The Body Shop brought suit in the summer of 1993 and won £276,000 in damages.

Although the company won their suit, the battle had focused attention on The Body Shop's ethical record and inspired additional criticism. Cosmetics competitor Goodebodies tried to distinguish themselves by pointing out that, unlike The Body Shop, they did not use any animal by-products, such as tallow from pigs to make soap. The Body Shop responded, however, that it only used by-products from the meat industry and that it provided customers with information in the store if they wished to choose products with no animal ingredients.

Questions about the company's integrity continued in the summer of 1994, when it was reported that the U.S. Federal Trade Commission was investigating The Body Shop for exaggerated claims of helping developing nations and for alleged pollution from a New Jersey warehouse. The investigation, combined with the company's slowing growth, led Franklin Research & Development, an investment fund that dealt only with socially responsible companies, to sell 50,000 shares. That in turn led to a stock price drop of 11 percent in the next two weeks. Although the stock price stabilized soon thereafter, the company remained in a defensive position.

In the mid-1990s, the company showed signs of changing some of its long-standing policies, such as its refusal to advertise. From 1976 until 1994, The Body Shop used window displays, catalogs, and point of purchase product descriptions to attract and inform customers. In 1994, however, Anita Roddick appeared in an American Express commercial, talking about the company's Trade Not Aid program. Later that year, the company placed its first "advertorial" in the magazine *Marie Claire.* This eight-page spread offered a discussion of the *Body Shop Book* on personal care techniques and products. In addition, the company was considering further "advertorials" or television "documercials" for the Trade Not Aid products, which would focus on the stories and people behind the products. Angela Bawtree, The Body Shop's head of investor relations, explained the company's apparent change of attitude toward advertising in an October 1994 *Advertising Age*: "It would be wrong for people to think we have some kind of moral problem with using advertising. But using glamorous images or miracle cure claims—those kinds of things you won't see us doing." As of late 1994, the company had no plans to hire an advertising agency.

In the mid-1990s, the company increased its focus on international expansion. Same-store sales in the United Kingdom, The Body Shop's most mature market, declined six percent in fiscal 1993 and were stagnant in fiscal 1994. New international stores seemed the key to continued growth, and Gordon Roddick specifically targeted Germany, France, and Japan for expansion. In early 1994, Germany had 39 stores and Japan had 17, and Roddick believed that each of these countries could support 200 stores. In addition, The Body Shop opened its first stores in Mexico in 1993.

"We think the limit for the number of stores we can have globally is more than 3,000," Gordon Roddick said to *Working Woman* in 1994. He also commented that "in three years we will see the company's worth hit $1 billion." This statement was supported by a 1994 report from NatWest Securities, which expressed "confidence that the international growth potential (over 2,000 stores in year 2,000) cannot only be realized, but also translated into healthy profits."

Further Reading:

Colin, Jennifer, "Survival of the Fittest," *Working Woman,* February 1994, pp. 28–31, 68–69, 73.

Jacob, Rahul, "What Selling Will Be Like in the '90s," *Fortune,* January 13, 1992, pp. 63–64.

Siler, Charles, "Body Shop Marches to Its Own Drummer," *Advertising Age,* October 10, 1994, p. 4.

Zinn, Laura, "Whales, Human Rights, Rain Forests—And the Heady Smell of Profits," *Business Week,* July 15, 1991, pp. 114–15.

—Susan Windisch Brown

C.H. ROBINSON COMPANY

C. H. Robinson, Inc.

8100 Mitchell Road
Eden Prairie, Minnesota 55344-2248
U.S.A.
(612) 937-8500
Fax: (612) 937-7809

Private Company
Incorporated: 1905 as C. H. Robinson Company
Employees: 1,500
Sales: $1.16 billion
SICs: 4731 Freight Transportation Arrangement; 5148 Fresh
   Fruits and Vegetables

C. H. Robinson, Inc. operates the largest fresh fruits and vegetables distribution network in North America and manages a freight transportation system with more than 100 offices worldwide. Privately held by more than half of its employees, C. H. Robinson began as a small brokerage business, functioning as intermediary between buyer and seller. However, with the development of the interstate highway system in the 1950s, the Minnesota company steadily evolved into a full-service transportation management supplier. By the mid-1990s, C. H. Robinson served the wholesale, retail, and foodservice markets in a variety of roles, including packer, shipper, sales agent, exporter/importer, and information provider. C. H. Robinson also carried its own line of produce, which it marketed under the label The Fresh 1.

The company traces its origin to the early 1900s, when Charles H. Robinson established a small brokerage firm in Grand Forks, North Dakota, to ship produce to customers throughout the Red River Valley region of northeastern North Dakota and northwestern Minnesota. In May 1905, Robinson formed a partnership with Grand Forks-based Nash Brothers, the forerunner of the Nash Finch Company and the leading wholesaler in North Dakota. The partnership was incorporated as C. H. Robinson Co., and Robinson was named the company's first president. According to popular legend, related by Lee Egerstrom in St. Paul's *Pioneer Press,* Robinson "sold out a couple of years later and ran off with Annie Oakley, the showgirl shootist of Buffalo Bill Cody's Wild West Show fame," dying shortly thereafter in 1909. However, historical evidence has showed that if such a relationship existed, it would have concluded before 1905. Moreover, Robinson did not die in 1909, nor were

his shares in the company acquired by the Nash brothers and Harry Finch at that time. Nevertheless, by 1913 the partnership had ended, and the principals of Nash Finch Company were the sole owners of C. H. Robinson Co.

The Robinson subsidiary served primarily as a produce procurement vehicle for Nash Finch and expanded rapidly by establishing branch offices in Minnesota, Iowa, Wisconsin, Illinois, and Texas—virtually everywhere that Nash had established its own warehouses. In 1918, Minneapolis became Robinson's headquarters, from which the company continued to expand until the war effort intervened some two decades later.

During the early 1940s, Robinson also faced action by the Federal Trade Commission (FTC), which concluded that the subsidiary and Nash Finch were in violation of the Robinson-Patman Act because of the price advantage Nash received over that of other wholesalers. As later explained in the *Chronicle* (Fall 1988): "Rather than taking the case to court, C. H. Robinson Co. was split into two separate companies. The first company, C. H. Robinson Co., was formed by all offices selling produce to Nash-Finch warehouses, and the ownership of this company was sold to all Robinson employees. The other company, C. H. Robinson, Inc., was comprised of the remainder of the offices and was still owned by Nash-Finch Co."

Up until this time, Robinson, like its competitors, was limited to rail transport for the majority of its shipments. However, massive funding of the interstate highway system was about to alter that. The Federal Highway Act of 1956 catapulted Robinson into the trucking business. Initially working through its Omaha branch office, C. H. Robinson began capitalizing on opportunities for truck brokerage, launching what may have been the first such brokerage operation in the country. This involvement in managing the transport of "exempt" commodities (perishables that were exempt from government regulation) spread to ten branches by the 1960s. Around mid-decade C. H. Robinson Co. and C. H. Robinson, Inc. consolidated their operations under the name C. H. Robinson Co. Wholesaler Nash Finch still held a minority stake of approximately 25 percent in the brokerage company, with Robinson employees owning the remainder.

This structural arrangement led to a natural conflict of interests, with Nash requesting more Robinson dividends to invest in its own operations and Robinson wishing to retain more earnings in order to accelerate the company's growth. Finally, in 1976, both companies were satisfied when all remaining Nash shares were bought out and Robinson Co. became an entirely employee-owned business. A year later, Sid Verdoorn was installed as company president, and Looe Baker was named chairman of the board. "With this new leadership in place," recorded the *Chronicle,* "Robinson remained on its successful path—with a new commitment to data processing, and a continued dedication to the expansion of transportation and produce branch offices."

In 1980, the federal government deregulated the transportation industry through the Motor Carrier Act, which effectively broadened competition in the field. Robinson responded by establishing a contract carrier program and promoting itself not only as a purveyor of food products but as a freight contractor, or middleman sourcing operation, for virtually all shippable goods. In just five years, the company's average annual growth, measured by truckloads, doubled. The company was now posting more than $700 million in sales, with roughly 40 percent generated by truck brokerage and most of the remainder through produce sales. Commenting on Robinson's evident edge in the truck contracting industry, John J. Oslund, of the Minneapolis *Star Tribune*, wrote, "Unlike most of its competitors, who are relative newcomers, Robinson has developed its expertise over more than 50 years in the dicey and competitive world of produce delivery."

In January 1988, in a concentrated effort to become a full-service, multiple carrier provider, the company launched its Intermodal Division (intermodal denotes truck and rail shipping). As explained in the *Chronicle* (Winter 1994), "By combining its truck strengths with the recently improved service of rail carriers, Robinson saves customers significant dollars on long-distance shipments." In a number of moves since that time, Robinson has increasingly solidified its reputation as a well-rounded, globally positioned transportation and logistics company. For example, in addition to systematically opening a number of new branch offices each year, in 1990, the company expanded its international service through the formation of C. H. Robinson de Mexico. And, in 1992, international freight forwarding and air freight operations were added through the acquisition of the oldest and largest freight forwarder, C. S. Green International Inc.

During 1993, a particularly dynamic year for the company, C. H. Robinson made its first foray into the general food and beverage business with the acquisition of New York-based Daystar International Inc., a $40 million distributor of fruit juice concentrates. As vice-president Looe Baker III told Tony Kennedy, in an interview for the *Star Tribune:* "It's a big deal for us, and you'll see us make more moves. . . . [We're] searching for ways to expand into diversified segments of the food market."

During this time, C. H. Robinson continued to rely primarily on a vast network of independent truck operators, who together offered some 730,000 pieces of equipment, from containers on flatcars to refrigerated vans. Nevertheless, the company began to relax its policy of operating as a non-asset-based service firm by acquiring trucking fleets of its own. In early 1993, Robinson bought a trucking operation based in Sioux Falls, South Dakota, in order to service Carlisle Plastics, whose Western Division was also based there. Other fleet purchases, designed "to provide customer-specific service to large, heavy-volume accounts like Frito Lay" and to create greater flexibility for the company, included 100 48-foot refrigerated containers and 90 48-foot insulated containers. During this time, Robinson worked with over 14,000 shippers and moved more than 500,000 separate shipments annually.

Before the end of 1993, the company enhanced its European presence by acquiring a 30 percent stake in Transeco, a French motor carrier; Robinson later acquired the remaining shares for full ownership of Transeco. Other international activity included the opening of offices in Mexico City; Santiago, Chile; and Valencia, Venezuela. In 1994, on the verge of celebrating its ninetieth anniversary, Robinson expanded its intermodal strategy with two purchases, Atlanta-based Commercial Transportation Services Inc. and Boston-based Bay State Shippers Inc., both for undisclosed amounts. The company also had plans to broaden its The Fresh 1 line to include more value-added items. Annual volume for the 28-item line numbered between six and eight million packages. Careful not to underestimate the potential of the brand, Robinson believed it may yet become "as recognizable to the trade and consumers as the likes of Dole, Del Monte and Chiquita."

Although produce was still "the company's strong suit," and transportation—at a healthy 15 percent growth rate—represented another primary source of income, distribution logistics were expected to prove critical to the company's future development. As company president Sid Verdoorn stated in the company document *3 on C. H. Robinson:* "We have been very successful partially because many Fortune 500 companies have been outsourcing their logistics needs to us. . . . This has been a part of our growth and we look for more of that in the future. My vision is that the produce industry will catch up on that, and that being a trading and information company there is a possibility and potential for Robinson to do outsourcing for various companies in the industry at the retail purchasing, distribution, and warehousing ends of the business."

Principal Subsidiaries: Action Produce Company; CHR Financial Services, Inc.; CHR Greene International Company; C. H. Robinson Co. Chile International S.A. Ltda.; C. H. Robinson Company (Canada) Ltd.; C. H. Robinson de Mexico, S.A. de C.V.; C. H. Robinson International, Inc.; Cityside Loan & Savings; Cityside Indirect; Combined Transport Group, Inc.; Daystar-Robinson, Inc.; The Fresh 1 Marketing, Inc.; Hillcrest Sales, Inc.; Payment & Logistics Services, Inc.; Professional Logistics, Inc.; T-Chek Systems, Inc.; Wagonmaster Transportation Company.

Further Reading:

Beal, Dave, "Robinson Celebrates a Big Year," *Pioneer Press* (St. Paul), September 12, 1992.
C. H. Robinson Company: Multimodal Capabilities, Minneapolis: C.H. Robinson Company, 1993.
"C. H. Robinson Sells Robco Name, Assets to Atlanta Transport Firm," *Star Tribune* (Minneapolis), September 3, 1986, p. 1M.
Chronicle (Minneapolis), Fall 1988; Winter 1994.
"Company News," *Star Tribune* (Minneapolis), March 27, 1990, p. 8D.
Egerstrom, Lee, "Annie Oakley Key Figure in Company Legend," *Pioneer Press* (St. Paul), October 6, 1986; "Food, Transport Broker Enjoys Life in the Middle," *Pioneer Press* (St. Paul), October 6, 1986.
Kennedy, Tony, "Robinson Co. Acquires N.Y. Juice Firm," *Star Tribune* (Minneapolis), May 18, 1993, p. 3D.
"Marketplace Pulse," *Star Tribune* (Minneapolis), September 3, 1986, p. 1M.
Oslund, John J., "Trucking Broker Rolls over Stereotypes," *Star Tribune* (Minneapolis), December 16, 1985, pp. 1M, 7M.
3 on C. H. Robinson, Eden Prairie, Minnesota: C. H. Robinson Company, 1994.

—Jay P. Pederson

Cadence Design Systems, Inc.

555 River Oaks Parkway
San Jose, California 95134
U.S.A.
(408) 943-1234
Fax: (408) 943-0513

Public Company
Incorporated: 1988
Employees: 2,400
Sales: $368.62 million
Stock Exchanges: New York
SICs: 7372 Computer Software

Cadence Design Systems, Inc. is the world's leading developer of electronic design automation (EDA) software, maintaining a 18 percent market share in 1993. EDA software is a form of computer-aided design and engineering (CAD/CAE) software specifically geared towards automating the design of electronic systems and integrated circuits (ICs). Cadence Design's clients are companies that manufacture computer chips and circuits used in computer components, telecommunications equipment, television sets, video game systems, pagers, watches, fax machines, bar code scanning systems, and pacemakers, among other devices. Cadence's clients include IBM, Apple Computer, Motorola, Sharp Electronics, and Hitachi.

Computer-aided design of ICs was a rapidly growing field when Cadence started operations. As chip manufacturers tried to fit increasingly many tiny transistors on each chip, the complex layout of the chip's design and its verification came to depend on design automation software.

Cadence Design Systems Inc. was incorporated in June 1988 as the new company resulting from the merger of CAD software companies, ECAD Inc. and SDA Systems Inc. ECAD, based in Santa Clara, California, developed and sold CAD/CAE software to accelerate the design of ICs, including both the schematic design and the testing phases. The company's specialty was design-verification software, in which it was a technology leader. The company's largest clients were Digital Equipment, NCR, Data General, National Semiconductor, and Advanced Micro Devices.

ECAD was founded in August 1982 by Glen M. Antle, who held the posts of chairperson and chief executive officer until

the SDA merger. Antle had worked on ICs and semiconductors since 1959 at Texas Instruments, ITT, Teledyne, and Data General. Until founding ECAD, Antle had headed the micro-electronics products division of Systems Engineering Laboratories (SEL) in Sunnyvale, California. When SEL began developing a 32-bit computer, the company's CAD team devised an extremely fast algorithm for testing the new design. This new CAD testing technology would become the basis of ECAD's software products. In 1982, SEL was acquired by Gould Inc., and the Sunnyvale facility was shut down. Gould/SEL granted Antle the marketing rights to the CAD technology plus $25,000 in funding for the new software technology, in exchange for completing some unfinished work on an operating system on which Antle and his team were working. Thus, Antle incorporated his own company, ECAD Inc., and operations began in January 1983.

ECAD began selling its first CAD integrated software package, Dracula, in April 1983. Dracula was a set of programs for integrated-circuit layout verification, which ran many times faster than the software of its competition. The package included a design-rule checker, an electrical rule checker, and a layout-versus-schematic consistency checker among other programs. In April 1984, ECAD acquired Simon Software, which produced the Simon Simulator, the only circuit-simulation program on the market developed especially for the MOS (metal oxide semiconductor) technique of chip design. ECAD's second major product family, SYMBAD, provided the automation of layout design of ICs. In August 1987, ECAD entered the printed circuit board design and layout market with its acquisition of the product line of Omnicad Corp.

Unlike most other CAD companies, ECAD provided only software, and its software was designed in versions to run on different kinds of hardware. ECAD's software was made available for computers manufactured by IBM, Sun Microsystems, Apollo, Gould, Ridge, and Elxsi. ECAD also had original equipment manufacturer (OEM) contracts to sell its software as part of the CAD/CAE systems supplied by Daisy Systems, Control Data, and VIA systems.

ECAD had made a profit every year since 1983, and its sales and profits increased steadily. Its 1986, revenues were $16.59 million, and profits were $1.5 million. The following year, sales rose to $23.90 million, and profits more than doubled to $3.16 million. The company went public on June 10, 1987 with a sale of 1.5 million shares of common stock, raising $11.3 million in capital. Moreover, ECAD had begun marketing overseas, targeting Taiwan, Hong Kong, and western Europe. By 1987, the company had subsidiaries in France, West Germany, the United Kingdom, and Hong Kong; a research and development center in Taiwan; and a licensed distributor in Japan.

SDA Systems Inc., located in San Jose, California, developed and sold computer-aided engineering software for the physical design of semiconductor chips. SDA was founded in 1983 by James Solomon, a product manager at National Semiconductor Corp. Solomon started his own company, with National Semiconductor's support, in order to attract the specific engineering talent needed for developing design software.

SDA received start-up financing from National Semiconductor and General Electric Co., of $1.5 million each, by establishing special corporate sponsor/client partnerships with these companies. Similar sponsorship relationships were subsequently established with Harris Corp. and L. M. Ericsson Telephone Co., also yielding contributions of $1.5 million each. In April 1987, SDA signed similar technology partnerships with Toshiba Ltd. of Japan and SGS Corp. of Italy. These types of alliances yielded more financing for less equity than funding from venture capital firms, yet, unlike straight sales contracts, they also brought in up-front cash. Although they owned equity, none of the corporate sponsors had any direct control of SDA. SDA did not mind having to share its technology, because the close relationship with its clients helped the company provide better products to serve its clients' needs.

SDA's primary technological innovation was its design framework architecture, which permitted designers to link software tools from various vendors in a common user interface and database. In 1985, SDA was the first software company to commercially introduce such a framework product. Like ECAD, SDA also distinguished itself from its competitors at the time by providing versions of its software that could run on different computer hardware platforms, such as workstations from Sun Micrososytems, Digital Equipment, and Apollo Computer.

In 1984, 33-year-old Joseph B. Costello joined SDA as vice president of customer service. He held a number of positions, and in March of 1987 became SDA's president and chief operating officer. Costello had received an M.A. in physics from Yale University and had begun Ph.D studies at the University of California at Berkeley before becoming a research and development manager at National Semiconductor. Upon Costello's appointment, Solomon retained the posts of chairperson and chief executive.

In 1986, SDA had about $6 million in sales, which jumped to $18 million the following year, allowing the company to turn a profit. Having raised an additional $8.3 million in the sale of preferred stock, the company filed for initial public stock offering of 3.4 million shares at $7.50 to $9 per share in September 1987. However, the October 19, 1987 stock market collapse caused those plans to be canceled.

In February 1988, an agreement was reached for ECAD Inc. to acquire SDA Systems Inc. for a stock swap of $72 million. At the time, ECAD had 197 employees, and SDA had 161. The merger was completed on May 31, and a new company, Cadence Design Systems, Inc., was incorporated on June 1. Although Antle was originally to become co-chair and chief executive officer of the merged company, he did not stay after the merger. Similarly, ECAD's president and chief operating officer, James Hill, had resigned following the decision to merge in February. Thus, Costello became Cadence's chief executive officer as well as president. Costello was credited with helping to facilitate the merger through his communication efforts among all the employees.

For the year ending December 31, 1988, Cadence's sales were $78.61 million, net income was $15.96 million, and the company had 433 employees. In August 1989, Cadence raised $1.6 million in an additional stock offering, increasing the public share of Cadence's stock. Until that time, corporate sponsors of former SDA still owned sizable stakes in the company, such as Harris Corp. with ten percent.

Cadence continued its strategy of offering software for multiple computer platforms. In addition to versions for Sun Microsystems, Digital Equipment, and Apollo computers, Cadence began making software available for Hewlett-Packard, Sony, and NEC computers in 1989 and 1990. Meanwhile, its competitors, Mentor Graphics Corp., Daisy Systems Corp., and Valid Logic Systems Inc., continued to bundle software with computer hardware for turnkey systems. Software portability was already common for various applications, but it did not become common for CAD software until the early 1990s.

Cadence soon became the world's leading supplier of IC, or chip, design software. In 1989, Cadence had a 15.4 percent market share, ahead of Seiko Instrument and Electronics with 11.5 percent (mostly in Japan), and Mentor Graphics Corp. with 8.4 percent, according to the market research firm Dataquest Inc. A year later, Dataquest put Cadence's market share at 44.2 percent.

Cadence was able to hold the largest share of the international IC design software market by becoming a dominant supplier to the large Japanese market. In 1989, Japan was producing 40 percent of the world's semiconductors, and Cadence was serving nine of the top ten Japanese chip makers, earning 30 percent of its 1989 revenues from Japan. Cadence attained its success in the Japanese market in part by implementing its predecessor SDA's practice of partnering with firms instead of merely contracting distributors. In April 1989, a subsidiary, Cadence Design Systems K.K. was established in Tokyo. This subsidiary served as more than just a sales office by also handling marketing, finance, and research and development.

Cadence began implementing a new product strategy in 1989, expanding into systems design software, used for the overall design of an electronic product such as a computer, instead of merely IC chip design. This involved providing software that could handle mechanical design, computer-aided manufacturing, and documentation, among other tasks. Although Cadence was the leading chip CAD provider, the chip design market in 1989 was only $179 million, compared to the $880 million systems-design market, which was the largest component of the overall $1.05 billion EDA market. In 1989, the EDA software industry was growing at 25 percent annually. Costello aspired to make Cadence into the leading EDA company by 1992, up from fourth place in 1989, and was determined that the company would first have to become at least the second-largest supplier of system-design tools.

To this end, Cadence acquired three other CAD companies with complementary technologies. In March 1989, Cadence acquired Tangent Systems Corp., a subsidiary of Intergraph Inc. based in Santa Clara, California. Tangent supplied gate-array products, integrated circuit layout design software. In November 1989, Cadence acquired Gateway Design Automation Corp. of Lowell, Massachusetts. Gateway's strength was in simulation software, and the company's main product was the Verilog line of logical simulation software. In April 1990, Cadence acquired

Automated Systems Inc., a supplier of printed circuit board design software and fabrication services located in Milwaukee, Wisconsin.

Cadence also invested heavily in research and development at the unusually high ratio of 21 percent of revenues, or $29 million, in 1989. To focus on the systems design market, the company formed new divisions devoted to systems design and analog design. Cadence introduced a full systems-design software package, Amadeus, in September 1990.

At the end of 1989, Cadence's sales had nearly doubled from $78.61 million in 1988 to $142.84 million, while net income jumped from $15.96 million to $27.78 million. Moreover the company's work force increased from 433 to 978 within the year. The following year, sales reached $231.4 million, and Cadence became the second leading EDA supplier, following Mentor Graphics Corp.

By late 1990, Cadence was developing CAD software based on a new systems-design methodology, which enabled designers to portray their ideas in a high-level hardware description language (HDL), instead of in gate-level engineering, in what was known as a "top-down" approach to systems design, the latest trend.

Cadence's Verilog-XL simulator software, that of acquired Gateway Design Automation, already used an HDL of its own. In May 1990, Cadence announced its intention to make the HDL of Verilog available in the public domain for custom and third-party software development. Cadence subsequently sponsored the formation of the Open Verilog International committee to oversee file compatibility with Verilog's HDL and to promote the adoption of Verilog HDL as a standard by the Institute of Electronics and Electrical Engineers. While Cadence gained some backers from among its competitors for Verilog HDL, others in the industry preferred the existing VHDL standard. In May 1992, Cadence called for the interoperability of Verilog HDL and VHDL. Finally, by 1993, Cadence introduced a product based on the VHDL industry standard, a simulator called Leapfrog.

In December 1991, Cadence acquired and merged with Valid Logic Systems Inc., the third-ranking EDA supplier, in exchange for $200 million in stock. Valid president and chief operating officer L. George Klaus was made executive vice-president and chief operating officer of Cadence, and Valid chairperson and CEO W. Douglas Hajjar became vice-chairperson. Valid was a developer of EDA software especially for electronic systems and printed circuit boards, and its product lines were merged into those of Cadence's over the course of 1992. Thus Cadence entered 1992 as the leading EDA supplier, surpassing Mentor Graphics, with a 24 percent market share.

Although Cadence's revenue was slightly higher in 1991 over 1990, the company recorded a net loss of $22.4 million, largely due to $49.9 in million restructuring costs and $1.7 in merger costs associated with the merger with Valid Logic Systems. In the months following the merger, ten percent of Cadence's employees were laid off in an effort to eliminate redundancies. Sales growth also slowed in the first half of 1991, due to a weaker economy.

In July 1993, Cadence acquired Comdisco Systems Inc., a subsidiary of Comdisco, Inc., for $13 million in stock. Comdisco Systems was the leader in design software for digital signal processing and communications applications, with an estimated 70 percent market share. Comdisco's technology had brought design to a higher level of abstraction than currently available. The company had pioneered system-level design in 1988 with the introduction of its signal processing worksystem. Cadence thus gained the leading position in the growing markets of block-diagram digital signal processing design tools and in network analysis tools. The unit was renamed the Alta Group in June 1994 with the acquisition of Redwood Design Automation.

After record revenue and profits in fourth quarter 1992, the company experienced a decline in revenue of 35 percent and an operating loss in first quarter 1993. Lower sales were attributed to a change in product strategy which confused customers and to poor economic conditions, especially in the Japanese market.

In response to the surprisingly lower sales, Cadence introduced a re-engineering plan in April 1993. This involved focusing on improving financial results, the hiring of new managers, including a new chief operating officer and a new chief financial officer, and the strengthening of international sales operations. The restructuring yielded immediate positive results, as revenues increased each quarter of 1993, and there were no operating losses in the succeeding quarters. The year still ended in a net loss of $12.78 million, due to $13.5 million in restructuring costs.

Lower revenues in 1993 were also seen as part of an industry trend confronting both of the larger EDA companies, Cadence and Mentor. In addition to financial losses, both companies also suffered defections of engineers and executives to start-up firms. A perception had emerged that the broad-line suppliers of EDA software were no longer on the cutting edge of technology in the fields of electronics systems design and high-level design automation. Furthermore, the EDA market had matured and was nearing saturation at the higher end, according to some industry observers.

One area in which Cadence did have an advantage over smaller start-ups was in its ability to provide a full array of support and consulting services. In 1991, Cadence formed a consulting services group as part of its new systems division. The group advised EDA users on selecting and developing tools for their design environments. In 1993, Cadence established its Spectrum Services consulting group, which soon began to be used by some of Cadence's largest software customers. Although income from sales of products declined in 1993, revenue from maintenance services increased by $23.9 million that year. In December 1993, Cadence sold its Automated Systems division, manufacturer of complex printed circuit boards, which the company had acquired in 1990.

By early 1994, Cadence already appeared on its way back to recovery after the slump in 1993. With sales of IC design software once again growing, sales of systems design also began to show life after falling from $100 million in 1990 between $35 and $40 million in 1993. Cadence's test equipment subsidiary, Integrated Measurement Systems Inc., was predicted to grow eight percent in 1994. The new consulting group, Spectrum Services, was forecast to grow 40 percent in 1994 and is eventually expected to comprise up to 50 percent of Cadence's overall business.

Principal Subsidiaries: Cadence Design Systems (Canada) Ltd.; Cadence Design Systems, S.A. (France); Cadence Design Systems GmbH (Germany); Cadence Design Systems Asia, Ltd. (Hong Kong); Cadence Design Systems (Israel) Ltd.; Cadence Design Systems S.r.l. (Italy); Cadence Design Systems K.K. (Japan); Integrated Measurement Systems Inc.

Further Reading:

Burrows, Peter, "Cadence Shoots for the Top," *Electronic Business,* October 29, 1990, pp. 36–40.

Card, David, "SDA Says it's Not Just Another CAE Start-Up," *Electronic Business,* May 1, 1987, p. 124.

Caruso, Denise, "Startup ECAD Thinks Big in CAD/CAE Marketplace," Dorsch, Jeff, "Surviving CAE Evolution," *Electronic News,* June 14, 1993, p. 1.

"ECAD to Buy SDA Systems in $72M Deal," *Electronic News,* February 29, 1988, pp. 1, 30.

Goering, Richard, "Cadence Acquires Comdisco Systems," *Electronic Engineering Times,* July 12, 1993, p. 1.

Hof, Robert D., "Sure, He's Wild and Crazy—Like a Fox," *Business Week,* October 30, 1989, p. 132.

Holden, Daniel, "Cadence Snubs VHDL International, Pushes Verilog for ASIC Design," *Electronic News,* June 15, 1992, p. 13.

Jones, Stephen, "High-Tech Firms ECAD and Impact Systems Seek Public Money," *San Jose Business Journal,* May 18, 1994, p. 6.

Jones, Stephen, "SDA Systems Inks Alliances with a Japanese and Italian Firm," *San Jose Business Journal,* May 4, 1987, p. 13.

Kerr, John, "Breaking into Japan: Small U.S. Companies Show How It's Done," *Electronic Business,* November 13, 1989, pp. 72–76.

McLeod, Jonah, "Going the Distance with Mergers, Acquisitions," *Electronics,* December 1989, p. 86.

McLeod, Jonah, "Why Cadence Is the Top Dog in the IC Design Pack," *Electronics,* June 1989, pp. 121–22.

Ricciuti, Mike, "Cadence Design Systems Inc.," *Datamation,* June 15, 1992, p. 142.

Stitt, Wendy, "And in This Corner . . . : Cadence Design Systems Continues to Trade 'Friendly' Punches with Mentor Graphics," *San Jose Business Journal,* March 18, 1991, p. S12.

Wiegner, Kathleen K., "The Hot Box Syndrome," *Forbes,* April 17, 1989, pp. 178–80.

—Heather Behn Hedden

Chiat/Day Inc. Advertising

340 Main Street
Venice, California 90291
U.S.A.
(310) 314-5000
Fax: (310) 396-1273

Private Company
Incorporated: 1968
Employees: 850
Gross Billings: $932 million
SICs: 7311 Advertising Agencies

Daring, controversial, and visionary from its inception, Chiat/ Day Inc. Advertising ranks 16th in gross earnings among U.S. ad agencies, according to *Advertising Age,* and is nevertheless regarded as leader in its field. The private company's notorious successes (which include the commercial spoofs featuring the Energizer Bunny and the slick Nissan fantasy campaigns) have come neither easily nor with any long-term guarantees. Of course, such is the nature of highly competitive, big-name advertising, but with Chiat both the rewards and the losses somehow seem magnified. To paraphrase one industry observer: Chiat's list of clients it has *lost,* let alone *won,* over the years would be enough to satisfy even the hungriest of its competitors—and equally enough to put most any other agency out of business. The secret to the dynamism, staying power, and uniqueness of the company is, according to many, the personality and drive of founder/chairperson Jay Chiat. As Christy Marshall observed, in *Business Month* magazine: "One of the few independents left in an industry dominated by mega-agencies, Los Angeles-based Chiat/Day is the personification of its founder and chief executive officer—a place where success breeds arrogance, where enthusiasm borders on fanaticism and where intensity looks suspiciously like neurosis. It is also a bone in the throat of Madison Avenue, which derides its inventive, often riveting ads as irresponsible and ineffective—and then mimics them."

Chiat/Day was established when two competitors combined their talents to take on the bigger agencies in the Los Angeles area. Jay Chiat & Associates, founded in 1962, had billings of $3 million when Guy Day of Faust/Day Advertising, a $5 million agency, proposed a merger. Chiat agreed with Day to pool their creative and financial resources, and, by October 1968, Chiat/Day was in operation. Day, after winning a coin toss, became company president.

From the beginning, the agency eschewed standard practices and created its own, unique brand of advertising. Chiat/Day was among the first to use the English concept of "account planners," liaisons between the agency and targeted consumers who travelled the country conducting individual and group interviews. Account planners not only gauged audience response and understanding of ads, but also served as a crucial link between the client and the buying public. A second Chiat/Day innovation was the requirement that clients actively participate in the creative process by attending an initial brainstorming or strategy session, as well as a subsequent planning session. Chiat/Day turned away business when clients refused this interaction. Third, Chiat/Day believed all staff members should be involved in a campaign via a "task force" approach. But Chiat/ Day's greatest innovations were the ad campaigns themselves, work that demonstrated the agency's relentless pursuit of quality and its unflagging ambition to unequivocally create the best ads in the industry.

After the two merging agencies combined their existing accounts and dropped any conflicts of interest, Chiat/Day was ready to take the advertising world by storm. In 1969, the agency picked up Western Harness Racing as client by betting its president they could raise attendance 15 percent with their ads. Another account included a public service ad, addressing racism, for the Los Angeles County Commission on Human Relations. Chiat/Day's "My Hero, the Pimp" ads of 1970 raised large amounts of money for Direction Sports, an organization involved in helping urban youth. In short, Chiat/Day pushed the public's buttons as it grew in both recognition and billings.

Jay Chiat's now classic maxim "Good enough is not enough" emerged as a defining concept for the company and a testament to Chiat's vision of advertising. With a pronounced ability to stir things up, according to Day and others, Chiat traditionally drove his creative teams to the "breaking point," the point where desperation often gave way to sudden inspiration. The enormous dedication called for among Chiat/Day employees engendered a corporate maxim perhaps just as popular and defining as Chiat's: "Chiat, Day and night." In 1971, the company hired Lee Clow, who would prove to best embody the creative soul of the agency in the years to come. While serving as the architect of many of Chiat/Day's most memorable campaigns, Clow rose through the ranks to become president and executive creative director worldwide. According to Karen Stabiner in *Inventing Desire,* the rare chemistry between Jay Chiat and Lee Clow, perhaps as much as anything, propelled Chiat/Day into the limelight.

Throughout the 1970s, Chiat/Day experimented in style and substance, employing psychedelic colors in its ads for Viviane Woodard Cosmetics, scenic wonders for Rancho California, offbeat ads for KNBC and Motel 6, and a series of breakthrough ads for Honda's new automobiles. However, in 1975, Honda, responsible for half of Chiat/Day's billings and three-quarters of its income, left for another ad agency. This proved the first of many blows to the fledgling agency, as small accounts would become giants thanks to Chiat/Day's ads and then abandon the company for bigger, "full-service" agencies.

The following year, Chiat/Day ran a series of trade ads targeting the food, airline, pet, and motorcycle industries. These ads paid off, and Chiat soon landed clients including Yamaha, Suntory Royal Whiskey's Midori Melon Liqueur, Alaska Airlines, and the Olympia Brewing Company. During this time, Guy Day, wishing to spend more time with his family and pursue his interest in writing, sold his agency holdings and left Chiat/Day in his partner's hands. By the end of the decade, Chiat/Day had opened an office in New York and had purchased an established agency in San Francisco. In 1980, the company was named Agency of the Year by *Advertising Age* magazine, which would again bestow that title on Chiat/Day later in the decade.

In 1981, as Chiat/Day was hitting its stride and becoming one of the fastest growing privately-held agencies in the United States, Guy Day rejoined the company to help steer its course. Also during this time, the foundation for what many consider the greatest ad in history was laid. Chiat/Day was steadily garnering attention for Apple Computer, a client of the agency's San Francisco office, through a series of popular ads. Then, in 1983, the agency began work on a TV spot introducing the Macintosh, a computer destined to revolutionize the industry, scheduled to air during the third quarter of the January 1984 Super Bowl. Using an abandoned print ad, staffers worked around the slogan "Why 1984 won't be like *1984*." Apple liked the idea, and the British film director Ridley Scott was hired for the filming. However, the disturbingly Orwellian commercial, featuring an athletic-looking young woman (symbolizing Macintosh) hurling a sledgehammer at a Big Brother TV screen (IBM), proved too brash a statement even for Apple's executives, and, before air-time on Super Bowl Sunday, a reluctant Apple tried to pull the plug, finally insisting that Chiat/Day sell the air time. Fortunately, only half of the scheduled time could be sold, and the "1984" ad was run. Chiat/Day held its collective breath and waited for the fallout.

"The commercial changed advertising; the product changed the ad business; the technology changed the world," wrote Bradley Johnson of *Advertising Age* in a January 1994 retrospective. "It turned the Super Bowl from a football game into advertising's Super Event of the year," Johnson contended, "and it ushered in the era of advertising as news." Costing a total of $900,000 to produce and air, "1984" resulted in millions for both Apple and Chiat/Day, as the spot was rebroadcast during evening newscasts and on *Entertainment Tonight.* "1984" not only swept the year's awards, winning the Grand EFFIE, the Cannes Gold, the Belding Sweepstakes, and the Clio, but it was later dubbed *Advertising Age*'s Commercial of the Decade. "This is what happens," Johnson concluded, "when breakthrough technology is given the benefit of the greatest TV commercial ever made."

In the wake of this success, Chiat/Day secured many new accounts, including Nike, Porsche, and Pizza Hut. The ads Chiat/Day produced for Pizza Hut spawned a lawsuit from competitor Godfather's Pizza. Setting an industry precedent, a California state court enjoined Chiat/Day from sharing confidential information learned while bidding previously for the Godfather account. The court also forbade any agency staffers

who worked on the Godfather pitch from working on rival Pizza Hut's account. In November 1984, an appellate court struck down the second part of the ruling, a victory for Chiat/Day and all ad agencies. Yet the remaining injunction seemed a moot point, since agency standards precluded the use of confidential information anyway.

In 1986 and 1987, Chiat/Day continued to prosper, with dynamic media ads for California Coolers, Nike, Worlds of Wonder's Teddy Ruxpin, and celebrity spots for Mitsubishi's 35-inch television by creative legends Bob Fosse, Jim Henson, John Huston, and Martin Scorsese. But with the highs came more lows, as both Apple and Nike (like Honda before them) departed for other agencies. According to *The Economist:* "No other agency has got so big while maintaining such a fine reputation for cutting-edge work. But nor has any been so sharply criticized for putting self-indulgent 'creativity' ahead of selling products. That has made for a history of stunning ads—and devastating client defections." After six years, Guy Day would also leave the agency again, this time for good.

Yet 1987's acquisition of the Nissan Motor Co. account heralded a new era for Chiat/Day. Not only did Nissan consolidate its regional marketing with the agency in 1988 (adding another $90 million in billings), but it helped catapult the agency into the big time. With gross billings of $500 million, Chiat/Day was now ranked among the industry's top 25 agencies. To handle the influx of new business, Chiat hired almost 200 additional staffers and recapitalized to pay off senior executives and other equity holders by borrowing in excess of $50 million in 1988. By the end of 1988 and throughout 1989, the agency had expanded by acquiring a design firm, two public-relations operations, a direct-marketing company, and a sales-promotion firm. The pinnacle of Chiat's growth during the 1980s came with the purchase of Mojo MDA Group Ltd., Australia's largest advertising agency, with $180 million in billings.

One of Australia's savviest agencies, Mojo was at its peak when the merger came through in 1989. Renaming the conglomerate Chiat/Day/Mojo, Jay Chiat was intent on building the world's premier advertising and communications firm, a full-service provider that could become "big" without sacrificing its reputation for innovation. To facilitate the necessary restructuring and to ease an eventual transition in management, Chiat removed himself from direct involvement with the company and appointed Bob Wolf to take his place. However, amidst internal dissension and severe economic pressures, according to Stabiner in *Business Month,* Chiat returned to the helm the following year.

Chiat/Day's billings hit $1.2 billion in 1991, with Toshiba, Reebok, American Express, The Boston Company, and Microsoft all signing on. Next in line was Nissan's Australian accounts, which Chiat believed would be brought in with ease, given Mojo's reputation and connections. However, Mojo failed to deliver Nissan or other international accounts, and instead began losing clients. Moreover, Shearson Lehman Brothers ($20 million), Chemical Manufacturers Association ($10 million), and AmEx Green Card ($60 million) all deserted Chiat. The industry was rife with speculation about Chiat/Day's debt load, wondering how the agency would handle its rising interest payments. With heavy losses and the recession hitting

Chiat/Day hard, the agency seemed at a dangerous crossroads, readying itself for massive layoffs or even acquisition.

By November 1992, Chiat/Day had unloaded Mojo to rival Foote, Cone & Belding Communications for an undisclosed sum. "It was a mix of cultures that wouldn't marry," original Mojo founding partner Alan Morris (the "Mo" of Mojo) told Tony Burrett of *Adweek* magazine. Jay Chiat, on the other hand, was more circumspect, telling the *Wall Street Journal* that "The initial reason for being in Australia and New Zealand was to service international accounts. But none of that has been fruitful, and it was time to move on." Nevertheless, Chiat remained optimistic about further international growth, noting: "All our expansion plans have been opportunistic. If those situations exist again, we'll explore them." In October 1992, just one month before deciding to sell off Mojo, Chiat/Day received some good news: Nissan Motor Co. offered the agency its Infiniti division, worth approximately $90 million in billings. One year later, according to Larry Armstrong of *Business Week,* Chiat had an estimated $850 million in billings, more than 40 percent of which were due to Nissan alone.

Although recent years for Chiat had been tumultuous, 1993 proved more so, as the agency executed some bold moves in preparation for the future and unprecedented losses struck at its core. Two initiatives went from drawing board to implementation. First was Project Chrysalis, a think tank designed to propel the agency away from its current restraints of time and space. Chrysalis developed the blueprint for the industry's first "virtual" office, a fully portable, organic workplace that broke with traditional concepts of office use and featured state-of-the-art communications technology. The second initiative involved Chiat/Day's push to replace standard 90-day termination clauses with three-year pacts. The move triggered debate across the country, as East Coast agencies attacked the idea and West Coasters embraced it. Though most agencies craved the security and stability a three-year pact guarantees, few clients were prepared to sign into such a fixed-term contract. Simon Bax, Chiat/Day's executive vice-president and chief operating officer, saw advantages for both sides: "The most difficult conversation between client and agency is compensation," he told *Advertising Age* in May 1993, noting that "if you can introduce an element that isn't financial, you can focus on the relationship."

While Chiat/Day began preparations for its virtual move and the celebration of its twenty-fifth anniversary, another string of heavy account losses struck the company. This time the defectors were *TV Guide* and National Car Rental Systems. Then, in September 1993, the agency was unceremoniously bounced from the $80 million Reebok account, which it had won back after a similar dumping in 1991. The account was given to Chicago rival Leo Burnett, as was the $60 million European portion of the billings, which had only recently been won by Euro RSCG agency.

Although David Ropes, Reebok's vice-president of worldwide marketing services, extolled Chiat/Day's virtues, he found the agency lacking in global terms: "We made this decision because we need better global resources. We want to tap into Burnett's world-wide network to drive our sales world-wide." With characteristic aplomb and irreverence, Chiat/Day took out

full-page ads in both the *Los Angeles* and *New York Times* that read "Now we know how Dan felt," referring to Dan O'Brien, who had failed to qualify for the Olympics. O'Brien had been featured in Chiat/Day's $30 million Reebok campaign, which centered on the rivalry between decathletes O'Brien and Dave Johnson. The agency had to scramble and developed an ad heralding the glory of the athlete featuring O'Brien. It was a public relations coup with coverage in all the major press.

Like O'Brien, who went on to shatter a world record, Chiat/Day came back with a vengeance, snagging the Cherry Coke ad campaign, consolidating all of NYNEX's media spending (the agency had previously scored with a popular campaign of stylish and humorous NYNEX yellow pages "human cartoons" ads), and adding the Starter Rugged Terrain shoes campaign. These full-page ads ended with a teaser, an apt motto for Chiat/Day: "You haven't heard the last of us, either."

"The key to this agency," Chiat had told *Business Month* in 1988, "is the premise that it is very important never to peak, because once you do, you're down the other side of the mountain." Indeed, Chiat/Day's commitment to innovation remained intact into the mid-1990s. On the cutting edge of style and architecture, the agency's corporate headquarters in Venice stood as a monument to Jay Chiat's inimitable style and determination. Valued at $20 million and designed by Frank Gehry, the odd collection of buildings included the Main Street corridor, the Fish (a meeting room resembling the belly of a whale), and the Boat and Tree wings, spectacularly joined by a three-story pair of binoculars created by Claes Oldenburg and Coosje Van Bruggen. Moreover, in keeping with Chiat's maverick reputation, extensive renovations were nearly complete for Chiat's new "virtual" workspace.

Investing nearly $8 million in technology alone, Chiat/Day's move to virtual reality was also regarded as innovative. "The technology is the easy part," remarked Laurie Coots, senior vice-president of administration and new business development. "The hardest part is intellectual, thinking through how people feel and work," she told *Advertising Age*. On January 3, 1994, the agency officially implemented its concept; traditional desks and cubicles were replaced by electronic calendars and e-mail, lockers, laptops, beepers, and cellular phones. "What we're trying to do is kill all the antiquated habits," Chiat explained in *Forbes ASAP,* noting that "we're trying to reinvent the way we work." Among the new features were SBUs (strategic business units) for conferences and pitches; computerized editing studios; a CD-ROM library; and the newly christened Student Union, with giant television screens, punching bags, a pool table, and a diner. Almost every square foot was wired for portable Macintoshes and phones—the agency's tools of the trade. "It's not for everybody," Karen Knowles, an assistant producer at Chiat/Day, told Betsy Sharkey of *Adweek* in May 1994, a few months after going virtual, "but it's always been survival of the fittest at Chiat/Day, and now it's more intensely that way."

Industry response has been, at best, reserved. "It's been debated, deified and debunked," Sharkey commented of Chiat/Day's virtual move. Chiat himself concurred: "If [J. Walter] Thompson had done it, there'd be less skepticism." As of 1993, staffers were adapting, and Chiat/Day's chief operating officer,

Adelaide Horton, believed their newfound flexibility would "reduce our real estate costs per employee as much as 50 percent." In June 1994, the New York office made its own leap into new quarters on Maiden Lane, adjacent to the South Street Seaport area. The work space has garnered interest from IBM, Arthur Anderson, Price Waterhouse, Citibank, and others as they begin implementation of their own versions of virtual offices.

Another innovative move for Chiat/Day was its move towards infomercials. Jay Chiat told the *Wall Street Journal* that while infomercials were not "part of the traditional agency make-up, we have the opportunity to do some interesting projects. More and more companies are interested in the infomercial form." Competitors DDB Needham and Interpublic Group were already producing infomercials with in-house units. In a related move, Jay Chiat with Jim Robinson invested $50,000 to acquire a minority stake in Interactive Connection, a struggling online service available through Internet.

Although Chiat/Day has probably had more than its share of ups and downs, the company's top executives, including Chiat, Wolf, Clow, and Bob Kuperman, remained a potent force in the ad business. According to *Adweek,* when the International Advertising Association (IAA) was planning its thirty-fourth annual World Advertising Congress, they had an idea: they would invite David Ogilvy, Jay Chiat, and Mike Ovitz to speak as the quintessential advertising entrepreneurs of the century. David Ogilvy would represent the past, Chiat the present, and Ovitz the future of the industry. But perhaps such pigeonholing, at least in Chiat's case, was premature. "I deal with today and tomorrow because I can't remember yesterday," Chiat told *Adweek.*

Principal Subsidiaries: Chiat/Day Communications Inc. Public Relations; Chiat/Day Direct Marketing-New York; Venice Operating Corp.

Further Reading:

"Agency Report," *Advertising Age,* April 13, 1994, pp. 16, 24.

Aho, Deborah, "Jay Chiat Gets Ready to Log onto Internet," *Advertising Age,* June 20, 1994, p. 74.

Alter, Stewart, "Fallout Lingers from Godfather's-Chiat Suit," *Advertising Age,* May 13, 1985, p. 60.

Armstrong, Larry, and Geoffrey Smith, "It's Reebok Out—and Nissan In," *Business Week,* October 4, 1993, p. 38.

"Brand New Day," *The Economist,* June 19, 1993, pp. 70–71.

Burrett, Tony, "FCB Has Got Mojo Working Again," *Adweek,* May 2, 1994, p. 46.

Elliott, Stuart, "Chiat/Day to Handle Benetton Campaign," *New York Times,* June 28, 1994, p. D18.

Farrell, Greg, "Chiat's End Game," *Adweek,* July 12, 1993, pp. 26–34.

Goldman, Kevin, "Chiat/Day Pulls Up Down Under, Selling Mojo Shop to Foote Cone," *Wall Street Journal,* November 11, 1992, p. B11; "Chiat/Day to Make Infomercials through a Joint-Venture Deal," *Wall Street Journal,* November 23, 1993, p. B10; "Reebok Fires Chiat/Day and Hires Burnett," *Wall Street Journal,* September 15, 1993, p. B7.

Horton, Cleveland, and Melanie Wells, "Chiat Pushes 3-Year Pacts for New Clients," *Advertising Age,* May 10, 1993, p. 4.

Horton, Cleveland, "A Day in the 'Virtual' Life of a Chiat/Day Executive," *Advertising Age,* March 14, 1994, pp. 19–20.

"How Agencies Fared Around the World," *Adweek Special Report,* March 20, 1989, p. N34.

Johnson, Bradley, "10 Years After '1984,' " *Advertising Age,* January 10, 1994, pp. 1, 12–14.

Kessler, Stephen, *Chiat/Day: The First Twenty Years,* New York, Rizzoli International Publications, 1990.

Landler, Mark, "Chiat/Day is Winning, After Losing, After Winning . . . ," *Business Week,* December 2, 1991, p. 120.

Levin, Gary, "Chiat Tries Direct Marketer Role in Infomercials," *Advertising Age,* May 16, 1994, p. 8.

Marshall, Christy, "Smart Guy," *Business Month,* April 1988, pp. 32–35.

Rapaport, Richard, "Jay Chiat Tears Down the Walls," *Forbes ASAP,* October 25, 1993, pp. 25–28.

Sharkey, Betsy, "Chiat/Day Comes of Age," *Adweek Special Report,* March 20, 1989, pp. N8–9, N12.

Sharkey, Betsy, "Going Virtual," *Adweek,* May 16, 1994, pp. 28–35.

Stabiner, Karen, *Inventing Desire,* Simon & Schuster: New York, 1993.

Stroud, Ruth, "Guy Day Cheers on His Namesake," *Advertising Age,* April 24, 1989, p. 64.

"The 30 Hottest Agencies of 1988," *Adweek Special Report,* March 20, 1989, p. N14.

Tilsner, Julie, "But Will They Get Their Own Water Coolers?," *Business Week,* July 19, 1993, p. 32.

Wells, Melanie, "Behind Scenes, Chiat Talks of HQ Sale," *Advertising Age,* April 28, 1993, p. 50.

"Working without Walls," *Advertising Age,* November 22, 1993, p. 8.

Yeoung, Mary, "If It's in There, It's Outrageous," *Marketing & Media Decisions,* August 1989, pp. 26–27.

—Jay P. Pederson and Taryn Benbow-Pfalzgraf

Chrysler Corporation

12000 Chrysler Drive
Highland Park, Michigan 48288-0001
U.S.A.
(313) 956-5741
Fax: (313) 956-1462

Public Company
Incorporated: 1925
Employees: 128,000
Sales: $43.6 billion
Stock Exchanges: New York London
SICs: 3711 Motor Vehicles and Car Bodies; 3714 Motor
Vehicle Parts and Accessories; 6141 Personal Credit
Institutions; 5511 New and Used Car Dealers; 6311 Life
Insurance; 7510 Automotive Rentals, No Drivers

With famous lines of passenger cars, numerous major manufacturing subsidiaries, and a variety of important interests in foreign countries, the Chrysler Corporation is a strong, viable company, a formidable force in the international automobile market. In the late 1970s and throughout the 1980s, however, Chrysler was fighting for its life. It took a massive injection of government and private capital, extremely careful management, and some brilliant marketing to restore the ailing giant, a resurgence that was not completed until the mid-1990s.

The company was incorporated in 1925 by Walter Percy Chrysler, a former vice-president of General Motors. Resigning from GM over policy differences, Chrysler went on to restore the Maxwell Motor Corporation to solvency; in the process, he designed Maxwell's Chrysler automobile. First exhibited in 1924, the car was an immediate success, and before year's end the company sold 32,000 cars at a profit of more than $4 million.

The enthusiasm with which the vehicle was met encouraged Walter Chrysler to design four additional models for the coming year: the 50, 60, 70, and Imperial 80. These model numbers referred to the maximum velocity that the cars could reach on a level stretch of road. Until that time, Ford's Model T had enjoyed the reputation of the fastest car, achieving a modest 35 mph. Alarmed by Chrysler's technological breakthrough, the Ford Motor Company closed its doors for nine months and emerged with a replacement for the Model T. However, by 1927 the Chrysler Corporation (as it had been called since 1925) had

firmly established itself with a sale of 192,000 cars, becoming the fifth largest company in the industry.

Walter Chrysler realized that in order to exploit his firm's manufacturing capacities to their fullest, he would have to build his own plants. Since he could not afford the estimated $75 million to achieve this, he approached the New York banking firm of Dillon Read and Company. Dillon Read had bought the Dodge Corporation of Detroit from the widows of the Dodge brothers and was happy to reach an agreement with the now highly regarded Walter Chrysler. In July 1928, Dodge became a division of the Chrysler Corporation; overnight, the size of the company increased fivefold.

Walter Chrysler, carefully avoiding the dangers associated with rapid growth, discontinued his policy of manufacturing as many parts as possible for his cars. While he paid more for components than other car makers, he was able to maintain greater flexibility in models and designs. This proved to be extremely important in an age of rapid technological advance. Indeed, Walter Chrysler's farsightedness helped the company to survive the Great Depression far better than most in the industry, and his strategy of spending money on research, "no matter how gloomy the outlook," may have been responsible for his firm's sound financial standing until well into the 1940s.

Along with the rest of Detroit's motor industry, Chrysler converted to war production during World War II. The manufacture of its Chrysler, Dodge, and Plymouth cars was put on hold while the corporation specialized in defense hardware such as small arms ammunition and submarine nets. But chief among its war products were B-29 bomber engines and anti-aircraft guns and tanks. Chrysler's wartime service earned it a special Army-Navy award for reliability and prompt delivery.

The corporation's problems started in the immediate postwar period. The ambition and spirit which drove the company to constant innovation and experimentation in the early days had been lost. The auto market had exhausted fundamental engineering breakthroughs, and American tastes had changed. It seemed that the public was more excited by the sleeker, less traditional, and sometimes less reliable models being produced by Chrysler's rivals. In short, the car industry was becoming a "marketer's game," and Chrysler's management wasn't playing.

In 1950, L. L. Colbert, a lawyer hired by Walter Chrysler in 1929, became the corporation's president. By this time, some major overhauling was necessary, and Colbert hired the management consulting firm of McKinsey and Company. Three reforms were instituted: Chrysler developed international markets for its cars, its management was centralized, and the role of the engineering department was redefined.

Colbert's reforms did little to revive the company's flagging fortunes, and two years later there was another change of management. Lynn Townsend, the new corporate head, proved to be more effective. He consolidated the Chrysler and Plymouth car divisions, closed some unproductive plants, and generally tightened operations; he also reduced the work force and installed an IBM computer system to replace 700 members of the clerical staff. Most importantly, he enhanced sales by improving the quality of the Chrysler automobile, introducing the best warranty the industry had yet seen and instituting a more aggressive marketing policy. In less than five years, Townsend had revitalized the corporation.

Success led to expansion: a space division was formed, and Chrysler became the prime contractor for the Saturn booster rocket. By the end of the 1960s, Townsend's international strategy yielded plants in 18 foreign countries. But before the decade was over, the domestic market was undergoing major changes. Inflation was taking its toll on U.S. auto manufacturers, imports of foreign vehicles had substantially increased, and the price of crude oil had risen drastically. Chrysler's troubles were compounded by internal factors: it was more concerned with competing against Ford and General Motors than in adapting itself to the rapidly changing market; it did not produce enough of its popular compact cars to meet consumer demand; and it had an overstock of larger vehicles.

The corporation reported a $4 million loss in 1969 and was operating at only 68 percent of its capacity; the previous year, it had earned profits of $122 million. Car prices were substantially reduced, but this did little to solve the underlying problems. John J. Riccardo, an accountant, succeeded to the presidency and immediately set about reducing expenses. Salaries, work force, and budget were all cut, and the company experimented with the marketing of foreign-made cars.

Unfortunately, Chrysler seemed incapable of reading the public mood: it narrowed and shortened Dodge and Chrysler models to bring prices down, but sales also tumbled; it continued to make Imperials long after Cadillacs and Lincolns had demonstrated their superiority in the luxury market; and it greeted the 1973–74 Arab oil embargo with a large inventory of gas-guzzlers. 1974 losses totalled a massive $52 million, and the next year's deficit was five times that amount.

The company experienced a brief respite in 1976 and 1977. Its trucks were in demand and foreign subsidiaries turned in good results, but domestic car sales remained a problem. Riccardo further consolidated North American operations and increased manufacturing capacity for compact cars. However, by the time Chrysler became a significant contender in that market, American car buyers were showing a distinct preference for the reliable and relatively inexpensive Japanese compacts. The days of United States manufacturing hegemony appeared to be over.

A loss of $205 million in 1978 led many industry watchers to wonder if Chrysler's rollercoaster finances could rebound from this latest big dip. The syndicate of banks (with Manufacturers Hanover Trust in the vanguard), which for years had been pouring money into Chrysler, panicked. Incredibly, many of the smaller banks had agreed to virtually unlimited lines of credit on the assumption that the company would never need to use them.

But complex and highly charged negotiations eventually saved Chrysler from bankruptcy. The federal government agreed to guarantee loans up to $1.5 billion, provided Chrysler raised $2 billion on its own. However, politicians could not justify such a massive bail-out without changes in Chrysler's management. Riccardo, who had diligently fought against heavy odds, had to go.

It was left to the charismatic Lee Iacocca to preside over Chrysler's comeback. An ex-Ford man with a flair for marketing and public relations, Iacocca took Chrysler's problems to the people, explaining that the company's failure would mean the loss of hundreds of thousands of jobs and could seriously damage the economy of the state of Michigan. Despite popular mythology and the near-adulation of Iacocca in some quarters, many observers suggested that Riccardo was largely responsible for forging the agreement that gave Chrysler a new lease on life.

Nevertheless, Iacocca's skills as a superb television salesman were of crucial importance. Under his stewardship, Chrysler battled back, and the road to recovery was a difficult one, demanding the closure of several plants and the reduction of the company's work force. In late 1987, Chrysler announced the temporary lay-off of employees at two assembly plants, then in 1988 closed an assembly plant in Wisconsin. Two additional plants were closed the following year, coinciding with a company-wide restructuring that cost Chrysler $577 million and left it with $359 million in net earnings for the year, significantly lower than the $1.05 billion recorded the year before. Once restructured, Chrysler scrapped its plans to diversify and divested the Gulfstream Aerospace unit it had purchased five years earlier, selling to a New York investment firm for $825 million in early 1990. Two other units in the company's Chrysler Technologies subsidiary—Electrospace Systems and Airborne Systems—were slated for divestiture as well, which underscored Iacocca's intent to create a leaner, more sharply focused company.

Reorganized as such, Chrysler entered the 1990s braced for a full recovery, but the economy did not cooperate. The decline in automotive sales during the fourth quarter of 1989—the company's first fourth quarter decline since 1982—portended a more crippling slump to come, as an economic recession gripped businesses of all types, both domestically and abroad. Net income in 1990 slipped to $68 million, then plunged to a $795 million loss the following year, $411 million of which was attributable to losses incurred by the company's automotive operations. The precipitous drop in earnings for 1991 was the latest in a nearly decade-long series of declines that saw Chrysler's earnings fall each year from the $2.3 billion generated in 1984 to 1991's disappointing loss. Mired in an economic downturn, Chrysler appeared destined for more of the same, rather than headed toward recovery as Iacocca had hoped, but part of the reason for 1991's losses also led to the company's first step toward genuine recovery.

Partly to blame for the $795 million loss in 1991 were the high pre-production and introduction costs associated with Chrysler's new Jeep Grand Cherokee and increased production costs at the company's St. Louis minivan plant. These two types of vehicles—minivans and sports-utility vehicles—represented the key to Chrysler's recovery. The popularity of these vehicles, coupled with significant price advantages over Japanese models, fueled Chrysler's resurgence. In 1992, when Chrysler's rival U.S. manufacturer, Ford, registered a $7.38 billion loss, Chrysler turned its $795 million loss the year before into a $723 million gain. It was a signal achievement, accomplished in Iacocca's last year as chief executive officer, but still the debilitative economic climate clouded the company's future, tempering hopes that the company could expect further earnings growth.

Aside from the stifling economic conditions, there were challenges unique to Chrysler that needed addressing before the company's management could be optimistic. In the first quarter of 1993, Chrysler recorded a $4.4 billion charge for retiree health benefits, which led to a $2.5 billion loss for the year, a staggering financial blow but one irrespective of the company's ability to successfully sell automotive vehicles. That ability was demonstrated in the first quarter of 1994, when Chrysler posted $938 million in profits, the most recorded in the company's history and the greatest amount since the $801 million recorded in the second quarter of 1984.

Driven by the widespread demand for sports-utility vehicles and the waning prowess of Japanese car manufacturers, who were hobbled by the dollar's strength against the yen, Chrysler entered the mid-1990s in a decidedly positive direction. As it charted its future, expectations for a recovery that had taken nearly a decade to realize were nearly complete, buoying hopes for a profitable conclusion to the 1990s and a strengthened position for the twenty-first century.

Principal Subsidiaries: Automotive Financial Services, Inc.; Acuflight, Inc. (67%); American Motors Pan American Corp.; Beaver Dam Products Corp.; Chrysler Corporation Fund; Chrysler International Corp.; Chrysler Pentastar Aviation, Inc.; Chrysler Technologies Corp.; Chrysler Transport, Inc.; Dealer Capital, Inc.; Jeep International Corp.; Chrysler Foreign Sales Corp.; AMC de Venezuela, CA; American Motors Overseas Corp.; Chrysler Canada Ltd.; Chrysler International SA; Chrysler Motors de Venezuela, SA; Chrysler Overseas Trading Co. Ltd.; Jeep Africa, Ltd. (51%); Jeep Australia, Pty. Ltd.; Jeep of Canada Ltd.; Jeep Japan, Ltd.; Chrysler de Mexico, SA (99.9%).

Further Reading:

Abodaher, David, *Iacocca,* New York: Macmillan, 1982.

Gorden, Maynard M., *The Iacocca Management Technique,* New York: Dodd Mead, 1985.

Iacocca, Lee, with William Novak, *Iacocca: An Autobiography,* New York: Bantam, 1984.

Kerwin, Kathleen, ''The Big Three Are Learning to Hold a Lead,'' *Business Week,* April 26, 1993, p. 29.

Kujawa, Duane, *International Labor Relations Management in the Automotive Industry: A Comparative Study of Chrysler, Ford, and General Motors,* New York: Praeger, 1971.

Langworth, Richard M., and Jan P. Norbye, *The Complete History of Chrysler Corporation, 1924–1985,* New York: Beekman House, 1985.

Moritz, Michael, and Barrett Seaman, *Going for Broke: The Chrysler Story,* New York: Doubleday, 1981.

Pomice, Eva, ''Can Detroit Hold On?,'' *U.S. News and World Report,* April 15, 1991, p. 51.

Reich, Robert B., and John D. Donahue, *New Deals: The Chrysler Revival and the American System,* New York: Time, 1985.

Taylor, Alex, ''The New Golden Age of Autos,'' *Fortune,* April 4, 1994, p. 50.

Thomas, Charles M., ''Big 3 Picture Brightens after '89 Plunge,'' *Automotive News,* February 19, 1990, p. 1.

—updated by Jeffrey L. Covell

Cirrus Logic, Incorporated

3100 West Warren Avenue
Fremont, California 94538
U.S.A.
(415) 226-2259
Fax: (415) 226-2240

Public Company
Incorporated: 1984
Employees: 748
Sales: $544.1 million
Stock Exchanges: NASDAQ

Cirrus Logic, Incorporated is a leading producer of semiconductors. While the company designs and writes software for microchips for use in a wide variety of specialized applications, it is an industry leader in the areas of mass storage management, VGA graphics, audiovisual conversion, and communications.

Cirrus Logic traces its origins to a small company called Patil Systems, which was founded in Utah in 1981 by Suhas Patil, a former Massachusetts Institute of Technology (MIT) professor then teaching at the University of Utah. While at MIT, Patil had developed a microchip-level software system for controlling computer hard disk drives, which he called Strategic/Logic Array (S/LA). The S/LA system represented a substantial improvement in the management of hard drive functions, since it behaved more consistently and was easier to design than existing systems. Patil gathered together several associates and formed Patil Systems to market his new product.

Over the next three years, however, the company's efforts produced little commercial success. "I made the rounds and couldn't give it away," Patil would later recall in *Upside*. For help with the marketing and management of his tiny, eleven-employee company, Patil contacted Michael Hackworth, a former marketing executive for Fairchild Industries and Motorola who was senior vice-president of Signetics, the Sunnyvale, California-based semiconductor subsidiary of North American Philips, in 1984.

The prospect of working with Patil sparked Hackworth's interest. Although a prominent executive at Signetics, he was unhappy with the way the company operated, and especially with the inefficiency with which it introduced new products. When Patil first contacted him, Hackworth thought that S/LA software might be of use to Signetics. But then, as he later remarked in *Upside,* "When I got in and met the people and understood what they had, it hit me like a ton of bricks that his could be the basis for a new kind of chip company." Hackworth perceived that Patil's S/LA system could be used to develop a wide range of highly specialized semiconductors in a relatively short time. All the development process would require was a systems engineer who could program and arrange the chips to facilitate whatever function the product was supposed to carry out.

Instead of absorbing Patil Systems into Signetics, Hackworth left Signetics to join Patil Systems. He became president and CEO, while Patil assumed the posts of chairman and executive vice-president of products and technology. The company reincorporated in California in 1984 under the name Cirrus Logic, Incorporated, and moved its headquarters to Fremont, in the northern half of the state. The company's new name came when Hackworth decided that Patil Systems needed a new name, but one that did not dip into the alphabet soup of Greek prefixes and suffixes in which the Silicon Valley seemed to swim. One of his daughters came up the idea of renaming the company after cirrus clouds, the highest clouds in the sky, as a way of expressing the elevated complexity of its products.

Under Hackworth, Cirrus Logic pursued a strategy that emphasized developing peripheral devices in which the company's semiconductors were used. This emphasis stemmed in part from Hackworth's experience at Signetics, which had developed a 2650 microprocessor only to see it fail because its application in peripheral devices had not been taken into account during the design process. Under this plan, Cirrus Logic would use the versatility of the S/LA system in an opportunistic manner, jumping into new peripheral markets as they emerged. The company bought raw microchips from outside foundries to avoid the burden of running its own fabrication operations.

When major opportunities presented themselves, Cirrus Logic did not ignore them. Originally, Hackworth's master plan had envisioned the company developing products for microcomputers, but not the microcomputers themselves. But in the mid-1980s, the boom in personal computers began. Cirrus Logic responded with a neat product development sidestep, simply applying the concepts it had intended for peripherals to the emerging PC market instead.

The company's first major effort in marketing its hard drive controller resulted in its first major success. Though it faced daunting competition from more established companies such as Adaptec and Western Digital, Cirrus Logic had an advantage: it had developed the first controller chip that could be mounted inside the drive mechanism, rather than on a card outside it. This innovation would eventually lead to more compact hard drives. At first, Cirrus Logic's product was too advanced to sell easily; an official from prominent hard drive manufacturer Seagate Technology told Hackworth that the Cirrus Logic controller was five years ahead of what his company wanted. But Cirrus Logic modified the chip to fit Seagate's needs and received a contract from them. Conner Peripherals, which made hard drives for Compaq Computer PCs, soon followed with orders of their own.

Cirrus Logic's successful entry into the PC hard drive market paved the way for future successes. While its hard drive controller chip drove sales, accounting for as much as 80 percent of total revenues, the company developed new graphics- and communications-related products. In 1987, IBM unveiled Video Graphics Array (VGA), its new technology standard for graphics display. This started a scramble among chipmakers to develop products to conform to the new standard, a competition that Cirrus Logic won, producing the first fully compatible VGA controller microchip. In 1989, the company developed a VGA controller for flat-panel liquid crystal diode (LCD) displays, barely anticipating the boom in notebook computers, which used such displays.

Also in 1989, Cirrus Logic went public. It used the cash raised to finance a series of acquisitions that broadened its technological expertise. In 1990, it acquired Data Systems Technology, which specialized in data compression and error-correction algorithms for modems. The next year it purchased a controlling interest in Pixel Semiconductor, a video-imaging technology firm with expertise in the multimedia field, from Visual Information Technologies. It later absorbed Pixel Semiconductor's operations into its own. In 1992, it acquired R. Scott Associates, a modem software company, and Acumos, which specialized in high-integration desktop graphics. In 1993, it acquired Pacific Communication Sciences, a leading developer of Cellular Digital Packet Data communications technology. Also in 1993, Cirrus Logic announced that it would produce custom microchips for companies licensed by Apple Computer to manufacture Apple's Newton personal digital assistant.

In its first fifteen years, Cirrus Logic grew from a tiny company struggling to raise a few million dollars in capital to an important presence in the microchip industry with well over $500 million in annual sales. At the same time that its sales skyrocketed, it broadened its technological expertise with similar rapidity. But its rapid growth brought problems as well as benefits, and in the wake of its rapid string of acquisitions in the early 1990s problems in incorporating these new subsidiaries became apparent. Difficulties in communication sometimes produced delays in developing and delivering new products. Consequently, the company embarked on a reorganization in 1993 designed to decentralize and streamline operations at the same time.

Cirrus Logic's growing importance as a supplier of semiconductors also increased concern over continued access to sufficient quantities of raw chips. Cirrus Logic had not only taken pride in its ''fablessness,'' its lack of chip fabrication operations and consequent need to rely on outside foundries, but considered it a necessity. ''We will never eliminate the fabless approach,'' Michael Hackworth declared in 1993. ''The foundry thing has provided us with enormous flexibility that we would never ever have if we had to drag our own clean room [for fabricating raw chips] around with us. The chances of us doing a [brand-new] clean room on our own are zero or none.'' But the production glut in raw chips that had made life easy for Cirrus Logic and similar fabless chipmakers began to dry up in the 1990s at the same time that demand for the company's products began to pick up from levels that were already quite high. In 1993, Cirrus Logic signed agreements with its suppliers to buy a set number of chips over three years in return for guarantees of foundry capacity, but even this did not prove entirely satisfactory.

Fortunately, Hackworth had not ruled out a joint fabrication venture with another semiconductor company with which it was not in direct competition. And so in 1994, Cirrus Logic took a first tentative step toward fabrication by signing a joint venture with IBM. Under the terms of the agreement, the two companies would refurbish an under-used IBM plant in East Fishkill, New York, that once manufactured chips for mainframe computers. Even with IBM's help, Cirrus Logic estimated that the project would cost it tens of millions of dollars.

That Cirrus Logic has experienced growing pains should not cause surprise or alarm. Its growth has been so rapid that it should have been expected. Keeping agile in an industry in which change is quick and consistent is the challenge for the company as it grows.

Principal Subsidiaries: Cirrus Logic K. K. (Japan); Cirrus Logic, Gmbh (Germany); Data Systems Technology; Data Pump International; Acumos Incorporated; Crystal Semiconductor; Pixel Semiconductor; R. Scott Associates.

Further Reading:

Arnold, Bill, ''Cirrus Takes the PC Market By Storm,'' *Upside,* August 1993.
Hof, Robert D., '' 'Real Men Have Fabs,' '' *Business Week,* April 11, 1994.

—Douglas Sun

Cisco Systems, Inc.

170 West Tasman Drive
San Jose, California 95134-1706
U.S.A.
(408) 526-4000
Fax: (408) 526-4100

Public Company
Incorporated: 1984
Employees: 2,262
Sales: $1.24 billion
Stock Exchanges: NASDAQ
SICs: 3577 Computer Peripheral Equipment, Not Elsewhere
   Classified

Cisco Systems, Inc. is the world's leading supplier of high-performance internetworking products for a growing market in which computer and telecommunications technologies converge. The company's product line includes routers, bridges, switches, protocol translators, internetwork management software, and communication servers, all of which link together geographically dispersed local area networks (LANs) and wide area networks (WANs) of computers. In particular, Cisco is the world leader in multi-protocol routers, which permit the linkage of different kinds of networks with different data communications protocols. Cisco maintained over 50 percent market share in multi-protocol routers in the eight years since introducing them in 1986 and still had a 40 percent share in 1994. In its first ten years, Cisco has sustained uninterrupted high growth in sales and profits.

Cisco Systems was founded in December 1984 in Menlo Park, California, by a husband and wife team from Stanford University, Leonard Bosack and Sandra Lerner. Bosack was the manager of the computer science department's laboratory, and Lerner oversaw the computers at the graduate school of business. At Stanford, Bosack devised a way to connect the two local area networks in the respective departments where he and his wife worked, 500 yards across campus.

Lerner and Bosack initially tried to sell the internetworking technology that Bosack had developed to existing computer companies, but none were interested. They then decided to start their own business, Cisco Systems, based on this technology. Bosack and Lerner were joined by colleagues Greg Setz, Bill Westfield, and Kirk Lougheed, as cofounders. Stanford Univer-

sity later tried to obtain $11 million in licensing fees from the new company, because Bosack had developed the technology while an employee at the university, but eventually the university settled for $150,000 and free routers and support services.

The company was established on a very tight budget. In fact, Bosack and Lerner had to mortgage their house, run up credit card debts, and defer salaries to their friends who worked for them in order to get the venture off the ground, and, even after two years of business, Lerner maintained an outside salaried job to supplement the couple's income.

Cisco's primary product from the beginning was the internetworking router, a hardware device incorporating software that automatically selects the most effective route for data to flow between networks. Cisco's routers pioneered support for multiple protocols or data transmission standards, and could therefore link together different kinds of networks, those having different architectures and those built on different hardware, such as IBM-compatible personal computers, Apple Macintosh computers, UNIX workstations, and IBM mainframes. Cisco thus became the first company to commercially provide a multi-protocol router when it shipped its first product in 1986, a router for the TCP/IP (Transmission Control Protocol/Internet Protocol) protocol suite. A year later, Cisco was selling $250,000 worth of routers per month. Sales for the fiscal year ending July 1987 were $1.5 million, and the company had only eight employees at the time.

Cisco initially marketed its routers to universities, research centers, the aerospace industry, and government facilities by contacting computer scientists and engineers via ARPANET, the precursor to what was later known as the Internet. These customers tended to use the TCP/IP protocols and UNIX-based computers. In 1988, the company began to target its internetworking routers at mainstream corporations with geographically dispersed branches that used different networks. To that end, Cisco developed routers serving an even greater array of communications protocols and subsequently distinguished its routers by enabling them to support more protocols than those of any other router manufacturer. By the late 1980s, when the commercial market for internetworking began to develop, Cisco's reasonably priced, high-performance routers gave it a head start over the emerging competition.

Although Cisco had a high rate of sales growth, the young company was still short of cash, and, in 1988 Bosack and Lerner were forced to turn to a venture capitalist, Donald T. Valentine of Sequoia Capital, for support. Valentine, however, required that the owners surrender to him a controlling stake in the company. Valentine thus became chairperson and then hired an outsider, John Morgridge, as the company's new president and chief executive officer. Morgridge, who had an M.B.A. from Stanford University, was chief operating officer at a laptop computer manufacturer GRiD Systems Corp. and prior to that had spent six years as vice-president of sales and marketing at Stratus Computer. Morgridge replaced several Cisco managers, who were friends of Bosack and Lerner, with more qualified and experienced executives. In February 1990, Cisco went public, after which Bosack and Lerner began selling their shares. Sales for the fiscal year ending July 1990 were $69.78 million, net income was $13.90 million, and the company had 254 employees.

Under Morgridge, Bosack had been given the title of chief scientist and Lerner was made head of customer service. However, Lerner reportedly did not get along well with Morgridge, and, in August 1990, she was fired, whereupon Bosack also quit. When they left the company, Bosack and Lerner sold the remainder of their stock for $100 million, for a total divestiture of about $200 million. The couple subsequently gave away the majority of their profits to their favorite charities.

Meanwhile, Morgridge built up a direct sales force to market the products to corporate clients. At first, Cisco's corporate clients were the scientific department of companies which already maintained large internal networks. Later, Cisco was able to market its products to all kinds of major corporations to help them link the computer systems of their headquarters, regional, and branch offices. As Cisco's client base grew, the company's greatest challenge became meeting customer support service needs. The large size of the network systems for which Cisco supplied products made the user support task especially complex.

The company grew at a tremendous rate as its market rapidly expanded. In the early 1990s, companies of all sizes were installing local area networks of personal computers. As such, the potential market for linking these networks, either with each other or with existing minicomputers and mainframe computers, also grew. Cisco's sales jumped from $183.18 million in fiscal 1991 to $339.62 million in 1992, and net income grew from $43.19 million to $84.39 million over the same year. In 1992, *Fortune* magazine rated Cisco as the second fastest growing company in the United States. As the leading internetworking router provider, Cisco could redefine and expand the market as it grew.

As new communications technologies became widespread, Cisco adapted and added the capabilities of handling new protocols to its products. In fall 1992, Cisco introduced Fiber Distributed Data Interface (FDDI) and Token-Ring enhancements to its high-end router. Around the same time, the company also introduced the first Integrated Services Digital Network (ISDN) router for the Japanese market.

Until 1992, Cisco's products had not addressed IBM's System Network Architecture (SNA), a proprietary network structure used by IBM computers. However, in September 1992, after IBM announced plans to license its Advanced Peer-to-Peer Networking (APPN) protocol used for SNA, Cisco responded by announcing plans for a rival Advanced Peer-to-Peer Internetworking (APPI) protocol for supporting SNA. By August 1993, Cisco had decided not to develop a rival protocol, because IBM made it clear that APPN would be a more open, multi-vendor protocol than originally intended. Cisco then went on to work with IBM on further defining the APPN standard and bought a license to use APPN technology.

The emergence of asynchronous transfer mode (ATM) technology as a new standard method for multi-protocol data communications posed a challenge to Cisco and the router industry. ATM is a cell-switching technique that can provide high-speed communications of data, voice, video, and images without the use of routers. In early 1993, Cisco entered into a joint development project with AT&T and StrataCom to develop standards that would ensure that ATM operated within existing Frame Relay networks. Cisco also became one of the four founding members of the ATM Forum to help define the emerging standard. In February 1993, Cisco announced a strategy to include ATM among the protocols supported by its products. In fiscal 1994, Cisco introduced its first ATM switch.

In January 1993, Cisco introduced a new flagship product, the Cisco 7000 router, which featured a 50 percent improvement in performance over the AGS +, Cisco's existing high-end router. In June of that year, Cisco introduced a new low-end, lower priced product line, the Cisco 2000 router family. The Cisco 2000 was aimed at companies desiring to link their smaller, remote branches or even remote individual employees, but unwilling to pay a premium price. Also during this time, the first network with over 1,000 Cisco routers was created.

International sales became an important part of Cisco's business. Subsidiaries were established in Japan and Australia, and a European Technical Assistance Center was established in Brussels, Belgium. In March 1993, Cisco Systems (HK) Ltd. became a new subsidiary in Hong Kong. International sales steadily increased, accounting for 35.6 percent of sales in fiscal 1991, 36 percent in fiscal 1992, 39 percent in fiscal 1993, and 41.9 percent in fiscal 1994. Most of Cisco's international sales were through distributors, whereas in the United States the majority of sales (65 percent in early 1994) were made directly to the end-users.

Cisco also began to market its technology, especially its software, more aggressively to long-distance telephone companies, as the deregulation of U.S. telephone carriers enabled these companies to provide more kinds of data communications products and services. For example, Cisco entered into a joint marketing agreement with MCI International to integrate Cisco's routers into end-to-end data networks over telephone lines. In 1992, Cisco entered new distribution agreements with Bell Atlantic Corp. and U.S. West Information Systems Inc. Cisco also signed marketing agreements in fiscal 1993 with Pacific Bell, whereby Cisco became a preferred router supplier for the company's network systems.

Cisco similarly began contracting with major European telecommunications companies at about the same time. British Telecom became an Original Equipment Manufacturer (OEM) client of all of Cisco's products. Other European telecommunications companies that entered into OEM relationships with Cisco included Alcatel of France and Siemens A.G. of Germany. Olivetti of Italy agreed to market Cisco's products under a Value-Added Reseller agreement late in 1992.

Cisco made other strategic alliances to position itself better in the maturing internetworking market. To reach out to less technical clients, Cisco entered into joint agreements with Microsoft Corp. to market Cisco's first PC-based router card with Microsoft's Windows NT Advanced Server networking software through Microsoft's marketing channels. Similarly, Cisco established a partnership with Novell to integrate Cisco's routers with Novell's Netware network software so as to provide links between Netware and UNIX-based networks. Additionally, Cisco began working with LanOptics Ltd. to develop remote-access products.

In September 1993, Cisco made its first acquisition. For $100 million, it acquired Crescendo Communications, which had pioneered products for a new technology called Copper Distributed Data Interface (CDDI). Crescendo's development of ATM technology was also a leading reason for the acquisition. Crescendo Communications was renamed the Workgroup Business Unit, and its switching technologies under development were later incorporated into Cisco's routers. Cisco made its second acquisition, that of Newport Systems Solutions for $90.8 million in stock, in August 1994. Newport Solutions sold the LAN2LAN product line, software used in linking local area networks.

Early in 1994, Cisco announced a new networking architecture, CiscoFusion, to provide clients with an gradual transition from routers to the new switched internetworking technologies of ATM and LAN switching. CiscoFusion allowed users to take advantage of both routing and switching techniques. As part of this architecture, several new switching products were introduced in March 1994, including the ATM Interface Processor and the Catalyst FDDI-to-Ethernet LAN switch. The latter was the first new product of the Workgroup Businesses Unit since the acquisition of Crescendo.

During this time, Cisco moved its headquarters from one end of Silicon Valley to the other, from Menlo Park to a newly constructed office building complex in San Jose, California. The growing size of the company had necessitated larger office space. The company's work force had grown from 1,451 in July 1993 to 2,262 in July 1994, as Cisco hired talent from smaller, struggling internetworking companies which were laying off personnel.

In fiscal 1994, Cisco topped $1 billion in sales, ending the year on July 31, 1994, with $1.24 billion in net sales, a 92 percent increase over the previous year, and $314.87 million in net income, 83 percent more than fiscal 1993. Industry observers noted that in the internetworking business, clients tended to stick with a given vendor for all their internetworking products and that the companies that had entered the router business early tended to be the ones to survive and grow stronger; Cisco thus seemed poised for continued success.

Principal Subsidiaries: Cisco Systems Canada Limited; Cisco Systems de Mexico S.A. de C.V.; Cisco Systems Europe s.a.r.l. (France); Cisco Systems GmbH (Germany); Nihon Cisco Systems K.K. (Japan); Cisco Systems Hong Kong, Ltd.; Cisco Systems Australia Pty., Ltd.

Further Reading:

Carlsen, Clifford, "Rolling on the Info Superhighway," *San Francisco Business Times,* August 20, 1993, p. 6A.
Emigh, Jacqueline, "Cisco Unveils ATM Interfacing Router," *Telephony,* February 1, 1993, pp. 24+.
Musich, Paula, "Cisco Chief Plots Router Course: Outlines Plans for ATM Technology," *PC Week,* September 13, 1993, pp. 49+.
Musich, Paula, "Cisco Revamps Router Strategy: Shifts Product, Distribution Tactics for Maturing Market," *PC Week,* November 22, 1993, p. 123.
Musich, Paula, "Cisco, Wellfleet Ride Router Market to Success," *PC Week,* December 14, 1992, pp. 163+.
Pitta, Julie, "Long Distance Relationship," *Forbes,* March 16, 1992, pp. 136+.

—Heather Behn Hedden

CompuAdd

CompuAdd Computer Corporation

12337 Technology Blvd.
Austin, Texas 78727
U.S.A.
(512) 250-1489
Fax: (512) 250-3658

Private Company
Incorporated: 1982
Employees: 300
Sales: $233.4 million
SICs: 3571 Electronic Computers; 3575 Computer Terminals;
 5961 Catalog and Mail Order Houses

One of the world's leading direct marketers of computers and peripheral equipment, CompuAdd Computer Corporation manufactures its own line of personal computers and PC-based point-of-sale terminals. CompuAdd also sells software and provides a full range of support services for the products it markets. By selling to its customers directly, primarily through mail-order, the company has kept its products' prices among the lowest in the industry. The vast majority of the CompuAdd's customers are businesses or government agencies. About one quarter of its business comes from government contracts, while large businesses account for 29 percent. About 17 percent of the company's customers are small or medium-sized businesses.

For the first twelve years of its existence, CompuAdd was essentially a one-man show run by founder Bill Hayden. Hayden, a mechanic's son who grew up in San Antonio, Texas, moved up the road to Austin for college and stayed there after graduating. He began his career as an engineer at Texas Instruments. To fulfill his entrepreneurial dreams, Hayden quit Texas Instruments in 1981 and launched CompuAdd in April 1982. Using as seed money $100,000 he had earned selling real estate on the side, Hayden started selling disk drives and other peripheral equipment out of the trunk of his aging orange Chevy Chevette. The name CompuAdd came from Hayden's idea to sell add-on equipment for computers. The company's first sale was made after Hayden ran a small ad in a computer magazine. After that initial breakthrough, orders began pouring in, and by the fall of 1982 Hayden's monthly receipts had reached $30,000. Before long, he was able to move CompuAdd's base of operations out of his shabby car and into a shabby office known as "the cave."

Hayden's initial plan for CompuAdd was relatively modest. He hoped to establish a successful mail-order operation that would sell computer equipment made by others at a significant discount and offer superior customer service. His original intention was to keep the product line small and the operation simple. By 1983, however, the business had grown so much that he and his wife, Connie, could no longer handle all of CompuAdd's affairs by themselves. With sales approaching $2 million, Hayden hired his first batch of managers. The three young men he brought on board were all in their twenties and were either recent college graduates or still in school. Under Hayden supervision, John Hutchison handled purchasing and advertising; Frank Taylor worked on shipping, quality control, and technical support; and Tom Irby managed CompuAdd's earliest forays into retail sales.

By 1984 CompuAdd was selling a full range of products for personal computers, including the PCs themselves. The company's growth during the next few years continued to accelerate, and by 1985 CompuAdd had about 80 employees and annual sales of about $25 million. In spite of CompuAdd's meteoric growth, Hayden was adamant that the company retain certain small business characteristics. As additional layers of management became necessary, communication between them remained old-fashioned. Inter-office memos were few and far between, and nobody, including Hayden himself, had a secretary. Business was conducted face-to-face, and everybody answered their own phones.

Sales at CompuAdd soared to the $100 million range by 1987. By this time, CompuAdd was marketing its own line of PCs, low-cost IBM clones that were sold mostly through mail-order catalogs and ads featuring the company's toll-free 800 number. Price and customer service remained CompuAdd's main hook for customers, and its direct marketing methods allowed the company to consistently undercut the competition. In 1989 Hayden decided to increase the role of retail outlets in the company's scheme. That year, the number of CompuAdd stores was increased from 15 to 71. The stores were warehouse-like, with little in the way of decoration or styling. Toshiba laptops and a few select brands of printers and other peripherals were stocked in addition to CompuAdd products. Hayden saw the stores as a way to tap further into the small business and individual computer-users market. At the same time, the company gained a retail presence without having to deal with the difficult task of breaking into the big computer retail chains. Despite the company's focus on in-store sales, telephone and mail-order sales accounted for 80 percent of the company's revenue for 1988. For the year, CompuAdd more than doubled its sales to $241 million.

CompuAdd's manufacturing capabilities began to grow more sophisticated in the late 1980s. When IBM abandoned some of its Austin-area operations, Hayden leased a 250,000-square-foot plant it had vacated, and hired a handful of former IBM and TI executives to help run it. These moves enabled CompuAdd to start designing its own computer systems from scratch, rather than merely assembling PCs from ready-made components. The company was able to design a new PC from the ground up in five months. CompuAdd's small size made it more agile than its larger competitors; the same task took 18 months at IBM. Leading the team was CompuAdd president Edward D.

Thomas, a 26-year IBM veteran who had worked with great success on the low-end versions of that company's popular PS/2 computer line.

The company entered the international marketplace by opening facilities for both sales and assembly in the United Kingdom in 1988. Hayden continued to expand CompuAdd's retail division with breathtaking speed in 1989. As many as three stores were opened in a single week during this period. By the end of the year, a total of 88 CompuAdd stores were in operation. The pace of the company's retail expansion slackened somewhat in 1990, as the Austin assembly plant struggled to coordinate its production with the needs of the outlets. This was balanced in part by the further growth of its international operations. Outposts were established during 1990 in Germany, France, and Mexico.

CompuAdd experimented with a telephone support line called the Direct Help service. While most computer hotlines were designed to provide support for a particular manufacturer's line of products, CompuAdd's 900-number differed by offering problem-solving assistance for virtually any PC-related snag, regardless of whose equipment was involved. By the end of 1990, CompuAdd's sales had reached $516 million, a 500 percent increase over 1987's figure.

In December of 1990, CompuAdd received a rush order from the Defense Department for $30 million worth of personal computers and laptops to be used in Operation Desert Shield and Desert Storm. Facing a close deadline, Hayden was able to convince many workers to put in huge amounts of overtime, and because of CompuAdd's nimble structure, resources and personnel were easily diverted from other projects. Although only a third of the necessary parts were on hand when the order came in, the computers were delivered on time. A letter sent to CompuAdd headquarters by an Army commander attests to the battle performance of the equipment. The letter, displayed prominently at the Austin home office, tells of a CompuAdd 486 computer blown completely through a wall by the explosion of an Iraqi missile. The only damage the computer sustained was to a circuit board. The case remained intact, and after a board transplant the computer was returned to service.

CompuAdd expanded its retail business in 1991, opening 32 new stores. The company's 120 stores were now located in 37 states, stretching to both coasts of the country. Customers at the stores paid the same prices as did those who ordered directly from the factory. By this time, retail and non-retail operations each accounted for about half of the company's sales.

In June of 1991, Hayden surprised everybody by announcing a major reorganization of CompuAdd's structure. The reorganization included the spin-off of the company's price-sensitive mail-order business, its original backbone, from corporate mail-order and retail operations. The spin-off was completed in September. The new company, called CompuAdd Express, was moved into a building across the street from CompuAdd's headquarters. Hayden was so adamant about the two companies having separate identities that no CompuAdd employees were allowed to set foot in the Express building, though Express was allowed to recruit personnel from among CompuAdd's work force. The separation was apparently successful, since Compu-

Add Express quickly began stealing customers from its mother company by establishing lower prices. To Hayden, it was obviously preferable to lose customers to another company he owned than to another upstart mail-order firm. Spinning off this key piece of its mail-order business enabled CompuAdd to operate without the burden of supporting the high-cost of retail operations. CompuAdd continued to grow without its mail-order business; its sales totaled $514 million in 1991.

In 1991, CompuAdd was awarded one of the largest government computer contracts ever, a deal worth about $400 million in the first year alone, to deliver 300,000 computers to the Air Force. The Desktop IV contract, which was shared with Sysorex Information Systems of Falls Church, Virginia, was immediately challenged by eight companies whose bids were passed over. The group of protesters included many industry heavyweights, including Apple Computer, General Motors' Electronic Data Systems Corporation unit, IBM, and Zenith. The contract was declared invalid due to the way new government contract procedures were implemented, and CompuAdd came out of rebidding among the losers.

In December of 1991, however, CompuAdd won a $53 million contract from Sears, Roebuck and Co. to supply 28,000 computerized cash registers, beating out such industry giants as IBM and NCR Corporation. The terminals were assembled by CompuAdd using the 386SX microprocessor made by Intel Corporation. The company's speed and agility impressed Sears' officials when CompuAdd was able to demonstrate a working prototype within days of submitting a proposal.

By the beginning of 1992, CompuAdd had 1,500 employees—and not one of them was a secretary. Hayden, by now listed as one of the wealthiest men in Texas, still marked his own calendar. In March of that year, Hayden spun off another chunk of the company in order to keep it streamlined. CompuAdd Information Systems was created as a separate entity specializing in custom programming for large companies. The new firm's first customer was Sears, which needed ongoing software support for its new point-of-sale terminals. Hayden also adjusted the mother company's corporate structure again, dividing it into two autonomous divisions. The Retail/International Division, headed by former Texas Instruments executive James Moore, took control of CompuAdd's stores and its overseas sales operations. John Conn, hired from Harris Corporation, became general manager of the Systems and Technology Division, in charge of government and large corporate accounts. The positions of president and chief operating officer, formerly held by Edward Thomas, were eliminated altogether.

Although CompuAdd's growth in its first ten years of operation could be described as spectacular, it did not match that of crosstown rival Dell Computer Corporation during the same period. As Hayden admitted to Stephanie Anderson Forest of *Business Week,* this was partly due to his reluctance to give up control of the company. After going public in 1988, Dell saw its sales balloon to nearly $2 billion a year by 1992. CompuAdd, on the other hand, relied completely on cash flow and bank loans to pay for the cost of its expansion. As Hayden told Forest in early 1993: ''I don't even have a savings account. All the money I have is sitting in this company.'' Dell's lead over CompuAdd was especially evident in the area of international sales. While

36 percent of Dell's business was generated overseas by 1992, sales abroad were bringing in only about ten percent of Compu-Add's revenue.

CompuAdd launched its first national television advertising campaign in the summer of 1992 in an effort to achieve better public name recognition. Price wars and fierce competition among computer stores, especially superstores like CompUSA, led Hayden to rethink his planned retail expansion. Instead of surging ahead, CompuAdd began scaling back its retail operations, getting out of some markets entirely. There were also plans to convert several stores into CompUSA-like superstores. For 1992, the company's sales grew only about three percent to $524 million, far short of the billion dollar mark that the Air Force contract had led Hayden to believe would be cracked. In March of 1993, CompuAdd announced it was fleeing the retail arena altogether, and would concentrate solely on direct sales in the future. The closures meant the elimination of about 600 jobs. The task of closing all of the retail stores created a host of complications, especially squabbles with landlords. Pressure from them and from other creditors forced CompuAdd to seek Chapter 11 bankruptcy protection in June of 1993 to smooth its withdrawal from retail sales and protect its viable mail-order business.

Bankruptcy did not slow the company's product development efforts, however. In June 1993, CompuAdd also launched a new line of Centura personal computers that completely supplanted its existing PC line.

CompuAdd emerged from bankruptcy in November of 1993. As part of the process, 75 percent ownership of the company was transferred to unsecured creditors, with Hayden retaining 20 percent and the remainder held for employees. Within a few weeks of CompuAdd's emergence from bankruptcy, Hayden announced his resignation from the company and went on to form three start-up ventures. The chief executive officer position was taken over by Richard Krause, the company's president and chief operating officer. Immediately, CompuAdd began looking for a buyer to assume controlling interest in the company. In July of 1994, CompuAdd announced that it would be bought by Dimeling, Schrieber & Park, a private Philadelphia investment company that specialized in purchasing companies emerging from bankruptcy. The acquisition, which included a significant infusion of capital and a new lending group, was completed in September of 1994.

Throughout the bankruptcy and shift in ownership, the company continued rolling out new products. Eleven new multimedia computer models were unveiled; a new line of Pentium-based PCs was introduced; and the line of notebook computers was expanded. Whether CompuAdd's new ownership can restore the company's momentum remained unclear in the mid-1990s, but CompuAdd's reputation for customer service and selling quality products at reasonable prices remained intact.

Principal Subsidiaries: CompuAdd Computers (U.K).

Further Reading:

Annin, Peter, and John Schwartz, "Making PCs, Texas Style," *Newsweek,* January 6, 1992, p. 35.
Bartimo, Jim, "No One Can Say CompuAdd Thinks Small," *Business Week,* November 13, 1989, p. 102E.
Biesada, Alexandra, "Austin's Other Upstart," *Financial World,* March 17, 1992, p. 38.
Forest, Stephanie Anderson, "A Little Computer Company That Could—Until Lately," *Business Week,* February 15, 1993, pp. 104B–C.
Francis, Bob, "The Datamation 100," *Datamation,* June 15, 1992, p. 125; June 15, 1993, p. 106.
Kapp, Sue, "CompuWho? Rolls Out 1st National Campaign," *Business Marketing,* July 1992, pp. 30–31.
Ladendorf, Kirk, "Investor Group to Buy CompuAdd," *Austin American-Statesman,* July 20, 1994.
Lancaster, Hal, "U.S. Cancels Contract with CompuAdd and Sysorex after Large Rivals Protest," *Wall Street Journal,* January 8, 1991, p. B2.
Lewis, Peter H., "CompuAdd Moves Up to the First Tier," *New York Times,* November 11, 1991, p. F9.
Pool, Claire, "CompuAdd's Price War," *Forbes,* April 27, 1992, pp. 158–159.
Pope, Kyle, "CompuAdd Seeks Chapter 11 Shield as Its Stores Close," *Wall Street Journal,* June 23, 1993, p. B7.
——, "Hayden Quits as the CEO of CompuAdd," *Wall Street Journal,* November 24, 1993, p. B3.
Posner, Bruce G., "Holding Your Own," *Inc.,* December 1989, pp. 171–172.

—Robert R. Jacobson

**INFORMATION
TECHNOLOGY
CONSULTING**

CTG, Inc.

800 Delaware Avenue
Buffalo, New York 14209
U.S.A.
(716) 882-8000
Fax: (716) 887-7246

Public Company
Incorporated: 1966 as Marks-Baer, Inc.
Employees: 4,132
Sales: $295 million
Stock Exchanges: New York Amsterdam
SICs: 7372 Prepackaged Software; 8742 Management
    Consulting Services

Computer Task Group Inc. (CTG, Inc.) is one of the largest providers of professional services related to computer information technology. The company contracts with many of the largest companies in the United States and Canada to develop computer software, and offers consulting services for managing and maintaining computer systems. CTG is one of a handful of top competitors in this area in the North American market, and has established a presence in the European market as well.

CTG began in 1966 in Buffalo, New York, when two employees of IBM decided to start their own company, offering a relatively new service. Randy Marks had been an account representative for IBM, and he was responsible for marketing in the new company, which was then called Marks-Baer Inc. (MBI). His partner, G. David Baer, had held technical and management positions at IBM, and he initially provided the technical consulting services MBI offered. The two men each invested $4,000 to found the company, and together they borrowed $16,000 as starting capital. When MBI started up, it was unusual for companies to employ outside consultants for help with their data processing needs, but computers were rapidly becoming more powerful, and software more complex. Randy Marks and David Baer correctly predicted that professional computer consulting services would become more necessary and common. Their company provided programmers, designers, and managers to clients who lacked the expertise to set up their own computing systems.

MBI's initial market was the medical industry, since both founders had experience in that area. But the medical market alone could not sustain the company, and MBI quickly branched into other areas. The company lost nearly $14,000 in its first year. MBI struggled to open markets for itself in Buffalo and around New York State, but sales gradually increased. By 1968, sales volume was $471,000, and the company opened a branch in New York City. Staff had grown to 20, and Marks-Baer Inc. changed its name to Computer Task Group Inc. (CTG). CTG went public in 1969, and by then the company's fortunes seemed clearly on the upswing. The initial public offering was oversubscribed in spite of the fact that the stock market had reached a ten year low and investor interest was supposed to be down. But the young firm was already listed in the top 70 software companies in the country, and it was the largest in New York State outside of New York City. Sales had grown significantly, to $704,000, and the company soon opened new branch offices in Syracuse and Toronto, and established a central data center in Cheektowaga, New York.

CTG had a list of impressive clients, including IBM, Union Carbide, Chemical Bank, Hooker Chemical, Rockefeller University, and Atlas Steel. And in 1970, the company increased its revenue significantly by adding two major accounts, the City of Buffalo Police Department and the New York State Job Bank. The Job Bank account was CTG's biggest; it accounted for half the company's 1970 revenue. The Job Bank matched jobs and job-seekers by computer, and it acquired the honor of becoming one of the biggest Xerox installations in the world, second only to the Pentagon. With these two large accounts, CTG sales surpassed $1 million for the first time, though profits were still low.

Despite increasing sales, the company closed its New York City, Syracuse, and Toronto branch offices because they had become a heavy cash drain. Nevertheless, CTG continued to grow. In 1971, the company gained two more major contracts with the city of Buffalo, one to automate data on criminal case flow for the Buffalo City Court, and the other to work with the city's Rodent Control Program. The company also explored a new market, tabulating Buffalo area election results for the news media, in alliance with a local firm that had previously relied on tabulating by adding machine. CTG also pioneered a software program called Basic Update Generator, or BUG, that automatically designed, coded, and generated COBOL computer programs up to 95 percent faster than normal COBOL. With these advances, the company was able to reestablish its Syracuse branch, and open a new branch in Rochester, New York.

CTG continued to find clients in the New York State area in the early 1970s. The company developed several software packages for use in different industries, including a number of medical systems, a grade reporting system for secondary schools, and a narcotics control system. The company began to diversify as well. In 1972, CTG acquired Paperwork Data-Comm Services Inc., a computer services company based in Syracuse. This company was easily integrated into CTG, as it was in the same line of business. In the same year, CTG bought an office supply company, United Office Products. Renamed CTG-United, in 1974 it became CTG's Furniture Division. This business was not successful because it was outside CTG's area of expertise, and in 1975 it was completely divested.

The company decided to stick closer to its core business in future ventures. In 1975 it attempted to capitalize on the growing mini-computer market by becoming the local dealer for BASIC/FOUR, a California manufacturer of small business computers. CTG opened BASIC/FOUR dealerships in Buffalo, Syracuse, and Pittsburgh, and became expert in the programming and installation of BASIC/FOUR equipment at small and medium-sized area companies. CTG also expanded its systems and programming operations to Chicago and Baltimore.

By 1976, the company's clients were primarily large national corporations and financial institutions. One major client was Bethlehem Steel, which put CTG in charge of automating its steel processing operations. Bethlehem set CTG to work at several different sites, including Baltimore, Maryland, and Gary, Indiana. CTG's management realized that to fully serve companies like Bethlehem, CTG too would have to have national reach.

Though expansion plans were laid, CTG's period of growth did not really begin until 1980, when it acquired Cleveland-based Neoterics Inc. Neoterics was a professional services firm with almost 180 employees and branches in Cleveland, Columbus, Pittsburgh, Toledo, Raleigh, and Charlotte. The company focused on large IBM mainframe operations, and had been founded, like CTG, by former IBM employees. The acquisition had immediate benefits for CTG. The company gained a strong base in industrial automation, it increased its presence in the Southeast through Neoterics' Raleigh and Charlotte branches, and it added nearly $10 million to its 1980 revenues.

The ambitious acquisition of Neoterics marked the beginning of a period of rapid expansion for CTG. The company had sales of $37 million in 1981, had opened its own Institute for Technical and Management Training to train new employees, and had continued to penetrate new markets such as the transportation industry and community mental health centers. Despite its expansion, the company's internal growth was deterred because its branch offices were located in states with less than half the computers in the country. The company decided it had to grow through acquisitions in order to open up the top 20 markets. It was reaching only ten percent of the Fortune 500 companies, at a time when the computer services industry was still expanding. To expand, CTG first targeted specific geographic areas, then sent out an acquisitions team to survey companies that might be good additions. Between 1980 and 1985, CTG made 15 acquisitions, giving it a network of outposts in 45 different cities.

CTG moved into large urban markets all across the United States, acquiring firms such as Data Structures Inc. in New York City, Holvick Corp. in Detroit, United Software Consultants Inc. in Chicago, and Amtec Systems Corp. in Los Angeles. In 1985 CTG bought three computer service firms in the West, Data Force Inc. of Seattle, Central Computer Systems Inc. of San Francisco, and Documentation Resources of Phoenix. CTG quickly integrated these new companies into its corporate structure. Although management of the acquired company was usually left intact, CTG took care of small details such as printing new business cards for its new employees.

CTG's revenues leaped upwards as a result of its expansion program. During the fourth quarter of 1983, revenues increased 62 percent over the same period a year earlier, and in 1984 the company comfortably predicted revenue growth of 50 percent. CTG's clients in this period included such major companies as Campbell Soup, U.S. Steel, Xerox, Citicorp, and Westinghouse.

CTG made its first overseas acquisition in July of 1986 when it bought Shubrooks International Ltd., a software consulting firm based in Chertsey, England. Several more international acquisitions followed. By 1986, CTG boasted 75 of the Fortune 100 companies on its client list, and its stock moved from over-the-counter to the prestigious New York Stock Exchange. CTG was working for Ford Motor Company, UNISYS, Baxter Healthcare and USX, and it was named as one of Wall Street's top 500 growth companies. By 1988, CTG had spent $37 million to acquire 19 companies. Sales stood at $220 million, and the company had behind it 20 consecutive quarters of profitable revenue growth.

Approximately five percent of CTG's revenue came from projects run by IBM. When IBM spent $21 million to acquire a 15 percent stake in CTG in June of 1989, CTG management was jubilant. CTG CEO David Campbell referred to the investment as "the most significant event in the history of CTG," because the arrangement had several benefits for the smaller company. IBM was given the right of first refusal on acquiring CTG if anyone else was to make an offer for the company, and in an era of hostile take-overs and increasing consolidation among computer companies, this was something of an assurance to CTG. The previous year, a Dutch holding company had purchased close to nine percent of CTG, and the company quickly enacted a shareholders' rights plan in the event of an unwelcome takeover. Clearly CTG was more comfortable with IBM, a company with which it had a long relationship, in case it should lose its independence. The arrangement would also serve to give CTG earlier access to IBM's technology. And CTG hoped to double the amount of business it got from IBM. Several months after IBM announced its purchase of CTG stock, IBM gave CTG a ten-year contract to run a new data processing plant for Bank South of Atlanta, and CTG negotiated to develop software for Kodak, another major IBM client.

After the stock purchase by IBM, CTG felt financially secure, and relatively sure of its future independence. CTG had penetrated into 80 percent of the top U.S. computer markets, fulfilling the goal it had set itself a decade earlier when the company began its expansion program. Prodded by a dropping net income, CTG reorganized and consolidated its U.S. operations, and formulated a plan for growth into the next decade. CTG consolidated some branches and streamlined its administration in the fourth quarter of 1989, ultimately reducing its workforce by 300. CTG also sold its Amtec subsidiary, as well as the Ottawa branch of its Canadian subsidiary. The company had to charge $13.6 million against earnings in order to effect these changes, but the result was lowered operating costs. The positive effect of the reorganization was felt almost immediately. Net earnings in 1990 reached $7.2 million on sales of $244 million, whereas the company had lost $7.8 million on similar sales the year before.

CTG continued to make strategic investments and acquisitions in 1990 to bring the company into new markets and to keep up with cutting edge technology. To increase its presence in Europe, CTG bought Rendeck International, a computer services firm headquartered in Amsterdam. That company had revenues of $24 million in 1989, and it served Western Europe through branches in Belgium, the Netherlands, and Denmark, as well as the United Kingdom. Following this purchase, CTG listed itself on the Amsterdam Stock Exchange. CTG also made agreements with the European companies Volmac Software and SAP to market SAP software in the United States.

CTG broadened it expertise when it bought the Massachusetts firm Connolly Data Systems, which had expertise in the growing field of "client/server" computer systems. CTG had worked primarily with the mainframe computer systems promulgated by IBM, so the acquisition of Connolly broadened CTG's technological base. Similarly, CTG bought a stake in a company that manufactured imaging technology, Image Business Systems Corp., to have a toe hold in that increasingly important market area.

CTG enjoyed its most profitable six months ever in 1990, as profits tripled in the second quarter. Revenues rose by 16.9 percent in 1991, but the cost of its recent acquisitions as well as increases in tax provisions led earnings to drop drastically, and the company embarked on another restructuring project. CTG had 65 branch offices worldwide by 1991. The company decided to divide itself less along geographic lines and set itself up instead as an umbrella of eight "practices" representing different technologies. These new divisions included a Communications Systems practice, for networking and telecommunications technology; the Migration Services practice, to help clients move applications and databases to new operating systems; a Database Consulting practice; an Image Systems practice; Information Engineering; Information Media; Project Management; and Industrial Systems Integration.

The new set-up changed the focus of the company somewhat. Instead of bidding to do a one-time project for a company, CTG aimed to take over full responsibility for its clients' computing needs through long-term contracts. The new approach slowed sales, but management expected to reap higher profits as soon as longer-term contracts began to pay off. Revenues rose only six percent in 1992, to $302.7 million. The next year, revenues dropped to $295 million, and earnings were below expectation.

CTG decided to restructure again in 1993, dividing its business into two interrelated business areas, Professional Software Services and Information Technology Consulting. Professional Software Services comprised short-term contracts for professional staffing, the core business upon which CTG was founded. This area accounted for more than 70 percent of CTG's profit in 1993. Through Information Technology Consulting, the company offered complete solutions for a client's computing needs. North American operations were pared down from over 60 branches to six regional centers for Professional Software Services and a single center for Information Technology Consulting. The new arrangement streamlined the company considerably, and management believed it would help CTG compete.

Further streamlining occurred in 1994. The company divested itself of two subsidiaries so that it could focus on its two new main business areas. In June CTG sold Profimatics, Inc., a petroleum industry engineering and software subsidiary it had acquired as part of a larger deal in 1987, to Honeywell Inc. In July of 1994, Sage Technologies bought CTG's Network Systems Integration Group. In December of 1994, CTG repurchased IBM's minority interest in the group in a program designed to enchance shareholder value.

CTG aimed to achieve greater local market share in 1994, and to return to its earlier high levels of profitability. The company still saw growth potential in the North American market, and the slightly smaller European market offered continuing opportunities as well. While the beginning of the 1990s did not prove as stellar as the 1980s for CTG, the company showed itself to be willing to make changes, again and again if necessary, in order to keep abreast of changing market conditions.

Principal Subsidiaries: CTG of Canada, Inc.; CTG Europe B.V.

Further Reading:

"The Company that Acquisition Built," *Management Review,* November 1989, p. 19.
Computer Task Group, A 25-Year Retrospective, Buffalo, New York: Computer Task Group, 1991.
"Comp. Task Group Buys Service Firms," *Electronic News,* October 7, 1985, p. 38.
"IBM Adds Investment," *Electronic News,* June 12, 1989, p. 15.
Laberis, Bill, "Acquisition a Viable Route to Corporate Growth," *Computerworld,* November 28, 1983, p. 145.
Margolis, Nell, "CTG Investment Sustains IBM Trend," *Computerworld,* June 5, 1989, p. 81.
Mead, Tim, "Computer Task Group Inc.," *Datamation,* June 15, 1991, pp. 124–125.
Miller, Michael, "Planned Investment in Software Concern by IBM Shows Its Move to Specialization," *Wall Street Journal,* June 1, 1989, p. B4.
Ryan, Alan J., "BankSouth Agrees to Cede Control of Data Center to IBM," *Computerworld,* October 9, 1989, p. 22.
Semich, J. William, "Computer Task Group Inc.," *Datamation,* June 15, 1992, pp. 149–150.
——, "Computer Task Group Inc.," *Datamation,* June 15, 1993, p. 121.
Wilder, Clinton, "Kodak Focuses on Next Outsourcing Frontier," *Computerworld,* August 28, 1989, p. 4.

—A. Woodward

Datapoint Corporation

8400 Datapoint Drive
San Antonio, TX 78229-8500
U.S.A.
(210) 593-7000

Public Company
Incorporated: 1968 as Computer Terminal Corp.
Employees: 1,777
Sales: $208.3 million
Stock Exchanges: New York
SICs: 3571 Electronic Computers; 7372 Prepackaged
    Software

Datapoint Corporation has a proud history as one of the most innovative American computer companies, and today, despite its weak reputation in the United States, it is the leading marketer of telephone-computer integration in Europe. Datapoint specializes in networking computers, and pioneered the local area network (LAN) and MINX, a device that integrated data, voice, and video communications. Datapoint was one of the first computer corporations to realize the importance of linking computer software to telecommunications, and some of the company's leading products are automatic call distributors for incoming calls, power dialers for outgoing calls, and other call management software. Datapoint produces a computer networking technology called ARCNET that is recognized as an industry standard. The company also owns significant patents in networked video products. Over 80 percent of Datapoint's sales are in Europe, and the company maintains a second headquarters in Paris.

Datapoint Corporation was created in 1968 by two engineers, Phil Ray and Gus Roche, who had acquired cutting-edge knowledge of computer technology through their work on various NASA projects. They both worked for General Dynamics' Dynatronic Division in Florida, which was assigned to assist the U.S. space program's goal of putting a man on the moon. Ray and Roche feared that once that goal was reached their engineering skills would be less in demand, and they determined to go into business for themselves before that happened. On the advice of one of Ray's former professors at the University of Texas, they decided to manufacture a generic computer terminal that could be hooked into a mainframe computer. At the time, mainframe computers were room-sized monstrosities, and a

terminal that fed it data required a noisy teletype that printed tape. Roche and Ray designed a terminal that would have a television screen instead of a teletype, would be quiet, and could be plugged into any mainframe and immediately be on line.

After finding financial backers in the San Antonio area, the two engineers incorporated there in July 1968 as Computer Terminal Corporation. The new terminal depended on a silicon chip, which was just then being developed by Texas Instruments. An industrial designer in New York created an elegant, streamlined casing for the machine, and by January 1969 Computer Terminal Corp. had built three working prototypes. The new machine was named the Data Point 3300, with the number indicating an advance on the current popular model of teletype, the ASR 33. The initial chips proved problematic: they usually burnt out after only half an hour of use. However, the Data Point 3300 clearly struck a new direction in computer hardware. The machine was an immediate hit at that year's national computer show, and orders soon swamped the new company. As orders outpaced the company's production capabilities, some of the early models had to be put together in housings made by a San Antonio motorcycle helmet manufacturer; soon, however, Computer Terminal established mass production facilities. By August 1969, the fledgling company had raised more than $4 million in an initial public offering on the over-the-counter market. Less than a year later, the initial shares, which had sold for $8 a piece, were selling at $45 a share.

With the startling success of the Data Point 3300, Computer Terminal's engineers decided to make a more sophisticated product, a terminal that would have some of its own memory and processing power. To do this, they first had to design what later became the first computer microprocessor. Two of Computer Terminal's engineers, Victor D. Poor and Harry Pyle, got the inspiration for this new silicon chip over a Thanksgiving dinner, achieving the technical breakthrough that made the small size of personal computers possible. However, Computer Terminal was still a small young company, and at first it had great difficulty convincing any one established in the industry to try to manufacture the new chip. Eventually Intel agreed to work on the new chip, which became its enormously successful Intel 8080.

Computer Terminal Corp. used the new chip in its Data Point 2200 terminal. The 2200 had many problems and did not do all it was designed to do. Strangely enough, it also did more than any one thought it could. In 1971 Victor Poor, one of the 2200's inventors, went on a trip to an Alabama chicken ranch owned by Pillsbury, where the managers had invited him to see their terminal at work. Poor was not terribly interested in the machine, until he asked his hosts to what mainframe the terminal was hooked. The Pillsbury people told the engineer that the terminal worked by itself. Poor tried to explain that the 2200 required a computer modem and a telephone line connecting the terminal to a mainframe, but his hosts finally convinced him that theirs did not work that way.

Poor realized that he and his partners had unwittingly created the first personal computer and that Computer Terminal had a chance to lead the industry. Unfortunately, because no one at the company had the necessary skills to manage the finances of the growing company, money was already running out.

Founders Roche and Ray considered selling the company and soon worked out a deal with a leading electronics firm, TRW Inc. However, after a TRW vice-president arranged the acquisition, the company's president balked, afraid that he would end up competing directly with IBM. Instead, TRW agreed to invest in Computer Terminal Corp. in exchange for exclusive rights to manufacture the company's products overseas. At the time, this deal seemed fine to Computer Terminal's owners, and TRW, along with several New York financial firms, gave Computer Terminal $7 million to develop a new product.

In spite of this large cash injection, Computer Terminal Corp. was still in financial trouble. The new investors had assigned someone to look over the company's books, and what they found did not please them. As a result, the company's first chairman, San Antonio insurance salesman Gerald Mazur, who had put together the company's first financing, resigned. Computer Terminal hired a new chairman, Harold O'Kelley, who had an engineering background and had been a vice-president of the electronics firm Harris Corp. He took over the firm, now renamed Datapoint Corporation, in 1973, and immediately set to work getting the company in order.

O'Kelley's first major step was to renegotiate the company's contract with TRW, which allowed them to manufacture Datapoint's products overseas. O'Kelley found the original agreement potentially devastating. If Datapoint's new terminal was successful, nothing could stop TRW from making it abroad and then importing it to the United States, forcing Datapoint to compete against itself. After protracted legal wrangling, O'Kelley signed a new agreement that let TRW have the overseas distribution of Datapoint products for ten years, without the manufacturing rights. O'Kelley's next accomplishment was to raise another $8 million for Datapoint on Wall Street. In 1973, Datapoint's sales were $18 million, and O'Kelley planned to raise that to $100 million in five years.

Harold O'Kelley had positioned Datapoint for years of astonishing growth. Between 1973 and 1981, revenues grew at close to 40 percent a year, and sometimes more. Sales surpassed the $100 million mark in 1977, and by 1981 were almost $450 million. The Datapoint 2200 Version II, which could operate without a mainframe, was only one of the company's many innovative products. A concept called Datashare let many terminals communicate with each other independent of a mainframe. In 1976, Datapoint introduced a machine that automatically routed outgoing telephone calls onto the cheapest available line. It introduced telephone directory software and word processing programs, as well as electronic mail functions. Its Attached Resource Computer (ARC), introduced in 1977, was the first of what became known in the industry as LAN (Local Area Network), which the major computer companies, such as Xerox, IBM, and Wang, soon imitated. All the different Datapoint technologies could be linked together, each single piece was relatively inexpensive, and the company provided free software, with frequent updates. Once a customer bought one piece of the Datapoint line, it was easy to sell more. Datapoint's vision was the Integrated Electronic Office, an "office of the future" where typewriters, filing cabinets, telephones, and mailroom would all be replaced with electronic devices that could be operated from a single terminal. By 1981,

Datapoint was estimated to control 21 percent of the distributed data processing industry.

During these growth years, Datapoint had attracted large institutional investors, such as union pension funds and mutual funds, and, by 1980, these made up at least 50 percent of the company's stockholders. Wall Street analysts generally predicted great things for the company, flagging Datapoint as a leader in the computer industry. The stock rose to a high of $67.50 a share in 1981, and in early 1982 it sold close to $50. Chairman O'Kelley worried that the stock price was actually too high and that analysts were projecting earnings for the company without taking into account enough factors. When the stock market began to slow in early 1982, the computer industry as a whole found business conditions worsening. Datapoint had had record earnings of 66 cents a share for its 1981 fourth quarter; earnings declined to 54 cents a share in the next quarter. When the company announced in February 1982 that its second quarter earnings would be only slightly better, the stock market reacted with panic. Large investors dropped the stock. Nearly 2 million shares were traded in two days, and in ten days, the stock had lost a third of its value.

The stock sank even deeper, and by May the stock that had been close to $50 in February was trading at $13. Datapoint announced that it would no longer make revenue and earnings forecasts, thinking that it had already said too much, but investors interpreted this to mean that more poor earnings were on the way. The poor business climate led Datapoint to lay off workers, further spooking Wall Street, and, in April 1982, the company announced its first loss after 39 consecutive quarters of gains. Some of the loss the company attributed to a reversal of $15 million worth of sales from prior quarters. The company had apparently been overstating its sales by reporting shaky orders as done deals, a practice said to be widespread in the industry; however, outraged shareholders threatened lawsuits. Fiscal 1982 ended with sales of $508 million, a slight increase over 1981, but profits had dropped to a bare $2.4 million, down from $48.7 million only a year earlier.

Flagging customer confidence, shaken by Datapoint's drastic plunge in earnings, added to the company's difficulty in recovering from the crisis of 1982. Harold O'Kelley vowed to concentrate on selling Datapoint's minicomputers and to let the "office of the future" go. The company sold its Communications Management Products Division in 1983, shedding itself of its promising PBX telephone system, because further technical development of the system was too expensive. However, the breadth of its products had been one of Datapoint's strongest selling points; the company had difficulty competing with its bigger rivals without it.

Datapoint limped along with small profits until more bad news hit the company. With its stock still selling at under $20, the company became the target of a buy-out. New York investor Asher B. Edelman announced in December 1984 that he had bought up 8 percent of the company, and his share soon increased to more than 10 percent. Edelman had already bought out three other companies, only to dismantle and liquidate them for a profit. When Edelman disclosed that he was interested in Datapoint, other investors began buying up the stock, hoping to cash in. Datapoint's customers began to fear that the company would not be around much longer, making them less likely to buy their products. January 1985 saw Datapoint's second quarterly loss since the 1982 debacle. By March, Edelman had gained control of the company through a proxy fight, Harold O'Kelley resigned, and various divisions of Datapoint were up for sale.

However, Asher Edelman soon announced that the company would not be liquidated. Incredulous investors felt misled, but Edelman insisted that Datapoint had many viable products and that the company would soon be profitable again. He spun off Datapoint's service division, but the rest of the company remained. However, Edelman's new leadership was not enough to turn the company around, leading him to appoint Doris Bencsik president in 1987. She undertook an expensive scaleback of the company that led to a slight improvement in the overall financial picture, but Datapoint was still far from what it had been. The company put out some new products and increased its advertising and trade show attendance, and in 1988 it had its first profitable year since 1984. Nevertheless, revenues were not impressive, and profits were eaten up in dividends paid to preferred shareholders.

In 1989, Datapoint was the target of another buy-out, when investor Martin Ackerman tried to wrest control of the company away from Asher Edelman. Ackerman bought close to 5 percent of Datapoint's stock, then launched a proxy fight, accusing Edelman of mismanaging the company. Ackerman failed to replace Edelman on the board, however, after Edelman upped his share in Datapoint to almost 40 percent. However, the fight cost the company, not only in legal fees but also in further customer uncertainty. Datapoint lost $13 million in the quarter Ackerman's bid surfaced, as sales declined by almost a third.

Troubles continued at Datapoint. The company lost $29.2 million in 1989. In 1990, a federal court of appeals reversed an earlier decision in a patent infringement suit brought against Datapoint by Northern Telecom Inc., resulting in $82.8 million in losses that year. Datapoint closed its U.S. sales division and opened headquarters in Paris, because by that time at least 80 percent of the company's sales were in Europe. In 1992, Datapoint premiered an enhanced version of one of its leading products, the ARCnet Plus, a computer networking system. This introduction promised better sales, especially in Europe. However, Datapoint continued in the red. The final settlement of the patent suit with Northern Telecom in 1992 left Datapoint liable for a $7.5 million cash payment, with additional payments contingent on profitability over the next ten years.

Datapoint had significant patents of its own in video conferencing technology, which, in 1993, it sued to protect. The company believed it had a strong future in video networking technology, since it was a natural extension of its other computer networking product lines. Despite its fallen reputation in the American market, Datapoint was a market leader in telephone-computer integration in Europe. In 1993, Datapoint entered into agreements with several other computer companies to distribute new computerized telephone equipment worldwide or in Europe.

A 1987 survey by *Computerworld* magazine had found that only five Wall Street analysts were following Datapoint, and those the magazine reached disavowed any interest in the company. Those quoted claimed that the company was no longer a force in the computer industry, and that once Edelman had taken over, Datapoint was only of interest to arbitrageurs. Edelman's reputation as a corporate raider hurt Datapoint substantially, and the second takeover attempt in 1990 only increased the doubt of Datapoint's customers that the company would continue to be around to serve them. However, in spite of Datapoint's long slide, the company was still coming out with new products in the mid-1990s. A core business of computer networking systems was still in place, though mostly in Europe. Though Datapoint in the mid-1990s was a far cry from its former prominence and was still plagued with troubles, it continued to fight for a position in the industry.

Principal Subsidiaries: Datapoint International, Inc.; Inforex International, Inc.; Datapoint International Exports, Inc.; Datapoint International Holdings, Inc.; Datapoint Disc, Inc.; Datapoint Development Center, Inc.; Datapoint Corporation Pty. Ltd. (Australia); Datapoint Belgium, S.A.; Datapoint S.A. (France); Datapoint Deutschland GmbH (Germany); Datapoint Italia S.p.A. (Italy); Datapoint Vastgoed, B.V. (Netherlands); Datapoint Beheer, B.V. (Netherlands); Datapoint Nederland B.V. (Netherlands); Datapoint Corp. (N.Z.) Ltd. (New Zealand); Point Data Sistemas Informaticos S.A. (Portugal); Datapoint Iberica S.A. (Spain); Datapoint Svenska AB (Sweden); Datapoint Switzerland (Schweiz) AG (Switzerland); Datapoint Holdings Ltd. (United Kingdom); Datapoint (U.K.) Ltd. (United Kingdom); Inforex Ltd. (United Kingdom); Datapoint International Headquarters, S.A.R.L. (France); Datapoint Far East Ltd. (Hong Kong).

Further Reading:

Blumenthal, Karen, "Datapoint Corp.'s Chairman Buys 30 Percent of Its Stock," *Wall Street Journal,* September 13, 1989, p. A6.

Chakravarty, Subrata N., "Elephant Walk," *Forbes,* October 12, 1981, p. 188.

Cohen, Tedd A., "In the Valley of the Giants," *Forbes,* December 10, 1979, pp. 70–72.

"Datapoint Corp. Begins Offer to Exchange Preferred Stock," *Electronic News,* March 23, 1992, p. 23.

"Datapoint Corp. Loses Appeal in Patent Case; Financial Impact Seen," *Wall Street Journal,* July 9, 1990, p. B5.

"Datapoint Corp. Posts Profit of $8.1 Million for Fiscal 4th Period," *Wall Street Journal,* September 3, 1987, p. 10.

"Datapoint Could Take an Even Deeper Bath," *Business Week,* July 5, 1982, p. 30.

"Datapoint in Black for Six," *Computerworld,* September 26, 1988, p. 107.

"Datapoint Leapfrogs into the Office," *Business Week,* December 10, 1979, p. 93.

"Datapoint Loses $13M, Seeks Buyer," *Electronic World,* December 18, 1989, p. 21.

"Datapoint Loses $82M in FY 1990," *Electronic News,* September 24, 1990, p. 34.

"Datapoint Mans the Barricades," *Business Week,* January 28, 1985, p. 100.

"Datapoint's Shrinking Office of the Future," *Business Week,* May 30, 1983, p. 37.

"Edelman Takes Aim at Datapoint," *Business Week,* December 24, 1984, p. 34.

"Edelman Takes Control of Datapoint," *Computerworld,* March 25, 1985, p. 82.

"Edelman's Moves at Datapoint," *Business Week,* September 16, 1985, p. 38.

Erickson, Richard, "Inside Datapoint," *San Antonio Light,* September 14–21, 1986.

Francis, Bob, "Datapoint Corp.," *Datamation,* June 15, 1992, p. 152.

"From Zero to $94 Million in Five Years," *Infosystems,* April, 1976, p. 22.

Harris, Marilyn A., "Asher Edelman Is Already Carving Up Datapoint," *Business Week,* April 1, 1985, pp. 35–36.

"Humble Pie May Nourish Datapoint," *Business Week,* November 29, 1982, p. 96.

"Investor Edelman Says He Controls 8 Percent Stake in Datapoint Corp.," *Wall Street Journal,* December 11, 1984, p. 8.

Lewis, Geoff, et al., "A Raider Tries to Beat Asher Edelman at His Own Game," *Business Week,* September 25, 1989, p. 50.

Marcial, Gene G., "A Battered Datapoint Lures Speculators," *Business Week,* May 17, 1982, p. 114.

Martin, James A., "Firm Strives to Regain Strength," *Computerworld,* March 9, 1987, p. 113.

Mason, Todd, Geoff Lewis, and Marilyn A. Harris, "Raider Asher Edelman Gets Trapped in the Executive Suite," *Business Week,* September 23, 1985, p. 115.

Moffett, Matt, and Timothy J. Carroll, "Datapoint Says Bid by Edelman Added to Financial Woes; Quarterly Loss Seen," *Wall Street Journal,* January 25, 1985, p. 9.

Pastore, Richard, "Firm Relocation Brings Woes," *Computerworld,* January 7, 1991, p. 6.

Ryan, Kimberly, "Datapoint Corp.," *Datamation,* June 15, 1993, pp. 126–27.

Scredon, Scott, "Asher Edelman Gets a 'Dear John' from the Street," *Business Week,* May 6, 1985, pp. 46–47.

Thomas, Paulette, "Datapoint Posts 2nd-Period Loss, Plans to Revamp," *Wall Street Journal,* March 2, 1987, p. 4.

—A. Woodward

The Davey Tree Expert Company

1500 N. Mantua Street
Kent, Ohio 44240-5193
U.S.A.
(216) 673-9511
Fax: (216) 673-5408

Private Company
Incorporated: 1909
Employees: 5,000
Sales: $200 million
SICs: 0782 Lawn & Garden Services; 0783 Ornamental
Shrub and Tree Services

The Davey Tree Expert Company pioneered the commercialized care of large trees through company founder John Davey's invention of tree surgery. The company's philosophy—''Do it right or not at all''—has fueled its research and development division's continued scientific advancements toward the improved care of plants for over a century. Operating in the United States and Canada, the company provides tree, shrub, lawn, and groundskeeper care services, interior plant care, and utility line clearing. It also runs a tree farm. Family-owned until 1979, the company has become one of the nation's largest and most successful employee-owned firms.

The Davey Tree Expert Company traces its history to John Davey's creation of the new science of tree surgery (now known as arboriculture). John Davey migrated from England to the United States in 1873, and, after working in a variety of jobs, he moved to Kent, Ohio, to become caretaker of the Standing Rock Cemetery. Davey thought of the cemetery as a laboratory where he could experiment with his notions about the care and conservation of trees. Through trial and error, he found scientific ways to heal sick, infected trees. One of his methods included carving decay out of a tree's cavity, disinfecting and waterproofing it, and supporting the hollow space with an intricate combination of concrete sections, three-ply tarpaper, and steel bracing, a practice that continued into the 1990s with a few modifications, including the use of plastic foam filling. Convinced of the importance of his discovery, Davey left his job at the cemetery to pursue work as a tree surgeon. Evidence of the quality of Davey's work proliferated around Kent and Warren, Ohio, and in 1904 there was enough work to keep Davey and two of his sons, Jim and Wellington, busy.

While his tree care and landscaping business grew, Davey lectured and wrote about the proper care of trees. In 1901, in order to publish his book, *The Tree Doctor,* he went $7,000 in debt. Although a risky venture, the book expanded demand for Davey's expertise throughout Ohio, Pennsylvania, New York, and Washington, D.C., as well as in Toronto and Ottawa, Canada. The book sold particularly well in the Hudson Valley region and Boston, where there were many large estates. Moreover, Martin, John Davey's son, sold the book to about 25 percent of Warren's residents. The demand for tree surgery services was growing so quickly that Davey and his sons could not possibly service all their requests. As a result, John and Wellington organized the Davey School of Practical Forestry to train others in the science of tree surgery.

As the business expanded, Davey called upon his son Martin to organize work in the East. Martin's flair for sales and organization made him ultimately responsible for the company's commercial viability. In 1907, Martin left college at the age of 23 to become a full partner in his father's business, which was then $25,000 in debt. After solving many of the management problems in the New York office, Martin began taking over responsibility for the entire company, as his father devoted more time to lecturing and writing. In 1909, the company was incorporated as The Davey Tree Expert Company.

The biggest challenge facing the company when Martin assumed the reigns was the seasonality of its work. Martin took two steps to combat this problem: he expanded business into the southern states, and he opened the Davey Institute of Tree Surgery in 1909. Although the company's southern operations would not be profitable for many years, the institute helped the company build a pool of workers to serve as foremen, supervisors, and salesmen and also kept the company from having to retrain crews at the beginning of each season.

Run much like a college, the institute proved intimidating to some. A rigorous academic curriculum that included botany, entomology, and plant pathology was taught by educators recruited from leading colleges and universities, and a vigorous athletic program kept the students in shape throughout the winter. To persuade workers to attend the institute, Martin offered them a raise, effective the following season, of a dollar a day. Twenty men accepted the offer and entered the first three-month course of study.

To further the commercial success of the firm, Martin employed the power of advertising. As cited in Robert E. Pfleger's *Green Leaves: A History of The Davey Tree Expert Company,* Martin maintained that ''in spite of the tremendous value of the service that we render the public in saving trees and in the improvements we made in the training and techniques of our men, our business could not have reached sizeable proportions without the powerful and constructive influence of advertising.'' The magazine *American Forester* carried the first Davey advertisement in its fall issue of 1910.

The company was also one of the first to use radio for advertising. In 1929, the company initiated the ''Davey Hour,'' which reached 24 stations from Boston to Kansas City. The program featured popular music of the past. Martin reasoned, according to Pfleger, that by using older music ''he could tap people's memories and associate the company with pleasant past experiences, enjoyed by listeners.'' The radio program was continued until it fell victim to the Great Depression in 1932.

The company started some of its most profitable ventures during the 1920s. With the acquisition of a power rig, it began spraying in 1921. In 1926, the company marketed its ability to transplant large trees; one of its most unusual orders for tree moving was from the Sterling and Welch Company, a department store in Cleveland, which displayed a four-story-high live Christmas tree each year from 1935 into the 1960s. But the company's decision to serve utilities became its most significant undertaking. While serving as Kent's Commissioner of Shade Trees in 1921, John Davey's youngest son Paul suggested that The Davey Tree Expert Company be employed to trim trees for the Northern Ohio Power and Light Company, which sought to cut trees to install new power lines. Although Martin and John initially did not want the company to be associated with utilities, because of the latter's historic disregard for the environment, clearing branches away from utility lines soon made up a large portion of the company's work. By 1960, utility work accounted for $7.05 million out of the company's $11.83 million total volume. By the 1990s, Davey cleared the lines of more than 200 utility companies in the United States and Canada.

In 1932, the company suffered a drop in volume from $3 million to $700,000, and, the following year, it faced some unlikely competition: President Roosevelt's Works Progress Administration (WPA). The WPA program lured trained workers away from the company by offering tree surgeons a wage of $1.20 per hour, which was significantly higher than the Davey wage of $0.70 per hour. After Martin and his chief competitor, F. A. Bartlett, addressed Roosevelt about the wage imbalance, Roosevelt instructed WPA administrator Harry Hopkins to emend the situation. Hopkins arranged for the government to lower its wage to $0.80 per hour, and this solution allowed both Davey and Bartlett's companies to stay in business.

The company had to adjust to new laws and a shortage of workers during the 1940s. In 1940, a new federal wage and hour law established a 42-hour work week for line clearing crews and required time and a half pay for overtime. Davey struggled with this new law at a time when it needed to expand its work force but was offering lower wages than war related industries and was no longer running the institute to attract workers. During the war years, Davey's tree surgeons were generally either old or very young men, or women. As the war came to a close, the company constructed a plan for retraining veterans and expanding the company's services.

In 1946, shortly after Martin Davey, Jr. returned from war, Martin Sr. died of a heart attack. Not only had Martin Sr. made his family's company a success, but he had also served his community for several years as mayor, congressman, and governor of Ohio. At age 28, Martin Jr. became president of the company. A Yale University graduate with a major in botany and a minor in business administration, as well as an experienced tree surgeon, Martin came prepared for his position's responsibilities. He also had the unique insights left to him by his father, who had explained his business philosophy in a letter to his son. Some of Martin Sr.'s insights included: ''Treat your employees as human beings. Good men are ambitious, frugal

and trustworthy. . . . Watch your credit with a jealous eye. . . . Never do anything while you are angry. . . . Don't do something merely because a competitor does it.''

Martin took his father's advice and lead the company to new levels of success. His first year of leadership ended with sales volume reaching a new high of $3.94 million, $800,000 more than the previous high in 1929. In addition to expanding company sales, Martin modified and reopened the Davey Institute of Tree Surgery. Because the company no longer needed to occupy its workers in the winter, since it had utilities work, the school term was shortened from three months to six weeks, the courses were limited to tree surgery, and the athletic program was eliminated.

Martin's first decade of management steadily increased company sales over 150 percent to $10 million. Under his leadership the company changed its main client base from large estate owners to utilities and commercial clients needing chemical brush control and mist spraying. Davey employees assessed their president in a 1956 report, saying, according to Pfleger, that ''Our President, during these past ten years, has managed well by seeming to manage little and above all has been prudent and thrifty with human material.'' Martin remained president until his son-in-law, Alexander M. Smith, took over. Smith lead the company through another period of growth, raising sales from $25.79 million in 1970 to $38.13 million in 1974.

In 1979, however, five years after the Internal Revenue Service began recognizing employee-owned companies through the Employee Retirement Income Security Act, The Davey Tree Expert Company was purchased by its employees. Since the concept of employee ownership was still new, the family did not see the employees as purchasers when they put it up for sale. Nevertheless, when the employees offered to buy the company, they were regarded as the preferred buyers, who could maintain the family's old-fashioned business strategies. After just over 16 months of friendly negotiation, 113 employees bought stock directly and 400 participated in an Employee Stock Ownership Plan, which held company stock in a trust for employees as a retirement benefit. The pioneering efforts of the Davey employees made it one of the largest and most successful employee-owned companies in the United States, recording 15 years of growth since its transition of ownership. In 1992, the company had sales of $200 million, according to *Crains Cleveland Business*. Davey president R. Douglas Cowan credited the company's success to its employee ownership, telling the *Record-Courier* that ''nothing motivates employees like having a little personal stake in every sale.'' In 1993, over 2,600 of its 5,000 employees were shareholders of the company.

The Davey Tree Institute became more prestigious under employee ownership. Instead of a lure to keep employees during the winter months, it became a selective four-week seminar that offered the top 50 Davey employees courses on subjects ranging from tree physiology to customer service. Company executive Roger C. Funk told *Crains Cleveland Business* that ''upon completion of their course work, graduates should be climbing the corporate ladder as well as they climb trees.''

Throughout its history, the company's structure has evolved to accommodate its growth. When the company was incorporated in 1909 its structure focused on function, dividing it into sales, finance, field personnel, technical development, and support services segments. As Davey expanded throughout the United States and its services diversified from tree surgery to utility line clearing, nursery, national landscaping, and lawn care services, it met the needs of customers on a geographic basis through regional management by 1974. In 1991, the company reorganized its regional structure to provide services to public utility, commercial, governmental, and residential customers through nationally coordinated efforts that were regionally arranged by customer or market group. The 1991 reorganization allowed the company to address the needs of each client base, while tailoring its marketing to the needs of different regions.

As The Davey Tree Expert Company expanded it carried on John Davey's commitment to the environment. By the early 1990s, the company's research and development team had patented nearly two dozen new products that helped the environment. Some of the products included No Leach/No Burn Fertilizer Arbor Green, a commercial fertilizer that would not damage plants and was easily used by plants so the fertilizer did not leach into the soil, and water-retaining soil additives, polymers that reduced the need for irrigation by up to 50 percent.

Though it has been quick to make use of new technologies, the company has watched the effects of those new technologies on the environment. In 1988, the company announced that it would reduce its usage of pesticides and herbicides by 75 percent, or by 30,470 gallons. To reduce the harmful effects of chemical overuse, the company created products that would control the amount of chemicals applied to plants and eliminate the use of large batches of pre-mixed pesticide solutions. Moreover, the company developed a "raindrop" nozzle, which allowed technicians to control the amount of pesticides and fertilizers being applied, and a proprietary "piggyback line" called the Davey Customizer, which eliminated the need for pre-mixing pesticide solutions in a large tank and allowed the company to more easily provide custom treatments. The Davey Plant Health Care program also helped reduce the use of chemicals by emphasizing the holistic care of plants. In 1993, the company had reached a 75 percent reduction in the use of traditional tree pesticides and a 50 percent reduction in traditional lawn care pesticides. Continually striving to improve its services, the company set another goal, to achieve a 95 percent reduction in traditional pesticide use by 1995.

Davey also affiliated itself with dozens of associations that promoted environmental concerns. One such affiliation started in 1989, when Davey started supporting the American Forestry Association's National Register of Big Trees Program and Global Releaf. Company president Cowan told *American Forests* that "we believe that our support of the Big Tree program will benefit forest conservation in a significant way. In addition, the Global Releaf message that individual action can make a difference is a premise our founder, John Davey, believed in, and it remains an important part of our company philosophy today." The company was also affiliated with the Audubon Society, Nature Conservancy, Sierra Club, Society of American Foresters, National Urban Forest Council, and Wilderness Society.

Principal Subsidiaries: Davey Tree Surgery Company; Davey Tree Expert Company of Canada, Ltd.; High Tree Services, Ltd.; Plantasia, Inc.; Canadian Shade Tree Service; Vancouver Tree People, Ltd.

Further Reading:

Gangloff, Deborah, "The Davey Connection," *American Forests,* July/August 1989.

Geiger, Peter, "Davey Tree to Trim Pesticides' Use by 75 Percent," *Beacon Journal* (Akron, Ohio), March 1, 1988.

Gorisek, Sue, "A Man Ahead of His Moment," *Ohio Magazine,* October 1992.

Harrison, Kimberly P., "Davey Staff Out on Limb on Climb Career Ladder," *Crains Cleveland Business,* March 8, 1993, p. 17.

Pfleger, Robert E., *Green Leaves: A History of The Davey Tree Expert Company,* Chester, Conn.: Pequot Press, 1977.

Urey, Craig, "Davey Owners Enjoy Fruits of Labor," *Record-Courier,* March 20, 1994, p. B1.

—Sara Pendergast

PAPER COMPANY

Dillard Paper Company

3900 Spring Garden Street
Greensboro, North Carolina 27407
U.S.A.
(910) 299-1211
Fax: (910) 852-8925

Wholly Owned Subsidiary
Incorporated: 1926
Employees: 1,800
Sales: $600 million
SICs: 5111 Printing & Writing Papers; 5112 Stationery and
    Office Supplies; 5113 Industrial and Personal Service
    Papers; 5084 Industrial Equipment; 5085 Industrial
    Supplies; 5087 Service Establishment Equipment and
    Supplies; 5162 Plastic Materials; 5169 Chemicals

Dillard Paper Company, one of North Carolina's largest privately owned corporations, has long been a major distributor of paper, packaging materials and equipment, and such related products as sanitary maintenance equipment and supplies, and graphic arts equipment and supplies. Its primary market has been the Southeast, where, in the mid-1990s, it maintained 24 distribution centers in seven states—Virginia, North Carolina, South Carolina, Tennessee, Alabama, Georgia, and Florida. Dillard Paper also owns a chain of retail paper stores called If It's Paper (with more than 40 offices in the Southeast), as well as two "converting" companies—Dillard Plastics (converter/manufacturer of plastic bags) and Dillard Converting (which converts jumbo roll stock paper into specialized paper products). In 1991, Dillard Paper was purchased by International Paper Company, a multibillion-dollar corporation, which wanted to expand its own distribution business. Dillard Paper, however, was allowed to continue to operate as an autonomous company.

Dillard Paper Company was named for its founder, Stark S. Dillard, who was born in 1894 in Lynchburg, Virginia. His father died when Dillard was just three years old, leaving Dillard's mother alone with 12 children. As a result, Dillard and his siblings had to find work at an early age. When he was 11 years old, Dillard took his first job—folding boxes for Old Dominion Box Company, which was owned by his older brother David. Over the next few years, Dillard's work load at Old Dominion increased to 11 hours a day, six days a week.

However, in 1910, Dillard was fired by the company's general manager, another older brother. Reportedly, Dillard had become close friends with a railroad engineer who regularly passed by the box company in his train. "He'd toot and I'd wave," Dillard later explained, noting that "my brother thought I was killing time and decided to make an example out of me."

Dillard, just 15 years old, then went to work for Hughes Buggy Company, where he initially performed odd jobs and was later promoted to a sales position. It was in sales that Dillard would find his talents. Four years later, he and a friend, Evans Caskie, found jobs as salesmen for the Alling and Cory Paper Company, headquartered in Rochester, New York. They both worked for Alling and Cory for three years, and, after gaining this additional experience, the two men decided to go into business for themselves, forming Caskie-Dillard Paper Company in Lynchburg. Begun with Caskie's money, the new company opened in November 1916 and over the next few years experienced remarkable success.

Even so, Dillard and Caskie began to disagree over where the company should expand. Caskie wanted to keep the business in the North Carolina town of Charlotte and the Virginia town of Lynchburg, while Dillard wanted to open a division in Greenville, a town in the northwestern part of South Carolina. Although remaining friendly with one another, Dillard and Caskie decided to end their business relationship in the fall of 1925. Meanwhile, Joseph J. Stone, owner of a large printing company in Greensboro, North Carolina, was encouraging Dillard to establish a paper distribution center there. Dillard agreed to do so, and in 1926 he moved to Greensboro, borrowed $25,000, rented a building in the downtown area, and opened his new business, which he called Dillard Paper Company. "I had no dreams of building a paper empire or being a rich man," Dillard confessed. "I just wanted enough to keep my wife from having to work in a dime store and to give my children a few more advantages than I had," he wrote.

At first, Dillard Paper was largely a solo operation. Dillard said of the early years, "I ordered the paper, unloaded it, wrapped it up, delivered it, collected for it, deposited the money in the bank and bought more paper." Its first product was printing paper, with most of its deliveries going to printers, such as Stone, but, in 1930, Dillard Paper added industrial paper to its inventory. As the owner of his own company, Dillard was able to make the most of his great talent in sales, and orders of his products boomed, so much so that in 1929 the company had to move into a larger facility, located on West Lee Street. A growing number of salesmen were also employed by the company. Then, in 1934, Dillard opened a branch in Greenville, the location where he had hoped to expand at Caskie-Dillard. Additional offices would be opened in Charlotte (1936) and in the Virginia cities of Roanoke (1941) and Bristol (1944).

The year 1936 has special significance for the company. On the evening of Friday, April 2, a tornado spun toward Greensboro, causing extensive property damage and killing 13 people. The Dillard Paper facility on West Lee Street was also hit, and its supply of paper was taken up by the storm and spread across several counties. Much of it landed on a farm about 40 miles away. Dillard, who was in Greenville during the tornado, rushed back to Greensboro to find his building in ruins. He began cleanup operations right away, moved his business temporarily into a warehouse on Davie Street, and ordered a new supply of paper. He borrowed additional money to pay the costs. A few days later, however, this paper, too, was ruined when the warehouse leaked during a thunderstorm. The company managed to survive the disasters, and Dillard would come to see them as a blessing, noting that ''It united the organization. The boys jumped in and worked night and day.'' The founder also kept his sense of humor. A woman told Dillard that during the tornado she was riding in a streetcar in Greensboro when suddenly a case of toilet paper came flying through a window. Dillard responded, ''Ma'am, that's just the kind of service we try to provide.''

After World War II, Dillard Paper entered a period of great expansion, in part through acquisitions of other companies. The company began by purchasing Cape Fear Paper Company of Wilmington, North Carolina, in April 1947, followed by the acquisitions of Bibb Paper Company of Macon, Georgia (April 1950); Volunteer Paper Company of Knoxville, Tennessee (also April 1950); Palmetto Paper Company of Columbia, South Carolina (May 1950); and Standard Paper Company of Augusta, Georgia (October 1951). Then, in March 1952, the company opened a new branch in Raleigh, North Carolina.

In the early 1950s, Dillard suffered two heart attacks, and, although he was able to continue his work at a somewhat slower pace, many were concerned about his health. During this time, ''D'' Month, a sales contest held each May, was established by the company's management in 1950 in honor of Dillard. The contest had two parts. The first was an intercompany competition for the Stark S. Dillard trophy (a large silver Paul Revere bowl), awarded to the salesperson who had the greatest percentage increase over his or her personal quota. Second and third place finishers were also recognized, as was the top finisher in each division. The second part of the contest, called ''D'' Month, involved Dillard's key suppliers and included cash and merchandise awards based on sales of specified products (later the company would establish competitions for employees not directly involved in sales). Despite the awards, the true prize in the contest was the prestige of being a top seller, and the contest did prove to be a strong incentive for boosting sales, a goal that all members of the company—even those in the warehouse or in purchasing—were expected to work toward. As a result, May, which had traditionally been a period of slow sales, consistently became the year's most successful sales month, and the ''D'' Month contest has been repeated each year into the 1990s, becoming an important part of Dillard Paper's corporate culture. In addition, about every four years ''D'' month has been followed by a sales conference in which management, salespeople, and representatives of mills came together to meet one another and plan for the future.

While the company was thus increasing its sales through various employee incentives, including the Stark S. Dillard award and ''D'' Month contests, it was accomplishing the same goal through additional acquisitions. These included Sommerville/Seybold Paper Company of Atlanta, Georgia (February 1953); Kelley Paper Company of Winston-Salem, North Carolina (November 1953); Piedmont Plastics of Thomasville, North Carolina (September 1959); and Southern Paper and Supply of Richmond, Virginia (September 1960). A new branch was also opened in Birmingham, Alabama, in March 1957. With its 16 branches (including its headquarters) in 1960, Dillard Paper had become the largest paper distributor in the Southeast, employing about 600 people.

Dillard Paper was also becoming more than just a paper distributor. The company's purchase of Piedmont Plastics, renamed Dillard Plastics, allowed it to enter the field of converting jumbo roll stock plastic material into new products, such as plastic bags. The company previously had difficulty finding the various types and sizes of plastic bags requested by its customers. Some new products were complements to existing ones. For example, Dillard Paper, which sold paper towels, also came to sell towel racks and soap. An important service provided by the company was the converting of jumbo roll stock paper into new products. Large rolls of paper were cut into smaller ones, for instance, and paper and cardboard were cut into specific shapes and sizes for numerous products, including the insert board found inside packages of women's hosiery. Most of the products, however, the company distributed rather than produced, and, beginning in the 1960s, the tens of thousands of items passing through Dillard's warehouses were monitored by an increasingly more sophisticated computer system. By 1969, sales had reached about $60 million, and the company was employing some 700 people.

During the 1960s, Stark Dillard remained the company's chairperson, while two of his nephews held the post of president. The first, Edwin Rucker Dillard, became president in 1959 and remain in that position for six years until his death in 1965 at the age of 40. Replacing him was John H. Dillard, who would hold the post from 1965 to 1986. A believer in the future of plastics, John Dillard was committed to continuing the company's program of expansion and diversification. Under his leadership, for example, Dillard Paper opened six new branches or divisions, beginning in July 1971 with the acquisition of Old Dominion Paper Company of Norfolk, Virginia, followed in 1975 by the opening of Dillard Converting, located in Greensboro, which converted paper into specialized products. Also that year, Stark Dillard died. In 1978, Dillard Paper acquired Flowers Paper Company, a small industrial paper house.

The 1980s saw several new divisions of Dillard Paper. The first, established in Greensboro in 1983 as Dillard Packaging Systems, sold packaging equipment, supplies, and parts. The company's reason for entering the field of packaging was simple. Its customers needed these products. Also that year, Dillard Paper created its own trucking operations, Dillard Transportation, also headquartered in Greensboro. This allowed the company to lower the cost of transporting its large and varied supply of products. In 1984, Dillard Paper established a new distribution branch in Lynchburg, notable in part because it was the hometown of the company's founder. Later, Dillard Paper opened a branch in Charleston, South Carolina, in 1986. In 1988, the Mudge Paper Company became a member of the Dillard family. Mudge eventually took on the Dillard name in the early 1990s but became a part of the Northeast Region and ResourceNet International. Another branch was opened in Montgomery, Alabama, in 1990. Also in 1990, Dillard Paper acquired Chattanooga Paper and Woodenware Co. of Chattanooga, Tennessee which operates under the Dillard name.

Thus, by 1990 the company had offices and warehouses in more than 20 cities in the Southeast, spanning from Virginia in the north to Alabama and Georgia in the south. Sales had reached some $500 million. At this time the company also had a small number of offices in Maryland and Pennsylvania. Meanwhile, a much larger corporation, International Paper Company, with sales of some $13 billion, was undertaking its own program of acquisitions. International Paper's empire was enormous and involved the manufacture or distribution of paper, packaging, office supplies, graphic arts products, wood products, and various other items, such as natural gas and photographic film, with divisions in more than 20 countries. However, International Paper lacked a good distribution network in the southeastern and mid-Atlantic regions of the United States, and for this reason it decided to approach Dillard Paper with an offer to buy the company. By March 1991, an agreement was reached allowing International Paper to acquire Dillard Paper, though the agreement also specified that Dillard Paper would continue to operate as an autonomous company.

The merger had immediate advantages for both companies. For International Paper, it expanded distribution business by 25 percent. Similarly, Dillard Paper gained access to International Paper's wholesale and retail distribution branches, which numbered some 250 at the time of the merger. Geoffry Clark, then chairman and CEO of Dillard Paper, explained Dillard Paper's willingness to be purchased: "International Paper approached us and made us quite an attractive offer that got our attention. Dillard Paper was never for sale. We acted in the best interest of our shareholders." He then went on to point out: "Customers and employees will see no change. The culture of the company will not change. The name will not change. We will operate independently. We feel this merger has enhanced our long term position."

It was not long, in fact, before the first visible benefits of the merger were seen. In 1992, for example, International Paper, which had purchased Palmer Paper Company of Florida, placed that company's four branches—located in Jacksonville, Tampa, Orlando, and Miami—under the control of Dillard Paper, thus expanding Dillard Paper's already extensive distribution network in the Southeast. Also at this time, Caskie Paper Company merged into Dillard Paper. Dillard Paper's future success was also linked with that of the paper industry, which operated on a small margin of profit and was intensely competitive. In 1993 Geoffry Clark moved into another position within International Paper and Newell Holt became president of Dillard Paper. Especially important was having a well-trained and hardworking sales force committed to identifying, meeting, and satisfying the customers' needs, and focused on maintaining and developing supplier relationships.

Principal Subsidiaries: Dillard Plastics; Dillard Converting; Dillard Packaging Systems; Palmer Paper Company; Dillard Transportation.

Further Reading:

"Dillard Paper Merges with International Paper," *PICA Scanner* [publication of Printing Industry of the Carolinas, Inc.], April 1991, p. 5.

"International Paper Says It Will Purchase Dillard Paper Co.," *Wall Street Journal,* March 13, 1991, p. B5.

"Paper Wholesaler Simplifies Its Cost Allocation," *Communications News,* November 1991, p. 8.

Thomas, Jan, "It Huffed & Puffed," *The State* [regional magazine of North Carolina], August 8, 1959, p. 14.

Wolter, Beverly, "A $60 Million Middleman," *Winston-Salem Journal and Sentinel,* February 9, 1969, p. D11.

Wright, W. B., "Little Stories about Business," *The State,* January 15, 1966, p. 23.

—Thomas Riggs

D&B SOFTWARE

Dun & Bradstreet Software Services Inc.

3445 Peachtree Road NE
Atlanta, GA 30326
U.S.A.
(404) 239-2000
Fax: (404) 239-2220

Wholly Owned Subsidiary of Dun & Bradstreet Corp.
Incorporated: 1990
Employees: 2,500
Sales: $475.6 million
SICs: 7372 Prepackaged Software

Dun & Bradstreet Software Services Inc. is one of the world's leading distributors of software for financial, human resource, distribution, and manufacturing applications. The company has over 12,000 customers worldwide and serves approximately 75 percent of the Fortune 500 companies. Dun & Bradstreet Software derives revenue primarily from licensing its software products and from maintenance fees and consulting fees related to their use. The company began by offering software primarily for companies using mainframe computer systems. Mainframe applications remain a substantial part of Dun & Bradstreet Software's business, though the company is committed to bringing out new products to be used with smaller, personal computer-based (''client-server'') systems. Dun & Bradstreet Software's products are installed on a range of computer hardware made by such principal computing companies as IBM, Digital Equipment Corporation, Fujitsu, and Hewlett-Packard. The company also works in partnership with such software firms as Microsoft, Powersoft, and Sybase to meet the complex computing requirements of its customers. Dun & Bradstreet Software also operates a worldwide customer support network, offering its clients 24-hour access to technical experts for assistance with product problems. The company maintains a European headquarters in Brussels and an Asia/Pacific headquarters in Sydney, Australia. Approximately 30 percent of the company's total revenues come from sales outside the United States.

Dun & Bradstreet Software resulted from the merger of two smaller companies, Management Science America, Inc., and McCormack & Dodge. McCormack & Dodge had been owned by Dun & Bradstreet Corp. since 1983. Management Science America (MSA) had been the principal competitor of Mc-

Cormack & Dodge throughout the 1980s, and the two companies were major players in mainframe applications software. In 1989, McCormack & Dodge controlled about 12 percent of the market for accounting applications, whereas MSA held 15.5 percent, and the two companies likewise controlled about 7 percent and 14 percent respectively of the human resource management software market. The two companies were fierce rivals, and executives from both companies admitted at the time of the merger that their sales forces had frequently sabotaged each other with such underhanded techniques as canceling their competitors' hotel and plane reservations. Nevertheless, the mainframe application market was consolidating rapidly through mergers and acquisitions, and it seemed wise for the two enemies to work together. Management Science America turned down a $191 million buyout offer from another principal competitor, Computer Associates International, in 1988, but the next year it agreed to better terms from Dun & Bradstreet. Dun & Bradstreet offered $333 million for MSA, which came to $18.50 a share for stock that had been trading on the over-the-counter market for only $10 to $11. The transaction was completed in January 1990, and Dun & Bradstreet combined its two software subsidiaries into Dun & Bradstreet Software Services Inc.

McCormack & Dodge and MSA had similar product lines, both principally serving clients with IBM and IBM compatible mainframe systems. Dun & Bradstreet announced at the time of the merger that it would continue both companies' products and maintain two sets of headquarters, MSA's in Atlanta and McCormack & Dodge's in Natick, Massachusetts. The president of MSA, John P. Imlay, became chairman and chief executive officer of the new company, and his counterpart at McCormack & Dodge, Frank Dodge, was to become vice-chairman. However, shortly after the merger was officially completed, Dodge left to form his own new company, and a former McCormack & Dodge vice-president, John Landry, took Dodge's place at Dun & Bradstreet Software. Landry was responsible for research and development initiatives. By the end of the first year of the new company, software revenues had risen about 10 percent, to $538.6 million.

Nevertheless, by early 1991 it was clear that Dun & Bradstreet Software needed to make changes in order to maintain profitability. The company's president, Henry Holland, conceded in March that the U.S. market for mainframe products was saturated and D&B Software would need to focus on managing its existing accounts rather than depending on new sales. In an effort to restructure, the company fired 300 people, mostly in the Atlanta and Massachusetts headquarters, bringing its worldwide work force down to 3,400. When parent company Dun & Bradstreet Corp. suffered a 5.5 percent decline in net income in its 1991 second quarter, part of the blame went to sluggish sales at the company's software division. Shortly after the second quarter statement of revenues, Dun & Bradstreet Software announced that it was embarking on a major new design initiative.

The company decided to follow the growing trend away from mainframe computing and make its software compatible with cheaper and easier-to-use personal computers. Personal computers linked to accomplish what a large mainframe could was known in the computer industry as a ''client-server'' system. Much of the actual computing was done on the ''client,'' usually a personal computer or workstation. The client computer requested information from a "server," which could be a mainframe, a midrange computer, or a powerful personal computer. This system had several advantages: the client-server system on the whole was cheaper than a mainframe, and many smaller or downsizing companies were interested in it for that reason. The client-server arrangement could also be used to automate many business procedures. For example, a financial manager might need to look over extensive weekly printouts using a mainframe computer, but with a client-server system, the server could send records directly to a personal computer at the manager's desk and note which records required immediate action. The personal computer could also be used as a traditional word processor and automatically send out letters to customers regarding late payments, for example. However, despite the new system's advantages, the software was extremely complicated and to a certain extent untested. Many customers were committed to their mainframe software, which cost between $100,000 and $200,000.

Dun & Bradstreet Software had the difficult task of pleasing its old customers while perfecting new software designs in an area in which the company admittedly did not have much expertise. The company contracted to work with a company called Powersoft to develop client-server software, meanwhile assuring its more than 10,000 mainframe customers that it would continue to support its traditional products. Dun & Bradstreet Software at first planned to bring out its initial client-server products in 1993, but the company pushed the deadline to 1992. The cost of developing the new technology dragged down profits, and in 1991 revenues rose less than 2 percent. The company enrolled Cognos Corp. and Sybase Inc. to help get the new software ready, and the company's chairman John Imlay announced that he expected client-server programs to totally replace mainframe systems as Dun & Bradstreet Software's major product over the next few years.

Dun & Bradstreet Software announced its new client-server product line in March of 1992. Its Smartstream, Financial Stream Analysis, and InterQ let mainframe users access information from a personal computer workstation, though the new products could not yet do everything that the traditional mainframe technology could. However, in the face of rapidly developing competition, releasing the first products was crucial. Small companies that focused exclusively on client-server software were quick to move into Dun & Bradstreet Software's market. A new company, PeopleSoft, Inc., made significant inroads in the human resource applications computing area with its new client-server programs, and other companies like SAP AG, Tesseract Corp., and Oracle Corp. also pushed ahead with client-server applications.

Dun & Bradstreet Software's president Henry Holland predicted in early 1992 that 40 percent of the company's mainframe customers would move to Dun & Bradstreet client-server systems over the next five years, but in the meantime revenues fell. 1992 sales stood at $533.5 million, a 4 percent drop from a year earlier, and profits dropped by over $24 million, to $18.7 million. Sales of mainframe applications were declining not only in the United States but in Canada, the United Kingdom, and Australia, though sales in Latin America, Europe, and the Asia/Pacific area offset this somewhat. Because fewer staff members were needed as mainframe sales shrank, the company laid off another 400 employees in 1992 and closed two of its development laboratories. The company also sold a subsidiary company targeted to the education market, Information Associates Inc., in order to focus more tightly on building client-server applications.

In 1993, Dun & Bradstreet Software stepped up its new product shipments to keep pace with the increasing number of competitors. The company brought out a new wave of financial application software in February and introduced new human resources tools and decision support applications in the next few months. As new companies, such as Walker Interactive Systems and The Dodge Group (headed by former McCormack & Dodge chairman Frank Dodge), rolled out more client-server products, Dun & Bradstreet Software tried to hold on to its established customers by offering them an easier path from mainframe to the new technology. The company announced in May 1993 that it would incorporate some software from Microsoft Corp. into some of its client-server systems, which was expected to yield a superior product. To upgrade its product for the manufacturing market, the company decided in February 1994 to work with a small Atlanta company, Industrial Computer Corp., on its Manufacturing Stream software. In May 1994, Dun & Bradstreet Software announced the availability of its new SmartPath program, a software system designed to ease its customers' transition from mainframe applications to client-server networks. SmartPath was able to automate 75 percent of the effort of migrating from the old system to the new, which could amount to significant customer savings, both of time and money.

Dun & Bradstreet Software initially planned to charge customers a usage fee for SmartPath as part of its professional services offering, instead of licensing it outright. Some customers complained, according to an article in *ComputerWorld* magazine, that the company should be offering more free assistance with the migration to client-server. However, many companies in the industry were unsure how to negotiate this tricky area, which only emphasizes the uncertainty surrounding Dun & Bradstreet Software's future fortunes, embarking on such a new direction in the computer industry.

The company named a new president and CEO in June 1994, when R. Douglas MacIntyre succeeded Henry Holland. MacIntyre claimed to see tremendous revenue opportunities for the company in the next few years as Dun & Bradstreet Software continued to improve its client-server offerings. Although revenues dropped slightly each year since the company was formed, it does not seem unreasonable to predict that as client-server technology becomes more entrenched, Dun & Bradstreet Software will achieve growth in years to come.

Further Reading:

Ballou, Melinda-Carol, "D&B Software to Cut Staff by 13 Percent," *ComputerWorld,* December 7, 1992, p. 117; "Microsoft, D&B Align on NT Applications," *ComputerWorld,* May 3, 1993, p. 8.

Bulkeley, William M., "Computers: D&B to Change Software Design to Use PC More," *Wall Street Journal,* July 30, 1991, p. B1.

Cafasso, Rosemary, "Migration Costs Stoke User Angst," *ComputerWorld,* May 16, 1994, p. 1.

Cortese, Amy, "Merger-Weary Users Turn Wary," *ComputerWorld,* December 4, 1989, p. 1.

Cusack, Sally, "D&B Pitches Client/Server Plan," *ComputerWorld,* March 30, 1992, p. 20; "D&B Software to Increase Services," *ComputerWorld,* December 17, 1990, p. 95; "D&B's Direction Focus of User Concern," *ComputerWorld,* January 27, 1992, p. 29.

"D&B Swallows More Software," *Business Week,* December 4, 1989, p. 42.

Hooper, Laurence, "D&B to Acquire Software Maker for $333 Million," *Wall Street Journal,* November 21, 1989.

"Is D&B a Late Guest at a Crowded Party?," *Datamation,* December 15, 1992, p. 31.

Margolis, Nell, and Amy Cortese, "D&B Unites Software Rivals," *ComputerWorld,* November 27, 1991, p. 1.

Nash, Kim S., "Financial Applications to Do Battle," *ComputerWorld,* February 15, 1993, p. 12.

Ricciuti, Mike, "Dun & Bradstreet Software Services Inc.," *Datamation,* June 15, 1992, pp. 121–22; "Dun & Bradstreet Software Services Inc.," *Datamation,* June 15, 1993, p. 101–2; "Dun & Bradstreet's Big Play in Client/Server," *Datamation,* December 15, 1992, p. 29–34.

Stedman, Craig, "D&B Software to Play Manufacturing Odds," *ComputerWorld,* February 7, 1994, p. 20.

—A. Woodward

DUTY FREE INTERNATIONAL, INC.

Duty Free International, Inc.

63 Copps Hill Road
Ridgefield, Connecticut 06877
U.S.A.
(203) 431-6057
Fax: (203) 438-1356

Public Company
Incorporated: 1983
Employees: 2,100
Sales: $376.44 million
Stock Exchanges: New York
SICs: 5182 Wines and Distilled Alcoholic Beverages; 5194
    Tobacco and Tobacco Products; 5122 Drugs, Drug
    Proprietaries, and Druggist's Sundries; 5145 Confectionery

Duty Free International, Inc. operates the largest chain of duty free stores in the world. Selling merchandise through 158 shops, located primarily near U.S. border crossings and in airports, the company is also the leading supplier of goods to foreign diplomats as well as ships engaged in international travel.

The duty free, or tax free, industry emerged following World War II. As international travel became increasingly popular during the late 1940s and 1950s, an international system was developed allowing travelers to purchase foreign goods free of all duties, sales taxes, and excise taxes. Under the system, customers were typically able to save between 20 and 60 percent on their purchases, making duty free goods extremely attractive. As a result of the duty free system, however, many countries began imposing additional fees or limits on the total value of merchandise travelers brought back to their home countries.

David Couri and John Bernstein, two duty free industry veterans, started Duty Free International in 1983. Couri had gained exposure to the business during his youth, as his father had founded a duty free company (the first, in fact, to offer goods other than liquor and cigarettes). As a teenager, Couri worked part-time in his family's duty free shop in New York's Kennedy Airport. In 1963, Couri graduated from Syracuse University with a degree in economics, and then served two years in the Army before taking a sales job. After several years in the floor covering business, Couri saw his chance to strike out on his own. On his way to Japan from Kennedy International Airport,

he noticed that there was no duty free shop in the Northwest Airlines terminal. By 1972, Couri had obtained a permit to open a duty free concession in the terminal, thus launching DFI International, Inc.

Bernstein was also exposed to the duty free business as a youth. At Samuel Meisel & Co., a Maryland-based duty free wholesaler, Bernstein worked summers in one of the company's two duty free shops in Washington, D.C., which catered to foreign diplomats. After receiving a B.A. in political science from Johns Hopkins in 1957, Bernstein went to work full-time on the sales staff at Meisel. Twenty-five years later, he was running the company. By this time, Couri's venture had expanded into a six store chain at Kennedy International Airport.

In 1983, Couri and Bernstein joined forces to start Duty Free International. They were aware that duty free sales along the Canada/U.S. border had been growing at a rate of ten to 15 percent annually, but they felt that the existing shops were failing to capitalize on the full potential of the market. "We looked at these [Canadian border] stores," Couri recalled in the August 19, 1991 issue of *Forbes,* "and many of them were dilapidated." Couri and Bernstein used some of their own money and borrowed heavily from banks to finance the $4.7 million buyout of 19 border stores and one airport shop in Maine, New York, and Vermont. They then spent an additional $4 million to revitalize the lagging outlets. As a result, sales volume at the stores doubled almost immediately. Amazingly, the fledgling business paid off most of its acquisition debt after only two years of operation.

Encouraged by their early success, Couri and Bernstein quickly acquired 11 more shops in small towns along the Canadian border. After considerable renovation, these stores were generating healthy profits by the mid-1980s. The border stores offered Duty Free an excellent opportunity to break into the industry quickly. Although those establishments lacked the prestige of airport shops and did not have access to a steady stream of well-heeled business travelers and tourists, border shops proved easier to open, since obtaining a concession license in an airport usually involved an expensive and complicated bidding process.

In 1986, Couri and Bernstein expanded the scope of Duty Free by purchasing Bernstein's old employer, Meisel. Meisel gave the company a dominant position in the niche market for merchandise sold to foreign diplomats. Indeed, embassies and consulates in Washington, D.C. and New York bought liquors and fine wines by the case from Meisel in order to avoid hefty taxes on those items. Duty Free also continued to buy border properties and to seek licenses for airport shops. By 1988, just five years after its inception, Duty Free International was racking up $69 million in annual sales and generating earnings of nearly $6 million. By 1989, the chain included several stores on the eastern U.S./Canadian border that operated under the name AMMEX Tax & Duty Free Shops and generated 46 percent of company sales. Several high-volume airport shops made up about 30 percent of revenues, and the Meisel division represented the remainder of receipts.

In the late 1980s, however, the company's plans for further expansion were stalled by a lack of investment capital. To obtain more cash for growth, Couri and Bernstein tried to take their company public in 1987. Indeed, all of the details for a Duty Free public stock offering had been worked out by October of that year. However, the morning of the pricing meeting, during which traders and underwriters hammer out the per-share price of the stock, Couri turned on the radio and learned that stock prices were slipping precipitously. Less than a week later, on a day known as "Black Monday," the market crashed, dashing any hopes of a successful offering for Duty Free.

Nevertheless, Couri (who became chief executive of Duty Free while Bernstein served as chairperson) rallied back to the market in 1989 with a stock sale that generated $22.6 million. Rather than have the money wired into the company's account, Couri requested a check for the full amount. He placed a framed copy of the check on his office wall next to a letter of apology from the underwriter of the failed 1987 issue. The fresh injection of capital, combined with funds from successive offerings, bankrolled a period of rapid growth for Duty Free International, which continued into the early 1990s. The company's earnings increased more than 100 percent in 1989, to about $10 million, as sales spiraled upward to $86 million. In anticipation of even faster growth, Couri and Bernstein moved Duty Free into a new, 100,000-square-foot, $5.5 million headquarters building.

The strategy behind Duty Free's strong performance during the 1980s and early 1990s was relatively simple. It grew by acquiring underperforming duty free shops and improving their performance with sound management. The company also offered a more profitable product mix than many of its competitors, following the example set by Couri's father; besides cigarettes and other highly taxed merchandise, Duty Free emphasized the sale of luxury items, such as leather goods, perfume, and cosmetics, all of which offered relatively high profit margins. Moreover, the company augmented border store acquisitions with lucrative airport shops. As the company swelled in size, economies of scale were achieved through bulk purchases and consolidated distribution and marketing operations.

In addition to solid management techniques that allowed Duty Free to gain on its industry peers, the company benefitted from favorable economic and demographic trends, particularly during the early 1990s. During that period, the value of the U.S. dollar dropped, making domestic goods a relative bargain for most foreigners. A $41 carton of cigarettes, for example, could be had at a Duty Free shop for just $15, and a bottle of American scotch whiskey that sold for $26 dollars in Canada cost less than half that when purchased duty free. As a result, the "capture rate," or number of border crossers that would stop at a duty free shop, increased from two percent in 1983 to ten percent in 1989, and then to 13 percent in 1991. Furthermore, the average sale at Duty Free's border stores climbed nearly 20 percent between 1989 and 1991, to $31.5 million. Similarly, airport store performance improved. Japanese travelers, for example, purchased an average of $125 worth of goods apiece when they visited the shops.

Duty Free's sales reached $105 million during 1990, about $15 million of which was netted as income, and Duty Free's stock price soared five-fold after its initial offering to about $29 by early 1991. During that year, moreover, Duty Free's revenues rose dramatically to $187 million as a result of new acquisitions and higher sales at existing stores. In an effort to sustain the explosive growth rate, Couri and Bernstein began searching for ways to diversify Duty Free and extend its geographic presence. In 1992, Duty Free purchased UETA Inc., a chain of duty free shops along the U.S./Mexican border that had 1991 sales of $150 million. Duty Free also launched multimillion-dollar advertising campaigns in Canada and Mexico and added stores along the western U.S./Canada border. By the early 1990s, Duty Free was accounting for 90 percent of all duty free sales made along the U.S./Canada border.

Largely as a result of the pivotal UETA merger, Duty Free's sales rose to $362 million in 1992, while net earnings surged to more than $30 million. The company continued to branch out along the Canadian and Mexican borders during 1992 and 1993, eventually amassing a force of 60 stores in the North and 28 shops in Texas, Arizona, and California. Duty Free also expanded its airport operations to include 85 retail and duty free shops in 14 international airports across the United States and Canada, and in Puerto Rico. Sales from its shops continued to be augmented by Duty Free's Meisel division.

By 1993, Duty Free had organized its sprawling operations into three succinct divisions; airport, border, and diplomatic and wholesale. Under the name Fenton Hill American Limited, the airport division operated traditional duty free stores, as well as several specialty shops aimed at foreign buyers of perfume, cosmetics, sports clothing, and jewelry. Its America-To-Go stores, for example, emphasized uniquely American products, such as regional foods and housewares. Moreover, Fenton Hill oversaw the operations of several premium brand boutiques, such as Chanel, Elizabeth Arden, and Christian Dior.

Duty Free's border division was separated into north and south operations. Stores in the North operated under the AMMEX Tax & Duty Free name and were located along the Canadian/U.S. border from Maine to the state of Washington. Several of those stores also offered gas stations, convenience stores, and currency exchanges. Shops in the South, located along the Mexican/U.S. border, all operated under the UETA name. They also offered a full line of luxury items in addition to popular tobacco and alcohol products.

Duty Free's diplomatic and wholesale division operated through three subsidiaries: Samuel Meisel & Company, Inc.; Lipschutz Bros., Inc.; and Carisam International Corp. Besides handling Duty Free's warehousing and distribution tasks, these subsidiaries provided upscale merchandise to diplomats primarily in the New York City and Washington, D.C. areas. The division also provided merchandise to cruise and merchant ships departing from Baltimore, Philadelphia, New York, Seattle, Los Angeles, and Miami.

Economic downturns and new government regulations in Canada caused sales from Duty Free's important north border division to drop in 1992 and 1993, reflecting the sensitivity of the duty free industry to outside economic and political influences. Nevertheless, Duty Free's diversification strategy paid off during this time, as gains in sales were realized in shops along the southern border. In fact, by 1993, UETA revenues had surpassed sales in the once dominant AMMEX stores near Canada. As a result, Duty Free was turning its attention toward greater expansion near Mexico. Sluggish sales in the north were also offset by steady gains in the diplomatic and wholesale division, and particularly in the lucrative airport division—those two segments made up about 40 percent of company revenues in 1993.

Despite an overall sales slowdown from its border operations, Duty Free revenues increased four percent in 1993, reaching $376 million. Net income slipped to a still healthy $27 million. During this time, Couri continued to penetrate new marketing channels and to diversify regionally. In 1993, for example, Duty Free entered into an agreement with McDonald's Corporation to form Chicago Aviation Partners, a joint venture designed to develop concessions at Chicago's O'Hare International Airport.

Early in 1994, Duty Free purchased Inflight Sales Group Limited, a New York-based concessionaire that sold merchandise on over 20 airlines. Inflight would provide more than $100 million in additional annual revenues to the Duty Free organization, and the buyout ensured Duty Free's status as the largest provider of duty free merchandise in the world. With operational efficiency, a light debt load, and dominance in its core market segments, Duty Free expected continued success throughout the 1990s.

Principal Subsidiaries: Fenton Hill American Ltd; AMMEX Tax & Duty Free Shops; UETA, Inc.; Samuel Meisel & Company, Inc.

Further Reading:

Cutro, Dyan C., "Duty Free International Reports Fourth Quarter and Fiscal Year 1993 Sales and Earnings," *Business Wire,* February 25, 1993.

Cutro, Dyan C., "Duty Free International to Acquire Inflight Sales Group," *Business Wire,* March 30, 1994.

Higgins, Carol B., "When Government Taxes Sin, Firm's Duty Is Clear," *Intercorp,* July 21, 1989, p. 16.

Lehren, Andrew W., "Partnership of N.Y., Chicago Firms Undergoes Biggest Changes," *Philadelphia Business,* June 17, 1994, p. 13.

Lynch, Mickey, "Duty Free Restructures UETA Inc.," *Daily Record,* June 25, 1992, p. 3.

Lyons, James, "Border Merchants," *Forbes,* August 19, 1991, pp. 56–57.

Myers, Randy, "Behind Clinton's Take Hike Plan, Duty Free Finds a Silver Lining," *Warfield's Business Record,* April 23, 1993, p. 3.

Roberts, Dan, "Doing Their Duty at Duty Free Shops," *Central New York Business Journal,* January 1988, p. 20.

Shopping Opportunities for the International Traveler, Ridgefield, Conn.: Duty Free International, Inc., 1993.

Williams, Elisa, "Duty Free Warehouse Makes Way for Growth," *Washington Times,* September 18, 1990, p. C1.

—Dave Mote

ECHLIN

Echlin Inc.

100 Double Beach Road
Branford, Connecticut 06405-4906
U.S.A.
(203) 481-5751
Fax: (203) 488-0370

Public Company
Incorporated: 1959
Employees: 20,600
Sales: $2.22 billion
Stock Exchanges: New York
SICs: 3714 Motor Vehicle Parts and Accessories; 3315 Steel
Wire and Related Products

Echlin Inc., founded by the Echlin brothers in 1924, is a leading manufacturer of automotive replacement parts, including brake parts, engine parts, and transmissions. The company made numerous acquisitions after 1964, establishing subsidiaries across the United States and in eight foreign countries. Despite the corporate trend to diversify, most of Echlin's expansions have been within the low-profile and often volatile automotive parts business.

Jack and Earl Echlin founded Echlin and Echlin in San Francisco in 1924. They made pistons, piston pins, and similar parts at first but then turned to manufacturing replacement parts such as ignitor gears and oil pump gears. Eventually, they bought the ignition business of another company and went on to become one of the leading U.S. ignition manufacturers.

While Earl established a small machine shop, Jack appointed himself salesman of the firm and attended a night class to learn the rudiments of his job. Soon thereafter, he devised a one-evening sales clinic for salesmen of auto parts stores whose training had been largely neglected. Salesmen from out of town began asking for the class, and soon Jack was traveling to cities across the country conducting his one-evening workshop. Jack Echlin expanded his class into a technical as well as a sales clinic, in which students were taught the value of replacement parts. His workshop and his company thus achieved a national reputation, and his classes became the cornerstone of Echlin's marketing program.

In 1928, the company signed a contract to supply oil pump and ignition gears to the National Automotive Parts Association

(NAPA) which, in turn, distributed those parts to garages across the country. The contract proved lucrative, and soon Echlin began supplying ignition parts as well. The company and the association, which continued to work together into the 1990s, grew faster than the industry as a whole, and NAPA became recognized as one of the most efficient distributors in the automotive parts market.

Continuing to demonstrate their understanding of the industry's needs, the Echlin brothers commenced publication of an ignition catalogue in 1929. It was the first time an entire list of ignition parts was listed within a single *Car Guide* and proved to be a boon to mechanics. The brothers followed this innovation with another—the Echlin Visumatic Business System, a specially designed cabinet in which a mechanic could organize a small inventory of popular replacement parts. This device (in effect, an inventory management system) moved automotive parts into the repair facility, where the mechanic had immediate access to them. The cabinet was used by Echlin ever since and was the model for parts cabinets made by other manufacturers.

Echlin struggled through the Depression, an era when many people decided that buying replacement parts for their car was less expensive than acquiring a new one. But the high costs of operating in San Francisco forced the company to move to New Haven, Connecticut, in 1939.

During World War II, the company profited by manufacturing parts for aircraft automatic pilots. Jack Echlin served on the advisory boards of the War Production Board and the Office of Price Stabilization. When the war ended, sales rose dramatically after the years of parts shortages.

Jack Echlin remained as head of the company until 1969. He established a consistent annual sales growth rate of 15 percent, while adhering to a policy that kept the firm from expanding into unrelated areas. But within the field of automotive parts, Echlin made a number of acquisitions and developed new product lines. The most important of these were hydraulic brake parts, which became the second largest product line of the company, with sales in 1985 of $308.6 million. Management next added fuel systems parts, thus providing a more efficient service for its customers.

Echlin acquired Ace Electric Company in 1970, a manufacturer of components for alternators, generators, and starters. Soon the company was producing electronic voltage regulators, the first electronic product to appear in automobiles. Despite warnings to stay out of the voltage regulator business because the new units would supposedly have a very long life, Echlin continued to produce replacement units. It was a wise decision since the original voltage regulators did not prove to be as durable as some had anticipated. Echlin then introduced replacement parts for electronic ignition systems, which were standardized by all car manufacturers in 1975.

Echlin's acquisition in 1971 of the Berg Manufacturing Sales Company, a small producer of air brakes for trucks, also paid off handsomely. Initially, it allowed Echlin to broaden its base in the truck and trailer service industry. Then, in the mid-1970s, the federal government imposed safety regulations mandating stopping distance and straight line braking requirements on heavy-duty trucks and truck trailer rigs. Those stopping requirements could only be met through the use of advanced, electronically controlled anti-skid systems. A joint venture between Berg and Italy's Fiat led to the development of an anti-skid system that became standard equipment on a number of truck trailers.

Another successful acquisition was that of Lift Parts Manufacturing, a producer and distributor of parts for industrial lift trucks. This acquisition provided the company with a foothold in the off-road equipment and construction markets.

Echlin remedied its neglect of high-performance ignition systems with a program started in the 1970s. Racing quality ignition parts were marketed under the brand name ACCEL which, despite fierce competition, soon became the leading name in its field. Echlin backed up its ignition parts business with high performance clutches and a turbocharger for both car and truck engines. The popular turbocharger, first marketed for just $700, provided extra horsepower and improved efficiency.

Echlin recognized the importance of foreign markets and, beginning in 1969, established subsidiaries in West Germany, England, Australia, Canada, South Africa, Brazil, Venezuela, and the Virgin Islands. In 1986, Echlin agreed to a joint venture with Lucas Girling of Birmingham, England, to manufacture and distribute brake parts for heavy-duty applications in Europe. Management had remained mindful of what Joe Scott, a president of Echlin, had said in 1976: "The growth in both passenger car and truck registrations outside the United States is about three times the rate of growth in North America. We view our international operations as money in the bank, ready to bring us increasing returns as our markets expand well beyond those of 1975."

The success of Echlin's policies were amply demonstrated by its revenues. Income climbed from $204.5 million in 1976 to $771.4 million in 1985. Profits over the same period rose from $13.2 million to $45.6 million.

The company relied on sales of its products to warehouse distributors; its other major customers were mass merchandisers, oil companies, truck and trailer manufacturers, and other auto parts replacement manufacturers. Its broad product line during the mid-1980s was divided into four categories: engine systems, brake parts, hard parts, and non-automotive parts. Engine systems included condensers, distributors and distributor caps, ignition coils, rotors, carburetor and emission control parts, fuel pumps, catalytic converters, and other items. The brake parts category comprised hydraulic brake master cylinders, items for both drum and disc brake systems, hoses and controllers for electrical brakes, and a variety of parts for the heavy-duty brake market. Hard parts consisted of clutches, transmission parts, and water pumps. In the nonautomotive category, Echlin produced small engine parts, fork lift truck replacement parts, security access control products, and industrial wire and cable products.

Entering the 1990s, Echlin faced an assortment of challenges, none more difficult than an economic recession that depressed U.S. automotive aftermarket sales and sent the economies of numerous foreign countries in which Echlin operated into a tailspin. Exacerbating matters, retailing in the United States was undergoing dramatic changes, as large, nationally-operated wholesale outlets forced smaller retail outlets out of business,

squeezing Echlin's profit margins. The decline of fully equipped service stations, which began in the 1970s and proceeded into the 1990s, was part of this trend, but their disappearance was trailed slowly by consolidation among jobbers and warehouse distributors, leading to what many industry pundits perceived as excess capacity at the auto parts distributor level.

In response to the changing conditions in the 1990s automotive aftermarket, Echlin slowed its pace of acquiring companies and consolidated its existing operations in an effort to increase profits margins and heighten efficiency. Vera Imported Parts, a U.S. importer and distributor of replacement parts for imported cars, was merged into the company's Beck/Arnley Worldparts, a move that compressed seven distribution facilities into four, and additional consolidations were effected in Europe. Net income slipped in 1991, falling from $47.2 million recorded the year before to $41.6 million on essentially flat sales, but the decline represented the worst the recession had to offer, and net income grew prodigiously over the next two years, more than doubling to $93.5 million.

This growth was attributable to several factors, including a recovery of the U.S. economy that spurred consumer confidence and increased industrial output, which led to more goods being hauled and, consequently, to more heavy trucks requiring maintenance, as well as the increasing age of the average car on the road. Encouraged by the company's financial growth, but mindful of the need to continue consolidating operations, Echlin's management pursued further growth, acquiring several companies as earnings climbed. In September 1992, Echlin acquired Sprague Devices, Inc., then in 1993 concluded the purchase of three additional properties, Mr. Gasket Company in May, Frictiontech Inc. in June, and the German hydraulic brake and clutch division of FAG Kugelfischer in October. The first three acquisitions, each of which generated between $20 million to $50 million in annual sales, strengthened the company's U.S. position, while the purchase of FAG Kugelfischer's division, a $135 million producer in annual sales, represented a significant move toward fueling Echlin's growth in Europe.

As Echlin entered the mid-1990s, U.S. sales continued to climb, but its international business, spread across six continents and conducted through 42 subsidiaries and divisions, continued to falter. The economic downturn that hobbled the U.S. economy in the early 1990s continued to depress Echlin's foreign markets in the mid-1990s, particularly in Germany, France, and Italy, where industrial output flagged and automotive replacement part sales dipped. Adding to the company's international financial woes were declining sales in Australia and Mexico, but a resurgence of sales in South America and a slowly recovering economy in the United Kingdom did provide a spark of hope. In Europe, where roughly 20 percent of the company's sales were generated, the vehicle population was growing three times as fast as in North America, suggesting robust growth once the overseas economic picture brightened. With established facilities in Europe poised to take advantage of a revitalized European economy and a growing presence in Eastern Europe, where the company opened the first Western-style auto parts store in Moscow in early 1994, adding to the geographic scope of its operations, Echlin stood well-positioned for growth throughout the 1990s.

Principal Subsidiaries: Ace Electric Company, Inc.; Automotive Controls Corp.; Automotive Brake Company Inc.; Blackstone Manufacturing Co., Inc.; Brake Parts, Inc.; BWD Automotive Corp.; Echlin International, V.I., Inc.; Echlin-Ponce, Inc.; The Echlin Sales Company; Pacer Industries, Inc.; Midland Brake, Inc.; Ristance Corp.; Sierra International Inc.; Tekonsha Engineering Company; Beck/Arnley Worldparts Corp.; BWD Automotive of Puerto Rico (70%); Distex Industries Inc.; EAP Automotive Products, Inc.; Echlin Argentina SA; Echlin Asset Funding Corp.; Echlin Australia (Pty.) Ltd.; Echlin Ltd. (Bermuda; 99%); Echlin Canada Inc.; Echlin Europe Ltd.; Echlin Holding Deutschland Gmbh (Germany); Frictiontech Inc.; Echlin Mexicana; Mr. Gasket, Inc.; Sprague Devices, Inc.; United Brake Systems Inc.; W.M. Holding Co., Inc.; Windsor Products Company, Inc.

Further Reading:

''Corporate Profiles: Raybestos/Brake Parts,'' *Automotive Marketing,* December 1993, p. 30.
Mehlman, William, ''Auto Aftermarket Recovery Indicated in Echlin Results,'' *The Insiders' Chronicle,* April 20, 1992, p. 1.
Mehlman, William, ''Echlin Inc.,'' *The Insiders' Chronicle,* November 5, 1990, p. 2.
''Parts Makers Merge,'' *Automotive News,* September 28, 1992, p. 21.
''Raybestos,'' *Automotive Marketing,* April 1993, p. 40.

—updated by Jeffrey L. Covell

EL CAMINO RESOURCES INTERNATIONAL, INC.

El Camino Resources International, Inc.

21051 Warner Center Lane
Woodland Hills, California 91367
U.S.A.
(818) 226-6600
Fax: (818) 226-6794

Private Company
Incorporated: 1979
Employees: 300
Sales: $504.37 million
SICs: 7377 Computer Rental & Leasing; 5045 Computers,
    Peripheral Equipment & Software; 5734 Computers &
    Computer Software; 6159 Miscellaneous Business Credit
    Institutions

El Camino Resources International Inc., through its primary operating company, El Camino Resources, Ltd., is a leading reseller and lessor of mainframe and midrange computers, with IBM mainframes as its core business. El Camino ranks as the second largest U.S. computer lessor after publicly-held Comdisco, Inc. and is also among the fastest growing private companies in the United States. The company has increased its revenues and profits every year since its founding in 1979. Even as the mainframe market matured in the early 1990s, El Camino continued to expand through acquisitions of other lessors and software companies. El Camino's value-added strategy in computer sales and leasing has distinguished itself from the competition.

El Camino was founded in 1979 in Northridge, California, by David E. Harmon and David A. Wolff, to provide independent, customer-oriented sales and leases of used mainframe computers in what is known as the resale market. Harmon became the new company's president and later assumed the additional titles of chief executive officer and chairperson, while Wolff became vice-president of trading and, later, executive vice-president of portfolio management. The two founders were joined by a third principal, Mel Kleinman, who later became executive vice-president of sales.

Mainframe computers are such large and expensive systems that their corporate use often does not justify the capital expenditure of an outright purchase of a new computer. Instead,

computer users often prefer either to lease mainframes or to buy used ones, and those companies that purchase new ones can recoup some of their expenses by selling the computers back into the resale market. While computer manufactures have handled such leasing and resale services, the founders of El Camino saw the opportunity to provide better service and be more responsive to the market in the capacity of an independent and purely wholesale and retail company. El Camino also provided customer financing from the beginning as part of its services.

El Camino began its business with the leasing and selling of used IBM mainframe computers and peripherals, such as printers and terminals, directly to corporate clients. A year after its founding, the company also began selling and leasing some new computer equipment. In 1983, El Camino diversified into non-IBM computers by offering VAX computers from Digital Equipment Corp. (DEC). Later El Camino established a DEC Division in Irvine, California. In addition to VAX computers, this division traded in communications and office equipment, bank point-of-sale systems, and CAD/CAM systems.

In the mid-1980s, El Camino began offering disaster recovery services. When one of its client's computer rooms was flooded after heavy rains caused its roof to collapse, El Camino was able to deliver and install a $1.5-million computer system within a week. As other companies began to request similar disaster recovery services, El Camino responded by developing a disaster recovery plan that involved a monthly fee and guaranteed the replacement of IBM 4300 computers and peripherals within five working days. Among the clients who called upon El Camino to help restore computer systems after damage to buildings were Mazda Motors of America Inc., whose U.S. data center was destroyed in a storm, and health and welfare benefits administration firm U.S. Administrators, which had a regional office destroyed in a fire.

The expansion of the corporate computing market fueled El Camino's growth. The company's revenues grew from under $40 million in 1984 to $165 in 1988, with a growth rate of nearly 80 percent between 1987 and 1988. In early 1988, the company diversified into reselling IBM mini- and microcomputers. El Camino established a midrange, or minicomputer, leasing division, El Camino Application Solutions Co., as an IBM business partner to sell IBM's newly launched AS/400 midrange computer series. El Camino correctly perceived that midrange computers would be a faster growing sector of the computer industry. The AS/400 turned out to be one of the most popular general-purpose midrange computers of the late 1980s and 1990s.

Selling IBM AS/400 computers under an Industry Remarketer relationship with IBM required that El Camino provide value-added software and implementation services in addition to meeting strict technical and financial standards. As with hardware, El Camino was not a developer or manufacturer of software but contracted to resell software developed by other vendors. After IBM introduced its RS/6000 RISC-based workstation 1990, the Application Solutions division began marketing this computer as well.

Also in 1988, El Camino entered the microcomputer leasing market with a $1.2-million contract with Nynex Business Centers, permitting Nynex to lease the computers. As such, El Camino began indirectly marketing hundreds of IBM PS-2 microcomputers annually to corporations.

In addition to financing and disaster recovery, El Camino had also added installation, software integration, training, maintenance, and on-site support. These services were enhanced when, in 1988, El Camino acquired Infinite, an engineering firm that reconfigured IBM and DEC computers and offered some maintenance services. The acquired company became a subsidiary of El Camino, Infinite Computer Group Inc.

In June 1989, El Camino formed a new disaster recovery firm, El Camino Recovery Services, as a joint venture with Global Marine Inc. of Houston, Texas. Subscribing companies could immediately use the computers at the Houston site if their own systems were damaged. El Camino Recovery Services also provided computer systems in trailers that could be brought to a client's site to handle short-term needs. El Camino also promised replacement of damaged computers within seven days and offered rates for use of disaster recovery services that were lower than that of the competition. The demand for disaster recovery services had grown in the 1980s, due to new regulations requiring banks and financial institutions to be running again within 72 hours of a computer failure.

El Camino began looking for an investment partner in the late 1980s. A relationship with General Electric was pursued but never completed. Then, in spring 1990, two Japanese companies—Japan Leasing Corp. and Applied Technology Corp.— offered substantial investment capital. Each company purchased a 12.5 percent stake in El Camino, and Japan Leasing appointed a representative to El Camino's board of directors. The deal enabled El Camino to boost its annual lease volume and also increased El Camino's opportunities for sales and leases of used computers in Japan. Japan Leasing's stake in El Camino was later increased to 25 percent.

Revenues for the fiscal year ending April 30, 1990, increased 62 percent to $254.95 million, net income rose nine percent to $3.33 million, and leased assets rose 33 percent to $186.28 million. At the same time, many competitors were reducing or liquidating their leased asset portfolios. El Camino's revenues for the fiscal year ending April 1991 rose almost eight percent to $274.47 million, and net after-tax earnings rose nearly eight percent to $3.59 million. In 1991, El Camino was earning 30 percent of its revenues from leasing.

By the early 1990s, the leasing business began growing at a faster rate than previously. The increasing rate of computer technological obsolescence made leasing much more attractive than buying, because lease agreements were typically structured to allow frequent hardware upgrades. The leasing business also fared well during the recession of 1990–91, as leasing became a more affordable alternative to purchasing computers for many companies.

At the same time that the leasing market was expanding, El Camino also began to take a more aggressive approach to the market. Previously El Camino had been more cautious, leasing equipment only when price and volume guaranteed a predict-

able used equipment market. With a strong financial backing from Japan Leasing and a strategy of seeking other investors, El Camino could afford to lease and sell more new computers whose success in the market was still unknown. This proactive approach helped El Camino expand its market share as the leasing industry consolidated.

In January 1991, El Camino acquired 80 percent of the entire leasing portfolio of Econocom USA, Inc. of Memphis, Tennessee, more than doubling the number of El Camino's equipment leases. El Camino thus opened a Memphis branch and employed several former Econocom sales representatives. The acquisition gave El Camino, whose strength continued to be in mainframe computers, a broader leasing portfolio in IBM midrange computers, the System/32X and the AS/400. The acquisition also gave El Camino markets in cities in the southeastern part of the United States, where El Camino had previously not had a strong presence, and, thus, the company's number of offices across the country grew to fourteen. Ten months later, El Camino became a Master Value-Added Reseller to DEC with an agreement between El Camino, DEC, and software developer MCBA Inc. to sell DEC computes with MCBA software with El Camino's financing and technical support services.

By 1991, through its El Camino Application Solutions Co. division, El Camino was providing midrange computers bundled with software applications specialized for customers in nine different industries. These included retailers, hotels, hospitals, lending institutions, building material suppliers, and telephone and utility companies. At this time, the three-year-old midrange division was accounting for about ten percent of El Camino's business.

Although the software El Camino sold, like its hardware, was acquired from other vendors, in November 1991 El Camino began to take on the development of proprietary, industry-specific software when it acquired assets of Darcor, a New Orleans-based developer of application programs for IBM System/36 and AS/400 midrange computers. A new Darcor Products Division of El Camino Application Solutions Co. was created, which brought software development in-house for El Camino for the first time. Darcor's primary products were the "Woodstock" program, which provided automated management of wholesale and retail sales management for lumber and building supply companies, and the "InvenTrac" program, which automated inventory control for warehouses. The acquisition also gave El Camino its first New Orleans office.

In March 1992, El Camino acquired from Bell Atlantic a majority share of Applied Technology Corp. (Europe), based in London, and thus expended its business into the European market. Through the acquisition by El Camino, Applied Technology's business of selling high-end IBM computers was augmented to include leasing activities.

Revenues for fiscal 1992 jumped to $337.34 million, and net income grew to $4.18 million. In fiscal 1993, revenues rose 33 percent to $447.47 million and net income rose 12 percent to $4.67 million, with substantial growth in retail sales of used computer equipment. As client companies downsized their computer operations, El Camino's midrange business expanded.

El Camino's IBM midrange computer reseller and software division, El Camino Application Solutions Co., changed its name to REAL Applications Ltd. in January 1992. In June 1993, this division was made into a subsidiary, and under this subsidiary two new divisions were formed, REAL Solutions Integrators and REAL Software Systems. Existing divisions under REAL Applications Ltd. were Level One Technical Support, the operating system support group for IBM midrange computers; and REAL South Division, the new name for the Darcor Products Division. REAL Applications was the IBM Industry Remarketer firm with the highest revenue in 1993 and as such was named a Premier Business partner by IBM.

Meanwhile, the REAL Applications Ltd. subsidiary expanded its software offerings through additional acquisitions in the early 1990s. In August 1992, it acquired assets of Management Computing Consultants Inc. of New Orleans, a developer of industry-specific software for the IBM System/36 and AS/400 computers. The product line was merged into that of the REAL's Darcor Products Division, more than doubling Darcor's product offerings. In March 1993, REAL acquired two more midrange software development companies: Glenn A. Barber & Associates, developer of Generation II accounting and distribution management software, and Entertainment Software Solutions, which provided software for motion picture and television distribution companies for their management of licensing agreements, royalties, and film product distribution.

At the end of 1992, El Camino's breakdown of products was estimated at between 30 to 40 percent in new and used IBM mainframe computers using the MVS operating system; 18 to 20 percent direct access storage device (DASD) peripherals; seven to ten percent IBM AS/400 midrange and RS/6000 workstation computers; seven to ten percent computer communication controllers; five to eight percent DEC computers; and the remainder being peripherals, CAD/CAM systems, and miscellaneous equipment.

In November 1992, the expanding companies, both El Camino and its REAL Applications subsidiary, relocated from Northridge to a new, larger facility in Woodland Hills, California. In 1993, El Camino had 26 sales offices in 19 states in addition to international operations. In the fiscal year ending April 1994, El Camino's annual revenues topped $500,000.

The mainframe business—especially in the resale and leasing markets—remained strong into the 1990s. Although midrange computers, workstations, and personal computers were becoming increasingly common in enterprises of all sizes, certain companies that had huge volumes of data processing needs continued to rely on mainframes. As their data processing requirements became ever greater, IBM continued to introduce new mainframe computers, such as the 9121 and 9021 series in 1993, which El Camino added to its product line.

IBM's corporate downsizing meant even more business opportunities for El Camino, for IBM began encouraging third-party computer system offerings which it was no longer taking on itself. For example, in spring 1994, REAL Applications cooperated with software company Cynosure Inc. to offer information database management software for the publishing industry bundled with the AS/400 computer in a program supported by IBM.

Nevertheless, new challenges faced El Camino in the mid-1990s. The cycle of computer product introductions was accelerating, and client demands were growing. Companies increasingly wanted total information system solutions, instead of simply data processing systems. Unlike the computer manufacturers, however, El Camino's line of business would allow it to be more flexible in responding to such changes in the market.

Principal Subsidiaries: El Camino Resources, Ltd.; REAL Applications, Ltd.; The Infinite Computer Group Inc.; El Camino Resources Canada Ltd.; Applied Technology Corporation (Europe) Limited (U.K.); ATC Systems Leasing GmbH (Germany); ATC (Asia) Pte. Ltd. (Singapore).

Further Reading:

Borowsky, Mark, ''Econocom Sells Bulk of Business to California Firm,'' *Memphis Business Journal,* February 4, 1991, pp. 1, 24.

''El Camino Application Solutions Acquires Assets of Darcor, New Orleans-Based Software Producer,'' *Business Wire,* November 22, 1991.

''El Camino Exec Addresses MIT Forum,'' *MIDRANGE Systems,* July 23, 1991, p. 7.

''El Camino Resources Ltd., Applied Technology Corp. Announce New European Business Affiliation,'' *Business Wire,* March 18, 1992.

''El Camino Resources Reports Fifth Annual Increase in Operating Results,'' *Business Wire,* September 25, 1991.

Harmon, David E., ''Mapping Out the New Direction of Information Systems,'' *The El Camino Advisor,* Fall/Winter 1993, pp. 3–4.

Holmes, Roger E., ''El Camino Resources Buys Most of Computer Leases of ECONOCOM-USA,'' *Business Wire,* February 6, 1991.

Homes, Roger E., ''Investment by Japanese Firms to Triple Computer Leasing Business of El Camino Resources Inc.,'' *Business Wire,* May 1, 1990.

Krivda, Cheryl D., ''The Art of the Deal,'' *MIDRANGE Systems,* April 7, 1992, p. 39.

McNelis-Ahern, Margret, ''Northridge Firm Expands Disaster Recovery Service,'' *Los Angeles Business Journal,* June 19, 1989, p. 26.

Panoe, Joe, ''Cynosure Signs Real Deal,'' *MIDRANGE Systems,* March 25, 1994, p. 3.

Shipley, T., ''El Camino—A New Competitor Among Large Lessors,'' *GartnerGroup Research Note,* November 9, 1992.

—Heather Behn Hedden

Eli Lilly & Company

Lilly Corporate Center
Indianapolis, Indiana 46285
U.S.A.
(317) 276-2000
Fax: (317) 276-3492

Public Company
Incorporated: 1901
Employees: 28,000
Sales: $6.45 billion
Stock Exchanges: New York Boston Cincinnati NASDAQ
    Philadelphia Basel Geneva Zurich
SICs: 2834 Pharmaceutical Preparations; 2835 Diagnostic
    Substances; 3841 Surgical and Medical Instruments; 5122
    Drugs, Proprietaries, and Sundries; 3845 Electromedical
    Equipment; 2948 Prepared Feed, Not Elsewhere Classified

Eli Lilly & Company discovers, develops, manufactures, and
markets ethical drugs in 14 plants and facilities in the United
States and in 25 plants in 19 countries around the world. The
company's products are sold in more than 120 countries. Although Lilly was embroiled in controversy and became the
target of numerous lawsuits related to its products in the early
1990s, the Indianapolis-based giant still ranked among the leaders in the pharmaceutical industry in the early 1990s. In 1993,
for the first time in its history, Lilly was led by an executive who
had not had a career with the venerable drug company. Chairperson and CEO Randall L. Tobias launched a strategic restructuring of the troubled company that year in the hopes of returning Lilly to its former glory.

Despite its huge domestic and international operations, Lilly
continued to maintain a close allegiance to the American Midwest and wielded significant influence in its native city. For
instance, in 1971 *Forbes* magazine prepared a profile of the
company, but because Lilly did not want the article published,
an Indianapolis newspaper refused to sell *Forbes* photographs
of the Lilly family.

Much of this community loyalty stems from Lilly's long history
of paternalism and generosity. In 1876, Colonel Eli Lilly, a
Civil War veteran, acquired a laboratory in Indianapolis and
began to manufacture drugs. The business established itself
successfully with the innovation of gelatin-coated capsules,
and it wasn't long before Colonel Lilly used company profits to

benefit the community. He donated money to build a children's
hospital and chaired a committee that helped the indigent during
the financial panic of 1893.

This civic consciousness was inherited by the second generation
of Lilly management. During the Depression, the Colonel's
grandson, Eli Lilly, refused to lay off any employees. Instead,
he had them help with general maintenance of the facility until
they could return to their normal jobs.

Lilly established the Lilly Endowment to provide financial support for educational institutions. The family donated $5 million
worth of rare books to Indiana University and later donated a
coin collection worth $5.5 million to the Smithsonian Institu-
tion. The foundation also funded new buildings, music schools,
student centers, and laboratories in every college and university
in Indiana and in several around the country.

Lilly also laid the foundations for its reputation for marketing
ingenuity in those early years. After the 1906 San Francisco
earthquake, Lilly did not wait for requests for medicine to
arrive; the company sent as much of its stock as it could to the
disaster area. Since then the ready availability of Lilly's products has been central to its marketing strategy. That and aggressive advertising campaigns, plus its large, eager sales force,
have been the keys to its marketing success.

Besides being a pioneer in pharmaceutical marketing, Lilly was
known for its development of many important drugs. In the
1920s, the company developed insulin from a hormone extracted from the pancreas of pigs; Lilly would remain the
leading manufacturer of insulin, commanding at least 75 percent of the American market in the early 1990s. Later in the
1920s, the company produced a liver extract for the treatment of
pernicious anemia. In the 1930s, Lilly laboratories synthesized
barbituric acids, essential to the production of drugs used in
surgery and obstetrics. In 1955, Lilly manufactured 60 percent
of the Salk polio vaccine. But the company's greatest contribution to human health was in production of penicillins and other
antibiotics that revolutionized the treatment of disease.

Throughout this era of innovation and expansion, and up until
the late 1980s, Lilly's management remained a constant. Every
president and almost every member of the board of directors
was either a direct descendant of Colonel Lilly or a native of the
Midwest, if not of Indiana. After the Colonel's death in 1898,
his son, Josiah Lilly, ran the company for the next 34 years. He
was succeeded by son Eli and later by Josiah Jr. During the 16-
year presidency of Eli Lilly, sales rose from $13 million in 1932
to $117 million in 1948. After Eli relinquished his executive
powers to his brother, he became the titular chairperson of the
company. Upon his death at age 91, he had lived to see the
company reach $1 billion in sales.

Josiah Jr.'s presidency marked the last reign of a direct family
descendant. Richard Wood, who advanced to the CEO position
in 1973, was only the second of six presidents to be an "outsider." He was, of course, born and raised in Indiana and was a
longtime Lilly employee.

Not only was the company's clannishness evident in the executive branch, it was also apparent in Lilly's management style.
In 1971, members and descendants of the Lilly family owned

$1 billion of the $4 billion in company stock, while the Lilly Endowment (controlled by the family) owned another $900 million. Furthermore, the foundation resisted making large disbursements, and it was not until the 1969 Tax Reform Act that the foundation was forced to loosen its 25 percent hold on stock. Still, in 1979 the foundation continued to hold 18.6 percent of company shares.

Lilly's conservative management paralleled its outspoken ideology. During the 1960s, the Lilly Endowment professed a specific political mission. The foundation was to support an understanding of "anti-communism, free enterprise, [and] limited government." Despite what some have called an anachronistic approach to business, no one can dispute Lilly's financial success. In the 1970s, while the rest of the drug industry was depressed, Lilly doubled in size. When the pharmaceutical business was hit hard by competition from generic drugs that flooded the marketplace after the expiration of patents for drugs discovered in the 1950s and 1960s, Lilly diversified into agricultural chemicals, animal-health products, medical instruments, and beauty-care products.

Meanwhile, Lilly increased its expenditure on research and development of pharmaceuticals, spending $235 million in those areas in 1981 alone. The immediate result was three new drugs: Ceclor, an oral cephalosporin antibiotic; Dobutrex, a heart-failure treatment; and Mandol, an injectable cephalosporin effective against a broad spectrum of hospital-acquired infections. The release of the new cephalosporins represented a significant step for Lilly. The company had always been dominant in the antibiotic market, but competition from Merck, SmithKline, and foreign drug companies threatened Lilly's supremacy. With the new drugs, the company was able to recapture hegemony of the cephalosporin market; of the $3.27 billion in company sales in 1985, $1.05 billion was from the sale of antibiotics.

A similar success story resulted after the company bought Elizabeth Arden for $38 million in 1971. At first glance, the purchase of the beauty-care company seemed an unwise move. Elizabeth Arden had been a money loser and continued to lose money for five years after Lilly acquired it. Lilly management seemed to have no idea of the intense competition in the beauty industry. But, in an unusual move, Lilly hired outsiders to fill its subsidiary's top executive positions, and by 1982 Elizabeth Arden's sales were up 90 percent from 1978, with profits doubling to nearly $30 million.

The introduction of several new drugs in the late 1970s increased Lilly's sales and challenged the market boundaries of competing products. Lilly released Nalfon, an anti-inflammatory drug, to compete with Merck's top selling Indocin. In addition, the company introduced Cinobac, an antibacterial agent used to treat urinary-tract infections; Eldisine, a treatment for childhood leukemia; Moxam, a potent new antibiotic licensed from Shionogi, a Japanese drug company; and Benoxaprofen, an antiarthritic introduced in the United Kingdom. Moreover, using groundbreaking recombinant DNA technology, Lilly was among the first to produce human insulin from bacteria. This breakthrough promised to protect Lilly's majority share of the insulin market.

During this time, the initial flurry over the possible hazardous side effects of a popular analgesic called Darvon seemed to have subsided. Critics had charged that the drug was both ineffective and had the dangerous potential for abuse, but Lilly mounted an educational campaign on proper use of the drug and continued to hold 80 percent of the prescription analgesic market. Darvon generated annual sales of $100 million.

With a 19 percent increase in sales in 1978, a 24 percent return on equity, and impressive results from Wood's foreign-market campaign, Lilly's prospects seemed excellent. Then, however, company growth began to fall short of projected figures. In 1982, a miscalculation of inventory and expected sales caused Lilly to produce far more Treflan (a soybean herbicide) than it could sell. With the patents expiring on Treflan and two animal products, and with the overproduction of Treflan, income from agricultural products suddenly did not look as promising as it once had. Furthermore, profits from Moxam had to be shared with Shionogi, the Japanese partner in the joint venture. And the patent on Keflin, an injectable cephalosporin that had been generating $100 million in sales, expired in November 1982.

Lilly's diversification into medical instruments through the acquisition of IVAC Corporation—a manufacturer of systems that monitored vital signs and equipment for intravenous fluid infusion—and Cardiac Pacemaker—a manufacturer of heart pacemakers—cost Lilly $286 million in stock, a significant investment with an unknown potential for profits. And since the combined assets of its medical instrument subsidiaries and Elizabeth Arden represented only 20 percent of the entire company, their projected profits were not expected to have a substantial effect on company profits as a whole. Elizabeth Arden was, in fact, later sold to Fabergé, Inc. for $657 million in 1987.

Of more concern, however, was the re-emerging specter of Darvon's addictive qualities. Ralph Nader's consumer-advocacy group demanded a ban on Darvon because of its alleged associations with suicides, overdoses, and misuse by addicts. Joseph Califano, the U.S. Secretary of Health, Education, and Welfare, harshly criticized the sincerity of Lilly's educational campaign and went so far as to recommend that Darvon and other propoxyphene products not be prescribed "unless there really isn't an alternative, and then only with care." The FDA charged that Lilly's educational campaign actually amounted to ingenious marketing, in that Lilly sales representatives not only gave doctors educational material that emphasized the drug's positive attributes but also conveniently left samples.

To the company's dismay, Darvon was not the only drug to cause a controversy. Oraflex, the American version of Benoxaprofen, was withdrawn from the market in August 1982. Only one month after the FDA approved Oraflex, a British medical journal documented five cases of death due to jaundice in patients taking the drug. The FDA accused Lilly of suppressing "unfavorable research findings." Initial warnings about the possibility of inconsequential side effects were later amended to include the threat of jaundice, but only after the company had already applied for FDA approval.

At a time when drug-regulation reform would have allowed companies to interpret the results of their own lab tests, the Oraflex controversy represented a major disaster. Furthermore, publicity for the drug, which was projected to be a $100 million seller (prescriptions for Oraflex increased by 194,000 in just one month), had been unwittingly distorted. Reports from outside the company had falsely claimed that the drug could cure arthritis.

On August 21, 1985, the Oraflex controversy culminated when the U.S. Justice Department filed criminal charges against Lilly and Dr. William Ian H. Shedden, the former vice-president and chief medical officer of Lilly Research Laboratories. The Justice Department accused the defendants of failing to inform the government about four deaths and six illnesses related to Oraflex. Lilly pleaded guilty to 25 criminal counts, which resulted in a $25,000 fine. Shedden pleaded no contest to 15 criminal counts and was fined $15,000. All 40 counts were misdemeanors; there was no charge against Lilly of intentional deception.

Lilly was cited as a defendant in a lawsuit filed against drug manufacturers and distributors of diethylstilbestrol (DES). The drug, which was prescribed to pregnant women during the 1940s and 1950s to prevent miscarriages, caused vaginal cancer and related problems in the children of the patients. Lilly was the first and largest manufacturer of DES, and it was estimated that 40 percent of the drug came from Lilly production facilities. In 1981, a court ordered the company to pay $500,000 in damages to one plaintiff, and in 1985 Lilly was ordered to pay $400,000 to the first male seeking damages in a DES-related case. Other claims asked for damages totaling in the billions of dollars.

In the midst of these legal wranglings, chairperson and CEO Richard Wood began acquiring manufacturers of medical devices and diagnostic equipment. Lilly added both Physio-Control Corp. and Advanced Cardiovascular Systems Inc. through share exchanges in 1980 and 1984, respectively. Intec Systems Inc., a manufacturer of cardiac defibrilators, was acquired in 1985. Hybritech, a California diagnostic products company, was purchased for $350 million in 1986. Lilly added Devices for Vascular Intervention, Inc. and Pacific Biotech, Inc. in 1989 and 1990. These companies (along with Origin Medsystems, a 1992 acquisition) constituted Lilly's Medical Devices and Diagnostics Division, which contributed about 20 percent of the pharmaceutical corporation's annual revenues in the early 1990s. But even this new business interest had its problems, not the least of which was intense competition from Abbott Laboratories.

While Wood concentrated on these domestic acquisitions, Lilly's competitors had expanded internationally, where two-thirds of the world's pharmaceutical market awaited. And although Lilly's top two drugs, Ceclor (an antibiotic) and Prozac (an antidepressant) were highly profitable, the company's $1 billion annual investment in research and development did not yield any blockbuster new breakthroughs.

In 1991, Wood abdicated Lilly's chief executive office and chose Vaughn D. Bryson, a longtime executive, as his successor. Lilly's employees reportedly appreciated Bryson's management style, which was much less formal than his predecessor. Unfortunately for Bryson, however, patent expirations, a

dearth of new drugs, and general volatility in the pharmaceutical industry combined to thwart his stint at the top. The company lost over 30 percent of its market value during his 18-month tenure. Worse, the corporation recorded the first quarterly loss in its history in the fall of 1992. Wood, who had retained Lilly's chairmanship, orchestrated a ''boardroom revolt'' to oust his protegé in 1993.

In June of that year, Randall Tobias was selected CEO and chairperson. Unlike all his predecessors, Tobias was recruited from outside Lilly's employee roster. The former vice-chairperson of American Telephone and Telegraph Co. had served on Lilly's board since 1986 and was by his own admission inexperienced in pharmaceuticals. Nonetheless, after just six months at Lilly's helm, Tobias announced a reorganization of the venerable drug company.

His plan included divestment of the profitable, but distractive Medical Device and Diagnostics Division, through which he hoped to raise $550 million. A cost-reduction program included the elimination of 4,000 employees through early retirement. Tobias planned to use these savings to acquire the distributors needed in a pharmaceutical industry that was increasingly influenced by budget-conscious managed care organizations. In line with this focus, Lilly announced its plan to acquire PCS Health Systems Inc., America's largest pharmacy benefit manager, from McKesson Corp. for $4 billion in mid-1994. Tobias, who had orchestrated AT&T's overseas expansion, also worked to expand Lilly's international sales from their 1993 level of about 39 percent of total revenues.

Tobias' plan also focused Lilly's research and development on five broad disease categories: central nervous system diseases, endocrine diseases (including diabetes and osteoporosis), infectious diseases, cancer, and cardiovascular diseases. In line with these strategic imperatives, Lilly looked forward to releasing Lys-Pro, a new type of insulin for the treatment of diabetes, in 1995, and olanzapine, indicated for schizophrenia, in 1996.

Principal Subsidiaries: Eli Lilly International Corporation; Eli Lilly Interamrica, Inc.; Eli Lilly de Centro America, S.A. (Guatemala); Eli Lilly Compania de Mexico, S.A. de C.V.; Dista Mexicana, S.A. de C.V.; EPCO; Eli Lilly Industries, Inc.; Eli Lilly & Company (Taiwan), Inc.; CBI Uniforms, Inc. (50%); ELCO Management Corp.; Eli Lilly S.A. (Switzerland).

Further Reading:

Clark, Roscoe Collins, *Threescore Years and Ten: A Narrative of the First Seventy Years of Eli Lilly & Company,* Chicago: R.R. Donnelly, 1946.
''Eli Lilly Puts Another Notch in Health Care's Belt,'' *Corporate Growth Report,* July 25, 1994, pp. 7363, 7374.
Greising, David, ''Randall Tobias Takes a Pruning Hook to Lilly,'' *Business Week,* January 31, 1994, p. 32.
Hass, Nancy, ''Serious Medicine,'' *Financial World,* November 9, 1993, pp. 32–34.
Teitelman, Robert, ''Wilting Lilly,'' *Financial World,* May 3, 1988, pp. 36–39.

—updated by April Dougal Gasbarre

Emge Packing Co., Inc.

W. Red Bank Road
Fort Branch, Indiana 47648
U.S.A.
(812) 753-3214
Fax: (812) 753-3248

Wholly Owned Subsidiary of Excel Corporation
Incorporated: 1947
Employees: 325
Sales: $260 million
SICs: 2011 Meat Packing Plants

The Emge Packing Co., Inc. provides packaged meats, including bacon, sausage, ham, and lunch meats, to grocery stores throughout the Midwest. Overseen by members of the Emge family for 90 years, the company was sold in 1990, becoming a division of the Kansas-based meat packing company Excel Corporation, which oversees plants primarily in the Southwest and is a wholly owned subsidiary of Cargill Inc.

The Emge family entered the meat business in the late nineteenth century, when Peter Emge began working at the sausage market of his uncle, John Knapp, in the southwestern Indiana town of Fort Branch. There, Emge learned the slaughtering and processing trades, and, in March of 1900, he and his wife Barbara purchased their own butcher shop in Fort Branch, at 110 North Railroad Street. After their first four years of operating a successful retail business, the Emges funded the construction of a new, brick building on the site of their original shop, portions of which were designated for the meat shop and the Fort Branch post office, while the Emge family moved into apartments upstairs.

During this time, the company also began a small wholesale operation, supplying shops in nearby Princeton and Oakland City with Emge sausage, bologna, and wieners, which were delivered via horse and wagon, or by rail in inclement weather. In 1906, Peter Emge purchased 40 acres of land on the southwest edge of town, to which all the company's operations would eventually be moved.

In 1910, Peter Emge's sole proprietorship was redesignated a partnership, called Peter Emge & Sons. The following year, the Emges began construction of a feed barn and two silos on the land Peter Emge had purchased, and, in 1914, the first Emge

slaughtering and manufacturing facility was erected on that site. The emerging complex of buildings featured the most modern construction techniques available at that time, including the use of concrete blocks, which had to be poured at the building site. Moreover, the Emge facilities were equipped with modern machinery, such as the company's first refrigeration system, which consisted of state of the art "ice machines." Further additions over the next several years included a building designated for curing meats as well as a brick home, completed in 1917, where the Emge family established permanent residence. During this time, Peter Emge & Sons became Fort Branch's largest employer, a legacy that would continue into the 1990s.

In September of 1922, a fire broke out at the Emge complex, destroying much of the original plant. Operations were halted completely until January of the following year, when processing began on a limited basis, as rebuilding efforts neared completion. During this time, the company began to focus increasingly on wholesale operations; the retail shop on North Railroad Street was closed in the spring of 1924, and a sales staff of two employees was established to concentrate on bringing Emge meat products to the larger Indiana communities of Vincennes and Evansville.

As a result, Emge meats became widely popular in southwestern Indiana. In 1925, the company, consisting of nine partners, shortened its name to Emge & Sons. Facing increased demand in a widening sales territory, the company made plans to update its facilities so that operations would comply with standards set by the Federal Meat Inspection Act. Meat inspection for companies engaged in interstate commerce had become mandatory in 1906, and, as Emge considered the potential for marketing its products outside of Indiana, it had to ensure that its facilities would meet with federal requirements and standards. Toward that end, the company employed a Chicago architect skilled in the layout and design of packing plants, and, in June of 1928, construction began on a new plant.

In addition to the main plant, other new buildings were erected, including an inspection office and a facility in which administrative and personnel duties could be performed. By 1935, Emge's facilities were in compliance with federal regulations, and the right to government inspection was granted. That year, the inspection process began, and Emge meats bearing "Federal Inspection No. 205" stamps became eligible for sale throughout the United States. Emge's first move outside of Indiana was to establish sales territories and delivery routes in southern Illinois and western Kentucky.

By 1941, Emge & Sons had expanded to include 17 partners. During World War II, Emge saw its workforce significantly depleted as large numbers of employees left to serve in the armed forces. Meat rationing among civilians went into effect in the spring of 1943, and Emge remained in business, shifting operations to accommodate the demand for packaged meat among U.S. soldiers abroad. After the war, production for domestic consumption resumed in full. Emge sales territories were expanded in Illinois and Kentucky and were established for the first time in Tennessee.

In December of 1946, Emge obtained Articles of Incorporation from the State of Indiana, and in January of the following year, the company began doing business as the Emge Packing Co., Inc. with Peter Emge's son Oscar serving as the company's first president. In 1949, Emge expanded its operations, purchasing an existing meat packing plant in Anderson, Indiana. Much of this plant was torn down, and new buildings were subsequently erected, providing increased space for the cattle and hog slaughtering, rendering, and manufacturing processes. Both the Anderson and Fort Branch plants were continually updated and added to over the next two decades, as product lines expanded and demand increased.

In 1973, Oscar Emge handed his responsibilities as president over to his son Walter, while retaining a seat on the company's board of directors, until heart problems forced him to retire ten years later. Under the leadership of Walter Emge, the company survived the effects of a national meat boycott organized by consumer groups in response to rapidly increasing food prices. Despite the boycott, employment at Emge's two plants had increased to 950, and the company began serving retail customers in Ohio and Michigan in addition to its established sales territories in Indiana, Kentucky, Illinois, and Tennessee. Moreover, a fleet of 85 trucks was maintained to deliver Emge meats to the increased customer base, among whom Emge sliced bacon and cured and smoked hams became especially popular. In Fort Branch, some 2,400 acres of land near the Emge complex was designated for farm use, and grain crops were raised to feed up to 1,000 head of cattle.

In the late 1980s, however, Emge Packing began experiencing some financial setbacks. The meat packing industry, in general, faced increased competition from newer companies that had implemented state-of-the-art production lines. Using high-tech instrumentation to speed up production with a lower wage scale and decrease a company's dependance on human labor, such new systems led to an overcapacity in many of the country's meat packing plants, according to some industry analysts. Moreover, economic recession during this time resulted in a sluggish market for meat products, and sales at Emge fell.

In the fall of 1989, Emge management announced that it was entering into sales negotiations with Dinner Bell Foods, Inc., a northwestern Ohio supplier of pork and beef to retail outlets and food service operations. Under a preliminary sales agreement, signed by the two companies on October 9, 1989, Emge proposed to sell its plants in Fort Branch and Anderson. One week later, Emge's 900 employees received notices of termination, indicating the company's intention of ceasing operations at the end of the year. As a result, rumors began to circulate that the company would be forced to close its Fort Branch plant, a move that would have devastated the town of Fort Branch, where 440 of the 2,500 residents were employed by Emge.

Officials at Dinner Bell were quick to respond to the growing public concern, stating that the notices of termination simply represented Emge's compliance with the Federal Worker Adjustment and Retraining Notification Act. In fact, Dinner Bell executives indicated that they would maintain the plants, moving only the cattle slaughtering operations, which would be consolidated with established plants in Ohio. However, Emge's negotiations with Dinner Bell broke down in December of that year, as Dinner Bell had not complied with a term of the sales agreement specifying that the deal be completed before January 1, 1990.

The future of Emge remained uncertain through much of 1990. The company was forced to lay off 100 of its Fort Branch workforce, after closing down the beef slaughtering facilities there. While slightly improved market conditions allowed the company to recall 19 of the 100 employees in May, the likelihood of future recalls and a return to the stability and success of previous years remained doubtful.

Then, in September of that year, Emge management announced that the company would be sold to Excel Corp. for an undisclosed sum. Excel, a meat processing and marketing company with $5 billion in annual sales, ranked third in the country among packers of beef products and fourth among pork producers. Since Excel was then primarily involved in supplying bulk meats to retailers, Emge would become Excel's first name brand product line.

Upon taking over Emge's operations on November 19, 1990, Excel focused on streamlining operations and cutting costs. More than half of the work force was not rehired after the takeover, and employment was cut from 400 to around 150 at each of the two plants. Emphasis was also placed on improving the packaging techniques at Emge, which, the company hoped, would allow for a longer shelf-life for Emge products, which would, in turn, enable wider distribution. Toward that end, Excel suspended Emge's slaughtering operations, while plans were made to modernize the facilities. In 1991, these plans were forestalled by another downturn in the meat market and inflated prices of pork.

Having sold the Fort Branch farm property and buildings at public auction on January 25, 1991, the Emge family discontinued its ties with the Emge Packing Company. However, as a division of Excel Corp., the company continued to produce meat products under the Emge name, which remained popular in midwestern supermarkets.

Further Reading:

Derk, James S., ''Gimme Emge!,'' *Indiana Business Magazine,* June 1, 1990.

DeWitte, Dave, ''Emge Owners Work on Package while Waiting on Meat Market,'' *Courier and Press* (Evansville, Indiana), October 20, 1991.

——, ''Sale of Emge Brings Sigh of Relief in Fort Branch,'' *Courier and Press* (Evansville, Indiana), September 18, 1990.

Leer, Steve, ''Excel Plans Nov. 19 Start-Up at Emge,'' *Anderson* (Indiana) *Herald,* October 25, 1990.

—Tina Grant

Enesco Corporation

One Enesco Plaza
Elk Grove Village, Illinois 60007
U.S.A.
(708) 640-5200
Fax: (708) 640-6151

Wholly Owned Subsidiary of Stanhome Inc.
Incorporated: 1958
Employees: 4,159
Sales: $300 million
SICs: 3999 Manufacturing Industries, Not Elsewhere
    Classified

A designer, manufacturer, and wholesaler of giftwares and collectibles for over 35 years, Enesco Corporation has become a world leader in the giftware industry. The company is best known for its Precious Moments Collection, whose pastel-tinted porcelain figurines of children with teardrop-shaped eyes are the number one collectible in United States. Enesco designs and manufactures numerous other collectible lines and giftware; their catalog contains more than 7,000 items, over half new each year. A subsidiary of Stanhome Inc., Enesco contributes more than half of its parent company's earnings.

Originally a part of the N. Shure Company, a wholesale merchandising catalog company, Enesco was established in 1958 as a small import division. When N. Shure was sold shortly thereafter, the division reorganized as a separate company. It created its name from the phonetic spelling of its parent company's initials: N.S.Co. The new Chicago-based company began marketing a line of imported giftware.

Enesco owes much of its success to Eugene Freedman, who in 1994 was president and chief executive officer of both Enesco Worldwide Giftware Group and Enesco Corporation and executive vice-president of parent company Stanhome Inc. Freedman was a driving force behind the company since its inception in 1958. Born in Philadelphia and raised in Milwaukee, Freedman enlisted in the Navy early in World War II, receiving his naval officer's commission at Notre Dame University. In the early 1950s, he started a company that made injection molded plastics and decorative figures, and, in 1958, he sold that business to his partner in order to join Enesco as manager of sales and overseas product development.

One of Freedman's earliest ideas became one of Enesco's most enduring marketing techniques. In the mid-1960s, Freedman established two large shows a year, the Pre-Show and the Spring Fling, which were by invitation only. The private shows gave buyers an opportunity to view Enesco's lines for the coming year. The Pre-Show was scheduled for late September through Thanksgiving and showcased the company's gifts and collectibles for the first half of the coming year as well as all-occasion selections. Spring Fling, in February, displayed Halloween and Christmas gifts and collectibles as well as the company's introductions for the second half of the year. The shows were a success and became an industry tradition over the next 30 years; by the mid-1990s, they attracted hundreds of buyers each day.

In 1978, Enesco began the line that would help it progress from a modestly successful giftware company to a leading manufacturer of collectibles: the Precious Moments collection. On a trip through California, Freedman ran across some greeting cards with inspirational messages and drawings of teardrop-eyed children, images he felt would translate well into porcelain bisque figurines. The creator of the cards, Samuel Butcher, had originally drawn the children as gifts for family and friends. He later began marketing greeting cards and posters featuring his drawings only as a way to support his seven children. When Freedman approached him with his idea for a figurine line, Butcher was afraid of commercializing the religious and inspirational aspects of his drawings.

Freedman took samples of Butcher's artwork to sculptors in Japan, Yasuhei Fujioka and Hitomi Kuwashita. The figurine they created, entitled "Love One Another," showed two children sitting together on a tree stump. Butcher was so impressed with the sample, he licensed Enesco to produce the first Precious Moments series. Seventeen figurines composed the initial Enesco offering in 1978, and four more were added early in 1979. The response from consumers when the figures were available for sale in 1979 was overwhelming.

Enesco took several steps to ensure that the Precious Moments phenomenon was not a fad. The first was the formation of the Precious Moments Collectors' Club in 1981. More than 69,000 people had joined by the end of the charter year, and by 1994 the club had over 500,000 members registered. In 1985, the company created the Enesco Precious Moments Birthday Club to involve children in collecting the figurines. In addition, certain Precious Moments figures were retired each year, thus limiting the number in circulation and enhancing their collectibility and value. Others were suspended to make room for new items; taken out of production, they might be manufactured again at a later date.

Enesco continued to produce the figurines by sending Butcher's original artwork to Japan, eventually establishing the Precious Moments Design Studio in Nagoya. At the studio, the drawings were translated into three dimensional models, from which plaster molds were made. The molds were cast with porcelain bisque materials, hand assembled, fired, hand painted, then refired. The original sculptor, Fujioka, continued to oversee the artisans who made the figurines, while Butcher and Freedman maintained strict control over the collection, making all the major decisions. In addition to porcelain bisque figurines, the collection expanded over the years to include plates, bells, ornaments, photo frames, crystal figurines, and musicals.

In 1983, Enesco was bought by Stanhome Inc. of Westfield, Massachusetts, owner of Stanley Home Products. The next year, the company consolidated its operations into new buildings. Since 1975, Enesco's headquarters had been housed in two office buildings and a warehouse in Elk Grove Village, Illinois. The company's new headquarters included 30,000 square feet of offices, a 455,000 square foot warehouse, and a 35,000 square foot showroom where Enesco's two yearly shows for buyers began to take place. In addition, Stanhome maintained 12 permanent showrooms for Enesco across the nation.

The National Association of Limited Edition Dealers (NALED), an industry association, recognized Enesco and the Precious Moments Collection with several awards in the late 1980s and early 1990s. For three consecutive years, from 1991 to 1993, the Precious Moments Collectors' Club was named by NALED as the Collector's Club of the Year. In 1992, two ornaments from the Precious Moments Collection, a doll and miniature, won awards in their respective categories. The same year, Samuel Butcher was recognized as Artist of the Year. NALED's Ornament of the Year was awarded to the Precious Moments Collection in 1993. Most significantly, in 1988, Freedman received the Lee Benson Award, NALED's highest honor, for his lifetime contributions to the collectibles industry.

Although the Precious Moments Collection was Enesco's most popular line, the company also produced several other well-known lines of giftware and collectibles, including a line of action musicals, the Enesco Small World of Music Collection. Established in 1981, the Small World attracted a strong following, generating its own collectors group in 1991. In 1988, the company introduced a line that quickly rose into the ranks of the top ten collectibles, the Memories of Yesterday Collection. Featuring figurines of chubby children from the 1920s and 1930s, the collection was based on the work of British artist Mabel Lucie Attwell. As of 1994, the associated club boasted 40,000 members. The company's fastest growing line in the mid-1990s was the Enesco Treasury of Christmas Ornaments, a collection of Artplas ornaments. An associated club started in 1993; in its first six months it attracted 10,000 members. The company also gained licenses from such popular cartoonists and artists as Walt Disney; Priscilla Hillman, the creator of Calico Kittens and Cherished Teddies; and Jim Davis, the creator of the cartoon cat Garfield.

As the number of its various collections grew, Enesco organized its U.S. sales force into two divisions: Enesco Designed Giftware and Enesco Gift Gallery. The Designed Giftware division took responsibility for the Precious Moments Collection, the Enesco Treasury of Christmas Ornaments, the Sisters & Best Friends line, Sesame Street giftware, the Sports Impressions line, other special collections, and Valentine's Day, St. Patrick's Day, Easter, and spring product lines. The Gift Gallery division began handling general giftware and certain other lines and collections, including the Cherished Teddies Collection, Laura's Attic items, the From Barbie With Love line, the Star Trek line, the Mickey & Co. line, and Disney giftware.

Enesco International (Hong Kong) Ltd., the company's first overseas operation, was started in 1985. Since that time, the company aggressively added overseas subsidiaries, including Enesco Imports GmbH, in Germany, which oversaw the music box company Heinz Deichert KG; N. C. Cameron & Sons, Ltd., a leading Canadian giftware importer and distributor in Mississauga, Ontario; and Enesco Ltd., headquartered in Carlisle, England. In 1988, Stanhome created the Enesco Worldwide Giftware Group to encompass Enesco Corporation and its global giftware operations.

The Enesco Worldwide Giftware Group continued to acquire giftware and collectibles manufacturers. In 1989, it bought the Tomorrow-Today Corporation of Westfield, Massachusetts, a designer and producer of decoupage gifts and decorative accessories. Its most significant contribution to the Enesco product line was its figurine collection based on the art of Bessie Pease Gutmann. Rather than maintaining the company as a subsidiary, Enesco assimilated its products into the Enesco line. However, when the group acquired Via Vermont Ltd., a designer and producer of fine art glass giftware in 1991, the Norwich, Vermont-based company continued to operate as an independent company. It continued to produce its own lines of music boxes, photo frames, jewelry boxes, vanity trays, display cases, and other hand-crafted art glass items.

Also in 1991, the Enesco Worldwide Giftware Group bought Sports Impressions, a producer of limited-edition porcelain collector plates, figurines, and other sports-related memorabilia featuring major figures in baseball, football, basketball, golf, and other sports. Sports Impressions became a division of Enesco Corporation. In 1994, the company diversified its product line further by acquiring Otagiri Mercantile Co. A veteran of the giftware industry for 47 years, Otagiri contributed home decor items, musicals, gift accessories, and mugs. In particular, the acquisition helped Enesco strengthen its relationships with retailers interested in home decor products. Enesco's success prompted parent company Stanhome to buy two related companies in the United Kingdom in the summer of 1994: Lilliput Group plc, the maker of the Lilliput Lane sculptured cottages, and Border Fine Arts, a manufacturer of collectible animal sculptures and figurines.

In 1987, Enesco became a National Corporate Sponsor of the National Easter Seal Society. From 1989 to 1994, the company raised over $15 million to help children and adults with disabilities. In 1994, it raised $3.4 million, its highest contribution to date. Although the company held numerous fund-raising events, its most fruitful method involved an annual commemorative Precious Moments figurine and a limited-edition nine-inch figurine, both designed by Samuel Butcher. Sales representatives donated their commissions from the commemorative figurine, and Enesco donated all of the proceeds it received from the nine-inch figurine.

Enesco played an increasingly important role in the health of its parent company in the early 1990s. Stanhome's revenues from its traditional direct sales products—home care and personal care items sold at Famous Stanley Hostess Parties—fell in the late 1980s and early 1990s due to changing demographics and consumer preferences. Enesco's growth helped make up the slack in Stanhome's performance during the recession of the late 1980s. By 1991, Enesco contributed 46 percent of Stanhome's operating revenues and 56 percent of earnings. That year, giftware sales reached $329 million, and operating profits for the giftware group hit $48.7 million. Collectible giftware was the strongest category, with the Precious Moments Collection alone accounting for one quarter of Stanhome's revenues.

Further Reading:

"Collectible Stock," *Forbes,* June 22, 1992, p. 245.

Hughes, Janet, "The Story behind 'Precious Moments' Figurines," *The Saturday Evening Post,* November/December 1993, pp. 38–39, 86–87.

"A Profile of Enesco Corporation," Elk Grove Village, Ill.: Enesco Corporation, 1994.

"The Success Story of the Enesco Precious Moments Collection," Elk Grove Village, Ill.: Enesco Corporation, 1994.

Wyatt, Edward A., "No Party Pooper: After a Pause, Stanhome's Ready to Resume Its Growth," *Barron's,* February 24, 1992, p. 14.

—Susan Windisch Brown

Enterprise Oil plc

Grand Buildings
Trafalgar Square
London WC2N 5EJ
United Kingdom
(071) 925 4000
Fax: (071) 925 4321

Public Company
Incorporated: 1982
Employees: 657
Sales: £546 million
Stock Exchanges: London New York
SICs: 6711 Holding Companies; 1311 Crude Petroleum and
    Natural Gas

Enterprise Oil plc is the largest independent oil exploration and production company in the United Kingdom. With a significant presence in the North Sea and interests in 17 countries overall, primarily concentrated in Italy, the Black Sea, Australia, and Southeast Asia, the company is a growing force in the discovery, development, and acquisition of oil and gas reserves worldwide. Enterprise Oil was formed in 1983 (although it was officially incorporated at the end of 1982) as a government initiative by the secretary of state for energy to take on the oil-producing activities of the British Gas Corporation just prior to that state-owned organization's privatization. The fledgling company was given a good start by its government parent, launched free of debt and protected by tax breaks in the 1983 budget, allowing it to write off over 80 percent of its exploration costs against taxes on existing production. Floated on the London Stock Exchange in 1984, Enterprise was the inheritor of several interests in the North Sea, including five commercial oil fields, a stake in 11 fields where oil had already been found, and a share in 14 other possible sites. In the next decade, Enterprise substantially widened its inherited interests in the North Sea and created an increasing portfolio of international interests.

The United Kingdom Continental Shelf (UKCS) in the North Sea remained the company's strongest area; as of the end of 1993 Enterprise held interests in 113 blocks in the region, equating to a net acreage of 4,704 sq. km., from which the company drew 72.8 percent of its total production. Almost from its inception, Enterprise concentrated on strengthening its U.K. interests through acquisition and exploration. In its first full year

of operations, 1985, the company purchased Tanks Oil and Gas, agreed a farm-in deal with Conoco, and acquired Saxon Oil. Two years later the company enhanced its position considerably with the acquisition of Imperial Chemical Industries' (ICI) international oil and gas interests. This coup, however, was to be overshadowed by another venture Enterprise was simultaneously—and secretively—planning: the Nelson project. Convinced by a combination of seismic data and sheer intuition of the great potential of one of the blocks in which it had acquired an interest through its earlier deal with Conoco, Enterprise completed a complicated series of swaps with other oil companies—all unsuspecting of Enterprise's objective—to achieve 100 percent ownership of the block, some 180 kilometers to the east of Aberdeen. The company's maneuvers, described in retrospect by the Independent as "little short of brilliant," were vindicated when in 1988 Enterprise announced its discovery of one of the largest oil finds of the decade. (The project was named after the famous British admiral Horatio Nelson, with whom Enterprise, with its head office in London's Trafalgar Square, claims an affinity.) Enterprise subsequently reduced its stake in the Nelson field to a 31.57 percent interest. However, it retained its position as operator of the £1.1 billion project, becoming the first independent U.K. company to operate a major North Sea oil field. The operation came on stream in February 1994.

In 1989 Enterprise further consolidated its position in the UKCS by acquiring the non-U.S. interests of Texas Eastern. In 1991, through a joint arrangement with the French company Elf Aquitaine, Enterprise acquired all of Occidental Overseas Ltd.'s North Sea license interests; as a result, the company also obtained a one-third interest in Elf Enterprise Petroleum Ltd. (EEP), the holding company of Occidental's former U.K. assets. Among other important UKCS interests is Enterprise's stake in the Scott oil field, which began production in 1993.

Enterprise's activities in the North Sea include projects in Norway as well. The company's operations on the Norwegian Continental Shelf began in 1989, when it formed Enterprise Oil Norge Ltd. with the Norwegian interests it had acquired from Texas Eastern. Over the next four years, Enterprise built up its presence in the area, holding interests, as of the end of 1993, in 24 blocks totaling 1,201 sq. km. Early in 1994 the company clinched a deal to finance a three-year Norwegian North Sea exploration in exchange for the right to farm in to three licenses held by Esso Norge—thus increasing its net acreage on the Norwegian Continental Shelf by 25 percent.

The North Sea has historically been and still remains Enterprise's primary area of operations, but the company is increasingly developing international interests as well. It first targeted Italy for exploration in 1985, with successful results. Enterprise opened a Rome office in 1988 and within four years had discovered three promising sites for exploitation: Monte Alpi, Tempa Rossa, and Cerro Falcone. With Enterprise holding interests in 27 licensed blocks in the region, Italy is the company's largest concern outside of its core area. Pursuing what the company terms a "geographically focused" policy, Enterprise also holds smaller but growing interests in Bulgaria, Romania, Australia, Cambodia, Indonesia, Laos, Vietnam, Ireland, Turkey, Kazakhstan, Malaysia, Taiwan, the Seychelles, and Equatorial Guinea. Perhaps an indication of Enterprise's future development may be deduced from those countries in which it has opened an overseas office: the first seven listed above.

Enterprise's enviable success with the Nelson field coincided, ironically, with a slump in industry prices which, in 1993/94, reached their lowest level in 20 years. In response, the company has instituted cost-cutting measures in equipment and procedures and restricted its activities to newer fields where modern, cost-efficient production facilities are in place and thus operating costs are lower. In this effort Enterprise is in line with the industry as a whole, which, it was reported in 1994, has formed a government-supported initiative, Cost Reduction in the New Era (Crine). Some 36 U.K. offshore operators are members of Crine, which aims to reduce the capital costs of new North Sea developments by standardizing equipment and procedures. In the past each project was developed with its own individually tailored—and thus highly expensive—engineering plan; oil companies, including Enterprise, are now recognizing that a more standardized approach to development can be much less costly and just as effective. The standardization of procedures and an increasing use of automation where possible also help to reduce costs, as does increasing cooperation among offshore operators.

Enterprise Oil has established a solidly favorable reputation over the years: the *Independent* claimed in 1994 that Enterprise "has been a showcase of inspired management and leadership in a difficult market," and the *Financial Times* agreed, saying Enterprise "has built a reputation for strong management and far-sightedness." It was thus considered more the pity that the company should have become embroiled in an almost farcical—and ultimately unsuccessful—takeover bid for a rival independent oil and gas company, London and Scottish Marine Oil (Lasmo).

The two companies "started out as the Tweedledum and Tweedledee of the UK oil industry," according to the *Financial Times,* but their fortunes soon diverged dramatically. At one time Lasmo was the more successful and enjoyed the status of the United Kingdom's leading independent oil and gas company; indeed, in 1986 the company actually owned a substantial stake of Enterprise (some 30 percent), and speculation was rife that Lasmo would attempt a takeover. Enterprise, however, greatly strengthened its position, first through its acquisition of ICI's worldwide interests and then with the great leap forward of the Nelson coup, and thus became clearly too powerful for takeover.

Lasmo, on the other hand, found its fortunes declining, reaching the nadir following a disastrous 1991 takeover of another oil and gas company, Ultramar. Financial pundits delighted in repeating the joke of Lasmo's strange arithmetics: how to add a £1 billion company to another £1 billion company and end up with—a £1 billion company. Losing money, seriously strapped for cash, and staggering under a backlog of debt, Lasmo appeared ripe for takeover—or so Enterprise thought.

Its bid got off to an unfortunate start when Enterprise was forced to show its hand before it was ready; leaked information had caused Lasmo's share price to rise dramatically, prompting the watchdog Takeover Panel, in an unusual move, to require Enterprise to publicly clarify its intentions. Over the next few months, a media battle ensued. Enterprise was accused of megalomania, Lasmo of monumental incompetence. Enterprise was charged with dubious accounting practices, Lasmo with staggering incompetence. Enterprise was denounced for offering Lasmo shareholders a poor deal, mere "junk paper," Lasmo for really quite astonishing incompetence. Gleeful city commentators speculated that the only reason the mud-slinging was not even worse was that the chairmen of the two companies were socially quite friendly, often hunting wildfowl together. In July 1994, Enterprise's bid for Lasmo failed.

Enterprise wanted Lasmo because it believed that the two companies would dovetail together neatly. Simply put, Enterprise had significant cash reserves but relatively poor long-term development prospects, whereas Lasmo enjoyed potentially profitable assets but, debt-ridden as it was, had little cash to exploit them. The two companies to some extent overlapped geographically, but Enterprise was stronger on the oil side whereas Lasmo had more gas reserves. Acquiring Lasmo would have roughly doubled Enterprise's size, but Enterprise's assertion that the company needed to be one of the "big boys" to compete in the oil business was widely ridiculed; even had the Lasmo takeover been accomplished, it could not have brought Enterprise into the league of the real big boys, such as Shell and Esso.

Enterprise suffered some damage to its reputation during the course of its failed bid, but the harm would probably be short-lived for a company that enjoyed a reputation for making good, solid deals prior to that fiasco. More importantly, the media spotlight trained on the company during the bid process highlighted questions about Enterprise's future. Riding high in 1994, thanks particularly to the handsome payoffs of the Nelson and Scott developments, Enterprise faced potential difficulties as the decade progressed. In the oil industry a company is only as good as its last discovery. The production of Enterprise's star players, Nelson and Scott, would have peaked by 1995 or 1996, and industry commentators stressed that the challenge for Enterprise would be to discover or acquire new profitable sources. With oil prices so low, however, it was risky to invest significant capital in exploration, even for the financially healthy Enterprise; in 1993 drilling levels had fallen to their lowest in the company's history.

Prudent management and disciplined control of costs placed Enterprise in a strong position in the mid-1990s. Satisfying revenue from its high-profile projects left the company financially robust, despite falling oil prices. Its healthy cash base, however, needed to be invested, and invested wisely. Financial analysts may have been divided over whether Enterprise's takeover of Lasmo would have been a good thing or not, but clearly the company had to acquire or discover new oil-producing assets in the near future.

Principal Subsidiaries: Enterprise Oil Exploration Ltd. (various countries); Enterprise Oil Indonesia Ltd.; Enterprise Oil Italy Ltd.; Enterprise Oil Norge Ltd. (Norway); Enterprise Petroleum Ltd.; Saxon Oil Ltd.

Further Reading:

"A Bid Too Far for the Starship Enterprise," *The Times,* May 21, 1994.
"Cash Flow Booms for Enterprise," *The Times,* March 11, 1994.

"A Decade-Long Dance Draws towards a Close," *Independent,* April 29, 1994.

"Enterprise, but Not Enough to Get Lasmo," *Guardian,* June 25, 1994.

"Enterprise Flushed Out as Lasmo Stalker," *Guardian,* April 28, 1994.

"Enterprise Oil Ready to Spend War Chest," *Lloyds List,* January 10, 1994.

"Gloves Off in Pounds 1.4bn Battle for Lasmo," *Observer,* June 12, 1994.

Key Facts 1994, London: Enterprise Oil, 1994.

Lascelles, David, and Peggy Hollinger, "Analysts Fear the Errors of Over-Ambition," *Financial Times,* April 28, 1994.

"Lasmo, the Perfect Fit for Enterprise," *Independent,* April 28, 1994.

Mortished, Carl, "Enterprise's 1.5bn Bid for Lasmo Flops," *The Times,* July 2, 1994, p. 21.

"Nelson's New Success Is the Result of Enterprise," *Daily Telegraph,* February 19, 1994.

"North Sea Turns Rough for Britain's Oil Industry," *The Times,* March 8, 1994.

"Oil Wars," *Daily Telegraph,* May 21, 1994.

"Reserve Judgment," *Economist,* June 23, 1983, pp. 79–80.

—Robin DuBlanc

Esselte Pendaflex Corporation

71 Clinton Road
Garden City, New York 11530
U.S.A.
(516) 741-3200
Fax: (516) 747-7476

Wholly Owned Subsidiary of Esselte AB
Incorporated: 1882 as Charles S. Jonas and Brother
Employees: 1,426
Sales: $300 million
SICs: 2675 Die-Cut Paper & Paperboard & Cardboard; 2782
   Blankbooks, Looseleaf Binders & Devices

Esselte Pendaflex Corporation is one of the oldest American manufacturers of office filing supplies and a North American market leader. The company makes general filing products and filing supplies, labeling systems and supplies, report covers and portfolios, bound books, binders and loose-leaf supplies, plastic office accessories, and document binding systems and supplies. Well known for its Oxford brand of filing supplies and for its Pendaflex hanging folders, Esselte Pendaflex also markets other leading brands such as Boorum & Pease, Amberg, and Dymo. Approximately 90 percent of the company's products are manufactured at the company's own production facilities in Syracuse, New York; Parsippany, New Jersey; Union, Missouri; Los Angeles, California, and other U.S. cities, as well as in Toronto, Canada. Owned by the Swedish company Esselte AB, one of the three largest suppliers of office products in the world, Esselte Pendaflex accounts for approximately 17 percent of its parent company's sales. Esselte Pendaflex markets primarily in the United States and Canada, though its presence in the Mexican market is increasing. A small percentage of the company's sales include exports to the Caribbean, South and Central America, the Middle East, and Asia.

The company was founded in Manhattan in 1882 by two brothers, Charles S. Jonas and Richard A. Jonas. Their company, Charles S. Jonas and Brother, at first operated in the specific field of paper ruling, providing the service of ruling lines on paper provided by its customers. After the turn of the century, businesses began to keep files using index cards and file folders, and Charles S. Jonas and Brother began to manufacture these items. This was the company's first venture in making its own products. The product line, at first limited to index cards and

guides, gradually expanded, and sales began to cover a larger territory. The company was renamed Record Card Company in 1909, reflecting the new manufacturing bent.

In 1918, the Record Card Company first registered the Oxford brand name. The success of Oxford led the company to change its name in 1921 to the Oxford Filing Supply Company. The firm continued to specialize in filing supplies, introducing many new items which contributed to the growth of the filing industry. In 1929, the company began making expanding envelopes and introduced the convenience of file folder labels in rolls, as well as corrugated board transfer files in a drawer style. The company's most significant advance, however, was the Oxford Pendaflex hanging file folder. This was the now familiar filing pouch that hooked over the sides of a file drawer. Smaller files placed inside the hanging file allowed the drawer to be easily subdivided. The company called its Pendaflex hanging file the greatest development in filing since the evolution of the filing folder. The Pendaflex added significantly to the Oxford product line.

Oxford Filing Supply gradually expanded its operations beyond the New York City environs, establishing a midwestern base in 1934, with a factory in St. Louis. Its main plant moved in 1948 from Brooklyn to Garden City, New York. The company built a West Coast manufacturing facility in 1953 in Los Angeles, and the St. Louis and Los Angeles plants were expanded several times in the 1960s. Also during this time, the company opened new facilities in Augusta, Georgia, and in East Rutherford, New Jersey, while establishing an equipment division in Long Island, which later moved to larger quarters in Moonachie, New Jersey.

Oxford Filing Supply Company changed its name in 1969 to reflect its leading brand, and the company became the Oxford Pendaflex Corporation. Business continued to grow, and, during the early 1970s, Oxford Pendaflex expanded its New Jersey, Missouri, Georgia, and California facilities. By 1976, the company had subsidiaries in Mexico, Costa Rica, and Venezuela, employed a work force of 1,200, and had a marketing organization supplying approximately 5,500 dealers and 60 wholesalers across the United States and Canada.

The company's comprehensive North American marketing organization was an attractive asset, and, in 1976, the Swedish office supply firm Esselte AB made a lucrative offer for Oxford Pendaflex. Oxford Pendaflex shares had been trading on the New York Stock Exchange for between $13 and $14 a share, and Esselte offered $23 a share to take over the American company. The two companies announced an agreement in March, and Oxford Pendaflex became part of the Swedish company's Esselte Business Systems group. Esselte was a much larger firm than Oxford Pendaflex, with 1975 sales of approximately $350 million, compared to an estimated $60 million for the American firm. Esselte was founded in Sweden in 1913 from the merger of ten small printing works. The company expanded into office supplies and equipment, which it marketed internationally, and in Sweden the company also engaged in printing, publishing, and consumer packaging. Esselte began an acquisition spree in 1974, buying up eleven companies including one in West Germany, one in England and another in Brazil, before acquiring Oxford Pendaflex in 1976. Esselte had positioned itself as one of the world's leading companies in office equipment, and it was willing to pay a high price for Oxford Pendaflex in order to gain access to the American and Canadian market.

Sales grew in the years after the takeover, reaching close to $75 million by 1978. That year Oxford Pendaflex, backed by parent company Esselte, took over the California company Dymo Industries, which was well known for its Dymotape labelling equipment. Dymo had revenues of close to $210 million, and more than half of its sales came from foreign operations. Esselte AB already distributed some of the Dymo line in Europe, and it paid out $43.5 million for the company. Although Dymo initially resisted the takeover, by July 1978 Oxford Pendaflex controlled 94 percent of Dymo's stock. Oxford took over the Dymo product lines, which included Ideal accounting books and the Sten-C-Labl addressing system in addition to Dymo-tape.

The next year, Oxford Pendaflex changed its name to Esselte Pendaflex Corporation and continued to expand through acquisitions. In 1981, Esselte Pendaflex took over the operation of its parent's U.S. pricemarking division by integrating with the Esselte subsidiary Esselte Meto. Esselte Meto had been formed out of the pricemarking operations of Dymo and that of a 1980 acquisition, Primark. The company's next major addition was the Boorum & Pease Company in 1985. Boorum & Pease, based in Elizabeth, New Jersey, manufactured and marketed office supplies, record-keeping supplies, and information storage and retrieval products, and was a leading manufacturer of blank books and looseleaf binders. The company had revenues of $70 million in 1985, and Esselte Pendaflex paid $40 million for it. That year, Esselte Pendaflex also acquired a Los Angeles firm called Universal Paper Goods. This company had a West Coast business manufacturing custom order folders and office supplies.

Esselte Business Systems, of which Esselte Pendaflex was a division, continued to pursue growth through acquisition. The company bought up nine firms in 1987 alone, with a total combined annualized sales of around $85 million. The three divisions of Esselte Business Systems, which included Esselte Pendaflex for office supplies, a division specializing in graphic arts supplies, and a retail supply division, posted record sales and profits in 1987. Esselte Pendaflex also named a new president that year, Theodore V. Kachel.

In the early 1990s, however, the U.S. market for office supplies weakened significantly. Parent company Esselte AB was forced to institute a stringent cost-cutting plan that included large bouts of lay-offs in 1990 and 1991, in order to make up for the deteriorating market conditions in the United States, as well as in some European markets. Sales for Esselte Pendaflex dropped off steeply between 1989 and 1990, and revenue remained relatively static over the next few years. Operating income also shrank drastically between 1989 and 1990, and in 1993 the company posted a loss.

The company's difficulties were attributed in part to changes in the North American office supply market overall. Distribution became more concentrated as stores consolidated through mergers and acquisitions and new superstores became more important players. Competition was intense between the large distributors, and prices overall were forced down. By 1993, Esselte Pendaflex had a smaller pool of customers than in past years, though the customers on the whole were larger. Another change in the market lay in the declining number of white collar workers within major corporations. And though more people were working from their homes, with an estimated 39 million home offices in 1992, this did not altogether offset the loss of corporate workers.

Esselte Pendaflex was aware of these changing conditions and took steps to keep pace. However, the company's operating costs were very high in the early 1990s, and many of its products had low profit margins. This led to a disappointing drop in income. The company appointed a new divisional president in April 1993, Alan Wood. His mission was to reorganize the company for cost efficiency. Esselte Pendaflex expected to make major transitions through 1993 and 1994. Despite recent changes in the market, the company still saw opportunity for growth and predicted improved profitability over the coming years.

Further Reading:

Dullforce, William, "Esselte Buys Control of Oxford Pendaflex," *Financial Times,* March 31, 1976, p. 28.
"Dymo's Defense," *Business Week,* May 29, 1978, p. 36.
"Esselte AB Subsidiary Sets $40 Million Offer for Boorum & Pease," *Wall Street Journal,* June 28, 1985, p. 26.
"Esselte AB," *Wall Street Journal,* June 26, 1991, p. A6.
"Esselte Business Systems Inc.," *Barron's,* February 22, 1988, p. 56.
"Esselte Business Systems Inc.," *Wall Street Journal,* May 4, 1988, p. 30.
"Esselte Business Systems Lifts Initial Issue to 3 Million Shares," *Wall Street Journal,* August 22, 1984, p. 38.
Lascelles, David, "Swedish Take-Over Bid for Dymo Inds," *Financial Times,* May 16, 1978, p. 35.
"Oxford Pendaflex Merger Pact Signed," *Journal of Commerce,* March 31, 1976, p. 4.
"Shipper Profiles: Esselte Pendaflex Corp.," *Global Trade,* October 1991, p. 40.
"Sweden's Esselte AB to Buy Remainder of Its U.S. Subsidiary," *Wall Street Journal,* November 9, 1989, p. A8.

—A. Woodward

Fiat S.p.A.

Corso Marconi 10-20
10125 Turin
Italy
011-39-11-65651
Fax: 11-68.37.591

Public Company
Incorporated: 1906 as Societa Anonima Fabbrica Italiana di
    Automobili
Employees: 171,000
Sales: L60 billion
Stock Exchanges: New York
SICs: 3711 Motor Vehicles & Car Bodies; 3537 Industrial
    Trucks & Tractors; 3541 Machine Tools—Metal Cutting
    Types; 8711 Engineering Services; 3743 Railroad
    Equipment

Fiat S.p.A., one of Europe's largest companies, is perhaps best
known as a manufacturer of automobiles. However, the company also produces commercial vehicles, construction machinery, thermomechanics and telecommunications equipment,
metallurgical products, engine components, railroad stock, tractors, and airplanes. Fiat has interests in bioengineering, transportation, and financial services companies and also owns one
of Italy's leading newspapers, *La Stampa.*

Fiat was founded in 1899 by Giovanni Agnelli, an ex-cavalry
officer, and a few other Turin businessmen. The city of Turin,
often known as "Italy's Little Detroit," was developed with
Fiat money; in the 1990s, half of its population, either directly
or indirectly, remained dependent on Fiat for its livelihood.

The company began manufacturing automobiles and engine
parts for the automotive industry very early in the twentieth
century. With the advent of World War I, however, Fiat significantly expanded its production line, and as the years passed, the
company became a conglomeration of various manufacturing
enterprises. By the early postwar years, Fiat was manufacturing
so many products that Agnelli felt it was time to improve central
administration.

To help him in his reorganization efforts, Agnelli hired Vittorio
Valletta, a university professor and former consulting engineer,
in 1921. Their aim was to control all of the manufacturing
processes as completely as possible, thus reducing their dependence on foreign suppliers. Soon, Fiat was pouring its own steel

and producing its own plastics and paints. Thus, the company
became even more diverse, and in a further reorganization,
Agnelli formed a holding company, the IFI (Industrial Fiduciary
Institute), in 1927. In the 1990s, IFI remained one of the wealthiest and most influential holding companies in Europe. It also
remained a closed company, owned and operated by Agnelli's
heirs.

In its first two decades, Fiat produced only two types of automobile: the basic, limited options model and the deluxe model. The
company had little incentive to offer other models since it was
protected by the Italian government's high tariff policy (known
as "kept capitalism"); as a result, imported cars were far
beyond the reach of the average Italian. Indeed, more than 80
percent of all the cars sold in Italy were Fiats, and much of the
remaining 20 percent of the country's car sales consisted of
expensive Italian-made Lancias and Alfa Romeos.

Finally sensitive to Italian complaints that Fiat's "cheap" car
was too expensive, the company developed the Topolino, or
"Little Mouse," a four-cylinder, 16 horsepower two-seater
which averaged 47 miles per gallon. It was an immediate
success and accounted for 60 percent of the Fiats sold in Italy up
until the mid-1950s.

Fiat flourished in World War II as it had in World War I, and
profits increased significantly under Mussolini's much heralded
modernization program. But the company's production of
planes, cars, trucks, and armored vehicles for the European and
African campaigns of the Axis forces made its plants prime
targets for Allied bombing raids.

Fiat faced the postwar era with war-torn plants and antiquated
production facilities, and at the height of its disarray, in 1945,
Giovanni Agnelli died. Valletta was named president and managing director and immediately set about reviving the company's fortunes, aided by Agnelli's grandson, Giovanni Agnelli
II, who became a senior vice-president.

Once the Allied effort to rebuild postwar Europe was under
way, Valletta applied to the U.S. government for a loan to
renovate and modernize company facilities. He reasoned that
Fiat was crucial to Italy's recovery and should therefore be
entitled to special help. Well aware of the political benefits of a
strong Italy, the Americans granted Fiat a $10 million, six-
month revolving loan. Other loans soon followed, and the company was back in business, gearing up for full production ahead
of most of its West European competitors. By 1948, Fiat's
holdings represented six percent of Italy's industrial capital.

But fewer people were able to buy cars than before the war, and
Fiat, like other car manufacturers, felt the effects of a smaller
market. In response, to reduce its production costs substantially,
Fiat built a plant for its 600 and 1300 models in Yugoslavia
which was able to produce about 40,000 automobiles yearly.
Other foreign expansion followed rapidly. Additionally, the
company managed to secure a lucrative manufacturing contract
from NATO.

Fiat's foreign forays were a mixed blessing; its Italian workers
began to fear for their jobs and worker agitation became a
severe problem. On a few occasions Valletta was held prisoner
in communist-led worker uprisings in Turin. The political situation did not cease until the mid-1950s when the U.S. govern-

ment tied an anti-communist clause to its $50 million offshore procurement contracts with Fiat. This resulted in the firing, relocation, and political reeducation of many Fiat employees, as well as improvements in the company's already elaborate (by U.S. standards) social welfare program. The Italian workers formed three unions, the largest of which cooperated closely with company management.

Valletta spent $800 million in expansion and modernization in the 15 years following World War II and built the most impressive steelworks in Italy. By 1959, Fiat sales reached $644 million, representing one third of its country's mechanical production and one tenth of its total industrial output. The price of Fiat's stock quintupled between 1958 and 1960; even so, Fiat did not reduce the relative price of its cars.

Still running the company in 1960 at the age of 76, Valletta was a keen supporter of Italy's membership of the European Economic Community. He was sure that Italian companies were strong enough to survive direct competition from the other five members. Fiat itself had the advantage of a highly trained staff, the swiftest production lines in Europe, and listed assets of $1.25 billion. But Italy's organization of manufacturers, Confindustria, opposed EEC membership, believing that France and Germany would quickly dominate the market. Nevertheless, by the end of the first year of membership, Italian companies made 283 deals with companies in other EEC countries; the only deal involving the giant Fiat was a sales arrangement with the French automaker Simca.

Valletta's confidence in his company's competitiveness within the EEC was seriously questioned when, in 1961, intra-community tariffs were lowered and import quotas were dropped. At the same time, American automakers such as General Motors, Ford, and Chrysler were significantly expanding their European operations. It quickly became apparent that Fiat had underestimated the potential sales of foreign-made cars in Italy. Unwilling to wait months for delivery of a Fiat, or simply tired of its models, Italians were more than ready to consider the increasing array of foreign vehicles. Moreover, Fiat misjudged its domestic market and failed to introduce a model that might appeal to the many Italians moving from the lower to the middle income bracket. In three years, from 1960 to 1963, Fiat's domestic sales dropped a massive 20 percent, from 83 to 63 percent.

The company filled the gap in its product line with its 850 sedan, and by 1965, Italian car imports had dropped to 11 percent. But part of the revival in Fiat's domestic sales was effected by less positive means: the company launched a vigorous campaign against car imports enlisting the aid of its newspaper, *La Stampa*. This campaign was aided and abetted by the Italian government which angered car exporting countries by imposing a supposedly non-discriminatory anti-inflation tax on automobiles.

Meanwhile, Fiat's exports improved and sales to underdeveloped nations flourished. In addition to its assembly plants in Germany and Austria, the company built plants in numerous other countries, including India, Morocco, Egypt, South Africa, Spain, and Argentina. Fiat also signed an agreement with the Soviet Union in 1965 for a facility capable of producing 600,000 units a year by 1970.

After running Fiat for 21 years, Vittorio Valletta was succeeded in 1966 by Giovanni Agnelli II, the founder's grandson. Under Agnelli's leadership, the company's annual sales came close to $2 billion by 1968, and for a short time Fiat edged out Volkswagen as the world's fourth largest automaker. At that time, Fiat's cooperative arrangement with the French car maker Citroen made it the world's sixth largest non-American firm; the company operated 30 plants and employed 150,000 workers. Agnelli candidly credited Fiat's success to the company's near monopoly of its domestic market for half a century, but he warned that more sophisticated production methods were required if Fiat was to survive in the international market. He imposed a schedule for new models of two years from drawing board to assembly line and standardized many car parts to allow more interchange between models.

Agnelli also sought further to diversify Fiat's products to lessen its dependence on autos and trucks which accounted for 86 percent of its revenue. At the same time, he set about improving the company's flagging sales performance in underdeveloped countries, and in 1969 he made two notable acquisitions. Fiat took full control of the Italian car manufacturer Lancia and announced a merger with Ferrari, the famous Italian racing car company. When Ferrari's problems had surfaced in 1962, owner Enzo Ferrari had turned down the Ford Motor Company but accepted financial backing from Fiat. Further losses forced Ferrari to sell, and his company was reconstructed as Fiat's racing car division.

While the Ferrari and Lancia acquisitions were good for Fiat's image both at home and abroad, its domestic situation worsened. The company had to contend with Italy's 7.3 percent inflation rate and a series of strikes; 1972 production fell short by 200,000 vehicles. For the first time in its history, Fiat failed to show a profit or pay an interim dividend. Fortunately, news from abroad was good. Agnelli's younger brother, Umberto, who had doubled sales at Fiat France in 1965–70 and constructed successful plants in Argentina and Poland, had gone on to direct American sales. The number of Fiats sold there doubled between 1970 and 1972 and Fiat cars became the fourth largest selling import in the U.S. Umberto returned to Italy as second-in-command to help his brother with the pressing problems at home.

However, Fiat's domestic fortunes deteriorated to the point where the company seemed a likely candidate for partial state ownership. In 1973, Fiat slipped $30 million into the red, and after a three-month strike in 1974, Italy's Socialist Labor Minister granted the union a monthly pay increase significantly higher than Fiat's final offer. Amidst Fiat's loud protests, the government also imposed ceilings on the prices the company could charge for its automobiles—and this at a time when sales were down 45 percent because of worldwide apprehension over the energy crisis. Finally, it seemed, the days of government protection for Fiat were over; the politicians were having to listen to their constituents, many of whom, at that time, viewed the industrial bosses as enemies of the people. Fiat's case was not helped by the Agnelli brothers' refusal to reveal the value of IFI, the family-owned holding company whose funds—in Swiss banks—were beyond Italian government scrutiny.

However, Fiat's foreign holdings continued to offset its severe troubles on the home front, and the company thrived in the less saturated markets of Eastern Europe, Turkey, and South America. Its largest overseas investment was an $86 million plant in Brazil, which became operational in 1976. Other foreign ventures included a project with the American Allis Chalmers company, an important manufacturer of earth-moving equipment with units in the United States, Italy, and Brazil, and under an arrangement with Colonel Khadafi in 1976, Libya acquired a ten percent interest in Fiat. This purchase cost Moammar Khadafi $415 million, and Fiat shares immediately rocketed on the Milan Exchange. Since Libya paid almost three times the market price, serious questions were raised about Khadafi's long-term motives. But Fiat had no such qualms; Khadafi's purchase eased its cash flow at a time when the company earned less than $200,000 on sales of about $4 million and had dipped into reserves in order to pay shareholders.

Meanwhile, the company's domestic woes continued. In 1974, with a heavy backlog of unsold cars to keep it going, Fiat fired all of its Italian workers with violent records. A year later, the company laid off a massive 15 percent of its Italian work force and was able to weather the ensuing strike.

Fiat's management was convinced that it could beat its powerful competitors by producing cars at the lowest possible price. Through its subsidiary Comau, a leader in the automation field, Fiat retooled and partially robotized its factories and standardized yet more Fiat car parts. The assembly robots provided the company with much greater flexibility on production lines, since the machines could easily be programmed to perform a variety of tasks on a variety of models. Further worker layoffs were justified by Fiat by the rise in production rates. Annual output per worker in 1979 was 14.8 units; in 1983 the output was up to 25 units per worker.

Fiat's bold and successful moves to modernize were matched by major changes abroad. The company entirely removed itself from the U.S. market, choosing not to compete against General Motors, Ford, Chrysler, and Japanese imports. In South America, the company closed operations in Uruguay, Chile, Colombia, and Argentina, retaining only its facility in Brazil. Fiat's international operations were also brought under the aegis of a new holding company, the Fiat Group.

Although it had retreated from several large international markets, conceding in part its role as an export-oriented company, Fiat had led the way in Europe toward factory automation during the early 1980s, a move that several of Europe's other volume car makers—Volkswagen, General Motors, Renault, Peugeot—copied. In 1986, Fiat purchased Alfa Romeo, paying state-owned Finmeccanica $1.75 billion to acquire the luxury car manufacturer. The following year, the first Alfa Romeo car, the 164, to appear under Fiat ownership made its debut, selling strongly in Italy but recording disappointing sales elsewhere. The dismal sales performance of the 164 was the first of many difficulties Fiat would experience with Alfa Romeo, as sales and production volume dipped throughout the remainder of the 1980s and into the early 1990s. By 1993, the number of cars manufactured under the Alfa Romeo name had slipped to slightly over 100,000, roughly the same number produced in 1970 and considerably less than the number of cars manufactured before Fiat's takeover.

In 1989, Fiat acquired part of another luxury car manufacturer, paying $120 million for a 49 percent interest in Maserati S.p.A., then four years later purchased the remaining 51 percent from De Tomaso Industries for $51.2 million. The addition of Alfa Romeo and Maserati to Fiat's automobile operations broadened the company's collection of automobile lines, bringing two luxury brand names to the company's established Ferrari, Innocenti, and Lancia-Autobianchi models. Despite the less than robust sales performance of Fiat's Alfa Romeo unit, annual sales grew prodigiously throughout the latter half of the 1980s, more than doubling between 1985, a year in which merger discussions with Ford Motor Company collapsed, and 1990. Fiat's ability to generate additional income from the increase in its revenues also met with considerable success, providing resounding evidence that the company had recovered from the financial malaise that characterized its operations during the early 1980s. In 1981, Fiat's income as a percentage of sales was a miserable 0.4 percent; by 1986 the company was realizing 7.2 percent of its annual sales as profit and its pioneering move into factory automation appeared to be paying dividends.

In 1990, however, Fiat's growth came to a stop. A global recession that crippled the economies of many countries hit the European car market particularly hard, exacerbating the traditional problems—high labor costs and industry overcapacity—that plagued European car makers. Fiat's profits plummeted 51 percent in 1990, and its income as a percentage of sales slipped to 2.8 percent. The recession continued to hamper sales throughout the early 1990s as Fiat struggled to withstand the debilitative effects of the dwindling demand for automobiles. By the mid-1990s, the European car market was showing some signs of recovery but continued to be stifled by depressed economic conditions, inhibiting Fiat's ability to reap the rewards that, under more favorable conditions, would be derived from its enviable share of the European car market. For the future, a return to more robust economic conditions in Europe and abroad prefigured Fiat's full recovery and its return to the highly profitable late 1980s.

Principal Subsidiaries: IHF S.A.; Iveco B.V.; Fiat-Allis B.V.; Bioengineering International B.V.; Fiat France S.A.; Deutsch Fiat GmbH.; Fiat do Brasil S.A.; Fiat Concord S.A.; Fiat USA; Fiat Financing Holding B.V.; Fiat Auto S.p.A.; Fiat Trattori S.p.A.; Teksid S.p.A.; Fiat Componenti S.p.A.; Comau Finanziaria S.p.A.; Fiatimpresit S.p.A.; Fiat Ferroviaria Savigliano S.p.A.; Fiat Aviazione S.p.A.; Fiat TTG S.p.A.; Telettra S.p.A.; Ventana S.p.A.; Itedi S.p.A.; Fidis S.p.A.

Further Reading:

Biagi, Enzo, *Il signor Fiat: Una biografia,* Milan: Rizzolii, 1976.
Castronovo, Valerio, *Giovanni Agnelli: La Fiat dal 1899 al 1945,* Turin: Einaudii, 1977.
''Fiat Auto Buys All of Maserati,'' *Automotive News,* May 24, 1993, p. 2.
''Fiat Performs CPR to Revive Alfa Romeo,'' *Automotive News,* May 16, 1994, p. 26.
Kurylko, Diane T., ''Mercedes, Fiat Discuss Joint Venture,'' *Automotive News,* April 18, 1994, p. 45.

—updated by Jeffrey L. Covell

First Commerce Corporation

210 Baronne Street
P.O. Box 60279
New Orleans, Louisiana 70160-0279
U.S.A.
(504) 561-1371
Fax: (504) 561-1923

Public Company
Incorporated: 1971
Employees: 3,400
Sales: $.50 billion (total interest income plus fee income)
Stock Exchanges: NASDAQ
SICs: 3100 Capital and Debt Management; 8100 Financial
    Services Industry; 8120 Retail Banking Services

With $6.7 billion in assets in 1993, First Commerce Corporation was the largest multibank holding company in Louisiana. First Commerce offers complete banking and related financial services to commercial clients and individuals in Louisiana and southern Mississippi. It operates through five banks and several service subsidiaries, although its primary holding is First National Bank of Commerce in New Orleans.

Although it was not incorporated until 1971, First Commerce Corp. traces its roots to 1831. The Louisiana Purchase had been consummated only 28 years earlier, and the renowned Battle of New Orleans (1815) had recently been fought. On March 5, 1831, the New Orleans Canal and Banking Company was founded as a means of securing capital for the construction of a canal—banks during that era could only receive a charter from the Louisiana State Legislature if they agreed to fund specific improvements. Maunsel White and Beverly Chew, the founders of the new bank, agreed to build a canal that would allow waterborne commerce from the Gulf of Mexico to reach New Orleans' port facilities.

The six-year construction and financing of the New Basin Canal became a monumental task. Because slave labor from the plantations was too costly, Irishmen escaping from the potato famine were hired to do most of the digging. Each receiving just $20 per month plus an allotment of liquor, they built the canal using shovels and wheelbarrows. Over 8,000 died from disease and sunstroke before it was completed in 1838. Although the total cost of the canal was a whopping $1.2 million, the bank earned $405,563 during its first year of operation from tolls paid by the shippers that used the waterway. Ownership of the canal was eventually transferred to the state of Louisiana.

After establishing itself in the New Orleans financial community, the Canal Bank (as it was named in 1895) flourished during the middle and late 1800s. It opened branches in four neighboring communities in 1839 and became a leading financial institution in burgeoning southern Louisiana. The bank's progress was especially impressive considering the hardships it endured during that century. In 1845, for example, its headquarters building burned to the ground. Many of its debtors were killed off by repeated yellow fever epidemics that plagued the region, particularly during the early 1850s. Finally, the Civil War and Reconstruction threatened to extinguish the bank in the late 1800s.

Also rising to prominence in the Louisiana banking industry during the 1800s was Citizens Bank, which was chartered in 1833 and dominated the Louisiana banking scene during most the century. Although Citizens was larger than Canal Bank throughout most of the 19th century—Citizens and Canal had assets worth $6.8 million and $4 million, respectively, in 1861—Citizen's capital base had shrunk to only $1.4 million by the end of the 1920 recession. Canal, on the other hand, had grown to become the 31st largest bank in the world by 1920. To house its thriving operation, in fact, Canal added an eleventh floor to its "skyscraper" in the early 1920s. Canal also continued to acquire other banks in the 1920s, as it had throughout much of the late 1800s.

In a landmark merger of the time, Canal Bank and Citizens Bank converged in 1924, substantially boosting the resultant Canal Bank and Trust's assets. Canal merged again in 1928, with Marine Bank and Trust Co. By the end of the 1920s, following nearly a century of acquisitions, mergers, and customer growth, it appeared as though Canal was poised for continued expansion and dominance of the regional banking industry. The stock market crash of 1929, however, changed that expectation. As many weaker banks quickly failed, Canal scrambled during the early 1930s to survive a steady decline in deposits and a glut of unpaid loans. Unable to stay afloat, Canal closed its doors and forfeited control of its operations to a government-appointed liquidator in 1933.

Three months after Canal Bank and Trust's directors and officers lost control of the bank, they opened the National Bank of Commerce. Through an agreement with the U.S. government the new bank was able to assume a portion of the deposits and liabilities of Canal Bank and Trust Co. In addition, former Canal bank managers literally knocked on the doors of their former depositors, asking them to deposit any funds distributed to them by Canal Bank liquidators into the National Bank of Commerce. Many of their depositors were understandably miffed at the former Canal Bank operators, as they had lost most of their deposits—canvassing solicitors for the new bank were often greeted by profanity or gunfire.

Despite a rocky start, the National Bank of Commerce was able to rally $3 million in start-up capital. Although National took over all 20 of Canal's branches in 1933, it immediately closed 15 of them. By the end of its first year of operation, the bank had attracted $21 million in deposits and had made loans totaling $6 million. By 1936, moreover, it had accrued $48 million in deposits, which grew to $91 million by 1943. Growth was disrupted by World War II, during which 34 of the bank's staff were called to active duty. National also contributed to the war effort by setting up military banking facilities and managing gas and food rationing programs. Despite a brief slowdown, by 1949 National Bank had $134 million in deposits and was generating annual income of $582,000.

National bank enjoyed a relatively peaceful period of solid growth during the 1950s under the direction of President Dale Graham. Before Graham's death in 1958, National completed a pivotal merger with Louisiana Bank & Trust (founded 1933), opened several new branches, and boosted its total deposits more than $100 million. By 1958, in fact, National Bank of Commerce boasted deposits of more than $230 million and annual net income of nearly $1.4 million.

Graham's successor, John A. Oulliber, was a well-known local sports star and had been with the bank since 1935. During his ten years of leadership the bank increased its deposits to more than $350 million and bolstered income to over $2.5 million. Importantly, however, Oulliber and his management team led National through a metamorphosis of the banking industry during the 1960s. Certificates of deposit, a key financial instrument that helped to buoy lagging bank deposits, emerged during that period. In addition, the industry experienced a transition from manual data and bookkeeping techniques to computerized information and data processing systems.

In 1968 Oulliber, sensing sour markets in the near future and wishing to divert the problems he had witnessed during the 1930s, set a goal for the bank of 41 percent liquidity by the early 1970s. Seeking a more aggressive approach to growth, the board elected 39-year-old James H. Jones as president and moved Oulliber to chairman of the board. Jones' aggressive growth strategy included reorganizing the National Bank of Commerce as a one-bank holding company in 1970. The holding company arrangement became popular during the 1970s as a way for banks to increase their income from various fee services—a holding company simply operated a bank as a subsidiary, thereby overcoming certain federal restrictions on banking activities.

First Commerce Corp. was established on November 17, 1970, as a holding company for National Bank of Commerce and several smaller subsidiaries. Ownership shares in National were simply converted into stock in First Commerce Corp. To reflect the change in organizational structure, National Bank of Commerce's title was changed to First National Bank of Commerce (First NBC) in 1971. In addition to First NBC, other subsidiaries of First Commerce included First Commerce Financial Corp., which provided various real estate services; First Investment Advisors, which managed fee income from real estate investment trusts; First Bancard, Inc., a credit card business; and First Investors Management Corp., an investment advisory service.

Under Jones' aggressive expansion tactics, National ballooned in size during the early 1970s. Total deposits grew from $338 million in 1969 to a stunning $840 million by 1974. Assets, moreover, leaped from $328 million to over $1 billion during

the same period. Phenomenal growth in assets and deposits, however, belied serious structural problems in the First Commerce organization. As Oulliber had predicted in the late 1960s, shifting financial markets, combined with U.S. economic problems, had placed much of the banking industry in a precarious position by the middle 1970s.

In an effort to buoy lagging profit margins, which were aggravated by the rising cost of money for banks, First Commerce had engaged in a relatively risky lending strategy during the late 1960s and early 1970s. It had invested its deposits in loans for illiquid assets, such as real estate, and had emphasized growth of high-cost deposits. As inflation and recession stumped deposit growth and margins during the mid-1970s, many beleaguered banks suffered immense losses. First Commerce was battered by the industry shakeout, and its financial health was placed into question by bank regulators. Earnings plummeted from $5.6 million in 1973 to a miserable $151,000 in 1975.

Jones left for California in 1975, ceding his position as president to Rodger J. Mitchell. With a mountain of problem loans and weak performance of its fee income subsidiaries, the company began retrenching in 1977. It slashed staff, jettisoned many of its fee-for-services operations, and sold its ownership share in its headquarters building. Dissatisfied with Mitchell's rate of progress, however, the board replaced him in 1978 with an interim president, Francis C. Doyle. Doyle was an American success story. He started as a messenger with Canal Bank in 1920 at the age of 14. Through a combination of hard work and a friendly demeanor, he had elevated himself to president at the age of 72. He smoothed the transition into a new era for First Commerce, led by Thomas G. Rapier.

Rapier, an attorney, became president of First Commerce Corp. in 1978. He spent his first two years shoring up the holding company's problem loans, reorganizing staff and operations, and liquidating the nonbank subsidiaries. Taking advantage of federal deregulation initiatives that were implemented in the early 1980s, Rapier launched an aggressive marketing campaign to bring in new funds through money market deposits. Between 1978 and 1982, First Commerce's deposits recovered from $694 million to $935 million. Net income, moreover, jumped from $3 million to a record $13.4 million. One of Rapier's greatest achievements was the successful merger of First Commerce with the Bank of New Orleans (BNO), which added $500 million in deposits and a network of new branch offices to First Commerce Corp.'s holdings.

To the dismay of First Commerce's directors and employees, Rapier died one week after the BNO merger. He was replaced by Chief Financial Officer Ian Arnof. Arnof, a Harvard MBA, continued Rapier's efforts at restoring First Commerce's grandeur. Importantly, in 1984 Arnof reorganized First Commerce from a one-bank holding company into a multibank holding company. This move, which was allowed under a new Louisiana law, permitted First Commerce to operate banks on a statewide basis, thereby increasing its ability to compete with nonbank financial institutions.

In a bold move to expand its reach and strength in Louisiana, First Commerce conducted a buying spree during 1984 and 1985. By 1985, the holding company had announced the acquisition of four major subsidiaries: City National Bank of Baton Rouge; Rapides Bank & Trust Company in Alexandria; The First National Bank of Lafayette; and The First National Bank of Lake Charles. First Commerce continued to acquire new banks and service subsidiaries during the mid-1980s, usually merging the banks into its five principal subsidiaries.

As a result of its massive expansion, deposits in First Commerce Corp.'s banks swelled to $1.8 billion in 1984, to $3 billion by 1988, and to a stunning $3.9 billion by 1991. Furthermore, despite huge losses incurred from write-offs of loans that were made in the 1970s, the company managed to keep its annual net income relatively steady at about $20 million throughout the 1980s. In addition, despite the successful implementation of labor-saving automation during the decade, First Commerce's work force surged from 1,860 in 1983 to 3,400 by the early 1990s.

First Commerce's growth during the 1980s may have appeared torrid and even excessive to the casual observer, particularly given the company's boom-and-bust history. In actuality, however, its expansion reflected a dominant trend toward consolidation in the U.S. banking industry during the decade. Indeed, as smaller banks found themselves under increasing pressure to compete against nonbank financial institutions that were encroaching on their traditional turf, the number of banking entities in the United States plunged from about 13,000 in 1983 to less than 10,000 by 1990. Meanwhile, the number of multibank holding companies grew from about 300 to around 1,000. Furthermore, Arnof strived for safe and conservative growth during the decade, foregoing opportunities to harvest large returns in anticipation of even greater payoffs during the 1990s.

Despite a nasty U.S. and global recession that began in the late 1980s and lingered into the early 1990s, First Commerce continued to expand its operations and increase its revenue and earnings. In 1992, the company beat out 34 other bidders to acquire Pelican Homestead and Savings, of Metairie, Louisiana. This acquisition was announced shortly after First Commerce assumed the leading position in the Louisiana banking industry (based on earnings growth and capital strength) in January of 1992. The Pelican purchase, which added approximately $1.5 billion in deposits, was lauded by analysts as a shrewd buy.

Although the failed Pelican savings and loan (S&L) was purchased from the U.S. government, the move did not reflect a strategy of buying shaky banks in order to expand First Commerce's reach in Louisiana. "Very few banks have been able to use an S&L acquisition to enter a market. . . ." Arnof explained in a February 1992 issue of New Orleans City Business. "Our basic approach is to try to acquire customers that we can serve primarily through our existing infrastructure."

In addition to acquisition efforts, First Commerce was striving to bolster its bottom line in the early 1990s through new services and advanced marketing techniques. For example, it was placing an increasing emphasis on direct marketing, which allowed it to advertise specialized offerings to target markets. It was utilizing direct mail, for instance, to sell automobile loans and to retain depositors in new bank acquisitions. "You'll be seeing more specific ads about consumer products—loans, credit cards, automatic teller machines, deposit products—in

addition to the traditional image advertising we've always had," predicted Barry Mulroy, director of advertising, in a November 1992 issue of New Orleans City Business.

First Commerce's growth and earnings strategies paid off in the early 1990s, as assets, deposits, and income soared. Net income, in fact, jumped from $22 million in 1990 to $34 million in 1991. In 1992, moreover, net income rocketed to $73 million before reaching a record $95 million in 1993. Deposits tracked income growth, swelling from $3.5 billion in 1990 to a weighty $5.2 billion by 1993. This growth was accompanied, however, by an unfortunate rise in First Commerce's debt ratio (a measure of a firm's ability to service its debt).

In an innovative move, First Commerce formed a nonprofit company in 1993 to augment its long list of financial services subsidiaries. The First Commerce Community Development Corporation (FCCDC) was established to increase the number of homes accessible to low- and middle-income residents in regions that it served. The FCCDC combines bank money with government grants to purchase land on which low-cost housing is built or existing homes are renovated. The company hoped to eventually establish a revolving fund that would be replenished each time a FCCDC property was sold. "This is an effort to address a major need in our communities," said Kathleen Laborde, executive director of the program.

As it entered the mid-1990s, First Commerce planned to continue to expand its services and regional coverage. Evidencing its focus on growth, First Commerce acquired First Acadiana National Bank in January of 1994, merging it with The First National Bank of Lafayette. The company was also striving to increase the quality of its loans and to minimize its exposure to the forces that had nearly destroyed the company earlier in the century. These objectives were highlighted in the company's statement of direction in 1994, which included four chief tenants: a commitment to quality; a market-driven, customer-oriented philosophy; a high-performance strategy; and positive corporate citizenship.

Principal Subsidiaries: City National Bank of Baton Rouge; First National Bank of Commerce; The First National Bank of Lafayette; The First National Bank of Lake Charles; Rapides Bank & Trust Company in Alexandria.

Further Reading:

Finn, Kathy, "Banking Industry Seeks Stability, Profits and Public Trust," *New Orleans City Business,* January 14, 1991, Sec. 1, p. 1; "First Commerce Spends a Little, Gains a Lot in Pelican Deal," *New Orleans City Business,* February 10, 1992, Sec. 1, p. 1.

McClain, Randy, "First Commerce, Others Take Steps to Address Affordable Housing Issue," *New Orleans City Business,* Sec. 1, p. 26; "Direct Response Advertising Is Hot Topic Among Bank Marketers," *New Orleans City Business,* November 16, 1992, Sec. 1, p. 24; "FNBC, Others Try for a Share of Pelican Deposits," *New Orleans City Business,* March 9, 1992, Sec. 1, p. 26.

Thompson, E. Graham, "First Acadiana Joins First Commerce Banking Family," *Business Wire,* June 30, 1993.

White, Joseph C., *Eulogies in Bronze: The Story of First National Bank of Commerce,* 1983.

—Dave Mote

First Empire State Corporation

One M&T Plaza
P.O. Box 223
Buffalo, New York 14240-0223
U.S.A.
(716) 842-5445
Fax: (716) 842-5177

Public Company
Incorporated: 1969 as First Empire State Corporation
Employees: 4,275
Assets: $10.36 billion
Stock Exchanges: American
SICs: 6712 Bank Holding Companies; 6021 National
    Commercial Banks

A major banking force in New York State, First Empire State Corporation is the holding company for two primary banking subsidiaries, Manufacturers and Traders Trust Company, and The East New York Savings Bank. Headquartered in Buffalo, New York, First Empire concentrated its expansion in upstate New York throughout the 1980s and early 1990s, intent on first consolidating its position in already established markets before broadening its geographic scope of influence to new markets. By the 1990s, this methodical approach toward growth had extended the company's presence southward from upstate New York to New York City, where its East New York Savings Bank operated 19 branch offices. Through its Manufacturers and Traders Trust Company, First Empire maintained 106 branch offices throughout western New York State, 13 offices in the Hudson Valley region, as well as offices in New York City, Albany, Syracuse, and Nassau, the Bahamas.

More than a century before First Empire was incorporated, one of its predecessor, Manufacturers and Traders Bank, began operating in New York under a charter granted in 1856. Manufacturers and Traders Bank would eventually operate under the charter granted Fidelity Trust & Guaranty Co. in 1892 in Buffalo, New York. A series of name changes ultimately resulted in the adoption of Manufacturers and Traders Trust Company (M&T) name in 1933. With these name changes came several mergers with other banks in upstate New York—all occurring the 1920s—that saw M&T bolster its presence in the Buffalo and Niagara Falls region. By the early 1930s, after nearly 80 years of existence, M&T had established only a modest record

of growth, acquiring two banks—Central Park Bank of Buffalo and the Riverside National Bank of Buffalo—and completing two mergers. Before the decade was through, M&T would make an additional acquisition, the Falls National Bank of Niagara Falls in 1939. Its first great surge of expansion, however, would wait until after the conclusion of World War II, when, in the first three years following the war, M&T merged with eight banks.

Aside from any particular strategy for growth each generation of M&T management may have employed, there was one legal barrier applicable to M&T that effectively restrained even the most aggressive acquirer: a New York state law stipulated that a bank could not expand through the acquisition of other banks outside its home district. Adopted in the early 1930s, the restrictive district legislation divided New York into nine banking districts; M&T was confined to one, legally bound to limit its acquisitions to the region surrounding Buffalo and barred from extending its presence beyond the state's boundaries. A few statewide banking concerns did exist at the time, operating under holding companies formed before the early 1930s, such as Marine Midland Corp., based in Buffalo. However, for the majority of the state's banks, widespread growth was essentially impossible.

In 1961, the dynamics guiding bank growth changed with the promulgation of a state law authorizing, once approved by the New York State banking department and federal regulators, the formation of statewide bank holding companies. M&T was one of the first banks to seek such authorization, joining, in 1961, six other banks in a bid to form a holding company. Led by Morgan Guaranty Trust Co., the seven banks gained approval by the New York State banking department, but their union was rejected on anticompetitive grounds by the Federal Reserve Board.

Though unsuccessful, the proposition led to further holding company proposals by other banks throughout the state, as large and small groups of banks banded together and then waited for the all-important nod of approval from the appropriate governing bodies. Three of the banks included in the group headed by Morgan Guaranty combined with other banks to successfully form a holding company, and four such companies were formed in the two years leading up to M&T's next chance at creating a holding company, in 1967. That year, M&T announced its intentions to join with two other banks, National Commercial Bank & Trust Co., based in Albany, New York, and First Trust & Deposit Co., of Syracuse, New York, to form a holding company with the name First Empire State Corporation.

M&T at that time was Buffalo's second largest bank, ranking behind Marine Midland Corp., which had been operating statewide for roughly the past 30 years. With 61 banking offices, more than $1 billion in resources, and approximately $850 million in deposits, M&T was the largest of the three now seeking state and federal approval, closely followed by National Commercial and far ahead of First Trust & Deposit. Six months after the announcement, in May 1968, a fourth bank joined the bid for approval, the First National Bank of Yonkers, with $112 million in deposits, roughly equal to the financial magnitude of First Trust & Deposit. Although small in comparison to the much larger deposit totals held by M&T and National Commercial, the addition of First National brought the total deposits of the four banks to $1.95 billion, which would make First Empire State Corporation the fourth largest bank holding company in New York and the seventh largest in the United States.

Slightly more than a year later, however, in August 1969, the Federal Reserve Board rejected First Empire's bid, citing the same concerns that had derailed M&T's first attempt eight years earlier. Ruling against the combination in a four-to-three vote, the Federal Reserve Board stated, as reported by the *Wall Street Journal,* that the proposed First Empire State Corp. "would foreclose significant potential competition in upstate areas of New York." In addition, the four board members who voted against it stated that if either of the two larger banks were excluded from the proposal then the merger "would be highly desirable." Three months later First Empire was incorporated as a holding company, not as a combination of banks, but solely for the purpose of acquiring M&T, the two earlier bids having dissuaded M&T's management from seeking a merger suitable to the Federal Reserve Board. First Empire then acquired the outstanding shares of M&T before the year was through.

M&T served as First Empire's principal operating subsidiary and held two small, wholly owned subsidiaries itself: M&T Capital Corporation, a business investment company, and M&T Discount Corporation, a dealer in banker's acceptances and certificates of deposits. First Empire first used its ability to acquire banks outside its home district in 1972, when it acquired Hambro American Bank & Trust Co., with $157 million in assets, from Hambros Bank Ltd., based in London. The Hambro purchase gave First Empire a foothold in the New York City market, where the Hambro name was changed to First Empire Bank—New York, and extended First Empire's presence into Europe, where Hambro had operated an office in Paris. Later that year First Empire acquired First National Bank of Highland, with $80 million in assets and five branch offices. The acquisition gave the rapidly growing holding company, now three years after its creation, a solid position in three of New York's nine banking districts.

Though it took several years for First Empire to assume the role of acquirer, the purchases completed in 1972 sparked an expansionary period that increasingly made the company an international banking concern. In 1973, First Empire opened a subsidiary of First Empire Bank—New York, named First Empire Bank International N.V., on Curacao in the Netherland Antilles. Later that year the company formed First Empire Overseas Corporation and two other overseas subsidiaries, First Empire Financial Services, Ltd., and First Empire Development Company, Ltd.

As First Empire increased its international presence, lending more money overseas and widening its geographic scope, an individual who would play an integral role in First Empire's future also was focusing on the international aspects of banking. The future chairman, president, and chief executive officer of First Empire, Robert G. Wilmers, was heading the efforts of the venerable J. P. Morgan & Co. in international private banking, a position he had been promoted to after running Morgan's bank in Belgium. Wilmers left J. P. Morgan in 1980, after ten years of service there, to start his own investment and consulting firm. It was through the course of this work that he first came in contact with First Empire.

What brought First Empire to Wilmers' attention did not bode well for the bank, now fully involved in international lending: Wilmers was conducting a search for under-performing banks possessing assets between $1 billion and $3 billion, criteria applicable to First Empire. By 1982, two years into his stint as an investor and consultant, Wilmers had become a director of First Empire, a company plagued by heavy international loan losses. When the chief executive of First Empire resigned the following year, as the pernicious effects of the loan losses mounted, the company's board of directors elected Wilmers, known for his conservative approach in financial matters, chairman of First Empire.

Wilmers responded to the bank's troubles by taking the bank in a different direction, a direction that started overseas and pointed back to upstate New York. In the course of a decade, First Empire, confined for more than a century to one banking district in northern New York, had expanded considerably beyond its original boundaries of operation, becoming a bank with decided international ambitions. This expansion, however, led to the bank's current troubles, the solution for which, as Wilmers perceived it, was to revert First Empire to strictly a regional banking concern. By 1985, no more than two years after his election as First Empire's chairman, Wilmers had realized his goal of taking the company back to its roots; now First Empire stood as a bank sharply focused on mortgage lending in northern New York.

This new strategy, a revamped version of M&T's operating philosophy, called for market consolidation before entry into new markets, an approach that enabled First Empire to bar out-of-state banks and the larger banks located downstate in New York City from entering its core area of activity. In 1987, an acquisition that represented an exception to this rule, the purchase of East New York Savings Bank, gave First Empire branch offices in New York City and added $1.6 billion in deposits. The addition of East New York Savings, which now became, along with M&T, one of First Empire's two primary subsidiaries, was an integral contribution to the company's growth during the late 1980s. During that span the holding company doubled its assets from roughly $4.5 billion in 1985 to $9 billion by the beginning of the 1990s.

As First Empire was recording this robust growth, other banks, particularly savings and loan institutions, were nearing a point of crisis that would predicate First Empire's expansion in the early 1990s. The late 1980s and early 1990s witnessed the devastation of the savings and loan industry, engendered by imprudent lending practices and exacerbated by a nationwide recession. Conversely, First Empire, under the conservative stewardship of Wilmers, stood on solid ground during these turbulent years, as several financial institutions within its region of operation collapsed. Poised to capitalize during a time characterized by a glut of properties and a limited number of buyers, First Empire did so, acquiring three failed savings and loan institutions in the first two years of the 1990s.

The first acquisition came in early 1990, the purchase of failed Monroe Savings Bank, with branch offices in Buffalo and Rochester. The absorption of Monroe Savings added $482 million in deposits to First Empire's deposit total, a figure that increased considerably with the company's next acquisition, in

September 1990, of Empire of America. Empire of America gave First Empire an additional $1.2 billion in deposits from an acquisition unlike any of the company's recent purchases. The acquisition of Empire of America was made through a joint bid with one of First Empire's major competitors, Albany-based KeyCorp, and led to another, much larger First Empire-KeyCorp acquisition the following year of Goldome, a savings bank with $11.4 billion in assets. First Empire's share of the Goldome purchase brought the company $2.1 billion in deposits, 14 branch offices, and significantly reshaped the banking market in northern New York. Before the addition of Goldome's resources, First Empire controlled 23.1 percent of the banking market in Erie and Niagara counties, a market share that jumped to 34.6 percent after the purchase and vaulted First Empire from the second largest depositor in the area to the number one position.

First Empire's acquisitive activity continued in 1992, still fueled by a depressed market filled with failed banks and few buyers. In July, the company completed another joint bid acquisition, this time with Syracuse-based Onbancorp Inc., that divided four bank subsidiaries owned by Midlantic Corp. between First Empire and Onbancorp. First Empire's share of the $201 million bid gave the company two commercial banks, Central Trust Company and Endicott Trust Company, both of which were merged into M&T. Central Trust, based in Rochester, increased First Empire's deposit total by $1 billion, and Endicott Trust, based in Endicott, New York, a property First Empire had originally attempted to purchase in 1988 and now obtained for $50 million below the 1988 asking price, added eight branch offices and $276 million in deposits.

First Empire nearly doubled in size between 1990 and 1992, a frenetic period of growth that made 1993 the first year since 1989 that the company completed a year with the same corporate structure with which it had begun. At the conclusion of 1993, First Empire's deposits had reached $7.35 billion, its assets had climbed to $10.36 billion, and the company's net income had soared from $41.3 million in 1989 to $102 million in 1993. Strengthened considerably by an economic climate that had negatively affected many other financial institutions during the late 1980s and early 1990s, First Empire charted its course for the remainder of the 1990s, emboldened by the results of the company's transformation into a more regionally focused network of banks.

Principal Subsidiaries: Manufacturers and Traders Trust Company; The East New York Savings Bank; M&T Capital Corporation; M&T Mortgage Corporation; M&T Securities, Inc.; M&T Financial Corporation.

Further Reading:

"First Empire State Corporation," *Wall Street Transcript,* January 1, 1973, pp. 31, 345.

"First Empire State's Holding Firm Plan Is Spurned by Federal Reserve Board, 4–3," *Wall Street Journal,* August 27, 1969, p. 7.

"Fourth New York Bank Agrees to Join Planned Upstate Holding Firm," *Wall Street Journal,* May 22, 1968, p. 4.

Hartley, Tom, "Rochester Expansion Ends M&T, Key 'Marriage of Convenience,' " *Business First,* March 2, 1992, p. 1; "Two Banks Become Darlings of Wall Street," *Business First,* June 17, 1991, p. 17; "The Verdict Is In on Takeover of Goldome, Empire," *Business First,* December 2, 1991, p. 3.

"Holding Company Set by 3 Upstate New York Banks," *Wall Street Journal,* December 7, 1967, p. 13.

Leander, Tom, "First Empire's Wilmers: Blunt Talk, Big Profits," *American Banker,* December 10, 1991, p. 1.

McNatt, Robert, "Parental Help Turns into Profits for Thrift," *Cain's New York Business,* April 13, 1992, p. 39.

McRae, Ron, "First Empire Emerging from KeyCorp's Shadow," *American Banker,* March 18, 1992, p. 9.

—Jeffrey L. Covell

First Financial Management Corporation

3 Corporate Square
Suite 700
Atlanta, Georgia 30329
U.S.A.
(404) 321-0120
Fax: (404) 633-2412

Public Company
Incorporated: 1971
Employees: 12,600
Sales: $1.6 billion
Stock Exchanges: New York

The First Financial Management Corporation is a leading provider of information services, with the largest share of the U.S. merchant credit card processing business. The company's merchant services unit also provides check verification and debt collection. Other units of First Financial provide health care data management services and data imaging capabilities. Overall, First Financial encompasses 185 business subsidiaries throughout North America. The company got its start processing checks and grew rapidly, diversifying its operations through a rapid series of acquisitions in the 1980s.

First Financial was founded in 1971 as the data processing unit of the First Railroad and Banking Company of Georgia. The enterprise was set up to process checks by electronically following them through the banking system. By 1983, this operation was reaping $24 million in revenues. At that time, First Federal was spun off from its corporate parent. When the company's president, Patrick H. Thomas, sold stock in First Financial to investors, he promised them that he would use their capital to raise First Financial's revenues to $100 million a year within four years. This rate of growth required that companies be acquired, rather than developed from scratch. Beginning in 1984, First Federal went on a buying streak that lasted for the rest of the decade.

In March 1984, First Federal paid $2 million for United Computer Services, Inc., based in Marion, Illinois. One month later, the company bought Financial Systems, Inc. In May, First Federal paid $200,000 for certain assets of First American National Bank-Eastern. In August, the company rounded out its first year of acquisitions with the purchase of Financial Computer Services, Inc., for three quarters of a million dollars.

In expanding its operations through acquisition, First Federal sought to become a major player in the commercial transaction industry. First Federal's executives believed that the wave of the future in banking and commerce lay with electronics and computerized information, not with cumbersome paper slips and forms. The company wanted to become the middleman for a wide variety of exchanges in which electronic data was manipulated, acting as a support system for the financial industry of the future.

To attain this status, First Federal continued its rapid pace of acquisitions in 1985, buying four computer data services during that year. In February, it paid $135,000 for assets of the Data One Corporation, and in June an interest in Financial Data Services, Inc., was acquired for $2.75 million. In the following month, Decimus Data Services joined the First Financial family of companies, and in December the company paid $229,000 for Bob White Computing Services.

In making acquisitions, First Federal sought out relatively small entrepreneurial firms, which were important because they helped First Federal to increase its list of clients. Because it was cumbersome and time consuming to win new customers in the financial services field, First Federal had found it more economical simply to buy a small company than to individually recruit each of its customers. When First Financial purchased a small firm, the company did not, however, insist that the smaller company's operations be broken down and merged with those of First Financial. Instead, the company left them intact in the same location, with the same management, culture, and individual style. First Financial had a decentralized management philosophy, and, though there was ample overlap in its operations, the company did not attempt to institute central marketing or sales operations. Former owners of properties that had been bought were encouraged through stock deals to stay and work for First Financial, because their ownership in First Financial could only be liquidated over time.

After a brief pause, First Financial resumed its acquisitions at the end of 1986, buying the customer base of American Information Services, Inc., for $2.5 million, in August. In the following month, the company bought American Data Technology, Inc., for $2.2 million, and in October 1986, First Financial acquired Mid-Continent Computer Services for $23 million. These purchases were designed to strengthen First Financial by building up its revenues. In March of the following year, First Financial bought Tel-A-Data Limited for $8.2 million, and the Confidata Corporation, for half a million dollars. Four months later, First Financial also purchased American Automated and its On-Line Terminal Services for $4.3 million.

In the last four months of 1987, First Financial made three purchases that moved it strongly into a new field and nearly tripled the size of its operations. In October 1987, the company bought the National Bancard Corporation (NaBanco) of Fort Lauderdale, Florida, for $48 million. With the acquisition of this company, First Financial moved aggressively into the market for credit card transaction processing. Later that month, First Financial added to its holdings in this area when it purchased

Endata, Inc., of Nashville, Tennessee. With these moves, First Financial became one of the three largest merchant credit card processors in the country. The company decided to enter this field after its examination of why banks were unable to make money on their credit card operations. First Financial found that banks lost money when they had to collect and manipulate paper credit card receipts from merchants. By installing electronic terminals at cash registers, the company was able to eliminate this step and make credit card transaction processing much more lucrative.

In addition to its credit card operations, First Financial also purchased the First Data Management Company of Oklahoma City at the end of 1987, and Midwest Com of Indiana, Inc., for which it paid $400,000. At the end of this year, First Financial reported revenues of $175 million, which yielded profits of $11.6 million. Thomas had met and nearly doubled his goal of three years ago.

In 1988, First Financial built on these strong returns by embarking on further acquisitions. The company continued its expansion into the credit card business by purchasing the retail merchants credit card processing contracts of Manufacturers Hanover Trust Company in February 1988. In December of that year, First Federal enhanced its computer operations when it bought Appalachian Computer Services, a company based in Kentucky, for $46.5 million. ''We're continuing on our path to be a significant financial-transaction company, and this rounds out one of our services,'' First Financial's chief financial officer told the *Atlanta Business Chronicle*.

By this time, First Financial had accumulated more than 25,000 customers, including over 1,500 financial institutions. This total had been achieved through the company's 27 acquisitions, which came, on average, once every three months. First Financial ended 1988 with revenues of $423.7 million, an increase of more than 100 percent from the previous year. Profits reached $29.3 million. Nearly half, by far the largest part, of this income was contributed by First Financial's credit card processing operations.

Early in 1989 First Financial announced that it would branch out beyond its core transaction processing businesses to acquire a Georgia savings and loan association, despite the fact that this industry had been in a severe and protracted slump. The company took this step in order to protect its lucrative credit card processing operations. Concerned that the major credit card companies might one day issue rules that would prevent third party companies, such as First Financial, from processing transactions, First Financial decided to buy into the credit card industry in order to gain some say over how the accounts were handled. In order to become a credit card issuer, it was necessary to own a financial institution. By buying Georgia Federal Bank in May 1989 for $234 million, First Financial became the issuer of over a hundred thousand credit cards. In addition, Georgia Federal boasted 11 percent of all deposits in its Atlanta market, where it was the largest thrift institution. Despite its size and strategic importance, Georgia Federal's acquisition by First Financial left the financial community worried about the company's prospects, and First Financial's stock price began to fall.

Following this unorthodox move, First Financial bought a company in its traditional line of business: Data Preparation, Inc., which was acquired in July 1989. In addition, The Computer Company, which processed Medicaid claims, was purchased in September for $38 million. With this acquisition, First Financial took a tentative step into the enormous market for management of health care data. In the last month of the year, First Financial made another large acquisition, paying $118 million for the MicroBilt Corporation. This company provided information processing systems for small, niche markets. The company combined standard hardware with specialized software to create unique systems for transaction-intensive industries.

At the start of 1990, First Financial announced that it would switch its stock listing from the over-the-counter market to the New York Stock Exchange. In this way, the company hoped to shore up its financial reputation and increase its attractiveness to foreign investors. Just a few days later, First Financial also announced that it had reorganized its Financial Services Group into a subsidiary and changed its name to BASIS Information Technologies, Inc. This new entity comprised First Financial's original business operations, which provided check-clearing services to independent, local banks, and 16 acquisitions in this field. With this restructuring along functional lines, the company hoped that BASIS would be better equipped to compete for the business of small financial institutions through its 24 data processing centers around the United States. By the end of its first quarter in business as a separate entity, however, BASIS was reporting only a 10 percent profit margin, half of what First Financial executives had predicted.

This news, combined with an announcement that the federal government would investigate the real estate holdings of First Financial's thrift institution and general jitteriness about the savings and loan industry, combined to push First Financial's stock price into a steep drop in the spring of 1990. Because the company used its stock to finance acquisitions, this drop in the value of its stock curtailed the number of purchases it could make.

By the start of the summer, First Financial's stock price had begun to recover, and the company announced in August that it had finalized its purchase of two Atlanta businesses, Nationwide Credit and Online Financial Communication Systems, which meshed with the company's Microbilt subsidiary. With its purchase of the first company, First Financial entered the debt collection business. With the purchase of the Zytron Corporation the same month First Financial enhanced its Endata operations. The company also bought the Electro Data Corporation of Denver and the Bank of Boston's credit card contracts. In December 1990, First Financial announced that it had also acquired the credit card contracts of the Southeast Bank of Florida, which had one of the ten largest merchant contract portfolios. Shortly before this, the company had completed its acquisition of the same operations from the Bank of New York, bringing a total of 12,000 new merchant customers to the company's credit card subsidiary. NaBanco, First Financial's credit card subsidiary, had become the nation's largest credit card processing company, notching annual growth of 40 percent.

Although First Financial's pace of acquisitions slowed in 1991, its revenues nevertheless climbed to $1.2 billion. In the following year, First Financial made a number of key purchases. In July 1992, the company augmented its credit verification operations by buying TeleCheck Services, Inc., and its subsidiary, the Payment Services Company, for $156 million. Shortly, First Financial would expand its ownership of TeleCheck franchises to 97 percent.

Three months earlier, First Financial had moved further into the health care field, acquiring ALTA Health Strategies, Inc., which it renamed FIRST HEALTH Strategies. This Utah-based enterprise was the largest independent health care management company in the United States. With this acquisition, First Financial signaled that it planned to move from its strength in bank processing to a dominant position in the automated medical claims processing field.

As part of this shift in corporate direction, First Financial divested itself of its savings and loan subsidiary, selling the Georgia Federal Bank, and its subsidiary, First Family Financial Services. After a planned sale of this property in the summer of 1992 fell through, First Financial petitioned the Georgia state banking regulators for permission to form a credit card bank, called the First Financial Bank. After transferring Georgia Federal's data processing business to this new subsidiary, the sale of the thrift was completed, as the First Union Corporation paid $153 million for the property. This move, long urged by the financial community, was expected to lift the price of First Financial's stock.

At the end of 1992, First Financial also announced that it would sell its BASIS Information Technologies subsidiary, the company's original business, which now contributed only 10 percent of First Financial's revenues. This move came on the heels of a $150 million lawsuit filed in October 1992 against the International Business Machines Corporation (IBM), alleging that IBM had failed to properly implement a new computer system, which had damaged the company's operations. After receiving a cash settlement from IBM, First Financial completed the sale of BASIS to FIServe, Inc., for $96 million in February 1993.

In July of that year, First Financial activated the First Financial Bank as a credit card issuer, making it the sponsoring bank on customer contracts for the NaBanco processing operation. In addition, the company moved more aggressively into the health care field, purchasing Hospital Cost Consultants and VIPS, which marketed a Medicare claims processing system. First Financial also took a step into a new industry in 1993 when it purchased International Banking Technologies, Inc., for $47 million. This company had helped extend banking operations to supermarkets by negotiating agreements between grocers and financial institutions. With this move, First Financial hoped to introduce its own services to a wider market. By the end of the 1993, First Financial's revenues had grown to $1.67 billion.

During the course of 1993, First Financial had also completed a reorganization of the company's infrastructure. In this way, First Financial hoped to prepare itself for effective action as the company moved into the late 1990s. With its record of rapid growth and strong financial performance, First Financial appeared to be well situated to thrive in the coming years.

Principal Subsidiaries: First Image Management Company; TeleCheck Services, Inc.; MicroBilt Corporation; Nationwide Credit, Inc.; National Bancard Corporation; First Health Services; First Health Strategies.

Further Reading:

Bean, Ed, ''An Empire in the Making,'' *Georgia Trend,* October 1989.
''The Bum Rap,'' *Georgia Trend,* August 1990.
King, Jim, ''First Financial Credit Card Bank Ok'd,'' *Atlanta Journal and Constitution,* November 26, 1992; ''First Union Will Buy Georgia Federal,'' *Atlanta Journal and Constitution,* December 21, 1992.
Lee, Shelley, ''FFMC Expands at Blistering Pace,'' *Business Atlanta,* December 1991.
Morrison, Cindy, ''FFMC Expects to Net a Big One Next Month,'' *Atlanta Business Chronicle,* November 21, 1988.

—Elizabeth Rourke

First Hawaiian, Inc.

1132 Bishop Street
Honolulu, Hawaii 96813
U.S.A.
(808) 525-7000
Fax: (808) 525-8831

Public Company
Incorporated: 1858 as Bishop & Co.
Employees: 2,600
Sales: $.51 billion (interest income + operating income)
Stock Exchanges: NASDAQ
SICs: 8100 Financial Services

With assets of $7.3 billion in 1994, First Hawaiian, Inc., is the second largest bank holding company in Hawaii. Its primary subsidiary is First Hawaiian Bank. Through that bank and four other subsidiaries, the holding company operates about 90 bank branches, provides various financial services, and leases and finances commercial equipment and vehicles. First Hawaiian Bank is one of the oldest and largest U.S. banks west of the Rocky Mountains.

The institution that would become First Hawaiian Bank was founded in 1858 in Honolulu by Charles Reed Bishop and William A. Aldrich. The Bishop Co. Savings Bank opened its doors on August 17 after advertising the venture in the local newspaper: "Bishop & Co.'s Savings Bank! The undersigned will receive money at their Savings Bank upon the following terms: On sums of $300 or under, from one person, they will pay interest at the rate of 5 per cent per annum from date of receipt." At the end of its first day of operation, Bishop and Aldrich were in business with $4,784.25 in deposits.

Bishop, an upstate New Yorker, had stopped in Honolulu on his way to Oregon in 1846 and stayed, although he would later return to the United States to build another fortune in San Francisco. Bishop soon became a respected business and civic leader in the Kingdom, which was ruled by King Kamehameha IV. He started out as a partner in a small drygoods store. After three years on the island, he obtained citizenship in the Kingdom and left the drygoods store to become collector of customs. In 1850, he married Princess Bernice Pauahi, who later inherited a wealth of Kamehameha land.

Bishop and his associate, Aldrich, recognized a need for a local bank in Hawaii during the 1850s. Whaling had grown into a big industry by that time, creating a need for a dependable place for people to store money, make payments to customers and employees, and to borrow money to start and grow businesses. Established to serve those needs, Bishop & Co. became the second bank to open west of the Rocky Mountains. It was headquartered in a small waterfront building that the cofounders shared with another tenant.

Bishop ran the bank for more than 30 years, during which he and his bank became a respected and important part of the Hawaiian community. For example, Bishop cofounded and helped run the Royal Hawaiian Agricultural Society, was a member of the King's Privy Council (cabinet) for over 30 years, was a lifetime member of the House of Nobles (upper legislative house), and played a pivotal role in the development of the sugar industry following the important Reciprocity Treaty with the United States in 1875. Among other accomplishments, Bishop received Japan's highest award, the Order of the Rising Sun First Class, from Emperor Meiji. After nearly 50 years in Hawaii, Bishop returned to the United States in the 1890s.

Despite Bishop's absence, Bishop & Co. continued to grow during the early and mid-1900s. In 1919 its name was changed to The Bank of Bishop and Co., Ltd. As population and commerce ballooned, the bank's name changed several times as Hawaii switched from a monarchy to a provisional republican government, to a U.S. territory (1900), and finally to the 50th state of the Union (1959). To house its expanding operations, the bank erected a two-story headquarters building on Bishop Street (in Honolulu) in 1925. In 1929, its name was changed to Bishop First National Bank of Honolulu before switching again in 1933 to Bishop First National Bank of Hawaii at Honolulu. The bank became Bishop National Bank of Hawaii in 1956 before switching to First National Bank of Hawaii in 1960, one year after Hawaii became a state. Finally, in 1969, it was titled First Hawaiian Bank.

Bishop experienced relatively steady growth during the 1900s, with the exception of temporary setbacks encountered during the Great Depression and during World War I and World War II. Its greatest era of expansion occurred during the 1960s and 1970s, following Hawaii's passage into statehood. During that period, tourism generated a massive economic boom that pumped up the bank's deposits and created a huge need for construction, business, and mortgage loans. To keep up with the surge in business, the bank built a new headquarters facility in the early 1960s. Located on Bishop and King Streets, near its existing building, the structure was the first major high-rise on the Honolulu skyline.

John D. Bellinger took over as chief executive of First Hawaiian Bank in 1969. He presided over a 20-year expansion of the organization that would take it far beyond what its founder had envisioned. Although First Hawaiian experienced record growth under Bellinger during the 1970s, and even before Bellinger during the 1960s, the bank was joined by a slew of competitors that were gunning for a share of First Hawaiian's customers. Notable was the entrance in 1960 of heavy-hitter Hawaii National Bank. On its opening day, First Hawaiian's new competitor captured $6.3 million in deposits, a national record for first-day deposits.

First Hawaiian faced competition during the 1970s and 1980s from an influx of new banks as well as from established competitors, such as Pioneer Federal Savings Bank. Pioneer was founded in 1890 and by the 1970s had become a leader in the residential mortgage market. Nevertheless, First Hawaiian rapidly enlarged its assets and customer base during the 1970s. It also expanded through acquisition. In 1975, for example, First Hawaiian purchased a financial services company to broaden its strength in both consumer and commercial credit markets, renaming the subsidiary First Hawaiian Creditcorp, Inc.

The banking industry as a whole suffered during the late 1970s and early 1980s from a variety of economic factors that caused a metamorphosis of U.S., and even global, financial markets. A combination of inflation and high interest rates diminished profit opportunities for First Hawaiian and its industry counterparts. Furthermore, banks came under increasing pressure from other financial institutions that were offering competing financial services. By the mid-1980s, however, a surging economy was pulling many U.S. banks out of the doldrums.

Hawaii, particularly, benefited from the economic boom of the 1980s. Besides heavy investment from the continental United States, First Hawaiian benefited from explosive economic growth in Japan. As that country's economic machine shifted into high gear during the 1980s, Japanese individuals and companies, eager to invest in the United States, began dumping billions of dollars per year into Hawaii's economy. In 1989 alone, in fact, Japan invested more than $4.4 billion in Hawaii. As other foreign dollars poured in, a massive commercial construction boom ensued. Healthy tourism, home building, and agricultural markets augmented First Hawaiian's expansion during the decade.

By the late 1980s, First Hawaiian was generating over $400 million annually in interest income on its loans and investments and was garnering over $40 million per year from its other services and operating activities; its actual net income in 1989 reached $57 million. Besides enhancing its reputation and financial strength in the region during the 1980s, First Hawaiian had also established a role as an innovator in the local banking industry. It was the first institution, for example, to introduce full-service automated teller machines or to offer telephone home banking services. Also during the 1980s, it introduced debit cards for gasoline purchases and created the first locally available variable-rate consumer loans.

After nearly a decade of unprecedented growth, it was clear to many observers that the economic boom of the mid- and late 1980s was coming to an end. First Hawaiian recognized the first signs of slowing growth in 1989. Investments from Japan and most other countries appeared to be fading, and the U.S. mainland was slipping into what appeared to be a recession. Coincidentally, Bellinger died in 1989 after 30 years of service, leaving First National in the hands of younger managers. Hoping to duplicate or even improve the performance the bank had achieved since its inception, First Hawaiian's board selected Walter A. Dods, Jr., to run the company.

Dods' appointment occurred at an opportune time. Although First Hawaiian did not know it at the time (nor did any other industry analysts), the nation was entering into a recession in 1989 that would linger through the early and even into the mid-1990s. The 50-year-old Dods, who had been with the company for 20 years, quickly installed a new management team, most of which still had 15 to 20 years of potential service left to the company. He decentralized the company's management structure by creating five separate divisions, each under the direction of a strong leader—Dods himself assumed a less controlling role than his predecessor. Dods also began to push for greater diversification and acquisitions. Diversification was an attempt to reduce First Hawaiian's dependence on traditional banking activities that were under increasing competitive pressures.

As the rest of the nation spiraled into recession, Hawaii managed to sustain moderate growth during 1989 and the early 1990s. In fact, the organization increased its interest and operating income to $523 million and $61 million, respectively, as net income surged about 40 percent to $81.7 million. Much of First Hawaiian's gains were the result of its 1991 acquisition of First Interstate of Hawaii, Inc., a commercial bank holding company with $900 million in assets. The bank also benefited from the relatively conservative lending strategy that it had employed during the 1980s. By the early 1990s, First Hawaiian's nonperforming assets totaled a comparatively low $39 million. In April of 1992, *Business Week* ranked First Hawaiian Bank the tenth safest lender in the nation.

Although it was delayed, Hawaii began to feel the effects of the global recession in 1992. Importantly, Japan fell into a deep slump during that period, all but halting serious investments from that country into Hawaii. Tourism was off too; Hawaii's visitor count plummeted about 6 percent in both 1992 and 1993, largely as a result of fewer mainland travelers. It was the largest decline since 1949. In addition, the tourists that were coming were spending less and not staying as long. Tourism, foreign investment, and agricultural markets continued to slide in 1993, resulting in lackluster lending opportunities. Although First Hawaiian's revenue and net income increased in 1992 to about $557 million and $87 million, respectively, those figures slipped to $511 million and $81.9 million in 1993.

In an effort to increase its efficiency by spreading its overhead amongst a larger customer base, Dods continued his acquisition strategy in 1993 by purchasing Pioneer Federal Savings Bank. Pioneer brought $650 million in assets to the organization, increasing the total base of assets under First Hawaiian, Inc.'s corporate umbrella to more than $7 billion. Pioneer also added 19 branches on four Hawaiian islands, boosting First Hawaiian's number of branches to 92. Dods oversaw the purchase of Phoenix Financial Services in 1993, as well, reflecting the bank's newfound emphasis on fee-based financial services. Phoenix specialized in mortgage financing.

First Hawaiian's portfolio of nonperforming assets doubled in 1992 to more that $70 million before declining slightly in 1993. Furthermore, its ranking in *Financial World* fell from 72 in 1991 to 217 in 1992. Nevertheless, it remained a very healthy bank by industry standards. In addition, Hawaii was still one of the healthiest business environments in the United States—the unemployment rate was only four percent in 1993—and First

Hawaiian enjoyed a rock-solid local reputation. Besides the company's relatively strong financial position and sticking power, the management team assembled by Dods seemed to be performing admirably.

A good example of First Hawaiian's management depth was Lily Yao, chief executive of the holding company's Pioneer subsidiary. Yao grew up in China, moved to Taiwan, and then relocated to Hawaii in 1968 where she went to work as a teller at Pioneer. While she earned her business degree at night, Yao climbed the corporate ladder. She quickly moved from teller to branch manager and up into the executive ranks. In 1984, Pioneer's board of directors selected her to head the company. Pioneer's sales jumped from $432,000 in 1984 to $6.1 million in 1993. Yao stayed with First Hawaiian after the buyout, and was even instrumental in transferring ownership to the well-heeled holding company. First Hawaiian also hoped to use Yao to secure business in burgeoning Asian markets.

In addition to branching into new foreign and financial markets in 1994, First Hawaiian declared its long-term growth intentions with the construction of a new, world-class headquarters build-ing. Scheduled for completion in 1996, the proposed building would be a $240 million, 30-story high-rise on Bishop street. The plaza level of the building, with its 40-foot ceilings, had been dedicated to house The Contemporary Art Museum. "First Hawaiian has been committed to Hawaii for 134 years, and our decision to build [the First Hawaiian Center] is a statement of our faith in the future of this state and our continued dedication to meeting the financial and community needs of Hawaii's people," proclaimed Dods on August 21, 1992, *PR Newswire.*

Principal Subsidiaries: First Hawaiian Bank; First Hawaiian Creditcorp, Inc.; First Hawaiian Leasing, Inc.; FHI Interna-tional, Inc.; Pioneer Federal Savings Bank.

Further Reading:

"Bank Bullish on Big Isle Future," *Pacific Business News,* October 4, 1993, p. A9.

Favorite, Monica, "Yao Says Yes: Pioneer Federal's Sale to First Hawaiian Is the Latest Feather in the Cap of Hawaii Finance's Sole Woman CEO," *Hawaii Business,* September 1993, Sec. 1, p. 18.

The First Hawaiian Bank, Honolulu: First Hawaiian Bank, 1969.

Halvorson, Lisa, "First Hawaiian Bank to Build New Banking Center with the Downtown Branch of the Contemporary Art Museum," *PR Newswire,* August 21, 1992.

Ma, Libya, "More of the Same? What's the Outlook in 1993?," *Hawaii Business,* Sec. 1, p. 55.

Ohira, Rod, "Dods' Quarterback Is a Woman: The Banker Says He Couldn't Survive without Audrey Mitsuda," *Honolulu Star-Bulle-tin,* March 9, 1993, Sec. BUS.

Wiles, Greg, "Hawaii Bank Companies Slip in Quality Rankings," *Honolulu Advertiser,* December 16, 1992, Sec. BUS.

—Dave Mote

First Security Bank

First Security Corporation

79 South Main Street
Salt Lake City, Utah 84111
U.S.A.
(801) 246-5647
Fax: (801) 359-6928

Public Company
Incorporated: 1928
Employees: 6,318
Sales: $7.50 billion
Stock Exchanges: NASDAQ
SICs: 6712 Bank Holding Companies; 6021 National
  Commercial Banks; 6022 State Commercial Banks

First Security Corporation, the oldest multistate bank holding company in the United States, operated 245 full-service banking offices in six states—Utah, Idaho, New Mexico, Oregon, Nevada, and Wyoming—and owned various non-bank subsidiaries during the mid-1990s. Based in Salt Lake City, Utah, First Security possessed $10.21 billion in consolidated assets in 1993, derived primarily from the company's three largest bank subsidiaries, First Security Bank of Utah, N.A., with $2.34 billion in deposits, First Security Bank of Idaho, N.A., with $1.18 billion in deposits, and First Security Bank of New Mexico, with $294 million in deposits. Through these subsidiary banks and those located in Oregon, Nevada, and Wyoming, combined with its non-bank subsidiaries, First Security represented a powerful force in the intermountain West.

First Security wielded considerable economic influence throughout Utah and its neighboring states for much of the 20th century, first by organizing a consortium of banks under the then-novel concept of a holding company, and later by expanding this assortment of financial institutions into one of the leading economic empires in the region surrounding the Rocky Mountain range. Early in its history, the influence exerted by First Security's leaders extended well beyond the confines of the intermountain West. These leaders, the principal figures responsible for the formation of First Security, assumed much larger roles, roles that would contribute significantly to the design and administration of several key federal departments that, in turn, would shape much of the nation's economic policy and structure for the 20th century. These men were Marriner S. Eccles, Elbert G. Bennett, and George S. Eccles.

The roots of First Security stretch back to the father of Marriner and George Eccles, David Eccles, who arrived in Utah with his parents, after emigrating from Glasgow, Scotland, in 1863. Converted to Mormonism, the Eccles clan settled in Utah, with David emerging as the most financially successful of the seven Eccles children. By the time of his death in 1912, David Eccles had amassed a small fortune through several investments, including a founding interest in Utah International, a portion of Amalgamated Sugar, and two banks. These investments and the two banks were bequeathed to his nine children, the eldest of whom, Marriner, then 22 years old, immediately ascended to the position of family patriarch and oversaw the family's business interests.

Over the course of the next 13 years, the family's banking interests became intertwined with another family's investments, the Browning family. In 1925, a watershed year for the future First Security Corporation, Marriner and George Eccles, together with Marriner A. Browning, the Browning family's representative, decided to increase their investments in banking, which at this point totaled six banks. To accomplish this, the three partners solicited the assistance of Elbert G. Bennett, a businessman from Idaho Falls, Idaho, who proved to be the correct addition for the task at hand. By 1928, the Eccles-Browning banking organization comprised 17 banks and one building and loan company, largely through the acquisitive talents of Elbert Bennett. In June of that year the Eccles made another fateful decision, organizing the 18 financial companies under a holding company, naming it First Security Corporation.

Because it emerged on the eve of the nation's greatest financial disaster, First Security almost immediately faced formidable challenges. The Great Depression would claim as victims scores of the country's businesses and, during its first four years, would cause the collapse of nearly 11,000 of the nation's banks, but First Security would not be one of them. In fact, to a certain extent, the fledgling banking concern prospered during the Depression's most deleterious years: it acquired failing banks, staved off runs at its banks, and, surprisingly, helped rival banks to keep their customers from withdrawing funds, thereby forestalling a run on the banks' deposits.

Marriner Eccles, First Security's chairmen and chief executive officer, was chiefly responsible for mitigating the financial situation in Utah and guiding First Security through the first years of the Depression. His achievements in Utah, combined with his innovative ideas concerning the restoration of the nation's economy, caught the attention of federal officials in Washington, D.C., and Eccles was offered the temporary appointment of Special Assistant to the Secretary of the Treasury. He left Utah in early 1934 to accept the position, then later that year was appointed to the Federal Reserve Board and designated its chairman by President Franklin D. Roosevelt. Eccles played a key role in designing and implementing several New Deal programs and departments, most notably the establishment of the Federal Housing Administration.

Marriner Eccles was not the first First Security official to leave the bank's base of operations in Ogden, Utah, for Washington: Bennett had left a year earlier, in 1933, to help establish the Federal Deposit Insurance Corporation (FDIC). One of three men appointed to such a post, Bennett eventually became responsible for ascertaining the solvency of 8,000 of the nation's banks to determine their suitability for FDIC membership.

With the elder Eccles and Bennett in Washington, leadership of First Security devolved to George Eccles. Before the two men left, however, they had bolstered First Security's position by acquiring Deseret National Bank during a 1932 bank panic in Salt Lake City. Founded in 1871 by Brigham Young, who led an exodus of the Mormons from Illinois to their permanent home in Salt Lake City, Deseret National not only strengthened First Security's ties to the Mormon community, but also extended First Security's presence into Salt Lake City, where the company would be headquartered for the next sixty years and beyond.

Marriner Eccles and Elbert Bennett would eventually return to First Security after their work in Washington was completed—Eccles remained chairman of the Federal Reserve Board until 1948, then continued as a governor for another three years—but dating from their departure forward, for roughly the next half century, the banks included under First Security's umbrella would be led by Marriner's younger brother, George Eccles. During his long tenure, George Eccles left an indelible mark on First Security's history, presiding over the bank with an authoritative air, delegating little responsibility to his branch managers, and slowly transforming First Security into a network of banks that concentrated heavily on providing real estate loans. Despite, or perhaps because of, his omnipotent grip on the daily operations of First Security, George Eccles earned the reverence of his employees. A looming, respected figure, he was responsible for the bank's emergence as one of the largest financial institutions of its kind in the United States. Although he remained in Utah while his brother and Bennett gained national prominence in Washington, George Eccles would assume leadership roles in arenas broader in scope than First Security as well. He later headed the Association of Reserve City Bankers and the Association of Registered Bank Holding Companies and served as a financial consultant to the Economic Cooperation Association, which gave him a contributing role in the implementation of the Marshall Plan.

Early in his career, however, George Eccles' greatest achievement was guiding First Security through the Depression, a decade-long span of financial trials for a bank in its first decade of existence. Through the strength of centralized management and credit controls inherent in First Security' corporate structure, the company withstood several runs on its deposits and survived the most economically pernicious decade in U.S. history. By the end of the Depression, First Security had acquired two additional banks in Salt Lake City and combined them with Deseret National to form First National Bank of Salt Lake. With strong lead banks in Ogden, Utah, and Boise, Idaho, First Security entered the 1940s as a healthy consortium of financial institutions prepared for the economic expansion and population growth following World War II.

By the conclusion of World War II , the western United States had been settled for approximately a century, but many regions remained sparsely populated. As the population expanded after the war and more Americans possessed the financial means to relocate, these regions would become more densely populated. The area surrounding First Security's growing empire of banks

was such a region, a prime location for the infusion of a new generation of Americans. Although the effects of population expansion in First Security's region would not appear overnight, the economic force of a burgeoning population, more people in the region seeking real estate loans, would fuel the company's growth during the latter half of the 20th century.

By 1965, roughly 15 years into the post-war economic expansion, First Security maintained $650 million in deposits, nearly double what it held in the previous decade. In addition to the general economic forces that combined to bolster First Security's position, the area served by First Security's banks proved to be rich in natural resources, drawing agricultural, mining, and energy companies to the region.

Five years later, in 1970, the bank's deposits had increased to $865 million. George Eccles nephew, Spencer F. Eccles, who later would become First Security's chairman and chief executive officer, moved from Idaho that year to become executive vice-president of First Security Company. The position gave him responsibility for the development of the bank's non-banking subsidiaries and a key role in enhancing the bank's operational programs. At that time, First Security was the only bank system in the area to possess computer operations and the first to participate in a credit card program, adding to its already considerable strength in the region. Through four banks and 108 branch offices, First Security controlled approximately 32 percent of the total banking resources in Utah and Idaho, and stood poised for further growth. Its loan portfolio described a company still heavily invested in the real estate growth of the area and benefiting from the commercial and industrial growth pervading Utah and Idaho, growth partly attributable to the region's oil and natural gas reserves. Commercial loans totaled $225 million, real estate loans accounted for $202 million, mortgage loans a robust $273 million, and installment loans an additional $181 million.

During the 1970s, the region's natural resource-related boom period reached its peak, driving First Security's growth. By the end of the decade, First Security Corporation comprised 13 banks and 153 branch offices scattered throughout Utah, Idaho, and Wyoming, and possessed $3.4 billion in assets, making it the 59th largest bank in the nation. Oil and natural gas development, combined with copper and silver mining, predicated economic growth in Utah, Wyoming, and Idaho, which was further buoyed by the opening of aerospace and electronics manufacturing plants in the area. Quickly though, First Security's fortunes were reversed, engendered by the collapse of the region's natural resource-based economy and brought to light by the death of George Eccles in 1982.

George Eccles 48th year of leading First Security, his last, was concurrent with the rapid decline of the agriculture, mining, and energy industries in the region. Land values plummeted as a consequence, making many First Security customers unable to stay current on their real estate loans, the payments for which the bank was heavily dependent upon. The economic collapse of First Security's service area rocked the foundation on which the bank had rested for the previous half century, and now, with the autocratic presence of George Eccles gone, the bank's future appeared suddenly uncertain.

The inheritor of this precarious situation was Spencer Eccles, president of First Security before his uncle George's death, and now the person entrusted with transforming First Security into the healthy financial institution it had once been. In addition to handling the instability of the bank, Eccles also had to restore First Security's vitality in the tall shadows cast by the bank's former leaders, the nationally known and highly reputable triumvirate of Marriner and George Eccles and Elbert Bennett. Spencer Eccles' approach was significantly different than the approach employed by his uncle, indeed the only approach known in First Security's history. Spencer Eccles immediately ceded more authority to First Security's branch managers, imploring them to spend less time managing and spend more time selling, and began to steer the bank away from real estate loans toward consumer and small commercial loan business.

Four years later, in 1986, First Security's rebound still had not materialized, and, if anything, the bank's financial condition had worsened. The region's natural resource market reached its nadir that year, the state of Utah ruled that out-of-state banks could purchase troubled Utah banks, and financially powerful Citicorp entered First Security's service area. Against this backdrop, Spencer Eccles announced First Security's 1985 earnings, yet another disappointing result. However, the bank's earnings finally began to rise in the late 1980s, primarily as a result of the measures put into place by Spencer Eccles.

A return to more financially robust times enabled First Security to increase the number of banks operating in the First Security system, something the bank did with considerable speed in the late 1980s and early 1990s. From 1989 to 1993, First Security acquired 18 financial institutions in five states, adding nearly $3 billion to its assets. In 1993, the most prodigious year of First Security's acquisitive activity, it completed nine bank purchases, setting the tone for the bank holding company's future in the 1990s. In August of that year, First Security bought Nevada Community Bank, then in November completed the largest acquisition in its history, purchasing the First National Bank in Albuquerque for $193 million. With deposits totaling $1.18 billion, First National added 26 branch offices, including 3 in New Mexico, to First Security's rapidly growing empire. Later that same month, First Security acquired Continental National Bank, with deposits of $264.5 million, then merged it with Nevada Community Bank to form First Security Bank of Nevada.

Entering the mid-1990s, First Security continued to search for additional financial institutions to add to its banking system, fully recovered from the ills that afflicted the bank holding company during the early 1980s. The pace of the company's expansion and the price paid for it, particularly the $193 million paid for First National Bank in Albuquerque, led some critics to contend that it was too rapid and potentially damaging to First Security's financial resources. Whether this evaluation bore any validity or not stood as the pivotal question as First Security and the Eccles family moved toward the 21st century.

Principal Subsidiaries: First Security Bank of Utah, N.A.; First Security Bank of Idaho, N.A.; First Security Bank of Oregon; First Security Bank of Rock Springs, Wyoming; First Security Investment Management, Inc.; First Security Investor Services; First Security Insurance, Inc.; First Security Life Insurance Co. of Arizona; First Security Leasing Co.; First Security Mortgage Co.; First Security Information Technology, Inc.; First Security Service Co.; First Security Business Investment Corp.

Further Reading:

"Bank and Insurance Stocks," *The Commercial and Financial Chronicle,* May 27, 1965, p. 22.
Button, Graham, "Strong Genes," *Forbes,* May 25, 1992, p. 12.
"First Security Corp.," *The Wall Street Transcript,* November 16, 1970, pp. 22, 325.
Heins, John, "The Decline and Fall of the House of Eccles," *Forbes,* March 10, 1986, p. 75.
Weberman, Ben, "Letting George Do It," *Forbes,* July 7, 1980, p. 49.

—Jeffrey L. Covell

First Tennessee National Corporation

165 Madison Avenue
Memphis, Tennessee
U.S.A.
(901) 523-4352
Fax: (901) 523-4354

Public Company
Incorporated: 1864 as First National Bank of Memphis
Employees: 8,000
Assets: $10.4 billion
Stock Exchanges: NASDAQ
SICs: 6712 Bank Holding Companies; 6021 National
   Commercial Banks; 6411 Insurance Agents, Brokers &
   Service

One of the 58 largest banking companies in the United States
and the largest bank holding company in Tennessee, First Tennessee National Corporation has provided banking services to
Tennesseans since the Civil War, when the company's oldest
and primary subsidiary, The First National Bank of Memphis,
was organized. By the 1990s, First Tennessee operated over 200
branch banking offices throughout Tennessee and owned more
than 100 offices involved in mortgage banking and consumer
lending for customers in 25 states.

During the Civil War, many southern cities, including Memphis, experienced the destructive and dissolutive effects of war.
Once a bustling center of commerce, Memphis had fallen victim
to the war in 1862, when Union troops gained control of the city
and placed it under military rule. Two years into this military
occupation, a resident named Frank S. Davis decided to form a
bank. Davis was convinced that Memphis would need additional banking and credit facilities, once a national system of
banks regulated by the federal government emerged, a prospect
ensured by the passage of the National Banking Act of 1863. To
that end, he organized a meeting to be convened on March 10,
1864 to discuss the possibilities of organizing a nationally
chartered bank. That day, Davis and several other Memphis
residents drafted the articles of association for such an enterprise and filed an application for a national charter. The charter
was granted on March 25, 1864, marking the formal beginning
of the city's new bank, The First National Bank of Memphis.

With Davis serving as the bank's president, and all those attending the first meeting selected as directors, First National began
operations during the last year of the Civil War, operating
initially out of one rented room, then moving, two months later,
to larger space, for which the bank paid $75 in monthly rent.
Despite the pernicious economic climate in which it emerged,
the bank survived its first year, proving to be enough of a viable
venture to merit the purchase of a two-story building in 1865.

The purchase of First National's new banking quarters coincided roughly with the end of the war and, it was hoped, a return
to the economic vibrancy the city had once enjoyed. However,
the resumption of a healthy business climate was slow in
coming; Memphis reconstruction did not begin in earnest until
the summer of 1866, when railroads leading in and out of the
city were rebuilt and funding for public improvement programs
was approved. During this time, many former Memphis residents returned home after relocating during the war. Thousands
poured into the city over the next ten years, bringing the city's
population to 45,000 and restoring economic prosperity to
Memphis. First National, a fledgling banking concern, was
inextricably wed to the prosperity of the community it served.
By the time Davis retired in 1882, after presiding over the bank
for 18 years, the calamities engendered by war, and ensuing
outbreaks of yellow fever, had come to end, and the bank stood
on solid ground.

Deposits at First National eclipsed $1 million in 1897 by virtue
of a rare acquisition completed that year, the purchase of the
German Bank, which increased deposits from $700,000 to
roughly $1.15 million. In 1913, the bank earned the distinction
of being selected to execute the implementation of the Federal
Reserve Act. Named as one of five banks in one of the 12
banking districts created by the Federal Reserve Act, First National assisted in the incorporation of the Federal Reserve Bank
of St. Louis, of which the Federal Reserve Bank of Memphis
was a branch.

In 1926, First National completed the first merger in its history,
joining with one of Memphis' most respected banking institutions, the Central-State National Bank. According to the terms
of the merger, First National would retain its name and charter—then in its 62nd year of existence—while the new bank's
leadership would be drawn from Central-State. As a result,
Central-State president S. E. Ragland became president of First
National. The merger proved timely, occurring before the onset
of the Great Depression, during which half of the nation's banks
failed, and predating a period in which Memphis experienced a
significant rise in population.

Better equipped after the merger to handle the increasing banking needs of a rapidly growing population, First National used
its new financial resources to expand the scope of its operations.
While America's entry into World War II forestalled First National's plans for significant expansion until the 1950s, some
physical growth was recorded, such as the establishment of a
suburban branch, the Crosstown Branch, in 1942. During the
1940s, Memphis continued to grow, entering the decade as the
nation's 32nd largest city and ranking 26th by 1949, commen-
surately increasing the bank's need to expand. By 1952, First
National operated seven branch offices in the region surrounding Memphis, and the bank's leadership began to look for a new

site for First National's headquarters, which were in need of expansion.

In 1961, plans were announced for the construction of a 25-story bank and office building to replace existing accommodations. Three years later, the building was finished, and First National moved in, opening six additional branch offices at the same time. While First National remained largely a regional bank, its area of service was wide enough to warrant further expansion, making it, by 1967, the largest bank in the Mid-South. In 1969, as First National was evolving into a statewide banking concern, a one-bank holding company, First National Holding Company, was formed. Two years later, the structure of the holding company was changed, becoming a multi-bank holding company to enable the bank to acquire other banks throughout Tennessee. Concurrent with the structural change of First National's holding company, a name change was effected, turning First National Holding Company into First Tennessee National Corporation.

First Tennessee, with its principal subsidiary, First National Bank of Memphis, began acquiring Tennessee-based banks at a rapid pace. Five banks were purchased in 1972, with more to follow throughout the decade, as First Tennessee extended its presence outside of Memphis and into other regions within the state. In 1974, First Tennessee's management selected a common name for the banks absorbed by the holding company, naming each First Tennessee Bank, a process concluded in 1977, when First National Bank of Memphis, the name selected by Frank S. Davis and other Memphis residents back in 1864, became First Tennessee Bank.

First Tennessee continued to acquire Tennessee-based banks throughout the 1980s. As it solidified its presence in markets outside of Memphis, the bank also acquired several non-banking financial institutions, gradually diversifying beyond its retail and commercial banking core. This diversification would become more important when First Tennessee effected a strategic shift in the early 1990s toward a greater interest in bonds and mortgage lending, but by the early 1980s the holding company had already begun to invest its energies in business lines apart from retail and commercial banking. In 1981, First Tennessee established First Express, a nationwide check clearing service, and, the following year, First Tennessee became the first bank in the Southeast to offer discount brokerage services.

As it entered the 1990s, after restructuring its banking organization in 1987 to give its regional departments more autonomy, First Tennessee's leadership decided a more profitable future could be realized in nontraditional banking areas. The holding company's retail and commercial banking operations would continue to provide a substantial earnings, generating, along with its credit card, trust services, check clearing, and transaction processing businesses, approximately 80 percent of its annual pre-tax income during the early 1990s. However, as bank acquisitions became increasingly expensive and First Tennessee's market share throughout the state became more entrenched, it became apparent that a greater return on investments could be achieved by strengthening its bond and mortgage lending businesses.

Between 1990 and 1993, First Tennessee's bond division, involved in purchasing and selling fixed income securities, more than doubled its volume of business, jumping from $66 billion worth of securities bought and sold in 1990 to $147.8 billion by 1993. This rate of growth, 30.8 percent compounded annually, was eclipsed by First Tennessee's mortgage expansion, an increase primarily realized through two important acquisitions in 1993. That year, the holding company purchased Maryland National Mortgage Corporation and SNMC Management Corporation, which added more than $6 billion to First Tennessee's mortgage origination total and positioned the company as one of the 10 largest mortgage originators in the nation. The addition of Maryland National and SNMC (raising First Tennessee's mortgage origination total from $700 million to $7.2 billion) enabled the holding company to record an annually compounded growth rate of 55.3 percent in mortgage originations between 1990 and 1993.

Increased activity in the bond and mortgage markets also meant increased activity at the national level. By 1993, the company's First Express business was operating in 43 states, and its bond division was serving customers in every state. Moreover, the company became a member of several national and international automated teller machine (ATM) service programs in more than 100,000 locations.

In the mid-1990s, First Tennessee was the dominant retail and commercial banking institution throughout much of Tennessee, ranking as the leader in deposit share in three of the state's five metropolitan areas. The holding company looked to expand beyond Tennessee's borders and beyond the traditional banking arena, striving to become a more diversified, nationally-oriented financial institution. In January of 1995, First Tennessee announced that the company had acquired Carl I. Brown and Company, headquartered in Kansas City, Missouri. With the completion of this acquisition, First Tennessee ranks among the top 10 retail and wholesale mortgage originators in the country, with mortgage offices in 25 states.

Principal Subsidiaries: First Tennessee Bank, N.A.; Check Consultants Incorporated; First Tennessee Brokerage, Inc.; First Tennessee Capital Assets Corporation; First Tennessee Equipment Finance Corporation; Hickory Venture Capital Corporation; Maryland National Mortgage Corporation; Atlantic Coast Mortgage Company; Sunbelt National Mortgage Corporation; Peoples and Union Bank; Hickory Capital Corporation; Highland Capital Management Corp.; Norlen Life Insurance Company; Carl I. Brown and Company.

Further Reading:

First Tennessee National Corporation, *The First Hundred Years: A History of the First National Bank of Memphis,* Memphis: First Tennessee National Corporation, n.d.
Roosevelt, Phil, "First Tennessee Buying Its Way into the Industry's Big Leagues," *American Banker,* December 3, 1993, p. 10.
"Why 1st Tennessee Decided to Join the Big Leagues in Home Lending," *American Banker,* September 3, 1993, p. 10.
Yawn, David, "First Tennessee Sees Growth in Bond, Trust Divisions," *Memphis Business Journal,* December 17, 1990, p. 43.

—Jeffrey L. Covell

FIRST USA

First USA, Inc.

2001 Bryan Tower
Dallas, Texas 75201
U.S.A.
(214) 746-8700
Fax: (214) 746-8556

Public Company
Incorporated: 1985 as MNet
Employees: 1,800
Total Assets: $5.49 billion
Stock Exchanges: New York
SICs: 6712 Bank Holding Companies; 6022 State
    Commercial Banks

First USA, Inc. is one of the largest credit card companies in the United States. Through its First USA Bank subsidiary, the company serves over 7.8 million credit card users throughout the nation, managing about $8.9 billion in credit card loans. All of the credit cards issued by First USA are either Visa (84 percent) or MasterCard (16 percent). Of those, more than half are premium accounts such as gold cards, and 70 percent bear the First USA brand name. The company also issues affinity cards in affiliation with a variety of organizations. In addition to providing credit cards, First USA is also a leading processor of credit card transactions for merchants. Through its First USA Merchant Services, Inc. subsidiary, the company processed over 304 million credit card transactions worth $17.3 billion during the fiscal year ending in June 1994. Another subsidiary, First USA Capital Markets, is responsible for locating funding sources for First USA Bank. First USA Capital Markets also handles the bank's investment portfolio and manages the investments of some of the company's agent banks, which offer First USA products to their customers.

First USA was established in 1985 as MNet, a subsidiary of Dallas-based financial holding company MCorp. MCorp had been formed a year earlier upon the merger of two major Texas financial concerns, Southwest Bancshares Inc. and Mercantile Texas Corporation. Executives at MCorp felt that the creation of an umbrella company for its emerging batch of consumer financial operations would enhance profits in those areas by consolidating their management in one place. MNet was formed as a holding company, and John C. Tolleson was named its first chairman and chief executive.

Under Tolleson, former CEO of MBank Austin, MNet immediately took control of MCorp's entire retail banking structure, which included a network of 63 banks. Among MNet's initial activities were credit cards, traveler's checks, mortgage banking, insurance, discount stock brokerage, and point-of-sale systems for retailers. The company also provided marketing support for these operations. Credit cards were issued through MBank USA, with headquarters in Wilmington, Delaware. MNet was charged with the task of developing new consumer banking products, as well as more efficient ways of marketing them. By the time MNet was established, MCorp already had 1.2 million credit cards issued, with outstanding loans worth $400 million on them.

Over the next year, MNet was one of the few bright spots for MCorp, which reported a loss of $91 million for the first nine months of 1986. Desperate for an infusion of capital, MCorp began looking to sell off one or more of its subsidiaries. In November 1986, MNet was purchased for $300 million by Dallas-based Lomas & Nettleton Financial Corporation, the second largest mortgage banking firm and largest independent mortgage banker in the United States. Lomas & Nettleton was attracted by MNet's huge new customer base, to whom Lomas' broad range of financial services could now be marketed. By the time of the sale, MNet had total assets of $900 million. Over two-thirds of that was in credit card loans through MCorp's 62-bank network and through 575 affiliated outside banks. MNet also had a thriving credit card processing business for 22,000 merchants. In addition, the company had a $700 million mortgage servicing portfolio. MNet also brought to Lomas its insurance business and its 26,000-customer discount brokerage service. Tolleson and the rest of MNet's upper management team moved to Lomas in the deal as well.

As part of the Lomas & Nettleton empire, MNet's name was changed to Lomas Bankers Corporation, while MBank USA, the Delaware-based credit card bank, was renamed Lomas Bank USA. By 1988 Lomas Bank had one million active credit card accounts, and was one of the 20 largest credit card issuers in the United States. Its assets were worth $1.2 billion. Much of the company's growth during this period came through the purchase of other banks' credit card portfolios, part of an overall consolidation trend in the credit card business. In the spring of 1988, Lomas bought a portfolio of nearly 100,000 Visa and MasterCard accounts from Dollar Dry Dock Savings Bank, ranked 92nd among the nation's credit card companies. The price was $107 million. Another major portfolio purchase took place that fall. In October, Lomas completed the acquisition of 35,000 credit card accounts with a total outstanding balance of $22.5 million from Bright Banc of Dallas.

Lomas Bank was the thirteenth largest credit card company by 1989. That year, parent company Lomas Financial Corporation (formerly named Lomas & Nettleton) ran into its own problems as the housing and real estate industries in the Southwest began to collapse. In desperate need of cash, Lomas Financial announced that its rapidly growing credit card unit was up for sale. An agreement was announced in June of 1989 to sell Lomas Bankers to an investment group led by Merrill Lynch Capital Partners Inc. and included members of Lomas Bank's upper management corps. The $500 million buyout was completed in August, and the company, now the nation's eleventh largest credit card issuer with 1.7 million active accounts and receivables totaling $1.35 billion, was on its own.

Lomas Bankers became First USA, Inc., following the buyout, while principal subsidiary Lomas Bank USA was renamed First USA Bank. Throughout the company's series of ownership changes, its management stayed relatively constant. Tolleson remained the only chairman and chief executive officer in the company's history. Richard Vague, president of First USA Bank, was also a holdover from the company's genesis at MCorp.

As the 1990s began, First USA's impressive growing spree did not slow. By early 1990 the company had $1.5 billion in credit card receivables. First USA began to cultivate its merchant services more actively; in 1990 the company signed a 10-year contract worth over $50 million for computerized credit card processing with Electronic Data Systems Corporation, a unit of General Motors. The First USA Merchant Services Inc. subsidiary was by this time processing credit card transactions for about 50,000 customers.

First USA continued to grow, and by the end of 1991 it had outstanding credit card loans of $2.2 billion from purchases and cash advances on three million accounts. In early 1992, First USA began exploring the possibility of reducing its leverage through an initial public stock offering. The company's original plan called for the sale of 6 million shares at $16 to $18 a share. That notion was quickly dropped because of weak market conditions. A few months later, however, a scaled-down version of the stock offering was completed. The company raised $41 million from the sale of 4.5 million shares of First USA stock, which was listed on the New York Stock Exchange. Those shares amounted to 20 percent of the company. Merrill Lynch continued to hold a majority interest of 51 percent, and company management retained control of ten percent of its stock. The offering made First USA one of only three independent credit card companies, including Advanta Corporation and MBNA Corporation, to go public up to that time.

Gold cards featuring low finance charges and no annual fees played a growing role in First USA's plans as the 1990s continued. As competition among credit card company's stiffened, the company concentrated on the most profitable segment of the market—namely, those cardholders who carried over sizable balances on their accounts from month to month, thereby generating interest income. Marketing efforts were focused on this group rather than on those who tended to pay off their entire bill each month. The company also sought to stay at the forefront of the industry in its use of technology. Its investment in state-of-the-art equipment improved efficiency and reduced long-term costs in a number of areas, including application processing, security, and billing.

Toward the end of 1992, First USA announced that it was joining a trend among credit card issuers by introducing variable-rate cards. Floating rates protect the company against sharp rises in interest rates. In addition, variable-rate credit cards usually begin at a lower rate than fixed-rate cards, making them more attractive to new customers. For the year, First USA added 570,000 new credit card accounts, 66 percent more than had been added the year before. The sales volume of merchant transactions processed by the company grew 67 percent to $5.9 billion.

First USA more than doubled its net income to $39 million in 1993. The company's performance played so well on Wall Street that the per share price of its stock increased 270 percent between the beginning and end of fiscal 1993, from $11¼ to $41⅝. Stock offerings in February and August brought in over $72 million, further reducing the debt incurred during the buyout from Lomas a few years earlier. Merrill Lynch still owned about 30 percent of the company's stock after these offerings.

Over a million new credit card accounts were opened during 1993. Late in the year, First USA introduced a new product, a no-fee gold card with a 6.9 percent variable interest rate. This was to become the primary product in the company's upcoming marketing efforts. In November First USA completed the acquisition of MAGroup Inc., a credit card processing service based in Tucson, Arizona. MAGroup, a private firm with 6,000 clients, was made part of First USA Merchant Services Inc., although it continued to operate under its own name and out of its Tucson offices.

Another 300,000 credit card accounts were opened with First USA in the first three months of fiscal 1994. By this time, the company had honed its risk evaluation process to such a degree that only 2.8 percent of its accounts were delinquent, compared with a 4.6 percent average for the industry as a whole. First USA rejected about half the credit card applications it received.

In 1994 First USA was ranked seventh in the industry in managed credit card loans at $5.4 billion. It was also in the top four among merchant processors of credit card transactions. The company's growth no longer came from acquiring portfolios from other companies as it had in the past. Most of its expansion came from direct marketing of First USA's own branded products. The company continued to focus on no-fee, low interest rate Visa and MasterCard accounts, marketed to customers whose histories showed a pattern of good credit and revolving balances, the best sources of profit. Another stock offering in March of 1994 reduced the company's debt even further.

As 1994 continued, things kept getting better at First USA. The company earned $27 million in the third quarter alone, and another half million credit cards were issued. In May, Peter Bartholow became chief financial officer. Prior to his arrival the position was held by Pamela Patsley, who continued to serve as president of First USA Merchant Services, Inc. There was an irony to the selection of Bartholow; a former CEO of MCorp, he oversaw First USA's birth as a subsidiary.

Meanwhile, First USA began to pay even more attention to the merchant services side of the operation. In July of 1994, the company announced that it had acquired two more independent processing outfits: the New York-based Electronic Processing Source Inc. and NationalCard Processing Systems Inc. of Englewood, New Jersey. Both companies were folded into the First USA Merchant Services subsidiary. The addition of those companies not only gave First USA a greater presence on the East Coast, but also gained it access to proprietary software developed for certain niche markets, including performing arts organizations, upscale retail stores, restaurants, and luxury hospitality.

As the credit card industry entered the mid-1990s, consolidation of card issuing with merchant processing seemed assured, and First USA appeared to be in a strong position to continue taking advantage of the trend. As long as the use of credit cards in the United States continues to expand, the pool of potential customers for companies like First USA is sure to grow.

Principal Subsidiaries: First USA Financial, Inc.; First USA Bank; First USA Merchant Services, Inc.; First USA Capital Markets, Inc.; First USA Management, Inc.

Further Reading:

Apcar, Leonard M., "MCorp Agrees to Sell Retail Bank Unit to Lomas & Nettleton for $300 Million," *Wall Street Journal,* November 18, 1986, p. 20.

Block, Valerie, "First USA Buys Two Processing Sales Agents," *American Banker,* July 19, 1994, p. 13.

——, "First USA Hires CEO of MCorp, its Former Parent, as Finance Chief," *American Banker,* May 18, 1994, p. 16.

Blumenthal, Karen, "Lomas Financial Agrees to Sell Off Credit-Card Lines," *Wall Street Journal,* June 9, 1989, p. A4.

Guenther, Robert, and Karen Blumenthal, "Lomas Financial Puts Credit-Card Unit on Block at a Price Under $700 Million," *Wall Street Journal,* May 16, 1989, p. B2.

Gullo, Karen, "First USA Signs with EDS," *American Banker,* February 28, 1990, p. 3.

Homa, Lynn, "Pair of Texas Banks Take New Names," *American Banker,* October 13, 1989, p. 16.

Iida, Jeanne, "First USA Expanding Scope of Card Document System," *American Banker,* July 17, 1992, p. 3.

Kleege, Stephen, "First USA Moves to Variable Rates," *American Banker,* December 14, 1992, p. 2.

——, "First USA Putting Its Own Brand on the Industry," *American Banker,* April 7, 1994, p. 14.

Kutler, Jeffrey, "Dollar Dry Dock Sells Credit Card Portfolio to Lomas Bank," *American Banker,* April 1, 1988, p. 12.

LaGesse, David, "Dallas' MCorp Gets $300 Million for Sale of MNet Unit to Lomas," *American Banker,* November 18, 1986, p. 1.

"Lomas Financial Sells its Credit-Card Line to Merrill Lynch Unit," *Wall Street Journal,* August 10, 1989, p. C14.

Mathews, Gordon, "First USA's Showing Bodes Well for Spinoffs," *American Banker,* July 16, 1992, p. 10.

"MCorp Establishes MNet Subsidiary to Sell Consumer Financial Services," *American Banker,* June 13, 1985, p. 3.

Quint, Michael, "Profits Are Slowing in Credit Cards, but First USA Does Well," *New York Times,* November 12, 1993, p. D6.

Schoultz, Donald, "Lomas to Sell Retail Banking Unit for $500 Million," *American Banker,* June 9, 1989, p. 3.

Siegel, David, "First USA Lowers Sights for Public Offering," *American Banker,* May 19, 1992, p. 16.

Weinstein, Michael, "MNet Set to Manage MCorp's Retail Concerns," *American Banker,* October 11, 1985, p. 11.

—Robert R. Jacobson

First Virginia Banks, Inc.

6400 Arlington Boulevard
Falls Church, Virginia 22042-2336
U.S.A.
(703) 241-4000
Fax: (703) 241-3090

Public Company
Incorporated: 1949 as Mt. Vernon Insurance Agency, Inc.
Employees: 5,621
Total Assets: $7.9 billion
Stock Exchanges: New York Philadelphia
SICs: 6712 Bank Holding Companies; 6022 State
    Commercial Banks

First Virginia Banks, Inc. is the oldest registered bank holding company headquartered in Virginia, with 23 separately-chartered member banks throughout Virginia, Maryland, and Tennessee. In addition to over 350 branch banking offices, the holding company has insurance, advertising, and mortgage subsidiaries with operations in seven states. The regional institution's stronghold lies in the affluent and stable metropolitan corridor extending from Baltimore to Washington, D.C. and south to Norfolk. This territory, with its concentration of government agencies and the highest average household income level of any major metropolitan area in the United States, has been characterized as "the most recession-resistant area in the country." In 1993, First Virginia claimed 12.7 percent of Virginia's banking offices and 9.4 percent of the state's total deposits. First Virginia characterizes itself as a "Super Community Bank," which "successfully combines the best aspects of a large, nationally-recognized bank with the best aspects of a small, hometown bank." The firm is consistently ranked as one of the nation's safest, strongest, and most responsible financial institutions.

The company's history may be traced to Edwin T. Holland, who, in 1944, became the director and shareholder of Old Dominion Bank, a small Arlington, Virginia, institution with three branches in the greater Washington, D.C. area. Holland was instrumental in transforming Old Dominion from a strictly commercial, industrial bank into a retail, consumer-oriented institution. He accomplished the shift by extending bank hours for the convenience of working customers, offering premiums with new accounts, and utilizing aggressive advertising cam-

paigns including direct mail. Advertising would continue to occupy an important niche in the First Virginia strategy into the 1990s.

After World War II, as automobile sales increased dramatically, Holland created the Mt. Vernon Insurance Agency to insure bank customers' car loans in 1949. Banking regulations prohibited Old Dominion from providing the capital for founding the insurance venture, so Holland incorporated Mt. Vernon himself and "donated" all its stock to the bank. The insurance company was then used as a vehicle for growth in the restrictive, but stable and prosperous, U.S. banking environment of the postwar era. Mt. Vernon acquired controlling interests in the Bank of Annandale and National Bank of Manassas in the early 1950s. When Congress passed the Bank Holding Act mid-decade, Mt. Vernon was reorganized as First Virginia Corporation, a bank holding company that was authorized to purchase and operate other banks within the state. Although banking was clearly the primary function of the firm, it continued to offer a variety of life, group, credit life, and property/casualty insurance products through its insurance subsidiaries into the 1990s.

By 1960, First Virginia had four banks with eight branch offices and $68 million in assets. The continuing relaxation of state and federal banking regulations encouraged an unprecedented surge of bank mergers. First Virginia's financial holdings grew eight-fold over the course of that decade, as it added eight banks in the state's largest metropolitan areas. Over 100 branches made banking more convenient to First Virginia's growing customer base. By the beginning of the 1970s, the bank had captured six percent of the state's commercial deposits. The firm acquired a mortgage subsidiary in 1968 to originate, package, and sell conventional and government-insured first mortgages.

During the 1970s, like most other bank holding companies, First Virginia dabbled in some of the riskier schemes it would later condemn. Real estate investment trusts (REITs) had started to gain popularity after 1960, when Congress improved the tax advantages of these investment vehicles. First Virginia sponsored formation of one of them during their early 1970s peak, when they were the primary financing method used for commercial construction loans. The collapse of the commercial real estate market mid-decade left many banks, including First Virginia, holding bad loans. During this period, First Virginia also purchased a consumer loan finance company. When the pitfalls of these sidelines proved deeper than the payoffs, First Virginia got out and swore off "non-traditional opportunities that promised to pay big dividends."

Barriers to intra- and then interstate banking continued to dissolve in the ensuing decades, encouraging industry consolidation that would continue through the 1990s. While First Virginia took advantage of opportunities for growth through acquisition, it did not expand at the breakneck pace of some of its competitors. First Virginia continued its careful acquisition and merger strategy in the 1970s, trading its own shares for ownership of ten independent banks and establishing five others. Consolidation culminated in a roster of 21 banks with 168 offices in 1980. By that time, First Virginia had access to over two-thirds of the state's population and had accumulated over $1 billion in assets. The pace of acquisition intensified in the 1980s, as the bank holding company brought 20 more banks into the fold and expanded into Maryland and Tennessee. In 1986, First Virginia ventured north, acquiring The Commercial Bank in Bel Air, Maryland. The company's first Tennessee acquisition came just one year later, with the purchase of Tri-City Bancorp, Inc. through an exchange of stock.

While regarded as overly conservative by some of its faster-moving competitors, First Virginia maintained its characteristic conservatism, which protected it from the speculative real estate loans, Third World debt, and other pitfalls that brought down hundreds of banks in the 1980s. The company's chairperson and CEO, Robert H. Zalokar, would later tell *Bank Management* magazine that First Virginia's strategy had been rather simple: ''We stayed out of [bad assets] by hewing to the standard principles of banking, by requiring equity on the part of the borrowers, and not advancing reserves or interest payments like so many of [our competitors] did.'' Cautious investment standards endowed the bank with an enviable portfolio of assets in the early 1990s. In 1993, as rivals struggled to unload commercial real estate holdings gone bad, First Virginia held no foreclosed property in the Washington/Baltimore region and had no foreign or highly leveraged transactions in its portfolio. In fact, the holding company's nonperforming assets as a percentage of total assets stood at less than one half of one percent ''an astoundingly low figure'' by *Bank Management*'s standards.

During this time, the Federal Reserve reduced the prime interest rate to its lowest level in decades, which was both good and bad news for First Virginia. While the bank's net interest income (the difference between income from earning assets and interest paid on deposits and borrowed funds) benefited, many customers moved their funds from low-interest savings accounts to mutual funds and other higher-performing financial services.

After two decades of acquisitions, First Virginia itself became the subject of takeover rumors. In 1990, company president Paul Geithner, Jr. conceded that ''we've been mentioned by everyone and his mother as a possible takeover target,'' but emphasized that ''the way to remain independent is to be a superior earner.'' Since the ''super-regionals'' were unable to acquire First Virginia outright, they brought intense competition to bear: in the last decade of the twentieth century, NationsBank and First Union, two of America's ten largest banks, began to encroach on First Virginia's stronghold.

First Virginia countered by continuing to emphasize superior customer service, expense control, and offered new products (including annuities, a discount brokerage, and an assest allocation account using mutual funds). The firm began to be called a ''Super Community Bank,'' referring to its blending of both the ideals and names of super-regionals and small community institutions. First Virginia maintained this corporate culture through a very decentralized management structure: each of the holding company's member banks and subsidiaries had its own board of directors, chief executive officer, and loan authority up to the legal limit of the bank. This organizational strategy kept each of the holding company's 20 banks in touch with local needs and helped lower the number of nonperforming loans. Moreover, the federation of the banks maximized economies of scale, with centralized, on-line computer processing and other more efficient administrative functions. In 1993, First Virginia's 56 percent efficiency ratio (a comparison of non-interest overhead to net operating revenue) was significantly better than the industry average of over 60 percent.

While First Virginia professed no grand growth aspirations, it did expect to acquire more banks in central and southern Maryland and east Tennessee before the end of the twentieth century. Criteria for acquisition included clean loan portfolios and a compatible corporate culture. In 1993, First Virginia recorded its 17th consecutive year of dividend increases, and its capital ratio (a key banking indicator) ranked first in the top five percent of the United States' largest banking companies. Moreover, as rising interest rates, intensifying competition from several angles, and regulatory challenges converged in the last decade of the twentieth century, the institution's top executives hinted in 1993's annual report that they may be inclined to take some risks in the years to come but will continue to adhere to its primary goal of operating a safe and sound banking institution while providing a good return to shareholders.

Principal Subsidiaries: First Virginia Bank—Central Maryland; First Virginia Bank—Maryland; First Virginia Bank—Central; First Virginia Bank—Colonial; First Virginia Bank—Commonwealth; First Virginia Bank—South Hill; First Virginia Bank of Tidewater; First Virginia Bank—Shenandoah Valley; First Virginia Bank—Clinch Valley; First Virginia Bank—Franklin County; First Virginia Bank—Highlands; First Virginia Bank—Piedmont; First Virginia Bank—Southside; First Virginia Bank—Southwest; Bank of Madisonville; First Virginia Bank—Mountain Empire; Tri-City Bank and Trust Co.; First Virginia Mortgage Co.; First General Mortgage Co.; First Virginia Life Insurance Co.; First Virginia Insurance Services Inc.; First Virginia Services, Inc.; Northern Operations Center, Inc.; Eastern Operations Center, Inc.; Southwest Operations Center, Inc.; Tennessee Operations Center Inc.; Springdale Advertising Agency, Inc; United Southern; First Knoxville Bank; Farmers Bank of Maryland; Atlantic Bank and Caroline County Bank.

Further Reading:

Feinberg, Mark, ''Whose Heads Are on the Bank Takeover Block?,'' *Bankers Monthly,* March 1990, pp. 19–24.
First Virginia Banks, Inc., *A World of Difference,* Falls Church, Virginia: First Virginia Banks, Inc., 1994.
Rice, Harvey, ''Tried and True First Virginia,'' *Bank Management,* September 1993, pp. 31–37.
Stillinger, Richard I., ''Riches Among the Ruins,'' *Bankers Monthly,* October 1990, pp. 74–79.

—April Dougal Gasbarre

Firstar Corporation

777 East Wisconsin Avenue
Milwaukee, Wisconsin 53202
U.S.A.
(414) 765-4321
Fax: (414) 765-6040

Public Company
Incorporated: 1853 as Farmers and Millers Bank
Employees: 8,720
Total Assets: $13.79 billion
Stock Exchanges: New York
SICs: 6712 Bank Holding Companies; 6021 National
    Commercial Banks

Firstar Corporation is the largest bank holding company head-quartered in Wisconsin. Much of its history has been dominated by acquisitions and mergers with other banks, often resulting in name changes. Founded in 1853 as a small, store-front bank, its original name was Farmers and Millers Bank. By 1919, it was known as First Wisconsin National Bank of Milwaukee, and, in 1929, the bank was placed administratively under the bank holding company Wisconsin Bankshares Corporation, which itself would be renamed First Wisconsin Bankshares Corporation in 1960, First Wisconsin Corporation in 1974, and Firstar Corporation in 1989. Aided by relaxed government regulations on interstate banking, Firstar had by 1994 become a regional power in the Midwest, boasting some 200 offices in Wisconsin, Illinois, Minnesota, and Iowa. It also maintained a small number of offices in Arizona and Florida.

Although regarded officially as part of the United States beginning in 1783, Wisconsin did not become a state until 1848. Most of the new settlers lived in the state's southwestern corner, where large deposits of lead had been discovered. In the southeast, however, settlers had formed a small village on Lake Michigan at the site of an Indian trading post. Called Milwaukee, the village experienced rapid population growth, expanding from fewer than a dozen settlers in the early 1830s to some 25,000 in 1853. New industries included machinery, shoes, and beer, and soon the city became a center for farm products, in particular wheat and hogs. A city bulletin during this time, however, pointed out that "our moneyed facilities are by no means commensurate with our needs."

During this period of great expansion and high hopes, Farmers and Millers Bank, the predecessor of Firstar, was organized. Founded by six stockholders and six bondsmen—led by Newcomb Cleveland, a Milwaukee business leader—the bank opened its doors for business on June 2, 1853. With total capital of $50,000, the bank initially operated out of a rented storefront located on East Water Street that was equipped with a newly installed "strong box." Four years later, the bank moved around the corner to a new location on Wisconsin Avenue.

With Cleveland as its first president, Farmers and Millers Bank helped provide financial stability for the new city. The 1850s were a difficult decade for banks, especially during the financial panic of 1857, which began after railroads defaulted on their bonds. Soon afterward, the Civil War brought great currency fluctuations, and, in 1861, bank riots occurred in Milwaukee. Despite these problems, Farmers and Millers Bank, according to one history of the city, had quickly become "a power financially, as well as a general favorite with the public."

The bank underwent its first reorganization in 1863, when the federal government passed the National Bank Act. The Act provided for a national currency and implemented guidelines for establishing a network of federally supervised national banks, measures, it was hoped, that would calm the troubled financial times. Farmers and Millers, the first bank in Wisconsin to apply for a national charter, became a national bank on September 19 of that year and was renamed First National Bank of Milwaukee.

After the Civil War, Milwaukee would become increasingly an industrial center. Its population also continued to grow rapidly, in part from an influx of Italian and Polish immigrants in the 1890s. With the growth in the city's industry and population came a corresponding rise in the bank's assets, from just $1.5 million in 1873 to more than $29 million in 1913. Part of this increase was the result of its 1894 merger with Merchants Exchange Bank, which had been founded in 1870 as Home Savings Bank and had undergone two previous mergers before becoming part of First National. Growth also prompted First National to seek larger facilities. Construction began on a 16-story structure on the corner of North Water Street and East Mason in 1912. Opened two years later, the new building housed the bank's main office until 1973.

It was not long before the bank made another huge jump in assets, this time through a merger with Wisconsin National Bank, which had been formed in 1892. Effective on June 30, 1919, the merger created an immense new organization, First Wisconsin National Bank of Milwaukee, with assets surpassing $100 million. This new bank then set about expanding across the city, in part through opening up branch locations, and, in 1928, it merged with yet another institution, Second Ward Savings Bank (founded in 1855), boosting assets to $177 million.

The following year, the directors of the bank founded Wisconsin Bankshares Corporation, a bank holding company (defined as a corporation owning at least two banks), which became the owner of First Wisconsin. This administrative change allowed for greater legal flexibility in acquisitions, and, by the end of 1930, this new corporation would acquire 23 additional Wisconsin financial institutions—such as Union National Bank in Eau Claire and First National Bank in Madison—giving the company a total of 16 national banks, 27 state banks, three trust companies, and seven other companies. All of Wisconsin Bankshares acquisitions maintained their original officers and board of directors, and First Wisconsin remained the lead bank.

When the stock market crashed in 1929, sending the financial industry into a tailspin, Wisconsin Bankshares was in a strong position and, unlike many of its competitors, was able to maintain healthy growth throughout 1930 and 1931. As the Depression dragged on, however, the company would find its fortunes diminished. Many banks, in an effort to become more efficient and avoid closure, were merging, and Wisconsin Bankshares soon found itself forced down the same path. By the end of 1932, it had reduced the number of national banks under its control to 11 and the number of state banks to 25. One piece of good news came from Wisconsin's state government, which responded to the crisis by lifting the freeze on branch banking, in effect since 1909.

In the early months of 1933, the financial situation deteriorated even further as nervous depositors began to pull their money out of banks. On March 5, 1933, with financial collapse imminent, the newly elected U.S. President Franklin D. Roosevelt had little choice but to close all banks nationally for a "bank holiday." Lasting ten days, this cooling-off period gave federal officials time to investigate banks and helped restore some confidence among consumers. Wisconsin Bankshares, meanwhile, continued efforts toward greater efficiency. It transformed some of its banks into branches of First Wisconsin, for example, eliminating their boards and reducing the number of officers in the process. Bookkeeping was also consolidated. The company, moreover, began to sell off some of its financial institutions, and, by the end of 1944, with World War II nearing an end, Wisconsin Bankshares had been streamlined to just five national banks, in addition to First Wisconsin Trust Company (founded in 1894 and the oldest trust company in the state) and five other institutions. Overall, these moves resulted in a stronger, more financially sound company, which was able to boost its bank assets from $301 million in 1931 to $666 million in 1944.

After World War II, Wisconsin Bankshares benefited from a robust economy. Also during this time, however, the state of Wisconsin decided to restore the freeze on branch banking. This move made it difficult for Wisconsin Bankshares to respond to a commercial trend in which shopping centers proliferated, drawing consumers away from the traditional shopping areas where most of the company's banks and branches were located. New regulations imposed by the Bank Holding Company Act of 1956, passed by Congress, also limited the company's flexibility. As a result, Wisconsin Bankshares, the largest bank holding company in the state, was prevented from both setting up branches and acquiring new banks, two of the most effective means of growth. It was, however, able to establish new banks (such as Southgate National Bank of Milwaukee in 1958), a slow and costly process, and to move some of its existing branches to more profitable locations.

In 1960, the company was renamed First Wisconsin Bankshares Corporation. Regulatory barriers, designed to protect small banks and to slow the consolidation of bank assets, would continue to frustrate the company until the late 1960s, when regulations began to be relaxed. In 1967, the company was allowed to acquire State Bank of Waunakee, and, in the next few years, it would start up new banks in such growing markets as Waukesha, West Green Bay, and Mequon. During the early 1970s, First Wisconsin became more involved in banking-related activities, forming, for example, First Wisconsin Financial Corporation (a commercial finance company) and First Wisconsin Mortgage Trust. It also established First Wisconsin International Bank, headquartered in New York. International loans would eventually produce a large percentage of its profits. In 1973, the company became even more prominent in Milwaukee with the completion of its new corporate headquarters, First Wisconsin Center, a 42-story facility near Lake Michigan and the tallest building in the state. The following year, because of its moves toward new types of services, the company decided to change its name to First Wisconsin Corporation.

In the late 1970s, Wisconsin's state government agreed to allow branch banking on a limited basis, giving First Wisconsin additional options for growth. The company quickly took advantage of its new freedom, and, by the mid-1980s, it had opened 19 new branches, expanding its total to 33. The company also continued to acquire existing banks across the state, helping to boost total assets to $4.75 billion in 1982 and $7.1 billion in 1986. During the same period, however, its profitable venture in international loans began to sour, resulting in large writeoffs (especially for loans to developing countries) and in a net loss of $49 million in 1987.

Reset on a more conservative, steady course, First Wisconsin was given a boost by a new state law that took effect on January 1, 1987. Reflecting similar changes across the country, the law allowed Wisconsin banks to acquire or be acquired by other banks in eight neighboring states—Illinois, Minnesota, Ohio, Michigan, Iowa, Indiana, Missouri, and Kentucky—provided those states made similar laws themselves. First Wisconsin wasted little time in making its first out-of-state purchase, buying DuPage Bank & Trust Co. in Glen Ellyn, Illinois, on April 29, 1987. This was followed by additional purchases in Illinois, Iowa, and Minnesota (in the Twin Cities area), all states contiguous with Wisconsin. Among its most significant acquisitions were Naper Financial Corp. in Illinois (1987), Shelard Bancshares, Inc., in Minnesota (1987), and Banks of Iowa, Inc. (1991). By the end of 1993, total assets had reached $13.79 billion, $9.3 billion of which was in Wisconsin. The company's share of bank deposits was 15.6 percent in Wisconsin, 6.7 percent in Iowa, and 2 percent in Minnesota. In Illinois, where it had about $1 billion in bank deposits, all in the Chicago suburbs, its share was only .55 percent. The company also had three offices in Arizona and two in Florida.

The company became Firstar Corporation in 1989. For the first time neither banking nor Wisconsin was mentioned in its name, reflecting its status as a multistate, diversified financial corporation. The banks themselves were also renamed Firstar, though this did not occur in Wisconsin until 1992. Similarly, its corporate headquarters became Firstar Center.

By this time, Firstar had left its troubles of the mid-1980s far behind, and it was being widely praised for its sound management, led from 1991 by Roger L. Fitzsimonds, chairperson and chief executive officer. In particular, Firstar had made great gains in its fee-generating services—such as credit cards, brokerage, check collection, insurance, and investment management—which tended to be less affected by economic downturns. These services were promoted not only through its numerous branches (some 200 by 1994), but also through more than 1,000 "correspondent banks"—generally independent banks too small to offer their own fee-based services.

On October 18, 1994, Firstar issued 1,801,577 shares of common stock to complete the acquisition of the $423 million First Southeast Banking Corp. First Southeast Banking Corp. is a bank holding company with two banks and 23 offices in the Racine/Kenosha area. The transaction was accounted for as a pooling of interests.

Ironically, the company's success placed it in jeopardy of becoming a takeover target, a threat that would become even more serious with the introduction of national interstate banking, expected in the mid-1990s. Even so, Firstar appeared more preoccupied with its own plans for acquisitions and seemed to benefit from a clear statement of purpose, summarized in 1993 by Fitzsimonds: "Firstar is not in the banking business. We are in the financial services business. . . . We focus on the consumer, small business and commercial middle markets. We also provide operating services to the large corporate segment. There's nothing that we can't evolve to, acquire or change that won't meet these customers' needs."

Principal Subsidiaries: Firstar Bank Milwaukee; Firstar Corporation of Iowa; Firstar Bank of Minnesota; Firstar Trust Company; Elan Insurance Services, Inc.; Elan Investment Services, Inc.; Elan Life Insurance Company; Elan Title Services, Inc.; Firstar Community Investment Corporation; Firstar Development Corporation; Firstar Home Mortgage Corporation; Firstar Information Services Corporation; Firstar Investment Research and Management Co.

Further Reading:

Byrne, Harlan S., "Firstar Corp.: Bank Company, Formerly First Wisconsin, Pushes beyond State Lines," *Barron's,* January 16, 1989, pp. 39–40.
Byrne, Harlan S., "Shining Brighter," *Barron's,* June 20, 1994, p. 19.
Klinkerman, Steve, "Firstar's Chief Exec Says the Real Keys to Profits Are People, Not Technology," *American Banker,* January 13, 1994, p. 4.
Norman, Jack, "A Rising Star in the Midwest," *Milwaukee Journal,* September 13, 1992, pp. 1, 7.
"Peer Pressure (interview with Firstar chairman Roger Fitzsimonds)," *United States Banker,* September 1993, pp. 14–20.
Weier, Anita, "Firstar Builds on Expansion Plan with Acquisition of Iowa Group," *The Business Journal-Milwaukee,* August 13, 1990, p. 2.
Weier, Anita, "Firstar Consolidates Minnesota Banks," *The Business Journal-Milwaukee,* February 11, 1991, p. 2.

—Thomas Riggs

Fiserv Inc.

255 Fiserv Drive
Brookfield, WI 53045
U.S.A.
(414) 879-5000
Fax: (414) 879-5275

Public Company
Incorporated: 1984
Employees: 6,300
Sales: \$.46 million
SICs: 5240 Software & Systems; 8100 Financial Services;
  8302 Software & Computer Services

Fiserv Inc. is one of the three largest data processing firms in the United States. From its Brookfield, Wisconsin, base, the company provides data management systems and services for more than 2,500 financial institutions worldwide representing approximately 58 million customer accounts. A simple formula of hard work and good people produced rampant growth for Fiserv during the 1980s and early 1990s.

Fiserv is the progeny of George Dalton and Leslie Muma, who founded the company in 1984. Dalton and Muma, who each operated his own data processing company, had been trying to merge their operations since the late 1970s. The friends realized early on that to excel in their competitive industry they would need to form a large, national network of clients and service offerings. After purchasing their firms through management buyouts—Dalton and Muma had both been operating as subsidiaries of well-heeled parent companies—the partners joined forces in what would quickly become the fastest growing financial data processing firm in the country.

Dalton, who became CEO of the newly formed Fiserv, was experienced and well respected in the data processing industry. Although peers described him as a visionary, Dalton attributed much of his success to meticulous planning and old-fashioned hard work. One of Dalton's first jobs, for example, was at a Kroger grocery store. Between the ages of 14 and 16 he advanced from stock boy to butcher to journeyman, outpacing his counterparts. "I worked nights, weekends, and during the summers," recalled Dalton in a March 1993 issue of *Business Journal of Milwaukee*. "The lesson I learned: Hard work produces results."

Displaying his penchant for planning, Dalton began learning German as a junior in high school (1944) in anticipation of serving his country in World War II—to his chagrin, he was sent to the Spanish-speaking Panama Canal Zone. It was also during his high school years, however, that Dalton "fell in love with data processing" and began preparing for his future career. After the war, he returned home and attended Northwestern University from 1947 to 1948. He then dropped out of college to accept a position with Bell & Howell Co.'s data processing department, or tabulating department as it was called in those days.

Dalton's three eye-opening years at Bell and Howell confirmed his enthusiasm for data processing, which was evidenced by his quick mastery of the equipment with which he worked. Despite a dearth of banking knowledge, Dalton's enthusiasm helped him to land a position as head of Marine Bank's data processing division. It was during his twelve years at Marine that computers were introduced to the banking industry on a large scale. Dalton grasped the technology immediately.

Dalton's move to the head of Midland National Bank's data processing department in 1965 was one that would cement the foundation for his own future enterprise. Midland wanted Dalton to run the department as a separate profit center, a concept that remained untested. He quickly grew the business by expanding its services into nonbanking areas, particularly retail, and establishing a healthy contracting business. When First Bank Systems Inc., of Minneapolis, acquired Midland in 1977 it was not sure how to treat Dalton's unique operation. It eventually established First Data Processing Inc. as a subsidiary in 1982, with Dalton at the helm.

Having established an in-depth understanding of the fledgling financial data processing industry, by the late 1970s Dalton was ready to branch out on his own and begin testing his new ideas about information processing. His ally would be Leslie Muma, of Freedom Savings and Loan in Tampa, Florida. Muma had befriended Dalton in the 1970s when Dalton was looking for fellow bank data processing department heads to share software development costs. By pooling their resources, Dalton reasoned, he and his industry cohorts could reduce data processing bills by as much as 60 percent. Muma was the only one that initially bought into the novel experiment.

Although Muma was only in his mid-30s when he and Dalton began working together, he was extremely knowledgeable of data processing systems and services. Before acquiring his master's degree in business administration from the University of South Florida, in fact, Muma had majored in theoretical mathematics. He worked as a data processing consultant at an accounting firm for a few years before joining Freedom Savings and Loan Association in Florida in 1971. Freedom planned to develop a subsidiary, Sunshine State Systems, that would be similar to that operated by Dalton. Muma became president of that division in 1972.

By 1984, the subsidiaries headed by Dalton and Muma were serving more than 100 clients and generating annual revenues in excess of \$22 million. Frustrated by their inability to get the two subsidiaries merged under one corporate umbrella, they struck out on their own in a risky venture. With venture capital backing, Muma and Dalton purchased their companies from their parent corporations and formed a single entity called Fiserv. To accomplish this feat, they were forced to surrender 89 percent of the equity in their venture to the financiers. ''Eleven percent of something is worth more than 100 percent of nothing,'' noted Dalton in an April 1992 issue of *Forbes.*

Dalton and Muma, who was president of the start-up, planned to build a national data processing company based on the concept the two had been implementing since the late 1970s: increased efficiency through economies of scale. Up to that time, most companies developed and operated a separate data processing system in-house. They created their own software and managed their own systems, often at an enormous and constantly escalating cost. Fiserv would save money for these companies by contracting to handle some or most of their data processing activities. Because Fiserv could essentially use the same software and systems for its entire base of clients, it could significantly reduce their expenses. The partners planned to quickly grow their customer base by acquiring regional processing firms similar to Fiserv but smaller in size.

To finance Fiserv's strategy of purchasing companies with cash, rather than debt, the company began selling shares publicly in 1986. Although this strategy reduced the founder's ownership interest to only two percent each by the early 1990s, it allowed them to reduce their debt burden and sustain aggressive expansion efforts. As Dalton went searching for new acquisition candidates during the 1980s, Muma focused on developing a high-tech, efficient, customer-oriented operation that could smoothly integrate new acquisitions and the clients that accompanied them.

Fiserv's success at purchasing good companies and providing top-notch service soon paid off. Between 1984 and 1989 Fiserv acquired 16 companies, boosting annual company sales more than 3,000 percent to $700 million. Likewise, Fiserv's work force swelled from just 300 in 1984 to a whopping 2,300 by 1989. Going into the 1990s, Fiserv was processing data in 36 states through 20 data centers. It served more than 800 financial institutions representing 19 million individual accounts. Furthermore, in the few years since its inception the company had expanded its operations internationally to include clients in Europe, Australia, and Canada.

Fiserv's rapid growth during the 1980s was largely a corollary of a metamorphosis of U.S. financial markets. Indeed, as a result new technologies, tax laws (i.e. the Tax Reform Act of 1986), increased competition, an easing of interstate banking regulations, and other factors, prospective Fiserv customers were increasingly seeking reduced costs associated with centralized, automated data processing. As a result, the data processing industry, in general, experienced growth and consolidation throughout the 1980s and early 1990s.

In addition to favorable industry trends, however, much of Fiserv's prosperity and dominance was attributable to its savvy management style. For example, Fiserv practiced extreme caution when it purchased new companies—of 600 acquisition candidates that it considered in 1992, it purchased only six. Besides examining a candidate's information systems, financial condition, and customer base, Dalton carefully considered the quality of its employees. When he finally decided to purchase a company, he did so with the intent of keeping the company's top management on board for at least three years. Furthermore, Dalton allowed the company's management to continue operating with a relatively high degree of autonomy.

Muma and other members of Fiserv's operations team complemented Dalton's prudent growth strategy with a near obsession with customer service. ''Fiserv is very professional, very current, and up-to-date on all the new advances in the computer and financial services industry,'' extolled a Fiserv client in a November 1989 issue of *Business Journal of Milwaukee.* ''They are extremely responsive to our concerns and to incorporating our direction into the system.'' Indeed, Fiserv was credited with maintaining a range of specialized products and services unmatched in the industry.

Another element of Fiserv's quest for market share was flexibility. Unlike many of its competitors, for instance, Fiserv did not push its new customers to utilize its software. Instead, Fiserv adapted its services to work with the institution's existing systems. Fiserv also worked with a range of account sizes; whereas industry leaders Electronic Data Systems (EDS) and Systematics Inc. concentrated on larger customers, Fiserv was willing to work with credit unions and other small institutions.

Although EDS and Systematics both served a broader customer base than that assisted by Fiserv, the latter's focused management style allowed it to assume the leading growth position (among established competitors) in the data processing industry during the late 1980s and early 1990s. Of the three leaders, in fact, Fiserv was the only one that concentrated solely on serving financial institutions. ''It's the best managed company of its kind because its got a clear focus on what its business actually is,'' explained investment analyst Paul Shain in a July 1992 issue of *Business Journal of Milwaukee.* ''It's a simple strategy of offering banks more sophisticated financial services and better customer service than they could otherwise afford.''

Fiserv's strategy benefited shareholders during the early 1990s, as assets, revenues, and clients ballooned. Indeed, after ingesting its first 16 companies between 1984 and 1989, Fiserv stepped up its growth plans with 15 additional purchases during 1990 and 1991. New buys included a major acquisition of a Citicorp data processing division for $49 million; the new subsidiary brought an additional 400 clients to Fiserv.

The Citicorp purchase reflected the growing size of the companies in Fiserv's client base. Although the company had targeted smaller and mid-size companies prior to 1990, it began serving several customers with sales of $1 billion-plus in the early 1990s. By 1991, Fiserv was serving more than 1,400 banks, savings and loans, and credit unions of all sizes. Its sales, moreover, vaulted to a whopping $281 million, from which $18.3 million in profit was gleaned.

In addition to continued acquisition and client growth during 1992 and 1993, Fiserv also shifted its operational focus. It had previously served most of its customers via modem through mainframes connected to its clients' terminals. To serve its larger customers, however, Fiserv in the early 1990s began literally taking over entire data processing departments at large companies. It hired much of the existing staff and operated the data processing facility on-site using Fiserv technical know-how. This strategy, combined with continued increases in its number of smaller clients, helped the company to grow its customer base to more than 5,400 in 1992 as its workforce swelled to 4,800. Likewise, revenues shot up an impressive 15 percent to $332 million, and earnings grew 27 percent, to $23 million.

Fiserv sustained its aggressive growth tactics in 1993. Among its acquisitions early in that year were two data processing businesses owned by Mellon Bank. This purchase brought about 200 new clients to Fiserv worth an estimated $70 million per year in revenues. Furthermore, most of these new clients had assets of more than $300 million, much more than the average for Fiserv's existing client base. Most notable during 1993, however, was Fiserv's addition of its largest buyout ever, Basis Information Technologies, Inc., which added 1,000 new workers to the Fiserv's payroll.

Although Dalton and Muma were aging going into the mid-1990s, their zeal for continued growth and innovation was reflected in pursuits outside their business. Muma, in fact, was known for his high energy and strong work ethic. To prepare for his 12-hour workday that began at 6:30 a.m., he jogged six miles. An avid runner since the age of 32, he began competing in marathons to overcome a smoking habit. Also a hard worker, Dalton filled his free hours by cruising on his 1990 Harley-Davidson motorcycle. He was an avid automobile enthusiast, as well. Despite outside interests, however, both men were admitted workaholics. "We don't bowl on Saturdays," said Muma, in the April 27, 1992, issue of *Forbes*, "We come to work."

Fiserv posted record growth in 1993; sales ballooned an impressive 38 percent, as income spiraled to more than $30 million. Furthermore, the company was poised for healthy expansion throughout the remainder of the 1990s. Dalton and Muma reflected on the Fiserv's rampant rise in the company's 1993 annual report: ". . . with the dedication and hard work of Fiserv people, we have grown this organization from two data process-ing centers in Milwaukee and Tampa employing less than 300 professionals to a company with locations in 61 cities supported by more than 6,300 industry professionals. We've grown from providing full-service processing for 170 clients in 1984 to over 2,500 clients in 1993. . . . We've built a strong foundation on which to base our future, and have in place a focused plan to direct that future."

Principal Subsidiaries: First Trust Corporation; Sendero Corporation.

Further Reading:

Banker, John, "Big Competitors Can't Keep Pace with Fiserv," *Business Journal of Milwaukee,* August 7, 1993, Sec. 1, p. 7.

Barthel, Matt, "Fiserv's Strategy for Rapid Growth," *American Banker,* August 27, 1993.

Dalton, George D., "Fiserv, Inc. and Mellon Bank Corp. Announce Agreement for Sale of Two Mellon Outsourcing Businesses for Bank Processing and Related Services," *Business Wire,* August 2, 1993.

Dries, Michael, "Shades of CEO: Heart and Soul—How Who They Are Plays a Role in How they Lead: George Dalton," *Business Journal of Milwaukee,* March 27, 1993, Sec. 3, p. 8; "Hot Shots—Wisconsin's Best-Performing Public Companies: Fiserv Inc.," *Business Journal of Milwaukee,* July 31, 1993, Sec. 3, p. 12.

Elliot, Suzanne, "Fiserv Plans Move to Cheaper Offices for Ex-Mellon Subs," *Pittsburgh Business Times & Journal,* August 16, 1993, Sec. 1, p. 1.

Higgins, Terry, "Fiserv Inc.," *Business Journal of Milwaukee,* July 25, 1992, Sec. 3, p. 12.

Palmeri, Christopher, "We Don't Bowl on Saturdays," *Forbes,* April 27, 1992, p. 104.

Snell, Ned, "Fiserv Inc.," *Datamation,* June 15, 1993, p. 120.

"The CEOs of Wisconsin: George Dalton," *Business Journal of Milwaukee,* March 27, 1993, Sec. 3, p. 15.

Weier, Anita, "Muma's Marathon Pace Keeps Fiserv on Growth Track," *Business Journal of Milwaukee,* November 20, 1989, Sec. 1, p. 10.

—Dave Mote

FMC

FMC Corporation

200 East Randolph Drive
Chicago, Illinois 60601-6401
U.S.A.
(312) 861-6000
Fax: (312) 861-6148

Public Company
Incorporated: 1928 as the John Bean Manufacturing
   Company
Employees: 20,696
Sales: $2.08 billion
Stock Exchanges: New York Boston Cincinnati NASDAQ
   Philadelphia Pacific
SICs: 3795 Tanks and Tank Components; 3812 Search and
   Navigation Equipment; 2812 Alkalis and Chlorine; 3523
   Farm Machinery and Equipment; 3061 Mechanical Rubber
   Goods; 2879 Agricultural Chemicals, Not Elsewhere
   Classified; 1041 Gold Ores; 3599 Industrial Machinery,
   Not Elsewhere Classified; 3711 Motor Vehicles and
   Passenger Car Bodies; 2819 Industrial Inorganic
   Chemicals, Not Elsewhere Classified; 3556 Food Products
   Machinery; 3489 Ordnance and Accessories, Not
   Elsewhere Classified

FMC Corporation is a leading producer of industrial and specialty chemicals and maintains interests in defense systems,
gold mining, and its historical base, machinery and equipment.
Having grown to include a diverse group of products and
industries in the early 1990s, the conglomerate was struggling
to achieve better organization and healthier returns from its
businesses.

The roots of the FMC Corporation lie in the John Bean Spray
Pump Company established in California in 1884 when Bean
invented the hand spray pump. Over the next 34 years, he built
his product into the preferred pump in the region. Another
prosperous local firm in the 1920s was Frank L. Burrell's
cannery. The two merged in 1928 to form the John Bean
Manufacturing Company, which changed its name to the Food
Machinery Corporation the next year. From this manufacturer
of simple food production equipment the diverse FMC was
to grow.

Bean, not a businessman by nature, passed the management of
the company on to his son-in-law, David Christian Crummey, at

a fairly early point in time. Upon the merger, control passed on
to his son, John David Crummey. While the younger Crummey
was a strong voice leading the firm, the hand of another man
was evident in the company's actions. This man was Paul L.
Davies, Crummey's son-in-law, who left a banking vice-presidency to become vice-president of Food Machinery. The policies of growth which Davies put into effect kept the company
financially healthy throughout the Depression. Davies recognized the cyclical nature of purely agricultural businesses; they
depended too much on crop fluctuations. In 1933, therefore, the
firm began to expand by purchasing the Peerless Pump Company, whose inexpensive pumps were in high demand during
these lean years. This was the beginning of a policy of diversification which was to bring the company into increasingly varied
and prosperous areas.

Food Machinery not only survived the Depression, it prospered,
and emerged in the early 1940s prepared for the consistent
growth which was to characterize it under Davies. An aggressive and energetic man who worked 12 hour days, Davies used
diversification as both a means of expanding the company's
market and a hedge against cyclical weakness in any one
branch. In 1943, the company made its first foray into the
chemical market by acquiring the Niagara Sprayer and Chemical Company, a strong independent manufacturer of insecticides and fungicides. This move was followed by the 1948
acquisition of Westvaco Chemical Corporation, which produced industrial chemicals. The Niagara merger left Food Machinery in the position of producing not only sprayers and
pumps, but the chemicals to put through them; the later merger,
upon which the company became the Food Machinery and
Chemical Corporation, expanded their chemical product line
even more.

Alongside this chemical expansion, Food Machinery's equipment division prospered in the 1940s due to the Second World
War. Some months before the United States entered the war,
Food Machinery began producing the "Water Buffalo," an
amphibious tank which provided important troop mobility over
the next crucial years. Other products were adapted for wartime
uses as well, such as the orchard sprayer, which was to be used
for decontamination purposes if necessary, and nailing machines which produced ammunition boxes at an exceedingly
high rate.

After the war, the company's production line returned to its
earlier emphasis, although defense contracts continued to play
an important role in FMC's operations throughout the twentieth
century. With the war ended, however, the company was at no
loss for customers. Wartime reductions produced a market for
expensive and technologically advanced food processing equipment, and Food Machinery's business grew. Other existing
products were adapted to peacetime uses as they had been in
war, with sprayers, for example, being turned to firefighting
uses. A drop in earnings occurred the year after the Westvaco
acquisition, but by 1950 the company was back on its prosperous track. Davies continued to put money both into diversification and into research and engineering which led to new products and continued growth.

Every year between 1950 and 1966 the Food Machinery and
Chemical Corporation (which changed its name to the FMC

Corporation in 1961) showed a financial gain, and the company was a favorite of investors. Their trend toward diversification continued, most notably with the purchase of the American Viscose Corporation in 1963, despite opposition from the antitrust division of the Justice Department. Davies' vigor, vision, and talent for profitable purchases provided a strong center for the company's rather loose management through 1966. In this year, Davies decided to retire. His strategy was to avoid overstaying his productive years and to leave a strong successor. The man who replaced him as chief executive officer, who had assumed the presidency some few years back, was engineer James M. Hait. It was Davies' intent to leave this hand-picked officer to continue the company's expansion and growth.

In 1967, FMC's financial growth came to an abrupt halt. While Hait would remain chairperson until 1971, he was replaced as chief executive officer in 1967 by Jack M. Pope. This year also marked the company's relocation of its headquarters to Chicago and its acquisition of the Link-Belt Corporation, an equipment manufacturer which quickly proved to have antiquated plants and serious financial difficulties. This purchase, along with the 1963 Avisco acquisition, became a draining point for FMC's finances, instead of increasing its profitability.

In 1968, with Pope as its leader, FMC did show a brief resumption of its upward growth trend. However, this improvement on the books proved largely due to an accounting change, and the health of the company was not restored. The growth which had paid off so strongly for Paul Davies was too much for his successors. Even toward the end of Davies' administration, the loose reins under which he had run the company had been a bit too loose for its ever-increasing size. Now, under new management, the control necessary for an improved financial condition was lost. The status of the company declined among investors as its finances weakened. By 1973, FMC stock had fallen from $44 per share to $15.

By the end of the decade, Paul Davies' company was experiencing severe financial difficulties. Its management was unable to maintain profitability. The synthetic fiber branch was losing money, and the recession of 1970–71 caused even the strong machinery division to suffer. FMC's profits fell to $39 million from their 1968 level of $75 million. It was at this point that the company appointed a third successor to Davies, one who would finally bring FMC back to financial prosperity. This successor was a Harvard Business School graduate who had been with FMC for 20 years, Robert H. Malott.

From the time that Malott took control of FMC, it was clear that it would not be an easy task to revive the company. Obviously a change in management strategy was called for in order to turn around the company's decline. For Malott, that change began with a recentralization of management. The company's size and relatively loose management procedures had contributed to its decline, so Malott reorganized FMC by consolidating the many branches of the company into two groups for better administrative control.

Realizing that the mere continuation of former company policy was an unworkable strategy, Malott approached his first years as chief executive officer with a different set of policies. Between 1972 and 1978, FMC disposed of 20 product lines that were either immediate financial drains or were soon to be in danger. This was one step that Hait and Pope had apparently been unwilling to take, but it gave new life to the company. Chief among these sales and closings was the 1976 sale of the fiber division. Price cutting in the synthetics market and competition from cotton and polyester (FMC produced primarily rayon) had made this one of the chief money drains and one of Davies' few untimely purchases. Malott ended this losing struggle by selling the division to the newly-formed Avtex Fibers Inc. He also made other timely decisions, such as the 1976 closing of a pulp mill in Alaska, in the face of strict environmental controls that were about to be imposed. His evaluation of these branches and concentration on the three core areas of industrial chemicals, defense equipment, and machinery provided the first step toward FMC's recovery.

Malott's financial policies also began to revive FMC during this period. One such policy was his refusal to reduce prices when faced with competition. Instead, Malott cut production, keeping profit margins up. Another keynote of Malott's financial management was his aggressive capital spending. His outlays in research and development made it possible for new products to be developed. In addition, in the two years prior to 1976, FMC put $400 million into high growth areas, such as petroleum equipment and specialty chemicals. The profitability of Malott's policies was almost immediately apparent; by the spring of 1976, with a personnel increase of only 1,000 workers, Malott raised sales from $1.3 billion to $2.3 billion, a much-needed $1 billion increase.

By 1976, FMC's great comeback was obvious. In an April article, *Forbes* magazine called the corporation "a stronger, better run company than it was in its heyday." Even with the company well on the road to full recovery, however, Malott continued to revise FMC policy. In 1977, Malott began to decentralize the administrative control of the company in order to facilitate faster growth. The diversification of the company itself suggested somewhat decentralized management, now that it was financially stable. Malott divided the company into nine well-defined groups, centering around their chemical, equipment, and specialty products. The situation differed from earlier times in that final decisions still rested with top management and close communication was to be maintained. Lower managers were being trained to think in terms of a world-wide market. This restructuring was to lead the company into its next significant period of growth and expansion.

The years between 1977 and 1980 were not, however, marked solely by unchecked growth. As in any industry, fluctuations were seen in the demand for FMC products. Four of the nine groups remained the strongest: defense equipment, petroleum equipment, industrial chemicals, and agricultural chemicals. Much of the strength of this last category came from the sales of Furadan, a popular pesticide for protecting corn, sugar cane, and some 18 other crops. Fluctuations in chemical markets were one reason that FMC, by 1980, was not reporting a financial return at hoped-for rates.

While management was bringing FMC back to prosperity, there were also periods of intense public scrutiny. As the government became more interested in environmental issues, for example, some of FMC's procedures were called into question. Alleged pollution from such chemicals as carbon tetrachloride gave rise to cease-and-desist orders and plant closings throughout the mid- to late 1970s. FMC was also involved in the major controversy over phosphates during the first half of the decade. In 1970, the company was the second largest producer of the chemicals, which caused premature aging of natural water sites. Court battles on the subject continued through 1975, when a Chicago ordinance banning the chemicals was upheld. Such environmental conflicts, while not damaging the company directly, forced additional internal changes in production.

FMC also became the primary contractor for an advanced armed personnel carrier called the Bradley Fighting Vehicle, developed during the 1970s to counter the introduction of a similar but less sophisticated Soviet model called the BMP. In the early 1980s, the Bradley was criticized for a lack of battlefield survivability. FMC and Pentagon officials responded that even the most heavily armored tanks were not impervious to attack, but nonetheless began to investigate ways to improve the Bradley. About 3,000 Bradleys were delivered, each capable of defeating enemy tanks and other fighting vehicles while moving at high speeds in any kind of weather.

Despite such conflicts, FMC continued its growth and expansion during the 1980s. Plans for new acquisitions were announced in 1984, and, the following year, FMC's stock standing was upgraded to "attractive" by an analyst specializing in chemicals firms, who had for a decade seen the field as only a fair risk. Profits and returns increased to record levels and long-term debt was insubstantial, an equation that drew the attention of corporate raiders in the 1980s. Amid concerns about a possible hostile takeover, CEO Malott planned a general restructuring of the entire company. Management's recapitalization effected a leveraged buyout. The company borrowed $1.8 million against its own assets, and paid public shareholders (who owned about 82 percent of FMC) $80 cash each in exchange for a 15 percent stake in the company. Management declined the cash to raise their cumulative share to 35 percent. The plan, which was okayed by shareholders in May 1986, saved FMC from outside takeover but saddled it with debt.

At the same time, FMC became embroiled in the insider trading scandal of 1986, when investor Ivan Boesky used illegally gained information about FMC's restructuring to turn a profit of $975,000. In the process, according to the company, his influence cost FMC some $225 million in additional recapitalization costs.

In the late 1980s, Malott expanded FMC into gold mining. While prospecting for antimony, a flame retardant chemical, the corporation discovered gold and elected to develop the resources under a new subsidiary, FMC Gold. In 1989, the company acquired Meridian Gold from Burlington Resources through an exchange of stock. By the end of the decade, FMC Gold contributed 25 percent of the conglomerate's annual reve-

nues and helped offset declining defense income as the Cold War ended.

Malott retired in 1991 at the age of 65, turning over a business he regarded as "dull" to FMC President Robert Burr. In the 1990s, industrial chemicals (26 percent of 1993 revenues and 17 percent of operating income) were sluggish, as detergent manufacturers continued to remove FMC's phosphates from their products. The defense segment (25 percent of sales and 43 percent of income) continued to suffer as well, as competition from a cheaper Russian tank combined with Defense Department cutbacks to herald FMC's halting exit from that industry. Early in 1994, FMC created United Defense, L.P., a joint venture with Harsco Corporation's Combat Systems, to control its defense unit. FMC Gold's primary mine "played out" in 1993, and in spite of the precious metal's strong performance that year, the subsidiary ran in the red, losing $50 million on operations. FMC's remaining machinery business contributed 23 percent of revenues but just two percent of operating income in 1993.

Specialty or "performance" chemicals were FMC's mainstay, contributing 23 percent of sales and 25 percent of operating income. FMC continued to lead the world in the production of cellulose gel, a fat replacement for food products marketed under the Avicel and Novagel brands. The company was also the leading manufacturer of agarose, a product used in genetic research, as well as phosphate ester flame retardants.

In May 1994, Dyan Machan, writing for *Forbes,* characterized FMC as "an untidy conglomeration of disparate businesses." She also quoted analyst Paul Rayman, of S.G. Warberg Securities, who called FMC "a hangover from the 1960s—a company with little strategic focus, betting on losing businesses." Nevertheless, Burt outlined three "fundamental strengths and future strategies" in his 1993 letter to shareholders: "strong positions in attractive markets"; "high returns and excellent cash flow through the economic cycles of the markets in which we operate"; and "a long-term strategy to increase FMC's historic growth rates by making investments that will increase growth in our major markets at returns above the cost of capital."

Principal Subsidiaries: FMC Foret, S.A.; FMC Gold; United Defense, L.P. (60%); Kongsberg Offshore Services, a.s.; SOFEC, Inc.

Further Reading:

Berss, Marcia, "FMC Corp.: Marching to Its Own Drummer," *Forbes,* September 17, 1990, pp. 95, 98.
Machan, Dyan, "The Strategy Thing," *Forbes,* May 23, 1994, pp. 113–114.
Wood, Andrew, "FMC: Expanding Its Chemical Universe," *Chemical Week,* December 23–30, 1992, pp. 24–26.

—updated by April Dougal Gasbarre

Ford Motor Company

The American Road
Dearborn, Michigan 48121-3236
U.S.A.
(313) 322-3000
Fax: (313) 322-7896

Public Company
Incorporated: 1919
Employees: 322,213
Sales: $108.52 billion
Stock Exchanges: New York Boston Pacific Midwest
   Toronto Montreal London
SICs: 3711 Motor Vehicles and Car Bodies; 3714 Motor
   Vehicles Parts and Accessories; 6159 Miscellaneous
   Business Credit Institutions; 6141 Personal Credit
   Institutions; 6035 Federal Savings Institutions; 6331 Fire,
   Marine, and Casualty Insurance; 7515 Passenger Car
   Leasing

One of a handful of companies that contributed significantly to
the growth of the United States, Ford Motor Company repre-
sents a more than $100 billion multinational empire. Known
primarily as a manufacturer of automobiles, Ford also holds a
considerable stake in financial services, which by themselves
generated more than $1 billion in income. With these vast
resources in banking-related assets complementing its storied
record of automobile production, Ford stood as formidable economic force.

Henry Ford, the founder of the Ford Motor Company, was born
on a farm near Dearborn, Michigan, in 1863. He had a talent for
engineering, which he pursued as a hobby from boyhood, but it
was not until 1890 that he commenced his engineering career as
an employee of the Detroit Edison Company. In his spare time,
Ford constructed experimental gasoline engines and in 1892
completed his first "gasoline buggy." Dissatisfied with the
buggy's weight, he sold it in 1896 to help fund the construction
of a new car. Ford's superiors at the electric company felt his
hobby distracted him from his regular occupation, and despite
his promotion to chief engineer, he was forced to quit in 1899.

Shortly afterwards, with financial backing from private investors, Ford established the Detroit Automobile Company. He
later withdrew from the venture after a disagreement with
business associates over the numbers and prices of cars to be

produced. Ford advocated a business strategy which combined a
lower profit margin on each car with greater production volumes. In this way, he hoped to gain a larger market share and
maintain profitability.

Working independently in a small shed in Detroit, Henry Ford
developed two four-cylinder, 80-horsepower race cars, called
the "999" and the "Arrow." These cars won several races and
helped to create a new market for Ford automobiles. With
$28,000 of capital raised from friends and neighbors, Henry
Ford established a new shop on June 16, 1903. In this facility, a
converted wagon factory on Mack Avenue in Detroit, the Ford
Motor Company began production of a two-cylinder, eight-
horsepower design called the Model A. The company produced
1,708 of these models in the first year of operation.

The Ford Motor Company was sued by the Licensed Association of Automobile Manufacturers, an industrial syndicate
which held patent rights for "road locomotives" with internal
combustion engines. Ford responded by taking the matter to the
courts, arguing that the patent, granted to George B. Selden in
1895, was invalid. During the long process of adjudication,
Ford continued to manufacture cars and relocated to a larger
plant on Piquette and Beaubien Streets. A Canadian plant was
established in Walkerville, Ontario, on August 17, 1904.

Henry Ford and his engineers designed several automobiles,
each one designated by a letter of the alphabet; these included
the small, four-cylinder Model N (which sold for $500), and the
more luxurious six-cylinder Model K (which sold poorly for
$2500). The failure of the Model K, coupled with Henry Ford's
persistence in developing inexpensive cars for mass production,
caused a dispute between Ford and his associate Alexander
Malcolmson. The latter, who helped to establish the company in
1903, resigned and his share of the company was acquired by
Henry Ford. Ford's holdings then amounted to 58 and one-half
percent. In a further consolidation of his control, Ford replaced
John S. Gray, a Detroit banker, as president of the company
in 1906.

In October 1908, despite the continuing litigation with the
Selden syndicate, Ford introduced the durable and practical
Model T. Demand for this car was so great that Ford was forced
to enlarge its production facilities. Over 10,000 Model Ts were
produced in 1909. Able to vote down business associates who
favored more conventional methods of production, Henry Ford
applied his "assembly line" concept of manufacturing to the
Model T.

In developing the assembly line, Ford noted that the average
worker performed several tasks in the production of each component, and used a variety of tools in the process. He improved
efficiency by having each worker specialize in one task with one
tool. The component on which the employee worked was conveyed to him on a moving belt, and after allowing a set time for
the task to be performed, the component was moved on to the
next operation. Slower workers thus needed to increase their
work rate in order to maintain production at the rate determined
by the speed of the belts.

Ford's battle with the Selden group led to a decision by the
Supreme Court in 1911, eight years after the initial suit. The
Court ruled that the Selden patent was invalid. The decision

freed many automobile manufacturers from costly licensing obligations; it also enabled others to enter the business.

When the United States became involved in World War I (April 1917), the Ford Motor Company placed its resources at the disposal of the government. For the duration of the war, Ford Motor produced large quantities of automobiles, trucks, and ambulances, as well as Liberty airplane motors, Whippet tanks, Eagle ''submarine chasers,'' and munitions.

In 1918, Henry Ford officially retired from the company, naming his son Edsel president and ceding to him a controlling interest. But, in fact, Henry continued to direct company strategy and spent much of his time developing a farm tractor called the Fordson. He also published a conservative weekly journal, *The Dearborn Independent.* Edsel, who was more reserved and pragmatic than his father, concerned himself with routine operations.

At the end of the war Henry and Edsel Ford disagreed with fellow stockholders over the planned expenditure of several million dollars for a large new manufacturing complex at River Rouge, near Detroit. The Fords eventually resolved the conflict by buying out all the other shareholders. Their company was re-registered as a Delaware corporation in July 1919. The River Rouge facility, built shortly afterward, was a large integrated manufacturing and assembly complex which included a steel mill of substantial capacity.

Between January 1 and April 19, 1921, the Ford Motor Company had $58 million in financial obligations due, and only $20 million available to meet them. Convinced that Ford Motor would be forced into bankruptcy, representatives of several large financial houses offered to extend loans to the company, on the condition that the Fords yield financial control. When the offer was refused, the bankers retreated, certain that they would soon be called upon to repossess the company.

With little time available, Henry Ford transferred as many automobiles as possible to his dealerships, who were instructed to pay in cash. Almost immediately, this generated $25 million. Next, Ford purchased the Detroit, Toledo & Ironton railroad, the primary medium of transportation for his company's supplies. By rearranging the railroad's schedules, Ford was able to reduce by one-third the time that automotive components spent in transit. This allowed him to reduce inventories by one-third, thereby releasing an additional $28 million. With additional income from other sources, and reduction in production costs, Ford had $87 million in cash by April 1, $27 million more than he needed to pay off the company debts.

The Ford Motor Company's only relationship with banks after this crisis was as a depositor. And despite poor financial management, Ford maintained such strong profitability that it offered to lend money on the New York markets, in competition with banks. With large quantities of cash still available, Ford acquired the financially troubled Lincoln Motor Company in 1922.

Edsel Ford was more enthusiastic about the development of the aircraft industry than his father, and in 1925 persuaded his fellow shareholders (all family members) to purchase the Stout Metal Airplane Company. His close friend William Stout, who

was retained as vice-president and general manager of the company, developed a popular three-engine passenger aircraft known as the Ford Trimotor. 196 of these aircraft were built during its production run.

After 18 years producing the Model T, the Ford Motor Company faced its first serious threat from a competitor. In 1926, the General Motors Corporation introduced its Chevrolet automobile, a more stylish and powerful car. Sales of the Model T dropped sharply. After months of experimenting with a six-cylinder model, Ford decided to discontinue the Model T in favor of the new Model A. On May 31 1926, Ford plants across the country were closed for six months while assembly lines were retooled.

That year Ford voluntarily reduced its work week to five days declaring that workers should also benefit from the success of the company. Ford was also one of the first companies to limit the work day to eight hours, and to establish a minimum wage of $5 per day. At Henry Ford's own admission, these policies were instituted more to improve productivity than to appease dissatisfied (and unrepresented) workers.

The British Ford Company was formed in 1928 and shortly thereafter the German Ford Company was founded. Henry Ford recognized the Soviet Union as a market with great potential, and like a number of other American industrialists, he fostered a relationship with officials in the Soviet government. Later, Ford participated in the construction of an automobile factory at Nishni-Novgogrod.

The economic crisis of October 1929, which led to the Great Depression, forced many companies to close. Ford Motor managed to remain in business, despite losses of as much as $68 million per year. By 1932, economic conditions became so difficult that the Ford minimum wage was reduced to $4 per day. But for its Model A, which sold 4.5 million units between 1927 and 1931, Ford's situation would have been much worse.

The economy of Detroit was heavily dependent on large, locally based industrial manufacturers and when companies less successful than Ford were forced to suspend operations, a banking crisis developed. The Ford Motor Company, and Edsel Ford personally, extended about $12 million in loans to these banks in an effort to maintain their solvency. But these efforts failed and the banks were forced to close in February 1933. Ford lost over $32 million in deposits and several millions more in bank securities. The principal Ford bank, Guardian National, was subsequently reorganized by Ford interests as the Manufacturers National Bank of Detroit. Ford's largest business rival, General Motors, having suffered a similar crisis, emerged with control over the National Bank of Detroit.

The implementation of President Roosevelt's ''New Deal,'' made conditions more favorable to the organization of labor unions. But Henry Ford, who had supported President Hoover in the election, advised his workers to resist union organization, and in 1935 raised the company's minimum wage to $6 per day.

In 1937, the United Automobile Workers union began a campaign to organize Ford workers by sponsoring the employee occupation of a Ford plant in Kansas City. The conflict was resolved when Ford officials agreed to meet with union representatives. That same year, there was trouble at the River Rouge complex. Several men distributing UAW pamphlets at the gates were severely beaten by unidentified assailants, believed to have been agents of the Ford security office. Following an investigation by the National Labor Relations Board, Ford was cited for numerous unfair labor practices. The finding was contested, but eventually upheld when the Supreme Court refused to hear the case.

In 1940, Henry Ford, who opposed American involvement in World War II, cancelled a contract (arranged by Edsel) to build 6000 Rolls-Royce Merlin aircraft engines for the British Royal Air Force, and 3000 more for the United States Army. In time, however, public opinion led Ford to change his mind. Plans were made for the construction of a large new government-sponsored facility to manufacture aircraft at Willow Run, west of Dearborn.

Unionization activities climaxed in April 1941 when Ford employees went on strike. The NLRB called an employee election, under the terms of the Wagner Act, to establish a union representation for Ford workers. When the ballots were tabulated in June, the UAW drew 70 percent of the votes. Henry Ford, an avowed opponent of labor unions, suddenly altered his stand. He agreed to a contract with union representatives which met all worker demands.

The company devoted its resources to the construction of the Willow Run Aircraft plant. Eight months later, in December 1941, the Japanese bombing of Pearl Harbor resulted in a declaration of war by the United States against Japan, Germany, and Italy. Willow Run was completed the following May. It was the largest manufacturing facility in the world, occupying 2.5 million square feet of floor space, with an assembly line three miles long. Adjacent to the plant were hangars, covering 1.2 million square feet, and a large airfield. The airplanes produced at this facility were four-engine B-24E Liberator bombers, the Consolidated Aircraft version of the Boeing B-24. Production of aircraft got off to a slow start, but after adjustments the rate of production was raised to one plane per hour, 24 hours a day. During the war, other Ford Motor plants produced a variety of engines, as well as trucks, jeeps, M-4 tanks, M-10 tank destroyers, and transport gliders. The company also manufactured large quantities of tires, despite the removal of its tire plant to the Soviet Union.

Edsel Ford died unexpectedly in May 1943 at the age of 49. At the time of his death, Edsel was recognized as a far better manager than his father. Indeed, Henry Ford was often criticized for repeatedly undermining his son's efforts to improve the company, and the managerial crisis which occurred after Edsel's death is directly attributable to Henry Ford's persistent failure to prepare capable managers for future leadership of the company.

Edsel had been responsible for much of the company's wartime mobilization and his absence was deeply felt by his aging father, who was forced to resume the company presidency. In need of assistance, Henry Ford sought a special discharge from the Navy for Edsel's son Henry II. The navy complied, citing the special needs of Ford management during wartime. Henry Ford vigorously prepared his grandson to succeed him. By the

end of the war, when the Willow Run plant was turned over to the government, Ford had produced 8600 B-24E bombers and over 57,000 aircraft engines.

In September 1945, Henry Ford II, aged 28, was named president of the Ford Motor Company. The inexperienced man could not have started at a worse time. No longer supported by government contracts, the company began to lose money at a rate of $10 million per month. The source of the problem was Henry Ford I's financial management policy, specifically designed to perplex the Internal Revenue Service and discourage audits. The severe economic conditions after the war made Ford's finances an albatross.

Unable to bring the company's finances under control, Henry II hired Ernest R. Breech, a General Motors executive and past chairperson of Bendix, in 1946. Breech was placed in charge of two groups—a managerial group and a financial one. The first one was comprised of several managers hired away from General Motors, and the second group was made up of ten talented financial experts who had served with the Air Force Office of Statistical Control. The Air Force group included Robert S. McNamara, J. Edward Lundy, Arjay Miller, and Charles "Tex" Thornton; they spent several years reconstructing the company's system of financial management.

Henry Ford I, who had retained the title of chairperson since 1945, died in April 1947 at the age of 83. Henry II and Ernest Breech were then able to implement their own strategies for recovery, and these included the adoption of the proven General Motors management structure, and the decision to establish the Ford Motor Company in foreign markets. In its first year under Breech, the company registered a profit and it continued to gain strength in the late 1940s and early 1950s. Breech's top priority was strict adherence to a financial plan with strong profit margins; unfortunately, this proved to be at the expense of developing automobiles for an increasingly complex market.

Over the previous two decades, the Ford Motor Company had been a notable pioneer and achiever in the industry, and it was the first company to cast a V-8 engine block (1932). Ford had produced its 25 millionth automobile in 1937 and the following year, its Lincoln Division introduced the Mercury line which proved highly successful in the growing market for medium-priced automobiles. Ford's good image had been further enhanced by its contributions to the Allied effort in World War II; even Josef Stalin had kind words for the enterprising American company.

Before he died, Henry Ford I had created two classes of Ford stock. The B Class was reserved for family members and constituted the controlling 40 percent voting interest. The ordinary common shares were to be retained by the company until January 1956, when they were to be offered to the public for the first time.

Two years after Henry I's death, in 1949, the company unveiled a number of new automatic styles. But while the cars were practical, and to a degree fashionable, the company no longer appeared to be a pioneer; indeed it gained a reputation, not wholly justified, as being an imitator of General Motors.

Regaining its initiative, the Ford Motor Company decided to introduce a new model to fill a gap in the market between the Ford and Lincoln-Mercury lines. In 1958, the much heralded 410 horsepower Edsel made its debut. It was a terrible flop. Ford's market researchers had been very wrong; there was no gap in the market for the Edsel to fill. After just two years, production of the ill-fated car ceased. 110,847 units had been produced, at a loss of some $250 million.

The 1960s saw many changes at Ford: dissatisfied with his secondary role in the company decision-making, Henry Ford stripped Breech of his power, replacing him with Robert McNamara. But McNamara left the Ford Motor Company in 1961 to serve as Secretary of Defense in the Kennedy administration. Many of McNamara's duties were taken over by Arjay Miller, who succeeded the interim president, John Dykstra, in 1963.

The Ford Motor Company purchased the Philco Corporation in 1961 and established a tractor division in 1962. The following year, Ford introduced its highly successful Mustang; more than 500,000 of these cars were sold in 18 months. The man most responsible for developing the Mustang was a protégé of Robert McNamara named Lee Iacocca.

In another move intended to assert his authority over management, Henry Ford dismissed Arjay Miller in 1968 and named Semon E. Knudsen as president. Knudsen, a former executive vice-president at General Motors, known for his aggressive personality, found himself in constant conflict with Henry Ford, and after 19 months he was replaced by Lee Iacocca. Iacocca was a popular figure, highly talented in marketing and sales, but like Knudsen, he frequently disagreed with Henry Ford.

Ford Motor Company subsidiaries in Europe entered a period of strong growth and high profitability in the early 1970s, and these subsidiaries produced components for the Pinto, a subcompact introduced in the U.S. in 1971. Pinto models from 1971 to 1976 and similarly configured Bobcats from 1975 to 1976 drew a great deal of attention after several incidents in which the car's gas tank exploded in rear-end collisions. The unfavorable publicity from news reports damaged Ford's public image, as did the wrongful death litigation.

In April 1977, Henry Ford II reduced Iacocca's power by creating a new executive triumvirate. Iacocca was a member of this, along with Ford himself and Philip Caldwell. But a year later, Ford added his brother William Clay Ford to the group and relegated Iacocca to a subordinate position; then within a few months, Ford suddenly fired Iacocca and installed Caldwell as president. Henry Ford was battling stockholder allegations of financial misconduct and bribery at the time and his dismissal of Iacocca made him more unpopular than ever.

Henry Ford made a critical decision and a very misguided one. He cancelled development of a small car which had been proposed by Iacocca and which was intended to succeed the aging Pinto. Thus, as the Japanese compacts became increasingly popular in the United States, Ford found itself quite unable to compete. Adding to its woes, Ford, along with other U.S. car manufacturers, was obligated by Congressional legislation (particularly the Clean Air Act) to develop automobiles which would emit less pollutants.

Henry Ford relinquished his position as chief executive officer to Philip Caldwell in October 1979. The following March, Ford retired and gave the chair to Caldwell, while retaining his seat on the board of directors.

The Ford Motor Company encountered severe economic losses as a result of a reduction in market share, as well as the high costs incurred by labor contracts and the development of automobiles that met the new federal standards. In 1980, the company lost $1.54 billion, despite strong profits from the truck division and European operations. Ford lost a further $1.06 billion in 1981 and $658 million in 1982 while trying to effect a recovery; its market share fell from 23.6 percent in 1978 to 16.6 percent in 1981.

Company officials studied Japanese methods of industrial management, and worked more closely with Toyo Kogyo, the Japanese manufacturer of Mazda automobiles (Ford gained a 25 percent share of Toyo Kogyo in November 1979, when a Ford subsidiary merged with the company). Ford imported Mazda cars and trucks, and in many ways treated Toyo Kogyo as a small car division until the Escort, its successor to the Pinto, reached the showrooms. This new compact was modelled after the Ford (Europe) Erika; another version of it, the Lynx, was produced by Ford's Lincoln-Mercury division.

Caldwell transferred the talented manager Harold Poling from the European division to the United States in an attempt to apply successful European formulas to the American operation. In the restructuring which followed several plants were closed and more than 100,000 workers were dismissed. Ford's weakness in the market was a major concern of the unions; consequently, the company inaugurated a policy of employee involvement in plant operations and was able to secure more favorable labor contracts. Productivity improved dramatically.

In 1984, with costs reduced, Ford started to repurchase 30 million shares (about ten percent of the company's stock). Its production of cars in Mexico was increased, and through its interest in Kia Motors, output was stepped up in South Korea. The following year, Ford introduced the Taurus (another version, the Salde, was produced by its Mercury division), a modern full-size automobile which had taken five years to develop at a cost of $3 billion. The Taurus proved highly successful and won several design awards.

Sales and profits reached record levels in 1984, and in 1986 Ford surpassed General Motors in income for the first time since 1924. In addition, Ford's market share increased to just under 20 percent. Ford Motor purchased several companies in the mid 1980s, including the First Nationwide Financial Corporation and the New Holland tractor division of Sperry, which was later merged with Ford Tractor. Ford also purchased a 30 percent share of Otosan, the automotive subsidiary of the Turkish Koc Group. The attempted acquisition of the Italian car maker Alfa Romeo in 1986 failed, due to a rival bid from Fiat.

The diversification into financial services that began in the mid-1980s continued in earnest throughout the rest of the decade, as each of the major U.S. car manufacturers sought to insulate themselves against the cyclical nature of their business. Ford spent $5.5 billion acquiring assets for its financial services group during the latter half of the decade, including a $3.4 billion purchase in 1989 of the Associates, a Dallas-based finance company. That acquisition, completed the same year Ford purchased the venerable British car manufacturer, Jaguar Cars Ltd., for $2.5 billion, made Ford the country's second largest provider of diversified financial services, ranking only behind Citicorp. With plans to eventually derive 30 percent of the company's profits from financial service-related business, Ford entered the 1990s with $115 billion worth of banking-related assets, a portfolio that provided the company's only bright moments during the otherwise deleterious early 1990s.

An economic recession crippled U.S. car manufacturers during the early 1990s, and Ford bore the brunt of the financial malaise that stretched around the globe. Domestically, car sales faltered and abroad, particularly in Great Britain and Australia, Ford's international sales plummeted. In 1991, Ford's worldwide automotive operations lost an enormous $3.2 billion after recording a $99 million profit the year before. In the United States, automotive losses reached an equally staggering $2.2 billion on the heels of a $17 million loss in 1990. The losses struck a serious blow to Ford, which as recently as 1989 had generated $3.3 billion in net income, but the financial results of 1991 would have been worse without the company's strategic diversification into financial services. For the year, Ford's financial services group registered a record $927 million in earnings, up from the previous year's total of $761 million, which left the company with a $2.25 billion loss for the year, an inauspicious record in Ford's nearly 90-year history.

The financial disaster of 1991, however, was just a prelude to more pernicious losses the following year, as the global recession reached its greatest intensity. In 1992, with revenue swelling to slightly more than $100 billion, Ford posted a crushing $7.38 billion loss. Although 1992 represented one of the bleakest years in Ford's history, the worst was over, and as the economic climate improved, the company emerged with renewed vitality. Against the backdrop of successive financial losses, Ford had increased its presence in the truck and minivan market niche, which represented the fastest growing segment of the broadly defined automotive market. Roughly 200,000 minivans and sports-utility vehicles were sold in the United States a decade earlier and now, as consumers once again returned to car dealers' showrooms, more than 2.3 million opted for minivans and light trucks, a trend that bolstered Ford's financial position and predicated its return to a profitable future.

In 1993, Ford generated $2.52 billion in net income from $108.5 billion in revenue during a year in which the company actually lost money on passenger car sales, yet recouped the losses through minivan and truck sales. By 1994, such vehicles accounted for 50 percent of Ford's automotive sales, a prodigious increase from the preceding decade and the primary engine driving the company's growth.

Despite the losses suffered several years earlier, there was justifiable hope for further growth as Ford entered the mid-1990s. The gap separating Japanese and American car manufacturers' production standards had narrowed considerably, with the U.S. manufacturers emerging from the early 1990s in a more envia-

ble position—Ford included. As the technological and managerial race between U.S. car manufacturers and their Japanese counterparts tightened, the importance of prudent product development and effective distribution networks increased. Toward this end, Ford reorganized its production and distribution operations in mid-1994 to better respond to the changing economic structure of the numerous countries in which Ford operated facilities. Regional trading areas, rather than nation states, would represent the primary focus of Ford's future efforts, a direction the company moved toward with its worldwide reorganization in 1994 and a direction that promised to redefine its style of operation for the twenty-first century.

Principal Subsidiaries: Ford Electronics and Refrigeration Corp.; Ford Export Corp.; Ford International Capital Corp.; Ford International Finance Corp.; Ford Holdings, Inc.; Ford Motor Credit Co.; Ford Leasing Development Co.; Ford Motor Land Development Corp.; First Nationwide Financial Corp.; First Nationwide Savings; Ford Motor Company Ltd. (England); Ford Motor Credit Company Ltd. (England); Ford-Werke A.G. (Germany); Ford Credit Bank A.G. (Germany); Ford Motor Company of Canada Ltd.; Ensite Ltd. (Canada); Ford Glass Ltd. (Canada); Ford Motor Company of Australia Ltd.; Ford Motor Company of New Zealand Ltd.; Ford Brasil S.A. (Brazil); Ford Motor de Venezuela; Ford France S.A.; Ford Motor Company (Belgium) N.V.; Ford Credit N.V. (Belgium); Ford Italiana S.p.A. (Italy); Ford Credit S.p.A. (Italy); Ford Leasing S.p.A. (Italy); Ford Motor Argentina S.A.; Ford Motor Company AS (Denmark); Ford Motor Company S.A. (Mexico); Ford Nederland B.V. (Netherlands); Ford Espana S.A. (Spain); Ford Credit S.A. (Spain); Ford Leasing S.A. (Spain); Ford Credit A.B. (Sweden); Ford Credit S.A. (Switzerland); Transcom Insurance Ltd. (Bermuda); Mazda Motor Corporation (Japan); Ford Motor Company (Japan) Ltd.; Ford Lio Ho Motor Company Ltd. (Taiwan); Jaguar Ltd.

Further Reading:

Beynon, Huw, *Working for Ford,* London: Penguin, 1984.
Dubashi, Jagannath, ''Ford: Looking Beyond the Shadows,'' *FW,* February 6, 1990, p. 23.
Gelderman, Barbara, *Henry Ford, the Wayward Capitalist,* New York: Dial Press, 1981.
Keatley, Robert, ''Ford Reorganizes to Stay Competitive and Reach New Markets in the World,'' *Wall Street Journal,* July 22, 1994, p. A4.
Lewis, David L., *The Public Image of Henry Ford: An American Folk Hero and His Company,* Detroit: Wayne State University Press, 1976.
Meyer, Stephen, *The Five Dollar Day: Labor Management and Social Control in the Ford Motor Company 1908–1921,* Albany: State University of New York Press, 1981.
Moreau, Dan, ''Instant Prosperity: Behind Ford's Fast Turnaround,'' *Kiplinger's Personal Finance Magazine,* July 1993, p. 28.
Nye, David E., *Henry Ford: 'Ignorant Idealist,'* Port Washington: Kennikat Press, 1979.
Reiff, Rick, ''Slowing Traffic Ahead,'' *Forbes,* April 30, 1990, p. 82.
Thomas, Charles M., ''Ford Loses a Record $2.3 Billion,'' *Automotive News,* February 17, 1992, p. 4.

—updated by Jeffrey L. Covell

Forest Laboratories, Inc.

909 Third Avenue
New York, New York 10022
U.S.A.
(212) 421-7850
Fax: (212) 750-9152

Public Company
Incorporated: 1956
Employees: 1,300
Sales: $.36 billion
Stock Exchanges: American
SICs: 8641 Pharmaceuticals

Forest Laboratories, Inc., develops, manufactures, and sells both brand name and generic prescription and nonprescription drugs in the United States, Europe, and Puerto Rico. Although the company operated in relative obscurity during the 1960s and 1970s, it became one of the fastest growing pharmaceutical firms in the United States during the late 1980s and early 1990s.

Forest Laboratories was founded in 1956 as a small laboratory service company. It helped larger pharmaceutical companies, which had hefty research and development funds, to create new drugs. After Forest developed a drug, it would hand the new product off to its client, who would then market, sell, and distribute the offering. Forest achieved a degree of success in its niche and found a steady demand for its services during the late 1950s and early 1960s. In addition, the company swerved slightly from its pharmaceuticals focus by diversifying into other markets: it invested particularly heavily in food businesses. Its foray into other ventures was an attempt to bolster the company's bottom line and to protect it from risks associated with the drug industry.

Forest continued to enjoy the greatest amount of success in its core drug development business. One of its most successful achievements was its creation of a controlled-release technology, called Synchron, that allowed an ingested drug to be slowly released inside the body. It was this penchant for exploiting profitable niches that would later become the base of the company's meteoric rise.

In the mid-1970s, Forest Lab's management elected to jettison its lagging food businesses and to focus on the pharmaceutical market. It called on Howard Solomon, who was serving as outside counsel for Forest, to handle the divestiture. Solomon not only sold the food businesses but assumed a leadership role in the company that would eventually result in his becoming president of Forest Laboratories. Solomon's key contribution would be helping the company make the transition from a service firm to a company that actually manufactured and sold its own pharmaceuticals.

Recognizing that the big profits in the drug industry were garnered from the marketing and sale of new drugs, Forest's management had been looking for a way to break into that side of the business. The company lacked the vast resources, however, that were necessary to fund the development, testing, marketing, and distribution of an entirely new drug. Indeed, it was entirely feasible that, even if Forest could gather enough capital to fund a new drug, the venture could go bust for any number of reasons and force the company into bankruptcy. For example, a newly developed drug could fail to pass federal approval, rendering it commercially useless, or the drug could simply fail to achieve commercial appeal.

Rather than trying to develop and market new drugs, Solomon decided to steer the company toward the drug marketing business through a sort of back door—generics. Generic drugs (drugs that perform the same essential function as the brand name drugs they mimic, but cost less) were becoming increasingly popular during the late 1970s as an alternative to expensive brand name pharmaceuticals. Because generics lacked patent protection, however, profits were typically elusive—the first company to introduce the drug could make big profits for a short time, until lower-priced generics from competing companies entered the market.

Solomon was able to successfully exploit the limited opportunities offered in the generics business by focusing on Forest's controlled-release Synchron technology. Forest had already succeeded in applying the technology to drugs for several major pharmaceutical companies. Solomon correctly suspected that a viable market existed for controlled-released versions of several popular drugs. As a result, the company shifted its corporate focus to generics, realizing sound revenue and profit growth during the late 1970s and early 1980s.

Despite its success with generics, Forest Lab's management in the early 1980s was still eager to participate in the potentially lucrative business of marketing brand name, patented drugs. It had most of the tools necessary to compete in the industry—it maintained a talented research and development arm, which had long been one of its core competencies, and had accrued a degree of manufacturing, sales, and distribution knowledge through its generics business. However, Forest still lacked the resources it needed to go toe-to-toe with the industry giants.

Forest embarked on a new corporate strategy in the mid-1980s that it hoped would allow it to market and sell proprietary drugs without having to face pharmaceutical industry leaders. It would look for branded drugs that had already been developed and marketed by larger companies, but served very small customer niches. If it found a drug that it felt was under-valued, it would purchase or receive license to the product and increase its value through aggressive marketing. The reasoning behind the strategy was that the big companies tended to ignore their smaller drugs, focusing their resources instead on popular, high-profile, high-profit offerings.

The only weapon needed to carry out the new strategy that was still missing from Forest Lab's armory was a sales force. So, in 1984 Forest purchased the assets of O'Neal, Jones & Feldman Inc., a St. Louis, Missouri-based pharmaceuticals company. O'Neal, Jones & Feldman Inc. was put on the block after its president and another executive were convicted and jailed for selling a drug that had not been approved by the Food and Drug Administration (FDA). Tragically, 27 infant deaths were linked to the misbranded drug before the company pleaded guilty to 17 violations.

Forest paid $8.3 million for its new acquisition and assumed an additional $1.5 million in debt. In what turned out to be a savvy purchase, Forest immediately gained an established 71-member sales force. In a carefully plotted stratagem, the company began tagging new drugs on to its existing line of generics and branded drugs, some of which had belonged to O'Neal, Jones & Feldman Inc. For example, the company bought a drug called Esgic, a stress headache remedy, and was able to significantly boost its sales. Forest also purchased other small pharmaceutical companies, continually increasing the size and scope of its sales force and gaining access to new proprietary drugs. All the while, the company's generics business remained strong.

Forest's growth strategy during the late 1980s and early 1990s was relatively simple and straight-forward, yet few other firms were successfully implementing the same tactics. Before it purchased an undervalued drug, it would make sure that the product was a good match with the company's existing product line. By emphasizing a small number of therapeutic categories, such as asthma and headache relief, Forest was able to increase the potency of its sales force and achieve a higher number of prescriptions written per sales call. Indeed, whereas many pharmaceutical firms would send salespeople to general practitioners, offering them a range of drug lines, most Forest salespeople focused on a few groups of specialists, particularly allergists, internists, and pulmonary physicians.

Forest's knack for turning an under-valued drug into an industry over-achiever was evidenced by its 1986 purchase of Aerobid, an asthma drug, from industry giant Schering-Plough Corp. Although Aerobid sales totaled only $2.3 million annually at the time of purchase, Forest was able to generate huge returns from the drug. By 1991, in fact, Aerobid revenues had exploded to $30 million annually. Furthermore, bolstered by independent research that recommended increased use of the drug in certain applications, sales of Aerobid were expected to eventually rocket as high as $100 million. Aerobid, along with Forest's other two major drugs (Tessalon, a cough medication, and Propranolol, a generic used to treat high blood pressure), would account for over 40 percent of the company's sales by 1993.

By the early 1990s it was clear that Forest Lab's new strategy was a shrewd one, and would likely continue to produce fantastic results. Indeed, the company's annual revenues had ballooned since the mid-1980s to about $133 million by 1990, of which $30 million was profit. Sales increased to $176 million in 1991 as income leapt to approximately $40 million. Importantly, Forest's sales force had swelled to more than 500, in-

cluding more than 50 salespeople employed by subsidiaries acquired in Europe. "The large sales force is really helping the company pick up drugs that fall through the cracks," observed industry analyst Martin Bukoll in a November 1991 issue of *Crain's New York Business.*

The strength of Forest's overall operations was exhibited by a setback that it encountered in 1991. Forest had purchased a license to market a new drug called Micturin, which it hoped would become one of its primary offerings with over $100 million in annual sales. Unfortunately, the FDA, citing negative side effects, chose not to approve the drug. Although the company's stock price plummeted 30 percent, within a few months it had regained most of its value on expectations of growth from other segments of Forest's operations. Furthermore, growth of Forest's sales, earnings, and equity value continued unabated through 1991 and 1992.

As Forest Labs continued to acquire low-profile underachievers that were being ignored by the major manufacturers, sales mushroomed throughout 1993 and 1994. "We can do things that large companies can't do," explained Solomon in an October 1993 issue of the *St. Louis Post Dispatch.* "Large companies are not interested unless a product can do $100 million per year in sales." Solomon watched his company's sales jump to $239 million in 1992, $285 million in 1993, and to an amazing $348 million in 1994 (fiscal year ending March 31, 1994). Likewise, net income tracked revenue growth, soaring more than 30 percent in 1992 to $50 million, to $64 million during 1993, and then to a whopping $80 million in 1994. The company's work force had multiplied to about 1,300 worldwide.

To accommodate the company's 100 percent sales growth in less than three years, Forest hurriedly expanded its U.S. and overseas facilities. Its major St. Louis subsidiary, Forest Pharmaceuticals Inc., which accounted for roughly two-thirds of company sales in 1993, was consolidated into a newly renovated 87,000-square-foot facility replete with high-tech manufacturing and distribution systems. The company added 65,000 square feet to a manufacturing operation in Cincinnati, and boosted its New York production facility, which manufactured generics, to 150,000 square feet. Forest was also completing a major new production facility in Ireland in 1994, which would be used to supply its eastern and western European clients.

Although Forest's established brand name drugs and generics had provided consistent growth for the company since the mid-1980s, it was forced to continue its search for new acquisitions that would supplant its fading superstars. Indeed, many of the brand name drugs that it had licensed had only a few years of patent protection remaining before generics would diminish their profit margins. As a result, Forest was reliant on new additions to its pharmaceutical arsenal to sustain its rampant growth. Reflecting the company's intent to introduce new products was its growing emphasis on research and development (R&D)—annual R&D expenditures by Forest increased from $10 million in 1990 to nearly $30 million during 1993.

One of Forest's most promising new drugs going into the mid-1990s was Infasurf. Yet to be approved by the FDA in 1994, Infasurf would be used to treat and prevent respiratory disease syndrome (RDS), an affliction that occurs in 60,000 to 80,000 infants annually and can cause death or physical abnormalities. Forest had licensed the drug in 1991 and was investing large sums in testing and FDA approval. Initial tests indicated that it was more effective than existing products in treating RDS.

In addition to several new potential performers, Forest also had high hopes for Cervidil C.R., a uteril insert designed to ease births requiring artificially induced labor. The high-tech insert contained a small polymer chip infused with a drug that would essentially accelerate the birth process. Early studies showed that the device successfully induced labor in 70 percent of patients, resulting in delivery of the baby an average of ten hours earlier than patients not using the drug. Forest applied for FDA approval in December of 1993.

Although increased federal entanglement in the U.S. healthcare system threatened to stifle Forest Laboratories and its pharmaceutical industry contemporaries going into the mid-1990s, forecasts for the competitor's continued expansion were otherwise rosy. In addition to its proven strategy, Forest would continue to rely on its talented team of employees to carry it into the next century. "Our operating results and consistent growth are not based on good fortune," wrote Solomon in the company's 1993 annual report. "They are based on steady, intelligent hard work by our employees, sales and marketing personnel, scientists, and financial and administrative staffs. All our strategies would be useless without them . . . we are confident of our continued success."

Principal Subsidiaries: Forest Pharmaceuticals, Inc.; Inwood Laboratories, Inc.; Pharmax Limited (United Kingdom); Tosara Group (United Kingdom).

Further Reading:

Colwell, Carolyn, "Firm Buys Hazeltine Building," *Newsday,* March 18, 1994, Sec. 1, p. 1.
"Forest Gambit Pays Off," *European Chemical News,* September 20, 1993, p. 16.
"Forest Gets Some High Marks for Its Slate of New products," *Chemical Marketing Reporter,* January 4, 1993, p. 7.
Kamen, Robin, "Unwanted Drugs a Powerful Elixir," *Crain's New York Business,* November 4, 1991, Sec. 1, p. 3.
Steyer, Robert, "Flu Season: Firm Brings Out Drug for Epidemic," *St. Louis Post Dispatch,* October 18, 1993, p. E3BP.

—Dave Mote

IV FOURTH FINANCIAL CORPORATION

Fourth Financial Corporation

100 N. Broadway
Wichita, Kansas 67202
U.S.A.
(316) 261-4444
Fax: (316) 261-2195

Public Company
Incorporated: 1968
Employees: 3,500
Total Assets: $7.65 billion
Stock Exchanges: NASDAQ
SICs: 6021 National Commercial Banks; 6712 Bank Holding
   Companies; 6311 Life Insurance; 6321 Accident and
   Health Insurance

Fourth Financial Corporation is the largest bank holding company in Kansas. Operating more than 150 banking offices through its primary subsidiaries, Bank IV Kansas and Bank IV Oklahoma, Fourth Financial entered a period of rapid expansion in 1985 that led to large-scale company reorganizations in the early 1990s.

The history of Fourth Financial may be traced to the founding of the Fourth National Bank of Wichita, one of the oldest banks in Kansas, established by George C. Strong in 1887. By 1968, Fourth National was one of the 300 largest banks in the nation, with $290 million in assets. That year, Fourth Financial was created as a one-bank holding company, with Fourth National Bank as its sole asset, and Jordan L. Haines, executive vice-president of Fourth National, was named president of the new company. A native Kansan, Haines was noted for leading by example and for his ability to draw talented managers into the company. Haines sustained the Bank of Wichita's legacy of fiscal conservatism, which had helped it to endure bank industry crises earlier in the century.

Prior to the creation of Fourth Financial, the Bank of Wichita and other U.S. banks were bound by restrictions that hampered their growth. Strict banking regulations had been passed as early as 1933, when the Federal Banking Act of 1933 was passed in reaction to the thousands of bank failures during the Great Depression. A series of laws restricting the activities of banks and bank holding companies ensued, including the pivotal Bank Holding Company Act of 1956, which required bank holding companies to refrain from all non-banking related oper-

ations and to seek state permission before branching out into other states.

Prompted by the Federal Reserve Board as well as by complaints from members of the banking industry, Congress enacted new laws in 1966 that were designed to eliminate restrictions and create more favorable tax laws for banks. In anticipation of still more deregulation, Haines and fellow executives formed Fourth Financial in 1968. By moving to a holding company format, Fourth Financial was able to conduct certain activities from which it would otherwise be barred. Importantly, new legislation in 1970 allowed multi-bank holding companies to operate in several non-banking financial markets.

Fourth Financial realized sound, steady growth during the 1970s and early 1980s under Haines' direction, despite general banking industry malaise. Indeed, the industry experienced increasing competition during that period from other financial institutions and investment vehicles that were draining deposits out of traditional banks. Furthermore, Fourth Financial was constrained by state laws that kept it from expanding outside of Wichita. Although Fourth Financial was able to attract new clients through such instruments as Certificates of Deposits (CDs), expanding its asset base three-fold between 1968 and 1982 to about $1 billion, profit margins slipped.

Fourth Financial's rapid rise during the 1980s was triggered by state legislation signed by Kansas Governor John Carlin in 1982. In an effort to project a more progressive business image for his state, Carlin passed a law allowing bank holding companies to purchase as much as 25 percent interest in other banks. In addition, another bill was pending that would allow holding companies to start buying 100 percent of other banks. Haines and fellow executives viewed the deregulation as an opportunity to begin expanding their organization statewide. Broadening Fourth Financial's scope, they reasoned, would eventually allow them to reduce costs through economies of scale and become more competitive with other financial institutions, thus increasing market share and boosting profit margins.

Between 1982 and 1985, Haines and his team purchased the maximum allowable shares of five Kansas banks as part of a carefully conceived strategy. The banks in which Fourth Financial invested had several characteristics in common. Each was located in a community with more than 10,000 residents and was a county seat. In addition, all the banks were near an institution of higher learning and had assets of $80 million to $100 million. Fourth Financial's management team believed that those traits would ensure high-quality assets. Assuming that the pending bill would also pass, Fourth Financial arranged for each of the banks to allow it to ultimately assume 100 percent ownership.

By 1985, Fourth Financial had $1.35 billion in assets, representing a 35 percent increase since passage of the 1982 legislation. When Kansas passed the multi-bank holding company laws in July 1985, Fourth Financial was positioned for even more rapid growth. The company immediately assumed full control of its five subsidiary banks, and within nine months it had purchased three more banks. By March 1986, Fourth Financial was the largest bank in the state, with assets totaling $2.5 billion. That year, the company renamed all of its subsidiaries

"BANK IV" to promote a sense of unity and to simplify marketing tasks. Over the next four years, moreover, Fourth Financial would bring 16 more institutions into the BANK IV fold, raising its total base of assets to more than $4 billion and cementing its role as a regional banking powerhouse.

While Fourth Financial's growth was exemplary in the banking industry, it also reflected a dynamic trend of consolidation within the U.S. banking industry during this time. As smaller banks faced increasing competitive pressures from less-regulated, non-bank financial institutions, the percentage of U.S. assets held by commercial banks dropped from about 37 percent in the late 1970s to 25 percent by the early 1990s. Furthermore, computers and electronic banking devices were making it easier for banks to operate across broad regions. As a result, the number of independent banking entities in the United States plunged from about 13,000 in 1983 to less than 10,000 by 1990. At the same time, the number of multi-bank holding companies grew through acquisition from about 300 to around 1,000.

In 1985, Haines selected Ron Baldwin to oversee Fourth Financial's aggressive buyout program. The 37-year-old Baldwin had started working for the bank in the early 1970s while he was a student at Wichita State University. Although he took a job in Dallas after graduation, he returned to his home state in 1976 to work for Fourth Financial. Baldwin rose quickly through the ranks. After being assigned head of the acquisition squad, Baldwin assembled a group of managers with expertise in targeting, analyzing, and negotiating buyouts. When the 1985 laws were passed, Baldwin and team advanced. "Every year we sit down and look at what kind of banks we want to buy, what cities we would like to be in, and what the best banks are within those cities, and we kind of plan an attack," Baldwin explained in the July 16, 1990 issue of *Wichita Business Journal*.

Between 1985 and 1990, Baldwin supervised the purchase of 24 banks at an average rate of one every 75 days. This pace surged to one per month during 1990, when Fourth acquired several troubled savings and loan institutions at rock-bottom prices. Analyzing a plethora of potential deals, Baldwin selected only those that would complement the overall organization. After Baldwin and his crew completed a new purchase, they were then charged with overseeing its integration into the BANK IV network, which meant streamlining computer systems, allaying customer concerns, and absorbing the new institution's financial products into their own portfolio of offerings.

By 1990, the original Fourth National Bank of Wichita organization had become part of a massive $4.2 billion corporation, only 30 percent of which was attributable to the pre-acquisition Bank of Wichita. After presiding over a 28-year era of growth and prosperity for Fourth Financial, 21 of which were served as president or chairperson, Haines announced his retirement in 1990. Before he left, however, he initiated a reorganization of the company to prepare for it for its next phase of expansion, slated to begin in July 1992. Indeed, new legislation was pending in Kansas which, when passed, would allow Fourth Financial and its Kansas peers to extend their reach into other states. The passage of this law would prove timely, as Fourth National was just a few acquisitions away from hitting a ceiling on the amount of deposits a single bank could control under Kansas laws.

Before his departure, Haines wanted to organize and streamline Fourth Financial. Toward that end, he consolidated many management functions into the holding company headquarters and assembled a non-banking division to manage Fourth Financial's services, including credit card, mortgage, and insurance-related services. Haines also merged several of the company's holdings into a subsidiary called BANK IV Kansas City. During this time, acquisition activity continued; in June 1990, Fourth Financial picked up Anchor Savings, a thrift with six branches and $565 million in assets.

Among Haines' most important acts, before his departure, was that of bringing in outsider Darrell G. Knudson as chief executive. Knudson assumed the leadership role in July 1991 and immediately intensified Haines' restructuring efforts. One month after taking the helm, Knudson announced 250 layoffs as part of a plan to cut annual expenses by $15 million. Moreover, the following month, he combined all of the holding company's 13 separately chartered bank divisions into one subsidiary, BANK IV Kansas. "I didn't come here to manage what was. I came here to create what can be," Knudson responded to his critics in the September 27, 1991 issue of *Wichita Business Journal*. Knudson also slowed the company's acquisition pace. Nevertheless, in April 1992, Fourth Financial picked up two more banks with about $120 million in assets.

Some insiders were surprised to see Knudson, a Minnesota banker, brought in to run one of the state's biggest and oldest financial institutions. However, Knudson's resume included a long list of credentials that were highly applicable to Fourth Financial's situation. Knudson had spent 32 years with Minnesota-based First Financial System Inc., a multi-state holding company that mirrored the interstate institution that Fourth Financial was striving to become. During the late 1980s, Knudson had orchestrated more than 2,000 layoffs, managed the integration of several large out-of-state banking systems into First Financial System, and conducted a massive cost-cutting effort that restored the organization's profitability.

Knudson picked up many of the skills that had made him successful in the banking industry while growing up in Centerville, South Dakota, a town of 1,200 people 35 miles south of Sioux Falls. On weekends, Knudson accompanied his father, an insurance salesman, on sales calls. "He would always give me tips and ideas about why the customer needed the insurance coverage," Knudson recollected in the September 27, 1991 *Wichita Business Journal*. An avid sports fan, Knudson eventually abandoned his plans for coaching in favor of career in business. Nevertheless, he maintained his competitive mindset; "The game we play is creating value every day for customers," Knudson related.

In 1992, shortly after Kansas passed its interstate banking laws, the reorganized Fourth Financial launched its assault on the Oklahoma banking market. The company purchased three banks in the Tulsa area with $780 million in assets and organized all of their branches into a single subsidiary, BANK IV Oklahoma. Moreover, having found a way to get around the deposit ceiling in Kansas, Fourth Financial also picked up five new banking systems in the state, with $430 million in assets. By the end of 1992, in fact, Fourth Financial had grown into an interstate, multi-bank holding company with $6 billion in assets, 2,600 employees, and nearly 100 offices in 30 communities. The bank's net income topped $50 million in 1992 from total revenues of about $275 million.

Although Fourth Financial greatly increased its debt load in 1992, the company was able to reduce its portfolio of bad loans left over from the most recent recession and to achieve marked profitability gains. Furthermore, Fourth Financial was successfully expanding most of its existing operations by bolstering customer service and emphasizing a range of new financial services. For example, Fourth Financial became the fifth largest investment brokerage house in Kansas in 1993 and increased its fee income from annuity sales to more than $2 million. The company also expanded efforts in mortgage, consumer finance, and trust services.

Besides buying banks, cutting costs, and stressing fee services, Fourth Financial boosted its profitability in the early 1990s with the implementation of the latest technology. A high-tech database marketing system, for instance, allowed staffers to organize and track thousands of varied transactions on a daily basis. The system helped the marketing department pinpoint the most profitable customers and market products targeted at their specific needs. Similarly, in 1994, Fourth Financial unveiled a new automated teller machine that perform virtually any transaction normally handled by a teller.

As profitability climbed in 1993 and 1994, Fourth Financial continued to fortify its stronghold in the Oklahoma and Kansas markets. The company completed nine more buyouts in 1993, mostly in Oklahoma, bringing the organization's total asset base to more than $6.7 billion. A string of new acquisitions early in 1994, moreover, increased Fourth Financial's assets to more then $8 billion, making it nearly dominant in its key Oklahoma markets, Oklahoma City and Tulsa. Total net income rose 20 percent in 1993, to $76 million, as the company's work force reached approximately 3,500. In less than ten years, the bank had blossomed from a mid-sized Wichita-based institution into a regional banking powerhouse. "We've made good time, and we're going the distance," asserted Knudson in Fourth Financial's 1993 annual report.

Principal Subsidiaries: Bank IV Kansas, N.A.; Bank IV Oklahoma, N.A.

Further Reading:

Bumgarner, Kevin, "Darrell Knudson: New Chairman Leads Bank IV System Through Sea of Change," *Wichita Business Journal,* September 27, 1991, p. 11.

Bumgarner, Kevin, "Wichita Banks Take Different Paths Toward Interstate," *Wichita Business Journal,* November 29, 1991, p. 1.

Curtis, Bruce, "Fourth Financial Income Up," *Tulsa World,* April 15, 1994, p. B1.

"Defining the Financial Field of Play," *Wichita Commerce,* September 1991, p. 12.

Gilliam, Carey, "Fourth Financial Merger Creates State's Largest Bank," *Kansas City Business Journal,* August 30, 1991, p. 21.

Gilmore, Casey, "Fast-Growing Fourth Licks Lips for Interstate Banking," Kansas City Business Journal, April 24, 1992, p. 1.

History of Fourth Financial Corporation, Wichita, KS: Fourth Financial Corporation, 1994.

Mullins, Jesse, "Fourth's Team Handles All Acquisitions," *Wichita Business Journal*, July 16, 1990, p. 21.

Mullins, Jesse, "Haines Departure Only One Element of Fourth Changes," *Wichita Business Journal,* December 17, 1990, p. 1.

Mullins, Jesse, "Ron Baldwin: Fourth Financial Operations Chief Oversees Company's Aggressive Acquisition Policy," *Wichita Business Journal,* July 16, 1990, p. 8.

Thomas, James H., *A History of the Fourth National Bank and Trust Company,* Oklahoma City: Western Heritage Books, Inc., 1980.

"Who's Doing It and Why," *Wichita Business,* March 1986, p. 21.

—Dave Mote

Franklin Quest Co.

2200 West Parkway Blvd.
Salt Lake City, UT 84119
U.S.A.
(801) 975-1776
Fax: (801) 977-1431

Public Company
Incorporated: 1983 as Franklin Institute, Inc.
Employees: 2,000
Sales: $216 million
Stock Exchanges: New York
SICs: 8310 Consulting

Franklin Quest Co. is a leading provider of time management training seminars and products. The company's offerings are based on its comprehensive "Franklin System," which is designed to help individuals identify goals and prioritize tasks. Franklin Quest has sales offices on four continents, operates more than 50 retail stores in North America, and sells its own software applications.

Franklin Institute, Inc., was officially founded in 1983 by Hyrum W. Smith, Dick Winwood, Dennis Webb, and Lynn Webb—Senator Robert F. Bennett joined the company the following year as chairman of the board. However, the company was actually started by Smith in 1981. The 37-year-old Smith, a graduate of nearby Brigham Young University, decided to start a business providing management seminars. He set up shop in his basement and was soon providing his homemade management courses to groups of business executives.

Benjamin Franklin served as the inspiration and guiding philosophy for the courses. In fact, Smith attributes his own achievements and the success of his company to Franklin's ideas about human values and quality of life. It was after reading Franklin's autobiography that Smith decided he would build his own time management program based on Franklin's proven self-improvement philosophy. Smith interpreted Franklin's philosophy to mean that peoples' happiness and inner peace do not come from owning things, but from identifying what is important to them and then making their life conform with those goals.

"Time is the stuff life is made of," Franklin is quoted as saying, and few Americans have used time as effectively as Franklin. In his 84 years of living, Franklin rose from apprentice to statesmen, making valuable contributions along the way in the areas of science, social philosophy, education, and the arts. Franklin achieved greatness, in part, through his homemade self-improvement and time management system. The program was based on a checklist of 13 virtues, which included frugality, industry, sincerity, and temperance. "If you're not doing what you value, you don't value yourself, so you won't value your time and make good use of it," Smith posited in the December 1992 issue of *Success*.

Smith developed, based on Franklin's ideas, a time management and motivational seminar program. The program's basic goal was relatively simple: to help people realize what they really want to accomplish, to help them do things for the right reasons, and to motivate them toward action. Although he targeted his courses primarily to corporate groups and business executives, he engaged in relatively little formal marketing after he started giving his seminars. Instead, he focused on creating an excellent product and allowing word-of-mouth to do the rest. Franklin Institute's guiding tenets became "How many people can we reach?" and "Do we have a product that works?"

After joining forces with Franklin Institute's co-founders in 1983, Smith and his team began giving their seminars all over the United States to just about anybody that would listen. In an effort to build a reputation, Smith accepted every opportunity to speak. Sometimes he found himself tutoring groups of only three or four people after expecting to work with a gathering of 30 or more. Smith would later calculate that between 1983 and 1990 he had spent four-and-a-half years either on a plane or in a hotel room. However, it was Franklin Institute's efforts in those early years that provided the foundation for its rapid rise during the late 1980s and early 1990s.

Franklin introduced the Franklin Day Planner in 1984 as a means of helping its seminar participants to better implement the Franklin time management system. The Day Planner consisted of a ring-binder with paper planning aids, monthly and annual calendars, and various personal management aids. Besides boosting revenue from its seminars, Franklin benefited by selling refill materials every year to its growing base of customers. In fact, Franklin estimated that approximately 90 percent of the people that purchased the planners through the seminar later bought refill materials or other products related to the Day Planner, a figure which still holds true.

In addition to using the Franklin Day Planner to add value to its time management seminars, Franklin Institute also offered the Planner and several related time management products beginning in 1984 through a catalog. The catalog represented Franklin's strategy of maintaining strict control over all distribution and customer service operations. By ensuring that its customers interacted only with trained Franklin employees, management reasoned that it could achieve much greater customer loyalty than it could if it sold its products through independent retailers.

Franklin's management seminars and Day Planner achieved immediate market penetration. By 1985, in fact, people that had heard about the Franklin System and wanted to try it provided a steady stream of walk-in traffic into Franklin's warehouse and catalog distribution facilities, demonstrating the company's growing reputation. As a result, Smith and his co-managers decided to experiment by opening a local retail store that sold the Day Planner and a growing inventory of related Franklin merchandise. The initial success of the store prompted the company to initiate an aggressive outlet store program. Staffed by trained Franklin Institute employees, the stores would be situated in high-traffic areas, such as malls, that would attract walk-in customers. Because many of them would be unfamiliar with the Franklin System, the stores would also serve as a marketing tool for the company's seminars.

Franklin Institute realized fast growth in its product sales during the early 1980s. However, its Franklin System training services remained the focus of its efforts during that period, only later giving way to the popularity of the Day Planner. Although the company relied heavily on word-of-mouth advertising, it also marketed its seminars by means of a direct sales force to institutions and the general public. Franklin, over time, developed a seminar entitled ''Increasing Personal Productivity Through Effective Time Management.'' The ''consultants'' that administered the seminars were certified by Franklin only after a rigorous training program. Attendees received a Franklin Planner along with instructional materials and order forms for new filler materials.

Franklin often worked with institutional clients beforehand to create a tailored seminar that would emphasize the particular goals of that organization. During the 1980s, Franklin developed an impressive list of seminar clients, including MCI, Intel, Procter & Gamble, Eastman Kodak, and the Internal Revenue Service. It also offered those customers its Franklin Flex Training (FFT) service, whereby employees of those institutions were trained and certified to give video presentations of Franklin's seminars to in-house employees. Franklin reached individuals and smaller companies through standardized public seminars that it offered in selected cities throughout the United States, and later in Hong Kong, Canada, and the United Kingdom.

The 1980s proved to be a perfect time for Franklin Institute to enlarge its fledgling time management company. Indeed, as U.S. corporations suffered from intense foreign competition and slowing domestic market growth during that decade, they began to search for ways to increase productivity and efficiency. In addition to laying off millions of middle managers, U.S. corporations and institutions turned to consultants like Franklin Institute to get more out of their decision makers. Franklin offered a seemingly perfect solution to much of what ailed corporate America. Through one or a series of simple seminars, it would essentially show a management team or group of individuals how to achieve a higher set of goals in a shorter span of time. Furthermore, it would boost their morale by helping them to focus on what they really wanted out of life. Franklin would even give them the tools they needed, such as the Day Planner, to make it happen.

By the end of the 1980s, Franklin Institute was garnering more than $10 million annually from its seminars. Importantly, however, sales of its Day Planner and related time management products had taken off. As seminar revenues swelled to $10.5 million in 1989, sales of Franklin's products ballooned to a whopping $20.3 million. Although much of the growth in product shipments was a result of increased first-time catalog and

retail sales, Franklin was also starting to benefit from its strategy of cultivating customer loyalty. While Franklin steadily attracted new customers through seminars, its old customers continued to purchase annual refills for their planners and to buy new Franklin offerings.

The strong growth of Franklin Institute and some of its competitors during the 1980s prompted many analysts to dismiss the popularity of time management systems as a corollary of the go-go 1980s. According to the critics, daily planners and motivational management seminars were simply a fad, destined to fade away when people realized the planners often consumed more time than they actually saved. Franklin rejected these appraisals outright, believing that its system offered a truly unique and effective method of giving greater meaning to the lives of its customers. Franklin's patrons supported their convictions—as the United States plunged into a deep recession during the late 1980s and early 1990s, Franklin's revenue and profit growth accelerated.

To augment sales from its profitable catalog and seminar divisions, Franklin decided to significantly expand its retail store operations in the early 1990s. It began opening stores, mostly in shopping malls, in areas that already had many Franklin clients. They hoped that existing buyers would supplement new customer sales. The strategy was extremely successful. From just $710,000 in retail store sales in 1987, revenues vaulted to more than $34 million by 1993 from a chain of 28 outlets in 14 states. Furthermore, catalog sales ballooned at a record rate during that period, pushing total sales of Franklin products to $60.5 million in 1991 and to a staggering $130 million in 1993. Revenues from seminars gained at a slower, though still healthy pace, reaching $35.5 million by 1993.

In 1992, Franklin Institute, Inc., went public, selling five million shares on the New York Stock Exchange at a price of $15.50 per share. The company also changed its name to Franklin Quest Co., reflecting its ongoing diversification into markets other than training and seminars. The public offering was performed, in large part, to raise $23 million in cash for Franklin's planned purchase of three separate companies that provided training, business communication, and various consulting services. Franklin expected the acquisitions, which would be completed in 1994, to enable it to penetrate a range of new markets and to bolster the presence of its existing divisions. The price of the shares nearly doubled by late 1993 to more than $30.

In addition to market diversification, Franklin's growth plan in the early 1990s included a steady stream of new product introductions. The new merchandise would allow it to capitalize on a loyal base of customers already comfortable with purchasing its goods. One of its most successful entries was the pocket planner. Introduced in 1992, the planner was designed to fit in a suit coat pocket or small purse while offering the same features as the popular Franklin Day Planner. After only one year Franklin had shipped more than 70,000 pocket planners for a gain of $7 million. Similarly, the company brought out a line of decorative filler pages for its planners; they were highlighted in floral patterns to coincide with the seasons of the year. Sales of that line topped a surprising $1.6 million during the first five months of 1993.

Perhaps Franklin's most notable new endeavor during the early 1990s was its foray into personal information management (PIM) computer software. In late 1991, Franklin unveiled its ASCEND software program, which was designed to be used in conjunction with the paper-based Day Planner or as a stand-alone time management system. The program was offered in a complete package with time management guide books and audio cassette tapes. ASCEND represented Franklin's effort to capture a piece of the burgeoning market for computer-based time management devices, such as personal digital assistants (hand-held electronic personal information devices).

Going into 1994, Franklin Quest continued to expand into new markets and to increase sales of its existing products and seminars. Since 1987, Franklin had trained more than one million people, including 280,000 during 1993. Franklin had overseas sales offices in Taiwan, Great Britain, Hong Kong, Japan, and Australia, and was targeting several new foreign markets. Furthermore, during the first six months of 1994 Franklin opened 11 new retail stores and had developed plans to start several more before the end of the year. As if the company itself were a testament to the effectiveness of the Franklin System used by its managers, Franklin's sales and profit growth continued to accelerate into 1994. The 3 million people that were regularly using the Franklin System suggested a rich future for the company.

Further Reading:

''A Plan for Success,'' *Success*, December 1992.

O Laughlin, Lynette, and Karey Worton, ''A Look at Franklin Quest Corp.,'' *Daily Herald*, October 10, 1993, Sec. BUS.

Prospectus: 2,500,000 Shares Franklin Quest Common Stock, New York: Merrill Lynch & Co., Smith Barney Shearson Inc., January 24, 1994.

Putnam, Richard, ''Franklin Quest Co. Acquires Shipley Associates, a Leading Business Communication Training and Consulting Firm,'' *PR Newswire*, December 21, 1993.

—Dave Mote

Fujitsu-ICL Systems Inc.

5429 LBJ Freeway
Dallas, Texas 75420
U.S.A.
(214) 716-8300
Fax: (214) 716-8586

*Joint Subsidiary of ICL PLC (80 percent) and Fujitsu (20
    percent)*
Incorporated: 1977 as ICL Inc.
Employees: 1850
Sales: $240 million
SICs: 7372 Prepackaged Software

Fujitsu-ICL Systems Inc. is the leading supplier of supermarket scanning systems in North America. The company provides information technology to specific retail markets, mainly large specialty stores, such as the well-known Pier 1 Imports chain, home center stores, and supermarkets. Fujitsu-ICL is also the third largest supplier of automated teller machines in the U.S. market, and holds a worldwide market share of over ten percent. Other major products include hand-held computer terminals. Fujitsu-ICL's major parent, the British computer company ICL PLC, has been a leader in the "open systems" movement in Europe, providing standardized software which can be used on many different computer systems, and Fujitsu-ICL Systems Inc. is similarly a leading supplier of open systems in the United States, particularly to the retail market.

The current company was formed out of a 1992 merger of ICL's North American operations with those of the Fujitsu company. ICL is the largest British computer firm, and one of the largest information technology firms in Europe. A long-time rival of IBM overseas, ICL first attempted to crack the American market in the early 1970s. Its first American subsidiary, called ICL (USA) was founded in 1974, but its business was confined exclusively to the New York metropolitan area. In three years ICL (USA) installed only 20 computer systems, and in 1977 the company was scrapped. ICL regrouped its North American operations that year, putting together a larger firm out of a merger with the Singer company. ICL acquired Singer's Cogar Corp. subsidiary and some of the manufacturing facilities of Singer's Business Machines division. Cogar had a line of intelligent data entry systems, and manufactured "point-of-sale" (POS) terminals, which were computers for use by retailers.

The new American ICL subsidiary, called ICL Inc., moved its headquarters from New York City to East Brunswick, New Jersey, and concentrated its manufacturing and software development operations in Utica, New York. Unlike ICL's earlier American effort, the new company was headed largely by British executives. ICL Inc. intended to market the new products it had acquired from Singer, but it would emphasize sale of ICL mainframe computer systems imported from England. The new company planned to double its marketing force and expand beyond the New York area.

Over the next few years, ICL Inc. developed a network of over 40 dealers. It opened a Distributive Systems Division headquartered in Irving, Texas, and an Advanced Systems Division in Falls Church, Virginia. New product announcements focused on the company's small-to-medium size business systems, meant to compete with IBM's System/34 and System/8. The small-to-medium sized business systems market was crowded; it included products from IBM as well as Burroughs, NCR, Univac, Basic Four, Qantel, Wang Laboratories, Cado, and Jacquard. ICL Inc.'s product line included both its System 10, which it had taken over from Cogar, and the ME29, imported from England.

Beginning in 1981, ICL Inc.'s British parent had been collaborating with the Japanese firm Fujitsu to upgrade the quality of ICL's mainframe computers. Fujitsu supplied ICL with its state-of-the-art semiconductor technology, which ICL badly needed in order to keep up with its rival IBM. So by the mid 1980s, ICL Inc.'s management was convinced that its small-to-midsize systems were technologically as good as IBM's, yet the American market was still very difficult to penetrate. The company made a decision not to try to compete across the board with a wide range of products, but to focus on specific market areas. The company concentrated on vertical market applications of small business computers, but it also eyed what seemed to be a broader market in multifunction workstations. Despite the apparent wisdom of this approach, a 1985 *ComputerWorld* article characterized the company's existence as "stop-and-go."

Nevertheless, the company kept itself in business, and over the next few years found a flourishing marketing niche, as retailing became ICL Inc.'s fastest growing area. In the late 1980s, the company's business in that area grew by 40 percent a year. ICL had a five percent market share by 1988, primarily selling to large home center stores. Sales in the retail niche totalled about $60 million a year in 1988. In that year, business increased significantly through a merger when parent company ICL PLC spent $90 million to purchase a company called Datachecker Systems from the National Semiconductor Corp.

Datachecker, a California company, sold laser scanners, POS terminals, and small computers and software to retailers. It sold mainly to home centers and specialist retailers, but its principal product was scanning systems for supermarkets. The company had sales of about $200 million in 1988, and it had been profitable for twelve years, though around the time of the merger with ICL it had been losing money. Intense competition with the ubiquitous IBM and another company, NCR, had caused Datachecker to lose ground. Datachecker became part of ICL's Retail Systems Division based in Stamford, Connecticut, almost doubling the size of that already growing business, and the name was changed to ICL/Datachecker.

ICL/Datachecker became the third largest company competing in the U.S. market, holding a market share of about 35 percent of supermarkets with installed point of sale systems. Even though the total number of supermarkets in the United States was declining, automation was becoming more important at the end of the 1980s, as stores installed more complicated and expensive programs. ICL/Datachecker positioned itself to sell the most advanced systems available. One new product the company marketed was a system of electronic shelf labels that displayed the product identification and price. These labels could be automatically updated by one central personal computer, and though the cost of installation was high, it would save the user money in labor. ICL/Datachecker also worked on ways to network existing supermarket software systems. And where the old Datachecker systems had run only on Datachecker hardware, ICL/Datachecker modified its product to run on IBM-compatible machines, making it a viable choice for many former IBM customers.

The next big change in ICL's U.S. operations came in 1992. In 1990 Fujitsu, which had already been involved in joint ventures with ICL, decided to buy 80 percent of the British company. Fujitsu had a hands-off attitude toward its new subsidiary, and ICL management maintained its independence to a large degree. But in 1992 the two companies consolidated some of their operations. Fujitsu took control of 80 percent of ICL's marketing operation in Australia, New Zealand, and the South Pacific, and in exchange, ICL gained 80 percent control of the new company that emerged when the North American operations of ICL and Fujitsu were combined. The new company, Fujitsu-ICL Systems Inc., put together ICL's retail systems operations with two divisions of Fujitsu called Fujitsu Systems of America and Fujitsu Customer Service of America. The combined companies had mostly retail-related computer sales. Fujitsu-ICL's annual retail sales almost doubled after the merger, to $350 million, though the company remained in the number three spot in the U.S. retail systems market, still behind IBM and NCR.

The combination was a logical one. Fujitsu Systems of America was a competitor of ICL, but it had carved out its own special niche in the retail market, focussing on specialty stores, especially apparel shops. Its customers included chains such as the County Seat clothing stores, the chain of Barney's department stores in New York, and the large paint store Sherwin-Williams. Its leading product, the Atrium 9000, was designed for specialty stores, mass merchandisers, and department stores, and it doubled as both point of sale register and personal computer. Fujitsu System's other big product was automated teller machines. The automated teller machine market was dominated by NCR Corp. and InterBold, which was a joint venture of IBM and Diebold, but Fujitsu had major customers such as the CombiNet banks in Boston. Some of Fujitsu's machines had special features, such as a machine for drive-through banks that adjusted itself to the height of each passing car and machines for the blind with voice guidance and braille indicators.

In 1993 Fujitsu-ICL entered an agreement with Applied Communications Inc. to explore further technological developments of self-service banking machines. The company gained further inroads in the financial service market by supplying machines to Meridian Bancorp in Pennsylvania, one of the country's largest owners of automated tellers, and winning a contract in 1994 to provide automated banking services at many of America's major airports. With sales of about 1,500 terminals, Fujitsu-ICL lagged far behind its two main competitors in automated teller sales worldwide, as InterBold shipped over 18,000 terminals in 1993 and NCR shipped over 26,000. But when only the U.S. market was considered, Fujitsu-ICL did much better; 1,200 of its automated teller machines were for the domestic market, compared to about 4,000 for InterBold and 5,000 for NCR. And there were signs that Fujitsu-ICL was gaining ground. In June of 1994 the company signed an exclusive deal with the Star Banc Corp. to supply approximately 100 teller machines a year for three years. The contract was noteworthy not only because it was worth approximately $6 million to Fujitsu-ICL, but also because Cincinnati-based Star Banc was in the heart of rival territory—both NCR and InterBold were Ohio-based companies. The newly-formed Fujitsu-ICL aimed to increase its presence in the retail market, and the Star Banc deal was perhaps an indicator of the company's success.

Further Reading:

Barthel, Matt, ''California Federal Buys Fujitsu ATMs for Disabled,'' *American Banker,* May 28, 1991, p. 3.

Bartolik, Peter, ''European Firms Take Varied Aim at U.S. Market,'' *ComputerWorld,* July 1, 1985, p. 1.

Fallon, James, ''National Agrees to Sell Datachecker to ICL for $90M,'' *Electronic News,* December 19, 1988, p. 10.

''Fujitsu, ICL Set Three Units,'' *Electronic News,* February 24, 1992, p. 1.

''Fujitsu-ICL's ATMs in Airline Clubs,'' *American Banker,* May 9, 1994, p. 13A.

Hooper, Laurence, ''Fujitsu, ICL to Consolidate Some Businesses,'' *Wall Street Journal,* February 21, 1992, p. 7A.

''ICL, Fujitsu Join Forces to Pool Efforts, Technology around Globe,'' *Supermarket Business,* March 1992, p. 17.

''ICL, Inc., Brings ME29 CPU to U.S. Market,'' *Electronic News,* June 16, 1980, p. 18.

''ICL (U.S.) Offers Upgraded System 10,'' *Electronic News,* January 21, 1980, p. 30.

''Independence as a State of Mind,'' *Economist,* April 10, 1993, p. 67.

McLean, Joe, ''ICL Regroups U.S. Staff in New Marketing Effort,'' *Electronic News,* January 10, 1977, p. 32.

''Meridian Bancorp Picks Fujitsu as Principal Source of ATMs,'' *American Banker,* February 18, 1993, p. 3.

Moran, Robert, ''OS/2 Suits Barney's for Point-of-Sale Net,'' *ComputerWorld,* August 21, 1989, p. 41.

Murphy, Liz, ''Fujitsu Sells Its Way into the Race,'' *Sales & Marketing Management,* May 14, 1984, pp. 41–44.

Savage, J. A., ''National Semi Sells Datachecker Division,'' *ComputerWorld,* December 19, 1988, p. 71.

Schneidman, Diane, ''Technology Drives Today's Financial Marketing Plans,'' *Marketing News,* April 24, 1987, p. 14.

Simmons, Tim, ''Big Front-End Changes Coming as Aging Systems Are Replaced,'' *Supermarket News,* May 22, 1989, p. 14.

Tucker, Tracy, ''Star Banc and Fujitsu in Exclusive ATM Deal,'' *American Banker,* June 17, 1994, p. 17.

''U.S. ATM Market Grows Better, Not Much Bigger,'' *Bank Technology News,* May 1994, p. 8.

''Weighing a Self-Service Future,'' *Bank Systems & Technology,* November 1993, p. 56.

—A. Woodward

GAYLORD ENTERTAINMENT COMPANY

Gaylord Entertainment Company

2802 Opryland Drive
Nashville, Tennessee 37214
U.S.A.
(615) 885-1000
Fax: (615) 871-5732

Public Company
Incorporated: 1925 as the Oklahoma Publishing Company
Employees: 4,600
Sales: $.62 billion
Stock Exchanges: New York
SICs: 4833 Television Broadcasting Stations; 4841 Cable and
   Other Pay Television Services; 7996 Amusement Parks
   and Hotels

Gaylord Entertainment Company is a diversified entertainment and communications company. Through its entertainment, cable network, broadcasting, and television companies, Gaylord focuses on serving the country music market. Its chief source of revenue is Opryland USA in Nashville, Tennessee, which includes the Grand Ole Opry and the Opryland Hotel.

The Gaylord and Dickinson families began what would become the Gaylord Entertainment Company in the Oklahoma Territory in 1903—Oklahoma would not become a part of the Union until 1907. The company was created as a newspaper publishing business to capitalize on the increasing demand for news in the burgeoning region. The two families incorporated the business in 1925 as the Oklahoma Publishing Company.

Realizing the future potential of radio, which was still in its infancy during the early 1920s, the Gaylords and Dickinsons branched out into the broadcasting industry in 1928 with the purchase of WKY-AM, a station in Oklahoma City. WKY, which started broadcasting in 1920, was the first radio station to operate west of the Mississippi and is the second oldest station in the United States. Shortly after Oklahoma Publishing bought it, WKY gained stature as a "beacon of hope" in the Oklahoma Dust Bowl during the Great Depression. Interestingly, another radio station of import to Oklahoma Publishing's future was getting its start in the mid-1920s: WSM-AM, of Nashville, began broadcasting in 1925. It was WSM's announcer, George D. Hay, that gave birth to the renowned Grand Ole Opry with his country music radio show.

Under the direction of cofounder Edward King Gaylord, Oklahoma Publishing Company prospered during the early and mid-1900s with its radio and publishing operations. Beginning in the late 1940s, the company made a seemingly natural progression into the television broadcasting industry. In fact, television became a primary focus of the company during 1950s and 1960s. Gaylord snapped up several stations, including KTVT in Dallas, WVTV in Milwaukee, Houston's KHTV, and KSTW in Seattle; at one point, the company was operating seven stations. Oklahoma Publishing Company's television and radio operations were organized under its wholly owned Gaylord Broadcasting subsidiary.

By the early 1970s, Oklahoma Publishing Company was a multimillion-dollar mini-conglomerate primarily comprising radio, television, and newspaper companies. Because the company was privately owned by the Gaylord family, financial and operating data was generally not made available to the public. Furthermore, the Gaylords led relatively private lives and had a reputation for keeping a firm grip on the company. Amazingly, Edward King Gaylord, who had helped start the company in 1903 at the age of 32, was still actively managing the company in the early 1970s. Edward King died in 1974 at the age of 101. His son, Edward L., became chief executive. An Oklahoma billionaire, Edward was described in the media as rich, ultra conservative, and reclusive.

Gaylord continued to successfully oversee the publishing and broadcasting business founded by his father. The company still owned its original radio station and newspapers and had added another television station the year of Edward King's death. But Gaylord also tried branching out into several new ventures. In the mid-1980s, for example, he made an unsuccessful bid to purchase the Texas Rangers baseball organization—because of his disdain for reporters, Gaylord had his Oklahoma newspapers carry stories (about the failed acquisition) from a Dallas newspaper. The business foray that would bring Gaylord the greatest amount of success and would thrust his company into the national spotlight was his 1983 purchase of Nashville-based Grand Ole Opry and the Opryland Hotel.

Opryland was the culmination of over 50 years of the Grand Ole Opry, which began in WSM-AM radio. Although the Opry was dealt a nearly lethal blow by the popularity of television and rock music during the 1950s, by the mid-1960s the show was regaining its appeal to a mainstream audience. By the late 1960s, in fact, interest in the Opry was surging to such an extent that WSM Inc., its owner, elected to build a new complex to replace the decaying Ryman Auditorium. It also wanted to capitalize on the Opry's popularity by offering related tourist attractions. WSM purchased a 406-acre site and broke ground on an Opry theme park in 1970. The theme park, a musical show park that emphasized live country music, opened in 1972. Two years later, the Grand Ole Opry moved into its new home not far from the theme park. In 1977, moreover, WSM opened the Opryland Hotel to accommodate a growing supply of tourists.

Opryland's vigorous expansion during the late 1970s and early 1980s caught the eye of Gaylord, who viewed the Opry's broadcasting and entertainment operations as a comfortable fit with Gaylord Broadcasting. When WSM's parent corporation went hunting for a buyer for the Opry complex, Gaylord made himself available. In September of 1983, Gaylord purchased the Opry properties for $250 million; the transaction would later be called one of the entertainment industry's better bargains. Gaylord renamed the complex Opryland USA. He also maintained the savvy management team that directs the enterprise and develops a strategy designed to help the Opry exploit the rising popularity of country music. Although Nashville locals feared that Dallas-based Gaylord Broadcasting might start selling off Opry properties, Gaylord soon allayed their worries.

Gaylord assumed a minimal role in the management of Opryland, choosing to leave E. W. "Bud" Wendell in charge of the complex. Wendell had started out selling insurance for WSM's parent corporation. After a series of transfers and promotions, the 56-year-old Wendell found himself in charge of WSM's Grand Ole Opry in the late 1960s. Wendell served as general manager of the complex during its development and was promoted to president of WSM in 1978. He began reporting to Gaylord after the 1983 acquisition. In addition to Wendell, several other executives that had helped build the enterprise were retained by Gaylord. For example, Tom Griscom, who had been with WSM since 1950, remained as head of the Opry's broadcast operations. Hal Durham, a 20-year Opry veteran, retained his role as manager of the Grand Ole Opry, and Julio Pierpaili remained manager of the Opryland theme park.

Two figures instrumental in the early success of the important Opryland Hotel also stayed with Opryland. Mike Dimond and Jack Vaughn had left coveted positions in the mid-1970s to join the Opryland team and to try to position the complex as a heavyweight convention and tourism center. Vaughn abandoned his leadership spot at the Century Plaza in Los Angeles and Dimond left a good job at Hyatt. Those two, like many of their co-managers at the Opry complex, had put their reputations on the line in an effort to build what they viewed as an innovative and promising venture. "Most people thought [Dimond] was crazy to leave such a stable background with Hyatt to come to Nashville and build a hotel in a cow pasture," said Jerry Wayne, vice president of marketing at the hotel in an October 1993 issue of *Nashville Business Journal.*

The Opryland Hotel achieved a healthy 78 percent occupancy rate during its first year of operation and grew at a rapid pace during the 1980s. One of Vaughn's and Dimond's savviest moves after the Gaylord acquisition was the creation of the Country Christmas, which brought country music stars in for a special, seasonal event. That program boosted lagging December hotel occupancy, which had historically lagged at 30 percent, to more than 90 percent. As a result of growth, the hotel continued to add new rooms and expand related facilities. Indeed, although it was originally planned to be a 250-room complex, the Opryland Hotel ballooned in size during the 1980s and early 1990s to almost 2,000 rooms, making it one of the largest and most successful hotels in the world.

The success of the Opryland Hotel was as much a reflection of the overall growth of Opryland USA as it was the ability of its managers. Indeed, as Gaylord beefed up the Opryland complex and stepped up promotional activities, attendance at the Grand Ole Opry and the theme park mushroomed. In addition, Gaylord began extending Opryland's reach in several other directions in an effort to build an entire Opryland enterprise founded on

country music. In 1983, Gaylord started beaming The Nashville Network (TNN), an advertiser-supported cable television network featuring country lifestyles and entertainment. By 1993, TNN was reaching a whopping 59.2 million American households and generating sales of nearly $200 million. In 1985, moreover, Gaylord opened the 1,200 passenger General Jackson riverboat, the largest paddlewheel showboat in the world.

Gaylord's success in Nashville prompted him to focus his organization's efforts on Opryland during the late 1980s. Nevertheless, his television operations boosted income during that period. In fact, Gaylord was able to unload one of his television stations in 1987 for a high $365 million. He even saved $100 million in taxes on the deal by selling it to a minority-owned company. An unfortunate corollary of that tax break was that he had to roll the proceeds over into a media-related purchase within two years. Gaylord beat the deadline by acquiring a California cable television company for a pricey $418 million.

In 1990, Gaylord Broadcasting and its subsidiaries garnered $512 million in sales. However, only $6.5 million of that amount was netted as income, largely because of the heavy debt load incurred by Gaylord when he purchased the lagging cable division. The debt was burdening his balance sheet and eating away at his profits. Lowering Gaylord's $550 million debt, among other objectives, prompted the media mogul to take his company public in October of 1991. Although he sold 22 percent of the equity in his company, he kept more than 60 percent and structured the offering in such a way that he retained voting control of the company. Oklahoma Publishing Company remained a separate company, but all of its broadcasting and entertainment holdings were folded into a new holding company, Gaylord Entertainment Company. The entity's headquarters were moved closer to its base of profits, Nashville.

Gaylord's stock offering in 1991 drew skepticism from some stock brokers who viewed the company as a large, but marginally profitable, concern dominated by an aging, out-of-step executive. "This company does a lot of revenues and doesn't make much money," exclaimed a Nashville stock broker in the October 14, 1991, issue of *Nashville Business Journal,* "I will not spend a lot of time cruising through that prospectus." Other analysts predicted that the move signaled the likely exit of Gaylord and his family from ownership of the company.

Despite some negative speculation about Gaylord Entertainment's stock sale, Gaylord continued to focus on bolstering the company's strength in country-related enterprises. In 1991 the company purchased a controlling interest in Country Music Television (CMT), a cable television station similar to TNN but geared toward country music videos. In 1992, Gaylord went international with CMT Europe, which offered the network's videos to viewers primarily in the United Kingdom and Scandinavia. By 1993, CMT Europe was also reaching viewers in Czechoslovakia, Poland, and Slovenia, among other nations. The company also initiated several major expansion projects related to its hotel and theme park and announced plans to renovate the old Ryman Auditorium.

To the dismay of Gaylord's detractors, Opryland management's aggressive, long-term growth efforts during the 1980s and early 1990s began to bear fruit. Gaylord's sales rose to $524 million in 1991 before jumping eight percent in 1992 to $564 million. Furthermore, 1992 net income gushed to nearly $30 million and Gaylord's total long-term debt tumbled to a manageable $300 million. Gaylord's performance in 1993 accelerated—sales bolted to $622 million and net income topped $27 million. By the end of 1993, Gaylord Entertainment had become a diversified media and entertainment conglomerate that was on the road to becoming virtually dominant in the country music industry.

As he prepared to lead his company into the mid-1990s, the 72-year-old Gaylord showed no signs of slowing down. Gaylord maintained an active management and ownership role going into 1994. Wendell restructured the company in 1993 to prepare it for more aggressive expansion, separating the company into four divisions: attraction, communications, music, and production. In addition, the company embarked on a number of new ventures that complemented its country music core. In 1994, Gaylord opened Wildhorse Saloon, a nightclub, restaurant, and television production studio. Gaylord hoped to expand the club internationally. It also initiated several other undertakings, including golf courses, river taxis, new convention facilities, and sports programming. As the popularity of country music increased going into the mid-1990s, Gaylord's continued success seemed assured in the short term and likely into the 21st century.

Principal Subsidiaries: Opryland USA; The Nashville Network.

Further Reading:

Chappel, Lindsay, "An Interview With E. W. Wendell," *Advantage,* January 1985, Sec. 1, p. 34.

Form 10-K: Gaylord Entertainment Company, Washington, D.C.: Securities and Exchange Commission, 1994.

Hall, Alan, "Gaylord Entertainment Co. Announces Reorganization," *Business Wire,* September 23, 1993; "Gaylord Entertainment Co. Names Chief Operating Officer," *Business Wire,* February 19, 1993.

Hall, Joe, "Gaylord Eyes Global Chain of Saloons," *Nashville Business Journal,* November 1, 1993, Sec. 1, p. 1; "Gaylord Execs Quieted Second-Guessing," *Nashville Business Journal,* October 4, 1993, Sec. 1, p. 6.

Hawkins, Chuck, "If Ed Gaylord Is So Private, Why Is He Going Public," *Business Week,* September 30, 1991, pp. 85–86.

London, Terry, "Gaylord Entertainment Co. Announces 1991 Results," *Business Wire,* February 11, 1992.

Oliver, Valeri, "Analysts Unexcited by Gaylord Stock Offer," *Nashville Business Journal,* October 14, 1991, Sec. 1, p. 1.

Serwer, Alan E., "Stand by Your Core Franchise," *Fortune,* January 25, 1993, p. 104.

—Dave Mote

General Nutrition Companies, Inc.

921 Penn Avenue
Pittsburgh, Pennsylvania 15222
U.S.A.
(412) 288-4600
Fax: (412) 288-2099

Public Company
Incorporated: 1935
Employees: 6,400
Sales: $.55 billion
Stock Exchanges: NASDAQ
SICs: 8390 Retail Stores; 8641 Pharmaceuticals

General Nutrition Companies, Inc., is the largest specialty retailer of vitamin, mineral, and sports nutrition supplements in the world. It is also a leading supplier of personal care, fitness, and other health-related products. It garners most of its earnings from its General Nutrition, Inc., subsidiary, which operates more than 1,500 General Nutrition Center retail stores. After sporadic growth since its inception in 1935, GNC experienced explosive expansion during the late 1980s and early 1990s.

Analysts questioned Jerry Horn's sanity when he, in 1985, accepted an invitation to serve as president of the troubled General Nutrition Inc. (GNI). Horn had just performed an impressive six-year stint as president of Seattle-based Recreational Equipment, Inc. (REI), and had previously completed 20 successful years with Sears. In short order, Horn had virtually turned REI around, essentially obliterating its debt problems and boosting the company's profits 40 percent within three years, to $10.8 million. At his last assignment with Sears, moreover, Horn had revived the retailers ailing San Francisco store, increasing its sales by 23 percent and making it the top profit contributor in Sear's western region—all within one year.

Now, having paid his dues and positioned himself to assume a number of high-profile, well-paid positions, Horn had chosen to attach himself to lagging health food and vitamin retail chain of relatively ill repute. Indeed, national news publications of the early 1980s carried such headlines as ''Under Attack: General Nutrition Inc. Is Besieged with Suits Over Bold Sales Tactics,'' and ''Reliance on Fads Take Toll.'' The federal Food and Drug Administration (FDA) had become a regular detractor of the organization's vitamin offerings, and the Federal Trade Commission (FTC) was pressuring the organization about alleged

false advertising claims related to its diet supplements. Furthermore, one of several lawsuits against GNI was filed by a group of shareholders, who claimed that the company was artificially inflating its stock price through questionable sales of faddish products.

GNI's condition by 1985 followed 50 years of hard work and success achieved by the company's founder, David Shakarian. Shakarian, in 1935, opened the first of what would eventually become a successful chain of GNI health food and vitamin stores. His innovative health concept flourished in the steel-making town of Pittsburgh during the mid-1900s, prompting him to eventually open 30 other stores in that city. He also began adding vitamins and other health supplements to his product line, and expanding operations into other cities, such as New York.

Shakarian's success peaked during the 1970s. Demand for vitamins and a new generation of ''miracle'' products, which claimed to improve both body and mind, emerged, and GNI experienced rampant expansion across the United States. As sales of the store's original core health food offerings continued to rise during the 1970s, shipments of vitamins and other supplements ballooned to represent about 50 percent of company sales. GNI's move into shopping malls bolstered its bottom line and gave the company a more progressive image. The lack of any competitors in GNI's niche, moreover, allowed the company to expand unfettered throughout the decade.

Shakarian profited handsomely during the 1970s by expanding the number and size of his stores, emphasizing an evolving line of trendy products, and developing and manufacturing his own proprietary products. He opened factories in Pennsylvania, North Dakota, South Carolina, and Minnesota. He also began selling his products by mail-order, substantially boosting access to less-populated areas and bolstering recognition of his specialty stores. By the early 1980s, Shakarian had grown the GNI chain from a single shop to a national network of 1,300 outlets. Because his Fortune 400 enterprise was still family owned, he and many of his relatives had amassed sizable fortunes.

GNI's profitability began to wane in the early 1980s, for a variety of reasons. Importantly, GNI began to face stiff competition from supermarkets and drug stores. Supermarkets cut into GNI's food business by capitalizing on the increased demand for health food. Whole wheat bread, rice cakes, tofu, and other items popular with the health crowd became commonplace in most grocery stores, thus eliminating much of GNI's singularity. Likewise, both supermarkets and drug stores vastly increased their vitamin offerings, which diminished GNI's sales and profit margins on nonproprietary supplements.

In addition to increased competition, GNI was also hampered by debatable management decisions that it had made during the 1970s. It had over-expanded its product line to include a huge number of goods, many of which were performing poorly or were cannibalizing sales of related offerings. In addition, its stores were still dedicating a disproportionately large share of their floor space to relatively low-margin food items. In fact, many stores in the chain were unprofitable and had become a drag on GNI's bottom line—in some instances, GNI had placed stores too close to one another. Furthermore, GNI was failing to capitalize on the emerging fitness boom that would dominate the market for health-related products during the 1980s, and it was ignoring younger, health-conscious consumers.

Augmenting GNI's woes were the numerous lawsuits and complaints that had surfaced during the previous 10 to 15 years, ranging from allegations of false claims about its vitamins to fiscal impropriety. Its public image was out of step with a more upbeat, energetic 1980s mentality—GNI was suffering from its reputation as a hard-sell, hippie-style granola shop that, on the side, pedaled a dubious mix of new-age snake oil cures. "In the 1960s and 1970s, it was our classic situation," said Gary M. Giblen, industry analyst, in an August 1993 issue of the *Pittsburgh Post-Gazette*. "You went in and everybody looked unhealthy. The biggest joke about health stores was that the help there looked like they were dying from starvation."

Shakarian died in 1984, just as the company was reaching a historic slump. Although the GNI's stock price had vacillated wildly during the past few decades, often rising after the introduction of a faddish new vitamin supplement, it was selling for a pitiful $5 per share when its founder died—$25 less than its price 12 months earlier. And problems continued to mount. GNI's factories were operating at only 30 percent capacity, and Shakarian's will, which included much of GNI's stock, was contested by his survivors. The company fired long-time president Gary Daum and fellow manager Bart Shakarian (David's brother) and brought in Horn in 1985 to clean up the mess.

Although GNI lost more than $15 million in 1985, Horn believed that the enterprise was a sleeper that offered excellent potential for long-term growth. He would build a new GNI based on its strengths of manufacturing and dominance of the U.S. "self care" market. He would also change the focus of the company from products to consumers, and transform GNI outlets from health stores into "health management centers." "What's happened at GNI is very normal, it's classical," explained Horn in the July 1986 issue of *Executive Report*. "We were product-driven as opposed to customer-driven. . . . GNI tended to seize the latest fad. It was part of the original entrepreneurial spirit that built the company . . . but this sort of zeal was becoming its undoing."

One of Horn's first moves was to dump the chain's languishing stores. He also earmarked $20 million to renovate its profitable outlets and change their layout and product mix to reflect consumer preferences. Although GNI would still emphasize the development and sale of new items, Horn eliminated 30 percent of GNI's offerings and established a system of routing out nonperformers. GNI's confusing array of food products was organized into eight major categories, defined by their health attributes; high fiber, low sodium, low calorie, and low cholesterol products, for example, were arranged in identifiable groups.

Virtually every item sold in GNI stores, including vitamins, was repackaged in an effort to streamline its products. Floor plans were changed to appear cleaner and less cluttered, and new sections were added to exploit a growing demand for nonedible health products, such as skin and hair care goods. The company also bolstered offerings to body builders and other serious athletes with over-the-counter energy and weight-gain supplements. To generate cash for expansion, the company sold its mail-order business and spotlighted its retail outlets.

Horn also made a concerted effort to appease critical federal regulators and to clean up the company's reputation. He initiated communication with the FDA, for example, seeking to establish a collaborative relationship. In addition, the company kicked off a new advertising campaign targeted more toward fitness-conscious consumers, including body-builders. Although Horn closed nearly 200 GNI stores in 1986, he opened 30 new ones and was planning to open many more before the close of the decade. Horn also set a goal of utilizing 88 percent of the company's manufacturing capacity, a strategy that would be achieved by augmenting sales through GNI stores with shipments to third-party retailers.

Horn's most prolific strategic initiative was a franchising program. Started in 1987, the program was created to help finance expansion and to infuse a new spirit of entrepreneurialism in the organization. GNI helped its franchisees, many of whom were former employees, by financing the stores and supporting owners with a high-quality marketing program. Existing stores that had been converted to franchises typically experienced sales increases of 60 percent during their first year of private ownership. As a result, GNI stepped up its franchising efforts throughout the late 1980s and early 1990s.

Although GNI struggled to regain profitability during the late 1980s, Horn had successfully put the company on a new path toward growth and prosperity. After closing down more than 300 stores and spending $46 million to settle lawsuits between 1985 and 1989, the GNI organization comprised over 1,100 outlets and was ringing up annual sales of more than $300 million. The streamlined nature of the new GNI reflected Horn's personality and management style. Out of the gym and behind his desk by 7:45 a.m., Horn stressed effort, team work, and a customer orientation.

William E. Watts replaced Horn as president of GNI in late 1988. Horn retained his position as Chief Executive Officer and was later elected Chairman of the Board. Shortly after the management change in 1989, GNI was purchased by Thomas H. Lee Company, a Boston investment firm whose holdings included Playtex Co. Lee created a new company, General Nutrition Companies, Inc. (GNC), which operated GNI as its major subsidiary. Although GNC was saddled with debt following the leveraged buyout, its management sustained the efforts initiated by Horn and was able to slowly boost sales. By 1992, the first year in which Lee realized a quarterly profit from the acquisition, GNC was operating about 1,125 stores and generating over $380 million in annual sales.

Lee eliminated much of GNC's debt burden in 1993 by making a new public stock offering. In fact, its slashed GNC's total debt from $380 million to just $180 million. With its new cache of capital, GNC aggressively pursued a new overall growth strategy. Having successfully restructured its organization and cut much of the fat from the old GNI, GNC was prepared to concentrate on replicating its proven manufacturing, distribution, and retail strategy. GNC planned to expand its retail store base and boost market share by opening stores in new metropolitan areas and by stepping up its franchise efforts.

GNC retained its emphasis on vitamins and minerals (which represented about 40 percent of revenues) and sports nutrition supplements (30 percent of sales), but it also began sporting new lines of apparel and exercise equipment. In addition, the company significantly increased its marketing budget and initiated several new advertising promotions. For example, customers who signed up for the company's Gold Card membership, which cost $15 annually, received 20 percent discounts on the first Tuesday of each month. Expenditures on television advertising more than doubled during 1992.

GNC's cash position and revised growth strategy allowed it to become one of the fastest growing retail chains in the nation during the early 1990s. As most other retailers struggled to retain sales and profits during a lingering recession, GNC expanded its organization to include 1,216 stores by the end of 1992 and 1,553 by the end of 1993. Revenue gains ensued; receipts shot up to $454 million and $546 million in 1992 and 1993, respectively. Furthermore, the average total floor space and sales-per-square-foot of its outlets soared as GNC continued to emphasize the development of self care "SuperStores." SuperStores consisted of a series of boutiques within the shop, each of which sported separate product categories, such as herbs, vitamins, apparel, or food.

As it prepared to enter the mid-1990s, GNC was hoping to increase its already brisk rate of growth—it planned to open 225 new stores in 1994. Still unchallenged by competitors in its market niche, moreover, GNC also planned to extend its reach internationally. To this end, it created an international franchise division in 1994. It was already active in four South and Central American countries by 1994, but was awarding new franchises in Western Europe, the Far East, and the Middle East. Indeed, GNC aimed to increase sales to more than $1 billion by the end of the decade. "GNC is one of the truly world class operators that is a category killer," Giblen said about GNC's prospects in the August 31, 1993 *Pittsburgh Post-Gazette* article. "It's like Toys 'R' Us is the place to get toys—It's totally dominant in the vitamin industry."

Principal Subsidiaries: General Nutrition, Inc.; General Nutrition Corporation; General Nutrition Products, Inc.

Further Reading:

Carlsen, Clifford, "GNC Pepping Up Expansion; Bay Fit for 10 More Stores," *San Francisco Business Times,* October 29, 1993, Sec. 1, p. 8.
"Franchising Program in High Gear," *Chain Store Age Executive,* September 1993, pp. 26–27.
Kamen, Robin, "Nutrition Chain Getting Physical in New York," *Crain's New York Business,* October 19, 1992, Sec. 1, p. 3.
Marano, Ray, "Saudi Venture a Go for GNC," *Pittsburgh Business,* August 20, 1990, Sec. 1, p. 1.
Rouvalis, Christina, "Studies Giving General Nutrition Healthy Outlook," *Pittsburgh Post-Gazette,* September 19, 1993, p. J8; "More Than Granola as General Nutrition Revamps Merchandise and Store Design," *Pittsburgh Post-Gazette,* August 31, 1993, p. B8.
Securities and Exchange Commission Form 10-K; General Nutrition Companies, Inc., Washington, D.C.: Securities and Exchange Commission, 1994.
Slom, Stanley H., "GNC to Pull More Weight in the 90s," *Chain Store Age Executive,* June 1992, pp. 21–22.
Tascarella, Patty, "Will Jerry Horn's Prescriptions Cure GNC?", *Executive Report,* July 1986, Sec. 1, p. 20; "GNC's Horn Opts for New Marketing Plan," *Pittsburgh Post-Gazette,* July 22, 1985, Sec. 1, p. 13.
Varnas, Carol, "General Nutrition Announces National Expansion Plan for 1993," *Business Wire,* September 14, 1992.

—Dave Mote

THE **GEON** *COMPANY*

The Geon Company

6100 Oak Tree Blvd.
Cleveland, Ohio 44131
U.S.A.
(216) 447-6000
Fax: (216) 447-6408

Public Company
Incorporated: 1993
Employees: 1,930
Sales: $972.5 million
Stock Exchanges: New York
SICs: 2821 Plastics Materials and Resins

The Geon Company is the world's largest producer of vinyl compounds and a leading North American producer of polyvinyl chloride (PVC) resins, with 13 manufacturing plants in the United States, Canada, and Australia. When it was spun off from The BFGoodrich Company in March of 1993, Geon became the only North American public company dedicated solely to the development, production, and marketing of vinyl, the second most widely used plastic in the world. Geon distinguished itself from its competitors by emphasizing high-end markets and specialty vinyl plastics used for such products as computers, appliance housings, and automotive parts. While with Goodrich, Geon spent heavily on research and market development, but since parting ways it has aggressively trimmed costs to ensure profitability. Bill Patient, president and CEO of Geon, told *Chemical Week*, " 'Our costs were out of line with global industry. And we needed to start using our own technology. The truth is we were licensing better than we were practicing.' "

BFGoodrich was founded in 1870 by Dr. Benjamin Franklin Goodrich in Akron, Ohio. The original Goodrich product was a cotton-covered fire hose. Research and development was always given a high priority at Goodrich, and within its first 20 years, the company became known as the rubber industry problem-solver. The first rubber research laboratory in the United States was set up by Charles Cross Goodrich, son of the founder, in 1895. The Goodrich inventors improved on all types of products, including golf balls. In addition, they developed an efficient rubber reclamation process which would be used by the industry for decades.

Polyvinyls were the fortuitous result of the Goodrich policy of research and development. A company scientist working on developing a rubber product that adhered to metal discovered a chemical product that did just the opposite. In addition, the new product did not deteriorate when exposed to rubber-damaging processes. By pioneering polyvinyl chloride in 1926, Goodrich founded the vinyl plastic industry. Early PVC applications included waterproof raincoats and umbrellas. The company's polyvinyls became known as Geon and Koroseal and the versatile materials, which could be used in soft or hard form, eventually found their way into a variety of commonly used products, including electrical insulation, floor tiling, garden hoses, draperies, and luggage.

In the 1930s Goodrich scientific developments included the first airplane De-Icer, the endless band vehicle track used for farm and military vehicles, and the first commercial production of synthetic rubber. Of these developments, company president John Lyon Collyer saw great potential in and put great emphasis on the production of synthetic rubber. There was an enormous market for U.S.-made rubber because, prior to World War II, the nation was importing 90 percent of its rubber supply from the Far East. During the war Goodrich became heavily involved in rubber production for the military.

Though Goodrich focused on rubber, it also saw potential in its chemical business. The Goodrich Chemical Company was established in 1943 and built the first commercialized PVC plants. Its main products were vinyl materials (Geon), plasticizers, special-purpose rubbers, rubber manufacturing chemicals, and general chemicals. In 1948 a new research center was opened to further pure science, as well as applications, in the fields of rubber, chemicals, plastics, chemurgy, and the new field of nuclear energy.

By the early 1950s the company's largest division was tires, but the company could not seem to capitalize on its research and creativity. After inventing the first radial tires in the 1960s, Goodrich could not sell them to car manufacturers or American consumers. Five years later, French tire manufacturer Michelin successfully introduced radial tires. Goodrich's marketing ineptness, which wasted its pioneering research, was recognized throughout the industry. "Long the tire industry research leader," *Forbes* contributor Robert J. Flaherty wrote, ". . . Goodrich has been the butt of a joke repeated in Akron for four decades: Goodrich invents it, Firestone copies it and Goodyear sells it."

A bitter takeover attempt in 1969 forced the Goodrich board to make some changes. In 1972 O. Pendleton Thomas, an oil company executive, took over command of Goodrich and restructured, closing money losing plants and modernizing others. Thomas also implemented cutbacks on the types of tires produced and moved toward greater emphasis on chemicals and plastics. Thomas timed the company's shift away from tires well, for the 1970s marked the downfall of the American tire industry.

In 1979, when John D. Ong took over as chair and CEO, Goodrich was fourth among tire manufacturers, behind Goodyear, Firestone, and Michelin. The recession years of the early 1980s were some of the worst in history for the tire industry. In

1981 Goodrich dropped out of the original-equipment tire market, no longer selling directly to the automobile manufacturers, and instead concentrated on the higher-margin replacement tire market. In spite of the recession, the company was able to break even.

In the wake of the tire industry downfall, Ong expanded Goodrich's PVC business. By the end of 1981, 51 percent of total assets and one-third of the company's $3 billion in sales were attributable to Goodrich's chemical group. The 100-year-old tire manufacturer was on its way to becoming a chemical company. Goodrich focused on one product group, polyvinyl chloride resins and compounds, an area in which it had already become a dominant supplier. Uniroyal, another American tire manufacturer, was also moving in the direction of chemicals, creating a broad product mix of chemicals and elastomers (a plastic and rubber combination). Other tire manufacturers, pressed by foreign competition and the longer lasting radial tire, were also increasing their chemical production, but not in the sweeping way in which Goodrich and Uniroyal were proceeding.

Unfortunately, excess capacity and poor pricing plagued the PVC business in the early 1980s, when the industry was in its deepest decline since the Depression. Total PVC production in the United States fell by 6.6 percent from 1981 to 1982, dropping plant capacity to 55 percent. In 1982 general-purpose PVC was selling at 25 cents a pound, two cents below the industry recognized break-even point for PVC manufacturers. That year Goodrich lost more than $30 million.

By the spring of 1983 the PVC market was in an upswing and Goodrich increased its PVC prices eight cents per pound in April. Goodrich had about 23 percent of the market at the time and was the only fully integrated PVC supplier in the world, with seven plant sites in production. The company was not only twice the size of second-ranked Tenneco but was also the low-cost producer. Even though Goodrich was increasing its debt load to expand its PVC business, buyers on Wall Street seemed to approve, with the stock reaching a 14-year high. The company recorded profits of $35 million on revenues of $3.2 billion. From 1979 to 1983 Ong had cut the workforce by 30 percent to 30,000 and put $1.3 billion into operations. He was also touting PVC as the basis of the company's growth. Capacity utilization was up to 80 percent in the plants.

The 1983 upswing in the PVC industry was short-lived, leaving a glut of the product from industry-wide plant expansions. In 1984, 200 jobs, or 25 percent of salaried employees, were cut from Goodrich's Chemical Group. The industry had adequately adjusted to the cyclical nature of its business. Low-margin commodity resins (providing the seasonal construction industry with pipes, siding, flooring coverings, and other building uses) were the mainstay of the industry, using almost 50 percent of all PVC. To establish steadiness for Goodrich's PVC business, Ong pursued production of finished PVC products such as bottles—a potentially huge market.

Goodrich's strategy in the mid 1980s was to expand specialty chemical activities and increase investment in aerospace activities. The company made four chemical manufacturer purchases and four aerospace acquisitions in three years. Goodrich also increased its research and development expenditures and created separate sales forces for the three specialty chemical units. In the second quarter of 1984, specialty-resins, which were enhanced with heat stabilizers and other additives, accounted for 55 percent of Goodrich's PVC sales, significantly more than the industry-wide average of 40 percent.

In 1984, however, *Business Week* claimed that Goodrich was experiencing a high turnover of management and that the Geon division, with two operating chiefs in three years, was experiencing low employee morale. Market miscalculations and management mistakes had plagued Geon for some time. The $700 million sunk into the PVC division from 1979 to 1984 had yielded an operating income of only $131 million. With its staff of applications researchers and marketers, Goodrich found itself competing with bare-bones operations such as Formosa Plastics and Shintech.

In the mid 1980s Goodrich tried to streamline its PVC production. Goodrich closed an outmoded, high-cost PVC resin facility, eliminating 170 million pounds per year of capacity. Nevertheless, Goodrich remained the largest PVC producer in the United States, with more than one billion pounds per year. The company also sold its unprofitable Convent, Louisiana, plant. The $250 million ethylene dichloride plant, completed in 1981, was part of the company's move toward backward integration into chemicals that were used to produce PVC. The Convent project was begun when it was cheaper to produce intermediate products due to scarcity of raw materials and high inflation. A predicted long-term chemical shortage failed to materialize and elevated gas prices boosted the energy cost to run the plant. In addition, PVC growth was overestimated and the price of low-grade resin, which made up a large segment of the market, was unstable. A total of $500 million in assets were divested in the restructuring. Those pieces of the business consisted of 25 percent of 1984 revenues generated, but operated at a loss of $22 million. After restructuring, Goodrich was down more than a billion in sales from its sales peak of $3.3 billion in 1984. But PVC was still the world's second-largest-selling plastic and the Geon Vinyl Division remained the largest producer of PVC in North America, grossing $865.8 million in 1985.

Specialty chemicals and aerospace were the clear focus of the company in the late 1980s because of their fast growth potential. Ann Slakter wrote in 1986, "Goodrich is heavily committed to the PVC business; its product line includes general- and special-purpose resins, special-purpose vinyl chloride monomer and caustic soda." In 1987 Geon Vinyl Division had sales of $1.06 billion and an operating income of $143.5 million. PVCs consisted of 49 percent of the company's total sales of $2.17 billion, with specialty chemicals bringing in 32 percent of sales, aerospace 15 percent, and industrial products four percent. While over 50 percent of the company's revenues had been from tires in the early 1980s, Goodrich moved further from its tire roots in 1986 by entering into a 50–50 joint venture with Uniroyal that combined their tire operations. When U.S. demand for PVC was high and export demand strong due to a weak dollar in 1988, Goodrich sold its 50 percent stake in Uniroyal-Goodrich Tire, leaving Goodrich with core businesses of polyvinyl chloride, special chemicals, and aerospace.

In 1989 William Patient, a chemical industry vice-president forced into early retirement, was hired to run the Geon division. In 1991 Goodrich entered the PVC recycling business by becoming one of three partners in the first large commercial PVC recycling facility, located in Hamilton, Ontario. Goodrich was responsible for purchasing and recompounding the PVC that was reclaimed. In another recycling partnership, the company introduced the first blow-molded bottles using recycled PVC. But in 1991 the Geon division lost $135 million on $1.2 billion in revenues. Patient saw that Goodrich was pushing itself as a specialty chemical maker but really was a high-cost producer of a commodity product. Goodrich was spending a lot on research and development instead of cutting costs.

In 1993 Geon was spun off from Goodrich, with Patient staying on as president, CEO, and chairman. Patient told *Forbes,* " 'We took a clean sheet of paper and started over.' " During the week following the announcement of the initial public offering, Goodrich stock plummeted some 18 percent. Goodrich had been selling itself as a PVC and chemical company and the impending sale came as a surprise to shareholders and analysts who had foreseen a strong resurgence in the PVC industry and had bought Goodrich shares as a value play. While the Geon Division had produced 35 percent of sales and consisted of 50 percent of the company's assets, it also had experienced six quarters of loses since 1991. Geon sold at $18 per share in April in the first of two offerings. The second public offering in November sold at $20 per share. Goodrich raised $700 million in the sale and planned to increase its investments in aerospace and specialty chemicals.

Geon, now a newly independent company, was the third largest PVC resin supplier in North America, with 1.94 billion pounds of capacity. Shintech had 2.3 billion pounds of capacity per year, followed by OxyChem with 2.1 billion. At the time of the sale the PVC maker had 2,500 employees; 14 businesses with resin-making compounding sites in the United States, Canada, and Australia; and a 50 percent share in a PVC compounding plant in England. Shintech was the low-cost resin and compounding company.

In a strategy designed to make Geon the recognized low-cost provider in the industry, product offerings in both resins and compounds were reduced and consolidated. The number of raw materials needed for manufacturing processes was also reduced. While this was being accomplished, Geon began targeting high-performance custom-molded compounds for future growth, thereby shifting the company away from some of the volatility in the PVC resins business.

In 1993 the U.S. PVC industry sold a record 10.5 billion pounds on the heels of eight consecutive years of six percent average growth. The upswing was led by an improved housing market and construction demand for residential siding, windows, and flooring. The industry was again at a high rate of capacity and the year ended unusually, with price increases and no typical year-end slowdown.

Due to the economic recession in Europe and Japan, though, world growth in PVC was weak in 1993, at five percent, and U.S. exports were flat. The majority of Geon PVC sales, 87 percent, were in North America. The Far East PVC growth was twice that of North America but Geon had only a small part of that market. The company's fiscal 1993 debt-to-capital ratio was 32 percent. Revenues broke down with 52 percent coming from vinyl resins, 39 percent from vinyl compounds, nine percent from vinyl chloride monomer, licensing, and other income. The number of employees had fallen by 35 percent since 1991 and was at 1,930 by year-end. Three high-cost resin plants had been closed, eliminating 500 million pounds or 25 percent of 1991 total resin production capability.

In 1994 Geon announced plans to increase vinyl chloride monomer (VCM) capacity in one of its plants at least 50 percent by 1996. The move would make the company less dependent on competition for raw materials while providing the raw material for PVC production at a lower cost than could be obtained by purchasing it from an outside supplier. Due to environmental concerns, chlorine use was declining in the paper industry, which lowered demand for one of the raw materials which Geon continued to purchase. In terms of future capacity, 1.5 billion pounds of U.S. PVC capacity was predicted to come onstream by mid-1996, causing a possible shift in demand and pricing.

Forbes contributor Dyan Machan wrote, "(Geon) is . . . , under Patient, a splendid example of how a producer of a commodity product can be run profitably." In 1991 the company was losing money and was a high-cost commodity producer. By the end of 1993 the company was trimmer, more focused, and in the black, with Geon stock reflecting a healthy 32 percent total return since the initial public offering. According to Geon's third quarter report of 1994, compound shipments were up 15 percent for the first nine months of the year and net income stood at $38.5 million (compared with net income for 1993 of $5.6 million). With 50 years of experience as a technological leader and its new-found independence, Geon could retain its position as a world-class competitor in the industry it created.

Principal Subsidiaries: Geon Canada; Geon Australia.

Further Reading:

Alperowicz, Natasha, "U.S. Buyers Possible for EVC, Europe's Largest PVC Maker," *Chemical Week,* April 13, 1994, p. 13.

"Behind the Revolving Door at B.F. Goodrich," *Business Week,* October 15, 1984, pp. 150–53.

Berman, Phyllis, "Here We Go Again," *Forbes,* July 15, 1985, pp. 32–33.

Brockinton, Langdon, and W. David Gibson, "From the Tire Industry: Growth in Chemicals," *Chemical Week,* August 31, 1988, pp. 26–29.

Byrne, John A., "A New Act in Akron," *Forbes,* November 21, 1983, pp. 78–79.

Coeyman, Marjorie, "Geon Learns to Stand on Its Own," *Chemical Week,* December 15, 1993, pp. 45–46.

Coeyman, Marjorie, Maurice Martorella, and Emily Plishner, "Geon VMC Expansion Will End Its Merchant Buying," *Chemical Week,* March 30, 1994, p. 9.

——, and Ian Young, "Healthy Demand Spurs U.S. Plastics Growth," *Chemical Week,* June 1, 1994, pp. 25–28.

Collyer, John Lyon, *The B.F. Goodrich Story of Creative Enterprise: 1870–1952,* New York: Newcomen Society, 1952.

Flaherty, Robert J., "Harvey Firestone Must Be Spinning in His Grave," *Forbes,* September 15, 1980, pp. 158–164.

"Geon Reports for First Time," *Chemical Marketing Reporter,* July 19, 1993, p. 24.

Hairston, Deborah W., "A Retreading for Goodrich," *Chemical Week,* June 26, 1985, pp. 8, 10.

Kimelman, John, "Ohio Nocturne," *Financial World,* June 7, 1994, pp. 40–41.

Kindel, Stephen, "Goodrich and Geon: Who Needs This Deal?" *Financial World,* May 11, 1993, p. 18.

Leaversuch, Robert D., "BFGoodrich Is Exiting PVC Supply; Vinyl Div. to Become Independent," *Modern Plastics,* March 1993, pp. 20–21.

Lodge, Charles, "PVC Bottles Get Frosted Glass Look," *Plastics World,* May 1988, p. 87.

Machan, Dyan, "Starting Over," *Forbes,* July 4, 1994, pp. 53–56.

Plishner, Emily S., "Geon Deal Triggers Bloodbath in Goodrich Stock," *Chemical Week,* March 3, 1993, p. 9.

Roberts, Michael, "Chlorine and PVC Demand to Increase Despite Green Pressures," *Chemical Week,* June 8, 1994, p. 20.

Schiller, Zachary, "Goodrich: From Tires to PVC to Chemicals to Aerospace . . . ," *Business Week,* July 18, 1994, pp. 86–87.

——, "Goodrich: 'Something Very Drastic . . . Had to Be Done,' " *Business Week,* July 1, 1985, p. 27.

Shapiro, Lynn, "Goodrich Expects Fourth Quarter Loss," *Chemical Marketing Reporter,* January 13, 1992, p. 16.

Slakter, Ann, "A New President for a 'New' Goodrich," *Chemical Week,* October 8, 1986, pp. 30–34.

——, "BFGoodrich Tires of Tires," *Chemical Week,* January 6–13, 1988, pp. 13–14.

Smock, Doug, "Reclaim Company to Build First Commercial PVC Recycle Plant," *Plastics World,* April 1991, p. 25.

"Tire Companies Beef up Chemicals," *Chemical Week,* May 4, 1983, pp. 30–34.

"VCM Gets Tighter Thanks to PVC Boom," *Chemical Marketing Reporter,* April 4, 1994, pp. 3, 12.

—Jay P. Pederson

Green Tree Financial Corporation

1100 Landmark Towers
345 St. Peter Street
St. Paul, Minnesota 55102-1639
(612) 293-3400
Fax: (612) 293-5746

Public Company
Incorporated: in 1975 as Green Tree Acceptance Inc.
Employees: 2,000
Revenues: $366.7 million
Stock Exchanges: New York Pacific
SICs: 6153 Short-term Business Credit; 6159 Miscellaneous
    Business Credit Institutions

Green Tree Financial Corporation is the only company in the
United States to specialize in manufactured home loans. As
such, it captured over 25 percent of that business by 1993. The
corporation originates, pools, sells, and services manufactured
home loans using a vehicle known in the industry as conditional
sales contracts. Green Tree offers point-of-sale financing
through its network of 2,800 dealers in all 50 states, support via
43 offices nationwide, and a centralized dealer service center in
St. Paul, Minnesota. Patrick Burton, an analyst for Piper Jaffray
Inc. characterized Green Tree as "a dominant player in a market
that's growing" to *American Banker* in July 1994. The company also makes home improvement, consumer products (such
as watercraft, motorcycles, sport utility trailers, and certain
musical instruments), commercial finance (over-the-road trucks
and aircraft), and used manufactured home loans, and sells
property, casualty, and mortgage life insurance to its customers.
Green Tree emerged from legal troubles in the late 1980s to
record outstanding earnings growth throughout the 1990s.

Green Tree was founded by Lawrence Coss, a 36-year-old who
approached Midwest Federal Savings & Loan Association (then
one of America's 30 largest savings and loans) in 1975 with a
proposal for a new subsidiary. The former car salesman convinced the traditional home mortgagor to begin offering higher-
yielding manufactured home loans through Green Tree Acceptance, Inc. the following year.

The new entity faced competition in its small but financially
significant market from regional banks, consumer finance companies, and savings and loans; however, its exclusive concentration in the industry gave it a distinct advantage. Green Tree

quickly cultivated a reputation for excellent service among
manufactured home dealers. It was often able to conduct thorough credit checks in 24 to 48 hours, and its efficient paperwork
allowed dealers to process loans in an astounding 10 minutes.
This speed, however, did not preclude judicious lending. Green
Tree also became known for its tough credit standards: 40
percent of applicants were rejected, and the company's loan
delinquency rate ran under 2.25 percent, well below an industry
average of over 4 percent.

Green Tree increased its share of the fragmented market for
manufactured home loans from about 7.5 percent in 1982 to 15
percent by 1986. The firm entered the recreational vehicle loan
segment (lending primarily for motorcycles) in 1984 and captured 10 percent of that business in just two years.

Green Tree pioneered the securitization of manufactured home
loans in the mid-1980s, when it became independent of Midwest Federal. The company transformed the funding dynamics
of the industry by pooling and packaging the loans it held and
selling them to private institutional investors like pension funds
and insurance companies. Loans guaranteed by the Federal
Housing Administration and Veteran's Administration were
converted into Government National Mortgage Association certificates issued by Green Tree and sold on the secondary market.
Green Tree makes its money on the difference between the rate
it charges manufactured home buyers and the rate it pays on the
securities. The firm's strict credit standards made its securities a
safe investment. The company also continues to service the
loans after it sells them, thereby garnering income from loan
servicing fees as well.

Former parent Midwest Federal became one of Green Tree's
first securities customers, purchasing $800 million in manufac-
tured home loans in addition to paying about $190 million for a
significant portion of Green Tree's future projected loan servicing cash flows relating to loans originated from 1985 to 1988.
The relationship soured in 1988, however, when Midwest Federal sued Green Tree, charging that the former subsidiary had
sold it $57 million in loans of "inadequate quality and docu-
mentation" and asserting that the loan servicing cashflows had
been overvalued. Midwest blamed Green Tree for its loss of
$100 million on the transactions. Green Tree countersued, but
Midwest's subsequent failure and takeover by the federal Resolution Trust Corporation (RTC) eliminated half of Green Tree's
loan servicing income. In 1988, the company suffered a $12
million loss.

Not surprisingly, the legal imbroglio erupted in what *American
Banker* reported as a "nasty feud" between Harold W. Greenwood, then chairman of Midwest and Green Tree, and Lawrence Coss, president and chief executive officer. When Greenwood stepped down from Green Tree's top post in 1987, Coss
took on the third title, which he would continue to hold into the
1990s. As chairman, Coss negotiated an annual bonus of 2.5
percent of Green Tree's annual pretax income, placing his
salary in the "executive compensation stratosphere," as
Forbes' Gretchen Morgenson noted in a May 1990 piece. In
1993, Coss' salary had vaulted to $14 million.

Manufactured home sales also slumped in the late 1980s as an
overabundance of rental units made renting more attractive. The

number of manufactured units sold annually declined by 30 percent from 1985 to 1990 to about 200,000 per year. Wall Street quickly lost faith in Green Tree—its stock dropped from $37 per share in 1987 to $7 in 1989. Some competitors, including Valley Federal of California and Financial Services Corporation of Michigan also gave up on the industry and stopped making manufactured home loans during this difficult period. Their exit would give Green Tree the opportunity to increase its market share to 20 percent—double its nearest competitor—by 1992.

In spite of its legal troubles and depressed stock price, Green Tree's per-share earnings increased an average of 36 percent annually from 1987 to 1992. Loan originations increased one and a half times over the same period, from $878 million to $1.32 billion. Having sewn up a significant portion of the new manufactured home loan market, Coss began to shift Green Tree's growth focus to new niches. The company applied its proven strategies to the home-improvement loan market. By 1991, it had established a network of 1,200 contractors and loaned over $112 million. Profits in that segment alone increased 43 percent in 1992. Green Tree also started to make loans for previously owned manufactured homes, an estimated market of 500,000 units suitable for Green Tree's lending purposes. Because the majority of these homes were not sold through dealers, Green Tree created its own sales force to make contacts with sellers, brokers, and manufactured housing community managers.

Green Tree's conflict with Midwest Federal and the RTC was not settled until 1992, when the former subsidiary agreed to repurchase $388 million of its manufactured home loans (at a $20 million discount) and $102 million of its own preferred stock still held by Midwest. A subsequent debt swap lowered Green Tree's interest costs and lengthened maturities and raised the company's debt ratings to investment grade. Green Tree changed its name that year, exchanging ''Acceptance Inc.'' for ''Financial Corporation.''

Debt restructuring and the resolution of Green Tree's conflict with the RTC combined to earn the financial services company more favorable credit ratings and open the door to unparalleled financial growth. Net earnings increased 111 percent, equity rose 83 percent, and assets grew 49 percent from 1992 to 1993. In a 1994 *American Banker* article, Chief Financial Officer John Brink counted the geographical diversity of Green Tree's loans as a key to the company's success, noting that, ''No more than 10 percent of Green Tree's loans come from any one state. No more than 1 percent comes from one ZIP code. No more than 1 percent comes from any one dealer. All of that helps insulate Green Tree against any economic downturns in any one area.'' The company's share of manufactured home loans advanced to 27 percent on a record $2.7 million in loan originations in 1993, and it was recognized at the National Manufactured Housing Congress as the ''Lending Institution of the Year.'' Wall Street responded favorably as well, pushing Green Tree's stock up to $57 per share before a June 1994 two-for-one split.

Early in 1993, Green Tree began to diversify the types of ''special products'' or recreational vehicles it financed to include snowmobiles, personal watercraft (jet skis) and all-terrain vehicles. An agreement to provide ''the nation's largest boat manufacturer'' (unnamed in the 1993 annual report) with consumer financing launched the company into the $5 billion marine products market the following year.

At the end of 1993, Green Tree ranked as the world's fourth-largest issuer of asset-backed securities and carried over $700 million in liquid assets that Coss was eager to lend. *American Banker* analyst John Engen forecasted that the company would have borrowers through the mid-1990s: shipments of new manufactured homes grew 21 percent in 1993, and Engen predicted 20 percent annual increases for the industry. It has often been noted that manufactured housing accounts for 25 percent of new single-family homes sold in the United States. However, as interest rates began to rise in late 1993, it was certain that Green Tree would begin to feel a margin squeeze on its securities issues.

As of 1994, there did not appear to be any significant threat to Green Tree's continued success. Lawrence Coss, known as a tough leader who had forged an equally tough executive team, was only 55 years old. Growing acceptance of factory-built homes—indicated in part by their increased placement on private land instead of mobile home parks—portended well for Green Tree's primary market. And the company's entry into new markets showed that it was not about to rest on its laurels.

Principal Subsidiaries: Green Tree Financial Corp. (Kentucky); Green Tree Financial Corp. (Louisiana); Green Tree Financial Corp. (Mississippi); Green Tree Financial Corp. (North Carolina); Green Tree Financial Corp. (Ohio); Green Tree Financial Corp. (Texas); Green Tree Credit Corp.; Green Tree Consumer Discount Co.; Consolidated Acceptance Corp.; Rice Park Properties Corp.; Woodgate Consolidated Inc.; Woodgate Utilities Inc.; Woodgate Place Owners Association; Green Tree Finance Corp. One; Green Tree Finance Corp. Two; Green Tree Finance Corp. Three; Green Tree Finance Corp. Four; Green Tree Finance Corp. Five; Green Tree Agency, Inc.; Green Tree of Montana, Inc.; Green Tree of Nevada, Inc.; GTA Agency, Inc.; Green Tree Life Insurance Co.; Consolidated Casualty Insurance Co.; Green Tree Guaranty Corp.; Green Tree Vehicles Guaranty Corp.; Mahcs Guaranty Corp.

Further Reading:

Button, Graham, ''Conventional Thinking,'' *Forbes,* May 24, 1993, p. 12.
Byrne, Harlan S., ''Green Tree Financial,'' *Barron's,* July 27, 1992, pp. 31–32.
Byrnes, Nanette, ''Green Tree Financial: Growing Like a Weed,'' *Financial World,* May 11, 1993, pp. 20–21.
Engen, John, ''Green Tree of Minn. Becomes a Power as Lender for Manufactured Homes,'' *American Banker,* July 13, 1994, p. 4.
Morgenson, Gretchen, ''Are the Tree's Roots Withering?'' *Forbes,* May 28, 1990, pp. 76–82.
Parker, Marcia, ''Bail-out by Ginnie Mae,'' *Pensions & Investment Age,* July 13, 1987, pp. 1, 39.

—April Dougal Gasbarre

Grumman Corporation

1111 Stewart Avenue
Bethpage, New York 11714-3580
U.S.A.
(516) 575-3369
Fax: (516) 575-2164

Public Company
Incorporated: 1929
Employees: 21,200
Sales: $3.24 billion
Stock Exchanges: New York
SICs: 3721 Aircraft; 3728 Aircraft Parts and Equipment, Not
Elsewhere Classified; 7374 Data Processing and
Preparation; 3812 Search and Navigation Equipment; 3713
Truck and Bus Bodies; 3699 Electrical Equipment and
Supplies, Not Elsewhere Classified

The manufacturer of the U.S. Navy's F-14 "Top Gun" fighter
aircraft, Grumman Corporation was acquired by Northrop Corporation, another U.S. aerospace manufacturer, in 1994, ending
65 years as producer of military aircraft and electronic surveillance equipment and beginning a new era as a component of
Northrop's organization. In addition to manufacturing aircraft
and military hardware, Grumman manufactured postal and firefighting vehicles.

Leroy Grumman left the Navy in 1920 to become a test pilot and
chief engineer for Grover and Albert Loening, who manufactured an airplane called the Fleetwing. In 1923, Vincent Astor's
New York-Newport Air Service Company lost one of its Fleet-
wings over the ocean. Cary Morgan (a nephew of J.P. Morgan)
was killed in the accident, which a later investigation revealed
was caused when Morgan fell asleep with his foot obstructing
the pilot's controls. Nevertheless, bad publicity surrounding the
accident put Astor's company out of business. Grumman and a
fellow worker named Leon Swirbul purchased the airline from
Astor and later transformed it into a manufacturing company,
building amphibious floats for Loening aircraft.

Unlike other aircraft manufacturers who entered the business as
barnstormers or hobbyists, Leroy Grumman was a graduate of
the Cornell University engineering school. Leon Swirbul was a
product of the disciplined military aviation program. Both men
continued to work for the Loening brothers while operating
their own company, which they had named Grumman Aircraft

Engineering. However, when Keystone Aircraft purchased
Loening Aeronautical in 1928, the entire operation was moved
to Keystone's headquarters in Bristol, Pennsylvania. Grumman
and Swirbul decided to remain in Long Island and operate their
own company.

After building a number of experimental airplanes, Grumman
Aircraft manufactured its first fighter, designated the FF-1, for
the Navy in 1932. This design was improved upon in subsequent models and led to the development of the successful F4F
Wildcat, Grumman's first fighter with folding wings. With
folded wings, twice as many airplanes could be stored on an
aircraft carrier as before. The company also manufactured a line
of "flying boats" called the Goose and the Duck.

Coincidentally, a second factory for manufacturing warplanes
was dedicated by Grumman on the morning of December 7,
1941, as the Japanese were bombing Pearl Harbor. At the outset
of the war Grumman had an advantage over non-military manufacturers because the company didn't require retooling. Automobile manufacturers, for instance, had to be converted from
the production of cars and trucks to battle tanks and airplanes,
assembly lines for sewing machines had to be refitted to produce machine guns. Grumman's only task was to increase its
output and develop new airplane designs.

During the war, Grumman developed new aircraft such as the
amphibious J4F Widgeon, the TBF Avenger naval attack
bomber, and a successor to the Wildcat called the F6F Hellcat.
The Hellcat was developed in response to the Mitsubishi Zero, a
highly maneuverable Japanese fighter with a powerful engine.
Grumman aircraft were used almost exclusively in the Pacific
war against Japan, and provided the American carrier forces
with the power to repel many Japanese naval and aerial attacks.
U.S. Secretary of Navy Forrestal later said, "In my opinion,
Grumman saved Guadalcanal."

No other aircraft manufacturer received such high praise from
the military. Grumman was the first company to be awarded an
"E" by the U.S. government for excellence in its work. The
award further increased the high morale at Grumman. The
Grumman company turned out over 500 airplanes per month.
To maintain that level of productivity the company provided a
number of services to its workers, including day care, personnel
counseling, auto repair, and errand running. In addition, employees were substantially rewarded for their efficient work.
The company had always had an excellent relationship with its
employees, largely as a result of policies set down by Leon
Swirbul, who oversaw production and employee relations while
Grumman involved himself in design, engineering, and financial matters. By the end of the war, Grumman had produced
over 17,000 aircraft.

The sudden termination of government contracts after the war
seriously affected companies such as Boeing, Lockheed, and
McDonnell Douglas, as well as Grumman. Many aircraft companies first looked to the commercial airliner market as an
opportunity to maintain both their scale of operation and profitability. The market suddenly became highly competitive. Although Grumman manufactured commercial aircraft, it elected
to remain out of the passenger transport business. Those companies which did manufacture commercial transports lost money,

and some even went out of business. Grumman continued to conduct most of its business with the Navy. In addition to its F7F Tigercat and F8F Bearcat, the company developed a number of new aircraft, including the AF-2 Guardian and the F9F Panther and F10F Jaguar, Grumman's first jet airplanes.

During the 1950s, Grumman developed two new amphibious airplanes called the Mallard and Albatross; new jets included the Tiger, Cougar and Intruder. It also diversified its product line by introducing aluminum truck bodies, canoes and small boats. In 1960, Grumman's co-founder Leon Swirbul died.

Grumman created a subsidiary in 1962 called Grumman Allied. The subsidiary was established to operate and coordinate all of the company's non-aeronautical business, and allow management to concentrate on its aerospace ventures. When the National Aeronautics and Space Administration (NASA) completed its Mercury and Gemini space programs, it turned its attention to fulfilling the challenge made by the late President Kennedy, namely, landing a man on the moon before 1970. The Apollo program called for several moon landings, each using two spaceships. The command modules, manufactured by McDonnell Douglas, were intended to orbit the moon while the lunar modules, built by Grumman, landed on the moon. Grumman's contract with NASA specified construction of 15 lunar modules, ten test modules and two mission simulators. Only 12, however, were actually built.

Design problems already faced by Grumman engineers were compounded by their limited knowledge of the lunar surface. The lunar modules had to meet unusual crisis-scenario specifications, such as hard landings, landings on steep inclines, and a variety of system failures. Nine thousand Grumman personnel were devoted to the lunar module project, representing a reorientation of the company's business—Grumman had entered the aerospace industry.

The United States made its first manned moon landing in July 1969, with several more to follow through 1972. Grumman's spaceships performed almost flawlessly and represented a new and special relationship between the company and NASA. Grumman was later chosen by NASA to build the six-foot thick wings for the agency's space shuttles.

Through the 1950s and 1960s, Grumman maintained a good relationship with the Pentagon. While that relationship continued to be good during the 1970s, it was marked by a serious disagreement over the delivery of 313 of Grumman's F-14 Tomcat fighter jets. At issue was who was to pay for cost overruns on a government-ordered project—the company or the taxpayer? Grumman was losing $1 million per F-14 and refused to deliver any more to the Navy until its losses were covered. The company pleaded its case in full-page advertisements in the *New York Times, The Wall Street Journal,* and the *Washington Post.* Grumman argued that completion of the contract under the present terms would bankrupt the company. The matter was later resolved when the Defense Department agreed to cover Grumman's losses, and the company agreed to a new contract procedure which would automatically review project costs on an annual basis and make adjustments when necessary.

Grumman's swing-wing F-14s became operational in 1973 and soon established itself as the standard carrier-based fighter jet for the U.S. Navy. Assigned to intercept attacking jets and protect carrier battle groups, the Tomcat had variable geometry wings that swept back when it was sprinting and swept out when it was landing. It could independently track 24 targets and destroy six of them at a time. F-14s performed successfully in intermittent raids and dogfights with Libyan pilots over the Gulf of Sidra.

In addition to the F-14, Grumman manufactured the E-2C Hawkeye, an early warning airborne command center able to track over 600 objects within three million cubic miles of airspace. The Israeli Air Force used E-2Cs to direct its air battles with Syrian pilots over Lebanon's Bekaa Valley in 1982. During those battles, Syria lost 92 of its Soviet-built MiGs while Israel lost only two of its jets. In the Falkland Islands War, Britain's HMS Sheffield was sunk by an Exocet missile launched from an Argentine Super Etendard attack jet. U.S. Navy Secretary John Lehman asserted that if the British had an E-2C in the Falklands, they would have had unchallenged air superiority and would not have lost any ships to Exocet missiles. Both examples illustrated the value of the Hawkeye.

The Navy's A-6 Intruder attack bomber and EA-6B Prowler radar jammer were also manufactured by Grumman, which also re-manufactured 42 General Dynamics F-111 bombers for the U.S. Air Force. The new aircraft, designated EF-111, was designed to jam enemy radar surveillance "from the Baltic to the Adriatic." According to Grumman's chairperson Jack Bierwirth, "it's one of the great exercises to fly this plane against the E-2C." This volley of electronic countermeasures showed the extent to which Grumman's only competition for a long time was itself.

The electronic sophistication of Grumman's aircraft invited criticism from military reformers who argued that modern weapons had become too complex and therefore unmanageable. In the 1970s, these reformers, led by Gary Hart, widely publicized this view. The ultimate success of their movement could have had disastrous effects for Grumman. Following the costly disagreement over the F-14, the company's long term viability was threatened even more by these reformers under the Carter Administration.

Continued attempts to sell F-14s to foreign governments failed, as did lobbying efforts to sell more of the jets to the U.S. Navy. Consequently, Grumman made an effort to diversify its product line. The strategy was ambitious but failed. The company's Dormavac freight refrigerators had no market (losing $46 million), and its Ecosystems environmental management and research venture was unable to turn a profit, resulting in losses of $50 million.

In 1978, Grumman acquired the curiously named Flxible bus division from Rohr Industries. Many of the buses developed cracked undercarriage components, prompting some customers (such as the City of New York) to pull all of their Flxible buses out of service. Grumman filed a $500 million suit against Rohr, alleging that details of design flaws were not revealed prior to the sale. The suit was dismissed in court. Grumman's losses in this venture approached $200 million before the entire division was sold to General Automotive in 1983 for $41 million.

In 1981, Grumman faced a hostile takeover from LTV Corporation, a steel, electronics, and aircraft conglomerate based in Texas. Grumman's workers mobilized an enthusiastic demonstration of support for their company's resistance to LTV. Leroy Grumman, who retired from the company in 1972, raised employee morale when he voiced his support of the opposition to the LTV takeover attempt. A U.S. Court of Appeals later rejected LTV's bid to take over Grumman on the grounds that it would reduce competition in the aerospace and defense industries.

Leroy Grumman died the following year after a long illness. It was widely reported that Grumman was blinded in 1946 by a severe allergic reaction to penicillin administered during treatment of pneumonia. In fact, Grumman was not blinded. His eyesight did, however, begin to deteriorate many years later as his health began to wane.

The Grumman Corporation faced another threat when it became involved in a scandal involving illegal bribes to government officials in Iran and Japan. After the Lockheed Corporation was accused of such improprieties, the sales practices of other defense contractors such as Grumman came under scrutiny. During the investigation of Grumman, a Japanese official named Mitsuhiro Shimada committed suicide.

After the investigations subsided, the companies in question were free to concentrate all their efforts on more constructive matters. Grumman engineers, however, had something highly unconventional on their drawing boards. Grumman's chairperson, Jack Bierwirth, was credited with saying, "If you don't invest in research and development, you damned well aren't going to accomplish anything." With that in mind, Grumman, in conjunction with the Defense Advanced Research Projects Agency, developed a special jet called the X-29 specifically to demonstrate the company's advanced technology. The revolutionary feature of the X-29 was that its wings swept forward, appearing to have been mounted backwards. This feature gave the X-29 superior maneuverability. To counteract the inherent instability of such a design, the X-29 was equipped with a Honeywell computer system which readjusted the canards (wing controls) 40 times a second, maintaining stable flight.

The X-29 was tested under the auspices of NASA during 1984 and 1985. Never intended for mass production, only one X-29 was built as a "technology demonstrator." Bierwirth described projects such as the X-29 as "marrying electronics with computer programming, then putting wings on it."

John Cocks Bierwirth, a former naval officer, became Grumman's chairperson and chief executive officer in 1976. Regarding his mission as "essentially building the corporation of the future," Bierwirth divided Grumman's operations into nine divisions under centralized management. According to Bierwirth, Grumman's future was with aircraft, space, and electronics. However, work on such projects as a new post office truck were designed to maintain a stable and diverse product line. Bierwirth claimed, "We think we are a good investment for people who are interested in the long term and are willing to grow with the company; Grumman is not a three month in-and-out investment."

Grumman's investments in research projects, however, did not prove as successful as Bierwirth hoped. Throughout the 1980s, with the notable exceptions of contracts for F-14 fighters and A-6 attack aircraft, Grumman was hobbled by research projects and product introductions that failed miserably. The company's diversification into the production of buses began the decade's string of failures, portending further mishaps to follow. The 851 Flxible buses purchased by New York's Metropolitan Transport Authority in 1980 were withdrawn from service three years later after repeated breakdowns, a failed venture for which Grumman paid $40 million in 1988 to settle legal claims against it. Other problems riddled the company, none larger nor more damaging in the long-term than its overwhelming dependence on government-funded military contracts. As Grumman's debt rose, exacerbated by research projects that swallowed vast amounts of cash and generated little profit, the company increasingly weakened, staggering, by the end of the decade, on untenable ground.

In 1988, the company named a new chief executive officer, John O'Brien, whose selection augured a return to more profitable days. O'Brien later became chairperson but resigned in 1990 amid allegations of illegal activities. He later plead guilty to bank fraud stemming from an investigation into bribery and political corruption, adding the public relations scandal and the financial charges that followed to Grumman's host of troubles. O'Brien's replacement was Renso L. Caporali, a Grumman employee since 1959, who began steering the embattled company in a positive direction.

Under Caporali's stewardship, Grumman experienced wholesale changes. The company's debt, which had risen to as high as $884 million in 1989, was trimmed 60 percent in the first three years of his tenure, payroll was reduced from a peak of 33,700 in 1987 to 21,000 by 1993, and Grumman's headquarters staff was cut by more than half. Perhaps more important, Caporali attempted to wean Grumman away from subsisting on military aircraft contracts by tapping the company's established expertise in data technology to produce tax processing systems for the Internal Revenue Service. Also, Caporali used the company's knowledge of integrating electronics and data systems. Caporali thus oversaw one of Grumman's few success stories in the past decade when the company's work on the Joint Surveillance Target Attack Radar System (JSTARS) program met with high praise in the Persian Gulf in 1991. Although Grumman could not expect to garner any profit from its involvement with the JSTARS project until 1994, the success of the project, triumphantly hailed by General Norman Schwarzkopf, was a public relations boon for company plagued by scandals and misfortune.

Although Grumman's condition was improving, it continued to rely on the federal government for the bulk of its revenues. In 1992, Grumman derived roughly 90 percent of its $3.5 billion in revenues from the government, an alarming percentage for a market sector experiencing little growth. Seemingly entrenched in this unenviable position, Grumman, pundits speculated, either needed to acquire additional business or be acquired itself. The latter occurred, leading to a bidding war for Grumman between the Martin Marietta Corporation and Northrop Corporation, which reached its climax in mid-1994, when

Northrop emerged as the winner and acquired Grumman for $2.1 billion.

With its acquisition, Northrop gained the electronic surveillance expertise of Grumman as well as its established ties with the U.S. Navy, which complemented Northrop's long history of conducting business with the U.S. Air Force. Merged together, Northrop and Grumman, under the stewardship of Northrop's chief executive officer and chairperson, Kent Kresa, represented a larger force to navigate the turbulent waters characterizing the aerospace industry in the post-Cold War era.

Principal Subsidiaries: Grumman Aerospace Corp.; Grumman Allied Industries, Inc.; Grumman Data Systems Corp.

Further Reading:

Biddle, Wayne, ''Meditations on a Merger: Grumman-Northrop, Etc.,'' *The Nation,* June 20, 1994, p. 87.
''Fighting Fit: Martin Marietta and Grumman,'' *The Economist,* March 12, 1994, p. 75.
Grover, Ronald, and Dean Foust, ''Firefight in the Defense Industry,'' *Business Week,* March 28, 1994, p. 31.
Norman, James R., ''Ninth Life?,'' *Forbes,* April 26, 1993, p. 72.
Pellegrino, Charles R., and Joshua Stoff, *Chariots for Apollo: The Making of The Lunar Module,* New York: Atheneum, 1985.
Ropelewski, Robert, ''Grumman Corp: Destined for Diversification,'' *Interavia Aerospace World,* March 1993, p. 18.
''Shooting Star; Grumman,'' *The Economist,* May 25, 1991, p. 76.
Thruelsen, Richard, *The Grumman Story,* New York: Praegeri, 1976.

—updated by Jeffrey L. Covell

Guardian Royal Exchange Plc

Royal Exchange
London EC3V 3LS
United Kingdom
(071) 283 7101
Fax: (071) 621 2599

Public Company
Incorporated: 1968
Employees: 14,600
Sales: £3.36 billion
Stock Exchanges: London
SICs: 6711 Holding Companies; 6311 Life Insurance; 6321
    Accident and Health Insurance; 6324 Hospital and Medical
    Service Plans; 6331 Fire, Marine, and Casualty Insurance;
    6799 Investors, Not Elsewhere Classified

Guardian Royal Exchange plc is one of the largest composite
insurers in the United Kingdom, with a portfolio including life
insurance, private motor and household insurance, health care,
property, and marine business. Internationally, the company
competes in the insurance markets of Germany, the United
States, Canada, Ireland, and Asia, and has representation in over
50 countries in all. Guardian also operates an active program of
corporate investment as a significant part of its activities.

Guardian Royal Exchange was created in 1968 from the merger
of two venerable insurance institutions, Royal Exchange Assurance and the Guardian Assurance Company. Royal Exchange
was founded in 1720 and was one of the first two insurance
companies to receive legal status by Royal Charter. Originally
established for marine business, the company expanded within a
year to include fire and life insurance as well, thereby becoming
Britain's first composite insurer.

Royal Exchange expanded rapidly, both in domestic and foreign
business and was a well-established firm by the time of the
Guardian's creation in 1821. Guardian, founded as a fire and life
insurer, also grew quickly throughout Britain and in foreign
markets. The company achieved composite status in 1893,
when it was granted new powers of underwriting and investment by Act of Parliament. In 1902, the name was changed
from Guardian Fire & Life to Guardian Assurance to reflect the
company's new interests in theft and burglary insurance, employers' liability, and general accident. The Royal Exchange,
too, had expanded its cover, moving into personal accident

(1898), employers' liability and fidelity guarantee (1899), burglary insurance (1900), and accident insurance. In 1917, the
company added auto insurance to its portfolio by merging with
the motor insurer Car and General.

Both the Royal Exchange and the Guardian built up profitable
overseas businesses, first through foreign agents and later
through branch offices. In the years 1890 to 1912, for example,
the Royal Exchange opened branches in the United States,
Canada, South Africa, New Zealand, India, Egypt, and South
America, as well as establishing a substantial presence in continental Europe.

Guardian Assurance and the Royal Exchange, then, both prospered during the nineteenth century, no small achievement at a
time when the insurance industry—mostly unregulated and
highly speculative—was notoriously volatile. The two companies emerged in the twentieth century with respectable reputations for sound, conservative business practices.

Over the years, both companies fueled their expansion as much
by strategic mergers and amalgamations as by organic growth.
Such insurance alliances were generally viewed favorably in the
industry, as a broader financial base tended to be a stronger one
and therefore of most benefit to policy holders. After World
War II, insurance mergers became even more common and
popular, and it was thus considered sensible strategy that the
Royal Exchange and Guardian Assurance should merge, a move
undertaken in 1968. Finalizing the merger was a long and
complicated process. The integration of two work forces, the
harmonization of different working practices and procedures,
and the monumental task of converting all documents and
records to the same system all required years to complete.

The result was the Guardian Royal Exchange, Britain's fifth
largest composite insurer. The company's business embraced
three primary areas: non-life insurance, life insurance, and
corporate investment. Taken as a whole, Guardian's non-life
insurance business, dominated by personal, motor, and household business, was the company's most lucrative. Indeed,
Guardian's U.K. business in this category was significant, accounting for some 43 percent of the company's premium income. In the 1990s, Guardian sought to strengthen its non-life
portfolio through acquisitions and additions. In 1993, the company purchased the health care and personal lines insurance
business of Orion Insurance, establishing the U.K. subsidiaries
Orion Healthcare Ltd. and Orion Personal Insurances Ltd. The
acquisition, particularly its health care aspect, filled a void in
Guardian's insurance range. Both new enterprises were relatively small but had successful records. Guardian did not intend
them to compete with the major insurers in their field, but hoped
rather to establish and slowly build up a niche market for the
two. The new business quickly accounted for a significant proportion of Guardian's non-life U.K. insurance business.

Guardian also moved into the direct telesales market with the
establishment of Guardian Direct in 1993. Direct sales of car
and household insurance policies were increasingly popular in
the United Kingdom, and Guardian hoped to reap its share of
the profits from this new and rapidly expanding market.

Guardian's overseas operations in non-life insurance was less
successful. In Germany, where the group operated Albingia,

conditions were difficult for a number of years, due largely to the recession and to significant increases in claims rising from household burglaries, car theft, and arson. Guardian attempted to offset such vicissitudes with several measures designed to improve its position—restructuring its portfolio, insisting on rigorous underwriting policies, and exercising strict financial control of costs—but had met with limited success in most overseas operations in the early 1990s.

The picture was somewhat brighter in the U.S. market, however, where Guardian was set on expansion. In 1993, the company acquired another non-standard motor insurer, American Ambassador Casualty Company, to complement the operations of a similar existing American subsidy, Globe American. Both companies offered car insurance to the ''non-standard'' driver—older drivers, drivers with poor records, and drivers of specialty vehicles. While Guardian historically approached the U.S. market with caution, American Ambassador had a healthy record of profit-making over the years, and the company was quietly confident that its acquisition would continue to perform well.

Guardian had non-life insurance operations in many other countries as well, including Canada, Ireland (where it was the country's largest motor insurer), South Africa, France, Holland, Portugal, and several Asian countries, where the company planned further expansion.

Guardian's position in the life insurance market was generally viewed as less secure than its niche in non-life markets. This was due in part to less favorable conditions in the market industry-wide. The selling of life insurance products was heavily linked to the mortgage market, which had been severely depressed in the recession of the early 1990s.

Guardian's corporate investment was largely in equities and properties in the United Kingdom and Germany. Over the years, this was generally a profitable area for Guardian, but it was, of course, a field subject to much fluctuation. Guardian included realized and unrealized investment gains in its profit figures for the first time in 1993, two years before such reporting was due to become compulsory for the insurers. The volatility of the corporate investment market was such that the new reporting could be a welcome boost to Guardian's figures, as it was in 1993, or a disquieting loss, as in the first six months of 1994.

In the early 1990s, Guardian was been beset by a string of misfortunes, some shared by the insurance industry as a whole and others uniquely the company's own. The year 1990 was a particularly disastrous one for all the big insurers in the United Kingdom. Years of progressively ruthless competition among the insurance companies, fighting desperately to retain their market shares, had resulted in pricing and underwriting decisions that proved unrealistic and unsustainable. This state of affairs, coinciding as it did with the recession and a higher than usual incidence of claims (many resulting from the natural disasters that hit the country at this time), had a devastating effect on the industry. Guardian itself plunged to a record loss, the company's first operating loss since the group's formation.

Guardian acted quickly to redeem the loss, instituting what the company termed ''remedial'' measures, including a rigorous review and overhaul of its underwriting policies, careful conser-

vation of capital, strict control of expenses, and a sharpened focus of what kind of business the company meant to attract and to retain. A corporate philosophy of attracting as wide a range of business as possible, and doing whatever necessary to keep it, had led Guardian and the other big insurers to an unwise—and ultimately calamitous—competition; Guardian's new policy led to decisions to jettison some aspects of its business in order to concentrate on higher quality, higher profit business. Premiums were raised, even at the risk of losing customers.

Guardian's strategies were successful, as the company climbed from a loss of some £210 million in 1991 to a 1992 profit of £3 million. The company was one of only two of the big composite insurers to return to profit and in so doing performed significantly better than financial analysts had predicted: Guardian ''deserves credit for playing itself back into the game,'' the *Financial Times* allowed. Guardian's 1993 pre-tax profit figures were still more impressive, reaching one of the highest levels in Guardian's history, even discounting the new inclusion of investment gains.

Other troubles plagued the company, however, as Guardian found itself at the center of several controversies. Guardian's propriety was first called into question in 1987, when the company's chief tax accountant, Charles Robertson, fired for alleged misconduct, protested to an industrial tribunal. Robertson claimed that the true cause of his dismissal was his investigation of irregular transactions between Guardian and some of its overseas subsidiaries and his insistence that he must inform the Inland Revenue of these transactions. The tribunal found in Robertson's favor and recommended (it hadn't the power to order) his reinstatement. The company refused, and later gave Robertson a settlement of £91,000 in compensation.

Guardian was also widely excoriated for its dubious connection with businessman Vinodchandra Manubhai Patel, a star salesman of the company in the 1980s whose ambitious forays into property investment were financed by loans (of some £80 million) from Guardian. Patel's bankruptcy in 1991 let to allegations that Guardian had acted, if not actually improperly, then certainly unwisely.

Further scandal was aroused by allegations that ''tied agents'' (not directly employed by Guardian but engaged in selling Guardian insurance products) had ''mis-sold'' insurance policies in 1990 and 1991, prompting an investigation by the Life Assurance and Unit Trust Regulatory Organisation and a great deal of bad publicity for the company. Guardian also found itself the target of legal actions in 1993 brought by several ex-agents who alleged that the company had failed to pay them the commissions to which they were entitled on policies they sold in the late 1980s. Guardian maintained that the trouble was due largely to a new computer system installed at that time.

It was perhaps in response to such setbacks—both to its finances and its image—that Guardian modified its name. Known as Guardian Royal Exchange since the 1968 merger of Guardian Assurance and Royal Exchange Assurance, the company sought a new image to boost public awareness and confidence. A team of corporate identity consultants, working in great secrecy for some seven months, finally unveiled the new image in 1993. While officially remaining Guardian Royal Exchange, the company would be known henceforth simply as Guardian, represented by the new logo of an owl, symbolizing the company's attributes of stability, dignity, and awareness.

Some analysts have suggested, however, that it will take more than a new name and logo to fully resuscitate Guardian's fortunes. Though one of the United Kingdom's largest corporate insurers, Guardian was frequently viewed as one of the weakest, particularly in the area of life insurance. In response, the company brought in a new management team for its life insurance business in 1992. Guardian's expansion policies were also criticized, particularly its purchase in the late 1980s of an Italian motor insurer; Guardian sold the company a year after buying it, at a loss of some £68 million.

Nevertheless, many of Guardian's efforts to counteract the industry-wide disasters of 1990 were met with approval, especially its unexpected turnaround from dramatic loss to decent profit in the early 1990s. Acquisitions such as the Orion companies were cautiously welcomed as sound strategy. Given time, Guardian seemed likely to bolster its reputation and services.

Principal Subsidiaries: Albingia Lebensversicherungs-Aktiengesellschaft (Germany; 86%); Albingia Versicherungs-Aktiengesellschaft (Germany; 86%); American Ambassador Casualty Co. (U.S.A.); Atlas Assurance Co., Ltd.; Caledonian Insurance Co.; Globe American Casualty Co. (U.S.A.); GRE Insurance Ltd. (Ireland); GRE Orion Healthcare Ltd.; Guardian Assurance plc; Guardian Direct Ltd.; Guardian Royal Exchange Assurance plc; Orion Personal Insurances Ltd.; The Royal Exchange Assurance; Union Insurance Society of Canton Ltd. (Hong Kong).

Further Reading:

Bagnall, Sarah, "GRE Investment Fall Wipes out Trading Profit," *The Times* (London), August 26, 1994, p. 23.

"Composites Face Up to Direct Challenge," *Lloyds List,* February 28, 1994.
Cook, Lindsay, "Guardian Goes Astray," *The Times* (London), August 27, 1994, p. 23.
"GRE Buys US Motor Insurer for Dollars 100m," *Financial Times,* November 16, 1993.
"GRE Could Pay Pounds 30m in Fraud Aftermath," *Daily Mail,* August 20, 1993.
"GRE Counts the Cost of Funding One Man's Empire," *Independent,* March 5, 1993.
"GRE in Dramatic Swing Back to Profit," *Lloyds List,* March 4, 1993.
"GRE Settles with Sacked Whistleblower," *Accountancy,* December 1988, p. 8.
"GRE to Launch Direct Insurance Operation," *Financial Times,* August 25, 1993.
"GRE Will Come Back to Earth with a Bump," *Evening Standard,* December 30, 1992.
"Guarded Confidence," *The Times* (London), August 26, 1994, p. 25.
"Guardian Royal Jumps to Pounds 751m," *Financial Times,* February 23, 1994.
"Insurer Faces Pay-Out Claims," *Financial Times,* November 5, 1993.
"The Lex Column: Guardian Royal," *Financial Times,* August 27, 1993.
"Retrenchment at GRE Pays Off," *Financial Times,* March 4, 1993.
"Sacked Accountant Denied Reinstatement," *Accountancy,* February 1988, p. 8.
Thomson, I.D., *Guardian Royal Exchange Worldwide: A Brief History of the Guardian Royal Exchange Companies' Contribution to the Development of International Insurance,* London: Guardian Royal Exchange, n.d., 86 p.
"UK Turnaround Drives Sharp Recovery at GRE," *The Times* (London), August 27, 1993.
"Whistleblower to Sue over Pension," *Accountancy,* June 1989, p. 8.

—Robin DuBlanc

H. J. Heinz Company

U.S. Steel Building
P.O. Box 57
600 Grant Street
Pittsburgh, Pennsylvania 15230-0057
U.S.A.
(412) 456-5700
Fax: (412) 456-6128

Public Company
Incorporated: 1900
Employees: 35,700
Sales: $7.05 billion
Stock Exchanges: New York Pacific Boston Philadelphia
SICs: 2033 Canned Fruits and Vegetables; 2091 Canned and
   Cured Fish and Seafoods; 2047 Dog and Cat Food; 2032
   Canned Specialties; 2037 Frozen Fruits and Vegetables;
   2099 Food Preparations, Not Elsewhere Classified; 2046
   Wet Corn Milling; 2035 Pickles, Sauces and Salad
   Dressings; 2038 Frozen Specialties, Not Elsewhere
   Classified

Perhaps best known for its ketchup, the H. J. Heinz Company
manufactures thousands of food products in plants on six continents and markets these products in over 200 countries and
territories. In the United States in the 1990s, Heinz ranked first
in ketchup, vinegar, relish. Moreover, the company's StarKist
brand tuna led its market with a 40 percent share, and its Ore-
Ida label held a segment-leading 48 percent share of frozen-
potato sales. The company was also a major presence in the
baby food, canned-bean, and pet food markets.

The origins of this vast food empire may be traced to Pennsylvania, where eight-year-old Henry John Heinz began selling
produce from his family's plot to nearby neighbors. At ten he
used a wheelbarrow, and, by the time he was 16, Heinz had
several employees and was making three deliveries a week to
Pittsburgh grocers. Born in 1844 to German immigrant parents,
Heinz was the oldest of nine children. He grew up in Sharpsburg, Pennsylvania, near Pittsburgh, and, after graduating from
Duff's Business College, he became the bookkeeper at his
father's brickyard. At age 21, he became a partner. (Heinz
retained an interest in bricks all his life—he personally supervised the buying and laying of brick for his company's buildings, and his office desk was often piled with brick samples

acquired on his travels.) In 1869, Heinz and L. C. Noble formed
a partnership called Heinz, Noble & Company in Sharpsburg to
sell bottled horseradish. Their product line soon expanded to
include sauerkraut, vinegar, and pickles.

Following the panic of 1873 and subsequent economic chaos,
the business failed in 1875, but Heinz quickly regrouped, and
the following year started afresh with the determination to repay
his creditors. With his brother John and cousin Frederick as
partners and himself as manager, Heinz formed the partnership
of F&J Heinz to manufacture condiments, pickles, and other
prepared food. The business prospered, and Heinz made good
on his obligations. In 1888, the partnership was reorganized as
the H.J. Heinz Company. Soon Heinz was known throughout
the country as the "pickle king."

Small, energetic, and ambitious, Heinz was a cheerful man with
courtly, old-fashioned manners. He exuded enthusiasm,
whether for work, family, travel, religious activities, or good
horses, and had a passion for involving others in his interests.
According to his biographer, Robert C. Alberts, Heinz once
installed an 800-pound, 14½-foot, 150-year-old live alligator in
a glass tank atop one of his factory buildings so that his employees might enjoy the sight as much as he had in Florida.

In the late 1800s, the typical American diet was bland and
monotonous, and the Heinz Company set out to spice it up with
a multitude of products. The phrase "57 Varieties" was coined
in 1892. Tomato soup and beans in tomato sauce were quickly
added to the product line. Even as "57 Varieties" became a
household slogan, the company already had more than 60 products. At the World's Columbian Exposition in Chicago in 1893,
Heinz had the largest exhibit of any American food company.

By 1900, the H.J. Heinz Company occupied a major niche in
American business. It was first in the production of ketchup,
pickles, mustard, and vinegar and fourth in the packing of
olives. Overall the company made more than 200 products.
Still, Heinz liked the lilt of his original slogan and in 1900 put it
up in lights in New York City's first large electric sign, at Fifth
Avenue and 23rd Street. Twelve hundred lights illuminated a
40-foot-long green pickle and its advertising message.

Heinz's clever merchandising won him a reputation as an advertising genius, but he did not allow his ambitions to overshadow
his religious convictions; during his lifetime, in deference to the
Sabbath, Heinz's advertisements never ran on Sundays. Heinz
Company factories were considered models in the industry,
both in their facilities and their treatment of workers. The
company received many awards, and Harry W. Sherman, grand
secretary of the National Brotherhood of Electrical Workers of
America, remarked after visiting a Heinz plant that it was "a
utopia for working men."

In 1886, Henry Heinz went to England carrying a sample case,
and came home with orders for seven products. By 1905, the
company had opened its first factory in England. The following
year, the Pure Food and Drug Act was vigorously opposed by
most food manufacturers, but Heinz, who understood the importance of consumer confidence in the purity of processed
foods, was all for it, and even sent his son to Washington, D.C.
to campaign for its passage.

Henry Heinz died at age 75 in 1919. At that time, the company had a work force of 6,500 employees and maintained 25 branch factories. Heinz was succeeded as president of the company by his son, Howard, who began his career with H.J. Heinz as advertising manager in 1905 and became sales manager in 1907. Howard Heinz remained president until his death in 1941. In 1939, *Fortune* estimated total sales for the still privately owned company at $105 million.

By the time Howard's son H. J. Heinz II (known as Jack) became president of the company at his father's death, he had worked in all the company's divisions, from the canning factories to the administrative offices. He chose to launch his career as a pickle-salter for $1 a day in the Plymouth, Indiana, plant. Later he became part of the cleanup staff, then a salesperson for H.J. Heinz Company, Ltd. in England. In 1935, fresh out of Cambridge University, Jack Heinz was sent by his father to establish a plant in Australia. Heinz-Australia later became that country's biggest food processing plant.

From 1941, when Jack took over, to 1946, H. J. Heinz's sales nearly doubled. That year, Heinz made its first public stock offering and revealed that its net profit was over $4 million. Foreign sales of baked beans and ketchup, particularly in England, contributed substantially to the company's success. During World War II, Jack Heinz was active in food relief and personally made four wartime trips to England to examine food problems there. The company insignia went to war too; the 57th Squadron of the 446th Army Air Force chose for its emblem a winged pickle marked "57."

Jack Heinz's tenure was marked by expansion of the company, both internationally and at home. Subsidiaries were launched in the Netherlands, Venezuela, Japan, Italy, and Portugal. In 1960 and 1961, the H.J. Heinz Company acquired the assets of Reymer & Bros., Inc. and Hachmeister, Inc. StarKist Foods was acquired in 1963 and Ore-Ida Foods, Inc. in 1965.

During the 25 years that H. J. Heinz II was chief executive, the food industry changed greatly. The era was marked by the rise of supermarket chains and the development of new distribution and marketing systems. In 1966, H. J. Heinz II stepped down as president and CEO, though he retained his position as chairperson until his death in February 1987.

In 1969, R. Burt Gookin, then CEO of Heinz, made Anthony (Tony) J. F. O'Reilly president of the company's profitable British subsidiary. O'Reilly, who was managing director of the Irish Sugar Company at the time, shook up the company by working 14-hour days and stressing a policy of winning through effort. O'Reilly was an uncommon executive; he was, among other things, a world-class rugby player. In 1973, O'Reilly was named president of the parent company, and in 1976 he became CEO. Shortly after the death of H. J. Heinz II, he was also made chairperson. From the beginning, O'Reilly stressed the importance of strong financial results. Some critics claimed that this emphasis created too stressful an atmosphere; in 1979, it was learned that managers of several subsidiaries had for years been misstating quarterly earnings in order to meet their target goals and impress top management.

Overall, O'Reilly's achievements were impressive, however. The timely acquisition of Hubinger Company in 1975 put Heinz

in a position to cash in on the demand for high-fructose corn syrup when the price of sugar soared. In 1978, O'Reilly acquired Weight Watchers International, just ahead of the fitness craze that swept America.

At the same time that the company was branching out into new products, O'Reilly was cutting back on traditional businesses. By 1980, Heinz had increased volume, while cutting its number of plants from 14 to seven and reducing employment by 18 percent. O'Reilly also gave up the battle with Campbell Soup Company for the retail soup market. And when generic products hit the supermarket shelves, Heinz countered not by producing for the generics industry but by "nickel and diming it," as he said. For example, Heinz switched to thinner glass bottles that cut the cost not only of packaging but also of transportation. When imports began to undersell StarKist tuna, StarKist decreased the size of the tuna can, just as Hershey had downsized its chocolate bar when cocoa prices soared. This ploy netted StarKist $7 million in savings. Other nickel-and-dime cost savings came from eliminating back labels from bottles, reclaiming heat, and reusing water.

O'Reilly's strategy in the 1980s was to pare costs to the bone and to use the savings to beef up marketing, primarily advertising, in an effort to increase market share. At the same time, Heinz pursued a cautious acquisition policy. By the mid-1980s, the company had spent $416 million to acquire more than 20 companies. Return on equity increased from nine percent in 1972 to 23.3 percent in 1986.

O'Reilly's cost-cutting war included a threat to go to contract manufacturers rather than his own plants if the same products could be purchased elsewhere for less. Such tough talk elicited substantial concessions from labor unions in 1986. O'Reilly's hard-nosed, bottom-line strategies won Heinz recognition as one of the country's five best-managed companies in 1986. When H.J. Heinz died the following year, O'Reilly became the first non-family member to advance to Heinz's chair.

In 1988, Heinz bid $200 million for Bumble Bee Seafoods, the third largest tuna company in the country. The purchase would have given Heinz, whose StarKist brand already ranked number one, more than 50 percent of the domestic tuna market. Accordingly, the Justice Department prevented the purchase on antitrust grounds. Also in 1988, Heinz reorganized StarKist Foods into StarKist Seafood and Heinz Pet Products in order to strengthen seafood operations for a push abroad. In pet foods, Heinz, already a leading canned cat food producer, strengthened its dog food position through the acquisition of several regional brands.

In overseas markets, Heinz has also begun to expand into the Third World. It became the first foreign investor in Zimbabwe when it acquired a controlling interest in Olivine Industries, Inc. in 1982. Heinz also has joint ventures in Korea and China, and in 1987 the company bought a controlling interest in Win-Chance Foods of Thailand. Win-Chance produced baby food and milk products, and, of course, Heinz planned to add ketchup to the line.

O'Reilly's strategies succeeded in the 1980s. Heinz's sales doubled from $2.9 billion in 1980 to $6.1 billion in 1990, and net profits quadrupled to $504 million during the period. The

CEO had hoped to increase Heinz's annual revenues to $10 billion by 1994, then retire at the close of his contract in 1995. However, recession and competition from private-label products in the early 1990s thwarted that plan and held the company's sales to $7 billion in 1993 and 1994. As Heinz's growth slowed from its double-digit pace of the previous decade, the company's stock declined as well—30 percent from 1992 to 1994—in spite of continuously rising dividends. As a result, O'Reilly postponed his retirement and embarked on a reorganization.

Divestments (most significantly, of the Hubinger subsidiary) in 1993 totaled $700 million. Internal cost-cutting measures included work force and management staff reductions as well as achievement of manufacturing efficiencies. In America, O'Reilly cut brand advertising by 40 percent from 1990 levels and resorted to discounting to reverse 1991's market share losses to private labels. He shifted the company's domestic sales focus to the high-margin food service sector, acquiring J.L. Foods from Borden Inc. in 1994 for $500 million.

But domestic operations were little more than half of Heinz's operations in the 1990s. O'Reilly pinned his expectations for future growth on overseas markets, targeting baby food, in particular, for expansion. Heinz controlled 29 percent of the global infant food market in 1994 and completed the acquisition of Farley's baby food of Great Britain and Glaxo Holdings plc's baby food interests in India that year. Previously unchallenged in international baby food sales, Heinz faced a serious threat from the U. S. leader, Gerber, which was acquired by Swiss pharmaceutical giant Sandoz Ltd. and groomed for international expansion that year as well. Heinz also buttressed its interests in the Asia/Pacific region with the purchase of New Zealand's Wattie's Limited. O'Reilly characterized the new addition as a "mini-Heinz" in a 1994 address to the New York Society of Securities Analysts. Heinz marked its 125th year in business with flat sales that O'Reilly himself characterized as disappointing.

O'Reilly's employment contract expired in 1995, when he would likely be replaced by one of four Heinz executives: William R. Johnson of Pet Products; David W. Sculley of Weight Watchers; William C. Springer of Heinz U.S.A.; or CFO David R. Williams. Gene G. Marcial of *Business Week* speculated that Heinz's relatively low stock price might prompt a takeover bid. Despite the company's difficulties, however, there was no denying its strong stable of brands. And in his 1994 letter to shareholders, O'Reilly asserted that Heinz remained "one of the world's most profitable food companies in terms of operating and net profit margins."

Principal Subsidiaries: Heinz U.S.A.; Ore-Ida Foods, Inc.; Star-Kist Foods, Inc.; Weight Watchers International, Inc.; Weight Watchers Food Company; Crestar Food Products, Inc.; H.J.Heinz Company of Canada Ltd.; Heinz Bakery Products; Heinz Service Company; Alimentos Heinz C.A. (Venezuela); H.J. Heinz Company, Limited (England); Heinz Italia S.p.A. (Italy); H.J. Heinz Central Europe S.A. (Belgium); Star-Kist Europe, Inc. (France); Heinz Iberica, S.A. (Spain); IDAL (Industrias de Alimentaçao, Lda.) (Portugal); Copaix Canning Industry S.A. (Greece); Magyar Foods Limited (England); H.J. Heinz Company (Ireland) Limited; Custom Foods Limited (Ireland); H.J. Heinz Company C.I.S. (Russia); H.J. Heinz (Botswana) Proprietary Ltd.; Olivine Industries (Private) Limited (Zimbabwe); Cairo Foods Industries SAE (Egypt); H.J. Heinz Australia Ltd.; Wattie's Limited (New Zealand); Heinz Japan Ltd.; Heinz-UFE Ltd. (China); Seoul-Heinz Ltd. (South Korea); Heinz Win Chance Ltd. (Thailand).

Further Reading:

Alberts, Robert C., *The Good Provider,* Boston: Houghton Mifflin, 1973.
Alexander, Keith L., and Stephen Baker, "The New Life of O'Reilly," *Business Week,* June 13, 1994, pp. 64–66.
In Good Company: 125 Years at the Heinz Table, Warner Books, 1994.

—updated by April Dougal Gasbarre

HEALTH SYSTEMS
INTERNATIONAL, INC.

Health Systems International, Inc.

225 North Main Street
Pueblo, Colorado 81003
U.S.A.
(719) 542-0500
Fax: (719) 542-4921

Public Company
Incorporated: 1985 as Qual-Med, Inc.
Employees: 2,367
Sales: $1.96 billion
Stock Exchanges: New York
SICs: 6324 Hospital and Medical Service Plans

Health Systems International, Inc. (HSI) was formed in January 1994 by the merger of QualMed and Health Net, two leading managed health care providers. Serving about 1.4 million members in several western states, particularly California and Colorado, the company benefitted from the innovative and aggressive operational strategies of QualMed and Health Net.

QualMed was founded by Dr. Malik M. Hasan, a neurologist from Pakistan. The son of a wealthy Pakistani family, Hasan was discouraged from pursuing a professional career. Nevertheless, his entrepreneurial nature emerged early; he made his first fortune as a teenager by purchasing undeveloped land and selling it at a large profit when the Pakistani government announced plans to add infrastructure near his property.

Hasan soon abandoned his business ventures to study medicine, attending school in Pakistan before traveling to London to receive training in neurology. After returning to Pakistan, he became frustrated with what he perceived as limited intellectual opportunities and an inferior health care system, and, in 1970, he and his wife moved to Chicago, where he practiced medicine for five years. In 1975, Hasan and his family moved to Pueblo, Colorado, where Hasan joined a small, profitable neurological practice. The money he made there during the late 1970s and early 1980s, in addition to some smart investments, secured his financial future.

Besides accruing medical and business knowledge at his group neurology practice, Hasan was also exposed to the management dynamics of larger health care organizations, serving as a director on the boards of a hospital and a major regional medical society. During this time, the cost of medical care was increas-

ing dramatically, and demand surfaced for a new type of care provider better able to contain costs. One popular alternative to traditional indemnity health insurance was the health maintenance organization (HMO). Under HMO plans, members were provided with medical services in exchange for subscription fees paid to the plan sponsor. Because HMO plans offered more efficient administrative and management services than those traditionally overseen by the health care provider, and worked to eliminate unnecessary treatments, the HMO was generally better able to contain costs.

In 1985, Hasan and six other physicians decided to become involved in this increasingly popular trend. With $100,000 in start-up capital, they formed QualMed, a company that then purchased the Pueblo-based San Luis Valley HMO, which had about 6,000 members. QualMed began operations in 1986 under the direction of Hasan and his partners. From the onset, Hasan focused on offering an alternative to traditional HMOs, which, he believed, limited a patient's choice of doctors and left critical decisions about health care in the hands of business people and bureaucrats rather than doctors and patients. While other HMOs controlled costs by relying heavily on clerks and nurses, rather than physicians, to review diagnoses and recommend treatment, Hasan's HMO emphasized physician-intensive management and improved communication between doctors.

Realizing that better medical care could be provided at a lower cost, Hasan soon became enamored by the business aspect of the operation. ''The best medical care is actually the cheapest,'' Hasan explained in the January 31, 1991 *Denver Post,* noting that ''we [physicians] know more about managing it than anybody else.'' Recognizing the market potential for physician-managed HMOs, Hasan began devising a strategy to expand QualMed. Eight more physicians joined the QualMed HMO in the late 1980s, bringing with them a larger client base, and, with an additional $2 million in capital, much of which came from Hasan, the company's services and membership expanded.

In 1987, QualMed purchased Health Dimensions of Colorado Springs. That acquisition, along with a general increase in the membership of its existing operations, made QualMed the eighth largest HMO in Colorado. Two years later, QualMed acquired HMO operations in Oregon, Washington, and New Mexico from Foundation Health Plan Inc., boosting QualMed's membership by 105,000. Foundation, a leading U.S. managed care provider, had experienced financial difficulty during the late 1980s typical of that faced by the entire managed care industry; a downturn in the health insurance underwriting industry had caught many competitors off guard. In fact, during 1987 and 1988, fewer than one-third of all U.S. HMOs turned a profit, enrollment growth practically stagnated, and many HMOs filed for bankruptcy.

Despite the industry shake-out, QualMed achieved a comparatively healthy financial performance during the late 1980s. Its losses in 1987 and 1988 were largely attributable to start-up costs and acquisition expenses. In 1989, QualMed posted its first profit—$3.24 million from sales of about $74 million—making it one of the few industry participants to realize a profit during that year. The purchase of Foundation's HMOs played a significant role in QualMed's success. Although some analysts had questioned the wisdom of the buyout, QualMed quickly improved the management and profitability of the Foundation holdings.

Entering the 1990s, Hasan's unique approach to the HMO was clearly a success. Among QualMed's innovations was its intense review process, particularly concerning patient referrals for specialty care. QualMed medical administrators reviewed every request for specialty procedures, averaging one administrator for every 25,000 members, a high ratio in the industry. Moreover, the company was unique in its focus on effective lines of communication between physicians and the company. While most competitors were forced to wait until after care had been provided before determining whether it had been necessary, QualMed's strategy allowed it to cut potentially unnecessary costs before treatment. Specifically, QualMed physicians communicated with each other and with plan administrators before providing many nonemergency treatments and were provided with continuous feedback in the form of quarterly reports that compared each doctor's use of medical services and costs per member served. "What we're after is the sentinel effect," Hasan stated in the *Denver Post* article, "making physicians think twice before they order a test or deliver a service."

The effectiveness of QualMed's savings strategy was reflected in its medical loss ratio, which was one of the lowest in the HMO industry. QualMed's medical loss ratio—the percentage of premium revenues that are spent to pay medical bills—was about ten percent lower than the industry average in the early 1990s. Furthermore, QualMed's members had one of the lowest per capita hospitalization rates in the nation, 30 percent below the managed care average. Both measures were regarded as important indicators of HMO efficiency.

While many managed care providers retrenched in the late 1980s and early 1990s, QualMed sought to expand and diversify. In 1990, for example, Hasan led the buyout of contracts from the Greater Oregon Health Service, an indemnity insurer, representing a deviation from the core health care operation. Also in 1990, Hasan spearheaded the acquisition of HEALs Health Plan, an HMO based in Oakland, California, with nearly 100,000 members. As a result of expansion, QualMed's sales doubled in 1990 to $142 million, as its net income rose to $4.6 million. At the same time, QualMed's long-term debt load was kept to a healthy $6 million.

Inspired by the success of the flourishing company, Hasan took QualMed public in 1991 to raise cash for faster expansion. The stock offering put $43 million into QualMed's account. One month later, QualMed offered to purchase Health Net, the second largest HMO in California. However, this offer, as well as a second bid of $340 million plus $60 million in preferred stock, was rejected. Nevertheless, QualMed succeeded in picking up several other prime HMO properties in 1992. The company purchased PCA Health Plans, for instance, a 26,000-member HMO in Sacramento, and acquired Preferred Health work, another California managed care provider. QualMed also purchased two other HMO providers with about 86,000 members, and acquired Great Northern Insurance Annuity Corp., a Seattle-based indemnity insurer.

As a result of this aggressive expansion, QualMed experienced dramatic revenue gains; sales doubled in 1991 and again rose

the following year, while profits also surged. By the end of 1992, QualMed's HMO work spanned six western states and served 327,000 members, revenues rose to over $450 million, and profits approached the $30 million mark. Furthermore, QualMed had bid for a $600 million military contract and had initiated plans to acquire several other managed care organizations. Also in 1992, QualMed moved into a new $2.4 million corporate headquarters building in Pueblo.

Hasan's expansion tactics were focused on purchasing financially troubled HMOs that he believed his QualMed managers could turn around within six months. Toward that end, QualMed's advanced information systems and medical management techniques, as well as its proven medical cost containment procedures, were all adapted for each new acquisition. Hasan purchased the indemnity insurers as a means of attracting larger employers to its system and to get new business from existing HMO clients, which consisted primarily of small and medium-sized employers.

During this period of rapid growth, QualMed became involved in several lawsuits and earned a reputation within the industry as overly aggressive, a "bully" by some accounts, in its expansionist pursuits. QualMed had filed suits on several occasions in an effort to protect its interests. The company sued Blue Cross and Blue Shield of Colorado, for example, claiming predatory pricing and unfair competition, and had tried to sue the state of Colorado for breaking a contract with QualMed.

QualMed's most prolific legal initiative was its action against Health Net, the giant HMO it had tried to purchase in 1991 in a $400 million hostile takeover. Health Net, which was founded in 1977, had operated as a nonprofit health care provider up until 1992, when its status changed to for-profit. QualMed sued Health Net for refusing to accept the offer, and Health Net countered with a suit charging that QualMed was squandering its corporate assets. As Health Net struggled to maintain its independence and QualMed sought to take over the company and expand its presence in California, the two companies became embroiled in a nasty court battle that was widely covered in the press.

To the surprise of industry analysts, Health Net and QualMed came to terms in mid-1993, announcing a merger of the two competitors into a new entity, which would be managed and run by both teams. While Health Net represented a huge addition to QualMed's operations, bringing about 900,000 new members to the company and promptly making QualMed a leader in the important California HMO market, Health Net also benefitted from QualMed's access to capital, operational strengths, and presence in markets outside of California. The merger resulted in the fifth largest managed care provider in the United States.

Pursuant to the agreement hammered out by Hasan and Health Net CEO Roger F. Greaves, the two companies joined to become Health Systems International, Inc. in January of 1994. In a unique arrangement, Hasan and Greaves each assumed the titles of "co-chairman, co-president, and co-chief executive officer." Together, the companies oversaw an organization with about 1.4 million members, 40,000 doctors, and about 400 member hospitals. HSI generated a staggering $1.96 billion in 1993 sales, representing an increase from $1.66 billion garnered by the two companies during 1992. Although net income slipped nearly 50 percent to $23.8 million, largely because of one-time costs associated with the merger, this figure was expected to rebound in 1994.

HSI continued to benefit from strong demand and increased interest in managed health care. Although critics cited HSI's unproven track record for growing the customer base of its existing operations, HSI management pointed to the company's relatively low debt load, strong operational skills, and cutting edge information and cost-containment systems as testimony to its long-term growth potential. "We think we are a national model for delivering health care more efficiently," Hasan related in the January 31, 1993 *Denver Post,* adding that "There are almost irresistible societal forces working in our favor."

Principal Subsidiaries: Health Net; QualMed.

Further Reading:

Brock, Kathy, "QualMed Toddles Toward Profitability," *Business Journal-Portland,* September 23, 1991, p. 1.

Colem Benjamin, "Health Will Merge with Colorado-Based HMO," *Los Angeles Business Journal,* September 6, 1993, p. 11.

Crain, Jan, "Health Care—QualMed Inc.: Dr. Malik M. Hasan, Chairman, President, and CEO," *Colorado Business,* August 1993, p. 29.

Davis, Gerald L., "QualMed Merger Approved; HMO Now Operating in 21 Northern California Counties," *Business Wire,* January 5, 1993.

Graham, Judith, "Audit Finds QualMed Problems," *Denver Post,* November 11, 1993, p. C1.

Graham, Judith, "QualMed Rattles Health Care Industry," *Denver Post,* January 31, 1993, p. H1.

Hicks, L. Wayne, "American Dream a Reality for QualMed," *Denver Business Journal,* August 13, 1990, p. 1.

Hicks, Wayne, and Kathy Brock, "QualMed Inc. Plans to Go Public with Stock Offering," *Business Journal-Portland,* April 8, 1991, p. 5.

Lee, Don, "Rivals Health Net, QualMed Agree to Merge," *Los Angeles Times,* August 31, 1993, p. D1.

Neurath, Peter, "Tough Assignment, But QualMed Gets it Done," *Puget Sound Business Journal,* December 10, 1990, p. 10.

Simpson, Bill, and Matt Nesland, "1993 Entrepreneur of the Year Award: Malik Hasan," *Denver Business Journal,* June 18, 1993, p. B6.

—Dave Mote

HOSPITALITY FRANCHISE SYSTEMS, INC.

Hospitality Franchise Systems, Inc.

339 Jefferson Road
P.O. Box 278
Parsippany, New Jersey 07054-0278
U.S.A.
(201) 428-9700
Fax: (201) 428-7307

Private Company
Incorporated: 1990
Employees: 1,600
Sales: $257 million
Stock Exchanges: New York
SICs: 7011 Hotels and Motels; 5812 Eating Places; 6794
   Patent Owners and Lessors

Hospitality Franchise Systems, Inc., (HFS) is the world's largest hotel franchiser, as measured by number of rooms and properties. Its chief franchise systems include Days Inns, Ramada, Howard Johnson, Super 8, Park Inns, and Village Lodges. It is also engaged in the gambling industry and offers various lodging-related fee services. The company's short history is characterized by rampant growth.

HFS was formed in 1990 by The Blackstone Group, a New York-based investment bank. Blackstone hired 50-year-old Henry Silverman, an attorney and investment banker with experience in the lodging industry, to run its merchant banking group. Blackstone formed HFS with the intent of purchasing ailing or undervalued franchise brands or the rights to those chain's brand names. It planned to generate profits by charging its member hotels up-front and annual franchise fees; Rather than own the hotels, it would simply provide marketing, reservation, and other value-added administrative services. In addition, it would target hotels that offered moderate- and low-priced rooms.

To the casual observer, Blackstone's entry into the lodging market may have seemed poorly timed. The U.S. hotel industry had just experienced its greatest period of expansion in history. By the early 1990s, in fact, there were more than three million hotel rooms in the nation, and about 30 percent of those had been built since the early 1980s. By the late 1980s it was clear to hotel industry participants that the market was quickly fading. Indeed, after increasing at a rate of approximately four percent a year throughout the middle and late 1980s, the number of newly

constructed hotel rooms plummeted. By the early 1990s the growth rate had plunged to less than one percent, and most of the new rooms were built in the Las Vegas area.

The decline of the U.S. lodging industry was the result of several factors. First, the Tax Reform Act of 1986 gradually diminished the tax-favored status of commercial real estate developments, such as hotels, and decreased investment capital for new construction. Second, and more important, was a decline in demand. As the economy slowed in the late 1980s and early 1990s, both business and personal traveling declined. Many hoteliers that had expanded their chains during the 1980s with expectations of high demand and a preferred tax status suddenly found themselves burdened with half-empty, unprofitable properties that they could not sell.

By forming HFS, The Blackstone Group hoped to exploit what it viewed as opportunities amidst turmoil in the lodging industry. Fewer than one-third of all U.S. hotels going into the 1990s were affiliated with a national or regional chain. As a result, their operating costs were generally very high compared to members of national chains, which benefited from economies of scale. National chains could provide national advertising campaigns, centralized and automated reservation and billing departments, quality assurance programs, administrative support, and management training. Furthermore, HFS believed that the majority of the hotels that were affiliated with a chain could benefit from joining an even larger organization. Because so many hoteliers were strapped for cash by the early 1990s, HFS reasoned that it could sell large numbers of franchised rooms at low prices and profit, despite sluggish demand for hotel rooms.

In July of 1990, HFS made its first acquisitions by purchasing the Howard Johnson franchise system and the rights to operate the domestic U.S. Ramada franchise system. HFS bought the troubled properties from Prime Motor Inns for a scant $170 million. Prime Motor Inns was one of the fastest growing hotel chains in the nation during the 1980s and had accrued an impressive list of holdings by the end of the decade. However, it had also racked up over $500 million in debt, causing it to seek refuge in bankruptcy court when the market finally soured. The profitability of its Ramada and Howard Johnson subsidiaries had deteriorated significantly by 1990—the Ramada chain was even losing money.

With its first purchase, HFS immediately became a major player in the U.S. lodging industry. The Ramada chain brought 472 hotels with more than 77,608 rooms under HFS's corporate umbrella. Howard Johnson added 417 properties with about 51,786 rooms. HFS incurred about $91 million in debt during its first year of operation, but was able to recoup approximately $50 million in franchise fees for a net loss of about $1.9 million—not a bad outcome considering the company's start-up costs. HFS lost about $5 million in 1991 as it bolstered marketing efforts for its chains, began to establish a consolidated infrastructure that could also support future acquisitions, and pared its debt by about 15 percent.

In addition to trying to improve the efficiency of the hotels already in its chain, HFS sought to generate additional profits by adding independent hotels, other chain's hotels, and new construction to the Ramada and Howard Johnson chains. During

1990 and 1991, in fact, HFS added about 22,000 rooms to the two hotel chains. It profited immediately from the additions of these properties because hotel owners that joined the franchises paid HFS an up-front fee, typically around $20,000 to $30,000. In addition, the owners agreed to pay an annual franchise fee of six percent to ten percent of gross receipts. The hotel owners benefited, of course, from access to a brand name and the reservation and marketing support proffered by HFS.

HFS's initial success prompted its second major acquisition in January of 1992. Also in January of that year it purchased Days Inn of America, Inc., from the troubled Tollman-Hundley Lodging Corp. for $259 million. Days Inn was started by Cecil B. Day in 1970 and had quickly grown into the third largest hotel brand in the world by 1992. It added about 1,220 hotels with about 133,127 rooms to HFS, thus almost doubling HFS's size. The Days Inn purchase proved to be a savvy buy for Silverman and his management team. Although HFS piled up a load of debt, it posted its first profit in 1992—net income (after-taxes) leaped to more than $20 million from revenues of about $200 million. By the end of 1992, HFS's three chains included almost 2,500 hotels with about 300,000 rooms. After fewer than three years of operation, HFS had become one of the largest hotel franchisers in the world.

In addition to praise from many of its investors, Silverman and HFS also drew criticism following their rapid climb in 1992. The Days Inn acquisition represented the third time that a group associated with Silverman had purchased the chain in less than eight years, resulting in a profit of more than $100 million for he and his investors. The first purchase occurred in 1984 by an investment fund headed by Silverman and supported by felons-to-be Ivan Boesky, Michael Milken, and Victor Posner. They sold part of the chain to public investors at a 200 percent profit, bought it back in 1988 following the 1987 stock market crash, and then sold it a year later to Tollman-Hundley for a large profit. Now, Silverman was borrowing heavily, critics said, to buy the chain again.

Although Silverman's deals were all legal, his detractors argued that HFS was engaging in questionable strategies. For example, its practice of growing quickly by lowering franchise fees to attract independent hotels into the chain (instead of building new ones) suggested a possible lowering of chain standards in order to generate short-term royalties. In addition, critics derided HFS's financing strategy, claiming that it benefited certain top executives but reduced the long-term viability of the organization.

Despite criticism from a few analysts, HFS management and investors alike placed faith in the franchiser's growth strategy. The company's success throughout 1992 and into 1993 seemed to support their optimism. In April of 1993, in fact, HFS edged out Holiday Inns as the largest corporate hotel chain operator in the world when it purchased the rights to hotels owned by Super 8 Motels, Inc. Super 8 comprised 971 hotels totaling 59,532 rooms, for which HFS paid $125 million. Super 8 focused on serving government, senior, and family travelers, thus augmenting HFS's strength in the economy/limited service hotel niche. Because most of its franchises were located in the Midwest, HFS believed it offered significant potential for expansion into other regions of the United States.

The business strategy adopted by HFS in the early 1990s was to significantly expand each of its franchise systems while maintaining or improving their reputation and to offer high-quality, value-added services to each chain. By accomplishing these goals, HFS expected to continually increase revenues from franchise fees, thus generating capital for new acquisitions and forays into related businesses. An integral component of HFS's overall strategy was its state-of-the-art national reservation systems. Customers that called any of HFS's chains were channeled to one of four national clearinghouses, where an operator would process the hotel reservation and also link customer travel requests with related services, such as airlines and rental cars. HFS provided each of its franchisees with specialized reports tracking call patterns and reservation trends, thus allowing them to improve occupancy.

In addition to its reservation system, HFS boosted the value of its franchises through marketing programs. Each of its companies had a separate marketing team to research and develop national and regional marketing initiatives, but the teams all benefited from lower shared costs related to volume purchases of printed materials and media advertising. HFS developed a quality assurance program to complement its marketing efforts by insuring that all franchise members adhered to brand-specific quality controls that created consistency for all hotels within each brand. HFS's training system educated each of its franchisees on how to get the most out of its reservation system and marketing programs.

One of the most important means of luring new hotels into its franchise system was its preferred vendor arrangements. Through volume buying, HFS allowed many of its franchise members to slash costs related to goods and services for everything from toilet paper to food. HFS also provided telephone support, via toll-free numbers, for each of its franchisees. In addition, it assisted existing hotels that were converting to a franchise with the design and construction services necessary to bring the unit up to its standards. The end result of HFS's various support services was that its hotel owners were typically able to improve occupancy and reduce operating costs, thus improving profitability compared to most independent hoteliers.

In June of 1993, shortly after acquiring Super 8, HFS added Park Inn International to its line-up. With 39 properties and 4,683 rooms in 13 states, Park Inn was a relatively small chain. HFS planned to market Super 8 and Park Inn chains separately and hoped to realize strong national growth for both brand names. Its expansion strategy resulted in an increase in the number of Super 8 franchisees of more than 12 percent during 1993, to more than 1,060. Meanwhile, HFS successfully enlarged its other chains, as well. The Ramada chain, for example, swelled to 676 hotels with 107,000 rooms by the end of 1993, and Howard Johnson increased to 566 properties with 63,000 rooms. Days Inn grew similarly, expanding to 1,441 hotels with 145,000 rooms.

By the end of 1993, HFS had 3,783 hotels with 383,931 rooms in its systems. Although it had accrued a weighty $350 million in long-term debt, HFS managed to boost sales 27 percent in 1993, to $257 million, as net income climbed 34 percent to $21.5 million. Also during 1993, Silverman and co-managers took HFS truly public, selling all ownership shares held by The

Blackstone Group on the stock market. It also increased the average occupancy rate of its hotels and was able to boost royalty fees for new members of its franchises.

HFS continued to grow each of its franchises early in 1994; by April it had about 4,000 hotels sending franchise fees to the home office. Furthermore, the company began branching out into new arenas. It formed several strategic alliances with transportation and food service companies in 1993 and 1994, such as Greyhound, Pizza Hut, and Carlson Hospitality Group, which owned several restaurants and hotels. The agreements provided services to franchise members, such as free in-room pizza delivery and reduced bus rates for HFS franchise guests. Also notable was HFS's entry into the gaming (gambling) market in 1993 and 1994. It began using its existing infrastructure to provide marketing and financing services to casino operators. In addition to those services, HFS was investing in several gambling-related ventures.

In late 1994, HFS formed National Gaming Corp. to handle the company's casino and entertainment projects. National Gaming will be responsible for the financing, development, and operation of casino gaming and entertainment facilities.

As it entered the mid-1990s, HFS appeared positioned to benefit from a projected increase in hotel room rates resulting from a dearth of new development in the early 1990s. Future demographics also boded well for long-term growth, as noted in the company's annual report: ''Our basic business plan is driven by an inescapable demographic fact: the American population is getting older, and as people age, they tend to travel more for leisure than business and to trade down to lower price points; the hotels, motels, and casinos under the HFS umbrella.''

Principal Subsidiaries: Days Inns of America, Inc.; Howard Johnson Franchise Systems, Inc.; Ramada Franchise Systems, Inc.; Super 8 Motels, Inc.; Parks Inns International, Inc.; Villager Franchise Systems, Inc.; HFS Gaming Group.

Further Reading:

Braue, Marilee Laboda, ''N.J. Hotel Giant Always Has Room for More,'' *Record,* January 7, 1993, Sec. BUS.

DeMarrais, Kevin G., ''No. 1 in Hospitality,'' *Record,* July 7, 1993, Sec. BUS.

Form 10-K: Hospitality Franchise Systems, Washington, D.C.: Securities and Exchange Commission, 1994.

Heyl, Eric, and Richard Gazarik, ''HFS Wants to Be High Roller in Gambling Industry Growth,'' *Tribune Review,* April 10, 1994, p. A10.

Holmes, Stephen P., ''Hospitality Franchise Systems Reports Record 1993 Results,'' *Business Wire,* February 10, 1994.

Prior, James T., ''Hospitality Franchise Systems—A NJ Gem,'' *New Jersey Business,* April 1993, Sec. 1, p. 22.

Sloan, Alan, ''Once Again, It's Checkout Time,'' *New York Newsday,* September 13, 1992, Sec. 1, p. 4.

Woody, Laura, ''Econo Lodge to Become Ramada,'' *Stuart News,* April 3, 1993, Sec. BUS.

—Dave Mote

Huntington Bancshares Inc.

Huntington Center
Columbus, Ohio 43287
U.S.A.
(614) 476-8300
Fax: (614) 480-5485

Public Company
Incorporated: 1905 as the Huntington National Bank of
    Columbus
Employees: 8,395
Sales: $1.1 billion
Stock Exchanges: NASDAQ
SICs: 6712 Bank Holding Companies; 6021 National
    Commercial Banks; 6022 State Commercial Banks; 6035
    Federal Savings Institutions

Huntington Bancshares Inc. is one of the 40 largest multibank
holding companies in the United States. With about $16.5
billion in assets in 1994, Huntington operated 350 offices in
eight states, mostly in Ohio and other midwestern states. It also
provided various financial services through several subsidiaries.
Huntington's rich history spans more than 125 years.

P. W. Huntington formed the Huntington National Bank in
1866. He had to do something big. After all, P. W. was one of
the most recent additions to a long line of Huntington's that had
helped shape the United States of America. In 1633 Simon and
Margaret Huntington left Norwich, England, with their daughter and four sons to settle in the tiny town of Roxbury, Massachusetts. Simon died of smallpox during the voyage, but the
family prospered, married, and multiplied. Benjamin Huntington, P. W.'s great grandfather and the descendent of one of
Margaret's sons, helped to start the Revolutionary War by calling the first revolutionary meeting in Norwich, Connecticut, in
1774. Another Huntington, Samuel, was president of the Continental Congress from 1779 to 1781, signed the Declaration of
Independence, and helped construct the Constitution; some historians have even referred to Samuel as the nation's true first
president. The Huntington after which P. W. was named,
Pelatiah Webster, was a well-known political economist, au-
thor, and teacher during the late 1700s.

P. W. himself was born 1836, went to work at the age of 14 on a
whaling vessel that sailed to Russia, and began a job as a
messenger in a Columbus, Ohio, bank when he was 17. After

working for 13 years in the rapidly growing Columbus banking
industry, P. W. started his own banking enterprise, P. W. Huntington & Company. The bank grew quickly. P. W. built a five-
story building in 1878, Columbus' first "skyscraper," and began to get his sons involved with the bank's operations. Four of
P. W.'s five sons became partners during the 1890s and early
1900s, eventually assuming executive management positions.
The bank was incorporated in 1905 as the Huntington National
Bank of Columbus.

Huntington moved to a new, larger building in 1916 to house its
burgeoning operations. P. W. died in 1918 shortly after turning
the bank over to his sons. By the time of his death, however, he
had built the bank into a leading financial institution in Columbus. Francis, or "F. R.," became president and provided active
leadership for fourteen years. One of F.R.'s most important
contributions during his short term as president was the initiation of an acquisition program; in 1923, Huntington purchased
State Savings Bank and Trust Co. and the Hayden Clinton
National Bank, thus swelling its capital base considerably.

As a result of its acquisitions, Huntington became active in the
trust business. In fact, by 1930 the bank's trust assets totaled
more than all its other banking assets combined. F. R. died in
1928 at the age of 52, but not before constructing a large
addition onto the bank's existing building. The grand complex
received world-wide attention when it was unveiled in 1926.
Shortly thereafter, F. R.'s brother, Theodore, or "T. S.," assumed the presidency. One year later, the Great Depression
began.

Fortunately for the bank's investors, T. S. maintained the strict,
low-risk banking strategy during 1928 and 1929 that had been
initiated by his father and followed by F. R. P. W. believed in
high liquidity, large cash reserves, and cautious investments.
P. W. had once turned away a giant $500,000 deposit from a
railroad, saying to one of his sons, "We should not owe that
much money to anyone." P. W. was also known for collecting
sticks on his walk to work in the morning—He burned them in
the company's fireplaces to save money on heating fuel. Like
his father, F. R. carefully avoided the urge to invest in the
plethora of speculative opportunities that arose during the
"Roaring Twenties."

As a result of its discipline, Huntington survived the Depression
while many of its industry peers shrank into oblivion. T. S.
guided the company for only four years before stepping aside
for health reasons. He handed the company off in 1933 to the
youngest Huntington brother, B. Gwynne, or B. G. Known for
his almost limitless energy, B. G. successfully guided the bank
through the perilous Depression and World War II years before
ceding his duties as president and becoming chairman of the
board in 1949. B. G. served as chairman during Huntington's
rapid postwar expansion. His death in 1958 marked the end of
92 years of guidance for Huntington National by the men of the
P. W. Huntington family. Exemplifying their leadership during
that period was the motto carved into the stone in the bank's
main lobby, "In Prosperity Be Prudent; In Adversity Be
Patient."

B. G. Huntington was succeeded as president by John E. Stevenson. Stevenson, who had worked in the Columbus banking

industry since 1907 and had come to Huntington by way of the 1923 mergers, was a strong and decisive leader. One of his most notable achievements as chief executive of Huntington was extending the bank's reach through the addition of branches. During the early 1960s, Huntington built several branches and acquired a number of banks that it turned into Huntington branches. Stevenson also oversaw Huntington's entry into new services, namely installment and mortgage loans and retail lending. Noted for his emphasis on loyalty, Stevenson is recorded in company annals as having told a colleague, ''Run the place as though you owned it, but never fool yourself into thinking that you do.'' Clair E. Fultz assumed Stevenson's duties as president in 1963.

Although the Huntington National Bank benefited from an astute, dedicated management team during its 1950s and 1960s growth years, much of its success was attributable to the healthy expansion of the local economy. Indeed, Columbus' population soared from 70,000 in 1940 to a whopping 376,000 by 1950 and to 471,000 by 1960, making it the second largest city in Ohio. The boom in housing, industry, and retail sectors created huge opportunities for Huntington to increase its lending activities and attract a steady supply of deposits. Huntington flourished. Between 1958 and 1966, in fact, its assets doubled. By the mid-1960s, the bank was separated into eight major division, was operating 15 offices in the Columbus area, was lending money for all types of consumer and business needs, and had implemented computer systems to reduce its escalating load of paperwork.

1966 marked Huntington's 100th anniversary. It also signaled the start of a new era of expansion for the bank that occurred during the late 1960s and 1970s. By 1965, Huntington's trust division had grown so large that a separate building, connected to the main bank by an underground tunnel, was created to separately house that operation. In 1966, Huntington created an international banking division that would eventually provide important financial services for foreign banks and companies. Among other accomplishments, in 1972 Huntington National became the first bank in the United States to open a 24-hour, fully automated banking office. Called the ''Handy Bank,'' the concept was soon copied around the world.

Importantly, Huntington National formed Huntington Bancshares Inc. in 1966 as a means of extending its reach into other parts of Ohio that were previously off limits under federal banking laws. Huntington Bancshares became the parent of Huntington National Bank and subsequently conducted a string of acquisitions during the late 1960s and 1970s. Under the direction of a new president, Arthur D. Herrmann, who took office in 1975, Bancshares created new financial services divisions to place under its corporate umbrella. In 1976, for instance, the Huntington Mortgage Company was founded—by 1979 it was the largest construction lender in central Ohio. The Huntington Leasing Company was started in 1977, and doubled its assets by 1979. By 1979, in fact, Huntington Bancshares Inc. had assets of nearly $2.5 billion (up from just $400 million in 1966) and was operating 97 offices through 15 affiliated banks.

State deregulation of the banking industry in 1979 provided new opportunities for Huntington to enlarge its already ballooning organization. Under the direction of Frank A.

Wobst, who became president of Huntington in 1981, Huntington National opened new branches in Kayton, Akron, and Cincinnati. Those gains were augmented by several new acquisitions by Bancshares, including two pivotal purchases in 1982: Reeves Banking and Trust Company of Dover and, more importantly, Union Commerce Corporation of Cleveland. As a result of expansion and acquisition, Huntington Bancshares became Ohio's fourth largest bank holding company in 1982, with $5 billion in assets, 176 branch offices, and operations in 94 Ohio cities.

Huntington was again aided by deregulatory efforts in 1985, but this time at the federal level. Congress approved interstate banking regulations in that year that allowed Huntington Bancshares and other multibank holding companies to become active in other states. Huntington's management determined that its national expansion objectives could best be achieved by establishing separate holding companies in different states. It formed Huntington Bancshares Indiana, Inc., for example, and set up similar holding companies in Kentucky and Michigan. Huntington completed four major acquisitions of banks in those three states, and also extended operations of some of its subsidiaries into Florida, Delaware, New Jersey, Pennsylvania, and several other states. All the while, Huntington continued to strengthen its presence in its core Ohio markets.

Although Huntington's rampant growth during the 1970s and 1980s may appear to reflect a divergence from the cautious growth strategies employed by the Huntington family, it was really more symbolic of industry trends dominant during that period. Indeed, as smaller U.S. banks found themselves under increasing pressure to compete against nonbank financial institutions that were encroaching on their traditional turf, the number of banking entities in the United States plunged from about 13,000 in 1983 to less than 10,000 by 1990. Meanwhile, the number of multibank holding companies, like Huntington Bancshares, grew from about 300 to around 1,000. Huntington did increase its exposure to risk, but it pursued a generally safe strategy during the 1980s.

Huntington's shakiest move was its $2 billion 1982 Union Commerce acquisition. Although it doubled Huntington's size, the purchase left the company loaded with debt that took six years to pare. Wobst and his colleagues learned from the troubled 1982 acquisition, and pursued a less aggressive growth plan throughout the remainder of the 1980s. Nevertheless, a steady stream of purchases combined with the Huntington's expansion into a range of new financial services generated strong asset, revenue, and profit growth for the holding company during most of the decade. By 1989, Huntington boasted $10.9 billion in assets and 248 offices in 11 states. Furthermore, the bank was gearing up for faster growth in the 1990s.

Although industry trends favored Huntington's rapid rise during the latter half of the 1900s, the primary source of its success was sound management. After all, many of Huntington's competitors had suffered irreversible defeats during the late 1970s and early 1980s, and many others had engaged in risky investment strategies that were about to damage them severely in the early 1990s. In contrast, Huntington remained comparatively healthy. It refused to be drawn into imprudent growth tactics to compete with its faster growing peers, such as industry leader Banc One.

"In the 1960s and 1970s they (Banc One) made a lot more money than we did. . . ," Wobst acknowledged in the September 13, 1993 issue of *Forbes.* "If we had tried to grow as fast as they did, we wouldn't be around anymore."

The chief executives that had provided Huntington's sound management during the 1980s represented an eclectic mix of skills and backgrounds. Wobst was born in Germany, studied law, and immigrated to the United States in 1934 when he was 24. Unable to speak English, Wobst learned the language and worked his way up to the presidency of the company after being in the United States for only 23 years. Wobst became chairman and chief executive in 1984, ceding his presidential duties to 40-year-old Zuheir Sofia. Sofia, a native of Lebanon, came to the United States as a teenager and joined Huntington's start-up international division in 1971. By 1984 he was practically running the company.

During the early 1990s Wobst and Sofia sustained, and even accelerated, the expansion rate they had achieved in the 1980s. They also succeeded in strengthening the holding company's balance sheet and improving its productivity and profitability. Huntington celebrated its 125th anniversary by offering a range of new financial and banking services. It began sponsoring low-income community development loan programs, for example, and started offering cut-rate, at-home banking for low- and moderate-income customers. Huntington also hopped into the surging mutual fund and insurance markets, offering its own proprietary products. Importantly, the bank continued to expand through cautious acquisitions.

Perhaps Huntington's greatest accomplishment during the late 1980s and early 1990s was its development and implementation of cutting-edge information systems that were slashing its labor costs and improving service. It poured millions of dollars into, for example, a system that allowed customers to pay bills through a touch-tone telephone. It also created a service that let customers talk to staff to make investments, loan inquiries, or account transactions by phone, 24 hours per day. It worked to developed a telephone with a screen that would let its customers pay bills, book airline tickets, and access other Huntington services. In 1994, Huntington opened a $4 million operations center in West Virginia, where it planned to consolidate its account management operations. "We have used technology very smartly," Sofia said in an August 1993 issue of *Columbus Dispatch,* "and all of the sudden it is beginning to pay off for us."

Other aspects of Huntington's operations were also paying off in the early 1990s. In 1992, Huntington Bancshares' earnings surpassed $50 million before rocketing almost 50 percent in 1993 to $103 million. Furthermore, the holding company's total base of assets ballooned to $16 billion. By early 1994, its assets had risen to a staggering $18 billion, a rise of more than 60 percent since 1989. Huntington had become the 40th largest bank in the United States (by assets) by 1994, and was operating more than 450 banking and financial services offices in 17 states. Befitting the legacy of fiscal propriety initiated by P. W. Huntington in the 1860s, the company's financial health was among the best in the industry going into the mid-1990s. In addition, its stock price surged more than 25 percent during 1993, reflecting Huntington's potential for future expansion.

Principal Subsidiaries: The Huntington National Bank.

Further Reading:

Amatos, Christopher A., "Banker Sees Technology as Source of Profits," *Columbus Dispatch,* December 29, 1992, Sec. BUS; "Huntington COO Sees Long-Range Plans Paying Off," *Columbus Dispatch,* August 9, 1993, Sec. BUS.

Form 10-K: Huntington Bancshares Inc., Columbus, Ohio: Huntington Bancshares, Inc., 1994.

Foster, Pamela E., "Bad Loans Prompt Huntington to Trim Jobs," *Business First-Columbus,* June 22, 1992, Sec. 1, p. 3; "Huntington Bank Gets High Marks for Customer Service, Technology," *Business First-Columbus,* December 14, 1992, Sec. 1, p. 6.

Fultz, Clair E., *Huntington: A Family & a Bank,* Columbus, Ohio: Huntington Bancshares Inc., 1989.

Hohmann, George, "Huntington Banks Building $4 Million Fairmont Facility," *State Journal,* May 1994, Sec. 1, p. 22.

"Huntington Celebrates 125th Anniversary with Lasting Contributions," *Columbus Dispatch,* February 16, 1992, Sec. BUS.

Novack, Janet, "A Nice, Boring Bank," *Forbes,* September 13, 1993, pp. 56–57.

Phillips, Cynthia, "The Huntington National Bank Introduces Visa Check Card as the New Shape of Checking," *PR Newswire,* April 4, 1994.

—Dave Mote

IDB Communications Group, Inc.

10525 West Washington Boulevard
Culver City, California 90232
U.S.A.
(213) 870-9000
Fax: (213) 870-3400

Public Company
Incorporated: 1983 as IDB Communications
Employees: 430
Sales: $310.7 million
Stock Exchanges: NASDAQ
SICs: 4899 Communications Services, Not Elsewhere
  Classified; 4813 Telephone Communications Except
  Radiotelephone

The fourth largest U.S.-based international long-distance carrier and the largest U.S.-based international private line carrier, IDB Communication Group, Inc., emerged as a rising giant in the telecommunications industry during the late 1980s and early 1990s, giving chase to telecommunications heavyweights AT&T Co., MCI Communications Corp., and Sprint Corp. 1 Originally founded as a mobile satellite services company, IDB diversified during the 1980s, branching into several broadcasting niches through its four subsidiaries, IDB Systems, IDB Broadcast, IDB Mobile, and IDB WorldCom. Together, these subsidiaries offered a variety of services to international and domestic customers and made IDB a company of special interest to both investors and competitors in the telecommunications industry.

When he was 13 years old, Jeffrey P. Sudikoff prophetically buried telephone wire beneath the lawns surrounding his Newton, Massachusetts, neighborhood. Though technicians from the telephone company were perplexed when they later unearthed the wires, Sudikoff's idea was clear: he wanted to connect his friends to a battery-operated telephone system that would allow them to talk to each other whenever they wished. The plan showed innovative thinking and an enterprising will unusual for a 13 year-old, attributes Sudikoff would rely on 15 years later, when, at age 28, he created IDB Communications with not much more than he had at his disposal when he was a telecommunications-minded teenager.

Several years after he graduated from Dartmouth College in 1977, Sudikoff began working as a rock music promoter in Los

Angeles, taking care of logistical details for Jackson Browne, Neil Diamond, Fleetwood Mac, and other music groups. In 1983, a banner year for Sudikoff, his job took him to San Bernadino, a county near Los Angeles, where a three-day concert was planned. Organizers of the concert approached him before the event, wanting to know if he could arrange to have the concert broadcast live to radio stations throughout the country. It was a defining moment for Sudikoff and IDB, not only because it launched the former toward enormous success and the latter into being, but also because it provided an early indication of the manner in which both would flourish.

Put simply, this approach could be defined in one word: "yes," the answer Sudikoff gave to the concert organizers in San Bernadino and the answer he would give to almost any proposal during IDB's first decade of existence. His willingness to provide whatever a potential customer wanted—no matter whether a project called for untested technological techniques or required equipment and other resources his company did not possess—gave IDB a foothold in markets eschewed by larger, more established competitors and proved to be instrumental in its quick rise to the upper echelon of the global telecommunications industry.

For his first project, the live broadcast of the three-day concert to radio stations across the country, Sudikoff lacked the necessary equipment and the resources to purchase such equipment, fundamental factors that did not deter him from agreeing to provide satellite link-up. To overcome this first hurdle, Sudikoff took out a $15,000 automobile loan, purchased a mobile transmitter with the money, then hauled it himself to the venue, and provided for the live broadcast. Left with the mobile transmitter after the concert was over and facing payments on his loan, Sudikoff decided to pursue the market for live concert broadcasts further and created IDB Communications to facilitate such an endeavor.

Several concerts followed, then later that year Sudikoff became involved in broadcasting sports events live, carrying radio broadcasts for major-league baseball. These broadcasts were the first step in IDB's development into the largest independent transmitter of sports events in the country. The next step in this direction was taken the following year, a busy year for IDB, when Sudikoff decided to construct the company's first major 24-hour up-link facility, the Los Angeles Teleport. The construction of the Los Angeles Teleport occurred contemporaneously with perhaps the largest sports spectacle in the world, the Olympic Games, held in Los Angeles in 1984 and fatefully arriving as Sudikoff was honing his fledgling company's skills at transmitting sports events. Then not more than a year old, IDB garnered a contract to transmit the 1984 Olympic Games live to radio stations nationwide, adding a prestigious client to a corporate resume that was quickly increasing in length.

Perhaps the most important event for the company's future occurred in 1984 before the windfall announcement of IDB's contract for the Olympic Games and before the construction of the Los Angeles Teleport, when AT&T was ordered to break-up and the telephone industry was deregulated. Coming when it did, less than a year after the formal creation of IDB, the dismantling of the enormously powerful AT&T provided a significant and considerable boost to a young company striving to compete in a field dominated by a leviathan corporation. In the aftermath of AT&T's break-up, the demand for satellite transmissions escalated exponentially; IDB was well positioned to provide satellite transmissions of programming previously sent via long distance phone lines. By the end of the year, the combined forces of the Olympic Games and the weakening of AT&T had fortuitously given IDB a firm foundation from which it could grow and had added measurably to the company's revenue total of $1.5 million at year end.

The following year, IDB constructed a system of fixed earth stations located in 36 cities in the United States called the Sports Satellite Interconnect system and later named Digital Sports Interconnect. The company's sales volume continued to increase, leading to preparations for IDB to become a publicly held company. Instrumental in this shift from private to public ownership was Edward R. Cheramy, a former partner with accounting firm Price Waterhouse, who joined IDB in 1986. Cheramy also figured prominently in matters beyond engineering the transition toward public ownership, functioning as a sometimes necessary voice of reason and prudence rebutting Sudikoff's unflagging desire to do anything, anywhere. So, with a former Price Waterhouse accountant and a former rock-and-roll promoter leading the way, IDB went public in 1986, with an initial share price of $6.

The same year, IDB broadened its scope by introducing television transmission services. Revenues by the end of the year totaled $6.3 million, as the company funneled as much money as possible toward expansion. A second major teleport modeled after the Los Angeles Teleport was constructed in New York in 1987 and named the Staten Island Teleport. Voice and data transmission services were also introduced that same year, a year that witnessed one of the most peculiar and formidable projects taken on by IDB. At various points in his company's history, Sudikoff's penchant for undertaking unique projects led to several inspired arrangements, including floating a satellite on a barge to Antarctica for Korean television, contracting with wedding parties to transmit the ceremonies to overseas relatives, and providing mobile communications for Allied troops during the Persian Gulf War. Now, in 1987, Sudikoff's former passion and his current one dovetailed, when the former rock-and-roll promoter was asked to transmit Billy Joel's concert in Leningrad back to radio stations in the United States.

Back at IDB, the company's management was creating a genuine corporate structure, forming subsidiaries by combining acquisitions, and adjusting for the added corporate weight these acquisitions produced. In 1988, IDB Systems was formed and established in Dallas, Texas, to focus on designing and constructing satellite networks in such countries as Chile, Argentina, Portugal, and the Philippines, countries largely ignored by the larger telecommunications companies. Intended to be used by U.S. companies with facilities in such countries and by the foreign governments themselves, the creation of IDB Systems strengthened IDB's international ties and opened a vast market for the company's future ventures.

In 1988 revenues totaled $20.1 million and would treble the following year, when IDB entered the television business by acquiring Hughes Television Network (HTN), a broadcaster of sports and horse racing, for $36 million. The acquisition of

HTN gave IDB long-term leases controlling the scheduling of 37 transponders on nine satellites, as well as some needed experience from a pioneer of television transmission and scrambling. With the acquisition, IDB formed a second subsidiary, IDB Broadcast, to provide domestic and international services for major network, cable, syndication, pay-per-view, sports, and remote special events. In 1989, IDB bought CICI, a division of Cantel Corp., for $21 million. The acquisition gave the expanding company private voice and data transmission services between the United States and more than 120 countries, which were to serve the U.S. government and corporations with international operations.

By the close of the 1980s, however, IDB's bright prospects began to fade and the company appeared headed for trouble. The recent acquisitions had added weight—divergent corporate structures and new employees inculcated with a much different business philosophy, in sometimes a much older corporate environment—to a company that owed its success largely to nimbleness and flexibility, to quickly taking advantage of a particular situation in a particular market niche. IDB was slow to assimilate these new employees and various corporate structures, and the company began to suffer, particularly from the HTN acquisition, which crimped the company's profits. Superfluous layers of management had also been added, clogging IDB's communications channels and further slowing its decision-making abilities. Finally, to exacerbate matters, several of the company's early acquisitions had been fueled by junk bonds, which raised IDB's debt to a dangerous level. These factors combined to send IDB's stock cascading downward from a high of $18 a share to $6, the original price of stock when the company went public in 1986.

Consequently, as IDB entered the 1990s it appeared headed for trouble, or at least for slower growth. To effect a recovery and a return to the exponential growth the company had known since its creation, Sudikoff and Cheramy readjusted the company's strategic focus. Its debt was reduced to a more comfortable level, and, perhaps more important, the company began to pursue a course that would make it primarily a telecommunications company, rather than a broadcasting company, returning Sudikoff to his childhood roots, when he created a battery-operated telephone system for his suburban neighborhood.

In 1991, IDB began offering international public switched telephone capacity between the United States and more than 70 overseas destinations, organizing these services under IDB&T. The following year the company bolstered its telecommunications interests with the acquisition of World Communications, Inc., an international private line and long distance telephony provider, from TeleColumbus AG, a Baden, Switzerland-based telecommunications company. The purchase of World Communications gave IDB precisely what its strategic shift called for, an extensive fiber optic network and a significant presence in Europe that strengthened considerably its position in the international telecommunications field. Concurrent with the World Communications acquisition, IDB purchased Houston International Teleport, Inc., the holding company of Satellite Transmission and Reception Specialist Company (STARS), both of which were U.S. subsidiaries of TeleColumbus. The company then formed IDB WorldCom, an amalgamation of IDB&T,

IDB International, World Communications, STARS, and Houston International Teleport.

Through IDB WorldCom, IDB offered international private line and public switched long-distance telephone services, and facsimile and data connections to a global customer base. By the following year, 1993, the results of the company's shift toward telecommunications were easily discernible. IDB continued to be involved in broadcasting—the company transmitted television and radio broadcasts for more than 13,000 sports events in 1993 alone—but the proportion of revenue generated by its broadcasting business had decreased in relation to the amount of revenue generated by its telecommunications business. In 1992, WorldCom accounted for 27 percent of IDB's total revenues and in 1993 it accounted for more than 50 percent, whereas the company's broadcasting total fell from 49 percent in 1992 to roughly 25 percent in 1993.

In December 1993, IDB further strengthened IDB WorldCom's position by purchasing TRT Communications, Inc., a provider of international telephone, private leased circuit, facsimile, telex, packet switching, and messaging services, from Pacific Telecom, Inc. The acquisition established the company's international digital communications subsidiary as the largest U.S. international private line carrier and the fourth largest provider of international public switched long distance telephone service, ranking behind AT&T, MCI, and Sprint. Revenues for the year were indicative of IDB's strong presence in a growing market and marked an end to the problems that plagued the company in the late 1980s. In 1992, revenues totaled $155.3 million, an encouraging rise from the $105.4 million recorded the previous year; however, 1993's total surpassed the most optimistic expectations, soaring to $310.7 million, a 100 percent increase in one year.

As IDB entered the mid-1990s, its telephone services generated three to four times as much revenue as its broadcasting, and it continued to augment its presence in the international long distance field through agreements with telephone companies in Italy, Belgium, and the United Kingdom. In 1994, WorldCom announced that it signed an agreement with British Telecom, which would allow IDB to provide direct-dial telephone service in the United Kingdom and thereby increase its international telephone services considerably. With the international telecommunications market valued at $10 billion for U.S. carriers in 1994 and expected to grow 15 percent annually throughout the decade, IDB's acquisitions had positioned it to take advantage of this lucrative market.

Principal Subsidiaries: IDB WorldCom; IDB Broadcast; IDB Systems; IDB Mobile.

Further Reading:

Ferguson, Tim W., "Showtime Is Anytime in This Phone Company's Book," *Wall Street Journal,* September 28, 1993, p. A19.

Harmon, Amy, "Peeking at the Future," *Los Angeles Times,* April 26, 1994, p. 26.

Jones, John A., "IDB Communications Expands Global Telephone Network," *Investor's Business Daily,* February 28, 1994, p. 46.

Murray, Kathleen, "Jeffrey Sudikoff: Technology's Everyman," *Upside,* April 1994, p. 40; "A Satellite Dish Here, Some Cable There," *New York Times,* December 26, 1993, p. 30.

Petruno, Tom, "Is Opportunity Calling in Form of Phone Book," *Los Angeles Times,* October 27, 1993, p. D1.

Tosi, Umberto, "Growth Gurus," *California Business,* September 1993, p. 26.

—Jeffrey L. Covell

Illinois Central Corporation

455 North Cityfront Plaza Drive
Chicago, Illinois 60611
U.S.A.
(312) 755-7500
Fax: (312) 755-7920

Public Company
Incorporated: 1851
Employees: 3,300
Sales: $.56 million
Stock Exchanges: New York
SICs: 4011 Railroads—Line-Haul Operating; 4013 Switching
   & Terminal Services; 6719 Holding Companies, Nec

Illinois Central Corporation owns and operates the oldest land-grant railroad in the United States, the Illinois Central Railroad. That rail system encompasses 2,700 miles of freight railroad lines, traverses six states between Chicago and the Gulf of Mexico, and is the tenth largest railroad in the nation. The Illinois Central Railroad played a prominent and enduring role in the evolution of the United States.

The Illinois Central (IC) Railroad was built between 1852 and 1856, following the Senate's passage of the Douglas Land Grant Bill. That bill essentially gave the state of Illinois the right to use federal lands for the construction of a north-south railroad system. As one of his first assignments as a lawyer, Abraham Lincoln served as counsel for IC during the early 1850s and helped the company to secure land rights. Interestingly, Lincoln had to sue IC for his $5,000 fee, the largest he had ever received, but he was kept on retainer with the railroad until 1960.

The IC railroad and others like it were a corollary of the rugged individualism and pioneer spirit that characterized the United States during the mid-1850s. Americans were still trying to achieve their "manifest destiny," and most people viewed the railroad as the best way to accomplish that vision. As immigration and a high birth rate raised the U.S. population past 23 million in 1850, the push west escalated along with the need for an efficient means of traversing the enormous territory. Before construction was started on the IC line the United States had only 9,000 miles of rail in operation, most of which was in the Northeast. By 1860, however, more than 30,000 miles of rail had been laid.

The actual construction of the IC Railroad during the 19th century is, perhaps, the most colorful aspect of the company's history. The work was grueling, and, because the land grants often required sections of track to be completed within a specific time frame, work usually progressed at a feverish rate. Between 1852 and 1856 rail crews working for IC laid 706 miles of track in Illinois, making its line the longest rail line in the world. At a cost of $25 million, the first 706-mile span of the railroad was the most expensive and among the most grand projects ever attempted in the United States.

Laborers poured in from all corners of the globe to help build the railroad, as the momentous project immediately absorbed the regional labor supply. In fact, workers were in such demand that IC recruited European immigrants straight off incoming ships. It also hired agents to find large numbers of immigrants and ship them to Illinois—one New York agency shipped 1,500 Germans to the project in 1853, only to be one-upped by the Irish Emigrant Society, which supplied an even larger group a few months later. "Wanted! 3,000 Laborers on the 12th Division of the Illinois Central Railroad. Constant employment for two years or more give. Good board can be obtained at two dollars per week. This is rare chance for persons to go West...," read an advertisement distributed in New York. Workers received $1.25 for a full 12-hour work day—good wages during that period.

Construction of the first 706-mile span of track was accomplished under the direction of taskmaster Colonel Roswell B. Mason, engineer-in-chief of the IC Railroad. A race in 1855 between Mason and Bill Mattoon, a contractor at an Indiana railroad company demonstrated the fervor with which the rail was constructed. Mattoon was building a section of track from Indiana to Illinois that was to join a leg being constructed by Mason. As legend has it, Mattoon challenged Mason to a bet to see which team could reach the specified meeting point first. Mason refused to wager for moral reasons, but agreed to name the new town at the crossing point after the man that reached it first. Both teams doubled their efforts. Mason won by a close margin, but was so grateful to his competitor for contriving the contest and speeding up construction that he renamed the town "Mattoon."

By 1855, with only 600 miles of rail in service, IC generated a staggering $1.3 million in revenues. A surprising half of that sum came from passenger service rather than freight. IC also entered into the steamboat transportation business in the 1850s on the Mississippi River, employing a young pilot named Samuel Clemens (Mark Twain) to guide one of its riverboats. All of IC's operations combined generated sales of $13 million between 1851 and 1860. The company showed a loss of only $5 million during that decade, despite enormous start-up costs. More importantly, IC had accomplished a construction feat arguably unsurpassed in the history of the nation.

Although the Civil War posed problems for IC during the early 1860s, such as a shortage of labor, it also resulted in huge profits for the company. As demand for freight and passenger service ballooned in the midst of the war, IC's revenues climbed from about $4 million annually in 1861 to almost $8 million by 1865. In addition, IC expanded its lines during the 1860s and early

1870s to include a total of 1,107 miles of rail reaching all the way from Chicago to New Orleans. During the same period, the total mileage of operating rail in the U.S. swelled to 53,000. Because it spanned the entire nation, north to south, Illinois Central became known as the "Main Line of Mid-America."

IC Railroad continued its rapid rise in the late 1800s and early 1900s as the U.S. population soared and the industrial revolution generated a massive demand for freight services. In fact, it was during that period that railroads reached their pinnacle of influence in North America. IC and its peers had a virtual lock on intercity commercial transport, and their monopoly of freight and passenger traffic became so dominant after 1900 that Congress chose to enact extensive restraints on the industry. Through new construction and acquisitions of smaller rail lines, IC expanded its system throughout Iowa, Illinois, and Mississippi. By 1890, in fact, the total IC system encompassed 2,874 miles of track. That figure rose to 3,845 by 1900 and then to a record 4,736 in 1910.

As IC's size increased, so did its sales. Revenues between 1900 and 1910 totaled $575 million, more than double the total during the previous decade. Likewise, net income surged from $36 million during the 1890s to $92 million from 1900 to 1910. Revenues and income grew to $1 billion and $116 million during the 1910s, moreover. The total number of people employed by the massive corporation reached about 60,000 by 1920. By that year, the miles of IC rail in service was approaching 5,000, while the total miles of track laid in the United States had surpassed 250,000. However, IC realized its most explosive period of growth during the "Roaring Twenties," as a red hot economy put IC's rails to work. Sales during the decade neared $2 billion as total track miles in service reached a pre-1972 peak of 6,721 in 1929.

IC suffered immensely during the Great Depression. As freight and passenger demand slowed, IC and other railroads were forced to reduce service, delay maintenance, and dismiss workers. IC's total work force, in fact, plummeted from 60,000 to only 25,000 between 1922 and 1933. Even IC's electric rail service in Chicago, which it had started in the 1920s, floundered. IC's total revenues during the 1930s dropped to just over $1 billion. It posted a discouraging net loss for period of $15 million. The tables were turned in 1939 by the advent of World War II, however, which spawned huge temporary sales and profit gains for IC.

Despite IC's recovery during World War II and even into the late 1940s and early 1950s, the railroad industry as a whole was beginning to feel the repercussions of more permanent trends that had begun in the 1910s and 1920s. Most importantly, new modes of transportation began challenging the railroad industry's unmitigated dominance. More efficient means of water transportation on rivers, canals, and lakes posed an early threat. However, that means of delivery soon began to give way to more high-tech transportation methods, such as the automobile and large trucks. By the 1950s even the casual observer could see that railroad companies like IC were going to face a serious threat from large trucks, proliferating networks of pipelines, and maybe even airplanes.

Wayne Andrew Johnston served as president of Illinois Central Railroad from 1945 to 1966, years in which the railroad industry entered a stage of maturity. Despite industry malaise, however, his keen management kept the company on a profitable course. Having served the longest term of any other IC president, Johnston is credited with having as great an impact on the company as any other individual. His leadership style reflected his personality—spartan and conservative. He worked long hours and always answered his own telephone at work. Johnston was known for giving up his seat on the ride to work to passengers riding on his train. A lifetime of public service was punctuated by his Sunday morning sermons from pulpits throughout mid-America; "You've got to put back as much or more than you take out," Johnston said about life.

Under Johnston's direction, IC's revenues grew a respectable 25 percent between 1945 and 1960, to about $295 million. For comparison, average industry growth during that period was about 19 percent. However, that steady growth belied serious railroad industry problems. By the late 1960s trucks and planes were rapidly eroding rail's share of the freight market. In addition, passenger service had all but disappeared as a result of the massive interstate highway system constructed during the post-WW II era, which made long-distance automobile and bus transportation possible. Ironically, much of the growth that IC was able to achieve during the 1960s and 1970s was from transporting new cars. By 1970, IC was making about $24 million in profits annually, operating 6,520 miles of track, and employing a work force of 17,000—the reduced work force was primarily the result of automation and a dearth of new construction activity.

One of Johnston's last moves as president was to create Illinois Central Industries (ICI), a holding company with Illinois Central Railroad as its primary subsidiary. ICI would provide a means of diversifying the company's activities to achieve greater returns—by the mid-1960s, the railroad industry was delivering the worst investment return of all the regulated trafficking industries, by far. Although IC had toyed with activities in other industries, such as real estate, prior to forming ICI, it stepped up its efforts after Johnston retired in 1966. The first new member of the ICI family was Waukesha Foundry Company, a producer of castings and pumps.

By the early 1970s, ICI boasted major holdings in several industries, including industrial products, consumer products, real estate, and financial services. It also put renewed effort into enlarging its rail service: In 1972, IC Railroad merged with Gulf, Mobile & Ohio to become the Illinois Central Gulf Railroad. The resultant carrier had almost 10,000 miles of track in 13 states. Nevertheless, in 1972 ICI's railroad operations furnished less than 30 percent of its pretax income. ICI continued to diversify throughout the decade, investing in everything from Midas International (Midas Muffler) to Pepsi Cola, and steadily diminishing the importance of its rail services.

By the late 1970s, the railroad industry was staggering. Competing transportation services had all but snuffed out some of its most important market niches. Furthermore, much of the massive rail network that had been created during the past century was in dire need of replacement. IC, for example, was forced to rebuild most of its lines during the late 1970s and early 1980s at an enormous expense, thus worsening the subsidiary's financial performance. In the early 1980s, ICI even started looking for a buyer for the lagging division. As it broadened its reach into food service, automobile repair, and aerospace, ICI began selling off chunks of Illinois Central Gulf, eventually reducing it to a 3,000-mile freight rail system by 1988. Finally, ICI, which by then was a $4 billion conglomerate, found a way to jettison its rail operations.

In 1989, ICI, which became Whitman Corporation in 1988, sold Illinois Central to The Prospect Group, Inc., an investment company. Prospect eventually paid a total of $560 million for the railroad, which basically consisted of a 3,000-mile system of rails between Chicago and New Orleans. It created a holding company called Illinois Central Corporation with Illinois Central Railroad Company as its chief subsidiary. Prospect made Edward Moyers president of Illinois Central. In fact, it was Moyers who had masterminded Prospect's buyout of IC and had devised a plan to return the ailing carrier to profitability.

The 62-year-old Moyers, a Mississippi native, had started his career with Illinois Central in the 1940s. He swept floors during his summer high school breaks and then joined the company full time after college. The would-be entrepreneur rose sluggishly through the ranks, developing a contempt for IC's bureaucracy. "I was hardheaded," Moyers recalled in a December 1990 issue of *Forbes*. "I spoke up about things I thought ought to be done and was told to go home and be quiet." Moyers left IC in 1977 and joined a smaller railroad where he could have an impact. He eventually ran the smaller railroad. In the late 1980s Moyers began eyeing the ailing Illinois Central as a potential takeover target and approached Prospect with the idea.

Moyers, to the dismay of IC's old guard, immediately transformed IC into a streamlined money machine. Moyers accomplished the spectacular feat through a series of innovative moves that, in retrospect, appeared quite simple. First, he fired all the department heads except one and replaced them with under-40 managers—"All their counterparts at other [railroad] companies are about 103," Moyers jested in the *Forbes* article. Next, Moyers removed one of the side-by-side tracks that connected Chicago and Illinois for northbound and southbound traffic. Every 12 miles he left a 3.4-mile siding where a train could move off of the track while an oncoming train passed. He sold the withdrawn rails and fittings for $50 million and used the remaining materials to cut IC's supply budget by $70 million over four years. He also installed a $20 million automated signaling and scheduling system that saved IC about $100 million.

As Moyers restructured IC's rail system, he went to work slashing the fat out of IC's management and labor force. In his first few months he eliminated 650 of 3,800 employees for a $24 million savings. He also dry-docked one-third of the company's 600 locomotives for an additional $12.6 million boost. In a savvy financial maneuver, Moyers purchased fuel contracts before the Persian Gulf War and saved the company about $1 million per month during the conflict. Moyers' productivity gains allowed IC to drop its grain-hauling prices 15 percent, thus regaining much of that market which had been lost during

the previous decade. The end result of Moyers efforts was that IC's operating income rose from $18 million in 1989 to a whopping $87 million in 1990, despite an ugly U.S. recession. Furthermore, IC was recognized as one of the most efficient carriers in the industry in 1990 after being labeled as one of the least productive just one year earlier.

Moyers continued to dispose of IC's unneeded assets and to whittle away at the carrier's overhead during the early 1990s. Total employment, for example, decreased from 3,688 in 1991 to 3,306 by 1993. Although sales remained level at about $550 million, costs steadily declined and profits improved. IC's income (before taxes) ballooned to $148 million in 1993. Its productivity continued to improve at a rapid pace, earning it the status of most efficient rail carrier in the United States between 1990 and 1993. Furthermore, by 1993 Moyers had eliminated about two-thirds of the debt that the company had accrued during the 1989 buyout.

After restoring the carrier's health and earning a multimillion-dollar personal fortune, Moyers stepped aside as president of IC in 1993. He was succeeded by E. Hunter Harrison, a board member with extensive industry experience. When Harrison assumed the presidency, IC shifted into "Phase II" of an eight-year plan started by Moyers in 1989. The first four-year phase focused on reducing operating costs and improving service. The second phase, to be administered by Harrison, would emphasize a lowering of debt and an increase in revenues through market share gains. IC's three stated goals going into 1994 were to increase annual sales by $100 million by the end of 1995, reduce operating costs, and cut annual interest expenditures (on debt) by $10 million. Harrison and co-managers had already achieved healthy progress toward those goals during 1993 and early 1994.

Illinois Central had declined significantly in stature since its glory days early in the 20th century. However, it entered the mid-1990s as a robust railroad company with long-term industry sticking power—a tribute to the great Americans that had helped to build it during the past 150 years. The company's future as it moved into the 21st century was as much dependent on government regulation, labor relations, and transportation trends as it was on the will of IC's management.

Principal Subsidiaries: Illinois Central Railroad Company.

Further Reading:

Bennett, Julie, "IC Poised for Growth in Food Biz," *Crains Chicago Business,* May 16, 1988, Sec. 1, p. 28.
Camp, Barry R., "Ed Moyers: 'A Good Railroad Man' and a New Captain of Industry," *Jackson Journal of Business,* July 1989, Sec. 1, p. 34.
Elstrom, Peter J. W., "Railroad Stock Revs Up," *Crains Chicago Business,* August 27, 1990, Sec. 1, p. 54.
Eubanks, Ben, "Pet, Hussman Lead IC Industries' Firms," *St. Louis Business Journal,* March 9, 1987, Sec. 1, p. 12A.
Form 10-K: Illinois Central Corporation, Washington, D.C.: Securities and Exchange Commission, 1993.
Machan, Dyan, "Mr. Moyers' List," *Forbes,* December 10, 1990, pp. 39–40.
Scott, Chris, "ICG Traffic Sails Past Stuck Barges," *Crains Chicago Business,* July 25, 1988, Sec. 1, p. 3.

Scott, Jonathon, "Investors' Central Station Plan a Whopper," *Memphis Business Journal,* November 8, 1993, Sec. 1, p. 1.

Snyder, David, "Bays Embraces Strategy, Culture at IC Industries," *Crains Chicago Business,* June 29, 1987, Sec. 1, p. 3.

Stover, John F., *History of the Illinois Central,* New York: Macmillan Publishing Co., Inc., 1975.

Thoma, Ann G., "Illinois Central Corp. Names Harrison Chief Executive Officer and Lamphere Chairman," *Business Wire,* February 19, 1993.

—Dave Mote

Infinity Broadcasting Corporation

600 Madison Ave
New York, New York 10022
U.S.A.
(212) 750-6400
Fax: (212) 888-2959

Public Company
Incorporated: 1972
Employees: 675
Sales: $232.42 million
Stock Exchanges: NASDAQ
SICs: 4832 Radio Broadcasting Stations

Infinity Broadcasting Corporation, the largest company in the United States exclusively engaged in radio broadcasting, owns 26 radio stations serving 13 of the nation's largest radio markets. The company expanded during the 1980s and early 1990s by acquiring existing stations and successfully cultivating high-profile radio personalities.

Infinity was created by partners Michael Wiener and Gerald Carrus, who formed the company in order to purchase KOME, an FM radio station broadcasting in San Jose that also served the San Francisco area. KOME had just received its license to broadcast from the Federal Communications Commission (FCC) in 1971 before Wiener and Carrus assumed ownership in 1973. At the time, FM radio was a burgeoning medium, still struggling to catch up with the long-popular AM band. As FM gained in popularity during the 1970s, Wiener and Carrus achieved notable success with KOME, eventually expanding it into one of the most successful rock-and-roll stations in its geographic niche.

During the 1970s, Infinity embarked on an acquisition program informed by the strategy that had made KOME profitable; it purchased developing or underperforming radio stations in major markets and then turned them around with improved programming and management. Infinity eventually sold many of these concerns as a way of ''trading up'' to larger stations. In 1979, Wiener and Carrus brought another FM station under the Infinity umbrella that, like KOME, would stay with the company through the mid-1990s. They purchased WBCN, an under-performing station in Boston that the two believed had the potential to become a local ratings leader. Wiener and Carrus planned to shape WBCN in the image of KOME, making it an album-oriented rock station geared towards males between the ages of 18 and 30.

In 1981, Wiener and Carrus brought in Mel Karmazin to serve as company president and to oversee day-to-day operations. The 38-year-old Karmazin, a young, aggressive radio executive, agreed to accept the position with New York-based Infinity for a $125,000 annual salary and an opportunity to own part of the company should he prove responsible for significant growth. His only condition was that he was given total control of its operations. ''You can't have three people run a company,'' Karmazin explained in the November 30, 1992 issue of *Broadcasting*.

Under Karmazin's direction, Infinity experienced steady, rapid growth during the 1980s. During his first year, in fact, he managed buyouts of two New York stations, WXRK-FM and WZRC-AM. He also picked up WYSP-FM in Philadelphia. In 1983, moreover, Infinity absorbed KXYZ-AM in Houston and WJMK-FM and WJJD-AM in Chicago. Those purchases substantially boosted the company's revenues and made it a contender in the upper ranks of the national radio broadcasting industry. Adhering to the company's original strategy of seeking undervalued companies, Karmazin nevertheless changed Infinity's direction by accruing a large portfolio of stations, the value of which he intended to increase over the long term.

Although Karmazin had significantly increased Infinity's assets and revenues with the string of early 1980s acquisitions, the company was strapped for cash by mid-decade. In a bid to raise investment capital for continued growth, Karmazin took Infinity public in 1986. Within a year, he had purchased five more stations: KROQ-FM in Los Angeles, WJFK-FM in Washington, D.C., WQYK-FM and WQYK-AM in Tampa, and KVIL-FM and KVIL-AM in Dallas. Then, in 1988, Karmazin and three other company executives borrowed more money in order to repurchase Infinity's stock and take the enterprise private again, reasoning that the stock market had undervalued the company and that they could profit in the future by selling off the repurchased stock. Despite the company's surging debt, management borrowed funds to procure three more stations during the late 1980s: WOMC-FM in Detroit and both WLIF-FM and WFJK-AM in Baltimore.

Infinity's critics during the late 1980s cited the company's high debt load and weak profit performance as evidence of its lackluster potential. However, many analysts believed that the company was a better investment than it appeared. Indeed, by the end of the 1980s, Infinity had positioned itself as a market-niche leader in several major broadcasting regions, a status achieved largely through a formula of developing unique and popular programs aimed at specific demographic groups, which boosted the stations' potential ad revenues. Infinity had been successful in purchasing key sports broadcasting rights, for example, and had cultivated several popular radio personalities, such as New York station WXRK's Howard Stern. Moreover, all of Infinity's stations provided nonentertainment programming, such as news or public affairs broadcasts.

Under Karmazin, stations acquired by Infinity were subjected to a rigorous regimen of financial reporting requirements and cost controls designed to improve their profit margins. In addition,

Karmazin's team would adjust a new station's promotional strategy, usually by emphasizing local, rather than national, advertising sales. The overall programming and promotional initiatives usually resulted in high listener loyalty and healthy cash flow for most of Infinity's member stations.

Karmazin became known during the 1980s for his disciplined, hands-on management style. He met several times each week with his management team and continued to personally check up on local advertising accounts as he had since his days as a salesman. He also kept a heavy hand on all of Infinity's larger deals, such as the negotiation of rights to sports broadcasts. Karmazin's penchant for efficiency started at the top; Infinity's entire corporate staff in the early 1990s consisted of six people; Karmazin, a chief financial officer, an administrative assistant, and a three-person accounting office.

Infinity's spartan corporate staff was made possible by the autonomy that Karmazin afforded his local radio affiliates, as long as their ratings continued to rise. An important element of Karmazin's strategy was decentralized local management. Infinity relied on a system of performance-based financial incentives to motivate its workers and attract high-quality personnel, which were well-compensated by industry standards. General managers earned money for increasing cash flow, for example, and program directors were rewarded for higher ratings. Karmazin was particularly proud of Infinity's pay scale for advertising salespeople, which was a straight six percent commission with no limit on total earnings. Many salespeople earned more than $100,000 annually, with a few topping the $300,000 mark. "If a salesperson is going to get rich on a six percent commission," Karmazin stated in a *Broadcasting* article, "the company is going to get very rich on the other 94 percent."

Karmazin's management talents were perhaps most apparent in the example of Jim Hardy, whom Karmazin hired to serve as general manager of KOME, the first division acquired by Infinity in 1973. Raised in a Colorado goldmining town, before the onset of television, Hardy became interested in radio at a young age. He got his start in the business in the 1960s, working for his college radio station, one of the first FM stations in Colorado. In 1970, he went on to work for the first all-rock station in the United States, Denver's KLZ-FM. Hardy then served a long stint as a salesman at KWFM in Arizona until the infamous 1982 assassination of that station's disk jockey, Bob Cook, by a fanatic listener. Hardy then became manager of the station and soon thereafter was spotted by Karmazin as a capable candidate for the general management slot at KOME. After accepting the job, Hardy moved KOME to a new facility and began to reposition its programming and promotional operations. Citing consistent support from Infinity and the freedom afforded him in making critical decisions as contributing factors to his success, Hardy successfully increased the station's ratings and advertising revenue. By the late 1980s, KOME was the top-rated medium-market radio station by readers of *Rolling Stone Magazine* and was finishing tops in the important 25 to 54-year-old demographic ratings. "Gold mining is just like radio," Hardy noted in the April 2, 1990, issue of *Business Journal-San Jose,* in that "you dig a lot of dirt and hope you strike gold."

Despite the success of KOME and several other member stations, Infinity's performance lagged following the stock buy-back of 1988. In addition to the company's huge debt load, which topped $450 million in 1989, poor advertising revenues during the U.S. recession damaged Infinity's bottom line. While sales increased slowly to $123 million in 1989 and then to $135 million in 1991, the company posted successive net losses totaling more than $100 million during that period. Nevertheless, Infinity retained its strength in core markets and managed to sustain a healthy cash flow, an important measure of health for radio stations.

In an effort to slash its debt and continue acquiring new stations, Infinity elected to go public again in 1992, earning $100 million in the offering, much of which was used to buy WFAN-AM in New York. Early in 1993, Infinity again borrowed money to purchase three additional stations—WUSN-FM in Chicago, WZLX-FM in Boston, and WZGC-FM in Atlanta—for a total of $100 million. Of all its acquisitions, the WFAN purchase garnered the most criticism from industry analysts, who regarded Infinity's payout of $70 million as excessive for an AM station, particularly a station that was not ranked in the top ten in its locale. Nevertheless, Karmazin viewed the addition as complementary to his strategy of focusing on radio sports; WFAN was an all-sports station.

In 1992, Infinity began to rebound, as sales increased about 29 percent and net losses were cut to about $9.4 million, largely the result of a general economic recovery. In mid-1993, the company initiated another stock offering in order to help pare its debt. Perhaps most importantly, many of Infinity's marketing strategies were beginning to pay off during this time. Having cultivated what was possibly the most impressive assemblage of high-profile talk and sport show talent in the business, Infinity was prepared when the popularity of talk and sports radio experienced a re-birth. Among its most notable local celebrities were: Don Imus (WFAN); Doug "The Greaseman" Tracht, whom Infinity had hired away from another station and planned to syndicate nationally; G. Gordon Liddy, attorney and talk show host on WJFK; and Mike Francesa (WFAN), who had become well-known on CBS-TV.

Foremost among Infinity's talk show staff was Howard Stern, an outspoken, controversial morning radio personality. After Stern had achieved a huge following on New York's station WXRG, Infinity began syndicating Stern's show to other stations for $300,000 per year during the early 1990s. Stern soon became one of Infinity's most coveted assets, generating an estimated $15 million annually in sales and capturing as much as $2,000 per 30 second advertising slot. Stern's key attribute was his appeal to white-collar men aged 18 to 34, the most difficult-to-reach and lucrative demographic group sought by advertisers. Of that group, in fact, Stern attained higher ratings in the massive New York market than the highest-rated prime-time television shows.

However, Infinity's success in the rapidly growing talk show market came at a price. Several of its stations' most popular hosts had drawn the attention of regulatory agencies, who cited them for crude and deviant behavior on the air. As a result, some premier advertisers had been scared away from those stations. Although the FCC had loosened restrictions on material it viewed as repulsive, Stern and several other hosts continued to push the boundaries. In 1992, "The Greaseman" was under investigation for indecencies allegedly committed before his move to Infinity, and Infinity's KROQ-FM in Los Angeles came under fire for broadcasting a controversial murder hoax. Howard Stern generated the most controversy, drawing criticism not only from the FCC but also from a wide range of special interest groups. Karmazin's emphatic defense of these talk show hosts earned him a reputation among some observers as a staunch advocate of what he viewed as First Amendment rights, while other analysts were not so favorably impressed.

As the economy improved and Infinity's programming and management strategies began to pay off, the company's financial performance improved. Of import to Infinity's bottom line was its move in 1992 to begin syndicating more of its talk shows nationally. Syndication allowed the company an entirely new means of profiting from its most popular programs. In addition, in 1992, the FCC amended its restrictions, increasing the total number of U.S. stations allowed per operator from 24 to 36 and boosting the number that an operator could own on each band (AM and FM) in one city from one to four. Late in 1993, Infinity added WIP-AM, an all-sports station in Philadelphia, bringing its total number of holdings to 22.

In 1993, with revenues up more than 35 percent to $234 million, Infinity posted its first positive net income—$14 million—since the mid-1980s. The company was also experiencing strong gains in the value of its stock and reported operating profit margins of 45 percent, a full ten percentage points higher than the industry average. Acquisitions that year cemented Infinity's position as the largest company solely engaged in radio broadcasting. From just a few rock-and-roll stations in the early 1980s, Infinity had grown into a diversified industry leader with stations providing sports, oldies, country music, talk show, and even Spanish-language programming. Karmazin picked up the company's 23rd station early in 1994, acquiring KRTH-FM, an oldies station in Los Angeles, for $110 million, the largest sum ever paid for a U.S. radio station. Taking advantage of the FCC's new, more permissive ownership regulations, the company expected to make several more acquisitions during the 1990s.

Principal Subsidiaries: WXRK-FM, WZRC-AM, WFAN-AM, KROQ-FM, KRTH-FM, WJMK-FM/WJJD-AM, WUSN-FM, KOME-FM, WIP-AM, WYSP-FM, WOMC-FM, KVIL-FM/AM, WJFK-FM, WBCN-FM, WZLX-FM, KXYZ-AM, WZGC-FM, WLIF-FM, WJFK-AM, WQYK-FM/AM.

Further Reading:

Barry, David, "Jim Hard: He Played a Part in How the West Was Won—By FM Radio," *Business Journal-San Jose,* April 2, 1990, p. 12.

Breznik, Alan, "In IPO, Infinity Pitching WFAN to Street," *Crains New York Business,* January 6, 1992, p. 4.

Farhi, Paul, "Bad Taste, Good Business: To His Employer, Howard Stern Easily Passes a Classic Cost-Benefit Test," *Washington Post,* March 27, 1994, p. H1.

Flint, Joe, "Infinity No Stranger to FCC Complaints," *Broadcasting,* November 30, 1992, p. 37.

Kanter, Bruce, "Westwood One and Infinity Broadcasting Enter Into Letter of Intent for Westwood One to Acquire Unistar Radio Networks," *Business Wire,* October 11, 1993.

Lippman, John, "New Notch for Infinity: KRTH Acquisition Continues Radio Group Owner's Trend," *Los Angeles Times,* June 18, 1993, p. D1.

Mirabella, Alan, "Is Summit Kissing WRKS Goodbye?", *Crains New York Business,* December 6, 1993, p. 1.

"The Infinite Possibilities of Radio," *Broadcasting & Cable,* September 6, 1993, pp. 32–33.

Viles, Peter, "Infinity Unbowed," *Broadcasting,* November 30, 1992, pp. 4+.

—Dave Mote

Ingram Industries, Inc.

One Belle Meade Place
4400 Harding Road
Nashville, Tennessee 37205
U.S.A.
(615) 298-8200
Fax: (615) 298-8242

Private Company
Incorporated: 1938 as Wood River Oil and Refining
    Company
Sales: $4.6 billion
SICs: 5045 Computers, Peripherals & Software; 7822 Motion
    Picture & Tape Distribution; 4449 Water Transport of
    Freight, Nec; 3533 Oil & Gas Field Machinery

Ingram Industries, Inc., is one of the largest privately held American companies, with a broad array of activities. The company is the leading distributor of books and computer equipment; it also wholesales videocassettes, magazines, and other materials. Ingram is the third largest player in the inland waterway transportation industry, owning and operating more than 1,500 barges. The company also has a variety of energy holdings and an insurance subsidiary.

Ingram got its start in the energy industry, which dominated company activities until the 1980s. Ingram's genesis was an outgrowth of another great fortune. The Ingram family first derived their money from the Weyerhauser timber company, which was founded in part by O. H. Ingram's grandfather. With the proceeds from the block of stock in Weyerhauser that he inherited, O. H. Ingram established himself as a successful oil refiner in the 1930s. In 1938, he and a partner formed the Wood River Oil and Refining Company, which operated a refinery near St. Louis. Although the refinery was later sold to the Sinclair company, Ingram used this base to branch out into other related areas. In 1946, the company began operating barges to bring crude oil to its St. Louis refinery.

In the 1950s, Ingram formed the Ingram Oil & Refining Company. In 1963, he died, and the family business was taken over by his two sons, Frederic and Bronson, who changed the company's name to the Ingram Corporation. Under the stewardship of Frederic and Bronson, the Ingram holdings grew dramatically over the next three decades. The brothers began by focus-

ing their efforts on the company's inland barge company, which at that time was losing $2 million a year.

To finance expansion, the company borrowed money from bankers who were impressed by the Ingrams' reputations. The Ingrams bought properties that related to their father's legacy of barging and petroleum activities, and also acquired a number of other companies based in Tennessee. A year after their father's death, for instance, the Ingrams bought the Tennessee Book Company. This company was a textbook depository for the public school systems of Tennessee.

Also in the mid-1960s, Ingram moved into the insurance industry for the first time, buying the Tennessee Insurance Company. This company, which had been established in 1930, was purchased as an adjunct of the company's other businesses. The Ingram brothers had realized that the extensive physical assets of their holdings and their marine operations required substantial outlays for property, liability, and marine insurance. Rather than give that money to an outsider, they decided to buy a company that would then provide cost-effective insurance for other Ingram properties. Tennessee Insurance not only sold insurance directly to Ingram affiliates, it also reinsured those risks with Lloyds of London and other insurance brokers around the world.

Throughout the 1960s, Ingram continued to expand its holdings in petroleum and related fields. The company acquired assets in oil and chemical trading and transporting, oil refining, pipeline construction, and barging. Ingram relied on its status as a private company to move quickly and decisively in sealing pacts. These strengths assisted the Ingram brothers in making a number of important deals with foreign companies. By the end of the 1960s, these activities had allowed Ingram to build the world's third largest offshore company, which it subsequently sold to McDermott, Inc.

Although Ingram's primary focus throughout the 1960s lay in the energy industry, at the end of the decade, the company's book distribution unit began to demonstrate unexpected growth. After the arrival of a new company president in 1969, the distributor, which had been making about $3 million in trade sales, began a series of innovative programs.

In 1970, Ingram formed the Ingram Book Company to handle the company's trade book distribution operations. Taking advantage of new technologies, Ingram introduced personalized ordering, rapid shipments, toll-free telephone lines, and deep wholesaler discounts. The company took as its slogan, "Remember . . . with Ingram . . . the bookseller comes first," and soon won a host of satisfied customers. In 1972, Ingram Book built on these gains by developing a microfiche system that provided weekly inventory updates to booksellers. In addition, the company later rolled out co-op advertising programs with its clients; a separate catalogue showcasing mass paperback titles, called Paperback Advance; and special procedures for supplying inventory to stores that were just starting.

Throughout that time, Ingram's other divisions were also growing. In 1970, the company made tentative plans to sell stock to the public in order to finance further expansion, but those plans were dropped in June. With this decision, Ingram also withdrew from arrangements to merge with a pipeline company. However, in 1973, Ingram did form a joint venture to build an oil refinery in Louisiana with Northeast Petroleum Industries, Inc. This project, which became the largest refinery ever constructed from scratch in the United States, was eventually sold to Marathon Oil.

In 1974, Ingram acquired Tampimex Oil, a London-based petroleum broker with revenues of $680 million. Two years later, Ingram's aggressive pursuit of revenue growth dropped the company into hot water, when the brothers were accused of participating in a $1.3 million kickback scheme to win a sludge-hauling contract from the city of Chicago for its barge line. Chicago had awarded Ingram a $43 million contract for the job in 1971, which was renewed in 1973, and the indictment charged that these awards had not been subject to a competitive bidding process. In 1977, the Chicago Metropolitan Sanitary District also sued the company for illegal operations.

Despite these legal entanglements, the Ingrams forged ahead with their program of expansion. In 1975, the company formed a joint venture to develop petroleum in Iran. In the following year, Ingram entered negotiations to buy the U.S. Lines shipping company and also began a move into the coal market. Eventually, Ingram came to broker over 2 million tons of coal annually, most of it to a large Ohio utility. Ingram also became a leading transporter of coal, particularly on the lower Ohio river.

By the end of 1976, Ingram's book distribution unit had also become the predominant American wholesaler of trade books after revolutionizing the book distribution industry. Company sales had risen to exceed $60 million a year, as Ingram pushed ahead with further technological developments and geographic expansion. From its base in Nashville, the company had added an east coast distribution center in Jessup, Maryland, and had also purchased the Raymar Book Corporation, giving it two west coast centers. In October 1976, gross monthly orders reached $1 million for the first time.

Ingram Book followed up on these advances by forming the Ingram Retail Advisory Council, made up of independent booksellers, at the 1977 convention of the American Booksellers Association. With the advice of this group, the company set out to develop a computer system for bookstore management, which was unveiled two years later under the name INVOY.

In 1978, the Ingrams rearranged the corporate structure of their holdings, and changed the name of their company from Ingram Corporation to Ingram Industries, Inc. This change better conveyed the increasingly diverse nature of the company's activities. In 1981, Ingram Book branched out from wholesaling to purchase the John Yokley Company, a commercial printer. Despite the success of this division, the Ingram Barge Company remained the largest subsidiary of the company. In 1984, Ingram moved to double the size of this operation when it purchased two U.S. Steel Corporation barge lines. In December, Ingram announced that it would pay $81 million for Ohio Barge Lines, Inc., and the Mon-Valley Transportation Company. In this way, the company expanded its inland waterways operation from Pittsburgh to Houston. In addition, Ingram added the capacity to carry coal, steel, and chemicals to its other barge operations, which moved stone, grain, and petroleum.

At this time Ingram was rebuffed in its effort to take over the Corroon & Black company. Ingram had offered $253 million to buy the 92.2 percent of Corroon & Black's stock which it did not already own, but this offer was rejected by the company's board. In 1985, however, Ingram announced a substantial investment in its petroleum wellhead equipment manufacturer and supplier. The company changed its subsidiary's name from Gulco Industries, Inc., to Ingram Petroleum Services, Inc., and spent over $10 million to move the company from its position as a mid-sized on-shore Oklahoma City firm, serving the middle region of the United States, to an international off-shore supplier.

Four years later, Ingram also augmented its barge operations when it bought the marine assets of the American Barge and Towing Company of St. Louis. The company purchased 319 barges and eight tugboats from American Barge, expanding its own fleet by 30 percent. Ingram planned to operate these barges, designed to carry wheat, on the upper Mississippi river. Ingram also announced that it would buy 23 barges and 5 tugboats from System Fuels, Inc. These properties were customized for the transport of liquids.

Despite these moves and Ingram's prominent place in the inland transportation industry, by the end of the 1980s rapid growth in the company's distribution activities meant that they had begun to contribute the lion's share of Ingram's revenues. Over the course of that decade, the balance of earning power within the conglomerate had gradually shifted away from heavy industrial activities toward the distribution of consumer products. The company had expanded its book distribution arm to include magazines and videotapes. In addition, Ingram Computer had been established to distribute computers and peripheral supplies from a warehouse in Buffalo, New York.

Ingram's move toward distribution got a significant boost when Ingram took over Micro D, Inc., a southern California personal computer distributor, in which Ingram had owned a majority interest for three years. Micro D had been the leading player in the personal computer distribution industry, which had grown dramatically in size during the 1980s, from $1.6 billion in sales in 1985, to $4.8 billion in 1989. Micro D's revenues during that time had shot up to $553 million in 1988. Ingram combined Micro D with Ingram Computer and called the new company Ingram Micro D, which was later shortened to Ingram Micro. It held 20 percent of the computer distribution market, twice as much as its nearest competitor. However, the consolidation of the two companies proved somewhat rocky, as the southern California ethos clashed with that of its new Eastern owner. A number of key executives left Micro D, and the company lost two major accounts in the two months after the merger.

In July 1989, Ingram made another acquisition in the consumer goods field when it purchased the Permanent General Companies, Inc., and made it a subsidiary of the Tennessee Insurance Company. This enterprise provided auto insurance to high-risk drivers in Tennessee and financing services to help customers pay premiums. With more than 40 percent of the Tennessee market for high-risk auto policies, the company planned to expand further into other southeastern markets.

Despite the early management difficulties at Ingram Micro, the company continued to dominate the computer distribution field, and by the start of the 1990s, Ingram could boast that it owned the largest player in both this field and book distribution. One computer publication reported that 90 percent of Ingram's total income of more than $2.5 billion came from its distribution activities. By 1991, Ingram executives were predicting that the company's biggest arena for growth in the 1990s would be global expansion of the microcomputer market. The company made efforts to establish a beachhead in Europe, starting up operations in the United Kingdom to prepare for broader activities as Europe unified its markets.

In March 1992, Ingram strengthened its distribution operations further when the company purchased the Commtron Corporation, a videocassette wholesaler, and merged it with its Ingram Entertainment, Inc. subsidiary, which also distributed videocassettes. After this merger, the two companies controlled an estimated one-third of the market.

By the end of 1993, Ingram Entertainment's fellow distributor, Ingram Micro, was still contributing a substantial portion of the company's revenues. Overall, the Ingram conglomerate encompassed 54 different units, spanning industries from petroleum refining to book distribution. With its record of strong growth and its toehold in the burgeoning computer industry, the company seemed assured of future success in the late 1990s.

Principal Subsidiaries: Ingram Distribution Group, Inc.; Ingram Micro, Inc.; Ingram Book Company; Ingram Entertainment, Inc.; Ingram Barge Company; Ingram Production Company; Tennessee Insurance Company; Permanent General Companies.

Further Reading:

Carey, Christopher, ''Firm Here Sells Fleet of Barges,'' *St. Louis Post Dispatch,* February 23, 1989.
''The Hungry Millionaires,'' *Forbes,* November 1, 1976.
''Ingram Continues to Expand Its Services,'' *Publishers Weekly,* November 15, 1976.
Olmos, David, ''Verdict Still Out on Micro D,'' *Los Angeles Times,* May 30, 1989.
Redlond, Kristen, ''Q & A: The Elusive Man at the Helm of Ingram Micro Parent,'' *Computer Reseller News,* September 9, 1991.
Snow, Nick, ''Despite Down Market, Ingram Will Expand,'' *The Oil Daily,* November 18, 1985.

—Elizabeth Rourke

International Telephone and Telegraph Corporation

1330 Avenue of the Americas
New York, New York 10019-5422
U.S.A.
(212) 258-1000
Fax: 489-5099

Public Company
Incorporated: 1968
Employees: 98,000
Sales: $22.76 billion
Stock Exchanges: New York London Paris Basle Bern
    Frankfurt Tokyo Vienna Geneva Lausanne Brussels
    Antwerp Zurich Boston Cincinnati NASDAQ Philadelphia
    Pacific
SICs: 6331 Fire, Marine and Casualty Insurance; 3714 Motor
    Vehicle Parts and Accessories; 6141 Personal Credit
    Institutions; 3812 Search and Navigation Equipment; 2611
    Pulp Mills; 3674 Semiconductors and Related Devices;
    3594 Fluid Power Pumps and Motors; 6153 Short-Term
    Business Credit Institutions, except Agricultural; 6321
    Accident and Health Insurance; 6311 Life Insurance; 3679
    Electronic Components, Not Elsewhere Classified; 3494
    Valves & Pipe Fittings, Not Elsewhere Classified; 7011
    Hotels and Motels

Once known primarily as a telecommunications company, the International Telephone and Telegraph Corporation (ITT) has interests in financial and business services, the manufacture of automotive and defense products, and hotels. ITT's history is interwoven with the lives of three men: Col. Sosthenes Behn, Harold Geneen, and Rand V. Araskog. Behn founded the company in 1920 with the intention of creating an international telephone system modeled after American Telephone and Telegraph. Geneen later took over the corporation and, believing that diversity facilitated growth, molded ITT into one of the world's largest conglomerates. Araskog, who inherited a sprawling, debt-ridden giant, whittled ITT down and divested its namesake telecommunications interests.

When Lt. Col. Louis Richard Sosthenes Behn and his brother Hernand founded ITT in 1920, they expected to take advantage of an industry market that barely existed outside of the United States. In 1920, the U.S. reported 64 phones per 1,000 inhabi-

tants, while Germany was estimated to have nine phones per 1,000 inhabitants, Britain five per 1,000 and France three per 1,000. At that time, three companies, Siemens, Ericsson, and AT&T, dominated what there was of the world market.

Although theirs was a small company, the Behns were well-positioned to compete in the growing international market. They had operated South Puerto Rico Telephone Company since 1905 and Cuban Telephone Company since 1916, and in both cases they used ingenuity and skill to transform inefficient companies into well-run, profitable operations with good service records. Sosthenes Behn's tour of duty with the American Expeditionary Force in World War I (where he gained the rank of Lieutenant Colonel) set in motion his vision for an international telephone system. Behn intended to achieve this international system via ITT, which he and his brother Hernand formed in 1920 as the holding company for their existing companies and for those they would acquire.

The way ITT expanded into the European market provided an example of the way it would conduct business during most of the Behn era. The combined effects of good timing, well-placed connections, and Sosthenes' charm brought ITT the concession for telephone service in Spain in 1924. Timing was crucial due to the fact that before 1924 ITT's securities were a questionable issue on Wall Street. However, the company's consistent growth and steadily expanding earnings, coupled with the support of National City Bank, provided Wall Street analysts with a good reason to support ITT's venture into the Spanish telephone market. Behn provided the rest by placing influential Spaniards on the board of ITT's new company, CTNE, and charming the appropriate members of the Spanish government.

The Spanish concession, operated by CTNE, furnished ITT with an entrance into the European market, one that Behn wasted no time in expanding. Upset with the quality of equipment available to him, he began to search for an equipment manufacturing company to purchase. Timing and connections again helped ITT. In 1925, the U.S. government was pressuring AT&T to divest its overseas operations, which included International Western Electric Company, a European-based manufacturer of telephonic equipment. A National City banker arranged a meeting between Walter Gifford, chairperson of bank customers at AT&T, and Sosthenes Behn, which resulted in the sale of the company to ITT on September 30, 1925, along with temporary use of some of AT&T's patents.

After ITT acquired the Spanish concession and the International Western Electric Company, it entered a period of rapid growth. ITT became one of the most highly valued stocks in the bull market of the period, enabling it to acquire numerous companies, mostly in the telecommunications field. Behn's dream for the international telephone system came closer to reality, and his reputation as a cosmopolitan and shrewd businessman increased.

ITT had become an international company holding manufacturing companies and operating concessions in France, Germany, Britain, and much of Latin America. National citizens ran ITT's subsidiaries in every country with a facility, while corporate headquarters in New York played a passive management role.

The search for additional companies continued, though Behn's acquisition program placed ITT heavily in debt. The debt seemed manageable in the thriving world economy of the late 1920s, and ITT continued to be a popular stock despite the fact that a recession would hurt the company.

Yet if a recession would hurt ITT, the Great Depression nearly put it out of business. The debt accumulated during the 1920s was only part of ITT's problems, as the very nature of the company's business exacerbated its financial difficulties. As a holding company ITT earned money through dividends and profits remitted by its subsidiaries, most of which were foreign. Most ITT clients were either governments or quasi-nationalized telephone operating companies. However, in the restrictive trade atmosphere of the early part of the Depression, many foreign nations refused to allow American-based ITT to repatriate earnings from its subsidiaries. ITT was therefore deprived of significant revenues and threatened with bankruptcy through much of the Depression, despite eliminating dividends to shareholders. To make matters worse, ITT lost a good manager when Hernand Behn died in 1933.

At the beginning of World War II, in Argentina, Spain, and elsewhere, ITT's holdings were in danger of being taken from the company by governments sympathetic to Germany. Profits again became impossible to repatriate. Behn's business acumen enabled him to sell some of ITT's holdings (in Rumania, for instance) and helped avoid having others (particularly SEG and Lorenz in Germany) taken from the company at a time when foreign operations of other major American manufacturers were not treated as well. As much a factor in these matters was Behn's penchant for employing mostly nationals, of whom the head of SEL had some influence with Hitler. Still, these events earned ITT the ire of many Americans, and after the war it was one of several companies accused of collusion with Hitler, an accusation that would linger long afterwards.

ITT's difficulties in the Depression and World War II made Behn determined to reduce its dependence on its non-U.S. companies. Behn abandoned the international telephone system and established ITT's new goal: to derive two-thirds of its revenues from American companies.

This goal was difficult to achieve. ITT had consolidated some operations within the United States in response to the war, centered around the earlier acquisition of Federal Electric. Federal's electronics and military contracts made it a significant revenue earner during the war, and Behn hoped the company could gain a portion of the postwar market for consumer electronics and durables. Such efforts were mixed at best and, as a result, Behn looked to merge ITT with one of several large U.S. companies, including Sylvania, Raytheon, the American Broadcasting Co. (ABC), and RCA in order to realize his postwar goal of a company earnings distribution. None of the larger mergers materialized, but those that did, such as Coolerator and Capehart-Farnsworth, drained capital and performed poorly, keeping ITT's stock low in a bull market.

Such domestic difficulties weakened ITT and Behn's position as leader. Although ITT was once again profitable, the dividend was not restored, and stockholders began to challenge Behn's decisions. A boardroom battle for power occurred, which Behn eventually lost, despite having reinstated the dividend in 1951. He remained chairperson until he died in 1956, though his power was largely symbolic after 1953.

During this time, the company's emphasis was on overseas operations, although even the European subsidiaries were posting smaller than expected profits. Some observers commented that the three years spanning Behn's death and Harold Geneen's accession at ITT saw nothing more significant than a change of logo from IT&T to ITT.

If there was a lull in company growth and productivity, it ended in 1959 when Harold Sydney Geneen took over as head of ITT. Geneen's management abilities had been showcased at such firms as American Can, Bell & Howell, Jones & Laughlin, and Raytheon, and at ITT he became almost a synonym for excellence in management. The Geneen method of "Management by Meetings" was popularized and widely imitated.

Geneen had drive, ambition, and seemingly endless energy. He also believed firmly that companies should aim at both short and long-term growth, not stability. He first reorganized ITT with a management shake-up and thorough cost-cutting measures. In his first five years, over 30 percent of the company's executives were replaced, though in keeping with ITT tradition few were fired. Instead, executives regarded as lacking the necessary skills were worked to the point where they would quit. As one executive remarked, "Nothing matters to him but the job—not the clock, not your personal life, nothing." So many executives would come and go during the Geneen era that ITT was compared to a revolving door, and a *Forbes* magazine reporter gave it the title of Geneen University.

Geneen instituted his changes to redirect a corporation that, in his mind, evoked the question "how long it would have gone on before it cracked wide open." This was not an entirely accurate perception; ITT was a growing company, even if it fell short of its earnings potential. Part of the problem stemmed from the Behn legacy, including the almost complete lack of cohesion among subsidiaries. Geneen worked to correct this and increased headquarters' role in the affairs of subsidiaries through yearly meetings and required reports.

In 1963, ITT began to make a significant number of acquisitions, averaging one company a month. Geneen promoted the notion of a diversified company as a strong company, one able to weather downturns in a particular sector of the economy through its holdings in other sectors. Such strength made a diversified company the best vehicle for corporate growth, assets could be transferred to the appropriate divisions, and the company would be less dependent on individual clients as well as cyclical markets.

His purchases emphasized U.S. operations over European ones, with an aspiration that 55 percent of ITT's revenues come from U.S. subsidiaries. When he set out, the ratio was 60/40 in favor of international operations. Several factors influenced his decision, including French and British advocacy of nationalization of certain ITT subsidiaries, Fidel Castro's expropriation of ITT's Cuban Telephone, and intensifying competition in the European telecommunications market.

Geneen achieved his objective through the frenetic acquisition of 350 companies from 1959 to 1979. In the early 1960s, acquisitions averaged one per month. Purchases included: Avis, Inc. (car rentals); Continental Baking Co. (Wonder bread, Twinkies); Sheraton Corp. of America (hotels); Grinnell Corp. (vending machines, foodservice); Bobbs-Merrill (publishing); Levitt Homes (suburban residential construction); Eason Oil Company (heating oil); W. Atlee Burpee Co. (seeds); Pennsylvania Glass Sand Co., and many others. Geneen's cost-cutting measures and his complementary acquisition program helped ITT meet his first five-year goal, namely, to double earnings and income. In this way, ITT became a billion dollar corporation in 1962, and by 1969 it had quadrupled in size. Under Geneen, ITT's revenues increased from $800 million to $22 billion, and the conglomerate became the fourth largest employer in America with 368,000 employees on its payrolls.

ITT made its move into the U.S. market at the same time as a number of other companies, part of a merger trend that due to its size and complexity caused a large amount of consumer distrust. In a decade that would become increasingly anti-big business, multinationals and especially conglomerates became targets of frequent attacks in the nation's press, fueled by books such as *Up the Corporation*. Some people thought that ITT symbolized what was wrong with big business.

Questionable actions in the United States and abroad did nothing to allay those perceptions. The first of a stunning series of setbacks came in 1968, when the conglomerate lost its bid to acquire the American Broadcasting Co. when the U.S. Justice Department challenged the takeover on antitrust grounds. The Justice Department made several more moves against ITT, including litigation attempting to prevent its takeover of Hartford Fire Insurance in 1970. ITT agreed to divest assets equal to those of Hartford's—including Avis, Levitt, Canteen, and Grinnell—and pledged not to acquire any companies with assets over $100 million until 1981. Much negative publicity arose from these confrontations with the Justice Department.

ITT's image with the U.S. public was further damaged in 1971. That year, ITT was accused of bribing Republican officials into locating the 1968 Republican National Convention at the Harbor Beach Sheraton in San Diego. At the same time, Chilean officials accused ITT of interfering in that country's elections. The corporation allegedly hoped to prevent election of a leftist president who threatened to nationalize ITT's business interests there.

These incidents alone would have cast a shadow over Geneen's final years as head of ITT. But to make matters worse, of his hundreds of acquisitions, only the Pennsylvania Glass Sand Company was an immediate source of profits for ITT. Additionally, the purchase of Levitt Homes would eventually prove a disaster. Writing in 1992 for *Business Horizons,* Danny Miller compared Geneen's managerial style to Icarus of Greek mythology—both characters' greatest assets led to their demise.

In 1978, Geneen, aged 67, stepped down from the chair of ITT, although he remained on the board until 1983. His immediate successor did not remain long and was soon replaced with the little known Rand Vincent Araskog. Araskog was a West Point graduate who had worked at Honeywell before joining ITT in 1968. The new leader was promoted from within ITT and was expected to be Geneen's pawn, but this proved a misconception. At first, Araskog boldly declared that ITT would return to its telecommunications roots and compete directly with AT&T in the domestic market. But economic realities, including the massive debt racked up during Geneen's tenure, soon thwarted that plan. In 1979, ITT had over $4 billion in debt—more than 40 percent of its capitalization. Instead, Araskog embarked on what *Financial World* later called "a gigantic corporate garage sale the likes of which the world will probably never see again."

From 1979 to 1983, Araskog sold off businesses worth $200 million each year and used the proceeds to pay down ITT's debt. By the end of 1984, the company had divested 69 subsidiaries totaling nearly $2 billion. Araskog did his job so well, in fact, that his slimmed-down, cash-rich corporation became one of the first high-stakes takeover targets of the 1980s. While fighting off hostile overtures from three corporate raiders—Jay A. Pritzker, Philip Anschutz, and Irwin Jacobs—Araskog continued to liquidate ITT's holdings, selling over 100 subsidiaries by 1986. The CEO's focus on retaining a profitable core of market leaders in insurance, finance, and automotive and industrial engineering conspicuously left out ITT's historical base: telecommunications. In 1986, after long negotiations, Araskog sold a majority stake in ITT's overseas telecommunications business to Cie Générale d'Electricité (which later became Alcatel Alsthom Compagnie Générale d'Electricité) for $2 billion to form a joint venture, Alcatel N.V. Abandoning the U.S. portion of the business precluded a $105 million write-off that year.

By the end of the decade, ITT's debt was below 30 percent of capital, and Araskog was credited with paring the company down to a profitable core. The CEO was paid generously ("lavishly," in *Business Week's* 1994 estimation) for his achievements: over $5 million in salary alone in 1989. But Wall Street seemed not to appreciate the changes at ITT. The corporation's stock trailed Standard & Poor's 500 index by 36 percent from 1979 to the end of 1991. Institutional investors, especially the California Public Employees' Retirement System (CalPERS) revolted against ITT when, in 1990, Araskog's salary doubled to $11.4 million in spite of a 20 percent decline in the corporation's stock price and a 30 percent drop in income from operations. Under fire from CalPERS, Araskog and ITT's board agreed to tie executive compensation to stock performance.

From 1992 to 1994, ITT's stock price rose 46 percent, to nearly 85 cents a share, driven in part by new asset sales. In 1992, the company sold off its 37 percent interest in Alcatel to its partner for $3.6 billion. Late in 1993, Araskog announced the pending spin-off of forest products subsidiary ITT Rayonier Inc. to shareholders. Araskog's pending retirement (in 1996, at age 65) and the resurgence in divestments combined to fuel speculation that the CEO might break ITT up into three independent companies. Araskog did nothing to dispel those rumors. In fact, *Business Week* quoted him calling that option "not outlandish," and the company announced that it was exploring the possibility early in 1994.

Principal Subsidiaries: ITT Hartford; ITT Financial Corporation; ITT Communications and Information Services, Inc.; ITT

Automotive Inc.; ITT Defense & Electronics, Inc.; ITT Fluid Technology Corporation; ITT Sheraton Corporation.

Further Reading:

Araskog, Rand, ''How I Fought Off the Raiders,'' *Fortune,* February 27, 1989, pp. 110–118.

Burns, Thomas S., *Tales of ITT: An Insider's Report,* Boston: Houghton Mifflin, 1974.

Deloraine, Maurice, *When Telecom and ITT Were Young,* New York: Lehigh, 1976.

Geneen, Harold, and Alvin Moscow, *Managing,* New York: Avon, 1993.

Lesly, Elizabeth, ''While ITT Lumbers, Its Stock Has Legs,'' *Business Week,* May 30, 1994, pp. 98–103.

Miller, Danny, ''The Icarus Paradox: How Exceptional Companies Bring About Their Own Downfall,'' *Business Horizons,* January/February 1992, pp. 24–35.

Sampson, Anthony, *The Sovereign State of ITT,* New York: Stein and Day, 1973.

Sobel, Robert, *ITT: The Management of Opportunity,* New York: Times, 1982.

Spero, Joan E., *The Politics of International Economic Relations,* New York: St. Martin's Press, 1985.

—updated by April Dougal Gasbarre

Invacare Corporation

899 Cleveland Street
P. O. Box 4028
Elyria, Ohio 44036
U.S.A.
(216) 329-6000
Fax: (216) 366-9008

Public Company
Incorporated: 1971
Employees: 3,040
Sales: $365 million
Stock Exchanges: NASDAQ
SICs: 3842 Surgical Appliances and Supplies; 2599 Furniture Fixtures, Nec

Invacare Corporation, one the leading manufacturers of home medical equipment in the world, focuses on supplying medical equipment and mobility products to people with disabilities and those who require home health care. Its product line ranges from commodes and electric beds to crutches and home respiratory systems. Invacare's innovative products have fueled its success. It was the first firm to produce a motorized wheelchair with computerized controls.

Incorporated in 1971 as a subsidiary of Technicare, a Cleveland-based medical equipment firm, Invacare mainly manufactured wheel chairs. But Invacare's slow sales, muddled management, and lack of new product development resulted in the company becoming a financial drain on Technicare. When Johnson & Johnson purchased Technicare in 1978, it decided to sell Invacare. The initial group of investors that arranged to purchase Invacare was frustrated in their attempt due to a squabble over the amount of control requested by the new chief executive officer. Then Malachi Mixon appeared on the scene.

Mixon, a 39-year-old head of marketing CT scanners for Technicare, former Marine Corps artillery officer who served in Vietnam, and Harvard Business School graduate, immediately decided to buy Invacare when he heard it was for sale. But with only $10,000 of his own money to invest, financing the acquisition of a company that cost $7.8 million seemed almost impossible. Undeterred, Mixon arranged for two real estate brokers to purchase Invacare's facility on Taylor Street, and then lease it back to the company. Then, Mixon arranged for a $4.3 million loan from First Chicago Bank. The remainder of the needed

money came from his own resources, loans from friends, and issuing shares of stock to various local investors. While structuring the financing of Invacare, Mixon included a 15 percent interest in the company for himself.

When Mixon and his group officially assumed control of Invacare on January 2, 1980, the company had a low standing within the health care products industry. Sales were stagnant at approximately $20 million, far lower than the $124 million sales figure of its chief competitor, Everest & Jennings. Furthermore, Mixon's leveraged buyout resulted in a $6.5 million debt, and the high interest rate of nearly 25 percent was devouring Invacare's modest $1.2 million profits.

During the first year as chief executive officer at Invacare, Mixon devoted a significant amount of time to studying the company's product line. After eliminating the manufacture of those items that were either obsolete or unprofitable, he pushed Invacare's engineering department to develop highly innovative products. Mixon believed that Everest & Jennings, which had over an 80 percent share of the world's wheelchair market, was not only growing complacent with its position within the industry but was losing touch with its customers.

In 1982, Mixon's emphasis on new product development paid off when Invacare was the first in the industry to introduce a motorized wheelchair with computerized controls. Invacare's computer controls could be easily adapted to suit the individual needs and requirements of the severely disabled. The wheelchair quickly became an industry standard, and Invacare suddenly found itself in an intense competition with Everest & Jennings for the larger share of the wheelchair market.

Everest & Jennings responded to Invacare by reducing its prices, but cost-effective production methods enabled Invacare to match its competitor's prices. At the same time, Mixon had worked hard to improve Invacare's distribution network: inexpensive financing, volume discounts, 48-hour delivery, funds for cooperative advertising, and prepaid freight convinced more than 6,000 home health care dealers in the United States that Invacare was the better of the two companies. In a short time, Invacare had equaled and then surpassed Everest & Jennings' share of the wheelchair market. Invacare's ever-expanding product line, which now included items such as cardiovascular exercise equipment and oxygen concentrators, and its policy of stocking parts for the products of its competitors, soon placed the company in a league of its own.

In the beginning of 1984, it appeared that Invacare's rapid growth and enviable financial success would continue unabated. During that year, Mixon decided to enter the European market for home health care products, and acquired a British firm that manufactured wheelchair and patient aids and a West German producer of wheelchairs. Mixon also determined that it was an appropriate time to take the company public in order to underwrite the expenditures for Invacare's quick growth, offer employee stock options that would attract highly qualified managers, and provide Invacare's original group of investors with some liquidity for their initial stake in the company.

Later in 1984, however, Invacare was hurt by a series of unexpected events. When the company discovered it had less inventory than was reported in its books, it was forced to take a charge against earnings which resulted in a financial loss for the fiscal year of 1984. In addition, because of manufacturing defects in the company's oxygen concentrator, Invacare was forced to recall the product and suffered a loss of approximately $1.5 million in sales. To compound company problems, in 1985 the U.S. government changed its formulas for Medicare reimbursement. The new requirement led wheelchair dealers to sell more chairs than they leased, which resulted in a disincentive for dealers to purchase better built, but more expensive, reusable wheelchairs. Invacare's sales dropped precipitously, and its profitability was threatened. Not surprisingly, the company's initial stock, offered at $11 per share just one year earlier, plummeted to less than $4 by mid 1985.

Mixon was convinced that a significant part of Invacare's problems could be attributed to a lack of manufacturing efficiency and quality control problems. He was determined never to allow another Invacare product to suffer the embarrassment of a recall by the federal government. Mixon hired J. B. Richey, a former associate at Technicare and general manager of that company's magnetic resonance division, to rectify the manufacturing problems at Invacare. First, Richey concentrated on finding Invacare's quality control problems. The company's sales force was required to submit monthly reports detailing customer complaints about its products. With these reports, Richey then began to correct the problems which occurred during production.

Simultaneously, Richey implemented a program in statistical process control methods for company employees. Another quality control measure involved sending Invacare's own certified representatives to check the plants of its suppliers; this policy led to a reduction in the number of suppliers but a higher and more consistent quality of product parts. Richey's strategy paid off handsomely as Invacare reduced the rejection rate of its supplier's parts to less than two percent. But Richey had said numerous times that Invacare's goal should be to measure rejection rates as Japanese companies do—in parts per million. One of the most important aspects of Invacare's determination to improve the quality control of its products involved a switch from purchasing to manufacturing the electronic control systems on its motorized wheelchairs. Richey went directly to the National Aeronautic and Space Administration's (NASA) Lewis Space Center and purchased much of the equipment NASA used to tests its controls on the space shuttles. The result of employing such sophisticated quality control equipment led to the perception that Invacare's power wheelchairs were the most reliable in the industry.

With all its improvements in quality control, Invacare was well-prepared to meet an unexpected challenge in 1986. Wheelchair manufacturers in Taiwan started to sell their products in the United States that year at nearly 20 percent below the normal price structure. Invacare's response was to construct a new manufacturing plant in Reynosa, Mexico, in addition to its facilities in Elyria, Ohio. Although Mixon denied that there was a plan to shut down the Elyria plant or relocate jobs to Mexico, the consequence was that Elyria employees became more productive and efficient in light of the prospect of losing their jobs. Invacare's new plant in Mexico produced wheelchairs at a much lower cost and almost eliminated the Taiwanese manufacturers from the U.S. domestic market. With its quality control prob-

lems solved and no other company to challenge its dominance of the wheelchair market, Invacare grew quickly. In 1986, the company reported profits of $3.4 million on revenues of $111 million.

By 1989, Invacare's revenues jumped to over $186 million. An important aspect of its success was the decentralized management structure emphasized by Mixon. Each of the key officers in the company was given complete authority to make the changes necessary for the respective divisions they supervised to meet their sales goals. This organizational setup encouraged a fast-paced, high-pressure work environment, but management was given full authority to meet the dual responsibilities of efficiency and productivity. In addition, Invacare not only hired disabled people to help design and test its products, but the company provided a stock sharing plan for its employees that helped create a sense of ownership, empowerment, and accountability.

The next two years, 1990 and 1991, were watershed years for Invacare. In 1990, the company introduced a total of 53 new products, including significant innovations in wheelchair design with the introduction of microprocessors for power wheelchairs and the first wheelchair designed for use on airliners. Invacare also created its Action Technology division in which highly flexible wheelchairs made of light composite materials were designed for active users. By 1991, Invacare stock had climbed to $25 per share. That year, the company launched an advertising campaign to sell its products directly to consumers. Although still relying heavily on dealers to market its products, Mixon successfully anticipated that a large segment of the disabled population was looking for products allowing them to lead a more active life. Invacare reported revenues of more than $263 million for the fiscal year ending 1991. Invacare's successes made it one of top 50 firms to invest in during the decade of the 1990s, according to *U.S. News and World Report.*

In 1992, Invacare was known by industry analysts as the leader in manufacturing wheelchairs and home care medical equipment. The company was manufacturing a comprehensive line of wheelchairs, including pediatric and sports models, quad canes, scooters, and walkers in the most up-to-date ultralight materials. With its oxygen concentrators, medical beds, nebulizers, cushions and positioning systems, Invacare produced the broadest line of items in the home health care industry. The company had expanded to include 19 manufacturing facilities in the United States and over 10,000 dealers distributing its products throughout the world, including Mexico, Canada, New Zealand, and Europe. In 1992, international sales accounted for approximately 23 percent of Invacare's total revenues.

Invacare experienced another banner year in 1993. Sales increased to $365 million while earnings were reported at over $22 million. From 1979 through 1993, the company had achieved an annual growth rate of over 23 percent and was listed in *Forbes* as one of the 200 best small companies in America and in *Business Week*'s "250 Companies on the Move." From October of 1991 to the end of 1993, Invacare made seven major acquisitions, including Canadian Posture and Seating Centre, Hovis Medical, Perry Oxygen, Poirier, Top End, Dynamics Controls, and Geomarine Systems, Inc. Although Dynamic Controls, a manufacturer of power controls for wheel chairs, and Geomarine Systems, a manufacturer of low air loss therapy mattress replacement systems, were important in expanding the company's product line and increasing the cost effectiveness of its manufacturing operations, it was the purchase of Top End Wheelchair Sports that was most significant. Top End products included road racing and tennis wheelchairs, and a water ski for disabled people. Top End Action wheelchairs were used in over 200 sports events during 1993, including the National Veterans Wheelchair Games, NBA-sponsored wheelchair basketball games, Easter Seals wheelchair tennis camps, and numerous other competitive and recreational sports events. The acquisition of Top End gave Invacare valuable exposure to the growing active user wheelchair market.

Invacare has been at the forefront of the debate on health care reform and Medicare reimbursement policy. Mixon has testified extensively before committees in both the Senate and the House of Representatives to lobby in favor of the economic and medical benefits of home care as opposed to institutional care. Of the 70 health care reform bills pending Congressional approval in 1993, 69 of them included legislation on the various services and equipment of home health care. Mixon admitted that passage of health care reform bills would directly benefit Invacare, but he cited statistics that convey a message other than self-interest: the cost to care for an infant born with feeding and breathing problems is $61,000 in a hospital and $20,000 at home; more than 90 percent of all people surveyed reported that they would rather be taken care of at home rather than at a hospital or institution; and demographic surveys taken by the U.S. Census Bureau indicate that there will be an ever-increasing demand for home health care equipment due to the fact that one out of every eight people in America is over the age of 65 during the 1990s—in contrast to one out of 25 over the age of 65 during the 1920s.

Invacare had six operating divisions in 1993: Home Care division, Rehab division, Aftermarket Parts division, Canadian division, European division, and Invacare Technologies division. The firm continued to hold the greater share of the home health care products market, but was seeing competition in the sports wheelchair market from Quickie Designs, a manufacturer of ultralightweight sports wheelchairs and a subsidiary of Sunrise Medical Inc. Despite the growing competition in the domestic and international wheelchair markets, industry analysts gave high marks to Mixon's management of Invacare and maintained that it was still the pre-eminent company in home health care products.

Further Reading:

Bendix, Jeffrey, "Invacare Rolls to Number 1," *Cleveland Enterprise,* Spring 1991.
Freeman, Anne M., "The Energizer," *Medical Industry Executive,* February/March 1992, pp. 28–31.
Palmeri, Christopher, "Wheel-To-Wheel Combat," *Forbes,* February 15, 1993, pp. 62–64.
Peric, T.S., "Mixonian Alchemy," *Cleveland Magazine,* 1993 Reprint.

—Thomas Derdak

Istituto per la Ricostruzione Industriale S.p.A.

Via V. Veneto, 89
I-00187 Rome
Italy
(06) 47271
Fax: (06) 47272308

State-Owned Company
Founded: 1933
Employees: 366,471
Sales: $50.48 billion
SICs: 6712 Bank Holding Companies; 6719 Holding
    Companies Not Elsewhere Classified

Istituto per la Ricostruzione Industriale S.p.A. (IRI), once the largest non-oil producing company in the world outside the United States, was by the mid-1990s a company in decline. Established in 1933 as a prop for failing Italian banks, the state-owned holding company grew over the years to encompass over 1,000 businesses, employ over 500,000 people, and produce everything from highways to telephone equipment to ice cream. IRI is credited with spurring the phenomenal growth of the Italian economy that occurred in the late 1950s and early 1960s, but by the 1980s the company appeared hopelessly out of date in a Europe that was rushing to privatize formerly state-owned businesses. When the Italian government quit funding IRI's debt in the early 1990s, the company instigated a wave of sell-offs and divestments; its future remained uncertain in 1994.

When the 1929 U.S. stock market crash initiated the worldwide depression of the 1930s, few countries were as adversely affected as Italy. Italian banks had a history of purchasing substantial interests in Italian industry, and when those industries began to fail it appeared that the nation's banking system might well collapse. The Fascist government of Benito Mussolini created IRI in January 1933 to bail out Italy's three largest banks—Banco di Roma, the Banca Commerciale, and the Credito Italiano. As a result, wrote Stuart Holland in *The State as Entrepreneur; New Dimensions for Public Enterprise: The IRI State Shareholding Formula,* "the new state holding company found itself responsible for major proportions of the main industrial and service sectors in the economy. These ranged from some half of iron and steel production, two thirds of telephone services, a quarter of electricity generation and distribution,

four-fifths of shipbuilding, and just less than a sixth of other engineering production."

IRI, created as a temporary solution to a problem, soon became the largest company in Italy and in 1937 was given a permanent legal structure. According to Ernesto Rossi, co-author of *Nationalization in France and Italy,* IRI became "an instrument for the furtherance of the industrial policy of the Fascist state" and "proceeded to invest in the industrial areas that were being developed by the Fascist policies of self-sufficiency (in cellulose, synthetic rubber, chemicals), as well as to expand the capacity of those industries that were specifically devoted to war production." In the 1930s, IRI created several of its major subsidiaries by merging companies it controlled to create STET, a holding company for three telephone operations, in 1933; FINMARE, a holding company for four shipping interests, in 1936; and FINSIDER, a holding company to manage IRI's steel holdings, in 1936.

World War II left IRI devastated, for its large industrial facilities had been the target of Allied bombers seeking to stem the flow of arms coming out of Italian factories. Consequently, steel production capacity was reduced by between 80 and 99 percent, shipyard capacity by 60 percent, and aircraft manufacturing capacity effectively destroyed. This destruction, and the lack of any coherent plan for IRI's growth now that it was controlled by a democratic rather than the Fascist regime, left IRI floundering through the late 1940s. Despite these problems, however, IRI reorganized its engineering interests under the holding company FINMECCANICA in 1948 and came to contribute to Italy's resurgent economy in the 1950s.

Once the ravages of wartime were overcome, Italy's economy expanded dramatically. Italian Gross National Product (GNP) grew at an average yearly rate of between 5.6 and 5.8 percent between the years 1952 and 1970, faster in some years than the economies of West Germany and France. Though such growth was called an economic miracle, IRI's growth was even more miraculous: while Italian GNP rose 130 percent between 1948 and 1962, IRI output rose by nearly 350 percent, according to M. V. Posner and S. J. Woolf, authors of *Italian Public Enterprise.* By 1962, IRI alone accounted for nearly four percent of Italian GNP. For a time, many of the economies of Europe looked to the "IRI formula" as a model for effective cooperation between private and state-owned business.

IRI's successes during the postwar years were notable. Among the most important achievements was the creation of modern integrated steel production facilities, which served both political and social functions in Italy. Between the years 1937 and 1953, IRI developed the steel industry from one which could not compete in European, let alone world, markets to one that allowed Italy admittance into the European Coal and Steel Community, and later the European Common Market, thus making Italy a full member in the newly revitalized Europe. Moreover, IRI's commitment to developing the steel industry in the southern, or Mezzogiorno, region of the country solved the long-standing social tension between prosperous, industrialized northern Italy and backward, agricultural southern Italy. IRI's proponents claimed that the company healed the nation.

IRI continued to engage in activities that would benefit the nation throughout the 1950s. In 1956, it proposed the construction of the Milan-Rome-Naples motorway, raised the necessary funds in the financial markets, and supervised construction over some of the most difficult terrain in Italy. In 1959, IRI rationalized the diverse Italian shipbuilding industry into a separate holding company, FINCANTIERI, thus assuming the burden of a struggling but important industry. The Italian government further invested its national identity in IRI when, in 1952, it transferred an absolute majority of shares in RAI, the national broadcasting company, to IRI. Moreover, the company took control of ALITALIA, the national airline, in 1957.

During the years of its intense growth, IRI behaved unlike any corporation seen before. Because it served the interests of the state, it did not have to concern itself with profits. Thus IRI could sink millions of lire into enterprises, like steel and roadbuilding, that profit-driven companies shied away from. The effect of such government investment was to create markets in which other companies could then compete, thereby expanding the economy as a whole. Instead of using tax-breaks and incentives, as did the U.S. government, Italy employed IRI. Not only did IRI create economic markets, it did so in areas that were thought to be most beneficial to the country as a whole or in areas that were of strategic importance.

IRI also avoided the pitfalls of most state-run businesses. The problem with most state-run businesses, especially in communist countries, was that there were few incentives to be productive or efficient. Thus, state-run companies often became notorious for mismanagement, creating unnecessary jobs and spending public money unwisely. IRI avoided these pitfalls by creating some distance between itself and its subsidiary holding companies. IRI's subsidiaries were encouraged to behave as if they were private enterprises; they were told to be entrepreneurs, while the small core of IRI management acted as investors, backed by the financial might of the Italian government. While IRI was 100 percent government owned, the subholdings were not, and thus these subholdings could attract private investment as well.

When IRI was working well, it combined the dynamism of entrepreneurial capitalism with the social guardianship of the most benevolent socialism. The success that IRI had in the 1950s and 1960s soon made it the model for governmental involvement with industry around the world. In the 1960s, Great Britain, France, Australia, Canada, Sweden, and West Germany all initiated programs that were based at least in part on the IRI formula of mixed state/private investment.

When IRI reached its zenith in the late 1960s, its reach extended to nearly every area of the Italian economy. As long as that economy expanded, so did IRI. But when the bottom dropped out of the world economy in the early 1970s, the IRI formula for success quickly turned out to be a recipe for failure. Though IRI's decline in the 1970s was initiated by the recession, it was compounded by internal weaknesses in the organization that had been hidden by economic prosperity. When times were good, IRI provided the impetus for growing companies to expand. But by the mid 1970s, noted *Euromoney,* "IRI had become the dumping ground for all the flagging companies which private industrialists no longer had the resources or the inclina-

tion to support." As IRI became increasingly burdened with unprofitable companies, private investment declined and the public sector's share of ownership crept from 51 percent to between 80 and 100 percent. "The state companies were saddled with large quantities of expensive bank debt," wrote *Euromoney,* "and were used as political vehicles for providing jobs and winning votes."

According to company literature, during the 1970s "IRI was compelled to undertake more difficult and varied tasks: promoting the economy in the South, investing against recession, maintaining employment, and supervision of areas of vital importance to the nation's economy, often with no sound economic criteria underlying these efforts." As it tried to hold the Italian economy together, IRI mushroomed in size until, in 1982, it consisted of 1,000 companies with more than 500,000 employees, three percent of Italy's total employment. According to *Business Week,* "losses topped $2 billion a year. IRI had $24.3 billion in debt in 1982, and its borrowing for the year was equal to 12 percent of all debt taken on by Italian households and companies." IRI had become, said one executive, a "garbage pail" for unprofitable companies, and it was losing over $5 million a day.

In November 1982, the Italian government appointed a new chairperson to run the ailing industrial giant. Romano Prodi, a professor of industrial organization at Bologna University, took charge of IRI, determined to shake things up. Within four years, Prodi had returned IRI to profitability by exploiting a changing political climate and a reviving Italian and world economy. In a world economic climate in which capitalism was the clear victor over socialism, Prodi attempted to renegotiate the ties between the state and the economy. Prodi's methods—privatization and professionalization—created profits while changing the role of IRI. Under Prodi, the world's largest state-run business would operate only in areas of strategic importance to the state.

Change within IRI could not have occurred had politicians not realized that their great experiment was no longer working. Swollen with ten years worth of failed businesses and staffed by employees whose jobs had been created by politicians seeking votes, IRI had become a great drain on the Italian economy. "Things were so bad that the politicians finally realized that without drastic change they were risking their own jobs," a senior manager at IRI's aerospace unit was quoted in *Business Week.* Throughout Europe the consensus was building that the solution to the problem was privatization. Although Italy was not ready to follow the lead of Prime Minister Margaret Thatcher of Great Britain, who urged privatization on a grand scale, it too recognized that if it wanted to compete with the United States, Japan, and West Germany, it would have to allow profits—and not social planning—to determine the direction of the economy.

Among Prodi's first actions was replacing the politicians with professional managers. To this end, Prodi replaced 70 percent of the top managers at IRI headquarters and half of the senior staff within the subholding companies, and introduced a merit-based pay system, according to *Business Week.* He also won concessions from Italy's radical labor unions that allowed him to abolish 60,000 jobs in the first four years of his tenure. Such tactics were successful in turning around Italtel, a telecommunications company controlled by IRI's STET division. Italtel reduced employment by 30 percent, completely revamped its product line, and, in just four years, tripled its sales. *Euromoney* lauded the Italtel case as an example of the benefits of business rationalization.

Equally important in Prodi's scheme was the privatization of non-strategic businesses. "The state ought not to make ice cream," Prodi once said, and he explained to *Euromoney* that "an optimal allocation of resources should require state intervention in very few industries. In any case where the private entrepreneur is able to do it, we should study the opportunity for privatization." Prodi did more than study the opportunity; by 1988, he had privatized 29 different companies, including the car maker Alfa Romeo and the commercial bank Mediobanca. During the first three years of Prodi's tenure, sales of shares in IRI companies raised $1 billion from the market. By 1986, IRI was breaking even, and, in 1987, the company turned its first profit in over a decade, earning $150 million on sales of $43 billion.

As the 1980s came to an end, slowing economic growth and political pressures combined to slow the pace of change at IRI. In a booming economy, many investors chose to place their money in the stock market, purchasing the stock of IRI companies. As the economy slowed, small investors left the stock market and only a handful of powerful industrialists continued to purchase stock. The politicians who oversaw IRI feared allowing too much control to fall into the hands of these few, and slowed privatization. Moreover, the small Milan Stock Exchange was becoming flooded with IRI stock, which at times accounted for as much as 25 percent of the activity on the exchange. Such dominance of the stock market ran counter to IRI's strategy of decreasing its role within the Italian economy.

Politics also played a part in slowing IRI's growth rate. According to the *Economist,* privatization was "fiercely resisted by politicians who have built up power bases on their ability to channel the flow of public money." This was especially true in a slowing economy, in which politicians sought to preserve for their constituents all available jobs. Another political factor was favoritism; when Prodi arranged for the sale of SME, IRI's food group, to the Buitoni food group, owned by Carlo De Benedetti, the sale was blocked by prime minister Bettino Craxi, De Benedetti's political enemy. Similarly, an attempt to merge Italtel with Telettra, a company controlled by Fiat, to form a internationally-competitive telecommunications manufacturer failed when the Socialist Party insisted that a member of their party serve as managing director. Though IRI's managers sought to run the company for profit, the company's real managers, the politicians, made sure that the company still functioned as a tool to dispense the power of the state.

By 1989, Prodi left IRI. "It was known that various parties and politicians, whose interests required maintaining the status quo, had exerted great pressure to make him leave," wrote *Europe* contributor Niccolò d'Aquino. Within a year, IRI was back in debt, and, in 1992, the company reported losses of $2.9 billion. Compounding its difficulties was the arrest of new chairperson Franco Nobili on corruption charges. In 1993, *Business Week* contributor John Rossant wrote, "At a time when Italy's post-war political and financial institutions are under fire as never

before, IRI's problems are adding to the deep sense of crisis that is pervading the country."

The crisis in Italy and at IRI was compounded in the early 1990s by pressure from the European Community (EC), whose blueprints for monetary union required drastic changes in the Italian economy. Admittance to the EC, deemed crucial to Italy's economic survival in the next century, required that public debt be no larger than 60 percent of annual gross domestic product and fiscal debt no larger than three percent of GDP. In 1992, those figures stood at 103 percent and ten percent, respectively, according to the *Wall Street Journal.* In 1991, seeking to meet these requirements, the state ended subsidies for IRI, forcing the company to seek private investment after years of dependence on the government. However, private investors were wary of IRI's unprofitable companies, and the company went even further into debt. Losses at ILVA, IRI's steel-making subsidiary, topped $1.8 billion in 1992, while losses at Iritecna, IRI's construction arm, topped $1.6 billion.

In 1993, new Italian prime minister Carlo Azeglio Ciampi turned again to Romano Prodi to rescue IRI. The reluctant Prodi accepted, insisting that this time privatization must occur even faster than it had occurred under his previous tenure. Prodi's motto would be "Either we privatize or we die," according to d'Aquino. "You can't have a conglomerate just because it's owned by the government," Prodi told the *Wall Street Journal Europe,* noting that "this is not a time for conglomerates—this glue must fade away. And IRI must fade away with it." Prodi was given some assistance in 1992 by former prime minister Guiliano Amato, who had transformed Italy's public holding companies, including IRI, into joint stock companies under the control of the Treasury, which, according to *Business Week,* was "considered the cleanest and most technically competent branch of the government." The article suggested that "For the first time in a century, . . . IRI will be subject to corporate legal rules making them more accountable to shareholders and the public."

Though Prodi insisted that all of IRI was for sale, his first task was to sell off the banks Banca Commerciale Italiana (BCI) and Credito Italiano. IRI's offering of shares in Credito Italiano in the fall of 1993 was a great success, as was the sale of shares in BCI in the spring of 1994. Plans to sell food group SME also progressed in 1993, as international food companies Nestle S.A. and Unilever and Italian companies Parmalat and Cragnotti expressed interest in portions of SME. Prodi also initiated plans to sell off ILVA and SIP, the telephone services sector. "When you have so many companies, the important thing is not to have a rigid order in selling them," Prodi told the *Wall Street Journal Europe*. Prodi noted that "The point is not to sell one or the other first, but to adapt to market needs."

In the 1990s, IRI faced the difficult task of adapting to market needs even as it dismantled itself. Investors were most interested in the IRI holdings that were profitable, such as SME, STET, and Finmeccanica, its engineering group. However, IRI needed the revenues produced by these companies so that it could restructure the unprofitable holdings, mainly ILVA and Iritecna, which IRI hoped to sell. This was Prodi's paradox: in order to dismantle one of the world's largest companies, he must first bring it back to profitability, piece by piece. Prodi insisted that his job was made easier the second time by the support—or at least the lack of interference—of the Italian government. "Resistance is 1/10 of what it was before," he told the *Wall Street Journal Europe,* commenting that "we've completely canceled political appointees from the board. I don't get calls any more, no one stops by."

When the conservative government of prime minister Silvio Berlusconi took over in 1994, Prodi again announced that he would leave IRI. But the new government quickly dispelled any rumors that IRI would go back to its old ways by assuring investors that whoever they appointed would be expected to continue the job that Prodi started. What remained a matter of speculation was the form, if any, that IRI would take by the year 2000. Between 1993 and 1994, IRI shrank from the seventh largest company in the world, with $67,547 million in sales and 400,000 employees, to the sixteenth largest company, with $50,488 million in sales and 366,471 employees, according to *Fortune.* If this trend continued, the "remnants of IRI should become seven or eight strong public companies, the perfect counterweight in a corporate scene which is still dominated by family-owned companies," according to the *Economist.* For most of the twentieth century, the fate of IRI was the fate of the Italian economy; in the mid-1990s, with IRI's role in the economy greatly reduced, some analysts suggested that Italians might finally find out what it means to compete in the world market.

Principal Subsidiaries: Iritecna; Ilva; STET (52%); Finmeccanica (86%); SME (62%); Alitalia (86%).

Further Reading:

Bannon, Lisa, "Carte Blanche: IRI's New Chairman Puts Whole Company into Privatization Play," *Wall Street Journal Europe,* June 21, 1993, pp. 1, 10.
Carrington, Tim, "Italy Braces for Privatization Measures," *Wall Street Journal,* June 12, 1992, p. A5.
d'Aquino, Niccolò, "Romano Prodi," *Europe,* February 1994, p. 38.
Einaudi, Mario, Maurice Byé, and Ernesto Rossi, *Nationalization in France and Italy,* Ithaca, NY: Cornell University Press, 1955.
"Fortune's Global 500," *Fortune,* July 26, 1993.
"Fortune's Global 500," *Fortune,* July 25, 1994.
Holland, Stuart, ed., *The State as Entrepreneur; New Dimensions for Public Enterprise: The IRI State Shareholding Formula,* White Plains, NY: International Arts and Sciences Press, 1972.
"Industry Brief: Back to Basics at IRI," *Economist,* March 1, 1986, pp. 76–77.
"Italy: A Profitable Public Sector," *Euromoney,* July 1988, pp. 20–21.
"Italy: State Sector," *Euromoney,* June 1985, pp. 56–63.
Kirkland, Richard I., Jr., "The Biggest Bosses: Lessons from a Master," *Fortune,* August 3, 1987, pp. 34–35.
"On Sale in Italy," *Economist,* October 16, 1993, p. 17.
"Open Drains," *Economist,* May 23, 1981, pp. 28–34.
Posner, M. V., and S. J. Woolf, *Italian Public Enterprise,* Cambridge, MA: Harvard University Press, 1967.
"Privatization in Fits and Starts," *Economist,* February 27, 1988, pp. 28–32.
"Prodding a Dinosaur," *Economist,* September 14, 1985, pp. 22–24.
"Prodi Discharges His Patients," *Euromoney,* December 1985, pp. 99–102.
"Professor at Work," *Economist,* January 7, 1989, pp. 59–60.
"The Role of State Enterprise," *Euromoney,* July 1987, pp. 56–60.
Rossant, John, " 'Dr. Subtle' Is Ready for Emergency Surgery," *Business Week,* July 27, 1992, pp. 42–43.
Rossant, John, "Privatize the Beast," *Business Week,* May 24, 1993, p. 54.
Sarti, Roland, *Fascism and the Industrial Leadership in Italy, 1919–1940: A Study in the Expansion of Private Power under Fascism,* Berkeley: University of California Press, 1971.
"Signor Prodi Sets Up His Store," *Economist,* October 2, 1993, pp. 75–76.
"State Sector's New Order," *International Management,* September 1992, pp. 52–53.
Symonds, William C., "The Turnaround Sparking a New Italian Renaissance," *Business Week,* March 2, 1987, pp. 60–61.

—Tom Pendergast

IVAX Corporation

8800 Northwest 36th Street
Miami, Florida 33178
U.S.A.
(305) 590-2200
Fax: (305) 590-2810

Public Company
Incorporated: 1985 as IVAX Inc.
Employees: 6,000
Sales: $1 billion
Stock Exchanges: American
SICs: 2869 Industrial Organic Chemicals, Nec; 2834
    Pharmaceutical Preparations; 2835 Diagnostic Substances;
    6719 Holding Companies, Nec

IVAX Corporation is a holding company primarily engaged in the development, manufacture, and marketing of pharmaceuticals. Its diversified subsidiaries are also involved in specialty chemicals, personal care products, and medical diagnostic equipment, among other goods. IVAX achieved meteoric growth during the late 1980s and early 1990s by acquiring other companies and introducing new products.

IVAX Corporation is the creation of dermatologist and deal maker Dr. Philip Frost. Frost formed IVAX Inc. in 1985 as a holding company. Its principal subsidiary, IVACO Industries Inc., was an $11 million (in sales) specialty chemicals manufacturer based in New Jersey. IVAX also owned major shares of two small, ailing pharmaceutical companies. To the casual observer, IVAX may have seemed a rather odd organization with limited potential. However, Frost had big plans for the fledgling operation. In fact, many analysts also expected big things from Frost's peculiar venture based on his past successes.

After finishing his residency at the University of Miami in the late 1960s, Frost's performance earned him a spot on the school's faculty. He left in 1970 to found the dermatology department at Miami Beach's Mt. Sinai Medical Center, where he served as chairman of the department until 1990. In addition to his professional activities during the 1970s, the high-energy Frost exercised his entrepreneurial bent through a variety of innovative ventures. Shortly after moving to Mt. Sinai, for example, Frost opened a fish farm in the everglades; a drought dried up the ponds and killed the fish, but the land appreciated in value and Frost profited from the undertaking.

Of all Frost's business exploits, the one that would eventually garner him the greatest amount of respect (and profit) was his 1972 purchase of Key Pharmaceuticals, Inc. By 1972, Frost had created a number of medical-related inventions, such as his disposable biopsy punch, and he wanted to use Key as a vehicle to take his ideas to market. Frost and partner Michael Jaharis purchased the struggling Key for a paltry $100,000. Jaharis became the detail man, directing the day-to-day operations of the start-up enterprise, while Frost handled the big picture.

Rather than using Key to launch new products, Frost eventually decided to develop and market new delivery systems for proven drugs. He believed that he could eliminate the time, costs, and risk associated with developing entirely new drugs. True to his entrepreneurial nature, Frost kept an open mind about Key during the 1970s and early 1980s. He adjusted its goals and struck dozens of deals along the way with industry big-wigs like Pfizer Inc., Mitsubishi Chemical Industries Ltd., and several European drug companies. Largely as a result of Frost's savvy deal making, Key Pharmaceuticals went from $65,000 in losses in 1972 to a staggering $22.1 million in profits by 1984.

Frost's supreme deal related to Key transpired in March of 1986. In a hurried transaction, pharmaceutical giant Schering-Plough purchased Key for an incredible $800 million. Because Frost and Jaharis still owned 30 percent of the company, Frost pocketed $150 million from the sale, cementing his position as one of the wealthiest individuals in Miami. Frost also got a five-year consulting contract with Schering that paid a cool half million dollars annually. Importantly, Frost, without tipping off Schering's management, negotiated a very favorable non-compete clause with Schering's attorneys. It essentially allowed him to remain active in the pharmaceutical industry, even if he competed with Schering.

The Schering buyout came at an opportune time for Frost. Although he had enjoyed transforming the company, by the mid-1980s he was also itching to try his hand at a new type of venture; rather than just market existing pharmaceuticals, he wanted to create and sell new drugs, an activity that offered a potentially greater opportunity for profit. Toward that end, Frost started assembling IVAX. Besides purchasing Ivaco Inc., in 1986 he bought Diamedix, a medical diagnostic kit manufacturer, and Pharmedix, a pharmaceutical company. Ivaco was a profitable company operating in a mature industry. Diamedix and Pharmedix, in contrast, more closely resembled pre-1972 Key Pharmaceuticals—both were relatively small and losing money when Frost purchased them. In December of 1987, Frost merged the three concerns into IVAX Corp.

Although IVAX's three companies were a strange mix, they reflected a shrewd strategy conceived by Frost to make IVAX into a major developer, manufacturer, and seller of proprietary drugs. Frost planned to use Ivaco as a cash cow to fund capital-intensive, pharmaceutical-related initiatives in a three-phase growth strategy: First, IVAX would buy drugs that already had passed the expensive and time-consuming regulatory approval process. Second, cash flow from those drugs would be used to purchase drugs that were not yet approved but had shown promise in preliminary clinical trials. Finally, earnings from those drugs would be devoted to the internal development of new drugs by IVAX's own scientists.

IVAX maintained its general strategy in the late 1980s, though Frost continued to seize new opportunities and adjust to market changes. IVAX acquired several companies during its first two full years of operation, including Baker Cummins Pharmaceuticals Inc. and Harris Pharmaceuticals Ltd., and developed its existing businesses into more profitable enterprises. By 1990, IVAX Corp.'s third full year of operation, the company had revenues of $60 million annually. It was still losing money, but IVAX had positioned itself for future growth: it had established a healthy cash flow and had plenty of money reserved for future acquisitions and development of new drugs. Importantly, in 1990 IVAX acquired Norton Healthcare Ltd., a leading British generic drug producer with more than 200 products. That purchase set the stage for IVAX's rampant growth during the early 1990s.

Frost's love of, and knack for, cutting shrewd deals had been a part of his personality since childhood. Born and raised in Philadelphia, Frost developed a strong work ethic and an appreciation of salesmanship in his father's shoe store. "I always liked that [selling shoes]," Frost reminisced in the May 1992 issue of *Florida Trend*. "You know when you've done it right, and you don't have to wait a long time to find that out." Aside from business, another of Frost's interests and talents was science. As a result of a scholarship offer, he enrolled in New York's Albert Einstein College of Medicine following high school. Even there, his bent for business came out. In fact, Frost was known by his roommates for always knowing where the bargains were.

Norton Healthcare turned out to be a very good bargain for IVAX. In 1991, IVAX's first full year of operation with Norton under its corporate umbrella, IVAX achieved its first year of profits. It earned $11.1 million on $181 million in sales. However, Frost made an even smarter purchase in December of 1991, when he bought Goldline Laboratories Inc. Goldline was one of the largest generic drug distributors in the United States, with marketing networks reaching hospitals, nursing homes, retail drug chains, and all other major sectors of the healthcare industry. It brought 490 employees and 1,600 new products to the IVAX organization.

Generic drugs, which accounted for the majority of IVAX's sales in the early 1990s, are basically molecular copies of branded drugs. They perform the same function as the drugs they mimic, but do not benefit from patent protection. As a result, they provide lower profit margins and are susceptible to competing generic products. Although Goldline achieved prominence in the industry during the 1980s, bad press about generics contributed to the company's slide in the early 1990s. Goldline lost $20 million in 1990 and 1991. Nevertheless, Frost saw potential in the lagging distributor and snapped it up. He jettisoned a troubled manufacturing plant and stepped up restructuring efforts. The results of his efforts were immediate, as Goldline began posting profits shortly after the acquisition.

Primarily as a result of its buyouts of Goldline and Norton, IVAX's revenues spiraled upward in 1991 to $180 million and then to a big-league $450 million in 1992. Furthermore, net income rocketed to about $16 million in 1991 and then to roughly $49 million in 1992. However, in 1993 Frost's acquisition of Goldline began to really pay off for IVAX. In August of

1992, IVAX, through Goldline, introduced Verapamil, a breakthrough generic heart disease treatment priced 25 percent lower than comparable brand name drugs. Massive demand made Verapamil the largest selling generic in the history of the drug industry. In 1993, in fact, IVAX captured revenues of $645 million, 23 percent of which were directly attributable to Verapamil. Furthermore, net income exploded to $85 million, a gain of almost 75 percent over 1992.

Verapamil's staggering success during 1993 was augmented by steady gains attained through numerous other product introductions and acquisitions conducted by IVAX in the early 1990s. As sales and cash flow increased, in fact, the pace of Frost's purchases accelerated. In September of 1992, for example, IVAX added H N Norton Co., a U.S. manufacturer of generic and over-the-counter drugs. Prior to that, in April, IVAX acquired Waverly Pharmaceutical Limited, a European maker of eye drops, lens solutions, and other fluid health care products. That same month, IVAX branched out into veterinary products with its buyout of DVM Pharmaceuticals, Inc. In 1993, IVAX entered into two joint ventures in China to furnish pharmaceuticals to that massive market.

IVAX's dizzying acquisition pace was not limited to the pharmaceuticals industry. As Frost jetted around the globe in search of new deals, IVAX added a number of non-drug companies to its portfolio. In 1991, for instance, it bought Delta Biologicals S.r.l., an Italian manufacturer of diagnostic equipment. In 1992, IVAX bought out Flori Roberts, Inc., which sold a line of cosmetics for dark-skinned women. A more lucrative purchase was Frost's takeover of Johnson Products Co., Inc. in 1993. Johnson, a developer and marketer of African American personal care products, was recognized as one of the most successful black-owned businesses in the United States. IVAX also added to its original specialty chemicals division in 1993 with its purchase of Elf Atochem North America, Inc., a major producer of industrial cleaning and maintenance products.

IVAX's crowning acquisition was completed early in 1994, when it picked up McGaw Inc. for $440 million. California-based McGaw was the third-leading U.S. supplier of intravenous solutions and related equipment. The company brought 30 national distribution centers to the IVAX organization and represented a major new source of revenue. In fact, had IVAX owned McGaw during 1993 its total revenue would have been nearly $1 billion (as opposed to $645 million). A drawback of the merger was that it earned IVAX a risky credit rating. Credit analyst Standard & Poor's noted IVAX's heavy debt load, excessive use of equity financing, and heavy reliance on Verapamil, which was facing stiff competition from other generics in 1994.

Despite analyst's doubts concerning IVAX's long-term prospects, Frost and his management team viewed massive growth during the early 1990s as part of their original growth strategy. Indeed, now that IVAX had accumulated a mass of profitable, cash-producing holdings, including several pharmaceutical concerns, it was prepared to enter stage three of its long-term plan—the introduction of internally produced, proprietary drugs that would generate large profit margins. Even without future plans for new drugs, IVAX was able to point to its (admittedly short) track record of success with its diversified core of businesses.

Going into 1994, IVAX continued to stress growth through acquisition and improvement of its existing holdings. It still had not introduced any of its own patented pharmaceuticals on a broad scale, but it had a pipeline of new drugs that it had been readying for market for several years. One of its most promising inventions was Elmiron, a drug that had already been approved in Canada as a treatment for a debilitating women's bladder disease. Elmiron was in the final stages of FDA approval early in 1994. Likewise, IVAX's Nalmefene, which could potentially treat a variety of afflictions, was also in the latter stages of development and was nearing FDA approval for some applications, such as reversal of drug overdoses. Other promising IVAX pharmaceuticals in 1994 included Ossirene, Azene, Naloxone, Scriptene, Nitric Oxide Vasodilator, and Taxol.

IVAX's long-term staying power remained a question going into the mid-1990s, but there was no uncertainty about the amazing short-term success the company had achieved since 1987. In less than seven years, IVAX had bolted from a awkward start-up to a $1 billion corporation listed in the Fortune 500. The personal success of IVAX's driving force, Frost, was just as impressive—Frost still owned nearly 20 percent of the company in 1994 and was serving as chairman, chief executive, and president.

Critics, citing IVAX's mediocre credit rating, feared that IVAX might end up like Frost's failed 1970s fish farm, or worse. However, Frost's past performance, combined with expected growth in the healthcare industry, indicated otherwise. In a February 1993 issue of *Miami Review* analyst Richard M. Lilly asserted, ''Phil Frost and the group around him, whatever their sins may have been, have created a more successful and more profitable company than anyone else in the business.''

In July of 1994 IVAX acquired the majority interest in Galena a.s., one of the oldest and best established pharmaceutical companies in Eastern Europe. A month later, IVAX announced the beginning of a merger with Zenith Laboratories, Inc. of North-vale, New Jersey. In October of 1994, IVAX established a joint venture with Knoll AG and BASF Aktiengesellschaft for the manufacture and marketing of generic pharmaceutical products in Europe. With this joint venture and the acquisition of Galena and Zenith Laboratories, IVAX would become the world's largest international generic pharmaceutical company.

Principal Subsidiaries: Baker Norton Pharmaceuticals, Inc.; Baker Cummins Dermatologicals, Inc.; Delta Biologicals, S.r.l. (Italy); Diamedix Corporation; DVM Pharmaceuticals, Inc.; H.N. Norton & Co., Limited; IVAX Industries, Inc.; Goldline Laboratories, Inc.; Goldcaps, Inc.; McGaw, Inc.; Johnson Products Co., Inc.; Norton Healthcare Limited (United Kingdom); Waverly Pharmaceuticals Limited (United Kingdom); Zenith Laboratories, Inc.; Galena a.s.

Further Reading:

Anderson, Veronica, ''Bidder a Stark Contrast to Lagging Johnson,'' *Crains Chicago Business,* June 21, 1993, Sec. 1, p. 3.

Form 10-K: IVAX Corporation, Washington, D.C.: Securities and Exchange Commission, 1994.

Guinta, Peter, ''Frost Is Building Another Drug Firm,'' *South Florida Business Journal,* December 7, 1987, Sec. 1, p. 1.

Hagy, James R., ''The Thrill of the Deal,'' *Florida Trend,* May 1992, Sec. 1, p. 58.

Hosford, Christopher, ''Following Frost's Footsteps,'' *South Florida Business Journal,* November 23, 1992, Sec. 1, p. 1A.

Miracle, Barbara, and Janice G. Sharp, ''The Florida CEO: Who Delivers—and Who Doesn't,'' *Florida Trend,* June 1994, Sec. 1, p. 39.

Mowatt, Twig, ''IVAX, Finally Has Seen the Competition,'' *Miami Daily Business Review,* April 4, 1994, p. A1.

Poppe, David, ''IVAX Acquisitions, Not Development, Pay the Way,'' *Miami Review,* February 5, 1993, p. A12.

Rubinger, Robert S., ''United-Guardian to Market Products in Mainland China,'' *Business Wire,* June 2, 1993.

Stieghorst, Tom, ''IVAX Completes Buyout, Gains S&P Rating,'' *Sun-Sentinel,* March 29, 1994, p. D3; ''Gold as Goldline: Fort Lauderdale Generic-Drug Distributor Poised for Growth,'' *Sun-Sentinel,* October 9, 1992, Sec. BUS.

—Dave Mote

The J.M. Smucker Company

Strawberry Lane
Orrville, Ohio 44667
U.S.A.
(216) 682-3000
Fax: (216) 684-3370

Public Company
Incorporated: 1921
Employees: 2,600
Sales: $511.5 million
Stock Exchanges: New York
SICs: 2033 Canned Fruits and Vegetables; 2037 Frozen
     Fruits and Vegetables; 2099 Food Preparations, Nec

The J.M. Smucker Company is America's top producer and marketer of jams, jellies, and preserves. Operating in the United States, Canada, Great Britain, and Australia, it also manufactures and markets peanut butter, ice cream toppings, and fruit drinks and syrups. The familiar corporate trademark, "With a name like Smucker's, it has to be good," alludes both to the company's founding family and its reputation for high-quality products. The firm is also known for its insistence on independence: family members maintain a controlling interest in their namesake company and fiercely guard their majority stake.

The company was founded in 1897 by Jerome Monroe Smucker, a Mennonite from the small agricultural community of Orrville, Ohio, about 45 minutes south of Cleveland. The Mennonites' traditional disdain for modernization did not keep Smucker from rational and efficient business practices. He applied his education from a two-year business course at a nearby academy to the management of four farms and a creamery that shipped butter as far as New York City. The success of his businesses allowed him to expand operations around the turn of the century, when Smucker bought a cider mill and began pressing apples from an orchard planted in the early nineteenth century by Johnny Appleseed. To even out the seasonality of apple cider sales, Smucker began to make apple butter from his Pennsylvania Dutch grandfather's recipe. Smucker's steam-powered press and secret method for capturing the vapors usually lost in cooking gave the spread a unique flavor that soon drew more customers than the cider mill and creamery. Smucker staked his name and reputation on each crock of apple butter, hand-signing the paper lid on every package.

The family-owned business prospered. J.M. Smucker's eldest son Willard began delivering the 25-cent, half gallon tubs in a wagon at the age of ten. By 1915, the first year for which records are available, the business was bringing in nearly $60,000 and netting almost $3,000 annually. And by the time it was incorporated in 1921, Smucker's offered a full line of preserves (generally made from whole fruit or large pieces of fruit) and jellies (made from strained, pure fruit juice). Sales topped $147,000 the year The J.M. Smucker Company, Inc. was capitalized at $100,000. J.M. Smucker owned 94 percent of the private company's stock; his sons and daughters split the remainder. The company had grown to such a scale that in 1928 the Pennsylvania Railroad built a special siding to the Smucker plant, as the company's products were distributed in ever-increasing volume throughout Ohio, Pennsylvania, and Indiana.

Sales continued to grow in spite of the October 1929 stock market crash, nearing $319,000 in 1931. But the company did not emerge from the crisis unscathed: it recorded two consecutive years of losses in 1932 and 1933. Throughout this period, J.M. Smucker began to delegate authority to Willard, who directed the establishment of Smucker's first facility outside Ohio in 1935. The plant was located in the state of Washington, chosen for its high-quality, low-priced apples, which were pre-processed, then shipped to Orrville for cooking. The move set Smucker's up for national distribution and marked the first step toward the vertical integration that would become a company hallmark.

Packaging and marketing were taken for granted at Smucker's until 1938, when Willard decided that the traditional crockery was too heavy and awkward to ship. He wanted to shift to a more modern glass package without losing the Smucker reputation for "old-fashioned" quality. The glass jar he designed and later trademarked reflected the old crock, and its label, showing a pioneer woman boiling up a batch of apple butter over an open fire, reinforced Smucker's quaint image. The new package was a success; after its introduction, sales surpassed the $1 million mark in 1939. The new jar and label also garnered the company an award from the National Packaging Show for best packaging design success.

The war years at Smucker's were characterized by labor, glass, and fruit shortages, but the company withstood such hardships to celebrate its fiftieth anniversary in 1947. Founder J.M. Smucker, too, endured just long enough to see his business through five decades: he passed away at the age of 90 the following year.

The second generational transfer of power at Smucker's began in the late 1950s, when son Paul joined Willard in drawing up a plan for future growth and diversification. Like his father, Paul had started working in the family business at a young age. From the age of 13, according to the *Wall Street Journal*, "... after school and during the summer months, he did everything from janitorial work to assisting the cook." Paul earned a business degree from Miami (Ohio) University in 1939, then returned to Orrville to work full-time as a cost accountant at a salary of $100 per month. After marrying and serving in the Navy for three years during World War II, Paul was put in charge of a recently-acquired applesauce factory. Despite the venture's failure, Paul's responsibilities increased: he was promoted to corporate secretary in 1946, treasurer in 1949, and executive vice-president in 1954.

In 1961 Paul became president of Smucker's. In spite of merger offers from such respected giants of the food industry as Quaker Oats, Ralston Purina, Beatrice Foods, and Borden, the family opted to remain independent. They offered one-third of the company to the public, raising $2.3 million for capital investments. At the time, Smucker's had annual sales of $11.4 million and earnings of $812,000. The family business legacy under Paul Smucker included an aversion to long-term debt and "an almost obsessive concern for avoiding any move that might adulterate his company's products or blemish the corporate image," according to the *Wall Street Journal.*

Paul Smucker lead a two-decade period of dramatic growth through increasing vertical integration, product diversification, acquisition, and national advertising and market penetration that culminated in the company's 1980 dominance of the fruit spread market. From early in its history, the company sought control of all aspects of production. Contracting directly with farmers for fruit crops precluded buying produce on the open market and empowered Smucker's to control production from seed to jam. Along with this vertical integration came vertical quality control. Beginning in 1946, Smucker's paid U.S. Department of Agriculture inspectors to oversee every aspect of its production, earning the company the designation "U.S. Grade A Fancy." This evidence of quality assurance allowed Smucker's a higher markup and better shelf placement.

Smucker's maintained its quality control as it expanded. The company opened a manufacturing plant in Salinas, California, that increased production capacity by 40 percent in 1960. Acquisitions, including $4 million (annual sales) West Coast jam and jelly maker Mary Ellen's, Inc. and Pennsylvania peanut-butter manufacturer H.B. DeViney Company, Inc., helped extend Smucker's geographical reach, augmented its annual sales volume, and increased product variety. Smucker's most successful and innovative internally-developed product was a candy-cane-striped mixture of peanut butter and jelly dubbed "Goober Jelly." The company expanded its product line to over 100 varieties, including ice cream toppings, which accounted for 20 percent of sales by 1960. By the late 1960s, jellies, jams, and preserves comprised less than two-thirds of sales. Product acquisitions and internal developments helped diversify the company's offerings, but not all new product launches and acquisitions were successful. The 1965 purchase of Wooster Preserving Company and the 1966 purchase of H.W. Madison Co., both pickle concerns, became an oft-noted example of failure.

In spite of Willard Smucker's general disdain for advertising, the company hired Wyse Advertising of Cleveland to produce radio spots in 1961. The agency thought up the enduring "With a name like Smucker's, it has to be good" slogan the following year. Family members didn't relish the thought of making fun of their own name at first, but the tagline's phenomenal success on the West Coast convinced them to use it for the brand's New York launch in the later years of the decade.

Sales doubled from $14.6 million in 1961 to $30 million in fiscal 1965. Smucker's stock more than tripled from its $20 issue price to $67.50 in 1965, when it was split 3-for-1 and listed on the New York Stock Exchange. Despite its growth, the company ranked second to grocery chain A & P's Ann Page store brand at the end of the decade. Smucker's increased its advertising budget to $1.3 million to accommodate network television, and continued to push for first place.

Profits more than tripled to $3 million between 1959 and 1969, then dropped almost 13 percent in the 1970 fiscal year in spite of a sales increase. The company continued to have troubles throughout the decade. Not able to increase prices as fast as inflation boosted overhead, the Smuckers steadfastly refused to compromise quality to pad earnings. As a result, profit margins shrunk from 16 percent in 1964 to 11 percent in 1970. Smucker's instituted cost cutting measures, including the consolidation of three packing operations into two and corresponding workforce reductions that reduced the payroll by 15 percent by from 1973 to 1984. The 1969 and 1971 acquisitions of manufacturing operations in Oregon, Tennessee, and California enhanced economies and enabled Smucker's to sell its excess fruit to competitors.

Still the number two jelly manufacturer (now to Welch's) in 1974, Smucker's launched a concerted effort to dominate the industry. The company broadened its institutional markets and rounded out consumer jelly lines with the introduction of "Smucker's For Kids," a lower-priced line, as well as low-calorie and all-natural products. The combination of increased advertising and more thorough market penetration (especially in the South) catapulted Smucker's to the number one spot among jelly and jam manufacturers, with over one-fourth of the market, in 1980. Over the course of the decade, sales increased almost three times to $145.8 million, and profits nearly doubled to $5.9 million.

The 1970s also saw the ascent of Smucker's fourth generation of family leadership, when Timothy Smucker was appointed vice-president of planning. The assignment marked a new, more modern approach to strategic, tactical, and operational planning, as the company began to rival some of the world's largest food companies in its specialized niche. Timothy refined the "Basic Beliefs" first outlined by his father in 1967, including commitments to quality, personal and business ethics, growth, and independence. He incorporated them into a detailed blueprint for the company's future. Timothy was promoted to president and chief operating officer and brother Richard earned the title chief administrative officer in addition to executive vice-president in 1981.

As the leader of the highly competitive, but slow growing, jam and jelly market, Smucker's found itself ever more dependent on heavy advertising expenditures, acquisitions, and product launches to increase sales and earnings in the 1980s. A four-year plant expansion program was announced in 1982 on the heels of a 39 percent year-to-year earnings gain. Magic Shell brand ice cream toppings were purchased from Foremost-McKesson in 1980 and Knudsen & Sons, Inc., a manufacturer of pure fruit juices, joined the family of companies in 1984. The 1987 purchase of R-Line Foods complimented Smucker's institutional operations.

Smucker's began international efforts in the late 1980s. In 1988, it acquired Canada's Good Morning brand marmalade (citrus jelly made of small pieces of fruit) and Shirriff ice cream toppings, as well as Elsenham Quality Foods, Ltd., a British manufacturer of specialty preserves, marmalades, and fruit chutneys. Henry Jones Foods, producer of "one of Australia's oldest and best-known labels," IXL preserves and jams, was purchased the following year. Sales more than doubled from $151 million in 1980 to $367 million in 1989, and earnings quadrupled during the same period from $6.7 million to $27.6 million. By 1993, international sales comprised almost eight percent of Smucker's annual total.

Smucker's entered the 1990s with 38 percent of the domestic jam and jelly market. The fourth-generation leaders set an even loftier goal for their namesake brand and company: a 70 percent share. But with tenacious, experienced branded rivals like Kraft and Welch as well as locally strong store brands, the company had its work cut out for it. In 1994, Smucker's ended its 35-year relationship with Wyse Advertising in favor of Leo Burnett Co., an agency company executives believed could support the brand's aspirations.

In the early 1990s, members of the Smucker family continued to control over half of the company's stock, and evinced no intentions of relinquishing that majority rule. As consolidation within the food industry gained momentum, the family shored up its takeover defenses by creating a new class of nonvoting stock. This allowed older members (Paul Smucker, for example) to plan their estates without relinquishing influence. From 1990 to 1993, sales increased over 16 percent to $491.31 million, as Smucker's sought to increase per capita consumption of its products, as well as increase its market share in each category.

Principal Subsidiaries: H.B. DeViney Company, Inc.; The Dickinson Family, Inc.; Elsenham Quality Foods Limited; JMS Specialty Foods, Inc.; Knudsen & Sons, Inc.; Mary Ellen's, Incorporated; A.F. Murch Company; Santa Cruz Natural Incorporated; Henry Jones Foods Pty. Ltd.; Smucker Australia, Inc.; J.M. Smucker (Canada), Inc.; Smucker International, Ltd.; Juice Creations Co.; Mrs. Smith's, Inc.; After the Fall Products, Inc.

Further Reading:

Brown, Paul B., "A Bread-&-Butter Business," *Forbes,* January 30, 1984, p. 77.

Byrne, Harlan S., "J.M. Smucker Co.: 'Why Can't We Be Like a Gerber?' Asks Jam Company," *Barron's,* April 9, 1990, p. 60.

Ellis, William Donohue, *"With a Name Like . . . ,"* Orrville, OH: The J.M. Smucker Company, 1987.

"False Teeth and Jelly," *Forbes,* November 1, 1968, pp. 21–22.

Groseclose, Everett, "The Scions: Paul H. Smucker Takes Great Pains to Preserve His Products' Quality," *Wall Street Journal,* February 3, 1975, pp. 1, 21.

"Increased Ad Spending, New Executives Boost Smucker Market Share," *Wall Street Journal,* December 26, 1979, p. 2.

The J.M. Smucker Company: An Introduction, Orrville, OH: The J.M. Smucker Company, 1990.

Kirk, Jim, "Smucker Jells for Burnett," *Adweek* (Midwest Edition), March 28, 1994, pp. 1, 5.

Phalon, Richard, "Closely Guarded Honey Pot," *Forbes,* November 25, 1991, pp. 48–50.

"Quality Image Gains Sales for Top Jam Maker," *New York Times,* September 13, 1980, pp. L27, L30.

"Recipe for Success at J.M. Smucker Accents Quality as Key Ingredient," *Barron's,* May 1, 1967, p. 22.

"The Savvy Saleslady of Strawberry Lane," *Sales Management,* September 1, 1971, p. 21.

"Smucker Spreads Out beyond Jam and Jelly," *Business Week,* November 13, 1965, pp. 194–195.

—April Dougal Gasbarre

Jefferson-Pilot Corporation

P.O. Box 21008
Greensboro, North Carolina 27420
U.S.A.
(910) 691-3000
Fax: (910) 691-3938

Public Company
Incorporated: 1907 as Jefferson Standard
Employees: 1,250 (home office, not including independent
   agents)
Sales: $1.25 billion
Stock Exchanges: New York Midwest Pacific
SICs: 8100 Financial Services; 8210 Life and Health
   Insurance; 8330 Broadcasting and Telecommunications

Jefferson-Pilot Corporation is a major U.S. provider of life and
health insurance, annuities, pension plans, and mutual funds for
individuals and groups. It also sells commercial casualty and
title insurance and invests in various broadcasting ventures.
Active primarily in the southern and southwestern United
States, Jefferson-Pilot possesses a rich history characterized by
shrewd, conservative growth.

Jefferson Standard Life Insurance was founded on August 7,
1907, in Raleigh, North Carolina. Although it set up operations
in a relatively modest second-story office in the state's capital
city, Jefferson Standard began with half a million dollars in
capital. In fact, it was heralded as the largest corporation ever to
have been established in North Carolina. The company was
patriotically named after Thomas Jefferson, the third U.S. president and the framer of the Declaration of Independence. ''A
Jefferson Standard Policy is a Declaration of Independence for
the Family,'' was Jefferson Standard's official slogan.

Jefferson Standard enjoyed immediate acceptance by the local
community. Only 111 life insurance companies existed in the
entire country when it opened its doors (compared to about
2,000 in the early 1990s) and people were eager to take advantage of the promise of security proffered by the fledgling
insurance industry. After only five months of operation, Jefferson Standard had about $1 million of insurance in force and was
finding strong demand in other parts of North Carolina and even
outside of the state.

Jefferson Standard's quick start was concocted by brothers P. D.
and Charles W. Gold, members of a prominent newspaper
family from Wilson, North Carolina. The Gold's had inherited
an entrepreneurial bent from their father and had access to a
pool of capital to back their ideas. In addition to their desire to
create a new enterprise, the Golds were driven by another force.
The sting of the Civil War and Reconstruction was still wearing
off and the Golds wanted to make their contribution to the New
South. Recognizing that large financial institutions, including
insurance companies, in the North were draining vital development capital from the South, the Golds wanted to form an
institution that could fund local industrial growth.

The Golds and 22 like-minded associates began Jefferson Standard with the intent of developing it into a regional insurance
powerhouse. Charles Gold's daughter came up with the name of
the company and P. D. Gold crafted a logo that would serve the
organization for decades to come. However, these superficial
activities were secondary to the primary mission of Jefferson
Standard's founders—to create a regional insurance company,
operated with uncompromising ethics, that could withstand national fiscal upheavals and enhance the economic stability of
North Carolina. Evidencing this goal and foreshadowing the
philosophy that would dominate Jefferson Standard's future
was this quote from the board minutes of 1910: ''The future . . .
is fraught with difficulties. The way to profit is long, the task is
arduous, and the cost is great.''

Eager to expand its reach and increase its capital strength,
Jefferson Standard completed mergers with two other companies in 1912. It absorbed Security Life and Annuity Company,
and Greensboro Life Insurance Company—and subsequently
transferred its headquarters to Greensboro. 1912 also marked
the beginning of an era of expanding prosperity for Jefferson
Standard under the direction of Julian Price, who was working
for Greensboro Life before the merger. Although he did not
officially become president until 1919, when the last of the
aging Gold brothers stepped down, Price played a pivotal role in
the company's progression throughout the 1910s and until his
death in 1946.

The 1912 mergers brought Jefferson Standard's total base of
assets to a stunning $3.6 million and its total insurance in force
to more than $37 million. Having established a firm footing and
acquired a sizable sales force, the company stepped up its
marketing efforts and worked at creating a more sophisticated
investment program for its flourishing reserve of capital. In fact,
Jefferson realized stunning growth after the mergers, swelling
its assets to almost $10 million by 1919 and boosting total
insurance sales to more than $81 million. ''The record is a
success unparalleled in the history of southern life insurance
companies, and one beyond our most sanguine expectations,''
reported the board of directors during that period.

Much of Jefferson's success in its early years stemmed from the
devotion and persistence of its sales force. It was that group that
actually went out to the farms and met with small-town business
owners to educate them about the concept of life insurance and
to sell them on the Jefferson Standard name. The agents often
were not paid in cash and had to barter for their commissions.
According to company annals, one salesman, after being paid
with a bull yearling, fattened up his commission and sold the
bull for twice its value the following year.

By the late 1910s, Price was pushing hard for faster growth—And he got it. Notwithstanding setbacks incurred during World War I, Jefferson Standard experienced its greatest year ever in 1918, when it boosted sales more than 50 percent and extended its operations into a total of 14 southern states. Price replaced George A. Grimsley as president of the company, gaining unfettered command of the organization. He quickly set Jefferson Standard on a course of expansion that would make it a national leader in the insurance industry and would make him one of the most respected CEOs in the United States. Noted as an articulate man of vision, Price combined top-notch skills in sales and finance with the deep sense of ethics originally prescribed by the company's founders.

Jefferson Standard, under Price, was still dedicated to its goal of building the South. It sought an aggressive lending strategy throughout the region, providing much-needed capital to farmers and industrialists. It also extended its sales activities throughout the Midwest and West during the 1920s in an effort to boost its reserves and generate new capital for regional investments. The company even authored a widely distributed book entitled *A Pattern for Southern Progress*. And at one point Price, as part of a marketing effort, had an artist superimpose a rendering of a cow on a U.S. map; the cow was being fed in the South and milked in the North, signifying the loss of southern capital to northern financial institutions.

As if to stake its claim on the future of the life insurance industry, Jefferson Standard erected a 17-story "skyscraper" in the early 1920s. Although the project was considered bold and nervy, particularly in a town of only 19,000 people, the marble-laden complex was completed in 1923 and was completely paid for before its doors were opened. When Jefferson moved into its new headquarters it boasted a record $200 million worth of insurance policies in force. Before the Great Depression hit, moreover, the company had boosted that figure to a striking $300 million and was unfurling a national sales force at a rate that awed many of its competitors.

Jefferson was battered during the Depression. Many of its debtors defaulted and its investments and sales soured. Nevertheless, it eventually emerged unscathed in comparison to most of its industry counterparts, the result of its conservative fiscal strategy and the determination of its managers. Price, particularly, was credited with guiding Jefferson through that trying era. Although some people, including some coworkers, castigated Price's cantankerous and outspoken personality, it was his assertiveness and grit that helped the company weather financial adversity and stay its course through the 1930s and even through World War II.

Besides, Price relished his reputation as a polite, though scrappy, man of principle and vision. He was admired and respected within his family, community, and industry. Shortly before his death in a car accident in 1946, the Greensboro newspaper, *The Democrat*, devoted almost an entire issue to Price. The paper offered some ideology and homespun common sense espoused by Price. It also gave some insight into his unconventional character. Price didn't own a home until he was 60 years old, for example, choosing instead to rent. "Fools build houses. Wise men live in them," he believed. Other gems of Price wisdom were recorded for posterity: "Stay out of debt. If you don't owe any money, you're able to look a man in the eye and tell him to go to Hell;" and his timeless "I like a fellow with his shoulders back and his head up. A fellow who looks like he is going somewhere, even if he isn't."

Price was succeeded as president of Jefferson Standard by his son, Ralph Clay, in 1946. Ralph Clay served for four years before the board of directors essentially forced him out of his leadership role and selected Howard Holderness as president. Holderness had been with Jefferson since the mid-1920s, first working there during the summers and then assuming a full-time job in 1925. His qualifications were impeccable. His father had helped found the company before sending his son to earn his Masters in Business Administration at Harvard. Holderness left Jefferson in 1945 and formed his own successful company before returning as president of Jefferson.

Holderness was the antithesis of Julian Price. A soft-spoken, easy-going man, Holderness never gave direct orders and prided himself on not interfering with his fellow managers' duties. Although his style was different, the results were much the same. One year after taking the helm at Jefferson, Holderness announced that the company had achieved $1 billion worth of life insurance in force. From there, Jefferson embarked on a journey of steady and rapid expansion that propelled it to the forefront of the insurance industry.

On its 50th anniversary, Jefferson achieved total insurance in force of $1.5 billion. Just a few years later, in 1960, that figure had ballooned to $2 billion. In 1967, the same year in which Holderness retired as president, Jefferson reached a record $3 billion of insurance in force and was approaching a staggering $1 billion in assets. By the late 1960s, in fact, Jefferson was providing insurance services to more than one million U.S. policyholders in 32 states, the District of Columbia, and Puerto Rico. Furthermore, Jefferson had managed to retain its prized reputation as a fiscally sound enterprise, garnering the admiration of life insurance industry leaders nationwide.

Although Jefferson Standard was known to the general public only as a life insurance company as it entered the 1970s, it was also active in several media ventures. Its interest in newspapers and broadcast companies could be traced back to the Gold and Price families, both of which owned newspapers at the time that Jefferson was founded. Price, having become fascinated with newspapers, had authorized a sizable loan to a local Greensboro newspaper in 1923. Recognizing the lack of capital available to aspiring newspaper publishers, Price advanced money to several start-up newspapers that went on to become major publications during the mid-1900s. Jefferson also purchased an interest in several radio stations and studios. The media division operated under a philosophy of "showmanship and citizenship" congruent with the purpose of the overall organization. Although Jefferson continued to focus on insurance, its media holdings were a profitable arm of its operations in the mid-1900s and particularly into the 1980s and early 1990s.

W. Roger Soles took the reins from Holderness in 1967 after 20 years of service to the company. Like Holderness, Soles was known as a soft-spoken, intuitive man with a knack for finance. But he also possessed the visionary traits that had made Price so successful as the company's leader. The 46-year-old Soles displayed his intent to achieve a new vision for Jefferson immediately after assuming leadership. To take advantage of tax laws and changing financial markets, Soles reorganized the organization into a holding company. Its name was changed to Jefferson-Pilot Corporation to reflect the integration of its major subsidiary, Pilot Life, into Jefferson Standard. Soles believed that the holding company structure would allow Jefferson-Pilot to achieve faster growth and greater diversification in evolving U.S. financial markets.

Soles was correct. Under his leadership, Jefferson experienced two decades of expansion unparalleled in its history. Soles brought a new emphasis on marketing to the organization and carried Jefferson-Pilot into the computer age by implementing vast automated systems. He also became a leader in the insurance industry, serving as the first chairman of the American Council of Life Insurers (ACLI), which is considered the highest management office in the industry. In fact, Soles is credited with changing the face of Jefferson-Pilot. Importantly, Jefferson entered a variety of new business and consumer markets during the 1970s, including tax sheltered annuities, retirement and pension programs, and numerous investment and financial planning services. Jefferson also restructured its sales force and developed new pay incentives for its agents.

By 1976, Jefferson-Pilot had more than $5 billion of insurance in force, reflecting rapid growth since Sole's selection as president. The company continued to expand in the late 1970s, boosting its insurance in force to a whopping $6 billion by 1978. Sales growth was augmented by increased investments in media ventures—Jefferson-pilot began to actually purchase newspapers and broadcasting companies. Despite its rampant increase in insurance and media revenues, however, Jefferson-Pilot's profit opportunities were diminished by widespread trends that were affecting the entire U.S. insurance industry. Specifically, rising interest rates and inflation in the late 1970s, combined with growing state and federal tax and regulatory pressures, crimped industry earnings.

While the overall life insurance industry suffered a general downturn during the late 1970s and early 1980s, Jefferson sustained moderate growth and remained financially healthy in comparison to most of its competitors. During the 1980s, Jefferson's operations continued to grow at a steady rate, though its growth lagged that of many of its life insurance company peers. Indeed, many insurers were able to reap huge investment gains during the 1980s by placing their reserves in real estate, junk bonds, and other high-risk vehicles that paid fantastic returns. Jefferson, in contrast, maintained its staid, conservative strategy of investing in low-risk, long-term, wealth-building instruments.

By 1989, Jefferson-Pilot had increased its life insurance in force to $37 billion, more than six times the amount of in-force insurance just ten years earlier. Although this growth belied the lack of a corresponding rise in profits from life insurance sales, Jefferson was able to bolster its bottom line during the decade by expanding into an array of complementary markets. While it earned about $109 million in net income during 1989 from life insurance, for example, it captured an additional $28 million from its casualty and title insurance activities, communications subsidiaries, and miscellaneous investment gains.

More important than Jefferson's steady revenue and profit gains during the 1980s was its successful strategy of conservatively investing its reserves. By the early 1990s, Jefferson's balance sheet stood out like a paradise island within the sea of red ink that swamped many of its competitors. Indeed, as new tax laws and an economic recession battered financial markets during the late 1980s and early 1990s, many insurers were teetering on the edge of bankruptcy or were, in fact, insolvent. "Jefferson-Pilot's got one of the best balance sheets in the business," said Myron Picoult, industry analyst, in the August 1992 issue of *Business-North Carolina*. "What they did was absolutely correct in terms of maintaining the integrity of their balance sheet, given the environment of the 1980s."

Despite Sole's success at keeping the company focused on long-term growth during the 1980s, he came under attack in the early 1990s from Louise Price Parsons, the daughter of Ralph Clay Price. Mrs. Parsons and her husband particularly wanted the board to remove Mr. Soles as president of the company. Among other things, they cited slow profit growth of the company in comparison to a few more successful insurers in the region.

While the Parsons did not succeed in their two-year effort to cause the company to remove Mr. Soles, they did reach a settlement with the company that mandated that the board implement certain corporate governance principles. Also in early 1993, Mr. Soles retired at the age of 71 and was followed by several other senior managers who had reached retirement age. During his last two years as president, Mr. Soles oversaw healthy income and profit gains; revenues rose to $1.20 billion in 1992 as net income rose an impressive 48 percent in three years to $195 million. David A. Stonecipher, who came from Life Insurance Company of Georgia, assumed the presidency in 1993, a year in which revenues rose to a record $1.25 billion. Stonecipher planned to pursue Jefferson-Pilot's long-practiced strategy of steady growth, responsible corporate citizenship, and fiscal conservatism—the same strategy initiated by the Gold brothers in 1907.

Principal Subsidiaries: Jefferson-Pilot Communications Company; Jefferson-Pilot Data Services, Inc.; Jefferson-Pilot Fire & Casualty Company; Jefferson-Pilot Investor Service, Inc.; Jefferson-Pilot Life Insurance Company; Jefferson-Pilot Title Insurance Company; JP Investment Management Company.

Further Reading:

Bailey, David, "Where There's a Will, There's a Way: After Inheriting 290,000 Shares of Jefferson Pilot Stock, an Heiress Sets Out to Make Its CEO Play by Her Rules," *Business-North Carolina*, August 1992, Sec. 1, p. 12.

Coleman, Kathleen, "The Pilot at JP Communications," *Business Journal-Charlotte*, November 13, 1989, Sec. 1, p. 8.

Fox, James F., *75 Years: 1907 to 1982; Jefferson Standard Life Insurance Company*, Greensboro, NC: 1982.

"The Jefferson Standard Story," *The Jeffersonian*, August 1982, pp. 14–17.

Marshall, Kyle, "JP Reaches Outside for Next CEO," *News & Observer*, August 12, 1992, Sec. BUS.

Still, John T., "Jefferson-Pilot and Parsons Group Settle Litigation," *PR Newswire*, April 5, 1993.

—Dave Mote

JONES APPAREL GROUP

Jones Apparel Group, Inc.

250 Rittenhouse Circle
Bristol, Pennsylvania 19007
U.S.A.
(215) 785-4000
Fax: (215) 785-1228

Public Company
Incorporated: 1975
Employees: 1,475
Sales: $545.12 million
Stock Exchanges: New York
SICs: 233 Women's, Misses' and Juniors' Outerwear; 6794
   Patent Owners and Lessers

Jones Apparel Group, Inc. is a leading U.S. designer and marketer of moderately priced women's sportswear, suits, and dresses. While most of its clothing is sold under the Jones New York label, other popular brands owned by Jones include Evan Picone and Rena Rowan for Saville. Jones Apparel Group was one of the fastest growing companies in the U.S. apparel industry during the late 1980s and early 1990s.

Jones Apparel Group was founded by Sidney Kimmel in 1975. A 20-year veteran of the women's clothing industry, Kimmel recognized a potentially lucrative void in the marketplace that he could fill by designing and marketing a line of clothing that mimicked extremely expensive designer fashions. Hoping to appeal to the middle-income market of working women, Kimmel decided that his apparel would be high in quality yet affordable.

By the time Kimmel started his Jones venture, he had already proven himself in the women's clothing industry. The son of a Philadelphia taxi driver, Kimmel had dropped out of college in the early 1950s to work in a knitting mill. Hard work and high energy, as well as his knack for developing and bringing to market popular clothing designs, earned Kimmel a top management spot at the mill by the 1960s, and he eventually became president of Villager, Inc., a top designer and manufacturer of women's sportswear.

Eager to build his own apparel line, Kimmel left Villager in 1969 to join W. R. Grace & Co. A diversified conglomerate, Grace & Co. was seeking to branch out into women's clothing and chose Kimmel to head up the new division. Kimmel brought with him his girlfriend, Rena Rowan, who had worked for him at Villager as a knitwear designer. Shortly after moving to Grace & Co., Kimmel and Rowan hit upon their idea of creating inexpensive, designer-look-alike clothing.

During this time, however, Grace's management decided their company didn't belong in the fashion business. Seeking a smooth way out of the undertaking, Grace jettisoned its new Jones division in 1975, selling it to Kimmel and Gerard Rubin, a Grace accountant. Kimmel and Rubin were pleased to get the business, along with its liabilities, for a relatively small cash investment. The two partners incorporated Jones Apparel Group, Inc. in Pennsylvania, and their staff soon consisted of Rowan and several other former Grace employees.

While there was no mistaking Kimmel's acuity in the fashion trade, his knowledge of finance was limited, as he recalled in the December 21, 1992 issue of *Forbes*: "I didn't know how to read a balance sheet." Even Rubin was unable to steer the fledgling company clear of fiscal distress, and, during its first five years of business, Jones Apparel was burdened by debt and short on cash. Nevertheless, Kimmel pursued an aggressive growth agenda, beginning several new labels and licensing the rights to other clothing lines.

The company did achieve a relatively high degree of success, particularly during the 1980s. Kimmel found a strong demand for many of his products among women who appreciated style and quality but didn't have a lot of money to spend on expensive designer wear. The Jones New York line, which featured career sportswear, suits, and dresses, was especially successful—for $100 to $300, women were able to purchase professional and casual wear that looked and felt like name brands selling for twice the price or more. Moreover, Kimmel was able to profit by outsourcing the manufacturing of his clothes to both U.S. and overseas producers. That tactic allowed Jones to focus on designing, marketing, and distributing its products, while at the same time bypassing hefty capital investments in manufacturing facilities.

Jones also gained on its industry peers during the 1980s by implementing the latest productivity-enhancing technology. Indeed, while many U.S. apparel producers succumbed to fierce foreign competition during the decade, Jones thrived. In 1981, for example, Jones became one of the first apparel designers in the United States to start using a computer-aided design (CAD) system and to employ a systems manager, Maureen Behl, in its design department. The new system saved large sums in wasted fabric, because it allowed designers to lay patterns out on a facsimile of the fabric (a process called marking), like pieces of a puzzle, before transferring the design and cutting the actual fabric.

CAD also slashed labor costs related to grading (shrinking a standard-size garment design to make other sizes). "There's really no comparison," Behl commented in the September 24, 1993 issue of *Philadelphia Business Journal*. "Doing it manually, it could take a day to do the marking and grading for one pattern. Now it takes a few hours." The improved turnaround time associated with the CAD system allowed Jones Apparel to provide better customer service. On short notice, Jones designers could get a sample of a design to a client within hours, and then quickly alter the computerized pattern to suit the client's needs.

Besides its keen market niche, low-cost manufacturing strategy, and advanced design program, Jones benefitted from economic and demographic trends during the mid-1980s. Generally healthy business expansion bolstered the demand for professional and casual wear in the United States. More importantly, the number of working women in the nation increased dramatically during the decade. As a result, the demand for suits and career sportswear flourished and the discretionary income available to women in Jones' key markets increased. Furthermore, diversifying into a range of apparel aimed at a variety of niche markets, the company purchased the rights to other clothing lines, including Gloria Vanderbilt Jeans, and thus enjoyed demand growth for products outside its core Jones New York line. By the mid-1980s, with annual sales of over $250 million, Jones had become the leading supplier of moderately-priced women's apparel, marketing its lines through retail establishments and catalogs throughout North America.

Kimmel continued to pursue new markets in an effort to increase sales, despite warnings from company accountants that Jones Apparel was growing too quickly. Moreover, Kimmel also engaged in several business deals that soured. Chief among such mishaps was his purchase of the marketing rights to Murjani's Gloria Vanderbilt. Kimmel neglected to secure any control over manufacturing costs, pricing, inventory, or delivery of the jeans, thus undermining his savvy marketing initiatives. That deal alone cost Kimmel $20 million by the late 1980s, severely crimping the company's profitability.

Largely as a result of the failed Murjani transaction—but also because of the heavy debt Jones had accrued during its start-up and rampant growth—Jones Apparel was on the verge of bankruptcy by 1987. As cash flow dried up and the cofounders were forced to spend much of their time putting out financial fires, sales and earnings plummeted. Sales topped $260 million in 1986, but Jones posted a distressing net loss of $4.6 million. In 1987, moreover, sales plunged 32 percent, to $177 million, for a net loss of $6 million.

Rather than seizing and liquidating the company, creditors offered Kimmel and Rubin an alternative. Kimmel and Rubin agreed to a strict reorganization plan designed to shore up Jones' balance sheet and restore the flailing company's profitability. To keep control of the operation, Kimmel and Rubin were forced to drop most of the labels Kimmel had licensed during the 1980s as add-ons to its core apparel lines. They also agreed to lay off many of their employees, scrap most of the companies 17 scattered divisions, and liquidate a major warehouse. Finally, both Kimmel and Rubin had to put their personal assets on the line by guaranteeing $8 million in loans made to the company. The aim of the shake-up was to help Jones Apparel Group focus on its most successful product line, Jones New York. Jones also retained a few of its profitable complementary brands, such as Christian Dior.

Jones reported a small profit as it wrapped up its reorganization in 1988, and, the following year, the company began to focus heavily on promoting and streamlining its Jones New York line. Weary from Jones' financial woes, Rubin bailed out of the

concern in 1989, selling his ownership interest to Kimmel. Unfortunately for Rubin, his departure marked the start of revenue and profit growth at Jones that would continue into the mid-1990s. Indeed, as the United States sank into a recession, demand for Jones New York apparel escalated. Many buyers abandoned expensive designer labels in favor of Jones' more practical attire; Jones' Giorgio Armani look-alike suit, for example, sold for only $240, or about $1,200 less than the Armani.

Kimmel augmented Jones' improved market appeal during the late 1980s with increased advertising and a new emphasis on cost control. Furthermore, he began to stress financial stability, working to pare the company's debt load and tighten its customer credit policies. As demand surged and operating costs fell, Jones posted a 25 percent sales gain in 1989, to $212 million, as net income soared to nearly $13 million. In 1990, moreover, income approached $30 million from revenues of $290 million. That year, to further reduce the company's liabilities, Kimmel took Jones Apparel Group public. By early 1993, the company's debt had been almost entirely eliminated and Kimmel still personally owned about 45 percent of the corporation.

Kimmel's financial recovery in the early 1990s was regarded in the business community as miraculous. Having faced the prospect of losing his company and much of his personal fortune, Kimmel rebounded, earning $185 million in cash during the 1991 stock offerings and reporting a net worth of nearly three-quarters of a billion dollars in the early 1990s. Expansion at Jones Apparel continued unabated, moreover, as Kimmel boosted Jones New York sales and extended the company's reach into complementary markets. Importantly, in 1991 Jones introduced its Rena Rowan for Saville line. Designed by and named after the woman that had driven the design success of the Jones New York line since 1970, the Rena Rowan line was a notch below Jones New York apparel in price and quality. By 1993, Rena Rowan clothing was accounting for about 15 percent of Jones' total receipts and was expected to lead sales growth into the mid-1990s.

In addition to making a bid for the lower-priced casual sportswear and dress market with the Rena Rowan line, Jones also expanded the Jones New York line, seeking to take advantage of four major niche markets: career sportswear, casual sportswear, suits, and dresses. Its Jones New York Sport line, created to penetrate the market for knit weekend and leisure sportswear, was bringing in about 20 percent of Jones revenue by 1993 and was expected to contribute much more in the future. Other additions to the Jones New York line included: Jones & Co., which offered "career casual" clothing to augment the Sport group; Jones New York Dress, which featured more casual business attire; and Jones New York Suits, a line of higher-priced career apparel. Jones also purchased the rights to use the Evan-Picone brand name in 1993 for $10.5 million in cash. This move illustrated its intent to break into the market for women's rainwear, coats, footwear, intimate apparel, hosiery, handbags, and other accessories.

Jones' prudent growth strategy continued to pay off in 1991 and 1992. Sales rose to $334 million in 1991 and then to $436 million one year later. Net income, moreover, rose more than 50 percent between 1990 and 1992 to over $41 million. Jones' solid profit growth reflected its huge profit margins, which, at about ten percent, were double the industry average. Income gains were also the result of Kimmel's cultivation of diverse distribution channels. For example, Jones began aggressively selling its merchandise through factory outlet stores in the early 1990s, opening more than 100 stores in outlet malls throughout the United States. By 1993, sales from the high-margin outlets had surpassed $55 million. Although department stores still made up more than 60 percent of company sales in the early 1990s, Jones had beefed up its distribution channels to encompass more than 8,000 locations in North America, including its direct mail catalog centers.

Going into the mid-1990s, Jones Apparel sustained its impressive growth rate. Sales increased 24 percent in 1993 to $541 million, from which nearly $50 million in net income was gleaned. Revenues were expected to jump to more than $600 million during 1994. Importantly, Jones' core market niches were expanding steadily, while its major competitors were losing ground. The company's negligible debt load, successful product introduction strategy, and lean organizational structure suggested continued expansion.

Further Reading:

Armstrong, Michael W., "Jones Apparel Seeks $58 million From IPO," *Philadelphia Business Journal,* April 22, 1991, p. 5.

Card Wesley R., "Jones Apparel Group, Inc. Reports Record Sales and Earnings for 1992," *PR Newswire,* February 10, 1993.

Davis, Jessica, "At Textile, Students Learn Computerized Design," *Philadelphia Business Journal,* September 24, 1993, p. 1.

Davis, Jessica, "Jones Apparel After Acquisition," *Philadelphia Business Journal,* May 3, 1993, p. 6.

Furman, Phyllis, "Jones, Like Liz, Outfitted to Grow," *Crains New York Business,* March 16, 1992, p. 35.

Longley, Alice Beebe, *Company Analysis: Jones Apparel,* New York: Donaldson, Lufkin & Jenrette, May 11, 1994.

Moukheiber, Zina, "Close Call," *Forbes,* December 21, 1992, p. 194.

—Dave Mote

create improved products, his mill became focused almost solely on the production of healthcare products. After the war, in fact, Kendall continued to chase the healthcare market. By the 1920s, Kendall was manufacturing hospital dressings, cheesecloth, sanitary gauze, and numerous coarse-mesh products. It sold its products under brand names that included Curity, Kendall, and Polyken.

The 1920s and 1930s represented an era of rapid growth for Kendall. It acquired other manufacturers of dressings and related healthcare products and also purchased additional spinning and weaving plants to meet the swelling demand for its products. Kendall even expanded outside of the United States in 1926, opening a subsidiary in Toronto, Canada. Kendall's early interest in foreign ventures would eventually result in nearly 20 percent of the company's revenues coming from cross-border operations. In 1928 the name of the company was changed to The Kendall Company.

World War II resulted in another period of huge growth for The Kendall Company, as the demand for Kendall's broad line of surgical dressings and first aid products ballooned. The company expanded its offerings during that period to include elastic stockings, nonwoven fabrics, and industrial tapes that utilized technology already implemented in some of its healthcare products. Examples of Kendall-manufactured goods included Curad adhesive bandages, Curity gauze bandages, Curity diapers and baby knits, Polyken plastic-coated electrical tape, and Curity Burn-a-lay (a burn relief cream).

Although The Kendall Company had to overcome a temporary reduction in shipments following World War II, it benefited during the 1950s and 1960s from the general expansion of the U.S. economy. As the population boomed, sales of its Curity diapers and other baby products shot up, as did shipments of its home first-aid products. Strong growth in the healthcare field boosted revenues from its gauzes, dressings, tapes, and ointments. Industrial and construction markets generated demand for Kendall's industrial adhesive tapes. Furthermore, U.S. government purchases bolstered Kendall's bottom line during the Korean War and the Vietnam War.

By the early 1970s, The Kendall Company had progressed from a small-town textile mill into a leading U.S. provider of hospital and home healthcare dressings and first aid products. Recognizing its market strength and future potential, The Colgate-Palmolive Company purchased Kendall in 1972. Kendall became a wholly-owned subsidiary of Colgate, and its products and brand names were swept into that massive U.S. conglomerate. Colgate owned Kendall and its products for 16 years, during which Curad, Curity, Polyken and other brands realized strong growth. Colgate's hefty capital backing and marketing savvy made many of Kendall's products household and hospital staples.

Until 1988, the subordinate Kendall was enveloped in the operations of its giant owner. In late 1988, however, a group of Colgate-Palmolive/Kendall managers, together with some outside vendors, formed Kendall International, Inc. as a holding company. Kendall International was created to purchase The Kendall Company and some related businesses and assets from Colgate-Palmolive. The management and investment group incurred $1 billion of debt during the acquisition. At the time of

Kendall International, Inc.

15 Hampshire Street
Mansfield, Massachusetts 02048
U.S.A.
(508) 261-8000
Fax: (508) 261-8353

Wholly Owned Subsidiary of Tyco International Ltd.
Incorporated: 1903
Employees: 8,500
Sales: $.83 billion
SICs: 8641 Pharmaceuticals; 8650 Electrical, Electronics, Instrumentation

Kendall International, Inc. manufactures, markets, and distributes disposable medical supplies and devices. It specializes in serving wound care, vascular therapy, and home healthcare markets, but also manufactures miscellaneous healthcare and industrial products. Although Kendall filed for bankruptcy in 1992, it restructured its organization and was able to resume the steady growth it has achieved since the beginning of the century.

The company that would become Kendall International was born in Walpole, Massachusetts in 1903. Henry P. Kendall, an entrepreneur with a knack for improving products and production processes, purchased the Lewis Batting Company, a small textile mill. The mill employed 80 people and produced cotton batts, carpet linings, and absorbent cotton. Kendall soon expanded that limited product line to include various cotton health and hygienic products, such as sterile wipes, surgical dressings, and protective tape coatings.

In 1916, Kendall purchased a cotton mill in Camden, South Carolina. In what would later be recognized as a shrewd innovation, Kendall became one of the first American companies to vertically integrate its production process; his company handled the spinning, weaving, and finishing of the broadwoven fabrics they made into dressings. The move allowed Kendall to boost earnings from his already growing business and to position his company to capitalize on a surge in demand for his medical products during the late 1910s.

World War I provided an opportunity for Kendall to serve his country by meeting a massive demand for his surgical dressings and cotton gauze. As he stepped up production and worked to purchase, Kendall was garnering about $650 million in annual sales. By that time it had increased its product lines to include numerous industrial coating products, medical supplies and devices, generic drugs, and personal healthcare products.

Shortly after Kendall regained its independence, the United States spiraled into a deep recession. Although many of Kendall's products were relatively unscathed by the downturn, growth fell short of projections, hurting the company's financial performance. Furthermore, three specific setbacks occurred in 1989 and 1990. First, the latex glove market collapsed as a result of industry overcapacity, stunting Kendall's margins in that important segment. Second, sales of oil pipeline coatings to Russia took a severe and unexpected downturn. Finally, Federal Food and Drug Administration (FDA) product approvals slowed to a near halt, forcing Kendall to sell its state-of-the-art generic drug facility and cede its share of that profitable market niche.

By 1990, Kendall International was buckling under its massive debt load. In an attempt to recover, the buyout team brought in a new chief executive, Dick Gilleland, a recognized "turn-around" expert in the healthcare industry. During 1990 and 1991, Gilleland worked to meet Kendall's debt payments. With sales falling below the projections made before the merger, he was forced to jettison a significant chunk of Kendall's assets for relatively low prices. Kendall raised $221 million, most of which came from the sale of its McGaw intravenous solutions division. Despite Gilleland's efforts, Kendall failed to meet its loan obligations. In June of 1992, Kendall International entered into a restructuring plan under Chapter 11 of the U.S. Bankruptcy Code.

As a result of Kendall's restructuring during 1992, which entailed a sale of company stock that raised $112 million, Kendall was able to reduce its debt payments to a manageable sum; further refinancing in response to low interest rates during 1993 improved the company's position. In addition, Kendall benefited from an uptick in the economy in 1992 and 1993 that allowed it to increase sales and profits. After rising to $688 million in 1990, Kendall's revenues climbed to $738 million in 1991, $775 million in 1992, and to $826 million in 1993. Likewise, net income increased to a healthy $52 million by 1993, the first positive figure since the company had secured its independence. Kendall appeared to be engaged in a healthy recovery.

The company was able to emerge from its debt load and the economic downturn largely through the efforts of its competent staff and managers. By the early 1990s, Kendall had about 8,500 people working in its organization, about 4,500 of whom were located in the United States. In addition to Gilleland, senior management included many seasoned industry veterans. For example, James S. Fraser, senior vice-president, had formerly served as president of Calcitek, a dental products manufacturer. Likewise, Kendall Healthcare Products Company President Richard J. Meelia had previously been president of Infusaid/Pfizer Hospital Group, a maker of implantable drug delivery products.

The company that emerged from the reorganization comprised four business units; Kendall Healthcare Products Company,

The Kendall-Futuro Company, Polyken Technologies, and the International Division. The smallest of these divisions was the Kendall-Futuro Company, which accounted for about 15 percent of company sales in the early 1990s. Kendall-Futuro manufactured and distributed home health care and first-aid products. Besides products under its popular Curad, Curity, Futuro, and Telfa brand names, the subsidiary produced a variety of miscellaneous goods, such as elastic supports and hosiery, wheelchairs and walkers, and diabetes management products.

Kendall's International Division accounted for approximately 17 percent of company receipts. It was responsible for manufacturing, marketing, and exporting Kendall products in more than 80 countries. It was primarily active in three regions: Europe, the Far East, and Latin America. However, Kendall also had operations in Australia, China, Thailand, Venezuela, and many other regions. Although the International Division focused on the sale of Kendall's hospital health care items, the company also used this division to procure raw materials for manufacturing.

Also making up about 17 percent of Kendall's shipments in the early 1990s was its Polyken Technologies subsidiary. Polyken manufactured and sold adhesive products and tapes for industrial and consumer applications worldwide. It sold such products as pipeline coatings, duct tape, and high-performance aerospace industry adhesives. Polyken also produced various goods for Kendall's medical product lines.

Kendall International's largest division was Kendall Healthcare Products Company, which generated more than 50 percent of the company's revenues in the late 1980s and early 1990s. That segment included various disposable medical, surgical, and vascular therapy products. Its three main product groups were: wound care supplies; urology and incontinent care, such as catheters and urine drainage devices; anesthesia products, such as airway management devices; and vascular therapy products, such as stockings and compression devices that reduce the risk of blood clots in immobilized patients. Kendall held an 80 percent share of the entire U.S. vascular compression market in 1993 and was experiencing its strongest demand for that line.

Despite tribulations during the late 1980s and early 1990s, Kendall International was relatively well positioned to take advantage of opportunities that were expected to arise during the middle and late 1990s. Importantly, Kendall held a solid leadership position in its key markets: it was at the head of both the U.S. wound care and vascular compression markets, and held the third leading spot in the urological industry. In addition, Kendall was recognized as maintaining state-of-the-art, efficient manufacturing operations. Kendall had established relationships with hospitals across North America and enjoyed a reputation for quality and service. Also to Kendall's credit were its respected consumer brand names. Finally, Kendall's chief competitor, Johnson & Johnson, was posing less of a threat to Kendall's profit margins going into the mid-1990s.

However, Kendall faced a range of obstacles that would likely hinder its success later in the decade. Healthcare initiatives proposed by Congress in 1994, for example, threatened to increase cost containment pressures on Kendall's largest customers—hospitals. Such efforts would likely reduce its already slipping profit margins from that market. Also, most of Kendall's businesses were in relatively mature, slow-growth areas that offered little chance of future expansion in the United States. Shorter hospital stays, less-invasive surgery techniques, and greater competition were a few of the major factors that were changing Kendall's market.

Only Kendall's important vascular compression product line proffered hope for hot growth in the 1990s. Sales of those items were expected to lurch from $86 million in 1992 to $167 million by 1996, providing the large majority of the gains for Kendall Healthcare. Unfortunately, Kendall severely underspent on research and development after its separation from Colgate-Palmolive. As a result, Kendall faced an uphill battle in sustaining its long-term leadership in some of its high-tech, high-profit niches. It would likely have to rely on acquisitions of other companies or products. Evidencing this likelihood was Kendall's announced buyout of Rhode Island-based Superior Healthcare Group, Inc., in 1994. Superior was a major producer of respiratory, urology, and nursing care products.

Going into the mid-1990s, Kendall, still under the direction of Gilleland in 1994, was making great strides in overcoming its debt problems. After boosting sales every year after Kendall International's formation in 1988, management was looking forward to continued growth as well as greater stability. At least one major market analyst predicted steady gains for Kendall through 1995 or 1996, when its reorganization would be complete. After that, its growth rate would likely slow to the single digit range. Kendall was looking to international expansion, increased demand for its vascular compression products, and continued dominance of its established brand names to drive future growth. In late 1994, Kendall was purchased by Tyco International Ltd. of Exeter, New Hampshire.

Principal Subsidiaries: The Kendall Company; The Kendall-Futuro Company; Kendall Healthcare Products Company; Polyken Technologies.

Further Reading:

Bacciocco, James S., "The Kendall Company Completes Financial Restructuring," *PR Newswire*, September 3, 1992; "Kendall International, Inc. Releases Year-End Results," *PR Newswire*, February 1, 1993.

Esquivel, Raul P., *Kidder Peabody Equity Research; Kendall International*, New York: Kidder, Peabody & Co., Inc., February 4, 1994.

Form 10-K; Kendall International, Washington, D.C.: Securities and Exchange Commission, 1994.

Hammers, Floyd, "Hammers Plastic Recycling Corp. Appoints Chief Operating Officer and Ends Negotiations for California Plant," *PR Newswire*, April 7, 1994.

Kendall, Mansfield, MA: The Kendall Company, 1993.

Kerry, Roger, "Kendall Changes Plans; Seeks Move from N. Ky.," *Greater Cincinnati Business Record*, April 19, 1993, Sec. 1, p. 3.

Schnaars, Nancy, "Kendall to Focus on Core, Health Care Businesses for Future Growth," *Business Wire*, June 13, 1990.

Schwarz, Lorraine, and Yolande Sylvestre, *Wertheim Schroder; Kendall International (KEND-42) Coverage Initiated with Buy Rating on Turnaround Hospital Supplier*, March 24, 1994.

—Dave Mote

KENETECH

Kenetech Corporation

500 Sansome Street
San Francisco, CA 94111
U.S.A.
(415) 398-3825
Fax: (415) 391-7740

Public Company
Incorporated: 1979 as U.S. Windpower
Employees: 1,200
Sales: $.25 billion
Stock Exchanges: NASDAQ
SICs: 1510 Energy Resources; 8340 Electric, Gas, and Water
  Utilities; 8370 Construction and Related Services

Kenetech Corporation is a leading developer and provider of
environmentally preferred electric power—principally wind,
biomass, and natural gas. It has installed more wind turbines
than any other company in the world and is a recognized technological leader in the field of wind energy. Kenetech also
builds and operates power production facilities on a fee basis.

Kenetech's precursor was founded in 1974 in Cambridge, Massachusetts. Stanley Charren and a group of forward-thinking
associates, recognizing the future potential of generating electric power by means other than fossil fuels, hoped to create an
energy company that utilized wind as its power source. The
company was incorporated in 1979 as U.S. Windpower to
design and sell wind turbines and wind power. During the early
1980s, U.S. Windpower designed and produced its first-generation wind turbine.

U.S. Windpower's entry into the alternative energy market was
made possible by the political and economic environment of the
1970s and early 1980s. Utilities during that period were predicting a long-term escalation of fossil fuel prices. As a result, the
federal government and certain state governments began offering financial incentives for companies to begin developing
new energy sources. Oil prices did, in fact, balloon at a feverish
pitch during the late 1970s and early 1980s in the wake of
efforts by the Organization of Petroleum Exporting Countries
(OPEC).

The Federal Government responded to the energy crunch by
bolstering its efforts to foster alternative power projects. In
addition to tax breaks for companies like U.S. Windpower, the

government also began requiring public utilities to purchase
power from qualifying energy producers, and it offered them
inducements to acquire and own non-fossil fuel energy projects.
Some states, particularly California, augmented federal initiatives with their own promotional programs. Besides offering
state tax breaks, the California Public Utilities Commission
required utilities to enter into long-term power purchase agreements with alternative suppliers that assured them fixed rates
for the energy they sold to the utilities.

Spurred by California's favorable regulatory environment, U.S.
Windpower relocated its operations to the San Francisco Bay
area. As oil prices continued to rise and alternative energy
projects achieved fad status, U.S. Windpower was able to ride
the industry wave. Between 1981 and 1984 the burgeoning
enterprise entered into power purchase agreements for approximately 420 megawatts of generating capacity in California—
one megawatt of capacity is roughly sufficient to power 350
households for one year. It also tried to market its windmills and
enter into agreements in a few other states.

During the early 1980s "wind farms" sprang up east of San
Francisco, as well as in many other regions of the country, by
the thousands. Windmill manufacturers, many of them under-
capitalized, rushed to the market. They erected hordes of relatively rudimentary turbines, many of which were powered by
simple helicopter blades. Sales of wind-powered electricity
soared from $21 million in 1981 to $748 million by 1985.
Spurred by its success, U.S. Windpower (and many of its
industry peers) even began seeking profits from other forms of
energy, such as biomass (burning plant material) and natural
gas.

Despite an influx of competitors during the early 1980s, U.S.
Windpower was able to assume a leadership role in the wind
power industry through technological prowess and sound management. Chairman and co-founder Charren, himself a graduate
of Brown University with a masters in engineering from Harvard University, was joined by an adept management and
technical team. For example, Gerald R. Alderson, a Harvard
M.B.A., became president and chief executive officer in 1981.
The board of directors also included several Harvard and Yale
graduates.

U.S. Windpower's technical competence was reflected in its
second-generation wind turbine system, the Model 56-100,
which it began marketing in 1983. That windmill represented a
vast improvement over helicopter blade-type systems and
proved to be more cost-effective than even the majority of the
most advanced turbines introduced during the early 1980s. During the mid-1990s, U.S. Windpower installed approximately
4,000 of those units, most of which were located in two locations 50 miles east of San Francisco. In most instances, U.S.
Windpower installed the turbines for third-party owners and
operated them in return for a percentage of energy sales. About
one-fifth of the units, though, were actually owned and operated
by U.S. Windpower.

Although the Model 56-100 was soon to be succeeded by
Kenetech's third generation turbine, it performed admirably
during the 1980s and contributed to U.S. Windpower's status as
an industry trend-setter. As advertised, the 56-100 units pro-

duced about 200 kilowatt-hours of power annually during the 1980s and achieved a mechanical availability rate of about 98 percent—good by industry standards. By the late 1980s, the Model 56-100 was generating about 25 percent of all the wind power being sold in California—wind power accounted for approximately 1.5 percent of that state's total power production.

Unfortunately for U.S. Windpower and other alternative energy pioneers, markets began to sour in the mid-1980s. By 1985, the Reagan administration had successfully dismantled many of the energy tax incentives created by President Carter. Most state enticements had also been withdrawn. Oil prices had fallen dramatically from the early 1980s highs, and new energy technologies were significantly boosting the efficiency of traditional power generating systems. As a result, the industry was beaten into submission by severely depressed markets. By 1988, in fact, wind power sales plunged over 1,000 percent from their 1985 peak to a measly $67 million per year. As visions of wind power grandeur faded, many companies were forced out of business.

U.S. Windpower was buoyed during the lean late 1980s by its guaranteed long-term contracts in California, the only state in which it was selling wind power during that period. More importantly, however, the company successfully supplanted lagging wind power revenue growth by emphasizing its diversification into energy-related ventures. It particularly stepped up its offerings of construction services, most of which were provided through its CNF Industries division; CNF provided engineering, procurement, and construction services for utility and industrial projects. Similarly, the company offered energy management services, including the development and implementation of cost-effectiveness programs for large industrial, commercial, and institutional energy users.

In 1988, U.S. Windpower reorganized its organization to reflect its growing diversification. It created Kenetech Corporation as a holding company for its subsidiaries, the most important of which remained Kenetech Windpower, or U.S. Windpower. Indeed, despite ailing alternative energy markets, Kenetech remained committed to the concept of wind power and believed that its future lay in that arena. Kenetech's senior management quickly steered the company into a new direction designed to continue the growth Kenetech had achieved since its inception.

Kenetech's reorganization was prompted, in part, by its recognition of the fact that earnings from its important wind power division were at risk. Despite the success of its Model 56-100, that turbine was no longer cost-competitive with many other means of generating electricity. Although Kenetech achieved 1988 sales of $148 million, the fixed-price purchase contracts it had signed in the mid-1980s were set to gradually expire by 1991, throwing doubt on the future of the company's core business. In response to the dilemma, Kenetech embarked on an ambitious venture in 1988 to develop a third-generation wind turbine that would allow it to compete with other energy sources on a level playing field, with government incentives.

After spending two years developing a new turbine, Kenetech began marketing its breakthrough Model 33M-VS in late 1991. Although the new windmill closely resembled the old 56-100—the Model 33M-VS stands 90–120 feet high, and has three

54-foot fiberglass blades—it is the gearing inside the giant turbine that makes it a major industry innovation. Prior to 1991, wind turbines operated at a single, constant speed. Regardless of how hard the wind blew, the rotor would spin at the same speed in order to deliver the required alternating current frequency of 50 or 60 hertz. As a result, high winds quickly wore out the machinery and significant wind energy was wasted.

The Model 33M-VS solved the problems of its predecessors. It used a variable-speed turbine that adjusted to the wind's speed, thus capturing more energy. Wear and tear was reduced, as was the costly maintenance required by traditional turbines. Furthermore, because the torque level was lower, the 33M-VS used less expensive parts and was about 25 percent less expensive to manufacture than the 56-100. The end result of Kenetech's efforts was that it had reduced the cost of generating a kilowatt-hour of electricity from $.075 to below $.05, suddenly making wind power cost-competitive with systems utilizing coal, natural gas, hydropower, or geothermal energy.

Kenetech invested nearly $40 million on research and development to create the Model 33M-VS. At the same time, its wind power revenues were coming under increasing pressure from falling natural gas and oil prices. Nevertheless, the company managed to stabilize its financial performance by increasing receipts from its management and construction services and by sustaining steady cash flow from its installed base of 56-100 turbines. In addition, Kenetech added a wood recycling subsidiary in 1991 and later constructed two biomass energy plants. As revenues swelled from $162 million in 1989 to $257 million in 1990, net income rose from $3.6 million to a hefty $15.4 million. Aggregate sales and income dipped in 1991, however, as Kenetech exited some of its long-term wind power contracts.

Kenetech's net income fell to $2.6 million in 1992 before tumbling to a net loss of $18.1 million in 1993. Energy sales fell 28 percent in 1993 and construction services sales dropped similarly as a result of lost wind power contracts. Nevertheless, Kenetech's management and investors were enthused about the company's performance; Kenetech began selling the 33M-VS system in 1993 and immediately realized a strong interest in the turbine. Windplant sales increased 267 percent in 1993, to about $17.7 million, despite the fact that the Model 56-100 had been completely phased out of production in the United States by 1992.

To fund its anticipated growth, Kenetech sold six million shares of stock in 1993 and raised $92 million for expansion. However, as interest and orders in its new generating system continued to rise, company management began to wonder if those new funds were enough to support the company's sudden growth. By 1993, the first year in which Kenetech had actually manufactured and installed the first of its commercial 33M-VS turbines, it had accrued more than $600 million in firm orders. Furthermore, Kenetech had been negotiating with numerous potential customers since 1992 to build and operate several massive projects. In short, Kenetech was poised on the brink of a major-league expansion of its business.

Kenetech was enjoying a huge interest in its new turbine by several states in the union after sweating out declining demand in its sole California market for more than a decade. In addition, the company was suddenly finding itself engaged in projects around the globe. In 1993, for example, Kenetech entered into an agreement to sell two windplant systems valued at $100 million to a Canadian utility. That project would entail construction of 150 to 200 turbines by 1995. Shortly before that deal was closed, Kenetech had entered into an agreement to supply a proposed $225 million wind power project in Maine.

Perhaps Kenetech's most ambitious project in the early 1990s was its construction of one of the largest wind energy facilities in the world. In 1993, Kenetech Windpower and a Ukrainian partner began building a 500-megawatt windplant on the Crimea Peninsula. It was designed to hasten the closing of the Chernobyl nuclear plant and provide power to about 400,000 Ukrainians. Interestingly, this particular project utilized Kenetech's old 56-100 turbines—Kenetech has formed a Ukraine-based joint venture to mass-produce 5,000 of the windmills, which it planned to install over a five-year period. In addition to the Ukrainian project, Kenetech had also cultivated business and had projects under development or in operation in Spain, Holland, the United Kingdom, Germany, Honduras, Costa Rica, New Zealand, India, China, Guatemala, and Egypt by 1993.

As Kenetech amassed contracts to manufacture, sell, and service its new Model 33M-VS, some critics observed that the technology was still unproved and threatened to hurt the industry's reputation. "There is a fear that they may be overselling what they have to offer," said David Torrey, assistant professor of electric power engineering at Rensselaer Polytechnic Institute, in the October 24, 1993, issue of Boston Globe. "They are the big name out there. If they fail, there is a good likelihood they will take the rest of the industry with them." Added wind power engineer, James Carter, "I don't think anyone has perfected this technology. . . . If they fall on their face, so will the rest of us."

Despite their detractors, Kenetech's managers remained optimistic going into the mid-1990s and were looking forward to massive growth. As Alderson pointed out in Kenetech's 1993 annual report, if the company transacted only the contracts that it was in the process of negotiating at the end of 1993 and no new customers were added, its revenues would explode from $250 million annually to more than $2 billion within a few years. To prepare for such growth, Kenetech was planning to double its work force during 1994 and to possibly double it again by 1995 or 1996.

"If we supplied just one percent of the world's electricity by the end of the century, we'd be trucking along at $3 billion to $4 billion in sales per year," Alderson estimated in a November 1993 issue of Business Week. Less than 1 percent of the United States' energy needs was supplied by wind power in 1993, making that estimation optimistic. Still, rising oil prices and increasing overseas energy demand in 1994 boded well for Kenetech's long-fought-for dream of making wind power an accepted technology.

Principal Subsidiaries: CNF Industries; Kenetech Energy Management; Kenetech Energy Systems; Kenetech Facilities Management; Kenetech Windpower (U.S. Windpower); Kenetech Resource Recovery.

Further Reading:

Allen, Scott, "Producing Profits Out of Thin Air," *Boston Globe,* December 18, 1993, Sec. 1, p. 29.

Carlsen, Clifford, "Wind Company in with $72 Million IPO," *San Francisco Business Times,* July 23, 1993, Sec. 1, p. 3.

Corporate Overview: Kenetech, San Francisco: Kenetech Corporation, 1994.

Davey, Tom, "Wind Power Company Spins Billion-Dollar Slate of Deals," *San Francisco Business Times,* Sec. 1, p. 4.

DePass, Dee, "NSP Signs Contract with Firm to Buy Wind-Generated Power," *Star Tribune,* October 30, 1993, Sec. BUS.

Howell-Skidmore, Linda, "The Winds of Canaan Valley," *Inter-Mountain,* July 21, 1992, Sec. BUS.

Kenetech Windpower: The 33M-VS Wind Turbine, San Francisco: Kenetech Corporation, 1994.

Lippman, Thomas W., "Future of Wind Power Gets a Lift," *Washington Post,* November 17, 1991, p. H1.

Prospectus: Kenetech, New York: Merrill Lynch & Co., April 28, 1994.

Shafroth, Mo, "U.S. Windpower Starts Work on Ukrainian Wind Farm," *San Francisco Business Times,* April 16, 1993, Sec. 1, p. 14.

Suber, Jim, "Winds of Change: Power Plants of the Future," *Topeka Capital-Journal,* January 20, 1994, Sec. BUS.

Sutherland, Billie, "Alternative Energy Firms Getting Their Second Wind," *San Diego Business Journal,* February 28, 1994, Sec. 1, p. 1.

Temes, Judy, "Catching a Second Wind: After Stumbling into Near Oblivion, the Wind Industry Attracts Renewed Interest in the Northeast," *Boston Globe,* October 24, 1993, p. A4.

—Dave Mote

Rampant growth in the oil industry boosted revenues during the late 1950s and early 1960s, as new oil wells and pumps were installed in record numbers throughout the southwest United States. In addition, Keystone began selling its valves in other markets, benefiting from the general postwar U.S. economic expansion. In fact, it was sales to these other markets, such as the chemical and utility industries, that helped Keystone weather the oil industry slowdown and shake-out of the 1960s and early 1970s. Created by mismanaged federal energy policies and flat oil prices, which resulted in a decline in the number of oil-producing companies from 30,000 in the early 1960s to just 13,000 by the early 1970s, the oil slowdown crushed valve demand by that industry.

The future of the Keystone company was also being shaped in the 1950s and 1960s by another company, Anderson, Greenwood & Co., which would later merge with Keystone to form the largest specialty valve company in the world. Like Keystone, Anderson, Greenwood was a Houston-based valve designer and manufacturer that was incorporated in 1947. Cofounders Marvin Greenwood, Ben Anderson, and Lomis Slaughter Jr. started the company with the intent of building small, private airplanes. They switched their focus to the aerospace industry in the early 1950s and eventually found themselves providing engineering services for a major defense missile project. The valves that Anderson, Greenwood designed for that project established its reputation as an innovator in the valve industry.

The company's premier innovation in the late 1950s was the pilot-operated safety relief valve, a low-maintenance, cost-efficient valve that could be used to relieve excess pressure in vessels, pipelines, and other equipment. Under the advice of a sharp new salesman, Frank Bright, the company began marketing a version of that valve to the oil industry in the early 1960s. Despite the energy industry recession that was occurring at the time, Anderson, Greenwood's valve was an instant hit in both the oil and gas industries.

Anderson, Greenwood & Co. again changed its emphasis in the mid-1960s, this time to the energy industry, and became a leader in the manufacture of energy-related valves during the 1970s and 1980s. "It was more fun than you can imagine, starting with a product that had zero sales," Bright recalled in the August 18, 1986, issue of *Houston Business Journal*. "Watching something grow is worth ten times more than going with a General Motors and trying to hold your own." Although it remained focused on the energy industry, the company stayed active in aerospace and other sectors. It also expanded moderately overseas, particularly in France; by the mid-1980s about 15 percent of its sales were to foreign buyers.

Keystone also grew internationally during the 1970s and 1980s, though under different management. Three years after taking the company public on the over-the-counter market in 1965, Stillwagon sold his share of Keystone to Systems Engineering and Manufacturing Company (SEMCO). SEMCO, a privately owned, Houston-based company, wanted to add Keystone's patented butterfly valves to its diversified product line. SEMCO's management team assumed some key positions at Keystone, but 39-year-old R. A. LeBlanc, who had been with Keystone since 1959, retained his leadership role.

Keystone International, Inc.

9600 West Gulf Bank Drive
Houston, Texas 77040
U.S.A.
(713) 466-1176
Fax: (713) 466-6328

Private Company
Incorporated: 1947 as The Keystone Tool Company
Employees: 4,200
Sales: $.52 billion
Stock Exchanges: New York
SICs: 3490 Valve Manufacturing

Keystone International, Inc., is the largest manufacturer and marketer of specialty valves and related products in the world. It operated 25 manufacturing facilities in 12 countries and garnered about 55 percent of its revenues from sales outside the United States in 1993. The company has grown since the 1950s through a strategy of creating quality products, acquiring other manufacturers, and fostering geographic and market diversification.

The Keystone Tool Company was founded in 1947 in Houston, Texas, by C. K. Stillwagon. During his first three years in business, Stillwagon designed, engineered, and patented his renowned "butterfly valve." In 1951, he began production of the valve that would be the foundation for his company throughout most of the 20th century. Stillwagon's butterfly valves were used primarily in the nearby oil fields for various oil flow control applications. As the oil industry grew during the 1940s and into the early 1950s, Keystone prospered.

Although Keystone Tool got off to a fast start, Stillwagon was stumped shortly after he began selling his breakthrough valve. The energy industry slumped into a cyclical downturn in the early 1950s, leaving the fledgling start-up hungry for new orders. Stillwagon survived the temporarily recessed market, but it was that early experience that convinced him to aggressively pursue a strategy of diversification that would protect his company from individual market fluctuations. His decision to diversify geographically in 1959, moreover, spurred Keystone's rapid growth during the 1960s and 1970s.

As Stillwagon expanded his line of butterfly valves and marketed his products to new industries, sales climbed steadily.

Following management changes by SEMCO, Keystone stepped up its geographic diversification efforts during the 1970s and 1980s, eventually broadening its reach into England, Holland, France, Italy, New Zealand, Korea, Japan, Brazil, and several other countries. Keystone's international strategy was relatively simple. Besides providing a unique, high-quality product, Keystone usually penetrated foreign markets by establishing a production facility and sales offices in the home country. Furthermore, it staffed the offices and facilities almost entirely with foreign nationals, from the president of the operation on down.

Keystone also elevated its market diversification efforts, particularly in the late 1970s and 1980s. It expanded sales to the chemical and power industries, for example, and started targeting a multitude of other industries, such as commercial construction, food and beverage, heavy equipment, water treatment, pulp and paper, and mining and minerals. Importantly, Keystone conducted a series of acquisitions of small companies during the late 1970s and early 1980s that broadened its product offerings to include actuator and control devices, among other things. Actuators, which are used to electrically or pneumatically trigger butterfly valves, fit well into the company's product line.

Some of Keystone's other acquisitions did not fit so well; it spun off an ailing trucking subsidiary in 1983 and jettisoned two other lagging subsidiaries in 1985 for a $381,000 loss. However, Keystone's general product and market diversification strategy seemed to be succeeding. Keystone's revenues broke $100 million in 1979, rising to $161 million in 1984 and then leaping to $192 million during 1985. Although that two-year gain was largely attributable to a strong economic recovery during that period, it also reflected the forward-thinking strategies that the company had been practicing since the 1950s and 1960s. Indeed, the faddish management gurus of the early and mid-1980s espoused theories on globalization and quality that Keystone had implemented years earlier. By 1985, for example, roughly half of Keystone's revenues came from overseas sales.

Anderson, Greenwood & Co. also enjoyed solid growth during the mid-1980s. Sales of its valves and related equipment jumped from $57.8 million in 1984 to a healthy $75.8 million in 1985. Anderson, Greenwood benefited during the late 1970s and early 1980s from the strongest oil and gas markets experienced in the U.S. since before the 1950s. In 1986, however, the company, along with many other U.S. valve producers, was stunned by another oil and gas industry downturn. As oil markets became glutted and prices plummeted, Anderson, Greenwood's orders slumped. The company was buoyed by shipments to its less-important petrochemical, food and beverage, and pulp and paper markets.

In 1986, Keystone acquired Anderson, Greenwood. At the same time, Keystone absorbed a major producer of industrial valves that significantly augmented both Keystone's and Anderson, Greenwood's product lines. Pennsylvania-based Yarway, with $70 million in 1985 sales, produced steam control valves and related products for power generation, chemical, pulp and paper, and a few other markets. The three-way merger created the largest producer of specialty valves and related products in the world.

The mergering of Keyston, Anderson, Greenwood, and Yarway became one of the largest mergers ever in the valve industry. Anderson, Greenwood realized that in order to avoid energy industry woes it would have to quickly expand into new industries and foreign markets. Keystone management believed that it could maximize sales of Anderson, Greenwood's respected valve lines through its potent and diverse U.S. and international sales and distribution networks. In addition, Keystone viewed the merger as a means of increasing its product and market diversity. It also wanted to utilize Anderson, Greenwood's excess production capacity to manufacture Keystone's breakthrough ''K-Lok'' high-performance butterfly valve, which it had recently introduced.

One drawback of the 1986 merger was that Keystone assumed a large amount of debt. In addition, the cost and time involved in merging the operations of the three companies exceeded Keystone's premerger expectations. Keystone, for instance, had to consolidate the group's 21 European sales offices into 10 nonoverlapping units. It also closed the least productive manufacturing facilities and had to condense the three company's research and development divisions. All the while the valve industry remained in a general slump, though Keystone and its talented management group were faring better than most of their competitors.

Despite postmerger pangs, Keystone realized immediate benefits. By 1987 the company was already achieving record sales levels, and by 1988 the company had accomplished the bulk of its global manufacturing and sales force consolidation initiatives. Importantly, Keystone eliminated more than $30 million in debt less than 12 months after the merger, thus slashing its interest payments and reducing its ratio of debt to capital by almost 50 percent. By 1989, Keystone was generating revenues of $376 million annually and netting income of $37 million. Its total debt had fallen from $124 million in 1986 to just $71 million.

Despite a nasty U.S. and global recession, Keystone managed to continue increasing its sales and income during the early 1990s. In fact, sales climbed steadily from $446 million in 1990 to $528 million in 1992 as net income fluctuated around the $43 million mark annually. Furthermore, Keystone managed to stabilize its debt load despite new acquisitions. In 1989, for instance, Keystone acquired valve operator and makers Vanessa and Biffi of Italy and Valvtron of Houston, a metal-seated valve manufacturer. In 1991, it purchased Kunkle Industries, a leading manufacturer of spring-operated valves. Besides those expenses, Keystone earmarked $22 million in 1992 for a complete restructuring of the company; the reorganization entailed assimilating the six companies and 11 major product lines that Keystone had acquired in recent years. Keystone also allotted $30 million to expand and upgrade its worldwide manufacturing network, particularly in Asia.

By 1993, Keystone International was truly a global, diversified manufacturer. It was operating 25 manufacturing facilities in 12 different countries and employing a worldwide work force of 4,200. Industrial valves, including the butterfly valve, remained the heart of Keystone's business. They accounted for 40 percent of 1993 shipments, followed by safety and environmental products, controls, and various specialty products. The company's geographic and customer markets were extremely diverse: 44 percent of Keystone's sales in 1993 were in the United States; 29 percent were in Europe, the Middle East, and Africa; 20 percent were in the Asia-Pacific region; and 7 percent were in Canada and South America. In addition, its sales were spread fairly evenly amongst 14 different sectors, the largest of which was chemicals (12 percent), followed by power generation (10 percent). No single customer accounted for more than 10 percent of the company's sales.

Despite Keystone's diversity and good reputation for quality and service, the global recession caught up with the manufacturer's balance sheet in 1993. Weak European and domestic demand, coupled with a strengthening U.S. dollar, contributed to a revenue slide of 2 percent in 1993, to $516 million. Net income, moreover, tumbled 8 percent to $39 million, partially as a result of restructuring and facility improvement expenditures. The fall was disheartening, especially given Keystone's average income growth rate of 10 percent since 1979.

Nevertheless, LeBlanc and his fellow managers remained optimistic. The company had positioned itself well to take advantage of recovering North American and European economies, and it was experiencing solid gains in burgeoning Asian markets, particularly in Korea and China. It continued to acquire new companies and products in 1993 and 1994 and to open and improve manufacturing facilities in different corners of the globe. "As the world's economies stabilize and begin to grow, we are optimistic that Keystone will achieve its goal of consistent earnings growth," LeBlanc stated in Keystone's 1993 annual report. His optimism was mirrored by the price of his company's stock going into the mid-1990s.

Principal Subsidiaries: Keystone Value USA, Inc.; Anderson, Greenwood & Co.; Keystone Controls, Inc.; Kunkle Industries, Inc.; Keystone Vanessa-Valvtron, Inc.; Keystone Vanessa, Inc.; Yarway Corporation.

Further Reading:

Brubaker, Laurel, "Keystone Orders Hit Record $74 Million," *Houston Business Journal,* May 25, 1987, p. 9A.
"Keystone Acquisitions Fortify Sales," *Houston Business Journal,* March 17, 1986, Sec. 1, p. 24.
Keystone: The Flow Control Company, Houston: Keystone International, Inc., 1994.
Klempin, Raymond, "Digesting a Double Merger," *Houston Business Journal,* March 24, 1986, p. 18B; "Anderson Greenwood: Airplanes and Pilot Valves," *Houston Business Journal,* August 18, 1986, p. 1A.
Lehren, Andrew H., "Keystone Buys Yarway for $100 Million," *Philadelphia Business Journal,* March 31, 1986, Sec. 1, p. 12.
McNamara, Victoria, "Stock Jump Stuns Keystone President," *Houston Business Journal,* January 8, 1990, Sec. 1, p. 1.
Schlegel, Darrin, "Keystone Expands Global Operations with $35 Million Spending Program," *Houston Business Journal,* May 10, 1993, Sec. 1, p. 4; "Keystone Acquires Australian Valve Maker," *Houston Business Journal,* October 11, 1993, Sec. 1, p. 8.

—Dave Mote

Kimco Realty Corporation

Kimco Realty Corporation

P. O. Box C
1044 Northern Boulevard
Roslyn, New York 11576
U.S.A.
(516) 484-5858
Fax: (516) 484-5637

Public Company
Incorporated: 1966 as Kimco Development Corporation
Employees: 130
Sales: $98.9 million
Stock Exchanges: New York
SICs: 6798 Real Estate Investment Trusts

Kimco Realty Corporation is one of the largest owners and operators of neighborhood and community shopping centers in the world. With 153 properties in 24 states in 1994, the company's growth was facilitated by its construction of new shopping centers as well as its acquisitions of established shopping centers, often with the use of innovative financing vehicles.

The Kimco Development Corporation was founded in 1966, when a group of real estate investors and shopping center owners combined their properties into a single entity with the intent of fusing their resources to build and manage new shopping centers. Among Kimco's founders was Martin S. Kimmel, who would remain chairperson of Kimco's board until the early 1990s. Another founder, Milton Cooper, would serve as president of Kimco during its steady growth in the 1970s, 1980s, and early 1990s.

Immediately after its inception, Kimco began building new shopping centers across the United States. In 1967, in fact, it erected facilities in Florida, Indiana, Ohio, and Utah. Throughout the late 1960s and early 1970s, Kimco focused on the construction of several shopping centers in Florida, while also adding several new centers in Pennsylvania, Illinois, New York, Ohio, Texas, and Virginia. By the mid-1970s, Kimco owned and operated about 50 shopping centers, most of which were located in Florida and the Midwest. Kimco funded most of its developments by borrowing, or through joint ventures with other investors or real estate developers.

Most of the shopping centers that Kimco built were relatively small in comparison to the regional malls that would become popular in the 1970s and 1980s. Kimco's projects were classified as neighborhood and community shopping centers and were designed to attract local customers seeking day-to-day necessities, rather than high-priced luxury items. Such centers were typically anchored by supermarkets, large drugstores, or discount department stores, including Winn-Dixie, Poston's World, Payday's Orlando, Save-A-Lot, and Hills Department Stores.

During this time, Kimco's development strategy was regarded as unique in the industry. Many development companies employed the services of real estate companies to serve specific functions in the development process, such as overseeing construction and financing or finding tenants to lease the property. Often, a development company would simply employ a property management and leasing company to handle the day-to-day operations of the property. Kimco, however, sought to profit by managing the entire process in-house, including construction, financing, legal and accounting functions, leasing, and maintenance. Cooper believed that total control of its holdings would allow the company to reduce costs, achieve higher quality projects, and build long-term wealth.

Throughout the 1970s, Kimco continued to add new projects to its list of holdings. While Florida remained a target market, Kimco also expanded into different northeastern, mid-atlantic, and midwestern states and engaged in a few projects in the West. Toward the end of the decade, however, the U.S. commercial real estate industry experienced a cyclical downturn, causing Kimco's development activity to continue at a much slower pace. Nevertheless, Kimco did generate a few new projects and, by 1981, the company owned and operated 77 shopping centers. Its total portfolio of properties would provide an important base of assets and cash flow that would contribute to Kimco's rapid growth during the next decade.

Real estate industry woes that lingered into the early 1980s prompted Cooper to shift Kimco's development strategy for the 1980s. For the past 15 years, Kimco had built most of its projects from the ground up; in 1981, only nine of its centers had been purchased after construction. However, Cooper found that ground-up construction had become too risky for developers seeking long-term profitability. "The theory was that if you developed anything new, you had to buy land, pay for construction, and have market rents," Cooper explained in the May 1992 issue of *Chain Store Age Executive,* adding that "The safety depended on the credit of the tenant." In addition, Kimco's executives thought that existing, undervalued properties were available for acquisition.

Bucking commercial real estate industry trends, Kimco embarked on a program of growth founded almost entirely on acquisitions. As the U.S. real estate development industry recovered and boomed in the mid- and late 1980s, office buildings and shopping centers were erected at a feverish pace as billions of investment dollars became available for new construction. Favorable tax laws, foreign investment, and deregulation of U.S. financial markets all contributed to the hot market for new projects. Nevertheless, Kimco stuck to its acquisition strategy, building less than five percent of the properties it would add to its portfolio throughout the decade.

Kimco's expansion activity remained low-key in the early 1980s. The company added a few shopping centers in New Orleans and Pennsylvania to its portfolio in 1983 and purchased a few undervalued centers in New York, New Jersey, Ohio, and West Virginia during 1984 and 1985. However, the following year, Kimco launched an aggressive growth initiative, prompted by strong capital markets and the boom in the real estate industry. Shifting its focus away from Florida, Kimco purchased a string of properties in Pennsylvania during 1986 and then began to focus on Ohio, where it would eventually amass about 30 properties. At the same time, Kimco continued to acquire new shopping centers throughout the eastern half of the country. By the late 1980s, Kimco had accumulated more than 150 properties and was generating annual sales of nearly $60 million. While about 90 percent of its revenues came from its core of community and neighborhood shopping centers, Kimco was also operating two regional malls.

By 1989, however, the real estate business was spiraling into a deep recession. Besides general U.S. economic malaise, most sources of lending for acquisitions and new construction had dried up, and the profitability of many existing projects was rapidly declining. Importantly, the Tax Reform Act of 1986 had dealt a deathly blow to the industry. That Act essentially wiped out many of the important tax advantages granted to investors in commercial real estate, including companies like Kimco. A result, Kimco and its industry peers had difficulty funding growth. Furthermore, the value, liquidity, and profitability of their existing properties was diminished.

Although Kimco's revenues climbed 11 percent in 1991, to $66 million, the company experienced a disappointing net loss of $15 million, which reached $16 million the following year. Despite setbacks, Kimco's problems were minor compared to those of most other developers, many of whom had relied on tax breaks and extreme financial leverage to achieve profits. Kimco's properties were relatively well managed, and the company had positioned itself for long-term growth and stable cash flow. As many other developers grappled for cash to meet their debt obligations, Kimco survived the downturn. It did suffer from an excessive debt load, however, which had swelled past a staggering $400 million by early 1991.

In an effort to diminish its burdensome liabilities and to generate cash for continued expansion, Cooper again bucked convention and pioneered a new growth strategy. Noting the plethora of vastly undervalued shopping centers on the market in the early 1990s, and the dearth of capitalized investors, he took Kimco public in 1991. A Real Estate Investment Trust (REIT) was created, containing most of Kimco's properties, and the sale of shares in that trust raised about $150 million. Kimco used most of this money to reduce its debt, which declined to about $290 million after the public offering. "Traditional real estate financing was over . . . ," Cooper recalled in the *Chain Store Age Executive* article, noting that "We saw that in order to have the kind of growth we wanted . . . we would have to become public, and have a permanent base of equity."

Kimco's move to a REIT was unique and influential. As a financing technique, the REIT was generally regarded as risky and had never been used on such a large scale to securitize shopping centers. Nevertheless, the REIT provided an important advantage in that its shares could easily be liquidated by sale on the stock market. In addition, REIT owners enjoyed tax advantages not available in other forms of real estate investing. Encouraged by Kimco's success, about 35 other developers created REITs during the next two years. "Before that, people thought it would be impossible to sell real estate stock," Cooper recollected in the September 27, 1993, issue of *Newsday*.

A corollary of Kimco's move to a REIT was the formation of KC Holdings, Inc. Kimco formed KC Holdings before the public offering and moved 45 of its 178 properties into that corporation's subsidiaries. The holdings consisted primarily of poorly performing shopping centers, projects that were joint ventures, and miscellaneous properties, such as a bowling alley. By removing those assets from under the Kimco umbrella, the company was able to offer a higher quality, lower risk REIT. The stock of the newly formed KC Holdings remained in the hands of Cooper and other Kimco stockholders prior to the public offering.

Pleased with their first stock sale, Kimco's management sold more shares in 1992 and 1993; the two offerings brought an additional $161 million to Kimco, most of which was used for new acquisitions. In fact, Kimco picked up 30 more properties during 1992 and 1993, raising its total asset base from about $400 million in 1991 to $450 million in 1992, and then to $650 million by the end of 1993. These gains were regarded as impressive, particularly since the company's total debt load remained below $300 million.

Kimco's savvy financing strategies during the early 1990s were lauded by industry analysts. Investors, too, were pleased, as Kimco's REIT shares rocketed more than 100 percent between 1991 and 1993. However, it was Kimco's continuing commitment to quality management and long-term growth that allowed it to survive the commercial real estate shake out of the early 1990s and then to prosper going into the mid-1990s. Indeed, as Kimco financiers jockeyed in financial markets, its operations team was busy streamlining the organization for improved efficiency and profitability in a changing real estate and retail environment. "The key to successful real estate investing is no longer 'location, location, location,' but 'management, management, management'," Cooper observed in Kimco's 1993 annual report.

Kimco's strengths were also reflected in its long-time commitment to sophisticated information systems, which were used to track and manage its properties and investment activities. Such integrated systems allowed small leasing staffs to easily access and track the entire portfolio of Kimco holdings. In addition, Kimco sustained its legacy of vertical integration, handling its leasing, acquisition, property management, accounting, architecture, and other functions in-house. Kimco accomplished those varied tasks with a small, highly efficient work force; about 80 people in its headquarters and 52 workers stationed at several of its larger properties managed the entire multimillion-dollar operation.

As Kimco bolstered its profit margins and increased its holdings, the U.S. economy began to recover. Kimco's revenues grew to $79 million in 1992, and it posted its first positive income figure, $19 million, since the late 1980s. In 1993, moreover, Kimco gleaned $35 million in profits from nearly $100 million in receipts and invested a record $164 million in new properties. Kimco continued to post solid gains early in 1994, raising an additional $150 million through two stock offerings, most of which was used to further pare its slimming debt load. The company also bought several more shopping centers, boosting its holdings to over 150 properties with about 20 million square feet of retail space in 24 states, figures which did not include the properties held by KC Holdings, Inc. Going into the mid-1990s, the company looked forward to what management believed would be the fastest period of expansion in the company's history.

Further Reading:

Colwell, Carolyn, ''REIT Rush: Real Estate Investment Trusts—Hot Property in a Revived Market,'' *Newsday,* September 27, 1993, p. 25.
Jochum, Glenn, ''Slicing Up LI's High Income Pie,'' *LI Business News,* May 9, 1994, p. 23.
McQuaid, Kevin L., ''Gambling Real Estate Futures on REITs,'' *Warfield's Business Record,* June 12, 1992, p. 1.
''Public Was the Way to Go at Kimco,'' *Chain Store Age Executive,* May 1992, pp. 102–03.
Talley, Karen, ''Kimco Planning Big Stock Sale,'' *LI Business News,* October 21, 1991, p. 3.

—Dave Mote

KLA Instruments Corporation

160 Rio Robles
P.O. Box 49055
San Jose, California 95161-9055
U.S.A.
(408) 434-4200
Fax: (408) 434-4268

Public Company
Incorporated: 1976
Employees: 1,000
Sales: $.17 billion
Stock Exchanges: NASDAQ
SICs: 3825 Instruments to Measure Electricity

KLA Instruments Corporation is a global leader in the design, manufacture, and marketing of yield management and process monitoring systems, which are used to reduce defects in integrated circuits. Although its market niche is relatively small, KLA dominates the burgeoning industry.

KLA was founded in 1975 by Kenneth Levy and Robert R. Anderson, entrepreneurs and pioneers in California's blossoming Silicon Valley. Levy and Anderson believed that they could use their knowledge of relatively new image processing technologies, as well as their marketing know-how, to open up completely new segments in the semiconductor industry. During the mid- and late 1970s, they went to work developing a first-generation manufacturing inspection system that could be used to improve the chip-making process.

During the semiconductor manufacturing process, multiple layers of material are grown or deposited on the surface of a thin wafer. The wafer is typically composed of silicon or gallium arsenide and is five to eight inches in diameter. A four-step procedure is generally followed: 1) deposition of film on the wafer; 2) impurity doping, when impurities are introduced that control conductivity; 3) lithographic patterning, which creates the geometric features and layout of the circuit; and 4) etching, which removes the film coating material to reveal the layout patterned in the lithographic process. These steps may be repeated numerous times, depending on the complexity of the device, before the semiconductor is separated into individual integrated circuits, or chips. Before the chips are assembled and packaged, a variety of tests may be conducted to weed out defective circuits.

In some cases, fewer than 50 percent (and sometimes fewer than 10 percent for more advanced chips) of the manufactured semiconductors are usable, making the production process for some types of chips extremely expensive and time consuming. As chips increased in layer number and became smaller and more intricate during the 1970s, moreover, the defect detection problem escalated. Bell and Levy hoped to tap a side of the industry that remained largely ignored even by the late 1970s: inspection equipment that would make defects easier to find and improve chip ''yields,'' thus reducing unnecessary manufacturing costs. The basic concept behind their efforts was to combine advanced optical technology with custom, high-speed digital electronics and proprietary software to replace conventional, rudimentary inspection systems that relied on the human eye and relatively low-tech visual aids.

When Levy and Anderson started KLA, the chip industry was still in its infancy. Bell Laboratories had introduced the solid-state transistor in 1947, but a significant demand for chips had not emerged until the 1960s. Commercial production of semiconductors did not begin on a significant scale until the 1970s. Importantly, Intel Corp.'s introduction of the memory integrated circuit in 1971 spawned a plethora of opportunities in the U.S. semiconductor industry, resulting in healthy growth during the mid- and late 1970s. That growth also spawned a demand for various complementary technologies, such as plasma etching and optical/image processing, the latter of which was KLA's forte.

KLA's first product was its reticle inspection system, named RAPID, which was introduced in the late 1970s. RAPID utilized advanced optical and image processing technology to test the ''stencils'' used to print circuit designs onto silicon wafers. Because a defective reticle, or template, can result in millions of ruined die, the system provided an important first step in ensuring high chip yields. RAPID was the first system of its kind to enter the market and was quickly accepted by the semiconductor industry. KLA's RAPID 210e series became the foundation on which KLA built its succeeding product lines. KLA went public in 1980, selling stock to raise cash for marketing its RAPID systems and to generate research and development funds to create new products.

KLA benefited from a ripe U.S. semiconductor manufacturing industry during the early 1980s, its sales leaping past $60 million by the middle of the decade. However, domestic demand began to sputter in the mid-1980s. Although the overall demand for chip-making equipment continued to increase, U.S. producers experienced continually rising pressure from efficient Japanese firms that were dominating the market for high-volume, commodity-like chip manufacturing systems. In fact, Japan increased its share of the world chip machine market from almost nothing in the late 1970s to nearly 50 percent by the late 1980s; U.S. producers supplied most of the remainder of demand. Fortunately for KLA, its systems enjoyed a paucity of competition, allowing it to expand internationally to pull up slack in domestic growth. By 1984, KLA was garnering 22 percent of its sales from Japan and Europe. That figure jumped to more than 40 percent by 1987.

Also bolstering KLA's growth during the mid-1980s was its introduction of the KLA 2000 series in 1984. The 2000 was an automated wafer inspection system, called WISARD, which found defects in wafers and looked for circuitry errors after the reticle pattern had been projected onto the wafer. KLA's WISARD systems represented the second step in ensuring high chip yields. Again, KLA's entry into the market niche was essentially uncontested, allowing it to enjoy almost immediate acceptance by the industry. As sales of 210e and 2000 systems increased, KLA's revenues steadily climbed to $82.5 million in 1986, $88 million in 1987, and then to a healthy $113 million in 1988, $8.8 million of which was netted as income. Overseas shipments accounted for the lion's share of those gains.

In addition to its WISARD and RAPID lines, KLA introduced automatic test equipment in the late 1980s, which represented the third stage of the inspection process. Its most important product in that category was its wafer probing system, a device that electrically tested completed chips before they were diced and packaged. KLA developed the wafer probe with Tokyo Electronic Corp. (TEL). Another important line of test equipment was KLA's emission microscope, which was used to discover electrical "leakage" between layers of a chip. Although KLA faced competition in the automatic test equipment market, primarily from General Signal Corp., its products were well received and accounted for about 30 percent of KLA's revenues by 1990—WISARD and RAPID each also accounted for about one-third of aggregate sales.

By 1990, KLA's revenues had ballooned to a whopping $161 million, about $9.5 million of which was net income. In contrast, however, the innovator's stock price had steadily slipped during the late 1980s, reflecting the investment market's lack of faith in KLA. The company's critics cited lagging profit growth and generally poor overall performance compared to earlier growth projections. In fact, KLA did suffer during the semiconductor industry downturn of the late 1980s—it cut its work force by about 4 percent and implemented salary cuts of up to 15 percent for the company's officers. It had also fallen short in achieving some of its own stated objectives.

On the other hand, KLA was relatively well positioned to take advantage of emerging trends in the chip industry going into the early 1990s. It already controlled about 70 percent of the wafer inspection equipment market and approximately 80 percent of the reticle inspection business. In addition, semiconductors were becoming increasingly complex, pushing the need for automated, high-tech devices that could detect even the most minuscule flaws. Furthermore, Levy and Anderson during the late 1980s had recognized the need for a new type of "in-line" monitoring equipment, which could be integrated as a step in the manufacturing process and provide immediate detection of defects, rather than having to test off-line and wait for results. To exploit the market potential for in-line systems, KLA had made hefty investments in research and development during the late 1980s to improve its existing products and create new equipment lines.

In the early 1990s, the U.S. semiconductor industry began to rebound, reflecting its new-found productivity and an emphasis on cutting-edge semiconductor manufacturing technologies. As the market picked up, KLA began to introduce the products that it had been working on since the late 1980s, a few of which it had intended to start selling before 1990. Most importantly, in

October 1990 KLA unveiled its second-generation wafer inspection systems, the 2100 series. The new systems, which were designed with in-line capabilities, offered greater sensitivity to defects and operated more than 100 times faster than the popular 2000 series. New and improved systems were added to the 2100 line during the early 1990s, resulting in more than 140 orders for 2100 systems by 1993. 2100 systems sold for $1 million to $2 million apiece.

In 1992, KLA updated its RAPID systems with the 300 series, which combined a reticle inspection system with a computer (the 30 Reference Data Computer) to form the KLA 331. The 331 offered the highest inspection sensitivity available in the world and provided numerous speed and flexibility improvements over the original 210e series. It was also designed for potential in-line use. Although initial sales of the new 331 systems were slow because of glitches in bringing them to market, KLA had shipped a total of 700 RAPID systems worldwide by 1993, including deliveries of its first generation systems. The 331 systems sold for $1.7 million to $2.6 million, depending on the options added.

In addition to updating its core WISARD and RAPID product lines, KLA also introduced important new products in its other testing categories. It made improvements to the KLA 5000 series, for example, which was used to increase the yield and performance of final integrated circuit devices. The 5000 series, or metrology line, sold for $300,000 to $550,000 per unit. Similarly, KLA's new SEMspec division brought out its new electron beam imaging systems, which offered improved sensitivity and measuring prowess compared to conventional laser optical systems. KLA also initiated KLA Acrotec Ltd. in the early 1990s, a venture with a Japanese company that used proprietary KLA technology to produce flat-panel displays, such as those utilized by portable computers.

To position itself for expansion in the wake of new product introductions, KLA restructured during the early 1990s. Levy, who had served as president and chief executive of KLA since he had founded it, moved to chairman and allowed Kenneth L. Schroeder to assume control of the company's day-to-day operations. Anderson ceded his position as chief financial officer and was effectively retired from KLA going into the mid-1990s. In 1992, Schroeder reorganized KLA into five operating segments: WRInG, which combined the WISARD and RAPID divisions; the Automated Test Systems Division; the Watcher Division, which encompassed new image processing systems that utilized advanced optical character recognition technology; the Metrology Division; the Customer Service Division; and the SEMSpec Division. He also cut 7 percent of the 1,100 member global work force and jettisoned KLA's emission microscopy business.

By the early 1990s, KLA was garnering about 60 percent of its total revenues from overseas sales. One of its most important markets, in fact, was Japan, where demand for yield management equipment was particularly strong. When the U.S. semiconductor industry emerged from its doldrums during the early 1990s, the Japanese industry suffered, as did KLA. Its sales to Japan dropped 9 percent between 1991 and 1993, whereas U.S. shipments climbed only 7 percent. So, although KLA's new systems were well received by the industry, its shipment growth was hindered by a serious downturn in Japan. In addition, delays in bringing some of its new systems to market, particularly the KLA 331, created a temporary dip in order volume. As a result, KLA's total revenues slipped about 8 percent in 1991, to $148 million, before bobbing up to $155 million in 1992 and $167 million in 1993.

KLA continued to pour cash into research and development during the early 1990s in an effort to get its new products to market. In fact, it spent a fat $64 million during 1991 and 1992 (22 percent of revenues). As a result, profits bottomed out in 1992 as KLA posted a depressing $14 million loss. By 1993, however, its major product introductions were almost complete, and the company was able to cut development costs to $24 million (14 percent of sales). Net income climbed to about $7 million.

The real payoff for KLA's hard work during the late 1980s and early 1990s began to occur in 1994. Sales began to rocket skyward early in that year as the global semiconductor industry improved and KLA's new products began to achieve widespread appeal. Importantly, the industry began showing a strong interest in KLA's in-line defect monitoring concept. As it entered the mid-1990s, KLA appeared positioned to capitalize on the industry niche that it controlled and had helped to create. Besides favorable industry and market trends, KLA's strong cash position and paltry debt load suggested continued dominance.

Further Reading:

Boehlke, Robert J., "Motorola MOS-11 Installs KLA 2110 Wafer Inspection System," *Business Wire,* November 14, 1991; "KLA Reports Operating Results for Fourth-Quarter and Year," *Business Wire,* July 30, 1992; "KLA Instruments Expects to Post Loss for 1992 Fiscal Year," *Business Wire,* July 9, 1992; "KLA Unveils Yield Management System for In-Line Process Control," *Business Wire,* July 9, 1992; "Robert R. Anderson Retires as Vice Chairman of KLA Instruments Corp.," *Business Wire,* March 25, 1994.
Form 10-K: KLA Instruments Corporation, Washington, D.C.: Securities and Exchange Commission, August 31, 1993.
KLA Instruments Corporation Common Stock, New York: Kidder, Peabody & Co., January 26, 1994.
Lasnier, Guy, "KLA Readies Products for 'New Market Nobody Owns Yet'," *Business Journal-San Jose,* September 7, 1987, Sec. 1, p. 3.
Moran, Susan, "KLA Instrument Starts Santa Clara Clean Room Expansion," *Business Journal-San Jose,* July 11, 1988, Sec. 1, p. 3.
Savitz, Eric J., "Every Little Bit Helps; Rebound in the Offing for KLA Instruments," *Barron's,* September 24, 1993, pp. 18–19.

—Dave Mote

KOMAG

Komag, Inc.

275 South Hillview Drive
Milpitas, California 95035
U.S.A.
(408) 946-2300
Fax: (408) 946-1126

Public Company
Incorporated: 1983
Employees: 3,600
Sales: $385.4 million
Stock Exchanges: NASDAQ
SICs: 3695 Magnetic & Optical Recording Media; 5045
    Computers & Computer Peripheral Equipment

Komag, Inc., is the world's leading manufacturer of magnetic thin-film disks for computer hard drives. The company's most important product is sputtered thin-film media, which are data storage components made by depositing successive layers of magnetic material on a disk, then covering it with a protective overcoat. The entire sputtering process must be done in a vacuum. Using this technique, Komag makes and markets thin-film products for several types of disk drives. The most common are the 5¼ inch, 3½ inch (by far the largest market), and the smaller, increasingly popular Winchester disk drive. Komag currently controls just over a quarter of the market for these products. The company's customer base is dominated by firms needing the highest capacity and performance available, including such major disk drive manufacturers as Hewlett-Packard, Conner Peripherals, and Seagate Technology. Komag's disks are among the highest density of their kind commercially available.

Through a joint venture with Japan's Asahi Glass Co., Ltd., Komag also controls Dastek, the world's third largest producer of thin-film recording heads, although changes in technology and market conditions make continued production of thin-film heads unlikely. Komag's product line also includes rewritable optical disks. Komag maintains important strategic connections with Asahi Glass and another Japanese company, Kobe Steel. Those two companies each control over ten percent of Komag's common stock. Komag operates production lines in three countries: ten in the United States, four in Japan, and one in Malay-

sia. Together, those facilities ship disks at a rate of over one a second.

Komag was founded in 1983 by Tu Chen and Scott Chen, who are not related to each other. Tu Chen, a former senior researcher at Xerox, served as chairman of the board from Komag's inception into the mid-1990s. He also served as the company's secretary in the mid-1990s. Another member of Komag's initial core group was Stephen Johnson, who joined the company a few months after its creation and held the position of president into 1994. Komag's early success can be attributed to Tu Chen's decision at the outset to manufacture thin-film disks instead of the oxide-coated disks that were more common during the early 1980s. To make thin film disks, an aluminum wafer is sprayed in a vacuum with very thin, uniform layers of a metallic film that retains data. Chen saw that the limited storage capacity of oxide-coated disks (five megabytes of data on two disks) would fall short of high-end customers' data storage needs within a few years. The use of thin-film components enabled Komag to produce disks capable of storing much more data than the standard oxide-coated variety could carry. The company was therefore able to seize a big share of the market for high-capacity disks at a relatively early stage in its corporate life.

By 1986 Komag was bringing in revenue in the range of $20 million a year. Around that time, an industry trend was taking place in which many large, well-established Japanese companies attempted to diversify by forming alliances with young, aggressive American firms. These cash-craving American upstarts were more than happy to receive the funding that such alliances would make available to them for further development. Komag launched this type of partnership with Asahi Glass Company in 1987. That year Komag, Asahi, and Vacuum Metallurgical Company, another Japanese concern, teamed up to form Asahi Komag Co., Ltd. (AKCL). Under the terms of the joint agreement, Komag received a 50 percent interest in the new subsidiary in exchange for use of its sputtered thin-film technology. The two Japanese partners each put up about $11 million to cover the costs of building a 50,000 square-foot production facility in Yonezawa, Japan. The plant sputtered its first disk in June 1988, and a second production line went into action a year later.

Komag's association with a major Japanese outfit like Asahi, which reported about $4 billion in sales in 1986, gave the company a rather smooth entry into the Japanese market, a difficult task without this sort of corporate escort. Although some of Komag's competitors, such as Lin Data Corp. and Akashic Memories, had already licensed their magnetic disk technology to Japanese companies for manufacture in Japan, Komag's arrangement was the industry's first to be set up as an equal partnership rather than simply a licensing agreement. For 1987, the year of its initial public stock offering, Komag reported sales of $47 million.

As the 1980s continued, Komag sought out further alliances with large Japanese companies, both to ensure its flow of capital for research and facilities and to solidify its market presence in that country. In 1988 Komag formed Komag Material Technology, Inc. (KMT), a wholly owned subsidiary whose purpose was to supply Komag with aluminum substrates used in the disk manufacturing process. Komag sold 45 percent interest in KMT to Kobe Steel in 1989 for $1.4 million. Because Kobe is one of the largest producers of aluminum substrate blanks in the world, this arrangement guaranteed KMT a reliable supply; Komag agreed to purchase KMT's entire finished substrate output. As a result of this alliance, Komag obtains over 80 percent of its necessary substrate from KMT and Kobe combined.

Between 1986 and 1988, Komag quadrupled its sales to $83.6 million. In 1988 the company turned a profit of $8.6 million. In January 1989 Asahi Glass paid $20 million for one million shares of newly issued Komag stock. The purchase agreement gave Asahi the right to buy additional shares on the open market sufficient to up its stake in the company to 20 percent. Kobe struck a similar deal the following year, paying the same price for the same amount of stock. The deals also assured that Komag would make every effort to get representatives from each of those companies elected to its board of directors. Komag's impressive growth rate stalled for one year in 1989, when sales inched to only $84.6 million. Much of the computer industry was mired in a slump during that time, and the dramatic slowdown in sales of minicomputers and workstations throughout the United States dragged the demand for Komag's wares down with it.

Komag entered the thin-film recording head business in 1990. Thin-film heads, a component used in manufacturing disk drives, had been in short supply for a year, and Komag planned to take matters into its own hands. That year, the company purchased the thin-film head facilities of Siemens AG, which was getting out of the disk drive business. By that time, Komag's growth was back in high gear. After losing $6 million the previous year, the company earned a record $13.4 million in 1990, as sales took a big jump to about $150 million.

A series of transactions beginning in late 1991 sharply increased Komag's presence in the thin-film recording head business. In December 1991 Komag merged with Dastek Inc., one of the three largest independent thin-film head producers in the world. Komag paid for the deal by issuing about $40 million in new common stock, and Dastek became a wholly owned subsidiary of the company. A few months after the merger, Dastek Holding Company (DHC) was created as an umbrella for Dastek and Komag's previously existing thin-film head development program, which mainly consisted of what the company had earlier bought from Siemens. Komag then sold 40 percent of DHC, worth about $60 million, to Asahi's American subsidiary.

By 1992 Komag's annual sales had reached $327 million. The majority of the company's net sales, 56 percent, were to firms based in the Far East. Thin-film media accounted for 86 percent of its sales, with thin-film heads making up the remainder. Although Komag's sales increased to over $385 million in 1993, the company lost nearly $10 million after earning a record $16.9 million the year before. The unexpected and rapid deterioration of Dastek's finances was the sole cause for this disappointing result. During 1993 Dastek fell victim to a steep erosion in thin-film head prices, caused in part by increased competition from newer metal-in-gap (MIG) recording heads. Dastek had deteriorated so badly that Komag announced late in 1993 that it would be withdrawing from thin-film head production once its existing orders had been filled. Dastek would then concentrate on developing a new generation of recording heads based on magnetoresistive (MR) technology, once funding for the necessary research could be secured.

In spite of Dastek's woes, Komag achieved a number of milestones in 1993. The company celebrated its tenth anniversary and shipped its 100 millionth disk. In addition, Komag's Malaysian plant began full production. The plant shipped 500,000 disks and turned a profit, the first one ever recorded by a Komag factory with only one active production line. Komag continued to lead the pack in high-capacity disk production. The transition taking place at the company's Dastek subsidiary in the mid-1990s was pivotal in determining Komag's future performance. If the transition to MR recording head production went smoothly, and if MR did indeed turn out to be a key technology in the next generation of data storage devices, then Komag was poised to maintain its strong position in the rapidly changing high-tech marketplace.

Principal Subsidiaries: Dastek, Inc. (60%); Komag Material Technology, Inc. (55%); Asahi Komag Company, Ltd. (Japan, 50%); Komag USA (Malaysia) Sdn.

Further Reading:

Barbosa, Jeff, ''Komag Celebrates Production of 100 Millionth Disk,'' *Milpitas Post,* November 17, 1993, p. 8.

Cochran, Thomas N., ''On the Fast Track,'' *Barrons,* March 12, 1990, p. 46.

''Dastek Charge Fuels Komag Losses,'' *Electronic News,* March 28, 1994, p. 16.

Gupta, Udayan, ''Small U.S. Firm to Form Venture with Asahi Glass,'' *Wall Street Journal,* December 2, 1986, p. 14.

Khermouch, Gerry, ''Komag to Buy Dastek in $42M Stock Deal,'' *Electronic News,* November 11, 1991, p. 11.

''Komag Hikes Thin-Film Head Presence,'' *Electronic News,* January 6, 1992, p. 17.

—Robert R. Jacobson

KU Energy Corporation

One Quality Street
Lexington, Kentucky 40507
U.S.A.
(606) 288-1155
Fax: (606) 288-1125

Public Company
Incorporated: 1912
Employees: 2,241
Sales: $.61 billion
Stock Exchanges: New York Pacific
SICs: 8340 Electric, Water, and Gas Utilities

KU Energy Corporation provides electric service to about 440,000 people in 77 Kentucky and 5 Virginia counties. Through its primary subsidiary, Kentucky Utilities Company, it operates seven power generating stations. A leading institution in the state, Kentucky Utilities Company has grown steadily during its 80-plus years of service to the region.

When Kentucky Utilities Company was formed in the early 1900s, the electric industry was still in its infancy. The first commercial power station, Thomas Edison's Pearl Street Station, had been installed in New York in 1883. Even 30 years later, however, most regions in the United States were without centralized electric service, and some rural communities had no electricity at all. Most towns in Kentucky got their electricity from small, local generators. The power was often costly and the service poor. The generators only ran from dusk to midnight, and, in a confusing arrangement, different generators often competed for customers within the same town.

It was this setting that lured Harry Reid from his New York home to the tiny town of Versailles, Kentucky. Having witnessed the success of central power stations in his home state, Reid saw an opportunity to bring the same type of service to Kentucky. So, with $200 in savings and the promise of credit from an east coast friend, the bespectacled Reid traveled by rail to Versailles. He arrived in 1905 with the intent of purchasing its small, run-down power plant.

Reid's plan was to eventually acquire a network of power generators that would serve the entire region, but his vision was dashed shortly after his arrival to the Blue Grass State. Although Reid was able to purchase the Versailles power station, his east coast friend died, leaving him strapped for cash. Unable to afford the expensive repairs needed to refurbish his dilapidated station, the local city council prepared to terminate his street lighting contract. The final blow came when Reid contracted typhoid fever and nearly expired.

Reid recovered and was able to rekindle his fading vision in 1912. He sold his power plant and led a group of like-minded entrepreneurs to form the Kentucky Utilities Company (KU), which began operations December 2, 1912. Reid was named general manager of the Lexington-based enterprise, which started out operating local electric systems and a few ice and water companies. With a hefty $2.7 million in capital, the company quickly purchased stations in eight surrounding areas (including Versailles), bringing its customer base to 4,277 and its first-year receipts to nearly $290,000.

KU continued to expand its operations aggressively throughout the decade and into the 1920s. By 1916, in fact, KU was serving 51 communities in the central and western regions of the state, many of which had never enjoyed access to electricity. By the early 1920s, KU was providing service to customers in eastern Virginia. Furthermore, KU benefited greatly from the burgeoning coal mining industry of that era. Besides consuming almost two-thirds of KU's electricity output by 1920, the local coal mines supplied a cheap source of fuel for KU's power plants. KU augmented its income from electricity operations by selling electrical appliances and charging people to wire their homes.

KU snapped up small power generators and even entire competing generation companies to build its network during the 1920s, and it erected poles and power lines throughout its service regions. The work was hard. Line crews traveled in wagons or trucks and lived out of tents for weeks on end. After falling the timber that was used for the poles, they used mules to drag the lumber from the forest. Even after the power lines were built and the generators were working, numerous problems plagued the systems. Aside from technical breakdowns, which occurred with frustrating regularity, high winds and ice often inflicted long-lasting damage to the company's fragile networks.

KU's early years were filled with telling examples of the type of ingenuity and perseverance that originally settled the region. One day, for example, the smokestack at KU's power plant in Richmond melted and folded in the middle, closing the draft necessary to keep the boilers operating. The manager of the plant grabbed his shotgun and a box of shells and started blasting holes in the stack. By the time he had emptied his gun the stack was again functioning properly. In another episode described in company annals, lightning struck and knocked out power at a KU plant two times during a storm, once even striking the plant operator. After a third bolt hit nearby, the operator turned the power off himself, exclaiming "If a Higher Power is going to run His light plant, I'm going to shut down mine."

KU persevered through the 1920s and was able to expand its reach significantly. Early in the decade, however, management realized that its disjointed network of plants and lines would soon be insufficient to handle the electricity demands that would arise in the near future. So, it began tying its operations together with the intent of creating one or two major power producing facilities that would distribute electricity to its broad customer base. To this end, the company constructed a 30,000-kilowatt power plant in Pineville, Kentucky in 1924. It served most of its central and southeastern markets. In the late 1920s, moreover, KU tapped into power provided by the massive Dix Dam. At 105 feet higher than Niagara Falls, the Dix hydroelectric dam was the tallest dam east of the Rocky Mountains at the time it was built.

By the end of the "roaring twenties," KU was providing electricity to over 250 communities, most of which had been added to the KU network since 1925. It had made large strides toward its goal of consolidating its systems, virtually redesigning and rebuilding the infrastructure in several service regions. KU had also initiated programs to take its service to small rural areas. In addition, its appliances division had grown into a surprisingly healthy sideline. Although the company's expansion was stumped in the five years following the Great Depression, growth resumed in the latter half of the 1930s. Importantly, KU absorbed competitors Lexington Utilities Company and Kentucky Power and Light Company in the early 1940s, making KU the dominant supplier in the state.

World War II delayed KU's construction of its gigantic Tyrone Plant until 1946. Completion of that facility in 1948 marked the beginning of a huge period of growth that would change the face of the fledgling power producer. Indeed, a vast supply of electricity would be needed to fuel the postwar U.S. economic boom. Recognizing the emerging need, KU decided to liquidate its varied operations—by the 1940s KU was operating water works, selling ice and appliances, and operating buses systems and trolleys—and focusing solely on developing an electrical supply network. In addition to the Tyrone plant, KU added its Green River Operating Station during that period.

During the 1950s KU became a truly statewide supplier of electricity, thus realizing its founder's original dream—Reid had stepped aside as president of the company in 1927. Demand for electricity soared during the 1950s and 1960s. Hundreds of manufacturing companies commenced operations in the state and the residential population boomed. Furthermore, the use of electrical appliances, such as water heaters and air conditioners, vastly broadened applications for electricity. Between 1960 and 1970, annual power consumption in Kentucky more than doubled. Despite government-supported utilities (i.e. the Tennessee Valley Authority (TVA) and rural electric cooperatives), which captured a significant share of the power generation market during the 1940s and throughout the mid-1900s, KU managed to sustain a healthy pattern of growth.

By the early 1970s, KU's generating capacity had soared to more than 1.2 million kilowatts (kw). Much of this increased capacity was the result of the first of a new generation of massive power generators that KU built in 1970 and 1971. Rated at 427,000 kw, the new Unit Three generator at KU's Brown Plant was capable of producing close to the total amount of KU electricity consumed annually just 15 years earlier. In 1974, KU added an even larger unit to its new station at Ghent on the Ohio River in northern Kentucky.

The Organization of Petroleum Exporting Countries (OPEC) in the Middle East slashed production in the mid-1970s, causing oil and gas prices to soar and resulting in what was referred to as an energy crisis. In response, KU and other utilities shifted their marketing strategies to emphasize conservation rather than increased consumption. Also during that period, dozens of tornadoes inflicted heavy damage on many of KU's facilities. The company was further strained by the winter of 1977–1978, during which extreme cold diminished local coal inventories. These problems, combined with general economic sluggishness in the region, nearly crippled KU by the late 1970s.

KU, under the direction of then-President William A. Duncan, Jr., withstood the crises of the 1970s and even managed to position itself for expansion during the coming decade. William B. Bechanan assumed Duncan's position in 1978, shortly before the company moved into its new nine-story corporate headquarters building in downtown Lexington. Early in the 1980s, KU completed construction of major new generation facilities. In addition, it opened a $6.6 million high-tech addition to its aging System Control Center, which served as a sort of central nervous system for KU's operations. The updated center greatly increased power generation efficiency and service.

Although several factors, such as the increasing popularity of natural gas heating in homes, detracted from the overall performance of the electric utilities industry during the late 1970s and early 1980s, KU managed to remain profitable and even to steadily enlarge its operations. To overcome lagging demand growth, KU initiated several programs during the early 1980s to increase consumption. Its economic development thrust, for example, helped state officials to attract major electricity-consuming manufacturers to Kentucky. Its Wise Choice Home program offered financial incentives to customers whose homes met energy efficiency guidelines, thus helping KU reclaim some of the residential energy market that it had lost to natural gas.

KU's growth during the 1970s and early 1980s represented a decline from the rate of expansion the company enjoyed during the boom years of the 1950s and 1960s. Nevertheless, it posted solid gains throughout much of that period. 1977 sales of $261 million, for example, swelled to $373 million in 1980 and to a whopping $512 million by 1983. Likewise, net income jumped from about $22 million to $27 million to $76 million in the same years. These figures reflected particularly strong growth in consumption by commercial and industrial sectors. KU's financial performance also reflected regulation of most of its rates by the Kentucky Public Service Commission, which served to protect consumers and restrict KU's profitability.

The power generation industry began to change in the 1980s. Alternative fuels, new energy technologies, slowing growth in demand, and a range of environmental issues diminished the industry's strength. KU, like many other traditional power generation companies, changed its focus during the decade away from expanding its generation capacity. Instead, it started to concentrate its efforts on increasing efficiency, boosting marketing efforts aimed at its most profitable niches, and improving customer service.

KU's increased emphasis on efficiency during the late 1980s merely augmented an already strong reputation for low-cost performance. Partly because of its reliance on coal, the company was already a low-cost leader in the U.S. power-producing industry. In 1987, in fact, the average residential electric bill in the United States for 500 kilowatt hours of energy was $40.21. KU customers, in contrast, paid only $27.02 for the same amount of power. KU was also a leader in its own state—competing TVA utilities charged $29.13. Furthermore, KU's emphasis on cost containment contributed to vastly improved performance by the 1990s. Indeed, as the national average increased to $48.25 by 1993, KU's price for 500 kilowatt hours actually fell to $25.33, a real victory for the company.

Thanks in part to cost control efforts and improved customer service, KU managed to stabilize its earnings and revenues during the middle and late 1980s, despite overall industry malaise. Consumption of KU's electricity increased only 22 percent between 1983 and 1987, and its actual sales almost stagnated, growing from $530 million in 1984 to only $531 million by 1987. Although profits dipped to $54 million in 1986, they bounced back to $65 million one year later.

KU, like many other large U.S. energy producers, continued to struggle during the late 1980s and early 1990s. Weak demand growth and an explosion of new environmental restrictions capped industry earnings and pummeled many competitors. KU was especially battered by the 1990 Clean Air Act Amendments, which instituted new restrictions on the amount of pollution that could be emitted by coal-burning power plants. Because over 99 percent of KU's energy was produced by coal-fired facilities, it faced major expenditures during the 1990s to bring its plants into compliance. The Kentucky Public Service Commission granted KU permission in 1994 to implement an environmental surcharge to help recover the costs of complying with the Clean Air Act amendments and any applicable federal, state, and local requirements that apply to coal combustion.

To bolster slacking profits, KU revised its growth strategy to take advantage of The National Energy Policy Act of 1992, industry deregulation enacted by Congress. The organization was restructured in 1991 as KU Energy Corporation with Kentucky Utilities Company as a wholly owned subsidiary. KU Energy's second wholly owned subsidiary, KU Capital Corporation, was created as a minor division to manage the organiza-

tion's nonutility, energy-related investments. Specifically, the company was focusing on investments in independent power projects encouraged by the new legislation.

Meanwhile, KU continued to strive toward greater productivity. The company implemented an array of high-tech information systems during the early and mid-1990s designed to increase efficiency and customer service. It also worked to ensure that its new and existing plants utilized state-of-the-art generation technology. Evidencing KU's success in the efficiency arena was a 1993 study conducted by a major investment banking firm. It ranked KU production costs second lowest of 80 investor-owned utilities. Despite these efforts, however, weak markets allowed KU to realize only tepid gains. Sales increased a measly ten percent between 1990 and 1993, to $607 million, as net income fluctuated between $75 million and $80 million annually.

Going into the mid-1990s KU faced ongoing obstacles to growth. Increased competition, lackluster demographic forecasts, and environmental difficulties would likely linger at least through the turn of the century. On the other hand, John T. Newton, KU Energy president since 1987, hoped that his company would benefit from industry deregulation and the company's subsequent activities related to independent power projects. Regardless of its performance in the future, KU Energy's customer base of 440,000 and its forceful presence in Kentucky almost ensured it a prominent role in the state's electric-generating community through the end of the century.

Principal Subsidiaries: Kentucky Utilities Company; KU Capital Corporation.

Further Reading:

Kentucky Utilities Company: A Pictorial History, Lexington, KY: KU Energy Corp., 1987.
Greene, Marvin, ''KU Affiliates with Power Plant Partnership,'' *Courier-Journal (Lexington, Kentucky),* April 5, 1994, p. B10.
Hershbert, Ben Z, ''Area Utilities Prepare for Greater Competition,'' *Courier-Journal (Lexington, Kentucky),* February 7, 1993, p. K9.

—Dave Mote

Kwik Save Group plc

Warren Drive
Prestatyn
Clwyd LL19 7HU
United Kingdom
(0745) 887111
Fax: (0745) 882504

Public Company
Incorporated: 1959 as Value Foods Ltd.
Employees: 23,000
Sales: £3 billion
Stock Exchanges: London
SICs: 5411 Grocers

The first and most successful grocery discounter to operate in the United Kingdom, Kwik Save developed the highly popular—and profitable—retailing strategy of selling a limited range of branded products very cheaply. This strategy, made possible through a combination of low overheads and strict central control, has resulted in a network of well over 870 unpretentious, conveniently located Kwik Save stores throughout the United Kingdom, all conforming to a simple, standardized pattern, and all boasting the Kwik Save "no nonsense" approach to grocery retailing.

Kwik Save was founded by Albert Gubay, a Welsh entrepreneur whose business ventures in the late 1950s already included Norwales Confectionery Ltd. and Norwales Development Ltd. Branching out cautiously into grocery retailing, Gubay at first rented market stalls and a small grocery shop in Rhyl, North Wales. Then in 1959 he established his own shop in Rhyl and with it a new private company, trading under the name Value Foods Ltd.

Although the company's early name indicates that Gubay was concerned from the outset with offering value for customers' money, he did not decide until 1965 to move into discount retailing—a concept unfamiliar in the United Kingdom at the time. A visit to the United States in late 1964 introduced Gubay first-hand to American-style discounting, with its hallmarks of low prices but high turnover for a limited range of brand-name products sold in simply designed and minimally decorated stores. Influenced by these American stores and inspired, as well, by the European model of discount retailing represented by the German supermarket chain Aldi, Gubay opened the first

Kwik Save Discount in Colwyn Bay in 1965. Although nothing like it had been seen in Britain before, the shop's success testified to the public's approval of the new concept: within two years there were 13 Kwik Save outlets operating in North Wales and Cheshire.

All of the Kwik Saves followed a similar simple format: basic, even spartan design promoting utility rather than aesthetics—or even comfort. Goods were offered still in their manufacturers' boxes, to be plucked out by customers, and were stacked high on the shelves to minimize warehouse and storage space. A very limited number of product lines—from 400 to 600—was available, but all of these were known manufacturers' brands, and all were sold at a very attractive price. Unlike other grocers, Kwik Save promoted no loss leaders, special offers, or sales on selected items—simply consistently low prices. No money was spent on inessentials such as individual price-tagging; prices were listed near the items for the customers' benefit, while checkout operators relied on a good memory. Wherever possible, Kwik Save stores also boasted another American-style feature quite unusual at the time in the United Kingdom: car parking facilities.

Clearly the company was filling a vacuum in grocery retailing, and during these early years expansion was swift and sure. Gubay's earlier ventures were now firmly harnessed to the Kwik Save cause; Norwales Confectionery functioned as a wholesaler for the retail operations, and Norwales Development, formerly a builder of bungalows, turned its energies to building, repairing, and converting properties for new Kwik Save stores. By 1970, when the newly renamed Kwik Save Discount Group Ltd. was converted to a public company, there were 24 Kwik Save stores, mostly congregated in the North Wales, Cheshire, and Shropshire areas. Kwik Save suffered a crisis of confidence in 1973 when Gubay sold his remaining shares in the company and abruptly left the country, but it was soon recognized that even without its founder Kwik Save was set on a course for success.

The 1970s and 1980s saw a revolution in Britain's retailing history: the rise of the superstores. A retailing culture traditionally revolving around the small High Street establishment or local neighborhood shop now witnessed the advent of edge-of-town and out-of-town "greenfield" sites being developed into huge grocery complexes. Provisions of all sorts were now available under one very large roof, and, as shelf space was no longer at a premium, the availability of product lines was limited only by food manufacturers' and grocers' imaginations. British shoppers at Sainsbury's, Tesco, Safeway, and the other new giant supermarkets were confronted, by the late 1980s, with a hitherto undreamed of choice.

Obviously unable to compete with the superstores on their own ground, Kwik Save quietly bucked the trend. Whereas before the company had chosen cheaper out-of-town sites for its stores, now it took every opportunity to move into the very areas being abandoned by other grocery retailers: town centers and residential areas. While the superstores were concentrating on creating, according to commentator Suzanne Bidlake, "atmosphere, leisure, excitement and ambiance," Kwik Save prosaically maintained that "shopping is a chore, and let's not pretend otherwise." "No fuss, no frills, we simply save you money at the tills,'' Kwik Save proclaimed—and Kwik Save kept its promise. Continuing its policy of pumping profits back into providing lower prices for customers, Kwik Save estimated that average shoppers could save 15 percent of their total grocery bill over a year's time by shopping at Kwik Save rather than at one of the superstores.

Kwik Save's smaller and simpler designs afforded it several advantages over the superstores. A Kwik Save, often a conversion of an already existing building of approximately 8,000 square feet, cost an average £1 million and could open within 10 days. A purpose-built superstore, of approximately 24,000 square feet, cost an estimated £25 million and could take up to three years to develop.

Nonconformist though it was in many respects, Kwik Save nonetheless saw the need to modify some of its strategies to compete with the superstore. The company's limited product range in comparison with the superstores' tremendous variety—viable in the 1970s when the difference was one of 600 versus 3,000—became worrying by the late 1980s when the superstores had boosted their range to approximately 15,000 products. Shoppers, of course, became increasingly accustomed to a wide choice, and many were reluctant to buy their cheap staples at Kwik Save only to have to go elsewhere for other products.

Thus in 1988 Kwik Save decided to widen its product range from its standard 600. Such a move meant that checkout operators could, of course, no longer memorize all product prices, so the company turned to technology for help. Almost from the outset of its history, Kwik Save had made extensive use of computer technology to ensure maximum efficiency, utilizing data-processing equipment as early as 1962. Therefore, the installation of laser scanners and computerized tills at the checkout was a natural progression. The system was capable of automatically recording sales volumes; it sent this information from individual outlets to central computers and even contacted regional distribution centers and suppliers for automatic stock replenishment. Kwik Save was thus able to stock "just enough" and "just in time"—essential for keeping operating costs down. By 1991 all of Kwik Save's outlets had been converted to the scanning system, and all stores stocked at least 1,500 different items, with many stocking up to 2,500, thus going some way to counter the disparity between choice at Kwik Save and at the superstores.

Image is a vital ingredient in any retail operation, and in this area, too, Kwik Save found itself at odds with the superstores. Kwik Save's market had historically been among the lower socio-economic groups. In addition, the stores tended to attract many older customers, who were alarmed by, or disapproved of, the new superstores and preferred the traditional walk-in High Street shop. The superstores, too, were simply out of reach for those without cars.

Kwik Save aimed to change this rather down-market image concurrently with its bid to move into the more affluent southeastern part of the country. The first London store opened in 1986, and in 1989 the company launched its first national advertising campaign designed to attract shoppers of all income levels. The timing was right; in a recession everyone welcomes the chance to save money where possible. By the mid-1990s 100 Kwik Save stores were operating in the Southeast, and the company had achieved some success in penetrating the middle socio-economic level. Although Kwik Save was unlikely ever to capture the market of status-conscious higher income groups who are able and prepared to pay for a greater range of choice in more comfortable surroundings, a niche appeared to exist for Kwik Save even in more affluent areas.

Competition with the superstores was not Kwik Save's only concern as it entered the mid-1990s; a challenge appeared at the other end of the market spectrum—rival discount retailers. The most prominent of these were foreign enterprises, particularly the German chain Aldi and the Danish Netto. American warehouse clubs, principally Costco, also entered the market. A few homegrown competitors emerged as well, attempting the best of both worlds by creating discount superstores, such as Food Giant, owned by Gateway, and Dales, the discount arm of ASDA.

Although a few individual Kwik Save outlets were forced into minor price wars by these competitors, on the whole the new ventures had not, as of the mid-1990s, proved significantly damaging to Kwik Save. Aldi and Netto, with foreign suppliers, suffered from poor brand recognition among U.K. shoppers; operations like Costco required customers to buy in bulk (not heretofore a British shopping preference) in order to save money; and the discount superstores, finding themselves somewhat of a contradiction in terms, had yet to take off.

Some analysts warned that, although Kwik Save may not yet have felt any disadvantage in operating between the superstores on one side and the new discount competition on the other, it soon would if it continued its present policy of being neither fish nor fowl. The argument runs that Kwik Save, obviously unable to compete in the superstore arena, has also come so far from its discount roots that it can no longer be classified as a discounter in the true sense. Indeed, in what may have been a tacit admission of this, the company quietly dropped the word "Discount" from its name in 1986, becoming simply Kwik Save Group plc.

Although the Kwik Save milieu is by no means as plush as a superstore's, the starkness of the earliest days has been softened, unlike such hard discounters as Aldi and Netto, which retain a distinctly warehouse-like atmosphere. In addition, Kwik Save, which built its reputation on a policy of selling only known branded goods, introduced its own "No Frills" brand in 1993, under pressure from the superstores, who had developed lower-priced "own-brand" products. The range was developed to complement, not to supplant, branded items, but critics maintain that the company's decision to provide more choice must of necessity result in higher prices; Kwik Save answers the charge by citing its efficient use of computer technology, which allows the stores to expand choice while retaining the lowest possible prices. In addition, Kwik Save, despite a broader product range and a slightly more up-market feel to the stores, remains true in the 1990s to the same strategies it developed in the 1960s. As the *Observer* succinctly described it in 1993: "Kwik Save chops prices, wins sales, gets better terms from suppliers, keeps costs down and grows profits, a virtuous circle.''

Certainly the company's healthily growing profits showed no cause for concern in the mid-1990s. Indeed, some analysts suspected that, if Kwik Save was moving toward a middle ground, perhaps a market for such a strategy existed. In the essentials of the grocery business, Kwik Save held the same principles it pioneered at the beginning of its history. The secret of Kwik Save's success was and remained its commitment—amounting almost to an obsession—to keep operating costs to an absolute minimum. The company maintains strict central control over its operations, which are standardized across the board. The surface simplicity of each Kwik Save store is backed by a highly sophisticated computerized system. Stock control is tightly regulated and administration, distribution, and store management are all kept as simple and streamlined as possible. Credit is not accepted at Kwik Save stores, thus keeping banking fees low. Customers soon learn that free bags will not be provided. Although its range is small, its products are high-volume staples, which have a quick and large turnover, giving Kwik Save strong buying power through bulk purchases; these lower prices from the manufacturers the company in turn recycles back into price savings for the consumer.

Kwik Save has always dealt strictly in non-perishable and semi-perishable items. Not wishing to diversify into areas where the company had no expertise but at the same time recognizing the importance of providing customers with one-stop shopping, Kwik Save developed the highly successful strategy of renting space in the stores to concessionaires providing meat, fruit and vegetables, and bakery goods. In 1981 the company acquired Colemans Ltd., to manage and monitor quality control of the franchises, all of which are run by local merchants. In 1991 the franchises were given brand names: Colemans (butchers); Gardeners (fruit and vegetables); Crumbs (bakery); and Petstop(pet supplies). Liquor sales are also available at many Kwik Saves; this, too, originated as a concession, but in 1991 the company acquired and integrated Liquorsave.

In the mid-1990s Kwik Save planed to continue to expand throughout the United Kingdom. After its successful foray into the Southeast, the company set its sights on Scotland. The first Scottish store opened in 1993 and a total of 100 were planned. A commentator in the *Guardian* wrote in 1993: "While Tesco, Sainsbury and Safeway have seduced most shoppers to their glistening temples on Britain's ring roads celebrating the joys of ready-washed salads and chilled fresh celery soup, Kwik Save has stuck to the long-abandoned . . . principle: stack things high and sell 'em cheap.'' In November of 1994, Kwik Save acquired the assets and business of Shoprite Group P.L.C. The Shoprite business includes 91 stores, 14 more stores under development, and two distribution centers.

With over 800 stores in 1994, Kwik Save was the largest discount grocery operator in the United Kingdom and by volume the third largest grocery retailer in general; clearly, its ''No nonsense, no frills'' approach had found favor with consumers.

Principal Subsidiaries: Colemans Ltd.; KS Insurance Ltd.

Further Reading:

''Attractive Policy,'' *Guardian,* November 26, 1970, p. 18.

Bidlake, Suzanne, ''King of the Discounts Invades the South,'' *Marketing,* September 13, 1990, pp. 38–41.

''Discounters Set the Alarm Bells Ringing,'' *Evening Standard,* March 31, 1993.

Ewer, Rhett, ''Computer Communications Lead Retail Expansion,'' *Management Services,* October 1991, pp. 16–19.

Gabb, Annabella, ''Kwik Save's Smaller Secret,'' *Management Today,* April 1986, p. 62.

''Gloves Come Off in Discounts Battle,'' *Scotsman,* May 18, 1993.

''Good Value at Kwik Save,'' *Observer,* November 28, 1993.

Grey, Sarah, ''Doing the Kwik-Step to Stay Ahead,'' *Accountancy,* December 1991, pp. 23–25.

''In No Man's Land—Neither a Hard Discounter nor Superstore,'' *Financial Times,* November 24, 1993.

''Kwik Save Moves into Own-Label,'' *Marketing,* May 6, 1993, p. 5.

''Kwik Save Moves into Scotland,'' *Financial Times,* February 5, 1993.

''Kwik Save Offer at 21s 6d,'' *Financial Times,* November 30, 1970, p. 28.

''Kwik Save off the Menu,'' *Daily Mail,* March 25, 1993.

''Kwik Save Stays at a Discount,'' *Observer,* May 2, 1993.

''Nagging Worries for Kwik Save,'' *Guardian,* April 30, 1993.

''Offer for Sale,'' *Financial Times,* November 30, 1970, pp. 34–35.

Sparks, Leigh, ''Spatial-Structural Relationships in Retail Corporate Growth: A Case Study of Kwik Save Group P.L.C.,'' *The Service Industries Journal,* January 1990, pp. 25–84.

—Robin DuBlanc

La Quinta Inns, Inc.

Weston Centre
112 East Pecan
P.O. Box 2636
San Antonio, Texas 78299-2636
U.S.A.
(210) 302-6000
Fax: (210) 302-6263

Public Company
Incorporated: 1968
Employees: 6,100
Sales: $272.85 million
Stock Exchanges: New York
SICs: 7011 Motor Inns; 8741 Hotel and Motel Management;
  6794 Franchises Selling or Licensing

With more than 220 inns in 29 states, La Quinta Inns, Inc. is one of the largest owner-operated hotel chains in the United States. Its properties, which are located primarily in Florida, California, and particularly Texas, are targeted toward cost-conscious business travelers. The hotel chain expanded rapidly during the 1980s by utilizing a variety of unique financing techniques.

La Quinta, which means "the country place" in Spanish, got its start in 1968 during HemisFair, the San Antonio, Texas world's fair. Across from the fairgrounds, entrepreneur Sam Barshop and his brother, Phil, built the first in what would become a successful chain of La Quinta Inns. After the fair, the Barshops used the hotel, as they would later describe the venture, to invent a new lodging industry niche: moderately priced accommodations that catered to the commercial business traveler.

By the time the Barshops built the first La Quinta Inn, they had racked up an impressive resume of experience in the real estate and lodging industries. Their family's successful real estate business had provided them with an adept understanding of finance and property transactions. That knowledge would later surface in a variety of innovative financing strategies, which they would use to fund the La Quinta chain. Moreover, during the early 1960s, the brothers started building and leasing hotels that were licensed by the Ramada Inn chain. Through their company, Barshop Motel Enterprises, they also obtained exclusive franchise rights for Rodeway Inns of America in Texas, Oklahoma, Arkansas, and Kansas. In the mid-1960s, in fact,

Sam and Phil Barshop made an unsuccessful bid to purchase the Rodeway chain.

Following their failed attempt to buy Rodeway, the Barshops opened La Quinta Inn. Recognizing the untapped potential of their new market niche, they began duplicating the La Quinta concept in neighboring areas. The Barshops used a variety of financing tools to pay for the construction of new hotels, including various partnership and joint-venture arrangements. They also expanded the chain by selectively licensing, or franchising, the La Quinta name and concept to unrelated third parties. By the late 1970s, La Quinta inns were springing up primarily across Texas, but also in a few other states. Phil Barshop left the company in 1977 to devote his attention to the family's real estate business, although he remained on the board of directors until 1994.

Aside from the Barshops' creative financing tactics, La Quinta's unique recipe for attracting travelers to its hotels allowed the chain to prosper during the 1970s and 1980s. La Quinta Inns were designed for male business travelers, especially those employed in sales jobs. Rather than striving to entertain guests, as Sam Barshop believed many of his competitors were trying to do, La Quinta simply provided its patrons with clean, comfortable rooms at low prices. Visitors typically enjoyed comparatively large rooms with large beds and ample space to work. The Barshops were able to undercut competing hoteliers, such as Holiday Inn and Rodeway, by eschewing such amenities as swimming pools, elaborate lounges, and restaurants that were of negligible interest to bustling businessmen. By focusing on its core market, La Quinta was able to accrue a large base of repeat customers that sought out La Quinta Inns during their travels.

The Barshops augmented the unique features associated with their individual hotels with a savvy marketing and organizational strategy. La Quinta's expansion came to be guided by the concepts of "clustering, adjacency, and filling in." In other words, the Barshops tried to build name recognition and secure regional market share by locating numerous inns in the same metropolitan areas, putting the hotels within no more than 300 miles of existing properties and then opening inns in smaller cities near established La Quinta markets. The proximity of the La Quintas in each market allowed the hotels to achieve economies of scale by sharing maintenance and purchasing expenses. In addition, Sam Barshop cultivated a reliable group of managers for his properties, hiring mostly ex-military or retired couples to run the hotels.

During this time, franchising had become a popular method of financing the growth of hotel chains because there was often little or no capital investment required by the parent organization. Rather, the parent earned various license and management fees from its franchise in lieu of direct operating profits. However, Barshop was wary of franchising. "You can't control a franchise. . . ," he remarked in the May 14, 1990 issue of *Hotel and Motel Management,* noting that franchises were "not maintaining control; they're not maintaining consistency." Reflecting his commitment to the stratagem of consistency through ownership of La Quinta properties, Barshop ended the company's franchising program in 1977. Barshop focused on building and operating hotels that were owned entirely, or mostly, by La Quinta Motor Inns, Inc.

To fund expansion of the La Quinta chain during the late 1970s and early 1980s, Barshop drew on his real estate and finance background to establish innovative deals that brought investment capital into the organization. In addition to selling stock, he formed joint ventures with well established financial institutions, particularly insurance companies. For hotels that it did not own completely, La Quinta Motor Inns, Inc. would earn fees for developing and managing the properties. The company would also keep a portion of the profits reflective of its ownership share in the projects, with the remainder of the income going to its partner. La Quinta typically maintained 40 percent to 80 percent ownership in the projects, although it retained as little as one percent of some hotels.

Integral to Barshop's financial strategy during the early 1980s was his use of a joint venture to fund the development of a new La Quinta Motor Inns, Inc. headquarters. Built in 1982 to house the hotelier's burgeoning operations, La Quinta Plaza in San Antonio resulted from a joint venture between La Quinta and Israel Fogiel, a local developer. La Quinta eventually purchased Fogiel's share of the complex during the mid-1980s, by which time it was involved in several deals with other investors. Importantly, by 1986 La Quinta had erected 40, or about one-quarter, of the hotels in its chain with the help of its most active partner, Prudential Insurance Company.

By 1986, La Quinta was operating 170 hotels, generating revenues of nearly $180 million and netting income of about $6 million. While most of its hotels were in Texas and Florida, the company had extended its reach into other regions of the South and Southwest as well. That year, however, Congress passed the Tax Reform Act (TRA), which essentially destroyed many of the valuable tax incentives apportioned to investors in commercial real estate projects and served to eventually diminish the liquidity and value of La Quinta's existing properties. Despite the apparent setback, Barshop characteristically tried to turn the new law into an opportunity.

Observers viewed the TRA of 1986 as a death knell for the formerly red-hot limited partnership market, in which limited partnerships allowed numerous smaller investors to invest in large development projects through publicly traded shares. However, Barshop became one of the first developers to establish a master limited partnership (MLP) under the new laws. He created a company called La Quinta Motor Inns Limited Partnership, placed 31 of his properties into the MLP, and then sold shares in the partnership to investors. La Quinta continued to operate the properties to garner management fees from the MLP. The deal resulted in about $75 million in cash that Barshop could use to build new hotels.

Barshop continued to expand the La Quinta chain during 1986 and 1987, using capital raised through various means. In 1987, for example, he formed two joint ventures with investment partnerships managed by CIGNA Investments, Inc. Those two endeavors produced nine hotels and six restaurants. La Quinta owned only one percent of the properties but secured long-term contracts to manage the inns on a fee basis. Between 1986 and 1990, La Quinta added a total of about 30 new properties to its holdings, including the properties held by the limited partnership. Steady growth, however, belied serious problems that

beset the lodging industry in the Southwest during the late 1980s and early 1990s.

By the end of the 1980s the U.S. economy had tailspinned into a recession, gutting market growth in the lodging industry. Hoteliers in the Southwest, in fact, had started suffering as early as 1988, and hotel and real estate industries across the United States were enduring the delayed effects of the TRA of 1986. Development of new hotels had virtually halted by the end of the decade as overbuilt markets scared away investors. While the average occupancy rate for hotels plummeted, many of La Quinta's peers struggled to avoid bankruptcy. The downturn signaled an end of the rapid expansion achieved by Barshop during the 1980s. Development of new La Quinta Inns slowed dramatically in 1990 and even into the mid-1990s.

Nevertheless, La Quinta managed to weather the storm with relatively minor difficulties. Importantly, the recession boosted corporate interest in lower-priced hotels. In fact, in 1991, La Quinta posted the highest occupancy rate, 75.7 percent, of any Texas hotel chain in the business-traveler category. Furthermore, La Quinta managed to get a jump on many of its competitors during the slump by updating and renovating its properties. Using the cash he had generated at the start of the recession, originally earmarked for new developments, Barshop refurbished his hotels and boosted La Quinta's share of a stagnating market. With characteristic optimism, Barshop used the recession as an opportunity to position La Quinta for growth in the 1990s. ''I think the golden years of this company will be the 1990s,'' he commented in *Hotel and Motel Management* magazine.

La Quinta bucked industry financial trends again in 1991 when it formed a new MLP, La Quinta Development Partners, L.P. The partnership, entered into with a Boston-based real estate firm, generated about $150 million in new working capital for the La Quinta organization. In addition, restructuring efforts initiated in the early 1990s were cutting La Quinta's overhead and increasing its operating margins. However, during this time, problems surfaced that would soon result in the resignation of many of La Quinta's executives and would later persuade Barshop to abandon the company he and his brother had founded.

In 1991, a group of shareholders based in Fort-Worth, lead by the Bass and Taylor families, attempted to gain control of the company. Rather than file for bankruptcy to avert the takeover, Barshop came to terms with the group. During the same period, a group of Connecticut investors filed suit against La Quinta Motor Inns Limited Partnership, alleging violations of securities law and mismanagement. Although Barshop denied the charges and fought the hostile takeover, the struggle resulted in the flight of several of his top managers, who were replaced by appointees of the Bass/Taylor Group. Barshop himself was forced out of his position as chief executive, although he retained his title of chairperson.

Gary L. Mead, a lodging industry veteran, assumed the presidency of La Quinta Motor Inns, Inc. in 1991. Although La Quinta's new management team sustained the chain's legacy of marketing toward business travelers, Mead instigated a reorganization of the company. Restructuring efforts were designed to transform La Quinta from an entrepreneurial-styled organization, which had served the company well during the 1970s and 1980s, into a more management-intensive, efficient corporate enterprise.

Under Mead's direction, La Quinta consolidated most of the holdings under its diverse partnerships and joint ventures into a unified chain of inns operated and owned, in full or in part, by the renamed La Quinta Inns, Inc. Mead also implemented vast staff cuts and slashed La Quinta's operating overhead—the company's work force plummeted from 6,800 in 1991 to about 6,100 by the end of 1993. In addition, during 1993 and 1994, La Quinta conducted a $50 million image-enhancement program to give its hotels a fresher, more contemporary appearance. The company also adopted a more progressive logo.

Although La Quinta quelled development of new hotels during the early 1990s, it managed to increase the number of rooms owned and operated by La Quinta Motor Inns, Inc. by about 40 percent, to more than 23,000. That feat was accomplished by purchasing La Quinta hotels from the limited partnerships and by acquiring and converting nearly 15 new properties between 1991 and 1994. As lodging markets began to recover and La Quinta's cost-cutting efforts began to pay off, the company started to prosper; after shouldering a net loss in 1992, La Quinta's earnings increased by $20.3 million from record sales of $272 million in 1993. Sales early in 1994, moreover, suggested improved performance. As evidenced by its move to a new corporate headquarters building in 1993, La Quinta was poised for a new era of expansion during the remainder of the decade.

Principal Subsidiaries: La Quinta Motor Inns Limited Partnership; La Quinta Inns Acquisition Corporation.

Further Reading:

Honeycutt, T. D., ''La Quinta Head Replaced,'' *San Antonio Light,* March 4, 1992.

Jusko, Jill, ''La Quinta Positioned for Future,'' *Hotel and Motel Management,* May 14, 1990.

Koss, Laura, ''Prognosis Good for La Quinta,'' *Hotel and Motel Management,* July 26, 1993, pp. 4+.

McCann, Nita Chilton, ''With Eye on 'Curb Appeal,' La Quinta Renovates Jackson Hotels,'' *Mississippi Business Journal,* November 22, 1993, p. 7.

Moore, Paula, ''FDIC Sues Barshop; La Quinta Battles Ronin in Court,'' *San Antonio Business Journal,* March 27, 1992, p. 3.

Moore, Paula, ''La Quinta Soars Despite Inner Upheaval,'' *San Antonio Business Journal,* October 25, 1991, p. 1.

Moore, Paula, ''Sources: La Quinta Moving Downtown,'' *San Antonio Business Journal,* May 21, 1993, p. 1.

Schmutz, John, ''La Quinta Inns, Inc., Initiates Negotiations to Acquire La Quinta Motor Inns Limited Partnership,'' *PR Newswire,* October 18, 1993.

Stableford, Joan, ''Stamford Group Mounts Hostile Bid for Inn Chain,'' *Fairfield County Business Journal,* October 21, 1991, p. 1.

—Dave Mote

Lam Research Corporation

4650 Cushing Parkway
Fremont, California 94538
U.S.A.
(510) 659-2935
Fax: (510) 490-5026

Public Company
Incorporated: 1980
Employees: 2,600
Sales: $493 million
Stock Exchanges: NASDAQ
SICs: 3550 Special Industry Machinery; 8650 Electrical,
    Electronics, Instrumentation Industries

Lam Research Corporation is a leading supplier of semiconductor manufacturing equipment to the global semiconductor industry. Through a combination of cutting-edge technological innovation and exemplary customer service, Lam became one of the fastest growing competitors in the worldwide industry during the late 1980s and early 1990s.

When Lam Research Corp. announced its sales and earnings figures for 1993, its stock price dropped more than 8 percent. Investors were disappointed: Lam had increased its sales only 92 percent compared to 1992, resulting in record earnings for the fast-growing supplier, and the company had just assumed the global lead in a pivotal chip fabrication technology. Shareholders were hoping for more, and, based on Lam's history of exceeding expectations, they expected it.

Lam Research was originally the brainchild of David Lam, a highly intelligent and restless player in the high-tech hotbed known as Silicon Valley. The son of Chinese refugees, Lam graduated from a Hong Kong high school and received a scholarship to study at the University of Toronto, Canada. He majored in physics and engineering and, at age 24, enrolled in Massachusetts Institute of Technology to study nuclear engineering. Because of a lack of funding for nuclear programs, Lam instead received a doctorate in chemical engineering with an emphasis in plasma, a specialty that would benefit him in the semiconductor industry.

Lam took a job in the early 1970s at Texas Instruments working with emerging semiconductor plasma technology. The semiconductor industry was still young; Bell Laboratories had only introduced the solid-state transistor in 1947, and a significant demand for chips had not emerged until the 1960s. Importantly, Intel Corp.'s introduction of the memory integrated circuit in 1971 spawned a plethora of opportunities in the U.S. semiconductor industry. True to his restless nature, Lam switched jobs several times during the 1970s, working for Xerox, Hewlett Packard, and finally as a salesman for Plasma-Therm.

Lam left Plasma-Therm in 1980 to form Lam Research Corp. With a loan from his mother, he developed plans to build his own prototype plasma-etching system, a technology used in the semiconductor, or chip, manufacturing process. Chipmaking entails a four-step procedure: 1) deposition of thin film on a (usually silicon) wafer; 2) impurity doping, when impurities are introduced that control conductivity; 3) lithographic patterning, which creates the geometric features and layout of the circuit; and 4) etching, which removes the film coating material to reveal the layout patterned in the lithographic process.

Lam used the start-up money from his mother to market his idea to venture capitalists. Citing his mastery of cutting-edge plasma-etching technology and a decade of sales and management experience, Lam was able to attract $800,000 in capital during his first year. Amazingly, by 1983 Lam Research was selling chip manufacturing systems and was sustaining a steady cash flow. "David had a great combination of skills in putting the company together, and he was always able to come up with financing in times of adversity," recalled Tom Nicoletti, Lam's chief financial officer during the mid-1980s, in a June 1990 issue of *San Francisco Business Times.* "He was outstanding in position and strategy, and he had an intuitive understanding of the industry."

Although Lam Research outshone many of its competitors during the early 1980s, its success was also attributable to the vast increase in semiconductor sales during the decade. Despite huge gains by Japanese companies during the 1980s that seriously weakened U.S. dominance of the global market, sales of chip manufacturing equipment grew strongly because of flourishing demand. Besides the massive personal computer market, chips were being integrated into products ranging from automobiles and stereos to dishwashers and telephones. Lam Research leveraged the demand growth by offering cutting-edge products and service.

Lam went public in 1984, garnering a hefty $20 million from the sale of stock. However, he was still not content staying in one place for any length of time. Just five years after founding the company that bore his name, Lam walked away from the highly successful venture to accept a position with Link Technologies; he would soon shift gears completely, trying his hand at developing computer software. The company, however, remained in excellent hands. In fact, the unprecedented growth that Lam Research would achieve in the coming decade would be a testament to the depth and proficiency of the management team that built a strong foundation for Lam Research.

The semiconductor manufacturing equipment industry fell on relatively rough times during the middle and late 1980s. Although demand for chip-making equipment continued to increase, U.S. producers experienced continuously rising pressure from efficient Japanese firms that were dominating the market for high-volume, commoditylike chip manufacturing systems. Japan increased its share of the world chip machine market from almost nothing in the late 1970s to nearly 50 percent by the late 1980s—U.S. producers supplied the remainder of demand. As a result, U.S. suppliers regrouped during the late 1980s by boosting productivity and concentrating on the development of high-volume, proprietary manufacturing technologies that they believed would benefit them in the 1990s.

Lam Research managed to prosper during the turbulent late 1980s by focusing on technological innovation, global expansion, market penetration, quality, and customer service. Its technological strength was achieved through heavy spending on research and development, which averaged about 10 percent of revenues, and the cultivation of a forward-thinking development team. Importantly, it broadened its product focus to include deposition equipment, another high growth segment in the service equipment industry. Specifically, Lam developed its breakthrough Integrity system, a chemical vapor deposition (CVD) system. Unveiled in 1990, the system integrated several manufacturing steps into a single process, thereby reducing production time and costs. The system won the *R&D Magazine* top product innovation award in 1991.

Lam's strategy of global expansion during the late 1980s and early 1990s emphasized the Pacific Rim and Europe. Since selling its first systems to Asian buyers in 1983, Lam had pursued a strategy of global growth, garnering about 50 percent of its revenues from overseas sales by the early 1990s. Of importance was its success in Japan. Lam entered a partnership with Japan's Sumitomo Metal Industries, Ltd. (SMI) in 1987 to help its renowned Rainbow etch product line in Japan. The two companies eventually stepped up joint research and marketing efforts. Lam opened its Lam Technology Center, a wholly owned subsidiary, near Tokyo in 1991 to support its increased activities in that region.

Thinking ahead, Lam management had long been pursuing growth in smaller markets, such as Taiwan and Korea. In fact, Lam had concentrated on Taiwan since the mid-1980s, but had also opened customer support centers throughout Europe, Japan, the United States, and several Asian countries. By the early 1990s, Lam had a strong foothold in such burgeoning markets as Korea, Singapore, and Taiwan, and it was beginning to set its sights on emerging demand in Malaysia, China, Israel, and several other emerging markets. By the early 1990s, Lam was engaged in, or considering, the establishment of development/demonstration or production facilities in Japan, Korea, Taiwan, and several other markets.

In addition to technological leadership and global expansion, Lam's insistence on quality and customer satisfaction bolstered its bottom line during the late 1980s and early 1990s. Its accomplishments in this area were evidenced by its attainment of the coveted VLSI Research Top Ten Award every year since the award's inception in 1988. VLSI Research Inc. bestows the award on only ten recipients after surveying 35,000 equipment users worldwide. The award is based primarily on customer satisfaction and product quality. "Lam's philosophy has always been to deliver equipment that works and to take responsibility for keeping it operating at optimum performance," said Dan

Hutcheson, president of VLSI. "It is this philosophy that has led to Lam's obvious success in customer satisfaction."

Lam was able to parlay its competencies into solid profit and revenue gains by the early 1990s, despite a global recession that had stumped many of its competitors. In 1991, in fact, Lam earned $6.1 million from $144 million in sales, 44 percent of which came from overseas shipments; however, this followed a loss of $5.8 million in 1990. Earnings topped $10 million from 1992 sales of $171 million, though, as the industry began to emerge from its doldrums. In addition to the improved economy, Lam and its U.S. counterparts were benefiting from a general revival in the competitiveness of the U.S. semiconductor equipment industry. Initiatives of the middle and late 1980s began to pay off as U.S. producers increased productivity and took the lead in important new technologies.

As of a result of steady growth, Lam's work force swelled to about 1,500 by the early 1990s, shadowing a rise in its production capacity. To house its growing operations, Lam announced plans in 1991 to expand its facilities by 58,000 square feet. It was already using more than 150,000 square feet and had the option of expanding onto a 50,000-square-foot parcel adjacent to its new location. In addition, in 1992 Lam applied for a 71,000-square-foot space in Korea, on which it planned to build an assembly plant. Reflecting its optimism, Lam also requested permission in its application to eventually expand the plant to as much as ten times that size.

Lam's success by the early 1990s was the direct result of its savvy management team, a collection of thinkers and doers gathered from all corners of the industry. For example, in 1992, David Lam transferred his responsibilities, becoming chief scientist, and Roger Emerick was recruited in as president to grow the company further. Dennis Key served as vice president of domestic sales before assuming leadership of global sales in 1992. Key brought more than 20 years of industry experience to his new post. Augmenting Key's efforts was Way Tu, head of Lam's Asian operations. Tu had been with Lam since 1983. Prior to that, the Stanford graduate had served a four-year stint with a leading semiconductor producer. Key, Tu, and other noted industry talents reported to chip-making veteran Roger Emerick, chief executive officer of the company.

Research, development, and marketing efforts implemented by Lam's talented management group during the 1980s began to bear fruit in the early 1990s, as the company introduced breakthrough etch and deposition technologies that were expected to reap big profits throughout the 1990s. After unveiling its Integrity CVD system in 1990, Lam launched its TCP 9400 polysilicon etch system, which was the first product to integrate Lam's patented Transformer Coupled Plasma (TCP) technology that it introduced in May of 1992. The second product in the series was the TCP 9600 metal etch system. The new TCP systems utilized advanced plasma-etch technology that was expected to allow greater production efficiency, chip quality, and chip uniformity.

In 1993, Lam released several products based on next generation technologies. The two new TCP products generated $33 million in sales in less than one year. Lam also introduced its new Epic system, a high-density CVD system offering capabilities no other system was capable of providing. These new products were helping the company start to achieve its stated goal of becoming a strong player in the deposition market. Management cited this goal as imperative to its survival in the increasingly integrated industry. "We are not doing this just to become a giant company," Emerick explained in the January 28, 1994, issue of *San Francisco Business Times.*

Because of its product introductions and sales growth in established product lines, Lam increased its sales 55 percent in fiscal 1993 (ending June 1993) to an impressive $265 million. Net income, moreover, ballooned 90 percent to nearly $19 million. "This has been a banner year for Lam," Emerick declared in Lam's year-end results, posted on *Business Wire* on August 10, 1993. "We have benefited from the semiconductor industry's strong growth in recent months, as well as from the market share gains made over the last several years."

Despite record sales and earnings growth during 1993 and 1994, Lam remained committed to expansion. It had been continuing strong research and development spending, leveling off to about 15 percent of its annual sales, and was aggressively seeking entry into new growth markets. In 1994, Lam received a $13.4 million contract from the United States Display Consortium (USDC) to develop an etch system for manufacturing FPDs. The system will be based on its TCP leap frog technology. Although the market for flat-panel displays was growing quickly and was expected to become huge by the end of the century, Japan served nearly 100 percent of global demand in 1993. Lam believed its existing next generation technology could be successfully applied in that burgeoning global industry.

Lam became the largest producer of etch equipment in the world in 1993, and increased its rank in the worldwide semiconductor manufacturing equipment market to fourth largest. It also acquired new land in Korea to build additional manufacturing capacity, which would be operational by the middle of 1995. Sizing up the company's future prospects, Emerick predicted in 1994 that Lam's sales would reach $1 billion before the turn of the century. The introduction of new technologies in 1994, stepped-up research and development efforts, and surging de-

mand going into the mid-1990s indicated the likelihood of Lam's robust growth in the evolving industry through the mid-1990s.

Further Reading:

Barry, David, and James S. Goldman, "Lam Research Inks Deal with Devcon Principals," *Business Journal-San Jose,* October 28, 1991, Sec. 1, p. 3.

Carlsen, Clifford, "David Lam's Career Path Winds to Presidential Commission Spot," *San Francisco Business Times,* June 18, 1990, Sec. 1, p. 12; "Lam Breaks Away from the Flock," *San Francisco Business Times,* January 28, 1994, Sec. 2, p. 5A; "Lam to Open Asian Offices," *San Francisco Business Times,* March 20, 1992, Sec. 1, p. 4.

Evenhuis, Henk, "Lam Reports Year-End Results; Record Revenues and Profits for Third Straight Year," *Business Wire,* August 10, 1993.

Goldman, James S., "Chip Boom to Boost Suppliers in '93," *Business Journal-San Jose,* Sec. 1, p. 1.

Hayes, Mary, "Lam Research Jumping into Flat-Panel Display Equipment," *Business Journal-San Jose,* September 20, 1993, Sec. 1, p. 5; "Applied and Lam May Build in Korea," *Business Journal-San Jose,* April 26, 1993, Sec. 1, p. 1.

McLennan, Karen, "Corporate Profile for Lam Research," *Business Wire,* December 28, 1992; "Lam and Sumitomo Metal Industries Expand Relationship to Bring Critical Next-Generation Technologies to Japanese Chipmakers," *Business Wire,* August 12, 1992; "Lam Announces Two New Executive Assignments," *Business Wire,* August 25, 1992; "Lam Attains Number One Position in Worldwide Dry Etch Market," *Business Wire,* January 26, 1991; "Lam Launches Breakthrough Etch Technology," *Business Wire,* May 11, 1992; "Lam Launches TCP 9400 Polysilicon Etch System," *Business Wire,* October 27, 1992; "Lam Names New Executive Director of Korean Operations," *Business Wire,* November 20, 1991; "Lam's Integrity CVD System Wins Coveted R&D 100 Award," *Business Wire,* September 19, 1991.

McLennan, Karen, and Carolyn Schwartz, "Lam Opens Technology Center in Japan; Names Vice President to Head New Operation," *Business Wire,* June 4, 1991; "Lam Listed Among World's 10 Best; Receives VLSI Research Award for Third Year Running," *Business Wire,* May 21, 1991.

—Dave Mote

Lechters, Inc.

1 Cape May Street
Harrison, New Jersey 07029
U.S.A.
(201) 481-1100
Fax: (201) 481-5493

Public Company
Incorporated: 1975
Employees: 3,040
Sales: $350 million
Stock Exchange: New York
SICs: 5719 Miscellaneous Home Furnishing Stores

Lechters, Inc., is the leading specialty retailer of housewares in the United States. The company runs nearly 600 stores, which sell a wide variety of kitchenware and other practical devices. Lechters started as a store designed for shopping malls and expanded dramatically throughout the 1980s. As overall mall business slowed, however, Lechters began to seek other places for its stores, opening outlets in cities and in outdoor strip shopping centers.

Lechters was founded in 1975 by Albert Lechter. The company ran housewares departments in leased space in two Valley Fair discount stores in New Jersey. The discount stores were owned by Donald Jonas, who had run a variety of retail outlets since entering the field in 1947 at age 18. In 1977, Jonas and Lechter decided to team up to open their own separate housewares store. Because many conventional department stores had shrunk or eliminated their housewares departments, the two businessmen felt that there was a gap in the market that they could fill with their store. In addition, they wanted to offer their goods in malls. Although these locations generally concentrated on clothing, shoes, and jewelry stores, Lechter and Jonas felt that their merchandise would also find a market there.

The two opened their prototype store in a mall in Rockaway, New Jersey. This store proved a complete failure. Not yet fully versed in the nature of their business, Lechter and Jonas had rented a large space, 6,500 square feet, in a far corner of the mall where there was very little foot traffic. In addition, relying on Jonas's experience in the clothing business, they had stocked their store with seasonal goods, such as picnic baskets in warm weather and holiday-themed kitchenware. When customers failed to buy the products at the appropriate time, they had to be marked down severely in order to be sold at all.

After two years, Lechter and Jonas had realized that they needed to adjust their formula. In 1979, Jonas bought out the bulk of Lechter's holdings in the company, and the two tried again. The second Lechters prototype was smaller than the first, with just 4,500 square feet. The company stocked this store with 4,000 different timeless, basic housewares, which never needed to be discounted.

By specializing in housewares, Lechters filled the gap between department stores, which offered a small selection of higher-priced items, and discount and variety stores, which considered housewares just one small part of a much larger variety of offerings. In addition, the company was moving into an area that had no dominant national retailer in place. Although housewares on the whole were not high-priced items, Lechters found that it could make money on a steady turnover of small, less expensive goods. The company instituted an everyday low-price policy, which matched the offerings of the discount stores and did not rely on special sales or promotions to bring customers into the stores.

By the end of the year, the new Lechters store had become profitable, and Jonas moved to expand his concept to other malls. The company grew rapidly in the early 1980s, in an effort to preempt any competitors who might decide to join Lechters in the niche it had created. By the end of 1980, Lechters had opened 30 stores in malls. By 1984, the company was expanding at a rate of 40 percent per year. In 1985, 83 Lechters stores had been opened. By the mid-1980s, Lechters' management was confident that they had a hot retail concept on their hands, and the company moved aggressively to capitalize on its success.

In 1986, Lechters raised $11 million in a private placement of stock, and the company used these funds to fuel even more rapid expansion. In the next three years, the company's number of stores more than doubled, to reach 297. In 1988, sales reached $120.7 million, and, in the following year, they grew to $150 million. The company's growing revenues and earnings were driven by the ever larger number of Lechters outlets taking their place in malls around the country.

In 1989, Lechters moved out of malls into the cut-throat retail environment of Manhattan for the first time. The company made this move with trepidation. "We weren't sure how people in Manhattan felt about Rubbermaid and cake plates," a Lechters' vice president later told *HFD,* a trade journal. However, the high density of customers, the relatively high income of the population, and the lack of any real competition made Lechters executives feel that the risk was worth it. The company shortly discovered that its experiment had been a success, as Lechters' Manhattan store began to turn in revenues twice as high as those of stores in suburban malls.

To fund further expansion, Jonas sold 35 percent of Lechters to the public in 1989. This offering of stock raised $53 million. Of this sum, $31 million was used to buy out previous investors and insiders, and the rest was dedicated to funding Lechter's growth. To direct this expansion, Lechters recruited seven senior executives from top retailers around the country in the late 1980s.

These managers were brought in to help Lechters move to the next stage of its development. The company had successfully invented and refined its concept, and it had rapidly expanded its format to a large number of locations. By the end of the 1980s, however, it was necessary for Lechters to invest in systems and controls to enhance the profitability of its existing operations.

By January of 1990, these operations comprised 280 separate Lechters stores. The company's sales had grown at a compound rate of 43 percent over the last five years. In that time, Lechters had come to dominate its housewares category, retailing gadgets, gifts, and frames, as well as basic cookware. Despite this success, one worrisome note was the company's reliance on new store openings for growth. Sales increases at individual stores had been minimal, rising just $20 per square foot over a two-year period.

In addition, the company experienced some difficulty with its Kitchen Place outlets. Along with its trademark stores, Lechters had moved into the burgeoning discount mall category, opening 13 Kitchen Place units. These stores were bigger than the typical Lechters and sold similar products at slightly lower prices. In its initial guise, this concept did not contribute strongly to Lechters' earnings, so the company revamped the idea to see if it would fly in strip malls. The new Kitchen Place store was envisioned as a more aggressively promoted, high-tech outlet, with lower prices and a higher profile. The company tested out this idea in a Price Club Plaza in North Haven, Connecticut.

In an effort to improve operations at its flagship chain, Lechters turned its attention to the consistency of its merchandise and to its distribution system. The company began testing new computers for sales and inventory control and also began to diagram more precisely where items should be displayed in each store. Without such planning, displays in Lechters' small stores sometimes became haphazard and disorganized. In addition, the company moved to pare down its offerings in some categories, after discovering that it had twice as many versions of some items as it needed. With these steps, the company hoped to position itself as a slightly more upscale retailer, with an average purchase slightly higher than its standard $6.

As part of this program, Lechters aggressively expanded its presence in Manhattan. In May 1990, the company opened a New York outlet, its 319th overall, and then in June a fourth Manhattan store was brought on line. By the end of the year, Lechters had a total of 364 units open. In an effort to reduce costs, the company had also started to import its products directly from overseas manufacturers. Lechters' sales for 1990 totaled $187.6 million.

As mall traffic began to slow, Lechters looked to a variety of store formats for further growth in 1991. The company had expanded its initial concept to include the Kitchen Place strip mall store, of which it planned to roll out 20 to 25 in the course of the year. In addition, Lechters resurrected a discount mall store called Famous Brands Housewares Outlets and introduced a mall ''superstore,'' which was much larger than a regular Lechters. The Kitchen Place stores and the Famous Brands

Outlets were to feature the same merchandise and price levels in different settings. Famous Brands merchandise would also be supplemented by excess inventory of manufacturers like Rubbermaid and Ekco.

Lechters' superstores had 50 percent more space than the regular stores. In their initial tests, in A&S Plaza in New Jersey and Newport Center in Jersey City, the Lechters superstores reported sales that grew by 50 percent when their size was expanded. New products offered in the bigger spaces included a wide variety of home decorations, such as ceramics, lamps, dried flowers, and brass and pewter objects.

In July 1991, Lechters rolled out a new prototype for its traditional stores, which featured more subtle shelving, wider aisles, and a bigger open space at the front of the store. In this way, the company hoped to relieve the crowding present in many of its smaller locations. In a test on Staten Island, these changes increased sales volume by 40 percent.

In addition to these changes, Lechters also planned to expand its urban operations by opening three more Manhattan stores and a first location in downtown Chicago. At the major intersection of 57th Street and Broadway in Manhattan, Lechters opened a two-level, 8,000-foot superstore. Called the ''Lechters Home Store,'' this outlet featured an expanded selection of merchandise. Despite Lechters' moves into the city and into strip malls, more than 80 percent of the company's revenues still derived from stores in malls by the end of 1992.

In January 1993, Lechters' sales reached the $234 million mark and earnings were at $13 million. This growth came despite a generally slowed economy. Rather than depress Lechters' earnings, the downturn appeared to have enhanced them, as people began to eschew expensive restaurant outings to eat more at home, which prompted them to buy more housewares.

Although Lechters' sales figures showed strong growth, trouble loomed on the horizon, as traffic in malls continued its steady drop. To counteract the effect this decline would have on its business, Lechter located just 20 of the 65 stores it opened in 1993 in malls. Despite this measure, the company reported falling profits in the first quarter of 1993, even though sales had risen. This trend continued throughout the year, and the company ended 1993 with sales up $44 million to $350 million, and profits down $4.3 million, to $11.1 million. This drop was attributed to weakness in the company's product selection and low levels of customer recognition. Without noticing it, Lechters had failed to establish any clear identity for the company in the public's mind.

To redress these problems, Lechters revamped its product presentation and increased the amount of information presented to customers, so that the store would become easier and more efficient to use. As part of this program, Lechters implemented a computerized ticket-scanning system at all of its cash registers. Lechters also opened its first distribution center in 1993, to serve its 100 west coast stores. Located in Las Vegas, this facility included 155,000 square feet of storage space. By the end of the year, the company's number of stores had reached 567, and Lechters executives estimated that there was room for at least 500 more stores in the years to come. Dominating a market niche that it had pioneered, Lechters looked forward to expanding its operations throughout the late 1990s.

Principal Subsidiaries: Lechters New York, Inc.; Lechters N.Y.C., Inc.; Lechters New Jersey, Inc.; Lechters California, Inc.; Lechters Texas, Inc.; Cooks Club, Inc.; Regent Gallery, Inc.; Lechter Investment Corporation.

Further Reading:

Erlick, June Carolyn, "Lechters Takes Manhattan," *HFD - The Weekly Home Furnishings Newspaper,* March 14, 1994.

Garbato, Debby, "Lechters New Manhattan Store Bows," *HFD - The Weekly Home Furnishings Newspaper,* June 29, 1992.

Gilbert, Les, "Lechters Fills Vacuum," *HFD - The Weekly Home Furnishings Newspaper,* January 22, 1990; "Lechters Speeds Up Expansion," *HFD—The Weekly Home Furnishings Newspaper,* November 11, 1991; "Lechters to Expand with Superstores Concept," *HFD - The Weekly Home Furnishings Newspaper,* May 4, 1992.

Guttner, Toddi, " 'You Can't Say No to Opportunity,' " *Forbes,* November 23, 1992.

—Elizabeth Rourke

Lee Enterprises, Incorporated

400 Putnam Building
215 N. Main Street
Davenport, Iowa 52801-1924
U.S.A.
(319) 383-2100
Fax: (319) 323-9608

Public Company
Incorporated: 1890 as the Ottumwa Daily Courier
Employees: 5,000
Sales: $372.91 million
Stock Exchanges: New York
SICs: 2711 Newspaper Publishing and Printing; 4833
    Television Broadcasting Stations

Lee Enterprises, Incorporated is a leading newspaper publisher and operator of television broadcasting stations. Besides publishing about 20 daily newspapers and more than 30 specialty publications, Lee owned and operated eight TV stations in 1994 and manufactured graphic arts systems that it sold to other publishers. Lee's engaging history spans more than a century.

The publishing venture that would become Lee Enterprises was started when A. W. Lee purchased the *Ottumwa* (Iowa) *Daily Courier* in 1890. By that time, the 32-year-old Lee had worked in the industry for several years in Chicago and Iowa and was eager to start running his own newspaper. So, for $16,000, which was most of his savings combined with money invested by family and friends, Lee bought the *Daily Courier* and began to shape it into what he believed a newspaper should be: a medium that served the local community and had a duty, as well as a right, to provide the most reliable and most provocative news available. Above all, Lee believed his newspaper should conform to a high ethical standard that would instill confidence in its readers.

Lee's vision for his newspaper was shaped by his conservative midwestern upbringing. After eloping in Philadelphia, Lee's parents moved to Iowa City and became pioneer farmers—Lee's mother abandoned her Quaker roots and his father left behind a family of aristocrats. Lee was exposed to both a strict upbringing and the newspaper business during his childhood. Besides working as a bookkeeper for the *Muscatine Journal,* Lee's father, John B., enjoyed writing and kept a detailed diary of the family's affairs. Even after his childhood, Lee would be

exposed to his father's stern business ethics and attention to detail while working under him as a bookkeeper.

Before Lee took a job with his father at the *Muscatine Journal,* he distinguished himself at the age of 13 by being the youngest student ever admitted to the State University of Iowa. He excelled at math, but Lee knew at that early age that he wanted to pursue a career related to writing and editing. He was a fan of Ralph Waldo Emerson and was heavily influenced by his writings. In fact, Lee was known for always carrying small pocket books with Emerson's essays printed on them wherever he went. Importantly, Lee subscribed to Emerson's motto, "Trust Thyself," which meant that individuals could improve their lives if they believed strongly in what they were doing and what they wanted to achieve.

A few years after graduating from college, Lee succeeded his father as head bookkeeper at the *Muscatine Journal.* But, because he wanted to write, he left that secure position to work for the *Chicago Times.* Following a two-year stint as a writer and part-time editor, he returned to Iowa and took over the *Ottumwa Daily Courier.* Lee's writing and editing skills, combined with his keen bookkeeping knowledge, allowed Lee to prosper with his new venture during the 1890s. Furthermore, his emphasis on integrity and journalistic responsibility, which is documented in company annals, permeated his organization and became a hallmark of the *Daily Courier.* Also during the 1890s, Lee's two sons died. To that tragedy was attributed Lee's noted determination to help other young men achieve success in his company.

Encouraged by the growth of the *Daily Courier,* Lee began seeking a way to expand his publishing operations near the turn of the century. In 1899 he purchased the *Davenport* (Iowa) *Times,* whose name he changed to the *Daily Times,* thus initiating a newspaper syndicate. He sent an associate and long-time *Muscatine Journal* employee, E. P. Adler, to help run the new concern. Lee had considered a number of potential acquisitions, but selected the *Davenport Times* because of its solid reputation, untapped readership potential, and advertising opportunities. It was soon clear that Lee's perception of the publication's potential was correct, as readership and revenues climbed.

Recognizing the potential to improve and then profit from other holdings, Lee bought his old hometown newspaper, the *Muscatine Journal,* from his brother-in-law in 1903. In 1907, moreover, he picked up the *Hannibal Courier-Post,* a nearby Missouri newspaper, and the *La Crosse* (Wisconsin) *Tribune,* which was just north of his Iowa operations. Lee achieved gains with those papers similar to those he had enjoyed with the *Daily Times.* His recipe for success was relatively straightforward: find a newspaper with promise in a small- to medium-sized town, increase its circulation and advertising sales, and hire an astute manager to operate it. An important element of Lee's strategy was management autonomy. The management team of each of his papers was allowed to run the organization almost as though it was their own business. Lee believed that each publication should be financially independent, without having to rely on resources from other Lee holdings to support it.

Shortly after launching his aggressive acquisition program, Lee died as a result of heart failure during a 1907 vacation in Europe. Because he had hired capable and independent managers, however, the company was in good hands. Adler was selected to head the Lee Syndicate, as it had become known, and co-worker Jim Powell became his vice-president. Adler, once described as "a fire-eating and adventurous but resourceful pioneer," complemented Powell's more cautious nature. Adler's colorful existence was evidenced by an attempt in 1917 to kidnap him from a hotel, stuff him in a trunk, and hold him for $40,000 ransom. Adler was able to escape from the two men who beat him and tried to stuff him in the trunk, and to capture one of the men with the help of passersby. All of his attackers were eventually convicted, and one hanged himself in jail. Immediately after the renowned event, Adler sent this telling radiogram message to his family: "Have suddenly become famous. Slightly injured. Nothing serious. Home tonight. Don't worry. —Dad."

Adler ran Lee Syndicate until 1947. During that period he perpetuated A. W. Lee's legacy of ethical reporting and community service. In addition, he sustained efforts to expand the company by acquiring other newspapers and improving their performance. In 1915 he purchased the *Democrat,* a Davenport, Iowa, newspaper. By 1930, in fact, he had added five newspapers to the Lee fold, including publications in Nebraska and Illinois. The company was organized as a holding company in 1928 under the name Lee Syndicate Company before postponing its acquisition activity during the Depression years. When it did resume expansion efforts, Adler took the company in a new direction.

In 1937 Lee purchased its first broadcasting unit, KGLO, a radio station in Mason City, Iowa. In 1941 it purchased interests in a Nebraska station, and in 1944 Lee bought WTAD, of Quincy, Illinois. Lee's extension into the broadcasting industry was lead by Lee P. Loomis, who had started with Lee in 1902 as a farm-to-farm subscription solicitor. Loomis was a nephew of A. W. Lee and had worked his way up to publisher of one of Lee's newspapers. Although Adler disagreed with Loomis about whether or not the company should get into radio, the company's policy of allowing its publishers autonomy prevailed. Loomis pioneered the foray into radio under Adler's condition that the investments begin to show a profit within two years. Despite several hurdles, Loomis achieved profitability in radio. Lee's radio holdings were eventually jettisoned, however, in response to Federal Communication Commission requirements regarding simultaneous ownership of radio and newspaper concerns.

Adler died in 1949 after 42 years of leadership and Loomis assumed the presidency. In 1950 all of Lee's holding were linked under a new corporate umbrella, Lee Enterprises, Incorporated. The company was reorganized and some of its newspapers were consolidated. Importantly, in 1953 Lee's first television station, KHQA-TV, began broadcasting to Hannibal and Quincy, Illinois. One year later, Lee started KGLO-TV in Mason City, Iowa. Loomis viewed the jump into television as a means of capturing the advertising market share that was shifting away from newspapers. He also continued to emphasize growth of Lee's core publications divisions. Just before retiring in 1960, in fact, Loomis oversaw the buyout of six Montana newspapers for $6 million. Also in 1960, all of Lee's holdings were officially consolidated under Lee Enterprises, Incorporated.

Loomis passed the baton to Philip Adler, the son of E. P. Adler. He had worked as a reporter, editor, and then publisher for Lee since 1926, but had also served as editor on both his high school and college newspapers during the 1920s. Like those before him, Adler maintained the company's emphasis on integrity and honesty. Earlier in his career, in fact, Adler was tested by several investigative pieces he wrote about a local businessman. Several readers canceled their subscriptions in protest, but Adler stuck to his story. After the businessman fled town with much of their money, most of those subscribers renewed. In addition to a pure code of ethics, Adler also worked to improve the quality of Lee's newspapers. He ended the practice of running many syndicated columns and press releases, for example, instead encouraging his publishers to generate copy in-house.

Adler served as president of Lee for ten years, during which he continued to increase its operations and holdings. In 1960, for example, KEYC-TV of Mankato, Minnesota, began telecasting. In 1967 the company moved all of its newspaper and broadcasting divisions to a new corporate headquarters in Davenport, and in 1969 Lee made its first public stock offering to raise cash for a new round of acquisitions. Shortly thereafter, Lee bought the publisher of the *Journal Times* in Racine, Wisconsin, and the *Corvallis Gazette-Times* of Corvallis, Oregon, for $2 million. It also completed the acquisition of a few newspapers in which it held a partial interest. By the time Adler retired in 1970, Lee was a diversified radio, television, and newspaper company active in ten upper-midwestern and western states.

David K. Gottlieb succeeded Adler. Gottlieb started working for Lee in 1936 and worked his way up through the ranks to vice-president of the entire company by 1967. He served only three years before he died unexpectedly of a heart attack in 1973. His most important contribution to Lee during that period was the initiation of a joint venture with Nippon Paint Co., Ltd, of Japan. In 1972 the two companies formed NAPP Systems Inc. to manufacture an advanced printing device for sale to the publishing industry. NAPP's innovative printing plates significantly sped up the plate-making process and reduced the number of people required to accomplish a specific task by as much as 50 percent. Also under Gottlieb's leadership, Lee purchased WSAZ-TV, an NBC affiliate in North Carolina, and WMDR-FM in Illinois.

Lloyd G. Schermer became president of Lee in 1973. The 46-year-old Schermer started with Lee in 1954 after receiving his masters degree in business administration from Harvard University. He moved from an advertising position to publisher of a Lee newspaper by 1961. Schermer was an avid outdoorsman and, like all of the Lee presidents before him, played a very active leadership role in local and regional volunteer programs. Schermer also emphasized reporting and broadcasting integrity as an integral tenant of the Lee Enterprises philosophy, and he sustained the steady expansion and acquisition activity that had made Lee a regional media contender. The first Lee purchase under Schermer's direction was KGMB-TV of Honolulu, Hawaii, in 1976. Lee also picked up KOIN-TV in Portland, Oregon, in 1977, and purchased the *Bismarck* (North Dakota) *Tribune* in 1978. In 1979 and 1980, moreover, the company absorbed newspapers in Illinois and Minnesota. Acquisitions of

TV stations in New Mexico, Arizona, and Nebraska followed in 1985 and 1986.

In addition to expanding Lee's holdings, Schermer drew on his Harvard-taught management techniques to whip the company's organizational structure into shape and boost its operating efficiency. Like A. W. Lee and his successors, Schermer believed in a relatively high level of autonomy for Lee's division managers, who knew better than central management how to serve their local markets. But Schermer brought a new emphasis on productivity to the company. Augmenting his technical style was an in-bred penchant for taking calculated risks. Schermer came from a family of entrepreneurs and was not afraid to test new waters at Lee. In 1983, for example, Schermer initiated Call-It Co. as a subsidiary of Lee. Research and development of the innovative venture, which was inspired by Schermer's interest in the ballooning market for telecommunications services, continued into the early 1990s.

In 1986, Schermer became chief executive officer of the company and Richard D. Gottlieb, son of David, took over as president. The two ran the company together, with Schermer slowly transferring supervision of day-to-day management duties to Gottlieb. Gottlieb had been with the company since 1964 and worked his way up to vice-president of newspapers by 1980. Known for his human relations and managerial skills, Gottlieb maintained the management style and growth strategy that had become a legacy of Lee enterprises. In 1990 he oversaw the acquisition of the *Rapid City* (Iowa) *Journal* and helped to complete the 100 percent purchase of NAPP Systems Inc. for $100 million.

By 1990, on its 100-year anniversary, Lee was operating 19 newspapers in small- to medium-sized towns, and six television stations in 13 states. It also owned and operated in excess of 30 specialty publications, most of which were magazine-like weeklies that carried classified advertisements in the upper Midwest. In addition, the company operated four printing facilities, NAPP Systems Inc., and Voice Response, Inc. (Call-It Co.). Despite heavy borrowing to feed its capital-intensive expansion program, the company was financially healthy and had succeeded in minimizing its debt load. Indeed, by 1990 Lee Enterprises was raking in $287 million annually and capturing $44 million per year in net income. As a result of 1990 acquisitions, moreover, Lee's revenues leapt to $346 million.

Despite Lee's financial successes, the newspaper industry, as well as most other media sectors, encountered setbacks during the economic recession of the late 1980s and early 1990s. As the economy slumped, advertising revenues sagged. Furthermore,

the newspaper industry, which accounted for the bulk of Lee's sales, was struggling under the pressure of increased competition from electronic media. Fortunately, however, Lee was able to endure the downturn unscathed compared to many of its industry peers. Its stability was largely a result of geography: most of its holdings were located in the economically healthy upper Midwest. Nevertheless, Lee's net income slipped to $31.5 million in 1991 before buoying back up to about $39 million in 1992.

As Lee slowly added new radio and television holdings to its portfolio during the early 1990s, its balance sheet began to reflect the economic recovery. Sales swelled to $373 million in 1993 as net income rose to about $41 million. Furthermore, the company anticipated receipts of about $400 million during 1994 based on surging sales early in the year. Under Gottlieb's direction, moreover, Lee was beginning to eye new markets for growth, such as electronic multi-media opportunities related to delivering information, farm magazines, and book publishing. Finally, Lee's NAPP subsidiary had developed and was selling a breakthrough photosensitive polymer printing plate that was receiving widespread market acceptance. As it focused on the remainder of the century, Lee continued to draw on many of the principles established by its founder to achieve prosperity and to serve as a responsible leader in the media industry.

Further Reading:

Bielema, Ross, "Times Makes an Effort to Recycle," *Quad-City Times,* December 28, 1992, sec. BUS.
Byrne, Harlan S., "Newspaper Tiger," *Barron's,* April 11, 1994.
Cross, Wilbur, *Lee's Legacy of Leadership,* Essex, CT: Greenwich Publishing Group, 1990.
Form 10-K: Lee Enterprises, Incorporated, Washington, DC: Securities and Exchange Commission, 1994.
Johnson, Charles S., "Lee Publishers, Governor Deny Making Sales-Tax Deal," *Missoulian,* May 25, 1993, sec. B., p. 1.
Marcial, Gene G., "Newspapers with Lots of Black Ink," *Business Week,* February 11, 1991, p. 70.
"Missoulian Editor Joins New Venture," *Missoulian,* May 7, 1994, sec. B, p. 1.
"Montana Magazine Purchased by Lee Enterprises," *Missoulian,* May 1, 1994, sec. B, p. 2.
Richgels, Jeff, "Burgess to Leave Journal," *Madison Capital Times,* April 1, 1993, sec. BUS.
Rondy, John, "Racine's Journal Times Takes the Flexographic Press Plunge," *Business Journal-Milwaukee,* February 12, 1994, sec. 2, p. 6A.
"Lee Enterprises Reports Earnings Slump," *Billings Gazette,* July 25, 1991, sec. C, p. 7.

—Dave Mote

Leggett & Platt, Incorporated

One Leggett Road
Carthage, Missouri 64836
U.S.A.
(417) 358-8131
Fax: (417) 358-6667

Public Company
Incorporated: 1901 as Leggett & Platt Spring Bed &
    Manufacturing Co.
Employees: 13,000
Sales: $1.52 billion
Stock Exchanges: New York Pacific
SICs: 2515 Mattresses & Bedsprings; 2511 Wood Household
    Furniture; 2514 Metal Household Furniture

Credited with launching the U.S. bedspring industry, Leggett &
Platt, Incorporated, one of the nation's largest manufacturers of
bedding and furnishing products, began operating in the late
19th century as the sole manufacturer of the coiled bedspring.
From this single product, invented and patented by one of the
company's founders, Leggett & Platt slowly expanded its product line to embrace a diverse assortment of products primarily
related to the furnishings industry. As the company's product
line evolved, so did the company, becoming a component supplier for other manufacturers rather than marketing and distributing its products at the retail level. Entering its second century
of business, Leggett & Platt's product line comprised four
product categories: bedding components, furniture components,
finished products, and diversified products, manufactured by
and distributed through a large network of strategically located
production and warehouse facilities.

Carthage, Missouri, in the late 19th century was home to two
men, each possessing distinct skills, who came together to
create a company that would outlive both them and their children, to flourish more than a century later. One of these men was
J. P. Leggett, an inventor who had achieved modest success
with several patented inventions, and the other was C. B. Platt, a
businessman and manufacturer, whose family owned a factory
in Carthage. By 1883, Leggett had developed an idea for a new
product and turned to Platt, his brother-in-law, to solicit his
manufacturing expertise and resources. Leggett's idea was innovative, a distinction that had already garnered him a patent,

and would literally support generations of Americans to come.
Leggett had invented the coiled bedspring.

Platt agreed to assist Leggett in manufacturing his invention,
and the two formed a partnership in 1883, using the Platt Plow
Works in Carthage as the production site for the first Leggett
bedsprings. Until Leggett had developed the coiled bedspring,
bedding in the United States generally consisted of cotton,
feather, or horsehair mattresses, with no added cushion beyond
that provided by the mattress material itself. Leggett's bedsprings were designed to be used as a foundation for these
mattresses, with the coils fabricated separately, then sold to
retail merchants and assembled in the backs of stores or on the
walkways in front.

For 12 years the Leggett and Platt partnership operated out of
the Platt Plow Works, forming the coils with belt-driven machinery and selling them to retail merchants. By 1895, the
partnership had its own factory and offices, a two-story building
that housed both sides of the young business's operations and
contained its entire work force, which at that point totaled seven
people, including the two founders. Before the decade was over,
another manufacturing plant was added in Louisville, Kentucky. Then, as if to formally recognize the recent expansion,
the partnership became a genuine corporation in 1901, incorporating under the name Leggett & Platt Spring Bed & Manufacturing Co., with Leggett serving as its first president.

The waning years of the century marked a rush of activity for
Leggett and Platt. The construction of two factories in five
years, after twelve years of production at Platt Plow Works, and
the incorporation of the growing concern appeared to fore-
shadow further expansion; however, the company would barely
exceed the pace of physical growth established between 1895
and 1900 in the 60 years following its incorporation. Moreover,
the first half century of Leggett's and Platt's business, from
1883 to 1933, would be almost entirely devoted to the production of a single product—Leggett's patented coil bedsprings.
So, from 1901 forward, the newly named Leggett & Platt Spring
Bed & Manufacturing Co. seemed resigned to fulfilling one
need with one product, with little effort expended toward expanding the company's scope. Leggett remained president until
1921, when Platt assumed the company's leadership and
oversaw the construction of a new factory in Carthage in 1925
to replace the now outdated original factory.

Platt's stewardship of Leggett & Platt devolved to Leggett's
son, J. P. Leggett, Jr., in 1929, a position he held for three years.
In that time he initiated the introduction of the company's first
new product in 50 years and its first diversification into another
market in 1933. Leggett & Platt began manufacturing springs
for innerspring mattresses that year, a product that would become increasingly integral to the company's operation. By this
time, Leggett & Platt had effected an important and defining
change in the way the company operated: it now sold its products to other manufacturers rather than to retailers, as the company had originally done. With a growing market for innerspring mattresses, the company found greater success and
greater profits selling springs to mattress manufacturers, who
then assembled a finished innerspring mattress with the springs
provided by Leggett & Platt. Perhaps equally important to the
evolution of Leggett & Platt into a diversified component spe-

cialist was its diversification into peripheral markets, specifically the manufacturing of coiled springs for the producers of upholstered furniture.

With these important changes behind it, and a rapidly growing market for springs waiting ahead, Leggett & Platt moved forward, past the Great Depression and toward the century's next notable event, the Second World War. A new factory was established in 1942, the first new location for a Leggett & Platt facility since the Louisville plant opened nearly 50 years earlier. Located in Winchester, Kentucky, the new factory absorbed the operations previously located in Louisville. Five years later, another new plant was established, this time in Ennis, Texas.

The addition of the Ennis plant concluded Leggett & Platt's physical growth until 1960, a pivotal year that would inaugurate for the company a new era of expansion and diversification, a new corporate strategy, and new leadership, transforming the modestly sized company into a formidable force in the furnishings industry. Chiefly responsible for this dramatic change in course was Harry M. Cornell, Jr., J. P. Leggett's grandson, who joined the company in 1950 and then became manager of the Ennis, Texas, plant in 1953. When he was appointed as the company's president in 1960, Cornell inherited from his father, H. M. Cornell, Sr., Leggett & Platt's president from 1953 to 1960, a company with three production plants and $7 million in annual sales.

The younger Cornell's plans for Leggett & Platt were entirely different than those actualized by each of the company's six previous presidents, who had limited Leggett & Platt's presence to a regional level. What Cornell saw after an examination of the U.S. furnishings industry was the opportunity for a company such as Leggett & Platt to capitalize on a highly fragmented market for finished furnishings products. This could be done, he theorized, by broadening Leggett & Platt's scope to a national level and by manufacturing and distributing components of furnishings products to manufacturers at a lower price than manufacturers could produce on their own. The first step in this direction was achieved during Cornell's first year as president, in October 1960, when the company acquired a small woodworking plant in Springfield, Missouri. Though the acquisition was small, it represented a move toward diversification, enabling Leggett & Platt to fabricate wood bed frames.

Additional acquisitions would follow, seven throughout the decade, as Leggett & Platt strategically added more facilities for manufacturing an increasing variety of bedding and furniture components. By the early 1970s, roughly a decade after the implementation of the company's new business philosophy, Leggett & Platt's growing network of manufacturing and distribution facilities comprised 17 manufacturing plants and five warehouses. Annual sales hovered around $50 million, reflecting a sales volume more than seven times greater than that recorded less than 15 years earlier. This growth translated into a 16.8 percent annual increase, a rate of percentage growth outpaced by the 25.5 percent annual increase recorded in the company's per share earnings since Leggett & Platt stock was first sold over-the-counter in 1967.

The company's growth and diversification fed upon its self. First, by bolstering its presence in the bedding and furnishings

market, the company increased its economies of scale, which proved to be Leggett & Platt's point of leverage in a fragmented industry. Secondly, the company had begun to vertically integrate, establishing production facilities that would supply its raw material needs. Through a joint venture with Armco Steel Corporation, Leggett & Platt constructed a wire mill in Carthage in 1970, enabling the company to satisfy virtually all of its wire needs within several years. Similarly, a wood saw mill was constructed in Naples, Texas, that same year, becoming operational the following year, to assure a steady source of lumber for the company's wood frame business.

Aside from Leggett & Platt's physical growth, progress was also being achieved in other areas, such as in the development of the company's products and in the machinery utilized to manufacture those products. At this point, in the early 1970s, the company had high hopes for a new and promising innerspring coil unit, the continuous coil spring, which required substantially less wire and less labor than the conventional coil assembly process. Also, new machinery for producing boxspring units was under development that would automate several manufacturing steps currently being performed by hand. All of these developments—the additional production facilities, the new products, the more sophisticated machinery—combined to increase and solidify Leggett & Platt's presence in the home-furnishings market, a market that was valued at $11 billion at the retail level, was growing 6 percent annually, and specifically contained $900 million worth of business for a company with Leggett & Platt's interests.

Concurrent with this growth, Leggett & Platt changed into a more diversified company, a change evinced by the proportional representation of the company's products in terms of the sales each product category generated. This shift was particularly evident in the early 1970s, when the production of bedding components began to contribute less to Leggett & Platt's sales volume. In 1970 bedding components accounted for 70 percent of the company's $40 million in sales; in 1974 the production of bedding components represented 43 percent of the company's $94 million in sales. This decline indicated significant diversification engendered by a greater focus on the company's finished furniture and upholstered furniture components product lines.

Entering the 1980s, Leggett & Platt's annual sales exceeded $250 million, having increased 18 percent annually from 1975 to 1980 despite a lackluster 1979. The company now had 60 manufacturing plants scattered throughout the United States that provided products for more than 10,000 large and small manufacturers. With 20 years of exponential growth behind it, the nation's largest independent supplier of components in the bedding industry continued to grow, doubling its sales volume by the mid-1980s to reach $500 million. This sales growth was even more remarkable considering the rest of the industry had suffered through three years of stagnant growth between 1980 and 1983. Leggett & Platt's continuous coil innerspring unit was partly responsible for the company's growth during an otherwise deleterious period for furnishings manufacturers. The product had inspired much confidence during the early 1970s, but had remained in a developmental stage for ten years and had finally been introduced in the mid-1980s.

Also contributing to the company's growth was a series of acquisitions, ten in the three-year period between 1983 and 1986, that, combined, had generated $164 million in sales before being acquired by Leggett & Platt. Two of these acquisitions in particular brought the company into the office furniture market, an arena in which the company wanted to increase its presence. Gordon Manufacturing Co., a Grand Rapids, Michigan, manufacturer of chair controls and steel bases for office furniture, was acquired in 1984, followed by the purchase of Northfield Metal Products, a leading manufacturer of similar products, a year later.

As part of a nationwide recession, Leggett & Platt experienced several years of less than robust growth in the early 1990s, posting a decline in sales between 1990 and 1991. Then the company began to show signs of recovery, recording a relatively small gain in 1992 of nearly $90 million to reach $1.17 billion in revenues. The company returned to its 30-year legacy of prodigious sales growth in 1993, registering $1.52 billion in sales. That same year it concluded two strategic acquisitions, adding to its network of 135 manufacturing facilities located throughout the United States and Canada. One of these was Hanes Holding Company, a converter and distributor of woven and non-woven industrial fabrics used in the construction of furniture and bedding. The other, Hickory, North Carolina-based VWR Textiles & Supplies, Inc., gave Leggett & Platt additional furniture and bedding fabric manufacturing re-

sources, strengthening its position in another market related to the furnishings industry. As of 1993 the company held 22 percent of the furniture and bedding components market, and, expecting to record 15 percent sales and earnings growth, Leggett & Platt anticipated garnering a an even greater share of various markets valued at an estimated $5.3 billion.

Principal Subsidiaries: Berkshire Furniture Co.; Collier-Keyworth Company.

Further Reading:

''Efforts to Integrate Operations Paying Off for Leggett & Platt,'' *Barron's*, August 2, 1971, p. 28.

Eidelman, David R., ''Leggett & Platt, Inc.,'' *Wall Street Transcript*, December 22, 1975, p. 42,325.

Gordon, Mitchell, ''Springing Ahead,'' *Barron's,* January 4, 1982, p. 41.

Langenberg, Oliver M., ''Leggett & Platt,'' *Wall Street Transcript,* August 14, 1972, p. 29,582.

''Leggett & Platt Says Appeals Court Reversed Antitrust-Suit Dismissal,'' *Wall Street Journal,* October 1, 1976, p. 32.

''Leggett & Platt Wins Dismissal of U.S. Suit on Antitrust Charges,'' *Wall Street Journal,* March 17, 1975, p. 14.

Our Hundredth Year 1883–1983. Carthage: Leggett & Platt, Incorporated, 1983.

''A Real Front-Runner: Leggett & Platt Outperforms Its Industry,'' *Barron's,* November 17, 1986, p. 58.

—Jeffrey L. Covell

Lennar Corporation

700 Northwest 107th Avenue
Miami, Florida 33172
U.S.A.
(305) 559-4000
Fax: (305) 226-4158

Public Company
Incorporated: 1969
Employees: 1,660
Sales: $666.9 million
Stock Exchanges: New York Boston Philadelphia
SICs: 6719 Holding Companies, Nec; 1521 Single-Family
    Housing Construction; 1542 Nonresidential Construction,
    Nec; 2431 Millwork; 6552 Subdividers & Developers, Nec

Florida's largest home builder and one of the largest residential builders in the country, Lennar Corporation began as a Miami-based residential home-building company, then later diversified into real estate investments and financial services to mitigate its dependence on a cyclical housing construction market. By the 1990s, Lennar was a full-service real estate company principally involved in designing, building, and selling all types of residential housing, but primarily focused on the market for first-time home buyers, or those homes selling for under $100,000. In addition to the company's considerable presence in the Florida home-building market, Lennar maintained a presence in Texas and Arizona as well. Lennar's financial services and investment businesses, operating as Lennar Financial Services, Inc., and the company's Investment Division, respectively, were national in scope and key contributors to the company's revenue total. Through its financial services subsidiary, Lennar originated or serviced mortgage loans in 48 states, provided title services, and operated a mortgage loan brokerage business, while the company's asset management business purchased and managed commercial real estate, including shopping centers, office buildings, warehouses, apartment properties, and mobile home parks.

Lennar's origins date to 1954, when Arnold P. Rosen, a home builder who had been involved in constructing residential homes in the Miami area for roughly ten years, founded F & R Builders, Inc. In 1956, shortly after the creation of F & R, an individual who would figure prominently Lennar's development moved to Florida, intent on utilizing his land development

and marketing skills. His name was Leonard Miller, a 23 year-old entrepreneur with $10,000 and 42 empty lots in Dade County, Florida.

Not long after his arrival in Florida, Miller participated in several joint ventures with Arnold Rosen and his fledgling construction company, adding his land management and marketing skills to Rosen's proven technical ability to build low- and medium-priced single-family homes. Soon, the business relationship between Rosen and Miller became a more permanent one, more than just an alliance for particular projects; Miller joined F & R Builders, devoting his energy to making the company a leader in the competitive Miami market.

By the mid-1960s, the partnership of Miller and Rosen had proved to be a boon to F & R Builders' growth, enabling the company to become the largest home builder in the greater Miami area in roughly a decade. As F & R Builders continued to expand, capturing a significant share of the low- and medium-price residential market, a market that included first-time home buyers and a growing number of new Florida residents looking to purchase retirement homes, Miller and Rosen decided to make their growing concern a publicly owned company. For the express intention of achieving this objective, Lennar Corporation was formed in 1969, with F & R Builders constituting its primary asset.

Lennar completed its underwriting and became a public company two years later, in 1971, when stock in the company was sold over the counter. It was listed on the American Exchange until 1972, when it began selling on the New York Stock Exchange. Using the funds from its stock sale, Lennar began to broaden its area of operation. Under the leadership of Miller, the company's chairman and president, and Rosen, its executive vice president, Lennar, still operating essentially as F & R Builders, expanded beyond Miami and the surrounding Dade County region. This expansion began in earnest in 1973, when Lennar entered the Phoenix, Arizona, market with the acquisition of Mastercraft Homes, Inc., for approximately $2 million, and Womack Development Company, both established home builders in the greater Phoenix area. Shortly thereafter, Lennar established housing operations in the midwestern United States by purchasing Bert L. Smokler & Company, based in Detroit, Michigan, and Dreyfus Interstate Development Corp., based in Minneapolis-St. Paul, Minnesota.

High inflation and a recession during the mid-1970s struck serious blows to the residential housing industry, which suffered from, among other problems, over-built inventories. Lennar was not immune to the negative conditions afflicting many home builders and incurred its share of losses; however, the downturn in housing construction starts did provide the company's management time to integrate the recent acquisitions into Lennar's operations and further develop the company's business philosophy. An intrinsic objective of this philosophy, created in part during F & R Builders' rise during the 1950s and strikingly germane during the downswing now restraining the company's growth, was the need for Lennar to develop a core earnings base unrelated to the frequently volatile housing construction market. As the company planned for the future, this objective became paramount, eventually leading to Lennar's diversification into other types of businesses and helping to ensure the company's solvency during future construction downturns.

By 1977 the U.S. housing industry had fully recovered from the difficulties hampering its growth during the mid-1970s, and so had Lennar, recording $83 million in sales for the year, up from $55 million registered the previous year. The following year, in 1978, revenues soared 60 percent, reaching $133 million, and earnings doubled to over $7 million. Florida still represented Lennar's primary market, accounting for 66 percent of its total housing deliveries, whereas its Midwest and Arizona markets accounted for 15 percent and 19 percent, respectively. By this time, in the late 1970s, the company was responding to changing consumer housing needs by constructing townhouses and condominiums. In addition, it was diversifying into other business activities as part of its plan to develop a core earnings base exclusive of the home-building market. Initially, Lennar gained entry into these other business sectors as a reward for its financially conservative and prudent management policies, which earned the respect of several lending institutions in Florida. These lending institutions asked Lennar to assume management responsibility for problem projects in their portfolios, leading, in many cases, to the acquisition of such projects by Lennar and signaling the beginning of the company's involvement in asset management.

In 1981, Lennar diversified further, entering the home mortgage business and originating what would later become Lennar Financial Services, Inc. The number of housing starts initiated by the company fell in 1981 and 1982, and a commensurate decline its earnings followed in the second year of the downturn. That year Lennar entered a joint property-development venture with Guaranty Properties Ltd., a subsidiary of Toronto-based Traders Group Ltd., to develop a 1,830-acre property in Orlando, Florida. Also in 1982, the company purchased H. Miller & Sons, Inc., for $24 million.

Lennar was able to assume the role of acquirer during such depressed economic periods partly because of its dependable management practices, but also because the addition of its asset management and home mortgage businesses had enabled a refinement of the company's long-standing conservative operating philosophy. Typically, during peak construction periods, home-building companies funneled their profits toward greater growth, buying additional land and constructing more homes, essentially attempting to capitalize on an expanding market. When the demand for home-building subsided, however, and the market plummeted into one of its capricious tailspins, many of these home builders found themselves over-extended and unable to survive the downturn. Lennar's management, on the other hand, approached robust periods of market growth differently, avoiding the impulse to expand rapidly when demand seemed insatiable. Instead, the company attempted to generate as much profit from each construction project as possible, then use the profit to lower the company's debt. When the home-building market once again slowed, Lennar was well positioned to reap the rewards of a depressed market—cheap and available land—at a time when a majority of its competitors were struggling to meet costs with their surplus land inventories.

This strategy served Lennar well as it progressed through the 1980s and into the 1990s, enabling it to increase its market share

in its areas of home building. Moreover, the company's additional investments in nonconstruction related businesses bolstered its revenue-generating ability during recessive financial periods, providing a hedge against the cyclicality of its primary business activity. In 1987, Lennar reorganized its financial services operations into Lennar Financial Services, Inc., the product of its entry into the home mortgage business six years earlier. By this time Lennar had withdrawn from the Midwest market and was considering an entrance into the Texas market, a location more consistent with its presence in other Sun Belt states. Still, however, the company's primary focus was on Florida, where Lennar controlled a significant portion of the home-building market. Its position in Florida was strengthened further with the acquisition of the home-building assets and operations of Richmond American Homes of Florida, Inc., in 1988 for approximately $18 million, and, in January 1989, with the purchase of M.D.C. for a similar price.

As Lennar entered the 1990s, the dynamics of the housing market in Florida were changing, engendered by rising construction prices, an economy that was beginning to show signs of deteriorating, and by changing demographics. Combined, these forces put an end to the rapid pace of construction experienced during the late 1980s, which was financed largely by the soon-to-fail savings and loan industry. The importance of several market niches increased, particularly the market for low- and medium-priced homes within reach of more pragmatic and cost-conscious consumers. Because Lennar had specialized in this market throughout its history, the company was positioned to capitalize on the changing business environment. However, a greater test of Lennar's operating strategy and financial resources was coming, as a nationwide recession gained momentum, and city, state, and regional economies soured.

The early 1990s were disastrous years for many home builders as orders for new construction evaporated, sending a considerable number of Lennar's competitors out of business or significantly reducing their ability to operate successfully. Lennar, however, posted its highest earnings gain in its history in 1991, recording a 56 percent leap to $8 million, despite a drop in revenues from $350.8 million in 1990 to $325.7 million. The company's sound operating philosophy, most apparent in a poor economic climate, had underpinned its profits as construction lagged and enabled it to become an acquirer at a time when other home builders were struggling to survive.

Lennar entered the Texas market in 1991, after four years of experimentation, and began construction in suburban Dallas. By the following year, the company had purchased 28,000 lots, primarily located in Florida, and opened a 1,400-home retirement complex in Phoenix. As part of this period of expansion, Lennar purchased the portfolio of a failed savings and loan institution, AmeriFirst Bank, formerly the largest in Florida, from the Resolution Trust Corporation for an estimated $450 million. Purchased in partnership with The Morgan Stanley Real Estate Fund, the AmeriFirst portfolio gave Lennar more than 1,100 commercial and residential properties and loans, including thousands of acres already approved for residential construction.

In 1993, as the U.S. economy began to recover, Lennar's revenues leaped 55 percent over the total recorded in 1992, reaching

$666.9 million. Earnings shot up as well, rising from $29.1 million in 1992 to 1993's total of $52.5 million, an 80 percent increase. By this time, the company had augmented its presence in Texas, adding Houston's housing market to its already established Dallas market. Together, the three states in which Lennar operated home-building operations generated $514 million in revenues, with Florida accounting for 80 percent of the total and Arizona and Texas accounting for 13 percent and 7 percent, respectively.

The company's subsidiary, Lennar Financial Services, originated $1.3 billion in new home mortgages during the year, bringing the value of the company's loan servicing portfolio to $3.4 billion. An equally strong performance was demonstrated by Lennar's Investment Division, largely because of two enormous acquisitions, the AmeriFirst purchase and an interest in a portfolio acquired in partnership with Westinghouse Electric Corporation and an affiliate of Lehman Brothers. These two acquisitions, concluded in the two years prior to 1993, gave Lennar an interest in real estate management assets valued at more than $4 billion, complementing an already solid combination of business interests that provided an enviable foundation for the company's future.

Principal Subsidiaries: Lennar Homes, Inc.; Lennar Homes of Arizona, Inc.; Lennar Homes of Texas, Inc.; Lennar Financial Services, Inc.; Universal American Mortgage Company; AmeriStar Financial Services, Inc.; Universal Title Insurors, Inc.; Lennar Funding Corp.; Loan Funding, Inc.; Lennar Commercial Properties, Inc.; Lennar Management Corp.; Universal American Realty Corp.

Further Reading:

Aschoff, Susan, "Rethinking the Home," *Florida Trend,* June 1992, p. 26.

Hackney, Holt, "Lennar: More Favorable Winds," *Financial World,* March 15, 1994, p. 20.

Johansen, Bert, "Lennar," *Wall Street Transcript,* April 16, 1973, p. 32,591.

"Lennar Bids for Easy Terms," *Florida Trend,* July 1992, p. 89.

"Lennar Corporation," *Wall Street Transcript,* November 5, 1972, p. 30,625.

"Lennar Corporation," *Wall Street Transcript,* May 14, 1979, p. 54,347.

"Lennar-Development Corp. Tie," *Wall Street Journal,* March 18, 1987, p. 5.

"Lennar Property Venture," *Wall Street Journal,* January 12, 1984, p. 36.

"Lennar to Buy Properties," *Wall Street Journal,* October 27, 1987, p. 25.

Palmer, Jay, "Bucking the Trend," *Barron's,* November 4, 1991, p. 12.

Poole, Claire, "Pyramiding Down," *Forbes,* July 6, 1992, p. 98.

Zipser, Andy, "After Andrew," *Barron's,* October 12, 1992, p. 20.

—Jeffrey L. Covell

Leucadia National Corporation

315 Park Avenue South
New York, New York 10010
U.S.A.
(212) 460-1900
Fax: (212) 598-4869

Public Company
Incorporated: 1969 as Talcott National Corporation
Employees: 4,372
Sales: $1.408.1 billion
Stock Exchanges: New York Pacific
SICs: 6719 Holding Companies, Nec; 6141 Personal Credit
   Institutions; 6153 Short-Term Business Credit; 6311 Life
   Insurance; 2434 Wood Kitchen Cabinets; 3089 Plastics
   Products, Nec; 3261 Vitreous Plumbing Fixtures

A holding company, Leucadia National Corporation owned an array of companies involved in diverse businesses, ranging from insurance to motivational services, to manufacturing. Although the roots of Leucadia National stretch back to 1854, the essence of the company in the 1990s reflected a truly modern creation: a company formed through the acquisition of various businesses, irrespective of their business lines. Leucadia began to grow through acquisitions in 1980, and from that year forward purchased companies that increased its financial magnitude. Through the course of the company's growth during the 1980s, it became heavily involved in the insurance business, specifically commercial and personal property and casualty insurance, as well as health and life insurance. In addition to these businesses, Leucadia National also owned significant interests in banking and lending, trading stamps, bathroom vanities manufacturing, and motivational services. By the early 1990s, the company had achieved encouraging results, raising its annual revenue total from $39 million in 1980 to $1.40 billion in 1993.

Both the Leucadia name and the corporate strategy that engendered its exponential increase in revenues emerged in 1980, but the foundation from which Leucadia was built was formed more than a century earlier, in 1854, when James Talcott, Inc. was established. James Talcott, Inc., incorporated 60 years after it was created as a factoring concern, generated revenue initially by accepting accounts receivable from companies involved in the textile industry and using those accounts as security to provide short-term loans. James Talcott, Inc.'s importance to Leucadia,

however, did not arise until the company evolved into a more diversified concern, when it began acquiring numerous financial institutions during the 1950s and 1960s, becoming, in 1968, Talcott National Corporation, a company engaged in commercial financing, real estate mortgage financing, equipment financing and leasing, factoring, and consumer financing.

Shortly after Talcott National came into being, the seeds for Leucadia's emergence were sown. In the early 1970s the company launched an imprudent diversification into insurance, fire engines, leather processing, and machine parts that led to a $20 million loss in 1972. Although the company attempted to recover, the losses resulting from the early 1970s saddled Talcott National with mounting debt. From 1972 to 1977 these losses amounted to $355 million, and the company began to flounder, reeling from successive, unprofitable years during the decade.

Although the company was on the brink of failure, several Utah businessmen, led by a Salt Lake City investor named Brooke Grant, believed they could extricate Talcott National from its financial malaise. The investors formed Uintah National Corp. in 1976 to purchase a controlling interest in Talcott National. They borrowed $6.9 million to buy 1.6 million Talcott National shares, which gave them a 53 percent stake in the company. Grant set out to rebuild Talcott National. Within a year of assuming control of the company, Grant enlisted the help of a young, respected businessman named Ian M. Cumming, who was president of a Utah-based land development company and who would soon become the chief architect of Leucadia's creation.

While working at New York-based Carl Marks & Co., a specialty Wall Street firm active in leveraged buyouts and venture capital, Cumming convinced his company to invest $1.5 million in a small land development company in Utah named Terracor. The company's investment, however, began to sour in the early 1970s, when a deteriorating market for second homes negatively affected Terracor's business, so the Wall Street investment firm sent Cumming to Utah in 1971 to help Terracor effect a recovery. Cumming became president of Terracor within several months after his arrival, then began cutting the company's expenses and repositioning its role in the housing market.

Although Terracor continued to lose money, incurring more than $100 million in debt during the decade, Cumming's talents gained Grant's attention, and he called Cumming, asking for his help in restoring Talcott National's financial health. Cumming was elected as Talcott National's chairman and president in mid 1978. Cumming's leadership of the company was open to much debate several years later, when two lawsuits were filed against him. Once Cumming assumed stewardship of the company, he decided against the plan he and Grant had originally formulated to sell a large group of Talcott National's assets to pay off its debt. Instead, he decided to sell the portfolios of the company's commercial loan offices piece by piece, enlisting the help of Carl Marks & Co. in New York, and recruiting a former Harvard Business School classmate and vice-president at Carl Marks & Co., Joseph S. Steinberg, to assist him in his endeavors at Talcott National.

Once Cumming and Steinberg were together at Talcott National they began engineering a plan to take the company over. They convinced Talcott National's creditor banks to approve a restructuring plan in 1979, then formed a partnership with Carl Marks & Co. and Stern & Stern Textiles, a textiles company that Steinberg had helped acquire while at Carl Marks & Co. Named TLC Associates, this partnership included Cumming, Steinberg, John W. Jordan II, a former Carl Marks vice-president, and Lawrence D. Glaubinger, Stern & Stern's chairman. After some initial disagreements between Cumming and Grant, TLC purchased Uintah and thereby a controlling interest in Talcott National, paying Grant slightly more than $900,000 and two of his remaining partners $28,000 to assume Uintah's $7.4 million in debt.

Several years later, in 1982, after Talcott National had become Leucadia and the company's stock began to soar, Grant filed a lawsuit against Cumming, accusing him of breach of contract and violations of fiduciary duty and security laws. Grant claimed he had not been paid the fair market value for his shares in Talcott National and that he had never received an additional payment he and Cumming had agreed upon in a peripheral deal during the TLC-Uintah negotiations, accusations that Cumming denied were true.

As this legal battle intensified, Cumming and TLC become the object of another lawsuit that same year, when Senior Corp., Terracor's main creditor, demanded Leucadia stock as partial payment of the more than $100 million debt Terracor owed. Senior Corp. charged that Cumming, who was still president of Terracor while he was working for Talcott National, had used Terracor funds to loan Grant $200,000 after his arrival at Talcott National, and had used Terracor time to negotiate for and acquire Talcott National, which entitled Senior Corp., according to its argument, to a portion of Leucadia.

Both of these cases were settled within the next two years. In the dispute with Grant, Cumming was ordered to pay $4.5 million, which he obtained from Leucadia, and in the lawsuit involving Senior Corp., Cumming and his associates retained their shares in Leucadia and gave Senior Corp. approximately half of the properties owned by Terracor, properties that were worth roughly $20 million at the time.

Part of the underlying reason both Grant and Senior Corp. had pursued their lawsuits against Cumming was attributable to the rapid success Leucadia had enjoyed during its first several years under Cumming's and Steinberg's guidance. From 1980 to 1984, the year the last of Cumming's legal disputes were concluded, the two partners had transformed Leucadia from a company with $39 million in annual revenues to a company that generated $232 million in annual revenues. Essentially all of this growth had been realized through acquisitions orchestrated by Cumming and Steinberg, something both were adept at and something they both began engaging in shortly after they gained control of Talcott National.

In 1980, after changing Talcott National's name to Leucadia National Corporation, Cumming and Steinberg sold the company's factoring unit, James Talcott Factors Inc., the 126 year-old remnant of James Talcott, Inc., to U.K.-based Lloyds & Scottish Ltd. for approximately $123 million. Once divested of

the company's factoring unit, Cumming and Steinberg set out to expand Leucadia's operations through acquisition, a strategy they would employ throughout the decade and one they first put into practice in December of 1980.

For Leucadia's first acquisition, Cumming and Steinberg selected American Investment Company, owner of a small-loan company and life insurance firm, which combined were much larger than Leucadia. To finance the acquisition, Leucadia arranged for American Investment to purchase the net assets of Leucadia's consumer finance company, for which Leucadia received $94 million, and then used the money obtained from this sale to purchase American Investment for $73.6 million. Leucadia then made three significant investments in 1982 by first purchasing a 57 percent interest in TFI Companies, Inc., then becoming a 50 percent partner in a newly formed private investment firm managed by John Jordan II, called The Jordan Company. The third investment was the acquisition of Terracor, the company that had originally brought Cumming to Utah. Leucadia purchased the remainder of Terracor after the settlement with Senior Corp. for $5.9 million.

By 1984, Leucadia's partnership in The Jordan Company had given it an interest in ten companies, which added $4.8 million to the company's profit total for the year. Its most profitable achievement for the year, however, and a striking example of Cumming's ability to generate profit through aggressive corporate tactics, involved an attempted acquisition of Avco Corp., a defense supplier as well as a financial concern. Over a five-month period, Leucadia spent $77.5 million to acquire a 12 percent stake in Avco, then made a $930 million bid for the company. Not wishing to sell, Avco's management decided to buy back the stock Leucadia had acquired for $100 million. This by itself gave Leucadia a $22.5 million profit, but Cumming had secured an agreement with Avco that stipulated if Avco was acquired by another company within a year, then it would pay Leucadia the per-share difference between the price Avco's acquirer paid and the price Avco paid Leucadia to buy back its stock. Within the agreed upon time frame, a company named Textron acquired Avco for $50-a-share, $14.25 more per share than Avco had paid Leucadia, which gave Cumming's company an additional $39.8 million in profit.

By the mid 1980s, among the host of companies Leucadia either owned or maintained an interest in, the company's two principal operations were a small-loan company named City Finance Company, which James Talcott, Inc. had purchased in 1966, and Charter National Life Insurance Company, an insurance firm that sold single-premium life policies. Leucadia's investments were strengthened considerably in 1988, when Leucadia increased its interest to 64 percent in PHLCorp, a company it became involved in during a failed takeover four years earlier. One of PHLCorp.'s main operating properties was The Sperry & Hutchinson Company, Inc., which was later divided into two divisions after Leucadia increased its ownership of PHLCorp. These two divisions were organized as a trading stamp business and motivation services business, which designed and managed incentive programs. The other main operating property belonging to PHLCorp., and the company that enriched Leucadia's insurance holdings, was Empire Insurance and its then-85 percent owned affiliate Allcity Insurance Co. Based in New York and primarily serving the New York City metropolitan area,

Empire wrote property and casualty policies, which broadened the scope Leucadia's insurance operations and added assets to the company valued at more than $200 million.

By this time, at the end of 1988, Leucadia was generating roughly $735 million in annual revenues and well on its way toward recording a $1 billion increase in its sales volume in a decade. An enormous step toward that direction was achieved in 1991, when the company acquired Colonial Penn Group Insurance Co. from FPL Group for $150 million. Leucadia's third insurance company, Colonial Penn was a direct marketing insurance company that became an integral component of the company's life insurance business and a nationwide provider of private passenger automobile insurance and homeowners insurance.

The addition of Colonial Penn helped elevate Leucadia's revenues to $1.57 billion in 1992, up from $1.08 billion recorded the year before, and a tremendous increase from the $39 million generated in 1980. By the conclusion of 1993, after 15 years of Cumming's and Steinberg's leadership, the value of Leucadia had increased considerably. The net worth of the company at year's end was $907.8 million, or $32.54 per share, compared to negative $0.22 in 1978 when Cumming and Steinberg assumed management of Talcott National. Leucadia's stock price also demonstrated commensurate growth, soaring from $0.16 in 1978 to $41 by 1993.

As the company planned for the future, it focused on increasing the profitability of its investments rather than increasing their market share or magnitude, a corporate philosophy that Cumming and Steinberg believed, as they wrote in a letter to the company shareholders in 1993, conformed to "the theory that the world can tolerate many mice, but few elephants." Operating according to this strategy, Leucadia looked for further growth in the 1990s.

Principal Subsidiaries: American Investment Bank, North America; American Financial; Charter National Life Insurance Company; Empire Insurance Group; Colonial Penn Life Insurance Company; Colonial Penn Insurance Company; CP Group; The Sperry & Hutchinson Company, Inc.; Allcity Insurance Co.; PHLCORP, Inc.; Charter National Life Insurance Company.

Further Reading:

"Colonial Penn Life, PA.," *Best's Review - Life-Health Insurance Edition,* June 1991, p. 122.

George, John, "Leucadia Buys Colonial Penn for $150 Million," *Philadelphia Business Journal,* April 15, 1991, p. 3.

"Package Deal," *Forbes,* April 1, 1976, p. 71.

Rosenberg, Hilary, "Elusive Leucadia," *Barron's,* November 11, 1985, p. 6.

Schwer, Robert B., "Hidden Value," *Barron's,* November 26, 1990, p. 16.

—Jeffrey L. Covell

Litton

Litton Industries, Inc.

360 North Crescent Drive
Beverly Hills, California 90210-9990
U.S.A.
(310) 859-5000
Fax: (310) 859-5940

Public Company
Incorporated: 1953 as Electro Dynamics Corp.
Employees: 29,000
Sales: $3.4 billion
Stock Exchanges: New York Zurich Amsterdam Boston
    Cincinnati NASDAQ Philadelphia Pacific
SICs: 3812 Search and Navigation Equipment; 3663 Radio
    and TV Communications Equipment; 3731 Ship Building
    and Repairing; 3550 Special Industry Machinery; 3699
    Electrical Machinery, Equipment and Supplies, Not
    Elsewhere Classified; 3571 Electronic Computers; 7373
    Computer Aided Systems Design

The U.S. conglomerate Litton Industries, Inc. has endured one of the American business world's most famous expansion odysseys. From its foundation in 1953 through the late 1960s, Litton's annual sales grew from $3 million to $1.8 billion as the company expanded from a relatively small electronics company to a far-flung aggregation of interests on the momentum of myriad acquisitions. Mounting debt, increasing bureaucracy, and other problems brought about an equally dramatic descent. By 1994, divestments whittled Litton down to two businesses: defense electronics and shipbuilding. The electronics segment included industry-leading electronic surveillance and aircraft guidance systems and missile cruisers. In the early 1990s, those high-tech electronic warfare products were in high demand around the world. Litton's Ingalls Shipbuilding subsidiary was one of America's largest and the world's most successful. It manufactured and repaired amphibious assault ships and guided missile cruisers. The U.S. Navy was one of Litton's best customers in both its business segments, and government contracts in general constituted over two-thirds of the company's revenues in the 1990s. The majority of Litton's operations were located in the United States, but the company also had plants in Germany, Canada, and Italy.

By the time he founded Litton in 1953, Charles "Tex" Thornton had compiled quite a resumé. Born to a family of modest means, Thornton made his first real estate investment at 14 and owned a filling station and car dealership at the age of 19. Thornton's reputation as an astute businessman was established during World War II when he designed a statistical control system that vastly improved the U.S. government's ability to procure and allocate military equipment.

Thornton and his associates, who included Robert S. McNamara, Arjay Miller, and Roy Ash, achieved fame during World War II as the Air Force's "Whiz Kids." After the war, the entire group was hired by Ford Motor Company. After two years at Ford, however, Thornton went to work for Howard Hughes and helped establish Hughes Aircraft Company in the semiconductor market. When Thornton tired of Hughes's eccentric business practices, he decided to form his own company.

When Thornton organized his company, he did not have any capital. However, he correctly believed that the U.S. Department of Defense would soon be seeking increasingly sophisticated weapons and that there would be room in the defense industry for another large electronics company. Due to the fact that small electronics firms tended eventually to be eliminated or absorbed by larger competitors, Thornton resolved that his company would grow and expand quickly, by making acquisitions if necessary. His company would have to be large if it was to compete with rivals like Howard Hughes.

Thornton believed that the success of his plan depended on surrounding himself with financially astute and technically proficient businessmen. Since he could not offer high salaries, he used stock options to induce people to join him. Over the years, the list of "Lidos" (Litton dropouts) read like a Who's Who of prominent American businessmen: Harry Gray built United Technologies Corporation; Dr. Henry Singleton founded Teledyne, Inc.(which later owned a significant stake in Litton); Arjay Miller became president of Ford Motor Company; and Robert McNamara became a Ford president, the U.S. Secretary of Defense, and head of the World Bank.

With the help of Roy Ash and Hugh Jamieson, Thornton formed a company called Electro Dynamics Corp., and immediately set out to find the small electronics company on which they would build their empire. Litton Industries, a vacuum tube manufacturer located near San Francisco, California, seemed the ideal choice. The only problem involved raising the $1.5 million necessary to purchase the firm from its founder, Charles Litton. After an agreement with Joseph Kennedy collapsed, Thornton and Ash approached Lehman Brothers, an investment firm. Lehman Brothers had followed Thornton's career since he was a vice-president at Hughes Aircraft and had decided to finance Thornton before he even requested assistance. Joseph Thomas from Lehman Brothers later said that their firm did not invest in Electro Dynamics as much as it invested in the ability of Thornton.

Using borrowed money, Thornton acquired Litton Industries in 1954 and purchased a few smaller electronics firms that same year. Thornton's strategy was to continue purchasing electronics companies with high growth potential and build Litton into a company that could meet almost any request for advanced technology.

Since Thornton knew Litton stock would eventually increase in value, he paid cash for companies whenever possible. Colleagues claimed that one of Thornton's techniques for arriving at a good price for a company was to continue the negotiations for as long as possible until physical exhaustion caused the other party to yield. After acquiring a company, Thornton allowed the original employees as much freedom as possible, so they could continue conducting the operations that made the company desirable in the first place.

When he purchased Litton Industries, Thornton promised Lehman Brothers that his company, with $8 million in sales, would have $100 million in sales by 1959. As it turned out, Litton Industries reached $120 million in sales by that year. In order to reach and exceed his goal, Thornton had merged with Monroe Calculating Machines. Monroe benefited from Litton's technological assets while Litton needed Monroe's sales and service outlets. Besides calculators, Litton was manufacturing inertial guidance systems for aircraft, potentometers, barratons, duplexers, klystroms, and other electronic products. During this period, almost 50 percent of Litton's business was with the U.S. government.

By 1961, Litton was the fastest growing company on the New York Stock Exchange. Litton's success during this time was attributed largely to Thornton's business acumen. Although Thornton had built Hughes Aircraft into a leader in the field of semiconductors, he kept his own company out of that market. The semiconductor market crashed in 1961, confirming Thornton's decision. Thornton also refrained from manufacturing transistors, which overcrowded the market in the early 1960s.

When Litton stock began selling at 33 times earnings (it was later to reach 75), some analysts suggested that the company would soon experience financial difficulties; Litton had acquired 23 companies in eight years. Thornton defended himself by pointing out that he purchased companies on the basis of how well they were managed and then provided the management with the money and freedom they needed to develop new products. The rate of growth for these companies, which averaged 50 percent a year, was produced internally as well as through acquisitions.

By 1963, sales reached $500 million. An article in *Fortune* magazine suggested that Litton's success lay in going against the current wisdom. For instance, in its defense work, Litton concentrated on procuring contracts for manned aircraft and let other contractors fight over missile contracts. The U.S. Air Force's need for aircraft turned out to be greater than anyone had previously suspected.

One of Litton's most important acquisitions was Ingalls Shipbuilding Corporation, the country's third largest private shipbuilder. The large but ailing company was purchased for $8 million in cash and the assumption of $9 million in debt. The appeal of the company was that it made submarines and oil-drilling equipment to which Litton's electronic controls could be added.

In the mid-1960s, Litton continued to sustain its high rate of growth, even after it passed the one billion dollar mark in sales. Although it continued to acquire more companies, Litton resisted defining itself as a conglomerate; instead, it referred to itself as a "technological company," or a multi-industry manufacturer of products whose common denominator was their technological complexity. Where Stouffer frozen foods and Royal typewriters fit into the picture was not clear. Yet Roy Ash spoke of the electronics empire as "a company that is meaningful as a whole" with "a coherent relationship between its different parts."

After 57 quarters of remarkable growth, Litton reported a decline in earnings of $11 million and, as a result, its stock plummeted. Investors incurred a paper loss of $2 million. The decline in profits would not have been such a catastrophe if Litton stock had not been selling at 40 times earnings, and if Litton had not conducted a certain type of publicity campaign. Critics charged that Litton's true innovations were in investor relations, rather than in high technology.

Forbes magazine described Litton's annual reports as "a feast for the eye and a famine for the mind." In fact, Litton used unusual, but not illegal, accounting techniques that exaggerated the company's growth. Litton convinced its stockholders to look at the company's "synergy" and its "meaning as a whole" rather than scrutinize figures that would have revealed some money losers among Litton's acquisitions. The company's highly publicized technological innovations and perceived advantage in the market was also exaggerated. For example, the license for Litton's microwave oven was owned by Raytheon, the company that invented it. It was revealed that Litton relied heavily on other companies' research and development of new products. Litton's success resulted from producing other companies' inventions inexpensively; when it had to depend on its own designs the company often ran into difficulties.

Part of Litton's failure to develop better products was attributed to the company's emphasis on short-term growth. Management often overlooked long-term research and development in favor of immediate financial gains. Although Litton executives envisioned themselves as part of a high technology conglomerate, according to *Business Week* magazine the company was "a mundane manufacturer of capital goods."

In 1972, Litton's credibility was further damaged by Roy Ash's claim that after three years of declining profits, Litton's sales would revive that year. Instead of sales reviving, however, the company recorded a $2.3 million deficit. The division most seriously affected was Ingalls Shipbuilding, which had recently built a large shipyard. Due to delays in building a number of container ships, Litton was forced to pay a total of $5 million in penalties. In addition, due to delays by the shipbuilder in meeting a $1 billion contract for landing helicopter assault ships, the U.S. Navy decided to reduce its initial order from nine to five ships.

In 1973, Fred O'Green, an engineer, was chosen by Thornton to replace the departing president Roy Ash. O'Green was instructed by Thornton to reduce Litton's holdings and improve its technological competence. O'Green was chosen because of his experience with Ingalls Shipbuilding. It was thought that O'Green could use his expertise to correct production and design problems at the shipyard.

O'Green began to analyze Litton's various businesses and separate the profitable ones from the money losers. In 1974, Litton reported $77 million in write-offs in the business systems division, which had lost money for two consecutive years. In 1979, the company sold its Triumph-Adler typewriter business, which had lagged far behind its competitors. The largest write-off, however, was the $333 million of cost overruns Ingalls Shipbuilding absorbed from the five disputed helicopter ships it had built for the U.S. Navy.

As Litton eliminated its losing businesses, the company's more successful ventures became apparent. Western Geophysical emerged as one of Litton's most profitable holdings; its seismic exploration services prospered during the 1970s oil crisis. Western Geophysical had compiled over 200,000 miles of logs charting seismic activity and these logs were a priceless source of information for oil drillers to pinpoint sources for oil. With 30 research ships collecting data around the world, Western Geophysical led the world in providing seismic information to the oil industry.

Another source of profit for Litton was its guidance and control business. Litton's most significant contribution to the high technology field was its inertial guidance system, which helped keep planes on their flight routes. As a direct result of the effectiveness of this system, Litton procured a $1.6 billion contract from the Saudi Arabian Air Force.

Problems at Ingalls Shipbuilding were eventually corrected. Profits increased from $44 million in 1979 to $78 million in 1983. Due to Litton's large capital investment in the shipyards, Ingalls' success was crucial to the financial stability of the company. The importance of Ingalls Shipbuilding to Litton was underscored when Western Geophysical's profits declined because of a decrease in oil exploration during the early 1980s.

During the 1980s, Litton finally became the high technology company it had always regarded itself. Orion Hoch, who took over as chief executive officer in late 1986, oversaw the divestment of 14 major unprofitable and non-related businesses representing over $1 billion in sales. Over the course of the decade, Litton exited business machines, publishing, medical products, office furniture, and its well-known microwaves to focus on its historical base in sophisticated electronics. Though earnings dropped in 1983, the company's earnings curve was much higher than it had been in the 1970s. In fact, Litton soon became a possible takeover candidate. The idea that Teledyne owned 26 percent of Litton's stock was not exactly reassuring to company management. Litton purposefully went deeper into debt to discourage potential buyers and to improve its cash reserves in the event of such a takeover.

In the early 1980s, Litton buttressed its electronics interests with the acquisition of Itek Corp., a defense electronics firm. The 1984 purchase of Core Laboratories Inc., a natural complement to Western Geophysical, seemed to indicate that Litton

would remain dedicated to the petroleum industry. After consolidating that division's interests in the late 1980s, however, Litton spun Western Atlas Inc. off to its shareholders in 1994. This move essentially split Litton's defense interests from its commercial interests.

Litton has not escaped controversy. In the early 1980s, the National Labor Relations Board investigating allegations that the parent company held to a centralized anti-union policy that filtered down to the subsidiaries. In addition, the U.S. Department of Defense suspended the company from bidding on new defense contracts when it was reported that a Litton subsidiary defrauded the government of $300 million. To make matters worse, the company's expanded capability radar warning system for the F-16 fighter jets failed operational tests.

Litton did enjoy the positive settlement of two lawsuits in the early 1990s, however. In 1993, Litton won a $1.2 billion jury award from competitor Honeywell Inc. The suit charged that Honeywell's ring laser gyroscope, a navigational system used in both military and commercial aircraft, breached Litton's manufacturing process patent. Later in the year, the federal government settled its suit against Litton regarding billing inconsistencies.

Hoch was succeeded in fiscal 1994 by John M. Leonis, a former senior vice-president. Litton's continuing dedication to the defense industry in spite of well-publicized cutbacks flouted conventional wisdom. But in his first annual report, Leonis asserted that "Litton is in the right place at the right time because we make products the U.S. needs now to meet its world peace-keeping role." Phil Friedman, an analyst with Morgan Stanley, told *Forbes* that Litton's positive cash position and low debt also boded well for the company.

Principal Subsidiaries: Ingalls Shipbuilding, Inc.; Litton Technology Corporation Ltd.; Litton Industrial Automation Systems, Inc.; Litton Systems, Inc.

Further Reading:

Jaffe, Thomas, "Litton After the Splitup," *Forbes,* April 11, 1994, p. 158.
Lay, Beirne, *Someone Has To Make It Happen: The Inside Story of Tex Thornton, The Man Who Built Litton Industries,* Englewood Cliffs, N.J.: Prentice Hall, 1969.
Lindorff, David, "US: When it's Time to Separate the Businesses," *Global Finance,* August 1993, pp. 15–16.
Miller, Danny, "The Icarus Paradox: How Exceptional Companies Bring About Their Own Downfall," *Business Horizons,* January/February 1992, pp. 24–35.
Velocci, Anthony L., Jr., "Litton Wins $1.2 Billion in Laser Gyro Patent Suit," *Aviation Week & Space Technology,* September 6, 1993, pp. 29–32.

—updated by April Dougal Gasbarre

Lockheed Corporation

4500 Park Granada Boulevard
Calabasas, California 91399-0610
U.S.A.
(805) 572-2974
Fax: (818) 876-2329

Public Company
Incorporated: 1916 as Loughead Aircraft Manufacturing
    Company
Employees: 83,500
Sales: $13.07 billion
Stock Exchanges: New York London Amsterdam Zurich
    Basle Lausanne Geneva
SICs: 3761 Guided Missiles and Space Vehicles; 3812
    Search and Navigation Equipment; 3663 Radio and TV
    Communications Equipment; 3721 Aircraft; 8711
    Engineering Services; 3760 Guided Missiles, Space
    Vehicles, Parts; 3670 Electronic Components and
    Accessories

One of the leading three defense contractors in the United States
during the 1990s, Lockheed Corporation was responsible for
producing the F-16, the F-117A stealth fighter, and the U-2 spy
plane, among other military aircraft and hardware for the U.S.
Department of Defense. In the pernicious economic climate
characterizing the aerospace industry in the post-cold war era,
Lockheed emerged as one of the strongest manufacturers of its
kind, intent on becoming the largest defense contractor in the
country.

The Lockheed Corporation has its origins with two brothers
named Allan and Malcolm Loughead. Allan, an auto mechanic,
first learned to fly in Chicago in 1912. When he returned home
to San Francisco later that year, he decided to build his own
airplane. He and Malcolm spent their evenings in a garage,
engineering and constructing a small ultralight seaplane they
called the Model G. This airplane was one of the first "tractor"
designs with a forward-mounted engine enclosed in the fuselage.

During this time, Allan flew as a barnstormer, but later gave it
up after some powerlines ensnared his Model G. The brothers
established the Alco Hydro-Aeroplane Company with financial
backing from Max Mamlock's Alco Cab Company and concentrated on building airplanes. Unfortunately, they couldn't sell

the airplanes, and the company was dissolved the following
year.

In 1916, the brothers started another new venture, the Loughead
Aircraft Manufacturing Company, based in Santa Barbara. Apparently tired of having their last name mispronounced as "lug
head," Allan and Malcolm changed the spelling to match the
pronunciation, "Lockheed." Likewise, the company's name
was changed to Lockheed. Malcolm left the company three
years later to sell hydraulic brakes. Still employed, however,
was a young engineer named Jack Northrop (later the founder of
the Northrop Corporation) who helped the brothers to develop
their twin-engine F-1 flying boat.

Northrop started a tradition of naming Lockheed airplanes after
celestial bodies. In 1927, he helped develop the Lockheed Vega
which became widely known as an explorer's airplane. When
Amelia Earhart crossed the Atlantic, she flew a Vega. In June
1928, Northrop left Lockheed to work for Avion, a subsidiary of
William Boeing's United Combine.

Lockheed was acquired by the Detroit Aircraft Corporation in
July 1929. An infuriated Allan Lockheed, who had little control
over the turn of events, resigned his post and sold all his
holdings in the company. Under new management, Lockheed's
engineers produced a number of new airplanes. Most notable
among them was a popular passenger transport called the Orion.

While Lockheed was still operating profitably two years into the
Depression, its parent company, Detroit Aircraft, was in poor
financial condition. When it went into receivership in 1932,
Lockheed was put up for sale. A group of investors, Robert
Gross and Lloyd Stearman among them, purchased the company for $40,000. The new owners wasted no time in develop-
ing a new airplane. In 1933, they introduced the Model 10
Electra. The Electra flew in the shadow of Douglas' DC-3, but
was still popular with Northwest and Pan Am as a complement
to their fleets of larger airplanes.

The following year, airmail legislation and other subsequent
congressional acts forced the breakup of a number of powerful
aviation combines. Lockheed, however, was small enough that
it remained largely unaffected.

One month after Germany annexed Austria in March 1938, a
British delegation toured the United States with the intention of
purchasing airplanes for the Royal Air Force. Lockheed engineers were given only five days notice to design the reconnaissance bomber in which the British were interested. They presented the "Hudson," a modified Model 14 Super Electra fitted
with more powerful engines, a bomb bay, and guns. For unknown reasons, the Hudson retained the Model 14's cabin
windows.

The British agreed to buy at least 200 Hudsons for $25 million.
It was the largest military contract awarded before the war and
marked a turning point in Lockheed's business. The Hudsons
were to be built by Lockheed's Vega subsidiary, predominantly
a manufacturer of military airplanes. By May 1943, Vega had
manufactured over 3,000 Hudsons.

As the United States became more involved in World War II,
Vega produced a number of new airplanes for the allied armies,

including the Ventura, the Harpoon, and variations of Boeing's B-17 bomber. Lockheed also introduced the P-38 Lightning, an effective and versatile triple hull interceptor. The company produced about 10,000 of these airplanes and its variations.

Because the War Department required so many different types of airplanes, Lockheed converted a number of commercial designs to perform military duties. Perhaps the most impressive among these conversions was the four engine C-69 Constellation. Originally, this airplane was secretly developed by Howard Hughes and Lockheed engineers for civilian service. However, after Pearl Harbor the government prohibited further production of commercial airplanes. Nevertheless, only 15 of these planes were delivered before the war ended.

When the war finally came to a close late in the summer of 1945, Lockheed had produced 19,297 aircraft for the military—nine percent of the total U.S. production. After the war, the company concentrated on meeting the demand for commercial airplanes caused by the various airlines' expansion plans. Thus, Lockheed resumed the civilian 049 Constellation project. Variously described as "beautiful" or "romantic," several versions of this distinctive triple-rudder airplane were manufactured. It was a commercial success for Lockheed; virtually every major airline in the world ordered at least one. Lockheed also remodeled its Electra, designated L-188, and fitted it with prop-jet engines.

After the war, Lockheed maintained numerous military contracts, many of them secret. One such project which the company and the armed forces had an interest in keeping quiet was the development of a jet fighter. Conventional piston-driven airplanes had propellers which simply pushed the air behind the airplane. Jets, on the other hand, sucked air into a chamber where at high pressures a spray of jet fuel was detonated. The rocket-like explosion of the fuel generated a powerful thrust. That thrust enabled an airplane to fly twice as fast as conventional airplanes. The newly created Air Force, now involved in the beginnings of the cold war, expressed great enthusiasm for the project.

Lockheed had become interested in developing a jet during 1939, the year the Germans first tested one. Two years later, the British designed and successfully built a jet. In 1943, Bell Aircraft built a jet called an Airacomet. All were test models and only Messerschmitt's Me.262 and Britain's Gloster F. 9/40 engaged in combat during World War II.

Kelly Johnson, the company's chief designer, led Lockheed's jet project at the secret Advanced Development Products (ADP) division. On January 8, 1944, the XP-80 Shooting Star was successfully flown over Muroc Dry Lake, Nevada. It later served as a prototype for more than 1,700 improved variations.

The XP-80 model jet arrived too late for World War II but was used when the Korean War broke out in 1950. Other Lockheed aircraft in action over Korea were the Neptune reconnaissance airplane, the F-94 Starfire interceptor, and the Constellation transport. "Korea," it was said, "was a Lockheed war."

The 1950s were a period of growth and innovation at Lockheed. With a steady flow of lucrative military contracts, the company expanded existing plants and built several new ones. It tested a

vertical take-off and landing (VTOL) airplane, as well as a ramjet, widely regarded as the propulsion mechanism of the next century. Lockheed even made plans for a nuclear-powered aircraft. In 1953, the company established its missiles and space division which produced satellites and submarine-launched missiles.

Lockheed built a number of variously designed fighter jets for testing and use by the Air Force. Their one failure was the F-104 Starfighter, which was sold to the West German Luftwaffe in 1959. The Germans called them "widowmakers" and "flying coffins." 175 of these jets crashed, killing a total of 85 pilots. Lockheed, which initially refused to acknowledge the design problems with Starfighter, paid the pilots' widows $1.2 million in compensation during 1975.

In the commercial market, Lockheed responded to Douglas' new DC-7 with an altered version of its Constellation, including new wings and a new name—the "Starliner." Two years later, in 1957, the company produced a small jet called Jetstar. These were to be Lockheed's last commercial ventures for 15 years.

In the early 1960s, Lockheed was closely associated with the Department of Defense. Robert and Courtland Gross, the company's chief executive officer and president, respectively, maintained low profiles and delegated much of their responsibility to subordinates. Even after Robert died in 1961 and Daniel Haughton was named president, the direction of the company remained the same.

In military ventures, the company developed transports such as the C-130 Hercules, the C-141 Starlifter, and the C-5 Galaxy, the largest airplane in the world. During this period, Lockheed's military products were consistently chosen over those of Boeing and Douglas for the award of Pentagon contracts.

In the 1960s, Lockheed developed two very important jets, the U-2 spy plane and the SR-71. The U-2 flew at altitudes over 70,000 feet loaded with remote sensing electronic equipment. After the Cuban missile crisis of 1962, Senator Barry Goldwater credited the U-2 alone, with its reconnaissance abilities, for providing President Kennedy with precise and accurate information regarding the location of missile sites in Cuba.

The SR-71 was designed in the early 1960s and has required no further improvement since; its aerodynamics were regarded by most engineers as nearly perfect. Called the "blackbird" because it was painted black, the SR-71 had a cruising speed of over 2,100 miles per hour and was able to fly at an altitude of over 85,000 feet. The SR-71's large engines created pockets of extremely low air pressure in front of the air intakes, drawing the aircraft forward. Acting like vacuums, the engines contributed to the forward motion of the airplane in this way.

In 1967, Courtland Gross stepped down as chairman, ending a 30-year era in the history of Lockheed. Daniel Haughton was promoted and Carl Kotchian was named president. These two men continued the conservative management tradition of the Grosses, but made one uncharacteristically risky venture in the commercial airline market. When Boeing announced the development of its 747 and Douglas its DC-10, Lockheed responded with a commercial wide body jetliner of its own, the 1011 TriStar. Lockheed's new jetliner first flew in November 1970.

However, the TriStar program was plagued with several major problems. Rolls-Royce, the manufacturer of the 1011's engines, went into receivership during February 1971. Several airline companies, principally Eastern, experienced numerous equipment failures with their TriStars. Sales of the airplane began to drop, and the company faced a liquidity crisis. Even after important modifications in the design of the aircraft and increased sales, production of the L-1011 continued to lose money for Lockheed.

Lockheed's decision to compete with the new generation of commercial jetliners nearly ruined the company. By 1971, Lockheed's financial position became so grave that it required a guaranteed government loan to remain financially afloat. After producing a total of about 250 TriStars, Lockheed discontinued the program in 1981.

Lockheed, like many of its competitors, always had a difficult time selling its jetliners in foreign markets. Their competitors were known to use bribery to procure lucrative contracts. Lockheed made no secret that it intended to challenge its competitors on similar terms when it informed the Securities and Exchange Commission in 1975 that it would resist that agency's efforts to halt Lockheed's "sales incentives." The SEC withheld any action against Lockheed because the guaranteed loan gave the government an active interest in the company's quick financial recovery.

Lockheed was accused of bribing officials in Iran, Indonesia, Italy, the Netherlands, and Japan. In 1976, a series of arrests in Japan culminated in the detention of the former prime minister, Kakuei Tanaka, whose government was brought down in the controversy. A month later, Prince Bernhard of the Netherlands was implicated in accepting Lockheed bribes. Questionable payments were made to officials in several other nations. Lockheed was successful in selling its planes, but now it was at the center of an international scandal.

The two men most closely associated with Lockheed's questionable practices were the company's president, Carl Kotchian, and chief executive officer, Daniel Haughton. Both men were compelled to resign in 1976 after details of the $30 million improprieties were publicized. Haughton, who consistently answered "no comment" to inquiries from the press, resigned peacefully. Kotchian had to be removed from his position during a four-hour board meeting.

The board named an interim chief executive officer, Robert Haack, to preside over a restructuring of the company. A former president of the New York Stock Exchange, Haack deserved much of the credit for rectifying Lockheed's management and marketing problems. At the same time, Lawrence Kitchen, a former vice-president, was promoted to president following the departure of Kotchian. His task in this position was less to administer than to improve the damaged reputation of the company. Eighteen months later, Lockheed's chief financial officer, Roy A. Anderson, replaced Haack as Lockheed's new chief executive officer.

By the late 1980s, Lockheed conducted its business through 18 subsidiaries in four principal divisions: the missiles, space and electronics systems group; the aeronautical systems group; the marine systems group; and the information systems group. Its major projects for the 1980s were primarily military hardware. They included building the F-19 stealth bomber and the Trident II submarine-launched missile, as well as maintaining the National Aeronautics and Space Administration's space shuttles. Because of its involvement in manufacturing so much military equipment, the company was regarded by the U.S. government as indispensable to the country's defense.

As Lockheed entered the 1990s, however, its future role as a primary supplier of military hardware and aircraft became an increasingly untenable position to occupy. With the end of the cold war and a dwindling defense budget promising little hope for robust growth, Lockheed entered into a new era for U.S. aerospace manufacturers that demanded sweeping changes to enable survival. The company gained new leadership to effect these changes in 1989, when Daniel M. Tellep was named chief executive officer and chairperson after managing the company's missile and space division for the previous four years. Under Tellep's stewardship, Lockheed initiated a diversification program to wean the company away from its overwhelming dependence on government-funded contracts. However, a more pressing problem also faced the new leader, as he fought to protect Lockheed from a hostile takeover.

Starting in 1988, a Dallas billionaire named Harold Simmons began amassing Lockheed stock, gaining control, by 1990, of slightly under 20 percent of the company. Simmons then waged a proxy battle that year, which failed but stirred shareholder unrest and diverted management's attention away from forging a new future for the company in the rapidly changing defense market. Lockheed lost the development contract for the U.S. antisatellite program during its struggle with Simmons, after spending the previous decade conducting much of the preliminary research, the fruits of which went to Rockwell International and left Lockheed with empty hands.

Simmons again initiated a proxy battle in 1991, but, as he had the year before, failed to muster the necessary support. Meanwhile, against the backdrop of this contentious struggle between Tellep and Simmons, Lockheed had begun to trim its operating expenses and diversify. Tellep cut Lockheed's work force by 9,500 during his first two years of leadership, transferred hundreds more from California to Georgia, and spearheaded the company's diversification. In 1990, he increased Lockheed's involvement in commercial aircraft maintenance, then maneuvered the company into conducting nuclear waste cleanup work for the Department of Energy and dismantling nuclear warheads in the United States and in the former Soviet Union.

By 1992, however, many of Lockheed's efforts at diversification had proven to be disappointments, unaided by a debilitative national economy. That year, Tellep changed course, moving away from the company's diversification program and toward further involvement in defense-oriented projects. Instead of moving away from manufacturing military hardware and aircraft, as many aerospace manufacturers were doing during the early 1990s, Tellep rushed toward acquiring additional defense-related assets, theorizing that with fewer manufacturers competing for government contracts, greater revenues could be gained by a select few companies.

Reflective of this corporate strategy, Lockheed gained an enviable asset in early 1993, when it concluded a deal to acquire General Dynamics Corporation's fighter aircraft division, maker of the high-performance F-16 fighter aircraft. In beating out Northrop Corporation for the coveted fighter aircraft unit, Lockheed executed a masterstroke, paying $1.5 billion for an additional $3 billion in sales and $13 billion in backlog orders, as well as adding the F-16 and the F-22 program to the company's established contracts to manufacture the F-117A stealth fighter, which was bolstered by the aircraft's laudable performance in the Persian Gulf two years earlier, and the U-2 spy plane.

The acquisition of General Dynamic's aircraft division fueled Lockheed's growth for the year, driving up its net income 21 percent from 1992's total and swelling revenues from $10.1 billion to $13.1 billion. As the company entered the mid-1990s, it continued to face the challenges of a leaner defense budget, but determinedly pursued its goal to become the largest defense contractor in the United States.

Principal Subsidiaries: Lockheed Air Terminal, Inc.; Lockheed Missiles & Space Company, Inc.; Lockheed Finance Corp.; Lockheed Engineering and Sciences Co.; Lockheed Space Operations Co.; Lockheed Support Systems, Inc.; Lockheed Canada, Inc.; Lockheed Commercial Electronics Co.; Lockheed Information Management Services Co.; Lockheed Sanders, Inc.; Mountaingate Data Systems, Inc.

Further Reading:

Banks, Howard, "Distracted," *Forbes,* November 26, 1990, p. 39.

Bilstein, Roger E., *Flight in America 1900–1983: From the Wrights to the Astronauts,* Baltimore: The Johns Hopkins University Press, 1984.

Blay, Roy, editor, *Lockheed Horizons,* Burbank, Calif.: Lockheed Corporation, 1983.

Boulton, David, *Lockheed: The Grease Machine,* New York: Harper, 1978.

Collingwood, Harris, "Now, Lockheed Is No. 2," *Business Week,* December 21, 1992, p. 42.

"Lockheed Buy Fuels 1993 Net, Sales Gain," *Electronic News,* February 14, 1994, p. 28.

Montgomery, Leland, "Lockheed: Still Climbing," *Financial World,* June 22, 1993, p. 16.

Newhouse, John, *The Sporty Game,* New York: Knopf, 1982.

Schine, Eric, "Lockheed: Oh, What a Difference a Year Makes," *Business Week,* February 25, 1991, p. 37.

—updated by Jeffrey L. Covell

Magma Power Company

4365 Executive Drive, Suite 900
San Diego, California 92121
U.S.A.
(619) 622-7800
Fax: (619) 622-7822

Public Company
Incorporated: 1981 as Magma Development Corporation
Employees: 340
Sales: $167.1 million
Stock Exchanges: NASDAQ
SICs: 4961 Steam & Air-Conditioning Supply

One of California's largest geothermal power companies, Magma Power Company explores for, develops, and sells or leases geothermal resources used to generate electric power. A pioneer in its field, Magma is largely responsible for creating the U.S. geothermal industry, first drilling for naturally produced steam in the mid-1950s. In addition to developing geothermal resources, the company also constructs and operates geothermal electric power plants using its proprietary process and production technologies, the success of which have enabled Magma to begin pursuing geothermal projects around the world.

Throughout much of the 20th century, the utilization of geothermal energy in the United States was virtually nonexistent, except for several isolated instances that were more curiosities than serious efforts to harness the steam created below the earth's surface. Elsewhere in the world, the beds of steam heated by molten rock, or magma, attracted more serious attention, beginning in 1904 with the construction of the world's first plant to generate electricity from geothermal steam in Larderello, Italy. Other countries began to explore the possibilities of tapping into these natural boilers as well, but in the United States, where energy needs were sufficiently met with low-cost coal and natural gas, geothermal steam was largely ignored as a commercially viable source of energy.

This indifference reigned until the 1960s, when rising coal and natural gas prices persuaded oil and utility companies, the likely investors in geothermal exploration, to examine alternative energy sources. What followed was a period of intense interest in geothermal steam; utility and oil companies hurried to find suitable locations for drilling, almost all of which were located in the western United States, where underground reservoirs of water were positioned closer to the Earth's surface. At that time, the nascent U.S. geothermal industry was attempting to effect the difficult transformation from a fragmented group of speculators, haphazardly selecting drilling sites and hoping for success and riches to follow, to an enterprise based on science and technology, an endeavor shed of its speculative risk and predicated on reliable and predictable methods. The oil industry had undergone the same evolution more than a half century earlier.

The sudden acceptance in the United States of geothermal energy as a feasible alternative to coal and gas in the late 1960s could be traced primarily to one individual, Barkman C. McCabe, a former stock broker from Los Angeles and the man many referred to as "the father of the geothermal industry." McCabe, by this time, had been drilling for geothermal steam through several joint ventures for more than decade and had already acquired most of the prime geothermal areas in the West, much to the dismay of those now willing to explore this alternative energy source. McCabe was drawn initially to a region in Sonoma County, California, 90 miles north of San Francisco, known as the Geysers. It was an inaccurate name for a region that contained no geysers, or water spouts, but did contain fumaroles, holes in the ground from which steam emanated; these fumaroles were sources of wonder for guests at a nearby resort during the 1920s and the objects of fear for a bear hunter who inadvertently came upon the area in 1847. Though it was known natural steam was below and that the steam could be used to generate electricity—the owners of the nearby resort had constructed a small generating plant, powered by two reciprocating steam engines, to supply their own electricity during the 1920s—the fumaroles were not used as useful indicators of geothermal steam located below until McCabe drilled his first well in 1955.

That year, McCabe and his lifelong friend and partner in a lumber business, Dan McMillan, purchased leases on 5,500 acres in the Geysers region and began drilling test wells. To finance their leasing and drilling operations, McCabe and McMillan each decided to form a drilling company and then sell stock, which served as the premise for McCabe's company, Magma Power Company, founded in 1955, and McMillan's company, Thermal Power Company, started a year later. After three years and six productive test wells, the two businessmen, in 1958, convinced Pacific Gas & Electric, the region's giant utility company, to purchase their steam and establish a pilot generating plant. This joint venture between Magma Power and Thermal Power became the first successful geothermal project in the United States. By 1960, the merits of generating electricity from geothermal steam had been sufficient to convince Pacific Gas & Electric to construct a turbine-powered geothermal plant, which began operation that year, specifically for the steam produced from McCabe's and McMillan's wells.

Encouraged by his initial success, McCabe formed a subsidiary company in 1961 to search for possible geothermal well sites beyond the Geysers region. Named Magma Energy Company, the subsidiary focused its efforts primarily in a southern California region known as Imperial Valley. Profits, however, were slow to develop, particularly in contrast to Magma's rapid expansion. Although the actual operation of the wells required little labor and incurred little cost, the construction costs were considerable, stifling Magma's ability to record any appreciable profit, an ability that was further reduced by the creation of Magma Energy and the expansion into Imperial Valley. Also, except for the association with Pacific Gas & Electric, business relationships with corporations boasting large reservoirs of cash were difficult to establish; geothermal energy continued to be a speculative risk, attracting few established investors.

This skepticism would change as the decade progressed and coal and natural gas prices rose, giving way to a dramatic increase in the interest directed toward geothermal energy. By the late 1960s, oil companies and other geothermal companies were scouting for suitable drilling sites, attempting to grab a share of what promised to be a lucrative market. One such newcomer, Union Oil Company of California, found a practiced partner to facilitate its entry into the geothermal market: Magma Power. For McCabe's company, the 1967 agreement with Union Oil, which gave the large oil concern a 50 percent stake in the portion of the Geysers region controlled by Magma and Thermal, infused the struggling geothermal company with much-needed working capital, albeit at a costly price. Magma, however, had essentially little choice. Now, as other interested parties searched for fumaroles and other signs of geothermal steam percolating underground, none looked as promising as those found in the region controlled by Magma, Thermal, and Union Oil.

The deal with Union Oil was costly for Magma partly because the agreement between the two ceded a share in the three wells now in operation in Imperial Valley, but primarily because the geothermal fields in Northern California were extremely valuable, the only successful fields in the United States despite the rash of geothermal projects sprouting up across the western states during the latter part of the decade. During the energy crisis in the early and mid-1970s, these fields would hold Magma in good stead and would continue to support the only geothermal project in the country to generate electricity. The energy crisis pushed the price of conventional fuels upward, increasing interest in geothermal energy, for which Magma's wells at the Geysers stood as a shining example. By the end of the decade, the geothermal leases held by Magma had become objects of considerable attention for companies wishing to claim a stake in the geothermal market. Aside from the 50 percent interest in the Geysers fields held by Union Oil, the oil concern also owned 9.2 percent of Magma itself, roughly the same percentage of Magma's stock that Dow Chemical Co. possessed. In addition to these investors, Natomas Co., a natural resource, energy, and transportation company based in San Francisco, owned a 25 percent interest in the Geysers fields, the same percentage held by Magma. Natomas augmented its investment in Magma, to the chagrin of McCabe and other members of Magma's management, by increasing its stake in the geothermal company to 7.5 percent in 1980.

With its purchase of additional Magma stock, Natomas announced that a greater investment in the company was imminent, that it was seeking to attain, as a company spokesperson related to the *Wall Street Journal*, "a significant minority investment" in Magma. For McCabe, his company's relationship with Union Oil was an association of necessity, essential to Magma's financial ability to continue drilling for geothermal

steam, and the increasing interest owned by Dow Chemical was received with open arms. However, he could not abide Natomas' bid to control a larger portion of Magma and flatly said as much, terming a possible merger between Natomas and Magma as "most undesirable." For its part, Natomas was not to be dissuaded from its objective and in March 1981 went well beyond its stated intent of attaining "a significant minority investment" by offering $390 million, or $42 a share to purchase Magma. McCabe responded by declaring, in the *Wall Street Journal*, that Natomas' offer was "totally inadequate" and that Magma's assets were worth at least $80 a share, or perhaps as much as $200 a share. The following month Natomas sued Magma, charging that McCabe had purposefully mislead Magma shareholders about the company's worth to prejudice their decision regarding Natomas' offer. Amid these charges of fraud, stock manipulation, and various other securities violations, McCabe announced he was actively engaged in seeking a more favorable offer, but his efforts were in vain, for one year later, in April 1982, Natomas completed its purchase of Magma for $45 a share.

Six months before the purchase was completed, in late 1981, when it became evident that the acquisition was indeed going to occur, another company was formed and incorporated as Magma Development Corp. Its purpose was to acquire all of the assets, excluding the geothermal assets connected with the Geysers, formerly owned by Magma Power. These properties, essentially all of Magma's geothermal assets in Southern California, were acquired in June 1982, two months after Magma Development had changed its name to Magma Power Company. In the end, Magma Power, with assets principally located in Northern California, had been absorbed into Natomas, and a new Magma Power had emerged, with geothermal assets principally located in Southern California's Imperial Valley, the region controlled by Magma Energy, the subsidiary formed in 1961.

Bereft of the valuable Geysers assets, the new Magma Power was smaller than the former Magma Power, recording slightly more than $3 million in revenues in 1984. Geothermal exploration and development continued to be a costly endeavor, and Magma, with a modest sales volume, needed greater financial resources to expand its operations in the Imperial Valley. Dow Chemical provided the solution, acquiring additional percentages of Magma stock during the mid-1980s, first in 1984, when its increased its stake in Magma to 20 percent, then in 1986, when it became a 25.5 percent owner of the company. Magma used the proceeds to finance work on a geothermal plant at East Mesa in the Imperial Valley and quickly watched its annual sales grow. In 1988, when Magma generated $26 million in revenues, it merged Magma Energy into the company and sold another subsidiary, Magma Electric Company, to an affiliate of Geothermal Resources International.

Magma's sales volume recorded encouraging jumps through the late 1980s, reaching $85.5 million by the beginning of the 1990s. Perhaps more important, the company's profit total enjoyed commensurate gains, the result of Magma's unrivaled experience in the geothermal development field and its efficient proprietary process and production technologies. In 1992, Magma announced its intent to purchase three geothermal power plants, located in the Imperial Valley, Nevada, and

Northern California, from Unocal Corp. for $225 million. The deal was completed the following year, in 1993, when annual sales reached $167.1 million, more than double the total recorded three years earlier. The three plants, which generated $70 million in annual sales before the acquisition, bolstered Magma's position in the Southern California market, where it provided geothermal steam to Southern California Edison, one of the region's utility companies. The acquisition was timely as well, putting Magma in an enviable position for gaining additional business later that year, when Southern California Edison and San Diego Gas & Electric were obliged under state regulations to seek bids for renewable energy supplies.

As Magma entered the mid-1990s, its future appeared bright. Remarkable gains in the company's sales volume—from $3 million to $167 million in less than a decade—were underpinned by equally robust increases in the company's earnings. In 1993, Magma earned 46 cents for every $1 generated in revenue, a ratio that ranked it as one of the leading performers in California industry and established it as a company for investors and competitors alike to monitor in the future.

Principal Subsidiaries: Imperial Magma; Vulcan Power Company; Desert Valley Company; Fish Lake Power Company; Salton Sea Power Company; Peak Power Corporation; Magma Netherlands B.V.; Vulcan/BN Geothermal Power Co. (50%).

Further Reading:

Bylin, James E., "Oil Concerns Vie in Western 'Steam Rush,' Tapping Boilers Stoked by Mother Nature," *Wall Street Journal,* June 10, 1968, p. 32.

Core, Richard, "Magma Purchase May Boost Profits by 40 Percent," *San Diego Business Journal,* December 21, 1992, p. 1.

"Dow Chemical Hikes Magma Power Stake," *Barron's,* December 3, 1984, p. 67.

"Dow Chemical Raises Magma Stake to 25.5%," *Wall Street Journal,* June 11, 1986, p. 42.

Loehwing, David A., " 'Nature's Teakettle': Geothermal Power Is Getting Up a Head of Steam," *Barron's,* August 13, 1973, p. 3.

"Magma Generates Powerful Margins," *California Business,* June–July 1993, p. 33.

"Magma Power Co.," *Wall Street Journal,* February 9, 1982, p. 47.

"Magma Power Co. Seeks Better Offer Than Natomas Co.'s," *Wall Street Journal,* April 7, 1981, p. 13.

"Magma Power Company," *Wall Street Transcript,* August 11, 1969, p. 17,604.

"Magma Power Company," *Wall Street Transcript,* December 21, 1970, p. 22,663.

"Natomas Lists 7.5% Magma Power Stake and May Seek More," *Wall Street Journal,* April 23, 1980, p. 8.

"Natomas Merger Completed," *Wall Street Journal,* April 26, 1982, p. 22.

"Natomas Suit Accuses Magma Power of Fraud in Acquisition Battle," *Wall Street Journal,* April 2, 1981, p. 45.

Summers, W. K., and Sylvia H. Ross, "Getting Up Steam," *Barron's,* November 17, 1969, p. 11.

—Jeffrey L. Covell

MAI Systems Corporation

9501 Jeronimo Road
Irvine, California 92718-2018
U.S.A.
(714) 580-0700
Fax: (714) 580-2378

Wholly Owned Subsidiary of BGLS Inc.
Incorporated: 1984 as MAI Basic Four, Inc.
Employees: 800
Sales: $115.29 million
SICs: 7373 Value-Added Resellers, Computer Systems

MAI Systems Corporation sells a wide range of computer equipment and related services to businesses throughout North America and Latin America. The company specializes in mid-range, multi-user computer systems and their system software, other network products, and application software designed for several specific industries. These industries include transportation, wholesale distribution, manufacturing, healthcare, retail, and hospitality and gaming. The company purchases and resells hardware platforms manufactured by others, marketing them under its proprietary ''MAI'' trademark or under a variety of vendor labels. MAI conducts its business through four independent operating units. The largest unit, MAI North America, markets OpenBASIC, a tool that allows software written in Business BASIC language to run on several different industry standard hardware platforms. This unit contributed about 69 percent of the company's total revenue in 1994. MAI's Computerized Lodging Systems Hospitality Group provides software systems for hotels, resorts, casinos, and other such businesses. MAI sells manufacturing software for the chemical, pharmaceutical, and food industries through its Sextant Corporation unit. The fourth business unit, MAI Latin America, markets hardware, software, and support services throughout Central and South America.

MAI's history can be traced to 1957, when Management Assistance Inc. was founded by Walter R. Oreamuno. Oreamuno, a native of Costa Rica, had landed his first job in the United States after winning an IBM problem solving contest. In forming Management Assistance Inc. (MAI), Oreamuno essentially invented the computer-leasing business. The business computer situation in the mid-1950s was completely dominated by IBM, which manufactured virtually all of the computers in use and leased them to the companies that used them. When IBM began to sell the computers in addition to leasing them in 1956 (under pressure from the Justice Department), Oreamuno recognized that a potentially lucrative role as middleman had opened up. Oreamuno and his associate, Jorge M. Gonzalez, approached IBM customers with an attractive offer: if the customer would buy the equipment from IBM, MAI would immediately buy it from the customer, then lease it right back to them at a rate lower than IBM was offering.

Oreamuno's novel idea was an immediate hit, and the company grew at a phenomenal rate through the early 1960s. Because IBM was depreciating its equipment very quickly, MAI was able to buy up used machines at a fraction of their original cost. In 1961, MAI offered its stock to the public, raising $300,000. The company continued to raise as much capital as quickly as it could, through private investments, loans, and further public offerings. Over a span of six years, MAI bought about $200 million worth of computer equipment. The company became a favorite on Wall Street, and its stock soared as high as $45 a share in 1966.

However, in the second half of the 1960s, MAI was challenged by a rapidly changing market. In 1965, IBM unveiled its third-generation 360 computer. The appearance of the 360 proved problematic for MAI, since it had already sunk so much of its money into older punch-card equipment. Since MAI's customers had two-year contracts with month-to-month cancellation options, the company was vulnerable to the emergence of vastly improved equipment that would make its own offerings obsolete. Nevertheless, Oreamuno continued buying up the older machines in the hope that the market for the IBM 360 would be very different from MAI's customer base. In 1967, after plans for a merger with Transamerica Corporation suddenly disintegrated, Oreamuno resigned as CEO. He was replaced by Luther Schwalm, a 37-year veteran of IBM who had recently come over to MAI.

Under Schwalm, MAI stopped buying additional punch-card equipment and began leasing peripheral items such as disk drives. By 1968, the errors of MAI's earlier ways became clear, and the company took a $17 million write-down on obsolete punch-card equipment. Customers were replacing the out-of-date IBM machinery so fast that MAI's cash flow sank into negative figures. While the company had $60 million in revenue in 1970, it maintained $140 million in debt and a net worth of negative $28 million. In 1971, MAI chief financial officer Raymond Kurshan took over as president of the company. Realizing that MAI's old business was crumbling, Kurshan sought to move the company into other areas while there was any company left to salvage. MAI was quickly reorganized into a holding company with several subsidiaries.

One of these subsidiaries was Basic/Four Corporation, headed by president Douglas K. Baker. Basic/Four was one of the first independent entrants into the small business computer system arena. It was also the entity that would survive to later form the core of the current version of MAI Systems. The other subsidiaries formed around the same time included Genesis One—whose purpose was to sell off or rent the aging equipment—and Sorbus, which serviced equipment made by other manufacturers. Basic/Four's first product, launched in 1971, was a line of business computer systems for small to medium-sized companies. The computers handled inventory control and general accounting. The high-end Model 500 was capable of accommodating up to eight work stations interacting with each other over telephone lines.

Both the Basic/Four and Sorbus subsidiaries did well enough to bring MAI back to life. Sorbus became profitable by using MAI's pre-existing 1,200-person maintenance staff as its core, and expanding from there. Basic/Four was a major success almost immediately. In 1972, Basic/Four introduced the first multi-user transaction processing mini-computer to use the Business Basic language. By 1975, Basic/Four's revenue had grown to $43 million, and it was contributing around two-thirds of MAI's total earnings.

Basic/Four and other small business computer system pioneers such as Microdata Corporation enjoyed explosive growth through the mid-1970s, as industry giants IBM and Hewlett-Packard fought to catch up with their smaller, more nimble competitors. By the latter part of the decade, in order to remain competitive, MAI began to focus increasingly on software. In 1977, the company acquired Wordstream Corporation, which produced word processing systems and IBM-compatible CRT terminals. Over the next several years, the company introduced several Business Basic-based business software packages that added up to a full set of tools for users of the company's computer systems. MAI's software offerings included EASY (an exception reporting system) and the Business Data data processing program.

In 1979, MAI launched DataWord II, a terminal that combined data and word processing capabilities. Around the same time, the company brought out a new workstation for its Wordstream shared-logic word processing systems. In spite of these advances, Wordstream became outmoded, as sophisticated word processing systems developed by Wang Laboratories and other companies became increasingly popular. MAI gave up on Wordstream in 1980, although the company continued to offer DataWord II through Basic/Four, as well as maintain support services for all of its word processing systems.

MAI shipped its 10,000th computer system in 1980. The market for business computers began to shift radically during this time, as many small companies were turning to cheaper, newly available personal computers instead of the mini-computers that had been Basic/Four's mainstay. Rather than buying a big computer and tailoring it to their needs with customized software, smaller firms were starting with low-priced PCs, buying application software off the shelf, and adding both hardware and software as it was needed. Although Basic/Four was still generating nearly two-thirds of MAI's revenue, it was becoming less profitable. For 1980, Basic/Four earned $14 million (a 39 percent drop) on sales of $304 million. In the wake of that performance, Theodore Smith was replaced by Stephen J. Keane as president of Basic/Four.

By 1982, it was clear that MAI had to seek a broader market for its goods in order to compete with IBM, Digital Equipment, and the rest. Revenue had grown to $358 million by that time (55 percent of which was contributed by Basic/Four), but net income had shrunk to $6.3 million. In 1983, the company intro-

duced its MAI 8000, a super-minicomputer nearly as powerful as a mainframe. Capable of serving up to 96 users at a time, the 8000 was MAI's attempt to attract larger businesses into its customer base, after serving mainly the small business system market for its entire history. The company also chose to intensify its quest for new customers in a handful of specific market niches, including pharmaceutical firms, sewing-goods companies, and non-profit agencies, fields that were already well represented among MAI's 20,000 customers. Basic/Four also expanded its global reach in 1983 with the formation of MAI Australia Information Systems. For fiscal 1983, Basic/Four reported an operating loss of $10.2 million.

By 1984, Basic/Four had a work force of 2,000. That year, New York-based investor Asher Edelman acquired 12 percent of MAI's stock. Edelman then began to wage a proxy war for control of the company, quickly securing four positions on MAI's ten-member board of directors. In the course of the proxy battle, Edelman received a settlement in the $1 million range following a libel suit filed against MAI concerning company advertisements. Meanwhile, structural changes were taking place within the company. In April 1984, MAI International Corporation, the company's worldwide marketing arm, was folded into Basic/Four. Basic/Four also absorbed another MAI division, MAI Applications Software Corporation.

Edelman managed to gain control of MAI's board in August 1984, when Kurshan resigned his positions as chair, chief executive officer, and president of the company. Once at the company's helm, Edelman immediately set out to liquidate MAI. By early 1985, most of the company's parts had been sold off. The Sorbus division was sold to a subsidiary of Bell Atlantic Corporation, while Basic/Four was purchased by investor Bennett S. LeBow in a leveraged deal worth about $100 million.

Now independent, Basic/Four inherited the initials of its former parent company, and was renamed MAI Basic Four, Inc. Prior to its purchase by LeBow, Basic/Four had been unprofitable. Weighted down by outdated technology and a marketing set-up that had never performed up to par, the company appeared to be failing. Under LeBow, the company's first move was to sell its Canadian subsidiary, MAI Canada Ltd., to Bell Atlantic for roughly $23 million. With cash from that sale, LeBow set out to reshape MAI by concentrating on its strengths, specifically its 27,000-customer base of Basic/Four computer users that was generally committed to the company's products. He also sought to exploit the company's 35-country distribution system and its overseas maintenance operation, which had been one of its few bright spots in recent years.

As a result, MAI enjoyed a renaissance that lasted for the next few years. While LeBow retained the company's chairmanship, the job of rebuilding MAI into a profitable company fell largely to William B. Patton, former president and CEO of Cado Systems Corporation. Accorded the same titles at MAI, Patton quickly took actions to cut MAI's costs dramatically. First, more than half the company's vice-presidents were let go. Then, in order to slash manufacturing costs, Patton began buying components from Asia, specifically Japan, Korea, Taiwan, and Singapore, rather than having them built at home. Realizing that the quality of the products was not enough to guarantee healthy sales, he also beefed up the company's direct sales staff. Under Patton, the company narrowed its sales focus to eight vertical markets, including hotels, retailing, apparel, manufacturing, and health care. The resurrection of MAI under Patton's guidance was rapid. For the fiscal year ending in September 1986, the company earned nearly $17 million on sales of $281 million. The company also went public again during that year.

By 1987, nearly two-thirds of MAI's total sales were coming from overseas, and half of the parts used in its manufacturing operations were from outside the company. Although MAI's installed customer base of 37,000 represented less than one percent of the worldwide mini- and microcomputer market, the company worked directly with independent software developers in each of its target industries to generate specific solutions for users of its computer systems. MAI introduced several new products during this period. In 1986, the company unveiled a mid-range computer system called the MAI 3000, which was followed up in 1987 by the MAI 4000, an expandable mid-range multi-user system. Both sales and profits at MAI took sizable leaps in 1987, reaching $22.8 million and $321 million, respectively.

With much of the debt from its leveraged buyout erased, MAI began buying up existing firms. By early 1988, the company had acquired 25 small software, distribution, and maintenance companies. It also bought back MAI Canada, the Canadian distribution subsidiary it had sold off to Bell Atlantic a few years earlier for much needed cash. Part of its former U.S. service subsidiary, Sorbus, which had been sold off by Edelman during liquidation, was also repurchased. Business peaked in 1988, when MAI earned net income of $24.5 million on $420 million in revenue.

Some setbacks occurred in 1989, however. Sales had begun to slip during the second half of 1988, and LeBow had announced that his controlling interest in MAI was available for purchase. When no buyers materialized, LeBow changed his strategy. In November 1988, MAI launched a surprise takeover bid for the much larger Prime Computer Inc., a Massachusetts-based rival. Meanwhile, the entire U.S. computer industry fell into a tailspin that saw sales decline across the board. In June 1989, in the thick of the bid for Prime, Patton suddenly resigned. The takeover bid eventually failed, after costing MAI $25 million over nine months in addition to a fair amount of bad publicity and hard feelings among customers. The emergence of multi-user personal computers continued to erode the company's sales as well.

In August 1989, MAI announced plans for a major restructuring of the company in order to cut costs and regain its momentum. An infusion of $55 million in cash came from Brooke Partners L.P., an investment group controlled by LeBow, giving Brooke a majority ownership in MAI. Sales continued to recede, however, and for 1989 the company suffered a net loss of $39 million on revenue of $397 million. In early 1990, Fred D. Anderson, with the company since 1978, became president and chief operating officer. William Weksel, who had been filling in as president and CEO, replaced LeBow as chairperson and remained CEO. LeBow's new position was chair of the board's executive committee.

In 1990, MAI developed Open BASIC, which enabled the company's software to run on a variety of operating systems. The company paid $1.9 million in April of that year for the outstanding stock of Computerized Lodging Systems, Inc., a maker of software systems for the hotel industry. Later in the year, the company's name was changed; Basic/Four was dropped in favor of MAI Systems Corporation. Weksel left the company in December to pursue other business interests, and LeBow returned to the posts of chairperson and chief executive of MAI. However, the red ink continued to flow through 1990, as the company recorded a net loss of $64 million on sales of $389 million.

With its core small computer market continuing to decline, MAI shifted its strategy radically in 1991. Around that time, the company began phasing out its manufacturing operations, transforming itself into a value-added reseller of equipment made by other companies. In May 1991, Peter Anderson was named to replace Fred Anderson as president and CEO of MAI. The company continued its cost-cutting efforts, reducing personnel and streamlining operations wherever possible. In spite of these efforts, MAI's finances continued to deteriorate, culminating in a loss of $182 million in fiscal 1992. In March 1993, a group of banks took control of MAI's European subsidiaries in exchange for the release of $84 million in debt. The company filed for Chapter 11 bankruptcy protection the following month while it concocted a reorganization plan.

MAI emerged from bankruptcy in November 1993 as a much leaner version of its former self. The company reported revenue of $115 million for 1993. Most of this dramatic reduction in sales stemmed from the elimination of its European subsidiaries. MAI entered 1994 on a high note, releasing several software products for its target industries in the first half of the year. Management at MAI hoped that the company, in its new streamlined form, was primed for yet another ascent.

Principal Subsidiaries: Computerized Lodging Systems, Inc.; Sextant Corporation.

Further Reading:

Carroll, Timothy J., "Big Investor in Management Assistance Gets Control of Board as Chairman Quits," *Wall Street Journal,* August 24, 1984, p. 4.
Deagon, Brian, "MAI Phasing Out Production in Shift to VAR," *Electronic News,* February 25, 1991, p. 14.
Deagon, Brian, "MAI Realigning, Seeks to Halt Sales Slide," *Electronic News,* August 28, 1989, p. 12.
Deagon, Brian, "MBF Seeks Buyer," *Electronic News,* August 29, 1988, p. 1.
"The Dramatic Rise and Fall of MAI," *Forbes,* September 1, 1969, pp. 19–21.
"First Items Bow at Basic/Four," *Electronic News,* July 5, 1971, p. 24.
Heins, John, "Sorry, Asher," *Forbes,* December 15, 1986, pp. 134–137.
Helm, Leslie, "The Merger Wave Bearing Down on Minicomputer Makers," *Business Week,* November 28, 1988, p. 36.
Jefferson, David J., "MAI's Patton Quits as Chief Executive, President Amid Duel for Prime Computer," *Wall Street Journal,* June 21, 1989, p. B13.
Kapp, Sue, "Fearless 'General' Patton," *Business Marketing,* December 1987, p. 8.

Lappen, Alyssa A., ''Thank You, Asher,'' *Forbes,* February 22, 1988, p. 8.

''MAI Will Merge Wordstream and Basic Four Subs,'' *Electronic News,* August 20, 1979, p. 22.

''Management Assist. Melds 2 Units,'' *Electronic News,* April 30, 1984, p. 26.

''MBF Expects Loss, Cites Prime Bid,'' *Electronic News,* August 14, 1989, p. 4.

McCusker, Tom, ''High Stakes Turn This Risk Taker Into a Miracle Maker,'' *Datamation,* September 15, 1988, p. 116.

McCusker, Tom, ''The Datamation 100,'' *Datamation,* June 15, 1992, p. 147; June 15, 1993, p. 122.

''Midsize Computer Makers Face a Midlife Crisis,'' *Business Week,* October 31, 1983, pp. 100B-D.

''A Squeeze on the Mini's Pioneers,'' *Business Week,* September 28, 1981, pp. 90–94.

Wiegner, Kathleen K., ''Caveat Raider,'' *Forbes,* June 12, 1989, p. 160.

''Where There's Life . . . ,'' *Forbes,* August 1, 1976, p. 38.

''Word/Data Terminal for Basic Four 410,'' *Electronic News,* October 22, 1979, p. 48.

—Robert R. Jacobson

MCDONNELL DOUGLAS

McDonnell Douglas Corporation

P.O. Box 516
St. Louis, Missouri 63166-0516
U.S.A.
(314) 232-0232
Fax: (314) 234-3826

Public Company
Incorporated: 1967
Employees: 70,016
Sales: $14.47 billion
Stock Exchanges: New York
SICs: 3721 Aircraft; 3728 Aircraft Parts and Equipment, Not
   Elsewhere Classified; 3761 Guided Missiles and Space
   Vehicles; 3724 Aircraft Engines and Engine Parts; 3812
   Search and Navigation Equipment; 3679 Electronic
   Components, Not Elsewhere Classified

The largest defense contractor in the United States, McDonnell
Douglas Corporation is also the world's largest builder of military aircraft, the third largest commercial aircraft maker in the
world, and the third largest National Aeronautics and Space
Administration (NASA) contractor. As McDonnell Douglas
fought to retain these enviable rankings in the 1990s, it faced a
host of new and formidable obstacles that represented some of
the most difficult challenges in its storied history.

Donald Douglas's interest in aviation can probably be traced
back to a Wright Brothers exhibition for the U.S. Army in 1908.
Douglas later entered the Naval Academy which, at the time,
was experimenting with seaplanes. After two years at the academy, he left to study mechanical engineering at the Massachusetts Institute of Technology. Douglas completed the four-year
curriculum in two years. Upon his graduation in 1915, he was
summoned to California by the designer Glenn Martin (later of
Martin Marietta). A year later, with the outbreak of war in
Europe, the United States government asked him to move to
Washington, D.C. in order to direct the aviation section of the
Signal Corps. After a few months, Douglas became frustrated
with Washington and returned to Martin's company, whose
headquarters had since moved to Cleveland.

Douglas left Martin in 1920 and established his own company
office behind a Los Angeles barber shop. With virtually no
capital at his disposal, Douglas persuaded a wealthy young
man, David R. Davis, to underwrite the costs of developing a

new aircraft design called the "Cloudster." With Davis's help,
Douglas had enough money to hire several engineers away from
Martin in order to build the Cloudster. This airplane was designed to fly coast to coast, stopping only to refuel. It also had a
service ceiling high enough to enable it to fly over mountain
ranges.

In 1921, the newly renamed Douglas Company produced a
torpedo plane for the Navy designated the "DT." The DT's
popularity established a reputation for Douglas in the War
Department which later led to an interest in Douglas's next
plane, the World Cruiser or "DWC." In a 1924 demonstration,
the World Cruiser was flown around the world in 15 days. This
accomplishment generated more interest in Douglas's small
company.

Douglas, no longer needing the financial support of Davis,
introduced a flying boat for the commercial market in 1928
called the Douglas Dolphin. In 1934 Douglas's rival, William
Boeing, secretly purchased a Dolphin which he allegedly used
to tender his yacht. It has been suggested that Boeing studied the
Dolphin's design and later incorporated some of this design into
the Boeing Company's flying boats.

When Jack Frye of TWA was unable to convince Boeing to sell
airplanes to his airline—Boeing chose to give top priority to the
airlines owned by his own United Company—he solicited several alternative aircraft companies for a new all-metal tri-motor
airplane capable of carrying 12 passengers at 145 miles per
hour. Douglas received one of Frye's written requests in August
1932. His small company was an unlikely candidate to supply
TWA with an airplane, but when Douglas submitted an airplane
design able to carry 14 passengers, capable of speed approxi-
mating 180 miles per hour, and fitted with only two engines,
Frye awarded him the contract. The airplane Frye agreed to
purchase was the DC-1 (DC stood for "Douglas Commercial"). Before more than one DC-1 could be produced, the
design was improved. The airplane finally delivered to TWA
was a revised version of the DC-1, redesignated the DC-2. With
the experience he had gained from the production of the DC-2,
Douglas began work on his next design, the DC-3. New airmail
legislation in 1934 increased the reliance of airlines on passenger business. As a result, the DC-3 was designed to meet new
specifications, making it the "first airplane to make money just
hauling passengers."

Airplane manufacturers were aware of the rising political ten-
sions in Europe. The likelihood of war was becoming increasingly apparent. Aircraft designers knew that the large commercial airplanes could easily be converted into bombers. Many
became suspicious when they learned that Hitler's Germany
was ambitiously building commercial planes for routes that
weren't yet charted. People wondered what Germany was doing
with so many planes, when the country in fact had no commercial airline. Douglas thought another war in Europe was inevitable, so the DC-3 was developed with a dual commercial/
military purpose in mind.

Douglas's DC-3 was more popular than Boeing's 247. At the
beginning of World War II, 80 percent of the airplanes in
commercial service were DC-3s. During the war, the DC-3
served as a personnel carrier, and in other design variations as

a B-18 bomber and a C-47 transport. Over 10,000 DC-3s of various configurations were built for service with the Army Air Corps. Douglas also produced a number of attack planes for the military, the A-20 Havoc and the SBD Dauntless among them. A squadron of Dauntless airplanes was instrumental in the defeat of the Japanese Navy at the battle of Midway Island.

Douglas's next plane, the DC-4, was put into military service (as a C-54) before it flew commercially. The DC-4 had four engines and was nearly three times larger than its predecessor. When it finally entered commercial service in 1946, it gained an undeserved reputation for accidents. Pilot error was most often determined to be the cause of the disasters.

When the war exposed the secret development of Lockheed's revolutionary designed "Constellation," Douglas was provided with a look at what his competition would be offering after the war. Douglas began work early on a response to Lockheed's airplane, and his DC-6 entered service after the war. An improved version, the DC-6B earned substantial revenues for the airlines. A further improvement, the DC-7, was the first commercial transport to cross the United States non-stop against prevailing winds. Over 1,000 airplanes in the DC-6/DC-7 series were produced. The first presidential aircraft were Douglas DCs; Roosevelt's "Sacred Cow" was a C-54, and Truman's "Independence" was a C-118, the military version of a DC-6.

Donald Douglas prepared his son, Donald Jr., for a leading position in the company, and appointed him president in 1958. The senior Douglas, however, continued to make the "important" decisions. One such important decision was to delay the development of a passenger jetliner. Unfortunately, it turned out to be a very costly decision. In Seattle, Boeing was flight testing its 707 when Douglas's DC-8 was just a model in the wind tunnel. Douglas was surprised when its most loyal customer, American Airlines, placed an order for Boeing 707s. Douglas accelerated development of its similarly configured DC-8, but Boeing's lead in designing and manufacturing a jetliner was insurmountable.

In a rather ironic turn of events, United Airlines, historically associated with Boeing, placed the first order for DC-8s. When the airplane finally became available, Douglas wasn't adequately prepared to meet the demand for its new jetliner, and a backlog of orders developed. The company lost some customers to Boeing and upset others by delaying delivery of the airplanes.

In 1965, the company introduced an improved jetliner designated the DC-9 in order to challenge Boeing's new 727. Once again these two airplanes were very similar. They were both designed with engines mounted on the rear of the fuselage, a feature first seen on the popular French-built Caravelle. The costly development of the DC-9 and the continuing backlog of orders resulted in a liquidity problem for Douglas. Douglas lost a great amount of money in 1966, and banks began to withhold their financial support of the company.

"Overwhelmed by prosperity," but unable to control costs, Douglas was quickly becoming a prime target for a takeover. In 1967, six companies submitted takeover bids for Douglas: General Dynamics, North American Aviation (later Rockwell International), Martin Marietta, Signal Oil & Gas, Fairchild, and McDonnell Aircraft. Douglas's board of directors voted for a

sale to McDonnell, which had a history of effective management as well as an innovative group of middle managers. McDonnell had expressed an interest in Douglas as early as 1963 but was unable to arrange a merger until Douglas's financial position had sufficiently deteriorated. The merger encountered no problems because McDonnell had recently split its operations into three separate divisions, all independently managed. The simple addition of Douglas as a fourth division was made without difficulty and without interruption of either company's business.

James Smith McDonnell's company began as an airplane manufacturer for the military shortly before World War II. It was a major manufacturer in St. Louis by the end of the war, but it gained significant recognition only with the production of its Phantom jets in 1946. McDonnell was primarily a manufacturer of military jets, including the F2H Banshee, F3H Demon, F-101 Voodoo, and the various F-4 Phantom designs. (James McDonnell had a fascination with the occult, which may explain the origin of the names he chose for his jets.) In addition, McDonnell built the Mercury and Gemini space capsules for NASA. Since that time, the company built a number of missile systems, but its business with NASA remained limited.

McDonnell had two sons, James III and John, as well as a nephew, Sanford. All three sat on the board of directors at McDonnell Douglas. Donald Douglas, Jr. was gradually excluded from the management of the company, and it became hard for him to work in the shadow of the McDonnell family. Sanford McDonnell was named chief executive officer of the company upon James McDonnell's retirement in 1971, but Sanford still took directions from his uncle.

Under the continuing domination of James McDonnell, McDonnell Douglas developed a wide body "jumbo" jetliner in order to compete with Boeing's 747 in the commercial airliner market. The 450-passenger 747 was certainly larger, but McDonnell Douglas' DC-10, with only three engines, was better suited for the needs of more airline companies. Boeing had a hard time selling 747s; the airplanes were regarded as too large. Soon the company was facing a financial crisis. Then, with modifications, the 747 began to garner substantial orders. The DC-10 entered the market just as the Boeing 747 was becoming popular. As a result, McDonnell Douglas had a difficult time selling the DC-10 and recovering its development costs.

More stable business came from the Pentagon. McDonnell Douglas was licensed to build Hawker Siddley's vertical take-off and landing Harrier "jump-jet," which played a prominent role in Britain's war in the Falkland Islands. The company also produced the popular F-4 Phantom, the F-15 Eagle, the A-4 Skyhawk, and the F-18A Hornet.

McDonnell Douglas risked losing its contract to manufacture F-15s in 1970 when the U.S. Civil Rights Commission reported racially discriminatory hiring and promotion practices at the company, particularly in regard to African American employees. By 1979, however, the company reported that the implementation of affirmative action programs had rectified the situation.

There were other problems for the company as well. In 1979, James McDonnell III and three other company officials were indicted on charges of bribing foreign officials. According to the indictment, McDonnell Douglas was paying bribes to influence the sales of its airplanes in Korea, Pakistan, Venezuela, Zaire, and the Philippines. Clark Clifford, a former secretary of defense, defended the company in court by arguing that these payments were made with the full knowledge of the U.S. government in "difficult sales environments." Nevertheless, a committee of directors recommended that nonmanagement executives should dominate the membership of the board of directors to prevent schemes such as this from happening again.

McDonnell Douglas wasn't the only company accused of paying bribes. Lockheed, desperate to sell the L-1011 TriStar, was similarly implicated, but its activities were believed to have been far more extensive. Both Lockheed and McDonnell Douglas admitted their guilt, but while McDonnell Douglas was merely ordered to pay a fine of $55,000 and a $1.2 million civil award, the Lockheed Corporation was nearly ruined.

It was a bad year for McDonnell Douglas in another way. On May 25, 1979, at Chicago's O'Hare Airport, an American Airlines DC-10 lost an engine during take-off, crashed, and killed all 273 people aboard. After a temporary grounding of DC-10s, the National Transportation Safety Board cited inherent design flaws and unapproved maintenance procedures for having caused the accident. In response, Sanford McDonnell issued a statement to remind DC-10 customers that American "damaged the plane severely by using a crude maintenance technique." Controversy persisted as the public continued to associate the DC-10 with the crash. The design problems were finally corrected, and all maintenance procedures were standardized. The DC-10 was updated, redesigned, and renamed the MD-11; the MD-11 looked very much like a DC-10 with the exception of small vertical winglets located on the tips of airplane's wings.

The MD-11 proved more fuel efficient, could carry 405 passengers, and required only a crew of only two. It also had a flying range of 8,870 miles. For these reasons, airlines showed significant interest in the airplane. It was uncertain, however, especially in light of intense competition from Boeing and Airbus, whether McDonnell Douglas could make the MD-11 project profitable.

During the 1980s, McDonnell Douglas attempted to compete in the commercial aircraft market without designing an entirely new jetliner. In addition to the MD-11, McDonnell Douglas offered an updated version of its DC-9, designated the MD-80 (the number ostensibly indicated the year of the design) to compete with Boeing's 757. This airplane seated 150 passengers and cost approximately half that of a new Boeing. In order to sell the MD-80, the company arranged to lend the jetliners to American Airlines with a later option to buy. Instead of the standard 18-year lease, the McDonnell Douglas-American contract had a five-year term.

As McDonnell Douglas entered the 1990s, however, the future prospects for government-funded projects—the perennial mainstay of the company—appeared bleak. For years, a steady supply of military contracts had driven the company's growth, fueling the development and operation of its commercial aircraft unit as well, but with the end of the cold war signalling reduced defense spending by the federal government, McDonnell Douglas quickly found itself without a predictable source of revenue. Moreover, the company's development of the MD-11 and several other programs had exhausted its cash reserves, sending America's largest defense contractor into the turbulent early 1990s strapped for cash.

Under the stewardship of a new leader, McDonnell Douglas fought to reposition itself for the difficult years to come. John F. McDonnell, the son of the company's founder, was selected as McDonnell Douglas' chief executive officer in 1988, and under his control the company headed toward the potentially deleterious early 1990s. Long-term debt tripled from 1986 to the beginning of the decade, swelling to an alarming $3.3 billion and putting the company on the brink of insolvency. McDonnell initiated a drastic restructuring program in mid-1990 to restore the company's financial health. He cut McDonnell Douglas's work force 40 percent, winnowed the company's operating costs by more than $700 million annually, and placed a stronger emphasis on its non-core, non-military businesses. Through such measures, McDonnell Douglas's debt was reduced by more than $1 billion, giving the company's management a much needed reprieve to target its long-term objectives for McDonnell Douglas's future growth.

Given the constraints of reduced defense spending, John McDonnell was forced to make the company's commercial airline business the engine for future growth. This formidable task was made more difficult because of several factors, including the pernicious economic climate during the early 1990s, the commanding lead of McDonnell Douglas's largest competitor in the airliner business, the Seattle-based Boeing Company, and the absence of vast reserves of cash to fund the development of new commercial aircraft. Boeing controlled a 55 percent share of the commercial airline order backlog in 1992, compared to 12 percent for McDonnell Douglas, a disparity resulting from Boeing's venerable history in the airliner business and its broader product line, which comprised five types of planes compared to the two models marketed by McDonnell Douglas. Of crucial importance to narrowing this gap and sparking the company's resurgence in the commercial airline business was the development of McDonnell Douglas's new plane, the MD-12, a widebody, jumbo jet designed to compete against Boeing's esteemed 747. Unlike years past, however, McDonnell Douglas needed a partner to help fund its development of the MD-12, and began courting both U.S. and foreign companies, particularly the Taiwanese government-backed Taiwan Aerospace Corp., to raise the roughly $5 billion necessary to put the MD-12 in the sky.

By 1993, however, McDonnell Douglas had effected a turnaround from the precarious position occupied several years earlier, assisted in large part by its success in garnering government-funded defense contracts. The same economic conditions that had hobbled McDonnell Douglas had damaged some of its competitors more severely, and from the rubble left in the aftermath of the industry-wide struggle for survival, with an assortment of mergers and divestitures leaving fewer companies competing for defense-related projects, McDonnell Douglas emerged revitalized. Earnings for the year soared 145 percent, up from a loss of $781 million in 1992 to $396 million in profit, despite a drop in revenues, while the company's debt continued to fall. As the company entered the mid-1990s, further cause for optimism arrived in early 1994, when Israel announced it would purchase 20 McDonnell Douglas F-15 fighter aircraft, a deal valued at $2 billion.

Although McDonnell Douglas's resurgence in the mid-1990s augured hope for the future, the transformation of its commercial airliner unit into the company's main profit engine remained the company's best hope for future long-term growth. During the early 1990s, the company's airliner unit remained in the black, but only through extreme cost-cutting measures. As the company charted its course for the remainder of the 1990s, away from the economic recession that hampered airliner sales earlier in the decade, much depended the performance of McDonnell Douglas in the commercial aircraft arena.

Principal Subsidiaries: McDonnell Douglas Financial Services Corp.; McDonnell Douglas Helicopter Co.

Further Reading:

Bilstein, Roger, *Flight in America 1900–1983: From the Wrights to the Astronauts,* Baltimore: The Johns Hopkins University Press, 1984.
Bowers, Peter M., *The DC-3: 50 Years of Legendary Flight,* Blue Ridge Summit: Tab Books, Inc., 1986.
''Dwindling Hopes,'' *Forbes,* June 8, 1992, p. 45.
Ellis, James E., ''Gone Is My Co-Pilot?,'' *Business Week,* July 6, 1992, p. 71.
Ellis, James E., ''McDonnell Douglas: Unfasten the Seat Belts,'' *Business Week,* February 14, 1994, p. 36.
Ingells, Douglas J., *The McDonnell Douglas Story,* Fallbrook: Aero Publishers, 1979.

—updated by Jeffrey L. Covell

Meditrust

197 First Avenue
Needham, Massachusetts 02194-9127
U.S.A.
(617) 433-6000
Fax: (617) 433-1290

Public Company
Incorporated: 1985
Employees: 44
Sales: $150.8 million
Stock Exchanges: New York Midwest Philadelphia
SICs: 6726 Investment Offices, Not Elsewhere Classified

The largest health care real estate investment trust company in the United States, Meditrust maintained investments in 233 health care facilities spread across 34 states. With $1.3 billion invested in the subacute sector of the health care industry, Meditrust ranked as the leader in health care real estate investment and as the second largest real estate investor in the country, regardless of the industry in which the investments were made. By focusing on investing in long-term care facilities, Meditrust expanded quickly during the late 1980s and early 1990s, its growth fueled by prudent management and by a rapidly expanding real estate investment industry, which in one year, from 1993 to 1994, doubled in financial magnitude form $20 billion to $40 billion.

In 1978, a wealthy Bostonian named Abraham D. Gosman purchased approximately 85,000 shares of a Massachusetts-based bank holding company called Multibank Inc. Multibank controlled seven banks scattered throughout the state, had assets of roughly $1 billion, and presented Gosman with what appeared to be a suitable investment opportunity. He later related to the *Wall Street Journal* that his acquisition of Multibank stock, which ceded him slightly more than a five percent stake in the holding company, was intended "purely as an investment." Quickly, however, Gosman's investment escalated into much more, evolving into what was heralded at the time as one of the most contentious bank battles in Massachusetts history, a struggle that indirectly led to the formation of Meditrust seven years later.

In the 50 years separating his birth and his acquisition of Multibank stock, Gosman had become a multi-millionaire, rising from his blue-collar roots as the son of a factory foreman to become an affluent member of Boston society, an ascension that began shortly after World War II, when Gosman finished his college education. After he graduated from the University of New Hampshire, Gosman used an $800 loan from his mother to start his own business—a company that laminated shoes—then used the proceeds to diversify his interests into the real estate development business. Gosman built apartment buildings and nursing homes in Massachusetts and in neighboring Connecticut, becoming enormously wealthy in the process. By the late 1970s, his ascension to the upper echelon of Massachusetts' business and social circles was complete, and he could count among his friends a prestigious collection of big-city mayors, U.S. senators, and influential business leaders. He was a triumphant success and not reticent to admit it. When asked by a *Wall Street Journal* reporter whether he was worth millions of dollars, Gosman replied, "Go on." When asked next if he was worth multi-millions, he invitingly responded, "You can go on some more."

Shortly after investing in Multibank, Gosman approached the holding company's president and chair, David L. Lynch, about becoming a director of the company, not an unusual request considering that Gosman's more than five percent stake in Multibank represented the largest held by a single shareholder. However, Lynch refused Gosman's request, later claiming he didn't know who Gosman was at the time of the request. This touched off the debacle that eventually led to the formation of Meditrust and more immediately led to a bitter struggle between Gosman and Multibank. Gosman was angered by Lynch's rebuff, then became enraged when he learned that no member of the Multibank board had ever even heard of him. The indignities became too much to bear, and Gosman quickly sought to make his presence known. Over the course of the next two months, he doubled his stake in Multibank, raising his interest to more than ten percent and returned to the company's board of directors, this time asking not for a directorship, but for Lynch's position as chairperson of the company. Not surprisingly, those attending the meeting who were not familiar with the name Abraham D. Gosman, now certainly were. The board rejected Gosman's attempted usurpation, declaring in the *Wall Street Journal* that Gosman's proposal was not "in the best interests of Multibank, its stockholders, or bank depositors." Gosman, however, was not deterred.

After the board's rejection, Gosman doubled his interest in Multibank again, controlling, by this time, roughly 23 percent of the company. Then Gosman began to enlist the support of some of his influential friends who were also Multibank shareholders, including former U.S. Senator Edward W. Brooke, the former mayor of Boston, John F. Collins, and New Hampshire's former bank commissioner, Vincent B. Dunn. With these reputable personalities behind him, Gosman charged, among various other allegations, that Multibank's dividend payments were too low. A legal imbroglio ensued; detective agencies were hired, public relations firms became involved, and charges and countercharges were filed, leading to an eventual resolution that gave Gosman an enviable return on what initially began as "purely an investment."

In the spring of 1981, Multibank's shareholders, after having voted against Gosman's takeover of the company, authorized the bank holding company to pay $30 per share to Gosman for the 353,241 shares he had acquired, many at $20 per share. With the profits realized from his rancorous association with Multibank, Gosman turned to a more familiar line of business, the development of nursing homes, and began acquiring nursing homes and other health care related properties. These properties would form the foundation for Gosman's new company, The Mediplex Group, Inc., a Wellesley, Massachusetts-based operator of nursing homes and other health care facilities.

Mediplex grew rapidly during the five years following its creation, with revenues climbing to roughly $80 million by the middle of the decade, representing a 32 percent compound annual increase from 1981's sales. By the mid-1980s, Mediplex's success had drawn the attention of Avon Products, Inc., an enormous cosmetics manufacturer that was diversifying into several other business lines, including health care. Avon's entrance in the health care field had begun in 1984, when the company acquired Foster Medical Corp., the country's largest home health care products and services company. After several smaller health care related acquisitions in 1984 and 1985, including Kagle Home Health Care and Retirement Inns of America, Inc., Avon acquired Gosman's Mediplex Group in 1986, adding the nursing home operator to the cosmetic company's burgeoning health care division in a transaction valued at roughly $250 million. Part of the deal between Gosman and Avon stipulated that Mediplex Group could remain under Gosman's stewardship; in fact, Avon encouraged Gosman to remain, offering him an additional $60 million if Mediplex Group achieved pre-determined profit objectives within a three-year period. Gosman opted to continue building his five-year old business, reasoning that Mediplex Group would benefit enormously under the benevolent and financially stable Avon corporate umbrella. However, he also had other business interests in addition to his five-year old Mediplex Group, one of which was his nearly one year-old trust company named Meditrust.

Meditrust had been formed in April 1985, eight months prior to Avon's acquisition of Mediplex Group, and its stock began trading in October. Established by Gosman as a business trust for Mediplex Group's health care properties, Meditrust invested in the health care facilities operated by Mediplex, then gradually developed a diversified clientele, becoming part of a soon-to-be rapidly growing niche in the real estate investment industry known as REITs, or Real Estate Investment Trusts. REITs like Meditrust owed their proliferation to the Real Estate Investment Act of 1961, which sought to encourage public investment in real estate and established rules for REIT operation. REITs operated essentially like other trusts, enabling a group of investors to invest in properties managed by appointed trustees. According to regulations established by the Real Estate Investment Act of 1961 and ensuing legislation, REITs had to distribute, among other qualification standards, at least 95 percent of their income—generated by developing or administering real estate property—to shareholders. By operating as such, REITs were exempt from corporate taxation, which provided Gosman with a financially prudent course to develop, finance, and administer Mediplex Group's growth.

Mediplex Group provided Meditrust with its initial business, but not long after the health care REIT's formation, it began investing in health care facilities operated by other health care companies and, in the process, spread its investments among various niches in the health care industry. Before the decade was through, Meditrust maintained investments in six types of health care facilities, the first type being, not coincidentally, long-term care facilities, the primary type of health care facilities operated by Mediplex Group. Other health care facilities in which Meditrust invested included rehabilitation hospitals, alcohol and substance abuse treatment facilities, psychiatric hospitals, retirement homes, and medical office buildings. The path toward attaining this diversification began when the company's stock was first listed on the New York Stock Exchange in October 1985, when Meditrust's management, the trustees headed by Gosman, began investing in facilities operated by Mediplex Group.

Through the proceeds gained from the issuance of stock in 1986, Meditrust acquired two alcohol and substance abuse treatment facilities and two long-term care facilities, all four of which were owned by Mediplex Group. In an arrangement similar to others that followed, Meditrust then leased these properties back to Mediplex Group, which, as it had before the sale to Meditrust, operated the facilities. The following year, Meditrust purchased a hospital company and a 172-bed long-term care facility from its familiar partner Mediplex Group. That same year, during which revenues reached $25.5 million, Meditrust became involved in a partnership to develop three rehabilitation hospitals, which, upon completion, were to be leased by Continental Medical Systems, Inc.

By mid-1988, after acquiring a long-term health care center from Integrated Health Services, Inc. in January, Meditrust's assets amounted to $428 million, a total that would more than double in the next four years despite the debilitative effects of a national recession. In June 1988, Meditrust acquired a long-term care facility in Medina, Ohio, the Riverbend Nursing Home in Grand Blanc, Michigan, a psychiatric hospital named Kentfield Rehabilitation Hospital, and a 90-bed psychiatric hospital in West Monroe, Louisiana. These acquisitions rounded out Meditrust's investment portfolio, which by this point included holdings in alcohol and substance abuse treatment centers, long-term care facilities, rehabilitation hospitals, psychiatric facilities, and retirement communities.

As Meditrust entered the 1990s, it stood on stable financial ground, having experienced considerable growth during its first five years of existence. Annual revenues had climbed to $89 million by 1990, up by nearly a quarter from the previous year's total, and net income had soared 35 percent, rising from $22 million to $29 million. Following these encouraging results, economic conditions throughout the country soured, forcing many industries to halt expansion and prepare for the potentially deleterious effects of a recession. Particularly hard hit was the real estate industry, but despite the economic climate Meditrust continued to demonstrate robust financial performance. With the closing of an $86 million mortgage financing deal in April 1992, nearly seven years to the day after the trust company's formation, Meditrust's real estate portfolio surpassed $1 billion in assets, 30 percent of which was invested in facilities operated by Mediplex Group. By then the largest of the ten REITs in the nation that specialized in health care investments, Meditrust maintained an interest in 142 health care facilities scattered throughout 25 states, from which the trust company generated $132 million in revenues and recorded $51 million in net income.

By the beginning of 1993, the number of health care facilities in which Meditrust maintained an investment had increased to 170 and its geographic scope had expanded to include four more states. A majority of these facilities—nearly 70 percent—were long-term care facilities, a segment of the health care industry in which Meditrust continued to increase its presence. After exploring more than $3.5 billion worth of investment opportunities during the year, Meditrust invested roughly $230 million in 30 health care facilities, 26 of which were long-term care facilities, catering to an increasingly aging U.S. population. Revenues surged forward again in 1993, reaching $150.8 million, while net income swelled to $63.6 million.

As Gosman and Meditrust's approximately 40 other employees searched for investment opportunities in 1994 and beyond, demographics of the U.S. population suggested a greater need for long-term care facilities in the future. In that direction the trust company charted its future, planing to increase its investments in long-term care facilities and complement those holdings with investments in the other five established areas of Meditrust's involvement.

Principal Subsidiaries: New England Finance Corp.; Pacific Finance Corp.; Mediplex of Queens, Inc.

Further Reading:

"Financing Business," *Wall Street Journal,* August 22, 1986, p. 27.

Gilpin, Kenneth N., "Vital Signs Improve for the Nursing Home Industry," *New York Times,* February 27, 1994.
"Health Care Trust Acquires 5 Facilities for $55 Million," *Wall Street Journal,* January 8, 1988, p. 30.
Lynch, Mitchell C., "Multibank Is Fighting Fiercely to Resist Quiet Multimillionaire's Bid for Control," *Wall Street Journal,* December 29, 1980, p. 15.
Marcom, John Jr., "Avon to Purchase Mediplex Group for $220 Million," *Wall Street Journal,* January 24, 1986, p. 8.
"Mediplex Group Sets Acquisition," *Wall Street Journal,* March 15, 1985, p. 3.
"Meditrust Acquires Four Specialty Health Facilities," *Modern Health Care,* June 17, 1988, p. 60.
"Meditrust Announces Offering of $175 Million of Equity and Convertible Debt," *Barron's,* February 15, 1993, p. 67.
"Meditrust Buys a Hospital Firm," *Wall Street Journal,* January 5, 1987, p. 24.
"Meditrust Buys 172-Bed Center," *Wall Street Journal,* October 6, 1987, p. 57.
"Meditrust Net Income, Cash Flow Jump in 1990," *Modern Health Care,* February 25, 1991, p. 38.
"Meditrust Raises $175 Million in Offering," *Modern Health Care,* February 15, 1993, p. 74.
"Meditrust Real Estate Assets Top $1 Billion," *Modern Health Care,* May 25, 1992, p. 39.
Marcial, Gene G., "Health Care Crunch, Hah!," *Business Week,* August 30, 1993, p. 70.
"Multibank Plan to Purchase Dissident's Stake Is Approved," *Wall Street Journal,* May 27, 1981, p. 18.
Suskind, Ron, "Head-Trauma Firm's Records Seized by Federal Agents in Fraud Inquiry," *Wall Street Journal,* October 28, 1992, p. A8.

—Jeffrey L. Covell

Mentor Graphics Corporation

8005 S. W. Boeckman Rd.
Wilsonville, Oregon 97070-7777
U.S.A.
(503) 685-7000
Fax: (503) 685-7985

Public Company
Incorporated: 1981
Employees: 1,900
Sales: $339.8 million
Stock Exchange: NASDAQ
SICs: 7372 Prepackaged Software; 7373 Computer Integrated
    Systems Design

Mentor Graphics Corporation is among the world leaders in electronic design automation (EDA), the use of computer software to design and analyze electronic components and systems. Mentor Graphics designs, manufactures, and markets software used in a number of industries, including aerospace, consumer electronics, computer, semiconductor, and telecommunications. Software produced by Mentor Graphics assists engineers in all of these industries in developing complex integrated circuits. Missile guidance systems, microprocessors, and automotive electronics are among the products designed with the help of Mentor Graphics software. Mentor Graphics also offers customers support and training in the use of its EDA systems.

Mentor Graphics was founded in 1981 by a group of young aggressive computer professionals at Tektronix, Inc., the largest electronics manufacturing company in Oregon. The main visionary in the group was Thomas Bruggere, a software engineering manager who had spent several years at Burroughs Corporation before joining Tektronix in 1977. Convinced that he could do better with his own company, Bruggere began assembling a core group of collaborators from among his associates at Tektronix. The group eventually consisted of seven members, who would meet after work to discuss what form a new company should take. Along with Bruggere, the group included Gerard Langeler, head of the Business Unit marketing department at Tektronix, and David Moffenbeier, the company's manager of operations analysis.

Initially, the company's pioneering group met in Bruggere's living room and had only a vague idea of what they would be producing. They decided that the area with the best prospects

for success was computer aided engineering, or CAE. Once startup financing was in place, members of the Mentor Graphics team traveled the country interviewing engineers to see what qualities were most important to them in a CAE system. For the company's initial product, Bruggere and company settled on a workstation that used their own software run on a powerful desktop computer manufactured by Apollo Computer, a Massachusetts-based company also in its infancy. The system was named the IDEA 1000, and represented a substantial improvement over anything already in use in the CAE field.

Once the system was conceived, its production became a race against time. The Mentor Graphics team believed that it was critical to have a working product finished in time to unveil at the June 1982 Design Automation Conference in Las Vegas, the industry's most important trade show. The IDEA 1000 made a big splash at the conference, and orders for the workstation began to pour in.

Throughout the planning stages, Bruggere and the others expected the company's principal competition to come from established industry heavyweights like Hewlett-Packard and alma mater Tektronix. However, during Mentor Graphics' first year of operation, two small companies, Daisy Systems and Valid Logic Systems, emerged in the Silicon Valley with CAE products and proved to be Mentor Graphics' stiffest competition. For several years the computer press generally lumped the three companies together, referring to them collectively by their first initials, DMV. Two things actually distinguished Mentor Graphics from the others. First, Mentor Graphics bought its computers from Apollo, while the Daisy and Valid Logic built their own hardware. This allowed Mentor Graphics to concentrate on the software side. Secondly, Mentor Graphics developed its software from scratch, in contrast to its competitors, whose software was either a hybrid or an adaptation of existing software packages. Because Mentor Graphics took the time following its conference success to develop its own database package rather than rely on the inferior one supplied by another company, Daisy gained a headstart in the race for customers. From the fall of 1982 until about 1985, Mentor Graphics and Daisy engaged in a brutal war for domination of the CAE business, with nearly every decision made at Mentor Graphics aimed at gaining market share from its rival.

In 1983 Mentor Graphics made its first acquisition of another company, California Automated Design, Inc. (CADI). CADI was developing software similar to Daisy's, and the purchase both strengthened Mentor Graphics' position against its chief rival and nipped another potential competitor in the bud. The results of the acquisition were mixed. Although the purchase gave Mentor Graphics an entrance into a new market segment, the two companies clashed philosophically. The relationship remained strained until 1986, when CADI founder Ning Nan stepped down from his position as vice chairman of Mentor Graphics' board. A more clear-cut success for Mentor Graphics in 1983 was the introduction of a new product called MSPICE, an interactive analog simulator. The first product of its kind on the CAE market, MSPICE made the process of designing and analyzing the behavior of analog circuits much more efficient.

1983 also marked Mentor Graphics' move into the international market with the formation of Mentor Graphics (UK) Ltd. Subsidiaries were added in France, Italy, the Netherlands, West Germany, Japan, and Singapore by the following year. By 1984, international sales were accounting for about 20 percent of the company's total. In September 1984 Mentor Graphics completed the acquisition of Synergy Dataworks, Inc., another young company based in Oregon. Mentor Graphics turned its first profit that year, reporting net income of $8.3 million after losing $221,000 in 1983. In addition, Mentor's initial public stock offering took place in January 1984. $51 million was raised through the sale of about 3 million shares of Mentor Graphics common stock.

Mentor Graphics' decision to use hardware produced outside the company in its workstations paid off handsomely in 1985. That year, archrival Daisy missed the deadline for its next generation of computer. Because Mentor Graphics' industry-standard workstations built by Apollo were experiencing no such delays in upgrading, Mentor Graphics was able to move into the industry lead for the first time. 1985 did not pass without major problems, however. The U.S. electronics industry suddenly encountered its worst recession in 20 years. One result was a glut in the semiconductor market, and semiconductor manufacturers were responsible for a quarter of Mentor Graphics' business. Mentor Graphics' net income for 1985 slipped to $7.99 million. The company was spared from worse devastation by the relative health of the aerospace and telecommunications industries, plus substantial growth in the company's international sales, which accounted for 37 percent of revenue for 1985.

By 1986, Mentor Graphics was releasing new products at the rate of one a month. The company's international operations continued to grow briskly, consisting by that time of 260 individuals working out of 17 offices in 13 countries. Their share of Mentor Graphics' revenue had reached 44 percent. One of the year's highlights was the debut of the Compute Engine Accelerator, a device capable of breaking through the computer bottlenecks often encountered by engineers during complex, multifaceted CAE operations. That year, Mentor Graphics' revenue reached $173.5 million. With both Daisy and Valid Logic losing money, Mentor Graphics' position at the top of the CAE industry was more or less cemented. In the broader design automation arena, Mentor Graphics was fourth largest.

The downturn in the computer industry had ended by 1987, and Mentor Graphics was able to increase its profits by 85 percent for the year. Sales were up to $222 million. 1988 was even better, as revenue passed the $300 million mark, and net income grew by another 65 percent. That year, Mentor Graphics was the most profitable among all design automation firms, earning more per share than such major players as IBM and McDonnell Douglas. In March 1988 Mentor Graphics absorbed the CAE business of Tektronix, paying $5 million for a business into which Tektronix had already sunk $200 million in development costs. By the middle of the year, Mentor Graphics controlled about a fourth of the $900 million market for electronic computer-aided design products, whereas the fading Daisy's share had dropped to 12 percent. About half the company's business was overseas by this time. Mentor Graphics was making an especially good showing in Japan, where the company held 60 percent of the market for CAE workstations.

Mentor Graphics' growth continued through 1989. The company's net income made another big jump, reaching $44.8 million on sales of $380 million. With everything looking rosy, the company embarked on an ambitious new project that year. Mentor Graphics announced its commitment to develop Release 8.0, a new generation of design automation software with capabilities far exceeding those of any existing product. This dream package was a bundle of 50 integrated programs designed into a framework that would allow a customer to move data freely among the various programs. It was hoped that Release 8.0 would cut months off the time required to design a new computer chip.

Several problems in 1990 combined to halt Mentor Graphics' dominance of the market. As Mentor Graphics' engineers continued incorporating new features into Release 8.0, the project became increasingly complex. Work on Release 8.0 fell months behind schedule. The company suffered from a faltering economy and customers who stopped buying Mentor Graphics' older products knowing that 8.0 was to be released soon. At the same time, new competition sprang up from Cadence Design Systems, a five-year-old company that sold only software rather than entire workstations. Whereas Mentor Graphics' products were essentially a closed system, incompatible with other software packages, Cadence was producing software that could run on a wide range of workstations and design more complex chips. Between the delays in 8.0 and the emergence of Cadence, Mentor Graphics hit a wall.

The company made several changes to protect its position in the newly heated up race for EDA preeminence. One was to strengthen its integrated circuit design capability by acquiring Silicon Compiler Systems, which was integrated as a division of Mentor Graphics. The company also adopted Sun Microsystems hardware as a second platform for its products. Toward the end of 1990, Mentor Graphics reorganized its command structure in an effort to get the 8.0 project back on track. The company was divided into three distinct product groups: Concurrent Engineering, headed by Philip Robinson, a former vice president at Tektronix, the Systems group, led by Langeler, whose previous titles of president and chief operating officer were eliminated, and World Trade, under David Moffenbeier, another member of Mentor Graphics' core founding group. Bruggere remained chairman and CEO.

One of the most important causes of Mentor Graphics' ills during this period was its reluctance to adapt to certain changes taking place in the electronic design automation industry. Prior to the 1990s, the bulk of Mentor Graphics' sales came from complete packages of workstations and software. Around 1991, however, most customers already had workstations they were comfortable with and were interested mainly in purchasing software that could run on whatever hardware platform they preferred.

In April 1991, Mentor Graphics reported a quarterly loss for the first time in its history as a public company. A few months later, the company announced a round of layoffs that eliminated 435 jobs, or about 15 percent of its work force. By the end of 1991, Cadence had passed Mentor Graphics in software revenues. Mentor Graphics finished the year by losing $61.6 million on sales of $400 million. The company's skid continued into

1992. When 8.0 was finally released early in the year, it performed more slowly than expected, and was plagued with bugs. Mentor Graphics' stock plummeted, diving as low as 5¼ in October. For 1992, the company's sales took another major plunge to $351 million, and the company reported a net loss of nearly $51 million.

Mentor Graphics' struggle to turn itself around continued in 1993. The rivalry between Mentor Graphics and Cadence became fierce, with each company aggressively courting the other's customers. Cadence won a three-year multimillion dollar contract from Tektronix, who had been a loyal Mentor Graphics customer for years. Mentor Graphics countered by forging a cooperative relationship with Harris Corporation, an early Cadence ally. The company underwent further restructuring in an effort to cut costs. Mentor Graphics still lost money in 1993 ($32 million on revenue of $340 million), but some of its business segments showed signs of recovery. A $17 million contract with Motorola contributed to the company's slightly improving prospects. The process of changing itself more completely into a software company continued.

In March 1994, Bruggere announced that he was stepping down as chairman to pursue other interests. After a short period during which the company's day-to-day operations were handled by president and chief executive Walden Rhines, Jon Shirley (a former Microsoft president) was named Mentor Graphics' new chairman. With adjustments in the company's approach to its products completed, the leadership at Mentor Graphics hoped that its offerings—once at the cutting edge of electronic design automation—had again caught up with the needs of its customers.

Principal Subsidiaries: Mentor Graphics (Canada) Limited; Mentor Graphics (Finland) OY; Mentor Graphics (France) SARL; Mentor Graphics (Deutschland) GmbH; Mentor Graphics Japan Co. Ltd.; Mentor Graphics (Netherlands) B.V.; Mentor Graphics Finance B.V.; Mentor Graphics (Singapore) PTE. Ltd.; Mentor Graphics (Scandinavia) AB; Mento Graphics (Schweiz) AG; Mentor Electronic Design SA; Mentor Graphics (Taiwan) Co. Ltd.; Mentor Graphics (UK) Ltd.; Mentor Graphics (Denmark); Mentor Graphics Far East Ltd. Pte.; SDL International, Inc.-Domestic; European Development Center, N.V.; Model Technology Incorporated; Anacad Computer Systems GmbH; CheckLogic Design Systems, Inc.

Further Reading:

"Chairman Will Resign From Mentor Graphics," *New York Times,* March 28, 1994, p. D3.

Hof, Robert D., "Mentor's Lessons in the School of Hard Knocks," *Business Week,* January 25, 1993, pp. 92–93.

Holden, Daniel, "EDA Prize Fight: Cadence vs. Mentor," *Electronic News,* March 16, 1992, p. 20.

Langeler, Gerard H., "The Vision Trap," *Harvard Business Review,* March–April 1992, pp. 46–55.

"Thriving on Change: A History of Mentor Graphics, 1981–1991," Wilsonville, Oregon: Mentor Graphics Corporation, 1991.

Wiegner, Kathleen K., " 'Things Are Too Quiet,' " *Forbes,* May 16, 1988, pp. 40–41; " 'We Have To Change,' " *Forbes,* September 30, 1991 p. 160.

Winkler, Eric, "Mentor Shifts President's Duties," *Electronic News,* December 3, 1990, p. 1.

Wyatt, Edward A., "Clever Mentor," *Barron's,* January 8, 1990, pp. 22–23.

—Robert R. Jacobson

Mercantile Bankshares Corp.

P.O. Box 1477
Baltimore, Maryland 21203
U.S.A.
(410) 237-5900
Fax: (410) 237-5703

Public Company
Incorporated: 1970
Employees: 1,500
Total Assets: $5.5 billion
Stock Exchanges: NASDAQ
SICs: 6712 Bank Holding Companies; 6022 State
 Commercial Banks; 6021 National Commercial Banks

Mercantile Bankshares, Inc. is a bank holding company that oversees 17 affiliate banks in Maryland, three in Virginia, and one in Delaware, as well as one Maryland-based mortgage company. Each affiliate is a traditional, community-orientated bank and keeps its own name, local management team, and historic ties to the community it serves. Mercantile's lead bank, Mercantile-Safe Deposit and Trust Company of Baltimore, is the largest trust company in Maryland with 66 percent of that state's personal trust business. Its community banks are primarily in the lending business, focusing on mortgages as well as installment, construction, and commercial loans. The company's holdings have grown profitable over the years through conservative lending practices and what Mercantile Bankshares chairperson and CEO Henry F. Baldwin called relationship banking, that is, developing strong relationships with customers, knowing their needs well, and providing for these needs. Mercantile has no credit card business and has avoided buying and selling market loans. Moreover, it is a very well capitalized company, with almost twice the amount of capital behind every dollar of assets than that of other U.S. banks. In 1993, *American Banker* ranked its Tier 1 capital ratio of 18.41 (tier 1 capital as a percentage of weighted risk assets) the highest of the top 100 bank holding companies in the United States. The company's total risk and leveraged capital ratio were ranked second and third, respectively.

Organized in 1969, Mercantile Bankshares Corp. was the first bank holding company in the state of Maryland. The corporation organized itself around the multi-bank structure, allowing member banks "to continue as separately chartered corporate

entities." In addition to keeping its traditional role in the community, each affiliate was individually responsible to government regulatory agencies, elected its own officers, and maintained its own board of directors.

Three banks were acquired by the new corporation in 1969: Mercantile Safe Deposit and Trust, Annapolis Banking and Trust Co., and Bellair National Bank. Intended as the lead bank, Mercantile Safe Deposit and Trust was Maryland's largest trust institution, created in 1953 through the merger of two Baltimore banks, Mercantile Trust Company and Safe Deposit and Trust Company.

These two banks shared similar origins. Safe Deposit and Trust Co. was organized in Baltimore in 1864, one year before the end of the Civil War and one year after the National Bank Act of 1863, which created a uniform national currency to replace currencies issued by various state banks. Quartered in the basement of the National Farmers and Planters Bank in Baltimore, the bank was founded by Farmers and Planters' president Enoch Pratt, an entrepreneur with holdings in shipping, railroad, and insurance companies. As the South began rebuilding after the Civil War, deposits grew steadily. By 1876, Safe Deposit was able to move into new quarters, a fire- and burglar-proof building in Baltimore. Also that year, Safe Deposit established the first corporate trust service in Maryland and one of the first in the United States.

Pratt also happened to be one of the founders of Mercantile Trust and Deposit, established in 1884. Mercantile Trust was organized under an innovative concept borrowed from the department stores in major cities, offering fiduciary services, checking accounts, loans, savings, foreign banking, and safekeeping facilities all under one roof. After the Civil War, Mercantile took on an important role in financing the reconstruction of the South, serving as underwriters of bonds issued by southern cities and raising capital to finance such infrastructures as the South Bond Railway Co., Charleston City Railway, and the Atlantic Gas and Light Company. Nearly three quarters of a century later, the two companies merged, creating Mercantile Safe Deposit and Trust, Maryland's largest trust institution.

When Mercantile Bankshares was organized in 1969, Mercantile Safe Deposit and Trust's director, Henry F. Baldwin, became president of the new company. In its first year, the corporation had aggregate deposits of $22.6 million. At the time, Maryland's second bank holding company, Maryland National Corp., a one-bank holding company for Maryland National Bank, had deposits of $931.3 million. Under Baldwin's direction, Mercantile Bankshares immediately began acquiring local banks. In 1970, it acquired Bank of Southern Maryland through a stock swap valued at about $4 million. The following year, it acquired the Chestertown Bank of Maryland, a bank with four branches and $15.9 million in deposits.

In 1973, Mercantile Bankshares formed MBC Financial Corp., a commercial financing subsidiary which specialized in inventory and receivables lending. 1973 net income totaled $9.1 million. By late 1974, with the acquisition of Fidelity Bank, Frostburg, Mercantile Bankshares' holdings comprised eight banks with total deposits of $463.1 million, plus MBC Financial and Mercantile Mortgage Corp. Net income dropped in 1974, to

$8.5 million, primarily due to poor results of its MBC Financial subsidiary. In 1975, Mercantile phased out MBC, and other subsidiaries absorbed its customers. 1975 net income dropped again, by 4.3 percent to $8.1 million.

Nevertheless, Baldwin's conservative leadership soon brought the banks back to profitability. Mercantile's strategy was to retain tight control of its lead bank and require that affiliate banks produce a minimum one percent return on assets. Further management consisted of offering affiliates guidelines on investments, as well as sharing expertise in trust services, corporate banking, loan pricing, and other areas where small banks would be less knowledgeable. According to the *Wall Street Transcript,* this management style was quite successful: "Provided with sophisticated techniques yet free from day-to-day control, these smaller banks [were] extremely competitive and responsive to local conditions."

Return on assets grew an average of 1.2 percent from 1977 to 1982. 1981 return on equity was 14 percent, "well above the profitability of the average regional bank," according to the *Wall Street Transcript.* Net income nearly doubled in that time to more than $100 million. Total assets among the 11 banking affiliates and one mortgage operation totaled $1.5 billion.

In 1987, Mercantile purchased Eastville Bank in Virginia for around $7.1 million. Assets had almost doubled over 1981 totals to $2.8 billion, and Mercantile's bad debt ratio was quite low. While other banks suffered from the housing and office glut of the early 1990s, which left them with a large number of bad loans, Mercantile remained profitable, with a 1.7 percent return on assets of $4 billion in 1990. Moreover, earnings totaled $68.8 million, a four percent rise over 1989. However, the region's continued economic downslide affected 1991's net income, which rose only two percent to $70.5 million.

Although the real estate slump continued through 1992, Mercantile posted an eight percent rise in earnings to $76.2 million. The company substantially increased its provision for loan losses, thereby offsetting a growing number of nonperforming loans. In 1992, a number of large national and multinational banks opened branches in Mercantile's traditional market areas,

providing a potential threat to the bank's profitability. In response, management made a decision to focus even more strongly on community banking, announcing in its 1992 Annual Report: "As this kind of . . . banking becomes more rare, we see an unprecedented window of opportunity for building our customer base."

As it approached the turn of the century, Mercantile faced enormous changes in the banking industry. Its strategy remained to acknowledge—but not participate in—industry-wide trends, while it continued its emphasis on community banking. "While some banks are gearing up to perform international currency swaps, we continue to focus on the people who are building a house, starting or expanding a business, or raising capital to finance public improvements," management remarked in the company's 1993 Annual Report. This strategy has proven successful in Mercantile Bankshares' relatively short history. Consolidated net income rose for the 18th consecutive year in 1994, to $82.4 million. Moreover, expansion continued as the company purchased Fredericksburg National Bancorp, parent company of National Bank of Fredericksburg, Virginia.

Principal Subsidiaries: Annapolis Bank and Trust Company; Baltimore Trust Company; Bank of Southern Maryland; Calvert Bank & Trust Company; Chestertown Bank of Maryland; Citizens National Bank; County Banking and Trust Company; The Eastville Bank; Farmers & Merchants Bank, Eastern Shore; Fidelity Bank; First National Bank of St. Mary's; Forest Hill State Bank; Fredericksburg Bancorp, Inc.; Frederickstown Bank and Trust Company; Mercantile Safe Deposit & Trust Company; Peninsula Bank; People's Bank of Maryland; Potomac Valley Bank; St. Michaels Bank; Westminster Bank & Trust Company; Mercantile Mortgage Corporation.

Further Reading:

The Wall Street Transcript, August 13, 1990, p. 98,144.
The Wall Street Transcript, July 5, 1982, p. 66,387.
The Wall Street Transcript, March 9, 1987, p. 84,828.

—Maura Troester

Merck & Co., Inc.

1 Merck Drive
P.O. Box 1000
White House Station, New Jersey 08889-0100
U.S.A.
(908) 423-1000
Fax: (908) 594-4459

Public Company
Incorporated: 1927
Employees: 47,100
Sales: $10.5 billion
Stock Exchanges: New York Boston Cincinnati Philadelphia
  Pacific NASDAQ
SICs: 2834 Pharmaceutical Preparations; 2833 Medicinals
  and Botanicals; 2879 Agricultural Chemicals, Not
  Elsewhere Classified; 2836 Biological Products Except
  Diagnostic; 2860 Industrial Organic Chemicals; 2899
  Chemicals and Chemical Preparations, Not Elsewhere
  Classified; 2869 Industrial Organic Chemicals, Not
  Elsewhere Classified

Merck & Co., Inc. is the largest pharmaceutical company in the
world and one of America's most admired firms. The company
also has interests in specialty chemicals. With manufacturing
operations in 24 countries, over half of Merck's sales are made
outside the United States.

Merck's beginnings can be traced back to Friedrich Jacob
Merck's 1668 purchase of an apothecary in Darmstadt, Germany called "At the Sign of the Angel." Located next to a
castle moat, this store remained in the Merck family for generations.

The pharmacy was transformed by Heinrich Emmanuel Merck
into a drug manufactory in 1827. His first products were mor-
phine, codeine, and cocaine. By the time he died in 1855, Merck
products were used worldwide. In 1857, Merck sent a representative, Theodore Weicker, to the United States. Weicker (who
would go on to own drug powerhouse Bristol-Myers Squibb)
was joined by George Merck, the 24-year-old grandson of
Heinrich Emmanuel Merck in 1891. In 1899, the younger
Merck and Weicker acquired a 150-acre plant site in Rahway,
New Jersey, and started production in 1903.

The manufacturing of drugs and chemicals at this site began in
1903. This same location housed the corporate headquarters of
Merck and Company and four of its divisions, as well as
research laboratories and chemical production facilities, into the
1990s. Once known as "Merck Woods," the land surrounding
the original plant was used to hunt wild game and corral
domestic animals. In fact, George Merck kept a flock of 15 to 20
sheep on the grounds to test the effectiveness of an animal
disinfectant. The sheep became a permanent part of the Rahway
landscape.

The year 1899 also marked the first year the *Merck Manual of
Diagnosis and Therapy* was published. In 1983, the manual
entered its fourteenth edition. A *New York Times* review rated it
"the most widely used medical text in the world."

During World War I, George Merck, fearing anti-German senti-
ment, turned over a sizable portion of Merck stock to the Alien
Property Custodian of the United States. This portion represented the company interest held by Merck's German cousins.
At the end of the war, Merck was rewarded for his patriotic
leadership; the Alien Property Custodian sold Merck shares,
worth $3 million, to the public. George Merck retained control
of the corporation, and, by 1919 the company was once again
entirely public-owned.

By 1926, the year George Merck died, his son George W.
Merck had been acting president for over a year. Over the next
25 years, the younger Merck initiated and directed the Merck
legacy for pioneering research and development. In 1933, he
established a large laboratory and recruited prominent chemists
and biologists to produce new pharmaceutical products. Their
efforts had far-reaching effects. En route to researching cures
for pernicious anemia, Merck scientists discovered vitamin
B12. Its sales, both as a therapeutic drug and as a constituent of
animal feed were massive.

The 1940s continued to be a decade of discoveries in drug
research, especially in the field of steroid chemistry. In the early
1940s, a Merck chemist synthesized cortisone from ox bile,
which led to the discovery of cortisone's anti-inflammation
properties. In 1943, streptomycin, a revolutionary antibiotic
used for tuberculosis and other infections, was isolated by a
Merck scientist.

Despite the pioneering efforts and research success under
George W. Merck's leadership, the company struggled during
the postwar years. There were no promising new drugs to speak
of, and there was intense competition from foreign companies
underselling Merck products, as well as from former domestic
consumers beginning to manufacture their own drugs. Merck
found itself in a precarious financial position.

A solution was found in 1953 when Merck merged with Sharp
& Dohme, Incorporated, a drug company with a similar history
and reputation. Sharp and Dohme began as an apothecary shop
in 1845 in Baltimore, Maryland. Its success in the research and
development of such important products as sulfa drugs, vac-
cines, and blood plasma products matched the successes of
Merck. However, the merger was more than the combination of
two industry leaders. It provided Merck with a new distribution
network and marketing facilities to secure major customers.

For the first time, Merck could market and sell drugs under its own name.

At the time of George W. Merck's death in 1957, company sales had surpassed $100 million annually. Although Albert W. Merck, a direct descendant of Friedrich Jacob Merck, continued to sit on the board of directors into the 1980s, the office of chief executive was never again held by a Merck family member.

In 1976, John J. Honran succeeded the eleven-year reign of Henry W. Gadsen. Honran was a quiet, unassuming man who had entered Merck as a legal counselor and then became the corporate director of public relations. But Honran's unobtrusive manner belied an aggressive management style. With pragmatic determination Honran not only continued the Merck tradition for innovation in drug research, but also improved a poor performance record on new product introduction to the market.

This problem was most apparent in the marketing of Aldomet, an antihypertensive agent. Once the research was completed, Merck planned to exploit the discovery by introducing an improved beta-blocker called Blocadren. Yet Merck was beaten to the market by its competitors. Furthermore, because the 17-year patent protection on a new drug discovery was about to expire, Aldomet was threatened by generic manufacturers. This failure to beat its competitors to the market is said to have cost the company $200 million in future sales. A similar sequence of events occurred with Indocin and Clinoril, two anti-inflammation drugs for arthritis.

Under Honran's regime, the company introduced a hepatitis vaccine, a treatment for glaucoma called Timoptic, and Ivomac, an antiparasitic for animals. And while Honran remained strongly committed to financing a highly productive research organization, Merck began making improvements on research already performed by competitors. In 1979, for example, Merck began to market Enalapril, a high-blood pressure inhibitor, similar to the drug Capoten, which was manufactured by Squibb. Sales for Enalapril reached $550 million in 1986. Honran also embarked on a more aggressive program for licensing foreign products. Merck purchased rights to sell products from Astra, a Swedish company, and Shionogi of Japan.

Honran's strategy proved very effective. Between 1981 and 1985, the company experienced a nine percent annual growth rate, and in 1985 the *Wall Street Transcript* awarded Honran the gold award for excellence in the ethical drug industry. He was commended for the company's advanced marketing techniques and its increased production. At the time of the award, projections indicated a company growth rate for the next five years of double the present rate.

In 1984, Honran claimed Merck had become the largest U.S. based manufacturer of drugs in the three largest markets—the United States, Japan, and Europe. He attributed this success to three factors: a productive research organization; manufacturing capability which allowed for cost efficient, high-quality production; and an excellent marketing organization. The following year, Honran resigned as chief executive officer. In 1986, his successor, P.R. Vagelos, was also awarded the ethical drug industry's gold award.

Although Merck's public image was generally good, it had its share of controversy. In 1974, a $35 million lawsuit was filed against Merck and 28 other drug manufacturers and distributors of diethylstilbestrol (DES). This drug, prescribed to pregnant women in the late 1940s and up until the early 1960s, ostensibly prevented miscarriages. The 16 original plaintiffs claimed that they developed vaginal cancer and other related difficulties because their mothers had taken the drug. Furthermore, the suit charged that DES was derived from Stilbene, a known carcinogen, and that no reasonable basis existed for claiming the drugs were effective in preventing miscarriages. (A year before the suit, the Federal Drug Administration banned the use of DES hormones as growth stimulants for cattle because tests revealed cancer-causing residues of the substance in some of the animals' livers. The FDA, however, did not conduct public hearings on this issue; consequently, a federal court overturned the ban.)

Under the plaintiffs' directive, the court asked the defendants to notify other possible victims and to establish early detection and treatment centers. More than 350 plaintiffs subsequently sought damages totalling some $350 billion.

Merck was not only beleaguered by the DES lawsuit. In 1975, the company's name was added to a growing list of U.S. companies involved in illegal payments abroad. The payoffs, issued to increase sales in certain African and Middle Eastern countries, came to the attention of Merck executives through the investigation of the Securities and Exchange Commission. While sales amounted to $40.4 million for that year in those areas of the foreign market, the report uncovered a total of $140,000 in bribes. Once the SEC revealed its report, Merck initiated an internal investigation and took immediate steps to prevent future illegal payments.

More recently, Merck found itself beset with new difficulties. In its attempt to win hegemony in Japan, the second largest pharmaceutical market in the world, Merck purchased more than 50 percent of the Banyu Pharmaceutical Company of Tokyo. Partners since 1954 under a joint business venture called Nippon Merck-Banyu (NMB), the companies used Japanese detail men (or pharmaceutical sales representatives) to promote Merck products.

However, when NMB proved inefficient, Merck bought out its partner for $315.5 million—more than 30 times Banyu's annual earnings. The acquisition was made in 1982, and Merck was still in the process of bringing Banyu into line with its more aggressive and imaginative management style in the early 1990s.

Problems in labor relations surfaced during the spring of 1985 when Merck locked out 730 union employees at the Rahway plant after failing to agree to a new contract. For three months prior to the expiration of three union contracts, involving 4,000 employees, both sides negotiated a new settlement. However, when talks stalled, the company responded by locking out employees. The unresolved issues involved both wages and benefits.

By June 5th, all 4,000 employees participated in a strike involving the Rahway plant and six other facilities across the nation. In West Point, Virginia, operations were halted when union picketers prevented non-striking employees from entering the plant. Merck, however, was able to win a court-ordered injunction limiting picketing.

The strike proved to be the longest in Merck's history; but after 15 weeks an agreement was finally reached. A company request for the adoption of a two-tier wage system which would permanently pay new employees lower wages was rejected, as was a union demand for wage increases and cost-of-living adjustments during the first year. Nevertheless, Merck's reputation as an exceptional, high-paying work place remained intact, and its subsequent contract agreements were amicable. In fact, Merck was ranked as one of the "100 Best Companies to Work for in America" and one of *Working Mother* magazine's "100 Best Companies for Working Mothers" since that ranking's 1986 inception.

During the late 1980s, double-digit annual sales increases catapulted Merck to undisputed leadership of the pharmaceutical industry. CEO Vagelos' research direction in the 1960s and 1970s laid the foundation for Merck's drug "bonanza" of the 1980s. Vasotec, a treatment for congestive heart failure, was introduced in 1985 and became Merck's first billion-dollar-a-year drug by 1988. Mevacor, a cholesterol-lowering drug, and ivermectin, the world's top-selling animal health product, also contributed to the company's impressive growth. In the late 1980s, Merck was investing hundreds of millions of dollars in research and development—ten percent of the entire industry's total. Over the course of the decade, Merck's sales more than doubled, its profits tripled, and the company became the world's top ranked drug company as well as one of *Business Week's* ten most valuable companies.

The company was also recognized for its heritage of social responsibility. In the 1980s, Merck made its drug for "river blindness"—a parasitic infection prevalent in tropical areas and affecting 18 million people—available at no charge. In 1987, the company shared its findings regarding the treatment of human immunodeficiency virus (HIV) with competitors. These efforts reflected George W. Merck's assertion that: "Medicine is for the patients. It is not for the profits. The profits follow, and if we have remembered that, they have never failed to appear. The better we have remembered it, the larger they have been."

Growth did slow in the early 1990s, however, as Merck's drug pipeline dried up. Although the company maintained the broadest product line in the industry, its stable of new drugs was conspicuously absent of the "blockbusters" that had characterized the previous decade.

In July 1993, Vagelos announced Merck's intention to acquire Medco Containment Services Inc. for $3.6 billion in cash, $2.4 billion in borrowings, and 112 new shares of stock. Medco was a mail-order distributor of drugs that was previously acquired by Martin Wygod in the early 1980s for $36 million. With the help of infamous investment banker Michael Milken, Wygod built Medco into a mass drug distribution system with $2.5 billion in revenues and $138 million in profits by 1992.

The wisdom of the purchase was debated among analysts. On one hand, it was regarded as making Merck more competitive in an American health care industry dominated by cost-cutting managed care networks and health maintenance organizations. On the other hand, some observers noted that Merck's newest subsidiary would necessarily distribute competitors' drugs and that it had been a major proponent of discounting, which threatened to cut into Merck's R&D funds.

The Medco acquisition also complicated Vagelos' plans for a successor. Vagelos' choice, Richard J. Markham, resigned unexpectedly in mid-1994, just months before the CEO's anticipated retirement. Some observers speculated that 54-year-old Wygod, with his cost-cutting tendencies and marketing forté, was a likely successor in the health-care industry of the 1990s.

Principal Subsidiaries: Chibret A/S; International Indemnity Limited (Bermuda); Kelco Specialty Colloids, Limited (Canada); Laboratories Prosalud S.A. (Peru); Medco Containment Services, Inc.; Merck and Company, Incorporated; Merck Capital Resources, Inc.; Merck Foreign Sales Corporation (Guam); Merck Foreign Sales Corporation Ltd.(Bermuda); Merck Holdings, Inc.; Merck Investment Co., Inc.; Merck Sharp & Dohme Inc. (Europe); Merck Sharp & Dhome Industria Quimica e Veterinaria Limitada (Brazil); Merck Sharp & Dohme, Limitada (Portugal); Merck Sharp & Dohme Limited (New Zealand); Merck Sharp & Dohme Overseas Finance N.V. (Netherland Antilles); Merck Sharp & Dohme S.A. (Panama); Merck Sharp & Dohme Scientific and Management Corp., Inc.; Merck Sharp & Dohme Limited (Zimbabe) (Private); MSD AGVET AG (Switzerland); MSD Co. (Japan).

Further Reading:

O'Reilly, Brian, "Why Merck Married the Enemy," *Fortune,* September 20, 1993, pp. 60–64.
Rudnitsky, Howard, "Anticipating Hillary," *Forbes,* August 30, 1993, pp. 44–45.
Weber, Joseph, "Merck is Showing its Age," *Business Week,* August 23, 1993, pp. 72–74.
Weber, Joseph, "Suddenly, No Heir is Apparent at Merck," *Business Week,* July 26, 1993, p. 29.

—updated by April Dougal Gasbarre

Meredith Corporation

1716 Locust Street
Des Moines, Iowa 50309-3023
U.S.A.
(515) 284-3000
Fax: (515) 284-2700

Public Company
Incorporated: 1902
Employees: 1,895
Total Assets: $864.47 million
Stock Exchanges: New York
SICs: 2721 Periodicals; 2731 Book Publishing; 4833
    Television Broadcasting Stations; 6794 Patent Owners &
    Lessors

Meredith Corporation is best known for publishing two of America's most popular magazines: *Better Homes and Gardens,* with a circulation of 7.6 million, and *Ladies' Home Journal,* with a circulation of five million. About 65 percent of the diversified media company's revenues come from its magazine business, which publishes 19 subscription magazines, more than 40 special interest publications, and a number of custom publications. The company also publishes about 175 different books, including the best-selling, red-and-white-checkerboard covered *Better Homes and Gardens Cookbook.* In addition, the company owns and operates five television stations and is involved in cable television and residential real estate. Even though Meredith has diversified into many areas of the media industry, all its products have a home and family slant. In 1994, women made up 61 percent of the company's employees.

The seeds that started the Meredith Corporation were given to Edwin Thomas (E. T.) Meredith as a wedding present. On E. T. Meredith's wedding day, his grandfather gave him several gold pieces, the controlling interest in his newspaper, and a note that said, "Sink or swim." After returning his grandfather's newspaper to profitability, Meredith sold it for a profit and began publishing a service oriented farm magazine called *Successful Farming* in 1902. The magazine grew quickly, from a starting circulation of 500 to over half a million subscribers by 1914. The company had grown proportionally, from five employees in 1902 to almost 200 in 1912. In 1994, the company had almost 2,000 employees and still occupied the same building that was established as company headquarters in 1912. The building

went through some expansion as well, including an $18 million renovation completed in 1980.

After serving a year as Woodrow Wilson's Secretary of Agriculture, E. T. Meredith returned to his company in 1920 and decided to publish more magazines. In 1922, the company purchased one magazine, *Dairy Farmer,* and launched another, *Fruit, Garden and Home.* Meredith tried to make the *Dairy Farmer* a national success for five years before merging it with *Successful Farming.* Unable to make a profit until 1927, *Fruit, Garden and Home,* a magazine similar to *Successful Farming* for the home and family, had start-up difficulties as well. At first, advertisers paid $450 per black-and-white page in *Fruit, Garden and Home,* as opposed to *Successful Farming*'s rate of $1,800 per black-and-white page. After a name change in 1924 to *Better Homes & Gardens,* the magazine's fortunes turned around, allowing it to command $1,800 per black-and-white page of advertising by 1925.

By E. T. Meredith's death in 1928, the year he was considered a candidate for the presidency, *Better Homes and Gardens* and *Successful Farming* had reached a combined circulation of 2.5 million. After World War II, *Better Homes and Gardens* had surpassed *McCall's, Good Housekeeping,* and *Ladies' Home Journal* to become the leading monthly magazine. Holding a circulation of about eight million for more than two decades, *Better Homes and Gardens* remained a powerful magazine into the 1990s, when it ranked fourth largest in the United States.

Meredith capitalized on the success of *Better Homes and Gardens* magazine and began publishing the *Better Homes and Gardens Cook Book* in 1930. Magazine subscribers received complimentary copies of the first edition, and book sales grew rapidly. The cookbook became one of the best-selling hardback books in America, with over 29 million copies sold by its tenth edition in 1992. The company has since used the *Better Homes and Gardens* name to further its profits, using it to sell special interest publications starting in 1937, to open a real estate service in 1978, and to offer garden tools at 2,000 Wal-Mart stores starting in 1994.

To raise the capital necessary to diversify its interests, the company began offering stock to the public in 1946. Over the next ten years, Meredith bought three television stations and opened a commercial printing business. By 1965, the company was listed on the New York Stock Exchange. By 1969, the company had had formed a printing partnership with the Burda family of West Germany, which would grow into one of the largest printing businesses in the United States.

In 1978, Meredith began a franchise-operated real estate business under the *Better Homes and Gardens* name. "It's a natural extension of the product franchise," Meredith chairperson Robert Burnett told *Advertising Age.* By 1985, the business challenged established realtors like Century 21 and Coldwell Banker, according to *Advertising Age.* The real estate business had grown to include about 700 firms, which owned and operated about 1,300 offices and had 24,000 sales associates by 1994. Company headquarters supplied the franchisees with marketing, management, and sales training information.

Although Meredith was publicly owned, it had a long history of cautiously seeking investors. In 1985, however, it turned into "a very different kind of company," Paine Webber analyst J. Kendrick Noble told *Advertising Age.* At that time, Meredith began welcoming interest in its operations. Meredith started sponsoring art exhibits in New York and giving presentations to security analysts. The change occurred to fuel a growth strategy, which helped make it a Fortune 500 company.

At the beginning of the 1980s, Meredith's interests included a printing business, a fulfillment system, a real estate franchise, four television stations, and three magazines: *Better Homes and Gardens, Metropolitan Home,* and *Successful Farming.* The company expanded quickly during the 1980s, entering the video market with Meredith Video Publishing, purchasing three television stations, launching seven new magazines, publishing a Korean edition of *Better Homes and Gardens* magazine (an Australian edition had been published since 1978), and purchasing *Ladies' Home Journal,* the sixth-largest women's service magazine when ranked by circulation at the time of the purchase in 1986. Despite its acquisitions and expansion, the company soon floundered. In 1992, Meredith had a net loss of $6.3 million.

In response, management decided to streamline Meredith, ridding the company of ancillary businesses. To soften the blow of a nationwide advertising slump it felt in its magazines and television stations, Meredith sold its 50 percent interest in the Meredith/Burda printing partnership to R. R. Donnelley & Sons Company of Chicago in 1990. Given the high costs of remaining competitive in the printing business, Meredith president Jack Rehm felt the sale was smart, telling *Business Record* that "we had to make a choice to either get bigger or else to get out. We felt we could better use our resources in our other businesses and depart the printing business." To further streamline, Meredith sold its fulfillment business to Neodata of Boulder, Colorado, in 1991, and two television stations were also sold off in 1993. Moreover, the company's work force was cut by seven percent, to 2,000, between 1992 and 1994.

Meredith's cuts and investments allowed it to focus on what it did best. E. T. Meredith III told *Business Week* in 1994 that "We're going back to what we were: a successful magazine and broadcasting company." Meredith planned to add three or four magazines per year. Realizing that advertising profits might never be as high as they were during the lucrative 1980s, the company earmarked $400 million for additional TV and magazine acquisitions, according to *Business Week.* In addition, the company developed customized marketing programs, which could create tailored packages of Meredith's magazine and book publishing, real estate service, and television stations for advertisers' specific needs. By 1994, company profits had started to climb again, jumping 23 percent over 1993 to $22.9 million on revenues of $799 million.

Meredith's streamlining helped the company take advantage of its unique niche, the home and family. Meredith sold its chic magazine, *Metropolitan Home,* to Hachette Filipacchi Magazines, the publishers of *Elle,* and introduced several new titles that targeted different domestic topics, such as *Country Home, Country America, WOOD, Midwest Living,* and *Better Homes and Gardens American Patchwork & Quilting.* Meredith's new magazines met with significant success, with growing circulations of 200,000 to one million. Shari Wall, senior vice-presi-

dent at J. Walter Thompson in Chicago, noted Meredith's fortuitous position in the market, telling *Business Week* that "their thrust of family and home is the hot thing for the 1990s." Meredith, too, eagerly publicized its area of focus. The company launched an advertising campaign for its magazine group in 1993, which asserted that "If it has to do with home and family, it has to be in Meredith." The campaign featured black-and-white pictures of real families having fun together.

Although Meredith promoted itself aggressively to advertisers, it relied most heavily on its subscribers, who fueled the company's rebound. Circulation for most of the company's magazines was up in 1993, but company president Jack Rehm told the *New York Times* that "the reason we have succeeded with so many magazine titles in the last several years is that we are able to get readers to really pay for the magazines. We must count much more on the reader to generate the revenue stream than the advertiser. Historically, that has not been true, and magazines who were overly dependent on advertising were the ones who really suffered." In 1993, Meredith's magazine subscription and newsstand revenues accounted for 32.2 percent of the company revenues, or $257.45 million, while magazine advertising revenues made up 29.6 percent, with $236.81 million.

Meredith's *Better Homes and Gardens* magazine proved a good example of the company's success in managing large publications. *Better Homes and Gardens* led the shelter magazine industry in ad revenues and pages in 1988, offering its advertisers an audience four times the size of its next competitor, according to *Marketing and Media Decisions.* A four-color page cost $103,480 in *Better Homes and Gardens*; in *Architectural Digest, Better Homes and Gardens*'s closest competitor in shelter magazines, a similar advertisement cost $28,490. According to some analysts, *Better Homes and Gardens'* fortunes can be traced to the trend toward home and hearth that started in the late 1980s and early 1990s; the magazine benefitted because it bridged the home and women's service categories.

Meredith took a conservative approach to changing its flagship magazine, refusing to bow to the shifting winds of publishing fashion. For example, when faced with "single, disenfranchised dropouts" at advertising agencies in the 1960s who were "insulted that we would continue to publish [*Better Homes and Gardens*] when [they] didn't think it should exist," Burnett told *Advertising Age,* "it was tempting to say, 'We've got to change *Better Homes and Gardens* and get with it'." However, Meredith remained committed to the magazine's focus on home and family.

To keep the magazine contemporary, Meredith continually made subtle changes, rather than doing major redesigns every five years like other magazines. According to Burnett, in an article in *Advertising Age,* rapid change was likely to alienate readers; Burnett commented that "the worst thing that could happen is for your best friend to show up with a changed personality; it's a shock and a negative." The magazine's enhancements for 1994 included the addition of puzzles and games for parents and their children. The company's strategy paid off, as *Better Homes and Gardens* continued to be a leader in its category.

In 1994, Meredith's several large circulation magazines and book clubs generated a subscriber database of 63 million, the largest database in the United States. Meredith began exploiting this database for profit in 1992, as the company's marketing department began using the database to give editors valuable feedback on their magazine's readership, as well as to cross-promote books and magazine spin-offs, target direct mail programs for advertisers, research new markets, and test new products. The company also used the database to aid in the launch of a new magazine called *Crayola Kids,* to insert specialized ads in targeted magazines for an auto advertiser, and to put in targeted editorials in *Better Homes and Garden* issues. The database also helped to turn around the fortunes of Meredith's book division. Despite its over 30 years of experience in database marketing, during which it had also used rented lists, Meredith did not consider itself a very sophisticated user of its own resource. Clem Svede, vice-president and director of consumer marketing, noted in *Direct* that "when someone asks how our database is doing, we say 'We think we're at the top of our class—but we're only in the first grade'."

In 1993, the company faced a challenge in the form of a natural disaster. Massive flooding in the Midwest that year, particularly in Iowa, reached the company's Des Moines headquarters, ruining the company's mainframe computer system. As a result, the company was forced to install a new desktop publishing network about eight months earlier than planned. Under the guidance of Robert Furstenau, director of production and technology for Meredith's magazines, the company converted to the new system in about two days. Meredith immediately purchased $400,000 worth of Macintosh computers and peripheral equipment, installed them in a rented space, and flew in software specialists from around the country to give 103 editorial employees two weeks of training information in a few hours. Despite the chaotic atmosphere, no deadlines were missed, and in the long run, the desktop system has reduced the company's pre-press production costs. Furstenau told the *Des Moines Register* that the flood "has got to be one of the better things that has happened to magazine production at Meredith in a long time."

In 1994, Meredith forecasted a strong future in the home and family marketplace. It planned to continue to focus on its most profitable divisions, magazines and television stations. The company expected to release a new gardening magazine in 1995, with a potential circulation of between 750,000 and one million, according to the *Des Moines Register.* The company also anticipated investing in new product development to enhance the performance of its book division. As its cable partnership proved financially draining, Meredith planned to sell or adjust the partnership's operations to achieve an acceptable level of financial performance. Finally, as a media company, Meredith was developing CD-ROM products for the information superhighway through Multicom Publishing Inc.

Principal Subsidiaries: Meredith Cable, Inc. (70%); Meredith Video Publishing Corporation; Meredith International, Ltd.

Further Reading:

Carmody, Deirdre, "A Focus on Home, Hearth and Profit," *New York Times,* October 4, 1993, p. C7.

Chase, Brett, "Meredith Leaves Printing behind, Looks to Future," *Business Record,* January 13, 1992, p. 2.

Cyr, Diane, "Database Magic at Meredith," *Direct: The Magazine of Direct Marketing Management,* February 1994.

Ebert, Larry Kai, "Meredith at 75: Multi-Media Expansion," *Advertising Age,* October 31, 1977, pp. 3, 78, 80.

Kasler, Dale, "Meredith Veteran Named New Better Homes Editor," *Des Moines Register,* April 6, 1993; "Meredith Will Launch 'Big' Gardening Magazine," *Des Moines Register,* July 4, 1994, p. 3; "The Talk of the Industry: Flood a Boon for Meredith," *Des Moines Register,* September 13, 1993.

Levin, Gary, "Meredith: Growing up with an '800-lb. Gorilla'," *Advertising Age,* March 11, 1985.

Melcher, Richard A., "Homes, Gardens—And a Tidy Turnaround," *Business Week,* August 22, 1994, pp. 55–56.

Podems, Ruth, "Serving Families for 77 Years," *Target Marketing,* September 1989, pp. 18–24.

Williams, Scott, "Realtor Links Up with Chain," *Seattle Times,* July 15, 1992, p. B4.

—Sara Pendergast

Meridian Bancorp, Inc.

35 North Sixth Street
P.O. Box 1102
Reading, Pennsylvania 19603
U.S.A.
(215) 655-2000
Fax: (215) 655-2452

Public Company
Incorporated: 1983
Total Assets: $14.1 billion
Employees: 7,000
Stock Exchanges: NASDAQ
SICs: 6712 Bank Holding Companies; 6022 State
    Commercial Banks

Meridian Bancorp is one of the largest and most venerable of
the regional financial services holding companies on the eastern
coast of the United States. Meridian was created in 1983 when
the boards of directors from Central Penn National Corp. of
Philadelphia, a traditional and rather conservative banking institution, and American Bancorp of Reading, a rapidly growing
rural bank, voted to consolidate their operations. Meridian owns
325 branch offices and 350 automated teller machines throughout eastern and central Pennsylvania, southern New Jersey,
and Delaware. The company's financial services include asset
management, mortgage financing for residential and commercial properties, brokerage services, and investment banking
services.

The Central Penn National Bank of Philadelphia opened for
business on July 14, 1828 under the name Bank of Penn Township. The bank was established to service the burgeoning business in and around Philadelphia during the early part of the
nineteenth century. During this time, Philadelphia was home to
over 30 cloth factories, ten sugar refineries, and a host of small
carpet, soap, glass, leather, paper, silverplate, and wallpaper
businesses. On the outskirts of Philadelphia lay Penn Township,
a district mostly populated by drovers, butchers, and market
people. Thirteen men from the Penn Township community
incorporated the bank with a capitalization of $150,000. The
original directors included six merchants, a carpenter, a drover,
a butcher, and two men who described themselves as "gen-
tlemen"; none, including the person chosen to serve as the
bank's first president, had any previous banking experience.

Nevertheless, in its early years the Bank of Penn Township was
a successful enterprise. The bank opened many individual accounts for customers living in the area and provided loans to the
Pennsylvania Canal & Railroad Company and the Germantown
& Norristown Railroad. By 1834, however, the bank began to
experience several challenges that threatened its survival.
Overdrafts became a serious problem and, due to the lack of
uniformity in design of a national currency, counterfeit paper
money proliferated. Moreover, in 1841, after examining the
books, the directors discovered that the cashier, first teller, and
second teller had stolen nearly $130,000 of the bank's money.
As a result, the bank was forced to reduce its activities and limit
business hours.

However, having made an excellent investment in the Pennsylvania Railroad in 1846, and with sound management through
the latter 1840s and early 1850s, the Bank of Penn Township
weathered these misfortunes as well as subsequent upheavals in
the banking industry, and, by 1858, it was once again operating
on a firm financial basis. When the Civil War began, the bank
began issuing loans to the U.S. federal government for the war
effort against the Confederacy. With the passage of the National
Bank Act of 1863, which among other things established a
uniform national currency, the directors of Penn recommended
that it be converted into a national bank. In 1864, the Bank of
Penn Township was officially renamed the Penn National Bank.
The bank's capitalization amounted to an impressive $500,000.

Every year, from the end of the Civil War in 1865 until 1873,
Penn National's net profits averaged 11 percent on net worth.
During this time, the bank loaned money primarily to shipping
companies, printing houses, and railroad operations. The failure
of the New York Securities & Warehouse Company, primarily
involved in financing new railroad ventures, led to a run on
other financial houses also involved in railroad securities. Penn
National lost much of its depository accounts and again scaled
back operations. However, management directed the bank
through the crisis, and, by the late 1880s, Penn National had
recouped its losses.

The financial crises of 1893 and 1907 were met by Penn
National with foresight and preparation, and the bank did not
suffer the losses typical of its earlier years. The bank prospered
and grew rapidly during World War I and was very active in the
federal government Liberty War Bond drive. Like other banks
listed on the New York stock exchange, Penn National prospered during the heady days of the 1920s. Just before the Wall
Street crash of October 1929, Penn National's assets amounted
to $21 million, while its profits exceeded $4 million. In 1929,
the bank split its stock ten for one, and its dividend rate was a
healthy 26 percent.

The Great Depression of the 1930s brought trouble once again
to Penn National. With ever decreasing deposits after a run on
the bank, and the unexpected death of the company president,
the directors at Penn National decided to merge with another
bank to ensure its long-term financial viability. In July of 1930,
Penn National consolidated its operations with Central National
Bank, an institution founded in 1864 to meet the needs of a
growing number of wealthy industrialists in the coal, machinery, and iron industries. The new bank, Central Penn National, had combined assets of over $70 million, and its strong

liquidity in the form of commercial paper helped offset the effects of the Depression on banking operations. Although deposits continued to decline, Central Penn was healthy enough to provide loans throughout the Depression to more needy banks in the Philadelphia area.

The bank expanded rapidly with the advent of World War II. By 1942, Central Penn's resources were over $100 million, and capital funds amounted to almost $11 million. In addition, the bank reported the largest number of commercial accounts in its entire history. Near the end of the war in 1945, the president and the board of directors recommended the approval of the Bretton Woods Agreement establishing the International Monetary Fund and the International Bank for Reconstruction and Development. Also that year, Central Penn collaborated with 36 other Philadelphia banks in order to create a $10 million loan fund for returning veterans, to be used primarily for commercial purposes; Central Penn provided the first loan out of this fund, enabling a veteran to open a printing shop in Philadelphia.

Over the next three decades, Central Penn continued its activity in the area of commercial banking, while expanding its base of operations by acquiring smaller local banks. In 1950, Central Penn purchased the Charter Bank, and, during 1952, the bank acquired both City National Bank and South Philadelphia National Bank. In 1955, Wyoming Bank and Trust Company was consolidated into Central Penn's operations, and both Newtown Bank and Trust and Peoples National Bank in Langhoma were acquired in 1958. In 1969, Central Penn became a wholly owned subsidiary of a new holding company, Central Penn Financial Corp., which was subsequently renamed Central Penn National Corp. By means of acquisition strategy, Central Penn expanded its branch network from four to seven counties, increased its services in consumer and instalment banking, and enlarged its base of deposits. By the time Central Penn merged with American Bank and Trust Co. to form Meridian in 1983, Central Penn reported over 30 years of ever-increasing deposits, capital accounts, commercial loans, and assets.

The history of American Bank and Trust Co. of Pennsylvania involved four community banks located in the city of Reading, Pennsylvania: Schuylkill Valley Bank, Colonial Trust Company, The Berks County Trust Company, and Northeastern Trust Company. Schuylkill Valley Bank opened for business on July 21, 1890, with initial resources of $50,000; Colonial Trust was opened on July 2, 1900, with resources of $375,000; The Berks County Trust Company opened approximately one year later, with resources of $375,000; Northeastern Trust Company opened in 1919, with original resources of $125,000. All of these banks provided banking services for individual customers as well as commercial accounts. Moreover, all four banks were heavily involved in providing loans for customers to build or purchase houses, securing capital for small business ventures, helping large manufacturing companies expand their facilities, and taking care of the large volume of deposits made by local farmers.

The growth of these banks was characterized not only by increasing assets but by constant mergers and acquisitions. In 1923, The Berks County Trust Company merged with Schuylkill Valley bank to form The Berks County Trust Company. In 1929, Colonial Trust Company and Northeastern Trust Com-

pany merged to form Colonial-Northeastern Trust Company. In 1932, at the height of the Great Depression, The Berks County Trust Company consolidated its operations with Colonial-Northeastern Trust Company in order to form Berks County Trust Company. With the resources from this merger, Berks County Trust not only survived the Depression but was designated as one of the two banks in Reading that was financially healthy enough to open for business after the "Bank Holiday" imposed by the Roosevelt administration in March 1933.

During World War II and the post-war economic boom in America, Berks County Trust did what it did best: merge with or acquire small banks. In 1941, the bank purchased Union National Bank and incorporated its branch network into its own operations. The strategy of an aggressive merger policy combined with new branch construction enabled Berks Country Trust to grow rapidly. Acquisitions such as Wyomissing Valley Bank of Mohnton, Temple State Bank, Mount Penn Trust Company, Reamstown Exchange Bank, and Schuylkill Trust Company in Pottsville increased both assets and branch operations. By 1964, Berks County Trust had grown from a small community bank into a large regional banking institution. That year, in order to reflect the rapid development in the scope of its services and operations, Berks County Trust changed its name to American Bank and Trust Co. of Pennsylvania. By the time of its merger with Central Penn in 1983, American Bank had established itself as a major presence in Pennsylvania. Between 1953 and 1983, the bank had either merged with or acquired over 20 financial institutions, expanding into eight counties of southeastern Pennsylvania and increasing its network of bank branches from four to 83.

On June 30, 1983, the board of directors at both American and Central Penn voted to consolidate their operations and form a new financial services holding company named Meridian Bancorp, Inc. American Bank and Central Penn National Bank were designated as wholly-owned subsidiaries under the auspices of Meridian. Upon its formation, Meridian reported assets of $3.6 billion and deposits amounting to $2.9 billion. The company recorded loans totaling $2.1 billion and just under $250 million in shareholder equity. Earnings for 1983, Meridian's first year of business, were $32.3 million. At the time, Meridian employed 2,794 people and operated 106 branches in 11 Pennsylvania counties.

In 1983, Meridian formed a mortgage subsidiary and also announced the establishment of discount brokerage services. The first major move after the consolidation, however, was during 1984 when Meridian purchased the First National Bank of Allentown. The acquisition of First National, founded in 1855, immediately made Meridian the dominant financial services provider in Pennsylvania's Lehigh Valley. Two years later, Meridian bought the First National Bank of Pike County, adding six branches to its already expanding network in northeastern Pennsylvania.

Continuing its expansion strategy, Meridian became the first Pennsylvania bank holding company to enter the Delaware market with its purchase of Delaware Trust Company in 1988. This acquisition added 24 branches to Meridian's banking network. From 1989 to 1993 Meridian focused on additional acquisitions, including Hill Financial Savings Association, Peoples Bancorp of Lebanon, Bell Federal Savings Bank, Liberty Bank, Commonwealth Bancshares, First National Bank of Bath, and four branch offices of Provident Federal Savings Bank in New Jersey. In 1993, Meridian entered the retail market in New Jersey by acquiring Cherry Hill National Bank.

In just ten years, from 1983 to 1993, Meridian had developed into a major regional financial services institution. The company's assets in 1993 shot up to over $14 billion, while deposits grew to more than $10 billion. During that year, Meridian reported $7.4 billion in loans and a shareholders equity amounting to $904 million. Earnings had increased to $157.8 million by 1993, and the company's work force numbered over 7,000 throughout southeastern Pennsylvania, New Jersey, and Delaware. With the June 1994 acquisition of Security Federal Savings Bank, Meridian Bank of New Jersey increased the number of its branch offices to 37 across the southern part of the state. This acquisition brought the total number of Meridian's branch offices to 325, with more than 350 automated teller machines located in 39 counties throughout a three state region. Meridian's primary business activities, including banking services, mortgage banking, asset management, and securities remained financially healthy and well-situated for future growth. In the mid-1990s, management had no intention of slowing down the pace of its acquisition strategy.

Principal Subsidiaries: Delware Trust Company; Meridian Asset Management, Inc.; Meridian Bank; Meridian Bank, New Jersey; Meridian Leasing, Inc.; Meridian Securitites, Inc.

Further Reading:

LaCerda, John, and Edward D. Maher, *This Is Our Story: Central Penn National Bank of Philadelphia,* Philadelphia: Allen, Scott & Lane, 1953.
Meridian Marks Tenth Anniversary as Financial Services Holding Company, Reading, Penn.: Meridian Bancorp, Inc., 1993.

—Thomas Derdak

Mesa Airlines, Inc.

2325 East 30th St.
Farmington, New Mexico 87041
U.S.A.
(505) 327-0271
Fax: (505) 326-4487

Public Company
Incorporated: 1983 as Mesa Air Shuttle, Inc.
Employees: 2,800
Sales: $353.6 million
Stock Exchanges: NASDAQ Chicago
SICs: 4512 Air Transportation, Scheduled; 4522 Air
   Transportation, Nonscheduled; 4581 Airports, Flying
   Fields and Services

Mesa Airlines, Inc., a group of airline and related companies operating in 26 states, own a fleet of 155 planes that provide commuter and regional service to more than 140 cities. These planes, flying under the Mesa Airlines name or such others as United Express, America West Express, Skyway Airlines, Air Midwest, USAir Express, or FloridaGulf Airlines, composed Mesa's commuter-airline empire, one of the largest of its kind in the world and the largest in the United States.

On the tenth anniversary of Mesa Airlines, Inc., Larry L. Risley must have experienced a sense of achievement mixed with disbelief. He and his wife Janie had started the regional/commuter airline company in 1980 with one small plane, seating five passengers, that flew between Farmington and Albuquerque, New Mexico. By its tenth year of existence Mesa Airlines had grown into one of the largest companies of its kind in the nation, belying both the airline's and Risley's modest beginnings.

By his own admission, Risley barely graduated from high school, having judged anything above a "C" grade "a wasted effort." He then enlisted in the U.S. Army and eventually obtained an aviation mechanic's license, aspiring to nothing more than emulating his two older brothers, who were employed as union mechanics for two major airline companies. However, following the career path chosen by his brothers proved difficult for Risley; he became a somewhat itinerant worker, securing employment at general aviation fields, then quickly losing his job or quitting in anger, a young aviation mechanic who disliked working under the supervision of any-

one. In between his stints as an aviation mechanic, Risley found employment where he could get it: selling burglar alarms, working as a janitor in a baby clothes factory, anything but the secure steady work as an aviation mechanic he had originally wanted. Later recalling this period of his life, Risley related, "I was really out of my element."

Risley's prospects brightened in 1970 when he found his first opportunity to work alone, unfettered by a supervisor. He opened an aircraft engine shop in Waxahachie, Texas, but this comfortable niche soon deteriorated. Several of his customers reneged on payments, debts mounted, and Risley's engine shop dissolved. It would be roughly another decade before an opportunity for success arrived, but when it did, Risley took hold and eventually entrenched himself in the industry that had for so long eluded him.

In 1979, through the assistance of his brother-in-law, Risley was hired by Four Corners Drilling Co., an oil company based in Farmington, New Mexico, to manage its charter airline service. Oil was a plentiful and lucrative commodity in the region during this period, and Risley was kept busy maintaining a fleet of 14 small planes that shuttled oil drillers to and from the desert. The oil boom era in the region was short lived, however, shuddering to a stop in 1980. The downward spiral of oil prices forced Four Corners Drilling to sharply reduce its oil drilling activities. The company's fleet of planes was sold as a consequence, but Risley convinced the company to keep one plane, a five-seat Piper, so he could try to establish a shuttle airline service between Farmington and Albuquerque.

With this one small plane, Risley established the foundation from which Mesa Airlines would evolve. He advertised on the local radio, placed signs along the roads surrounding Four Corners Regional Airport, and, perhaps most important, charged half the ticket price of his rival, Frontier Airlines Inc. After two years, during which time both husband and wife worked seven days a week maintaining and operating the shuttle service, the Risleys decided to purchase the plane, offering their pick-up truck and house as collateral against a $125,000 loan. The following year, in 1983, their fledgling enterprise was incorporated, initially named Mesa Air Shuttle, Inc.

From the beginning Risley's operating philosophy was to fly only small planes between cities and towns in need of additional airline service and to pay assiduous attention to the company's operating costs. Those costs largely resulted from aircraft maintenance, a task for which Risley was particularly well-suited considering his certification as an aviation mechanic. Keeping costs low also carried over into other areas, such as having the pilots of the shuttle service assist in loading passengers' baggage, reducing the number of gate crew at arrival and destination points, and keeping the number of reservation agents to a minimum. Risley's strategy was to have a comparatively small work force operating small planes that flew their routes with greater frequency—initially five times a day between Farmington and Albuquerque—than the company's competitors. If all reservation agents were busy booking flights, the incoming calls were directed to other Mesa employees, and if the entire staff was busy handling reservations, as they often were during Mesa's first decade of operation, Risley himself would answer the phone and book a passenger's flight.

Very early then, the characteristics that would set Risley's company apart from other regional/commuter airline companies were established, and the shuttle service prospered. From the single, five-seat Piper, the company's fleet gradually grew, with each new plane and each new service route enabling the company to generate greater revenues. With the exception of a small restated loss in 1984, Mesa recorded a profit throughout the 1980s and reached a financial level that enabled it to become an acquirer, thus broadening its presence in the southwestern United States.

A majority of Mesa's acquisitions in its first decade were not outright purchases of other airline companies, but instead were code-sharing agreements reached with major airline companies, a necessary arrangement for a small airline company following the deregulation of the airline industry in 1978. Code-sharing is essentially a marketing agreement with a larger carrier according to which the smaller company operates a particular region for the larger carrier, frequently adopting the corporate logo and colors of the larger carrier. A code-sharing agreement is a franchise of sorts that enables smaller airlines to benefit from the air traffic attracted by larger carriers without incurring the enormous marketing expense.

In the mid- and late 1980s, Mesa signed two such agreements, first with Midwest Express, then with United Airlines, and more were to follow. Generating nearly $5 million in sales in 1985, the company embarked on a five-year period of prodigious growth, elevating itself to the top ranks of the regional/commuter airlines in the United States. In 1986, Mesa forced a much larger airline company, Air Midwest, out of the New Mexico region, then, the following year, changed its name to Mesa Airlines, Inc., and became a publicly held corporation. The same year Mesa increased its sales volume to $14.3 million, nearly a 200 percent increase from two years earlier.

That year, 1987, proved to be a busy year for Risley's company, a year not without its disappointments. Mesa acquired the assets and the Denver, Colorado-based route system of Centennial Airlines, a purchase that resulted in a $250,000 loss for Mesa. The decision to acquire Centennial's service routes emanating from Denver and thereby compete against much larger, much more entrenched air carriers represented a step away from Risley's initial corporate strategy to only enter markets suffering from a dearth of established air carriers. Operating as an independent in a market occupied by airline companies possessing much larger financial resources, Mesa's approach of offering low air fares and more frequent service was not enough to wrest the grip held by the larger air carriers. The Centennial acquisition was a lesson for Risley and Mesa's management, a reminder that Mesa's strengths and the possibility for its future growth did not lay in competing in densely populated markets.

Mesa's entry into the Denver market emphasized the weakness of a small independent competing in a market dominated by major airlines. However, code-sharing's limitations were illustrated that same year, when Trans Colorado, operating under a code-sharing agreement with Continental Express, aggressively entered Mesa's Albuquerque market. The move by Trans Colorado essentially represented the opposite of Mesa's decision to enter the Colorado market, a small airline operating under a code-sharing agreement entering a market bereft of a major airline instead of a small airline entering a market dominated by a major airline. The result was inverse as well, this time in Mesa's favor. Trans Colorado was driven out of the Albuquerque market by a sharp reduction in Mesa's air fare prices, by a small airline company able to wield more control in a market without a major airline.

With these code-sharing lessons behind it, Mesa continued to expand. By 1989, the airline's annual sales had soared to over $22.5 million, more than four times the volume recorded four years earlier, and the mainstream press began to take notice. A year earlier *Inc.* magazine had named Mesa as one the country's fastest-growing small public companies. In 1989 Mesa formed Skyway Airlines as a wholly owned subsidiary to fly in conjunction with Midwest Express Airlines out of Milwaukee, Wisconsin, extending Mesa's reach northward. In the same year, the company became the only commuter airline in the world authorized by Pratt & Whitney, an aircraft engine manufacturer, to perform complete overhauls of the PT6, the primary type of engine used by Mesa's planes. The construction of the company's $1 million engine shop, which gained its certification from Pratt & Whitney, was indicative of Risley's focus on reducing aircraft maintenance costs. Within a year, the costs incurred from building the engine shop were recouped, positioning Mesa as one of the few vertically integrated commuter airlines in the world and paving the way for the company's celebration of its tenth anniversary.

Now ten years removed from the days when a single, five-seat plane flew between Farmington and Albuquerque, Risley could look back on a decade of enormous success. Mesa Airlines had quadrupled in size between 1985 and 1990, and doubled in size in roughly the five months preceding the company's tenth anniversary in October 1990 by acquiring Aspen Airway's United Express franchise at United's Denver hub. By letting each market dictate the size of the plane serving that market, Mesa had perennially recorded one of the lowest seat per mile costs in the industry and could efficiently operate its 33 planes. Mesa planes by this time serviced a considerable portion of the United States: its Skyway planes serviced Iowa, Wisconsin, Illinois, Indiana, Michigan, and New York; its United Express code-sharing agreement took Mesa planes throughout Colorado, Wyoming, Nebraska, and South Dakota; and its original route system, evolving from the company's Farmington to Albuquerque flight, now covered New Mexico, Arizona, Texas, and Colorado. All this was enough to make Mesa one of the ten largest commuter/regional airlines in the nation.

The airline's greatest growth, however, was still to come, and would arrive largely because of the influence of a new Mesa employee, Jonathan Ornstein, an airline financier who joined the company during its tenth year of operation. Ornstein had originally approached Risley to inquire about purchasing Mesa, an offer Risley declined, but the meeting eventually led to Ornstein's employment by Mesa. Once Ornstein arrived, he began prodding Risley to pursue purchases of additional airline-related assets and to increase Mesa's influence in the commuter/regional airline industry—to generally pursue aggressively a course Risley had pursued with moderation.

One year after Ornstein's arrival, Mesa acquired Air Midwest, Inc., an airline that operated under a code-sharing agreement with USAir Inc. The purchase extended Mesa's presence into Missouri by virtue of USAir's base operations in Kansas City and signaled the beginning of an era in which Ornstein and his desire to increase Mesa's magnitude would figure prominently. Later that year, in 1991, Mesa formed a new subsidiary, FloridaGulf Airlines, spreading the company's influence into the southeastern United States. By the conclusion of 1991, a disastrous year for many air carriers, particularly for Eastern, Pan-Am, and Midway Airlines, each of which ceased operations, Mesa continued to exhibit robust performance. The company posted a 39 percent increase in earnings from 1990, a 69 percent increase in revenues to $78 million, and a 50 percent increase in passengers from the previous year.

The following year, however, overshadowed 1991's encouraging results and, in fact, overshadowed all of Mesa's previous 12 years of existence in terms of growth. In May 1992, Mesa announced the completion of a merger combining Mesa Acquisition Corp., a wholly owned subsidiary of Mesa, with and into WestAir Holding Inc., California's largest regional airline. For Mesa the acquisition was enormous, doubling its size and vaulting the airline from the tenth largest in the country to the largest regional/commuter airline in the United States. WestAir Holding was organized as a wholly owned subsidiary after the merger and continued to operate under its code-sharing agreement with United Airlines as United Express, based in Fresno, California.

As Mesa entered the mid-1990s, it continued to look for additional acquisitions, guided by both Risley and Ornstein. In 1994, a year in which the company expected to post $354 million in sales, Risley was contemplating the purchase of CCAir Inc., a commuter airline based in Charlotte, North Carolina, for $32 million, as well as other, smaller, acquisitions, such as a $3 million acquisition of SunAir, an airline serving the Virgin Islands and Puerto Rico, and a 24 percent share in a small commuter carrier based in Britain. As the company continued to expand, succeeding where other airlines had failed, it was gaining the attention of investors and competitors alike, becoming, for some, the prototype of a regional/commuter airline for the future.

Principal Subsidiaries: Air Midwest, Inc.; America West Express; FloridaGulf Airlines; Four Corners Aviation, Inc.; San Juan Pilot Training Inc.; Skyway Airlines; WestAir Holding, Inc.; YV Services, Inc.

Further Reading:

"Commuter/Regional Airline of the Year," *Air Transport World,* February 1993, p. 35.
"Flight Leader," *Success,* January 1993, p. 30.
Frink, S., and Jack Hartsfield, "On the Wings of Eagles: The Air Industry," *New Mexico Business Journal,* February 1992, p. 26.
"Mesa Airlines Embraces Code Sharing," *Air Transport World,* September 1990, p. 178.
Reagor, Catherine, "Mesa Airlines Makes Offer to WestAir," *The Business Journal,* November 18, 1991, p. 1; "Woes of Big Airlines Mean Boom Times for Mesa, StatesWest," *The Business Journal,* October 21, 1991, p. 11.
Shine, Eric, "Is Mesa Airlines Flying Too High?," *Business Week,* May 9, 1994, p. 82.
"Temporary Downdraft," *Forbes,* June 22, 1992, p. 244.
Teitelbaum, Richard S., "Mesa Airlines," *Fortune,* May 4, 1992, p. 88.

—Jeffrey L. Covell

Kiewit Diversified Group, which oversaw the parent company's interests in telecommunications and incorporated MFS Communications' predecessor, Kiewit Communications Company, Inc., in 1987.

Led by James Q. Crowe, who would continue to oversee the company once it became MFS Communications, Kiewit Communications was founded to test a theory formulated by himself and other members of Kiewit's management regarding the rapidly changing telecommunications market, the dynamics of which were transforming in the wake of the consent decree that deregulated the telephone industry and ushered in a new era of competition. Before deregulation, they theorized, competition in the telecommunications industry had been predicated on technology, guided by regulation, and driven by expansion into new markets; a company's success was largely determined by its ability to extend the geographic boundaries of its operations. The emphasis had been on securing new markets essentially through technological sophistication and financial might, but, as with monopolized industries before it, the telecommunications industry paid little attention to marketing toward specific types of customers or developing diversified services to suit the divergent needs of its clientele.

This was the direction Crowe and others saw the telecommunications industry moving toward after deregulation: a market reorganized around customers, spawning specialized market niches that addressed the specific needs of specific customers. Indeed, many of the characteristics that defined the industry before deregulation would continue to characterize it in its new competitive era. Technology and market expansion would continue to be the foundation from which growth and success would develop, but in a more competitive arena customer satisfaction and loyalty would play a much larger role in determining success in the industry.

With this perspective in mind, Kiewit Communications was organized to provide telecommunications services to specific clientele: large corporations and government agencies. In so doing, the company carved a niche in the broadly defined telecommunications market as a bypass provider of telecommunication services, generating revenue by enabling its customers to place long-distance telephone calls without going through the local telephone utility, thereby avoiding additional connection fees charged by the local utility.

Initially targeting financial institutions—large banks and investment firms—as the company's primary type of customer, Kiewit Communications began operating in 1988 with an emphasis on building its presence in its newly created market niche at the expense of short-term profits, structuring its growth around particular customer types located in particular metropolitan areas. Six years later, the company still had not recorded a profit, but prodigious growth had been recorded, as each metropolitan area added to the company's network increased its presence and influence in the U.S. telecommunications market and limited its capability to post any profit.

Chicago was the first city in which Kiewit Communications provided telecommunication services through a fiber-optic network, beginning in April 1988. By the end of the following

MFS Communications Company, Inc.

One Tower Lane, Suite 1600
Oakbrook Terrace, Illinois 60181
U.S.A.
(706) 218-7200
Fax: (706) 218-1216

Public Company
Incorporated: 1987 as Kiewit Communications Company, Inc.
Employees: 654
Sales: $141.1 million
Stock Exchanges: NASDAQ
SICs: 4813 Telephone Communications Except Radiotelephone

A leading provider of communication services for businesses and government agencies in the United States, MFS Communications Company, Inc. competes with regional telephone companies by supplying such customers with telephone and data services through fiber-optic networks, enabling its customers to place long-distance telephone calls and transmit data without going through the local phone utility. Through five subsidiary companies, divided into two business segments, telecommunications services and network systems integration and facilities management, the company operated in 24 U.S. cities in 1994, with additional operations in the United Kingdom and Germany. Before the conclusion of the decade, MFS Communications planned to extend its service area to approximately 50 additional cities, an objective that included establishing service in ten international markets.

One of a new breed of telecommunication companies engendered by the deregulation of the telephone industry in the early 1980s, MFS Communications began operating in 1988 as a wholly owned subsidiary of Kiewit Diversified Group Inc., which in turn was a wholly owned subsidiary of Peter Kiewit Sons' Inc., one of the largest construction and mining companies in the United States. Peter Kiewit Sons' entered the telecommunications business as part of a diversification strategy the company effected during the early 1980s, engaging in a series of acquisitions that led to the formation of Kiewit Holdings Group in 1986. From Kiewit Holdings Group evolved year, seven more metropolitan areas were added, bringing Kiewit Communications' revenues for the year to $397,000. Its net loss, however, approached $18 million, significantly more than the $2.9 million recorded as a loss the previous year, evidence that the company's initial intent was not to operate at a profit, but to establish itself as a long-term participant in the telecommunications market through rapid growth. This strategy was made possible by the financial support of its parent company, Peter Kiewit Sons', and afforded Kiewit Communications an opportunity to grow more rapidly and pay less attention to the bottom line than other, newly emerging competitors.

Kiewit Communications focused on expansion, increasing the number of cities to which it provided long-distance and data transmission services to 12 by 1991—when Kiewit Communications became MFS Communications, Inc.—then to 14 the following year. In the course of this growth, the company's annual sales increased exponentially, rising from the $397,000 generated in 1989 to $10.6 million the following year, then soaring to $37.2 million by 1991 and $108 million in 1992. With robust revenue growth and market expansion, however, came further increases in MFS Communications' net losses, which peaked at $30.9 million in 1990, then slid to $13.1 million by 1992. As these losses mounted and growth continued unabated, the company, still operating as a second tier subsidiary of Peter Kiewit Sons', began to look for additional ways to finance its growth. The most obvious solution involved a public underwriting of MFS and a separation from Peter Kiewit Sons', which the company did the following year, in May 1993.

Once a publicly-held company, MFS Communications used the money raised from the sale of its stock—approximately $1 billion was realized in 1993 and early 1994—to begin marketing the company's services to a new class of customers: small and medium-sized businesses employing between five and 200 employees and using between one and 250 telephones. Before MFS Communications' efforts toward entering this much larger and virtually untapped market materialized, the company unveiled a revolutionary telecommunications service in August 1993, when it built the first nationwide Asynchronous Transfer Mode (ATM) network, enabling customers to transmit voice, video, and data signals simultaneously through a single telephone or cable-television line. The company's establishment of nationwide ATM service evidenced its ability to offer more sophisticated telecommunication services than other much larger rivals, such as AT&T, MCI, and Sprint, without recording any profit, an ability that enabled the company to compete in a market dominated by wealthier competitors and provided a springboard for further market penetration.

The springboard provided by the establishment of an ATM network carried MFS Communications overseas the following month, when the company received a telecommunications license from the British government to build and operate a local fiber-optic network. Also utilizing an ATM network, the company's expansion overseas initially led to an agreement with roughly 70 business customers, primarily U.S. and U.K. multinational companies that MFS Communications had served in the United States, and established a base of operations for further European expansion. Entry into the United Kingdom, where telecommunication regulations were most permissible

for such a foray, was also a suitable starting point because approximately 300 of the company's 800 business customers in the United States had operations in the United Kingdom. Building from this base, MFS Communications planned to operate additional telecommunication networks in Frankfurt and Paris in the imminent future, then expand to other areas in Europe within the next several years, drawing on its established clientele in the United States and in the United Kingdom to fuel its international growth.

As the company was defining itself in its new era of operations after becoming a public company, two strategic objectives were readily apparent: international expansion and the development of a small and medium-sized business clientele. The former was being executed through the construction and operation of a fiber-optic network in England under the purview of a subsidiary company, MFS International, Inc., while the latter was being executed through another of the company's subsidiary units, MFS Intelenet, Inc. Although plans were developing for both of these objectives as the company effected the transition from operating as a subsidiary of Peter Kiewit Sons' to becoming a publicly-held corporation, neither materialized in any substantive form until 1994, when the company's transatlantic audio, data, and video service began and it purchased Centex Telemanagement Inc. in a bid to accelerate the introduction of its fiber-optic network services to small and medium-sized businesses.

A San Francisco-based telecommunications management company with 11,000 customers, Centex was among the first businesses in the United States to manage local and long-distance telecommunication services for smaller business, giving MFS Communications valuable assets, experience, and talent in a market it hoped to considerably strengthen its presence. In addition to the Centex acquisition, MFS Communications also constructed two new fiber-optic networks in 1994 in Phoenix and San Diego, further broadening its service area in the United States, which by mid-1994 comprised 31 U.S. metropolitan areas either serviced or under development by MFS Communications' fiber-optic networks. Internationally, the company began offering telecommunication service in Frankfurt in July 1994, its first Continental European city of operation, and planned to begin offering service in Paris in September 1994. Positioned as such, the company entered the mid-1990s planning, as it had since its emergence in 1988, for further growth without expectations of posting a profit in the immediate future, but with considerable expectations of increasing its domestic and international presence.

Principal Subsidiaries: MFS Telecom, Inc.; MFS Network Technologies, Inc.; MFS Datanet, Inc.; MFS Intelenet, Inc.; MFS International, Inc.

Further Reading:

Andrew, Edmund L., ''Fiber Optic Rival in Phones Turns Its Sights on Europe,'' *New York Times,* May 25, 1994, p. D5.
Karpinski, Richard, ''Bellsouth's Atlanta Network is Carrier's Bright and Shining Star,'' *Telephony,* April 19, 1993, p. 8.
Karpinski, Richard, ''Texas-sized Regulatory Storm Brews in Lone Star State,'' *Telephony,* January 11, 1993, p. 8.

Naik, Gautam, "Initial Offer of MFS Communications Calls Up Good Response from Investors," *Wall Street Journal,* May 21, 1993, p. A5.

Naik, Gautam, "MFS to Offer Local Calling in Rochester," *Wall Street Journal,* May 19, 1994, p. B8.

Naik, Gautam, "MFS Will Offer Trans-Atlantic Audio, Data, Video," *Wall Street Journal,* May 25, 1994, p. B3.

Neumeier, Shelley, "Ringing Up Big Gains from Your Telecom Portfolio," *Fortune,* July 12, 1993, p. 19.

"A New Offer for Centrex is Accepted," *New York Times,* May 3, 1994, p. D5.

Pfeiffer, Deborah, "MFS Communications," *Telephony,* August 16, 1993, p. 8.

"Phone Concern to Construct Two Fiber-Optic Networks," *Wall Street Journal,* June 3, 1994, p. A5.

Wallace, Bob, "MFS Unveils Worldwide ATM Service," *Infoworld,* June 6, 1994, p. 43.

—Jeffrey L. Covell

Michigan National Corporation

27777 Inkster Road
P.O. Box 9065
Farmington Hills, Michigan 48333-9065
U.S.A.
(810) 473-3000
Fax: (810) 473-3086

Public Company
Incorporated: 1972
Employees: 5,900
Total Assets: $10 billion
Stock Exchanges: NASDAQ
SICs: 6712 Bank Holding Companies; 6021 National
   Commercial Banks; 6022 State Commercial Banks; 6035
   Federal Savings Institutions

Michigan National Corporation is a bank holding company for nationally and state-chartered commercial banks and federally-chartered savings and loan institutions. Its major subsidiaries operate in Michigan and California. In 1994, Michigan National's principal subsidiary, Michigan National Bank (MNB) had assets valued at $8.8 billion. It ranked as the 58th largest bank in the United States. MNB operated 189 branches and boasted one of the largest Automated Teller Machine (ATM) networks in Michigan, consisting of about 300 ATMs.

Michigan National Bank was founded in 1941, when Howard J. Stoddard consolidated six Michigan banks: First National Bank (Battle Creek), First National Bank (Grand Rapids), Lansing National Bank (Lansing), First National Bank (Marshall), First National Bank (Port Huron), and Saginaw National Bank (Saginaw). At the time, this was the second largest bank merger in the United States.

Stoddard, an innovative executive, earned a reputation for actively seeking out consumers and introducing many new services. Under his direction in 1946, MNB pioneered extended banking hours. Saturday banking was first offered in 1947, and Michigan's first drive-through window appeared in 1948. In 1955, MNB became the first Michigan bank to pay semi-annual interest on Certificates of Deposit. In 1960, it began offering ''Full-Time'' daily interest on savings accounts.

Stoddard's son, Stanford ''Bud'' Stoddard, who had begun working as a teller at age 14 during the 1940s, became president of MNB's flagship bank in Detroit in 1962. Following the elder Stoddard's sudden death in 1971, Stanford Stoddard moved into his father's office.

Regulatory changes led to the establishment of Michigan National Corporation in 1972. Prior to that year, Michigan state law did not permit banking institutions to own bank stocks, keeping statewide chains of affiliated banks from forming. The Stoddards, however, had circumvented the regulation by using employee pension funds (which were not subjected to the same regulatory prohibitions) and partnerships with investors to control related banks throughout the state. After regulatory modifications permitted the establishment of multiple-bank holding companies, Stoddard reorganized the MNB system establishing Michigan National Corporation.

The newly formed Michigan National Corporation, with Stanford Stoddard as president, immediately became the largest banking system in the state. Its five existing banks had a total of 360 offices. Stoddard led the company into an era of expansion. He worked to increase Michigan National's market share through the opening of new branches and by engaging in heavy promotion of innovative banking products such as mortgages for mobile homes. By 1981, Michigan National had grown to incorporate 27 affiliate banks.

Stoddard also pioneered the fields of credit cards and ATMs. Under his leadership, Michigan National developed one of the largest ATM networks in Michigan and became one of the leading credit card issuers in the nation.

The early 1980s, however, brought difficulties to Michigan National. The company purchased $200 million in bad loans from Oklahoma City's Penn Square Bank, which collapsed in 1982. As a result, Michigan National lost approximately one-third of its capital. In 1983, Michigan National failed to produce a profit. The U.S. Comptroller of the Currency expressed concern about the company's methods of accounting for its loans with Penn Square Bank and Continental Illinois Bank, and the negative attention led to regulatory sanctions. According to a report in *Bankers Monthly,* Michigan National returned to only modest profits in 1984.

In 1984, Stanford Stoddard resigned. The controversial resignation took place after charges of mismanagement were made by the U.S. comptroller, who accused Stoddard of having diverted bank money for his personal use. In addition, Stoddard faced Federal fraud charges claiming that he had leased a building in which he held partial ownership to Michigan National at rates higher than the market rate. Although Stoddard was initially convicted, the Federal fraud charge conviction was overturned and charges made by office of the comptroller were withdrawn. In addition, in 1993, Stoddard reached a $4 million settlement with Michigan National for damages suffered in the aftermath of his resignation.

Robert J. Mylod, former executive of Federal National Mortgage Association, became chairperson and chief executive officer of Michigan National in 1985. Immediately after attaining the office, Mylod faced multiple challenges including a hostile takeover attempt from a competitor, Comerica, Inc. His attempts to restore profitability included staff cuts and consolidating or selling some affiliate banks and branches. At the time

Mylod took over, Michigan National's system of 700 ATMs and 340 branches was the largest in the state. Under his direction, 140 branches were closed, the number of ATM's was cut in half, and employment was pared from 7,000 to 6,300.

Mylod's struggle to boost profitability by controlling expenses led to an improvement in Michigan National's overall financial picture. As a result, in 1986 regulatory sanctions were removed. Mylod also increased efforts aimed at promoting services to the consumer and commercial markets and expanding the company's mortgage operations. Mylod's management team focused on developing the company's core business in four areas which were identified as commercial, consumer, investment, and mortgage banking. According to information published in *Banker's Monthly,* the company's mortgage portfolio increased from $500 million in 1985 to $6 billion in 1988.

Michigan National's net income rose 36 percent in 1987. The number of nonperforming loans (non-accruing and renegotiated loans) dropped to 1.54 percent of total loans, compared with 1.97 percent in 1986. Return on equity, another measure of bank performance, was reached 14 percent, up from nine percent in 1985. By the end of 1988, return on equity had risen further to 17.18 percent. Michigan National's total earnings of $93.2 million in 1988 set a company record.

Despite these successes, the late 1980s also brought new challenges. In 1988, a change in Michigan's banking regulations allowed for mergers between Michigan banks and banks in other states. The new climate again raised the risk of hostile takeover and brought new rivals into the state. According to a statement made by Michigan National at the time, ''Michigan laws that allow reciprocal interstate banking with contiguous states and nationwide interstate banking have enlarged the banking market and heightened competitive forces.'' Michigan National took advantage of the regulatory changes by purchasing banks in California and Texas. Other acquisitions, however, yielded disappointing results. Michigan National purchased an investment advisory company and a commercial lending company, both of which sustained losses and were folded.

By establishing itself as a strong commercial lender, Michigan National found itself in a difficult position when the national economy suffered a downturn at the end of the 1980s. The company had increased commercial real estate lending by 73 percent during the last three years of the decade and suffered from the financial woes of its customers. According to a report in the *Detroit News,* commercial real estate accounted for 70 percent of Michigan National's bad loans. In addition, Michigan National had made risky loans to out-of-state commercial ventures.

In order to offset losses from commercial real estate loans, Michigan National sold its credit card operations. The sale resulted in a pre-tax gain of $225 million, a figure representing more than half the corporation's profits in 1989. Although the move drew controversy and criticism, Mylod defended it. According to his own projections, the credit card business faced increased competition not only among banks but from new corporate competitors such as General Motors Corp. Mylod expected the increased competition to lead to a reduction or elimination of annual fees making credit card operations less

profitable. By the early 1990s, some industry analysts conceded that Mylod's predictions had proved correct.

Another controversy occurred when Michigan National moved into new headquarters in Farmington Hills, Michigan, in 1989. The $30 million, 240,000-square-foot structure, built to accommodate 1,150 workers included athletic and dining facilities. In light of the company's poor profit picture, some critics regarded the building as excessive.

Michigan National turned to fee-generating services in an attempt to bolster profits. According to a *Forbes* report, in 1991 Michigan National spent $252 million to purchase mortgage servicing rights to a large group of mortgages. Under the agreement, Michigan National would collect and process mortgage payments on behalf of other lenders for a fee. The servicing rights were purchased with the expectation that Michigan National would collect processing fees over the long-term duration of the mortgages. When interest rates subsequently fell to 30-year lows, homeowners refinanced in droves. As a result, the potential income to be generated from processing fees was lost.

Other types of fee-generating activities, such as credit card processing and personal investment advising, were also explored. In 1991, Michigan National was the nation's 14th largest processor of credit-card purchases, processing retail charges totaling $3.2 billion. Personal investing services were conducted by a subsidiary, Independence One Capital Management. Independence One used ''pattern recognition'' models to make investment decisions based on past market behavior.

Another attempt to expand fee income involved the purchase of a Dallas-based software producer, BancA Corp. BancA's software package, POWER 1, was first used by Michigan National in 1989 to streamline commercial credit operations. POWER 1 provided the tools necessary for portfolio management and tracking customer profitability. The software enabled users to reduce expenses by implementing a uniform policy, working more efficiently with a reduced staff, and improving loan quality by weeding out applications that failed to meet pre-specified criteria. However, slower than expected software sales led to the 1993 decision to sell BancA's products to Andersen Consulting.

In 1993, Michigan National was ranked at the bottom of a list of Michigan's 18 largest banks. Rankings were made using standard industry measurements such as return on equity and growth in earnings per share. Moreover, according to an analysis made by Keefe, Bruyette & Woods, Michigan National's return on assets placed it last among U.S. banks with assets over $10 billion. While disgruntled stockholders began pushing for the sale of the company, Mylod insisted that the organization was committed to remaining independent.

Michigan National's earnings in 1993 fell to $23.8 million, down from the $66.1 million reported in 1992. A Memorandum of Understanding was then issued by the Office of the Comptroller of Currency, calling for Michigan National to review and improve its management structure, institute better policies for controlling risk management, and analyze its mortgage banking business.

Some of Michigan National's profit woes were directly related to its high expenses. According to report a in *Forbes,* Michigan

National's efficiency ratio, expressed as a percentage of expenses to revenue, stood at 77 percent. The figure was much higher than other banks in Michigan, which posted efficiency ratios averaging about 63 percent. Efficiency ratios at some of the nation's stronger banks were reported at less than 60 percent. In order to help reduce expenses and improve the corporation's profitability, Michigan National's management decided to refocus attention on its core businesses in Michigan. As a result, Michigan National began divesting itself of its diverse holdings. In 1993, some bank holdings in Texas were sold to the Lockwood Banc Group, Inc. for $16.7 million. Michigan National also announced plans to sell its remaining Texas affiliates.

As Michigan National entered 1994, its primary focus continued to be in mortgage banking and financial institutions. The company's Independence One Mortgage Corporation originated and serviced residential mortgage loans through 23 offices in ten states. Its servicing portfolio totaled $8.9 billion. Other operating subsidiaries included: Independence One Bank of California (IOBOC), a savings and loan association with five branches and three business lending offices. IOBOC had assets totaling $757 million. Its primary market was in Southern California. First Collateral Services, Inc. (FCSI), a mortgage warehouse lender and subsidiary of IOBOC, also operated in California. Independence One Brokerage Services, Inc. (IOBSI), a broker-dealer established to assist clients in achieving their financial goals, was licensed to do business in 13 states. Independence One Capital Management Corporation provided investment advice and managed assets of more than $6.5 billion. Executive Relocation Corporation (ERC) served Fortune 500 firms and assisted in relocating employees throughout the United States.

The fastest growing segment of Michigan National's loan portfolio, consumer loans, increased to $596.6 million in 1993, up $78.6 million over the previous year. In addition, consumer deposits grew. According to the company's 1993 annual report, checking and savings deposits increased from $192 million to $2.2 billion. Debit card processing provided another rising source of income. Michigan National reported that it handled approximately 75 percent of point-of-sale transactions in Michigan. Fees generated from debit card activities increased 74 percent in 1993 and were projected to continue to swell.

Continuing its tradition of innovation, Michigan National, in partnership with Microsoft Corp., introduced an electronic home banking system in 1994. Michigan National was one of only three banks across the nation to offer the new services. Using Microsoft's program Microsoft Money 3.0, users could access "Bank On-Line," which permitted them to review transactions, balance checkbooks, and communicate with the bank. "Pay On-Line" users could pay bills electronically. A third electronic service, "Quote On-Line" enabled investors to track stocks and keep a watchful eye on the value of their investment portfolios.

Despite its efforts, bank profitability remained marginal, and Michigan National announced further cost cutting measures including the closing of 12 additional branches. In a display of dissatisfaction, one-third of the company's shareholders voted against the slate of directors at the company's annual meeting held in 1994. Some demanded that the organization be sold. In June, the company announced that it planned to sell its mortgage subsidiary, Independence One Mortgage.

Michigan National reported some improvement in the second quarter of 1994. The company's quarterly net income increased to $63.3 million, compared with $8.9 million in the same quarter the previous year. Mylod attributed the improvement to refocused efforts in the Michigan market, higher net interest margins, lower mortgage servicing amortization, improved asset quality, and better performance in consumer and commercial banking sectors.

Amid much speculation about whether Michigan National's management would sell or merge the company, Mylod remained adamant in his commitment to independence. According to a published statement, the corporation claimed, "Our vision is to remain a strong, independent financial services company which is able to provide shareholders with a competitive return on their investment."

Principal Subsidiaries: Michigan National Bank; Independence One Bank of California; First Collateral Services, Inc.; Independence One Brokerage Services, Inc.; Independence One Mortgage Corporation; Independence One Capital Management Corporation; Executive Relocation Corporation.

Further Reading:

Fraser, Bruce, "Michigan National Takes Lead in Electronic Overhaul," *American Banker,* February 1, 1993.

Hellauer, Brian, "Anderson Acquires Software Unit from Michigan National," *American Banker,* October 21, 1993.

Klinkerman, Steve, "Michigan National Settles with Ex-Chairman for $4 Million," *American Banker,* May 13, 1993.

Koselka, Rita, "Under Siege," *Forbes,* May 23, 1994.

Kreuzer, Terese, "Born-Again Banks: Four Fabulous Turnarounds," *Bankers Monthly,* April 1989.

"Michigan National's Mortgage Unit Is for Sale," *New York Times,* June 21, 1994.

Roush, Matt, "Breaking New Ground," *Crains Detroit Business,* August 17, 1992.

Starkman, Eric M., "How Stanford Stoddard Fought Off the Regulators," *American Banker,* November 19, 1991.

Waldsmith, Lynn, "Bank Hires N.Y. Firm for Financial Advice," *Detroit News,* May 26, 1994.

Waldsmith, Lynn, "Michigan National to Close 12 Branch Offices, Cut Staff," *Detroit News,* January 20, 1994; "Michigan National to Offer At-Home Banking," *Detroit News,* January 12, 1994; "Sizing Up Michigan National," *Detroit News,* April 10, 1994.

Zweig, Phillip L., "The Rehabilitation of Michigan National," *Financial World,* November 17, 1987.

—Karen Bellenir

Micron Technology, Inc.

2805 East Columbia Road
Boise, Idaho 83706-9698
U.S.A.
(208) 368-4000
Fax: (208) 343-2536

Public Company
Incorporated: 1978
Employees: 5,300
Sales: $828.2 million
Stock Exchanges: New York
SICs: 3674 Semiconductors & Related Devices

Micron Technology, Inc., is a holding company for subsidiaries engaged in the design and production of semiconductors and other related products. One of the few U.S. manufacturers to remain in the market for DRAM (dynamic random access memory) chips, Micron competed against formidable foreign competition during the 1980s, when the global semiconductor market rapidly expanded into a $20 billion industry by the 1990s. Micron experienced considerable difficulties during its history, rising from a small design and consulting firm located in the basement of a dentist's office in Boise, Idaho to an internationally recognized and respected manufacturer of memory chips. It entered the mid-1990s exhibiting robust growth, confounding those convinced a comparably small semiconductor manufacturer based in Idaho could not effectively compete in a market dominated by powerful foreign competitors.

During the summer months of 1978, three design engineers left the employ of Mostek Corporation, a pioneer in the design and production of semiconductors, to join Inmos Ltd., a British-financed competitor. On the surface, the emigration of three employees to Inmos appeared insignificant, an unremarkable switch of employers by a small number of employees, but at Mostek tempers flared. These three engineers, Ward Parkinson, Dennis Wilson, and Douglas Pittman, were not the first employees to leave Mostek for better offers from Inmos. One former Mostek employee, in fact, had co-founded Inmos, and Mostek's management wanted to stanch the flow of additional employee departures, particularly if those employees were moving to Inmos. A legal battle ensued, with Mostek filing a suit against Inmos that called for a permanent injunction to stop further raids on its personnel. Mostek also attempted to enjoin Inmos

from starting operations, but both of these demands were dismissed, including charges that the three engineers took trade secrets from Mostek to Inmos.

Caught in the middle of these accusations, the three engineers made the summer's squabble moot in October, when, led by Ward Parkinson, they decided to leave Inmos and start their own design and consulting company, Micron Technology. Incorporated that month, five days after Parkinson left Inmos, the company established modest operations in the basement of a dentist's office in Boise, Idaho, performing essentially the same work for the same people as they had before the summer began. All three had been working on a 64 kilobit (K) random access memory (RAM) program while at Mostek, and now, after the dispute between Inmos and Mostek, the three contracted to design a 64K chip for Mostek, Micron's first and, it appeared, only customer.

The company had been formed with the intent of serving only Mostek; Parkinson told *Electronic News,* a trade publication, "We are not looking for other customers." However, the idea of working for Mostek on an exclusive basis was short-lived, falling apart the following year when United Technologies acquired Mostek. United Technologies canceled the contract with Micron, leaving the fledgling company, entirely dependent on Mostek for revenue, without any customers. The three design engineers, later joined by Parkinson's twin brother, Joseph L. Parkinson, a Wall Street lawyer and eventual leader of Micron, decided to continue designing the 64K chip on their own and began looking for investors to finance their endeavor.

The first of Micron's many struggles, the loss of the contract with Mostek tested the company's commitment to manufacture semiconductor chips in a market dominated by leviathan Japanese electronic companies. Success in the memory chip market was essentially determined by size: the smaller the size of the chip and the greater the size of its memory capabilities, the greater the manufacturer's profits and market share. In this race for smaller chips and greater memory, a race predicated on technology, the Japanese were well ahead, rivaled only by large American companies based typically in California's Silicon Valley, the U.S. bastion for semiconductor research and production. Industry pundits and, more important, loan officers and venture capitalists strongly believed no new U.S. memory chip manufacturer could enter the market as late as 1979 and hope to succeed—certainly not a tiny company based in Boise, Idaho. Consequently, Micron's entreaties for financing were met with disdain. As Ward Parkinson later related to *Forbes,* his typical response from investors "wasn't 'no,' it was 'Hell, no.'"

However, as was often true throughout its history, Micron's weaknesses were its strengths, or, more precisely, the company drew from characteristics regarded as weaknesses and used them to its advantage. With its decision to enter the memory chip manufacturing arena, Micron immediately inherited three weaknesses: its size, its location, and the late date of its entry into the memory chip market, all of which were adversely affecting its ability to secure financing. To solve this formidable problem, Micron drew upon one of its weaknesses, its location, and canvassed wealthy Idaho residents for an interest in Micron. There, at home, the company found success, enlisting the support of a machine shop operator, Ron Yanke, a wealthy sheep rancher, Tom Nicholson, and Allen Noble, a wealthy potato farmer—all Boise residents. Next came Micron's wealthiest supporter, John R. Simplot, a billionaire potato farmer and the largest supplier of potatoes to McDonalds. McDonalds in turn invested $1 million in Micron in 1980 and later poured tens of millions of dollars into Micron. With this distinctly Idahoan cadre of investors, Micron began operations, starting with $9 million in an industry that conventionally required at least a $100 million start-up investment.

Micron's location also served it well in other important areas that gave the company a much-needed boost in its transformation from a design and consulting firm to a manufacturer of memory chips. Land in Idaho was considerably cheaper than in Japan or in the Silicon Valley, which helped to reduce start-up costs. Labor was cheaper, and Idaho's hydroelectric power rates were roughly a third of those incurred by California memory chip manufacturers. With these advantages, Micron required less initial capital investment. In addition, its small size forced the company to closely examine the production methods currently employed by other manufacturers with the hope of identifying inefficiencies in conventional processes. This bare-boned approach to all aspects of the memory chip business enabled Micron to operate in an industry dominated by much larger and perhaps more complacent competitors, a cost-cutting approach that enabled the company to construct its first factory for $20 million, roughly one-quarter of the typical cost for a semiconductor manufacturing facility.

However, Micron could not control all aspects of the memory chip business. As Micron was effecting its transformation, Japanese electronic companies, such as Hitachi, NEC, and Fujitsu, had gained an early lead in the market for 64K DRAM chips, a key component of computers, video games, and telecommunications systems. By 1981, Japanese companies had secured 70 percent of the global market for 64K DRAM chips, without having to contend with any serious challenge from U.S. manufacturers. Finally, two U.S. companies, Texas Instruments and Motorola, began volume production of 64K chips the following year, whereas other American contenders, Intel, National Semiconductor, and Mostek did not begin production until late 1982. Before the year was through, however, the two strongest U.S. entries, Texas Instruments' and Motorola, did not prove to be serious forces in the global market—Motorola's chip, derogatorily known as the "postage stamp," was large and, consequently, expensive to manufacture, and Texas Instruments' chip suffered from temporary production problems in late 1982. For Micron, these developments were unfavorable because they strengthened Japan's grip on the market and kept worldwide attention, the attention of potential Micron customers, focused on Asia.

As it turned out, what Micron lacked in financial backing and timeliness of product entry, it made up for in product quality and innovation. Micron shipped over 1 million chips in 1982, not by itself a noteworthy achievement when compared to the production totals of its competitors, but notable in the quality and size of its chips. With bigger, easier-to-read memory cells than competing chips, Micron's chips were more reliable and were also remarkably small—40 percent smaller than Motorola's chip and 15 percent smaller than Hitachi's chip. In early 1983, Micron achieved a dramatic breakthrough when it further reduced the size of its chips, thus garnering the attention of semiconductor engineers and customers worldwide. Micron's 1982 chip measured 33,000 square mils (one mil equals 1/1000 of an inch), whereas the new chip measured 22,000 square mils, roughly half the size of Japan's leading chips and a third smaller than Texas Instruments' chip. As the size of Micron's chips decreased, so did the company's manufacturing costs, giving the company a significant advantage over its competitors and a springboard toward viability in the global semiconductor market.

The financial rewards of this innovation in memory chip production arrived the following year, in 1984, the same year Micron became a publicly held corporation. For the year, Micron earned $29 million in after-tax profit on revenues of $84 million, a profit-to-revenue ratio that ranked among the highest recorded by electronics companies worldwide. Micron used part of the proceeds from its success with its 64K chip to begin development of the industry's next benchmark semiconductor chip, the 256K chip, which the company began shipping in small quantities by the end of the year. However, earlier in the year, significant developments in the semiconductor industry had occurred that promised to radically change the industry's future and Micron's position in it. In September of that year, when worldwide demand for chips exceeded supply, Micron drastically reduced the price of its chips, selling each for $1.95, well below the international list price of $3.40. It was a move to strengthen the company's position in the memory chip market at the expense of profit margins, a temporary maneuver to increase its customer base and undercut its competitors. At the same time, several major U.S. manufacturers, such as Intel and AMD, retreated from the fierce competition of the Japanese companies and into the high-performance, specialty chip market, where competition was less intense. Micron had decided to stay in the conventional chip market, and its price reduction was an indication of its intent; however, its strategy was not without precedent, a strategy the Japanese had been employing for a year.

For Micron, its price reduction was a way of increasing business, but the ploy was only temporary because undercutting competitors' prices impinged on profits, leaving Micron without money it sorely needed. For the Japanese companies, however, price reductions could be adopted as a long-term strategy because their large reservoirs of cash could withstand significant reductions in profits. This the Japanese companies did, dropping their prices, and forcing U.S. competitors to exit the market for memory chips. National Semiconductor suspended plans to market a 256K chip in 1985, Intel announced it was closing all of its RAM production during the fall, and United Technologies closed Mostek's operations the same year.

The effect of this aggressive pricing strategy was disastrous for Micron. In 1985, the price of 64K chips plummeted from approximately $4 to 25 cents, and the price of 256K chips fell from $20 at the beginning of the year to $2.50 by its conclusion. Micron's earnings aped this pattern, falling from $28.9 million in 1984 to $154,000 in 1985. For Micron the worst was yet to come, the company had to cope without half of its work force, which was laid off in the spring of 1985, and without one of its two production lines, which also fell victim to the pernicious downward swing of memory chip prices. In 1986, the company lost $33.9 million and generated $48.8 million in revenue, significantly less than 1985's total of $75.8 million.

Micron responded by formally accusing the Japanese semiconductor industry in 1985 of creating the collapse of the U.S. industry by illegally flooding the U.S. market with products sold below manufacturing costs, a practice commonly known as "dumping," and, several months later, in the fall, filed a $300 million antitrust lawsuit against six Japanese electronics companies. The result of these and other, repeated dumping charges against the Japanese led to the signing of the Semiconductor Trade Agreement between the United States and Japan in 1986, which established fair prices for Japanese memory chips and, according to Micron's management, enabled the company to effect a recovery.

Before the recovery, Micron recorded another dismal year, equally as poor as 1986. The company lost $22.9 million in 1987, although total sales climbed to $91.1 million, but in 1988 both revenues and earnings recorded substantial leaps: revenues soared to $300.5 million and earnings jumped to $97.9 million, giving credence to the company's accusations of dumping. Now once again recording profits, Micron moved forward, still operating in a highly competitive market dominated by Japanese companies, something the Semiconductor Trade Agreement had not altered. Sales climbed to $446.4 million in 1989 and earnings increased modestly to $106.1 million. The following year demonstrated the volatility of the semiconductor market when the arrival of a nationwide recession caused sales to fall to $333 million and earnings to plummet to $4.9 million.

During the recessive early 1990s, revenues recorded modest gains, rising to $425.3 million in 1991, then reaching $506.3 million the following year, but earnings remained deleteriously low, rising to only $6.6 million by 1992. That year, Micron canceled its plans to develop microprocessors and decentralized its operations, dividing the company into five subsidiary companies with Micron Technology, Inc., serving as the parent company and Micron Semiconductor, Inc., as the core operating unit. In 1993, the semiconductor market once again demonstrated its volatility, but this time in a most agreeable manner, particularly for Micron shareholders. Revenues increased 63 percent, bringing the year's total to $828.3 million, but the most remarkable increase—a 1,470 percent increase—was recorded in Micron's profits, which soared to $104.1 million, nearly reaching the total generated before the recession in 1989.

As Micron charted its future, prognostications for the global semiconductor market appeared to be in the company's favor. Still enjoying an overwhelming lead in the memory chip market, Japanese semiconductor manufacturers, who controlled approximately 50 percent of the worldwide market for DRAMS in 1994, were beginning to suffer from rising capital costs, a financial constraint that forced many companies to reduce their chip production and consequently created a shortage of chips. Micron stood poised to fulfill this demand as it entered the mid-1990s, hoping to secure a greater portion of the market it had been nearly forced out of during the mid-1980s.

Principal Subsidiaries: Micron Semiconductor, Inc.; Micron Custom Manufacturing Services, Inc. (86%); Micron Communications, Inc. (86%); Micron Display Technology, Inc. (91.25%); Micron Computer, Inc. (77%); Micron Construction, Inc. (86%); Micron Systems Integration, Inc. (87.15%); Micron Investments, Inc.

Further Reading:

Brammer, Rhonda, "Back in the Chips?," *Barron's,* February 3, 1986, p. 16.

Chakravarty, Subrata N., "We've Heard All That Before," *Forbes,* December 31, 1984, p. 34.

Connelly, Joanne, "Micron Asks Dumping Duties on Korean Memories," *Electronic News,* April 27, 1992, p. 4.

Davis, Dwight B., "Micron's Formula: Be the First to Make Money," *Electronic Business,* March 1993, p. 59.

Fisher, Lawrence M., "The Rescue of a U.S. Chip Company," *New York Times,* April 6, 1988, p. D1.

Gianturco, Michael, "The Semiconductor Double Take," *Forbes,* April 2, 1990, p. 170.

Gilder, George, "Idaho's New Breed of RAMs," *Forbes,* March 14, 1983, p. 130.

Greenburg, Adam, and Brooke Crothers, "Micron, NEC Sign Memory Deal," *Electronic News,* June 8, 1992, p. 37.

Hershberger, Steven, "3 Engineers Exit Inmos, Form Firm," *Electronic News,* October 23, 1978, p. 1.

"Micron Splits into 5 Operating Firms, Shifts Execs, Drops Processor Effort," *Electronic News,* August 10, 1992, p. 23.

"Micron Technology Is Making Its Initial Public Offering," *Wall Street Journal,* June 4, 1984, p. 40.

Miller, Michael W., "Fallen Star: Precipitous Decline of Memory Chip Firm Shakes the Industry," *Wall Street Journal,* January 17, 1986, p. 1.

Pulliam, Susan, "Micron Probably Will Escape Serious Damage Even If Computer Sales Ease, Its Backers Say," *Wall Street Journal,* May 19, 1994, p. C2.

Waldman, Peter, "Micron, a Critic of Japan, Explored Takeover by Firm There, Sources Say," *Wall Street Journal,* March 23, 1987, p. 5; "Micron Technology Says Japanese Firms Still Violate Chip Pact," *Wall Street Journal,* March 19, 1987, p. 4.

Wrubel, Robert, "Micron Technology: Finally, Good News," *Financial World,* March 2, 1993, p. 15.

—Jeffrey L. Covell

Minerals Technologies Inc.

The Chrysler Building
405 Lexington Avenue
New York, New York 10174-1901
U.S.A.
(212) 878-1831
Fax: (212) 878-1801

Public Company
Incorporated: 1968 as the Special Minerals Division of
    Chas. Pfizer & Co.
Employees: 2,150
Sales: $428.3 million
Stock Exchanges: New York
SICs: 1411 Dimension Stone; 2819 Industrial Inorganic
    Chemicals, Not Elsewhere Classified

Minerals Technologies Inc. is a leading force in the international paper making industry, responsible in large part for transforming the process by which paper was produced in North America and creating a market niche, which it quickly dominated. The company is known for designing and implementing an innovative system to produce precipitated calcium carbonate, a filler and pigment used in the production of paper, as well as for manufacturing mineral-based monolithic refractory products, which are used primarily by the steel industry to resist the effects of high temperatures. Minerals Technologies also mines and processes various minerals.

The company traces its history to 1968, when pharmaceutical giant Pfizer Inc. formed and incorporated its special minerals division, which comprised an amalgamation of companies involved in the excavation of minerals—particularly limestone—that Pfizer had acquired earlier in its history. While some of the acquisitions dated back to the 1940s, a majority arrived during the 1960s, when the company began purchasing in earnest the properties that would eventually form its specialty minerals division. With these minerals excavation companies and minerals reserves, Pfizer produced various minerals—limestone, lime, talc, and calcium—for the building materials, steel, paints and coatings, and chemical industries, as well as other manufacturing industries, which together, composed one of three product lines that would fuel the division's growth throughout its existence under Pfizer's corporate umbrella.

The division's second product line was established seven months after its incorporation through the acquisition in September 1968 of New York City-based Quigley Company, Inc., a manufacturer of mineral-based refractory products used to resist the effects of high temperatures in manufacturing processes utilized by the steel, cement, and glass industries. With the addition of Quigley, Pfizer's specialty minerals division now offered two product lines—both sold chiefly to the steel industry—that provided a foundation for the division's growth and supported its existence for roughly the next two decades. Although refractory products and mineral mining and processing were integral contributors to Pfizer's mineral-related operations, the specialty minerals division's third product line, precipitated calcium carbonate (PCC), was the key to its success, vaulting first Pfizer then its spin-off, Minerals Technologies Inc., into a dominant position in the paper making industry.

Produced from a mixture of lime, carbon dioxide, and water, PCC was used primarily as a filler in alkaline process, wood-free paper and, to a lesser extent, as a specialty pigment to make coated and uncoated paper. Its use as an alternative to more expensive wood pulp and to other fillers, such as kaolin clay and titanium dioxide, had been known for years. Historically, however, North American manufacturers of wood-free paper utilized acid technologies, rather than alkaline technologies, significantly limiting the demand for PCC. Although manufacturing costs associated with producing PCC were low, drying and transporting the product were expensive processes, adding more than $100 per ton of filler and giving Canadian and American wood-free paper producers little incentive to convert to an alkaline-based process.

Pfizer's specialty minerals division would provide these manufacturers with the incentive to switch to an alkaline process, but not until roughly 20 years after its incorporation and not until a lengthy research and development program produced a solution to the prohibitive cost of PCC. As Pfizer's researchers perceived it, the problem with PCC was not how it was produced as much as where it was produced, so the specialty minerals division began developing a plan to manufacture PCC in proximity to the pulp and paper mills that would use the product. The concept, under development by 1982 at the company's research center in Easton, Pennsylvania, and its lime and limestone plant in Adams, Massachusetts, changed the way a majority of the paper was produced in North America and positioned Pfizer's specialty minerals division as a burgeoning force in the paper industry.

By producing PCC in plants adjacent to pulp and paper mills, the specialty minerals division eliminated both the need to dry PCC and the costs incurred from shipping it, yielding a delivered product that was substantially cheaper than purchasing PCC from an independent, "merchant" plant. Adjacent, or satellite plants, as designed by Pfizer's specialty minerals division, used carbon dioxide produced by the host paper mill, combined it with dissolved lime, then delivered the product in slurry form, saving the mill more than 50 percent in its PCC costs and creating a new niche in the paper filler market. Although innovative, the satellite PCC plant concept was suitable only for producers of alkaline-based paper, not for the vast majority of manufacturers who produced paper under acid conditions, but, while the satellite program was being refined during the early and mid-1980s, the price of fillers used in acid technologies, particularly the price of titanium dioxide, began to climb. Coupled with the innovative and relatively inexpensive satellite PCC plant concept developed by Pfizer's specialty minerals division, the rising cost of wood pulp, titanium dioxide, and other fillers provided sufficient incentive for paper makers employing acid technologies to seriously consider adopting the division's PCC system. The decision these producers made quickly transformed their industry, and along with it, the future of Pfizer's specialty minerals division.

The first satellite PCC plant, the first of many to follow, was dedicated in 1986, four years after the development program was initiated, marking the beginning of a new era for the specialty minerals division, then in its 18th year of operation. Before the first plant was completed, a $10 million facility constructed near Consolidated Papers, Inc.'s paper mill at Wisconsin Rapids, Wisconsin, plans were announced for another, this time in Ticonderoga, New York, adjoining International Paper Company's pulp and paper mill. Both of these facilities were owned and operated by Pfizer's specialty minerals division, an arrangement that was typical of the on-site facilities to follow, and each produced approximately 30,000 tons of PCC a year, affording paper mill operators substantial savings. Over the course of the next two years, from the end of 1986 to the end of 1988, three additional plants were constructed, then another 12 during the next two years, giving Pfizer 17 satellite PCC plants by the conclusion of 1990. By the end of the following year, the specialty minerals division's last full year as a subsidiary of Pfizer, the number of on-site PCC plants had swelled to 21, while conversely, Pfizer had begun to do the opposite, shedding itself of assets deemed inconsistent with its future plans.

Eight additional satellite PCC plants were put into operation in 1992, the greatest increase in one year since the specialty minerals division's on-site project had begun six years earlier. Against the backdrop of this prodigious expansion—which brought the total number of facilities in operation to 29 and cast Pfizer as the central agent of change in the paper making industry—larger, more defining issues were being discussed that led to the creation of a new company and ended Pfizer's long history of involvement in the specialty minerals business.

Like other U.S. health care companies, Pfizer Inc. spent the early 1990s re-examining its future role in an industry that appeared destined for dramatic, sweeping change. As the 1992 U.S. presidential election neared and the debate concerning national health care reform intensified, many health care executives maneuvered to anticipate the effects of widespread federal legislation, pinning the future success of their companies on decisions made in uncertain times. Among the larger, more diversified health care companies, a pattern emerged, as several multinational concerns began to shed assets unrelated to the health care market. One of these large, diversified health care companies was Pfizer Inc., a $7 billion corporation with wide-ranging interests in pharmaceuticals, hospital products, consumer health care products, chemicals, and minerals, among others.

During the early 1990s, Pfizer began divesting properties deemed inconsistent with the company's plans for its future,

which, as Pfizer's chairman William C. Steere, Jr. related to the *New York Times,* consisted of pursuing a "strategy of focusing on [Pfizer's] strengths as a research-based, diversified health care company." Toward this objective, Pfizer sold its citric-acid business in 1990, touching off a series of strategic divestitures over the course of the next two years that represented a loss of more than $1 billion in total sales and led to the divestiture of the company's specialty minerals division, a $359 million contributor to the company's 1991 annual sales.

In August 1992, Pfizer announced plans to sell the bulk of the company's interest in specialty minerals through the public offering of stock in a newly created company, Minerals Technologies Inc. Approximately 60 percent of Pfizer's interest in its specialty minerals division was sold by the end of October, and the remaining 40 percent was sold six months later, in April 1993, completing the full divestiture of Pfizer's specialty minerals division and beginning Minerals Technologies' first year of business as a manufacturer and marketer of PCC, refractory products, and other minerals.

Concurrent with Pfizer's initial announcement to spin-off its specialty minerals division in August 1992 was the selection of Minerals Technologies' chair and chief executive officer, Jean-Paul Vallès, who had joined Pfizer in 1967, one year before the specialty minerals division was incorporated. In the three years leading up to Pfizer's divestiture of its specialty minerals division, Vallès had been responsible for several of Pfizer's businesses, including the specialty minerals division that now represented Minerals Technologies. Vallès left his position as vice-chairman of Pfizer and assumed stewardship of Minerals Technologies' three business lines, the most promising of which continued to be its design and operation of satellite PCC plants.

Although Minerals Technologies' two other product lines figured less prominently in the company's future than its involvement in on-site PCC production, they nevertheless were essential contributors to the company's annual sales volume, providing diversity and stability to predicate the company's further expansion in its PCC business. Minerals Technologies' refractory product business, which generated $147.6 million in sales in 1993 compared to the $171.1 million derived from PCC sales, was operated through the company's subsidiary, Minteq International Inc. Minteq sold refractory products in North America, Europe, and Asia, giving the company the geographic breadth to help mitigate the product line's dependence on the historically capricious steel market. This involvement overseas was particularly important in Minerals Technologies' first year of existence, when sluggish steel markets in the United States and Japan were offset by Minteq's production facilities in South Korea, where steel production was robust, and in China, which, for the first time, produced more steel than the United States.

In addition to its presence in strong steel-producing regions, Minerals Technologies also owned minerals reserves in the eastern, midwestern, and western areas of the United States. From these reserves, estimated to last between 40 and 70 years, the company mined and processed limestone and talc as well as manufactured mineral-based and technology-based products, which combined, constituted Minerals Technologies' other mineral products line, a contributor of $109.6 million to the company's sales volume in 1993.

While refractory products and other mineral products together generated more than 50 percent of Minerals Technologies' total sales in 1993, the company's greatest expectations were invested in the expansion of its satellite PCC concept, the essence of the company's future. By the end of 1993, Minerals Technologies was operating 34 on-site PCC plants, which accounted for more than 90 percent of all satellite PCC production. Expansion had extended the company's presence into Europe, where Minerals Technologies operated an on-site plant in Saillat Sur Vienne, France, and three more plants in Finland. In Europe, where for years paper producers had manufactured their product under alkaline conditions, the company's focus was not on converting from acid to alkaline paper making as it was in North America, but on convincing European manufacturers to use PCC, rather than ground chalk or ground calcium carbonate. Toward this objective, Minerals Technologies announced a joint venture in August 1993 with Partek Corporation, an international industrial group based in Finland and Scandinavia's largest producer of lime, to produce PCC in the Nordic countries and in Eastern Europe.

With this European expansion bolstering the company's position in the global paper industry, Minerals Technologies entered 1994 looking to translate its success in the wood-free segment of the paper industry into success in the wood-containing segment. By this time, the company's development of satellite PCC plants had dramatically altered the wood-free segment of the paper industry, converting an industry that predominately had utilized acid-based technology to an industry in which 80 percent of the paper produced was made with alkaline technology. Efforts to effect a commensurate transformation of the wood-containing industry had been stalled by the tendency of wood-containing paper to darken in an alkaline environment. However, in 1993 Minerals Technologies successfully commercialized an acid-tolerant PCC, opening up a vast new market for the company's expertise in PCC production. As Minerals Technologies entered its first full year as a separate, independent company, expectations ran high, with plans to further solidify its position in the wood-free paper industry and to begin its involvement in the wood-containing paper industry, both of which promised to sustain the company's growth throughout the 1990s.

Principal Subsidiaries: Specialty Minerals Inc.; Barretts Minerals Inc.; Minteq International, Inc.; Mintech Japan K.K.; Minerals Technologies Holdings Ltd.; Minteq Australia Pty Ltd.; Specialty Minerals S.A.R.L.; Mintech do Brasil Commercial Ltda.; Minteq International GmbH; Minteq Europe Ltd.; Minteq Canada Inc.; Minteq Italiana S.p.A.; Minteq Korea Inc.; Minteq U.K. Ltd.; BYM Refractories Ltd.

Further Reading:
"Another Pfizer Lime Plant," *Chemical Week,* February 11, 1987, p. 20.
Freudenheim, Milt, "Pfizer Selling Off Control of Specialty Minerals Unit," *New York Times,* August 18, 1992, p. C4.
"Joint Venture Is Formed with Company in Finland," *Wall Street Journal,* August 13, 1993, p. B5.
Jones, John A., "Minerals Technologies Brings Cost Savings to Paper Mills," *Investor's Business Daily,* April 28, 1993, p. 28.
"Minerals Technologies Inc.," *Wall Street Journal,* March 1, 1993, p. B5.
"Minerals Technologies' Shares," *Wall Street Journal,* April 7, 1993, p. B10.
"Pfizer Board Clears Sale of Stake in Unit, Repurchase of Shares," *Wall Street Journal,* August 18, 1992, p. A12.
"Pfizer on Line," *Chemical Marketing Reporter,* July 21, 1986, p. 9.
"Pfizer Plans PCC Unit," *Chemical Marketing Reporter,* October 19, 1987, p. 9.
"Pfizer Takes Its Satellite Plants Overseas," *Chemical Week,* June 4, 1986, p. 5.
"Pfizer to Build Plant," *Chemical Marketing Reporter,* November 13, 1989, p. 9.
"Pfizer to Construct Calcium Carbonate Plant," *Chemical Marketing Reporter,* April 21, 1986, p. 3.
Plishner, Emily S., "Satellites Launch Minerals Technologies on Growth Trajectory," *Chemical Week,* June 9, 1993, p. 26.
Shapiro, Lynn, "Chemical Stocks Seen as Bargain," *Chemical Marketing Reporter,* December 14, 1992, p. 3.

—Jeffrey L. Covell

Minnesota Power & Light Company

30 West Superior Street
Duluth, Minnesota 55802
U.S.A.
(218) 722-2641
Fax: (218) 723-3960

Public Company
Incorporated: 1906 as Duluth Edison Electric Company
Employees: 2,587
Sales: $505.52 million
Stock Exchanges: American New York
SICs: 1221 Bituminous Coal and Lignite Surface Mining;
    2621 Paper Mills; 4911 Electric Services; 4924 Natural
    Gas Distribution; 4931 Electric & Other Services
    Combined; 4941 Water Supply

Minnesota Power & Light Company (MP&L), the second largest electric utility in Minnesota, provides power to the northern third of the state as well as electricity, water, and natural gas to neighboring northwestern Wisconsin. The company, throughout its long history, has been and remains closely linked to the development of the considerable natural resources in the Arrowhead region of Minnesota. Between 1991 and 1993, some 56 percent of the company's total electric revenue came from large taconite and wood products plants in the area. To offset this historically beneficial yet potentially limiting dependency, the utility has evolved into a successfully diversified company since the early 1980s, gaining national attention in the process. Through October of 1994 electric revenue accounted for 80 percent of the company's operating revenues in 1994. Water utility operations in Florida and the Carolinas; utility-related ventures such as coal mining, paper production, and pulp production; and investments in insurance, real estate, and securities comprised the remainder.

MP&L's roots go back to the late 1880s when small electric utilities were sprouting up across the nation. These early entrepreneurial ventures competed with each other to provide service to growing urban industrial and commercial areas. Duluth, Minnesota, at the southwestern tip of Lake Superior, was a port town receiving timber from the white pine forests of northeastern Minnesota and grain from the Red River Valley to the west. The electric utilities were eager to serve the lumber and ship-

ping businesses on the shore of the big lake and the city itself. To do so, they needed to create an infrastructure to carry the electricity to their customers—a difficult task in a city built on rock.

Alexander W. Hartman was one of the people who was instrumental in electrifying Duluth. As was typical with early utilities ventures, Hartman's efforts materialized in many mergers and acquisitions, ending with the formation of Duluth Edison Electric Company in 1906. The electric power retailer would be one of the principal companies that merged with other regional electric utilities to form Minnesota Power & Light Company.

While Hartman and other electric retailers were creating the systems of power lines to deliver the electric power, other visionaries were developing hydroelectric power from the area's abundant water resources. Investment banker Jay Cooke helped lay the groundwork for the construction of a dam on the lower St. Louis River which ran into Lake Superior. The Thomson Hydroelectric Station was constructed in 1907 by Great Northern Power Company, the second of the regional utilities which would form MP&L.

General Light and Power Co. in Cloquet, about 20 miles from Duluth, and the smallest of the four utilities to later form MP&L, had a history that is representative of the physical difficulties of electrifying the region. In Duluth, the utilities had trouble installing electric poles because of the rock bed on which the city was built. The Cloquet utility's problem with nature was the abundance of pine and aspen forests and the occurrence of devastating forest fires. Two such fires, one in the late nineteenth century and another in the early twentieth century, destroyed entire systems of lines and caused more than a thousand deaths. Nature, in northeastern Minnesota, brought disaster on the one hand and on the other provided plentiful resources that served the growing utility industry.

The last decade of the nineteenth century was marked by the discovery of rich iron ore deposits in northeastern Minnesota. The Minnesota Utilities Company was created in 1917 from smaller utilities vying to serve the booming mining industry; it ranked as the state's third largest supplier of electricity. Usage of electric power by iron mines quadrupled from 1918 to 1924 and quadrupled again by 1929 due to the electrification of the growing mines and the electrification of heavy mining-related equipment, such as locomotives and steam shovels. In 1922, the year before its consolidation with MP&L, the Minnesota Utilities Company was earning a profit on revenues of $544,000.

On October 23, 1923, Minnesota Power & Light was consolidated by Electric Bond and Share, a subsidiary of the Eastern electrical equipment manufacturer General Electric. The manufacturer, through its subsidiary, had been financially tied to small electric utilities in the area since the 1890s. By 1922, Electric Bond and Share Co., which provided capital for the small utilities, owned most of Duluth Edison Electric Co. and had a controlling interest in the Great Northern Power Company. Minnesota Utilities and General Light and Power entered into agreements with Electric Bond and Share that year. The consolidation of the four utilities was financed with 125,000 shares of preferred stock of American Power and Light Co., a holding company subsidiary, at a par value of $12.5 million. The sale was a complex one which would later be brought under federal scrutiny.

The federal government had encouraged the consolidation of utilities such as MP&L due to the massive needs of World War I, which helped foster the concept of the holding company, as well as the need to link up utility systems in order to provide an adequate supply of power. Herbert Hoover, as secretary of commerce in the early 1920s, promoted this ''super power'' idea, the networking of electric utilities. In addition, the 1920 Federal Power Act had given electric utilities the right of eminent domain in building and operating hydroelectric dams on rivers.

Not surprisingly then, the 1920s were years of expansion for the newly created Minnesota Power & Light Co. Construction of three dams and the linkage of the four existing utility systems by transmission lines highlighted the decade. Total capitalization rose from about $41 million at the time of consolidation to $70 million at the end of the decade. In those early years, MP&L sold the bulk of its electricity to northeastern Minnesota industries—mines, paper mills, and coal shipping docks. In 1927, 66 percent of its kilowatt hours (kwh) went to industrial customers, and over 50 percent of revenues were derived from fewer than 200 customers. The company ended the decade with $6 million in annual sales.

The Great Depression of the 1930s brought with it social and economic change, and, with the election of Franklin Delano Roosevelt in 1932, the climate for the electric utility holding companies was drastically altered. Legislation created the Tennessee Valley Authority and the Rural Electrification Administration, which were intended to bring power to distressed areas and farmers. In effect, the federally financed projects directly competed with the utilities. The Public Utilities Holding Company Act was also passed, calling for the breakup of the holding companies. And in Minnesota, in the region served by MP&L, a movement of local governments emerged to create publicly owned utilities in order to curb costs of electrifying their cities.

In spite of political and economic stresses brought on by the Depression and the accompanying recession in the iron and steel industries, MP&L survived the decade. Electric utilities were a growing industry at the time, and both commercial and residential use increased throughout the 1930s. Stock dividends were down and operations and wages cut back during the worst times, but by the end of the decade MP&L was back up to its 1929 revenue level.

The Roosevelt-era movement to change the face of electric utilities was put on hold in December 1941 when America entered World War II. As Bill Beck noted in *Northern Lights: An Illustrated History of Minnesota Power & Light,* ''The Sherman tanks rolling off assembly lines in Detroit, the airplanes being assembled in the California plants, the aircraft carriers sliding down the ways in East Coast shipyards—all were dependent upon the soft, red iron ore of the Mesabi Range.''

When the war ended, MP&L focused on recapitalization of its stock and reclassification of its accounts. The recapitalization

was due to the 1935 Public Holding Company Act, which required subsidiaries to be separated from their holding companies. The reclassification was the result of other federal action in the 1930s. During an investigation of electric holding companies, MP&L was found to have overvalued stock at the time of consolidation. The decade was also marked by MP&L's decision to move from hydroelectric generation of power to coal-fired steam generation. Coincidentally, the region was facing the worst drought in decades. Nevertheless, MP&L weathered the turmoil and finished the 1940s financially strong while setting new records for power usage.

MP&L entered the 1950s by terminating its affiliation with American Power and Light as its holding company. Thus the company began the new decade as a small utility serving the seasonal needs of the iron ore industry, with 58 percent of its power coming from hydroelectric sources and 42 percent through steam generation. It was a decade of increased defense needs due to the Korean War and a rapid increase of residential use due to widespread home modernization. MP&L's rapid construction of steam generating stations resulted in the first rate increase in its history. Economic diversification of the region helped MP&L grow. The St. Lawrence Seaway connected Duluth with the Atlantic Ocean, paper production in the city was expanded, and commercial ventures were on the rise. The 1950s also saw the advent of atomic power in utilities.

The 1960s marked the end of MP&L's relative isolation from other utilities when the company linked with the two other large utilities in the state, Northern States Power and Otter Tail Power. MP&L expanded its power pooling and transfer of bulk power through a regional grid when the Minnesota utilities joined those in Iowa and Wisconsin to form the Upper Mississippi Valley Power Pool in 1961. In 1963, the Midcontinental Area Power Planners linked 22 power suppliers in ten states and Canada.

The decade also proved a politically charged one for the utility, as it fought the expansion of federally funded electric cooperatives and pressure from Minnesota Senator Hubert H. Humphrey regarding MP&L's own rates. However, the company benefited from the passage of Minnesota's taconite amendment, which would revitalize the fading iron ore industry in the Arrowhead region. In 1968, the company decided to shift from high-sulfur Eastern coal to low-sulfur Western coal and began initiating extensive plant building and adapting of existing plants.

The 1970s was a growth decade for MP&L and the taconite industry, which unlike the iron ore industry demanded electric power 24 hours a day throughout the year. Revenues went from $50 to $281 million in the ten-year period. As the taconite plants grew MP&L kept pace by adding additional coal-fired generating stations. According to Beck, ''During the latter half of the decade, MP&L was perhaps the fastest growing electric utility in the United States.'' During the decade, the company also increased its power supply through a cooperative project with a utility in North Dakota. The Square Butte Electric Cooperative offered access to the area's vast lignite coal reserves through a 400,000 kw mine-mouth generating plant and sent power to Minnesota via a state-of-the-art AC/DC transmission line. On the political front MP&L was entering the era of federal and state environmental regulation. The 1970s also marked the end of a 40-year trend toward lower rates. The low point of 2.26 cents per kwh in 1967 doubled to 4.51 cents in 1979.

In 1980, the company changed its name to Minnesota Power and began the decade with legal proceedings, fighting a 30 percent severance tax on Montana coal and a 62 percent rate increase by Burlington Northern Railroad, its sole rail shipper. More foreboding for the utility, however, was the national economic recession. The recession hit the taconite industry hard and production of the low-grade ore fell 40 percent from 1979 to 1982. In an effort to cut costs the utility trimmed 15 percent of its work force between 1980 and 1985. Anthony Carideo, in an article for a November 1984 edition of the Minneapolis *Star Tribune,* observed that "Five years ago, Minnesota Power looked like a candidate for the poor house. Strapped with an $850 million construction program, the Duluth-based utility was at the door of the Minnesota Public Utilities Commission (PUC) for rate increases every year except one between 1976 and 1981. Faced with a nearly insolvent utility, state regulators allowed the company to bill consumers for millions of dollars in construction costs before the work was finished, a concession it had never made before to any utility and has allowed only once since." The company comeback was also served by the take-or-pay contracts it had entered into with the taconite companies when the industry was booming and they were building plants to keep up with the demand for power. Under such contracts, the companies had agreed to pay for a certain level of use each month whether they used it or not. However, by the mid-1980s, the taconite producers wanted out of the contracts.

Fortunately, Minnesota Power had by then built a profitable investment portfolio (stocks and bonds of other utilities) and had formed a subsidiary, Topeka Group, Inc., which owned a five-state telephone firm and a water and waste water treatment company in Florida. The utility was also embarking on a joint venture with St. Paul-based Pentair, Inc. to build a high-tech supercalender paper plant in Duluth. The plan was to keep investments in regulated and core support industries. Minnesota Power had used the post-construction cash buildup it had beginning in 1981 for its investments rather than give large stockholder dividends. By 1985, the company was looking at a 44 percent market return (stock movement plus dividends) according to Standard and Poor's, while the industry average was 25 percent. The company also exceeded the industry's five-year compound earnings growth and dividend growth with increases of 13 and eight percent, respectively. A December 1989 *Forbes* article reported that Minnesota Power had the second lowest electric utility rates in the country at 4.2 cents per kwh yet was among the most profitable with a five-year average return on equity of 15.8 percent. *Forbes* also reported that by the end of 1989 the utility had sold its telephone investment for three times the purchase price, expanded its water and waste water ventures, and purchased a coal mining venture to serve its North Dakota power generation interests. Minnesota Power also sold about 100 megawatts of surplus capacity—a problem since the taconite industry downturn—to a group of Wisconsin municipal utilities. The company still gained 57 percent of its $460 million in operating revenue from electric sales to industrial customers, compared with a 30 percent utility industry average.

The 1990s marked a change in the company's approach to its largest customer, the taconite industry. Jack Rowe, who led the company during the taconite hey days, had stood firm on the take-or-pay contracts. With Arend "Sandy" Sandbulte at the helm, the company began to renegotiate rates to the remaining taconite plants, giving a 20 to 30 percent decrease in rates and shortening the length of contracts. The company continued to look toward a future that was less dependent on the taconite industry with a goal of accelerating the contributions of non-electric businesses to over 60 percent of total revenue by the year 2000.

The 1990s also saw increased involvement by Minnesota Power in the economic development of the Arrowhead region. Minnesota Power not only provided funding for start-up businesses but offered financial support as part of a state package to attract a Northwest Airlines' maintenance base and reservations center to Duluth and the Iron Range. In another move to create usage for its core business of electric power, Minnesota Power created Synertec, a waste paper reclamation subsidiary. In partnership with four competing paper mills, Synertec opened a $76 million paper recycling plant in Duluth, named Superior Recycled Fiber Industries.

In spite of Minnesota Power's move toward decreased dependency on the taconite industry, the company's financial strength was still clearly tied to it. When National Steel Co., one of its largest customers, shut down its Keewatin plant indefinitely in the fall of 1993, Minnesota Power experienced a more than $2 a share fall on the stock market. The utility responded by actively working with other stakeholders in the taconite industry to facilitate the restarting of the Japanese-owned plant. By mid-1994, new corporate management at National's subsidiary had recommitted to fully integrated steel operations and was prepared to end the deadlock and resume operations, following various concessions and the approval of union steelworkers. National Steel Pellet and Minnesota Power arrived at a new electric rate deal in July 1994.

In January 1994, Minnesota filed for a rate increase of up to 25 percent for residential and commercial customers. The last rate increase Minnesota Power had filed for was in 1987, one which was successfully fought by the Minnesota Senior Federation's Northeastern Coalition. Subsequently, rates for homes and businesses had not risen in 12 years. The utility asserted in the filing that industrial users had been carrying an unfair share of the company's costs.

Also during this time, the company faced more changes on the regulatory front. The state of Minnesota began to require that utilities include environmental costs—such as air emissions of coal-burning plants—in the estimate of the costs of future plants. Moreover, Minnesota Power experienced a downturn in its strong investment portfolio. First quarter earnings fell 53 percent due mainly to poor performance of the company's securities investments. Nonetheless, Minnesota Power itself remained a proven performer, dedicated to its core business of providing electricity and other utility services to its more than 300,000 customers. The company was also uniquely situated to continue a program of diversification with benefits both to itself and the economies of the regions it served.

Principal Subsidiaries: BNI Coal, Ltd.; Heater Utilities, Inc.; Lake Superior Paper Industries (50%); Southern States Utilities, Inc.; Superior Water, Light & Power Company; Synertec, Inc.

Further Reading:

Beck, Bill, "Do You Know Your Company Roots?," *Electric Perspectives,* Winter 1986, pp. 63–64.

Beck, Bill, *Northern Lights: An Illustrated History of Minnesota Power,* Duluth: Minnesota Power, 1986.

Brissett, Jane, "Minnesota Power Passages," *Corporate Report Minnesota,* April 1988, pp. 115–16.

Carideo, Anthony, "Blindsided in Duluth," *Star Tribune* (Minneapolis), October 21, 1993, p. 1D; "LSPI's New Plant: A Thriving 1-Year-Old," *Star Tribune* (Minneapolis), March 20, 1989, p. 1D; "Minnesota Power Is Busy Generating Revenues," *Star Tribune,* November 11, 1984, p. 1D.

Cook James, "Deft Management," *Forbes,* December 11, 1989, pp. 96, 100, 105.

"The Good, The Bad, and Minnesota Power," *Corporate Report Minnesota,* March 1981, pp. 26–30.

"How Minnesota Power Deals with the Dreaded 'D Word,' " *Electrical World,* December 1990, pp. 20–21.

Lappen, Alyssa A., "Gene's Dream," *Forbes,* May 30, 1988, pp. 212–15.

Marcotty, Josephine, "Minnesota Power Charging Ahead," *Star Tribune* (Minneapolis), June 8, 1987, p. 1M.

Marx, Patrick, "Railroad Issue Threatens Utility's Coal Future," *Star Tribune* (Minneapolis), November 9, 1980, p. 1D.

McDonnell, Lynda, "Utility Navigates New Route," *Pioneer Press & Dispatch* (St. Paul), February 10, 1986, pp. 1, 10–11.

Meersman, Tom, "PUC Says Utilities Must Start Tallying Ecological Costs of Power Plants," *Star Tribune* (Minneapolis), February 5, 1994, p. 1B.

"Minnesota Power Posts 47% Drop in Quarterly Earnings," *Star Tribune* (Minneapolis), April 23, 1994, p. 2D.

Morse, Mary, "Pulp Romance," *Corporate Report Minnesota,* June 1986, pp. 80–83.

Morse, Mary, "There's No Place Like Home," *Corporate Report Minnesota,* April 1992, pp. 50–54.

Oakes, Larry, "Duluth Utility Requests Rate Increase," *Star Tribune* (Minneapolis), January 5, 1994, p. 2B; "9-Month Deadlock, 3-Day Solution; New Management Key to Keewatin Plant Agreement," *Star Tribune* (Minneapolis), June 28, 1994, p. 5B; "Officials Promise Iron Range Placement Assistance," *Star Tribune* (Minneapolis), October 23, 1993, p. 1B; "U.S. Union Leaders to Appeal to Tokyo Firm," *Star Tribune* (Minneapolis), January 15, 1994, p. 2B.

"People," *Electrical World,* September 1988, p. 29.

Peterson, Susan E., "New Paper Out of Old," *Star Tribune* (Minneapolis), October 6, 1993, p. 1D.

—Jay P. Pederson

Molex Incorporated

2222 Wellington Court
Lisle, Illinois 60532
U.S.A.
(708) 969-4550
Fax: (708) 969-1352

Public Company
Incorporated: 1938
Employees: 8,200
Sales: $964.1 million
Stock Exchanges: NASDAQ London
SICs: 3678 Electronic Connectors; 3643 Current-Carrying
   Wiring Devices

The second largest electronic connector company in the world, Molex Incorporated manufactures electrical and fiber optic interconnections systems, ribbon cable, switches, and application tooling. Through 41 plants in 19 countries, Molex manufactures more than 40,000 products sold primarily to manufacturers involved in the automotive, computer, business equipment, telecommunications, and home appliance/home entertainment industries. In the mid-1990s, the company derived more than 70 percent of its revenues from products manufactured and sold outside the United States.

The history of Molex is largely the story of the Krehbiel family, who had emigrated from their native Switzerland to Germany and then relocated again in the United States in the 1820s, in pursuit of a country that would honor the pacifist ideals set forth by their Mennonite religion. They settled in Newton, Kansas, where the patriarch of the family, John Jacob Krehbiel, built a wagon- and carriage-making business and became one of the founders and chairman of Bethel College. His son, Frederick Augustus Krehbiel, would become the first of four generations of Krehbiels who would be responsible for creating and building one of the largest electronic connector companies in the world.

After growing up in Newton, Frederick Krehbiel attended Cleveland's Armour Institute and then Cornell University. He moved back to Chicago, where he took a job with the Arnold Engineering Company before establishing his own business, Krehbiel Engineering. By the turn of the century, he had designed and built power plants for several large cities, including Cincinnati and Kansas City, earning, through the course of his

work, the esteem of his peers and clients. His reputation grew as the years passed by, elevating Krehbiel to a position of prominence in his field and drawing the attention of federal officials, who, as America prepared to enter World War I, desperately required the skills he possessed.

The U.S. government asked Krehbiel to design a refinishing plant to generate toluol, a byproduct of coal that was intrinsic to the production of TNT. Previously, the United States had purchased TNT from Germany, but now, as the country prepared to battle its supplier, it found itself without the production facilities required to meet its mounting needs. Krehbiel complied with the government's request, and a refinishing plant was designed and constructed in Terra Haute, Indiana, that immediately began processing coal to meet the nation's demand for TNT. It was while observing his plant in action that Krehbiel first began to develop ideas about the product that would eventually give Molex Incorporated its name and launch the Krehbiel family toward tremendous success.

Like many others who worked near the refinishing plant, Krehbiel observed piles of coal tar pitch, a waste product left over after the coal was refined and heated to produce the toluol vapors. Giant piles of the black waste material surrounded the plant, and Krehbiel made a note of it. Several years later in Canada, while helping to build superstructures of asbestos mines, Krehbiel noticed an equally worthless material gathered in giant piles: the fine, little strands of asbestos known as asbestos tailings. Krehbiel realized that if he used the coal tar pitch as a binder and the asbestos tailings as a filler, then combined them with limestone, which would serve as a reinforcing agent, he could create a new material—a plastic—that could be produced at a nominal cost. He dubbed the new material Molex, a low-cost product with good moisture resistance and properties that made it an excellent electrical insulator. In 1938, Krehbiel, then in his late 60s, formed a new company with the same name as the product he created. Later he enlisted his two sons as partners, and then began using Molex as a material to make casings for underground cables.

Seven years earlier, Krehbiel's son John had started his own business, the J. H. Krehbiel Company. John Krehbiel, then 26 years old, had created the company to fulfill a contract he had been awarded to manufacture fireproofing material for Commonwealth Edison stipulating that Edison would purchase 100,000 bags of the compound per year. Krehbiel borrowed the money to build a plant expressly for producing the material, then set out to satisfy the annual quota of the contract. However, the Depression, then reaching its greatest intensity, curtailed Edison's anticipated rate of consumption, and it took the company three years instead of one to use the first 100,000 bags of the fireproofing material. Forced to diversify into another business to offset the financial loss resulting from Edison's reduced fireproofing needs, John Krehbiel began manufacturing insulating material for underground and overhead high voltage cable, selling the material to various utility companies such as Commonwealth Edison, Public Service of North Indiana, Cleveland Electric Company, and Philadelphia Electric Company.

Due to this diversification, John Krehbiel was able to save his company from financial ruin and keep it growing. He next started another company, Illinois Manufacturing Chemists. His partners were his Hinsdale neighbors, the Regnery family. They produced nitrocellulose, an explosive made by treating cotton, a form of cellulose, with a mixture of nitric and sulfuric acids. Nitrocellulose was a highly flammable product, and it demonstrated its volatility on two separate occasions, blowing up the Illinois Manufacturing Chemists' factory twice in a five-year span. By the time the nitrocellulose factory exploded the second time, Frederick Krehbiel was urging John to assume a more active role in the family business, then roughly three years old and being run by Frederick and another son, Edwin Krehbiel.

With the outbreak of World War II, the U.S. War Production Board placed all established molding materials on restricted lists, forbidding their use in the manufacture of products deemed nonessential to the war effort and limiting their use for commercial purposes according to a government priority system. Virtually unknown, Molex appeared on no such lists, enabling the Krehbiels—Frederick, John, and Edwin—to use their patented material to manufacture whatever they wished. They worked first with the government to try and establish a use for the material in the military, but it was not of interest to the government. The potential uses for Molex were virtually unknown to the Krehbiels as well, leaving the three partners with a material and no obvious market in which to sell it. Since none of the established plastics were available for the production of nonessential, consumer products, the Krehbiels moved in that direction, attempting to fill the void created by the restriction of Bakelite, polystyrene, and other plastic substances that manufacturers had relied on before the war.

During this time, Molex Inc. began manufacturing toys. For those familiar with the Krehbiel family, the decision to manufacture toys represented an incongruous leap from the generating stations designed by Frederick Krehbiel and the nitrocellulose and electrical insulating material manufactured by John Krehbiel. Initially, Molex made toy submarines and toy pistols, then began making flower pots, salt dispensers for the Morton Salt Co., and clock casings manufactured for Hanson Manufacturing Co. These projects generated enough income for the fledgling company and the new plastic to survive the war years and also gave the Krehbiels the opportunity to explore the potential applications for Molex plastic. An important alteration was made in the production of Molex immediately after the war, when the limestone used to reinforce the material was replaced by fiberglass. The substitution of fiberglass greatly improved the product's strength and flexibility, and when Bakelite and polystyrene were taken off the government's restricted list and once again became available, they proved no match for the malleability and low cost of Molex, still essentially fabricated from scrap materials.

John Krehbiel by this time had assumed control of the company, as his brother Edwin, trained as an artist, preferred to spend his time designing the molds and equipment required to manufacture the products. His father, then nearing his 80s, was easing into retirement. The former manufacturer of electrical insulating material and nitrocellulose decided that Molex was best suited for electrical insulation, a pivotal decision that steered the company and the plastic toward the appliance market. The first product tooled and marketed with Molex was a molded terminal block for General Electric's Hotpoint range. Other, similar

products followed, manufactured for companies such as Whirlpool and Westinghouse. The decision to enter the appliance market proved sound, giving Molex its first viable, vast market.

Nevertheless, possessing a wide range of talents and interests, the Krehbiels frequently shifted the focus of their company. Shortly after marketing Molex as an electrical insulator and entering the appliance market, John Krehbiel steered the company in a new direction, realizing, through his contacts with appliance manufacturers, that a more lucrative future lay in the production of connectors used to link electronic components. The move propelled the company into the consumer electronics industry and dramatically transformed Molex from a materials company into a connector company, a decision that signalled the end of Molex, the material, and engendered the rebirth of Molex, the company.

Molex began manufacturing pin and socket connectors, designed by John Kriehbiel, to link electronic components in color television sets, a new product during the 1950s that, like the market in which it was sold, was headed toward enormous growth. By manufacturing connectors for companies such as Zenith, RCA, and Magnavox, Molex realized rapid growth, generating $1.06 million in annual sales in 1962, the first year the company eclipsed the $1 million mark. It had taken nearly a quarter of a century for Molex to reach the $1 million plateau, and now, with the exponential expansion of the consumer electronics industry fueling its growth, the company surpassed the $2 million mark three years later, garnering $2.4 million in 1965 and adding another million dollars to its sales volume the following year.

Although John Krehbiel was delighted with Molex's growth, his brother Edwin, a 40 percent owner of the company, was not. Edwin Krehbiel had no desire to build Molex into a larger company and already felt swamped by the number of projects the company was involved in, as his brother continued to canvass manufacturers in the electronics industry and broaden Molex's scope. By 1965, Edwin Krehbiel wanted to retire and began looking for investors to purchase his stake in Molex. One year later, he found some interested investors, a group of businessmen backed by A.G. Becker, a Chicago investment banking firm. John Krehbiel, however, was staunchly opposed to selling the company. With Edwin and John each owning 40 percent of the company, the deciding vote was cast by Marie Manette. She voted not to sell. Edwin went ahead and sold his share and retired. Marie Manette had worked with Fred Krehbiel as his secretary after graduating from high school. She remained at the Krehbiel Engineering Co. and then moved to Molex as Treasurer, retiring after a combined 50 years of service. Upon her death, she willed most of her stock to John Krehbiel's sons John Jr. and Frederick to ensure continued family control.

A.G. Becker held its share in Molex until 1972, when it was instrumental in Molex becoming a public company. Molex was taken public by William Blair & Co. In the intervening six years, developments had occurred that positioned Molex for even greater growth than the pace recorded during the early and mid-1960s. John H. Krehbiel, Jr., joined the company in 1959, and his brother Fred joined in 1967.

John Jr. had begun as Pricing Manager and then moved on to the position of Sales Manager. Looking for a place for his younger son, John Krehbiel Sr. suggested that Fred explore potential business opportunities for Molex overseas. The decision to send Frederick Krehbiel II overseas represented more of a solution to the uncertainty of the young graduate's future position within the company than a strategic decision to expand overseas. Nevertheless, its ramifications on the future of Molex were significant.

Given $25,000, from which he was expected to draw his salary, Frederick Krehbiel was charged with expanding Molex's business overseas. That year, he went to Japan and approached potential customers of Molex connectors, fortuitously entering the Japanese electronics industry at a time of rapid growth. Krehbiel encountered a country that was producing a tremendous number of electronic products, particularly television sets, which eventually would set the standard worldwide. Initially, he received several small orders from Matsushita Company and some orders from Europe, reporting a grand total of $54,000 in his first year of overseas business. With considerable advice from an outside consultant, Ed Frume, Fred continued to build on the modest beginning. The focus on local supply in Japan, however, demanded that Molex manufacture its products in Japan, where Japanese manufacturers could monitor the production of Molex connectors. Accordingly, the company's first plant outside the United States was constructed in Yamato City, Japan, opening in 1970. By the end of the year, Molex realized $776,000 in international sales, compared to the $8.9 million generated domestically.

During the early 1970s, the U.S. home entertainment industry started to experience strong competition from Japan, and, seeing this, John H. Krehbiel, Jr. determined that the U.S. company needed to find applications other than home entertainment and appliances. He saw the rapid gains in business machines and the emergence of computers and worked to build a position for Molex in these markets. This resulted in Molex gaining a share of these markets, and today Molex sells far more to these markets than to its customers in its traditional areas.

During this period, sales generated from international business continued to grow rapidly. An additional overseas plant was constructed in Ireland in 1971, paving the way for the prodigious geographic expansion that would take place during the decade. As Molex grew, a distinctive style of overseas management emerged, a style that largely developed from the company's unconventional direction of expansion. Typically, when a U.S. company began to establish operations outside the country's borders, it first went to Canada, then to Europe, and then, perhaps, to Asia. Molex, however, selected Japan as its initial proving ground, and this trial-by-fire in the world's most demanding market taught the company a great deal about how to meet the needs of demanding customers. Fred Krehbiel and others in the company's international division learned the merits of "being local" and adjusting to the culture of the region in order to meet the needs of the local customer, a lesson they would employ in expansion throughout Europe, South America, and Asia.

By 1979, domestic sales at Molex totaled $44.6 million, while its international sales reached $53.4 million, representing the first year the company's business overseas surpassed the total recorded domestically. The following year, Molex was the tenth largest connector company in the world, its growth fueled by the company's international expansion and its moving into the fast growing computer, computer peripheral, and business equipment markets. The 1980s would witness the rise of personal computers, and Molex would share in the billions of dollars garnered by the computer industry during the decade through the production of connectors used to link the electronic components of personal computers, as well as connectors for peripheral devices such as terminals, printers, and modems. Driven by the nearly insatiable demand for electronic connectors by computer and other electronics manufacturers during the decade, Molex prospered, recording $253 million in sales by 1985.

By 1991, Molex had become a genuine multinational company, a global company that was beating its competition by virtue of its early and aggressive expansion overseas and by sustaining the entrepreneurial spirit that originally had engendered its creation. Molex continued to expand its markets, moving into automotive electronics, telecommunications, and other markets such as instrumentation and medical electronics.

By the early 1990s, Molex was the second largest connector company in the world, ranking behind Amp, Inc., based in Harrisburg, Pennsylvania. With more than 40 manufacturing facilities operating in 19 countries, Molex derived 71 percent of its revenues from products manufactured and sold outside the United States. Nearly half the company's total sales volume was generated by its manufacturing and sales offices in the Far East, the fastest growing economic sector in the world during the early and mid-1990s. With this solid and broad geographic presence serving as the company's foundation for future growth, Molex anticipated eclipsing the $1 billion sales plateau by 1995, an objective that appeared well within the company's expansive grasp.

Principal Subsidiaries: Molex S.A. de C.V. (South America); Molex Far East Management Ltd. (Hong Kong); Molex Japan Co. Ltd.; Molex Singapore Pte., Ltd.; Molex Taiwan Ltd.; Molex B.V. (Netherlands); Molex Hong Kong Ltd.; Molex Electronics Ltd. (Canada); Molex Illinois S.A. (Switzerland); Molex Electronics Ltd. (U.K.); Molex Italia S.p.A. (96%); Molex Sweden; Molex, ETC. Inc. (90%); Molex Industrial Interfaces Inc.; Molex Caribe Inc.; Molex Ireland Ltd.; Molex Elektronik GmbH (Germany); Molex France SARL; Molex Nanco Ltd. (Hong Kong) (90%); Molex US Inc.; Molex Export Inc.; Molex International, Inc.; Molex Overseas Inc.

Further Reading:

Knight, Robert M., "How Molex Inc. Connected in World Markets," *Chicago Enterprise,* July/August 1994, p. 24.
Linn, Ed, and John H. Krehbiel Sr., *A Great Connection,* Chicago: Regnery Gateway, Inc., 1988, 229 p.
Yates, Ronald E., "From Electronic Connectors to Global Connections: Molex Incorporated," *Hemispheres,* April 1994, p. 39.
Yates, Ronald E., "Molex Puts Itself on the Map," *Chicago Tribune,* February 6, 1994.

—Jeffrey L. Covell

Montana Power Company

40 East Broadway
Butte, Montana 59701-9394
U.S.A.
(406) 723-5421
Fax: (406) 496-5099

Public Company
Incorporated: 1912
Employees: 4,089
Sales: $1.07 billion
Stock Exchanges: New York Pacific Boston Philadelphia
SICs: 4931 Electric & Other Services Combined; 1221
    Bituminous Coal & Lignite—Surface; 1311 Crude
    Petroleum & Natural Gas; 1321 Natural Gas Liquids; 4813
    Telephone Communications Except Radiotelephone

Montana Power Company is one of the largest utility companies
in the Northern Rockies area of the United States, serving
262,000 customers, including Yellowstone National Park, with
electricity and 126,000 with natural gas. In addition, Montana
Power owns and operates properties in non-utility businesses,
including coal mining, gas and oil exploration, development
and marketing, and technology, including electronic controls
and telecommunications. By the early 1990s, the utility's sales
had surpassed $1 billion, and its expansion had carried it into
four countries, making Montana's only company listed on the
New York Stock Exchange a recognizable and formidable force
in the U.S. utility industry.

To the sparsely populated area once known as Montana Territory, electricity arrived before statehood, preceding the region's
admittance as the 41st state by eight years, when the pioneering
denizens of the small silver mining town of Walkerville first
received electricity in 1880. The illumination of its famous
neighbor, Butte, marked the beginning of the electrification of
Montana and spawned a new breed of business competitors:
power companies intent on linking major industrial and manufacturing activities to hydroelectric generation on the Missouri
and Madison rivers with electrical transmission lines. During
the three decades following Butte's historic entrance into the
electrical age, eventually 40 small power companies serving
sundry small towns gradually joined together to form four
regional electric utilities, Butte Electric & Power Co., Madison
River Power Co., Billings Eastern Montana Power Co., and

Missouri River Electric & Power Co. When these four power
companies consolidated in late 1912, the consortium that
emerged represented Montana's newest and largest utility, the
Montana Power Company.

Chiefly responsible for the merger of the four power companies
was John D. Ryan, a prominent Montana businessman with
considerable power in the region's copper industry. In 1905, he
was elected president of Anaconda Copper Mining Company,
rising from the position of managing director, a post he had held
in several subsidiary companies owned by Anaconda's parent
company, Amalgamated Copper Company. Several years later,
Ryan would become president of Amalgamated Copper itself,
then gain national notoriety by railing against the implementation of anti-trust legislation in the copper industry. But, before
doing so, his most notable achievement was the formation of
Montana Power, the primary source of the copper industry's
power. In the years leading up to Montana Power's formation,
Ryan and several business partners purchased power sites along
the Missouri river, and then Ryan orchestrated the consolidation
of the four hydroelectric utilities. Four days after Montana
Power was incorporated, with capital stock amounting to
$7.7 million, Ryan was selected as the company's president, on
December 12, 1912.

Copper mining at Butte's "Richest Hill on Earth" and processing operations at Anaconda and Great Falls were a major source
of Montana Power's early business; railroad companies were
another, with the newly formed utility company providing the
power to fuel the electric locomotives that ferried people and
supplies to and from Montana. To carry current to the railroads
and to other customers, dams had to be constructed, generating
stations needed to be built, and transmission wire needed to be
strung, some of which had been accomplished before Montana
Power's formation, when small electric utilities populated the
state. However, a majority of the construction work would take
place after the utility's creation, and much of it under Montana
Power's purview. In 1915, Montana Power spent $3.4 million
on extending its service area, particularly to include the Chicago, Milwaukee & St. Paul Railroad. The utility registered
$4.3 million in revenue that year, up more than 15 percent from
1914's total, and served 32,000 customers.

By extending its service area to accommodate the utility's
industrial customers and leasing electric washers and ranges to
its residential customers, Montana Power grew, serving 70
towns and cities in Montana by 1922. Two additional dams
were brought on line during the 1920s, one at the decade's
beginning and the other at its conclusion, giving Montana
Power a total of 12 dams from which the utility derived power
to generate electricity. Half of these dams were constructed
before Montana Power's formation, beginning with Black Eagle Dam in 1890 and ending with the reconstruction of Hauser
Dam in 1911. Several of these pre-existing dams were products
of Ryan's early power site purchases along the Missouri River
before he coordinated the merger of the four utilities that would
form Montana Power, while the six dams constructed after the
utility's creation were built under Montana Power's supervision. The first of these dams built by Montana Power was
Thompson Falls Dam, which was completed in July 1915. Two
more dams were completed that year, the Ryan Dam the following month, and Hebgen Dam two months later in October. The

sixth and last dam completed during the decade, Holter Dam, was brought on line in 1918.

The 1920s represented a less prodigious period of dam construction, but the decade brought Montana Power into contact with a coal mining operation located at Colstrip, Montana, that would later become an integral contributor to the utility's revenue volume. Montana Power's first association with the coal mines at Colstrip occurred during the construction of Mystic Dam, a dam built to supply electricity to the coal mine's owner and operator at the time, Northern Pacific Railway. Completed in 1927, Mystic Dam enabled Montana Power to supply Northern Pacific with energy to run the railroad company's electrically operated coal mine, which was used to produce boiler fuel. Although it would be roughly 30 years until Montana Power assumed control of the rich Colstrip mines, the contract to supply Northern Pacific with electricity helped accelerate the utility's growth. Two years after the completion of Mystic Dam, Montana Power earned a profit of $666,390, nearly three times as much as it earned the year before, an increase that was attributable largely to the utility's electricity contracts with large operations in the mining and smelting industries.

Growth continued throughout the 1920s, with annual revenues eclipsing $10 million by 1928, up substantially from the $3 million recorded in 1922. In 1930, another dam was brought on line, the Morony Dam, but the decade would be remembered less for hydroelectric expansion and more for the arrival of a new type of fuel to the region, the advent of natural gas. In 1931, Montana Power signed contracts with Anaconda, the copper mining company, that entailed the expenditure of between $10 and $12 million for the construction of natural gas pipelines over the course of the coming year. Constructed chiefly to serve Butte and Anaconda and their industries with natural gas, the pipeline also brought natural gas to other areas included within Montana Power's service area. In July 1931, two months after pipeline construction began, natural gas arrived in Bozeman, Montana, from a separate line origination in southcentral Montana. A larger, southbound line originating from northern Montana natural gas fields wound through several other Montana towns, arriving in Helena, the state's capital, by the beginning of September and in Butte two weeks later. As it had with electricity, Montana Power offered gas appliances at low costs and initially for free to customers who signed up for gas service, then supported its natural gas service with a fleet of cars and salespeople. By 1932, Montana Power had 9,623 natural gas customers and considerably more electricity customers, giving the utility two foundations from which to further diversify.

The construction of dams did not stop in the 1930s, but progress was slowed appreciably by the debilitative economic conditions characterizing the decade. Construction of Kerr Dam was started in 1930, then halted the following year, resumed in 1936, and finally completed in 1938, as the utility fitfully proceeded through the decade. The 1940s brought few changes to the utility beyond meeting the increasing wartime needs of its residential and industrial customers. The 1950s, however, were replete with significant and sweeping changes that included Montana Power's diversification into non-utility businesses, its adoption of a different form of power generation, and the expansion of its burgeoning natural gas business.

Three signal events occurred early in the decade that dramatically altered Montana Power's future. In 1951, the utility completed construction of the Frank W. Bird plant located on the banks of the Yellowstone River in Billings, Montana. Fueled either by natural gas or oil, the Bird plant represented Montana Power's first fossil-fueled plant and augured the utility's strategic shift away from hydroelectric power to power generation from other fuels. Dwindling opportunities for hydroelectric development—the utility's last Missouri River dam, Cochrane, was completed during the decade—and the mounting energy needs of Montana's residents and businesses compelled Montana Power to begin exploring for alternative energy sources, a decision manifested in the construction of the Bird plant and one that induced the utility to form Western Energy Company in 1951. Years later in the 1960s, Western Energy would spearhead the utility's movement into coal mining and processing, a fuel Montana Power would rely on heavily to fuel its power generation plants. In 1952, Montana Power began receiving natural gas from Canada, which, in addition to broadening the scope of the utility's natural gas business, led to its diversification into oil and gas exploration in Canada, a venture conducted through Altana Exploration Company, a Canadian subsidiary formed in 1957.

Perhaps the most defining development, however, occurred at the decade's conclusion, when Montana Power secured much of its future fuel supply by purchasing the rights to the Rosebud Coal Mine and other mines located at Colstrip. The Colstrip reserves were vast—the Rosebud mine was regarded as one of the eight largest coal mines in the United States during the 1990s—and Montana Power spent much of the next decade incorporating its new fuel source into the utility's system. By 1968, the utility's first coal-fired generation plant was completed, located 100 miles west of Colstrip in Billings, where the Frank Bird plant was erected.

Efforts to market coal to other utilities were first successful in 1969 and 1970 and provided encouraging results. However, the utility's mainstay continued to be its involvement in supplying electricity, from which Montana Power derived 65 percent of its slightly more than $80 million in annual revenues recorded at the beginning of the 1970s. The balance was derived primarily from the utility's natural gas business, including both the provision and exploration of the fuel. Prospects for the immediate future brightened when one of the utility's major customers, Anaconda, announced plans for a multi-million dollar expansion program to increase its production volume, which for Montana Power meant a heightened need for power. An energy crises during the early and mid-1970s, however, tempered any hopes of widespread industrial expansion in the state and spawned a movement toward energy conservation. Montana Power's management accelerated its natural gas exploration efforts. In 1977, another Canadian subsidiary, Roan Resources Limited, was formed. Roan Resources, Altana (the other Canadian subsidiary created 20 years earlier), and a U.S.-based company named North American Resources, organized in 1980, made up Montana Power's oil division.

The 1970s also saw the beginning of development of the four Colstrip plants. Units 1 and 2 are 330 megawatt plants owned equally by Montana Power and Puget Sound Power and Light, and Units 3 and 4, at 700 megawatts each, are owned 30 percent by Montana Power, 25 percent by Puget Sound Power and Light, 15 percent by Washington Water Power, 20 percent by Portland General Electric, and 10 percent by PacifiCorp. These four plants represent the second largest coal-fired electric generating complex east of the Mississippi River.

After a decade filled with energy construction and conservation measures and widespread federal reform of the utility industry through the promulgation of the 1978 Public Utility Regulatory Act, Montana Power entered the 1980s intending to reposition itself for the future and increase its stake in non-utility ventures. Most of the changes initiated by the utility were organizational in nature and stemmed from developments during the 1970s as well as from earlier decisions that had steered Montana Power into non-utility businesses. It was the reorganization of these various non-utility businesses that Montana Power began to carry out once power plant construction began winding down in 1983. The following year, the utility formed a new subsidiary named Entech, Inc., which absorbed Western Energy, the company that operated Montana Power's coal properties, as well as the utility's oil exploration businesses, Altana Exploration, Roan Resources, and North American Resources Co. Entech, which essentially became an organizational umbrella under which Montana Power's non-utility interests were grouped, also absorbed two new businesses, Telecommunications Resources, Inc. and Tetragenics Company. Formed in 1982, Tetragenics sold electronic controls, while Telecommunications Resources, organized the following year, was involved, as its name suggested, in telecommunications.

An additional non-utility business, Special Resources Management, was formed in 1985, marking Montana Power's entrance into toxic waste handling and management. Special Resources Management was later sold in 1993. In 1988, the Montana Power completed another organizational move by creating the Independent Power Group (IPG) to manage Montana Power's long-term contracts for the sale of coal produced at Colstrip and to invest in non-utility electric generating plants.

Reshaped during the 1980s, the utility entered the 1990s supported by its three primary business units, Entech, IPG, and its utility division, the heart of Montana Power and the largest contributor to its annual sales volume. The utility registered $823 million in revenues in 1990, more than half of which was generated by its electric and natural gas service. By 1993, revenues had eclipsed the $1 billion plateau, and Montana Power's two newest business units, Entech and IPG, had extended the utility's geographic presence considerably beyond Montana's borders. Entech by this time held an investment interest in a gold mine in Brazil, while IPG maintained a stake in the world's largest co-generation plant in Teesside, England, assumed operational responsibility for a plant in Argentina, and

was involved in the development of a coal-fired project in China. In reaching its $1.07 billion in revenues for the year, Montana Power garnered $410.4 million from Entech's various business lines and $120.3 million from IPG's wholesale electricity sales, non-utility electric generation facility operation, and engineering and plant maintenance services.

In 1986, with the completion of the Colstrip Unit 4 and in light of an earlier decision by the Anaconda Company to exit the copper mining and refining business in Montana, Montana Power sold its 30 percent ownership in Colstrip Unit 4, leasing back the power that it has sold outside of Montana on long-term contracts.

As Montana Power charted its future in an industry governed by strict regulatory policies, cause for optimism existed in its enviable and considerable interests in non-utility and, therefore, non-regulated businesses. The coal division operating within Entech stood as one of the 12 largest coal producers in the nation during the mid-1990s, providing sufficient coal to fuel Montana Power's five enormous jointly owned coal-fired electric generating plants while still permitting the sale of coal to other utilities.

Principal Subsidiaries: Canadian-Montana Pipe Line Co.; Canadian-Montana Gas Co. Ltd.; Colstrip Community Services Co.; Glacier Gas Co.; Continental Energy Services, Inc.; Sunlight Development Co.; Pacific Northwest Power Co.; Entech, Inc.; Altana Exploration Co.; Entech Altamont, Inc.; Roan Resources Ltd.; North American Resources Co.; Tetragenics Co.; TRI Touch America, Inc.; Basin Resources, Inc.; Horizon Coal Services, Inc.; North Central Energy Co.; Northwestern Resources Co.; Trinidad Railway, Inc.

Further Reading:

"Butte to Get Natural Gas," *New York Times,* March 7, 1931, p. 32.
"Buys Natural Gas Fields," *New York Times,* May 16, 1931, p. 28.
Byrne, Harlan S., "Montana Power Co.," *Barron's,* January 28, 1991, p. 35.
Gannon, Bob, "The Montana Power Company Perspective," *Montana Business Quarterly,* autumn 1993, p. 11.
"Montana Power Company," *Wall Street Transcript,* September 7, 1970, p. 21, 648.
"Montana Power Earnings," *New York Times,* March 22, 1916, p. 15.
"Montana Power Names Engineer to Be Chief," *New York Times,* October 2, 1991, p. D4.
"Montana Power's Year," *New York Times,* March 20, 1924, p. 28.
"People," *Electrical World,* March 1992, p. 22.
Rowe, Bob, and Bob Anderson, "The Regulatory Compact," *Montana Business Quarterly,* autumn 1993, p. 7.
"Ryan Elected President of Anaconda," *New York Times,* June 20, 1905, p. 13.

—Jeffrey L. Covell

MORRISON RESTAURANTS INC.

Morrison Restaurants Inc.

4721 Morrison Drive
P.O. Box 160266
Mobile, Alabama 36625
U.S.A.
(334) 344-3000
Fax: (334) 344-3066

Public Company
Incorporated: 1928 as Morrison Cafeterias Consolidated, Inc.
Employees: 33,000
Sales: $1.21 billion
Stock Exchanges: New York NASDAQ
SICs: 750 Eating Places

One of the companies responsible for bringing the cafeteria concept of dining to the Southern United States, Morrison Restaurants Inc. evolved from one cafeteria in Mobile, Alabama, into a network of cafeterias and casual and family-dining restaurants composing a $1.2 billion food-service empire. Through one of its two main operating segments, the Ruby Tuesday Group, the company operates nearly 300 casual dining restaurants, known variously as Mozzarella's Cafe, Sweetpea's Restaurants, and Ruby Tuesday. The other segment, the Morrison Group, is comprised of more than 435 retail and health-care outlets, including the vestiges of the company's original line of business, Morrison's Cafeterias.

The first Morrison cafeteria opened during the fall of 1920 in Mobile, Alabama. A novel dining concept for the area, the cafeteria caused the proprietor, J. A. Morrison, more than the usual entrepreneurial nervousness associated with starting a new business. Aside from the fear that customers would not be willing to experiment with a new type of dining establishment, Morrison also had to impart his vision of how a cafeteria should look and operate to his initial staff of 40 employees, all unfamiliar with the concept. For the location of his new cafeteria, Morrison opted for the first floor of an existing building, and for the interior he supervised the installment of stamped tin to cover the ceilings, a material that also was used for the moldings. The floor was made of white rock maple that was scrubbed with beach sand and a deck broom to ensure it was "sanitary and vermin-proof" for the cafeteria's expected clientele, recently introduced to the dangers of bacteria.

With each employee trained by Morrison, the cafeteria opened on September 4, 1920, its success dependent on the judgment of Morrison's storeroom manager as much as it was on the arrival of customers through the doors. The storeroom manager, whose job it was to issue the correct amount of food from the cafeteria's refrigerated storeroom for the coming business day, dictated, to a large extent, the profits for the day. Once food was removed from the storeroom, it was either cooked or discarded, eroding profits as the food rotted because Morrison's business, unlike other Mobile restaurants, was predicated on volume. Initially, the cafeteria offered 73 different items with the typical meal costing $.31, a menu variety and cost structure Mobile residents immediately welcomed. Within a week, Morrison and his staff were serving lunch and supper to 1,000 patrons each day, assuaging any of Morrison's anxiety regarding the peculiarity of cafeteria-style dining for Mobile's citizens.

Morrison's success carried beyond the first week, as his inexpensive dining alternative attracted enough customers to sustain further growth. In 1928, Morrison incorporated his growing concern in Louisiana, naming the enterprise Morrison's Cafeterias Consolidated, Inc. Customers continued to frequent Morrison Cafeterias throughout the Great Depression—700,000 customers a year were eating at the company's cafeterias by 1938—with Morrison's dining concept extending into other Southern states as the number of cafeterias increased. By 1950, the last year Morrison Cafeterias would be entirely devoted to operating cafeterias, there were 17 such establishments, composing a modestly sized, prosperous company that had achieved more than a modicum of success in 30 years of operation and was destined to become much more.

In 1951, Morrison Cafeterias diversified into noncommercial feeding by providing meals on the set of the film *The Greatest Show on Earth*. The catering contract with the film's producers represented the first of many such contracts to follow, a line of business that would constitute one of the primary business segments of the company for the next 40 years. Another key contributor to the company's future growth was added the following year, when Morrison Cafeterias signed a catering agreement with Loyola University, paving the way for future education contracts and broadening the scope of the company's catering clientele. In 1953, the company signed a catering contract with Mound Park Hospital in St. Petersburg, Florida, adding the third arm of the company's catering business, health care. Before the close of the decade, Morrison Cafeterias, now structured as a catering and cafeteria company, made one more signal move by opening the company's first suburban cafeteria in Gentilly Woods, Louisiana, a harbinger of the direction the company would later follow, when it operated properties exclusively in shopping malls and other retail-oriented centers.

The company entered the 1960s with designs to further diversify, this time in nonfood related directions. Following the corporate trend of the era, Morrison Cafeterias embarked on a mission to become a vertically integrated company, acquiring assets that would supply its cafeteria and catering needs as well as steer the company away from food service altogether in a bid to become a multidimensional corporation. In 1968, Morrison Cafeterias Consolidated, Inc. changed its name to Morrison Incorporated. The new Morrison Inc. completed several acquisitions in the late 1960s and throughout the 1970s, adding to the company's corporate umbrella a motel chain, a china and small wares facility, an insurance carrier specializing in coverage for strip mines, a distribution company, and a breading plant. With each acquisition, Morrison replaced existing management with Morrison personnel, attempting to meld the disparate organizations into one corporate body.

Late in the 1970s, the company began to flounder, as its widespread interests had created bureaucratic layers that led to confusion and significantly lower profit margins. In 1980, the company selected a new chief executive, Ernest Eugene Bishop. Bishop had joined Morrison in 1947 at age 16, intent on earning money to help pay for a college education. He never entered college and instead stayed at Morrison, rising through the company's ranks from cafeteria counter worker, to district manager, and, ultimately, to Morrison's chief executive officer. Recognizing the problems that saddled the company, Bishop divested all of the company's nonrestaurant holdings, noting later to *Nation's Restaurant News* that the company's management "fell into the integration trap in the late 1960s and into the 1970s because it was in vogue." Bishop also realized that many of the company's top management and board of directors were too much alike, that the views and opinions expressed by the company's leadership were too similar, leading him to conclude that Morrison's management needed representation from outside the Morrison organization.

Bishop's new vision for Morrison was put the test in 1982, when the company completed the most important acquisition in its history, the 15-unit restaurant chain, Ruby Tuesday, Inc. Ruby Tuesday was founded in 1972 by five college students attending the University of Tennessee. This group of young entrepreneurs, led by Samuel E. (Sandy) Beall III, converted an old house on the University's campus in Knoxville into a small, casual-style dining establishment that featured barn wood walls and a hamburger served on an English muffin priced at $1.45. Beall, who had managed a Pizza Hut restaurant as an 18-year-old freshman at the university, then used a cash gift from one of the early developers of the Pizza Hut chain to start Ruby Tuesday. Like Bishop, Beall never completed his education, and instead, devoted his energies toward making his fledgling enterprise a success.

By 1982, Ruby Tuesday had grown into a 15-unit chain, roughly the size of Morrison Cafeterias when Bishop joined the organization. Bishop decided to acquire the budding restaurant chain, paying $15 million in a combination of cash and stocks, as he effected a strategic shift away from the cafeteria side of the company's business toward casual, inexpensively priced restaurants. The incorporation of the Ruby Tuesday organization into Morrison highlighted the significant differences between Bishop's management style and that of his predecessors, which led to confusion and rivalry among Morrison's various divisions before Bishop gained control of the company. With this acquisition, Bishop granted Beall and Ruby Tuesday's management virtual autonomy in controlling their organization instead of replacing them with Morrison personnel. Furthermore, he named Beall president of Morrison's newly created Specialty Restaurant Division, grooming him for an executive leadership position at Morrison's headquarters in Mobile. Beall remained in Knoxville until 1985, by which time he had been promoted to corporate executive vice-president in charge of the

company's specialty restaurant and cafeteria business. Two years later, Beall was named president and chief operating officer and was well on his way toward assuming control of Morrison.

Beall and Bishop increasingly worked in concert as Morrison increased its interests in the restaurant business. Within two years of the Ruby Tuesday purchase, the company added Silver Spoon Cafe and L&N Seafood Grill, both of which offered inexpensively priced menu items. In 1984, Morrison, through its food contract, cafeteria, and restaurant business, generated $464.4 million in annual revenue, a total that would triple in the coming decade largely because of the company's focus on its specialty restaurants.

The growth of this segment of the company's business was accelerated considerably by the acquisition of three contract food service companies in 1987, including the purchase of Pennsylvania-based Custom Management Corp., which lent its name to the formation of Morrison Custom Management, a division containing Morrison's food contracting businesses. Remaining a stable contributor to the company's overall revenue total, contract food accounts provided a consistent revenue base from which Morrison could invest in its higher-growth restaurant business. By 1988, this division serviced more than 800 accounts, ranging from providing meals for single tenants in large office buildings, to food service contracts with factories, universities, and health care facilities. This division would provide a solid foundation for the restructuring of Morrison in the early 1990s, as stewardship of the company passed from Bishop to Beall.

Beall was named chief executive officer of Morrison in 1992. This year also featured the reorganization of Morrison's various businesses into three primary divisions, Morrison's Family Dining Group, Casual Dining Group, and Hospitality Group. The oldest business segment and the former mainstay of Morrison Cafeteria, the Family Dining Group comprised the company's 147 cafeterias and Sadie's Buffet & Grill, Morrison's entry into the all-you-can-eat market. The Casual Dining Group included Ruby Tuesday, of which there were over 200 establishments, L&N Seafood Grill, and Silver Spoon Cafe units. Morrison's third business segment, its Hospitality Group, comprised all of the company's contract food service accounts, which were further divided into health care, business/industry, and education divisions. As the company planned for its future, an emphasis was placed on its Casual Dining Group, which contributed 29 percent of 1991's $970 million in total revenue, a percentage of gross sales eclipsed by its other two groups but a business segment that contributed significantly higher profits.

Morrison's strategy to distance itself from its cafeteria image and identify itself as a specialty restaurant and contract-feeding operator led to a name change in 1992, when the former Morrison Incorporated became Morrison Restaurants Inc. To bolster its presence in the specialty restaurant market, the core of its Casual Dining Group, Morrison attempted to acquire Uno Restaurants Corporation, an operator of a 110-unit Italian restaurant chain. Uno Restaurants agreed to the acquisition and signed a letter of intent in late 1992 but pulled out of the deal in early 1993 over a disagreement on the proposed purchase price. Left without an interest in the rapidly growing Italian restaurant market, a market Beall strongly believed Morrison should enter, the company began converting its Silver Spoon Cafe units into specialty Italian restaurants, which the company named Mozzarella's Cafe.

As the conversion of Silver Spoon units took place, the company opened a new type of cafeteria, called Morrison's Fresh Cooking, to bolster its Family Dining Group, which was phasing out the company's disappointing Sadie's Buffet & Grill units. Also added in 1993 were two new units of a Southern-theme specialty restaurant called Sweetpea's to further increase Morrison's investment in its Casual Dining Group. The company restructured its operations again in 1994, combining its Hospitality Group with its Family Dining Group to create the Morrison Group, and renaming its Casual Dining Group the Ruby Tuesday Group, providing a clear indication of the company's strategic priorities as it entered the mid-1990s.

Several months after reorganizing the company into two operating groups, Morrison sold all of its education and business/industry food service accounts to Gardner Merchant Ltd., an international contract food services company, leaving Morrison with only its health care food service contracts. Concurrent with its decision to lessen its interests in food service contracts, Morrison announced plans to phase out the company's L&N Seafood Grills and convert them to Ruby Tuesday Restaurants and Mozzarella's Cafes, two of its restaurant concepts that had proven to be more profitable and successful than the family dining restaurants. With 288 restaurants within its Ruby Tuesday Group and 163 family-dining units and food service contracts controlled by the company's Morrison Group, Morrison

entered the mid-1990s poised to strengthen its presence in the specialty restaurant market at the national level.

Principal Subsidiaries: Morrison International, Inc.; Custom Management Corp.; John C. Metz & Associates, Inc.; Manask Food Service, Inc.; Custom Management Corp. of Pennsylvania; Morrison Custom Management Corp. of Pennsylvania; Ruby Tuesday, Inc.

Further Reading:

Allen, Robin Lee, "Underpromising and Overdelivering," *Nation's Restaurant News,* March 28, 1994, p. 110.

Carlino, Bill, "Forging a New Identity," *Nation's Restaurant News,* March 28, 1994, p. 65.

Carlino, Bill, "Saddling Up the Workhorse," *Nation's Restaurant News,* March 28, 1994, p. 72.

Hayes, Jack, "Family Group 'Freshens' Focus, Growth Plans," *Nation's Restaurant News,* March 28, 1994, p. 104.

Hayes, Jack, "Stirring Up the Status Quo," *Nation's Restaurant News,* March 28, 1994, p. 120.

Howard, Theresa, "Morrison's, Uno Prepare to Tie the Knot," *Nation's Restaurant News,* December 21, 1992, p. 2.

Liddle, Alan, "Beating the Odds by Bucking Tradition," *Nation's Restaurant News,* March 28, 1994, p. 122.

"Morrison Rest. Inc. to Grow Southern Sweet Peas," *Nation's Restaurant News,* March 15, 1993, p. 2.

"Morrison's Aims to Update Image with Name Change," *Nation's Restaurant News,* April 27, 1992, p. 44.

Prewitt, Milford, "Morrison Realigns, Fuses Family, Hospitality Groups," *Nation's Restaurant News,* April 18, 1994, p. 14.

"Uno, Morrison's Deal Collapses Over Price Snag," *Nation's Restaurant News,* January 18, 1993, p. 2.

—Jeffrey L. Covell

Motorola, Inc.

1303 East Algonquin Road
Schaumburg, Illinois 60196-1079
U.S.A.
(708) 576-5000

Public Company
Incorporated: 1928 as Galvin Manufacturing Corporation
Employees: 120,000
Sales: $16.96 billion
Stock Exchanges: New York Midwest London Tokyo
SICs: 3674 Semiconductors and Related Devices; 3663
  Radio and TV Broadcasting and Communication
  Equipment; 3661 Telephone and Telegraph Apparatus;
  3571 Electronic Computers; 3694 Electrical Equipment for
  Internal Combustion Engines; 3812 Search and Navigation
  Equipment; 3670 Electronic Components and Accessories.

Electronic communications pioneer Motorola, Inc. ranked among the 25 largest companies in the world in the early 1990s. At that time, the corporation sold 45 percent of the world's cellular phones and an overwhelming 85 percent of its pagers. Motorola also commanded a very respectable third-place showing among the world's manufacturers of semiconductors. Over half of its sales were made outside the United States. Motorola also gained recognition over the years for its emphasis on quality, for which it garnered the first annual Malcolm Baldrige National Quality Award in 1988, and for its innovative employee welfare and training programs.

The story of Motorola was an American classic. It began during the 1920s, when a small-town Illinois boy, Paul Galvin, went to Chicago to seek his fortune. Galvin had returned from World War I with an interest in the technological changes of the time. In 1920 he worked for a Chicago storage-battery company, and one year later he opened his own storage-battery company with a hometown friend, Edward Stewart. After two years of rocky operations, the government closed the business for non-payment of excise taxes.

The former partners, undaunted by this setback, joined forces again three years later when Galvin bought an interest in Stewart's new storage-battery company. But with the rise of electric power, batteries lost popularity with the public. To keep their business afloat, Stewart created a device that allowed a radio to be plugged into an ordinary wall outlet, aptly named the "bat-

tery eliminator." Once again, the storage-battery company failed, though Galvin was able to buy back the eliminators at the company's public auction. Joe Galvin joined his brother Paul at this time to peddle the eliminators to various retail distributors, such as Sears, Roebuck and Company. In 1928 Paul formed the Galvin Manufacturing Corporation with five employees and $565, and continued making battery eliminators.

During the Great Depression, Galvin Manufacturing Corporation found itself burdened by inventory that it could not sell because of restricted market conditions and underselling by other manufacturers. To rectify this situation, Galvin began experimenting with the virtually untouched automobile-radio market. Before this time, automobile radios had been deemed impractical because they had very poor reception. The first commercially successful car radio came out of Galvin Manufacturing in 1930 under the brand name Motorola. The name, coined by Galvin, was a hybrid of "motor" and "victrola." The units sold for about $120 including accessories and installation, which compared favorably with the $200–$300 custom-designed units then available.

During the 1930s the company also established its first chain of distributorships (Authorized Motorola Installation Stations), began advertising its products in newspapers and on highway billboards, and started to research radios to receive only police broadcasts. The market for police radios appeared so promising that the company formed a police radio department. In 1937 Galvin Manufacturing entered the home-radio market, introducing the first push-button tuning features.

In 1936, after a tour of Europe with his family, Galvin returned home convinced that war was imminent. Knowing that war could provide new opportunities, he directed the company's research into areas he felt could be useful to the military. The Handie-Talkie two-way radio and its offspring, the Walkie-Talkie, resulted. Used by the United States Army Signal Corps, these were among the most important pieces of communications equipment used in World War II.

Galvin was always concerned with the welfare of his employees, and in 1947 he instituted a very liberal profit-sharing program that was used as a model by other companies. By this time, the company employed around 5,000 people and had formed an early human-relations department. The company's good labor relations enabled it to remain nonunion throughout its history. After Galvin's son Robert and Daniel Noble, an engineer who would eventually have a tremendous impact on the future of the company, joined the company in 1947, its name was officially changed to Motorola.

The first Motorola television was introduced that same year. It was more compact and less expensive than any competing models—Motorola charged $180, while its nearest competitor charged more than $300. The Motorola "Golden View" set became so popular that within months of its introduction the company was the fourth-largest seller of televisions in the nation.

Later in 1947, Motorola bought Detrola, a failing automobile-radio company that had manufactured car radios for the Ford Motor Company. The purchase was made on the condition that Motorola retain Detrola's contract with Ford. This deal greatly strengthened the company's automobile-radio business. Motorola subsequently supplied 50 percent of the car radios for Ford and Chrysler as well as all of the radios for American Motors.

The creation of the transistor in 1948 by Bell Laboratories marked a major turning point for Motorola. The company had concentrated on the manufacture of consumer products, and Paul Galvin felt that the company was unequipped to enter the transistor and diode field. However, with his son Robert and Dan Noble advocating the company's expansion into this new market, a semiconductor-development group was formed. The first Motorola product to result from this effort was a three-amp power transistor, and later a semiconductor plant was constructed in Arizona. Following this expansion, Motorola supplied transistors to other companies for use in products that Motorola also manufactured. In effect, Motorola found itself in the awkward position of supplying its competitors with parts.

During the 1950s, Motorola became involved in the Columbia Broadcasting System's failed entry into the color-television industry. Motorola used the CBS-designed and produced color tubes in its color-television sets. After a convoluted struggle for approval from the Federal Communications Commission (FCC), the CBS system was rejected in favor of a system developed by the Radio Corporation of America (RCA). Despite this setback, Motorola pioneered many new features in television technology, including a technique for reducing the number of tubes in black-and-white sets from 41 to 19.

By the middle of the decade, Paul Galvin realized that the company had become too large for one man to continue making all the decisions. He granted divisional status to various businesses, giving each its own engineering, purchasing, manufacturing, and marketing departments and regarding each as an individual profit center. This was the beginning of Motorola's famous decentralized-management scheme. As part of this reorganization, Robert Galvin became president and each divisional manager an executive vice-president. Paul Galvin became chairman of the board and CEO, which he remained until his death in 1959. Beginning in 1958, Motorola became involved in the American space program. Virtually every manned and unmanned space flight since that time utilized some piece of Motorola equipment.

Motorola made several acquisitions during the 1960s that left observers baffled. It purchased, and sold almost immediately, Lear Inc.'s Lear Cal Division, which manufactured aircraft radios. This was followed by the purchase and subsequent divestment of the Dalberg Company, a manufacturer of hearing aids. Acquisitions were also considered in the fields of recreation, chemicals, broadcasting, and even funeral homes. This trend continued into the 1970s and constituted a period of real adjustment for Motorola. However, three very important corporate strategies grew out of this floundering.

First, the company began to expand operations outside the United States, building a plant in Mexico and marketing Motorola products in eight countries, including Japan. An office in Japan was opened in 1961, and in 1968 Motorola Semiconductors Japan was formed to design, market, and sell integrated circuits. Second, Robert Galvin instituted several progressive management policies. In 1974, the company launched an employee training and involvement program that emphasized teamwork and empowered workers at all levels to make decisions. Such policies laid the groundwork for Motorola's much-touted quality and efficiency gains of the 1980s. Third, in the late 1970s, Motorola gradually began to discontinue its consumer-product lines in favor of high-tech electronic components.

Motorola's radio and television interests were the first to go. In 1974 Motorola sold its consumer products division, which included Quasar television, to the Matsushita Electric Industrial Company of Japan. Three years later the company acquired Codex Corporation, a data-communications company based in Massachusetts. In 1978 Universal Data Systems was added. Motorola began phasing out its car-radio business at the end of the decade, and made its last car radio in 1983. These maneuvers were intended to concentrate Motorola's activities in high technology.

Motorola's largest and most important acquisition came in 1982 with its purchase of Four-Phase Systems, Inc. for $253 million. A California-based manufacturer of computers and terminals, Four-Phase also wrote software for its own machines. The purchase puzzled observers because Four-Phase was in serious trouble at the time. Though Four-Phase did quite well in the 1970s, by the end of that decade its product line was aging, its computer-leasing base had grown too large, and its debt was tied to the rising prime rate. These problems had their origin in the company's insistence upon manufacturing its own semiconductors instead of purchasing commercially available components—an insistence that consumed time and money, and also meant that new product developments at Four-Phase were slow in coming. However, Motorola was looking for a custom-computer manufacturer and was impressed with the sales force at Four-Phase: Motorola's grand strategy was to branch into the new fields of office automation and distributed data processing.

Distributed data processing involved the processing of data through computers that were geographically distributed. The purchases of both Four-Phase and Codex made perfect sense when viewed in light of Motorola's intent to enter this field. The plan was simple: data processing provided by Four-Phase computers would be linked by data-communications equipment provided by Codex, and Motorola proper would provide the semiconductors and much of the communications equipment for the operation. The goal was to create a fully mobile data-processing system that would allow access to mainframe computers from a pocket unit. Motorola also figured that its experience in portable two-way radios and cellular remote telephone systems would prove valuable in this endeavor. Although Motorola was able to turn Four-Phrase around temporarily, Four-Phrase lost more than $200 million between 1985 and 1989.

The cellular remote telephone system was developed by American Telephone and Telegraph's Bell Laboratories in the early 1970s. The system functioned by dividing an area into units, or cells, each with a low-level transmitter that had 666 channels. As a driver using a phone moved from cell to cell, his call was carried on the transmitter in each successive cell. After he left a cell, the channel he was using became available for another call in that cell. (Earlier remote systems relied on a powerful transmitter covering a large area, which meant that only a few channels were available for the whole area.) Motorola aided in the design and testing of the phones and supplied much of the transmission-switching equipment.

Motorola's early estimates of the cellular phone market seemed astronomical—one million users by the early 1990s—though in fact there were more than 4 million users by 1989. However, the system developed major problems. There were massive licensing and construction problems and delays. Added to this were complaints about the quality and reliability of Motorola's phones compared to Japanese-manufactured remote phones. A surplus of phones, coupled with the desire to capture a large market share, soon prompted Japanese companies to cut their prices radically—some by as much as half. Motorola went straight to the U.S. government to request sanctions against the Japanese companies. In 1986 the commerce department declared that eight Japanese companies were in fact "dumping" their products (selling at a below-cost price) and were liable to pay special duties. This gave Motorola a new edge in the cellular-phone market—it soon became the world's top supplier of cellular phones, though the competition remained intense.

Motorola's relations with Japanese companies has been checkered. In 1980 it formed a joint venture with Aizu-Toko K. K. to manufacture integrated circuits in Japan. Two years later Motorola acquired the remaining 50 percent interest in the company from Aizu-Toko and created Nippon Motorola Manufacturing Company, a successful operation run along Japanese lines mostly by Japanese. Also in 1982, Motorola received a $9 million order for paging devices from Nippon Telegraph and Telephone. These ventures were followed by vigorous pleas from Robert Galvin for the U.S. government to respond in kind to Japan's trade tactics. In fact, Galvin was a founder of the Coalition for International Trade Equity. This organization has lobbied Congress for legislation that would impose tariffs on foreign companies that are subsidized by their governments. Motorola further called for a surcharge on all imports to reduce the U.S. trade deficit. Other major companies in the United States (Boeing and Exxon among them) have rejected these measures on the grounds that they would spark trade wars that would damage the position of U.S. companies doing business with Japan.

In 1986, Motorola made a groundbreaking deal with Japan's Toshiba to share its microprocessor designs in return for Toshiba's expertise in manufacturing dynamic random access memories (DRAMs). Prior to this arrangement, the Japanese had driven Motorola, along with nearly every other American semiconductor company, out of the DRAM market.

In 1988, Motorola took on the Japanese in another way: that year its Boynton Beach, Florida, plant began producing the company's Bravo model pocket pager in a fully automated factory. The prototypical facility used 27 small robots directed by computers and overseen by 12 human attendants. The robots could build a Bravo within two hours of the time an order was received at corporate headquarters in Schaumburg, Illinois; the process normally would take three weeks.

Motorola's adoption of "Total Quality Management" (TQM) principles during the 1980s furthered that push for quality and earned it the admiration of analysts and competitors alike.

Building on the foundation laid by his employee empowerment programs of the 1970s, Robert Galvin was able to instill a drive for continuous quality improvement in his teams of workers. From 1981 to 1986, Motorola reduced its defect rate by 90 percent. By 1992, the company had achieved "six sigma quality": less than 3.4 mistakes per million. The corporation did not sacrifice productivity for these quality improvements, either: from 1986 to 1994, sales per employee increased 126 percent, in spite of a net increase in the work force. Some divisions had achieved such high quality rates that they were striving to reduce error rates to defects per *billion* in the 1990s. The corporation's ongoing goals were to reduce error rates tenfold every two years and simultaneously reduce production time tenfold every five years. Motorola's campaign for quality was highlighted by its 1988 receipt of the first annual Malcolm Baldrige National Quality Award.

In 1989 Motorola introduced the world's smallest portable telephone, but soon found that its new product was excluded from the Tokyo and Nagoya markets, two cities that together represented more than 60 percent of the $750 million Japanese cellular phone market. When Motorola cried foul, the Japanese government agreed to allow adapted Motorola phones in Tokyo, but only for use in automobiles. This excluded the 90 percent of portable phones used on trains. In response to these restrictions, Motorola led the push to impose trade sanctions on certain Japanese imports. Then-President George Bush publicly accused Japan of being an unfair trading partner and threatened to take punitive action if the Japanese did not remove barriers to free trade.

The growth of the computer industry has provided both opportunities and challenges for Motorola. Throughout the 1980s, the company's most popular 68000 family of microchips powered personal computers (PCs) and workstations built by Apple Computer, Inc., Hewlett-Packard Company, Digital Equipment Corporation, and Sun Microsystems, Inc., among others. Upstart competitor Intel Corporation, whose chips were the cornerstone of International Business Machines Corporation (IBM) and IBM-compatible PCs, launched a successful campaign to capture the microchip market. Intel combined ever-increasing power and speed with aggressive marketing to win the semiconductor market from Motorola. Undaunted, Motorola teamed up with industry giants Apple and IBM to develop the PowerPC in the 1990s. As of 1993, Motorola ranked third among the world's semiconductor manufacturers, behind Intel and Japan's NEC Corp.

In many respects, however, Motorola's computer chip operations have been eclipsed by its communications interests. The company's 45 percent leading share of the global cellular phone market and whopping 85 percent of the world's pager sales forced it to place an increased emphasis on consumer marketing in the early 1990s. Accordingly, Motorola recruited market specialists from General Electric, Black and Decker, Apple, and (as *Fortune* put it in a 1994 article) "even Mattel." The company began selling its pagers at mass merchandisers and offering them in a variety of colors. Evidence of its re-entry into the consumer market after nearly twenty years came in the form of a 1993 television and print campaign targeted at women (especially mothers).

Over the course of the 1980s, Motorola's sales and profits tripled, to $9.6 billion and $498 million, respectively, in 1989. By 1993, sales vaulted over 56 percent to $16.96 billion and earnings more than doubled to over $1 billion. The company underwent its third transfer of power that year, when Robert Galvin "retired" to the office of chairman of the executive committee of the board at the age of 71. Gary L. Tooker, former president and chief operating officer, advanced to the chair and chief executive office, and Galvin's son Christopher assumed Tooker's responsibilities.

Although some analysts worried that Motorola, like many other large, successful corporations, would fall into complacency, that fear did not seem well founded. The company has earned a reputation for "self-obsolescence" that seemed likely to keep it in the vanguard of wireless communication. For example, the Motorola Integrated Radio Service (MIRS) combined features of cellular phones, pagers, and two-way radios in a system that could rival all three. Motorola hoped to undermine the cellular "duopolies" organized by the Federal Communications Commission by operating the system over Specialized Mobile Radio (SMR) frequencies that had been limited to use by taxis and tow trucks. Motorola also continued work on its multi-billion dollar "Iridium" project, a plan to wirelessly interconnect the entire globe through a system of low-earth-orbiting satellites (LEOS). The company hoped to complete the project by 1998.

Continuing globalization at Motorola focused on Asian, Eastern European, and Latin American markets in the early 1990s. In 1993, the company announced "Corporate America's biggest manufacturing venture in China": two plants for the manufacture of simple integrated circuits, pagers, and cellular phones. Motorola executives expected foreign revenues to constitute 75 percent of annual sales by the turn of the century, up from 56 percent in 1993.

Principal Subsidiaries: Codex Corporation; Motorola Credit Corporation; Motorola International Capital Corporation; Motorola International Development Corporation; Universal Data Systems; Motorola Australia Proprietary Ltd.; Motorola (China) Electronics Ltd.; Iridium, Inc.; Motorola International Sales, Inc.; Motorola Lighting, Inc.; Motorola Satellite Communications, Inc.; Motorola Telcarro de Puerto Rico, Inc.; Motorola A.S.; Motorola Electronique Automobile; Motorola S.A. (France); Motorola Electronic GmbH (Germany); Motorola B.V. (The Netherlands); Motorola Communications Israel Ltd.; Motorola Telephone Cellular Communication Ltd.; Motorola SpA (Italy); Nippon Motorola, Ltd. (Japan); Motorola Electronics Sdn. Bhd. (Malaysia); Embarc Communication Services, Inc.; Motorola Philippines, Inc.; Motorola Espana S.A.; Motorola A.B. (Sweden); Telcel S.A.; Motorola Foreign Sales Corp.; Motorola Componentes de Puerto Rico, Inc.; Motorola Portavoz de Puerto Rico, Inc.; Motorola Telcarro de Puerto Rico, Inc.; Motorola Canada Ltd.; Motorola Limited (United Kingdom); Motorola Semiconducteurs S.A. (France); Motorola GmbH (Germany); Motorola Asia Ltd. (Hong Kong); Motorola Semiconductors Hong Kong Ltd.; Motorola Israel Limited; Motorola Korea, Ltd.; Motorola Malaysia Sdn. Bhd.; Motorola Semiconductor Sdn. Bhd. (Malaysia); Motorola de Mexico, S.A.; Motorola Electronics Pte. Ltd. (Singapore); Motorola Electronics Taiwan, Ltd.

Further Reading:

Brown, Kathi, *A Critical Connection: The Motorola Service Station Story,* Rolling Meadows, Illinois: Motorola University Press, 1992.
Galvin, Robert W., *The Idea of Ideas,* Rolling Meadows, Illinois: Motorola University Press, 1993.
Henkoff, Ronald, "Keeping Motorola on a Roll," *Fortune,* April 18, 1994, pp. 67–78.
Petrakis, Harry M., *A Founder's Touch: The Life of Paul Galvin of Motorola,* New York, McGraw-Hill, 1965.

—updated by April Dougal Gasbarre

Multimedia, Inc.

305 S. Main St.
Greenville, South Carolina 29601
U.S.A.
(803) 298-4373
Fax: (803) 298-4424

Public Company
Incorporated: 1968
Employees: 3,500
Sales: $634.5 million
Stock Exchanges: NASDAQ
SICs: 2711 Newspapers; 4833 Television Broadcasting
   Stations; 4832 Radio Broadcasting Stations; 2741
   Miscellaneous Publishing; 2721 Periodicals; 4899
   Communications Services, Not Elsewhere Classified

One of the most profitable media communications companies in the United States, Multimedia, Inc. grew rapidly by acquiring an assortment of daily and non-daily newspapers, radio stations, and network-affiliated television stations, then established itself as a leading cable television operator in the 1980s. In the course of assembling its network of media properties, Multimedia developed an entertainment production company that owned the production and syndication rights for several of the country's most popular talk show hosts, including Phil Donahue, Sally Jessy Raphael, Jerry Springer, and Rush Limbaugh. By the 1990s, the company had organized all of its media assets into four subsidiary companies constituting the four operating divisions of Multimedia: Multimedia Newspaper Company, Multimedia Broadcasting Company, Multimedia Cablevision Company, and Multimedia Entertainment, Inc. In addition to these business groups, each generating roughly 25 percent of the company's total revenues, Multimedia also owned a residential security alarm service and a cable television advertising business.

Multimedia was formed on the first day of 1968, when three small southern U.S. companies merged. The Greenville News-Piedmont Company, owner of two Greenville, South Carolina, newspapers founded in the early 1800s—the *Greenville News* and *The Piedmont*—was the driving force behind the merger that combined a subsidiary company purchased in 1954 and the Southern Broadcasting Corporation. The subsidiary company,

the Asheville Citizen-Times Publishing Company, owned the two daily newspapers and radio station WWNC in Asheville, North Carolina, while the Southern Broadcasting Corporation owned and operated radio and television properties in South Carolina, Georgia, and Tennessee. When these three companies merged to form Multimedia, the resulting combination already represented a strong media communications company, with newspaper, radio, and television properties scattered throughout four states. Multimedia, however, would quickly become a much larger concern, its creation serving merely as a prelude to further growth.

Leadership of the newly created company was drawn from each of the three companies, with Roger C. Peace, the president and publisher of Greenville News-Piedmont Company, selected as Multimedia's first chairperson, and Robert A. Jolley, Sr., whose family owned a substantial percentage of Southern Broadcasting Corporation's stock, serving as the company's vice-chairperson. Guided by these two men and other representatives of the merged companies, Multimedia began acquiring additional newspaper, radio, and television properties to strengthen the company's market position in regions where it already maintained a presence and into new markets to widen the geographic scope of its operations. The first two acquisitions, the *Montgomery Advertiser* and *Alabama Journal*, were completed in early 1969, adding another state to Multimedia's area of operations and bringing two more daily newspapers to a company that owned six such publications, seven radio stations, and three television stations by the end of the decade.

In 1971, Multimedia became a publicly traded company, then began acquiring newspaper, television, and radio companies in earnest the following year, when it purchased television station WSJS for $7.5 million. Located in Winston Salem, North Carolina, the National Broadcasting Corporation (NBC) affiliate, which later became WXII, served the largest television market between Washington D.C. and Atlanta.

The following year, Multimedia purchased Leaf-Chronicle Co., Inc., publisher of the *Leaf-Chronicle,* the daily newspaper of Clarksville, Tennessee, providing Multimedia with a publishing base of operations that eventually would oversee the production of 13 daily and non-daily publications. Next, the company strengthened its broadcasting division considerably by purchasing four radio stations. Three of these were AM stations— WAKY in Louisville, KEEL in Shreveport, and KAAY in Little Rock—bringing the number of AM stations operated by Multimedia to seven, the maximum number one company could own according to Federal Communications Commission restrictions. The other station, KMBQ-FM, located in Shreveport, completed the purchase from LIN Broadcasting Corp. for a total of approximately $8.5 million.

Spread across eight southern states, Multimedia's properties included 11 radio stations, four television stations, and seven newspapers by the end of 1975. Moreover, an acquisition completed the following year would extend the company's presence beyond the southern United States, launch a new business division for the company, and rank as one of the most important moves of its history. The impetus for this acquisition, completed in the spring of 1976, was largely attributable to a new employee, Walter E. Bartlett, who joined Multimedia earlier that year to head the company's broadcast division. Shortly after his arrival, Bartlett convinced the company's chairperson, Wilson C. Wearn, one of the original Multimedia board members in 1968, that the company should enter the television programming market. Wearn agreed, and Multimedia purchased WLWT, a Cincinnati, Ohio-based NBC affiliate, for $16.3 million.

The acquisition of WLWT represented a signal move for the company. The television station served a market considerably larger than any of Multimedia's previous purchases and had made television history as the first NBC affiliate outside New York and the first television station in Ohio. However, its local live programming and original production capabilities, for which the station had earned recognition from the broadcast industry, were the qualities that set its acquisition apart from any of the company's other properties. In acquiring WLWT, Multimedia also gained the production and syndication rights for several television programs, including the highly profitable *Phil Donahue Show.*

By obtaining the rights to the talk show hosted by Phil Donahue just before the program became a tremendous national success (eventually broadcast in roughly 200 television markets throughout the country), Multimedia secured a position in the rapidly growing market for program production and syndication. Program production and syndication would eventually become the focus of the company's Multimedia Entertainment, Inc. subsidiary. In 1976, however, the company maintained three operating divisions: newspaper, radio and television, and the recently added program production and syndication segment, initially named Multimedia Program Productions.

In the late 1970s, cable television represented only a modestly sized market. Consumers had subscribed to cable television as a means to improve television reception, but this, the only attribute of cable service, had limited appeal, attracting a relatively small number of subscribers who typically lived in rural areas where television reception was poor. During this time, however, increasing numbers of cable subscribers were interested in the greater variety of television programming cable operators were providing, and Multimedia's management began looking for a way to enter the market. Such a way was found in 1979, when Multimedia purchased the Kansas State Network and Air Capital Cablevision, which together served more than 30,000 cable subscribers in Kansas and Oklahoma. Multimedia Cablevision Company was formed to guide the company's interests in cable television, adding the fourth principal subsidiary to the Multimedia organization and concluding a decade of prodigious growth.

Growth also occurred in the company's more traditional segments of business, as Multimedia bolstered its newspaper and broadcast divisions. Two FM radio stations were purchased—KEZQ in Little Rock and WEZW in Milwaukee—while eight newspapers were purchased, located in Arkansas, Florida, Virginia, West Virginia, and Ohio. With these additional newspapers, Multimedia owned 13 daily newspapers and 23 non-daily newspapers by the end of the decade, publications that comple-

mented Multimedia's 13 radio stations and five television stations located in many of the same markets.

Entering the 1980s, the company recorded exponential growth in the number of its cable television subscribers, increasing Multimedia Cablevision Co.'s roster of customers to 66,000 by the end of its first year of business, then gaining an additional 60,000 subscribers when it was awarded franchises in four suburban Chicago communities in 1980. The following year, Multimedia purchased a 20 percent stake in North Carolina-based Tar River Communications Inc., and later acquired the remainder of the cable operator's assets, giving the company 18 cable franchises and 50,000 subscribers. In 1982, Multimedia began offering home security alarm service in Witchita, Kansas, drawing on its financial and managerial expertise in providing cable television service. The company also traded two of its television stations, WXII in Winston Salem, North Carolina, and WFBC in Greenville, South Carolina, for KSDK in St. Louis, the 18th largest television market in the country. The acquisition of KSDK provided the testing ground for a new talk show developed by the company's Program Productions division, renamed Multimedia Entertainment, Inc. in 1983. Called the *Sally Jessy Raphael Show,* the new program was debuted in St. Louis and remained there for two years until it was syndicated nationally, becoming as successful as the company's *Donahue* program.

By the time *Sally Jessy Raphael* became a nationally distributed program, the growth and success Multimedia had achieved in the past 17 years had attracted the attention of potential buyers, leading to several hostile takeover attempts. In a bid to quell further takeover attempts, Bartlett, by this time Multimedia's chief executive officer, initiated a dramatic recapitalization of the company in 1985 that increased its debt tenfold. The recapitalization forced Multimedia to assiduously monitor its spending habits and greatly improve the efficiency of it operations to overcome the company's $576 million of negative net worth. Coming when it did, roughly five years before a national recession that would force other media communications companies to effect similar cost-cutting procedures, the constraints engendered by the recapitalization significantly improved Multimedia's position for the future, particularly during the recessive early 1990s.

During those debilitative years, Multimedia demonstrated its ability to post encouraging profits while other media communications companies, including Capital Cities/ABC, the Washington Post Company, and the Tribune Company, floundered under the effects of the harsh economic climate. From 1985 to 1993, the company's annual revenues nearly doubled, reaching $634.5 million. However, its earnings demonstrated the most impressive leap, particularly during the recessive early 1990s, when earnings soared from $45 million in 1990 to $99.8 million by 1993. This increase was largely due to the success and profitability of the company's entertainment division. In 1991, Multimedia Entertainment introduced a new daytime talk show, *Jerry Springer,* which by the following year was broadcast in 100 U.S. markets, covering 76 percent of the nation. *Sally Jessy Raphael* and *Donahue* by this time were broadcast in nearly 200 U.S. markets and aired in 14 foreign markets. In 1992, the company introduced its first late-night talk show, *Rush*

Limbaugh, which was soon broadcast in 98 percent of the country.

Complementing these successes were equally strong performances exhibited by Multimedia's cable television business, which, by 1993, served over 411,000 subscribers in Kansas, Oklahoma, Illinois, Indiana, and North Carolina. Multimedia Broadcasting Company, the subsidiary comprised of Multimedia's radio and television properties, now included five television stations, three of which were located in the 30 largest markets by population in the United States, and seven radio stations. Multimedia's newspaper assets included 12 daily and 49 non-daily newspapers, with the majority of the company's newspaper revenues derived from three daily newspapers in Asheville, Greenville, and Montgomery, Alabama.

Each of these four business segments contributed roughly a quarter of Multimedia's aggregate revenue as the company entered the mid-1990s. Planning for the future, the company was expected to rely heavily on the expansion of its entertainment and cable television businesses to fuel its growth. A step in this direction was taken in 1994 when Multimedia announced plans to invest $150 million in upgrading the coaxial cable utilized by its cable television business to fiber-optic cable, which would enable the company to increase the number of television channels offered through its cable service from 40 to as many 110. Intending to spend roughly $90 million between 1994 and 1996 to begin the conversion process, Multimedia appeared poised to strengthen its cable television business and to maintain its position as one of the strongest media communications companies in the 1990s.

Principal Subsidiaries: Multimedia Newspaper Company; Multimedia Boradcasting Company; Multimedia Entertainment Company; Multimedia Cablevision Company; Multimedia Security Service.

Further Reading:

''FCC OK's NBC Sale of WKYC-TV to Multimedia,'' *Broadcasting,* December 31, 1990, p. 37.
''Multimedia Plans,'' *Television Digest,* February 21, 1994, p. 6.
''Multimedia Sets Strategy for Converging Communications,'' *Editor & Publisher,* March 12, 1994, p. 37.
''Multimedia's $17 Million Man,'' *Forbes,* July 8, 1991, p. 124.
Taub, Stephen, ''Multimedia's Day of Reckoning,'' *Financial World,* February 20, 1990, p. 14.
Wrubel, Robert, ''Media Maven,'' *Financial World,* March 30, 1993, p. 30.

—Jeffrey L. Covell

NATIONAL HEALTH LABORATORIES
I n c o r p o r a t e d®

National Health Laboratories Incorporated

4225 Executive Square, Suite 800
La Jolla, California 92037
U.S.A.
(619) 454-3314
Fax: (619) 456-0688

Public Company
Incorporated: 1971 as DCL Health Laboratories, Inc.
Employees: 7,700
Sales: $760.5 million
Stock Exchanges: New York
SICs: 8731 Commercial Physical Research

One of the leading companies in the rapidly growing U.S. blood-testing industry, National Health Laboratories Incorporated provided clinical diagnosis services to physicians, hospitals, clinics, nursing homes, and other clinical laboratories through a national network of laboratories. National Health conducts tests of patients' blood, urine, and other bodily fluids and tissues, the results of which assist the medical profession in diagnosing and treating a broad range of diseases. As the clinical laboratory industry consolidated during the early 1990s, National Health emerged as one of the industry's leaders, poised to garner an appreciable share of an approximately $30 billion market and intent on increasing the size of its operations. By 1993, the company's network of facilities comprised 17 major laboratories, a national reference laboratory, and 662 patient service centers, which together served customers in 44 states.

In the summer of 1971, Revlon, Inc., a diversified manufacturer of cosmetics and ethical drugs, as well as a host of other, related products, purchased a small clinical laboratory business, founded three years earlier, called DCL BioMedical, Inc. DCL was incorporated as a subsidiary of Revlon that same year and its name changed to DCL Health Laboratories, Inc., the predecessor to the company that would later become National Health Laboratories Incorporated. Initially, DCL operated as a division within another Revlon subsidiary, USV Pharmaceutical Corporation, which oversaw Revlon's ethical pharmaceutical operations. DCL remained positioned as such, a second tier subsidiary, until roughly the end of the decade, but during the

intervening years the geographic scope of its operations widened and the variety of tests conducted by its laboratories increased.

Under the Revlon corporate umbrella, DCL benefitted from the stability and financial security provided by its much larger parent company, an enviable position for an independent laboratory to occupy in a fragmented and highly competitive industry. In the blood-testing industry, hospitals accounted for the bulk of the testing work performed, with individual doctors and independent laboratories performing the balance of the country's blood-testing. The market niche occupied by independent laboratories comprised scores of small laboratories scattered throughout the nation, each competing in their geographic regions for a share of the national blood-testing market. Even though some doctors conducted blood and tissue tests for their patients on their own premises and some hospitals operated their own diagnostic laboratories, independent laboratories such as DCL, had an interdependent rather than a purely competitive relationship with doctors and hospitals because they were independent laboratories' primary customers.

Positioned as such within the blood-testing industry, DCL subsisted on work supplied by doctors and hospitals, and competed against a bevy of small independent laboratories, each of which vied for a share of a decentralized market. Although DCL represented an appreciable force within the segment of the blood-testing market controlled by independent laboratories, the fragmented nature of the market meant that the leading laboratories garnered only a negligible percentage of the total blood-testing market. Accordingly, DCL was a prominent company during the early 1970s, but a company that generated relatively little revenue. Growth would come as the market consolidated and as DCL widened the scope of its operations and expanded its geographic presence, efforts made easier under the sponsorship of DCL's much larger parent company, Revlon.

In 1974, DCL underwent a name change, becoming National Health Laboratories Incorporated. After the name change, the company began to expand, operating clinical testing laboratories in 13 cities and maintaining auxiliary service centers and satellite laboratories in 15 other cities by 1977. The following year, National Health's expansion efforts received a considerable boost when Revlon purchased American Biomedical Corporation and fused its assets with National Health. The acquisition extended National Health's presence into the Southwest and gave the company valuable and sophisticated data processing technology that enabled it to improve the operating efficiency of its laboratories' test results through telecommunication capabilities.

By the beginning of the 1980s, organizational changes at Revlon had recast National Health's position in the network of subsidiaries owned by the parent company. Revlon's diagnostic products and services operations were conducted now through three subsidiaries instead of operating as an adjunct to the company's ethical pharmaceutical business. These three subsidiaries were National Health, Meloy Laboratories, Inc., and a 1980 Revlon acquisition, Technicon Corp. Each of these companies commanded one of the three subdivisions composing

Revlon's diagnostic products and services division, with National Health's subdivision constituting Revlon's interests in clinical diagnostic laboratories.

By this time, National Health operated one of the leading clinical diagnostic laboratory companies in the United States, but still garnered only a small portion of the independent clinical diagnostic laboratory business in the country, a portion excluding clinical testing performed by hospitals for their patients and by doctors on their own premises. To secure a greater stake in the market, National Health had continued to increase the number of its facilities, and, as it entered the 1980s, it operated 15 major laboratories, including two central reference laboratories in Vienna, Virginia, and Dallas, Texas, and 75 satellite laboratories and client service centers. Any dramatic market share increase, however, was dependent largely on the consolidation of the independent laboratory industry. Lacking the ability to control the forces that shaped the industry, National Health did what it could, strengthening its position in extant areas of operation and looking to expand into new regions.

Additional data processing and communications equipment was installed in 1982, concurrent with the introduction of six new test procedures, which augmented the battery of testing services National Health offered to the medical profession. That same year, the testing capabilities of the company's two reference laboratories were expanded and its regional laboratory in south Florida was relocated to a new 21,000 square foot facility.

The 1980s would be a decade of tremendous change for National Health, engendered by the significant changes effected by Revlon. In the mid-1980s, Revlon underwent sweeping organizational and structural changes, as the company adjusted its corporate strategy and prepared for a series of mergers that would devolve ownership of Revlon, Inc. to another corporate body. As part of this transformation, Revlon sold its ethical pharmaceutical business in 1986, and with it Meloy Laboratories, one of the three subsidiary companies through which Revlon conducted its diagnostic products and services operations. Plans were announced that year for the sale of Technicon Corp., also one of Revlon's diagnostic products and services subsidiaries, leaving National Health, by this time operating in 24 states through 15 major laboratories, as the sole operating company for Revlon's clinical services interests. While these divestitures and organizational changes were being effected, Revlon Group Incorporated purchased Revlon, Inc. in 1985 through a subsidiary created expressly for purchasing Revlon, Inc. The following year, New York-based MacAndrews & Forbes Holdings Inc. acquired approximately 32 percent of the outstanding voting shares of Revlon Group Incorporated, then purchased the remaining shares in 1987, making, after the developments of the previous two years, MacAndrews & Forbes Holdings Inc. the ultimate parent company of National Health.

In this new corporate hierarchy, National Health operated as a division of Revlon Health Care Group, but the clinical diagnostic laboratory would not remain in this position for long. In 1988, National Health filed with the Securities and Exchange Commission for an initial public offering of 9 million shares of common stock, then, three years later MacAndrews & Forbes

Holdings reduced its ownership in National Health to roughly 20 percent, giving the independent laboratory its first taste of independence.

Now essentially operating on its own for the first time, National Health faced its future in an industry that was demonstrating signs of appreciable growth potential. The reason for this optimism stemmed, in part, from an aging population, as the bulk of the country's citizens were reaching an age that portended greater medical difficulties. The early 1990s was also a period during which doctors were becoming increasingly apprehensive about the threat of malpractice lawsuits, apprehension that led them to be more cautious in their diagnosis and treatment of patients, which spurred the demand for blood and tissue tests. Adding to the demand for services provided by companies like National Health was the growing trend of organizations to test their employees for illegal drugs, coupled with the desire of individuals to monitor their medical conditions more assiduously.

All of these factors contributed to the growth of the blood-testing industry, which by the time National Health emerged on its own in 1991 represented a $26 billion business. Hospitals accounted for half of the test work completed, with doctors performing 25 percent and independent laboratories performing the balance. The independent laboratory niche of the market, however, was still highly fragmented. The largest five companies accounted for only 14 percent of the market controlled by independent laboratories, but this decades-old characteristic of the industry was changing during the early 1990s, educed, in part, by more restrictive federal government safety standards, which dramatically reduced the profitability of the country's smaller clinical laboratories. Market consolidation translated as greater profit potential for the industry's largest companies, such as National Health, that now competed in a significantly different business environment.

As this new era in the independent diagnostic laboratory industry began, the four largest companies were, in ranking order, SmithKline Beecham Clinical Laboratories, Corning Inc., National Health, and Damon Corporation, an order National Health hoped to alter. In June 1993, the company announced it had agreed to acquire Needham Heights, Massachusetts-based Damon Corporation, which operated 13 clinical laboratories in the United States and one in Mexico City. Combined with National Health's $721 million in sales in 1992, the addition of Damon would create a company with $1.2 billion in annual revenues and vault National Health to the industry's number two position behind SmithKline's $1.5 billion in annual revenues. The $260 million proposed acquisition was stalled, however, when Corning Inc., then the industry's second largest company, offered $368 million for Damon. Unwilling to pay such an amount for Damon, National Health withdrew from the bidding contest and Corning acquired Damon in mid-1993. National Health's president and chief executive officer, James R. Maher, reacted to the failed acquisition by responding to the *Wall Street Journal* that he "would have been pleased to acquire Damon, but not at the premium that the Corning offer required."

Although the purchase of Damon would have strengthened substantially National Health's position in the blood-testing industry, the disappointment surrounding the failed acquisition was overshadowed by a greater disappointment for National Health that year, which resulted in a prison sentence for Maher's predecessor, Robert E. Draper, the leader of National Health for the previous two decades. The legal turmoil began in 1990, when a grand jury investigation was launched in response to accusations made the year before that National Health had manipulated doctors into ordering unnecessary blood tests. During the investigation, the company's employees were questioned and reams of corporate documents were taken from National Health laboratories across the country. After reviewing the material, federal prosecutors were convinced that National Health had persuaded doctors from as far back as 1987 to order unnecessary blood tests by misleading them about how much the company was billing Medicare, the federally sponsored health care program.

As the evidence mounted and prosecutors were preparing to ask the grand jury for an indictment in 1992, settlement talks between the government's attorneys and National Health intensified, spurred by National Health's fear that it would face automatic exclusion from the Medicare program, a major source of the company's revenue. In December 1992, National Health plead guilty to two felony counts of submitting false claims to the Civilian Health and Medical Program for the Uniformed Services, which provided health care to military families. By admitting to such violations, National Health avoided automatic Medicare suspension, but was forced to pay $111.4 million as part of the settlement, which ranked as the largest Medicare fraud case in history. Following the settlement, Robert E. Draper, the president and chief executive officer of National Health, was sentenced to three months in prison in early 1993 and fined $500,000 for his involvement in the illegal activities, the maximum amount permissible.

The effect of the legal battle was severe, but if any optimism could be drawn from the losses incurred as a result of National Health's guilty plea, it was found in the fact that the company recorded $40 million in profit for the year, despite the $111.4 million settlement payment and a $136 million charge related to the settlement. With the resignation of Draper, National Health gained Maher, a former vice chairmen of First Boston Corp., who was selected for his history of managing successful acqui-

sitions and charged with increasing the scope of the company's operations. This he did in earnest, acquiring 34 clinical laboratories in 1993 and completing the purchase of Nashville, Tennessee-based Allied Clinical Laboratories Inc., one of the country's largest blood-testing companies, in mid-1994.

Entering the mid-1990s, National Health continued to look for additional properties, involved in both the blood-testing industry and unrelated industries, as a means for growth. In June 1994, the company's shareholders approved a resolution to reorganize National Health into a holding company to facilitate such acquisitions. As part of the company's restructuring, plans were announced to change its name to National Health Laboratories Holdings Incorporated, giving the company a new name and a new focus in an industry undergoing rapid change. With its legal difficulties behind it, National Health charted its future, intent on strengthening its position in the blood-testing industry.

Further Reading:

Adelson, Andrea, "2 New Consolidations in Blood-Testing Industry," *New York Times,* May 5, 1994, p. C3.
——, "Bid for Allied Clinical Is Cut after Investigation Widens," *New York Times,* June 9, 1994, p. D5.
"Holders Vote to Approve Change to Holding Company," *Wall Street Journal,* June 8, 1994, p. A8.
Moukheiber, Zina, "Dealing with Hillarynomics," *Forbes,* July 5, 1993, p. 52.
"National Health Labs' Former CEO Gets Prison Sentence, Fine," *Wall Street Journal,* April 6, 1993, p. A6.
"National Health Gets Time to Raise Offer for Damon," *Wall Street Journal,* July 1, 1993, p. B6.
Rundle, Rhonda L., "National Health Labs Reduces the Price of Tender Offer for Allied Clinical," *Wall Street Journal,* June 9, 1994, p. B7.
Rundle, Rhonda L. and Amy Stevens, "Investigators Intensify Crackdown on Fraud in the Health Industry," *Wall Street Journal,* August 16, 1993, p. A1.
Salomon, R.S. Jr., "Testing, Testing . . . ," *Forbes,* October 26, 1992, p. 300.
Sims, Calvin, "National Health Labs to Buy Rival," *New York Times,* June 22, 1993, p. D5.
"Testing Laboratory Files for Initial Public Offering," *Modern Healthcare,* July 1, 1988, p. 34.
Wilke, John R., "Damon Accepts Corning Buyout at $23 a Share," *Wall Street Journal,* July 6, 1993, p. B6.

—Jeffrey L. Covell

National Service Industries, Inc.

NSI Center
1420 Peachtree Street N.E.
Atlanta, Georgia 30309
U.S.A.
(404) 853-1000
Fax: (404) 853-1015

Public Company
Incorporated: 1928 as National Linen Service Corporation
Employees: 22,200
Sales: $1.8 billion
Stock Exchanges: New York
SICs: 1742 Plastering, Drywall & Insulation; 2677
    Envelopes; 2782 Blankbooks & Looseleaf Binders; 2789
    Bookbinding & Related Work; 2842 Polishes & Sanitation
    Goods; 3645 Residential Lighting Fixtures; 3646
    Commercial Lighting Fixtures; 6719 Holding Companies,
    Not Elsewhere Classified; 7213 Linen Supply

A diversified manufacturing and service company, National Service Industries, Inc. operates as a holding company for an amalgamation of companies involved in six divergent industries. Originally a linen supply and rental business, the company evolved into a conglomerate with substantial investments in lighting equipment manufacturing, textile rental, specialty chemicals, insulation service, envelope production, and marketing services, all businesses the company entered through three decades of acquisitions. Its three core businesses—lighting equipment, textile rental, and specialty chemicals—contributed the bulk of the company's $1.80 billion in revenues in 1993, a sales volume that ranked National Service as the 255th largest industrial company in the United States. Aside from owning the largest lighting fixture manufacturing company in North America, Lithonia Lighting, and the largest multi-service textile rental supplier in the United States, National Linen Service, the company represented one the few perennially successful U.S. conglomerates in a business community populated by narrowly focused, streamlined companies.

The history of National Service Industries may be traced to the formation of the National Linen Service, which rented linens and uniforms and was owned by a prominent Atlanta family named Weinstein. In 1928, National Linen Service was incorporated to acquire three Atlanta, Georgia-based companies:

Southern Linen Supply Corporation, the linen supply departments of Atlanta Laundries, Inc., and Laundry and Dry Cleaning Service, Inc.

Roughly 40 years separated the formation of National Linen Service and the creation of National Service Industries, a span during which National Linen Service developed into a formidable force in the linen supply industry. Positioned as one of the few large, publicly traded companies competing in a highly fragmented and densely populated industry, National Linen Service grew to such an extent that the U.S. Justice Department intervened in 1958, setting stringent restrictions on the company's further expansion. Although the company, then led by Milton N. Weinstein, would continue to acquire small linen supply companies, the ruling by the U.S. Justice Department led to its diversification into other business lines, marking a significant turning point in the company's history and forever changing the scope of its operations.

Other leading linen supply companies were diversifying too, enriched by the dramatic growth of the textile rental industry, which nearly doubled in size between the 1950s and the 1960s as the concept of renting rather than buying durable goods became popular following World War II. Of these other leading linen supply companies, perhaps none were as successful in their diversification efforts outside the industry as National Linen Service, which entered the 1960s entirely devoted to renting linen and uniforms and exited as a full-fledged conglomerate with multifarious investments in service and manufacturing. Instrumental to this transformation was a former neighbor of Milton Weinstein's named Erwin Zaban, the president of National Linen Service's first acquisition outside its field of expertise, Zep Manufacturing Company.

By the time National Linen Service acquired Zep Manufacturing Co., Zaban already had invested 26 years of his life in his family's business, a janitorial supplies company started by his father. Zaban began working for his father full-time at an early age, dropping out of high school at age 15 in 1936 to help his father's company withstand the debilitative effects of the Great Depression. The company survived, and by the early 1960s, with Zaban serving as its president, the company had expanded into selling cleaning and sanitation products. This was the company Milton Weinstein selected as National Linen Service's first non-linen supply acquisition, an acquisition that served as a model for future acquisitions and marked the beginning of a new era for National Linen Service and Erwin Zaban.

Growth would come quickly after the merger of Zep Manufacturing Co. and National Linen Service in 1962, but not at the expense of incurring potentially crippling debt. Virtually every acquisition that brought National Linen Service into a new business line was paid for through stock, the acquisition of Zep Manufacturing Co. being no exception. Zaban's company received 382,218 common shares of National Linen Service stock, giving Zaban and his company's management a vested interest in the future profitability of National Linen Service. This financial stake was particularly important to the future success of National Linen Service, because with each acquisition the acquired company's management was absorbed as well and granted virtual autonomy in the running of their company. Again, the acquisition of Zep Manufacturing Co. was no exception to this acquisitive philosophy. Not only was Zaban allowed to retain control of the successor to his father's business, but within four years he was selected as president of the parent company, by then known as National Service Industries.

The name change from National Linen Service Corporation to National Service Industries, Inc. occurred two years after the acquisition of Zep Manufacturing Co., in 1964, when National Linen Service acquired Atlanta Envelope Co. and Southern Envelope Manufacturers, Inc., which would form the foundation of the company's envelope manufacturing division. One month after acquiring these two companies, paid for with 116,000 common shares, National Linen Service effected the name change in recognition of its more diversified interests. These interests then represented three separate business lines: the mainstay linen supply business, Zep Manufacturing Co. (later organized as part of its chemical division), and the envelope manufacturing operations.

A fourth line was added in 1966, when National Service ceded 103,736 common shares to acquire North Brothers, Inc., an insulation service company. By this time, National Service was the largest linen supply company in the United States, with roughly $100 million in annual revenues, a total that was nearly twice as much as its closest competitor, F.W. Means & Company. Buoyed by its dominant position in the linen supply industry, National Service augmented its investment in insulation services, a business line entered into with the acquisition of North Brothers, Inc., by paying cash for Jackson, Mississippi-based Mid-South Insulation Co. in 1967.

The transition from linen supply to chemicals, envelopes, and insulation appeared void of any synergy, and, indeed, Zaban's intent was not to create an assortment of interdependent companies positioned to dominate a particular market, or even dominate four markets. Rather, he focused on acquiring profitable companies, regardless of their expertise, targeting companies with managements compatible with National Service's corporate philosophy, since more often than not acquired companies would continue to be led by extant executive officers.

With these criteria guiding National Service's diversification, the company continued to widen the range of its operations, purchasing Selig Chemical Industries with 88,667 common shares in 1968, which bolstered the company's chemical division. The following year, National Service made a pivotal acquisition, relinquishing $6.2 million and 419,156 shares to obtain Lithonia Lighting, Inc., a manufacturer of lighting fixtures. Lithonia formed National Service's fifth operating division, a division that would become the company's largest revenue contributor in the 1990s, when Lithonia became the largest lighting fixture manufacturer in North America. By 1970, the company's sixth division was added, as National Service gave 803,891 shares of its stock to acquire Southern Binders Inc., Brown Printing Co., Acme Display Co., Tufted Sample Co., and Southern Sample Service Inc., while forming a marketing services division to provide marketing aids for the carpet, home furnishing, and commercial printing markets.

As National Service entered the 1970s, each of the core business lines that would support the company in the 1990s were established. Diversification had also brought the company into

markets it would later abandon. Entering the furniture market in 1969, with the purchase of five furniture manufacturers, National Service formed its Duchess Furniture Division, which was discontinued in 1976. National Service also had formed a packaging division during the late 1960s, beginning with the acquisition of Flexi-Pak, Inc. in 1968 and strengthened by the addition of Color Wrap of Colorado the following year. This division also was sold, as were properties that represented other National Service business lines, including a furniture leasing division and a recreation division.

Many of these other companies were sold during the 1970s, although the company's furniture leasing division continued to grow and operate until 1986, and its men's apparel division, established in 1972, remained a part of the company until 1991. These acquisitions underscored Zaban's willingness to acquire any type of company, provided that company was profitable. Once a company became unprofitable it was divested; a simple strategy that meant National Service did not attempt to rescue floundering companies or acquire companies operating at a loss to increase market share in a particular market. Zaban sought only profitable, well-managed companies, which explained a history of acquisitions that otherwise appeared predicated on whimsy.

Those lines that proved most profitable were the five divisions established within the first eight years of his arrival at the company as well as the original line of business, textile rental. In the early 1970s, the company's textile rental division contributed the bulk of its revenues and profits. In 1972, its original linen business generated roughly 40 percent of the company's total revenues and more than 50 percent of its profits. However, the relative importance of this division would diminish somewhat as National Service augmented its investments in its other primary business lines.

In the late 1970s and early 1980s, National Service increased the magnitude of its lighting division with three acquisitions. In 1979, the company purchased the outdoor aluminum lighting pole business belonging to Kaiser Aluminum in Louisville, Kentucky. The following year, the company purchased the indoor lighting business of ITT Corp. And, in 1981, it purchased the assets of Major Corp., a Chicago-based supplier of anodized parts. Also during this time, National Service acquired a linen supply company, Champa Linen Service, and Robert P. Gillote & Co., a distributor of filing systems, which the company added to its envelope division. Subsequent additions to the lighting and insulation divisions included the Acme Manufacturing Co., a manufacturer of commercial and residential florescent lighting fixtures, and Extol of Georgia, a manufacturer of pipe covering and insulation materials.

As acquisitions continued unabated throughout the 1980s, National Service benefitted from the fundamental advantage of existing as a conglomerate, yet avoided the usual trap that stifled a conglomerate's growth. Its diverse business mix shielded it from pernicious economic cycles to a great degree, with one division compensating for losses suffered by another, giving the company the financial stability to enable further acquisitions. At the same time, its diversity did not engender superfluous, bureaucratic layers of management, as Zaban's emphasized maintaining profitability and retaining existing management.

In 1987, the company's stewardship passed from Zaban to Sidney Kirschner, who was selected as National Service's chief executive officer that year. Kirschner had joined the company in 1973 and, consequently, owned a substantial amount of National Service stock. After becoming chairperson in 1992, when Zaban retired due to health problems, Kirschner surprised many at National Service by abruptly resigning, giving up his positions as the company's president, chief executive officer, and chairperson. In an interview with the *Wall Street Journal,* Kirschner enigmatically related that his decision to leave National Service was "a choice I made that I'd rather do something else."

Zaban, by then 71 years old, came out of retirement to fill the void created by Kirschner's departure and served as the company's president, chief executive officer, and chair until a successor was found later that year. Elected as chief executive officer in January 1993, D. Raymond Riddle, National Service's banker for many years, assumed control of the company as it emerged from the economic recession of the early 1990s.

During this time, National Service generated the bulk of its revenue and profits from three of its six divisions: lighting equipment, textile rental, and chemicals. The greatest contributor, the company's lighting equipment division, generated 38.4 percent of National Service's total annual revenue and 29.4 percent of its operating income, while National Linen Service, the company's linen supply business, contributed 30.3 percent of National Service's total revenues for the year and 37.4 percent of its operating income. The company's chemical division, comprising Zep Manufacturing Co., Selig Chemical Industries, and National Chemical, supplied 17.6 percent of National Service's revenue and 25.4 percent of its operating income, more than three times the amount of income generated by National Service's three smaller divisions: insulation service, envelopes, and marketing services.

National Service thus entered the mid-1990s looking to strengthen its investments in each of its operating divisions rather than to diversify into new business lines. As it planned for the future, the company's management envisioned a greater presence in Europe, where it maintained a foothold in the European chemical market through Zep Manufacturing Co. This stake overseas was increased significantly in 1992, when the company acquired Graham Group, Europe's second-largest specialty chemicals company and National Service's first solo venture overseas. Graham Group was absorbed by National Service's chemical division, a business that demonstrated encouraging growth and was likely to be augmented in the future.

Principal Subsidiaries: NSI Holdings, Inc.; Selig Co. of Puerto Rico, Inc.; National St. Louis Redevelopment Corp.; Lithonia Lighting Products Co. of Arizona; Lithonia Lighting Products Co. of Georgia; Lithonia Lighting Products Co. of Nevada; NSI Insurance (Bermuda) Ltd.; Corisma Group, Inc.; South Insulation Co., Inc.; I.A. Enterprises, Inc.; Zep Europe B.V. (Netherlands); NUS, Inc.

Further Reading:

"National Service Chief and President Quits; Zaban Steps Up Again," *Wall Street Journal,* October 13, 1992, p. B8.

"National Service Stumbles," *Financial World,* November 7, 1973, p. 22.

"Profitable Services," *Financial World,* December 22, 1965, p. 14.

Smith, William, "Inside Georgia's Most Powerful Corporate Board," *Georgia Trend,* February 1994, p. 24.

"Throwing Away the Rule Book," *Forbes,* November 15, 1972, p. 67.

Willatt, Norris, "No Washday Blues," *Barron's,* September 27, 1965, p. 5.

Zipser, Andy, "Conglomerate and Proud of It!," *Barron's,* June 8, 1992, p. 18.

—Jeffrey L. Covell

NBD Bancorp, Inc.

611 Woodward Avenue
Detroit, Michigan 48226
U.S.A.
(313) 225-1000
Fax: (313) 225-2012

Public Company
Incorporated: 1933 as National Bank of Detroit
Employees: 17,993
Total Assets: $45 billion
Stock Exchanges: New York
SICs: 6712 Bank Holding Companies; 6021 National
    Commercial Banks; 6022 State Commercial Banks

NBD Bancorp, Inc. is the largest bank holding company in Michigan and the 18th largest such concern in the United States, with assets reaching $43 billion as of June 1994. The company's early success was built on commercial banking, particularly with the state's major automakers and their suppliers. In the 1980s, however, the company set a goal of expanding its consumer loan business and began a program of acquiring banks in other states, including Indiana, Illinois, and Ohio, as well as establishing the NBD Trust Company of Florida. Moreover, it has established foreign offices in England, Germany, Japan, Australia, Hong Kong, and Canada.

National Bank of Detroit was founded in the midst of a nationwide financial collapse. Although bank failures, especially of small institutions, were not infrequent during the 1920s, the stock market crash of October 1929 undermined the basic foundations of the U.S. banking system, resulting in 3,635 bank closings nationwide in 1930–31. Fearing the loss of their savings, consumers, both rich and poor, began to withdraw their money from banks, and, by early 1933, hoarding became rampant. In Detroit—the capital of the beleaguered automobile industry—even the major financial institutions, such as Guardian National Bank of Commerce and First National Bank of Detroit, were running out of liquid assets and nearing collapse.

Responding to pleas by Michigan bankers, the state's governor, William A. Comstock, declared a statewide "banking holiday" on February 14, 1933, effective immediately. Suddenly depositors were prohibited access to their accounts, giving the banks time to find a way to stabilize the system. The Michigan action was soon adopted in other states, and, on March 5, 1933, Frank-

lin D. Roosevelt, the newly elected president, ordered the closure of all banks across the nation.

For six weeks, Michigan was virtually without banking services. Revitalization of the system would come only with the help of the Reconstruction Finance Corporation (RFC), a U.S. government agency created in 1932 to assist financially troubled banks, railroads, and other businesses. The RFC began by establishing a plan to pay off small depositors, while also looking to start up new banks to replace those that could no longer be revived. Jesse H. Jones, a director (and soon-to-be chairperson) of the RFC, hoped to enlist the help of Henry Ford, head of Ford Motor Co., and Alfred P. Sloan, president of General Motors Corp., both of whom had a financial incentive in restoring order to Michigan's banking system. The arrangement with Ford fell through, and, on March 21, Sloan and Jones announced the founding of National Bank of Detroit, or NBD. Sloan explained that his company was merely performing its patriotic duty and that it would divest itself from the bank "as soon as the situation was stabilized."

According to the agreement, General Motors purchased all the bank's common stock for $12.5 million, while the RFC put up the same amount for the entire issue of preferred stock. The new bank also took over assets of First National of Detroit and Guardian National Bank of Commerce. To run NBD, the General Motors board wanted to find a banker from New York, while Sloan preferred someone from the Midwest. Finally chosen was Walter S. McLucas—formerly chairperson of Commerce Trust Company of Kansas City, Missouri—who would serve as NBD's president from 1933 to 1938 and as chairperson from 1938 to 1953.

The bank opened for business on March 24, 1933, in the First National Bank Building. Sidney Dowding, an NBD employee, described the first hours of operation: "When the day-gate to the main banking floor was lowered, a tremendous rush of people swarmed into the bank. They carried bundles of currency and coin wrapped in every conceivable way—in newspapers, paper and canvas bags, gunny sacks, cigar boxes, shoe boxes, and suit cases. Amounts ranged from a few hundred dollars to several hundred thousand dollars. Some individuals were accompanied by armed guards."

By March 31, some 4,000 people had deposited a total of $29 million in the bank, and in nine months that figure would jump to more than $189 million, making NBD, with 26 branch offices, the 23rd largest bank in the country. By early 1935, NBD not only began making new real estate mortgage loans but also paid its first dividends to investors (NBD, in fact, would continue to pay dividends each year into the 1990s). The success of its first years were not without criticism, however. On August 12, 1933, the editorial page of the *Detroit News* carried the following complaint: "While Roosevelt is busy making the Automotive Industry and other industries establish working codes ... the National Bank of Detroit, which is partially government owned, reduces salaries and thinks nothing of working their employees 16 hours a day."

Despite such criticism, NBD would have a stable and dominant presence in Detroit throughout the 1930s. Increases in deposits and loans would result in some $500 million in assets by the decade's end, with outstanding real estate loans reaching almost $14 million. The bank also opened its first drive-in window office in 1941. NBD's immense size would allow it to contribute greatly to the country's participation in World War II. NBD was a major seller of U.S. war bonds, for example, and it helped the U.S. government collect unpaid taxes. In 1942, Charles T. Fisher, Jr., the bank's president, took a leave of absence to become a director of the RFC, which was then involved in financing war production. With so many men off to war, NBD began to hire women in great numbers, not only as tellers but also for accounting positions. Women would form as much as 67 percent of NBD's work force during the war years.

The war's end brought a new era for NBD. On April 2, 1945, Sloan announced that "the time has now come—with the emergency long since over, and the institution solidly established—for General Motors to retire from the banking business." Sold a month later were General Motors' remaining 509,550 shares, along with 250,000 new shares offered by the bank, bringing thousands of new shareholders to NBD. Then, on January 6, 1947, the bank made its last payment to the RFC, ending that entity's involvement in the bank. Free from its two founders, NBD would continue to grow with the postwar economic boom, with assets reaching $1.4 billion by 1950. In 1948, the bank also became the first in the country to sell ten million U.S. savings bonds.

Up to this point, NBD's impressive growth had taken place entirely within Detroit's city limits. In the 1950s, NBD made a decision to expand its base by merging with banks in suburban Detroit, though none farther away than 25 miles from its downtown office, a limit established by Michigan law. These mergers would result in 32 new NBD branches during the 1950s, boosting the bank's total number of branches to 67 by the decade's end. In 1959, NBD moved its headquarters across the street to a newly built downtown office building designed by the noted industrial architect Albert Khan. The 12-story facility, located at 611 Woodward Avenue, cost the bank some $12 million and was the first multistory office building to be constructed in downtown Detroit in 25 years.

Meanwhile, NBD was undergoing numerous changes in management. McLucas, the bank's longtime chairperson, died in 1953 and was replaced by Fisher, who had been president of the bank since 1938. Fisher, however, died five years later, and Donald F. Valley, formerly the executive vice-president, was elected chair and chief executive officer. Regular turnover would continue with the election of bank CEOs Henry T. Bodman in 1964 and Robert M. Surdam in 1972.

NBD entered the 1960s with assets of nearly $2 billion and outstanding real estate mortgage loans of some $140 million. Like other banks during this time, NBD began to take major steps toward electronic banking, including, for example, imprinting magnetic ink ID numbers on its customers' checks. The bank also opened another 35 branches during the decade, mostly in suburban Detroit, raising the total number to 102. Moreover, steps were taken to expand its loan service to international markets. International Bank of Detroit, a wholly owned subsidiary of NBD, was established in 1963, and, in 1968, the bank opened its first overseas office, in London. This would be

followed by offices in Frankfurt (1972); Tokyo (1973); Nassau, Bahamas (1978); and other locations.

While the bank was thus looking to make loans far beyond its base, it was also being forced to pay closer attention to problems in Detroit. In July 1967, race riots flared across the city, causing extensive property damage and bringing the city's economy to a virtual standstill. Immediately afterward, new efforts to solve Detroit's long-standing social and economic problems were begun. NBD branch officers, for example, worked as task force volunteers for New Detroit, Inc.—a coalition of community, labor, and business leaders—in order to address the problems that led to the riots. NBD has since shown obvious pride in its various commitments to community service.

NBD underwent major restructuring during the early 1970s. In 1972, it formed National Detroit Corporation, a bank holding company (defined as a corporation that controls at least two banks), and, on January 1, 1973, this new entity was made the owner of NBD. Nationwide, numerous other banks had already undergone a similar administrative restructuring, largely because it allowed them to avoid various legal restrictions regarding where they could do business, while allowing them to enter new, though closely related, activities, which for NBD eventually included mortgage banking, insurance, trust services, leasing, consumer credit processing, securities brokerage, and community and economic development. Throughout the decade, the bank was also able to establish or acquire new Michigan banks outside the Detroit metropolitan area. The company's assets rose accordingly, from $4.7 billion in 1970 to $9.5 billion in 1980. In 1981, the holding company was renamed NBD Bancorp, Inc.

The 1980s saw even greater expansion, prompted by changes in state laws. The U.S. Bank Holding Company Act of 1956, known as the Douglas Amendment, had forbid bank holding companies from purchasing a bank in another state unless the other state explicitly allowed out-of-state ownership. In the early 1980s, states begin to pass such ownership laws. For NBD Bancorp, which was looking to lessen its dependence on the cyclical Detroit economy and especially on the automotive industry, this change brought great fortune. In 1986, NBD Bancorp began purchasing smaller bank holding companies in Indiana and Illinois, forming a ring of financial institutions around Lake Michigan. Its first out-of-state bank purchase was Midwest Commerce Corporation of Elkhart, Indiana. The following year, NBD Bancorp acquired the Illinois banking company USAmeribancs, based in Bannockburn, and State National Corporation, with branches in Evanston and Arlington Heights. NBD Bancorp soon entered the Ohio market as well.

The significance of these moves was reflected in NBD Bancorp's breakdown of deposits. At the end of 1973, a full 100 percent of its deposits came from the Detroit area. After it had begun to expand across the state, that figure had fallen to 97.5 percent in 1978 and 84.1 percent in 1983. In 1988, after a little more than two years of acquiring out-of-state banks, the company saw its Detroit area deposits drop to just 61.4 percent of the total. At the same time, the company was making its first push in consumer loans, which jumped from nine percent of the total in the early 1980s to 25 percent in 1992. NBD Bancorp's out-of-state forays were greatest in Indiana, where in 1992, for example, it purchased INB Financial Corp. of Indianapolis, a holding company with assets of $6.6 billion, six separate banks, and 124 offices. After this acquisition, NBD Bancorp had an estimated 17 percent share of the Indiana deposit market, about the same percentage it maintained in Michigan, making it the largest bank holding company in both states. This dramatic expansion was overseen by Charles T. Fisher III, who was chair, president, and chief executive officer of the company from 1982 until his retirement in 1993. He was replaced as chairperson and chief executive officer by Verne G. Istock, while Thomas H. Jeffs II became president and chief operating officer.

In the early 1990s, NBD Bancorp continued to expand both inside and outside Michigan, as well as abroad. By mid-1994, assets had reached $45.2 billion, making NBD the 18th largest bank holding company in the United States. Unlike many other fast-growing bank holding companies, NBD Bancorp managed to expand without taking on a large amount of uncollectible debt. Its writeoffs for bad loans typically occurred at a rate less than half the average for large regional banks. Also in 1994 the company's main subsidiary, NBD Bank, N.A., was making plans to discontinue its status as a national bank and to apply instead for a Michigan state charter. This move would likely save as much as $1.5 million in regulatory costs and give NBD Bancorp greater influence with the state legislature.

Various explanations have been given for the company's success, though commonly praised has been its conservative lending style. NBD Bancorp avoided relying on giant loans (its average loan in the early 1990s was about $500,000, with few over $50 million), and loans were approved only after an unusually extensive review process. Only in his capacity as chairman of the executive committee could Fisher be described as "personally involved." Moreover, despite the well-publicized economic problems of Detroit and Michigan, NBD Bancorp managed to do quite well in its home turf, in part because its dependence on the area's automotive industry has greatly diminished. In the early 1990s, only about ten percent of its corporate loans involved car-related businesses, and many of these were to manufacturers of products, such as tooling, that were not strongly affected by economic cycles. Meanwhile, NBD consumer loans in Michigan greatly benefited from labor contracts giving laid-off autoworkers 95 percent of their salary for up to a year. It was perhaps the company's familiarity with hard times—both from its origin in the Depression and its operation in an economically troubled state—that was ulti-

mately responsible for its successful, conservative strategy. Fisher, summarizing this approach, explained, "If it grows like a weed, it probably is a weed, because an oak doesn't grow that way. We're in the oak business."

Principal Subsidiaries: NBD Bank; NBD Bank, Canada; NBD Bank, FSB; National Bank of Detroit-Dearborn; NBD Brokerage Services, Inc.; NBD Community Development Corporation; NBD Financial Services of Michigan, Inc.; NBD Insurance Company; NBD Leasing, Inc.; NBD Mortgage Company; NBD Real Estate Services, Inc.; NBD Securities, Inc.; Charter Oak Insurance Agency of Michigan, Inc.; Corporate Funding, Inc.; NBD Equipment Finance, Inc.; NBD Equity Corp.; NBD Transportation Company; NBD Illinois, Inc.; NBD Indiana, Inc.; NBD Bank (Wheaton, Illinois); NBD Skokie Bank, N.A.; NBD Bank (Elkhart, Indiana); NBD Bank, N.A.; NBD Bank (Columbus, Ohio).

Further Reading:

Berg, Eric N., "A Quiet Bank in Detroit Is Charming Wall Street," *New York Times,* August 5, 1989, pp. 31, 33.

Berss, Marcia, "Bank by Fisher," *Forbes,* April 13, 1992, p. 52.

Byrne, Harlan S., "NBD Bancorp: Detroit-Based Holding Company, Helped by Strong Ratios, Accelerates Expansion," *Barron's,* June 22, 1992, pp. 49–50.

Cocheo, Steve, "If It Grows Fast, It's Probably a Weed," *ABA Banking Journal,* February 1991, p. 48.

"G.M.C. Will Open New Detroit Bank," *New York Times,* March 24, 1933, p. 31.

"GM to Sell Stock in Bank of Detroit," *New York Times,* April 3, 1945, p. 26.

Jones, Jesse H., *Fifty Billion Dollars: My Thirteen Years With the RFC (1932–1945),* New York: The MacMillan Company, 1951, pp. 33, 54–69, 529.

Kennedy, Susan Estabrook, *The Banking Crisis of 1933,* Lexington: University Press of Kentucky, 1973, pp. 77–102, 193–195.

Kleege, Stephen, "Big Detroit Banks Outpace Michigan Auto Industry," *American Banker,* January 10, 1992, p.12.

"NBD Bancorp: Log Cabin Virtues," *Financial World,* March 8, 1988, p. 14.

"New Detroit Bank Backed by R.F.C.," *New York Times,* March 22, 1933, p. 25.

"New Detroit Bank Gains in Deposits," *New York Times,* March 26, 1933, pp. 7, 12.

Rose, Barbara, "Bank Buy Vaults NBD to Top Tier," *Crain's Chicago Business,* April 1, 1991, pp. 3, 36.

"Stock Sale Today Shifts Control of the National Bank of Detroit," *New York Times,* April 5, 1945, pp. 29, 32.

—Thomas Riggs

Nevada Power Company

6226 West Sahara Avenue
Las Vegas, Nevada 89151
U.S.A.
(702) 367-5000
Fax: (702) 367-5615

Public Company
Incorporated: 1929 as Southern Nevada Power Company
Employees: 1,741
Sales: $651.7 million
Stock Exchanges: New York Pacific
SICs: 4911 Electric Services

One of the fastest growing electric utilities in the United States, Nevada Power Company provided electric service to more than 400,000 residential, business, and industrial customers in southern Nevada during the mid-1990s, the most notable of which were the operators of Las Vegas's many hotels and gambling casinos and their fluorescent signs. Although the brightly lighted streets of Las Vegas's "Strip" represented the most noticeable example of the utility's electrical service, Nevada Power's service area was considerably larger than the greater Las Vegas metropolitan area, comprising more than 4,500 square miles in portions of Clark and Nye counties. Nevada Power used 11,000 miles of transmission and distribution lines to serve its customers. As an integral contributor to the growth of the communities it served, Nevada Power represented an indispensable source of electricity for much of Nevada, fueling the development of the state's various industries and enabling the creation of one of the world's most popular gambling destinations.

At the turn of the twentieth century, Las Vegas was little more than a way station along a railroad line, a sparsely populated community consisting of a collection of tents and shacks. Situated in the desert near the California border, the town was surrounded by a vast and largely uninhabited portion of the southwestern United States that promised to be one of the richest mining regions in the country. Encouraged by such prospects, miners, their families, and those wishing to participate in the growth of a boom town rushed to Las Vegas, creating fierce competition for the town's prime building and business lots. For much of the century, Las Vegas would be referred to as one of the fastest growing communities in the nation as it

quickly emerged as a bustling center of trade and commerce from the dust of the Mojave Desert.

Fire proved to be an immediate problem in the rapidly growing town, whose residents lighted their homes and businesses with gasoline lamps, which posed considerable risk to the town's wood buildings and canvas-covered shacks. By 1906, shortly after the incorporation of the town, two fires had swept through the community, destroying nearly everything that had been constructed in the town's brief existence. The growing fear over fire led one local businessman, Charles P. Squires, to search for a solution, which he found in an idle direct current generator owned by a local company named Armour & Company. Power poles were constructed with wood from Squires' lumberyard, and copper wire was strung from the generator at Armour & Company into the center of Las Vegas, completing the initial transmission network of Las Vegas's new utility company, incorporated as Consolidated Power & Telephone Company on March 28, 1906.

Given the initial push by Squires and the financial support of a small group of other Las Vegas businessmen, Consolidated Power & Telephone began operating in the summer of 1906. From the outset, the company's two divisions, its electricity and telephone businesses, were essentially one, with the same management, workers, and equipment being used to serve the telephone and power needs of Las Vegas. These needs increased as the town's population grew, forcing the company to replace the Armour & Company generator with a more powerful, permanent generator.

This new generator, powered by a 90-horsepower, single-cylinder gasoline engine, became a fixture of Las Vegas life, reminding the town's residents of its existence every night. Referred to as "Old Betsy" by the local citizens, the engine was started every evening at dusk, emitting a coughing noise that, reportedly, could be heard a mile away all through the night. By 1912, however, the power supplied by Old Betsy was insufficient for the city's needs, and Consolidated Power & Telephone doubled its generating capacity with the addition of another engine, generator, and transformer. After six years of operation, Consolidated Power & Telephone had increased its generating capacity twice, a familiar theme throughout the utility's history and one that would be repeated as Las Vegas's only electric company continually struggled to keep pace with its community's electricity needs.

Two years after Consolidated Power & Telephone's generating capacity was doubled, the utility realized that it needed a larger power source and reached an agreement with Las Vegas's railroad shop (the San Pedro, Los Angeles, and Salt Lake Railroads had since arrived) to purchase all of the utility's electricity needs from the shop's power house. Using this source, the two business components of Consolidated Power & Telephone, still essentially operating as one, grew with the town, becoming larger as new arrivals poured into town.

In 1924, Consolidated Power & Telephone elected Edward W. Clark president of the company, five years before the beginning of the Great Depression and five years before Consolidated Power & Telephone was split in two. Clark had arrived in Las Vegas in 1905 and started a business called Clark Forwarding

Company that, as its name suggested, carried supplies to distant mining camps. In his venture, Clark was successful, becoming a prominent figure in Las Vegas social circles and a well-respected businessman, who was selected as president of the city's First State Bank three years after being elected president of Consolidated Power & Telephone. Under Clark's stewardship, Consolidated Power & Telephone was divided into two companies, Southern Nevada Power Company and Southern Nevada Telephone Company, in 1929, and began operating as such on the first day of 1930. But, as the two divisions had done in the previous 23 years, the telephone and electricity operations continued to share personnel, facilities, and equipment, a practice that would continue for another 25 years.

Once Consolidated Power & Telephone was split in two, Clark became president of Southern Nevada Power, a company whose future energy requirements had been secured in a pivotal agreement negotiated by Clark. Clark was instrumental in adding the "Nevada Amendments" to the Swing-Johnson Act, which gave the state of Nevada the right to share in the water and power distributed by one of the largest construction projects in U.S. history, the Hoover Dam. Southern Nevada Power became the first utility to distribute electricity from Hoover Dam in 1937, when the dam was completed, and would use the hydroelectric power generated from the dam to supply all of Las Vegas's electricity needs for roughly the next 20 years. In the interim, during the early and mid-1930s before power from the dam was available, Southern Nevada Power expanded its transmission system by constructing a 69-kilovolt line to accommodate the voltage coming from Hoover Dam, establishing a reliable transmission network for what was believed at the time to be a permanent source of power.

With the formidable force of the Hoover Dam behind it, Las Vegas increasingly became an all-electric city during the late 1930s, when many residences and businesses replaced their coal and kerosene-fired stoves with electric heating units. As the city was effecting this transition, the Second World War broke out, bringing with it a significant boost to the population of the region surrounding Las Vegas. Nellis Air Force Base, the largest air training base in U.S. history, was established outside of Las Vegas, substantially increasing the area's electricity needs and providing additional clientele for a number of new businesses that opened during the war years. One notable addition to the city's business community was the El Rancho Vegas, which opened in 1940 and sparked the construction of similar, luxury hotels that catered to the area's military personnel and to tourists, drawn to the region's major attraction, the Hoover Dam. Adding to this rush of activity were two other key contributors to the region's growth: the relocation of many workers from the Hoover Dam project, referred to as "Boulder Dam Holdovers," into Las Vegas and a steadily growing electro-chemical industry near Henderson, Nevada, which combined with the establishment of Nellis Air Force Base, created a much greater need for electricity and strengthened Southern Nevada Power's position considerably.

The greatest boost to Las Vegas's growth, however, was yet to come, occurring after the war in 1946, when Bugsy Siegel opened the Flamingo hotel and casino and launched Las Vegas's gaming industry. Similar resort hotels and casinos were soon to follow, increasing the pace of the city's growth dramati-

cally. By 1952, Southern Nevada Power's management realized the company's allocation of power from the Hoover Dam could no longer satisfy the electricity needs of its service area, so the company decided to construct a steam generating plant of its own.

This became the first unit of the utility's Clark Station, named after Edward W. Clark, who had negotiated the rights to Hoover Dam's power and in whose memory the utility now shifted away from Hoover Dam's power. The first unit was put into operation in 1955, but before it was completed, construction of a second unit was begun, which began operating in 1957. Before the decade was through, as Las Vegas underwent a transition from being a hydroelectric-powered city to a steam-generated-powered city, construction of a third unit was begun, which was in service by 1961. For the decade, Southern Nevada Power recorded prodigious growth, benefitting from the population increases of the 1940s and the popularity of Las Vegas as a gambling destination in the 1950s. The utility entered the decade with 12,360 customers and exited it with 35,000, a rate of increase that was eclipsed by its annual revenue totals, which soared from $1.8 million in 1950 to $9.2 million in 1959.

In 1961, Southern Nevada Power substantially increased its service area by merging with Elko-Lamoille Power Company, a northern Nevada utility company. The absorption of Elko-Lamoille's territory extended Southern Nevada Power's presence into Elko County, home to many of the state's largest livestock ranches, and led to a name change in June that year, when Southern Nevada Power Company became Nevada Power Company in recognition of its broader scope of operation.

Throughout the 1960s, the utility's growth was accelerated by its further involvement in the Atomic Energy Commission's research and production activities in Nevada, which began in 1956 when a 64-mile-long transmission line was constructed to serve nuclear test sites at Mercury and Indian Springs Air Force Base. Nevada Power provided the electricity for the Commission's nuclear testing and development of propulsion systems for space exploration.

Against this backdrop, Nevada Power began construction of the Reid Gardner Station in 1963, named for the president of the utility who died that year after nine years of guiding the company. Opened in 1965, the Reid Gardner Station represented a significant change in direction for Nevada Power, and, as it turned out, a prophetic one as well that helped the utility withstand the pernicious years that loomed ahead. Instead of oil, the Reid Gardner Station utilized coal as its fuel, coal supplied from underground mines in southern Utah. When the first unit of the station was completed in 1965, Nevada Power became the first utility in the state to operate a coal-burning generating station, a distinction that benefitted the company enormously when an energy crisis gripped the nation in the early and mid-1970s. Before the oil embargo that sparked the energy crisis occurred, however, Nevada Power strengthened its dependence on coal by adding a second unit to the Reid Gardner Station in 1968, then beginning construction of a third unit in the early 1970s while oil prices soared.

Bolstered by its early development of coal-burning generating stations, Nevada Power was able to mitigate the debilitative effects of the energy crisis at a time when the neon lights describing Las Vegas's gambling district were dimmed voluntarily for a five month period. The 1970s included other challenges for Nevada Power, as rising inflation and growing public opposition to rate increases inhibited the utility's growth after two decades of robust expansion. Despite the harsh economic times, Nevada Power was ranked as one of the fastest growing utilities in the country during the 1970s, growth that was partly attributable to the utility's early reliance on coal as an energy source for its generating stations. While other utility companies invested considerable sums in converting generating facilities to coal, Nevada Power was well on its way, obtaining, by the end of the decade, roughly 70 percent of its fuel requirements from coal, 27 percent from natural gas, four percent from hydroelectric power, and relatively little from oil.

Entering the 1980s, Nevada Power's area of service was focused largely in southern Nevada, its territory in Elko County having been exchanged for the service responsibilities for Henderson, Nevada, in a deal with California-Pacific Utilities in 1977. Henderson, situated in the region that had prospered from a rapidly growing electro-chemical industry during the 1950s, experienced a substantial surge in population during the 1980s, increasing nearly threefold, a growth trend imitated by other communities in Nevada Power's service area during the 1980s. This was true of Las Vegas's population during the decade, which nearly doubled. But equally as important, the city's popularity as a gambling and recreation destination for tourists grew, fueling the demand for more and more hotels to accommodate the continuous stream of people entering the city. As it had for much of the century, the growth of Las Vegas translated into growth for Nevada Power, which by mid-1980s collected roughly $360 million a year in revenues.

When it entered the 1990s, Nevada Power served approximately 350,000 customers, possessing slightly more than $1 billion in assets. These figures would climb, as would annual revenues, which amounted to $422 million in 1990 largely because of the continued population and construction growth in Las Vegas. In 1992, the U.S. Census Bureau reported that Las Vegas was the fastest growing metropolitan area in the country, which was encouraging news for Nevada Power's leadership, struggling to post higher revenues yet keep electricity rates low in an increasingly competitive business environment.

In 1993, Nevada Power recorded $651.7 million in electric sales, $326 million of which was derived from the utility's commercial and industrial customers, while $267 million was collected from its residential customers. Three major hotel facilities were opened that year, the MGM Grand Hotel, the Luxor, and the Treasure Island, creating an additional need of 65 megawatts of electricity to light the hotels' 10,000 rooms, an amount of electricity nearly equal to the generating capacity of the utility's Clark Station during the late 1950s. As Nevada Power charted its future in the mid-1990s, the addition of similarly enormous hotels, with their vast electricity needs, seemed to guarantee that the primary power for the bright lights of Las Vegas would continue to be supplied by Nevada Power Company well into its second century of business.

Principal Subsidiaries: Nevada Electric Investment Co.; Commsite Inc.

Further Reading:

"Growth Marks NPC's 75-Year History," *Livewire,* Nevada Power Company Publication, 1981.
"Nevada Power Co.," *Wall Street Journal,* January 31, 1992, p. B4.
"Nevada Power Early Retirement," *Wall Street Journal,* November 26, 1993, p. A10.
"Nevada Power Joins Los Angeles in Project to Shift Electricity," *Wall Street Journal,* August 6, 1993, p. A12.
"Nevada Power, LADWP Plan 500-kV Line," *Electrical World,* November 1993, p. 26.
"Nevada Power to Get Hearing on Recovery of Accident's Costs," *Wall Street Journal,* June 18, 1991, p. A14.
Stevens, Amy, "Nevada Power's Rate Rise Is 40% of Total Requested," *Wall Street Journal,* November 12, 1991, p. A10.

—Jeffrey L. Covell

New Plan Realty Trust

New Plan Realty Trust

1120 Avenue of the Americas
New York, New York 10036
U.S.A.
(212) 869-3000
Fax: (212) 302-4776

Public Company
Incorporated: 1961 as New Plan Realty Corporation
Employees: 125
Sales: $76.3 million
Stock Exchanges: New York Chicago
SICs: 6798 Real Estate Investment Trusts

The largest equity real estate investment trust in the United States, New Plan Realty Trust owns income-producing properties in 17 states. With a portfolio valued at more than $1 billion and comprised of shopping centers, garden apartments, and factory outlet centers, the trust company represents a model of success in the nation's real state investment community and is one of the strongest investment vehicles for small investors. New Plan Realty began its existence as a trust in 1972, then evolved into the largest company of its kind through the development and acquisition of regional shopping centers. In the early 1990s, it began investing in factory outlet centers, a strategic maneuver that positioned the company in one of the dynamic growth areas open to real estate investment trusts and renewed optimism for prodigious growth beyond the 1990s.

The roots of New Plan Realty stretch back to 1926, when Morris B. Newman opened an office in New York City as a certified public accountant and real estate broker. Morris Newman would be the first of two Newmans to launch the family name toward success in real estate investment. Morris Newman imparted his knowledge of the real estate business to his son, William, and thereby laid the foundation for New Plan Realty's future success. The elder Newman's business realized modest success during the first 15 years of its existence, but bore little resemblance to the type of company that would later achieve much more than modest success. That defining transformation came shortly after 1942, when Morris Newman developed an investment arrangement that enabled investors with limited resources to pool their money with other small investors and invest in large real estate properties. It was a signal decision that pointed

the Newman family in a new direction and led to the formation of New Plan Realty Corporation, which was the link connecting Morris Newman's real estate brokerage office and New Plan Realty Trust, the company that ranked in the 1990s as the largest real estate investment trust in the United States.

The investment arrangement Newman had devised, others had as well. In fact, since the turn of the century, debate had centered on the classification of such organizations and whether or not they were obligated to pay corporate tax. This debate, argued before the U.S. Supreme Court on numerous occasions and the subject of various legislative efforts and federal tax reforms, was not definitively settled until the promulgation of federal legislation nearly two decades after Newman began pooling investors together to invest in large-scale real estate properties. The investment organizations that Newman and others had created were the forerunners of what would be later called real estate investment trusts (REITs).

Historically, many of these early versions of REITs were located in Massachusetts, but a few, such as Newman's company, were located elsewhere. Although these "Massachusetts trusts," as they were called, differed in many respects to the REITs that emerged later, the essence of the organizations were identical: each provided an investment vehicle for the pooling of ownership in real estate. Part of the initial impetus for the formation of these business trusts was to circumvent early state laws that often prohibited corporate ownership of real estate. However, by the 1950s, the federal government, prodded by the lobbying efforts of business trusts, was looking for a way to encourage public investment in real estate.

Congress passed a REIT bill in 1956, but President Eisenhower vetoed the bill, hobbling efforts to fully legitimize and define syndicated real estate ownership. Several years later, however, the U.S. Treasury Department, initially opposed to REIT legislation, reversed its position and Congress passed a second REIT bill, which was signed by President Eisenhower in 1960 and put into effect on the last day of that year. With the promulgation of the Real Estate Investment Act of 1961, a new niche in the investment industry was formally created, enabling real estate trusts to avoid corporate tax provided they were structured and operated according to criteria established by federal legislators.

Although Morris Newman entered into this type of real estate syndication 20 years before REITs were defined through legislation, his company did not become organized as a trust until a decade after the passage of the Real Estate Investment Act of 1961. In the interim, Morris Newman expanded his real estate accounting and syndication firm through the acquisition of several New York City commercial properties.

In 1961, the same year federal legislation spawned the REIT industry, Newman's company was incorporated as New Plan Realty Corporation, and its leadership was devolved to William Newman, one of three of Morris Newman's sons who would join the company. William Newman, who began working for his father's company at age 15, was 35 years old when he assumed control of New Plan Realty, which became a public company the following year, in 1962. Under the stewardship of William Newman, who would lead New Plan Realty into the

1990s, lasting and defining changes occurred that dramatically altered the company's line of business and engendered its reorganization as a REIT. Prompted by external economic forces, the younger Newman redirected the company's focus; compelled by the capricious New York City real estate market in the early 1970s, he divested the company's real estate properties. Twelve Manhattan office buildings were sold, and then Newman began making acquisitions in smaller towns, accumulating a handful of shopping centers by the end of 1971.

The following year, the company was reorganized as a REIT, becoming New Plan Realty Trust, one of the smallest REITs at the time, but involved in a burgeoning area of investment that promised to enrich those with the foresight or luck to invest in its growth. In the ten years since the REIT industry had been formally launched, it had grown into a $6 billion business, a fraction of the dollar amount the industry would hold in assets during the early 1990s, when its asset total hovered around $50 billion. But at the onset of the 1970s, many such investment organizations were sinking their shareholders' dollars into the development or acquisition of shopping centers, a retail concept that would fuel much of the REIT industry's growth over the next two decades. For investment purposes, the country's 13,000 shopping centers, which accounted for half of total retail sales in the United States, afforded several attractive advantages to REITs. Typically containing food and drug stores as their major tenants, shopping centers were, if not recession-proof, then at least recession resistant, a desirable attribute for trusts accustomed to the otherwise cyclical nature of real estate. Moreover, small shopping centers in rural areas generally occupied relatively inexpensive property and faced a dearth of commensurate competition, further heightening their appeal to REITs, particularly small REITs such as New Plan Realty.

This was the direction Newman opted to take New Plan Realty as it forged its new future in the REIT industry. New Plan Realty acquired failing or near-failing regional shopping centers and strip malls, remodeled them, and then leased the retail space to financially stable tenants. The company thus amassed a collection of shopping centers and several apartment complexes over the next two decades to become the largest REIT in the country, its growth predicated on the prudent selection of real estate properties and its ability to carve a stable presence in the mid-Atlantic states.

By the early 1990s, however, New Plan Realty's record growth began to falter as a national recession loomed on the horizon, and the company's once robust portfolio showed signs of deterioration. Occupancy at New Plan Realty's 62 shopping centers dropped from 91 percent in July 1990 to 78 percent the following year, while 26 percent of the company's retail properties recorded occupancies below 80 percent, sending distress signal throughout the REIT's management.

Until this time, New Plan Realty had achieved remarkable, industry-leading success. Since 1976, the company had recorded earnings growth every year, and in every year since its reorganization as a REIT, the company's trustees had distributed dividends, at first monthly until 1976 and then on a quarterly basis for every fiscal period afterwards. So, while the early signs of trouble in the early 1990s were not overly significant by themselves, when juxtaposed with the enviable results that preceded them, the declining occupancy rates and the diminishing popularity of shopping centers were sufficient cause for alarm.

To stave off the portended losses, William Newman, by this point New Plan Realty's chair and chief executive officer, approved a plan developed by Arnold Laubich, the company's president and chief operating officer, to invest in factory outlet centers, which were proliferating as shopping centers struggled. The company invested in its first factory outlet center in January 1992, funneling more than $17 million into Sembler Company's outlet project in St. Augustine, Florida. The move into factory outlet centers represented a turning point for New Plan Realty, which historically had limited its investments to regional strip centers and apartment complexes, and it was a move reflective of the changing face of retailing in the United States, mirroring the shifting emphasis away from strip centers toward suburban centers, the so-called outlet malls. Other investments in factory outlet centers followed New Plan Realty's involvement in the St. Augustine project, one in Ossage Beach, Missouri, in January 1993, then three Factory Merchant Malls later that year in November. By mid-1994, the company had invested roughly $150 million in its five large factory outlet centers, which represented only eight percent of the New Plan Realty portfolio's assets but contributed between 15 to 20 percent of its net operating income.

By this point, the early signs of financial trouble in 1991 had become manifest. In 1992, New Plan Realty recorded its first decline in earnings growth since 1984. However, the decline did not stem from the dangerously low occupancy rates of its properties, but rather from the slide in earnings resulted from, of all things, an excess of cash. During the early 1990s, New Plan Realty had accumulated $400 million to effect a contemplated merger, and when the merger did not occur, the company was left with the cash just as interest rates began to plunge. Interest rates dropped from nine percent to three percent, and the company absorbed the loss, which led to 1993's financial stagnation and the end of the company's prestigious record of earnings growth.

Another hallmark of New Plan Realty's success, and a more genuine measure of a REIT's vitality, did, however, remain intact, assuaging some of the disappointment engendered by 1993's results. By 1994, the company had increased its cash distribution to shareholders for 14 consecutive years, an achievement that earned industry-wide recognition and elevated optimism for the future. As the trustees of New Plan Realty explored further investments in factory outlet centers and discussed plans to extend the company's presence in the West, its record of consistent growth and position as industry leader buoyed hopes for the future.

Principal Subsidiaries: New Plan Securities Corporation; New Plan Realty of Alabama, Inc.; Factory Merchants Malls, Inc.

Further Reading:

Hackney, Holt, "Cash 'N Carry," *FW*, July 24, 1990, p. 70.
Lazo, Shirley A., "Speaking of Dividends," *Barron's*, December 9, 1991, p. 50.

Leibowitz, David S., "Fiscal Attraction," *FW,* August 6, 1991, p. 80; "Two Misunderstood Opportunities," *FW,* January 4, 1994, p. 80; "When Cash Burns a Hole in Your Pocket," *FW,* September 15, 1992, p. 80.

McGough, Robert, "The REIT Stuff," *FW,* November 12, 1991, p. 38.

Oliver, Suzanne L., "Eat Your Heart Out, Donald," *Forbes,* October 29, 1990, p. 164.

Vinocur, Barry, "Have New Plan's Shares Finally Peaked," *Barron's,* March 2, 1992, p. 54; "These REITs Are Sound, but No Bargains," *Barron's,* December 14, 1992, p. 58; "New Plan Realty's New Look Fails to Fan Interest from Institutions," *Barron's,* July 25, 1994, p. 40.

—Jeffrey L. Covell

NINE WEST.

Nine West Group Inc.

9 West Broad Street
Stamford, Connecticut 06902
U.S.A.
(203) 324-7567
Fax: (203) 328-3550

Public Company
Incorporated: 1977 as Fisher Camuto Corporation
Employees: 2,302
Sales: $552 million
Stock Exchanges: New York
SICs: 3144 Women's Footwear Except Athletic; 5661 Shoe
   Stores; 5139 Footwear

Nine West Group Inc. is a leading designer, developer, and marketer of women's casual and dress footwear, offering a full collection of women's shoes in three retail price ranges starting from $25 for a pair of shoes and reaching $150 for a pair of the company's leather boots. The three market segments of the U.S. women's shoe market in which Nine West competes are classified by industry terms as "better," "upper moderate," and "moderate." Nine West has realized considerable success in both wholesale and retail operations; the company's footwear is available through more than 2,000 department, specialty, and independent stores as well as through more than 300 of the company's own retail outlets. In addition to its flagship Nine West label, the company's nationally recognized brands include Enzo Angiolini, Calico, 9 & Co., and Westies. In 1993, Nine West celebrated its first year of business as a publicly owned corporation, posting encouraging results in the wake of a national economic recession that had crippled many retail businesses. That year, revenues climbed more than 20 percent above the previous year's total, while profits surged 55 percent from $38.2 million in 1992 to $59.3 million in 1993.

The company commenced operations in May 1977, when Jerome Fisher and Vincent Camuto incorporated a wholesale women's shoe business named Fisher Camuto Corporation. The company was a logical extension of business ties the two founders had formed nearly a decade earlier with manufacturers in southern Brazil, where costs associated with production were relatively low. Specifically, raw materials were abundant in Brazil, labor was cheaper, and capital expenditures were minimal. Fisher Camuto Corporation's utilization of Brazilian man-

ufacturing facilities and personnel was a boon to the company, a hallmark of its success, and one not to be underestimated in understanding the history of the company's growth.

As the relationship with factory managers in Brazil matured and facilities there became more sophisticated, Fisher Camuto Corporation grew. The company generated $9 million in sales within its first year of business, a total that increased to more than $300 million over the course of the next decade. Although its design and marketing operations were based in the United States, and manufacturing was performed abroad, the Fisher Camuto Corporation nevertheless managed to maintain a production schedule commensurate with those of other U.S.-based shoe designers and manufacturers. Moreover, Fisher and Camuto proved adept at adjusting the company's designs to suit rapidly changing fashion trends.

In 1988, Fisher and Camuto formed Jervin Inc., a name derived by combining the first three letters of their first names. Jervin was established as a private-label concern engaged in arranging, on an agency basis, the sale of unbranded, or private-label, women's footwear manufactured in Brazil to retailers and wholesalers. The following year, when the company's annual sales were $338.7 million, Fisher and Camuto attempted to acquire the footwear division of U.S. Shoe Corporation, the assets of which several other companies had expressed interest. A bidding war ensued, with Merrill Lynch Capital Partners emerging as the leader. Although Fisher and Camuto were willing to better Merrill Lynch Capital Partners bid of $422.5, U.S. Shoe Corporation's financial adviser, Merrill Lynch Capital Markets, claimed that the terms of a binding contract between U.S. Shoe and Merrill Lynch expressly forbid U.S. Shoe from providing the wholesaler with any confidential material or allowing it to participate in the bidding process. Rebuffed, Fisher and Camuto were forced to turn their attentions elsewhere.

Nevertheless, over the next three years, Fisher and Camuto's company embarked on a period of prodigious growth. From 1989 to 1992, annual sales climbed modestly from $338.7 million to $461.6 million, while net income increased more than 60 percent, from $14.3 million to $38.2 million. These increases were particularly impressive given the business environment at the time. The late 1980s and early 1990s were deleterious years for women's specialty apparel and footwear retailers; overall sales had declined dramatically during a recession that stifled the nation's economy.

By the end of the 1980s, Fisher and Camuto's company was involved in both the wholesale and retail markets of the women's shoes business. On December 31, 1991, these concerns—Fisher Camuto Corporation, Fisher Camuto Retail Corporation, and Espressioni, Inc.—merged to form a new company, which was soon renamed Nine West Group Inc. Preparing to go public, Fisher and Camuto merged Jervin Inc. into the Nine West Group, of which it became a division in 1992. Once this transaction was completed, Nine West became a public corporation in early February 1993, selling shares of common stock on the New York Stock Exchange.

By this time, Nine West was operating 236 retail and outlet stores as well as designing and marketing branded and private-label shoes to more than 2,000 department, specialty, and independent store customers. Of its five nationally recognized brands, its Nine West brand was the most successful, having been redefined and repositioned in 1989 to compete in the $50 to $65 price range. The company's more moderately priced Calico brand represented its most traditionally styled shoe, typically selling for between $40 to $50. Nine West's Westies brand, sold only by independent retailers, competed in the under $40 market segment, while the Enzo Angiolini brand, the company's designer label, comprised leather shoes priced between $65 and $80. The company's fifth brand, 9 & Co., was created to attract a younger clientele and featured a line of junior footwear priced below $50, which was sold through the company's new retail store concept, also named 9 & Co.

In the wholesale side of its business, Nine West distributed private-label shoes to a host of large, nationally recognized customers, including J.C. Penney Company, Sears, Roebuck & Co., Thom McAn Shoe Company, and Kinney Shoes. Design, manufacturing, and sales operations of the private-label footwear were overseen the Nine West's Jervin division. The company's branded shoes were distributed to several of the largest department stores in the country, including The May Department Stores Company, R.H. Macy & Co., Federated Department Stores, Nordstrom, and Dillard Department Stores.

Nine West's success was largely dependent on its use of Brazilian manufacturing facilities. While these factories had initially manufactured 200 pairs of shoes per day for Fisher and Camuto, the production level had increased exponentially, reaching 130,000 pairs of shoes per day in 1993. During this time, the industry in Brazil employed a work force of over 39,000 and maintained cost-efficient factories, which operated their own tanneries. Moreover, through manufacturing arrangements with 25 independent Brazilian shoe manufacturers, which produced Nine West shoes in 40 factories, Nine West was able to deliver design specifications and receive completed products in an eight-week period, giving the company a supplier network that ranked among the best in the U.S. shoe industry.

Buoyed by this established supply network, Nine West capitalized on a fashion trend away from sneakers toward heavier, sturdier shoes, a trend widely embraced by younger consumers in late 1993 and early 1994. The shift in consumers' tastes caught several of the country's large athletic shoe manufacturers—Reebok International Ltd., Nike, Inc., and L.A. Gear, Inc.—by surprise, and their sales figures declined. However, Nine West and some other companies, such as Timberland Co., an outdoor apparel and shoe company, experienced a surge in profits. Nine West's stock price, which initially sold for $17.50 per share, shot up to more than $34 by the fourth quarter of the company's 1993 fiscal year.

As Nine West planned for the future, it focused on becoming a greater retail force in the U.S. shoe industry, a market segment that represented a $14 billion business in 1993. Toward this end, in 1994, the company planned to open 20 Enzo Angiolini stores, prompted by heightened consumer interest in elegant footwear. By 1997, Nine West's management hoped to derive half of its sales from the retail segment of its business, which during the mid-1990s recorded one of the highest sales-per-square-foot averages in the U.S. shoe industry at $555 per-square-foot a year. With more than 325 retail stores and its established wholesale business supplying more than 5,500 storefronts with women's shoes, Nine West expected to garner a greater share of the U.S. retail and wholesale market.

Principal Subsidiaries: Nine West Distribution Corporation; Nine West Footwear Corporation.

Further Reading:

Getler, Warren, ''Insiders Often Dump Shares Long Before Concerns Enter Bankruptcy, Study Says,'' *Wall Street Journal,* July 7, 1993, p. A5.

Hoffer, Richard, ''Wayne Weaver,'' *Sports Illustrated,* December 13, 1993, p. 64.

Marcial, Gene G., ''Nine West Has Put On Its Dancing Shoes,'' *Business Week,* May 31, 1993, p. 79.

''Market Basket,'' *Women's Wear Daily,* May 24, 1994, p. 8.

''Nine West Group,'' *Fortune,* May 3, 1993, p. 73.

Pereira, Joseph, ''Footwear Firms Hit by Fashion Change, Face Disappointing Quarterly Earnings,'' *Wall Street Journal,* January 17, 1994, p. A5.

Reilly, Patrick M., ''Nine West Group Prepares for Return of Sleek Footwear,'' *Wall Street Journal,* March 11, 1994, p. A4.

''U.S. Shoe Corp.,'' *Wall Street Journal,* March 15, 1989, p. C6.

—Jeffrey L. Covell

Nissan Motor Company, Ltd.

17-1, Ginza, 6-chome Chuo-ku
Tokyo 104
Japan
81-354 355 23

Public Company
Incorporated: 1933
Employees: 139,000
Sales: ¥5.8 trillion ($55.8 billion)
Stock Exchanges: Tokyo Osaka Niigata Nagoya Kyoto
    Fukuoka Supporo Frankfurt
SICs: 6719 Holding Companies, Nec; 3711 Motor Vehicles
    and Car Bodies; 3713 Truck and Bus Bodies; 3714 Motor
    Vehicle Parts and Accessories

Established in 1933, Nissan Motor Company, Ltd. was a pioneer in the manufacturing of automobiles. More than a half-century later, Nissan has become one of the world's leading automobile manufacturers, with annual sales of approximately ¥5.8 trillion and annual production of 2.9 million units, which represented 6.6 percent of the global market. In addition to cars and sport-utility vehicles, Nissan also produced textile machinery, forklifts, marine engines, watercraft, and even the solid-propellant launch vehicles used in Japan's space program.

In 1911 Masujiro Hashimoto, an American-trained engineer, founded the Kwaishinsha Motor Car Works in Tokyo. Hashimoto dreamed of building the first Japanese automobile, but lacked the capital. In order for his dream to come true, he contacted three men—Kenjiro Den, Rokuro Auyama, and Keitaro Takeuchi—for financial support. To acknowledge their contribution to his project, Hashimoto named his car DAT, after their last initials. In Japanese, "dat" means "escaping rabbit" or "running very fast."

The first DAT was marketed and sold as a 10-horsepower runabout. Another version, referred to as "datson" or "son of dat," was a two-seater sports car produced in 1918. One year later, Jitsuyo Jidosha Seizo Company, another Nissan predecessor, was founded in Osaka. Kwaishinsha and Jitsuyo Jidosha Seizo combined in 1926 to establish the Dat Jidosha Seizo Company. Five years later, the Tobata Imaon Company, an automotive parts manufacturer, purchased controlling interest in the company. Tobata Imaon's objective was to mass-produce

products that would be competitive in quality and price with foreign automobiles.

In 1932, "Datson" became "Datsun," thus associating it with the ancient Japanese sun symbol. The manufacturing and sale of Datsun cars was controlled by the Jidosha Seizo Company, established in Yokohama through a joint venture between Nihon Sangyo Company and Tobata Imaon. In 1934 the company changed its name to Nissan, and one year later the operation of Nissan's first integrated automobile factory began in Yokohama under the technical guidance of American industrial engineers.

However, Datsun cars were not selling as well as expected in Japan. Major American automobile manufacturers, such as General Motors Corporation and the Ford Motor Company, had established assembly plants in Japan during this time. These companies dominated the automobile market in Japan for 10 years, while foreign companies were discouraged from exporting to the United States by the Great Depression of 1929.

With the advent of World War II in 1941, Nissan's efforts were directed toward military production. During wartime, the Japanese government ordered the motor industry to halt production of passenger cars and instead produce much-needed trucks. After World War II, the Japanese auto industry had to be completely re-created. Technical assistance contracts were established with foreign firms such as Renault, Hillman, and Willys-Overland. In 1952 Nissan reached a license agreement with the United Kingdom's Austin Motor Company Ltd. With American technical assistance and improved steel and parts from Japan, Nissan became capable of producing small, efficient cars, which later provided the company with a marketing advantage in the United States.

The U.S. market was growing, but very gradually. Nonetheless, Nissan felt that Americans needed low-priced economy cars, perhaps as a second family car. Surveys of the American auto industry encouraged Nissan to display its cars at the Imported Motor Car Show in Los Angeles. The exhibition was noticed by *Business Week,* but as an analyst wrote in 1957, "With over 50 foreign car makers already on sale here, the Japanese auto industry isn't likely to carve out a big slice of the U.S. market for itself."

Nissan considered this criticism as it struggled to improve domestic sales. Small-scale production resulted in high unit costs and high prices. In fact, a large percentage of Datsun cars were sold to Japanese taxi companies. Yet Kawamata, the company's new and ambitious president, was determined to increase exports to the United States. Kawamata noted two principal reasons for his focus on exports: "Increased sales to the U.S.A. would give Nissan more prestige and credit in the domestic markets as well as other areas and a further price cut is possible through mass producing export cars."

By 1958 Nissan had contracted with two U.S. distributors, Woolverton Motors of North Hollywood, California, and Chester G. Luby of Forest Hills, New York. However, sales did not improve as quickly as Nissan had hoped. As a result, Nissan sent two representatives to the United States in order to help increase sales: Soichi Kawazoe, an engineer and former employee of GM and Ford; and Yutaka Katayama, an advertising and sales promotion executive. Each identified a need for the development of a new company to sell and service Datsuns in America. By 1960 Nissan Motor Company U.S.A. had 18 employees, 60 dealers, and a sales total of 1,640 cars and trucks. The success of the Datsun pickup truck in the U.S. market encouraged new dealerships.

Datsun assembly plants were built in Mexico and Peru during the 1960s. In 1966 Nissan merged with the Prince Motor Company Ltd., and two years later Datsun passenger cars began production in Australia. During the year of 1969 cumulative vehicle exports reached one million units. This was a result of Katayama and Kawazoe's efforts to teach Japanese manufacturers to build automobiles comparable to American cars. This meant developing mechanical similarities and engine capacities that could keep up with American traffic.

The introduction of the Datsun 240Z marked the debut of foreign sports cars in the American market. Datsun began to receive good reviews from automotive publications in the United States, and sales began to improve. Also at this time, the first robotics were installed in Nissan factories to help increase production. In 1970, Japan launched its first satellite on a Nissan rocket.

Only five years later, Nissan export sales reached $5 million. But allegations surfaced that Nissan U.S.A. was "pressuring and restricting its dealers in various ways: requiring them to sell at list prices, limiting their ability to discount, enforcing territorial limitations," according to author John B. Rae. In 1973 Nissan U.S.A. agreed to abide by a decree issued from the U.S. Department of Justice that prohibited it from engaging in such activities.

The 1970s marked a slump in the Japanese auto industry as a result of the oil crisis. Gasoline prices started to increase, and then a number of other difficulties arose. American President Richard Nixon devalued the dollar and announced an import surcharge: transportation prices went up and export control was lacking. To overcome these problems, Nissan U.S.A. brought in Chuck King, a 19-year veteran of the auto industry, to improve management, correct billing errors, and minimize transportation damages. As a result, sales continued to increase with the help of Nissan's latest model, the Datsun 210 "Honeybee," which was capable of travelling 41 miles on one gallon of gas.

In 1976 the company began the production of motorboats. During this time, the modification of the Datsun model to American styling also began. Additions included sophisticated detailing, roof racks, and air conditioning. The new styling of the Datsun automobiles was highlighted with the introduction of the 1980 model 200SX.

During the 1980s Nissan established production facilities in Italy, Spain, West Germany, and the United Kingdom. An aerospace cooperative agreement with Martin Marietta Corporation was also concluded, and the Nissan CUE-X and MID4 prototypes were introduced. In 1981, the company began the long and costly process of changing its name from Datsun to Nissan in the American market.

The new generation of Nissan automobiles included high-performance luxury sedans. They featured electronic control, vari-

able split four-wheel drive, four-wheel steering, an "intelligent" engine, a satellite navigation system, as well as other technological innovations. Clearly, the management of Nissan had made a commitment to increase expenditures for research and development. In 1986 Nissan reported that the company's budget for research and development reached ¥170 billion, or 4.5 percent of net sales.

During the late 1980s, Nissan evaluated future consumer trends. From this analysis, Nissan predicted consumers would prefer a car with high performance, high speed, innovative styling, and versatile options. All of these factors were taken into account to form "a clear image of the car in the environment in which it will be used," said Yukio Miyamori, a director of Nissan. Cultural differences were also considered in this evaluation. One result of this extensive market analysis was the company's 1989 introduction of its Infiniti line of luxury automobiles.

The use of robotics and computer-aided design and manufacturing reduced the time required for computations on aerodynamics, combustion, noise, and vibration characteristics, enabling Nissan to have an advantage in both the domestic and foreign markets. The strategy of Nissan's management during the late 1980s was to improve the company's productivity and thus increase future competitiveness.

By the start of the next decade, however, Nissan's fortunes began to decline. Profits and sales dropped, quelling hopes that the 1990s would be as lucrative as the 1980s. Nissan was not alone in its backward tumble, however: each of the major Japanese car makers suffered damaging blows as the decade began. The yen's value rose rapidly against the dollar, which crimped U.S. sales and created a substantial price disparity between Japanese and American cars. At the same time, America's three largest automobile manufacturers showed a surprising resurgence during the early 1990s. According to some observers, Japanese manufacturers had grown complacent after recording prolific gains to surpass U.S. manufacturers. In the more cost-conscious 1990s, they allowed the price of their products to rise just as U.S. manufacturers reduced costs, improved efficiency, and offered more innovative products.

In addition, the global recession that sent many national economies into a tailspin in the early 1990s caught Nissan with its resources thinly stretched as a result of its bid to unseat its largest Japanese rival, Toyota Motor Corporation. Toyota, much larger than Nissan and possessing deeper financial pockets, was better positioned to sustain the losses incurred from the global economic downturn. Consequently, Nissan entered its ninth decade of operation facing formidable obstacles.

The first financial decline came in 1991, when the company's consolidated operating profit plummeted 64.3 percent to ¥125 billion ($886 million). Six months later, Nissan registered its first pre-tax loss since becoming a publicly traded company in 1951—¥14.2 billion during the first half of 1992. The losses mounted in the next two years, growing to ¥108.1 billion in 1993 and ¥202.4 billion by 1994, or nearly $2 billion. To arrest the precipitous drop in company profits, Nissan's management introduced various cost-cutting measures—such as reducing its materials and manufacturing costs—which saved the company roughly $1.5 billion in 1993, with an additional $1.15 billion savings expected to be realized in 1994. But for Japan's second-largest car manufacturer and the world's fifth-largest, the road ahead still loomed ominously.

As the company prepared for the remainder of the 1990s, however, there were some positive signs to inspire hope for the future. Nissan's 1993 sales increased nearly 20 percent, vaulting the car maker past Honda Motor Company to reclaim the number-two ranking in import sales to the all-important U.S. market. Much of this gain was attributable to robust sales of the Nissan Altima, a replacement for its Stanza model, which was marketed in the United States as a small luxury sedan priced under $13,000. To the joy of Nissan's management, however, the Altima was typically purchased with various options added on, giving the company an additional $2,000 to $3,000 per car. Buoyed by the success of the Altima and encouraged by strong sales of its Quest minivan, Nissan entered the mid-1990s dispirited by its losses, but aspiring toward a profitable future.

Principal Subsidiaries: Nissan Aichi Machine Industry Co., Ltd.; Atsugi Motor Parts Co., Ltd.; Ikeda Bussan Co., Ltd.; Japan Automatic Transmissions Co., Ltd.; Japan Electronic Control Systems Co., Ltd.; Kanto Seiki Co., Ltd.; Kiriu Machine Mfg. Co., Ltd.; NDC Co., Ltd.; Nihon Radiator Co., Ltd.; Nissan Credit Corp.; Nissan Diesel Motor Co., Ltd.; Nissan Koki Co., Ltd.; Nissan Motor Car Carrier Co., Ltd.; Nissan Motorist Service Co., Ltd.; Nissan Motor Sales Co., Ltd.; Nissan Real Estate Co., Ltd.; Nissan Rikuso Co., Ltd.; Nissan Shatai Co., Ltd.; Nissan Trading Co., Ltd.; Rhythm Motor Parts Mfg. Co., Ltd., Tokyo Sokuhan Co., Ltd.; Tsuchiya Mfg. Co., Ltd.; Yokohama Transportation Co., Ltd.

Further Reading:

Chang, C.S., *The Japanese Auto Industry and the U.S. Market,* New York: Praeger, 1981.

Crate, James R., ''Japan's Big Five Atone for Sins of Late '80s: Drive to Cut Costs Focuses on Proliferation of Parts,'' *Automotive News,* May 17, 1993, p. 19.

Crate, ''Nissan Posts $273 Million Loss,'' *Automotive News,* November 1, 1993, p. 8.

Gross, Ken, ''Doomed to Niches?,'' *Automotive Industries,* May 1992, p. 13.

Gross, ''Learning from Mistakes,'' *Automotive Industries,* March 1994, p. 64.

Johnson, Richard, ''Nissan Loss Widens to Nearly $2 Billion,'' *Automotive News,* June 6, 1994, p. 6.

Maskery, Mary Ann, ''Nissan Gets First Taste of Red Ink,'' *Automotive News,* November 9, 1992, p. 6.

Miller, Karen Lowry, and Larry Armstrong, ''Will Nissan Get It Right This Time? After a Decade of Trouble, the Carmaker Is Making Major Changes,'' *Business Week,* April 20, 1992, p. 82.

''Nissan Earnings Dive 64.3 Percent,'' *Automotive News,* June 3, 1991, p. 4.

Sobel, Robert, *Car Wars: The Untold Story,* New York: Dutton, 1984.

—updated by Jeffrey L. Covell

Noble Affiliates, Inc.

110 West Broadway
P. O. Box 1967
Ardmore, Oklahoma 73402
U.S.A.
(405) 223-4110
Fax: (405) 221-1210

Public Company
Incorporated: 1969
Employees: 518
Sales: $286.5 million
Stock Exchanges: New York
SICs: 1311 Crude Petroleum & Natural Gas

One of the leading independent energy companies in the United States, Noble Affiliates, Inc. was involved in oil and gas exploration, development, and production through its principal subsidiary, Samedan Oil Corporation. Noble Affiliates' predecessor began drilling for oil in the United States during the 1920s, then, as the company grew, it expanded its operations into Canada, Tunisia, Equatorial Guinea, and Indonesia. By 1993, the company produced more than 19,000 barrels of oil per day and over 200 million cubic feet of natural gas per day.

The roots of Noble Affiliates stretch back to the 1880s, when two brothers, Sam and Ed Noble, moved to Ardmore, Indian Territory, roughly two decades before the region surrounding Ardmore entered the Union as the state of Oklahoma. Their relocation to Ardmore and the business they opened there, a hardware store, eventually led to the first association of oil with the Noble name, a relationship that would exist for much of the twentieth century, but one that did not begin until approximately 40 years after the two brothers opened their store.

In fact, Sam and Ed Noble would never know of the importance of oil to their family name. Shortly before they died, the two brothers received a farm as payment for a debt to their hardware store, a farm they left to their two widows, Hattie and Eva Noble. The farm itself represented little value, but when oil was discovered on the land its value soared exponentially and provided inspiration for Hattie's son, Lloyd Noble, then a college student, to enter the oil drilling business.

Lloyd Noble formed a partnership with a young oil driller named Arthur Olson and, after convincing Hattie Noble to co-

sign a $20,000 loan, the two partners purchased a used, steam-powered drilling rig for $14,000. Noble and Olson drilled their first well in 1921 for the Carter Oil Company, which later became part of Exxon Corporation, on the company's leased land in Carter County, Oklahoma. After two unprofitable years, their fledgling business began to prosper, thriving in the robust conditions characterizing the oil drilling business in Southern Oklahoma during the 1920s, and enabling the two partners to begin drilling in Alberta, Canada, where they became one of the first oil drillers in the Turner Valley Field in 1928. By the end of the decade, after accumulating 38 oil rigs, Noble and Olson decided to dissolve their partnership and form separate oil drilling companies, with each taking their share of the partnership's equipment. Their employees were allowed to select which man they wanted to work for, and the two former partners, who would soon be rivals, set out on their own, nine years after they had entered the oil drilling business.

For Lloyd Noble, the 1930s would be a decade of expansion for his company, Noble Drilling Corporation, and a decade that saw Noble broaden the scope of his operations beyond oil drilling to oil production. First Noble focused on increasing the geographic range of his drilling operations and began contracting for oil fields outside of southern Oklahoma in west and east Texas and in New Mexico, the origins of the company's West Texas division. In 1931, one year after Noble and Olson went their separate ways, an oil rig was moved to Worland, Wyoming, the company's first entrance into the Rocky Mountain region, and later that same year a rig was established in Bridger, Montana, where Noble developed a recently discovered oil field for the Ohio Oil Company. The following year oil rigs were established near Corpus Christi and Houston, Texas, and in 1933 the company's first operation on water was begun in southern Texas, where Noble's drilling equipment drilled a wildcat well for the Amerada Petroleum Company.

Further expansion followed throughout the decade, including a move into southern Louisiana in 1935 and the establishment of Noble's first rig on a submersible drilling barge in 1937, but earlier in the decade Noble had diversified into oil production to complement his interests as a drilling contractor and to operate the producing properties he had acquired during his first decade in the oil business. In 1932, Noble formed a second company, naming it Samedan Oil Corporation in tribute to his three children, Sam, Ed, and Ann. Samedan first began operating in Carter County, Oklahoma, the same county in which Noble and Olson had drilled their first well, in an oil field called Wildcat Jim. Production of other wells soon followed, when Samedan's presence was extended into Texas, and several other producing companies were formed and then either sold or merged into Samedan.

With these two companies, Noble Drilling Corporation and Samedan Oil Corporation, combined with the producing properties he had acquired, Lloyd Noble had created a small yet viable oil company, an independent in a market dominated by much larger oil concerns. The company prospered throughout the 1930s and into the 1940s. Noble's death in 1950 devolved ownership of much of Noble Drilling's and Samedan's stock, as well as all of Noble's producing properties, to The Samuel Roberts Noble Foundation, a charitable foundation Lloyd Noble had formed several years before his death and named in memory of his father.

After Noble's death, the two companies operated as wholly owned subsidiaries of the Noble Foundation, with the producing properties organized as a separate collection of assets. In accordance with tax law changes, the producing properties were transferred to Samedan in 1954, which bolstered Samedan's revenues and enabled the company to begin prospecting for oil and gas, an activity Samedan engaged in vigorously during the 1950s. Two years before the producing properties were transferred to Samedan, an exploration and production office was opened in Midland, Texas, and then three additional offices were established later in the decade, one in Lafayette, Louisiana, in 1955, and one each in Oklahoma City, Oklahoma, and Calgary, Canada, in 1958.

By the end of the 1950s, the properties controlled by the Noble Foundation were involved in oil and gas exploration, drilling, and production, giving the trustees of the foundation the synergism it needed to compete against much larger competitors. The complementary relationship between Noble Drilling and Samedan was strengthened in 1957, when the Noble Foundation purchased an interest in an oil field trucking company named B.F. Walker, Inc. that provided the Noble Foundation with a fleet of vehicles to move the drilling and production equipment utilized by Noble Drilling and Samedan. Three years later, B.F. Walker's remaining stock was purchased when the trucking company's founder retired, giving the Noble Foundation three subsidiary companies to chart its future in the oil industry.

As the foundation entered the 1960s, the oil industry was changing, and unfortunately for those parties with investments in it, change during this decade meant a change for the worse. Depressed oil and gas prices began to have a similar effect on the industry, signaling the end of the oil boom years during which Noble Drilling and Samedan had emerged and prospered. From 1955 to 1971 the number of active rotary drilling rigs in the country dropped by more than 60 percent, plummeting from 2,686 to 976, which hampered growth for many oil companies and particularly for small independent companies like Noble Drilling and Samedan. But Noble Drilling and Samedan enjoyed several benefits its larger competitors did not, the first being its size and the manner in which the companies operated. Division managers controlled, to a large extent, the field operations and exploration activities for both companies, giving Noble Drilling and Samedan enviable agility during a period when the ability to halt, relocate, or start operations quickly was crucial. Both companies also benefitted from their unique position as subsidiaries of a charitable organization, which allowed them to retain their equipment and continue exploration activities despite economic pressures that otherwise would have forced them to liquidate certain assets. Aside from the revenues generated by Noble Drilling, Samedan, and B.F. Walker, the Noble Foundation possessed sufficient producing assets to remain solvent without contributions from its oil interests, enabling each of the three oil and gas subsidiaries to withstand the debilitative effects of a depressed oil and gas market.

The 1960s, however, would be the last decade the three companies would be organized as such. In 1969, a tax reform provision passed by the U.S. Congress stipulated that charitable foundations could no longer own more than 20 percent of any corporation or commercial enterprise, which left the trustees of the Noble Foundation with two choices: either divest themselves completely of Noble Drilling, Samedan, and B.F. Walker, or combine their assets and then sell 80 percent of the stock to the public. The trustees opted for the latter, and formed Noble Affiliates, Inc. later that year, with the first public stock offering following three years later.

The Noble Foundation gradually relinquished the majority of its ownership of the three companies throughout the 1970s, a decade during which Noble Affiliates' annual revenues leaped from $38 million to $214 million, more than quintupling as each of the three subsidiary companies recorded encouraging physical and financial growth. Noble Drilling purchased 18 oil rigs during the decade, and Samedan made significant oil and gas discoveries, particularly in Texas, Oklahoma, and Alberta, Canada. Its offshore exploration activities, which began in 1968 in the Gulf of Mexico near Galveston, Texas, were strengthened considerably during the decade, extending the company's offshore presence from Louisiana to Corpus Christi, Texas. To support the company's larger geographic area of service, B.F. Walker purchased two trucking companies during the decade, which combined added 16 mideastern states and 16 western states to the company's licensed area of operation.

Although each of the companies demonstrated strong performances during the 1970s (B.F. Walker generated nearly as much revenue by itself at the end of the decade as all three companies had at the beginning of the decade), it would be the last decade all three operated under Noble Affiliates' purview. Influenced by changing conditions in the oil industry that made drilling increasingly expensive, Noble Affiliates' management decided to steer the company away from a diversified stake in the oil market and to concentrate primarily on its investments in oil and gas exploration and production. For Noble Drilling and B.F. Walker this decision appeared to portend the end of their existence as Noble Affiliate subsidiaries, as the parent company began to funnel the bulk of its resources toward Samedan. In 1983, after allocating approximately 90 percent of its capital expenditures to Samedan, Noble Affiliates derived nearly 70 percent of its revenues from oil and gas operations and the balance from contract drilling and its trucking operations. This was a significant shift in the parent company's distribution of capital outlays, which for the ten previous years had been roughly a 60 percent to 40 percent split between Samedan and Noble Drilling, and was indicative of the course Noble Affiliates would pursue in the future.

B.F. Walker was sold late that year, in December 1983, and Noble Drilling was spun-off to shareholders two years later, leaving Noble Affiliates with one principal subsidiary and one business line to pursue. After shedding Noble Drilling, the company strengthened its oil and gas reserves in 1986 by purchasing domestic oil and gas properties from eight subsidiaries of Texas Eastern Corporation for $176 million. These acquisitions helped lift Noble Affiliates' oil reserves ten percent and its natural gas reserves 23 percent for the year. Additional oil and gas acquisitions followed throughout the late 1980s, as the company endeavored to increase its stake in oil and gas exploration after dividing its energies and funds for the bulk of its existence. In 1988, Noble Affiliates entered into a joint venture with Apache Corp. to acquire Natural Gas Clearinghouse, an independent gas marketing company that sold roughly 2 billion cubic feet of gas per day at the time of the acquisition. The joint venture with Apache gave Noble Affiliates, through one if its subsidiaries, Noble Natural Gas, Inc., a 50 percent interest in Natural Gas Clearinghouse and a significant boost to the company's natural gas assets. After strengthening this segment of its business, Noble Affiliates increased its investments in oil the following year, when Samedan purchased an interest in four producing properties in the Gulf of Mexico for $8.1 million.

Noble Affiliates acquired interests in other oil and gas fields, purchasing domestic onshore and offshore properties as well as international properties located in Equatorial Guinea, Indonesia, and Tunisia, where the company began exploration activities during the 1970s. Part of the company's reason to concentrate on oil and gas exploration and production rather than drilling was the relatively lower costs involved in exploration and production. This was particularly true in the early 1990s, when some of the larger oil concerns, such as Amoco and Chevron, began selling domestic assets to finance international exploration. Operating as a medium-size, independent company, Noble Affiliates was able to strategically acquire such properties and bolster its holdings in natural gas and oil exploration and production.

Buoyed by this trend in the oil industry during the early 1990s, Noble Affiliates in 1993 eclipsed, for the first time, its revenue total recorded in 1984, the year before the Noble Drilling divestiture. After spinning-off Noble Drilling, Noble Affiliate's sales total fell from $270 million to $170 million, then slipped the following year, in 1986, to $122 million. From this level, the lowest in a decade, the company effected a slow recovery, fueled largely by the series of oil and gas acquisitions during the late 1980s, and reached $278 million by 1993, a year that also marked a substantial increase in the company's oil and gas reserves. The oil and gas reserves increase was the largest in the company's history. The company's natural gas reserves increased from 372.2 billion cubic feet to 691.5 billion cubic feet during the year and oil reserves jumped from 47.4 million barrels to 73 million barrels.

With these substantially improved reserves, Noble Affiliates entered the mid-1990s with plans to continue acquiring additional gas oil properties. The company spent $515 million on such acquisitions during 1993 and maintained sufficient cash balances to fund $100 million worth of acquisitions in 1994. As it charted its future, Noble Affiliates looked to increase its oil and gas reserves and production totals principally in the major basins of the Gulf of Mexico.

Principal Subsidiaries: Samedan Oil Corp.; Samedan Oil of Canada, Inc.; Samedan North Sea, Inc.; Samedan Oil of Indonesia, Inc.; Samedan Pipeline Corporation.

Further Reading:

Dorfman, John R., ''Oil Explorers' Pump Primed by Investors,'' *Wall Street Journal,* January 3, 1991, p. C1.
''Noble Affiliates, Apache Deal,'' *Wall Street Journal,* May 19, 1989, p. A7C.
''Noble Affiliates Inc.,'' *Wall Street Journal,* June 23, 1993, p. B4.
''Noble Affiliates, Inc.,'' *Wall Street Transcript,* October 29, 1984, p. 75,726.
''Noble Affiliates Reserves Rose,'' *Wall Street Journal,* February 9, 1987, p. 2.
Nully, Peter, ''Cashing In on the Big Oil Auction,'' *Fortune,* November 30, 1992, p. 30.
Solomon, Caleb, ''Two Oil Firms Weigh Buying U.S. Reserves,'' *Wall Street Journal,* March 19, 1992, p. A5.

—Jeffrey L. Covell

Nordson Corporation

28601 Clemens Road
Westlake, Ohio 44145
U.S.A.
(216) 892-1580
Fax: (216) 892-9507

Public Company
Incorporated: 1935 as U.S. Automatic Corporation
Employees: 3,281
Sales: $506.7 million
Stock Exchanges: NASDAQ
SICs: 3569 General Industrial Machinery, Not Elsewhere
    Classified

Nordson Corporation is a leading manufacturer of machines that apply liquid and powder coatings, adhesives, and sealants to a wide variety of consumer and industrial products during the manufacturing process. Nordson-built machines impact daily life around the world by making possible such products as pressure-sensitive labels, gender-specific diapers, sturdy cartons and boxes, and noncorrosive food and beverage cans. Nordson systems also bond together and apply finishes to automotive, appliance, furniture, and computer components. The company not only manufactures the machinery and equipment, but also develops the software and related control technologies needed to synthesize its equipment and systems with customers' operations. Nearly 60 percent of the company's annual sales come from exports through its 29 subsidiaries outside the United States, which market Nordson products to virtually every country in the world.

The firm traces its history to 1909 and the founding of U.S. Automatic Company in Amherst, Ohio, near Cleveland. The predecessor firm manufactured high-volume, low-cost screw machine parts for the emerging automobile industry. When the company went bankrupt in 1929, Walter G. Nord acquired control and in 1935 reorganized it as U.S. Automatic Corporation, shifting production emphasis to lower-volume precision parts, which proved vital to the U.S. army forces during World War II. In the years following the war, Walter and his sons, Eric Nord and Evan Nord, acquired patents for the "hot airless" method of applying paint, coatings, and adhesives, in which machines sprayed materials through tiny openings at high pressure.

Walter's sons, Eric, who joined the firm in 1939 after earning a degree in mechanical engineering from Case Institute of Technology, and Evan, formed the Nordson Division of U.S. Automatic in 1954 to produce and market airless spray equipment. Evan ran the operations of the businesses, while Eric searched for the proprietary technology of the airless spray equipment, which became the basis of the new Nordson Division.

The Nordson Division expanded into thermoplastic adhesion in the early 1960s. Machines developed during this period applied hot glue for such packaging as cartons and boxes as well as product assembly. Nordson soon emerged as a leader in this industry, which eventually became one of its primary businesses. The subsidiary grew quickly during the early years of the decade, establishing European marketing branches and absorbing parent U.S. Automatic in 1966. Walter G. Nord died the following year, leaving a legacy of beneficence in the Nordson Foundation, which was endowed with five percent of the corporation's pretax earnings.

Eric Nord advanced to the company's presidency, a position he occupied for 20 years. Eric Nord later was to be credited with guiding the company's growth and providing an example of innovative thinking; before he retired, Nord was granted more than 25 patents for inventions. One noteworthy Nordson innovation of the late 1960s was a device that recovered and recycled over-sprayed powder coatings, thereby eliminating solid waste and pollutants while simultaneously saving customers' money.

Nordson established a foothold in the burgeoning Japanese manufacturing market with the founding of Nordson K.K. in 1969 to distribute American-made machinery. Over the course of the 1970s, the corporation also increased its domestic packaging operations through the purchase of Domain Industries Inc., a manufacturer of packaging machinery, and the acquisition of a controlling interest in American Packaging Corporation, producer of Ampak brand flexible film and die-cutting equipment. Technological advances in hot melt adhesives and other thermoplastic compounds expanded Nordson's client base during the late 1970s and early 1980s. Soon the company's devices were modified for many applications within the automotive, off-road equipment, appliance, and woodworking industries for joining, caulking, and sealing.

Not all of Nordson's ventures were successful, however. In 1978, the company began manufacturing industrial robots. These spray-painting machines, which were less costly than human labor and could work in hazardous environments, were expected to become a high-growth venture. However, after six years of intense marketing, including a 1982 agreement with two Japanese firms, the program was dropped due to the industry's high rate of obsolescence.

A shift in management in the early 1980s brought public speculation that Nordson was a candidate for takeover. In 1982, James E. Taylor advanced to the presidency and chief executive office, while Eric Nord retired from day-to-day operations, retaining his seat at the head of the board of directors. Taylor divested two non-core businesses to focus corporate energies on what had become Nordson's most significant and promising businesses—packaging and assembly equipment to apply adhesives, sealants, caulking, and other thermoplastic substances, and liquid and powder coating technology. By 1984, the company had over $30 million in cash and had reportedly been plied with several takeover and/or merger proposals. Although the majority of Nordson's stock was very closely held—the Nord family owned 40 percent, the Nordson Foundation retained ten percent, and current and former managers held another ten percent—shareholders instituted anti-takeover measures.

Speculation increased in 1985, when Taylor resigned, bringing Eric Nord back to the offices of president and CEO. Taylor and Nordson cited "philosophical differences" for the departure; while Taylor preferred a centralized management scheme, Nord and the board of directors feared that tight controls would stifle the creativity necessary for the company to maintain its technological lead. Sales flattened out at $140 million in 1984 and 1985, while profits declined during the last year of Taylor's tenure from $11.3 million to $9.7 million.

After a six-month search, Nordson offered the top positions to William P. Madar, a 47-year-old executive of Standard Oil Co. (later renamed B.P. America, Inc.). Leaving a 20-year career at Standard Oil to capitalize on Nordson's untapped potential, Madar brought a new management style to the company, which he characterized as "professorial," that encouraged problem-solving through the Socratic method: Madar preferred not to give specific instructions, but to ask questions that would allow employees to arrive at their own conclusions. This corporate culture gave employees—over half of whom lived outside North America—freedom to customize the company's systems to accommodate local clients' needs.

Madar also moved immediately to revitalize his new employer, commissioning a 3-R (resource review and reallocation) study. The restructuring recommended in the review included decentralization through the creation of four geographical sales and service divisions for North America, Japan, Pacific/South America (including Brazil, China, and India), and Europe. A core manufacturing and product development division retained responsibility for product lines. Madar removed redundant management tiers and formed a business-opportunity group to seek out new applications for existing technologies.

In 1987, the company built a new, $9 million laboratory for product engineering and development near its Amherst headquarters and committed an average of five percent of sales annually to research and development. The investments kept Nordson ahead of its competition and marketplace needs through technology developments. Edward B. Keaney, an analyst with Newhard, Cook & Co. of St. Louis, told the *Cleveland Plain Dealer* in May 1988 that Nordson "tends to be the technology leader." This edge proved critical to the company's financial survival; had Nordson rested on its laurels, it would have quickly lost business. An estimated 20 percent of annual sales came from three- to four-year-old products, and by the late 1980s, Nordson employees held over 1,000 patents and patent applications worldwide.

In interviews, Madar often uses a "leap frog" analogy to describe Nordson's development of new products, likening the application of existing technologies to new, but closely related markets to "a frog leaping from one lily pad to the next." New markets, or lily pads, in turn, become the foundation from which to make another technological leap. For example, the company adapted an electrostatic powder painting technique, commonly used on household appliances and other metal parts, to the strategic application of a superabsorbent polymer powder to gender-specific disposable diapers. Similarly, with different technology, Nordson applies high-speed liquid-paint spraying techniques, generally used to spray adhesives on food cans, to computer circuit boards. The precisely applied coatings protect hundreds of delicate circuits from moisture and dirt each minute. By making such incremental leaps, Nordson augments its knowledge and technology while keeping financial risks in check.

In 1987, the company introduced a new adhesive process that impregnated a standard adhesive with an inert gas to make a sealant that foamed as it was applied. The compound reduced the amount of glue needed and thereby lessened manufacturing costs. Nordson customers who purchased the new machines could expect to recover their costs within two years.

The results of Madar's restructuring were virtually immediate: his first annual report, in 1986, registered a new sales record of $168.7 million, a 20 percent increase from 1985. Operating profit increased 44 percent, and Nordson's average annual return on equity of 29 percent was double that of the overall capital goods industry. Exports increased even faster than domestic sales, contributing 66 percent of total sales by the early 1990s, with noteworthy growth in Australia, Canada, Europe, the Far East, and South America. Nordson's 1993 decision to obtain ISO 9000 certification from the International Organization of Standardization in Switzerland promised increased global competitiveness as well. By that time, the company had established a manufacturing facility in its European market to better serve that geographic region and had invested in an international communications network.

Value Line responded to the improved results by giving the company's stock its highest recommendation. Annual sales tripled from 1986 to 1993 under Madar's direction, from $140 million to $461 million. Profits jumped 79 percent in fiscal 1987 alone, to $24.7 million, and peaked at $46.6 million in 1994. Nordson recorded its 31st consecutive year of increases in the cash dividend, and noted that "more than 70% of employees are shareholders" in the 1994 annual report. Analyst Timothy P. Burns, of First Boston Corp. in Chicago, ascribed most of Nordson's success during the period to "management's well-crafted strategy, long-term investments, and the ability to find new ways to apply new glues, adhesives and other advanced materials." External factors, including rising automobile and appliance sales, as well as a weak dollar, also contributed to Nordson's early 1990s earnings boom.

Nordson's corporate trademark encouraged prospective clients to "expect *more*." In 1994, company spokespersons indicated that they would expect more from themselves as well, predicting that earnings would more than double by the turn of the 21st century to over $1 billion. CEO Madar and Chairperson Nord prepared for this growth by setting up a "logical succession of leadership" and creating a new layer of management. Moreover, Nordson established the position of executive vice-president and chief operating officer, which was filled by Edward P.

Campbell. Analyst Maureen P. Lentz, of Roulson Research Corp. in Cleveland, told the *Cleveland Plain Dealer* that Nordson's plans to double sales in five years were "do-able . . . because of the recovery in overseas markets." The company also implemented a formal employee empowerment training program in an effort to maintain its innovative edge.

Principal Subsidiaries: Nordson Application Equipment, Inc. (Hong Kong); Nordson Australia Pty., Limited (Australia); Nordson Belgium N.V. (Belgium); Nordson do Brasil Industria y Comercio Ltda.; Nordson Canada, Limited; Nordson Corporation Representative Office (Peoples Republic of China); Nordson Corporation South Asia Regional Office (India); Nordson CS, spol.s.r.o (Czech Republic); Nordson Danmark A/S; Nordson Deutschland GmbH; Nordson Deutschland GmbH Representative Office (Russia); Nordson Engineering GmsbH (Germany); Nordson Finland Oy; Nordson France S.A.; Nordson GesmbH (Austria); Nordson Iberica, S.A. (Spain); Nordson Italia SpA; Nordson K.K. (Japan); Nordson (Malaysia) Sdn. Bhd.; Nordson de Mexico, S.A. de C.V.; Nordson Nederland B.V. (Holland); Nordson Norge A/S (Norway); Nordson Polska Sp.z.o.o.; Nordson Portugal Equipamento Industrial Lda.; Nordson Sang San Limited (South Korea); Nordson S.E. Asia (Pte.) Limited (Singapore); Nordson (Schweiz) AG (Switzerland); Nordson Sverige AB (Sweden); Nordson (U.K.) Limited; Mountaingate Engineering, Inc.; Slautterback Corporation; Electrostatic Technologies, Inc.

Further Reading:

Banks, Howard, "The World's Most Competitive Economy," *Forbes,* March 30, 1992, p. 84.

Benson, Tracy E., "Empowered Employees Sharpen the Edge," *Industry Week,* February 19, 1990, pp. 12–20.

"Eric Nord Is Retiring Today; Inventor, Founder of Firm," *Cleveland Plain Dealer,* October 30, 1983, p. 11E.

Fuller, John, "Production of Robots Spells a New Future for Two Ohio Firms," *Cleveland Plain Dealer,* October 7, 1980, pp. D1, D7.

Gleisser, Marcus, "Nordson Fires 95 in Restructuring," *Cleveland Plain Dealer,* November 13, 1986, p. 1C.

Gerdel, Thomas W., "Nordson's Search Ends in Board Room," *Cleveland Plain Dealer,* February 11, 1986, p. 4D; "Firm Applies Know-How to New, Related Markets," *Cleveland Plain Dealer*, May 7, 1988, 1E, 4-E; "Nordson Adopts Poison Pill Plan," *Cleveland Plain Dealer,* August 27, 1988, p. 1D; "Nordson Emphasizes Creativity," *Cleveland Plain Dealer,* July 11, 1989; "Ten Best in Ohio: Nordson," *Cleveland Plain Dealer,* June 1, 1992, p. 12F; "Nordson Takes Aim at $1 Billion in Sales," *Cleveland Plain Dealer,* March 11, 1994, p. 1C.

Henry, Fran, "William Madar," *Cleveland Plain Dealer,* November 29, 1992, p. 30S.

Karle, Delinda, "No Sale, Nordson Exec Says," *Cleveland Plain Dealer,* July 16, 1985, pp. 1E, 3E; "Nordson to Use Technology to Keep Profits Growing," *Cleveland Plain Dealer,* March 3, 1988, p. 3D.

"Nordson Expects Climb in Fiscal 1984 Results, Says Orders Are Strong," *The Wall Street Journal,* June 7, 1984, p. 55.

Robinson, Duncan, "Exporter Knows When to Hedge," *Journal of Commerce and Commercial,* April 26, 1991, p. 1A, 5A.

Teresko, John, "Running His Own Show," *Industry Week,* May 4, 1987, pp. 47–48.

—April Dougal Gasbarre

North West Water Group plc

Dawson House
Liverpool Road
Great Sankey
Warrington
Cheshire WA5 3LW
United Kingdom
(0925) 234000
Fax: (0925) 233361

Public Company
Incorporated: 1989
Employees: 8,013
Operating Revenues: £924 million
Stock Exchanges: London
SICs: 6711 Holding Companies; 4952 Sewerage Systems;
  4941 Water Supply

North West Water is the largest water and wastewater utility in the United Kingdom, supplying the water needs of 7 million customers. Originally state owned, the company was privatized in 1989 but the core business remains strictly regulated by the government because of its status as a monopoly utility. Since privatization, North West Water has diversified from its core business of water supply and wastewater treatment in the northwest region of England to become involved in a number of long-term foreign initiatives.

The harnessing of water resources in Britain began during the Industrial Revolution, when rapidly expanding urban centers demanded more water than local rivers and lakes could provide. In the northwest region of England, the needs of Manchester and Liverpool were paramount, and most noteworthy early schemes were constructed for the cities. In 1809 a private company, Manchester and Salford Waterworks, built Manchester's first reservoirs at Gorton, but these soon proved inadequate to meet ever-growing demand. Developers looked to the upland regions where water was plentiful: first to the Pennines, where during the mid-nineteenth century a network of reservoirs, flood water channels, and aqueducts was constructed, and then to the Lake District, where in 1885 work began at Thirlmere. Here one of the country's first dams was constructed: 58 feet high, 857 feet long, raising the water level in the lake by 54 feet. At the same time work progressed on an aqueduct to carry the water some 100 miles to the cities. A pioneering achievement of

engineering for its time, the aqueduct was mostly underground, with the water flowing naturally by the force of gravity. Significantly, the aqueduct was also designed to serve the needs of the communities that lay along its route, the first step toward a future regionwide network of water supply.

Following these landmark supply systems, development continued apace. The suppliers, whether private companies or local authorities, required in each instance an act of Parliament to carry out their schemes. Because each proposed development was considered in isolation from the others, a certain amount of inefficiency and confusion ensued, with no attempt to impose a rational, coherent policy on rival developments. As early as 1869 the problems inherent in such an unplanned system were recognized, and the Royal Commission on Water Supply mooted the idea of regional planning. No action was taken, however, until much later, in 1924, when the Ministry of Health, in conjunction with the water suppliers, established Regional Advisory Water Committees to coordinate development and operation.

Successive acts of Parliament solidified the central government's involvement with water supply, culminating in the Water Act of 1973, which put an end to the network of individual suppliers and created 10 regional Water Authorities in England and Wales, leaving only a handful of private water companies intact. The far-reaching act also encompassed river management and sewage disposal, operations that had hitherto been entirely separate from water supply, bringing all three related operations under common management. When the law came into full effect in 1974, well over 200 separate organizations were merged to become the North West Water Authority.

During the 1980s, the Conservative government led by Margaret Thatcher instituted a wide-ranging policy of privatizing public utilities and services: the North West Water Authority became North West Water Group plc in late 1989. Immediately after privatization, the company launched a drive to make its operations more cost effective. Some 1,700 jobs were shed as the company increased its use of advanced computerization and automation. A sophisticated database was developed to hold the region's maps in digitized form. New construction and development made use of computer-aided design. Routine water sampling was automated, with the results transmitted to the Central Laboratory and the Operational Control Centre. Many stations could now be activated or shut down by remote control, as needed.

Although it is privatized, North West Water Ltd. is a utility monopoly and as such remains subject to regulatory control by the government. The rate the company may charge its customers is determined by the Office of Water Services (Ofwat), the industry price regulator. In addition, the company must meet—and prove annually that it has met—both the stipulations of U.K. law and the standards of the European Commission regarding water quality and pollution control. Here the company finds itself in a somewhat difficult position. Constrained in how much it may charge, North West Water is also required by law to invest a considerable amount of capital each year (in 1994 the figure was some 425 million) into improving its infrastructure to comply with public health and environmental standards. Such investment is urgently needed—

and only a drop in the bucket. The company—in common with all the former water authorities—inherited an operation riddled with problems. Much of the region's equipment, so innovative in the water industry's Victorian heyday, has not been replaced or upgraded since then; North West Water has had to struggle with an antiquated system that is in parts both prone to breakdown and unfit to comply with current water quality and environmental standards.

Indeed, the water industry's record of environmental care is an appallingly poor one. Although water pollution has been a problem—and has been recognized as a problem—since the nineteenth century, remarkably little has been done over the years to combat it. Increasing levels of industrial waste and sewage filth led to the Rivers Pollution Prevention Act of 1876. The only antipollution legislation in effect for the better part of a century, the act ostensibly prohibited pollution but was in practice heavily weighted in favor of industrial interests: in effect, industrialists could dump their waste as they pleased simply by claiming there was no alternative. The act was emasculated, too, by administrative confusion; with several authorities responsible for different sections of a single river, a coordinated policy was next to impossible.

Further legislation began to be enacted from the mid-twentieth century, but the continuing poor quality of Britain's waterways is testimony to the lack of political will—and public funds—needed to confront the issue. (To take just one example, 9 out of 33 bathing beaches in the northwest region of England have been deemed by the European Commission, as of 1994, to be unsuitable for swimming.) This was North West Water's inheritance and, as the company itself stresses, it will take years to set the environmental mistakes and neglect of the past even partially right.

Pollution caused by wastewater is one side of the coin, water quality for consumption the other, and here the picture is rather brighter. North West Water takes numerous water samples each day (from treatment works, service reservoirs, and customers' taps) and could claim, in 1993, that over 99 percent of its samples met the water quality standards of the European Commission—the highest percentage yet.

North West Water derives its water mostly from reservoirs and lakes in the Lake District, the Pennines, the Peak District, and, although technically out of its region, North Wales. Water is also taken from rivers and streams and from water sources within rock strata. Underground water is the purest, usually requiring only chlorination to keep it free of bacteria. Water from other sources needs more complex treatment before it can meet the European Commission's standards relating to bacteria, chemicals, taste, odor, and color.

The water found in the northwest tends to be "soft," meaning it contains relatively few dissolved minerals. However, traces of dissolved iron, manganese, and aluminum do occur, and the water needs to be carefully filtered and treated with chemicals to be safe to drink. Another characteristic of water in the region is its mild acidity; such water may dissolve the lead in lead water pipes. Although North West Water ensures that water leaving its treatment works is lead-free, by the time it reaches consumers' taps it can possibly have a high lead content because

the old lead piping, much of which is in consumers' homes, has yet to be fully replaced. The company is able to alleviate this problem to some degree by adjusting acid levels, but it cannot be solved until new piping is installed. (Interestingly, water consumers themselves are complacent; when asked via a North West Water survey if they would voluntarily pay more for water services in order to accelerate needed improvements, the response was resoundingly negative.) Here again, North West Water is held strictly accountable, required to supply its water quality findings to the government-appointed Drinking Water Inspectorate, the local authorities, and the general public via the Drinking Water Register.

North West Water's involvement with environmental issues is not confined to pollution, nor does the company's duty to the public interest stop with the provision of good-quality water. As the largest landowner in the northwest region, North West Water owns some 140,000 acres of England's loveliest and most popular countryside, and must therefore be sensitive to issues of conservation and recreation. North West Water draws extensively on the Lake District, the Pennines, and the Peak District. Some 30 percent of North West Water's supply is taken from the world-famous Lake District, which, like the Peak District, is a national park; the North Pennine region and the Forest of Bowland are designated Areas of Outstanding Natural Beauty.

Historically, water industry development has been treated with deep distrust. The first excursion into the Lake District at Thirlmere, undertaken in 1885 by one of North West Water's predecessors, was greeted by the lake's owners with threats of unspecified but "very severe" measures to be taken against anyone suspected of being an agent of Manchester City Council. Subsequent development at Ullswater and Windermere faced similarly fierce opposition. Today North West Water makes it a policy to try to balance its needs with the conservation of the countryside, the wishes of the locals, the demands of the tourist trade, and the activities of countless recreational users of North West Water land. The company has connections with conservation and environmental groups, such as the British Trust for Conservation Volunteers and the Groundwork Trust. It has set up a special Conservation, Access and Recreation Department, guided by the regulations of the 1989 Code of Practice on Conservation, Access and Recreation. A portion of its annual capital expenditure is allocated for conservation projects, preservation of man-made heritage, and recreational facilities.

Despite the constraints of price controls and government-mandated improvements to its infrastructure, North West Water has returned steadily increasing profits each year since its privatization. Nonetheless, the company, in a bid to escape the regulators and seek a profit in the free market, has pursued a policy of diversification since 1990, just after its privatization. Indeed, all 10 of the former water authorities opted for diversifying, but North West Water has taken a more aggressive approach than most.

The company laid the groundwork for its plans during 1990 and 1991 by acquiring several process engineering and process equipment companies, both domestic and foreign. Acquisition of the U.K.-based Water Engineering and Edwards & Jones, the

U.S. firms Envirex and Wallace & Tiernan, and the Irish company Jones Environmental immediately and impressively expanded North West Water's expertise and experience in the design, manufacture, and installation of water and wastewater treatment equipment and services. Aside from generating business on their own account (just after Envirex was acquired, for example, the subsidiary undertook to supply sludge collection mechanisms to Boston as part of that city's efforts to clean up its harbor), the technological benefits these firms bring to North West Water can be applied both to the company's core domestic business and to its various ventures abroad. Its own regional experience thus bolstered by the know-how of its new subsidiaries, North West Water International undertook in the early 1990s several ambitious foreign projects.

Many countries, whose water and wastewater systems are less developed, are looking to foreign expertise to help them improve existing inadequate methods; most of North West Water's projects abroad involve designing and building a system, operating it for a specified period of time, and then handing it over to local authorities. In Mexico City, North West Water entered into a 10-year contract to provide water services for 5 of the city's 16 municipalities. In Malaysia the company signed a 28-year contract with a local consortium to upgrade the sewerage systems for 43 cities and towns. The Macau project commits North West Water to design, build, and operate a wastewater treatment plant and a sludge processing plant, and in Bangkok the company is installing a wastewater network and treatment facility for some 700,000 customers. Other contracts to design, build, and operate a water treatment plant were negotiated with authorities in Melbourne and in Sydney. With these projects still in their infancy in 1994, North West Water has seen little return as yet on its substantial investment, but the company is confident that foreign diversification will prove a lucrative enterprise.

Research and development is an important aspect of North West Water's operations, as the company aims to be a world leader in water management skills and technology. In 1993 the company acquired Ceramesh and ICI Membranes, developers of advanced membrane technology that helps in the filtering of water and wastewater.

The privatized water companies have been severely criticized by consumer groups because the cost of an average consumer's bill has risen dramatically, along with the company's profits and the earning level of top executives in the industry. North West Water is by no means the worst offender in terms of water bills; at £182 per year in 1994, the charge is the third lowest among the 10 former water authorities. (Still, this compares to a 1989 figure of £147; the increase has well exceeded the rate of inflation.) On the other hand, the salary increase of the then company's chairman is one of the highest of the 10: from £47,000 in 1989 to £338,000 in 1994. The Water Services Association, spokesman for the industry, cites the tremendous burden of financing the necessary improvements to systems and equipment as the reasons for higher bills, an argument rejected by those who feel the consumer should not be made to foot the bill for years of neglect while the industry was in the public sector.

In July of 1994, five years after privatization, Ofwat imposed new and more stringent restrictions on the water companies' profits, limiting price increases to an average of 1 percent above inflation for the 10-year period 1995–2005. It is likely that the companies will now be forced to borrow or drastically cut their operating expenses in order to fund environmental improvements.

In late November of 1994 North West Water announced a proposed worldwide partnership with the Bechtel Corporation. Both companies hope the establishment of this wide ranging business partnership will accomplish the following objectives: to vigorously grow water and waste water operations internationally; to develop a significant presence in the North American water and waste water market; through the proposed sale of North West Water Engineering to Bechtel to develop a world class design resource that will be available to support operations in the United Kingdom and internationally; and to challenge aggressively the cost of the capital works of North West Water's UK Utility.

Inheritor of a faulty and neglected system, North West Water still has far to go in implementing necessary improvements to the infrastructure of its core business. The company faces a challenging remit, as it struggles to balance the conflicts between consumers' pocketbooks and environmental standards—and its own financial imperative to return a profit to its shareholders. At the same time it is meeting further challenges as it seeks to raise its profile in the international arena. North West Water's future will be an interesting—and doubtless controversial—one, as it strives to provide at home and abroad what the company proudly terms "world class water."

Principal Subsidiaries: Consolidated Electric Co., Inc. (U.S.A.); Edwards & Jones Ltd.; Envirex Inc. (U.S.A.); North West Water Australia Pty Ltd.; North West Water Ltd.; North West Water (Malaysia); North West Water International Ltd.; NWW Canada Ltd.; U.S. Water Inc.; Wallace & Tiernan Inc. (U.S.A.); Wallace & Tiernan GmbH; Wallace & Tiernan de Mexico SA de CV; Wallace & Tiernan Pty Ltd.; Wallace & Tiernan Canada, Inc.; Wallace & Tiernan do Brasil SA; NWW Properties; Asdor Ltd.; General Filter Co. (U.S.A.); Edwards & Jones Ltd.; Indah Water Operations Sdn Bhd; Agua de Mexico, SA de CV; North West Water (Thailand).

Further Reading:

"British-Malaysian Venture Bags Sewerage Contract," *Business Times,* April 21, 1993.
"Diversification: The Case Is Still Unproven," *Investors' Chronicle,* May 7, 1993, p. 60.
First Report of Survey of Water Management and Use, Warrington: North West Water Authority, 1978.
Mortished, Carl, "Water Bills Will be Capped for 10 Years," *The Times,* July 29, 1994, p. 1.
Murray, Ian, "Ofwat Plans to Cut Flow of Profits to Water Industry," *The Times,* July 12, 1994, p. 7.
Norman, Margot, "Muddying the Waters," *The Times,* July 12, 1994, p. 16.
"North West Water Pledges to Keep on Cutting Its Costs," *Birmingham Post,* May 26, 1994.
"North West Water Wins Thai Contract," *Independent,* November 2, 1993.

Porter, Elizabeth, *Water Management in England and Wales,* Cambridge Geographical Studies, no. 10, Cambridge University Press, 1978, 178 p.

"Solid Performance for North West Water," *Investor's Chronicle,* May 28, 1993.

"U.K. Company News: Rulings, Relationships and Regulatory Regimes," *Financial Times,* May 25, 1993.

"Water Profits," *Guardian,* May 26, 1994.

"Water Profits under Pressure," *The Times,* July 7, 1994, p. 26.

Wilsher, Peter, "British Water Makes Waves Overseas," *Management Today,* October 1993, pp. 86–90.

"Work Flows in for North West Water," *Yorkshire Post,* May 27, 1993.

—Robin DuBlanc

Northrop Corporation

1840 Century Park East
Los Angeles, California 90067-2199
U.S.A.
(310) 553-6262
Fax: (310) 553-2076

Public Company
Incorporated: 1939
Employees: 29,800
Sales: $5.06 billion
Stock Exchanges: New York
SICs: 3721 Aircraft; 3812 Search and Navigation Equipment;
3761 Guided Missiles and Space Vehicles; 3769 Space
Vehicle Equipment, Not Elsewhere Classified; 3674
Semiconductors and Related Devices

The Northrop Corporation manufactures aircraft, including bombers and fighter jets that are sold to the U.S. military. Having absorbed the Grumman Corporation, another military aircraft provider, in April 1994, Northrop sought to recover revenues in the wake of some lost contracts in the mid- and late 1980s. Northrop's founder, Jack Northrop, worked as an engineer at various aviation companies in the United States for nearly 20 years before starting his own company. Donald Douglas said of Jack Northrop in the 1940s that "every major airplane in the skies today has some Jack Northrop in it." Douglas's observation remains true even in the last quarter of the twentieth century. Northrop's many discoveries and innovations are commonly used in jetliners manufactured by Boeing, McDonnell Douglas, Lockheed, and Airbus, as well as the company he founded.

John Knudsen Northrop was born in 1895. He served in the infantry during World War I and was later transferred to the Army Signal Corps, which was responsible for military aviation. In the Signal Corps he developed a skill for designing aircraft and, as a result, went to work for Donald Douglas in California after the war. As a draftsman, he helped to develop the airplanes that first established Douglas's firm as a leading aircraft manufacturer.

In 1927, he went to work for Allan Lockheed, where he led the development of the Vega, the airplane that made Lockheed a major company. The Vega was one of the first airplanes to have a "stressed skin" construction, meaning that the structural integrity of the outer shell of the aircraft was sufficient to eliminate the need for a weighty frame and struts. The design ushered in a new generation in aircraft design. Amelia Earhart flew a Vega on her solo flight across the Atlantic in 1932.

Northrop formed his own company in 1928, the Avion Corporation. Here he conducted research for the first all-metal aircraft and the "flying wing," a highly efficient boomerang-like aircraft with no fuselage. Two years later, Avion was purchased by Bill Boeing's United Aircraft and Transport Corporation.

Jack Northrop created a second company in 1932 as a division of Douglas Aircraft. Established as a partnership with Douglas, the Northrop Corporation developed an airplane for the Army Air Corps called the Alpha. Similar to the Vega, the Alpha had a single shell, or "monocoque," construction. However, because the plane was made of metal instead of wood, it was more durable and efficient. The Alpha made a new generation of aircraft possible for Douglas, namely the DC-1, DC-2, and the DC-3. Northrop's engineering success with this type of airplane set a new standard for manufacturers; biplanes, double-skin construction, and airplanes made of wood were relegated to the past.

In 1939, Jack Northrop left Douglas to establish his own company called Northrop Aircraft. When World War II erupted, Northrop devoted much of his company's resources to the development of a flying wing bomber. This revolutionary design was greeted with great skepticism. The advantage of the flying wing was that without the "baggage" of a fuselage or tail section, the entire mass of the airplane could be employed to produce the lift needed to keep it aloft. This allowed the possibility of much greater bomb payloads. In 1940, the company flew its first experimental flying wing designated the N-1M.

Northrop later developed the B-35 flying wing bomber and then an improved version called the B-49, which he hoped would be chosen as the primary bomber for the Air Corps. Yet the Army cancelled further development of Northrop's bomber because, as reported by the Army, the B-49 wasn't stable enough in the air and because it required powered rather than manual controls. Northrop, however, revealed shortly before he died that the Army cancelled the B-49 because he refused to merge his company with a manufacturer in Texas. Others have suggested that the Army dropped the flying wing when Northrop refused to allow other government-appointed companies to manufacture his design. Even today the real reason the B-49 was cancelled is not clear.

In spite of the B-49 fiasco, Northrop contributed to the war effort in many other ways. His company built the P-61 night fighter known as the Black Widow. He also established a prosthetics department at his company for dismembered veterans. He even employed disabled servicemen either at the plant or in their hospital beds for regular pay.

In 1952, Jack Northrop retired and relinquished his presidency to O. P. Echols. In 1958, the name of the company was changed to the Northrop Corporation, and the following year Thomas V. Jones took over as president. Jones led the company into a number of diversified subcontracting arrangements. Northrop built numerous airplane and missile parts, electronic control systems, and even became involved in construction.

During the 1950s and 1960s, Northrop produced the F-89 jet interceptor and the curiously named Snark missile system. The company continued to produce its own jet fighters, including the popular F-5 Freedom Fighter. A total of over 2200 F-5s were flown by 30 countries, including Nationalist Taiwan, Iran, and South Korea. The trainer version of the F-5, the T-38, was used by the U.S. Air Force and was also the jet chosen by the Thunderbirds acrobatic flying troupe.

In 1972, Jones made an illegal $50,000 contribution to the re-election campaign of President Nixon; he was fined $200,000 for this indiscretion. The scandal led to an investigation that revealed another more serious impropriety. The company admitted to paying $30 million in bribes to government officials in Indonesia, Iran, and Saudi Arabia, among other countries, in an effort to increase business.

An enraged stockholder sued the company and, as a result, won a settlement that forced Jones to resign his presidency but allowed him to remain as chairman. A further condition of the court ruling was that the board was required to seat four more independent directors, giving the non-management "outsiders" a majority. Into the 1990s, company policy held that 60 percent of the board seats had to be held by non-management personnel.

After the scandal, the company had considerably more trouble selling its products. David Packard, an assistant secretary of defense in the Nixon Administration, invited two finalists to compete for the job of producing America's next fighter jet; Northrop's F-17 Cobra competed against General Dynamics' F-16. Prototypes of the jets flew against each other in dogfights. In the end, the F-16 won the competition. The F-17, however, was later redesigned by Northrop in conjunction with McDonnell Douglas and renamed the F-18 Hornet.

The F-18 Hornet was to be produced in two versions in partnership with McDonnell Douglas. Douglas was the prime contractor for the F-18A carrier-based fighter, and Northrop was the prime contractor for the F-18L, a landbased version. Each company was supposed to serve as the other's subcontractor. A dispute erupted when McDonnell Douglas's F-18A outsold the F-18L, even in countries without aircraft carriers. According to Northrop, the company was being treated unfairly by McDonnell Douglas. The two companies brought legal action against each other, charging violation of their "teaming agreement," one of the first major competitor partnerships since World War II. In April 1985, the court settled in favor of Northrop and awarded the company $50 million. McDonnell Douglas, however, was awarded the prime contractor's role for all future F-18s, with Northrop designated as the subcontractor.

Northrop had another unpleasant experience when the Carter administration called for the development of an advanced fighter jet that was expressly intended for export. Too many foreign countries were showing interest in jets the government considered too technologically sophisticated for mass export. In response, Northrop, at its own expense, developed a less sophisticated fighter called the F-20 Tigershark. It was delivered ahead of schedule and below budget. The problem was that foreign governments still wanted the more sophisticated American jets. Northrop complained that the United States government wasn't promoting the F-20 vigorously enough. The government denied a large sale of F-20s to Taiwan because it was afraid the sale would upset mainland China. In November of 1986 the U.S. Air Force selected General Dynamics' F-16 over the F-20 as its main fighter for defense of the North American continent. As a result, Northrop announced that it would halt further work on the F-20.

Controversy continued to hound Northrop into the late 1980s, particularly Jones, who left the company amid a storm of accusations in 1989, ending his 30-year tenure and leaving the company in a precarious position. Jones had racked up an enormous debt during the decade, banking on the success of two projects, the U.S. Air Force's Advanced Tactical Fighter (ATF) and the B-2 stealth bomber, which represented, by the decade's end, the company's only opportunities for growth. To fund these and other projects, Northrop borrowed heavily, increasing its debt from $215 million in 1984 to an enormous $1.1 billion by 1989.

After Jones's departure, Kent Kresa, a former technology director and engineer, became Northrop's chief executive officer, assuming his post in January 1990. Shortly thereafter, the company plead guilty to 34 counts of fraud for falsifying test data on two military programs and paid a $17 million fine. Then, Kresa began effecting substantial changes in the size and operation of the company to further distance itself from the embarrassments of the 1980s. He replaced nearly half of the company's senior management, reduced the company's debt by selling its headquarters and idle production sites, and intensified the company's lobbying efforts to ensure the success of the ATF and B-2 programs, both of which seemed to be slipping away from Northrop's grip, yet represented the company's only true opportunity to arrest the financial slide begun several years earlier.

In 1991, when hopes for the future of the B-2 program were buoyed by the launching of Operation Desert Storm in the Persian Gulf, disaster again struck Northrop with the announcement by the Pentagon that it had selected Lockheed to manufacture the Air Force's ATF. Air Force Secretary Donald B. Rice noted that both Lockheed's and Northrop's supersonic stealth fighters had performed equally well, but Lockheed received the contract because of its proven track record to control costs and meet production schedules. The announcement represented a severe loss for Northrop, heaping all of the company's hopes for the future on the continued funding of the B-2 program, which accounted for 50 percent of the company's revenues.

Except for the 1992 acquisition of LTV Corp.'s Vought Aircraft Co. in a joint venture with the Carlyle Group, Northrop failed to secure a more viable and stable future for itself in the years following the loss of the AFT project. Support for the B-2 program continued to wane, and Northrop recorded a string of failed acquisitions, including unsuccessful attempts to purchase IBM's Federal Systems Division and General Dynamics' F-16 fighter business. With its debt reduced, however, and $1.3 billion in credit lines, the company continued to look for an acquisition to partly offset its reliance on funding for the B-2 program. An opportunity presented itself in early 1994, when

Northrop and Martin Marietta aggressively pursued Grumman Corporation, an aerospace and electronic surveillance manufacturer with ties to the U.S. Navy. Northrop won the bidding war for Grumman, eclipsing Martin Marietta's price of $1.9 billion with a $2.17 billion offer of its own. In April 1994, Northrop absorbed Grumman, making the combination a weak third in the industry behind Lockheed and McDonnell Douglas, but a stronger, more diversified organization, nevertheless.

With Grumman's experience and contacts with the U.S. Navy complementing Northrop's somewhat embattled relationship with the U.S. Air Force, the consolidation of the two appeared to produce a more stable corporate entity. Before their union, however, both companies were heavily dependent on government-funded contracts to fuel their growth, a characteristic that remained after their consolidation. Consequently, the future growth of Northrop Grumman Corporation rested on the federal government's appetite for military aircraft and hardware.

Principal Subsidiaries: Northrop Services, Inc.; Northrop Worldwide Services, Inc.; Wilcox Electric, Inc.

Further Reading:

Dade, George C., and George Vecsey, *Getting Off the Ground: The Pioneers of Aviation Speak for Themselves,* New York: Dutton, 1979.

Deady, Tim, "Future of Northrop Hangs in Balance of Proposed B-2 Cuts," *Los Angeles Business Journal,* August 6, 1990, p. 1.

"For Northrop, a Shot at Survival," *Business Week,* April 18, 1994, p. 52.

Schine, Eric, "Northrop's Biggest Foe May Have Been Its Past," *Business Week,* May 6, 1991, p. 30.

Wrubel, Robert, "Stay of Execution; Iraq May Save Northrop's B-2 Bomber, but the Defense Contractor's Problems Run Deep," *FW,* September 4, 1990, p. 4.

—updated by Jeffrey L. Covell

Helping Make Life a Little Better.

NovaCare, Inc.

1016 West Ninth Avenue
King of Prussia, Pennsylvania 19406
U.S.A.
(610) 992-7240
Fax: (610) 992-3341

Public Company
Incorporated: 1986 as InSpeech, Inc.
Employees: 4,600
Sales: $37.5 million
Stock Exchanges: New York
SICs: 8099 Health and Allied Services, Not Elsewhere
   Classified

NovaCare, Inc. is America's leading provider of contract rehabilitation services as well as orthotic supports and prosthetics.
The company's largest business group, Contract Services (constituting over two-thirds of revenues), coordinates speech, occupational, and physical therapists with over 1,900 health care
institutions—primarily nursing homes—in 39 states. NovaCare
is the largest non-government employer of rehabilitation therapists, and has a nine percent share of the orthotics and prosthetics field. Having grown dramatically through acquisition
and internal growth, the company reported average annual sales
and earnings increases from 1987 to 1992 of 70.2 percent and
74.6 percent, respectively. In 1993, John H. Foster, chairperson
and CEO, predicted that the firm would reach annual sales of
$3 billion by 1998.

NovaCare was founded in 1976 as InSpeech, Inc. by speech
pathologist Leslie Isenberg. However, the company's phenomenal growth was largely attributable to the direction of John H.
Foster. In 1980, Foster, a medical services entrepreneur,
founded Foster Medical Corp., a home health care services and
equipment company, which he took public two years later. In
1983, Foster sold his namesake venture to Avon Products Inc.
for $240 million in Avon stock. He then used the profits from
that sale to acquire InSpeech, Inc. through his Foster Management Co. venture capital firm in 1985.

Foster then began to make good on his goal of consolidating and
integrating rehabilitation services in America, using InSpeech
as his base. At the time, the highly fragmented industry was
dominated by thousands of local practices that Foster dis-
paragingly called "mom and pop franchises" in an October

1991 *Business Week* article. Foster foresaw the expansion of the
rehabilitation industry, as Americans (especially the "baby
boomer" generation) continued to age and advances in the
treatment of serious injuries resulted in physical impairment
rather than death. InSpeech also lobbied for legislation that
required nursing homes to provide therapy to residents, which
further boosted its potential market.

The rehabilitation industry offered inherently low overhead—
the therapists themselves represented the overhead and the assets—that would be further enhanced through consolidation.
Whereas nursing homes and hospitals often did not have
enough patients to justify employment of a full-time therapist
and suffered high turnover, InSpeech could staff more cost-
effectively than health care institutions, pay its employees
higher salaries on average than they made independently, and
still earn a high return on equity through economies of scale.
Foster also wanted to establish a strong market presence and
become a service sector "category killer."

With the backing of partners, Foster began immediately to
augment InSpeech through acquisitions of occupational and
physical therapy businesses. The May 1986 purchase of Irwin
Lehrhoff Associates gave InSpeech a national presence, and
acquisitions in Arizona, California, Colorado, Florida, Georgia,
Illinois, Minnesota, North Carolina, Virginia, and Wisconsin
followed within the year. Foster took InSpeech public in November and spent the next year integrating his purchases.

During this time, the significance of InSpeech's human assets—
its therapists—came to the fore, as InSpeech suffered a backlash from clinicians who perceived the company's integration
and economization methods as infringements on their ability to
provide quality care. Turnover at InSpeech soared to 56 percent
by the end of 1987, as therapists who could not make the
transition from their relatively autonomous working environment to a tightly controlled corporate culture left. Foster tackled
the crisis by making a survey of staff members throughout the
country. The employees who remained convinced the CEO to
renew and clarify InSpeech's emphasis on professionalism.
After six months and 250 drafts, the firm ratified a 16-page
statement of its "Purpose and Beliefs," which included the oft-
cited credo: "Helping Make Life a Little Better." Foster also
hired C. Arnold Renschler, M.D., a prominent nursing-home
executive, as president. Therapist turnover declined to 20 percent, below the industry's average, and, by fall 1991, the company was hiring about 100 new clinicians each month. In 1989,
Foster changed the company's name to NovaCare, Inc. to reflect
its diversification into occupational and physical therapy and
reorganized the firm into four geographical divisions.

In the early 1990s, NovaCare began to expand into freestanding
outpatient hospitals and community re-entry programs with the
acquisition of Rehab Systems Company's seven facilities in
1991. NovaCare also purchased Orthopedic Services, Inc.
(OSI), the country's largest manufacturer and fitter of custom
braces and prosthetics, in exchange for $265 million of its own
stock. OSI had been, not coincidentally, launched by Foster
Management Co. in 1987 at a cost of $.12 per share. OSI's
initial public offering drew $16 per share in 1990, and Nova-
Care paid the equivalent of $32 per share for it the following
year.

Similar inside transactions followed in 1993 and 1994. Nova-Care acquired Rehabilitation Hospital Corporation of America (RHCA), a chain of five freestanding hospitals and outpatient centers, which it merged into its newly formed NovaCare Medical Rehabilitation Hospital Group in October 1993. The $49 million cash transaction included $19 million in repayments of loans to Foster's partnerships. The following February saw NovaCare's acquisition of RehabClinics Inc., a 181-clinic, publicly traded group of outpatient centers, which was 42 percent controlled by Foster.

In the mid-1990s, Foster faced increasing criticism that his inside deals benefited him and his partners more than NovaCare and its shareholders, about half of whom were institutional investors. However, Foster insisted that Foster Management Co. was an investment arm of NovaCare. In November 1993, he told Janet Novack of *Forbes* that "NovaCare's board has determined that NovaCare is not in the venture capital business." In the same article, he pointed out that "the timing and price of deals between his companies [were] determined by outside directors using outside advisers." Neither critics nor investors could argue with the financial success of the deals: NovaCare's split-adjusted share price had tripled from $4.25 in 1986 to $13 in 1993.

However, some analysts cautioned that profit margins in the entire health care industry would shrink as social, corporate, and governmental pressure to control upwardly spiraling health care costs became vital to the Clinton administration. Moreover, others predicted that high health care earnings were due for a downward cycle, regardless of legislation. Nevertheless, such warnings seemed more applicable to segments of the health care industry other than that represented by NovaCare. The rehabilitation industry appeared limited only by the number of therapists available, as demand for therapy in nursing homes doubled from 1990 to 1992, while the number of clinicians only increased five percent per year. As Foster noted in his 1993 letter to shareholders, the field was "marked by excess demand, with many unserved patients and too few clinical professionals." NovaCare recruited a significant number of the therapists available, signing on a record 2,300 for a 46 percent increase in its clinical contract staff. Being a preferred employer in the field helped shield NovaCare from competition. Moreover, national health care reform remained a matter of debate in the mid-1990s, and rehabilitation and treatment in outpatient facilities like NovaCare's appeared a cost-effective alternative regardless of federal initiatives. Analysts also emphasized the continued growth potential of the rehabilitation market, which remained largely fragmented. NovaCare's reliance on Medicare and Medicaid for 34 percent of revenues put the company at the mercy of regulatory changes but also gave it a preferred position in the event that a single-payer health care system was adopted.

NovaCare has linked its future growth to managed care organizations, referring to them as the "customer of the future." Foster hoped to sell health management organizations (HMOs) a "seamless continuum of care," including hospital, nursing home, and outpatient care, thereby increasing and capturing the HMOs' investment in rehabilitation. Foster and his colleagues hoped to capture six percent of managed care insurers' annual rehabilitation services outlays by being the most cost-effective provider. They reasoned that NovaCare could move patients out of acute care hospitals and into its more efficient rehabilitation hospitals and nursing homes more quickly. Some analysts noted that such large health care groups had already been chosen by half of insured Americans and predicted that they would capture 90 percent of the health insurance market by the turn of the century. Toward that end, NovaCare began to quantify its recovery rates, enabling it to clearly and credibly illustrate its performance to such large clients.

In 1993, with revenues of $539.07 million, Foster predicted that NovaCare would be a highly profitable company with $3 billion in revenues by 1998 and that company stock would sell between $50 and $80 a share. Although compound growth of 40 percent annually would be necessary to reach that goal, this plan allowed for a slower growth rate than the previous five years' 70 percent average annual growth. If his expectations were realized, Foster and NovaCare would increase their net worth considerably; Foster's five percent share in NovaCare was worth about $30 million in 1993, according to *Forbes*.

Principal Subsidiaries: Ask Colorado Health Care Services, P.C.; Cannon & Associates, Inc.; CR Services Corp.; Craig & Ford Rehabilitation Services, Inc.; Farh Services Corp.; FD Capital Corp.; Heartland Rehabilitation, Inc.; Jana B. Mason Therapy Associates, Inc.; Jana B. Mason L.P.T., Inc.; Life Dimensions, Inc.; Life Dimension of California, Inc.; National Rehab Services; Ninth Avenue Capital Corp.; Northwest Rehabilitation, Inc.; NovaCare (Colorado), Inc.; NovaCare, Inc. (PA); NovaCare Management Co.; NovaCare Rehabilitation Agency of Northern California; NovaCare Rehabilitation Agency of Southern California; NovaCare Rehabilitation Agency of Tennessee, Inc.; NovaCare Rehabilitation Agency of Wisconsin, Inc.; NovaCare Services Corp.; NovaCare Speech Therapy & Audiology, Inc.; NovaCare (Texas), Inc.; Irwin Lehrhoff & Associates, Inc. (Illinois); Irwin Lehrhoff & Associates, Inc. (Oregon); Irwin Lehrhoff & Associates, Inc. (Texas); Irwin Lehrhoff & Associates, Inc. (Washington); Marilyn Hawker, Inc.; Marina Professional Services; Mitchell-Zoltowicz-Hotz & Associates, Inc.; Northside Physical Therapy Services, Inc.; Physio West Rehabilitation Services, Inc.; Prather & Associates, Inc.; SG Rehabilitation Agency, Inc.; SG Speech Associates Inc.; Western Rehabilitation Services, Inc.; Easton & Moran Physical Therapy, Inc.; NovaCare (Arizona), Inc.; NovaCare (Illinois), Inc.; Rehabilitation Systems of Illinois, Ltd.; Rehabilitation Systems, Inc.; Rehabilitation Systems Illinois Clinics, Inc.; Rehab Therapy, Inc.; Rehab Systems Co.; Rehab Systems Financial Corp.; Meridian Point Rehabilitation Hospital, Inc.; Arizona Rehabilitation Hospital, Inc.; Tri-State Regional Rehabilitation Hospital, Inc.; Rehabilitation Hospital of North Texas, Inc.; Tucson Regional Rehabilitation Hospital, Inc.; West Virginia Rehabilitation Hospital, Inc.; California Rehabilitation Systems, Inc.; NovaCare Orthotic & Prosthetics, Inc.; Applied Orthotic/Prosthetic Technologies, Inc.; Arizona Therapy Limb & Brace, Inc.; Barnhart Prosthetic & Orthotic Center, Inc.; Burge-Lloyd Surgical Company, Inc.; Coastal Orthopedics, Inc.; Commonwealth Prosthetics & Orthotics, Inc.; Custom Prosthetics Of Arizona, Inc.; Fillauer Orthotic & Prosthetic Services, Inc.; Florida Foot Care Centers, Inc.; Florida Orthotic & Prosthetic Centers of Broward, Inc.; Florida Orthotic & Prosthetic Centers of Palm Beach, Inc.; Gaines Brace & Limb, Inc.; Isle Acquisition, Inc.; Jim All, Inc.; Karg

Prosthetics, Inc.; Knoxville Orthopedic Appliance Co., Inc.; Lux Artificial Limb & Brace Co.; McFarlen & Associates, Inc.; McFarlen & Associates, I, II, II, & IV; Mobility Orthotic & Prosthetics, Inc.; Newport Orthopedic & Prosthetic Center, Inc.; Ortho-Care, Inc.; NovaCare Orthotics & Prosthetics West, Inc.; NovaCare Orthotics & Prosthetics East, Inc.; NovaCare Orthotics & Prosthetics Holdings, Inc.; Phoenix Limb Shop, Inc.; R.E. Huck Co.; Rehabilitation Services, Inc.; Rex McKinney, CPO, Ltd.; R. Press, Inc.; Savannah Orthotics, Inc.; Savannah Orthopedic, Inc. of Boulder; Webb's K.I. Karlson Co., Inc.; Young's Orthopedic Service, Inc.; Southwest Rehabilitation Hospital, Inc.; West Coast Rehab Systems Co.; New Jersey Rehab Systems Co.; Advanced O & P; Allied Limb & Brace; Aurora Orthopedics, Inc.; Bryco Fabrication, Inc.; Brywood Orthopedic Center, Inc.; Canoga Orthopedic; North Iowa Prosthetics; Oak Ridge Orthopedic Appliance Co.; Southside Orthopedic Specialties; Worcester Orthopedic Appliance Co.

Further Reading:

Bianco, Anthony, "Health Care's Busiest Empire Builder," *Business Week,* October 28, 1991, pp. 126, 128.
Novack, Janet, "Insider Trading," *Forbes,* November 8, 1993, pp. 118–120.

—April Dougal Gasbarre

Ohio Casualty Corp.

136 North Third Street
Hamilton, Ohio 45025-0001
U.S.A.
(513) 867-3000
Fax: (513) 867-3964

Public Company
Incorporated: 1919 as Ohio Casualty Insurance Corp.
Employees: 4,300
Operating Revenues: $56.5 million
Stock Exchanges: NASDAQ
SICs: 6331 Fire, Marine, and Casualty Insurance; 6311 Life
    Insurance; 6719 Holding Companies, Not Elsewhere
    Classified

Ohio Casualty Corp., which celebrated its 75th anniversary in 1994, ranks as one of the United States's top 35 stock insurance holding companies, with $3.8 billion in assets. The vast majority (97 percent) of the firm's business is in property-casualty insurance, including private passenger auto, homeowners, inland marine, workers' compensation, commercial auto, and general liability. Although Ohio Casualty had $5.3 billion in life insurance in force as of 1993, life insurance products constituted a very small segment of the corporation's business. All policies are sold and serviced through a combination of 4,000 independent agents and branch offices in 38 states. The insurer has chalked up nearly a half-century of consecutive annual dividend increases in spite of formidable obstacles in the early 1990s.

The Ohio Casualty Insurance Company was established in Hamilton, Ohio, a small industrial town located between Dayton and Cincinnati. Howard L. Sloneker, Sr., Samuel M. Goodman, and Ben D. Lecklider, all of whom were in the auto insurance business before World War I, opened an office in the Rentschler Building in November 1919. The new firm became Ohio's first stock insurance company to offer full coverage automobile policies—including allowances for property damage, personal liability, fire, theft, and tornado damage—and auto insurance was its only line of business. Lecklider advanced to the forefront of the organization, and Goodman oversaw the new company's finances as treasurer. Known as a "people person," Sloneker expanded the business through his posi-

tive relationships with agents, policyholders, employees, and investors.

The young company's premiums exceeded $400,000 within just a few years, but its success highlighted its risky emphasis on only one product in only one state. The company began to diversify in 1923, offering glass insurance for homeowners and businesses, and selling policies outside the state. Ohio Casualty established its first affiliate, the Inland Casualty Company, just two years later. Rapid growth necessitated the parent's third and final move to an office on Third Street in Hamilton in 1927. Although the buildings were remodeled and expanded over the years, that location remained Ohio Casualty's headquarters into the 1990s.

The insurer had added fidelity and surety lines, as well as burglary, forgery, and general liability insurance, to its product offerings by October 1929, when the stock market crash heralded the Great Depression. Surprisingly, Ohio Casualty managed to avoid laying off a single employee, and even achieved growth, throughout the Depression. The company established its first branch office, in Cleveland, in 1935; a second branch followed three years later in Detroit. The 1939 acquisition and subsequent merger of the Pennsylvania Indemnity Company expanded Ohio Casualty's reach eastward.

Co-founder Howard Sloneker, Sr. advanced to Ohio Casualty's presidency when Ben Lecklider died in 1940. Sloneker would continue in a leadership capacity through World War II and into the postwar era. As the number of vehicles and drivers increased during this time, Ohio Casualty began to segment its clients according to age, driving record, and other quantitative categories. The company insured only the statistically best candidates, known in the industry as "standard risks." Ohio Casualty acquired the firm that would long rank as its largest subsidiary, California's West American Insurance Company, in 1945.

Howard Sloneker's oldest son, Howard Jr., was named president of the company in 1953, and he oversaw daily operations in that position for a decade. He then became chairperson, following his father's death in 1963, while his brother, John, advanced to the presidency. The Sloneker family legacy drove Ohio Casualty's dramatic growth through acquisition in the 1960s. The company established its Ocasco Budget subsidiary at the outset of the decade. This operation provided premium financing for its own and other companies' clients, thereby easing the financial burden of large semiannual premium payments. The following year witnessed the charter of The Ohio Life Insurance Company, which offered personal and business life insurance, as well as pension and profit sharing programs. Just one year later, Ohio Casualty acquired another Hamilton-based firm, Ohio Security Insurance Company, and closed out the decade with the acquisition of American Fire and Casualty Company of Orlando, Florida, a firm that held out great growth potential through its southeastern network of agents. An insurance holding company, Ohio Casualty Corporation, was formed in 1969 to coordinate the activities of the six related companies.

During the 1960s, increasing loss costs shifted the auto insurance industry's profit center from underwriting to investing. An underwriting profit was measured by the combined operating ratio, which compares claims and overhead to premiums collected. A combined operating ratio of 100 or less indicated that a company's expenses equaled or were less than premiums collected, while a ratio of 107 signified a seven percent underwriting loss, indicating that premiums collected fell seven percent short of claims and operating expenses. Since the automobile insurance business began consistently recording losses on underwriting activities in the 1960s, most companies, including Ohio Casualty, made money through profitable investments.

Problems compounded in the insurance market of the 1970s, as soft markets, cash flow underwriting, and continuously increasing loss costs exacerbated negative combined ratios and reduced profitability. The industry averaged a seven percent annual loss on underwriting from the 1970s through the early 1990s. Ohio Casualty's underwriting loss from 1984 to 1993 was slightly below that average, at 6.3 percent. John Sloneker advanced to Ohio Casualty's board chair and chief executive office when brother Howard retired in 1978. Joseph Marcum, an Ohio Casualty employee since 1947, became the company's first president outside the Sloneker family in almost four decades.

Sloneker and Marcum lead Ohio Casualty to ever-higher premium growth, exceeding $1 billion in gross premiums written in 1985. When Sloneker retired from active management in 1988, Marcum advanced to the positions of chairperson and CEO. He served in that capacity until 1994, when Lauren Patch, then acting as president, added the duties of the chief executive office to his responsibilities.

The insurance industry overall suffered consumer backlash that came to fruition in the form of rate legislation in the late 1980s. The most notorious law, California's Proposition 103, mandated 15 percent cuts in auto insurance premiums and refunds to many customers after its 1988 ratification. At that time, Ohio Casualty's West American Insurance Company in that state contributed over one-fifth of the holding company's annual revenues. Nevertheless, the parent elected to withdraw from California in 1992. Legislative assessments and loss of premium revenues combined with decreasing investment yields resulted in an 11.7 percent decline in net income from $98.5 million in 1992 to $87 million in 1993. Gross premiums dropped 12.4 percent during the same period, as Marcum and Patch shifted the corporation's focus to the states of Ohio, Kentucky, Indiana, Illinois, and Tennessee. The leaders set a long-term goal of capturing at least five percent of each of those competitive markets, and at least one percent of each of the other 33 states in which it operated. Achieving these two seem-

ingly modest goals alone promised to double Ohio Casualty's premium writings, and would thereby salvage the revenues lost from exiting the California market.

Acknowledging that selling through independent agents had distanced the firm from its ultimate customers, the policyholders, Ohio Casualty attempted to remedy this situation through the creation of the its first formal marketing department and the implementation of a Total Quality Management program in the early 1990s. A new statement of purpose, issued in 1993, identified four key stakeholders: policyholders, shareholders, employees, and agents. More tangible changes included a corporate reorganization into four organizational areas: policyholder services, management support systems, human resources, and technology. Cost reduction strategies such as increased automation and consolidation of branch offices were implemented to curb historically high underwriting expenses.

The insurer also adopted several anti-takeover measures in the early 1990s, first reducing its cash position to virtually nothing in 1990, since cash-rich firms are often targeted for acquisition. At about the same time, the company created a shareholder protection rights plan that provided for the distribution of one common share purchase right for each outstanding common share in the event that a person or group acquired 20 percent or more of the insurer's common shares.

Marcum and Patch conceded that Ohio Casualty Corporation's financial performance was disappointing in 1993, but emphasized that, with its reputation for underwriting and claims servicing, the firm could expect better earnings in 1994 on the occasion of its 75th anniversary.

Principal Subsidiaries: Ohio Casualty Insurance Co.; West American Insurance Company; Ohio Security Insurance Co.; American Fire & Casualty Co.; Ohio Life Insurance Co.; Ocasco Budget, Inc.

Further Reading:

Gilbert, Evelyn, "Takeover Defenses Adopted," *National Underwriter,* January 29, 1990, pp. 9, 38–39.

Maturi, Richard I., "Prosperous Insurer: Ohio Casualty Excels in Premium Growth, Investments," *Barron's,* January 19, 1987, p. 39.

McCoy, Thomas A., "Ohio Casualty Marketing Plan: A Blend of Consistency and Innovation," *Rough Notes,* May 1993, pp. 40–41.

"Shareholder Rights Plans Set," *National Underwriter,* January 8, 1990, pp. 35, 39.

—April Dougal Gasbarre

CK OLD KENT

Old Kent Financial Corp.

One Vandenberg Center
Grand Rapids, Michigan 49506-0321
U.S.A.
(616) 771-5000
Fax: (616) 771-4698

Public Company
Incorporated: 1971
Employees: 5,130
Total Assets: $10.1 billion
Stock Index: NASDAQ
SICs: 6712 Bank Holding Companies; 6022 State
   Commercial Banks; 6021 National Commercial Banks

Old Kent Financial Corp. is one of the country's best performers, with 21 bank subsidiaries and over 200 branches in Michigan and suburban Chicago. The institution dominates western Michigan, with more than twice its nearest competitor's market share. Hallmarks of Old Kent's performance include dependable earnings and dividends as well as conservative, yet aggressive, growth strategies. Moreover, the bank's exceptional overhead ratio (a comparison of noninterest overhead to net operating revenue) has earned it a high rank among the most efficient banking companies in the United States. The holding company also operates five non-bank subsidiaries, offering mortgage, insurance, brokerage, and other financial services. These operations extend Old Kent's reach into Ohio, Indiana, Pennsylvania, Kentucky, and even farther south into Florida. The relatively little-known institution gained national recognition in the 1980s, when a spate of acquisitions nearly tripled its assets and catapulted it to the top of its home state's bank roster. The company's 16 affiliate banks and over 200 branches were considered a prime takeover target in the late 1980s and early 1990s, but John Canepa, chairperson, president, and CEO, asserted that Michigan's top-performing bank was not for sale.

Old Kent Financial Corp. was incorporated in 1971 to acquire the assets of Old Kent Bank & Trust Company, which traced its history to the establishment of the Daniel Ball Exchange Bank in 1853. At the time, any entrepreneur who met relatively lax minimum state requirements could open a financial institution. Thousands of banks were created and failed during this largely unregulated period before 1862, when Congress established a federal charter (with more stringent requirements) and national

currency. The industry was further reformed with the 1913 creation of the Federal Reserve System. Moreover, the banking crises of the Great Depression brought increasing regulation, separating commercial and investment services and permitting statewide branching for national banks for example. The cautious banking environment that lasted throughout World War II and into the postwar era provided the backdrop for the 1958 union of Michigan's Old National Bank and Kent State Bank.

Taking advantage of state legislation permitting the creation and expansion of bank holding companies in the early 1970s, Old Kent was incorporated in 1972. The firm acquired three banks—Peoples State Bank, Peoples Bank & Trust, N.A., and Central Michigan Bank and Trust—over the course of the decade.

The pace of acquisitions at Old Kent increased in the 1980s, especially after the 1982 ascension of John Canepa to the chief executive office. A Harvard graduate, Canepa had started his career in New York in the 1950s at Chase Bank, moved to American Financial Corporation in the 1960s, and started at Old Kent in the 1970s. Over the course of Canepa's first decade at its helm, the holding company took over 45 banks and virtually tripled its assets to $8.8 million. Old Kent added non-bank affiliates over the course of the 1980s as well, including a mortgage service, an insurance subsidiary, and other financial services. Canepa applied three basic criteria to potential acquisitions: good financial performance, a reliable management team, and especially stable assets. Old Kent's integration strategy centralized office processing functions of new affiliates for efficiency but encouraged local autonomy through maintenance of local boards of directors. In April 1992, Canepa told *Bank Management* that "our strictest merger standard is that every acquisition must increase shareholder value." Nevertheless, the holding company paid the Resolution Trust Corp. $1.7 million for St. Charles Federal Savings Association's $80 million portfolio of cash, residential mortgages, and other deposits in 1990. Consolidation resulted in a roster of 16 affiliate banks and over 200 bank branches by 1993.

Old Kent managed to avoid the speculative real estate loans, Third World debt, and other 1980s pitfalls that troubled many banks. The firm's conservative approach earned it a high credit rating and praise from Salomon Brothers. Efficiency was also a frequently cited factor in Old Kent's success. Although many banks made acquisitions their primary vehicle for achieving efficiency as well as growth, Old Kent relied on some time-tested methods for increasing profitability. While the banking industry's cost to service a single loan stood at $88 in 1992, Old Kent averaged only $60. The bank's overall efficiency, at less than 58 percent, also compared favorably with an industry average that consistently exceeded 60 percent. On a smaller scale, everyone, including the CEO, flew coach class on business trips. Management maintained that while this did not save significant amounts of money, it reinforced a spirit of efficiency. Old Kent also encouraged competition among its largely autonomous affiliates and subsidiaries through a monthly scorecard that ranked all 16 on a variety of standards.

Acquisitions slowed somewhat during the early 1990s. Old Kent bought eleven bank branch offices in 1991 and 1992, but negotiations for the acquisition of Hasten Bancorp, which would have taken Old Kent into Indiana, failed. Nevertheless, Canepa asserted that Old Kent was still "in the business of making acquisitions" and was constantly evaluating and negotiating prospective affiliates. In 1994, Old Kent increased its Chicago presence with the $62 million acquisition of EdgeMark Financial Corporation, a five-bank holding company with assets of $534 million. Future expansion targets included Indiana and Wisconsin.

As commercial loan demand declined rapidly during an early 1990s recession, Old Kent diversified its strategy to include more fee-based retail banking. Interest rates plummeted to their lowest levels in decades, and the bank turned to mortgage refinancing and mutual fund brokerage to bolster its asset base. In 1993 alone, Old Kent's consumer loans increased 20 percent, mortgage servicing revenues nearly doubled, and the proprietary Kent Funds swelled to over $2 billion in assets. A regional mortgage production office in Columbus, Ohio, was established that year to serve Ohio, Indiana, Michigan, Pennsylvania, and Kentucky. Old Kent further bolstered its mortgage service business and ventured outside the Midwest with an agreement to purchase Princeton Financial Corporation of Orlando, Florida. The acquisition, which was completed early in 1994, brought 13 origination offices and a comprehensive network of independent brokers into the Old Kent fold. The holding company shifted an extra $1 billion into its investment portfolio during this transitional period to maintain returns.

Old Kent Financial Corporation has articulated several core tenets of its business philosophy, including: maximizing shareholder value, customer service, employee enrichment, and corporate citizenship. The firm has reported increasing earnings per share in every year since its formation in 1972, and Salomon Brothers has characterized Old Kent as "an increasingly profitable franchise that is driven by prudent acquisition policy and superior credit quality." Through 1992, Old Kent's ten-year total return to investors ranked eighth among the 100 largest banks and 21st in *Fortune* magazine's ranking of the 500 largest services companies in the United States. In 1994, *U.S. Banker* rated Old Kent the top performing bank in Michigan and eleventh in the nation.

In 1993, the bank set up an organized transition of leadership, selecting David J. Wagner (president of the Old Kent Bank and Trust Company in Grand Rapids) to succeed John Canepa as president and CEO in 1995. Canepa planned to continue on in the capacity of board chairperson through 1997. As consolidation in the industry continued in the 1990s, Old Kent's appeal as a target for takeover remained a concern.

Principal Subsidiaries: Old Kent Bank & Trust Co.; Old Kent Bank (Illinois); Old Kent Bank-Central; Old Kent Bank-Grand Traverse; Old Kent Bank-Southwest; Old Kent Bank of Grand Haven; Old Kent Bank of Holland; Old Kent Bank-Southeast; Old Kent Bank of Brighton; Old Kent Bank of Gaylord; Old Kent Bank of Petoskey; Old Kent Bank of Big Rapids; Old Kent Bank of Cadillac; Old Kent Bank of Hillsdale; Old Kent Bank of St. Johns; Old Kent Bank of Ludington; Hartger & Willard Mortgage Associates, Inc.; Old Kent Bank Brokerage Services, Inc.; Old Kent Financial Life Insurance Co.; Vanguard Financial Service Corp.; Old Kent Mortgage Co.

Further Reading:

Byrne, Harlan S., "Old Kent Financial," *Barron's,* September 21, 1992, p. 34.
Cocheo, Steve, "Triumph Over Overhead," *ABA Banking Journal,* August 1992, pp. 52–56.
Feinberg, Mark, "Whose Heads Are on the Bank Takeover Block?," *Bankers Monthly,* March 1990, pp. 19–24.
Grennan, Gene, "Active Acquirer with a Conservative Accent," *Bank Management,* April 1992, pp. 18–20.
Hellauer, Brian, "New Weapon Puts Old Kent on Target," *American Banker,* August 2, 1993, p. 4A.
Klinkerman, Steve, "Old Kent Betting on Retail Strategy for Strength to Keep Acquirers at Bay," *American Banker,* December 15, 1993, p. 4.
Layne, Richard, "Old Kent Solves a Widespread Problem," *American Banker,* November 22, 1991, p. 16.
Meece, Mickey, "Old Kent Pumps New Life Into Issuing Side," *American Banker,* February 16, 1994, p. 12.
Zack, Jeffrey, "Old Kent's New Focus: Retail and Mortgages," *American Banker,* January 31, 1994, p. 1A.

—April Dougal Gasbarre

Garfield Casualty Company in 1923. In 1927, Garfield Casualty amended its charter to include life insurance and changed its name to Twentieth Century Life Company. The name Old Republic Life Insurance Company was adopted in 1930.

In 1931, Old Republic Life merged with Bankers Credit Life Insurance, and the corporate name Old Republic Credit Life Insurance Company was adopted. In 1955, the company returned to the name Old Republic Life Insurance Company. Old Republic Life pioneered consumer credit life insurance, focusing on providing policies to consumers through lending institutions and automobile dealerships. By the early 1990s, Old Republic Life was licensed to operate in 48 states, the District of Columbia, Puerto Rico, Hong Kong, Canada, Mexico, Philippine Islands, and U.S. Virgin Islands.

The flagship company of ORI's General Insurance Group, Old Republic Insurance Company, was incorporated in 1935 as Coal Operators Casualty Company. In 1955, Old Republic acquired an ownership interest in Coal Operators Casualty, and the organization's charter was amended permitting it to offer a broader range of insurance lines. In 1956, Old Republic entered the Canadian market, and, by the early 1990s, the company had grown and expanded its offerings to encompass a wide variety of underwriting and risk management services for commercial property and liability risks. These coverages included workers' compensation, general liability, and commercial automobile. The company specialized in serving targeted industries such as transportation, construction, forest products, and coal and other energy businesses. In 1994, A. M. Best Company reported that workers' compensation represented 60 percent of ORI's business. The company was licensed in all 50 states, the District of Columbia, Canada, Guam, Puerto Rico, and the Virgin Islands.

The Old Republic International Corporation (ORI) was organized in 1969 to serve as a holding company for diversified insurance, financial, and investment operations. Initially, all shares of Old Republic Life were converted to ORI common stock. Two years later in 1971, ORI also became the parent company of Old Republic Insurance.

In another action in 1971, ORI purchased Reliable Life Insurance Company, of Hamilton, Ontario (Canada). Reliable Life, incorporated in 1963, had been providing life and disability insurance through a predecessor organization since 1887 making it ORI's oldest operating subsidiary. Following its acquisition, Reliable Life continued to offer a limited amount of whole life, endowment, and term insurance, but the company's greatest growth came from group insurance policies such as student accident and long-term disability insurance. In 1993, Reliable Life received premiums totaling C$13.3 million. ORI projected that Reliable Life's greatest growth in 1994 would occur as a result of travel insurance programs.

During the early 1970s, ORI expanded its activities in mortgage guaranty insurance for lending institutions. Republic Mortgage Insurance Company was established in 1972 and began operations in 1973; Old Republic Mortgage Assurance Company was established in 1973 and began operations in 1974; and, Republic Mortgage Insurance Company of Florida was incorporated in 1974 and began operations in 1975.

Old Republic International Corp.

307 N. Michigan Avenue
Chicago, Illinois 60601
U.S.A.
(312) 346-8100
Fax: (312) 346-3248

Public Company
Incorporated: 1923
Employees: 6,100
Total Assets: $6.1 billion
Stock Exchanges: New York
SICs: 6331 Fire, Marine & Casualty Insurance; 6311 Life Insurance; 6361 Title Insurance; 6719 Holding Companies, Not Elsewhere Classified

Old Republic International Corporation, one of the 50 largest publicly held insurance organizations in the United States, is a holding company for a diversified array of insurance companies. Conducting business through 125 different corporate entities—including 30 autonomous insurance subsidiaries covering all 50 states and Canada—Old Republic International (ORI) specializes in lines of insurance marketed toward specific industries. The company's philosophy, as stated in its *1993 Annual Review,* is to "offer a limited line of coverages to relatively few industries at the core of the American economy." ORI also offers fee-based risk management services for self insurers. ORI's subsidiaries are organized into four groups. The General Insurance Group, one of the nation's 100 largest property and liability insurance groups, serves industrial, mining, transportation, and financial service organizations. The Title Insurance Group provides title protection to purchasers of property and mortgage lenders, holding a seven percent share of the U.S. market in 1993. The Old Republic Mortgage Guaranty Group insures financial institutions against default on first mortgages for single-family homes, typically those with low down payments of five to ten percent. The Life Insurance Group specializes in offering credit and term insurance to consumers through outlets such as lending institutions and automobile dealers.

The organization, which traces its origins to the 1920s, achieved much of its growth by purchasing troubled insurance carriers and redirecting them to create profitable subsidiaries. The first company in the ORI family was incorporated under the name

During the late 1970s, ORI continued its expansion. In 1978, the company purchased the Alabama Rural Fire Insurance Company, founded in 1972. The organization's name was changed to Capitol Fire and Marine Insurance Company in 1978, and the name Old Republic Union Insurance Company was adopted in 1992 during an initiative to have many key operating subsidiaries adopt ORI's new logo. As part of the program aimed at increasing national name recognition, some subsidiaries also changed their names to include an "Old Republic" appellation.

Another company to come under ORI ownership during the late 1970s was the Mississippi Valley Title Insurance Company. Mississippi Valley had been founded by the Taylor family in 1941 as a sideline to an existing law practice. Following World War II, the company enjoyed quick growth, since VA and FmHA loans required title insurance. By 1990, Mississippi Valley reported that it had achieved a 66 percent share of the market in Mississippi and served many clients in Alabama as well.

Several changes and expansions in ORI's reinsurance activities occurred during the late 1970s and early 1980s. Reinsurance, a process of obtaining insurance on the potential risk faced by an insurer under an existing insurance contract, helped limit the insurance carrier's risk exposure from any one incident. In 1977, ORI assumed complete financial control of International Business and Mercantile Reassurance Company, a corporation formed in 1960 as Motorists Beneficial Insurance Company. Old Republic Insurance, an ORI subsidiary, had acquired an ownership interest in the organization by purchasing its outstanding capital stock in 1961. American Business & Mercantile Insurance Mutual, Inc., a miscellaneous reinsurer for subsidiaries in the Old Republic Insurance Group, was incorporated in 1981 and began operation in 1982. In 1983, the name Inter Capital Assurance Company was adopted by ICS Assurance Company, another reinsurer that had been under direct or indirect ORI control since its inception in 1966. Inter Capital Assurance assumed its business (primarily auto liability, workers' compensation, and aircraft insurance) from Old Republic Insurance Company.

One of ORI's largest acquisitions occurred in 1985 when it merged with Bitco Corporation, previously known as Bituminous Holdings, Ltd. Bitco served as a holding company for Bituminous Casualty Corporation and Bituminous National Group Inc. Bituminous Casualty Corporation, established in 1928 as a successor to Bituminous Casualty Exchange, served as a specialty underwriter for forest products industries, gas and oil companies, and construction contractors. The company conducted its operations through 18 full-service branch offices and two claim service offices. Other subsidiary companies acquired in the transaction were Bituminous Fire & Marine Insurance Company and the Great West Companies.

Great West Insurance Company, which was incorporated in 1956 and changed its name to Great West Casualty Company in 1962, specialized in providing insurance coverage for mid-sized, long-haul trucking companies. Policies provided commercial automobile, workers compensation, general liability, and cargo insurance protection. The company also sold federal crop and hail insurance policies, lines it abandoned in 1993 to concentrate on the needs of the trucking industry.

Upper Peninsula Insurance Company, reinsurer of errors and omissions, and directors and officers insurance, was established in 1985. Upper Peninsula functioned as a wholly owned subsidiary of the Chicago Underwriting Group, Inc, which was 80 percent owned by ORI.

In 1986, ORI purchased an organization with a 50-year history and reorganized it as the Old Republic Surety Group, Inc. The original entity, Mutual Surety Company of Iowa, founded in 1936, was succeeded by State Surety in 1956, and State Surety was absorbed by Nebraska Surety Company in 1971. In 1978, 96 percent of its outstanding shares were acquired by Northwestern National Insurance and transferred to its wholly owned subsidiary Northwestern National Surety Company. Northwestern National Surety Company became Old Republic Surety Company, and its subsidiaries (Lawyers Surety Corporation and State Surety Company) were sold to ORI.

Acquisitions and reorganizations continued through the 1980s. Old Republic Standard Insurance Company, originally named Guaranty Re Insurance, was acquired by Old Republic Standard Underwriters, Inc. following the abandonment of a plan for a public offering in 1987. Old Republic Standard Underwriters was a joint venture formed in 1988, 86 percent owned by ORI, to provide specialty agriculture insurance products such as grain elevator coverage. In 1989, ORI acquired Lincoln Title Company, a title agency operating in the Los Angeles metropolitan area. In addition, ORI purchased USA Title Company, Inc. of Indianapolis, to increase its participation in the Midwest title market.

In 1989, ORI reported that most of its revenues were generated from general industry (31.3 percent). The real estate industry accounted for 23.7 percent; transportation, 13.9 percent; energy, 9.7 percent; financial services, 8.1 percent; contractors, 4.4 percent; agriculture, 3.9 percent; reinsurance assumed, 1.8 percent. All other industries accounted for 3.2 percent of revenues.

Two important milestones were achieved in 1990. In August, the company's common stock was listed on the New York Stock Exchange. And, at the year's end, ORI announced that its premium and fee revenues exceed $1 billion for the first time. In 1990, Old Republic Dealer Service Corporation was formed to direct the company's sales of credit life and disability insurance and extended warranty products through automobile dealers. In 1991, ORI acquired three additional title companies: The Title Insurance Company of North Carolina, Western States Title Company, and Conner Land Title. The newly formed ORI subsidiary Old Republic Security Holdings, Inc. acquired the Minnehoma Insurance Company in 1992. Minnehoma, a provider of automobile warranty, collateral protection, and credit insurance, had originally been incorporated in 1977 in Arizona. Prior to its acquisition by ORI, Minnehoma had been unprofitable due to poor performance in its non-standard auto and mortgage guaranty lines. Under ORI's leadership, these were discontinued, and Minnehoma was refocused to provide collateral protection to financial institutions and consumer auto warranty products that were offered exclusively through automobile dealers.

In 1992, ORI formed the Employers General Insurance Group, a property and liability insurer in Texas. The joint venture, 80 percent owned by ORI, began operation in 1993. It was established following the collapse of Employers Casualty, a 75-year-old Dallas-based insurer that had previously operated nine subsidiaries and held $650 million in assets. As a result of losses attributed to workers' compensation regulations during the late 1980s, the Texas Department of Insurance seized Employers Casualty in 1992. Under an agreement with officials in Texas, ORI agreed to purchase the company's records and three remaining subsidiaries. ORI planned to restore profitability by avoiding high-risk policies without adequate premiums and by focusing on a single line of business.

ORI's success in managing its assets was recognized in 1992 when three of its subsidiaries in the Old Republic Title Insurance Group became the first title companies to receive claims-paying ability ratings from an independent agency. Old Republic National Title, Mississippi Valley Title, and Old Republic General Title achieved A+ evaluations from Standard and Poor's rating service.

Other events of the early 1990s, however, brought new challenges to ORI's leaders. In 1992, natural disasters such as Hurricane Andrew, resulted in $7.1 million in losses from property exposure. Moreover, the company's Bituminous Casualty Corporation became engaged in a court battle regarding pollution coverage. Although the company was originally ordered to pay compensation to a landfill operator in Wisconsin by a lower court, the 5th U.S. Circuit Court of Appeals ruled that Bituminous Casualty could not be held liable for the costs because the policies under which the claim had been made could not be found. In another court action, Old Republic Insurance Company's exclusion of defense coverage for sexual harassment was upheld.

As the national economic picture shifted and ORI adjusted its mix of insurance companies, the balance of revenue-producing industries changed. In 1993, ORI reported that the real estate industry had assumed the position of the organization's largest revenue producer, accounting for 30.8 percent. The transportation industry generated 20.5 percent of its revenues; general industry, 16.5 percent; financial services, 8.0 percent; energy, 6.7 percent; contractors, 6.0 percent; forestry and timber, 3.6 percent; wholesale/retail, 3.0 percent; agriculture, 3.0 percent; reinsurance assumed, 1.0 percent; and others accounted for only 0.9 percent.

ORI expected continued increases in housing-related insurance needs through 1994. While company analysts predicted decreases in refinancing, they expected increases in the sales of new and existing homes. In addition, ORI planned to focus on increasing its market share in existing markets and to expand into new territories. Improvements, however, were expected to be modest as private sector mortgage insurance guarantors faced increased competition from the Federal Housing Administration's more lenient provisions.

Principal Subsidiaries: Bituminous Casualty Corporation; Great West Casualty Company; International Business & Mercantile Reassurance Company; Old Republic General Title Insurance Corporation; Old Republic Insurance Company; Old Republic Life Insurance Company; Old Republic National Title Insurance Company; Republic Mortgage Insurance Company.

Further Reading:

Andresky, Jill, ''Discipline Is All,'' *Forbes,* July 16, 1984.

Bradford, Michael, ''Policy Disappears; So Does Coverage,'' *Business Insurance,* November 23, 1992.

Byrne, Harlan S., ''Old Republic International: It's Fully Recovered from Mortgage-Insurance Debacle,'' *Barron's,* January 14, 1991.

Geschel, Christine, ''Insurers May Be on the Hook for Hazardous Waste Cleanup Costs,'' *The Business Journal-Milwaukee,* July 16, 1990.

Greenwald, Judy, and Gayin Souter, ''Harassment Defense Denied,'' *Business Insurance,* October 4, 1993.

''ITT Hartford to Acquire Crop Insurance Business,'' *New York Times,* August 11, 1993.

Jones, Kevin, ''Dominating a Market: How Mississippi Valley Title Keeps Two-Thirds of the Business,'' *Mississippi Business Journal,* July 30, 1990.

Preston, Darrell, ''New Insurer Launched from Employers' Ashes,'' *Dallas Business Journal,* January 1, 1993.

—Karen Bellenir

Overseas Shipholding Group, Inc.

1114 Avenue of the Americas
New York, New York 10036-1222
U.S.A.
(212) 869-1222
Fax: (212) 536-3776

Public Company
Incorporated: 1969
Employees: 2,060
Operating Revenues: $420.1 million
Stock Exchanges: New York Pacific
SICs: 4412 Deep Sea Foreign Transportation of Freight;
    4424 Deep Sea Domestic Transportation of Freight; 4481
    Deep Sea Passenger Transportation, Except Ferry

Overseas Shipholding Group, Inc. is one of the largest independent bulk shipping companies in the world. The company owns and operates a diversified fleet of over 60 domestic and international oceangoing tankers and bulk carriers, as well as 16 U.S. flag tankers (used in "flag trade" or coastal commerce among U.S. ports) and dry cargo vessels. The firm serves three segments: the international tanker markets (for both crude oil and oil products); the international dry bulk markets (primarily iron ore, coal, and grain); and the unsubsidized U.S. flag markets (mainly Alaskan crude). At the end of 1993, 51 percent of Overseas Shipbuilding's global bulk fleet consisted of oil tankers, 43 percent transported dry goods, and the remainder were combination carriers capable of transporting either wet or dry cargoes. Two-thirds of Overseas Shipholding's shipping revenues came from transporting petroleum and its derivatives in 1993. Although its domestic business often receives the most media attention, the shipper's international fleet is one of the largest in the world and contributed the majority (about 61 percent) of annual revenues on average in the 1990s.

Overseas Shipholding is one of only three oil tanker companies that are publicly traded in the United States. The company operates on a contract rather than common carrier basis, meaning that its vessels are not bound to specific ports of schedules. Freight rates are negotiated through a closely related brokerage firm, Maritime Overseas Corporation. Overseas Shipbuilding's domestic fleet consists entirely of "Jones Act" vessels. Established in 1920 to promote a national merchant marine and shipyard capacity in case of national emergencies, the Jones Act

required ships involved in U.S. flag trades to be built in American shipyards and without government subsidy, as well as to be owned and operated by Americans. The capital and operating costs resulting from these conditions nearly tripled international levels. Until the late 1980s, companies that met these criteria operated in a market largely protected from foreign and subsidized competition.

Created in 1969 through the merger of the ship holdings of five private businessmen, Overseas Shipholding Group (OSG) became the only publicly traded pure ocean shipping company in the United States. The union of Overseas Bulk Ships, Inc., Transoceanic Bulk Carriers, Inc., and United Steamship Corp. boasted a fleet of 32 ships at its founding. The owners sold one-third of their new company public at $12 per share and elected Morton P. Hyman, a 35-year-old attorney, as president. The early 1970s were boom years for the tanker business, and OSG's revenues doubled from $85 million to nearly $169 million between 1972 and 1974. Profits increased even faster, from $15.6 million to $38.4 million during the same period.

During this time, Hyman proved adept at anticipating demand; he had an enviable knack for ordering ships before they were needed and then contracting them before they even came into service. Mid-decade, however, recession and widely fluctuating shipping rates brought what *Forbes* magazine called "one of the stormiest periods ever in the bulk shipping business." Some of the United States's biggest public and private fleets were "crippled or sunk" during this difficult period. Still, while OSG's revenues declined seven percent, its profits rose almost 40 percent. Analysts attributed this market-defying performance to Hyman's commitment to reliable, but relatively low-return, long-term contracts (some of which would last until 1989). By 1977, Hyman had expanded the fleet to 49 ships—the largest independent fleet of U.S. flag tankers in operation. The fleet was modern as well as large, as, in 1977, the average ship age was seven years. Moreover, the opening of the Alaska pipeline in the late 1970s gave OSG's domestic tankers their first major source of consistent business: transporting crude oil from the West Coast terminus of the pipeline to the East Coast.

OSG recorded outstanding performance during its first ten years of business, as operating profits increased at an average compounded rate of over 20 percent per year. By 1979, sales reached $268 million, and profits neared $66 million. The company also achieved a 20 percent return on equity during that period, a rate almost unheard of in the shipping industry. Debt-to-equity, which averaged 2-to-1 for the high-overhead global shipping business, decreased to 1.2-to-1 at OSG from 1969 to 1980. With 15 tankers and two dry bulk carriers in domestic service in 1979, OSG held a ten percent share of all Jones Act tankers in operation at the time. In a 1980 *Barron's* profile, Hyman attributed OSG's growth to "a willingness to sacrifice the chance to maximize profits in periods of unusually high spot rates for long-term charters, assuring a steadier stream of rising earnings."

The 1980s, however, saw OSG's earnings decline sharply from $65.9 million in 1979 to a low of $31 million in 1985. The Iran-Iraq war brought years of unprecedented losses for OSG's international fleet, resulting in the destruction and damage of over 40 million tons of oil-transporting capacity. In fact, the

Persian Gulf became known in the industry as "Exocet Alley" after the missiles that terrorized tanker fleets there. Ironically, however, *Financial World* referred to the war "a drastic solution to the tanker glut"; in the late 1980s, the tanker supply tightened enough to encourage higher rates. Other factors in the last half of the decade helped OSG's revenues and earnings steadily recover to $349.9 million and $51.1 million, respectively, in 1989. Mid-decade, OSG garnered an auto transport contract with Toyota that extended until 1994. During the late 1980s, oil imports rose and aging ships throughout the industry were retired, further boosting OSG's recovery. Although the firm was not performing as well as it had in the 1970s, a 1987 *Financial World* profile noted that OSG still had "the strongest balance sheet in the business."

In the mid-1980s, the U.S. Maritime Administration reversed the policy that sheltered flag trade from foreign and subsidized competition. New policies began to allow several oil carriers built with construction subsidies to enter the Alaskan coastal trades after they repaid their subsidies. Finding that the competition presented by these carriers depressed freight rates and forced some smaller tanker operators out of business, OSG and other Jones Act tanker owners challenged the Maritime Administration's decision in the courts. In spite of judgments in their favor, the subsidized carriers were allowed to remain in the U.S. flag trades pending appeal.

Protection of the U.S. flag trades suffered another blow in the early 1990s, when a debate emerged over the interpretation of the Merchant Marine Act of 1936, which prohibited a recipient of government financial assistance from participating in domestic markets for its "full operational life." Subsidized tanker owners contended that the 1936 law referred not to the full life of the ship, but to its "economic life," 20 to 25 years. If the latter interpretation applied, subsidized tankers could potentially increase the total carrying capacity of the domestic tanker fleet by 12.3 percent from 1993 to 1996. The entry of the group of tankers on which subsidy contracts expired in the early 1990s threatened to erode shipping rates, especially since those vessels had inherently lower capital investments. OSG requested a review of the policy by the U.S. Department of Transportation in 1993, and the issue remained unresolved in 1994.

In 1990, following the massive oil spill on the Alaskan coast from the Exxon *Valdez,* Congress enacted the Oil Pollution Act, which phased in a requirement that all oil tankers entering U.S. waters have double-hulls by the year 2015. The Act also significantly increased the potential liability of tanker owners for environmental accidents in U.S. waters. OSG favored this legislation, as the company's commitment to ongoing fleet modernization put it in the vanguard of technology. In 1993, OSG focused on obtaining certification from the International Standards Organization to further bolster its reputation for quality.

OSG's annual report called 1992 "the most difficult year since the Company's formation in 1969." The global recession and overcapacity in the industry adversely affected all of the firm's business segments, bringing about the first pre-tax net loss in OSG's public history. From 1991 to 1992, revenues declined by over 15 percent, from $452 million to $383 million, and net income (after taxes) plummeted over 72 percent, from $56 million to $16 million.

In light of these competitive, regulatory, and market factors, OSG made its first major move to diversify in order to offset the effects of the cyclical shipping industry. In 1992, the firm formed a joint venture with The Chandris Group, a business with over 30 years of experience in the cruise market. OSG's $220 million investment earned it a 49 percent share of The Chandris Group, which operated two lines: Celebrity and Fantasy cruises. Celebrity's three ships catered to the upscale segment of the market, while the Fantasy line's two ships were positioned in the budget market. In its relatively brief four-year history, the Celebrity line had earned numerous industry awards. Readers of *Condé Nast Traveler* ranked the line as one of the world's top ten in 1991, 1992, and 1993. Berlitz gave the entire line its coveted five-star rating, and the International Cruise Passenger Association named it "Cruise Line of the Year." OSG's capital infusion was used to double the Celebrity line's capacity with the addition of three new ships before the end of the century. With average growth of ten percent per year from 1984 to 1993, the North American cruise industry offered OSG a relatively steady stream of income to offset the vagaries of the shipping industry.

OSG's key markets improved only slightly in the mid-1990s, as recession in Japan and Europe continued and total world oil demand remained flat. OSG's financial fortunes followed suit, as sales and profits rebounded slightly from the previous year to $420.1 million and $17.9 million, respectively.

Principal Subsidiaries: OSG Bulk Ships, Inc.; United Steamship Corp.; Trader Shipping Corp.; OSG International, Inc.; OSG Financial Corp.

Further Reading:

Cantwell, Alice, "Japan Automakers Renew U.S. Shipping Line Contracts," *Journal of Commerce and Commercial,* August 11, 1992, p. 8B.
Covey, Claudette, "Celebrity Officials Explain Line's Decision to Build Larger Vessels," *Travel Weekly,* April 15, 1993, p. 1.
Gordon, Mitchell, "Full Speed Ahead: Overseas Shipholding Plies in Growing Market," *Barron's,* June 23, 1980, pp. 31, 40.
Gordon, Mitchell, "Overseas Shipholding Steams Toward New Peak," *Barron's,* July 18, 1977, pp. 29–30, 42.
Kindel, Stephen, "The Economics of Exocet Alley," *Financial World,* August 25, 1987, pp. 22–23.
"Old Glory Sails Again," *Forbes,* February 1, 1977, pp. 34–35.
"Overseas Shipholding's Profit Plunges," *Journal of Commerce and Commercial,* May 21, 1993, p. 1B.
Pollack, Gerald A., and Lillian Nicolich, "The Business Economist at Work: Overseas Shipholding Group," *Business Economics,* July 1989, pp. 48–51.
Sansbury, Tim, "Carrier, Operators Clash on Use of Subsidized Ships," *Journal of Commerce and Commercial,* October 1, 1993, p. 1B.
Vail, Bruce, "Cancellation of Deal Between Overseas, American Trading Pleases BP Company," *Journal of Commerce and Commercial,* March 21, 1991, p. 8B.
Zipser, Andy, "Adventure on the High Seas," *Barron's,* October 7, 1991, pp. 40–41.

—April Dougal Gasbarre

PacifiCare®
Health Systems

PacifiCare Health Systems, Inc.

5995 Plaza Drive
Cypress, California 90630-5028
(714) 952-1121
Fax: (714) 220-3774

Public Company
Incorporated: 1983
Employees: 3,500
Revenues: $2.9 billion
Stock Exchanges: Nasdaq
SICs: 6324 Hospital and Medical Service Plans; 6411
   Insurance Agents, Brokers and Service

PacifiCare Health Services ranks among the biggest and best of America's health maintenance organizations. The billion-dollar company has over 1.4 million members, half of whom are in California, with the remainder in Oregon, Texas, Florida, Oklahoma, and Washington. In 1993, a survey of over 400 health maintenance organizations (HMOs) by Health Plan Management Services ranked PacifiCare among the ten best, and a 1994 *Fortune* poll named the company the second most-admired firm in the health care industry. Throughout its history, PacifiCare has scored financial successes along with these kudos, having reported the longest record of profitability of any for-profit HMO company. The company experienced dramatic growth during the 1980s, which began to slow somewhat in the early years of the 1990s.

PacifiCare was founded as a nonprofit corporation by Samuel J. Tibbitts of the Lutheran Hospital Society of Southern California in 1975 and became a federally qualified health maintenance organization (HMO) three years later. Unlike standard indemnity insurance plans, in which members are reimbursed for specified medical expenses on a fee-for-service basis, HMOs provide health care services for a prepaid fee (often assumed by the enrollee's employer) with no deductible. These organizations, which have existed since the late 1940s, are able to save themselves and their customers money by buying medical care "wholesale" from a limited pool of physicians, limiting unnecessary procedures, and encouraging prevention and fitness.

One way HMOs keep costs low is by restricting members' choice of doctors and hospitals. Physicians and facilities employed by the HMO are either salaried or they agree to accept "capitation" (fixed per-member) fees. Members who want to choose their own physicians must pay a premium for the privilege. A primary physician—either selected by the patient or assigned by the HMO—controls members' access to specialists and testing. Supporters of such "managed care" feel that the elimination of fee-for-service payments reduces the temptation to provide extraordinary, expensive treatments when a simpler, cheaper option exists. HMO detractors assert that beneficial procedures are sometimes not administered for the sake of cost-cutting. Managed health care organizations like PacifiCare typically attract younger, healthier members with their low out-of-pocket costs. When employers offer a choice between a traditional indemnity plan or an HMO, older workers with established physician relationships favor the freedom of choice afforded by indemnity plans. Some industry observers assert that this "self-selection" also contributes to HMOs' low cost structure—young, healthy members usually consume fewer health services than their aging counterparts.

PacifiCare was incorporated in 1983 and, like many other HMOs, switched to for-profit status the following year. The company made its initial public stock offering in May 1985, but less than 20 percent of its stock was actually sold to the public: 70 percent was held by UniHealth America (which had retained its non-profit status) and another 11 percent was owned by insiders. In its two decades in operation, PacifiCare has grown organically, by creating new subsidiaries and drawing new members, as well as through acquisitions.

In 1985, PacifiCare created its first subsidiary outside California: PacifiCare of Oregon. The group would eventually become Oregon's largest and fastest-growing HMO. PacifiCare also established Secure Horizons that same year. This subsidiary won California's first "risk-sharing" contract with Medicare (federal health benefits). Under its agreement with the government health care program, PacifiCare provided all Medicare-covered benefits in exchange for a monthly fee known as the "adjusted community rate." Statisticians determine the ACR based on the "adjusted average per capita cost" (AAPCC), which takes 122 demographic factors like age, sex, and Medicaid (low-income federal health benefits) into account. Because the ACR can never exceed the amount Medicaid would normally have paid a traditional fee-for-service plan, the government agency theoretically saves money.

Although older members were notorious for using more medical services than HMOs' traditional young customers, PacifiCare was able to make significant profits from the Secure Horizons division. By 1991, in fact, PacifiCare CEO and President Terry Hartshorn told *Barron's* that "the 20 percent of his members who are Medicare patients generate half of the company's revenues." Independent observers, however, warned that operations like Secure Horizons were bound by the rate increases dictated by Medicare, and couldn't make rate hikes at their own discretion.

PacifiCare grew rapidly during the mid-1980s, adding subsidiaries in Oklahoma and Texas and acquiring the Columbia General Life Insurance Company of Indiana (later renamed PacifiCare Life and Health) in 1986 alone. PacifiCare Life and Health was licensed to offer group life and health, supplemental life, and disability insurance in 34 states and the District of Columbia. That year, PacifiCare also jointly established Life-

Link, a behavioral health managed care company later renamed PacifiCare Behavioral Health (except in California, where it continued to be known as LifeLink), with Treatment Centers of America. A 1994 study by the American Academy of Actuaries endorsed the application of managed care's cost-cutting techniques to mental health care. The investigation found that per-patient mental health care costs at HMOs averaged only $45 to $75 annually, at least 60 percent less than traditional fee-for-service plans. Other acquisitions in the last half of the 1980s included MultiMed, an Oklahoma City HMO, and Oregon's McLean Clinic. Rapid growth compelled PacifiCare's move into a larger corporate headquarters in Cypress, California, in 1986.

Secure Horizons was expanded into Oregon and Texas during the late 1980s, and was designated America's fastest-growing health plan for Medicare beneficiaries by the federal Health Care Financing Administration in 1991. The plan became California's largest Medicare risk program in 1992, and went national as Secure Horizons USA the following year. The national effort used partnerships with other HMOs to plan, develop, and market Secure Horizons to senior citizens eligible for Medicare across the country. Although some analysts warned that President Bill Clinton's plans to cut the growth of Medicare and Medicaid spending by $180 billion from 1996 to 2001 would squeeze the margins of programs like Secure Horizons, the national group's president, Craig Schub, said in a September 1993 *Modern Healthcare* that "the potential volume of Medicare patients and new revenues could outweigh the effects of spending restrictions." The Medicare segment of PacifiCare's business already contributed one-third of its total enrollment and over half of its $2.2 billion in annual revenues by that time.

From 1980 to 1990, membership in American HMOs quadrupled to 36.5 million people, or about 15 percent of the population. One-third of Californians were members of managed care groups by that time. PacifiCare signed on its 500,000th member, accomplished a two-for-one stock split, and made a successful public offering of 1.7 million shares in 1989. The corporation's operating revenue increased an average of 63 percent each year from 1985 to 1990, rising from $87.9 million to $975.8 million.

PacifiCare formed HMO National Network (now known as Covantage), a system of regional HMOs created to serve multi-state employer groups, in 1991. The health care company increased its membership rolls by 18.7 percent and strengthened its California stronghold with the 1991 acquisition of one of the state's largest "independent physician association model" HMOs, Health Plan of America. This brand of managed care group, also known as a "group model HMO," employed physicians who had already banded together in partnership or as a professional organization. HMOs like Health Plan of America contracted with and paid the organization for services at a preset rate, and the association, in turn, paid its members. The addition of Health Plan of America brought PacifiCare's total membership to 825,000. The concurrent purchase of Execu-Fit Health Programs, a San Francisco-based national provider of on-site health education and wellness programs for businesses, gave PacifiCare one of the top programs of its kind. The company was renamed PacifiCare Wellness Company in 1993.

Mounting debt, which totaled nearly $200 million by the end of fiscal 1992 on September 30, compelled several changes in PacifiCare's stock. First, a recapitalization created a new class of nonvoting stock and each shareholder received one share of the issue for each share of the old. The company used the proceeds of two separate public offerings of 6.7 million shares of the new stock for debt repayment and general corporate purposes, including new products, services, and acquisitions.

In 1993, Alan Hoops replaced Terry Hartshorn as president and CEO. Hoops had worked at PacifiCare since 1977 and had quickly advanced to vice president of marketing and planning. With advanced degrees in psychology and health administration, he was named senior vice president in 1985 and executive vice president and chief operating officer the following year. Hartshorn stayed on as chairman in the early 1990s.

After a year of research and planning, PacifiCare's workers' compendsation subsidiary, COMPREMIER, teamed with Liberty Mutual Insurance Group, the United States's largest workers compensation insurer, to launch a workers compensation HMO product in 1993. The venture drew upon the aptitudes of each partner: PacifiCare brought its cost-cutting talents to the management of medical care for workers injured on the job, and Liberty Mutual offered rehabilitation case management, workplace safety programs, and indemnity benefit actuarial expertise. Liberty Mutual paid a local PacifiCare HMO a monthly per-employee fee on behalf of employer/clients, and PacifiCare agreed to provide any employee who filed a workers comp claim with a year of medical treatment. Long-term responsibility for employees' medical care then passed to Liberty Mutual. One unique cost-cutting aspect of the joint venture was a strictly monitored incentive bonus paid to doctors who encouraged patients to return to work as soon as possible.

In 1993 alone, PacifiCare acquired two healthcare companies in its home state—Freedom Plan and California Dental Health Plan—as well as Advantage Health Plans, Inc. (renamed PacifiCare of Florida), a Miami-based HMO. These acquisitions helped the company cross the one-million-member mark in 1993. Still, PacifiCare's revenue growth slowed from its hectic late 1980s pace to still-impressive 31.6 percent average annual increases in the early 1990s; revenue doubled from less than $1 billion in 1990 to $2.2 billion in 1993.

Late in 1993, UniHealth America reduced its stake in PacifiCare from 53 percent to 48.6 percent. Although the former parent would continue to be PacifiCare's single largest shareholder, it hoped that the divestment would allow the HMO more options when pursuing stock-swap acquisitions.

PacifiCare calls itself "an organization of dedicated people committed to improving the quality of those lives we touch." That corporate philosophy is reflected in programs designed for the society at large as well as the health care organization's own employees. In 1991, the company established PacifiCare Foundation, a nonprofit charitable and educational organization that, in keeping with the corporate focus, emphasized health, wellness, and welfare. The company was ranked among *Working Mother* magazine's 1992 list of the 100 best companies for working parents by virtue of its child care assistance and family leave programs. The following year, the firm responded to the needs of its corporate headquarters employees—75 percent of whom were women of child-bearing age—with the launch of the first corporate-sponsored child care facility in California's Orange County.

As social, corporate, and governmental pressure to control upwardly spiraling health care costs came to bear in the early 1990s, the entire industry anticipated fundamental changes. Despite its professed cost-cutting forte, PacifiCare came under criticism from U.S. Representative Fortney Stark for rate hikes in 1993. At the same time, some industry analysts predicted that high-flying health care earnings were due for a downward cycle under margin-squeezing pressure from physicians and hospitals demanding higher reimbursements, HMO members in search of more choices, and employers trying to decrease their share of the bill. Still, PacifiCare executives expressed confidence that the company would thrive in a government-regulated environment, asserting "plans to continue its strategy of controlled, national growth with the constant goal of being the market leader in whatever area it serves." John Persinos, an analyst for *Kiplinger's Personal Finance Magazine* added his vote of confidence when, in May 1994, he predicted that PacifiCare would prosper under health care reform.

The HMO's successful programs with federal agencies also indicated that it would do well in the event that a government-regulated health care system ever came into being. In 1993, PacifiCare established PacifiCare Military Health Systems, a subsidiary serving the Civilian Health and Medical Program for the Uniformed Services (CHAMPUS). Military Health Systems offered health benefits to military personnel and their dependents in 19 northeastern and midwestern states.

Although PacifiCare's financial performance was undeniably good in the early 1990s, the uncertainty imposed by industry forces made it impossible to predict the health maintenance organization's future prospects.

Principal Subsidiaries: PacifiCare of California; PacifiCare of Florida; PacifiCare of Oklahoma; PacifiCare of Oregon; PacifiCare of Texas; PacifiCare of Washington; Secure Horizons of California; Secure Horizons of Oklahoma; Secure Horizons of Oregon; Secure Horizons of Texas; Secure Horizons of Washington; California Dental Health Plan; PacifiCare Life & Health; PacifiCare Behavioral Health/LifeLink; PacifiCare Wellness Company; Covantage; Prescription Solutions; COMPREMIER; PacifiCare Military Health Systems; Preferred Health Resources, Inc.; Pasteur Health Plans.

Further Reading:

de Lafuente, Della, "UniHealth Planning to Relinquish Its Majority Stake in PacifiCare," *Modern Healthcare,* August 23, 1993, p. 7.
Kenkel, Paul J., "PacifiCare Unit to Boost Medicare Business," *Modern Healthcare,* September 20, 1993, p. 10.
"PacifiCare, Liberty Mutual in Work Comp Venture," *Business Insurance,* February 28, 1994, p. 17.
Paris, Ellen, "Marathon Man," *Forbes,* April 3, 1989, p. 166.
Savitz, Eric J., "No Miracle Cure: HMOs Are Not the Rx for Spiraling Health-Care Costs," *Barron's,* August 5, 1991, pp. 8–9, 21–23.
Shalowitz, Deborah, "PPO to Open Employee Child Care Center," *Business Insurance,* February 8, 1993, p. 6.

—April Dougal Gasbarre

Paging Network Inc.

4965 Preston Park Blvd.
Plano, Texas 75093
U.S.A.
(214) 985-4100
Fax: (214) 985-6711

Public Company
Incorporated: 1981
Employees: 3,900
Sales: $311.39 million
Stock Exchanges: NASDAQ
SICs: 4812 Radiotelephone Communications; 6719 Holding
    Companies, Not Elsewhere Classified

Paging Network Inc., known as PageNet, is the largest provider
of wireless digital messaging services in the United States with
more than 4.1 million pagers in service. According to PageNet's
1993 annual report, the company has a subscriber base three
times as large as that of its nearest competitor. PageNet operates
in all 50 states and the District of Columbia. Its combined local,
regional, and national service areas encompass more than 90
percent of the U.S. population.

PageNet was established in 1981 by George M. Perrin, who
served as president and chief executive until 1993. Perrin was
formerly the president of Gencom, Inc., a paging subsidiary of
Communications Industries Inc. Characterizing the industry as
comprising small companies using outdated equipment, Perrin
founded PageNet with the hope of building a more efficient and
less costly service. Start-up financing of $6 million was pro-
vided by a group of Chicago-based venture capitalists.

PageNet began operations in June 1982, with headquarters established in the Dallas suburb of Plano. That year, Terry L.
Scott, formerly with Arthur Young & Co., joined the company
as chief financial officer; Scott would succeed Perrin as president and chief executive officer in 1993. PageNet's first paging
systems were established in Detroit and Phoenix, and expansion
in Ohio and Texas quickly followed. Marketing efforts focused
on offering quality service at the lowest cost, and, by 1983,
PageNet's first full year of operation, the company reported net
revenues of $11.8 million.

By transmitting signals over radio frequencies controlled and
allocated by the Federal Communications Commission (FCC),

paging services allowed subscribers to receive messages
through the individual paging devices they carried. Early pagers
notified subscribers of incoming calls by sounding a tone; upon
hearing the tone, the subscriber would then use an established
telephone number to return the call.

However, technological advances soon led to the development
of numeric display pagers. To activate numeric display pagers, a
caller dialed a telephone number assigned to the paging service
subscriber. Using a touch tone phone, the caller could enter the
numeric code displayed on his pager. Most often the code
entered was a phone number at which the caller could be
reached. Pagers notified subscribers of incoming calls by vibrating or beeping and were often called "beepers." By the middle
of the decade, numeric display pagers had supplanted the tone-
only models as the most popular form of pager.

In 1987, PageNet introduced alphanumeric pagers. These
pagers had the ability to display alphabet characters as well as
numbers. Although they offered increased flexibility in messaging, alphanumeric pagers failed to gain widespread popularity due to the higher cost of the service, difficulties with the
technology, and the inconvenience callers experienced in trying
to input messages. PageNet reported that in 1993, 95 percent of
the company's customers continued to use numeric display
pagers.

During the early 1990s, PageNet continued to grow by adding
subscribers in existing market regions and by expanding into
new geographic territory. As pagers became more popular
among a wider range of customers, PageNet's subscriber base
grew. Customers included large and small businesses, government agencies, tradesmen, service providers, professionals,
models, flight attendants, salespeople, and even expectant fa-
thers. In 1991, the company signed up its one-millionth subscriber.

Up until this time, pagers had been leased or sold by a direct
sales force. In 1991, however, Pagenet added an indirect channel of distribution, offering its products and services through
retailers and other resellers. By 1993, about 40 percent of
PageNet's products were sold through a direct business-to-
business sales force. The remaining 60 percent of sales were
accomplished through indirect sellers.

During this time, PageNet entered a phase of expansion, which
it funded, in part, by going public. An initial public offering
(IPO) made in October 1991 raised $116 million. The move
made PageNet the first publicly traded independent paging
company in the United States. An additional $200 million was
subsequently raised through a public debt offering in May 1992.

PageNet entered 13 new territories in a multi-year expansion
program initiated in 1992. By the end of 1994, PageNet had
operations in virtually every major U.S. market. In entering
these new markets, PageNet followed a proven strategy that
offered high quality, low cost paging services. PageNet was
able to offer lower prices due to its size and the economies of
scale it could achieve. For example, PageNet purchased more
than a million pagers from Motorola annually. PageNet received a substantial discount on the large order, and, in turn,
passed along the savings to its customers. According to a report
in *Forbes,* PageNet's costs per subscriber were approximately

33 percent below the industry average, and prices charged to its subscribers were about 22 percent less than prices charged by its competitors. As a result, PageNet's operating cash flow, a measure commonly used to judge the financial health of paging services, produced a higher margin than could be attained by others.

PageNet also expanded into areas that complemented its paging service, including data transmission and voice messaging services. According to a company statement, any information capable of being digitized could be sent over the PageNet transmission system. Innovative technologies allowed subscribers to take advantage of news and stock quote updates, voice mail, fax forwarding, and data transmission to portable computers. PageNet's PageMail was an automated answering service that let callers hear a pre-recorded announcement and leave a numeric or voice message. Another new service, FaxNow, received and stored faxed transmissions. Subscribers alerted to an incoming fax were able to call from a touch tone phone and direct the fax to any convenient receiving device.

PageNet also became the first company to design and build a 900MHz system, which provided access to newly allocated radio frequencies. This helped to alleviate problems in urban markets caused by frequency congestion. In addition, the company expanded its customer service capability, and, by the end of 1992, PageNet had invested $12 million in a computer system able to handle all customer records.

Expansion continued in 1993 with the construction of two nationwide frequencies. The nationwide frequencies, constructed by identifying unused or little-used frequencies and obtaining the necessary FCC licenses, were added at a cost of $10 million. About 300 new transmitters were also erected, primarily in areas lacking local service. In 1994, the network was strengthened by the addition of 850 transmitters. PageNet's nationwide network has 1,750 transmitters, more than twice as many as any other paging carrier. Each of the two new frequencies held the capacity to serve 600,000 to 800,000 numeric display pagers.

Following its acquisition of the nationwide frequencies, PageNet launched PageNet Nationwide, which offered subscribers the lease of a pager, a personal 800 number, and the ability to receive pages anywhere in the nation without notifying the company of their movement. Although nationwide subscribers for all paging carriers represented only about two percent of paging customers, PageNet expected demand to increase because of its competitive rates and superior digital network. During its first month of availability, 7,700 subscribers signed up for PageNet Nationwide.

In 1993, PageNet reported net revenues of $311.4 million, an increase of 40.3 percent over 1992. In addition, 990,615 new pagers were brought into service. Of these, 70 percent were attributed to sales in areas serviced prior to 1992, indicating the success of the company's plan to increase its presence in existing markets. Such market penetration was associated, in part, with increased sales to nontraditional users; PageNet's 1993 annual report highlighted one innovative use of a PageNet pager by the family of an infant in need of a heart transplant. According-

ing to a PageNet statement, the company had a policy of donating paging services to prospective organ recipients.

In early 1994, PageNet entered into an agreement with Ameritech to market its nationwide paging service under the name Ameritech Nationwide. With Ameritech functioning as a national reseller, the subscriber base grew dramatically. By the end of the first quarter of 1994, the company reported more than 32,000 nationwide pagers in service.

That year, PageNet also announced an agreement with Hewlett-Packard to provide wireless data and messaging services for HP's StarLink product. StarLink supplied subscribers with services such as E-mail, voice and data messages, news, sports, and financial information via palmtop and notebook computers. The service was made possible using an innovative device called a PCMCIA receiver card, which could be inserted into a computer enabling it to receive wireless digitized data.

Moreover, PageNet began testing a new voice messaging product, VoiceNow, which was developed in partnership with Motorola. Operating as a portable answering machine small enough to carry in a purse or pocket, VoiceNow was made possible by PageNet's two-way transmission capabilities. Under the new system, the paging terminal received a voice mail message, located the receiver, and then transmitted a digitized voice message. Moreover, VoiceNow offered subscribers the option of replaying a message upon its receipt or storing it for retrieval at a later time. Although the concept of voice paging had emerged in the 1980s, early products proved inconvenient; improved technology, however, such as data compression and digital messaging, had allowed for service that took up less space on the frequency and featured better sound quality for a lower price. PageNet expects VoiceNow to be available during 1995 at about $20 per month, twice the cost of conventional numeric paging but still substantially less than cellular phone service.

In 1994, *The Wall Street Journal* estimated that pagers were used by approximately seven percent of the U.S. population. Almost 20 million units were in operation, and some analysts expected that number to grow by about 20 percent annually through the 1990s. New York industry analyst Salomon Brothers Inc. expected pager penetration to increase to 8.6 percent of the population by the end of 1994. PageNet estimated that its share of the domestic paging market stood at 16 percent, making it the largest single provider of paging services. The company attributed its success to its ability to simplify the process for consumers and to contain costs.

PageNet reported net revenues for the first quarter of 1994 exceeding $90 million, representing a 32 percent increase over the revenues for the first quarter of the previous year. Although the company reported a net loss of $7.7 million, its operating cash flow of $29.6 million represented an increase of 42.7 percent over the first quarter of 1993. In addition, PageNet products were offered by more than 4,000 resellers.

PageNet expected to continue its practice of growth through expansion and acquisition. In 1994, the company participated in FCC auctions to acquire narrowband personal communications services (PCS) frequencies. PageNet won three nationwide licenses—the maximum allowed. Moreover, Pagenet was anticipating increased sales following its introduction of advanced paging units, slated to debut in late 1994. These units were expected to operate more efficiently than the company's older pagers and to make better use of radio frequencies.

Principal Subsidiaries: Paging Network of St. Louis, Inc.; Paging Network of Louisiana, Inc.; Paging Network of Upstate New York, Inc.; Paging Network of Minnesota, Inc.; Paging Network of Oklahoma, Inc.; Paging Network of South Carolina, Inc.; Paging Network of Tennessee, Inc.; Paging Network of Wisconsin, Inc.; Paging Network of Hartford/Springfield, Inc.

Further Reading:

"Ameritech to Resell Pagenet's Nationwide Paging Service," *PR Newswire,* April 6, 1994.

Bates, Daniel, "Pager Firms Hear PageNet's Signal, Prepare for War," *Pittsburgh Business Times,* September 28, 1992.

Hill, Dee, "Industry Front-Runners Positioned for Explosive Growth," *Dallas Business Journal,* February 14, 1992.

Morgenson, Gretchen, "A Pager in Every Pocket?," *Forbes,* December 21, 1992.

Nethery, Ross, "PageNet Signals Investors to Buy, Buy, Buy," *Dallas Business Journal,* January 15, 1993.

"Paging Network Reports Record Growth in Net Revenues, Cash Flow and Pagers in Service," *PR Newswire,* April 28, 1994.

Pope, Kyle, "Motorola Plans a New Pager for Next Year," *The Wall Street Journal,* April 8, 1994.

Silbert, Lurie, "3 Meld, Biggest Paging Source Born," *HFD,* March 8, 1993.

—Karen Bellenir

Payless Cashways, Inc.

Two Pershing Square
2300 Main, P.O. Box 419466
Kansas City, Missouri 64141-0466
U.S.A.
(816) 234-6000
Fax: (816) 234-6361

Public Company
Incorporated: 1988
Employees: 18,000
Sales: $2.5 billion
Stock Exchanges: New York
SICs: 5211 Lumber and Other Building Materials; 5251
Hardware Stores; 5231 Paint, Glass, and Wallpaper Stores

Payless Cashways, Inc. ranks fourth among the United States' building supply retailers, after Home Depot, Inc., Lowe's Companies, Inc., and Sherwin-Williams Co. The chain's 197 stores operate in 26 states under the names Payless Cashways, Furrow Lumberjack, Hugh M. Woods, Somerville Lumber, and Knox Lumber. Seven decades in the building supply industry have seen Payless's customer base shift from professional tradesmen to lay "do-it-yourselfers" and back again. By 1993, professional customers comprised almost 50 percent of sales. Payless Cashways went public in 1993, after five years under private ownership. While the company's sales increased steadily in the early 1990s, its losses mounted to over $86 million in the first three years of the decade. The sale of 70 percent of its shares raised revenues for debt retirement and a reorganization that CEO David Stanley hoped would return Payless Cashways to profitability.

The building supplies chain was founded in 1930 by Sanford "Sam" Furrow, who had by that time accumulated 25 years of experience in lumberyards throughout Iowa and South Dakota. With help from sons Sanford and Vernon and a colleague, John Evans, Furrow raised $10,000 to buy a defaulted lumberyard in Pocahontas, Iowa. Although the Great Depression seemed an unfavorable time to go into business, Sam Furrow asserted that he "could not have gotten into the lumber business in a big way if times had been good." Indeed, banks were so desperate to recover any amount of money on foreclosed mortgages that Furrow was able to negotiate low purchase prices on two other lumberyards in the Iowa towns of Early and Webster City by mid-1932, thereby giving each of his sons a business to manage.

Sam Furrow continued to work for the Fullerton Lumber Company, with which he had been employed since 1912, and he named his Pocahontas business Kiefer-Wolfe Lumber Company to conceal the fact of his ownership. When the Fullerton Lumber Company discovered Sam's duplicity in 1933, he quit and went to work at the renamed Pocahontas Lumber Store. The three-store chain carried small selections, focusing primarily on lumber, paint, and builder's hardware in one 80- to 100-square-foot room. Furrow's lumberyards earned steady profits during the 1930s by establishing comprehensive contracts with insurance companies, which repossessed and repaired numerous dilapidated farms during the Depression.

Sam Furrow soon began challenging established business practices in the regional building materials industry, first taking on the Lumber Trust. This amalgamation of businesses was linked by a mutually beneficial price-fixing agreement that helped everyone but the customer. Furrow launched his Webster County Lumber Store in Fort Dodge, Iowa, in 1937 by advertising "Live and Let Live Prices" that were set without regard to the Lumber Trust. Delighted customers flocked to the business, substantiating Furrow's notion that high sales volume, and not the highest margin the market would bear, was the key to success in his chosen field. He gradually increased merchandise selections at his yards, adding plaster board, ceiling tiles, insulation, and asphalt shingles; by the end of the decade, Furrow's stores were offering over 200 products.

After World War II, John Evans and Sam Furrow split their partnership. Furrow kept all but the Fort Dodge and Webster City yards and, in 1947, he opened a new location in Iowa Falls, Iowa, to be managed by son Vern. There, Vern first experimented with the "cash-and-carry" policy that would later be applied chainwide. The change reflected shifts in the store's customer base and its terms. Before this time, most customers were professional contractors accustomed to making large orders on credit. After the war, however, many retail suppliers to construction outfits had trouble collecting on accounts receivable; rising lumberyard prices reflected those difficulties. At the same time, increasing numbers of laymen began to circumvent professional repairmen's high rates by tackling their own home repair and improvement projects. Low cash-and-carry prices, as well as more aggressive direct mail advertising, attracted this new class of do-it-yourselfers and bolstered the building suppliers' cash flow.

The loose-knit chain that would become Payless Cashways grew rather spontaneously during these early decades. The family members and long-time colleagues who opened new locations contributed to each new store's startup costs and were therefore entitled to a share of the profits. This arrangement fostered decentralization and self-motivation among individual store managers, considered a major element of the chain's early success. However, in the 1950s, the Furrows instituted several changes that made the loose-knit lumberyards more of a modern retail chain.

Having suffered a mild heart attack in 1950, Sam Furrow gradually turned the business over to his sons. In 1951, Vern and Sanford Jr. established a wholesale company, Iowa Lumber and Supply, to pool purchasing and distribution for the stores and thereby achieve economies of scale. Relinquishing management of their lumberyards to take more active roles in the management of the chain, Sanford and Vernon assumed the roles of president and vice president, respectively, at the new company, which had eight stores by 1954. Within a year, the Furrows brought all the chain's accounting under one firm and unified advertising and promotion. Under the name Payless Cashways, the stores adopted a logo featuring a curved red arrow and Payless Pete, a caricature of a lumberjack. By the end of the decade, the chain had added stores in Minnesota, Illinois, and Arizona.

When patriarch Sam Furrow and son Sanford died within a year of each other late in the 1950s, Vernon was unexpectedly left to head the chain. The 52-year-old had hoped to retire several years earlier but was instead thrust into a leadership role. In spite of his initial reluctance, Vern lead the company's expansion into New Mexico, Colorado, and Nebraska, before taking the company public as Payless Cashways, Inc. in 1969. Vernon was elected chairperson of the 16-store company, and Robert Lincoln, who had served as the company's first chainwide accountant, became president and treasurer. During its first year as a public entity, Payless recorded sales of $24 million and $.9 million in profits.

Four decades of active family management came to end in 1971, when Vernon Furrow retired. Robert Lincoln became chairperson, president, and chief executive officer. Flush with the infusion of funds from its initial public offering, Payless Cashways focused on growth in the 1970s, concentrating on establishing new stores, expanding and remodeling existing stores, and increasing each location's product line. The company also established its construction division, anticipating dramatic growth in that segment.

Moreover, a new tactic, dubbed invasion, established several stores in a single market for increased impact. Payless "attacked" Dallas and Kansas City, establishing four large-format suburban stores that featured 30,000 square-foot retail areas, 30,000 square-foot warehouses, and massive lumberyards on multiacre sites in each metropolitan area. Automotive and lawn-and-garden supplies were added to the stores' lines, which included over 13,000 items by the end of the decade. The chain's physical growth was suspended only in 1974, which *Time* magazine called "the year the building stopped." Housing starts declined by more than half that year, and many construction firms failed as a result. However, by this time, Payless catered primarily to do-it-yourselfers, who used the building hiatus to fix up and remodel rather than purchase new homes. That year, the chain's sales and profits actually increased by 34 and 21 percent, respectively.

By the end of the 1970s, Payless boasted 68 stores in 14 states and nine distribution centers. Sites in Texas, Oregon, Missouri, Kansas, Oklahoma, California, and Indiana were also added under the name of Furrow's, due to trademark conflicts in several markets. In 1976, Lincoln abdicated the top position, citing "operational conflicts," and longtime employee Stan Covey was elected chairperson and chief executive officer. The following year, corporate headquarters were moved to Kansas City, Missouri, a more central location. The company's growth was in no way impeded by the management upheaval: sales increased from $24 million to $316.1 million between 1969 and 1979. Profits rose even faster, from less than $1 million to $14.5 million, over the same period. This growth coincided with a six-fold increase in the do-it-yourself market, from just under $6 billion in 1970 to $35 billion in 1980. By 1981, Payless Cashways was the fifth largest chain in the industry, and its annual sales growth in the last half of the 1970s had doubled the industry average.

The 1980s brought the election of a new company president, former attorney and stockbroker David Stanley, who directed a shift from traditional rural markets to more urban and suburban markets in an effort to capture a bigger share of the still-fragmented do-it-yourself market. This change called for an alteration of Payless's store formula, distribution channels and methods, and corporate image. Smaller stores with a more locally targeted inventory would strive to supply "virtually all home building needs," as Stanley told *Business Week* in 1981. Payless's wholesale distribution arm only controlled about 17 percent of the chain's distribution, while managers ordered the remainder of their merchandise directly from vendors. Stanley challenged the persistent autonomy of Payless store managers by directing an increase in the chain's share of cooperative buying to capitalize on previously untapped economies of scale. Payless hoped to transform its corporate image along with its target audience by shifting its appeal from farmers, who had comprised 40 percent of the customer base, to white-collar persons engaged in building projects on the weekends.

One thing Stanley did not change, however, was the growth rate at Payless: the chain doubled in size from 1979 to 1984, adding 39 stores in 1984 alone, including 14 Prime Home Improvement Centers in Colorado and Nevada, as well as Somerville Lumber in Massachusetts. That year, while Payless topped the $1 billion sales mark, profits declined nine percent from the previous year to $37.4 million. Daniel McConville, an analyst for *Barron's,* attributed the earnings decline to "indigestion."

Later in the decade, a takeover attempt by Asher Edelman prompted yet another major change at Payless Cashways. In 1988, Stanley marshaled a unique group of investors, under the name PCI Acquisition, to take the company private. The assemblage included Payless executives, financial institutions, and such key suppliers as Masco, a major faucet vendor that contributed over 20 percent of the $909 million needed for the leveraged buyout. Although highly irregular, the deal with Masco was not considered an infringement on competition because the supplier didn't earn an unfair advantage over its rivals for its contribution.

Although the leveraged buyout saved Payless from takeover, it was not an unqualified success. The company did not have a single year of profitability during the five years it was private, as a recession in its core mid- and southwest markets, high debt from the buyout, and competition from up-and-coming "category killer" Home Depot, Inc. combined to slow sales growth, weaken margins, and depress operating earnings. With the help of a team of outside consultants, Stanley opted to sidestep competition with Home Depot and return Payless Cashways' focus to professional contractors, a customer group that was growing at a faster rate than do-it-yourselfers.

Stanley and his colleagues formulated a reorganization of everything from distribution and inventory systems to supplier relationships and strategic focus. The new Payless featured separate entrances for contractors, better credit terms than do-it-yourselfers, phone and fax ordering services, delivery, and even free coffee. Moreover, lawn mowers and outdoor furniture were dropped from the merchandise line and were replaced with high-quality—and high-margin—professional tools. In 1992, Payless opened eight Remote Contractor Sales Offices, which offered in-stock, high-demand products and next-day on-site delivery, opening 17 more such offices the following year to access underserved areas within 50 to 75 miles of existing stores.

In 1993, the company experimented with two new formats targeted at the professional home builder and remodeler: Home and Room Designs featured kitchen and bath finishing products, and Tool Site offered 6,500 professional tools. While Payless was not alone in offering many of these services, none of its competitors courted the professional customer so steadfastly. From 1987 to 1993, the company's sales to professionals increased from 25 percent of total revenues to 45 percent, compared to around 20 percent for market leader Home Depot. Sales increased to $2.6 billion in 1993, but the chain remained unable to turn a profit.

Nevertheless, Stanley was able to sell 70 percent of Payless back to the public in 1993, raising $350 million in debt-reduction funds and thereby eliminating almost $80 million in annual interest expenses. Stanley projected the addition of 28 new stores by 1998, and Payless also took advantage of the North American Free Trade Agreement, announcing a joint venture with Grupo Industrial Alfa, S.A. de C.V. to establish 25 stores in Mexico by the turn of the century. The building supplies industry remained fragmented in the early 1990s (the top ten chains comprised only 12 percent of total annual sales), affording Payless Cashways an opportunity to establish a stable position among the leaders as market consolidation continued.

Principal Subsidiaries: Somerville Lumber & Supply Co. Inc.

Further Reading:

Cianci, Gary, ''Supplier Sources Fund Payless Cashways' LBO,'' *Chain Store Age Executive,* November 1988, p. 94.
Furrow, Virginia Sugg, *Aged in Wood: The Story of Payless Cashways, Inc.,* Kansas City: Payless Cashways, Inc., 1984.
Gross, Lisa, ''Do It Yourself,'' *Forbes,* October 11, 1982, pp. 102–103.
Haller, Karl, ''Warehouse Stores Lead Home Improvement Push,'' *Chain Store Age Executive,* August 1993, pp. 25A–27A.
McConville, Daniel J., ''Lumbering Giant: Payless Cashways Squaring Away Acquisitions,'' *Barron's,* January 14, 1985, pp. 22, 24, 31, 45.
Palmeri, Christopher, ''Remodeling Your Business,'' *Forbes,* August 16, 1993, p. 43.
''Payless: Zeroing in on Suburbia,'' *Business Week,* September 7, 1981, pp. 104–105.
Pike, Helen, ''Think Profit,'' *Computerworld,* April 3, 1989, pp. 18–24.

—April Dougal Gasbarre

PECO Energy Company

2301 Market Street
P. O. Box 8699
Philadelphia, Pennsylvania 19101
U.S.A.
(215) 841-4000
Fax: (215) 841-4188

Public Company
Incorporated: 1902 as Philadelphia Electric Company
Employees: 7,400
Sales: $3.99 billion
Stock Exchanges: New York Philadelphia
SICs: 4931 Electric and Other Services Combined; 4923 Gas
   Transmission and Distribution

PECO Energy Company ranked among America's top 25 electric and gas utilities in terms of annual sales in 1994. With a service area of 2,475 square miles in southeastern Pennsylvania, including the city of Philadelphia, the company serves over three million customers. Known as Philadelphia Electric Company for most of the twentieth century, the utility changed its name to PECO Energy Company in 1994: it had long been referred to by the acronym. In the early 1990s, PECO prepared for a less regulated electric industry with a corporate reorganization.

The Philadelphia Electric Company was incorporated in 1902, but finds it origins in The Brush Electric Light Company of Philadelphia, which was formed in 1881. In 1880, Thomas Dolan convinced ten of Philadelphia's wealthiest entrepreneurs to invest in a company in "the business of manufacturing, procuring, owning and operating various apparatus used in producing light, heat, or power by electricity or used in lighting buildings." The new venture traded a 50 percent share, or $100,000, of its stock for a license of the Brush arc dynamo, an electric generator that was then considered the best way to generate power for lighting.

Electric utilities customarily focused on a particular product, such as street lighting or industrial applications, in the late 1800s. As its name implied, The Brush Electric Light Company was primarily involved in commercial and street lighting. The Brush Company's first president was Henry Lewis, a dry goods merchant who served until his death in 1886. Dolan, who had

been treasurer, chairman of the executive committee, and defacto head of the company, assumed the presidency at that time. He deflected early criticism of the Brush's poles and wires, oversaw the construction of its first permanent generating facility, and helped increase the company's capitalization to $1 million to finance construction and expansion.

Throughout this early stage in the history of electric utilities, competition and fragmentation characterized the industry. Within the same city, varying voltages, currents, and frequencies provided by a multitude of companies made it difficult to develop standardized products. Utilities began to consolidate near the end of the nineteenth century to end competition and coordinate service. Brush merged with its most powerful rival, The United States Electric Lighting Company of Pennsylvania, in 1885.

The merged companies secretly formed an "Electric Trust," known more commonly today as a holding company, in 1886. Secrecy was required because of the mistrust in which the public and politicians held such combines. The Trust soon acquired or controlled four more small local utilities, issuing $3.5 million in bonds as financial backing. But, as its existence came to light in the early 1880s, public and media criticism of the "monopoly" intensified. The Trust's "unpopularity stemmed from its very name. Its behind-doors management of the operating companies could never bring it goodwill," according to Nicholas B. Wainwright in his *History of The Philadelphia Electric Company, 1881–1961.*

Competition hurt Brush as well. Its competitor, the Edison Electric Light Company of Philadelphia, had grown to equal the Trust in profits by 1892. Around the same time, local entrepreneur Martin Maloney reentered the electric industry after a successful gas venture. Maloney hoped to eliminate wasteful competition by consolidating Philadelphia's electric companies and standardizing service. He chartered the Pennsylvania Heat, Light and Power Company in 1895 with a massive capitalization of $10 million and immediately began to acquire competitors, taking over Columbia Electric Light Company and courting the Philadelphia Edison Company. By March 1896, he had merged with Edison and earned a seat on its board of directors.

When Maloney's Pennsylvania Heat acquired the Electric Trust and all its subsidiaries later that year, Thomas Dolan joined its board of directors. Unlike the Electric Trust, Maloney's consolidation scheme proceeded relatively smoothly in part because of a good public perception of his goals, which he stated in his first annual report: "To secure that class of service that would enable the Company to furnish to its patrons electricity under such conditions that they could use it more generally and apply it in many ways that the high prices prevailing prevented, and to demonstrate to the citizens of Philadelphia that a corporation could work for the benefit of the public and its stockholders at the same time." Maloney did, in fact, cut residential rates to below the national metropolitan average.

In 1898, Maloney absorbed five of Philadelphia's eight remaining independent arc lighting companies. A threat to his progress arose the following year, with the formation of the $25 million

National Electric Company. This new entity immediately acquired the Southern Electric Light and Power Company, one of the few strong competitors remaining. Maloney negotiated a merger of the two big companies that year. The combination had assets of $19.9 million and net profits of $518,000. The companies incorporated as the Philadelphia Electric Company (PE) in 1902.

Maloney retired and was succeeded as president by 29-year-old Joseph B. McCall, who guided the company through the difficult period of legal, financial, and technical reorganization that ensued. Demand had risen rapidly, and by the turn of the century, it was clear that the utility would need a massive central generating station. When PE's Station A on the Schuylkill River was completed in 1903, it was the largest in the state, generating over 7,000 kilowatts (kw). Although PE standardized much of its service as alternating current, most of downtown Philadelphia, which was served by the Edison division, continued to operate on direct current until 1935 (reflecting Thomas Edison's conviction that alternating current was dangerous). PE moved to a new, larger headquarters at the corner of Tenth and Chestnut streets in Philadelphia in 1907. That location would remain the center of PE operations until 1973.

Many factors encouraged a dramatic expansion of the electric industry during the first two decades of the twentieth century. Larger, more efficient equipment was developed and service areas were expanded to include rural areas. Company-sponsored sales departments promoted appliances like the electric washer, iron, refrigerator, and vacuum cleaner to encourage increased use of electricity. As new applications for electric power developed, demand increased significantly. PE raised its generating capacity to meet this ever-expanding demand: each of the 30,000- and 35,000-kw units installed in 1915 and 1916 had a higher capacity than the entire PE system of 1903 (at 20,000 kw).

After the United States entered World War I the following year, the manufacture of munitions, ships, and steel in the Philadelphia area kept PE operating at capacity throughout the era. The company was often challenged by coal shortages and government rationing during the conflict. A centennial history published by PE in 1981 quoted an employee of the era who affirmed "the sigh of relief" felt at Schuylkill Station on Armistice Day.

By 1918, PE had 103,000 customers, a figure that nearly tripled within five years to 306,000 in 1923. During that period, the electric utility added twelve generators with a total capacity of over 300,000 kw. Joseph B. McCall advanced to the chairmanship of the company in 1924, and was succeeded as president by Walter H. Johnson, who served for four years. Later that decade, PE completed its first hydroelectric project on the Conowingo River in northeast Maryland. The company obtained land and financing, met political and regulatory requirements, and overcame construction obstacles to complete the unit in 1928. With a generating capacity of 252,000 kw, the hydroelectric dam ranked second only to the one at Niagara Falls. That same year, William H. Taylor assumed PE's presidency.

PE recorded another influential event during the prosperous decade of the 1920s; the Pennsylvania-New Jersey Interconnection was created in 1927. This cooperative linked Public Service Electric and Gas Company of New Jersey (which had had a partnership with PE since 1923) and Pennsylvania Power & Light Company (of Allentown) with Philadelphia Electric. The organization took advantage of regular fluctuations in each utility's power requirements to achieve economies of scale. For example, Allentown experienced morning peaks in October due to its coal mining activities, while Newark and Philadelphia scored highs in the December holiday season. The three original members were joined by the General Public Utilities Corporation and the Baltimore Gas and Electric Company in 1956, when the cooperative's name was changed to the Pennsylvania-New Jersey-Maryland Interconnection (PJM). The Potomac Electric Power Company (PEPCO), serving metropolitan Washington, D.C., joined in 1965. The cooperative promoted savings and reliability.

In the early twentieth century, Philadelphia Electric's service area was surrounded by three major electric and gas utility companies under the aegis of United Gas Improvement Company (UGI) (which, coincidentally, had Thomas Dolan as a board member in common with PE). In spite of the general public's suspicion of monopolies, the financial community viewed the consolidation of UGI and PE as ultimately inevitable and beneficial. UGI acquired a controlling stake in Philadelphia Electric in February, 1928, and the two merged on October 31, 1929, adding 1,380 square miles, 88,000 electric customers and 112,000 gas customers, as well as 78,000 kw of electric generating capacity and three gas producing plants to Philadelphia Electric's operations. PE was reorganized into the Philadelphia and five suburban operating and commercial divisions.

The effect of the Depression on Philadelphia Electric was characterized by company historian Nicholas Wainwright as "harassing but not crippling." Net income actually increased in spite of a steady decline in residential and industrial customers. There were no large-scale layoffs; PE relied on attrition to shorten its payrolls. The company was surviving well enough, in fact, that during the depth of the Depression in 1932, it ordered one of the era's largest generating units. The 165,000 kw machine known as "Big Ben" was the first in the country to burn pulverized coal and employ electrostatic emissions reducers. It ran from 1935 to 1977. In 1938, Horace P. Liversidge, who had first been employed by PE in 1898 as a wiring inspector, advanced to the company's presidency. Liversidge has been credited with shaping the company's modern history.

The Depression also brought Franklin D. Roosevelt's New Deal and with it the Securities and Exchange Commission, which regulated the activities of holding companies, in 1935. Electric utilities had been regulated since the 1910s, but holding companies were not regulated early in the twentieth century. Although some holding companies were legitimate structures created to coordinate associated industries, many were precarious "pyramids" of companies. The organizers of these corporate entities could use the combined value of subsidiaries to finance loans, then charge the subsidiaries outrageous rates for the redistributed funds. As the oldest public utility holding company in the world, UGI was reluctant to submit to a breakup order, but by

1943, Philadelphia Electric was once again an independent company. PE retained the suburban gas and electric utilities that had been merged into it in 1929.

World War II once again forced a concentration of manufacturing capacity on war production: Philadelphia produced ships, tanks, and armaments, and PE supplied the power to do so. Before the United States entered the war in December 1941, these preparations were made in addition to normal civilian production. Voluntary and mandatory restrictions on the use of power, as well as curtailment of civilian production, prevented a wartime power shortage.

The postwar era brought a new focus on PE's gas operations, especially after 1948, when the "Big Inch" and "Little Big Inch" interstate pipelines were converted from oil to natural gas transmission. Philadelphia Electric completed its conversion from manufacturing gas locally to purchasing gas produced in the Gulf states in 1964, and even undertook its own exploration and production efforts in the late 1970s.

R. George Rincliffe advanced through the executive ranks to PE's presidency in 1952. He assumed the company's chair and newly created chief executive office ten years later, holding those positions until his retirement in 1971. During his tenure, Rincliffe oversaw the unabated expansion of PE's capacity through a variety of methods, including traditional generators, hydroelectric plants, and nuclear power. The company brought its Eddystone plant, which featured the world's most efficient coal-fired generating unit, on line in 1960. A joint minemouth generation project among members of the PJM to create the Keystone plant in Indiana, Pennsylvania, was undertaken in 1962. Located at the fuel source, Keystone generated power and linked the PJM with other cooperative systems on the National Electric Reliability Council, a U.S./Canada grid which aided in the efficient supply of bulk power throughout North America. Keystone began running in 1967, the same year that Pennsylvania Electric's Muddy Run pumped-storage hydroelectric generating plant (the largest of its type) on the Susquehanna River began operation.

Philadelphia Electric first participated in studies on the feasibility of using nuclear energy to drive power plants as a member of the Atomic Power Development Associates, Inc., in 1952. Then, in 1958, the company joined over fifty other utilities to build a prototypical reactor dubbed Peach Bottom No. 1. It took almost a decade for the unit to go into production, but by that time, PE had committed itself to shares in four 1-million-kw nuclear units. The company regarded nuclear power generation as vital for two reasons. First, during the 1950s, demand for electricity rose sharply due to the advent of television, increased commercial and residential use of air conditioning, and industrial expansion. Second, the federal government established the first stringent emissions controls in 1960. The company reasoned that nuclear capabilities would enable it to maintain standards of service while conforming to clean air and water standards. PE's employment of nuclear energy seemed to be progressing well until 1968, when regulatory and other delays prevented completion of two wholly owned nuclear power plants at Limerick, Pennsylvania, until the mid and late 1980s.

Robert F. Gilkeson assumed PE's helm in 1971 at the outset of a decade characterized by federal, state, and local regulation of virtually every aspect of its business, from employment to environmental practices. Economic fluctuations influenced decisions about capital investment and rate increases. Gilkeson launched a Corporate Communications Department in 1975 to act as a liaison between the utility and the media, government agencies, and the general public. J. L. Everett, III succeeded Gilkeson in 1978, just in time to see Philadelphia Electric's total assets exceed $5 billion for the first time.

PE was faced with another series of regulatory and financial hurdles in the 1980s. The utility suffered one of the most damaging and traumatic episodes in its history when inspectors from the Nuclear Regulatory Commission (NRC) found a control room employee "inattentive to duty," or, as Amy Barrett of *Financial World* alleged in a May 1990 article, "operators were found playing video games and having rubber band fights in the control rooms" at the Peach Bottom nuclear facility. The plant was ordered closed within 24 hours and remained shut down for over two years. During that time, criticism from the NRC and the influential Institute of Nuclear Power and Operations poured in. Joseph F. Paquette, Jr. was called back to PE after a brief hiatus to accept the chair and chief executive office of the troubled company in 1988. He set out to transform the company by focusing on long-term strategic planning, human resource management, and downsizing.

Over the course of the 1980s and into the 1990s, the Pennsylvania Public Utilities Commission (PUC) executed several policy reversals with regard to Philadelphia Electric, its nuclear operations, and its rates. In 1982, the PUC refused to allow a rate hike to pay for the second phase of the plant and halted the project. Three years later, as Limerick's first phase was nearing completion, the Commission gave PE the green light on Limerick II, but set stringent time and financial limitations on the project. Although the plant came in almost $400 million under budget and nine months ahead of schedule, the PUC refused to increase rates to help cover capital costs, citing "excess reserve power capacity," and thereby implying that Limerick II was inherently wasteful. Earnings in the late 1980s and early 1990s reflected the rate ruling, as per share income plummeted from a high of almost $3 million in 1984 to $2.33 million in 1987 and $0.07 million in 1990. That year, CEO Paquette instituted cost-cutting measures that included an early retirement program, reduced advertising budget, and executive pay cuts of two percent to ten percent. Paquette himself took his second salary cut that year.

These cost-cutting efforts bore fruit before the middle of the decade, as per share earnings recovered somewhat to $2.45 million in 1993 on year-to-year revenue and profit increases of 0.6 percent (to $3.99 billion) and 23 percent (to $590.6 million), respectively. The importance of nuclear generation to Philadelphia Electric's operations was reflected in the fact that the nuclear segment of the company's total electric power output was 60 percent in 1993. A reorganization undertaken that year planned to create five strategic business units—Consumer Energy Services, Gas Services, Nuclear Generation, Power Generation, and Bulk Power Enterprises—by January 1995. Paquette and his team of executives hoped that the revision would prepare the company for the more competitive (and less regulated) environment anticipated by the electric industry in the 1990s.

Principal Subsidiaries: Conowingo Power Co.; Eastern Pennsylvania Development Corp.; Eastern Pennsylvania Exploration Co.; Philadelphia Electric Power Co.; The Susquehanna Electric Co.

Further Reading:

Barrett, Amy, ''The Luck of the Irish,'' *Financial World,* v. 159, May 29, 1990, pp. 28–29.

Bleiberg, Robert M., ''PECO's Woes,'' *Barron's,* v. 70, May 28, 1990, p. 12.

Laabs, Jennifer J., ''Plant Shutdown Forces Changes in Operations,'' *Personnel Journal,* v. 72, March 1993, pp. 112–122.

Philadelphia Electric Company, *Milestones: Philadelphia Electric Company, 1881–1981,* Philadelphia: Philadelphia Electric Company, [1981].

Wainwright, Nicholas B., *History of The Philadelphia Electric Company, 1881–1961,* Philadelphia: The Philadelphia Electric Company, 1961.

—April Dougal Gasbarre

The Pep Boys—Manny, Moe & Jack

3111 W. Allegheny Avenue
Philadelphia, Pennsylvania 19132
U.S.A.
(215) 229-9000
Fax: (215) 227-4067

Public Company
Incorporated: 1925 as Pep Auto Supply Co.
Employees: 15,000
Revenues: $1.24 billion
Stock Exchanges: New York
SICs: 5531 Auto and Home Supply Stores; 7538 General
   Automotive Repair Shops.

With close to 400 automotive aftermarket superstores in 29 states and plans to add 200 more stores and 8 more states to its roster by the end of 1997, The Pep Boys—Manny, Moe & Jack ranked as the nation's largest auto parts and service chain in early 1994. The chain underwent an intense, five-year period of expansion in the late 1980s and early 1990s that catapulted it from a successful regional competitor to a formidable national player. With its unsurpassed diversity in automotive retail, including tires, hard parts, accessories, and service, Pep Boys has succeeded in catering to both the "do-it-yourself" and (in a phrase often employed by CEO Mitchell Leibovitz) "do-it-for-me" markets. Advertised as "the three best friends your car ever had," the original Pep Boys launched their first auto parts store just as the automobile was coming of age.

Pep Boys was founded by Emanuel (Manny) Rosenfeld, Maurice (Moe) Strauss, Moe Radavitz, and W. Graham (Jack) Jackson, Philadelphians who met and became friends during their World War I stint in the U.S. Navy. In 1921, less than 15 years after mass production came to the auto industry, the four war buddies put up $200 each to open an auto supplies store in their hometown. Strauss, who had already made two unsuccessful attempts at entrepreneurship, started out as a silent partner—he was already employed at a competing store, and wasn't ready to give up the steady income.

The partners rented a small storefront in Philadelphia, so small that only the shortest of names would fit on its marquee. Corporate folklore tells of a brainstorming session that adopted the "Pep" from Pep Valve Grinding Compound, one of the shop's first product lines. Pep Auto Supply fit neatly above the

shop's front door, but there is more to the chain's christening. The tale goes on to tell of a street cop who, upon issuing equipment citations, would recommend that the motorists go to the "boys" at Pep for replacement parts. The three Pep Boys who remained after Moe Radavitz cashed out in the early 1920s tacked their own names on in 1923.

The corporate caricatures that would later become famous throughout the country were commissioned shortly thereafter and drawn by Harry Moskovitch. Manny, a now-reformed cigar smoker with a Charlie Chaplin mustache, was on the left. Moe, who would be known as "the father of the automotive aftermarket," was in the middle. Jack's grinning caricature made a brief appearance before being replaced with that of Moe's brother, Isaac (Izzy) Strauss, on the right. (The company name stayed the same despite the personnel changes—"Manny, Moe and Izzy" just didn't sound right.) As the chain grew, the Pep Boys were rendered in cotton on T-shirts, in ink on match books, and in cement as statues in front of stores. The bizarre but distinctive trademark was later joked about in Johnny Carson's *Tonight Show* monologue, parodied on *Saturday Night Live,* and came to life in Claymation for late 1980s television ads.

In the late 1920s, Manny Rosenfeld brought his brother, Murray, into the business and Izzy Strauss broke away to start his own automotive chain. The sometimes convoluted family ties at Pep Boys remained strong through the 1980s, and the Strauss and Rosenfeld families controlled one-fifth of the chain's stock into the early 1990s.

By 1928, Pep Boys had a dozen stores in the Philadelphia area, and Strauss began to feel the pull of the burgeoning California market. He had lived briefly in the state in the early 1920s, when he became convinced that it was an ideal location for an automotive retail business. In 1932, he sent Murray Rosenfeld, called "perhaps the most astute merchandiser of the Philadelphia group" by *Aftermarket Business* in 1991, out to the West Coast to launch what was commonly known as Pep Boys West. The first two California stores were opened in 1933 in Los Angeles. By that time, the chain had 40 Philadelphia outlets.

Although the founders had planned to operate both segments of the business in concert, the physical distance between them soon forced the division of primary merchandising functions. For example, intense competition compelled Pep Boys West to expand the size of, and selection at, those stores, whereas east coast outlets concentrated more on service. Manny Rosenfeld stayed in Philadelphia, his brother Murray ran the Los Angeles operation, and Moe Strauss commuted between the two.

During World War II, automotive production was curtailed while car companies focused on war production, and "Murray the merchandiser" stocked Pep Boys West shelves with nonautomotive products like work clothes, bicycles, and lawn and garden equipment. The west coast division also experimented with wholesaling and even exporting.

When the retailer went public in 1946, Manny Rosenfeld was named president and Moe Strauss was elected chairman of the board. For the next three decades, the company grew relatively slowly under what was later interpreted as a preponderance of caution—the company insisted on owning, rather than leasing, its stores, and doggedly avoided debt. Under the direction of

Moe Strauss, who assumed the additional responsibilities of president in 1960 after Manny Rosenfeld's death, the chain only grew by two net stores over the twenty-year period from 1964 to 1984. The fiscally conservative Strauss occupied both posts until 1973, when he relinquished the title of president to son Benjamin; however, he remained chairman through 1977. He was still a member of the board of directors at his death in 1982, over six decades after he helped found the business.

Ben Strauss advanced to chairman and CEO that year, and Morton (Bud) Krause, son-in-law of Moe Strauss, was named president. When he took an early retirement in 1984 at the age of 54, Ben Strauss shouldered the responsibilities of all three offices. In 1986, Strauss called on Mitchell Leibovitz to become Pep Boys' first president from outside the founding families. Leibovitz had joined the company at the age of 33 in 1978 as controller and was promoted to chief financial officer within a year. He had worked as a teacher and coach before earning an M.B.A. from Temple University by going to night classes. Leibovitz caught Ben Strauss' attention while employed as a CPA for the accounting firm that audited Pep Boys' books. From 1979 to 1984, Leibovitz was in charge of Pep Boys' eastern operations. He closed down 32 "small and stodgy" stores, then opened sixty stores in the ensuing two years. The east coast expansion was financed with an offering of $50 million in convertible debentures (bonds that can be converted to stock), a debt Moe Strauss would never have taken on.

By 1986, when Leibovitz assumed the presidency, Pep Boys was the second-largest chain in the highly fragmented, $100 billion automotive aftermarket industry, after Western Auto Supply Co. Its earnings had increased 18 percent annually from 1982 to 1986, but the new leader had even bigger plans for the retailer. As president, Leibovitz mapped out and executed a five-year plan to consolidate Pep Boys' headquarters and simultaneously expand its geographic reach, in the hopes of its becoming the Home Depot of the retail automotive aftermarket industry. In fact, Leibovitz enjoyed the counsel of Bernie Marcus, the executive who catapulted Home Depot to the upper echelon of the do-it-yourself home repair market. Leibovitz recognized the industrywide changes that could either launch Pep Boys to the top of the heap or see it acquired by a competitor by the end of the century.

During the 1980s, the traditionally fragmented retail automotive aftermarket industry became more competitive as larger chains began to emerge. Many neighborhood service garages were being transformed into convenience stores with gas stations, and some of the larger chains that had provided limited service, like J.C. Penney and K Mart, also started phasing out auto repairs. All the while, cars were growing increasingly complex and difficult for non-pros to fix.

In the face of these market shifts, Leibovitz set out a five-year plan for Pep Boys that encompassed six goals: store expansion, a refined merchandise mix, increased warehousing and distribution capacity, improved promotion of the service operations, modernization of systems support, and consolidation of the headquarters in Philadelphia. From February 1986 to February 1991, Pep Boys invested $477 million in the plan—almost as much as 1986's sales of $486 million.

During that period, the number of Pep Boys stores doubled to 337 and product offerings tripled from 9,000 items to 24,000. Individual locations were expanded into a "superstore" or "warehouse" format, with an average size of 23,000 square feet, and the company launched an "everyday low price" strategy. These larger stores also featured an increased number of service bays—a fairly unique feature in the industry—and services offered were expanded. Unlike many of its competitors, which would only install tires and batteries (if anything), Pep Boys' mechanics would perform practically any automotive service except body work and engine replacement. Pep Boys' new computerized merchandising and inventory control helped stores tailor their offerings to the local market. For example, rural stores might carry more truck parts, whereas urban stores might stock more foreign car parts. Weekends were added to the retailer's schedule, and hours were extended to 9 p.m. on weeknights.

To tout the service bays and increase emphasis on national brands, Leibovitz raised Pep Boys' advertising budget and began to divert funds from traditional, full-page newspaper ads to direct mail, catalogs, and electronic media. He also began phasing the Pep Boys caricature out of advertising and promotional material in an effort to modernize the company's image, even though "the boys" had ranked as one of the automotive aftermarket's five most recognized corporate symbols.

In 1991, as the company concluded its five-year plan and celebrated its 70th anniversary, it also topped $1 billion in annual sales, added 8 Sunbelt states to its geographic reach, and more than doubled corporate employment from 5,500 to 14,000. Leibovitz advanced to Pep Boys' chief executive office and the company was added to Standard & Poor's 500 Index in 1990. Although the young leader modestly deflected praise of his transformation of Pep Boys to the management team he had assembled, analysts gave him the lion's share of the credit for modernizing the chain.

Pep Boys is considered a noncyclical business, but its massive expenditures and assumption of debt combined with an early 1990s recession to depress profit growth. Net income declined from $42 million in 1989 to $32 million in 1990, then increased incrementally in 1991 and 1992. Pep Boys was able to begin fueling its continuing expansion and retire debt with cash flow in 1992. The company added 30 stores that year and took advantage of an "early conversion expiration" provision (also known as a "screw clause" to investors) to save $2.3 million in interest on a $75 million convertible debenture.

Pep Boys had long been known for its good working conditions and generous benefits, which helped the company attract and retain some of the industry's best employees for decades. Leibovitz instilled his employees with competitive fervor by staging ritual annihilations of competitors. Whenever competitive pressure from Pep Boys closed down a major rival's store, he added a photo of the closed-down outlet to his collection. Baseball caps bearing the vanquished competitors' corporate logos were incinerated, and Leibovitz videotaped the symbolic destruction for in-house pep rallies.

1993 saw the inauguration of yet another change at Pep Boys that was hailed by *Financial World* as "the final step in transforming the old-fashioned family-owned chain into a nation-wide leader.'' After a year of planning, Leibovitz put all his technicians and mechanics on commission in the hopes of attracting top employees and increasing their productivity. But just three months after he made the shift, consumer fraud inspectors in California, Florida, and New Jersey charged Sears Roebuck & Co.'s auto service division with systematically overcharging customers for unnecessary repairs. The allegations specifically cited Sears' commission program as the locus of the problem. Although chagrined at the negative publicity surrounding commissioned employees generally, Leibovitz confidently stuck with his plan, which incorporated several safeguards. The cornerstone of Pep Boys' system was an ethics policy that dictated termination of mechanics who made unnecessary repairs. Technicians, who are certified by the Institute for Automotive Service Excellence (ASE), also agreed to have their commission docked if their work had to be redone.

Even with commissions, Pep Boys' service cost 20 to 50 percent less than dealerships and independent garages. Service accounted for 13 percent of the retailer's total revenue in fiscal 1993, and income from that segment was increasing over 10 percent each year in the early 1990s. Sears' subsequent decision to cut back on auto service undoubtedly sent more business to Pep Boys' service bays.

Leibovitz worked to allay customers' ingrained apprehension about gouging in automotive repairs by offering a toll-free ''squeal line'' and postpaid comment cards addressed to the CEO. Complaints were categorized and tabulated to detect patterns of misconduct, and regional sales managers followed up each complaint with a personal contact. According to the chief, Pep Boys receives about 200 complaints and 200 compliments, out of about 5 million customers, each month. Commendations are reviewed and read on videotape for the firm's ''Customer Corner,'' a video presentation played back in company break rooms across the country.

Pep Boys emerged from the early 1990s recession with strong earnings and stock performance. Even though comparable store sales only increased 1 percent, profits grew by over 20 percent from 1992 to 1993, to $65.6 million and the share price jumped from less than $20 in early 1992 to over $30 by early 1994. Stock market observers predicted that Pep Boys' stock would increase 20 to 30 percent by the end of 1994. Future expansion was planned for new markets in Chicago, Ohio, Denver, Houston, the San Francisco Bay area, and New England. The chain also expected to increase its grip on existing markets in New York and New Jersey, Baltimore, Washington, D.C., Florida, and its historical strongholds in southern California and Philadelphia. Leibovitz projected that his company would cross the $2 billion sales mark by 1996.

Principal Subsidiaries: PBY Corp.; Pep Boys—Manny, Moe and Jack of California.

Further Reading:

Hass, Nancy, ''Truths of Commission,'' *Financial World,* January 19, 1993, pp. 28–29.

Johnson, Jay L., ''Pep Boys on the Fast Track,'' *Discount Merchandiser,* October 1990, pp. 18–25.

Kharouf, Jim, ''Pep Boys Speeding into Area,'' *Daily Southtown (Chicago),* June 22, 1994, pp. 1–2.

Levy, Robert, ''Manny, Moe & Jack on the Move,'' *Dun's Business Month,* July 1986, pp. 28–29.

Lubove, Seth, ''Retail Is Detail,'' *Forbes,* September 30, 1991, pp. 144, 146.

''Pep Boys: More Than an Industry Leader, an Institution,'' *Aftermarket Business,* December 1, 1991, pp. 17–39.

''Pep Boys Passes $1 Billion Mark,'' *Discount Merchandiser,* January 1992, pp. 14–17.

Silverthorne, Sean, ''Pep Boys' Mitchell Leibovitz: He Studied Industry Leaders to Recast Auto Parts Store,'' *Investor's Business Daily,* October 13, 1992, pp. 1–2.

Taylor, Alex III, ''How to Murder the Competition,'' *Fortune,* February 22, 1993, pp. 87, 90.

Wayne, Leslie, ''Pep Boys (Manny, Moe, and Jack) See Their Stock Climb,'' *The New York Times,* April 19, 1994.

Weiss, Gary, ''Beware the Turn of the Screw,'' *Business Week,* June 1, 1992, p. 108.

Werner, Thomas, ''Seeking No. 1: Pep Boys Expands Auto-Parts Chain by Big Leaps,'' *Barron's,* July 6, 1987, pp. 34–35.

—April Dougal Gasbarre

Policy Management Systems Corporation

One PMS Center
Blythewood, South Carolina 29016
U.S.A.
(803) 735-4000
Fax: (803) 735-5440

Public Company
Incorporated: 1980
Employees: 4,786
Sales: $435.1 million
Stock Exchanges: New York
SICs: 7372 Prepackaged Software; 7374 Data Processing and
    Preparation

Policy Management Systems Corporation (PMSC) provides computer software and information services that help property/casualty and life insurance companies manage their policies. The company's more than 90 software systems provide for the automation of many basic insurance processing functions such as underwriting, claims accounting, financial and regulatory reporting, and cash management. By 1994, PMSC had operations in 24 countries and 3,000 software systems licenses in force. The firm's consulting services include the design and management of automation packages for clients. PMSC's U.S. telecommunications network provides customers with the raw data necessary to set policy pricing and establish claims. After a brief foray into information services for health insurance companies, PMSC registered its first annual loss and exited that segment in 1993, due to uncertainty regarding health care reform.

PMSC began in 1966 as a division of Seibels, Bruce & Co., a South Carolina property casualty insurer. At that time, G. Larry Wilson, a sophomore majoring in business at the University of South Carolina, had a $100 per week internship at the firm. His assignment was to devise a method of automating the company's policy administration and claims processing functions. Although Wilson's experience with computers was limited, he worked diligently to acquire a greater understanding, often putting in eight-hour days at the company while maintaining a full course load at the university. Wilson's rewards were swift, impressive, and enduring. By the time he was a junior, he had advanced to director of the Seibels, Bruce & Co. systems and programming department. By 1970, the year he earned his M.B.A., Wilson was a vice-president.

The software programs Wilson helped develop automated premium calculation and billing procedures, and, as word of his computer-driven business solutions spread, other insurance companies became interested. In 1974, Seibels, Bruce began selling its programs to the entire property/casualty industry. Named for the basic mainframe system that was its primary product, PMSC went public in 1981, with Seibels, Bruce holding a controlling 82 percent stake. Wilson—who became president and chief executive officer of PMSC at the age of 35—and four colleagues retained a two percent interest in the company.

Throughout the early 1980s, PMSC grew by marketing long-term licenses of its proprietary insurance software systems and related automation support systems to property/casualty insurance companies. Moreover, the company augmented its business with the acquisitions of Mutual Data Inc. and Business Computer System Inc. in 1983. However, when the property/casualty segment of the insurance industry slumped mid-decade, PMSC's earnings flattened, and the company began to diversify its product offerings and target markets to protect itself from such downward cycles.

In 1985, PMSC began marketing information services to help underwriters and claims managers work more efficiently. PMSC expanded this business through product development and acquisition. It acquired regional information services—including Compuclaim Corp., Commercial Services, Inc., and Insurance Companies Inspection Bureau, Inc.—with the goal of amassing an electronic network that could gather and communicate data from all states and regions in the United States. PMSC achieved national coverage in the fields of motor vehicle reports (accident records), personal lines, and replacement costs by the end of 1986. Within two years, the company had also attained national coverage of premium audits and commercial lines inspections. The resulting information gathering network enabled PMSC to offer its clients the data necessary to make more informed assessments of risk selection, pricing, and claims adjusting. The diversification also reduced PMSC's dependence on software licensing revenues from almost 44 percent in 1985 to 16.5 percent by 1993. By 1991, database services brought in 30 percent of annual revenues.

PMSC's Series III platform was developed in the late 1980s as part of the company's information services business. PMSC invested over $100 million in the creation of this system, which integrated information and data gathering, processing, underwriting, claims handling, and reporting processes. The system's optical scanning and storage of typical insurance documents helped reduce clerical support and data entry, while its communications feature linked insurance agents, branch offices, and headquarters in what PMSC called "a seamless flow of information." Despite Series III's rather steep price—up to $50 million—by the end of 1990, PMSC had orders for the system from ten major insurance companies, including John Hancock Property & Casualty, Maryland Casualty, and five foreign insurers. Series III's customer base included 63 insurance companies in North America, Europe, and Australia by 1992.

PMSC's expansion of its target markets during the late 1980s added life and health insurance clients through acquisitions and joint ventures. The 1987 purchase of controlling interest in Aavant Health Management Group, Inc., of New Haven, Connecticut, brought a marketer of software for health maintenance organizations and preferred provider organizations. In 1989, PMSC invested over $16 million in the acquisition of Advanced System Applications, a Chicago-based premier supplier of systems and services to the group health insurance industry.

Over the course of the 1980s, Seibels, Bruce reduced its stake in PMSC and was replaced as a primary shareholder by International Business Machines Corp. (IBM). As part of an intensive campaign of equity investments in software companies, IBM offered to purchase 49 percent of PMSC stock in 1989. Worried that "Big Blue's" notorious bureaucracy would adversely affect PMSC, Wilson declined the proposal. He was, however, amenable to IBM's $116.8 million purchase of 19.8 percent of the stock. The alliance that resulted expedited software development and promoted the exchange of information between the two partners. IBM sales staff earned commissions for promoting PMSC's software, and PMSC was able to test insurance programs designed for IBM hardware while it was still in development.

In 1992, PMSC formed Inserv, a non-exclusive joint venture, with IBM subsidiary Integrated Systems Solutions Corp. Inserv was created to provide "outsourcing," or consultant-oriented automation services to property/casualty, life, and health insurers. While most analysts regarded this combination of the insurance industry's top hardware and software suppliers as fortuitous, some insisted that in-house information systems would continue to prevail. In response, Inserv's organizers promoted the financial and technological benefits of outsourcing to prospective clients. Wilson told *Computerworld* in March 1992 that the joint venture's niche would emerge from "the gap between [major insurance firms'] need for new technology and their [financial] ability to implement it."

Acquisitions in the early 1990s focused on gaining access to hospital medical records, attending physician statements, and personal history interviews for the life and health insurance industries. From 1988 to 1992, PMSC's annual revenues grew at an average rate of 23 percent, as sales doubled from $216.9 million to $497.1 million. During the same period, earnings increased at an average annual rate of 30.5 percent, nearly tripling from $20.5 million to $59.4 million. However, the company's impressive growth was forestalled in early 1993, as the company reported its first quarter of diminished earnings in its 12 years as a publicly traded company. In fact, PMSC's stock plummeted 41 points one day in April, losing nearly half its value in a precipitous drop from $84 to $43.

In a statement to *Datamation* in June 1993, Wilson attributed the tumble to the 1992 election of Bill Clinton, a Democrat whose campaign platform featured reform of the country's health care system. Uncertain of their future, many health insurers curtailed purchases of information services, effectively choking that segment of PMSC's business. Wilson noted that "as the industry became concerned about how changes in Washington would affect existing health companies, they cut back on purchases, and our quarterly earnings were down from $13.7 million in the previous quarter to around $10 million." The chairperson downplayed the effects of the health care crisis on future performance, noting that the majority of PMSC customers were in the policy/casualty segment. Nevertheless, the

episode Wilson characterized as "a little storm" early in the year soon prompted a reevaluation of PMSC's entire health insurance business.

In mid-1993, the company ascertained that that year's health insurance services revenues would only amount to half of those of 1992. As it became apparent that, either by government regulation or economic forces, the health care industry would be irrevocably changed, PMSC realized that insurers in that market would be reluctant to make a significant investment in its services "until the uncertainty regarding the ultimate outcome of reform was resolved." The company's decision to discontinue health insurance services resulted in a restructuring charge of $25.2 million, which contributed to 1993's net loss of $56.1 million, as sales declined 8.9 percent to $453.1 million.

Problems mounted as a group of shareholders brought a class action suit against the company. The litigation charged that PMSC had failed "to disclose certain information regarding, among other things, its business and prospects in violation of the Federal securities laws, the South Carolina Code and common law." PMSC denied the allegations, admitting to "errors in the application of accounting principles" in fiscal 1993's 10-K report submitted that December. The litigation remained unresolved in 1994.

During this time, PMSC created a new business to concentrate on life insurance services, acquiring the CYBERTEK Corporation of Dallas at a cost of almost $60 million. With a customer base of 100 companies, CYBERTEK was a top provider of information management systems and processing solutions for life insurance and financial services companies. PMSC focused on integrating this company's activities with its previously existing Series III software. PMSC also shifted its emphasis to international sales in the Australian, Canadian, and European markets. The company also formed an alliance with AT&T Global Information Solutions (formerly NCR Corporation) to develop a UNIX-based version of the Series III system. PMSC hoped to return to profitability through these new and developing businesses while remaining focused on the insurance industry.

Principal Subsidiaries: Policy Management Systems Canada Ltd.; Policy Management Systems International Ltd.; Policy Management Corp.; Policy Management Systems Netherlands BV; Policy Management Systems Barbados, ltd.; Policy Management Systems Europe Ltd.; P.M.S. Inc.; Policy Management Systems Australia Ptd. Ltd; Policy Management Systems Germany; Policy Management Systems Life, Inc.

Further Reading:

Geer, Carolyn Torcellini, "The Up & Comers: Insured Growth," *Forbes,* October 1, 1990, pp. 190–91.
Marcial, Gene G., "A Software Stock Rewards Faith," *Business Week,* October 14, 1985, p. 138.
Margolis, Nell, "Insurance Firms Doubt Big Blue Service Move," *Computerworld,* March 16, 1992, p. 12.
"Software Alliances," *IBM Directions,* Winter 1989/1990, pp. 29–35.
Strauss, Paul, "Datamation 100 North American Profiles: Policy Management Systems Corp.," *Datamation,* June 15, 1993, pp. 104, 107.

—April Dougal Gasbarre

Potter & Brumfield Inc.

200 S. Richland Drive
Princeton, Indiana 47671
U.S.A.
(812) 386-1000
Fax: (812) 362-2289

Wholly Owned Subsidiary of Siemens AG
Incorporated: 1933
Employees: 2,681
Sales: $290 million
SICs: 3625 Relays and Industrial Controls

Potter & Brumfield Inc. (P&B) is the leading manufacturer of electronic relays—devices that control the flow of electric current—in the United States. Vital components in a wide range of products, relays are found in small appliances, automobiles, furnaces and air conditioners, and vending machines. P&B also designs and markets timers, connectors, circuit breakers, input/output modules, and other mechanisms necessary in the transmission of electric power. A subsidiary of the German conglomerate Siemens AG since 1986, P&B focused on developing new products as well as consolidating and automating its production lines in the 1990s, in order to compete more effectively with Japanese relay manufacturers.

P&B's history may be traced to 1932, when Elbert E. Potter and Richard M. Brumfield established a small manufacturing business in their hometown of Princeton, in southwestern Indiana. At the time, the two young men were employed at the local Hansen Manufacturing Company, which produced small motors for clocks. There, Potter was a toolmaker, and Brumfield, who had studied engineering at Purdue University, worked in the design and drafting department and also operated a die cast machine. During 1932, however, both men were often out of work, as the company was forced to lay off large numbers of its employees in order to withstand the effects of the Great Depression. During these periods of unemployment, Potter and Brumfield decided to try developing a business of their own.

Potter invested $280 in the necessary tools, and together the men set up a small shop in a corner of Potter's basement, with the goal of manufacturing timer controls for stokers, machines that fueled furnaces. During their first year of business, the two men remained on the Hansen Manufacturing payroll, working there whenever possible and using off periods to work in their own shop. The following year, however, they left Hansen to focus exclusively on Potter & Brumfield Inc., which they incorporated in 1933.

In order to support themselves financially while they perfected the timer control, Potter and Brumfield took on various repair jobs for their friends and neighbors. In April 1933, for example, the company's ledger book listed income of 25 cents for fashioning a key, $1.70 for repairing a washing machine motor, and 65 cents for welding skates. By the fall of that year, however, the two men had sold their first timer control, to the Meier Electric and Machine Company of Indianapolis, which paid $31.75 for the device. At the end of their first full year of business, P&B reported a profit of $243.

Orders for the timer controls increased over the next few years. To meet the demand, Potter and Brumfield moved their operations into a small building in Princeton and hired their first employee. By 1936, the company's work force numbered eight, and its product line had expanded to include timing gears and the electronic relay, a product that would eventually become P&B's mainstay. During this time, Potter focused on product development, while Brumfield spent much of his time making sales calls and devising marketing strategies. In 1939, however, they hired Ralph Brengle to take over as chief sales representative.

As the company grew over the next several years, Brengle would oversee the expansion of the company's sales staff into a national organization. During World War II, while Brengle and many of the company's skilled laborers served in the U.S. armed forces, the demand for stoker timers declined dramatically but the need for electrical relays escalated, ensuring a brisk business for the company. Gradually, P&B began focusing exclusively on relay production.

When Brengle returned from overseas, he put together a deal that would forever change the nature of P&B. In 1947, he secured a contract to supply a manufacturer with $500,000 worth of relays within one year. This was by far the largest order P&B had ever received, and it led to a rift between the company co-founders. While Brumfield welcomed the increased business and looked forward to becoming a major player in the industry, Potter preferred that the company remain a modest, specialized firm. When it became apparent that they would never agree on the direction their company should take, Potter and Brumfield decided to sell the business. They first extended an offer to Brengle, and he accepted, purchasing a 100 percent interest in the company. Although the split was amicable, Potter left the company altogether, moving to south central Illinois, where he took up farming. Brumfield, on the other hand, took some time off; when he returned, he purchased a 37.5 percent interest in P&B from Brengle and remained as president of the firm.

Under Brengle and Brumfield, the company began realizing rapid growth, with production volume doubling annually over the next several years. In 1951, construction was completed on a new plant in Princeton, an 85,000-square-foot facility that housed a work force of around 200. By the mid-1950s, Potter & Brumfield was the country's largest manufacturer of electrical relays, producing over 50 varieties of the device, most of which were designed specifically for each customer. P&B relays were in demand from manufacturers of aircraft, submarines, and missiles, as well as makers of toys and household appliances, and the company's work force swelled to around 700.

In 1954, P&B was acquired by the American Machine and Foundry Co. (AMF), a New York-based sports and leisure manufacturer—best known for their bowling alley pinspotting machines—which was seeking to diversify its interests. Under its new parent, P&B was afforded a great deal of autonomy; Brumfield remained company president, Brengle was named vice-president and sales consultant, and both men were named to the board of directors.

In 1956, the company expanded its presence beyond Indiana, establishing a manufacturing facility in Franklin, a town in southwestern Kentucky. Later that year, however, P&B's growth rate and sales were curbed dramatically by a four-month-long strike among its unionized employees, during which research and production came to a halt. Once the strike was settled, P&B faced a backlog of orders and wavering consumer confidence, as well as heightened competition among the nearly 150 other relay manufacturers in the United States. As sales at P&B declined slightly and its backorders were eventually filled, the company's work force was scaled back to 300. Nevertheless, by maintaining its emphasis on engineering new relays to suit specific needs, P&B eventually regained its customer base. By the late 1950s, P&B had recovered its reputation as a leader in the industry and sales again surged. In 1958, P&B built a new plant in Ontario, Canada, and the following year, a second Kentucky manufacturing plant was opened, in the northwestern city of Marion.

During much of the 1960s and 1970s, P&B worked toward establishing a national presence. Its facilities in Princeton and Franklin were enlarged, while construction was completed on a new plant in Gainesville, Georgia, in 1966. In 1969, the company made its first acquisition, purchasing a relay manufacturer in San Juan Capistrano, California, where P&B also opened a new office from which representatives oversaw sales in the western states. A factory in Juarez, Mexico, was opened in 1971, and in 1973, the year that Richard Brumfield retired, P&B opened an eastern states sales office in Braintree, Massachusetts. Increased business prompted the company to construct a new distribution center in Princeton in 1975, and the following year a new, 111,000-square-foot, tri-level Administration and Engineering Building in Princeton became P&B headquarters.

Also during this time, P&B became known in the industry for its contributions to new relay and switching device technology. Among the company's innovations were the first magnetic latching relay, the first snap switches for television sets, and the only all-solid-state polarized telegraph relay, which replaced its electromechanical predecessor. P&B also produced the first military and aerospace relays capable of resisting large shocks and vibrations; as a result, virtually all space vehicles through the 1980s were equipped with P&B relays.

P&B's parent company, AMF, had also expanded during the 1960s and 1970s. However, its rapid growth rate through acquisition had engendered several problems. In the early 1980s, AMF's debt load was high, its energy division, which included interests in petroleum drilling and exploration, was experiencing heavy losses, and its stock prices were plummeting. In order to offset the effects of its high debt-to-equity ratio, AMF, led by chairperson W. Thomas York and president William P. Sovey, engineered stock swaps and public stock offerings, paying off some of its debt with the profits. By 1984, AMF had emerged a much healthier company, reporting a profit of $15 million on revenues of $1.1 billion. However, the company still maintained a small equity base, and its stock prices remained depressed. Moreover, some critics alleged, management had been neglectful of the company and had made some poor decisions. Thus, during this time, AMF became the object of a highly publicized hostile takeover by Minneapolis-based Minstar Inc., led by corporate raider Irwin L. Jacobs.

AMF initially rejected Jacobs' April 1985 offers to acquire a 50.5 percent interest in the company, and weeks of litigation ensued as AMF charged Jacobs with proposing "greenmail"— buying up the company's stock in order to resell it to the company at an inflated price—while Minstar charged AMF management with setting up "poison pills"—tactics, such as increasing the company's indebtedness, to deliberately devalue the company—in order to dissuade Jacobs. Eventually, however, AMF was forced to accept the Minstar takeover; Jacobs and his company paid a reported $563.8 million for AMF, a price just slightly over book value. As expected, Jacobs then dismantled much of AMF, and in the process Potter & Brumfield was sold to the German conglomerate Siemens AG for an undisclosed sum.

Siemens AG's primary business was electronics. Its holdings included companies prominent among Europe's telecommunications, automotive, and industrial markets. Moreover, Siemens was Europe's leading relay manufacturer. The new relationship between Siemens and P&B was regarded as mutually beneficial, since P&B could take advantage of Siemens' technological advances and financial resources, while Siemens gained better access to the U.S. market for relays. Furthermore, by joining forces the two companies stood a far better chance of competing effectively with Japanese relay manufacturers. When asked by a local news reporter to comment on the recent acquisition, Richard Brumfield remarked, "It's a good fit. Siemens is very familiar with the electric relay business. They're the General Electric of Europe."

Under Siemens, P&B underwent several changes, the first of which involved the overhaul of P&B's management. Roy H. Slavin, chief operating officer at Cerwin-Vega, Inc., an electronic equipment company, was named president, while Edward B. Prior, a former vice-president in acquisitions and mergers at Siemens, became P&B's executive vice-president. Slavin, who had considerable experience in bringing electronics companies to profitability, looked forward to directing P&B, which was already on solid financial ground yet faced possible extinction as foreign competition intensified. Under Slavin and Prior, P&B was provided with a new growth plan, which focused on research and development, expansion into foreign markets, and the consolidation and automation of its existing manufacturing facilities.

Exploring ways to improve the company's productivity, the new management team called for renovations to P&B's outdated facilities and modernization of its production lines. They also introduced new concepts such as "cell manufacturing," under which a team of workers oversaw every step of production for a specific assigned product, rather than just one stage of the assembly. This practice was intended to give workers a broader knowledge and a greater sense of responsibility for the product.

With the financial backing of Siemens, P&B was also able to invest more heavily in new product development. The automotive and telecommunications industries were regarded as holding the greatest potential for increased relay sales. Toward that end, P&B began developing new relays for use with circuit boards, a segment of the industry then controlled by Japanese relay manufacturers. Moreover, since most automobiles typically relied on more than 30 different types of relays to activate their electronic systems, P&B also stepped up efforts to custom-design relays for the country's major automobile manufacturers. In 1987, for example, the company designed and manufactured a relay used to trip the locking mechanism on some models of General Motors automobiles.

Automation of P&B assembly lines became an increasingly important part of management's new plan. According to a company spokesperson at the time, computer-controlled production lines ensured quality and eventually proved cost-effective. P&B spent millions to automate each of its plants in Indiana, Kentucky, and Mexico (having closed its Georgia and California plants in 1983 and 1985, respectively). Despite the increased reliance on computers and other machinery, P&B maintained a 1987 work force of 1,000 at its Princeton facilities, 300 in Marion, Kentucky, another 300 in Franklin, Kentucky, and 1,600 in Juarez, Mexico. Retraining programs were instituted to help some employees adapt to new roles as machine operators rather than assemblers, and benefit packages were improved.

As economic recession in the early 1990s hit automakers hard, P&B experienced some disappointing sales figures. Since projected growth had fallen short of expectations, P&B had to further consolidate its operations. Some of P&B's moves to ensure competitiveness proved upsetting to the company's hometown of Princeton, where P&B had been the largest employer for over 50 years. Between 1990 and 1995, the Princeton work force was cut significantly. In 1990, operations at the Princeton distribution center were transferred to Marion, Kentucky. Two years later, company officials announced a major restructuring, stating that they would be forced to eliminate more than 300 jobs at the Princeton plant and to transfer nearly 100 more from Princeton to the Franklin, Kentucky, facilities. In 1994, the last of the Princeton manufacturing operations were transferred to Kentucky. Nevertheless, as of early 1995, P&B's administrative and engineering headquarters remained in Princeton.

P&B had estimated annual sales of nearly $300 million in the mid-1990s, making it the leading supplier of relays to original equipment manufacturers in the United States. The company marketed over 100 models of electromechanical and solid state relays, and as new uses for the device emerged—particularly in computers, automobiles, and aerospace equipment—the company looked forward to continued growth as well as to securing a competitive ranking in foreign markets.

Further Reading:

Ash, Christopher, "Future Bright for Marion Firm," *Paducah (Kentucky) Sun,* July 26, 1987.
DeWitte, Dave, "Automation Leads to Potter Pullout," *Evansville (Indiana) Courier,* December 1, 1993.
DeWitte, "Potter & Brumfield Shift Not Based on Grant," *Evansville Courier,* March 21, 1992.
Forty-Five Years of Growth, company brochure, Princeton, Indiana: Potter & Brumfield, 1977.
Garnett, Anne Marie, "Potter & Brumfield Strives to Meet Goals," *Evansville Courier,* August 16, 1987, p. 15.
"How AMF Knocked Down Its Debt Load," *Business Week,* January 9, 1984, pp. 104–105.
"How to Stay a Growth Company," *Business Week,* September 12, 1959, pp. 188–94.
Kinney, Steve, "New Products Forecast at Princeton's P&B," *Evansville Courier,* January 30, 1986, p. 6.
Mangan, Tom, "Purchase of P&B Boosts Firm's Rank," *Evansville Courier and Press,* June 29, 1986, p. 19.
Ross, Irwin, "Irwin Jacobs Lands," *Fortune,* July 8, 1985, pp. 130–36.
Runge, Mel, "New Company, Small Town Delights P&B Chief Slavin," *Evansville Press,* January 31, 1986, p. 24.
Thompson, Bish, "Basement Shop to Giant of Industry," *Evansville Press,* December 13, 1957.

—Tina Grant

PowerGen PLC

Haslucks Green Road
Shirley
Solihull
West Midlands B90 4PD
United Kingdom
(021) 701-2000
Fax: (021) 701-2616

Public Company
Incorporated: 1989 as The Power Generation Company PLC
Employees: 4,185
Sales: £2.93 billion
Stock Exchanges: London
SICs: 4911 Electric Companies and Systems

PowerGen PLC is the smaller of the two electricity generating companies created from the breakup of the nationalized electricity industry in England and Wales. Carved out as a separate division of the Central Electricity Generating Board in 1989 while privatization loomed, PowerGen was incorporated as a public limited company in 1989 and the majority of its shares were sold to the public two years later. PowerGen and its larger rival, National Power, constituted a virtual duopoly of electricity generation in England and Wales, though that scenario was expected to change as more and more competition entered the industry. Perhaps in response to this inevitable shift in the status quo, the company increasingly became involved in allied ventures including forays into international power markets, the provision of combined heat and power, and, most significantly, investment in natural gas.

Electricity was first harnessed for practical use in the United Kingdom in the late nineteenth century with the introduction of street lighting in 1881. By 1921 over 480 authorized but independent electricity suppliers had sprung up throughout England and Wales, creating a rather haphazard system operating at different voltages and frequencies. In recognition of the need for a more coherent, interlocking system, the Electricity (Supply) Act of 1926 created a central authority to encourage and facilitate a national transmission system. This objective of a national grid was achieved by the mid-1930s.

The state consolidated its control of the utility with the Electricity Act of 1947, which collapsed the distribution and supply activities of 505 separate bodies into 12 regional Area Boards, at the same time assigning generating assets and liabilities to one government-controlled authority. A further Electricity Act, in 1957, created a statutory body, the Central Electricity Generating Board (CEGB), which dominated the whole of the electricity system in England and Wales. Generator of virtually all the electricity in the two countries, the CEGB, as owner and operator of the transmission grid, supplied electricity to the Area Boards, which they in turn distributed and sold on within their regions.

This situation continued for 30 years, until the government mooted the idea of privatizing the electricity industry in 1987. The proposal was enshrined in the Electricity Act of 1989, and a new organizational scheme was unveiled. The CEGB was splintered into four divisions, destined to become successor companies: PowerGen, National Power, Nuclear Electric, and the National Grid Company (NGC). PowerGen and National Power were to share between them England and Wales's fossil-fueled power stations; Nuclear Electric was to take over nuclear power stations; and the NGC was to be awarded control of the national electricity distribution system. The 12 Area Boards were converted, virtually unchanged, into 12 Regional Electricity Companies (RECs), and these were given joint ownership of the NGC. The RECs' shares were the first to be sold to the public, at the end of 1990. PowerGen and National Power's shares were offered for sale the following year.

In order to understand PowerGen's role within the electricity industry it is helpful to understand how the system operates. The provision of electricity consists of four components: generation, transmission, distribution, and supply. In England and Wales, generation is the province of PowerGen, National Power, and Nuclear Electric. Transmission is the transfer of electricity via the national grid, through overhead lines, underground cables, and NGC substations. Distribution is the delivery of electricity from the national grid to local distribution systems operated by the Regional Electricity Companies. Supply, a term distinct from distribution in the electricity industry, refers to the transaction whereby electricity is purchased from the generators and transmitted to customers. Under the terms of its licence, PowerGen has the right to supply electricity directly to consumers, but to date that right has been relatively little exercised. PowerGen's usual customers are the RECs, which in turn sell the electricity to the end users.

A new trading market was devised with the privatization scheme for bulk sales of electricity from generators to distributors—the pool. A rather complicated pricing procedure exists in the pool, according to which each generating station offers a quote for each half-hour of the day, based on an elaborate set of criteria including the operating costs of that particular plant, the time of day, the expected demand for electricity, and the available capacity of the station. The NGC arranges these quotes in a merit order and makes the decisions regarding which plant to call into operation when. The pool system is not relied upon exclusively, however, as the generators frequently make contractual arrangements with distributors for a specified period of time as a means of mutual protection against fluctuations in the pool price.

To view PowerGen's overall position in the industry, it is necessary to recognize its comparative status just prior to privatization, at the end of 1990. National Power, its bigger rival, boasted an aggregate Declared Net Capacity or Capability (DNC) of 29,486 megawatts (MW), where a megawatt was defined as the generating capacity of a power station in any given half-hour. PowerGen, in second place, had 18,764MW DNC. Nuclear Electric's figure was 8,357MW, the National Grid Company controlled 2,088MW, and British Nuclear Fuels PLC, the United Kingdom Atomic Energy Authority, and small independent generators together accounted for about 2,900MW. Another, though limited, source was provided by linkages with the Scottish and French electricity systems, with which import or export deals were sometimes made. PowerGen and National Power between them thus controlled some 78 percent of the electricity market in England and Wales, of which about 30 percent was held by PowerGen.

Privatization of the utility was designed to promote a beneficial result through the free play of market forces. The introduction of competition in power generation, it was argued, would lead both to greater efficiency within the industry and to lower prices for the consumer. Within a few short years, however, concerns had already arisen, as critics of the scheme had predicted from the start. A duopoly which at the time of its creation held such a significant majority of the electricity generating market was never likely to embody the purest form of free market operations.

In 1994 the industry watchdog, the Office of Electricity Regulation (Offer), expressed concern about PowerGen and National Power's continuing dominance of the market—and the fact that from June 1990 to January 1994 the wholesale price of electricity had risen by 50 percent. The market share of the big two had in fact declined since privatization, with National Power enjoying some 33 percent and PowerGen controlling less than 25 percent, but nonetheless rumors were rife that Offer would refer the duopoly to the Monopolies and Mergers Commission. Offer eventually stopped short of that proceeding, but the regulator did lay strictures on the two generating companies, requiring that they should sell a specified amount of generating plant capacity—in the case of PowerGen 2,000MW—and submit to price capping for a period of two years.

The demand to sell plant capacity was expected to cause little hardship to PowerGen; it was left to the company's discretion, provided it complied with Offer's deadline of December 31, 1995, which plant to sell and when. Much of the plant capacity disposed of was expected to be less-attractive coal-fired plants, some of which PowerGen would have closed anyway as unnecessary to its needs. In preference to an outright sale, it seemed possible that PowerGen might be able to arrange an asset exchange with a foreign power company.

The required price caps, ironically, appeared likely to prove a less onerous burden to PowerGen and National Power than to the state-owned Nuclear Electric and to small independents, both existing and potential. Nor would the new pricing rules result in lower electricity bills for the average household consumer—only for large corporate customers.

The government, apart from its concerns about fair competition and price, was particularly interested in resolving any controversy or questions regarding PowerGen and National Power, as it intended to sell its remaining 40 percent share (which it had retained at privatization) in each of the two companies. The sell-off to the public, scheduled to take place in February 1995, was expected to raise a welcome £4 billion for the government, £1.5 billion of which would be attributable to PowerGen.

PowerGen has followed the usual route of privatized companies in the United Kingdom by undertaking a rigorous program of cost-cutting, achieved primarily through improved efficiency, staff reductions, and plant closures. Employee redundancies have been dramatic: PowerGen's staff as of 1994 was less than half its 1990 level. Several power stations were closed outright, while others were put into indefinite reserve. The strategy proved a successful one, with the company's profits healthy despite a reduction in sales.

In the preparations for privatization, plans were laid to reorganize and modernize power generation, and during the 1990s the face of the industry accordingly changed. From a heavy reliance on coal-fired plants, PowerGen, like its rival National Power, began moving to a more diversified base. As of 1994 coal was still the dominant source—figures for 1993–1994 proved that PowerGen still relied very heavily on the resource, with coal accounting for a hefty 80.6 percent of total fuel used. Increasingly, coal was imported from abroad, as the foreign variety had a lower sulphur content than its British counterpart, obviating the need to fit special emission-reducing equipment to comply with environmental standards.

An emerging trend was toward combined cycle gas turbine plants (CCGT)—the so-called "dash for gas." Excess generating capacity in the 1980s made redundant some coal-fired capability, and more was jettisoned in favor of natural gas, the use of which had both economic and environmental advantages. The use of gas, while relatively small at 10.6 percent, should be compared to 1992–1993 figures, when gas accounted for only 3.6 percent. And clearly, PowerGen believed the future was in natural gas. Since privatization the company has invested in some 3,000MW of new CCGT plant capacity, generated by three power stations: Killingholme, in Humberside (completing its first full year of operations in 1993–1994); Rye House, Hertfordshire (finished in 1993); and Connah's Quay, in North Wales. The last-named, begun in 1993 and scheduled for completion in 1996, was expected to provide over half the electricity needs of Wales.

Thus a part of PowerGen's long-term plan was to broaden its interests in natural gas. As early as 1989, with privatization on the horizon but not yet effected, PowerGen, in a joint venture with Conoco UK Ltd., set up a gas trading company, Kinetica, to market gas downstream and construct gas transport pipelines. The venture became a clear success for PowerGen, and the company was confident that there would be ample scope for further development. The subsidiary PowerGen (North Sea) Ltd. constituted an investment for the company's future business. In 1993 PowerGen acquired from Monument Oil and Gas PLC a 3.9 percent stake in the Liverpool Bay development. This would supply gas to PowerGen's own Connah's Quay power station. Further widening its scope, PowerGen purchased in 1994 from a subsidiary of Lasmo an additional 5 percent of Liverpool Bay and a 12 percent interest in the Ravenspurn

North field as well as a 3.75 percent stake in Johnston field, both located in the Southern Gas Basin of the North Sea.

Since becoming a PLC, PowerGen has increasingly looked abroad for opportunities and advancement. In 1993–1994 the company undertook, as a member of a consortium with two U.S. companies—NRG Energy, Inc. and Morrison Knudson Co., Inc.—to operate lignite mining and power generation in the Leipzig region of Germany. As a future investment in the area, and again in cooperation with NRG Energy, the company bought a 400MW share in the 900MW Schkopau power station, under construction in 1994. At Tapada do Outeiro in Portugal, PowerGen became a member of a consortium charged to build and operate a 900MW CCGT power station. Although as yet a relatively small player on the international stage, PowerGen International aimed for growing participation in energy projects worldwide.

PowerGen began moving into the field of combined heat and power generation through its subsidiary PowerGen CHP. Its first project in this area, initiated in 1993–1994, was a 14MW co-generation plant commissioned by SmithKline Beecham. The subsidiary has also undertaken to provide energy for three paper mills in Kent. Small beginnings as yet, but PowerGen planned to explore other opportunities of a similar nature.

PowerGen's sorties into ventures related to but independent of its primary function as a U.K. power generator were necessary for the company to grow. Its share of the home electricity market was undeniably dwindling, from a post-privatization inheritance of 30 percent to some 24.5 percent in 1994; Nuclear Electric has edged out PowerGen as the second-largest power generator. PowerGen's market share was expected to sink yet further as the government's plan to increase competition in power generation came to fruition. Nonetheless, it seemed likely that PowerGen would continue to control a significant proportion of the industry. This, together with the company's increasing investment in natural gas, combined heat and power opportunities, and international projects, should secure Power-Gen a comfortable and continuing niche in the energy industry for the foreseeable future.

Principal Subsidiaries: Kinetica Ltd. (49.99 percent); Power-Gen CHP Ltd.; PowerGen (North Sea) Ltd.; Saale Energie GmbH (Germany; 50 percent).

Further Reading:

Butler, Daniel, ''Power at Play,'' *Management Today,* November 1990, pp. 54–59.

''Customers Set to Benefit by up to £500m,'' *Financial Times,* February 12, 1994.

''Electricity Generator May Swap Assets,'' *Financial Times,* June 10, 1994.

''Electricity Generators to Escape Monopolies Reference,'' *Financial Times,* February 11, 1994.

''The Generation Game,'' *Economist,* September 1, 1990, p. 29.

''Generators in Deal to Sell Plant and Reduce Prices,'' *Financial Times,* February 12, 1994.

''Generators Stake to Be Sold for £4bn,'' *London Times,* March 5, 1994.

''Government Announces Last of PowerGen Sell-Off,'' *Birmingham Post,* March 5, 1994.

''The Lex Column: Cash Power,'' *Financial Times,* June 10, 1994.

Main Prospectus: National Power PLC, PowerGen PLC, offers for sale by Kleinwort Benson Limited on behalf of the Secretary of State for Energy, 1991.

''Offer Proves a Party-Pooper for High-Flying Generators,'' *Independent,* January 5, 1994.

''PowerGen,'' *London Times,* November 16, 1994, p. 28.

''Power Generators Meet Offer to Head Off MMC Enquiry,'' *London Times,* January 24, 1994.

''PowerGen Looks for Role in Offshore Gas,'' *Lloyds List,* December 29, 1993.

''PowerGen Sees Live Chances on Overseas Circuit,'' *Evening Standard,* January 21, 1994.

''PowerGen Strengthens Gas Interests,'' *Birmingham Post,* December 12, 1993.

''Power Sell-off in February,'' *London Times,* September 30, 1994, p. 21.

''Special Report on Competitive Power,'' *Daily Telegraph,* March 11, 1994.

Tieman, Ross, ''Powerful 27 Percent Payout from PowerGen,'' *London Times,* November 16, 1994, p. 26.

—Robin DuBlanc

Praxair, Inc.

39 Old Ridgebury Road
Danbury, Connecticut 06810-5113
U.S.A.
(203) 837-2000
Fax: (203) 837-2454

Public Company
Incorporated: 1907 as Linde Air Products Co.
Employees: 16,766
Sales: $2.44 billion
Stock Exchanges: New York Pacific Cincinnati Midwest
SICs: 2813 Industrial Gases; 3479 Surface Technologies

With operations in 24 countries around the world, Praxair, Inc. is the Western Hemisphere's top supplier of industrial gases. The company's 10 percent share of the $23 billion global market for industrial gases ranks third behind that of L'Air Liquide (18 percent) and BOC (15 percent). Formerly the Linde Division of chemical giant Union Carbide Corporation, Praxair was spun off to shareholders in 1992 as an independent company. Over half of the new firm's sales are generated outside the United States.

Praxair's business interests are focused in two basic segments: industrial gases and surface coatings. The company's surface coatings business was developed in the 1950s to supply wear-resistant and high-temperature corrosion-resistant metallic and ceramic coatings and powders to many industries. Industrial gases by far constitute the greatest portion of Praxair's operations, contributing 91 percent of 1993 sales. Industrial gas products include atmospheric gases like oxygen, nitrogen, and argon, and process gases such as helium, hydrogen, and acetylene. Distribution of industrial gases occurs by one of four methods: pipeline, on-site systems (both cryogenic and non-cryogenic), merchant liquid, and packaged or cylinder gases. Many of Praxair's largest customers, and an increasing number of smaller volume customers, utilize on-site distribution, wherein a dedicated plant is built on or adjacent to the customer's site to supply the product directly. Pipeline and on-site delivery constituted about 24 percent of Praxair's 1993 sales. Merchant liquid delivery involves transportation of medium-sized volumes of gases by tanker truck or railroad tank car to on-site storage containers owned and maintained by Praxair. This segment contributed about 39 percent of the company's

1993 sales. Customers requiring small volumes of industrial gases receive them in metal cylinders or tanks. This "packaged gases" business constituted 28 percent of 1993 sales.

Praxair's origins may be traced back to nineteenth-century Germany, where a professor of mechanical engineering at the College of Technology in Munich started experiments in refrigeration. Karl von Linde's research came to fruition with the 1895 development of a cryogenic air liquefier. von Linde built his first oxygen production plant in 1902. His continuing research led to the establishment of the first plant for the production of pure nitrogen two years later. The entrepreneur/scientist went on to build air separation plants throughout Germany and Europe during the first decade of the twentieth century.

Karl von Linde's 1907 foundation of Linde Air Products Company in Cleveland, Ohio, established the first firm in the country to produce oxygen from air using a cryogenic process. Although oxygen distillation was relatively inexpensive—the raw material is, after all, free—the storage and transportation of gases in heavy containers was very costly. With its foundation in scientific inquiry, the Linde Air Products Company made research and development a priority. As a result, the industrial gas business evolved into a very capital-intensive enterprise; in 1992, *Chemical Week* estimated that every dollar of annual sales cost over a dollar in assets.

The Linde Company's relationship with Union Carbide started around 1911, when the two competitors undertook joint experiments regarding the production and application of acetylene. Union Carbide had been formed in 1898 to manufacture calcium carbide, a catalyst for the production of metal alloys. The partners had hoped that acetylene—a flammable, gaseous byproduct of alloying calcium carbide with aluminum—could be marketed for street and household lighting. While acetylene gas lighting was extensively used especially in rural areas and was also used for auto lights, Thomas Edison's invention and commercialization of electric incandescent light bulbs distracted some emphasis away from acetylene gas lighting. Fortunately, a French researcher's discovery that acetylene could be burned in oxygen to produce a hot, metal-cutting flame launched a whole new market for the gas.

In 1917, Linde pooled its resources with National Carbon Co., Inc., Prest-O-Lite Co., Inc., Electro Metallurgical Co., and Union Carbide Co. to form Union Carbide and Carbon Corporation. The new entity was organized as a holding company, with its five members acting relatively autonomously and cooperating where their businesses converged. As a subsidiary of one of the United States' largest chemical companies, Linde soon became one of the world's largest producer of such industrial gases as acetylene, hydrogen, and nitrogen, which formed the foundation of the petrochemical industry. The companies' combined research efforts coincided with a national push for new technologies to help win World War I, and new applications for industrial gases came in rapid succession. Cooperative research and development among Union Carbide companies used Linde's gases to facilitate production of corrosion and heat-resistant ferroalloys used in skyscrapers, bridges, and automobiles. Linde also earned a reputation as an innovator in the industrial gases industry by developing new applications for industrial gases, especially in conjunction with the growing chemicals operations of its parent. During the 1940s, for example, Linde participated in Union Carbide's contribution to the development of the atomic bomb. Linde scientists perfected a refining process for treating uranium concentrates through gaseous diffusion. In the late 1940s, Union Carbide executives attempted to centralize the traditionally autonomous nature of the corporation through a reorganization. The holding company arrangement was dissolved, and subsidiaries were transformed into divisions. Each division, however, retained the word "company" in its name, suggesting that a decentralized corporate culture still endured at Union Carbide.

The Linde Division benefited from Union Carbide's mid-1950s to mid-1960s globalization and retained its position as America's top producer of industrial gases through continuous innovation. The development of oxygen-fired furnaces for steel manufacture and application of nitrogen as a refrigerant increased Linde's markets during the 1960s. The industrial gas company was even able to benefit from the energy crisis of the 1970s, when the rapidly rising costs of traditional fuels made oxy-fuel an attractive alternative to air-fuel because one received maximum heat from fuel. Applications of industrial gases in the food industry during this period included the use of hydrogen in hydrogenated cooking oils and nitrogen to quick-freeze foods.

However, Linde's steady performance throughout the 1970s and 1980s was largely obscured by the succession of financial, environmental, and human disasters endured by Union Carbide. In the 1970s, "stagflation" and overcapacity hammered the company's commodities markets and decimated its profits. The parent was also targeted as an air polluter by consumer crusader Ralph Nader. A succession of company leaders lowered overhead, increased efficiency, and kept the global corporation afloat, but the infamous disaster at Union Carbide's pesticide plant in Bhopal, India, in December 1984, struck the corporation just as it was starting to earn steady profits. *Newsweek* magazine called the incident, which killed over 2,300 and injured another 10,000, "the worst industrial accident in history." Union Carbide's market value plummeted 75 percent to less than $3 billion in the aftermath, and the chemical giant was compelled to take on massive debt to repulse a takeover threat. Divestments scaled the parent company back to its three primary businesses (industrial gases, chemicals and plastics, and carbon products) in the late 1980s, but its debt load curbed research and development, diversification, and international expansion.

By the early 1980s, Linde was a $1 billion contributor to Union Carbide's $9 billion annual sales. However, over the course of the decade, Linde began to lose U.S. market share, particularly to American rival Air Products and Chemicals, Inc. By the late 1980s, Linde was ranked second in nitrogen and hydrogen production and distribution. Nevertheless, Linde maintained its reputation for innovation, including a small, profitable business segment with the development of such coatings processes as acetylene detonation, which metallurgically bonded protective coatings to metal surfaces. High-tech acetylene detonation and diffusion processes were used in aircraft engines and rolled steel, while also having applications in the automotive industry, most notably in Rolls Royce production. In 1989, the industrial gas company introduced a technological breakthrough in its primary market, air separation. Robert Reitzes, then an analyst with New York's C. J. Lawrence, predicted that the economical, non-cryogenic, vacuum pressure swing adsorption (VPSA) technology would consume 20 to 25 percent of the merchant market by the turn of the twentieth century. The company now estimates that more than 40 percent of the merchant liquid market will be served by non-cryogenic systems, both VSPA and Membrane.

In 1988, the Linde division was renamed Union Carbide Industrial Gases, and in June 1992 its shares were distributed to Union Carbide shareholders on the basis of one share of the new Praxair, Inc. for each share of the parent. The new company maintained some ties to its former parent; Union Carbide was still one of its largest customers, and the two continued to share a common headquarters.

Praxair emerged with over $2.5 billion in annual sales, more employees (18,600) than its former parent (16,000) and a debt-to-capital ratio of over 60 percent. Debt reduction was a high priority for CEO H. William Lichtenberger, who devised several corporate goals in the early 1990s: reducing overhead, doubling profitability, effecting 15 percent annual net income growth, and expanding Praxair's global presence, especially in Asia and South Africa. Expense reduction commenced immediately under a "work process improvement initiative," and the company's work force was reduced by ten percent in Praxair's first year of independence. The establishment of joint ventures in Indonesia and China was expected to help Praxair catch up quickly with its competitors in the region. Two joint ventures in Beijing and Shanghai were expected to "give Praxair the largest representation in China among industrial-gases companies."

In 1994, Praxair, Inc. earned one of the most comprehensive quality system certifications issued by the International Organization for Standardiation (ISO). Covered by the ISO 9002 certificate are all 54 bulk-gas operating sites, 12 customer service centers, distribution facilities including the company's North American Logistics Center, plant operations center and two pipeline control centers, and more than 250 on-site air separation plants in the U.S., Canada, and Puerto Rico.

Twenty-five additional ISO certifications have been earned by Praxair sites and businesses in Europe, Brazil, Mexico, Canada, and the U.S. since the company launched its certification effort four years ago.

Principal Subsidiaries: Altair Gases and Equipment; Amko Service Company; Gas Tech, Incorporated; Genex, Ltd.; Innovative Membrane Systems, Inc.; Jacksonville Welding Supply, Inc.; Linde de Mexico, S.A. de C.V.; Praxair Canada, Inc.; Praxair Puerto Rico, Inc.; Praxair Surface Technologies, Inc.; UCISCO Inc.; Praxair Argentina S.A.; S.A. White Martins (Brazil); Argon S.A. (Spain); Companhia Nacional de Oxigenio S.A. (Portugal); Indugas N.V. (Belgium); IGI-Italiana Gas Industriali S.p.A.; Praxair B.V. (The Netherlands); Praxair GmbH (Germany); Praxair Iberica S.A.; (Spain); Praxair N.V. (Belgium); Praxair S.A. (France); SIAD S.p.A. (Italy); Beijing Praxair Inc. (People's Republic of China); Praxair Asia, Inc. (Hong Kong); Praxair K.K. (Japan); Praxair Indonesia; Union Gas Company Limited (Korea); Oxigeno de Colombia; SAID Vertrieb Technischer Gase (Austria); Montkemijeka (Croatia);

SAID Technicke Plyny spol. (Czech Republic); Rivoira S.p.A. (Italy).

Further Reading:

"Carbide Industrial Gases Busy on Verge of Spin-Off," *Chemical Marketing Reporter,* June 1, 1992, pp. 5, 40.

"Cost-Cutting Shaped Linde's President," *Chemical Week,* January 6, 1982, pp. 54–55.

"Ethyl, Praxair Reorganize," *Chemical Marketing Reporter,* July 5, 1993, p. 5.

Hunter, David, Debbie Jackson, and Marjorie Coeyman, "Industrial Gases: Quickening Pace in the Americas," *Chemical Week,* April 7, 1993, pp. 21–23.

Hunter, David, "Industrial Gases: Focus on Costs, Mix, and Geography," *Chemical Week,* February 23, 1994, pp. 25–27.

Plishner, Emily S., "Breaking Free at Carbide: Hydrogen Propels Growth of Industrial Gases Unit," *Chemical Week,* May 13, 1992, pp. 56–57; "ISO 9000—Praxair: Learning From International Experience," *Chemical Week,* November 10, 1993, p. 73; "Mergers and Acquisitions Become Demergers and Spinoffs," *Chemical Week,* October 7, 1992, pp. 24–25; "Praxair Promises More Profits," *Chemical Week,* March 16, 1994, p. 13; "Reconstructing Balance Sheets," *Chemical Week,* October 7, 1992, pp. 22–24.

Shapiro, Lynn, "Checks and Balances in Executive Pay," *Chemical Business,* October 1993, pp. 11–12.

—April Dougal Gasbarre

PROGRESSIVE™

Progressive Corporation

6300 Wilson Mills Road
Mayfield Village, Ohio 44143
U.S.A.
(216) 461-5000
Fax: (216) 446-7603

Public Company
Incorporated: 1956 as Progressive Casualty Insurance
    Company
Employees: 7,300
Revenues: $2.3 billion
Stock Exchanges: New York
SICs: 6331 Fire, Marine, and Casualty Insurance; 6399
    Insurance Carriers, Nec; 6719 Holding Companies, Nec

By practically any measure, Progressive Corp. ranks among the United States' most successful property and casualty insurers. The holding company's primary subsidiary, Progressive Casualty Insurance Co., got its start by insuring "non-standard" or high-risk drivers. The firm's profits consistently outperform the industry: from 1970 to 1992, Progressive averaged a 3 percent annual profit on underwriting insurance, whereas its competitors averaged a 7 percent annual loss. From 1983 to 1993, the company's stock price increased twice as fast as Standard & Poor's 500 index. In 1992, Progressive became the nation's largest provider of automobile insurance through independent agents. In 1993, Progressive became the largest automotive insurer in its home state, Ohio. Although a publicly traded company, Progressive has remained a family-run enterprise: in 1994, the founding Lewis family owned 19 percent of its stock. Peter B. Lewis, son of a founder, was chief executive officer, president, and chairman of the board, and his younger brother, Daniel R. Lewis, served as a division president and treasurer.

The Progressive insurance organization was created in 1937 when Peter and Daniel's father, Joe, joined fellow Cleveland attorney Jack Green for a state-sponsored investigation of a group of door-to-door insurance salesmen. In the course of that operation, the partners discovered a profitable and (unlike the subjects of their investigation) legal niche in the insurance business. Too fill that niche, the two graduates of Western Reserve University School of Law first obtained insurance licenses. Using $10,000 borrowed from Lewis' mother-in-law, they acquired five small auto service companies and called their new venture Progressive Mutual Insurance Company. Lewis and Green established innovation as a hallmark of their enterprise at the outset. Before World War II, insurers customarily set premiums according to noncompetitive rate tables and required prepayment of policies. Progressive targeted blue-collar drivers with an inexpensive $25 policy, a monthly payment plan, and an industry first—the "one-and-one" policy. In the event of an accident, this coverage would pay up to $1000 to repair either the insured's or the other driver's car, at the policyholder's discretion. By virtue of its establishment in a garage, Progressive also offered its clients another unique convenience—drive-in claims services.

Lewis and Green wrote less than $10,000 in premiums that first year, and by 1939, Progressive's original capital had dwindled to less than $1,500. A Chicago consultant advised the partners to get out of insurance, but they struggled on through the early 1940s. Peter B. Lewis would later observe that "World War II saved Progressive. People finally had jobs and money, so they could afford cars and insurance, but gas was rationed so they couldn't drive and didn't have many accidents." The booming, car-crazy, postwar economy further accelerated Progressive's business: premium revenues reached $480,000 by 1946. The era saw Progressive expand into the related areas of fire, theft, and collision insurance, as well as some financing services.

A new market opened up in the 1950s as many leading insurers began to segment their clients according to age, driving record, and other quantitative categories. They then insured only the statistically best candidates, known in the industry as "standard risks." Progressive Casualty Insurance Company was created in 1956 to capture the growing "nonstandard" pool of drivers that didn't make it into the preferred category. The new subsidiary wrote $83,000 in premiums during its first year in operation.

Founder Joe Lewis had died just one year earlier, and son Peter Lewis joined the firm after graduating from Princeton University. The younger Lewis helped lead Progressive's expansion outside Ohio's boundaries after 1960. The company began writing policies in Michigan, Florida, Tennessee, Kentucky, Georgia, and Mississippi and, within three years, extra-Ohio premiums topped $5 million annually. The Progressive Corporation, an insurance holding company, was formed in 1965 upon Jack Green's retirement. It brought Progressive Casualty and three related insurance agencies under the Lewis family's control through a leveraged buyout. The new company's premium revenue totaled about $7.4 million during its first year of incorporation, which was also Peter Lewis' first year as president and chief executive officer.

In nearly four decades at its helm, Lewis left his personal imprint on Progressive. The avid art collector and patron started a corporate collection and commissioned a new artist to illustrate the company's annual report each year. By 1987, the corporate collection constituted over 1,000 pieces of award-winning contemporary art. Lewis was characterized as "a brilliant and unusual man" in a 1990 *Financial World* treatment, and has been credited with the managerial savvy that kept Progressive in the vanguard of auto insurance. Lewis established high employment standards early in his career. Progressive recruited employees at the country's top business schools on the assumption that only the best students are accepted at, and matriculated from, these institutions. Lewis prided himself on the "ruthless discipline" expected of his executives. In 1990, he told *Financial World* that "There are 15 people who used to work for us who we asked to leave who became presidents of other insurance companies."

Lewis took Progressive public in 1971 with the sale of 110,000 shares. That same year, the company formed a subsidiary, Progressive American Insurance Co., in Miami, Florida. Progressive and the property/casualty industry in general got a "wake-up call" in the mid-1970s, when years of consolidation, acquisition of major companies by noninsurance conglomerates, and depletion of reserves brought on the worst years since the Depression. During this crisis, Lewis set forth one of the company's most important goals: to always achieve an underwriting profit. That standard, measured in the insurance industry as the combined operating ratio, soon became one of Progressive's hallmarks. Most auto insurance companies are satisfied with a combined operating ratio of 100 or more—meaning that claims and expenses paid equaled or exceeded premiums collected. They make money not from selling insurance, but from making profitable investments. Progressive insists on keeping its combined ratio under 100 and therefore making an operating profit before investments. Since the 1960s, the auto insurance industry overall has consistently recorded losses on underwriting activities, but Progressive has done so very infrequently.

As one of the few nonstandard or high-risk insurance companies, Progressive grew virtually unchallenged in the late 1970s. From 1975 to 1978, premium income nearly quadrupled, from $38 million to $112 million, as standard auto insurers turned away and dropped their riskier customers. By 1979, the company wrote policies in 31 states. Ohio accounted for one-third of premiums.

One of the keys to Progressive's impressive results was its exacting actuarial standards. In the 1950s the company began to invest far more heavily than its competitors in collecting and analyzing accident data. Progressive's actuaries sought out the best of the bad risks and devised more accurate pricing policies. For example, actuaries at Progressive found that, of motorists arrested for driving while under the influence of alcohol, those with children were least likely to drive drunk again. These select customers were still charged higher-than-normal rates, but Progressive's "high-risk" premiums remained lower than competitors'.

These pricing policies helped the company's premium volume increase to $157.3 million by 1980. As business around the country increased, Progressive established regional offices in Sacramento, Tampa, Richmond, Colorado Springs, Austin, Omaha, and Toronto in the late 1970s and early 1980s. In 1986, the company wrote over $830 million in premiums, over five times as much as it had at the beginning of the decade.

After the 1987 stock market crash, Lewis ousted his investment team and brought Alfred Lerner, chairman of Equitable Bancorp, MNC Financial Inc., and MBNA Corp., on as chairman and director of investments. Upon his hiring, Lewis compared Lerner's investment expertise to basketball great Michael Jordan's athletic prowess. Lewis asked Lerner to invest $75 mil-

lion in Progressive to ensure the newcomer's vested interest in his new employer's financial performance.

The insurer celebrated its 50th anniversary in 1987 with its first $1 billion year and a listing on the New York Stock Exchange. Lewis told the *Cleveland Plain Dealer* that "We feel humble here because this could happen only in America."

Over the course of his five-year tenure at Progressive, Lerner appeared to have invested the firm's funds profitably. Then, late in 1992, the investor converted his $75 million bond into $244.5 million in Progressive stock and sold half of his holdings. Lewis resumed the responsibilities of the chair and control of the firm's investment strategy early in 1993, asserting that he simply had "the desire, time and comfort level necessary to reassume responsibility for the financial side of the business," in a February 1993 *Cleveland Plain Dealer* article.

The insurance industry overall suffered consumer backlash that took the form of rate legislation in the late 1980s. The most notorious law, California's Proposition 103, mandated 20 percent cuts in auto insurance premiums and refunds to many customers after its 1988 adoption. That year, $305 million, or 28 percent, of Progressive's business was in California. By 1993, Progressive had reduced its revenues from the state to $50 million and created a $150 million reserve to pay for rate rollbacks to 260,000 current and former policyholders. That year, Lewis reached an agreement with John Garamendi, California's insurance commissioner, to refund $51.2 million, or 18 percent of premiums paid on policies written between November 1988 and November 1989. The remaining $100 million in the contingency fund went to Progressive's coffers. Competition in the nonstandard segment also heated up in the late 1980s, as Allstate, Integon, American Premier (formerly Penn Central Corp.), and small local rivals followed Progressive's lead into this "risky business." Progressive responded to these challenges and instituted several operational changes.

Part of Progressive's claims strategy involved a five-year, $28 million overhaul of the company's information system with the goal of increasing profits, cutting costs, and improving customer satisfaction by expediting the settlement of claims. A computer system known as Pacman (for Progressive's Automated Claim Management), was implemented in July 1989.

The company also instituted Immediate Response claims service accessible using a toll-free, 24-hour hotline. Claims representatives may arrive in specially-marked claims vehicles, and are often able to settle claims on the spot. Cat personnel in vans equipped with cellular phones, fax machines, and link-ups to Pacman were often able to settle claims on the spot. In 1992, Progressive adjusters contacted over three-fourths of all claimants within 24 hours of their report. A television advertising campaign emphasized not only the speed, but the compassion, that Progressive's policyholders could expect by recounting an incident when a Progressive claims representative actually arrived at an accident site before the police. Lewis emphasized two bottom-line benefits of such efficient and empathetic claims adjusting in a 1990 *Financial World* article: "We have evidence that the person who doesn't go to a lawyer winds up with more money, and we wind up spending less. . . . [F]raud is [also] becoming an increasingly important aspect of insurance company costs. If you get there early, there's less fraud. And that eliminates costs." The company was widely praised for its extraordinarily customer-oriented approach to claims. Progressive reported that its company mission is to reduce the human trauma and economic costs of automobile accidents.

However, Progressive and its talented leader were not infallible. In 1986, the company began insuring long-haul truck and bus fleets. This segment grew from nothing to $175 million in premiums within two years. However, trucking companies wielded strong buying power, and insurance industry rivals' price cuts soon siphoned off Progressive's long-haul business. By 1992, the experiment had lost $84 million—an amount unheard of and unacceptable at Progressive—and was eliminated.

The combination of rollbacks in California, the misstep into transportation insurance, and drastically lower net income in 1991 (profits dropped from $93.4 million in 1990 to $32.9 million in 1991) created a "mini-crisis" that soured Wall Street on Progressive. The stock's price inched up just 6 percent in 1991, compared to its 35 percent increase the previous year. In response, Lewis reduced employment at Progressive the next year by 19 percent, or 1,300 workers. Lewis softened the blow for the remaining 5,600 employees by instituting a profit-sharing program, but admitted to *Fortune* magazine that the money-saving decision "destroyed morale." However, Progressive was able to cut costs enough to actually reduce premium rates in 18 states during 1993. After 1991's rather dismal results, profits nearly tripled to $153.8 million in 1992 and rose to $267.3 million the following year. Standard and preferred policies only constituted 4.5 percent of Progressive's private passenger auto premiums in 1993, but in 1993 and 1994 the company had established pilot programs in Texas, Florida, Ohio, Illinois, and Virginia to break into that market.

Analysts agreed that Progressive had taken "steps that are very positive," as Joyce L. Culbert, an analyst with Chicago Corp. judged in 1993. However, with continuing competition in the nonstandard segment, some industry observers wondered whether Progressive could continue to make the dramatic strides it had recorded in the past. In addition, after being led by Peter Lewis for nearly four decades, one writer noted that "Progressive's biggest risk is losing Lewis." Brother Daniel, 13 years Peter's junior, stood in the wings, but as of 1994 the elder Lewis, at 60, still occupied the company's top three positions.

Principal Subsidiaries: Airy Insurance Center, Inc.; Allied Insurance Agency, Inc.; Auto Insurance Solutions, Inc.; Classic Insurance Co.; Express Quote Services, Inc.; Gold Key Insurance Agency; Greenberg Financial Insurance Services, Inc.; Insurance Confirmation Services, Inc.; Lakeside Insurance Agency, Inc.; Mountain Laurel Assurance Co.; Mountainside Insurance Agency, Inc.; National Continental Insurance Co.; Pacific Motor Club; Paloverde Insurance Company of Arizona; PCIC Canada Holdings, Ltd.; Progressive Adjusting Company, Inc.; Progressive American Insurance Co.; Progressive Casualty Insurance Co.; Progressive Insurance Agency, Inc.; Progressive Investment Company, Inc.; Progressive Max Insurance Co.; Progressive Mountain Insurance Co.; Progressive Northern Insurance Co.; Progressive Northwestern Insurance Co.; Progressive Partners, Inc.; Progressive Preferred Insurance Co.; Progressive Premium Budget, Inc.; Progressive Risk Management Services, Inc.; Progressive Southeastern Insurance Co.; Richmond Transport Corp.; Tampa Insurance Services, Inc.; Progressive Agency, Inc.; Transportation Recoveries, Inc.; United Financial Casualty Co.; Village Transport Corp.; Wilson Mills Land Co.; Bayside Underwriters Insurance Agency Inc.; Garden Sun Insurance Services Inc.; Halcyon Insurance Co.; Marathon Insurance Co.; Ohana Insurance Company of Hawaii Inc.; Paragon Insurance Company of NY; Progressive Casualty Investment Company; Progressive NY Agency Inc.; Progressive American Life; Progressive Bayside Insurance Company; Progressive Casualty Insurance Company of Canada; Progressive County Mutual Insurance Company; Progressive Gulf Insurance Company; Progressive Life Insurance Ltd.; Progressive Premier Insurance Company of Illinois; Progressive Specialty Insurance Company; Progressive Universal Insurance Company of Illinois; Pro-West Insurance Company; The Paradyme Corporation; United Financial Adjusting Company.

Further Reading:

Bowler, William R., "High Risk's Reward: Progressive Corp. Writes Good Profits on Bad Drivers," *Barron's,* September 17, 1979, pp. 56–57.

David, Gregory, "Chastened?" *Financial World,* January 4, 1994, pp. 38–40.

Dumaine, Brain, "Times Are Good? Create a Crisis," *Fortune,* June 28, 1993, pp. 123–30.

Gleisser, Marcus, "Progressive Insurance Profits Hit $1 Billion," *Cleveland Plain Dealer,* February 6, 1988, p. 5B.

Greene, Jay, "Progressive Switches Control of Investments," *Cleveland Plain Dealer,* February 12, 1993, p. 1E; "Hard Choices Ensure Success," *Cleveland Plain Dealer,* June 7, 1993, p. 17G.

King, Julia, "Re-engineering Put Progressive on the Spot," *Computerworld,* July 15, 1991, p. 58.

McGough, Robert, "Like to Drink and Drive?" *Financial World,* November 27, 1990, pp. 26–28.

Mendes, Joshua, "Progressive: The Prince of Smart Pricing," *Fortune,* March 23, 1992, pp. 107–8.

Phillips, Stephen, "Bad Risks Are this Car Insurer's Best Friends," *Business Week,* November 12, 1990, p. 122.

—April Dougal Gasbarre

Racal-Datacom Inc.

1601 North Harrison Parkway
Sunrise, Florida 33323
U.S.A.
(305) 846-1601
Fax: (305) 846-3935

Wholly Owned Subsidiary of Racal Electronics PLC
Incorporated: 1955
Sales: $583 million
Employees: 2,500
SICs: 3661 Telephone and Telegraph Apparatus; 7372
   Prepackaged Software

Racal-Datacom Inc. is a leader in the ever-growing international market of data communications products and services. Concentrating primarily on offering solutions for local area networks (LANs) and wide area networks (WANs), the company provides a diverse array of network items, including Excalibur access devices, INTERNEXT intelligent hubs, Prem Net metropolitan fiber distribution systems, routers, multiplexers, and ALM high-speed modems. Racal-Datacom is also one of the world's leaders in local area network design and integration.

Founded in 1955 by Monroe A. Miller and based in Miami, Florida, the company originally manufactured electronics products under the name Milgo Electronic Corporation. Miller soon established close ties with the U.S. government and began making electronics items for the National Aeronautics and Space Administration (NASA). With the construction of Cape Canaveral in Florida, the company won many of the early contracts for manufacturing electronic equipment used in America's early, unmanned space flights.

As competition for government contracts, particularly in the field of space exploration, grew more intense, in 1966 Milgo decided to enter the burgeoning commercial communications market. The company's first contract included the design and construction of a modem (computer-telephone interconnecting device) that was capable of transmitting data over an ordinary telephone line at 2,400 bits per second in a bandwidth of 3,000 cycles per second. At the time, building a modem that could send data at such speed was regarded as highly unlikely. Yet the Milgo engineers surpassed the design specifications stipulated in the contract, and constructed a modem that transmitted data at 2,400 bits per second at 800 cycles per second, a significantly

narrower band of transmission. To put this achievement in perspective, commercial modems used in 1994 will soon meet an international standard to move data at a rate of 28,800 bits per second, or ten times faster.

Milgo's success in building this modem was revolutionary because it was considered next to impossible but also because other kinds of communications such as voice and teletype messages could now be sent over the same telephone line. Thus customers were able to communicate their data twice as fast over a telephone line which could also be used for other communications. The modems Milgo had designed and built, models 4400/24 and 4400/48 were initially sold to Western Union and soon became the standard modems in the industry. Milgo found itself in the enviable position of being the only company capable of manufacturing 2,400 bps (bits per second) modems that could operate on unconditioned switched telephone lines.

In 1969, Milgo began its relationship with Racal Electronics Ltd., a British-based manufacturer of radio communications products. With revenues over $140 million, Racal had already established an extensive network of manufacturing facilities in developing countries around the world. Racal approached Milgo and convinced Miller to create Racal-Milgo Ltd., a joint-venture company which would build and market Milgo's data communications products through Racal's international network. The joint venture proved so successful that it accounted for a large percentage of Milgo's revenues and profits within a few years. The arrangement with Milgo also made a significant contribution to Racal's revenues.

Less than a decade later, with Milgo's help Racal had developed into one of fastest growing and most profitable European companies in the communications industry. Building upon its manufacturing and marketing network in developing countries, Racal reported revenues of over $400 million. Racal's revenues were increasing at a compounded rate of 33 percent per year for the last five years, while profits were increasing at a rate of 37 percent per year and its exports at the impressive rate of 40 percent per year during the same period. The company offered developing nations and their military forces simplified versions of radio equipment previously designed and built for the Ministry of Defense in Britain. Racal dominated the emerging-nations market, and its exports were more than the total combined amount of all the other British radio manufacturers. The company's highly sophisticated international marketing organization, its product maintenance and service strategy, and its huge customer base enabled it to provide radio and communications equipment to over 130 governments worldwide.

Pleased with Milgo's contribution to Racal's success, management at Racal decided to acquire Milgo in 1977. At the same time, Digital Data Systems Company, a computer-terminal manufacturer located in Hauppage, New York, and only half Milgo's size, also decided to purchase Milgo. As a result, a bidding contest between Racal and Digital Data soon broke out. The head of Digital Data, Leeam Weathers-Lowin, purchased more than 200,000 shares of Milgo stock in 1967 to help the company through a severe financial crisis. Although almost all of these holdings were later sold, Weathers-Lowin never lost interest in Milgo and now wanted to parley his previous association with the company into a long-standing relationship. However, Milgo's founder and chairman, Monroe Miller, was more sympathetic to the Racal buyout and immediately indicated that a large group of managers at Milgo would tender all their shares to the British firm. In 1977, after a prolonged war with Digital Data, Racal purchased Milgo for $60 million. The company was then renamed Racal-Milgo.

By 1979, Racal-Milgo reported $100 million in sales for its parent company and was regarded as one of the industry leaders in modem supplies and equipment. Yet in spite of the fact that Racal-Milgo had recently introduced a highly innovative data-encryption device and a new product line of intelligent communications terminals, the parent company began to reduce its subsidiary's expenditures for research and development. Angry at what they perceived as British management's insensitivity to Racal-Milgo's potential for growth, almost all of Racal-Milgo's management team either was fired for communicating their grievance or soon resigned. Racal subsequently tightened its control of its subsidiary by absorbing it into a new Data Communications Group headquartered in England. The engineer who had been in charge of developing Milgo's first modem back in 1966, Edward Bleckner, Jr., was chosen as head of the new Racal-Milgo and reported to management in England.

Racal-Milgo began to experience declining profits during the early 1980s. In an attempt to restore its profitability to previous levels, Racal management decided to realign Racal-Milgo and divided the company into six divisions, including Office Networks, Network Components, Communications Network, Racal-Milgo Government Systems, Inc., and separate Sales and Service divisions. While the Office Networks division manufactured and marketed products such as protocol converters to large businesses, Racal-Milgo Government Systems, Inc. supplied products to the federal government, most notably to the U.S. Department of Defense. The Network Components division built modems, statistical multiplexers, data encryption devices and various sorts of data accessory items, and the Communications Network division focused on developing and marketing highly sophisticated advanced management and control systems and other software products. The company's Sales and Service divisions were completely revamped in order to provide a more efficient domestic and international distribution network.

In 1984, Racal established Racal-Vodaphone and entered the brand new cellular radio market in Britain. The firm's primary competition was from British Telecom, the national leader in the telecommunications industry. In order to gain a foothold in the cellular radio market, Racal began to develop specialized data communications systems for cellular radio under a program sponsored by the British government. As Racal's expansion in England and other countries continued, the company grew increasing dependent on its subsidiaries, especially American-based Racal-Milgo, for additional revenues. Fortunately, Racal-Milgo was having one of its most profitable years ever; the company's computer aided engineering unit added $30 million alone to parent Racal's revenues in 1984. In addition, Racal-Milgo began manufacturing various products and software for the growing local area network (LAN) market in the United States. Aimed at office automation for businesses and

defense applications, Racal-Milgo's entry into the local area network market was an immediate success.

During the late 1980s, Racal-Milgo concentrated on developing products and software for the implementation, management, and support of networks from relatively simple desktop computers to highly sophisticated and complex local area networks and wide area networks. The company also began to provide services such as network design and integration, and worldwide support and maintenance, for the needs of both national and multinational firms in the finance, retail, banking and health care industries.

Racal-Milgo was riding high at the start of the 1990s. The company's government systems division and its products for the local area network market were reaping high profits. The firm acquired Network Communications Associates, Inc. for approximately $28 million, and began offering a network solutions package through a joint marketing arrangement with MCI Communications Corporation. Yet parent Racal-Electronics was confronted with a vexing problem in regard to its mobile telephone business in England. The market had grown so rapidly that Racal's cellular telephone subsidiary had such an extremely high stock price and market valuation that it began to compete against its own parent company and consequently skewed the market value of other businesses in Racal. Racal management in England therefore decided to spin off the company's cellular telephone business in 1991. During the same time, to lessen redundant operations and services, parent company Racal Electronics consolidated its 15 separate data communications businesses under the title of the Racal-Datacom Group.

The Racal-Datacom Group included five core businesses, including Defense Radar and Avionics, Radio Communications, Special Businesses, Marine and Energy, and Datacom, the company's single largest operating division. Miami-based Racal-Milgo, now known as Racal-Datacom, continued to improve its standing as a leading worldwide supplier of data communications products and services by concentrating on local area networks, data security, and its traditional product of high speed modems. In 1992, Racal-Datacom joined BellSouth Corporation, a telecommunications holding company located in Atlanta, Georgia, to provide end-to-end network systems for BellSouth's customers. As a result of this agreement, BellSouth's private line and switched data services were linked with Racal-Datacom's T1 multiplexers and various other products. Total revenues for the Racal-Datacom Group at the end of fiscal 1994 were $553 million.

Racal-Datacom has been at the forefront in the development of data communications products, systems, and services from 1955 onward. During the 1950s, space communications technology inched forward at the same rate as teletype, approximately one word per second. By the start of the 1990s, however, the communications systems within America's space shuttles Columbia and Enterprise were capable of conveying data at a rate of 7.5 million words per second. With the increasing sophistication of its products, Miami-based Racal-Datacom intends to take advantage of the growing trend toward a national information network that will link every business, school, library, hospital, and government office in the United States.

Further Reading:

Antelman, Leonard, ''Racal Splits Milgo Subsidiary to Six Divisions,'' *Electronic News,* July 11, 1983, p. 11.

''The Hot Bidding War to Capture Milgo,'' *Business Week,* February 7, 1977, pp. 33–34.

Johnston, Marsha W., ''Racal Electronics PLC,'' *Datamation,* July 1, 1991, p. 74.

Kaye, Jon, ''Racal Electronics PLC,'' *Datamation,* July 1, 1992, p. 79.

''Racal Electronics PLC,'' *Datamation,* June 1, 1985, p. 127.

''Racal's Raid on the U.S. Market,'' *Business Week,* July 16, 1979.

Wehle, Jonathan, ''Racal Electronics: Eat or Be Eaten,'' *Financial World,* January 19, 1993, pp. 16–17.

—Thomas Derdak

Raytheon Company

141 Spring Street
Lexington, Massachusetts 02173-7899
U.S.A.
(617) 862-6600
Fax: (617) 860-2172

Public Company
Incorporated: 1922 as American Appliance Company
Employees: 60,000
Sales: $9.2 billion
Stock Exchanges: New York Boston Cincinnati NASDAQ
  Philadelphia Pacific
SICS: 3812 Search and Navigation Equipment; 3761 Guided
  Missiles and Space Vehicles; 3670 Electronic Components
  and Accessories; 3720 Aircraft & Parts; 1629 Heavy
  Construction, Nec; 3530 Construction and Related
  Machinery; 8711 Engineering Services; 3663 Radio and
  Television Broadcasting and Communication Equipment;
  3674 Semiconductors & Other Devices; 3721 Aircraft;
  3632 Household Refrigerators & Farm Freezers

Raytheon is one of the largest and most diversified companies in
the United States, with domestic facilities in 28 states and the
District of Columbia. Overseas facilities and representative
offices are located in 26 countries, principally in Europe, the
Middle East, and the Pacific Rim. International sales comprised
18.4 percent of revenues in 1993. Raytheon had four primary
business interests in the early 1990s: electronics, aircraft products, energy and environmental services, and major appliances.
The company ranked as America's fifth-largest defense contractor: approximately half of its business is conducted with the
United States government. Raytheon was also the country's
fifth-largest appliance manufacturer, with such consumer items
as Amana microwave ovens, Speed Queen washers and dryers,
and Caloric cooking ranges. The company's aircraft segment,
anchored by Beech Aircraft Corporation, boasted the broadest
line in general aviation.

Raytheon was founded in 1922 when a civil engineer named
Laurence Marshall was introduced to an inventor and Harvard
physicist named Charles G. Smith by Dr. Vannevar Bush.
Marshall proposed a business partnership with Smith and Bush
after hearing that Smith had developed a new method for
noiseless home refrigeration using compressed gases and no
moving parts. Marshall raised $25,000 in venture capital from
investors and a former World War I comrade and incorporated
the partnership in Cambridge, Massachusetts (near Bush's employer, the Massachusetts Institute of Technology) as the American Appliance Company.

Marshall and Smith never developed their refrigeration technologies for the market, but instead shifted their attention to vacuum tubes and other electronic devices. In 1924 Marshall made
a three-month tour of the United States to study the pattern of
growth in the electronics market. Noting rapidly growing consumer demand for radios, Marshall negotiated the purchase of
patents for the S-tube, a gas-filled rectifier that converted alternating current (AC) used in households to the direct current
(DC) used in radio sets (Ironically, the technology had been
developed by Smith and Bush some years earlier while they
worked for the American Research and Development Corporation). Up to that time, radios ran on an auto storage battery
called the A battery and a high voltage B battery which were
costly, cumbersome, messy, and relatively expensive to replace.

In 1925, shortly before S-tube production began, a firm in
Indiana laid claim to the American Appliance company name.
The partners decided to change their corporate moniker to
Raytheon Incorporated. Despite the fact that *raytheon* is Greek
for "god of life," the name was actually chosen for its modern
sound. By 1926, Raytheon had become a major manufacturer of
tube rectifiers and generated $321,000 in profit on sales of $1
million.

Virtually all the tubes produced by Raytheon were used in radio
sets whose design patents were held by RCA. In 1927 RCA
altered its licensing agreements with radio manufacturers to
stipulate that the radios could be built only with new rectifier
tubes (called Radiotrons) manufactured by RCA. Raytheon
was, in effect, denied access to its markets. The company was
forced to switch to the production of radio-receiving tubes, a
field in which more than 100 companies were engaged in fierce
competition.

Marshall's response to operating in this difficult environment
was to diversify. Raytheon acquired the Acme-Delta Company,
a producer of transformers, power equipment, and electronic
auto parts. Profits resulting from new products were immediately put back into research and development to improve products, particularly in industrial electronics and microwave communications.

Marshall also sought the support of the National Carbon Company (a division of Union Carbide Corp.) during this difficult
period. In 1929, National Carbon took a $500,000 equity posi-
tion in Raytheon and held an option to buy the remaining
portion of the company for an additional $19.5 million. Na-
tional Carbon knew that Raytheon rectifier tubes had originally
replaced its B battery business and was also convinced that its
battery distribution would do well handling replacement tubes
marked Eveready-Raytheon. Although the cooperative project
was unsuccessful, National Carbon's investment carried Raytheon through the Depression. National Carbon allowed its
option to acquire Raytheon to lapse in 1938.

With world war looming in 1940, U.S. President Franklin Roosevelt and British Prime Minister Winston Churchill authorized the joint development of new radar technologies by American and British institutions. Through the Radiation Laboratory at the Massachusetts Institute of Technology, Raytheon was chosen to develop the top-secret British magnetron, a microwave radar power tube. The technology would provide the range and clearer images required for successful detection and destruction of enemy planes, submarines (when they surfaced), and German warships. The new device had over 100 times the power of previous microwave tubes and was cited as one of the Allies' top secrets. However, Britain needed the United States' manufacturing capacity. In June 1941 Raytheon also won a contract to deliver 100 radar systems for navy ships.

Workers produced 100 magnetrons a day until plant manager Percy Spencer discovered a method, using punch presses, to raise production to more than 2,500 a day. Spencer's ingenuity won Raytheon an appropriation of $2 million from the U.S. Navy for the construction of a large new factory in Waltham, Massachusetts. By the end of the war, Raytheon magnetrons accounted for about 80 percent of the one million magnetrons produced during the war. By 1944, virtually every U.S. Navy ship was equipped with Raytheon radar. The company became internationally known for its reliable marine radar. The company also offered complete radar installations, with the help of subcontractors, and developed tubes for the VT radio fuse, a device that detonated fired shells when it sensed they were near solid objects. Over the course of the war, Raytheon's sales increased 55 times, from $3 million in 1940 to $168 million in 1945.

Raytheon was fortunate to be involved in a high-growth area of defense industry. When the war ended, companies specializing in high-technology military systems suffered less from cuts in the postwar defense budget than aircraft or heavy-vehicle manufacturers, or shipbuilders. Largely as a result of the war, Raytheon emerged as a profitable and influential, but still financially vulnerable, electronics company.

During the spring of 1945 Raytheon's management formulated plans to acquire several other electronics firms. As part of a strategy to consolidate independent component manufacturers into one company, in April the company purchased Belmont Electronics for $4.6 million. Belmont, located in Chicago, was a major consumer of Raytheon tubes and was developing a television for the commercial market. That October, Raytheon acquired Russell Electric for $1.1 million and entered merger negotiations with the Submarine Signal Company. Sub Sig, as the company was known, was founded in Boston in 1901 as a manufacturer of maritime safety equipment, including a depth sounder called the fathometer. Sub-Sig manufactured a variety of sonar equipment during the war and, like Belmont, was a major Raytheon customer. When the two companies agreed to merge on May 31, 1946, it was decided that Sub-Sig would specialize in sonar devices and that Raytheon would continue to develop new radar systems.

Despite Raytheon's strengthened position as a result of the mergers, the company faced severe competition in both the sonar and radar markets from companies like General Electric,

RCA, Westinghouse Electric, and Sperry. Belmont, which planned to bring its television to market in late 1948, suffered a crippling strike during the summer and, as a result, lost much of its projected Christmas business. Unstable price conditions the following spring created further losses from which the subsidiary was largely unable to recuperate.

Laurence Marshall, though a superb engineer, was generally regarded as a poor manager. His inability to effect positive changes within the company led him to resign as president in February 1948. The following December he resigned as CEO, but he remained chairman of the board until May 1950, when he resigned after failing to gain support for a proposed merger with International Telephone & Telegraph. Charles F. Adams, a former financial advisor who joined Raytheon in 1947, assumed Marshall's responsibilities.

The sudden resumption of military orders after the outbreak of the Korean War in June 1950 greatly benefited Raytheon, as Defense Department contracts enabled the company to develop new technologies with initially low profitability. That year, a "Lark" missile equipped with a Raytheon-designed guidance system made history when it intercepted and destroyed a Navy drone aircraft. Raytheon's advanced research center, called Lab 16, was designed to develop the Sparrow air-to-air and Hawk surface-to-air missiles. Raytheon became a partner in Selenia, a joint venture with the Italian firms Finmeccanica and Fiat that was established to develop new radar technologies. Raytheon's association with Selenia afforded it an opportunity to work with the Italian rocket scientist Carlo Calosi.

Raytheon's Belmont operation was re-formed in 1954, but two years later all radio and television operations were sold to the Admiral Corporation. Raytheon continued, however, to develop new appliances such as the Radarange microwave oven. In 1956 Charles Adams hired Harold S. Geneen, a highly innovative and dynamic manager, as executive vice-president. Three years later, however, Geneen left Raytheon to become chief executive of ITT. Richard E. Krafve (who once headed the Ford Motor Company's Edsel project) enjoyed only a short tenure as Geneen's successor; he disagreed frequently with Adams and was apparently unable to gain the respect of engineers. Thomas L. Phillips, manager of the Missile Division, replaced Krafve.

In 1956 and 1957, Raytheon and Minneapolis-Honeywell jointly operated a computer company called Datamatic. Raytheon soon sold its interest to Honeywell when Datamatic failed to compete effectively against IBM. Raytheon's joint-venture projects with Italian companies continued to expand, however. D. Brainerd Holmes, a former director of the American manned-space-flight program, joined Raytheon in 1963 to manage the company's military business, reporting to Phillips.

Raytheon's top managers began to recognize weaknesses in the company's organizational structure perhaps as early as 1962; Raytheon, they decided, had become too dependent on government contracts. So in 1964 Adams and Phillips, who had become chairman and president, respectively, conceived a plan that aimed to diversify the company's operations. Raytheon acquired Packard-Bell's computer operations and a number of small electronics firms. In 1965 Raytheon acquired Amana Refrigeration. Although Raytheon had invented the microwave oven twenty years earlier, it needed Amana to commercialize the technology. Caloric Corporation, a major manufacturer of gas ranges and appliances, was added in 1967. By 1967, Raytheon had absorbed a number of additional companies, including the E. B. Badger Co., Inc.; United Engineers and Constructors; D.C. Heath & Company; and a geological-survey company called the Seismograph Service Corporation.

Raytheon's association with Selenia became strained in 1967. Raytheon's directors concluded that its Italian partners were unwilling to reform the operations of Selenia and Elsi (a jointly operated electronics firm). They voted to sell Raytheon's share of the companies to its partners and end their association with Calosi. Nevertheless, the defense department selected Raytheon as the prime contractor for the new SAM-D missile.

The goal of reducing Raytheon's proportion of sales to the government from 85 percent to 50 percent was achieved on schedule in 1970. But, while Raytheon's sales continued to rise, profits began to lag. Intra-company discussions determined that, with the exception of D. C. Heath, Raytheon should dispense with its marginally performing educational-services units. In 1972, after several relatively small acquisitions, Raytheon purchased Iowa Manufacturing Company (now called Cedarapids, Inc.) a producer of road-building equipment.

When Charles Adams retired as chair in 1975, Tom Phillips was elected the new chairman and chief executive officer. Brainerd Holmes was promoted to president. Raytheon's financial performance during the mid-1970s was impressive: from 1973 to 1978 sales and profits grew at annual rates of 15 percent and 26 percent respectively. Acquisitions in the latter years of the decade included Switchcraft, Inc., an electronics manufacturer, Glenwood Range and Modern Maid gas range producers. The laundry products and kitchen appliance divisions of McGraw-Edison, which included the popular Speed Queen brand name, were added in 1979. The company's retained earnings were placed in high-yielding money-market accounts until needed to finance acquisitions.

In 1977 Phillips tried to acquire Falcon Seaboard, an energy-resources company involved primarily in strip mining coal, but withdrew the offer when favorable terms could not be reached. Instead, Phillips entered into negotiations to acquire Beech Aircraft, a leading manufacturer of single- and twin-engine aircraft. Raytheon acquired Beech in February of 1980 for $800 million. The new affiliate recorded annual losses in each of the ensuing seven years, finally turning a profit in 1988.

At this time Raytheon's business with the government consisted mainly of radar systems, solar systems, communications equipment, and the Hawk, Sparrow, Patriot (formerly SAM-D), and Sidewinder missiles, all of which totaled less than 40 percent of Raytheon's sales. Raytheon was now more widely exposed to commercial computer and consumer markets, but these markets had become unexpectedly competitive, leading Raytheon management to reconsider its trend of moving away from stable military contracts.

Raytheon's Data Systems division, created in 1971 through the merger of the company's information-processing and display units, established a small market by manufacturing terminals for airline reservation systems. Raytheon failed, however, to integrate Data Systems effectively with a word-processing subsidiary called Lexitron, which it acquired in 1978. As the computer-products market expanded, Data Systems found itself unable to compete. After mounting losses, the division was sold to Telex in 1984.

In January 1986 Raytheon acquired the Yeargin Construction Company, a builder of electrical and chemical plants, and the following October it acquired the Stearns Catalytic World Corporation, an industrial plant maintenance company.

When Brainerd Holmes retired on May 31, 1986, as he reached the traditional retirement age of 65, he was succeeded as president by R. Gene Shelley, who himself retired in July 1989 and was replaced by Dennis J. Picard. Picard succeeded Tom Phillips as chairman and chief executive of Raytheon in 1990, and Max E. Bleck rose to president.

While other major defense contractors moved to convert to civilian interests in the wake of post-Cold War defense budget cuts, Raytheon planned to buttress its position within its four business segments. In 1992, Picard announced a new five-year plan. Its goals included increasing foreign military sales from 20 percent to 40 percent of total defense revenues; doubling energy and environmental services' $1.7 billion sales; doubling Beech's $1.1 billion sales; and increasing appliance sales by 60 percent. The versatile Patriot missile—Raytheon's single most important product in the 1990s—was considered pivotal to an increase in the company's overseas sales. From the end of the Gulf War until late in 1994, Raytheon received nearly $2.5 billion in orders for the missiles from overseas customers. The corporation's environmental and energy service was consolidated to form Raytheon Engineers & Constructors International Inc. (RECI), one of the world's largest engineering and construction groups, in 1993. The acquisitions of Harbert Corp., Gibbs & Hill, and key segments of EBASCO Services, Inc., that year were intended to help boost RECI's annual sales. British Aerospace Corporate Jets was also purchased that year for $387.5 million. The acquisition helped expand Beech's penetration of the business aircraft market. An extensive overhaul of the appliance segment, including downsizing, consolidation, and the 1994 acquisition of UniMac Companies, helped increase that division's sales and profits.

CEO Picard noted in his 1994 annual report that Raytheon's goal was "to become a diversified *commercial* company with a strong defense electronics base." That year, Raytheon launched a new public relations campaign to emphasize this unified corporate image.

Principal Subsidiaries: Amana Refrigeration, Inc.; Beech Aircraft Corporation; Cedarapids, Inc.; Raytheon Engineers & Constructors, Inc.; Raytheon Service Company.

Further Reading:

Hughes, David. "Raytheon Targets Growth Within Four Core Groups," *Aviation Week & Space Technology*, v. 138, March 1, 1993, 52–53.

Schriener, Judy. "Blasting Off for Peacetime Targets," *ENR*, v. 232, April 18, 1994, 24–28.

Scott, Otto J. *The Creative Ordeal: The Story of Raytheon*, New York, Atheneum, 1974.

Smith, Geoffrey. "Raytheon's Strategy: Guns and Lots More Butter," *Business Week*, November 6, 1992, 96.

Suhrbier, Robin. "Raytheon Pushes Single Brand," *Business Marketing*, v.79, January 1994, 4, 40.

—updated by April Dougal Gasbarre

Republic New York Corporation

452 Fifth Avenue
New York, New York 10018
U.S.A.
(212) 525-6100
Fax: (212) 525-5569

Public Company
Incorporated: 1973
Employees: 4,900
Total Assets: $39.49 billion
Stock Exchanges: New York
SIC(s): 6712 Bank Holding Companies; 6021 National
    Commercial Banks; 6036 Savings Institutions Except
    Federal

Republic New York Corporation is a bank holding company for nationally chartered commercial banks and state-chartered savings banks, focusing its services in the areas of international private banking, retail banking, institutional banking, and domestic private banking. The corporation's principal subsidiary, Republic National Bank of New York, is one of the 15 largest banks in the United States, as ranked by shareholder equity, and has consistently been ranked by financial publications and analysts as one of the safest and most creditworthy banks in the world. Through Republic National Bank of New York and Republic New York's other major domestic banking subsidiary, Republic Bank of Savings, the corporation has more than 65 domestic bank branches and one of the largest retailing banking operations in the New York City area. Republic New York also has dozens of foreign offices and affiliates in North America, South America, Europe, the Middle East, and Asia and, as a licensed depository for four currency exchanges, operates one of the world's largest gold trading houses.

Republic New York Corporation traces its heritage to the 1966 formation of the Republic National Bank of New York, founded by Edmond Safra. Safra's family had a century-long tradition of leading conservative, international banking operations, having begun their banking operations during the Ottoman empire in the ancient town of Aleppo, Syria, where they traded precious metals and helped finance Middle East caravans. After the collapse of the empire following World War I, Safra's father moved his family to Beirut, Lebanon, where Edmond Safra was born. Following the establishment of Israel during the late

1940s, anti-Semitic riots swept through Beirut, and Edmond Safra—who never attended college—established a banking business in Italy, before moving his base to Sao Paulo, Brazil, a major refuge port for Aleppo Jews in flight from Syria. At the age of 24, in 1956, Safra established what would become known as the Geneva-based Trade Development Bank (TDB), which began providing private banking services to the wealthy fleeing the Middle East and soon flourished. In 1962, Safra sold his Brazilian bank to his brothers, and, two years later, he began organizing the Republic National Bank of New York, using the assets of his Geneva bank for financing.

On January 24, 1966, Senator Robert F. Kennedy officially opened the Republic National Bank during a ribbon-cutting ceremony at the bank's 18-story headquarters in the Knox Building on Manhattan's Fifth Avenue. The bank opened with what was the highest initial capitalization of any bank in the United States to date—$11 million—and 560 private shareholders from more than 30 states and a dozen countries. Safra was the bank's principal shareholder and was named its honorary chairperson. Peter White, a seasoned banker from Manufacturers Hanover Trust Company, became president, and well-known labor mediator Theodore W. Kheel was named chairperson. Like TDB (which initially acquired a 36 percent stake in the New York bank), Republic National Bank began operations with an emphasis on international banking and a targeted customer base that included foreign companies and domestic firms engaged in international trade. During its first month of operations, Republic National set a record for a New York City commercial bank, opening 20,000 accounts.

While maintaining the Safra family tradition of conservative risk-adverse banking, which thrives on a loyal customer base, during the late 1960s and early 1970s, Republic National launched innovative programs designed to boost the domestic side of its operations and attract new depositors. To compete for consumer savings account business, the bank began giving away television sets to its customers who brought in another person to open interest-bearing time savings accounts of $10,000 or more (laws prohibited the bank from giving such gifts in direct exchange to an individual opening an account). The television campaign was an immediate success, bringing in scores of new customers. Moreover, for a time, Republic National was the nation's leading color television set distributor and became known in New York as the "TV bank." Encouraged by the success of its television promotions, in 1970 Republic National began offering such gifts as motor bikes, refrigerators, dishwashers, and home entertainment centers as part of a program to attract new customers by way of a product called a Bonus Bond—a four-year certificate of deposit (CD). Rather than collecting interest at the CD's maturity, depositors received a merchandise gift, which they chose and which varied in value depending on the amount of the initial deposit.

Republic National's international business also grew during the bank's first five years, prompting the 1971 opening of its first foreign branch in London, where operations were initially focused on money market accounts, syndicated loans, and time deposits. In 1972, Republic National launched a five-year capital-building program and made an initial public offering of $15 million in convertible capital debentures. In September 1973, Republic New York Corporation (Republic) was established as a one-bank holding company for Republic National, which, in 1974, was merged with the Brooklyn-based Kings Lafayette Bank to create a subsidiary that included 18 former Kings Lafayette branches and expanded Republic National from a Manhattan bank to a city-wide bank with offices in Suffolk County, Queens, and Brooklyn. Kings Lafayette (founded in 1889) also provided Republic National with an established base of depositors and launched Republic National's commercial services by adding installment loan, mortgage, and trust departments to the expanded bank's activities.

Like previous Safra-family banks, Republic National was also involved in precious metals trading. It was the first American bank to be granted a license to sell gold for industrial purposes, becoming the largest seller of gold bullion to industry after the U.S. government stopped the practice of selling gold in 1968. In 1974, after the U.S. Treasury lifted the 41-year-old ban on private ownership of gold, Republic soon became the nation's leading importer of gold coins and profited from gold trading by capitalizing on the spread between bidding and asking prices for the gold it imported, housed, and sold to such customers as Wall Street commodities traders and Manhattan jewelers.

By the close of 1974, Republic National was the 100th largest bank in the United States and had assets of $1.1 billion and annual earnings of $13.5 million. In March 1975, Republic acquired American Swiss Credit Company, Ltd.—a former Franklin National Bank unit and a prominent international finance firm specializing in international loans—from the Federal Deposit Insurance Corporation (FDIC), the liquidator of the collapsed Franklin National. The acquisition of American Swiss represented a major step in Republic's history: it raised Republic National's annual revenues to more than $100 million, increasing shareholder equity to a level that allowed the bank to begin selling large denomination negotiable CDs on a regular basis.

In 1975, Kheel resigned as chair and was succeeded by White, who also continued serving as president until his retirement four years later. During the mid-1970s, Republic's assets, capital, and number of bank branches continued to grow, and the company rose quickly on the list of the nation's 100 largest banks. By the end of 1975, Republic was the 75th largest bank in the country.

In 1977, Republic—in the company's first issue of nonconvertible public debt—sold $50 million worth of preferred stock to an even mix of retail and institutional buyers, representing one of the first times institutional customers purchased preferred stock on such a large scale. The sale of preferred stock, coupled with a sale that year of $35 million in long-term debentures, helped the company complete its five-year plan to bring Republic National's capital to over $250 million.

Between 1977 and 1978, Republic expanded its client base by opening an office in Tokyo and creating the Miami-based subsidiary, Republic International Bank of New York, targeting a Latin American customer base. In 1977, Republic also broadened the scope of its business client services with the establishment of the subsidiary Republic Factors Corporation, created to offer corporate customers financing, collection and bookkeeping, data processing, and counseling services. Repub-

lic Factors helped Republic New York Corporation break into the middle market of retail banking and broaden the company's asset base while also serving as a source of referrals for banking operations. Beginning with a two-employee operation headed by Louis Moskowitz, whose book *Modern Factoring and Commercial Finance* was published by Dun & Bradstreet the year the subsidiary was created, Republic Factors, without the use of acquisitions, grew in less than two decades into the fifth largest concern of its kind in the United States.

Between 1979 and 1981, John A. Waage served as Republic chairperson before retiring and being replaced by Moskowitz. In 1980, Walter H. Weiner, Safra's attorney, was named president of the corporation, and, by 1981, he had also assumed the duties of Republic National Bank president. During this time, in 1980, Republic New York was listed on the New York Stock Exchange and made three public offerings—increasing its equity capital by selling $26 million worth of common stock, $25 million in preferred stock, and $75 million in sinking fund debentures—in order to support future expansion of the corporation. Also that year, the company expanded its branch network to 32 with the opening of a new branch in Manhattan's World Trade Center and the acquisition of a dozen Bankers Trust Company branches—ten in Manhattan, one in the Bronx, and one in Brooklyn—with the Bankers Trust branches holding a total of $130 million in deposits. In 1980, the company also expanded its banking opportunities on the West Coast and in the Far East with the establishment of a California subsidiary, Republic International Bank of New York.

Despite general economic instability, Republic's earnings, assets, and capital continued to grow during the early 1980s—largely because of a growth in interest income, an expanding spread in the volume of interest-earning assets, and a sizable increase in income generated from precious metals trading. By 1982, Republic National was the 25th largest bank in the country, and the following year the bank's assets topped $10 billion.

During the early 1980s, following the lifting of interest rate ceilings and the easing of banking regulations in the United States, Republic found itself in a more competitive financial market and responded with a family of money market products designed to compete with the services of both regulated and nonregulated financial businesses and institutions. One of the more successful of these products was Republic's Money Market 100 Account, requiring an initial $100,000 deposit while offering daily interest at money market rates and allowing depositors to borrow money from their own funds.

In 1983, investment banker Jeffrey C. Keil was named president of Republic New York. That year Safra—in what the Lebanese banker later told *Business Week* was his biggest mistake ever—sold his Trade Development Bank to the international banking unit of American Express, which was looking to capitalize on Safra's name and contacts and become a major player in private banking. Selling TDB for $520 million in cash and stock, Safra became the largest stockholder of American Express in a deal in which he also agreed to a five-year non-competition clause with that company. Known as a private man, Safra's style did not fit well with the bureaucracy of American Express, and the banker also became frustrated that that company's money-losing insurance company, Fireman's Fund, was quickly depreciating the value of his stock. In late 1984, Safra severed his short partnership with American Express and the following year sold his stock, which had plummeted $135 million in value since 1983. As part of a departure agreement, Safra bought back TDB's French operations and London-based banknote business, which were soon integrated into the Republic domain.

Building on those London and French operations and Safra's desire to become reinvolved in overseas international private banking, Republic began significantly expanding its London branch and private banking operations in other European locations. In 1984, the London branch assumed the former TDB banknote business and added private banking, bond trading, securities trading, options trading, and foreign exchange and currency swaps to its line of services and also began trading in precious metals. By 1986, Republic had also established foreign subsidiaries in France, Luxembourg, Gibraltar, and Guernsey, focusing on international banking products and funds placement and personal account services.

During the early 1980s, Republic became one of the first banking companies to take a conservative stance toward ongoing credit loans (initially made to Latin American countries during the early 1970s), as a debt crisis began to spread through that region in the 1980s. After Republic National began reducing its exposure to loan losses in Latin America by refusing to renew loans or broaden credit lines to the small group of banks, governments, and government agencies to which it had extended loans, Republic began placing Latin American loans on nonaccrual status (logging interest only after cash payments were received), signalling its more cautious attitude about loan repayment. The company also began setting aside larger loan-loss reserves and in 1986—in moves to reduce its exposure to Latin American losses—began selling portions of its portfolio of Latin American loans.

In 1986, Republic created a management team that would lead it into the following decade: Weiner was named chairperson of the corporation, succeeding Moskowitz, and Israeli-born Dov C. Schlein was named president of Republic Bank of New York, while Keil remained corporation president. In 1987, Republic acquired The Williamsburg Savings Bank with 13 branches, expanding the company's domestic operations to a 43-branch network and broadening its geographic coverage of the greater New York City area. After acquiring Williamsburg Savings, which brought $1.4 billion in mortgages and $2.2 billion in deposits to the company, Republic added new financial products targeting business and professional clients to Williamsburg Savings operations and infused $200 million in capital to the acquired bank, prompting Standard & Poor's to give Williamsburgh Savings the highest rating of any savings bank in the country.

Operating nine banking subsidiaries outside the United States in 1987, Republic registered to open a Swiss banking subsidiary the following year when Safra's non-competition clause with American Express expired. During this time, Safra was gearing up to start Republic National Bank of New York (Suisse) S.A., and 20 TDB executives left American Express to rejoin the Safra fold. Believing Safra might have broken his non-competition agreement, American Express personnel—in what evolved into a smear campaign—began collecting information on Safra,

trying to determine if the agreement had been broken and, if so, to what extent. American Express, in a futile attempt, also protested the formation of the new Safra Swiss subsidiary, which began operations in 1988.

In a larger restructuring of its European operations and expansion of its international private banking business, in 1988 Republic and Safra began preparing for the 1992 lifting of European Economic Community trade restrictions and organized a new Geneva-based holding company, Safra Holdings S.A. Edmond Safra became the chairperson and largest stockholder of the new corporation, while Republic, in exchange for its subsidiaries in Switzerland, Luxembourg, France, Guernsey and Gibraltar, received a 48.8 percent interest in Safra Holdings. Through an international offering of $500 million in shares—the largest in Republic's history and ironically led by Shearson-Lehman Hutton Inc., an investment bank 60 percent owned by American Express—the offering created a broad international shareholder base, raised public awareness of Republic's worldwide operations, and gave Republic the size and geographic diversity to compete for growing European business without forfeiting capital or diluting Republic's public stock.

By 1989, international newspapers had picked up on rumors spread by American Express personnel about Safra, including attempts to link the Lebanese banker to money laundering, drug smuggling, and illicit arms trading. Safra responded by hiring Stanley S. Arkin to investigate the origin of the smear campaign, and, by March 1989, Safra was convinced that the snowballing rumors had begun at American Express. Safra complained to American Express chairperson James D. Robinson III, who later apologized for a "shameful" and "baseless" campaign to discredit Safra's name (though not noting specifically where the rumors originated from) and agreed to donate $8 million to four of Safra's favorite charities in attempts to make amends.

In 1990, Republic acquired the 140-year-old Manhattan Savings Bank with 17 branches in New York City and Westchester County, New York, and $2.8 billion in deposits and $3.1 billion in assets. Manhattan Savings and Williamsburgh Savings were then merged into a single Republic subsidiary operating under the Manhattan Savings name (renamed Republic Bank for Savings in 1993), creating New York's fifth largest savings bank with assets of about $6 million from two formerly troubled financial institutions. In 1992, Republic expanded its retail banking operations with the acquisition of $678 million worth of FDIC-insured deposits in seven American Savings Bank branches (with those operations consolidated into four Republic branches) and also acquired Manhattan Savings Bank through a merger with the ten-branch SafraBank, N.A. Miami, which expanded Republic's operations into Florida and added $250 million in deposits to Manhattan Savings assets.

In the early 1990s, after increasing its retail deposit business with acquisitions, Republic began developing a line of fee-based investment products for retail customers and wealthy individuals in order to: fend off competitors targeting its customers, compensate for low interest rates squeezing the spread between what Republic paid customers and what it earned on investments, and attract "new" money customers as well as heirs to old world money seeking higher returns on their deposits. In late 1991, Republic, preparing to start a securities business, tapped former Shearson Lehman Brothers executive Louis Lloyd (who had left during a management shakeup at its parent American Express) to write a business plan for and serve as president and chief executive of Republic New York Securities Corporation. In 1992, Republic hired the former Shearson Lehman president Peter A. Cohen (who, like Lloyd, was ousted in an American Express management reorganization) to serve as chairperson of the new subsidiary Republic Securities, which began operations in November of that year. Republic Securities offered full-service brokerage, securities lending, and prime brokerage services for hedge funds (unregulated, private partnerships for the very wealthy and a fast growing Wall Street business) and securities credit products for wealthy individuals and institutional clients.

Cohen was also put in charge of another sister startup, Republic Asset Management Corporation, which began offering asset management services for wealthy private banking customers, retail depositors, and corporations in 1993. Early that year, Republic hired an experienced group of swaps and derivative products professionals so the company could begin dealing in those fee-based areas and foreign exchange trading; by mid-1993, an equity research group and retail sales unit for fee-based services was created. In November 1993, Republic Securities hired Lee Hennessee, a former Smith Barney Shearson consultant known for her expertise in hedge fund management, to run the new Republic Hedge Fund Select Group targeting wealthy individuals and institutions seeking help selecting hedge fund managers. In a unique brokerage service, Hennessee began creating investment manager portfolios for wealthy clients and matching hedge funds with potential clients with at least $10 million to invest.

In 1993, Republic acquired a $259 million-deposit branch from the Greater New York Savings Bank. That year, the corporation acquired SafraCorp California and its subsidiary (renamed Republic Bank California N.A.), a private banking services operation in Southern California. During late 1993, Republic hired Leslie E. Bains as executive vice-president in charge of a new division focusing on banking, trust custody, and investments for wealthy individuals. The corporation took a major step into the domestic private banking and global trust arenas, with domestic banking operations already in place to build on in three of the four principal markets for such services: Los Angeles, Miami, and New York.

Internationally, Republic made two key moves in 1993 to benefit from the North American Free Trade Agreement: it applied to establish a bank subsidiary in Mexico and acquired the financially troubled Bank Leumi of Canada, giving the company an entrance into the Toronto market and additional customers in Montreal. Later that year, Republic also acquired Citibank's World Banknote Services operations involved in the shipment of American dollars to and from banks worldwide, and Mase Westpac Limited (renamed Republic Mase Bank Limited), an authorized gold bullion bank and a member of the London Gold Fixing, which twice daily established benchmark prices for gold. The acquisition of Mase Bank, with offices around the world, expanded Republic's role as a world leader in precious metals, giving Republic's clients the ability to trade gold 24 hours a day and thereby substantially boosting Republic's gold dealing business for hedge funds and commodity traders.

Republic New York entered 1994 as the 13th largest bank in the United States. Early that year, Republic Securities received clearance from the Federal Reserve System to begin dealing in all forms of debt and equity securities. By April 1994, Republic Securities was profitable, having become prime broker for 15 hedge-fund managers running nearly 50 hedge funds while the subsidiary's balance sheet had in one year increased from an initial capitalization of $100 million to $1.9 billion. However, in a retrenchment move designed to reduce hedge fund financing, Republic Securities also began scaling back its activities and shutting down higher-risk products to focus on the company's bank client base, resulting in a demotion of Lloyd, who lost his Republic Securities chief executive title, and coinciding with the resignation of Cohen, who left Republic to start his own securities firm.

Republic moved into the mid-1990s expecting domestic private banking to pick up the slack left by reduced securities operations, which was redirected to become an arm of domestic banking operations. Targeting entrepreneurs who had accumulated large financial resources—those with at least $2 to $5 million in assets—Republic was counting on domestic private banking growth from four main products: lending, custody, trust and estates, and investment management services (including advisor or intermediary fee services to investors in search of hedge funds).

Republic expected domestic private banking to eventually provide the company with about one-fourth of its business. In the evolving financial marketplace, Republic's mission would be expanded from not only protecting depositors' funds, but to also include protecting their clients' capital and broadening their capital-earning potential through fee-based services. By moving from strictly banking to more fee-based operations providing higher returns than traditional banking services, Republic expected to earn dividends from such things as brokerage services for all of its client bases, foreign exchange funds for institutional and international private banking clients, and CDs for retail clients. Moreover, despite its expanded line of financial products and services, Republic still believed its customer-oriented philosophy would help distinguish it from other competitors, which had grown to include both financial institutions as well as brokerage firms and money managers. That philosophy, nurtured by Safra, had resulted in some powerful assets as well as significant dividends for the company's founder, who had become a billionaire. As noted in a March 1994 *Business Week* article, "no other major U.S. bank [had] so overpowering a capital position or so razor-thin a cost structure. And few approach[ed] its stellar share-price performance over the long term.... [And] no other major banker since the era of the Morgans and Rockefellers has been so successful as an entrepreneur—perhaps because none has quite so direct a stake in his bank."

Principal Subsidiaries: Republic National Bank of New York; Republic Bank for Savings; Republic Bank California N.A.; Republic Asset Management Corporation; Republic Factors Corp.; Republic Information and Communications Services, Inc.; Republic New York Mortgage Corporation; Republic New

York Securities Corporation; Republic New York Trust Company of Florida, National Association; Republic National Bank of New York International Limited (Gibraltar); Republic National Bank of New York (Cayman) Limited; Republic National Bank of New York (Canada); Republic National Bank of New York (Singapore) Ltd.; Republic New York (U.K.) Limited; Republic National Bank of New York (Uruguay) S.A.; Republic International Bank of New York; Republic Mase Bank Limited; Republic New York Investment Corporation; Republic Overseas Banks Holding Corporation; Safra Republic Holdings S.A. (48.8%).

Further Reading:

"Bank Offering Gifts Now Instead of Interest Later," *The Wall Street Journal,* March 31, 1970, p. 11.

Cooper, Ron, "Republic Securities: Make Way for the New Kid," *Investment Dealers' Digest,* November 23, 1992, pp. 14–20.

Forman, Craig, "Republic New York Restructures Units In Europe, Returning Safra to Spotlight," *The Wall Street Journal,* September 20, 1988, p. 4.

Glasgall, William, and John Meehan, with Blanca Riemer and Jon Friedman, "American Express Slings Mud—And Gets Splattered," *Business Week,* August 14, 1989, pp. 102–04.

Holland, Kelley, "Banking on Fees," *Business Week,* January 18, 1993, pp. 72–73.

Lappen, Alyssa A., "What Capital Squeeze?," *Forbes,* November 26, 1990, pp. 198–202.

Pratt, Tom, "Republic Names Lee Hennessee to Head New Hedge Fund Group," *Investment Dealers' Digest,* November 29, 1993, p. 10.

Siconolfi, Michael, "Republic New York Selects Peter Cohen for Vice Chairman," *The Wall Street Journal,* November 11, 1992, p. B8.

Stabler, Charles N., "A TV Spectacular Sets Off a 'Run' on New York Bank," *The Wall Street Journal,* April 11, 1973, p. 19.

Strauss, Cheryl Beth, and Gregory Zuckerman, "Republic Securities Launches Equity Research, Broker Units," *Investment Dealers' Digest,* July 26, 1993, p. 8.

Taylor, John, "Bank Shot: Edmond Safra Turns the Tables on American Express," *New York,* September 18, 1989, pp. 42–47.

Weiss, Gary, "Republic's Odd Couple Gets a Quickie Divorce," *Business Week,* May 23, 1994, p. 107.

Weiss, Gary, with Neal Sandler, "The Mystery Man of Finance: Inside the World of Billionaire Banker Edmond Safra," *Business Week,* March 7, 1994, pp. 98–105.

Woolley, Suzanne, "Republic, the Boring Bank, Breaks Out," *Business Week,* December 9, 1991, pp. 82–84.

—Roger W. Rouland

Riverwood International Corporation

3350 Cumberland Circle
Suite 1400
Atlanta, Georgia 30339
U.S.A.
(404) 644-3000
Fax: (404) 644-2921

Public Company
Incorporated: 1989
Employees: 8,500
Sales: $1.12 billion
Stock Exchanges: New York Boston Cincinnati Chicago San
   Francisco Philadelphia
SICs: 2621 Paper Mills; 2631 Paperboard Mills; 2657
   Folding Paperboard Boxes; 3565 Packaging Machinery;
   6719 Holding Companies, Not Elsewhere Classified

Riverwood International Corporation is an international paperboard, packaging, and packaging machinery holding company, whose subsidiaries produce coated unbleached kraft (CUK) paperboard, packaging products (including beverage carriers and folding cartons), packaging machinery, containerboard, linerboard, corrugated boxes, and lumber and plywood. Riverwood is a leading supplier of CUK paperboard—the thick, glossy paperboard used in secondary packaging—to the beverage industry. The company has a strong overseas presence, operating on four continents in more than a dozen countries, with a vertically integrated strategy that links its timberlands, papermills, packaging plants, and packaging machinery operations. Riverwood owns or manages timberland in the United States and Brazil, which supply a portion of its energy and pulp requirements for its paper and wood operations. The company also leases proprietary packaging machinery, which is designed by the company and which uses the company's CUK paperboard. In June 1992, Riverwood International completed an initial public offering of about 20 percent of its common stock, with the remainder of the company's stock held by Manville Corporation.

The foundation for Riverwood's integrated paper and packaging operations was laid in 1952, when Olin Mathieson Chemical Corp. acquired Frost Industries, Inc. Frost, which had begun in 1884 as an Arkansas sawmill company, owned five sawmills

and timberlands in Louisiana, Arkansas, and Texas, which Olin used to form a forest products division. Three years later, Olin Corp. acquired the Brown Paper Mill Company. Established in 1923, the Brown Paper Mill was the first American company to produce sheet brown kraft paper and Southern Pine kraft linerboard. During World War II, the mill also developed Victory Board, used in corrugated supply boxes that were dropped from Allied airplanes.

Olin consolidated Brown Paper Mill into its forest products division and moved the division's headquarters to West Monroe, Louisiana. Between 1956 and 1958, Olin Corp. acquired a Louisiana sawmill and a Brazil pulp and paper mill, while developing and producing the world's first on-machine clay-coated beverage carrierboard. During the 1960s, Olin Corp. developed the trademarked Marksman Packaging System for cans and bottles, installed the world's first paper machine specifically designed to produce the trademarked beverage carrierboard Aqua-Kote, and entered the plywood business. In 1967, Olinkraft, Inc. was established as a wholly owned subsidiary of Olin Corp. and that same year introduced the world's first solid unbleached sulfate (SUS) natural kraft folding cartonboard. In 1971, Olinkraft entered the particle board business, and, by the time Olinkraft was spun off as a separate public entity in 1974, the company had a diversified and integrated paper and wood products business that, in addition to particle board, was producing kraftpaper, paperboard, packaging products, and building materials.

In September 1978, the Johns-Manville Corp. initiated a bidding war for Olinkraft, despite the fact that Olinkraft had recently signed a merger agreement with Texas Eastern Corp. By October, Olinkraft had agreed to accept a higher offer from Johns-Manville. The following year, Olinkraft was merged into a Johns-Manville subsidiary, which was renamed Manville Forest Products Corporation shortly thereafter.

During this time, however, several lawsuits threatened to put Johns-Manville out of business. Specifically, the suits charged that asbestos building materials used in insulating fiber made by Manville had caused several serious illnesses, including lung disease, among employees and those who used the product. By 1981, around 400 lawsuits per month were being filed. That year, Johns-Manville was reorganized as a holding company, Manville Corporation, with Manville Forest Products serving as one of five wholly separate operating subsidiaries. The following year, Manville and its subsidiaries—even though still profitable at the time—filed petitions for reorganization under the Chapter 11 Federal Bankruptcy Code in a move to shield the company against losses it faced as a result of the lawsuits. By 1985, Manville had exited the asbestos-based product business entirely.

While the Manville Corporation was withdrawing from the asbestos business, it was also plunging money into equipment updates and capital improvements for other operations, including forest products, while absorbing and expanding upon former Olinkraft operations. Between 1983 and 1986, Manville Forest Products acquired a plywood and sawmill plant in Louisiana, a folding carton plant in Mississippi, and Eastex Packaging Inc., which brought three additional folding carton plants in Memphis.

In 1988, Manville emerged from bankruptcy under a landmark reorganization plan that established an independent trust, the Manville Personal Injury Settlement Trust, to which Manville would funnel as much as $3 billion to asbestos-injury victims over a 30-year period and which gave its victims majority control of Manville. In return for a shield against future asbestos-related litigation, Manville gave trust stockholders $2.5 billion in assets, mostly in the form of stock, and promised to pay its victims $75 million annually beginning in August 1991, plus 20 percent of Manville's annual income until all claims were settled.

In 1989, a holding company (later renamed Riverwood International Corporation) was created for Manville's forest products operations. The company then embarked on a plan to double its size over the next five to seven years. In September 1989, the company acquired Papelok S.A., a paper mill and corrugated container plant in Brazil. In November, Thomas H. Johnson—who had served as president of both the coated board and paperboard divisions of rival Mead Corp.—became president of Manville Forest Products.

In the early 1990s, Manville Forest Products relocated its headquarters from West Monroe, Louisiana, to Atlanta, and began plans to embark on an international expansion program. At the time, Manville Forest Products was still largely a domestic concern, with foreign operations limited to Brazil, where a new anti-inflation program was tightening profit margins. In 1990, Manville Forest Products began developing its international folding carton converting base by acquiring DRG Cartons Ltd. (renamed Riverwood International Cartons), Britain's third-largest folding carton concern serving the frozen food, confectionery, and detergent markets and reporting $60 million in annual sales. Manville Forest Products also acquired the assets of the Australian concern Visypack Pty. (renamed Riverwood Cartons Pty. Ltd.), a maker of lithographic folding cartons for the food, consumer products, and beverage industries, with five carton plants and annual sales of $140 million. Manville Forest Products also expanded its base of paperboard production operations with the purchase of Fiskeby Board AB of Sweden, a European producer/converter of recycled cartonboard.

In June 1991, the company's name was changed to Riverwood International Corporation after Manville became the holding company for two subsidiaries: Riverwood, which had grown into one of two major players in the beer and soft-drink cardboard packaging industry, and Manville Sales Corp. (renamed Schuller International, Inc. in 1992), an insulation, reinforcement, filtration, and building products concern.

In a move to strengthen the company's focus on the development of packaging machinery systems, Riverwood created a packaging machinery division in 1991. Around the same time, the company began signing customers to leases for high-speed proprietary packaging machinery and, in the process, became those customers, sole supplier of paperboard used to produce beverage cartons and cases. To further develop its machinery business, Riverwood made several acquisitions, including Minnesota Automation Inc., a global supplier of packaging machinery; the JAK-ET-PAK machinery system, which included machinery, technology, patents, trademarks, and trade names; the paperboard packaging and machinery systems manufactur-

ing operations of Jorba, S.A. and Syspack, S.A. (Syspack was later merged into Jorba), two privately held corporations located in Barcelona, Spain, with annual sales of more than $300 million; and M.E.A.D. Ltd., a Brazil company specializing in beverage packaging machinery. The company also entered a joint venture agreement with Rengo Company, Japan's leading producer of corrugated products, to market machinery-based packaging systems in Japan.

Between 1989 and 1991, a period of consolidation in the paper and packaging industry, Riverwood spent $250 million in acquisitions, as sales climbed from $774 million to $993 million, while earnings inched upward from $75 million to $89 million. By 1991, Riverwood controlled 25 percent of the overseas beverage packaging market and 45 percent of the American beverage market. Moreover, the company was the leading supplier of printed paperboard packaging to the domestic brewing industry and was second only to Mead Corp. in supplying packaging to the American soft-drink industry.

After expanding its international and machinery-lease operations, the company turned its attention to increasing its production of coated unbleached kraft (CUK) paperboard, used increasingly in the packaging industry by food and drink companies. By this time, Riverwood had successfully whittled out a profitable niche in CUK paperboard sales and was serving such customers as Anheuser-Busch, Miller Brewing Company, Coca-Cola, PepsiCo, Procter & Gamble, and Unilever.

In the spring of 1992, Riverwood announced it would offer about 20 percent of its common stock in an initial public offering designed to help finance the acquisition of Macon Kraft, Inc., a 525,000-ton linerboard mill in Macon, Georgia. As recent government allowances had granted certain banking companies reentry to the stock underwriting business, for the first time since the Depression, a bank—J. P. Morgan Securities—took the lead position in a stock offering, heading a Wall Street underwriters team that took Riverwood public.

In June 1992, Riverwood completed an initial public offering of 19.5 percent of its common stock for $172 million and raised an additional $400 million through its public debt offering. In July, Riverwood acquired Macon Kraft (renamed Riverwood International Georgia, Inc.) for $219 million, including the assumption of $169 million of debt, and began a two-year program to convert one of the two Macon plant's linerboard machines to produce Riverwood's proprietary CUK paperboard.

That year, 69 percent of Riverwood's revenues and 76 percent of its profits were generated from sales of specialized paperboard and leases of packaging machinery to beverage and consumer goods companies in more than a dozen countries. Although Riverwood's earnings rose to a record $1.18 billion, costs associated with the Macon Kraft acquisition and conversion, as well as the sluggish economy, led to an earnings decline, and Riverwood's profits fell to just $43.7 million. Before closing out the year Riverwood secured a $50 million line of back-up credit from Morgan Guaranty Trust Company.

During this time, Riverwood established a product development center in Atlanta for machinery-based packaging systems. The company also debuted its Twin-Stack packaging system, becoming the first company to offer a packaging innovation that could accommodate two-tiered can multiples of 12, 18, 24, 30, and 36. Riverwood's Twin-Stack system had numerous advantages over traditional slab packaging, offering beverage manufacturers better package graphics and expanded promotional and merchandising opportunities via paperboard pads separating two layers of cans. The new system also provided retailers improved utilization of shelf space and offered consumers a more compact and portable beverage container with handles and improved weight distribution. Working with PepsiCo, Riverwood began test marketing its Twin-Stack packaging. Four months after the first Twin-Stack pack appeared on store shelves, Mead joined the race for two-tiered packaging sales with its DuoStack system.

Riverwood continued its international expansion drive in 1993, forming a joint venture with Danapak Holding Ltd., the leader in Scandinavian carton converting, to serve the Scandinavian beverage market with packing machinery systems for beverage and foods. The venture was designed to provide beverage customers—in Denmark, Finland, Norway, Sweden, Iceland, Greenland, and the Faroe Islands—with multiple packaging beverage systems that used Riverwood's proprietary CUK paperboard, converted by Danapak into paperboard beverage cartons through Riverwood's packaging machinery.

In 1993, Riverwood also made several moves to improve its short-term financial condition, which was strained by the Macon conversion project and weak containerboard prices and international demand. Those moves included rescheduling debt payments and selling 60,000 acres of U.S. timberland for about $17 million. With earnings continuing to slide in late-1993, Riverwood undertook a series of capital-generating steps: it sold Manville additional stock which increased the parent company's stake in Riverwood from 80.5 to 81.5 percent and gave Riverwood a much-needed infusion of $50 million; it sold another $125 million in bonds in a public debt offering; it brought a former General Electric executive, George F. Varga, on board to assume the new position of chief financial officer; and it initiated a restructuring program aimed at cutting costs and streamlining and consolidating operations which had doubled in size since 1989. Nonetheless, a linerboard glut in the paper and pulp industry, coupled with conversion costs, squeezed Riverwood's profits; in 1993, profits plunged to $1.1 million on sales that remained essentially flat at $1.12 billion.

Riverwood expected its Macon conversion to be completed by late 1994. The new concern promised reduced exposure to commodity price fluctuations and would expand the company's ability to serve the growing and increasingly competitive beverage packaging industry. That year, the company's leases of proprietary machines and sales of twin-pack beverage-can packages were exceeding expectations, and the company's stock prices were climbing.

Moreover, five years of expansion efforts had left Riverwood well positioned to take advantage of three trends which began in the United States and began to develop in Europe in the 1990s: the increase in popularity of cans as the preferred form of primary beverage container packaging, the growth in popularity of CUK paperboard as a form of secondary packaging due to an increase in the size of container multipacks, and the rising popularity of CUK paperboard as a marketing and promotional

tool. With packaging never before so important an element in beverage promotions, Riverwood expected to capitalize on the industry trend of using packaging as a marketing tool; industry insiders predicted that the soft drink industry would launch a promotion a week by 1995, up from six promotions a year in the late-1980s.

Riverwood's future seemed increasingly dependant on dominating the niche market for beer and soft-drink packaging, both through machine leases and CUK paperboard production and sales. Future sales to the beverage industry were expected to be paced by growth of two-tiered packaging. Riverwood's Twin-Stack, which had become better known as Pepsi's Cube, 7-Up's Double Dozun, and Dr. Pepper's Double Decker, was expected to realize the greatest profits. Future company earnings related to CUK paperboard were expected to increase substantially after the Macon plant conversion was completed.

Riverwood moved into the mid-1990s as one of a few companies in the world that had operations in all three coated paperboard packaging segments: coated paperboard production, conversion systems, and machinery systems. Internationally, the company had a strong presence in North America and Europe and a growing presence in Latin America and Asia that was expected to help international sales eventually outpace domestic sales.

Domestically, by 1994 the company was producing 50 to 60 percent of all paperboard beer containers used in the United States and 20 to 30 percent of soft-drink containers. Mead produced most of the remaining containers and was expected to remain Riverwood's principal competitor, particularly in sales of two-tiered packaging, though another competitor, C. W. Zumbiel Company, began producing its version of double-tiered packaging in 1993. Riverwood, like others in the industry, expected two-tiered packaging systems to become the standard for packaging as beverage producers move away from slab packaging, giving the company reason to believe that its Twin Stack machines, which could also manufacture slab packaging, would be vital to the industry.

Riverwood's future as a Manville unit remained uncertain in 1994. Manville's two subsidiaries had grown into highly marketable, autonomous operations, with potential for a profitable sale or breakup in the event that the Manville Personal Injury Settlement Trust needed to liquidate its holdings in order to pay $2 billion or more in asbestos victim claims. Regardless of whether Riverwood remained part of Manville, was spun off, or was sold, the company appeared poised to cart away a substantial portion of domestic and international beverage packaging sales for years to come.

Principal Subsidiaries: Agrok Agro-Florestal Ltda. (Brazil); Fiskeby Board AB (Sweden); Fiskeby Board A/S (Denmark); Fiskeby Board Ltd. (U.K.); Fiskeby Board S.a.r.l. (France); Igaras Agro-Florestais Ltda. (Brazil); Jorba, S.A. (Spain); Riverwood Cartons Pty. Ltd. (Australia); New Materials, Ltd. (U.K.); P.C. Empreendimentos, Participacoes E Comercia Ltda. (Brazil); Papelok S.A. Industria E Comercia (Brazil); Pine Pipeline, Inc.; Riverwood International B.V. (Netherlands); Riverwood International Canada, Inc.; Riverwood International Corporation; Riverwood International Georgia, Inc.; Riverwood

International Japan KK; Riverwood International Limited (U.K.); Riverwood International Packaging, Asia Pacific, Limited (Hong Kong); Riverwood International S.A. (France); Riverwood International USA, Inc.; Riverwood Mehrstuckverpackungs GmbH (Germany); Riverwood Packaging Systems Pty. Ltd. (Australia); Riverwood Rengo Machinery Ltd. (Japan; 60%); Slevin South Company.

Further Reading:

Billips, Mike, "Co-Managers Work to Renovate Mill, Rebuild Labor Relations," *Macon Telegraph,* September 28, 1992.

Bleakley, Fred R., and Howard Hoffman, "A Long Hiatus: Morgan, a Bank, To Handle IPO," *The Wall Street Journal,* April 23, 1992, pp. C1, C17.

Charlier, Marj, "For Manville, a Sale or Breakup Appears Imminent," *The Wall Street Journal,* March 23, 1992, p. B4.

Charlier, Marj, "Life After Asbestos: Manville Tries to Build New Identity as a Firm Keen on Environment," *The Wall Street Journal,* May 31, 1990, pp. 1, A16.

Demarco, Edward, "Riverwood International Hopes to Box Up Greater Profits," *Denver Business Journal,* March 18, 1994, p. A13.

Jabbonsky, Larry, "Doubled Up," *Beverage World,* March 1994, pp. 94–98.

"Johns-Manville, Olinkraft Agree On Merger Plan," *The Wall Street Journal,* November 10, 1978.

"Johns-Manville Seeks 49% Stake in Olinkraft Inc.," *The Wall Street Journal,* September 26, 1978, p. 8.

Lee, Peter, "US Capital Markets: No Run-Of-The-Mill Deal," *Euromoney,* July 1992, pp. 9–10.

Leib, Jeffrey, "Manville: A New Identity, *The Denver Post,* November 3, 1991, p. G1.

McNaughton, David, "Riverwood International Corp.—Making a Case for Growth," *Atlanta Constitution,* February 3, 1993, p. D1.

Torres, Craig, "Riverwood's Fans Say Investors Should Look Beyond the Trees to See Paper Firm's Potential," *The Wall Street Journal,* May 28, 1993, p. B5C.

Zipser, Andy, "The Asbestos Curse: After Many Painful Years, Manville Is Exorcising It," *Barron's,* October 14, 1991, p. 12.

—Roger W. Rouland

Roche Biomedical Laboratories, Inc.

231 Maple Avenue
Burlington, North Carolina 27215
U.S.A.
(910) 229-1127
Fax: (910) 222-1755

Wholly Owned Subsidiary of Hoffman-La Roche, Inc.
Incorporated: 1982
Employees: 9,000
Sales: $600 million
SICs: 8071 Medical Laboratories

Roche Biomedical Laboratories (RBL), a subsidiary of Hoffman-La Roche, Inc., is one of the largest networks of clinical laboratories in the United States. With a system of 20 major laboratories across the country, supplemented by 350 other locations, RBL performs more than a million diagnostic medical tests every day.

RBL was created by Hoffman-La Roche, the American arm of Roche Holding, Limited, an international biomedical conglomerate based in Switzerland. In 1905, Hoffman-LaRoche began operations in the United States, with headquarters in Nutley, New Jersey. It was not until 1969, however, that the company entered the clinical laboratory business. At that time, it purchased the Kings County Research Laboratories, which were based in Brooklyn, New York. Throughout the 1970s, Hoffman-La Roche added to its research laboratory holdings. In 1982, the company made its most significant acquisitions in this area, buying two major independent clinical laboratory businesses, including Biomedical Reference Laboratories of North Carolina. In the following year, Hoffman-La Roche merged all of its laboratory properties into one company, which it called Roche Biomedical Laboratories.

The headquarters for the newly formed RBL were established in Burlington. This site was chosen because it was the home of Biomedical Reference Laboratories, the largest of the laboratories that Hoffman-La Roche had combined into RBL. Biomedical got its start in the late 1960s, when three brothers founded a clinical laboratory in the town of Elon College, North Carolina. In doing so, the brothers were joining a family tradition. Their father, Thomas Edward Powell, Jr., had taught biology at Elon College for 15 years early in the century. Unable to obtain suitable supplies for his students to perform their experiments,

he founded Carolina Biological Supply in 1927 to provide dissection specimens. During the Great Depression of the 1930s, when Elon College was unable to pay its faculty's salaries, Powell left the college and entered business full time. As the New Deal increased federal funding for education programs, Carolina Biological Supply prospered. In the 1960s, Powell handed down the family business to his son, Thomas Edward Powell III.

In 1969, Thomas Powell joined with his twin brothers, James B. Powell, a doctor, and John, to form Biomedical Reference Laboratories. With 16 employees, the lab performed testing for physicians, hospitals, researchers, and small companies in the nearby North Carolina Research Triangle. In 1970, the lab moved from its location at Elon College to an old empty hospital in Burlington. James Powell was in the army, stationed in Washington, D.C., and he came down on the weekends to work. During the 1970s, the lab grew quickly, as scientific research in the area surrounding it intensified.

In 1979, Biomedical sold stock to the public for the first time. The company offered $7.2 million worth of stock, which made the lab itself worth about $50 million. With this infusion of funds, Biomedical moved from its old quarters to a nearby office and laboratory complex called York Court. Three years after Biomedical went public, Hoffman-La Roche purchased the lab for $163.5 million. The company's original owners, the Powell brothers, became multimillionaires. Only one, James, was still involved with the company at that time, and he stayed on as its head.

By the early 1980s, the town where RBL was located had suffered a dramatic decline, as businesses fled to the suburbs. This exodus had left a large number of vacant buildings available, and RBL seized this opportunity to expand rapidly in Burlington. Although RBL comprised labs located all over the country, the North Carolina operations became the company's fastest-growing. In 1984, the U.S. Congress approved more stringent Medicare regulations, which forced testing laboratories to provide greater billing information. Because this change required more space for office work, RBL moved into larger quarters in Burlington, taking over an 80,000 square foot building rented from a hosiery company.

In addition to its clinical testing operations, RBL also conducted extensive research to develop quicker and more sensitive diagnostic assays. The company focused its efforts on products for which society seemed to have a growing need. "We follow the demands of the health-care system," Powell told *Business North Carolina* in 1993. "But we like to think that we are innovators also. We want to be more than just a service lab." To promote development of new products and procedures, RBL established a Center for Molecular Biology, which conducted research on promising ideas in Research Triangle, North Carolina.

In February 1987, RBL joined with Pragma Bio-Tech, Inc., a New Jersey-based company, to provide workplace drug and alcohol testing. Under the agreement, Pragma employees would take samples from employees at their jobs and then convey them to RBL, which would conduct sensitive gas chromatography/mass spectrometry tests to detect the presence of controlled substances. Results would be available within 48 hours. With this joint venture, RBL hoped to tap into the growing concern among employers about drug abuse.

With the help of such programs as the employee drug and alcohol testing, RBL's business continued to grow throughout the 1980s. In 1989, the company established a new division, the Roche Insurance Laboratory. This enterprise was set up to perform the tests required by insurance companies in determining whether to extend coverage or to pay a claim.

At the start of the 1990s, RBL consolidated geographically, selling its western regional operations in August 1990. Labs in Sacramento, California, and Denver, Colorado, were sold to the Unilab Corporation for $41 million. These facilities included clinical, anatomical, and cytology testing businesses. Under the terms of the sale, RBL retained its esoteric and specialty testing operations in those areas. Overall, however, it had withdrawn from participation in the west coast market.

In 1991, RBL used its newly developed DNA technology to help identify the remains of American soldiers killed in the Persian Gulf War. By examining the so-called genetic fingerprint of tissues, the lab was able to help the Armed Forces Institute of Pathology identify all of the missing combatants. Because of this work, Desert Storm was the first war in which no American fighter was buried at the Tomb of the Unknown Soldier. Bodies were also able to be returned to families as intact as possible.

In that same year, Roche expanded its operations by establishing its Consulting Physicians Network in May 1991. This service was established by a subsidiary of RBL, the Roche Insurance Laboratory. With this service, the company sought to provide access to a medical insurance board-certified physician to underwriting companies without a full-time physician on their staff. The doctors provided by RBL would perform risk selection, read EKGs, and review files within one to two days. "The Consulting Physicians Network complements our existing businesses and allows us to respond to the changing needs of the insurance industry," an RBL executive told the *Business Wire*.

By the end of 1991, RBL had become the second largest medical testing company in the United States, with revenues of more than $600 million. The company had more than 8,000 employees in 400 locations across the country. In February 1992, Hoffman La Roche purchased the CompuChem Corporation, based in North Carolina, for $75 million. When this company's operations were combined with those of RBL, the Roche laboratory became the second largest drug-screening provider in the United States. RBL had previously attained the position of the second-largest paternity tester, as well. In May 1992, RBL dedicated a new 94,000 square foot extension of the company's laboratory facilities in Burlington. With this addition, the RBL space became one of the world's largest clinical laboratories. More than 850 people worked at this location.

Also in May 1992, RBL announced that it would sell off CompuChem's environmental division. Despite the fact that CompuChem had spent several million dollars developing its environmental testing products, the company had discovered that the market for these expensive processes was small, as

confusion about state and local regulations left companies in doubt about whether they were necessary. "The environmental operations does not fit with our business," Powell told *Triangle Business* in explaining RBL's decision to seek a buyer for the unit.

In July 1992, RBL announced that its Raritan, New Jersey, and its North Carolina operations had been licensed by the New York City Department of Health to perform tests for the Human Immunodeficiency Virus (HIV). RBL was the first laboratory to receive this approval, of 59 that applied. Earlier, RBL had also been licensed by the State of New York to perform these tests. With this move, RBL stepped up its participation in the rapidly growing field of HIV testing. The company offered all of the available technologies for testing, including antibody tests and a sophisticated DNA test. The latter test involved the use of polymerase chain reaction technology, which duplicated one strand of DNA millions of times to reveal the presence of the virus. This test was particularly useful for detecting the presence of HIV in newborn babies, since their bodies often had not yet formed antibodies to the virus.

In September 1992, RBL made a breakthrough when it introduced the first automated allergy test that used histamine levels to determine sensitivities. The company planned to make this test commercially available and sell it to allergy clinics and allergists through 200 sales representatives. In addition, RBL planned to make presentations at professional meetings and send out brochures advertising the test. RBL's new product employed leukocyte histamines. Before, this test had been labor intensive and expensive, costing from $300 to $400 per antigen and requiring a large blood sample. With the new technology, however, physicians would be able to run 23 tests for $115, using only 2.5 milliliters of blood. During the test, allergens were mixed with the blood to see if a histamine reaction was provoked.

In October 1992, RBL made another technological advance that allowed it to fulfill a need in a rapidly growing market. At that time, the lab introduced a new test to detect the tuberculosis bacterium in just 48 hours—a vast improvement over the old test, which took three to six weeks. Because the advent of AIDS and antibiotic-resistant strains of tuberculosis had caused a resurgence of the disease, this product responded to a growing demand, as state and federal health officials struggled to control the outbreak of the disease. The new test was particularly helpful because it permitted treatment to begin earlier, thus shortening the period in which an infectious person might contaminate others while waiting for test results.

The new test achieved its rapid results by applying polymerase chain reaction technology in another context. Technicians duplicated DNA found in sputum and other samples of respiratory matter to detect the presence of tuberculosis. In announcing the test, Powell said that he expected it "to become a major weapon in the war against tuberculosis, which has increased in incidence by 15.5 percent in the U.S. since 1984," as the *Business Wire* reported.

In addition to the tuberculosis test and the HIV test based on polymerase chain reaction technology, RBL also offered a variety of other assays using this technology. These included tests for HTLV-1 and HTLV-2, viruses thought to cause certain leukemias and lymphomas; a screen for the Lyme disease agent, Borelia bungdorferi; and diagnostic procedures for the human papilloma virus and chlamydia trachomatis. In addition, this technology could be used to identify people, as had been done in the wake of the Gulf War.

At the end of 1992, RBL dedicated a new laboratory and patient service center in Greenville, North Carolina. This facility consolidated operations that had previously been conducted in two locations. By that time, RBL also ran facilities in 11 different office buildings in downtown Burlington.

Throughout 1993, RBL worked to enhance its testing procedures for HIV, cancer, heart disease, and other illnesses. At the company's Roche Image Analysis Systems center, located in the town of Elon College, the company refined a new approach to cancer screening that used computers to standardize interpretation of pap smear results. In addition, the company further developed its forensic uses of DNA testing and enhanced its already large share of the growing market for paternity testing.

In the spring of 1994, RBL updated its data management mechanisms to better manage reporting of laboratory results. With a leading position in a rapidly growing field and the backing of a multinational parent, RBL appeared assured of continuing success in the years to come.

Principal Subsidiaries: CompuChem, Inc.; Roche Insurance Laboratory.

Further Reading:

Bouchey, Lisa M., ''A Clinical Approach,'' *Business Life,* January 1993.
Chapman, Dan, ''From Textiles to Test Tubes,'' *Business North Carolina,* February 1993.
Mukherjee, Sougata, ''Roche May Sell RTP Unit,'' *Triange Business,* May 4, 1992.
''Rapid Detection Test for TB Now Available,'' *Business Wire,* October 8, 1992.
''Roche Insurance Laboratory Establishes Consulting Physicians Network,'' *Business Wire,* May 7, 1991.

—Elizabeth Rourke

Rockwell International Corporation

2201 Seal Beach Boulevard
Seal Beach, California 90740-8250
U.S.A.
(310) 797-3311
Fax: (310) 797-5690

Public Company
Incorporated: 1928 as North American Aviation
Employees: 78,685
Sales: $10.84 billion
Stock Exchanges: New York
SICs: 3823 Process Control Instruments; 3812 Search and
Navigation Equipment; 3764 Space Propulsion Units and
Parts; 3724 Aircraft Engines and Engine Parts; 3714
Motor Vehicle Parts and Accessories; 3861 Photographic
Equipment and Supplies; 3661 Telephone and Telegraph
Apparatus

One of five companies in the United States supplying the federal
government with military aircraft fighters and bombers during
the 1990s, Rockwell International emerged from the end of the
Cold War as an increasingly commercially-oriented company.
In addition to its aerospace and military hardware business,
Rockwell was a major manufacturer of high-speed modems and
factory automation products, business lines that predicated the
company's growth during the 1990s. These businesses were
complemented by Rockwell's involvement in manufacturing
newspaper printing presses, other graphic arts equipment, and
automotive vehicles. In a changing economic climate for military aerospace manufacturers, Rockwell represented a company
headed toward genuine diversification, away from government-
funded contracts, and one of the most successful companies of
its kind.

Charles Lindbergh's flight across the Atlantic in 1927 generated
such interest in aviation that suddenly even small aviation companies were deluged with money from investors. So much
capital was made available by investors (almost one billion
dollars by 1929) that holding companies created hundreds of
airlines and airplane manufacturers. Three companies in particular emerged in the late 1920s as the largest aeronautic concerns: the Aviation Corporation of the Americas (Avco), run by
Averell Harriman and the Lehman Brothers investment firm;
the Boeing/Rentschler consortium known as United Aircraft

and Transportation; and North American Aviation, the predecessor of Rockwell International, organized by a New York
financier named Clement Keys.

Once the engine manufacturer Pratt & Whitney had secured two
airplane manufacturers and a major airline, the United Aircraft
consortium, as exclusive customers, Clement Keys recognized
that his company needed a similar affiliation if it was to survive.
He finalized an arrangement wherein the Wright Engine Company became the exclusive supplier of engines for North American Aviation.

North American's major airline, National Air Transport, was
one of 45 aviation companies operated by Keys; the list also
included the Curtiss Aeroplane & Motor Company and Wright
Engine. Curtiss was a successful manufacturer of such airplanes
as the Condor, and Wright manufactured some of the highest
quality aircraft engines of the day. North American also owned
Eastern Air Lines, the pioneer of air service along the eastern
coast of the United States, and Transcontinental Air Transport.
These subsidiaries made the parent company's stock even more
attractive. Money continued to flow into North American from
investor groups, making the original stockholders (Keys among
them) extremely wealthy.

The bright future of the aviation companies came to an abrupt
end on October 24, 1929 when a financial disaster hit Wall
Street. Virtually all stocks were inflated in value and backed
only with borrowed funds. When investors realized that the
market could no longer support the inflated values of their
stock, they flooded brokerage houses with orders to sell. The
large number of claims led people, banks, and companies into
bankruptcy. The resulting stock market crash brought about a
ten-year world depression.

In 1930, North American lost its majority control of National
Air Transport to the United Aircraft company. The buyout
provided temporary relief to financially troubled North American, which was purchased by General Motors four years later.
General Motors was one of the few companies with capital
available to refinance a business which held such promise for
the future. General Motors acquired North American in an
attempt to diversify, since its own product was not selling well
during the Depression.

Keys retired from business in 1932 because of ill health, and
James Howard Kindelberger, who was with Donald Douglas
during development of the DC-1 and DC-2, was made president
of North American in 1935. He was trained as an engineer but
knew the automotive business so well that his managerial
acumen overshadowed his engineering skills.

General Motors, which held a substantial amount of stock in
Trans World Airlines, sold its holdings in that company in 1936.
In the same year, North American (still a subsidiary of General
Motors) sold its Eastern Air Lines unit to the airline's director,
Eddie Rickenbacker. The divestiture of airline companies from
airplane manufacturers was forced upon the three largest aeronautic conglomerates by Senator Hugo Black, who also advocated the break-up of numerous other monopolies. North American Aviation was no longer an airline company but merely a
manufacturer of airplanes and parts for airplanes.

During World War II, North American manufactured thousands of P-51 Mustangs for the U.S. Army Air Corps. The P-51, one of the last mass-produced piston engine airplanes, saw action in every theatre during the war. The company also built the B-25 Mitchell bomber and T-6 Texan trainer. The company built more airplanes for the U.S. military than any other company during the war years. The rapid expansion of the company was financed mostly by the government, which was North American's largest customer.

When the war ended, North American's military contracts also ended. Like the Grumman Corporation, North American opted to avoid entering the competitive commercial airliner market. Instead, the company focused its resources on the development of the next generation of military aircraft, namely, jets. Working from designs and prototypes of jet aircraft captured from the Germans after the war, North American built its first fighter jet called the F-86 Sabre. Because the Sabre's supersonic wings were developed from German designs, the company saved millions of dollars in research and development costs.

In the years after the war, North American attempted to enter the private airplane market, with a small four-passenger plane called the Navion. However, poor sales of the Navion convinced company management of the futility of entering the private market. In 1947, the design and production rights to the Navion were sold to Ryan Aeronautical.

North American continued to develop new equipment for the military. The company built a number of fighters and trainers for the Navy's aircraft carriers, in addition to a new jet called the F-100 Super Sabre. North American also constructed the first experimental supersonic aircraft, the rocket-powered X-15 and X-70.

When General Motors sold its share of the company in 1948, North American diversified its product line, becoming involved in the development of rockets, guidance systems, and atomic energy. It created Rocketdyne, Autonetics, and Atomics International as new divisions to pursue research in those individual fields. Here again, Rocketdyne was assisted by the Germans; much of its rocket and missile technology was acquired from captured German data.

Kindelberger, who had been promoted to chairperson, and the company's new president, J.L. Atwood, planned the company's diversification before the war ended. They both knew that in order for the company to survive the postwar environment, they would have to prove the company's worth to the government by leading the development of the newest defense systems. The government could then justifiably be asked to fund much of the costly development of any new systems.

The company's greatest success was in its Rocketdyne division, which produced the Thor, Jupiter, Redstone, and Atlas rockets. The research and development of an atomic-powered missile was abandoned when the system was declared impractical and unworkable. Research from the ambitious but ill-fated project was converted for use in the development of nuclear reactors.

When the Soviet Union put Yuri Gagarin into space in 1961, the U.S. space program was jolted into action. North American's Redstone rocket was used to launch Alan Shepard and Virgil

Grissom into space during the Mercury space program in 1961. Later, John Glenn was launched into orbit aboard a Mercury spacecraft perched on top of an Atlas rocket. North American Aviation enabled the United States to recover its technological edge in the space race with the Soviet Union.

In order to meet President Kennedy's challenge to land a man on the moon before 1970, the National Aeronautics and Space Administration (NASA) contracted North American to build the three-passenger Apollo space capsule. On January 27, 1967, a flash fire swept through a manned Apollo capsule during a ground test. Killed in the accident were Virgil Grissom, Edward White II, and Roger Chaffee. The astronauts' widows each received $350,000 in a legal settlement, but North American was still harshly criticized. Despite the fact that most of its business involved government contracts, the company suffered severe financial reverses which threatened it with bankruptcy. Within two months of the accident, North American Aviation was a prime candidate for a takeover.

Rockwell-Standard made a $922 million bid for North American Aviation in March of 1967. Rockwell was established in Wisconsin in 1919 as a manufacturer of truck axles. At the time of the bid, Rockwell was primarily a manufacturer of industrial machinery and light and heavy vehicle parts.

Under the terms of the merger, J.L. Atwood, president and chief executive officer of North American, would assume the same duties at the new company, while Colonel Willard Rockwell, of Rockwell-Standard, would serve as chairperson. The merger was delayed for a few months by the Justice Department, which argued that the merger would be anti-competitive. The problems were finally resolved and the smaller Rockwell, with sales of $636 million, took over North American, with sales of $2.37 billion.

Atwood said the merger was "in furtherance of North American's previously announced objective to diversify its activities into the commercial and industrial sector." What the company management really wanted was to improve its public image. Its association with the Apollo space capsule tragedy was never forgotten. The merger with the Rockwell company would recover the reputation of integrity that management thought North American deserved. It was clear that Colonel Rockwell would be firmly in charge of the new company, which was called North American Rockwell.

Rockwell's role in the U.S. space program continued, but the company maintained a low profile. It spent much of its first years after the merger manufacturing car and truck parts, printing presses, tools, industrial sewing machines, and electronic instruments for flight and navigation. The company devoted much of its resources to the development of space systems, including the enormous Saturn V rocket engines, which launched later Apollo missions to the moon. Later, the company was chosen as the primary contractor for NASA's space shuttles. During this time, it also became NASA's largest contractor, a position it continued to hold into the 1990s. In 1973, the company changed its name to Rockwell International when it was merged with another separate company created by Willard Rockwell Jr., the Rockwell Manufacturing Company.

Willard Rockwell, Jr., who took over from his father in 1967, retired in 1979, and Robert Anderson assumed the position of chairperson. Anderson had joined Rockwell in 1968 after he left the Chrysler Corporation. He was named president of Rockwell in 1970 and chief executive officer in 1974. Anderson's background in the automotive business made him a conservative and cautious manager. Generally regarded as an engineer more than as a financial manager, he had a strategy for the company's growth and expansion that was markedly different from that of his predecessor. Anderson himself later remarked, "it's fair to say that we disagreed on the direction of the company altogether."

Under the junior Rockwell, the company made some high risk acquisitions, stretching its balance sheet to an uncomfortable degree. At one point the company was reportedly losing a million dollars a day. Rockwell was trying to establish the firm's business in high profile consumer markets, like Admiral television, which Anderson sold in 1974.

Anderson, who was originally hired to smooth the transition of management and resources during the 1967 merger, had little tolerance for the waste usually associated with defense contracts. He introduced the General Motors policy, which required all company divisions to submit profit goals for various production periods. As a result of Anderson's strict management, Rockwell's debt-equity ratio (the company's debt divided by its net worth) fell from 99 percent in 1974 to 50 percent in 1977 and to nine percent in 1983.

Rockwell had initially planned to build the B-1 bomber, but in 1977 the Carter administration cancelled the program, favoring instead the development of Northrop's stealth bomber. By 1983, however, the Reagan administration had reactivated the B-1 project as part of its ambitious military program. Production of the B-1 bomber was expected to generate a profit of approximately $2 billion a year for Rockwell, but subsequent orders for more of the bombers ceased. Once again, Rockwell and its B-1 were summarily excluded from consideration for the production of the United States' next strategic bomber. The company still had other defense contracts, however: the MX "Peacekeeper" missile (designed to replace the nation's stock of aging minuteman missiles), five space shuttles, and a navigation satellite called Navstar.

Willard Rockwell, Jr. resigned as a consultant to Rockwell in 1984 due to a conflict of interest between the company and a separate concern he founded n 1979 called Astrotech. Astrotech was negotiating to purchase one or more of NASA's space shuttles in the belief that only private enterprise could make shuttle flights profitable.

That venture was indefinitely postponed by the explosion of the space shuttle Challenger in January 1986. An investigation of the accident later revealed that one of the booster rockets malfunctioned and caused the rocket to collide with the huge external fuel tank. The resulting explosion decimated the orbiter and killed all seven of its astronauts. A few months later President Reagan announced the order for a new shuttle from Rockwell to replace the Challenger.

Shortly before the accident Rockwell was implicated in a government investigation into illegal overcharges on various government contracts. The company was banned from further contract awards until Anderson himself convinced Air Force Secretary Vernon Orr to reinstate the company in December 1985. Anderson promised to fire senior managers involved in any illegal activities.

In 1985, Anderson oversaw the first major acquisition of his career at Rockwell with the $1.7 billion purchase of the Allen-Bradley Company of Milwaukee. Rockwell was suffering from a decrease in business after the cancellation of the B-1 bomber and the completion of the space shuttles. Allen-Bradley, a successful manufacturer of industrial automation systems, provided Rockwell with a steady profit from its operations and helped to reduce the company's dependence on government contracts.

Robert Anderson retired in 1988, relinquishing control of the company to its president, Donald R. Beall, who had been priming himself for Rockwell's leadership position for a decade. Ten years earlier, in 1978, when Beall was president of Rockwell's electronic division in Dallas, he reportedly spent one evening composing notes delineating what he would do if given control of Rockwell. Ten years and 14 pages later, he was given that opportunity and immediately set himself to the task of redefining the company's future.

A principal component of Beall's strategy was to reduce Rockwell's dependence on federal defense contracts and increase its presence in the electronics market. Specifically, this meant an expansion of Rockwell's telecommunications operations and a more significant role for the company's Allen-Bradley subsidiary, which Beall had encouraged Anderson to acquire. To make the company more responsive to customers, Beall granted company managers nearly autonomous control of their operations and then sharply reduced the bureaucratic layers of management that had accumulated over the years. Seven management levels were compressed into three, the company's headquarter staff was cut by more than half, and Rockwell's various businesses were reorganized into four major categories: electronics products, automotive products, a graphics unit (which manufactured high-speed newspaper presses), and aerospace.

Before Beall could complete his transformation of Rockwell, however, economic conditions soured, sending the national economy in a tailspin and shrouding Beall's efforts to create a more diversified, commercially-oriented company. Despite the economic downturn, Beall funnelled more than $250 million into Allen-Bradley to create a new generation of factory automation products, which, coupled with the company's commanding presence in the market for high-speed modems (a product of Rockwell's 1973 acquisition of Collins Radio Co.), provided two stable, commercially-oriented legs for the company to stand on once economic conditions improved.

When conditions did improve, the fruits of Beall's strategy were unveiled. Government-funded business, which as recently as 1988 had accounted for 50 percent of Rockwell's sales, contributed only 23 percent to the company's sales total in 1993, a span during which 40,000 government-funded jobs within the company had been eliminated. Conversely, Rockwell's commercial business had grown substantially, fueled by Beall's efforts to expand the company's telecommunication business and bolster

Allen-Bradley's market position. By 1994, Rockwell's tele-communications unit was manufacturing 80 percent of all modems in computers and fax machines sold throughout the world, while the company's investment in Allen-Bradley began paying dividends, buoyed by a more favorable economic picture. In early 1994, Allen-Bradley was recording $8.1 million in sales per day, the greatest amount in the company's history and cause for much optimism for Rockwell's future as a more dynamic player in the commercial electronics market.

With the changes effected by Beall driving Rockwell's growth, the aerospace and electronics manufacturer entered the mid-1990s pursuing additional changes. Rockwell's aerospace and defense businesses were expected to plateau in the wake of the Cold War, while its commercial businesses were expected to continue their expansion and profitability. As Rockwell charted its future, its products and corporate priorities reflected the demand of a marketplace gearing for the twenty-first century.

Principal Subsidiaries: Allen-Bradley Company, Inc.; Rockwell-Collins International Inc.; Rockwell Graphic Systems, Inc.; Rockwell International Finance Corp.; Rockwell International of Canada (Ontario), Ltd., Rockwell International Holdings, Ltd.; Rockwell International, Ltd. (England); Rockwell International Sales Corp.

Further Reading:

Bright, Charles D., *The Jet Makers: The Aerospace Industry from 1945–1972.* Lawrence: Regents Press of Kansas, 1978.

Cook, Nick, "Who's Winning the US Combat Airframe Battle," *Interavia Business & Technology,* May 1994, p. 22.

Deady, Tim, "Rockwell's Earning's Socked by Recession: But Northrop Corp. Is Given a Boost by B-2 Revenues," *Los Angeles Business Journal,* April 22, 1991, p. 8.

"Electronics Fuels Rockwell Net Rise; Sales Up Slightly," *Electronic News,* May 16, 1994, p. 10.

MacKnight, Nigel, *Shuttle.* Osceola, Fla.: Motorbooks International, 1985.

Mrozek, Donald J., "The Truman Administration and the Enlistment of the Aviation Industry in Postwar Defense," *Business History Review,* Spring 1974.

—updated by Jeffrey L. Covell

Rollins, Inc.

2170 Piedmont Road N.E.
Atlanta, Georgia 30324
U.S.A.
(404) 888-2000
Fax: (404) 888-2662

Public Company
Incorporated: 1948 as Rollins Broadcasting, Inc.
Employees: 10,000
Sales: $575.8 million
Stock Exchanges: New York Pacific Philadelphia Chicago
Boston
SICs: 7342 Disinfecting & Pest Control Services; 7382
Security Systems Services; 0782 Lawn & Garden Services;
0781 Landscape Counselling & Planning; 7389 Business
Services, Not Elsewhere Classified; 5992 Florists; 5191
Farm Supplies

Rollins, Inc. is a leading consumer service company in the
United States, providing termite and pest control, lawn care,
plantscaping and protective services to more than 1.6 million
residential and commercial customers. Rollins derives the majority of its revenues and profits from Orkin Pest Control, the
largest operation of its type in the world, with branches in 49
states, the District of Columbia, Canada, Mexico, and Puerto
Rico and one of only two national concerns in its field. Rollins'
other divisions include Rollins Protective Services, which custom designs, installs, maintains, and monitors wireless and
hardwired residential and commercial security systems; Orkin
Lawn Care, which provides fertilization, weed and insect control, seeding, aeration, and tree and shrub care services; and
Orkin Plantscaping, the second largest operation of its kind in
the country involved in the design, installation, and maintenance of plants it rents and sells to commercial customers.

Rollins, Inc. began as Rollins Broadcasting, Inc. in the 1940s,
though the company's Orkin Pest Control business is older, having been founded in 1901 and acquired by Rollins in the 1960s.
Rollins Broadcasting was co-founded by O. Wayne Rollins, who
was raised in rural Georgia and worked in a cotton mill during
the Depression era, and his brother, John Rollins. Together they
formed Rollins Broadcasting, a partnership based on a simple
strategy: Wayne Rollins would acquire a small Virginia radio
station that would advertise his brother's car dealership.

Wayne Rollins became president of Rollins Broadcasting and
guided an expansion of its media interests which by 1960
included six radio stations and three television stations in the
eastern United States. In 1961, the company went public and
was listed on the American Stock Exchange. Also that year, the
company began diversifying, acquiring Tribble Advertising
Company of Texas, which launched Rollins' outdoor adver-
tising/billboard business. In 1962, Rollins acquired its tenth
broadcasting station with the purchase of its first west coast
media operation, KDAY radio station in Los Angeles.

In 1963, Rollins expanded its outdoor advertising business further south when it acquired Vendors S.A., a Mexican company
which marked Rollins entry into international operations. During the first half of 1964, Rollins acquired Satin Soft Cosmetics
and also entered the citrus-fruit growing business, planting
groves on acreage it had acquired in south-central Florida
during the late-1950s.

In mid-1964, Wayne Rollins led what is believed to have been
the first leveraged buyout in history, when his rapidly diversifying company acquired Orkin Exterminating Company for
$62.4 million, a figure nearly seven times that of Rollins Broad-
casting's revenues that year. At the time of the Orkin acquisition, the family-run Atlanta-based pest control business was
beset with squabbles that at one juncture led family members to
commit the company founder, known as "Otto the Rat Man,"
to a mental institution. Though Wayne Rollins knew little about
pest control, he used his connections with Delaware's Du Pont
family to help secure financing from the Chase Manhattan Bank
and Prudential Insurance Company, which funded most of the
acquisition costs. With more than 800 offices in 29 states and
the District of Columbia, Orkin gave Rollins a service company
to which Rollins could apply advertising and merchandising
operations. For a time the buyout served as a case study at the
Harvard Business School, representing the first time that large
institutional investors backed a smaller firm buying a larger
company and lent money on the basis of potential earnings
rather on the base value of Orkin, setting the stage for an
acquisition that Wayne Rollins compared to "Jonah swallowing
the whale." The deal also became emblematic of other future
Rollins' acquisitions, with Rollins later acquiring several family-owned businesses based in southern states, which offered
cross-marketing opportunities.

Soon after acquiring Orkin, Rollins entered the professional
building maintenance service business with the acquisition of
another Atlanta-based business, L.P. Martin Maintenance Corp.
(renamed Rollins Services), with operations in ten southern
states. Between 1964 and 1965 Rollins also took over several
smaller pest control firms, including Dettlebach Pesticide Corp.,
a manufacturer of pesticides, insecticides, and rodenticides; and
Arwell, Inc., a midwestern termite and pest control firm.

With the name Rollins Broadcasting no longer reflecting the
company's scattered interests, in 1965 the company changed its
name to Rollins, Inc. By 1966, Orkin's operations had been
expanded to 1,000 offices and its recently acquired pest control
business had followed Rollins billboard business into Mexico.
The following year, Rollins, Inc. relocated its corporate offices
from Wilmington, Delaware, to the Orkin headquarters in Atlanta, and, in 1968, Rollins began trading on the New York

Stock Exchange. Moreover, the company also entered the wall-covering and decorating business with the purchase of the Atlanta-based wholesale distribution firm Dwoskin, Inc. and its subsidiary Dwoskin Decorating Company.

In 1968, the Federal Communications Commission (FCC) refused to renew the operating license of one of Rollins then-12 radio stations, WNJR in Newark, New Jersey—one of the first radio stations in the United States to tailor programming specifically to African American audiences. In failing to renew the license, the FCC cited gross misconduct and fraud by station managers who concealed the relationship between the station and an advertising agency and charged that home office officials failed to exercise adequate control and supervision over the station. The FCC ruling was later upheld when the U.S. Supreme Court refused to hear a Rollins appeal.

In 1969, Rollins sales rose above $100 million for the first time. By the end of the decade, the company had formed Rollins Protective Services (RPS), initially a subsidiary, which became a pioneer in the security field after developing one of the first affordable wireless early-warning burglar and fire alarm systems in the 1970s.

During the early 1970s Rollins continued diversifying by acquiring the consumer cooperative United Buying Service and the oil and gas field services operation of Patterson Services, a leading services supplier to oil and gas companies and drilling contractors in the Gulf Coast area. During the same period, Rollins also expanded its home-decorating operations with the acquisitions of Star Wallpaper & Paint Company, Carole Textile Company, and Marks Custom Draperies, Inc. In 1973, the company's Dwoskin division, which had become the country's largest wholesale distributor of wallcoverings, began serving as the sole distributor of Ultra-Ease, a prepasted vinyl-coated wallcovering developed by the Du Pont Company.

By the end of 1973—Rollins' 25th year in business—the company's media interests included a growing cable television system in Wilmington, Delaware (a state which had no commercial television station), as well as three television stations and six radio stations operating in Virginia, West Virginia, Alabama, Illinois, California, and New York. Rollins was also operating the nation's fourth largest outdoor advertising firm and an expanded collective buying service involved in the sale of such items as furniture, major appliances, cars, and boats and boasting one of the largest operations of its kind. Additionally, Rollins Services, the company's building maintenance division, was the largest such operation serving commercial and institutional customers in the Southeast and Southwest and had expanded its services to include janitorial, building management, security and polygraph, engineering, hospital laundry and carpet care, and air sanitization services. Moreover, Rollins' leading service business, Orkin, was the world's largest termite and pest control company, having grown to serve more than one million customers through offices in 35 states, Mexico, and Jamaica.

R. Randall Rollins, son of Wayne Rollins, succeeded his father as president in 1975 while the company co-founder remained as chairperson and chief executive. In 1975, the company sold

Dwoskin operations and closed the year recording revenues of $213 million and earnings of $19 million.

In early 1976, Rollins became the first American company to formally announce that it had made and would continue to make payoffs to local Mexican government officials (which was not illegal under U.S. law) in order to conduct business across the border. In a voluntary disclosure statement filed with the Securities and Exchange Commission (SEC), the company reported that it had paid Mexican officials $127,000 over a five-year period, helping Rollins' billboard business earn about $10 million. After receiving negative publicity from the disclosure, in late 1976 Rollins announced that it would discontinue questionable payments to Mexican officials.

In 1977, Rollins began operating its second cable television system, in New Haven, Connecticut, and about the same time the company completed a new, expanded Plattsburgh, New York, television station, which began broadcasting across the northern U.S. border to Montreal. In 1977, Orkin Pest Control, hoping to benefit from another cross-marketing opportunity, launched a lawn care operation to compete for business in that growing industry, while Rollins, between 1978 and 1981, abandoned its consumer cooperative, business services, and custom drapery operations by discontinuing the business of United Buying Service and selling Rollins Services, Carole Textile Company, and Marks Custom Draperies.

In 1980, Rollins annual sales surpassed $400 million for the first time—after nearly doubling in five years—as earnings rose above $35 million. In 1982, drawing on Orkin's history of serving residential customers in an environmentally sensitive markets, Rollins created a separate lawn care entity, Orkin Lawn Care, offering fertilization, weed and insect control, seeding, and aeration services.

During the early 1980s, Rollins began acquiring and operating numerous cable television franchises in Massachusetts and Rhode Island. In 1982, a local attorney representing Rollins in Danvers, Massachusetts, was convicted of offering a town official a $50,000 bribe to help Rollins secure a franchise there. Rollins was never implicated in the bribe, and, following the conviction, the Danvers Town Council voted to grant a franchise to Rollins, although the cable license was revoked in 1983 by a state consumer agency.

During this time, Rollins acquired about three million shares of its common stock as the Rollins family increased its stake in the company to about 43 percent. During the same period, Rollins' earnings, which had increased on an average of more than 20 percent per year since the company went public, dipped with falling profits from oil and gas services. In 1984, seeking increased shareholder value and expanded business opportunities for family members, Wayne Rollins split his company into three public units: a new Rollins, Inc., operating strictly as a consumer services business offering pest control, lawn care, and security services; a media business, Rollins Communications, Inc. (RCI), controlling television and radio stations and cable television franchises; and RPC Energy Services (RPC), focusing on oil and gas field services. RCI and RPC were then spun off to shareholders, with Rollins family members retaining significant stakes in each. Wayne Rollins remained chair and chief executive of Rollins, Inc. and became chair and chief executive of RCI; Randall Rollins became senior vice-chairperson of Rollins, chair and chief executive of RPC, and president of RCI; and Wayne Rollins' younger son, Gary, became president of Rollins, Inc., assuming the bulk of operational control over the new Rollins, Inc.

With the ability to channel capital, which its service divisions had earned, back into the company, Rollins, Inc. bought back more than a million of its shares for acquisition purposes and purchased companies operating in all three of Rollins' principal business segments. In 1985, RPS increased its scope of operations in Cincinnati, Columbus, Dallas, Houston, and St. Louis with the acquisition of Warner Amex Security Systems, a home security business that provided Rollins with a hardwired security system product line (generally used in commercial application) to add to the company's established line of wireless systems. Rollins' pest control business also expanded in 1985 through acquisitions, including that of Ace Pest & Termite Control Company, which gave Orkin an entrance into the southern California market.

Between 1984 and 1987, Orkin Lawn Care, in attempt to pull its operations out of the red, expanded its reach from the Southeast across seven sunbelt markets from North Carolina to Texas. In 1987, the lawn care division further extended operations into the Midwest and Northeast with the acquisition of Amcare, Inc., which gave Orkin Lawn Care an additional 24 branches and doubled the division's number of locations to more than 40.

Also that year, the company acquired two pest control firms, including Abalene, the largest operation in New York and New England. By this time, Orkin controlled about ten percent of the American pest control market—followed by Terminix with about six percent—and accounted for about 90 percent of Rollins revenues and earnings. After media properties became a hot commodity on Wall Street, the Rollins family sold its interest in RCI for $600 million, propelling Wayne Rollins into the ranks of the world's 400 wealthiest. Moreover, *Forbes* magazine named Rollins, Inc. the nation's leading service company in 1987.

During this time, however, the Federal Trade Commission (FTC) ruled that Orkin Exterminating had unfairly raised its renewal fees in 1980 (after earlier guaranteeing certain customers fixed fees). The company was ordered to roll back fees, although it was allowed to retain the $7.5 million it earned as a result of the increases. Orkin, which had cited inflation as the impetus for its fee hikes, appealed the decision, which was ultimately upheld when the Supreme Court let the FTC ruling stand. Two years after the initial FTC ruling, a federal court found Orkin guilty of improper use of pesticides during a home fumigation—which allegedly caused the death of a Virginia couple—and was fined $350,000. In 1988, Orkin's pest control operations were hurt by industry-wide regulatory changes after the U.S. Environmental Protection Agency banned Chlordane, a widely used termiticide. Rollins responded to the new regulations, which took effect in the midst of Orkin's research into a new foam termiticide, by establishing new customer relations and public relations departments which focused their efforts on public education.

During the late 1980s, Orkin Lawn Care acquired Village Green, Inc., operating in Connecticut and New York, and Easylawn, Inc., operating in South Carolina. Initially Orkin Lawn Care treated lawns with sprays, but in 1988 it converted its treatment process to a combination of wet and dry granular applications, allowing the company to change its vehicle fleet from tankers to smaller and more economical vans. Despite having expanded to a peak of 56 branches by 1988, Orkin Lawn Care had generated little profit since its formation six years earlier. Faced with an industry slump and increased competition, the lawn care division began consolidating some operations and added a complete tree and shrub program to its services. Continuing to persist in a goal of profitability, in 1989 the lawn care division entered the commercial market while pushing its territory westward, acquiring Yearound Lawn Care Experts, a West Coast company with branches in San Diego, Los Angeles, Sacramento, Portland, and Seattle.

During the late 1980s, RPS opened an expanded Technical Center in Atlanta, upgraded the computerized operating systems at its three alarm monitoring centers, acquired two security firms, and entered the Chicago residential security market. In 1989, Orkin—the only pest control business maintaining a continuous national television and outdoor advertising program—launched its "Exterminator" advertising campaign designed to reinforce the recognition of Orkin's name while using the robotic Exterminator to suggest that the firm was the service company of the future. For 1989, Rollins sales climbed above $400 million (for the first time since the 1984 spinoffs) while profits remained flat due to unusual weather conditions that reduced the termite swarm period and delayed the start-up season for lawn care.

During the slow-growth period of late 1980s, Rollins began focusing on lowering turnover among both customers and employees by initiating a program that increased employee recruiting, training, and compensation. Early the following decade, Rollins initiated a total quality improvement plan, beginning with corporate management and designed to eventually touch the company's entire work force with additional quality training.

Rollins entered the 1990s introducing a new division, a new foam termiticide, and new security systems. In 1990, Rollins formed Orkin Plantscaping to sell and rent flowering and green plants principally to commercial customers such as upscale hotels, office buildings, and shopping malls. Also that year, Orkin Termite and Pest Control division, after four years of development work, became the first business in its field to employ a foam termiticide. The pest control division, seeking ways to develop low-cost sales leads, also introduced a toll-free phone line—offering free termite inspections—in conjunction with its Exterminator commercials. In 1990, RPS launched a new automated alarm monitoring system and introduced the Rollins' System VI and the hardwired Vista LX System. The System VI, consisting of a network of alarm sensors and devices communicating directly with one of the company's three, 24-hour alarm monitoring centers, featured one-touch system activation, multiple zone security, and house lighting controls while the Vista LX system combined hardwired and wireless features.

In 1991, O. Wayne Rollins died unexpectedly after entering a hospital for a pacemaker implant. A near-billionaire and one of Florida's largest landowners and biggest cattle barons, Rollins had an estimated net worth of $930 million and had been one of Atlanta's most generous philanthropists. Randall Rollins succeeded his father as chairperson and chief executive while Gary Rollins remained president.

In 1991, the company launched a "Zero Pest" guarantee designed to attract premium commercial pest control accounts from sources such as upscale restaurants and major hotels as well as to complement the company's toll-free inspection hotline, which was generating increasing numbers of residential sales leads. In 1991, RPS introduced its Quality-Plus system, targeting the middle-income family and small business markets, and the following year the security division expanded its cross-marketing programs with other Rollins operations and opened new commercial offices. In 1991, Orkin Plantscaping acquired operations in Dallas, Nashville, and Denver and the following year purchased operations in Portland, San Diego, and Seattle, as it became the second largest plantscaping concern in the country. In 1992, with increased sales generated by three of its four divisions, Rollins' revenues rose more than $50 million and climbed above $500 million for the first time—to $528 million—while net income rose to $38 million.

While Rollins pest control, security, and plantscaping services were growing during the early 1990s, Orkin Lawn Care continued to struggle, resulting in further departures from unprofitable markets. In 1991, Orkin Lawn Care abandoned California and the following year bowed out of parts of the Northeast and Midwest. A slowing of industry growth and an increase in competition caused the lawn care operation to boost its prices and redirect marketing activities to focus on direct sales and forced the operation to retreat from some of its territory. By 1993, the lawn care division had been pared back to a 32-branch area, largely in territory familiar to Rollins: the Southeast and the sunbelt region.

In 1993, Orkin Plantscaping, then serving 16 states, opened a new Dallas distribution center to consolidate purchasing, warehousing, and distribution of plants and supplies. Also that year, Orkin Pest Control introduced a 24-hour hotline and launched a new agribusiness service designed to help dairy farmers in the control of the common fly. In September 1993, the Smithsonian National Museum of Natural History's insect zoo was renamed the O. Orkin Insect Zoo after the company donated $500,000 for its expansion and renovation. Taking aiming at its core residential market, RPS introduced a mid-priced security system product, Protector. Moreover, Orkin Lawn Care introduced its Total Lawn Care (TLC) service, an expanded all-inclusive lawn service, and began a training school for its lawn care technicians and managers. For 1993, Rollins—for the seventh consecutive year—was ranked by *Forbes* as the nation's best services company, as revenues rose to more than $575 million and net income increased to $44.5 million, marking the company's fourth consecutive year recording double-digit earnings increases.

Rollins, Inc. moved into the mid-1990s with the Rollins family owning in excess of 41 percent of the company's common stock and occupying three of the company's seven director seats. The Orkin Pest Control division continued to pace Rollins' revenues and earnings and had only one national competitor in the fragmented and growing near $4 billion pest control industry, which was still in the process of slowly consolidating. In looking to the future, Rollins anticipated increased acquisition activity—which had slowed considerably during the late 1980s and early 1990s due to high asking prices—particularly in the area of local and regional pest control operations and possibly those which could extend operations into Canada and Europe. Rollins Protective Services, generating about ten percent of the company's revenues, appeared to be gaining momentum as it increased cross-marketing programs with other company divisions and expanded its product line in both residential and commercial market segments. Rollins was also hoping that its plantscaping operation, generating about five percent of Rollins' annual sales, could become the first national concern of its kind and that the company's determination to continue in the lawn care business, generating about five percent of Rollins' revenues, would eventually become profitable. With continued attention to customer and employee retention paying dividends as the company neared the mid-decade mark, Rollins appeared to have sound reasons to believe it could reach its goal of becoming a billion-dollar company by the year 2000.

Further Reading:

Calonius, Erik, "Cable Conniving: Fight for TV Franchise in New England Town Elicits Big Bribe Offer," *The Wall Street Journal,* September 22, 1981, pp. 1, 8.

FCC Refuses to Renew a Radio License Of Rollins Unit, Charges Improper Moves," *The Wall Street Journal,* November 29, 1968, p. 4.

"Ghouls' Choice," *Forbes,* January 20, 1992, pp. 134–35.

Haddad, Charles, "O. Wayne Rollins Lets Go," *Georgia Trend,* November 1988, p. 42.

Hannon, Kerry, "Bugs, Burglars and Sod," *Forbes,* July 25, 1988, p. 168.

Ho, Rodney, "On the Prowl for Acquisitions," *Atlanta Constitution,* May 31, 1994, p. D1.

McKenna, Jon, "Rollins' Sons Absorbed Dad's Lessons: Steady, Careful Management," *Atlanta Business Chronicle,* October 21, 1991, p. 3A.

McKenna, Jon, "Wayne Rollins' Fortune: What's Charity's Stake in $930 Million," *Atlanta Business Chronicle,* November 11, 1991, p. 1.

Neill, Carol P., "For Rollins, A House Divided Is Good News," *Business Atlanta,* January 1986, p. 22.

"Nobody's Fool," *Forbes,* January 30, 1984, p. 46.

Paul, Bill, "Rollins Payoffs: Perils of Candor," *The Wall Street Journal,* October 1, 1976, p. 10.

"Rollins Broadcasting Plans to Buy Orkin, Pest-Control Firm, for $62.4 Million Cash," *The Wall Street Journal,* June 22, 1964, p. 7.

Schonbak, Judith, "Randall Takes Rollins' Reins," *Business Atlanta,* December 1991, p. 12.

—Roger W. Rouland

RUST

Rust International Inc.

100 Corporate Parkway
Birmingham, Alabama 35242-2928
U.S.A.
(205) 995-7878
Fax: (205) 995-7355

Public Company
Incorporated: 1988
Employees: 23,000
Sales: $1.24 billion
Stock Exchanges: New York
SICs: 8711 Engineering Services; 4953 Refuse Systems;
   1541 Industrial Buildings and Warehouses; 8742
   Management Consulting Services

With operations in North and South America, Europe, and the Pacific Rim, Rust International Inc. is the world's leading environmental restoration firm and America's largest provider of scaffolding and maintenance. The company helps other firms and governmental agencies become more efficient, conform to environmental standards, build new facilities and maintain old ones, dispose of waste, and remediate environmental hazard sites. By the mid-1990s, Rust International had cleaned up over 10,000 contaminated sites, including one-third of all commercial Superfund projects and 4,350 radioactive waste sites. The company emerged from a comprehensive reorganization in 1993. Touted as the "new Rust," this firm combined segments of three subsidiaries of WMX Technologies, Inc. (formerly Waste Management, Inc.), the world's largest waste handling company: Chemical Waste Management, Wheelabrator Technologies, and The Brand Companies. While the majority (52 percent) of Rust International's shares were owned by Chemical Waste Management, and another large stake (37 percent) was held by Wheelabrator Technologies, the company returned to the public arena in 1993 with the sale of 11 percent of its stock on the New York Stock Exchange.

Named for the three brothers who founded the company in Birmingham, Alabama, in 1905, the Rust Engineering Company built a reputation for high quality industrial and civil design. The company continued under the control of the Rust family through World War II, when it garnered contracts with the federal government to build armament facilities. By the end of the global conflict, Rust Engineering had offices in Birmingham, Pittsburgh, New York City, and Washington D.C. At this time, the company began shifting its focus from building the national arsenal to determining the disposition of war plants during peacetime. During the Cold War, Rust again applied its experience to the construction of several defense facilities.

Rust's defense work led to contracts with the National Aeronautics and Space Administration (NASA), created in 1958 to coordinate research and development in the country's "space race" with the Soviet Union. Beginning in 1961, Rust built facilities and provided consulting support services for NASA. Although government contracts contributed significantly to Rust's operations in the 1950s, the company also designed facilities for an increasingly diverse variety of industries, including steel and paper manufacturing. By the end of the 1970s, Rust had designed and built over 160 pulp, paper, and newsprint mills throughout the United States as well as in New Zealand, Mexico, Canada, and Turkey. Activity in this water-intensive industry also prompted the company's expansion into water pollution control facilities during this time.

Rust's acquisition by Litton Industries Inc., through a 1967 exchange of stock, launched a lengthy period of subsidiary status for the engineering company. In 1969, Rust secured the North American rights to the patented von Roll technologies, Swiss mechanical processes that Rust applied to highly efficient incinerator designs. The licensing agreement helped launch Rust's expansion into such environmental services as pollution control, cogeneration, and refuse-to-energy plants. One of a myriad of Litton acquisitions during the late 1960s, Rust was divested to Wheelabrator-Frye Inc. in 1972.

Rust became the primary operating business of Wheelabrator-Frye's Engineering and Erection Services division, which helped build the company's first waste-to-energy plant in Saugus, Massachusetts, and reported sales of over $80 million in 1974. Wheelabrator-Frye's acquisition of The M. W. Kellogg Company in 1978 doubled the Engineering division's revenues and quadrupled its earnings. When Kellogg Rust Inc., a holding company that directed the two subsidiaries' international activities, was formed in 1981, the division emerged as Wheelabrator's largest business segment and one of the world's top engineering and erection organizations.

The 1980s were characterized by corporate consolidation. In 1983, Wheelabrator merged with The Signal Companies and was renamed Signal Environmental Systems. Rust, as a result, became a part of a multi-tiered conglomerate. Kellogg Rust continued to grow, as it performed many of ultimate parent Signal's engineering functions. The development of cheaper, more efficient plant designs enabled Kellogg Rust to build its second waste-fueled plant during the first half of the decade.

In 1985, when The Signal Companies merged with chemical giant Allied Corporation, the new combine determined that Wheelabrator and its Kellogg Rust subsidiaries were among 35 non-core units that would be spun off. Wheelabrator took back its name, and the 35 businesses were combined under a holding company—The Henley Group—which was divested as a new conglomerate. The Kellogg Rust holding company was dissolved the following year and its construction activities were divided between the two primary entities. Wheelabrator and its Rust International Corp. subsidiary were spun off from The Henley Group through a public offering in 1987.

Throughout this period of corporate wrangling, landfill space dwindled and, therefore, grew more expensive. As a result, Rust's sophisticated incinerators became a more economically viable option for communities in need of large-scale waste disposal. For its part, parent Wheelabrator sponsored public hearings, worked with environmental advocacy groups, and lead tours of incinerators to demonstrate the environmental and economic advantages of incineration over landfills.

In the late 1980s, Wheelabrator and Rust forged a relationship with their former rival, Waste Management, Inc. By this time, Waste Management had grown from a Chicago-area private garbage hauler into the world's largest waste services company. However, Waste Management had also garnered a reputation for carelessness and even criminal irresponsibility. While the company had established an incineration division, its lack of engineering knowledge and experience, as well as its unfavorable public image, had hindered its progress in the incineration business. In 1988, Wheelabrator exchanged 22 percent of its equity for Waste Management's entire waste incineration business, thereby eliminating one of Wheelabrator's competitors and simultaneously associating Waste Management with the positive public image Wheelabrator had long cultivated. Waste Management Inc. increased its investment in Wheelabrator's carefully crafted reputation with the acquisition of a majority stake in 1990.

The new parent announced its plans to consolidate its remediation and construction capabilities as well as boost its stock value through the amalgamation of several subsidiaries in 1992. Called the "new Rust," the entity combined Rust International with segments of Chemical Waste Management Inc. (Waste Management's toxic waste abatement subsidiary) and The Brand Companies Inc. Rodney C. Gilbert, formerly president of Wheelabrator, was elected president and chief executive officer of the new entity. Gilbert had started with Rust in 1958, became president of the company in 1982, and had advanced to the leading post at Wheelabrator three years later. The reorganization created a "seamless organization" of six companies that could "address virtually any need in the areas of project management and environmental engineering as well as infrastructure design and environmental consulting," according to Waste Management chairperson and CEO Dean Buntrock. Under the reorganization, Rust Engineering Co. handled process and waste-to-energy engineering; Rust Environment & Infrastructure Inc., a new operation, was formed from the former SEC Donahue; and its counterpart, Rust Remedial Services Inc., performed chemical cleanups.

However, environment-related activities were only half of the new Rust's story. Rust Industrial Services evolved from The Brand Companies Inc., which was acquired by Waste Management in 1988. Formed in 1961 to manufacture insulation, Brand grew quickly on the basis of its asbestos removal services. In its new incarnation, Rust Industrial Services performed industrial cleaning, built scaffolding, and provided plant maintenance services. Rust Construction Services managed contractors and construction, and Rust Limited, based in London, oversaw international business. Moreover, a seventh unit, Rust Federal Services, was created late in 1993 to manage government contracts. The consolidation increased employment in the Rust organization almost sixfold, from 4,000 to 23,000 worldwide, calling attention to one of the company's few potential problems: integrating a varied work force.

In 1992, Rust International, Inc. generated $1.4 billion in revenue and commanded a backlog of $902 million. Anticipated annual environmental industry growth of 15 to 20 percent during this time necessitated internal development and acquisition of new technologies. Toward that end, Rust established a research center affiliated with Clemson University to investigate new methods of toxic and radioactive waste remediation. In addition, Rust used a $350 million loan from its new parent (renamed WMX Technologies in 1993) to embark on a global acquisition spree. The purchase or creation of seven engineering companies in Australia, Great Britain, Hong Kong, Sweden, Mexico, and Germany increased Rust's international work force from ten to 1,500 employees. By early 1994, Rust had established 20 principal offices outside the United States. Five domestic acquisitions in 1993 alone contributed primarily to the Industrial Services Division, and Rust's purchase of Sky Climber Inc.'s ten distribution centers brought that division into the commercial scaffolding market.

In the mid-1990s, Rust characterized itself as "a single-source provider of services for large, full-scale environmental projects." Its range of services, as well as its long history of government contracting, led to several significant government contracts within the first year after the reorganization, including two Total Environmental Restoration Contracts with the Army Corps of Engineers and a total of at least $940 million in Army and Air Force obligations. The Department of Energy, another frequent client, recognized Rust as its single most cost-effective contractor.

Although governmental contracts were likely to provide a lucrative source of income for Rust during the 1990s, CEO Gilbert planned to maintain an even balance between public and private sector contracts. Shortly after its formation, the new Rust won an important contract to reformulate processes at all seven of Hoechst Celanese Corp.'s American plants to produce more "environmentally friendly" products. In fact, Rust ranked as one of America's top ten design/build contractors, with expertise in aerospace, pulp and paper, chemicals, foods and beverages, manufacturing, metals, and petrochemicals. The company's prospects were considered very good in an era when global environmental concerns have become a top priority. Analysts predicted that remediation would be the fastest-growing portion of environmental industry in the last years of the twentieth century.

Principal Subsidiaries: Rust Engineering Co.; Rust Construction Services; Rust Environment & Infrastructure Inc.; Rust Remedial Services Inc.; Rust Industrial Services; Rust Limited; Rust Federal Services.

Further Reading:

Chakravarty, Subrata N., "Dean Buntrock's Green Machine," *Forbes,* August 2, 1993, pp. 96–100.
Powers, Mary B., and Debra K. Rubin, "Rust Gets a New Shine," *ENR,* June 14, 1993, pp. 22–26.

—April Dougal Gasbarre

Saab-Scania AB

S-581 88 Linkoping
Sweden
(46) 13-180000
Fax: (46) 13-181802

Public Company
Incorporated: 1937 as Svenska Aeroplan Aktiebolaget
Employees: 32,000
Sales: $6.00 billion
Stock Exchanges: Stockholm
SICs: 3711 Motor Vehicles & Car Bodies; 3713 Truck &
    Bus Bodies; 3721 Aircraft; 3761 Guided Missiles & Space
    Vehicles; 3541 Machine Tools—Metal Cutting Types

One of the world's oldest automobile manufacturers, as well as
a respected producer of aircraft, missiles, and energy systems,
Saab-Scania AB has faced significant challenges in the 1990s.
In 1989, as its inefficient automobile division continued to lose
money, Saab-Scania entered into a joint venture with General
Motors Corporation. The combined effort made important productivity improvements, but the company still sought to gain
ground in the highly competitive global automobile industry. In
1991, threatened by looser trade restrictions when Sweden
joined the European Community, industry baron Peter Wallenberg staged the largest leveraged buyout in Swedish history to
gain control of Saab-Scania. With all these changes, Saab-
Scania hoped to return to its long history of success.

In the early 1890s the English bicycle manufacturer Humber
built a factory in Malmo, Sweden, called the Svenska AB
Humber & Company. Near the turn of the century, the plant was
sold to Swedish interests and the name was changed to Masinfabriks AB Scania. Initially the plant manufactured vacuum
cleaners and paper machines as well as bicycles. New bicycle
models introduced in the early 1900s cost the average consumer
the equivalent of six months' wages, so ownership was limited
to the wealthy. At the time, the company was also manufacturing a primitive type of motor vehicle, consisting of a French
gasoline-powered engine with an English carburetor fastened to
a bicycle frame. The construction of this vehicle was important
in that it gave the company practical experience in combustion
engines.

In 1901 a new managing director, Hilding Hessler, and a new
plant manager, 23-year-old Anton Svensson, assumed control

of company operations. The two men began focusing on the
manufacture of automobiles. During 1901 and 1902 the company's best engineers, Fridolf Thorssin and Tomas Krause, built
at least three experimental models. All were constructed with
the engine and gearbox under the driver's seat. Svensson, however, believed that the engine should be placed in the front of
the car. This disagreement led to Thorssin's departure from the
company, at which time Svensson decided to establish a regular
production model based on his own ideas.

At the beginning of 1903 Scania offered three models: the four-
seat Model A, the two-seat Model B, and the Model C, a larger,
luxury car. The Scania automobiles featured one-, two-, and
four-cylinder engines, respectively, ranging from 4.5 to 24
horsepower. The engines were purchased from the Kemper
Motorenfabrik in Berlin, thus enabling Scania to concentrate on
the development of a chassis. The new vehicles were remarkably advanced for their time, featuring a track-rod steering system and central chassis lubrication. The Scania Model A featured a rear seat that could be converted into a small loading
platform.

In 1911 Scania merged with the Vagnfabriks Aktie Bolaget in
Sodertalje (Vabis), a railroad car manufacturer which had also
been producing automobiles since 1897. The new company,
Scania-Vabis, developed the world's first "purpose-built" bus.
In 1924 Scania-Vabis decided to concentrate its efforts on the
manufacture of larger trucks and buses, and in 1929 it discontinued automobile manufacture altogether. The company introduced its first diesel engine in 1936.

With the threat of another war in Europe, it became imperative
for Sweden to improve its defenses. Not least important was the
need for a domestic aircraft industry large enough to supply the
Swedish forces with military aircraft. This led to the formation
in April 1937 of the Svenska Aeroplan Aktiebolaget, abbrevi-
ated SAAB. Two years later, SAAB, with headquarters in
Trollhattan, took over the aircraft division of the Aktiebolaget
Svenska Jarnvagsverkstaderna, or Swedish Railroad Works, located in Linkoping. SAAB subsequently transferred its corporate headquarters and construction and design departments to
Linkoping.

Construction was accelerated at both the Linkoping and Trollhattan plants, which were building aircraft designed by Bristol,
Junkers, and Northrop. During this period work proceeded on
the first SAAB aircraft, the Svenska B-17 dive bomber, which
made its first flight in 1940. When war came to Europe, however, Sweden declared itself neutral. As a result the country was
spared from occupation by Nazi troops which had already taken
control of its Scandinavian neighbors Norway and Denmark.

Plans for car production at the SAAB plant at Trollhattan started
evolving as World War II neared an end, and management
sought to widen the production program to meet an expected
decline in military aircraft requirements. The success of small
European cars in the Swedish market just prior to the war
provided management with confidence that cars of the same
type would also prove popular in the future, and that demand
would be steady enough to ensure the success of a SAAB
automobile.

A talented aircraft engineer named Gunnar Ljungstrom was placed in charge of the development of the SAAB auto, the first prototype of which, the 92001, was ready by the summer of 1946. The body design, however, was neither practical nor aesthetically pleasing. The car was reintroduced in 1947 with an improved external design and was designated the 92002. The design of this model was to characterize SAAB automobiles for the next 30 years. Streamlining helped to reduce fuel consumption and engine wear, and enabled the car to reach speeds of 60 miles per hour. Despite a number of minor shortcomings, the car's road performance was excellent, and its appearance was stylish and popular.

Improved versions of Ljungstrom's original design appeared throughout the 1950s, and by 1955 SAAB automobiles had become the most popular in Sweden; one car left the assembly line every 27 minutes. In order to meet anticipated demand, more plant space was required, and a new factory was established at Goteborg to manufacture engines and gearboxes.

During the previous 20 years, Scania-Vabis developed and produced heavy vehicles, particularly trucks and buses. While somewhat less dynamic in character than SAAB, the company managed to make several innovations in Swedish industry, including the introduction of a turbocharged diesel engine in 1951.

SAAB continued to develop a variety of aircraft, particularly military fighter jets. The first of these was introduced in 1949, and production in various forms was maintained throughout the 1950s. The SAAB aircraft division also held licenses to manufacture foreign-designed aircraft and produce aircraft components for foreign manufacturers.

As early as 1953 SAAB management started exploring the possibility of selling cars in the United States, but hesitated to enter that market until 1956, when a more promising atmosphere had developed. Using New York City as a base of operations, an American subsidiary was created to import SAAB automobiles, and a depot was established near Boston to receive cars and store spare parts. It was a modest beginning for a small foreign company in the world's largest automobile market, and growth was difficult and slow.

During the 1960s the scope of SAAB's operations expanded from automobiles and aircraft into satellites, missiles, and energy systems. On May 19, 1965, as its business continued to grow, the company changed its name to Saab Aktiebolag (the acronym had become so popular as to warrant the elimination of the old name). Over the next four years, officials of Saab and Scania-Vabis began to investigate the viability of operating as a single corporation.

Saab and Scania-Vabis merged their operations during 1969, and absorbed two other military contractors, Malmo Flygindustri and Nordarmatur. All automotive operations of the new Saab-Scania AB were centered at the facility in Sodertalje, and the aircraft division headquarters, which produced the JAS-35 Draken and JAS-37 Viggen fighter jets, remained at Linkoping. Also in 1969, Saab-Scania, in cooperation with the Finnish company Oy Valmet AB, established an automobile factory at Uusikaupunki, Finland.

Saab-Scania decided to focus its efforts on competing for a significantly larger share of the American automobile market, the main goal being to define its cars as a better choice than those offered by BMW, Mercedes-Benz, and Volvo. These cars had been highly successful with more affluent American consumers. The expanded marketing campaign produced few results over the first half of the decade, but by 1978 began to pay off handsomely. The company's sales increased by 19 percent in America and by 17 percent in Scandinavia.

In 1980 the company introduced a new line of Scania trucks based on a unique method of modular construction. These trucks were primarily class 7 vehicles (26,001 to 33,000 pounds in gross vehicle weight), which became extremely popular in the United States. Meanwhile, the automotive division was preparing to introduce a restyled line of cars in its 9000 series; they were introduced in 1984 and proved to be popular. However, problems related to retooling production plants thwarted a planned expansion of production capacity by 10 percent during 1985.

Saab-Scania entered into a joint venture with Fairchild Industries of the United States in 1980 to develop a new 30–36 passenger commercial airliner called the SF340. However, a corporate restructuring of Fairchild forced the company's withdrawal from the project in 1985. Saab-Scania took complete control of the SF340 in November of that year and completed the project in 1986. The SF340 remained in service with a number of airline companies in the mid-1990s, providing connection services between small airports in outlying areas and major airports. The aircraft division also started development of the JAS-39 Gripen fighter jet, which was scheduled to enter service in 1992.

In the late 1980s, Georg Karnsund, Saab-Scania's president, placed greater emphasis on marketing programs in Europe, particularly in France and Italy, as well as in Australia and Japan. Karnsund believed that Saab's ability to develop advanced technology would give its cars a distinct advantage in increasingly competitive international markets.

For Saab-Scania, the 1980s ended with the conclusion of a pivotal deal that ceded half of its automobile operations to General Motors Corporation. Prior to the consummation of the 50–50 joint venture with Saab-Scania, General Motors had sought to acquire Jaguar Cars Ltd., a British manufacturer of luxury cars, but in November 1989 the U.S. car maker was beaten to the prize by rival Ford Motor Company. Still in the mood to acquire, and seeking to increase its presence in the European luxury car market, General Motors entered into its joint venture with Saab-Scania the following month, paying $600 million to gain 50 percent interest in the prestigious yet troubled car maker.

By the late 1980s, Saab-Scania's automobile segment was becoming a perennial financial loser, crippled by declining sales in the United States, the company's largest single market for car sales. The affiliation with General Motors was expected to ameliorate Saab-Scania's position overseas, but at home, larger, more formidable obstacles faced the company and its enormously powerful part-owner, Peter Wallenberg. In addition to holding a controlling interest in Saab-Scania, Wallenberg maintained sizable investments in many other large Swedish companies, including appliance maker Electrolux Corporation and L.M. Ericsson, Sweden's largest communications company. Wallenberg's empire accounted for a third of Sweden's $165 billion economy—a much-coveted portfolio when the country's economy was robust, but a financial nightmare when economic conditions soured as they did entering the 1990s. To make Wallenberg's position more precarious, by 1990 Sweden was prepared to join the European Community, which would force the country to drop its protective economic barriers. These barriers had insulated Wallenberg against foreign corporate raiders and thus enabled him to control companies that represented $55 billion in market value with only $5 billion in equity.

Fearing a hostile takeover, Wallenberg increased his ownership of Saab-Scania in 1990 from 36 percent to 58 percent, then initiated the largest leveraged buyout in Swedish history the following year after learning that outside investors were planning to acquire ten percent of the company's stock—purchasing all of Saab-Scania for $2.3 billion. Against the backdrop of Wallenberg's strategic maneuvers, Saab Automobile, the company's joint venture with General Motors, continued to lose money, recording a loss of $848 million in 1990, which translated into an alarming $9,200 loss for each car sold. Although the other segments of Saab-Scania compensated for the drag of its car sales, giving the company a $375 million profit for the year on $5.4 billion in sales, a revival of its automobile segment represented an integral component of the company's resurgence.

By 1992, it appeared that Saab Automobile was destined for a more profitable future, thanks in large part to the assistance of General Motors' management, who greatly improved the segment's manufacturing efficiency. When General Motors' management arrived at Saab-Scania's car operations in 1989, it took 100 hours to produce a single car, but by 1992 the hours required per car had been whittled down to 50 or 60 hours, cutting in half the production quota required to generate a profit. Although Saab-Scania and General Motors needed to effect further improvements to spark a complete resurgence of Saab automobiles, progress was being made. The introduction of a replacement for the 20-year-old Saab 9000 series in mid-1993 fueled hopes for a recovery of Saab's U.S. sales, a necessary ingredient in Saab-Scania's revitalization. Meanwhile the company's Saab 2000 aircraft, designed for regional airline service and introduced in 1994, added to management's optimism for the future.

Principal Subsidiaries: VAG Sweden Group (67 percent); Bill & Buss Group; Saab-Ana Group (Sweden); Saab-Scania of America, Inc.; Saab (Great Britain) Ltd.; Saab-Scania Combitech Group; Saab-Scania Enertech Group (Sweden); Oy Saab-Valmet AB (50 percent); Oy Scan-Auto AB (Finland; 50 percent); Scancars AG (Switzerland; 25 percent); Scania Nederland BV (Netherlands).

Further Reading:

Feast, Richard, ''Jaguar and Saab: Bullish on America; Ford and GM Patiently Groom Their Latest European Acquisitions for the Long Haul,'' *Automotive Industries,* May 1991, p. 14.

Flint, Jerry, ''Europe to the Rescue,'' *Forbes,* February 3, 1992, p. 19.

Johnson, Richard, ''Europeans Pinched, but Most Are Profitable in Market Dip,'' *Automotive News,* May 27, 1991, p. 2.

Kapstein, Jonathan, ''Fortress Wallenberg Is Showing Some Cracks,'' *Business Week,* December 10, 1990, p. 45.

Kapstein, ''Wallenburg's New Walls,'' *Business Week,* March 11, 1991, p. 46.

Templeman, John, ''Saab: Halfway through a U-Turn,'' *Business Week,* April 27, 1992, p. 121.

—updated by Jeffrey L. Covell

Seagull Energy Corporation

1001 Fannin Street
Suite 1700
Houston, Texas 77002-6714
U.S.A.
(713) 951-4700
Fax: (713) 951-4846

Public Company
Incorporated: 1973 as Seagull Pipeline Corporation
Employees: 682
Sales: $377.17 million
Stock Exchanges: New York
SICs: 4923 Gas Transmission and Distribution; 1311 Crude
    Petroleum and Natural Gas

Seagull Energy Corporation is an energy company with operations in the southwestern United States, Alaska, and Canada. The firm is primarily engaged in natural gas exploration and production, but it also transports, distributes, and markets natural gas, liquid products, and petrochemicals and is involved in natural gas processing. In its first two decades in business, Seagull evolved from a tiny gas gatherer with virtually no gas reserves of its own into a billion-dollar diversified gas producer with over 1.2 trillion cubic feet of natural gas reserves. Two basic factors account for the company's dramatic transformation: the deregulation of the natural gas industry and the leadership of Barry Gault.

Seagull Pipeline Corporation was created in 1973 as an interstate gas-gathering pipeline subsidiary of Houston Oil & Minerals Corp. Although not generally well known, Houston Oil & Minerals was a wildcatting legend among oilmen and investors in the 1970s. Under the leadership of Joseph C. Walter, Jr., Houston Oil & Minerals became a petrochemical industry prodigy. First, Walter created Seagull Pipeline Corporation to collect the "leftovers" from properties that larger gas and oil companies had determined were too small for them to waste time and money to explore. Using these wells as collateral, Walter borrowed money and embarked on his own exploration efforts. A combination of luck, skill, and audacity brought success: Houston Oil & Minerals, proved natural gas reserves doubled every year from 1970 to 1976. However, the company's debt grew almost as fast, as Walter mortgaged the reserves of one property to finance exploration of another.

Houston Oil & Minerals' capital expenditures ran at two to three times its annual cash flow, and its long-term debt quintupled from 1974 to 1977.

When the company's gas and oil reserves tumbled in 1978, its stock, which had increased from 74 cents in 1972 to $42 in 1977 (after numerous splits), lost 28 percent of its value in four days. Walter suffered a serious heart attack that November, and Executive Vice President F. Fox Benton, Jr. took charge. Benton (who advanced to president and chief executive officer shortly thereafter) reorganized Houston Oil & Minerals, cut its capital expenditures budget, and redirected the money to debt retirement. Exploration was severely curtailed as the company went from wildcatter to conservative within two years.

In September 1980, the company's financial devaluation was acknowledged when Allied Chemical proposed a merger. Houston Oil & Minerals declined, but soon sought a partner in Tenneco Inc., a diversified conglomerate. The two companies combined late in 1980; Seagull was spun off from its parent and listed on the New York Stock Exchange the following year. M. Allen Reagan was Seagull's first chairman and Dan H. Montgomery served as president. The firm's 1981 revenues totaled $62.6 million.

Seagull was taken independent during a tumultuous period for the natural gas industry. Federal regulation of natural gas had commenced in the 1950s, but shortages during the harsh winter of 1976–1977 were blamed on the artificial market forces imposed by government controls. Residential and industrial customers switched from gas to oil in droves. The Natural Gas Policy Act of 1978 launched the decontrol of the industry by placing it under the administration of the Federal Energy Regulatory Commission (FERC). The FERC set an irregular schedule for deregulation. For example, so-called "new gas," fuel discovered after 1977, was freed from price controls after 1985. The price of "old gas" was gradually increased during the interim until the two figures met. As a gas gatherer with comparatively low overhead and risk, Seagull was positioned to take advantage of changes in the industry. The newly independent company resumed the strategy that had made Houston Oil & Minerals' fortunes in the 1970s—it collected gas reserves that were too small for big companies to lay a pipeline to, processed the gas into higher-value natural gas liquids, and transported it to the interstate pipeline system for delivery to utilities and industry.

In June of 1981—just three months after becoming an independent company—the firm formed Seagull Energy Corporation, a subsidiary that would begin exploration and production (E&P). Seagull brought its first producing gas well on line in 1983, the same year shareholders voted to change the company's name from Seagull Pipeline Corporation to Seagull Energy Corporation. The subsidiary became known as Seagull Energy E&P Inc.

Another of Seagull's major projects was the "Seagull Offshore System," of which it owned 25 percent. Touted as "the largest intrastate offshore natural gas pipeline in the U.S.," the $300 million, 258-mile project was renamed the Seagull Shoreline System, and construction started in 1982. By the time the system was completed five years later, its accent on gas gathering in general had given way to an emphasis on E&P. Eventually, Seagull's interest in it was reduced to 19 percent.

E&P efforts, as well as acquisitions, accelerated after that year when Barry J. Galt, formerly of Williams Cos. (an Oklahoma pipeline and telecommunications company) became president, chief executive officer, and chairman. Although demand for gas in the United States declined steadily in the mid-1980s, Galt took a long view of the industry. For while domestic production capacity continued to slope downward in the second half of the decade, demand took a sharp turn upward. Other factors also augured well for natural gas. Many electric utilities, which traditionally burned coal to fire their generators, began to view natural gas as an economical option for new facilities. Growing governmental and public concern over air quality, acid rain, and the greenhouse effect also favored gas, which gives off far less carbon dioxide, nitrous oxide, and sulfuric oxide than oil or coal when burned. Research into the use of compressed natural gas as an automotive fuel, while still in experimental stages, also gave gas companies cause to look to the future with hope.

Galt anticipated an expanding market for natural gas and led Seagull's investment of nearly $1 billion from 1985 to 1993 in the acquisition of natural gas producers and their reserves. One of Galt's first moves was the 1985 purchase of ENSTAR Corporation, an Alaskan natural gas utility that had, at that time, 76,000 customers in Anchorage. The $65 million acquisition was financed, in part, with a stock offering and a bond issue. ENSTAR became Seagull's largest division, and Galt soon began using the utility's steady cash flow as an acquisition fund. Regulatory uncertainty and low demand during the decade motivated many companies to abandon natural gas, and Galt was able to pick up several "bargains." It was often cheaper to buy others' reserves than to invest in exploration and production to find your own.

Seagull traded $23 million in stock for Liberty Natural Gas Co., a Dallas gas gatherer, in 1987, thereby doubling gas volume on its pipelines to 280 million cubic feet per day. The company acquired former parent Houston Oil & Minerals Corporation's 45 oil and gas fields in 14 states from Tenneco for $13.8 million cash in 1988. Before the end of the decade, Seagull added the assets of the Houston Oil Trust at a cost of $68.3 million. Wacker Oil Inc. was purchased in 1990 for $73.4 million, which increased proved gas and oil reserves by 62 percent. Seagull formed its Mid-Continent Division for exploration and production by acquiring a portfolio of gas and oil properties, reserves, and undeveloped land parcels from Mesa Limited Partnership in 1991. Galt's largest purchase came in 1992, when Seagull took a controlling interest in Arkla Exploration Company (a subsidiary of Arkansas-Louisiana Gas). The Arkla acquisition doubled Seagull's proved reserves for the second time in five years and pushed the energy company over the $1 billion mark in assets. Arkla became the Mid-South division of E&P.

Each of the acquisitions was followed by a stock offering: six flotations raised $327 million over the years and kept debt at a manageable level. In spite of the dilution of Seagull's stock, cash flow per share more than doubled in the five years from 1988 to 1993. In fact, Seagull was able to offer stockholders a two-for-one stock split through a 100 percent dividend paid in 1993.

Growth during the 1980s also came from joint ventures. In 1983, a pact with Texaco saw the completion of a 280-mile, $80 million petrochemical pipeline on which Seagull transported others' gas supplies for a fee, and which also helped fund the acquisition of ENSTAR. A 1987 partnership with Amoco Gas Company called Cavallo Pipeline Company resulted in a 60-mile on- and off-shore gas delivery system. In 1989 Seagull contracted with Quantum Chemical Corporation to construct and operate a 73-mile petrochemical pipeline system along Texas' Gulf Coast. These joint ventures and the concurrent acquisitions fueled Seagull's growth during Galt's first decade at the helm, when the company's annual revenues increased 4.5 times, from $83.81 million in 1983 to $377.17 million in 1993.

Seagull and Galt suffered some criticism when the company moved into Canadian exploration and production with the 1993 acquisition of Novalta Resources Inc. for $194 million. Seagull's stock declined 30 percent in reaction to both declining oil prices (making that energy source more attractive) and news that the Novalta price tag totaled seven times its cash flow. Some analysts also worried that Seagull was following too closely in Houston Oil & Minerals' footsteps: its mounting debt amounted to 60 percent of capital in 1994. Galt refused to finance new purchases with stock issues at this low market price. Unperturbed, Galt vowed to continue his acquisition efforts—even if it meant taking on more debt—expressing continued confidence in the future of natural gas.

Early in 1994, Galt hinted to a *Forbes* reporter that one of Seagull's expansion targets was the burgeoning South American natural gas market. Deregulation and privatization of that country's natural gas industry combined with economic growth in the early 1990s to make the region an attractive candidate for expansion. While Seagull has yet to pursue opportunities in this region, the company is involved in an exploration venture in the United Kingdom.

With deregulation complete, industry observers have noted that gas producers can no longer rely on commodity price increases to improve their financial results. Instead, reserve replacement and growth as well as production growth will mark successful producers. Accordingly, in his 1993 letter to shareholders, Galt hoped for small price increases but emphasized the goal of "amassing as many natural gas reserves as possible," a plan that had begun as early as 1987, fueling the company's growth.

Principal Subsidiaries: Alaska Pipeline Co.; Arkoma Production Co.; Artex Exploration Co.; Cavallo Pipeline Co. (50%); Houston Oil & Minerals Corp.; Seagull Energy E&P Inc.; Seagull Industrial Pipeline Co.; Seagull Marketing Services, Inc.; Seagull Midcon, Inc.; Seagull Mid-South Inc.; Seagull Natural Gas Co.; Seagull Processing Co.; Seagull Transmission Co.; Wacker Oil Inc.

Further Reading:

Deffarges, Etienne H., and Luiz T. A. Maurer, "Growing Brazilian Demand to Spur Gas Network in South America," *Oil & Gas Journal,* January 18, 1993, pp. 34–38.
Keefe, Lisa M., "Sitting Pretty," *Forbes,* October 5, 1987, p. 172.
Palmeri, Christopher. "Gas Pains," *Forbes,* January 17, 194, p. 46.

"Seagull to Acquire Arkla Exploration," *Oil & Gas Journal,* November 23, 1992, p. 30.

Shaw, Susan, "The Outlook for Natural Gas," *Gas Energy Review,* September 1990, pp. 8–14.

Stuart, Alexander, "Why an Oil-Patch Legend Joined Tenneco," *Fortune,* January 18, 1981, pp. 48–52.

"Summary of Significant Events in History of Seagull Energy Corporation, 1981–1993," Houston: Seagull Energy Corporation, 1993.

Vogel, Todd, "Gas Is Cooking Now: The Long-Term Players Leap at Tenneco's Sale," *Business Week,* October 24, 1988, pp. 24–25.

Wagner, Stuart J., "Breaking Away," *Oil & Gas Investor,* November 1992, pp. 45–48.

—April Dougal Gasbarre

THE WORLD LEADER IN LOSS PREVENTION

Sensormatic Electronics Corp.

500 N. W. 12th Avenue
Deerfield Beach, Florida 33442
U.S.A.
(305) 427-9700
Fax: (305) 428-9253

Public Company
Incorporated: 1968
Employees: 4,000
Sales: $487.3 million
Stock Exchanges: New York
SICs: 3812 Search & Navigation Equipment; 3663 Radio &
   Television Communications Equipment

Sensormatic Electronics Corp. is the world's leading producer of electronic devices used to prevent theft in retail stores and other industries. In the 1970s, Sensormatic achieved substantial success by outfitting department stores with small, white, plastic tags attached to clothing that sound an alarm when passed through an exit gate. Since then it has grown into a world-wide source for a variety of security devices, including close circuit television and electronic access control systems. Its electronic and magnetic tags are now affixed to a myriad of objects ranging from filet mignon to wallpaper samples and even babies in hospital maternity wards. Customers included drug stores, supermarkets, and music and entertainment stores, as well as casinos, hospitals, manufacturing facilities, nuclear power plants, and office buildings.

Sensormatic's origins date to a hot July morning in 1965 when Ronald G. Assaf, the manager of a Kroger supermarket in Akron, Ohio, spied a husky young man walking out of the store without paying for the two bottles of wine he held under his arms. "Without thinking of the consequences," said Assaf in a company newsletter, "I took off chasing the shoplifter. As I was running after him, the thought occurred to me: if I caught him, I was probably in a great deal of trouble . . . he was seven inches taller and a good 50 pounds heavier." Assaf let the thief outrun him and returned to the store. Upon returning, the first person he saw was his cousin, John Welsh, an amateur inventor who loved to tinker with things in his garage. "Jack," the exasperated Assaf said to his cousin, "If you could invent something to stop shoplifting, you'd become a millionaire."

Welsh took the idea seriously. For over a year, the cousins met twice a week to discuss the possibilities of developing a theft prevention system that could be sold to retailers. Welsh decided it was wiser to track the movement of goods through the store than to use surveillance cameras, security guards, and other techniques to watch customers. He came up with the concept of an electronically activated tag that would sound an alarm when passed in front of a screen located at the store's exit. Sales clerks would remove the tags when a customer purchased the goods.

The cousins pooled their finances and hired two scientists from the University of Michigan to develop a prototype based on this concept. By 1966, the prototype, a large electronic receptor and a plastic disc the size of a dinner plate, was finished. Assaf and Welsh determined the size was too large to appeal to retailers; however, they were pleased with the concept, and continued to raise capital to finance more research. Within a year a more suitable system was created with four-inch paper tags that could easily be hidden on clothing and other goods. In 1967 the two took on James Rogers, a former union official, as a third partner and began marketing their product.

As Assaf later told *Dun's Review* the three "started out by making just about every mistake possible." Bordering on bankruptcy, the team raised $3 million in capital by selling marketing franchises nationwide. The original plan was that Sensormatic would act as a middleman between independent manufacturers of the system and its marketing franchises. Selling the system to retailers, however, proved to be difficult. When weeks had passed and Sensormatic's sales representatives had secured no orders, Assaf decided to go out and try selling the system himself. "The first week," he said, "I called on every retailer in Akron and found that they were not in the least bit interested in this new toy or gimmick. The second week I decided that if they wouldn't pay for the system, I would go out and give it to them so we could obtain the necessary experience of having the system in a store. I had no better results. We couldn't even give it away." Finally, Assaf found a shopping mall that was willing to install the system if Sensormatic would pay $300 per month for the inconvenience of attaching the tags to clothing.

After its first year of business, Sensormatic had installed only 20 systems nationwide, and, of those, only one store actually paid for the system. In 1969, the company went public, raising capital to buy back its floundering franchises. Although Sensormatic's early struggle was to overcome retailers' resistance to the concept of electronic article surveillance, the system itself also had defects. Originally plagued by false alarms and other malfunctions, Sensormatic kept improving the system until it actually proved too good at catching shoplifters. In one incident, the system was installed at a military PX and within a week had nabbed the wife of the base's commanding officer. Unwilling to encounter other similarly delicate situations, the base packed the system and called Sensormatic to remove it from the premises.

From this event, Assaf said he realized that retailers prefer to deter shoplifters, not actually catch them. One reason for this was that the actual cost of prosecuting shoplifters often outweighed the cost of the merchandise lost, and litigation was slow and time consuming. With this in mind, Sensormatic developed conspicuous white plastic tags that could only be removed using a special device. In 1970, with the fear of bankruptcy hanging over his head, Assaf moved the company to Deerfield Beach, Florida, where he set up Sensormatic's first manufacturing operations. This greatly reduced production costs and also allowed the company to focus on improving the quality of its electronic chips, a crucial component in the system.

Assaf also instituted a major marketing drive led by several former IBM executives that focused on the use of the system as a means of deterring shoplifters. The company relegated 25 percent of revenues to marketing and expanded its sales force to cover the globe. Sensormatic had one major rival in the field: Knogo Corp., which had introduced the concept of ''electronic article surveillance'' in 1965. Because Knogo was having some success selling to smaller boutiques and specialty stores, Sensormatic went after large department stores. Sensormatic's big breakthrough came in the early 1970s when Bloomingdale's department store in New York City and Famous-Barr in St. Louis ran successful trials of the system and agreed to install them. With two well-known stores as clients, Sensormatic's sales force found others more willing to purchase the system. After three years of near failure, sales finally began to climb.

1973 marked the company's first profitable year: sales were $3.8 million and earnings were $191,000. Sales took off with the introduction of the ''alligator tag,'' a thin white plastic tag that could be easily attached and removed from clothing by store personnel. The alligator tag became a common sight in department and clothing stores across the United States, and Sensormatic entered a ten-year stretch of record earnings. By 1977, sales were $7.7 million. Two years later they jumped to $27.6 million, with earnings of $4.4 million. By 1982 sales had exploded to over $67 million and earnings hit $15 million.

Analysts say the company's success was fueled more by an industrywide fear of shoplifting rather than by an actual increase in the number of crime incidents. Nevertheless, shoplifting cost an estimated $26 billion in lost revenues in the United States in 1981, and retailers were beginning to find that systems such as Sensormatic's not only helped prevent shoplifting by as much as 70 percent but might also reduce theft by in-store personnel.

By 1983, Sensormatic's continuously strong growth had made it a ''darling of Wall Street,'' and stocks were trading at three times earnings. The company held 80 percent of the U.S. market and 70 percent of the worldwide market for security tags, and analysts estimated that only 4.7 percent of the worldwide market for such goods had been penetrated. Sensormatic expanded its product line, developing Shopkeeper, a small system for boutiques that it hoped would sell well in Europe, and SensorGate, a surveillance system for hard goods. SensorGate was developed for retail outlets such as grocery, hardware, and liquor stores and used soft, magnetically sensitive labels which could be adhered to high priced items. Customers would pass through a gate and receive the purchased goods on the other side.

By 1984, however, Sensormatic's impressive growth had stalled. Sales of its much-touted SensorGate system were far below expectations, and orders from Sensormatic's traditional clothing retailers had also slackened. Quarterly earnings early that year plummeted from 20 cents to 6 cents per share. Sales were flat in 1985, at $24.9 million (compared to $24.8 million in 1984 and $51.2 million in 1983), and the company reported a loss of $4 million.

The company diversified slightly during this time, purchasing $2.5 million worth of convertible notes from Datavision Inc., a residential security company. This gave Sensormatic the potential to own 20 percent of Datavision if it chose to convert the notes into common shares. In 1985, the company purchased I.D. Systems, Inc., a small manufacturer of radio-wave article surveillance systems similar to Sensormatic's own line. I.D. Systems became a division of Sensormatic, and the company began marketing its products to smaller specialty stores. Also that year, Sensormatic entered into a joint venture with Allied-Signal to develop a new, computerized system to monitor hard goods called Identitech. The company began marketing Identitech to the retail sector while Allied-Signal began marketing it to the industrial customers.

Despite the company's financial woes, it still retained 70 percent of the worldwide market, far outstripping any of its competitors. In 1986, Allen Dusault, a company director since 1984, was appointed president and CEO. Assaf remained chairman of the board and oversaw development of new technology. Dusault, who was known as a turnaround wizard, set out to improve Sensormatic's finances. He immediately sold the company's new $9 million headquarters in Boca Raton, Florida, cut middle management by approximately 200 people, and moved a percentage of manufacturing from Florida to Puerto Rico. Dusault also improved operating margins, which had fallen from 37 percent in 1983 to 6 percent in 1986. Within a year, sales rose 10 percent to $95 million.

Once Dusault had gotten Sensormatic's finances back under control, Assaf resumed his position as CEO and began an extensive marketing campaign for two new systems. One was an improved, magnetic-field system of tracking goods in hardware stores and supermarkets. The other was a software package that combined close-circuit television systems with electronic ID door openers and was aimed at industrial customers seeking to reduce on-the-job theft and fraud. Sales resumed their upward trend, climbing from $95 million in 1987 to $239 million in 1991.

Foreign expansion fueled much of this growth. Sensormatic stepped up its overseas marketing, setting up a sales headquarters in Singapore and making headway into the newly opened Russian market. Another percentage of Sensormatic's growth came through the acquisition of new companies. In 1992, Sensormatic merged with BURLE Industries Inc., the leading manufacturer of close-circuit televisions and accessories in the United States. It also significantly increased its European market presence with the purchase of Automated Security (Holdings) PLC's electronic article surveillance and close circuit television businesses. Sensormatic merged the operations of both companies yet continued to market products under both the Automated Securities and BURLE names.

Having recovered from its problems in the mid-1980s, Sensormatic entered the second half of the 1990s on track for impressive growth. Its market share was unrivaled worldwide, with European sales alone totaling more than the combined sales of its two largest competitors. As it approached the turn of the century, Sensormatic was continuing to expand both through product introduction and through the acquisition of new companies. In 1993 Sensormatic purchased its largest European rival, Automated Loss Prevention Systems, a top manufacturer of electronic article surveillance and close-circuit television systems. Revenues neared the $500 million mark, and the company posted record earnings of $54 million.

Further Reading:

Crisafulli, Patricia, "Anti-Theft Devices Snare Overseas Markets," *The Journal of Commerce and Commercial,* May 5, 1992, p. 1.

"Knocking Down a Pyramid to Build Sales," *Sales and Marketing Management,* February 4, 1980, p. 13.

Nulty, Peter, "Sensormatic Collars the Shoplifter," *Fortune,* February 25, 1980, p. 114; "Cashing In on Security," *Fortune,* October 7, 1991, p. 113.

"Sensormatic Electronics Corporation (SNSR)" *The Wall Street Transcript,* November 27, 1989, pp. 95,558.

Taub, Stephen, "Why Crime Pays," *Financial World,* April 30, 1983, p. 54; "Follow the Leader: North and South: Sensormatic Canada Is Finally Coming to Life," *Financial World,* April 18, 1984, p. 28.

"They're Making Crime Pay at Sensormatic," *Dun's Review,* March 1980, p. 32.

Verespej, Michael J., Turnaround Junkie Who Doesn't Hipshoot," *Industry Week,* January 4, 1988, p. 43.

—Maura Troester

SIGNET®

Signet Banking Corporation

7 North 8th Street
Richmond, Virginia 23219-3301
U.S.A.
(804) 747-2000
Fax: (804) 771-7599

Public Company
Incorporated: 1962
Total Assets: $10.8 billion
Employees: 4,697
Stock Exchanges: New York Chicago Boston
SICs: 6712 Bank Holding Companies; 6021 National
   Commercial Banks; 6022 State Commercial Banks; 6099
   Foreign Currency Exchange; 6162 Mortgage Banks; 6211
   Security Brokers and Traders; 6411 Insurance Agents

Signet Banking Corporation is a registered multi-bank, multi-state holding company with 24-hour telebanking, 240 regional offices, and over 230 automatic teller machines (ATMs) located throughout Maryland, the District of Columbia, and Virginia providing a wide range of financial services to its customers and shareholders. With assets in excess of $10.8 billion, Signet is comprised of five financial groups, including consumer loans, commercial banking, real estate lending, security markets, and the largest and most successful of these lines—the credit card division. Due to the phenomenal growth of its bank card business in the early 1990s, Signet was ranked among the top 15 largest MasterCard and Visa credit card agents in the United States, with over four million cardholders and $6.6 million in outstanding managed debts. According to company literature, Signet's mission for the 1990s was "to maximize shareholder value by becoming widely regarded as among the best banks in the United States."

Signet's history has been one of continual expansion and diversification. The company originated in 1922, with an innovative financial institution called the Morris Plan Bank of Richmond, Virginia. Originally founded by Arthur J. Morris, Morris Plan banks filled a growing niche in the communities of the early 1900s, providing loans to individuals who were generally unable to secure funds elsewhere. Any consumer who could offer two cosigners or collateral and was of "good character" qualified for a Morris Plan loan.

During the next 20 years, the Morris Plan Bank of Richmond became the Morris Plan Bank of Virginia (1928) and the Bank of Virginia (1945). Then, on January 11, 1962, after acquiring the Bank of Henrico, the Bank of Occoquan, the Bank of Salem, and the Bank of Warwick, the organization was recreated as the Virginia Commonwealth Corporation. After merging with the Bank of Dinwiddie in 1963, the corporation acquired three more banks (Bristol Washington Trust & Savings Bank, Inc., Peoples National Bank of Pulaski, and the Bank of Nokesville), then merged once again with the Hallwood National Bank in 1964. After two further mergers—Guardian National Bank of Springfield and the Bank of Boydton—the company again altered its name and became Virginia Commonwealth Bankshares Inc. on October 10, 1966. The same year, the company merged with the National Bank of Rosslyn and acquired the Bank of Central Virginia.

The rest of the decade was marked by continued evolution, with five more acquisitions (National Bank of Commerce in Fairfax County, American National Bank of Fredericksburg, First Valley Bank in Weber City, First Colonial Bank of Virginia Beach, Security Bank and Trust Company of Danville) and six mergers (Bank of Lacrosse, Farmers Bank in Boydton, Peoples Bank of Reedville, the Peoples Bank of White Stone, the Russell County National Bank, Fidelity National Bank in Arlington).

During the 1970s, the company reached several important milestones beginning with regulatory approval in 1970 to form Virginia Commonwealth International. In October 1971, the company spent over $3.47 million for Canadian Factors Corp., acquired The Merchants and Farmers Bank of Galax, and formed two Bank of Virginia branches in Roanoke and Loudoun. During this time, Robert M. Freeman joined the company as vice-president in the main offices in Richmond. In 1972, after an exchange of stock, the Bank of Whaleyville and the Bank of Warren joined the Virginia Commonwealth's holdings, then an additional 60,965 common shares were proffered to acquire both Hanover Mortgage Corp. and Richmond Finance Corp. This year also marked the adoption of a more simple name: Bank of Virginia.

For the remainder of 1970s, the company reorganized its vast holdings, seeking to make the Bank of Virginia family both recognized and renowned in its market area and beyond. Significant acquisitions included the General Finance Service Corp. of Huntingdon, Pennsylvania, Cavanagh Leasing Corp., and Commonwealth Mortgage Company. The latter two were merged into the BVA Credit Corp. (originally formed in 1973), which later spawned the BVA Mortgage Corporation in 1974. After four years with the company, Robert Freeman was promoted to senior vice-president, and then in 1977, was named executive vice-president. In December of 1978, the nine banking affiliates owned by the Bank of Virginia Company were merged into today's Signet Bank/Virginia with the Bank of Virginia retaining 100 percent ownership of its stock.

The next dozen years were of growth, both internal and external. Several branches were brought under the Bank of Virginia umbrella, including four from the Northern Virginia Savings & Loan Association at the end of May 1982. By the end of 1982, the company acquired 92 percent of the Bank of Vienna, which was merged into Bank of Virginia holdings the next May. In

September 1983, assets of the General Finance Service Corp. (acquired March 30, 1973) were sold to the Security Pacific Corp. for $32 million.

On May 2, 1985, the company created the Corporate Finance Advisors, which would become Signet Financial Services, Inc. in 1992 and eventually Signet Investment Banking Company. In December of 1985, Union Trust Bancorp and its subsidiary, the Union Trust Bank of Maryland (later renamed Signet Bank/ Maryland), were acquired. Terms of the agreement stipulated that Union Trust's common stock be converted to 2.05 shares of the Bank of Virginia Company's common stock.

In March 1986, the company formed the BVA Investment Corp., which would later become part of the Signet Investment Banking Company. And, in another acquisition, the Security National Corp. of Washington, D.C. and its banking subsidiary, the Security National Bank, became a part of the Bank of Virginia Company. Finally, 1986 also marked the Bank of Virginia Company's move to the name Signet Banking Corporation, on July 14. The following year, two subsidiaries were added to the Signet conglomerate: the Signet Production Company and the Signet Loan Company of Pennsylvania. Reorganizing its assets in 1988, Signet sold Landmark Financial Services Inc. for $82 million to the MNC Financial Corp.

To raise capital, Signet sold 400,000 shares of common stock to European investors in 1988, shoring up stateside operations and strengthening its capital position. According to Signet, this decision gave the corporation necessary "liquidity, stability and greater resources," which were rerouted internally. This year also marked Signet's highest earnings yet—hitting $152.5 million—helped in part by the sale of Landmark Financial Services. In 1989, Signet scored an 11 percent gain in earnings, with net income of $123.3 million. Robert Freeman, who had become president and chief executive officer of Signet, continued to play a pivotal role in guiding the company's evolution.

In 1990, Freeman became chairperson and CEO, with Malcolm S. McDonald as president and chief operating officer. During this time, Signet developed its master plan to become one of the most respected and stable banking institutions in the country. The "Best Bank" blueprint, it was hoped, would vault Signet to the forefront of the industry by transforming its problematic, non-performing assets into healthy ones, and utilizing its "information-based strategy" to move Signet's computer network into the future. Net income for 1990 plummeted 66 percent to $41.4 million, due in part to fluctuations in the real estate market. The "Best Bank" vision then became crucial—and to stem losses, Signet announced the formation of the "Accelerated Real Estate Asset Reduction Program" in 1991.

Meanwhile, in Washington, D.C., the Federal Reserve Board pumped nearly $100 million into the failing Madison National Bank to no avail. After regulators seized the bank, Signet bought Madison's 12-branch franchise (ten branches were merged into Signet Bank N.A and the remaining two into Signet Bank/Virginia). By the end of 1991, Signet had managed to reduce nonperforming real estate assets by $400 million, but suffered an overall net loss of $25.7 million.

By placing greater emphasis on what Signet called its "credit culture" and giving employees carte blanche to develop and implement non-traditional methods for personalized products and services, Signet bounced back from 1991's heavy losses to a net income of $109.2 million. In 1993, Signet concerted efforts to promote internal growth and bring nonperforming assets to more acceptable levels. By consolidating commercial real estate activities and scaling down construction loans, commercial mortgages, and foreclosed properties to $934 million in outstandings (or less than shareholder equity), Signet terminated its Accelerated Real Estate Asset Reduction Program. Net income for 1993 grew 60 percent to $174.4 million, and earnings per share rose 56 percent from $1.96 to $3.06. Signet's annual report boasted a stock performance among the best in the industry with 54 percent appreciation in stock prices and dividends rising twice. The 1993 annual rate of $1.00 per share represented a 67 percent increase over 1992.

According to bank stock specialists Keefe, Bruyette & Woods, Signet's return on equity of 19.63 percent ranked fifth and their 1.50 percent return on assets was fourth best among the nation's largest 50 banks. Signet's capital base also grew to a robust 81.4 percent equity-to-assets ratio by the end of 1993. "Unquestionably, the success of our information-based strategy in the credit card business was the single most important contributor to our results in 1993," chairperson and CEO Freeman observed.

Credit card loans, including securitized receivables, accounted for more than 50 percent (and perhaps closer to 65 percent) of Signet's loan portfolio with approximately 1.5 million new accounts in 1993, adding $2.9 billion in receivables, which brought Signet's total managed assets to $5.1 billion. Signet issued $2.3 billion in asset-backed securities during 1993, which elevated their total securitized assets to a total of $3.3 billion, enabling the bank to obtain and offer highly competitive interest rates. Spending around $60 million annually on bank card promotion, Signet took a relatively small, competitive business in its immediate marketing area and created "a highly profitable national business driven by specialized target marketing."

In 1994, Signet merged with Pioneer Financial Corp., the parent company of the $400 million Pioneer Federal Savings Bank, located in Chester, Virginia. This year would mark exceptional second quarter growth for Signet's bank card portfolio, as net income climbed 25 percent to $50.4 million or 88 cents per share, up from the previous year's second quarter figures of $40.4 million and 71 cents per share. However, these figures were below analysts' predicted returns, and Signet stock sank 11 percent ($4.375) to $36.50 per share in composite NYSE trading. Net interest income also decreased four percent, shrinking the net interest margin to 5.01 percentage points, a 0.23 percentage point loss from 1994 first quarter figures, and 0.2 from the year before.

As one of five firms profiled in *Money* magazine's "Wall Street Newsletter," industry analysts cited Signet as one to watch for significant investment returns of 14–30 percent in 1995. Analysts Moshe A. Orenbuch, of Sanford C. Bernstein in New York City, and John A. Heffern of Baltimore's Alex. Brown & Sons, both believed Signet's earnings potential would reach 20 percent annually in 1995 and 1996, while delivering stock growth of as much as 25 percent or around $53 a share. "Signet was once a takeover target, but they've found a way to generate revenue and earnings growth on their own," said Heffern.

On July 27, 1994, Signet announced the spin-off its most profitable enterprise—its credit card portfolio—into a separate company. "In 1988, we began investing in technology that would enable us to become a state-of-the-art, unique provider of financial products and services. We successfully achieved this objective in our credit card division, and with the spin-off," Freeman contended, they would "be able to concentrate fully on improving the business strategies of our core bank."

Signet filed a registration statement with the SEC for an initial public offering of up to 19.9 percent interest in the newly formed corporation, to be completed by the fall of 1994. Stockholders were to be provided with a tax-free offering of the remaining shares in the new company by 1995, with about 57 million shares outstanding. "By spinning them apart," Freeman explained, "shareholders will have one of each and realize the full value."

The new credit card unit, called OakStone Financial Corporation—so named to reflect "its financial strength and stability" according to OakStone's newly appointed chairperson and CEO Richard D. Fairbank—was expected to apply for a New York Stock Exchange listing. Costs of creating the company and restructuring were expected to result in a one-time debit of between $60 and $70 million during the third quarter. Some industry analysts believed Signet would once again be a takeover target after the spin-off was complete. "We've been on [the] takeover list ever since I can remember," Freeman admitted to the *Wall Street Journal* as the news broke. "We believe, and the board believes, that we have the talent and management plans to remain independent." Freeman was equally candid about Signet's shortcomings and plans for the future: "It's a fair assessment to say that today, the core bank is underperforming. But therein lies the opportunity to reinvent the corporation." Signet's shares rose $1.75 to $39.25 on the NYSE after the spin-off news release.

Oakstone was slated to be headquartered in northern Virginia with offices in Richmond and Fredericksburg, Virginia. As the spin-off was finalized, Signet's core strength were expected to be put to the test. "We will reinvent Signet Bank one process and one product at a time," Malcolm S. McDonald, Signet president and COO, said in July 1994, "with the goal of delivering maximum long-term value to our customers and our shareholders."

Principal Subsidiaries: Signet Bank, N.A.; Signet Bank Ltd. (Bahamas); Signet Asset Management, Inc.; Signet Commercial Credit Corp.; Signet Equipment Company; Signet Financial Services Corp.; Signet Insurance Services, Inc.; Signet Investment Banking Company; Signet Leasing & Financial Corp.; Signet Lending Services, Inc.; Mortgage Corporation; Signet Second Mortgage Corporation; Signet Production Company; Signet Properties Company; Signet Realty, Inc.; Signet Strategic Capital Corporation; Signet Trust Company Inc.; 800 Building Corporation; Elgin Corporation; General Finance Service Corporation; Landexco Inc.; MH Utilities Corp.; Mystic Harbour Corp.; Second Eleutheran Investment Co., Ltd.; SM Corporation; St. Paul Realty, Inc.; The Budget Plan Company of Virginia; Wharton & Bennett, Inc.

Further Reading:

Dreman, David, "Where Are the Values?," *Forbes,* May 28, 1990.
Halper, Mark, "EDS/Signet Contract Shows Signs of Strain," *Computerworld,* June 15, 1992.
Lipin, Steven, "Signet Plans Restructuring, Sets Spinoff and Public Offering of Credit-Card Unit," *Wall Street Journal,* July 28, 1994.
"Signet Banking to Spin Off Credit Card Business," *New York Times,* July 28, 1994.
Sivy, Michael, "How to Earn 14%-Plus Profits on the Bank of the Future," *Money,* July 1994.
Yang, Catherine, and Dean Foust, "Disaster on a Watchdog's Doorstep," *Business Week,* June 3, 1991.

—Taryn Benbow-Pfalzgraf

Snapple Beverage Corporation

P.O. Box 9400
East Meadow, New York 11554
U.S.A.
(516) 222-0022

Public Company
Incorporated: 1972 as Unadulterated Food Products, Inc.
Employees: 230
Sales: $231.9 million
Stock Exchange: New York
SICs: 2086 Bottled and Canned Soft Drinks and Carbonated
  Waters

The Snapple Beverage Corporation is the leading American retailer of single-serving iced tea drinks and the second largest seller of fruit drinks. Started as a part-time business in the natural foods industry during the 1970s, Snapple grew dramatically after it introduced a new, better-tasting iced tea product in the late 1980s. Its subsequent explosion in growth, in which sales more than doubled every year, came as the American soft drink market shifted away from carbonated beverages toward a wider variety of noncarbonated drinks and fruit juices. This industrywide movement was fueled in part by Snapple's introduction of healthy, all natural products.

Snapple was founded in 1972 by Arnold Greenberg, Leonard Marsh, and Hyman Golden. Greenberg operated a health food store on the lower east side of Manhattan. His boyhood friend Marsh ran a window-washing service with his brother-in-law, Golden. In the early 1970s, the three founded Unadulterated Food Products, Inc., to sell pure fruit juices in unusual blends to health food stores. Products were bottled at a small plant in the New York metropolitan area. The partners ran the business in their spare time while all three kept their regular jobs, and the enterprise plodded along until the late 1970s.

In 1978, Unadulterated Foods began to market carbonated apple juice. The company called the product "Snapple," after purchasing the name for $500. In the first month of its introduction, Unadulterated sold 500 cases of apple juice. In the second month, the company sold another 500 cases of Snapple, and distributors started calling to request the product. When tops starting popping off bottles in the warehouse, Unadulterated realized that the growing popularity of Snapple might be related to the fact that the juice was fermenting.

Outside of this brief and unintended foray into the alcoholic beverage industry, however, Unadulterated's legitimate business had begun to grow. In 1979, the company hired its first salesman and began seeking out franchised distributors. "One day we woke up. We realized we had a business," Marsh later told *Newsday.* The partners began to step up their efforts. In 1980, Unadulterated expanded the Snapple line to include other all natural juices. In 1982, it added natural sodas. Despite their relatively high price of $1 a bottle, these products enjoyed some success in the New York, Boston, and Washington, D.C., areas in the early 1980s. The company's three founders spent much of their time thinking up new flavors and names for their drinks. Each new variety of Snapple took from six months to a year to develop, as alterations were made in taste, color, and name. The company strove for memorable names that were not too gimmicky, rejecting, for instance, "guava nagilah."

As a result of these efforts, in 1986 Snapple expanded its line to include fruit drinks. It was not until the following year, however, when the partners decided that Snapple needed a summertime drink, that the company hit upon the product that would allow its growth to take off: iced tea. In the past, iced teas had been manufactured in the same way that other drinks were, with flavor, derived from a concentrate, sugar, preservatives and soda. Unadulterated, however, spent three years working with a tea vendor and a bottler to perfect a method in which tea was bottled while hot, which allowed the preservatives to be eliminated. "We made the first ready-to-drink tea that didn't taste like battery acid," Greenberg later told the *New York Times.* "We came up with the first real brewed tea that was cooked."

In 1988, Snapple introduced a lemon-flavored iced tea made with the new process. This product proved to be so popular that its sales continued even after the hot weather was gone. "It blew everyone away," Marsh explained to *Newsday.* Driven by the popularity of the new iced tea product, which was soon supplemented by other flavors of tea, Snapple sales took off. By the end of 1988, Unadulterated's sales had increased by 60 percent over the previous 12 months, to $13.3 million. This strong growth continued in the following year. Unadulterated expanded the Snapple line to include 53 different flavors, and, in the first six months of 1989, the company's revenues from noncarbonated beverages increased by 600 percent.

By that fall, Snapple was unable to fulfill all the demand for its iced tea products, and the company had instituted an allocation system to distribute its drinks. Only after Unadulterated had contracted with a second bottling plant in upstate New York did it begin to catch up with demand. At the end of the year, total company sales had nearly doubled from the year before.

In 1990, Snapple built on these dramatic gains by introducing Snap-Up, its entrant in the isotonic sports drink market, which was rolled out in four flavors. In addition, in an effort to break out of the single-serving market, Snapple introduced a 32-ounce bottle of its beverages, to be sold in grocery stores and taken home. As sales of its flavored teas doubled over the course of 1990, Snapple became the market leader for this category in the New York area. In an effort to enhance that position, the company launched a $2 million advertising campaign featuring tennis star Ivan Lendl. The company hoped that Lendl's active and physically fit image would appeal to consumers of its all-natural products.

In 1991, Unadulterated moved its headquarters from Brooklyn to Long Island, where its three founders had long lived. With strong returns from flavors such as mint, cranberry, and decaffeinated iced teas, Snapple's revenues more than doubled to $95 million, with 55 percent of its sales in iced teas as the market for this product grew to $400 million. The company had attained a solid second place in this field with 19.3 percent of sales, behind long-time market leader Lipton, with 37.2 percent of the market, as it expanded its market beyond the East Coast, introducing Snapple products in California.

In order to expand its geographic reach further, Snapple needed an infusion of capital. Although the company had looked for a corporate partner for several years, its three founding partners were unwilling to relinquish control of Unadulterated, and they wished to keep all of the company's operations intact, rather than shedding the less successful non-iced-tea product lines. Finally, Snapple reached an agreement with a Boston-based investment banking firm, the Thomas H. Lee Company. In January 1992, Lee formed the Snapple Holding Corporation in Delaware. Then in April, the founders of Unadulterated, Marsh, Golden, and Greenberg, sold 70 percent of Unadulterated to this company for $45 million. In doing so, they received guarantees that they would remain in charge of the firm and that salaries of $300,000 a year would be paid to each of them through 1996, along with several multimillion dollar bonus payments at the time of the sale of stock.

With this deal, Snapple gained the resources to pay for nationwide distribution of its products. In addition, the company geared up for major competition from the leaders of the soft drink industry, Coca-Cola and Pepsi-Cola. Taking notice of the explosive growth of the iced tea industry, Coke had teamed up with Lipton, and Pepsi with Nestea to market their own iced tea products, and industry observers predicted that their entry into the market in full force in the summer of 1992 would bury upstart Snapple.

In an effort to counteract the Coke and Pepsi challenge, Snapple began running a new line of advertisements in May 1992, which featured its trademark "made from the best stuff on earth" line in ads that spoofed earlier beer and sports drinks promotions; the ads received low marks from advertising industry observers. In addition, the company used its $15-million-a-year advertising budget to pay for a long-lived series of live radio commercials featuring controversial disk jockeys Howard Stern and Rush Limbaugh. At the end of the summer of 1992, Snapple conducted a five-week search for a new advertising agency that could better convey its corporate identity in preparation for a wider national push. Later that year, Snapple also signed tennis player Jennifer Capriati to endorse its products.

Despite the competitive threat from Coke and Nestea, which released its product in February 1992, Snapple's market share continued to grow. In the first six months of 1992, the company sold nearly as much product as it had sold in all of the previous year. In an effort to expand its reputation for high-quality teas to its sports drink line, Snapple introduced tea-flavored Snap-Up, in August 1992.

With its infusion of new capital, Snapple had expanded its distribution to every major city in the United States by August 1992, and it signed new contracts with beverage distributors. The company owned no manufacturing facilities, but instead made agreements with more than 30 bottlers across the country. In this way, Snapple was able to keep its overhead low and its payroll short. The company administration consisted of just 80 employees, 50 of whom worked out of a modest office building on Long Island.

In addition to its efforts to expand domestic distribution, Snapple also began a push to sell its products in foreign markets in 1992. As a first step in this effort, the company began distributing its drinks to American military bases around the world. By the fall of that year, these moves had started to show fruit, as Snapple pulled ahead of Nestea to become the leader in the ready-to-drink iced tea market, earning 30 percent of all sales for the first eight months of the year.

With these strong results, Snapple announced that it would sell stock to the public for the first time in December 1992. In preparation for the stock offering, Snapple Holding merged into its subsidiary, becoming the Snapple Beverage Corporation. In the initial offering, 17 percent of Snapple's stock was offered to investors, with the bulk of the proceeds going to pay off debts incurred when the company was first purchased from its founders. On December 15, the stock was first offered, at $20 a share. The offering was an immediate hit, as the four million shares were snapped up, and the company's stock price was driven to $33. These results were reinforced at the end of the year, when the company posted annual revenues for 1992 of $231.9 million, more than double the previous year's tally. Within six months, Snapple stock had been split twice, as revenues continued to grow, and the company's founders had sold another eight percent of their holdings to take advantage of the bull market in the company's shares.

With the introduction of Lipton Original ready-to-drink tea in the late spring of 1993, however, Snapple faced a new and aggressive competitor. The company tripled its advertising budget and unveiled a new campaign in an effort to maintain its standing in the market. As Lipton ran radio ads charging that Snapple's product was made from reconstituted tea powder, it briefly passed Snapple in market share during the key summer months, before becoming unable to meet demand. By the fall however, Snapple had regained the lead in sales in larger supermarkets, earning a 39.4 percent share.

In addition to the threat from Lipton, Snapple's franchise as a health food purveyor was threatened when the U.S. Food & Drug Administration began to question the use of the words "all natural" on some company labels, and California regulators became suspicious of the designation "brewed" on the company's teas. In addition, Snapple confronted a bizarre series of rumors concerning its products. One tale had it that the company supported the Ku Klux Klan, perhaps because a small "K" on its labels indicated that its products were kosher, or because the background picture on its iced tea bottles, depicting the Boston Tea Party, with masked raiders in boats, had been misinterpreted. Another swift-moving rumor alleged that Snapple supported the extreme anti-abortion group Operation Rescue. Company officials guessed that the source of this misinformation was the product's long-time advertisements on the Rush Limbaugh show.

Despite these worries, Snapple's sales continued to boom. The company finished 1993 with sales up 119 percent from the previous year, as the company moved 55.6 million cases of beverage. This marked the third year in a row in which sales of Snapple drinks had more than doubled. One half of the company's revenues were still contributed by iced teas, with the remaining portion made up by its 10 flavors of fruit drinks (45 percent) and its 23 flavors of natural soda, fruit juices, and Snapple Sport drink.

These gains continued in the first quarter of 1994, as Snapple reported three-month sales that had doubled from the year before. In order to strengthen its market share, Snapple embarked on a program in 1994 to expand its product offerings and to shore up its distribution system. In April, the company rolled out eight new flavors, including Mango Tea, three new sodas, and four new fruit drinks, including diet versions of popular offerings, such as Pink Lemonade. The company also introduced a larger, 15.5 ounce can. With these steps, Snapple hoped to shore up its fruit juice category, which Coca-Cola had recently entered with a line of "Fruitopia" drinks.

In order to display its products more effectively, Snapple unveiled a new glass-fronted vending machine, which showed 54 different beverages at once. The company rolled out 1000 of these to begin with, with plans to add 9,000 more in locations across the country. Snapple believed that the glass front of the machine encouraged impulse buying.

Snapple took steps to gain greater control over its domestic distribution in June 1994. At that time, the company purchased two of its long-time distributors, Groux Beverage Corporation, of Orange County, California, and Trinity Beverage Corporation, based in Texas. In addition, Snapple purchased a half interest in the Haralambos Beverage Corporation, based in Los Angeles. With these investments, Snapple was able to increase its percentage of direct distribution, in which wholesalers sold and delivered Snapple products directly to stores, rather than to other middlemen who ran warehouses. In this way, the company hoped to gain greater control over its retail presentation and to get more shelf space, as distributors themselves actually stocked the shelves.

By the start of the summer of 1994, Snapple had moved to a new headquarters building and increased its staff to 230 people. In an effort to maintain the superior quality that it believed would support its market share, Snapple increased the size of its quality-control department rapidly. The company contracted with 28 bottlers in the United States and 2 in Canada to produce its beverages. Earlier that spring, Snapple had also expanded its international distribution to Japan. Previously, sales had begun in Canada, Mexico, the United Kingdom, Greece, Norway, and Hong Kong. The company looked to Australia, Singapore, and the Phillipines for further expansion late in 1994.

By July 1994, Snapple had solidified its position as the fastest growing beverage company in the world and the second largest seller of single-serving juices, growing steadily larger in a market that continued to rapidly expand. Although the company faced significant threats from large and powerful competitors, its record of introducing popular new products boded well for its future success.

Principal Subsidiaries: Trinity Beverage Company; Groux Beverage Company; Haralambus Beverage Company (50%).

Further Reading:

Blanton, Kimberly, "Big Score, '80's Style," *Boston Globe,* October 27, 1992.

Kelley, Kristine Portnoy, "*Beverage Industry,* November 1993.

Much, Marilyn, "Snapple's New Age Beverage Comes of Age," *Investor's Business Daily,* June 29, 1994.

Peneberg, Adam L., "Snapple Challenged in Wide Market," *New York Times,* July 10, 1994.

Prince, Grey W., "Snapple Offering Proves Unadulterated Success," *Beverage World Periscope Edition,* December 31, 1992.

Rigg, Cynthia, "Snapple, Misreading Tea Leaves, Prepares for Entries from Giants," *Crain's New York Business,* April 27, 1992.

Stevens, Jerry E., "The Fuss over Snapple," *Beverage Industry,* October 1993.

Wax, Alan J., "Snapple's Tea Party," *Newsday,* June 29, 1992.

—Elizabeth Rourke

SOTHEBY'S

Sotheby's Holdings, Inc.

1334 York Avenue
New York, NY 10021
U.S.A.
(212) 606-7507
Fax: (212) 606-7287

Public Company
Incorporated: 1983
Employees: 1,494
Sales: $235 million
Stock Exchanges: New York
SICs: 7389 Business Services Not Elsewhere Classified

Sotheby's Holdings, Inc. is the holding company for Sotheby's, one of the world's premier fine arts auction houses, with operations in more than 70 different collecting areas and offices established in 36 different countries. The company got its start in the mid-eighteenth century, focusing on the British book market. Later in the century, Sotheby's branched out into other markets. Sotheby's began to expand beyond its British base in the 1940s, and it had established a significant worldwide presence at the time of the art boom in the 1980s, which pushed its sales totals up dramatically.

The history of Sotheby's may be traced to 1744, when the English bookseller Samuel Baker held his first auction. During this time, book collectors had become increasingly interested in enhancing their holdings by purchasing works from the libraries of collectors who had died. Baker's first auction, in March 1744, featured 457 books previously belonging to Sir John Stanley. Baker sold the contents of Stanley's library for £826. Following this event, Baker and his associates became the premier auctioneers of British libraries. Baker auctioned the book collections of several famous clients, including Prince Talleyrand, John Wilkes, John Bright, the Marquess of Landsdowne, the Dukes of York, Buckingham, and Devonshire, and the Earls of Pembroke, Sunderland, and Hopetoun. One client, Richard Rawlinson, had amassed so many books that the only room left for him to sleep in was the hallway of his living quarters. At Rawlinson's death, it took Baker 50 days to disperse the collection.

In 1767, Baker took on a partner in his business, an accomplished auctioneer named George Leigh, who was noted for using props, such as a snuff box and an ivory gavel, in conducting sales of books. When Baker died in 1778, his estate was divided between Leigh and Baker's nephew John Sotheby.

Under the leadership of John Sotheby, the auction house expanded its activities beyond books for the first time, including the sale of prints, medals, coins, and rare antiquities. The company's staff also expanded, and, in 1842, Sotheby's senior accountant, John Wilkinson, was permitted to purchase a 25 percent share in the partnership. In 1861, the last member of the Sotheby family died, and Wilkinson took over as the company's leader. Three years later, Wilkinson promoted another long-time employee, Edward Grose Hodge, and changed the enterprise's name to Sotheby, Wilkinson, and Hodge, the name it would carry for the next 60 years.

In the late nineteenth century, Sotheby's dominated the book trade of London. Key to this success were the activities of Bernard Quaritch, a book dealer who purchased the property of such prominent figures of the day as Disraeli and Gladstone, both British prime ministers, and other leading cultural and political figures. Quaritch maintained a high profile, bringing free publicity and renown to Sotheby's and helping the company to maintain its preeminent spot in the industry.

In 1878, Thomas Hodge, the son of Edward Grose Hodge, joined the firm, and in 1896, as the previous generation retired, the younger Hodge became the sole active partner in the business. Over the course of his career, the Hodge developed a rich store of knowledge about the antiquities that Sotheby's sold. In addition to his concern for old things, Hodge was notorious for his attachment to old ways; for example, he loathed the telephone and insisted that all of his letters be handwritten, not typed.

When Edward Hodge died in 1907, his son sold three additional shares in the Sotheby's partnership. These were purchased by Montague Barlow, a lawyer and Member of Parliament; Felix Warre, a banker; and Geoffrey Hobson, an official in the British Foreign Service. The new partners undertook as one of their first major projects the sale of the Huth library. This property, which had taken 50 years and two generations to amass, took 12 sales over 11 years to disperse, netting £300,000.

In 1917, Sotheby, Wilkinson, and Hodge moved its business offices from Wellington Street in London, to 34/35 New Bond Street. At the time of the move, company employees carefully detached a black basalt bust of the lion-goddess Sekhmet, carved in ancient Egypt around 1320 B.C., from its place of honor in Sotheby's offices and installed it over the front entrance of the firm's new premises. The statue had come to the company in the 1800s as part of a collection of Egyptian artifacts and was sold for £40. When the object's buyer never appeared to collect it, the orphaned goddess was adopted by Sotheby's and became its muse, giving the company the oldest privately owned monument in London.

In the wake of World War I, a way of life for many of Britain's old landed families began to come to an end. As a result of the break-up of Britain's vast country estates, Sotheby's began to receive commissions to auction the contents of many country houses. At the suggestion of a young company employee, Sotheby's began to hold these sales on the premises of the estates. The first such sale was at Kinmel Park in Wales, where the sole surviving member of the manor's family lived alone in a house with 57 bedrooms. Sotheby's continued to hold on-site estate sales throughout the 1920s and 1930s.

During this time, Sotheby's began to see the bulk of its business shift away from books and literary property, in favor of paintings and other works of art. Nevertheless, Sotheby's did continue to conduct major sales of libraries. The Britwell collection took 21 separate sales to disperse and set a new record for the sums fetched by a library at auction. In addition, the company presided over the sale of Yates Thompson's collection of illuminated manuscripts, Anton Mensing's collection of early printed books, and the unpublished papers, containing three million words, of Sir Isaac Newton.

In 1937, Sotheby's conducted its most notable house sale of the pre-war era, when it dispersed the contents of 148 Piccadilly, formerly owned by the Rothschild family. The BBC broadcasted the auction live, and £125,000 was netted from the sale, an enormous sum for the time. Within two years of this sale, however, Britain had entered World War II, and the war-time economy naturally brought changes to Sotheby's activities.

After the war, Sotheby's experienced a boom in operations. In 1946, the company sold £1.5 million worth of goods, a figure that would not be equaled for the next eight years. As British regulations governing monetary exchanges were relaxed, Sotheby's was allowed to expand its operations beyond Great Britain for the first time in the late 1940s. With this new freedom, the company sought to become a dominant player in the international auction business.

A key step in this strategy was taken in 1955, when Sotheby's inaugurated American operations, opening an office in New York. With this move, along with gains in other areas, the company's receipts climbed to £1.7 million in that year. The most striking development in Sotheby's business in the late 1950s was the rapid increase in popularity and price of Impressionist and Modern art. In 1957, Sotheby's held its first auction devoted exclusively to these works, when it sold the Weinberg collection in London.

On October 15 of the following year, Sotheby's sold the famed Goldschmidt Collection. This group of seven paintings was sold at an evening auction, a black tie event attended by many celebrities and covered extensively by the press. In just 21 minutes, the works were sold for £781,000, the largest amount ever attained in a fine arts sale. The Paul Cézanne painting entitled *Garçon au Gilet Rouge* was sold to Paul Mellon for £220,000, more than seven times higher a price than any other modern painting had ever fetched. The auctioneer, Sotheby's president Peter Wilson, responded famously to this bid by asking, "What, will no one offer any more?" At the end of the Goldschmidt sale, the audience of 1,400 stood on their chairs and cheered for an extended period of time. With this event, an international boom in art sales was launched.

In June 1959, another major sale strengthened the market for art works, when Rubens' altarpiece *The Adoration of the Magi*, painted in 1634 for a Flemish convent, sold for £275,000, following two minutes of bidding. The painting was offered for sale by the Duke of Westminster, whose family had owned it since 1806. Because it measured 8 feet by 12 feet, Sotheby's had to winch the work into its West Gallery through a hole made in the floor and then break down two walls to get it into the main gallery for sale.

On the day after the Rubens sale, Sotheby's set another record, when it sold the Westminster Tiara for £110,000, twice as much as any other piece of jewelry had ever fetched. This diamond crown featured two enormous pearl-shaped diamonds, known as the Arcot Diamonds, surrounded by 1,240 smaller stones. It was purchased by Harry Winson, who reset the stones in different pieces of jewelry. By the end of 1959, with contributions from these two landmark sales, Sotheby's annual sales had reached £6 million.

Throughout the late 1950s and the early 1960s, the main thrust of Sotheby's growth was in markets outside the United Kingdom. In 1964, the company dramatically enhanced its foreign operations when it purchased Parke-Bernet in New York, the largest American fine art auction house. With this acquisition, Sotheby's became Sotheby Parke Bernet. The American arm of the firm reaped its most handsome profits from the sale of Impressionist and Modern pictures in the mid-1960s. In October 1965, for instance, Cézanne's *Maison à l'Estaque* brought a record $800,000.

With these strong returns from its American branch, Sotheby's increased its international presence in the late 1960s. In 1967, the company opened offices in Houston, Los Angeles, and Paris. The following year, operations in Toronto, Florence, and Melbourne were inaugurated, and, in 1969, Sotheby's added Edinburgh, Zürich, Munich, and Johannesburg. The company's Swiss location soon became a center of European jewelry sales.

In the 1970s, Sotheby's continued its expansion. In 1971, the company opened a second London showroom, in the section of the city known as Belgravia. This facility specialized in art from the Victorian and Edwardian eras. In 1973, Sotheby's moved overseas again, opening an office and showroom in Hong Kong, which soon handled the sale of the Chow collection of Ming and Qing porcelain. In the following year, the company expanded its European holdings, purchasing Mak van Waay, a Dutch seller of fine art. From this base, Sotheby's began to conduct annual sales of Flemish and Dutch Old Master paintings and drawings. Also in 1974, Sotheby's opened offices in Stockholm, Milan, Brussels, and Dublin. In January of the following year, Sotheby's expanded into that area of Europe controlled by the French customs service, signing an agreement to conduct auctions in Monaco. In this way, the company was better able to circumvent the French government's state control of all auctions. The company's first Monaco sale, held in the Winter Casino, was an auction of furniture and silver owned by Baron Guy de Rothschild. In 1976, Sotheby's expanded its Swiss operations to include winter jewel auctions held in the resort of St. Moritz. In May 1976, the company successfully auctioned the renowned Pink Diamond, for a record price of $1.09 million.

The following year, Sotheby's turned its attention to its home base, undertaking a significant expansion in Britain and Ireland. The company opened a salesroom outside London, in Billingshurst, Sussex, and also began to conduct auctions in Scotland.

Eventually, Sotheby's grew to include eleven offices and ten further representatives throughout Great Britain.

In the spring of 1977, Sotheby's decided to sell shares in the partnership to the public for the first time. The company's initial stock offering proved highly popular, and the price of shares had soon more than doubled. In the wake of this move, Sotheby's pushed on with its international expansion. At the end of the 1970s, the company opened a third Swiss office in Geneva. In 1979, Sotheby's also opened an office in Spain, which was inaugurated in May 1979, with the house sale of El Quexigal, a former residence of the Hohenlohe princes. The company had also opened offices in Rome and Hamburg by the end of the decade.

In 1980, Peter Wilson, Sotheby's long-time leader, stepped down from his post and was followed by a number of other executives in quick succession. In 1982, the company's chief expert on Chinese art was appointed head of Sotheby's International outside the United States. The following year, the company faced a major threat in the wave of corporate takeovers that swept the financial world in the early 1980s, when two investors amassed a large number of Sotheby's shares and attempted a hostile takeover of the company. In September 1983, the company was rescued by A. Alfred Taubman, an American businessman and patron of the arts, who formed Sotheby's Holdings, Inc., to purchase Sotheby Parke Bernet Group plc. With the approval of the company's leaders, Taubman purchased all of Sotheby's on November 9, 1983.

The sale and purchase of Sotheby's itself came as the business of selling things in general entered a boom period. The company set records for prices of art works sold at auction in 1983 and 1984 and recorded its highest annual totals of sales in 1984 and 1985. The dramatic growth rate continued throughout the following two years, and, in 1987, Sotheby's reported an 85 percent annual increase in auction sales, as the company passed the $1 billion mark for the first time. In that year, the company sold the Duchess of Windsor's jewels for £31 million and Van Gogh's *Irises* for $53.9 million, an astounding figure that was later revealed to have been enhanced by the auction house's offer of a loan to the buyer.

In 1988, Sotheby's fantastic success continued, as the company's annual sales rose to $1.81 billion, a three-fold increase over the last five years. That year, the company auctioned off a part of the Andy Warhol estate and also conducted sales in the Soviet Union and China for the first time. The following year, Sotheby's moved further afield, opening offices in Tokyo and Budapest and conducting an auction in Vienna. By the end of 1989, the company's sales had doubled again over just two years, with strong returns from contemporary and impressionist art. There seemed to be no end in sight to the boom, and, in July 1990, Sotheby's annual sales reached $3.2 billion.

By the start of 1991, however, the bubble had burst. A severe worldwide economic downturn, as well as anxiety surrounding the Persian Gulf War, brought an end to the auction returns of the late 1980s. The company's contemporary, modern, and impressionistic art sales were hurt particularly badly. By December 1991, annual sales had dropped to $1.1 billion. Sotheby's annual sales figures remained in the $1 billion range for the next few years. In January 1993, the company increased its buyer's premium, which helped to improve its profits. By 1994, improving prices in some areas, such as jewelry, began to indicate a slow recovery in the market. Given its illustrious history, wide range of operations, and expertise in the field of fine arts, Sotheby's was well situated to take advantage of any upturns in the art market.

Principal Subsidiaries: Sotheby's Inc.; Sotheby's Financial Services; Sotheby's International Realty

Further Reading:

Brown, Christie, "Revenge of the Philistines," *Forbes,* December 6, 1993.
Ebony, David, "Spring Auction Rollercoaster: Art Auctions," *Art in America,* July 1993.
Hughes, Robert, "Auctions in the Pits," *Time,* May 16, 1994.
Robinson, Walter, "Sizzle or Fizzle?" *Art in America,* January 1993.
Sivv, Michael, "Pricier Art Could Brighten Sotheby's Picture by 69%," *Money,* January 1994.

—Elizabeth Rourke

Southtrust Corporation

420 North 20th Street
Birmingham, Alabama 35203
U.S.A.
(205) 254-6616
Fax: (205) 254-5404

Public Company
Incorporated: 1887 as Birmingham Trust and Savings
   Company
Employees: 6,500
Total Assets: $15.1 billion
Stock Exchanges: NASDAQ
SICs: 6712 Bank Holding Companies; 6021 National
   Commercial Banks; 6022 State Commercial Banks

The SouthTrust Corporation is a multi-bank holding company with operations in six southeastern states. Based in Alabama, SouthTrust is the dominant banking company in that state and a prominent player in the region as a whole. The company was formed from four local banks in the early 1970s, and grew rapidly by acquiring other Alabama banks. In the late 1980s, state law began to permit interstate banking for the first time, and SouthTrust undertook a regional expansion, buying small local banks and fostering their growth through decentralized management.

Southtrust traces its origins to the Birmingham Trust and Savings Company, which opened its doors for business on December 9, 1887. The bank was headed by H. M. Caldwell and situated on Morris Avenue in Birmingham, Alabama. By the end of the century, deposits at Birmingham Trust had grown to $1 million. In 1902, the bank moved to a new location, on 20th Street in Birmingham. This new building contained a modern vault, for the safe storage of valuable possessions.

Within ten years of this move, Birmingham Trust's deposits had topped the $5 million mark, as the bank continued to prosper. In 1922, the company's assets had grown to $15 million. Birmingham Trust remained a local company, with an exclusive emphasis on serving the community of its hometown throughout the 1920s, 1930s, and the war years of the early 1940s.

In the wake of World War II, however, Birmingham Trust set its sights on a larger world for the first time. In 1946, the company sought a charter from the federal government and became a national bank. The company changed its name at this time to Birmingham Trust National Bank (BTNB).

Four years later, BTNB opened its first branch office, at 7524 First Avenue North in the town of East Lake. Further innovation came late in the 1950s, when BTNB introduced the first charge plan to be offered in the state of Alabama.

In 1963, BTNB expanded the scope of its activities further, when it merged with another financial institution, the Bank for Savings and Trusts. Five years later, the company restructured itself, forming a holding company called the BTNB Corporation. This company had as its assets the Birmingham Trust National Bank and comprised the first one-bank holding company in Alabama.

Also in 1968, BTNB became the first bank in Alabama to offer the BankAmericard charge card. Three years later, in 1971, the company again became a pioneer in the banking industry, when it installed the first automated central information system used in an American bank. In 1972, BTNB introduced the first electronic banking machines offered in Alabama. Called "Anytime Tellers," they offered basic banking services at any hour of the day.

In the early 1970s, BTNB began a period of strong growth. In 1972, the company formed a union of four banks, together with the First National Bank of Dothan, the Peoples National Bank of Huntsville, and the Commercial Guaranty Bank of Mobile. This new company took the name Alabama Financial Group, Inc.

Under the leadership of Wallace D. Malone, Jr., who had contributed his family bank in Dothan to the Alabama Financial Group pact, the company began to grow rapidly. Over the next 15 years, the Alabama Financial Group bought 28 financial institutions within its home state, to become one of Alabama's top four bank holding companies.

This process began in 1973, when the Alabama Financial Group purchased three banks—the Baldwin County Bank of Bay Minette, the Marion County Banking Company of Hamilton, and the First National Bank of Anniston. In 1974, the Alabama Financial Group purchased the Southern Bank of Lauderdale County, the Sand Mountain Bank of Boaz, the Citizens Bank and Trust Company of Selma, and the Southern Bank of Montgomery, N.A.

With this further expansion, the Alabama Financial Group changed its name once again, becoming the Southern Bancorporation of Alabama. With combined assets exceeding $1 billion, this company took its place in the upper ranks of the country's regional financial organizations.

In an effort to maintain that standing, Southern continued to purchase other financial institutions in the mid-1970s. In 1975, the company bought the stock of the Jackson Company, a leading mortgage bank. In addition, the Southern Bank of Lee County and the Southern Bank of Russell County were brought under the umbrella of the holding company.

Throughout this time, Southern's lead bank, BTNB, had also experienced strong growth. In 1977, BTNB reported that its assets exceeded $1 billion; it was the second bank in the state to reach this size. Two years later, BTNB also passed the $1 billion mark in deposits.

In 1980, Southern added another banking property, when the First National Bank of Etowah County became an affiliate of the company. The following year, the company again changed its name, this time to SouthTrust Corporation, and began to convert the names of all its affiliates to the new common identifier. Among the first banks to undergo this process was the Auburn Bank and Trust Company, which became affiliated with South-Trust, and then merged with the Southern Bank of Lee County, becoming the SouthTrust Bank of Lee County.

In 1982, SouthTrust's lead bank, the Birmingham Trust National Bank, officially became the SouthTrust Bank of Alabama, N.A. SouthTrust also bought the Muscle Shoals National Bank and merged it with the Lauderdale County Bank, renaming the resulting financial institution SouthTrust Bank of the Quad Cities. In addition, the company added the First National Bank of Piedmont, the Citizens Bank of Northport, and the Coosa Valley Bank of Gadsden.

In 1983, SouthTrust placed additional Alabama financial institutions on its roster of affiliates. The company bought the Midland State Bank, the First Bank of Alabaster, the Leeth National Bank, and the Bank of Hackleburg. In addition, South-Trust consolidated two of its other operations, merging the SouthTrust Bank of Piedmont into the SouthTrust Bank of Calhoun County.

In September 1983, SouthTrust purchased another Alabama bank holding company, the Citibanc Group, Inc., which had six affiliated banks and assets totaling $140 million. By this time, SouthTrust had grown to include 18 different bank subsidiaries, giving it assets of $2.6 billion. At the end of the year, South-Trust stood as Alabama's fourth largest banking company.

In 1984, SouthTrust completed the conversion of its affiliates' names, when its non-banking units also adopted the new corporate logo. Accordingly, the Jackson Company, SouthTrust's mortgage banking subsidiary, became the SouthTrust Mortgage Corporation. In a further consolidation, the SouthTrust Bank of Dale County merged with the SouthTrust Bank of Dothan, taking the latter's name. In addition, the Peoples Bank of Anniston was folded into the SouthTrust Bank of Calhoun County. By the end of the year, SouthTrust had overtaken its closest rival to become Alabama's third largest bank, with assets of $3.09 billion.

SouthTrust's rearrangement of its assets continued in 1985, when the SouthTrust Bank of Tuskegee merged into the South-Trust Bank of Auburn. At the same time, the Alex City Bank was added to the SouthTrust Bank of Coosa County, forming the SouthTrust Bank of Central Alabama.

The bank also renewed its practice of purchasing other financial institutions. After the Elba Exchange Bank became a South-Trust affiliate, its name was changed to SouthTrust Bank of Coffee County. Another acquisition, the First National Bank of Opp, was renamed the SouthTrust Bank of Covington County. In addition, SouthTrust bought the Peoples Bank and Trust Company in Sylacauga, Alabama, which became the South-Trust Bank of Talladega County, and it purchased the First

National Bank of the South, which was renamed the SouthTrust Bank of Covington County. With the completion of this string of mergers, SouthTrust had grown to become the second largest bank holding company in Alabama. Its assets had increased to $3.7 billion, and its properties included 22 financial institutions and seven bank-related affiliates.

In 1986, SouthTrust added three new banking affiliates, the Citizens Bank of Hartselle, the Bank of Ozark, and the South-Trust Bank of Cleburne County, and it also started a new bank, the SouthTrust Bank of Walker County. With these moves, SouthTrust passed the $5 billion mark in assets for the first time.

SouthTrust attributed its steady growth and continuing financial success to its policy of hands-off management. Rather than try to integrate all of its purchases thoroughly into one company, SouthTrust remained a loose federation of community-based banks. The company was noted for its policy of allowing local employees to make decisions about loans and other matters, and it often did not even require that a SouthTrust representative sit on the Board of Directors of the banks it had purchased.

These policies enabled SouthTrust to grow so steadily that the company required a new headquarters facility in 1986. At that time, SouthTrust moved its home base to the new SouthTrust Tower in Birmingham, the tallest building in the state. The company's identification with Alabama's tallest building was a physical representation of its literal condition within its home state. By 1987, SouthTrust had grown as much as it could grow within the borders of Alabama.

In order to continue its expansion, SouthTrust needed to look to other, more fertile markets. In July 1987, this became possible for the first time, when Alabama passed a regional banking law allowing financial institutions to run banks in the 12 southeastern states that made up the reciprocal interstate banking region. In response to this change in its business environment, South-Trust announced its intention to achieve assets of $10 billion by 1991 and to expand its operations into all 12 of the states available to it.

SouthTrust began its campaign to achieve these goals just days after passage of the new banking law, when it purchased the Central Bank of South Daytona Beach, in Volusia County in Florida, becoming, in the process, the first Alabama state to add a Florida financial institution to its roster. A string of other acquisitions followed, as SouthTrust went on a Florida buying binge. The company limited its purchases to central and northern Florida and concentrated on the segment of the financial market that it knew best: banks that served small-to-medium sized businesses, professional customers, and retailers in the immediate area of the branch office.

In 1987, SouthTrust took over the Vista Bank of Marion County, the Vista Bank of Volusia County, the First Bank of Mariana, and the Gulf/Bay Financial Corporation. In July, the company announced that it would buy the Bank of Florida Corporation, based in St. Petersburg, Florida. In the fall, South-Trust also purchased the First National Bank of Jacksonville.

On the whole, the banks that SouthTrust purchased in Florida had not demonstrated stellar financial returns. Analysts speculated that the company hoped to acquire money-losing properties cheaply and then make them profitable. With a total of seven acquisitions, the company had established a presence in three of Florida's main banking markets and two of its medium-sized markets within the first year of its entry into the state.

Also in the fall of 1987, SouthTrust made its first foray into Georgia, when the company petitioned federal regulators for permission to move the headquarters of its SouthTrust National Bank of Russell County across the state line to Columbus, Georgia. The company's interstate expansion continued in the following year, when SouthTrust acquired the Latta Bank and Trust, of Latta, South Carolina, which became the SouthTrust Bank of Dillon County. In addition, the company moved into Tennessee, opening the SouthTrust Bank of Middle Tennessee, based in Nashville.

In April 1988, SouthTrust reorganized its Florida holdings, the assets of which had grown to $500 million, by forming a new bank holding company, SouthTrust of Florida, Inc. This company was given jurisdiction over SouthTrust's seven Florida banks, with 23 branches. In this way, SouthTrust hoped to maintain its heavily decentralized structure, fostering a small bank culture, with the advantages of quick decision making, backed up by big bank resources.

SouthTrust enhanced its presence in the Florida market in 1989, establishing the SouthTrust Estate & Trust Company in St. Petersburg and opening the SouthTrust Bank of Sarasota County. The Bank of Washington County and the First Bank of Holmes County were also merged into the SouthTrust Bank of Northwest Florida, which had previously been formed by the merger of Florida Central Banks, Inc. and Florida Community Banks, Inc., with the SouthTrust Bank of Jackson County.

In addition, SouthTrust added a new bank in its home state, the Wiregrass Bank and Trust Company of Headland, Alabama. In South Carolina, SouthTrust opened the doors of a newly-founded bank, the SouthTrust Bank of Charleston. The company also enhanced its holdings in Georgia by buying Sentry Bank and Trust in Roswell, Georgia, which became the South-Trust Bank of Atlanta.

By early 1990, SouthTrust's steady growth had made it the largest bank based in Alabama, with assets of $7.5 billion. In February of that year, SouthTrust continued its incursion into the Florida banking market when it opened the SouthTrust Bank of Orlando. In addition, the company bought the Community National Bank of Cape Coral and changed its name to the SouthTrust Bank of Southwest Florida. The company also consolidated two of its northern Florida banks into one unit. In June 1990, SouthTrust also strengthened its Georgia operations when it bought the north Georgia banking division of the First Liberty Financial Corporation, which had more than 12 bank branches in the Atlanta area, and 22 former Fulton Federal Savings and Loan offices altogether. This gave SouthTrust 42 locations in the Atlanta market.

In 1991, SouthTrust moved into North Carolina, establishing the SouthTrust Bank of North Carolina. Later that year, the company also purchased three offices of the Barclays Banks of North Carolina. In addition, SouthTrust added to its Florida holdings, buying the Duval Savings and Loan company of Jacksonville and the Clearwater office of the Florida Bank of Commerce.

By the end of 1992, SouthTrust had more than doubled in size since the advent of interstate banking in 1987. The company had completed 18 acquisitions of small banks outside Alabama, bringing its assets to nearly $12 billion. One of the bank's primary focuses outside Alabama was Atlanta, a fast-growing market where SouthTrust acquired 90 branch offices in just three years, making it one of the city's largest banks. All together, SouthTrust had 336 offices across six states, and it had attained the status of a "mini super-regional bank."

At this stage of its growth, SouthTrust announced that it would limit further geographical expansion to concentrate instead on improving its market share in the areas where it had already established operations, along with a few new target markets. One of these key focus areas was Charlotte, North Carolina, where SouthTrust bought the 11 branch offices of the American Commercial Savings Bank, owned by American Bancshares, Inc., in January 1993. The company planned further expansion in this area.

In addition, SouthTrust made further inroads into the Orlando market, buying the Commercial State Bank of Orlando for $10.6 million. By the end of 1993, SouthTrust's assets had grown to $15.1 billion.

SouthTrust opened up another new territory for growth in May 1994, when it announced that it had purchased the First Jefferson Corporation, owner of the Jefferson Bank of Mississippi. Three months later, SouthTrust also made its debut in the Memphis, Tennessee market, starting from scratch instead of buying an existing property. This operation was added to SouthTrust's 39 existing banks, with more than 400 branch offices. With a steady record of strong growth and careful expansion, South-Trust appeared well situated to prosper as it expanded its reach in the coming years to include all of the southeastern United States.

Principal Subsidiaries: SouthTrust Bank of Alabama, N.A.; SouthTrust Bank of Calhoun County, N.A.; SouthTrust Bank of Dothan; SouthTrust Bank of Hartselle; SouthTrust Bank of Mobile; SouthTrust Bank of Northwest Florida; SouthTrust Bank of Ozark.

Further Reading:

Cline, Kenneth, "Alabama Banks Look Beyond Borders," *The American Banker,* June 21, 1989.
Cline, Kenneth, "SouthTrust's Malone Sets His Own Terms for Growth," *The American Banker,* October 27, 1992.
Flaum, David, "Expanding SouthTrust Opens Here Monday," *The Commercial Appeal,* August 7, 1994.
King, Jim, "Competitive SouthTrust," *The Atlanta Journal and Constitution,* October 4, 1992.
Kuhn, Brad, "Alabama Banks Spreading into Sunshine State," *Orlando Sentinel Tribune,* June 27, 1993.
Kuhn, Brad, "Thinking Small in a Big Way," *Orlando Sentinel Tribune,* January 8, 1990.
Livingston, Skip, "SouthTrust Bank Buys Sweep Across Florida," *The Business Journal—Jacksonville,* November 16, 1987.
Swasy, Alcia, "SouthTrust Forms New Florida Bank-Holding Firm," *St. Petersburg Times,* April 20, 1988.

—Elizabeth Rourke

🔳 ST. JUDE MEDICAL

St. Jude Medical, Inc.

One Lillehei Plaza
St. Paul, Minnesota 55117
U.S.A.
(612) 483-2000
Fax: (612) 482-8318

Public Company
Incorporated: 1976
Employees: 725
Sales: $252.6 million
Stock Exchanges: NASDAQ
SICs: 3842 Surgical Appliances and Supplies; 3840 Medical
    Instruments and Supplies

St. Jude Medical, Inc. (SJM) is the world's leading maker of
mechanical heart valves and serves physicians worldwide with
medical devices for cardiovascular applications. Based in St.
Paul, Minnesota, the company maintains additional operations
in Massachusetts, Canada, Puerto Rico, and Belgium. Approximately 1,500 medical centers in 75 countries actively use SJM
products.

In 1972, the bileaflet mechanical heart valve was developed at
the University of Minnesota. This new valve was made of
pyrolytic carbon, a hard, shiny material that did not cause blood
clots and could last for years in the human body. St. Jude
Medical, Inc. was formed and incorporated in 1976 to further
develop, market, and manufacture this valve. The company was
founded by Manuel A. Villafana, a businessman who began his
career at the helm of Cardiac Pacemakers, Inc., revolutionizing
that industry with the innovation of long-lasting lithium batteries. Two years before selling his company to Eli Lilly for
$127 million, Villafana formed SJM.

In February 1977, SJM made an initial stock offering at $3.50
per share. In October, the first human implant of the SJM
mechanical heart valve took place. Dr. Demetre Nicoloff performed the operation on Helen Heikkinen, a 69-year-old heart
patient, at the University of Minnesota Hospital.

A superb salesman, Villafana convinced so many heart surgeons to try the SJM heart valve that the company was criticized
for the emphasis placed on sales in what was supposedly a
clinical trial program. The Food and Drug Administration
(FDA) became involved, prompting Villafana's departure from

the company in 1981. Villafana would later establish Helix
Biocore, a competitor company.

In 1982, SJM received approval from the FDA to market its
mechanical heart valve in the United States. SJM's profits
began to ascend rapidly, rising from $2.3 million in 1982 to $4.3
million in 1983. By 1984, SJM had achieved revenues of almost
$35 million and profits of $5.3 million, solely from sales of its
mechanical heart valve. Twenty-five percent of the 100,000
artificial valves implanted in diseased hearts that year were SJM
valves. As a one-product company with a market value of $41
million, SJM could not afford any threat to the successful
manufacturing of that vital product.

However, a threat did come in 1984. The distinctiveness of
SJM's heart valve was found in the marriage of a bileaflet
design, created by St. Jude engineers, and its anti-blood clotting
carbon skin coating, produced and supplied to SJM by Carbo-
Medics, a subsidiary of Intermedics, Inc., a cardiac-pacemaker
company. In March 1984, the two companies were unable to
reach an agreement on a long-term supply contract and filed
countersuits.

The dispute had actually begun shortly after CarboMedics was
purchased by Intermedics in 1979. Intermedics's reputation in
the field was that of a tough player, and SJM executives began
to quietly look for a second-source supplier of the valve's
carbon coating. In addition, Villafana had launched a pace-
maker-development project, in hopes of diversifying the company. G. Russell Chambers, Intermedics's director, threatened
to raise the price of the carbon coating when he learned of the
pacemaker project. Pacemaker sales accounted for the majority
of Intermedics's profits. Chambers's threat worked; Villafana
dropped the pacemaker project.

At the same time, a company called Hemex was formed in
1979, selling a heart valve that was similar to SJM's. Observing
that Intermedics officers and directors owned stakes in Hemex
and that Chambers's son, Rusty Chambers, was Hemex's chairperson, SJM inferred that Intermedics was behind this new
competitor in the valve business.

Although Chambers denied any connection between the companies, SJM's new CEO, LaVerne Rees, was unconvinced. In
1981, Rees directed the company to take the necessary steps
toward development of its own carbon coating. When this
costly and ambitious project was announced in SJM's 1983
annual report, Chambers was outraged and demanded that SJM
halt all research efforts. According to *Business Week,* an SJM
consultant then attempted to purchase the carbon formula from
an employee of CarboMedics. In 1983, Chambers directed his
company to stop supplying SJM with carbon components. The
dispute became heated, and court depositions alleged that CarboMedics hired detectives to search SJM garbage cans for
stolen trade secrets.

CarboMedics charged SJM with patent infringement, while
SJM responded with breach of contract, antitrust, and restraint-
of-trade claims. Essentially, SJM alleged that Intermedics
sought to achieve a monopoly and to restrain trade in the heart
valve business. Each company accused the other of theft of
trade secrets and contract violation. In the fall of 1984, SJM's
board let Rees go, leaving Chairperson William Hendrickson

in command, with Thomas M. Garrett III—the attorney who drafted SJM's articles of incorporation—playing a greater role in advising the company.

The legal battle continued for two years and involved court cases in the United States as well as in Europe. Because CarboMedics refused to supply SJM during this period, SJM ran out of completed valves to sell, forcing doctors and patients to look elsewhere for supplies, and eroding the sales and stock market earnings of both companies. According to *Business Week,* in 1985 SJM produced only about one-third of the 25,000 heart valves it had produced in 1984. Intermedics lost approximately $20 million on an annual basis, and SJM sank from record revenues of $35 million in 1984 to $26 million in 1985. SJM's stock, which had previously been a high-rated investment, plummeted, as did that of CarboMedics. Meanwhile, competitors in the heart valve industry had a field day, as their sales—and their share of the market—increased.

In February 1985, SJM named Lawrence A. Lehmkuhl as its new president and CEO. Lehmkuhl, who had previously served as divisional president at American Hospital Supply Corp., made it his first priority to end the supplier boycott of SJM, which threatened to destroy the company's ability to produce and market its only product. Lehmkuhl was selected not only on the basis of his potential to resolve the dispute, but also as a leader who might broaden the company's product line, eliminating the vulnerability associated with being a one-product company. In September 1985, an agreement was signed by the two companies, allowing SJM to continue its carbon manufacturing research and development efforts and to produce limited quantities of pyrolytic carbon.

In 1986, the first SJM mechanical heart valve produced with the company's own pyrolytic carbon-coated components was implanted in a patient in Germany. SJM augmented its mechanical heart valve business in 1986 when it acquired BioImplant, expanding into tissue heart valves. However, the company only sold the tissue valves outside of the United States for several years. SJM implemented a 2-for-1 stock split, tripling its authorized common shares to 30 million. 1986 revenues rose to $60.5 million.

Once again, the company demonstrated consistent growth and stock market value. By 1988, SJM was again a favorite pick for investment specialists. Fiscal year 1987 had closed with a net profit of $17 million and $1.55 a share, with net income rising 44 percent over the prior year to $71.8 million and sales climbing 19 percent. Furthermore, the company had no debt. In fact, SJM's cash balance was an astonishing $65 million. In an article in *Barron's,* investment specialist Bing Carlin selected SJM as his favorite investment, citing competitor Baxter Travenol's suspension of its heart valves (due to possible malfunction) and the FDA's approval of SJM's new low-cost plant in Puerto Rico as optimistic factors for SJM. Another competitor, Pfizer, also experienced failure with its heart valve. In addition, SJM's decision to sell directly to hospitals, rather than working through distributors, meant that the company would retain more profits. The company achieved revenues of $114 million and $148 million in 1988 and 1989, respectively.

In 1990, SJM established its International Division, headquartered in Brussels, Belgium. SJM was still a top-rated pick for investors, and the company's stock was selling at 20 times its earnings. Other than the decline in profits in 1985, SJM had demonstrated revenue growth of 30 percent or more each year, with revenues of $175.2 million in 1990, and the company possessed over $150 million in cash. Over 300,000 SJM mechanical heart valves had been put to use.

One reason for SJM's success was that the average age of heart valve recipients had declined. Older patients favored non-mechanical heart valves, which were made of pig tissue and did not require anti-clotting medication. Such tissue valves had an average age of five years, and as the age of heart patients declined, the life expectancy after implant increased. This increased life expectancy created a greater demand for mechanical valves, since tissue valves would have to be replaced through open heart surgery after five years.

In addition, SJM had reached an agreement with CarboMedics, giving SJM the right to make increasing quantities of components until 1998 and to make all parts in-house beginning in 1998. The pricing structure contained within the agreement significantly reduced SJM's costs, in exchange for SJM's commitment to purchase decreasing percentages of carbon components over the next five years. Since Baxter Travenol's design flaw, SJM had faced virtually no serious competition. The heart valve market was not large enough to attract major pharmaceutical companies as competitors.

Under the leadership of Lehmkuhl, SJM had begun to make cautious acquisitions. Those acquisitions included a Canadian company that manufactured porcine valves that were sold internationally (while awaiting U.S. FDA approval), a company that made intra-aortic balloon pumps, and a centrifugal pump system. In addition, SJM had expanded its research department, funding vascular graft research. However, the core of SJM's operations remained its heart valve business. In 1991, SJM received FDA approval for two internally developed products: the BiFlex annuloplasty ring and the sterile aortic valved graft. SJM became the only heart valve manufacturer with two sources for pyrolytic carbon-coated components. Revenues rose again, to $209.8 million in 1991.

After five years with annual earnings growth of 59 percent and an 84 percent rise in shares in 1991, SJM's stock suddenly took another downturn in summer of 1992. The catalyst was the company's disclosure, on July 1, that second quarter sales and earnings had fallen short of analysts' projections. On July 2, investors pulled $285 million out of SJM, 16 percent of the company's market capitalization.

Lehmkuhl attributed the shortfall to aggressive promotion of tissue valves by two competitors, Medtronic and Baxter International. *Barron's* magazine also cited a decline in open heart surgeries in Los Angeles, one of SJM's largest markets, as a negative factor, along with an "inventory adjustment" by a Japanese customer and decreased sales in Poland. The shortfall was estimated to be only two percent of the domestic market (SJM controlled over 45 percent of the international market and 60 percent of the U.S. market). However, since 95 percent of the company's sales continued to be generated by the heart valve, even that small setback was enough to scare off investors who were wary of the risks of a one-product company.

The result was that SJM's shares, which had been priced at 55 and one-half cents in January of 1992, dropped dangerously to 27 and one-half cents. Ironically, sales climbed 3.5 percent over the previous year's second quarter to $57 million, and earnings per share rose from 45 cents to 52 cents. Moreover, the company would close 1992 with another dramatic increase, achieving $239.5 million in revenues.

Seeing competition from tissue valve companies as a major challenge, SJM began to work toward sales of tissue valves in the United States. The company already sold both tissue and mechanical valves in Europe, and it formed a partnership with Hancock Jaffe Laboratories to design and market a new bio-prosthetic tissue valve in the United States. Also during this time, SJM began construction of a new 65,000 square foot facility for manufacturing pyrolytic carbon-coated components. The facility would undergo FDA qualifications in 1994 and 1995.

Taking a long-anticipated step toward long-term stability, Lehmkuhl made his first aggressive maneuver toward an acquisition strategy when he hired John Alexander as vice-president for corporate development in July 1992. Alexander had previously spearheaded business development and strategy for Baxter International's diagnostics division. SJM had been criticized for being too conservative with its $300 million cash supply by observers who could not understand why the company did not diversify through acquisitions earlier. Lehmkuhl had been cautious, in part, because any acquisition would initially dilute SJM's tremendous earning power. Health-care company prices had dropped significantly since the beginning of 1992, and the time was seen as ripe for the beginning of an acquisition strategy.

Ronald Matricaria, formerly an executive with Eli Lilly & Co., replaced Lawrence Lehmkuhl as president and CEO in 1993, while Lehmkuhl remained as company chairperson. Matricaria was known as an aggressive competitor, having built Lilly's cardiac pacemakers unit from a failing business to a world leader. Matricaria breathed new life into the acquisition hunt, giving it the code name "Project Runner," and involving the company's top management in a process of self-examination and assessment. This process involved the identification of SJM's business strengths—the manufacture of implant devices and an intricate knowledge of blood flow and clotting—and the application of those strengths to potential areas of acquisition. The company studied 16 medical specialties fields in order to make its decision.

In the spring of 1993, the company signed an exclusive license and supply agreement with Telios Pharmaceuticals, Inc. to utilize Telios' proprietary cell adhesion technology. In August, SJM bought a large minority stake in InControl Inc., a company developing an implantable machine to stop atrial fibrillation (rapid pulsing of the heart's upper chambers). In December, SJM acquired Electromedics, a Colorado maker of blood management and blood conservation equipment and related disposable devices, in a $90 million deal. The company's stock fell 87.5 cents to 27 and three-quarters the day before the acquisi-

tion was announced. According to the *Wall Street Journal,* the industry was "on the rocks."

SJM's stock market decline was attributed to two primary factors: cost cutting by corporations and insurance companies and an uncertainty about the future nature of medical care created by President Clinton's health care plan. SJM faced other problems as well. The company's tax rate went up by almost five percentage points through the loss of tax benefits from manufacturing in Puerto Rico. And in September 1993, CarboMedics received approval to sell heart valves in the United States. SJM was not yet ready to promote the improved tissue valve being developed. Instead, the company continued its acquisition strategy, hoping to renew growth through diversification. Revenues continued to rise, with sales of $252.6 million at the end of 1993.

In June 1994, SJM announced that it was prepared to make a major acquisition. Project Runner had arrived at its conclusion—SJM would enter the expanding market for cardiac rhythm management. SJM would purchase the cardiac pacing device businesses of Siemens AG—the world's number two maker of pacemakers for slow heartbeats—for over $500 million. The acquisition would launch SJM as a top-tier company in the realm of pacing device manufacturers. Further, SJM would more than double its sales and triple its work force. In 1993, Siemens's cardiac rhythm management business demonstrated over $350 million in sales and retained 1,300 employees.

That year brought new developments in existing products as well. SJM announced the first U.S. implants of its stentless tissue heart valve, previously marketed internationally. The FDA granted SJM approval to market its new collagen-impregnated aortic valved graft in the United States. The company launched an alliance with Advanced Tissue Sciences to pursue the joint development of tissue engineered heart valves. And The Heart Valve Company (the joint venture between SJM and Hancock Jaffe Laboratories) made its first implant of the new bioprosthetic heart valve at Glenfield Hospital in Leicester, England. Finally, the company made a $12 million equity investment in Endo Vascular Technologies, Inc., a leading company in the development of products to less invasively repair damaged or diseased blood vessels. In mid-1994, SJM remained dependent largely on its mechanical heart valve, over 500,000 of which had been implanted. Nevertheless, the first steps toward diversification were underway and would undoubtedly change the nature both of SJM as a company and the cardiac business itself.

Principal Subsidiaries: St. Jude Medical, Inc., Cardiac Assist Division; St. Jude Medical Puerto Rico, Inc.; St. Jude Medical Sales Corp.; St. Jude Medical S.C., Inc; 151703 Canada Inc.; St. Jude Medical Ltd.; St. Jude Medical International, Inc.; St. Jude Medical U.K. LTD; St. Jude Medical France SA; St. Jude Medical GmbH; St. Jude Medical Espana SA; St. Jude Medical Europe, Inc.; S.A. St. Jude Medical Belgium NV; St. Jude Medical AG; St. Jude Medical Nederland BV; St. Jude Medical Medizintechnik GESMBH; St. Jude Medical Acquisition Corp.

Further Reading:

Barker, Robert, "All Heart: Examining a Bitter Corporate Feud," *Barron's,* February 11, 1985, pp. 14–30.

Burton, Thomas M., "St. Jude to Buy Siemens Cardiac Pacemaker Lines," *The Wall Street Journal,* June 28, 1994, pp. A3, A8.

Cochran, Thomas N., "Heartening Prospects," *Barron's,* June 6, 1988, p. 60.

Dorfman, John R., "St. Jude Medical Shares Will Reap Rewards for Long Term Investors, Some Managers Say," *The Wall Street Journal,* January 17, 1994, p. C2.

Forsyth, Randall W., "Too Good to Last?," *Barron's,* January 6, 1992, p. 35.

Gianturco, Michael, "Go with the Greats," *Forbes,* July 19, 1993.

Netzer, Baie, "These Health-Care Stocks Can Prosper Even in the Face of Cost-Cutting," *Money,* July 1990, pp. 55, 58.

Pitzer, Mary J., "The Bad Blood Over a Heart Valve," *Business Week,* May 13, 1985, pp. 141, 144.

"St. Jude Agrees to Buy Electromedics in $90 Million Deal," *The Wall Street Journal,* December 8, 1993, p. C14.

"St. Jude Medical Picks Lawrence Lehmkuhl as President and Chief," *The Wall Street Journal,* February 12, 1985, p. 47.

Wyatt, Edward A., "The Mugging of St. Jude," *Barron's,* August 31, 1992, pp. 17, 25.

Zipser, Andy, "Heart's Content," *Barron's,* September 3, 1990, p. 34.

Zipser, Andy, "Twelve Winning Months," *Barron's,* January 6, 1992, p. 34.

—Heidi Feldman

Standard Microsystems Corporation

80 Arkay Drive
Hauppauge, New York 11788
U.S.A.
(516) 273-3100
Fax: (516) 273-7935

Public Company
Incorporated: 1971
Employees: 728
Sales: $322 million
Stock Exchanges: NASDAQ
SICs: 3571 Electronic Computers; 3674 Semiconductors and
   Related Devices

Since being incorporated in 1971, Standard Microsystems Corporation has evolved from a semiconductor supplier to a leader in standards-based networking technology. In 1994 the company ranked as one of the world's largest suppliers of products that businesses and individuals use to connect personal computers over local area networks (LANs). The firm's System Products Division—which accounted for 82 percent of Standard Microsystem's revenues in 1994—designs, produces, and markets a variety of LAN switches, hubs, LAN adapters, and network management software. The company's Component Products Division designs and produces innovative complementary metal oxide semiconductor, large scale, and very large scale integrated circuits for the personal computer market. The company ranks number two in worldwide Ethernet adapter market share and boasts the number one spot in unmanaged hubs. With its growing share in Token Ring adapters and Ethernet intelligents hubs, SMC also figures as a major player in the rapidly expanding switch market.

In 1971 Paul Richman, educated as an engineer at Massachusetts Institute of Technology (MIT), and three other men interested in the rapidly growing and very lucrative field of computer technology formed Standard Microsystems Corporation as a spin-off of a company then owned and run by Herman Failkov. Failkov, an extremely successful venture capitalist, became the company's part-time chairman, and Richman headed its engineering and technological development unit. Though its headquarters were in Hauppauge, New York, the company opened a calculator microchip manufacturing facility in Silicon Valley to take advantage of the booming computer microchip market.

Unfortunately, one of the company's major customers, a Japanese firm, decided to cancel its order for chips in 1973. In addition, the company lost most of its investment in the West Coast venture and, as a consequence, revenues began to plummet. Standard Microsystems's stock, already trading on the OTC market, dropped precipitously to 40 cents a share.

In 1973 and immediately afterward, Standard Microsystems devoted itself to recapturing lost business. The focus of the company's activity was on designing and manufacturing metal oxide semiconductor large scale integrated (MOS/LSI) and very large scale integrated (MOS/VLSI) circuits, primarily employed in data transmission and telecommunications products. Developing this technology allowed the firm to begin licensing a number of major patents it received for breakthroughs in MOS and LSI circuitry. Hitachi, IBM, Fujitsu, and Western Electric started licensing Standard Microsystems's increasing portfolio of high-technology patents. In addition, by selling the company's ROM operation in Silicon Valley and deciding to remain on the East Coast, management also built an impressive base of eastern customers, including Digital Equipment Corporation, Data General Corporation, Burroughs, and Honeywell. Despite these accomplishments, the company lost approximately $1 million on revenues of only $3 million and reported total debts amounting to almost $1 million.

To correct its financial problems, Standard Microsystems appointed Morton Brozinsky, an executive with a long history of turning a profit, to the position of chief executive officer and chairman of the company. Brozinsky took over just as an especially intense price war in the semiconductor industry had ended. Brozinsky immediately brought small company tactics to the problems confronting Standard Microsystems. Paul Richman, still head of research and development at the company, had created a fundamental breakthrough in the industry with his COPLAMOS technology. The COPLAMOS process was used in designing N (Negative) channel metal oxide semiconductor (MOS) chips, which were significantly smaller and much quicker than the standard but older P (Positive) channel metal oxide semiconductor chips. Brozinsky licensed Richman's revolutionary technology to large companies that subsequently manufactured the product for the booming memory market in high volume numbers. With numerous companies signing agreements with Standard Microsystems to license its technology, Brozinsky shifted his attention to concentrate on smaller markets in which the company could easily compete.

Standard Microsystems also realigned its internal operations to provide more services to customers. Brozinsky's rationale was to let the larger companies provide standardized products in large volume, while Standard Microsystems would stress product innovation and customization. Most important, Richman and his team of engineers were able to conceive enough innovative product designs to keep ahead of other firms in an industry known for intense competition. Under Richman's direction, Standard Microsystems was the first company to manufacture a CRT controller and a synchronous data link controller.

Standard Microsystems had not only regained its old business, but it was also one of the few companies to experience a meteoric rise in the semiconductor industry during the mid- and late 1970s. From the time he was hired as chairman in December of 1974 until January of 1980, Brozinsky had reduced the company's debt to ten percent of its capitalization. Additionally, he had achieved an average return on equity of over 43 percent and had increased revenues to 3½ times more than when he first took over. Revenues at the end of fiscal 1979 were a reported $11.4 million. Licensing agreements were finalized with such giants as General Motors, ITT, and Texas Instruments to use Richman's highly innovative and lucrative COPLAMOS process. Stockholder equity had increased from $140,000 to $9 million during Brozinsky's tenure, and the company's stock was trading 24 times 1979 earnings on the OTC market. From the late 1960s through 1980, more than 40 start-up companies like Standard Microsystems had entered the semiconductor industry, but as the large corporations jockeyed to acquire semiconductor technology only 17 companies remained independent.

Although Standard Microsystems was spending a significant amount of money on research and development, Richman thought that it was imperative to commit even more funds to designing innovative products. In late 1979 and early 1980, however, it appeared that Brozinsky ran afoul of Richman when he indicated a reluctance to approve the increase in expenditures for research and development. Previous to this disagreement, Brozinsky had been stripped of his title as chief executive officer and Richman was appointed president of the company. In effect, Brozinsky and Richman were working in an uneasy partnership. By May of 1980, Brozinsky had stepped down as chairman of the company. Standard Microsystems was going through a management reorganization, Richman told the business press, and the slight decrease in both revenues and earnings had nothing to do with Brozinsky's departure.

As president and new chief executive officer of Standard Microsystems, Richman continued the policies that Brozinsky implemented, except he committed more money to research and development. The company concentrated on providing supplies for the minicomputer and microcomputer markets and built upon its reputation as a high-quality, dependable manufacturer of circuit controls for CRT video displays, local area networks, keyboards, printers, floppy disk drives, and floppy disk data separators. Nearly 75 percent of the firm's circuits were standard products during this time, while the remaining 25 percent were custom made circuit boards. Through its ability to specialize in such products, Standard Microsystems was able to avoid the deleterious price wars and intense competition that destroyed many firms in the semiconductor industry during the early 1980s. Revenues in 1982 jumped to $27 million, an increase of almost $8 million over the previous year. The company's stock, trading at $7 per share near the end of 1981, shot up to $18 per share by November of 1982. This prompted Richman to make a public stock offering in May of 1983. In just one month, Standard Microsystem stock was trading at $37 per share.

Much of the investor optimism was due to Richman's continuing commitment to expanding the company's research and development division and to the licensing of its technologies to other companies. Standard Microsystems was able to increase its royalties while spending its own money to design new products. In 1982 the company introduced 19 new products. Expenditures for research and development increased from $2.3

million in 1982 to $2.9 million in 1983. Just as important, in January of 1983, the company signed a licensing contract with National Semiconductor Corporation, and in February of the same year SMC and Nippon Electrical Corporation reached an agreement to cross-license their own patents of semiconductor products. Although the agreement with NEC took over four years to conclude, it was the most beneficial licensing arrangement that Standard Microsystems had ever finalized with a major semiconductor producer.

Although the early 1980s seemed to indicate that Standard Microsystems would continue its meteoric rise, this was not the case throughout the remainder of the decade. Revenues increased modestly from year to year largely on the strength of the company's domestic and foreign licensing agreements. But its stock price was overvalued and dropped to under $10 per share by the end of the decade. The company's lackluster financial performance, and the slowdown of new product introductions, led to an attempted hostile takeover in 1989 by SMC Acquisition Corporation. SMC Acquisition Corporation was a combination of investment firms, including C.B. Equities, Oxford Capital Management, both located in New York, and HSG Equities Limited Partnership from Chevy Chase, Maryland, that banded together with the purpose of purchasing Standard Microsystems. Fortunately for Richman, SMC Acquisition Corporation's tender of $9 per share for Standard Microsystems was ruled invalid under the auspices of a Delaware law that made hostile takeovers extremely tedious and very expensive. Standard Microsystems was protected by the ruling since it was originally incorporated in the state of Delaware.

Standard Microsystems reported revenues of $71.6 million for fiscal 1989, and early in 1990 the company signed manufacturing agreements with the Japanese companies Sharp and Sanyo Electric. But the firm had lost $2.5 million and appeared to be at a standstill in the semiconductor market. Having been with Standard Microsystems from its inception, Paul Richman stepped aside for new leadership to take control of the company, although he remained as chairman of the board of directors.

The new president and chief executive officer, Victor F. Trizzino, refocused the company's operations on supplying products for the rapidly growing field of local area networks (LANs), which link together personal computers, printers, disk drives, and other equipment and software. Even though the company had already entered the LAN market as one of the original suppliers of ARCNET products, Standard Microsystems had neither the product line nor the sales distribution to carve out a significant portion of the LAN market. Trizzino therefore decided to embark on a campaign to acquire companies that would provide Standard Microsystems with both the products and sales network it needed to become a major supplier for local area networks.

In October of 1991, Standard Microsystems purchased Western Digital's LAN business. In one move, Standard Microsystems more than doubled its size, expanded its share of the LAN market, incorporated newer technologies, and lowered its manufacturing costs through economies of scale. The company also implemented a strategy of vertical integration by acquiring the ability to produce its own semiconductor chips, whereas most of its competitors were purchasing theirs. The acquisition was immediately profitable. Standard Microsystems expanded Western Digital's Ethernet business by 40 percent in less than one year, and the firm's revenues dramatically increased to almost $133 million for the fiscal year ending 1992.

Continuing its acquisition strategy, Standard Microsystems purchased Sigma Network Systems in December of 1992. Sigma was known for its manufacture of a high-end enterprise switching hubs, and the acquisition allowed Standard Microsystems to move beyond adapters and hubs and provide an even broader range of products to its customers. The company's product line now included such items as network adapter cards, hubs/concentrators, network management software, and transceivers; Token Ring STP and UTP passive and intelligent multi-station access units; LAN switches; and ARCNET, one of the original LAN technologies including bus topology, unshielded twisted pair cabling operation, and supporting products including adapters, hubs, links, and various software products. Revenues for fiscal 1993 reached $250.5 million, an increase of 89 percent over the previous year. Revenues for fiscal 1994 reached $322.6 million.

By 1994 Standard Microsystems had developed into one of the world's largest providers of networking products. The company designs, manufactures, and markets network interface cards, hubs, LAN switches, and networking software for the Token Ring, Ethernet, FDDI, and its own ARCNET markets. Much of the company's success, however, can be attributed to a comprehensive realignment of its marketing and distribution strategy. With offices in Canada, Japan, Germany, Britain, Australia, France, and Singapore, international operations provided 44 percent of the company's total revenues. With its new Japanese subsidiary, Toyo Microsystems Corporation, and its forays into Latin America and Eastern Europe, Standard Microsystems is looking to increase its share of the LAN market.

Further Reading:

Sandomir, Richard, "Some Very Special Chips," *Financial World,* August 15, 1983, pp. 22–23.
Smith, Geoffrey, "When the Chips Are Down," *Forbes,* January 21, 1980, pp. 55–57.
Sullivan, Kristina B., "Ethernet Bid from SMC," *Personal Computer,* April 8, 1991, p. 39.

—Thomas Derdak

STAR BANC CORPORATION

Star Banc Corporation

425 Walnut Street
Cincinnati, Ohio 45202
U.S.A.
(513) 632-4000
Fax: (513) 632-5512

Public Company
Incorporated: 1973
Employees: 3,540
Total Assets: $7.64 billion
Stock Exchanges: NASDAQ
SICs: 6712 Bank Holding Companies; 6021 National
  Commercial Banks; 6022 State Commercial Banks

Star Banc Corporation is a bank holding company for nationally and state-chartered commercial banks in the tristate area of Indiana, Kentucky, and Ohio. The holding company oversees 198 bank branches, an automatic teller machine (ATM) network, and two 24-hour telephone systems, the Automated Voice Response line for general information and the Financial Services Center telemarketing unit, which handles loan applications and opens new accounts. Diversifying both its holdings and corporate plan in the 1990s, Star Banc became a leading provider of consumer, commercial, and financial trust services in the tristate region. The company also became known for creating new financial tools and experimenting with nontraditional investment products. The corporation, headquartered in Cincinnati, shares the 26-floor Star Bank Center with its largest subsidiary, Star Bank, N.A., which reported assets of $6.6 billion in 1993.

Star Banc's history began with the founding of the First National Bank of Cincinnati in 1863. Over the years, First National would engage in numerous acquisitions, mergers, personnel changes, and reorganizations. In 1957, Oliver Waddell, a law school graduate from the University of Kentucky, joined First National as a management trainee; his name would eventually become synonymous with both the First National Bank of Cincinnati and later Star Banc Corporation.

In January 1974, Star Banc's immediate predecessor, the First National Cincinnati Corporation, was formed as a bank holding company in Delaware to acquire assets of the First National Bank of Cincinnati. The following year, First National Cincinnati acquired Miami Deposit Bank of Yellow Springs, Ohio,

from the Midwestern Fidelity Corp. for over $3.56 million. Exactly one year later, on September 30, 1976, the holding company acquired two more Ohio banks, the First National Bank of Ironton for $7.05 million and the First National Bank & Trust Company of Troy for $9.23 million. Oliver Waddell, after little more than five years as vice-president, was appointed senior vice-president in 1976.

On December 1, 1977, the holding company acquired the Third National Bank of Circleville, Ohio, for $2.91 million, then the Commercial and Savings Bank of Gallipolis for $5.44 million in August 1979. The following year marked the ascension of Waddell to president and director, as well as the sizeable acquisition of Portsmouth Banking Company for $15.36 million on August 1. In March 1982, First National's vast holdings gained another bank, the Second National Bank of Hamilton, for its largest payout to date of $22.2 million. As president and chief executive officer, Waddell aggressively continued the holding company's expansion the next year with the March 1 acquisition of the Farmers & Traders National Bank of Hillsboro for $6.8 million in cash and notes. Three months later, in June, another $8.6 million in cash and notes acquired Banc One of Fairborn, to be quickly followed on July 1 by the $3.27 million purchase of the Peoples National Bank in Versailles. As a crowning point of the year, Waddell was named chairperson, in addition to his titles of president and CEO.

The next five years mirrored the previous as a time of immense growth and development for First National and its subsidiaries. In 1985 and 1986, there were five acquisitions (Preble County Bank of Eaton, Ohio; Ohio State Bank of Columbus; New Bancshares, Inc. of New Port, Kentucky; People's National Bancorp of America, Lawrenceville, Indiana; and the Second National Bank of Richmond, Indiana) through stock exchanges totaling approximately two million shares. While 1977 was a quiet year without buyouts or mergers, it was one of internal consolidation. By January of 1988, First National was back in the acquisitions game, with the First Sidney Banc Corp. (Sidney, Ohio) and Aurora First National Bank (Aurora, Indiana) coming on board as a pooling-of-interests for a combined stock exchange of 1.82 million common shares. February delivered a similar transaction for the Peoples Liberty Bancorporation of Covington, Kentucky, for 1.52 million shares, and July's pick-up of the First National Bancorp of Miamisburg, Ohio, for 892,000 shares.

Perhaps most notable that year was First National's reincorporation under the laws of Ohio and the amalgamation of all subsidiaries to the Star name, for what the company deemed "unified product development and marketing, to enhance convenience and customer service and to increase shareholder value." The company adopted the name Star Banc Corporation on April 12, 1989. Acquisitions over the next two years included all outstanding shares of Fir-Ban, Inc. in May of 1990, and the $393 million in total assets of the Kentucky Bancorporation Inc. in July 1991. By late 1991, Star Banc posted modest gains from 1980, with a net income of $65.83 million (up from $64.89 million) and $6.33 billion in total assets (up from $6.02 billion).

To shareholders and customers alike, 1992 was a pivotal year with many repercussions. Star Banc began strengthening its retail markets and continued expansion in Kentucky and the Cleveland area. As a solid outfit with steady growth, Star Banc became a perfect target for the consolidation craze sweeping the country. On April 16, 1992, Fifth Third Bancorp issued a $1.2 billion bid to take over Star Banc. The ensuing battle of wills often found Waddell and Star Banc's officers at odds with their own trust department, which had fiduciary responsibility to consider Fifth Third's offer on behalf of shareholders, regardless of the management's stance.

Despite Fifth Third's offer of $38 to $40 per share for Star Banc's 30 million shares (Star's stock was valued at $28.50 the day of Fifth Third's announcement, Fifth Third's at $46.75), Star Banc boardmembers unanimously refused the merger—sparking industry-wide debate and rumors of a hostile takeover between Cincinnati's two biggest banking firms. The furor also managed to split the city's generally close-knit financial community, many of whom had stock in both Star Banc and Fifth Third. Then City Councilman David Mann urged city officials to look into anti-trust implications, doubting "the public interest" would be served by allowing Fifth Third to completely dominate the Cincinnati market and become Ohio's fourth largest banking firm with $16 billion in assets.

Though Star Banc couldn't compete with Fifth Third's assets ($9.1 billion to Star Banc's $6.7 billion) and earnings ($138 million as compared to Star Banc's $65.8 million in 1991), Star Banc's strength in corporate markets and expansion in northern Kentucky were a major attraction in the merger. Yet Waddell and Star Banc's top brass didn't believe Fifth Third's stock would maintain its inflated value and were furious that their rival had broken an agreement not to go public without prior board approval. While insiders speculated about a "white knight" rescue of Star, Detroit-based NBD Bancorp officials came to town with the supposed intention of launching a bidding war for Star Banc. For those who wanted the merger between Star Banc and Fifth Third, one stumbling block was the inevitability of job losses when the two companies combined personnel and closed overlapping branches.

Though most analysts regarded Fifth Third's offer as too good to ignore, Star Banc hired advisers from Chicago and Washington, D.C. and remained steadfast—incurring ire and a class-action lawsuit on behalf of shareholder Thomas A. Abrahamson and others who felt Star Banc's rejection was wrong. As a last attempt to rein in Star Banc's board, without going directly to shareholders, Fifth Third increased its offer to $42 per share. Again, Waddell issued a flat denial, Fifth Third withdrew its offer, and the ordeal was finally over—though many believed Fifth Third would have gone even higher if Star Banc had indicated interest and entered into negotiations. In the attempted takeover's aftermath, Star Banc stock fell to under $32 and the directors were subject to sharp criticism.

To clean up their image and aggressively move Star Banc into the future, Waddell instituted "Project EXCEL," an extensive restructuring plan "designed to evaluate and examine every aspect of the corporation in an effort to enhance revenues, control costs and realize effiencies through elimination of duplicate functions and nonproductive systems." To prove its commitment to comprehensive change in the wake of the Fifth Third imbroglio, Star eliminated 450 positions by November 1992 for

a savings of $20 million. Despite the one-time restructuring charge of $3.96 million after taxes, 1992's total assets swelled to $7.17 billion, with a net income of $76.12 million, up 15.5 percent from 1991. This was due in part to the mid-1992 purchase of 28 Cleveland-area branches of Ameritrust Company, N.A., which had $238 million in securities, $111 million in loans and $937 million in deposits.

In 1993, first quarter net income was up 41.2 percent from the year before, reaching $24.9 million or 84 cents per share, with total assets of $7.4 billion. Then, in May, longtime chairperson and CEO Oliver Waddell stepped down from these posts, three years shy of his mandatory retirement at age 65. He was succeeded by 48-year-old Jerry A. Grundhofer, formerly of Security Pacific National Bank in Los Angeles and well-known in the industry as part of the largest bank merger in U.S. history—between Security Pacific and San Francisco giant BankAmerica Corp. for $6.2 billion in 1992. Waddell continued to serve on the board of directors and retained the title of CEO until June 15, when Grundhofer assumed full control of the corporation.

Under Grundhofer, Star Banc management underwent dramatic changes. High-level executives who had been appointed by Waddell were offered generous compensation packages to leave. Grundhofer then began importing key personnel from the West Coast, including David Moffett (executive vice-president and CFO), husband and wife team John (senior vice-president of sales) and Robin Nenninger (senior vice-president of customer service), Richard Davis (executive vice-president of consumer banking), and others.

In a 1993 letter to shareholders, Grundhofer referred to the year as "one of notable challenges, accomplishments and changes," which included several initiatives to help Star Banc gain market share. Among the new initiatives was the reduction of non-accrual loans and real estate holdings by 23.6 percent, and the development of more proprietary mutual funds and fee-based commercial services. Another 1993 project was the merger of ten independent Star Banc offices into three major banking units in Indiana, Kentucky, and Ohio. Star Banc further reorganized by separating its regional subsidiaries into two distinct groups: "Community" banks in smaller rural and urban areas and "Metropolitan" banks in larger cities. Metropolitan offices were divided into four groups: greater Cincinnati (with 45 branches); Cleveland (37); Columbus (17); and Dayton (28). Community markets were segmented into Indiana (with 20 offices); Kentucky (27); and Ohio (38), serving almost 500,000 area households. "We expect this realignment," Grundhofer said in the company's 1993 annual report, "to foster greater earnings for Star as each region division leverages its specific strengths."

Having become more sales oriented, more productive, and more cost effective, Star Banc saw its 1993 net income climb 31.7 percent to $100.27 million with a year-end market value of $35 per common share. To show their approval of Grundhofer's efforts, the board increased Star Banc's dividend by 20 percent or 35 cents per share. To coincide with the company's revitalized image, the company's logo was changed, symbolizing, according to the 1993 annual report, "new direction, new initiatives and renewed focus on sales, customer service and convenience in every area of our business." As part of this vision, Star Banc joined up with the MAC (Money Access Service Corp.) electronic network to increase access to its ATMs, while placing them inside Wal-Mart, Sam's Club, Super Kmart, and Twin Valu stores. Putting ATMs in popular retail facilities and supermarkets not only slashed start-up and general operating costs, but afforded Star Banc almost unlimited access to the public. "There seems to be a reinvigoration, an enthusiasm, throughout the bank," board member Thomas Klinedinst, Jr. told the *Cincinnati Business Courier* about Grundhofer's tenure as president, chairperson, and CEO. According to that publication, Grundhofer "charmed the investment community, won over several large institutional shareholders and inspired fierce loyalty from some employees" in the short amount of time he'd been at Star Banc.

Principal Subsidiaries: Star Bank, N.A.; First National Cincinnati Corporation; Miami Valley Insurance Company; Star Banc Center Corporation.

Further Reading:

Bolton, Douglas, "Star Banc Bid Scrutinized," *Cincinnati Post,* May 7, 1992.

Braykovich, Mark, "Sides Being Taken in Fifth Third's Takeover Bid," *Cincinnati Enquirer,* April 18, 1992.

Braykovich, Mark, "Failed Merger Stains Images of Both Banks," *Cincinnati Enquirer,* July 2, 1992.

Gallagher, Patricia, "Merger Would Net Two Insurers Millions," *Cincinnati Enquirer,* April 17, 1992.

Hellauer, Brian, "Star Gets an Overhaul to Boost Performance," *American Banker,* July 21, 1993.

Klinkerman, Steve, "Jerry Grundhofer Faces New Challenges at Star," *American Banker,* June 10, 1993.

Klinkerman, Steve, "Star Banc Shines, But It May Have to Do a Lot More to Stay Independent," *American Banker,* August 10, 1994.

Lipin, Steven, "Signet Plans Restructuring, Sets Spinoff and Public Offering of Credit-Card Unit," *New York Times,* July 28, 1994.

Mills, Robert L., "Helping Financial Achievers Achieve," *ABA Banking Journal,* November 1988.

Peale, Cliff, "Merger Proposal Came Too Quickly for Star," *Cincinnati Business Courier,* May 4, 1992.

Peale, Cliff, "New Star Boss Likes the Look of a Healthy Bank," *Cincinnati Business Courier,* May 24, 1993.

Sivy, Michael, "How to Earn 14%-Plus Profits on the Bank of the Future," *Money,* July 1994.

"Star Banc Corp. Names Jerry A. Grundhofer Its CEO and President," *Wall Street Journal,* May 13, 1993.

—Taryn Benbow-Pfalzgraf

Sterling Software, Inc.

8080 N. Central Expy.
Suite 1100
Dallas, TX 75206
U.S.A.
Phone: (214) 891-8600
Fax: (214) 739-0535

Public Company
Founded: 1981
Employees: 2,150
Sales: $259.2 million
Stock Exchanges: New York
SICs: 7372 Prepackaged Software; 7373 Computer Integrated
   Systems Design

Sterling Software, Inc., is a computer software company that is in the forefront of developing products for electronic data interchange, otherwise known as EDI. EDI's use of universal standards allows documents to be transmitted computer-to-computer from one business to another even though the businesses may use different software and hardware. Over 40,000 companies in the United States use EDI to communicate electronically, and EDI serves as the foundation for the Clinton administration's strategy to "reinvent government." As the leading EDI supplier, Sterling provides software for the banking, grocery, hardware, transportation, and retail industries, and the federal government. Of all the industries using this software application, however, Sterling has been most influential in the health care industry, where its market share is an impressive 88 percent.

The company was jointly founded in 1981 by Sam Wyly, Charles Wyly, Jr., Sterling Williams, and Philip Moore, but the driving force behind Sterling was Sam Wyly. Occasionally, a company that is led by a strong-willed chief executive officer or chairman of the board will reflect the characteristics of the person himself. This is what happened at Sterling. At the age of 28, Wyly started University Computing Company (later renamed Wyly Corporation), and built it into one of the first and largest of the data processing firms. After a number of years as head of University Computing, Wyly then decided to establish a telecommunications network called Datran. Competing directly with AT&T was too difficult, however, and after huge losses Wyly was forced to resign from the company in 1979.

After the unsuccessful venture with Datran, Wyly sold most of his holdings in Wyly Corporation and invested heavily in some less-than-successful enterprises, including Scott Instruments Corporation, a manufacturer of electronics equipment, and Bonanza International Corporation, a steak restaurant franchise. His greatest success came with Earth Resources Company, an operation he founded with his brother Charles for $10 million and subsequently sold to Mapco for $400 million in 1981. With a large cash reserve, and plenty of confidence, Wyly was ready to begin another public venture.

Along with his brother Charles, Wyly brought in Moore and Williams, who had worked for him at University Computing, to help set up Sterling Software. Wyly became chairman of the firm, his brother was appointed vice chairman, and Williams was chosen to act as Sterling's president and chief executive officer. Organized as a Dallas-based umbrella organization, the group's strategy was to grow quickly by means of acquisitions and internal research and development. Immediately, Sterling began to purchase small, independent computer software companies. While retaining the engineers from these firms, Wyly applied his financing and marketing know-how in order to promote Sterling's rapidly increasing software product line. By June 1983, Sterling was performing so well that Wyly decided to issue a public stock offering at $9 per share. After one week, Sterling stock shot up to $18 and at the beginning of August was trading at $23 per share. The Wyly brothers owned approximately 37 percent of the company, or 1.4 million shares.

Sterling was growing rapidly under Wyly's leadership. In 1985, Wyly and his management group decided to acquire Informatics General Corporation, a firm that developed mainframe utilities and end-user applications. What was surprising about the acquisition was the size of Informatics—the company was nearly 10 times larger than Sterling. Informatics' sales for 1984 were $191 million, as opposed to Sterling's $18.7 million. However, the size of the acquisition did not make Wyly hesitate in the least. Wyly knew that Informatics had not performed well financially in 1982 and 1983 and that earnings were down in 1984. He also knew the company had suffered constant change in both organizational structure and personnel over the same period. In fact, many of the executives who helped establish Informatics had recently resigned due to power struggles and personality clashes within the company.

Informatics fought back. Although the company was able to withstand an initial offer of $25 per share for its purchase, Informatics' management knew that time was growing short and that Wyly was not about to disappear. Walter F. Bauer, chairman of the board of directors at Informatics, enlisted the aid of Smith Barney, Harris Upham & Company to resist what had developed into a hostile takeover attempt. After another offer to acquire Informatics at $26 per share failed, Wyly and his management team made a final offer of $27 per share. Successful at last, Sterling purchased Informatics at the price of $126 million. In a management transition that was notable for its lack of problems, Sterling quickly incorporated Informatics' applications products into its own banking application software.

Sterling's acquisitions helped the company move aggressively into three of the fastest growing areas of the software industry: systems applications, professional services, and banking software. The company's legal software, which allowed lawyers quick and easy access to data bases for thousands of court cases, was so innovative that it developed a stranglehold on that sector of the market. In addition to the rising demand for its legal software, the company's software applications for accountants, real estate brokers, and other professionals began to sell beyond management's expectations. At the same time, Sterling also jumped into the big leagues by reaching agreements with such customers as General Motors and International Business Machines. IBM began marketing one of Sterling's programs that provides a database connection between mainframe computers and personal or microcomputers. Many industry analysts regarded it as a major step in Sterling's development when IBM agreed to sign a $900,000 contract and market Sterling's applications and programs on its own equipment in India.

Although revenues for Sterling jumped tenfold and reached $239 million shortly after its acquisition of Informatics, the company began to experience some difficulties. As the stock market boomed during the late 1980s, and as stocks of software companies began trading at 15 to 20 times their cash flow, Sterling gradually lost its ability to acquire new companies. In 1986, the Dallas-based firm lost a bidding war with other suitors for a California-based graphics company, Integrated Software Systems Corporation, and for Martin Marietta's software division. In addition, the company's earnings fell nearly 15 percent at the beginning of 1987, to $1.2 million on sales of almost $50 million. The decline in earnings was partially due to IBM's decision to suddenly terminate four out of nine programming contracts agreed upon during the previous two years. Sterling's stock fell precipitously and was trading at a price of $9 per share.

Throughout 1988 and 1989, Sterling's sales remained flat. Yet Wyly and his management team were working on a strategy to reinvigorate the company and increase sales. By 1990, Sterling was climbing its way back and reported sales of over $200 million. The Federal Systems group, which provided specialized technological services to the federal government, experienced its best year yet. One of the company's two largest divisions, the Federal Systems group accounted for nearly half of all revenues in 1990 and was awarded a five-year $210 million contract by the National Aeronautics and Space Administration (NASA). At the same time, the Systems Software group, the company's second largest division, which accounted for 37 percent of its revenue, implemented three new business ventures, including the Corporate Storage Management Initiative, the Corporate Applications Management Initiative, and the Corporate Data Communications Initiative.

The creation of the Electronic Data Interchange (EDI) group, however, signaled a promising future for Sterling. Established in 1990, the Electronic Data Interchange group soon became the fastest growing division of the company's business; in the group's first year, Sterling's EDI contracts experienced a 79 percent jump in revenue. The development and growth of Sterling's EDI group was partially due to the purchase of two leading EDI companies, Lakestone Systems, Inc., and Metro-Mark Integrated Systems Inc. With these two acquisitions, almost overnight the company became the leader in EDI software and the second largest supplier of EDI services. Not wasting any time, the EDI group began to take advantage of its market position and quickly expanded its international presence.

Due to Wyly's highly effective management, Sterling's revenues continued to grow during 1991. The company reported revenues of $228.9 million, an increase of 10.6 percent over the previous year's figure. With the major part of the debt from its acquisition of Informatics paid off, Sterling began purchasing software and information services firms once again. Knowledge Systems Concepts was acquired and merged into Sterling's Federal Systems group, and Redinet Services Division of Control Data Corporation, one of the largest suppliers of electronic data interchange services, was also acquired and subsequently merged with Sterling's EDI group. The company continued its plans for worldwide expansion by acquiring a software development facility in Tefen, Israel. This purchase gave Sterling a presence in the burgeoning information management services market in the Middle East. Because the majority of Sterling's revenues in 1991 was derived from repeat business, the company's strategy was to help its more than 90,000 customers develop their advanced-computing systems and to provide comprehensive client support.

Sterling had a watershed year in 1992. The company had clearly developed into one of the leading suppliers of storage management tools, data communication products, information management reporting applications, and software development items. Although the market in which its Federal Systems group operated had almost stopped growing, this news was more than offset by the rapid growth and phenomenal success of its EDI group. In both 1991 and 1992, the company's EDI revenues grew by more than 30 percent. More importantly, however, was that Sterling's EDI business amounted to approximately 20 percent of the entire market. Sterling had cornered the market in certain areas: the company provided services and products to over 90 percent of the total customer base in the pharmaceutical industry, to nearly 70 percent in the hardgoods industry, to over 50 percent in the insurance and healthcare industry, and to approximately 46 percent of the grocery stores in the United States. With the acquisition of Entity Software, a British firm, Sterling planned to move more aggressively in the European market for EDI services. The two most important acquisitions of the year included National Systems, a firm that specialized in EDI products for the banking industry, and Knowledge Systems Concepts, a supplier of professional engineering services to the United States's armed forces.

If 1992 had been a good year for Sterling, 1993 was even better. Revenues increased to $411.8 million while earnings per share jumped a whopping 336 percent to $1.22. The acquisition of Systems Center, Inc., a leading software supplier and one of Sterling's major competitors, was an important move for the company. Systems Center was one-half the size of Sterling, and dramatically increased Sterling's presence in the systems management and data communications software markets. The purchase of Systems Center led to a reorganization of the entire company: the Electronic Data Interchange (EDI) group was reconfigured into the Electronic Commerce group by adding both Sterling's and System Center's communication software product lines and broadening its approach to electronic communications; the Systems Software group was rechristened the New Enterprise Software group and concentrated on the company's systems software business; the Federal Systems group remained much as it had always operated; and the International group was established to coordinate the activities of Sterling's growing international operations.

Under Wyly's leadership, by the mid-1990s Sterling had grown into one of the largest software and computer services firms in the world. His uncanny ability to incorporate the services and product lines of firms that Sterling purchased was evidence of his managerial acumen. With 22 acquisitions since the company first started business, undoubtedly Wyly would continue to look for new opportunities to expand Sterling's business.

Further Reading:

Bagamery, Anne, ''Sam Wyly's Comeback,'' *Forbes,* August 1, 1983, page 42.

''The Datamation 100,'' *Datamation,* June 1991, June 1992, June 1993.

Klinkerman, Steve, and Scott Ticer, ''Mudslinging Comes to Software Country,'' *Business Week,* May 13, 1985, pp. 29–30.

Myers, Edith, ''Picking up the Pieces,'' *Datamation,* August 15, 1985, pp. 57–60.

Marcial, Gene G., ''Why Sterling's Software Stands Out in the Crowd,'' *Business Week,* July 14, 1986, page 61.

Mason, Todd, ''Sam Wyly: Will the Hunter Become the Hunted?,'' *Business Week,* July 13, 1987.

''Sterling Software, Inc.,'' in *Hoover's Handbook of Emerging Companies, 1993–1994,* page 334.

—Thomas Derdak

Stewart & Stevenson Services Inc.

2707 North Loop West
P.O. Box 1637
Houston, Texas 77251
U.S.A.
(713) 868-7700
Fax: (713) 868-7692

Public Company
Founded: 1902
Employees: 4,300
Sales: $982 million
Stock Exchanges: NASDAQ
SICs: 3511 Turbines and Turbine Generator Sets; 3799
    Transportation Equipment, Not Elsewhere Classified

Stewart & Stevenson is one of the world's leading suppliers of power systems and related mechanical equipment. The company manufactures gas turbine generator sets for electric power, as well as diesel and gas-powered equipment, which it supplies to all the branches of the U.S. military. The largest distributor of diesel engines worldwide, Stewart & Stevenson also produces such diverse items as: oil drilling and pumping products, aircraft and cargo tractors for the airline industry, diesel-powered refrigeration and air-conditioning units, and cable extractors for the communications industry.

In April 1903, C. Jim Stewart, a blacksmith working in Houston, Texas, joined Joe R. Stevenson, a woodworker with his own business, in order to form a partnership. Each of the young craftsmen contributed $300 of their own resources and signed a contract to establish a horse and buggy business, which they named Stewart & Stevenson Inc. Stewart contributed his blacksmith skills and Stevenson provided the woodworking skills— while the contract stipulated that "both shall do such things in and about said business which shall be necessary"—and the company began offering carefully crafted, handmade wagons, buggies, and carriages.

Within two years, the men had built their business into a highly profitable and respectable enterprise. A unique company for its time, the operation wasn't an ordinary horse stable but an indoor horseshoeing parlor. Managers worked next to the horses, and both managers and groomers wore three piece suits. Not surprisingly, the company's reputation grew as word spread

about the sturdiness and meticulous detail that went into every four-wheeled transport built.

In 1905, the Southern Motor Car Company heard of the growing reputation of Stewart & Stevenson and asked the two men to repair an "automobile." The automobile was a four cylinder, 24-horse powered roadster called the Dixie Flyer, which had almost been destroyed by fire. Since it gave them an opportunity to diversify and take advantage of the trend towards a new form of transportation, Stewart and Stevenson quickly signed a contract with Southern Motor. Rather than rebuilding the original body of the car, however, they decided to build a brand new four-door wooden body, which became the first four-door, touring car body in Houston.

As the automobile industry grew during the following years, Stewart & Stevenson became leaders in building bodies for four-door touring cars and two-door roadsters. At the same time, however, the company continued making buggies, wagons, and carriages for people living in the rural areas of Texas. At the onset of World War I, Stewart & Stevenson was contracted by the U.S. government to build horse-drawn wagons for the Army Medical Corps. By the end of the war, as automotive vehicles began to replace horse drawn transport along the Western Front in France, the company was asked to build more bodies for engine-powered cars and trucks.

During the 1920s, Stewart & Stevenson shifted production to meet the needs of customers, who demanded new, improved car designs. During this time, Stewart & Stevenson would purchase a truck or car chassis, for example, add engine and other parts from various manufacturers, and then customize the body to the requirements of the customer. In this way, the company provided a unique, customized design for car hoods, truck beds, and other components. Stewart & Stevenson also agreed to act as a franchise for the Detroit Diesel Corporation, and began to customize diesel engines according to the specific needs of companies within various industries. By 1930, the company was the largest distributor of customized diesel engines in the United States.

Throughout the 1930s, the market for customized car and truck bodies declined, due to decreases in demand caused by the Great Depression as well as competition from the automotive industry's assembly lines, which had developed more sophisticated techniques. To compensate for its declining business in this area, Stewart & Stevenson worked to develop the commercial market for customized diesel engines. In 1938, the company became a distributor for General Motors' new diesel engine. With confidence in its ability to customize General Motors' diesel engines, as it had with Detroit Diesel, Stewart & Stevenson created the Engine Division to market the new product. By the end of the decade, the company was selling its customized General Motors' diesel engines to run ice plants, cotton gins, and lumber mills.

Although World War II virtually eliminated the market for commercial diesel engines, Stewart & Stevenson was again called upon by the U.S. government, which wanted the firm to supply products for diesel-powered equipment. One of its first contracts called for Stewart & Stevenson to supply 35 mobile diesel generator sets with the capability of operating on Russian

M-4 heavy fuel and, most importantly, in temperatures ranging from −40 to −100 degrees Fahrenheit. The work for the U.S. government marked a turning point for the distributor of diesel engines and power units; during the war years, Stewart & Stevenson became the second largest supplier of diesel engines and diesel generator units under the auspices of the "Lend Lease Act."

Stewart & Stevenson was also asked by the government to reconfigure approximately 4,000 General Motors' model 6-71 diesel engines at the rate of 40 per day. The engines were designated for use in the U.S. Army's Sherman Tanks. When the terms of the contract were concluded and all the engines had been delivered, the company voluntarily returned over $1 million to the American government for what it regarded as excess profits.

The innovative engineering and management confidence that developed out of the company's work during the war years contributed to its success in the postwar era. The most important ingredient of Stewart & Stevenson's business was its concentration on the development of diesel power. Some of the more important products manufactured by the company at this time included: a vertical crankshaft diesel engine designed specifically for deep-well turbine pumps; one of the first lightweight power generator sets to operate at −125 degrees Fahrenheit and at elevations of 10,000 feet or more, designed for and used by the U.S. armed forces for many years; and the first winterized, gasoline engine, aircraft support units developed for and used by the U.S. Air Force.

Although C. Jim Stewart and Joe R. Stevenson were no longer making decisions for the company, Stewart & Stevenson continued its history of success into the 1950s. New management, some of it comprised of family members and some hand-chosen by the two founders, proved equally skilled at developing new markets. In the early 1950s, the company made a significant expansion into the marine market by selling and distributing its General Motors' diesel engines to the work boats employed off the Gulf Coast. The company was one of the participants in what has come to be known as the "Dieselization" of work boats in the Gulf Coast waters. Moreover, Stewart & Stevenson entered the market for oilwell and petroleum products equipment during this time by supplying hydraulic control equipment for drilling rigs and providing highly sophisticated diesel pumps for oil production units. In 1956, the company constructed the first diesel power engines with 1,000 horsepower, which doubled the horsepower of the Detroit Diesel engine product line. In 1958, the firm expanded into the growing market for airline ground support equipment and introduced an innovative diesel powered, self-propelled, ground power unit, which supplied commercial aircraft with electrical power while being serviced on the ground.

During the early 1960s, the company began to design and construct heavy equipment using gas turbine engines. Toward that end, the company used and adapted General Motors' Allison gas turbines; during the decade Stewart & Stevenson received 15 awards for its applications of the turbines. The company also used and adapted Garrett and General Electric turbine engines for various industrial applications. The company continued to develop diesel and turbine power applications for the airline support, marine, oilfield and defense industries. In the late 1960s, the company developed the DIESELDRIVE, a compact, high-speed diesel engine to be used for stern-driven pleasure boats. Soon, Stewart & Stevenson began to apply gas turbine engines for use in pleasure craft, and launched a campaign to become one of the largest suppliers of propulsion packages for such vessels as trawlers, shrimp boats, and offshore oil rig supply boats.

In the early 1970s, Stewart & Stevenson procured a lucrative contract from the U.S. Navy to supply turbine engines for powering medium-sized ships and smaller boats, particularly vessels that formed the fleet of the U.S. Coast Guard. While the company also moved into the market for gas-fired generators, the nascent cogeneration market eventually became the focal point of its activity. The business began to boom with the passage of the 1978 federal energy deregulation law. Deregulation required utility companies to purchase power from cogenerators, which were industrial facilities or plants that used steam and natural gas-powered generators to generate electricity for sale to other businesses as well as for use in their own operations. This turn of events created a new market for electrical power, and Stewart & Stevenson rapidly positioned itself to become a leading worldwide supplier. By providing gas-fired generators ranging between 20 to 50 megawatts, the company began to supply power to numerous electric utility companies, as well as cogenerator plants, around the world. As a result, Stewart & Stevenson quickly became the leading supplier to developing nations in the Pacific Rim, Middle East, and Latin America.

Much of the company's success during the 1960s and 1970s was directly related to the burgeoning oil industry in the United States. When the industry collapsed in the early 1980s, Stewart & Stevenson was hit hard. While most of the firm's customized diesel engines and parts were sold to drilling rigs and offshore supply vessels, management was still forced to write off $26 million in losses. Moreover, in just two years, from 1981 to 1983, revenues were cut in half to $237 million, a significant part of the labor force was laid off, and executive pay was lowered by 20 percent. In an attempt to adapt to the shrinking oilfield market, the company expanded its presence in the aircraft ground maintenance market and extended its distribution operations by becoming a franchisee for both Perkins Diesel Engines and John Deere industrial equipment.

During the mid-1980s, Stewart and Stevenson reached an agreement with General Electric Corporation—at that time the leading international manufacturer of aircraft engines—to package its most popular aircraft engine throughout the United States and Canada. Stewart and Stevenson also signed a contract with the Gas Research Institute to design and manufacture modification technology that would convert oil-burning diesel engines to compressed natural gas for buses and other commercial vehicles. Additional attempts to offset losses in the oilfield industry involved competing for larger contracts to build all-purpose trucks for the U.S. Navy and Marines, and manufacturing gas-turbine pumping systems for oil pipelines in Saudi Arabia.

Bolstered by expansion into new markets and its reputation for flexibility, Stewart & Stevenson was able to compete in a rapidly changing manufacturing environment. From 1986 to

1989, the company's revenues almost doubled, with gas-turbine sales accounting for nearly 50 percent of the growth. While most of the remaining revenues came from supplying custom-built diesel generators, the company's market share of aircraft ground maintenance equipment, and its distribution of John Deere construction equipment, began to contribute substantially to company profits.

In both 1985 and 1988, Stewart & Stevenson made bids to design and build a new generation of trucks for the U.S. Army. The Army asked the prospective contractors to submit designs based on its specifications and, in order to save funds, requested that widely available commercial components be used to build the truck. With a history of adapting the designs of other manufacturers, Stewart & Stevenson's design team had soon built a truck with cab parts from an Australian company, a transmission from Allison, an engine from Caterpillar, an axle from Rockwell, and tires from Michelin, a French company. While the company drew criticism regarding its use of a foreign tire manufacturer for the original truck parts, award of the contract was granted in 1991, and Stewart & Stevenson received a five-year, $1.2 billion deal to build 11,000 trucks. When Stewart &

Stevenson discovered that the U.S. Army hadn't redesigned its trucks since the time of the Korean war, management made a commitment to pursue new orders from the Army, Navy, and Air Force, and American allies such as Israel and Kuwait. Management also decided to adapt the truck to meet the needs of customers in the construction, oilfield, and utility industries.

Stewart & Stevenson's sales rose from just under $400 million in 1987 to $686.4 million in 1991. During the same period, earnings rose from $15 million to $35.7 million, and, by 1994, sales had increased to $982 million. The company seemed well positioned as one of the world's leaders in harnessing power.

Further Reading:

Boisseau, Charles, "An Engine For Profits," *The Houston Chronicle,* 1991.
Capability Transcends the Years: Stewart & Stevenson, Houston: Stewart & Stevenson, 1990.
Cook, James, "We're Still Harnessing Power," *Forbes,* May 29, 1989.
Palmeri, Christopher, "Off-The-Shelf And Onto The Road," *Forbes,* July 18, 1994.

—Thomas Derdak

Stryker Corporation

2725 Fairfield Road
Kalamazoo, Michigan 49002
U.S.A.
(616) 385-2600
Fax: (616) 385-1062

Public Company
Incorporated: 1946
Employees: 3,951
Sales: $557 million
Stock Exchanges: NASDAQ
SICs: 3841 Surgical and Medical Instruments; 3842 Surgical
   Appliances and Supplies

The Stryker Corporation is a leading niche producer of medical supplies, including endoscopic systems, orthopedic implants, powered surgical instruments, hospital beds and stretchers, and physical therapy centers. Founded by a surgeon in the early 1940s, Stryker remained a small family-owned business for nearly 40 years. In the late 1970s, the company went public under new management, and Stryker subsequently achieved a remarkable record of steady growth, facilitated by a strategy of cautious innovation, the perfection of existing technologies, and expansion of its markets to include customers on five continents.

Stryker was founded in 1940 by Dr. Homer Stryker, an orthopedic surgeon who practiced medicine in Kalamazoo, Michigan. In 1941, Stryker hired his first employee, and began to market his first two products, a walking heel, and a frame that allowed a patient to be turned in bed. The young company's most important product came four years later, when Dr. Stryker introduced a device to cut plaster casts, easing their removal, which would soon become standard throughout the orthopedics field. In the year following this breakthrough, 1946, Stryker incorporated his fledgling business.

Over the years, the company brought several other medical advances to market. In 1955, Stryker introduced its 1300 Series of electric motor powered instruments for use in orthopedic surgery. Also that year, L. Lee Stryker, Homer's son, took over the management of the company. In 1959, Stryker introduced the Circ-O-lectric Bed, which made long-term immobilization less uncomfortable for patients. Invented by Homer Stryker, this bed featured a mattress suspended between two large metal rings, which allowed the angle of the bed to be adjusted to a wide variety of different settings. Gradually, Stryker earned a reputation as a leader in its field.

Five years later, Stryker continued its innovation in the hospital bed field when it introduced a hydraulic stretcher, its Model 390. In 1966, Stryker updated its electric motor powered surgical instruments with its 1400 Series of pneumatic powered instruments. The following year, the company came out with a line of very small, micro-powered instruments, for use in more delicate surgery.

In the 1970s, Stryker continued to offer customized stretcher beds for use in hospitals and nursing homes. The company's InstaCare/SurgiBed Series was introduced in 1974. Stryker also introduced its first pulsating lavage, a pump used to clean wounds during surgery. In 1975, Stryker embarked on its first drive to expand its markets beyond U.S. borders.

Stryker remained a family-owned and operated company until 1977. At that time, L. Lee Stryker, who had been president and chief executive of the company, died. He was replaced by John W. Brown, an executive with the Squibb Corporation, another medical equipment company. When Brown joined Stryker, the company was a middle-of-the-pack medical equipment maker, which sold products primarily to the American market. Brown agreed to become president of the company with the understanding that Stryker's board of directors would authorize a stock offering to the public, so that the company could upgrade its product line to become more competitive and also step up its expansion beyond the United States.

One of the first initiatives Stryker undertook at Brown's direction was the company's entry into the arthroscope market. Brown was attending a medical conference when he saw a display of orthopedics instruments that allowed surgeons to make a small cut in the skin, and insert a narrow, optical tube into the knee to inspect soft tissue and determine whether surgery was necessary to repair an injury. Previously, surgeons had needed to make a six-inch diagnostic incision in order to inspect ligaments and muscles, which did not show up on X-rays. In addition to permitting diagnosis of knee injuries, arthroscopic tools could also be used during operations to repair problems.

At the time that Brown discovered arthroscopic devices, several other companies had already entered the field. Nevertheless, Stryker proceeded with its own product development. Stryker made it a policy to perfect or modify existing technology, rather than make risky pathfinding breakthroughs. Assured that there was a future in arthroscopy, the company created its own three-inch long, three ounce microcamera, which transmitted images from inside the body to a video screen in the operating room. This made surgery easier and also allowed operations to be videotaped, as a safeguard against malpractice suits. Sports medicine proved a fruitful ground for sales of arthroscopic equipment, and the technique gained free publicity with each big-name athlete who underwent the procedure. Soon, sales of arthroscopic equipment were growing at a rate of 25 percent per year, providing one-fifth of Stryker's earnings.

In accordance with its agreement with Brown, Stryker announced its initial public offering of stock at the end of March

1979, when shares in Stryker were offered on the market for $6 each. In May 1980, Homer Stryker died at the age of 85, leaving the title of company chairperson to Brown. Stryker's principal product became its motor-powered surgical instruments, and the company made the bulk of its profits by replacing instruments used in the United States and also looked for strong growth in demand for its devices overseas.

Later that year, the company used the proceeds of its stock sale to purchase the Osteonics Corporation, a start-up company which had created a unique design for artificial hip joint replacements. With replacement hips produced by Stryker's competitor, surgeons had to speculate on which size would fit the patient before the surgery took place. Stryker's product, however, allowed surgeons to switch different sizes of the hip socket once part of the implant had been put in place. This allowed for greater flexibility and a better fit with the existing bones. Stryker began to market its universal head replacement for artificial hips in 1980, and the company was able to seize a significant part of the market for artificial joints from its larger competitors.

During this time, Stryker sought to market products to fulfill narrow needs within the medical community. "We're a 'niching' company," Brown explained to the *New York Times,* noting that "We have special niches in our marketplace. As long as you're offering a superior product, there's going to be a place for you." By 1983, Stryker's continued growth had driven the value of its stock from $6 to $39.50. The following year, however, concerns about changes in health care regulations had caused that price to drop by half. Although Stryker's arthroscopic and bone implant businesses were growing steadily, 40 percent of its income was derived from more conventional medical equipment, such as stretchers. In the uncertain climate, demand for these standard items had flattened.

Nevertheless, in the mid-1980s, Stryker began to expand its product line through a series of acquisitions. On the first day of 1985, the company purchased Favro B.V., which it renamed Temfa Stryker. Also in that year, Stryker began to fund a long-term effort to create human osteogenic protein, a substance that helped the body to create bone. In 1986, Stryker acquired the video camera properties of SynOptics, Inc., augmenting its operations in the arthroscopic optics field. By the end of the year, Stryker's sales had reached $121 million, yielding earnings of $10 million.

In March 1987, Stryker purchased Adel Medical Limited, a privately-held company that manufactured hospital maternity beds. Paying $8.5 million for Adel, Stryker hoped to strengthen its standing in the specialty bed market. One month later, Stryker also acquired the Hexcel Medical Corporation. Hexcel, based in California, was developing carbon composites and polymers that could be absorbed by the body for use in orthopedics devices. This purchase was intended to complement Stryker's Osteonics Corporation and provide a boost to its efforts in the reconstructive bone products market. Stryker believed that demand in this market was shifting from products made of metal alloys to devices made of polymers, which provided superior elasticity, and better compatibility with the body's own tissues. Stryker's osteonics group introduced its first total knee implants in 1987.

While Stryker augmented its osteonics operations, the company's medical supplies branch experienced difficulties and started to slip in growth. This unit, which accounted for 20 percent of Stryker's revenues, produced specialty beds and stretchers purchased by hospitals. One of its beds, an electric bed designed for use in intensive care units, was found to have some flaws in its design, and, from 1987 to 1988, Stryker redesigned the entire bed and replaced all existing units of the product.

In 1988, Stryker moved into a new field, when it began to distribute the dental implant line of Quintron, Inc., in conjunction with its own line of powered oral surgery instruments. Two years later, Stryker bought Driskell Bioengineering, the subsidiary of Quintron which made these products. With this move, the company strengthened its standings in the rapidly growing dental implant market. By the end of 1988, Stryker's earnings had risen to $15.9 million on revenues of $178.6 million.

The following year, those figures rose again, as Stryker recorded sales of $225.9 million and earnings of $19.2 million. By this time, Stryker had seen 13 straight years of earnings growth that topped 20 percent, as the company stuck to its strategy of entering niche markets and developing superior products for those needs. "What we're good at is ascertaining the needs of the markets and responding to them," Brown told *Investor's Daily.* In doing so, Stryker relied on a combination of internal development and small, carefully-chosen acquisitions. Among Stryker's strongest lines of business were its osteonics products, where it held eight percent of the $900 million market.

Stryker continued its strong growth in 1990. The company's endoscopy division, which had previously concentrated on devices for use in joint surgery, began to market its products for use in abdominal surgery as well, primarily for gall bladder removals, representing a dramatic increase in the potential market for these tools.

At the end of 1990, Stryker received notification from the U.S. Food and Drug Administration (FDA) that it would be permitted to sell a new hip stem implant, which was coated with a special substance that aided bone fusion. This product had been in use in Europe for four years and had been undergoing tests in the United States for two years. During this time, Stryker's financial results were strengthened by the settlement of a patent infringement suit, in which Zimmer Inc. paid Stryker $10 million. Among Stryker's more innovative offerings during this time were physical therapy facilities, called "work hardening centers," which the company began to open in the southeastern United States.

Stryker funded further product innovations with $20.7 in research spending in 1990 alone. "We grow by cranking out product innovations," Brown told *The Detroit News,* observing that the company experienced "not revolutionary changes, but evolutionary ones, like you see in the auto industry. The idea is to improve performance. We're not always the first on the market with a product, but we're seldom last. What we try to do is get a good feel for whether something is a good idea or not. A lot of new designs fail. We like to stay one fad behind."

That policy, combined with a long-term research effort, paid off for Stryker in November 1991, when the company received

FDA approval to begin clinical trials in humans of its new bone-growth implant. This device, a joint project of Stryker Biotech and Creative BioMolecules, Inc., a Massachusetts biopharmaceutical research company, combined OP-1, a human recombinant osteogenic protein, with a carrier that could be absorbed by the body. If successful, this device, a natural extension of the company's hip and knee replacement business, promised to product high sales for a long time to come.

By the end of 1991, Stryker was enjoying a strong boom in growth, as the market for endoscopic tools took off. Sales of Stryker's endoscopy division grew by more than 60 percent to $70 million. Stryker had become the second largest American maker of arthroscopic tools, as well as the second largest maker of powered surgical instruments, the second largest manufacturer of hospital emergency room beds, and the fourth largest producer of orthopedic implants. In addition, the company had made substantial progress in its effort to become an international supplier, as 31 percent of its sales came from areas outside the United States. Stryker ended 1991 with sales of $364.8 million, which yielded earnings of $33.1 million.

Stryker continued to expand its product line in 1992, when the company's French subsidiary purchased the spinal implant business of Dimso, S.A., and its subsidiaries in France and Spain, known collectively as the Dimso Group. Stryker paid $13 million for these properties. This company became a part of Stryker's European subsidiary.

Another Stryker alliance with a European company went awry a year later, when Haemocell, a British maker of a blood-cleansing machine, terminated Stryker's exclusive American license to distribute the product, after sales targets failed to be met. Despite this setback, Stryker ended 1993 with sales of $557 million, and earnings of $60 million. For the seventeenth year in a row, Stryker's management had met its target of 20 percent annual growth in earnings.

Among the initiatives Stryker took in order to meet this target was the culmination of a two-year program to produce a general hospital bed, which the company named the MPS Primary Acute Care Bed. Along with the company's initiative in spinal implants, this marked the second new area of business Stryker entered in 1993, in an effort to assure future growth, despite general anxiety about high health care costs. In addition, Stryker restructured its manufacturing process for artificial hips and knees, in order to increase output and lower costs by eliminating several layers of management. To produce future savings, Stryker also invested in high-tech manufacturing equipment for its other divisions.

In June 1994, Stryker announced that it had purchased 31 percent of its Japanese distribution partner, Matsumoto Medical Instruments. This followed the company's August 1993 purchase of 20 percent of Matsumoto, bringing Stryker's share to 51 percent. The company paid $90 million for controlling ownership in the company, which was based in Osaka. By the middle of the year, Stryker was predicting 1994 sales of $640 million. With its remarkable record of growth and a strong portfolio of products, Stryker appeared well-situated to continue its strong success in the coming years.

Principal Subsidiaries: Osteonics Corporation; Physiotherapy Associates, Inc.; Stryker Deutschland GmbH (Germany); Stryker France; Stryker Japan K.K.; Stryker Far East, Inc.; Stryker Canada, Inc.; Stryker Sales Corporation.

Further Reading:

"Bigger Niche at Stryker," *New York Times,* December 16, 1980.
Jones, John A., "Stryker Keeps Moving With Strong Research Commitment," *Investor's Business Daily,* January 20, 1992.
Kramer, Farrell, "Stryker Becomes Synonym for Consistency," *Investor's Daily,* July 6, 1990.
Rogers, Doug, "Stryker Skillfully Handles a Steady Run of New Products," *Investor's Daily,* March 21, 1991.
Seebacher, Noreen, "Stryker Products: Just What the Doctor Ordered," *Detroit News,* May 6, 1991.
Stavro, Barry, "The Hipbone's Connected to the Bottom Line," *Forbes,* December 3, 1984.
Stroud, Michael, "Stryker: Another Play on Endoscopy Boom," *Investor's Business Daily,* October 25, 1991.

—Elizabeth Rourke

Sumitomo Corporation

2-2, Hitotsubashi 1-chome
Chiyoda-ku, Tokyo 100
Japan
(03) 217-5082
Fax: (03) 217-5128

Public Company
Incorporated: 1919 as Osaka North Harbor Co., Ltd.
Employees: 9,212
Sales: ¥17 trillion ($165.05 billion)
Stock Exchanges: Frankfurt Tokyo Osaka Nagoya
SICs: 5051 Metals Service Centers and Offices; 5052 Coal
and Other Minerals and Ores; 5084 Industrial Machinery
and Equipment; 5169 Chemicals and Allied Products, Not
Elsewhere Classified; 5172 Petroleum and Petroleum
Products Wholesalers except Bulk Stations and Terminals

With interests in everything from chemicals to consumer goods,
Sumitomo Corporation ranked among the oldest and largest
surviving business ventures in the world. The firm was characterized as a *keiretsu* (banking conglomerate), a family of businesses linked through Japanese history and tradition, as well as
cross-shareholdings and interlocking directorates. This scheme
provided Sumitomo affiliates with common and well-known
brand names, access to credit, and protection from hostile takeovers. The Sumitomo *keiretsu* was organized around the Sumitomo Bank, Ltd., which was the world's second-largest bank (in
terms of profitability), and Sumitomo Corp., the second-largest
diversified trading company in the world. The Sumitomo
guruupu, or group, included such well-known affiliates as:
Sumitomo Electric Industries Ltd. (Japan's largest manufacturer of electric wires and cables); NEC Corp. (one of the
world's top manufacturers of semiconductors); Sumitomo
Chemical Co. Ltd. (Japan's third-largest chemical manufacturer); and Sumitomo Rubber Industries, Ltd. (one of the
world's largest tire manufacturers).

Sumitomo's business interests in the early 1990s focused on
metals (about 38 percent of annual revenues), machinery (about
31 percent of annual revenues), and chemicals and fuels (about
15 percent of annual sales). Other interests extended to motor
vehicles (under the Mazda and Nissan labels), media, real
estate, insurance, textiles, and foodstuffs. Although such massive business concerns typically developed reputations for be-

ing impersonal, Sumitomo has historically shown concern for
the well-being of employees and customers. In 1994, Sumitomo
Corporation President Tomiichi Akiyama's letter to shareholders reemphasized that consideration: ''Valuing our customers' trust above all, and with foresight, flexibility, and an
entrepreneurial spirit, we will deal with the changing times.''
The Sumitomo companies adhered closely to basic principles of
conduct in which harmony and patriotism were emphasized.

The ''spiritual pillar'' of the Sumitomo Corporation was
Masatomo Sumitomo, the first head of the family and founder
of the business. He was born just north of Kyoto in 1585 and
became a Buddhist priest. At the age of 45 he opened a small
medicine and book shop called the Fujiya. There he established
a set of highly moralistic principles for conducting business
which were passed down through subsequent generations to
form the basis for the modern Sumitomo company charter.

Since Masatomo's marriage had produced no sons, his brother-
in-law Riemon Soga was adopted into the family. Masatomo
and Riemon were also related by a common lineage to the noble
Heike family. When Masatomo died in 1652, Riemon Soga
became head of the House of Sumitomo. As a young man,
Riemon worked as an apprentice in a copper refinery. In 1590,
at 18, he opened his own shop in Kyoto called the Izumiya,
literally the ''Fountainhead Shop.'' For the company's logo he
adopted the *igeta,* the ancient character for ''well frame.''
Twentieth-century annual reports noted that the character
''symbolizes the fresh, sparkling water gushing from a fountainhead, which forms a mighty river and finally flows into the
vast ocean.'' The *igeta* would become a metaphor for Sumitomo's own growth over the ensuing centuries.

Japanese refineries at this time lacked the technology to remove
small, naturally occurring quantities of gold and silver from
copper. These precious metals were sold to foreign traders as
copper and were later extracted overseas at a great profit.
Riemon Soga, however, learned about a refining procedure used
by the foreigners (who were called *nanban-jin,* or ''southern
barbarians'') which involved adding lead to molten copper and
smelting with charcoal to remove silver from copper, and later
lead from silver. This method, known as *nanban-buki,* made
Riemon and the Izumiya very successful. Contrary to what may
have been expected of an entrepreneur, Soga unselfishly
instructed his competitors in the *nanban-buki* method.

When Riemon Soga died in 1636, the Izumiya passed to his
second son, Chubei. His first son, Tomomochi, married
Masatomo's daughter and was adopted by the Sumitomo family. He established a separate copper refinery and crafting shop
which was also named Izumiya.

At the age of 16 Tomomochi moved his business from Kyoto to
Osaka, which was recovering from damage incurred during a
war between Tokugawa and Toyotomi armies. Tomomochi's
competitors welcomed him to Osaka in a demonstration of their
gratitude to his father. The Izumiya expanded quickly and later
absorbed both the Fujiya and the original Izumiya operated by
his brother. By the time of Tomomochi's death in 1662, the
Izumiya in Osaka had become the center of the Japanese copper
industry.

Tomomochi's fifth son, Tomonobu, became the third head of the Sumitomo family at the age of 15. In 1680 he gained permission from the Tokugawa Shogunate to rehabilitate the Yoshioka Copper Mine, which had been worked to exhaustion over a period of centuries. Shortly after Sumitomo commenced revitalization of the Yoshioka mine in 1684, it was discovered that Tomonobu's younger brother Tomosada had committed several serious errors in the management of the family brokerage house, which subsequently was forced to liquidate. This placed the entire family enterprise in jeopardy and the following year obliged Tomonobu, who was a partner in the brokerage operation, to resign all his posts at the age of only 38. He was succeeded as head of the family by his 15-year old son Tomoyoshi. The Izumiya endured several more years of hardship, but eventually recovered. In the meantime, restoration of the Yoshioka site continued.

In June of 1690 the manager of the Yoshioka mine, Jyuemon Tamuke, was approached by a man from the island of Shikoku who quite unexpectedly confided in Jyuemon that he had discovered a promising rock formation on the side of the mountain opposite the Tatsukawa Copper Mine, where he was employed as a miner. An expedition was ordered to investigate the area. The results immediately convinced the Sumitomo family to apply to the Shogunate for permission to mine the site, called Besshi. A permit was granted the following May, and digging commenced in December. Despite a fire in 1694 which claimed the lives of 133 people, Besshi was ambitiously developed and over the next one hundred years produced more copper than any other mine.

The Besshi and Tatsukawa mines continued to operate on both faces of the same mountain but were prevented from coordinating their operations because the Shogunate was opposed to giving one family control over such a large natural resource. In 1749 representatives from both mines convinced the government that the failing Tatsukawa mine could only remain viable if it was placed under Sumitomo management. By 1762 Tatsukawa was again faced with closure unless its operations were fully integrated with Besshi. That year the government permitted the Sumitomo family to purchase the mine.

During the next century the Sumitomo family remained involved in a variety of business activities. The primary trade, around which all other ventures revolved, was copper production. While the Sumitomos' wealth increased, no innovations were made in the smelting process and no real business acumen was displayed. The Besshi mine became a liability, dependent on government subsidies. In 1867 the family business was renamed Sumitomo Honten (head office) and designated as the central office for all Sumitomo activities.

During 1865 armed forces of the Choshu clan initiated a military campaign against the Tokugawa government, with whom the Sumitomo family had cultivated close ties. Despite its relationship with the Tokugawa Shogunate, the Besshi subsidies were suspended and the Sumitomo family was ordered to remit substantial amounts of money in war taxes to help fund government counteroffensives. Three years later the Choshu were joined by the Tosa and Satsuma clans, and together they succeeded in overthrowing the Shogunate and restoring the Meiji Emperor.

In the process, the Besshi mine was sealed by Tosa forces and the Sumitomo copper warehouses at Osaka were occupied by the Satsuma. Saihei Hirose, who had just been appointed general manager of the Besshi mine, met with the leader of the Tosa forces, Ganyemon Kawada (later president of the Bank of Japan). He persuaded Kawada to evacuate the Sumitomo properties after convincing him that the family unwillingly supported the Shogunate.

Still, the company was in very poor financial condition. The defeated warlords of the Shogunate defaulted on loans from the Sumitomo financial office, and the currencies it held greatly decreased in value. In addition, the Besshi mine had degenerated to the point where it was nearly unworkable. At this point there was strong pressure from within the family to sell the mine.

Hirose was determined to rehabilitate the Besshi mine. He secured new sources of food for the employees, constructed new housing, and even established a day care center. After he settled an ownership dispute with the government, Hirose proceeded with the modernization of the mine. Hirose managed to obtain numerous loans which required him to mortgage most of the family's property. In 1873 he hired a French engineer named Louis Larroque to prepare a study on Besshi with recommendations for its modernization. Hirose did not extend Larroque's two-year contract, but instead sent two of his own employees to Europe to study French methods of mining and metallurgy.

Hirose introduced a number of technological innovations to Japanese mining in 1880, including the use of dynamite and jackhammers. He purchased a steam-powered ship and train engine, and incorporated the substitution of coke for charcoal in the smelting process. He established his own sales and supply branches, including an export office. Large areas of woodland were purchased for lumber, and a machine manufacturing and repair shop was established. The productivity of the Besshi mine rose quickly; annual copper production increased from 420 tons in 1868 to over 1800 tons in 1888.

Saihei Hirose was regarded as the most important figure in Sumitomo's modern history. In addition to being given credit for saving the family enterprise, he successfully asserted the independence of the business from the government and contributed greatly to the development and growth of Osaka. He retired in 1894 and died 20 years later at the age of 86.

Hirose was replaced by his nephew, Teigo Iba, who continued to emphasize the modernization of Besshi, but also advocated the diversification of the Sumitomo family enterprise. Iba formalized the family banking operations in 1895 when he established the Sumitomo Bank.

Iba stepped down in 1904, proclaiming that only younger, more dynamic managers possessed the imagination and courage to implement new strategies and take risks. He was succeeded by Masaya Suzuki, who led the company until his death in 1922. During his tenure Sumitomo was reorganized as a limited partnership, and renamed Sumitomo So-Honten in 1921. Suzuki also re-emphasized Masatomo's founding precepts of moralistic and trustworthy conduct. He was remembered as a highly principled manager who expected nothing less than strict adherence to ethical business practices.

Between 1922 and 1930 two more men served briefly as the top executive, Kinkichi Nakata and Kanchiki Yukawa. During their leadership Sumitomo branched out into several more fields with the creation of new subsidiaries. By this time Sumitomo had grown to become one of Japan's largest industrial concerns. It was one of the country's few but powerful *zaibatsu,* or "money cliques," which emerged after the Meiji Restoration. Unlike the other *zaibatsu,* Mitsui, Mitsubishi, and Furukawa, Sumitomo did not become involved in the purchase of high-growth "model" industries which were established by the Meiji government and later turned over to private enterprise. Sumitomo's prominence had been gained purely on the virtues of its existing operations.

In 1930 Sumitomo appointed Masatune Ogura to serve as director general. He supervised the company's incorporation as Sumitomo Honsha (trading company), Ltd. in 1937. But his 11 years as chief executive were complicated by right-wing nationalists operating within the military. They gained influence in Japanese politics through intimidation and assassination and openly attacked the *zaibatsu* for their preoccupation with self-interest and "lack of sympathy" for the masses. However, of the *zaibatsu,* Sumitomo was spared most often from militarist terrorism. Whatever his political beliefs, Ogura was drafted into the militarist government in 1941 to serve as a cabinet minister.

Later that year Japan began a full-scale war of conquest in Asia aimed at establishing a regional economic order centered around Japan. For Sumitomo's new chairman, Shunnosuke Furuta, it was an extremely difficult period. He was required to make special efforts in order to keep the company's various divisions together; the unusual circumstances of war had forced Sumitomo's subsidiaries to adopt a more autonomous, presidential form of management. Additionally, the company and its 200,000 employees were not fully prepared for the wartime mobilization.

Japan's fortunes in World War II began to change during 1942. Within the year American bombers were within range of targets on the Japanese mainland. Since Sumitomo was a large industrial concern, and therefore essential to the Japanese military, its factories were exposed to frequent bombings. When the war ended in September of 1945, virtually all of Japan's industrial capability had been destroyed.

Japan was placed under the administration of a military occupation authority called SCAP, an acronym for the Supreme Commander of Allied Powers. SCAP imposed a variety of American-style commercial laws, including an anti-monopoly law, which mandated the complete dissolution of all *zaibatsu.* Despite strong criticism from some quarters, Shunnosuke Furuta complied with the edict and supervised the breakup of the Sumitomo Honsha, or parent company, into several fully independent firms, all of which were forbidden to use the *igeta* logo.

In the following months thousands of Japanese citizens, including Sumitomo employees who were posted overseas, returned to Japan. It was extremely demoralizing for those who had been fortunate enough to avoid areas of battle. Furuta worked very hard to ensure that all his employees could remain employed and healthy.

The *Honsha* was reorganized in November of 1945. Furuta made the difficult decision to set the company on a new course of business. Under its new name, the Nihon Kensetsu Sangyo, Ltd., was established as a general trading company, or *sogo shosha.*

In the years following World War II, particularly during the Korean War, the restrictive commercial laws were gradually relaxed. The former Sumitomo companies began to establish affiliations through the Sumitomo Bank and limited cross-ownership of stock. The *igeta* came back into use and a monthly meeting, the *Hakusui-kai,* or "White Water Club," was established so that the individual heads of the affiliated Sumitomo companies could coordinate business strategies. This did not, however, mark the reformation of the *zaibatsu,* which had a more disciplined, autocratic management style.

On June 1, 1952, the company officially changed its name to Sumitomo Shoji Kaisha, literally the "Sumitomo Commercial Affairs Company." It became the trading house for the various Sumitomo affiliated companies at a time when Japan was experiencing a period of phenomenal economic growth. As Japan grew in economic importance, Sumitomo Shoji established a number of foreign offices. Products handled by the company soon included iron and steel, non-ferrous metals, electrical and industrial equipment, chemicals, textiles, fuel, agricultural and marine products, and real estate. Sales transactions rose from $254 million in 1955 to $2.3 billion in 1965, then to over $26 billion in 1975, and reached nearly $74 billion by 1985.

The *keiretsu* organizational scheme emerged from this phenomenal growth, which was accompanied by an accumulation of debt. Majority holdings of virtually all affiliates were maintained within the *keiretsu,* thereby preventing hostile takeovers when share prices of a given member slipped dangerously low. If, for instance, Sumitomo Heavy Industries was in danger of being purchased by a competitor, the affiliated Sumitomo companies would collectively refuse to sell their controlling interest.

Sumitomo's fortunes, as well as the Japanese economy, declined in the late 1980s and early 1990s. Falling demand in Sumitomo's all-important metals and chemicals sectors combined with a "strong-yen recession" to effect steady revenue shortfalls—from ¥20 trillion in 1991 to ¥17 trillion in 1994. After four years of sector-leading profits, Sumitomo Bank fell to second place among the world's leaders. Its difficulties included bad loans to affiliate Itoman and to the former Soviet Union that culminated in the 1990 resignation of the bank's chairman.

In spite of such setbacks, the group was able to invest in several promising new ventures in the early 1990s. Media investments captured the most attention, especially a joint cable television venture with America's Tele-Communications, Inc. Other new enterprises included: a chain of Western-style drugstores called TomoD's; marketing of such American clothing brands as Eddie Bauer and Gotcha; creation of a digital communications system in Russia; filmmaking; and environmentally friendly products.

As Sumitomo approached the end of its fourth century in business, it maintained offices in 43 Japanese cities and 93 principal cities worldwide, as well as trading subsidiaries in 60 major cities globally. Its list of principal subsidiaries and associated companies numbered nearly 200.

Principal Subsidiaries: Asahi Breweries, Ltd.; NEC Corp.; Nippon Sheet Glass Co., Ltd.; Sumitomo Bank, Ltd.; Sumitomo Cement Co., Ltd.; Sumitomo Chemical Co., Ltd.; Sumitomo Coal Mining Co., Ltd.; Sumitomo Construction Co., Ltd.; Sumitomo Corp.; Sumitomo Electric Industries, Ltd.; Sumitomo Forestry Co., Ltd.; Sumitomo Heavy Industries, Ltd.; Sumitomo Life Insurance Co.; Sumitomo Light Metal Industries, Ltd.; Sumitomo Marine & Fire Insurance Co., Ltd.; Sumitomo Metal Industries, Ltd.; Sumitomo Metal Mining Co., Ltd.; Sumitomo Realty & Development Co., Ltd.; Sumitomo Rubber Industries, Ltd.; Sumitomo Trust & Banking Co., Ltd.; Sumitomo Warehouse Co., Ltd.

Further Reading:

"The Mighty Keiretsu," *Industry Week,* January 20, 1992, pp. 52–54.
Neff, Robert, "For Bankrupt Companies, Happiness Is a Warm Keiretsu," *Business Week,* October 26, 1992, pp. 48–49.
Young, Alexander, *The Soga Shosha: Japan's Multinational Trading Company,* Boulder, Colorado: Westview Press, 1979.

—updated by April Dougal Gasbarre

SunAmerica Inc.

1 SunAmerica Center
Century City
Los Angeles, California 90067-6022
U.S.A.
(310) 772-6000
Fax: (310) 772-6564

Public Company
Incorporated: 1890 as Sun Life Insurance Company
Employees: 1,000
Total Assets: $13.39 billion
Stock Exchanges: New York
SICs: 6311 Life Insurance; 6282 Investment Advice; 6719
    Holding Companies, Not Elsewhere Classified

SunAmerica Inc., among the nation's largest life insurers, is also a financial services company, offering retirement planning and savings products as well as retirement annuities. SunAmerica began as a subsidiary of a house building company that sought to diversify its activities and cushion the impact of cyclical financial trends on its business. Over time, SunAmerica evolved from a general life insurance provider to a specialist in retirement planning. In the late 1980s, the company was separated from the home building business, and it grew rapidly as a purely financial business.

The earliest incarnation of SunAmerica was the Sun Life Insurance Company of America, which was founded in 1890 in Baltimore. This company started on the path that led to the formation of SunAmerica on November 19, 1971, when it was purchased by the Kaufman and Broad Building Company. Kaufman and Broad had been started in 1957 by Eli Broad, who joined with Detroit-area builder Donald Kaufman to form a housing construction firm. Kaufman and Broad prospered during the 1960s boom years in the housing market, and by the end of the decade, the company was looking for ways to diversify its operations and protect itself from downswings in the volatile housing market. In addition to its life insurance operations, Kaufman and Broad also operated its own financial services company, which provided funds for mortgages for buyers of Kaufman and Broad homes.

In 1973, two years after Kaufman and Broad purchased Sun Life, Eli Broad left the company. He returned, however, in 1975, after the crash of the housing market in the previous year

threatened the survival of the company. In August of that year, as Kaufman and Broad's building operations struggled to regain profitability, Sun Life pulled out from a $38 million bid to buy the Colonial Life Insurance Company from the Chubb Corporation. Sun abandoned its offer to take over Colonial, which specialized in policies for low-income families, after the company's six-month profit dropped from $1.8 million to $277,000, indicating that the business was in a severe slump.

Despite this setback, however, Kaufman and Broad persevered in its attempt to diversify more fully into the financial services industry in the late 1970s. In February 1978, the company purchased 79 percent of the Coastal States Corporation, which owned the Coastal States Life Insurance Company, based in Atlanta, for $17.9 million. Three months later, Kaufman and Broad completed its acquisition of the company, bringing the price to $23 million.

Kaufman and Broad saw its life insurance operations as a synergistic partner to its building business, which was highly susceptible to the vicissitudes of the financial markets. "Life insurance is the perfect complement to our housing operations," Broad told *Business Week* the following year, adding that "When interest rates are high, the life insurance operations can [invest premiums collected] in higher yields for long periods."

In addition to its purchase of Coastal States, Kaufman and Broad actively sought other life insurance properties. The company planned to double the values of the policies it had written from 1979 to 1983, hoping to attain a level of $7 billion. To reach that goal, Kaufman and Broad intended to concentrate their insurance efforts on the southeastern United States, where the population was growing rapidly. In addition, the company planned to market products for newly emerging demographic sectors of the population, such as working women.

In May 1980, Kaufman and Broad was once again frustrated in its attempts to expand insurance holdings through acquisitions, when it made a hostile bid to take over the Standard Life Insurance Company of Indiana. Although Kaufman and Broad already owned 4.1 percent of Standard's stock and had a commitment to purchase an additional 7.8 percent, the company was beaten out by the INA Corporation, a financial services conglomerate based in Philadelphia, which bid $5 more for Standard's stock.

In June 1980, however, Kaufman and Broad tried again, paying $16 million for a one-quarter interest in the Biscayne Federal Savings and Loan Association, based in Miami. This move partially satisfied the company's goal of diversifying into the thrift industry. Unfortunately, however, the moment that Kaufman and Broad chose to enter this field couldn't have been less auspicious, as the thrift collapsed in 1982. "Our timing was impeccably bad," Broad told *Forbes,* and Kaufman and Broad was forced to write off its $18 million investment in the savings and loan after its portfolio of mortgage loans went bad.

Despite this setback, the contribution made by financial services to Kaufman and Broad's bottom line continued to grow throughout the early 1980s. In 1983, Sun Life inaugurated an annuity marketing division, as the company began to shift its emphasis toward retirement savings plans. "We don't want hot annuity money that can get in and go out as rates go up or down,'' Broad told *Forbes,* explaining the company's new direction. Rather, he asserted, ''We want it to be serious retirement money that is going to persist.'' In this way, the company hoped that the stability of this business would offset the vicious cycles that beset its housing operations.

In addition, Kaufman and Broad hoped to tap into the same demographic segment of the population with which it had first grown to prominence. After building houses for the generation of ''baby boomers'' throughout the 1960s and 1970s, the company now hoped to help them prepare for retirement by offering tax-deferred savings products. As a vast portion of the American populace approached old age, demand for these retirement investment instruments was expected to increase markedly. ''We served them [the baby boomers] with their first home,'' Broad told *Business Week,* ''and now, 30 years later, we're helping them plan for retirement.''

To create a financial services company specializing in retirement planning, Kaufman and Broad instituted a practice of ''cherry-picking,'' that is, choosing the parts of other bankrupt financial institutions that had money-making potential. Using this philosophy, the company made a series of acquisitions from other struggling companies, often acquiring assets at bargain-basement prices.

In 1985, Kaufman and Broad made its first major advance into the annuity business, when it paid $16 million for $550 million worth of annuities owned by Capital Life Insurance Company, a struggling Denver firm. Although Kaufman and Broad had the right to purchase all of Capital's business, the company was careful to take on only the aspects of its portfolio that it regarded as sound. By fiscal 1985, life insurance revenues accounted for 54 percent of the company's overall sales, beating out Kaufman and Broad's housing revenues for the first time.

In January 1986, Kaufman and Broad agreed to purchase the bankrupt Anchor National Life Insurance Company of Phoenix, with assets of $1.6 billion. With this move, Kaufman and Broad entered the variable annuity market for the first time. In addition, the company purchased Anchor National Financial Services, Inc., an affiliated broker-dealer. Kaufman and Broad paid the Washington National Corporation $75 million for the properties. Anchor promised to add $180 million a year to its parent's life insurance revenues.

Kaufman and Broad also sought to enhance its insurance portfolio by purchasing the insurance policies issued by a failed insurer, Baldwin-United. This company had invested the premiums paid by its retirement annuities customers in other businesses it owned, and had, as a result, been shut down by insurance regulators in Indiana and Arkansas, where the company operated. Although other members of the insurance industry, led by the Metropolitan Life Insurance Company, had put together a plan to purchase the annuities and rescue the victimized customers of Baldwin, Kaufman and Broad's Sun Life Group of America stepped in with a bid at the last minute, in an effort to win the remains of the defunct company and thereby double the size of its insurance business at half the cost of developing the business from scratch.

This bid was rejected by the courts in Indiana in April 1986, but the company persisted in its bid for $3.2 billion worth of business based in Arkansas, forming an Arkansas subsidiary to handle the matter in an effort to curry favor with Arkansas insurance regulators. Kaufman and Broad hoped not only to win new business for their insurance subsidiary, but to further insulate their company from the volatile interest rate cycle that plagued its housing operations, by now limited to California and France. Annuity premiums were particularly valuable in this respect, since they were invested in government securities and high-quality utility and corporate bonds. Unfortunately Kaufman and Broad failed in its attempt to win the Arkansas Baldwin business.

In 1987, however, Kaufman and Broad succeeded in enhancing its insurance business when it bought the First SunAmerican Life Insurance Company, based in New York. Following this purchase, the company began to streamline its life insurance activities, withdrawing from all mortality-based life insurance activities over the course of an 18-month period, in order to get into the faster-growing single premium annuity business. As part of this program, Kaufman and Broad sold its interest in the Coastal States Life Insurance Company, and the annual premium universal life insurance business of its Anchor subsidiary in 1987. Instead, Kaufman and Broad bought the Harris Annuity company, Harris Financial, Inc., and the Financial Network Marketing Company. At the end of the year, Kaufman and Broad's financial services companies once again accounted for more than half of the company's revenues.

In 1988, Kaufman and Broad continued to restructure its financial holdings. The company sold its interest in the Universal Guaranty Life Insurance Company, Anchor's term life insurance subsidiary, and Sun Life's Career Division for $111 million. Because of the costs of these adjustments, however, Kaufman and Broad's life insurance operations lost money over the course of 1988.

At the end of that year, distressed about the low value of his company in the stock market, Eli Broad came out of retirement for the second time to take control of the company that bore his name. On December 5, 1988, Kaufman and Broad unveiled a new plan to make the most of the company's assets. The company announced that it would sell off its housing operations and rename the remaining financial properties—which would remain in the hands of Eli Broad—Broad, Inc. In this way, the company would present to the stock market two single-activity companies, rather than one company that had operations in two very diverse areas. In addition, Kaufman and Broad hoped to move its new financial services company into mutual funds, consumer finance, and the savings and loan industry, despite its last disastrous brush with thrifts. All in all, the company hoped to double its level of assets in the next five years and thereby revive its sagging fortunes.

In March 1989, Kaufman and Broad completed its corporate transformation. The home-building property was separated from the financial services company, which retained assets of $7 billion. The new company marketed a variety of financial instruments under the name SunAmerica. Within six months, this move had proved profitable, as Broad, Inc. doubled its stock price and improved its stock rating by six levels.

In mid-1989, Broad was able to increase its mutual fund sales force through the purchase of the bankrupt Southmark company, an organization of 1,300 brokers. In late September, the company moved further in its effort to restructure, selling Sun Life's General Agency Division for $28 million.

In January 1990, Broad took another important step in its transformation when it bought $2.2 billion in annuities, $1.75 billion in private accounts and a mutual fund, and a broker/dealer with 3,000 representatives from Integrated Resources, Inc., acquiring $4 billion in assets for $95 million. Integrated had originally acquired these properties from the Capital Life Insurance Company of Denver, which Kaufman and Broad had earlier bought part of as well. Because Integrated was on the verge of bankruptcy and did in fact expire in the wake of the sale to Broad, this move initially depressed the price of the company's stock, but it expanded Broad's portfolio from $7 billion to $11 billion and enabled the company to add mutual funds, investment counseling, retirement trust services, and a second broker-dealer organization. In this way, Broad was able to better position itself within the fast-growing financial planning market.

In 1991, Broad continued to enhance its operations in the retirement planning field. The company acquired a second group of struggling mutual funds and another distribution arm for these funds from the bankrupt Equitec Financial Group for $680 million, as it moved towards its goal of a dominant place in the single-premium annuity industry. By July 1991, Broad's assets in insurance and mutual funds had increased to $13 billion.

In 1993, Broad once again changed its name, seeking to unify its corporate and marketing aspects. The company now became SunAmerica, Inc. After a number of successful stock offerings, SunAmerica had amassed $800 million, sufficient funds to pay for further acquisitions. In June 1993, the company announced that it would put these funds to work by buying a one-third stake in the successor to a bankrupt Los Angeles insurer, the Executive Life Insurance Company. This was, in effect, a consolation prize, after SunAmerica lost out in its October 1991 attempt to be awarded the company's assets by the California insurance regulator. Despite this setback, however, SunAmerica's assets had increased to $17 billion and its stock price had risen from $3 a share to $28 a share by the middle of 1993.

In July 1993, SunAmerica returned, in a limited fashion, to the business it had left just four years ago, announcing that it would develop, with a partner, 1,200 homesites in Phoenix, Arizona. This real estate venture was designed to complement the company's other investment instruments.

In addition, SunAmerica embarked on a program to push its number of broker/dealers, or "financial planners," who sold its various investment products, to 5,000 before the end of 1995. This work force had reached 4,000 by the middle of 1994, as the company became the second largest financial planning vendor, after American Express, with an asset total of $23 billion.

Along with an expansion in its sales force, SunAmerica also planned to introduce new financial products and services and to inaugurate alliances with banks, which could market these instruments. The company also planned to acquire further properties in the mutual fund field to strengthen its offerings in that area. These plans came as SunAmerica completed a four-year period in which the company's operating income had more than doubled. With a record of strong growth behind it, and an ever-growing market to look forward to, SunAmerica appeared to be well-situated for continued expansion and success in the late 1990s.

Principal Subsidiaries: SunAmerica Asset Management Corporation; SunAmerica Corporation; Sun Life Insurance Company of America; Anchor National Life Insurance Company; Royal Alliance Associates, Inc.; Resources TrustCompany; First SunAmerica Life Insurance Company; Anchor National Financial Services, Inc.; SunAmerica Securities, Inc.

Further Reading:

Barrett, Amy, "Still Dealing After All These Years," *Business Week,* March 29, 1993.
Heins, John, "The Virtues of Restraint," *Forbes,* June 2, 1986.
Laderman, Jeffrey M., "Two Life Insurers Fight Over Baldwin-United's Remains," *Business Week,* April 28, 1986.
"Sawing Off Markets and Diversifying Faster," *Business Week,* October 29, 1978.
Schifrin, Andrew, "Cherry-Picking," *Forbes,* July 8, 1991.
Toy, Stewart, "Eli Broad Moves Away From Home," *Business Week,* December 19, 1989.

—Elizabeth Rourke

SunGard Data Systems Inc.

1285 Drummers Lane
Wayne, Pennsylvania 19087-1586
U.S.A
(610) 341-8851
Fax: (610) 341-8739

Public Company
Incorporated: 1982
Employees: 2,300
Sales: $381.4 million
Stock Exchanges: NASDAQ London
SICs: 7373 Computer Integrated Systems Design; 7374 Data
Processing and Preparation

SunGard Data Systems Inc. is one of the largest firms in the information services industry and is a leading provider of disaster recovery services, proprietary investment management software, and data processing services. SunGard's predecessor, Sun Information Systems, pioneered the development of disaster recovery services for banks and other companies that relied heavily on computers for daily operations. The company's investment management software systems are designed for trust and investment accounting, securities trading and accounting, portfolio management, employee benefit plan management and international banking. SunGard also provides remote access data processing and automated mailing services.

SunGard began as a subsidiary of the oil giant Sun Co. In the mid-1970s, Sun Information Services (SIS) had served as the data processing arm of Sun Co. and also provided data processing services to companies in the greater Philadelphia area. As Sun's business became increasingly dependent on the use of computers, SIS President John Ryan noted that the company could lose up to $3 million by the third day if its computer system failed. His division developed a disaster contingency plan for Sun, in which daily transactions were recorded on backup tapes and stored at an off-site area. Should Sun's mainframe computer fail, these could then be loaded into an alternate mainframe and business could continue running as usual.

In 1978, SIS received a request for a proposal from a group of Philadelphia businesses searching for a similar disaster recovery system. Based on its own program, SIS then presented itself as a "commercial hot site vendor," offering subscriptions to data storage and emergency off-site data processing on an IBM

370/158 mainframe computer. According to the program, should a disaster prevent a subscriber from accessing its computer system, SIS would load the subscriber's back-up data into its system and allow access to its computers so that business could begin running as usual the next day. SIS won the contract and immediately began soliciting subscriptions from other businesses. Within the first year, 80 companies had subscribed to the service. By 1980, SIS had 110 subscribers, each paying between $3,500 and $12,000 per month for services.

In the late 1970s, having diversified into several non-oil related businesses, Sun Co. maintained four computer-related subsidiaries—SunGard Services Co., Applied Financial Systems Inc., Catallactics Corp., and NMF Inc.—in addition to SIS. When oil prices hit $30 a barrel in the early 1980s, Sun decided to spin off a number of its subsidiaries and asked SIS president Ryan to search for potential buyers. Convinced that SIS and these four companies could form a profitable business, Ryan and a group of venture capitalists arranged to purchase an 80 percent share of the five subsidiaries for $19.5 million in cash and notes in 1983.

That proved to be a fortuitous year for the spin-off company. In 1983 the Comptroller of the Currency began requiring national banks to have a testable backup plan should their computer systems fail. SunGard and a rival firm, Comdisco Disaster Recovery Services Inc., were the only two companies in the United States offering emergency backup services. Thanks to the new banking regulations, SunGard's disaster recovery customer base more than doubled to 280 subscribers. Each company paid upwards of $50,000 in subscriptions fees, plus an additional user fee of $25,000 or more for use of SunGard's computer systems. By 1985, disaster recovery services brought in 49 percent of the company's $58.5 million total revenues; financial processing software and services accounted for 47 percent.

In March 1986, the company went public on the NASDAQ exchange under the name SunGard Data Systems Inc. Its disaster recovery services became a wholly owned subsidiary under the name SunGard Recovery Services Inc. The initial public offering raised $23.7 million dollars. SunGard paid its debts to Sun Co. and other venture capital firms that financed the spin-off, reinvesting the remaining $10.2 million. Profits that year totaled $5.5 million, on revenues of $69 million.

During this time, SunGard sought to improve its offerings in the data processing arena, acquiring a total of 27 companies between 1986 and 1994, primarily in the investment support services arena. SunGard made four acquisitions in 1987, the largest of which was Devon Systems International, a provider of software for currency and interest rate options trading, purchased for $20 million in cash, notes, and common stock. That year, profits rose 50 percent to $8.2 million on revenues of $91.1 million. Fifty percent of revenues came from software sales and operation, and 50 percent were attributable to disaster recovery services.

By 1988, SunGard Recovery had "hot sites" in Chicago, San Diego, Philadelphia, St. Paul, and London. That year, the company also began offering downtime services, which allowed customers to cope with lost time caused by more regular computer failures in communications and processor systems. The following year, SunGard entered a joint venture with STM Systems Corp., a Toronto-based firm, to provide disaster recovery services in Canada under the name STM-SunGard Recovery Services.

In 1989, another competitor entered the disaster recovery arena. International Business Machines Corporation (IBM), whose mainframe computers SunGard used to backup client data at its hot sites, began offering backup services for many of its own systems, including System/36, System/38 and AS/400 computers. SunGard issued a press release welcoming IBM's entry into the industry and told *American Banker* that competition with IBM would ''make us a better company.'' At that time, SunGard Recovery and Comdisco had penetrated less than 50 percent of the disaster recovery market. Both believed there was room for a third competitor.

IBM initially captured some big accounts from SunGard's customers who worked with large IBM systems. However, SunGard took measures to prevent further sales erosion, and, by 1991, had curtailed the loss of customers to its new competitor. Despite increased competition, disaster recovery sales grew by over 30 percent in 1990, fueled by the earthquakes that shook California as well as several other natural disasters across the United States. In 1990, company-wide sales hit $262 million, up 59 percent from 1988.

In 1989, SunGard merged with Daytron Corp., a large supplier of bank data processing software, and also purchased Warrington Financial Systems, Inc., a British supplier of bank treasury software, for $65.3 million in cash. Following this acquisition, the company formed a new division, SunGard Financial Systems, which included subsidiaries Warrington, Devon Systems International Inc., Wismer Associates Inc., Money Management Systems Inc. and SunGard Investment Systems Inc. In 1990, SunGard expanded into the securities trading management arena, purchasing Phase3 Systems, Inc., a supplier of ''integrated, real-time securities transaction processing systems for equity and fixed-income instruments'' for undisclosed terms. Phase3 served about 35 corporate customers across the United States.

SunGard's growth in investment support services soon began to outpace its disaster recovery division. In 1991, investment support services brought in approximately 58 percent of the $262 million in sales. Following its long string of mergers and acquisitions, SunGard sought to pare down some of its services, selling its Daytron Mortgage Systems Division to Stockholder Systems Inc. in 1991 for an undisclosed price. It then acquired Shaw Data Services, a top supplier of portfolio management services to banks and other institutional investors., for approximately $35 million. This was all in keeping with what Richard C. Tarbox, vice-president of corporate development, said was SunGard's growth strategy: ''to provide investment support on a service basis . . . [and have] something to offer all managers of money.''

By its tenth anniversary in 1993, SunGard had firmly established itself as leading provider of investment management software and disaster recovery services. That year, SunGard shares began trading on the London Stock Exchange and earnings rose 49 percent from 1992, to $38 million on revenues of $381 million. Astute acquisitions and a solid marketing strategy formed the cornerstone of its growth, and the company seemed well prepared to address an ever-expanding market for its services.

Principal Subsidiaries: Shaw Data Services, Inc.; SunGard Capital Markets Inc.; SunGard Computer Services Inc.; SunGard Financial Systems Inc.; SunGard Investment Systems Inc.; SunGard Mailing Services; SunGard Planning Solutions Inc.; SunGard Recovery Services Inc.; SunGard Shareholder Systems Inc.; SunGard Trust Systems Inc.; SunGard Digital Solutions Inc.; SunGard Business Systems Inc.

Further Reading:

Koselka, Rita, ''Blue-Chip Backup,'' *Forbes,* January 26, 1987, p. 80.
Millman, Joel, ''The Great Escape, *Forbes,* November 11, 1990, p. 234.
Tyson, David O., ''IBM to Compete with Major Vendors in Disaster Recovery Market,'' *American Banker,* April 5, 1989, p. 9.
Zipser, Andy, ''SunGard Shines Again: After a Dull Year, It's Set for Fresh Growth,'' *Barron's News and Investment Weekly,* October 21, 1991, p. 15.

—Maura Troester

Sunrise Medical Inc.

2355 Crenshaw Blvd., #150
Torrance, California 90501
U.S.A.
(310) 328-8018
Fax: (310) 328-8184

Public Company
Incorporated: 1983
Employees: 2,625
Sales: $319 million
Stock Exchanges: New York
SICs: 3842 Surgical Appliances and Supplies; 2599 Furniture
Fixtures, Nec

Sunrise Medical Inc. is the second largest supplier of home health care products in the world, next in sales only to Invacare. The company is the world's leading manufacturer of customized lightweight wheelchairs, and is Invacare's only significant competitor in the market for ultralight sports wheelchairs, designed to be used by disabled individuals in playing tennis, basketball, baseball, competing in marathons, and other rigorous athletic activities. Sunrise manufactures and markets an extremely wide variety of items, including customized manual and electric wheelchairs, patient-room beds, specialty mattresses, and ambulatory safety aids.

Sunrise Medical was founded in 1983 by Richard H. Chandler. Chandler had graduated magna cum laude from Princeton University in 1964, and received an MBA from the University of Chicago in 1966. After graduate school, Chandler worked his way up the management ladder to vice-president of marketing for DeVry, Inc., Bell and Howell Company's education division. Chandler then worked in various management positions at Sara Lee Corporation from 1974 to 1979. In 1979, he became president of Abbey Medical, Inc., one of the leading chains of home health care stores in the United States. One of the original investors who purchased Abbey Medical from Sara Lee Corporation, Chandler and his investment group sold the company in 1981 to American Hospital Supply.

Chandler knew that the population within the United States was aging rapidly and that important changes were on the horizon for government health care reimbursement programs such as Medicare. He was also aware that there was a growing demand for wheelchairs and home health care products that would only grow in the future. Recognizing that no one company was dominating the health care product market, Chandler decided to start his own firm. On January 18, 1983, Chandler incorporated his company under the name Sunrise Medical Inc., with an initial capitalization of $50,000. During the spring of that year, Chandler arranged lines of credit at various banking institutions and raised supplementary venture capital. On May 1, Sunrise opened for business, and ten days later the company not only held its first meeting of the board of directors but received notification of a $5 million additional investment in venture capital.

With the new investment, Chandler purchased five medical equipment companies over a three month period: Joerns, Trans-Aid, A-BEC Mobility, BEC Mobility from the United Kingdom, and Guardian products. A management team, salesforce, and distribution network were set in motion, and the company began selling the home care products of its acquisitions. In November, Sunrise raised approximately $11 million in an initial public offering as its stock began trading on the NASDAQ exchange. In June of 1984, at the end of its first fiscal year, Sunrise reported earnings of $1.6 million on revenues of $52 million.

In the mid-1980s, Sunrise continued to expand through acquisitions. In August of 1984, the company acquired American-based Tru-Trac Therapy Products and its British affiliate, manufacturers of physical therapy equipment such as treatment tables and traction machines. In April of 1985, Sunrise bought W. R. Breen Company, a manufacturer of seat lift chairs, along with its affiliate located in Ontario, Canada. This Canadian acquisition was rechristened Sunrise Medical Canada, and a salesforce was quickly formed to market all the company's products in the country. In August the company purchased Bio-Clinic, a hospital products company well known as a supplier of foam mattress overlays. In October, Sunrise acquired NTRON, a maker of electric therapy devices; in November, the company purchases J. E. Nolan, a producer of bath tub and swimming pool seats; and in December, it acquired a British manufacturer of motorized stair lifts, Minivator Ltd.

Other acquisitions included Walton Manufacturing, a producer of fitness products for home health care dealers; Motion Designs, a manufacturer of lightweight manual wheelchairs; MAI Inc., a maker of rowers and treadmills for disabled people; and Safety Rehab, a builder of pediatric wheelchairs. Sunrise management established a comprehensive system of bookkeeping, inventory control, and product coordination to fold these companies into its framework. Sunrise now functioned like a mini-conglomerate, with economies of scale and an expanding marketing and sales force.

Despite all the new products lines incorporated into the company, Sunrise profits began to fall precariously in 1986. Freedom Technology, a direct marketing unit previously created to sell electric scooters, suffered continuous losses and its operations were closed. When the company's other operating divisions experienced decreasing profits on revenues of $140 million for the fiscal year of 1986, Chandler decided to do two things: establish a sales and distribution operation in Germany to take advantage of the growing European market for home health care products, and travel to Japan in order to learn about their ideas on managerial and corporate success.

While attending a trade show in Japan, Chandler devoted a large amount of time to visiting companies such as Toyota and Matsushita and studying Japanese management style. When he returned to the United States, Chandler implemented the lessons he had learned. He quickly put a halt on the company's acquisition strategy, sold non-performing acquisitions, divisions, and product lines, and reorganized the Sunrise employees into autonomous, self-directed teams. He revised the company's procedure on inventory control, keeping only those parts required for the day's production and shipping the product to dealers and customers as soon as it was completed. Chandler also initiated an 18-month period of restructuring and consolidation. Nolan and Trans-Aid were subsumed under Guardian, while Sunrise Medical Ltd. incorporated Minivator. Motion Designs was renamed Quickie Designs and established its own marketing and salesforce.

The most important changes at Sunrise, however, involved the creation of a unique corporate culture. The Sunrise Pursuit of Excellence Program encouraged a relation between employer and employee that dramatically changed the company. To reduce waste, Sunrise implemented an idea known as "sharing rallies," where employees on the factory floor are recognized for their suggestions to improve production. If an employee makes a suggestion, then management has to respond within 72 hours and let the employee know what is being done about the suggestion. Sunrise also adopted a statement of Corporate Values espousing such goals as Product Superiority, Service to Customers, Individualism, Teamwork, Performance, Citizenship, and Corporate Character. The description of Corporate Character reads: "We believe that great corporations, like great individuals, always act with integrity and character. When faced with moral choices, they do the right thing."

The pursuit of excellence extended to sales and manufacturing as well. For example, the company discovered that when a medical-supply house phoned to order a product, they had to wait an average of 4½ minutes to place an order. During the time they were on hold, approximately 23 percent of the customers refused to wait and decided to hang up. When Sunrise pushed the hang-up rate down to a mere two percent, its growth rate boomed to 30 percent a year. To increase sales, Sunrise improved its production techniques so that expensive options on wheelchairs, for example, became standard features. The company's most popular wheelchair is offered in a dizzying number of permutations: it is produced in one-inch increments of back height, seat depth, and seat width, just to name a few. Essentially, Sunrise created a customized wheelchair fitted to a user's specific needs and requirements.

Sunrise's reorganization plan continued into 1988. A-BEC Mobility was merged into Quickie Designs and relocated its operations to Fresno, California. Safety Rehab was then subsumed under Quickie as one of its operating divisions. During the summer of that year, Chandler decided to sell the company's holdings in physical therapy and fitness products, including Tru-Trac, Akron, and NTRON. For the fiscal year of 1988, although revenues amounted to $140 million, the company recorded a loss of $10.9 million on discontinued operations.

Nonetheless, the company's five core businesses, Bio-Clinic, Guardian, Quickie, Joerns, and Sunrise Medical Ltd., all posted over $25 million in sales for the year and were recognized as market leaders in their respective fields.

The company's adaptation of Japanese team-building management techniques was most evident in the events of 1989. Chandler started the firm's first "Corporate Growth Conference," which brought together top-level management from sales, marketing, customer service, and product development. The purpose of the conference was to generate new ideas for increasing sales more rapidly. The strategy worked. By the end of fiscal 1989, Sunrise revenues had risen to just over $152 million. During the same year, Sunrise acquired Brentwood Sales, the Canadian distributor of Quickie's wheelchairs, and combined it with Sunrise Medical Canada. The company also purchased the product line of fitness mats from Rib-Cor and subsumed it under Bio-Clinic.

During 1990 and 1991, Sunrise developed long-term strategic plans and more company team-building activities. Each division was required to draw up a plan to clarify its goals until the year 2000, and describe precisely how it would become the global market leader in recovery and rehabilitation products. Part of this long-term strategic planning included securing a $70 million multi-currency bank credit line to prepare for international acquisitions. Another part of it included combining all the company's management, financial, and human resources information systems to assure quicker and more efficient communication for the anticipated growth over the next five years. In the area of team-building, Chandler established awards for exceptional performance and for corporate teamwork in order to encourage and reward employees for their contributions to the company's success. Everything Chandler had done up until this time—from the acquisition strategy to the employee awards—could be described as a foundation for the future.

Sunrise had a watershed year in 1992. In the beginning of the year, Sunrise expanded into Europe with the major acquisitions of Sopur in Germany and Talleres Uribarri in Spain, both wheelchair manufacturers, and the establishment of Sunrise Medical S.A.R.L. in France, and Sunrise Medical B.V. in the Netherlands, both distribution operations. In the United States, additional acquisitions included Hoyer; Dufco Electronics, a firm already supplying Quickie with power controls; Magic in Motion, a specialty wheelchair manufacturer; and RVH, the French distributor of Sopur's wheelchairs. Company revenues shot up to $243 million, a 72 percent rise since 1988, while earnings were reported at over $12 million. During the summer, Sunrise stock was listed on the New York Stock Exchange, and by September its shares underwent a two-for-one split. For its accomplishments, *Forbes* magazine included Sunrise in its list of the top 200 emerging growth companies in the United States.

Sunrise also developed social responsibility programs in 1992. With large amounts of corporate support, Sunrise created the Winners On Wheels (WOW) Foundation, a not-for-profit organization promoting personal growth and development for children in wheelchairs. Sunrise also supported numerous wheelchair marathons across the United States, and sponsored a wheelchair team for the Barcelona Paralympics. For its contributions in the field of social activism, Sunrise was profiled along with 11 other companies in a book entitled *Companies with a Conscience: Intimate Profiles of Twelve Firms that Make a Difference.*

Although all of Sunrise's divisions were growing, Quickie Designs led the company. Quickie introduced its original, U.S.-made power wheelchair in 1990 and since that time has continuously produced more and more innovative wheelchairs. One of its best sellers was the Quickie 2, an aluminum model weighing 25 pounds with a highly functional rear wheel that shifted forward for greater maneuverability in sports, or shifted backward to provide the stability needed for normal wheelchair use. Quickie quickly became the leader in custom-designed wheelchairs made with the most advanced technologies and lightweight materials; with a Quickie wheelchair quadriplegics, ordinarily dependent upon others, were able to operate a power wheelchair by the movement of their head or through breath controls.

In 1991, Quickie acquired the pediatric wheelchair product line from Luconex, and in 1992, it acquired the Shadow athletic equipment product line. The addition of Shadow products gave Quickie access to a whole new market, including bikes, water skis, snow skis, and racing wheelchairs for disabled athletes. In 1992, sales of Quickie power wheelchairs jumped 84 percent, and in 1993 sales climbed 92 percent. With Quickie leading the way, Sunrise's 1992 earnings totaled $14 million on revenues of $244 million, and in 1993 earnings increased slightly while revenues climbed to $319 million.

Sunrise acquired DeVilbiss Health Care, Inc. in 1993 for $130 million. At the time, it was the largest acquisition in the history of the home health care products industry. DeVilbiss manufactured the world's most reliable and best selling compressor nebulizer, the most widely used oxygen concentrator, and was a leading supplier of sleep therapy products. The strategy behind the acquisition was to combine the two companies' international marketing and distribution networks and expand the Sunrise product line in health care recovery and rehabilitation products. Chandler hoped DeVilbiss would help Sunrise become a billion dollar company by the year 2000.

With approximately 50 percent of the market for manual and customized wheelchairs and sales continuing to rise, Sunrise is well on the way to achieving its goal of becoming a billion dollar company. As long as Chandler remains head of Sunrise, cultivating a unique team-building corporate culture, the company can continue to build on its previous success.

Further Reading:

Autry, Ret, "Sunrise Medical," *Fortune,* February 25, 1991, p. 92.
Barrier, Michael, "Re-Engineering Your Company," *Nation's Business,* February 1994.
Hartman, Curtis, "Six Stocks that Will Benefit Your Portfolio and Your Conscience," *Worth Magazine,* December/January 1994.
Jaffe, Thomas, "Will Sunrise also Rise?," *Forbes,* May 13, 1992, p. 152.
Sunrise Medical, *Sunrise Medical: The First Ten Years,* 1993.

—Thomas Derdak

Synopsis, Inc.

700 East Middlefield Road
Mountain Valley, California 94043
U.S.A.
(415) 962-5000
Fax: (415) 965-8637

Public Company
Incorporated: 1986 as Optimal Solutions, Inc.
Employees: 590
Sales: $108 million
Stock Exchanges: NASDAQ
SICs: 7372 Prepackaged Software

Synopsis, Inc. is the leading developer of high-level design automation models and software for designers of integrated circuits and electronic systems. The company is perhaps best known for pioneering the commercial development of synthesis technology, which became the basis of the company's high-level design methodology. Synopsis has subsidiary offices in continental Europe, Japan, and the Pacific Rim.

Beginning in the 1970s, electronic design automation (EDA) software became a key factor in the dramatic advances of the electronics industry. Increasingly complex integrated circuits (ICs) and electronic systems, coupled with a scarcity of qualified IC engineers, created a need for software that could reduce the time to market and product design and development costs, while facilitating the design of reliable, high-speed, high-density ICs.

EDA design methods changed rapidly, with three new generations of enabling technologies. The 1970s brought the first generation of EDA: computer-aided design (CAD). Computer-aided engineering (CAE) was the technology of the 1980s, representing an even greater improvement over the archaic, manual design methods. CAE made great progress in automating the design of complex integrated circuits, but engineers were still spending needless hours connecting the thousands of nodes (or gates) used on silicon chips. CAE could not keep up with the fast-paced changes of the electronics industry, and increasing circuit complexity led to an opening for a third generation design method in the 1980s. It was at the crossroads of the third generation of EDA technology that Synopsis emerged.

Aart de Geus, who led a work team at General Electric Microelectronics Center, developed a set of ideas for a new software technology called Synthesis. With Synthesis, engineers would be able to "write" the functionality of a circuit in computer language, rather than describing it in terms of individual gates. The software would automatically create the logic synthesis, saving design time and freeing engineers to focus on creative design solutions rather than manual implementation. Synthesis would create circuit designs from hardware languages (such as VHDL and, later, Verilog), supporting the new generation of EDA technology, hardware language design automation (HLDA).

In 1986, de Geus and several other engineers received support from General Electric and formed Optimal Solutions, Inc., dedicating themselves to the development of Synthesis software. After building the initial prototype, the company relocated to Mountain View, California, renaming itself Synopsis (SYNthesis OPtimization SYstems). In 1987, EDA entrepreneur Harvey Jones became president and CEO of the company, leaving Daisy Systems, where he had been president, CEO, and co-founder.

From 1986 until 1990, the company focused on becoming "The Synthesis Company," as well as on changing the methodology of modern electronic design. Synopsis quickly jumped to the forefront of top-down design companies, launching an era that would be defined by top-down design. In fact, Synopsis had virtually no competitors in the synthesis market.

Synopsis was successful in marketing its new synthesis technology by demonstrating improved circuit design quality through advances in timing optimization. Sales in the 1980s, and in fact throughout Synopsis's history, demonstrated dramatic increases each year. In 1987, Synopsis's revenues were $130,000. The next year, revenues rose by over 700 percent, to $976,000. An even more dramatic increase occurred in 1989, when revenues skyrocketed by another 700 percent, to $7.3 million. The company entered the 1990s with a 204 percent increase, ending the fiscal year 1990 with $22.1 million in revenues.

Recognition of the vital importance of hardware description languages (HDLs) led the company to broaden its focus in the 1990s. In 1990, Synopsis purchased a VHDL simulator from Zycad Corp. and introduced test synthesis products, anticipating the acceptance of VHDL as the computer language of choice. While other companies had used HDLs, including VHDL, before Synopsis entered the market, usage was primarily to meet Department of Defense documentation regulations. Synopsis offered the first synthesis technology that was well supported and marketed, spawning widespread reliance on HDL as a productivity tool. In 1991, Synopsis ended its fiscal year with a 55 percent increase in sales, and revenues of $40.5 million.

By 1992, Synopsis counted among its customers nine of the top ten computer makers, the top 25 semiconductor companies, and many other prominent businesses. Using synthesis, companies including NCR Corp. cut their custom-chip design time by 30 percent. Synopsis's $50 million operation owned over 75 percent of the logic synthesis tools market, which was EDAs hottest growth area. In 1992 and 1993, Synopsis would introduce both design-for-test products and Design-Ware methodology for smart design reuse.

Although clearly the industry leader, Synopsis faced its first real competitive challenge in 1992. Vantage Analysis Systems, Inc., the leading VHDL simulator vendor, based in Fremont, California, organized an alliance with eight synthesis vendors. Vantage joined broad-based EDA suppliers including Mentor Graphics, Cadence Design Systems, Racal-Redac, and Viewlogic, who purchased synthesis technology in a joint effort to unseat Synopsis as the synthesis market leader. Although Synopsis no longer had a monopoly on the synthesis market, the company remained in control of over 50 percent.

Since capital budgets were loosening and only approximately five percent of electronics designers used HDLs at all in 1992, some companies looked to displace Synopsis. Cadence Design Systems and Mentor Graphics emerged as Synopsis's primary competitors. Both companies possessed greater financial, technical, and marketing resources, as well as larger installed customer bases than Synopsis. Synopsis's profits had fallen sharply, largely due to a five-fold increase in the cost of software license revenues (from $722,000 in fiscal 1990 to $3.6 million in fiscal 1991).

In 1992, Peter Schleider, an analyst with Wessels, Arnold & Henderson, predicted that Synopsis's market share would fall to the 40 percent range, in an interview with *Electronic Business.* Amidst talk that the company might be bought by a larger competitor, Synopsis announced that it would go public in spring of 1992. Synopsis president Harvey Jones announced, in an interview with *Electronic Business,* ''We have no interest in being a tool vendor in someone else's strategy. We feel we can drive a paradigm shift all on our own.''

Three corporate shareholders sold stock in Synopsis's 1992 initial public offering: Harris Corp., Sumitomo Corp., and Zycad. Synopsis was also backed by three venture capital firms, none of whom participated in the stock offering: Oak Hill Investment Partners, investment funds affiliated with Technology Venture Investors, and Merrill, Pickard, Anderson & Eyre IV. Synopsis announced the sale of two million shares of stock, at an initial selling price between $13 and $15 per share. The expected $19.6 million proceeds would be used for working capital and general corporate activity, including strategic acquisitions.

Also during the spring of 1992, Synopsis announced that it would link its suite of high level design tools with Mentor Graphics Corp.'s Falcon framework. This announcement was a surprise to Cadence Design Systems, whose executives had expected their own framework to be chosen for the linkage. According to *Electronic News,* Synopsis's senior product marketing manager, Kevin J. Kranaen, attributed the selection of Mentor's framework over Cadence's to flaws in Cadence's interface, ''based on intermediate files with shallow integration.''

In June 1992, Synopsis introduced yet another breakthrough in synthesis technology: version 3.0 of its synthesis tools. The new tools further accelerated sequential timing of electric circuits, using a path-based timing verifier. Designers could take advantage of the new tools in applying synthesis to increasingly common multi-clock, multi-cycle, and multi-phase communica-

tions designs. In addition, timing-driven design of electronic circuits could be maintained throughout the design process. While other companies owned products capable of sequential design, Synopsis's version 3.0 was the first product that could optimize sequentially in a timing-driven fashion, by manipulating data through a timing verifier.

In September 1992, Synopsis introduced DesignWare, a new product area that would facilitate the ''smart re-use'' of electronic designs through methodologies, tools, and libraries. Synopsis entered into a cooperative agreement with Texas Instruments and Comdisc Systems, using DesignWare to link TI's custom digital signal processing (DSP) architectures to Comdisc's Signal Processing Worksystem. To increase the quality of its customer support, in 1993 Synopsis introduced SOLV-IT!, a 24-hour customer service that combined the company's complete design knowledge database with information retrieval technology.

Synopsis signed on as a supporter of a new initiative sponsored by Cadence in early 1993. The new effort, VHDL Initiative Toward ASIC Libraries (Vital), initially made Synopsis wary, when it seemed that Vital was focused on tying Verilog libraries into the VHDL language. Verilog, a competing hardware description language, was developed by a company that was later acquired by Cadence. Synopsis initially withdrew its support, not wanting to participate in the development of an initiative that could become competitive with its own products. However, it became apparent that support of Vital could promote Synopsis as a leading vendor and that, without Synopsis, Vital would not succeed. In January 1993, Synopsis announced that it would support Vital with technical expertise and experience in ASIC libraries for synthesis, simulation and test tools. This support was provided with the stipulation that the group must encourage the development of a VHDL ASIC library standard.

A new high-level design tool marked the expansion of Synopsis's line of electronic designs in January 1993. The FPGA Compiler was introduced, featuring architecture-specific logic optimization and mapping and state machine optimization to increase performance of FPGA designs. FPGA represented a major growth area for Synopsis, as the complexity and performance requirements of the FPGA marketplace demanded more efficient design methodologies, and only ten to 20 percent of the people who could be using high-level FPGA design tools were actually using them.

Five years after its spinoff from General Electric Co., Synopsis held a 70 percent share of its chief market, specialized software to speed chip design. Synopsis's HLDA software was used by almost every major chip designer, from Intel Corp. to NEC Corp., as well as by such computer makers as Apple, Sun Microsystems, and Sony. In fiscal 1992, Synopsis's sales had skyrocketed, jumping by 56 percent to $63 million. Profits doubled, reaching $7.1 million, and Synopsis's stock closed at 36 and one-half in January of 1993, 50 times its projected 1993 earnings.

One reason for Synopsis's success in fiscal 1992 was a 73 percent increase over the previous year in international revenue. This growth was achieved through two major investments. First, Synopsis restructured its European offices. Continental

Europe was emerging as a center of electronic design, and Synopsis established its European headquarters in Munich, Germany. The company continued to cover the continent with additional offices in France and England. This restructuring allowed Synopsis to secure important contracts in growth industries, including three of its top ten clients. Second, Synopsis acquired an 82 percent interest in its former Japanese distributor, Nihon Synopsis, in July 1992. Synopsis maintained Nihon Synopsis offices in Tokyo and Osaka, along with Asia/Pacific offices in Korea and Taiwan. Moreover, two of Synopsis's top ten clients were located in Japan.

In March 1993, Synopsis filed a lawsuit against Cadence, charging misappropriation of trade secrets in connection with the new Leapfrog VIIDI simulator developed by Cadence. In a related complaint, Synopsis had filed suit against Seed Solutions, Inc., and its co-founders Paul M. Hubbard and Greg M. Ordy. Hubbard and Ordy served as employees of Zycad Corp. and Endot, a company acquired by Zycad, before founding Seed Solutions in 1988. From 1988 to 1990, they worked as consultants to Zycad in developing VIIDI simulation software. In 1990, Zycad sold the rights to simulation software to Synopsis. Synopsis claimed that Hubbard and Ordy had intentionally concealed information and misled Synopsis (and its Zycad subsidiary) about the best path for future software development. The day after Hubbard and Ordy's contract with Synopsis/Zycad was terminated, in October 1990, Seed Solutions had distributed a detailed business plan for Seed Solutions' ''new'' product: VIIDI simulation software which would compete directly with the software Synopsis had purchased from Zycad. In 1992, Cadence acquired the rights to Seed's software, leading to the 1993 lawsuit.

In June 1993, Synopsis joined Sunrise Test Systems in the purchase of a failed company, ExperTest. ExperTest had been founded in 1988, and although its fiscal operations failed, its technological advancements were valuable. In the joint purchase of the automatic test pattern generation (ATPG) technology, both companies integrated the technology into their own design-for-test-product lines.

In November 1993, Synopsis expanded its VIIDI System Simulator (VSS) line, introducing the VSS Professional and the VSS Expert. These products would help system designers reduce the number of simulators used in design creation. Synopsis targeted the VIIDI simulation market as its fastest growing segment. Synopsis identified three factors behind the accelerating sales growth of its simulation products: the market momentum designating VHDL as an industry standard for high-level design, Synopsis's ability to provide increased simulation speed and productivity for all phases of the design process, and the fact that Synopsis's VHDL simulator was the first to achieve application-specific integrated circuit (ASIC) signoff.

Due to both the expansion of its technological focus and the success of its international business in the Japanese market, Synopsis crossed the $100 million mark in sales in fiscal year 1993, closing the year at $108 million (a 71 percent increase over the previous year). In addition, Synopsis almost doubled its cash position between 1992 and 1993.

Synopsis began the new year in 1994 with the acquisition of Logic Modeling, a company that marketed a library of software models for more than 12,0000 commercially available ICs, as well as a line of hardware modeling systems. The acquisition was achieved in March through a stock swap with a value of $116 million and was structured as a pooling of interests. Logic Modeling was established as a ''differentiated business unit'' in Beaverton, Oregon. The relationship was structured as a ten-year partnership with the goal of bridging a developing gap between EDA tools and ASIC process technology.

Later in 1994, Synopsis continued to expand its design re-use operations, acquiring CADIS GmbH of Aachen, Germany, an innovative company specializing in digital signal processing (DSP) design. CADIS was acquired for approximately $4 million, in a strategic move to take Synopsis into the digital signal processing market with second generation technology.

In March 1994, Synopsis signed a marketing deal with Quickturn Design Systems, allowing the companies to jointly design and market products and to provide each other with software to speed product integration. In 1994, Synopsis also began the process of selling its synthesis, VIIDI, simulation, test, and design re-use software and services to Texas Instruments. Another connection was strengthened when Synopsis made it possible for users of Altera's programmable logic devices (PLDs) to use Synopsis's DesignWare and VIIDI System Simulator (VSS). The companies had been working closely together since 1991, with more than 100 mutual clients, but only in 1994 could Altera users perform timing-driven synthesis by specifying clock frequencies and path delays using Synopsis's automation tools.

In what was referred to as the ''Blockbuster Video approach to design tools'' (by Bill Hood, a program manager at Locklead Sanders), Synopsis lent its expertise to a new plan to rent software over the Internet in April 1994. The rental idea was developed to appeal to military contractors who often needed additional capacity during some phases of a project, but for whom purchase of software would be inefficient in the long-term.

Other new developments in 1994 included the announcement of Behavioral Compiler, a synthesis tool that simplified IC design by cutting specification time by five to ten times, allowing designers to use a higher level of programming and facilitating modification and reuse. For the first time, Synopsis announced that bus interface would become available in DesignWare, a kit that can be configured and synthesized into an ASIC design, through an agreement with Intel Corporation to offer Peripheral Component Interconnect (PCI) Local Bus solutions for the systems market.

In the mid-1990s, Synopsis was intent upon establishing itself as a leader in its three technological areas: synthesis, simulation, and test. The company's HLDA tools were marketed to a worldwide network of key accounts and were widely used on UNIX workstations, including Sun Microsystems, Hewlett-Packard, IBM, Digital Equipment Corporation, Solbourne, MIPS, and Sony. Synopsis provided customer service, training, and support as a component of its HLDA offerings. Synopsis had license agreements with over 250 customers, including the world's leading semiconductor, computer, communications, and military and aerospace companies. In addition, Synopsis had invested in developing and maintaining cooperative market development relationships with leading semiconductor vendors worldwide. As electronics technology continued to experience fastpaced advances in the 1990s, Synopsis expected to continue doing what it does best—creating and marketing solutions that allow engineers to maximize their creative time while taking advantage of the latest technology.

Principal Subsidiaries: Synopsis GMBH; Synopsis (Northern Europe) Ltd.; Synopsis SARL; Nihon Synopsis K.K.; Synopsis Korea, Inc.; Synopsis International, Inc.; Synopsis Technology, Inc.

Further Reading:

Dorsch, Jeff, "Synopsis Sues Cadence Design over VHDL Flap," *Electronic News,* March 15, 1993, p. 4.

Dorsch, Jeff, "Synopsis in $116M Deal to Buy Logic Modeling," *Electronic News,* January 10, 1994, pp. 1, 21.

"Entire Synopsis Line Supports Altera PLDs," *Electronic News,* April 11, 1994, p. 46.

Hof, Robert D., "Chip-Design Shortcuts are Synopsis' Long Suit," *Business Week,* January 25, 1993, p. 93.

"LSI Logic, Synopsis Spurred by User Integrations," *Electronic News,* May 2, 1994, p. 56.

"Quickturn, Synopsis Sign Marketing Deal," *Electronic News,* March 7, 1994, p. 22.

"Sequential Timing Version Added to Synopsis Tool Line," *Electronic News,* June 22, 1992, p. 20.

"Synopsis Endorses ASIC Initiative," *Electronic News,* January 11, 1993, p. 10.

"Synopsis Introduces FPGA Design Tool," *Electronic News,* January 18, 1993, p. 10.

"Synopsis Joins RASSP; Will Rent Software," *Electronic News,* April 25, 1994, p. 44.

"Synopsis Set to Buy Logic Modeling," *Electronic News,* January 10, 1994, p. 21.

"Synopsis Software Recycles Design Elements," *Electronic News,* September 21, 1992, p. 18.

"Synopsis, Sunrise Buy ExperTest Tech," *Electronic News,* June 7, 1993, p. 12.

"Synopsis Surprises Cadence, Picks Mentor for High-End Link," *Electronic News,* April 27, 1992, p. 15.

"Synopsis Tries to Stay #1 with IPO," *Electronic News,* February 24, 1992, p. 21.

"Synopsis Unveils VHDL Software Aimed at Cutting Simulator Count," *Electronic News,* November 22, 1993, p. 14.

—Heidi Feldman

T. Rowe Price Associates, Inc.

100 East Pratt Street
Baltimore, Maryland 21202
U.S.A.
(410) 547-2000
Fax: (410) 539-7645

Public Company
Incorporated: 1947 as T. Rowe Price & Associates
Employees: 1,665
Operating Revenues: $310 million
Stock Exchanges: NASDAQ
SICs: 6282 Investment Advice; 6289 Services Allied with
   the Exchange of Securities or Commodities, Not
   Elsewhere Classified; 6211 Security Brokers, Dealers, and
   Flotation Companies

T. Rowe Price Associates, Inc. is a Baltimore-based investment management firm that provides a broad range of investment services in mutual funds, real estate partnerships, discount brokerage, venture capital, and international investment programs. In addition to serving as investment adviser to the growing T. Rowe Price family of mutual funds, the firm offers a full spectrum of investment advice on equity, bond, and money market securities. The company's diverse client base ranges from individual investors to institutions, including pension, profit sharing, and other employee benefit plans, endowments, and foundations. As of September 1994, T. Rowe Price managed $60 billion in more than three million investor accounts.

Such a grand scale was hardly part of T. Rowe Price's design when the firm's namesake founder set the groundwork for his own investment counsel firm in the mid-1930s. Mr. Price's original goal was to provide stock investors with a new and virtually unavailable service, which he called "investment counseling." Price's idea was to recommend investment picks and strategies by applying sound research, basing his fees on expertise, not on standard commission income. With that goal in mind, the young entrepreneur founded Price Associates, a financial counseling business, in 1937, and incorporated as T. Rowe Price & Associates ten years later.

If Price's idea to market financial advice was novel, then the growth stock theory of investing that he championed was unheard of. Price was not satisfied with the common treatment of stocks as cyclical investments, which rise and fall in value according to prevalent economic trends and should be bought or sold at the right time to make a profit. Instead, he believed that investor interests were best served by a long-term view of the investment process—one by which a financial advisor helped clients identify stocks in well-managed companies that would grow over a long period of time. Rather than buying and selling stocks for speculative profits, Price emphasized the value of investing in growing businesses and sticking with them "through thick and thin." Price believed that true growth companies—identified with careful research—would enjoy earnings growth that would augment both market value and growth of dividend income over the long haul.

Price's early experience and some of his distinct personality traits helped prepare him for the rigors of starting his own firm—especially one that would initially run against the grain of generally accepted investment practices. After studying for a career as an industrial chemist and landing two short-lived jobs in that field, he decided to turn his energies toward his real passion: investing. Brief stints at a brokerage house and a small bond house in the early 1920s provided him with enough experience to land a more permanent position in finance. In 1925, he became a stockbroker at the Baltimore investment firm Mackubin, Goodrich & Co. (later known as Mackubin, Legg & Co. and ultimately as Legg, Mason & Co. by the late 1980s). There, he climbed the corporate ladder, becoming head of the bond department and, by 1930, head of the investment management department.

By 1934, Price had convinced senior management at Mackubin, Goodrich to let him start up an investment management department at the firm. Several factors were working against Price, however. First, his growth-stock philosophy met with unusual resistance from many principals at the firm. In addition, the residual effect of the Great Depression still cast somber light on investing in general. Finally, Price was reputed as iron-willed and often difficult to work with, adding some disfavor to his already unprofitable department. By 1937, the principals of MacKubin, Goodrich decided to phase out the investment management program altogether, prompting Price to set out on his own. Several of Price's closest colleagues joined his entrepreneurial venture. Marie Walper, Isabella Craig, Walter Kidd, and Charles Schaeffer comprised the original "Associates" of the newly established partnership, T. Row Price & Associates.

Price's fledgling investment management firm struggled through its early years. Even in the best of financial markets, such a business depended on the time-consuming and uncertain process of winning client confidence. From the late 1930s right through the 1950s, moreover, financial markets were unfavorable. For several years, T. Rowe Price & Associates boasted few individual and no institutional clients. The partners accepted irregular salaries and exchanged actual pay for shares in the new enterprise. Fortunately, Price's wife had the financial resources to bankroll many of the firm's early losses. Even though Price's initial objective—that of building a company with 25 employees and $60 million in assets under management—was reasonable, it remained dubious for nearly the first decade in operation.

By the late 1940s, however, T. Rowe Price's growth-style of investing had started to chalk up a few of the successes that would give the firm forward momentum. The key was careful research, on which T. Rowe Price placed tremendous importance. For example, the firm would only invest in stock of a company whose president had been carefully interviewed by a T. Rowe Price analyst. The result was several winning stock picks between 1938 and 1949: Sharp & Dohme, the pharmaceutical company, jumped 468 percent over that period; Abbott Laboratories (334 percent); USF&G Corporation, the insurance provider (198 percent); Addressograph-Multigraph (140 percent). In the late 1930s and early 1940s, the company's investments in companies like Minnesota Mining and Manufacturing (later 3M Corp.) and IBM Corp. also proved invaluable.

Despite the tremendous odds facing T. Rowe Price before the end of World War II, the company managed to expand at a reasonable rate. According to records kept by Walter Kidd, director of research, total assets under management increased from $2.3 million in 1938 to $28 million in 1945 and $42 million in 1949. That year marked an important milestone: 12 years after the company's inception, T. Rowe Price finally broke into the black.

The 1950s marked an overall transition into a faster rate of growth and change for the company. In 1950, the firm converted from a three-person partnership to a corporation. Also that year, T. Rowe Price contracted its first institutional client, American Cyanamid, which remained a major account into the 1990s. In 1950, Price also introduced the Growth Stock Fund, the firm's first mutual fund. At that time, mutual funds were still not in vogue. Price regarded the new fund merely as a service to clients who wanted to capitalize on the Uniform Gift to Minors Act. Recently passed by Congress, the act permitted parents to manage trusts for their children and pay taxes at a relatively negligible rate. Moreover, the fund charged no "load," or sales charge, adding extra appeal to its subscribers. Though the Growth Stock Fund began as a low-profile product, it ultimately showcased the success of T. Rowe Price's growth-stock strategy in action; by 1960, Weisenberger's fund-rating service rated it as the country's best performer for the ten-year period.

The success of the Growth Stock Fund through the 1950s reflected an improved investment environment. With the exception of some economic fallout from the Korean War—such as a new Excess Profits Tax—the 1950s was a period of strong economic growth and low inflation. Growth stocks made a comeback, and Mr. Price stood in the limelight, claiming center stage through a series of articles he contributed to *Forbes* magazine on a regular basis. Meanwhile, a vigorous market for pension funds had taken shape, and T. Rowe Price jumped on the bandwagon. In all, economic recovery and a turnaround in growth stocks set the groundwork for an upcoming decade of new institutional clients and a broader range of mutual fund offerings, including pension funds.

One such fund was the New Horizons Fund, which Price introduced in 1960 in order to capitalize on the growth potential of so-called emerging growth companies, or small, rapidly growing companies in the early stage of corporate development. Some of the first stocks in New Horizon Fund's portfolio of investments included Texas Instruments, Hertz, and Haloid-Xerox, the precursor of Xerox Corp. To manage New Horizons (and a projected progeny of other mutual funds to follow) Price

founded Rowe Price Management, which he headed while remaining at the helm of the parent company.

The New Horizons Fund, like T. Rowe Price itself, suffered difficult beginnings. In fact, the fund not only lagged in the 1961 bull market but also when the market turned bearish in 1962: New Horizons dropped by 29 percent, versus a decline of nine percent for the Standard and Poore's (S&P) 500—a common index of leading company performance. Not surprisingly, critics coined derogatory variations on the fund's forward-looking name: "New Horizontal," "Blue Horizons," and "Lost Horizons."

By 1965, yet another market correction worked in favor of small growth companies, and the New Horizons Fund lived up to its real name. The fund's total return leaped 44 percent in one year, compared to 12 percent for the S&P 500. Such success attracted new investors, and both New Horizons and T. Rowe Price snowballed; by the end of 1965, the firm had topped the $1 billion mark. In fact, emerging growth stocks grew so heated that Price decided to temporarily step back. Price thought shareholders might be ill-served if the New Horizons Fund continued to invest new assets in an overvalued growth. From October 1967 to June 1970 and from March 1972 to September 1974, Price closed the fund to new investors. As John Train suggested in *The Money Masters,* Price was clearly not driven by short-term greed but had the best interest of his shareholders in mind through these maneuvers. Meanwhile, the Growth Stock Fund also rode the wave and would continue to do so into the 1970s. From 1966 through 1972, shares of that fund appreciated 80 percent, assuming reinvestment of dividends and capital gains.

As T. Rowe Price grew in the 1960s, Mr. Price's relationship with the firm loosened and a new generation of leaders began to move toward the helm. Employing roughly 200 personnel and offering new and diverse products and services required a more formal administrative structure. Price's various colleagues gradually moved away from their multiple-chore posts and into more specialized cadres. Mr. Schaeffer gravitated toward public relations; Mr. Kidd became the equivalent of chief operations officer; while other associates like E. Kirdbride Miller and John Ramsay became senior investment counselors. In 1968, Price relinquished presidency of the Growth Stock Fund, and he resigned as president of New Horizons Fund the following year. In addition, in 1968, he sold the remaining shares of Rowe Price Management (RPM) to T. Rowe Price Associates, which held a controlling interest in RPM since 1966.

Along with his responsibilities at the company, Price's overall economic outlook began to change. He foresaw the onset of a bleak "new era" in which the dollar would decline, inflation would rage, natural resources would diminish, and growth stocks would suffer. In near antipathy to his previous growth theories, he told *Forbes* in 1969 that "People will not want paper dollars. They will want tangible property: land, natural resources, timber, minerals in the ground. They will want investments in companies that can increase their profits faster than the decline in the value of the dollar."

To accommodate such a shift, Price founded the New Era Fund in 1969. The fund's portfolio of investments emphasized natural resource companies (gold, silver, uranium, copper, and forest products), while mixing in some technology and a measure of more traditional growth stocks. As was often the case with Price's initiatives, the New Era Fund performed badly at first and eventually proved itself. In the early 1970s, growth stocks held up well, and the New Era Fund lost ground. When the oil embargo aggravated economic recession until the end of 1974, the New Era Fund and its growth-driven cousins all suffered comparable pains. By the late 1970s and early 1980s, however, rampant inflation finally paid off for Price's ''Anti-Inflation Fund,'' as he had originally intended to call the New Era Fund. Between 1978 and 1981—with inflation approaching the 20 percent mark and the price of gold topping $800 an ounce—New Era jumped almost 130 percent. A key lesson that the firm derived from New Era's performance was that its traditional growth strategy could be effectively combined with other strategies to best accommodate economic change.

Starting in the 1970s—and to a much greater degree in the 1980s and onward—T. Rowe Price Associates began diversifying its strategies and its products. Indeed, Price's retirement in 1971 marked just one of many momentous changes. In 1971, George J. Collins was hired to start a fixed-income division. By the end of 1973, Collins had created New Income Fund, a balanced, fixed-income mutual fund. Though the new bond fund was not an immediate eye-opener, it soared when interest rates increased dramatically in the latter half of the decade; by 1977, New Income ranked as the third largest corporate bond fund in the United States.

When Congress passed legislation permitting tax-free municipal bond funds, Collins launched the Tax-Free Income Fund in 1976. By 1978, that fund boasted $215 million in assets and ranked third among more than 40 rivals. By the early 1990s, T. Rowe Price's lineup of tax-free mutual funds offered nearly every maturity category, as well as an insured fund for investors seeking extra credit protection and a high-yield fund for the more risk-tolerant.

A combination of socio-political and technological advances in the late 1970s and early 1980s greatly facilitated international trade and investing, virtually turning the financial world into a global marketplace. In 1979, T. Rowe Price's joint venture with Robert Fleming Holdings Ltd., a London-based merchant bank, rode the wave. Meanwhile, the growing popularity of mutual funds throughout the 1980s gave individual investors the resources to invest globally—through fund managers with the ability to conduct international research, probe credit and currency risk, and employ sophisticated hedging techniques. By 1994, Rowe Price-Fleming International, Inc. had become one of the largest managers of overseas assets in the United States, with approximately $17 billion under management.

In addition to new vigor in the international investment arena, myriad other influences prompted T. Rowe Price to diversify its financial services and products. Entering the 1980s, the rapidly growing firm had struck a delicate balance between its past growth tradition and a wide slew of new investment alternatives. Indeed, in 1984—the year after Mr. Price passed away—George J. Collins stepped up as president. The man who had brought bond investing to the exclusively growth-stock-driven firm 13 years earlier was now in command. Responding to greater competition in the financial services field—largely spurred by deregulation in the early 1980s—the company launched numerous new types of stock and bond funds.

Special emphasis was placed on retirement funds for both large institutional clients and small retail investors. After Congress created tax incentives for individuals to establish retirement accounts, T. Rowe Price correctly anticipated a decline in defined benefit retirement programs—pension plans in which a retired worker was assured a fixed income. Instead, the firm began developing funds geared toward 401(k) plans, funds sponsored by an employer in which workers can invest money tax-free until it is withdrawn after age 59. Although T. Rowe Price barely placed among the top ten mutual fund companies in assets by October 1993, it stood third in the 401(k) market, according to Leslie Wayne in a 1993 *New York Times* article.

In an effort to diversify its services, T. Rowe Price also made available innovative limited partnerships starting in the early 1980s. In 1983, the Threshold Limited Partnership was formed to help finance select private companies expected to go public within 12 to 18 months. T. Rowe Price eventually joined the bandwagon itself; it went public in 1986, and—disregarding a slight dip in 1990—enjoyed steadily rising earnings into the early 1990s. The New Frontier Fund Limited Partnership was also introduced to help non-U.S. clients invest in very small U.S. public companies.

Applying many of the venture-capital techniques from its limited partnership dealings, T. Rowe Price moved into real estate in 1984. That year, it developed the first real estate limited partnership available to investors nationwide with no sales commission. According to the company's 1986 annual report, the real estate business was ''an excellent source of diversification and improved long-term returns for all investors.'' Consequently, a real estate management subsidiary was formed.

The early 1990s saw continued efforts to diversify in order to compete in an increasingly ferocious investment market. In 1992, for example, the company acquired six mutual funds managed and distributed by USF&G Corporation. Then in 1993, T. Rowe Price, the CUNA Mutual Insurance Group, and the Credit Union National Association & Affiliates formed a joint venture to provide a family of proprietary no-load mutual funds for credit union members.

These and other initiatives called for more effective programs in customer support. By the late 1980s, the company had already implemented a sophisticated computerized telephone system—Tele*Access—with which customers could use a touch-tone phone to access their accounts 24 hours-a-day, or to buy, sell, and exchange shares in the T. Rowe Price fund family. The company also implemented advanced administrative tools, such as PAS, a computerized record keeping system for defined contribution retirement plans.

Meticulously planned marketing campaigns also helped support T. Rowe Price's services into the 1990s. In 1989, the company first introduced its Retirement Planning Kit and Retirees Financial Guide, designed for both employed people planning ahead and retired investors seeking advice. While other financial houses offered similar free guides, Price's stood out for their lucid language and current details on tax and Social Security laws, according to Susan Antilla in a 1992 *New York Times* article. Accompanying Retirement Planning Kit software was described as "friendly to the point of being verbose, but its price makes it a package to consider," by *PC Magazine*. By 1994, when the company offered new editions, investors had requested more than one million kits.

T. Rowe Price advertising was consistent with a low-key, honest approach. In September 1993, for example, the company introduced its first corporate campaign designed to burnish its corporate image rather than specific products. The broadcast and print campaign, by McCaffrey & McCall New York, carried the slogan, "Invest with confidence." The campaign was intended to correspond with the company's product-oriented promotions, which have been consistently noted for their lucidity and usefulness by such independent rating agencies as Morningstar, Inc.

From its beginning, in fact, T. Rowe Price tried to eschew catchy marketing and yield-driven investment strategies in favor of a moderate approach. As the 1993 annual report explained, the company's primary objective is always to "make sure our shareholders . . . understand the risk and reward trade-offs each investment involves." In order to do so amidst shifting markets, the firm had to adapt to a changing financial climate. Over the course of 60 years, it changed from a three-person partnership to a multinational corporation; from an exclusive growth-stock house to a leader in limited partnerships, real estate management, money market funds, and mutual funds ranging from growth stocks to tax-free municipal bonds and emerging markets. Indeed, between January 1 and December 31 1993, the company introduced 11 new mutual funds to its roster of dozens.

To be sure, the company faced momentous changes in the worldwide financial landscape of 1994—including passage of the North American Free Trade Agreement and the Federal Reserve's multiple interest-rate hikes designed to temper incipient inflation in the U.S. But as Mr. Price habitually remarked, change remains "the investor's only certainty."

Principal Subsidiaries: TRP Finance, Inc.; TRP Finance MRT, Inc.; Rowe Price-Fleming International, Inc. (50%); TRP Suburban, Inc.

Further Reading:

Antilla, Susan, "Does Little Pay off a Lot? T. Rowe Price Does," *New York Times,* June 17, 1992, p. C15.
Eliott, Stuart, "To a Company that Sells Mutual Funds, a Return on its Image is the Goal of a New Campaign," *New York Times,* September 7, 1993, p. C6.
"History of T. Rowe Price," Baltimore: T. Rowe Price Associates, 1987.
Michaels, James W., "Thomas Rowe Price 1898–1983," *Forbes,* November 21, 1983, p. 51.
Train, John, *The Money Masters,* New York: Harper & Row, 1979, pp. 139–157.
Trivette, Don, "T. Rowe Price Retirement Planning Kit (Software Review)," *PC Magazine,* November 24, 1992, p. 596.
"T. Rowe Price and USF&G Corporation Announce Plans for T. Rowe Price to Acquire Six Mutual Funds," *PR Newswire,* April 16, 1992.
Wayne, Leslie, "T. Rowe Price Sticks With Its Niche," *New York Times,* October 18, 1993, p. C1.

—Kerstan Cohen

Talbots

The Talbots, Inc.

175 Beal Street
Hingham, Massachusetts 02043
U.S.A.
(617) 749-7600
Fax: (617) 741-4369

Public Company
Incorporated: 1947
Employees: 5,000
Sales: $736 million
Stock Exchanges: New York
SICs: 5621 Women's Clothing Stores; 5961 Catalog and
    Mail-Order Houses

The Talbots, Inc., is a leading niche retailer of women's apparel and related products, with 367 stores and a catalog operation. The company got its start in New England in the 1940s and remained a small regional chain for nearly 30 years before it was purchased by General Mills, which undertook a nationwide expansion. In the late 1980s, Talbots was sold to a Japanese retail conglomerate, which funded further growth for the company. In the 1990s, Talbots expanded both its product offerings and its geographical scope, as it began to open stores overseas.

Talbots was founded in 1947 by Rudolf and Nancy Talbot. The couple inherited a store in Hingham, Massachusetts, a suburb of Boston, from Rudolf's father and named it "The Talbots." Over time, the company became popularly known simply as Talbots. The couple stocked their store with classic women's apparel. In their first year in business, sales totaled $18,000. During their second year in business, the Talbots branched out from in-store retailing, launching a catalog operation. After buying a list of subscribers to *The New Yorker* magazine, they distributed 3,000 black-and-white fliers featuring illustrations of Talbots clothing to these potential customers.

By 1950, the Talbots's business had outgrown its first location, and they moved to a two-story colonial frame house that had been built in the seventeenth century in Hingham. The first floor was given over to sales, and the second floor was converted into office space. The front door of this building was lacquered a bright red, and this architectural touch later became a hallmark of the Talbots chain. Five years after this expansion, Talbots opened its first branch store, in Duxbury, Massachusetts, a town south of Hingham. In the following years, stores were also opened in Lenox, Massachusetts; Hamden, Connecticut; and Avon, Connecticut.

Throughout the social and cultural upheavals of the 1960s, Talbots maintained its focus on classic styles and traditional clothing for an affluent, well-educated customer. By the end of the decade, the company's growth in store number and size, along with expanding catalog sales, necessitated larger facilities. In 1970, Talbots moved its business headquarters and mail-order operations to a new location in Hingham. By this time, the company's staff had grown to include 71 employees, who worked in the five New England Talbots stores.

By 1973, the original black-and-white Talbots brochure had evolved into four yearly full-color catalogs, which, combined with the company's five retail outlets, brought in $8 million in annual revenues. This success attracted the attention of larger companies, and, that year, the Talbots sold their chain of stores to consumer goods giant General Mills.

After purchasing the chain, General Mills began a program of limited regional expansion. Over the next seven years, Talbots opened eight new stores in locations throughout New England. In 1980, the company moved outside New England for the first time, inaugurating outlets in New York, Pennsylvania, and Delaware. With these new locations, Talbots's payroll swelled to include 800 people. Also in 1980, Talbots established a toll-free telephone number to make it easier for customers to order from its catalog. The company also expanded its headquarters facility from 80,000 to 200,000 square feet.

Throughout the 1980s, with a heavy infusion of funds from General Mills, Talbots expanded its chain of stores dramatically. The company grew from less than 20 stores to 126 stores in just eight years. With each new store that it opened, Talbots implemented its retailing strategy. The company strove to give all of its outlets the residential feel of the company's original seventeenth-century Hingham home. Interiors were decorated with maple floors and wainscotting, and walls were hung with traditional botanical and equestrian prints, to simulate the atmosphere of a gracious English home. In addition, each store was fitted with a bright red door and, wherever possible, matching red awnings over the windows.

In 1984, Talbots expanded the range of its merchandise offerings when it introduced clothing in petite sizes in both its stores and catalog. In this way, the company hoped to tap into the sizable market of women who needed professional and sophisticated clothing in smaller sizes. The following year, Talbots expanded its efforts in this area, opening a Talbots Petites store in Cambridge, Massachusetts.

By 1988, Talbots had expanded its primary store concept to 25 states, and the company was taking in $350 million annually in sales. Of those revenues, 40 percent were derived from catalog sales. The company's 24 annual glossy and colorful brochures were distributed to 70 million customers throughout the world. To better serve catalog customers, Talbots opened a new catalog fulfillment and merchandise distribution center in Lakeville, Massachusetts, in January 1988. The 555,000 square foot facility processed an average of 20,000 items a day and was capable of completing two-and-a-half times as many during peak periods, such as the holiday shopping season.

At the start of 1988, General Mills announced that it was divesting itself of its clothing retail operations, in order to concentrate fully on its food-related businesses. Talbots's corporate parent put it up for sale along with Eddie Bauer, Inc., an outdoor clothing company that also maintained catalog operations. Although industry observers were hesitant about General Mills's asking price of $250 million for each chain and were also concerned about difficulties in the mail-order business overall, several companies indicated interest in purchasing Talbots, among them Sears, Roebuck & Company, and Spiegel, Inc., another women's clothing cataloger.

Ultimately, however, General Mills sold the chain to the Jusco Group, a leading Japanese retailer which was the core company of the AEON Group. AEON brought together approximately 150 different international retail properties, led by Jusco, a major chain of Japanese department stores. Jusco purchased Talbots for $350 million in June 1988. At the time of this sale, Talbots also acquired a data processing center in Tampa, Florida, owned by General Mills.

Talbot's new owner planned to use the company as a first step towards American retailing operations and also hoped to successfully expand the Talbots concept in Japan. Although Talbots's president had resigned when General Mills announced that it was selling the chain, its second-in-command remained, and Jusco put him in charge of running its new purchase.

At the time, Talbots's rapid expansion had left it with some problems in its operation. At the catalog sales telemarketing center, frequent computer breakdowns forced employees to write out orders by hand, a cumbersome process. In addition, customers often had difficulty getting through on the phone. Moreover, systems in Talbots stores also needed improvements. For instance, employees had no way of monitoring stock at stores, so that they could recommend that customers seek certain items at other locations. Jusco spent $50 million implementing new computer systems in an effort to fix these and other problems.

In addition, Talbots refocused its merchandise offerings. Rather than relying on other clothing manufacturers' labels for 75 percent of its merchandise, the company decided to rely almost exclusively on its own private label. In this way, it was able to keep more of the money it made on clothing and was also able to maintain strict control over the quality of the clothes it sold. Under this new program, 95 percent of the clothes sold in Talbots stores carried the Talbots label.

Talbots also decided to emphasize its retail outlets over its catalog operations. Under this strategy, the company began to use its catalog primarily as a market indicator of the most potentially profitable parts of the country. By opening a store in a given area, Talbots was able to increase its sales dramatically, without doing heavy damage to its catalog sales. Once mail-order sales were running at $100,00 to $150,000 within a given zip code, Talbots learned, a store located in that area would draw $1 million to $1.5 million in annual sales, while only cutting catalog sales by 25 percent. With this in mind, Talbots set out to open a large number of stores in areas across the nation. In addition, Talbots embarked on a multifaceted program to expand beyond women's clothing into other related lines of merchandise. Despite its overall push to concentrate on stores rather than catalogs for the bulk of its sales, Talbots did open a second telemarketing center in Knoxville, Tennessee, in April 1989. This facility augmented the operations at the company's original Hingham, Massachusetts, telemarketing location.

At the same time, Talbots also inaugurated its first overseas operation, establishing Talbots International Retailing Limited, Inc., in Hong Kong. This office was responsible for overseeing manufacture in the Far East of many Talbots private-label products, including quality control, design, and testing. It also provided a communications link between the company's Asian manufacturers and its American Product Development and Merchandising offices.

In July 1989, Talbots introduced a catalog devoted entirely to children's clothing called "Talbots Kids." With this line of goods, the company hoped to capitalize on the brand loyalty of mothers who bought Talbots merchandise for themselves, hoping they would also want to do so for their children. When the Talbots Kids catalog proved successful, the company went on to open the first two Talbots Kids stores, in Westport, Connecticut, and Charlotte, North Carolina. These stores were placed right next to existing Talbots stores, to make a block of stores carrying the Talbots line. The children's stores featured bright colors, whimsical fixtures, and fun children's furniture. About 80 percent of the goods they offered carried the Talbots brand name.

As Talbots made the transition from the ownership of General Mills to AEON and tried to retool itself for further growth in the 1990s, the company experienced several challenges. In 1990, for instance, Talbots introduced clothing in more trendy, less traditional colors, stocking stores with blouses and skirts in avocado and gold, rather than the traditional navy blue and red. Customers were less than pleased with this development, and operating profits dropped by 40 percent, as the chain suffered a loss for the year of $7 million. In response to these poor results, Talbots returned to its more traditional styles, and the chain's sales soon began to recover.

In November 1990, Talbots also branched out into its first non-clothing line of merchandise, when it began to market "Talbots," a white floral perfume. The company offered the scent in five different forms, including lotion, powder, and gel. By the end of 1990, Talbots had also begun to roll out the expansion of its Talbots Petites stores, opening locations next to previously established Talbots outlets. Further extension of Talbots's line of products came in July 1991, when the company began to offer underwear and sleepwear through its fall catalog. This line was designed to compete with the market that Victoria's Secret had pioneered, but in a more traditional vein.

Also that year, Talbots launched its first international effort, creating Talbots Canada, Inc., a subsidiary headquartered in Toronto. In September 1991, the first Canadian Talbots stores opened in three separate Toronto locations. Seven Talbots stores had already been opened in Japan, but these were directly owned by the company's Japanese parent and thus were not run by the American subsidiary. By the end of the year, Talbots ran 240 stores of its own, 43 of which had been opened in the preceding 12 months. Overall, Talbots sales from these locations and its catalog operation, which made up one-third of the whole, totaled more than $500 million.

Part of Talbots's strategy for maintaining its profitability was to resist the lure of constant discounting to pump up sales. The company conducted four annual mark-downs and otherwise sold all merchandise at full price. In addition, Talbots benefited from a strong demand for its traditionally-styled clothing among those who rejected other emerging fashion trends, including grunge and the baby-doll look, from the rest of the fashion industry.

Talbots continued its strong showing in 1992. The company began to team up with other niche retailers, such as the Gap, to open stores in mini-malls, which offered lower rents than larger suburban malls. In addition, the company pushed forward with its policy of clustering the different stores in its line, including Talbots Kids and Talbots Petites, for greater selling power.

In October 1992, Talbots introduced a new member of its retail family, when freestanding Talbots Intimates stores were opened in Austin, Texas; St. Louis, Missouri; and Troy, Michigan. In addition, the company opened in-store boutiques in existing outlets in Boston; Chicago; Pittsford, New York; and Short Hills, New Jersey. Each of these locations was designed to look like a New England summer cottage, with lots of light and whitewashed wood. The stores offered perfume, books, and an assortment of gifts, as well as lingerie and sleepwear. About half of the merchandise carried the Talbots label, a lower percentage than the company's other operations. Talbots Intimates goods were also offered through a separate catalog.

By the end of 1992, Talbots sales had increased 23 percent over the 12-month period, to reach $642 million, and the company continued to open new stores at a brisk pace. In May 1993, Talbots opened a Midwest flagship store on Michigan Avenue in Chicago. With its location in a popular shopping area, the outlet was expected to become the company's highest grossing store. In addition, Talbots moved forward with its Canadian expansion, opening four new stores in the fall of 1993, in Ottawa and Vancouver, British Columbia.

In September 1993, Talbots's Japanese parent announced that it would sell shares in the company to the public. The initial public offering of 11 million shares, which took place in November 1993, reaped $242 million, with AEON Group retaining 67 percent ownership in the company. In the first day of trading, the company's stock proved to be extremely popular with investors, and its price quickly rose by 20 percent, as buyers re-

sponded favorably to Talbots strong brand name and image. With the money from the sale of stock, Talbots paid off some debts and repurchased some trademark rights from AEON's European arm.

At the time of its sale to the public, Talbots had grown to comprise 313 stores in 44 states, which included eight Talbots Surplus stores, where the company sold outdated merchandise at discounted prices. By the end of 1993, Talbots sales had risen to $737 million, a gain of 15 percent. The company's net income also rose, to $35 million. Overall, earnings had grown by sevenfold since the start of the 1990s.

In April 1994, Talbots opened three more stores in Canada and announced plans for a major push into Europe. Anticipating that its current rate of growth, in which around 50 new Talbots stores were opened each year in the United States, would saturate the market in seven years, the company turned to foreign shores for future growth. On the basis of its strong success in Canada, Talbots chose England as its next target. In September 1994, the company opened a test store in a London suburb. Pending the results from the London store, Talbots planned to open 30 stores in the United Kingdom and 170 stores in other parts of Europe and Mexico.

In addition, Talbots entered a new merchandise field when it began distributing a catalog focusing on shoes and accessories. In the same way that it had previously used other catalogs to test the market for children's clothing and lingerie, Talbots hoped in this way to fine tune its entry into yet another retail category. With a solid base of loyal customers, a trusted brand name, and a tested retail strategy, Talbots appeared well-situated to prosper in the years to come.

Principal Subsidiaries: Talbots Canada, Inc.

Further Reading:

Barmash, Isidore, ''General Mills to Pick Bids for Two Units,'' *New York Times,* May 10, 1988.
Biddle, Frederic M., ''Talbots: Master of Nice Retailing,'' *Boston Sunday Globe,* August 2, 1992.
Fallon, James, ''Talbots Revs Up Expansion Plans in Europe,'' *Women's Wear Daily,* June 23, 1994.
Feldman, Amy, ''Basics for the Nineties,'' *Forbes,* May 9, 1994.
Neale, Stacy, ''Talbots Inc. is Set to Try on Europe for Size,'' *Boston Business Journal,* May 20–26, 1994.
Schmeltzer, John, ''Talbots Has Red-Letter Day on Michigan Ave.,'' *Chicago Tribune,* May 15, 1993.

—Elizabeth Rourke

tellabs

Tellabs, Inc.

4951 Indiana Avenue
Lisle, Illinois 60532
U.S.A
(708) 969-8800
Fax: (708) 852-7346

Public Company
Incorporated: 1975
Employees: 2,000
Sales: $320 million
Stock Exchanges: NASDAQ
SICs: 3661 Telephone & Telegraph Apparatus; 3613
    Switchgear & Switchboard Apparatus; 3669
    Communications Equipment, Not Elsewhere Classified

An international company that designs, manufactures, markets, and services telecommunications equipment, Tellabs, Inc. has become an innovative force in the ever-expanding telecommunications industry. Tellabs's customers include the regional Bell companies and their subsidiaries, long-distance companies such as MCI and Sprint, international service providers, and businesses and governmental organizations with private voice and data networks. The company's sales network covers North America, Asia, and Europe, with manufacturing plants in Illinois, Texas, Ireland, and Finland, and international sales offices in Ireland, England, Belgium, Sweden, Finland, Hong Kong, Australia, New Zealand, South Korea, Beijing, Munich, and the United Arab Emirates. Sales topped $320 million in 1993, with profits of $32 million.

Tellabs was founded in 1975, when six men, all with various degrees of experience in electrical engineering and sales, got together around a suburban Chicago kitchen table, "drinking coffee and brainstorming." (Of the six, two would stay with the company for over 20 years: Michael Birck, CEO and president, and Chris Cooney, vice president of sales.) The group planned to form a telecommunications company that did not fit traditional corporate molds, one that offered customers products and services that met their specific needs.

Between them, the six partners raised start-up capital of $110,000 and incorporated Tellabs in the spring of 1975. The company's research and development department consisted of one man, a handmade wooden workbench, a used soldering machine (purchased for $25 dollars), and an outdated oscillo-

scope. Its sales force consisted of two men and two used Chrysler New Yorkers, chosen for their large trunks. Within months, the company began marketing its first product, an echo suppressor intended for independent telephone companies, such as Continental Telephone and GTE.

During this time, the founding members drew no salaries. Family members supported the new company by going back to work, mortgaging homes, cleaning Tellabs offices on weekends—even posing as assembly line workers when potential customers were taken through the "plant." By December 1975, Tellabs was enjoying a bit of success. It had 20 permanent employees and sales of $312,000. Soon the company landed an account with Western Union, its first major customer. By 1977, Tellabs was able to move into a permanent facility in Lisle, Illinois, and its sales force had quadrupled to eight. That year, annual sales jumped to $7.8 million.

Tellabs's expansion continued with the opening of its first subsidiary, Tellabs Communications Canada, Ltd., in 1979. The following year, the company expanded its market to the south, with the opening of its Tellabs Texas manufacturing facility, and also became public, trading on the NASDAQ exchange. The company put more money into research and development, developing complex networking systems, as well as a line of digital communications systems for telephone companies and large computer systems. In 1983, with the opening of Tellabs's fourth facility in Puerto Rico, it seemed Tellabs growth would continue uninterrupted. Then, in 1984, the monolithic Bell System was dissolved, and several regional "Baby Bell" companies emerged.

Prior to the break-up, the Bell System had designed its own products through its subsidiary Bell Laboratories and produced them through Western Electric, AT&T's manufacturing division. Suddenly, through the divestiture, the previously closed Bell market was wide open. Although analysts had predicted that companies like Tellabs would benefit substantially from the new market, the new arrangement prompted intense competition as a large number of new companies emerged to compete for contracts with the Baby Bells. Regional Bell companies no longer had the financial resources of Ma Bell to rely upon and began looking for the lowest possible bidder when making new purchases. Competition became fierce, and although Tellabs's sales hit $100 million in 1985, gross profit margin dropped from 50 percent in 1984 to 35 percent in 1985.

Company management thus decided to make some internal changes in order to compete more effectively. Tellabs implemented a progressive management system, incorporating the Japanese just-in-time inventory management system, new employee training programs, and replacing traditional manufacturing lines with manufacturing cells, with each employee skilled in a number of interchangeable functions. The company also increased its research and development expenditures by about 40 percent and began developing such products as the $100,000 CROSSNET digital interchange product, CT1 multiplexer, that brought in much higher profit margins than Tellabs's early $200 echo suppressor. As private communications networks sprang up, Tellabs began to customize products to meet their needs. The company's increased efficiency in bringing new products to the market also allowed it to effectively win a bid against Bell

Labs and Western Electric for an ongoing contract to supply AT&T with networking multiplexers, an integral component in AT&T's communications operations.

By 1987, Tellabs was back on the road to profitability, with improved sales to regional Bell companies as well as to long-distance service providers. That year, the company signed a $10 million contract with the long-distance carrier Sprint to supply its entire optical fiber network with digital echo cancellers. Sales for 1987 rose 18 percent to $136.1 million; net income rose 27 percent to $10.7 million.

Also that year, Tellabs began boosting efforts to penetrate foreign markets. "We didn't have the staff or the right products to address foreign markets before," CEO Birck told share-holders the following year, noting that "in 1987 we felt we were big enough and had a sufficient array of products to make a real commitment overseas." Birck then predicted that overseas sales, which accounted for one percent of revenues in the early 1980s, would rise to 30 percent by 1990. By 1988, Tellabs had opened sales offices in London, Australia, and Hong Kong and had expanded its Canadian operations.

In 1989, the company made a significant step towards increasing its European presence with the acquisition of Delta Communications in Shannon, Ireland. Renamed Tellabs Ltd., the subsidiary supplied signaling and conversion systems for Europe's E1 telecommunications markets, a venue previously untapped by Tellabs. By 1992, Tellabs's foreign sales network expanded to cover Belgium, New Zealand, Korea, and Mexico, where government monopolies on telecommunications systems were beginning to dissolve. The following year, the company acquired Martis Oy, a Finnish telecommunications supplier purchased for approximately $70 million. This acquisition further solidified Tellabs's European market presence and gave the company the impetus to expand into other international markets.

Tellabs's marketing efforts worldwide were boosted by an array of new, state-of-the art technologies, such as the TITAN 5500 digital cross-connect system introduced in 1991 and a line of digital echo cancellers designed to work in conjunction with new fiber optics systems. By 1992, Tellabs's sales of digital echo cancellers totaled $40 million, second only to AT&T. Also in 1992, Tellabs entered the race to market high-bit-rate digital subscriber line (HDSL) equipment, a much anticipated technol-ogy which converted ordinary copper telephone lines into high-capacity digital lines. Fueled by an expanded TITAN line, Tellabs's total sales soared in 1993, up 90 percent over the previous year to a record high of $320 million with earnings of $32 million. Tellabs was a darling on Wall Street, as stock prices jumped from $21 per share to just over $69 per share.

On the eve of its 20th anniversary, Tellabs's growth seemed to have paralleled that of the booming North American telecom-munications industry. Sensing that sales in North America had begun to plateau, Tellabs branched out to new growth markets worldwide with the hope of competing with European giant Ericsson, AB. Moreover, as the telecommunications industry found new applications for its technology in fields such as cable television, Tellabs seemed well poised to benefit; in 1994, Tellabs introduced a new asynchronous transfer mode product, Alta 2600, and the CABLESPAN 2300 Universal Telephony Distribution System. Ultimately, the company's future in all markets depended on its ability to deliver the right technology at the right time, and Tellabs was proving itself capable: first-half sales in 1994 topped $200 million, and continued growth seemed likely. In fact, sales of $345 million for the first nine months exceeded the total for the year 1993. Tellabs was headed toward its ninth successive year of improvement in gross margins and second consecutive year over 50 percent.

Principal Subsidiaries: Tellabs Operations, Inc.; Tellabs Com-munications Canada Ltd.; Tellabs Ltd.; Martis Oy.

Further Reading:

Murphy, H. Lee, "Phone Company Competition Dampens Tellabs' Optimism," *Crain's Chicago Business*, May 5, 1986, p. 57; "Phone Lines Dial Up Dollars for Tellabs," *Crain's Chicago Business,* May 2, 1988, p. 35; "Tellabs Bets on Upturn from New Products," *Crain's Chicago Business,* May 6, 1985, p. 56.

Quintanilla, Carl, "As Domestic Growth Eases, Tellabs Sees Europe as Next Site for Expansion," *The Wall Street Journal,* February 14, 1994, p. B6.

Slutsker, Gary, "Goliath, Meet Michael Birck," *Forbes,* December 7, 1992, p. 156.

Yates, Ronald E., "Tellabs Tough on Indifference: Company Makes Its Workers Feel Part of the Action," *Chicago Tribune,* April 17, 1994, Sec. 7, p. 1.

—Maura Troester

Teradyne, Inc.

321 Harrison Avenue
Boston, Massachusetts 02118
U.S.A.
(617) 482-2700
Fax: (617) 422-2910

Public Company
Incorporated: 1960
Employees: 4,100
Sales: $554 million
Stock Exchanges: New York
SICs: 3699 Electrical Equipment and Supplies, Not
    Elsewhere Classified

Teradyne, Inc. is a leading producer of systems to test electronic and computer components while they are being manufactured in factories around the world. The company was founded in the early 1960s, when the semiconductor industry was in its infancy, and Teradyne pioneered many early testing systems, becoming the dominant player in its field. By the mid-1970s, however, the company had lost some of its technological edge, and it began to suffer inroads on its market share from competitors. In the 1980s, the increasing globalization of the semiconductor industry put Teradyne under further pressure. The company responded by investing heavily to update its products and to establish a worldwide presence.

Teradyne was founded in 1960 by two 32-year-old graduates of the Massachusetts Institute of Technology, Nicholas DeWolf and Alexander V. d'Arbeloff. The two had first met as students when they lined up alphabetically in a Reserve Officer Training Corps class. After graduation, DeWolf became an engineer at Transitron, a company located in Wakefield, Massachusetts, that worked in the fledgling semiconductor industry. In the 1950s, DeWolf gained widespread renown in his field for his innovative applications work and use of germanium diodes and other components.

By the end of the decade, however, DeWolf had become bored with the security and routine of corporate life. He quit his job, planning to start another company but with no firm plans as to how. In the fall of 1960, he hooked up with his old college classmate d'Arbeloff, and the two decided to go into business together. To begin, they chose a name for their venture. "It had to have a 'D' in it, DeWolf later told *The New Englander*. He

continued: " 'Tera' is the prefix for 10 to the 12th power and 'dyne' is a unit of force. To us, the name meant rolling a 15,000-ton boulder uphill."

Once they had chosen a name, DeWolf and d'Arbeloff chose a location for their business, taking care that both men would be able to walk to work and that they would be near the center of mass transit lines, so that factory workers could commute easily. The space they chose was a loft over Joe & Nemo's hot dog stand in downtown Boston. After raising $250,000 in financing, of which $25,000 came from their own savings, the partners opened their doors early in 1961.

The first product Teradyne created was a "go/no-go" diode tester. The partners spent all their capital designing and producing this device and then tried to sell it to their friends in the diode industry. Initially, the product met with some resistance. "That's a pretty low point. When your *friends* not only say 'no,' they say 'no' and 'we feel *sorry* for you',"" DeWolf later recalled in *The New Englander*. By the end of the year, however, Teradyne had sold one of its devices to the Raytheon company, reaping $5,000. Altogether, Teradyne had grown to include nine employees.

The work force included 20 people by the end of 1962, and the company had sold an additional 18 diode testers. Growth continued in the following year, when Teradyne sold 59 testers, worth $431,000, and the staff rose to 35 people. This rapid growth was a testament to the success of the unique business philosophy of DeWolf and d'Arbeloff. Rather than attempting to meet customer demands, they undertook to understand what their customers were doing as well as the customer did, then built a machine that their clients needed and taught them how they could use the new device.

The product that DeWolf invented was a diode tester that enabled manufacturers to produce diodes more cheaply. At the time that Teradyne first marketed this product, sophisticated testing devices were limited to the laboratory, while factory floors got by with crude, slow, and inexact hand-testers. Teradyne's innovation was to bring high-quality diode testers from the laboratory to the manufacturing process.

On the strength of this advance, Teradyne experienced rapid growth in the early 1960s. It soon branched out from diode testing to other kinds of component testing, including resisters, transistors, integrated circuits, and zener diodes. Its list of semiconductor manufacturing clients also expanded.

In 1966, Teradyne introduced a new product, which created an entire market that the company then virtually owned for the next ten years. As more circuits and transistors were crowded onto tiny slivers of silicon, picking out bad chips in semiconductors manually became impossible. After DeWolf realized that testing routines for some sophisticated components had become too complicated to program by hand, Teradyne began to implement minicomputers in its testing devices, thereby creating the automated testing equipment (ATE) industry. The use of ATE proved essential to further industrial development in semiconductor design and manufacture.

Initially, Teradyne purchased minicomputers from the nearby Digital Equipment Corporation, becoming that supplier's largest customer at one point. Eventually, however, DeWolf designed his own minicomputer for use in Teradyne's products. One such early effort, the J259, a computer-controlled integrated circuit tester, "made Teradyne the company it is," DeWolf told *The New Englander*. Although it did not perform highly sophisticated tests, it did basic, essential processes very reliably. "We wanted to build a company with a reputation for doing simple things well," DeWolf elaborated.

With the growth in demand for ATE, Teradyne's facilities over the hot dog stand also expanded. In 1967, the company moved to a nearby eight-story building that had previously been a leather market. By the end of the 1960s, Teradyne had doubled its sales for six of its first ten years in existence. In 1969, the company's sales exceeded $15 million, and profits topped $1.2 million. The following year, Teradyne sold stock to the public for the first time.

Despite Teradyne's success in the 1960s, the spring of 1970 brought the first of many cyclical downturns in the semiconductor industry, as both computer makers and the military cut back on consumption. This, in turn, cut down on orders for Teradyne's equipment. From April 1970 to April 1971, the company did not receive one order from the customers to whom it had previously sold 80 percent of its products. With its rapid growth, Teradyne had neglected to diversify its customer base sufficiently, and the company began to lose money.

In the summer of 1970, Teradyne began to take steps to prevent further crashes in its market. The company was reorganized into seven different product groups, and it started work on four new areas. Among the initiatives it got underway were test systems for semiconductor users as well as makers, since customers had started to inspect the electronics products they bought more carefully.

In addition, Teradyne hired a direct sales force, instead of relying on manufacturers' representatives, in hopes of increasing sales. Despite these moves, however, the company was forced to lay off 15 percent of its work force, or 100 employees, in the fall of 1970.

By the summer of 1971, the semiconductor industry appeared to be recovering, and DeWolf decided that he would depart from Teradyne, which, like his last employer, had grown too large and bureaucratic to hold his interest. He left the company in the hands of his partner, d'Arbeloff, and, by the end of that year, Teradyne appeared to have weathered the semiconductor depression. The severe cutback in production had created a temporary semiconductor shortage, so manufacturing, and demand for Teradyne's products, boomed briefly.

In addition, diversification meant that half of Teradyne's products were now sold to new customers. To further broaden its customer base, Teradyne began a program in 1972 to develop a testing device for telephone systems, called 4Tel.

The expansion in the scope of Teradyne's activities in the early 1970s lead to expansion of company facilities. Teradyne established a connector manufacturing division in Lowell, Massachusetts; a wire-wrapping operation in Schaumburg, Illinois; and a digital integrated circuit testing division in Chatsworth, California. In addition, the company purchased a 225,000

square-foot building to accommodate further expansion in Boston. By the fall of 1974, the company's payroll had grown to include 1,300 people.

This number soon shrank, however, as Teradyne suffered the effects of its failure to make the transition from specialized testing equipment to general-purpose devices, and also as the semiconductor industry went into a slump. In October 1974, the company cut its work force, and, in November, it was forced to temporarily shut down most manufacturing operations and further lay off employees. The following year, Teradyne laid off another 15 percent of its workers.

By 1976, the market was once again looking robust, and Teradyne's sales rose to $54 million, with profits of $2 million. The company's financial returns continued to improve throughout the 1970s, as revenues reached $165 million, and earnings hit $11 million.

Despite this outward growth, however, Teradyne's long-term prospects were growing dimmer, as the company rested on its laurels in the mid-1970s. Rather than aggressively seeking to develop new products for the ever-changing semiconductor industry, Teradyne relied on earlier product innovations to maintain its market share.

By the late 1970s, the damage had been done. Teradyne had ignored the development of digital large-scale integrated circuits (LSI), which meant that it missed out on an ATE market that expanded by 35 percent every year of the decade. In addition, because of this omission, the company was way behind in bringing state-of-the-art testing systems to market. In an effort to redress this error, d'Arbeloff began an aggressive program to develop new products in 1976. Over the next four years, Teradyne's spending on research and development grew dramatically, from $5 million to $17 million.

Despite these steps, Teradyne relinquished its dominance in the ATE market in 1978 to arch-rival Fairchild Camera and Instrument Corporation. With this ominous sign, amid a general perception that Teradyne had missed the boat, important managers and salespeople began to leave the company. One group of ex-employees brought out their own testing device and gained half of the market Teradyne had previously held.

In the early 1980s, Teradyne continued its quest to regain market share through new product development, even as its financial results slipped. Although an industry-wide recession cut the company's sales by three percent in 1980, and earnings dropped from $11 million to $4 million in 1981, Teradyne raised research spending to $20 million. By 1982, research spending had reached $25 million, or 14 percent of sales. In order to pay for this effort, the company went into debt, racking up $66 million in long-term notes.

The centerpiece of Teradyne's costly development program was a tester for the next generation of semiconductors, very large scale integrated (VLSI) circuits, called the J941 logic test system. In late 1982, Teradyne received an early vote of confidence on this offering when it won a $1 million contract from the Intel Corporation.

In addition, Teradyne had developed several products to appeal to a broader customer base, as part of its perennial effort to lessen the impact of cyclical depressions in the chip market. One focus was the telecommunications industry, where the company had installed five of its 4Tel systems by 1977. In 1981, Teradyne netted its largest ever contract in this area, when the GTE Corporation signed on to buy a $35.6 million 4TEL system.

By 1983, Teradyne's effort to introduce a new generation of products had started to pay off. Sales for that year increased by 42 percent, to $250 million, and income multiplied by four, to $21 million. Despite these gains, the company still faced stiff competitive threats from others in its industry, primarily Takeda Riken, a Japanese chip testing company.

Within two years, aggressive price-cutting by Japanese microchip manufacturers, combined with lowered demand for personal computers, had once again depressed Teradyne's fortunes. In August 1985, the company laid off 140 workers; 1986 also proved to be a year of poor financial returns. In 1987, Teradyne racked up $21.1 million in losses, marking the first time in its history that it had lost money for two years in a row.

Teradyne found itself trapped in a market that had changed forever and was forced to adapt to the new conditions. The Japanese had successfully captured much of the U.S. semiconductor industry, and the remaining American players were locked in a protracted recession, which had eliminated profit margins for all of them. Teradyne began to compete for business in ways it had never before found necessary. The company started trying to undercut its competitors on price and also relied heavily on its diversified line of products, which included mixed-signal test systems, analog test systems, and memory test systems. In addition, Teradyne worked hard to sell its products in Japan.

On the strength of these areas, Teradyne managed to cut its losses to $3.29 million in 1988. Only 65 percent of the company's revenues that year came from its ATE business; the rest were derived from other areas, which included a computer-aided engineering (CAE) group created through the purchase of the Aida Corporation (for $29 million) and Case Technologies, Inc. (for $18 million), the previous year.

By 1989, Teradyne had returned to profitability, as the company earned $10 million on sales of $483.5 million, despite the continued overall slump in its industry. Analyzing this situation, d'Arbeloff prioritized competition on a global level as his company's best chance for ultimate survival. While the overcrowded ATE industry kept margins narrow in Teradyne's main business sector, the company profited from its thriving telecommunications unit and its connection systems business, a big defense contractor.

Unfortunately, the defense industry proved a weak customer as the 1990s began. In October 1990, Teradyne undertook a round of layoffs, as its sales to the military plummeted. In April 1991, the company continued its cost-cutting efforts, implementing salary freezes and briefly suspending production, while also buttressing its overseas operations in its drive to return to profitability.

By the end of the following year, Teradyne's restructuring had resulted in strong financial returns. The company reported sales of $529.6 million and earnings of $22.5 million. In 1993, the good news continued. In August, Teradyne's efforts to become a global player paid off, as the company won a massive $63 million contract to supply test equipment to the German national telephone system. Exports accounted for 40 percent of Teradyne's sales by this time.

In addition, Teradyne introduced a new generation of ATE, which tested application-specific integration circuits, enabling chip manufacturers to produce semiconductors more cheaply. This development came as the demand for computer chips increased dramatically following a new wave of personal computers which met the industry's diminished capacity. Teradyne ended 1993 with a record backlog of orders for its equipment. Overall, sales had risen to $554.7 million, and earnings had reached $35.2 million. The company looked forward to garnering continued strong returns.

Principal Subsidiaries: Teradyne Assembly GmbH Ltd. (Germany); Teradyne GmbH Ltd. (Germany); Teradyne International, Ltd.; Teradyne Ireland Ltd.; Teradyne Japan, Ltd.; Teradyne K.K. (Japan); Zehntel Holdings, Inc.

Further Reading:

Burrows, Peter, ''Teradyne: Yankee Conservative Makes its Hunches Pay Off,'' *Electronic Business,* January 8, 1990.

Day, John, ''Teradyne: The House that Nick and Alex Built,'' *The New Englander,* November 1974.

Fisher, Maria, ''Back on the Fast Track,'' *Forbes,* May 7, 1984.

''How Teradyne is Spending its Way to Recovery,'' *Business Week,* September 27, 1982.

Jones, John A., ''Teradyne Recovers with Boom in Semiconductor Test Gear,'' *Investor's Business Daily,* February 22, 1994.

Kiely, Thomas, ''Teradyne's Paradox,'' *New England Business,* June 1990.

—Elizabeth Rourke

Texas Instruments Inc.

P.O. Box 655474
13500 North Central Expressway
Dallas, Texas 75243-1108
U.S.A.
(214) 995-2011
Fax: (214) 995-4360

Public Company
Incorporated: 1930 as Geophysical Service, Inc.
Employees: 59,400
Sales: $8.52 billion
Stock Exchanges: New York London Switzerland Boston
   Cincinnati NASDAQ Philadelphia Pacific
SICs: 3674 Semiconductors and Related Devices; 3812
   Search and Navigation Equipment; 3625 Relays and
   Industrial Controls; 7372 Prepackaged Software; 7371
   Computer Programming Services; 3577 Computer
   Peripheral Equipment, Not Elsewhere Classified

The history of Texas Instruments Inc. (TI) was intimately related to the history of the American electronics industry. TI was one of the first companies to manufacture transistors, and it introduced the first commercial silicon transistors. It was a TI engineer who developed the first semiconductor integrated circuit in 1958, and TI's semiconductor chips helped fuel the modern electronics revolution. After a disappointing performance in the 1980s, the corporation abandoned its long-held, but unfulfilled dream of becoming a consumer electronics powerhouse in favor of specialization in high-tech computer components.

Texas Instruments's roots can be traced to Geophysical Service, a petroleum-exploration firm founded in 1930 by Dr. J. Clarence Karcher and Eugene McDermott. Headquartered in Dallas, Geophysical Service used a technique for oil exploration developed by Karcher. The technique, reflection seismology, used underground sound waves to find and map those areas most likely to yield oil. When Karcher and McDermott opened a research and equipment manufacturing office in Newark, New Jersey—to keep their research and their seismography equipment operations out of view of competitors—they hired J. Erik Jonsson, a mechanical engineer, to head it.

Toward the end of the 1930s, Geophysical Service began to change its business focus because of the erratic nature of the oil exploration business. The company was reorganized: an oil company, Coronado Corporation, was established as the parent company; and a geophysical company, Geophysical Service, Inc. (GSI), was formed as a subsidiary. McDermott and Jonsson, along with two other GSI employees, purchased GSI from Coronado in 1941. During World War II, oil exploration continued, and the company also looked for other business opportunities. The skills GSI acquired producing seismic devices were put to use in the development and manufacture of electronic equipment for the armed services. This experience revealed marked similarities in design and performance requirements for the two kinds of equipment. Jonsson, encouraged by GSI's expansion during the war, helped make military manufacturing a major company focus. By 1942 GSI was working on military contracts for the U.S. Navy and the Army Signal Corps. This marked the beginning of the company's diversification into electronics unrelated to petroleum exploration.

After the war, Jonsson coaxed a young naval officer named Patrick E. Haggerty—a man of exceptional vision—to join GSI. At a time when many defense contractors had shifted their focus from military manufacturing to civilian markets, Haggerty and Jonsson firmly believed that defense contracts would help them establish GSI as a leading-edge electronics company. They won contracts to produce such military equipment as airborne magnetometers and complete radar systems. Haggerty, who was general manager of the Laboratory and Manufacturing (L & M) division, also set about turning GSI into a major electronics manufacturer. He and Jonsson soon won approval from the board of directors to build a new plant to consolidate scattered operations into one unit. The new building opened in 1947.

By 1951 the L & M division was growing faster than GSI's Geophysical division. The company was reorganized again and renamed General Instruments Inc. Because its new name was already in use by another company, however, General Instruments became Texas Instruments that same year. Geophysical Service Inc. became a subsidiary of Texas Instruments in the reorganization, which it remained until early 1988, when most of the company was sold to the Halliburton Company.

The next major change came late in 1953 when Texas Instruments went public by merging with the almost-dormant Intercontinental Rubber Company. The merger brought TI new working capital and a listing on the New York Stock Exchange, and helped fuel the company's subsequent growth. Indeed, the postwar era was a heady time for Texas Instruments. In 1953 alone, TI acquired seven new companies. Sales skyrocketed from $6.4 million in 1949 to $20 million in 1952 to $92 million in 1958, establishing TI as a major electronics manufacturer.

A major factor in TI's astronomical growth in the 1950s was the transistor. In 1952, TI paid $25,000 to Western Electric for a license to manufacture its newly patented germanium transistor. Within two years, TI was mass-producing high-frequency germanium transistors and had introduced the first commercial silicon transistor. The silicon transistor was based on research conducted by Gordon Teal, who had been hired from Bell Laboratories to head TI's research laboratories. Teal and his research team had developed a way to make transistors out of silicon rather than germanium in 1954. Silicon had many advantages over germanium, not least of which was its resistance to high temperatures. The silicon transistor was a critical breakthrough.

It was Patrick Haggerty who was convinced that there was a huge market for consumer products that used inexpensive transistors. In 1954 TI, together with the Regency division of Industrial Engineering Associates, Inc., developed the world's first small, inexpensive, portable radio using the germanium transistors TI had developed. The new Regency Radio was introduced in late 1954 and became the hot gift item of the 1954 Christmas season. The transistor soon usurped the place of vacuum tubes forever.

During all this, Haggerty and Mark Shepherd Jr.—then manager of TI's Semiconductor Components division and later chairman of TI—had been trying, with little success, to persuade IBM to make TI a supplier of transistors for its computers. But Thomas Watson Jr., president and founder of IBM, was impressed with the Regency Radio, and in 1957 IBM signed an agreement that made TI a major component supplier for IBM computers. In 1958, Patrick Haggerty was named to succeed Jonsson as president.

From 1956 to 1958, Texas Instruments's annual sales doubled from $46 million to $92 million. In 1957 TI opened its first manufacturing facility outside the United States—a plant in Bedford, England, to supply semiconductors to Britain and Western Europe. And in 1959, TI's merger with Metals and Controls Corporation—a maker of clad metals, control instruments, and nuclear fuel components and instrument cores—gave TI two American plants as well as facilities in Mexico, Argentina, Italy, Holland, and Australia.

One of Texas Instruments's most important breakthroughs occurred in 1958 when a newly hired employee, Jack S. Kilby, came up with the idea for the first integrated circuit. The integrated circuit was a pivotal innovation. Made of a single semiconductor material, it eliminated the need to solder components together. Without wiring and soldering, components could be miniaturized, which allowed for more compact circuitry and also meant huge numbers of components could be crowded onto a single chip.

To be sure, there were manufacturing problems to be overcome. The chips had to be produced in an entirely dust-free environment; an error-free method of ''printing'' the circuits onto the silicon chips had to be devised; and miniaturization itself made manufacturing difficult. But Texas Instruments realized the chip's potential and, after two years of development, the company's first commercial integrated circuits were made available in 1960. Although the electronics industry initially greeted the chip with skepticism, integrated circuits became the foundation of modern microelectronics. Smaller, lighter, faster, more dependable, and more powerful than its predecessors, the chip had many advantages, but it was expensive—$100 for small quantities in 1962. But integrated circuits were ideally suited for use in computers, and together, chips and computers experienced explosive growth.

Semiconductors quickly became a key element in space technology, too, and early interest by the military and the U.S. space program gave TI and its competitors the impetus to improve

their semiconductor chips and refine their production techniques. Under Jack Kilby, TI built the first computer to use silicon integrated circuits for the air force. Demonstrated in 1961, this ten-ounce, 600-part computer proved that integrated circuits were practical.

Chip prices fell to an average of $8 per unit by 1965, making the circuits affordable enough to use in consumer products. Another important breakthrough came in 1969, when IBM began using integrated circuits in all its computers. Soon the government was no longer TI's main customer, although defense electronics remained an important part of its business. Within ten years of Kilby's discovery, semiconductors had become a multi-billion-dollar industry. Early on, TI's management anticipated a huge world demand for semiconductors, and in the 1960s the company built manufacturing plants in Europe, Latin America, and Asia. TI's early start in these markets gave the company an edge over its competitors.

In 1966 Haggerty was elected chairman of TI's board when Jonsson left to become mayor of Dallas. Haggerty had already challenged a team of engineers to develop a new product—the portable, pocket-sized calculator—to show that integrated circuits had a place in the consumer market. In 1967, TI engineers invented a prototype hand-held calculator that weighed 45 ounces. It was four years before the hand-held calculator hit the stores, but once it did, it made history. Within a few years, the once-ubiquitous slide rule was obsolete.

In 1970 TI invented the single-chip microprocessor, or microcomputer, which was introduced commercially the next year. It was this breakthrough chip that paved the way not only for small, inexpensive calculators but also for all sorts of computer-controlled appliances and devices. TI formally entered the consumer-electronic calculator market in 1972 with the introduction of a four-ounce portable calculator and two desktop models, which ranged in price from $85 to $120. Sales of calculators soared from about 3 million units in 1971 to 17 million in 1973, 28 million in 1974, and 45 million in 1975.

Despite this early success, TI was to learn many bitter lessons about marketing to the American consumer. Even early success was hard won. Bowmar Instruments had been selling a calculator that used TI-made chips since 1971. In 1972, when TI entered the calculator market and tried to undercut Bowmar's price, Bowmar quickly matched TI and a price war ensured. TI subscribed to learning-curve pricing: keep prices low (and profits small) in the early stages to build market share and develop manufacturing efficiencies, and then competitors who want to enter the market later will find it difficult or impossible to compete. But after a few years, competitors did begin to make inroads into TI's business; by 1975, as increased competition in the market led to plummeting prices, the calculator market softened, leading to a $16 million loss for TI in the second quarter.

But TI rebounded and again sent shock waves through the consumer-electronics world in 1976 when it introduced an inexpensive, reliable electronic digital watch for a mere $19.95. Almost overnight, TI's watches grabbed a large share of the electronic watch market at the expense of long-established watch manufacturers. A little more than a year later, TI cut the price of its digital watch to $9.95.

When low-cost Asian imports flooded the market in 1978, however, Texas Instruments began to lose its dominant position. TI also failed to capitalize on liquid crystal display (LCD) technology, for which it held the basic patent. It had not anticipated strong consumer demand for LCD watches, which displayed the time continuously rather than requiring the user to push a button for a readout. When sales of LCD watches exploded, TI could not begin mass-production quickly enough. The company's digital-watch sales dropped dramatically in 1979, by the end of 1981 TI had left the digital watch business.

Meanwhile, in TI's mainstay business, semiconductor manufacturing, orders for chips became backlogged. Texas Instruments had spread its resources thinly in order to compete in both the consumer and industrial markets, and worldwide chip demand had soared at the same time. Despite these problems, TI grew at a rapid rate during the 1970s. Defense electronics continued to be highly profitable and semiconductor demand remained strong, buoyed by the worldwide growth in consumer-electronics manufacturing. The company reached $1 billion in sales in 1973, $2 billion in 1977, and $3 billion in 1979.

Mark Shepherd was named chairman of the board upon Patrick Haggerty's retirement in 1976, and J. Fred Bucy, who had worked in almost all of TI's major business areas, was named president and remained chief operating officer. Haggerty continued as general director and honorary chairman until his death in 1980.

In 1978, Texas Instruments introduced Speak & Spell, an educational device that used TI's new speech-synthesis technology, which proved quite popular. That same year, TI was held up as *Business Week*'s model for American companies in the 1980s for its innovation, productivity gains, and phenomenal growth and earnings records.

In mid-1979 TI introduced a home computer, which reached the market that December. Priced at about $1,400, the machine sold more slowly at first than TI had predicted. In 1981 sales began to pick up, though, and a rebate program in 1982 kept sales—and sales predictions—very strong. In April 1983, TI shipped its one millionth home computer.

But suddenly, sales of the TI-99/4A fell off dramatically. By October, TI's overconfident projections and failure to predict the price competitiveness of the market had driven the company out of the home computer business altogether. By the time the 99/4A was withdrawn from the market, TI's usual competitive-pricing strategy had reduced the computer's retail price below the company's production cost, causing TI's first-ever loss, $145 million, in 1983.

TI's consumer electronics never managed to become a consistent money-maker. The company was often accused of arrogance—of trying to find mass markets for new TI inventions rather than adapting its product lines to accommodate customers' needs—and TI's aggressive price-cutting was often insensitive to dealers and customers alike. In addition, TI's pursuit of both consumer and industrial markets often caused

shortages of components resulting in backlogged or reduced shipments.

After experiencing its first loss, TI found regaining its former footing difficult. A slump in semiconductor demand during the recession of the early 1980s made TI's heavy losses in home computers particularly painful. Cost-cutting became a high priority, and TI trimmed its work force by 10,000 employees between 1980 and 1982. In addition, management decided that its matrix management structure was strangling the company and so began to modify the system to revive innovation. Although the company's engineers continued to lead the semiconductor field in innovations, increased competition both in the United States and overseas meant that technological superiority was no longer a guarantee of success. The company recorded yet another $100 million-plus loss in 1985.

TI President Fred Bucy was roundly criticized for being abrasive and autocratic, and the disappointments of the early 1980s hastened his departure. In May 1985 Bucy abruptly retired and Jerry Junkins was elected president and CEO. Junkins, a lifetime TI employee with a much cooler and more conciliatory management style, proved a popular chief executive.

TI's aggressive defense of its intellectual property rights—the exclusive use of the patented technological developments of its employees—highlighted activities in the late 1980s. In 1986 TI filed suit with the International Trade Commission against eight Japanese and one Korean semiconductor manufacturers who were selling dynamic random-access memories (DRAMs) in the United States without obtaining licenses to use technology that belonged to TI. TI reached out-of-court settlements with most of the companies but, more importantly, demonstrated that infringements on its patents would not be tolerated. Royalties from these decisions proved an important source of revenue (over $250 million annually) for TI.

In late 1988 Texas Instruments announced plans to join Japan's Hitachi, Ltd. in developing 16-megabit DRAM technology. Although this decision came as quite a surprise to the electronics industry given TI's successful Japanese subsidiary and its manufacturing plant there, TI explained that the move was necessary to spread the mounting risks and costs involved in producing such an advanced chip.

In 1977, TI had boldly set itself a sales goal of $10 billion by 1989; not long after, it upped the ante to $15 billion by 1990. The company actually entered the 1990s some $9 billion short of that extraordinary goal. After watching its share of the semiconductor market slide from 30 percent to a meager 5 percent over the course of the decade, Junkins took a decisive step. In 1989, the CEO inaugurated a strategic plan to radically reshape Texas Instruments, dubbed ''TI 2000.'' A key aspect of the plan was to loosen the corporation's traditionally tight corporate culture and encourage innovation. This fundamental change was intimately linked to a shift in manufacturing focus from cheap, commodity-based computer chips to high-margin, custom-designed microprocessors and digital signal processors. For example, in 1989 TI embarked on a partnership with Sun Microsystems Inc. to design and manufacture microprocessors, sharing engineering personnel and proprietary technology in the process. TI garnered vital contracts with Sony Corporation,

General Motors Corporation, and Swedish telecommunications powerhouse L.M. Ericsson. The company promoted its repositioning with new business-to-business advertising. From 1988 to 1993, the specialty components segment increased from 25 percent of annual sales to nearly 50 percent. In 1993, Junkins told *Business Week* that TI was "looking for shared dependence" in these partnerships. He also hoped to parlay technological gains into mass sales.

Under Junkins, TI also increased its global manufacturing capacity through a number of joint ventures in Europe and Asia. A 1990 partnership with the Italian government allowed the shared construction expenses of a $1.2 billion plant. By 1992, TI had forged alliances with Taiwanese manufacturer Acer, Kobe Steel in Japan, and a coterie of companies in Singapore. Texas Instruments planned to invest $1 billion in Asian plants by the turn of the century. Joint ventures with Samsung Electronics Co., Ltd. and Hitachi, Ltd. in 1994 split the costs of building semiconductor plants in Portugal and the United States, respectively. TI 2000 also set a goal of increasing the company's high-margin software sales five times, to $1 billion, by the mid-1990s.

Although Texas Instruments recorded net losses in 1990 and 1991, the company's sales and profits rebounded in 1992 and 1993. Profitability, in terms of sales per employee, increased dramatically from $88,300 in 1989 to $143,240 in 1993. In 1992, the firm won the coveted Malcolm Baldrige National Quality Award in manufacturing and adopted the Baldrige criteria as its quality standards. Wall Street noticed the improved performance: TI's stock price more than doubled from 1991 to early 1993.

Principal Subsidiaries: JMA Information Engineering Ltd.; Texas Instruments Deutschland GmbH (Germany); Texas Instruments Equipamento Electronicl Lda. (Portugal); Texas Instruments France S.A.; Texas Instruments Holland B.V.; Texas Instruments Italia SpA; Texas Instruments Japan Ltd.; Texas Instruments Ltd.; Texas Instruments Malaysia Sdn. Bhd.; Texas Instruments Inc. (Philippines); Texas Instruments Singapore (Pte) Ltd.; Texas Instruments Taiwan Ltd.

Further Reading:

Burrows, Peter, "TI Is Moving Up in the World," *Business Week,* August 2, 1993, pp. 46–47.

Lineback, J. Robert, "Rebuilding TI," *Electronic Business Buyer,* March 1994, pp. 52–57.

Rogers, Alison, "Texas Instruments: It's the Execution that Counts," *Fortune,* November 30, 1992, pp. 80–83.

—updated by April Dougal Gasbarre

Thames Water plc

14 Cavendish Place
London W1M 9DJ
United Kingdom
(071) 636 8686
Fax: (071) 436 6743

Public Company
Incorporated: 1989
Employees: 10,352
Sales: £1.04 billion
Stock Exchanges: London
SICs: 6711 Holding Companies; 4941 Water Supply; 4971
   Irrigation Systems

Thames Water is the largest of the United Kingdom's privatized water industries, providing some 7 million customers with water and serving the sewerage needs of nearly 12 million in London and the Thames Valley. In the public sector for years, Thames was privatized in 1989 but remains subject to government regulation as a regional monopoly supplier of an essential utility. Since becoming privatized, the company has widened its portfolio by diversifying into specialist water and wastewater services and long-term management projects abroad.

Water suppliers to London and the surrounding area had been operating on a small scale for centuries, but not until the nineteenth century did modern water management systems come into being to meet the growing demands of the urban center. Increasing population and the phenomenal rise of industry meant that the city was no longer able to satisfy its water needs from local sources. Throughout the Victorian period and well into the twentieth century, a network of supply systems sprang up, with both private waterworks companies and local authorities constructing technologically advanced dams, reservoirs, and aqueducts to meet the ever-increasing demand.

Water projects were regulated in the sense that each required a separate act of parliamentary approval to proceed, but because each proposal was considered in isolation of the others, no attempt was made to implement a coherent, interlocking system of water supply. As early as 1869 the problems inherent in such an unplanned system were recognized, and the Royal Commission on Water Supply mooted the idea of regional planning. No action was taken, however, until much later, in 1924, when the Ministry of Health, in conjuction with the water suppliers,

established Regional Water Committees to coordinate development and operation. Successive acts of Parliament solidified the central government's control of the water industry, culminating in the Water Act of 1973, which put an end to the network of individual suppliers and created 10 regional water authorities in England and Wales. The far-reaching act also encompassed river management and sewage disposal, operations which had hitherto been entirely separate from water supply. All three related operations were thus brought under common management.

Thames Water can claim a role in the water authorities' conversion to plcs through the activities and lobbying of its chairman, Roy Watts. Appointed in 1983 (and serving until his death 10 years later), Watts had already instituted streamlining measures at the water authority (including reducing the board of directors from 62 members to 15) "because I tend to think old companies get fat." Bringing his commercial background to bear, Watts cut costs to the extent that the authority was able to contain tariff increases to 3 percent—whereas the government favored an increase of 10 percent. The disagreement became public, leading to a House of Commons debate and, eventually, the government's decision to privatize all the water authorities. In 1989 Thames Water Authority became Thames Water plc.

The newly privatized water industry remained strictly subject to governmental control. The Office of Water Services (Ofwat), the industry price regulator, set a ceiling on the amount the new company could charge its customers. In addition, it was stipulated that Thames must meet—and annually prove that it has met—both the requirements of U.K. law and the standards of the European Commission regarding water quality and pollution control. These regulations place the company in a somewhat delicate position. Constrained in how much it may charge, Thames is also required by law to invest a considerable amount of capital each year into improving its infrastructure to comply with public health and environmental standards.

Such investment is urgently needed, as Thames, in common with the other former water authorities, inherited a faulty and antiquated system whose myriad inadequacies had been too long ignored. As of 1994, significant investment is necessary to upgrade or replace systems and equipment if they are to be acceptable to current water quality and environmental standards. It will take years, in the opinion of both Thames Water and independent observers, to rectify the mistakes and neglect of the past. These improvements will also take a great deal of money, and how this money is to be obtained is a source of great controversy.

Although Thames's customers' water bills are lower on average than those of any other of the former water authorities, the company reaps its share of the general public disapproval of the privatized companies' performance. To what extent this sense that consumers are not receiving value for money is justified is debatable. Certainly water bills have risen well in advance of inflation since 1989 and certainly high-ranking executives in all the water companies are commanding salaries substantially higher than those they had received while the industry remained in the public sector. (In Thames's case, the chairman's salary rose from £41,000 in 1989 to £317,400 in 1994.) On the other hand, Thames, along with the other former authorities, has had to invest huge amounts of capital to improve its legacy of a defective and outmoded infrastructure to meet increasingly stringent environmental and public health standards. Nor has Thames raised its prices to the highest limit allowed it under the rules established at privatization.

Wherever one chooses to assign blame, it is perhaps inevitable that a monopoly supplier of an essential utility will be viewed with some suspicion. Thames Water attempts to counteract this negative image by producing a flurry of informational material for better public understanding and by initiating an active program of market research to determine just what its market will bear. The company undertook such a study in 1992, explaining to customers that it faced two kinds of financial obligations, mandatory and discretionary. Mandatory spending, by far the lion's share, included all the improvements to its systems and equipment that Thames must finance if the company is to satisfy the requirements of the European Commission. Thames outlined three possible scenarios for the future balancing of water purity and environmental concerns with water rates customers will be obliged to pay by the year 2000. If Thames Water meets the minimum requirements demanded of it now, and no more, the average consumer bill (£162 in 1994) will be £200 in 2000. If Thames were to take what the company terms the "pure and green" route, meaning doing all within its power to ensure the purest possible water quality and the most environmentally healthy treatment of wastewater, the average bill will be £440 per year. If Thames takes a middle ground, the bill is likely to be around £315 per year. Thames's market research found that, overwhelmingly, customers preferred the lowest cost option. Similarly, with regard to discretionary spending, which Thames defined as desirable but not essential spending to accelerate solutions to such problems as interruption to water supply, poor supply pressure, flooding from sewers, and odors from sewage works, customers were willing to pay more only to prevent sewers from actually flooding. The provision of water services, Thames's report concluded, is "taken for granted" and "customers find it hard to imagine what money is actually being spent on."

In July of 1994, five years after privatization, Ofwat imposed new and more stringent controls on the water companies' profits, limiting price increases to an average of 1 percent above inflation for the 10-year period 1995–2005. It is likely that the water companies will have to borrow or drastically cut their operating expenses in order to finance environmental improvements.

Like the other privatized water companies, Thames Water has attempted to escape the government's regulations by diversifying into non-core activities where it may operate in a freer market. Thames has been active internationally since well before privatization, largely in consultancy and training roles, but since 1989 the company has widened its scope to include projects in water process engineering and specialist treatment products. The company's international portfolio includes projects in the privatization of existing utility organizations, the management and operation of water and wastewater utilities, process design and construction, the management of water distribution systems, project financing, demand forecasting and conceptual designs, and feasibility studies.

In 1989 Thames acquired Portals Water Treatment (now PWT Worldwide), a leading water process contractor through which Thames designs and constructs water and wastewater treatment plants. The subsidiary has undertaken projects in Pakistan, Hong Kong, Nigeria, Japan, Singapore, Australia, India, the United Kingdom, and the United States. Discussions initiated in 1990 resulted in a significant 1993 agreement whereby a consortium led by Thames will design and build a water treatment plant at Izmit, Turkey. The subsidiary Thames Water International, the technical and managerial services arm of the Thames group, will then operate the finished project for a period of 15 years before relinquishing it to the management of local authorities. Also in 1993 Thames acquired the environmental engineering business of Simon Engineering, which allows the company additional scope for wastewater treatment projects. The German Utag was acquired in 1992 for its expertise in consulting, contracting, and the construction of environmental products.

Despite such an ambitious international portfolio, Thames has had little success in its non-core activities: indeed the *Evening Standard* stated bluntly in 1994: "The company seems accident prone overseas. . . . After five years abroad, Thames has yet to make a penny profit outside Britain," and in the same year the *Financial Times,* alluding to Thames's overseas activities, called it the "worst performing water company since privatization." Thames Water defends its record, citing the monumental costs of restructuring its foreign acquisitions and unwise contracts entered into by its subsidiaries prior to their acquisition by Thames. The company insists that its overseas strategies must be taken in a long-term context, and that its unprofitable foreign ventures will be breaking even by 1994–95 and bringing in profits thereafter.

Thames has a better record in its primary function as a U.K. utility. The company's brightest star is the London Water Ring Main, needed to alleviate pressure on the city's antiquated pipe system, which was in danger of leaking or even bursting. Eighty kilometers long (longer than the Channel Tunnel) and 40 meters deep (deeper than most London Underground lines), the £250 million project was built to supply half of London's drinking water. Thames completed the project in 1994, to budget and two years ahead of schedule.

Other significant successes for Thames include its 1993 completion of a five-year modernization program at the 140-year-old Hampton water treatment works, and a £400 million investment to install advanced water treatment (AWT) facilities at its plants to filter out pesticides. The company also points to its success in containing leakage. At privatization the company was losing 25 percent of its water through leaks; this loss had been reduced, as of 1993, through a technologically sophisticated system of leakage detection and solution, to 17 percent, obviating the need to build new reservoirs. Such improvements—and others involving better water clarification systems, safer sewage plants with improved odor control, and more efficient sludge management systems—point to the company's active research and development team.

Scope for improvement remains, however; in 1992–93 the company was successfully prosecuted four times by the National Rivers Authority for improper treatment and disposal of sewage. Much work remains to be done on Thames's nearly 400 sewage treatment works, virtually all of which were in an inadequate condition at privatization.

Thames Water is required by the government Code of Practice on Conservation, Access and Recreation to report regularly on the company's sensitivity to these issues. Some 20 percent of Thames-owned land is in designated Areas of Outstanding Natural Beauty. Furthermore, as the Thames region encompasses a high proportion of densely populated urban centers, the need for conservation and recreational areas is particularly acute. In compliance, Thames liaises with dozens of conservation, environmental, and community groups and is involved in numerous projects to protect the region's natural and man-made heritage and to improve recreational access to its land.

Privatization almost always results in staff cuts and more rigorous cost controls, and the privatization of Thames was no exception. Personnel numbers have been reduced by some 6.6 percent since 1989 and the company has cut operating costs where possible—replacing, for instance, the authority's 25 small laboratories dotted throughout the region with two large central ones in London and Reading. In addition, the company sought to improve its level of customer service, building a new centralized customer service center in Swindon. The status of a privatized but still closely regulated utility is in many respects a problematic one. Like the other water companies, Thames has seen its share of controversy as it tries to strike the balance between the public duty of a monopoly utility and the profit motive of the private sector. It has also (at least to date) seen its share of disappointment in its diversifications abroad. Perhaps it is as well to keep in mind one simple statistic so often taken for granted by supporters and detractors alike—over 99 percent of the water Thames supplies to its millions of customers meets all the stringent requirements of both the United Kingdom and the European Commission.

Principal Subsidiaries: PCI Membrane Systems Ltd.; PWT Worldwide Ltd.; Simon-Hartley Ltd.; Simon Waste Solutions Inc. (U.S.A.); Thames Water Environmental Services Ltd.; Thames Water International Services Holdings Ltd.; Thames Water Utilities Ltd.

Further Reading:

"Dangerous Waters," *Evening Standard,* June 15, 1994.
Kay, Helen, "Thames Water Makes Waves," *Management Today,* July 1991, pp. 34–39.
"Keep Taking the Waters," *The Times,* June 16, 1994.
"The Lex Column: Thames Water," *Financial Times,* June 16, 1994.
Mortished, Carl, "Water Bills Will Be Capped for 10 Years," *The Times,* July 29, 1994, p. 1.
Murray, Ian, "Ofwat Plans to Cut Flow of Profits to Water Industry," *The Times,* July 12, 1994, p. 7.
Norman, Margot, "Muddying the Waters," *The Times,* July 12, 1994, p. 16.
"Of Wealth and Water," *Economist,* October 6, 1990, pp. 39–40.
Porter, Elizabeth, *Water Management in England and Wales,* Cambridge Geographical Studies, no. 10, Cambridge University Press, 1978.
Taking Care of the Future: Thames Water Market Plan, London: Thames Water plc, 1993.
"Technology: Stopping the Flood," *Financial Times,* March 4, 1994.
"Thames Drops to Pounds 242m after Costs," *Daily Telegraph,* June 16, 1994.
"Thames Looks for Growth with 'Dirty Water' Industry," *Yorkshire Post,* January 13, 1993.
"Thames Water Shares Take a Dive," *Independent,* June 16, 1994.
"Thames Water to Lead Dollars 700m Turkish Project," *Financial Times,* February 4, 1993.
"Water Profits under Pressure," *The Times,* July 7, 1994, p. 26.
Wilsher, Peter, "British Water Makes Waves Overseas," *Management Today,* October, 1993, pp. 86–90.

—Robin DuBlanc

Thermo Instrument Systems Inc.

Thermo Instrument Systems Inc.

504 Airport Road
Santa Fe, New Mexico 87504-2108
U.S.A.
(617) 622-1111
Fax: (617) 622-1207

Public Company
Incorporated: 1986
Employees: 4,033
Sales: $584 million
Stock Exchanges: New York
SICs: 3826 Analytical Instruments; 3829 Measuring and
    Controlling Devices; 8734 Testing Laboratories

Thermo Instrument Systems Inc., a majority-owned subsidiary of Thermo Electron, is an international leader in developing and manufacturing analytical instruments used to detect and measure air pollution, nuclear radioactivity, complex chemical compounds, toxic metals, and other elements. In addition, the company provides specialized environmental analysis and engineering services throughout the United States. Facilities are located throughout North America, Europe, and Asia, with representatives and distributors serving more than 50 countries. The company's customer base includes industrial companies, utilities, government agencies, and research laboratories. Thermo Instrument Systems has been extremely profitable, largely due to its success in acquiring promising but failing businesses and turning them around. The company is ranked in the top ten of all instrument companies in the world based on sales, earnings, and return on stockholders' equity.

The history of Thermo Instrument Systems is inextricably linked to that of its majority owner, Thermo Electron, a Massachusetts-based company specializing in high-technology products. With $800 million in annual sales, Thermo Electron is renowned for its innovative spin-off strategies. Thermo Electron has nine majority-owned spin-offs, including Thermo Instrument Systems, and several wholly owned subsidiaries. Thermo Electron is led by the vision of its founder and CEO, Dr. George Hatsopoulos.

Born in Athens, Greece, Hatsopoulos was the son of the chief operating officer of Greece's electric rail system. Hatsopoulos attended the National Technical University in Greece, where he studied electrical engineering and thermodynamics. He then completed his studies in the United States, earning Bachelor's and Ph.D. degrees in thermodynamics at the Massachusetts Institute of Technology. As a graduate student at M.I.T., Hatsopoulos became fascinated by the concept of converting heat into electricity, and he began to work on the creation of a thermionic energy converter. While completing his doctoral research, he sought a means of marketing the products described in his dissertation, and, in 1956, with the support of a Greek shipping company, Hatsopoulos founded Thermo Electron.

Thermo Electron was unique for several reasons, all of which have contributed to its success in an industry in which many companies have struggled or gone bankrupt. Specifically, Thermo Electron sought to reward risk-takers and innovators, creating opportunities for them to pursue unusual research projects with commercial potential. Research projects that proved commercially viable were then made into subsidiary companies and spun off to the public. Generally, these subsidiaries were managed by the engineers and scientists who originated the research. This aspect of Thermo Electron's managerial structure was highly unusual in a field which typically provided very little in the way of upper-level advancement opportunities for engineers.

In 1970, Hastopoulos hired Arvin Smith to manage the direct energy conversion and electronics group of the company's Research and Development/New Business Center. Prior to joining Thermo, Smith had worked as an engineer and engineering manager in the aerospace industry for 16 years. In the early years of the space program, Smith worked at NASA's Jet Propulsion Laboratory and then relocated to Washington's Office of Advanced Research and Technology, where he became chief of solar and chemical power systems.

Shortly after Smith joined Thermo Electron, the company established a department within the R&D center to develop air pollution monitoring instruments. Smith was selected to head this new department. In 1977, Thermo Electron formed a new Environmental Instrument Division, appointing Smith as president. Under Smith's leadership, the division became one of Thermo Electron's most profitable businesses. In 1986, Thermo Instrument Systems Inc. was spun off and incorporated as a majority-owned subsidiary, and Smith became its president. The company's revenues for its first year were $85.8 million.

Thermo Instrument Systems enjoyed tremendous financial success from the outset. Like its parent company, Thermo Instrument maintained a group of division presidents who were technically knowledgeable engineers. Each division president was given financial goals, with a cumulative goal of 30 percent earnings growth for the company each year. In the years from 1986 to 1994, the company and its divisions reached their goals each year.

Two strategies in particular secured growth for the company: acquisitions and internal development. Through nine acquisitions between 1986 and 1994, the company achieved new technologies, distribution channels, markets, personnel, and opportunities to improve margins and profitability. In every acquisition, the company expanded margins and profitability, positioning each business for long-term dependable growth.

A 1994 management study of Thermo Instrument Systems by Raymond James & Associates found the company's propensity to transform a failing business into a profitable one to be "nothing short of extraordinary." Acquisitions were made with a three-prong approach, emphasizing earnings over revenue growth. First, the company de-emphasized lower margin products, increasing the price to the point where a reasonable gross margin could be earned. If the product did not sell at that price, it was discontinued. At the same time, the company developed technically superior products which could command a price premium of five to ten percent. Because the first two strategies were not always possible, the third focused on improving productivity. In 1994, Thermo Instrument Systems displayed the highest productivity of any company in a comparable group. The company's revenue per employee was $200,000, while the industry standard was $160,000 to $170,000.

In 1989, Thermo Instrument Systems made its first important acquisition, purchasing LDC Analytical for $21.2 million. LDC Analytical manufactured an analytical instrument known as the high performance liquid chromatograph (HPLC). This acquisition provided the company with new technology that facilitated the separation, isolation, and purification of complex molecular mixtures. This technology was used in the pharmaceutical, biotechnology, and chemicals industries.

1990 marked the beginning of a new era of expansion for Thermo Instrument, as it merged with Thermo Environmental Corporation, which had been formed in 1987 when Thermo Analytical merged with Thermo Water Management. Thermo Environmental, an 80 percent subsidiary of Thermo Electron, was acquired by Thermo Instrument Systems in 1990. Thermo Environmental was then divided into several wholly owned subsidiaries, including Thermo Analytical Inc., Thermo Consulting Engineers, Bettigole Andrews and Clark Inc., and TMA/Normandeau Associates. The acquisition of Thermo Environmental was a key move for Thermo Instrument Systems Inc., allowing the company to expand by adding laboratory, consulting, and engineering services to complement its core analytical instruments business. This merger/acquisition paved the way for Thermo Instrument's expansion into operations beyond instrument manufacturing in the 1990s. The company's year-end revenues for 1989 (refigured to include the merger) were $184.7 million.

Thermo Instrument Systems made a strategic decision to enter the market for mass spectrometers in 1990. That fall, the company acquired Finnigan Corporation, the world's leading manufacturer of mass spectrometers. Often referred to as "the mother of all detection technologies," mass spectrometers were unsurpassed by any analytical instrument in their ability to provide information on the molecular weight of a chemical/biological compound and the amount of compound present in a sample. The market for mass spectrometers—one of the fastest growing segments of the analytical instruments market—would grow at approximately ten percent each year.

In 1990, the Clean Air Act was passed, with emission monitoring rules mandating the installation of continuous emission monitoring systems on boilers for utilities and industry. This legislation would become important in the early 1990s, as regulations became finalized and spending to bring boilers in

line began to occur. The company achieved revenues of $285.4 million in 1990 (accounting for 40 percent of Thermo Electron's revenue) and $338.8 million in 1991.

Another important acquisition was made in 1992, when Thermo Instrument Systems purchased Gas Tech, Inc., a California manufacturer of worker safety instruments and systems that detected and monitored toxic and combustible gases. Prior to the acquisition, Thermo Instrument Systems sold air monitoring instruments through its Thermo Environmental Instruments subsidiary. However, the purchase of Gas Tech, Inc. opened new markets to the company, because while the instruments sold by Thermo Environmental were driven by EPA rules, Gas Tech was governed by OSHA (worker safety) standards.

Also in 1992, the company acquired new technology with the purchase of Nicolet Instrument Company. With 1992 revenues of $139 million, Nicolet was Thermo Instrument's largest acquisition, and its assimilation represented the greatest challenge in the company's history. Fourier Transform Infrared Spectrometry (FTR), an analytical instrument technology that identified organic compounds and determined their concentration, presented excellent potential for monitoring air pollutants. Recognizing that FTR technology would become an important segment of the analytical instruments market, Thermo Instrument Systems again positioned itself to reach that market through the acquisition of Nicolet, the world's leader in the market. Thermo Instruments closed the 1992 fiscal year with sales of $423 million, a 25 percent increase over the previous year.

In 1993, for the third year in a row, Thermo Instrument was named one of America's 1,000 most valuable companies by *Business Week*. Thermo Instrument was the only New Mexico-based company on the list, and was placed at number 638 on the basis of its stock market value of $1.15 billion. Earnings per share had risen 25 percent, from 92 cents in 1991 to $1.15 in 1992. According to *Financial World*, a $100 investment in the company in 1987 would have been worth $429 by the end of 1992. By 1993, Thermo Instrument's revenue increased to $584 million (primarily due to the 1992 acquisitions), a remarkable 38 percent increase over the previous year.

In 1994, the company acquired several of the businesses that formed the envirotech measurement and controls group of Baker Hughes Incorporated. The company also joined forces with Thermo Process Systems, forming an environmental services company entitled Thermo Terra Tech. Under the agreement, Thermo Instrument would contribute its environmental service business, and Thermo Process would contribute its environmental laboratory business. This joint venture brought Thermo Instrument back to its origins as an instrument manufacturer.

In 1994, Thermo Instrument's business plan for the next few years continued to project 30 percent growth, with the source of growth split evenly between internal development and acquisitions. During the early 1990s, the majority of growth came from acquisitions, with only four to five percent real growth in sales. The company also expected to achieve greater internal development through maintenance of its competitive position within existing, growing product lines and through accelerated development of new products, as it strove to become a leader in each of four areas of business: analytical instruments, monitoring instruments, process monitoring, and environmental services. With a broad customer base that included industrial companies, government agencies, utilities, and private research laboratories, a growing market in universities, and exceptional stock market value, Thermo Instrument Systems was likely to meet its goals.

Principal Subsidiaries: Finnigan; Nicolet Instrument Corporation; Thermo Jarrell Ash; LDC Analytical; Thermo Environmental Instruments, Inc.; Gas Tech, Inc.; Eberline; National Nuclear; Reactor Experiments; Xetex; Eberline Ltd.; Thermo Analytical Inc.; Bettigole Andrews and Clark, Inc.; Thermo Consulting Engineers; TMA/Normandeau Associates; Envirotech Measurement and Controls Group of Baker Hughes.

Further Reading:

David, Gregory E., "Thermo Instrument: It Measures Up," *Financial World,* October 26, 1993, p. 20.

Feder, Barnaby J., "The Spinoff Stratagem," *The New York Times,* November 11, 1990, p. 4.

Miller, Christopher, "Santa Fe Company Stays on Elite List," *Albuquerque Journal,* April 9, 1993.

"Not By Technology Alone," *Chief Executive,* April 1993.

"Thermo Electron Says Two Subsidiaries Buy Baker Hughes Lines," *Wall Street Journal,* February 1, 1994, p. B2.

"The 200 Best Small Companies in America," *Forbes,* November 12, 1989, p. 234.

—Heidi Feldman

Thomas&Betts

Thomas & Betts Corp.

1555 Lynnfield Road
Memphis, Tennessee 38119
U.S.A.
(901) 682-7766
Fax: (901) 685-1988

Public Company
Incorporated: 1917 as Thomas & Betts Co.
Employees: 8,000
Sales: $1.07 billion
Stock Exchanges: New York
SICs: 3643 Current-Carrying Wiring Devices; 3644
    Noncurrent-Carrying Wiring Devices; 3678 Electronic
    Connectors

Thomas & Betts Corp. (T&B) is a global manufacturer of electrical and electronic connectors, components, and systems. As the computer age has created an ever-growing need for new electrical and electronic products, and as international markets have opened up, the company has diversified its products worldwide. Its facilities and marketing activities are concentrated in North America, Europe, and the Far East, and its diverse product line includes fittings and accessories for electrical raceways, crimp and mechanical connectors for small wires and power cables, wire fastening devices and markers, insulation products, fiber optic connectors, networking interconnection systems for voice and data communications, ceramic chip capacitors, flat cables, connectors, and accessories for electronic applications. These and other products are used in a wide array of markets, including automobile manufacturing, telecommunications, residential construction, and power utilities. Within these markets, the company serves the maintenance and repair segments, as well as original equipment manufacturers (OEMs).

From its earliest years in business, T&B demonstrated an ability to transform electrically charged business ideas into readily marketable products. In 1898, Robert M. Thomas and Hobart D. Betts, both engineering graduates from Princeton University, established an agency in New York City for selling electrical conduit. Within a year, they were joined by Adnah McMurtrie, another engineer whose in-house designs added to the fledgling agency's list of salable products. As early as 1906, T&B's innovative products changed the electric industry. The Erickson coupling, for example, permitted electricians to join two con-

duits without having to rotate either, or to separate conduit without disassembling the whole conduit run. These early patents set industry standards and were still widely used in the 1990s. Such products made for healthy sales around the turn of the century.

To push their young firm's growth up to the next level, however, the three colleagues realized that they had to begin manufacturing the goods they designed and sold. To that end, in 1912 they purchased the Standard Electric Fittings Company of Stamford, Connecticut. The following year, they solicited the expertise of Robert Thomas's nephew, George C. Thomas, Jr., who pushed the company's manufacturing capabilities to unprecedented levels. With design, manufacturing, and sales efforts all advancing at a healthy rate by 1917, it was time to centralize resources and consolidate operations. That year, Thomas & Betts sales agency and the Standard Electric Fittings Company were merged to form one, new corporation, Thomas & Betts Co. Central headquarters were established on Butler Street in Elizabeth, New Jersey, a site that remained T&B's largest manufacturing facility into the 1990s.

Following its incorporation, T&B entered a period of diversification and geographic expansion that would last uninterrupted until the outbreak of World War II. In 1928, G. C. Thomas, Jr. rose to the position of chief executive officer, a tribute the importance of the manufacturing initiatives he had managed over the previous decade and would continue to expand into the 1970s. Under Thomas Jr.'s leadership, T&B also pushed into broader markets, founding Thomas & Betts Limited in order to sell products in Canada.

The onset of World War II forced T&B into product development that it may have otherwise neglected. The military's drive to reduce weight in aircraft, for example, spurred the firm's development of the first successful compression lugs for connecting aluminum conductors. This breakthrough led to the development of a complete line of color-coded compression connectors, as well as hand and hydraulic tools and dies. After the war, these and other innovations served numerous civilian applications, adding significantly to the company's product line.

Product changes were accompanied by organizational changes as the company entered the 1960s. T&B became a public company in 1959 and was first listed on the New York Stocks Exchange in 1962. Meanwhile, in 1960, Thomas Jr. Jr. retired as CEO and was replaced by Nestor J. MacDonald, the former vice-president of marketing.

Early in MacDonald's tenure, T&B continued to stride assiduously into new, international markets. Building on its existent Canadian presence, a new international division was established in 1962. By 1963, the company emphasizing closer field contact with licensees in Great Britain, Europe, and Mexico. In order to speed up the development of European markets, the company also established a new European subsidiary, Thomas & Betts of Belgium, S.A. in June of that year. By 1983, a Luxembourg facility had been established to produce electronic connectors for even broader European markets. Moreover, Ouest Electronic Connecteurs, a French maker of electronic connectors and custom components of which T&B had acquired 80 percent in 1982, provided additional R&D and manufacturing capabilities in Europe. Other international points of contact included an Australian location to supply the South Pacific.

While delving into foreign markets in the 1960s and 1970s, T&B also began to push aggressively beyond its traditional expertise in electric supplies and into electronic components. Its initial forays in that direction were bolstered by the purchase of Arthur Ansley Manufacturing Company in 1966 and Digital Sensors, Inc. (DSI) in 1968. After J. David Parkinson—former head of the company's electrical business—succeeded Mac-Donald as CEO in 1974, electronic product development was stepped up yet again. In 1975, T&B merged its Ansley and DSI divisions into Ansley Electronics Division (subsequently renamed Thomas & Betts electronics division in 1981).

Progress in electronics built on a solid foundation of innovation that had already distinguished T&B as a market leader in the electrical market. Through the 1980s, many of the company's past developments were still considered milestones in the industry at large: conduit fitting with integrally insulated throats in 1954; new cable ties and straps in 1959; use of steel in rigid conduit fittings line in 1968; new designs in floor boxes in 1970; heat shrinkable insulating covers and caps in 1974; and a line of flat conductor cable for under carpet wiring systems in 1980. That list was supplemented by a growing of electronic interconnection products for professionals in electronic engineering, telecommunications, and automotive electronics. Some of T&B's best performers included: the FLEXPAC Termination system, consisting of flexible conductor cables, jumpers, and circuits; connectors for leadless chip carriers, designed for multilayer printed circuit boards in advanced computer systems; and dual in-line package (DIP) sockets for interconnecting integrated circuits (ICs).

Through the late 1980s, T&B continued to aggressively seek out new markets. The firm began a series of strategic acquisition under the guidance of T. Kevin Dunnigan—a seasoned veteran who had progressed from Canadian sales in the 1960s to president and COO in 1980, and finally to CEO in 1985. In 1987, the company acquired Vitramon, Inc., a manufacturer of surface-mount ceramic chip capacitors (an integral part of the power management process in all electronic systems). Vitramon's surface-mount technology permitted direct soldering of the chips onto printed circuit boards, thereby simplifying the manufacturing process and saving space. This acquisition was quickly followed by the 1988 acquisition of Nevada Western Supply Co., specializing in voice and data wiring products that could be easily and cost-effectively installed using ordinary telephone wiring. Both these acquisitions were a step away from T&B's core line of electrical and electronic connectors, and both were intended to capitalize on new demands related to computer and communications networking.

The 1989 acquisition of Holmberg Electronics Corp., a manufacturer of electronic connectors, was more in line with T&B's historical field of specialty. The effect of that acquisition on core business was soon eclipsed, however, by the largest acquisition in the company's history. On January 2, 1992, T&B acquired FL Industries Holdings, Inc., known in the electrical industry as American Electric. The corporation's electrical business and American Electric were merged into a new Thomas & Betts Electrical Division, which, along with the existing corpo-

rate headquarters, was relocated to Memphis, Tennessee, on the site of the former American Electric. By the first quarter of 1994, T&B's Electronics Division headquarters also moved to Memphis, thereby joining the newly energized core.

Critical to that core was the competitive edge that American Electric would contribute to T&B. Founded in 1958, American Electric had undergone a series of transformations and buyouts. In 1968, when American Electric still focused on its original business of manufacturing lighting and related products to the utility market, it was acquired by ITT Corp. After becoming the nation's largest street light manufacturer, American Electric was sold to Forstmann-Little, a leveraged buyout firm, in June 1985. Under that management, the company began a rapid chain of acquisitions, including the Electrical Products Division of Midland-Ross Corp., the Lighting Division of North American Phillips, Anchor Metals, and American Pole. With such a dynamic range of constitutive parts, American Electric was better suited to give T&B "a broader market presence, and [to] function more effectively as a single global unit," as chairperson and CEO Dunnigan remarked in the 1993 letter to shareholders.

T&G's acquisition of American Electric triggered a series of other strategic moves and organizational changes designed to consolidate operations and optimize efficiency of the larger company. On January 1, 1994, Clyde R. Moore became president and COO. He brought to the post experience as previous president of Thomas & Betts Electrical Division and president of American Electric before the acquisition. Six months later, T&B sold Vitramon—the manufacturer of ceramic chip capacitors it had acquired in 1987—to Vishay Intertechnology, Inc. The move represented an effort to focus on T&B's core businesses of electrical and electronic connectors, components, and systems. In continuation of that process, on September 16, 1994 the company announced pre-tax charge of approximately $90 million to cover the costs for various initiatives to "optimize operations," according to a T&B press release on that date. According to Dunnigan, "the actions covered by these charges are expected to result in savings of approximately $8 million in 1995 and over $20 million annually in subsequent years."

In the effort to optimize operations, one of the first areas of concentration was quality control. Starting in 1987, the firm launched its Total Quality Excellence (TQE) program, involving all employees in an ongoing effort to improve product quality and reduce costs. T&B began implementing statistical quality control and just-in-time manufacturing techniques in all its plants, as well as computer-aided design and manufacturing. The program's ultimate goal was to provide "each customer with the right product, on time delivery, zero defects, and competitive pricing," according to Jim Dailey, vice-president of marketing for the T&B electrical division, in a July 1990 *Industrial Distribution* article.

Declaring in its promotional literature that "the era of electronic commerce has arrived," T&B also dedicated significant resources to marketing strategies employing electronic data interchange with its customers. In an effort to optimize customer service for its electrical distributors, T&B's largest single market, the company designed SIGNATURE SERVICES, a marketing package that sped up the order entry process and reduced paperwork for shipping billing. Taking that system a step further in 1993, T&B implemented DISTRIBUTOR/MANUFACTURER INTEGRATION, an interactive system that made inventory management a responsibility—and ideally a simple one—shared by both the distributor and the company. A similar service, Easy Access, was designed for electronics customers. Distributors and buying manufacturers in that market could check T&B's inventory and pricing, the status of their orders, while corresponding instantaneously via electronic mail. These state-of-the-art systems represented important steps toward reducing costs while increasing direct contact with market trends via the company's customers.

The combination of such interactive customer support systems and its diversifying product line set the stage for continued expansion into the twenty-first century. The direction of such expansion would depend in large part on the directions of the electric and electrical component markets. Still, T&B was positioned to gain from a wide array of possible scenarios. With tens of thousands of components, accessories, and sub-assemblies in its inventory, the company offered useful products wherever wires and other electrical conductors were used. In the early 1990s, the firm gained a Fortune 500 listing, and, in April 1994, *Fortune* magazine ranked T&B 351 in sales and 220 in profits against the largest U.S. industrial corporations.

Principal Subsidiaries: FL Industries Holdings, Inc.; Quelcor, Inc.; Thomas & Betts Caribe, Inc.; Thomas & Betts FSC, Inc. (U.S. Virgin Islands); Thomas & Betts Industries Co., Ltd. (Taiwan, R.O.C.); Thomas & Betts International, Inc.

Further Reading:

Beaty, Wayne, "Mergers Bring Problems and Opportunities," *Electric Light and Power,* April 1993, p. 31.
"Connectors and Terminations (1991–92 Electrical Products Yearbook Issue)," *EC&M Electrical Construction & Maintenance,* November 15, 1991, p. 62.
Fodor, George M., "Shared Data Fosters Quality; Distributors and Suppliers Work Together to Improve Service," *Industrial Distribution,* July 1990, p. 43.
Shepard, Scott, "Building a Better Hub: Thomas & Betts Uses Its New Corporate Culture to Get Product to Market Quickly," *Memphis Business Journal,* December 21, 1992, p. 3.
"Thomas & Betts Announces Special Charge to Optimize Operations," *Business Wire,* September 16, 1994.
"Vishay Completes Acquisition of Vitramon Multi-Layer Ceramic Chip Capacitor Business," *PR Newswire,* July 19, 1994.

—Kerstan Cohen

3Com Corp.

5400 Bayfront Plaza
Santa Clara, California 95052-8145
U.S.A.
(408) 764-5000
Fax: (408) 764-5001

Public Company
Incorporated: 1979
Employees: 2,300
Sales: $1,013.7 million
Stock Exchanges: NASDAQ
SICs: 3577 Computer Peripheral Equipment, Not Elsewhere
   Classified

3Com Corp. is the world's leading provider of Ethernet network adapters, circuit boards added to personal computers that permit them to operate on local area networks. The company holds a 29 percent share in the $1.8 billion Ethernet network adapter business, which it pioneered. 3Com is also a significant provider of other network equipment, such as network hubs (central switching devices for network communication lines), internetworking routers (devices that automatically select the most effective routes for data being transmitted between networks), and access servers that foster teleworking. Thus 3Com, unlike its competitors, offers its clients complete network or internetworking systems.

3Com Corp. was founded in 1979 by Robert M. Metcalfe as a consulting firm for computer network technology. The name 3Com was derived from its focus on the computer, communication, and compatibility. Bob Metcalfe, an M.I.T.-educated engineer, originally established the firm as a consultancy because the market for computer network products had not yet emerged. Six years earlier at Xerox's Palo Alto Research Center, Metcalfe had led a team that invented Ethernet, one of the first local area network (LAN) systems for linking computers and peripherals (printers, scanners, modems, etc.) within a building. In 1979, after attending an M.I.T. alumni seminar on starting one's own business, the 32-year-old Metcalfe quit Xerox to start his own consulting firm. Later that year, he incorporated 3Com, with the participation of college friend Howard Charney, an engineer-turned-patent attorney, and two others as co-founders.

In 1980, the group of four decided the time was ripe to convert their company into a LAN equipment manufacturing business using the Ethernet technology. It was at this time, following Metcalfe's encouragement, that Xerox had decided to share its Ethernet patent with minicomputer manufacturer Digital Equipment Corp. and microprocessor manufacturer Intel Corp. in order to establish Ethernet as a LAN industry standard. As a manufacturer, 3Com was still a little ahead of its time; although there were very few enterprises that had multiple computers, most having only one mainframe or at most a couple of minicomputers, Metcalfe foresaw that personal computers would someday become commonplace.

The group began approaching California venture capital firms in October 1980 for financing in order to begin developing products. 3Com's business plan emphasized a strategy of letting market demand determine its rate of growth, taking the risk that the market might run away, and focusing on long-term growth, rather than short-term market share. Despite the initial slow growth predications, three venture capitalists contributed a total of $1.1 million in the first round of financing, largely on the strength of its founders' reputations.

In March 1981, Metcalfe recruited L. William Krause, who then was general manager of Hewlett-Packard's General Systems Division, to become 3Com's president. Metcalfe retained the positions of chief executive officer and chairperson and assumed the additional title of vice-president of engineering. Bill Krause was also given a nine percent share in the company, second in size only to Metcalfe's 21 percent. 3Com then had only nine employees, but Krause had visions of a much larger company. Also that month, 3Com began shipping its first hardware product, its first Ethernet transceiver and adapter. Krause soon hired a vice-president of sales and a vice-president of marketing, and, a few months later, he hired someone else to assume Metcalfe's position of vice-president of engineering.

Krause had a conservative, risk-averse management style. When sales of 3Com's interim product were not as high as expected in summer 1981 and a cash flow problem loomed, Krause initiated a survival plan that involved a hiring freeze, a pay cut for all employees and officers, and a specific list of objectives. Even so, 3Com was not in serious difficulty. Sales for the year ending May 31, 1982 were $1.8 million. A second round of financing totaling $2.1 million came in January 1982. At the June 1982 board meeting, the board compelled Metcalfe to relinquish his title of CEO to Krause, who had really been in charge since he came to 3Com. Metcalfe then took on a new, more active role in the position of vice-president of sales and marketing.

3Com's sales took off in the summer months of 1982, not long after IBM introduced its 16-bit personal computer. The young company became profitable in 1983, and, in March 1984, 3Com went public, raising $10 million. By then it was expanding by approximately 300 percent annually, having grown from $4.7 million to $16.7 million in sales for the fiscal year ending May 1984. Earnings that year were $2.3 million, and the company had a 15 percent operating profit. Two years later, for fiscal year ending May 31, 1986, revenues reached $64 million.

The company was doing well selling adapter cards to value-added resellers and to original equipment manufacturers, which were large computer manufacturing companies. However, the market was rapidly maturing, as computer manufacturers, including IBM and Digital Equipment Corp., were beginning to integrate their own networking functions into their computers. In 1986, 3Com held eight percent of the LAN market, while computer manufacturer IBM had captured 28 percent of the market by including LAN hardware and software within its computers.

In response to the trend, 3Com decided to move in the direction of providing more complete computer network systems. In 1984, Metcalfe had started a new software division to develop advanced network software, and the company shipped its first network operating system software, 3+, two years later. Also during this time, 3Com began marketing its own computer called the 3Server to function as a network server, a computer on a network whose data is accessed by multiple desktop computers in a configuration known as client-server. By spring 1986, servers accounted for 32 percent of 3Com's sales. To complete the system, 3Com also wanted to offer computers that functioned as clients. Therefore, in early 1986, it pursued a merger with Convergent Technologies Inc., which manufactured UNIX-based workstations. However, two days before the scheduled shareholder approval in March 1986, 3Com's investment banker advised against being acquired by Convergent. On its own, 3Com then began selling systems that included modified personal computers, referred to as network stations, which operated only within its networks.

In 1987, 3Com began marketing itself more as a workgroups computing company that made and marketed PC-network systems. As such, it emphasized products that improved the productivity of workgroups. Several product introductions were made that year, including new network servers, software, and industry-standard network adapter cards. With this market strategy, however, 3Com was running into competition with Novell, Inc., which offered similar products. One important difference, however, was that 3Com targeted niche markets of more sophisticated users.

In September 1987, 3Com made a significant acquisition by purchasing Bridge Communications Inc. for $151 million. Bridge was a provider of internetwork gateways and multiple-protocol bridges, devices that link different networks together on a corporate level. Thus Bridge's products complemented 3Com's, and the largest independent networking manufacturer at that time was formed.

Integration of the two companies, however, was not without difficulties. Bridge was completely merged into 3Com by March 1988, but it was not until the end of 1989 that its new internetworking products were introduced. Bridge co-founder William Carrico was appointed president of 3Com, with Krause remaining as CEO, but differences in management styles and corporate cultures prompted Carrico to resign in May 1988, and Krause regained the presidency. At the same time, Bridge Communications Division General Manager Judy Estrin, another co-founder of Bridge, also resigned.

The integration of the sales forces also caused problems, since 3Com had focused on value-added resellers, whereas Bridge was more involved in direct sales. Therefore, a Cooperative Selling Program was launched whereby sales representatives earned commissions on sales to value-added resellers just as they did for direct sales. However, the buildup of a direct sales force angered some of 3Com's traditional dealers, and sales of LAN Manager suffered.

Also in 1987, 3Com had entered into a joint effort with Microsoft Corp. to develop and market LAN Manager network software for the OS/2 operating system. 3Com sold LAN Manager under a license agreement with Microsoft, and, beginning in 1988, it also marketed 3+Open, its own version of LAN Manager. However, LAN Manager was a direct competitor of Novell's product, NetWare, and OS/2 eventually proved less popular an operating system than expected.

3Com's sales for the year ending May 31, 1988 were $252 million, up from $156 million in the previous year, and earnings had risen from $16.2 million to $22.5 million. By 1988, 3Com was the leading company specializing in computer networks. As a provider of networks, it was second only to Digital Equipment Corp., and was ahead of IBM.

Then, in the summer of 1989, revenue growth began to slow seriously for the first time, partly due to the poor sales of LAN Manager. 3Com had its first annual drop in earnings for the year ending May 1990. The company was also losing in its battle against rival Novell's NetWare, which by 1990 had 65 percent of the network operating system market share. In 1989, 3Com shipped 14,000 copies of its 3+ and 3+Open software, whereas Novell shipped 181,000 copies of NetWare. Meanwhile, internetworking products, the specialty of the acquired Bridge Communications, were being neglected.

Krause responded by implementing a "New Renaissance Plan" beginning in January 1990 to reorganize and refocus the company. 3Com began marketing itself as a "network integrator" and a "network systems supplier," as a single source for network hardware and applications software compatible with multiple vendors' systems. Client/server networking was de-emphasized, and the focus shifted to comprehensive networking and inter-network connections. 3Com thus gave up going head-to-head against Novell, and 3Com's hardware henceforth supported both LAN Manager and its former competitor, NetWare. The marketing of LAN Manager, meanwhile, was left to Microsoft.

Krause also centralized the company by reducing the number of divisions from five to three: product development, internal operations, and sales. New executive vice-presidents were named to head each division, replacing the authority of Metcalfe's vice-presidency. Krause then removed himself from daily operations and began looking for someone else to replace him as CEO.

In April 1990, 3Com appointed Eric Benhamou, who had been the new executive vice-president of product development, as president and chief operating officer. Benhamou had been one of the cofounders of the acquired Bridge Communications company. A month later, founder Metcalfe resigned from his posts as vice-president of marketing and boardmember, after being passed over for the position of president. In August 1990, Krause himself resigned as both chairperson and CEO of 3Com, and Benhamou assumed those posts as well. Krause remained only as chairman of the board, leaving management satisfied with his accomplishments in building 3Com into a significant company of 2,000 employees.

Benhamou continued the process of refocusing the company along the lines of Krause's Renaissance plan. 3Com began investing more in technically innovative products such as network adapters, software, network-management, and internetworking. Increasing emphasis was also put on the cohesiveness of its products. To that end, in November 1990, two new divisions were created to replace four previous product-oriented groups. A Network Adapter Division was created to sell the company's Ethernet cards, replacing the former Transmission Systems Division, and a Network Systems Division, headed directly by Benhamou, assumed the responsibilities of the former Enterprise Systems Division, distributed Systems Division, and the Management, Messaging and Connectivity Division. Some mid-level mangers were also removed in the process.

In January 1991, 3Com further redefined its business objectives. The company completely gave up the network operating system software business, which had been providing the software packages LAN Manager, 3 +, and 3 + Open, since the LAN Manager royalty contract with Microsoft had become a financial burden. Under the contract, 3Com had to pay Microsoft royalties even if the computer servers it sold did not include LAN Manager but 3Com's 3 + Open instead. Moreover, when LAN Manager was sold independently, not bundled with 3Com hardware, 3Com still had to pay the expense of customer support for LAN Manager, and thus was losing money. 3Com's exit from the network operating system business freed the company from its royalty contract with Microsoft, and all marketing and support of LAN Manager was turned over to Microsoft. 3Com's LAN operating system, which had been losing market share to Novell's NetWare for the past three years, held only 14 percent of the market when the company dropped out.

The restructuring also involved steering away from providing client and server computers in order to focus on the networks themselves. Benhamou's redirection and reorganization of the company also involved putting two businesses up for sale. Communications Solutions Inc., a manufacturer of connectivity products beyond LANs which had been acquired in 1988, was sold to Attachmate Corp. The workgroup business, that which sold servers and workstations, however, could not find a buyer, and was gradually eliminated. While workgroup-related hardware and software had contributed $113 million, almost one quarter, of 3Com's revenues in 1990, this figure had dropped to 11 percent in 1991. The reorganization also involved laying off of 234 employees, or 12 percent of the work force, and a $67 million restructuring charge.

Thereafter, the company refocused on its successful LAN adapter line and internetworking products, such as bridges, hubs, adapters, and routers. 3Com had begun to depend increasingly on sales from its internetworking business, that of the acquired Bridge Communications company, after neglecting it for three years. 3Com had seen its market share in bridges and routers fall from 29 percent in 1988 to 19 percent in 1990, although it was still the third ranking company in the field, following Cisco Systems Inc. and Vitalink Communications Corp. Network adapters, meanwhile, came to account for 72 percent of sales in the second half of 1991. 3Com further

concentrated on improving its core adapter product line with the development of adapters for wireless notebook computers and adapters for higher speed network systems.

The initial results of the restructuring included lower revenues due to fewer product lines. For calendar year 1991, sales declined 15 percent to $370 million, and the company suffered a loss of $33 million, compared to a $24 million profit the previous year. Lower profits were also partly due to the more competitive nature of the LAN adapter market that had emerged in the early 1990s. By the end of 1991, 14 percent of the company's work force had been laid off, leaving a total of 1,676 employees. However, by 1992, the company was back on track, with sales rebounding to $423.8 million for the fiscal year ending May 31, 1992 and earnings becoming positive at $7.96 million.

For its other LAN components, 3Com came to rely increasingly on licensing or acquiring third party technology. The company bolstered its hub business by acquiring the Data Networks business of U.K.-based BICC PLC, one of Europe's largest hub manufacturers, in January 1992. This gave 3Com the Link-Builder ECS, an Ethernet chassis hub. In September 1992, 3Com introduced LinkBuilder 3GH, a high-end switching hub licensed from Synernetics Inc., a manufacturer of LAN switches. In a move to expand beyond Ethernet LAN structures, in 1993 3Com acquired Star-Tek Inc., which produced hubs for the Token-Ring network architecture. 3Com introduced a multi-function hub, LinkBuilder MSH, which could support both Ethernet and Token-Ring LANs in spring 1993. In December of that year, 3Com purchased wireless communications technology from Pacific Monolithics Inc. Early in 1994, 3Com acquired Synernetics, a manufacter of LAN switches, and Centrum Communications Inc., which provided products for remote network access. In September 1994, 3Com purchased ATM innovator NiceCom Ltd., a subsidiary of Nice Systems based in Tel Aviv, Israel.

3Com's product strategy and acquisitions under Benhamou helped the company reach $827 million in sales in fiscal 1994, nearly double that of two years prior. Optimism in the company resulted in a record high stock price of $68.25 per share in August 1994, compared with a low of under $6 in 1990. By the mid-1990s 3Com was facing more challenging competition from the 1994 merger of the largest hub provider Synoptics with the second largest router provider Wellfleet and from the entry of chip-maker Intel into the adapter business. As long as 3Com was prepared to meet its challenges, however, it could look forward to continued growth in the ever-expanding network market.

Principal Subsidiaries: 3Com Asia Limited (Hong Kong); 3Com Canada Inc.; 3Com China Ltd.; 3Com Europe Limited (United Kingdom); 3Com GmbH (Germany); 3Com Ireland; 3Com Asia Ltd.

Further Reading:

Barney, Cliff, "Sales and Profit Gains Ease the Pain of the 3Com/Bridge Merger," *Electronic Business,* November, 15, 1988, pp. 54–56.

Burke, Steven, "3Com Recharts Networking Course," *PC Week,* January 14, 1991, pp. 1, 8.

Flynn, Laurie, "As Networks of Computers Grow, 3Com Stock Surges," *New York Times,* August 31, 1994, pp. C1, C4.

Goldstein, Mark L., "Bill Krause Changes Course," *Industry Week,* June 1, 1987, p. 55.

Kerr, Susan, "3Com Corp.," *Datamation,* June 15, 1992, p. 141.

Lewis, Jamie, "3Com's Pulse Strong After Years of Change," *PC Week,* January 25, 1993, p. 64.

Moad, Jeff, "On the Road Again," *Datamation,* May 1, 1986, pp. 31–37.

Ould, Andrew, "3Com Reorganizes Divisions; Key Executive Departs," *PC Week,* November 5, 1990, p. 181.

Richman, Tom, "Growing Steady," *Inc.,* September 1984, pp. 69–81.

Richman, Tom, "Who's in Charge Here?," *Inc.,* June 1989, pp. 36–46.

Shao, Maria, "3Com's 'New Renaissance' Hasn't Ended its Dark Ages," *Business Week,* April 23, 1990, pp. 118–19.

—Heather Behn Hedden

Tidewater Inc.

1440 Canal Street
New Orleans, Louisiana 70112
U.S.A.
(504) 568-1010
Fax: (504) 566-4582

Public Company
Incorporated: 1956 as Tidewater Marine Service, Inc.
Employees: 6,864
Sales: $475.5 million
Stock Exchanges: New York
SICs: 4492 Towing and Tugboat Services; 3563 Air and Gas
Compressors

Tidewater Inc. has grown from one small boat operating in the Gulf of Mexico to a fleet of nearly 500 boats ranging from the waters of the Caspian Sea to the Gulf of Tonkin off the Vietnam coast. With offices located in New Orleans, Louisiana, the company's marine division runs the world's largest fleet of vessels serving the international offshore gas and oil industry. In addition to its offshore marine support and transportation services, Tidewater's compression division ranks as one of the largest suppliers of natural gas and air compression equipment and services for numerous industries in the United States and South America.

Tidewater's development parallels the discovery of oil in the Gulf of Mexico and the development of the offshore oil industry. The first offshore oilfield in the Gulf of Mexico was found in 1938, a little more than one mile from Cameron Parish, Louisiana. By the mid 1940s, petroleum geologists were estimating that there was between 10 and 12 billion barrels of oil waiting to be recovered in the Gulf. After fixed platforms were built and large-scale drilling operations started in 1946, a new industry developed around what was termed an "oil rig."

Oil rigs were manned 24 hours a day, with living and eating facilities, a galley, and even recreation areas. Although they seemed self-sufficient, the rigs were entirely dependent on the supply boats that brought food, water, and drilling equipment, and transported crews back and forth from the mainland. The first vessels to serve the oil rigs were old Navy boats and reconfigured shrimp boats. It soon became clear, however, that a special type of boat designed specifically for supplying offshore oil rigs was needed.

Alden J. "Doc" Laborde, a retired Navy officer who was chairman and president of Ocean Drilling and Exploration Company (ODECO), one of the first firms to drill for oil in the Gulf, was convinced that the offshore oil industry needed a specialty supply boat with a revolutionary design. His own design put the boat's pilot house forward, and the crew's quarters and wheelhouse forward in the bow. The boat's deck was entirely flat in order to easily lay various piping and supplies, yet still had a clear afterdeck for any towing that was required. Laborde organized a meeting with nine other men—including his older brother, C.E. Laborde, Jr., a marine operator, an owner of a towing business, an engineer, an accountant, and a few of his closest personal friends—and sought their support in forming a marine supply service for offshore oil rigs. Contributing $10,000 each toward the construction of the first boat, the men incorporated the Tidewater Marine Service Corporation in Louisiana on July 8, 1954.

Tidewater's first boat, the steel-hulled *Ebb Tide*, was built and launched in 1955. A request from ODECO to lease the boat resulted in Alden Laborde's decision to withdraw from involvement in Tidewater to avoid an apparent conflict of interest. Authority for all company decisions was left up to C.E. Laborde, Jr., Ed Kyle, and Don Durant. When the Shell Oil Company heard about the new boat and contacted Tidewater to charter a similar vessel, Laborde, Jr. decided to form a second corporation for the purpose of constructing and operating another supply boat. A third corporation was also formed when Phillips Petroleum wanted to charter a boat. As the demand for its vessels grew, the initial investors in Tidewater began to discuss an expansion program and the possibility of additional financing. Arrangements were made through Rheinholdt & Gardner, an investment firm with close ties to the offshore oil industry, and Whitney National Bank of New Orleans to provide the necessary funding, including loans and an initial public stock offering. On February 7, 1956, a parent organization, Tidewater Marine Service, Inc., was incorporated under the state laws of Delaware.

Throughout its initial period of development, Tidewater's management was informal. There was no main office, records were kept haphazardly, business commitments were made by any one of the original ten investors without regard to formal contracts or agreements, and the company's only employee worked out of his own house. Realizing that Tidewater's rapid expansion necessitated a professional management team, Laborde, Jr. consulted with the other investors and agreed to ask his younger brother, John, to accept the position of president. The younger Laborde, a graduate of Louisiana State Law School who had served as an adjutant on the staff of General Douglas MacArthur during World War II, accepted the offer. Although he knew absolutely nothing about boats, John Laborde was very familiar with the oil industry and its operations in the Gulf of Mexico.

Laborde went to work immediately: he rented office space, hired secretarial and bookkeeping help, sorted out the little documentation there was on the company, and met with the original investors and convinced them it was his responsibility alone to make agreements and arrange contracts for Tidewater. Not long after he started, Laborde was notified by the U.S. Coast Guard that one of Tidewater's vessels was in violation of marine regulations. The fine amounted to nearly $168,000. Knowing that Tidewater faced bankruptcy if the full amount of the fine were to be paid, Laborde explained the circumstances of the violation, which was due to a lack of knowledge on the part of the crew, and negotiated a settlement of $2,000 with the Coast Guard. This exchange with the Coast Guard led Laborde to educate himself on all aspects of marine laws and regulations so that he could formulate operating procedures for Tidewater.

During its first fiscal year, Tidewater recorded a loss of $10,027. Yet Laborde remained optimistic, largely because of a gross revenue amounting to over $400,000. The company's fleet expanded to eleven vessels. Near the end of 1957, Tidewater became the first offshore marine transportation business located in the Gulf of Mexico to make a foray into foreign waters. Laborde reached an agreement with a small boat company, Semarca, to transport supplies for an over-water oil and gas firm operating on Lake Maracaibo in Venezuela. By the end of the second fiscal year Laborde's optimism was rewarded: Tidewater doubled its gross revenues to $851,156, while net earnings jumped to over $97,000.

Tidewater grew rapidly during its first decade of operation. In 1961, just five years after the company's first boat was launched, Tidewater had already made a major acquisition by purchasing the Offshore Transportation Corporation. By taking over OTC's fleet, Tidewater increased the number of its revenue-producing vessels to 56. The Venezuelan venture was contributing nearly 40 percent of the company's total earnings. Individual stockholders in the company had grown from under 50 to over 800. Most importantly, the company reported gross revenues of $4,887,208 for 1961, but net revenues of $584,444, an increase of 59 percent over the previous year.

In 1962, Tidewater suffered a small decrease in revenues from the previous year, but the Venezuelan venture continued to be very profitable and the company expanded its operations to include the coastal waters off California and Trinidad. One year later, Tidewater continued the development of its American West Coast operation by initiating business in Alaska and by locating a base at Santa Barbara, California. In 1964, the company's fleet of vessels was working regularly in the Red Sea, the Gulf of Suez, the North Sea, Lake Maracaibo in Venezuela, the Gulf of Mexico, off the coastal waters of Trinidad, and along the entire U.S. Pacific coast. Having purchased T. J. Falgout, a Galveston, Texas-based competitor in the Gulf of Mexico, Tidewater's fleet amounted to 104 vessels. That same year, Tidewater passed one of its most important milestones; it increased profits to over $1,000,000. Gross revenues were reported at $7,625,698, a leap of almost 50 percent over the previous year.

By the end of its first decade, company operations had expanded to the Persian/Arabian Gulf, and plans were being implemented to provide marine services to Nigeria, Iran, Canada, and Australia. More boats were added to the Tidewater fleet, some newly constructed and some purchased used, which brought the total to 180 vessels. And, not surprisingly, revenues and profits continued their upward spiral. In 1966, Tidewater revenues soared to $19,733,881, an increase of 90 percent over the previous year. Profits jumped 30 percent over the previous year, and were now close to $3,000,000.

In order to capitalize on its success, during the following years Tidewater's strategy was to concentrate on diversifying and expanding its operations. In 1968, Tidewater merged with Twenty Grand Marine Services, Inc., its closest competitor in the Gulf of Mexico. This acquisition brought in Twenty Grand's tugboats and other vessels, and Tidewater's fleet increased to a total of 358. Tidewater also purchased Sandair Corporation, a leader in the air and gas compressor market; entering the air and gas compressor business was regarded by Tidewater management as a logical extension of its specialized services for the offshore oil industry. Foreign partnerships were established in the Netherlands and Iran. In 1969, the company acquired Hamer Hammer Service, Inc., a firm that supplied both equipment and personnel for the on-shore and offshore driving of oil well casings, and South Coast Gas Compression Company, Inc., a provider of natural gas compression equipment and services for the offshore oil industry.

The decade of the 1970s was just as successful for Tidewater as the company's early years. In 1970, Tidewater reported revenues of over $50 million, and over $5 million in profits. In May of the same year, Tidewater joined the select list of 1,300 companies listed on the New York Stock Exchange. In 1971, Tidewater acquired interests in offshore oil production in Indonesia, Java, and Sumatra. At the same time, the company created Pental Insurance Company, Ltd., a Bermuda-based firm insuring all of Tidewater's vessels. The company was soon providing services in the Adriatic Sea, and its large supply and towing-supply vessels were commanding higher and higher rates wherever they operated. Hillard Oil and Gas Company, Inc., an American oil and gas exploration firm, was purchased in 1977, the same year the board of director's decided to change the name of the Tidewater Marine Services to Tidewater, Inc. Tidewater, Inc., reorganized to function as a parent organization for its many subsidiaries, formed six divisions, including: Marine Services, Compression Services, Oil & Gas, Insurance, Real Estate, and Contractor Services. By 1979, total revenues shot past the $200 million mark, and profits exceeded $30 million.

Revenues and profits continued their meteoric rise during the early 1980s. However, when the oil and gas industry was sent into an historic decline by plummeting oil prices, Tidewater's fortunes went spinning downward. The company's position was exacerbated by an inundated supply boat market, and a sudden decrease in day rates for its vessels. The most significant threat to Tidewater, however, came from hostile takeover attempts. In 1984, Irwin L. Jacobs, a corporate raider, purchased enough Tidewater stock to attempt to take control of the company. When Jacobs's first offer was rejected by Tidewater's board of directors, he engaged in a complicated series of corporate and legal maneuverings over the next five years to wrest control of the company from the directors. Frustrated by his inability to acquire Tidewater by legal means, in 1989 Jacobs made another offer to purchase Tidewater at $11 per share. With John Laborde still providing sound leadership, Tidewater's board of directors sidestepped Jacobs by agreeing to facilitate the sale of Jacobs's stock and arranging a registered secondary stock offering. As a result, Jacobs withdrew his offer to acquire Tidewater and disposed of his shares with a handsome profit.

The takeover attempts and the continuing slump in the oil and gas industry had deleterious effects on Tidewater. In 1985, the company reported it first loss since 1957, and by 1987 losses amounted to a record $56 million. With losses continuing to mount, John Laborde proved his leadership with a calm, confident demeanor and astute decision-making skills. Although Tidewater was losing money, Laborde's earlier decision to enter the natural gas compression business seemed prescient. During the worst years of the oil and gas industry recession, Tidewater's compression business provided a steady flow of revenue that kept the company afloat. Laborde also decided to sell all of the company's Indonesian oil interests. In 1987, Laborde restructured debt payments with Tidewater's primary lenders, and by 1990 had pared downed over $60 million of the company's senior debt. During the same year, Laborde convinced Tidewater's board of director's to make a public offering of over five million shares of common stock. With revenues starting to increase, Laborde thought it best to continue expanding Tidewater's international operations by placing 41 pieces of towing equipment in and around West Africa.

Perhaps the most important of Laborde's decisions involved the acquisition of Zapata Gulf Marine Corporation in 1992. Tidewater's biggest rival, Zapata was an amalgamation of the company's four most important competitors. By consolidating Zapata's vessels with its own, Tidewater doubled its marine fleet. For Laborde, the timing of this acquisition could not have been better; after one of the worst freezes of the century in the Gulf of Mexico, a spring thaw led to a doubling of day rates for workboats. With the largest fleet in the Gulf, Tidewater took advantage of this opportunity to put all of its newly acquired vessels from Zapata into service.

By the end of fiscal year 1994, Tidewater had completely recovered from the recession of the offshore oil industry, increased its fleet to 594 vessels, and expanded its overseas ventures. Over 70 percent of Tidewater's fleet operated in foreign waters. With nearly 85 percent of its revenues from marine operations and the remainder from compression operations, Tidewater reported total revenues amounting to $522 million. A good cash-flow and increasing offshore marine contracts from around the world enabled the company to eliminate its entire debt. In light of the revitalization of the company, John Laborde decided to retire in October of 1994 after serving 38 years as president of Tidewater. His replacement, William C. O'Malley, the former chief executive officer of Sonat Offshore Drilling Inc., can only hope to match Laborde's legacy of astute management and financial success.

Further Reading:

Dufour, Charles, L., *Taken at the Flood: The Story of Tidewater,*
Hartley, Lynn, ''U.S. Service Sector Follows Majors Abroad,'' *Platt's Oilgram News,* July 2, 1992, p. 3.

—Thomas Derdak

Tomkins plc

East Putney House
84 Upper Richmond Road
London SW15 2ST
United Kingdom
(081) 871 4544
Fax: (081) 877 9700

Public Company
Incorporated: 1925 as F. H. Tomkins Buckle Co. Ltd.
Employees: 45,496
Sales: £3.24 billion
Stock Exchanges: London
SICs: 6711 Holding Companies; 3524 Garden Tractors and
   Lawn and Garden Equipment; 3484 Small Arms; 5084
   Industrial Machinery and Equipment; 5072 Hardware;
   3432 Plumbing Fixture Fittings and Trim

Tomkins plc is a multinational conglomerate, overseeing a variety of manufacturing companies in diverse industries. With the corporate motto "Working for Shareholders," Tomkins purchases underperforming businesses and turns them into healthy, profitable companies. These results are achieved through the application of a strict regime of efficient management, commitment of capital for development where necessary, and exacting financial control. Tomkins' constituents are carefully selected to represent a wide array of firms and products so as to minimize risk to the profitability of the conglomerate as a whole. The result is a company whose product range encompasses faucets, footwear, bicycles, bread, guns, and garden equipment.

Tomkins traces its history to the 1925 founding of the F. H. Tomkins Buckle Company Ltd., a manufacturer of buckles and fasteners operating from England's West Midlands. Buckles and fasteners largely remained the company's focus until 1983, when Tomkins underwent a dramatic metamorphosis and emerged as an international conglomerate.

The company's sudden change in direction was largely due to the vision of one man, Gregory Hutchings, who in 1983 acquired a 22.9 percent stake in Tomkins. Becoming chief executive of Tomkins in January 1984, Hutchings assembled a management team and set about transforming the company through an aggressive acquisition strategy aimed primarily at companies based in the United Kingdom and the United States. In quick but

carefully phased succession, Tomkins acquired Ferraris Piston Service (1984), Hayters, a manufacturer of garden tools (1984), Pegler-Hattersley, a maker of taps, valves, plumbing fittings, and heating control systems (1986), Smith & Wesson, the well-known gun manufacturers (1987), and Murray Ohio, a lawn-mower and bicycle company (1988).

During this time, Tomkins was creating and solidifying its careful and conservative approach to business, "control" being the company's watchword. Implicit in Tomkins' success as a conglomerate was its unwavering belief that any business, no matter what its end product, would respond to the basic business tenets to which Tomkins subscribed: stringent financial control fortified by tough and realistic budgetary planning; efficient, waste-reducing management procedures; and judicious use of capital as and when dictated by the needs of the business.

The company's acquisition policy also emphasized selectivity. Tomkins favored what it termed "low-risk" technology businesses—those that produced and/or distributed products not subject to rapid technological change or frequent development and improvement. Moreover, the company was reluctant to purchase any concern that would hinder the conglomerate's earnings even temporarily; new acquisitions were chosen with the expectation that they would contribute to the firm's profits in their first year. Finally, Tomkins' policy was to fully integrate one acquisition into the company as a whole before moving on to the next. Consequently, Tomkins made only eight major acquisitions between 1983 and 1993.

Each of the companies acquired by Tomkins was afforded considerable autonomy in regards to its management and operations, provided that the company conform to the parent company's strict financial regime. Subsidiaries were expected to strive to become the lowest-priced and most efficient supplier in their particular market. In turn, Tomkins was willing to provide capital for new plants and equipment, product development, management training, advertising campaigns, or whatever was regarded as necessary to achieving that goal.

Seeking to build an empire whose broad base ensures continued profitability even if one sector of the company should suffer a setback, Tomkins also sought to achieve geographical balance among its enterprises. The company's ideal ratio was to have 40 percent of its business based in the United Kingdom, 40 percent in the United States, and 20 percent elsewhere.

Hutchings' strategies proved phenomenally successful. In 1983, Tomkins, wholly reliant on the fastener business, controlled seven companies, employed a work force of 400, and made a pre-tax profit of £1.6 million, mostly in the United Kingdom. In 1994, however, the company boasted 73 companies, supported 45,000 employees, and enjoyed a pre-tax profit of over £257 million garnered from businesses operating in the United Kingdom, North America, Europe, and Australia, with no one product accounting for a disproportionate amount of Tomkins' profits.

In 1994, the company's business fell roughly into five categories: fluid controls; services to industry; professional, garden, and leisure products; industrial products; and Rank Hovis Mc-Dougall, a food manufacturer acquired by Tomkins in 1992. The fluid controls business comprised the manufacture and international distribution of water, heating, ventilating, and air conditioning valves, taps, radiators, and plumbing fittings. Tomkins' firms in this category, based in the United Kingdom, the United States, and Canada, included Ruskin, Air System Components, Pegler, and Guest & Chrimes.

The services to industry category, a more varied group, included Totectors, a U.K. supplier of safety footwear; the automotive components distributor Ferraris Piston Service; the Belgian valve and pipeline equipment firms Prometal and Dutch UBEL; as well as U.S. manufacturers of conveyor and material handling systems such as Mayfran and Dearborn Fabricating & Engineering. The services to industry category also included distribution of an array of high specification valves, the supply of fasteners to clients in the United Kingdom and Europe, the provision of spring steel and heat treatment, and the printing of business forms.

The highest-profile business in Tomkins line of professional, garden, and leisure products was the U.S.-based Smith & Wesson, the largest producer of handguns in the world. Another U.S. firm, Murray Ohio, manufactured high-quality lawnmowers and bicycles. Also included in this category was the original Tomkins—F. H. Tomkins Buckle Company—which continued to supply a variety of buckles for both the U.K. and foreign markets.

Tomkins' industrial products were largely low-risk technology products such as plastic and fiberglass moldings, doors, windows, wheels, axles, rubber components, coated textiles, control instrumentation, metal pressings, precision turned parts, industrial disc brakes, clutches, and flexible couplings. Lasco Bathware, Philips Products, manufacturer of aluminum doors and windows for recreational vehicles and manufactured housing, Dexter Axle, Northern Rubber, and Premier Screw were among the Tomkins companies in the industrial products line.

Rank Hovis McDougall (RHM), a substantial and controversial acquisition of 1992, made and distributed bread and a range of private-label and other brand-name food products for consumers and for catering and food manufacturing markets in the United Kingdom, Europe, and the United States. Among RHM's well-known brand names were Hovis, Mothers Pride, Mr Kipling and Cadbury's cakes, Bisto, and Paxo.

Tomkins frequently came under fire for its eclectic acquisition strategy, and never more so than in 1992, when the company bought the bread maker and distributor Rank Hovis McDougall. Although it was no surprise that the company should make a bid for a large U.K. concern—at the time only 17 percent of its profits were coming from the United Kingdom, an undesirable ratio to Tomkins—this move "from guns to buns," as the city's pundits delighted in terming it, was viewed by financial analysts and stockbrokers as inexplicable, unwise, and potentially disastrous. To diversify so drastically from Tomkins' usual business was considered a risk, but to diversify into the volatile and oversaturated bread market was regarded as foolhardy.

At the time of the purchase, RHM was in second place in the British baking market, holding approximately 33 percent in comparison to the 36 percent controlled by Associated British Foods, with the remaining market share divided among smaller, independent bakeries. Moreover, although consumption of

bread had dropped, production had not, leading to ruthless price wars in the market. In 1989, RHM had pulled a profit of £69 million from milling and baking; by 1992 that figure had dwindled to £20 million. Many analysts saw further cause for alarm in that with this acquisition Tomkins charged the cost to its balance sheet rather than following its usual strategy of writing off the cost in the profit-and-loss account. Stock market doubts were fueled by Tomkins' reluctance to discuss the purchase. Although the company's policy was to keep its own council about a new acquisition until its first full year, no news in this case was seen as bad news, and Tomkins' share price dropped. Even *The Financial Times,* a fairly conservative journal, remarked that it was indeed "perplexing" that Tomkins should invest good money into a "seeming quagmire."

Undeterred, Tomkins set out to prove the analysts wrong, instituting a £90 million program of restructuring and rationalization. The company cut RHM bakery capacity by ten percent and well over 2,000 jobs, all without diminishing RHM's market share. Tomkins then instituted an ambitious marketing campaign to reinforce an already-high brand recognition for the new subsidiary's bakery and other food items. Over 300 new food products were developed, including specialty items such as sun-dried tomato bread. Responding to fads popular among children at the time, the bakery also began producing "dinosaur bread" in 1993.

When Tomkins finally lifted its veil of secrecy in 1994, it revealed that while the bakery business remained troubled, it had performed very creditably in the food industry as a whole, better, in fact, than had been expected. Moreover, Tomkins as a whole boasted a 50 percent rise in profits. Nevertheless, the damage to Tomkins' reputation through its purchase of RHM purchase, seemed to linger. Financial analysts remained skeptical and wary of Tomkins, and, in 1994, the company's share price had not returned to its pre-RHM high.

Some analysts attributed this problem to the fact that Tomkins was out of financial fashion. In the mid-1990s, not only was the food industry regarded as unpromising, but the concept of conglomerates was falling out of favor. "We keep on scoring goals," remarked Hutchings, "but still end up bottom of the league." According to the *Guardian,* however, such an experience was "nothing new for Mr Hutchings, who has had difficulty in the past persuading sceptical investors that he knows what he is doing, is capable of doing it and will go on to do even more."

Nevertheless, Tomkins continued to seek new acquisitions, purchasing the Outdoor Products and Dynamark Plastics businesses of the Canadian Noma Industries in 1994. Tomkins intended Outdoor Products, which made and distributed lawnmowers and snowblowers, to enhance Murray Ohio's range of garden equipment as well as to help balance seasonal sales by offering a product used in the winter months. Dynamark Plastics, an injection molder, was integrated into the company's industrial products sector.

Fortified by a strong cash base, the company appeared set to continue its aggressive but selective acquisition policy. Despite faltering share prices and broker confidence, Tomkins entered the mid-1990s with a record of consistently growing profits every year since 1983, even during the worst of the recession. As Hutchings told Kirstie Hamilton: "There is really no difference between food and lawnmowers. It is about innovation, imagination, attacking costs and introducing new products."

Principal Subsidiaries: Air System Components (U.S.A.); ASL (Canada); Dearborn Fabricating & Engineering Co. (U.S.A.); Ferraris Piston Service Ltd.; F. H. Tomkins Buckle Co. Ltd.; Guest & Chrimes Ltd.; Hayter Ltd.; Mid-West Conveyor Co., Inc. (U.S.A.); Murray Ohio Manufacturing Co. (U.S.A.); Murray Outdoor Products (U.S.A.); Northern Rubber Co. Ltd.; Premier Screw & Repetition Co. Ltd.; Rank Hovis Ltd.; Ranks Meel BV (Holland); Red Wing Co., Inc. (U.S.A.); RHM Foods Ltd.; Ruskin (U.S.A.); Smith & Wesson Corp. (U.S.A.); Totectors Ltd.

Further Reading:

"Bank on Hutchings as Heat Stays on RHM," *Sunday Times,* May 16, 1993.

Bögler, Daniel, "Tomkins 50pc Surge Fails to Impress City," *Daily Telegraph,* July 12, 1994.

Bose, Mihir, "Mr Kipling Goes to War," *Director,* October 1993, pp. 44–48.

"Careful Wording Is Not Enough," *Independent,* May 11, 1993.

Dunham, Robin, "Tomkins: Giving Companies a New Lease of Life," *Accountancy,* May 1989, pp. 130, 132.

Gilchrist, Susan, "Tomkins Defies Critics with 50% Profit Rise," *The Times,* July 12, 1994, p. 25.

Hamilton, Kirstie, "Hutchings' Dough Fails to Rise," *Sunday Times,* July 17, 1994.

"Moving up the Ranks," *The Times,* July 12, 1994, p. 27.

Pangalos, Philip, "RHM Adds Grist to Tomkins Mill," *The Times,* July 11, 1994.

"Resilient Tomkins," *Financial Times,* January 12, 1993.

"Sceptical City Chewing over Tomkins Classic Pudding Mix," *Guardian,* January 11, 1994.

"Tomkins—a Snip," *Independent on Sunday,* March 13, 1994.

"Tomkins Buys Rival Lawnmower Maker," *Independent,* March 12, 1994.

"Tomkins Goes to Mow in Canada," *Evening Standard,* March 11, 1994.

"Tomkins Steady in Nervous Times," *Daily Telegraph,* September 18, 1993.

"Tomkins to Wield Axe in Ranks Shake-Up," *Daily Telegraph,* May 11, 1993.

"Tomkins Uses Loaf to Tap Dino-Market," *Birmingham Post,* July 7, 1993.

—Robin DuBlanc

TOYOTA

Toyota Motor Corporation

1, Toyota-cho
Toyota City, Aichi Prefecture 471
Japan
(0565) 28-2121
Fax: (0565) 23-5800

Public Company
Incorporated: 1937
Employees: 108,000
Sales: ¥9.36 trillion ($94.6 billion)
Stock Exchanges: Tokyo NASDAQ
SICs: 3711 Motor Vehicles and Car Bodies; 5012
   Automobiles and Other Motor Vehicles; 3448
   Prefabricated Metal Buildings

Toyota Motor Corporation was Japan's largest car company and the world's third largest in the mid-1990s. The company produced over 4 million units annually and controlled 9.5 percent of the global market for automobiles. Although its profits declined substantially during the global economic downturn of the early 1990s, Toyota responded by cutting costs and moving production to overseas markets. The company represented one of the true success stories in the history of manufacturing, its growth and success reflective of Japan's astonishing resurgence following the Second World War.

In 1933 a Japanese man named Kiichiro Toyoda traveled to America, where he visited a number of automobile production plants. Upon his return to Japan, the young man established an automobile division within his father's loom factory and in May 1935 produced his first prototype vehicle. General Motors and Ford were already operating assembly plants in Japan, but U.S. pre-eminence in the worldwide automotive industry did not deter Toyoda.

Since Japan had very few natural resources, the company had every incentive to develop engines and vehicles that were highly fuel efficient. In 1939, the company established a research center to begin work on battery-powered vehicles. This was followed in 1940 by the establishment of the Toyoda Science Research Center (the nucleus of the Toyota Central Research and Development Laboratories, Inc.) and the Toyoda Works (later Aichi Steel Works, Ltd.). The next year Toyoda Machine Works, Ltd. was founded for the production of both machine tools and auto parts.

As Japan became embroiled in World War II, the procurement of basic materials for automobile manufacturing became more and more difficult. At one point Toyoda was manufacturing trucks with no radiator grills, brakes only on the rear wheels, wooden seats, and a single headlight. Pushing toward the limits of resource conservation as the course of the war began to cripple Japan's economy, the company started piecing together usable parts from wrecked or worn-out trucks in order to build "recycled" vehicles.

When the war ended in August of 1945 most of Japan's industrial facilities had been wrecked, and the Toyoda (or Toyota as it became known after the war) production plants had suffered extensively. The company had 3,000 employees but no working facilities, and the economic situation in Japan was chaotic. But the Japanese tradition of dedication and perseverance proved to be Toyota's most powerful tool in the difficult task of reconstruction.

Just as the Japanese motor industry as a whole was beginning to recover, there was mounting concern that American and European auto manufacturers would overwhelm the Japanese market with their economic and technical superiority. Japan's automakers knew that they could no longer count on government protection in the form of high import duties or other barriers as they had before the war.

Since American manufacturers were concentrating their efforts on medium-sized and larger cars, Toyota's executives thought that by focusing on small cars the company could avoid a head-on market confrontation. Kiichiro Toyoda likened the postwar situation in Japan to that in England. "The British motorcar industry," he said, "also faces many difficulties, but its fate will be largely determined by how strongly American automakers feel they should concentrate on small cars." It was January 1947 when Toyota engineers completed their first prototype for a small car: its chassis was of the backbone type—never used before in Japan; its front suspension relied primarily on coil springs; and its maximum speed was 54 miles per hour. After two years of difficulties the company seemed headed for success.

However, this was not to be accomplished as easily as expected. Two years later, in 1949, Toyota suffered its first and only serious conflict between labor and management. Nearly four years had passed since the end of the war, but Japan's economy was still in poor condition: goods and materials of all kinds were in short supply; inflation was rampant; and worst of all, people in the cities were forced to trade their clothing and home furnishings for rice or potatoes in order to keep themselves alive. That year the Japanese government took measures to control runaway inflation in ways that severely reduced consumer purchasing power and worsened the already severely depressed domestic automotive market. Japanese auto manufacturers found themselves unable to raise the funds needed to support their recovery efforts, for the new governmental policy had discontinued all financing from city banks and the Reconstruction Finance Corporation.

Under these conditions the company's financial situation deteriorated rapidly. In some months, for example, the company produced vehicles worth a total of ¥350 million while income from sales reached only ¥250 million. In the absence of credit sources to bridge the imbalance, Toyota was soon facing a severe liquidity crisis. Largely because of wartime regulations and controls, Toyota had come to place strong emphasis on the production end of the business, so that in the early postwar years not enough attention had been paid to the proper balance between production and sales. The Japanese economy at that time was suffering from a severe depression, and because the Toyota dealers were unable to sell cars in sufficient quantities, these dealers had no choice but to pay Toyota in long-term promissory notes as inventories kept accumulating.

Finally, Toyota was unable to meet its regular payroll. Delayed payments were followed by actual salary reductions and then by plans for large-scale layoffs—until April of 1949, when the Toyota Labor Union went on strike. Negotiations between labor and management dragged on with the union leaders bitterly opposed to any layoffs. As a result, Toyota was compelled to reduce both production and overhead. Workers staged demonstrations to press their demands, and all the while Toyota kept falling further into debt, until the company finally found itself on the verge of bankruptcy.

Production dropped to 992 vehicles in March of 1949, to 619 in April, and to 304 in May. Crucial restructuring efforts included a proposal to incorporate Toyota's sales division as a separate company, leading eventually to the formation of Toyota Motor Sales Company Ltd. in April 1950. Toyota Motor Sales Company handled all domestic and worldwide marketing of Toyota's automotive products until July of 1982, when it merged with Toyota Motor Company.

In the meantime, discussions between labor and management finally focused on whether to admit failure, declare bankruptcy, and dissolve the company, or to agree on the dismissal of some employees and embark upon a rebuilding program. In the end management and labor agreed to reduce the total work force from 8,000 to 6,000 employees, primarily by asking for voluntary resignations. At the management level, President Kiichiro Toyoda and all of his executive staff resigned. Kiichiro, Toyota's founder and a pioneer of the Japanese automotive industry, died less than two years later.

Not long after the strike was settled in 1950, two of the company's new executives, Eiji Toyoda (now chairman of Toyota Motor Corporation) and Shoichi Saito (later chairman of Toyota Motor Company), visited the United States. Seeking new ideas for Toyota's anticipated growth, they toured Ford Motor Company's factories and observed the latest automobile production technology. One especially useful idea they brought home from their visit to Ford resulted in Toyota's suggestion system, in which every employee was encouraged to make suggestions for improvements of any kind. However, on their return to Japan the two men inaugurated an even more vital policy that remained in force at Toyota through the 1990s—the continuing commitment to invest in only the most modern production facilities as the key to advances in productivity and quality. Toyota moved quickly and aggressively in the 1950s, making capital investments in new equipment for all the company's production facilities. Not surprisingly, the company began to benefit from the increased efficiency almost immediately.

Along with improvements in its production facilities, Toyota also worked to develop a more comprehensive line of vehicles in order to contribute toward the growing motorization of Japanese society. During 1951, for example, Toyota introduced the first four-wheel-drive Land Cruiser. Moreover, as the domestic demand for taxis rapidly increased, production of passenger cars also rose quickly, from 50 units per month to 250 units per month by 1953.

In production control, Toyota introduced the "Kanban" (or "synchronized delivery") system during 1954. The idea was derived from the supermarket system, where "consumers" (those in the later production stages) took "products" (parts) from the stock shelves, and the "storekeepers" (those in the earlier production stages) replenished the stock to the degree that it was depleted. The Kanban system became the basis for Toyota's entire production system.

By the early 1950s, just as Toyota had anticipated, the Japanese market was crowded with vehicles from the United States and Europe. It soon became apparent that to be competitive at home and abroad, Toyota would not only have to make additional investments in manufacturing facilities and equipment, but also undertake a major new research and development effort. This was the reasoning behind Toyota's decision in 1958 to build a full-scale research center for the development of new automobiles (which was also to become Japan's first factory devoted entirely to passenger-car production). Toyota also began to offer a more complete line of products. Beginning with the Crown model, introduced in 1955, Toyota quickly expanded its passenger-car line to include the 1000-cubic-centimeter Corona, then added the Toyo-Ace (Japan's first cab-over truck) and a large-sized diesel truck.

Throughout these years Toyota was also working hard on another important, if less conventional, approach to adapting itself to the rapid motorization of Japan, brought about by a remarkable increase in national income. When, for example, Toyota Motor Sales was capitalized at ¥1 billion, 40 percent of that amount (¥400 million) was immediately invested to establish an automobile driving school in an effort to help citizens acquire driver's licenses. Through this and similar efforts, Toyota made a major contribution to Japan's growing motorization in the years following 1965, a trend that was to lead to a mass domestic market for automobiles.

In 1955, ten years after its defeat in World War II, Japan became a member of the General Agreement on Tariffs and Trade (GATT); but automobiles remained one of Japan's least-competitive industries in the international arena. Toyota, foreseeing the coming age of large-scale international trade and capital liberalization in Japan, decided to focus on lowering its production costs and developing even more sophisticated cars, while at the same time attempting to achieve the highest possible level of quality in production. This was a joint effort conducted with Toyota's many independent parts suppliers and one which proved so successful that ten years later, in 1965, Toyota was awarded the coveted Deming Prize for its quality-control achievements. That was also the year that the Japanese government liberalized imports of foreign passenger cars. Now Toyota was ready to compete with its overseas competitors—both in price and quality.

In subsequent years Japan's gross national product expanded rapidly, contributing to the impressive growth in auto sales to the Japanese public. The Toyota Corolla, which went on sale in 1966, quickly became Japan's most popular family car and led the market for autos of its compact size. Toyota continued to make major investments in new plants and equipment in order to prepare for what it believed would be a higher market demand. In 1971 the government removed controls on capital investment. In the wake of this move, several Japanese automakers formed joint ventures or affiliations with U.S. automakers.

Two years later, the 1973 Middle East War erupted and the world's economy was shaken by the first international oil crisis. Japan, wholly dependent upon imports for its oil supply, was especially affected. The rate of inflation increased and demand for automobiles fell drastically. Yet, in the face of the overall pessimism that gripped the industry and the nation, Toyota's chairman Eiji Toyoda proposed a highly aggressive corporate strategy. His conviction was that the automobile, far from being a "luxury," had become and would remain a necessity for people at all levels of society. As a result, Toyota decided to move forward by expanding the company's operations.

The 1973 oil crisis and its aftermath were valuable lessons for Toyota. The crisis demonstrated the necessity for a flexible production system that could easily be adapted to changes in consumer preferences. For example, Toyota did away with facilities designed exclusively for the production of specific models, and shifted instead to general-purpose facilities which could be operated according to changes in market demand for the company's various models.

In December of 1970 the U.S. Congress passed the Muskie Act, which set limits on automobile engine emissions. In the United States the enforcement of this law was eventually postponed, but in Japan even stricter laws were promulgated during the same time with no postponement of enforcement deadlines. When the Muskie Act was first proposed, automakers all over the world were opposed to it. They argued that it would actually prohibit the use of all internal combustion engines currently used, and they requested that the enforcement of the law be postponed until new technology, able to meet the law's requirements, could be developed.

Notwithstanding these developments, Toyota moved forward on its own to develop a new generation of cleaner and more fuel-efficient engines. After studying all the feasible alternatives—including catalytic systems, rarefied combustion, rotary engines, gas turbine and battery-powered cars—Toyota settled on the catalytic converter as the most flexible and most promising, and succeeded in producing automobiles that conformed to the world's toughest emissions-control standards. (Meanwhile, imported cars were given a three-year grace period to conform to Japan's strict emissions-control standards.)

In 1980 Japan's aggregate automobile production was actually better than that of the United States. In the same year, Toyota ranked second only to General Motors in total number of cars produced. Although Toyota made efforts over the years to improve the international cooperation between automakers, in such ways as procuring parts and materials from overseas manufacturers, Japan's successes in the world auto market nonetheless resulted in the Japanese automobile industry becoming a target of criticism.

Shoichiro Toyoda, president of Toyota during the mid- and late 1980s, possessed a solid understanding of American culture. Toyoda reportedly believed that Toyota's future success depended in part on the way it handled public relations with the United States, a nation that he perceived to be extremely bitter about losing trade battles with Japanese industry. By means of intense advertising and controlled public relations under Toyoda's direction, Toyota tried to elevate the principle of free competition in the minds of the American people. At the same time, Toyoda carefully committed his company to greater international cooperation in both technological and managerial areas.

In 1984, for example, Toyota entered into a joint manufacturing venture with American giant General Motors called New United Motor Manufacturing, Inc. (NUMMI). This state-of-the-art facility allowed Toyota to begin production in the United States cautiously at a time of increasing protectionism, as well as learn about American labor practices. At the same time, it provided General Motors with insight into Japanese production methods and management styles. The plant was slated to build up to 50,000 vehicles a year. In the fall of 1985, moreover, Toyota announced that it would build an $800,000 production facility near Lexington, Kentucky. The plant, which was expected to begin assembling 200,000 cars per year by 1988, created approximately 3,000 jobs.

By the end of the 1980s, Toyota's position as a powerful, exceptionally well-run car company was nearly unassailable. After a decade of prodigious growth, the company stood atop the Japanese automobile industry and ranked number three worldwide, a position it had held since 1978 and strengthened in the ensuing years. By the beginning of the 1990s, Toyota commanded an overwhelming 43 percent of the Japanese car market, and in the United States it sold, for the first time, more than one million cars and trucks. Aside from these two mainstay markets, Toyota was solidifying its global operations, particularly in Southeast Asia, and carving new markets in Latin America, where the burgeoning demand for cars promised much growth. Toyota also spearheaded the Japanese automobile industry's foray into the luxury car market, leading the way with its Lexus LS400 luxury sedan, which by the mid-1990s was outselling market veterans BMW, Mercedes-Benz, and Jaguar.

Despite these favorable developments, all of which pointed toward further growth and underscored the car company's vitality, Toyota's management continued to strive for improvements. In 1990, for example, when the company was posting enviable financial results and its manufacturing processes provided a model for other companies to follow, Shoichiro Toyoda eliminated two layers of middle management, effected substantial cuts in the company's executive staff, and reorganized Toyota's product development. With the highest operating margin of any car maker in the world, Toyota was a formidable force.

Toyota had little control over external forces, however, and as the 1990s progressed, a global economic downturn brought the prolific growth of Japan's largest car manufacturer to a halt. The recession stifled economic growth throughout the world, while a rising yen made Japanese products relatively more expensive in overseas markets. Toyota's profits declined for four consecutive years between 1991 and 1994, falling to the lowest level in more than a decade. Midway through Toyota's net income slide, the company gained new leadership when Totsuro Toyoda succeeded his brother in September 1992. Under Totsuro Toyoda's stewardship, a cost-cutting program was enacted that reduced expense account budgets 50 percent, limited travel expenditures, and eliminated white-collar overtime. Toyoda also continued the trend toward moving production to less-expensive overseas markets by ordering the construction or expansion of six assembly plants in Great Britain, Pakistan, Thailand, Turkey, the United States, and Japan.

As Toyota's profit decline continued, however, the mounting losses persuaded Toyoda to intensify his cost-cutting measures. Design changes in the company's vehicles coupled with reductions in manufacturing and distribution costs saved Toyota ¥150 billion in 1993, and another ¥100 billion in savings was expected to be realized in 1994. In 1994, the fourth consecutive year of negative net income growth, Toyota recorded ¥125.8 billion in consolidated net income, just over a quarter of the total posted in 1990, when the company earned ¥441.3 billion. Although Toyota's financial prospects remained bleak as it entered the mid-1990s, the recovery of Japan's economy and a return to more robust economic times in Europe meant that relief was in sight. Solidly positioned to take advantage of this expected economic revitalization, Toyota continued with its decades-long emphasis on becoming and remaining the world's premier car maker.

Principal Subsidiaries: Toyoda Automatic Loom Works, Ltd.; Aichi Steel Works, Limited; Toyoda Machine Works, Ltd.; Toyota Auto Body Co., Ltd.; Toyota Tsusho Corporation; Aisin Seiki Co., Ltd.; Nipponsdenso Co., Ltd.; Toyoda Spinning & Weaving Co., Ltd.; Towa Real Estate Co., Ltd.; Toyota Central Research & Development Laboratories, Inc.; Kanto Auto Works, Ltd.; Toyoda Gosei Co., Ltd.; Hino Motors, Ltd.; Daihatsu Motor Co., Ltd.

Further Reading:

Butler, Steven, "Toyota Puts It on the Line: Stung by Recession, the Auto Maker Embarks on Deep Cost Cutting," *U.S. News and World Report,* August 23, 1993, p. 47.

Kamiya, Shotaro, with Thomas Elliott, *My Life with Toyota,* Toyota City: Toyota Motor Sales Co., 1978.

Pollack, Andrew, "Toyota Profit Declines for a Fourth Year; Loss Had Been Feared; Future Called Brighter," *New York Times,* August 26, 1994, p. C2.

Spindle, William, "Toyota Retooled: Profits and Global Output Are Up, and New Models Are on the Way," *Business Week,* April 4, 1994, p. 54.

Taylor, Alex, "A Back-to-Basics U-Turn in Japan," *New York Times,* August 26, 1994, p. C1.

—updated by Jeffrey L. Covell

Transatlantic Holdings, Inc.

80 Pine Street
New York, New York 10005
U.S.A.
(212) 770-2000
Fax: (212) 248-0965

Public Company
Incorporated: 1986 as PREINCO Holdings, Inc.
Employees: 248
Total Assets: $3.2 billion
Stock Exchanges: New York
SICs: 6331 Fire, Marine, and Casualty Insurance; 6719
   Holding Companies, Not Elsewhere Classified

Transatlantic Holdings, Inc. (TRH) is an insurance holding company that provides property and casualty reinsurance to other insurance and reinsurance firms in the United States and internationally through its Transatlantic Reinsurance Company and Putnam Reinsurance Company subsidiaries. As of 1993, over 45 percent of TRI's stock was held by American International Group, Inc., the leading U.S.-based international insurance organization and the country's largest underwriter of commercial and industrial coverages. With $631 million in 1993 net premiums written, TRH ranked as the seventh-largest reinsurance organization in the United States. At that time, one-fifth of the company's 1993 premiums were non-U.S. risks. The company's principal lines of reinsurance include general, professional, and automobile liability, medical malpractice, and workers' compensation in the casualty segment. Moreover, the growth of environmentally-focused businesses has encouraged the company to offer specialty coverages of the environmental liabilities of remediation contractors, asbestos abatement contractors, and toxic waste treatment, storage, and disposal facilities. TRH's property lines emphasize fire and inland marine coverages. Casualty reinsurance, which protects the insured against losses arising due to an obligation to others, has historically constituted the majority of the company's annual premiums written. The company has been characterized as a cautious investor: the majority of its investments (approximately 65 percent) were in municipal bonds at the end of 1993.

Reinsurance is essentially an agreement between two insurance companies, whereby the reinsurer assumes all or part of the liabilities of another insurer or reinsurer (known in the industry as the ceding company). This reduced obligation on individual policies can permit ceding firms to underwrite more policies than their assets would otherwise allow. Reinsurance also helps protect primary insurers from catastrophic losses and their devastating financial consequences. Reinsurance agreements are provided in one of two forms: pro rata, or proportional, and excess of loss, or nonproportional. In a pro rata reinsurance contract, the reinsurer and the ceding company share the premiums and the losses in an agreed-upon proportion. Excess of loss reinsurance stipulates that the reinsurer will assume losses within certain limits (for example, amounts over $10,000 on a $100,000 policy).

TRH was formed by American International Group (AIG) in June 1986 as PREINCO Holdings, Inc., a private company. The new company's chairperson, M. R. Greenberg, who had served as AIG's president since 1967 and chief executive officer since 1969, was named chairperson of PREINCO. AIG contributed all the common stock of an inactive subsidiary, Putnam Reinsurance Company, to the new entity, along with additional consideration in exchange for a 20 percent interest in PREINCO. Over 70 percent of PREINCO's early business reinsured AIG and its subsidiaries, and PREINCO was given the right of first acceptance of virtually all of AIG's reinsurance requirements since that time. Eventually, PREINCO's dependance on AIG would decline; while, in its first full year of business, the new company derived over 70 percent of its gross premiums from AIG, that figure declined to 61 percent in 1988 and held steady at 54 percent in 1989 and 1990. All of PREINCO's stock was held institutionally for the first four years of its existence—founding shareholders included AIG (with over 40 percent), American Express Company, Lambert Brussels Financial Corporation, Transatlantic Reinsurance Co., among other companies.

PREINCO was launched during an up cycle in the reinsurance industry, when low capacity coincided with high demand to effect rising premiums. As more companies entered the market, however, competition ensued. PREINCO's revenues declined from $169.88 million in 1987 to $145.66 million in 1988. Nevertheless, the company's conservative investment strategy kept its profits on a strong upward trend, from $8.01 million to $11.97 million. Property and casualty insurance in the late 1980s and early 1990s was also characterized by record catastrophic losses. Almost annual natural disasters, including Hurricane Hugo and a devastating earthquake in California, plagued underwriting ratios. Still, PREINCO's revenues from 1988 to 1989 rose 28 percent, to $186.6 million, and profits grew more than 60 percent, to $19.4 million.

In April 1990, PREINCO acquired the Transatlantic Reinsurance Company. Transatlantic had been launched in 1953 and acquired by AIG in 1967; just prior to the time its acquisition by of PREINCO, Transatlantic was 49.99 percent owned by AIG. Transatlantic was the first non-Japanese professional reinsurer to be licensed in that country, and the company also boasted offices in London, Hong Kong, and Toronto. Moreover, the addition of Transatlantic more than tripled the holding company's annual revenues and profits over 1989, which topped $580.10 million and $61.9 million, respectively, for the 1990 fiscal year. To reflect the international activities of its new and substantially larger subsidiary, PREINCO changed its name to

Transatlantic Holdings, Inc. (TRH). The company also then gained a listing on the New York Stock Exchange, selling about 35 percent of its shares to the public.

TRH's prudent underwriting and conservative investing helped it thrive in an insurance market besieged by natural and financial catastrophes in the early 1990s. Typhoons in Japan, a hurricane in the eastern United States, and devastating fires in Oakland, California, took their toll on property insurers. However, TRH's emphasis on casualty (rather than property) underwriting helped offset its share of these losses. Around the same time, companies throughout the insurance industry were taken to task for gambling assets on junk bonds and other risky investments. Although the ensuing bad publicity affected the public image of the industry as a whole, TRH profited from the "flight to quality" that followed. By the end of fiscal 1991, it ranked as the second largest publicly traded reinsurance group based in the United States, with revenues of $618.75 million and profits of $70.55 million. The following year, the insurance industry experienced its worst losses in history, estimated at $23 billion. Hurricanes Andrew and Iniki were the most damaging and cost TRH $20 million. TRH's revenues declined slightly from 1991 to 1992, but its net income actually rose to $71.66 million.

During this time, such major competitors as Transamerica and Continental Reinsurance began exiting the difficult property and casualty reinsurance market. Analyst Graham Tanaka of Tanaka Capital Management praised TRH's conservative underwriting, noting that the company hadn't "chased after the kinds of risky business that others have" in a 1992 *Business Week* article. Wall Street recognized TRH's growth and stability as well; the company's stock rose 44 percent from 1991 to 1992 to over $56. Analysts surmised that other U.S. and foreign rivals would abandon the segment as well, leaving TRH to choose the best risks left behind. Moreover, problems at Lloyd's of London opened the door to more business for the holding company's United Kingdom office, which more than doubled its premiums from 1991 to 1992. In that year, the London operations led foreign branch premium growth of over 50 percent, as Transatlantic targeted the global reinsurance market for growth. In 1993, the company established an office in Miami to increase Latin American business.

Although TRH counted its relationship with AIG as a strength, the larger company's contribution to annual premium income continued to decline from about 50 percent in 1991 to 40 percent in 1992 and 32 percent in 1993. TRH had made impressive strides in the reinsurance market; its annual revenues quadrupled, and profits multiplied sixteen-fold from 1986 to 1993. The company outperformed the S&P Property-Casualty Insurance Index by 110 percent and the S&P 500 Index by 104 percent in the early 1990s, as its share value (with dividends reinvested) nearly doubled from mid-1990 to year end 1993.

Principal Subsidiaries: Transatlantic Reinsurance Co.; Putnam Reinsurance Co.

Further Reading:

Marcial, Gene G., "Transatlantic is Cruising," *Business Week,* December 28, 1992, p. 78.

"Transatlantic Cites Impact of Cat Losses," *National Underwriter,* March 15, 1993, p. 23.

"Transatlantic Holdings Posts Record Net Income," *National Underwriter,* April 13, 1992, p. 23.

—April Dougal Gasbarre

TriMas Corp.

315 East Eisenhower Parkway
Ann Arbor, Michigan 48108
U.S.A.
(313) 747-7025
Fax: (313) 747-6565

Public Company
Incorporated: 1986 as Campbell Industries Inc.
Employees: 3,400
Sales: $.43 billion
Stock Exchanges: New York
SICs: 8600 Manufacturing Industries; 8660 Metals and
    Metalworking

TriMas Corp., through its diversified subsidiaries, is a leading manufacturer of fasteners, towing systems, specialty container products, and other miscellaneous products. During its short history the company has achieved meteoric growth through cautious acquisitions and a hands-off management style.

TriMas is the indirect progeny of Masco Corp. of Ann Arbor, Michigan. Founded in 1929 just before the Great Depression, Masco realized stunning growth during the 1960s, 1970s, and 1980s, making it one of the largest 150 companies (by sales volume) in the United States by the early 1990s. In fact, Masco increased its revenues at an average annual rate of 19 percent between 1957 and 1989, and its net income rocketed at an average of 22 percent each year. By the 1990s, Masco was capturing more than $4 billion in annual revenues.

An understanding of Masco's distinctive style during its growth years grants insight into the success of its stepchild, TriMas Corp. Masco flourished during the middle 1900s by purchasing a multitude of small and medium-sized manufacturing companies, most of which were leaders in their market niche. Unlike many other holding companies, Masco did not strive to profit by purchasing undervalued or underperforming companies that it believed it could turn around. Instead, it purchased healthy, innovative companies. It would then simply allow the companies to continue doing whatever they did best.

In addition to its hands-off management approach, Masco operated an extremely efficient, streamlined operation. Despite its size and strength in several industries—it owned several recognized manufacturing companies, such as Delta and Peerless

faucets, Drexel Heritage, and Henredon—Masco's headquarters was a relatively small, low-profile facility located among a string of industrial parks west of Detroit. Just a few hundred employees managed one of the country's largest holding companies, earning Masco a reputation as one of the leanest, best-run corporations in the world.

A chief contributor to Masco's rampant expansion was Brian Campbell. Campbell joined Masco in 1974, bringing with him a decade of valuable experience in the investment banking industry. He served as vice president of business development for Masco for 12 years, during which the conglomerate bolted from $250 million to more than $1.5 billion in annual sales. Campbell played an integral role in fostering internal growth. More importantly, however, he helped build an aggressive acquisitions program. Campbell also developed a reputation as an astute, people-oriented businessman.

After his successful stint at Masco, Campbell indulged his entrepreneurial bent by breaking away in 1986 to form his own holding company, Campbell Industries, Inc. With $10 million in financial backing from Masco, Campbell started his company with the purchase of Lake Erie Screw Corp., of Cleveland, Ohio. Shortly afterward, he bought Di-Rite Company in nearby Lakewood, Ohio. The start-up was generating profits of about $9.5 million annually from sales of $100 million by 1988. In addition to his two Ohio gems, Campbell developed a list of more than 100 companies that became potential targets for his takeover team.

Campbell had access to credit that he could have used during the late 1980s to add some of those 100 manufacturers to his portfolio. Instead, he surprised analysts by sitting on the sidelines during the takeover binge of that period. In what Campbell later called a feeding frenzy, institutions and investment funds poured huge dollars into corporate buyouts during the late 1980s, thus over-inflating the value of many of Campbell's prospective acquisitions. His patience during that period reflected the aversion to risk that had characterized his endeavors at Masco. "People expected Brian to go out acquiring from day one," said John Nicholls, TriMas's treasurer, in a July 1990 issue of *Detroit News*, "but he practiced extreme caution."

Although Campbell Industries did not engage in any takeovers during the late 1980s, it did significantly expand its holdings through a deal with Campbell's business partner and former employer, Masco Corp. Actually, Campbell cut a deal with Masco Industries, a subsidiary of Masco Corp. Masco Corp. created that subsidiary during the 1980s as a way to more efficiently operate and run several of its smaller holdings. Then, in 1988, Masco Industries used Campbell Industries to serve a similar purpose. Since its inception in 1984, Masco Industries had grown through acquisition to $1.5 billion in annual sales. In an effort to jettison some of the smaller companies to which it felt it could no longer devote sufficient attention, Masco Industries arranged for Campbell to buy them.

In 1988, Campbell purchased ten divisions of Masco Industries. Campbell Industries Inc. was dissolved and renamed TriMas Corp. The new organization immediately had $300 million in sales. It also had less debt, more investment capital, and much more profit potential. In return for its holdings, Campbell agreed to transfer $200 million in cash and debt to Masco Industries. The end result of the sale was that Masco Corp. and Masco Industries owned a total of 71 percent of TriMas stock, while Masco Corp. shareholders divided another 25 percent. Campbell himself retained the remaining four percent ownership share of TriMas, effectively making his company an independent division of Masco Corp.

Through a single transaction Campbell had broadened his company from a maker of industrial screws and fasteners to a manufacturer of heat treating equipment, tooling machines, gas cylinders, and various defense-related metal products. TriMas was particularly focused on the production of metal industrial fasteners, which are used to connect and bind parts in cars, tractors, airplanes, furniture, and a plethora of other products. It also produced a large amount of towing systems for cars, trucks, and heavy equipment. Although it would later reduce its emphasis in this market, TriMas garnered most of its revenues immediately following the Masco deal from the manufacture of defense products, such as rocket motors, missile casings, and various ordinance components.

During 1989 Campbell and his talented staff worked to consolidate and streamline TriMas's new group of companies and to prepare for new acquisitions in the 1990s. Campbell planned follow the same trail he had blazed at Masco. He would continue to buy undervalued, well-run manufacturing companies with profit margins of 15 percent or more, allowing their managers to continue to run them autonomously. He would then use their strong cash flows to service debt on new acquisitions. Like Masco, TriMas would function with an almost skeletal staff. Before it purchased the Masco companies, in fact, Campbell ran the entire operation with just three other coworkers. That number jumped to a still-meager 13 by 1989. The overall strategy seemed to be paying off as TriMas's sales climbed from $100 million in 1988 to $221 million in 1989 and net income also doubled to $18.6 million.

Almost four years after his first acquisition, Campbell again fired up his buyout machine in 1990. The United States had fallen into a deep recession and the takeover binge of the late 1980s had faded. Prices on several of the acquisition candidates targeted by Campbell had plummeted more than 20 percent. He purchased three more companies from Masco in January of 1990: Compac Corp., Reese Products Co., and Fulton Manufacturing Co. These new purchases increased his reach into Australia and Canada. In June, moreover, Campbell bought Draw-Tite Inc., a trailer-hitch manufacturer with annual sales of more than $50 million.

The new additions to TriMas's portfolio all had several characteristics in common. Campbell looked for low-tech market leaders that had minimal research and development requirements and were less susceptible to technical obsolescence than high-tech firms. He also sought organizations that lacked the deep pockets necessary to implement needed improvements, such as increased manufacturing automation or better information systems. Campbell also wanted the managers of his subsidiaries to have an entrepreneurial attitude and philosophy congruent with his own. "You develop over the years an intuitive feel when you walk through a factory and talk to

management," Campbell related in a July 1990 issue of *Detroit News*. "It's sort of an art form."

Campbell's treatment of two of his new purchases exhibited his unique treatment of his subsidiary companies. Both Draw-Tite Inc. and Reese Products Co. were leading U.S. manufacturers of trailer hitches and related accessories. Despite the fact that the two companies were battling toe-to-toe with one another, TriMas did not interfere with their management styles or their fiercely competitive rivalry. "I don't want to take away that competitive edge," explained Campbell in the *Detroit News* article. "The key is that TriMas doesn't come in and force a lot of changes here," added Draw-Tite president James Mellow.

Despite a sporadic string of acquisitions during the latter half of 1990 and throughout the early 1990s, some observers were still puzzled by the seemingly slow rate at which TriMas was adding new manufacturers to its portfolio. However, Campbell sustained his extremely disciplined expansion approach, citing his aversion to unnecessary risks. Besides, TriMas was achieving remarkable internal growth by increasing the efficiency of its holdings and by taking advantage of market and economic trends that were increasing the value of many of its subsidiaries. For instance, TriMas was able to substantially increase fastener sales with minor labeling and marketing changes. It had also invested large amounts of cash into improving the manufacturing efficiency of several of its subsidiaries through increased automation.

Campbell's efforts bore fruit during the early 1990s, surprising many analysts that doubted his ability to grow TriMas without relying heavily on a steady stream of new acquisitions. Sales increased about 50 percent to $328 million in 1990 as a result of new purchases. Revenues continued to climb steadily to $388 million during 1992, from which a healthy $17 million in profit was gleaned. Importantly, TriMas was making strides in several areas that would set the stage for future growth and acquisitions. It announced plans to significantly expand several of its manufacturing facilities, for example. It also pared its heavy debt load down to a manageable 45 percent of its total capital by 1992.

By 1993, TriMas was a fast-growing, truly diversified international manufacturing company. It owned 15 manufacturing subsidiaries with operations in Mexico, Canada, Australia, and throughout the United States. Although it focused on only four relatively specific product categories, its revenues were somewhat evenly spread across a healthy variety of markets, including construction, transportation, chemical, and maintenance. Although the staff at TriMas's headquarters remained bare in comparison to most holding companies its size, the number of workers employed by its subsidiaries had ballooned to nearly 3,500 going into 1994. Furthermore, its assets had swelled to a big-league $490 million.

The largest of its four product divisions was specialty containers, which manufactured containers and dispensers for various fluids and gases. Companies in that division included Lamons Metal Gasket Co., Norris Cylinder Company, and Rieke Corp. Towing systems contributed the second greatest share of TriMas revenues. Companies in this important division included Draw-Tite, Inc., Fulton Performance Products, Inc., and Reese Products. TriMas's specialty fasteners branch included industry leaders Commonwealth Industries, Eskay Screw Corporation, Lake Erie Screw Corporation, and Monogram Aerospace Fasteners, Inc. Finally, TriMas held six miscellaneous companies that manufactured fiberglass insulation, industrial tape, and precision cutting tools.

As each of its divisions continued to post healthy gains, TriMas's revenues surged during 1993 to $443 million, reflecting average annual growth of 35 percent since 1988. Likewise, net income soared to $38 million by 1993—a 58 percent jump over 1992 earnings. In addition, as evidenced by its 1993 purchase of Lamons Metal Gasket, TriMas's cautious acquisition strategy was still intact going into the mid-1990s. At least one major investment house predicted that TriMas's sales would increase a minimum of 20 percent in 1994 and would likely stay a similar course throughout the decade. When asked about the possibility of his retirement in an April 1990 issue of *Crains Detroit Business*, the 53-year-old Campbell replied, "It's unlikely, because I'm having too much fun. . . . The ability to find good companies goes on and on. They're always there."

Principal Subsidiaries: Commonwealth Industries; Compac Corporation; Draw-Tile, Inc.; Eskay Screw Corp.; Fulton Performance Products, Inc.; Keo Cutters and Kee Services; Lake Erie Screw Corp.; Lamons Metal Gasket Co.; Monogram Aerospace Fasteners, Inc.; Norris Cylinder Company; Punchcraft Company; Reese Products, Inc.; Reska Spline Products Co.; Richards Micro-Tool, Inc.; Rieke Corp.

Further Reading:

Barkholz, David, "A Vanished Acquisition? TriMas Boss Knows When to Say 'No'," *Crains Detroit Business*, April 19, 1993, Sec. 1, p. 2; "TriMas President Plans Growth Through Acquisition," *Crains Detroit Business*, February 13, 1989, Sec. 1, p. 1.

Johnson, Mark W., "TriMas Corp.," *Bloomington Research Associates Economic and Investment Research*, April 4, 1994.

King, Angela, "Masco Stock, Earnings on Big Rebound," *Crains Detroit Business*, May 18, 1992, Sec. 1, p. 1; "After Idle '89, TriMas Readies for Buying Binge," *Crains Detroit Business*, April 9, 1990, Sec. 1, p. 1.

Matz, Kristin, "Clinton County Has 'Blue Chip' Businesses," *Lafayette Business Digest*, September 9, 1993, p. C3.

McBride, Michael A., "Acquisitive Spirit—A Word of Advice from Masco: Buy the Best," *Michigan Business*, October 1989, Sec. 1, p. 30.

Price, Caroline, "On-the-Road Warrior: Masco's Export Expert Blazes New Trails for International Sales," *Michigan Business*, June 1990, Sec. 1, p. 22.

Vlasic, Bill, "Shopping Around: Feeding Frenzy Over, TriMas Moves into Marketplace," *Detroit News*, July 9, 1990, p. F1.

Zagoudis, George, "TriMas Corp.," *Bloomington Research Associates Economic and Investment Research*, April 4, 1994.

—Dave Mote

Triton Energy Corporation

6688 North Central Expressway
Suite 1400
Dallas, Texas 75206
U.S.A.
(214) 691-5200
Fax: (214) 987-0571

Public Company
Incorporated: 1962
Employees: 490
Sales: $.11 billion
Stock Exchanges: New York, Toronto
SICs: 8510 Petroleum; 1300 International Trade and Foreign
    Investment

Triton Energy Corporation is one of the largest U.S. independent oil and natural gas exploration and production companies. It is distinguished from its U.S. peers by its emphasis on overseas operations. Triton's roller coaster ride to success was punctuated by infighting, brushes with bankruptcy, allegations of fraud, and high-risk ventures.

Triton was founded in Dallas by L. R. Wiley in 1962, just as the oil industry was entering a decade of defeat. Although many "wildcat" oil and gas exploration firms in the southwest of the United States had reaped huge profits from the booming energy industry during the 1950s and early 1960s, most of the 1960s and early 1970s were fraught with obstacles to success. As mismanaged federal energy policies and flat oil prices stumped producers, the number of oil and gas exploration industry participants plummeted from 30,000 in 1960 to a beleaguered group of 13,000 by the early 1970s.

Despite industry woes, Triton managed to survive, and even profit, during the 1960s and early 1970s by finding and exploiting large reserves. Like many other companies of that era, Triton augmented its U.S. activities with overseas exploration and drilling, resulting in several important oil and gas discoveries. In 1971, for example, a well drilled in the Gulf of Thailand encountered natural gas zones that promised as much as 29 million cubic feet of natural gas per day—a major find. Typical of many overseas energy ventures, however, political roadblocks kept Triton from capitalizing on the find until the 1990s.

Just as it had done in the 1960s, when it built its company amidst the ruins of many of its competitors, Triton displayed its maverick bent again in the mid-1970s. During the early 1970s, the Organization of Petroleum Exporting Countries (OPEC) began limiting its oil production in a bid to boost profits. As oil prices vaulted to $30 per barrel, many U.S. exploration and production companies began to focus on developing domestic reserves in lieu of more risky overseas ventures. Triton bucked this trend by continuing to engage in high-risk, though potentially lucrative, foreign endeavors.

During the 1970s and 1980s Triton stuck its neck out in almost every corner of the globe. Scavenging for untapped reserves of oil and natural gas, Triton opened subsidiaries and invested in ventures in Australia, Indonesia, Thailand, Malaysia, Europe, Argentina, New Zealand, Canada, and other places. As the company bypassed less perilous domestic opportunities that it viewed as offering relatively low returns, it became known as a savvy industry maverick with a knack for scouting out and exploiting international profit opportunities.

Although the company suffered several defeats, its few big winners provided enough income to allow it to continue searching for new reserves and to gain favor on Wall Street. Indeed, by the early 1990s the company boasted at least eight major discoveries totaling more than 2.5 billion barrels of oil and ten trillion cubic feet of gas. The find in the Gulf of Thailand, for example, offered potentially large returns if Triton could overcome the political stalemate between Thailand and Malaysia concerning the reserves. Similar successes that brought more immediate returns were achieved in the United Kingdom, Canada, and Australia.

One of Triton's most prolific triumphs during the 1970s and 1980s was its foray into France. In 1980, Triton became the first independent U.S. oil company to obtain an onshore exploration permit in that country. It teamed up with France's Total Exploration S.A. in a venture that yielded important discoveries in the Paris Basin of north central France. Those French oil reserves, 50 percent of which were owned by Triton, swelled to more than 15 million barrels in 1985, representing a significant portion of Triton's total reserves going into the mid-1980s. "This accomplishment, which started from just an idea, is the result of good planning, geology, geophysics, engineering, politics, and also a little good luck," exclaimed Mike McInerny, vice president of corporate planning, in a July 1985 issue of the *Dallas Business Journal.*

Triton's success in France reflected its ability to detect and cultivate opportunities that had been overlooked by its competitors. Indeed, both large and small U.S. oil firms had ignored the Paris Basin because of deceptive geological characteristics, which made it appear that the region was not worth drilling. In contrast, Triton, suspecting that the neglected area could hide large reserves, was willing to risk failure. After actually discovering a healthy supply of oil, moreover, Triton benefited from extremely low production costs, which were less than 20 percent of those in the United States. "They are the only company that is doing what they're doing in their particular way," noticed oil analyst Lincoln Werden in the *Journal* article.

By the mid-1980s, Triton was producing oil or owned reserves in France, Australia, New Zealand, Colombia, Thailand, Great Britain, West Africa, the United States, Canada, and the North Sea. Furthermore, it was planning to drill new wells in Nepal, Gabon, and several new regions in the countries in which it was already active. Largely as a result of its breakthrough discovery in France, Triton's assets had ballooned to about $200 million by 1985. Likewise, revenues jumped 100 percent during fiscal 1985 (ending in June) to roughly $50 million. Profits jumped similarly. Furthermore, Triton management expected sales in 1986 to surge to nearly $90 million. In addition, the company planned to drill an additional 200 wells worldwide during that year.

Although its future seemed bright as it entered the latter half of the 1980s, Triton began to experience financial setbacks. The entire oil industry, in fact, began to spiral into a down cycle in 1986 as the oil market became glutted and oil and gas prices plunged. Triton's sales continued to grow, but slimming profit margins were diminishing the concern's ability to fund expansion or to even remain profitable. Although the company realized an increase in revenues to $68 million in 1987, it posted a crushing loss of $7.8 million. In 1988, moreover, Triton realized a similar loss after boosting sales more than 100 percent.

To alleviate the negative influence of oil and gas prices on its bottom line, Triton stepped up its efforts to diversify into related businesses. For example, it accrued a major ownership share of Input/Output, Inc., a Houston-based manufacturer of seismic equipment, and bolstered investments in its domestic pipeline system. In 1988, Triton purchased two airport service operations, one in Texas and one in Oklahoma, in a bid to establish itself as a leading supplier of aviation fuels and services. The company, through its Triton Aviation subsidiary, planned to sell its crude oil to refineries in exchange for aviation fuel, thereby eliminating the cost of operating its own refinery. The two 1988 acquisitions, along with smaller purchases, quickly propelled Triton to the status of major player in the aviation services industry. "They'll have to prove themselves," cautioned Greg Wheeler, vice president of competing Avfuel, in a May 1988 issue of *Dallas Business Journal*.

Triton's efforts at diversification only seemed to exacerbate its problems. As profits continued to lag into the late 1980s and early 1990s, management struggled to find a way out of the ever-deepening hole into which it had fallen; unable to profit from its devalued oil and gas reserves or its sinking subsidiaries, the company was having trouble stabilizing its earnings and generating sufficient cash for an aggressive exploration and development program. Furthermore, Triton stammered under the pressure of an entirely unrelated set of problems that followed the company through the late 1980s and early 1990s like a lost puppy.

Triton was forced to battle an array of allegations in the early 1990s that it had falsified accounting records during the 1980s. A Triton official confirmed the problem when he acknowledged that the company had made payoffs to officials in Indonesia that had led to "creative" accounting methods. Company employees admitted to routinely overstating expenses, altering bookkeeping entries, and bribing auditors. Triton's accounting firm resigned amidst controversy.

The blow-up over Triton's Indonesian affairs followed on the heels of a more costly problem. Jimmy Janacek, who worked at Triton from 1981 to 1989 and served as controller, filed suit against Triton for wrongful termination. Janacek claimed that Triton had fired him for refusing to violate state and federal securities laws in fulfilling the company's reporting requirements. The jury agreed with Janacek and elected to award him $124 million—a potentially deathly blow for his former employer. Stunned Triton officials, who had turned down a $5 million settlement just days before the award, paid $9.4 million while Triton's insurers paid an unspecified reduced settlement.

As Triton floundered into the 1990s, it experienced increasing pressure from shareholders to start producing some results. One major investor, in a move that smacked of a takeover threat, actually sent a letter to Triton executives in 1990 encouraging them to liquidate their major assets. Although Triton had already begun to restructure, it stepped up its reorganization efforts in an attempt to appease investors and improve its performance. It cut 25 employees from its Dallas headquarters, announced plans to dump the majority of its non-oil subsidiaries, and decided to shuck major portions of its underperforming overseas oil and gas operations.

Battered by slumping oil prices, a U.S. recession, legal battles, the effects of inconsistent management practices, and failed attempts at diversification, Triton slouched wearily into 1991. Management believed that the company was undervalued on the stock market and that its long-term outlook was generally positive, especially given the fact that oil and gas prices would likely recover in the near future. Nevertheless, detractors shunned the organization as a sloppy, overweight, unfocused corporation whose high-risk strategy had finally caved in.

Critics' suspicions were supported by Triton's inability to move some of its holdings—when it tried to sell its European subsidiary for $200 million, the highest bid came in at $100 million and Triton chose not to sell. Furthermore, Triton losses had increased to $12.5 million in 1989 and to a whopping $54 million in 1990. Triton's bleak condition was reflected in articles about the company's woes. A *Barron's* article, for example, referred to Triton as "a wisp of an oil-exploration firm" that was "burdened by self-dealing and impropriety."

After a five-year period of torment and suffering, Triton blasted its critics and turned its entire organization around with a single, momentous breakthrough. In July of 1991, elated Triton executives confirmed rumors that the company was on the verge of a major oil strike in central Columbia. In the most meteoric rise of a U.S. energy stock since the 1970s, the price of a Triton share rocketed from a 52-week low of $4 to nearly $50 by the end of August. Analysts estimated that the new discovery could yield three billion barrels or more of oil, making it the most important find in the Americas since Prudhoe Bay in the Arctic Circle.

Triton had been actively searching for oil in Columbia since the summer of 1981. Convinced that there was oil to be found, Executive Vice President John Tatum initiated years of fruitless efforts and hefty capital investments. Finally, in 1987, Triton and its partner, British Petroleum (BPX), found an area that they believed might produce oil. In an extremely risky venture, Triton and BPX began drilling in one of the most geographically and socially challenging regions of the world. To reach the jungle-covered oil, they had to drill holes two miles deep at a cost of $27 million per hole; each hole required six to ten months to drill.

Worse yet, the region in which they were drilling was brimming with danger. Three separate groups of Marxist guerrillas, organized criminals seeking to protect their interests in nearby emerald mines, and other violent elements combined to produce a murder rate averaging 80 per day—ten times the U.S. per-capita average. Bullet proof vests could not protect the drillers from the equally distressing threat of kidnapping, a relatively common practice in Columbia.

Triton's assumption of risk reaped major rewards in the early 1990s. Although the company's losses continued to mount, its stock price soared as enthusiastic investors sought a piece of the action. Triton's losses were attributable primarily to its investments in the Columbian drilling operation, which would not begin to produce positive cash flow until at least 1995. Triton's losses swelled to $94 million in 1992 and to about $90 million in 1993.

Triton's revenues also plummeted. Indeed, when the magic bullet that Triton managers had hoped for finally arrived, they began a rapid reorganization plan that emphasized development of the Columbian drilling operations. After all, in just one year the percentage of Triton's proved reserves (the amount of oil still underground to which it had rights) represented by its Columbian division rocketed from zero to 68, making the importance of its holdings in all other regions of the globe comparatively negligible. To carry the company into a new era of profitability, Triton moved William Lee, who had served as president since 1966, to the position of chairman of the board. Lee was succeeded as president by Thomas G. Finck, an engineer and industry veteran.

As a result of its new focus, Triton decided to shed all of its non-oil subsidiaries, liquidate its U.S. and Canadian oil and gas reserves, and "reassess" its development prospects in France. Its reduction of working operations contributed to a decline in sales from $209 million in 1991 to $125 million in 1992 and $110 million in 1993. At the same time, however, the company's total proved reserves increased from 83 million net equivalent barrels (a measure that incorporates both oil and natural gas reserves) to 130 million, boding well for Triton's future.

As though the sun was finally breaking through the clouds that had darkened Triton's balance sheet during the late 1980s and early 1990s, recovering gas and oil prices accelerated in 1994 and were expected to rise through at least 1995. Estimates that the Columbian operations would be producing 150,000 barrels per day by the end of 1995 and 900,000 barrels per day by the end of the decade suggested potentially enormous profits for Triton. Furthermore, Triton's ongoing exploration in other regions, such as Argentina, could yield more surprise additions to the company's reserves.

In keeping with its long-time strategy of engaging in high-risk, long-term international exploration and development ventures, Triton entered the mid-1990s determined to sustain its search for new reserves. "As our future lies in creating value through exploration, management must look beyond the current development projects to the future," stated Finck in the company's 1993 annual report. "Large-scale, high-potential international exploration projects take many years to develop. Triton must identify and pursue attractive opportunities."

Principal Subsidiaries: Crusader Limited (Australia) (49.9%); Triton Argentina, Inc. (Argentina); Triton Colombia, Inc. (Columbia); Triton Indonesia (Indonesia); Triton Oil and Gas Corp.; Triton Oil Company of Thailand (Thailand).

Further Reading:

Fine, Jennifer, "Triton Energy Hits It Rich with Finds Near City of Lights," *Dallas Business Journal,* July 29, 1985, Sec. 1, p. 1.

Lampman, Dean, "Triton Aviation Fuels Expansion Effort with Acquisitions," *Dallas Business Journal,* May 30, 1988, Sec. 1, p. 5.

Majors, Stephana, "Triton: Columbian Well Big; Country May Take 50 Percent," *Dallas Business Journal,* July 12, 1991, Sec. 1, p. 6; "Investors Gambling on Triton Oil Strike," *Dallas Business Journal,* July 5, 1991, Sec. 1, p. 17.

Manning, Stuart, "Triton Canadian Unit to Sell Natural Gas to Massachusetts Utility," *Dallas Business Journal,* November 14, 1988, Sec. 1, p. 6.

Preston, Darrell, "Triton Attacks Lawyer over Huge Jury Award," *Dallas Business Journal,* July 24, 1992, Sec. 1, p. 1; "Justice Department Launches Probe of Triton Energy," *Dallas Business Journal,* March 26, 1993, Sec. 1, p. 3.

Steffy, Loren, "Big Investor Urges Triton to Divest Bulk of Its Operations," *Dallas Business Journal,* August 31, 1990, Sec. 1, p. 3; "Axed Whistle Blower Sues Triton," *Dallas Business Journal,* July 9, 1990, Sec. 1, p. 1; "Colombia Gusher, Fires Triton Stock," *Dallas Times Herald,* August 24, 1991, p. B1.

Totty, Michael, "Triton Nudged to Drop Production Companies," *Dallas Times Herald,* August 28, 1990, p. B2.

Zipser, Andy, "Trials of Triton," *Barron's,* July 26, 1993, pp. 14–15.

—Dave Mote

TRW Inc.

1900 Richmond Road
Cleveland, Ohio 44124-3719
U.S.A.
(216) 291-7000
Fax: (216) 291-7758

Public Company
Incorporated: 1916 as The Steel Products Co.
Employees: 61,200
Sales: $7.95 billion
Stock Exchanges: New York Boston NASDAQ Philadelphia
    Pacific
SICs: 3714 Motor Vehicle Parts and Accessories; 2399
    Fabricated Textile Products, Not Elsewhere Classified;
    3764 Space Propulsion Units and Parts; 3769 Electronic
    Components, Not Elsewhere Classified; 3761 Guided
    Missiles and Space Vehicles; 361 Pumps and Pumping
    Equipment; 3494 Valves and Pipe Fittings, Not Elsewhere
    Classified; 3812 Search and Navigation Equipment; 3769
    Space Vehicle Equipment, Not Elsewhere Classified; 7370
    Computer and Data Processing Services; 7323 Credit
    Reporting Services

After eight decades of highly praised management and growth, TRW Inc.'s unique combination of mundane and high-tech products ran into roadblocks in the late 1980s and early 1990s. Its space and defense division had been a major manufacturer of satellites and an important contractor in the U.S. Department of Defense's Strategic Defense Initiative program (better known as "Star Wars"). Virtually every car manufactured featured a TRW part, whether it was a seat belt, steering system, or engine valve. And at least half of America's citizens were registered in its credit reporting system. But when the late 1980s brought the end of the Cold War, a global recession, and intense competition, TRW found itself with lagging sales, lackluster earnings, and a stagnant stock price. A new chief executive officer, Joseph T. Gorman, brought a restructuring plan and a renewed commitment to the corporation's historic emphasis: automotive parts.

TRW's conglomerate structure grew out of the company's history. The company was founded in 1901 as the Cleveland Cap Screw Company to manufacture and supply bolts for early automotive engines. Name changes, to Electric Welding in 1908 and Steel Products Company in 1915, reflected the firm's expansion into a wider variety of auto parts. During the 1920s,

Charles E. Thompson, a welder at the company, conceived of a new method of valve manufacture that catapulted the parts company into the vanguard of global valve making. The firm was renamed Thompson Products in 1926 in recognition of his vital breakthrough.

By the early 1950s the company had made a name for itself in automotive and had expanded into aircraft engine parts. It had also become well known by sponsoring the famed Thompson Trophy Race, the aeronautical equivalent of auto racing's Indianapolis 500. But in the postwar era, the company faced a decline in manned aircraft and saw opportunities in aerospace and electronics. J. David Wright, the company's general manager, and Horace Shepard, a vice president, thought the auto valve and steering component maker needed more technical sophistication and looked to acquisition to get it.

To break into the budding high-tech industry, Wright and Shepard tried to buy Hughes Aircraft Co. Hughes was willing to listen to bids but scoffed at the Thompson offer, which was thought to be ten times too low. Just a few months later, two of Hughes Aircraft's top scientist-executives, Simon Ramo and Dean Woolridge, decided to leave Hughes to form a new electronic systems company, and Thompson put up $500,000 to bankroll the venture. Not long afterward, Ramo-Woolridge Corporation was established in Los Angeles and quickly gained solid standing in the advanced technology business, being awarded the systems engineering and technical direction contracts for such important missile programs as Atlas, Minuteman, Titan, and Thor.

By 1958 Thompson Products had invested $20 million—20 percent of its net worth at the time—for a 49 percent interest in Ramo-Woolridge, and the two operations were merged as Thompson-Ramo-Woolridge. Though united on paper, the company maintained separate corporate headquarters, with Woolridge president in Los Angeles and Wright chairman in Cleveland. Ramo and Shepard, a former chief of production procurement for the Air Force, also had an active role in management.

The merger could hardly have started less auspiciously. In the midst of a recession, the Cleveland-based group was hit with a 14 percent drop in automotive business and a 34 percent drop in manned aircraft business. When business improved for the Cleveland division, Los Angeles got into trouble. Its venture into semiconductors collapsed in 1961, and the McNamara era was beginning at the Pentagon.

The West Coast scientists, who had only known cost-plus-fixed-fee contracts, had to learn how to go from spending money to making it. This education was hampered by hard feelings between the two groups. The electronics end was not living up to its promise of being the business of the future. In its first four years following the merger, profit margins that had been at the 4 percent-plus level in the mid-1950s dropped to an average of barely 2 percent.

With the company facing such mundane tasks as cost-cutting, Woolridge, who reportedly never really wanted to be a businessman anyway, resigned in 1962. As Woolridge was getting settled in at his new job as a professor at the California Institute of Technology, Shepard was promoted to president and Ramo was named vice-chairman. With Cleveland now in control of the company, the Los Angeles scientists were quickly reassured when the new management team instituted a number of reforms to get the company back on its feet, including writing off $3 million in inventory.

In 1963, Shepard and Wright began pruning unprofitable divisions. They sold most of the unprofitable Bumkor-Ramo computer division to Martin Marietta. The company retained partial ownership in Bumkor-Ramo but no longer played a large role in the company's plans. Shepard and Wright continued hammering out the company's plans for long-term growth, seeking specifically to raise profit margins. To this end, in 1964 they sold the microwave division and the division that made high fidelity components, intercoms, and language laboratories.

To shore up the company's auto parts division, they bought Ross Gear & Tool, a maker of mechanical and power steering units, and Marlin-Rockwell, a ball bearings manufacturer. The 7 percent profit margin of the new acquisitions, which had combined profit of $5.7 million on sales of $76.5 million, helped boost TRW's overall margin to 4 percent in 1964, up a percentage point from a year earlier.

In 1965, in another look toward the future, Thompson-Ramo-Woolridge adopted a shorter, less cumbersome name, the now instantly recognizable initials TRW. Also that year the company's investment in aerospace and electronics was becoming increasingly clear. In the previous decade, sales in space and electronics shot up from $14 million to $200 million. But despite that dramatic growth, the company's earnings still came mostly from its oldest business, auto parts. New and replacement parts accounted for 34 percent of TRW's $553 million in sales and 40 percent of its earnings. Chief among those products were its steering linkages, valves, and braking devices that it sold to General Motors, Ford, and Chrysler.

Things improved for TRW in 1966. An auto parts boom was helping the company's profitability. The Cleveland-based automotive group had a return of 6 percent on sales of $350 million. The equipment group, also in Cleveland, had an increase of sales to $200 million in aerospace and ordinance technology, but lower profit margins because of start-up costs for unexpected demand in commercial aircraft. The Los Angeles-based TRW Systems had $250 million in sales and a 3 percent profit margin building and designing spacecraft and doing research. Totals were up to $870 million in sales for TRW, producing $36 million in profit for a 4.2 percent return. Even with the upturn in sales, the company was relying less on government contracts, down to about 44 percent from 70 percent ten years earlier. With the company's financial picture on the upturn, the wrangling between Los Angeles and Cleveland declined. As *Business Week* reported, the discord was "under control, if not cured."

The company continued its tightening of operations in 1966. It bought United Car with $122 million in sales and sold its one consumer business, a hi-fi manufacturer. Nevertheless, TRW had grown into a conglomerate, a term disliked by company management. In 1969 TRW operated six groups that, in turn, administered 55 divisions. The company derived 32 percent of its revenues from aerospace products and computer software, 28 percent from vehicle components for autos and trucks, 23 percent from electronic components and communication, and 17 percent from industrial products ranging from mechanical fasteners to automated controls.

To manage the increasingly far-flung company, TRW maintained strict management control over all operations. By encouraging communication between all levels of management and holding monthly manager meetings, TRW avoided the problems that had plagued Gulf & Western, which had grown into a rambling giant. Another of TRW's successful management styles caught *Fortune*'s eye in 1966. The magazine covered in depth the happenings of a TRW management meeting in Vermont, where 49 of the company's top executives had gathered annually since 1952 at an old farmhouse to think about the company's future.

The next year TRW continued beefing up its auto parts business, acquiring Globe Industries, a Dayton-based maker of miniature AC and DC electric motors. At the same time, TRW's electronics group had grown to more than 20 plants in the United States, Canada, and Mexico. The company continued to evade problems that had plagued other conglomerates, posting a slight pre-tax gain of 16.4 percent, above the industry average of 13.3 percent.

In 1969 TRW named a new president, Ruben F. Mettler. One of his first big projects was a contract for a laboratory that NASA would send on the Viking probe to Mars. TRW won the challenge to provide one black box weighing 33 pounds with complex instruments capable of making biological and chemical tests to detect the most primitive forms of life. The NASA contract was only worth $50 million, not a big financial risk for a multi-billion dollar company like TRW, but the job was important for the company's prestige.

The auto parts business, in the meantime, was once again proving to be immune to cyclical trends in car output. The market for new parts was in a slump, but it was made up for by the accompanying increase in demand for replacement cars as consumers kept their cars on the road longer. TRW also parlayed the computer programming expertise it had garnered along the way into another business, credit reporting. This "sideline" would eventually record the credit ratings of over half of the U.S. population.

The company's sound financial condition was unmistakable. For the five years preceding 1970, the company had average earning jumps of 27 percent annually and an average 23 percent annual increase in sales. But company officials conceded that TRW—which had acquired 38 companies through 1968—could not keep growing at that rate forever. The company looked for future growth to run about 10 percent.

TRW's skillful management again became apparent in 1971, when the company was forced to make cuts because of an aerospace recession. Its TRW Systems division had to cut the number of employees by 15 percent. Managers were not spared cuts either; 18 percent of the professional staff was laid off. The company's open management style enabled TRW to build a strong enough relationship with its employees that two-thirds of them were non-union, perhaps preventing labor squabbles that had appeared in other companies.

TRW made a risky venture in 1976, entering the tricky market of electronic point-of-sale (POS) machines. Those machines had boosted profits for retailers, but not for manufacturers. Its proposed 2001 system aimed at the general market and cost $4,000 per unit, similar to competitors. TRW's move into POS machines was largely a defensive tactic. The electronic credit authorization business it had pioneered in the 1960s was coming under increasing competition. Competitor NCR, the overall leader in POS machines, launched a POS system that incorporated a credit check in 1975. TRW attempted to enter the market with an established customer base by acquiring the service contracts for the 65,000 customers Singer had built up during its short, ill-fated move into the POS market. TRW remained cautious, however, only delivering 200 to 300 machines in 1976, mostly to the May Co. Altogether that year non-food retailers ordered 24,500 POS terminals worth $94 million, and the market was picking up.

In 1976 TRW achieved the moment of glory it had long awaited with Viking's historic landing on Mars. The company took out full-page newspaper ads proclaiming, "That lab is our baby." Appropriately, Mettler, 52, who had pushed for TRW to compete for the Viking contract, was named to succeed Horace Shepard as chairman and chief executive officer when Shepard retired the next year.

Aerospace ventures continued to play an important role in the company's finances. In 1977 TRW was still the chief engineer for U.S. intercontinental ballistic missiles. Aerospace and government electronic revenues were providing a cool $60 million in profits on revenue of $440 million. The electronics division had $300 million in sales. The data communications unit was also doing well with over $150 million in sales. It had established a retail credit bureau and a business credit system, and was an international maker of data equipment. But auto and commercial parts were still accounting for twice as much in sales and five times as much in earnings.

In 1980 TRW and Fujitsu Ltd., Japan's largest computer maker, formed a joint venture that aimed to grab a large share of the U.S. market. TRW had a 3,000-person service organization, reportedly the largest independent network in the U.S. for data processing maintenance, with a special team to develop software. Each company invested $100 million, with Fujitsu keeping a 51 percent share and TRW 45 percent. TRW initiated the venture, seeking a foreign partner to perform maintenance work for its POS machines. Fujitsu, which obtained 68 percent of its revenue from data processing, was eager to expand overseas to increase its economy of scale to compete with IBM back home. Fujitsu named a majority of the directors of the new company so it could qualify for Japanese export and financing tax breaks, but TRW took charge of running it. One of new company's first moves was to buy TRW's ailing POS and automated teller machine (ATM) division. The company, hoping in the beginning to capture a large segment of the small and medium-sized computer market, predicted sales of $500 million to $1 billion by the decade's end.

Despite TRW's careful planning, the POS and Fujitsu deals both proved unsuccessful. The competition from established POS makers, particularly IBM and NCR, was too great. And to make matters worse, evidence that the company's traditionally high ethical standards were eroding surfaced mid-decade. The credit reporting group, for example, violated its own code of ethics by gathering non-credit information on consumers for use in direct mail. TRW also plead guilty to charges of conspiring to overcharge the federal government on contracts for military aircraft engines, and agreed to pay $14.8 million in penalties and refunds.

Joseph T. Gorman, a 22-year veteran of TRW, advanced to the conglomerate's chief executive office in 1988 upon Ruben Mettler's retirement. Unfortunately for Gorman, however, he took the helm just as the end of the Cold War gutted federal defense and space spending, a global recession squeezed profits for auto makers and their suppliers, and competition in the credit information industry froze TRW's sales, earnings, and stock price. To make matters worse, the corporation's most encouraging business, automobile air bags, was plagued by seemingly unshakable losses and a 1990 plant explosion that hampered shipments.

Gorman called in a series of consultants, including Jim Womack, one of the authors of *The Machine That Changed the World.* According to Robin Yale Bergstrom, editor-at-large of *Production,* Womack told TRW's management at their annual retreat that the venerable manufacturer was hopeless. Nonetheless, Gorman decided to base TRW's restructuring on Womack's book, which detailed Toyota's "lean production system." TRW management wrote its own 3.5-pound "total quality management bible," titled *The Lean Production System, Principles and Techniques,* and began applying its concepts in December 1991, after TRW lost $140 million on sales of $7.9 billion.

The restructuring's financial goals included a 20 percent return on equity and positive cash flow. To achieve these standards, Gorman shifted TRW's emphasis back to its historic strength in automotive parts, emphasizing air bags. TRW invested $500 million in this segment, whose sales were boosted by growing consumer demand for such safety restraints. The company aggressively pursued international markets, especially those in Europe and Japan. As a result, sales to Japanese automakers increased from $50 million in 1988 to $600 million in 1992.

Proceeds from divestments totaling about $475 million in 1992 and 1993 were used to pay down corporate debt, which was reduced to its lowest level in five years by 1993. Gorman pronounced the restructuring complete in his 1993 annual letter to shareholders. That year, the company reported its first net profit—$195 million on sales of $7.9 billion—of the 1990s.

Principal Subsidiaries: TRW U.K. Ltd.; ESL Inc.; TRW Vehicle Safety Systems Inc.; TRW Automotive Products Inc.; TRW Steering Systems Japan Co. Ltd.; TRW Canada Limited; TRW Components International Inc.; TRW Italia SpA; TRW Title Inc.; TRW France S.A.; TRW Koyo Steering Systems Co. (51%).

Further Reading:

Bergstrom, Robin Yale, "Reinvention in the Rustbelt: An Essay," *Production,* October 1993, pp. 50–52.

England, Robert Stowe, "Less Sizzle, More Steak," *Financial World,* August 4, 1992, pp. 20–21.

Mettler, Ruben F., *The Little Brown Hen That Could: The Growth Story of TRW Inc.,* New York: Newcomen Society, 1982.

—updated by April Dougal Gasbarre

Vail Associates, Inc.

600 Lionshead Mall
Vail, Colorado 81657
U.S.A.
(303) 476-5601
Fax: (303) 845-5728

Private Company
Incorporated: 1961
Employees: 600 to 4,100 (seasonal)
Operating Revenues: $370 million
SICs: 7999 Amusement and Recreation, Not Elsewhere
    Classified; 6531 Real Estate Agents and Managers; 7011
    Hotels and Motels; 5812 Eating Places; 5813 Drinking
    Places

Vail Associates, Inc., is the owner of Vail Mountain, the largest
and most popular ski area in the United States; company headquarters are at the base of the Vail resort, some 8,200 feet above
sea level in the Colorado Rockies. The company also owns
Beaver Creek and Arrowhead, two nearby ski resorts, as well as
land, lodges, restaurants, and other property in the Vail Valley.
Its ski school alone employs more than 1,300 instructors. In
1985, Vail Associates was purchased by Gillett Holdings Inc.,
and when Gillett Holdings filed for bankruptcy in 1991, Vail
Associates came under the control of Apollo Ski Partners LP of
New York.

The Vail Valley, also known as Gore Creek Valley, lies in west-
central Colorado near the Continental Divide. Cut off at one end
by a pass of 10,600 feet and at the other by a canyon about the
width of a horse, the valley long maintained an obscure presence in Colorado. For generations it was a place where native
Utes would come to escape the summer heat. After the Civil
War, white settlers pushed into the valley, among the first of
whom were miners searching for gold and silver, as well as map
surveyors, who charted its canyons, cliffs, and other features.
The land was settled by a small number of ranchers, but the
steep terrain and cold climate eventually drove most of them
away, leaving the area to sheepherders, who used the valley as
pastureland during the spring and summer.

During World War II, the U.S. Army set up a training center,
Camp Hale, in another isolated valley about 23 miles from Vail.
There, the army trained ski troopers of the Tenth Mountain
Division, who were later sent to fight in the Apennine mountains of northern Italy. Pete Seibert, one of these troopers, was
lucky to have made it through the war alive. Hit by small-arms
fire and two mortar shells, Seibert was badly wounded, and one
of the shells had blown off his right kneecap. Doctors told him
he would never again be able to ski. A few years later, however,
Seibert was working as a ski instructor at Aspen, the famous
Colorado resort, and in 1950 he made the U.S. ski team, though
torn ligaments kept him from competing. During the next few
years he studied at a hotel school in Lausanne, Switzerland.

Like many others in Colorado during the 1950s, Seibert was
dreaming of a way to establish his own resort, though perhaps
with a bit more zeal. "I had first started thinking of running a
resort when I was 12 years old," Seibert explained, noting
"there was nothing I wanted more in my life than to start a ski
area." In this endeavor, Siebert would have considerable help
from Earl Eaton, another Camp Hale veteran. Born not far from
the present Vail resort, Eaton had become a uranium prospector,
and, one day, while searching for uranium in Gore Creek
Valley, he arrived at the ridge of an unnamed mountain. Looking south his eyes fell upon a vast expanse of treeless slopes,
later called the "back bowls," some of the most famous ski
terrain in the United States. In March 1957, Eaton took Seibert
to the mountain, and they both trudged seven hours through
deep snow up to the ridge. When they arrived, Seibert, too, was
stunned by the back bowls, as well as the view of the towering
peaks of Gore Range.

Their first step was buying land. Although unable to purchase
the mountain itself, which was owned by the U.S. Forest
Service, they were able to purchase a 500-acre ranch at the base
for $55,000 in 1957. Funded by six partners (mostly from
Denver), Siebert and Eaton bought the land under the guise of a
new company, Transmontane Rod and Gun Club, a name they
used to keep their plans a secret from the local residents. During
this time, they also searched for a name for their new resort. One
suggestion was Shining Mountains, the Ute phrase for the
western Colorado region. However, "when mountains shine,"
Seibert pointed out, "it means they're icy." So they settled on
Vail, the name of the pass at the eastern end of the valley,
named for Charles D. Vail, a former chief engineer of the
Colorado highway department.

Next, Siebert and Eaton applied for a "Conditional Special Use
Permit." However, the U.S. Forest Service turned them down,
claiming there were already enough ski resorts in the White
River National Forest. Undeterred, the group appealed the decision, and, a year later, they received the permit, allowing them
to attract 21 new investors, some from as far away as Texas
and New York, and to found a new company, Vail Corp., which
was used to raise additional funds. In 1960, again through
Transmontane Rod and Gun Club, the group purchased an
adjacent property, also of 500 acres. Finally, in 1961, after the
group brought in 100 limited partners (each putting up
$10,000), Vail Associates, Inc., was born.

Vail Associates got the go-ahead from the U.S. Forest Service
in December 1961, and the company wasted no time in developing the foundations of the resort. Ski lifts were ordered, bull-
dozers pushed the snow out of the way to make room for
construction, and trails on the mountain were cut. The mountain's front side was ideal for the kind of gentle, treelined slopes

appropriate for beginners and intermediates, while the back bowls were the draw for advanced and expert skiers. Some of the trail names emerged from the early ski experiences of the Vail Associates group. The "Forever" trail in the back bowls, for example, was named one spring day when snow conditions were so perfect that a number of people skied down the back of the mountain; without a ski lift, the walk back up the mountain seemed to last forever.

With about $2 million slated for development, the group was able to cut the necessary trails and construct a nearly two-mile gondola (including a building at its base), two double chair lifts (holding two persons per chair), a beginner's surface lift, a lodge at midmountain ("Mid-Vail"), a ski patrol shack at the top, and a bridge across Gore Creek. Bob Parker, also from the Tenth Mountain Division and a former editor of *Skiing* magazine, became the marketing director of Vail Associates, and his contributions included the setting up of numerous crowd-gathering events. Especially important was an agreement by the U.S. ski team to hold an Olympic training camp at Vail, an event that began on December 23, 1961, just eight days after the resort opened.

Opening day was hardly indicative of the resort's future greatness. With no snow at the base, and snow only about ankle deep at the top, the resort sold a small number of $5 lift tickets, only a few of which actually went to skiers. Most of the tickets were purchased by area residents, who wanted the novelty of riding the lifts up and down the mountain. Three weeks later, on January 10, 1963, the resort managed to draw just 12 skiers, bringing in a total of $60 from lift tickets.

The resort's fortunes soon improved, however. Its large amount of gentle terrain attracted families, and its more fearsome back bowls became legendary among experienced skiers. Closer to Denver than its soon-to-be archrival Aspen, Vail began to draw tourists. More importantly, however, Vail also benefited from a tremendous increase in the sport's popularity during the 1960s and 1970s. The 1960 Winter Olympics, held at Squaw Valley, California, encouraged many Americans to try skiing, as did the new Head metal skis, which made the sport easier. Other important developments included safer ski bindings; "stretch" ski pants, which were more fashionable than the traditional bulky skiwear; heavy promotions by airlines, which saw in skiing a new market for themselves; and legal changes that made condominium ownership more practical and appealing.

As a result, Vail took off, growing faster than even the most optimistic hopes of its founders. By 1964, the company had developed enough new terrain to triple skier capacity, and trails and lifts would continue to spread east and west across the mountain. Its Golden Peak and Lionshead ski areas opened in 1967 and 1969, respectively. For the base area, the company followed its master plan, which called for an Austrian-style village, complete with winding lanes, foot bridges, arcades, and a clock tower, while avoiding such distractions as neon lights. Each building in the town offered unique features, while conforming to the general style. In 1966, however, when the town of Vail was incorporated, the company lost control of the town's development, though new projects continued to spill across both sides of the valley. At this point, Vail Associates

was plenty busy with expanding and improving the mountain's ski terrain and facilities.

To help pay for the development, costing some $13 million by 1969, the company sold part of its land in the valley as commercial and residential lots, and, in 1966, it began to offer its stock over the counter, a move that left Seibert as chairperson while effectively reducing his power. In 1971, the company also spent $4.4 million to purchase 2,200 acres of land ten miles down the road, which would later become the site of its Beaver Creek resort. By 1973, Vail Mountain had some 800 acres of skiable terrain, two gondolas, nine chairlifts, and four restaurants (two on the top of the mountain and two on the bottom). Total revenues were about $7 million.

Even more attention was focused on Vail in 1974, when Gerald Ford took over the U.S. presidency from the resigning Richard Nixon. Ford, in addition to being the first "skiing president," frequently took vacations at Vail and owned a three-bedroom condominium in the center of town. His first Vail ski vacation while president took place in December 1974, but for security reasons he rented out the home of Harry W. Bass, a Texas multimillionaire and Vail board member. Some began to dub this rented home the "Western White House."

Vail's next major source of publicity was the result of a tragic accident. On March 26, 1976, a frayed cable on the Lionshead gondola got caught in one of the lift towers, causing the passing cars to bounce and shake. Two cars then fell off, plummeting 125 feet to the ground, while the rest of the lift came to a halt. Although the ski patrol was able to rescue those trapped in the stalled lift, four people died and eight others were injured, at the time the worst accident at a U.S. ski resort.

The tragedy was bad publicity for Vail, and, worse, prompted a wave of lawsuits totaling more than $50 million. Fearing its liability in the accident, the board decided to sell the company, and, in late 1976, Harry Bass was able to gain controlling interest in Vail Associates for some $13 million. Soon afterward, Seibert was forced out of the company, reportedly because of a personality clash with Bass. Ironically, Vail Associates eventually settled all the lawsuits out of court for only a fraction of the total claim.

During this time, the company's Beaver Creek site was chosen to host the downhill event for the Winter Olympics, scheduled to take place in Colorado in 1976. However, the Olympic offer was turned down by Colorado voters, and the games were instead held at Innsbruck, Austria. Initially seen as a setback, the loss of the Olympic games gave the company more time to plan Beaver Creek; in fact, the planning alone would take seven years and cost $50 million. Ultimately Beaver Creek became not merely a ski resort but an elegant, truly luxurious, all-season resort area, which included facilities for conventions and conferences. Opened on December 14, 1980, Beaver Creek initially offered 450 acres of skiable terrain, boosted to some 1,000 acres by the decade's end. During this period, Vail Associates was also marketing the valley as a summer vacation area, where people could hike, raft, ride the gondola, shop at the more than 200 stores, or golf at one of the four 18-hole courses.

By 1982, Vail Associates had assets of nearly $100 million and revenues of $43.7 million—$31 million from its ski resorts and another $12 million from real estate operations. Vail Mountain was without a doubt one of the country's premier ski resorts, and Beaver Creek, though small, had built a reputation for opulence. All boded well for the company save two developments. First, the popularity of skiing in the United States had declined dramatically, and sales of the Beaver Creek properties were dismal. By the mid-1980s, real estate prices in the valley had collapsed, causing the near failure of Vail Associates. Second, problems for the company were further complicated in 1984 by a confrontation between Bass and his children, whose trust, established by Bass, owned enough Vail stock to oust him from the chairmanship.

In the summer of 1985, Vail Associates was purchased for $115 million by George Gillett, head of Gillett Holdings Inc., which at the time owned nine television stations, 21 newspapers, two radio stations, and a meatpacking plant. George Gillett had been a customer at Vail since 1963 and was an enthusiastic skier prepared to make large capital investments. His appraisal of the resort's recent past, however, was harsh. He noted that Vail was not making money and that it had over six years of condo inventory in Beaver Creek. Gillett also criticized the company for maintaining an entire department devoted to real estate development, when there was no demand. Employee attitudes towards the customers were cited as poor, and the people who owned many of the businesses in town viewed skiers as intruders on their peaceful lifestyle.

Gillett set out to change this environment, emphasizing the simple principle "the customer is king." One of the first areas he attacked was training. Gillett personally led every employee training program at the Vail resort, as well as additional training programs for city employees, restaurant workers, bus drivers, and cab companies. He arranged to have television crews follow several families on a Vail vacation—from the moment they made their reservations until they left the resort for home—and then showed a film of these trips to Vail's management. Among the problems they discovered was the lack of a central reservations system; the high incidence of lost baggage at the airport; long lines at ticket windows and lifts; and the lack of children's activities after skiing.

From 1985 to 1989, the company invested $60 million in capital improvements. Part of this sum went to the China Bowl Expansion, which opened up an immense new area of advanced terrain on the back side of the mountain, in the process doubling the resort's skiable terrain to 3,787 acres. With the addition of China Bowl, Vail became the country's largest ski resort, surpassing the former leader, Mammoth Mountain in California. By 1989, it had also installed six high-speed quad lifts (with four-person chairs), which, though costing several million dollars each, considerably reduced lift lines. For children, the company opened a kids-only hill, which included Ft. Whippersnapper, an adventure park with mock hunting camps and an Indian village. Remarkably, by 1989, all the condominiums in Beaver Creek were occupied.

The readers' poll of *Ski* magazine rated Vail the top resort in North America three years in a row—1989, 1990, and 1991—and the company also set attendance records, with some 1.5 million "skier visits" each year at Vail Mountain and more than 400,000 at Beaver Creek. Capital improvements contin-

ued, as Vail constructed a public bobsled course in 1990 and installed its tenth high-speed quad in 1992. By 1993, it had 4,020 acres of skiable terrain and a total of 25 lifts. Vail was also the host of the 1989 World Alpine Ski Championships, an event that hadn't been held in the United States since 1950. The event gave Vail extensive international press coverage, which Vail Associates hoped would encourage skiers from other countries to visit the resort.

However, while Vail thrived, its parent, Gillett Holdings, was collapsing under the weight of failed junk bonds (high-risk, high-yielding debt certificates), issued in the 1980s to finance its acquisitions. The holding company filed for bankruptcy on June 25, 1991, and its eventual reorganization transferred the ownership of Vail Associates to Apollo Ski Partners LP of New York, a company headed by Leon Black, a former Drexel Burnham banker. Nevertheless, George Gillett continued to serve as chairman of Vail Associates.

Despite the financial complications of its parent company, the day-to-day operations of Vail Associates remained profitable, and the company continued to make ambitious expansion plans. In 1993, Vail sought approval from the U.S. Forest Service to develop a giant, north-facing bowl, which would almost double the resort's already huge amount of skiable terrain. Farther west, the company had purchased Arrowhead, a new, small ski resort next to Beaver Creek, and plans were underway to connect the two resorts with a chair lift. The many projects taken on by Vail Associates, however, were also reflected in the price of Vail Mountain's daily lift ticket, which jumped from $30 in 1986 to $46 in 1994.

Vail Associates was not alone in its plans for expanding terrain and upgrading facilities, nor in its raising of lift ticket prices. Many other resort owners—noting that Americans were increasingly going to the biggest and best-equipped ski areas—were also investing in expansion projects, while small ski areas, unable to compete, were failing at a rapid rate. Vail Mountain had managed to remain at the top of North American ski resorts, though not without competition. Nearby Aspen, for example, with its four separate ski mountains, continued to benefit from its reputation as a more "authentic," culturally sophisticated town. Moreover, several Utah resorts offered drier snow and steeper terrain. Farther north, Whistler and Blackcomb, contiguous resorts in British Columbia, both had a considerably larger vertical drop (the difference in elevation between the base and the summit) and, when viewed as a single ski area, a greater amount of skiable terrain. But while other resorts could claim to be the best in certain categories, Vail Mountain was frequently rated the finest all-around North American ski resort, a position Vail Associates was working hard to maintain.

Further Reading:

"Apollo Ski's Vail Unit Agrees to Purchase a Resort in Colorado," *Wall Street Journal*, September 1, 1993, p. A5.

"Aspen and Vail Combine Efforts to Lure International Ski Market," *Travel Weekly*, June 22, 1992, p. 17.

"Beaver Creek: The Beverly Hills of Resorts," *Colorado Business*, February 1981, pp. 83–84.

Brizzolara, Kim, "Riding the Seesaw," *Skiing*, October 1991, pp. 26–27.

Charlier, Marj, "Vail, Miffed at Loss of No. 1 Ranking in Skier Survey, Printed Fake Ballots," *Wall Street Journal,* February 22, 1993, p. A5.

Gillett, George, "George Gillett, Director of Quality Control," *Colorado Business Magazine,* November 1989, p. 44.

Johnson, William Oscar, "A Vision Fulfilled: From One Man's Dream, Vail Has Grown into America's Biggest Ski Resort," *Sports Illustrated,* January 30, 1989, pp. 70–82.

May, Clifford D., "Sampling New Terrain at Vail," *New York Times,* January 15, 1989, Sec. 10, p. 8.

Metz, Robert, "Market Place: A Skiing Lesson for Wall Street," *New York Times,* May 30, 1973, p. 52.

Parker, Bob, "Looking Back on Vail," *Skiing,* December 1982, p. 42.

Purdy, Penelope, "Success Sampler: Three of the Best," *Colorado Business,* May 1983, p. 40.

Simonton, June, *Vail: Story of a Colorado Mountain Valley,* Dallas: Taylor Publishing Co., 1987.

Sterba, James P., "Vail, Colo., Tries to Stay Calm While It Awaits a Special Skier," *New York Times,* December 15, 1974, p. 59.

Stern, Richard L., "Bailing Out Vail," *Forbes,* May 27, 1991, p. 16.

Stern, Richard L., "Downhill Bracer," *Forbes,* May 27, 1991, pp. 55–64.

Walter, Claire, "Vail Parent in Chapter 11," *Skiing Trade News,* September 1991, p. 12.

—Thomas Riggs

Vodafone Group plc

The Courtyard
2-4 London Road
Newbury
Berkshire RG13 1JL
United Kingdom
(0635) 33251
Fax: (0635) 45713

Public Company
Incorporated: 1985 as Racal Telecommunications Group Ltd.
Employees: 2,200
Sales: £6.64 billion
Stock Exchanges: London New York
SICs: 6711 Holding Companies; 4811 Telephone
Communication (Wire or Radio); 4899 Communication
Services, Nec; 5999 Miscellaneous Retail Shops, Nec;
7394 Equipment Rental and Leasing Services; 7399
Business Services, Nec

During its brief but eventful history, Vodafone has been a leading force in the mobile telecommunications revolution. Launched in 1985, Vodafone established the first cellular phone network in the United Kingdom and since then has presided over an industry with a phenomenal growth rate. The company's subsidiaries have played an important role in advancing related technologies, such as Vodapage's nationwide radio-paging service and Paknet's national public data communications network.

Vodafone was the brainchild of Racal Electronics Ltd., a modestly prosperous U.K. electronics firm, and Millicom, a U.S. communications company. Developed as a joint venture during the early 1980s, Vodafone was granted a license to develop a cellular network in the United Kingdom and was introduced under the auspices of Racal in January of 1985. The new subsidiary's success was stunning. The corporate sector was quick to appreciate the advantages of mobile telecommunications, and individuals were equally quick to spot the status symbol potential of the new technology; fueled by business need and Yuppie culture, the demand for mobile phones skyrocketed.

Vodafone found itself one of only two entrants in the United Kingdom in a virtually unregulated new industry; the other member of the duopoly was Cellnet, still Vodafone's principal

competitor in the mid-1990s. Throughout the 1980s the company created much of the technology—and enjoyed most of the profits—of this rapidly expanding field. Racal Telecommunications' profit and loss history from 1985 to 1989 succinctly describes the matter: in the year of its creation, Vodafone was operating at a loss of £10 million; by the end of the decade pretax profits were over £84 million. Racal soon developed allied divisions, including Vodac, Vodata, and Vodapage, to expand the number and type of services the company offered.

By 1988 Racal Telecommunications Group Ltd., as Vodafone and the related subsidiaries were officially known, was by far the most successful player on the Racal Electronics team. The parent company, fearing that the Telecommunications Group was hampered on the stock market by its subsidiary status, and wishing, in addition, to enhance other aspects of its business with profit from Vodafone stocks, proposed a partial flotation of the subsidiary. The move was opposed by Millicom, the second largest shareholder, who lobbied for a complete sell-off; in the end, only 20 percent of the share capital of Racal Telecom was offered on the market. Three years later, however, Racal Electronics reconsidered, and Racal Telecom was separated from its parent company in 1991, at which time the name was changed to Vodafone Group Ltd.

Vodafone has been market leader in the United Kingdom since its inception. Its main competitor, Cellnet, jointly owned by British Telecom and Securicor, was also granted its license in 1985 and grew as steadily as Vodafone. However, it always remained a step or two behind, with Vodafone generally enjoying some 56 percent of the market. The two remained the only companies on the scene for approximately eight years. Although an industry regulator, Oftel, existed, frequent rumors that the duopoly would be subjected to some sort of price regulation never materialized—on the grounds, it is thought, that further competition in such an obviously lucrative industry was bound to eventually appear. As the Daily Mail commented in early 1993, "Profits from mobile phones have been mouthwatering." Such competition did appear when Mercury, in a joint venture between Cable & Wireless and the telephone company US West, issued its challenge in 1993.

Amid much publicity and a flurry of marketing, Mercury's Personal Communications Network, called One-2-One, was launched. Mercury's advertising campaign hammered home a message of lower costs. By offering low prices and even free off-peak local calls, Mercury forced the two telecommunications giants into a price war—but only in the London area, where Mercury's operations began.

One-2-One was seen primarily as a bid for the private market of mobile telephone users, whereas the majority of Vodafone's customer base was in the corporate sector, where demand and the tariffs charged were historically higher. Despite Vodafone's focus on business customers, the company was clearly not unmindful of the competitors' interest in the vast untapped private market. It first responded to the threat of Mercury's introduction with its own countermarketing. After One-2-One was operating, Vodafone introduced new options such as Low Call, which, with its lower rental costs but higher call charges, was targeted at individuals who use their phones less frequently than business customers. Another new initiative, MetroDigital, a service begun in 1993 that allowed subscribers low rates when calling from an urban "home cell," was aimed at least in part at the personal user market.

Mercury's One-2-One employed the new digital technology rather than the analog systems used until then by Vodafone and Cellnet. Digital technology represented a significant advance in the industry, as its use allowed for higher quality, better security, and lower costs. Not to be outdone, Vodafone too was expanding its digital network, and the company expected operations to be fully digital by the end of the 1990s.

As of the mid-1990s it was too soon, of course, to assess the ramifications of Mercury's entry into the market, or indeed that of newcomer Hutchison Microtel, which began operating its Orange network in 1994. Most financial analysts predicted, however, that there was room for all in a market so ripe for expansion; increased competition would thus have little effect on profit margins.

Although Vodafone Ltd. is clearly its flagship company, the Vodafone Group as a whole comprises several wholly owned subsidiaries that support or complement the activities of Vodafone Ltd. Vodac is the group's service provider, buying cellular airtime wholesale from Vodafone and selling it, equipment, and services to customers via service centers, retail outlets, dealers, mail order, and special corporate accounts. Another subsidiary, Vodapage, operates a nationwide radiopaging network; among the services if offers are Healthcall Medical Answerline Service; Neighbourhood Watch Information Line, a crime prevention service; and even the Rare Bird Alert News Service. Paknet, a radio-based national public data communications network, has a client base of banks, retailers, utilities, alarm companies, and others, and has a variety of applications. Country councils have used it to handle traffic measurements; British Rail uses it for credit card authorization.

Vodafone has been involved as well in a number of other specialized applications of its capabilities. "SafeLink," introduced in 1992 in conjunction with the West Yorkshire Police, gives potential crime victims fast access to the police via the Vodafone network. The "Callsafe" service, developed the same year, allows stranded motorists to contact the Automobile Association. Perhaps the company's highest profile special application, however, came in 1993 when it provided the emergency mobile phone service to environment rescue workers following the wreck of the tanker Braer in the Shetland Islands.

Vodata, another crucial subsidiary, develops and markets new products and services for Vodafone and Vodapage customers. The company has pioneered information services for users, such as the Automobile Association's "Roadwatch" and the Financial Times' "CityLine." "Recall," the world's largest voice messaging service, was introduced in 1992. "Vodastream" fax allows customers access to up-to-date macro-economic statistics compiled by the Central Statistical Office; "Met fax" gives the latest weather bulletins; and "Vodafax Broadcast" allows the facsimile transmission of information to several different destinations simultaneously.

Vodafone Group International is a rapidly growing component of the group. Active in seeking opportunities and implementing projects abroad, Vodafone International looks likely to one day be as important to the group as Vodafone Ltd. itself. In 1993 the company was awarded a license in Australia to operate that country's third digital mobile telephone network. In the same year consortia of which Vodafone is a member received similar licences to operate in Greece and Germany. Vodafone also has substantial interests in France, Scandinavia, Hong Kong, Fiji, Malta, and Mexico. Although start-up costs for foreign ventures are obviously high, the field is very lucrative, and Vodafone is continually on the lookout for new possibilities. Analysts predict that Vodafone will increase its investments with the aim of acquiring more foreign associates and, eventually, subsidiaries.

In the 1990s a digital system that allows international calls between participating countries was developed. Called the Global System for Mobile Communications (GSM), it was first used by Vodafone, whose introduction of EuroDigital in 1991 allowed customers to "roam" throughout Europe and Scandinavia. In 1994 the company acquired a 10 percent stake in Globalstar, an international consortium formed to develop a satellite-based network that will allow mobile telecommunications to operate everywhere in the world (except the polar ice caps) by 1998.

As of 1994, Vodafone operated one the world's largest cellular networks, with over one million subscribers. This, combined with the company's increasingly high international profile, made it a safe bet that Vodafone would continue its prominent role in the expanding mobile telecommunications industry. The Mail on Sunday confidently predicted in 1993: "We're on the verge of a communications explosion. By 2000, nearly all of us will have a phone in our pocket." And it is highly likely that for many, that phone will be a Vodafone.

Principal Subsidiaries: Vodac Ltd.; Vodafone Asia Pacific Ltd. (Hong Kong); Vodafone Pty Ltd. (Australia; 95 percent); Vodafone Europe Holdings B.V. (Netherlands); Vodafone Group Services Ltd.; Vodafone Ltd.; Vodafone SA (France); Vodapage Ltd.; Vodata Ltd.; Paknet Ltd.; Telecell Ltd. (Malta; 80 percent).

Further Reading:

Brown, Malcolm, "Slow March of the Mobiles," *Management Today,* December 1993, pp. 54–57.
"Calling the Masses," *Sunday Times,* June 20, 1993.
"Crossed Lines over Survey," *Sunday Times,* March 28, 1993.
Ferguson, Anne, "Securing Racal's Future," *Management Today,* August 1988, pp. 30–31.
"Harrison's Happy Ending," *Daily Telegraph,* June 9, 1993.
"The Lex Column: Mobile Market," *Financial Times,* June 8, 1994.
"A Line to the Future," *Mail on Sunday,* February 7, 1993.
"Stay Well Connected for the Phoney War," *Daily Mail,* February 3, 1993.
"Upwardly Mobile," *Economist,* August 13, 1988, pp. 62–64.
"Vodafone: Casting a Worldwide Network," *Investors' Chronicle,* January 7, 1994.
"Vodafone Move Fuels Price War," *Financial Times,* June 17, 1993.
"Vodafone: On Line for a Breakthrough," *Investors' Chronicle,* October 22, 1993.
"Vodafone Signs up for Dollars 1.8bn Satellite Telecoms Venture," *Independent,* March 25, 1994.

—Robin DuBlanc

Volkswagen A.G.

Postfach 3180 Berlinger Ring 2
Wolfsburg, 1
Germany
(0049) 6361-90
Fax: (0049) 5361-928282

Public Company
Incorporated: 1938
Employees: 283,000
Sales: $45.6 billion
Stock Exchanges: Berlin Dusseldorf Frankfurt Hamburg
  Munich Stuttgart Zurich Basle Geneva Vienna Brussels
  Antwerp Luxembourg Amsterdam
SICs: 3711 Motor Vehicles and Car Bodies; 3714 Motor
  Vehicle Parts and Accessories; 5012 Automobiles and
  Other Motor Vehicles

Volkswagen A.G., a company born in the shadow of Nazism, rose to become the world's fourth-largest automobile company. It produced 3.5 million vehicles annually in the early 1990s to control 7.8 percent of the global market. Volkswagen has long been the industry leader in Germany, and it claimed the top position in European sales with 17 percent market share. But the company also led the trend among automakers to locate production facilities in emerging international markets such as China, eastern Europe, and Latin America: by the mid-1990s it maintained plants in the United States, Brazil, Mexico, South Africa, Nigeria, Yugoslavia, Argentina, and Belgium. In addition to its automotive subsidiaries, Volkswagen owned computer and office equipment concerns. Yet, however large and diverse the company became, it was always strongly associated with the idea behind its name, "the people's car."

Volkswagen was founded in 1937 as the Company for the Development of the German Volkswagen. It embodied the dreams of two men: Ferdinand Porsche and Adolf Hitler. Porsche, an engineer, had designed powerful luxury automobiles for Austro-Daimler, but had been dreaming of a small, low-priced car for the ordinary consumer since the early 1920s. Porsche had tried in vain to find financiers for his venture. Always interested in technical innovation, Porsche had designed a rear-engined, air-cooled vehicle with independent suspension. The radical design had to be perfected, however, and Porsche's first sponsor had little patience for torsion bars that

exploded under pressure and engines that malfunctioned after a few miles.

Porsche's meeting with Hitler in 1934 changed everything. By 1938 his roundish, odd-looking car had become the center of a plan to build an ideal worker's city, and a factory was started at Wolfsburg. During the war, however, the Volkswagen plant produced vehicles for the German military, largely with the slave labor of prisoners. By the end of the war the factory had been virtually destroyed by bombing. Hitler's "people's car" never materialized.

The Volkswagen factory was operated by the British occupation forces from 1945 to 1949. The company became the focus of an effort to rebuild the German auto industry, and within a decade Volkswagen was producing half of Germany's automobiles. Ironically, it was the British administrators of Volkswagen who started the production of passenger rather than military vehicles, and thus made the dream of the people's car a reality.

The company came under the control of the German federal government and the state of Lower Saxony in 1949. The man the British selected to head the company, Heinz Nordhoff, was largely responsible for Volkswagen's impressive recovery and the conversion of a reminder of Nazi aspirations into the most popular car ever built. His success was the more surprising given that he was no fan of Volkswagen prior to his arrival there. Nordhoff, an engineer, had been employed by the Adam Opel Company, owned by General Motors, before and during the war. Opel management resented Hitler's Volkswagen because they were hoping to develop a similar automobile of their own.

Unlike Porsche, it was not Nordhoff's skill as an engineer (though he was responsible for innovations) but his managerial ability that made such a contribution to the success of Volkswagen. (Porsche was unable to take part in the realization of his dream; his health was ruined by nearly two years spent in a French prison on charges of war crimes for which he was later acquitted. Porsche died in 1951.) Nordhoff was able to assemble around him a talented team of executives, and he inspired his sometimes despairing and hungry workers. He actually slept in the factory for six months, and instituted the quite novel practice of addressing the work force on a regular basis. Nordhoff, however, also gained a reputation for being autocratic and even arrogant, perhaps due to his unrelenting managerial approach.

Success came slowly, particularly in the United States. Nordhoff sorely needed U.S. dollars, but his first trip to the United States in 1949 was a failure, and only 330 Volkswagens were sold there in 1950. The car's Nazi associations continued to haunt it. Though American interest in foreign cars grew during the mid-1950s, it was really not until 1959, when the firm of Doyle Dane Bernbach took over the advertising for the car, that it began to appeal to large numbers of Americans. Doyle Dane Bernbach coined the name "Beetle" for the Volkswagen. In a series of award-winning advertisements, the ad agency took what had been the car's drawbacks and turned them into selling points with such slogans as "Think Small" and "Ugly Is Only Skin-deep." Even the car's apparently invariable design from year to year was exploited, with an advertisement that had no photography at all and claimed there was nothing new to display about the more recent models. Changes were made internally, however, and the Volkswagen became renowned for its durability. The Beetle eventually had a record production run of over 40 years, during which over 20 million cars were produced, making it the best-selling car in the world. During the 1960s, the Volkswagen Beetle became a counterculture symbol in the United States and helped imports to gain an important foothold in the American market for the first time.

In 1960 Volkswagen was, in essence, denationalized, with the sale of 60 percent of its stock to the public. The remaining 40 percent of the stock was divided evenly between the German government and the government of Lower Saxony. A foundation was also established to promote research in science and technology, and it received all dividends paid to the two governments. These measures settled the disagreement between the federal government and Lower Saxony over the ownership of the company. Nordhoff was glad to have an end to the question, but he did not benefit directly since he and other Volkswagen executives in high income brackets were not eligible to purchase stock under the terms of the sale.

Annual production of the Beetle peaked in 1968 at 400,000 units, and by the early 1970s the Beetle was finally regarded as outdated. In 1974 Volkswagen was brought to the brink of bankruptcy. Diminishing sales, rising labor costs, increasing competition from Japanese automakers, and the end of fixed exchange rates had all contributed to the dramatic decline. New models were introduced, but they suffered from a poor reputation.

A development program was instituted to create a successor to the Rabbit, the company's major automobile after the Beetle. Meanwhile in 1981 Volkswagen's U.S. work force was cut from 10,000 to 6,000, and a plant in Michigan was sold to Chrysler. In 1983 the company lost $144 million in the United States alone.

When the new Golf was finally unveiled, it looked very much like the Rabbit but had a larger engine, more interior space, and better overall performance. The changes paid off: sales rose 25 percent in 1985, profits doubled, and Volkswagen became the leading European auto manufacturer. The Golf GTI was named "Car of the Year" by *Motor Trend* in 1985. In the luxury car market sales of the Audi were up 50 percent for a second straight record year (Volkswagen had acquired Audi in 1965). Even more remarkable was that sales of the Jetta, a model costing about $1,000 more than the Golf, jumped 120 percent.

From the company's point of view, it was significant that the gap between Volkswagen and the competition had been narrowed. It used to be that German cars cost 20 percent more than their Japanese rivals, but the base price of the Golf eventually went below those of competing vehicles from Honda and Toyota. These gains were due in part to Volkswagen's policy of automating its factories. The company spent $194 million on its Halle 54 at the Wolfsburg factory (the largest single automobile factory in the world), where 25 percent of final assembly was performed by robots. The automation provided a time savings of 20 percent.

Not everything looked promising for Volkswagen, however. The company recalled 77,000 Golf and GTI models because the innovative high-density polycarbonate fuel tank which fit under the rear seat and over the axle failed to meet crash test requirements. The cost of the recall could run as high as $18 million. Additionally, 18,000 Vanagons and Campers were recalled for a potential problem with the latches on their sliding doors. Finally, the New York attorney general and two consumer groups asked the Transportation Department to recall 200,000 Audi 5000s, claiming that the cars could suddenly accelerate when shifted out of the park position. Volkswagen maintained that the accidents reported were the result of driver error, but it also replaced some damaged cars or paid repair costs.

Volkswagen sales fell in the first quarter of 1986, at least partially because of a drop in the value of the U.S. dollar. And while the Westmoreland, Pennsylvania, plant was operating at half capacity, there was an order backlog for Golfs in Europe. A plan was considered to produce 21,000 to 30,000 Jettas at the Westmoreland plant, which would allow the European operation to increase its capacity, but it would take a year to retool the factory. Without such an adjustment the Westmoreland factory, where 18,000 workers were already on layoff, could face further cuts. There was talk of building Subarus at Westmoreland with Fuji Heavy Industries, but discussions were suspended. Plans were also made to close a West Virginia parts plant and substitute parts from Mexico and Brazil, where auto workers collected an hourly wage of $2 compared to about $20 for unionized American workers.

In 1986 the company sold Royal Business Machines, one of its office equipment subsidiaries, and purchased a majority interest in Spain's Sociedad Española de Automobiles del Turismo S.A. (SEAT), which had been a money-losing venture. The Spanish government agreed to absorb the company's $1 billion debt and to provide a cash infusion of $114 million. With SEAT, Volkswagen could acquire 25 percent of the Spanish car market.

Volkswagen made agreements with East Germany and China for the production of 300,000 and 100,000 automobile engines, respectively, with options for Volkswagen to buy back some of the engines to help alleviate its capacity problems. The company also negotiated with the Soviet Union to build an engine plant and entered into a licensing agreement with Nissan for the production of kits to build Nissan Santanas. A possible production merger was discussed by Ford Argentina and Volkswagen of Brazil in order to increase capacity by 30 percent and meet consumer demand. With Renault, Volkswagen planned development of a four-wheel-drive/automatic transmission system. Almost every Volkswagen model brought out between the mid-1980s and the end of the decade was slated to be available with a four-wheel-drive option. The company also had ambitious plans to compete with Yugoslavia's Yugo and South Korea's Hyundai Excel by introducing a Brazilian-built, low-priced car, referred to initially as Project 99. Volkswagen hoped sales of this car would reach 100,000 cars per year. Meanwhile, the company continued its Golf design, but its Scirocco sports model, introduced in the early 1980s, was to be replaced with a car along the lines of the Porsche 944.

Volkswagen chairman Carl C. Hahn, who worked under Heinz Nordhoff, stressed German engineering and advanced technology as the key to the company's competitiveness. He set his sights on rebuilding the public's confidence in Volkswagen in the United States and hoped to boost the company's return on sales from 1 percent to 3 percent to match the U.S. automakers. Hahn also aimed to cut costs and raise profit margins by making use of newly acquired SEAT and other Volkswagen operations in developing countries. Capital spending was expected to increase 25 percent by the early 1990s, with $13 billion aimed at operations outside Germany. It was uncertain what labor's reaction would be to the increasing use of foreign resources; the German auto industry was plagued by strikes in 1984.

Hahn gained valuable experience in the American market by heading up the Volkswagen operation in the United States during the Beetle's heyday. Later Hahn became chief of continental Gummi Werke, where he turned a money-losing business into an industry leader. Like his predecessor, Hahn seemed capable of taking forceful steps where necessary to control the direction of the company, and he appeared more than willing to circumvent the inflexible, bureaucratic corporate culture that frequently afflicted large German firms.

Hahn's strategy for Volkswagen's resurgence, though it included cost-cutting measures, essentially involved the expenditure of vast sums to build or acquire production facilities and thereby broaden the company's geographic scope. Capital spending, which had been increasing gradually during the latter half of the 1980s, picked up pace, reaching prodigious proportions by the beginning of the 1990s. Hahn spent $3.3 billion to increase production capacity at a plant in Zwikau in eastern Germany, plowed an additional $3.3 billion into SEAT, and invested a massive $6 billion to acquire a 31 percent interest in the Czechoslovakian Skoda automobile plant in 1991—all part of an enormous $34 billion capital-spending program set to take place in the first half of the 1990s. A cost-reduction plan initiated in 1987 had saved, by this point, $2.6 billion, but the expenditures far outweighed the savings. Hahn, whose retirement was scheduled to begin in 1991, was given a two-year extension to oversee the denouement of his bold and costly plan.

Hahn, however, was gone by the following year, forced to resign in 1992 after presiding over Volkswagen's rise from fourth to first place in European market share during his decade-long tenure. Despite this laudable success, Hahn's strategy had proven too ambitious. Volkswagen's U.S. operations continued to cede market share to Japanese and U.S. car manufacturers and the profit margins realized from sales elsewhere were alarmingly low. The person partly responsible for Hahn's ouster and also selected to replace him was Ferdinand Piech, grandson of Volkswagen's founder Ferdinand Porsche. Piech had served as the top development manager at Audi during the 1980s, then became its chairman in 1988. He rose through the ranks to gain overall control of Volkswagen in January 1993, a company he described to *Automotive News* as "a duck grown too fat to fly."

To trim the excess fat from Volkswagen, Piech announced he would cut 12,500 of Volkswagen's 127,000 German jobs by 1998 and initiate substantial restructuring of all company operations in an effort to save Volkswagen more than $5 billion, the figure he calculated would enable the company to avoid a loss for the year. Although substantial changes were effected, financial loss was not avoided, and Volkswagen recorded a $1.15 billion loss for 1993, abetted by poor performances of the company's North American operations, Audi A.G., and SEAT.

Entering 1994, Volkswagen's management held the modest hope of breaking even for the year, as a lingering recession hampered European car manufacturers' ability to steer their companies toward a more profitable future. At Volkswagen, spirits were raised by a relatively robust second quarter in 1994, when profits reached DM 133 million ($86.1 million), compared to 1993's second quarter loss of DM 335 million. The gain was attributed to the cost-cutting measures of previous years and a return to manufacturing less-expensive cars. As Volkswagen's management planned for an increasingly competitive future, the prospects were foreboding. But through continued cost-cutting programs and prudent product development, Piech and those surrounding him hoped to remain Europe's largest car manufacturer into the 21st century.

Principal Subsidiaries: AUDI A.G. (99 percent); V.A.G. Kredit Bank GmbH; V.A.G. Leasing GmbH; VOTEX GmbH; VW KRAFTWERK GmbH; VW Siedlungsgesellschaft GmbH; InterRent Autovermietung GmbH; V.A.G. Marketing Management Institut GmbH

Further Reading:

Choi, Audrey, "European Auto Makers Show Signs of Bouncing Back; Cost Cutting and Shift toward Less-Expensive Cars Brighten Outlook," *Wall Street Journal,* September 15, 1994, p. B4.

Feast, Richard, "Cutting Cost at VW," *Automotive Industries,* September 1993, p. 37.

Flint, Jerry, "Eastward Ho," *Forbes,* November 26, 1990, p. 291.

Hopfinger, K.B., *The Volkswagen Story,* Cambridge: R. Bentley, 1971.

Kurylko, Diana T., "Lopez Sees VW Return to U.S. Glory of the '70s," *Automotive News,* March 29, 1994, p. 8.

Nelson, Walter H., *Small Wonder: The Amazing Story of the Volkswagen,* Boston: Little Brown, 1967.

"The People's Car," *Economist,* March 7, 1992, p. 74.

Sawyer, Arlena, "VW Merges U.S., Canada Units," *Automotive News,* August 8, 1994, p. 1.

Templeman, John, "Carl Hahn's High-Octane Growth Plan for VW," *Business Week,* March 18, 1991, p. 46.

—updated by Jeffrey L. Covell

West One Bancorp

101 South Capital Blvd.
Boise, Idaho 83702
U.S.A.
(208) 383-7000
Fax: (208) 383-3864

Public Company
Incorporated: 1867 as First National Bank of Idaho
Employees: 4,900
Total Assets: $8.1 billion
Stock Exchanges: NASDAQ
SICs: 6712 Bank Holding Companies; 6021 National
    Commercial Banks; 6022 State Commercial Banks

West One Bancorp is Idaho's oldest and largest banking concern; with more than 200 offices in Idaho, Washington, Oregon, and Utah, West One is also the eighth largest agricultural lender in the United States. Founded in 1867 to serve the area's early miners, the company has since played an important role in Idaho's economic development, particularly in agriculture. Its original name was First National Bank of Idaho, and, by 1941, it was known as Idaho First National Bank. In 1981, the bank was placed administratively under a holding company—Moore Financial Group Inc.—which provided the legal means for it to expand, largely through acquiring existing banks, into the states of Washington, Oregon, and Utah. The holding company, along with its banks, was renamed West One in 1989.

Idaho in the 1800s was a rough, largely undeveloped area. Trappers and fur traders had arrived early in the century and were followed by missionaries and small numbers of farmers. In 1860, gold was discovered in northern Idaho, bringing a rush of hopeful settlers. Among these gold seekers were the bank's founders, Chistopher W. Moore and Benjamin M. DuRell. Previously, Moore had farmed with his family in Oregon and had worked as a cattle dealer on the Pacific Coast, but, in 1862, at the age of 27, he followed his dreams of gold and moved to Idaho. DuRell, meanwhile, had undertaken a number of businesses in Oregon, most of which ended in disaster. Near Portland, for example, he built a flour mill and a sawmill, which burned down in 1857. Next, he went to Salem, where he constructed a pork-packing plant, shipped produce to California, and built another sawmill. When this sawmill also burned

down, he rebuilt the mill, only to watch it be washed away in a flood during the winter of 1861–62.

Moore and DuRell became acquainted while both were working as gold prospectors in Idaho. Realizing he was unlikely to make a fortune in gold, DuRell soon decided that there were great opportunities in hauling supplies to the mines, and he was able to convince Moore to help him. Their first and only shipment in 1862 was from Walla Walla, Washington, to Auburn, a town in eastern Oregon, after which they traveled to the coast for the winter. The next spring, hearing rumors of large gold finds in southwestern Idaho, they set out with supplies to Boise Basin, arriving around July 1. They began by selling goods from their wagons, and within a year they had set up general stores both in Boise, a city that DuRell helped found, and in nearby Ruby City. By 1865, one of their services was safekeeping "deposits" of gold dust and nuggets, as well as analyzing the gold itself. They also extended credit to miners for supplies, and for this they relied only on their judgment of character.

During this time, gold dust and then gold bars were the main forms of currency in mining towns. That would change after Congress passed the National Bank Act (1863), which authorized a national currency and provided guidelines for establishing a network of federally supervised national banks. Among other things, the Act required that a national bank be incorporated by no fewer than five people and with no less than $100,000 in capital. DuRell and Moore, eager to jump on the bandwagon, found three other investors and set up an organizational meeting to be held in November 1866. DuRell, with 550 shares, was named president of the new enterprise, and Moore, with 315 shares, was elected cashier. The other investors were William Roberts (75 shares); David W. Ballard (50 shares), the governor of the Idaho territory; and Joel Fithian (10 shares). Their application, however, was initially denied by the U.S. government, as the entire $300 million in bank notes had already been assigned to other banks. A tenacious man, DuRell responded by traveling to New England, where he found a bank to sell him $65,000 of its notes, and then approached the government again. On March 11, 1867, DuRell finally received a charter for his new business, First National Bank of Idaho. It was, in fact, the first national bank to be established in the Idaho territory and the second west of the Rocky Mountains.

Opened on June 6, 1867, the bank operated out of a back room of the Boise general store, B.M. DuRell & Co. It contained a 4,200-pound safe; bank notes in denominations of $1, $2, and $5; and scales to weigh gold. By July 1, the bank had loans of $43,369 and deposits of $24,866—by modern standards a poor ratio of loans to deposits—and not until the 1873 or 1874 did total deposits match total loans. Still, DuRell and Moore proved to be good judges of character, and the bank, by helping to introduce bank notes as the main form of currency, played an important role in stabilizing Idaho's economy and in facilitating its trade with other regions.

The bank soon showed outward signs of growth. Not long after it opened, it moved into its own building at 633 Main Street. A banking "agency," or branch, was then established in Idaho City, and for a number of years another was maintained in Silver City. Despite this growth, DuRell decided in 1872 to sell his shares to Moore and two other stockholders, and, afterward, the board elected one of these two, B. F. Channell, the new president. The office of presidency, however, was demoted to a part-time position, and Moore continued to run the day-to-day operations. DuRell, who later attempted new ventures in Salt Lake City and elsewhere, would never again find lasting business success.

Over the next two decades Idaho, which became a state in 1890, and the bank experienced a period of growth tempered by instability. The so-called Panic of 1873, set off by financial crises in Vienna, led to an economic slowdown across the globe and was felt even in Idaho. Construction of railroads, for example, which had boosted the territory's economy, was cut back, and some businesses, including banks, were forced to close. During this time, the board of First National Bank of Idaho also underwent many changes. Possibly the result of a disagreement with John Huntoon, one of the shareholders, Moore resigned his position in 1876 and sold his shares. After March 15 of that year, the bank was controlled by Huntoon and eight new board members, with Huntoon acting as cashier. Moore, however, continued to have allies on the new board, and, a year later, he again purchased shares of First National. On January 8, 1889, he was elected president by the board, which had also reinstated that office as a full-time position with authority over the cashier. Moore would remain the head of the bank until his death in 1916.

Although the country's economy was badly shaken by financial panics in 1893 and 1907, Idaho was relatively unscathed. While some Idaho banks failed, First National had little trouble remaining solvent, though not without having to reduce earnings and salary increases. First National had already outgrown its old facilities by 1890—when it moved to the Post & Bilderback Building on the corner of 8th and Main—and, in 1903, the completion of an elegant three-story structure, built on the same site, provided the bank's customers with visible evidence of its financial stability. During this period, mining remained a focus of the bank's services, but Idaho's growing agricultural industry was also seeking loans for development. First National would greatly benefit from an increasing state population, which jumped from 161,772 in 1900 to 325,594 in 1910, pushing deposits beyond the $1 million mark in 1906. A separate savings department was established in 1912, when deposits hit $1.7 million.

Amid this great expansion was the nagging problem of government regulation. As a national bank, First National operated under the jurisdiction of the U.S. comptroller of the currency and was required to disclose its finances. Moore—as well as his son Crawford, who became president in 1916—resented this interference and generally dragged their feet in complying with federal regulations, resulting in regular confrontations between the bank and the comptroller. The comptroller, for example, was displeased by the high number of past due loans, reaching 40 percent in 1913. To circumvent the problem, the bank's directors formed The Western Loan and Investment Company, which was charged with various responsibilities, including buying and selling mortgages, stocks, and notes. As it was not a national bank and thus not supervised by the comptroller, The Western Loan and Investment Company was also where the directors could make loans that the government would find questionable. The feud with the comptroller would eventually become a major liability for the bank.

Nevertheless, First National experienced profitable years during World War I. In 1915, the completion of the Arrowrock Dam, located near Boise, helped boost the state's agricultural industry, as did the war itself. First National responded by investing more heavily in farming and livestock, including in irrigation projects. When the postwar economy took a downturn in 1920, the bank was in excellent financial shape, which could not be said of many other Idaho banks, 27 of which failed between 1920 and 1922. Under the guise of The Western Loan and Investment Company, First National's directors were able to purchase numerous failed banks, which they recapitalized and reopened as state banks.

Again becoming too large for its facilities, First National moved in 1928 to the Empire Building, an impressive, six-story structure (to which the bank attached another building) located outside the center of town at 10th and Idaho streets. The move, accomplished in October 1928, was done under intense security. Even so, the plan broke down at a critical juncture, and in the old bank as much as $600,000 was left unguarded in an open safe. Fortunately, the money was discovered by Crawford Moore, who had a janitor help him stuff the bills into garbage cans, cover the money with wastepaper, and place the cans in his car. With no protection, Moore then drove off to the bank's new location.

The completion of the Empire Building seemed to presage another era of growth, but, in 1929, when the stock market crashed, the economy began a steady downward spiral. Hit particularly hard was Idaho, where farm income dropped 57 percent between 1929 and 1932. The state's other two major industries, mining and lumber, did not fare much better. Depositors, who had experienced a financial crisis less than a decade earlier, became frightened and began to pull their money out of banks, thereby guaranteeing the disaster they hoped to avoid. The number of banks in Idaho fell from 106 in 1929 to 68 in 1933. In Boise, one of the three largest banks, Boise City National, failed in July 1932 after its depositors began draining its funds. First Security Bank, another of the top three, managed to survive, though only with the help of the Reconstruction Finance Corporation (RFC), a U.S. government agency established that year to help financially troubled banks, railroads, and other businesses. First National, the last of the big three, was still stubbornly independent and initially showed no interest in federal assistance. Its independence, however, did not stop depositors from withdrawing their money, and when deposits reached a dangerously low level, First National had little choice but to approach the RFC and the Federal Reserve Bank for help. Moore, however, had only a small amount of time in which to maneuver, and he was unable to strike an agreement he found acceptable. So on August 31, 1931, First National, the state's oldest bank, simply shut its doors.

First National would remain closed for two months, during which time the bank was reorganized under the direction of Harry W. Morrison, a friend of Moore's and owner of the worldwide construction firm Morrison-Knudsen Company, Inc. Morrison was asked to head the Reorganization Committee by Moore and the RFC. The eventual restructuring would force the

Moore family to surrender half of its stocks, allow bank customers to purchase stock with frozen assets, free up accounts with less than $200, and permit all other depositors to withdraw one-fourth of their money at the bank's opening and an additional one-fourth at six-month intervals. The RFC, moreover, loaned the bank $1.86 million. Moore remained president, but active management of the bank was handed over to Homer Pitner—formerly an officer at Pacific National Bank of San Francisco—who was named executive vice-president.

After the bank reopened on October 31, 1932, it followed a conservative strategy, keeping much of its assets "liquid"— that is, not tied up in loans and available for withdrawal. As a result, profits fell. However, by 1934, deposits rebounded to $9,945,000, with only $1,501,000 in outstanding loans. The bank was even able to free up accounts more quickly than planned. The Banking Act of 1933, which provided for deposit insurance and branch banking, would be a boon for First National. First National was then legally allowed to purchase the seven Idaho banks owned by The Western Loan and Investment Company and convert them into branch outlets. In 1934, however, as the bank was just recovering, Pitner was drowned in an accident, leaving the bank temporarily without a leader. He was replaced by John A. Schoonover, president of the Regional Agricultural Credit Corporation in Spokane, Washington. After Moore resigned as president on December 31, 1938, Schoonover was also elevated to that post, which he held until 1960.

During the 1930s, the state's economy was given a boost by federal grants and loans, such as for rural electrification projects, which together totaled $321 million between 1933 and 1939. As the state's health improved, First National also began to flourish. Deposits ballooned to $24 million by 1939, and that year loans reached $7.5 million. Unlike past leaders of the bank, Schoonover was eager to take advantage of new government programs. For example, he gained approval for the bank to participate in the Federal Housing Authority Title II program, which allowed First National to greatly increase its involvement in real estate loans. Under Schoonover, the bank would also expand to 15 branches by 1940, mostly through acquisitions of existing banks. One acquisition was Lewiston National Bank, located in the northern Idaho town of Lewiston. Because there was a competing institution in that town called the First National Bank of Lewiston, First National decided in 1936 to rename itself Idaho First National Bank of Boise, shortened in 1941 to Idaho First National Bank.

During World War II, Idaho First's deposits, aided by government funds and a booming economy, soared from $32 million in 1942 to more than $100 million in 1945. Loans, however, lagged behind, in part because farmers, benefiting from higher prices for their crops, earned greater profits and became less dependent on credit. Such losses were partially offset by the bank's holdings in government bonds, and the bank was able to make its final repayment to the RFC on December 28, 1944.

Idaho First thus entered the postwar years with great strength. The country's wartime production had been immediately shifted to consumer goods, and demand suddenly increased for loans on houses, cars, furnishings, and other goods. Farmers also sought credit for new and more advanced machinery, and

Idaho First was well positioned to serve them with its many branches, which had jumped to 33 by 1957. As a result, Idaho First's loans, just $10 million in 1942, jumped to $44 million in 1950 and $112 million in 1960, when deposits reached some $233 million. In 1955, the bank opened its first drive-in facility, built next to the home office in Boise.

Although these were profitable years, administratively the bank experienced turmoil. Schoonover, long the bank's leader, was increasingly attacked for his independent style of management, which he conducted largely at the expense of the board. Laurence Bettis, a director and a member of the Moore family, was his chief opponent and, in 1960, Bettis and his board allies were able to elect William E. Irvin as president. Though Schoonover was then given the title chairman of the board, his power was much reduced, and he resigned in 1962. Irvin, who did much to improve the bank's public relations, would hold the post of chairperson from 1962 to 1971, when he retired and was replaced by Thomas C. Frye. Frye, in turn, would be replaced by Fred C. Humphreys in 1977.

Throughout the 1960s and 1970s, Idaho First remained actively involved in the state's agricultural industry, which did well during most of these years. In contrast, the timber and mining industries began to show weaknesses that would worsen into the 1980s. Taking up some of the slack would be the state's expanding manufacturing base and its tourism and recreation industries. Idaho First was involved in the development of many new businesses, such as food processors, fertilizer plants, and manufacturers of irrigation and agricultural equipment. In recreation it was involved, for example, in funding the first ski lift at the Bogus Basin resort. During this period, the bank began to rely more heavily on automated machinery, especially in data processing, and was able to greatly increase its number of branches, spurred by reduced government regulation. Growth would finally cause the bank to move once more, this time to a newly constructed, 19-story building called Idaho First Plaza. Opened in 1978 and dominating the Boise skyline, the new building was located at 101 South Capital Boulevard, just a block from the bank's original 1867 location.

Changes in government regulations in the 1960s, 1970s, and 1980s, both at the state and national levels, would help reshape Idaho First. In particular, Idaho's state government in the early 1980s began to allow bank holding companies (that is, corporations owning at least two banks) to purchase banks in other states. To take advantage of this change, the directors of Idaho First decided to create their own holding company, Moore Financial Group Inc., established in 1981. The following year, the new company began to acquire banks in Utah, and soon thereafter it expanded into Oregon (beginning in 1983) and Washington (1988), both in the Seattle and Spokane areas. Much of this expansion was done under the direction of Daniel R. Nelson, who came to Moore Financial in 1984 to coordinate the subsidiaries in Utah and Oregon. Nelson was named president and chief operating officer in 1985, becoming chairperson and chief executive officer the following year. In 1989, both the company and its banks took on a new name, West One Bancorp.

By 1994, West One had become a regional power, with more than 200 offices in Idaho, Washington, Oregon, and Utah. Strongest in Idaho, where its share of the commercial banking market was around 40 percent, West One was, however, thriving in all four states, where economic growth was considerably higher than the national average. Agriculture and mining continued to be important to West One's lending strategy in Idaho, as was the defense industry, American Express's processing center, and the Delta Airlines hub in Utah; forest products, agriculture, and electronics in Oregon; and Boeing Company in Washington. Moreover, tourism was important in all four states.

Still, West One's primary borrowers were consumers and midsized businesses, and, in the early 1990s, its average commercial loan was less than $100,000. To capitalize on this, West One began taking extraordinary steps to improve its customer relations. In 1987, in Idaho, for example, it conducted the "Idaho Wants You" campaign, in which the bank agreed to donate a portion of every new deposit or loan until the total reached $500,000, which was then given to economic development projects. Moreover, during the campaign bank employees were sent out to visit every home and business in the state. Also notable was West One's willingness to carry higher salary expenses to fully staff its branch banks. Because of such heavy investments in customer service, West One was not always able to offer the lowest rates. "We probably wouldn't win a bidding war," admitted Nelson, but that seemed to matter little, as the bank continued to report strong growth and earnings. Its suc-

cess, however, has made it one of the most attractive takeover targets in the western United States.

Principal Subsidiaries: West One Bank, Idaho; West One Bank, Washington; West One Bank, Oregon; West One Bank, Oregon, S.B.; West One Bank, Utah; Idaho First Bank; West One Trust Company, Washington; West One Financial Services; West One Life Insurance Company.

Further Reading:

Anderson, Eloise H., *Frontier Bankers,* Caldwell, Idaho: The Caxton Printers, Ltd., 1981.
Byrne, Harlan S., "West One Bancorp: Acquisitions, Northwest's Economy Spur a Rebound," *Barron's,* August 24, 1992, pp. 35–36.
Moser, Michael J., "Bankers Go Door-to-Door to Reap Idaho Goodwill," *Bank Marketing,* November 1989, pp. 16–17.
Neurath, Peter, "West One Bank Chief Builds on Old Rainier Ties," *Puget Sound Business Journal,* December 11–17, 1992, pp. 1, 36–37.
Tanja, Lian, "Putting Together the Pieces of Service Quality," *Bank Marketing,* April 1994, pp. 28, 30.
Taylor, John H., "No More White Telephones," *Forbes,* January 18, 1993, p. 43.
Zuckerman, Sam, "West One Bancorp's Chief Rides High in the Saddle," *American Banker,* February 23, 1993, p. 1.

—Thomas Riggs

Wherehouse Entertainment Incorporated

19701 Hamilton Avenue
Torrance, California 90502
U.S.A.
(310) 538-2314
Fax: (538) 538-8698

Private Company
Incorporated: 1970 as Integrity Entertainment Corporation
Employees: 7,000
Sales: $380 million
SICs: 5735 Record & Prerecorded Tape Stores; 5734
   Computer & Software Stores

Wherehouse Entertainment Incorporated oversees one of the country's largest chains of retail outlets engaged in selling audio and video recordings. Despite strong competition from industry leader Blockbuster Entertainment Corporation, the company's stores, called The Wherehouse, have maintained a top position in its primary market, California. In fact, Wherehouse maintains over 300 stores in the western United States, the majority of which are located in California. In the early 1990s, The Wherehouse also began selling and renting video game cartridges, as well as marketing books on audio tape and used music compact discs.

Wherehouse was founded in 1970 in Gardena, California, a suburb southwest of Los Angeles, by Leon Hartstone. Hartstone named the parent company of his fledgling chain Integrity Entertainment Corporation, while the stores themselves were called The Wherehouse. The Wherehouse chain grew quickly, and at the end of its first decade in business, over 100 stores were in operation across most of its current geographical territory.

At the same time, however, Integrity Entertainment was also losing money. Thus, in 1979, Hartstone turned to Louis Kwiker, a one-time lawyer and investment banker who was then running a music industry consulting firm in Chicago. Hartstone initially hired Kwiker as a marketing and management consultant. Kwiker sold his firm, came to Los Angeles, and within a year had made such an impression on Hartstone that the company's founder appointed him president in 1980.

Two years later, however, Hartstone died after undergoing heart surgery, and, under the terms of his will, his estate was directed to sell Integrity Entertainment's assets for cash. Hoping to acquire the company himself, Kwiker formed an employee stock ownership trust, and, while Hartstone's estate negotiated unsuccessfully with potential buyers, Kwiker secured a $7 million loan for the trust, enough to cover the entire purchase price of the company, from Bank of America. The trust then stepped in and acquired all of Integrity Entertainment, using its assets to secure the debt. Kwiker retained a 37 percent interest for himself, enough to maintain control of the company, and he immediately became CEO.

Under Kwiker, the company's name was changed to Wherehouse Entertainment Corporation and headquarters were moved to the nearby suburb of Torrance. The company also embarked on a program of expansion. At the time of Hartstone's death, The Wherehouse had 130 stores; by the end of fiscal 1985, that number had grown modestly, to 142. That year, *Business Week* named Wherehouse Entertainment one of the 100 best companies in the United States with annual sales of less than $150 million. Two years later, however, The Wherehouse had more than doubled in size, to 295 stores, and sales reached $225 million. At the same time, the chain proved quick to adapt to radical shifts in recording technology, phasing out long-playing records as compact discs became the wave of the future. The company also moved into sales and rental of videotaped movies, and, by 1987, it had become one of the two largest video retailers in the nation, vying with the East Coast-based Erol's Video Club chain.

Perhaps just as impressive as its growth rate was the fact that Wherehouse Entertainment expanded dramatically while remaining relatively fussy about its choice of real estate. In order to keep up with shifts in entertainment software media, the company insisted on maintaining relatively large facilities. Therefore, unlike most chain retailers, The Wherehouse shied away from locations in regional malls, preferring sites that were either freestanding or in strip malls.

The overhead costs associated with rapid growth and higher effective tax rates began to depress company profits in 1986, and depressed stock prices left the company vulnerable to attempts at leveraged buyouts and hostile takeovers. In October 1987, Shamrock Holdings, an investment company based in the Los Angeles suburb of Burbank and headed by Roy Disney, nephew of Walt Disney, announced that it was offering $113.5 million for the 93 percent of Wherehouse Entertainment stock that it had not already acquired on the open market.

Shamrock Holdings claimed that its ownership of four television and fourteen radio stations gave it expertise that "could substantially contribute to the success of Wherehouse," as Shamrock president Stanley Gold noted in a letter to Kwiker. Wherehouse Entertainment, however, regarded Shamrock's bid as a hostile takeover, and, after two months of fending off Shamrock, the company turned to New York-based leveraged buyout firm Adler & Shaykin, which agreed to acquire Wherehouse Entertainment for $118 million, or $14 per share.

However, the white knight that Kwiker had courted soon proved his undoing. In March 1988, Kwiker was forced to leave the company by Adler & Shaykin. Kwiker had lately been criticized by investors for allowing the costs associated with expansion to depress company profits. Such criticism grew more intense after the company's bondholders learned that Adler & Shaykin's buyout package would pay them only half of the face value of their securities. In interviews Kwiker had regarded himself as a team-builder who favored the Japanese trend of consensus-based management. However, while analysts and former executives praised Kwiker as a brilliant manager, they also described him as an egotist whose management style led to conflicts with other executives.

Kwiker was replaced as CEO by Scott Young. Under Young's management and Adler & Shaykin's ownership, Wherehouse Entertainment realized some immediate benefits from privatization. Soon after taking over the company, Young drastically changed The Wherehouse's merchandise mix, increasing the number of videocassettes of popular movies fourfold. The move paid off; more customers came to The Wherehouse once they realized that the chain was certain to have copies of the movies they most wanted to rent. Moreover, the move might not have occurred had the company not gone private. As Young observed: "Woe to the CEO of a publicly held company that diverges from Wall Street's expectations, if even for a quarter.... Having only a small group of sophisticated owners made us a little more courageous." Young also felt that privatization helped improve employee morale, since executives, spared of the need to mollify shareholders, could spend more time communicating with them.

In the long run, however, the benefits of privatization did not entirely outweigh the burden of the leveraged buyout. In the early 1990s, fiscal problems created by stiff competition from Blockbuster Video and recession in the California economy were only made worse by the high interest payments that Wherehouse Entertainment had incurred through the Adler & Shaykin buyout. Video rentals also dropped in 1991, as the nation became transfixed by the war in the Persian Gulf. Moreover, Adler & Shaykin admitted that it faced considerable problems of its own when its largest subsidiary, retail chain Best Products, filed for Chapter 11 bankruptcy in January 1991.

Not surprisingly, Adler & Shaykin were forced to sell Wherehouse Entertainment in 1992. The buyer, a group of senior management backed by Merrill Lynch Capital Partners, paid $250 million for Wherehouse, $131.4 million of which went to pay down Wherehouse's existing debt. Merrill Lynch Capital Partners received a controlling interest in the company and hinted that it would eventually take Wherehouse Entertainment public again. Scott Young remained CEO.

However, the Merrill Lynch deal did not solve the company's longer-term fiscal dilemma any more effectively than had the Adler & Shaykin buyout. Where Merrill Lynch's financial package had provided $131.4 million to pay down debt, it had also created another $220 million in obligations through taking out bank loans and issuing bonds. Wherehouse Entertainment continued to lose money throughout the following year, due to continuing recession in California, competition from the Blockbuster empire, and interest payments on its long-term debt.

Looking for a way to increase sales and customer traffic, and unable to overtake Blockbuster in video rentals, the company shifted emphasis in 1993. The company's decision to begin buying and selling used compact discs brought both opportunity and controversy. The market for second-hand music recordings had a long history, and the small stores that had always traded used records and cassettes had already started retailing used CDs. However, The Wherehouse was the largest chain to enter the business. Wherehouse had first experimented with selling used CDs in 1991, when, concerned by customer discontent over high CD prices, it began allowing customers to return CDs for full refund for any reason. Alarmed by The Wherehouse's new policy and similar moves by other retailers, Sony's music distribution arm stopped allowing retailers to return CDs for which the packaging had been opened. Unable to return Sony CDs, The Wherehouse instead sold them at reduced prices, much to the delight of consumers.

The market for used CDs, however, presented the music industry with a threat that used album sales never had. Second-hand records had offered consumers a trade-off: reduced price for reduced sound quality caused by wear and tear on the recording. However, CDs didn't suffer much from use, since they required no mechanical parts, such as tape heads or phonograph needles, that grated against the recording during playback. Therefore, large quantities of good-as-new CDs could be passed between an infinite number of owners without any revenue going to the record companies or artists.

The record companies and the musicians they represented wasted little time in responding. In May 1993, the distribution arms of four of the six largest record companies—Sony, Warner Music, Capitol-EMI, and MCA—announced that they would withhold cooperative advertising money from any retailer selling used compact discs. In June of that year, country-western superstar Garth Brooks announced that he would not allow his recordings to be distributed to stores that retailed used CDs. But if, as Scott Young said at the time, the record industry giants expected Wherehouse Entertainment to retreat, they were wrong. In July, the company retaliated with a lawsuit alleging that the four major distributors had violated anti-trust laws, claiming that their refusal to provide advertising support constituted an unreasonable restraint of trade and commerce. Moreover, the suit charged that distributors were acting to protect CD prices that were "artificially high." The Independent Retailers Music Association (IRMA) immediately voiced its support for the suit, although neither IRMA nor any of its members joined in the legal proceedings.

Whatever ill will the company may have engendered in the record industry with its lawsuit, Wherehouse Entertainment reaped a huge publicity windfall from the controversy. It also scored a significant victory in September 1993, when Capitol-EMI settled with the company, agreeing to resume cooperative advertisement. In return, Wherehouse Entertainment dropped Capitol-EMI from the suit and agreed not to sell used CDs of recordings currently being supported by cooperative ad funds.

While Capitol-EMI's capitulation provided Wherehouse Entertainment with at least a psychological boost, it did not solve the problems presented by its substantial debt load and intense competition from major rivals in its field, which, by this time, included Blockbuster Video, Musicland, and Tower Records. Nevertheless, Wherehouse had coped well with the challenges of a retailing sector that had undergone major changes and had always managed to keep pace with its competition, if not stay a step ahead.

Principal Subsidiaries: The Wherehouse.

Further Reading:

Armstrong, Larry, ''What's Wrong With Selling Used CDs?,'' *Business Week,* July 26, 1993.

Bates, James, ''Kwiker Out at Wherehouse Entertainment,'' *Los Angeles Times,* March 25, 1988.

Duffy, Thom, ''Merrill Lynch to Buy Wherehouse,'' *Billboard,* May 16, 1992.

''Louis Kwiker: Nothing Can Take the Place of Dumb Luck,'' *Chain Store Age Executive,* October 1985.

Peltz, James F., ''Shamrock Bids $113.5 Million for Wherehouse,'' *Los Angeles Times,* October 14, 1987.

Razzano, Rhonda, ''The Philosophy of the Ant and the Elephant,'' *Chain Store Age Executive,* September 1987.

—Douglas Sun

INDEX TO COMPANIES AND PERSONS

Listings are arranged in alphabetical order under the company name; thus Eli Lilly & Company will be found under the letter E. Definite articles (The) and forms of incorporation that precede the name (A.B. and N.V.) are ignored for alphabetical purposes. Company names appearing in bold type have historical essays on the page numbers appearing in bold. Updates to entries that appeared in earlier volumes are signified by (upd.). The index is cumulative with volume numbers printed in bold type.

A.A. Housman & Co., **II** 424
A.A. Mathews. *See* CRSS Inc.
A & C Black Ltd., **7** 165
A. Ahlström Oy, **IV** 276–77
A&K Petroleum Co., **IV** 445
A & M Instrument Co., **9** 323
A&N Foods Co., **II** 553
A&P. *See* The Great Atlantic & Pacific Tea Company, Inc.
A&P Water and Sewer Supplies, Inc., **6** 487
A&W Root Beer Co., **II** 595
A.B. Chance Co., **II** 20
A-B Nippondenso, **III** 593
A-BEC Mobility, **11** 487
A.C. Nielsen Co., **IV** 605
A.D. International (Australia) Pty. Ltd., **10** 272
A. Dager & Co., **I** 404
A. Dunkelsbuhler & Co., **IV** 20–21, 65; **7** 122
A.E. Fitkin & Company, **6** 592–93
A.E. LePage, **II** 457
A.G. Becker, **II** 259–60; **11** 318
A.G. Edwards & Sons, Inc., **8** 3, 5
A.G. Edwards, Inc., 8 3–5
A.G. Industries, Inc., **7** 24
A.G. Spalding & Bros., **I** 428–29
A.G. Stanley Ltd., **V** 17, 19
A. Gettelman, Co., **I** 269
A. Goertz and Co., **IV** 91
A.H. Belo Corporation, IV 605; **10** 3–5
A.H. Robins Co., **I** 366; **9** 356; **10** 70
A.I. Credit Corp., **III** 196
A.J. Caley and Son. Ltd., **II** 569
A.J. Oster Co., **III** 681
A. Johnson & Co. *See* Axel Johnson Group.
A.M. Collins Manufacturing Co., **IV** 286
A.O. Smith Corporation, 11 3–6
A.O. Smith Data Systems, **7** 139
A-1 Steak Sauce Co., **I** 259
A-1 Supply, **10** 375
A.R. Pechiney, **IV** 173
A. Roger Perretti, **II** 484
A.S. Abell Co., **IV** 678
A.S. Aloe, **III** 443
A.S. Cameron Steam Pump Works, **III** 525
A/S Titan, **III** 418
A. Schulman, Inc., 8 6–8
A.V. Roe & Co., **I** 50; **III** 508
A.V. Roe Canada, **III** 508
A.W. Bain Holdings, **III** 523
A.W. Shaw Co., **IV** 635
A-Z International Cos., **III** 569
AA Development Corp., **I** 91
AA Energy Corp., **I** 91
Aachen & Munich. *See* Aachener und Münchener Gruppe.
Aachener und Münchener Feuer-Versicherungs-Gesellschaft, **III** 376
Aachener und Münchener Gruppe, **III** 349–50
Aachener Union, **II** 385
Aalborg, **6** 367
Aalto, Alvar, **IV** 276

Aansworth Shirt Makers, **8** 406
AAR Ltd., **III** 687; **IV** 60
Aargauische Portlandcement-Fabrik Holderbank-Wildegg, **III** 701
Aaron, Daniel, **7** 90
Aartz, Peter F., **I** 143
Aavant Health Management Group, Inc., **11** 394
AB Dick Co., **II** 25
AB-PT. *See* American Broadcasting-Paramount Theatres, Inc.
ABA. *See* Aktiebolaget Aerotransport.
Abacus Fund, **II** 445
ABB ASEA Brown Boveri Ltd., II 1–4; **IV** 109
Abbate, Mario, **III** 208
Abbatoir St.-Valerien Inc., **II** 652
Abbe, Ernst, **III** 445–46
Abbey Life Group PLC, **II** 309
Abbey Medical, Inc., **11** 486
Abbey National Life, **10** 8
Abbey National Mortgage Finance, **10** 8
Abbey National PLC, 10 6–8
Abbey Rents, **II** 572
Abbey Road Building Society, **10** 6–7
Abbott, E., **I** 265
Abbott Laboratories, I 619–21, 686, 690, 705; **II** 539; **10** 70, 78, 126; **11** 7–9 (upd.), 91, 494
Abbott, Proctor & Paine, **II** 445
Abbott, Wallace Calvin, **I** 619; **11** 7
Abboud, A. Robert, **II** 285–86
ABC. *See* American Broadcasting Co. *and* Capital Cities/ABC Inc.
ABC Appliance, Inc., 10 9–11
ABC Records, **II** 144
ABC Warehouse, **10** 9–11
ABD Securities Corp., **II** 239, 283
Abdoo, R. A., **6** 603
Abdson, Lester, **I** 227; **10** 181
ABECOR. *See* Associated Banks of Europe Corp.
Abegg, Carl J., **II** 547; **7** 382
Abekawa, Sumio, **II** 277
Abeles, Peter, **IV** 651; **V** 523–25; **7** 390
Abell, William H., **III** 217–18
Abenius, Håkan, **IV** 336
Abercom Holdings, **IV** 92
Aberconway (Lord). *See* Henry D. McLaren.
Abercrombie & Fitch, **V** 116
Abernathy, K. Brooks, **III** 444
Abernathy, Roy, **I** 136
Aberthaw Cement, **III** 671
Abex Aerospace, **III** 512
Abex Corp., **I** 456; **10** 553
Abex Friction Products, **III** 512
ABF. *See* Associated British Foods PLC.
ABI, **I** 289
Abitibi Paper Co. Ltd., **IV** 246–47
Abitibi Power & Paper Co. Ltd., **IV** 245–46
Abitibi Pulp & Paper Co. Ltd., **IV** 245
Abitibi-Price Inc., IV 245–47, 721; **9** 391
Abko Realty Inc., **IV** 449
Ablah, George, **IV** 449

Ablon, R. Richard, **6** 151, 153
Ablon, Ralph E., **I** 512–14; **6** 151
ABN. *See* Algemene Bank Nederland N.V.
Abodaher, David, **I** 145
ABR Foods, **II** 466
Abraham & Straus, **V** 168; **8** 443; **9** 209
Abraham, Claude, **6** 380
Abraham Schaaffhausenscher Bankverein, **IV** 104
Abrahamson, Thomas A., **11** 466
Abramson, Leonard, **6** 194–95
Abri Bank Bern, **II** 378
Abs, Hermann J., **II** 279
Abu Dhabi Co. for Onshore Oil Operations, **IV** 364
Abu Dhabi Gas Liquefaction Co. Ltd., **IV** 364
Abu Dhabi Investment Corp., **IV** 397
Abu Dhabi Marine Areas Ltd., **IV** 363–64
Abu Dhabi Marine Operating Co., **IV** 364
Abu Dhabi National Oil Co. for Distribution, **IV** 364
Abu Dhabi National Oil Company, IV 363–64
Abu Dhabi National Tankers Co., **IV** 364
Abu Dhabi Oil Co. Ltd., **IV** 476
Abu Dhabi Petroleum Co., **IV** 363–64
Abu Qir Fertilizer and Chemical Industries Co., **IV** 413
Academic Press, **IV** 622–23
Access Technology, **6** 225
Accessory Network Group, Inc., **8** 219
Accident and Casualty Insurance Co., **III** 230–31
ACCO Canada Ltd., **7** 4–5
ACCO International, **7** 4
ACCO Products, Inc., **7** 3–4
ACCO USA, **7** 4–5
ACCO World Corporation, 7 3–5
ACCO-Rexel Group Holdings, PLC, **7** 5
Accor SA, 10 12–14
Accountants on Call, **6** 10
Accounting and Tabulating Corporation of Great Britain, **6** 240
Accuralite Company, **10** 492
Accurate Forming Co., **III** 643
Accuride Corp., **IV** 179
Ace Electric Co., **I** 156
Ace Refrigeration Ltd., **I** 315
Acer America Corporation, **10** 257
Acer Group, **6** 244
Acheson, Edward, **8** 396
Acheson Graphite Corp., **I** 399; **9** 517
Acheson, Lila Bell. *See* Wallace, Lila Acheson.
ACI Holding Inc., **I** 91
Aciéries et Minières de la Sambre, **IV** 52
Aciéries Réunies de Burbach-Eich-Dudelange S.A., **IV** 24–26
Acker, Edward, **I** 116
Ackerley, Barry A., **9** 3–5
Ackerley Communications, Inc., 9 3–5
Ackerman, Martin, **11** 69
Ackerman, Martin S., **9** 320
Acklin Stamping Company, **8** 515

ACLC. *See* Allegheny County Light Company.
ACLI Government Securities Inc., **II** 422
Acme Boot, **I** 440–41
Acme Can Co., **I** 601
Acme Carton Co., **IV** 333
Acme Corrugated Cases, **IV** 258
Acme Quality Paint Co., **III** 744
Acme-Delta Company, **11** 411
Acorn Computer, **III** 145
Acoustics Development Corporation, **6** 313
Action, **6** 393
Acton Bolt Ltd., **IV** 658
Acumos, **11** 57
Acuson Corporation, 9 7; **10 15–17**
Acxiom, **6** 14
Ad Astra Aero, **I** 121
AD-AM Gas Company, **11** 28
Adam Opel AG, 7 6–8
Adam Opel Company, **11** 549
Adam, Ray C., **10** 435
Adams and Co., **II** 380, 395; **10** 59
Adams, Aret, **IV** 474
Adams, Charles F., **II** 86–87; **11** 412–13
Adams, Charles Francis, **III** 312
Adams, Charles Francis, Jr., **V** 530
Adams Childrenswear, **V** 177
Adams Express Co., **II** 380–81, 395–96; **10** 59–60
Adams, Harland, **7** 266
Adams, John (Sgt.), **III** 272
Adams, K.S. (Boots), **IV** 521–22
Adams, Morton, **7** 105
Adams, William W., **III** 424
Adaptec, **11** 56
Adar Associates, Inc. *See* Scientific-Atlanta, Inc.
ADC Advanced Fiber Optics Corp., **10** 19
ADC Incorporated, **10** 18
ADC Telecommunications, Inc., 10 18–21
Adco Products, **I** 374
Addinsell, Harry M., **II** 402
Addis, Charles, **II** 297
Addison Wesley, **IV** 659
Addressograph-Multigraph, **11** 494
Adelphi Pharmaceutical Manufacturing Co., **I** 496
Ademco. *See* Alarm Device Manufacturing Company.
Adenauer, Konrad, **II** 257; **IV** 589
Adger Assuranceselskab, **III** 310
Adhere Paper Co., **IV** 252
Adia S.A., 6 9–11; 9 327
Adia Services, Inc., **6** 9–11
Adiainvest S.A., **6** 9, 11
Adidas AG, **8** 392–93
Adjemian, Harry, **III** 568
Adler and Shaykin, **III** 56; **11** 556–57
Adler, Carl, **7** 140
Adler, E.P., **11** 251–52
Adler, Frederick, **8** 137
Adler Line. *See* Transatlantische Dampfschiffahrts Gesellschaft.
Adler, Mortimer, **7** 167
Adler, Philip, **11** 252
ADM. *See* Archer-Daniels-Midland Co.
Admiral Co., **II** 86; **III** 573
Admiral Cruise Lines, **6** 368
Adnan Dabbagh, **6** 115
ADNOC. *See* Abu Dhabi National Oil Company.
Adobe Systems Incorporated, 10 22–24

Adolph Coors Company, I 236–38, 255, 273
Adonis Radio Corp., **9** 320
Adria Steamship Company, **6** 425
Adriatico Banco d'Assicurazione, **III** 206, 345–46
Adsega, **II** 677
Adtel, Inc., **10** 358
Advance Publications Inc., **IV 581–84**
Advanced Communications Engineering. *See* Scientific-Atlanta, Inc.
Advanced Entertainment Group, **10** 286
Advanced Medical Technologies, **III** 512
Advanced Micro Devices, Inc., 6 215–17; **9** 115; **10** 367; **11** 308
Advanced MobilComm, **10** 432
Advanced System Applications, **11** 395
Advanced Technology Laboratories, Inc., 9 6–8
Advanced Telecommunications Corporation, **8** 311
ADVANTA Corp., 8 9–11; 11 123
ADVANTA Mortgage Corp. USA, **8** 10
Advantage Company, **8** 311
Advantage Health Plans, Inc., **11** 379
Advertising Unlimited, Inc., **10** 461
Advo, Inc., 6 12–14
Advo Publications, Inc., **6** 13
AEA. *See* United Kingdom Atomic Energy Authority.
AEA Investors, **II** 628
AEG A.G., I 151, **409–11; II** 12, 279; **III** 466, 479; **IV** 167; **6** 489
AEG Kabel A.G., **9** 11
AEG-Daimler, **I** 193
AEG-Telefunken, **II** 119
Aegis Group plc, 6 15–16
Aegis Insurance Co., **III** 273
AEGON N.V., III 177–79, 201, 273
AEL Ventures Ltd., **9** 512
AEON, **V** 96–99; **11** 498–99
AEP. *See* American Electric Power Company.
AEP-Span, **8** 546
Aeppli, Otto, **II** 268
Aer Lingus, **6** 59
Aeritalia, **I** 51, 74–75, 467
Aero Engines, **9** 418
Aero Mayflower Transit Company. *See* Mayflower Group Inc.
Aero O/Y, **6** 87–88
Aero-Coupling Corp., **III** 641
Aero-Portuguesa, **6** 125
Aeroflot Soviet Airlines, I 105, 110, 118; **6 57–59**
Aerojet, **8** 206, 208
Aerojet-General Corp., **9** 266
Aerolíneas Argentinas, **I** 107; **6** 97
Aeroquip Automotive, **V** 255
Aeroquip Co., **V** 255
Aeroquip Corp., **III** 640–42
Aerospace Avionics, **III** 509
Aerospatiale, I 41–42, 46, 50, 74, 94; **7 9–12**
AES China Generating Co. Ltd., **10** 27
The AES Corporation, 10 25–27
Aetna Accident and Liability Co., **III** 181
Aetna Business Credit Inc., **II** 236
Aetna Casualty and Surety Co., **III** 181–82
Aetna Fire Insurance Co., **III** 180
Aetna Insurance Co., **III** 223, 226
Aetna Life and Casualty Company, II 170–71, 319; **III** 78, **180–82,** 209, 226,

254, 296, 298, 305, 313, 329; **III** 389; **IV** 123, 703
Aetna Life and Casualty Insurance Company, **10** 75–76
Aetna Life Insurance Co., **III** 180–82
Aetna Oil Co., **IV** 373
AFC. *See* America's Favorite Chicken Company, Inc.
AFCO, **III** 241
AFCO Industries, Inc., **IV** 341
Afcol, **I** 289
AFE Ltd., **IV** 241
Affiliated Enterprises Inc., **I** 114
Affiliated Products Inc., **I** 622
Affiliated Publications, **6** 323;
Affiliated Publications, Inc., 7 13–16
AFG Industries Inc., **I** 483; **9** 248
AFLAC Inc., 10 28–30 (upd.). *See also* American Family Corporation.
AFLAC Japan, **III** 187–88
AFP. *See* Australian Forest Products.
African and European Investment, **IV** 96
African Coasters, **IV** 91
African Explosive and Chemical Industries, **IV** 22
AG&E. *See* American Electric Power Company.
AGA, **I** 358
Agar Manufacturing Company, **8** 267
Agee, William A., **I** 68, 142–43; **7** 357
Agee, William J., **7** 356
AGEL&P. *See* Albuquerque Gas, Electric Light and Power Company.
Agence France Presse, **IV** 670
Agency, **6** 393
AGF, **III** 185
AGFA, **I** 310–11
Agfa-Ansco Corp., **I** 337–38
AGFA-Gevaert, **III** 487
Agiba Petroleum, **IV** 414
Agip Mineraria, **IV** 420–21
Agip Nucleare, **IV** 421
Agip/Phillips, **IV** 472
Agip SpA, **IV** 454, 466, 472–74, 498. *See also* Azienda Generale Italiana Petroli.
AGLP, **IV** 618
Agnelli family, **III** 209, 347
Agnelli, Giovanni, **I** 161; **11** 102
Agnelli, Giovanni, II, **I** 161–62; **11** 102–03
Agnelli, Umberto, **I** 162; **11** 103
Agnew, Jonathan, **II** 423
Agnew, Rudolph, **7** 125
AGO, **III** 177, 179, 310
AGO General Insurance Co., **III** 179
AGO Holding Co., **III** 179, 273
AGO Life Insurance Co., **III** 179
Agor Manufacturing Co., **IV** 286
AGRAN, **IV** 505
Agrawal, S.K., **IV** 144
AgriBank FCB, **8** 489
Agrico Chemical Company, **IV** 82, 84, 576; **7** 188
Agricultural Insurance Co., **III** 191
Agricultural Minerals Corp., **IV** 84
Agrifan, **II** 355
Agrigenetics Corp., **I** 361
Agrippina Versicherungs AG, **III** 403, 412
Agroferm Hungarian Japanese Fermentation Industry, **III** 43
AGTL. *See* Alberta Gas Trunk Line Company, Ltd.
Aguila (Mexican Eagle) Oil Co. Ltd., **IV** 657

Aguilo, Miguel, **6** 97
Agway, Inc., 7 17–18
Ahlman, Einar, **IV** 300
Ahman, Fritiof, **6** 87
Ahmanson. *See* H.F. Ahmanson &
  Company.
Ahmanson Bank, **II** 182
Ahmanson Bank and Trust Co., **II** 181
Ahmanson, Howard Fieldstead, **II** 181; **10**
  342
Ahmanson Mortgage Co., **II** 182; **10** 343
Ahmanson Trust Co., **II** 182
Ahmanson, William A., **II** 181
Ahold's Ostara, **II** 641
AHP. *See* American Home Products.
Ahronovitz, Joseph, **II** 204
AHSC Holdings Corp., **III** 9–10
AIC. *See* Allied Import Comapny.
Aichi Bank, **II** 373
Aichi Kogyo Co., **III** 415
Aichi Steel Works, **III** 637
Aida Corporation, **11** 504
Aidekman, Alex, **II** 672–74
Aidekman, Ben, **II** 672
Aidekman, Sam, **II** 672
AIG Data Center, Inc., **III** 196
AIG Energy, **III** 197
AIG Entertainment, **III** 197
AIG Financial Products Corp., **III** 197
AIG Oil Rig, Inc., **III** 196–97
AIG Political Risk, **III** 197
AIG Risk Management, Inc., **III** 196
AIG Specialty Agencies, Inc., **III** 197
AIG Trading Corp., **III** 198
AIGlobal, **III** 197
Aiken, Edmund, **II** 284
Aikoku Sekiyu, **IV** 554
AIM Create Co., Ltd., **V** 127
Ainslie, Michael L., **9** 344
**Air & Water Technologies Corporation,
  6 441–42**
Air Afrique, **9** 233
Air BP, **7** 141
Air Brasil, **6** 134
Air Canada, 6 60–62, 101
Air Co., **I** 298
Air France, **I** 93–94, 104, 110, 120; **II**
  163; **6** 69, 95–96, 373; **8** 313
Air Inter, **6** 92–93; **9** 233
Air Lanka Catering Services Ltd., **6**
  123–24
Air Liberté, **6** 208
Air Micronesia, **I** 97
Air Midwest, Inc., **11** 299
Air Nippon Co., Ltd., **6** 70
**Air Products and Chemicals, Inc., I
  297–99**, 315, 358, 674; **10 31–33
  (upd.); 11** 403
Air Reduction Co., **I** 297–98; **10** 31–32
Air Southwest Co. *See* Southwest Airlines
  Co.
Air Spec, Inc., **III** 643
Air-India, 6 63–64
Airborne Accessories, **II** 81
Airborne Express. *See* Airborne Freight
  Corp.
Airborne Express Japan, **6** 346
Airborne Freight Corp., 6 345–47 345
Airbus, **10** 164
Airbus Industrie, **6** 74; **7** 9–11, 504; **9** 418.
  See also G.I.E. Airbus Industrie.
AirCal, **I** 91
Aircraft Marine Products, **II** 7
Aircraft Services International, **I** 449

Aircraft Transport & Travel Ltd., **I** 92
Airlease International, **II** 422
Airmec-AEI Ltd., **II** 81
Airport Ground Service Co., **I** 104, 106
Airstream, **II** 468
Airtel, **IV** 640
AirTouch Communications, 10 118; **11
  10–12**
Airtours International GmbH. and Co.
  K.G., **II** 164
Airways Housing Trust Ltd., **I** 95
Airwick, **II** 567
Airwork. *See* AirEgypt.
Aisin (Australia) Pty. Ltd., **III** 415
Aisin (U.K.) Ltd., **III** 415
Aisin America, Inc., **III** 415
Aisin Asia, **III** 415
Aisin Deutschland, **III** 415
Aisin do Brasil, **III** 415
Aisin Seiki Co., Ltd., III 415–16
Aisin U.S.A. Manufacturing Co., **III** 415
Aisin-Warner Ltd., **III** 415
Aitken, W. Max (Lord Beaverbrook), **III**
  704; **IV** 208; **6** 585
AITS. *See* American International Travel
  Service.
Aivaz, Boris, **IV** 260
Aizu-Toko K.K., **II** 62
Ajax, **6** 349
Ajax Iron Works, **II** 16
Ajinomoto Co., Inc., II 463–64, 475; **III**
  705
Ajinomoto Frozen Foods, **II** 463
Ajisaka, Mutsuya, **I** 636
Ajman Cement, **III** 760
Ajroldi, Paolo, **6** 47–48
Akane Securities Co. Ltd., **II** 443
Akashi, Teruo, **II** 325
Akashic Memories, **11** 234
Akema, Terayuki, **V** 727
Akerman, Jack, **IV** 685
Akers, John, **III** 149; **6** 252
Akiyama, Takesaburo, **II** 67
Akiyama, Tomiichi, **11** 477
AKO Bank, **II** 378
Akron Brass Manufacturing Co., **9** 419
Akron Corp., **IV** 290
Akseli Gallen-Kallela, **IV** 314
Aktiebolaget Aerotransport, **I** 119
Aktiebolaget Electrolux, **III** 478–81
Aktiebolaget SKF, III 622–25; IV 203
Aktiengesellschaft für Berg- und
  Hüttenbetriebe, **IV** 201
Aktiengesellschaft für Maschinenpapier-
  Zellstoff-Fabrikation, **IV** 323
Aktiv Placering A.B., **II** 352
Akzo, **I** 674; **II** 572; **III** 44
Al Copeland Enterprises, Inc., **7** 26–28
al Sulaiman, Abd Allah, **IV** 536
al-Badri, Abdallah, **IV** 455
al-Banbi, Hamdi, **IV** 413
al-Marri, Jaber, **IV** 525
al-Mazrui, Sohal Fares, **IV** 364
al-Thani, Abdulaziz bin Khalifa (Sheikh),
  IV 524
al-Thani family, **IV** 524
al-Thani, Khalifa bin Hamad (Sheikh), **IV**
  524
Alaadin Middle East-Ersan, **IV** 564
Alabaster Co., **III** 762
Aladdin's Castle, **III** 430, 431
Alais et Camargue, **IV** 173
Alamito Company, **6** 590
Alamo Engine Company, **8** 514

Alamo Rent A Car, Inc., 6 348–50
Alarm Device Manufacturing Company, **9**
  413–15
Alascom, **6** 325–28
Alaska Air Group, Inc., 6 65–67; 11 50
Alaska Airlines. *See* Alaska Air Group.,
  Inc.
Alaska Co., **III** 439
Alaska Hydro-Train, **6** 382; **9** 510
Alaska Natural Gas Transportation System,
  V 673, 683
Alaska Pulp Co., **IV** 284, 297, 321
Alba, **III** 619–20
Albany and Susquehanna Railroad, **II** 329
Albany Assurance Co., Ltd., **III** 293
Albany Felt Company. *See* Albany
  International Corp.
Albany Felt Company of Canada, **8** 13
Albany International Corp., 8 12–14
Albarda, Horatius, **I** 108
Albeck, Andy, **II** 148
Albee, Mrs. P.F.E., **III** 15
Albemarle Paper Co., **I** 334–35; **10** 289
Albers Brothers Milling Co., **II** 487
Albers, William, **II** 643
Albert, Carl, **9** 205, 207
Albert E. Reed & Co. Ltd., **7** 343
Albert Heijn NV, **II** 641–42
Albert, King (Belgium), **I** 395
Albert, Kurt, **I** 392
Albert Nipon, Inc., **8** 323
Alberta Distillers, **I** 377
Alberta Gas Trunk Line Company, Ltd., **V**
  673–74
Alberta Sulphate Ltd., **IV** 165
Alberthal, Lester M., **III** 138
Alberto, **II** 641–42
Alberto-Culver Company, 8 15–17
Alberts, Robert C., **II** 507
Albertson, Joe, **II** 601–04; **7** 19–21
Albertson's Inc., II 601–03, 604–05, 637;
  7 19–22 (upd.); 8 474
Albi Enterprises, **III** 24
Albion, **III** 673
Albion Reid Proprietary, **III** 673
Albrecht, R.A., **I** 254
Albright & Friel, **I** 313; **10** 154
Albright & Wilson Ltd., **I** 527; **IV** 165
Albright, Joseph, **IV** 683
Albright, Josephine, **IV** 683
Albu, George, **IV** 90
Albu, Leopold, **IV** 90
Albuquerque Gas & Electric Company. *See*
  Public Service Company of New
  Mexico.
Albuquerque Gas, Electric Light and Power
  Company, **6** 561–62
Albury Brickworks, **III** 673
Alcan Aluminium Limited, II 415; **IV
  9–13**, 14, 59, 154
Alcan Aluminum Corp., **IV** 11; **9** 512
Alcan Australia Ltd., **IV** 155
Alcantara and Sores, **II** 582
Alcatel, **II** 13, 69; **7** 9; **9** 32; **11** 59
**Alcatel Alsthom Compagnie Générale
  d'Electricité, 9 9–11; 11** 198
Alcatel Bell, **6** 304
Alcatel N.V., **9** 9–10
Alchem Capital Corp., **8** 141, 143
Alco Cab Co., **I** 64
**Alco Health Services Corporation, III
  9–10**
Alco Hydro-Aeroplane, **I** 64
Alco Oil & Chemical Corp., **I** 412

**Alco Standard Corporation, I 412–13;
III** 9; **9** 261
Alcoa. *See* Aluminum Company of
America.
Alcock, John (Sir), **I** 81
Alcon Laboratories, **II** 547; **7** 382; **10** 46,
48
Alcudia, **IV** 528
Aldama (Marquis of), **II** 197
Alden, George I., **8** 395
Alden, Robert, **I** 32
Aldermac Mines Ltd., **IV** 164
Alderson, Gerald R., **11** 222, 224
Alderton, Charles C., **9** 177
Aldi, **11** 240
Aldine Press, **10** 34
Aldred, Edward, **III** 27
Aldrich Chemical Co., **I** 690
Aldrich, William A., **11** 114
Aldrich, Winthrop W., **II** 247–48, 397; **10**
61
Aldus Corporation, 10 34–36
Aldwarke Main & Car House Collieries, **I**
573
Alen, Charles, **I** 701
Alenia, **7** 9, 11
Aler, I.A., **I** 108
Alessio Tubi, **IV** 228
Alex & Ivy, **10** 166–68
Alexander (Lord), **II** 335
Alexander & Alexander Services Inc., III
280; **10 37–39**
Alexander & Baldwin,
Alexander & Baldwin, Inc., I 417; **10
40–42**
Alexander, Douglas, **II** 9
Alexander, Evelyn, **II** 664
Alexander Grant & Co., **I** 481, 656
Alexander Hamilton Life Insurance Co., **II**
420
Alexander, Herbert George Barlow, **III**
228–29
Alexander Howden, **III** 280
Alexander Howden Group, **10** 38–39
Alexander, James, **III** 247
Alexander, John, **11** 460
Alexander Martin Co., **I** 374
Alexander, Samuel T., **10** 40–41
Alexander, Tsar (Russia), **I** 271
Alexander, Wallace, **10** 40–41
Alexander, Walter, **7** 322
Alexander, William, **III** 247
Alexander's Inc., **10** 282
Alexanderson, Ernst, **II** 29
Alexis Lichine, **III** 43
Alfa Romeo, **I** 163, 167; **11** 102, 104, 139,
205
Alfa Trading Company, **8** 380
Alfa-Laval AB, III 417–21; IV 203; **8**
376
Alfa-Laval Co., **III** 419–20
Alfa-Laval Contracting, **III** 420
Alfa-Laval Engineering, **III** 420
Alfa-Laval Inc., **III** 420
Alfa-Laval Lté., **III** 420
Alfa-Laval Separation A/S, **III** 420
Alfa-Laval Service, **III** 420
Alfiero, Salvatore H., **7** 296–98
Alfinal, **III** 420
Alfonsín, Raúl, **IV** 578
Alfred Hickman Ltd., **III** 751
Alfred Marks Bureau, Ltd., **6** 9–10
Alfred Nobel & Co., **III** 693
Alfred Teves, **I** 193

Alfried Krupp von Bohlen und Halbach
Foundation, **IV** 89
ALG. *See* Arkla, Inc.
Algemeene Bankvereeniging en Volksbank
van Leuven, **II** 304
Algemeene Friesche, **III** 177–79
N.V. Algemeene Maatschappij tot
Exploitatie van
Verzekeringsmaatschappijen, **III** 199
Algemeene Maatschappij van
Levensverzekering en Lijfrente, **III** 178
Algemeene Maatschappij voor
Nijverheidskrediet, **II** 304–05
Algemeene Nederlandsche Maatschappij ter
begunstiging van de Volksvlijt, **II** 294
**Algemene Bank Nederland N.V., II
183–84,** 185, 239, 527; **III** 200
Algoma Steel, **8** 544–45
Algoma Steel Corp., **IV** 74
Algonquin Energy, Inc., **6** 487
Algonquin Gas Transmission Company, **6**
486
Alhadeff, Victor D., **9** 194–95
Alibrandi, Joseph F., **I** 544–45
Alidata, **6** 69
Aligro Inc., **II** 664
Alimentana S.A., **II** 547
Alitalia—Linee Aeree Italiana, SpA, I
110, 466–67; **6** 96, **68–69**
Alix, Jay, **10** 420
Alken, **II** 474
Oy Alkoholiliike Ab, **IV** 469
Alkor-Oerlikon Plastic GmbH, **7** 141
All American Airways, **I** 131. *See also*
USAir Group, Inc.
All American Aviation, **I** 131. *See also*
USAir Group, Inc.
All Nippon Airways Company Limited, I
106, 493; **6 70–71** 118, 427; **9** 233
Allaire, Paul A., **III** 173; **6** 290
Allami Biztosito, **III** 209
Allan, G.W., **III** 260
Allbritton, Joe, **IV** 684
Allders International, **III** 502
Allders Stores, **III** 502
Alleanza & Unione Mediterranea, **III** 208
Alleanza-Securitas-Esperia, **III** 208
Alleghany Corporation, II 398; **IV**
180–81; **10 43–45**
Alleghany Financial Corporation, **10** 44
Allegheny Airlines, **I** 131. *See also* USAir
Group, Inc.
Allegheny Beverage Corp., **7** 472–73
Allegheny County Light Company, **6**
483–84
Allegheny International, Inc., **III** 732; **8**
545; **9** 484
Allegheny Ludlum, **I**, 307; **II** 402
Allegheny Ludlum Corporation, 8 18–20
Allegheny Ludlum Industries Inc., **8**
19–20; **9** 484
Allegheny Ludlum Steel Corporation, **8**
18–20
Allegheny Power System, Inc., V 543–45
Allegheny Steel and Iron Company, **9** 484
Allegheny Steel Company, **9** 484
Allegis, Inc., **6** 129; **9** 283; **10** 301. *See
also* UAL, Inc.
Allegmeine Transpotmittel
Aktiengesellschaft, **6** 394
Allen & Co., **I** 512, 701; **II** 136
Allen & Hanbury's, **I** 640
Allen, B.R., **I** 320
Allen, Charles, **8** 395–97

Allen, Charles, Jr., **I** 512–13, 701
Allen, Darryl F., **III** 642
Allen, Fred, **II** 151
Allen, Gracie, **II** 133, 151
Allen, Harold G., **III** 329
Allen, Hart, Franz and Zehnder, **III** 204
Allen, Howard P., **V** 714, 717
Allen, James L., **10** 172–74
Allen, Kim, **9** 462
Allen, Paul, **6** 257–59
Allen, Paul G., **10** 57
Allen, Ralph, **V** 496
Allen, Ronald W., **6** 82
Allen, Roy, **I** 109
Allen, Wells P., Jr., **6** 535–36
Allen, William, **7** 558–59
Allen, William M. (''Bill''), **I** 48; **10** 163
Allen-Bradley Co., **I** 80; **II** 110; **III** 593;
11 429–30
Allen-Bradley/TDK Magnetics, **II** 110
Allen-Leversidge Ltd., **I** 315
Allende, Salvador, **I** 464
Aller, H.L., **6** 545
Aller, Howard, **6** 597
Allergan, Inc., 10 46–49
Allgemeine Deutsche Creditanstalt, **II** 211,
238, 383
Allgemeine Eisenbahn-Versicherungs-
Gesellschaft, **III** 399
Allgemeine Elektricitäts-Gesellschaft. *See*
AEG A.G.
Allgemeine Rentenstalt Lebens- und
Rentenversicherung, **II** 258
Allgemeine Versicherungs-Gesellschaft
Helvetia, **III** 375
Alliance Agro-Alimentaires S.A., **II** 577
Alliance Amusement Company, **10** 319
Alliance Assurance Co., **III** 369–73
Alliance Brothers, **V** 356
Alliance Insurance Co., **III** 224
Alliance Marine, **III** 373
Alliance Mortgage Co., **I** 610
Alliance Paper Group, **IV** 316
Alliance Tire and Rubber Co., **II** 47
Alliant Techsystems, Inc., 8 21–23
Allianz AG, **III** 186; **IV** 222
Allianz AG Holding, II 257, 279–80; **III
183–86,** 250, 252, 299–301, 347–48,
373, 377, 393
Allianz Allgemeine
Rechtsschutzversicherungs-AG, **III** 185
Allianz Insurance Co., **III** 185
Allianz International Insurance Co. Ltd.,
III 185
Allianz Lebensversicherungs-AG, **III** 184,
186, 200, 301
Allianz Lebensversicherungsbank-AG, **III**
183
Allianz Ultramar, **III** 185
Allianz Versicherungs-Aktien-Gesellschaft,
I 411, 426; **II** 239; **III** 183–85
Allibert, **III** 614
Allied Bakeries Ltd., **II** 465–66
Allied Breweries Ltd., **I** 215; **III** 105; **IV**
712
Allied Chemical, **I** 310, 332, 351–52; **8**
526; **9** 521–22
Allied Chemical & Dye Corp., **I** 414; **7**
262; **9** 154
Allied Color Industries, **8** 347
Allied Container Corp., **IV** 345
Allied Corp., **I** 68, 141, 143, 414, 534; **III**
118, 511; **6** 599; **7** 356; **9** 134; **11** 435

Allied Crude Vegetable Oil Refining Co., **II** 398; **10** 62
Allied Dunbar, **I** 427
Allied Engineering Co., **8** 177
Allied Food Markets, **II** 662
Allied Gas Company, **6** 529
Allied Grape Growers, **I** 261
Allied Health and Scientific Products Company, **8** 215
Allied Import Company, **V** 96
Allied Maintenance Corp., **I** 514
Allied Mills, Inc., **10** 249
Allied Oil Co., **IV** 373
Allied Overseas Trading Ltd., **I** 216
Allied Polymer Group, **I** 429
Allied Safety, Inc., **V** 215
Allied Signal, **V** 605
Allied Signal Engines, 9 12–15
Allied Steel and Wire Ltd., **III** 495
Allied Stores, **II** 350, 611–12
Allied Stores Corporation, **V** 25–8; **9** 211; **10** 282
Allied Structural Steel Company, **10** 44
Allied Supermarkets, Inc., **7** 570
Allied Suppliers, **II** 609
Allied Telephone Company. *See* Alltel Corporation.
Allied Tin Box Makers Ltd., **I** 604
Allied Towers Merchants Ltd., **II** 649
Allied Van Lines Inc., **6** 412, 414
Allied Vintners, **I** 215
Allied-Lyons plc, I 215–16, 258, 264, 438; **IV** 721; **9** 100, 391; **10** 170
Allied-Signal Inc., **I** 141, 143, **414–16**; **III** 511; **6** 599–600; **9** 519; **11** 444
Allis-Chalmers Corp., **I** 163; **II** 98, 121; **III** 543–44; **9** 17; **11** 104
Allison, **9** 417
Allison Gas Turbine Division, 9 16–19; **10** 537; **11** 473
Allison, James A., **9** 16
Allison, John P., **6** 523
Allison, Robert, Jr., **10** 83
Allmanna Svenska Elektriska Aktiebolaget, **II** 1; **IV** 66
Allmänna Telefonaktiebolaget L.M. Ericsson, **V** 334
Allnatt London & Guildhall Properties, **IV** 724
Allnet, **10** 19
Allo Pro, **III** 633
Allor Leasing Corp., **9** 323
Alloy & Stainless, Inc., **IV** 228
Alloys Unlimited, **II** 82
The Allstate Corporation, 10 50–52
Allstate Insurance Co., **I** 23; **III** 231–32, 259, 294; **V** 180, 182
Allstate Insurance Venture Capital Group, **6** 12
Alltel Corporation, 6 299–301
Alltel Mobile Communications, **6** 300
Alltel Publishing, **6** 300
Alltel Supply, Inc., **6** 300
Allyn, E.H., **9** 303
Allyn, Stanley, **6** 265–66
Allyn, Stanley C., **III** 151
Almac Electronics Corporation, **10** 113
Almaden Vineyards, **I** 377–78
Almanij. *See* Algemeene Maatschappij voor Nijverheidskrediet.
Almay, Inc., **III** 54
Almon, William, **6** 231
Almours Security Co., **IV** 311
Alocer, Alberto, **II** 198

Aloha Airlines, **I** 97; **9** 271–72
Alpen-Elektrowerke Aktiengesellschaft, **IV** 230
Alpert, Leon, **8** 338; **9** 323
Alpex Computer Corp., **III** 157
Alpha Beta Co., **II** 605, 625, 653
Alphonse Allard Inc., **II** 652
Alpina Versicherungs-Aktiengesellschaft, **III** 412
Alpine, **IV** 234
Alpine Electronics, **II** 5
Alps Electric Co., Ltd., II 5–6
Alric Packing, **II** 466
Alsen-Breitenbury, **III** 702
Alsons Corp., **III** 571
Alsthom, **II** 12
Alsthom-Atlantique, **9** 9
Alston, James O., **III** 765
Alta Gold Co., **IV** 76
ALTA Health Strategies, Inc., **11** 113
Alta Holidays Ltd., **I** 95
Altamil Corp., **IV** 137
Altan, Ozer, **IV** 563–64
Alte Leipziger, **III** 242
Altec Electronics, **I** 489–90
Alter, Dennis, **8** 9–11
Alter, J.R., **8** 9
Alter, Stewart, **I** 35
Alternate Postal Delivery, **6** 14
Althoff KG, **V** 101
Althoff, Theodor, **V** 100–02
Althouse Chemical Company, **9** 153
Althouse, Nathan, **9** 153
Althus Corp, **I** 361
Alton & Eastern Railroad Company, **6** 504
Alton Box Board Co., **IV** 295
Altos Computer Systems, **6** 279; **10** 362
Altschul, Selig, **I** 116
Aluma Systems Corp., **9** 512
Alumax, Inc., **I** 508; **III** 758; **IV** 18–19; **8** 505–06
Alumina Partners of Jamaica, **IV** 123
Aluminate Sales Corp, **I** 373
Aluminio de Galicia, **IV** 174
Aluminium Co. of London, **IV** 69
L'Aluminium Francais, **IV** 173
Aluminium Ltd., **IV** 9–11, 14, 153
Aluminium Plant and Vessel Co., **III** 419
Aluminium-Oxid Stade GmbH, **IV** 231
Aluminum Can Co., **I** 607
Aluminum Co. of Canada Ltd., **II** 345; **IV** 10–12, 154
Aluminum Company of America, **I** 373, 599; **II** 315, 402, 422; **III** 490–91, 613; **IV** 9–12, **14–16**, 56, 59, 121–22, 131, 173, 703; **6** 39
Aluminum Cooking Utensil Co., **IV** 14
Aluminum Forge Co., **IV** 137
Aluminum Norf GmbH, **IV** 231
Aluminum of Korea, **III** 516
Aluminum Seating Corp., **I** 201
Alun Cathcart, **6** 357
Alup-Kompressoren Pressorun, **III** 570
Alusaf, **IV** 92
Alusuisse, **IV** 12
Alva Jams Pty., **I** 437
Alvarez, Isidoro, **V** 51–53
Alyeska Pipeline Service Co., **IV** 522, 571
Alyeska Seafoods Co., **II** 578
ALZA Corporation, 10 53–55
Alzheimer, Alois, **III** 300
Alzwerke GmbH, **IV** 230
AM Acquisition Inc., **8** 559–60
Am-Par Records, **II** 129

Amadeo of Savoy, Luigi (Duke of the Abruzzi), **III** 346
Amagasaki Co., **I** 492
Amagasaki Spinners Ltd., **V** 387
Amagasaki Steel Co., Ltd., **IV** 130
Amalgamated Chemicals, Ltd., **IV** 401
Amalgamated Dental Company Limited, **10** 271
Amalgamated Dental International, **10** 272
Amalgamated Distilled Products, **II** 609
Amalgamated Press, **IV** 666; **7** 244, 342
Amalgamated Roadstone Corp., **III** 752
Amalgamated Weatherware, **IV** 696
Amana Refrigeration, **II** 86; **11** 413
Amano, Chiyomaru, **III** 656–57
Amarillo Railcar Services, **6** 580
Amarin Plastics, **IV** 290
Amato, Guiliano, **11** 205
AMAX Aluminum Group, **IV** 18
AMAX Chemical Corp., **IV** 18
AMAX Coal Co., **IV** 18
AMAX Inc., **I** 508; **IV** 17–19, 171, 239, 387; **6** 148
AMAX Petroleum Corp., **IV** 18
AMAX Potash Corp., **IV** 18
Amazôna Mineracao SA, **IV** 56
Ambac Industries, **I** 85
AmBase Corp., **III** 264
Ambridge, Douglas W., **IV** 246
Ambros, Otto, **I** 349
Ambrose Shardlow, **III** 494
AMCA International Corporation, **8** 545
AMCA International Finance Corporation, **7** 513
AMCA International, Ltd., **8** 545; **10** 329
Amchem Products Inc., **I** 666
Amcor Fibre Packaging, **IV** 250
Amcor Limited, **IV** 248–50
Amcor Packaging (Europe) Ltd., **IV** 250
AMD. *See* Advanced Micro Devices, Inc.
Amdahl, Burgee, **8** 490
Amdahl Corporation, **III** 109–11, 140; **6** 272
Amdahl, Gene M., **III** 109–10, 140
AME Finanziaria, **IV** 587
AMEC, **I** 568
Amedco, **6** 295
Amelio, Gilbert F., **6** 263
Amerada Corp., **IV** 365, 657
Amerada Hess Corporation, **IV** 365–67, 454, 522, 571
Amerada Hess Norge A/S, **IV** 367
Amerada Minerals Corp. of Canada Ltd., **IV** 367
Amerada Petroleum Company, **11** 353
Amerada Petroleum Corp., **IV** 365–66, 400, 522, 658
Amerco, 6 351–52
America Japan Sheet Glass Co., **III** 714
America Latina Companhia de Seguros, **III** 289
America Online, Inc., 10 56–58, 237
America West, **6** 121
America West Airlines, 6 72–74, 121
American Agricultural Chemical Co., **IV** 401
American Airlines, **I** 30–31, 48, 71, **89–91**, 97, 106, 115, 118, 124–26, 130, 132, 512, 530; **III** 102; **6** 60, 81, **75–77** **(upd.)**, 121, 129–31; **9** 271–72; **10** 163; **11** 279
American Airways Company, **II** 32; **6** 75
American Alliance Co., **III** 191
American Alliance Insurance Co., **III** 191

American Allsafe Co., **8** 386
American Amusements, Inc., **III** 430
American Appliance Co., **II** 85; **11** 411
American Arithmometer Company, **III** 165. *See also* Burroughs Corporation.
American Asiatic Underwriters, **III** 195
American Association of Retired Persons, **9** 348
American Automated, **11** 111
American Automobile Insurance Co., **III** 251
American Aviation and General Insurance Co., **III** 230
American Avitron Inc, **I** 481
American Bancorp, **11** 295
American Bancshares, Inc., **11** 457
American Bank, **9** 474–75
American Bank Note, **IV** 599
American Bankcorp, Inc., **8** 188
American Banker/Bond Buyer, **8** 526
American Barge and Towing Company, **11** 194
American Beet Sugar Company, **11** 13–14
American Bell Telephone Company, **V** 259
American Beryllium Co., Inc., **9** 323
American Beverage Corp., **II** 528
American Biodyne Inc., **9** 348
American Biomedical Corporation, **11** 333
American Biscuit Co., **II** 542
American Box Co., **IV** 137
American Brake Shoe and Foundry, **I** 456
American Brands Corporation, **7** 3–4
American Brands, Inc., **II** 468, 477; **IV** 251; **V** 395–97, 398–99, 405; **9** 408
American Bridge Co., **II** 330; **IV** 572; **7** 549
American Broadcasting Co., **I** 463–64; **II** 89, 129–33, 151, 156, 170, 173; **III** 188, 251–52; **6** 157–59, 164; **11** 197–98. *See also* Capital Cities/ABC Inc.
American Broadcasting Cos., **II** 130; **III** 214
American Broadcasting-Paramount Theatres, Inc., **II** 129
American Builders, Inc., **8** 436
American Building Maintenance Industries, Inc., **6** 17–19
American Cable Systems, Inc. *See* Comcast Corporation.
American Cablesystems, **7** 99
American Cafe, **I** 547
American Can Co., **IV** 36, 290; **8** 476;**10** 130; **11** 29, 197. *See also* Primerica Corp.
American Carbide Corporation, **7** 584
American Cash Register Co., **III** 150; **6** 264
American Casualty Co., **III** 230–31, 404
American Casualty Co. of Dallas, **III** 203
American Cellular Network, **7** 91
American Cellulose and Chemical Manufacturing Co., **I** 317
American Central Insurance Co., **III** 241
American Cereal Co., **II** 558
American Chicle, **I** 711
American Chocolate & Citrus Co., **IV** 409
American Chrome, **III** 699
American Clay Forming Company, **8** 178
American Clip Company, **7** 3
American Commercial Bank, **II** 336
American Commonwealths Power Corporation, **6** 579
American Community Grocers, **II** 670

American Continental Insurance Co., **III** 191–92
American Cotton Oil Co., **II** 497
American Credit Corp., **II** 236
American Crystal Sugar Company, **7** 377; **11** 13–15
American Cyanamid, **I** 300–02, 619; **III** 22; **IV** 345, 552; **8** 24–26 (upd.); **10** 269; **11** 494
American Dairy Queen Corporation, **10** 373
American Data Technology, Inc., **11** 111
American Distilling Co., **I** 226; **10** 180–81
American District Telegraph Co., **III** 644
American Eagle Fire Insurance Co., **III** 240–41
American Education Press, **10** 479
American Electric Co., **II** 27
American Electric Power Company, **II** 3; **IV** 181; **V** 546–49; **6** 449; **11** 516
American Electric Power Corporation, **6** 524
American Empire Insurance Co., **III** 191
American Emulsions Co., **8** 455
American Envelope Co., **III** 40
American Equipment Co., **I** 571
American Export Steamship Lines, **I** 89
American Express Bank, Ltd., **II** 398; **10** 62
American Express Company, **I** 26–27, 480, 614; **II** 108, 176, 309, 380–82, **395–99,** 450–52, 544; **III** 251–52, 319, 340; **IV** 637, 721; **6** 206–07, 409; **8** 118; **9** 335, 343, 391, 468–69, 538; **10** 44–45, **59–64** (upd.); **11** 41, 532
American Express Corp., **II** 398; **III** 389; **10** 62
American Express Field Warehousing Co., **II** 397; **10** 62
American Express International Banking Corp., **II** 398; **10** 62; **11** 416–17
American Express International Banking Corp., **II** 398; **10** 62; **11** 416–17
American Express Travel Related Services, **II** 398; **III** 252; **10** 62–63
American Factors Ltd., **I** 417, 566
American Family Corporation, **III** 187–89. *See also* AFLAC Inc.
American Family Life Assurance Co., **III** 187–88
American Feldmühle Corp., **II** 51
American Filtrona Corp., **IV** 260–61
American Finance Systems, **II** 349
American Financial Corporation, **II** 596; **III** 190–92, 221; **8** 537; **9** 452
American Financial Insurance Co., **III** 191
American Financial Insurance Group, **III** 191–92
American Flavor & Fragrance Company, **9** 154
American Food Management, **6** 45
American Fore Group, **III** 241–42
American Fore Loyalty Group, **III** 242
American Foreign Insurance Assoc., **III** 223, 226
American Forest Products Co., **IV** 282; **9** 260
American Gage Co., **I** 472
American Gas & Electric. *See* American Electric Power Company.
American Gasoline Co., **IV** 540
American General Capital Corp., **I** 614
American General Corporation, **III** 193–94; **10** 65–67 (upd.); **11** 16
American General Finance Corp., **11** 16–17

American General Insurance Co., **III** 193–94
American General Investment Corp., **III** 193
American General Life Insurance Company, **6** 294
American Greetings Corporation, **7** 23–25
American Greetings Publishers, **7** 23
American Grinder and Manufacturing Company, **9** 26
American Harvester, **II** 262
American Heritage Savings, **II** 420
American Hoist & Derrick Co., **8** 544
American Home Assurance Co., **III** 196–97
American Home Assurance Co. of New York, **III** 203
American Home Products, **I** 527, **622–24,** 631, 676–77, 696, 700; **III** 18, 36, 444; **8** 282–83; **10** 68–70 (upd.), 528; **11** 35
American Home Shield, **6** 46
American Home Video, **9** 186
American Honda Motor Co., **I** 174; **10** 352
American Hospital Association, **10** 159
American Hospital Supply Corp., **I** 627, 629; **III** 80; **10** 141–43; **11** 459, 486
American I.G. Chemical Corp., **I** 337
American Impacts Corporation, **8** 464
American Independent Oil Co., **IV** 522, 537. *See also* Aminoil, Inc.
American Industrial Manufacturing Co., **I** 481
American Information Services, Inc., **11** 111
American Instrument Co., **I** 628
American Insurance Agency, **III** 191, 352
American Insurance Co., **III** 251
American International Assurance Co., **III** 195
American International Group, Inc., **II** 422; **III** 195–98, 200; **6** 349; **10** 39; **11** 532–33
American International Healthcare, Inc., **III** 197
American International Insurance Co. of Ireland, Ltd., **III** 196
American International Life Assurance Co. of New York, **III** 196
American International Reinsurance Co., Inc., **III** 196–97
American International Travel Service, **6** 367
American International Underwriters, **III** 195
American International Underwriters Assoc., **III** 196
American International Underwriters Overseas, Ltd., **III** 196
American Iron and Steel Manufacturing Co., **IV** 35; **7** 48
American Jet Industries, **7** 205
American Ka-Ro, **8** 476
American La-France, **10** 296
American Laboratories, **III** 73
American Learning Corporation, **7** 168
American Life Insurance Co., **III** 195–96
American Light and Traction. *See* MCN Corporation.
American Lightwave Systems, Inc., **10** 19
American Limestone Co., **IV** 33
American Linseed Co, **II** 497

American Machine and Foundry Co., **II** 7;
 III 443; **7** 211–13; **11** 397
American Machine and Metals, **9** 23
American Machinist Press, **IV** 634
American Magnesium Products Co., **I** 404
**American Management Systems, Inc., 11
 18–20**
American Manufacturers Mutual Insurance
 Co., **III** 269, 271
American Medi-cal Enterprises, **III** 73
American Medical Holdings, Inc., **III**
 73–74
**American Medical International, Inc., III
 73–75**, 79
American Medical Services, **II** 679–80
American Medicorp., **III** 81; **6** 191
American Merchants Union Express Co., **II**
 396
American Metal Climax, Inc., **III** 687; **IV**
 18, 46
American Metal Co. Ltd., **IV** 17–19, 139
American Metal Products Corp., **I** 481
American Metals Corp., **III** 569
American Microsystems, **I** 193
American Milk Products Corp., **II** 487
The American Mineral Spirits Company, **8**
 99–100
American Motorists Insurance Co., **III** 269,
 271
American Motors Corp., I 135–37, 145,
 152, 190; **II** 60, 313; **III** 543; **6** 27, 50;
 8 373; **10** 262, 264
American Movie Classics Co., **II** 161
American National Bank and Trust Co., **II**
 286
American National Can Co., **III** 536; **IV**
 173, 175
American National Corp., **II** 286
American National Fire Insurance Co., **III**
 191
American National General Agencies Inc.,
 III 221
American National Insurance and Trust
 Company. *See* American National
 Insurance Company.
**American National Insurance Company,
 8 27–29**
American National Life Insurance
 Company of Texas, **8** 28–29
American Natural Resources Co., **I** 678;
 IV 395
American Newspaper Publishers
 Association, **6** 13
American of Philadelphia, **III** 234
American Oil Co., **IV** 369–70; **7** 101
American Oil Pipe Line Co., **IV** 370
American Olean Tile Co., **III** 424
American Optical Co., **I** 711–12; **III** 607;
 7 436
American Overseas Holdings, **III** 350
American Paging, **9** 494–96
American Petrofina, Inc., **IV** 498; **7**
 179–80
American Photographic Group, **III** 475; **7**
 161
American Physicians Service Group, Inc., **6**
 45
American Platinum Works, **IV** 78
American Postage Meter Co., **III** 156
American Potash and Chemical Corp., **IV**
 95, 446
American Power & Light Co., **6** 545,
 596–97

**American Premier Underwriters, Inc., 10
 71–74**
American President Companies Ltd., III
 512; **6 353–55**
American President Domestic Company, **6**
 354
American President Lines Ltd., **6** 353–54
American Protective Mutual Insurance Co.
 Against Burglary, **III** 230
American Publishing Co., **IV** 597
American Pure Oil Co., **IV** 497
American Radiator & Standard Sanitary
 Corp., **III** 663–64
American Radiator Co., **III** 663–64
American Railway Express Co., **II** 382,
 397; **10** 61
American Railway Publishing Co., **IV** 634
American Re Corporation, 10 75–77
American Re-Insurance Co., **III** 182
American Record Corp., **II** 132
American Ref-Fuel, **V** 751
American Refrigeration Products S.A, **7**
 429
American Republic Assurance Co., **III** 332
American Research and Development
 Corp., **II** 85; **III** 132; **6** 233
American Residential Holding Corporation,
 8 30–31
**American Residential Mortgage
 Corporation, 8 30–31**
American Resorts Group, **III** 103
American River Transportation Co., **I** 421;
 11 23
American Robot Corp., **III** 461
American Rolling Mill Co., **IV** 28; **8**
 176–77
American Royalty Trust Co., **IV** 84; **7** 188
American RX Pharmacy, **III** 73
American Safety Equipment Corp., **IV** 136
American Safety Razor Co., **III** 27–29
American Sales Book Co., Ltd., **IV** 644
American Satellite Co., **6** 279
American Savings & Loan, **10** 117
American Savings Bank, **9** 276
American Sealants Company. *See* Loctite
 Corporation.
American Seating Co., **I** 447
American Seaway Foods, Inc, **9** 451
American Sheet Steel Co., **IV** 572; **7** 549
American Smelters Securities Co., **IV** 32
American Smelting and Refining Co., **IV**
 31–33
American Standard Inc., III 437, **663–65**
American States Insurance Co., **III** 276
American Steamship Company, **6** 394–95
American Steel & Wire Co., **I** 355; **IV**
 572; **7** 549
American Steel Foundries, **7** 29–30
American Steel Hoop Co., **IV** 572; **7** 549
American Stock Exchange, **10** 416–17
American Stores Company, II 604–06
American Technical Services Company.
 See American Building Maintenance
 Industries, Inc.
**American Telephone and Telegraph
 Company, I** 462; **II** 13, 54, 61, 66, 80,
 88, 120, 252, 403, 430–31, 448; **III** 99,
 110–11, 130, 145, 149, 160, 162, 167,
 246, 282; **IV** 95, 287; **V 259–64**,
 265–68, 269, 272–75, 302–04, 308–12,
 318–19, 326–30, 334–36, 341–342,
 344–346; **6** 267, 299, 306–07, 326–27,
 338–40; **7** 88, 118–19, 146, 288, 333; **8**
 310–11; **9** 32, 43, 106–07, 138, 320,

321, 344, 478–80, 495, 514; **10** 19, 58,
 87, 97, 175, 202–03, 277–78, 286, 431,
 433, 455–57; **11** 10, 59, 91, 183, 185,
 196, 198, 302, 500–01
American Telephone and Telegraph
 Technologies Inc., **V** 339
American Television and Communications
 Corp., **I** 534–35; **II** 161; **IV** 596, 675; **7**
 528–30
American Textile Co., **III** 571
American Tin Plate Co., **IV** 572; **7** 549
American Title Insurance, **III** 242
American Tobacco Co., **I** 12–14, 28, 37,
 425; **V** 395–97, 399, 408–09, 417–18,
 600
American Tool & Machinery, **III** 420
American Totalisator Corporation, **10**
 319–20
American Tourister, Inc., **10** 350
American Tractor Corporation, **10** 379
American Trading and Production
 Corporation, **7** 101
American Transport Lines, **6** 384
American Trust and Savings Bank, **II** 261
American Trust Co., **II** 336, 382
American Ultramar Ltd., **IV** 567
American Viscose Corp. *See* Avisco.
American Water Works & Electric
 Company, **V** 543–44
**American Water Works Company, 6
 443–45**
American Woolen, **I** 529
American Yearbook Company, **7** 255
American-Marietta Corp., **I** 68, 405
American-Palestine Trading Corp., **II**
 205–06
American-South African Investment Co.
 Ltd., **IV** 79
American-Strevell Inc., **II** 625
**America's Favorite Chicken Company,
 Inc., 7 26–28**
AmeriFirst Bank, **11** 258
Amerifirst Federal Savings, **10** 340
Amerimark Inc., **II** 682
Amerisystems, **8** 328
Ameritech, V 265–68; 6 248; **7** 118; **10**
 431; **11** 382
Ameritech Development, **V** 265–68
Ameritech Information Systems, **V** 265,
 268
Ameritech Mobile Communications, Inc.,
 V 265–68
Ameritech Publishing Inc., **V** 265–68
Ameritrust Corporation, **9** 476
Amerman, John W., **7** 306
Amerotron, **I** 529
Amersil Co., **IV** 78
Ames, C.B., **7** 409
Ames, Charles W., **7** 580
Ames Department Stores, Inc., V
 197–98; **9 20–22**; **10** 497
Ames, Jack, **8** 268
Ames, Oakes, **V** 529
Ames, Oliver, **V** 529
Ames Worsted Textile Company, **9** 20
Amesh, Salem Mohammed, **IV** 453
AMETEK, Inc., 9 23–25
N.V. Amev, III 199–202
AMEV Australia, **III** 200
AMEV Finance, **III** 200
AMEV Financial Group, **III** 200
AMEV General Insurance, **III** 200
AMEV Holdings, **III** 201
AMEV Inc., **III** 200

AMEV International, **III** 199, 201
AMEV Levensverzekeringen, **III** 200–01
AMEV Life Assurance, **III** 200
AMEV Maatschappij voor belegging in aandelen NV, **III** 201
AMEV Nederland, **III** 199, 201
AMEV Schadeverzekering, **III** 201
AMEV South East Asia, **III** 200–01
AMEV Venture Management, **III** 200
AMEV Verzekeringen, **III** 200
Amey Roadstone Corp., **III** 503
Amey Roadstone Corporation, America, **7** 209
Amfac Inc., **I 417–18**, 566; **IV** 703; **10** 42
Amfas, **III** 310
Amgen, Inc., **I** 266; **8** 216–17; **10 78–81**
Amherst Coal Co., **IV** 410; **7** 309
Amiga Corporation, **7** 96
Aminoil, Inc., **IV** 523. *See also* American Independent Oil Co.
AMISA, **IV** 136
Amitron S.A., **10** 113
AMK Corporation, **II** 595; **7** 85
Ammentorp, Kjeld, **III** 737–38
Ammo-Phos, **I** 300; **8** 24
L'Ammoniac Sarro-Lorrain S.a.r.l., **IV** 197
Amoco Canada, **II** 376; **IV** 371
Amoco Chemicals Corp., **I** 202; **IV** 370–71
Amoco Corporation, **I** 516; **IV 368–71**, 412, 424–25, 453, 525; **7** 107, 443; **10** 83–84
Amoco Fabrics & Fibers Co., **IV** 371
Amoco Gas Company, **11** 441
Amoco International Oil Co., **IV** 370–71
Amoco Iran Oil Co., **IV** 371
Amoco Performance Products, **III** 611
Amory, Jean-Pierre, **IV** 499
Amos, Bill, **III** 187–88; **10** 28–29
Amos, Daniel P., **III** 188–89; **10** 29–30
Amos, John B., **III** 187–89; **10** 28–30
Amos, Paul S., **III** 187–89; **10** 30
Amos, Shelby, **III** 187; **10** 28
Amoseas, **IV** 453–54
Amoskeag Company, **6** 356; **8 32–33**; **9** 213–14, 217
AMP, Inc., **II 7–8**; **11** 319
AMP Special Industries, **II** 7
AMPAL. *See* American-Palestine Trading Corp.
AMPCO Auto Parks, Inc. *See* American Building Maintenance Industries, Inc.
AMPEP, **III** 625
Ampex Corp., **III** 549; **6** 272
Ampol Exploration Ltd., **III** 729
Ampol Ltd., **III** 729
Ampol Petroleum Ltd., **III** 729
AMR Corp., **I** 90–91; **6** 76; **8** 315
AMR Information Services, **9** 95
AMRE, **III** 211
Amrep S.A., **I** 563
Amro. *See* Amsterdam Rotterdam Bank N.V.
AMS Trading Co., **III** 112
Amstar Sugar, **II** 582; **7** 466–67
Amsted Industries Incorporated, **7 29–31**
Amstel Brewery, **I** 257
Amsterdam Bank, **II** 183–85
Amsterdam-Rotterdam Bank N.V., **II** 184, **185–86**, 279, 295, 319; **III** 200
Amstrad International (Hong Kong), **III** 112
Amstrad plc, **III 112–14**
Amtec Systems Corp., **11** 65

Amtech. *See* American Building Maintenance Industries, Inc.
Amtel, Inc., **8** 545; **10** 136
Amtliches Bayerisches Reisebüro, **II** 163
Amtrak, **II** 2; **10** 73
AmTrans. *See* American Transport Lines.
Amway (Japan) Ltd., **III** 14
Amway Corporation, **III 11–14**
Amway de Mexico, **III** 13
Amway Sales Corp., **III** 11–12
Amway Services Corp., **III** 11–12
Amylum, **II** 582
ANA Enterprises, Ltd., **6** 70
Anacomp, Inc., **11** 19
Anaconda Aluminum, **11** 38
Anaconda Co., **III** 644; **IV** 33, 376; **7** 261–63
Anaconda-Jurden Associates, **8** 415
Anadarko Petroleum Corporation, **10 82–84**
Analog Devices, Inc., **10 85–87**
Analytic Sciences Corporation, **10 88–90**
Anamax Mining Co., **IV** 33
AnAmo Co., **IV** 458
ANB Bank, **I** 55
Anchor Bancorp, Inc., **10 91–93**
Anchor Cable, **III** 433
Anchor Financial Corporation, **10** 92
Anchor Mortgage Resources, Inc., **10** 91
Anchor Mortgage Services, Inc., **10** 92
Anchor National Financial Services, Inc., **11** 482
Anchor National Life Insurance Company, **11** 482
Anchor Oil and Gas Co., **IV** 521
Anchor Records, **II** 130
Anchor Savings Bank F.S.B., **10** 91–93
Anchor Savings Bank F.S.B. New Jersey, **10** 92
Anchor-Hocking, **I** 609–10
Ancienne Mutuelle, **III** 210
Ancienne Mutuelle du Calvados, **III** 210
Ancienne Mutuelle Transport de Bétail, **III** 210
Anderer, Joseph, **III** 55
Anderheggen, Erwin, **IV** 198
Anders, William A., **10** 318
Andersen, Anthony L., **8** 239–40
Andersen, Arthur Edward, **10** 115–16
Andersen Consulting, **9** 344; **11** 305
Andersen Corporation, **10 94–95**
Andersen, Elmer, **8** 237–39
Andersen, Fred, **10** 94
Andersen, Hans Jacob, **10** 94
Andersen, Herbert, **10** 94
Anderson & Kerr Drilling Co., **IV** 445
Anderson, A.D., **II** 515
Anderson, Abraham, **III** 479; **7** 66
Anderson and Campbell, **II** 479
Anderson, Arthur, **V** 490–91
Anderson, Ben, **11** 225
Anderson Box Co., **IV** 342; **8** 267
Anderson, Charles A., **10** 379
Anderson Clayton & Co., **II** 560
Anderson, Donald, **V** 492
Anderson, Ed, **10** 233
Anderson, Fred, **8** 183; **11** 275
Anderson, Fred D., **11** 275
Anderson, Gene, **IV** 119–20
Anderson, Gerald, **8** 35–36
Anderson, Greenwood & Co., **11** 225–26
Anderson, Harlan, **III** 132–33
Anderson, Harland, **6** 233–34
Anderson, Harold, **III** 670

Anderson, James L., **IV** 445
Anderson, Noble, **11** 25
Anderson, O. Kelley, **III** 313
Anderson, Pamela K., **III** 84
Anderson, Peter, **11** 275
Anderson, Ray C., **8** 270–72
Anderson, Richard, **II** 262
Anderson, Robert, **I** 79–80; **11** 429
Anderson, Robert O., **IV** 375–76
Anderson, Robert R., **11** 231–32
Anderson, Roger, **II** 262
Anderson, Roy A., **I** 66; **11** 268
Anderson Testing Company, Inc., **6** 441
Anderson, Truman E., **10** 102
Anderson, Warren, **I** 400–01; **9** 518
Anderson, William S., **III** 152; **6** 266
Anderton, **III** 624
Anderton, James, **IV** 39
Andes Candies, **II** 520–21
Andian National Corp. Ltd., **IV** 415–16
Ando, Norinago, **III** 405
Ando, Taro, **IV** 726–27
Ando, Toyoroku, **III** 718
Andrae, Herman, **II** 421
André Courrèges, **III** 47; **8** 342–43
Andreas Christ, **6** 404
Andreas, Dwayne O., **I** 420–21; **11** 22–23
Andreas, Michael, **11** 23
Andress, James, **10** 359
Andrew Corporation, **10 96–98**
Andrew Jergens Co., **III** 38
Andrew, Victor J., **10** 96
Andrew Weir & Co., **III** 273
Andrews, C.F., **IV** 218
Andrews, Clark & Company, **IV** 426; **7** 169
Andrews, Cliff, **8** 178
Andrews Group, Inc., **10** 402
Andrews, Matthew, **8** 346
Andrews, Samuel, **IV** 426–27; **7** 169–70
Andrews, T. Coleman, III, **10** 561
Andrus, Major, **10** 377
Anfor, **IV** 249–50
Angele Ghigi, **II** 475
Angelo's Supermarkets, Inc., **II** 674
Angerstein, John Julius, **III** 278
ANGI Ltd., **11** 28
Angiulo, Gennaro J., **II** 208
Anglo. *See* Anglo American Corporation of South Africa Limited.
Anglo American Construction, **IV** 22
Anglo American Corporation of South Africa Limited, **I** 289, 423; **IV 20–23**, 56–57, 64–68, 79–80, 90, 92, 94–96, 118–20, 191, 239–40; **7** 121–23, 125
Anglo American Investment Trust, **IV** 21
Anglo American Paper Co., **IV** 286
Anglo Company, Ltd., **9** 363
Anglo Energy, Ltd., **9** 364
Anglo Mexican Petroleum Co. Ltd., **IV** 657
Anglo-American Chewing Gum Ltd., **II** 569
Anglo-American Clays Corp., **III** 691; **IV** 346
Anglo-American Oil Company Limited, **IV** 427; **7** 170
Anglo-American Telegraph Co., **IV** 668
Anglo-Belge, **II** 474
Anglo-Canadian, **III** 704
Anglo-Canadian Mining & Refining, **IV** 110

Anglo-Canadian Telephone Company of Montreal. *See* British Columbia Telephone Company.
Anglo-Dutch Unilever group, **9** 317
Anglo-Egyptian D.C.O., **II** 236
Anglo-Elementar-Versicherungs-AG, **III** 185
Anglo-Huronian Ltd., **IV** 164
Anglo-Iranian Oil Co., **IV** 379, 419, 435, 450, 466, 559; **7** 57, 141
Anglo-Lautaro Nitrate Corporation, **9** 363
Anglo-Palestine Bank, **II** 204
Anglo-Palestine Co., **II** 204
Anglo-Persian Oil Co., **IV** 363, 378–79, 381, 429, 450, 466, 515, 524, 531, 557–59; **7** 56–57, 140
Anglo-Swiss Condensed Milk Co., **II** 545
Anglo-Thai Corp., **III** 523
Anglo-Transvaal Consolidated, **IV** 534
Anglund, Joan Walsh, **IV** 622
Angot, Pierre, **IV** 544
Angus Hill Holdings, **IV** 249
Angus, M.R., **II** 590
Angus, Michael, **9** 318
Anheuser, Eberhard, **I** 217; **10** 99
Anheuser-Busch Company, Inc., I 32, **217–19**, 236–37, 254–55, 258, 265, 269–70, 290–91, 598; **IV** 624; **6** 20–21, 48; **9** 100; **10 99–101 (upd.)**, 130; **11** 421
ANIC Gela, **IV** 421
Anikem, **I** 374
Anitec Image Technology Corp., **IV** 287
Anker, Peter, **IV** 711–12
Annabelle's, **II** 480–81
Annenberg, Moses, **IV** 629
Annenberg, Walter, **IV** 629
AnnTaylor, **V** 26–27
Annuaries Marcotte Ltd., **10** 461
Anonima Infortunia, **III** 208
Ansa Software, **9** 81
Ansaldo, **II** 191
Anschütz & Co. GmbH, **III** 446
Anschutz, Philip, **V** 517–18; **11** 198
Anschütz-Kaempfe, **III** 446
Ansell, **I** 215
Ansell, Joseph, **I** 215
Ansell Rubber Company, **10** 445
Ansett Airlines, **6** 73
Ansett, Reginald (Sir), **IV** 651; **V** 523; **7** 390
Ansett Transport Industries Limited, **V** 523–25
Anson, Frank H., **IV** 245
Ansonia Brass and Battery Co., **IV** 176–77
Ansonia Manufacturing Co., **IV** 176
Ant Nachrichtentechnik GmbH., **I** 411
Anta Corporation, **6** 188
Antar group, **IV** 544, 546
Antares Electronics, Inc., **10** 257
ANTEX. *See* American National Life Insurance Company of Texas.
Anthes Imperial Ltd., **I** 274
Anthes Industries Inc., **9** 512
Anthony, Barbara Cox, **IV** 596–97
Anthony, Garner, **IV** 596–97
Anthony Stumpf Publishing Company, **10** 460
Antico, Tristan (Sir), **III** 728–29
Antillaase Bank-Unie N.V., **II** 184
Antle, Glen M., **11** 45–46
Antoine Saladin, **III** 675
Antwerp Co., **IV** 497

ANZ. *See* Australia and New Zealand Banking Group Ltd.
Anzon Ltd., **III** 681
AOE Plastic GmbH, **7** 141
Aoi, Chuji, **V** 127–28
Aoi, Joichi, **I** 535
Aoi, Tadao, **V** 127–28
Aoki Corporation, **9** 547, 549
AON Corporation, III 203–05
Aon Reinsurance Agency, **III** 205
AON Risk Services, **III** 205
AP. *See* Associated Press.
AP&L. *See* American Power & Light Co.
AP-Dow Jones, **10** 277
AP-Dow Jones/Telerate Company, **10** 277
APAC, Inc., **IV** 374
Apache Corp., 10 102–04; 11 28
Apache Petroleum Company, **10** 103
Apex Financial Corp., **8** 10
Apex Smelting Co., **IV** 18
Apita, **V** 210
APL. *See* American President Lines Ltd.
APL Associates, **6** 353
APL Corporation, **9** 346
APL Information Services, Ltd., **6** 354
APL Land Transport Services Inc., **6** 354
APM Ltd., **IV** 248–49
Apogee Enterprises, Inc., 8 34–36
Apollo Computer, **III** 143; **6** 238; **9** 471; **11** 284
Apollo Ski Partners LP of New York, **11** 543, 545
Apollo Technologies, **I** 332
Apotekarnes Droghandel A.B., **I** 664–65
Appalachian Computer Services, **11** 112
Appel, Daniel F., **III** 313
Appel, Uranus J. (Bob), **III** 73
Appell, Louis J., **8** 509
Appell, Louis J., Jr., **8** 509–10
Apple Computer, Inc., II 6, 62, 103, 107, 124; **III** 114, **115–16**, 121, 125, 149, 172; **6 218–20 (upd.)**, 222, 225, 231, 244, 248, 254–58, 260, 289; **8** 138; **9** 166, 170–71, 368, 464; **10** 22–23, 34, 57, 233, 235, 404, 458–59, 518–19; **11** 45, 50, 57, 62, 490
Apple Container Corp., **III** 536
Apple Europe, **6** 219
Apple Pacific, **6** 219
Apple Products, **6** 219
Apple USA, **6** 219
Appleseed, Johnny, **11** 210
Appleton & Cox, **III** 242
Appleton Papers, **I** 426
Appleton Wire Works Corp., **8** 13
Appliance Buyers Credit Corp., **III** 653
Les Applications du Roulement, **III** 623
Applied Bioscience International, Inc., 10 105–07
Applied Color Systems, **III** 424
Applied Communications, Inc., **6** 280; **11** 151
Applied Data Research, Inc., **6** 225
Applied Digital Data Systems Inc., **II** 83; **9** 514
Applied Engineering Services, Inc. *See* The AES Corporation.
Applied Komatsu Technology, Inc., **10** 109
Applied Learning International, **IV** 680
Applied Materials, Inc., 10 108–09
Applied Power, Inc., 9 26–28
Applied Solar Energy, **8** 26
Applied Technology Corp., **11** 87
Approvisionnement Atlantique, **II** 652

Appryl, **I** 303
Apps, Frederick L., **III** 274
APS. *See* Arizona Public Service Company.
Apura GmbH, **IV** 325
APUTCO, **6** 383
Aqua Glass, **III** 570
Aqua Pure Water Co., **III** 21
Aqua-Chem, Inc., **I** 234; **10** 227
Aquarius Group, **6** 207
Aquila, **IV** 486
Aquila Energy Corp., **6** 593
Aquino, Corazon, **6** 106–07
Aquitaine. *See* Société Nationale des Petroles d'Aquitaine.
AR-TIK Systems, Inc., **10** 372
ARA Holding Co., **II** 608
ARA Services, II 607–08
Arab Contractors, **III** 753
Arab Japanese Insurance Co., **III** 296
Arab Petroleum Pipeline Co., **IV** 412
Arabian American Oil Co., **I** 570; **IV** 386, 429, 464–65, 512, 536–39, 552, 553, 559; **7** 172, 352. *See also* Saudi Arabian Oil Co.
Arabian Gulf Oil Co., **IV** 454
Arabian Oil Co., **IV** 451
Arai, Akira, **IV** 656
Arakawa, Masashi, **7** 220–21
Araki, Yoshiro, **II** 293
Aral, **IV** 487
Aramco. *See* Arabian American Oil Co. *and* Saudi Arabian Oil Company.
de Araoz, Daniel, **6** 95
Araskog, Rand Vincent, **I** 462, 464; **11** 196, 198
Aratsu Sekiyu, **IV** 554
ARBED Finance S.A., **IV** 26
ARBED S.A., **IV** 24–27, 53
ARBED-Felten & Guilleaume Tréfileries Réunies, **IV** 26
d'Arbeloff, Alexander V., **11** 502–04
Arbitron Corp., **III** 128; **10** 255, 359
Arbor Living Centers Inc., **6** 478
Arbuckle, Ernest C., **II** 382
Arbuckle, Fatty, **II** 154
Arbuthnot & Co., **III** 522
Arby's, **II** 614; **8** 536–37
ARC Ltd., **III** 501
ARC Materials Corp., **III** 688
Arcadian Marine Service, Inc., **6** 530
Arcata National Corp., **9** 305
Arcelik, **I** 478
Arch Mineral Corporation, **IV** 374; **7 32–34**
Archbold, John D., **IV** 428, 488; **7** 171
Archer Daniels Midland Chemicals Co., **IV** 373
Archer Drug, **III** 10
Archer, George A., **I** 419; **11** 21
Archer, James, **6** 558
Archer, Shreve M., Jr., **I** 420; **11** 22
Archer-Daniels Linseed Co., **I** 419
Archer-Daniels-Midland Co., I 419–21; **7** 432–33; **8** 53; **11 21–23 (upd.)**
Archers Gilles & Co., **II** 187
Archibald, Nolan D., **III** 437
ARCO. *See* Atlantic Richfield Company.
ARCO Alaska, **IV** 376
ARCO Chemical Company, **IV** 376–77, 456–57; **10 110–11**
ARCO Coal Co., **IV** 376
Arco Electronics, **9** 323
ARCO International, **IV** 376

ARCO Oil and Gas, **IV** 376; **8** 261
ARCO Products Co., **IV** 376–77, 456
Arco Societa Per L'Industria Elettrotecnica, **II** 82
ARCO Solar, **IV** 376–77
ARCO Transportation, **IV** 376
Arctic, **III** 479
ARD. *See* American Research & Development.
Ardal og Sunndal Verk AS, **10** 439
Ardbo, Martin, **9** 381
Ardell, William, **7** 488
Arden, Elizabeth, **8** 166–68
Ardent Computer Corp., **III** 553
Ardic, Furuzan, **IV** 563
Ardrey, Alex H., **II** 230
Areal Technologies, **III** 715
Areces Rodriguez, Ramón, **V** 51–53
Arend, Francis, **III** 419
Argbeit-Gemeinschaft Lurgi und Ruhrchemie, **IV** 534
Argo Communications Corporation, **6** 300
Argonaut, **I** 523–24; **10** 520–22
Argos, **I** 426
Argus, **IV** 22, 611
Argus Chemical Co., **I** 405
Argus Corp., **IV** 272
Argus Energy, **7** 538
Argyll Foods, **II** 609
Argyll Group PLC, I, 241; **II 609–10,** 656
Arison, Micky, **6** 367–68
Arison, Ted, **6** 367–68
Arizona Copper Co., **IV** 177
Arizona Edison Co., **6** 545
Arizona Public Service Company, **6** 545–47
Ark Securities Co., **II** 233
Arkady Co., **I** 421
Arkady Co., Ltd., **11** 23
Arkansas Breeders, **II** 585
Arkansas Chemicals Inc., **I** 341
Arkansas-Louisiana Gas, **11** 441
Arkansas Louisiana Gas Company. *See* Arkla, Inc.
Arkansas Power & Light, **V** 618
Arkay Computer, **6** 224
ARKE, **II** 164
Arkla Exploration Company, **11** 441
Arkla, Inc., V 550–51
Arkwright, Preston, **6** 446–47
Arledge, Roone, **II** 130
Arlesey Lime and Portland Cement Co., **III** 669
Arlington Corporation, **6** 295
Arlington Motor Holdings, **II** 587
Armacost, Samuel, **II** 228
Armani, Georgio, **8** 129
Armaturindistri, **III** 569
ARMCO, **11** 5
Armco Financial Corp., **IV** 29
Armco Financial Services Corp., **IV** 28–29
Armco Inc., III 259, 721; **IV 28–30,** 125, 171; **10** 448
Armco Steel Corp., **IV** 28–29; **11** 255
Armco-Boothe Corp., **IV** 29
Armin Corp., **III** 645
Armin Poly Film Corp., **III** 645
Armitage Shanks, **III** 671
Armor Elevator, **11** 5
Armour & Company, **8** 144
Armour Dial, **I** 14
Armour family, **IV** 372

Armour Food Co., **I** 449–50, 452; **II** 494, 518
Armour, J. Ogden, **6** 510–11
Armour Pharmaceutical Co., **III** 56
Armour-Dial, **8** 144
Armsby, George, **7** 131
Armsby, J.K., **7** 131
Armstrong Advertising Co., **I** 36
Armstrong Air Conditioning Inc., **8** 320–22
Armstrong Autoparts, **III** 495
Armstrong, Brother & Co., Inc., **III** 422
Armstrong, Charles Dickey, **III** 422–23
Armstrong Communications, **IV** 640
Armstrong Cork Co., **III** 422–23
Armstrong, F. Wallis, **I** 36
Armstrong, Neil, **II** 89
Armstrong Nurseries, **I** 272
Armstrong Rees Ederer Inc., **IV** 290
Armstrong, Thomas Morton, **III** 422
Armstrong, Whitworth & Co. Ltd., **I** 50; **III** 508; **IV** 257
Armstrong, William W., **III** 291, 316, 337
Armstrong World Industries, Inc., III 422–24; 9 466
Armstrong-Siddeley Co., **III** 508
Armstrong-Siddeley Development, **III** 508
Armtek, **7** 297
Army Cooperative Fire Insurance Company, **10** 541
Army Signal Corps Laboratories, **10** 96
Arnao, Charles, Jr. **10** 102
Arnault, Bernard, **10** 399
Arndale, **IV** 696
Arno Press, **IV** 648
Arnof, Ian, **11** 106
Arnold Foods Co., **II** 498
Arnold, Matthew, **7** 166
Arnold Thomas Co., **9** 411
Arnoldo Mondadori Editore S.p.A., IV 585–88, 675
Arnotts Ltd., **II** 481
Aro Corp., **III** 527
Aromat Corporation, **III** 710; **7** 303
Aron, Adam, **III** 97
Arpet Petroleum, **III** 740; **IV** 550
Arpic, **III** 426
Arrigoni, Louis, **9** 160
Arrison, Clement R., **7** 296–98
Arrow Electronics, Inc., 10 112–14
Arrow Food Distributor, **II** 675
Arrow Oil Co., **IV** 401
Arrow Oil Tools, **III** 570
Arrow Pump Co., **I** 185
Arrow Radio, **10** 112
Arrow Specialty Co., **III** 570
Arrowsmith & Silver, **I** 428
A.B. Arsenalen, **II** 352
Artec, **III** 420
Artesian Manufacturing and Bottling Company, **9** 177
Artex Enterprises, **7** 256
Arther, William, **6** 38
Arthur Andersen, **III** 143; **6** 244; **10** 174
Arthur Andersen & Company, Société Coopérative, 10 115–17
Arthur D. Little, **IV** 494; **10** 139, 174–75
Arthur Ovens Motor Freight Co., **6** 371
Arthur Tappan & Co., **IV** 604
Arthur Young, **IV** 119. *See also* Ernst & Young.
Arthur Young & Company, **10** 386
Arts & Entertainment Network, **IV** 627
Artzt, Edwin L., **III** 53

Arvey Corp., **IV** 287
Arvida Corp., **IV** 703
Arvin Heater Company, **8** 37
Arvin Industries, Inc., 8 37–40
Arvin, Richard Hood, **8** 37
ASAB, **III** 480
Asada, Shizuo, **I** 105
Asahi Breweries Ltd., I 220–21, 282, 520
Asahi Chemical Industry Co., **I** 221; **III** 760; **IV** 326
Asahi Glass Company, Limited, I 363; **III 666–68; 11** 234–35
Asahi Kasei Industry Co. Ltd., **IV** 476
Asahi Komag Co., Ltd., **11** 234
Asahi Kyoei Co., **I** 221
Asahi Manufacturing, **III** 592
Asahi Milk Products, **II** 538
Asahi National Broadcasting Company, Ltd., 9 29–31
Asahi Oil, **IV** 542
Asahi Processed Glass, **III** 667
Asahi Real Estate Facilities Co., Ltd., **6** 427
Asahi Seiko, **III** 595
Asahi Shimbun, **9** 29–30
Asahi Special Glass, **III** 667
Asahi Trust & Banking, **II** 323
Asai, Koji, **II** 361
Asano Group, **III** 718
Asano, Ryozo, **IV** 162
Asano, Shuichi, **III** 486
Asano, Taro, **V** 679
ASARCO Incorporated, I 142; **IV 31–34**
ASARCO Mexican, S.A., **IV** 33
ASB Agency, Inc., **10** 92
ASB/NJ Agency, Inc., **10** 92
Aschaffenburger Zellstoffwerke AG, **IV** 323–24
Ascom AG, 9 32–34
Ascometal, **IV** 227
ASD, **IV** 228
ASDA, **11** 240
Asda Group PLC, II 611–12, 513, 629
Asda Stores Ltd., **II** 611–12
ASEA A.B., **II** 1–4; **III** 427; **IV** 204, 300
Asea Brown Boveri. *See* ABB ASEA Brown Boveri Ltd.
ASEA-ATOM, **II** 2
Asean Bintulu Fertilizer, **IV** 518
A.B. Asesores Bursatiles, **III** 197–98
ASF. *See* American Steel Foundries.
Ash Company, **10** 271
Ash, Mary Kay, **9** 330–31
Ash, Roy, **I** 484–85; **II** 33; **11** 263–64
Ashburton, Lord, **7** 58
Ashcroft, Ken, **III** 114
Ashe, William J., **I** 406
Asher, Garland, **6** 244
Ashford, James K., **10** 380
Ashitaka Rinsan Kogyo, **IV** 269
Ashland Chemical Co., **IV** 373; **8** 99; **9** 108
Ashland Coal, Inc., **IV** 198, 374
Ashland Exploration, Inc., **IV** 374
Ashland Iron and Mining Co., **IV** 28
Ashland Oil & Refining Co., **I** 420; **IV** 373, 453
Ashland Oil Canada Ltd., **IV** 373–74
Ashland Oil Company, **7** 32–33
Ashland Oil, Inc., IV 71, 366, **372–74,** 472, 658; **11** 22
Ashland Refining Co., **IV** 372–73
Ashland Services Co., **IV** 374
Ashley, Richard C., **I** 332

Ashton, Alan, **10** 556–57
Ashton Joint Venture, **IV** 60, 67
Ashton Mining, **IV** 60
Ashton-Tate Corporation, **9** 81–82; **10** 504–05
Asia Life Insurance Co., **III** 195–96
Asia Oil Co., Ltd., **IV** 404, 476
Asia Television, **IV** 718
Asia Terminals Ltd., **IV** 718
Asiain, Jose Angel Sanchez, **II** 195
Asiana Airlines, **9** 233
Asiatic Petroleum Co., **IV** 434, 530
Asil çelik, **I** 479
ASK Group, Inc., 9 35–37
ASK Micro, **9** 35. *See also* Software Dimensions, Inc.
Asland SA, **III** 705, 740
Asmussen, Henry F., **7** 580
Aso Cement, **III** 705
Aso, Yutaka, **III** 705
Aspdin, Joseph, **III** 669
Aspen Mountain Gas Co., **6** 568
Aspen Skiing, **II** 170
Asquith, Henry, **II** 318
Asquith, Herbert, **III** 521
Assaf, Ronald G., **11** 443–44
Assam Co. Ltd., **III** 522–23
Assam Oil Co., **IV** 441, 483–84
L'Assicuratrice Italiana, **III** 346–47
Assicurazioni Generali Austro-Italiche, **III** 206–09
Assicurazioni Generali S.p.A., II 192; **III 206–09**, 211, 296, 298
Associated Anglo-Atlantic Corp., **III** 670
Associated Aviation Underwriters, **III** 220
Associated Banks of Europe Corp., **II** 184, 239
Associated Biscuit Co., **II** 631
Associated Book Publishers, **8** 527
Associated Bowater Industries, **IV** 258
Associated Brewing Co., **I** 254
Associated British Foods PLC, II 465–66, 565, 609; **11** 526
Associated British Maltsters, **II** 500
Associated British Picture Corp., **I** 531; **II** 157
Associated City Investment Trust, **IV** 696
Associated Communications Corporation, **7** 78
Associated Cooperative Investment Trust Ltd., **IV** 696
Associated Dairies and Farm Stores Ltd., **II** 611
Associated Dairies Ltd., **II** 611
Associated Dry Goods, **V** 134
Associated Electrical Industries, Ltd., **II** 25; **III** 502
Associated Employers General Agency, **III** 248
Associated Food Holdings Ltd., **II** 628
Associated Fresh Foods, **II** 611–12
Associated Fuel Pump Systems Corp., **III** 593
Associated Gas & Electric Company, **V** 621, 629–30; **6** 534
Associated Gas Services, Inc., **11** 28
Associated Grocers, Incorporated, 9 38–40
Associated Grocers of Arizona, **II** 625
Associated Grocers of Colorado, **II** 670
The Associated Group, **10** 45
Associated Hospital Service of New York, **III** 245–46
Associated Iliffe Press, **IV** 666

Associated Indemnity Co., **III** 251
Associated Insurance Cos., **III** 194
Associated Lead Manufacturers Ltd., **III** 679, 680–81
Associated London Properties, **IV** 705
Associated Madison Insurance, **I** 614
Associated Milk Producers, Inc., 11 24–26
Associated National Insurance of Australia, **III** 309
Associated Natural Gas Corporation, 11 27–28
Associated Newspapers, **IV** 686
Associated Octel Company Limited, **10** 290
Associated Oil Co., **IV** 460
Associated Pipeline Contractors, **III** 559
Associated Piping & Engineering Corp., **III** 535
Associated Portland Cement Manufacturers (1900) Ltd., **III** 669–71
Associated Press, **IV** 629, 669–70; **7** 158; **10** 277
Associated Pulp & Paper Mills, **IV** 328
Associated Spring, **III** 581
Associated Television, **7** 78
Associated Timber Exporters of British Columbia Ltd., **IV** 307
Associated TV, **IV** 666
Associates Investment Co., **I** 452
Assubel, **III** 273
Assurances du Groupe de Paris, **III** 211
Assurances Generales de France, **III** 351
AST Holding Corp., **III** 663, 665
AST Research, Inc., 9 41–43; 10 459, 518–19
Asta Pharma AG, **IV** 71
Asta Werke AG, **IV** 71
Asteroid, **IV** 97
Astley & Pearce, **10** 277
Astor family, **IV** 687
Astor, John Jacob, **II** 312; **III** 247
Astor Trust Co., **II** 229
Astor, Vincent, **I** 61; **11** 164
Astra A.B., I 625–26, 635, 651; **11** 290
Astrolac, **IV** 498
Astrotech, **11** 429
Aswell, Edward, **IV** 636
Asylum Life Assurance Co., **III** 371
Asymetrix, **6** 259
AT&T. *See* American Telephone and Telegraph Company.
AT&T Communications, **V** 262–63
AT&T Global Information Solutions, **11** 395
AT&T Microelectronics, **II** 125
AT&T Network Systems International, **V** 262–63
AT&T Ricoh Co., **III** 160
AT&T Technologies, **V** 262–63; **7** 289
Ataka & Co., **I** 433; **II** 361
Atari Corporation, II 176; **III** 587; **IV** 676; **6** 244; **7** 395–96; **9 44–47**; **10** 284, 482, 485
Atatürk, Kemal, **I** 478
ATC, **III** 760
Atchison, Topeka and Santa Fe Railroad, **V** 507–08
ATD Group, **10** 113
ATE Investment, **6** 449
Atelier de Construction Electrique de Delle, **9** 9
ATEQ Corp., **III** 533
Atex, **III** 476; **7** 162; **10** 34

ATH AG, **IV** 221
Atha Tool Co., **III** 627
Athalon Products Ltd., **10** 181
Athens National Bank, **III** 190
Athens Piraeus Electricity Co., **IV** 658
Atherton, Frank C., **9** 275
Atherton, Henry, **I** 415
Atherton, James B., **III** 433
Atherton, Joe, **II** 490
ATI, **IV** 651; **7** 390
Atkins, Orin, **IV** 374; **7** 32–33
Atlanta Braves, **II** 166
Atlanta Gas Light Company, 6 446–48
Atlanta Hawks, **II** 166
Atlanta Paper Co., **IV** 311
Atlantic Acceptance Corporation, **7** 95
Atlantic Aircraft Corp., **I** 34
Atlantic and Pacific Telegraph Company, **6** 338
Atlantic Cement Co., **III** 671
Atlantic City Electric Company, **6** 449
Atlantic Energy, Inc., 6 449–50
Atlantic Energy Technology, Inc., **6** 449–50
Atlantic Generation, Inc., **6** 449–50
Atlantic Gulf and Caribbean Airways, **I** 115
Atlantic Import, **I** 285
Atlantic Light and Power Company, **6** 449
Atlantic Precision Works, **9** 72
Atlantic Records, **II** 176
Atlantic Refining Co., **III** 497; **III** 498; **IV** 375–76, 456, 504, 566, 570
Atlantic Richfield Canada, **IV** 494
Atlantic Richfield Company, I 452; **II** 90, 425; **III** 740; **IV 375–77**, 379, 435, 454, 456–57, 467, 494, 522, 536, 571; **7** 57, 108, 537–38, 558–59; **8** 184, 416; **10** 110
The Atlantic Seaboard Dispatch. *See* GATX.
Atlantic Securities Ltd., **II** 223; **III** 98
Atlantic Southern Properties, Inc., **6** 449–50
Atlantic Surety Co., **III** 396
Atlantic Wholesalers, **II** 631
Atlantic-Union Oil, **IV** 570
Atlantis Ltd., **II** 566
AB Atlas, **III** 425, 480
Atlas Assurance Co., **III** 370
Atlas Chemical Industries, **I** 353
Atlas Copco AB, III 425–27; IV 203
Atlas Copco Airpower, **III** 427
Atlas Copco MCT, **III** 427
Atlas Copco Tools, **III** 427
Atlas Corp., **I** 58, 512; **10** 316
Atlas Diesel, **III** 426
Atlas Hotels, Inc., **V** 164
Atlas Petroleum Ltd., **IV** 449
Atlas Powder Co., **I** 343–44
Atlas Shipping, **I** 285
Atlas Steel & Spring Works, **I** 572
Atlas Steel Works, **I** 572
Atlas Steels, **IV** 191
Atlas Supply Co., **IV** 369
Atlas Tag & Label, **9** 72
Atlas Works, **I** 531
Atlas-Werke AG, **IV** 88
Atle Byrnestad, **6** 368
Atmos Lebensmitteltechnik, **III** 420
Atnip, Michael G., **11** 16
ATO Chimie, **I** 303; **IV** 560
Atochem S.A., I 303–04, 676; **IV** 525, 547; **7** 484–85

Atom-Energi, **II** 2
ATR, **7** 9, 11
ATS. *See* Magasins Armand Thiéry et
    Sigrand.
ATT Microelectrica España, **V** 339
Attachmate Corp., **11** 520
Attali, Bernard, **6** 93
Atterbury, Frederick, **7** 216
Atterbury, William D., **8** 157
Attlee, Clement Richard (Earl), **IV** 704
Attwell, Mabel Lucie, **11** 95
Attwood, James, **III** 306–07
Atwater, H. Brewster, Jr., **II** 502; **10** 323
Atwater McMillian, **III** 357
Atwood, Donald J., **II** 35
Atwood, J.L., **I** 79; **11** 428
Au Printemps S.A., V 9–11
Auberger, Bernard, **II** 266
Aubert, Alexander, **III** 371
Aubin, Christian, **II** 117
Aubrey G. Lanston Co., **II** 301
Aubrey, James, **II** 133, 149; **6** 158
Auchan, **10** 205
Audi, **I** 202; **IV** 570
Audio Development Company, **10** 18
Audio/Video Affiliates, Inc., **10** 468–69
Audiotronic Holdings, **III** 112
Auerbach, Norbert, **II** 148
Aufina Bank, **II** 378
Aufschläger, Gustav (Dr.), **III** 693
Aug. Stenman A.B., **III** 493
Augé, Claude, **IV** 614
Aughton Group, **II** 466
Augsburger Aktienbank, **III** 377
Auguri Mondadori S.p.A., **IV** 586
August Max Woman, **V** 207–08
August Thyssen-Hütte AG, **IV** 221–22
Auguste Metz et Cie, **IV** 24
Augustine, Norman R., **I** 69
Aunor Gold Mines, Ltd., **IV** 164
Aunt Fanny's Bakery, **7** 429
Aurell, Ernst, **III** 479
Aurora Products, **II** 543
Ausilio Generale di Sicurezza, **III** 206
Ausimont N.V., **8** 271
AUSSAT Ltd., **6** 341
Aussedat-Rey, **IV** 288
Austin & Son Company, Samuel. *See* The
    Samuel Austin & Son Company.
Austin, Albert E. (Dr.), **IV** 674; **7** 527
The Austin Company, 8 41–44
Austin, J. Paul, **I** 234; **10** 227
Austin, John H., Jr., **V** 696
Austin, Jonathan, **9** 274
Austin Motor Company, **I** 183; **III** 554; **7**
    458
Austin Nichols, **I** 248, 261, 280–81
Austin, Samuel, **8** 41–42
Austin, Shirley P., **6** 483
Austin, T. L., Jr., **V** 724
Austin, Wilbert J., **8** 41–42
Austin-Morris, **III** 494
Austral Waste Products, **IV** 248
Australasian Paper and Pulp Co. Ltd., **IV**
    248
Australasian Sugar Co., **III** 686
Australasian United Steam Navigation Co.,
    III 522
Australia and New Zealand Bank Ltd., **II**
    187, 189
Australia and New Zealand Banking
    Group Ltd., II 187–90
Australia and New Zealand Savings Bank
    Ltd., **II** 189

Australia Gilt Co. Group, **II** 422
Australia National Bank, Limited, **10** 170
Australian Airlines, **6** 91, 112
Australian and Kandos Cement (Holdings)
    Ltd., **III** 687, 728
Australian and Overseas
    Telecommunications Corporation, **6**
    341–42
Australian Associated Press, **IV** 669
Australian Automotive Air, Pty. Ltd., **III**
    593
Australian Bank of Commerce, **II** 188
Australian Blue Asbestos, **III** 687
Australian Consolidated Investments,
    Limited, **10** 170
Australian Forest Products, **I** 438–39
Australian Guarantee Corp. Ltd., **II** 389–90
Australian Gypsum Industries, **III** 673
Australian Iron & Steel Co., **IV** 45
Australian Metal Co., **IV** 139
Australian Mutual Provident Society, **IV**
    61, 697
Australian Paper and Pulp Co. Ltd., **IV** 248
Australian Paper Co., **IV** 248
Australian Paper Manufacturers Ltd., **IV**
    248
Australian Paper Mills Co. Ltd., **IV** 248
Australian Telecommunications
    Corporation, **6** 342
Australian United Corp., **II** 389
Australian Window Glass, **III** 726
Austrian Industries, **IV** 485, 486
Austrian National Bank, **IV** 230
Austrian, Neil A., **I** 31
Austro-Americana, **6** 425
Austro-Daimler, **I** 138, 206; **11** 31
Auto Coil Springs, **III** 581
Auto Shack. *See* AutoZone, Inc.
Auto Strop Safety Razor Co., **III** 27–28
Auto Union, **I** 150
Auto-Flo Co., **III** 569
Auto-Flo Corp., **III** 569
Autodesk, Inc., 10 118–20
Autolite, **I** 29, 142; **III** 555
Automat, **II** 614
Automated Building Components, **III** 735
Automated Communications, Inc., **8** 311
Automated Loss Prevention Systems, **11**
    445
Automated Security (Holdings) PLC, **11**
    444
Automated Wagering Systems, **III** 128
Automatic Data Processing, Inc., III
    117–19; 9 48–51 (upd.), 125, 173
Automatic Fire Alarm Co., **III** 644
Automatic Manufacturing Corporation, **10**
    319
Automatic Payrolls, Inc., **III** 117
Automatic Retailers of America, **II** 607
Automatic Sprinkler Corp. of America, **7**
    176–77
Automatic Telephone & Electric, **II** 81
Automatic Vaudeville Arcades Co., **II** 154
Autombiles Citroen, **11** 103
Automobile Insurance Co., **III** 181–82
Automobiles Citroen, I 162, 188; III 676;
    IV 722; V 237; 7 35–38
Automotive Components Group
    Worldwide, **10** 325
Automotive Diagnostics, **10** 492
Autonet, **6** 435
Autophon AG, **9** 32
AutoTrol Technology, **III** 111
AutoZone, Inc., 9 52–54

Autry, Ret, **6** 244
Auyama, Rokuro, **I** 183
Avana Group, **II** 565
Avco. *See* Aviation Corp. of the Americas.
Avco Corp., **11** 261
Avco National Bank, **II** 420
Avecor, **8** 347
Avedon, Richard, **10** 69
Avendt Group, Inc., **IV** 137
Avenir, **III** 393
Averill, D.R., **III** 744
Averill, Dr. George G., **9** 304
Avery Adhesive Label Corp., **IV** 253
Avery Dennison Corporation, IV 251–54
Avery International Corp., **IV** 251–54
Avery Paper Co., **IV** 253
Avery Products Corp., **IV** 253, 327
Avery, R. Stanton (Stan), **IV** 252–53
Avery, Sewell, **III** 762–63; **V** 146–47; **10**
    172
Avery, Waldo, **III** 762
Avesta Steel Works Co., **I** 553–54
Avfuel, **11** 538
Avgain Marine A/S, **7** 40
Avia Group International, Inc., **V** 376–77
Aviacion y Comercio, **6** 95–96
AVIACO. *See* Aviacion y Comercio.
Aviation Corp. of the Americas, **I** 48, 78,
    89, 115, 530; **III** 66; **9** 497–99; **10** 163;
    11 427
Aviation Corporation (AVCO), **6** 75
Aviation Power Supply, **II** 16
Avieny, R.W., **IV** 140
Avion Coach Corp., **III** 484
Avion Corp., **I** 76; **11** 363
Avions Marcel Dassault-Breguet
    Aviation, I 44–46; 7 11; 7 205; 8 314
Avis Europe PLC, **6** 357
Avis, Inc., I 30, 446, 463; II 468; III 502;
    IV 370; 6 348–49, 356–58, 392–93; 8
    33; 9 284; 10 419; 11 198
Avis, Warren E., **6** 356
Avisco, **I** 317, 365, 442–43; **V** 359
Avisun Corp., **IV** 371
Avnet, Charles, **9** 55
Avnet Inc., 9 55–57; 10 112–13
Avnet, Lester, **9** 55
Avon Cosmetics, Ltd., **III** 15; **8** 329
Avon Products Inc., III 13, 15–16, 62; 9
    331; 11 282, 366
Avon Publications, Inc., **IV** 627
Avoncraft Construction Co., **I** 512
Avondale Industries, Inc., 7 39–41
Avondale Marine Ways, Inc., **I** 512–14; **7**
    39
Avondale Mills, Inc., **8** 558–60; **9** 466
Avondale Shipyards, Inc., **7** 39
Avondale Technical Services, **7** 40
Avondown Properties Ltd., **IV** 711
Avro, **I** 81
AVS, **III** 200
Avtex Fibers Inc., **I** 443; **11** 134
Avunduk, Uzeyir, **I** 478
Award Foods, **II** 528
Aweida, Jesse, **6** 275–76
AXA, III 209, 210–12
AXA Assurances, **III** 211
AXA-Midi, **III** 209, 211
Axel Johnson Group, I 553–55
Axel Springer Gesellschaft für Publizistik
    KG, **IV** 590
Axel Springer Verlag AG, IV 589–91
Axelrod Foods, **II** 528
Axene, Harry, **10** 372

Axon Systems Inc., **7** 336
Ayco Corp., **II** 398; **10** 62
Ayers, Richard H., **III** 628–29
Ayerst, **I** 623
Äyräpää, Matti, **II** 302
Ayshire Collieries, **IV** 18
Ayukawa, Yoshisuke, **IV** 475
Azaria, Pierre, **9** 9
Azienda Generale Italiana Petroli, **IV** 419–21. *See also* Agip SpA.
Azienda Metanodotti Padani, **IV** 420
Azienda Nazionale Idrogenazione Combustibili, **IV** 419–22
AZL Resources, **7** 538
AZP Group Inc., **6** 546
Azuma Leather Co. Ltd., **V** 380
Azuma Shiki Manufacturing, **IV** 326
Azusa Valley Savings Bank, **II** 382

B & O. *See* Baltimore and Ohio Railroad.
B&Q, **V** 106, 108
B&W Diesel, **III** 513
B. B. & R. Knight Brothers, **8** 200
B.C. Rail Telecommunications, **6** 311
B.C. Sugar, **II** 664
B. Dalton Bookseller, **10** 136
B.F. Ehlers, **I** 417
B.F. Goodrich Co., **I** 28, 428, 440; **II** 414; **III** 118, 443
B.F. Walker, Inc., **11** 354
B. Perini & Sons, Inc., **8** 418
B.R. Simmons, **III** 527
B.S. Bull & Co., **II** 668
B. Stroh Brewing Co., **I** 290
B.T.I. Chemicals Ltd., **I** 313; **10** 154
BA. *See* British Airways.
BAA plc, 10 121–23
Babangida, Ibrahim Badamasi (Gen.), **IV** 473
Babbage's, Inc., 10 124–25
Babbitt, Isaac, **I** 158
Babbitt, Jack, **8** 183–84
Babcock & Wilcox Co., **III** 465–66, 516, 559–60; **V** 621
Babcock, George Herman, **III** 465
Babcock, Havilah, **III** 40
Baby Furniture and Toy Supermarket, **V** 203
Babybird Co., Ltd., **V** 150
BAC. *See* Barclays American Corp.
Bacall, Lauren, **II** 175
Bache, **III** 340
Bache & Company, **8** 349
Bachrach Advertising, **6** 40
Backe, John D., **II** 133; **6** 158
Backer & Spielvogel, **I** 33
Backer, Bill, **I** 18
Backroom Systems Group, **II** 317
Backstrand, Clifford J., **III** 423
Bacon & Matheson Drop Forge Co., **I** 185
Bacon, Edwin Munroe, **7** 13
Bacot, J. Carter, **II** 216, 218
Bader, Alfred R., **I** 690–91
Bader, Théophile, **V** 57–58
Badger Co., **II** 86
Badger Illuminating Company, **6** 601
Badger Paint and Hardware Stores, **II** 419
Badham, Henry, **7** 572
Badin, Adrien, **IV** 173
Badische Analin & Soda Fabrik A.G., **I** 305
Badovinus, Wayne, **9** 190
Baer, A.M., **IV** 191
Baer, Francis S., **II** 230

Baer, G. David, **11** 64
BAFS. *See* Bangkok Aviation Fuel Services.
Bagley, James W., **10** 109
Bahia de San Francisco Television, **IV** 621
Bailey Controls, **III** 560
Bailey, E.E., **I** 124
Bailey, Irving W., II, **III** 218
Bailey, Ralph E., **IV** 401–02
Bailey, William O., **III** 182
Bailly, Jean, **III** 705
Bain & Co., **III** 429; **9** 343
Bain, Neville, **V** 357
Bains, Leslie E., **11** 418
Bainum, Robert, **6** 187
Bainum, Stewart, **6** 187–89
Bainum, Stewart, Jr., **6** 189
Baird, **7** 235, 237
Bakelite Corp., **I** 399; **9** 517
Baker & Co., **IV** 78
Baker & Crane, **II** 318
Baker & McKenzie, 10 126–28
Baker & Taylor, **I** 548
Baker, Bobby, **II** 181
Baker Casing Shoe Co., **III** 429
Baker, Charles H., **6** 565
Baker Cummins Pharmaceuticals Inc., **11** 208
Baker, David, **IV** 45
Baker, Dexter F., **10** 31, 33
Baker, Douglas K., **11** 273
Baker, Edward, **III** 699
Baker, Edwin G., **IV** 645
Baker, George, **7** 266
Baker, George L., **III** 272
Baker Hughes Incorporated, III 428–29; 11 513
Baker Industries, **III** 440
Baker Industries, Inc., **8** 476
Baker International Corp., **III** 428–29
Baker, LaVern, **II** 176
Baker, Looe, **11** 43
Baker, Looe III, **11** 44
Baker, Lorenzo Dow, **II** 595; **7** 84
Baker, Melvin, **10** 421–22
Baker Oil Tools, **III** 428–29
Baker, Reuben C. (Carl), **III** 429
Baker, Robert B., **III** 485
Baker, Russell, **10** 126–27
Baker, Samuel, **11** 452
Baker, Ted, **I** 97
Bakersfield Savings and Loan, **10** 339
Bakery Products Inc., **IV** 410
Bakke, Dennis, **10** 25–27
Bakken, Earl, **8** 351–53
Balaban, Barney, **II** 155
Balair Ltd., **I** 122
Balazs, Endre, **I** 665
Balco, Inc., **7** 479–80
Balcor Co., **II** 398; **IV** 703
Balcor, Inc., **10** 62
Baldi, Gene, **7** 339
Baldwin, Arthur, **IV** 634
Baldwin, E. Colin, **III** 745
Baldwin, Frank, **10** 41
Baldwin Hardware Manufacturing Co., **III** 570
Baldwin, Henry F., **11** 287
Baldwin, Henry P., **10** 40–41
Baldwin, Paul C., **IV** 330
Baldwin, Robert, **II** 432
Baldwin, Ron, **11** 145
Baldwin-United Corp., **III** 254, 293
Baldwins Ltd., **III** 494

Bålforsens Kraft AB, **IV** 339–40
Balfour Beatty, **III** 433–34
Balfour, Lord (of Burleigh), **II** 308
Balfour, St. Clair, **7** 487
Balikpapan Forest Industries, **I** 504
Balke, Julius, **III** 442
Balke, Julius, Jr., **III** 443
Ball & Young Adhesives, **9** 92
Ball brothers, **I** 597
Ball, C.A., **I** 223
Ball Computer Products Division, **I** 598; **10** 130
Ball Corporation, I 597–98; 10 129–31 (upd.)
Ball, Edmund F., **I** 597; **10** 129
Ball, Edward, **8** 485–87
Ball, George, **10** 43
Ball-Bartoe Aircraft Corp., **I** 598; **10** 130
Balladur, Edouard, **II** 233; **10** 347
Ballam, Sam, **6** 444
Ballantine, **6** 27
Ballantine & Sons Ltd., **I** 263
Ballard & Ballard Co., **II** 555
Ballard, David W., **11** 552
Ballard, Robert D. (Dr.), **III** 138
Ballin, Albert, **6** 397
Ballmer, Steven A., **6** 260
Bally Distributing Co., **III** 430
Bally Distribution, **10** 375
Bally Manufacturing Corporation, III 430–32; 6 210; **10** 375, 482
Bally Systems, **III** 431
Bally's Park Place, **III** 430–31
Baltensweiler, Armin, **I** 121–22
AB Baltic, **III** 418–19
Baltimore & Ohio, **I** 584; **III** 329; **V** 438–40
Baltimore Aircoil Company, **7** 30–31
Baltimore Gas and Electric Company, V 552–54; 11 388
Baltimore Paper Box Company, **8** 102
Balzaretti-Modigliani, **III** 676
Bamberger's of New Jersey, **V** 169; **8** 443
Banana Republic, **V** 61–62
Banc One, **11** 181
Banc One Corporation, 9 475; **10 132–34**
Banca Brasiliana Italo-Belga, **II** 270
Banca Coloniale di Credito, **II** 271
Banca Commerciale Italiana SpA, I 368, 465, 467; II 191–93, 242, 271, 278, 295, 319; **III** 207–08, 347
BancA Corp., **11** 305
Banca d'America e d'Italia, **II** 280
Banca Dalmata di Sconto, **II** 271
Banca de Gottardo, **II** 361
Banca di Genova, **II** 270
Banca Internazionale Lombarda, **II** 192
Banca Italiana di Sconto, **II** 191
Banca Italo-Cinese, **II** 270
Banca Italo-Viennese, **II** 270
Banca Jacquet e Hijos, **II** 196
Banca Luis Roy Sobrino, **II** 196
Banca Nazionale de Lavoro, **II** 239
Banca Nazionale dell'Agricoltura, **II** 272
Banca Nazionale di Credito, **II** 271
Banca Unione di Credito, **II** 270
BancItaly Corp., **II**, 226–27, 288, 536
Banco Aleman-Panameno, **II** 521
Banco Bilbao Vizcaya, S.A., II 194–96
Banco Central, II 197–98; III 394; **IV** 397
Banco de Albacete, **II** 197
Banco de Barcelona, **II** 194
Banco de Bilbao, **II** 194–96

Banco de Castilla, **II** 194
Banco de Comercio, **II** 194
Banco de Fomento, **II** 198
Banco de Vizcaya, **II** 194–96
Banco di Roma, **I** 465, 467; **II** 191, 257, 271
Banco di Santo Spirito, **I** 467
Banco do Brasil S.A., II 199–200
Banco Español de Credito, **II** 195, 198; **IV** 160
Banco Industrial de Bilbao, **II** 195
Banco Italo-Belga, **II** 270, 271
Banco Italo-Egiziano, **II** 271
Banco Nacional de Cuba, **II** 345
Banco Nacional de Mexico, **9** 333
Banco Popolar, **III** 348; **6** 97
Banco Santander, **III** 271, 294
Banco Trento & Bolanzo, **II** 240
Banco Vascongado, **II** 196
BancOhio National Bank in Columbus, **9** 475
Bancroft, Hugh, **IV** 601–02
Bancroft, Jane Barron, **IV** 601–02
Bancroft Racket Co., **III** 24
BancSystems Association Inc., **9** 475, 476
Banesto. *See* Banco Español de Credito.
Banexi, **II** 233
Bangkok Airport Hotel, **6** 123–24
Bangkok Aviation Fuel Services Ltd., **6** 123–24
Bangor and Aroostook Railroad Company, **8** 33
Bangor Punta Corp., **I** 452, 482; **II** 403
Bangs, George, **9** 406
Bangs, Samuel, **10** 3
Bank Brussels Lambert, II 201–03, 295, 407
Bank Bumiputra, **IV** 519
Bank CIC-Union Européenne A.G., **II** 272
Bank Européene de Credità Moyen Terme, **II** 319
Bank for International Settlements, **II** 368
Bank für Elektrische Unternehmungen. *See* Elektrowatt AG.
Bank für Gemeinwirtschaft, **II** 239
Bank Hapoalim B.M., II 204–06
Bank Leu, **I** 252
Bank Leumi, **II** 205
Bank Mizrahi, **II** 205
Bank of Adelaide, **II** 189
Bank of America, **I** 536–37; **II** 226–28, 252–55, 280, 288–89, 347, 382; **III** 218; **6** 385; **8** 94–95; **9** 50, 123–24, 333, 536. *See also* BankAmerica Corporation.
Bank of America National Trust and Savings Assoc. (NT & SA), **I** 536; **II** 227, 288. *See also* BankAmerica Corporation.
Bank of America of California, **II** 226, 288
Bank of Antwerp, **IV** 497
Bank of Asheville, **II** 336
Bank of Australasia, **II** 187–89
The Bank of Bishop and Co., Ltd., **11** 114
Bank of Boston, **7** 114
Bank of Boston Corporation, II 207–09
Bank of Boston National Assoc., **II** 208
Bank of British Columbia, **II** 244, 298
Bank of British Honduras, **II** 344
Bank of British North America, **II** 220
Bank of California, **II** 322, 490
Bank of Canada, **II** 210, 376
Bank of Central and South America, **II** 344
Bank of Chicago, **III** 270
Bank of China, **II** 298

Bank of Chosen, **II** 338
Bank of Commerce, **II** 331
Bank of England, **II** 217, 235–36, 306–07, 318–19, 333–34, 357, 421–22, 427–28; **III** 234, 280; **IV** 119, 366, 382, 705, 711; **10** 8, 336
Bank of Finland, **III** 648
Bank of France, **II** 232, 264–65, 354; **III** 391
Bank of Hamilton, **II** 244
Bank of Hindustan, **IV** 699
Bank of Israel, **II** 206
Bank of Italy, **I** 536; **II** 192, 226, 271–72, 288; **III** 209, 347; **8** 45
The Bank of Jacksonville, **9** 58
Bank of Japan, **I** 519; **II** 291, 325
Bank of Kobe, **II** 371
Bank of Liverpool, **II** 236
Bank of London and South America, **II** 308
Bank of Manhattan Co., **II** 247–48
Bank of Montreal, II 210–12, 231, 375
Bank of New Brunswick, **II** 221
Bank of New England, **9** 229
Bank of New England Corporation, II 213–15
Bank of New Orleans, **11** 106
Bank of New Queensland, **II** 188
Bank of New South Wales, **II** 188–89, 388–90
Bank of New York and Trust Co., **II** 218
Bank of New York Company, Inc., II 192, **216–19,** 247
Bank of New York, N.B.A., **II** 217–18
Bank of Nova Scotia, II 220–23, 345; **IV** 644
Bank of Nova Scotia Trust Co., **II** 221
Bank of Ontario, **II** 210
Bank of Osaka, **II** 360
Bank of Ottawa, **II** 221
Bank of Pasadena, **II** 382
Bank of Queensland, **II** 188
The Bank of Scotland. *See* The Governor and Company of the Bank of Scotland.
Bank of Spain, **II** 194, 197
Bank of the People, **II** 210
Bank of the United States, **II** 207, 216, 247
Bank of the West, **II** 233
Bank of Tokyo, Ltd., II 224–25, 276, 301, 341, 358; **IV** 151
Bank of Toronto, **II** 375–76
Bank of Upper Canada, **II** 210
Bank of Wales, **10** 336, 338
Bank of Western Australia, **II** 187
Bank of Winterthur, **II** 378
Bank Powszechny Depozytowy, **IV** 119
Bank voor Handel en Nijverheid, **II** 304
BankAmerica Corporation, II 226–28, 436; **8 45–48 (upd.),** 295, 469, 471. *See also* Bank of America *and* Bank of America National Trust and Savings Assoc.
Bankers and Shippers Insurance Co., **III** 389
Bankers Co., **II** 230
Bankers Investment, **II** 349
Bankers Life and Casualty Co., **10** 247
Bankers Life Association, **III** 328
Bankers Life Co., **III** 328–30
Bankers Life Equity Management Co., **III** 329
Bankers Life Equity Services Corp., **III** 329
Bankers National Bank, **II** 261

Bankers National Life Insurance Co., **II** 182; **10** 246
Bankers Trust Co., **II** 229–30; **10** 425; **11** 416
Bankers Trust Co. of South Carolina, **II** 337
Bankers Trust New York Corporation, I 601; **II** 211, **229–31,** 330, 339; **III** 84–86
Bankhaus IG Herstatt, **II** 242
Bankhead, Tallulah, **II** 155
Banks, David R., **III** 76–77
Banks, Howard, **I** 95
BankVermont Corp., **II** 208
Banner Life, **III** 273
Banque Belge et Internationale en Egypte, **II** 295
Banque Belge pour l'Etranger, **II** 294
Banque Belgo-Zairoise, **II** 294
Banque Bruxelles Lambert. *See* Bank Brussels Lambert.
Banque Commerciale du Maroc, **II** 272
Banque Commerciale-Basle, **II** 270
Banque d'Anvers/Bank van Antwerpen, **II** 294–95
Banque de Bruxelles, **II** 201–02, 239
Banque de Credit et de Depot des Pays Bas, **II** 259
Banque de l'Indochine et de Suez, **II** 259
Banque de l'Union Européenne, **II** 94
Banque de l'Union Parisienne, **II** 270; **IV** 497, 557
Banque de la Construction et les Travaux Public, **II** 319
Banque de la Société Générale de Belgique, **II** 294–95
Banque de Louvain, **II** 202
Banque de Paris, **II** 259
Banque de Paris et des Pays-Bas, **II** 136, 259; **10** 346
Banque de Reports et de Depots, **II** 201
Banque du Congo Belge, **II** 294
Banque Européenne pour l'Amerique Latine, **II** 294
Banque Française et Espagnol en Paris, **II** 196
Banque Francaise pour le Commerce et l'Industrie, **II** 232, 270
Banque Génerale des Pays Roumains, **II** 270
Banque Générale du Luxembourg, **II** 294
Banque Indosuez, **II** 429
Banque Internationale à Luxembourg, **II** 239
Banque Internationale de Bruxelles, **II** 201–02
Banque Italo-Belge, **II** 294
Banque Italo-Francaise de Credit, **II** 271
Banque Lambert, **II** 201–02
Banque Nationale de Crédit, **II** 232
Banque Nationale de Paris S.A., II 232–34, 239; **III** 201, 392–94; **9** 148
Banque Nationale Pour le Commerce et l'Industrie, **II** 232–33
Banque Nationale pour le Commerce et l'Industrie (Afrique), **II** 232
Banque Nordique du Commerce, **II** 366
Banque Orea, **II** 378
Banque Paribas, **II** 192, 260; **IV** 295
Banque Rothschild, **IV** 107
Banque Sino-Belge, **II** 294
Banque Stern, **II** 369
Banque Transatlantique, **II** 271
Banque Worms, **III** 393

Banquet Foods Corp., **II** 90, 494
Bantam Books, Inc., **III** 190–91
Bantam Doubleday Dell Publishing Group, **IV** 594
Bantle, Louis F., **9** 533–34
Banyu Pharmaceutical Co., **I** 651; **11** 290
BAPCO, **III** 745
Barach, Philip G., **V** 208
Barat. *See* Barclays National Bank.
Barbakow, Jeffrey, **II** 149–50
Barbanson, Gustave, **IV** 24
Barber (Lord), **II** 358
Barber, Anthony, **III** 739
Barber, Charles, **IV** 33
Barber, Nicholas, **6** 417
Barber, Red, **III** 52
Barber, Walter C., **V** 753
Barbera, Joe, **II** 148
Barberet & Blanc, **I** 677
Barbero, Ronald D., **III** 340
Barbier, Aristide, **V** 236
Barclay & Co., Ltd., **II** 235
Barclay & Fry, **I** 604–05
Barclay Group, **I** 335; **10** 290
Barclay, James, **II** 235
Barclay, Kenneth, **8** 544–45
Barclay, Robert, **I** 604
Barclays American Corp., **II** 236
Barclays Bank (Canada), **II** 244
Barclays Bank (D.C.O.), **II** 236
Barclays Bank (Dominion, Colonial & Overseas), **II** 236
Barclays Bank International, **II** 236; **IV** 23
Barclays Bank of California, **II** 236, 383
Barclays Bank of New York, **II** 236
Barclays Bank S.A., **II** 237
Barclays, Bevan & Tritton, **II** 235
Barclays de Zoete Wedd, **II** 237, 429; **11** 30
Barclays Merchant Bank Ltd. de Zoete, **II** 237
Barclays National Bank, **II** 237; **IV** 23
Barclays PLC, I 604; **II** 202, 204, **235–37,** 239, 308, 319, 333, 422; **III** 516; **IV** 722; **7** 332–33; **8** 118; **11** 29
Barclays, Tritton, Ransom, Bouverie & Co., **II** 235
BarclaysAmerican Corporation, **11** 29
BarclaysAmerican Mortgage Corporation, 11 29–30
Bard, Charles Russell, **9** 96
Bard, Thomas, **IV** 569
Barden Cablevision, **IV** 640
Bardot, Brigitte, **III,** 46
Bardou, Jean-Pierre, **I** 188
Barell, Emil C., **I** 642–43
Barents, Brian, **8** 315
Barfoot, Henry Charles, **III** 334
Baring Brothers, **III** 699
Baring, Francis, **III** 372
Barker & Dobson, **II** 629
Barker, James, **10** 50
Barklay, Norman A., **I** 483
Barlow, Charles, **I** 422–23
Barlow, Ernest (Maj.), **I** 422
Barlow, Montague, **11** 452
Barlow Rand Ltd., I 288–89, **422–24; IV** 22, 96
Barlow, Robert, **I** 604–05
Barlow, William (Sir), **III** 434
Barmer Bankverein, **II** 238, 241
Barnato, Barney, **IV** 64; **7** 121
Barnato Brothers, **IV** 21, 65; **7** 122
Barnes & Noble, Inc., 10 135–37

Barnes, Charles Montgomery, **10** 135
Barnes Group, **III** 581
Barnes, J. David, **II** 316
Barnes, James E., **IV** 459
Barnes, John, **10** 136
Barnes, Leslie O., **V** 505
Barnes, Robert J., **9** 203
Barnes, William R., **10** 135
Barnes-Hind, **III** 56, 727
Barnet, Herbert, **I** 277; **10** 451
Barnetson, William (Lord), **IV** 686
Barnett Banks, Inc., 9 58–60
Barnett Banks of Florida, Inc., **9** 58
Barnett, Bion, **9** 58
Barnett Brass & Copper Inc., **9** 543
Barnett Equity Securities, **9** 59
Barnett First National Bank of Jacksonville, **9** 58
Barnett, Frank, **V** 531
Barnett, Hoares and Co., **II** 306
Barnett National Securities Corporation, **9** 58
Barnett, William Boyd, **9** 58
Barnett, William D., **9** 58
Barnette, Curtis H., **7** 51
Barnetts, Hoares, Hanbury and Lloyds, **II** 306
Barnevik, Percy, **II** 2–4; **IV** 204
Barney, Ashbel H., **II** 381
Barney, Danforth, **10** 59
Barney, Danforth N., **II** 380–81, 395
Barney, Hiram, **III** 239
Barney, J.W., **IV** 601
Barney, Lawrence D., **I** 643
Baron, Stanley Wade, **I** 219, 255, 270, 292
Baroncini, Gino, **III** 208
Barr & Stroud Ltd., **III** 727
Barr, David W., **IV** 645
Barr, John J. (Jack), **6** 443
Barr, Kenneth J., **7** 107–08
Barranquilla Investments, **II** 138
Barratt American Inc., **I** 556
Barratt Developments plc, I 556–57
Barratt, Lawrie, **I** 556
Barratt Multi-Ownership and Hotels Ltd., **I** 556
Barrera, Antonio, **V** 338
Barret Fitch North, **II** 445
Barrett Burston, **I** 437
Barrett Co., **I** 414–15
Barrett, J. Patrick, **6** 357
Barrett, Tom H., **V** 247–48
Barriger, John, **I** 472–73
Barringer, John H., **III** 151; **6** 265
Barron, Clarence, **IV** 601
Barron family, **IV** 602
Barron, Jessie, **IV** 601
Barrow, Richard Cadbury, **II** 476
Barrow, Thomas D., **7** 263; **10** 262
Barry & Co., **III** 522
Barry Wright Corporation, **9** 27
Barrymore, John, **II** 175
Barsab, **I** 288–89
Barshop, Phil, **11** 242
Barshop, Sam, **11** 242–43
Barsotti's, Inc., **6** 146
Barstow & Company, W. S., **6** 575
Bartels, Peter, **7** 183–84
Barth Smelting Corp., **I** 513
Bartholomew, Guy, **IV** 666
Bartholomew, H.G., **7** 342
Bartlett, F.A., **11** 72
Bartlett, Walter E., **11** 331
Barton Brands, **I** 227; **II** 609; **10** 181

Barton, Bruce, **I** 28
Barton, Duer & Koch, **IV** 282; **9** 261
Bartz, Carol A., **10** 118
Baruch, Edgar, **II** 415
BASF A.G., I 305–08, 309, 319, 346–47, 632, 638; **II** 554; **IV** 70
BASF Corp., **IV** 71
BASF Wyandotte Corp., **I** 275
Basic American Retirement Communities, **III** 103
Basic Resources, Inc., **V** 725
BASIS Information Technologies, Inc., **11** 112–13, 132
Baskin-Robbins Ice Cream Co., **I** 215; **7** 128, 372
Basle A.G., **I** 632–33, 671–72; **8** 108–09
Basle Air Transport, **I** 121
Basler and Zürcher Bankverein, **II** 368
Basler Bank-Verein, **II** 368
Basler Bankverein, **II** 368
Basler Depositen-Bank, **II** 368
Bass & Co., **I** 142
Bass, Arthur C., **6** 389–90
Bass Charington, **I** 222; **9** 99
Bass, Ed, **I** 418
Bass family, **II** 173; **6** 175, 192–93
Bass, Gordon M., **9** 548
Bass, Harry W., **11** 544–45
Bass, Lee, **I** 418
Bass, Michael, **I** 222
Bass, Michael Thomas, **I** 222
Bass plc, I 222–24; III 94–95; **9** 425–26
Bass Ratcliffe & Gretton, **I** 222
Bass, Robert M., **I** 418; **9** 63–64
Bass, Sid, **I** 418
Bass, William, **I** 222
Bassett, Allen L., **III** 337
Bassett Foods, **II** 478
Bassett, Marcus, **9** 408
Bassett-Walker Inc., **V** 390–91
Bassins Food Chain, **II** 649
Bastian, Bruce, **10** 556–57
BAT. *See* British-American Tobacco Co., Ltd.
BAT Industries plc, I 425–27, 605; **II** 628; **III** 66, 185, 522; **9** 312
Bataafsche Petroleum Maatschappij, **V** 658
Batchelors Ltd., **I** 315
Bateman Eichler Hill Richards, **III** 270
Bateman, Giles H., **V** 164
Bates & Robins, **II** 318
Bates, Albert D., **I** 254
Bates Chemical Company, **9** 154
Bates, Edward B., **III** 238
Bates Manufacturing Company, **10** 314
Batesville Casket Company, **10** 349–50
Bath & Body Works, **11** 41
Bathurst Bank, **II** 187
Baton Rouge Gas Light Company. *See* Gulf States Utilities Company.
Batson, Homer Ward, **III** 216–17
Battelle, Annie Norton, **10** 138
Battelle, Gordon, **10** 138–39
Battelle Memorial Institute, Inc., 6 288; **10 138–40**
Batten Barton Durstine & Osborn, **I** 25, 28–31, 33
Batten, George, **I** 28
Batten, Jim, **IV** 630
Batterson, James G., **III** 387–88
Battle Creek Toasted Corn Flake Co., **II** 523
Battle Mountain Gold Co., **IV** 490
BATUS Inc., **9** 312

Bauborg, **I** 560–61
Baudhuin, F.J., **8** 553
Baudhuin, Ralph J., **8** 553
Baudhuin-Anderson Company, **8** 553
Bauer, Eddie, **9** 188–89
Bauer, Heinrich, **7** 42
Bauer, Heinz, **7** 42
Bauer, Louis, **7** 42
Bauer Publishing Group, 7 42–43
Bauer, Robert F., **9** 266
Bauer, Walter F., **11** 468
Bauersfeld, Walther, **III** 446
Baugh, John, **II** 675
Baulieu, Etienne-Emile, Dr., **8** 452
Bauman, Robert P., **III** 66–67
Baumann, Paul, **I** 349–50
Baumgardner, Russ, **8** 34–36
Bausch & Lomb Inc., III 446; **7 44–47**;
    10 46–47
Bausch & Lomb Optical Co., **7** 44
Bausch, Edward, **7** 44
Bausch, John Jacob, **7** 44
Bavarian Railway, **II** 241
Bawtree, Angela, **11** 42
Bax, Simon, **11** 51
Baxter, Donald, **I** 627; **10** 141
Baxter Estates, **II** 649
Baxter International Inc., I 627–29; 9
    346; **10 141–43** (upd.), 198–99; **11**
    459–60
Baxter, L. D. M., **V** 737
Baxter Laboratories, **I** 627
Baxter Travenol Laboratories, **I** 627
Baxter Travenol Laboratories, Inc., **8** 215;
    11 459
Bay Area Review Course, Inc., **IV** 623
Bay Cities Transportation Company, **6** 382
Bay City Cash Way Company, **V** 222
Bay Colony Life Insurance Co., **III** 254
Bay Petroleum, **I** 526
Bay Ridge Savings Bank, **10** 91
Bay State Glass Co., **III** 683
Bayazit, Rifat, **IV** 563
Bayer A.G., I 305–06, **309–11**, 319,
    346–47, 350; **II** 279
Bayer, Friedrich, **I** 309
Bayer S.p.A., **8** 179
Bayerische Aluminium AG, **IV** 230
Bayerische Disconto- und Wechsel Bank,
    II 239
Bayerische Flugzeugwerke, **I** 73
Bayerische Handelsbank, **II** 241
Bayerische Hypotheken- und Wechsel-
    Bank AG, II 238–40, 241–42; **IV** 323
Bayerische Kraftwerke AG, **IV** 229–30
Bayerische Landesbank, **II** 257–58, 280
Bayerische Motoren Werke A.G., I 75,
    138–40, 198; **II** 5; **III** 543, 556, 591; **11**
    31–33 (upd.)
Bayerische Rückversicherung AG, **III** 377
Bayerische Rumpler Werke, **I** 73
Bayerische Staatsbank, **II** 239, 242
Bayerische Stickstoff-Werke AG, **IV**
    229–30
Bayerische Vereinsbank A.G., II 239–40,
    241–43; III 401
Bayerische Versicherungsbank, **II** 238; **III**
    377
Bayerische Wasserkraftwerke
    Aktiengesellschaft, **IV** 231
Bayerische Zellstoff, **IV** 325
Bayernwerk AG, IV 231–32, 323; **V**
    555–58, 698–700
Bayless, Charles E., **6** 591

Bayon Steel Corp., **IV** 234
Bayou Boeuf Fabricators, **III** 559
Bays, Karl D., **10** 554
Bayside National Bank, **II** 230
Bayview, **III** 673
BBC. *See* British Broadcasting Corp.
BBC Brown, Boveri Ltd., **II** 1, 3–4, 13;
    III 466, 631–32
BBC World Service, **7** 52, 54
BBDO. *See* Batten Barton Durstine &
    Osborn.
BBME. *See* British Bank of the Middle
    East.
BC Mobile Ltd., **6** 310
BC TEL. *See* British Columbia Telephone
    Company.
BC TEL Mobility Cellular, **6** 311
BC TEL Mobility Paging, **6** 311
BCal. *See* British Caledonian Airways.
BCE, Inc., V 269–71; 6 307; **7** 333
BCI. *See* Banca Commerciale Italiana SpA.
BCI (Suisse), **II** 192
BCI Funding Corp., **II** 192
BCI Holdings Corp., **II** 468
BDB Corp., **10** 136
BDDP. *See* Wells Rich Greene BDDP.
Beach, Morrison H., **III** 389
BeachviLime Ltd., **IV** 74
Beacon Manufacturing, **I** 377
Beacon Oil, **IV** 566
Beacon Participations, **III** 98
Beacon Publishing Co., **IV** 629
Beal, David, **11** 30
Beal, Orville E., **III** 338–39
Beal, Thaddeus, **6** 458
Beal, William K., **6** 458
Beale, John Field (Sir), **III** 493–94
Beale, Leonard T., **I** 382
Beale, Samuel (Sir), **III** 494
Beall, Donald, **I** 80
Beall, Donald R., **11** 429–30
Beall, Ingrid, **10** 127
Beall, Samuel E., III, **11** 324
Beals, Vaughn, **7** 212–13
Beam, C. Grier, **6** 369–70
Beam, Dewey, **6** 369–70
Bean, Francis Atherton, **7** 241–42
Bean, John, **I** 442; **11** 133
Bean, Leon Leonwood, **10** 388–89
Beane, Alpheus, Jr., **II** 424
Bear Automotive Service Equipment
    Company, **10** 494
Bear, Joseph, **II** 400; **10** 144
Bear Stearns & Company and Subsidiaries,
    10 144
Bear, Stearns & Company, Inc., **II** 400; **10**
    144–45
Bear Stearns Companies, Inc., II
    400–01, 450; **10 144–45 (upd.)**, 382
Beard & Stone Electric Co., **I** 451
Bearden, C. Ray, **9** 111–12
Beardsley, Albert R., **I** 653
Beardsley, Andrew Hubble, **I** 653
Beardsley, Charles S., **I** 653
Beardsley, Paul R., **I** 199; **10** 492
Bearings Co. of America, **I** 158–59
Beath, Hugh R., **6** 13
Beatrice Cheese, **II** 467
Beatrice Companies, **II** 468; **6** 357
Beatrice Company, I 353; **II 467–69**,
    475; **III** 118, 437; **9** 318
Beatrice Creamery Co. of Nebraska, **II** 467
Beatrice Foods Co., **I** 440–41; **II** 467
Beatrice/Hunt Wesson, **II** 467

Beatty, Chester (Sir), **IV** 21
Beauharnois Power Company, **6** 502
Beaulieu Winery, **I** 260
Beaumont, Ernest, **IV** 261
Beaumont-Bennett Group, **6** 27
Beaupre, T.N., **IV** 272
Beauvais, Edward R., **6** 72–73
Beaver, Hugh E.C. (Sir), **I** 251
Beaver Lumber Co., **I** 274
Beaverbrook (Lord). *See* Aitken, W. Max.
Beazer Plc., **7** 209
Beazer USA, Inc., **7** 207
Bebber, Rolf, **I** 111
Bébéar, Claude, **III** 209–11
Beber, Frank, **I** 656
Bechanan, William B., **11** 237
Becherer, Hans W., **III** 464
Bechtel Corporation, **6** 148–49, 556
Bechtel Group Inc., I 558–59, 563; **III**
    248; **IV** 171, 576
Bechtel, Stephen, **I** 558
Bechtel, Stephen D., **8** 415
Bechtel, Stephen, Jr., **I** 558–59
Bechtel, Warren A., **I** 558
Bechtolsheim, Andreas, **7** 498–99
Beck & Gregg Hardware Co., **9** 253
Beck, Dave, **I** 169
Beck, Eckardt C., **6** 441
Beck, Marshall, **III** 438
Beck, Robert, **III** 340
Beck, Sir Adam, **6** 541
Becker Paribas Futures, **II** 445
Becker Warburg Paribas, **II** 259
Becket, Fredrick M. (Dr.), **I** 399
Beckett, John R., **I** 537; **II** 147
Beckjord, Walter C., **6** 466
Beckley-Cardy Co., **IV** 623–24
Beckman, Arnold O., **I** 694
Beckman, Charles, **9** 433
Beckman Instruments, **I** 694
Becky, Kermit, **7** 505
Becton, Dickinson & Company, I
    630–31; IV 550; **9** 96; **11 34–36 (upd.)**
Becton, Henry P., **I** 630; **11** 34
Becton, Maxwell W., **I** 630; **11** 34
Bedford Chemical, **8** 177
Bedford, Thomas Edward, **II** 496–97
Bedford-Stuyvesant Restoration Corp., **II**
    673
Bedrosian, John, **III** 87
Bee Chemicals, **I** 372
Bee Gee Shoe Corporation, **10** 281
Bee Gee Shrimp, **I** 473
Beebe, Frederick, **I** 415
Beebe, Palmer, **9** 435
Beebe, W.T., **I** 100; **6** 82
Beeby, Robert, **7** 473
Beech Aircraft, **II** 87
Beech Aircraft Corporation, 8 49–52,
    313; **11** 411, 413
Beech Holdings Corp., **9** 94
Beech, Olive Ann, **8** 49–51
Beech, Walter Herschel, **8** 49–50, 90
Beech-Nut Corp., **I** 695; **II** 489
Beecham Group Ltd., **I** 626, 640, 668; **II**
    331, 543; **III** 18, 65–66; **9** 264
Beecham, Henry, **III** 65
Beecham, Joseph, **III** 65
Beecham Research Laboratories Ltd., **III**
    65
Beecham, Thomas, **III** 65
Beecham's Pills, **III** 65
Beeching, Richard, **V** 422
de Beer, Tom, **IV** 92

Beerman, Arthur, **10** 281–82
Beerman Stores, Inc., **10** 281
Beers, Henry, **III** 181
Beeson, R.C., **7** 266
Begelman, David, **II** 136
Begelman, Mark, **8** 405
Beggs, John I., **6** 601–02
Beghin Say S.A., **II** 540
Behl, Maureen, **11** 216
Behn, Hernand, **I** 462–63; **11** 196–97
Behn, Sosthenes (Col.), **I** 462–63; **11** 196–97
Behr-Manning Company, **8** 396
Behrakis, George, **I** 667
Behrens, Herman A., **III** 229
Beijerinvest Group, **I** 210
Beijing Machinery and Equipment Corp., **II** 442
Beise, Clark, **II** 227
Beit, Alfred, **IV** 94
Beitz, Berthold, **IV** 88–89
Bejam Group PLC, **II** 678
Beker Industries, **IV** 84
Bekkum, Owen D., **6** 530
Belairbus, **I** 42
Belasco, Warren I., **III** 94
Belcher New England, Inc., **IV** 394
Belcher Oil Co., **IV** 394
Belden Corp., **II** 16
Belding, Don, **I** 12–14
Belfast Banking Co., **II** 318
Belfrage, Kurt-Allan, **III** 426–27
Belgacom, 6 302–04
Belgian De Vaderlandsche, **III** 309
Belgian Rapid Access to Information Network Services, **6** 304
Belgian Société Internationale Forestière et Minière, **IV** 65
Belgochim, **IV** 499
Belgrano, Frank N., **II** 289
Belize Sugar Industries, **II** 582
Belk Stores Services, V 12–13
Belk, William Henry, **V** 12
Belknap, Hobart, **9** 96
Bell, **III** 674
Bell & Howell, **I** 463; **IV** 642
Bell, A. Scott, **III** 361
Bell Aerospace, **I** 530
Bell Aircraft, **I** 529; **11** 267
Bell, Alexander Graham, **II** 97; **IV** 663; **6** 338, 341; **9** 366–67; **10** 377
Bell, Alexander Melville, **6** 305
Bell and Howell Company, 9 33, 61–64; 11 197
Bell, Andrew, **7** 165
Bell Atlantic Corporation, V 272–74; 9 171; 10 232, 456; 11 59, 87, 274
Bell Canada, 6 305–08
Bell Canada Enterprises Inc. See BCE, Inc.
Bell, Charles H., **II** 501–02; **10** 323
Bell, David, **9** 281–82
Bell, Donald J., **9** 61
Bell, Drummond, **I** 378
Bell, Glen, **7** 505–06
Bell, Gordon, **III** 132, 134; **6** 234–35
Bell, Griffin, **I** 490
Bell, James S., **II** 501; **10** 322
Bell, Joseph M., Jr., **6** 534–35
Bell Laboratories, **II** 33, 60–61, 101, 112; **8** 157; **9** 171; **11** 327, 500–01
Bell, Lawrence D., **I** 529
Bell Resources, **I** 437–38; **III** 729; **10** 170
Bell System, **II** 72, 230; **6** 338–40; **7** 99, 333; **11** 500

Bell Telephone Company, **I** 409; **6** 332, 334
Bell Telephone Company of Pennsylvania, **I** 585
Bell Telephone Company of Canada, **V** 269, 308–09. See also Bell Canada.
Bell Telephone Laboratories, Inc., **V** 259–64; **10** 108
Bell Telephone Manufacturing, **II** 13
Bell, Thaddeus F., **8** 274
Bell, Tim, **I** 33
Bell, Tom, **IV** 246
Bell, William, **I** 300–01; **8** 24–25
Bell's Asbestos and Engineering, **I** 428
Bell-Northern Research, Ltd., **V** 269–71
Bellamy, Francis, **6** 582
Belle Alkali Co., **IV** 409; **7** 308
Belledune Fertilizer Ltd., **IV** 165
Bellefonte Insurance Co., **IV** 29
Bellemead Development Corp., **III** 220
Belli, Melvin, **I** 400
Bellinger, John D., **11** 114–15
Bellisario, Marisa, **V** 326
Bellman, Harold, **10** 7
Bellonte, Maurice, **V** 471
BellSouth Corporation, V 276–78; 9 171, 321; 10 431, 501
Belmont Electronics, **II** 85–86; **11** 412
Belmont Savings and Loan, **10** 339
Belmont Springs Water Company, Inc., **I** 234; **10** 227
Belo, Alfred H., **10** 3
Belo Productions, Inc., **10** 3, 5
Beloit Corporation, **8** 243
Beloit Woodlands, **10** 380
Belridge Oil Co., **IV** 541
Belzberg family, **III** 424
Belzberg, Hyman, **III** 763
Belzberg, Samuel, **II** 661; **III** 763
Belzberg, William, **III** 763
Belzburg family, **10** 422
Belzer Dowidat, **IV** 199
Belzer group, **IV** 198
Bembridge, B.A., **I** 715
Bemis, A. Farwell, **8** 54
Bemis Company, Inc., 8 53–55
Bemis, F. Gregg, **8** 54
Bemis, Judson (Sandy), **8** 54–55
Bemis, Judson Moss, **8** 53–54
Bemis, Stephen, **8** 54
Bemrose group, **IV** 650
Ben & Jerry's Homemade, Inc., 10 146–48
Ben Franklin, **V** 152–53; **8** 555
Ben Franklin Savings & Trust, **10** 117
Ben Hill Griffin, **III** 53
Ben Johnson & Co. Ltd., **IV** 661
Ben Line, **6** 398
Bencsik, Doris, **11** 69
Bendelari, Arthur, **8** 156
Bender, John, **7** 434
Bender, Marglin, **I** 116
Bender, Robert E., **V** 156, 158
Bendetsen, Karl, **IV** 264
Bendicks, **I** 592
Bendix Aviation Corp., **I** 141; **II** 33; **9** 16–17; **10** 260
Bendix Corp., I 68, 141–43, 154, 166, 192, 416; III 166, 555; 7 356; 8 545; 10 279; 11 138
Bendix Helicopters Inc., **I** 141
Bendix Home Appliances, **I** 141
Bendix, Vincent, **I** 141
Beneduce, Alberto, **I** 465

Benedum, Mike L., **IV** 415
Beneficial Corporation, II 236; 8 56–58, 117; 10 490
Beneficial Finance Corporation. See Beneficial Corporation.
Beneficial National Bank USA, **II** 286
Beneficial Standard Life, **10** 247
Benetton, **8** 171; **10** 149
Benetton, Carlo, **10** 149
Benetton, Gilberto, **10** 149
Benetton, Giuliana, **10** 149
Benetton Group S.p.A., 10 149–52
Benetton, Luciano, **10** 149–50, 152
Benetton U.S.A. Corporation, **10** 150–51
Bengal Iron and Steel Co., **IV** 205–06
Benhamou, Eric, **11** 519–20
Benjamin Allen & Co., **IV** 660
Benjamin, Curtis G., **IV** 635–36
Benjamin, John, **III** 114
Benjamin, Robert, **II** 147
Benn Bros. plc, **IV** 687
Bennack, Frank A., Jr., **IV** 627
Bennet, Richard J., **I** 684
Bennett Biscuit Co., **II** 543
Bennett, Clarence F., **III** 627
Bennett, Donald, **7** 450–51
Bennett, Elbert G., **11** 117–19
Bennett, F.I., **III** 508
Bennett, Floyd, **I** 54
Bennett, Martin, **I** 196
Bennett, Peter, **III** 554–55; **V** 212
Bennett, R. B., **6** 585
Bennett, Richard Bedford, **I** 285
Bennett, Robert F., **11** 147
Bennett, T.R.G., **I** 714
Bennett, W.S., **III** 697
Bennett, William, **IV** 308
Bennett, William G., **6** 203–05
Bennigan's, **II** 556–57; **7** 336
Benny, Jack, **II** 132, 151
Bensinger, Benjamin, **III** 443
Bensinger, Bob, **III** 443–44
Bensinger, Moses, **III** 442–43
Bensinger, Ted, **III** 443–44
Bensly, Bob, **III** 509
Benson & Hedges, **V** 398–99
Benson, Chris, **IV** 712
Benson, Craig, **10** 193–94
Benson, Donald, **9** 40
Benson family, **IV** 421
Benson, Kevin, **10** 531
Benson Wholesale Co., **II** 624
Bentham, William, **III** 359
Bentley Mills, Inc., **8** 272
Bentley Motor Ltd., **I** 194
Bentley Systems, **6** 247
Benton & Bowles, **I** 33; **6** 20, 22
Benton, F. Fox, Jr., **11** 440
Benton, William, **6** 22; **7** 167
Benxi Iron and Steel Corp., **IV** 167
Benz, Carl, **I** 149
Benzina, **IV** 487
Benzinol, **IV** 487
N.V. Benzit. See N.V. Gemeenschappelijk Benzit van Aandeelen Philips Gloeilampenfabriken.
Berard, Mario, **II** 200
Berchtold, Walter, **I** 121
Bere, James, **III** 440
Berec Group, **III** 502; **7** 208
Berg Manufacturing Sales Co., **I** 156
Berg, Paul, **9** 7
Berg, William, **IV** 386
Berg- und Metallbank, **IV** 139–40

Bergdorf Goodman, **I** 246; **V** 30–31
Bergedorfer Eisenwerk, **III** 417–20
Bergen Bank, **II** 352
Bergen Brunswig Corporation, **I** 413; **V** 14–16, 152
Bergen Brunswig Drug Company, **V** 14–16
Bergen, Candice, **10** 491
Bergen, Edgar, **II** 133, 151
de Bergendal, Diego du Monceau, **V** 65
Bergenthal, August, **7** 546–47
Bergenthal, August K., **7** 547
Bergenthal, Bruno, **7** 547
Bergenthal, William, **7** 546
Berger, Donald, **6** 390
Berger Jenson and Nicholson, **I** 347
Berger, Julius, **I** 560
Berger, Robert J., **9** 409
Bergerac, Michel, **III** 56
Bergische-Markische Bank, **II** 278
Bergius, Friedrich, **I** 349; **IV** 534
Bergland, Robert, **II** 616
Berglen, **III** 570
Bergman, Klaus, **V** 544
Bergmann & Co., **II** 27
Bergner, Carl, **III** 418
Bergstresser, Charles M., **IV** 601, 603
Bergstresser family, **IV** 601
Bergstrom Paper Company, **8** 413
Bergswerksgesellschaft Hibernia, **I** 349; **IV** 194
Bergvik & Ala, **IV** 336, 338–39
Berkeley Computers, **III** 109
Berkeley, Norborne, **II** 252
Berkeley, Stephen M., **10** 458–59
Berkey Photo Inc., **I** 447; **III** 475
Berkshire Cotton Manufacturing Co., **III** 213
Berkshire Fine Spinning Associates, **III** 213
Berkshire Hathaway Inc., **III** 29, **213–15**
Berkshire International, **V** 390–91
Berkshire Partners, **10** 393
Berleca Ltd., **9** 395
Berlex Laboratories, **I** 682; **10** 214
Berlin Exchange, **I** 409
Berlin Göring-Werke, **IV** 233
Berlin, J.L., **II** 601; **7** 19
Berlin, Richard, **IV** 627
Berliner Bank, **II** 256
Berliner Bankverein, **II** 278
Berliner Handels- und Frankfurter Bank, **II** 242
Berliner Union, **I** 409
Berlinische Bodengesellschaft, **I** 560
Berlitz International Inc., **IV** 643; **7** 286, 312
Berlusconi, Silvio, **IV** 587–88; **6** 16; **11** 206
Berman, Joshua M., **III** 643
Bernardi, Robert, **10** 455
Bernbach, Bill, **I** 30–31, 36
Berner, T. Roland, **7** 263; **10** 261–63
Berner, Ted, **9** 14
Berner, Thomas R., **10** 263
Bernhard, Prince (Netherlands), **I** 66; **11** 268
Bernhardt, Sarah, **II** 154
Berni Inns, **I** 247
Bernina, Pfaff, **II** 10
Bernstein, Alex, **II** 139
Bernstein, Alexander, **II** 138
Bernstein, Carl, **IV** 672, 689
Bernstein, Cecil, **II** 138
Bernstein, Jeffrey G., **10** 455

Bernstein, John, **11** 80–81
Bernstein Macauley, Inc., **II** 450
Bernstein, Sidney, **II** 138–39
Bernström, Erik (Capt.), **III** 419
Bernström, John, **III** 418–19
Bernström, Richard, **III** 419
Berry, Antony, **9** 327
Berry Bearing Company, **9** 254
Berry, H. Seymour, **III** 493
Berry Industries, **III** 628
Berry, Marcellus, **II** 396; **10** 60
Berry, Norman, **I** 26
Berry, William W., **V** 598
Berryman, John, **IV** 622
Bersticker, Albert C., **8** 179
Bert L. Smokler & Company, **11** 257
Berta, Ruben, **6** 133
Bertea Corp., **III** 603
Bertelsmann AG, **IV** **592–94**, 614–15; **10** 196
Bertelsmann, Carl, **IV** 592
Bertelsmann, Friederike, **IV** 592–93
Bertelsmann, Heinrich, **IV** 592–93
Bertelsmann Verlag, **IV** 592–93
Bertrand Michel, **II** 266
Bertron Griscom & Company, **V** 641
Berzelius Metallhütten Gesellschaft, **IV** 141
Berzelius Umwelt-Service, **III** 625; **IV** 141
Bess Mfg., **8** 510
Bessborough (Earl of), **III** 493
Besse, Georges, **I** 190; **IV** 174
Bessemer Gas Engine Co., **II** 15
Bessemer Limestone & Cement Co., **IV** 409
Bessemer Steamship, **IV** 572; **7** 549
Besser Vibrapac, **III** 673
Besserdich, William R., **7** 416
Besso, Giuseppe, **III** 206–07
Besso, Marco, **III** 206–07
Best Apparel, **V** 156
Best Buy Co., Inc., **9** **65–66**; **10** 305
Best, C.W., **III** 450–51
Best, Charles Lorenz, **I** 269
Best, Daniel, **III** 450
Best Foods, Inc., **II** 496–97
Best, M. O., **6** 545
Bestwall Gypsum Co., **IV** 281; **9** 259
Beswick, **II** 17
Beswick (Lord), **I** 52
Betancourt, Belisario, **IV** 417
Béteille, Roger, **I** 41–42
Bethesda Research Labs, **I** 321
Bethlehem Steel, **11** 65
Bethlehem Steel Corporation, **IV** **35–37**, 228, 572–73; **6** 540; **7** **48–51 (upd.)**, 447, 549–50
Beton Union, **III** 738
Bettencourt, Liliane, **III** 47–48; **8** 131, 342, 344
Better Communications, **IV** 597
Bettis, Laurence, **11** 554
Betts, Hobart D., **11** 515
Betulander, G. A., **V** 331
Betz de Mexico, **10** 154
Betz Environmental Engineers, **10** 154
Betz International, Inc., **10** 154
Betz, John Drew, **I** 312; **10** 153–54
Betz, L. Drew, **I** 312; **10** 153–54
Betz Laboratories, Inc., **I** **312–13**; **10** **153–55 (upd.)**
Betz, William H., **I** 312; **10** 153
Bevan and Wedd Durlacher Mordaunt & Co., **II** 237

Bevan, Francis Augustus, **II** 235
Bevan, Silvanus, **II** 235
Bevan, Timothy, **II** 236
Beverly Enterprises, Inc., **III** **76–77**, 80
Beverly Hills Savings, **II** 420
Bevis, Herman W., **9** 423
Beynon, Huw, **I** 168
Bezair, Dave, **10** 192
BFGoodrich Chemical Company, **V** 232
BFGoodrich Company, **V** **231–33**; **8** 80–81, 290; **9** 12, 96, 133; **10** 438; **11** 158
BG&E. *See* Baltimore Gas and Electric Company.
BGC Finance, **II** 420
Bharat Coking Coal Ltd., **IV** 48–49
Bharat Petroleum Ltd., **IV** 441
Bhaskar, Krish, **I** 196
BHC Communications, **9** 119
BHP. *See* Broken Hill Proprietary Company Ltd.
BHP Gold Mines Ltd., **IV** 47
BHP Steel, **IV** 46
Bi-Lo Inc., **II** 641; **V** 35
Biagi, Enzo, **I** 163
Bialek, Fred, **II** 64
BIC Corporation, **8** **59–61**
Bic Pen Corp., **III** 29
BICC Cables, **III** 433
BICC North America, **III** 433
BICC PLC, **III** **433–34**; **11** 520
BICC Technologies, **III** 433
Bich, Bruno, **8** 60
Bich, Marcel, **8** 59–60
Bickett, Thomas J., **I** 406
Bickmore, Lee S., **II** 543
Bicoastal Corporation, **II** **9–11**
Bide, Austin, **I** 640; **9** 264
Biederman, Paul, **I** 103, 127, 130
Biegler, John C., **9** 423
Biehl, Hans-Reiner, **IV** 199
Bien, William, **I** 218; **10** 100
Bienfaisance, **III** 391
Bierbrauerei Wilhelm Remmer, **9** 86
Bierce, Ambrose, **IV** 625
Bierich, Marcus, **I** 193
Bierwirth, Jack Cocks, **11** 165–66
Bierwith, Jack, **I** 62–63
Bierwith, James, **I** 377–78
Bierwith, John Cocks, **I** 63
Big Boy, **III** 102–03
Big Horn Mining Co., **8** 423
Big M, **8** 409–10
Big Rivers Electric Corporation, **11** **37–39**
Big Three Industries, **I** 358
Bigelow, Charles H., **III** 355–56
Bigelow, Frederic, **III** 356
Biggam, Robin, **III** 434
Biggart, Nicole W., **III** 11
Biggs, Alfred B., **6** 341
Bilbao Insurance Group, **III** 200
Biles, John, **10** 46
Bilfinger & Berger Bau A.G., **I** **560–61**
Bilfinger, Paul, **I** 560
Billboard Publications, Inc., **7** 15
Biller, Karl, **II** 621
Billerud, **IV** 336
Billig, Erwin H., **III** 570
Billingsley, Case, **III** 370
Billiton Metals, **IV** 56, 532
Bill's Casino, **9** 426
Bilstein, Roger E., **I** 49, 66, 72

Biltwell Company, **8** 249
Bilzerian, Paul, **II** 9–11
Binder, Bernhard (Sir), **IV** 685
Binder, Gordon M., **10** 79
Binder Hamlyn, **IV** 685
Bindley, Bill, **9** 67–68
Bindley Western Industries, Inc., 9 67–69
Bing Crosby Productions, **IV** 595
Binger, James H., **II** 42
Bingham, Hiram, **9** 367
Binghamton Container Company, **8** 102
Binney & Smith, **II** 525; **IV** 621
Binns, James H., **III** 423
Binns, R. H., **6** 483
Binny & Co. Ltd., **III** 522
Binny, Anthony, **III** 670–71
Binny's, **III** 522
Binter Canarias, **6** 97
Bio/Dynamics, Inc., **10** 105, 107
Bio-Clinic, **11** 486–87
Bio-Toxicological Research Laboratories, **IV** 409
Biofermin Pharmaceutical, **I** 704
Biogen, **I** 638, 685; **8** 210
Biokyowa, **III** 43
Biological Research, **III** 443
Biological Technology Corp., **IV** 252
Biomedical Reference Laboratories of North Carolina, **11** 424
Biomet, Inc., 10 156–58
Biondi, Frank J., **7** 223
BioSensor A.B., **I** 665
Biotechnica International, **I** 286
Bioteknik-Gruppen, **I** 665
Bioter S.A., **III** 420
Bioter-Biona, S.A., **II** 493
Biotherm, **III** 47
Birch, Peter, **10** 7
Birch, Stephen, **7** 261–62
Birck, Michael, **11** 500–01
Birdsall, Inc., **6** 529, 531
Birdseye, Clarence, **II** 530–31; **7** 272–74, 277
Birfield Ltd., **III** 494
Birgi, Sahap (Dr.), **IV** 562
Birk, Roger, **II** 425
Birkbeck, **10** 6
Birkeland, Kristian, **10** 437
Birkin, Derek, **IV** 192
Birmingham & Midland Bank, **II** 318
Birmingham Joint Stock Bank, **II** 307
Birmingham Screw Co., **III** 493
Birmingham Slag Company, **7** 572–73, 575
Birnbaum, Hans, **IV** 201
Birnbaum, Melvin, **I** 620; **11** 8
Birtman Electric Co., **III** 653
Biscayne Federal Savings and Loan Association, **11** 481
Biscuiterie Nantaise, **II** 502; **10** 323
Biscuits Belin, **II** 543
Biscuits Delacre, **II** 480
Biscuits Gondolo, **II** 543
Bishop & Babcock Manufacturing Co., **II** 41
Bishop & Co. Savings Bank, **11** 114
Bishop, Charles Reed, **11** 114
Bishop Co., **11** 114
Bishop, Ernest Eugene, **11** 324
Bishop First National Bank of Honolulu, **11** 114
Bishop National Bank of Hawaii, **11** 114
Bishopsgate Insurance, **III** 200

Bisignani, Giovanni, **6** 69
Bismarck, Otto von, **II** 241
Bissell, Anna, **9** 70–71
BISSELL, Inc., 9 70–72
Bissell, John M., **9** 72
Bissell, Melville, III, **9** 71
Bissell, Melville, Jr., **9** 71
Bissell, Melville R., **9** 70–71
Bittner, John, **7** 429
Bitumax Proprietary, **III** 672
Bitumen & Oil Refineries (Australia) Ltd., **III** 672–73
Biver, Hector, **III** 676
BizMart, **6** 244–45; **8** 404–05
Bizot, Henry, **II** 233
Björkenheim, Gösta, **IV** 299, 301
Björkenheim, Robert, **IV** 301
Björknäs Nya Sågverks, **IV** 338
Björnberg, C.G., **IV** 348
Björnberg, Claes, **IV** 347
Björnberg family, **IV** 349
BKW, **IV** 229
BL Ltd., **I** 175; **10** 354
Black & Decker Corporation, I 667; **III** 435–37, 628, 665; **8** 332
Black & Decker Manufacturing Co., **III** 435–37; **8** 349
Black, Adam, **7** 165
Black Arrow Leasing, **II** 138
Black, Charles, **7** 165
Black, Conrad, **7** 253–54; **8** 347
Black, Eli, **II** 595–96; **7** 84–85
Black Flag Co., **I** 622
Black Hawk Broadcasting, **10** 29
Black Hawk Broadcasting Group, **III** 188
Black, Hugo, **I** 78, 84; **10** 536; **11** 427
Black, James W., **I** 693
Black, Kenneth E., **III** 263
Black, Leon, **7** 200; **11** 545
Black, Robert D., **III** 436
Black, S. Duncan, **III** 435–36
Black, Sir Douglas, **6** 452–53
Black Spread Eagle, **II** 235
Black, Theodore, **III** 527
Blackburn, **III** 508
Blackburn, Charles L., **7** 309–10
Blackhawk, **9** 26
Blackhorse Agencies, **II** 309
Blackler, F.H.M., **I** 211
Blackmer, Harry M., **6** 539
Blackmer Pump Co., **III** 468
Blackstone Capital Partners L.P., **V** 223; **6** 378
The Blackstone Group, **II** 434; **IV** 718; **11** 177, 179
Blackstone National Bank, **II** 444
Blackwell, David, **8** 449
Blackwell, Hubert C., **6** 466
Blades, A. T., **6** 421
Blaine Construction Company, **8** 546
Blaine, James G., **IV** 647
Blair and Co., **II** 227
Blair, F.W., **III** 51
Blair, Ledyard, **IV** 180
Blair Paving, **III** 674
Blair Radio, **6** 33
Blair, S. Robert, **V** 673–75
Blake, Frank, **9** 275
Blake, Isaac Elder, **IV** 399
Blakenham (Lord), **IV** 659
Blakiston Co., **IV** 636
Blanchar, Carroll, **6** 556
Blanchard, Noah, **III** 337
Blancke, Harold, **I** 318–19

Bland, John Randolph, **III** 395, 397
Bland, R. Howard, **III** 396
Blane Products, **I** 403
Blank, Arthur, **V** 75
Blankley, Walter E., **9** 24
Blaschke, Heribert, **III** 695
Blatz Breweries, **I** 254
Blaupunkt-Werke, **I** 192–93
Blaustein family, **IV** 369
Blaustein, Louis, **7** 101
Blauvelt, Howard W., **IV** 401
Blay, Roy, **I** 66
Blazer, Paul, **IV** 372–73
Blazer, Rex, **IV** 373
BLC Insurance Co., **III** 330
BLC National Insurance Co., **III** 330
Bleck, Max E., **11** 413
Bleckner, Edward, Jr., **11** 409
Bleiberg, Robert, **IV** 602
Bleichröder, **II** 191
Bleicken, Gerhard D., **III** 267
Bleight, Samuel, **III** 342
Blendax, **III** 53; **8** 434
Bleriot, Louis, **7** 9
Bless, James F., **9** 222
Blinn, A. C., **V** 676
Blitz, Gérard, **6** 206
Bloch, Henry, **9** 268–70
Bloch, Marcel-Ferdinand, **I** 44
Bloch, Richard, **9** 268–70
Blochman Lawrence Goldfree, **I** 697
Block, Alexander, **8** 62
Block Drug, **6** 26
Block Drug Company, Inc., 8 62–64
Block, James A., **8** 63
Block, Joseph, **IV** 113
Block, Joseph L., **IV** 115
Block, L.E., **IV** 113–14
Block, Leonard, **8** 62–63
Block, Macy T., **10** 502
Block Medical, Inc., **10** 351
Block, Phillip D., **IV** 113–14
Block, Phillip D., Jr., **IV** 115
Block, Thomas, **8** 63
Blockbuster Entertainment Corporation, II 161; **IV** 597; **9** 73–75, 361; **11** 556–58
Blockson Chemical, **I** 380
Bloedel, Julius Harold (J.H.), **IV** 306–07
Bloedel, Prentice, **IV** 306–08
Bloedel, Stewart & Welch, **IV** 306–07
Blohm & Voss, **I** 74
Blood, Howard K., **III** 439
Bloomingdale, Joseph, **9** 209
Bloomingdale, Lyman, **9** 209
Bloomingdales, **I** 90; **III** 63; **IV** 651, 703; **9** 209, 393; **10** 487
Bloomquist, Al, **11** 15
Blough, Roger M., **IV** 573–74; **7** 550
Blount Inc., **I** 563
Blount, Orison, **III** 290
Bluck, Duncan, **6** 79–80
Bludhorn, Charles, **III** 745
Blue Arrow PLC, **II** 334–35; **9** 327
Blue Bell, Inc., **V** 390–91
Blue Chip Stamps, **III** 213–14
Blue Circle Aggregates, **III** 671
Blue Circle Industries PLC, III 669–71, 702
Blue Circle Southern Cement Ltd., **III** 673
Blue Cross and Blue Shield Association, 10 159–61
Blue Cross and Blue Shield of Colorado, **11** 175

Blue Cross and Blue Shield of Greater New York, **III** 245, 246
Blue Cross Association, **10** 160
Blue Cross Commission, **10** 159
Blue Cross of Northeastern New York, **III** 245–46
Blue Funnel Line, **I** 521; **6** 415–17
Blue Line Distributing, **7** 278–79
Blue Metal Industries, **III** 687
Blue Mountain Arts, **IV** 621
Blue Ribbon Beef Pack, Inc., **II** 515–16
Blue Ribbon Sports, **V** 372
Blue Ribbon Sports. *See* Nike, Inc.
Blue Ridge Grocery Co., **II** 625
Bluebird Inc., **10** 443
Bluffton Grocery Co., **II** 668
Bluhdorn, Charles George, **I** 451–53; **II** 155–56; **IV** 289
Bluhm, Neil, **IV** 702–03
Blum, Léon, **I** 44; **II** 12; **IV** 558; **10** 347
Blumenthal, W. Michael, **I** 142; **III** 166; **6** 282–83
Blumkin, Rose, **III** 214–15
Blunt Ellis & Loewi, **III** 270
Bly, Stanley, **10** 46
Blyth and Co., **I** 537
Blyth Eastman Dillon & Co., **II** 445
Blyth Eastman Paine Webber, **II** 445
Blyth Merrill Lynch, **II** 448
Blythe Colours BV, **IV** 119
BMC Industries Inc., **6** 275
BMG Music, **IV** 594
BMI Ltd., **III** 673
BMO Corp., **III** 209
BMW. *See* Bayerische Motoren Werke.
BMW of North America, **I** 139
BNA. *See* Banca Nazionale dell'Agricoltura.
BNCI. *See* Banque Nationale Pour le Commerce et l'Industrie.
BNE. *See* Bank of New England Corp.
BNP. *See* Banque Nationale de Paris S.A.
BOAC. *See* British Overseas Airways Corp.
BOAC Cunard Ltd., **I** 93
Boada, Claudio, **I** 460
Boardman, Thomas, **II** 334–35
Boardwalk Regency, **6** 201
Boart and Hard Metals, **IV** 22
Boase Massimi Pollitt, **6** 48
Bob Evans Farms, Inc., 9 76–79; 10 259
Bobbs-Merrill, **11** 198
Bobingen A.G., **I** 347
Bobst, Elmer Holmes, **I** 642–43, 710–11; **10** 549–51
BOC Group plc, I 314–16, 358; **11** 402
Bochumer Verein für Gusstahlfabrikation, **IV** 88
Bock Bearing Co., **8** 530
Bock, Edward J., **I** 366; **9** 356
Bodcaw Co., **IV** 287
Bodegas, **8** 556
Bodenstein, Walter, **II** 516
Bodman, Henry T., **11** 340
Bodman, Samuel, **8** 79
The Body Shop International PLC, 11 40–42
Boeing Air Transport Co., **I** 47, 96, 128; **6** 128; **10** 162
Boeing Aircraft and Transportation Company, **10** 162
The Boeing Company, I 41–43, **47–49**, 50, 55–56, 58, 61, 67–68, 70–72, 74, 77, 82, 84–85, 90, 92–93, 96–97, 100,

102, 104–05, 108, 111–13, 116, 121–22, 126, 128, 130, 195, 489–90, 511, 530; **II** 7, 32–33, 62, 442; **III** 512, 539; **IV** 171, 576; **6** 68, 96, 130, 327; **7** 11, 456, 504; **8** 81, 313, 315; **9** 12, 18, 128, 194, 206, 232, 396, 416–17, 458–60, 498; **10** **162–65 (upd.)**, 262, 316, 369, 536; **11** 164, 267, 277–79, 363, 427
Boeing, William, **I** 47, 64, 70, 76, 84, 96, 125, 128; **6** 128; **9** 12, 416; **10** 162–63, 536; **11** 266, 277, 363
Boeke & Huidekooper, **III** 417
Boel, Baron Rene, **I** 395
Boenisch, Peter, **IV** 590
Boerenbond, **II** 304
Boeschenstein, Harold, **III** 720
Boeschenstein, William, **III** 721–22
Boesky, Ivan, **I** 202, 252, 444; **II** 408; **IV** 523; **7** 309–10; **11** 135
Boettcher & Co., **III** 271
Bofors, **9** 380–81
Bofors Nobel, **9** 381
Bogan, Ralph, **I** 448
Bogardus, John, Jr., **10** 38
Bogart, Humphrey, **II** 175
Böhme-Fettchemie, Chenmitz, **III** 32
Bohn Aluminum & Brass, **10** 439
Boileau, Oliver, **I** 59; **10** 317
Boise Cascade Corporation, I 142; **III** 499, 648, 664; **IV 255–56**, 333; **6** 577; **7** 356; **8 65–67 (upd.)**, 477
Boise Payette Lumber Co., **IV** 255; **8** 65
Bokaro Steel Ltd., **IV** 206
Bol, P.J., **III** 199
Bolands Ltd., **II** 649
Boldrini, Marcello, **IV** 419–21
Boles, Edgar H., **III** 258
Bolger, John J., **11** 17
Boliden Mining, **II** 366
Bolinder, Robert D., **II** 601–02; **7** 20
Bolinder-Munktell, **I** 209; **II** 366
Bolingbroke, Robert A., **III** 22
Bolitho Bank, **II** 235
Bölkow GmbH, **I** 74
Bölkow, Ludwig, **I** 74–75
Bolles & Houghton, **10** 355
The Bolsa Chica Company, **8** 300
Bolter, James, **III** 387
Bolton, August, **6** 397
BOMAG, **8** 544, 546
The Bombay Company, Inc., III 581; **10 166–68**
Bon Appetit, **II** 656
The Bon Marche, **V** 25; **9** 209
Bonanza, **7** 336; **10** 331
Bonaparte, Josephine, **II** 260; **III** 676
Bonaparte, Napoleon, **I** 271, 293; **II** 199, 260; **III** 178, 391, 402; **11** 13
Bonaventura, **IV** 611
Bonaventure Liquor Store Co., **I** 284
Bond, Alan, **10** 169–71
Bond Corporation Holdings Limited, I 253, 255; **10 169–71**
Bond, James, **IV** 79
Bonde, Peder, **III** 420
Bondex Company, **8** 454
Bondex International, **8** 456
Bonehill, Thomas, **IV** 52
Bonfield, Peter, **6** 242
Bonham, Derek C., **7** 209
Bonhoeffer, Dietrich, **IV** 593
Boni, Robert, **10** 38
Boni, Robert E., **IV** 29–30

Bonifiche Siele, **II** 272
Boniger, Melchior, **I** 671
Bonimart, **II** 649
Bonnange, Claude, **6** 47
Bonnell, John, **10** 328
Bonner, Robert, **IV** 308
Booge, James E., **6** 523
Booher, Edward, **IV** 636
Book-of-the-Month-Club, **IV** 661, 675; **7** 529
Bookmasters, **10** 136
Bookout, John F., **IV** 541
Bookstop, **10** 136
Boot, Jesse, **V** 17–18
Booth Fisheries, **II** 571
Booth, H.C., **III** 478
Booth, I. MacAllister, **III** 609; **7** 438
Booth, Inc., **I** 420
Booth Leasing, **I** 449
Booth, Wallace, **II** 596
Booth-Kelly Lumber Co., **IV** 281; **9** 259
Boots Company PLC, V 17–19
Boots Opticians, **V** 17, 19
Boots Pharmaceutical Co., **I** 640, 668, 708; **II** 650; **8** 548
Boots the Chemists, **V** 17, 19
Booz Allen & Hamilton Inc., 10 172–75
Booz, Edwin G., **10** 172–73
Boral Bricks (Victoria), **III** 673
Boral Bricks Proprietary, **III** 673
Boral Cyclone, **III** 673
Boral Limited, III 672–74
Boral Resources (Queensland), **III** 672
Boral Resources (South Australia) Proprietary, **III** 673
Boral Resources (Victoria) Proprietary, **III** 672–73
Boral Steel Ltd., **III** 673
Borax Holdings, **IV** 191
Bordas, **IV** 615
Borden Co., **II** 471–72
Borden Condensed Milk Co., **II** 470–71
Borden, Gail, **II** 470, 486, 545; **7** 380
Borden, Henry Lee, **II** 470
Borden, Inc., II 470–73, 486, 498, 538, 545; **IV** 569; **7** 127, 129, 380; **11** 173
Borden Inc. International, **II** 472
Borden, John Gail, **II** 470
Borden's Cheese & Produce Co., Inc., **II** 471
Borden's Dairy Products Co., Inc., **II** 471
Borden's Food Products Co., Inc., **II** 471
Borden's Ice Cream and Milk Co., Inc., **II** 471
Border Fine Arts, **11** 95
Borders Books & Music, **9** 361
Borders Inc., **10** 137
Borg & Beck Co., **III** 438–39
Borg, Charles W., **III** 438
Borg, George, **III** 438–39
Borg-Warner Acceptance Corp., **III** 440
Borg-Warner Australia, **III** 596
Borg-Warner Corporation, I 193, 339, 393; **III** 428, **438–41**
Borick, Louis L., **8** 505
Borland International, Inc., 6 255–56; **9 80–82**; **10** 237, 509, 519, 558
Borman, Frank, **I** 90, 102–03; **9** 368
Borman's, **II** 638
Born, Allen, **IV** 19
Borneo Airways. *See* Malaysian Airlines System BHD.
Borneo Co., **III** 523
Borrmann, Fritz, **II** 621

Borsheim's, **III** 215
Borstein, Michael L., **9** 453
Bosack, Leonard, **11** 58–59
Bosanquet, Salt and Co., **II** 306
Bosch. *See* Robert Bosch GmbH.
Bosch, Carl, **I** 349
Bosch, Robert, **I** 192
Boschert, **III** 434
Bose, **II** 35
Bosert Industrial Supply, Inc., **V** 215
Boso Condensed Milk, **II** 538
Bosshard, Gottfried, **III** 403
Bossier, Albert L., **7** 39
Bossier, Albert L., Jr., **7** 40
Bostich, **III** 628
Boston Casualty Co., **III** 203
Boston Co., **II** 451–52
Boston Consulting Group, **I** 532; **9** 343
Boston Distributors, **9** 453
Boston Fruit Co., **II** 595
Boston Gas Company, **6** 486–88
Boston Globe, **7** 13–16
Boston Herald, **7** 15
Boston Industries Corp., **III** 735
Boston Marine Insurance Co., **III** 242
Boston News Bureau, **IV** 601
Boston Overseas Financial Corp., **II** 208
Boston Whaler, Inc., **V** 376–77; **10** 215–16
Boswell, James, **II** 306; **IV** 636
BOTAS, **IV** 563
Botha, Pieter, **I** 423
Botsford, Constantine & McCarty, Inc. *See* Botsford Ketchum, Inc.
Botsford Ketchum, Inc., **6** 40
Botto, Rossner, Horne & Messinger, **6** 40
Botts, Guy W., **9** 58
Bottu, **II** 475
Boudreau, Donald, **9** 139–40
Bougainville Copper Pty., **IV** 60–61
Boulet Dru DuPuy Petit Group, **6** 48. *See also* Wells Rich Greene BDDP.
Boulton, David, **I** 66
Boulware, Lemuel, **II** 29
Boundary Gas, **6** 457
Bouquet, **V** 114
Bourgois, Christian, **IV** 615
Bourgois, Jean-Manuel, **IV** 615
Bourke, William, **IV** 187
Bourne, F.G., **II** 9
Bourne, Richard, **V** 490
Boussena, Sadek, **IV** 425
Boussois Souchon Neuvesel, **II** 474; **III** 677
Bouygues, I 562–64
Bouygues, Francis, **I** 562–63
Bouygues, Nicolas, **I** 563
Bouyssonnie, Jean Pierre, **II** 117
Bouzan Mines Ltd., **IV** 164
Bovaird Seyfang Manufacturing Co., **III** 471
Bovis, C.W., **I** 588
Bovis Ltd., **I** 588
Bowater Containers, **IV** 339
Bowater Corporation, **7** 208
Bowater, Eric (Sir), **IV** 257–59
Bowater Industries plc, **IV** 259
Bowater Paper Corp., **IV** 258
Bowater PLC, III 501–02; **IV 257–59; 8** 483–84
Bowater, Thomas Vansittart (Sir), **IV** 257
Bowater, William Vansittart, **IV** 257
Bowater-Scott Corp., **IV** 258–59
Bowden, A. Bruce, **II** 316

Bowen, Charlie, **10** 173–74
Bowen, Henry C., **III** 239
Bowen, Jack, **V** 739
Bowen, Kenneth E., **6** 470–71
Bower, Marvin, **9** 343
Bower Roller Bearing Co., **I** 158–59
Bowerman, William, **8** 391
Bowers, Geoffrey, **10** 127
Bowers, Peter M., **I** 72
Bowery and East River National Bank, **II** 226
Bowery Savings Bank, **II** 182; **9** 173
Bowes Co., **II** 631
Bowes, Joseph (Jos), **7** 410
Bowes, Walter, **III** 156
Bowie, David, **9** 30
Bowlby, Joel M., **8** 156–57
Bowles, Chester, **6** 22
Bowman, James (Sir), **IV** 39
Bowmar Instruments, **II** 113; **11** 506
Bowring, Peter, **III** 283
Box Office Attraction Co., **II** 169
BoxCrow Cement Company, **8** 259
Boxer, Leonard, **8** 329
Boyce, H.H. (Col.), **IV** 677
Boyd, J. Mitchel, **7** 475
Boyd, Joseph, **II** 37–38
Boyd, Morton, **III** 217
Boyd, William, **III** 665
Boyer, Augustin, **IV** 614
Boyer, Herbert, **I** 637; **8** 209
Boykin Enterprises, **IV** 136
Boyle, Peyton, **7** 580
Boyoud, Emile, **IV** 173
Boz, **IV** 697–98
Bozel, Électrométallurgie, **IV** 174
BP. *See* British Petroleum Company PLC.
BP America, **IV** 379, 525
BP Benzin und Petroleum Aktiengesellschaft, **7** 141
BP Benzin und Petroleum GmbH, **7** 141
BP Canada Inc., **IV** 495
BP Chemicals PlasTec GmbH, **7** 141
BP Chemie GmbH, **7** 141
BP Chimie, **I** 303
BP Handel GmbH, **7** 142
BP Marine, **7** 141
BP Minerals, **IV** 57, 192; **7** 289
BP Oil, **7** 58–59
BP Oiltech GmbH, **7** 141
BP Tankstellen GmbH, **7** 142
BPB, **III** 736
BPI Communications, Inc., **7** 15
BR. *See* British Rail.
Braas, **III** 734, 736
Brabant, **III** 199, 201
Brabazon, **III** 555
Brace, Donald C., **IV** 622
Bradbury Agnew and Co., **IV** 686
Braddock, Richard, **9** 347
Braddock, Robert, **III** 258
Braden, Glen T., **7** 409
Bradford District Bank, **II** 333
Bradford Insulation Group, **III** 687
Bradford Pennine, **III** 373
Bradham, Caleb D., **I** 276; **10** 450
Bradlee, Benjamin, **IV** 689
Bradlees, **II** 666–67
Bradley, F. K., **V** 140
Bradley Lumber Company, **8** 430
Bradley, Milton, **III** 505
Bradley Producing Corp., **IV** 459
Bradshaw, Charles J., **II** 679
Bradshaw, Thornton F., **II** 90; **IV** 375–76

Bradstreet, Ann, **IV** 604
Bradstreet Co., **IV** 604–05
Bradstreet, John, **IV** 604
Bradstreet, Simon, **IV** 604
Brady, Anthony, **V** 679
Brady, William, **II** 497
Brady, William V., **III** 239
Bragge, William, **I** 572
Bragussa, **IV** 71
Brahs, Stuart J., **III** 330
Brainard, Morgan Bulkeley, **III** 181–82
Brainerd, Andrew, **10** 126
Brainerd, Paul, **10** 34–35
BRAINS. *See* Belgian Rapid Access to Information Network Services.
Bramalea Ltd., 9 83–85; 10 530–31
Brambles Industries, **III** 494–95
Bramco, **III** 600
Bramono, Bambang, **IV** 492
Bramwell Gates, **II** 586
Bran & Lübbe, **III** 420
Branch, Ben, **I** 324; **8** 148
Branch, Taylor, **IV** 672
Brand Companies, Inc., **9** 110; **11** 436
Brandeis, **IV** 174
Brandeis, Louis, **II** 205
Brandenburgische Motorenwerke, **I** 138
Brandino, Joseph, **I** 496
Brandner, J. William, **IV** 624
Brando, Marlon, **II** 143, 175
Brandon, Dave, **8** 550
Brandon, David, **8** 551
Brandt, Joe, **II** 135
Brandt, John, **II** 535–36
Braniff Airlines, **I** 97, 489, 548; **II** 445; **6** 119–20
Braniff International Airlines, **6** 50, 120
Branigar Organization, Inc., **IV** 345
Brascade Resources, **IV** 308
Brascan, Ltd., **II** 456; **IV** 165, 330
Brase, Bertus, **I** 54
Braspetro, **IV** 454, 501–02
Brass Craft Manufacturing Co., **III** 570
Brasseries Kronenbourg, **II** 474–75
Bratt, Ivan, **I** 625
Brauerei Beck & Co., 9 86–87
Brauerei C.H. Haake & Co., **9** 86
Braun, **III** 29
Braunig, V.H., **6** 473–74
Braunkohlenwerk Golpa-Jessnitz AG, **IV** 230
Brazilian Central Bank, **IV** 56
Brazos Gas Compressing, **7** 345
Breakstone Bros., Inc., **II** 533
Breakthrough Software, **10** 507
Bredel Exploitatie B.V., **8** 546
Bredell Paint Co., **III** 745
Bredero's Bouwbedrijf of Utrecht, **IV** 707–08, 724
Breech, Ernest, **11** 138–39
Breech, Ernest R., **I** 141–42, 166–67; **11** 138
Breed, Richard E., **V** 546
Breedband NV, **IV** 133
Breen, John G., **III** 745
Brega Petroleum Marketing Co., **IV** 453, 455
Brégou, Christian, **IV** 615
Breguet Aviation, **I** 44
Breguet, Louis, **I** 45
Breitenburger Cementfabrik, **III** 701
Breitschwerdt, Werner, **I** 151
Breitweiser, Stanley, **IV** 392
Bremner Biscuit Co., **II** 562

Brenda Mines Ltd., **7** 399
Brengel, Fred L., **III** 535
Brengle, Ralph, **11** 396
Brennan, Bernard, **V** 148
Brennan, Edward, **V** 182
Brennan, Patrick, **8** 125
Brenner, Joseph D., **II** 8
Brenninkmeyer, August, **V** 23
Brenninkmeyer, Clemens, **V** 23
Brenntag AG, 8 68–69, 496
Brenntag Eurochem GmbH, **8** 69
Brentano's, **7** 286
Breslube Enterprises, **8** 464
Bressler, Richard M., **10** 190
Brestle, Daniel J., **9** 204
Breton, Louis, **IV** 617–18
Brett, Bruce Y., **7** 286
Brett, George Edward, **7** 285
Brett, George Platt, **7** 285
Brett, George Platt, Jr., **7** 285
Brett, Herbert, **III** 697
Brewer, Gene, **IV** 264
Brewster, J. Christopher, **7** 375
Brewster Lines, **6** 410
Breyer Ice Cream Co., **II** 533
Brezhnev, Leonid, **I** 313
BRI Bar Review Institute, Inc., **IV** 623
Brian Mills, **V** 118
Bricker, William H., **IV** 409–10; **7** 309
Brickwood Breweries, **I** 294
Bridge Oil Ltd., **I** 438
Bridge Technology, Inc., **10** 395
Bridgeman Creameries, **II** 536
Bridgeport Brass, **I** 377
Bridges, Harry, **IV** 541
Bridgestone (U.S.A.), Inc., **V** 235
Bridgestone Corporation, V 234–35
Bridgestone Cycle Co., Ltd., **V** 235
Bridgestone/Firestone, Inc., **V** 235
Bridgestone Liquefied Gas, **IV** 364
Bridgestone Ltd., **V** 234
Bridgestone Sports Co., Ltd., **V** 235
Bridgestone Tire Co., Ltd., **V** 234
Bridgeway Plan for Health, **6** 186
Bridgman, Thomas, **10** 127
Brier Hill, **IV** 114
Briggs & Stratton Corporation, III 597;
    8 70–73
Briggs, Alky, **II** 247
Briggs, Asa, **I** 216
Briggs, Guy, **7** 462
Briggs, Roger, **I** 441
Briggs, Stephen F., **III** 597–98
Briggs, Stephen Foster, **8** 70–71
Briggs-Shaffner Division, **8** 476
Brigham, Dwight S., **9** 304
Bright, Charles D., **I** 80
Bright, Frank, **11** 225
Brighton Federal Savings and Loan Assoc.,
    II 420
Brill, Ronald, **V** 75
Brill, Sol, **II** 169
Brimsdown Lead Co., **III** 680
Brin, Arthur, **I** 314
Brin, Leon Quentin, **I** 314
Brin's Oxygen Co., **I** 314
Brinckman, Donald W., **8** 462–64
Brinco Ltd., **II** 211
Brink, John, **11** 163
Brink's Home Security, Inc., **IV** 182
Brink's, Inc., **IV** 180–82
Brinker International, Inc., 10 176–78
Brinker, Norman E., **10** 176–78
Brinsfield, Shirley D., **10** 262–63

BRIntec, **III** 434
Brinton Carpets, **III** 423
Brisbane Gas Co., **III** 673
Bristol Aeroplane, **I** 50, 197; **10** 261
Bristol, Henry, **III** 17; **9** 88
Bristol Laboratories, **III** 17
Bristol, Lee, **III** 17; **9** 88
Bristol PLC, **IV** 83
Bristol, William, Jr., **III** 17; **9** 88
Bristol, William McLaren, **III** 17; **9** 88
Bristol-BTR, **I** 429
Bristol-Myers Co., **I** 26, 30, 37, 301, 696,
    700, 703; **III** 17–19, 36, 67; **IV** 272; **6**
    27; **7** 255; **8** 282–83
Bristol-Myers Squibb Company, III
    17–19; 8 210; **9 88–91 (upd.); 10** 70;
    11 289
Bristol-Siddeley Ltd., **I** 50
Britannia Airways, **8** 525–26
Britannica Software, **7** 168
Britches of Georgetowne, **10** 215–16
British & Commonwealth Shipping
    Company, **10** 277
British Aerospace Corporate Jets, **11** 413
British Aerospace plc, I 42, 46, **50–53,**
    55, 74, 83, 132, 532; **III** 458, 507; **V**
    339; **7** 9, 11, 458–59; **8** 315; **9** 499
British Aircraft Corp., **I** 50–51
British Airways Ltd., **IV** 658
British Airways plc, I 34, 83, **92–95,** 109;
    IV 658; **6** 60, 78–79, 118, 132
British Aluminium, Ltd., **II** 422; **IV** 15
British American Cosmetics, **I** 427
British American Insurance Co., **III** 350
British American Nickel, **IV** 110
British American Tobacco Co. See BAT
    Industries plc.
British and Dominion Film Corp., **II** 157
British and Foreign Marine, **III** 350
British and French Bank, **II** 232–33
British Bank of North America, **II** 210
British Bank of the Middle East, **II** 298
British Borneo Timber Co., **III** 699
British Broadcasting Corporation, III
    163; **IV** 651; **7 52–55**
British Caledonian Airways, **I** 94–95; **6** 79
British Can Co., **I** 604
British Celanese Ltd., **I** 317
British Cellulose and Chemical
    Manufacturing Co., **I** 317
British Chrome, **III** 699
British Coal Corporation, IV 38–40
British Columbia Forest Products Ltd., **IV**
    279
British Columbia Packers, **II** 631–32
British Columbia Resources Investment
    Corp., **IV** 308
British Columbia Telephone Company,
    IV 308; **6 309–11**
British Columbia Telephone Company,
    Limited. See British Columbia
    Telephone Company.
British Commonwealth Insurance, **III** 273
British Commonwealth Pacific Airways, **6**
    110
British Continental Airlines, **I** 92
British Credit Trust, **10** 443
British Dyestuffs Corp., **I** 351
British Dynamite Co., **I** 351
British Engine, **III** 350
British European Airways, **I** 93, 466
British Executive, **I** 50
British Fuels, **III** 735
British Gas Corporation, **11** 97

British Gas plc, II 260; **V 559–63; 6**
    478–79
British General, **III** 234
British Goodrich Tyre Co., **I** 428
British Home Stores, **II** 658
British Hovercraft Corp., **I** 120
British India and Queensland Agency Co.
    Ltd., **III** 522
British India Steam Navigation Co., **III**
    521–22
British Industrial Solvents Ltd., **IV** 70
British Industry, **III** 335
British Insulated and Helsby Cables Ltd.,
    III 433–34
British Insulated Cables, **III** 433
British Insulated Callender's Cables Ltd.,
    III 433–34
British Insulated Wire Co., **III** 433
British Isles Transport Co. Ltd., **II** 564
British Land Company, **10** 6
British Leyland, **I** 175, 186; **III** 516, 523
British Linen Bank, **10** 336
British Marine Air Navigation, **I** 92
British Metal Corp., **IV** 140, 164
British Motor Corporation, **III** 555; **7** 459
British Motor Holdings, **7** 459
British National Films Ltd., **II** 157
British National Oil Corp., **IV** 40
British Newfoundland Corporation, **6** 502
British Nuclear Fuels PLC, I 573; **6**
    451–54
British Overseas Airways Corp., **I** 51, 93,
    120–21; **III** 522; **6** 78–79, 100, 110,
    112, 117
British Oxygen Co. See BOC Group.
British Petroleum Company PLC, I 241,
    303; **II** 449, 563; **IV** 61, 280, 363–64,
    378–80, 381–82, 412–13, 450–54, 456,
    466, 472, 486, 497–99, 505, 515,
    524–25, 531–32, 557; **6** 304; **7 56–59**
    (upd.), 140–41, 332–33, 516, 559; **9**
    490, 519; **11** 538
British Plasterboard, **III** 734
British Portland Cement Manufacturers, **III**
    669–70
British Printing and Communications
    Corp., **IV** 623–24, 642; **7** 312
British Printing Corp., **IV** 641–42; **7**
    311–12
British Prudential Assurance Co., **III** 335
British Rail, **III** 509; **V** 421–24; **10** 122
British Railways, **6** 413
British Railways Board, V 421–24
British Road Services, **6** 413
British Royal Insurance Co., Ltd., **III** 242
British Satellite Broadcasting, **10** 170
British Shoe Corporation, **V** 178
British South Africa Co., **IV** 23, 94
British South American Airways, **I** 93
British South American Corporation, **6** 95
British Steel Brickworks, **III** 501; **7** 207
British Steel Corp., **III** 494–95; **IV** 41–43
British Steel plc, IV 40, **41–43,** 128
British Sugar Corp., **II** 514, 581–82
British Tabulating Machine Company, **6**
    240
British Telecom, **8** 153; **11** 185, 547
British Telecommunications plc, I 83,
    330; **II** 82; **V 279–82; 6** 323; **7** 332–33;
    9 32; **11** 59
British Thermoplastics and Rubber. See
    BTR plc.
British Timken Ltd., **8** 530
British Tyre and Rubber Co., **I** 428

British United Airways, **I** 94
British Vita Pensions Trust Limited, **9** 92
British Vita PLC, **9** 92–93
British Zaire Diamond Distributors Ltd., **IV** 67
British-American Tobacco Co., Ltd., **V** 396, 401–02, 417; **9** 312
Britoil, **IV** 380
Britt Airways, **I** 118
Britt Lumber Co., Inc., **8** 348
Brittain, Alfred III, **II** 229, 230–31
Brittains Bricks, **III** 673
Brittan, Leon (Sir), **IV** 528–29
Britton Lee, **10** 504
BRK Electronics, **9** 414
Broad, Eli, **8** 284; **11** 481–82
Broad, Inc., **11** 482
Broad River Power Company, **6** 575
Broadcom Eireann Research, **7** 510
Broadhead, James, **V** 624
BroadPark, **II** 415
Brock, Horace, **I** 116
Brock, Jeffry Hall, **III** 260
Brock Residence Inn, **9** 426
Brockway Glass, **I** 524
Broderbund Software, **10** 285
Brodeur, Paul, **III** 706
Brodsky, Julian, **7** 90
Brody, Alexander, **I** 37
Brody, Herb, **II** 672–74
Broederlijke Liefdebeurs, **III** 177
Broglie (Duc de), **III** 676
Broida, Dan, **I** 690–91
Broken Hill Associated Smelters Proprietary Co., **IV** 45, 58
Broken Hill Proprietary Company Ltd., **I** 437–39; **II** 30; **III** 494; **IV** 44–47, 58, 61, 171, 484; **10** 170
Broken Hill South Blocks Co., **IV** 58
Bronfman, Charles, **I** 286
Bronfman, Edgar, **I** 285–86, 329; **8** 152
Bronfman, Edward, **II** 456; **IV** 165; **10** 529–30
Bronfman family, **IV** 308, 721; **9** 391
The Bronfman Group, **6** 161, 163
Bronfman, Harry, **I** 284
Bronfman, Peter, **II** 456; **IV** 165; **10** 529–30
Bronfman, Sam, **I** 240, 284–85; **10** 529
Bronfman, Yechiel, **I** 284
Brooke Bond, **II** 590
Brooke, Edward W., **11** 281
Brooke Partners L.P., **11** 275
Brooker, Robert E., **V** 147
Brookes, Raymond (Sir), **III** 494
Brookhuis, John, **I** 347
Brooklyn Borough Gas Company, **6** 456
Brooklyn Edison, **6** 456
Brooklyn Flint Glass Co., **III** 683
Brooklyn Gas Light Company, **6** 455
Brooklyn Trust Co., **II** 312
Brooklyn Union Gas, 6 455–57
Brooks Brothers, **V** 26–7
Brooks, Dwight, **IV** 306–07
Brooks, Garth, **11** 557
Brooks, Harvey & Co., Inc., **II** 431
Brooks, John G., **I** 481, 483
Brooks, John W., **I** 318
Brooks, Lewis, **6** 571
Brooks, Sam A., **III** 78
Brooks, Scanlon & O'Brien, **IV** 306
Brooks, Shoobridge and Co., **III** 669
Brooks, William, **9** 303
Brooks-Scanlon Lumber Co., **IV** 306

Brookstone, **II** 560
Brookstone, Arnold, **IV** 334
Brookville Telephone Company, **6** 300
Brookwood Health Services, **III** 73
Brotman, Jeffrey H., **V** 36
Brough, D.W., **I** 605
Brower, Charlie, **I** 28–29
Brower, Horace W., **I** 537
Brown & Dureau Ltd., **IV** 248–49
Brown & Root, **III** 498–99, 559
Brown and Williamson, **I** 426
Brown, Bennett, **10** 426–27
Brown Bibby & Gregory, **I** 605
Brown Boveri. *See* BBC Brown Boveri.
Brown Boveri International, **II** 3
Brown Boveri Kent, **II** 3
Brown, Charles, **III** 402, 631–32; **9** 304
Brown, Chester M., **I** 415
Brown Co., **I** 452; **IV** 289
Brown, Colon, **10** 422
Brown Corp., **IV** 286
Brown, Curtis, **8** 514
Brown, David A., **10** 458–59
Brown Drug, **III** 9
Brown, Edward Eagle, **II** 285
Brown, Edward J., **8** 53–54
Brown Foundation, **III** 498
Brown, Frank, **I** 683–84; **III** 395
Brown, George, **IV** 697
Brown, George Andrews, **II** 592
Brown, George Garvin, **I** 225; **10** 179–81
Brown, George Warren, **V** 351–52
Brown Group, Inc., **V** 351–53; **9** 192; **10** 282
Brown, Howard, **8** 173
Brown Instrument Co., **II** 41
Brown, Jack E., **III** 763
Brown, John, **I** 572; **9** 228, 407
Brown, John T., **10** 379
Brown, John Thomson, **IV** 248
Brown, John W., **11** 474–75
Brown, John Y., Jr., **6** 200; **7** 265–66
Brown, L.H., **III** 706–07; **7** 291–92
Brown, Michael, **8** 525, 527; **10** 362
Brown Oil Tools, **III** 428
Brown, Owsley, II, **10** 182
Brown Paper Mill Co., **I** 380
Brown, Raymond, **II** 83
Brown, Richard, **II** 41
Brown, Roy (Capt.), **III** 507
Brown Shoe Company, **V** 351–52
Brown, Stephen L., **III** 268
Brown, Vandiver, **III** 706; **7** 291
Brown, W.L. Lyons, **I** 227
Brown, W.L. Lyons, Jr., **10** 181–82
Brown, Walter Folger, **I** 115, 125
Brown, Werner, **I** 344–45
Brown, Willard, Jr., **II** 442
Brown, William, **II** 208
Brown, William Folger, **10** 536
Brown, Wilson M., Jr., **9** 475
Brown-Forman Corporation, **I** 225–27; **10** 179–82 (upd.)
Brown-Forman Distillers Corp., **I** 225; **III** 286; **10** 179–81
Brown-Forman Distillery, **10** 179
Brown-Service Insurance Company, **9** 507
Brown-Shipley Ltd., **II** 425
Browne & Nolan Ltd., **IV** 294
Browne, H.J.C. (John), **6** 79
Browne, W. Herman, **IV** 645
Brownell, Francis H., **IV** 33
Brownell, Kenneth, **IV** 33
Browning, Jack, **10** 46

Browning Manufacturing, **II** 19
Browning, Marriner A., **11** 117
Browning, Peter C., **10** 423
Browning-Ferris Industries, Inc., V 749–53; **8** 562; **10** 33
Broyhill Furniture Industries, Inc., **III** 528, 530; **10** 183–85
Broyhill, James Edgar, **10** 183
Broyhill, Tom, **10** 183
Brozinsky, Morton, **11** 462–63
BRS Ltd., **6** 412–13
Bruederer, Willy, **IV** 559
Brufina, **II** 201–02
Bruggere, Thomas, **11** 284, 286
Brumfield, Richard M., **11** 396–97
Brundage, Percival F., **9** 423
Brüning, Friedrich, **I** 349
Brunner, Eugenio, **III** 346
Brunner family, **III** 347
Brunner, John, **I** 351
Brunner Mond and Co., **I** 351
Bruno, Angelo, **7** 61
Bruno, Joe, **7** 60
Bruno, Ronald, **7** 61
Bruno's Inc., 7 60–62
Brunswick, Benedict, **III** 443
Brunswick Corporation, **III** 442–44, 599; **9** 67, 119; **10** 262
Brunswick, David, **III** 442
Brunswick, Emanuel, **III** 442
Brunswick, Hyman, **III** 442
Brunswick, John Moses, **III** 442–43
Brunswick, Joseph, **III** 442
Brunswick Panatrope & Radio Corp., **III** 443
Brunswick Pulp & Paper Co., **IV** 282, 311, 329; **9** 260
Brunswick Tire Co., **III** 443
Brunswick-Balke-Collender Co., **III** 442–43
Brunswig, Lucien Napoleon, **V** 14–15
Brunton, Gordon, **8** 527
Brunzell, George, **6** 597
Brush, Alvin G., **I** 622; **10** 68
Brush, Charles F., **I** 399; **III** 508
The Brush Electric Light Company, **11** 387
Brush Electrical Machines, **III** 507–09
Brush Moore Newspaper, Inc., **8** 527
Bruson, Herman, **I** 392
Bryan Bros. Packing, **II** 572
Bryan, John H., **II** 572–73
Bryan, William Jennings, **IV** 625
Bryant, George A., **8** 42
Bryant Heater Co., **III** 471
Bryce & Co., **I** 547
Bryce Grace & Co., **I** 547
Brydges, Charles J., **6** 359
Brymbo Steel Works, **III** 494
Bryson, John, **V** 717
Bryson, Vaughn D., **11** 91
BSB, **IV** 653; **7** 392
BSC (Industry) Ltd., **IV** 42
BSkyB, **IV** 653; **7** 392
BSN Groupe S.A., II 474–75, 544
BSN-Gervais-Danone, **II** 474–75
BSR, **II** 82
BT. *See* British Telecommunications, plc.
BT Credit Co., **II** 230
BT New York Corp., **II** 230
BTI Services, **9** 59
BTM. *See* British Tabulating Machine Company.
BTR plc, I 428–30; **III** 185, 727; **8** 397
Buccleuch (Duke of), **III** 358

Bucerius, Gerd (Dr.), **IV** 592
Buchan, Carl, **V** 122
Buchanan, **I** 239–40
Buchanan Electric Steel Company, **8** 114
Buchner, Edouard, **I** 391
Buck, Pearl S., **IV** 671
Buckeye Union Casualty Co., **III** 242
Buckingham Corp., **I** 440, 468
Buckler Broadcast Group, **IV** 597
Buckley, Peter, **I** 246, 279
Buckley, R.M. (Mike), **IV** 342
Buckley, Robert J., **8** 19; **9** 484
Bucknell, Earl, **III** 329
Bucy, J. Fred, **II** 114; **11** 507
Bucyrus-Erie Company, **7** 513
The Budd Company, IV 222; **8 74–76**
Budd, Edward, **8** 74–75
Budd, Edward G., Jr., **8** 75
Budd, Edward H., **III** 389
Budd, Ralph, **V** 427, 428
Budd Wheel, **III** 568
Buderus AG, **III** 692, 694–95
Buderus, Georg, **III** 694
Buderus, Georg, I, **III** 694
Buderus, Georg, II, **III** 694
Buderus, Georg, III, **III** 694
Buderus, Hugo, **III** 694
Buderus, Johann Wilhelm, I, **III** 694
Buderus, Johann Wilhelm, II, **III** 694
Buderus'sche Eisenwerke, **III** 694–95
Budge, Alexander G., **II** 491
Budget Rent a Car Corporation, I 537; **6** 348–49, 393; **9 94–95**
Buegler, Larry, **8** 490
Buell, Margaret, **III** 40
Buena Vista Distribution, **II** 172; **6** 174
Buetow, Herbert, **I** 500
Buffalo Forge Company, **7** 70–71
Buffalo Insurance Co., **III** 208
Buffalo Mining Co., **IV** 181
Buffets, Inc., 10 186–87
Buffett Partnership, Ltd., **III** 213
Buffett, Warren, **III** 29, 190, 213–15
Buffington, A.L., **7** 496
Buhler, Hans, **I** 410
Buick, David, **I** 171; **10** 325
Buick Motor Co., **I** 171; **III** 438; **8** 74; **10** 325
Builders Square, **V** 112; **9** 400
Buitoni SpA, **II** 548
Buley, R. Carlyle, **III** 266
Bulgarian Oil Co., **IV** 454
Bulkeley, Eliphalet, **III** 180, 236
Bulkeley, Morgan G., **III** 180–81
Bull. *See* Compagnie des Machines Bull S.A.
Bull, Frank, **10** 378
Bull, Fredrik Rosing, **III** 122
Bull HN Information Systems, **III** 122–23
Bull, M.W.J., **I** 288
Bull Motors, **11** 5
Bull S.A., **III** 122–23
Bull, Stephen, **10** 377
Bull Tractor Company, **7** 534
Bull-GE, **III** 123
Bulldog Computer Products, **10** 519
Bullis, Henry, **II** 501; **10** 322
Bullock, L.C., **I** 714
Bullock, Thomas A., **6** 142, 144
Bullock's, **III** 63
Bulolo Gold Dredging, **IV** 95
Bulova Watch Co., **I** 488; **II** 101; **III** 454–55
Bulova-Citizen, **III** 454

Bumble Bee Seafoods, Inc., **II** 491, 508, 557
Bumkor-Ramo Corp., **I** 539
Bumpus, James N., **6** 560
Bumstead, Albert, **9** 367
Bunawerke Hüls GmbH., **I** 350
Bund, Karlheinz, **IV** 195
Bunker, Arthur H., **IV** 18
Bunker, George, **I** 67–68
Bunker, Gerald, **III** 228
Bunker Ramo Info Systems, **III** 118
Buntrock, Dean, **11** 436
Buntrock, Dean L., **V** 752
Bunyan, John, **I** 293
Bunzl & Biach, **IV** 260–61
Bunzl & Biach (British) Ltd., **IV** 260
Bunzl family, **IV** 260–61
Bunzl, G.G., **IV** 261
Bunzl, Hugo, **IV** 260
Bunzl PLC, IV 260–62
Bunzl Pulp & Paper Ltd., **IV** 260
Burbank, James C., **III** 355
Burberry's Ltd., **V** 68; **10** 122
Burbidge, Frederic, **V** 430
Burbridge, F. B., **6** 539
Burda family, **11** 292
Burda, Franz, **IV** 590–91
Burda, Frieder, **IV** 590–91
Burden, John, III, **V** 27
Burdines, **9** 209
Bureau de Recherches de Pétrole, **IV** 544–46, 559–60; **7** 481–83
Burger Boy Food-A-Rama, **8** 564
Burger Chef, **II** 532
Burger King Corporation, I 21, 278; **II** 556–57, **613–15**, 647; **7** 316; **8** 564; **9** 178; **10** 122
Burger, Ralph, **II** 637
Burger, Warren, **9** 368
Burgess, Carter, **I** 126
Burgess, Ian, **III** 688
Burgess, Ray, **8** 238
Burill, William, **II** 424
Burke, Daniel, **II** 131
Burke Dowling Adams Advertising Agency, **I** 29
Burke, Edmund S., **8** 291
Burke, James, **III** 36–37; **8** 282–83
Burke, Richard, **9** 524
Burke Scaffolding Co., **9** 512
BURLE Industries Inc., **11** 444
Burlesdon Brick Co., **III** 734
Burlington, **8** 234
Burlington Air Express, Inc., **IV** 182
Burlington Coat Factory Warehouse Corporation, 10 188–89
Burlington Industries, Inc., V 118, **354–55**; **9** 231
Burlington Northern Air Freight, **IV** 182
Burlington Northern, Inc., V 425–28; **10** 190–91
Burlington Northern Railroad, **11** 315
Burlington Resources Inc., 10 190–92; **11** 135
Burmah Castrol PLC, IV 381–84
Burmah Engineering, **IV** 382
Burmah Industrial Products, **IV** 382
Burmah Oil Company, **IV** 378, 381–83, 440–41, 483–84, 531; **7** 56
Burmah-Castrol Co., **IV** 382
Burmah-Shell, **IV** 440–41, 483
Burmeister & Wain, **III** 417–18
Burn & Co., **IV** 205
Burn Standard Co. Ltd., **IV** 484

Burnards, **II** 677
Burnett, Clinton Brown, **III** 707; **7** 292
Burnett, Leo, **I** 22, 36
Burnett, Robert, **11** 292–93
Burnham and Co., **II** 407–08; **6** 599; **8** 388
Burnham, Daniel, **II** 284
Burnham, Donald, **II** 121
Burnham, Duane L., **11** 9
Burnham, I.W. "Tubby", **II** 407–08; **8** 388–89
Burns & Wilcox Ltd., **6** 290
Burns, C.F., **7** 104
Burns Cos., **III** 569
Burns, Ed, **7** 104
Burns Fry Ltd., **II** 349
Burns, George, **II** 133, 151
Burns International, **III** 440
Burns, John, **IV** 392
Burns, John, Jr., **10** 45
Burns, M. Anthony, **V** 505
Burns, Robin, **9** 203
Burns, Thomas S., **I** 464
Burpee Co. *See* W. Atlee Burpee Co.
Burr & Co., **II** 424
Burr, Aaron, **II** 217, 247
Burr, Donald C., **I** 117–18, 123–24
Burr, Robert, **11** 135
Burrill & Housman, **II** 424
Burritt, Arthur W., **IV** 252
Burroughs Adding Machine Co., **III** 165–66
Burroughs Corp., **I** 142, 478; **III** 132, 148–49, 152, 165–66; **6** 233, 266, 281–83. *See also* Unisys Corporation.
Burroughs, Silas M., **I** 713
Burroughs Wellcome & Co., **I** 713; **8** 216
Burroughs, William Seward, **III** 165; **6** 281
Burrows, Daniel, **III** 282
Burrows, Harold, **8** 34–35
Burrows, Marsh & McLennan, **III** 282
Burry, **II** 560
Bursley & Co., **II** 668
Burt Claster Enterprises, **III** 505
Burt, Wayne, **7** 288–89
Burthy China Clays, **III** 690
Burtis, Theodore A., **IV** 550
Burton, Ed, **I** 96
Burton Group plc, V, 20–22
Burton J. Vincent, Chesley & Co., **III** 271
Burton, John, **10** 395
Burton, Montague, **V** 20–21
Burton, Parsons and Co. Inc., **II** 547
Burton Retail, **V** 21
Burton, Richard, **II** 176
Burton Rubber Processing, **8** 347
Burton's Gold Metal Biscuits, **II** 466
Burton-Furber Co., **IV** 180
Burtsell, B.W, **III** 651
Bury, David, **III** 509
Bury Group, **II** 581
Busch, Adolphus, **I** 217–18; **10** 99
Busch, Adolphus, III, **I** 218; **10** 100
Busch, August A., Sr., **10** 99
Busch, August, III, **I** 218; **10** 100
Busch, August, Jr., **I** 218; **10** 100
Buschmann, Siegfried, **8** 76
Busemann, Ernst, **IV** 140
Bush, A.G., **I** 499–500; **8** 369–70
Bush Boake Allen Ltd., **IV** 346
Bush, George, **IV** 489; **8** 165; **9** 545; **10** 539
Bush, Vannevar, **11** 411
Bushnell, Nolan, **9** 44–46
Business Depot, Limited, **10** 498

Business Men's Assurance Co. of America, **III** 209
Business Software Association, **10** 35
Business Software Technology, **10** 394
BusinessLand, **10** 235
Businessland Inc., **III** 153; **6** 267
Bussan, Mitsui, **V** 383
Busse Broadcasting, **7** 200
Büssing Automobilwerke AG, **IV** 201
Bustello, Carlos, **I** 460
Buster Brown, **V** 351–52
Busti, Dennis, **III** 197
Butano, **IV** 528
Butcher, Samuel, **11** 94–95
Butcher, Willard C., **II** 248
Butler Cox PLC, **6** 229
Butler, Harold, **10** 301
Butler, I.G., **III** 681
Butler, James, **V** 674
Butler, Louis F., **III** 388
Butler, Thomas, **7** 202
Butler, William E., **10** 280
Butterbrodt, John, **11** 24
Butterfield & Swire, **I** 469, 521–22; **6** 78
Butterfield Brothers, **I** 521
Butterfield, John, **II** 380–81, 395; **10** 59
Butterfield, Richard Shackleton, **I** 521
Butterfield, Wasson & Co., **II** 380, 395; **10** 59
Butterley Company, **III** 501; **7** 207
Butterworth & Co. (Publishers) Ltd., **IV** 641; **7** 311
Butterworth, William, **III** 462
Buttfield, Alfred, **7** 573
Buttfield, William J., **7** 573
Butz, Albert, **II** 40
Butz, Earl, **11** 24
Butz Thermo-Electric Regulator Co., **II** 40
Buxton, **III** 28
Buxton, Winslow, **7** 420
Buz, Carl, **III** 561
Buz, Heinrich, **III** 561
Buzick, William A., Jr., **II** 572
Buzzard Electrical & Plumbing Supply, **9** 399
BVA Investment Corp., **11** 447
BVA Mortgage Corporation, **11** 446
Byerly, Russell W., **II** 669
Byers, William N., **6** 558
Byllesby, Henry Marison, **V** 670; **6** 516–17
Byng, Gustav, **II** 24
Byrd, Richard, **I** 54
Byrd, Richard E., **9** 367
Byrne, John J., **III** 214, 252
Byrnes Long Island Motor Cargo, Inc., **6** 370
Byron, Fletcher L., **I** 354–55
Byron, George, **III** 345
Byron Jackson, **III** 428, 439
Bystedt, Gösta, **III** 479
Bytrex, Inc., **III** 643

C & O. *See* Chesapeake and Ohio Railway.
C.&E. Cooper Co., **II** 14
C.&G. Cooper Co., **II** 14
C.A. Pillsbury and Co., **II** 555
C.A. Reed Co., **IV** 353
C.A. Swanson & Sons, **II** 479–80; **7** 66–67
C&A Brenninkmeyer KG, V 23–24
C&E Software, **10** 507
C&S Bank, **10** 425–26
C&S/Sovran Corporation, **10** 425–27

C. Bechstein, **III** 657
C. Brewer, **I** 417
C.D. Haupt, **IV** 296
C.D. Kenny Co., **II** 571
C.D. Magirus AG, **III** 541
C.E.T. *See* Club Européen.
C.F. Mueller Co., **I** 497–98
C. Francis, Son and Co., **III** 669
C.G. Conn, **7** 286
C.H. Robinson, **8** 379–80
C.H. Dexter & Co., **I** 320
C.H. Knorr Co., **II** 497
C.H. Musselman Co., **7** 429
C.H. Robinson, Inc., 11 43–44
C-I-L, Inc., **III** 745
C. Itoh & Co., I 431–33, 492, 510; **II** 273, 292, 361, 442, 679; **IV** 269, 326, 543; **10** 500
C. Itoh & Co. Ltd., **7** 529
C. Itoh Energy Development Co., **IV** 516
C.J. Devine, **II** 425
C.J. Lawrence, Morgan Grenfell Inc., **II** 429
C.J. Smith and Sons, **11** 3
C.L. Bencard, **III** 66
C. Lee Cook Co., **III** 467
C.M. Barnes Company, **10** 135
C.O. Lovette Company, **6** 370
C.R. Bard Inc., IV 287; 9 96–98
C. Reichenbach'sche Maschinenfabrik, **III** 561
C. Rowbotham & Sons, **III** 740
C.S. Rolls & Co., **I** 194
C.T. Bowring, **III** 280, 283
C.V. Buchan & Co., **I** 567
C.V. Gebroeders Pel, **7** 429
C.V. Mosby Co., **IV** 677–78
C.W. Holt & Co., **III** 450
C.W. Zumbiel Company, **11** 422
Cable and Wireless (Hong Kong). *See* Hongkong Telecomminications Ltd.
Cable and Wireless plc, IV 695; V 283–86; **7** 332–33; **11** 547
Cable and Wireless Systems Ltd. *See* Hongkong Telecommunications Ltd.
Cable Communications Operations, Inc., **6** 313
Cable News Network, **II** 166–68; **6** 171–73; **9** 30
Cablec Corp., **III** 433–34
Cableform, **I** 592
Cabletron Systems, Inc., 10 193–94; 10 511
Cablevision Systems Corporation, 7 63–65
Cabot Corporation, 8 77–79
Cabot, Godfrey, **8** 77
Cabot, Godfrey Lowell, **8** 77–78
Cabot, Samuel, **8** 77
Cabot Shops, Inc., **8** 77
Cabot, Thomas, **8** 77
Cacharel, Jean, **8** 129
Cadadia, **II** 641–42
Cadagan, C.C., **10** 41
Cadbury, Adrian, **II** 477–78
Cadbury, Benjamin, **II** 476
Cadbury Beverages, **9** 178
Cadbury Brothers Ltd., **II** 476; **III** 554
Cadbury, Dominic, **II** 478
Cadbury family, **II** 476
Cadbury Fry, **II** 476
Cadbury, George, **II** 476
Cadbury, John, **II** 476, 478
Cadbury Ltd., **II** 476, 592

Cadbury, Richard, **II** 476
Cadbury Schweppes Canada Inc., **II** 631
Cadbury Schweppes PLC, I 25–26; II 476–78, 510, 512; **6** 51–52
Cadence Design Systems, **6** 247; **10** 118
Cadence Design Systems, Inc., 11 45–48, 285, 490–91
Cadence Industries Corporation, **10** 401–02
Cadillac Automobile Co., **I** 171; **10** 325
Cadillac Fairview Corp., **IV** 703
Cadillac Plastic, **8** 347
Cadisys Corporation, **10** 119
Cadman, John, **IV** 379; **7** 57, 59
Cadogan, Bill, **10** 19–20
Cadoricin, **III** 47
CAE Systems Inc., **8** 519
Caesar, Orville, **I** 448–49
Caesar, William J., **9** 422
Caesar-Wollheim-Gruppe, **IV** 197
Caesars New Jersey, **6** 200
Caesars Palace, **6** 199–200
Caesars Tahoe, **6** 201
Caesars World, Inc., 6 199–202
Caetano, Marcelo, **IV** 506
Café Grand Mère, **II** 520
Caflisch, Albert, **I** 643
CAFO, **III** 241
Cagliari, Gabriele, **IV** 422
Cagney, James, **II** 175
Cagni, Umberto, **III** 346
Cahn, Jacob, **10** 489
Cahn, Miles, **10** 219
Cahn, William, **III** 237
Cahners, **IV** 667
Cahouet, Frank, **II** 317
Cailler, **II** 546
Cain Chemical, **IV** 481
Cain, George, **I** 686
Cain, Gordon, **I** 402
Cain, Victor M., **7** 479
Cairns, John C., **III** 628
Caisse Commericale de Bruxelles, **II** 270
Caisse de dépôt et placement du Quebec, **II** 664
Caisse des Dépôts, **6** 206
Caisse National de Crédit Agricole, **II** 264–66
Caja General de Depositos, **II** 194
Calarco, Vincent, **9** 154
Calazans, Camilo, **II** 200
Calcined Coke Corp., **IV** 402
Calco, **I** 300–01
Calculating-Tabulating-Recording Company. *See* International Business Machines Corporation.
Calcutta & Burmah Steam Navigation Co., **III** 521
Caldbeck Macgregor & Co., **III** 523
Calder, Alexander (Sandy), **IV** 344–45
Calder, Alexander (Sox), Jr., **IV** 345
Calder, Lou, **IV** 345
Caldera, Rafael, **IV** 507
Caldwell, Edward, **IV** 634–35
Caldwell, H.M., **11** 455
Caldwell, James, **III** 613
Caldwell, James H., **6** 465
Caldwell, Philip, **I** 167; **8** 449; **11** 139
Caldwell, William S., **6** 465
Caledonian Airways. *See* British Caledonian Airways.
Caledonian Bank, **10** 337
Caledonian Paper plc, **IV** 302
Calédonickel, **IV** 107

Calgary Power and Transmission Company Limited. *See* TransAlta Utilities Corporation.
Calgary Power Company. *See* TransAlta Utilities Corporation.
Calgary Power Ltd. *See* TransAlta Utilities Corporation.
Calgary Water Power Company, **6** 585
Calgon Corporation, **6** 27
Calhoun, Chad, **IV** 121
Calhoun, Lawton, **7** 466
Califano, Joseph, **I** 646; **III** 246
California Arabian Standard Oil Co., **IV** 536, 552
California Automated Design, Inc., **11** 284
California Bank, **II** 289
California Cooler Inc., **I** 227, 244; **10** 181
California First, **II** 358
California Institute of Technology, **9** 367
California Insurance Co., **III** 234
California Oilfields, Ltd., **IV** 531, 540
California Perfume Co., **III** 15
California Petroleum Co., **IV** 551–52
California Plant Protection, **9** 408
California Portland Cement Co., **III** 718
California Steel Industries, **IV** 125
California Telephone and Light, **II** 490
California Test Bureau, **IV** 636
California Texas Oil Co., **III** 672
California Tile, **III** 673
California Woodfiber Corp., **IV** 266
California-Western States Life Insurance Co., **III** 193–94
Caligen, **9** 92
Call, C.J., **II** 605
Call-Chronicle Newspapers, Inc., **IV** 678
Callaghan & Company, **8** 526
Callaghan, James, **I** 51
Callahan, T. M., **V** 90
Callard and Bowser, **II** 594
Callaway Wines, **I** 264
Callebaut, **II** 520–21
Callender, D.E., **6** 602
Callender, William M., **III** 433
Callender, William Ormiston, **III** 433
Callender's Cable and Construction Co. Ltd., **III** 433–34
Callies family, **III** 122–23
Calloway, Cab, **III** 443
Calloway, D. Wayne, **I** 279; **7** 267; **10** 453
Calloway, Wayne, **7** 435
Calma, **II** 30
Calman, Robert F., **IV** 76
CalMat Co., **III** 718
Calmic Ltd., **I** 715
Calor Group, **IV** 383
Caloric Corp., **II** 86
Calosi, Carlo, **II** 86; **11** 412–13
Calpine Corp., **IV** 84
Calsil Ltd., **III** 674
Caltex, **7** 483
Caltex Oil Refining (India) Ltd., **IV** 441
Caltex Petroleum Corp., **II** 53; **III** 672; **IV** 397, 434, 440–41, 479, 484, 492, 519, 527, 536, 545–46, 552, 560, 562, 718
Calumet & Arizona Mining Co., **IV** 177
Calumet Electric Company, **6** 532
Calvano, James F., **6** 356
Calvert & Co., **I** 293
Calvet, Jacques, **I** 188, 233
Calvin Bullock Ltd., **I** 472
Calvin Klein Cosmetics Corporation, **9** 203
Cambria Steel Company, **IV** 35; **7** 48

Cambridge Applied Nutrition Toxicology and Biosciences Ltd., **10** 105
Cambridge Interactive Systems Ltd., **10** 241
Camco Inc., **IV** 658
Camden, John, **III** 738–40
Camden Wire Co., Inc., **7** 408
CAMECO, **IV** 436
Cameron, C.C., **10** 298
Cameron Iron Works, **II** 17
Cameron Oil Co., **IV** 365
Cameron-Brown Company, **10** 298
CAMI Automotive, **III** 581
Camicia, Nicholas T., **IV** 181
Camintonn, **9** 41–42
Camm, Sydney, **III** 508
Cammarata, Bernard, **V** 197
Camp family, **IV** 345
Camp Manufacturing Co., **IV** 345; **8** 102
Campbell Box & Tag Co., **IV** 333
Campbell, Brian, **11** 534–36
Campbell, Calvin A., Jr., **7** 108–09
Campbell, Chesser, **IV** 683
Campbell, Daniel W., **10** 557
Campbell, David, **11** 65
Campbell, Edward J., **10** 381
Campbell, Edward P., **11** 358
Campbell Enterprises, **II** 481
Campbell, Gordon, **IV** 177
Campbell, Gordon A., **9** 114, 116
Campbell Industries, Inc., **11** 534
Campbell, Joseph, **II** 479; **7** 66
Campbell, Joseph S., **II** 479
Campbell, Keith, **II** 389
Campbell, Robert E., **III** 37; **8** 283
Campbell, Robert, Jr., **II** 388
Campbell Soup Co. Ltd., **II** 479
Campbell Soup Company, **I** 21, 26, 31, 599, 601; **II** 479–81, 508, 684; **7** 66–69 (upd.), 340; **10** 382; **11** 172
Campbell Taggart Inc., **I** 219
Campbell, Willis, **III** 353
Campbell's Soups Ltd., **II** 479
Campbell's Soups S.p.A., **II** 479
Campbell-Ewald Co., **I** 16–17
Campeau Corporation, **IV** 721; **V** 25–28; **9** 209, 211, 391
Campeau, Robert, **IV** 721; **8** 160; **9** 211
Campion, Robert, **I** 481–83
CAMPSA. *See* Compañia Arrendataria del Monopolio de Petróleos Sociedad Anónima.
Camu, Louis, **II** 202
Camuto, Vincent, **11** 348–49
Canada & Dominion Sugar Co., **II** 581
Canada Cable & Wire Company, **9** 11
Canada Cement, **III** 704
Canada Cement Lafarge, **III** 704–05
Canada Cup, **IV** 290
Canada Development Corp., **IV** 252
Canada Dry, **I** 281
Canada Packers Inc., **II** 482–85
Canada Packers Ltd., **II** 482
Canada Safeway Ltd., **II** 650, 654
Canada Trust. *See* CT Financial Services Inc.
Canada Tungsten Mining Corp., Ltd., **IV** 18
Canada Wire & Cable Company, Ltd., **IV** 164–65; **7** 397–99
Canadair, **I** 58; **7** 205
Canadian Airlines International Ltd., **6** 61–62, 101
Canadian Bank of Commerce, **II** 244–45

Canadian British Aluminum, **IV** 11
Canadian Cellucotton Products Ltd., **III** 40
Canadian Copper, **IV** 110
Canadian Copper Refiners, Ltd., **IV** 164
Canadian Dominion Steel and Coal Corp., **III** 508
Canadian Eastern Finance, **IV** 693
Canadian Fina Oil, **IV** 498
Canadian Forest Products, **IV** 270
Canadian Fuel Marketers, **IV** 566
Canadian General Electric Co., **8** 544–45
Canadian Government Merchant Marine, **6** 360–61
Canadian Gridoil Ltd., **IV** 373
Canadian Imperial Bank of Commerce, **II** 244–46; **IV** 693; **7** 26–28; **10** 8
Canadian International Paper Co., **IV** 286–87
Canadian Keyes Fibre Company, Limited of Nova Scotia, **9** 305
Canadian National Railway System, **6** 359–62
Canadian Northern Railway, **I** 284; **6** 359–60
Canadian Odeon Theatres, **6** 161
Canadian Pacific Enterprises, **III** 611
Canadian Pacific Limited, **V** 429–31; **8** 544–46
Canadian Pacific Railway, **I** 573; **II** 210, 220, 344; **III** 260; **IV** 272, 308, 437; **6** 359–60
Canadian Packing Co. Ltd., **II** 482
Canadian Petrofina, **IV** 498
Canadian Radio-Television and Telecommunications Commission, **6** 309
Canadian Telephones and Supplies, **6** 310
Canadian Transport Co., **IV** 308
Canal Bank, **11** 105
Canal Plus, **III** 48; **7** 392; **10** 195–97, 345, 347
CanAmera Foods, **7** 82
Cananwill, **III** 344
Cancell, Benton R., **8** 429
Candler, Asa G., **I** 232–33; **10** 225–26
Candler, Charles Howard, **I** 233, 235
Candy, John, **II** 173
Canepa, John, **11** 371–72
Caner, John, **10** 432
Canfield, Brian, **6** 310
Canfor Corp., **IV** 321
Canfor Pulp Sales, **IV** 321
Canhedo, Wagner, **6** 134
Canion, Joseph R. (Rod), **III** 124–25; **6** 221–22, 230
Canion, Rod. *See* Canion, Joseph R.
Canning, Fred F., **V** 219–20
Cannon Assurance Ltd., **III** 276
Cannon, Charles, **9** 214–15
Cannon, James William, **9** 214
Cannon, Joseph, **7** 193–95
Cannon Mills, Co., **9** 214–16
Canon Camera Co. Ltd., **III** 120
Canon Europa, **III** 120
Canon Inc., **I** 494; **II** 103, 292; **III** 120–21, 143, 172, 575, 583–84; **6** 238, 289; **9** 251; **10** 23
Canon Sales Co., **II** 459; **III** 533
Canpet Exploration Ltd., **IV** 566
Cans Inc., **I** 607
Canteen Corp., **I** 127; **II** 679–80
Cantel Corp., **11** 184
Canton Chemical, **I** 323; **8** 147
Canton Railway Corp., **IV** 718
Cantor, Eddie, **II** 151–52

Cantor Fitzgerald Securities Corporation, **10** 276–78
Cap Rock Electric Cooperative, **6** 580
CAPCO. *See* Central Area Power Coordination Group.
Capcom Co., **7** 396
Cape Cod-Cricket Lane, Inc., **8** 289
Cape Horn Methanol, **III** 512
Cape May County Electric Company, **6** 449
Cape May Light and Power Company, **6** 449
Cape Wine and Distillers, **I** 289
Capehart-Farnsworth, **11** 197
Capehart-Farnworth, **I** 463
Capex, **6** 224
AB Capital & Investment Corporation, **6** 108
Capital Airlines, **I** 128; **III** 102; **6** 128
Capital and Counties Bank, **II** 307; **IV** 91
Capital Cities/ABC Inc., **II** 129–31; **III** 214; **IV** 608–09, 613, 652; **11** 331. *See also* American Broadcasting Co.
Capital Cities Communications, Inc., **II** 131; **III** 214
Capital Financial Services, **III** 242
Capital Holding Corporation, **III 216–19**
Capital Life Insurance Company, **11** 482–83
Capitol Film + TV International, **IV** 591
Capitol Radio Engineering Institute, **IV** 636
Capitol Records, **I** 531–32
Capitol-EMI, **11** 557
Caporali, Renso L., **11** 166
Capp, Al, **IV** 672
Capper Pass, **IV** 191
Cappy, Joseph E., **I** 136
Capra, Frank, **II** 135, 175
Capseals, Ltd., **8** 476
Capsugel, **I** 712
Car-lac Electronic Industrial Sales Inc., **9** 420
Car-X, **10** 415
Caracas Petroleum Co., **IV** 565
Caracas Petroleum Sociedad Anónima, **IV** 565–66
Caracas Petroleum US Ltd., **IV** 566
Caracciolo, Carlo, **IV** 586–88
Carando Foods, **7** 174–75
Carat Group, **6** 15–16
Carbide Router Co., **III** 436
Carbis China Clay & Brick Co., **III** 690
Carbocol, **IV** 417
Carboline Co., **8** 455
CarboMedics, **11** 458–60
Carbon Research Laboratories, **9** 517
Carborundum Co., **III** 610
Carcelle, Yves, **10** 399
Carcin, Jérome, **IV** 618
Cardboard Containers, **IV** 249
Cardem Insurance Co., **III** 767
Cárdenas, Lázaro, **IV** 512
Cardiac Pacemaker, **I** 646; **11** 90
Cardiac Pacemakers, Inc., **11** 458
Cardinal Distributors Ltd., **II** 663
Cardone, Albert A., **III** 246
Caremark International Inc., **10** 143, **198–200**
CarePlus, **6** 42
Carey Canada Inc., **III** 766
Carey, William, **7** 486
Carey-McFall Corp., **V** 379
Cargill Brothers, **II** 616

Cargill, David, **IV** 381
Cargill Elevator Co., **II** 616
Cargill Grain Co., **II** 617
Cargill, Inc., **II** 494, 517, **616–18**; **11** 92
Cargill, James, **II** 616
Cargill, John (Sir), **IV** 381
Cargill, Samuel, **II** 616
Cargill, William S., **II** 616
Cargill, William Wallace, **II** 616
CARGOSUR, **6** 96
Cariani Sausage Co., **II** 518
Caribair, **I** 102
Caribbean Chemicals S.A., **I** 512
Caribe Co., **II** 493
Caribe Shoe Corp., **III** 529
Cariboo Pulp & Paper Co., **IV** 269
Carintusa Inc., **8** 271
CARIPLO, **III** 347
Carita, **III** 63
Carkner, James W., **I** 277; **10** 451
Carl Byoir & Associates, **I** 14
Carl Marks & Co., **11** 260–61
Carl, William, **10** 331
Carl Zeiss, **III** 445–47, 583
Carl's Superstores, **9** 452
Carl-Zeiss-Stiftung, **III 445–47**
Carlan, **III** 614
Carlberg, Anders, **9** 381
Carless Lubricants, **IV** 451
Carleton Financial Computations Inc., **II** 317
Carlgren, Matts, **IV** 318
Carli, Guido, **II** 403
Carlin Gold Mining Company, **7** 386–87
Carlin, John, **11** 144
Carling O'Keefe Breweries, **7** 183
Carling O'Keefe Ltd., **I** 218, 229, 254, 269, 438–39
Carlingford, **II** 298
Carlisle Companies Incorporated, **8 80–82**
Carlo Erba S.p.A., **I** 635
Carlow, Michael, **10** 171
Carlsberg, **I** 247
Carlsberg A/S, **9 99–101**
Carlsberg Biotechnology, **9** 100
Carlsberg Finans A/S, **9** 100
Carlsberg Foundation, **9** 99
Carlsberg-Tetley P.L.C., **9** 100
Carlson, Chester, **III** 171; **6** 288
Carlson Companies, Inc., **6 363–66**
Carlson, Curtis L., **6** 363–65
Carlson, Edward E., **I** 129; **6** 129; **9** 548–49
Carlson, Jan, **I** 120
Carlson, LeRoy T., **9** 494–96, 527
Carlson, Robert J., **10** 380
Carlson, Ted, **9** 494–96
Carlsson, Sven, **I** 625
Carlstedt, Sven, **III** 478
Carlton and United Breweries Ltd., **I 228–29**, 437–39; **7** 182–83
Carlton, Richard, **I** 500; **8** 370
Carlton, William J., **I** 19
Carlyle Group, **11** 364
Carmalt, Caleb, **III** 342
Carmeda AB, **10** 439
Carnation Company, **II 486–89**, 518, 548; **7** 339, 383, 429; **10** 382
Carnation Corp., **I** 269
Carnation Milk Products Co., **II** 486–87
Carnaud Basse-Indre, **IV** 228
Carnegie, Andrew, **III** 379; **IV** 35, 572–73; **7** 549–50

Carnegie Brothers & Co., Ltd., **9** 407
Carnegie, Dale, **IV** 671
Carnegie Steel Co., **II** 330; **IV** 572; **7** 549
Carney, Dan, **7** 434
Carney, Dennis J., **7** 587–88
Carney, Frank, **7** 434
Carney, Robert, **I** 14
Carney, Robert J., **I** 123
Carney, Thomas P., **I** 687
Carnival Cruise Lines, Inc., **6 367–68**
Carnot family, **I** 388; **10** 470
Carol Moberg, Inc., **6** 40
Carol-Braugh-Robinson Co., **II** 624
Carolco Pictures Inc., **III** 48; **10** 196
Carolina Biological Supply, **11** 424
Carolina Coin Caterers Corporation, **10** 222
Carolina Energies, Inc., **6** 576
Carolina First National, **II** 336
Carolina Freight Corporation, **6 369–72**
Carolina Power & Light Company, **V 564–66**
Carolina Telephone and Telegraph Company, **10 201–03**
Carolina Telephone Long Distance, **10** 203
Carothers, Wallace H., **I** 329; **8** 152
Carpenter, Candice M., **9** 429
Carpenter, Edmund, **9** 251
Carpenter, Leslie, **IV** 667
Carpenter Paper Co., **IV** 282; **9** 261
Carpenter, Richard M., **III** 59
le Carpentier, Jacques-Théodore, **III** 210
Carpets International of Georgia, Inc., **8** 270
Carpets International Plc., **8** 270–71
Carr family, **IV** 650
Carr Fowler, **III** 673
Carr, Fred, **III** 253, 254
Carr, John, **II** 207
Carr, Jonathan Dodgson, **II** 594
Carr, William, **III** 338; **7** 389
Carr, William (Sir), **IV** 650
Carr, William H.A., **III** 224
Carr's of Carlisle, **I** 604; **II** 594
Carr-Union Line, **6** 397
Carrefour SA, **II** 628; **8** 404–05; **10 204–06**
Carreras, **V** 411–12
Carrico, William, **11** 519
Carrier Air Conditioning Company of America, **7** 71
Carrier Air Conditioning Corp., **I** 85; **III** 329
Carrier Corporation, **7 70–73**
Carrier Engineering Corporation, **7** 71
Carrier, Willis Haviland, **7** 70–71
Carrigg, James A., **6** 536
Carroll County Electric Company, **6** 511
Carroll, Earl, **III** 195–96
Carroll, John, **7** 418
Carroll Reed Ski Shops, Inc., **10** 215
Carroll, Wallace, **I** 472–73
Carroll's Foods, **7** 477
Carrus, Gerald, **11** 190
Carse, Henry, **I** 57–58; **10** 315–16
Carson, Chester, **10** 139
Carson, Jack, **II** 152
Carson, Johnny, **III** 506
Carson Pirie Scott and Co., **II** 669; **9** 142
Carson, Rachel, **I** 366; **IV** 671
Carte Blanche, **9** 335
Cartensen, Fred V., **I** 182
Carter & Co., **IV** 644
Carter Automotive Co., **I** 159
Carter, Berlind, Potoma & Weill, **II** 450

Carter, Berlind, Weill and Levitt, Inc., **II** 450
Carter, Edward, **V** 29–30
Carter, George L., **IV** 180
Carter Hawley Hale Stores, **I** 246; **V** 29–32; **8** 160
Carter Holt Harvey, **IV** 280
Carter, James E., **I** 142, 530–31; **III** 166, 527; **IV** 596; **11** 429
Carter, Jimmy, **8** 164
Carter, John, **III** 249; **IV** 644
Carter, John Samuel, **8** 83
Carter Medicine Company, **8** 83
Carter Oil, **IV** 171
Carter Oil Company, **11** 353
Carter Products, Inc., **8** 84
Carter, Rice & Company, **8** 382
Carter-Wallace, **6** 27
Carter-Wallace, Inc., **8** 83–86
Carteret Bancorp, **III** 264
Carteret Mortgage, **III** 264
Carteret Savings Bank, **III** 263; **10** 340
Cartier Monde, **IV** 93; **V** 411, 413
Cartier Refined Sugars Ltd., **II** 662–63
Cartiera F.A. Marsoni, **IV** 587
Cartiere Ascoli Piceno, **IV** 586
Cartiers Superfoods, **II** 678
Cartillon Importers, Ltd., **6** 48
de Carvalho, Erik, **6** 133
Carworth Inc., **I** 630; **11** 34
Cary, Frank, **III** 149; **6** 252
Cary, R.O., **III** 507
Cary-Davis Tug and Barge Company. *See* Puget Sound Tug and Barge Company.
CASA, **7** 9
Casa Bonita, **II** 587
Cascade Lumber Co., **IV** 255; **8** 65
Cascade Natural Gas Corporation, **6** 568; **9** 102–04
Case Manufacturing Corp., **I** 512
Case, Pomeroy & Co., Inc., **IV** 76
Case, Stephen M., **10** 56
Case Technologies, Inc., **11** 504
Case, Weldon W., **6** 299–300
Casein Co. of America, **II** 471
Caserio, Martin J., **II** 34
Casey, Albert V., **I** 90; **6** 76
Casey, Edward F., **9** 133
Casey, J. Joseph, **I** 566
Casey, James J., **9** 190
Casey, Jim, **V** 533
Casey, John, **I** 90
Casey, William, **I** 559
Cash, C.A., **IV** 409–10; **7** 309
Cashel, William S., Jr., **II** 481
Casino, **10** 205
Casio Computer Co., Ltd., **III** 448–49, 455; **IV** 599; **10** 57
Caskie, Evans, **11** 74
Casler, Lon, **8** 545
Caspary, Delo, **7** 282
Cassa Generale Ungherese di Risparmio, **III** 207
Cassady Broiler Co., **II** 585
Cassatt, **II** 424
Cassatt, Alexander Johnston, **10** 72
Cassel, Ernest (Sir), **IV** 54
Cassidy, L.M., **III** 707; **7** 292
Casson, Bob, **II** 672
Casson, John, **II** 568
Cassoni, Vittorio, **III** 145; **6** 290
Castiglioni, Camillo, **I** 138; **11** 31
Castle & Cooke Foods, **II** 492

Castle & Cooke, Inc., **I** 417; **II** 490–92; **9** 175–76; **10** 40
Castle Brewery, **I** 287
Castle, Samuel Northrup, **II** 490
Castle Tretheway Mines Ltd., **IV** 164
Castlemaine Tooheys, **10** 169–70
Castrén, Fredrik, **IV** 300
de Castro, Edson, **III** 133; **6** 234
Castro, Fidel, **I** 463; **II** 208, 345; **III** 196; **IV** 82; **11** 14, 197
Castrol Ltd., **IV** 382–83
Castronovo, Valerio, **I** 163
Castrorama, **10** 205
Casual Corner, **V** 207–08
Catacosinos, William J., **V** 654
CATCO. *See* Crowley All Terrain Corporation.
Catell, Robert B., **6** 457
Cater, J.R., **I** 241
Cater, Richard, **6** 80
Caterpillar Belgium S.A., **III** 452
Caterpillar Inc., **I** 147, 181, 186, 422; **III** 450–53, 458, 463, 545–46; **9** 310; **10** 274, 377, 381, 429; **11** 473
Caterpillar of Canada Ltd., **III** 452
Caterpillar Tractor Co., **III** 450, 451–53
Caterpillar Tractor Co. Ltd., **III** 451
Cates, Louis S., **IV** 177
Cathay Insurance Co., **III** 221
Cathay Pacific Airways Limited, **I** 522; **II** 298; **6** 71, 78–80
Cathcart, James, **III** 258
Cathcart, Silas S., **III** 519
Catherine, Queen (England), **II** 466
Catlin, Sheldon, **III** 224
Cato Oil and Grease Co., **IV** 446
Catto (Lord), **II** 428–29
Catto, Thomas (Sir), **II** 428; **IV** 685
CATV, **10** 319
Caudill, Bill, **6** 142
Caudill Rowlett. *See* CRSS Inc.
Caudill Rowlett Scott. *See* CRSS Inc.
Caulo, Ralph D., **IV** 624
CAV, **III** 554–55
CAV-Bosch, **III** 555
Cavallier, Camille, **III** 677
Cavallo Pipeline Company, **11** 441
Cavedon Chemical Co., **I** 341
Cavendish International Holdings, **IV** 695
Cavendish Land, **III** 273
Cavenham Ltd., **7** 202–03
Cawoods Holdings, **III** 735
Cawthorn, Robert, **I** 668
Caxton Holdings, **IV** 641
CB&I, **7** 76–77
CB&Q. *See* Chicago, Burlington and Quincy Railroad Company.
CBC Film Sales Co., **II** 135
CBI Industries, Inc., **7** 74–77
CBM Realty Corp., **III** 643
CBS Inc., **I** 29, 488; **II** 61, 89, 102, 129–31, **132–34**, 136, 152, 166–67; **III** 55, 188; **IV** 605, 623, 652, 675, 703; **6** 157–60 **(upd.)**; **11** 327
CBS Records, **II** 103, 134, 177; **6** 159
CBS/FOX Company, **II** 133; **6** 158
CBS/Sony, **II** 103
CBT Corp., **II** 213–14
CBWL-Hayden Stone, **II** 450
CC Soft Drinks Ltd., **I** 248
CCAir Inc., **11** 300
CCG. *See* The Clark Construction Group, Inc.
CCH Computax, **7** 93–94

CCH Legal Information Services, **7** 93
CCI Electronique, **10** 113
CCP Insurance, Inc., **10** 248
CCS Automation Systems Inc., **I** 124
CCT. *See* Crowley Caribbean Transport.
CdF-Chimie, **I** 303; **IV** 174, 198, 525
CDI Corporation, **6** 139–41
CDMS. *See* Credit and Data Marketing Services.
CE-Minerals, **IV** 109
Ceat Cavi, **III** 434
Ceco Doors, **8** 544–46
CECOS International, Inc., **V** 750
Cedar Engineering, **III** 126
Cedarapids, Inc., **11** 413
Cedarleaf, Edwin, **7** 502
Cederroth International AB, **8** 17
Cefis, Eugenio, **I** 369; **IV** 421–22
Cegedur, **IV** 174
CEIR, **10** 255
Celanese Corp., **I** 317–19, 347
Celestial Seasonings, **II** 534
Celfor Tool Company, **8** 114. *See also* Clark Equipment Company.
Celite Co., **III** 706; **7** 291
Celite Corporation, **10** 43, 45
Cella Italian Wines, **10** 181
Celler, Emanuel, **II** 230
Cellnet, **11** 547
Cellonit-Gesellschaft Dreyfus & Cie., **I** 317
Cellular America, **6** 300
Cellular One, **9** 321
Cellulosa d'Italia, **IV** 272
Cellulose & Chemical Manufacturing Co., **I** 317
Cellulose & Specialties, **8** 434
Cellulose du Pin, **III** 677, 704
Celotex Corp., **III** 766–67
Celsius Energy Company, **6** 569
CELTEX, **I** 388–89
Celtex. *See* Pricel.
Cementia, **III** 705
Cemij, **IV** 132
CenCall Communications, **10** 433
Cenco, Inc., **6** 188; **10** 262–63
Cenex Cooperative, **II** 536
Cengas, **6** 313
Centel Business Systems, **6** 313
Centel Cable Television, **6** 314
Centel Communications Systems, **6** 313
Centel Corporation, **6** 312–15, 593; **9** 106, 480; **10** 203
Centel Information Systems, **6** 313
Centerior Energy Corporation, **V** 567–68
Centex Cement Enterprises, **8** 88
Centex Construction Company, **8** 87
Centex Corporation, **8** 87–89, 461
Centex Custom Homes, **8** 88
Centex Development Company, **8** 88
Centex Mortgage Banking, **8** 88
Centex Real Estate Corporation, **8** 87
Centex Telemanagement Inc., **11** 302
CentraBank, **II** 337; **10** 426
Central and South West Corporation, **V** 569–70
Central Area Power Coordination Group, **V** 677
Central Arizona Light & Power Company, **6** 545
Central Bancorp of Cincinnati, **II** 342
Central Bank for Railway Securities, **II** 281
Central Bank of Italy, **II** 403

Central Bank of London, **II** 318
Central Bank of Oman, **IV** 516
Central Bank of Scotland, **10** 337
Central Coalfields Ltd., **IV** 48–49
Central Computer Systems Inc., **11** 65
Central Covenants, **II** 222
Central Electric & Gas Company. *See* Centel Corporation.
Central Electric and Telephone Company, Inc. *See* Centel Corporation.
Central Finance Corp. of Canada, **II** 418
Central Foam Corp., **I** 481, 563
Central Hankyu Ltd., **V** 71
Central Hardware, **III** 530
Central Hudson Gas and Electric Company, **6** 458
Central Hudson Gas And Electricity Corporation, 6 458–60
Central Illinois Public Service Company. *See* CIPSCO Inc.
Central Independent Television plc, 7 78–80
Central India Spinning, Weaving and Manufacturing Co., **IV** 217
Central Indiana Power Company, **6** 556
Central Japan Heavy Industries, **III** 578–79; **7** 348
Central Maine Power, 6 461–64
Central Maloney Transformer, **I** 434
Central Mining and Investment Corp., **IV** 23, 79, 95–96, 524, 565
Central National Bank, **9** 475
Central National Life Insurance Co., **III** 463
Central Nebraska Packing, **10** 250
Central Newspapers, Inc., 10 207–09
Central Pacific Railroad, **II** 381
Central Park Bank of Buffalo, **11** 108
Central Penn National Corp., **11** 295
Central Planning & Design Institute, **IV** 48
Central Point Software, **10** 509
Central Public Service Corporation, **6** 447
Central Savings and Loan, **10** 339
Central Solvents & Chemicals Company, **8** 100
Central Soya Company, Inc., 7 81–83
Central Soya Feed Co., **7** 82
Central Telephone & Utilities Corporation, **6** 313–14. *See also* Centel Corporation.
Central Telephone Company, **6** 312–13. *See also* Centel Corporation.
Central Terminal Company, **6** 504
Central Transformer, **I** 434
Central Trust Co., **II** 313; **11** 110
Central Union Trust Co. of New York, **II** 313
Central West Public Service Company. *See* Centel Corporation.
Centran Corp., **9** 475
Centre de Dechets Industriels Group, **IV** 296
Centre Lait, **II** 577
Centrum Communications Inc., **11** 520
CenTrust Federal Savings, **10** 340
Centura Software, **10** 244
Century Bank, **II** 312
Century Cellunet Company, **9** 106
Century Communications Corp., 10 210–12
Century Savings Assoc. of Kansas, **II** 420
Century Telephone Enterprises, Inc., 9 105–07
Century Tool Co., **III** 569

Century 21 Real Estate, **I** 127; **II** 679; **III** 293; **11** 292
CEPCO. *See* Chugoku Electric Power Company Inc.
CEPSA. *See* Compañia Española de Petroleos S.A.
CEPSA Compania Portuguesa, **IV** 397
Cera Trading Co., **III** 756
Ceramesh, **11** 361
Ceramic Supply Company, **8** 177
Cerberus Limited, **6** 490
Cereal Industries, **II** 466
Cereal Partners Worldwide, **10** 324
Cerebos, **II** 565
Cerex, **IV** 290
Ceridian Corporation, **10** 257
Cermalloy, **IV** 100
Cerro Corp., **IV** 11, 136
Cerro de Pasco Corp., **IV** 33
CertainTeed Corp., **III** 677–78, 621
CertainTeed Products Corp., **III** 762
Certanium Alloys and Research Co., **9** 419
Certified Laboratories, **8** 385
Certified TV and Appliance Company, **9** 120
Certus International Corp., **10** 509
Cerveceria Polar, I 230–31
Cessna, **III** 512
Cessna Aircraft Company, 8 49–51, 90–93, 313–14
Cessna, Clyde V., **8** 49, 90–91
Cessna-Roos Company, **8** 90
Cetus Corp., **I** 637; **III** 53; **7** 427; **10** 78, 214
Cevallos, Rodrigo Borja, **IV** 510–11
Ceylan, Rasit, **IV** 563
Cézanne, Paul, **11** 453
CF AirFreight, **6** 390
CF Industries, **IV** 576
CF&I Steel Corporation, **8** 135
CFM. *See* Compagnie Française du Méthane.
CFP. *See* Compagnie Française des Pétroles.
CFP (Algérie), **IV** 560
CFS Continental, **II** 675
CG&E. *See* Cincinnati Gas & Electric Company.
CGCT, **I** 563
CGE, **II** 117
CGM. *See* Compagnie Générale Maritime.
CGR-MeV, **III** 635
Chace, Kenneth V., **III** 213–14
Chace, Malcolm, **V** 662
Chaco Energy Corporation, **V** 724–25
Chadbourne, H.W., **IV** 164
Chadwick, Don, **8** 256
Chadwick's of Boston, **V** 197–98
Chaffee, Roger, **I** 79; **11** 428
Chaine, Jacques, **9** 148
Chalandon, Albin, **IV** 546–47; **7** 484
Challenge Corp. Ltd., **IV** 278–79
Challenger Minerals Inc., **9** 267
Chalmers, Floyd S., **IV** 639
Chalmers, Rich, **9** 435
Chamberlain, Joseph, **III** 493
Chamberlain, Neville, **I** 81
Chambers, Anne Cox, **IV** 596–97
Chambers Corporation, **8** 298
Chambers, G. Russell, **11** 458
Chambers, Maurice R., **III** 529–30
Chambers, Rusty, **11** 458
Chambers, Sydney, **I** 287
Champin, Marcel, **IV** 558

Champion Coated Paper Co., **IV** 263
Champion Engineering Co., **III** 582
Champion Fibre Co., **IV** 263
Champion, Inc., **8** 459
Champion International Corporation, III 215; **IV 263–65,** 334
Champion Paper and Fibre Co., **IV** 263–64
Champion Spark Plug Co., **II** 17; **III** 593
Champion Valley Farms, **II** 480
Champlin Petroleum Company, **10** 83
Champlin Refining and Chemicals, Inc., **IV** 393
Chance Bros., **III** 724–27
Chance Vought Aircraft Co., **I** 67–68, 84–85, 489–91
Chancellor, Christopher (Sir), **IV** 259, 669
Chanco Medical Industries, **III** 73
Chandler, Alfred D., Jr., **I** 330; **III** 626; **IV** 379
Chandler, Colby H., **III** 476–77; **7** 162
Chandler Evans, **I** 434
Chandler, Marvin, **6** 529
Chandler, Richard H., **11** 486–87
Chandon de Briailles, Pierre-Gabriel, **I** 271
The Chandris Group, **11** 377
Chang, C.S., **I** 184
Channel Master, **II** 91
Channell, B.F., **11** 553
Chantiers de l'Atlantique, **9** 9
Chaparral Steel Company, **8** 522–24
Chapin, Dwight, **I** 20
Chaplin, Charlie, **I** 537; **II** 146–47
Chaplin, Merle, **9** 304
Chapman, Alvah H., Jr., **IV** 629–30
Chapman, Frank, **7** 466
Chapman, James C., **III** 599–600
Chapman, Joseph, **7** 87
Chapman Valve Manufacturing Company, **8** 135
Chapman, William, **V** 124
Chapman, William H., **V** 641
Chargeurs, 6 373–75
Chargeurs Réunis, **6** 373–74, 379
Charise Charles Ltd., **9** 68
Charisma Communications, **6** 323
Charles A. Eaton Co., **III** 24
Charles B. Perkins Co., **II** 667
Charles Hobson, **6** 27
Charles I, Emperor (Hapsburg), **III** 207
Charles I, King (Spain), **IV** 527
Charles II, King (England), **II** 466
Charles III, King (Spain), **IV** 527
Charles Luckman Assoc., **I** 513
Charles of the Ritz Group Ltd., **I** 695–97; **III** 56
Charles Pfizer Co., **I** 96
Charles Phillips & Co. Ltd., **II** 677
Charles Schwab, **II** 228
Charles Schwab Corp., 8 94–96
Charles Scribner's Sons, **7** 166
Charles VI, King (Hapsburg), **III** 206
Charleston Consolidated Railway, Gas and Electric Company, **6** 574
Charleston Electric Light Company, **6** 574
Charleston Gas Light Company, **6** 574
Charlestown Foundry, **III** 690
Charley Brothers, **II** 669
Charmin Paper Co., **III** 52; **IV** 329; **8** 433
Charming Shoppes, Inc., 8 97–98
Charney, Howard, **11** 518
Charpie, Robert A., **8** 78–79
Charren, Stanley, **11** 222
Charrington & Co., **I** 223
Charrington United Breweries, **I** 223

Chart House, **II** 556, 613–14
Charter Bank, **II** 348
Charter Club, **9** 315
Charter Consolidated, **IV** 23, 119–20
Charter Corp., **III** 254
Charter National Life Insurance Company, **11** 261
Charter Oil, **II** 620
Charter Security Life Insurance Cos., **III** 293
Chartered Bank, **II** 357
Chartered Bank of India, Australia, and China, **II** 357
Chartered Co. of British New Guinea, **III** 698
Chartered Mercantile Bank of India, London and China, **II** 298
Charterhouse Petroleum, **IV** 499
Chartwell Associates, **9** 331
Chartwell Association, **III** 16
Chartwell Land, **V** 106
Chas. A. Stevens & Co., **IV** 660
Chase & Sanborn, **II** 544
Chase Corp., **II** 402
Chase Drier & Chemical Co., **8** 177
Chase, Harris, Forbes, **II** 402
Chase Manhattan Bank N.A., **II** 248
Chase Manhattan Corporation, **I** 123, 334, 451; **II** 202, 227, 247–49, 257, 262, 286, 317, 385; **IV** 33; **6** 52; **9** 124
Chase National Bank, **II** 247–48, 256, 397, 402; **III** 104, 248; **10** 61
Chase, Salmon P., **II** 217, 247
Chase Securities Corp., **II** 247, 397; **10** 61
Chase, Stephen, **II** 382
Chasen, Melvin, **6** 199
Chassagne, Yvette, **III** 393
Chastain-Roberts, **II** 669
Chateau Cheese Co. Ltd., **II** 471
Chateau Grower Winery Co., **II** 575
Chater, Catchik Paul, **IV** 699–700
Chater, Sir Paul, **6** 498–99
Chatfield & Woods Co., **IV** 311
Chatfield, Glen F., **10** 394
Chatfield Paper Co., **IV** 282; **9** 261
Chatham and Phenix National Bank of New York, **II** 312
Chatham Bank, **II** 312
Chattanooga Gas Company, Inc., **6** 577
Chattanooga Gas Light Company, **6** 448
Chaux et Ciments de Lafarge et du Teil, **III** 703–04
Chaux et Ciments du Maroc, **III** 703
Chavez, Cesar, **I** 243; **II** 655
Chazen, Jerome, **8** 329
Cheatham, Owen, **IV** 281; **9** 259
Checchi, Alfred, **6** 104–05
Checker Holding, **10** 370
Checker Motors Corp., **10** 369
Cheek, Joel, **II** 531
Cheeld, Chuck, **I** 98
Cheesman, Walter Scott, **6** 558
Chef Boyardee, **10** 70
Chef Pierre, **II** 572
Chef's Orchard Airline Caterers Inc., **I** 513
Chef-Boy-Ar-Dee Quality Foods Inc., **I** 622
Cheil Sugar Co., **I** 515
Cheil Wool Textile Co., **I** 515
Chelan Power Company, **6** 596
Chelberg, Bruce, **10** 555
Chellgren, Paul W., **9** 344
Chem-Nuclear Environmental Services, Inc., **9** 110

Chem-Nuclear Systems, Inc., **9** 109
Chemap, **III** 420
Chemcentral Corporation, **8** 99–101
Chemcut, **I** 682
Chemetron Process Equipment, Inc., **8** 545
Chemex Pharmaceuticals, Inc., **8** 63
Chemical Bank, **II** 250; **9** 124
Chemical Bank & Trust Co., **II** 251
Chemical Bank Home Loans Ltd., **II** 234
Chemical Bank New Jersey, **II** 252
Chemical Banking Corporation, **II** 250–52, 254; **9** 361
Chemical Coatings Co., **I** 321
Chemical Corn Exchange Bank, **II** 251
Chemical National Assoc., Inc., **II** 251
Chemical National Bank of New York, **II** 250–51
Chemical National Co., Inc., **II** 251
Chemical New York Corp., **II** 251
Chemical Process Co.
Chemical Process Co., **IV** 409; **7** 308
Chemical Realty Co., **II** 252
Chemical Specialties Inc., **I** 512
Chemical Waste Management, Inc., **V** 753; **9** 108–10; **11** 435–36
Chemins de fer de Paris à Lyon et à la Méditerranée, **6** 424
Chemins de fer du Midi, **6** 425
Chemins de Fer Fédéraux, **V** 519
Chemisch-Pharmazeutische AG, **IV** 70
Chemische Fabrik auf Actien, **I** 681
Chemische Fabrik Friesheim Elektron AG, **IV** 229
Chemische Fabrik vormals Sandoz, **I** 671
Chemische Fabrik Wesseling AG, **IV** 70–71
Chemische Werke Hüls GmbH. *See* Hüls A.G.
Chemise Lacoste, **9** 157
Chemmar Associates, Inc., **8** 271
Chempump, **8** 135
Chemurgic Corporation, **6** 148
Chemway Corp., **III** 423
Chen, Scott, **11** 234
Chen, Steve S., **III** 130
Chen, Tu, **11** 234
Chen Yaosheng, **IV** 389
Chenery, Christopher T., **6** 577
Cheng, Yu Tung (Dr.), **IV** 717
Cheong, Liang Yuen, **IV** 717
Cheplin Laboratories, **III** 17
Cheramy, Edward R., **11** 184
Cherokee Insurance Co., **I** 153; **10** 265
Cherry Co., **I** 266
Cherry Hill Cheese, **7** 429
Cherry, Wendell, **III** 81–82
Cherry-Burrell Process Equipment, **8** 544–45
Chesapeake and Ohio Railroad, **II** 329; **10** 43
Chesapeake and Ohio Railway, **V** 438–40
Chesapeake Corporation, **8** 102–04; **10** 540
The Chesapeake Corporation of Virginia, **8** 102
Chesapeake Packaging Company, **8** 102
Chesapeake Pulp & Paper Company, **8** 102
Chesapeake Wood Treating Co., **10** 540
Chesapeake-Camp Corporation, **8** 102
Chesebrough, Robert, **8** 105
Chesebrough-Pond's Inc., **II** 590; **7** 544; **9** 319
Chesebrough-Pond's USA, Inc., **8** 105–07

Cheshire Wholefoods, **II** 528
Chester, Colby M., **II** 531
Chester Engineers, **10** 412
Chester G. Luby, **I** 183
Chester Oil Co., **IV** 368
Chesterfield, Tom, **III** 670
Chetwynd (Lord), **III** 370–71
Cheung Kong (Holdings) Limited, **I** 470; **IV** 693–95
Chevalier, Alain, **I** 272; **10** 398–99
Chevalier, Jean, **10** 347
Chevalier, Maurice, **II** 155
Chevrolet Motor Division, **V** 494; **9** 17
Chevron Corporation, **II** 143; **IV** 367, 385–87, 452, 464, 466, 479, 484, 490, 523, 531, 536, 539, 721; **9** 391; **10** 119
Chevron International, **IV** 563
Chevron USA Inc., **IV** 387
Chew, Beverly, **11** 105
Cheyne, James A., **III** 358
CHF. *See* Chase, Harris, Forbes.
Chiang K'aishek, **IV** 388
Chiapparone, Paul, **III** 137
Chiat, Jay, **11** 49–52
Chiat/Day Inc. Advertising, **11** 49–52
Chiat/Day/Mojo, **9** 438
Chiba, Kazuo, **IV** 321–22
Chiba Riverment and Cement, **III** 760
Chibu Electric Power Company, Incorporated, **V** 571–73
Chicago & Calumet Terminal Railroad, **IV** 368
Chicago and Alton Railroad, **I** 456
Chicago and North Western Holdings Corporation, **6** 376–78
Chicago and North Western Railway Co., **I** 440
Chicago and North Western Transportation Company. *See* Chicago and North Western Holdings Corporation.
Chicago and Southern Airlines Inc., **I** 100; **6** 81
Chicago Bears, **IV** 703
Chicago Bridge & Iron Company, **7** 74–77
Chicago Burlington and Quincy Railroad, **III** 282; **V** 425–28
Chicago Chemical Co., **I** 373
Chicago Corp., **I** 526
Chicago Cubs, **IV** 682–83
Chicago Directory Co., **IV** 660–61
Chicago Edison, **IV** 169
Chicago Flexible Shaft Company, **9** 484
Chicago Heater Company, Inc., **8** 135
Chicago Motor Club, **10** 126
Chicago Pacific Corp., **I** 530; **III** 573
Chicago Pneumatic Tool Co., **III** 427, 452; **7** 480
Chicago Radio Laboratory, **II** 123
Chicago Rawhide Manufacturing Company, **8** 462–63
Chicago Rock Island and Peoria Railway Co., **I** 558
Chicago Steel Works, **IV** 113
Chicago Sun-Times Distribution Systems, **6** 14
Chicago Times, **11** 251
Chicago Title and Security Union, **10** 44
Chicago Title and Trust Co., **III** 276; **10** 43–45
Chicago Title Insurance Co., **10** 43
Chicago Tribune. *See* Tribune Company.
Chichester, J.H.R., **III** 272
Chick, Joseph S., **6** 510
Chicopee Manufacturing Corp., **III** 35

Chief Auto Parts, **II** 661
Chiers-Chatillon-Neuves Maisons, **IV** 227
Chifley, Ben, **II** 389
Chifley, J.B., **IV** 58
Chilcott Laboratories Inc., **I** 710–11
Children's World, **II** 608; **V** 17, 19
Chiles Offshore Corporation, 9 111–13
Chiles, William E., **9** 111–12
Chili's, **10** 331
Chillicothe Co., **IV** 310
Chilton Corp., **III** 440
Chiminter, **III** 48
Chimio, **I** 669–70; **8** 451–52
China Airlines, **6** 71; **9** 233
China Borneo Co., **III** 698
China Canada Investment and
    Development Co., **II** 457
China Coast, **10** 322, 324
China Electric, **II** 67
China Foreign Transportation Corporation,
    6 386
China Industries Co., **II** 325
China International Trade and Investment
    Corporation, **II** 442; **IV** 695; **6** 80
China Light & Power, **6** 499
China Mutual Steam Navigation Company
    Ltd., **6** 416
China National Automotive Industry
    Import and Export Corp., **III** 581
China National Aviation Co., **I** 96
China National Chemicals Import and
    Export Corp., **IV** 395
China National Machinery Import and
    Export Corporation, **8** 279
China Navigation Co., **I** 521
China Orient Leasing Co., **II** 442
China Zhouyang Fishery Co. Ltd., **II** 578
Chinese Electronics Import and Export
    Corp., **I** 535
Chinese Metallurgical Import and Export
    Corp., **IV** 61
**Chinese Petroleum Corporation, IV
    388–90,** 493, 519
Chinese Steel Corp., **IV** 184
Chino Mines Co., **IV** 179
Chinon Industries, **III** 477; **7** 163
CHIPS and Technologies, Inc., 6 217; **9
    114–17**
Chiquita Brands, Inc., **II** 595–96; **III** 28
**Chiquita Brands International, Inc., 7
    84–86**
Chirac, Jacques, **II** 117, 260; **IV** 227
Chiro Tool Manufacturing Corp., **III** 629
Chiron Corporation, 7 427; **10 213–14**
Chisholm, Hugh, **7** 166
Chisso Chemical, **II** 301
Chiswick Polish Co., **II** 566
Chiswick Products, **II** 566
Chiswick Soap Co., **II** 566
Chita Oil Co., **IV** 476
Chivers, **II** 477
Chiyoda Bank, **I** 503; **II** 321
Chiyoda Chemical, **I** 433
Chiyoda Fire and Marine, **III** 404
Chiyoda Kogaku Seiko Kabushiki Kaisha,
    III 574–75
Chiyoda Konpo Kogyo Co. Ltd., **V** 536
Chiyoda Mutual, **II** 374
Chloé Chimie, **I** 303
Chloride S.A., **I** 423
Cho, Choong-Hoon, **6** 98–99
Choay, **I** 676–77
Chobei, Ohmiya, **I** 704
Chocolat Ibled S.A., **II** 569

Chocolat Poulait, **II** 478
Chocolat-Menier S.A., **II** 569
Chogoku Kogyo, **II** 325
Choice Hotels International, Inc., **6** 187,
    189
Chopin, Frederic, **III** 366
Chorlton Metal Co., **I** 531
Chosen Sekiyu, **IV** 554
Chotin Transportation Co., **6** 487
Chow Tai Fook Jewellery Co., **IV** 717
Chris-Craft Industries, Inc., II 176, 403;
    III 599–600; **9 118–19**
Christal Radio, **6** 33
Christensen Company, **8** 397
Christensen, Frank A., **III** 241
Christensen, Roy E., **III** 76
Christian Bourgois, **IV** 614–15
Christian Dior, **I** 272
Christians, Wilhelm, **II** 280
Christiansen, Russell E., **6** 524
Christie, Agatha, **IV** 671
Christie, H. Merlyn, **7** 344
Christie, M.F., **III** 261
Christie, Mitchell & Mitchell, **7** 344
Christienne, Charles, **I** 46
Christopherson, Weston, **II** 605
Chrysler Corp., I 10, 17, 28, 38, 59, 79,
    136, **144–45,** 152, 162–63, 172, 178,
    182, 188, 190, 207, 504, 516, 525, 540;
    II 5, 313, 403, 448; **III** 439, 517, 544,
    568, 591, 607, 637–38; **IV** 22, 449, 676,
    703; **7** 205, 233, 461; **8** 74–75, 315,
    505–07; **9** 118, 349–51, 472; **10** 174,
    198, 264–65, 290, 317, 353, 430; **11
    53–55 (upd.),** 103–04, 429
Chrysler Financial Corp., **II** 420
Chrysler Realty Corp., **IV** 449
Chrysler, Walter Percy, **I** 144; **11** 53
Chu Ito & Co., **IV** 476
Chubb and Son PLC, **II** 84; **III** 190,
    220–21, 368
Chubb Corporation, III 220–22; 11 481
Chubb Custom Market, **III** 220–21
Chubb Life Insurance Co. of America, **III**
    221
Chubb, Percy, **III** 220
Chubb, Percy, II, **III** 220
Chubb, Thomas, **III** 220
Chubu Electric Power Co., **IV** 492
Chugai Pharmaceutical Company, **8**
    215–16; **10** 79
Chugai Shogyo Shimposha, **IV** 654–55
**Chugoku Electric Power Company Inc.,
    V 574–76**
Chung, Dal Ok, **7** 234
Chung, Ju Jung, **III** 515–16
Chung, Ju Yung, **7** 231–32, 234
Chung, Po, **6** 385
Chung, Se Yung, **7** 234
Chung, Seyoung, **III** 515
Chuo Koronsha, **IV** 632
Chuo Trust & Banking Co., **II** 373, 391
Church, Goodman, and Donnelley, **IV** 660
Church's Fried Chicken, Inc., **I** 260; **7**
    26–28
Churchill Insurance Co. Ltd., **III** 404
Churchill, Winston (Sir), **I** 107, 223, 388;
    II 85; **III** 698; **IV** 378, 381, 621; **7** 342;
    9 367; **10** 357
Churchman, Joseph B., **III** 9
Churny Co. Inc., **II** 534
Ciba Chemical & Dyestuff Company, **9**
    153

Ciba Consumer Pharmaceuticals, **10** 54
Ciba Ltd., **I** 632; **8** 108–10
Ciba-Geigy Corporation, **8** 63
Ciba-Geigy Ltd., I 625, **632–34,** 671,
    690, 701; **III** 55; **IV** 288; **8 108–11
    (upd.),** 376–77; **9** 441; **10** 53, 213
CIBC. *See* Canadian Imperial Bank of
    Commerce.
CIBC Securities Europe Ltd., **II** 245
CICI, **11** 184
CIDLA, **IV** 504–06
Cie Continental d'Importation, **10** 249
Cie des Lampes, **9** 9
Cie Générale d'Electro-Ceramique, **9** 9
Cifra, **8** 556
CIGNA Corporation, III 197, **223–27,**
    389; **10** 30
CIGNA Investments, Inc., **11** 243
Cii-HB, **III** 123, 678
Cilag-Chemie, **III** 35–36; **8** 282
Cilbarco, **II** 25
Cillon, Andre, **IV** 615
Cilva Holdings PLC, **6** 358
Cimarron Utilities Company, **6** 580
Ciments d'Obourg, **III** 701
Ciments de Chalkis Portland Artificiels, **III**
    701
Ciments de Champagnole, **III** 702
Ciments de l'Adour, **III** 702
Ciments Lafarge France, **III** 704
Ciments Lafarge Quebec, **III** 704
Cimino, Michael, **II** 148
Cimos, **7** 37
Cincinnati and Suburban Bell Telephone
    Company. *See* Cincinnati Bell.
Cincinnati Bell, Inc., 6 316–18
Cincinnati Chemical Works, **I** 633
Cincinnati Edison Electric Company, **6** 465
Cincinnati Electric Company, **6** 465
Cincinnati Electronics Corp., **II** 25
**Cincinnati Gas & Electric Company, 6
    465–68,** 481–82
Cincinnati Gas, Light & Coke Company, **6**
    465
Cineamerica, **IV** 676
Cinecentrum, **IV** 591
Cinema International Corp., **II** 149
Cinemax, **IV** 675; **7** 222–24, 528–29
Cineplex Odeon Corporation, II 145, **6
    161–63**
Cintel, **II** 158
Cipa, Walter (Dr.), **I** 411
CIPSCO Inc., 6 469–72, 505–06
Circle A Ginger Ale Company, **9** 177
Circle K Corporation, II 619–20; V 210;
    7 113–14, 372, 374
Circle K Food Stores, Inc., **II** 619
Circle Plastics, **9** 323
Circuit City Stores, Inc., 9 65–66,
    120–22; 10 235, 305–06, 334–35,
    468–69
Circus Circus Enterprises, Inc., 6 201,
    203–05
Cirrus Logic, Incorporated, 9 334; **11
    56–57**
Cisco Systems, Inc., 11 58–60, 520
Cisler, Walker, **V** 593
CIT Alcatel, **9** 9–10
CIT Financial Corp., **II** 90, 313; **8** 117
Citadel General, **III** 404
CITGO Petroleum Corporation, II
    660–61; **IV 391–93,** 508; **7** 491
Citibanc Group, Inc., **11** 456

Citibank, **II** 227, 230, 248, 250–51, 253–55, 331, 350, 358, 415; **III** 243, 340; **6** 51; **9** 124; **10** 150; **11** 418

CITIC. *See* China International Trade and Investment Corporation.

Citicorp, **II** 214, **253–55**, 268, 275, 319, 331, 361, 398, 411, 445; **III** 220, 397; **7** 212–13; **8** 196; **9 123–26 (upd.)**; **10** 469; **11** 140

Citicorp Capital Investors, **9** 441

Citicorp Venture Capital Ltd., **III** 10; **10** 463

Cities Service Co., **IV** 376, 391–92, 481, 575

Citinet. *See* Hongkong Telecommunications Ltd.

Citivision PLC, **9** 75

Citizen de Mexico, **III** 454

Citizen Jewelry, **III** 454

Citizen Kohatsu, **III** 455

Citizen Latinamerica, **III** 455

Citizen Manufacturing (UK), **III** 455

Citizen Systems, **III** 455

Citizen Trading Co., **III** 454

Citizen Uhrenfabrik, **III** 455

Citizen Watch Co., Ltd., **III 454–56**, 549

Citizen Watch Co. of America, **III** 455

Citizen's Electric Light & Power Company, **V** 641

Citizen's Federal Savings Bank, **10** 93

Citizen's Fidelity Corp., **II** 342

Citizens and Southern Bank, **II** 337; **10** 426

Citizens Bank, **11** 105

Citizens Bank of Hamilton, **9** 475

Citizens Bank of Savannah, **10** 426

Citizens Federal Savings and Loan Association, **9** 476

Citizens Gas Co., **6** 529

Citizens Gas Fuel Company. *See* MCN Corporation.

Citizens Gas Light Co., **6** 455

Citizens Gas Supply Corporation, **6** 527

Citizens National Bank, **II** 251

Citizens National Gas Company, **6** 527

Citizens Savings & Loan Association, **9** 173

Citizens Trust Co., **II** 312

Citizens Utilities Company, **7 87–89**

Citizens' Savings and Loan, **10** 339

Citroën. *See* Automobiles Citroen.

Citroen, Andre, **7** 35–36

Citroen Gear Company, **7** 35

Citroen SA, **7** 36

Citrus Corporation, **6** 578

City and St. James, **III** 501

City and Suburban Telegraph Association, **6** 316

City and Suburban Telegraph Association and Telephonic Exchange, **6** 316–17

City and Village Automobile Insurance Co., **III** 363

City Auto Stamping Co., **I** 201

City Bank Farmers' Trust Co., **II** 254; **9** 124

City Bank of New York, **II** 250, 253

City Brewery, **I** 253

City Centre Properties Ltd., **IV** 705–06

City Finance, **10** 340

City Finance Company, **11** 261

City Ice Delivery, Ltd., **II** 660

City Investing Co., **III** 263; **IV** 721; **9** 391

City Light and Traction Company, **6** 593

City Light and Water Company, **6** 579

City Mutual Life Assurance Society, **III** 672–73

City National Bank of Baton Rouge, **11** 107

City National Leasing, **II** 457

City of London Real Property Co. Ltd., **IV** 706

City Products Corp., **II** 419

City Public Service, **6 473–75**

City Savings, **10** 340

Cityhome Corp., **III** 263

Civil & Civic Contractors, **IV** 707–08

Civil Service Employees Insurance Co., **III** 214

Cizik, Robert, **II** 16–17

Claiborne, Elisabeth ''Liz'', **8** 329–30

Clairmont, Maurice, **II** 136

Clairol, **III** 17–18

Clairton Steel Co., **IV** 572; **7** 550

CLAM Petroleum, **7** 282

Clapp, Joseph, **V** 503

Clapp, Norton, **IV** 356; **9** 551

Clapper, J.S., **7** 534

Clare, David R., **III** 36; **8** 282–83

Clares Equipment Co., **I** 252

Clark & Co., **IV** 301

Clark & Rockefeller, **IV** 426

Clark, A. James, **8** 112–13

Clark, Allen, **II** 81–82

Clark Bros. Co., **III** 471

Clark, C. Spencer, **9** 102

Clark, Charles B., **III** 40

Clark, Charles F., **IV** 604

Clark, Charles Heath, **III** 696–98

Clark, Charles M., **IV** 604

The Clark Construction Group, Inc., **8 112–13**

Clark, Dick, **II** 129

Clark, Dietz & Associates-Engineers. *See* CRSS Inc.

Clark, Donald, **II** 420

Clark, E.H., **III** 428

Clark, E.H. (Hubie), Jr., **III** 429

Clark, Edward, **II** 9

Clark, Edward W., **11** 342–43

Clark Equipment Company, **I** 153; **7** 513–14; **8 114–16**; **10** 265

Clark, Ernest E., **III** 328

Clark Estates Inc., **8** 13

Clark, Eugene, **8** 114–15

Clark, Geoffry, **11** 76

Clark, George, **IV** 92

Clark, Henry, **II** 492

Clark, Homer P., **7** 580

Clark, Howard L., **10** 61–62

Clark, Howard L., Jr., **II** 397–98, 452; **9** 469–70

Clark, James, **9** 471–72

Clark, Jim. *See* Clark, A. James.

Clark, John, **II** 81–82

Clark Materials Handling Company, **7** 514

Clark, Maurice, **IV** 426

Clark, Michael, **II** 81–82

Clark Motor Co., **I** 158; **10** 292

Clark, Noah, **IV** 488

Clark, Paul F., **III** 266

Clark, R.T., **7** 53

Clark, Roscoe Collins, **I** 647

Clark, W. H., **I** 374

Clark, W. Van Alan, **III** 15

Clark, William, **III** 286

Clarke, David H., **7** 209

Clarke, Ian M., **I** 353

Clarke, Neil, **IV** 119–20

Clarke, Richard, **V** 686

Clarke, Robert F., **9** 276

Clarkson International Tools, **I** 531

CLASSA. *See* Compañia de Líneas Aéreas Subvencionadas S.A.

Claude, Georges, **I** 357–58

Clausen, A.W. (Tom), **II** 228; **8** 47

Clausen, Leon R., **10** 378

Clavel, Alexander, **I** 632

Clavel, Rene (Dr.), **I** 317

Clawson, Dud, **8** 177–78

Clayton & Dubilier, **III** 25

Clayton, G., **III** 272

Claytor, Robert, **V** 485

Claytor, W. Graham, **V** 485

Clean Window Remodelings Co., **III** 757

Cleanaway Ltd., **III** 495

Cleancoal Terminal, **7** 582, 584

Clearing Inc., **III** 514

Clearwater Tissue Mills, Inc., **8** 430

Cleary, Michael, **III** 323

Cleary, Russell, **I** 254–55

Clef, **IV** 125

Cleland, Hance H., **V** 711

Clemenceau, George, **IV** 557

Clement, John, **II** 587; **V** 118

Clements Energy, Inc., **7** 376

Clements, Leon, **III** 86

Clemm, Carl, **IV** 323

Clemm, Michael von, **II** 268

Cletrac Corp., **IV** 366

Cleveland and Western Coal Company, **7** 369

Cleveland Electric Illuminating Company. *See* Centerior Energy Theodor.

Cleveland, Grover S., **II** 329–30; **III** 247, 302; **IV** 604

Cleveland, Newcomb, **11** 127

Cleveland Oil Co., **I** 341

Cleveland Paper Co., **IV** 311

Cleveland Pneumatic Co., **I** 457; **III** 512

Cleveland Twist Drill, **I** 531

Clevepak Corporation, **8** 229

Clifford, Clark, **I** 72; **11** 279

Climax Molybdenum Co., **IV** 17–19

Clinchfield Coal Corp., **IV** 180–81

Cline, Richard G., **6** 531

Cline, Robert S., **6** 346

Cline, Walter B., **V** 682

Clinical Assays, **I** 628

Clinical Science Research Ltd., **10** 106

Clinton, Bill, **10** 16, 199, 540

Clinton Pharmaceutical Co., **III** 17

Clinton, William, **9** 8–98

Clipper, Inc., **IV** 597

Clipper Manufacturing Company, **7** 3

Clipper Seafoods, **II** 587

Clone, Alan, **I** 426

Clore, Alan, **I** 668

Clore, Charles, **IV** 706; **V** 177

Clorox Chemical Co., **III** 20, 52; **8** 433

Clorox Company, **III 20–22**

Clough, DeWitt, **I** 619; **11** 7

Clouterie et Tréfilerie des Flandres, **IV** 25–26

Clover Leaf Creamery, **II** 528

Clover Milk Products Co., **II** 575

Clovis Water Co., **6** 580

Clow, Lee, **11** 49, 52

Club Aurrera, **8** 556

Club Européen du Tourisme, **6** 207

Club Med. *See* Club Méditerranée SA.

Club Med, Inc., **6** 49, 207–08

Club Méditerranée SA, **I** 286; **6 206–08**

Clubhôtel, **6** 207
Cluett Peabody, **II** 414
Cluett, Peabody & Co., Inc., **8** 567–68
Clyde Iron Works, **8** 545
Clydebank Engineering & Shipbuilding
    Co., **I** 573
Clyne, John Valentine, **IV** 307–08
Clyne Maxon Agency, **I** 29
CM Industries, **I** 676
CM&M Equilease, **7** 344
CMB Acier, **IV** 228
CMB Packaging, **8** 477
CML Group, Inc., 10 215–18
CMS, **IV** 23; **8** 466
CMS Energy Corporation, V 577–79
CN. *See* Canadian National Railway
    System.
CN Exploration, **6** 361
CN North America, **6** 361
CNA Financial Corporation, I 488; **III**
    228–32
CNA Health Plans, **III** 84
CNA Nuclear Leasing, **III** 231, 339
CNA Realty, **III** 231
CNCA. *See* Caisse National de Crédit
    Agricole.
CNEP. *See* Comptoir National d'Escompte
    de Paris.
CNG. *See* Consolidated Natural Gas
    Company.
CNN. *See* Cable News Network.
CNN Radio, **II** 166–67
Co-Axial Systems Engineering Co., **IV** 677
Co. Luxemburgeoise de Banque S.A., **II**
    282
Co. of London Insurers, **III** 369
Co-Steel International Ltd., **8** 523–24
Coach Leatherware, 10 219–21
Coach Specialties Co., **III** 484
Coad, Roy, **I** 576
Coal India Limited, IV 48–50
Coast-to-Coast Stores, **II** 419
Coastal Coca-Cola Bottling Co., **10** 223
Coastal Corporation, IV 394–95
Coastal States Corporation, **11** 481
Coastal States Gas Corporation, **IV** 394; **7**
    553–54
Coastal States Gas Producing Co., **IV** 366,
    394
Coastal States Life Insurance Company, **11**
    482
Coastal Valley Canning Co., **I** 260
Coating Products, Inc., **III** 643
Coats Patons, **V** 356–57
Coats Viyella Plc, V 356–58
CoBank. *See* National Bank for
    Cooperatives.
Cobb, Inc., **II** 585
Cobden, Richard, **10** 6
Cobrin, Marilyn, **II** 664
Coburn, Charles, **I** 89
Coburn Optical Industries, **III** 56
Coburn Vision Care, **III** 727
Coca-Cola Bottling Co. Consolidated, 10
    222–24
Coca-Cola Bottling Co. of Los Angeles, **II**
    468
Coca-Cola Bottling Company of Mid-
    Carolinas, **10** 222
Coca-Cola Bottling Company of West
    Virginia, Inc., **10** 222
Coca-Cola Bottling Midwest, **II** 170
The Coca-Cola Company, I 17, **232–35**,
    244, 278–79, 286, 289, 440, 457; **II**

103, 136–37, 477–78; **III** 215; **IV** 297;
    6 20–21, 30; **7** 155, 383, 466; **8** 399; **9**
    86, 177; **10** 130, 222–23, **225–28**
    (upd.); **11** 421, 450–51
Coca-Cola Enterprises, Inc., **10** 223
Coca-Cola Export Corp., **I** 248
Coca-Cola Nestlé Refreshment Company, **7**
    383
Cochery, Adolphe, **V** 471
Cochran, Henry J., **II** 230
Cochran, Josephine, **8** 298
Cochrane Corporation, **8** 135
Cock, Gerald, **7** 53
Cockerell, H.A.L., **III** 334
Cockerill Group, **IV** 51–53
Cockerill, John, **IV** 51
Cockerill Sambre Group, **IV** 26–27, **51–53**
Cockerill Sambre S.A., **IV** 51–53
Cockerill, William, **IV** 51
Cockerill-Ougrée, IV 52
Cockerill-Ougrée-Providence, **IV** 52
Cockwell, Jack, **10** 529
Coco's, **I** 547
Codere, Charles F., **III** 356
Codex Corp., **II** 61
Codville Distributors Ltd., **II** 649
Coe, E. H., **6** 545
Coffin, Arthur, **I** 320
Coffin, Charles A., **II** 27
Coffin, David L., **I** 320–21
Coffin, Dexter, **I** 320
Coffin, Herbert, **II**, **I** 320
Coffin, Herbert R., **I** 320
COFINA, **III** 347
COFIRED, **IV** 108
Cofrin, Austin Edward, **8** 197
Cofrin, John, **8** 197
Cogéma, **IV** 108
COGEMA Canada, **IV** 436
Cogentrix Energy, Inc., 10 229–31
Coggeshall, James, **II** 402
Cognos Corp., **11** 78
Cohen, Abraham, **10** 391
Cohen, Ben, **10** 146
Cohen, Emanuel, **II** 155
Cohen, Israel (Izzy), **II** 634–35
Cohen, John Edward (Jack), **II** 677
Cohen, Leonard, **III** 87
Cohen, Maurice, **10** 391
Cohen, Nehemiah Myer (N.M.), **II** 633–35
Cohen, Norman, **10** 391
Cohen, Peter, **II** 450–52; **9** 469
Cohen, Peter A., **11** 418
Cohen, Philip, **10** 391
Cohen, Samuel, **6** 200–01
Cohen, Stanley N., **I** 637
Cohn, Harry, **II** 135–36
Cohn, Jack, **II** 135
Coinamatic Laundry Equipment, **II** 650
Cojuangco, Antonio, **6** 106
Coker, Charles, Jr., **8** 476
Coker, Charles W., **8** 476
Coker, Charles Westfield, **8** 475
Coker, James, Jr., **8** 475
Coker, James L. (Maj.), **8** 475
Coker, James Lide III, **8** 475–76
Colaccino, Frank, **7** 113–15
Colbert, Claudette, **I** 448; **II** 155
Colbert, Jean Baptiste, **III** 675
Colbert, L.L., **I** 144; **11** 53
Colbert Television Sales, **9** 306
Colburn, Irwin, **III** 640
Colby, Gerard, **I** 330
Colchester Car Auctions, **II** 587

Coldwell, Banker & Company, **IV** 715; **V**
    180, 182; **11** 292
Coldwell Banker Commercial Group, Inc.,
    IV 727
Cole & Weber Inc., **I** 27
Cole, Francis W., **III** 388
Cole, Glen W., **III** 683
Cole, Walton, **IV** 669
Colebrook, James, **III** 370
Coleco Industries, **III** 506
Coleman & Co., **II** 230
The Coleman Company, Inc., III 485; **9**
    127–29
Coleman, Dennis, **10** 507
Coleman, James, **I** 244; **7** 156
Coleman, John, **III** 165; **6** 281
Coleman, Sheldon, **9** 128
Coleman, Thomas, **I** 328; **8** 151
Coleman, William Coffin, **9** 127–28
Colemans Ltd., **11** 241
Coles, **V** 35
Coles, A.W., **V** 33
Coles Book Stores Ltd., **7** 486, 488–89
Coles, E.B., **V** 33
Coles, Fossey, **V** 35
Coles, George James, **V** 33
Coles Myer Ltd., V 33–35
Colgate & Co., **III** 23
Colgate, Bayard, **III** 23
Colgate, Bowles, **III** 23
Colgate, Samuel, **III** 23
Colgate, William, **III** 23
Colgate-Palmolive Company, I 260; **II**
    672; **III 23–26**; **IV** 285; **9** 291; **11** 219
Colgate-Palmolive-Peet, **III** 23; **9** 317
Colijn, H, **IV** 132
Colin, Oswaldo R., **II** 199
College Construction Loan Insurance
    Assoc., **II** 455
College Survival, Inc., **10** 357
Collegiate Arlington Sports Inc., **II** 652
Collender, H.M., **III** 442
Collens, Clarence, **9** 439
Collett Dickenson Pearce, **I** 33
Collier, Abram, **III** 313–14
Collier, Geoffrey, **II** 428
Collier, Harry, **IV** 537
Collin, Fernand, **II** 304–05
Collins & Aikman Corp., **I** 483
Collins, George J., **11** 495
Collins, Jack W., **II** 21, 22
Collins, Jackie, **IV** 672
Collins, John, **9** 539
Collins, John F., **11** 281
Collins Radio, **III** 136
Collins Radio Co., **11** 429
Collins, Ron, **6** 15
Collins, Sammy, **IV** 66–67; **7** 123–24
Collinson, Joseph, **I** 530
Collomb, Bertrand, **III** 705
Collyer, John L., **V** 232
Collyer, John Lyon, **11** 158
Colman, James, **II** 566
Colman, Jeremiah, **II** 566; **III** 233
Colo-Macco. *See* CRSS Inc.
Colodny, Edwin, **I** 131–32; **6** 131–32
Cologne Reinsurance Co., **III** 273, 299
Colonia, **III** 273, 394
Colonial & General, **III** 359–60
Colonial Air Transport, **I** 89, 115
Colonial Airlines, **I** 102
Colonial Bancorp, **II** 208
Colonial Bank, **II** 236
Colonial Container, **8** 359

Colonial Food Stores, **7** 373
Colonial Insurance Co., **IV** 575–76
Colonial Life Assurance Co., **III** 359
Colonial Life Insurance Co. of America, **III** 220–21
Colonial Life Insurance Company, **11** 481
Colonial National Bank, **8** 9
Colonial National Leasing, Inc., **8** 9
Colonial Penn Group Insurance Co., **11** 262
Colonial Penn Life Insurance Co., **V** 624
Colonial Rubber Works, **8** 347
Colonial Stores, **II** 397
Colonial Sugar Refining Co. Ltd., **III** 686–87
Colony Communications, **7** 99
Color Corporation of America, **8** 553
Color-Box, Inc., **8** 103
Colorado Belle Casino, **6** 204
Colorado Cooler Co., **I** 292
Colorado Electric Company. *See* Public Service Company of Colorado.
Colorado Gathering & Processing Corporation, **11** 27
Colorado Interstate Gas Co., **IV** 394
Colorcraft, **I** 447
Colorfoto Inc., **I** 447
Colossal Pictures, **10** 286
Colson Co., **III** 96; **IV** 135–36
Colt Industries Inc., I 434–36, 482, 524; **III** 435
Colt Pistol Factory, **9** 416
Colt, S. Sloan, **II** 230
Colt, Samuel Pomeroy, **9** 228–29
Columbia, **II** 135
Columbia Broadcasting System. *See* CBS Inc.
Columbia Chemical Co., **III** 731
Columbia Electric Street Railway, Light and Power Company, **6** 575
Columbia Forest Products, **IV** 358
Columbia Gas & Electric Company, **6** 466. *See also* Columbia Gas System, Inc.
Columbia Gas Light Company, **6** 574
Columbia Gas of New York, Inc., **6** 536
Columbia Gas System, Inc., **V** 580–82
Columbia Gas Transmission Corporation, **6** 467
Columbia General Life Insurance Company of Indiana, **11** 378
Columbia House, **IV** 676
Columbia Insurance Co., **III** 214
Columbia News Service, **II** 132
Columbia Paper Co., **IV** 311
Columbia Phonograph, **II** 132
Columbia Phonograph Broadcasting System, **II** 132
Columbia Pictures Corp., **II** 135; **10** 227
Columbia Pictures Entertainment, Inc., **II** 103, 134, **135–37**, 170, 234, 619; **IV** 675; **10** 227
Columbia Pictures Television, **II** 137
Columbia Railroad, Gas and Electric Company, **6** 575
Columbia Recording Corp., **II** 132
Columbia River Packers, **II** 491
Columbia Savings & Loan, **II** 144
Columbia Steel Co., **IV** 28, 573; **7** 550
Columbian Chemicals Co., **IV** 179
Columbian Peanut Co., **I** 421; **11** 23
Columbus & Southern Ohio Electric Company (CSO), **6** 467, 481–82
Columbus Savings and Loan Society, **I** 536
Columbus-Milpar, **I** 544

Com Ed. *See* Commonwealth Edison Company.
Com-Link 21, Inc., **8** 310
Com-Link 21, Inc. of Tennessee, **8** 310
Comalco Fabricators (Hong Kong) Ltd., **III** 758
Comalco Ltd., **IV** 59–61, 191. *See also* Commonwealth Aluminium Corp.
Comat Services Pte. Ltd., **10** 514
Comau, **I** 163
Combined American Insurance Co. of Dallas, **III** 203
Combined Casualty Co. of Philadelphia, **III** 203
Combined Communications Corp., **II** 619; **IV** 612; **7** 191
Combined Insurance Co. of America, **III** 203–04
Combined International Corp., **III** 203–04
Combined Mutual Casualty Co. of Chicago, **III** 203
Combined Registry Co., **III** 203
Combs, Harry, **8** 314–15
Combustiveis Industriais e Domésticos. *See* CIDLA.
Comcast Corporation, 7 90–92; **9** 428; **10** 432–33
Comdisco Disaster Recovery Services, **9** 131
Comdisco Disaster Recovery Services Inc., **11** 484
Comdisco Equities, Inc., **9** 131
Comdisco Financial Services, Inc., **9** 130
Comdisco, Inc., 9 130–32; **11** 47, 86, 490
Comdor Flugdienst GmbH., **I** 111
Comer, Gary, **9** 314
Comer Motor Express, **6** 370
Comerco, **III** 21
Comet, **II** 139; **V** 106–09
Cometra Oil, **IV** 576
ComFed Bancorp, **11** 29
Comfort, Harold W., **II** 472
Comforto GmbH, **8** 252
Cominco, **IV** 75, 141
Comitato Interministrale per la Ricostruzione, **I** 465
Comm-Quip, **6** 313
CommAir. *See* American Building Maintenance Industries, Inc.
Commander Foods, **8** 409
Commander-Larabee Co., **I** 419
Commentry, **III** 676
Commerce and Industry Insurance Co., **III** 196, 203
Commerce Clearing House, Inc., 7 93–94
Commerce Group, **III** 393
Commerce Union, **10** 426
Commercial & General Life Assurance Co., **III** 371
Commercial Alliance Corp. of New York, **II** 289
Commercial Aseguradora Suizo Americana, S.A., **III** 243
Commercial Assurance, **III** 359
Commercial Bank of Australia Ltd., **II** 189, 319, 388–89
Commercial Bank of London, **II** 334
Commercial Bank of Tasmania, **II** 188
Commercial Banking Co. of Sydney, **II** 187–89
Commercial Bureau (Australia) Pty., **I** 438
Commercial Credit Company, 8 117–19; **10** 255–56

Commercial Credit Corp., **III** 127–28
Commercial Exchange Bank, **II** 254; **9** 124
Commercial Filters Corp., **I** 512
Commercial Insurance Co. of Newark, **III** 242
Commercial Life, **III** 243
Commercial Life Assurance Co. of Canada, **III** 309
Commercial National Bank, **II** 261; **10** 425
Commercial National Bank & Trust Co., **II** 230
Commercial National Bank of Charlotte, **II** 336
Commercial Ship Repair Co., **I** 185
Commercial Union plc, II 272, 308; **III** 185, **233–35**, 350, 373; **IV** 711
Commerz- und Credit-Bank, **II** 257
Commerz- und Disconto-Bank, **II** 256–57
Commerz- und Privatbank, **II** 256
Commerzbank A.G., II 239, 242, **256–58**, 280, 282, 385; **IV** 222; **9** 283
Commerzbank Bankverein, **II** 257
Commerzfilm, **IV** 591
Commes, Thomas A., **III** 745
Commodity Credit Corp., **11** 24
Commodore Business Machines Ltd., **7** 95
Commodore Computers, **II** 6; **III** 112; **7** 532
Commodore Corporation, **8** 229
Commodore International, Ltd., 6 243–44; **7** 95–97; **9** 46; **10** 56, 284
Commodore Portable Typewriter Co., Ltd., **7** 95
Commonwealth & Southern Corporation, **V** 676
Commonwealth Aluminium Corp., Ltd., **IV** 122. *See also* Comalco Ltd.
Commonwealth Bank, **II** 188, 389
Commonwealth Board Mills, **IV** 248
Commonwealth Edison, II 28, 425; **III** 653; **IV** 169; **V** 583–85; **6** 505, 529, 531
Commonwealth Hospitality Ltd., **III** 95
Commonwealth Industries, **III** 569; **11** 536
Commonwealth Insurance Co., **III** 264
Commonwealth Land Title Insurance Co., **III** 343
Commonwealth Life Insurance Co., **III** 216–19
Commonwealth Mortgage Assurance Co., **III** 344
Commonwealth National Financial Corp., **II** 316
Commonwealth Oil Refining Company, **II** 402; **7** 517
Commtron, **V** 14, 16
Commtron Corporation, **11** 195
Communication Services Ltd. *See* Hongkong Telecommunications Ltd.
Communications Data Services, Inc., **IV** 627
Communications Properties, Inc., **IV** 677
Communications Solutions Inc., **11** 520
Communicorp, **III** 188; **10** 29
Community Direct, Inc., **7** 16
Community HealthCare Services, **6** 182
Community Hospital of San Gabriel, **6** 149
Community Medical Care, Inc., **III** 245
Community National Bank, **9** 474
Community Power & Light Company, **6** 579–80
Community Public Service Company, **6** 514
Community Savings and Loan, **II** 317
Comnet Corporation, **9** 347

Compac Corp., **11** 535
Compactom, **I** 588
Compagnia di Assicurazioni, **III** 345
Compagnia di Genova, **III** 347
Compagnie Auxiliaire de Navigation, **IV** 558
Compagnie Bancaire, **II** 259
Compagnie Belge pour l'industrie, **II** 202
Compagnie Continentale, **I** 409–10
Compagnie d'Assurances Générales, **III** 391
Compagnie d'assurances Mutuelles contre l'incendie dans les départements de la Seine Inférieure et de l'Eure, **III** 210
Compagnie d'Investissements de Paris, **II** 233
Compagnie de Compteurs, **III** 617
Compagnie de Five-Lille, **IV** 469
Compagnie de Mokta, **IV** 107–08
Compagnie de Navigation Mixte, **III** 185
Compagnie de Reassurance Nord-Atlantique, **III** 276
Compagnie de Recherche et d'Exploitation du Pétrole du Sahara, **IV** 545
Compagnie de Saint-Gobain, **8** 395, 397
Compagnie de Saint-Gobain S.A., **II** 117, 474–75; **III 675–78**, 704
Compagnie de Suez, **III** 677
Compagnie de Transport Aerien, **I** 122
Compagnie des Glaces, **III** 675
Compagnie des Machines Bull S.A., **II** 40, 42, 70, 125; **III 122–23**, 154; **IV** 600. *See also* Groupe Bull.
Compagnie des Messageries Maritimes, **6** 379
Compagnie des Produits Chimiques d'Alais et de la Camargue, **IV** 173
Compagnie des Produits Chimiques et Électrométallurgiques d'Alais, Froges et Camargue, **IV** 173–74
Compagnie du Midi, **III** 209, 211
Compagnie du Nord, **IV** 108
Compagnie Européenne de Publication, **IV** 614–15
Compagnie Financiere Alcatel, **9** 10
Compagnie Financiere de Paribas, **II** 192, **259–60**; **III** 185
Compagnie Financiere de Paris et des Pays-Bas, **II** 259
Compagnie Financière de Suez, **III** 394
Compagnie Française de Distribution en Afrique, **IV** 559
Compagnie Française de Raffinage, **IV** 558–60
Compagnie Française des Lubricants, **I** 341
Compagnie Française des Minerais d'Uranium, **IV** 108
Compagnie Française des Mines de Diamants du Cap, **IV** 64; **7** 121
Compagnie Française des Pétroles, **II** 259; **IV** 363–64, 423–24, 454, 466, 486, 504, 515, 544–46, 557–60; **7** 481–83
Compagnie Française des Produits d'Orangina, **I** 281
Compagnie Française du Méthane, **V** 626
Compagnie Française Thomson-Houston, **I** 357; **II** 116
Compagnie Générale d'Électricité, **I** 193; **II 12–13**, 25; **IV** 174, 615; **9** 9–10
Compagnie Generale de Cartons Ondules, **IV** 296
Compagnie Generale de Radiologie, **II** 117
Compagnie Generale de Telegraphie Sans Fils, **II** 116

Compagnie Générale des Eaux, **V** 632–33; **6** 441
Compagnie Générale des Établissements Michelin, **V 236–39**
Compagnie Générale Maritime (CGM), **6** 379–80
Compagnie Générale Maritime et Financière, **6 379–81**
Compagnie Générale Transatlantique (Transat), **6** 379–80
Compagnie Industriali Riunite S.p.A., **IV** 587–88
Compagnie Internationale de l'Informatique, **III** 123
Compagnie Internationale Pirelli S.A., **V** 249
Compagnie Navale Des Pétroles, **IV** 558
Compagnie Parisienne de Garantie, **III** 211
Compagnie Pneumatique Commerciale, **III** 426
Compagnie Tunisienne de Ressorts a Lames, **III** 581
Companhia Brasileira de Aluminio, **IV** 55
Companhia Brasileira de Mineracão e Siderugica, **IV** 54
Companhia de Diamantes de Angola, **IV** 21
Companhia de Minerales y Metales, **IV** 139
Companhia de Pesquisas Mineras de Angola, **IV** 65; **7** 122
Companhia de Seguros Argos Fluminense, **III** 221
Companhia Siderúrgica de Tubarao, **IV** 125
Companhia Siderúrgica Mannesmann S.A., **III** 565–66
Companhia Siderúrgica Nacional, **II** 199
Companhia Uniao Fabril, **IV** 505
Companhia Vale do Rio Doce, **IV 54–57**
Compañía Arrendataria del Monopolio de Petróleos Sociedad Anónima, **IV** 396–97, 527–29
Compañía de Investigacion y Exploitaciones Petrolifera, **IV** 397
Compañia de Líneas Aéreas Subvencionadas S.A., **6** 95
Compañia Española de Petroleos S.A., **IV 396–98**, 527
Compañia Minera La India, **IV** 164
Compañia Nacional Minera Petrólia del Táchira, **IV** 507
Compañía Telefónica Nacional de España S.A., **V** 337
Compaq Computer Corporation, **II** 45; **III** 114, **124–25**; **6** 217, **221–23 (upd.)**, 230–31, 235, 243–44; **9** 42–43, 166, 170–71, 472; **10** 87, 232–33, 366, 459, 518–19
Compass Group, plc, **6** 193
Compeda, Ltd., **10** 240
Competition Tire East, **V** 494
Competition Tire West, **V** 494
Compex, **II** 233
Components Agents Ltd., **10** 113
Composite Craft Inc., **I** 387
Comprehensive Resources Corp., **IV** 83
Compressed Industrial Gases, **I** 297
Compression Labs, **10** 456
Comptoir d'Escompte de Mulhouse, **II** 232
Comptoir des Textiles Artificielles, **I** 122, 388–89
Comptoir Métallurgique Luxembourgeois, **IV** 25

Comptoir National d'Escompte de Paris, **II** 232–33, 270
Compton Communications, **I** 33
Compton Foods, **II** 675
Compton, George E., **I** 653
Compton, Ronald E., **III** 182
Compton, Walter Ames, **I** 653, 655
Compton's MultiMedia Publishing Group, Inc., **7** 165
Compton's New Media, Inc., **7** 168
CompuAdd Computer Corporation, **11 61–63**
CompuAdd Express, **11** 62
CompuAdd Information Systems, **11** 62
CompuChem Corporation, **11** 425
CompuCom Systems, Inc., **10 232–34**, 474
Compugraphic, **III** 168; **6** 284
Compumotor, **III** 603
CompUSA, **11** 63
CompUSA, Inc., **10 235–36**
CompuServe Incorporated, **9** 268–70; **10 237–39**
Computax, **6** 227–28
Computer Associates International, Inc., **6 224–26**; **10** 394
The Computer Company, **11** 112
Computer Consoles Inc., **III** 164
The Computer Department, Ltd., **10** 89
Computer Depot, **6** 243
Computer Discount Corporation. *See* Comdisco, Inc.
Computer Dynamics, Inc., **6** 10
Computer Plaza K.K., **IV** 542–43
Computer Power, **6** 301
Computer Research Corp., **III** 151; **6** 265
Computer Sciences Corporation, **6** 25, **227–29**
Computer Shoppe, **V** 191–92
Computer Terminal Corporation, **11** 67–68
ComputerCity, **10** 235
Computerized Lodging Systems, Inc., **11** 275
ComputerLand Corporation, **6** 243; **9** 116; **10** 233, 563
Computervision Corporation, **6** 246–47; **7** 498; **10 240–42**; **11** 275
Computing Scale Company of America, **III** 147. *See also* International Business Machines Corporation.
Computing-Tabulating-Recording Co., **III** 147
Compuware Corporation, **10 243–45**
Compuware Corporation Do Brasil, **10** 244
Compuware Japan Corporation, **10** 244
Comsat, **II** 425
Comstock Canada, **9** 301
Comstock, William A., **11** 339
Comte, **I** 121
Comyn, D.G., **III** 751–52
Con Ed. *See* Consolidated Edison of New York, Inc.
Con-Ferro Paint and Varnish Company, **8** 553
ConAgra, Inc., **II 493–95**, 517, 585; **7** 432, 525; **8** 53, 499–500
ConAgra Turkey Co., **II** 494
Conahay & Lyon, **6** 27
Concord International, **II** 298
Concordia, **IV** 497
Concrete Industries (Monier) Ltd., **III** 735
Conde, Mario, **II** 198
Condé Nast Publications, Inc., **IV** 583–84
Cone, Bernard, **8** 121

Cone, Caesar, **8** 120–21
Cone, Fairfax, **I** 12–15
Cone, Herman, **8** 120
Cone, Julius, **8** 120–21
Cone Mills Corporation, 8 120–22
Cone, Moses, **8** 120
Conestoga National Bank, **II** 316
Confaloniere, Fedele, **IV** 588
Confederation of Engineering Industry, **IV** 484
Confidata Corporation, **11** 111
Confindustria, **I** 162
Congas Engineering Canada Ltd., **6** 478
Congdon, R. C., **6** 447
Congressional Information Services, **IV** 610
Conic, **9** 324
Conifer Group, **II** 214
Conill Corp., **II** 261
Coniston Partners, **I** 130; **II** 680; **III** 29; **6** 130; **10** 302
Conkling, Edgar, **8** 155
Conkling, Stephen, **8** 155
Conley, Kelvin, **III** 728
Conn, John, **11** 62
CONNA Corp., **7** 113
Connally, John, **11** 25
Connecticut Bank and Trust Co., **II** 213–14
Connecticut General Corp., **III** 223, 225–26
Connecticut General Life Insurance Co., **III** 223, 225–26
Connecticut Life Insurance Co., **III** 314
Connecticut Mutual Life Insurance Company, III 225, **236–38**, 254, 285
Connecticut Telephone Company. *See* Southern New England Telecommunications Corporation.
Connecticut Trust and Safe Deposit Co., **II** 213
Connecting Point of America, **6** 244
Connelly, John F., **I** 601–02
Conner, Finis F., **6** 230–31
Conner Peripherals, Inc., 6 230–32; 10 403, 459, 463–64, 519; **11** 56, 234
Conner Technology, Inc., **6** 231
Connie Lee. *See* College Construction Loan Insurance Assoc.
Connolly Data Systems, **11** 66
Connolly, John, **III** 603
Connolly, Walter J., Jr., **II** 214–15
Connor, John T., **I** 415
Connor, Joseph E., **9** 423
Connor, William, **7** 342
Connors Brothers, **II** 631–32
Conoco, **6** 539; **11** 97
Conoco Chemicals Co., **I** 402; **IV** 401
Conoco Coal Development Co., **IV** 401
Conoco, Ecuador Ltd., **IV** 389
Conoco Inc., I 286, 329, 346, 402–04; **II** 376; **IV** 365, 382, 389, **399–402**, 413, 429, 454, 476; **7** 346, 559; **8** 556
Conoco Oil, **8** 152, 154
Conoco UK Ltd., **11** 400
Conorada Petroleum Corp., **IV** 365, 400
Conover Furniture Company, **10** 183
Conover, James, **6** 465
Conrad, Anthony L, **II** 90
Conrad International Hotels, **III** 91–93
Conrail. *See* Consolidated Rail Corporation.
Conseco Capital Management, Inc., **10** 247
Conseco Capital Partners, **10** 247

Conseco Capital Partners II, L.P., **10** 248
Conseco Entertainment Inc., **10** 248
Conseco Inc., 10 246–48
Consgold. *See* Consolidated Gold Fields of South Africa Ltd. *and* Consolidated Gold Fields PLC.
Considine, Frank, **I** 608
Consolidated Aircraft Corporation, **9** 16, 497
Consolidated Aluminum Corp., **IV** 178
Consolidated Cable Utilities, **6** 313
Consolidated Cement Corp., **III** 704
Consolidated Cigar Co., **I** 452–53
Consolidated Coal Co., **IV** 82, 170–71
Consolidated Coin Caterers Corporation, **10** 222
Consolidated Controls, **I** 155
Consolidated Denison Mines Ltd., **8** 418
Consolidated Diamond Mines of South-West Africa Ltd., **IV** 21, 65–67; **7** 122–25
Consolidated Distillers Ltd., **I** 263
Consolidated Edison, I 28; **6** 456
Consolidated Edison Company of New York, Inc., **V 586–89**
Consolidated Electric & Gas, **6** 447
Consolidated Foods Corp., **II** 571–73, 584; **III** 480
Consolidated Freightways, Inc., V 432–34; 6 280, 388
Consolidated Gold Fields of South Africa Ltd., **IV** 94, 96, 118, 565, 566
Consolidated Gold Fields PLC, **II** 422; **III** 501, 503; **IV** 23, 67, 94, 97, 171; **7** 125, 209, 387
Consolidated Grocers Corp., **II** 571
Consolidated Insurances of Australia, **III** 347
Consolidated Marketing, Inc., **IV** 282; **9** 261
Consolidated Mines Selection Co., **IV** 20, 23
Consolidated Mining and Smelting Co., **IV** 75
Consolidated National Life Insurance Co., **10** 246
Consolidated Natural Gas Company, V 590–91
Consolidated Oatmeal Co., **II** 558
Consolidated Papers, Inc., 8 123–25; 11 311
Consolidated Power & Light Company, **6** 580
Consolidated Power & Telephone Company, **11** 342
Consolidated Press Holdings, **8** 551
Consolidated Rail Corporation, II 449; **V 435–37**, 485; **10** 44
Consolidated Rand-Transvaal Mining Group, **IV** 90
Consolidated Steel, **I** 558; **IV** 570
Consolidated Temperature Controlling Co., **II** 40
Consolidated Tyre Services Ltd., **IV** 241
Consolidated Vultee, **II** 7, 32
Consolidated Zinc Corp., **IV** 58, 122, 189, 191
Consolidated Zinc Proprietary, **IV** 58–59
Consolidated-Bathurst Inc., **IV** 246–47, 334
Consolidation Coal Co., **IV** 401; **8** 154, 346–47
Consoweld Corporation, **8** 124
Constable, Archibald, **7** 165

Constance, S.J., **I** 288
Constantineau, Richard, **II** 652
Constar International Inc., **8** 562
Constellation, **III** 335
Constellation Insurance Co., **III** 191
Constellation Reinsurance Co., **III** 191–92
Construcciones Aeronauticas S.A., **I** 41–42
Construcciones y Contratas, **II** 198
Construtora Moderna SARL, **IV** 505
Consumer Value Stores, **V** 136–37; **9** 67
Consumer's Gas Co., **I** 264
Consumers Cooperative Association, **7** 174
Consumers Distributing Co. Ltd., **II** 649, 652–53
Consumers Electric Light and Power, **6** 582
The Consumers Gas Company Ltd., 6 476–79
Consumers Power, **V** 577–79, 593–94
Contact Software International Inc., **10** 509
Contadina, **II** 488–89
Container Corp. of America, **IV** 295, 465; **V** 147; **7** 353; **8** 476
Container Transport International, **III** 344
Containers Packaging, **IV** 249
Contech, **10** 493
Contel Cellular, Inc., **6** 323
Contel Corporation, **II** 117; **V** 294–98
Contherm Corp., **III** 420
ContiCommodity Services, Inc., **10** 250–51
Continental AG, **9** 248
Continental Airlines, I 96–98, 103, 118, 123–24, 129–30; **6** 52, 61, 105, 120–21, 129–30
Continental Aktiengesellschaft, V 240–43, 250–51, 256; **8** 212–14
Continental American Life Insurance Company, **7** 102
Continental and Commercial National Bank, **II** 261
Continental and Commercial Trust and Savings Bank, **II** 261
Continental Assurance Co., **III** 228–30
Continental Assurance Co. of North America, **III** 228
Continental Baking Co., **I** 463–64; **II** 562–63; **7** 320–21; **11** 198
Continental Bancor, **II** 248
Continental Bank and Trust Co., **II** 251
Continental Bank Corporation, II 261–63; **IV** 702. *See also* Continental Illinois Corp.
Continental Blacks Inc., **I** 403
Continental Cablevision, Inc., 7 98–100
Continental Can Co., **I** 597; **II** 34, 414; **III** 471; **10** 130
Continental Carbon Co., **I** 403–05; **II** 53; **IV** 401
Continental Care Group, **10** 252–53
Continental Casualty Co., **III** 196, 228–32
Continental Cities Corp., **III** 344
Continental Corporation, III 230, **239–44**, 273; **10** 561
Continental Cos., **III** 248
Continental Divide Insurance Co., **III** 214
Continental Express, **11** 299
Continental Fiber Drum, **8** 476
Continental Gas & Electric Corporation, **6** 511
Continental Grain Company, 10 249–51
Continental Group Co., **I 599–600**, 601–02, 604–05, 607–09, 612–13, 615; **IV** 334
Continental Group, Inc., **8** 175, 424

Continental Gummi-Werke, **9** 248

Continental Gummi-Werke Aktiengesellschaft, **V** 241

Continental Illinois Corp., **I** 526; **II** 261–63, 285, 289, 348. *See also* Continental Bank Corporation.

Continental Illinois National Bank and Trust Co. of Chicago, **II** 261

Continental Illinois Venture Co., **IV** 702

Continental Insurance Co., **III** 239–42, 372–73, 386

Continental Insurance Cos., **III** 242

Continental Insurance Cos. of New York, **III** 230

Continental Investment Corporation, **9** 507

Continental Life Insurance Co., **III** 225

Continental Medical Systems, Inc., 10 252–54; **11** 282

Continental Milling Company, **10** 250

Continental Motors Corp., **I** 199, 524–25; **10** 521–22

Continental National American Group, **III** 230, 404

Continental National Bank, **II** 261; **11** 119

Continental National Bank and Trust Co., **II** 261

Continental Oil & Transportation Co., **IV** 399

Continental Oil Black Co., **IV** 400

Continental Oil Co., **IV** 39, 365, 382, 399–401, 476, 517, 575–76

Continental Radio, **IV** 607

Continental Reinsurance, **11** 533

Continental Risk Services, **III** 243

Continental Savouries, **II** 500

Continental Securities Corp., **II** 444

Continental Telephone Company, **V** 296–97; **9** 494–95; **11** 500

Continental-Caoutchouc und Gutta-Percha Compagnie, **V** 240

Continental-Emsco, **I** 490–91

Continental-National Group, **III** 230

Continentale Allgemeine, **III** 347

Control Data Corporation, **III** 118, **126–28**, 129, 131, 149, 152, 165; **6** 228, 252, 266; **8** 117–18, 467; **10** 359, 458–59; **11** 469

Control Data Systems, Inc., 10 255–57

Controls Company of America, **9** 67

Convair, **I** 82, 121, 123, 126, 131; **II** 33; **9** 18, 498

Convenient Food Mart Inc., **7** 114

Convergent Technologies, **III** 166; **6** 283; **11** 519

Converse, Edmund C., **II** 229

Converse Inc., **III** 528–29; **V** 376; **9** **133–36**, 234

Converse, Marquis M., **9** 133

Conway, Michael J., **6** 72–74

Conway, William E., **8** 383

Conycon. *See* Construcciones y Contratas.

Conzinc Riotinto of Australia. *See* CRA Limited.

Cook, Bob, **11** 191

Cook, C.W., **II** 532

Cook Data Services, Inc., **9** 73

Cook, David, **9** 73

Cook, Donald C., **V** 548

Cook Industrial Coatings, **I** 307

Cook, J. Michael, **9** 168

Cook, Jane Bancroft, **IV** 602

Cook, Jerry, **10** 331

Cook, John Mason, **9** 503–04

Cook, Lodwrick M., **IV** 376; **10** 111

Cook, Paul, **8** 446

Cook, Sandy, **9** 73

Cook, Thomas, **9** 503–04

Cook United, **V** 172

Cook, William R., **10** 155

Cooke, Alison, **I** 95

Cooke, Amos S., **10** 40

Cooke, Amos Starr, **II** 490

Cooke, Clarence, **9** 275

Cooke, E. H., **6** 539

Cooke, Jack Kent, **IV** 684; **6** 323; **8** 525

Cooke, Jay, **11** 313

Cooke, Joseph P., **10** 40

Cooke, Nelson M., **IV** 635

Cooke, Richard, **9** 275

Cookson America, Inc., **III** 681

Cookson, Clive, **III** 680–81

Cookson Group plc, **III** **679–82**

Cookson Industrial Materials, **III** 679

Cookson, Isaac, **III** 679

Cookson, Isaac, III, **III** 679

Cookson, Norman, **III** 679–80

Cookson, Roland, **III** 681

Cookson, William Isaac, **III** 679–80

Coolerator, **I** 463

Cooley, Richard P., **II** 382–83; **9** 195

Coolidge, Calvin, **II** 151, 315

Coolidge, Thomas Jefferson, **8** 32

Coolidge, William, **II** 28

Cooling, Parke, **6** 409

Cooney, Chris, **11** 500

Coope, George, **I** 215

Coope, Octavius, **I** 215

Cooper, Barry, **II** 34

Cooper, Charles, **II** 14, 16

Cooper, Charles Gray, **II** 14

Cooper, Dan, **I** 113; **6** 104

Cooper, Elias, **II** 14

Cooper, Francis D'Arcy, **II** 589; **7** 543

Cooper, Gary, **II** 155

Cooper, Harris, **10** 373–74

Cooper Industries, Inc., **II** **14–17**

Cooper, Ira J., **8** 126

Cooper Laboratories, **I** 667, 682

Cooper LaserSonics Inc., **IV** 100

Cooper, Mathew, **I** 75

Cooper McDougall & Robertson Ltd., **I** 715

Cooper, Milton, **11** 228–29

Cooper, Owen, **8** 183–84

Cooper Tire & Rubber Company, **8** **126–28**

Cooper, William, **9** 137

Cooper, William I., **9** 222

Cooper-Bessemer (U.K.), Ltd., **II** 16

Cooper-Bessemer Corp., **II** 14–16

Cooper-Bessemer of Canada, **II** 15

Cooper-Weymouth, **10** 412

Cooperative Grange League Federation Exchange, **7** 17

Coopers & Lybrand, **9** **137–38**

CooperVision, **7** 46

Coordinated Caribbean Transport. *See* Crowley Caribbean Transport.

Coors, Adolph Herman Joseph, **I** 236

Coors, Adolph, III, **I** 237

Coors, Adolph, Jr., **I** 236

Coors, Bill, **I** 237

Coors Company. *See* Adolph Coors Company.

Coors, Jeffrey, **I** 237

Coors, Joe, **I** 237

Coors, Peter, **I** 237

Coors Porcelain Co., **I** 237

Coorsh and Bittner, **7** 430

Coos Bay Lumber Co., **IV** 281; **9** 259

Coosa River Newsprint Co., **III** 40

Cooymans, **I** 281

Copeland, Al, **7** 26–28

Copeland Corp., **II** 20

Copeland, Lammont duPont, **I** 329; **8** 152

Copeland, William, **I** 265

Copland Brewing Co., **I** 268

Copley Real Estate Advisors, **III** 313

Copolymer Corporation, **9** 242

Coppée, Evence Dieudonné, **III** 705

Coppée, Evence, IV, **III** 705

Copper Queen Consolidated Mining Co., **IV** 176–77

Copper Range Company, **IV** 76; **7** 281–82

Copper, Robert, **7** 430

Coppers, George, **II** 543

Copperweld Steel Co., **IV** 108–09, 237

Coppi, Antonio, **IV** 588

Coppola, Joseph R., **10** 330

Copycat Ltd., **8** 383

Cora Verlag, **IV** 590

Coral Drilling, **I** 570

Coral Leisure Group, **I** 248

Coral Petroleum, **IV** 395

Corby, Brian (Sir), **III** 334–36

Corco. *See* Commonwealth Oil Refining Company.

Corcoran, David, **I** 699

Corcoran, Tom, **I** 699

Cord, E.L., **I** 89, 125; **9** 497

Cordell, Joe B., **III** 765

Cordier, Gabriel, **IV** 173

Cordon & Gotch, **IV** 619

Cordon Bleu, **II** 609

Cordovan Corp., **IV** 608

Core Laboratories, **I** 486

Core Laboratories Inc., **11** 265

Corey, H.H., **II** 505

Corey, Jim, **9** 439

Corfield, Kenneth, **III** 163

Cori, Tom, **I** 691

Corinthian Broadcast Corporation, **10** 4

Corinthian Broadcasting, **IV** 605

Corley, Kenneth, **III** 556

Cormack, James A., **I** 678

Cormetech, **III** 685

Corn Exchange Bank, **II** 316

Corn Exchange Bank Trust Co., **II** 251

Corn Exchange National Bank, **II** 261

Corn, Jack, **7** 444–45

Corn Products Co., **II** 496

Corn Products Refining Co., **II** 496–97

Corn Sweeteners Inc., **I** 421; **11** 23

Cornelis, Francois, **IV** 499

Cornelius, Martin P., **II** 229

Cornelius, W. E., **V** 742

Cornell, Harry M., Jr., **11** 255

Cornell, Robert, **III** 602

Cornerstone Direct Marketing, **8** 385–86

Cornerstone Title Company, **8** 461

Corness, Colin, **III** 734–35

Cornhill Insurance Co., **I** 429; **III** 185, 385

Cornhusker Casualty Co., **III** 213

Corning Asahi Video Products Co., **III** 667

Corning, Erastus, **8** 12; **10** 71

Corning Flint Glass Co., **III** 683

Corning Glass Works Inc., **I** 609; **III** 434, 667, 683–85, 720–21

Corning Incorporated, **III** **683–85**; **8** 468; **11** 334

Corning, Parker, **8** 12

Corning-BICC, **III** 434

Cornog, Robert A., **7** 480
Cornvelle, Herbert C., **I** 566
Cornwallis (Lord), **IV** 666
Coronado Corp., **II** 112
Coronet Industries, **II** 90
Corp. d'acquisition Socanav-Caisse Inc., **II** 664
Corp. of Lloyd's, **III** 278–79
Corporacion Estatal Petrolera Ecuatoriana, **IV** 510–11
Corporación Venezolana de Petroleo, **IV** 507
Corporate Microsystems, Inc., **10** 395
Corporate Software Inc., 9 139–41
Corpoven, **IV** 508
Corr, Joseph, **I** 127
Corrado Passera, **IV** 588
Corral Midwest, Inc., **10** 333
Correll, A.D., **9** 261
Corrèze, Jacques, **8** 129, 131
Corroon & Black, **III** 280
Corrugated Paper, **IV** 249
Corry, Charles A., **IV** 574; **7** 551
Cortina, Alberto, **II** 198
Corvallis Lumber Co., **IV** 358
Cory Canada, Inc., **II** 608
Cory Corp., **II** 511
Cory Food Services, Inc., **II** 608
Cory, William, **6** 417
Cosby, Bill, **I** 38
Cosden Petroleum Corp., **IV** 498
Cosgrave, Ronald F., **6** 66–67
Cosgrove & Co., **III** 283
Cosgrove, W. L., **6** 446
Cosmair Inc., III 47–48; **8 129–32,** 342–44
Cosmo Oil Co., Ltd., IV 403–04
Cosmopolitan Productions, **IV** 626
Cosorzio Interprovinciale Vini, **10** 181
Coss, Lawrence, **11** 162–63
Costa Apple Products, **II** 480
Costa e Ribeiro Ltd., **IV** 504
Costain, **III** 495
Costco, **11** 240
Costco Wholesale Corporation, V 36; 10 206
Costello, Albert J., **8** 26
Costello, Joseph B., **11** 46
Costello, Richard, **6** 47
Coster, Frank D., **I** 496
Costes, Dieudonné, **V** 471
Cosulich, Antonio, **III** 208
Côte d'Or, **II** 521
Cott Beverage Corporation, **9** 291
Cottees General Foods, **II** 477
Cotter & Company, V, 37–38
Cotter, John, **V** 37–38
Cotterill, F.W., **III** 493
Cotting, James, **10** 430
Cottingham, Walter H., **III** 744–45
Cotton, Jack, **IV** 706
Cotton, Joseph, **II** 143
Coty, **I** 662
Coty, François, **10** 347
Coulam, Robert F., **I** 60
Counsil, William G., **V** 724
Country Kitchen Foods, **III** 21
Country Music Television, **11** 153
Country Poultry, Inc., **II** 494
Country Store of Concord, Inc., **10** 216
Countryman, Fred, **7** 131–32
Countryman, Jack, **7** 131
Countway, Francis A., **9** 317
County Bank, **II** 333

County Fire Insurance Co., **III** 191
County Market, **II** 670
County NatWest, **II** 334–35
County NatWest Securities, **II** 334
County Perfumery, **III** 65
County Seat Stores Inc., II 669; **9** **142–43**
County Trust Co., **II** 230
Cour des Comptes, **II** 233
Courage Brewing Group., **I** 229, 438–39; **III** 503
Courcoux-Bouvet, **II** 260
Couri, David, **11** 80–82
Courrèges Parfums, **III** 48; **8** 343
The Courseware Developers, **11** 19
Court House Square, **10** 44
Courtauld, Samuel, **V** 359–61
Courtaulds Plc, I 321; **IV** 261, 670; **V** 356–57, **359–61**
Courtney Wines International, **II** 477
Courtot Investments, **II** 222
Courtyard by Marriott, **9** 427
Coussmaker, Arthur, **IV** 118–20
Cousteau, Jacques-Yves, **9** 367
Coutts & Co., **II** 333–34
Couvrette & Provost Ltd., **II** 651
Couvrette, Bernard, **II** 651
Couvrette, Jacques, **II** 651
Covantage, **11** 379
Covenant Life Insurance, **III** 314
Coventry Co., **III** 213
Coventry Machinists Company, **7** 458
Coventry Ordnance Works, **I** 573
Coventry Union Banking Co., **II** 318
Covey, Roger E., **10** 513
Covey, Stan, **11** 385
Covidea, **II** 252
Cow & Gate Ltd., **II** 586–87
Cowan, R. Douglas, **11** 72–73
Coward, Noel, **IV** 671
Cowdray (first Viscount). *See* Pearson, Weetman Dickinson (first Viscount Cowdray).
Cowdray (second Viscount). *See* Pearson, Harold (second Viscount Cowdray).
Cowdray (third Viscount), **IV** 658–59
Cowe, Roger, **III** 509
Cowell, Casey, **9** 514
Cowham Engineering, **III** 704
Cowham, W.F., **III** 704
Cowles Communications Co., **IV** 648
Cowles, Gardner, **I** 129; **6** 129
Cowles Media, **IV** 613; **7** 191
Cownie, James, **II** 160–61
Cox & Co., **II** 236, 307–08
Cox, Anne. *See* Chambers, Anne Cox.
Cox, Barbara. *See* Anthony, Barbara Cox.
Cox, Benjamin H., **8** 155
Cox Broadcasting Corp., **IV** 595–96; **6** 32
Cox Cable Communications Inc., **IV** 595–96
Cox, Charles, **7** 262
Cox Communications, **9** 74
Cox Enterprises, Inc., IV 595–97; 7 327
Cox family, **IV** 595–96
Cox, Gilbert, **10** 42
Cox, Guy W., **III** 266
Cox In-Store Advertising, **IV** 597
Cox, James M., **IV** 595
Cox, James M., Jr., **IV** 595–96
Cox, James W., Jr., **8** 12
Cox Newsprint, Inc., **IV** 246
Cox, Robert, **10** 127
Cox, William J., **7** 166

Cox Woodlands Co., **IV** 246
Coy, George, **6** 338
Coykendall, Joe G., **6** 590
Cozad, James W., **10** 554
Cozen, Willibald Hermann, **I** 683–84
Cozens-Hardy, Edward (Lord), **III** 725–26
Cozens-Hardy, Hope, **III** 725
Cozens-Hardy, Peter, **III** 726
CP. *See* Canadian Pacific Limited.
CP Air, **6** 60–61
CP National, **6** 300
CPC Foodservice, **II** 498
CPC International Inc., II 463, **496–98**
CPL. *See* Carolina Power & Light Company.
CRA Limited, IV 58–61, 67, 192; **7** 124
Crabtree Electricals, **III** 503; **7** 210
Crabtree, John, **III** 503
Cracker Barrel Old Country Store, Inc., **9** 78; **10 258–59**
Craft House Corp., **8** 456
Crafts, James F., **III** 251
Craib, Donald F., Jr., **10** 51
Craig, David, **III** 672
Craig, Isabella, **11** 493
Craig, Jenny, **10** 382
Craig, Kyle, **7** 267
Craig, Sid, **10** 382–83
Cramer Electronics, **10** 112
Cramer, Ernst, **IV** 590–91
Cramer-Klett, Theodor, **III** 299
Crandall, Robert, **I** 90; **6** 76–77, 130
Crane and Brother, R.T., **8** 133
Crane Brothers Manufacturing Company, **8** 134
Crane, Charles, **8** 133–34
Crane Co., 8 133–36, 179
Crane Elevator Company, **8** 134
Crane, Keith, **III** 24–25
Crane, Richard T., **8** 133–34
Crane, Richard T., Jr., **8** 134
Crane, Stanley L., **V** 435–36
Crane Supply Company, **8** 135
Cranor, John M., **7** 267–68
Cranston, Alan, **I** 243
Crate and Barrel, 9 144–46
Craven, John, **II** 268, 429
Craven Tasker Ltd., **I** 573–74
Crawford and Watson, **IV** 278
Crawford, Bruce, **I** 29
Crawford, Christina, **I** 277
Crawford, Duncan A., **6** 447
Crawford, George W., **V** 611
Crawford Gosho Co., Ltd., **IV** 442
Crawford, Harry, **7** 443
Crawford, Joan, **I** 277; **II** 176; **10** 287, 451
Crawford Supply Company, **6** 392
Crawford, W. Donham, **6** 495–96
Crawford, William, **7** 494
Craxi, Bettino, **11** 205
Cray Computer Corp., **III** 129–30
Cray, Ed, **I** 173
Cray Research, Inc., III 126, 128, **129–31; 10** 256
Cray, Seymour, **III** 126, 129–30
CRD Total France, **IV** 560
Cream City Railway Company, **6** 601
Cream of Wheat Corp., **II** 543
Creamola Food Products, **II** 569
Crean, John C., **III** 484
Creasy Co., **II** 682
Creative Artists Agency, **10** 228
Creative Forming, Inc., **8** 562
Creative Homes, Inc., **IV** 341

Crédit Agricole, II 264–66, 355
Credit and Data Marketing Services, **V** 118
Credit Clearing House, **IV** 605
Credit du Nord, **II** 260
Credit Factoring International SpA, **II** 271
Crédit Foncier, **II** 264
Crédit Général de Belgique, **II** 304
Credit Immobilier, **7** 538
Crédit Liégiois, **II** 270
Crédit Lyonnais, **II** 242, 257, 354; **6** 396;
   7 12; **9 147–49**
Credit Mobilier, **II** 294
Crédit National S.A., 9 150–52
Credit Service Exchange, **6** 24
Crédit Suisse, **II 267–69**, 369–70,
   378–79, 402–04. *See also*
   Schweizerische Kreditanstalt.
Credit Suisse First Boston. *See* Financière
   Crédit Suisse-First Boston.
Creditanstalt-Bankverein, **II** 242, 295
CrediThrift Financial, **11** 16
Credithrift Financial of Indiana, **III** 194
Credito de la Union Minera, **II** 194
Credito Italiano, **I** 368, 465, 567; **II** 191,
   270–72; **III** 347
Credito Italiano International Ltd., **II** 272
Creed, Eddie, **9** 237–38
Creedon, John J., **III** 293–94
Creighton, John, **IV** 356; **9** 551
Crelinger, Otto, **III** 399
Crellin Holding, Inc., **8** 477
Crellin Plastics, **8** 13
Creole Petroleum Corporation, **IV** 428; **7**
   171
Cresap, Mark, **II** 121
Crescendo Productions, **6** 27
Crescent Chemical, **I** 374
Crescent Niagara Corp., **II** 16
Crescent Vert Co. Ltd., **II** 51
Crescent Washing Machine Company, **8**
   298
Cressbrook Dairy Co., **II** 546
Cressey Dockham & Co., **II** 682
Cresson, Edith, **10** 472
Crest Service Company, **9** 364
Crestbrook Forest Industries Ltd., **IV** 285
Creusot-Loire, **II** 93–94
Critchley (Gen.), **III** 670
Criterion Casualty Company, **10** 312
Criterion Life Insurance Company, **10** 311
Critikon, Inc., **III** 36
Crocker, Jack J., **II** 669–70
Crocker National Bank, **II** 226, 317, 319,
   383
Crockett Container Corporation, **8** 268
Crockett, Ward, **8** 566
Croda International Ltd., **IV** 383
Croll, George, **III** 698
Cromer (Earl of), **III** 280
Crompton & Knowles Corp., **I** 633; **9
   153–55**
Crompton & Knowles Loom Works, **9** 153
Crompton & Knowles Tertre, **9** 153
Crompton Loom Works, **9** 153
Crompton, William, **9** 153
Cromwell, Oliver, **I** 293
Cronje, Frans J.C. (Dr.), **I** 288
Cronkite, Walter, **III** 353
Crop Production Services, Inc., **IV** 576
Crosby, Bing, **II** 151, 155, 533
Crosby, Joseph, **I** 370; **9** 500
Crosby, Oscar T., **6** 552
Croscill Home Fashions, **8** 510
Crosfield, James, **III** 697

Crosfield, Joseph, **III** 696
Crosfield, Lampard & Co., **III** 696
Cross & Trecker Corporation, **10** 330
Cross, A. E., **6** 585
Cross, Geoff, **6** 241
Crossair, **I** 121
Crosse and Blackwell, **II** 547
Crossett Lumber Co., **IV** 281; **9** 259
Crossland Capital Corp., **III** 293
Crothall, **6** 44
Crouse-Hinds Co., **II** 16
Crow Catchpole, **III** 752
Crow, Trammell, **8** 326, 532–34
Crowe, James Q., **11** 301
Crowell, Henry Parsons, **II** 558–59
Crowell Publishing Co., **IV** 310
Crowell-Collier Publishing Company, **7**
   286
Crowley All Terrain Corporation, **6** 383
Crowley American Transport, Inc. *See*
   Crowley Maritime Corporation.
Crowley Caribbean Transport, **6** 383
Crowley Environmental Service, **6** 383
Crowley Foods, Inc., **II** 528
Crowley Launch and Tugboat Company.
   See Crowley Maritime Corporation.
Crowley, Leo, **I** 681, 683
Crowley Marine Services, Inc. *See*
   Crowley Maritime Corporation.
**Crowley Maritime Corporation, 6
   382–84**; **9** 510–11
Crowley Maritime Salvage, **6** 383
Crowley, Thomas B., Sr., **6** 382–83
Crown Aluminum, **I** 544
Crown Can Co., **I** 601
Crown Center Redevelopment Corp., **IV**
   621
**Crown Central Petroleum Corporation,
   7 101–03**
Crown, Cork & Seal Co., I 601–03
Crown Cork International Corp., **I** 601
Crown Drugs, **II** 673
Crown Forest Industries, **IV** 279
Crown, Henry, **I** 58; **10** 316–17
Crown Life Insurance Company, **III** 261; **6**
   181–82
Crown Oil and Refining Company, **7** 101
Crown Publishing, **IV** 584
Crown Zellerbach Corp., **IV** 290, 345; **8**
   261
Crownx Inc., **6** 181–82
CRS. *See* CRSS Inc.
CRS Design. *See* CRSS Inc.
CRS Design Associates. *See* CRSS Inc.
CRS Group. *See* CRSS Inc.
CRS Production, Inc. *See* CRSS Inc.
CRS Sirrine, Inc. *See* CRSS Inc.
CRS Supervision, Inc. *See* CRSS Inc.
CRSS Capital, Inc. *See* CRSS Inc.
CRSS Inc., 6 142–44
CRTC. *See* Canadian Radio-Television and
   Telecommunications Commission.
Crucible Steel, **I** 434–35
Crude Oil Pipe Line Co., **IV** 400
Cruden Investments Pty Ltd., **IV** 651; **7**
   390
Crull, Timm F., **II** 489
Crum & Forster, **II** 448; **III** 172; **6** 290
Crummey, David Christian, **I** 442; **11** 133
Crummey, John David, **I** 442; **11** 133
Crump E & S, **6** 290
Crump Inc., **I** 584
Crüsemann, C. A., **6** 397
Crush International, **II** 478; **III** 53

Crushed Stone Sales Ltd., **IV** 241
Crutchfield, Edward E., Jr., **10** 298–99
Cruzeiro do Sul Airlines, **6** 133
Cryomedics Inc., **I** 667
Crystal Brands, Inc., 9 156–58
Crystal Oil Co., **IV** 180, 548
CS First Boston Inc., **II** 269, **402–04**; **III**
   289. *See also* First Boston Corp.
CS First Boston Pacific, **II** 402, 404
CSA Press, **IV** 661
CSC. *See* Computer Sciences Corporation.
CSC Credit Services, **6** 25
CSC Industries, Inc., **IV** 63
CSE Corp., **III** 214
CSFB. *See* Financière Crédit Suisse-First
   Boston.
CSK, **10** 482
CSO. *See* Columbus & Southern Ohio
   Electric Company.
CSR Chemicals, **III** 687
CSR Limited, **III 686–88**, 728, 735–36;
   IV 46
CSX Commercial Services, **9** 59
CSX Corporation, **V 438–40**, 485; **6** 340;
   9 59
CSY Agri-Processing, **7** 81–82
CT Financial Services Inc., **V** 401–02
CT&T. *See* Carolina Telephone and
   Telegraph Company.
CTA. *See* Comptoir des Textiles
   Artificielles.
CTG, Inc., 11 64–66
CTNE, **I** 462
CTR. *See* International Business Machines
   Corporation.
CTX Mortgage Company, **8** 88
Cub Foods, **II** 669–70
Cuban American Nickel Co., **IV** 82; **7** 186
Cuban American Oil Company, **8** 348
Cuban Telephone Co., **I** 462–63
Cuban-American Manganese Corp., **IV** 81;
   7 186
Cubitts Nigeria, **III** 753
Cuccia, Enrico, **III** 208; **IV** 586
Cuckler Steel Span Co., **I** 481
Cudlipp, Hugh, **IV** 666; **7** 342
Cugat, Xavier, **II** 543
Culbreath, H. L., **6** 583
Cullen, Michael, **II** 644
Culligan, Emmett J., **I** 373
Culligan International, **I** 373; **II** 468
Culligan, John W., **I** 623–24; **10** 70
Cullinan, Joseph S., **IV** 551
Cullinan, Thomas, **IV** 65; **7** 122
Cullinet Software Inc., **6** 225
Cullman, John, **I** 270
Cullum Companies, **II** 670
Culver, Bernard, **III** 241
Culver, David, **IV** 11–12
Cumberland Newspapers, **IV** 650; **7** 389
Cumberland Paper Board Mills Ltd., **IV**
   248
Cumberland Pipeline Co., **IV** 372
Cumberland Property Investment Trust
   Ltd., **IV** 711
Cumming, Ian M., **11** 260–62
Cummings, Bart, **I** 24, 38
Cummings, Homer, **IV** 15
Cummings, Hugh, **7** 105
Cummings, John J., Jr., **9** 229
Cummings, Nathan, **II** 571
Cummings, Walter J., **II** 261
Cummins, **IV** 252
Cummins, Clessie L., **I** 146

Cummins Engine Corp., I 146–48, 186;
III 545; **10** 273–74
CUNA Mutual Insurance Group, **11** 495
Cunard Steamship Co., **I** 573
Cuneo, Joseph, **I** 536
Cunliffe-Owen, Hugo (Sir), **I** 425–26
Cunningham, Calder, **II** 83
Cunningham, Harry Blair, **V** 111
Cunningham, James E., **III** 559–60
Cunningham, John F., **III** 170; **6** 286
Cunningham, Mary, **I** 68, 142; **7** 356
Cupples Products Co., **IV** 15
Curcio, John, **I** 178–79
Curie, Marie, **I** 395
Curler, Howard, **8** 54–55
Curlett, John, **7** 315
Curley, James, **7** 14
Curley, John, **IV** 612–13; **7** 190–91
Curme, George O. (Dr.), **I** 399; **9** 16
Current, Inc., **7** 137, 139
Currie, Bill, **10** 539
Currie, George, **IV** 308
Currie, John H., **II** 470
Currie, Malcolm, **II** 34
Currie, William Crawford, **V** 491
Curry, W. Roger, **6** 390
Currys Group PLC, **V** 49
Cursenir, **I** 280
Curtice, Edgar, **7** 104
Curtice, Simeon, **7** 104
Curtice-Burns Foods, Inc., 7 17–18,
104–06
Curtin, John, **IV** 45
Curtis, Charles, **III** 312
Curtis Circulation Co., **IV** 619
Curtis, Elwood, **III** 462–63
Curtis, James, **9** 462
Curtis, Tony, **II** 143
Curtiss Aeroplane & Motor Company, **11**
427
Curtiss Candy Co., **II** 544
Curtiss, Cyrus H.K., **I** 19
Curtiss, Glenn H., **10** 260
Curtiss-Wright Corporation, I 524; III
464; **7** 263; **8** 49; **9** 14, 244, 341, 417;
10 260–63
Curver Group, III 614
Curver-Rubbermaid, III 615
Curzon, George (Lord), **IV** 219, 386
Cushman, Harry D., **8** 176–77
Cushman Motor Works, III 598
Cusin, Vidal Benjamin, III 206
Custom Electronics, Inc., **9** 120
Custom Expressions, Inc., **7** 24
Custom Metal Products, Inc., III 643
Custom Organics, **8** 464
Custom Products Inc., III 643
Cuthbert, Lawrence "Ben" Ferguson, **9**
373–74
Cuthbert, Tom, **II** 601; **7** 19
Cuthbert, William R., **9** 374–75
Cutler, Joseph A., III 535
Cutler-Hammer Inc., **I** 155; III 644–45
Cutter Laboratories, **I** 310
Cutting, Allen B., **10** 243
Cutting, Francis, **7** 130
Cutting, Ralph H., **9** 305
CVL Inc., **II** 457
CVN Companies, **9** 218
CVS. *See* Consumer Value Stores.
CWM. *See* Chemical Waste Management,
Inc.
CWM Remedial Services, Inc., **9** 110
Cybernet Electronics Corp., **II** 51

Cybernex, **10** 463
CYBERTEK Corporation, **11** 395
CyberTel, **IV** 596–97
Cycle Video Inc., **7** 590
Cyclo Chemical Corp., **I** 627
Cyclo Getriebebau Lorenz Braren GmbH,
III 634
Cyclone Co. of Australia, III 673
Cyclops Corporation, **10** 45
Cyclops Industries Inc., **10** 45
Cymbal Co., Ltd., **V** 150
Cynosure Inc., **11** 88
Cyphernetics Corp., III 118
Cypress Insurance Co., III 214
Cypress Semiconductor, **6** 216
Cyprus Minerals Company, 7 107–09
Cyrix Corp., **10** 367
Cyrus J. Lawrence Inc., **II** 429
Czapor, Edward, **II** 35
Czapski, Siegfried, III 446

D & P Studios, **II** 157
D & W Food Stores, Inc., **8** 482
D'Alessandro, Angelo, **10** 38
D'Anonima Grandine, **III** 208
D'Arcy Advertising Agency, **I** 233–34; **10**
226–27
D'Arcy MacManus Masius. *See* D'Arcy
Masius Benton & Bowles.
D'Arcy Masius Benton & Bowles, Inc., 6
20–22
D'Arcy, William C., **6** 20
D'Arcy, William Knox, **IV** 378, 381; **7** 56,
59
D'Arcy-McManus. *See* D'Arcy Masius
Benton & Bowles.
D'Arcy-McManus & Masius. *See* D'Arcy
Masius Benton & Bowles.
D'Arcy-McManus International. *See*
D'Arcy Masius Benton & Bowles.
D&N Systems, Inc., **10** 505
D.B. Marron & Co., **II** 445
D.C. Heath & Co., **II** 86; **11** 413
D.C. National Bancorp, **10** 426
D. Connelly Boiler Company, **6** 145
D.E. Makepeace Co., **IV** 78
D.E. Winebrenner Co., **7** 429
D. Hald & Co., III 417
D.M. Osborne Co., III 650
Dabah, Ezra, **8** 219–20
Dabah, Haim, **8** 219–20
Dabah, Isaac, **8** 219–20
Dabah, Morris, **8** 219–20
Dabney, Charles H., **II** 329
Dabney, Morgan & Co., **II** 329
Dacre (Lord). *See* Trevor-Roper, Hugh.
Dade, George C., **I** 77
Dade Wholesale Products, **6** 199
DADG. *See* Deutsch-Australische
Dampfschiffs-Gesellschaft.
Dae Won Kang Up Co., III 581
Daejin Shipping Company, **6** 98
Daesung Heavy Industries, **I** 516
Daewoo Corp., III 457–58
Daewoo Electronics, III 457
Daewoo Group, I 516; **II** 53; III **457–59**,
749
Daewoo Heavy Industries, III 457–59
Daewoo Investment and Finance, III 459
Daewoo Motor, III 457
Daewoo Securities, III 459
Daewoo Shipbuilding and Heavy
Machinery, III 457–59
DAF, **I** 186; III 543; **7** 566–67

Dage-Bell, **II** 86
Daggett, Samuel S., III 321
Dagincourt, III 675
Dagsbladunie, **IV** 611
Daher, Charles, III 703
Dahl, Harry, **I** 254
Dahl, Robert, **6** 354
Dahlgren, **I** 677
Dai Nippon Brewery Co., **I** 220, 282
Dai Nippon Ink and Chemicals, **I** 303
Dai Nippon Mujin, **II** 371
Dai Nippon Printing Co. (Singapore) Ltd.,
IV 600
Dai Nippon Printing Co., Ltd., IV
598–600, 631, 679–80
Dai Nippon X-ray Inc., **II** 75
Dai Nippon Yuben Kai, **IV** 631–32
Dai Nippon Yuben Kai Kodansha, **IV**
631–32
Dai-Ichi. *See also* Daiichi.
Dai-Ichi Bank, **I** 507, 511; **IV** 148
Dai-Ichi Kangyo Bank Ltd., II 273–75,
325–26, 360–61, 374; III 188
Dai-Ichi Kangyo Bank of California, **II**
274
Dai-Ichi Kangyo Trust Co., **II** 274
Dai-Ichi Kokuritsu Ginko, **II** 273
Dai-Ichi Mokko Co., III 758
Dai-Ichi Mutual Life Insurance Co., **II**
118; III 277, 401
Dai-Nippon. *See also* Dainippon.
Daido Electric Power Co., Ltd., **IV** 62
Daido Electric Steel Co., Ltd., **IV** 62
Daido Spring Co., III 580
Daido Steel Co., Ltd., IV 62–63
Daido Trading, **I** 432, 492
Daiei, V 11, **39–40**
Daihatsu Motor Company, Ltd., 7
110–12
Daiichi. *See also* Dai-Ichi.
Daiichi Atomic Power Industry Group, **II**
22
Daiichi Bussan Kaisha Ltd., **I** 505, 507
Daiichi Fire, III 405
Daijugo Bank, **I** 507
Daiken Co., **I** 432, 492
Daikin Air Conditioning (Thailand) Co.,
Ltd., III 461
Daikin Europe N.V., III 460
Daikin Industries, Ltd., III 460–61
Daikyo Oil Co., Ltd., **IV** 403–04, 476
Dailey & Associates, **I** 16
Dailey, Jim, **11** 516
Daily Chronicle Investment Group, **IV** 685
Daily, F.R., Jr., **7** 375
Daily Mirror, **IV** 665–66
Daily Press Inc., **IV** 684
Daimaru, V 41–2, 130
Daimler Airway, **I** 92
Daimler, Gottlieb, **I** 149; III 541
Daimler, Paul, **I** 149
Daimler-Benz A.G., I 138, **149–51**,
186–87, 192, 194, 198, 411, 549; **II**
257, 279–80, 283; III 495, 523, 562,
563, 695, 750; **7** 219; **10** 261, 274; **11**
31
Daimler-Motoren-Gesellschaft, **I** 149
Dain, Joseph, III 462
Daina Seikosha, III 620
Daini-Denden Kikaku Co. Ltd., **II** 51
Dainippon. *See also* Dai-Nippon.
Dainippon Celluloid, **I** 509; III 486
Dainippon Ink & Chemicals, Inc., **IV** 397;
10 466–67

Dainippon Shurui, **III** 42
Dainippon Spinning Company, **V** 387
Daio Paper Corporation, IV 266–67,
269. *See also* Taio Paper Manufacturing
Co.
Dairy Farm, **I** 471
Dairy Farm Ice and Cold Storage Co., **IV**
700
Dairy Maid Products Cooperative, **II** 536
Dairy Mart Convenience Stores, Inc., 7
113–15
Dairy Mart de Mexico, **7** 115
Dairy Queen National Development
Company, **10** 372
Dairy Supply Co., **II** 586; **III** 418, 420
Dairyland Food Laboratories, **I** 677
Dairymen, Inc., **11** 24
Daishowa Paper Manufacturing Co., Ltd. **II**
361; **IV 268–70,** 326, 667
Daishowa Paper Trading Co., Ltd., **IV** 268
Daishowa Pulp Manufacturing Co., Ltd.,
IV 268
Daishowa Uniboard Co., Ltd., **IV** 268
Daishowa-Marubeni International Ltd.,
IV 268
Daisy/Cadnetix Inc., **6** 248
Daisy Systems Corp., **11** 46, 284–85, 489
Daiwa (Switzerland) Ltd., **II** 406
Daiwa Bank, Ltd., II 276–77, 347, 438
Daiwa Europe N.V., **II** 406
Daiwa International Capital Management
Co., Ltd., **II** 406
Daiwa Investment Trust and Management
Co., Ltd., **II** 405
Daiwa Securities (Hong Kong) Ltd., **II** 406
Daiwa Securities America Inc., **II** 406
Daiwa Securities Company, Limited, II
276, 300, **405–06,** 434; **9** 377
Daiwa Singapore Ltd., **II** 406
Dakota Power Company, **6** 580
Dakotah Mills, **8** 558–59
Dalberg Co., **II** 61
Dale, Henry, **I** 714
Dalgety and Co. Ltd., **II** 499
Dalgety, Frederick, **II** 499
Dalgety Inc., **II** 500
Dalgety, PLC, II 499–500; III 21
Dalian Cement Factory, **III** 718
Dalian Huaneng-Onoda Cement Co., **III**
718
Dallas Airmotive, **II** 16
Dallas Lumber and Supply Co., **IV** 358
Dallas Power & Light Company, **V** 724
Dallas Southland Ice Co., **II** 660
Dallas-Fort Worth Suburban Newspapers,
Inc., **10** 3
Dalle, François, **III** 46–47; **8** 341–43
Dalloz, Désiré, **IV** 615
Dalsey, Adrian, **6** 385
Dalton, George, **11** 130–32
Daly, Edward J., **10** 560
Dalzell, Robert (Col.), **III** 369
Damar, **IV** 610
Damm, Alexander, **I** 97
Dammann Asphalt, **III** 673
Dammeyer, Rod, **9** 297
Damodar Valley Corp., **IV** 49
Damon Corporation, **11** 334
Damon, Ralph, **I** 89, 126
Dan, Takuma, **I** 503–07; **II** 325, 328; **III**
295; **IV** 147
Dana, Charles A., **I** 152; **10** 264
Dana Corporation, I 152–53; 10 264–66
(upd.)

Danaher Controls, **7** 117
Danaher Corporation, 7 116–17
Danair A/S, **I** 120
Danapak Holding Ltd., **11** 422
Danat-Bank, **I** 138
Dancer Fitzgerald Sample, **I** 33
Dandison, B.G., **IV** 636
Dane, Max, **I** 30
Danforth, Donald, **II** 561–62
Danforth, Douglas, **II** 122
Danforth, William Henry, **II** 561–63
Dangerfield, Rodney, **I** 270
Daniel International Corp., **I** 570–71; **8**
192
Daniel P. Creed Co., Inc., **8** 386
Daniel, R. Ronald, **9** 343
Daniell, Robert, **10** 538
Daniell, Robert F., **I** 86; **7** 72; **9** 417
Daniels, Draper, **I** 24, 38
Daniels, Edwin F., **IV** 169
Daniels, Fred H., **8** 395
Daniels, John, **I** 420; **11** 22
Daniels, John W., **I** 419; **11** 21
Daniels Linseed Co., **I** 419
Daniels, Thomas L., **I** 420; **11** 22
de Daninos, Alessadro, **III** 346
Danish Almindelinge Brand-Assurance-
Compagni, **III** 299
Danks, Harvey, **III** 285
Danley Machine Corp., **I** 514
Danner, Ray, **7** 474–75
Dannon Co., **II** 468, 474–75
Dansk Bioprotein, **IV** 406–07
Dansk International Designs Ltd., **10** 179,
181
Dansk Metal, **III** 569
Dansk Rejsebureau, **I** 120
Danzansky, Joseph B., **II** 634
Danzas, Emile Jules, **V** 441
Danzas Group, V 441–43
Danzas, Louis, **V** 441
DAP, Inc., **III** 66
Dapples, Louis, **II** 546–47; **7** 381–82
Darigold, Inc., 9 159–61
Darling and Hodgson, **IV** 91
Darling, Jay, **II** 614
Darmstadter, **II** 282
Darnell, Donald, **I** 570
Darracq, **7** 6
Dart & Kraft, **II** 534; **III** 610–11; **7** 276
Dart Group Corp., **II** 645, 656, 667, 674
Dart Industries, **II** 533–34; **III** 610; **9**
179–80
Dart, Justin, **II** 533–34; **V** 218; **7** 275–76
Dart Truck Co., **I** 185
Darval, Roger, **II** 189
Das Gupta, Mr., **I** 395
DASA. *See* Deutsche Aerospace Airbus.
Dassault, Marcel, **I** 44–45
Dassault, Serge, **I** 46
Dassault-Breguet. *See* Avions Marcel
Dassault-Breguet Aviation.
Dastek Inc., **10** 464; **11** 234–35
DAT GmbH, **10** 514
Dat Jidosha Seizo Co., **I** 183
Data Base Management Inc., **11** 19
Data Business Forms, **IV** 640
Data Card Corp., **IV** 680
Data Card Japan, **IV** 680
Data Corp., **IV** 311
Data Documents, **III** 157
Data Force Inc., **11** 65

Data General Corporation, II 208; **III**
124, 133; **6** 221, 234; **8 137–40; 9** 297;
10 499
Data One Corporation, **11** 111
Data Preparation, Inc., **11** 112
Data Resources, Inc., **IV** 637
Data Structures Inc., **11** 65
Data Systems Technology, **11** 57
Data 3 Systems, **9** 36
Datachecker Systems, **II** 64–65; **III** 164;
11 150
Datacraft Corp., **II** 38
Datamatic Corp., **II** 41, 86
Datapoint Corporation, 11 67–70
Datapro Research Corp., **IV** 637
Dataquest Inc., **10** 558
Datas Incorporated, **I** 99; **6** 81
Datastream, **IV** 605
Datastream International, **10** 89
Datavision Inc., **11** 444
Date, Munenari, **III** 383
Datext, **IV** 596–97
Datran, **11** 468
Datsun. *See* Nissan Motor Company, Ltd.
Datteln, **IV** 141
Daubrée, Edouard, **V** 236
Daugherty, J. Arthur, **III** 325
Daum, Gary, **11** 156
Dauphin Distribution Services. *See* Exel
Logistics Ltd.
Dauzier, Paul, **10** 347
Davant, James W., **II** 444–45
Davenport & Walter, **III** 765
Davenport, O.L., **III** 765
Davey, Jim, **11** 71
Davey, John, **11** 71–72
Davey, Martin, Jr., **11** 72
Davey, Martin, Sr., **11** 71–72
Davey, Paul, **11** 72
The Davey Tree Expert Company, 11
71–73
Davey, Wellington, **11** 71
David Brown, Ltd., **10** 380
David Crystal, Inc., **II** 502; **9** 156; **10** 323
David, George, **10** 538
David, Nelson, **6** 66
David Sandeman Group, **I** 592
David Sassoon & Co., **II** 296
David Williams and Partners, **6** 40
David-West, Tam, **IV** 473
Davidson, Alfred, **II** 389
Davidson, Andrew, **III** 360
Davidson, Arthur, **7** 211
Davidson Automatic Merchandising Co.
Inc., **II** 607
Davidson, Charles, **II** 389
Davidson, Davre, **II** 607
Davidson, Henrik, **II** 351
Davidson, Nigel, **7** 245
Davidson, Richard K., **V** 531
Davidson, Walter, **7** 211
Davidson, William G., **7** 211–12
Davies, David J., **I** 471; **IV** 120
Davies, F.A., **IV** 536
Davies, Joseph, **IV** 672
Davies, Marion, **IV** 626
Davies, Paul L., **I** 442–43; **11** 133–34
Davies, R.E.G., **I** 114
Davies, Ralph K., **6** 353
Davies, Robert, **I** 371; **9** 358, 501
Davies, William Ltd., **II** 482
Davila, William S., **7** 570
Davis & Henderson Ltd., **IV** 640
Davis, A.C., **III** 670

Davis, A. Dano, **II** 684
Davis and Geck, **I** 301
Davis, Arthur Vining, **IV** 10, 14
Davis, Bette, **II** 143, 175–76
Davis, Bob, **8** 518
Davis, Charles S., **III** 438–39
Davis Coal & Coke Co., **IV** 180
Davis, Culver M., **II** 669
Davis, D.W., **II** 654
Davis, David R., **I** 70; **11** 277
Davis, Delmont A., **10** 130
Davis, Donald D., **II** 501; **10** 322
Davis, Donald W., **III** 628–29
Davis, E. Asbury, **III** 396
Davis, Edmund (Sir), **IV** 21
Davis, Edward K., **IV** 10–11, 14
Davis, Edwin Weyerhaeuser, **8** 429
Davis, Erroll, **6** 606
Davis Estates, **I** 592
Davis, Frank S., **11** 120
Davis, George Ade, **6** 539
Davis, J.E., **II** 683–84
Davis, J. Luther, **6** 588–89
Davis, Jacob, **II** 644
Davis, Jefferson, **10** 268
Davis, Jim, **11** 95
Davis, John, **II** 158–59; **IV** 381
Davis Manufacturing Company, **10** 380
Davis, Martin S., **I** 451, 453; **II** 156
Davis, Marvin, **II** 170–71
Davis, Nathanael V., **IV** 11–12
Davis, Norman, **III** 738
Davis, Peter, **IV** 667
Davis, Richard, **11** 466
Davis, Robert D., **II** 684
Davis Wholesale Company, **9** 20
Davis, William, **IV** 686
Davis, William M., **II** 683
Davis-Standard Company, **9** 154
Davison Chemical Corp., **IV** 190
Davison, Ian Hay, **III** 280
Davison, Robert Park, **9** 506–07
Davison, Stanley, **II** 211
Davy Bamag GmbH, **IV** 142
Davy McKee AG, **IV** 142
Dawnay Day, **III** 501
Dawson Mills, **II** 536
Day & Zimmerman, **6** 579
Day & Zimmermann Inc., 9 162–64
Day Brite Lighting, **II** 19
Day, Cecil B., **11** 178
Day, Charles, **9** 162
Day, Doris, **II** 175
Day, Guy, **11** 49–50
Day International, **8** 347
Day, William, **III** 247–48
Day-Glo Color Corp., **8** 456
Day-Lee Meats, **II** 550
Day-N-Nite, **II** 620
Dayco Products, **7** 297
Days Corp., **III** 344
Days Inn of America, **III** 344
Days Inn of America, Inc., **11** 178
Daystar International Inc., **11** 44
Daystrom, **III** 617
Daytex, Inc., **II** 669
Dayton Citizens' Electric Co. *See* Dayton Power & Light Company.
Dayton Engineering Laboratories, **I** 171; **9** 416; **10** 325
Dayton Flexible Products Co., **I** 627
Dayton, George Draper, **V** 43–44

Dayton Hudson Corporation, V 43–44; 8 35; **9** 360; **10** 136, 391–93, 409–10, 515–16
Dayton Lighting Co. *See* Dayton Power & Light Company.
Dayton Power & Light Company, **6** 467, 480–82
Dayton Walther Corp., **III** 650, 652
Daytron Mortgage Systems, **11** 485
DB. *See* Deutsche Bundesbahn.
DCA Food Industries, **II** 554
DCL BioMedical, Inc., **11** 333
DCMS Holdings Inc., **7** 114
DDI Corporation, 7 118–20
De Angelis, Anthony "Tino", **II** 398; **10** 62
De Beers Botswana Mining Company Limited, **IV** 66; **7** 124
De Beers Consolidated Mines Limited / De Beers Centenary AG, I 107; **IV** 20–21, 23, 60, **64–68**, 79, 94; **7 121–26 (upd.)**
De Beers Industrial Diamond Division, **IV** 66
De Benedetti, Carlo, **II** 295; **III** 144–45; **IV** 587–88, 615; **11** 205
De Benedetti, Franco, **III** 144–45
De Campi, John Webb, **I** 196
de Castro, Esdon, **8** 137–39
De Chalmont, Guillaume, **I** 399
De Grenswisselkantoren NV, **III** 201
De Groote Bossche, **III** 200
De Havilland, **7** 11
De La Rue PLC, 10 267–69
De Laurentiis Entertainment Group, **III** 84
De Laval Chadburn Co., **III** 419, 420
De Laval Cream Separator Co., **III** 418–19
De Laval Dairy Supply Co., **III** 419
De Laval Separator Company, **7** 235–36
De Laval Steam Turbine Company, **III** 419; **7** 235
De Laval Turbine Company, **7** 236–37
De Leuw, Cather & Company, **8** 416
De Lorean, John Z., **I** 173
De Nederlandse Bank, **IV** 132
De Payenneville, Gaston, **III** 210
De Pree, D.J., **8** 255–56
De Pree, Hugh, **8** 256
De Pree, Max, **8** 256
De Ster 1905 NV, **III** 200
De Tomaso Industries, **11** 104
De Trey Gesellchaft, **10** 271
De Villiers, Wim (Dr.), **IV** 90, 92
De Vos, Richard M., **III** 11–14
De Walt, **III** 436
De-sta-Co., **III** 468
Dealer Equipment and Services, **10** 492
Dealey, George Bannerman, **10** 3
DeAllesandro, Joseph P., **III** 197
Deamer, Adrian, **IV** 651; **7** 390
Dean & Barry Co., **8** 455
Dean, Clarence R., **V** 652
Dean Foods Company, 7 127–29
Dean, Howard M., **7** 127–28
Dean, R. Hal, **II** 562
Dean, Sam, Sr., **7** 127
Dean Witter & Co., **II** 445; **IV** 186
Dean Witter Financial Services Group Inc., **V** 180, 182
Dean Witter Reynolds, **7** 213
Dean-Dempsy Corp., **IV** 334
Dear, Albert, **IV** 582
Dear, Walter, **IV** 582
Dearden, William E., **II** 511

Deary, William, **8** 428
Deasy, Henry (Maj.), **III** 508
Deasy, W.J., **7** 356
DeBartolo, Edward J., **8** 159–61
DeBartolo, Edward J., Jr., **8** 161
Debenhams, **V** 20–22
Debron Investments Plc., **8** 271
DEC. *See* Digital Equipment Corp.
Decca Ltd., **II** 81, 83
Decca Records, **II** 144
Decherd, Robert, **10** 4
Decision Base Resources, **6** 14
Decker, Alonzo G., **III** 435–36
Decker, Alonzo G., Jr., **III** 436
Decker, William C., **III** 683
Decoflex Ltd., **IV** 645
Dedeurwaerder, Jose, **I** 136, 190
Dee Corp., **I** 549; **II** 628–29, 642
Dee, Robert F., **I** 692
Deeds, Edward, **III** 151; **6** 265; **9** 416
Deeks McBride, **III** 704
Deely, J. T., **6** 474
Deep Oil Technology, **I** 570
Deep Rock Oil Co., **IV** 446
Deep Rock Oil Corp., **IV** 446
Deep Rock Water Co., **III** 21
Deepsea Ventures, Inc., **IV** 152
Deepwater Light and Power Company, **6** 449
Deer Park Spring Water Co., **III** 21
Deere & Company, I 181, 527; **III** **462–64**, 651; **10** 377–78, 380, 429; **11** 472
Deere & Mansur Works, **III** 462
Deere, Charles, **III** 462
Deere, John, **III** 462; **10** 377
Deere-Hitachi Construction Machinery, **III** 464
Deering Co., **II** 330
Deering, Ernest, **IV** 118
Deering Harvester Co., **IV** 660
Deering Milliken, **8** 13
Deering-Milliken, **V** 366–67
Defense Plant Corp., **IV** 10, 408
Defforey, Denis, **10** 204–05
Defforey, Jacques, **10** 205
Defforey, Louis, **10** 204–05
DeForest, Lee, **III** 534
Deft Software, Inc., **10** 505
DEG. *See* Deutsche Edison Gesellschaft.
Degener, Carl, **II** 163
Degener, Herbert, **II** 164
Degolia, E.B., **9** 548
DeGolyer, Everette, **IV** 365
DeGroat, C.H., **10** 328
Degussa AG. *See* Degussa Group.
Degussa Carbon Black Corp., **IV** 71
Degussa Corp., **IV** 71
Degussa Group, I 303; **IV 69–72**, 118
Degussa s.a., **IV** 71
Deihl, Richard H., **II** 182; **10** 343
Deikel, Ted, **9** 218–19, 360
Deinhard, **I** 281
Dejouany, Guy, **V** 633–34
DeKalb AgResearch Inc., **9** 411
Dekker, Nicholas, **III** 241–42
Dekker, Wisse, **II** 80
Del Monte Corporation, II 595; **7 130–32**
del Valle Inclan, Miguel Angel, **V** 415
Del-Rey Petroleum, **I** 526
Delagrange, **I** 635
Delahye Ripault, **II** 356
Delaney, Don, **6** 79

Delaware Charter Guarantee & Trust Co., **III** 330
Delaware Lackawanna & Western, **I** 584
Delaware Management Holdings, **III** 386
Delaware North Companies Incorporated, 7 133–36
Delbard, **I** 272
Delbrück, Adalbert, **I** 410
Delchamps, **II** 638
Delco, **6** 265
Delco Electronics, **II** 32–35; **III** 151
Deledda, Grazia, **IV** 585
Delestrade, René, **III** 393
Delfont, Bernard, **I** 532
Delhaize Freres & Cie, "Le Lion," **II** 626
Delhi Gas Pipeline Corporation, **7** 551
Delhi International Oil Corp., **III** 687
Dell Computer Corp., 9 165–66; **10** 309, 459; **11** 62
Dell, Michael, **9** 165
della Vida, Samuel, **III** 206
Dellwood Elevator Co., **I** 419
Delmar Chemicals Ltd., **II** 484
Delmar Paper Box Co., **IV** 333
Delmarva Properties, Inc., **8** 103
Delmonico Foods Inc., **II** 511
Delmonico International, **II** 101
Deloitte & Touche, 9 167–69, 423
Deloitte, Haskins, & Sells. *See* Deloitte & Touche.
Deloitte Touche Tohmatsu International, **9** 167–68
Deloitte, William Welch, **9** 167
DeLong Engineering Co., **III** 558
DeLong-McDermott, **III** 558
Deloraine, Maurice, **I** 464
DeLorean Motors Company, **10** 117
Delorme, Jean, **I** 358
Delorme, Paul, **I** 357
Delort, Jean-Jacques, **V** 10
Delphax, **IV** 252
Delprat, **IV** 58
Delprat, Guillaume, **IV** 44–45
Delta Air Corporation. *See* Delta Air Lines, Inc.
Delta Air Lines Inc., I 29, 91, 97, **99–100**, 102, 106, 120, 132; **6** 61, **81–83 (upd.)**, 117, 131–32, 383
Delta Air Service. *See* Delta Air Lines, Inc.
Delta Apparel, Inc., **8** 141–43
Delta Biologicals S.r.l., **11** 208
Delta Communications, **IV** 610
Delta Faucet Co., **III** 568–69
Delta Lloyd, **III** 235
Delta Manufacturing, **II** 85
Delta Mills Marketing Company, **8** 141, 143
Delta Motors, **III** 580
Delta Savings Assoc. of Texas, **IV** 343
Delta Steamship Lines, **9** 425–26
Delta Woodside Industries, Inc., 8 141–43
DeLuxe Check Printers, Inc., **7** 137
Deluxe Corporation, 7 137–39
DeLuxe Laboratories, **IV** 652
Delvag Luftürsicherungs A.G., **I** 111
DelZotto, Angelo, **9** 512
DelZotto, Elvio, **9** 512–13
DelZotto, Leo, **9** 512
Demag AG, **II** 22; **III** 566; **IV** 206
DeMille, Cecil B., **II** 154–55
Deminex, **IV** 413, 424
Deming Company, **8** 135
Deming, W. Edward, **8** 383

Deming, William Edwards, **III** 61, 545, 548; **IV** 162
Demka, **IV** 132–33
Demonque, Marcel, **III** 703–04
Dempsey & Siders Agency, **III** 190
Dempsey, Jerry E., **V** 753
Den Fujita, **9** 74
Den, Kenjiro, **I** 183
Den norske Creditbank, **II** 366
Den Norske Stats Oljeselskap AS, IV 405–07, 486
Den-Tal-Ez, **I** 702
Denain-Nord-Est-Longwy, **IV** 227
Denault Ltd., **II** 651
Denenberg, Herbert, **III** 326
Deneuve, Catherine, **10** 69
Denison Corp., **III** 628
Denison, Merrill, **I** 275
Denius, Homer, **II** 37–38
Denki Seikosho, **IV** 62
Denney-Reyburn, **8** 360
Dennison, Aaron, **IV** 251
Dennison and Co., **IV** 251
Dennison, Andrew, **IV** 251
Dennison Carter, **IV** 252
Dennison, Charles, **IV** 251
Dennison, Eliphalet Whorf (E.W.), **IV** 251–52
Dennison, Henry B., **IV** 251
Dennison, Henry Sturgis, **IV** 251–52
Dennison Manufacturing Co., **IV** 251–52, 254
Dennison National, **IV** 252
Denny, Arthur, **9** 539
Denny, Charles, **10** 18–20
Denny's, **II** 680; **III** 103
Denny's Japan, **V** 88–89
Denshi Media Services, **IV** 680
Dent & Co., **II** 296
Dent, Hawthorne K., **III** 352–53
Dental Houses/Dentsply, **10** 272
The Dentists' Supply Co. *See* Dentsply International Inc.
Dentsply International Inc., 10 270–72
Dentsu Inc., I 9–11, 36, 38; **9** 30
Dentsu, Ltd., **6** 29
Denver Chemical Company, **8** 84
Denver Consolidated Electric Company. *See* Public Service Company of Colorado.
Denver Gas & Electric Company, **IV** 391; **6** 558
Denver Gas & Electric Light Company. *See* Public Service Company of Colorado.
Denver Gas Company. *See* Public Service Company of Colorado.
Department Stores International, **I** 426
Depew, Chauncey M., **10** 72
Deposito and Administratie Bank, **II** 185
Depositors National Bank of Durham, **II** 336
Depuy Inc., **10** 156–57
Der Anker, **III** 177
Deramus, William N., **6** 400
Deramus, William N., III, **6** 400–01
Derby Commerical Bank, **II** 318
Derbyshire Stone and William Briggs, **III** 752
Dercksen, Gerrit Jan, **III** 308
Derr, Kenneth, **IV** 387
Deruluft, **6** 57
Derwent Publications, **8** 526
Des Moines Electric Light Company, **6** 504

Des Voeux, William (Sir), **IV** 699
DESA Industries, **8** 545
DesBarres, John P., **V** 740
Deseret National Bank, **11** 118
Desert Partners, **III** 763
Design Craft Ltd., **IV** 640
DeSimone, L.D., **8** 371
Desmarais Frères, **IV** 557, 559
DeSoto, Inc., **8** 553
Desoutter, **III** 427
Despret, Maurice, **II** 202
Destray, Ellen, **10** 383
Det Danske Luftartselskab, **I** 119
Det Norske Luftartselskab, **I** 119
Deterding, Henri, **IV** 379, 530–31
Detra, Ralph W., **III** 643
Detroit Aircraft Corp., **I** 64; **11** 266
Detroit Automobile Co., **I** 164
Detroit Chemical Coatings, **8** 553
Detroit City and Gas Company. *See* MCN Corporation.
Detroit City Gas Company. *See* MCN Corporation.
Detroit Copper Co., **IV** 176
Detroit Copper Mining Co., **IV** 177
Detroit Diesel Allison. *See* Detroit Diesel Corporation.
Detroit Diesel Corporation, V 494–95; **9** 18; **10 273–75**; **11** 471
Detroit Edison Company, I 164; **V** 592–95; **7** 377–78; **11** 136
Detroit Fire & Marine Insurance Co., **III** 191
Detroit Gaslight Company. *See* MCN Corporation.
Detroit Gear and Machine Co., **III** 439
Detroit Radiator Co., **III** 663
Detroit Red Wings, **7** 278–79
Detroit Steel Products Co. Inc., **IV** 136
Detroit Toledo & Ironton Railroad, **I** 165
Detroit Vapor Stove Co., **III** 439
Detroit-Graphite Company, **8** 553
Detrola, **II** 60
Deupree, Richard R., **III** 52; **8** 432
Deutsch Erdol A.G., **IV** 552
Deutsch, Felix, **I** 410
Deutsch Shea & Evans Inc., **I** 15
Deutsch-Australische Dampfschiffs-Gesellschaft, **6** 398
Deutsch-Luxembergische Bergwerks und Hütten AG, I 542; **IV** 105
Deutsch-Österreichische Mannesmannröhren-Werke Aktiengesellschaft, **III** 564–65
Deutsch-Skandinavische Bank, **II** 352
Deutsche Aerospace Airbus, **7** 9, 11
Deutsche Airbus, **I** 41–42
Deutsche Allgemeine Versicherungs-Aktiengesellschaft, **III** 412
Deutsche Anlagen Leasing GmbH, **II** 386
Deutsche Babcock & Wilcox Dampfkessel-Werke AG, **III** 465
Deutsche Babcock AG, II 386; **III 465–66**
Deutsche Babcock Energie-und Umwelttechnik, **III** 465
Deutsche Babcock Handel, **III** 465
Deutsche Babcock-Borsig, **III** 465
Deutsche Bank (Asia), **II** 280
Deutsche Bank A.G., I 151, 409, 549; **II** 98, 191, 239, 241–42, 256–58, **278–80**, 281–82, 295, 319, 385, 427, 429; **III** 154–55, 692, 695; **IV** 91, 141, 229, 232, 378, 557; **V** 241–42

Deutsche Bank Capital Corp., **II** 280
Deutsche BP Aktiengesellschaft, 7 140–43
Deutsche Bundespost Telekom, V 287–90
Deutsche Bundesbahn, V 444–47; 6 424–26
Deutsche Edelstahlwerke AG, **IV** 222
Deutsche Edison Gesellschaft, **I** 409–10
Deutsche Erdol Aktiengesellschaft, **7** 140
Deutsche Gold-und Silber-Scheideanstalt vormals Roessler, **IV** 69, 118, 139
Deutsche Hydrierwerke, **III** 32
Deutsche Industriewerke AG, **IV** 230
Deutsche Länderbank, **II** 379
Deutsche Lufthansa A.G., I 94, **110–11,** 120; **6** 95
Deutsche Marathon Petroleum, **IV** 487
Deutsche Mineralöl-Explorationsgesellschaft mbH, **IV** 197
Deutsche Nippon Seiko, **III** 589
Deutsche Petroleum-Verkaufsgesellschaft mbH, **7** 140
Deutsche Reichsbahn, **V** 444. *See also* Deutsche Bundesbahn.
Deutsche Schiff-und Maschinenbau Aktiengesellschaft "Deschimag," **IV** 87
Deutsche Shell, **7** 140
Deutsche Spezialglas AG, **III** 446
Deutsche Strassen und Lokalbahn A.G., **I** 410
Deutsche Texaco, **V** 709
Deutsche Union, **III** 693–94
Deutsche Union-Bank, **II** 278
Deutsche Wagnisfinanzierung, **II** 258
Deutsche Werke AG, **IV** 230
Deutsche-Asiatische Bank, **II** 238, 256
Deutsche-Nalco-Chemie GmbH., **I** 373
Deutscher Aero Lloyd, **I** 110
Deutscher Automobil Schutz Allgemeine Rechtsschutz-Versicherung AG, **III** 400
Deutsches Reisebüro DeR, **II** 163
Deutz AG, **III** 541
Deutz-Allis, **III** 544
Deutz-Fahr-Werk, **III** 544
Devcon Corp., **III** 519
Development Finance Corp., **II** 189
Devenow, Chester, **I** 202
Deveshwar, Yogesh, **6** 64
DeVilbiss Company, **8** 230
DeVilbiss Health Care, Inc., **11** 488
Deville, Henri Sainte-Claire, **IV** 173
Devitt, James, **III** 306
DeVries, J., **IV** 708
DeVry Technical Institute, Inc., **9** 63
Dewar, Joe, **III** 739
Dewars Brothers, **I** 239–40
Dewey & Almy Chemical Co., **I** 548
Dewey, Thomas, **I** 29; **III** 335
DeWitt, J. Doyle, **III** 388–89
DeWolf, Nicholas, **11** 502–03
Dexter, Charles Haskell, **I** 320
Dexter Corp., I 320–22
Dexter, Seth, **I** 320
Dexter, Seth, II, **I** 320
Dexter, Thomas, **I** 320
DFS Dorland Worldwide, **I** 35
DFW Printing Company, **10** 3
DG&E. *See* Denver Gas & Electric Company.
DH Compounding, **8** 347
DHI Corp., **II** 680
DHL. *See* DHL Worldwide Express.
DHL Airways, **6** 385–86
DHL Budapest Ltd., **6** 386

DHL Corp., **6** 385–86
DHL International Ltd., **6** 385–86
DHL Sinotrans, **6** 386
DHL Worldwide Express, 6 385–87
Di-Rite Company, **11** 534
Dia Prosim, S.A., **IV** 409
Diagnostics Pasteur, **I** 677
The Dial Corp., 8 144–46
Dial, Morse G., **9** 517
Dialog Information Services, Inc., **IV** 630
Diamandis Communications Inc., **IV** 619, 678
Diamang, **IV** 65, 67
Diamedix, **11** 207
Diamond Alkali Co., **IV** 408–09; **7** 308
Diamond Black Leaf Co., **IV** 409
Diamond Communications, **10** 288
Diamond Corporation Ltd., **IV** 21, 66; **7** 123
Diamond Corporation Sierra Leone Ltd., **IV** 66–67; **7** 123
Diamond Corporation West Africa Ltd., **IV** 66
Diamond Development Company Ltd., **IV** 66; **7** 123
Diamond, Frank, **10** 473
Diamond International, **IV** 290, 295
Diamond Oil Co., **IV** 548
Diamond, Richard, **IV** 583
Diamond Savings & Loan, **II** 420
Diamond Shamrock Chemical Co., **IV** 409, 481
Diamond Shamrock Coal, **7** 34
Diamond Shamrock Corp., **IV** 409–11; **7** 308–09
Diamond Shamrock, Inc., IV 408–11; 7 309, 345
Diamond Shamrock Natural Gas Marketing Co., **IV** 411
Diamond Shamrock Offshore Partners Ltd., **IV** 410
Diamond Shamrock Oil and Gas Co., **IV** 409
Diamond Shamrock R&M, Inc., **IV** 410
Diamond/Sunsweet, **7** 496–97
Diamond Trading Company, **IV** 66–67; **7** 123
Diamond Walnut Growers, **7** 496–97
Diamond-Star Motors Corporation, **9** 349–51
Díaz, Porfirio, **IV** 657–58
Diaz-Verson, Sal, **III** 188; **10** 29
Dickens, Charles, **IV** 617; **10** 355
Dickenstein, Avraham, **II** 205
Dickerman, **8** 366
Dickerman, Robert S., **8** 365–66
Dickey, Charles, **IV** 330
Dickey, Umberto M., **9** 159–60
Dickhoner, William H., **6** 467
Dickins, George, **7** 215
Dickinson, Arthur Lowes, **9** 422
Dickinson, Fairleigh, Jr., **11** 34–35
Dickinson, Fairleigh S., **I** 630; **11** 34
Dickinson, Fairleigh S., Jr., **I** 630–31
Dickinson, R.S., **II** 493
Dickson, Leonard, **III** 360
Dickson, Robert L., **I** 476
Dictaphone Corp., **III** 157
Didier Werke AG, **IV** 232
Diebold, Albert H., **I** 698–99
Diebold Bahmann & Co. *See* Diebold, Inc.
Diebold, Charles, **7** 144
Diebold, Inc., 7 144–46
Diebold Safe & Lock Co. *See* Diebold, Inc.

Diehl Manufacturing Co., **II** 9
Diemakers Inc., **IV** 443
Diemand, John A., **III** 224–25
Diener, Royce, **III** 73–74
Diesel, Rudolf, **I** 146; **III** 426, 561, 630; **IV** 86
Diesel United Co., **III** 533
AB Diesels Motorer, **III** 425–26
Diet Center, **10** 383
Dieterich, Charles F., **I** 399
Dieterich Standard Corp., **III** 468
Dietler, Cortlandt S., **11** 27
Dietrich Corp., **II** 512
Dietrich, Marlene, **II** 155
Dietrich, Noah, **I** 126; **II** 32
Dietrich's Bakeries, **II** 631
Dietz, Lawrence, **I** 279
DiFranza Williamson, **6** 40
Digi International Inc., 9 170–72
DiGiorgio Corp., **II** 602
Digital Audio Disk Corp., **II** 103
Digital Data Systems Company, **11** 408
Digital Devices, Inc., **III** 643
Digital Equipment Corporation, II 8, 62, 108; **III** 118, 128, **132–35,** 142, 149, 166; **6** 225, **233–36 (upd.),** 237–38, 242, 246–47, 279, 287; **8** 137–39, 519; **9** 35, 43, 57, 166, 170–71, 514; **10** 22–23, 34, 86, 242, 361, 463, 477; **11** 46, 86–88, 274, 491, 518–19
Diligent Engine Co., **III** 342
Dill & Collins, **IV** 311
Dill, C.W., **8** 99
Dill, Orville, **8** 99
Dillard Department Stores, V 45–47; 10 488; **11** 349
Dillard, Edwin Rucker, **11** 75
Dillard, John H., **11** 75
Dillard Paper Company, 11 74–76
Dillard, Stark S., **11** 74–75
Dillard, William, **V** 45–47
Dillard, William, II, **V** 46
Diller, Barry, **II** 155–56, 171; **9** 428–29
Dillingham, Benjamin Franklin, **I** 565
Dillingham Corp., I 565–66
Dillingham Holdings Inc., **9** 511
Dillingham, Lowell, **I** 566
Dillingham, Walter F., **I** 565–66
Dillon Cos., **II** 645
Dillon, George, **III** 709; **7** 294
Dillon, H. G., **V** 712
Dillon Paper, **V** 288
Dillon, Read and Co., Inc., **I** 144, 559; **III** 151, 389; **6** 265; **11** 53
Dillon, Tom, **I** 29
DiMatteo, Dominick, Jr., **9** 451–52
DiMatteo, Dominick, Sr., **9** 451
Dime Banking and Loan Association of Rochester, **10** 91
Dime Savings Bank of New York, F.S.B., 9 173–74
Dimeling, Schrieber & Park, **11** 63
Dimond, James T., **8** 9–10
Dimond, Mike, **11** 153
Dineen, Robert, **III** 323
Diners Club, **II** 397; **9** 335; **10** 61
Diners Club of America, **6** 62
Dingman, Michael, **6** 599–600
Dingman, Michael D., **III** 511–12
Dinner Bell Foods, Inc., **11** 93
de Dion, **III** 523
Dionne, Joseph L., **IV** 637
Dirección General de Correos y Telecomunicaciones, **V** 337

Dirección Nacional de los Yacimientos Petrolíferos Fiscales, **IV** 577–78
Direct Mail Services Pty. Ltd., **10** 461
Direct Spanish Telegraph Co., **I** 428
Direction Générale de la Poste, **V** 471
Direction Générale des Télécommunications, **V** 471
Directorate General of Telecommunications, 7 147–49
Dirr's Gold Seal Meats, **6** 199
Disco SA, **V** 11
Discol SA, **V** 11
Disconto-Gesellschaft, **II** 238, 279
Discount Bank, **II** 205
Discover, **9** 335
DiscoVision Associates, **III** 605
Disney Channel, **6** 174–75
Disney Co. *See* Walt Disney Company.
Disney, Elias, **II** 172
Disney, Roy, **II** 172–73; **11** 556
Disney Studios, **II** 408; **6** 174, 176
Disney, Walt, **II** 147, 172–73; **11** 95
Disney-MGM Studios, **6** 176
Disneyland, **6** 175
Dispatch Communications, **10** 432
Display Components Inc., **II** 110
Displayco Midwest Inc., **8** 103
Disposable Hospital Products, **I** 627
Distillers and Cattle Feeders Trust, **I** 376
Distillers Co. Biochemical, **I** 240
Distillers Co. Ltd., **I** 239–41; **IV** 70
Distillers Co. plc, I 239–41, 252, 284–85; **II** 429, 609–10
Distillers Corp., **I** 284
Distillers Corp.-Seagrams Ltd., **I** 240, 263, 284
Distillers Securities, **I** 376
Distinctive Printing and Packaging Co., **8** 103
Distinctive Software Inc., **10** 285
Distribution Centers Incorporated. *See* Exel Logistics Ltd.
Distribution Services, Inc., **10** 287
District Bank, **II** 333
District Cablevision, **II** 160
District News Co., **II** 607
Distrigas, **IV** 425
DITAS, **IV** 563
Ditmore, Robert, **9** 524
Ditzler Color Co., **III** 732
DIVAL, **III** 347
Dively, George, **II** 37–38
Diversey Corp., **I** 275, 333
Diversified Agency Services, **I** 32
Diversified Retailing Co., **III** 214
Diversified Services, **9** 95
Diversifoods Inc., **II** 556
Dix, Bill, **6** 112
Dixie Hi-Fi, **9** 120–21
Dixie Home Stores, **II** 683
Dixie Paper, **I** 612–14
Dixie Power & Light Company, **6** 514
Dixie Yarns, Inc., **9** 466
Dixie-Narco, Inc., **III** 573
Dixieland Food Stores, **II** 624
Dixon, George, **8** 80
Dixon, James, **10** 232
Dixon, Jeane, **10** 287
Dixon, John W., **9** 182–83
Dixon, R.C., **10** 82
Dixon, Robert, **9** 287
Dixon, Wendell L., **11** 16
Dixons Group plc, II 139; **V** 48–50; **9** 65; **10** 45, 306

Dixons U.S. Holdings, Inc., **10** 306
Dixwell, John James, **II** 207
Djerassi, Carl, **I** 701–02
DKB. *See* Dai-Ichi Kangyo Bank Ltd.
DLC. *See* Duquesne Light Company.
DMB&B. *See* D'Arcy Masius Benton & Bowles.
DMP Mineralöl Petrochemie GmbH, **IV** 487
DNAX Research Institute, **I** 685
DNEL-Usinor, **IV** 227
DNP DENMARK A/S, **IV** 600
Doan, Lee, **I** 324; **8** 148
Doan, Ted, **I** 324; **8** 148
Dobbs House, **I** 696–97
Dobrin, Melvyn, **II** 662–64
Dobrin, Mitzi Steinberg, **II** 664
Dobrolet, **6** 57
Dobson, Roy, **III** 508–09
Doctors' Hospital, **6** 191
Documentation Resources, **11** 65
Dodd, Amzi, **III** 302–03
Dodd, Edwin D., **I** 610
Dodge Corp., **I** 144; **8** 74; **11** 53
Dodge, Frank, **11** 77
The Dodge Group, **11** 78
Dodge, Kern, **9** 162
Dodge Manufacturing Company, **9** 440
Dodge, William, **IV** 176
Dods, Walter A., Jr., **11** 115
Dodwell & Co., **III** 523
Doerig, Hans Ulrich, **II** 268
Doerr, John, **10** 507
Doetsch, Heinrich, **IV** 189
Dofasco Inc., IV 73–74
Doheny, Edward L., **IV** 512
Doherty Clifford Steers & Sherfield Inc., **I** 31
Doherty, Henry L., **IV** 391–92; **6** 558–59
Doherty, Mann & Olshan. *See* Wells Rich Greene BDDP.
Dohm, Robert, **II** 257
Doko, Toshiwo, **I** 534
Dolan, Beverly, **I** 530; **9** 499
Dolan, Charles F., **7** 63–65
Dolan, Thomas, **11** 387–88
Dolan, Tom, **11** 5
Dole Food Company, Inc., 9 175–76; **I** 565; **II** 492
Dole, James Drummond, **9** 175–76
Dole, Jim, **I** 565; **II** 491
Dole Philippines, **II** 491
Dole, Sanford B., **I** 565
Doll, Henri, **III** 616–17
Dolland & Aitchison Group, **V** 399
Dollar, R. Stanley, **6** 353
Dollar Rent A Car, **6** 349
Dollar, Robert, **6** 353
Dollar Steamship Lines, **6** 353
Domagala, Thomas, **8** 355
Domain Technology, **6** 231
Domaine Chandon, **I** 272
Dombrico, Inc., **8** 545
Dome Laboratories, **I** 654
Dome Petroleum, Ltd., **II** 222, 245, 262, 376; **IV** 371, 401, 494
Domestic Electric Co., **III** 435
Domestic Operating Co., **III** 36
Dominick's Finer Foods, **9** 451
Dominion Bank, **II** 375–76
Dominion Bridge Company, Limited, **8** 544
Dominion Cellular, **6** 322
Dominion Dairies, **7** 429

Dominion Engineering Works Ltd., **8** 544
Dominion Far East Line, **I** 469
Dominion Foundries and Steel, Ltd., **IV** 73–74
Dominion Hoist & Shovel Co., **8** 544
Dominion Life Assurance Co., **III** 276
Dominion Mushroom Co., **II** 649–50
Dominion Ornamental, **III** 641
Dominion Paper Box Co. Ltd., **IV** 645
Dominion Resources, Inc., V 591, **596–99**
Dominion Securities, **II** 345
Dominion Steel Castings Co. Ltd., **IV** 73
Dominion Steel Foundry Co., **IV** 73
Dominion Stores Ltd., **II** 650, 652
Dominion Tar & Chemical Co. Ltd., **IV** 271–72
Dominion Terminal, **7** 582, 584
Dominion Terminal Associates, **IV** 171
Dominion Textile, Inc., **V** 355; **8** 559–60
Domino's Pizza, Inc., 7 150–53; **9** 74
Domtar Inc., IV 271–73, 308
Don Baxter Intravenous Products Co., **I** 627
Donac Company, **V** 681
Donahue, John D., **I** 145
Donahue, Phil, **11** 330
Donald Arthur Girard, **III** 580
Donald, D.W.A., **III** 361
Donald L. Bren Co., **IV** 287
Donaldson, Lufkin & Jenrette, **II** 422, 451; **III** 247–48; **9** 115, 142, 360–61
Doncaster Newspapers Ltd., **IV** 686
Donegani, Guido, **I** 368
Dong-A Motor, **III** 749
Dong-Myung Industrial Co. Ltd., **II** 540
Dongbang Life Insurance Co., **I** 515
Dongil Frozen Foods Co., **II** 553
Dongsu Industrial Company, **III** 516; **7** 232
Donley, Edward, **I** 298–99; **10** 32
Donnahoe, Alan S., **7** 326–27
Donnell, James, **IV** 574; **7** 551
Donnelley, Gassette & Loyd, **IV** 660
Donnelley, Gaylord, **IV** 661
Donnelley, James R., **IV** 661
Donnelley, Loyd & Co., **IV** 660
Donnelley, Naomi Shenstone, **IV** 660–61
Donnelley, Reuben H., **IV** 660–61
Donnelley, Richard Robert (R.R.), **IV** 660–61; **9** 430
Donnelley, Thomas Elliot, **IV** 660–61; **9** 430
Donnelly, Joseph L., **6** 496
Donovan, Hedley, **IV** 674–75; **7** 528
Donovan, J.J., **IV** 306
Donzi Marine Corp., **III** 600
Dooner Laboratories, **I** 667
Door-to-Door, **6** 14
Dopchie, Jacques, **V** 65
Döpke, Carl, **V** 744–45
Dorado Beach Development Inc., **I** 103
Dordrecht, **III** 177–78
Doré, Gustave, **IV** 617
Dorfman, Henry, **7** 523–24
Dorfman, Joel, **7** 524
Doriot, Georges (Gen.), **III** 132; **6** 233
Dorman Long & Co. Ltd., **IV** 658
Dornier, **I** 46, 74, 151
Dornier-Merkur, **I** 121
Dorothy Perkins, **V** 21
Dorrance, Arthur, **II** 479
Dorrance, Arthur C., **II** 479; **7** 66
Dorrance, John T., Jr., **II** 481
Dorrance, John Thompson, **II** 479; **7** 66

Dorsey, Tommy, **II** 143
Dortch, Oscar L., **8** 264
Dortmund-Hörder Hüttenunion, **IV** 105
Dortmunder Union, **IV** 103, 105
Dortmunder-Union-Brauerei, **II** 240
Doser, Wulf, **10** 127
Dothée family, **IV** 51
Doubleday, **IV** 636
Doubleday Book Shops, **10** 136
Doubleday, George, **III** 526
Doubleday-Dell, **IV** 594
Douce, Jacques, **10** 347
Douce, William, **IV** 523
Dougherty, Charles, **V** 742
Dougherty, Philip, **I** 18
Dougherty, William, **8** 296–97
Douglas Aircraft Co., **I** 48, 70, 76, 96, 104, 195; **II** 32, 425; **III** 601; **9** 12, 18, 206; **10** 163
Douglas, Donald, **I** 67, 70–71, 73, 76, 78, 89, 125, 529; **III** 601; **9** 417; **11** 277–78, 363, 427
Douglas, Donald, Jr., **I** 71; **11** 278
Douglas, Edwin, **I** 320
Douglas, H.A., **11** 13
Douglas, James, **IV** 176
Douglas, Kenneth J., **7** 127–28
Douglas, Kirk, **II** 143
Douglas, Lewis, **III** 306
Douglas Oil Co., **IV** 401
Douglas, Paul W., **IV** 82–83, 182; **7** 186–87
Douglas, Stephen, **IV** 682
Douglas, Walter, **IV** 177
Douglas-Dahlin Co., **I** 158–59
Douglass, Benjamin, **IV** 604
Douglass, Robert Dun, **IV** 604
Douglass, Sam P., **6** 294
Doulton Glass Industries Ltd., **IV** 659
Doumani, Edward M., **6** 210
Douwe Egberts, **II** 572
Dove International, **7** 299–300
Dove, Percy, **III** 349
Dover Corporation, III 467–69
Dover Diversified, **III** 467–68
Dover Elevator International, **III** 467–68
Dover Industries, **III** 467–68
Dover Resources, **III** 467–68
Dover Sargent, **III** 468
Dover Technologies, **III** 467–68
Dow, Alex, **V** 592
Dow, Charles Henry, **IV** 601–03
Dow Chemical Co., I 323–25, 334, 341–42, 360, 370–71, 708; **II** 440, 457; **III** 617, 760; **IV** 83, 417; **8 147–50** **(upd.)**, 153, 261–62, 548; **9** 328–29, 500–501; **10** 289; **11** 271
Dow Corning, **II** 54; **III** 683, 685
Dow family, **IV** 601
Dow Financial Services Corp., **II** 457
Dow, Herbert, **I** 323–24; **8** 147–48
Dow, J.B., **III** 360–61
Dow, James R., **III** 290
Dow, Jones & Co., **IV** 601–02
Dow Jones & Company, Inc., IV 601–03, 654, 656, 670, 678; **7** 99; **10** 276–78, 407
Dow Jones Telerate, Inc., 10 276–78
Dow, Willard, **I** 323–24; **8** 147–48
Dowd, Clement, **II** 336
Dowdings Ltd., **IV** 349
Dowell Australia Ltd., **III** 674
Dowell Schlumberger, **III** 617
Dowidat GmbH, **IV** 197

Dowidat-Werke Saar GmbH, **IV** 197
Dowlais Iron Co., **III** 493
Dowling, Robert, **III** 263
Down, Alastair, **IV** 382–83
Downingtown Paper Company, **8** 476
Downs, W. Findlay, **9** 162
Downyflake Foods, **7** 429
Doxat, Edmund, **II** 499
Doyle Dane Bernbach, **I** 9, 20, 28, 30–31, 33, 37, 206; **11** 549
Doyle, Donald E., **7** 267
Doyle, Francis C., **11** 106
Doyle, J.C., **I** 14
Doyle, Ned, **I** 30
DP&L. *See* Dayton Power & Light Company.
DPCE, **II** 139
DPL Inc., 6 480–82
DQE, **6 483–85**
DR Holdings, Inc., **10** 242
Dr Pepper/7Up Companies, Inc., 9 177–78
Dr. Miles' Medical Co., **I** 653
Dr. Pepper Co., **I** 245; **IV** 477
Dr. Richter & Co., **IV** 70
Dr. Tigges-Fahrten, **II** 163–64
Drabinsky, Garth, **6** 161–63
Drackett, **III** 17
Dragados y Construcciones S.A., **II** 198
Dragon, **III** 391
Drake Bakeries, **II** 562
Drake Beam Morin, Inc., **IV** 623
Drake, Carl B., **III** 356–57
Drake, Earl G., **II** 312
Drake, Eric (Sir), **IV** 379
Drake, Harrington, **IV** 605
Drake, James, **II** 421
Drake, Sir Arthur Eric Courtney, **7** 58–59
Drake, William P., **I** 382–83
Drake-Beam & Associates, **IV** 623
Draper & Kramer, **IV** 724
Draper, E. Linn, **6** 496
Draper, Robert E., **11** 335
Draper, Simeon, **III** 290
Drathen Co., **I** 220
Dravo Corp., **6** 143
Draw-Tite, Inc., **11** 535
Drayton Corp., **II** 319
Drayton, Harold Charles (Harley), **IV** 686
Drennen, Michael, **II** 417
Dresden Bankhaus, **II** 281
Dresdner Bank A.G., I 411; **II** 191, 238–39, 241–42, 256–57, 279–80, **281–83**, 385; **III** 201, 289, 401; **IV** 141
Dresdner Feuer-Versicherungs-Gesellschaft, **III** 376
Dresser Industries, Inc., I 486; **III** 429, **470–73**; 499, 527, 545–46
Dresser Manufacturing Co., **III** 471
Dresser Manufacturing Co., Ltd., **III** 471
Dresser, Paul, **8** 104
Dresser Power, **6** 555
Dresser, Solomon, **III** 470
Dresser Vaduz, **III** 472
Dresser-Rand, **III** 473, 527
Drever, Thomas, **7** 30
Drew, Daniel, **II** 395; **10** 59
Drew, William, **II** 593
Drewry Photocolor, **I** 447
Drews, Rudolph, **I** 496
Drexel and Company, **II** 329–30, 407; **8** 388
Drexel, Anthony J., **II** 329, 407
Drexel Burnham, **9** 346

Drexel Burnham and Company, **II** 407; **8** 388
Drexel Burnham Lambert Incorporated, **II** 167, 330, **407–09**, 482; **III** 10, 253, 254–55, 531, 721; **IV** 334; **6** 210–11; **7** 305; **8** 327, 349, 388–90, 568. *See also* New Street Capital Inc.
Drexel Firestone Inc., **II** 407; **8** 388
Drexel, Francis Martin, **II** 407; **8** 388
Drexel, Harjes & Co., **II** 329
Drexel Heritage, **11** 534
Drexel Heritage Furniture, **III** 571
Drexel Morgan & Co., **II** 329, 430
Drexler, Millard Mickey, **V** 60–62
Dreyer's Grand Ice Cream, Inc., **10** 147–48
Dreyfus, Camille E. (Dr.), **I** 317–18
Dreyfus, Henri (Dr.), **I** 317
Dreyfus Interstate Development Corp., **11** 257
Dreyfus, Ludwig, **II** 414
Dreyfus, Pierre, **I** 189–90
DRI. *See* Dominion Resources, Inc.
Dribeck Importers Inc., **9** 87
Drinkwater, Terrell, **I** 96
Driscoll, Alfred, **I** 710–11; **10** 549–50
Drohan, Thomas E., **I** 497
Dromer, Jean, **III** 393
Drott Manufacturing Company, **10** 379
Drouot Group, **III** 211
Drown, L.M., **91**
Drug City, **II** 649
Drug House, **III** 9
Drug, Inc., **III** 17
Drumheller, Roscoe, **9** 531
Drummond, Gerard K., **7** 376–77
Drummond Lighterage. *See* Puget Sound Tug and Barge Company.
Druout, **I** 563
Dry Milks Inc., **I** 248
Dryden and Co., **III** 340
Dryden, Forrest, **III** 337–38
Dryden, John F., **III** 337–38
Dryfoos, Orvil E., **IV** 648
Drysdale Government Securities, **10** 117
DSC Nortech, **9** 170
DSM N.V., I 326–27; **III** 614
DST Systems Inc., **6 400–02**
Du Bain, Myron, **I** 418
Du Bouzet, **II** 233
Du Mont Company, **8** 517
Du Pont. *See* E.I. du Pont de Nemours & Co.
Du Pont, Alfred I., **I** 328; **IV** 311
Du Pont Chemical Company, **11** 432
Du Pont, Coleman, **III** 247
Du Pont de Nemours, Alfred, **I** 328
Du Pont de Nemours, Eleuthère Irenée, **I** 328
Du Pont de Nemours, Henry, **I** 328
Du Pont, Eugene, **I** 328
Du Pont Fabricators, **III** 559
Du Pont family, **11** 431
Du Pont Glore Forgan, Inc., **III** 137
Du Pont Photomask, **IV** 600
Du Pont, Pierre S., **I** 328
Du Pont, Richard C., **I** 131; **6** 131
Du Pont Walston, **II** 445
Dubin, Ronald N., **10** 235
Dublin and London Steam Packet Company, **V** 490
Dubose, Lori, **I** 117
Dubreuil, Audouin, **7** 35–36
Dubreuil, Haardt, **7** 35–36

Dubrule, Paul, **10** 12–14
Ducat, D., **I** 605
Ducatel-Duval, **II** 369
Duck Head Apparel Company, Inc., **8** 141–43
Ducon Group, **II** 81
Dudley, Alfred E., **8** 180
Duerden, Peter, **III** 350
Duerksen, Christopher J., **I** 325
Duff Bros., **III** 9–10
Duff, Tom, **8** 561
Duffield, Edward D., **III** 338
Duffy, Ben, **I** 28–29
Duffy, Edward W., **III** 763
Duffy-Mott, **II** 477
Dugan, Allan E., **6** 290
Duisberg, Carl, **I** 305, 309
Duke, James, **8** 24
Duke, James Buchanan (Buck), **I** 300, 425; **IV** 10; **V** 395, 408, 417, 600; **9** 312, 533
Duke Power Company, **V** 600–02
Duke, William Meng, **I** 544
Dulles, John Foster, **I** 507
Dumaine, F.C. "Buck", Jr., **8** 32; **9** 213
Dumaine, Frederic C., Sr., **8** 32–33; **9** 213
Dumez, **V** 655–57
Dumont Broadcasting Corporation, **7** 335
Dumont, Francois, **IV** 226
Dumont, Victor, **IV** 226
Dun & Bradstreet Corporation, **I** 540; **IV** 604–05, 643, 661; **8** 526; **9** 505; **10** 4, 358
Dun & Bradstreet Cos. Inc., **IV** 605
Dun & Bradstreet, Inc., **IV** 605
Dun & Bradstreet Software Services Inc., **11** 77–79
Dun, Robert Graham, **IV** 604
Dunbar, Michael, **I** 427
Duncan, Alexander E., **8** 117
Duncan, Daniel, **III** 96–97
Duncan Foods Corp., **I** 234; **10** 227
Duncan, James H., **8** 188
Duncan, James S., **III** 651
Duncan, John C., **7** 107–08
Duncan, John W., **6** 446
Duncan Mackinnon, **III** 521
Duncan Macneill, **III** 522
Duncan, Sherman & Co., **II** 329
Duncan, Val, **IV** 191–92
Duncan, William (Sir), **I** 83
Duncan, William A., Jr., **11** 237
Duncanson, Thomas S., **IV** 645
Dundee Cement Co., **III** 702; **8** 258–59
Dunham, Sylvester, **III** 387–88
Dunhams Stores Corporation, **V** 111
Dunhill, **IV** 93
Dunhill Holdings, **V** 411
Dunkin' Donuts, **II** 619
Dunlevy, George, **6** 348
Dunlop, **V** 250, 252–53
Dunlop Holdings, **I** 429; **III** 697
Dunlop Japan, **V** 252
Dunlop, John Boyd, **10** 444
Dunlop, Robert G., **IV** 549–50; **7** 414
Dunlop Tire (USA), **I** 429
Dunn, Frank H., Jr., **10** 299
Dunn, Henry, **IV** 604
Dunn, J.H., **IV** 409; **7** 309
Dunn Paper Co., **IV** 290
Dunn, Vincent B., **11** 281
Dunne, James E., **III** 216
Dunnett, Peter J.S., **I** 196
Dunnigan, T. Kevin, **11** 516
Dunning, Harrison, **IV** 330

Dunoyer, **III** 675
Dupar, Frank A., **9** 547
Dupar, Harold E., **9** 547
Dupil-Color, Inc., **III** 745
Dupol, **III** 614
duPont, Alfred I., **8** 151, 485–86
Dupont Chamber Works, **6** 449
DuPont Chemical Company, **7** 546
duPont de Nemours, Éleuthère Irenée, **8** 151
duPont, Pierre S., **8** 151
Duquesne Enterprises, **6** 484
Duquesne Light Company, **6** 483–84
Duquesne Systems, **10** 394
Dura Corp., **I** 476
Dura-Vent, **III** 468
Duracell International Inc., **9** 179–81
Durand & Huguenin, **I** 672
Durand, Ariel, **IV** 671
Durant, Don, **11** 522
Durant, Thomas C., **V** 529
Durant, Will, **IV** 671
Durant, William, **I** 171; **10** 325
Durante, Jimmy, **II** 151
Durban Breweries and Distillers, **I** 287
Dureau, David Henry, **IV** 248
DuRell, Benjamin M., **11** 552–53
Durfee, Dorothy, **IV** 252
Durham Chemicals Distributors Ltd., **III** 699
Durham, Fred D., **III** 467
Durham, Hal, **11** 153
Durham Raw Materials Ltd., **III** 699
Durkee Famous Foods, **II** 567; **8** 222
Durkee Foods, **7** 314
Durkee-French, **II** 567
Durr, Emil, **III** 762
Dürr, Heinz, **I** 411
Dürrer, Robert, **IV** 233
Durstine, Roy, **I** 28
Dusault, Allen, **11** 444
Dusseldorp, Gerard J., **IV** 707–09
Dusto, Fred, **9** 287
Dutch Boy, **II** 649; **III** 745; **10** 434–35
Dutch Crude Oil Company. *See* Nederlandse Aardolie Maatschappij.
Dutch East Indies Post, Telegraph and Telephone Service, **II** 67
Dutch Nuts Chocoladefabriek B.V., **II** 569
Dutch Pantry, **II** 497
Dutch State Mines. *See* DSM N.V.
Duthie, John, **III** 670
Dutilh, Danilo, **III** 345
Dutschke, Rudi, **IV** 590
Dutt, James, **II** 468
Dutton Brewery, **I** 294
Duty Free International, Inc., **11** 80–82
Duval Corp., **IV** 489–90
Duval Texas Sulfur Co., **7** 280
Duvall, William, **8** 326
DWG Corporation. *See* Triarc Companies, Inc.
Dwiggins, William, **IV** 661
Dworkin, Elliot, **V** 172
Dworkin, Marc, **V** 172–73
Dworkin, Sidney, **V** 171–73
Dwyer, Andrew T., **9** 300–01
Dyckerhoff, **III** 738
Dyer, Henry K., **IV** 251
Dyer, William A., **10** 208
Dyke, F.J., Jr., **7** 372
Dykstra, John, **I** 167
Dynaco Inc., **III** 643
Dynamatic Corp., **I** 154

Dynamic Controls, **11** 202
Dynamic Microprocessor Associated Inc., **10** 508
Dynamit AG, **III** 693–94
Dynamit Nobel AG, **III** 692–95
Dynapar, **7** 116–17
Dynatron/Bondo Corporation, **8** 456
Dynell Electronics, **I** 85
Dyonics Inc., **I** 667
DYR, **I** 38

E & H Utility Sales Inc., **6** 487
E & J Gallo Winery, **I** 27, **242–44**, 260; **7 154–56 (upd.)**
E. & B. Carpet Mills, **III** 423
E.A. Miller, Inc., **II** 494
E.A. Pierce & Co., **II** 424
E.A. Stearns & Co., **III** 627
E&B Company, **9** 72
E.B. Badger Co., **11** 413
E.B. Eddy Forest Products, **II** 631
E. de Trey & Sons, **10** 270–71
E.F. Hutton Group, **I** 402; **II** 399, 450–51; **8** 139; **9** 469; **10** 63
E. Gluck Trading Co., **III** 645
E.H. Bindley & Company, **9** 67
E.I. du Pont de Nemours & Company, **I** 21, 28, 305, 317–19, 323, **328–30**, 334, 337–38, 343–44, 346–48, 351–53, 365, 377, 379, 383, 402–03, 545, 548, 675; **III** 21; **IV** 69, 78, 263, 371, 399, 401–02, 409, 481, 599; **V** 360; **8** 151–54 (upd.), 485; **9** 154, 216, 352, 466; **10** 289
E.J. Brach, **II** 521
E. Katz Special Advertising Agency. *See* Katz Communications, Inc.
E.L. Phillips and Company, **V** 652–53
E.M. Warburg, **7** 305
E.N.V. Engineering, **I** 154
E.R. Squibb, **I** 695
E.S. Friedman & Co., **II** 241
E-Systems, Inc., **I** 490; **9 182–85**
E-II Holdings, **II** 468; **9** 449
E.W. Bliss, **I** 452
E.W. Oakes & Co. Ltd., **IV** 118
E.W. Scripps Company, **IV** 606–09; **7 157–59 (upd.)**
E.W.T. Mayer Ltd., **III** 681
Eadie, William E., **IV** 381
Eagle Credit Corp., **10** 248
Eagle Electric & Plumbing Supply, **9** 399
Eagle Industries, **8** 230
Eagle Oil Transport Co. Ltd., **IV** 657
Eagle Printing Co. Ltd., **IV** 295
Eagle Snacks Inc., **I** 219
Eagle Square Manufacturing Co., **III** 627
Eagle Star Insurance Co., **I** 426–27; **III** 185, 200
Eagle Supermarket, **II** 571
Eagle Travel Ltd., **IV** 241
Eagle-Lion Films, **II** 147
Eagle-Picher Industries, Inc., **8 155–58**
Eamer, Richard K., **III** 87
Eames, Alfred W., Jr., **7** 132
Eames, Charles, **8** 255–56
Eames, Ray, **8** 255
Earhart, Amelia, **I** 64, 76, 125; **8** 313; **11** 266, 363
Earle, George (Sir), **III** 670–71
Earth Resources Co., **IV** 459
Easco Hand Tools, Inc., **7** 117
Eason Oil Company, **6** 578; **11** 198
East Chicago Iron and Forge Co., **IV** 113

East India Co., **I** 468; **III** 521, 696; **IV** 48
East Japan Heavy Industries, **III** 578–79; **7** 348
East Japan Railway Company, **V 448–50**
East Midlands Electricity, **V** 605
The East New York Savings Bank, **11** 108–09
East of Scotland, **III** 359
East Texas Pulp and Paper Co., **IV** 342, 674; **7** 528
Easter Enterprises, **8** 380
Eastern Airlines, **I** 41, 66, 78, 90, 98–99, **101–03**, 116, 118, 123–25; **III** 102; **6** 73, 81–82, 104–05; **8** 416; **9** 17–18, 80; **11** 268, 427
Eastern Associated Coal Corp., **6** 487
Eastern Bank, **II** 357
Eastern Carolina Bottling Company, **10** 223
Eastern Coal Corp., **IV** 181
Eastern Coalfields Ltd., **IV** 48–49
Eastern Corp., **IV** 703
Eastern Enterprises, **IV** 171; **6 486–88**
Eastern Gas and Fuel Associates, **I** 354; **IV** 171
Eastern Indiana Gas Corporation, **6** 466
Eastern Kansas Utilities, **6** 511
Eastern Operating Co., **III** 23
Eastern States Farmers Exchange, **7** 17
Eastern Telegraph, **V** 283–84
Eastern Texas Electric. *See* Gulf States Utilities Company.
Eastern Tool Co., **IV** 249
Eastern Wisconsin Power, **6** 604
Eastern Wisconsin Railway and Light Company, **6** 601
Eastex Pulp and Paper Co., **IV** 341–42
Eastham, Edward, **6** 548
Eastham, William K., **III** 59
Eastman Chemical Products, Inc. **III** 475; **7** 161; **8** 377
Eastman Co., **III** 474; **7** 160
Eastman Dry Plate and Film Co., **III** 474; **7** 160
Eastman Dry Plate Co., **III** 474; **7** 160
Eastman, George, **III** 474–76; **7** 160–62; **9** 422
Eastman Kodak Company, **I** 19, 30, 90, 323, 337–38, 690; **II** 103; **III** 171–72, **474–77**, 486–88, 547–48, 550, 584, 607–09; **IV** 260–61; **6** 288–89; **7** **160–64 (upd.)**, 436–38; **8** 376–77; **9** 62, 231; **10** 24
Eastman Photographic Materials Co., **III** 474; **7** 160
Eastman Radio, **6** 33
Eastman Technology, **III** 475
Eastmaque Gold Mines, Ltd., **7** 356
Eaton Axle Co., **I** 154
Eaton, Bob, **7** 462
Eaton, Cole & Burnham Company, **8** 134
Eaton Corporation, **I** 154–55, 186; **III** 645; **10 279–80 (upd.)**
Eaton, Cyrus, **6** 605; **7** 446
Eaton, Earl, **11** 543
Eaton, Frank, **9** 92
Eaton, Joseph Oriel, **I** 154; **10** 279
Eaton, Robert, **7** 461
Eaton Yale & Towne, **I** 154
Eavey Co., **II** 668
Eayres, Ellen Knowles, **IV** 622
Ebamsa, **II** 474
EBASCO. *See* Electric Bond and Share Company.

Ebasco Service Inc., **V** 612
Ebasco Services, **III** 499; **IV** 255–56
Ebbers, Bernard, **8** 310
EBC Amro Ltd., **II** 186
Eberhard Foods, **8** 482
Eberle, William D., **III** 664–65
Eberstadt, Rudolph, Jr., **8** 366–67
Ebert, Horatio B., **III** 613
EBIC. *See* European Banks' International Co.
Eble, Charles, **V** 587–88
EBS. *See* Electric Bond & Share Company.
EC Erdolchemie GmbH, **7** 141
ECC Construction, **III** 689
ECC Construction Materials, **III** 689
ECC Group plc, **III 689–91**
ECC International Ltd., **III** 689–91
Eccles, George S., **11** 117–19
Eccles, Marriner S., **11** 117–18
Eccles, Samuel, **I** 267
Eccles, Spencer, **11** 119
Echevarrieta, Horacio, **6** 95
Echigoya Saburobei Shoten, **IV** 292
Echlin Corp., **I 156–57**
Echlin, Earl, **I** 156; **11** 83
Echlin Inc., **11 83–85 (upd.)**
Echlin, Jack, **I** 156; **11** 83
Echo Bay Mines Ltd., **IV 75–77**
Echols, O.P., **I** 76; **11** 363
Les Echos, **IV** 659
Eckel, Paul, **I** 28
Ecker, Frederick H., **III** 292
Ecker, Frederick W., **III** 292
Eckerd College, **9** 187
Eckerd Corporation, **9 186–87**
Eckerd Family Youth Alternatives, **9** 187
Eckerd, J. Milton, **9** 186
Eckerd, Jack, **9** 186
Eckerd Optical, **9** 186
Eckert, J. Presper, **III** 165
Eckert, Wesley E., **9** 161
Eckert-Mauchly Corp., **III** 166
Eckhouse, Joseph L., **7** 202
Eckman, John, **I** 666–68
Ecko Products, **I** 527
Ecko-Ensign Design, **I** 531
Eckrich, Donald P., **7** 82
Eclipse Machine Co., **I** 141
Ecolab Inc., **I 331–33**
Economics Laboratory. *See* Ecolab Inc.
Economo family, **III** 347
Economy Book Store, **10** 135
Economy Grocery Stores Corp., **II** 666
Ecopetrol. *See* Empresa Colombiana de Petróleos.
EcoSystems Software, Inc., **10** 245
Ecusta Corporation, **8** 414
Eddie Bauer Inc., **9 188–90**; **9** 316; **10** 324, 489, 491; **11** 498
Eddie Bauer Ltd., **II** 503; **V** 160
Eddins, H.A. "Tex", **7** 410
Eddy Paper Co., **II** 631
Edeka Co-op Bank, **II** 621–22
Edeka Import and Export, **II** 621
Edeka Zentrale A.G., **II 621–23**
Edelman, Asher, **11** 274
Edelman, Asher B., **I** 170; **6** 146; **7** 514; **11** 68–69
Edelstahlwerke Buderus AG, **III** 695
Edelstein, Michael, **I** 471, 522
Edenhall Group, **III** 673
EDF. *See* Electricité de France.
Edgar, Jim, **6** 201
Edgar, N.S., **IV** 75

Edgars, **I** 289
Edgcomb Metals, **IV** 576
Edgcomb Steel Co., **IV** 575
Edgell Communications Inc., **IV** 624
Edgell, Robert L., **IV** 623–24
Edgerly, Martin Van Buren (Col.), **III** 285
Edgerly, William, **8** 492
Edgerton, David, **II** 613
Edgerton, Harold E., **8** 163
Edgewater Hotel and Casino, **6** 204–05
Edinburgh (Duke of), **IV** 708
Edison Brothers Stores, Inc., **9 191–93**
Edison Co., **III** 433
Edison Electric Appliance Co., **II** 28
Edison Electric Co., **I** 368; **II** 330; **6** 572
Edison Electric Illuminating Co., **II** 402; **6** 595, 601
Edison Electric Light & Power, **6** 510
Edison Electric Light Co., **II** 27; **6** 565, 595; **11** 387
Edison General Electric Co., **II** 27, 120, 278
Edison, Harry, **9** 191–92
Edison, Irving, **9** 192
Edison Machine Works, **II** 27
Edison Phonograph, **III** 443
Edison, Sam, **9** 192
Edison, Thomas, **11** 402
Edison, Thomas A., **I** 409, 597; **II** 27–28, 120; **III** 683; **V** 695; **6** 465, 483, 555, 574, 595; **9** 274; **10** 115
Editions Albert Premier, **IV** 614
Editions Bernard Grasset, **IV** 618
Editions Dalloz, **IV** 615
Editions Nathan, **IV** 615
Editorial Centro de Estudios Ramón Areces, S.A., **V** 52
Editoriale L'Espresso, **IV** 586–87
Editoriale Le Gazzette, **IV** 587
EdK. *See* Edeka Zentrale A.G.
Edman, Jan, **II** 366
Edmond Garin, **III** 418
Edmonston, D.C., **II** 297
Edmonton City Bakery, **II** 631
Edmunds, Henry, **I** 194
Edogawa Oil Co., **IV** 403
EdoWater Systems, Inc., **IV** 137
Edper Equities, **II** 456
EDS. *See* Electronic Data Systems Corporation.
Edstrom, J. Sigfrid, **II** 1–2
Education Funds, Inc., **II** 419
Education Systems Corporation, **7** 256
Educational & Recreational Services, Inc., **II** 607
Educational Credit Corporation, **8** 10
Educational Supply Company, **7** 255
EduQuest, **6** 245
Edward Ford Plate Glass Co., **III** 640–41, 731
Edward J. DeBartolo Corporation, **V** 116; **8 159–62**
Edward Lloyd Ltd., **IV** 258
Edward Smith & Company, **8** 553
Edward VII, King (England), **I** 251
Edwardes, Michael (Sir), **I** 429; **7** 332
Edwards & Jones, **11** 360
Edwards, Albert Gallatin, **8** 3–4
Edwards, Albert Ninian, **8** 4
Edwards, Benjamin Franklin, **8** 3–4
Edwards, Benjamin Franklin, III, **8** 3–5
Edwards Dunlop & Co. Ltd., **IV** 249
Edwards Food Warehouse, **II** 642
Edwards, Garth W., **III** 628

Edwards George and Co., **III** 283
Edwards, George Lane, **8** 4
Edwards Industries, **IV** 256
Edwards, Presley W., **8** 4
Edwards, William L., Jr., **III** 530
Eerste Nederlandsche, **III** 177–79
Eff Laboratories, **I** 622
Effectenbank, **II** 268
Efnadruck GmbH, **IV** 325
EG&G Incorporated, 8 163–65
EGAM, **IV** 422
Egan, Michael S., **6** 348–49
Egerton Hubbard & Co., **IV** 274
Eggermont, Lodewijk, **6** 303
Egghead Inc., 9 194–95; 10 284
EGPC. *See* Egyptian General Petroleum
  Corporation.
Eguchi, Tomonaru, **7** 111
EGUZKIA-NHK, **III** 581
Egyptair, I 107; **6 84–86**
**Egyptian General Petroleum
  Corporation, IV 412–14**
Egyptian Petrochemicals Co., **IV** 413
EHAPE Einheitspreis Handels Gesellschaft
  mbH. *See* Kaufhalle AG.
Ehinger, Charles E., **10** 263
Ehrentheil, Emanuel, **III** 207
Ehrhardt, Heinrich, **9** 443–44, 446
Ehrlichman, Ben S., **9** 531
Ehrnrooth, Casimir, **IV** 300–01
Eichenrode, Wilfried Hertz, **IV** 590
Eickhoff, Dennis R., **8** 10
Eidgenössische Bank, **II** 378
Eidgenössische Versicherungs-Aktien-
  Gesellschaft, **III** 403
84 Lumber Company, 9 196–97
Eiichi, Shibusawa, **III** 490
Eilers, Anton, **IV** 32
Eilers, Karl, **IV** 32
EIMCO, **I** 512
Einstein, Albert, **I** 395
EIS Automotive Corp., **III** 603
Eisen-und Stahlwerk Haspe AG, **IV** 126
Eisen-und Stahlwerk Hoesch, **IV** 103
Eisenhauer, Robert S., **I** 530
Eisenhower, Dwight D., **I** 29, 84, 233; **III**
  52; **IV** 115, 392, 621; **10** 226; **11** 345
Eisenhower Mining Co., **IV** 33
Eisner, Michael, **II** 156, 173–74; **6** 174–76
Eiszner, James R., **II** 498
EKA A.B., **I** 330
EKA AB, **8** 153
Eka Nobel AB, **9** 380
Eklund, Coy, **III** 248–49
Ekman, Elon V., **III** 479
El Al Israel Airlines, **I** 30
**El Camino Resources International, Inc.,
  11 86–88**
El Corte Inglés, S.A., V 51–3
El Dorado Investment Company, **6** 546–47
El Paso Natural Gas Co., **10** 190; **11** 28
Ela, Richard, **10** 377
ELAN, **IV** 486
Elan Corp. plc, **10** 54
Elco Motor Yacht, **I** 57
Elda Trading Co., **II** 48
Elder, Alexander Lang, **I** 438
Elder Dempster Line, **6** 416–17
Elder Johnston Company. *See* Elder-
  Beerman Stores Corp.
Elder, Robert, **10** 281
Elder Smith Goldsbrough Mort Ltd., **I**
  437–38; **7** 182
Elder, Thomas, **10** 281

Elder's Insurance Co., **III** 370
**Elder-Beerman Stores Corporation, 10
  281–83**
Elders IXL Ltd., I 216, 228–29, 264,
  437–39, 592–93; **7** 182–83
Electra Corp., **III** 569
Electralab Electronics Corp., **III** 643
Electric Boat Co., **I** 57–59, 527; **II** 7; **10**
  315
Electric Bond & Share Company, **V**
  564–65; **6** 596
Electric Energy, Inc., **6** 470, 505
Electric Fuels Corp., **V** 621
Electric Heat Regulator Co., **II** 40
Electric Iron and Steel, **IV** 162
Electric Light and Power Company, **6** 483
Electric Light Company of Atlantic City.
  See Atlantic Energy, Inc.
Electric Thermostat Co., **II** 40
Electrical Lamp Service Co., **I** 531
Electricité de France, I 303; **V 603–05,**
  626–28
Electro Dynamics Corp., **I** 57, 484; **11** 263
Electro Metallurgical Co., **I** 400; **9** 517; **11**
  402
Electro Refractories and Abrasives
  Company, **8** 178
Electro-Alkaline Co., **III** 20
Electro-Chemische Fabrik Natrium GmbH,
  IV 69–70
Electro-Flo, Inc., **9** 27
Electro-Mechanical Research, **III** 617
Electro-Motive Engineering Company, **10**
  273
Electro-Nite International N.V., **IV** 100
Electro-Optical Systems, **III** 172; **6** 289
Electrobel, **II** 202
ElectroData Corp., **III** 165; **6** 281
Electrolux A.B., **6** 69
Electrolux Corp., **III** 479–80; **11** 439
Electrolux Group, II 69, 572; **III** 420,
  478–81; IV 338
Electromedics, **11** 460
Electronic Arts Inc., 10 284–86
Electronic Arts Victor Inc., **10** 285
Electronic Banking Systems, **9** 173
Electronic Data Systems, **11** 131
Electronic Data Systems Corporation, I
  172; **II** 65; **III 136–38**, 326; **6** 226; **9**
  36; **10** 325, 327; **11** 62, 123
Electronic Rentals Group PLC, **II** 139
Electrorail, **II** 93
Electrowatt Engineering Services Limited,
  6 491
Electrowatt Finance (BVI) Limited, **6** 491
Electrowerke AG, **IV** 230
Elektra, **III** 480
Elektriska Aktiebolaget, **II** 1
Elektrizitäts-Gesellschaft Laufenburg, **6**
  490
Elektrizitätswerk Westfalen AG, **V** 744
Elektro-Watt Elektrische und Industrielle
  Unternehmungen AG. *See* Elektrowatt
  AG.
Elektro-Watt Ingenieurunternehmung AG,
  6 490
Elektrobank. *See* Elektrowatt AG.
ElektroHelios, **III** 479
Elektromekaniska AB, **III** 478
Elektromekano, **II** 1
Elektrowatt AG, 6 489–91
Eleme Petrochemicals Co., **IV** 473
Elettrofinanziaria Spa, **9** 152
Eleventh National Bank, **II** 373

Elf. *See* Société Nationale Elf Aquitaine.
Elf Aquitaine. *See* Société Nationale Elf
  Aquitaine.
Elf Enterprise Petroleum Ltd., **11** 97
Elgin Blenders, Inc., **7** 128
Eli Lilly & Co., I 637, **645–47**, 666, 679,
  687, 701; **III** 18–19, 60–61; **8** 168, 209;
  9 89–90; **10** 535; **11** 9, **89–91 (upd.)**,
  458, 460
Eli, Walters, **9** 275
Elias Brothers Restaurants, **III** 103
Eliot, Samuel, **III** 312
Eliot, T.S., **II** 307; **IV** 622
Elish, Herbert, **IV** 238
Elit Circuits Inc., **I** 330; **8** 153
Elite Microelectronics, **9** 116
Elite Sewing Machine Manufacturing Co.,
  III 415
Elizabeth Arden, **I** 646, **III** 48; **9** 201–02,
  428, 449
Elizabeth Arden Co., 8 166–68, 344; **11**
  90
Elizabeth I, Queen (England), **I** 285, 312;
  II 236
Elizabeth II, Queen (England), **III** 105, 163
Eljer Industries, **II** 420
Elk River Resources, Inc., **IV** 550
Elka, **III** 54
Elke Corporation, **10** 514
Elko-Lamoille Power Company, **11** 343
Ellenville Electric Company, **6** 459
Eller, Karl, **II** 619–20
Eller, Tim, **8** 88
Ellerson, H. Watkins, **8** 102
Ellesse International, **V** 376
Ellice-Clark, Edward Badouin, **I** 314
Ellinger, Leo, **IV** 139–40
Ellington, Duke, **III** 443
Elliot, John, **V** 421
Elliott Automation, **II** 25
Elliott, Byron K., **III** 267
Elliott, Frederic (Dr.), **III** 245
Elliott, John D., **I** 437–39; **7** 182–84
Elliott Paint and Varnish, **8** 553
Elliott, T.R., **I** 714
Elliott, Thomas, **I** 205
Elliott-Automation, **6** 241
Ellis Adding-Typewriter Co., **III** 151; **6**
  265
Ellis Banks, **II** 336
Ellis, Chafflin & Co., **IV** 310
Ellis, Charles, **I** 572–73
Ellis, Davis W., **10** 51
Ellis, George Holland, **I** 317
Ellis, Gilbert, **II** 419–20
Ellis, Gordon, **7** 430
Ellis, Harry W., **III** 534–35
Ellis, John Devonshire, **I** 572
Ellis, Perry N., **7** 39
Ellis, Ray, **II** 34
Ellis, Reuben M., **V** 405
Ellis, William B., **V** 668–69; **9** 344
Ellis, William Henry, **I** 572
Ellison, Eugene, **III** 224
Ellison, Lawrence J., **6** 272–74
Ellos A.B., **II** 640
Ellwood, Paul, **9** 524
ELMA Electronic, **III** 632
Elmendorf Board, **IV** 343
Elmer, Charles W., **7** 425
Elrick & Lavidge, **6** 24
Elsbury, David, **II** 84
Elsevier Business Press, **IV** 610
Elsevier family, **IV** 610

Elsevier Information Systems Inc., **IV** 610
Elsevier NV, IV 610–11, 643, 659
Elsevier Opleidingen, **IV** 611
Elsevier Realty Information, Inc., **IV** 610
Elsevier Science Publishers BV, **IV** 610–11
Elsevier Vendex Film CV, **IV** 611
Elsevior, **7** 244
Elsi, **II** 86
Elsner, David M., **I** 24
ELTO Outboard Motor Co., **III** 597
Eltra, **I** 416, 524
Elving, Rudolf, **IV** 299
Elwerath, **IV** 485
Elwinger, L. Arling, **I** 665
Ely, Joseph, II, **9** 214, 216
Elyria Telephone Company, **6** 299
Email Ltd., **III** 672–73
Emballage, **III** 704
Embankment Trust Ltd., **IV** 659
Embassy Book Co., Ltd., **IV** 635
Embassy Hotel Group, **I** 216; **9** 426
Embassy Suites, **9** 425
Embry-Riddle, **I** 89
Emco, **III** 569
Emerald Coast Water Co., **III** 21
Emerald Technology, Inc., **10** 97
Emerick, Roger, **11** 246
Emerson Drug, **I** 711
Emerson, Edward Octavius, **IV** 548
Emerson Electric Co., II 18–21, 92; **III** 625; **8** 298
Emerson Electric Manufacturing Co., **II** 18
Emerson, John Wesley, **II** 18
Emerson-Brantingham Company, **10** 378
Emery Air Freight, **6** 345–46
Emery Air Freight Corporation, 6 386, **388–91**
Emery Express, **6** 389
Emery Group, **I** 377; **III** 33
Emery, John C., Jr., **6** 388–90
Emery, John Colvin, Sr., **6** 388–89
Emery Worldwide. *See* Emery Air Freight Corporation.
Emeryville Chemical Co., **IV** 408
Emge & Sons, **11** 92
Emge, Oscar, **11** 93
Emge Packing Co., Inc., 11 92–93
Emge, Peter, **11** 92
Emge, Walter, **11** 93
Emhart Corp., **III** 437; **8** 332
EMI Ltd., **I** 531; **6** 240
Emmanuel, Victor, **9** 497–98
Emmerich, Fred, **I** 415
Emmett, Martin, **8** 512–13
Empain, **II** 93
Empain, Edouard, **II** 93
Empain-Schneider, **II** 93
Empire Blue Cross and Blue Shield, III **245–46**; **6** 195
Empire Brewery, **I** 253
Empire Co., **II** 653
Empire Cos., **IV** 391
Empire District Electric, **IV** 391
Empire Gas & Fuel, **IV** 391
Empire Hanna Coal Co., Ltd., **8** 346
Empire Inc., **II** 682
Empire Life and Accident Insurance Co., **III** 217
Empire National Bank, **II** 218
Empire of America, **11** 110
Empire Pencil, **III** 505
Empire Savings, Building & Loan Association, **8** 424

Empire State Group, **IV** 612
Empire State Petroleum, **IV** 374
Empire Trust Co., **II** 218
Employers Reinsurance Corp., **II** 31
Employers' Liability Assurance, **III** 235
Empresa Colombiana de Petróleos, IV **415–18**
Empresa Nacional de Electridad, **I** 459
Empresa Nacional del Petroleo, **IV** 528
Empresa Nacional Electrica de Cordoba, **V** 607
Empresa Nacional Hidro-Electrica del Ribagorzana, **I** 459; **V** 607
Empresa Nacional Hulleras del Norte, **I** 460
Emprise Corporation, **7** 134–35
Ems-Chemi, **III** 760
Enagas, **IV** 528
ENCASO, **IV** 528
ENCI, **IV** 132
Encyclopaedia Britannica Educational Corporation, **7** 165, 167
Encyclopaedia Britannica Films, Inc., **7** 167
Encyclopaedia Britannica International, **7** 167
Encyclopaedia Britannica North America, **7** 167
Encyclopedia Britannica, Inc., 7 165–68
Endata, Inc., **11** 112
Enders, Thomas O., **III** 180
ENDESA Group, V 606–08
Endevco Inc., **11** 28
Endiama, **IV** 67
Endicott Trust Company, **11** 110
Endo Vascular Technologies, Inc., **11** 460
Endrich, Ekkehard, **I** 122
Endsor, Alan, **III** 739
ENECO. *See* Empresa Nacional Electrica de Cordoba.
ENEL. *See* Ente Nazionale per l'Energia Elettrica.
Enercon, Inc., **6** 25
Energen Corp., **6** 583
Energie-Verwaltungs-Gesellschaft, **V** 746
Energizer, **9** 180
Energy Corp. of Louisiana, **V** 619
Enesco Corporation, 11 94–96
Enesco Ltd., **11** 95
Engel, Friedrich Wilhelm, **IV** 105
Engelhard, Charles, **IV** 78–80, 99
Engelhard, Charles, Jr., **IV** 78
Engelhard Corporation, II 54; **IV** 23, **78–80**
Engelhard family, **IV** 79–80
Engelhard Hanovia, **IV** 79–80
Engelhard Industries, **IV** 78–79
Engelhard Minerals & Chemicals Corp., **IV** 79–80
Engelhorn, Frederick, **I** 305
Engellau, Gunnar, **I** 209; **7** 566
Engen, **IV** 93
Engineered Polymers Co., **I** 202
Engineering Co. of Nigeria, **IV** 473
Engineering Company, **9** 16
Engineering for the Petroleum and Process Industries, **IV** 414
Engineering Plastics, Ltd., **8** 377
Engineering Research Associates, **III** 126, 129
England, Frank W., **III** 518
Englander Co., **I** 400
Engländer, Sigismund, **IV** 668
Englehart, Jacob, **IV** 437

English, Calvin, **III** 274
English China Clays Ltd., **III** 689–91
English Clays Lovering Pochin & Co., **III** 690–91
English Condensed Milk Co., **II** 545
English Electric Co., **I** 50; **II** 25, 81; **6** 241
English family, **III** 762
English, Floyd, **10** 97
English Mercantile & General Insurance Co., **III** 376
English Property Corp., **IV** 712
English, Scottish and Australian Bank Ltd., **II** 187–89
ENHER. *See* Empresa Nacional Hidro-Electrica del Ribagorzana.
ENI. *See* Ente Nazionale Idrocarburi.
EniChem, **IV** 413, 422
EniChimica, **IV** 422
ENIEPSA, **IV** 528
Enimont, **IV** 422, 525
Enman, Horace L., **II** 221
Ennand, Alastair, **I** 593
Ennerfelt, Göran, **I** 554
d'Ennetières (Marquis), **II** 201
Ennia, **III** 177, 179, 310
Eno Proprietaries, **III** 65
Enocell Oy, **IV** 277
Enogex, Inc., **6** 539–40
Enpetrol, **IV** 528
Enquirer/Star Group, Inc., 10 287–88
Enrico, Roger, **I** 279
Enron Corp., III 197; **V** 609–10; **6** 457, 593
Enseco, **III** 684
Ensearch Corp., V 611–13
Ensidesa, **I** 460
Ensign Oil Company, **9** 490
Enskilda Fondkommission, **II** 353
Enskilda S.A., **II** 353
Enskilda Securities, **II** 352–53
Enso. *See* Enso Träsliperi AB.
Enso Träsliperi AB, **IV** 274–77
Enso-Gutzeit Osakeyhtiö, **IV** 275
Enso-Gutzeit Oy, IV 274–77
Enstar Corp., **IV** 567
ENSTAR Corporation, **11** 441
Enström, Axel, **IV** 339
Ensys Environmental Products, Inc., **10** 107
ENTASA, **IV** 528
Ente Gestione Aziende Minerarie, **I** 466
Ente Nazionale di Energia Elettrica, **I** 466
Ente Nazionale Elettricità, **IV** 421
Ente Nazionale Idrocarburi, I 369; **IV** 412, **419–22**, 424, 453, 466, 470, 486, 546; **V** 614–17
Ente Nazionale Metano, **IV** 420
Ente Nazionale per l'Energia Elettrica, V 614–17
Entenmann's, **I** 246, 712; **10** 551
Entergy Corp., V 618–20; **6** 496–97
Enterprise Cellular Inc., **6** 393
Enterprise Diversified Holdings, **V** 701–03
Enterprise Leasing, 6 392–93
Enterprise Metals Pty. Ltd., **IV** 61
Enterprise Oil Norge Ltd., **11** 97
Enterprise Oil plc, 11 97–99
Enterprise Rent-A-Car, **6** 392–93
Entity Software, **11** 469
Entrada Industries Incorporated, **6** 568–69
Entré Computer Centers, **6** 243–44
Entremont, **I** 676

Entreprise de Recherches et d'Activités
  Pétrolières, **IV** 453, 467, 544, 560; **7**
  481, 483–84
**Entreprise Nationale Sonatrach, IV
  423–25**; **V** 626, 692; **10** 83–84
Entrex, Inc., **III** 154
Envirex, **11** 361
ENVIRON International Corporation, **10**
  106
Environmental Defense Fund, **9** 305
Environmental Planning & Research. *See*
  CRSS Inc.
Environmental Systems Corporation, **9** 109
Environmental Testing and Certification
  Corporation, **10** 106–07
Enwright Environmental Consulting
  Laboratories, **9** 110
Enzyme Technologies Corp., **I** 342
Eon Productions, **II** 147
Eon Systems, **III** 143; **6** 238
Ephlin, Donald, **7** 461–62, 464
Les Epiceries Presto Limitée, **II** 651
Epoch Systems Inc., **9** 140
Eppert, Ray, **III** 165–66; **6** 281
Eppler, Guerin & Turner, Inc., **III** 330
Eppley, **III** 99
Epsilon Trading Corporation, **6** 81
Epstein, Max, **6** 394
Epstein, Robert, **10** 504
Equator Bank, **II** 298
EQUICOR-Equitable HCA Corp., **III** 80,
  226
Equifax Canada Inc., **6** 25
Equifax Europe, **6** 25
Equifax, Inc., 6 23–25
Equifax Insurance Systems, **6** 25
Equitable Equipment Company, **7** 540
Equitable Gas Company, **6** 493–94
Equitable General Insurance, **III** 248
**Equitable Life Assurance Society of the
  United States**, **II** 330; **III** 80, 229, 237,
  247–49, 274, 289, 291, 305–06, 316,
  329, 359; **IV** 171, 576, 711; **6** 23
Equitable Life Leasing, **III** 249
Equitable Life Mortgage Realty Trust, **III**
  248
Equitable Resources, Inc., 6 492–94
Equitable Trust Co., **II** 247, 397; **10** 61
Equitec Financial Group, **11** 483
Equity & Law, **III** 211
Equity Corp. Tasman, **III** 735
Equity Corporation, **6** 599
Eramet, **IV** 108
Eramet-SLN, **IV** 108
ERAP. *See* Entreprise de Recherches et
  d'Activités Pétrolières.
Erasco, **II** 556
Erburu, Robert, **IV** 677–78
Erdal, **II** 572
Erdölsproduktions-Gesellschaft AG, **IV** 485
Erftwerk AG, **IV** 229
Erhard, Ludwig, **IV** 193; **V** 165–66
Erhart, Charles, **I** 661; **9** 402
Erhart, William, **I** 96
Erho, Eino, **IV** 469
Ericson, Thorsten, **II** 2
Ericson Yachts, **10** 215
Ericssan, AB, **11** 501
Ericsson, **9** 32–33; **11** 196. *See also* L.M.
  Ericsson.
Ericsson, Lars Magnus, **V** 334
Erie and Pennyslvania, **I** 584
Erie County Bank, **9** 474
Erie Railroad, **I** 584; **II** 329; **IV** 180

Erikson, Evans W., **7** 504
Eriksson, Per-Olof, **IV** 204
Eritsusha, **IV** 326
ERKA. *See* Reichs Kredit-Gesellschaft
  mbH.
d'Erlanger, Emile (Baron), **IV** 668; **10** 346
Erlick, Everett, **II** 129
Ernest Oppenheimer and Sons, **IV** 21, 79
Erni, Paul, **I** 634
Ernst & Ernst, **I** 412
Ernst & Whinney. *See* Ernst & Young.
Ernst & Young, 9 198–200, 309, 311; **10**
  115
Ernst, A.C., **I** 412
Ernst, Alwin C., **9** 198
Ernst, Friedrich (Count of Solms-Laubach),
  III 694
Ernst, Henry, **IV** 574; **7** 551
Ernst, Theodore C., **9** 198
Erol's, **9** 74; **11** 556
Eroll (Lord), **IV** 259
ERPI, **7** 167
Errera-Oppenheim, Jacques, **II** 201
Erskine, Massena, **10** 377
Erste Allgemeine, **III** 207–08
Ertan, Ismail, **IV** 563
Ertegun, Ahmet, **II** 176
Erving Distributor Products Co., **IV** 282; **9**
  260
Erwin Wasey & Co., **I** 17, 22
Erzbergbau Salzgitter AG, **IV** 201
ES&A. *See* English, Scottish and
  Australian Bank Ltd.
Esanda, **II** 189
Esau, Abraham, **III** 446
ESB Inc., **IV** 112
Esbjerg Thermoplast, **9** 92
Escambia Chemicals, **I** 298
Escamez, Alfonso, **II** 198
Escanaba Paper Co., **IV** 311
Escarra, Eduard, **9** 148
Escaut et Meuse, **IV** 227
L'Escaut, **III** 335
Escher, Alfred, **II** 267; **III** 375, 410
Escher Wyss, **III** 539, 632
Eschweiler Bergwerks-Verein AG, **IV**
  25–26, 193
Esco Trading, **10** 482
Escoffier, Auguste, **9** 455
Escoffier Ltd., **I** 259
Esdon de Castro, **8** 137
ESE Sports Co. Ltd., **V** 376
ESGM. *See* Elder Smith Goldsbrough
  Mort.
ESI Energy, Inc., **V** 623–24
Eskay Screw Corporation, **11** 536
Eskilstuna Separator, **III** 419
Eskin, Gerald, **10** 358
Esmark, Inc., **I** 441; **II** 448, 468–69; **6** 357
Esperance-Longdoz, **IV** 51–52
ESPN, **II** 131; **IV** 627
Esprit de Corp., 8 169–72
La Espuela Oil Company, Ltd., **IV** 81–82;
  7 186
Esquire Inc., **I** 453; **IV** 672
Esrey, Bill, **9** 478–80
Esrey, William T., **V** 346
Esselte AB, **11** 100
**Esselte Pendaflex Corporation, 11
  100–01**
Essener Reisebüro, **II** 164
Essex Outfitters Inc., **9** 394
Esso, **I** 52; **II** 628; **III** 673; **IV** 276, 397,
  421, 423, 432, 441, 470, 484, 486,

  517–18, 531; **7** 140, 171. *See also*
  Standard Oil Company of New Jersey.
Esso Chemical, **IV** 439
Esso Eastern Inc., **IV** 555
Esso Exploration and Production Australia,
  III 673
Esso Exploration Turkey, **IV** 563
Esso Libya, **IV** 454
Esso Norge, **11** 97
Esso Production Malaysia, **IV** 519
Esso Sirte, **IV** 454
Esso Standard, **IV** 46
Esso Standard Eastern Inc., **IV** 555
Esso Standard Sekiyu K.K., **IV** 432–33,
  555
d'Estaing, Giscard, **II** 265; **IV** 618–19
Estée Lauder Inc., **I** 696; **III** 56; **8** 131; **9**
  201–04; **11** 41
Estel N.V., **IV** 105, 133
Estenfelder, L.G., **9** 243
Estes, Eleanor, **IV** 622
Esteva, Pierre, **III** 393
Estlow, Edward W., **IV** 608; **7** 159
Eston Chemical, **6** 148
Estrin, Judy, **11** 519
ETA Systems, Inc., **10** 256–57
Etablissement Mesnel, **I** 202
Etablissement Poulenc-Frères, **I** 388
Etablissements Pierre Lemonnier S.A., **II**
  532
Eteq Microsystems, **9** 116
Ethan Allen, Inc., **III** 530–31; **10** 184
Ethicon, Inc., **III** 35; **8** 281; **10** 213
Ethyl Corp., **I** 334–36, 342; **IV** 289; **10**
  289–91 (upd.)
Etimex Kunststoffwerke GmbH, **7** 141
L'Etoile, **II** 139
Etos, **II** 641
ETPM Entrêpose, **IV** 468
Eubanks, Gordon E., Jr., **10** 507
Euclid, **I** 147
Euclid Chemical Co., **8** 455–56
Eugster, Jack W., **9** 360–61
Euler, Rudolf, **IV** 140
Euralux, **III** 209
Eurasbank, **II** 279–80
Eureka, **III** 478, 480
Eureka Insurance Co., **III** 343
Eureka Specialty Printing, **IV** 253
Eureka Tent & Awning Co., **III** 59
Eureka X-Ray Tube, Inc., **10** 272
Euro Disney, **6** 174, 176
Euro-Pacific Finance, **II** 389
Euro-RSCG, **10** 345, 347
Eurobel, **II** 139; **III** 200
Eurobrokers Investment Corp., **II** 457
Eurocan Pulp & Paper Co. Ltd., **III** 648;
  IV 276, 300
Eurocard France, **II** 265
Eurocopter Holding, **7** 11
Eurocopter SA, **7** 9, 11
Eurogroup, **V** 65
Euromarché, **10** 205
Euromarket Designs Inc., **9** 144
Euromissile, **7** 9
Euronda, **IV** 296
Europa Metalli, **IV** 174
Europaischen Tanklager- und Transport
  AG, **7** 141
Europcar Interrent, **10** 419
European and African Investments Ltd., **IV**
  21
European Banking Co., **II** 186

European Banks' International Co., **II** 184–86, 295
European Coal and Steel, **II** 402
European Investment Bank, **6** 97
European Periodicals, Publicity and Advertising Corp., **IV** 641; **7** 311
European Petroleum Co., **IV** 562
European-American Banking Corp., **II** 279, 295
Europeia, **III** 403
Europemballage, **I** 600
Europensiones, **III** 348
Eurotec, **IV** 128
Eurotechnique, **III** 678
Eurovida, **III** 348
Evaluation Associates, Inc., **III** 306
Evan Picone, **III** 55
Evans, **V** 21
Evans, Bob, **9** 76
Evans, D. G., **6** 602
Evans, E.P., **7** 286
Evans, Emerson E., **9** 76
Evans, Harold, **IV** 652; **7** 391
Evans, Harry, **IV** 59
Evans, Henry, **III** 240–41
Evans, James S., **7** 327
Evans, John, **11** 384
Evans, John J., **III** 422
Evans, Marshall, **II** 121
Evans, Mary, **10** 124
Evans, Maurice, **IV** 620
Evans, Mike, **I** 196
Evans, P. Wilson, **I** 373
Evans, R.S., **8** 135–36
Evans, Raymond F., **IV** 408–10; **7** 308–09
Evans, T. Mellon, **7** 286
Evans, T.R., **IV** 408; **7** 308
Evans, Thomas Mellon, **8** 135
Evans-Aristocrat Industries, **III** 570
Eve of Roma, **III** 28
Evelyn Haddon, **IV** 91
Evelyn Wood, Inc., **7** 165, 168
Evence Coppée, **III** 704–05
Evening News Association, **IV** 612; **7** 191
Evenson, Terry, **9** 360
L'Evèque, Edouard, **V** 441
Ever Ready Label Corp., **IV** 253
Ever Ready Ltd., **7** 209; **9** 179–80
Everaert, Pierre J., **II** 642
Everest & Jennings, **11** 200
Everest, C.M., **IV** 463; **7** 351
Everest, Hiram Bond, **IV** 463; **7** 351
Everest, Larry, **I** 401
Everett, J.L., III, **11** 389
Everett, James, **V** 696
Everett, Robert G., **9** 452
Evergreen Resources, Inc., **11** 28
Everhart, Rodney L., **10** 407
Everingham, Lyle, **II** 645
Eversharp, **III** 28
Evian, **6** 47, 49
Evill, William, **II** 476
Evinrude Motor Co., **III** 597–99
Evinrude, Ole, **III** 597–98; **8** 71
Evinrude, Ralph, **III** 598
Evinrude-ELTO, **III** 597
Evins, Dan, **10** 258–59
Evren, Kenan (Gen.), **I** 479
Ewald, Earl, **V** 672
Ewald, J.A., **III** 15
Ewaldsen, Hans, **III** 466
Ewart, Peter, **III** 359
Ewell Industries, **III** 739
Ewing, Matthew, **IV** 463; **7** 351

Ewing, Wayne T., **10** 448
Ewo Breweries, **I** 469
Ex-Cell-O Corp., **IV** 297
Exacta, **III** 122
Exatec A/S, **10** 113
Excaliber, **6** 205
Excel Corporation, **11** 92–93
Excelsior Life Insurance Co., **III** 182
Excerpta Medica International, **IV** 610
Exchange & Discount Bank, **II** 318
Exchange Bank of Yarmouth, **II** 210
Exchange Oil & Gas Corp., **IV** 282; **9** 260
Exco International, **10** 277
Execu-Fit Health Programs, **11** 379
Executive Income Life Insurance Co., **10** 246
Executive Life Insurance Co., **III** 253–55; **11** 483
Executive Life Insurance Co. of New York, **III** 253–55
Executive Systems, Inc., **11** 18
Exel Logistics Ltd., **6** 412, 414
Exeter Oil Co., **IV** 550
Exide Electronics, **9** 10
Exley, Charles E., Jr., **III** 152–53; **6** 266
Exors. of James Mills, **III** 493
Expercom, **6** 303
Experience, **III** 359
Exploitasi Tambang Minyak Sumatra Utara, **IV** 492
Explosive Fabricators Corp., **III** 643
Export-Import Bank, **IV** 33, 184
Express Dairies, **I** 247–48
Express Foods Inc, **I** 248
Express Newspapers plc, **IV** 687
Extel Corp., **II** 142; **III** 269–70
Extel Financial Ltd., **IV** 687
Extendicare Health Services, Inc., III 81; **6 181–83**
Extendicare Ltd., **6** 181
Extracorporeal Medical Specialties, **III** 36
Exxon Chemicals, **V** 605
Exxon Co. USA, **IV** 428
Exxon Corporation, I 16–17, 360, 364; **II** 16, 62, 431, 451; **IV** 171, 363, 365, 403, 406, **426–30**, 431–33, 437–38, 454, 466, 506, 508, 512, 515, 522, 537–39, 554; **7 169–73 (upd.)**, 230, 538, 559; **9** 440–41; **11** 353
Exxon Research and Engineering Co., **IV** 554
Eyde, Sam, **10** 437
Eyeful Home Co., **III** 758
Eyelab, **II** 560
Eyton, Trevor, **II** 456; **10** 529–30
EZ Paintr Corporation, **9** 374
Ezell, John Samuel, **IV** 445
Ezra, Derek (Sir), **IV** 40

F & R Builders, Inc., **11** 257
F. & F. Koenigkramer Company, **10** 272
F.& J. Heinz, **II** 507
F. & M. Schaefer Brewing Co., **I** 253, 291, **III** 137
F. & M. Schaefer Corp., **III** 137
F & M Scientific Corp., **III** 142; **6** 237
F.A. Ensign Company, **6** 38
F.A.I. Insurances, **III** 729
F.A.O. Schwarz, **I** 548
F&G International Insurance, **III** 397
F. Atkins & Co., **I** 604
F.E. Compton Company, **7** 167
F.F. Dalley Co., II 497

F.F. Publishing and Broadsystem Ltd., **IV** 652; **7** 392
F.H. Tomkins Buckle Company Ltd., **11** 525
F. Hoffmann-La Roche & Co. A.G., **I** 637, 640, **642–44**, 657, 685, 693, 710; **7** 427; **9** 264; **10** 80, 549
F.J. Walker Ltd., **I** 438
F.K.I. Babcock, **III** 466
F. Kanematsu & Co., Ltd., **IV** 442
F.L. Industries Inc., **I** 481, 483
F.L. Moseley Co., **III** 142; **6** 237
F.N. Burt Co., **IV** 644
F. Perkins, **III** 651–52
F.S. Smithers, **II** 445
F.W. Dodge Corp., **IV** 636–37
F.W. Means & Company, **11** 337
F.W. Sickles Company, **10** 319
F.W. Williams Holdings, **III** 728
F.W. Woolworth Co., **II** 414; **IV** 344; **V** 225–26
Fabergé, Inc., **II** 590; **III** 48; **8** 168, 344; **11** 90
Fabius, Laurent, **II** 117, 260; **10** 195
Fabrica de Cemento El Melan, **III** 671
Facchin Foods Co., **I** 457
Facit, **III** 480
Fadiman, Clifton, **IV** 671
FAG Kugelfischer, **11** 84
Fagersta, **II** 366; **IV** 203
Fahr AG, **III** 543
Fahrni, Fritz, **III** 633
Fahrzeugwerke Eisenach, **I** 138
FAI, **III** 545–46
Faid, Mustapha, **IV** 425
Failkov, Herman, **11** 462
Faina, Carlo, **I** 368–69
Fair, James G., **II** 381
Fairbank, Richard D., **11** 448
Fairbanks, Douglas, **I** 537; **II** 146–47
Fairbanks Morse Co., **I** 158; **10** 292
Fairbanks Morse Weighing Systems, **I** 434–35
Fairbanks Whitney Co., **I** 434
Fairchild Aircraft, Inc., 9 205–08, 460; **11** 278
Fairchild Camera, **6** 262
Fairchild Camera and Instrument Corp., **II** 50; **III** 110, 141, 455, 618; **6** 261; **7** 531; **10** 108; **11** 503
Fairchild Communications Service, **8** 328
Fairchild, Frank L., **II** 14
Fairchild Industries, **I** 71, 198; **11** 438
Fairchild Photographic, **II** 63
Fairchild Semiconductor Corporation, **II** 44–45, 63–65; **III** 115; **6** 215, 247; **10** 365–66
Fairchild, Sherman, **9** 205
Fairclough Construction Group plc, I 567–68
Fairclough, Leonard, **I** 567
Fairclough, Leonard Miller, **I** 567–68
Fairey Industries Ltd., **IV** 659
Fairfax, **IV** 650
Fairfax, Edward, **7** 251
Fairfax, James Oswald, **7** 251
Fairfax, James Reading, **7** 251
Fairfax, John, **7** 251
Fairfax, Warwick, **7** 251–53
Fairfax, Warwick, Jr., **7** 253
Fairless, Benjamin F., **IV** 573; **7** 550
Fairmont Foods, **7** 430
Fairmount Glass Company, **8** 267
Faisal, King (Saudi Arabia), **I** 559

Falck, Alexander D., **III** 683
Falcon Oil Co., **IV** 396
Falcon Seaboard Inc., **II** 86; **IV** 410; **7** 309
Falconbridge, Ltd., **IV** 165–66
Falconbridge Nickel Mines Ltd., **IV** 111
Falconet Corp., **I** 45
Falk, Ralph, **I** 627; **10** 141
Falkingham, R.P., **7** 252–53
Fall, Albert B., **IV** 688
Fallon, Edmund H., **7** 17
Fallon, Walter A., **III** 476; **7** 162
Falls National Bank of Niagara Falls, **11** 108
Falls Rubber Company, **8** 126
Famalette, Joseph P., **11** 15
Family Health Program, **6** 184
Family Life Insurance Co., **II** 425
Family Mart Company, **V** 188
Family Mart Group, **V** 188
Famosa Bakery, **II** 543
Famous Players, **I** 451; **II** 154; **6** 161–62
Famous Players in Famous Plays, **II** 154
Famous Players-Lasky Corp., **II** 154
Fannie Mae. *See* Federal National Mortgage Association.
Fantus Co., **IV** 605
Fanuc Ltd., III 482–83
Far East Airlines, **6** 70
Far East Machinery Co., **III** 581
Far West Restaurants, **I** 547
Faraday, Michael, **III** 679
Faraday National Corporation, **10** 269
Farben. *See* I.G. Farbenindustrie AG.
Farbenfabriken Bayer A.G., **I** 309
Farbwerke Hoechst A.G., **I** 346–47; **IV** 486
Fargo, Charles, **II** 381
Fargo, James C., **II** 395–97; **10** 60–61
Fargo, William G., **II** 380–81, 395–96; **10** 59–60
Farine Lactée Henri Nestlé, **II** 545
Farinon Corp., **II** 38
Farley, James, **III** 307; **10** 174
Farley, Laurence, **III** 437; **V** 152
Farley Northwest Industries Inc., I 440–41
Farley, Raymond F., **III** 59
Farley, William Francis, **I** 441; **8** 201–02, 568
Farm Credit Bank of St. Louis, **8** 489
Farm Credit Bank of St. Paul, **8** 489–90
Farm Electric Services Ltd., **6** 586
Farm Power Laboratory, **6** 565
Farman, Henri, **7** 9
Farmers and Merchants Bank, **II** 349
Farmers Bank of Delaware, **II** 315–16
Farmers National Bank & Trust Co., **9** 474
Farmers Regional Cooperative, **II** 536
Farmers' Loan and Trust Co., **II** 254; **9** 124
Farmland Foods, Inc., 7 174–75
Farmland Industries, **IV** 474; **7** 17, 174–75
Farnam Cheshire Lime Co., **III** 763
Farquhar, Percival, **IV** 54
Farrar, Straus & Giroux, **IV** 622, 624
Farrell, David, **V** 134
Farrell, Roy, **6** 78
Farrington, George, **III** 355
Farrington, John, **III** 355
Farwell, Simeon, **8** 53
Fasco Industries, **III** 509
Faserwerke Hüls GmbH., **I** 350
Fashion Bug, **8** 97
Fashion Bug Plus, **8** 97

Fashion Co., **II** 503; **10** 324
Fasquelle, **IV** 618
Fasson, **IV** 253
Fasson Europe, **IV** 253
Fast Fare, **7** 102
Fata, **IV** 187
Fatjo, Tom, Jr., **V** 749
Fatt, Arthur, **6** 26–27
Fatum, **III** 308
Fauber, Bernard M., **V** 112
Faugere et Jutheau, **III** 283
Faulkner, Dawkins & Sullivan, **II** 450
Faulkner, Eric O., **II** 308–09
Faulkner, Harry, **III** 420
Faulkner, Harry G., **III** 420, 479
Faulkner, William, **I** 25; **IV** 586
Faust, Levin, **7** 502
La Favorita Bakery, **II** 543
Fayette Tubular Products, **7** 116–17
Fazio, Carl, **9** 451–52
Fazio, Frank, **9** 451
Fazio, John, **9** 452
FBC. *See* First Boston Corp.
FBO. *See* Film Booking Office of America.
FCBC, **IV** 174
FCC. *See* Federal Communications Commission.
FCC National Bank, **II** 286
FDIC. *See* Federal Deposit Insurance Corp.
Fearn International, **II** 525
Fechheimer Bros. Co., **III** 215
Fechheimer, Samuel, **V** 207
Federal Barge Lines, **6** 487
Federal Bearing and Bushing, **I** 158–59
Federal Bicycle Corporation of America, **11** 3
Federal Coca-Cola Bottling Co., **10** 222
Federal Communications Commission, **6** 164–65; **9** 321
Federal Deposit Insurance Corp., **II** 261–62, 285, 337
Federal Express Corporation, II 620; **V 451–53**; **6** 345–46, 385–86, 389
Federal Home Life Insurance Co., **III** 263; **IV** 623
Federal Home Loan Bank, **II** 182
Federal Insurance Co., **III** 220–21
Federal Lead Co., **IV** 32
Federal Light and Traction Company, **6** 561–62
Federal Mining and Smelting Co., **IV** 32
Federal National Mortgage Association, **II 410–11**
Federal Pacific Electric, **II** 121; **9** 440
Federal Packaging and Partition Co., **8** 476
Federal Paper Board, **I** 524
Federal Paper Board Company, Inc., 8 173–75
Federal Paper Mills, **IV** 248
Federal Signal Corp., 10 295–97
Federal Steel Co., **II** 330; **IV** 572; **7** 549
Federal Trade Commission, **6** 260; **9** 370
Federal Yeast Corp., **IV** 410
Federal-Mogul Corporation, I 158–60; **III** 596; **10 292–94 (upd.)**
Federale Mynbou, **IV** 90–93
Federale Mynbou/General Mining, **IV** 90
Federated Department Stores Inc., IV 703; **V** 25–28; **9 209–12**; **10** 282; **11** 349
Federated Development Company, **8** 349
Federated Metals Corp., **IV** 32
Federated Publications, **IV** 612; **7** 191

Federated Timbers, **I** 422
Federico, Corrado, **8** 170–71
Fedmart, **V** 162
Feehan, John, **6** 449
Fehlmann, Heinrich, **III** 403
Feikes & Sohn KG, **IV** 325
Feinblech-Contiglühe, **IV** 103
Feith, Marc, **6** 295
Feizal, King (Iraq), **IV** 558
Felco. *See* Farmers Regional Cooperative.
Feldberg, Stanley, **V** 197
Feldberg, Sumner, **V** 197
Feldman, Alvin L., **I** 98
Feldman, Elliot J., **I** 53
Feldmühle AG, **II** 51; **III** 692–93
Feldmühle Cellulose Factory, **III** 692
Feldmühle Corp., **III** 693
Feldmühle Kyocera Elektronische Bauelemente GmbH., **II** 50
Feldmühle Nobel AG, III 692–95; **IV** 142, 325, 337
Feldmühle Paper and Cellulose Works AG, **III** 692–93
Feldmühle Silesian Sulphite and Cellulose Factory, **III** 692
Felker, G. Stephen, **8** 558–60
Felker, George W., III, **8** 558
Felker, George W., Jr., **8** 558
Felten & Guilleaume, **IV** 25
Femtech, **8** 513
Fendel Schiffahrts-Aktiengesellschaft, **6** 426
Fenestra Inc., **IV** 136
Feninger, Claude, **III** 99
Fenner & Beane, **II** 424
Fenwal Laboratories, **I** 627; **10** 141
Fergusen, Sydney, **IV** 311
Ferguson, Archibald, **IV** 604
Ferguson, C.C., **III** 260
Ferguson, Daniel C., **9** 374–75
Ferguson, Daryl, **7** 89
Ferguson, Francis, **III** 323–24
Ferguson, Harry, **III** 651
Ferguson, Harry S., **I** 415
Ferguson, Jerry, **10** 156, 158
Ferguson, Leonard, **9** 374–75
Ferguson Machine Co., **8** 135
Ferguson, Malcolm P., **I** 142
Ferguson Radio Corp., **I** 531–32
Ferguson, Robert R., **9** 223
Ferguson, Robert R., Jr., **9** 223
Fergusson, E.B., **III** 372
Ferienreise GmbH., **II** 164
Ferland, E. James, **V** 703
Fermentaciones Mexicanas, **III** 43
Fernandez, Ronald, **I** 86
Fernando Roqué, **6** 404
Ferngas, **IV** 486
Ferrand, Camilo, **IV** 507
Ferranti, Basil de, **6** 241
Ferranti Ltd., **II** 81; **6** 240
de Ferranti, Sebastian, **III** 433
Ferrari, **I** 162; **11** 103
Ferrari, Enzo, **I** 162; **11** 103
Ferrier Hodgson, **10** 170
Ferris, Richard, **I** 129–30; **6** 129–30
Ferro (Holland) B.V., **8** 178
Ferro Brazil, **8** 177
Ferro Corporation, 8 176–79; **9** 10
Ferro Enamel & Supply Co., **8** 176
Ferro Enamel S.A., **8** 177
Ferro Enameling Company, **8** 176
Ferro Enameling Company (England) Limited, **8** 176

Ferro Enamels (Pty.) Ltd., **8** 177
Ferro Enamels Ltd., **8** 177
Ferro France, **8** 177
Ferro Manufacturing Corp., **III** 536
Ferruzzi, **I** 369
Ferruzzi Agricola Finanziario, **7** 81–83
Ferry, Jules, **IV** 614
Fery, John, **IV** 256; **8** 66–67
Fesca, **III** 417–18
Fetzer Vineyards, **10** 182
FHP, Inc., **6** 185
**FHP International Corporation, 6
184–86**
FHP Life Insurance Company, **6** 185
Fiat Avianzione, **9** 418
Fiat Group, I 154, 157, **161–63**, 459–60,
466, 479; **II** 280; **III** 206, 543, 591; **IV**
420; **11** 104, 139
Fiat S.p.A., 9 10; **11 102–04 (upd.)**
Fiber Chemical Corporation, **7** 308
Fiberglas Canada, **III** 722
Fibermux, **10** 19
Fibiger, John A., **III** 314
Fibre Containers, **IV** 249
Fibreboard Containers, **IV** 249
Fibreboard Corp., **IV** 304
FibreChem, Inc., **8** 347
Fibro Tambor, S.A. de C.V., **8** 476
Fichtel & Sachs, **III** 566
Fidata Corp., **II** 317
Fidelco Capital Group, **10** 420
Fidelity and Casualty Co. of New York,
III 242
Fidelity and Guaranty Fire Corp., **III** 396
Fidelity and Guaranty Insurance Co., **III**
397
Fidelity and Guaranty Insurance
Underwriters, **III** 396
Fidelity and Guaranty Life Insurance Co.,
III 396–97
Fidelity Brokerage Services Inc., **II** 413; **8**
194
Fidelity Federal Savings and Loan, **II** 420
Fidelity Fire Insurance Co., **III** 240
Fidelity Institutional Services, **II** 413
Fidelity Insurance of Canada, **III** 396–97
Fidelity International, **II** 412
Fidelity Investments, II 412–13; **III** 588
Fidelity Investments, **9** 239. *See also* FMR
Corp.
Fidelity Investments Southwest, **II** 413
Fidelity Life Association, **III** 269
Fidelity Management and Research Co., **II**
412
Fidelity Management Trust Co., **II** 413
Fidelity Marketing Co., **II** 413
Fidelity Mutual Insurance Co., **III** 231
Fidelity National Financial, **II** 413
Fidelity National Life Insurance Co., **III**
191
Fidelity Oil Group, **7** 324
Fidelity Savings and Loan Co., **II** 420
Fidelity Service Co., **II** 412
Fidelity Systems Co., **II** 413
Fidelity Title and Trust Co., **II** 315
Fidelity Trust Co., **II** 230
Fidelity Union Life Insurance Co., **III** 185
Fidelity-Phenix Fire Insurance Co., **III**
240–42
Field, Almeron, **9** 266
Field, Cyrus W., **III** 228
Field Enterprises, **IV** 672
Field, Kenneth, **9** 83–84
Field, Marshall, **IV** 629, 672; **9** 213

Field Oy, **10** 113
Fieldcrest Cannon, Inc., 8 32–33; **9
213–17**
Fieldcrest Mills. *See* Fieldcrest Cannon,
Inc.
Fieldhouse, William, **IV** 248
Fielding, Charles (Sir), **IV** 190
Fielding, Thomas, **III** 278
Fields, Bill, **IV** 194
Fields, Ernest S., **6** 466
Fields, Michael S., **6** 274
Fields, W.C., **I** 20; **II** 155
Fields, William R., **8** 556
Fieldstone Cabinetry, **III** 571
Fife, William J., Jr., **10** 329–30
Fifteen Oil, **I** 526
Fifth Generation Systems Inc., **10** 509
Fifth Third Bancorp., **9** 475; **11** 466
Figgie, Harry E., Jr., **7** 176–78
Figgie International Inc., 7 176–78
Figgins, David, **I** 585
Figi's Inc., **9** 218, 220
Filene, Lincoln, **IV** 252
Filene's, **V** 132, 134
Filer, John H., **III** 182
Filkowski, Walter J., **III** 86
Fill, Dennis C., **9** 7–8
Filles S.A. de C.V., **7** 115
Fillon, René, **IV** 107
Film Booking Office of America, **II** 88
Filtrol Corp., **IV** 123
Fin. Comit SpA, **II** 192
FINA, Inc., 7 179–81
Financial Computer Services, Inc., **11** 111
Financial Corp. of Indonesia, **II** 257
Financial Data Services, Inc., **11** 111
Financial Investment Corp. of Asia, **III**
197
Financial Network Marketing Company, **11**
482
Financial News Ltd., **IV** 658
Financial Security Assurance, **III** 765
Financial Services Corp., **III** 306–07
Financial Services Corporation of
Michigan, **11** 163
Financial Systems, Inc., **11** 111
Financière Crédit Suisse-First Boston, **II**
268, 402–04
Financière de Suez, **II** 295
Financière Saint Dominique, **9** 151–52
FinansSkandic (UK), **II** 352
FinansSkandic A.B., **II** 353
Finast, **II** 642
Finazzo, Paul, **9** 272
Fincantieri, **I** 466–67
Finch, Harry, **8** 379–80
Fincham, Allister, **IV** 66
Finck, Thomas G., **11** 539
Finck, Wilhelm, **III** 183
Findlater, John, **8** 448
Findus, **II** 547
Fine Fare, **II** 465, 609, 628–29
Fine, William C., **III** 745
Finelettrica, **I** 465–66
Fingerhut Companies, Inc., I 613; **V** 148;
9 218–20
Fingerhut, Manny, **9** 218
Fininvest Group, **IV** 587–88
Fink, Henry, **V** 484; **6** 520
Fink, Peter R., **I** 679
Finkelstein, David, **7** 335
Finkelstein, Edward S., **V** 169–70; **8**
443–45
Finland Wood Co., **IV** 275

Finlay Forest Industries, **IV** 297
Finlayson, David, **II** 188
Finley, Peter, **III** 673
Finmare, **I** 465, 467
Finmeccanica, **II** 86
Finn, Richard G., **8** 107
Finnair Oy, I 120; **6 87–89**
Finnforest Oy, **IV** 316
Finnie, Charles, **6** 349
Finnigan Corporation, **11** 513
Finnish Cable Works, **II** 69
Finnish Fiberboard Ltd., **IV** 302
Oy Finnish Peroxides Ab, **IV** 300
Finnish Rubber Works, **II** 69
Finniston, Monty (Sir), **IV** 43
Oy Finnlines Ltd., **IV** 276
Finsa, **II** 196
Finservizi SpA, **II** 192
Finsider, **I** 465–66; **IV** 125
Fire Association of Philadelphia, **III**
342–43
Fireman, Paul B., **9** 436–37
Fireman's Corp., **III** 250–51
Fireman's Fund American Insurance Cos.,
III 251
Fireman's Fund Corp., **III** 252
Fireman's Fund Indemnity Co., **III** 251
Fireman's Fund Insurance Co. of Texas,
III 251
Fireman's Fund Insurance Company, I
418; **II** 398; **III** 214, **250–52**, 263; **10**
62
Fireman's Fund Mortgage Corp., **III** 252
Fireman's Fund of Canada, **II** 457
Firemen's Insurance Co. of Newark, **III**
241–42
Firestone Tire and Rubber Co., **III** 440,
697; **V** 234–35; **8** 80; **9** 247
The First, **10** 340
First Acadiana National Bank, **11** 107
First American Bank Corporation, **8** 188
First American National Bank-Eastern, **11**
111
First and Merchants, **10** 426
First Bancard, Inc., **11** 106
First Bank and Trust of Mechanicsburg, **II**
342
First Bank of the United States, **II** 213,
253
First Bank Systems Inc., **11** 130
First Boston Corp., **II** 208, 257, 267–69,
402–04, 406–07, 426, 434, 441; **9** 378,
386. *See also* CS First Boston Inc.
First Boston Inc., **II** 402–04
First Boston, London Ltd., **II** 402
First Brands Corporation, 8 180–82
First Capital Financial, **8** 229
First Chicago Corporation, II 284–87
First City Bank of Rosemead, **II** 348
First Colony Farms, **II** 584
First Colony Life Insurance, **I** 334–35; **10**
290
The First Commerce Community
Development Corporation, **11** 107
First Commerce Corporation, 11 105–07
First Commerce Financial Corp., **11** 106
First Commercial Savings and Loan, **10**
340
First Consumers National Bank, **10** 491
First Dallas, Ltd., **II** 415
First Data Corp., **10** 63
First Data Management Company of
Oklahoma City, **11** 112
First Delaware Life Insurance Co., **III** 254

First Deposit Corp., **III** 218–19
First Deposit National Bank, **III** 219
First Empire Bank International N.V., **11** 109
First Empire Overseas Corporation, **11** 109
First Empire State Corporation, 11 108–10
First Engine and Boiler Insurance Co. Ltd., **III** 406
First Executive Corporation, III 253–55
First Federal Savings & Loan Assoc., **IV** 343; **9** 173
First Federal Savings and Loan Association of Crisp County, **10** 92
First Federal Savings and Loan Association of Hamburg, **10** 91
First Federal Savings and Loan Association of Fort Myers, **9** 476
First Federal Savings and Loan Association of Kalamazoo, **9** 482
First Federal Savings Bank of Brunswick, **10** 92
First Fidelity Bank, N.A., New Jersey, 9 221–23
First Financial Bank, **11** 113
First Financial Management Corporation, 11 111–13
First Florida Banks, **9** 59
First Hawaiian Creditcorp, Inc., **11** 115
First Hawaiian, Inc., 11 114–16
First Health, **III** 373
FIRST HEALTH Strategies, **11** 113
First Heights, fsa, **8** 437
First Industrial Corp., **II** 41
First Insurance Co. of Hawaii, **III** 191, 242
First International Trust, **IV** 91
First Interstate Bancorp, II 228, 288–90; 8 295; **9** 334
First Interstate Bank Ltd., **II** 289
First Interstate Bank of California, **II** 289
First Interstate Bank of Colorado, **II** 289
First Interstate Bank of Texas, **II** 289
First Interstate Discount Brokerage, **II** 289
First Investment Advisors, **11** 106
First Investors Management Corp., **11** 106
First Jersey National Bank, **II** 334
First Liberty Financial Corporation, **11** 457
First Line Insurance Services, Inc., **8** 436
First Mid America, **II** 445
First Mississippi Corporation, 8 183–86
First National Bank, **10** 298
First National Bank (Revere), **II** 208
First National Bank and Trust Company of Kalamazoo, **8** 187–88
First National Bank and Trust of Oklahoma City, **II** 289
First National Bank in Albuquerque, **11** 119
First National Bank of Akron, **9** 475
First National Bank of Allentown, **11** 296
First National Bank of Azusa, **II** 382
First National Bank of Boston, **II** 207–08, 402
First National Bank of Carrollton, **9** 475
First National Bank of Chicago, **II** 242, 257, 284–87; **III** 96–97; **IV** 135–36
First National Bank of Commerce, **11** 106
First National Bank of Harrington, Delaware. *See* J.C. Penny National Bank.
First National Bank of Hawaii, **11** 114
First National Bank of Highland, **11** 109
The First National Bank of Lafayette, **11** 107

The First National Bank of Lake Charles, **11** 107
First National Bank of Lake City, **II** 336; **10** 425
First National Bank of Mexico, New York, **II** 231
First National Bank of New York, **II** 254, 330
First National Bank of Raleigh, **II** 336
First National Bank of Salt Lake, **11** 118
First National Bank of Seattle, **8** 469–70
First National Bank of York, **II** 317
First National Boston Corp., **II** 208
First National Casualty Co., **III** 203
First National City Bank, **9** 124
First National City Bank of New York, **II** 254; **9** 124
First National City Corp., **III** 220–21
First National Insurance Co., **III** 352
First National Life Insurance Co., **III** 218
First National Supermarkets, Inc., **II** 641–42; **9** 452
First Nationwide Bank, **8** 30
First Nationwide Financial Corp., **I** 167; **11** 139
First Nitrogen, Inc., **8** 184
First of America Bank Corporation, 8 187–89
First of America Bank-Monroe, **9** 476
First of Boston, **II** 402–03
First Penn-Pacific Life Insurance Co., **III** 276
First Railroad and Banking Company, **11** 111
First Republic Bank of Texas, **II** 336
First RepublicBank, **II** 337; **10** 426
First RepublicBank Corporation, **10** 425
First Savings and Loan, **10** 339
First Savings and Loan of Oakland, **10** 339
First Seattle Dexter Horton National Bank, **8** 470
First Security Bank of Idaho, N.A., **11** 117
First Security Bank of Nevada, **11** 119
First Security Bank of New Mexico, **11** 117
First Security Bank of Utah, N.A., **11** 117
First Security Corporation, 11 117–19
First Signature Bank and Trust Co., **III** 268
1st State Bank & Trust, **9** 474
First SunAmerican Life Insurance Company, **11** 482
First Tennessee National Corporation, 11 120–21
First Texas Pharmaceuticals, **I** 678
First Trust and Savings Bank, **II** 284
First Union Corporation, 10 298–300
First Union Mortgage Corporation, **10** 298
First Union Trust and Savings Bank, **II** 284–85; **11** 126
First United Financial Services Inc., **II** 286
First USA, Inc., 11 122–24
First Virginia Banks, Inc., 11 125–26
First Westchester National Bank of New Rochelle, **II** 236
First Western Bank and Trust Co., **II** 289
Firstamerica Bancorporation, **II** 288–89
Firstar Corporation, 11 127–29
FirstMiss, Inc., **8** 185
FirstRepublic Corp., **II** 383
Fischbach & Moore, **III** 535
Fischbach Corp., **III** 198; **8** 536–37
Fischer, Alois, **II** 163
Fischer, Franz, **IV** 534

Fischer, Hermann, **IV** 104
Fischer, Jürgen, **II** 163
Fischer, William, **7** 128
FISCOT, **10** 337
Fiserv Inc., 11 130–32
Fisher & Company, **9** 16
Fisher, A.R., **III** 707; **7** 292
Fisher Body Company, **I** 171; **10** 325
Fisher, Carl, **III** 220; **9** 16
Fisher, Charles, **9** 451
Fisher, Charles T., III, **11** 341
Fisher, Charles T., Jr., **11** 340
Fisher Corp., **II** 92
Fisher, Donald G., **V** 60–62
Fisher, Doris F., **V** 60–62
Fisher, Edwin, **II** 236
Fisher, Ellwood, **9** 451
Fisher Foods, Inc., **II** 602; **9** 451, 452
Fisher, George, **10** 431
Fisher, Henry (Sir), **III** 280
Fisher, Jerome, **11** 348–49
Fisher, John W., **I** 597–98; **10** 129, 130, 133
Fisher, Kenneth G., **10** 240
Fisher, L.G., **IV** 344
Fisher, Manning, **9** 451
Fisher Marine, **III** 444
Fisher, Richard, **II** 432
Fisher Scientific Co., **III** 512
Fisher Scientific Group, **III** 511–12
Fisher, Shelton, **IV** 636
Fisher-Price Toy Co., **II** 559–60
Fishers Agricultural Holdings, **II** 466
Fishers Nutrition, **II** 466
Fishers Seed and Grain, **II** 466
Fishery Department of Tamura Kisen Co., **II** 552
Fishman, Katherine Davis, **III** 117
Fishman, William, **II** 607–08
Fisk, James, **II** 329
Fisk, James, Jr., **9** 370
Fisk, Kirby H., **I** 415
Fisk Telephone Systems, **6** 313
Fiske, Haley, **III** 266, 291–92
Fison, Packard, Prentice and Co. *See* Fisons plc.
Fisons, James, **9** 224
Fisons Ltd. *See* Fisons plc.
Fisons plc, 9 224–27
Fitchburg Daily News Co., **IV** 581
Fitchell and Sachs, **III** 495
Fitel, **III** 491
Fites, Donald V., **III** 453
Fitzgerald, Edmund, **III** 323
Fitzgerald, Ernest A., **II** 33
Fitzgerald, Frederick, **IV** 437
Fitzgibbons, James, **9** 217
Fitzhugh, Gilbert, **III** 292–93
Fitzpatrick, Don, **10** 238
Fitzsimonds, Roger L., **11** 129
Fjestul, Dean, **8** 22
FL Industries Holdings, Inc., **11** 516
Flachglass A.G., **II** 474
Flagler, Henry, **IV** 426–27; **7** 169–70
Flagler, Henry M., **8** 486–87
Flagstar Companies, Inc., 10 301–03
Flamson, Richard, III, **II** 349–50
Flanagan (Capt.), **IV** 415
Flanagan McAdam Resources Inc., **IV** 76
Flannery, Joseph, **9** 119
Flatbush Gas Co., **6** 455–56
Flavin, Joseph, **II** 10
Fleck, Alexander (Sir), **IV** 38
Fleer Corporation, **10** 402

Fleet (Lord Thomson of). *See* Thomson, Roy (Lord of Fleet).
Fleet Call, Inc., **10** 431–32
Fleet Financial Group, Inc., 9 228–30
Fleet Holdings, **IV** 687
Fleet/Norstar Financial Group, **9** 229
Fleetway, **7** 244
Fleetwood Credit Corp., **III** 484–85
Fleetwood Enterprises, Inc., III 484–85
Fleischmann Co., **II** 544; **7** 367
Fleischmann Malting Co., **I** 420–21; **11** 22
Fleming, Alexander, **I** 661; **III** 65
Fleming Co. Inc., **II** 624
Fleming Companies, Inc., II 624–25, 671; **7** 450
Fleming, Douglas, **7** 82
Fleming Foods Co., **II** 624
Fleming, Ian, **IV** 79
Fleming, James D., **III** 644
Fleming Machine Co., **III** 435
Fleming, Ned, **II** 624
Fleming, O.A., **II** 624
Fleming-Wilson Co., **II** 624
Flender, P., **III** 239
Fletcher, Andrew, **IV** 278
Fletcher Brothers Ltd., **IV** 278
Fletcher Challenge Canada Ltd., **IV** 279
Fletcher Challenge Ltd., IV 250, **278–80**
Fletcher Construction Co. Ltd., **IV** 278–79
Fletcher Fishing, **IV** 280
Fletcher Holdings Ltd., **III** 687; **IV** 278–79
Fletcher, Hugh, **IV** 279–80
Fletcher, James, **IV** 278–79
Fletcher, James C., **IV** 279
Fletcher, John, **IV** 278
Fletcher Trust and Investment Ltd., **IV** 279
Fletcher, William, **IV** 278
Fleuve Noir, **IV** 614
Flexi-Van Corp., **II** 492
Flexible Packaging, **I** 605
FLGI Holding Company, **10** 321
Flick, Friedrich Christian, **III** 695
Flick, Friedrich Karl (Dr.), **I** 150, 548–49; **II** 280; **III** 692, 695
Flick, Gert Rudolf, **III** 695
Flick Industrial Group, **II** 280, 283; **III** 692–95
Flight Transportation Co., **II** 408
FlightSafety International, Inc., 9 231–33
Flint and Walling Water Systems, **III** 570
Flint, Charles Ranlett, **III** 147; **6** 250
Flint Eaton & Co., **I** 627
Le Floch-Prigent, Loïk, **I** 389–90; **IV** 547; **7** 484–85; **10** 471–72
Floden, Per, **I** 665
Flood, James, **II** 381
Florescue, Barry W., **II** 614
Florey, Howard, **I** 661
Flori Roberts, Inc., **11** 208
Florida Cypress Gardens, Inc., **IV** 623
Florida East Coast Railway Company, **8** 486–87
Florida Gas Transmission Company, **6** 578
Florida National Banks of Florida, Inc., **II** 252
Florida Power & Light Co., **V** 623–24
Florida Power Corp., **V** 621–23
Florida Presbyterian College, **9** 187
Florida Progress Corp., V 621–22
Florida Telephone Company, **6** 323
FloridaGulf Airlines, **11** 300
Florsheim, Harold, **9** 234–35
Florsheim, Irving, **9** 234

Florsheim, Milton, **9** 234
Florsheim Shoe Company, III 528–29; **9** 135, **234–36**
Flower Gate, **I** 266
Flowerree, Robert, **IV** 282; **9** 260
Floyd West & Co., **6** 290
Floyd West of Louisiana, **6** 290
Fluor Corporation, I 569–71, 586; **III** 248; **IV** 171, 533, 535, 576; **6** 148–49; **8 190–93 (upd.)**
Fluor Daniel Inc., **8** 190, 192
Fluor, J. Robert, **I** 570–71; **8** 191–92
Fluor, J. Simon, **8** 190–91
Fluor, J. Simon, Jr., **8** 190–91
Fluor, John Simon, **I** 569–70
Fluor, John Simon, Jr., **I** 569–70
Fluor, Peter Earl, **I** 569–70; **8** 190–91
Flushing National Bank, **II** 230
Flying Tiger Line, **V** 452; **6** 388
Flymo, **III** 478, 480
Flynn, Dennis T., **7** 409
Flynn, Donald, **9** 73
Flynn, Errol, **I** 175
FMC Corp., I 442–44, 679; **II** 513; **11 133–35 (upd.)**
FMR Corp., II 412; **8 194–96**
FMR Investment Management Service Inc., **II** 412
FN Life Insurance Co., **III** 192
FNC Comercio, **III** 221
FNCB. *See* First National City Bank of New York.
FNMA. *See* Federal National Mortgage Association.
Focke Wulf, **III** 641
Fodens Ltd., **I** 186
Fokker. *See* Koninklijke Nederlandse Vliegtuigenfabriek Fokker.
Fokker Aircraft Corporation of America, **9** 16
Fokker, Anthony H.G., **I** 54, 56, 73
Fokker V.F.W., **I** 41–42
Foley, Harold, **IV** 307
Foley, Milton Joseph (Joe), **IV** 307
Foley, Patrick, **6** 386
Foley, Paul, **I** 17
Folgers, **III** 52
Folland Aircraft, **I** 50; **III** 508
Folley, Clyde, **III** 527
Follis, R. Gwin, **IV** 386
Fonda, Henry, **II** 143
Fonda, Peter, **II** 136
Fondiaria Group, **III** 351
Fonditalia Management, **III** 347
Font & Vaamonde, **6** 27
Font Vella, **II** 474
FONTAC, **II** 73
Fontana Asphalt, **III** 674
Food City, **II** 649–50
Food Giant, **II** 670
Food Investments Ltd., **II** 465
Food Lion, Inc., II 626–27; **7** 450
Food Machinery and Chemical Corp. *See* FMC Corp.
Food Machinery Corp. *See* FMC Corp.
Food Marketing Corp., **II** 668
Food Town Inc., **II** 626–27
Food-4-Less, **II** 624
FoodLand Distributors, **II** 645, 682
Foodland Super Markets, **II** 625
Foodmaker, Inc., **II** 562
Foodstuffs, **9** 144
Foodtown, **II** 626; **V** 35
Foot Locker, **V** 226

Foote Cone & Belding Communications Inc., I 12–15, 28, 34; **11** 51
Foote, Emerson, **I** 12–13
Foote Mineral Company, **7** 386–87
Foote, Robert, **7** 547–48
Foote, W. A., **V** 577
Forages et Exploitations Pétrolières, **III** 617
Forbes, Allan, **8** 492
Forbes, David, **IV** 189
Forbes, John, **V** 426
Ford Aerospace, **9** 325
Ford, Burdette E., **I** 263
Ford, Edsel, **I** 128, 165–66, 337; **6** 128; **11** 137–38
Ford, Edward, **III** 641
Ford, George, **III** 744
Ford, Gerald R., **III** 13; **IV** 16; **9** 186; **11** 544
Ford, Henry, **I** 128, 164–66, 174, 189, 499; **II** 33; **III** 601; **6** 128, 523; **7** 7, 211; **8** 448–49; **10** 465; **11** 136–38, 339
Ford, Henry, II, **I** 166–67; **8** 448; **11** 138–39
Ford, James, **II** 501; **10** 322
Ford, Joe T., **6** 299–300
Ford, John, **II** 143
Ford, John B. (Capt.), **III** 641, 731
Ford, Larry J., **10** 514
Ford Motor Co., I 10, 14, 20–21, 136, 142, 145, 152, 154–55, 162–63, **164–68,** 172, 183, 186, 201, 203–04, 280, 297, 337, 354, 423, 478, 484, 540, 693; **II** 7–8, 33, 60, 86, 143, 415; **III** 58, 259, 283, 439, 452, 495, 515, 555, 568, 591, 603, 637–38, 651, 725; **IV** 22, 187, 722; **6** 27, 51; **7** 377, 461, 520–21; **8** 70, 74–75, 117, 372–73, 375, 505–06; **9** 94, 118, 126, 190, 283–84, 341–43; **10** 32, 241, 260, 264–65, 279–80, 290, 353, 407, 430, 460, 465; **11** 53–54, 103–04, **136–40 (upd.),** 263, 326, 339, 350, 528–29
Ford Motor Credit Co., **IV** 597
Ford Transport Co., **I** 112; **6** 103
Ford, William Clay, **I** 167, 349; **11** 139
Fordyce Lumber Co., **IV** 281; **9** 259
Foreman State Banks, **II** 285
Foremost Dairy of California, **I** 496–97
Foremost-McKesson, **11** 211
Foremost-McKesson Inc., **I** 496–97, **III** 10
Forenza, **V** 116
Forest Laboratories, Inc., 11 141–43
Forest Products, **III** 645
Forethought Group, Inc., **10** 350
Forex Chemical Corp., **I** 341
Forex-Neptune, **III** 617
Forgan, James B., **II** 284
Forges d'Eich–Le Gallais, Metz et Cie, **IV** 24
Forges de la Providence, **IV** 52
Forget, Louis-Joseph, **6** 501
Forman, James, **II** 220
Forman, John, **I** 225; **10** 179
Formenton, Cristina Mondadori. *See* Mondadori, Cristina.
Formenton family, **IV** 587–88
Formenton, Luca, **IV** 587
Formenton, Mario, **IV** 586–87
Formica Ltd., **10** 269
Forming Technology Co., **III** 569
Formosa Plastics, **11** 159
Formosa Springs, **I** 269

Formularios y Procedimientos Moore, **IV** 645

Forney Fiber Company, **8** 475

Forrest, Joseph K.C., **IV** 682

Forrest, Ron, **10** 38

Forrestal, Don, **I** 365

Forsakrings A.B. Volvia, **I** 20

Forsberg, Carl, **6** 605–06

Forster, Peter C., **8** 113

Forstmann Little & Co., **I** 446, 483; **II** 478, 544; **III** 56; **7** 206; **10** 321

Forsyth, Cecil, **9** 237

Fort Associates, **I** 418

Fort Dummer Mills, **III** 213

Fort Howard Corporation, 8 197–99

Fort, John F., **I** 645

Fort Mill Manufacturing Co., **V** 378

Fort William Power Co., **IV** 246

Forte, Charles (Lord). *See* Monforte, Carmine.

Forte, Rocco, **III** 105–06

Forte's Holdings Ltd., **III** 104–05

Fortier, Charles, **III** 534

Fortuna Coffee Co., **I** 451

Forum Hotels, **I** 248

Foseco plc, **IV** 383

Foshay, W.B., **7** 87

Foss Maritime Co., **9** 509, 511

Foss, Martin M., **IV** 634

Foss, Thea, **9** 511

Foster & Kleiser, **7** 335

Foster & Marshall, **II** 398; **10** 62

Foster, Alfred, **III** 313

Foster and Braithwaite, **III** 697

Foster, David, **III** 23, 24

Foster, Dwight, **III** 312

Foster Grant, **I** 670; **II** 595–96

Foster, John H., **11** 366

Foster Management Co., **11** 366–67

Foster Medical Corp., **III** 16; **11** 282

Foster, R.R., **I** 228

Foster, W.M., **I** 228

Foster Wheeler, **I** 82

Foster Wheeler Australia Pty. Ltd., **6** 145

Foster Wheeler Corporation, 6 145–47

Foster Wheeler Energy Corporation, **6** 146

Foster Wheeler Enviresponse, Inc., **6** 146

Foster Wheeler Environmental Services, Inc., **6** 146

Foster Wheeler France, S.A., **6** 145

Foster Wheeler Iberia, **6** 145

Foster Wheeler Italiana, S.p.A., **6** 145

Foster Wheeler Limited (Canada), **6** 145

Foster Wheeler Power Systems, Inc., **6** 146

Foster Wheeler USA Corporation, **6** 146

Foster, William E., **10** 499

Foster's Brewing Group Ltd., 7 182–84

Fotomat Corp., **III** 549

Fouad I, King (Egypt), **III** 701

Foundation Health Plan Inc., **11** 174

Four Seasons Hotels Inc., 9 237–38

4 Seasons, Inc., **II** 531

Four Seasons Nursing Centers, Inc., **6** 188

Four Winns, **III** 600

Four-Phase Systems, Inc., **II** 61; **11** 327

Fournier, Bernard, **10** 205

Fournier, Marcel, **10** 204–05

Fourth Financial Corporation, 11 144–46

Fourtou, Jean-René, **I** 390; **10** 472

Fouse, Winfred E., **8** 212

Foussard Associates, **I** 333

Fowler Road Construction Proprietary, **III** 672

Fowler, Stuart A., **II** 390

Fowler, Theodore M., Jr., **10** 331–32

Fowler-Waring Cables Co., **III** 162

Fownes, Henry, **7** 309

Fox & Jacobs, **8** 87

Fox Broadcasting Co., **II** 156; **IV** 608, 652; **7** 391–92; **9** 428

Fox, Edward A., **II** 453

Fox Film Corp., **II** 146–47, 154–55, 169

Fox, Fowler & Co., **II** 307

Fox Glacier Mints Ltd., **II** 569

Fox Grocery Co., **II** 682

Fox, J. Carter, **8** 103

Fox, John, **II** 595

Fox, Michael, **III** 342

Fox Paper Company, **8** 102

Fox Photo, **III** 475; **7** 161

Fox, Stephen, **I** 18, 38

Fox, William, **II** 169

Foxmeyer Corporation, **V** 152–53

Foy, Fred, **I** 354–55

FP&L. *See* Florida Power & Light Co.

FPL Group, Inc., V 623–25

Fraenckel, Louis, **II** 365

Fraley, John L., **6** 370–71

Fram Corp., **I** 142

Fram Group, **I** 567

Framatome, **9** 10

Frame, Alistair, **IV** 192

Frame, Clarence, **7** 538

France Cables et Radio, **6** 303

France 5, **6** 374

France Telecom Group, V 291–93, 471; **9** 32

France-Loisirs, **IV 615–16, 619**

Francesa, Mike, **11** 191

Francis II, Emperor (Austria), **I** 271

Francis, Kay, **II** 155

Francke, D.O., **III** 425

Fränckel, Eduard, **III** 425

Franco, Francisco (Gen.), **I** 459–60; **II** 194–95, 197–98; **IV** 190, 396–97, 527–28

Franco-American Co., **I** 428

Franco-American Food Co., **II** 479

Francois, Albert, **IV** 95

François, Alfred, **III** 703–04

Francois Dalle, **8** 129

François-Poncet, Michel, **II** 260

Frank & Hirsch, **III** 608

Frank & Schulte GmbH, **8** 496

Frank Dry Goods Company, **9** 121

Frank J. Rooney, Inc., **8** 87

Frank Wheaton, Jr., **8** 572

Fränkel & Selz, **II** 239

Frankel, Albert J., **8** 355

Frankenberry, Laughlin & Constable, **9** 393

Frankford-Quaker Grocery Co., **II** 625

Frankfort Oil Co., **I** 285

Frankfurter Allgemeine Versicherungs-AG, **III** 184

Franklin Assurances, **III** 211

Franklin Baker's Coconut, **II** 531

Franklin, C. Anson, **IV** 624

Franklin Container Corp., **IV** 312

Franklin Institute. *See* Franklin Quest Co.

Franklin Life Insurance Co., **III** 242–43; **V** 397

Franklin Mint, **IV** 676; **9** 428

Franklin National Bank, **9** 536

Franklin Quest Co., 11 147–49

Franklin Rayon Yarn Dyeing Corp., **I** 529

Franklin Research & Development, **11** 41

Franklin Resources, Inc., 9 239–40

Franklin, Roger, **I** 60

Franklin Steamship Corp., **8** 346

Franks Chemical Products Inc., **I** 405

Franks, Oliver, **II** 308

Frantz, Jacob F., **10** 270

Franz and Frieder Burda, **IV** 661

Franz Foods, Inc., **II** 584

Franz Josef, Emperor (Austria), **I** 138

Franz Ströher AG, **III** 69

Franz Ströher OHG, **III** 68

Franz Ströher-Rothenkirchen, **III** 68

Frasch, Herman, **IV** 81; **7** 185

Fraser, Carlyle, **9** 253

Fraser Cos. Ltd., **IV** 165

Fraser, James S., **11** 220

Fraser, Peter M., **III** 238

Fraser, Tom, **V** 422

Fratelli Manzoli, **IV** 585

Fratelli Treves, **IV** 585

Fraternal Assurance Society of America, **III** 274

Frayssinous, Denis (Monsignor), **IV** 617

Frazee, Rowland, **II** 345

Frazer, Joseph, **IV** 121

Frazer, Robert E., **6** 481–82

Fre Kote Inc., **I** 321

Freame, John, **II** 235

Frears, **II** 543

Freas, Guy, **8** 173

Fred Harvey, **I** 417

Fred Meyer, Inc., II 669; V 54–56

Fred S. James, **III** 280

Fred S. James and Co., **I** 537

Fred Sammons Co., **9** 72

Fred Sands Realtors, **IV** 727

Fred Schmid Appliance & T.V. Co., Inc., **10** 305

Frederick Miller Brewing Co., **I** 269

Frederick, Robert R., **II** 90

Frederick William IV, King (Prussia), **II** 385

Fredholm, Ludwig, **II** 1

Freedman, Eugene, **11** 94–95

Freedman, Louis, **IV** 704–05

Freedom Technology, **11** 486

Freedom-Valvoline Oil Co., **IV** 373

Freeland, Michael, **II** 176

Freeman, Bill, **III** 737

Freeman, Gaylord, **II** 285

Freeman, Robert H., **6** 487

Freeman, Robert M., **11** 446–48

Freeman, W. Winans, **6** 466

Freeman, Y. Frank, **II** 155

Freemans, **V** 177

Freeport Asphalt Co., **IV** 81

Freeport Chemical Co., **IV** 82; **7** 186

Freeport Gold Co., **IV** 82–84; **7** 187

Freeport Indonesia, Inc., **IV** 82; **7** 186

Freeport Itaolin Co., **7** 188

Freeport Kaolin Co., **IV** 82–83; **7** 186

Freeport McMoRan Australia Ltd., **IV** 84; **7** 188

Freeport McMoRan Energy Partners, Ltd., **IV** 83; **7** 188

Freeport Minerals Co., **IV** 81–83; **7** 185–87

Freeport of Australia, **IV** 82; **7** 186

Freeport Oil Co., **IV** 82

Freeport Spain, **7** 188

Freeport Sulphur Co., **IV** 81–82, 111, 146; **7** 185–86

Freeport Sulphur Transportation Co., **IV** 81

Freeport Terminal Co., **IV** 81; **7** 185

Freeport Texas Co., **IV** 81–82; **7** 185–86

Freeport Townsite Co., **IV** 81; **7** 185
Freeport-McMoRan Gold Co., **IV** 83–84; **7** 188
Freeport-McMoRan Inc., IV 81–84; 7 185–89 (upd.)
Freeport-McMoRan Oil and Gas Royalty Trust, **IV** 83
Freeport-McMoRan Resource Partners, L.P., **IV** 84, 576; **7** 188
Freezer House, **II** 398; **10** 62
Freezer Shirt Corporation, **8** 406
Freiberger Papierfabrik, **IV** 323
Freiburghouse, Robert A., **10** 499
Freightliner, **I** 150; **6** 413
FreightMaster, **III** 498
Freiherr, Felix, **II** 281
Frejlack Ice Cream Co., **II** 646; **7** 317
Frelinghuysen, Frederick, **III** 303
Fremlin Breweries, **I** 294
Fremont Butter and Egg Co., **II** 467
Fremont Canning Company, **7** 196
Fremont Savings Bank, **9** 474–75
French and Richards & Co., **I** 692
French Bank of California, **II** 233
French, John Russell, **II** 389
French Kier, **I** 568
French Petrofina, **IV** 497
Frequency Sources Inc., **9** 324
Frère, Albert, **IV** 499
Frere, Henry Bartle (Sir), **III** 521
Freshbake Foods Group PLC, **II** 481; **7** 68
Fresnel, Augustin, **I** 394
Fretter, Howard O., **10** 306
Fretter, Inc., 9 65; **10** 9–10, **304–06**, 502
Fretter, Oliver L., **10** 304, 306
Freudenberger, Kent W., **6** 345
Frey, Donald N., **9** 63
Freyssinet, Eugène, **I** 562
Frialco, **IV** 165
Fribourg, Jules, **10** 249
Fribourg, Michel, **10** 249–51
Fribourg, Paul, **10** 251
Fribourg, Simon, **10** 249
Frick, Henry Clay, **9** 370
Fricke, Richard, **III** 306
Frictiontech Inc., **11** 84
Friden, Inc., **II** 10
Friderichs, Hans, **II** 283; **IV** 141
Fridy-Gauker & Fridy, **I** 313; **10** 154
Fried. Krupp AG, **IV** 86–88
Fried. Krupp GmbH, II 257; **IV** 60, **85–89**, 104, 128, 203, 206, 222, 234
Fried. Krupp Hüttenwerke AG, **IV** 89
Friedholm, Roger, **I** 290
Friedley, David, **8** 519
Friedman family, **III** 215
Friedman, Gary, **9** 296–97
Friedman, W. Robert, **III** 86
Friedrich, Albrect, **II** 504
Friedrich Flick Industrial Corp., **I** 548
Friedrich Flick Industrieverwaltung KGaA, **III** 692
Friedrich Krupp in Essen, **IV** 85
Friedrich Roessler Söhne, **IV** 69
Friedrich Wilhelm IV, King (Prussia), **III** 399
Friedrichshütte, **III** 694
Friend, Hugh M., Jr., **III** 96
Friendly Ice Cream Corp., **II** 511–12
Fries, William, **7** 130–31
Friesch-Groningsche Hypotheekbank, **III** 179
Frigessi, Arnoldo, **III** 346–47
Frigessi family, **III** 347

Frigidaire, **III** 572
Frigo, **II** 587
Friguia, **IV** 165
Frisbee, Don C., **7** 376
Frisia Group, **IV** 197–98
Frist, Thomas F., **III** 78
Frist, Thomas F., Jr., **III** 78–80
Frito-Lay, **I** 219, 278–79; **III** 136
Fritz, Johan, **IV** 92
Fritz Thyssen Stiftung, **IV** 222
Fritz W. Glitsch and Sons, Inc. *See* Glitsch International, Inc.
Fritzsche Dodge and Ollcott, **I** 307
Friz, Max, **I** 138; **11** 31
Froebel-Kan, **IV** 679
Froehlke, Robert F., **III** 248
Froelich, Eugene, **III** 86
Frohman, Dov, **II** 44; **10** 366
Fromageries Bel, **II** 518; **6** 47
Frome Broken Hill Co., **IV** 59
Fromm & Sichel, **I** 285
Fromstein, Mitchell S., **9** 326–27
Frondizi, Arturo, **IV** 578
Frontier Airlines, **I** 97–98, 103, 118, 124, 129–30; **6** 129
Frontier Airlines Inc., **11** 298
Frontier Oil Co., **IV** 373
Frost, Philip, **11** 207–09
Frost, Sydney C., **II** 221
Frost, Tom, **II** 334
Fru-Con Corp., **I** 561
Fruchtenbaum, Ed, **7** 24
Fruehauf, August, **I** 169
Fruehauf Corp., I 169–70, 480; **II** 425; **III** 652; **7** 259–60, 514
Fruehauf, Harvey, **I** 169
Fruehauf, Roy, **I** 169–70
Fruehauf Trailer Co., **I** 169
Fruehauf Trailer Corporation, **7** 513–14
Fruit of the Loom, Inc., 8 200–02
Fry, George, **10** 172–73
Fry, John, **I** 604
Fry's Diecastings, **III** 681
Fry's Metal Foundries, **III** 681
Frydman, Jean, **8** 343
Frye Copy Systems, **6** 599
Frye, Jack, **I** 70, 96, 125–26, 338; **II** 32; **11** 277
Frye, Thomas C., **11** 554
Fuchs, Michael J., **II** 167; **7** 223
Fuel Pipeline Transportation Ltd., **6** 123–24
Fuel Resources Development Co., **6** 558–59
Fuel Resources Inc., **6** 457
Fuelco. *See* Fuel Resources Development Co.
FuelMaker Corporation, **6** 569
Fuente, David, **8** 404–05
Fuhrman, Peter, **6** 69
Fuji Bank & Trust, **II** 292
Fuji Bank, Ltd., I 494; **II 291–93**, 360–61, 391, 422, 459, 554; **III** 405, 408–09
Fuji Diesel, **II** 22
Fuji Electric Co., Ltd., II 22–23, 98, 103; **III** 139
Fuji Heavy Industries, **I** 207; **III** 581; **9** 294
Fuji International Finance, **II** 292
Fuji Iron & Steel Co., Ltd., **I** 493; **II** 300; **IV** 130, 157, 212
Fuji Kaolin Co., **III** 691
Fuji Kleinwort Benson, **II** 292

Fuji Paper, **IV** 320
Fuji Photo Film Co., Ltd., III 172, 476, **486–89**, 549–50; **6** 289; **7** 162
Fuji Seito, **I** 511
Fuji Television, **7** 249; **9** 29
Fuji Trust & Banking Co., **II** 363
Fuji Xerox, **III** 172. *See also* Xerox Corporation.
Fuji Yoshiten Co., **IV** 292
Fujihara, Ginjiro, **IV** 320–21
Fujikoshi Kozai, **III** 595
Fujimoto Bill Broker & Securities Co., **II** 405
Fujimoto Bill Broker and Bank, **II** 405
Fujimoto, Ichiro, **IV** 125
Fujimoto, Sibei, **II** 405
Fujimura, Masaya, **III** 713
Fujioka, Kiyotoshi, **III** 581
Fujioka, Yasuhei, **11** 94
Fujisawa Pharmaceutical Co., I 635–36; **III** 47; **8** 343
Fujisawa Shoten, **I** 635
Fujisawa, Takeo, **I** 174; **10** 352
Fujisawa, Tomokichi, **I** 635
Fujita Airways, **6** 70
Fujitsu, **11** 308
Fujitsu Fanuc Ltd., **III** 482
Fujitsu Limited, I 455, 541; **II** 22–23, 56, 68, 73, 274; **III** 109–11, 130, **139–41**, 164, 482; **V** 339; **6** 217, 240–42; **10** 238; **11** 542
Fujitsu-ICL Systems Inc., 11 150–51
Fujiyi Confectionery Co., **II** 569
Fukuhara, Shinzo, **III** 62, 64
Fukuhara, Yoshiharu, **III** 64
Fukuhara, Yushin, **III** 62
Fukuin Electric Works, Ltd., **III** 604
Fukuin Shokai Denki Seisakusho, **III** 604
Fukuju Fire, **III** 384
Fukumitsu, Shoji, **V** 71
Fukuoka Paper Co., Ltd., **IV** 285
Ful-O-Pep, **10** 250
Fulcrum Communications, **10** 19
Fulgoni, Gian, **10** 358
Fuller Brush Co., **II** 572
Fuller Co., **6** 395–96
Fuller, Harvey Benjamin, Jr., **8** 237–38
Fuller, Jane, **IV** 261
Fuller Manufacturing, **I** 154
Fuller Manufacturing Company. *See* H.B. Fuller Company.
Fullerton, R. Donald, **II** 245
Fulton Co., **III** 569
Fulton Insurance Co., **III** 463
Fulton Manufacturing Co., **11** 535
Fulton Municipal Gas Company, **6** 455
Fulton Performance Products, Inc., **11** 535
Fulton, Robert F., **9** 112
Fulton, S.Q., **III** 762
Fultz, Clair E., **11** 181
Funai-Amstrad, **III** 113
Fund American Cos., **III** 251–52
Funk & Wagnalls, **IV** 605
Funk, Roger C., **11** 72
Funk Software Inc., **6** 255
Fuqua Industries Inc., I 445–47, 452; **8** 545
Fuqua, John Brooks, **I** 445–47
Furalco, **IV** 15
Furek, John, **I** 261
Furihata, Minao, **IV** 555
Furlaud, Richard M., **I** 695–97; **III** 19; **9** 6–7, 90
Furniss, James P., **8** 228

Furr's Inc., **II** 601
Furrow, Sanford "Sam", **11** 384–85
Furrow, Sanford, Jr., **11** 384–85
Furrow, Vernon, **11** 384–85
Furstenau, Robert, **11** 294
Furth, Jacob, **6** 565
Furukawa Aluminum Co., **III** 490–91
Furukawa Electric Co., Ltd., **II** 22; **III** 139, **490–92**; **IV** 15, 26, 153
Furukawa, Ichebei, **III** 490
Furukawa Kogyo, **III** 490
Furukawa Metal Industry, **III** 491
Furukawa, Shuichi, **V** 209
Furukawa-Oxford Magnet, **III** 491
Furumoto, Jiro, **III** 667
Furuta, Norimasa, **9** 342
Furuta, Shunnosuke, **I** 519–20; **IV** 215; **11** 479
Fusanosuke Kojima, **III** 539
Fusee, Fred, **III** 16
Fusi Denki, **II** 98
Fuso Marine Insurance Co., **III** 367
Fuso Metal Industries, **IV** 212
Fuss, Karl, **II** 163
Futagi Co., Ltd., **V** 96
Futagi, Hidenori, **V** 98
Futagi, Kazuichi, **V** 96
Futami, Tomio, **7** 221
The Future Now, **6** 245
Fuyo Group, **II** 274, 291–93, 391–92, 554
FWD Corporation, **7** 513
Fysh, William Hudson, **6** 109–10
Fyshe, Thomas, **II** 220

G & H Products, **III** 419
G.A.F., **I** 337–40, 524–25, 549; **II** 378; **III** 440; **8** 180
G.A. Serlachius Oy, **IV** 314–15
G&G Shops, Inc., **8** 425–26
G&L Albu, **IV** 90
G. and T. Earle, **III** 669, 670
G&R Pasta Co., Inc., **II** 512
G.B. Lewis Company, **8** 359
G.C.E. International Inc., **III** 96–97
G.C. Murphy Company, **9** 21
G.C. Smith, **I** 423
G.D. Searle & Co., **I** 365–66, **686–89**; **III** 47, 53; **8** 343, 398, 434; **9** 356–57; **10** 54
G.H. Rinck, NV, **V** 49
G.H. Wetterau & Sons Grocery Co., **II** 681
G. Heileman Brewing Co., **I 253–55**, 270; **10** 169–70
G.I.E. Airbus Industrie, **I 41–43**, 49–52, 55–56, 70, 72, 74–76, 107, 111, 116, 121; **9** 458, 460; **11** 279, 363
G.L. Rexroth GmbH, **III** 566
G.P. Putnam's Sons, **II** 144
G. R. Kinney Corp., **V** 226, 352
G. Riedel Kälte- und Klimatechnik, **III** 420
G. Washington Coffee Refining Co., **I** 622
Gabelli, Mario, **9** 106
Gable, Clark, **I** 25; **II** 143, 148
Gable House Properties, **II** 141
Gabor, Eva, **III** 506
Gabor, Zsa Zsa, **III** 92
Gabriel Industries, **II** 532
Gabrielsson, Assar, **I** 209; **7** 565–66
Gabrielsson, Börje, **I** 625
GAC Corp., **II** 182; **III** 592
GAC Holdings L.P., **7** 204
Gadsen, Henry W., **I** 650; **11** 290
GAF Corp., **9** 518
Gagarin, Yuri, **I** 79; **11** 428

Gage, Edwin C., III, **6** 365
Gage, Lyman, **II** 284
Gaherty, Geoffrey, **6** 585
Gail Borden, Jr., and Co., **II** 470
Gaillard, André, **II** 576
Gain Technology, Inc., **10** 505
Gaines, Charles, **III** 167; **6** 283
Gaines Dog Food Co., **II** 531
Gainey, Daniel C., **7** 255
Gainsborough Craftsmen Ltd., **II** 569
Gair Paper Co., **I** 599
Gairns, Catherine, **II** 592
Gaisman, Henry J., **III** 27–28
Galaxy Energies Inc., **11** 28
Galbraith, John Kenneth, **I** 355; **IV** 252
Gale, Michael, **6** 320
Gale Research Inc., **8** 526
Gale, Stephen F., **V** 425
Galeries Lafayette S.A., **V 57–59**
Galesburg Coulter Disc Co., **III** 439–40
Gall, Robert (Dr.), **I** 218; **10** 100
Gallagher, Bernard P., **10** 212
Gallagher, Robert, **6** 555–56
Gallaher Limited, **IV** 260; **V 398–400**
Gallaher, Tom, **V** 398
Gallatin, Albert, **II** 312
Gallatin Bank, **II** 312
Galletas, **II** 543
Gallier, Frédéric, **I** 357
Galliker, Franz, **II** 370
Gallimard, **IV** 618
Gallo. *See* E & J Gallo.
Gallo, David, **I** 244; **7** 156
Gallo, Ernest, **7** 154–56
Gallo, Joseph, **I** 242, 244; **7** 155–56
Gallo, Julio, **I** 242–44, **7** 154–56
Gallo, Robert, **I** 244; **7** 156
Gallup, George, **I** 25
Galor, **I** 676
GALP, **IV** 505
Galpin, Rodney, **II** 358
Galt, Barry J., **11** 441
Galvanizing Co., **IV** 159
Galveston *Daily News*, **10** 3
Galvin, Christopher, **11** 329
Galvin, Joe, **II** 60
Galvin Manufacturing Corp., **II** 60; **11** 326
Galvin, Paul, **II** 60–61; **11** 326–27
Galvin, Robert, **II** 60–62; **11** 326–29
Gambill, Malcolm W., **8** 247
Gamble, Bertin, **10** 44
Gamble, James, **III** 50–51, 53; **8** 431–32
Gamble, James Norris, **III** 50–51; **8** 431–32
Gamble, Theodore, **7** 429–30
Gamesa, **II** 544
GAMI. *See* Great American Management and Investment, Inc.
Gamlestaden, **9** 381–82
Gamlestadens Fabriker, **III** 622
Gandhi, Mohandas (Mahatma), **II** 9; **IV** 218
Gandhi, Rajiv, **9** 381
Gandois, Jean, **I** 389–90; **IV** 174; **10** 471
Gandolfi, Enrico (Dr.), **IV** 422
Gang-Nail Systems, **III** 735
Gannett Co., Inc., **III** 159; **IV 612–13**, 629–30; **7 190–92 (upd.)**; **9** 3
Gannett, Frank, **IV** 612–13; **7** 190–91
Gannett, Henry, **9** 367
Gannett National Service, **IV** 612
Gannett News Service, **IV** 612
Gannett Outdoor, **IV** 612
Gantt, H.L., **IV** 622

Gantz, William H., **I** 629
Gaon, Benny, **II** 48
Gap, Inc., **V 60–62**; **9** 142, 360; **11** 499
Garberding, Larry, **6** 531
Garbo, Greta, **II** 143
Garden Botanika, **11** 41
Garden State Life Insurance Company, **10** 312
Gardenia, **II** 587
Gardiner, Gregory John, **7** 252–53
Gardini, Raul, **IV** 422
Gärdlund, Torsten, **III** 425
Gardner & Harvey Container Corporation, **8** 267
Gardner Advertising. *See* Wells Rich Green BDDP.
Gardner, LeRoy U. (Dr.), **III** 707; **7** 292
Gardner Merchant, **III** 104
Gardner Merchant Ltd., **11** 325
Gardner, Walter, **IV** 140
Gardner, Walter J., **10** 461
Gardner-Denver Co., **II** 16
Garfield, James R., **IV** 428
Garlock, **I** 435
Garner, James, **II** 173
Garnier, **III** 47
Garnier, Jules, **IV** 107
A.B. Garnisonen, **II** 352
Garrard Engineering, **II** 82
Garrett, **9** 18; **11** 472
Garrett AiResearch, **9** 18
Garrett, Cliff, **9** 12–14
Garrett, David, **I** 100; **6** 82
Garrett, John W., **V** 438
Garrett Poultry Co., **II** 584
Garrett, Thomas M., III, **11** 459
Garrett, Wilbur, **9** 368
Garrett-Buchanan, **I** 412
Garrick, George, **10** 359
Garrison, Edwin, **9** 501
Garrison, Michael, **10** 47
Garrison, Walter R., **6** 139–40
Garrison, William Henry, **10** 541
Garrison, William Lloyd, **III** 312
Garros, Roland, **I** 54
Garry, Fred W., **9** 459–60
Gartley, Alonzo, **9** 274–75
Gartrell White, **II** 465
Garuda, **I** 107
Garuda Indonesia, **6 90–91**
Garvan, Francis P., **I** 698
Gary, Elbert Henry, **IV** 572–73; **7** 549–50
Gary Industries, **7** 4
Gary-Wheaton Corp., **II** 286
Gas Authority of India Ltd., **IV** 484
Gas Corp. of Queensland, **III** 673
Gas Energy Inc., **6** 457
Gas Group, **III** 673
Gas Light and Coke Company. *See* British Gas plc.
Gas Light Company. *See* Baltimore Gas and Electric Company.
Gas Machinery Co., **I** 412
Gas Service Company, **6** 593
Gas Supply Co., **III** 672
Gas Tech, Inc., **11** 513
Gas Utilities Company, **6** 471
Gassette, Norman T., **IV** 660
Gaston, Don F., **I** 453
Gaston Paper Stock Co., Inc., **8** 476
Gasunie. *See* N.V. Nederlandse Gasunie.
GATC. *See* General American Tank Car Company.
Gate City Company, **6** 446

Gate City Gas Works, **6** 446
Gates, Alfred, **II** 586
Gates, Charles, **II** 586
Gates, Charles Arthur, **II** 586
Gates, Charles C., **8** 314
Gates, Charles, Jr., **9** 242
Gates, Charles, Sr., **9** 241–42
The Gates Corporation, 9 241–43
Gates, John, **9** 241
Gates, Leonard, **II** 586
Gates Radio Co., **II** 37
Gates, Thomas S., Jr., **II** 407
Gates, Walter, **II** 586
Gates, William, **II** 586; **6** 257–59
Gateway, **11** 240
Gateway Corporation Ltd., II 612,
    628–30, 638, 642; **10** 442
Gateway Foodmarkets, **II** 628
Gateway 2000, Inc., 10 307–09
Gatliff Coal Co., **6** 583
GATX, 6 394–96
GATX Capital Corporation, **6** 394–96
GATX Leasing, **6** 395
GATX Terminals Corporation, **6** 394, 396
Gaucher, Michel, **II** 664
Gaudette, Francis J., **6** 260
Gaughler, Mr., **I** 301
de Gaulle, Charles, **I** 44–45, 189; **III** 122;
    IV 544–46, 559; **7** 481–84
Gault, Stanley C., **III** 614; **V** 248
Gaumont-British, **II** 157–58
Gauntlet Developments, **IV** 724
Gauntlett, John, **III** 737
Gaut, Norman, **10** 455
Gauthier, C. J., **6** 529–31
Gavilan Computer Corp., **III** 124; **6** 221
Gay-Lussac, Joseph Louis, **III** 676
Gaylord, Bill, **III** 137
Gaylord Broadcasting, **11** 152–53
**Gaylord Container Corporation, 8
    203–05**
Gaylord Container Corporation Mid-
    America Packaging Division, **8** 204–05
Gaylord, Edward King, **11** 152
Gaylord, Edward L., **11** 152–54
**Gaylord Entertainment Company, 11
    152–54**
Gaz de France, IV 425; **V 626–28**
Gaziano, Joseph P., **III** 643–45
Gazit, Giora, **II** 206
Gaztelu, Candido Velazquez. *See*
    Velazquez Gaztelu, Candido.
GB Papers, **IV** 290
GB-Inno-BM, **II** 658; **V** 63
GBL, **IV** 499
GCFC. *See* General Cinema Finance Co.
GDF. *See* Gaz de France.
GE. *See* General Electric Company.
GE Aircraft Engines, 9 244–46
GE Fanuc Automation, **III** 483
GE Solid State, **II** 39
Geach, Charles, **II** 318
Gearhart Industries, **III** 499
Gearmatic, **I** 185
Geary, John, **IV** 437
Gebauer, Antonio, **II** 331
Gebrüder Kiessel GmbH, **IV** 197
Gebrüder Sulzer Aktiengesellschaft. *See*
    Sulzer Brothers Limited.
Gebrüder Volkart, **III** 402
Gebrueder Ahle GmbH, **III** 581
GEC. *See* General Electric Company PLC.
GEC Alsthom, **9** 9, 10
GEC Alsthom Electromotors, **III** 509

GEC plc, **9** 9
Geckle, Jerome W., **V** 496
GECO, **III** 618
Geco Mines Ltd., **IV** 165; **7** 398
Geddes, Auckland (Sir), **IV** 190–91
Geddes, Ford, **V** 492
Gee, Edwin, **IV** 287
Geer Drug, **III** 9–10
GEGC, **III** 434
Geginat, Hartwig, **III** 695
Gehry, Frank, **11** 51
GEICO Corporation, III 214, 248, 252,
    273, 448; **10 310–12**
Geier, Philip, **I** 18
Geisse, John F., **V** 134
Geist, Jerry, **6** 563–64
Geithner, Paul, Jr., **11** 126
Geitz, William D., **9** 522
Gelatin Products Co., **I** 678
Gelb, Arthur, **10** 88–89
Gelb, Richard, **III** 17–19; **9** 89–90
Gelderman, Barbara, **I** 168
Gellatly, Hankey and Sewell, **III** 521
Geller, Laurence, **III** 97
Gelotte, Beril, **I** 665
Gelsenberg, **IV** 454
Gelsenberg AG, **7** 141
Gelsenberg Bergwerks AG, **I** 542; **IV**
    194
Gelsthorpe, Edward, **III** 28; **7** 404
Gem State Utilities, **6** 325, 328
GEMA Gesellschaft für Maschinen- und
    Apparatebau mbH, **IV** 198
Gemcolite Company, **8** 178
N.V. Gemeenschappelijk Benzit van
    Aandeelen Philips Gloeilampenfabriken,
    II 79
Gemey, **III** 47
Gemina, **I** 369
Gemini Computers, **III** 109
Genbel Investments Ltd., **IV** 92
Gencor Ltd., I 423; **IV 90–93**
GenCorp Automotive, **8** 206–08
GenCorp Inc., 9 247–49
GenCorp Polymer Products, **8** 206–08
Gendex Corp., **10** 270, 272
Gene Reid Drilling, **IV** 480
Geneen, Harold S., **I** 462–64; **II** 86; **III**
    99, 163; **11** 412
Geneen, Harold Sydney, **11** 196–98
Genentech Inc., I 628, **637–38**; **III** 43; **8
    209–11 (upd.)**, 216–17; **10** 78, 80, 142,
    199
General Accident & Employers Liability
    Assurance Association Ltd., **III** 256
General Accident Fire and Life Assurance
    Corp., **III** 256–57
General Accident plc, III 256–57, 350
General America Corp., **III** 352–53
General American Oil Co., **IV** 523
General American Tank Car Company, **6**
    394–95
General Aniline Works Inc., **I** 337–39
General Artificial Silk Co., **IV** 310
General Automotive, **I** 62
General Automotive Parts Corp., **9** 254
General Aviation Corp., **I** 54; **9** 16
General Battery Corp., **I** 440–41
General Binding Corporation, 10 313–14
General Binding Corporation Canada, Ltd.,
    10 313
General Box Corp., **IV** 342
General Brewing Corp, **I** 269

General Bussan Kaisha, Ltd., **IV** 431–32,
    555
General Cable Co., **IV** 32; **7** 288; **8** 367
General Casualty and Surety Reinsurance
    Corp., **III** 258
General Casualty Co., **III** 343, 352, 404
General Casualty Co. of Illinois, **III** 343
General Chemical Co., **I** 414
General Chocolate, **II** 521
General Cinema Corp., I 245–46; **II** 478;
    IV 624
General Cinema Finance Co., **II** 157–58
General Co. for Life Insurance and
    Superannuation, **III** 309
General Corporation, **9** 173
General Credit Ltd., **II** 389
General Crude Oil Co., **II** 403; **IV** 287
General Dynamics Corporation, I 55,
    57–60, 62, 71, 74, 77, 482, 525, 527,
    597; **6** 79, 229; **7** 520; **8** 51, 92, 315,
    338; **9** 206, 323, 417–18, 498; **10**
    315–18 (upd.), 522, 527; **11** 67, 165,
    269, 278, 364
General Electric Broadcasting Company, **6**
    32
General Electric Co. Ltd., **II** 24
General Electric Company, I 41, 52,
    82–85, 195, 321, 454, 478, 532, 534,
    537; **II** 2, 16, 19, 22, 24, **27–31**, 38–39,
    41, 56, 58–59, 66, 82, 86, 88–90,
    98–99, 116–17, 119–21, 143, 151–52,
    330, 431, 604; **III** 16, 110, 122–23, 132,
    149, 152, 154, 170–71, 437, 440, 443,
    475, 483, 502, 526, 572–73, 614, 655;
    IV 66, 203, 287, 596, 675; **V** 564; **6** 13,
    27, 164–66, 240, 261, 266, 288, 452,
    517; **7** 123, 125, 161, 456, 520, 532; **8**
    157, 262, 332, 377; **9** 14–18, 27, 128,
    162, 244, 246, 352–53, 417–18, 439,
    514; **10** 16, 241, 536–37; **11** 46, 313,
    318, 422, 472, 490
General Electric Company, PLC, I 411,
    423; **II** 3, 12, **24–26**, 31, 58, 72, 80–83,
General Electric Credit Corp., **II** 30, 349;
    III 340
General Electric Venture Capital
    Corporation, **9** 140; **10** 108
General Electronics Co., **III** 160
General Europea S.A., **V** 607
General Felt Industries, **I** 202
General Film Distributors Ltd., **II** 157
General Finance, **11** 16
General Finance Corp., **II** 419; **III** 194,
    232
General Finance Service Corp., **11** 447
General Fire and Casualty, **I** 449
General Fire Extinguisher Co., **III** 644
General Foods Corp., **I** 26, 36, 608, 712; **II**
    414, 463, 477, 497, 502, 525, 530–34,
    557, 569; **III** 66; **V** 407; **7** 272–74; **10**
    323, 551
General Foods, Ltd., **7** 577
General Foods of Mexico S.A., **II** 532
General Furniture Leasing Co., **III** 200
General Gas Co., **IV** 432
General Growth Properties, **III** 248
General Health Services, **III** 79
General Host, **7** 372
General Instrument Corporation, II 5,
    160; **10 319–21**
General Instruments Inc., **II** 112
General Insurance Co. of America, **III**
    352–53
General Jones, **I** 438

General Learning Corp., **IV** 675; **7** 528
General Life Insurance Co. of America, **III** 353
General Merchandise Company, **V** 91
General Milk Co., **II** 487; **7** 429
General Milk Products of Canada Ltd., **II** 586
General Mills, Inc., **II** 493, **501–03**, 525, 556, 576, 684; **III** 505; **7** 547; **8** 53–54; **9** 156, 189–90, 291; **10** 177, **322–24** (upd.); **11** 15, 497–98
General Mining and Finance Corp. Ltd., **I** 423; **IV** 90–93, 95
General Mining Metals and Minerals Ltd., **IV** 93
General Mining Union Corp. Ltd., **IV** 90–91
General Mortgage and Credit Corp., **II** 256
General Motors Acceptance Corp., **II** 268; **10** 325; **11** 29
General Motors Corp., **I** 10, 14, 16–17, 54, 58, 78–80, 85, 101–02, 125, 136, 141, 144–45, 147, 154–55, 162–63, 165–67, **171–73**, 181, 183, 186–87, 203, 205–06, 280, 328–29, 334–35, 360, 448, 464, 481–82, 529, 540; **II** 2, 5, 15, 32–35, 431, 608; **III** 55, 136–38, 292, 442, 458, 482–83, 536, 555, 563, 581, 590–91, 637–38, 640–42, 760; **6** 140, 256, 336, 356, 358; **7** 6–8, 427, 461–64, 513, 565, 567, 599; **8** 151–52, 505–07; **9** 16–18, 36, 283, 293–95, 341, 343, 344, 439, 487–89; **10** 198, 232, 262, 264, 273–74, 279–80, 288–89, **325–27 (upd.)**, 419–20, 429, 460, 537; **11** 5, 53, 103–04, 137–39, 339, 350, 427–29, 437–39, 471–72, 528, 530
General Nucleonics Corp., **III** 643
General Nutrition Companies, Inc., **11** **155–57**
General Nutrition, Inc., **11** 155–56
General Petroleum and Mineral Organization of Saudi Arabia, **IV** 537–39
General Petroleum Authority, **IV** 412
General Petroleum Co., **IV** 412
General Petroleum Corp., **IV** 431, 464; **7** 352
General Portland, **III** 704–05
General Precision Equipment Corp., **II** 10
General Printing and Paper, **II** 624–25
General Property Trust, **IV** 708
General Public Utilities Company, **6** 579
General Public Utilities Corporation, **V** **629–31**; **6** 484, 534; **11** 388
General Public Utilities, Inc., **6** 579–80
General Railway Signal Company. *See* General Signal Corporation.
General Re Corporation, **III** **258–59**
General Reinsurance Corp., **III** 258–59, 276
General Rent A Car, **6** 349
General Seafoods Corp., **II** 531
General Sekiyu K.K., **IV** **431–33**, 555
General Sekiyu Refining Co., **IV** 432
General Sekiyu Seisei Co. Ltd., **IV** 555
General Signal Corporation, **III** 645; **9** **250–52**; **11** 232
General Supermarkets, **II** 673
General Telephone and Electronics Corp., **II** 47; **V** 295, 345–46
General Telephone Corporation, **V** 294–95; **9** 478, 494

The General Tire & Rubber Company. *See* General Tire, Inc.
General Tire, Inc., **8** 206–08, **212–14**; **9** 247–48
General Transistor Corporation, **10** 319
General Utilities Company, **6** 555
Generale Bank, **II** **294–95**
Générale Biscuit S.A., **II** 475
Générale de Banque. *See* Generale Bank.
Générale de Mécanique Aéronautique, **I** 46
Générale des Eaux Group, **V** **632–34**
Générale Occidentale, **II** 475; **IV** 614–15
Generali. *See* Assicurazioni Generali.
Generali Belgium, **III** 209
AB Generali Budapest, **III** 209
Generali France, **III** 209
Generali Lebensversicherung, **III** 209
GenerComit Gestione SpA, **II** 192
Genesee Iron Works, **V** 221
Genesis, **II** 176–77
Genet, Arthur, **I** 449
Genetic Systems Corp., **I** 654; **III** 18
Genetics Institute, Inc., **8** **215–18**; **10** 70, 78–80
Geneva Pharmaceuticals, Inc., **8** 549
Geneva Steel, **7** **193–95**
Genex Corp., **I** 355–56
GENIX, **V** 152
Genix Group. *See* MCN Corporation.
de Genlis, Jean de Waubert, **III** 703
Genossenschaftsbank Edeka, **II** 621–22
Genstar Gypsum Products Co., **IV** 273
Genstar Stone Products, **III** 735
Gentry, Conrad M., **6** 409
Gentry International, **I** 497
Genuine Parts Company, **9** **253–55**
Genung's, **II** 673
Geo. W. Wheelwright Co., **IV** 311
Geodynamics Oil & Gas Inc., **IV** 83
Geomarine Systems, **11** 202
The Geon Company, **11** **158–61**
Geophysical Research Corp., **IV** 365
Geophysical Service, Inc., **II** 112; **III** 499–500; **IV** 365
George A. Hormel and Company, **II** **504–06**; **7** 547
George A. Touche & Co., **9** 167
George Batten Co., **I** 28
George, David Lloyd, **IV** 685
George Fischer, Ltd., **III** 638
George H. Dentler & Sons, **7** 429
George, Harold, **II** 33
The George Hyman Construction Company, **8** 112–13
George I, King (England), **III** 370
George K. Smith & Co., **I** 692
George Kent, **II** 3
George Newnes Company, **7** 244
George Newnes Ltd., **IV** 641
George Peabody & Co., **II** 329, 427
George R. Newell Co., **II** 668
George R. Rich Manufacturing Company, **8** 114. *See also* Clark Equipment Company.
George V, Prince (Wales), **III** 256
George, Valassis, **8** 550
George VI, **I** 285, 312
George, W.H. Krome, **IV** 15–16
George W. Neare & Co., **III** 224
George Weston Limited, **II** 465, **631–32**, 649
Georges, John, **IV** 287–88
Georges Renault, **III** 427
Georgetown Steel Corp., **IV** 228

Georgia Credit Exchange, **6** 24
Georgia Federal Bank, **I** 447; **11** 112–13
Georgia Gulf Corporation, **IV** 282; **9** **256–58**, 260
Georgia Hardwood Lumber Co., **IV** 281; **9** 259
Georgia International Life Insurance Co., **III** 218
Georgia Kraft Co., **IV** 312, 342–43; **8** 267–68
Georgia Natural Gas Company, **6** 448
Georgia Natural Gas Corporation, **6** 447
Georgia Power, **6** 447
Georgia Power & Light Co., **V** 621
Georgia Power Co., **V** 624; **6** 537
Georgia Public Utilities Company, **6** 447
Georgia Railway and Electric Company, **6** 446–47
Georgia Railway and Power, **6** 447
Georgia-Pacific Corporation, **IV** **281–83**, 288, 304, 345, 358; **9** 256–58, **259–62** (upd.)
Georgia-Pacific Plywood & Lumber Co., **IV** 281; **9** 259
Georgia-Pacific Plywood Co., **IV** 281; **9** 259
Georgie Pie, **V** 35
Georgius, John R., **10** 299
Geosource Inc., **III** 182
Geothermal Resources International, **11** 271
Gepp, Herbert (Sir), **IV** 249
Gérard, Max-Leo, **II** 202
Gerber Childrenswear, Inc., **7** 196–98
Gerber, Daniel, **7** 196–98
Gerber, David, **II** 149
Gerber, Dorothy, **7** 196
Gerber, Frank, **7** 196
Gerber, Fritz, **III** 412
Gerber Products Co., **II** 481; **III** 19; **7** **196–98**, 547; **9** 90; **11** 173
Geren Associates. *See* CRSS Inc.
Gerevas, Ronald E., **10** 383
Gerin, Gaston, **II** 93
Gerlach, John B., **8** 307
Gerlach, John B., Jr., **8** 308–09
Gerling of Cologne, **III** 695
Gerlinger family, **IV** 357
Gerlinger, George, **IV** 357–58
Gerlinger, Louis, **IV** 357
Germain, Henri, **9** 147–48
Germaine Monteil Cosmetiques Corp., **I** 426; **III** 56
German Cargo Service GmbH., **I** 111
German Mills American Oatmeal Factory, **II** 558
German-American Car Company. *See* GATX.
German-American Securities, **II** 283
Germania Refining Co., **IV** 488–89
Germehausen, Kenneth J., **8** 163
Germplasm Resource Management, **III** 740
Gerresheimer Glas AG, **II** 386; **IV** 232
Gerrity Oil & Gas Corporation, **11** 28
Gershwin, George, **IV** 671
Gerstacker, Carl, **I** 324–25; **8** 148
Gerstel, Martin, **10** 53
Gerstner, Louis V., Jr., **II** 544; **9** 344
Gervais Danone, **II** 474
GESA. *See* General Europea S.A.
Gesbancaya, **II** 196
Geschke, Charles, **10** 22, 24
Gesellschaft für Chemische Industrie im Basel, **I** 632

Gesellschaft für den Bau von Untergrundbahnen, I 410
Gesellschaft für Linde's Eisenmachinen, I 581
Gesellschaft für Markt- und Kühlhallen, I 581
Gesparal, III 47; 8 342
Gestettner, II 159
Gestione Pubblicitaria Editoriale, IV 586
Getchell, J. Stirling, I 12–13
Gething, Jack, 6 79
Gettier, Glen, III 249
Getty, Gordon, IV 490
Getty, J. Paul, IV 460, 489–90
Getty Oil, 8 526; 11 27
Getty Oil Co., II 448; IV 367, 423, 429, 461, 479, 488, 490, 551, 553
Getty Synthetic Fuels, 6 457
Getz Corp., IV 137
Getz, Oscar, I 227; 10 181
de Geus, Aart, 11 489
Geyser Peak Winery, I 291
Geysers Geothermal Co., IV 84, 523; 7 188
GFS. See Gordon Food Service Inc.
GFS Realty Inc., II 633
GHH, II 257
Ghormley, A.M., II 488
GI Communications, 10 321
Giacco, Alexander, I 344–45
Giannichesi, Angelo, III 345–46
Giannikesis, Angelos. See Giannichesi, Angelo.
Giannini, A.H., II 157
Giannini, Amadeo Peter, I 536; II 226–28, 288–89; 8 45–47
Giannini, Lawrence Mario, II 227
Giannini, Peter Amadeo, I 536
Giant Construction Co., II 633
Giant Food Inc., II 633–35, 656
Giant Food Markets Inc., II 627
Giant Food Properties, II 633
Giant Food Shopping Center Inc., II 633
Giant Food Stores Inc., II 641
Giant Resources, III 729
Giant Retail Bakery, II 633
Giant Stores, Inc., 7 113
Giant Tire & Rubber Company, 8 126
Giant Wholesale, II 625
GIB Group, V 63–6
Gibbons, Green, Van Amerongen, II 605; 9 94
Gibbons, J.P., 10 222
Gibbs, Anthony, II 298
Gibbs Automatic Molding Co., III 569
Gibbs Nathaniel, IV 259
GIBCO Corp., I 321
Giblin, S. Burke, I 711; 10 550
Gibraltar Casualty Co., III 340
Gibraltar Financial Corp., III 270–71
Gibson (Lord), IV 659
Gibson Greetings, 7 24
Gibson, Robert, 7 534
Giddings & Lewis, Inc., 8 545–46; 10 328–30
Giddings, George, 10 328
Gidnitz, Betsy, I 120
Gidwitz, Gerald, 8 253
Gienow, Herbert (Dr.), IV 128
Gifford, Kathie Lee, 6 367
Gifford, Michael, II 159
Gifford, Nelson S., IV 252, 254
Gifford, Walter, I 462; 11 196
Gifford, Walter S., V 261

Gilbert, Carl, III 28
Gilbert, Grove Karl, 9 367
Gilbert, John, I 692
Gilbert, L. S., 6 24
Gilbert Lane Personnel, Inc., 9 326
Gilbert, Paul, I 588
Gilbert, Rodney C., 11 436
Gilbert, S. Parker, II 432
Gilbert-Ash Ltd., I 588
Gilchrist, Finlay, III 699
Gilchrist, James, 10 295
Gilchrist, John, 10 295
Gilchrist, P., IV 24
Gilde-Verlag, IV 590
Gilde-Versicherung AG, III 400
Gildon Metal Enterprises, 7 96
Giles, Zena, 9 77
Gilkeson, Robert F., 11 389
Gilkey Bros. See Puget Sound Tug and Barge Company.
Gill and Duffus, II 500
Gill, Daniel, 7 45–46
Gill Industries, II 161
Gill, Tony, III 556
Gilleland, Dick, 11 220–21
Gillespie, Robert W., 9 475–76
Gillet, Andre, 7 242–43
Gillet family, 10 470
Gillet, John, II 619
Gillet, Nicolas, I 388
Gillett, George, 11 545
Gillett, George, Jr., 7 199–201
Gillett Holdings, Inc., 7 199–201; 11 543, 545
Gillett, Horace W., Dr., 10 138
Gillette Company, III 27–30, 114, 215; IV 722; 8 59–60; 9 381, 413
Gillette, King, III 27–28; 8 60
Gillette Safety Razor Co., III 27
Gilliam Manufacturing Co., 8 530
Gilliand, Merle, II 342
Gillilan, William J., 8 88
Gillman, Richard, III 431
Gillum, Jack, III 96–97
Gilman & Co., III 523
Gilman Fanfold Corp., Ltd., IV 644
Gilman, George Francis, II 636
Gilman, Irving, 9 20
Gilman, Milton, 9 20
Gilman, Norman, 9 16–17
Gilmartin, Raymond V., 11 36
Gilmore Brother's, I 707
Gilmore, Donald S., I 707; 8 547
Gilmore, Jim, 7 150
Giltspur, II 587
Gimbel's, 8 59
Gimbels, I 426–27
Gindick Productions, 6 28
Ginn & Co., IV 672
Ginna, Robert E., 6 572
Ginnie Mae. See Government National Mortgage Association.
Gino's, III 103
Giordani, Francesco, I 465
Giordano, Richard, I 316
Giorgio, Inc., III 16
Girard, Alexander, 8 255
Girard Bank, II 315–16
Girard Bank Delaware, II 316
Girard Savings Institution, II 315
Girard, Stephen, II 315
Girling, III 556
Girling, Lucas, 11 84
Girolami, Paul, I 640; 9 264

Girotti, Raffaele, IV 422
Giroux, Robert, IV 622
Gist-Brocades Co., III 53
The Gitano Group, Inc., 8 219–21
Gitano, Inc. See The Gitano Group, Inc.
Giugiaro, Giorgetto, III 516
Giuily, Eric, 6 380
Giuntini, Philip M., 11 19
Giussani, Camillo, III 208
GK Technologies Incorporated, 10 547
GKN (Midlands), III 494
GKN (South Wales) Ltd., III 494
GKN Automotive Components Inc., III 494
GKN Autoparts, III 495
GKN Bolts and Nuts Ltd., III 495
GKN Chep, III 494
GKN Dowlais, III 494
GKN International Trading, III 494
GKN Kwikform, III 495; 9 512
GKN Ltd., III 494; IV 658
GKN plc, III 493–96, 554, 556. See also Guest, Keen and Nettlefolds plc.
GKN Steel Co., III 494
GKN Transmission, III 595–96
Glaceries de Sain-Roch, III 677
Glaces de Boussois, II 474–75
Glacier Park Co., 10 191
Gladieux Corp., III 103
Gladstone, William, III 334–35
Glaser, Herbert O., 10 282
Glasier, Robert, 6 248
Glasrock Home Health Care, I 316
Glass, Alexander, 7 586
Glass, Charles, I 287
Glass Containers Corp., I 609–10
Glass, David D., V 217; 8 556–57
Glass Fibres Ltd., III 726
Glass, John O., III 422
Glasser, James, 6 395
GlasTec, II 420
Glatfelter, P.H., II, 8 413
Glatfelter, P.H., III, 8 413
Glatfelter, Philip H., 8 412–13
Glatfelter, William L., 8 413
Glatfelter Wood Pulp Company, 8 413
Glaverbel, III 667
Glaxo Holdings plc, I 639–41, 643, 668, 675, 693; III 66; 9 263–65 (upd.); 10 551; 11 173
Glaxo, Incorporated, 6 346
Gleed, Thomas, I 129; 6 129
Glen & Co, I 453
Glen Cove Mutual Insurance Co., III 269
Glen Iris Bricks, III 673
Glen Line, 6 416
Glendale Federal Savings, IV 29
Glenn, B. Duke, Jr., 10 112
Glenn, John, I 79, 338; III 475, 575; 11 428
Glens Falls Insurance Co., III 242
GLF-Eastern States Association, 7 17
Glickman, Louis, IV 581
The Glidden Company, 8 222–24
Glidden, Francis Harrington, 8 222
Glidden Paint, I 353
Glieg, George, 7 165
Glitsch International, Inc., 6 146
Global Energy Group, II 345
Global Engineering Company, 9 266
Global Marine Inc., 9 266–67; 11 87
Global Natural Resources, II 401; 10 145
Global Transport Organization, 6 383
Globe & Rutgers Co., III 195

Globe & Rutgers Insurance Co., **III** 196
Globe Co. **I** 201
Globe Electric Co., **III** 536
Globe Files Co., **I** 201
Globe Grain and Milling Co., **II** 555
Globe Industries, **I** 540
Globe Insurance Co., **III** 350
Globe Life Insurance Co., **III** 187; **10** 28
Globe National Bank, **II** 261
Globe Newspaper Co., **7** 15
Globe Petroleum Ltd., **IV** 401
Globe-Union, **III** 536
Globe-Wernicke Co., **I** 201
Globetrotter Communications, **7** 199
La Gloria Oil and Gas Company, **7** 102
Gloria Separator GmbH Berlin, **III** 418
Gloster Aircraft, **I** 50; **III** 508
Glovatorium, **III** 152; **6** 266
Gluck, Fred, **9** 344
Gluck, Henry, **6** 201
Gluck, W.J., **I** 275
Glucksman, Lew, **II** 451; **9** 469
Glyn, Mills and Co., **II** 308
Glyn, Sidney, **I** 588
**GM Hughes Electronics Corporation, II
32–36; 10** 325
GMAC Mortgage Corporation, **10** 93
GMARA, **II** 608
GMFanuc Robotics, **III** 482–83
GMFanuc Robotics Europa, **III** 483
GNB International Battery Group, **10** 445
GND Holdings Corp., **7** 204
GNMA. *See* Government National
   Mortgage Association.
Goal Systems International Inc., **10** 394
Gobel, George, **I** 14
Goddard, Paul B., **III** 518
Godeffroy, Adolf, **6** 397
Godfather's Pizza, **II** 556–57; **11** 50
Godfrey, Arthur, **I** 14
Godfrey Co., **II** 625
Godfrey L. Cabot, Inc., **8** 77
Godiva Chocolatier, **II** 480
Godo Shusei, **III** 42
Godowsky, Leopold, **III** 443
Godsell, **10** 277
Goebbels, Joseph, **IV** 589
Goebel & Wetterau Grocery Co., **II** 681
Goebel, Frederick, **II** 681
Goehst, John, **10** 295
Goeken, John, **V** 302
Goering, Hermann, **I** 107; **II** 282
Goering Werke, **II** 282
Goertz, Adolf, **IV** 90
Goertz, Albrecht Graf, **I** 139; **11** 32
Goessel, William, **8** 243
Goetting, Adolf, **III** 15
Goffart, Albert, **IV** 52
Gohda, Shigeru, **III** 635
Göhner AG, **6** 491
Goit, Kenneth, **7** 534
Goizueta, Roberto, **I** 234; **10** 227
Gokey's, **10** 216
Gold Bond Stamp Co., **6** 363–64
Gold, Charles W., **11** 213
Gold Crust Bakeries, **II** 465
Gold Dust Corp., **II** 497
Gold Exploration and Finance Co. of
   Australia, **IV** 95
Gold Fields American Development Co.,
   IV 95
Gold Fields Australian Development Co.,
   IV 95

Gold Fields Mining and Development
   Corp., **IV** 96
Gold Fields Mining Corp., **III** 501
Gold Fields of South Africa Holdings, **IV**
   97
Gold Fields of South Africa Ltd., I 423;
   IV 91, **94–97**
Gold Kist, **7** 432
Gold Mines of Australia, **IV** 95
Gold, P.D., **11** 213
Gold Seal, **II** 567
Gold, Stanley, **8** 305; **11** 556
Gold, Stanley P., **7** 82
Gold Star Foods Co., **IV** 410
Goldberg, Arthur, **10** 369–70
Goldberg, Avram J., **II** 666–67
Goldberg, Carol, **II** 666–67
Goldberg, Michael L., **III** 709
Goldblatt Bros., **IV** 135
Golden, **III** 47
Golden Corral Corporation, 10 331–33
Golden Eagle Exploration, **IV** 567
Golden Eagle of Canada, **IV** 566
Golden Eagle Refining Co., **IV** 566
Golden Grain Macaroni Co., **II** 560
Golden Hope Rubber Estate, **III** 697, 699
Golden, Hyman, **11** 449
Golden Nugget, **III** 92, 431
Golden Nugget Company. *See* Mirage
   Resorts, Inc.
Golden Partners, **10** 333
Golden Sea Produce, **10** 439
Golden Skillet, **10** 373
Golden State Bank, **II** 348
Golden State Newsprint Co. Inc., **IV** 296
Golden State Sanwa Bank, **II** 348
Golden Tulip International, **I** 109
Golden Wonder, **II** 500; **III** 503
Goldenberg, Bernhard, **V** 708
Goldenlay Eggs, **II** 500
Goldenson, Leonard, **II** 129, 131
Goldfarb, Jacob (Jack), **8** 200–01
Goldfarb, Leo, **II** 662
Goldfeder, Howard, **V** 27; **9** 211
Goldfinger, Auric, **IV** 79
Goldfish, Samuel, **II** 154
Goldfus, Don, **8** 35–36
Goldkuhl & Broström, **III** 419
Goldline Laboratories Inc., **11** 208
Goldman, Charles, **IV** 581
Goldman, Henry, **II** 414
Goldman, Marcus, **II** 414
Goldman, Sachs & Co., II 11, 268, 326,
   361, **414–16**, 432, 434, 448; **III** 80, 531;
   IV 611; **9** 378, 441; **10** 423
Goldman, Sachs, Ltd., **II** 415
Goldman Sachs Trading Corp., **II** 414–15
Goldome, **11** 110
Goldsbrough Mort & Co., **I** 437
Goldsmith, Harold, **8** 362
Goldsmith, James (Sir), **I** 600; **II** 609; **IV**
   290, 615; **7** 202–03
Goldsmith, Robert, **9** 460
Goldsmith's, **9** 209
Goldstar Co. Ltd., **II** 5, 53–54; **7** 233
Goldstar Electronics, **II** 54; **III** 517
Goldston, Mark, **8** 305
Goldwater, Barry, **I** 65; **10** 287; **11** 267
Goldwell, **III** 38
Goldwyn Picture Corp., **II** 148
Goldwyn, Samuel, **II** 146–48, 154
Golhan, Mehmet, **IV** 563
Golub, Harvey, **9** 344; **10** 63
Gomez, Alain, **II** 116, 117

Gómez, Juan Vicente (Gen.), **IV** 507, 565
Gompertz, Benjamin, **III** 373
Gonda, Keiji, **III** 638
Gonzalez, Emilio, **6** 96
Gonzalez, Jorge M., **11** 273
Good, Brent, **8** 83
Good Foods, Inc., **II** 497
The Good Guys!, Inc., 10 334–35
Good, Harry, **8** 83
Good, Kenneth, **7** 538
Good Times, Inc., **8** 303
Good Weather International Inc., **III** 221
Goodbody & Co., **II** 425
Goodby, Berlin & Silverstein, **10** 484
Goodebodies, **11** 41
Goodenough, Frederick Crauford, **II**
   235–36
Goodenough, William Macnamara, **II** 236
Gooderham and Worts, **I** 216, 263–64
Goodes, Melvin R., **10** 551
Goodheart, William, **II** 143
Goodlass, Wall & Co., **III** 680–81
Goodlass Wall & Lead Industries, **III**
   680–81
Goodman, Benny, **II** 543; **III** 443
Goodman, Ed, **IV** 620
Goodman Fielder, Wattie's, Ltd., **II** 565; **7**
   577
Goodman, Martin, **10** 400–01
Goodman, Samuel M., **11** 369
Goodnight, James, **10** 476
Goodrich, **V** 240–41
Goodrich, Benjamin Franklin, **V** 231; **11**
   158
Goodrich, Charles Cross, **V** 231; **11** 158
Goodrich, Enid, **10** 207
Goodrich, Henry, **8** 267–68
Goodrich, Henry C., **6** 577
Goodrich, M. Keith, **IV** 646
Goodrich Oil Co., **IV** 365
Goodrich, Tew and Company, **V** 231
Goodrich Tire Company, **6** 27
Goodson, R. Eugene, **7** 418
Goodwin, Jacob, **I** 60
Goodwin, James, **III** 236–37
Goodwin, Leo, **10** 310
Goodwin, W. Richard, **III** 707–08; **7**
   292–93
Goodyear Aerospace Corp., **8** 339; **9** 324
Goodyear, Charles, **V** 244; **8** 290
Goodyear Tire & Rubber Company, I
   21; **II** 304; **III** 452; **V** 244–48; **8** 81,
   291–92; **9** 324; **10** 445
Gookin, R. Burt, **II** 508; **11** 172
Göransson, Anders Henrik, **IV** 202
Göransson family, **IV** 203
Göransson, Göran Fredrik, **IV** 202
Göransson, Karl Fredrik, **IV** 202–03
Gorden, Maynard M., **I** 145
Gordon A. Freisen, International, **III** 73
Gordon B. Miller & Co., **7** 256
Gordon, Ben, **8** 225–26
Gordon Capital Corp., **II** 245
Gordon, Donald, **6** 361
Gordon Food Service Inc., 8 225–27
Gordon, Frank, **8** 225–26
Gordon Investment Corp., **II** 245
Gordon Manufacturing Co., **11** 256
Gordon, Peter, **IV** 209
Gordon Publications, **IV** 610
Gordon, William Bingham (Bing), **10** 284
Gordon-Van Cheese Company, **8** 225
Gore, Albert, Jr., **10** 238
Gore Newspapers Co., **IV** 683

Göring, Hermann, **IV** 200
Gorley, Dennis J., **10** 293
Gorman, Joseph T., **11** 540, 542
Gorman, Leon A., **10** 389
Gorman, Paul A., **IV** 287
Gorman, Willis A., **III** 355
Gormully & Jeffrey, **IV** 660
Gorr, Ivan, **8** 127
Gorst, Vernon, **I** 47, 128; **6** 128
Gorton's, **II** 502; **10** 323
Goschen, G.J., **III** 278
Gosho Co., Ltd., **IV** 442
Gosho Corp., **IV** 442
Gosho Trading Co., Ltd., **IV** 442
Gosman, Abraham D., **11** 281–83
Goss, Dick, **I** 288
Goss, Wesley P., **7** 288
Gosse, Henry, **II** 476
Gossett, William T., **II** 170
Gossler, Phillip G., **6** 466
Gotaas-Larsen Shipping Corp., **6** 368
Götabanken, **II** 303, 353
Göteborgs Handelsbank, **II** 351
Göteborgs Handelskompani, **III** 425
Göth, Elis, **I** 665
Gothenburg Light & Power Company, **6** 580
Gothenburg Tramways Co., **II** 1
Goto, Shimpei, **V** 448
Goto, Yasuo, **III** 406
Gotoh, Keita, **V** 199, 510, 526–27
Gotoh, Konsuke, **V** 528
Gotoh, Noboru, **V** 527–28
Gotoh, Shinpei, **III** 454
Gott Corp., **III** 614
Gott, Edwin H., **IV** 574; **7** 551
Gott, Rodney C., **7** 211
Götte, Klaus, **III** 563
Gottlieb, David K., **11** 252
Gottlieb, Myron, **6** 162–63
Gottlieb, Richard D., **11** 253
Gottstein, Kurt (Dr.), **III** 693
Gottstein, L., **III** 692
Gottwald, Bruce C., **10** 291
Gottwald, Floyd, **I** 334; **10** 289–90
Gottwald, Floyd, Jr., **I** 334; **10** 290–91
Goudefroy, Hans, **III** 184–85
Goulard and Olena, **I** 412
Goulart, João, **IV** 55
Gould, Bruce, **I** 56
Gould, Charles N., **IV** 391
Gould Inc., **III** 745; **11** 45
Gould, Irving, **7** 95–97
Gould, Jay, **II** 329; **V** 529–30; **6** 338; **9** 370
Gould, William R., **V** 716
Goulding Industries Ltd., **IV** 295
Gourmet Foods, **II** 528
Gousseland, Pierre, **IV** 19
Government Bond Department, **9** 369
Government Employees Insurance Company. *See* GEICO Corporation.
Government National Mortgage Assoc., **II** 410
The Governor and Company of the Bank of Scotland, **II** 422; **III** 360; **V** 166; **10** 336–38
Gowen, Franklin Benjamin, **9** 407
Gower, Bob, **IV** 456–57
GP Group Acquisition Limited Partnership, **10** 288
GPU. *See* General Public Utilities Corporation.
Graber Industries, Inc., **V** 379

Grable, Errett M., **III** 613
Grabowsky, Ian, **6** 79
Grace. *See* W.R. Grace & Co.
Grace Drilling Company, **9** 365
Grace, Elliot, **10** 372
Grace, Eugene G., **IV** 35–36; **7** 48–49
Grace, J. Peter, **I** 547–49
Grace, James, **I** 547
Grace, Jim, **10** 372
Grace, Joseph, **I** 547
Grace, Michael P., **I** 547; **III** 525
Grace, Robert, **I** 584
Grace, William R., **I** 170, 547; **III** 525
Gradco Systems, Inc., **6** 290
Grade, Jeffery T., **8** 243
Grade, Lew (Sir), **I** 531
Gradmann & Holler, **III** 283
Graebner, Wolfgang, **II** 242
Graef & Schmidt, **II** 54
Graf Bertel Dominique/New York, **6** 48
Graf, Robert J., **V** 711
Gräff, Leo, **I** 542
de Graffe, Robert F., **IV** 671
Gragg, Williford, **III** 397
Graham, Ann, **I** 575
Graham, Billy, **10** 58
Graham Container Corp., **8** 477
Graham, D.M., **II** 261
Graham, Dale, **11** 106
Graham, Donald, **IV** 690
Graham family, **IV** 688, 690
Graham, Florence Nightingale. *See* Arden, Elizabeth.
Graham, Ford, **7** 280–82
Graham, Katharine Meyer, **IV** 689–90
Graham Page, **III** 568
Graham, Peter, **II** 358
Graham, Philip, **IV** 689–90
Graham, William B., **I** 627–28; **10** 141–42
Grahams Builders Merchants, **I** 429
Grainger, Isaac, **II** 251
Grainger, William W., **V** 214
Gralla, **IV** 687
Grambling, John A., Jr., **V** 674
Gran Central Corporation, **8** 487
Granada Computer Services, **II** 139
Granada Computer Services International, **II** 139
Granada Group Limited, **II** 138
Granada Group PLC, **II** 70, **138–40**
Granada Group Services, **II** 139
Granada Hospital Group, **II** 139
Granada Microcomputer Services, **II** 139
Granada Motorway Services, **II** 138
Granada Overseas Holdings, **II** 139
Granada Overseas Limited, **II** 138
Granada Royale Hometels, **9** 426
Granada Television, **II** 138–39
Granada Television International, **II** 138
Granada Theatres Limited, **II** 138
Grand Metropolitan plc, **I** 247–49, 259, 261; **II** 555–57, 565, 608, 613–15; **9** 99
Grand Rapids Carpet Sweeper Company, **9** 70
Grand Rapids Gas Light Company. *See* MCN Corporation.
Grand Rapids Wholesale Grocery Company, **8** 481
Grand Trunk Corp., **6** 359–61
Grand Trunk Pacific, **6** 360
Grand Union Company, **II** 637, 662; **7** 202–04; **8** 410
Grand Union Holdings Corp., **7** 204
Grand Union Tea Co., **7** 202

Grand Valley Gas Company, **11** 28
Grand-sons of Francois de Wendel, **IV** 226
Granda Cable and Satellite, **II** 139
Grandell, Leonard, **6** 88
Grandell, Leonard (Lt. Gen.), **III** 647
Grandi, Alberto, **IV** 422
Grandmet USA, **I** 248
de Grandpre, A. Jean, **V** 269–70
Grands Magasins L. Tietz, **V** 103
Granger, William, Jr., **II** 468
Gränges, **III** 480
Granica, Pablo, **II** 198
Granier de Lilliac, René, **IV** 560
Grant, A. A., **6** 561
Grant, Alexander, **II** 592–93
Grant, Alistair, **II** 609–10
Grant, Allen (Sir), **I** 574
Grant, Arthur W., **8** 290
Grant, Brooke, **11** 260–61
Grant, Margaret, **II** 593
Grant, Norman, **III** 738
Grant Oil Tool Co., **III** 569
Grant, Robert McVitie, **II** 592–93
Grant Street National Bank, **II** 317
Grant, Ulysses S., **III** 247; **IV** 604
Grant, William F., **10** 539
Graphic Controls Corp., **IV** 678
Graphic Services, **III** 166; **6** 282
Graphic Systems, **III** 169; **6** 285
Graphics Systems Software, **8** 519
Graphite Oil Product Co., **I** 360
Grass, Alex, **V** 174, 176
Grass Valley Group, **8** 518, 520
Grasselli Dyestuffs Corp., **I** 337
Grasset, **IV** 618
Grasset-Fasquelle, **IV** 617
Grattan, **V** 160
Grau, August, **7** 546–47
Grava, Alfred, **I** 202
Graves, Bob, **IV** 492
Graves, J. P., **6** 596
Gray, A.A. **I** 715
Gray, Bowman, **V** 409
Gray, Bowman, Jr., **V** 409
Gray, Byron A., **III** 529
Gray Dawes & Co., **III** 522–23
Gray Dawes Bank, **III** 523
Gray Dawes Travel, **III** 523
Gray Drug Stores, **III** 745
Gray Dunn and Co., **II** 569
Gray, Elisha (Bud), **II**, **III** 653–54
Gray, George, **III** 359
Gray, Harold, **I** 452
Gray, Harry, **I** 68, 85–86, 143; **III** 74; **9** 418; **10** 537–38; **11** 263
Gray, Jim, **II** 167
Gray, John S., **I** 164; **11** 136
Gray, Latimer W., **II** 208
Gray Mackenzie & Co., **III** 522–23
Gray, R.F., **II** 505
Gray, Seifert and Co., **10** 44
Grayarc, **III** 157
Grayburn, Vandeleur, **II** 297
Grayrock Capital, **I** 275
Greaseater, Ltd., **8** 463
Greaseaters of Ireland, **8** 464
Great American Corp., **III** 191
Great American First Savings Bank of San Diego, **II** 420
Great American Holding Corp., **III** 191
Great American Indemnity Co., **III** 191
Great American Insurance Co., **III** 190–92
Great American Life Insurance Co., **III** 190–92

Great American Management and Investment, Inc., 8 228–31
Great American Mortgage and Investment, **8** 228
Great American Reserve Insurance Co., **IV** 343; **10** 247
Great American Tea Co., **II** 636, 666
Great Atlantic & Pacific Tea Company, Inc., II 636–38, 629, 655–56, 666
Great Beam Co., **III** 690
Great Eastern Railway, **6** 424
Great 5¢ Store, **V** 224
Great Halviggan, **III** 690
Great Lakes Bancorp, 8 232–33
Great Lakes Bankgroup, **II** 457
Great Lakes Chemical Corp., I 341–42; 8 262
Great Lakes Corp., **IV** 136
Great Lakes Pipe Line Co., **IV** 400, 575
Great Lakes Steel Co., **8** 346
Great Lakes Steel Corp., **IV** 236
Great Land Seafoods, Inc., **II** 553
Great Northern, **III** 282
Great Northern Import Co., **I** 292
Great Northern Nekoosa Corp., **IV** 282–83, 300; **9** 260–61
Great Northern Paper Co., **IV** 282
Great Northern Railway Company, **6** 596
Great Universal Stores P.L.C., V 67–9
Great Western Billiard Manufactory, **III** 442
Great Western Corporation, **10** 339
Great Western Financial Corporation, 10 339–41
Great Western Railway, **III** 272
Great Western Savings and Loan, **10** 339
Great Western Savings Bank. *See* Great Western Financial Corporation.
Great Western Savings of Central California, **10** 339
Great Western Tea Co., **II** 643
Great-West Life Assurance Co., **III** 260–61
Great-West Lifeco Inc., III 260–61
Greatamerica Corp., **I** 489; **10** 419
Greater All American Markets, **II** 601; **7** 19
Greater New York Film Rental Co., **II** 169
Greaves, Roger F., **11** 175
Grede, William, **10** 379
Greehey, William, **7** 553–54
Greeley, A.W., **9** 366
Greeley, Horace, **IV** 647
Green, Adolphus, **II** 542–43; **7** 365–66
Green Bay Food Company, **7** 127
Green Cross K.K., **I** 665
Green, Cyril K., **V** 55
Green Giant, **II** 556
Green Island Cement (Holdings) Ltd. Group, **IV** 694–95
Green, Jerome K., **10** 380
Green, John Jefferson, **7** 490–91
Green, Lawrence, **6** 592
Green, Lemuel K., **6** 592–93
Green, Michael D., **6** 278
Green, Owen (Sir), **I** 429
Green, Philip, **8** 502
Green Power & Light Company. *See* UtiliCorp United Inc.
Green, Ralph, **6** 592–93
Green, Richard, **6** 593
Green, Richard, Jr., **6** 593–94
Green River Electric Corporation, **11** 37
Green, Roger E., **10** 112

Green Thumb, **II** 562
Green Tree Financial Corporation, 11 162–63
Greenall, Peter, **III** 724
Greenawalt, Richard A., **8** 10
Greenaway, Peter, **IV** 611
Greenbaum, Leon C., **9** 283
Greenberg, Alan (Ace), **II** 401; **10** 145
Greenberg, Arnold, **11** 449
Greenberg, Frank S., **V** 355
Greenberg, Jeffrey W., **III** 197
Greenberg, M.R., **11** 532
Greenberg, Maurice R., **III** 196–97
Greenberg, Robert, **8** 303–05
Greene, Copley, **III** 312
Greene, Hugh, **7** 54
Greene, Jacob L., **III** 237
Greene, Stewart, **6** 50
Greenfield, Albert M., **9** 448
Greenfield, Jerry, **10** 146
Greenleaf Corp., **IV** 203
Greensboro Life Insurance Company, **11** 213
Greenville Insulating Board Corp., **III** 763
Greenwald, Jim, **6** 32
Greenwalt, Clifford L., **6** 471
Greenway, Charles, **IV** 378–79; **7** 56–57, 59
Greenwell Montagu Gold-Edged, **II** 319
Greenwich Capital Markets, **II** 311
Greenwood, Harold W., **11** 162
Greenwood, Marvin, **11** 225
Greenwood Publishing Group, **IV** 610
Gregg, Frederick, Jr., **9** 320
Gregg Publishing Co., **IV** 636
Gregory, Marion, **7** 480
Gregory, Robert, **V** 391
Gregory, Robert, Jr., **8** 220
Gregory, Vincent, **I** 393
Greiner, Louisa, **III** 442
Grenfell and Colegrave Ltd., **II** 245
Grenfell, Edward, **II** 427–28
Gresham Fire and Accident, **III** 272
Gresham Life Assurance, **III** 200, 272–73
Gresham, Thomas, **II** 236
Gressens, Otto, **IV** 170
Gretton, John, **I** 222
Gretton, John, Jr., **I** 222–23
Greve, Einar, **6** 589–91
Grey (fourth Earl), **III** 104
Grey Advertising, Inc., I 175, 623; **6 26–28; 10** 69
Grey Direct, **6** 27
Grey Entertainment & Media Subsidiary, **6** 27
Grey, Henry, **IV** 35
Grey Medical, **6** 27–28
Grey Public Relations, **6** 27
Grey, Rex B., **III** 163
Grey Reynolds Smith, **6** 27
Grey Strategic Marketing, **6** 27
Grey Studios. *See* Grey Advertising, Inc.
Grey United Stores, **II** 666
Grey/2, **6** 27
Greyhound Corp., I 448–50; II 445; **6** 27; **8** 144–45; **10** 72
Greyhound Dial, **8** 145
Greylock Mills, **III** 213
Grezel, Pierre, **IV** 174
Gribben, George, **I** 37
GRiD Systems Corp., **II** 107
Grier, Herbert E., **8** 163
Griesheim Elektron, **IV** 140
Grieve, Pierson M., **I** 332–33

Grieveson, Grant and Co., **II** 422–23
Griffin and Sons, **II** 543
Griffin, Elton, **III** 672–73
Griffin, Marcus, **6** 109
Griffin, Marvin, Jr., **10** 222
Griffin, Matthew, **9** 194–95
Griffin, Merv, **9** 306
Griffin Pipe Products Co., **7** 30–31
Griffin Wheel Company, **7** 29–30
Griffin, William, **10** 287
Griffith, D.W., **I** 537; **II** 146
Griffith, Franklin, **6** 548–49
Griffith-Boscawen, Arthur, **I** 288
Griffiths, Edgar H., **II** 90
Griffiths, G. Findley, **8** 273–74
Grigg, C.L., **9** 177
Grigg, James, **I** 223
Griggs, Herbert, **II** 217
Grillet, Charles, **I** 488
Grillet, Nicolas, **10** 470
Grimshaw, Norman, **9** 92
Grindlays Bank, **II** 189
Gringoir/Broussard, **II** 556
Grinnell Corp., **III** 643–45; **11** 198
Grinstead, Stanley, **I** 247
Grinstein, Gerald, **V** 428
Grip Printing & Publishing Co., **IV** 644
Grisanti, Eugene P., **9** 292
Griscom, Tom, **11** 153
Grisewood & Dempsey, **IV** 616
Grissom, Virgil, **11** 428
Grissom, Virgil I., **I** 79
Griswald, Gordon, **6** 456
Grocer Publishing Co., **IV** 638
Grocery Store Products Co., **III** 21
Grocery Warehouse, **II** 602
Groebler, Alfred, **III** 694
Groen Manufacturing, **III** 468
Grogan-Cochran Land Company, **7** 345
Grolier, **IV** 619
Grones, Alex, **I** 186
Grönfeldt, Mr., **I** 664
Groot-Noordhollandsche, **III** 177–79
Groovy Beverages, **II** 477
Grosch, Ernst, **III** 695
Gross, Courtland, **11** 267
Gross, Courtlandt, **I** 65
Gross, Patrick W., **11** 18
Gross, Robert, **I** 64–65; **III** 601; **11** 266–67
Gross Townsend Frank Hoffman, **6** 28
Grosset & Dunlap, Inc., **II** 144; **III** 190–91
Grossman, M.J., **III** 375–76
Grossmith Agricultural Industries, **II** 500
Grosvenor, Edwin, **9** 366
Grosvenor, Gilbert H., **9** 366–67
Grosvenor, Gilbert M., **9** 367–68
Grosvenor Marketing Co., **II** 465
Grosvenor, Melville Bell, **9** 367
Grotoh, Keita, **V** 487
Groton Victory Yard, **I** 661
Grotrian, Herbert (Sir), **IV** 685
Group Hospitalization and Medical Services, **10** 161
Groupe AG, **III** 201–02
Groupe Air France, 6 92–94
Groupe Ancienne Mutuelle, **III** 210–11
Groupe Barthelmey, **III** 373
Groupe Bull. *See* Compagnie des Machines Bull.
Groupe Bull, **10** 563–64
Groupe de la Cité, IV 614–16, 617
Groupe de la Financière d'Angers, **IV** 108

Groupe Salvat, **IV** 619
Groupe Victoire, **III** 394
Groupement des Exploitants Pétroliers, **IV** 545
Grousbeck, Irving, **7** 98–99
Groux Beverage Corporation, **11** 451
Grove, Andrew, **II** 44–46; **10** 365–67
Grove, Ernest L., Jr., **10** 306
Grove Manufacturing Co., **I** 476–77; **9** 393
Grover, Lewis C., **III** 302
Grow, Robert, **7** 193–94
Growmark, **I** 421; **11** 23
Grua, Rudolph, **10** 314
Grubb, L. Edward, **IV** 111
Gruene Apotheke, **I** 681
Gruhl, Alfred, **6** 602
Grum, Clifford, **IV** 343
Grumman Corp., **I** 58–59, **61–63**, 67–68, 78, 84, 490, 511; **7** 205; **8** 51; **9** 17, 206–07, 417, 460; **10** 316–17, 536; **11** **164–67 (upd.)**, 363–65, 428
Grumman, Leroy, **I** 61–63, 490; **11** 164, 166
Grün & Bilfinger A.G., **I** 560–61
Grün, August, **I** 560
Grundhofer, Jerry A., **11** 466–67
Grundig, **I** 411; **II** 80, 117
Grundig, Max, **II** 117
Grune, George, **IV** 664
Grunenthal, **I** 240
Gruner + Jahr, **IV** 590, 593
Gruntal and Co., **III** 263
Gruntal Financial Corp., **III** 264
Grupo Corvi S.A. de C.V., **7** 115
Grupo Industrial Alfa, **II** 262; **11** 386
Grupo Televisa, S.A., **9** 429
Grupo Tudor, **IV** 471
Grupo Zeta, **IV** 652–53; **7** 392
Gruppo IRI, **V** 325–27
Grusin, Harry Jack. *See* Gray, Harry.
GSG&T, **6** 495
GSI. *See* Geophysical Service, Inc.
GSU. *See* Gulf States Utilities Company.
GTE Corporation, **II** 38, 47, 80; **V** **294–98**; **9** 49, 478–80; **10** 19, 97, 431; **11** 500. *See also* British Columbia Telephone Company.
GTE Data Services, **9** 171
GTE Products Corp., **III** 475
GTE Sprint Communications, **9** 478–79
GTE Telenet Information Services, **III** 118
GTO. *See* Global Transport Organization.
Guangzhou M. C. Packaging, **10** 130
Guaranty Federal Savings & Loan Assoc., **IV** 343
Guaranty Federal Savings Bank, **IV** 343
Guaranty Properties Ltd., **11** 258
Guaranty Savings and Loan, **10** 339
Guaranty Trust Co. of New York, **II** 329–32, 428; **IV** 20
Guardian, **III** 721
Guardian Federal Savings and Loan Association, **10** 91
Guardian Mortgage Company, **8** 460
Guardian National Bank, **I** 165; **11** 137
Guardian Royal Exchange, **III** 350
Guardian Royal Exchange Plc, **11** **168–70**
Gubanich, John A., **6** 444
Gubay, Albert, **11** 239
Guber, Peter, **II** 137, 149
Guelph Dolime, **IV** 74
Guerney, Samuel, **III** 372
Guernsey Banking Co., **II** 333

Guest, Charlotte (Lady), **III** 493
Guest, John, **III** 493
Guest, Josiah (John) (Sir), **III** 493
Guest, Keen & Co., **III** 493
Guest, Keen & Nettlefolds Ltd., **III** 493–95
Guest, Keen and Nettlefolds plc, **III** 495. *See also* GKN plc.
Guest Keen Baldwins Iron and Steel Co., **III** 493–94
Guest, Keen Iron and Steel Co., **III** 494
Guest, Keen, Williams Ltd., **III** 493
Guest, Thomas, **III** 493
Gueyraud et Fils Cadet, **III** 703
Gueyraud, Felix, **III** 703
Gugelmann, Fritz, **I** 122
Guggenheim Brothers, **IV** 32
Guggenheim, Daniel, **IV** 31–33
Guggenheim family, **IV** 31–32, 176; **7** 261
Guggenheim, Isaac, **IV** 32
Guggenheim, Meyer, **IV** 31
Guggenheim, Murry, **IV** 32
Guggenheim, Simon, **IV** 32–33
Guggenheim, Solomon, **IV** 32
Guilford Industries, **8** 271
Guilford Mills Inc., **8 234–36**
Guilford of Maine, Inc., **8** 270, 272
Guiliani, Rudolph, **II** 408
Guillaumat, Pierre, **IV** 544–47, 560; **7** 482–84
Guillichsen, Alex, **IV** 277
Guimet, Emile, **IV** 173
Guimet, Jean-Baptiste, **IV** 173
Guinn, Donald, **V** 319
Guinness, Adelaide, **I** 251
Guinness, Arthur, **I** 250
Guinness, Arthur Edward, **I** 250
Guinness, Arthur, II, **I** 250
Guinness, Benjamin Lee, **I** 250
Guinness, Edward Cecil, **I** 250–51
Guinness, Hosea, **I** 250
Guinness Peat, **10** 277
Guinness plc, **I** 239, 241, **250–52**, 268, 272, 282; **II** 428–29, 610; **9** 100, 449; **10** 399
Gujarat State Fertilizer Co., **III** 513
Gulbenkian, Calouste, **IV** 363, 515, 557–58
Gulco Industries, Inc., **11** 194
Güldner Aschaffenburg, **I** 582
Güldner, Hugo, **I** 582
Gulez, Turgut, **IV** 562
Gulf + Western Inc., **I** 418, **451–53**, 540; **II** 147, 154–56, 177; **III** 642, 745; **IV** 289, 672; **7** 64
Gulf + Western Industries, **10** 482
Gulf Air, **6** 63
Gulf Canada Ltd., **I** 216, 262, 264; **IV** 495, 721; **6** 478; **9** 391
Gulf Caribbean Marine Lines, **6** 383
Gulf Corp., **IV** 385–87, 421, 510, 538. *See also* Gulf Oil Corp.
Gulf Engineering Co. Ltd., **IV** 131
Gulf Exploration Co., **IV** 454
Gulf, Mobile & Ohio, **11** 187
Gulf Mobile and Northern Railroad, **I** 456
Gulf Mobile and Ohio Railroad, **I** 456
Gulf of Suez Petroleum Co., **IV** 412–14
Gulf Oil Corp., **I** 37, 584; **II** 315, 402, 408, 448; **III** 225, 231, 259, 497; **IV** 198, 287, 392, 450–51, 466, 470, 472–73, 476, 484, 508, 512, 531, 565, 570, 576. *See also* Gulf Corp.
Gulf Plains Corp., **III** 471

Gulf Public Service Company, **6** 580
Gulf States Paper, **IV** 345
Gulf States Steel, **I** 491
Gulf States Utilities Company, **6 495–97**
Gulf United Corp., **III** 194
Gulfstream Aerospace Corp., **7 205–06**
Gulfstream Banks, **II** 336
Gullichsen, Alexander, **IV** 274–75
Gulliver, James, **II** 609–10, 628
Gulton Industries Inc., **7** 297
Gumbiner, Robert, **6** 184–86
Gummi Werke, **I** 208
Gump's, **7** 286
Gumucio, Marcelo, **III** 131
Gund, John, **I** 253
Gunda, John, **III** 323
Gundy, Richard H., **9** 142
Gunfred Group, **I** 387
Gunns Ltd., **II** 482
Gunpowder Trust, **I** 379
Gunst, Robert A., **10** 335
Gunter Wulff Automaten, **III** 430
Gunther, Hans, **I** 349
Gunther, John, **I** 15
Gunther, S.A., **8** 477
Gupta, Rajat, **9** 343
Gupte, Subbash, **6** 64
Gurneys, Birkbeck, Barclay & Buxton, **II** 235
Gusswerk Paul Saalmann & Sohne, **I** 582
Gustav Schickendanz KG, **V** 165
Gustav V, King (Sweden), **I** 448; **III** 28
Gustavus A. Pfeiffer & Co., **I** 710
Gut, Rainer, **II** 268
Gutehoffnungshütte Aktienverein AG, **III** 561, 563; **IV** 104, 201
Gutfreund, John, **II** 448, 449
Guth, Charles G., **I** 276–77; **10** 451
Guth, W., **IV** 141
Guthrie Balfour, **II** 499–500
Guthrie, Giles, **I** 93
Gutman, Eugene, **II** 281
Gutmann, Bessie Pease, **11** 95
Gutmann, Max, **10** 281–82
Gutta Percha Co., **I** 428
Gutzeit. *See* AB W. Gutzeit & Co. *and* W. Gutzeit & Co.
Gutzeit, Hans, **IV** 274
Guy Carpenter & Co., **III** 282
Guy Salmon Service, Ltd., **6** 349
Guzzle, Timothy L., **6** 583
GW Utilities Ltd., **I** 264; **6** 478
Gwathmey & Co., **II** 424
Gwillim, Russell A., **8** 463
Gwilt, George, **III** 361
Gwinn, Robert P., **7** 167
Gwinn, W.P., **I** 85; **10** 537
Gwynn, William, **V** 552
Gyllenhammar, Pehr G., **I** 210–11; **7** 566
Gypsum, Lime, & Alabastine Canada Ltd., **IV** 271
Gysler, Friedrich, **III** 402

H & R Block, Incorporated, **9 268–70**
H N Norton Co., **11** 208
H.A. Job, **II** 587
H.B. Claflin Company, **V** 139
H.B. Fuller Company, **8 237–40**
H.B. Reese Candy Co., **II** 511
H.B. Viney Company, Inc., **11** 211
H.C. Christians Co., **II** 536
H.C. Frick Coke Co., **IV** 573; **7** 550
H.C. Petersen & Co., **III** 417

H.D. Lee Company, Inc. *See* Lee Apparel Company, Inc.
H.D. Pochin & Co., **III** 690
H. Douglas Barclay, **8** 296
H.F. Ahmanson & Company, II 181–82; 10 342–44 (upd.)
H.F. Ahmanson Co., **II** 181
H. Fairweather and Co., **I** 592
H.G. Anderson Equipment Corporation, **6** 441
H. Hackfeld & Co., **I** 417
H. Hamilton Pty, Ltd., **III** 420
H.I. Rowntree and Co., **II** 568
H.J. Green, **II** 556
H.J. Heinz Co., Ltd., **II** 508; **III** 21
H.J. Heinz Company, I 30–31, 605, 612; **II** 414, 480, 450, **507–09**, 547; **7** 382, 448, 576, 578; **8** 499; **10** 151; **11 171–73 (upd.)**
H.K. Ferguson Company, **7** 355
H.L. Green Company, Inc., **9** 448
H.L. Judd Co., **III** 628
H.L. Yoh Company, **9** 163
H.M. Byllesby & Company, Inc., **6** 539
H.M. Goush Co., **IV** 677–78
H.M. Spalding Electric Light Plant, **6** 592
H. Miller & Sons, Inc., **11** 258
H.O. Houghton & Company, **10** 355
H.P. Foods, **II** 475
H.P. Hood, **7** 17–18
H.P. Smith Paper Co., **IV** 290
H.R. MacMillan Export Co., **IV** 306–08
H. Reeve Angel & Co., **IV** 300
H.V. McKay Proprietary, **III** 651
H.W. Heidmann, **I** 542
H.W. Johns Manufacturing Co., **III** 706; **7** 291
H.W. Johns-Manville Corp., **III** 663, 706–08; **7** 291
H.W. Madison Co., **11** 211
H. Williams and Co., Ltd., **II** 678
Haab, Larry D., **6** 507
Haack, Robert, **I** 66; **11** 268
Häagen-Dazs, **II** 556–57, 631; **10** 147
Haagn, Ernst (Dr.), **IV** 99
Haake-Beck Brauerei AG, **9** 86
Haas, Carl, **IV** 323
Haas Corp., **I** 481
Haas, Earle, **8** 511
Haas, James, **V** 152
Haas, John, **I** 392–93
Haas, Otto, **I** 391–92
Haas, Robert D., **9** 344
Haas, Rudolf Christian, **IV** 323
Haas, Walter, **V** 363
Haase, Alfred, **III** 185
Haber, Fritz, **I** 349
Haber, Ludwig F., **I** 369
Haberer, Jean Yves, **II** 260; **9** 148
Habib, Philip, **I** 559
Habirshaw Cable and Wire Corp., **IV** 177
Habkirk, Lon, **9** 144
Hachette, IV 614–15, **617–19**, 675
Hachette Filipacchi Magazines, **11** 293
Hachette, George, **IV** 617
Hachette, Louis, **IV** 617–18
Hachette Première, **IV** 619
Hachette S.A., **10** 288
Hachette-Littérature, **IV** 617
Hachirobei, Takatoshi, **II** 325
Hachisuka, Mochiaki, **III** 383
Hachmeister, Inc., **II** 508; **11** 172
Hackbarth, Ed, **7** 505
Hackblock, W.H., **I** 287

Hacker-Pschorr Brau, **II** 242
Hackfeld, Heinrich, **I** 417
Hackworth, Michael, **11** 56–57
Hadden, Briton, **IV** 673; **7** 526
Hadleigh-Crowther, **I** 715
Haebler, William T., **9** 290
Haemocell, **11** 476
Hafez Insurance Co., **III** 242
Haffner, Charles C. (Gen.), Jr., **IV** 661
Haft family, **II** 656
Hagan, Ward S., **I** 711–12; **10** 550–51
Hagel, Raymond C., **7** 286
Hagen, James A., **V**, 436
Hagen, Torstein, **6** 405
Häggert, Carl Erick, **I** 664
Haggerty, Joseph, **10** 421
Haggerty, Patrick E., **II** 112–14; **11** 505–07
Haggie, **IV** 91
Haggin, James Ben Ali, **I** 527; **10** 527
Haglund, Philip, **8** 448
Haglund, Wilhelm, **IV** 203
Hagstrom, Tony, **V** 332
Hagura, Nobuya, **II** 274
Hahn, Carl C., **I** 207–08; **11** 550
Hahn, T. Marshall, Jr., **IV** 282–83; **9** 260–61
Hahnemann, Paul, **I** 139
Haid, Paul, **III** 241
Haig, Alexander, **I** 86, 559; **10** 538
Hain Pure Food Co., **I** 514
Hainaut-Sambre, **IV** 52
Haines, Jordan L., **11** 144–45
Hait, James M., **I** 442–43; **11** 134
Hajjar, W. Douglas, **11** 47
Hakkarainen, Niilo, **IV** 349–50
A.B. Hakon Swenson, **II** 639
Hakuhodo Advertising America, **6** 30
Hakuhodo, Inc., 6 29–31, 48–49
Hakuhodo Newspaper and Magazine Advertising, **6** 29
HAL Inc., 9 271–73
Halaby, Najeeb, **I** 116
Halbou, Alphonse, **IV** 52
Halcon International, **IV** 456
Haldeman, H.R., **I** 20
Hale, Charles, **I** 314
Hale, Prentis, **V** 29–30
Haley, Roy W., **11** 17
Halfords, **V** 17, 19
Halfords Ltd., **IV** 382–83
Halifax, **III** 309
Halifax (Lord), **I** 107
Halifax Banking Co., **II** 220
Halifax Timber, **I** 335
Hall & Levine Agency, **I** 14
Hall, A. Rupert, **I** 715
Hall and Co., **III** 737
Hall and Ham River, **III** 739
Hall, Arnold (Sir), **I** 51; **III** 509
Hall, Arthur Fletcher, **III** 274–75
Hall Bros. Co., **IV** 620–21; **7** 23
Hall, Charles Martin, **IV** 14
Hall Containers, **III** 739
Hall, Donald, **IV** 620–21
Hall, Edward Smith, **II** 388
Hall, Floyd, **I** 102
Hall, Harold, **V** 485
Hall, John, **III** 285
Hall, John R., **IV** 374
Hall, Joseph, **II** 644
Hall, Joyce C., **IV** 620–21
Hall, Perry, **II** 431
Hall, Robert C., **6** 483

Hall, Rollie, **IV** 620
Hall, Ronald E., **IV** 392–93
Hall, Wilfred, **IV** 271–72
Hall, William, **IV** 620
Hall, William W., **9** 274
Hallamore Manufacturing Co., **I** 481
Hallas-Moller, Gudrun, **I** 658
Hallas-Moller, Knud, **I** 658–59
Halle, Pentti, **IV** 276
Haller, Raymond & Brown, Inc., **II** 10
Halliburton Company, II 112; **III** 473, **497–500**, 617; **11** 505
Halliburton, Erle Palmer, **III** 497–98
Halliburton Oil Well Cementing Co., **III** 497–98
Halliburton, Vida, **III** 497
Hallivet China Clay Co., **III** 690
Hallman, Michael, **6** 260
Hallmark Cards, Inc., IV 620–21; **7** 23–25
Hallmark Chemical Corp., **8** 386
Hallstein, D. Wayne, **III** 526
Hallward, Hugh G., **7** 488
Haloid Company. *See* Xerox Corporation.
Haloid Xerox. *See* Xerox Corporation.
Halpern, Ralph, **V** 2
Halpin, James, **10** 236
Halsey, Brenton S., **IV** 289–90
Halsey, Stuart & Co., **II** 431; **III** 276
Halske, J.G., **II** 97
Halstead, Ronald (Sir), **III** 66
Halsted, G.A. (Capt.), **III** 278
Ham, Arthur, **II** 418
Hamada, Hiroshi, **III** 160
Hamada Printing Press, **IV** 326
Hamanaka, Shoichiro, **V** 479
Hamashbir Lata'asiyah, **II** 47
Hambleton, Bert, **9** 39–40
Hambrecht & Quist, **10** 463, 504
Hambro American Bank & Trust Co., **11** 109
Hambro Life Assurance, **I** 426
Hambros, **II** 422
Hamburg-Amerikanische-Packetfahrt-Actien-Gesellschaft, **6** 397–98
Hamburg Banco, **II** 351
Hamburg-Amerika, **I** 542
Hamburger Flugzeubau GmbH., **I** 74
Hamer Hammer Service, Inc., **11** 523
Hamersley Holdings, **IV** 59–61
Hamersley Iron, **IV** 59–60
Hamilton Aero Manufacturing, **I** 47, 84; **10** 162
Hamilton, Alex D., **IV** 272
Hamilton, Alexander, **II** 207, 216
Hamilton, Anthony, **9** 55–56
Hamilton Beach/Proctor-Silex, Inc., **7** 369–70
Hamilton Blast Furnace Co., **IV** 208
Hamilton Brown Shoe Co., **III** 528
Hamilton, Carl, **10** 172–73
Hamilton, David, **III** 522
Hamilton, George (Lord), **IV** 217
Hamilton, Keith, **6** 100, 117
Hamilton, Lloyd N., **IV** 536
Hamilton Malleable Iron Co., **IV** 73
Hamilton Oil Corp., **IV** 47
Hamilton, Richard W., **IV** 645
Hamilton Standard, **9** 417
Hamilton Steel and Iron Co., **IV** 208
Hamilton, Thomas, **9** 416
Hamilton, William, **III** 369
Hamish Hamilton, **IV** 659; **8** 526
Hamlet, Kenneth, **III** 94–95

Hamlyn, Paul, **IV** 667
Hammamatsu Commerce Bank, **II** 291
Hammarsforsens Kraft, **IV** 339
Hammer, Armand, **IV** 392, 480–82; **8** 262; **10** 379
Hammer, Frances, **IV** 480
Hammerich & Lesser, **IV** 589
Hammermill Paper Co., **IV** 287
Hammers Plastic Recycling, **6** 441
Hammerson, Lew, **IV** 696
Hammerson Property and Investment Trust, **IV** 696–97
Hammerson Property Investment and Development Corporation PLC, IV 696–98
Hammerstein, Oscar, II, **IV** 671
Hammond Corp., **IV** 136
Hammond, John Hays, **IV** 95
Hammond Lumber Co., **IV** 281; **9** 259
Hammond, Mike, **10** 307
Hammond's, **II** 556
Hammonton Electric Light Company, **6** 449
Hamomag AG, **III** 546
Hampton Inns, **9** 425–26
Han Kook Fertilizer Co., **I** 516
Hanafy, Amin, **10** 15
Hanbro Life Assurance Ltd., **III** 339
Hanbury, Taylor, Lloyd and Bowman, **II** 306
Hanburys and Lloyds, **II** 306
Hancock, Frederick, **8** 395
Hancock Jaffe Laboratories, **11** 460
Hancock, Lang, **IV** 59
Hancock, Walter, **I** 428
Hand in Hand, **III** 234
Hand, John, **IV** 660
Hand, Learned (Judge), **I** 698; **IV** 15
Handelsbank of Basel, **III** 375
Handelsfinanz Bank of Geneva, **II** 319
Handelsmaatschappij Montan N.V., **IV** 127
Handelsunion AG, **IV** 222
Handler, Elliot, **7** 304
Handler, Ruth, **7** 304–05
Handley Page Transport Ltd., **I** 50, 92–93
Handy Dan, **V** 75
Hanes, Bill, **I** 379–80
Hanes Corp., **II** 572–73; **8** 202, 288
Hanes Holding Company, **11** 256
Hang Lung Bank, **IV** 717
Hang Seng Bank, **II** 298; **IV** 717
Hanigan, Jack, **III** 443–44
Hanil Development Company, **6** 98
Hanjin Group, **6** 98
Hanjin Sightseeing Bus Company, **6** 98
Hanjin Transportation Co., **6** 98
Hankook Tyre Manufacturing Company, **V** 255–56
Hanks, Tom, **II** 144, 173
Hankuk Glass Industry Co., **III** 715
Hankuk Safety Glass Co., **III** 715
Hankyu and Toho Group, **V** 70
Hankyu Corporation, V 454–56
Hankyu Department Stores, Inc., V 70–71
Hankyu Ings Co., Ltd., **V** 71
Hanley, H.L., **6** 504–05
Hanley, John W., **I** 366; **9** 356
Hanlin, H. Carey, **III** 332–33
Hanman, Gary, **7** 339
Hanmi Citizen Precision Industry, **III** 455
Hanna, Daniel R., **8** 345
Hanna, David B., **6** 360
Hanna, Howard Melville, **8** 345

Hanna, Howard Melville, Jr., **8** 345–46
Hanna Iron Ore Co., **IV** 236
Hanna, Leonard, **8** 345
Hanna, Leonard Colton, **8** 345
Hanna, Marcus Alonzo, **8** 345
Hanna Mining Co., **8** 346–47
Hanna, William, **II** 148
Hanna-Barbera, **7** 306
Hannah, Daryl, **II** 173
Hannen Brauerei GmbH, **9** 100
Hannevig, Christoffer, **8** 102
Hannifin Corp., **III** 602
Hannon, John W., **II** 231
Hannoversche Bank, **II** 278
Hanold, Terrance, **II** 556
Hanover Bank, **II** 312–13
Hanovia Co., **IV** 78
Hanrstoffe-und Düngemittelwerk Saar-Lothringen GmbH, **IV** 197
Hans Grohe, **III** 570
Hansard, Luke Graves, **7** 215–16
Hansberger, Robert V., **IV** 255–56; **8** 65–66
Hanseco Reinsurance Co., **III** 343
Hansen, Harald R., **10** 299
Hansen, Kenneth, **6** 44
Hansen, Zenon C.R., **I** 178–79
Hanson, Clarence B., Jr., **IV** 582
Hanson family, **IV** 582
Hanson, Harry, **8** 448
Hanson Industries, Inc., **III** 501–03; **IV** 169, 173; **7** 207–09
Hanson, James Edward, (Lord), **III** 501–03; **7** 207–10
Hanson, John K., **7** 589–91
Hanson, John V., **7** 589–90
Hanson Lighting, **III** 501
Hanson Lighting Group, **7** 207
Hanson PLC, III 501–03; IV 94, 97, 169, 171, 290; 7 207–10 (upd.); 8 224
Hanson, Robert, **III** 463
Hanson Trust, **I** 438, 475, 477; **II** 319; **III** 501–02, 506; **IV** 23; **7** 207
Hanta, Edward H. *See* Edward H. Hunter.
Hanta, Ryutaro, **III** 513
Hapag. *See* Hamburg-Americanische-Pacetfahrt-Aktien-Gesellschaft.
Hapag-Lloyd Ag, 6 397–99
Happy Eater Ltd., **III** 106
Haralambos Beverage Corporation, **11** 451
Harald Quant Group, **III** 377
Harb, Talaat, **6** 84
Harben, Henry, **III** 334–35
Harben, Henry Andrade, **III** 335
Harbison, Leslie, **II** 417–18
Harbison-Walker, **III** 472
Harbor Tug and Barge Co., **6** 382
Harborlite Corporation, **10** 45
Harcourt (Lord), **II** 428
Harcourt, Alfred, **IV** 622
Harcourt, Brace & World, Inc., **IV** 622
Harcourt, Brace and Co., **IV** 622
Harcourt, Brace and Howe, **IV** 622–23
Harcourt Brace Jovanovich, Inc., II 133–34; III 118; IV 622–24, 642, 672; 7 312
Harcros Chemical Group, **III** 699
Harcros Investment Trust Ltd., **III** 698–99
Hardee's, **II** 679; **7** 430; **8** 564; **9** 178
Hardin, John R., **III** 303
Harding, James W., **III** 271
Harding, Warren G., **II** 315–16; **III** 302; **IV** 252, 595, 688
Hardison & Stewart Oil, **IV** 569

Hardison, Wallace, **IV** 569
Hardman Inc., **III** 699
Hardman, John, **II** 611–12
Hardwick Stove Co., **III** 573
Hardy, Jim, **11** 191
Hardy, Joe, Jr., **9** 196
Hardy, Joseph A., Sr., **9** 196–97
Hardy, Maggie, **9** 196–97
Hardy, Maurice, **9** 397
Hardy, N.E., **I** 268
Hardy Spicer, **III** 595
Hardymon, James F., **II** 20
Hare, Archdeacon, **7** 284
Harima Shipbuilding & Engineering Co., Ltd., **I** 511, 534; **III** 513, 533
Harima Zosenjo, Ltd., **IV** 129
Harker, Ronald W., **I** 83, 196
Harkins, Robert, **10** 82
Härkönen, Aarne, **III** 648–49
Harlan, Neil, **I** 497
Harlem Globetrotters, **7** 199, 335
Harlequin Enterprises Ltd., **IV** 587, 590, 617, 619, 672
Harley, William S., **7** 211
Harley-Davidson Inc., III 658; 7 211–14
Harlow, James G., Jr., **6** 540
Harlow, Jean, **III** 46
Harlow Metal Co. Ltd., **IV** 119
Harman, Pete, **7** 265
Harmon, David E., **11** 86
Harmon, Mark, **I** 12
Harmsworth, Alfred, **7** 341–43
Harmsworth, Alfred (Lord Northcliffe), **IV** 257, 665, 685
Harmsworth, Arthur, **7** 342
Harmsworth, Harold (Lord Rothermere), **IV** 257, 665–66, 685; **7** 341–42
Harnden, William, **II** 395; **10** 59
Harness, Edward G., **III** 52; **8** 433
Harnischfeger Corp., **I** 186; **IV** 130
Harnischfeger, Henry, **8** 241–42
Harnischfeger, Henry II, **8** 242–43
Harnischfeger Industries, Inc., 8 241–44
Harnischfeger, Walter, **8** 242
Haroff, Ray, **10** 156, 158
Harold A. Wilson & Co., **I** 405
Harper & Row, **IV** 652; **7** 391
Harper, Brad, **10** 166
Harper, Charles, **II** 494
Harper, I.W., **II** 407
Harper, J.C., **IV** 607
Harper, John, **IV** 15
Harper, Marion, **I** 16–17, 36
Harper, Paul, **I** 31
HarperCollins Publishers, **IV** 652; **7** 389, 391
Harpo Productions, **9** 307
Harpole, Murray, **7** 419–20
Harrah, Bill, **9** 426
Harrah's, **9** 425–27
Harrell International, **III** 21
Harriman, Averell, **I** 78, 89; **11** 427
Harriman Co., **IV** 310
Harriman, E. H., **V** 427, 517–18, 530–31
Harriman, E. Roland, **V** 530
Harriman, Edward H., **II** 381
Harriman, Henry, **V** 662
Harriman, Ripley and Co., **II** 407
Harriman, W. Averell, **V** 530–31
Harrington, Michael, **I** 355
Harris Abattoir Co., **II** 482
Harris, Alanson, **III** 650
Harris Automatic Press Co., **II** 37
Harris Bankcorp, **II** 211

Harris, Billy Bob, **I** 491
Harris Corporation, II 37–39; 11 46, 286, 490
Harris Daishowa (Australia) Pty., Ltd., **IV** 268
Harris, Dave, **IV** 480
Harris Financial, Inc., **11** 482
Harris, George James, **II** 568–69
Harris, Harold R., **I** 113; **6** 104
Harris, Hollis L., **6** 61
Harris, Irving, **9** 413
Harris, J. Ira, **II** 448; **IV** 137
Harris, James M., **III** 124; **6** 221–23
Harris Laboratories, **II** 483
Harris, Mike, **7** 333
Harris, Monroe, **III** 707; **7** 292
Harris, Neison, **9** 413
Harris Pharmaceuticals Ltd., **11** 208
Harris, Robert, **II** 315; **V** 426
Harris, Robert T., **10** 543
Harris, Shearon, **V** 565–66
Harris/3M Document Products, Inc., **II** 39
Harris Transducer Corporation, **10** 319
Harris-Intertype Corp., **II** 37–38
Harris-Seybold-Potter Co., **II** 37
Harrisburg Bank, **II** 315
Harrisburg National Bank and Trust Co., **II** 316
Harrison & Sons (Hanley) Ltd., **III** 681
Harrison, Benjamin, **I** 323
Harrison, Daniel, **III** 696
Harrison, E. Hunter, **11** 188
Harrison, Ernest, **II** 83–84
Harrison, Fairfax, **V** 485
Harrison, George, **III** 334
Harrison, Godfrey, **I** 576
Harrison, J.B., **10** 222
Harrison, Joseph, **III** 696
Harrison, Perry, **II** 668
Harrison, Richard D., **II** 624–25
Harrison, Russell E., **II** 245
Harrison, Smith, **III** 696
Harrison, Terry, **7** 456
Harrison, Thomas G., **II** 668
Harrison, William, **IV** 685
Harrisons & Crosfield Ltd., **III** 696–99
Harrisons & Crosfield plc, III 696–700
Harrisons, King and Irwin, **III** 697–98
Harrow Stores Ltd., **II** 677
Harry F. Allsman Co., **III** 558
Harry Ferguson Co., **III** 651
Harry N. Abrams, Inc., **IV** 677
Harsco Corporation, 8 245–47; 11 135
Harshaw Chemical Company, **9** 154
Harshaw/Filtrol Partnership, **IV** 80
Hart, Alex W., **9** 334, 335
Hart, Claude E., **8** 126
Hart, Gary, **I** 62; **11** 165
Hart, George P., **III** 627
Hart Glass Manufacturing, **III** 423
Hart, Harry, **8** 248
Hart, John M., **9** 304
Hart, Lorenz, **IV** 671
Hart, Max, **8** 248
Hart, Milledge A. (Mitch), **III** 136–37
Hart, Ralph A., **I** 260
Hart, Schaffner & Marx, **8** 248–49
Hart Son and Co., **I** 592
Hart, William H., **III** 626–28
Harte & Co., **IV** 409; **7** 308
Harter BanCorp., **9** 474
Harter Bank & Trust, **9** 475
Hartford Container Company, **8** 359
Hartford Fire Insurance, **11** 198

Hartford, George Huntington, **II** 636–37
Hartford, George, Jr., **II** 636–37
Hartford Insurance, **I** 463–64
Hartford, John, **II** 636–37
Hartford Trust Co., **II** 213
Hartford-Connecticut Trust Co., **II** 213
Hartley, Fred, **IV** 570–71
Hartley, John, **II** 37
Hartley, Milton E., **10** 282
Hartley's, **II** 477
Hartman, Alexander W., **11** 313
Hartmann & Braun, **III** 566
Hartmarx Corporation, 8 248–50
Hartnack, Carl, **II** 349
Hartshorn, Terry, **11** 378–79
Hartstone, Leon, **11** 556
Hartt, Stanley, **V** 28
Hartunian, Gordon, **10** 9–11
Hartwright, Tim, **III** 739
Harvest International, **III** 201
Harvestore, **11** 5
Harvey Aluminum, **I** 68
Harvey Benjamin Fuller, **8** 237–38
Harvey, George, **III** 158
Harvey, James R., **I** 537; **II** 148; **6** 598
Harvey Lumber and Supply Co., **III** 559
Harvey-Bailey, Alex, **I** 196
Harvey-Jones, John (Sir), **I** 353
Hasan, Malik M., **11** 174–76
Hasbro Bradley Inc., **III** 506
Hasbro Canada, **III** 504
Hasbro, Inc., III 504–06; IV 676; **7** 305, 529
Hasbro Industries, **III** 504–06
Hascal, Adolfo, **IV** 504
Hasegawa, Kaneshige, **I** 398
Hashida, Tanzo, **II** 293
Hashimoto, Keizaburo, **IV** 554
Hashimoto, Masujiro, **I** 183; **11** 350
Hashimoto, Ryutaro, **9** 379
Haskell, Amory, **I** 328
Haskell, Clinton, **II** 467–68
Haskell, George, **II** 467
Haskell, Jabez, **I** 320
Haskins, Christopher, **10** 442–43
Haslam, Robert (Sir), **IV** 40
Hasler Holding AG, **9** 32
Hassel, Karl E., **II** 123
Hassenfeld, Alan, **III** 505–06
Hassenfeld Brothers (Canada) Ltd., **III** 504
Hassenfeld Brothers Inc., **III** 504
Hassenfeld, Harold, **III** 504–05
Hassenfeld, Henry, **III** 504
Hassenfeld, Herman, **III** 504
Hassenfeld, Hilal, **III** 504
Hassenfeld, Merrill, **III** 504–05
Hassenfeld, Stephen D., **III** 505–06
Hassler, Russell, **9** 276
Hasten Bancorp, **11** 371
Haswell, Ernest Bruce, **III** 50
Hata, Itsuzo, **V** 380
Hata, Kenjiro, **III** 289
Hatch, Calvin, **IV** 21
Hatch, H. Clifford, **I** 263–64
Hatch, Harry C., **I** 262–63
Hatch, Orrin, **III** 188
Hatfield, Robert, **I** 500
Hathaway Manfacturing Co., **III** 213
Hathaway Shirt Co., **I** 25–26
Hatlen, Roe, **10** 186–87
Hatori, Sachio, **IV** 163
Hatry, Clarence, **II** 421
Hatsopoulos, George, **7** 520–21
Hatsopoulos, George, Dr., **11** 512

Hatsopoulos, John, **7** 520
Hatt, Fritz, **V** 442
Hatt, Hans, **V** 442
Hatton, Frank, **IV** 688
Hattori (Hong Kong) Ltd., **III** 620
Hattori (Thailand) Ltd., **III** 621
Hattori, Genzo, **III** 619–20
Hattori, Ichiro, **III** 620–21
Hattori, Kentaro, **III** 620–21
Hattori, Kintaro, **III** 619
Hattori Overseas (Hong Kong) Ltd., **III** 620
Hattori, Reijiro, **III** 621
Hattori Seiko Co., Ltd., **III** 455, 619–21
Hattori, Shoji, **III** 620
Haub, Evrian, **II** 638
Hauer, Jacob, **8** 412
Hauge, Gabriel, **II** 313
Haugh, Robert J., **III** 357
Haughton, Daniel, **I** 65; **11** 267–68
Hauptfuhrer, Robert, **7** 414–15
Havas, **IV** 616
Havas, Auguste, **10** 345
Havas, Charles, **IV** 668–69; **10** 345
Havas, SA, 10 195–96, **345–48**
Haven Automation International, **III** 420
Havens, Joshua P., **III** 224
Haverty, Harold, **7** 137, 139
de Havilland Aircraft Co., **I** 82, 92–93, 104, 195; **III** 507–08
Havilland, Olivia de, **II** 175
Hawaii Electric Company, **9** 276
Hawaii National Bank, **11** 114
Hawaiian, Airlines, **6** 104
Hawaiian Airlines Inc., **9** 271–73
Hawaiian Dredging & Construction Co., **I** 565–66
Hawaiian Electric Company, **9** 274. *See also* Hawaiian Electric Industries, Inc.
Hawaiian Electric Industries, Inc., 9 274–77
Hawaiian Electric Renewable Systems, **9** 276
Hawaiian Fertilizer Co., **II** 490
Hawaiian Insurance Group, **9** 276–77
Hawaiian Pineapple Co., **II** 491
Hawaiian Tug & Barge, **9** 276
Hawaiian Tuna Packers, **II** 491
Hawke, Robert, **I** 439; **IV** 652; **7** 391
Hawker Aircraft, **I** 50
Hawker, Cyril, **II** 357–58
Hawker de Havilland, Ltd., **III** 509
Hawker, Harry G., **III** 507–08
Hawker Siddeley Aircraft Co. Ltd., **I** 41–42, 50, 71, 470; **III** 507–08
Hawker Siddeley Group Public Limited Company, III 507–10; 8 51
Hawkes, Michael, **II** 423
Hawkeye Cablevision, **II** 161
Hawkins, William M., **III** (Trip), **10** 284–86
Hawkins, William Waller, **IV** 607–08
Hawkrigg, Melvin, **II** 456
Hawks, Rex, **IV** 445
Hawley & Hazel Chemical Co., **III** 25
Hawley, Philip, **V** 30–31
Haworth, Gerrard W., **8** 251
Haworth Inc., 8 251–52
Haworth, Richard, **8** 251–52
Hawthorn Company, **8** 287
Hawthorn family, **III** 680
Hawthorn-Mellody, **11** 25
Hawthorne Appliance and Electronics, **10** 9–11

Hawthorne Mellody, **I** 446
Haxton, Henry, **7** 166
Hay, Bill, **10** 529–30
Hay Group, **I** 33
Hay, Ray, **I** 490–91
Hayakawa Electrical Industries, **II** 95–96
Hayakawa Metal Industrial Laboratory, **II** 95
Hayakawa, Tokuji, **II** 95–96
Hayaku Zenjiro, **III** 408
Hayama Oil, **IV** 542
Hayashi Kane Shoten, **II** 578
Hayashi, Kazuo, **IV** 476
Hayashi, Senjuro, **II** 291
Hayashi, Suehiko, **III** 405
Hayashi, Tomoyuki, **III** 405
Hayashi, Torao, **III** 591–92
Hayashikane Gyogyo K.K., **II** 578
Hayashikane Reizo K.K., **II** 578
Hayashikane Shoten K.K., **II** 578
Hayden, Bill, **11** 61–63
Hayden Clinton National Bank, **11** 180
Hayden, Julius, **6** 446
Hayden, Robert L., **9** 452
Hayden Stone, **II** 450; **9** 468
Hayes, Charles (Chuck), **8** 234–35
Hayes, Clarence B., **7** 258
Hayes, Geoff, **6** 47
Hayes, John P., **10** 422–23
Hayes Microcomputer Products, **9** 515
Hayes, Peter, **I** 308, 311, 348
Hayes, Rutherford B., **IV** 688
Hayes Wheel Company, **7** 258
Hayford, Warren, **8** 203
Haynie, Roscoe, **I** 489
Hays, Charles Melville, **6** 359–60
Hays Petroleum Services, **IV** 451
Hayssen, Herman, **7** 269
Hayward, Keith, **I** 53
Hazard, **I** 328
Hazard, Ebenezer, **III** 223
Hazard, Robert C., Jr., **6** 188–89
HAZCO International, Inc., **9** 110
Hazel Bishop, **III** 55
Hazel-Atlas Glass Co., **I** 599
Hazell Sun Ltd., **IV** 642; **7** 312
Hazeltine, Inc., **II** 20
Hazelwood, William, **8** 515
Hazen, Paul, **II** 383
Hazlenut Growers of Oregon, **7** 496–97
Hazlitt, William, **7** 165
HBO. *See* Home Box Office Inc.
HCA Management Co., **III** 79
HCA Psychiatric Co., **III** 79
HCI Holdings, **I** 264
HCL America, **10** 505
HCL Sybase, **10** 505
HDR Inc., **I** 563
Heads and Threads, **10** 43
Healey & Baker, **IV** 705
Healey, Thomas G., **6** 446
Health & Tennis Corp., **III** 431
Health Care Corp., **III** 79
Health Maintenance Organization of Pennsylvania. *See* U.S. Healthcare, Inc.
Health Maintenance Organizations, **I** 545
Health Plan of America, **11** 379
Health Plan of Virginia, **III** 389
Health Products, Inc., **I** 387
Health Services, Inc., **10** 160
Health Systems International, Inc., 11 174–76
Health Way, Inc., **II** 538
HealthAmerica Corp., **III** 84

HealthCare USA, **III** 84, 86
HealthTrust, **III** 80
Healy, Robert, **I** 17
Hearst Corporation, IV 582, 596, 608, **625–27**
Hearst family, **IV** 627
Hearst, George, **IV** 625
Hearst, William Randolph, **IV** 581, 625–27, 682–83, 688; **6** 32; **10** 287
Hearthstone Insurance Co. of Massachusetts, **III** 203
Heartland Building Products, **II** 582
Heartland Components, **III** 519
Heat Transfer Pty. Ltd., **III** 420
Heatcraft Inc., **8** 320–22
Heath, Barrie (Sir), **III** 494
Heath, C.E., **III** 279
Heath Co., **II** 124
Heath, Edward, **IV** 379, 532; **6** 241
Heath, Peter, **III** 523
Heath Steele Mines Ltd., **IV** 18
Heath, William C., **11** 4
Heather, Dick, **V** 496
Hebrew National Kosher Foods, **III** 24
Hecht, Abraham L., **9** 120–21
Hecker-H-O Co., **II** 497
Heckett Technology Services Inc., **8** 246–47
Heckett Yugoslavia Ltd., **8** 247
Heckman, William "Guy," **7** 32–34
Heco Envelope Co., **IV** 282; **9** 261
Hedges, Charles E., **6** 523
Hedges, D. T., **6** 523
Hedien, Wayne E., **10** 51
Hedrick, Frank E., **8** 50–51
Heekin Can, Inc., **10** 130
Heerensperger, David J., **9** 399–400
Heffern, Gordon E., **9** 475
Hegeman, John Rogers, **III** 291–92
Hegg, Oscar T., **III** 518
HEI Investment Corp., **9** 276
Heiberg, Herman, **IV** 275
Heidelberg, **III** 701
Heidelburger Drueck, **III** 301
Heidi Bakery, **II** 633
Heights of Texas, fsb, **8** 437
Heijn, Albert, **II** 741
Heike family, **I** 518
Heikkilä, Oskari, **8** 294
Heikkinen, Helen, **11** 458
Heil-Quaker Corp., **III** 654
Heilbronn, Max, **V** 57–58
Heilbronner, Henry, **7** 546
Heileman Brewing Co. *See* G. Heileman Brewing Co.
Heileman, Gottlieb, **I** 253
Heileman, Johanna, **I** 253–54
Heilemann, Willy, **III** 574
Heilicher, Amos, **9** 360
Heilicher, Dan, **9** 360
Heiligbrodt, L. William, **6** 295
Heimat, **III** 403
Heimstatt Bauspar AG, **III** 401
Heine, Andrew, **8** 537
Heineken, Alfred, **I** 257–58
Heineken, Charlene, **I** 258
Heineken, Gerard Adriaan, **I** 256
Heineken, H.P., **I** 256–57
Heineken N.V., I 219, **256–58**, 266, 288; **II** 642
Heineman, Ben W., **I** 440–41; **6** 377; **8** 367
Heiner, Lawrence E., **7** 378
Heinkel Co., **I** 74

Heinrich Bauer North America, **7** 42–43
Heinrich Koppers GmbH, **IV** 89
Heinrich Lanz, **III** 463
Heinrichs, T.H., **I** 654
Heins, John, **9** 137
Heinz Co. *See* H.J. Heinz Company.
Heinz Deichert KG, **11** 95
Heinz, Frederick, **II** 507; **11** 171
Heinz, H.J., II, (Jack), **II** 508; **11** 172
Heinz, Henry John, **II** 507; **11** 171–72
Heinz, Howard, **II** 508; **11** 172
Heinz, John, **II** 507; **11** 171
Heinz, Noble & Co., **II** 507
Heinz Pet Products, **II** 508
Heinz-Australia, **II** 508
Heisers Inc., **I** 185
Heiwa Sogo Bank, **II** 326, 361
Heizer Corp., **III** 109–11
HEL&P. *See* Houston Electric Light & Power Company.
Helbut, Philip, **III** 370
Heldring, Ernst, **6** 403
Helemano Co., **II** 491
Helena Rubenstein, Inc., **III** 24, 48; **8** 343–44; **9** 201–02
Helene Curtis Industries, Inc., I 403; **8 253–54**
Helfferich, Emil, **6** 398
Helford, Irwin, **10** 544–46
Helix Biocore, **11** 458
Hellberg, Franz, **V** 708
Hellbruegge, Heinrich, **IV** 233
Hellefors Jernverk, **III** 623
Heller Financial Corporation, **7** 213
Heller, Joseph, **IV** 672
Heller, Simon, **II** 593–94
Heller, Walter E., **II** 319
Heller, William, **III** 55
Hellman, I.W., II, **II** 382
Hellman, I.W., III, **II** 382
Hellman, Isaias W., **II** 381–82
Hellman, Warren, **8** 230
Hellschreiber, **IV** 669
Helm, Harold, **II** 251
Helme, William, **6** 446
Helms, Richard, **I** 559
Helmsley Enterprises, Inc., 9 278–80
Helmsley, Harry Brakmann, **9** 278–80
Helmsley, Leona, **9** 278–80
Helmsley-Spear Inc., **9** 278–80
Helmut Delhey, **6** 428
Helmuth Hardekopf Bunker GmbH, **7** 141
Help-U-Sell, Inc., **III** 304
Helson, Michel, **IV** 226
Helton, Bill D., **6** 581
Helvetia General, **III** 376
Helvetia Milk Co., **II** 486
Helvetia Milk Condensing Co., **7** 428
Helvetia Schweizerische Feuerversicherungs-Gesellschaft St. Gallen, **III** 375
Hely Group, **IV** 294
Hemelinger Aktienbrauerei, **9** 86
Hemex, **11** 458
Hemingway, Ernest, **IV** 586
Hemlo Gold Mines Inc., 9 281–82
Hemma, **IV** 616
Hemmeter, Chris, **III** 97
Hemminghaus, Roger R., **IV** 410
A.B. Hemmings, Ltd., **II** 465
Henderson, Byrd, **II** 418–19
Henderson, Denys, **I** 353
Henderson, Ernest, **III** 98–100
Henderson, George, **III** 98

Henderson, M.J.G., **III** 681
Henderson, Monty, **7** 433
Henderson, Rupert, **7** 252
Henderson's Industries, **III** 581
Henderson-Union Electric Cooperative, **11** 37
Hendrick, John, **9** 275
Hendrickson, William, **11** 458
Hendrie, Gardner C., **10** 499
Hendrix, Gary, **10** 507
Henijean & Cie, **III** 283
Henke, Harry, Jr., **9** 38
Henkel, **9** 382
Henkel & Cie., **III** 31
Henkel, Fritz, **III** 31, 33
Henkel, Fritz, Jr., **III** 31
Henkel Group, **III** 31–34
Henkel, Hugo, **III** 31–32
Henkel, Jost, **III** 32–33
Henkel KGaA, **III** 21, **31–34**, 45; **IV** 70
Henkel, Konrad, **III** 33
Henle family, **III** 542
Henle, Günter, **IV** 127–28
Henle, Jörg A., **IV** 128
Henley Drilling Company, **9** 364
Henley Group, Inc., **I** 416; **III** **511–12**; **6** 599–600; **9** 298; **11** 435
Henley, Jeffrey, **6** 274
Henley Manufacturing Corp., **III** 512
Henley Properties, **III** 512
Henley, W.T., **III** 433
Henne, Ernst, **I** 138; **11** 31
Hennebech, Ralph, **IV** 34
Hennessee, Lee, **11** 418
Hennessey, Jack, **II** 268
Hennessy, Edward L., **I** 143; **6** 599
Hennessy, Edward L., Jr., **I** 415–16; **III** 511; **9** 521
Henny, Carel, **III** 308, 310
Henny, Christiaan Marianus, **III** 308–09
Henredon, **11** 534
Henredon Furniture Industries, **III** 571
Henry, Glenn, **9** 165
Henry Grant & Co., **I** 604
Henry Holt & Co., **IV** 622–23
The Henry Jones Co-op Ltd., **7** 577
Henry Jones Foods, **11** 212
Henry Jones IXL Ltd., **I** 437–38, 592; **7** 182
Henry L. Doherty & Son, **IV** 391
Henry, Leonard & Thomas Inc., **9** 533
Henry Pratt Company, **7** 30–31
Henry S. King & Co., **II** 307
Henry Tate & Sons, **II** 580
Henry Telfer, **II** 513
Henry Waugh Ltd., **I** 469
Henske, J.M., **I** 381
Henson, Joe M., **10** 394
Henthy Realty Co., **III** 190
Hepburn, Harry M., **9** 275
Hepburn, Katharine, **II** 32
HEPCO. *See* Hokkaido Electric Power Company Inc.
Hepworth, Mr., **I** 604
Her Majesty's Stationery Office, **7** **215–18**
Heraeus Edelmetalle GmbH, **IV** 99
Heraeus Electro-Nite, **IV** 100
Heraeus family, **IV** 99
Heraeus, Heinrich, **IV** 98
Heraeus Holding GmbH, **IV** **98–100**, 118
Heraeus Instruments GmbH, **IV** 100
Heraeus, Johannes, **IV** 98
Heraeus, Jürgen (Dr.), **IV** 100

Heraeus Kulzer GmbH, **IV** 100
Heraeus Ltd., **IV** 100
Heraeus Quarzglas GmbH, **IV** 100
Heraeus Vakuumschmelze, **IV** 99
Heraeus, Wilhelm, **IV** 98–99
Heraeus, Wilhelm Carl, **IV** 98
Herald and Weekly Times, **IV** 650, 652; **7** 389, 391
Heralds of Liberty, **9** 506
Herbert, Anthony E., **II** 133
Herbert, Edwin (Sir), **IV** 565
Herbert, Gavin, Jr., **10** 46–47
Herbert, Gavin S., Sr., **10** 46–47
Herbert W. Davis & Co., **III** 344
Herco Technology, **IV** 680
Hercofina, **IV** 499
Hercules Filter, **III** 419
Hercules Inc., **I** **343–45**, 347
Hercules Nut Corp., **II** 593
Hercules Powder Co., **I** 343, **III** 241
Herd, J. Victor, **III** 241–42
Herff Jones, **II** 488
Heritage Bankcorp, **9** 482
Heritage Communications, **II** 160–61
Heritage Federal Savings and Loan Association of Huntington, **10** 92
Heritage House of America Inc., **III** 81
Heritage Life Assurance, **III** 248
Heritage National Health Plan, **III** 464
Herman Miller, Inc., **8** 251–52, **255–57**
Herman's World of Sporting, **I** 548; **II** 628–29
Hermannshütte, **IV** 103, 105
Hermes Kreditversicherungsbank, **III** 300
Hermundslie, Palmer, **8** 351
Héroult, Paul, **IV** 173
Herrhausen, Alfred, **II** 280
Herrick, Kenneth G., **8** 514–15
Herrick, Myron T., **6** 559
Herrick, Ray W., **8** 514–15
Herrick, Todd, **8** 515
Herring, James, **II** 644–45
Herring, Leonard, **V** 122
Herring-Hall-Marvin Safe Co. of Hamilton, Ohio, **7** 145
Herrington, John S., **IV** 624
Herrington, L. B., **6** 513
Herrmann, Arthur D., **11** 181
Hersch, Stuart A., **9** 306
Hersey Products, Inc., **III** 645
Hershey Bank, **II** 342
Hershey Canada Inc., **II** 512
Hershey, Catherine, **II** 510
Hershey Chocolate Co., **II** 510–11
Hershey Foods Corporation, **I** 26–27; **II** 478, 508, **510–12**, 569; **7** 300; **11** 15
Hershey, Milton S., **II** 510–12
Hertford Industrial Estates, **IV** 724
Hertie Family Foundation, **V**, 73
Hertie Siftung, **V** 73
Hertie Waren- und Kaufhaus GmbH, **V** **72–74**
Herts & Beds Petroleum Co., **IV** 566
The Hertz Corporation, **6** 52, 129, 348–50, 356–57, 392–93; **9** **283–85**; **10** 419; **11** 494
Hertz Equipment Rental Corporation, **9** 283
Hertz, John, **I** 125; **9** 283
Hertz Rent-a-Car Co., **I** 130; **II** 90
Hertz Technologies, Inc., **9** 283
Hertz-Penske Leasing, **V** 494
Hervey, Fred, **II** 619
Heskett, David, **7** 324
Heskett, R.M., **7** 322–24

Hess, Hans, **III** 183–84
Hess, Leon, **IV** 366
Hess, Mores, **IV** 366
Hess Oil & Chemical Corp., **IV** 366
Hessische Berg- und Hüttenwerke AG, **III** 695
Hessische Landesbank, **II** 385–86
Hessische Ludwigs-Eisenbahn-Gesellschaft, **6** 424
Heublein, Gilbert, **I** 259
Heublein Inc., **I** 226, 246, 249, **259–61**, 281; **7** 266–67; **10** 180
Heublein, Louis, **I** 259
Heuga Holdings B.V., **8** 271
L'Heureux, Willard, **10** 531
Heuss, Theodor, **III** 446
Hewitt & Tuttle, **IV** 426
Hewitt, Anderson F., **I** 25
Hewitt, Edward R., **I** 177
Hewitt Motor Co., **I** 177
Hewitt, William A., **III** 462
Hewlett, Walter B., **III** 143; **6** 238
Hewlett, William, **III** 142–43; **6** 237–38
Hewlett-Packard Company, **II** 62; **III** 116, **142–43**; **6** 219–20, 225, **237–39** **(upd.)**, 244, 248, 278–79, 304; **8** 139, 467; **9** 7, 35–36, 57, 115, 471; **10** 15, 34, 86, 232, 257, 363, 404, 459, 464, 499, 501; **11** 46, 234, 274, 284, 382, 491, 518
Hexatec Polymers, **III** 742
Hexcel Medical Corporation, **11** 475
Heyden Newport Chemical Corp., **I** 526
Heyke, John, **6** 456
Heyl, Frederick W., **I** 707; **8** 547
Heyman, J., **I** 549
Heyman, Phillip, **9** 99
Heyman, Samuel, **8** 180; **9** 518
Heyman, Samuel J., **I** 339; **III** 440
Heymann, Walter M., **IV** 135
HFC. *See* Household Finance Corporation.
HFC Leasing, **II** 420
HG Hawker Engineering Co. Ltd., **III** 508
HGCC. *See* Hysol Grafil Composite Components Co.
HI. *See* Houston Industries Incorporated.
Hi-Bred Corn Company, **9** 410
Hi-Mirror Co., **III** 715
Hi-Tek Polymers, Inc., **8** 554
Hiatt, Arnold, **8** 502–03
Hibbing Transportation, **I** 448
Hibernia & Shamrock-Bergwerksgesellschaft zu Berlin, **I** 542–43
Hibernian Banking Assoc., **II** 261
Hickenlooper, Andrew, **6** 465
Hickey, Frank G., **10** 320
Hicklin, W., **III** 15
Hickorycraft, **III** 571
Hicks & Greist, **6** 40
Hicks & Haas, **II** 478
Hicks, Leslie H., **9** 275–76
Hicksgas Gifford, Inc., **6** 529
Hidaka, Teru, **II** 459
Hiebert, Mark, **I** 700
Higaki, Bun-ichi, **III** 406
Higby, Larry, **7** 506
Higdon, E.G., **III** 572
Higgins, Milton P., **8** 395–96
Higginson et Hanckar, **IV** 107
Higgs & Young Inc., **I** 412
High Point Chemical Corp., **III** 38
High Retail System Co., Ltd., **V** 195
Highland Container Co., **IV** 345

Highland Superstores, **9** 65–66; **10** 9–10, 304–05, 468
Highland Telephone Company, **6** 334
Highlands Insurance Co., **III** 498
Highmark International, **I** 109
Hightower, Dwight, **10** 126
Highveld Steel and Vanadium Corp., **IV** 22
Higo Bank, **II** 291
Higuchi, Hirotaro, **I** 221
Higuchi, Minoru, **IV** 713–14
Hijikata, Takeshi, **I** 398
Hilbert, Stephen C., **10** 246–48
Hilbun Poultry, **10** 250
Hilco Technologies, **III** 143; **6** 238
Hildén, Aarne, **IV** 276
Hilex Poly Co., Inc., **8** 477
Hill & Knowlton Inc., **I** 21; **6** 53. *See also* WPP Group PLC.
Hill, George Washington, **I** 12–13, 28, 37; **V** 397
Hill, James, **11** 46
Hill, James J., **IV** 355; **V** 427; **9** 550
Hill, John A., **III** 78, 182; **IV** 634
Hill, Leslie, **7** 79
Hill, Merritt D., **10** 379
Hill, Percival S., **V** 396, 417
Hill, Philip, **III** 65
Hill Publishing Co., **IV** 634
Hill, Richard, **II** 208
Hill, Rowland, **V** 496–97, 501
Hill Samuel, **II** 379; **IV** 711–12
Hill Stores, **II** 683
Hill-Rom Company, **10** 349–50
Hillard Oil and Gas Company, Inc., **11** 523
Hillards, PLC, **II** 678
Hillary, Sir Edmund, **8** 288
Hillblom, Larry, **6** 385
Hille, Fritz, **I** 139; **11** 32
Hillebrecht, Robert R., **IV** 623
Hillenbrand, August (Gus), **10** 350–51
Hillenbrand, Daniel A., **10** 349
Hillenbrand, George C., **10** 349
Hillenbrand Industries, Inc., **6** 295; **10** 349–51
Hillenbrand, John A., **10** 349
Hillenbrand, John W., **10** 349
Hillenbrand, William A., **10** 349
Hiller Aircraft Company, **9** 205
Hilles, Rick, **10** 47
Hillhaven Corp., **III** 76, 87–88; **6** 188
Hillin Oil, **IV** 658
Hillman, **I** 183
Hillman, Priscilla, **11** 95
Hillman, William, **7** 458
Hills & Dales Railway Co. *See* Dayton Power & Light Company.
Hills Brothers Inc., **II** 548; **7** 383
Hills Department Stores, **11** 228
Hills, Lee, **IV** 628–30
Hills Pet Products, **III** 25
Hills, Robert C., **IV** 82; **7** 186
Hillsborough Holdings Corp., **III** 765–67
Hillsdale Machine & Tool Company, **8** 514
Hillsdown Holdings, PLC, **II** 513–14
Hillsdown International B.V., **II** 514
Hillshire Farm, **II** 572
Hilo Electric Light Company, **9** 276
Hilton, Anderson and Co., **III** 669
Hilton, Anderson, Brooks and Co., **III** 669
Hilton, Conrad N., **III** 91–92; **9** 548
Hilton Gravel, **III** 670
Hilton Hotels Corporation, **II** 208; **III** 91–93, 98–99, 102; **IV** 703; **6** 201, 210; **9** 95, 426

Hilton Hotels, Inc., **III** 91
Hilton Hotels International, **I** 127, 130; **II** 142, 679–80; **III** 92
Hilton, Hugh, **IV** 209
Hilton International Co., **6** 385
Hilton, James, **IV** 671
Hilton, William Barron, **III** 92–93
Himmelman, Lynn P., **9** 548–49
Himmler, Heinrich, **II** 279
Himolene, **8** 181
Hinde & Dauch Ltd., **IV** 272
Hinde & Dauch Paper Co., **IV** 352
Hindell, J.W., **II** 611
Hindell's Dairy Farmers Ltd., **II** 611–12
Hinds, Ernest, **10** 541
Hinds, Hayden & Eldredge, **10** 135
Hindustan Petroleum Corp. Ltd., **IV** 441
Hindustan Shipyard, **IV** 484
Hindustan Steel Ltd., **IV** 205–07
Hines, John, **IV** 702
Hinkle, Samuel, **II** 511
Hinman, Brian L., **10** 455
Hinman, Edward B., **IV** 286–87
Hinman family, **IV** 286
Hinman, John, **IV** 286
Hino Motors, Ltd., **7** 219–21
Hinode Life Insurance Co., Ltd., **II** 360; **III** 365
Hinomaru Truck Co., **6** 428
Hinton, Sir Christopher, **6** 451
Hip Hing Construction, **IV** 717
Hipercor, S.A., **V** 52
Hiraiwa, Gaishi, **V** 732
Hiram Walker Resources Ltd., **I** 216, 262–64; **IV** 721; **9** 391
Hiram Walker-Consumers' Home Ltd. *See* Consumers' Gas Company Ltd.
Hiram Walker-Gooderham & Worts Ltd., **6** 478
Hirano, Fubito, **III** 592–93
Hirano, Tomijo, **III** 532
Hirata, Kusuo, **III** 487
Hirl, J. Roger, **IV** 481
Hirohito, Emperor of Japan, **7** 248
Hirose, Saihei, **I** 519; **IV** 215; **11** 478
Hirose, Sukesaburo, **III** 318
Hirsch, Gary, **7** 204
Hirsch, Harold, **I** 233
Hirsch, Larry, **8** 88
Hirsch, Leon, **10** 533–35
Hirsch, Moritz, **6** 424
Hirsch, Neil S., **10** 276–77
Hirschfield, Alan J., **II** 136, 170–71
Hirsig, Alan R., **10** 111
Hirst, Hugo, **I** 24
Hirzel, Marie Louise, **III** 631
Hispanica de Petroleos, **IV** 424, 527, 546
Hispano Aviacion, **I** 74
HISPANOBRAS, **IV** 55
Hispanoil. *See* Hispanica de Petroleos.
Hispeed Tools, **I** 573
Hisshin-DCA foods, **II** 554
Hit, **II** 164
Hit or Miss, **V** 197–98
Hitachi Ltd., **I** 454–55, 494, 534; **II** 5, 30, 59, 64–65, 68, 70, 73, 75, 114, 273–74, 292–91; **III** 130, 140, 143, 464, 482; **IV** 101; **6** 238, 262; **7** 425; **9** 297; **11** 45, 308, 507
Hitachi Magnetics Corp., **IV** 101
Hitachi Metals America, Ltd., **IV** 101
Hitachi Metals Europe GmbH, **IV** 101
Hitachi Metals Industries Ltd., **IV** 101

Hitachi Metals International (U.S.A.), Ltd., **IV** 101
Hitachi Metals, Ltd., **IV** 101–02
Hitachi Metals North Carolina, Ltd., **IV** 101
Hitachi Shipbuilding, **III** 513
Hitachi Shipbuilding and Engineering, **III** 513–14
Hitachi Zosen Clearing Inc., **III** 514
Hitachi Zosen Corporation, **III** 513–14
Hitachi Zozen, **8** 449
Hitchcock, Alfred, **II** 143
Hitchcock, Peter, **9** 439
Hitchcock, Ruben, **9** 439
Hitco, **III** 721–22
Hitler, Adolf, **I** 70, 73, 110, 138, 192, 206, 306, 309, 346–47, 349, 463, 465, 560; **III** 184, 208, 300, 338, 601; **IV** 88, 104, 221, 260, 348, 536, 591, 593, 651; **7** 391, 452; **11** 31, 197, 277, 549
Hixon, Carl, **I** 24
Hiyama, Hiro, **I** 493
Hjalmar Blomqvist A.B., **II** 639
Hjelt, August, **II** 302
Hjelt, Otto, **II** 302
HL&P. *See* Houston Lighting and Power Company.
HLH Products, **7** 229
HMO-PA. *See* U.S. Healthcare, Inc.
HMT Technology Corp., **IV** 102
HMV, **I** 531
Ho, Sin-Hang (Dr.), **IV** 717
Ho, Tim, **IV** 717
Hoag, David, **I** 491
Hoak, James, Jr., **II** 160–61
Hoare Govett Ltd., **II** 349
Hobart Corp., **II** 534; **III** 610–11, 654; **7** 276
Hobart Manufacturing Company, **8** 298
Hobbes Manufacturing, **I** 169
Hobbes Trailer and Equipment, **I** 169–70
Hobson, Geoffrey, **11** 452
Hobson, Laura Z., **IV** 672
Hobson, Robert, **IV** 208
Hobson, Taylor, **II** 158
Hoch, Jan Ludvik. *See* Maxwell, Robert.
Hoch, Orion, **I** 486; **11** 265
Hochschild, Berthold, **IV** 17
Hochschild, Kohn Department Stores, **II** 673
Hochschild, Zachary, **IV** 139–40
Hochstein, Louis, **IV** 581, 582
Hock, Dee Ward, **9** 536–37
Hockaday, Irvine O., **6** 401
Hockaday, Irvine O., Jr., **IV** 621
Hoden Oil, **IV** 478
Hodes, Robert, **9** 323
Hodge, Edward, **11** 452
Hodge, Edward Grose, **11** 452
Hodge, Thomas, **11** 452
Hodgens, Edward, **IV** 437
Hodgens, Thomas, **IV** 437
Hodgkin, Barnett, Pease, Spence & Co., **II** 307
Hodnett, Byron E., **10** 299
Hodowal, John R., **6** 508
Hoechst A.G., **I** 305–06, 309, 317, 346–48, 605, 632, 669–70; **IV** 451; **8** 262, 451–53
Hoechst Celanese Corp., **8** 562; **11** 436
Hoeganaes Corporation, **8** 274–75
Hoenecke, Karl F., **10** 295–96
Hoerner Waldorf Corp., **IV** 264
Hoesch & Co., **IV** 323

Hoesch AG, IV 103–06, 128, 133, 195, 228, 232
Hoesch, Albert, **IV** 103–04
Hoesch Dortmund, **IV** 133
Hoesch, Eberhard, **IV** 103
Hoesch Hohenlimburg AG, **IV** 103
Hoesch, Leopold, **IV** 103
Hoesch Stahl AG, **IV** 103
Hoesch, Viktor, **IV** 103
Hoesch Werke AG, **IV** 105
Hoesch, Wilhelm, **IV** 103
Hoevels, Werner, **IV** 197–98
Hoff, Hubert, **IV** 25
Hoff, Ted, **II** 44; **10** 365
Hoffman, Edwin, **II** 420
Hoffman, Felix, **I** 309, 698
Hoffman, Mark, **10** 504
Hoffman, Paul, **II** 448–49
Hoffman, R. C., **6** 447
Hoffman, Ulrich, **I** 349
Hoffman-La Roche, Inc., **11** 424–25
Hoffmann, Emanuel, **I** 642
Hoffmann, Fritz, **I** 642
Hoffmann, Lukas, **I** 642
Hoffmann-La Roche & Co. *See* F. Hoffmann-La Roche & Co.
Hoffmeister, B.M., **IV** 307
Hofmann, Philip, **III** 36; **8** 282
Hofmeyer, Murray B., **I** 289
Hofstad, Ralph, **II** 536
Hogate, Kenneth Craven (Casey), **IV** 601–02
Högbo Stål & Jernwerks, **IV** 202
Hoge, James, **IV** 684
Högforsin Tehdas Osakeyhtiö, **IV** 300
Hogg, Christopher (Sir), **IV** 670
Hogg, Russell E., **9** 333
Hoglund, William E., **7** 462; **10** 420
Hokkaido Butter Co., **II** 575
Hokkaido Colonial Bank, **II** 310
Hokkaido Dairy Cooperative, **II** 574
Hokkaido Dairy Farm Assoc., **II** 538
Hokkaido Electric Power Company Inc., V 635–37
Hokkaido Forwarding, **6** 428
Hokkaido Rakuno Kosha Co., **II** 574
Hokkaido Takushoku Bank, **II** 300
Hokoku Cement, **III** 713
Hokoku Fire, **III** 384
Hokuetsu Paper Manufacturing, **IV** 327
Hokuriku Electric Power Company, V 638–40
Hokusin Kai, **IV** 475
Hokuyo Sangyo Co., Ltd., **IV** 285
Holbrook Grocery Co., **II** 682
Holcombe, W.J., **7** 236–37
Holcroft & Company, **7** 521
Holden, Edward, **II** 318
Holden Group, **II** 457
Holden, Hale, **V** 427
Holden-Brown, Derrick (Sir), **I** 216
Holderbank Financière Glaris Ltd., III 701–02; 8 258–59
Holderbank Franciere Glaris S.A., **8** 456
Holdernam Inc., **8** 258–59
Holderness, G.A., **10** 201–02
Holderness, H. Dail, **10** 202
Holderness, Howard, **11** 214
Holdredge, William, **III** 250
Holdsworth, Trevor (Sir), **III** 494–95
Holiday Corp., **I** 224; **III** 94–95; **9** 425–26
Holiday, Harry, **IV** 29
Holiday Inn Worldwide, **III** 94–95

Holiday Inns, Inc., III 94–95, 99–100; **6** 383; **9** 425–26; **10** 12; **11** 178, 242
Holiday Inns of America, **III** 94
Holiday Rambler Corporation, **7** 213
Holladay, Ben, **II** 381
Holland America, **6** 397
Holland America Line, **6** 368
Holland America Westours, **6** 368
Holland, Edwin T., **11** 125
Holland Hannen and Cubitts, **III** 753
Holland, Henry, **11** 77–78
Holland House, **I** 377–78
Holland, John, **I** 57; **8** 201–02; **10** 315, 336
Holland, Stuart, **I** 467
Holland van 1859, **III** 200
Holland, William, **8** 545–46
Hollandsche Bank-Unie, **II** 184–85
Hollerith, Herman, **III** 147; **6** 240, 250
Holley Carburetor, **I** 434
Holliday, Cyrus K., **V** 507
Holliday, Raymond, **III** 428
Hollingsworth & Whitney Co., **IV** 329
Hollingsworth, B.B., Jr., **6** 294–95
Hollis, Mark, **7** 441
Hollostone, **III** 673
Holly Farms Corp., **II** 585; **7** 422–24
Hollywood Pictures, **II** 174
Hollywood Records, **6** 176
Holm, Johan, **IV** 202
Holman, Currier J., **II** 515–16
Holmen Hygiene, **IV** 315
Holmen S.A., **IV** 325
Holmens Bruk, **IV** 317–18
Holmes à Court, Robert, **I** 437–38; **7** 78, 253; **8** 551; **10** 169
Holmes, Brainerd, **11** 413
Holmes, Dyer Brainerd, **II** 86–87; **11** 412
Holmes Electric Protective Co., **III** 644
Holmes, Thomas, **III** 527
Holmes, William, **6** 510
Holmsund & Kramfors, **IV** 338
Holnam Inc., III 702; **8 258–60**
Holst, Gilles, **II** 78
Holt, Alfred, **6** 415
Holt, Charles, **III** 450–51
Holt, Christian, **IV** 274
Holt, Don, **9** 215
Holt, Herbert S., **6** 501–02, 585
Holt, John, **10** 90
Holt Manufacturing Co., **III** 450–51
Holt, Philip, **6** 415
Holt, Rinehart and Winston, Inc., **IV** 623–24
Holtback, Roger, **7** 567
Holte, Johan B., **10** 438
Holton, Earl, **7** 331
Holton, I.J., **II** 505
Holtrop, M.W., **IV** 132
Holtzclaw, Jack G., **V** 597
Holtzman, Don, **6** 392
Holtzmann, Jacob L., **I** 512
Holvick Corp., **11** 65
Holzer and Co., **III** 569
Holzverkohlungs-Industrie AG, **IV** 70
Homart Development, **V** 182
Home & Automobile Insurance Co., **III** 214
Home Box Office Inc., II 134, 136, 166–67, 176–77; **IV** 675; **7 222–24**, 528–29; **10** 196
Home Capital Services, **III** 264
Home Charm Group PLC, **II** 141

Home Depot, Inc., V 75–76; 9 400; **10** 235; **11** 384–86
Home Furnace Co., **I** 481
Home Group, **III** 263–64
Home Indemnity Co., **III** 262
Home Insurance Company, I 440; **III 262–64**
Home Insurance Cos., **III** 264
Home Oil Company Ltd., **I** 264; **6** 477–78
Home Reinsurance Co., **III** 263
Home Savings of America, **II** 181–82; **10** 342–43
Home Shopping Club, **V** 77
Home Shopping Network, Inc., V 77–78; 9 428
Home Shopping Spree, **V** 77
Home Telephone and Telegraph Company, **10** 201
Home Telephone Company. *See* Rochester Telephone Corporation.
Homebase, **II** 658
Homécourt, **IV** 226
HomeFed Bank, **10** 340
Homemade Ice Cream Company, **10** 371
Homer, Arthur B., **IV** 36; **7** 49
Homer, Charles, **8** 552
Homer McKee Advertising, **I** 22
Homer, Sidney, **II** 448
Homestake Mining Co., **IV** 18, 76
Homewood Stores Co., **IV** 573; **7** 550
Homewood Suites, **9** 425–26
Hominal Developments Inc., **9** 512
Hompe, A.W., **7** 493
Honam Oil Refinery, **II** 53
Honcho Real Estate, **IV** 225
Honda Motor Co., I 9–10, 32, **174–76**, 184, 193; **II** 5; **III** 495, 517, 536, 603, 657–58, 667; **IV** 443; **7** 212–13, 459; **8** 71–72; **9** 294, 340–42; **11** 33, 49–50, 352
Honda Motor Company Limited (Honda Giken Kogyo Kabushiki Kaisha), 10 352–54 (upd.)
Honda, Soichiro, **I** 174; **10** 352–53
Hondo Oil & Gas Co., **IV** 375–76
Honeywell Bull, **III** 123
Honeywell Heating Specialities Co., **II** 41
Honeywell Inc., I 63; **II** 30, **40–43**, 54, 68; **III** 122–23, 149, 152, 165, 535, 548–49, 732; **6** 266, 281, 283, 314; **8** 21; **9** 171, 324; **11** 198, 265
Honeywell Information Systems, **II** 42
Honeywell, Mark, **II** 41
Hong Kong Aircraft Engineering Co., **I** 522; **6** 79
Hong Kong Airways, **6** 78–79
Hong Kong and Kowloon Wharf and Godown Co., **IV** 699
Hong Kong Island Line Co., **IV** 718
Hong Kong Resort Co., **IV** 718
Hong Kong Telecommunications Ltd., V 285–86; **6 319–21**
Hong Kong Telephone and Cable. *See* Hong Kong Telecommunications Ltd.
Hong Kong Telephone Co., **IV** 700. *See also* Hong Kong Telecommunications Ltd.
Hong Leong Corp., **III** 718
Hongkong & Kowloon Wharf & Godown Co., **I** 470
Hongkong and Shanghai Bank of California, **II** 298
Hongkong and Shanghai Banking Co., **II** 296

Hongkong and Shanghai Banking Corporation Limited, II 257, **296–99**, 320, 358; III 289
Hongkong Bank of Canada, II 298
Hongkong Electric Company Ltd., 6 498–500
Hongkong Electric Holdings, IV 695, 700
Hongkong Land Co., IV 700
Hongkong Land Holdings Ltd., I 470–71; **IV 699–701; 6** 499
Hongkong Land Investment and Agency Co. Ltd., IV 699–700; **6** 498
Hongkong Telecom. *See* Hong Kong Telecommunications Ltd.
Hongkong Telecom Foundation. *See* Hong Kong Telecommunications Ltd.
HongkongBank. *See* The Hongkong and Shanghai Banking Corporation Limited.
HongkongBank of Australia, II 298
Honig-Copper & Harrington, I 14
Honjo Copper Smeltery, III 490
Honkajuuri, Mauri, II 303
Honolulu Oil, II 491
Honolulu Sugar Refining Co., II 490
Honran, John J., I 650–51; **11** 290
Honshu Container Co. Ltd., IV 285
Honshu Paper Co., Ltd., IV 268, **284–85**, 292, 297, 321, 326
Hood, Bill, **11** 491
Hood, Clifford F., IV 573; **7** 550
Hood, Raymond, IV 635
Hood Sailmakers, Inc., **10** 215
Hooglandt, J.D., IV 134
Hoogovens. *See* Koninklijke Nederlandsche Hoogovens en Staalfabricken NV.
Hoogovens IJmuiden, IV 133–34
Hooiberg, I 256
Hook, Bud, **9** 67
Hook, Charles, IV 28
Hook, Harold S., **11** 16
Hook, Harold Swanson, III 193–94; **10** 66
Hook's Drug Stores, **9** 67
Hooker Chemical, IV 481
Hooker Petroleum, IV 264
Hooker, Richard, III 181
Hooley, E. Purnell, III 751
Hooley family, II 669
Hooper, Franklin, **7** 166
Hooper, Frederick, II 477
Hooper, Horace E., **7** 166
Hoops, Alan, **11** 379
Hootnick, Lawrence R., **10** 404–05
Hoover Ball and Bearing Co., III 589
Hoover Co., II 7; III 478
Hoover, Herbert, I 165; II 151, 316; IV 20, 634; **7** 323; **11** 137, 314
Hoover Industrial, III 536
Hoover, William R., **6** 227–29
Hoover-NSK Bearings, III 589
Hope, Bob, I 14; II 147, 151; III 55
Hope, C.C., **10** 298
Hope, Frank, II 444
Hope, George T., III 239–40
Hopfinger, K.B., I 208
Hopkins, Claude, I 12, 25, 36; **9** 70
Hopkins, Harry, **11** 72
Hopkins, John Jay, I 58; **10** 316
Hopkinson, David, III 699
Hopkinson, Edward, Jr., II 407
Hopper, Dennis, II 136
Hopper, Wilbert, IV 494, 496
Hopson, Howard C., V 629–30
Horace Young, **8** 395
Horizon Bancorp, II 252

Horizon Corporation, **8** 348
Horizon Travel Group, **8** 527
Hormel Co. *See* George A. Hormel and Company.
Hormel, George A., II 504–05; **7** 525
Hormel, Jay C., II 504–05
Hormel Provision Market, II 504
Horn & Hardart, II 614
Horn, Heinz, IV 195
Horn, Jerry, **11** 155, 156
Horn, John F., I 113; **6** 104
Horn, Marty, **10** 464
Horn Silver Mines Co., IV 83; **7** 187
Hornacek, Rudy, **9** 527–28
Hornaday, Harold, **9** 215
Hornaday, James, **8** 234
Hornblower & Co., II 450
Horne, Edgar, III 335
Horne, Edmund, IV 164; **7** 397
Horne, Henry, III 670
Horne, William Edgar, III 335
Horne's, I 449
Horner, H. Mansfield, I 85
Horner, Jack, **9** 417; **10** 537
Hornery, S.G., IV 708–09
Hornsberg Land Co., I 553
Horsley, Alec, **10** 441–42
Horsley, Nicholas, **10** 442
Horten, II 622
Horton, Dexter, **8** 469–71; **9** 539
Horton, George, **7** 74–75
Horton, Horace B., **7** 76
Horton, Horace Ebenezer, **7** 74–75
Horton, Jack K., V 716
Horton, Robert, IV 380; **7** 58–59
Horwitz, Martin, **7** 360
Hospital Affiliates International, III 79
Hospital Corporation of America, II 331; **III 78–80**
Hospital Cost Consultants, **11** 113
Hospital Products, Inc., **10** 534
Hospital Service Association of Pittsburgh, III 325
Hospitality Franchise Systems, Inc., 11 177–79
Host International, III 103
Hostetter, Amos, **7** 98–100
Hot Shoppes Inc., III 102
Hotchkiss, William Roy, **7** 137–38
Hotchkiss-Brandt, II 116
Hoteiya, V 209–10
Hotel Scandinavia K/S, I 120
Hotta, Shozo II 360–61
Houdry Chemicals, I 298
Houdry, Eugene, IV 549
Hough, William J., **8** 99–100
Houghton & Haywood, **10** 355
Houghton, Alanson B., III 683
Houghton, Amory, III 683
Houghton, Amory, Jr., III 683–84
Houghton, Arthur A., III 683
Houghton, Arthur A., Jr., III 683
Houghton, Henry Oscar, **10** 355–56
Houghton Mifflin Company, 10 355–57
Houghton, Osgood & Company, **10** 356
Houldsworth, Hubert (Sir), IV 38
House and Land Syndicate, IV 710
House of Windsor, Inc., **9** 533
Household Commercial Financial Services, II 420
Household Finance Corp., I 31; II 417; **8** 117
Household Flight Credit Corp., II 419

Household International, Inc., II **417–20**, 605; **7** 569–70; **10** 419
Household Products Inc., I 622; **10** 68
Houser, Robert N., III 330
Housman, Arthur, II 424
Housman, Clarence, II 424
de Houssoy, Robert Meunier, IV 618
Houston, David, III 306
Houston, Edwin, II 27
Houston, Effler & Partners Inc., **9** 135
Houston Electric Light & Power Company, V 641
Houston, Frank, II 251
Houston General Insurance, III 248
Houston Industries Incorporated, V **641–44; 7** 376
Houston International Teleport, Inc., **11** 184
Houston Lighting and Power Company, V 641–44
Houston Natural Gas Corp., IV 395; V 610
Houston Oil & Minerals Corp., **11** 440–41
Houston Oil Co., IV 342, 674
Houston Oil Trust, **11** 441
Houston, Sam (Gen.), IV 456
Houston, Stewart, IV 638
Housz, A.H. Ingen, IV 132
Housz, Ingen, IV 133
Hoveringham Group, III 753
Hovis-McDougall Co., II 565
Howaldtswerke-Deutsche Werft AG, IV 201
Howard, Charles, **10** 226
Howard Hughes Medical Institute, II 33, 35
Howard, J. Don, **6** 605
Howard, Jack R., IV 608; **7** 158–59
Howard, John, I 293
Howard Johnson, **11** 177–78
Howard Johnson Co., III 94, 102–03; **6** 27; **7** 266
Howard, Nat R., IV 607–08
Howard Printing Co., III 188; **10** 29
Howard, Ron, II 144, 173
Howard, Roy H., IV 607
Howard, Roy W., **7** 158
Howard Smith Paper Mills Ltd., IV 271–72
Howden. *See* Alexander Howden Group.
Howdy Company, **9** 177
Howe and Brainbridge Inc., I 321
Howe, Bruce, IV 308
Howe, C. D., V 737
Howe, Elias, II 9
Howe Sound Inc., IV 174
Howe Sound Pulp and Paper Ltd., IV 321
Howe, Wesley J., I 630–31; **11** 34–35
Howe, Will D., IV 622
Howell, Albert S., **9** 61–62
Howell, Harley, V 496
Howell, William, I 270
Howerton, J. A., **6** 325
Howerton, Norman, **6** 325
Howland, Henry Stark, II 244
Howlett, William, II 571–72
Howmet Aluminum Corp., IV 174
Howmet Turbine Components Corp., IV 174
Howson, Robert, III 560
Hoya Corp., III 715
Hoyt Archery Company, **10** 216
Hoyt, Charles, **8** 84
Hoyt, Frank L., IV 581
Hoyt, Harry, Jr., **8** 84

Hoyt, Harry, Sr., **8** 83–84
Hozier, Henry, **III** 279
HQ Office International, **8** 405
H2O Plus, **11** 41
Huaneng Raw Material Corp., **III** 718
Huang, Peter C.A., **III** 263
Hubachek, Frank, **II** 417–18
Hubbard Air Transport, **10** 162
Hubbard, Baker & Rice, **10** 126
Hubbard, C.B., **III** 228
Hubbard, Edward, **I** 47, 97; **10** 162
Hubbard, Elizabeth, **8** 166
Hubbard, Gardiner Greene, **9** 366
Hubbard, Paul M., **11** 491
Hubbard, Westervelt & Motteley, **II** 425
Hubbell, Harvey, II, **9** 286
Hubbell, Harvey, III, **9** 286–87
Hubbell Incorporated, 9 286–87
Hubbs, Ronald M., **III** 356
Hubinger Co., **II** 508; **11** 172
Huchon, Jean Paul, **II** 266
Huddart Parker, **III** 672
Hudiburg, John J., **V** 624
Hudler, Donald, **7** 463
Hudnut, **I** 710
Hudson, Edward J., **III** 559
Hudson Engineering Corp., **III** 559
Hudson, Harold, Jr., **III** 259
Hudson Motor Car Co., **I** 135, 158; **III** 568; **10** 292
Hudson Packaging & Paper Co., **IV** 257
Hudson River Railroad, **II** 396
Hudson River Rubber Company, **V** 231
Hudson Scott & Sons, **I** 604
Hudson, Tom, **6** 241
Hudson Underground Telephone Company, **6** 299
Hudson's, **V** 43–44. *See also* Dayton Hudson Corporation.
Hudson's Bay Company, I 284; **IV** 400, 437; **V 79–81; 6** 359; **8** 525
Hudson's Bay Oil and Gas Co., **IV** 400–01
Hue International, **8** 324
Hueppe Duscha, **III** 571
Huettmann, Fred, **II** 418
Huey, Ward, **10** 4
Huff Daland Dusters, **I** 99; **6** 81
Huff, Willard, **II** 41
Huffco, **IV** 492
Huffman, Horace, Jr., **7** 225
Huffman, Horace M., **7** 225
Huffman Manufacturing Company, **7** 225–26
Huffy Corporation, 7 225–27
Hughes Aircraft Co., **I** 172, 484, 539; **II** 32–35; **III** 428, 539; **7** 426–27; **9** 409; **10** 327; **11** 263, 540
Hughes, Charles Evans, **II** 88; **III** 291, 316, 337
Hughes Electric Heating Co., **II** 28
Hughes, Howard, **III** 428; **6** 81; **9** 266; **10** 316; **11** 263, 267
Hughes, Howard, Jr., **I** 58, 64, 99, 125–27, 484; **II** 32–34, 130, 146, 425; **III** 428
Hughes, James A., **IV** 409
Hughes Television Network, **11** 184
Hughes Tool Co., **I** 126; **II** 32; **III** 428–29
Hughes, William M., **IV** 45
Hugo Stinnes A.G., **I** 542
Hugo Stinnes AG, **8** 69
Hugo Stinnes GmbH, **8** 494–95
Hugo, Victor, **IV** 617
Huguenot Fenal, **IV** 108
Huh family, **II** 53

Huizenga, Wayne, **V** 752; **9** 73–74
Hulbert, Thomas, **II** 417–18
Hulce, Josh T., **III** 709; **7** 294
Hulett, Anthony, **III** 740
Hulett, William, **8** 499–500
Hull, Barry, **II** 211
Hull, H.C., **IV** 20–21
Hull, Latham, **8** 187–88
Hull, Roger, **III** 306
Hull, William, **I** 263
Hüls A.G., I 349–50
Humana Inc., III 79, **81–83; 6** 28, 191–92, 279
Humason Manufacturing Co., **III** 628
Humber, **I** 197
Humble Oil & Refining Company, **III** 497; **IV** 373, 428; **7** 171
Humboldt AG, **III** 541
Humboldt-Deutz-Motoren AG, **III** 541–42, 543; **IV** 126
Hume, Joseph, **10** 6
Hummel, **II** 163–64
Hummel, Joseph, Jr., **8** 156
Hummel-Hummel, **II** 163
Hummel-Reise, **II** 164
Humphrey, George M., **8** 346
Humphrey George M., II, **8** 347
Humphrey, Gilbert W., **8** 346
Humphrey, Hubert, **10** 287
Humphrey, Hubert H., **11** 24, 314
Humphrey Instruments, **I** 693
Humphrey, Stephen, **10** 423
Humphrey's Estate and Finance, **IV** 700
Humphreys & Glasgow Ltd., **V** 612
Humphreys, Arthur, **6** 241
Humphreys, Fred C., **11** 554
Hunco Ltd., **IV** 640
Hungária Biztositó, **III** 185
Hungarotex, **V** 166
Hunsucker, Robert D., **V** 692
Hunt, Alfred E. (Capt.), **IV** 10, 14
Hunt, Andrew M., **6** 523
Hunt, Bunker, **7** 229
Hunt, H.L., **7** 228–29
Hunt, Haroldson Lafayette. *See* Hunt, H.L.
Hunt, Herbert, **7** 229
Hunt Investment and Woodbine Development Co., **7** 229
Hunt, L.B. (Dr.), **IV** 119
Hunt Lumber Co., **IV** 358
Hunt Oil, **IV** 367, 453–54
Hunt Oil Company, 7 228–30
Hunt, P.J., **IV** 706
Hunt Petroleum, **7** 378
Hunt Production Co., **7** 228
Hunt, Ray, **7** 229–30
Hunt, Roy, **IV** 10, 14–15
Hunt, Tom, **7** 229
Hunt, William H., **IV** 304–05
Hunter, Croil, **I** 112–13; **6** 103
Hunter, Donald F., **IV** 640
Hunter, Edward H., **III** 513
Hunter Engineering Co., **IV** 18
Hunter, Evan, **IV** 672
Hunter family, **IV** 640
Hunter, Horace T., **IV** 638–39
Hunter, James, **II** 484
Hunter, Oakley, **II** 411
Hunter, P.V., **III** 434
Hunter, Samuel, Dr., **8** 352–53
Hunter, W.W., **III** 65
Hunter, William, Jr., **10** 281
Hunter-Douglas, **8** 235
Hunter-Hayes Elevator Co., **III** 467

Hunters' Foods, **II** 500
Hunting Aircraft, **I** 50
Hunting, David D., **7** 493
Huntington, B. Gwynne, **11** 180
Huntington Bancshares Inc., 11 180–82
Huntington, David L., **6** 596
Huntington, Francis R., **11** 180
Huntington Leasing Company, **11** 181
Huntington Mortgage Company, **11** 181
Huntington National Bank, **11** 180–81
Huntington National Bank of Columbus, **11** 180
Huntington, P.W., **11** 180, 182
Huntington, Robert W., **III** 225
Huntington, Theodore S., **11** 180
Huntley and Palmer Foods, **II** 544
Huntley Boorne & Stevens, **I** 604
Huntoon, John, **11** 553
Huntsman Chemical Corporation, 8 261–63
Huntsman Container, **9** 305
Huntsman, Jon Meade, **8** 261–62
Hupp Motor Car Company, **8** 74; **10** 261
Hupp Motor Car Corp., **III** 601
Hurcomb, Cyril, **V** 421
Hurd & Houghton, **10** 355
Hurd, G. David, **III** 330
Hurd, Melancthon M., **10** 355
Hurlburt Paper Co., **IV** 311
Hurley, John B., **10** 306
Hurley, Roy T., **10** 260–61
Hürlimann, Erwin, **III** 376
Hurst, Emmett, **8** 123
Hurst, Peter F., **III** 641
Hurwitz, Charles, **II** 492; **8** 349
Husbands, Sam, **II** 410
Huskisson, William, **III** 373
Husky Oil Ltd., **IV** 454, 695; **V** 673–75
Hussein, Saddam, **IV** 651; **7** 390
Hussman Corp., **I** 457–58
Hussmann Refrigerator Co., **7** 429–30
Hussmann Corporation, **10** 554
Huston, John, **II** 175
Huston, Walter, **II** 155
Hutchcraft, A. Steven, Jr., **IV** 123
Hutchings, Gregory, **11** 525–27
Hutchins, Robert Maynard, **7** 167
Hutchins, Stilson, **IV** 688
Hutchins, Pemberton, **7** 584
Hutchinson Wholesale Grocery Co., **II** 624
Hutchinson-Mapa, **IV** 560
Hutchison, **I** 470
Hutchison, John, **11** 61
Hutchison Microtel, **11** 548
Hutchison Whampoa, **IV** 694–95
Huth Manufacturing Corporation, **10** 414
Hüttenwerk Oberhausen AG, **IV** 222
Hüttenwerk Salzgitter AG, **IV** 201
Huttig Sash & Door Company, **8** 135
Hutton, E.F. *See* E.F. Hutton.
Hutton, Edward F., **II** 531; **7** 273
Hutzler, Morton, **IV** 447–48
Huxley, Thomas Henry, **7** 166
Huyck Corp., **I** 429
Huyghebaert, Jan, **II** 305
Hwack, Shin Hyon, **III** 748
Hyams, Harry, **IV** 712
Hyatt Bearing, **9** 17
Hyatt Corporation, II 442; **III** 92, **96–97; 9** 426
Hyatt Development Corp., **III** 97
Hyatt Hotels Corp., **III** 96–97; **IV** 135
Hyatt International, **III** 97

Hyatt Medical Enterprises, **III** 73
Hyatt Roller Bearing Co., **I** 171–72; **10** 326
Hybridtech, **III** 18
Hyde, Charles F., **9** 393–395
Hyde, Charles H., **II** 670
Hyde Company, A.L., **7** 116–17
Hyde, Douglas W., **9** 393, 395
Hyde, Henry Baldwin, **III** 247
Hyde, James Hazen, **III** 247–48
Hyde, Joseph R., III, **9** 52–53
Hydraulic Brake Co., **I** 141
Hydro Electric Power Commission of Ontario, **6** 541
Hydro-Aire Incorporated, **8** 135
Hydro-Carbon Light Company, **9** 127
Hydro-Electric Power Commission of Ontario, **9** 461
Hydro-Quebec, 6 501–03
Hydrocarbon Services of Nigeria Co., **IV** 473
Hydroponic Chemical Co., **III** 28
Hydrox Corp., **II** 533
Hygeia Sciences, Inc., **8** 85, 512
Hygienic Ice Co., **IV** 722
Hygrade Containers Ltd., **IV** 286
Hygrade Foods, **III** 502; **7** 208
Hyland Laboratories, **I** 627
Hyland, Lawrence, **II** 33
Hyman, George, **8** 112–13
Hyman, Morton P., **11** 376
Hyndley (Lord), **IV** 38
Hyosung Group, **III** 749
Hyper Shoppes, Inc., **II** 670
Hyperion Press, **6** 176
Hypermart USA, **8** 555–56
Hyplains Beef, **7** 175
Hypo-Bank. See Bayerische Hypotheken-und Wechsel-Bank AG.
Hypobaruk, **III** 348
Hypro Engineering Inc., **I** 481
Hysol Corp., **I** 321
Hysol Grafil Composite Components Co., **I** 321
Hyster, **I** 424
Hyster-Yale Materials Handling, Inc., **7** 369–71
Hystron Fibers Inc., **I** 347
Hyundai America, **III** 515; **7** 231
Hyundai Cement Co., **III** 515; **7** 231
Hyundai Corp., **III** 515–16; **7** 231–32
Hyundai Electrical Engineering Co., **III** 516; **7** 232
Hyundai Electronics Industries Corporation, **III** 517; **7** 233; **10** 404
Hyundai Engine and Machinery Co., **III** 516; **7** 232
Hyundai Engineering & Construction Co., **III** 515–17; **7** 231, 233
Hyundai Group, I 207, 516; **II** 53–54, 122; **III** 457–59, **515–17**; **7 231–34 (upd.)**
Hyundai Heavy Industries Co., **III** 516–17; **7** 232
Hyundai Housing and Industrial Development Co., **III** 516; **7** 232
Hyundai Information Systems, **7** 234
Hyundai Merchant Marine Co., **III** 516; **7** 232
Hyundai Mipo Dockyard Co., **III** 516; **7** 232–33
Hyundai Motor America, **7** 234
Hyundai Motor Co., **III** 515–17, 596; **7** 231, 233; **9** 350

Hyundai Precision & Industry Co., **III** 516; **7** 232
Hyundai Shipbuilding and Heavy Industries Co., **III** 516; **7** 232
Hyundai Wood Industries Co., **III** 516; **7** 232

I.C.H. Corp., **I** 528
I.C. Johnson and Co., **III** 669
I.D. Systems, Inc., **11** 444
I.G. Chemie, **I** 337
I.G. Dyes. See IG Farben.
I.G. Farben. See I.G. Farbenindustrie AG.
I.G. Farbenindustrie AG, **I** 305–06, 309–11, 337, 346–53, 619, 632–33, 698–99; **II** 257; **III** 677, 694; **IV** 111, 485
I.J. Stokes Corp., **I** 383
I.M. Pei & Associates, **I** 580; **III** 267
I.M. Singer and Co., **II** 9
I. Magnin Inc., **8** 444
I/N Kote, **IV** 116
I/N Tek, **IV** 116
I.R. Maxwell & Co. Ltd., **IV** 641; **7** 311
I-T-E Circuit Breaker, **II** 121
Iacocca, Lee, **I** 145, 167, 188; **III** 544; **7** 205; **11** 54, 139
Iba, Teigo, **I** 519; **II** 360; **IV** 215; **11** 478
Ibe, Kyonosuke, **II** 361
Iberdrola, **V** 608
Iberia, **I** 110
Iberia, Compañia Aérea de Transportes, S.A. See Iberia Líneas Aéreas de España S.A.
Iberia Líneas Aéreas De España S.A., 6 95–97
Ibero-Amerika Bank, **II** 521
Iberstein, Robert, **III** 258
Iberswiss Catering, **6** 96
Ibex Engineering Co., **III** 420
IBH Holding AG, **7** 513
IBJ. See The Industrial Bank of Japan Ltd.
IBJ International, **II** 301
IBM. See International Business Machines Corporation.
IBM Credit Corp., **II** 440
IBM Japan, **III** 139; **6** 428
IBM World Trade Corp., **III** 148
Ibn Saud, King (Saudi Arabia), **IV** 386, 536–37
IBP, inc., II 515–17; **7** 525
Ibstock Johnsen, **III** 735
Ibuka, Masaru, **II** 101–02
Ibuki, Kazuo, **II** 322
IC Industries Inc., I 456–58; **III** 512; **7** 430; **10** 414, 553
ICA AB, II 639–40
ICA Banan A.B., **II** 640
ICA Eol A.B., **II** 639
ICA Essve A.B., **II** 639
ICA Frukt och Grönsaker A.B., **II** 639
ICA Hakon A.B., **II** 639
ICA Mortgage Corporation, **8** 30
ICA Rosteri A.B., **II** 640
ICA Technologies, Ltd., **III** 533
ICA-förlaget A.B., **II** 640
Icahn, Carl, **I** 123, 127, 426; **II** 408; **IV** 523, 553, 574; **7** 551; **8** 106
ICE, **I** 333
Ichihara, Akira, **V** 143
Ichikawa, Shinobu, **I** 492
Ichimura, Kiyoshi, **III** 159; **8** 278
ICI. See Imperial Chemical Industries plc.
ICI Americas, Inc., **8** 179, 222

ICI Colours, **9** 154
ICI Membranes, **11** 361
ICI Paints, **8** 222
Ickes, Harold L., **IV** 121, 552
ICL plc, II 65; **III** 141; **6 240–42**; **11** 150
ICL-KMECS, **6** 242
ICM Mortgage Corporation, **8** 436
ICOA Life Insurance, **III** 253
ICS. See International Care Services.
ICX, **IV** 136
ID, Inc., **9** 193
Idaho Frozen Foods, **II** 572–73
IDB Broadcast, **11** 183–84
IDB Communications Group, Inc., 11 183–85
IDB Mobile, **11** 183
IDB Systems, **11** 183–84
IDB WorldCom, **11** 183–85
Ide, Chandler, **6** 353
Ide Megumi, **III** 549
Ideal Basic Industries, **III** 701–02; **8** 258–59
Ideal Corp., **III** 602
Ideka, Mochimasa, **III** 383–84
Idema, Walter D., **7** 493–94
Idemitsu Petrochemicals, **8** 153
Idemitsu & Co., **IV** 434
Idemitsu Geothermal Development Co. Ltd., **IV** 435–36
Idemitsu Japanese Sea Oil Development Co. Ltd., **IV** 435
Idemitsu, Keisuke, **IV** 435
Idemitsu Kosan K.K., II 361; **IV 434–36**, 476
Idemitsu Myanmar Oil Exploration Co. Ltd., **IV** 519
Idemitsu Oil & Gas Co. Ltd., **IV** 435
Idemitsu Oil Development Co. Ltd., **IV** 435, 519
Idemitsu Petrochemical Co. Ltd., **I** 330; **IV** 435, 519
Idemitsu, Sazou, **IV** 434–35
Idemitsu Tanker Co. Ltd., **IV** 435
Idestam, Knut Fredrik, **IV** 314
IDG Communications, Inc, **7** 238
IDG World Expo Corporation, **7** 239
IDO. See Nippon Idou Tsushin.
Idris, King (Libya), **IV** 480–81
IEL. See Industrial Equity Ltd.
IFI, **I** 161–62; **III** 347
IFS Industries, **6** 294
IG Farben, **8** 108–09
IG Farbenindustrie AG, **11** 7
IGA, **II** 624, 649, 668, 681–82; **7** 451
Iggesund Bruk, **IV** 317–18
IGT-International, **10** 375–76
IGT-North America, **10** 375
Ihamuotila, Jaakko, **IV** 471
IHI, **I** 534
IHI Granitech Corp., **III** 533
Iida & Co., **I** 493
Iida, Seizo, **II** 439; **9** 384
Iida, Shinshichi, **V** 193
Iiguchi, Jiro, **V** 680
IinteCom, **III** 169
IISCO-Ujjain Pipe and Foundry Co. Ltd., **IV** 206
Ikawa family, **IV** 266
IKEA Group, V 82–84
IKEA International A/S of Denmark, **V** 82
IKEA-Belgium, **V** 65
Ikeda, Ichiro, **II** 277
Ikeda, Kikunae, **II** 463
Ikeda, Nariaki, **II** 291

Ikeda, Seihin, **I** 507
Ikeda, Shigeaki, **II** 325
Ikeura, Kisaburo, **II** 301
Ikuta, Hiizu, **I** 220
Ilitch, Marian, **7** 278–79
Ilitch, Michael, **7** 278–79
Illia, Arturo, **IV** 578
Illinois Bell Telephone Co., **IV** 660
Illinois Central Corporation, 11 186–89
Illinois Central Gulf Railroad, **I** 456, 584;
  11 187
Illinois Central Industries, **11** 187
Illinois Central Industries, Inc., **I** 456; **8**
  410; **10** 553
Illinois Central Railroad Company, **11** 188
Illinois Electric and Gas Company, **6** 470
Illinois Glass Co., **I** 609
Illinois Iowa Power Company, **6** 505
Illinois IP Inc., **6** 506
Illinois Merchants Trust Co., **II** 261
Illinois National Bank & Trust Co., **III**
  213–14
Illinois Power & Light Corporation, **6**
  504–05
Illinois Power Company, 6 470, **504–07**
Illinois Power Finance Company N.V., **6**
  506
Illinois Power Fuel Company, **6** 506
Illinois Steel Co., **IV** 572; **7** 549; **8** 114
Illinois Terminal Company, **6** 504
Illinois Tool Works Inc., III 518–20
Illinois Traction Company, **6** 504
Illinois Trust and Savings Bank, **II** 261
Ilmor Engineering of Great Britain, **V** 494
Ilse-Bergbau AG, **IV** 229–30
Ilselder Hütte, **IV** 201
Ilwaco Telephone and Telegraph Company.
  See Pacific Telecom, Inc.
IMA Holdings Corp., **III** 73–74
Image Business Systems Corp., **11** 66
Imaoka, Yasuo, **II** 109
Imasa Group, **IV** 34
Imasco Foods Corp., **I** 514
Imasco Limited, II 605; **V 401–02**
Imatran Voima Osakeyhtiö, **IV** 469
IMC Drilling Mud, **III** 499
IMC Fertilizer Group, Inc., 8 264–66
Imcera Group, Inc., **8** 264, 266
IMED Corp., **I** 712; **III** 511–12; **10** 551
Imetal S.A., IV 107–09
IMI plc, 9 288–89
IMI Radiators, **III** 593
Imigest Fondo Imicapital, **III** 347
Imlay, John P., **11** 77–78
Immunex Corp., **8** 26
Immuno Serums, Inc., **V** 174–75
Imo Delaval, Inc., **7** 235
Imo Industries Inc., 7 235–37
IMO Ltd., **III** 539
Impala Platinum Holdings, **IV** 91–93
Imperial Air Transport, **I** 92
Imperial Airways, **I** 92; **6** 109–10, 117.
  See also AirEgypt.
Imperial Bank of Canada, **II** 244–45
Imperial Bank of Persia, **II** 298
Imperial British East Africa Co., **III** 522
Imperial Business Forms, **9** 72
Imperial Chemical Industries, **11** 97
Imperial Chemical Industries plc, I 303,
  351–53, 374, 605, 633; **II** 448, 565; **III**
  522, 667, 677, 680, 745; **IV** 38, 110,
  698; **7** 209; **8** 224; **9** 288; **10** 436
Imperial Fire Co., **III** 373
Imperial Goonbarrow, **III** 690

Imperial Group, **II** 513; **III** 503; **7** 209
Imperial Life Co., **III** 288, 373
Imperial Marine Insurance Co., **III** 384,
  405–06
Imperial Metal Industries Ltd. *See* IMI plc.
Imperial Oil Co., Ltd., **IV** 437–38, 494
Imperial Oil Limited, IV 428, **437–39**
Imperial Pneumatic Tool Co., **III** 525
Imperial Premium Finance, **III** 264
Imperial Savings Association, **8** 30–31
Imperial Smelting Corp., **IV** 58
Imperial Tobacco Co., **I** 425–26, 605; **IV**
  260
Imperial Tobacco Limited, **V** 401
Imprimis, **8** 467
Impulse, **9** 122
Imreg, **10** 473–74
IMS International, Inc., **10** 105
Imus, Don, **11** 191
In-Sink-Erator, **II** 19
INA Corp., **II** 403; **III** 79, 208, 223–25,
  226; **11** 481
INA Wälzlager Schaeffler, **III** 595
INA-Naftaplin, **IV** 454
Inaba, Seiuemon, **III** 482–83
Inabata & Co., **I** 398
Inamori, Kazuo, **II** 50–51; **7** 118–19
Inayama, Yoshihiro, **IV** 158
Incasso Bank, **II** 185
Inchcape (Baron, of Strathnaver). *See*
  James Lyle Mackay.
Inchcape (first Earl of). *See* James Lyle
  Mackay.
Inchcape (Lord), **V** 491–92
Inchcape (third Earl of), **III** 522–23
Inchcape & Co. Ltd., **II** 233; **III** 521,
  522–23
Inchcape PLC, III 521–24
Incheon Iron & Steel Co., **III** 516
Inchon Heavy Industrial Corp., **IV** 183
Inclan, Miguel Angel del Valle. *See* del
  Valle Inclan, Miguel Angel.
Inco Limited, IV 75, 78, **110–12**
Incola, S.A., **II** 471
InControl Inc., **11** 460
Ind Coope, **I** 215
Ind, Edward, **I** 215
Indemnité, **III** 391
Indemnity Insurance Co., **III** 224
Independent Breweries Company, **9** 178
Independent Grocers Alliance. *See* IGA.
Independent Grocers Alliance Distribution
  Co., **II** 649
Independent Metal Products Co., **I** 169
Independent Oil & Gas Co., **IV** 521
Independent Power Generators, **V** 605
Independent Warehouses, Inc., **IV** 180
La India Co., **II** 532
India General Steam Navigation and
  Railway Co., **III** 522
India Life Assurance Co., **III** 359
India Rubber, Gutta Percha & Telegraph
  Works Co., **I** 428
Indian, **7** 211
Indian Airlines Corporation. *See* Air-India.
Indian Iron & Steel Co. Ltd., **IV** 49,
  205–07
Indian Oil Co., **IV** 440–41
Indian Oil Corporation Ltd., IV 440–41,
  483
Indian Point Farm Supply, Inc., **IV** 458–59
Indian Refineries Ltd., **IV** 440–41
Indiana Electric Corporation, **6** 555
Indiana Gas & Water Company, **6** 556

Indiana Group, **I** 378
Indiana Oil Purchasing Co., **IV** 370
Indiana Power Company, **6** 555
Indiana Refining Co., **IV** 552
Indianapolis Air Pump Company, **8** 37
Indianapolis Brush Electric Light & Power
  Company, **6** 508
Indianapolis Cablevision, **6** 508–09
Indianapolis Light and Power Company, **6**
  508
Indianapolis Motor Speedway Company, **9**
  16
Indianapolis Power & Light Company, **6**
  508–09
Indianapolis Pump and Tube Company, **8**
  37
Indianhead Truck Lines, **6** 371
Indo-Asahi Glass Co., Ltd., **III** 667
Indo-China Steam Navigation Co., **I** 469
Indola Cosmetics B.V., **8** 16
Indonesia Petroleum Co., **IV** 516
Induban, **II** 196
Industria Gelati Sammontana, **II** 575
Industria Metalgrafica, **I** 231
Industria Raffinazione Oli Minerali, **IV** 419
Industrial & Trade Shows of Canada, **IV**
  639
Industrial Acceptance Bank, **I** 337
Industrial Bancorp, **9** 229
Industrial Bank of Japan (Switzerland), **II**
  301
Industrial Bank of Japan, Ltd., II
  300–01, 310–11, 338, 369, 433, 459
Industrial Bank of Scotland, **10** 337
Industrial Bio-Test Laboratories, **I** 374, 702
Industrial Cartonera, **IV** 295
Industrial Circuits, **IV** 680
Industrial Computer Corp., **11** 78
Industrial Development Corp., **IV** 22, 92,
  534
Industrial Development Corp. of Zambia
  Ltd., **IV** 239–41
Industrial Engineering, **III** 598
Industrial Engineering Associates, Inc., **II**
  112
Industrial Equity Ltd., **I** 438
Industrial Fuel Supply Co., **I** 569
Industrial Gas Equipment Co., **I** 297
Industrial Mutual Insurance, **III** 264
Industrial National Bank, **9** 229
Industrial Publishing Company, **9** 413
Industrial Reorganization Corp., **III** 502,
  556
Industrial Resources, **6** 144
Industrial Trade & Consumer Shows Inc.,
  IV 639
Industrial Trust Company, **9** 228
Industrial Vehicles Corp. B.V., **III** 543–44
Industrias y Confecciones, S.A. **V** 51
Industrie Regionale du Bâtiment, **IV** 108
Industrie-Aktiengesellschaft, **IV** 201
Industriegas GmbH., **I** 581
Industrionics Control, Inc., **III** 643
Industrivärden, **II** 366
Induyco. *See* Industrias y Confecciones,
  S.A.
Inelco Peripheriques, **10** 459
Inexco Oil Co., **7** 282
Infinity Broadcasting Corporation, 11
  190–92
INFLEX, S.A., **8** 247
Inflight Sales Group Limited, **11** 82
Infobase Services, **6** 14
Infonet Services Corporation, **6** 303

Informatics, **III** 248
Informatics General Corporation, **11** 468
Informatics Legal Systems, **III** 169; **6** 285
Information Associates Inc., **11** 78
Information Consulting Group, **9** 345
Information, Dissemination and Retrieval Inc., **IV** 670
Information Resources, Inc., 10 358–60
Information Unlimited Software, **6** 224
Informix Corp., 10 361–64, 505
Informix Software Inc., **10** 362
Infrasud, **I** 466
Ing. C. Olivetti & C., S.p.A., **III** 122, **144–46**, 549, 678; **10** 499
Ingalls, George A., **II** 7
Ingalls Quinn and Johnson, **9** 135
Ingalls Shipbuilding Corp., **I** 485; **11** 264–65
Ingear, **10** 216
Ingells, Douglas J., **I** 49, 72
Ingelmann, Björn, **I** 665
Ingenegeren, W.P., **III** 199
Ingersoll, Ralph, **IV** 674; **7** 527
Ingersoll, Robert, **III** 439–40
Ingersoll Rock Drill Co., **III** 525
Ingersoll, Roy, **III** 439
Ingersoll, Simon, **III** 525
Ingersoll, Stephen, **III** 439
Ingersoll-Rand Company, **III** 473, **525–27**; **10** 262
Ingersoll-Sergeant Rock Drill Co., **III** 525
Inglis, Brian (Sir), **IV** 250
Inglis, John B., **9** 423
Inglis Ltd., **III** 654
Ingram Barge Company, **11** 194
Ingram Book Company, **11** 193
Ingram, Bronson, **11** 193
Ingram Computer, **11** 194
Ingram Corp. Ltd., **III** 559; **IV** 249
Ingram Entertainment, Inc., **11** 195
Ingram, Frederic, **11** 193
Ingram Industries, Inc., 11 193–95
Ingram Micro, **10** 518–19; **11** 194–95
Ingram, O.H., **11** 193
Ingram Oil & Refining Company, **11** 193
Ingram Petroleum Services, Inc., **11** 194
AB Ingredients, **II** 466
Ingredients Technology Corp., **9** 154
Ingres Corporation, **9** 36–37
Ingwerson and Co., **II** 356
INH. *See* Instituto Nacional de Hidrocarboros.
Inhalation Therapy Services, **III** 73
INI. *See* Instituto Nacional de Industria.
Inland Box Co., **IV** 342; **8** 267
Inland Container Corporation, **IV** 311, 341–42, 675; **7** 528; **8** 267–69**
Inland Iron and Forge, **IV** 113
Inland Lime and Stone Co., **IV** 114
Inland Pollution Control, **9** 110
Inland Specialty Chemical Corp., **I** 342
Inland Steamship Co., **IV** 113
Inland Steel Co., **IV** 113–16
Inland Steel Industries, Inc., **II** 403; **IV** **113–16**, 158, 703; **7** 447
Inland Steel Services, **IV** 116
Inland Steel Urban Development Corp., **IV** 115
INMOS, **I** 532
Inmos Ltd., **11** 307
Inno-France. *See* Societe des Grandes Entreprises de Distribution, Inno-France.
Innovative Pork Concepts, **7** 82
Innovative Software Inc., **10** 362

Inns and Co., **III** 734
Innwerk AG, **IV** 229
Innwerk Bayerische Aluminium AG, **IV** 229
Ino, Kinji, **I** 10
Inoue, Choichi, **6** 70
Inoue Electric Manufacturing Co., **II** 75–76
Inoue, Jiro, **V** 96
Inoue, Kaoru, **I** 502, 505–06
Inoue, Masaru, **V** 448
Input/Output, Inc., **11** 538
INSCO, **III** 242
Insilco Corp., **I** 473
Insinger, M.S., **6** 403
Inskeep, John, **III** 223
Insley Manufacturing Co., **8** 545
Insta-Care Pharmacy Services, **9** 186
Instant Milk Co., **II** 488
Institut de Sérothérapie Hémopoïétique, **I** 669
Institut für Gemeinwohl, **IV** 139
Institut Merieux, **I** 389
Institut Ronchese, **I** 676
Institute for Scientific Information, **8** 525, 528
Instituto Nacional de Hidrocarboros, **IV** 528
Instituto Nacional de Industria, **I** **459–61**; **V** 606–07; **6** 95–96
Instituto per la Ricostruzione Industriale, **V** 614
Instone Airline, **I** 92
Instrumentation Laboratory Inc., **III** 511–12
Insulite Co. of Finland, **IV** 275
Insull family, **IV** 372
Insull, Martin, **6** 555, 605
Insull, Samuel, **V** 583–84, 587, 670; **6** 524, 532, 555, 602, 604–05; **10** 115–16, 295
Insull, Samuel, Jr., **6** 532
Insurance Co. against Fire Damage, **III** 308
Insurance Co. of North America, **III** 190, 223–25, 367
Insurance Co. of Scotland, **III** 358
Insurance Co. of the State of Pennsylvania, **III** 196
Insurance Corp. of Ireland (Life), **III** 335
INTEC, **6** 428
InteCom Inc., **6** 285
Integon Corp., **IV** 374
Integrated Data Services Co., **IV** 473
Integrated Genetics, **I** 638; **8** 210
Integrated Health Services, Inc., **11** 282
Integrated Resources, Inc., **11** 483
Integrated Software Systems Corporation, **6** 224; **11** 469
Integrated Systems Operations. *See* Xerox Corporation.
Integrated Systems Solutions Corp., **9** 284; **11** 395
Integrated Technology, Inc., **6** 279
Integrity Life Insurance, **III** 249
Intel Corporation, **II** **44–46**, 62, 64; **III** 115, 125, 455; **6** 215–17, 222, 231, 233, 235, 257; **9** 42–43, 57, 114–15, 165–66; **10 365–67** (upd.), 477; **11** 62, 308, 328, 490, 503, 518, 520
Intelicom Solutions Corp., **6** 229
IntelliCorp, **9** 310
Intelligent Electronics, Inc., 6 243–45
Inter IKEA Systems B.V., **V** 82

Inter Island Telephone, **6** 326, 328
Inter State Telephone, **6** 338
Inter-American Development Bank, **IV** 55
Inter-American Satellite Television Network, **7** 391
Inter-City Gas Corp., **III** 654
Inter-City Western Bakeries Ltd., **II** 631
Inter-Comm Telephone, Inc., **8** 310
Inter-Mountain Telephone Co., **V** 344
Interactive Systems, **7** 500
Interamericana de Talleras SA de CV, **10** 415
Interbake Foods, **II** 631
InterBold, **7** 146; **11** 151
Interbrás, **IV** 503
Intercity Food Services, Inc., **II** 663
Interco Incorporated, **III** **528–31**; **9** 133, 135, 192, 234–35; **10** 184
Intercolonial, **6** 360
Intercomi, **II** 233
Intercontinental Apparel, **8** 249
Intercontinental Breweries, **I** 289
Intercontinental Hotels, **I** 248–49
Intercontinental Mortgage Company, **8** 436
Intercontinental Rubber Co., **II** 112
Intercontinentale, **III** 404
Interedi-Cosmopolitan, **III** 47
Interessen Gemeinschaft Farbenwerke. *See* IG Farben.
Interface Asia-Pacific, Inc., **8** 271
Interface Europe, Inc., **8** 271
Interface Flooring Systems, Inc., **8** 271
Interface, Inc., 8 270–72
Interfinancial, **III** 200
InterFirst Bancorp, Inc., **9** 482
Interfood Ltd., **II** 520–21, 540
Intergraph Corporation, **6 246–49**; **10** 257
Interhandel, **I** 337–38; **II** 378
INTERIM Services, Inc., **9** 268, 270
The Interlake Corporation, **8 273–75**
Intermagnetics General Corp., **9** 10
Intermed, **I** 429
Intermedics, **III** 633; **11** 458–59
Intermedics Intraocular Inc., **I** 665
Intermoda, **V** 166
Intermountain Broadcasting and Television Corp., **IV** 674
International Aero Engines, **9** 418
International Agricultural Corporation, **8** 264–65
International Assurance Co., **III** 195
International Bank, **II** 261
International Bank of Moscow, **II** 242
International Banking Corp., **II** 253; **9** 123
International Banking Technologies, Inc., **11** 113
International Brotherhood of Pulp, Sulphite and Paper Mill Workers, **9** 304
International Business Machines Corporation, **I** 26, 455, 523, 534, 541; **II** 6, 8, 10, 42, 44–45, 56, 62, 68, 70, 73, 86, 99, 107, 113, 134, 159, 211, 274, 326, 379, 397, 432; **III** 9, 109–11, 113–18, 121–28, 130, 132–34, 136, 139–43, 145, **147–49**, 151–52, 154–55, 157, 165–72, 200, 246, 313, 319, 326, 458, 475, 549, 618, 685; **IV** 443, 711; **6** 51, 218–25, 233–35, 237, 240–42, 244–48, **250–53** (upd.), 254–60, 262, 265, 269–71, 275–77, 279, 281–89, 320, 324, 346, 390; **7** 145–46, 161; **8** 138–39, 466–67; **9** 36, 41–42, 48, 50, 114–15, 131, 139, 165–66, 170–71,

184, 194, 284, 296–97, 310, 327, 463–64; **10** 19, 22–24, 58, 119, 125, 161, 194, 232, 237, 243–44, 255–56, 309, 361–62, 366–67, 394, 456, 463, 474, 500–01, 505, 510, 512–13, 518–19, 542; **11** 19, 45, 50, 59, 61–62, 64–65, 68, 86–88, 150, 273–74, 285, 364, 395, 469, 485, 491, 494, 506, 519
International Care Services, **6** 182
International Cellucotton Products Co., **III** 40
International Commercial Bank, **II** 257
International Computers, **II** 82
International Computers and Tabulators, Ltd., **6** 240–41
International Computers, Ltd., **II** 81; **III** 164; **6** 241. *See also* ICL plc.
International Controls Corporation, **10 368–70**
International Credit Card Business Assoc., **II** 436
International Dairy Queen, Inc., **7** 266; **10 371–74**
International Data Group, **7 238–40**
International Development Bank, **IV** 417
International Digital Communications, Inc., **6** 327
International Egyptian Oil Co., **IV** 412
International Engineering Company, Inc., **7** 355
International Equities Corp., **III** 98
International Factoring Corp., **II** 436
International Factors, Limited, **II** 208
International Flavors & Fragrances Inc., **9 290–92**
International Foods, **II** 468
International Game Technology, **10 375–76**
International Graphics Corp., **IV** 645
International Harvester Co., **III** 473, 650, 651; **10** 264, 280, 378, 380, 528. *See also* Navistar International Corporation.
International Healthcare, **III** 197
International Hydron, **10** 47
International Income Property, **IV** 708
International Learning Systems Corp. Ltd., **IV** 641–42; **7** 311
International Lease Finance Corp., **III** 198; **6** 67
International Light Metals Corp., **IV** 163
International Marine Oil Co., **IV** 363
International Mercantile Marine Co., **II** 330
International Milling, **II** 493; **7** 241–42
International Mineral & Chemical, Inc., **8** 265–66
International Multifoods Corporation, **7 241–43**
International News Service, **IV** 626–27
International Nickel Co. of Canada, Ltd., **III** 677; **IV** 78, 110–12
International Pacific Corp., **II** 389
International Paper & Power Co., **IV** 286
International Paper Company, **I** 27; **II** 208, 403; **III** 693, 764; **IV** 16, 245, **286–88**, 289, 326; **8** 267; **11** 76, 311
International Parts Corporation, **10** 414
International Petroleum Co., Ltd., **IV** 415–16, 438, 478. *See also* International Petroleum Corp.
International Petroleum Corp., **IV** 454, 484. *See also* International Petroleum Co., Ltd.
International Publishing Corp., **IV** 641, 666–67; **7** 343

International Sealants Corporation, **8** 333
International Shoe Co., **III** 528–30
International Silver, **I** 30
International Standard Electric, **II** 66–68
International Stores, **I** 427
International Telcell Group, **7** 336
International Telephone & Telegraph Corporation, **I** 434, 446, **462–64**, 544; **II** 13, 66, 68, 86, 130, 331; **III** 99, 162–64, 644; **V** 334–35, 337–38; **6** 356; **8** 157; **10** 19, 44, 301; **11 196–99 (upd.)**, 337. *See also* ITT Corp.
International Terminal Operation Co., **I** 513
International Time Recording Company, **III** 147. *See also* International Business Machines Corporation.
International Trust and Investment Corp., **II** 577
International Trust Co., **II** 207
International Utilities Corp., **IV** 75–76; **6** 444
International Western Electric Co., **I** 462; **II** 66; **III** 162; **11** 196
International Wind Systems, **6** 581
International Wine & Spirits Ltd., **9** 533
International Wire Works Corp., **8** 13
Internationale Industriële Beleggung Maatschappij Amsterdam BV, **IV** 128
InterNorth Corp., **II** 16
InterNorth, Inc., **V** 610
Interocean Management Corp., **9** 509–11
Interpac Belgium, **6** 303
Interprovincial Pipe Line Ltd., **I** 264; **IV** 439
Interpublic Group Inc., **I 16–18**, 31, 36; **6** 53
Intersil, **II** 30
Interstate & Ocean Transport, **6** 577
Interstate Bag, **I** 335
Interstate Bakeries, **7** 320
Interstate Brick Company, **6** 568–69
Interstate Electric Manufacturing Company. *See* McGraw Electric Company.
Interstate Finance Corp., **11** 16
Interstate Financial Corporation, **9** 475
Interstate Power Company, **6** 555, 605
Interstate Public Service Company, **6** 555
Interstate Stores Inc., **V** 203
Interstate Supply and Manufacturing Company. *See* McGraw Electric Company.
Interstate Supply Company. *See* McGraw Electric Company.
Interstate United, **II** 679; **III** 502
Intertype Corp., **II** 37
Interunfall, **III** 346
Intervideo TV Productions-A.B., **II** 640
Interweb, **IV** 661
Intrac Handelsgesellschaft mbH, **7** 142
Intradal, **II** 572
Intraph South Africa Ltd., **6** 247
IntraWest Bank, **II** 289
Invacare Corporation, **11 200–02**, 486
Invep S.p.A., **10** 150
Inveresk Paper Co., **III** 693; **IV** 685
Invergordon Distillers, **III** 509
Inversale, **9** 92
Investors Diversified Services, Inc., **II** 398; **6** 199; **8** 348–49; **10** 43–45, 59, 62
Investors DS, **10** 44
Investors Group, **III** 261
Investors Management Corp., **10** 331
Investors Overseas Services, **10** 368–69

Invista Capital Management, **III** 330
Iolab Corp., **III** 36
Ionpure Technologies Corporation, **6** 486–88
Iowa Beef Packers, **II** 515–16; **IV** 481–82
Iowa Beef Processors, **II** 516–17
Iowa Light, Heat and Power, **6** 523
Iowa Manufacturing, **II** 86
Iowa Power, **6** 525
Iowa Public Service Company, **6** 524–25
Iowa Resources, Inc., **6** 523
IP Gas Supply Company, **6** 506
IP Services, Inc., **IV** 597
IP Timberlands Ltd., **IV** 288
IP&L. *See* Illinois Power & Light Corporation.
Ipalco Enterprises, Inc., **6 508–09**
IPC Magazines Limited, **IV** 650; **7 244–47**
Ira J. Cooper, **8** 127
Iran Air, **6** 101
Iran Pan American Oil Co., **IV** 466
Irani, Ray, **IV** 481
Iranian Offshore Oil Co. of the Islamic Republic, **IV** 467
Iranian Oil Exploration and Producing Co., **IV** 466–67
Iranian Oil Refining Co., **IV** 466
Iraq Petroleum Co., **IV** 363, 386, 429, 450, 464, 558–60
Irby, Tom, **11** 61
Irby-Gilliland Company, **9** 127
Ireland, Charles, **10** 44
Ireland, Charles Lincoln, **7** 572, 575
Ireland, Charles T., **II** 133; **6** 158
Ireland, Charles W., **7** 573
Ireland, Norman, **IV** 259
Irgens, Finn T., **III** 598
IRI. *See* Instituto per la Ricostruzione Industriale.
IRIS Holding Co., **III** 347
Irish Paper Sacks Ltd., **IV** 295
Irish Sugar Co., **II** 508
Iron and Steel Corp., **IV** 22, 41, 92, 533–34
Iron Ore Company of Canada, **8** 347
Iroquois Gas Corporation, **6** 526
Irvin, Tinsley, **10** 38
Irvin, William E., **11** 554
Irving Bank Corp., **II** 192
Irving, David, **7** 578
Irving, John, **III** 372
Irving Trust Co., **II** 257
Irvington Smelting, **IV** 78
Irwin Lehrhoff Associates, **11** 366
Irwin, Will G., **I** 146
Irwin, William G., **9** 274
Iscor. *See* Iron and Steel Corporation.
Isenberg, Eugene M., **9** 364
Isenberg, Leslie, **11** 366
Isetan Company Limited, **V 85–87**
Isetan Finance Company, Ltd., **V** 87
Isetan Research Institute Company, Ltd., **V** 87
Iseya Tanji Drapery, **V** 85
Isham, Ralph H. (Col.), **IV** 636
Ishibashi, Kanichiro, **V** 234
Ishibashi, Shojiro, **V** 234
Ishida, Taizo, **III** 637
Ishigami, Minoru, **IV** 298
Ishii, Susumu, **9** 379, 386
Ishikawajima Airplane Manufacturing Co., **III** 532

Ishikawajima Automobile Manufacturing Co., **III** 532
Ishikawajima Automobile Manufacturing, Ltd., **9** 293
Ishikawajima Heavy Industry Co., Ltd., **III** 513, 532–33
Ishikawajima Hirano Shipyard, **III** 532
Ishikawajima Shibaura Turbine Co., **III** 532
Ishikawajima Shipyard Co., Ltd., **III** 532
Ishikawajima Systems Technology Co., **III** 533
Ishikawajima-Harima Heavy Industries Co., Ltd., **I** 508, 511, 534; **II** 274; **III** 532–33
Ishimoto, Shizue, **IV** 147
Ishizaki Honten, **III** 715
Ishizuka, Yozo, **III** 604–05
Isis Distributed Systems, Inc., **10** 501
Island Holiday, **I** 417
Isobe, Ritsuo, **6** 30
Isoda, Ichiro, **II** 361
Isolite Insulating Products Co., **III** 714
Isosceles PLC, **II** 628–29
Isover, **III** 676
ISS International Service System, Inc., **8** 271
Issenmann, Nico, **6** 11
Istanbul Fertilizer Industry, **IV** 563
Istituto per la Ricostruzione Industriale, **I** 207, 459, **465–67**; **II** 191–92, 270–71; **IV** 419
Istituto per la Ricostruzione Industriale S.p.A., **11** 203–06
Istock, Verne G., **11** 341
Isuzu Motors, Ltd., **II** 274; **III** 581, 593; **7** 8, 219; **9** 293–95; **10** 354
IT International, **V** 255
Itabira Iron Ore Co. Ltd., **IV** 54
ITABRASCO, **IV** 55
Itakura, Joji, **II** 326
Italcarta, **IV** 339
Italcementi, **IV** 420
Italiatour, **6** 69
Italmobiliare, **III** 347
Italstate. *See* Societa per la Infrastrutture e l'Assetto del Territorio.
Italtel, **V** 326–27
Itaú Winterthur Seguradura S.A., **III** 404
Itek Corp., **I** 486; **11** 265
Itel Corporation, **IV** 64; **III** 512; **6** 262, 354; **9** 49, **296–99**
Ithaca Gas & Electric. *See* New York State Electric and Gas.
Ithaca Gas Light Company, **6** 534
ITM International, **IV** 239
Ito Bank, **II** 373
Ito Carnation Co., **II** 518
Ito, Denzo, **II** 518
Ito Food Processing Co., **II** 518
Ito Gofuku Co. Ltd., **V** 129
Ito Ham Co. Ltd., **II** 518
Ito Ham Provisions Co. Ltd., **II** 518
Ito, Jirozaemon, **V** 130
Ito, Kenichi, **II** 518
Ito, Masatoshi, **V** 88
Ito Meat Processing Co., **II** 518
Ito, Morimatsu, **V** 129
Ito Processed Food Co., **II** 518
Ito, Tatsuji, **IV** 714
Ito, Yasuhisa, **V** 89
Ito, Yudo, **V** 129
Ito-Yokado Co., Ltd., **II** 661; **V** 88–89
Itoh. *See* C. Itoh & Co.

Itoh, Chubei, **I** 431, 492
Itoh, Chubei, II, **I** 431, 492
Itoh, Junji, **I** 106
Itoham Foods Inc., **II** 518–19
Itokin, **III** 48
ITT. *See* International Telephone and Telegraph Corporation.
ITT Corp., **III** 98, 164, 166, 645, 684; **9** 10–11, 324; **11** 516. *See also* International Telephone & Telegraph Corporation.
ITT Sheraton Corporation, **III** 98–101
ITW. *See* Illinois Tool Works Inc.
Iue, Kaoru, **II** 91–92
Iue, Satoshi, **II** 92
Iue, Toshio, **II** 55, 91–92
Iue, Yuro, **II** 91
IVAC Corp., **I** 646; **11** 90
IVACO Industries Inc., **11** 207
Ivanhoe, Inc., **II** 662, 664
IVAX Corporation, **11** 207–09
Iveagh (Earl of), **I** 251
Iveco, **I** 148
Iverson, F. Kenneth, **7** 400–02
Ives, **I** 623
Ives, J. Atwood, **I** 245; **6** 487–88
Ivory, James, **III** 360
Ivy, Robert E., **I** 682
Iwadare, Kunihiko, **II** 66–67
Iwai & Co., **I** 492, 509–10; **IV** 151
Iwai, Bunsuke, **I** 509
Iwamura, Eiro, **IV** 125
Iwasa, Yoshizane, **II** 292
Iwasaki family, **II** 57; **III** 577
Iwasaki, Koyata, **I** 503
Iwasaki, Toshiya, **III** 666
Iwasaki, Yanosuke, **I** 265, 503; **IV** 713
Iwasaki, Yataro, **I** 363, 502–03, 506; **II** 57; **III** 577, 666, 712; **IV** 713; **7** 347
Iwata Air Compressor, **III** 427
Iwata, Kohachi, **V** 149–50
Iwatsuki, Tatsuo, **III** 592
Iwazaki, Shoshichi, **V** 735
Iwerks, Ub, **II** 172
Iyanaga, Kyojiro, **III** 121
IYG Holding Company of Japan, **7** 492
d'Izarn, André Sahut, **III** 210–11
Izod Lacoste, **II** 502–03; **9** 156–57; **10** 324
Izumi Fudosan, **IV** 726
Izumiya, **V** 477

J Sainsbury PLC, **II** 657–59, 677–78; **10** 442; **11** 239, 241
J&J Colman, **II** 566
J&J Corrugated Box Corp., **IV** 282; **9** 261
J&L Specialty Products Corp., **IV** 228
J&L Steel, **I** 490
J. Aron & Co., **II** 415
J.B. Williams Company, **8** 63
J.B. Lippincott, **IV** 652
J.B. McLean Publishing Co., Ltd., **IV** 638
J.B. Williams, **III** 66
J. Bibby & Sons, **I** 424
J. Byrons, **9** 186
J.C. Penney Company, Inc., **I** 516; **V** 90–92; **6** 336; **8** 288, 555; **9** 156, 210, 213, 219, 346–94; **10** 409, 490; **11** 349
J.C. Penney National Bank, **V** 92
J.D. Powers & Associates, **9** 166
J.E. Baxter Co., **I** 429
J.E. Nolan, **11** 486
J.E. Sirrine. *See* CRSS Inc.
J.F. Corporation, **V** 87

J.F. Lauman and Co., **II** 681
J. Fielding & Co., **IV** 249
J.G. McMullen Dredging Co., **III** 558
J. Gadsden Paper Products, **IV** 249
J. George Leyner Engineering Works Co., **III** 525–26
J.H. Stone & Sons, **IV** 332
J.H. Whitney & Company, **9** 250
J.I. Case Company, **I** 148, 527; **10** 377–81
J.I. Case Plow Works Co., **III** 651
J.I. Case Threshing Machine Company, **10** 378
J.K. Armsby Co., **7** 130–31
J.K. Starley and Company Ltd, **7** 458
J.L. Kraft & Bros. Co., **II** 532
J.L. Shiely Co., **III** 691
J. Lyons & Co., **I** 215
J.M. Brunswick & Balke Co., **III** 442
J.M. Brunswick & Brother, **III** 442
J.M. Brunswick & Brothers, **III** 442
J.M. Horton Ice Cream Co., **II** 471
J.M. Jones Co., **II** 668
J.M. Kohler Sons Company, **7** 269
The J.M. Smucker Company, **11** 210–12
J.M. Tull Metals Co., Inc., **IV** 116
J-Mass, **IV** 289
J. Muirhead Ltd., **I** 315
J.P. Stevens, **8** 234
J.P. Heilwell Industries, **II** 420
J.P. Morgan & Co. Incorporated, **II** 281, **329–32**, 407, 419, 427–28, 430–31, 441; **III** 237, 245, 380; **IV** 20, 180, 400; **9** 386
J.P. Morgan Securities Inc., **II** 331; **11** 421
J.P. Morgan Securities Ltd., **II** 331
J.P. Wood, **II** 587
J.R. Geigy S.A., **I** 632–33, 635, 671; **8** 108–10
J.R. Parkington Co., **I** 280
J.R. Wyllie & Sons, **I** 437
J. Ray McDermott (Venezuela), C.A., **III** 559
J. Ray McDermott & Co., **III** 558–59
J.S. Fry & Sons, **II** 476
J.S. Morgan & Co., **II** 329, 427
J. Sainsbury Ltd., **II** 657
J. Sanders & Sons, **IV** 711
J. Sears & Company (True-Form Boot Company) Ltd., **V** 177
J.T. Wing and Co., **I** 158
J.W. Bateson, **8** 87
J.W. Buderus and Sons, **III** 694
J.W. Higman & Co., **III** 690
J. Walter Thompson Co., **I** 9, 17, 25, 37, 251, 354, 623; **10** 69; **11** 51
J. Weingarten Inc., **7** 203
J. Wiss & Sons Co., **II** 16
J. Zinmeister Co., **II** 682
Jaatinen, Rafael, **IV** 299
Jacintoport Corporation, **7** 281
Jack Daniel Distillery, **10** 180
Jack Houston Exploration Company, **7** 345
Jackling, Daniel Cowan, **7** 261
Jackson & Curtis, **II** 444
Jackson, A.B., **III** 356
Jackson, Bo, **8** 393
Jackson Box Co., **IV** 311
Jackson, C.D., **IV** 674; **7** 527
Jackson, Carl, **I** 448
Jackson, Carlton, **I** 450
Jackson, Derek, **IV** 650; **7** 389
Jackson, Harry A., Jr., **7** 179
Jackson, Henry, **I** 48; **10** 163

Jackson, J.L., **IV** 410
Jackson, Jesse, **I** 261
Jackson Marine Corp., **III** 499
Jackson, Michael, **I** 278–79; **II** 134; **10** 452
Jackson National Financial Services, Inc., **8** 277
Jackson National Life Co., **III** 335–36
Jackson National Life Insurance Company, 8 276–77
Jackson Purchase Electric Cooperative Corporation, **11** 37
Jackson, Robert, **I** 91, 114
Jackson, Robert W., **6** 471
Jackson, T. K., **6** 539
Jackson, Thomas, **II** 296
Jackson, W. Graham, **11** 391
Jackson, Walter M., **7** 166
Jackson, William, **III** 610
Jacksonville Shipyards, **I** 170
Jacob, P.L. Justman, **IV** 133
Jacob, Solon, **7** 572
Jacobs Brake Manufacturing Company, **7** 116–17
Jacobs, Charles, **7** 133–34
Jacobs Coffee Co., **II** 520
Jacobs Engineering Company, **6** 148–49
Jacobs Engineering Group Inc., 6 148–50
Jacobs, Irwin, **IV** 523
Jacobs, Irwin L., **II** 492; **III** 15–16; **11** 198, 397, 523
Jacobs, J. M., **6** 546
Jacobs, Jeremy, **7** 134–35
Jacobs, Johann, **II** 520
Jacobs, Joseph J., **6** 148–50
Jacobs, Klaus, **II** 520–21
Jacobs, Klaus J., **6** 11
Jacobs, Lawrence, **7** 135
Jacobs, Louis, **7** 133–34
Jacobs, Marvin, **7** 133–34
Jacobs, Max, **7** 134–35
Jacobs Suchard AG, II 520–22, 540, 569
Jacobs, Walter, **II** 520
Jacobs, Walter L., **9** 283
Jacobsen, Arne, **I** 658
Jacobsen, Carl, **9** 99
Jacobsen, J.C., **9** 99
Jacobsen, Jake, **11** 25
Jacobson, Allen, **I** 501
Jacobson, Ishier, **7** 88
Jacobson, Jerome, **I** 142
Jacobsson, Gunnar, **III** 425–26
Jacoby, Robert, **I** 33
Jacor Communications, **6** 33
Jacotett, Carl Maurice, **I** 672
Jacques Borel International, **II** 641; **10** 12
Jacques Fath , **III** 47
Jacuzzi, Inc., **7** 207, 209
JAF Pampryl, **I** 281
Jaffe, Thomas, **6** 244
Jaffré, Philippe, **II** 266
Jagenberg AG, **9** 445–46
Jaguar, **III** 439, 495
Jaguar Cars Ltd., **11** 140
Jaharis, Michael, **11** 207
Jahnke, Charles B., **II** 15
Jahr (G & J), Gruner, **7** 245
JAI Parabolic Spring Ltd., **III** 582
Jaicks, Frederick G., **IV** 115
Ab Jakobstads Cellulosa-Pietarsaaren Selluloosa Oy, **IV** 302
Jakopp, Heinrich, **III** 543
Jaluzot, Jules, **V** 9

Jamaica Gas Light Co., **6** 455
Jamaica Plain Trust Co., **II** 207
Jamaica Water Supply Company. *See* JWP Inc.
JAMCO, **III** 589
James A. Ryder Transportation (Jartran), **V** 505
James Bay Development Corporation, **6** 502
James Beam Distilling Co., **I** 226; **10** 180
James, Daniel, **IV** 176
James, Elliott, **6** 248
James Ericson, **III** 324
James Fison and Sons. *See* Fisons plc.
James Fleming, **II** 500
James Gulliver Associates, **II** 609
James Hardie Containers, **IV** 249
James Hartley & Son, **III** 724
James, Henry, **III** 380
James, Howard (Bud), **III** 99
James, John V., **III** 472–73
James, Leland, **V** 432
James Lyne Hancock Ltd., **I** 428
James Magee & Sons Ltd., **IV** 294
James, Marquis, **III** 291
James McNaughton Ltd., **IV** 325
James O. Welch Co., **II** 543
James R. Osgood & Company, **10** 356
James River Corporation of Virginia, **IV** 289–91; **8** 483
James River Graphics, **IV** 289; **8** 483
James Stedman Ltd., **II** 569
James Talcott, Inc., **11** 260–61
James, Thomas W., **I** 360
James Thompson, **IV** 22
James, William, **IV** 165–66; **7** 399
James Wrigley & Sons, **IV** 257
Jamesway Co. Ltd., **IV** 136
Jamesway Incubator Corp., **IV** 136
Jamieson, Hugh, **I** 484; **11** 263
Jamna Auto Industries Pvt. Ltd., **III** 581
Jämsänkoski Oy, **IV** 347
Janacek, Jimmy, **11** 538
Jane's Information Group, **8** 525
Janesville Electric, **6** 604
Janet Frazer, **V** 118
Jann, Adolf W., **I** 643
Jannott, E. (Dr.), **III** 400
Jannott, Horst K., **III** 300
Janssen Pharmaceutica, **III** 36; **8** 282
Janssen-Kyowa, **III** 43
JANT Pty. Ltd., **IV** 285
Jantscha, Robert, **III** 465–66
Jantzen Inc., **V** 391
Janus Capital Corporation, **6** 400–02
Japan Acoustics, **II** 118
Japan Air Filter Co., Ltd., **III** 634
Japan Air Lines Co., I 104–06; **6** 70–71, 118, 123, 386, 427
Japan Asia Airways Co., **I** 106
Japan Beer Brewing Co., **I** 220
Japan Brewing, **I** 265
Japan Broadcasting Corporation (Nippon Hoso Kyokai), **I** 586; **II** 66, 101, 118; **7 248–50**
Japan Cable Television, **9** 31
Japan-California Bank, **II** 274
Japan Commerce Bank, **II** 291
Japan Copper Manufacturing Co., **II** 104; **IV** 211
Japan Cotton Co., **IV** 150
Japan Creative Tours Co., **I** 106
Japan Credit Bureau, **II** 348
Japan Dairy Products, **II** 538

Japan Day & Night Bank, **II** 292
Japan Development Bank, **II** 300, 403
Japan Dyestuff Manufacturing Co., **I** 397
Japan Electricity Generation and Transmission Company (JEGTCO), **V** 574
Japan International Bank, **II** 292
Japan International Liquor, **I** 220
Japan Iron & Steel Co., Ltd., **IV** 157
Japan Leasing Auto Corporation, **8** 279
Japan Leasing Corporation, 8 278–80; **11** 87
Japan LP Gas Meter Lease Company, **8** 278
Japan Machinery Leasing and Sales Company, **8** 279
Japan National Oil Corp., **IV** 516
Japan National Railway, **V** 448–50; **6** 70
Japan Oil Development Co., **IV** 364
Japan Petroleum Development Corp., **IV** 461
Japan Petroleum Exploration Co., **IV** 516
Japan Pulp and Paper (SP) Pte. Ltd., **IV** 293
Japan Pulp and Paper (U.S.A.) Corp., **IV** 293
Japan Pulp and Paper Co. (H.K.), Ltd., **IV** 293
Japan Pulp and Paper Company Limited, IV 292–93, 680
Japan Pulp and Paper GmbH, **IV** 292
Japan Reconstruction Finance Bank, **II** 300
Japan Satellite Broadcasting Corp., **7** 249; **9** 31
Japan Special Steel Co., Ltd., **IV** 63
Japan Steel Manufacturing Co., **IV** 211
Japan Steel Works, **I** 508
Japan Telecom, **7** 118
Japan Tobacco Incorporated, V 403–04
Japan Trust Bank, **II** 292
Japan Try Co., **III** 758
Japanese and Asian Development Bank, **IV** 518
Japanese Electronic Computer Co., **III** 140
Japanese Enterprise Co., **IV** 728
Japanese National Railway, **I** 579; **III** 491
Japanese Victor Co., **II** 118
Japex Oman Co., **IV** 516
Japonica Partners, **9** 485
Jarcho Brothers Inc., **I** 513
Jardine Fleming, **I** 471
Jardine Matheson Holdings, I 468–71, 521–22, 577, 592; **II** 296; **IV** 189, 699, 700
Jardine Strategic Holdings, **IV** 700
Jardine, William (Dr.), **I** 468
Jarman, Nathaniel, **III** 371
Jarratt, Alex, **IV** 667
Jartran Inc., **V** 505
Järvenpään Kotelo Oy, **IV** 315
Jarvis, W.H.R., **I** 268
Jas, Hennessy & Co., **I** 272
JASCO Products, **III** 581
Jasper Corp., **III** 767
Jato, **II** 652
Java-China-Japan Line, **6** 403–04
Javelin Software Corporation, **10** 359
Javex Co., **IV** 272
Jax, **9** 452
Jay Cooke and Co., **III** 237; **9** 370
Jay, Ken, **9** 12
Jay's Washateria, Inc., **7** 372
Jay-Ro Services, **III** 419
Jaywoth Industries, **III** 673

JCJL. *See* Java-China-Japan Line.
Jean Lassale, **III** 619–20
Jean Nate, **I** 695
Jean Pagées et Fils, **III** 420
Jean Prouvost, **IV** 618
Jeanne Piaubert, **III** 47
Jeanniot, Pierre J., **6** 61
Jeckel, Norman, **9** 97
Jefferson Chemical Co., **IV** 552
Jefferson, Edward G., **I** 330; **8** 153
Jefferson Fire Insurance Co., **III** 239
Jefferson, John, **II** 660–61
Jefferson National Life Group, **10** 247
Jefferson Smurfit & Sons Ltd., **IV** 294
Jefferson Smurfit Corp., **IV** 295
Jefferson Smurfit Group Ltd., **IV** 294–95
Jefferson Smurfit Group PLC, **IV** 294–96
Jefferson Standard Life Insurance, **11** 213–14
Jefferson, Thomas, **II** 312
Jefferson Warrior Railroad Co., **III** 767
Jefferson-Pilot Corporation, **11 213–15**
Jeffery Sons & Co. Ltd., **IV** 711
Jeffrey Galion, **III** 472
Jeffrey, Walter J., **III** 396
Jeffs, Thomas H., II, **11** 341
JEGTCO. *See* Japan Electricity Generation and Transmission Company (JEGTCO).
Jell-O Co., **II** 531
Jellicoe, Lord, **II** 582
Jellinek, Emil, **I** 149
Jellinek, Mercedes, **I** 149
Jenaer Glaswerk, **III** 447
Jenaer Glaswerk Schott & Genossen, **III** 445
Jenkins, Benjamin P., **10** 299
Jenkins, Clive, **6** 58
Jenkins, George W., **7** 440–41
Jenkins, Hugh, **III** 336
Jenkins, Mike, **7** 336
Jenkins, Robert L., **8** 322
Jenkins, William M., **8** 471
Jenks, Frank W., **I** 181
Jenn-Air Co., **III** 573
Jenney, William Le Baron, **III** 262
Jennie-O Foods, **II** 506
Jennings, S. Edmunds, **6** 370
Jenny Craig, Inc., **10 382–84**
Jenrette, Richard, **III** 248–49
Jensen, Arlo, **9** 434
Jensen, Harry A., **III** 423
Jensen Salsbery, **I** 715
Jenson, Kenneth, **8** 22
JEORA Co., **IV** 564
Jephcott, Harry, **I** 639–40; **9** 263
Jeppesen Sanderson, **IV** 677
Jeppson, John, **8** 395–96
Jepson Corporation, **8** 230
Jerome Increase Case Machinery Company, **10** 377. *See also* J.I. Case Company
Jeroushi, Mohammed, **IV** 453
Jerrold Corporation, **10** 319–20
Jersey Paper, **IV** 261
Jersey Standard. *See* Standard Oil Co. of New Jersey.
Jesse L. Lasky Feature Play Co., **II** 154
Jesselson, Ludwig, **IV** 80
Jessup & Moore Paper Co., **IV** 351
Jet America, **I** 100
Jet America Airlines, **6** 67, 82
Jet Capital Corp., **I** 123
Jet Petroleum, Ltd., **IV** 401
Jet Research Center, **III** 498

Jetley, Rajan, **6** 64
Jetway Systems, **III** 512
Jeumont-Industrie, **II** 93
Jeumont-Schneider, **II** 93–94; **9** 10
Jewel Companies, **II** 605; **6** 531
Jewel Food Stores, **7** 127–28
Jewell Ridge Coal Corp., **IV** 181
Jewett, George F., **8** 429
Jiffee Chemical Corp., **III** 21
Jiffy Convenience Stores, **II** 627
Jiffy Lube International, Inc., **IV** 490
Jim Walter Corp., **III** 765–67
Jim Walter Papers, **IV** 282; **9** 261
Jim Walter Resources, **III** 766
Jitsugyo no Nihon-sha, **IV** 631
Jitsuyo Jidosha Seizo Co., **I** 183
JLA Credit, **8** 279
JMB Development, **IV** 703
JMB/Federated Realty Associates, **IV** 703
JMB Institutional Realty, **IV** 703
JMB Realty Corporation, **IV 702–03**
JNR. *See* Japan National Railway.
Joannes Brothers, **II** 668
João (Dom), **II** 199
Job, Peter, **IV** 670
Jobe, Edward, **10** 76
Jobe, John B., **III** 707; **7** 292
Jobs, Steve, **III** 115–16, 121, 172
Jobs, Steven, **6** 218–19, 289
Joe B. Hughes, **III** 498
Joel, Solly, **IV** 65; **7** 122
Joh. Parviaisen Tehtaat Oy, **IV** 276
Johann Jakob Rieter & Co., **III** 402
Johannesburg Consolidated Investment Co. Ltd., **IV** 21–22, 118
Johannsmeier, Karl, **10** 15
Johansen, Ralph T., **I** 254
John A. Frye Co., **V** 376
John A. Frye Shoe Company, **8** 16
John Alden Life Insurance, **10** 340
John Bean Spray Pump Co., **I** 442
John Blair & Company, **6** 13
John Blair Marketing, **6** 13
John Brown plc, **I 572–74**
John Bull, **II** 550
John Crosland Company, **8** 88
John de Kuyper and Son, **I** 377
John Deere. *See* Deere & Company.
John Deere Credit Co., **III** 463
John F. Jelke Company, **9** 318
John F. Murray Co., **I** 623; **10** 69
John Fairfax Holdings Limited, **7 251–54**
John Gardner Catering, **III** 104
John Govett & Co., **II** 349
John Gund Brewing Co., **I** 253
John Hancock Financial Services, **III** 265
John Hancock Income Securities Group, **III** 267
John Hancock Mutual Life Insurance Company, **III 265–68**, 291, 313, 332, 400; **IV** 283
John Hancock Reinsurance Co., **III** 343
John Hill and Son, **II** 569
John Holroyd & Co. of Great Britain, **7** 236
John L. Wortham & Son Agency, **III** 193
John Labatt Ltd., **I** 267; **II** 582; **8** 399
John Laing plc, **I 575–76**, 588
John Lewis and Company, Ltd., **V** 94
John Lewis Partnership plc, **V 93–95**
John Lucas Co., **III** 745
John Lysaght, **III** 493–94
John Lysaght (Australia), **III** 495

John M. Hart Company, **9** 304
John Macfarlane and Sons, **II** 593
John Mackintosh and Sons, **II** 568
John Mackintosh and Sons. Ltd., **II** 569
John McLean and Sons Ltd., **III** 753
John Morrell and Co., **II** 595–96
John Nicholls & Co., **III** 690
John Nuveen & Co., **III** 356
John Oster Manufacturing Company, **9** 484
John R. Figg, Inc., **II** 681
John Rogers Co., **9** 253
John Strange Paper Company, **8** 358
John Swire & Sons Ltd., **I** 521–22; **6** 415
John, Thomas, **IV** 474
John Walker & Sons, **I** 239–40
John Williams, **III** 691
John Wyeth & Bro., **I** 713
John Yokley Company, **11** 194
Johns, Henry Ward, **III** 706; **7** 291
Johns Perry, **III** 673
Johns-Manville Corp., **III** 708; **7** 293; **11** 420
Johnsen, Arve, **IV** 406
Johnson. *See* Axel Johnson Group.
Johnson & Johnson, **I** 301; **II** 582; **III** 18, **35–37**; **IV** 285, 722; **7** 45–46; **8** **281–83 (upd.)**, 399, 511–12; **9** 89–90; **10** 47, 69, 78, 80, 534–35; **11** 200
Johnson & Johnson Hospital Services, **III** 36
Johnson & Johnson Ltd., **III** 35
Johnson, A. Clark, **9** 522
Johnson, Abbot L., **III** 438
Johnson, Al, **II** 151
Johnson and Patan, **III** 671
Johnson and Sons Smelting Works Ltd., **IV** 119
Johnson, Antonia, **I** 554
Johnson, Axel, **I** 553–54
Johnson, Axel, II, **I** 553–54
Johnson, Axel, III, **I** 554
Johnson, B.J., **III** 23
Johnson, Bruce W., **9** 421
Johnson, Carruthers & Rand Shoe Co., **III** 528
Johnson, Charles B., **9** 239–40
Johnson, Charles E., **I** 199; **10** 492
Johnson, Clarence, **III** 440
Johnson, Claude, **I** 194; **7** 455
Johnson Controls, Inc., **III 534–37**
Johnson, Dale A., **10** 494
Johnson, Darwin W., **III** 216
Johnson, Dave, **11** 51
Johnson, David W., **II** 481; **7** 68
Johnson, Dennis, **8** 490
Johnson Diversified, Inc., **III** 59
Johnson, Donald M., **III** 182
Johnson, Earvin "Magic", **9** 135
Johnson, Edward C., II, **II** 412–13; **8** 194
Johnson, Edward C., III (Ned), **II** 412–13; **8** 194–96
Johnson, Edward Mead, **III** 35; **8** 281
Johnson Electric Service Co., **III** 534
Johnson, F. Ross, **II** 544; **V** 410; **7** 367
Johnson family, **8** 194, 196
Johnson, Guy, **V** 90
Johnson, H. C., **V** 422–23
Johnson, Hank, **10** 490
Johnson, Herbert F., **III** 58
Johnson, Herbert F., Jr., **III** 58–59
Johnson, J. Seward, **III** 35; **8** 281
Johnson, Jackson, **III** 528
Johnson, James, **10** 222

Johnson, James Wood, **III** 35; **8** 281
Johnson, Joe, **7** 479–80
Johnson, John G., Jr., **8** 465
Johnson, Josephine, **IV** 671
Johnson, Kelly, **I** 65, 73; **11** 267
Johnson, Kevin "KJ", **9** 135
Johnson, Lady Bird, **9** 368
Johnson, Larry, **9** 135
Johnson, Lyndon, **11** 25
Johnson, Lyndon Baines, **I** 97, 172, 415;
    III 169; **IV** 178, 489, 522, 583
Johnson, Matthey & Co. Ltd., **IV** 117–19
Johnson Matthey Bankers Ltd., **II** 390; **IV**
    119
Johnson Matthey PLC, IV 23, **117–20**
Johnson Motor Co., **III** 597–99
Johnson, N. Baxter, **II** 251
Johnson, Oscar, **III** 528
Johnson, Paul, **I** 199
Johnson, Percival, **IV** 117, 119–20
Johnson, Phil, **I** 48; **10** 163
Johnson Products Co., Inc., **11** 208
Johnson, Ralph, **9** 276
Johnson, Robert, **III** 35–36
Johnson, Robert E., **8** 322
Johnson, Robert H., **III** 526
Johnson, Robert Wood, **III** 35–36; **8** 281
Johnson, Rupert, **9** 239
Johnson, S. Curtis, III, **III** 59
Johnson, Samuel, **II** 306
Johnson, Samuel C., **III** 58–59
Johnson, Samuel Curtis, **III** 58
Johnson Service Co., **III** 534–36
Johnson, Stephen, **11** 234
Johnson Systems, **6** 224
Johnson, Theodore, **10** 379
Johnson, Thomas B., **9** 59
Johnson, Thomas H., **11** 421
Johnson, Truman, **6** 363–64
Johnson, Walter H., **11** 388
Johnson, Warren Seymour, **III** 534–35
Johnson Wax. *See* S.C. Johnson & Son,
    Inc.
Johnson Wax Associates, **III** 59
Johnson, William, **I** 496; **10** 414, 553–54
Johnson, William B., **I** 496; **7** 430; **9** 457
Johnson, William E., **6** 336–37
Johnson, William J., **9** 363
Johnson, William R., **11** 173
Johnsson, Erik, **III** 427
Johnston, Don, **I** 20–21
Johnston Evans & Co., **IV** 704
Johnston Foil Co., **IV** 18
Johnston Harvester Co., **III** 650
Johnston, John C., **III** 321
Johnston, John H., **III** 321
Johnston, Percy H., **II** 251
Johnston, Russell, **10** 281
Johnston, Wayne Andrew, **11** 187
Johnstone, Glenn W., **I** 700
Joiner, Columbus, **7** 228
Jointless Rim Ltd., **I** 428
Jokisch, **II** 556
Joklik, G. Frank, **7** 263
Jolley, Robert A., Jr., **11** 330
Jolly, J.H., **III** 494
Jolson, Al, **I** 20; **II** 175; **III** 25
Jonas, Charles S., **11** 100
Jonas, Donald, **11** 248
Jonas, Richard A., **11** 100
Jonathan Backhouse & Co., **II** 235
Jones & Laughlin Steel Corp., **I** 463,
    489–91; **11** 197
Jones, Alan, **V** 524

Jones Apparel Group, Inc., 11 216–18
Jones, B.F., **II** 342
Jones, Bradley, **I** 491
Jones Brothers Tea Co., **7** 202
Jones, Charles, **7** 202
Jones, Charles S., **IV** 375
Jones, Cyrus, **7** 202
Jones, David, **III** 81–82
Jones, David R., **6** 448
Jones, Dean, **II** 173
Jones, Edward, **IV** 601, 603
Jones Environmental, **11** 361
Jones, Fletcher, **6** 227–28
Jones, Frank, **7** 202
Jones, George, **IV** 647
Jones, Harrison, **I** 233
Jones, Harvey, **11** 489–90
Jones, Henry (Sir), **I** 437
Jones, Isaac, **II** 250
Jones, Jenkin, **III** 371–72
Jones, Jesse H., **11** 339
Jones, John Quinton, **II** 250–51
Jones, Joseph L., **III** 424
Jones, Kennedy, **7** 341
Jones, Lang Wootton, **IV** 697
Jones, Lawrence M., **9** 128–29
Jones, Leroy P., **I** 517
Jones, Lewis D., **9** 422
Jones Motor Co., **10** 44
Jones, O. Marshall, **9** 102
Jones, Oakah, **6** 477
Jones, Reginald, **II** 30
Jones, Richard M., **10** 159
Jones, Roderick, **IV** 669
Jones, Thomas V., **I** 76–77; **11** 363–64
Jones, W. Alton, **IV** 392–93
Jonker Fris, **II** 571
Jonsson, J. Erik, **II** 112–13; **11** 505–06
The Jordan Company, **11** 261
Jordan, Eben, **7** 13
Jordan, Edward G., **V** 435
Jordan Marsh, **III** 608; **V** 26; **9** 209
Jordan, Michael, **8** 393–94, 526; **9** 134
Jordan, Michael H., **9** 344
Jorndt, L. Daniel, **V** 220
Jos. A. Bank Clothiers, **II** 560
Josaphat, Israel Beer. *See* Reuter, Julius.
Josef Meys, **III** 418
Joseph Bellamy and Sons Ltd., **II** 569
Joseph Campbell Co., **II** 479; **7** 66
Joseph Campbell Preserve Co., **II** 479; **7**
    66
Joseph Crosfield, **III** 31
Joseph E. Seagram & Sons, **I** 266, 285
Joseph, Frederick, **II** 408
Joseph Garneau Co., **I** 226; **10** 180
Joseph, Keith (Sir), **I** 51
Joseph Leavitt Corporation, **9** 20
Joseph Lucas (Cycle Accessories), **III** 555
Joseph Lucas (Industries) Ltd., **III** 555
Joseph Lucas & Son, **III** 554–56
Joseph Magnin, **I** 417–18
Joseph, Maxwell, **I** 247–48
Joseph Nathan & Co., **I** 629–40
Joseph Rank Limited, **II** 564
Joseph, Samuel, **I** 588
Joseph T. Ryerson and Son Inc., **IV** 114
Josephine, Empress (France). *See*
    Bonaparte, Josephine.
Josephson, Marvin, **IV** 623
Joshu Railway Company, **6** 431
Joslyn, Harriet, **7** 406
Josselyn, Benage, **6** 548
Josten, Otto, **7** 255

Jostens Inc., 7 255–57
Jostens Learning Corporation, **7** 255
Jostens Learning Systems, **7** 256
Jostens Manufacturing Company, **7** 255
Jostens Travel, **7** 256
Jourdan, James H., **V** 455–56
Jouven, Pierre, **IV** 174
Jovan, **III** 66
Jovanovich, Peter William, **IV** 624
Jovanovich, William, **IV** 622–24, 672
Jove Publications, Inc., **II** 144; **IV** 623
Jovi, **II** 652
Joy, Bill, **7** 498
Joy, James F., **V** 425–26
Joy Manufacturing, **III** 526
Joy Planning Co., **III** 533
Joy Technologies, **II** 17
Joyce, Adrian D., **8** 222
Joyce, Dwight P., **8** 222
Joyce, James, **IV** 295
Joyce, John, **III** 27
Joyce, William B., **III** 395
JP Household Supply Co. Ltd., **IV** 293
JP Information Center Co., Ltd., **IV** 293
JP Planning Co. Ltd., **IV** 293
JPC Co., **IV** 155
JPT Publishing, **8** 528
JT Aquisitions, **II** 661
Juan Carlos, King (Spain), **I** 460
Juan N nez Anchustegui, **I** 197
Judah, Theodore D., **V** 516
Jude Hanbury, **I** 294
Judelson, Robert, **IV** 702–03
Judson, Arthur, **II** 132; **6** 157
Jugo Bank, **II** 325
Juice Bowl Products, **II** 480–81
Jujo Kimberly, **IV** 297–98
Jujo Paper Co., Ltd., IV 268, 284–85,
    292–93, **297–98,** 321, 326, 328, 356
Julin, Richard, **I** 625
Julius Berger-Bauboag A.G., **I** 560–61
Jung-Pumpen, **III** 570
Junghans Uhren, **10** 152
Junkers, **6** 87–88
Junkers Luftverkehr, **I** 110, 197
Junkins, Jerry, **II** 114; **11** 507
Jurenka, Robert, **III** 465
Jurgens, **II** 588–89
Jurgens, Anton, **II** 589
Jurgovan & Blair, **III** 197
JUSCO Co., Ltd., V 96–99; **11** 498
Justus, Samuel, **IV** 488
JVC. *See* Victor Company of Japan, Ltd.
JVC America, **II** 119
JWP Inc., 9 300–02
JWT Group Inc., I 9, **19–21,** 23; **6** 53.
    See also WPP Group plc.
Jylhävaara, **IV** 348

K Line. *See* Kawasaki Kisen Kaisha, Ltd.
K&L, **6** 48
K & R Warehouse Corporation, **9** 20
K-C Aviation, **III** 41
K.C.C. Holding Co., **III** 192
K.F. Kline Co., **7** 145
K-H Corporation, **7** 260
K. Hattori & Co., Ltd., **III** 454–55,
    619–20
k.k. Staatsbahnen, **6** 419
K-III Holdings, **7** 286
Ka Wah AMEV Insurance, **III** 200–01
Kachel, Theodore V., **11** 101
Kaduna Refining and Petrochemicals Co.,
    IV 473

Kaestner & Hecht Co., **II** 120
Kafescioglu, Ismail (Dr.), **IV** 563
Kafka, Franz, **III** 207
Kaga Forwarding Co., **6** 428
Kagami Crystal Works, **III** 714
Kagami, Kenkichi, **III** 384–85; **V** 482–83
Kagle Home Health Care, **11** 282
Kahan and Lessin, **II** 624–25
Kahn, Albert, **V** 57
Kahn, Ely Jacques, **I** 235
Kahn, Leo, **10** 496
Kahn, Philippe, **9** 80–81
Kahn's Meats, **II** 572
Kai Tak Land Investment Co., **IV** 717
Kaifa, Hachiroh, **I** 511
Kairamo, Kari, **II** 69–70
Kaiser Aluminium Europe, **IV** 123
Kaiser Aluminum & Chemical Corporation, IV 11–12, 15, 59–60, **121–23**, 191; **6** 148
Kaiser Aluminum Corp., **IV** 121, 123; **8** 348, 350
Kaiser Bauxite Co., **IV** 122
Kaiser Cargo, Inc., **IV** 121
Kaiser Cement, **III** 501; **IV** 272
Kaiser Cement and Gypsum, **III** 760
Kaiser Company, **6** 184
Kaiser, Edgar F., **IV** 123
Kaiser, Eduard, **III** 694
Kaiser Energy, Inc., **IV** 123
Kaiser Engineering, **IV** 218
Kaiser, Henry J., **I** 565–66; **IV** 15, 121–23
Kaiser Industries, **III** 760
Kaiser International, **IV** 122–23
Kaiser Permanente, **6** 279
Kaiser Steel, **IV** 59
Kaiser Trading Co., **IV** 123
Kaiser-Frazer Corp., **IV** 121
KaiserTech Ltd., **IV** 123
Kaisha, Senshu, **IV** 655
Kaizosha, **IV** 632
Kajaani Oy, **II** 302; **IV** 350
Kajii, Takeshi, **II** 67
Kajima Corp., I 577–78
Kajima, Iwakichi, **I** 577
Kajima, Morino, **I** 578
Kajima, Seiichi, **I** 578
Kajima, Shoichi, **I** 578
Kajima, Ume, **I** 578
Kaku, Ryuzaburo, **III** 120–21
Kalamazoo Paper Co., **IV** 281; **9** 259
Kalbfleish, **I** 300
Kalinske, Thomas, **10** 483
Kalkkinen, Ilmari, **IV** 315
Kalms, Charles, **V** 48
Kalms, Stanley, **V** 48–50
Kalua Koi Corporation, **7** 281
Kalumburu Joint Venture, **IV** 67
Kamaishi, **IV** 157
Kamerbeek, G.J., **7** 509
Kametaka, Sokichi, **IV** 131
Kameyama, Shunzo, **III** 385
Kaminski, Ken, **8** 299
Kamioka Mining & Smelting Co., Ltd., **IV** 145, 148
Kamiya, Kenichi, **II** 326
Kamiya, Shotaro, **I** 205; **III** 637
Kampen, Emerson, **I** 341–42
Kamprad, Ingvar, **V** 82
Kanagawa Bank, **II** 291
Kanaoka, Matazacman, **V** 638
Kanda, Nobusuke, **7** 119
Kandall, David, **IV** 262
Kane Financial Corp., **III** 231

Kane Foods, **III** 43
Kane Freight Lines, **6** 370
Kane, Jasper, **I** 661; **9** 402
Kane, M. L., **6** 447
Kanebo Spinning Inc., **IV** 442
Kanegafuchi Shoji, **IV** 225
Kaneko, Naokichi, **I** 509; **V** 380
Kaneko, Toshi, **II** 292
Kanematsu Corporation, IV 442–44
Kanematsu, Fusijaro, **IV** 442
Kanematsu New York Inc., **IV** 442
Kanematsu Trading Corp., **IV** 442
Kanematsu-Gosho Ltd., **IV** 442–43
Kangaroo. *See* Seino Transportation Company, Ltd.
Kangol Ltd., **IV** 136
Kangos, Ed, **9** 168
Kangyo Bank, **II** 300, 310, 361
Kanhym, **IV** 91–92
Kanji, Wada, **IV** 403
Kankaanpää, Matti, **III** 649
Kann, Peter R., **IV** 603
Kansai Electric Power Co., Inc., IV 492; **V 645–48**
Kansai Seiyu Ltd., **V** 188
Kansai Sogo Bank, **II** 361
Kansallis Banken, **II** 302–03
Kansallis Banking Group, **II** 302
Kansallis-Osake-Pankki, II 242, **302–03**, 366; **IV** 349
Kansas City Electric Light Company. *See* Kansas City Power & Light Company.
Kansas City Gas Works, **6** 510
Kansas City Light & Power Company. *See* Kansas City Power & Light Company.
Kansas City Power & Light Company, 6 510–12, 592
Kansas City Southern Industries, Inc., 6 400–02
Kansas City Southern Railway (KCSR), **6** 400–02
Kansas Fire & Casualty Co., **III** 214
Kansas Gas and Electric Company, **6** 512
Kansas Power and Light Company, **6** 504
Kansas Power Company, **6** 312
Kansas Utilities Company, **6** 580
Kanto Steel Co., Ltd., **IV** 63
de Kantzow, Sydney, **6** 78–79
Kanzaki Paper Manufacturing Co., **IV** 285, 293
Kao Co. of America, **III** 38
Kao Corporation, III 38–39, 48
Kao Infosystems, **III** 38
Kao Soap Co., Ltd., **III** 38, 44
Kaohsiung Refinery, **IV** 388
Kaolin Australia Pty Ltd., **III** 691
Kapioltas, John, **III** 100
Kaplin, D.P., **I** 124
Kapnick, Harvey, **10** 116–17
Kapor, Mitchell D., **6** 254–54
Kappel, Frederick, **IV** 287
Kapy, **II** 139
Karafuto Industry, **IV** 320
Karatz, Bruce, **8** 285
Karcher, J. Clarence, **II** 112; **IV** 365; **11** 505
Karg, Georg, **V** 73
Karg, Hans-Georg, **V** 73
Karg'sche Familienstiftung, **V** 73
Karman, James A., **8** 455
Karmanos, Peter, **10** 243
Karmazin, Mel, **11** 190–92
Karmel, Kenneth, **I** 342
Karmelkorn Shoppes, Inc., **10** 371, 373

Karnes, William, **II** 468
Karnsund, Georg, **I** 198; **11** 438
Karp, Allen, **6** 163
Karp, Harvey L., **7** 361
Karpeles, Emil, **6** 425
Karpeles, Moritz, **6** 424–25
Karrels, Ed, **7** 199
Karstadt AG, **V** 101
Karstadt Aktiengesellschaft, V 100–02
Karstadt, Rudolph, **V** 100–02
Kartasamita, Indra, **IV** 492
Kasado Dockyard, **III** 760
Kasai, Junpachi, **III** 717
Kasai Securities, **II** 434
Kasai, Shinzo, **III** 717
Kaset Rojananil, **6** 123
Kashio, Kazuo, **III** 448
Kashio, Tadao, **III** 448
Kashio, Toshio, **III** 448
Kashio, Yukio, **III** 448
Kaske, Karlheinz, **II** 99
Kaskel, Carl Freiherr von, **II** 281
Kasmarov, **9** 18
Kasputys, Joseph E., **10** 89
Kasriel, Bernard, **III** 705
Kast Metals, **III** 452
Kaster, Robert L., **8** 353
Katada, Tetsuya, **III** 546
Katalco, **I** 374
Kataoka Electric Co., **II** 5
Kataoka, Katsutaro, **II** 5
Kataoka, Masagi, **V** 679–80
Kataoka, Otogo, **II** 439; **9** 384
Katayama, Nihachiro, **II** 59
Katayama, Yutaka, **I** 183–84; **11** 350
Katelise Group, **III** 739–40
Kates, Henry E., **III** 304
Kathleen Investment (Australia) Ltd., **III** 729
Katies, **V** 35
Kativo Chemical Industries Ltd., **8** 239
Kato, Benzaburo, **III** 42
Kato, Yogoro, **II** 109
Kataoka, Masataka, **II** 6
Katy Industries Inc., I 472–74
Katz Agency. *See* Katz Communications, Inc.
Katz Communications, Inc., 6 32–34
Katz Drug, **II** 604
Katz, Emmanuel, **6** 32
Katz, Eugene, **6** 32
Katz, George R., **6** 32
Katz, Nathan, **I** 665
Katzenberg, Jeffrey, **6** 176
Katzman, James A., **6** 278
Kauffman, Erwing Marion, **I** 648–49; **9** 328
Kauffman-Lattimer, **III** 9–10
Kaufhalle AG, **V** 104
Kaufhof, **II** 257
Kaufhof Holding AG, V 103–05
Kaufhof Mode und Sport GmbH, **V** 104
Kaufman and Broad Home Corporation, 8 284–86; 11 481–83
Kaufman, Armin, **III** 645
Kaufman, Don, **8** 284
Kaufman, Donald, **11** 481
Kaufman, Henry, **II** 448
Kaufman, Mitchell B., **9** 133
Kaufman, Stephen, **10** 113
Kaufman, Victor, **II** 137
Kaufmann, Abraham, **III** 290
Kaufmann's, **V** 132–33
Kaufmann's Department Stores, **6** 243

Kaukaan Tehdas Osakeyhtiö, **IV** 301
Oy Kaukas Ab, **IV** 300–02
Kaukas Oy, **IV** 302
Kaunda, Kenneth D., **IV** 18, 239–41
Kauppaosakeyhtiö Kymmene Aktiebolag, **IV** 299
Kauppiaitten Oy, **8** 293
Kautex Werke Reinold Hagen AG, **IV** 128
Kautex-Bayern GmbH, **IV** 128
Kautex-Ostfriedland GmbH, **IV** 128
Kawachi Bank, **II** 361
Kawada, Ganyemon, **I** 519; **11** 478
Kawai, Ryoichi, **III** 545–46
Kawai, Yoshinari, **III** 545
Kawakami, Gen'ichi, **III** 657
Kawakami, Kaichi, **III** 657
Kawamata, **11** 350
Kawamata, Katsuji, **I** 183
Kawamoto, Nobuhiko, **10** 354
Kawamura, Teijiro, **V** 473
Kawanto, Nobuhiko, **III** 549
Kawasaki Aircraft Co., **III** 539
Kawasaki Aircraft Heavy Industries, **III** 539
Kawasaki Denki Seizo, **II** 22
Kawasaki Dockyard Co., Ltd., **III** 538–39; **IV** 124
Kawasaki Heavy Industries, Ltd., **I** 75; **II** 273–74; **III** 482, 513, 516, **538–40**, 756; **IV** 124; **7** 232; **8** 72
Kawasaki Kisen Kaisha, Ltd., **V** 457–60
Kawasaki Rolling Stock, **III** 539
Kawasaki, Shozo, **III** 538; **IV** 124
Kawasaki Steel Corporation, **I** 432; **II** 274; **III** 539, 760; **IV** 30, **124–25**, 154, 212–13
Kawasaki, Yaemon, **6** 430
Kawasaki Zosenjo, **V** 457–58
Kawase, Jiro, **III** 715
Kawashima, Hiroshi, **III** 658
Kawashima, Kiyoshi, **I** 175
Kawashimaya Securities Co., **II** 433
Kawashimaya Shoten Inc. Ltd., **II** 433
Kawazoe, Soichi, **I** 183–84; **11** 350
Kawecki Berylco Industries, **8** 78
Kawneer Aluminum GmbH., **IV** 18
Kawneer Co., **IV** 18
Kawneer G.m.b.H., **IV** 18
Kawsmouth Electric Light Company. *See* Kansas City Power & Light Company.
Kay County Gas Co., **IV** 399
Kay, Jean, **I** 45
Kay's Drive-In Food Service, **II** 619
Kay-Bee Toy and Hobby Shops, Inc., **V** 137
Kaye, Marvin, **III** 504
Kayex, **9** 251
Kaynar Manufacturing Company, **8** 366
Kayser Agricultural Chemicals, **8** 229
Kayser Aluminum & Chemicals, **8** 229
Kayser-Roth, **8** 288
Kaysersberg, S.A., **IV** 290
Kazan, Elia, **II** 175
Kazarian, Paul B., **9** 485
KBLCOM Incorporated, **V** 644
KC Holdings, Inc., **11** 229–30
KCPL. *See* Kansas City Power & Light Company.
KCSI. *See* Kansas City Southern Industries, Inc.
KCSR. *See* Kansas City Southern Railway.
KDT Industries, Inc., **9** 20
Keady, William L., **III** 763
Kean, Bruce R., **III** 674

Keane, Stephen J., **11** 274
Kearns, David T., **6** 290
Keating, Charles, **III** 191; **9** 199; **10** 340
Keating, Paul, **IV** 652; **7** 391
Keaton, Buster, **II** 146
Keay, John (Sir), **III** 690–91
Keck, Donald, **III** 684
Keck, George, **I** 129; **6** 128–29
Keebler Co., **II** 594
Keebler, Godfrey, **II** 594
Keefe Manufacturing Courtesy Coffee Company, **6** 392
Keefe, Thomas J., **8** 322
Keeler, William, **IV** 522–23
Keen, Arthur, **III** 493
Keen, Arthur T., **III** 493
Keen, Robinson and Co., **II** 566
Keene, W.C.L., **III** 272
KEG Productions Ltd., **IV** 640
Kehrl, Howard, **7** 461
Kei, Hara, **III** 408
Keiffer, E. Gene, **9** 183–84
Keihan JUSCO, **V** 96
Keil Chemical Company, **8** 178
Keil, Jeffrey C., **11** 416–17
Keio Teito Electric Railway Company, **V** 461–62
Keir, John S., **IV** 252
Keisei Electric Railway, **II** 301
Keiser, Robert, **7** 415
Keith, John, **V** 401
Keith, Kenneth, **I** 82
Keith, Max, **I** 233; **10** 226
Keith, Minor, **II** 595
Keith of Castleacre (Lord), **III** 164
Keith, Robert J., **II** 556
Keith, William H., **9** 222
Keith-Albee-Orpheum, **II** 88
Kekkonen, Urho (Dr.), **IV** 469
Kelce, David, **7** 33
Kelce, Merl, **IV** 170; **7** 32
Kelce, Russell, **IV** 170; **10** 447–48
Kelce, Ted, **IV** 170
Kell, Eliza, **I** 267
Kelleher, Herbert D., **6** 119–21
Keller, Gottfried, **III** 376, 410
Keller, Mark, **9** 112
Kelley, Gaynor N., **7** 425, 427
Kelley, Jack, **8** 256
Kelley, Wendell J., **6** 506–07
Kelley, William V., **7** 29
Kellock, **10** 336
Kellogg, Amherst W., **III** 321
Kellogg Company, **I** 22–23; **II** 463, 502–03, **523–26**, 530, 560; **10** 323–24
Kellogg Food Co., **II** 523
Kellogg, John Harvey, **II** 523
Kellogg, John L., **II** 523–24
Kellogg, Leonard Lamb, **6** 523
Kellogg, Robert H., **III** 237–38
Kellogg Toasted Corn Flake Co., **II** 523
Kellogg, Will Keith, **II** 523–25
Kellum, John, **9** 369
Kellwood Asia Ltd., **8** 289
Kellwood Company, **V** 181–82; **8** 287–89
Kelly & Associates, **III** 306
Kelly & Cohen, **10** 468
Kelly Assisted Living Services, Inc., **6** 37
Kelly, Donald, **I** 441; **II** 468–69
Kelly, Douglas and Co., **II** 631
Kelly, Edwin S., **8** 290
Kelly Girl Service, Inc. *See* Kelly Services Inc.
Kelly Health Care, **6** 36–37

Kelly Home Care. *See* Kelly Health Care.
Kelly, James, **IV** 682
Kelly, James B., **I** 584
Kelly, Richard, **6** 35
Kelly, Russell. *See* Kelly, William Russell.
Kelly Services, Inc., **6** 35–37, 140; **9** 326
Kelly, Walt, **IV** 672
Kelly, William Russell, **6** 35–36
The Kelly-Springfield Tire Company, **8** 290–92
Kelm, Erwin, **II** 617
Kelman, Bryan, **III** 687, 737–39
Kelsey, Harold, **9** 245
Kelsey, John, **7** 258
Kelsey Wheel Company, **7** 258
Kelsey-Hayes Corp., **I** 170; **III** 650, 652; **7** 258–60
Kelsey-Hayes Group of Companies, **7** 258–60
Kelsey-Hayes Wheel Company, **7** 258
Kelso & Co., **III** 663, 665
Kelty Pack, Inc., **10** 215
KemaNobel, **9** 380–81
KemaNord, **9** 380
Kemi Oy, **IV** 316
Kemira, **III** 760
Kemira, Inc., **6** 152
Kemira-Ube, **III** 760
Kemoularia, Claude de, **II** 259
Kemp's Biscuits Limited, **II** 594
Kemp-Welch, John, **II** 476–77
Kempe, Carl, **IV** 317–18
Kempe, Erik, **IV** 318
Kempe, Frans, **IV** 317
Kempe, J.C., **IV** 317
Kemper Clearing Corp., **III** 271
Kemper Corporation, **III** 269–71, 339
Kemper Financial Cos., **III** 269, 271
Kemper Financial Services, **III** 270
Kemper Group, **III** 270–71
Kemper, Heinz P., **IV** 195; **8** 68, 495
Kemper Insurance and Financial Cos., **III** 270
Kemper Investors Life Insurance Co., **III** 270
Kemper, James S., **III** 269–70
Kemper, James S., Jr., **III** 269–71
Kemper Motorenfabrik, **I** 197
Kemper National Insurance Cos., **III** 271
Kemper Reinsurance Co., **III** 269
Kemperco Inc., **III** 269–70
Kempinski Group, **II** 258
Kemps Biscuits, **II** 594
Ken-L-Ration, **II** 559
Kenan, Norman G., **6** 465
Kendall Co., **I** 529; **III** 24–25; **IV** 288
The Kendall Company, **11** 219
Kendall, Donald M., **I** 277–79; **10** 452
Kendall Healthcare Products Company, **11** 220
Kendall, Henry P., **11** 219
Kendall International, Inc., **11** 219–21
The Kendall-Futuro Company, **11** 220
Kenealy, Alexander, **7** 342
Keneko, Saichiro, **IV** 297
Kenetech Corporation, **11** 222–24
Kenetech Windpower, **11** 223
Kenna, E. Douglas, **8** 80
Kennametal, **IV** 203
Kennan, George, **9** 366
Kennecott Copper Corp., **III** 248; **IV** 33–34, 79, 170–71, 179, 380; **7** 288; **10** 448

Kennecott Corporation, **IV** 192, 576; **7** **261–64**; **10** 262
Kennedy, Bruce R., **6** 67
Kennedy, Charles F., **6** 535
Kennedy, David M., **II** 261
Kennedy, Donald S., **6** 539
Kennedy, Edward, **I** 490, 687; **10** 287
Kennedy, Gary D., **6** 273
Kennedy, George, **7** 258–59
Kennedy, J.R., **8** 173–74
Kennedy, James C., **IV** 597
Kennedy, John E., **I** 12
Kennedy, John F., **I** 29, 58, 62, 65, 79, 97, 167, 172; **II** 152; **III** 248; **IV** 115, 573, 602, 636; **7** 249, 551; **11** 165, 428
Kennedy, John H., **III** 9
Kennedy, John R., Jr. (Jack), **8** 173–75
Kennedy, Joseph P., **I** 484; **II** 88
Kennedy, Julian, **IV** 217
Kennedy, Laurence S., **III** 283
Kennedy, Robert D., **9** 519
Kennedy, Robert F., **I** 268; **11** 415
Kennedy, Taylor, **III** 704
Kenner, **II** 502; **10** 323
Kenner Parker Toys, Inc., **II** 503; **9** 156; **10** 324
Kenrick, Timothy, **II** 306
Kent Drugs Ltd., **II** 640, 650
Kent Fire, **III** 350
Kent, Rockwell, **IV** 661
Kent, Sidney R., **II** 169
Kent-Moore Corp., **I** 200; **10** 492–93
Kentland-Elkhorn Coal Corp., **IV** 181
Kentucky Bonded Funeral Co., **III** 217
Kentucky Electric Power Company, **6** 514
Kentucky Fried Chicken, **I** 260–61; **II** 533; **III** 78, 104, 106; **6** 200; **7** 26–28, 433; **8** 563. *See also* KFC Corporation.
Kentucky Power and Light Company, **11** 237
Kentucky Securities Company, **6** 514
Kentucky Utilities Company, **6** **513–15**; **11** 37, 236, 238
Kenway, **I** 155
Kenwood, **I** 532
Kenworth Motor Truck Corp., **I** 185–86
Kenworthy, Donald F., **6** 409
Kenyon, Art, **9** 434
Kenyon Sons and Craven Ltd., **II** 593–94
Keo Cutters, Inc., **III** 569
Keoughan, S.H., **IV** 399–400
KEPCO. *See* Kyushu Electric Power Company Inc.
Ker, William, **I** 592
Kerby, William, **IV** 602
Kerkorian, Kirk, **II** 136, 149–50, 167
Kerlick, Switzer & Johnson, **6** 48
Kerlyn Oil Co., **IV** 445–46
Kern, Adolph, **7** 573
Kern, Alfred, **I** 671
Kern County Land Co., **I** 527; **10** 379, 527
Kern, Herbert A., **I** 373
Kern, Jerome, **IV** 671
Kernite SA, **8** 386
Kernkraftwerke Lippe-Ems, **V** 747
Kernridge Oil Co., **IV** 541
Kerr, David, **IV** 166; **7** 399
Kerr Glass Manufacturing Co., **III** 423
Kerr Group Inc., **10** 130
Kerr, James, **V** 738
Kerr, James R., **9** 498–99
Kerr, Robert S., **IV** 445
Kerr-Addison Gold Mines, **IV** 165
Kerr-Addison Mines Ltd., **IV** 165

Kerr-McGee Chemical Corp., **IV** 446
Kerr-McGee Coal Corp., **IV** 446
Kerr-McGee Corporation, **IV** **445–47**
Kerr-McGee Nuclear Corp., **IV** 446
Kerr-McGee Oil Industries, Inc., **IV** 446
Kerridge, John, **9** 225–26
Kerrigan, James, **I** 450
Kerzner, Sol, **I** 288
Keski-Suomen Tukkukauppa Oy, **8** 293
Kesko Ltd (Kesko Oy), **8** **293–94**
Kesselman, Joseph, **7** 266
Kessler, G.A., **IV** 132
Kessler, George, **10** 3
Kessler, J.B. August, **IV** 530
Keswick, Henry, **IV** 700
Keswick, James Johnstone, **IV** 699–700
Keswick, John, **I** 469–71
Keswick, Maggie, **I** 471
Keswick, Simon, **I** 469–71
Keswick, Thomas, **I** 468
Keswick, Tony, **I** 469
Keswick, William, **I** 468
Ketchikan International Sales Co., **IV** 304
Ketchikan Pulp Co., **IV** 304
Ketchikan Spruce Mills, Inc., **IV** 304
Ketchum and MacLeod Advertising Agency. *See* Ketchum Communications Inc.
Ketchum, Carlton, **6** 38
Ketchum Communications Inc., **6** **38–40**
Ketchum, George, **6** 38
Ketchum, Inc. *See* Ketchum Communications Inc.
Ketchum, MacLeod & Grove, Inc. *See* Ketchum Communications Inc.
Ketchum Publicity, Inc. *See* Ketchum Communications Inc.
Ketelsen, James Lee, **10** 380, 527–28
Ketelson, James Lee, **I** 527–28
Ketner and Milner Stores, **II** 683
Ketner, Brown, **II** 626
Ketner, Ralph W., **II** 626–27
Kettering, Charles F., **I** 171; **II** 34; **III** 150–51; **6** 264–65; **10** 273, 325
Keumkang Co., **III** 515; **7** 231
Kewanee Public Service Company, **6** 505
Key, Dennis, **11** 246
Key, James L., **6** 446–47
Key Markets, **II** 628
Key Pharmaceuticals, Inc., **11** 207
KeyCorp, **8** **295–97**; **11** 110
Keyes Fibre Company, **9** **303–05**
Keyes Fibre Sales Corporation, **9** 304
Keyes, James H., **III** 536–37
Keyes, Martin, **9** 303–04
Keynes, John Maynard, **II** 318; **IV** 622
Keys, Clement, **I** 78, 101, 128; **6** 128; **11** 427
Keys, Derek, **IV** 92–93
Keystone Aircraft, **I** 61; **11** 164
Keystone Custodian Fund, **IV** 458
Keystone Foods Corporation, **10** 443
Keystone Franklin, **III** 570
Keystone Franklin, Inc., **9** 543
Keystone Gas Co., **IV** 548
Keystone International, Inc., **11** **225–27**
Keystone Life Insurance Co., **III** 389
Keystone Paint and Varnish, **8** 553
Keystone Pipe and Supply Co., **IV** 136
Keystone Savings and Loan, **II** 420
The Keystone Tool Company, **11** 225
KFC. *See* Kentucky Fried Chicken.
KFC Corporation, **7** **265–68**; **10** 450

Khadafi, Moammar, **I** 163; **IV** 453, 481; **11** 104
Khalda Petroleum Co., **IV** 413
Khan, Reza, **IV** 379
KHD AG. *See* Klöckner-Humboldt-Deutz AG.
KHD group. *See* KHD Konzern.
KHD Industrieanlagen AG, **III** 543
KHD Konzern, **III** **541–44**
KHD Luftfahrttechnik GmbH, **III** 544
KHD Nederland, **III** 543
Kheel, Theodore W., **11** 415–16
KHL. *See* Koninklijke Hollandsche Lloyd.
Khomeini, Ruholla (Ayatollah), **I** 261; **III** 137
Khoo, Tan Sri, **II** 358
Khosla, Vinod, **7** 498
Khrushchev, Nikita, **I** 277
Kia Motors, **I** 167
Kianka, Frances, **I** 46
Kidd, Walter, **11** 493–94
Kidde Inc., **I** **475–76**; **III** 503; **7** 209
Kidde, John, **I** 476
Kidde, Walter, **I** 475–76
Kidder, C. Robert, **9** 179–80, 344
Kidder, Peabody & Co., **II** 31, 207, 430; **IV** 84; **7** 310
Kidder Press Co., **IV** 644
Kids "R" Us, **V** 203–05; **9** 394
Kidston Mines, **I** 438
Kiekhaefer Corp., **III** 443
Kienzle Apparate GmbH, **III** 566
Kiernan, Peter D., **9** 229
Kierulff Electronics, **10** 113
Kiewit Diversified Group Inc., **11** 301
Kiewit, Peter, **8** 422–24
Kifer, E. H., **6** 473
Kikawada, Kazutaka, **V** 730–31
Kikkoman, **I** 9
Kikuchi, Minori, **III** 386
Kikuchi, Shojiro, **V** 483
Kikumoto, Naojiro, **II** 325
Kilbourne, E. C., **6** 565
Kilburn & Co., **III** 522
Kilby, Jack S., **II** 113; **11** 506
Kilgo Motor Express, **6** 370
Kilgore, Barney, **IV** 602
Kilgore Ceramics, **III** 671
Kilgore Federal Savings and Loan Assoc., **IV** 343
Kilgour, Charles H., **6** 316
Killam, Izaak Walton, **6** 585–86
Killen, Robert, **6** 481
Kilmartin, John, **10** 409
Kilmer, Fred B., **III** 35; **8** 281
Kilmer, Joyce, **III** 35
Kilpatrick, Robert D., **III** 226
Kilsby Tubesupply, **I** 570
Kim, Suk Joon, **III** 749
Kim, Suk Won, **III** 748–50
Kim, Sung Kon, **III** 747–48
Kim, Woo Choong, **III** 457–59
Kimball, David, **III** 644; **9** 251
Kimball, Frederick, **V** 484
Kimball, Justin Ford, Dr., **10** 159
Kimbell Inc., **II** 684
Kimberley Central Mining Co., **IV** 64; **7** 121
Kimberly & Clark Co., **III** 40; **IV** 648
Kimberly, Clark & Co., **III** 40
Kimberly, John A., **III** 40
Kimberly-Clark Australia Ltd., **IV** 249

Kimberly-Clark Corporation, **I** 14, 413; **III** 36, **40–41**; **IV** 249, 254, 297–98, 329, 665; **8** 282
Kimco Realty Corporation, **11 228–30**
Kimes, Beverly Rae, **I** 151
Kimmel, Martin S., **11** 228
Kimmel, Sidney, **11** 216–18
Kindelberger, James, **I** 78–79
Kindelberger, James Howard, **11** 427–28
Kinden Corporation, **7** 303
Kinear Moodie, **III** 753
King, Albert E., **III** 360
King, Alexander, **IV** 672
King, Cecil Harmsworth, **IV** 666; **7** 342–43
King, Charles, **9** 306
King, Chuck, **I** 184; **11** 351
King Cullen, **II** 644
King, Don, **6** 211
King Features Syndicate, **IV** 626
King Fook Gold and Jewellery Co., **IV** 717
King, Frank, **II** 289
King, J.B., **III** 162
King, John (Lord), **I** 94
King, Mackenzie, **6** 360
King, Martin Luther, Jr., **I** 420, 449; **II** 634
King, Michael, **9** 306
King, Olin, **9** 463–64
King, Roger, **9** 306–07
King, Rollin, **6** 119
King, W. Frank III, **6** 255
King World Productions, Inc., **9 306–08**
King World's Camelot Entertainment, **9** 306
King-Seeley Thermos, **II** 419
Kingfisher plc, **V 106–09**; **10** 498
Kingly, William C., **II** 312
Kings County Lighting Company, **6** 456
Kings County Research Laboratories, **11** 424
Kingsbury, J.E., **III** 162
Kingsford Corp., **III** 21
Kingsford-Smith, Charles (Sir), **I** 54
Kingsin Line, **6** 397
Kingsley, Darwin, **III** 316
Kingsley, Francis G., **V** 139–40
Kingsmill, W.H. (Lt. Col.), **IV** 723
Kingsport Pulp Corp., **IV** 310
Kinki Nippon Railway Company Ltd., **V 463–65**
Kinnear, Thomas C., **II** 344
Kinnevik, **IV** 203–04
Kinney, Alva, **II** 493
Kinney, E. Robert, **II** 502–03; **10** 323–24
Kinney National Service Inc., **II** 176; **IV** 672
Kinney, Samuel, **IV** 346
Kinney Services, **6** 293
Kinney Shoe Corporation, **V** 226; **11** 349
Kinoshita Sansho Steel Co., **I** 508
Kinross, **IV** 92
Kinsella, John, **I** 23
Kintec Corp., **10** 97
Kintigh, Allen E., **6** 536
Kipfmuller, Emil, **II** 163
Kirby, **III** 214
Kirby, Allan, Jr., **10** 44
Kirby, Allan P., **IV** 180; **10** 43–44
Kirby Forest Industries, **IV** 305
Kirby, Fred, **10** 43
Kirby, Fred, II, **10** 44–45
Kirby, Fred M., **V** 224–25
Kirby, Robert, **II** 121–22
Kirch Group, **10** 196

Kirch, Leo, **IV** 591
Kircher, Donald P., **II** 10
Kircher, John, **IV** 401
Kirchner, Moore, and Co., **II** 408
Kirchoff, Donald J., **II** 491–92
Kirdorf, Adolph, **I** 542
Kirdorf, Emil, **I** 542
Kirin Brewery Co., **I** 258, **265–66**, 282; **10** 78, 80
Kirin-Seagram Ltd., **I** 266
Kirk, Desault B., **II** 14
Kirk-Stieff Co., **10** 181
Kirkstall Forge Engineering, **III** 494
Kirkwood, Robert C., **V** 225
Kirman, Ernest, **II** 594
Kirn, W.H., **I** 622
Kirsch Co., **II** 16
Kirschner, Sidney, **11** 338
Kirstein, Louis, **V** 26
Kirwan, Thomas, **III** 249
Kishimoto & Co., **I** 432, 492
Kishimoto Shoten Co., Ltd., **IV** 168
Kissel, R., **IV** 140
Kissel, Wilhelm, **I** 138; **11** 31
Kissinger, Henry, **II** 248; **III** 197
Kisskalt, Wilhelm, **III** 300
Kistler, Lesh & Co., **III** 528
Kistler, William, **III** 429
Kistner, Erik, **I** 625
Kita Karafunto Oil Co., **IV** 475
Kita Nippon Paper Co., **IV** 321
Kitagawa & Co. Ltd., **IV** 442
Kitagawa, Yohei, **IV** 442
Kitaura, Kiichiro, **II** 440; **9** 385
Kitchen, Lawrence, **I** 66; **11** 268
KitchenAid, **III** 611, 653–54; **8 298–99**
Kitchenbell, **III** 43
Kitchens of Sara Lee, **II** 571–73
Kittinger, **10** 324
Kittredge, Rufus J., **9** 61–62
Kittredge, William, **IV** 661
Kivekas, Lauri, **II** 302
Kiwi Packaging, **IV** 250
Kjøbenhavns Bandelsbank, **II** 366
KJPCL. *See* Royal Interocean Lines.
KKK Shipping, **II** 274
KKR. *See* Kohlberg Kravis Roberts & Co.
KLA Acrotec Ltd., **11** 232
KLA Instruments Corporation, **11 231–33**
Klamon, Lawrence P., **I** 445–47
Klauber, Ed, **II** 132; **6** 157
Klaus, L. George, **11** 47
Kleiner & Perkins, **6** 278
Kleiner, Eugene, **6** 278
Kleiner, Perkins, Caufield & Byers, **I** 637; **10** 15, 504
Kleinman, Mel, **11** 86
Kleinwort, Alexander, **II** 421
Kleinwort Benson Australia, **II** 422
Kleinwort Benson Cross Financing, **II** 422
Kleinwort Benson Energy, **II** 422
Kleinwort Benson Government Securities, **II** 292–93, 422
Kleinwort Benson Group PLC, **II** 379, **421–23**; **IV** 191
Kleinwort Benson Lonsdale, **II** 422
Kleinwort Grieveson Securities, **II** 423
Kleinwort, Sons & Co., **II** 414, 421
Kleist, Dale, **III** 720
Kline, Mahlon, **I** 692
Kline Manufacturing, **II** 16
Kline, Richard, **II** 605
Klinedinst, Thomas, Jr., **11** 467

KLM. *See* Koninklijke Luftvaart Maatschappij N.V.
Klöckner, **IV** 127
Klöckner & Co., **III** 542; **IV** 126, 232
Klöckner & Co. AG, **IV** 126
Klöckner, Peter, **III** 541, 542; **IV** 126, 127, 128
Klöckner-Ferromatik GmbH, **IV** 127
Klöckner-Humboldt-Deutz AG, **I** 542; **III** 541–44; **IV** 126–27
Klöckner-Werke AG, **IV** 43, 60, **126–28**, 201
Klopman, William A., **V** 355
Kloth-Senking, **IV** 201
Kluckman, Revone, **II** 124
Klug, Norman, **I** 269
Kluge, John W., **6** 168–69; **7** 335–36
Klugman, Jack, **III** 121
Klugt, Cornelis van der, **II** 80
Klusen, Karl, **II** 279
Kluwer, **IV** 611
Klynveld Main Goerdeler, **10** 387
Klynveld Peat Marwick Goerdeler. *See* KPMG Peat Marwick.
KM&G. *See* Ketchum Communications Inc.
KM&G International, Inc. *See* Ketchum Communications Inc.
Kmart Corporation, **I** 516; **V** 35, **110–12**; **6** 13; **7** 61, 444; **9** 361, 400, 482; **10** 137, 410, 490, 497, 515–16
Kmart Sporting Goods, **V** 111
KMP Holdings, **I** 531
KN. *See* Kühne & Nagel Group.
Knape, Eldon, **I** 301
Knapp & Tubbs, **III** 423
Knapp Communications, **II** 656
Knapp, George O., **I** 399
Knapp, John, **11** 92
Knapp, Joseph F., **III** 290–91
Knauf, **III** 721, 736
Knickerbocker Toy Co., **III** 505
Knife River Coal Mining Company, **7** 322–25
Knight, Charles F., **II** 19–20
Knight, Charles Landon (C.L.), **IV** 628
Knight, Goodwin J., **II** 181
Knight, James L., **IV** 628–30
Knight, John S., **IV** 628–30
Knight, Lester, **II** 20
Knight Newspapers, **7** 191
Knight Newspapers, Inc., **IV** 613, 628–29
Knight Paper Co., **III** 766
Knight, Peter O., **6** 582
Knight, Philip H., **8** 391–94
Knight-Ridder, Inc., **III** 190; **IV** 597, **628–30**, 670; **6** 323; **10** 407
Knight-Ridder Newspapers, Inc., **IV** 628–30; **7** 191, 327
Knobloch, Carl W., **8** 229
Knoff-Bremse, **I** 138
Knogo Corp., **11** 444
Knoll International Holdings, **I** 202
Knoll Pharmaceutical, **I** 682
Knomark, **III** 55
Knorr Co. *See* C.H. Knorr Co.
Knorr-Bremse, **11** 31
Knott, **III** 98
Knowledge Systems Concepts, **11** 469
KnowledgeWare Inc., **9 309–11**
Knowles, Bill, **6** 79
Knowles, Lucius J., **9** 153
Knowlton, Richard L., **II** 504, 506
Knox, Edward, **III** 686

Knox, Edward Ritchie, **III** 687
Knox, Edward William, **III** 686–87
Knox, Seymour Horace, **V** 224–25
KNSM. *See* Koninklijke Nederlandsche
  Stoomboot Maatschappij.
Knudsen & Sons, Inc., **11** 211
Knudsen, C. Calvert, **IV** 308
Knudsen, Morris Hans, **7** 355
Knudsen, Semon E., **I** 167; **11** 139
Knudson, Darrell G., **11** 145–46
Knudson, Gene, **IV** 358
Knutange, **IV** 226
Kobayashi, Ichizo, **V** 70, 454–55
Kobayashi, Jun'ichiro, **IV** 284, 297, 321
Kobayashi, Keita, **V** 526–28
Kobayashi, Kohei, **V** 456
Kobayashi, Koji, **II** 67–68
Kobayashi, Koshiro, **V** 462
Kobayashi, Tomijiro, **III** 44
Kobayashi Tomijiro Shoten, **III** 44
Kobayashi, Toshimine, **V** 154
Kobayashi, Yonezo, **V** 455
Kobe Copper Products, **IV** 130
Kobe Precision Inc.., **IV** 130
Kobe Shipbuilding & Engine Works, **II** 57
Kobe Steel, **11** 234–35
Kobe Steel America Inc., **IV** 131
Kobe Steel Asia Pte Ltd., **IV** 131
Kobe Steel Australia Pty. Ltd., **IV** 131
Kobe Steel Co., **IV** 129
Kobe Steel Europe, Ltd., **IV** 131
Kobe Steel, Ltd., **I** 511; **II** 274; **IV** 16,
  129–31, 212–13; **8** 242
Kobe Steel USA Inc., **IV** 131
Kobe Steel Works, Ltd., **IV** 129–30
Kobelco Middle East, **IV** 131
Kober, Roger W., **6** 572
Koç Holdings A.S., **I** 167, **478–80**; **11** 139
Koç, Rahmi, **I** 479
Koç, Vehibi, **I** 478–79
Koç-American Bank, **I** 480
Koch, Charles, **IV** 448–49
Koch, David, **IV** 449
Koch Engineering, **IV** 449
Koch family, **IV** 448–49
Koch, Fred C., **IV** 448–49
Koch, Frederick, **IV** 448–49
Koch, Harry, **7** 39
Koch, Henry, Jr., **7** 546
Koch Industries, Inc., **IV** 448–49
Koch, William, **IV** 449
Koci, L.F., **10** 274
Kockos Brothers, Inc., **II** 624
Kodak. *See* Eastman Kodak Company.
Kodama, Kazuo, **III** 636
Kodama, Yoshi, **IV** 224
Kodansha International/USA, Ltd., **IV** 631,
  633
Kodansha Ltd., **IV** 631–33
Ködel & Böhn GmbH, **III** 543
Koehring, **8** 545
Koehring Company, **8** 545
Koehring Cranes & Excavators, **7** 513
Koei Real Estate Ltd., **V** 195
Koepchen, Arthur, **V** 708
Koepff, Heiner, **I** 679
Koffler, Murray, **9** 237–38
Koga, Yoshine, **III** 756
Kogan, Herman, **I** 621
Kogura, Koshin, **V** 536
Kogure, Gobei, **I** 11
Koh, Byung Woo, **III** 749
Kohl's Corporation, **9** 312–13
Kohl's Food Stores, **I** 426–27

Kohlberg, Jerome, Jr., **9** 180
Kohlberg Kravis Roberts & Co., **I** 566,
  609–11; **II** 370, 452, 468, 544, 645,
  654, 656, 667; **III** 263, 765–67; **IV**
  642–43; **V** 55–56, 408, 410, 415; **6** 357;
  7 130, 132, 200; **9** 53, 180, 230, 469,
  522; **10** 75–77, 302
Kohler Bros., **IV** 91
Kohler Company, **7** 269–71; **10** 119
Kohler, Herbert, **7** 270–71
Kohler, Herbert, Jr., **7** 271
Kohler, John Michael, **7** 269
Kohler, Walter, **7** 269–70
Kohner Brothers, **II** 531
Koholyt AG, **III** 693
Koike Shoten, **II** 458
Koivisto, Mauno (Dr.), **IV** 470
Kojima, Masashi, **V** 307
Kojiro Matsukata, **V** 457–58
Kok, Bessel, **6** 304
Kokomo Gas and Fuel Company, **6** 533
Kokuei Paper Co., Ltd., **IV** 327
Kokura, Fusazo, **IV** 554
Kokura Sekiyu Co. Ltd., **IV** 554
Kokura Steel Manufacturing Co., Ltd., **IV**
  212
Kokusai Kisen, **V** 457–58
Kokusaku Kiko Co., Ltd., **IV** 327
Kokusaku Pulp Co., **IV** 327
Kolb, Hans Werner, **III** 695
Kolbenschmidt, **IV** 141
Kolber, Leo, **6** 163
Kolff, Willem, **I** 627; **10** 141
Kolker Chemical Works, Inc., **IV** 409; **7**
  308
The Koll Company, **8** 300–02
Koll, Donald M., **8** 300
Komag, Inc., **11** 234–35
Komag Material Technology, Inc., **11** 234
Komatsu America Corp., **III** 546
Komatsu Dresser Co., **III** 470, 473, 545
Komatsu Heavy Industry, **III** 470
Komatsu, Koh, **II** 361–62
Komatsu Ltd., **III** 453, 473, **545–46**
Komatsu Trading International, **III** 546
Komatsu, Yasushi, **II** 361
Kommanditgesellschaft S. Elkan & Co., **IV**
  140
Kommunale Energie-
  Beteiligungsgesellschaft, **V** 746
Kompro Computer Leasing, **II** 457
Konan Camera Institute, **III** 487
Kondo, Mitchitaka, **6** 30
Kondo, Rempei, **V** 482
Kondo, Takeo, **I** 504
Kongl. Elektriska Telegraf-Verket, **V** 331
Kongo Bearing Co., **III** 595
Konica Business Machines U.S.A., **III** 549
Konica Corp. (USA), **III** 549
Konica Corporation, **III** 547–50
Konica Manufacturing U.S.A., **III** 550
Konica Technology, **III** 549
König, Friedrick, **III** 561
Koninklijke Ahold N.V., **II** 641–42
Koninklijke Distilleerderijen der Erven
  Lucas Böls, **I** 226
Koninklijke Hollandsche Lloyd, **6** 403
Koninklijke Java-China Paketvaart Lijnen.
  See Royal Interocean Lines.
Koninklijke Luchtvaart Maatschappij
  N.V., **I** 55, **107–09**, 119, 121; **6** 95, 105,
  109–10

Koninklijke Nederlandsche Hoogovens
  en Staalfabrieken NV, **IV** 105, 123,
  132–34
Koninklijke Nederlandsche Maatschappig
  Tot Exploitatie van Petroleumbronnen in
  Nederlandsch-indie, **IV** 530
Koninklijke Nederlandsche Petroleum
  Maatschappij, **IV** 491
Koninklijke Nederlandsche Stoomboot
  Maatschappij, **6** 403–04
Koninklijke Nederlandse
  Vliegtuigenfabriek Fokker, **I** 46,
  54–56, 75, 82, 107, 115, 121–22
Koninklijke Nedlloyd Groep N.V., **6**
  403–05
Koninklijke Paketvaart Maatschappij, **6**
  403–04
Koninklijke PTT Nederland NV, **V**
  299–301
Koninklijke Wessanen N.V., **II** 527–29
Koninklijke West-Indische Maildienst, **6**
  403
Koniphoto Corp., **III** 548
Konishi Honten, **III** 547
Konishi Pharmaceutical, **I** 704
Konishi, Shinbei, **I** 705
Konishiroku, **III** 487, 547–48
Konishiroku Honten Co., Ltd., **III** 547–49
Konishiroku Photo Industry (Europe), **III**
  548
Konishiroku Photo Industry Co., **III** 548
Kono, Shunzi, **III** 386
Konoike Bank, **II** 347
Konoike family, **II** 347
Koo, Cha-Kyung, **II** 53–54
Koo, In-Hwoi, **II** 53
Koolsbergen, Hein, **7** 537
Koontz, Raymond, **7** 145
Koopman & Co., **III** 419
Koor Industries Ltd., **II** 47–49
Koortrade, **II** 48
Kop-Coat, Inc., **8** 456
Koper, Danis, **I** 478
Koppens Machinenfabriek, **III** 420
Kopper, Hilmar, **II** 280
Kopper United, **I** 354
Koppers Company, **6** 486
Koppers Inc., **I** 199, **354–56**; **III** 645, 735
Korab, William, **7** 431
Korbel, **I** 226
Korda, Alexander, **II** 147, 157–58
Korea Development Leasing Corp., **II** 442
Korea Steel Co., **III** 459
Korea Telecommunications Co, **I** 516
Korea Vehicle Transportation, **6** 98
Korean Air Lines Co. Ltd., **II** 442; **6**
  98–99
Korean Development Bank, **III** 459
Korean Institute of Aeronautical
  Technology, **6** 99
Korean National Air Lines, **6** 98
Korean Tungsten Mining Co., **IV** 183
Kornbluth, Jesse, **I** 279
Korshak, Sidney, **III** 92
Kortbetalning Servo A.B., **II** 353
Kortgruppen Eurocard-Köpkort A.B., **II**
  353
Koryeo Industrial Development Co., **III**
  516; **7** 232
Koryo Fire and Marine Insurance Co., **III**
  747
Koskelo family, **IV** 349
Kosset Carpets, Ltd., **9** 467
Kosuge, Kuniyasu, **V** 87

Kosuge, Tanji, **V** 85–86
Kosuge, Tanji, II, **V** 85
Kosuge, Tanji, III, **V** 86–87
Kotchian, Carl, **I** 65, 493; **11** 267–68
Kotilainen, V.A., **IV** 275–76
Kotobukiya Co., Ltd., V 113–14
Kowa Metal Manufacturing Co., **III** 758
Koyama, Goro, **II** 326
Koyo Seiko, **III** 595–96, 623–24
Kozaki, Zenichi, **III** 711; **7** 303
Kozmetsky, George, **I** 523; **10** 520
KPM. *See* Koninklijke Paketvaart
   Maatschappij.
KPMG Peat Marwick, **7** 266; **10** 385–87
KPMG Worldwide, 10 115, **385–87**
Kraft, Charles, **II** 532
Kraft Cheese Co., **II** 533
Kraft Cheese Co. Ltd., **II** 533
Kraft Foods Co., **II** 533, 556
Kraft, Fred, **II** 532
Kraft General Foods, Inc., II 530–34; V
   407; **7 272–77 (upd.)**, 339, 433, 547; **8**
   399, 499; **9** 180, 290, 318; **11** 15
Kraft, Inc., **II** 129, 530–34, 556; **III** 610; **7**
   274–76
Kraft, James L., **II** 532–33; **7** 274–75
Kraft, John, **II** 532
Kraft, Neil, **8** 171
Kraft, Norman, **II** 532
Kraft-Phenix Cheese Corp., **II** 533; **7**
   274–75
Kraft-Versicherungs-AG, **III** 183
Kraftco, **II** 533
Kraftwerk Union, **I** 411; **III** 466
Krafve, Richard E., **II** 86; **11** 412
Kral, Richard, **9** 156–58
Kramer, **III** 48
Krämer & Grebe, **III** 420
Kramp, Horst, **I** 682
Kranaen, Kevin J., **11** 490
Krannert, Herman C., **IV** 342; **8** 267
Krapek, Karl, **10** 538
Krasnoff, Abraham, **9** 396–97
Krause, Morton, **11** 392
Krause, Tomas, **I** 197
Krause, William, **11** 518–20
Krauss-Maffei AG, **I** 75; **II** 242; **III** 566,
   695
Kraut, H.B., **10** 328–29
Kravco, **III** 248
Kravis, Henry R., **9** 180
Krebs, Roland, **I** 219
Kredietbank (Suisse) S.A., **II** 305
Kredietbank N.V., II 295, **304–05**
Kredietbank S.A. Luxembourgeoise, **II**
   304–05
Kredietbank voor Handel en Nijverheid, **II**
   304
Kreditanstalt für Wiederaufbau, **IV** 231–32
Kreft, **III** 480
Krehbiel, Edwin, **11** 318
Krehbiel, Frederick A., II, **11** 319
Krehbiel, Frederick Augustus, **11** 317–18
Krehbiel, John H., Sr., **11** 317–18
Krema Hollywood Chewing Gum Co. S.A.,
   II 532
Kremers-Urban, **I** 667
Kremp, Herbert, **IV** 590
Kresa, Kent, **11** 167, 364
Kresge Foundation, **V** 110
Kresge, Sebastian Spering, **V** 110–11
Kreuger & Toll, **IV** 338
Kreuger, Ivar, **II** 365–66; **IV** 338; **V**
   334–36

Krieble, Robert, **8** 332–33
Krieble, Vernon, **8** 332–33
Kriegschemikalien AG, **IV** 229
Kriegsmetall AG, **IV** 229
Kriegswollbedarfs AG, **IV** 229
Krim, Arthur, **II** 147–48
Krim, Arthur B., **6** 167–69; **7** 336
Krislex Knits, Inc., **8** 235
Krispy Kitchens, Inc., **II** 584
Kroc, Ray, **II** 613, 646–47; **III** 63; **7**
   317–18, 505
Kroger, Bernard H., **II** 643, 645
Kroger Company, II 605, 632, **643–45**,
   682; **III** 218; **6** 364; **7** 61
Kroger Grocery and Baking Co., **II**
   643–44
Kroger, Joseph, **III** 167; **6** 283
Krogh, Harry, **9** 394
Krohn, Irwin, **V** 207
Krohn-Fechheimer Shoe Company, **V** 207
Kroll, Alex, **I** 37–38
Krone, Helmut, **I** 30
Krones A.G., **I** 266
Kropotkin, Pyotr, **7** 166
Kropper, Jon A., **III** 170; **6** 286
Krovtex, **8** 80
Krugman, Stan, **6** 148
Krumm, Daniel J., **III** 572–73
Krupp. *See* Fried. Krupp GmbH.
Krupp, Alfred, **IV** 85–87
Krupp, Bertha, **IV** 86
Krupp, Friedrich Alfred, **IV** 86–87
Krupp, Friedrich Nicolai, **IV** 85
Krupp, Hermann, **IV** 87
Krupp, Margarethe, **IV** 87
Krupp, Therese, **IV** 85
Krupp von Bohlen und Halbach, Alfried,
   IV 88
Krupp von Bohlen und Halbach, Arndt, **IV**
   88
Krupp von Bohlen und Halbach, Gustav,
   IV 86–87
KSSU Group, **I** 107–08, 120–21
KTR. *See* Keio Teito Electric Railway
   Company.
KU Capital Corporation, **11** 238
KU Energy Corporation, 6 513, 515; **11**
   236–38
Kubitschek, Juscelino, **IV** 502
Kubo, Masataka, **III** 635
Kubo, Tomio, **9** 349
Kubota Corporation, I 494; **III 551–53**;
   10 404
Kubota, Gonshiro. *See* Gonshiro Oode.
Kubota Iron Works, **III** 551–52
Kubota Ltd., **III** 551–53
Kubota, Toshiro, **III** 551
Küch, Richard (Dr.), **IV** 99
Kuechle, Urban, **11** 5
Kuehn, Ronald L., Jr., **6** 578
Kuhara, Fusanosuke, **IV** 475
Kuhara Mining Co., **IV** 475
Kuhlmann, **III** 677; **IV** 174
Kuhn Loeb, **II** 402–03
Kühne & Nagel Group, **V** 466–69
Kühne & Nagel Holding, Inc., **V** 466
Kühne & Nagel International AG, V
   466–69
Kühne, Alfred, **V** 466–68
Kühne, August, **V** 466
Kühne, Klaus-Michael, **V** 468
Kühne, Werner, **V** 466
Kuhnke, Hans-Helmut, **IV** 195
Kuhns, George, **III** 328–29

Kuhns, William, **V** 630–31
Kuitu Oy, **IV** 348
Kujawa, Duane, **I** 145
KUK, **III** 577, 712
Kukje Group, **III** 458
Kullberg, Duane, **10** 117
Kulmobelwerk G.H. Walb and Co., **I** 581
Kum-Kleen Products, **IV** 252
Kumagai Gumi Co., I 579–80
Kumagai, Santaro, **I** 579
Kumagai, Taichiro, **I** 580
Kumagai, Tasaburo, **I** 579–80
Kume, Hiroshi, **9** 30
Kumm, Roy E., **I** 254
Kumsung Industry Co. Ltd., **III** 748
Kumsung Shipping Co., **III** 748
Kumsung Textile Co., **III** 747
Kumura, Seita, **V** 380
Kunett, Rudolf, **I** 259
Kunisch, Robert D., **V** 496
Kunst und Technik Verlag, **IV** 590
de Kunwald, C.M., **I** 664
Kunzel, Herbert, **9** 297
Kuo International Ltd., **I** 566
Kuperman, Bob, **11** 52
The Kuppenheimer Company, **8** 248–50
Kurabayashi, Ikushiro, **I** 705
Kurata, Chikara, **I** 454; **IV** 101
Kurata, Okito, **IV** 148
Kureha Chemical Industry, **I** 675
Kureha Textiles, **I** 432, 492
Kuriki, Kan, **IV** 148
Kurosawa Construction Co., Ltd., **IV** 155
Kurosawa, Torizo, **II** 574
Kurose, **III** 420
Kuroyanagi, Tetsuko, **9** 30
Kurshan, Raymond, **11** 273
Kurt Möller Verlag, **7** 42
Kurtzig, Ari, **9** 35
Kurtzig, Sandra, **9** 35–37
Kurushima Dockyard, **II** 339
Kusin, Gary M., **10** 124–25
Kuter, Lawrence S., **I** 49
Kuusankoski Aktiebolag, **IV** 299
Kuwait Foreign Petroleum Exploration Co.,
   IV 451
Kuwait International Petroleum Investment
   Co., **IV** 451
Kuwait Investment Office, **II** 198; **IV** 380,
   452
Kuwait National Petroleum Co., **IV**
   450–51
Kuwait Oil Co., **IV** 450–522
Kuwait Oil Tanker Co., **IV** 451–52
Kuwait Petroleum Co., **IV** 141, 450
Kuwait Petroleum Corporation, IV 364,
   450–52, 567
Kuwait Petroleum International, **IV** 451–52
Kuwaiti Petroleum Lubricants, **IV** 452
Kuwashita, Hitomi, **11** 94
Kuykendall, Jerome, **I** 526; **10** 526
Kwaishinsha Motor Car Works, **I** 183
Kwalwasser, Edward A., **9** 371
Kwik Save Discount Group Ltd., **11** 239
Kwik Save Group plc, 11 239–41
Kwiker, Louis, **11** 556–57
KWIM. *See* Koninklijke West-Indische
   Maildienst.
Kwolek, Stephanie, **I** 329; **8** 152
KWV, **I** 289
Kyd, George, **III** 256
Kygnus Sekiyu K.K., **IV** 555
Kylberg, Lars V., **III** 420–21
Kyle, Ed, **11** 522

Kymi Paper Mills Ltd., **IV** 302
Kymmene Aktiebolag, **IV** 299
Kymmene Corporation, **IV** 276–77, **299–303**, 337
Kymmene France S.A., **IV** 302
Kymmene Oy. *See* Kymmene Corporation.
Kymmene U.K. plc, **IV** 302
Kymmene-Strömberg Corp., **IV** 300
Kyocera (Hong Kong) Ltd., **II** 51
Kyocera America, Inc., **II** 51
Kyocera Corporation, **II 50–52**; **III** 693; **7** 118
Kyocera Electronics, Inc., **II** 51
Kyocera Europa Elektronische Bauelemente GmbH, **III** 693
Kyocera Feldmühle, **III** 693
Kyocera International, Inc., **II** 50–51
Kyocera Mexicana, S.A. de C.V., **II** 51
Kyodo Dieworks Thailand Co., **III** 758
Kyodo Gyogyo Kaisha, Limited, **II** 552
Kyodo Kako, **IV** 680
Kyodo Oil Co. Ltd., **IV** 476
Kyodo Securities Co., Ltd., **II** 433
Kyodo Unyu Kaisha, **I** 502–03, 506; **IV** 713; **V** 481
Kyoei Mutual Fire and Marine Insurance Co., **III** 273
Kyoritsu Pharmaceutical Industry Co., **I** 667
Kyosai Trust Co., **II** 391
Kyoto Bank, **II** 291
Kyoto Ceramic Co., **II** 50–51
Kyoto Ouchi Bank, **II** 292
Kyowa Chemical Research Laboratory, **III** 42
Kyowa Hakko Kogyo Co., Ltd., **III 42–43**
Kyowa Sangyo, **III** 42
Kytölä, Viljo A., **IV** 315
Kyusha Refining Co., **IV** 403
Kyushu Electric Power Company Inc., **IV** 492; **V 649–51**
Kyushu Oil Refinery Co. Ltd., **IV** 434
KYZ International, **9** 427

L'Air Liquide, **I** 303, **357–59**; **11** 402
L'Air Reduction Co., **I** 358
L'Oréal, **8** 129–31; **341–44 (upd.)**; **11** 41
L'Unite Hermetique S.A., **8** 515
L.A. Darling Co., **IV** 135–36
L.A. Gear, Inc., **8 303–06**; **11** 349
L&W Supply Corp., **III** 764
L.B. DeLong, **III** 558
L. Bamberger & Co., **V** 169; **8** 443
L.C. Bassford, **III** 653
The L.D. Caulk Company, **10** 271
L.H. Parke Co., **II** 571
L.J. Knowles & Bros., **9** 153
L.L. Bean, Inc., **9** 190, 316; **10 388–90**
L.M. Electronics, **I** 489
L.M. Ericsson, **I** 462; **II** 70, 82, 365; **III** 479–80; **11** 46, 439
L.M. Ericsson Telephone Co., **II** 1, 81
L-N Glass Co., **III** 715
L-N Safety Glass, **III** 715
L-O-F Glass Fibers Co., **III** 707; **7** 292
L.S. DuBois Son and Co., **III** 10
L. Straus and Sons, **V** 168
L.W. Hammerson & Co., **IV** 696
La Barge Mirrors, **III** 571
La Cerus, **IV** 615
La Choy, **II** 467–68
La Cinq, **IV** 619
La Concorde, **III** 208

La Crosse Telephone Corporation, **9** 106
La Cruz del Campo S.A., **9** 100
La Gorce, John Oliver, **9** 367
La Quinta Inns, Inc., **11 242–44**
Laaf, Wolfgang (Dr.), **III** 695
Laakirchen, **IV** 339–40
Laan, Adriaan, **II** 527
Laan, Dirk, **II** 527
Laan, Jan, **II** 527
Laan, Raymond, **II** 528
Laan, Remmert, **II** 527
LAB. *See* Lloyd Aereo de Bolivia.
LaBakelite S.A., **I** 387
Labatt Brewing Co., **I 267–68**
Labatt, Ephraim, **I** 267
Labatt, Hugh, **I** 267–68
Labatt, John Kinder, **I** 267
Labatt, John, II, **I** 267
Labatt, John, III, **I** 267–68
Labatt, Robert, **I** 267
Labaz, **I** 676; **IV** 546
Labelcraft, Inc., **8** 360
LaBelle Iron Works, **7** 586
LaBonté, C. Joseph, **10** 383
LaBonte, Jovite, **III** 191
LaBoon, Joe T., **6** 448
Labor für Impulstechnik, **III** 154
Laboratoire Michel Robilliard, **IV** 546
Laboratoire Roger Bellon, **I** 389
Laboratoires d'Anglas, **III** 47
Laboratoires Goupil, **III** 48
Laboratoires Roche Posay, **III** 48
Laboratoires Ruby d'Anglas, **III** 48
Laboratorios Grossman, **III** 55
Laboratory for Electronics, **III** 168; **6** 284
Laborde, Alden J. "Doc," **11** 522
Laborde, C.E., Jr., **11** 522
Laborde, John, **11** 522–24
LaBour Pump, **I** 473
LaBow, Haynes Co., **III** 270
Labrunie, Gérard. *See* Nerval, Gerard de.
de Lacharrière, Marc Ladreit, **III** 47–48
Lachine Rapids Hydraulic and Land Company, **6** 501
Lachman, Charles R., **III** 54
Lachner, Grete, **V** 165–66
Lackawanna Steel & Ordnance Co., **IV** 35, 114; **7** 48
Lacombe Electric. *See* Public Service Company of Colorado.
Lacquer Products Co., **I** 321
Ladbroke City & Country Land Co., **II** 141
Ladbroke Group PLC, **II** 139, **141–42**
Ladbroke Group Properties, **II** 141
Ladbroke Retail Parks, **II** 141
Ladd, Alan, Jr., **II** 149, 170
Ladd, Howard, **II** 92
Ladd Petroleum Corp., **II** 30
LADECO, **6** 97
Ladenso, **IV** 277
Lady Foot Locker, **V** 226
Laeisz, Ferdinand, **6** 397
Laemmle, Carl, **II** 135
Lafarge, Auguste Pavin de, **III** 703
Lafarge Canada, **III** 704
Lafarge Cement of North America, **III** 704
Lafarge Coppée S.A., **III** 702, **703–05**, 736; **8** 258; **10** 422–23
Lafarge Corp., **III** 705
Lafarge, Edouard, **III** 703
Lafarge, Edouard, II, **III** 703
Lafarge family, **III** 704
Lafarge, Joseph, **III** 703
Lafarge, Leon, **III** 703

Lafarge, Paul, **III** 703
Lafarge, Raphaël, **III** 703
Lafayette Radio Electronics Corporation, **9** 121–22
Lafitte, Pierre, **IV** 618
Laflin & Rand, **I** 328
Laflin & Rand Powder Co., **I** 328; **III** 525
LaForge, Abiel T., **V** 168; **8** 442
LaFrankie, James V., **6** 444
LAG&E. *See* Los Angeles Gas and Electric Company.
Lagardère, Jean-Luc, **IV** 617–19
Lagoven, **IV** 508
LaGuardia, Fiorello, **IV** 582
Laguionie, Gustave, **V** 9
Laidlaw, Sir Christophor, **6** 241–42
Laidlaw Transportation, Inc., **6** 410
Laing, **IV** 696
Laing, David, **I** 575
Laing, Hector, **II** 593–94
Laing, James, **I** 575
Laing, James Maurice, **I** 576
Laing, John, **I** 575
Laing, John William, **I** 575–76
Laing, Martin, **I** 575–76
Laing, R. Stanley, **III** 152; **6** 266
Laing, William Kirby, **I** 576
Laing's Properties Ltd., **I** 575
Laird, Melvin, **10** 287
Laister, Peter, **I** 52
Laitaatsillan Konepaja, **IV** 275
Lake Arrowhead Development Co., **IV** 255
Lake Central Airlines, **I** 131; **6** 131
Lake, Charles W., Jr., **IV** 661
Lake Erie Screw Corp., **11** 534, 536
Lake, Pete, **7** 228
Lake Superior Consolidated Iron Mines, **IV** 572; **7** 549
Lakeland Fire and Casualty Co., **III** 213
Läkemedels-Industri Föreningen, **I** 664
Laker Airways, **6** 79
Laker Airways Skytrain, **I** 94
Laker, Freddie (Sir), **I** 94, 117, 120
Lakeside Laboratories, **III** 24
The Lakeside Publishing and Printing Co., **IV** 660
Lakestone Systems, Inc., **11** 469
Lalley, John, **V** 496
Lam, David, **11** 245
Lam Research, **IV** 213
Lam Research Corporation, **11 245–47**
Lam Technology Center, **11** 246
Lamb, George C., Jr., **V** 534
Lamb, Larry, **IV** 651; **7** 391
Lamb, Roland O., **III** 266
Lamb Technicon Corp., **I** 486
Lamb-Weston, **II** 417
Lambert, Allan, **II** 456
Lambert Brothers, Inc., **7** 573
Lambert Brussels Financial Corporation, **11** 532
Lambert Brussels Witter, **II** 407
Lambert family, **II** 407
Lambert, Gerard, **III** 28
Lambert, Henri, **II** 201
Lambert, Hope, **I** 143
Lambert, James (Sir), **III** 370
Lambert Kay Company, **8** 84
Lambert, Léon, **II** 201, 407
Lambert Pharmacal Co., **I** 710–11; **III** 28
Lambert, Samuel, **II** 201
Lamkin Brothers, Inc., **8** 386
Lamm, Oscar, **III** 417–18, 425
Lamm, Oscar, Jr., **III** 417

Lamond, Pierre, **II** 64; **6** 262
Lamons Metal Gasket Co., **III** 570; **11** 535
Lamont, Robert P., **7** 29–30
Lamont, Thomas, **II** 330
Lamontagne Ltd., **II** 651
LaMothe, William E., **II** 525
Lampard, Arthur, **III** 696–97
Lamport, Hiram H., **III** 239–40
Lamprecht, J.I., **IV** 372
Lamson Bros., **II** 451
Lamson Corporation, **7** 145
Lamson Industries Ltd., **IV** 645
Lamson Store Service Co., **IV** 644
Lancashire, **III** 350
Lancashire, Ben, **8** 268
Lancaster, Beverly, **8** 315
Lancaster Caramel Co., **II** 510
Lancaster Colony Corporation, 8 307–09
Lancaster Cork Works, **III** 422
Lancaster National Bank, **9** 475
Lancia, **I** 162; **11** 102
Lancôme, **III** 46–48; **8** 342
Land, Edwin H., **III** 475, 607–09; **7** 162,
   436–38
Land O'Lakes Creameries, Inc., **II** 535
Land O'Lakes, Inc., II 535–37; **7** 339
Land Securities Assets Co. Ltd., **IV** 704
Land Securities Investment Trust Ltd., **IV**
   704–06
Land Securities PLC, IV 704–06
Land-Wheelwright Laboratories, **III** 607; **7**
   436
Landau, Basil, **IV** 92
Landau, Jacob, **I** 409
Lander Alarm Co., **III** 740
Länderbank, **II** 282
Landesbank für Westfalen Girozentrale,
   Münster, **II** 385
Landis, Dick, **7** 132
Landis International, Inc., **10** 105–06
Landmark Banks, **10** 426
Landmark Financial Services Inc., **11** 447
Landmark Target Media, **IV** 597
Lando, Barry, **II** 133
Landon, Alf, **IV** 626
Landon, Jervis, Jr., **V** 439
Landor Associates, **I** 94
Landry, John, **11** 77
Lands' End, Inc., 9 314–16
Landsdowne, Helen, **I** 19
Lane Bryant, **V** 115–16
The Lane Co., Inc., **III** 528, 530
Lane, Frank, **6** 117
Lane, Fred, **IV** 530
Lane, John, **IV** 601
Lane Processing Inc., **II** 585
Lane Publishing Co., **IV** 676; **7** 529
Lane, Robert H., **V** 246
Lane Rossi, **IV** 421
Lane, William N., **10** 313
Laneco, Inc., **II** 682
Lang, James, **II** 593
Langdon, Jervis, Jr., **10** 73
Lange, Maxwell & Springer, **IV** 641; **7**
   311
Langeler, Gerard, **11** 284
Langen, Dieter von, **II** 164
Langen, Eugen, **III** 541
Langford Labs, **8** 25
Langmuir, Irving, **II** 28–29
Langrand-Dumonceau, A. (Count), **III** 177
Langton, Bryan, **III** 95
Langworth, Richard M., **I** 145
Lanier Business Products, **8** 407

Lanier Business Products, Inc., **II** 39
Lanier, George, **8** 566
Lanier, Hicks, **8** 406
Lanier, John Hicks, **8** 407–08
Lanier, Joseph, Jr., **8** 567
Lanier, Lafayette, **8** 566
Lanier, Sartain, **8** 406–08
Lanier, Tommy, **8** 406–07
Lanier Voice Products, **II** 39
Lanier Worldwide, Inc., **II** 39
Lanigan, Robert, **I** 610
Lanne, Adolphe, **III** 210
Lanners, Fred T., **I** 331
Lannig, Charles, **I** 382
Lano Corp., **I** 446
Lansdowne (Lord), **III** 521
Lansi-Suomen Osake-Pankki, **II** 303
Lansing, Sherry, **II** 170
Lanson Pere et Fils, **II** 475
Lanterman, Joseph B., **7** 30
Lantic Industries, Inc., **II** 664
Lantic Sugar Ltd., **II** 664
Lanvin, **I** 696; **III** 48; **8** 343
Lanz, Kurt, **I** 348
Lanza, A.J. (Dr.), **III** 706; **7** 291
Lanza, Frank, **9** 323
Lanzafame, Samuel, **7** 408
LAPE. *See* Líneas Aéreas Postales
   Españolas.
Lapensky, Joseph M., **I** 113; **6** 104
Lapin, Raymond H., **II** 411
Lapine Technology, **II** 51
Laporte, **I** 303
Laporte Industries Ltd., **IV** 300
LaPorte, William F., **I** 622, 624; **10** 68, 70
Lapp, **8** 229
Larche, John, **9** 281–82
Large, Judson, **6** 312
Larimer, William, **II** 315
Larkin, Frederick, Jr., **II** 349
Laroche, Guy, **8** 129
Laroche Navarron, **I** 703
Larousse Group, **IV** 615
Larousse, Pierre, **IV** 614
Larousse-Nathan, **IV** 614–15
Larroque, Louis, **I** 519; **IV** 215
Larsen & Toubro, **IV** 484
Larsen Company, **7** 128
Larsen, Ralph S., **III** 37; **8** 283
Larsen, Roy E., **IV** 674; **7** 527
Larson, Elwin S., **6** 455–57
Larson, Gary, **III** 13; **6** 386
Larson, Gustav, **I** 209; **7** 565–66
Larson Lumber Co., **IV** 306
Larwin Group, **III** 231
Lasala, Joseph, **II** 316
LaSalle National Bank, **II** 184
LaSalles & Koch Co., **8** 443
Lasell, Chester, **II** 432
Oy Läskelä Ab, **IV** 300
Lasker, Albert, **I** 12–13, 25, 36
Lasky, David, **10** 263
Lasky, Jesse, **II** 154
Lasky's, **II** 141
Lasmo, **IV** 455, 499
Lasser, J.K., **IV** 671
Lassila, Jaakko, **IV** 349
Latécoère, Pierre, **V** 471
Lathière, Bernard, **I** 41
Latrobe, Ferdinand C., **III** 395
Latrobe Steel Company, **8** 529–31
Lattès, Jean-Claude, **IV** 617, 619
Latzer, John, **7** 428–29

Latzer, Louis, **7** 428–29
Latzer, Robert, **7** 429
Laubach, Gerald, **I** 663; **9** 404
Lauder, Estée, **9** 201–02, 290
Lauder, Evelyn, **9** 202, 204
Lauder, Joseph, **9** 201–03
Lauder, Leonard, **9** 201–04
Lauder, Ronald, **9** 202–04
Lauder, William, **9** 204
Lauer, John N., **V** 233
Laughlin, James, **II** 342
Lauman, J.F., **II** 681
Laura Scudder's, **7** 429
Lauren, Ralph, **III** 55; **8** 130–31, 408
Laurentien Hotel Co., **III** 99
Laurenzo, Vince, **III** 652
Lauson Engine Company, **8** 515
Lautenberg, Frank, **III** 117–18
Lautenberg, Frank R., **9** 48
de Laval, Carl Gustaf Patrik, **7** 235
de Laval, Gustaf, **II** 1; **III** 417–19
Laval, Gustaf de. *See* de Laval, Gustaf.
Lavanchy, Henri-Ferdinand, **6** 9
Laventhol, David, **IV** 678
Lavin, Leonard H., **8** 15–17
Lavine, Larry, **10** 176
LaVoisier, Antoine, **I** 328
Law Life Assurance Society, **III** 372
Lawn Boy, **7** 535–36
Lawn Boy Inc., **8** 72
Lawrence, Harding, **I** 96–97
Lawrence, John, **III** 472
Lawrence Manufacturing Co., **III** 526
Lawrence, T.E., **I** 194
Lawrence Warehouse Co., **II** 397–98; **10**
   62
Lawrenceburg Gas Company, **6** 466
Lawrenceburg Gas Transmission
   Corporation, **6** 466
The Lawson Co., **7** 113
Lawson, Dominic, **III** 503
Lawson Milk, **II** 572
Lawson-Johnston, Peter, **9** 363
Lawyers Cooperative, **8** 528
Lawyers Cooperative Publishing Company,
   8 527
Lawyers Trust Co., **II** 230
Laxalt, Paul, **III** 188
Lay, Beirne, **I** 486
Lay, Herman, **I** 278; **III** 136; **10** 452
Layne & Bowler Pump, **11** 5
Layton, F.D., **III** 229
Layton, Joseph E., **8** 515
Lazard Bros. & Co., **IV** 658–59
Lazard Frères, **II** 268, 402, 422; **IV** 23, 79,
   659; **7** 287, 446; **10** 399
Lazard Freres and Company, **6** 356
Lazarus, Charles, **V** 203–06
Lazarus, Fred, **V** 26–27
Lazarus, Fred, Jr., **9** 209–10
Lazarus, Hyman (Judge), **IV** 581–82
Lazarus, Ralph, **V** 26; **9** 210–11
Lazarus, Wilhelm, **III** 206
Lazell, H.G. Leslie, **III** 65–66
Lazenby, Robert S., **9** 177
LBS Communications, **6** 28
LDDS Communications, Inc., **7** 336
LDDS-Metro Communications, Inc., 8
   310–12
LDX NET, Inc., **IV** 576
Le Brun and Sons, **III** 291
Le Buffet System-Gastronomie, **V** 74
Le Courviour S.A., **10** 351
Lea & Perrins, **II** 475

Lea County Gas Co., **6** 580
Lea, R.W., **III** 707; **7** 292
Lead Industries Group Ltd., **III** 681; **IV** 108
Leadership Housing Inc., **IV** 136
Leaf River Forest Products Inc., **IV** 282, 300; **9** 261
Leahy, Patrick, **III** 188
Leaman, June, **9** 202
Leamington Priors & Warwickshire Banking Co., **II** 318
Lear Inc., **II** 61; **8** 49, 51
Lear, John, **I** 662; **9** 403
Lear Romec Corp., **8** 135
Lear Siegler Inc., **I** 481–83; **III** 581
Lear Siegler Seating Corp., **III** 581
Lear, William Powell, **8** 313–16
Lear-Siegler Inc., **8** 313
Learjet Inc., **8** 313–16; **9** 242
Learned, Stanley, **IV** 522
Leasco Data Processing Equipment Corp., **III** 342–44; **IV** 641–42; **7** 311
Lease International SA, **6** 358
Leaseway Transportation, **V** 494
Leatherdale, Douglas W., **III** 357
Leavey, W.M., **IV** 708
Leblanc, Nicolas, **I** 394
LeBlanc, R.A., **11** 225, 227
LeBow, Bennett S., **11** 274–75
Leca, Dominique, **III** 393
Lecerf, Olivier, **III** 704–05
Lechmere Inc., **10** 391–93
Lechter, Albert, **11** 248
Lechters, Inc., **11** 248–50
Lecklider, Ben D., **11** 369
Leclerc, Edouard, **10** 204
Ledder, Edward J., **I** 619–20; **11** 7–8
Ledebur, Adolf, **IV** 156
Lederle Laboratories, **I** 300–02, 657, 684
Lederle Labs, **8** 24–25
Ledoux, Fréderic, **IV** 107
Lee, A.W., **11** 251–53
Lee Apparel Company, Inc., **8** 317–19
Lee, Archie, **I** 233; **10** 226
Lee Brands, **II** 500
Lee, Byung-Chull, **I** 515–16
Lee Company, **V** 390–92
Lee Enterprises, Incorporated, **11** 251–53
Lee, Frank A., **6** 145–46
Lee, George, **9** 105–06
Lee Hecht Harrison, **6** 10
Lee, Henry David, **8** 317–18
Lee, Kun-Hee, **I** 516
Lee, Kyung Hoon, **III** 458
Lee, Quo Wei, **IV** 717
Lee, Sung Won, **III** 749
Lee Telephone Company, **6** 313
Lee, W. S., **V** 601
Lee, Wallace L., **6** 447–48
Lee Way Motor Freight, **I** 278
Lee, William, **11** 539
Lee, William S., **V** 601–02
Leeds & County Bank, **II** 318
Leeds & Northrup Co., **III** 644–45
Leeman, Hermann, **I** 671–72
Lees, David, **III** 495
Lefaucheux, Pierre, **I** 189
LeFauve, Richard G., **7** 462
Lefebre, Pierre, **I** 188
Lefébure, Charles, **I** 395
Lefebvre, Andre, **7** 36
Lefebvre, Gordon, **II** 15
Lefeldt, **III** 417, 418

Lefeldt, Wilhelm, **III** 417
Lefevre, Jacques, **III** 705
Lefrak Organization, **8** 357
Legal & General Assurance Society, **III** 272–73
Legal & General Group plc, **III** 272–73; **IV** 705, 712
Legal & General Life Assurance Society, **III** 272
Legal & General Netherlands, **III** 273
Legault and Masse, **II** 664
Legent Corporation, **10** 394–96
Legg, Mason & Co., **11** 493
Leggett & Platt, Incorporated, **9** 93; **11** 254–56
Leggett, J.P., **11** 254
Leggett, J.P., Jr., **11** 254
Leggett, Will, **V** 12
Lehigh Railroad, **III** 258
Lehman Bros., **I** 78, 125, 484; **II** 259, 448; **6** 199; **10** 63; **11** 263–64
Lehman Bros. Kuhn Loeb, **II** 192, 398, 450–51; **10** 62
Lehman, Clarence, **7** 592
Lehman, Fred, Jr., **9** 411
Lehman, John, **I** 59, 62, 527; **11** 165
Lehman, Robert, **I** 89
Lehmer Company, **6** 312. *See also* McGraw Electric Company.
Lehmkuhl, Joakim, **7** 531
Lehmkuhl, Lawrence A., **11** 459–60
Lehn & Fink, **I** 699
Lehnkering AG, **IV** 140
Lehr, Lewis, **I** 500; **8** 371
Lehrman Bros., **III** 419
Lehrman, Jacob, **II** 633–34
Lehrman, Samuel, **II** 633
Lehtinen, William, **III** 276–77
Leibovitz, Mitchell, **11** 391–93
Leigh, Claude Moss, **IV** 710–11
Leigh, George, **11** 452
Leigh, R. Walter, **11** 13
Leigh, Vivien, **II** 148, 175
Leigh-Pemberton, Robin, **II** 334
Leighton, Charles M., **10** 215
Leinenkugel, **I** 253
Leipsner, Steven, **7** 472–73
Leisen, Mitchell, **II** 155
Leisenring, E.B., **7** 582
Leisenring, Edward B., Jr., (Ted), **7** 583–84
Leisure Lodges, **III** 76
Leitz, **III** 583–84
Leland, Glenn, **8** 517
Leland, Henry, **I** 171; **10** 325
Leland, Marc, **9** 112
Lemaire, Raymond, **10** 482
Leman, Paul H., **IV** 11
LeMasters, Kim, **II** 134; **6** 159
LeMay, Curtis, **9** 368
Lemmen, Harvey, **7** 331
Lena Goldfields Ltd., **IV** 94
Lenard, Phillip, **I** 349
Lenc-Smith, **III** 430
Lend Lease Corporation Limited, **IV** 707–09
Lend Lease Development Pty. Ltd., **IV** 708
Lendrum, Jim, **III** 704–05
Lengnick, Lewis W., **9** 276
Lenhartz, Rudolf, **IV** 198
Lenin, Vladimir, **IV** 299, 480; **9** 148
Lennar Corporation, **11** 257–59
Lennar Financial Services, Inc., **11** 257–59
Lennings, Manfred, **III** 563

Lennon's, **II** 628
Lennox, Dave, **8** 320
Lennox Furnace Company, **8** 320
Lennox Industries (Canada) Ltd., **8** 321
Lennox Industries Inc., **8** 320–22
Lennox International Inc., **8** 320–22
Lenoir Chair Company, **10** 183
Lenoir Furniture Corporation, **10** 183
Lenox Awards, **7** 256
Lenox Inc., **I** 227; **10** 179, 181
Lens Crafters, **V** 207–08
Lent, John A., **IV** 583
Lentheric, **I** 426
Lenton, Aylmer, **IV** 259
Lenz, Randolph W., **7** 513–14
Leo, **I** 665
Leo Burnett Co., **I** 22–24, 25, 31, 37; **11** 51, 212
Leonard Development Group, **10** 508
Leonard Express, Inc., **6** 371
Leonard, H.S., **III** 669
Leonardo Editore, **IV** 587
Leonberger Bausparkasse, **II** 258
Leone, William, **8** 349–50
Leonis, John M., **11** 265
Léopold II (Belgium), **II** 201
Lepco Co., **III** 596
Leppart, John, **I** 379
Lepper, David, **IV** 332
Lern, Inc., **II** 420
Lerner Plastics, **9** 323
Lerner, Sandra, **11** 58–59
Lerner Stores, **V** 116
Leroux, Charles, **IV** 107
Les Chantiers de l'Atlantique, **II** 13
Lesch, George H., **III** 23
Lesch, James, **III** 428
Lescure, Pierre, **10** 195
Leser, Lawrence A., **IV** 608
Lesher, John L., **10** 174
Leshner, Zane, **7** 506
The Leslie Fay Companies, Inc., **8** 323–25
Leslie, Jim, **6** 111
Leslie Paper, **IV** 288
de Lespaul, Adolphe Demeure, **IV** 498–99
Lessard, Pierre, **II** 652
Lesser-Goldman, **II** 18
Lester B. Knight & Associates, **II** 19
Lestrem Group, **IV** 296
Let op Uw Einde, **III** 199
Letts, Arthur, **V** 29
Leucadia National, **6** 396
Leucadia National Corporation, **11** 260–62
Leuna-Werke AG, **7** 142
Leutwiler, Fritz, **II** 4
Level, Jacques, **IV** 173–74
N.V. Levensverzekering Maatschappji Utrecht, **III** 199–200
Léveque, Jean-Maxime, **9** 148
Lever Brothers Company, **I** 17, 21, 26, 30, 333; **II** 497, 588–89; **III** 31; **7** 542–43, 545; **9** 291, 317–19
Lever, James, **II** 588; **9** 317
Lever, William Hesketh, **II** 588–89; **7** 542; **9** 317
Leverhulme, Lord. *See* Lever, William Hesketh.
Leverone, Nathaniel, **10** 301
Levésque, René, **III** 708
Leveton, Richard, **9** 181
Levi, Masino, **III** 206–07

Levi Strauss & Co., **I** 15; **II** 634, 669; **V** 60–61, **362–65**; **9** 142
Levi-Strauss, Claude, **IV** 586
Levin, Meyer, **IV** 672
Levine, Dennis, **II** 408
Levine, Huntley, Vick & Beaver, **6** 28
Levine, Jack, **II** 663
Levine, Robert, **10** 193–94
Levitt & Sons, **IV** 728
Levitt Homes, **I** 464; **11** 198
Levy Bakery Goods, **I** 30
Levy, Ben, **II** 447–48
Levy, Gustave, **II** 415
Levy, Ira, **9** 202
Levy, Irvin L., **8** 385–86
Levy, Kenneth, **11** 231–32
Levy, Lester A., **8** 385
Levy, Milton P., **8** 385
Levy, Milton P., Jr., **8** 385
Levy, Ruth, **8** 385–86
Lew, Solomon, **V** 34
Lewellyn, Gary V., **10** 474
Lewinsky, Herbert (Dr.), **IV** 234
Lewis and Marks, **IV** 21–22, 96
Lewis Batting Company, **11** 219
Lewis Construction, **IV** 22
Lewis, David, **I** 58–59; **10** 316–17
Lewis, Drew, **V** 531
Lewis, Essington, **IV** 45–46
Lewis, George T., **I** 382
Lewis, George T., Jr., **10** 229
Lewis Grocer Co., **II** 669
Lewis, Henry, **11** 387
Lewis, John C., **III** 110–11; **10** 558
Lewis, John Spedan, **V** 93–95
Lewis, L. Ben, **II** 383
Lewis, Marilyn Ware, **6** 444
Lewis, Morris, Sr., **II** 669
Lewis, O.F., **10** 328
Lewis, Robert, **III** 373
Lewis, Robert E., **7** 426
Lewis, Roger, **I** 58; **10** 316
Lewis, Salim L. (Cy), **II** 400–01; **10** 144–45
Lewis, Sinclair, **IV** 622
Lewis, Tony, **III** 740
Lewis, William R., **10** 383
Lewis's, **V** 178
Lewis's Bank, **II** 308
Lewis-Howe Co., **III** 56
Lewisohn, Adolph, **IV** 31
Lewisohn brothers, **IV** 31
Lewisohn, Leonard, **IV** 31
Lex Electronics, **10** 113
Lex Service, **10** 113
Lexington Broadcast Services, **6** 27
Lexington Furniture Industries, **III** 571
Lexington Ice Company, **6** 514
Lexington Insurance Co., **III** 197
Lexington Utilities Company, **6** 514; **11** 237
Lexitron, **II** 87
Lexmark International, Inc., **9** 116; **10** 519
Ley, Hellmut, **IV** 141
Leybold AG, **IV** 71
Leyland and Birmingham Rubber Co., **I** 429
Leyland Motor Corporation, **7** 459
LFC Financial, **10** 339
LFE Corp., **7** 297
LG&E Energy Corp., **6 516–18**
LG&E Energy Systems Inc., **6** 518
LG&E Power Systems Inc., **6** 518
Lhomme S.A., **8** 477

Li Ka-shing, **I** 470; **IV** 693–94, 695
Liaoyang Automotive Spring Factory, **III** 581
Libbey, Edward D., **III** 640
Libbey-Glass Co., **I** 609; **III** 640
Libbey-Owens Sheet Glass Co., **III** 640–41, 731; **IV** 421
Libbey-Owens-Ford Glass Co., **III** 640–42, 707, 714–15, 725–26, 731
Libby, **II** 547; **7** 382
Libby McNeil & Libby Inc., **II** 489
Libeltex, **9** 92
Libenson, Richard M., **V** 164
Liberty Bank of Buffalo, **9** 229
Liberty Brokerage Investment Company, **10** 278
Liberty House, **I** 417–18
Liberty Life, **IV** 91, 97
Liberty Mexicana, **III** 415
Liberty Mutual Insurance Co., **I** 28
Liberty Mutual Insurance Group, **11** 379
Liberty National Bank, **II** 229
Liberty National Insurance Holding Co., **9** 506, 508
Liberty National Life Insurance Co., **III** 217; **9** 506–07
Liberty Natural Gas Co., **11** 441
Libman, Robert H., **V** 674
Libra Bank Ltd., **II** 271
Librairie de Jacques-Francois Brétif, **IV** 617
Librairie Fayard, **IV** 618
Librairie Générale Francaise, **IV** 618
Librairie Larousse, **IV** 614–16
Librairie Louis Hachette, **IV** 617–18
Librairie Nathan, **IV** 614, 616
Librairie Victor Lecou, **IV** 617
Libyan Arab Airline, **6** 85
Libyan Arab Foreign Bank, **IV** 454
Libyan Arab Foreign Investment Co., **IV** 454
Libyan General Petroleum Corp., **IV** 453
Libyan National Oil Corporation, **IV 453–55**
Libyan-Turkish Engineering and Consultancy Corp., **IV** 563
Lichtenberg, Paul, **II** 257
Lichtenberger, H. William, **11** 403
Lichtman, Al, **II** 146
Liddy, G. Gordon, **11** 191
Lidköpings Mekaniska Verkstad AB, **III** 623
Liebe, Bodo, **III** 543–44
Lieberman, Leonard, **II** 674
Liebert Corp., **II** 20
Liebknecht, Otto, **IV** 70
Liebling, A.J., **IV** 582
Liedtke brothers, **IV** 489–90
Liedtke, J. Hugh, **IV** 488–90
Liedtke, William, **IV** 489
Life and Casualty Insurance Co. of Tennessee, **III** 193
Life Assoc. of Scotland, **III** 310
Life Fitness Inc., **III** 431
Life Insurance Co. of Georgia, **III** 310
Life Insurance Co. of Scotland, **III** 358
Life Insurance Co. of Virginia, **III** 204
Life Insurance Securities, Ltd., **III** 288
Life Investors, **III** 179
Life of Eire, **III** 273
Life Savers Co., **II** 129, 544; **7** 367
Life Science Research, Inc., **10** 105–07
Life Technologies Inc., **I** 321
Lifecycle, Inc., **III** 431

LifeLink, **11** 378
Lifemark Corp., **III** 74
LIFETIME, **IV** 627
Lift Parts Manufacturing, **I** 157
Ligand Pharmaceutical, **10** 48
Liggett & Meyers, **V** 396, 405, 417–18
Liggett Group, **I** 248; **7** 105
Light Corrugated Box Co., **IV** 332
Light, Frank, **7** 496–97
Light-Servicos de Eletricidade S.A., **II** 456
Lightel Inc., **6** 311
Lighting Corp. of America, **I** 476
Lightner, Milton, **II** 9–10
LIGHTNET, **IV** 576
Lightwell Co., **III** 634
Lignum Oil Co., **IV** 658
Liguori, Frank N., **6** 42–43
LILCO. *See* Long Island Lighting Company.
Liliuokalani, **I** 565
Lillard, John, **IV** 703
Lillehei, C. Walton, **8** 351
de Lilliac, René Granier. *See* Granier de Lilliac, René.
Lillie, John M., **6** 355
Lilliput Group plc, **11** 95
Lilly & Co. *See* Eli Lilly & Co.
Lilly, David, **7** 534–35
Lilly, Eli, **I** 645; **11** 89
Lilly, Eli, Jr., **11** 89
Lilly, Josiah, **I** 645; **11** 89
Lilly, Josiah, Jr., **I** 645; **11** 89
Lillybrook Coal Co., **IV** 180
Lillywhites Ltd., **III** 105
Lily Tulip Co., **I** 609, 611
Lily-Tulip Inc., **8** 198
Limbaugh, Rush, **11** 330
Limburger Fabrik und Hüttenverein, **IV** 103
Limited Express, **V** 115
Limited, Inc., **V 115–16**; **9** 142
Limmer and Trinidad Ltd., **III** 752
LIN Broadcasting Corp., **II** 331; **6** 323; **9 320–22**; **11** 330
Lin Data Corp., **11** 234
Lincoln, Abraham, **II** 247, 284; **III** 239, 275, 315, 505; **IV** 604, 647, 668, 682; **8** 222; **11** 186
Lincoln American Life Insurance Co., **10** 246
Lincoln Benefit Life Company, **10** 51
Lincoln Electric, **II** 19
Lincoln Electric Motor Works, **9** 439
Lincoln First Bank, **II** 248
Lincoln Income Life Insurance Co., **10** 246
Lincoln, John, **9** 439
Lincoln, Leroy A., **III** 292
Lincoln Liberty Life Insurance Co., **III** 254
Lincoln Life Improved Housing, **III** 276
Lincoln Motor Co., **I** 165
Lincoln National Corporation, **III 274–77**; **6** 195; **10** 44
Lincoln National Life Insurance Co., **III** 274–76
Lincoln Philippine Life Insurance Co., **III** 276
Lincoln Property Company, **8 326–28**
Lincoln, Robert, **11** 385
Lincoln, Robert Todd, **III** 274
Lincoln Savings, **10** 340
Lincoln Savings & Loan, **9** 199
LinCom Corp., **8** 327

Lindbergh, Charles A., **I** 78, 89, 125; **II** 151; **III** 27, 251; **IV** 370; **7** 35; **9** 416; **11** 427
Lindblom, C.G., **III** 478
Linde A.G., **I** 297–98, 315, **581–83**; **10** 31–32
Linde Air Products Co., **I** 582; **9** 16, 516; **11** 402
Linde Company, **11** 402–03
Lindemann, Karl, **6** 398
Lindemann's, **I** 220
Linden, Arthur, **II** 2
Linder, David, **V** 442
Lindex, **II** 640
Lindh, Björnz-Eric, **I** 211
Lindner, Carl Henry, **I** 453; **II** 596, 619; **III** 190–92; **7** 84–86; **8** 537; **9** 452; **10** 73
Lindner, Carl, **III**, **10** 74
Lindner, Richard E., **III** 190
Lindner, Robert D., **III** 190
Lindsay Parkinson & Co., **I** 567
Lindustries, **III** 502; **7** 208
Linear Corp., **III** 643
Líneas Aéreas Postales Españolas, **6** 95
Linehan, Joel, **III** 430
Linen, James A., III, **IV** 674; **7** 527
Linen, Jonathon, **9** 470
Linfood Holdings Ltd., **II** 628–29
Ling Electric Co., **I** 489
Ling Electronics Inc., **I** 489
Ling, James J., **I** 489–91
Ling-Temco-Vought. *See* LTV Corporation.
Linjeflyg, **I** 120
Link, Gordon, **6** 16
Link House Publications PLC, **IV** 687
Link-Belt Corp., **I** 443; **IV** 660
Linkletter, Art, **IV** 83; **7** 187
Lint, Amos, **I** 201
Lintas Worldwide, **I** 18; **6** 30
Linton, Robert E., **II** 407–08; **8** 388–89
Lintott Engineering, Ltd., **10** 108
Lion Corporation, **III 44–45**
Lion Dentrifice Co., Ltd., **III** 44
Lion Fat & Oil Co., Ltd., **III** 44
Lion Manufacturing, **III** 430
Lion Oil, **I** 365
Lion Products Co., Ltd., **III** 44
Lion Soap Co., Ltd., **III** 44
Lion's Head Brewery, **I** 290
Lipman, Frederick, **II** 382
Lipper, Kenneth, **I** 631
Lippincott & Margulies, **III** 283
Lippincott, Philip E., **IV** 330–31
Lipson, Norman S., **II** 649
Lipton, **11** 450
Liptons, **II** 609, 657
Liquid Carbonic, **7** 74, 77
Liquor Barn, **II** 656
Liquorland, **V** 35
Liquorsave, **II** 609–10
LIRCA, **III** 48
Lisbon Coal and Oil Fuel Co., **IV** 504
Liscaya, **II** 196
Lissarrague, Pierre, **I** 46
Lister, Joseph, **III** 35
Litchfield, Paul W., **V** 244–46
Litco Bancorp., **II** 192
Litho-Krome Corp., **IV** 621
Litronix, **III** 455
Little, Arthur D., **IV** 92
Little, Brown & Company, **IV** 675; **7** 528; **10** 355

Little Caesar International, Inc., **7 278–79**; **7** 278–79
Little Chef Ltd., **III** 105–06
Little General, **II** 620
Little Giant Pump Company, **8** 515
Little, Royal, **I** 529–30; **8** 545
Little Tikes Co., **III** 614
Little, W. Norris, **9** 466
Littlewoods Mail Order Stores, **V** 117
Littlewoods Organisation PLB, **V 117–19**
Littlewoods Warehouses, **V** 118
Litton, Charles, **I** 484; **11** 263
Litton Industries Credit Corp., **III** 293
Litton Industries Inc., **I** 85, 452, 476, **484–86**, 523–24; **II** 33; **III** 473, 732; **IV** 253; **6** 599; **10** 520–21, 537; **11 263–65** (**upd.**), 435
Litton Resources Group, **III** 473
Litwin Engineers & Constructors, **8** 546
Livanos, **III** 516
Lively, Tom, **8** 87–88
Liverpool (Lord), **II** 306
Liverpool and London and Globe Insurance Co., **III** 234, 350
Liverpool and London Fire and Life Insurance Co., **III** 349
Liverpool Fire and Life Insurance Co., **III** 350
Liversidge, Horace P., **11** 388
Livesey, George, **V** 559–60
Livia, **I** 154; **10** 279
Livia, Anna, **IV** 295
Living Videotext, **10** 508
Livingston Communications, **6** 313
Livingston, Crawford, **II** 395; **10** 59
Livingston, Fargo and Co., **II** 380, 395; **10** 59
Livingston, Homer, **II** 284
Liz Claiborne, Inc., **8 329–31**
Ljungberg, Erik Johan, **IV** 336
Ljungström, Gunnar, **I** 197; **11** 438
LKB-Produkter AB, **I** 665
Llewellyn, John S., Jr., **7** 404
Lloyd A. Fry Roofing, **III** 721
Lloyd Adriatico S.p.A., **III** 377
Lloyd Aereo de Bolivia, **6** 97
Lloyd, Charles, **II** 306
Lloyd, Charles, II, **II** 306
Lloyd, Edward, **III** 278; **IV** 257
Lloyd, Harold, **II** 155, 307, 309
Lloyd, Ian, **I** 196
Lloyd Italico, **III** 351
Lloyd, James, **II** 306
Lloyd, John, **III** 508
Lloyd, Louis, **11** 418
Lloyd, Sampson Samuel, **II** 306–07
Lloyd, Sampson, II, **II** 306–07
Lloyd, Sampson, III, **II** 306
Lloyd Webber, Andrew, **6** 162
Lloyd's of London, **III** 234, **278–81**; **9** 297; **10** 38; **11** 533
Lloyd-Smith, Parker, **IV** 673; **7** 526
Lloyds Abbey Life, **II** 309
Lloyds and Bolsa International Bank, **II** 308
Lloyds and Co., **II** 306
Lloyds Bank Europe, **II** 308
Lloyds Bank International, **II** 308–09
Lloyds Bank Ltd., **II** 307
Lloyds Bank PLC, **II 306–09** 319, 334, 358
Lloyds Bank Property Co., **II** 308
Lloyds Banking Co. Ltd., **II** 306

Lloyds, Barnetts and Bosanquets Bank Ltd., **II** 306
Lloyds Leasing, **II** 309
Lloyds Life Assurance, **III** 351
Lloyds Merchant Bank, **II** 309
LM Ericsson. *See* Telefonaktiebolaget LM Ericsson.
LME. *See* Telefonaktiebolaget LM Ericsson.
LNG Co., **IV** 473–74
Lo-Cost, **II** 609
Lo-Vaca Gathering Co., **IV** 394; **7** 553
Loadometer Co., **III** 435
Lobitos Oilfields Ltd., **IV** 381–82
Loblaw Cos., **II** 632
Loblaw Groceterias, **II** 631
Local Data, Inc., **10** 97
Locations, Inc., **IV** 727
Locke, Charles, **I** 371–72; **9** 358–59, 501
Locke, Lancaster and W.W.&R. Johnson & Sons, **III** 680
Lockhart Catering, **III** 104
Lockhart, Charles, **IV** 375
Lockheed Aircraft Company, **9** 12
Lockheed, Allan, **9** 12; **11** 266, 363
Lockheed Corporation, **I** 13, 41, 48, 50, 52, 54, 61, 63, **64–66**, 67–68, 71–72, 74, 76–77, 82, 84, 90, 92–94, 100, 102, 107, 110, 113, 121, 126, 195, 493–94, 529; **II** 19, 32–33; **III** 84, 539, 601; **IV** 15; **6** 71; **9** 17–18, 272, 417, 458–60, 501; **10** 163, 262–63, 317, 536; **11** 164, 166, **266–69 (upd.)**, 278–79, 363–65
Lockheed, Malcolm, **11** 266
Lockheed Missiles and Space Company, **6** 149
Lockwood Banc Group, Inc., **11** 306
Lockwoods Foods Ltd., **II** 513
Loctite Corporation, **8 332–34**
Lodder, Bryan, **8** 234–35
Lodding Engineering, **7** 521
Lodestar Group, **10** 19
Lodge-Cottrell, **III** 472
Loeb, Carl M., **IV** 17
Loeb Rhoades, **II** 450
Loeb Rhoades, Hornblower & Co., **II** 451; **9** 469
Loening Aeronautical, **I** 61; **11** 164
Loening, Albert, **I** 61; **11** 164
Loening, Grover, **I** 61; **11** 164
Loew, Marcus, **II** 148, 154
Loew's Consolidated Enterprises, **II** 154
Loewi Financial Cos., **III** 270
Loews Corporation, **I** 245, **487–88**; **II** 134, 148–49, 169; **III** 228, 231
LOF Plastics, **III** 642
LOF Plastics, Inc., **8** 124
Lofficier, Jean-Charles, **III** 704
Loffland Brothers Company, **9** 364
Lofgren, Nils, **I** 626
Loft Inc., **I** 276; **10** 451
Logged Off Land Co., **IV** 355–56
Logic Modeling, **11** 491
Logistics, **III** 431
Logistics Management Systems, Inc., **8** 33
Logitech, Inc., **9** 116
Loiseau, John E., **6** 559
Lolli, Ettore, **III** 347
Lomas & Nettleton, **III** 249
Lomas & Nettleton Financial Corporation, **11** 122
Lomas Financial Corporation, **11** 122
Lomb, Henry, **7** 44
Lombard, Carole, **II** 155

Lombard North Central, **II** 442
Lombard Orient Leasing Ltd., **II** 442
Lombardi, Maurice, **IV** 386
London & Hull, **III** 211
London & Leeds Development Corp., **II** 141
London & Midland Bank, **II** 318
London and County Bank, **II** 334
London and Hanseatic Bank, **II** 256
London and Lancashire Insurance Co., **III** 350
London and Scottish Marine Oil, **11** 98
London and Westminster Bank, **II** 333–34
London Asiastic, **III** 699
London Assurance Corp., **III** 278, 369–71, 373
London Brick Co., **III** 502; **7** 208
London Brokers Ltd., **6** 290
London Buses Limited, **6** 406
London Chartered Bank of Australia, **II** 188
London Clermont Club, **III** 431
London County and Westminster Bank, **II** 334
London County and Westminster Bank (Paris), **II** 334
London County Freehold & Leasehold Properties, **IV** 711
London, County, Westminster & Parrs, **II** 334
London, Edinburgh and Dublin Insurance Co., **III** 350
London Film Productions Ltd., **II** 157
London General Omnibus Company, **6** 406
London Guarantee and Accident Co., **III** 372
London Insurance Co., **III** 373
London Joint Stock Bank, **II** 318, 388
London Life Assoc., **IV** 711
London Life Insurance Co., **II** 456–57
London Passenger Transport Board, **6** 407
London, Provincial and South Western Bank, **II** 235
London Regional Transport, 6 406–08
London Transport. *See* London Regional Transport.
London Underground Limited, **6** 406
London Weekend Television, **IV** 650–51; **7** 389
Lone Star and Crescent Oil Co., **IV** 548
Lone Star Brewing Co., **I** 255
Lone Star Gas Co., **V** 611
Lone Star Gas Corp., **V** 609
Lone Star Industries, **III** 718, 729, 753; **IV** 304
Lone Star Northwest, **III** 718
Lone Star Steel, **I** 440–41
Long Distance Discount Services, Inc., **8** 310
Long Distance/USA, **9** 479
Long, George, **IV** 355
Long, Gerald, **IV** 669–70
Long Island Airways, **I** 115
Long Island Cable Communication Development Company, **7** 63
Long Island Daily Press Publishing Co., **IV** 582–83
Long Island Lighting Company, V 652–54; 6 456
Long Island Trust Co., **II** 192, 218
Long, Joseph, **V** 120–21
Long Lac Mineral Exploration, **9** 282
Long Manufacturing Co., **III** 439
Long, Robert, **V** 121

Long, Thomas, **V** 120–21
Long-Airdox Co., **IV** 136
Long-Term Credit Bank of Japan, Ltd., **II** 301, **310–11**, 338, 369
Longfellow, Henry Wadsworth, **IV** 617
Longfield, William H., **9** 98
Longines-Wittenauer Watch Co., **II** 121
Longman Group Ltd., **IV** 611, 658
Longmat Foods, **II** 494
Longs Drug Stores Corporation, V 120
Longstreth, Bevis, **I** 370; **9** 500
Longview Fibre Company, 8 335–37
Longwy, **IV** 227
Lonrho Plc, **IV** 651–52; **10** 170
Lonsdale Investment Trust, **II** 421
Lonvest Corp., **II** 456–57
Loombe, Cecil, **II** 564
Loomis, James Lee, **III** 238
Loomis, Lee P., **11** 252
Loomis, Sayles & Co., **III** 313
Loomis, Simeon, **III** 262
Looney, Wilton, **9** 254
Loose Leaf Metals Co., Inc., **10** 314
Lopez, Joseph E., **III** 241
Loral Corporation, II 38; **7** 9; **8 338–40;** **9 323–25**
Loral Qualcomm Satellite Services, **9** 325
Lorber, Matthew, **10** 85
Lord & Thomas, **I** 12–14; **IV** 660
Lord Ashfield, **6** 407
Lord Baltimore Press, Inc., **IV** 286
Lord Chetwynd's Insurance, **III** 370
Lord Inchcape, **V** 491–92
Lord Onslow's Insurance, **III** 370
Lorentz, Francis, **III** 123
Lorenz, **I** 463
Lorenz, William, **8** 338; **9** 323
Lorenzo, Frank, **I** 98, 103, 123–24, 130; **6** 129
Lorillard, **V** 396, 407, 417
Lorillard Industries, **I** 488
Lorimar Telepictures, **II** 149, 177
Lorman, William, **V** 552
Lorraine-Escaut, **IV** 227
Lorrell, Mark A., **I** 43
Lortie, Pierre, **II** 652
Lorvic Corp., **I** 679
Los Angeles Can Co., **I** 599
Los Angeles Gas and Electric Company, **V** 682
Los Angeles Steamship Co., **II** 490
Los Gaitanes (Count of), **II** 197
Los Nietos Co., **IV** 570
Lothian (Marquis of), **III** 358
Lothringer Bergwerks- und Hüttenverein Aumetz-Friede AG, **IV** 126
Lothringer Hütten- und Bergwerksverein, **IV** 126
Lotus Development Corp., IV 597; **6** 224–25, 227, **254–56,** 258–60, 270–71, 273; **9** 81, 140; **10** 24, 505
Lotus Publishing Corporation, **7** 239
Lotus Radio, **I** 531
Loucks, Hoffman & Company, **8** 412
Loucks, Vernon R., **I** 628
Loucks, Vernon R., Jr., **10** 142–43
Loughead Aircraft Manufacturing Co., **I** 64
Loughead, Allan, **I** 64, 76
Loughead, Malcolm, **I** 64
Loughhead, Robert L., **IV** 237
Louis B. Mayer Pictures, **II** 148
Louis C. Edwards, **II** 609
Louis, J.C., **I** 235, 279
Louis Marx Toys, **II** 559

Louis Philippe, King (France), **III** 616; **IV** 226
Louis Rich, **II** 532
Louis Vuitton, I 272; **10 397–99**
Louis Vuitton Moët Hennessy, **III** 48; **8** 343
Louis XIV, King (France), **II** 474; **III** 675
Louis XVIII, King (France), **IV** 617
Louisiana Bank & Trust, **11** 106
The Louisiana Land and Exploration Company, IV 76, 365, 367; **7 280–83**
Louisiana Land Offshore Exploration Co., **7** 281
Louisiana-Pacific Corporation, IV 282, **304–05; 9** 260
Louisville Cement Co., **IV** 409
Louisville Gas and Electric Company. *See* LG&E Energy Corporation.
Lourle, Donald B., **II** 559
Louthan Manufacturing Company, **8** 178
Love, Howard M. (Pete), **V** 152–53
Love, J. Spencer, **V** 354
Lovelace, Griffin M., **III** 238
Lovering China Clays, **III** 690
Lovering family, **III** 690–91
Low, Abiel A., **III** 240
Lowe Bros. Co., **III** 745
Lowe, James, **V** 122
Lowe, L. S., **V** 122
Lowe, Leo, **I** 661
Lowe, William C., **7** 206
Lowe's Companies, Inc., V 122–23; 11 384
Lowell Bearing Co., **IV** 136
Lowell, John, **III** 312
Löwenbräu, **I** 220, 257; **II** 240
Lowenstein, Louis, **II** 673–74
Lowney/Moirs, **II** 512
Lowry, Edward, **III** 258
Lowry, Grosvenor, **II** 27
Loyalty Group, **III** 241–42
Loyalty Life, **III** 243
Loynd, Richard B., **III** 531; **9** 134
Lpuschow, Gunter, **I** 138
LRL International, **II** 477
LSI. *See* Lear Siegler Inc.
LTA Ltd., **IV** 22
LTV Corporation, I 62–63, **489–91; 7** 107–08; **8** 157, 315; **10** 419; **11** 166, 364
Luberef, **IV** 538
Lubert, Ira, **10** 232
Lubitsch, Ernst, **II** 155, 175
Lubrizol Corp., **I 360–62**
Lucander, Bruno Otto, **6** 87
Lucas Aerospace, **III** 555–56
Lucas Applied Technology, **III** 556
Lucas Automotive, **III** 556
Lucas Battery Co., **III** 556
Lucas Bols, **II** 642
Lucas Defence Systems, **III** 556
Lucas, Donald L., **6** 272–73
Lucas Electrical Co., **III** 554–55
Lucas, George, **II** 144
Lucas Girling, **I** 157
Lucas, Harry, **III** 554
Lucas Industrial Systems, **III** 556
Lucas Industries Plc, III 509, **554–57**
Lucas Instruments, **III** 556
Lucas, John H., **6** 510
Lucas, Joseph, **III** 554
Lucas, Oliver, **III** 554–55
Lucas, William F., **I** 226–27; **10** 180–81
Lucasfilm, **9** 368, 472

Lucchini, **IV** 228
Luce, Charles F., **V** 588
Luce, Clare Boothe, **IV** 674; **7** 527
Luce, Henry, III, **IV** 675; **7** 528
Luce, Henry Robinson, **IV** 661, 673–75; **7** 526–28
Luciano, R.P., **I** 685
Lucier, Francis P., **III** 436
Lucking, W.T., **6** 546
Luckman, Charles, **I** 513
Lucks, Roy, **7** 131
Lucky Chemical Co., **II** 53–54
Lucky Continental Carbon, **II** 53
Lucky Lager Brewing Co, **I** 268
Lucky Stores, **II** 605, 653
Lucky Stores Inc., **6** 355; **8** 474
Lucky Strike, **II** 143
Lucky-Goldstar, **II** 53–54; **III** 457
Ludlow Corp., **III** 645
Ludlow, Daniel, **II** 247
Ludmer, Irving, **II** 663–64
Ludvigsen, Elliot, **I** 154; **10** 279
Ludwick, Andrew K., **10** 510, 512
Ludwig, Daniel K., **IV** 522, 570
Ludwig I, King (Bavaria), **II** 238, 241
Ludwig II, King (Bavaria), **II** 241
Luecke, Joseph E., **III** 270–71
Lüer, Carl, **IV** 140
Luerssen, Frank, **IV** 115
Lufkin Rule Co., **II** 16
Luft, Klaus, **III** 155
Luftag, **I** 110
Lufthansa. *See* Deutsche Lufthansa A.G.
Lufthansa A.G., **6** 59–60, 69, 96, 386
Luigs, C. Russell, **9** 266
Luisi, Marie, **I** 21
Luiso, Anthony, **7** 242–43
Lukas, Stephen **I** 678
Luke, David, **IV** 351
Luke, David L., III, **IV** 353–54
Luke, David L., Jr., **IV** 351–53
Luke, John, **IV** 351
Luke, John A., **IV** 354
Luke, Thomas, **IV** 351
Luke, William, **IV** 351
Lukey Mufflers, **IV** 249
Lukman, Rilwanu, **IV** 473–74
Lum's, **6** 199–200
Lumac B.V., **I** 387
Lumbermen's Investment Corp., **IV** 341
Lumbermens Mutual Casualty Co., **III** 269–71
La Lumière Economique, **II** 79
Lummus Co., **IV** 469
Lumonics Inc., **III** 635
Lundberg, Kenneth, **IV** 576
Lundberg, William, **I** 136
Lundeen, Robert, **I** 325; **8** 149, 519
Lundqvist, Bengt, **I** 626
Lundqvist, Emil, **IV** 336
Lundy, J. Edward, **I** 166; **11** 138
Lunevale Products Ltd., **I** 341
Lunn Poly, **8** 525–26
Luntey, Gene, **6** 457
Luotto-Pankki Oy, **II** 303
Lurgei, **6** 599
LURGI. *See* Metallurgische Gesellschaft Aktiengesellschaft.
Lurgi Paris S.A., **IV** 141
Luria Bros. and Co., **I** 512–13
Luria Brothers, **6** 151
Lurie, Robert, **8** 229–30
Lurton, H. William, **7** 255–56
Lutens, Serge, **III** 63

Luter, Joseph W., III, **7** 477
Luther's Bar-B-Q, **II** 556
Luthringer, Marshall S., **6** 470
Lutteroth, Herman (Baron), **III** 345
Lutz, Norman E., **7** 479
Lux, **III** 478
Lux, John H., **9** 24
Lux Mercantile Co., **II** 624
Lux, Samuel, **II** 624
Luxor, **II** 69; **6** 205
Luyt, Louis, **I** 289
LVMH, **I** 272
LVO Cable Inc., **IV** 596
Lyall, G. Hudson, **I** 714
Lyberg, Bengt, **IV** 318
Lybrand, William M., **9** 137
Lydex, **I** 527
Lygo, Raymond, **I** 52
Lykes Bros. Steamship Co., **I** 490–91
Lykes Corp., **I** 490
Lyle, Abraham, III, **II** 580–81
Lyle, Charles, **II** 581
Lyle, J. Irvine, **7** 70–71
Lyle, Oliver, **II** 581
Lyle, Philip, **II** 581
Lyle, Robert, **II** 581
Lynch, Charles A., **6** 386
Lynch, Dale L., **II** 655–56
Lynch, David L., **11** 281
Lynch, Edmund, **II** 424
Lynch, Peter, **II** 413; **8** 195
Lynn, James T., **III** 182
Lynn, Mitchell, **V** 164
Lynn, Robert, **IV** 445–46; **6** 385
Lynx Express Delivery, **6** 412, 414
Lyon & Healy, **IV** 660
Lyon, Alfred, **V** 406
Lyon, Edward F., **I** 158; **10** 292
Lyon, Wayne B., **III** 570
Lyon's Technological Products Ltd., **III** 745
Lyondell Petrochemical Company, **IV** 377, **456–57**; **10** 110
Lyonnaise Communications, **10** 196
Lyonnaise des Eaux-Dumez, **I** 576; **V** **655–57**
Lyons. *See* J. Lyons & Co. Ltd.
Lyons, William, **6** 535–36
Lypho-Med, **IV** 333
Oy Lypsyniemen Konepaja, **IV** 275–76
Lysaght's Canada, Ltd., **IV** 73
Lystads, **I** 333
Lyttelton, Oliver, **IV** 140

M & S Computing. *See* Intergraph Corporation.
M and G Fund Management, **III** 699
M Stores Inc., **II** 664
M.A. Hanna Company, **8** **345–47**
M.A.N., **III** 561–63
M&M Limited, **7** 299
M&T Capital Corporation, **11** 109
M&T Discount Corporation, **11** 109
M.D.C., **11** 258
M.E.P.C. Ltd., **IV** 711
M. Guggenheim's Sons, **IV** 31
M.H. McLean Wholesaler Grocery Company, **8** 380
M. Hensoldt & Söhne Wetzlar Optische Werke AG, **III** 446
M.J. Brock Corporation, **8** 460
M. Loeb Ltd., **II** 652
M. Lowenstein Corp., **V** 379
M-1 Drilling Fluids Co., **III** 473

M.P. Pumps, Inc., **8** 515
M. Polaner Inc., **10** 70
M. Samuel & Co., **II** 208
M.W. Kellogg Co., **III** 470; **IV** 408, 534
MA/Com, Inc., **6** 336
Ma. Ma-Macaroni Co., **II** 554
Maabed, Muhammed, **IV** 413
Maakauppiaitten Oy, **8** 293–94
Maakuntain Keskus-Pankki, **II** 303
Maakuntain Pankki, **II** 303
Maas, Myrtil, **III** 391
MaasGlas, **III** 667
Maass, Adolf, **V** 466–67
Maatman, Gerald L., **III** 271
MABAG Maschinen- und Apparatebau GmbH, **IV** 198
Mabley & Carew, **10** 282
Mac Tools, **III** 628
MacAllister, Jack A., **V** 341–43
MacAndrews & Forbes Holdings Inc., **II** 679; **III** 56; **9** 129; **11** 334
MacArthur, Douglas (Gen.), **I** 492, 503; **II** 224; **III** 63, 295, 319, 385, 409, 552, 710, 713, 741; **IV** 145, 148, 632, 655; **6** 106; **7** 45, 302
MacArthur, John, **6** 348
Macauley, Walter, **6** 10–11
MacAvoy, Thomas C., **III** 684
MacBain, Gavin K., **III** 17–18; **9** 88
MacBeth, William, **8** 515
Maccabees Life Insurance Co., **III** 350
MacComber, John, **I** 318
Macdonald, Alexander, **III** 260
Macdonald, B.W., **III** 522
Macdonald, Ewan, **7** 132
MacDonald, Halsted, and Laybourne, **10** 127
Macdonald Hamilton & Co., **III** 522–23
MacDonald, Harold, **II** 419
MacDonald, John A., **6** 359
MacDonald, Nestor J., **11** 515
MacDonald, Peter, **II** 593
Macdonald, Ray, **III** 166; **6** 282
MacDonald, Reynold C., **8** 274–75
MacDonald Taylor, **I** 715
MacDougall, A. Kent, **I** 32
MacDougall, Alexander, **II** 216
Mace, Garry, **IV** 279
Macey Furniture Co., **7** 493
Macfarlane, Don B., **IV** 250
Macfarlane, Frederick, **9** 274
Macfarlane, James, **II** 593
Macfarlane, John, **II** 593
Macfarlane, John E., **II** 593
Macfarlane, John, Jr., **II** 593
Macfarlane Lang & Co., **II** 592–93
Macfarquhar, Colin, **7** 165
MacGregor, Ian K. (Sir), **IV** 18–19, 40, 43
MacGregor Sporting Goods Inc., **III** 443
Machine Vision International Inc., **10** 232
Machiz, Leon, **9** 55–57
MacInnes, William, **6** 582
Macintosh, **6** 219
MacIntyre, Malcolm, **I** 102
MacIntyre, R. Douglas, **11** 78
Macioce, Thomas, **V** 26
Mack, Augustus, **I** 177
Mack Bros. Co., **I** 177
Mack, Jack, **I** 177
Mack Trucks Inc., **I** 147, **177–79**; **9** 416
Mack, Walter, **I** 246, 279
Mack, Walter S., Jr., **I** 277; **10** 451
Mack, Wilbur, **I** 679
MacKay, Donald, **IV** 307

Mackay, James Lyle. *See* Lord Inchcape.
Mackay, James Lyle (first Earl of Inchcape), **III** 521–22
Mackay, John, **II** 381; **8** 546
MacKay-Shields Financial Corp., **III** 316
Macke, Kenneth, **10** 515
MacKenzie & Co., **II** 361
Mackenzie Hill, **IV** 724
MacKenzie, John D, **IV** 33
Mackenzie Mann & Co. Limited, **6** 360
Mackenzie, Robert, **III** 521
Mackenzie, William, **6** 360
Mackersy, L.S., **II** 245
Mackey Airways, **I** 102
Mackey, Frank, **II** 417–18
Mackie, R.W., **7** 416
Mackinnon Mackenzie & Co., **III** 521–22
Mackinnon, William (Sir), **III** 521–22
Mackintosh, Harold, **II** 569
Mackintosh, John, **II** 569
Macklem, Stanley, **7** 105
Macklin, Gordon S., **10** 416–17
Macknett, Charles S., **9** 222
MacKnight, Nigel, **I** 80
Mackworth-Young, William, **II** 428
Maclaren Power and Paper Co., **IV** 165
MacLaurin, Ian, **II** 677–78
MacLean, Alexander, **III** 286
MacLean, Basil C., **10** 160
Maclean, Hugh, **IV** 638
Maclean Hunter Cable TV, **IV** 640
Maclean Hunter Limited, IV 638–40
Maclean, John Bayne (Col.), **IV** 638–40
Maclean Publishing Co. Ltd., **IV** 638–39
Maclean-Hunter Publishing Co., **IV** 639–40
Macleans Ltd., **III** 65
Maclellan, Hugh, **III** 332
Maclellan, R.L., **III** 332
Maclellan, Robert J., **III** 331–32
Maclellan, Thomas, **III** 331
MacLeod, Norman, **6** 38
MacMarr Stores, **II** 654
MacMillan & Bloedel Ltd., **IV** 307
Macmillan & Co., Ltd., **7** 284–85
Macmillan, Alexander, **7** 284–85
MacMillan, Bloedel and Powell River Ltd., **IV** 307
MacMillan Bloedel Building Materials, **IV** 309
MacMillan Bloedel Limited, IV 165, 272, **306–09**, 721; **9** 391
MacMillan, Cargill, **II** 616
Macmillan Company, **7** 285
Macmillan, D. & A., **7** 284
Macmillan, Daniel, **7** 284
MacMillan, Donald B., **II** 123
Macmillan, Frederick, **7** 285
Macmillan, George A., **7** 285
Macmillan, Harold, **IV** 41
MacMillan, Harvey Reginald (H.R.), **IV** 306–08
MacMillan, Inc., IV 637, 641–43; **7** **284–86**, 311–12, 343; **9** 63
MacMillan, John Hugh, **II** 616
MacMillan, John, Jr., **II** 616–17
Macmillan, Maurice, **7** 285
MacMillan, Whitney, **II** 616–17
MacMurray, Fred, **II** 173
Macnaughton Blair, **III** 671
MacNaughton, Donald S., **III** 79, 339–40
MacNaughton, Malcolm, **II** 491
Macneill & Barry Ltd., **III** 522
Macneill & Co., **III** 522

Macomber, John R., **II** 402
Macon Gas Company, **6** 447
Macon Kraft Co., **IV** 311; **11** 421
Maconochie Bros., **II** 569
Macquarie, Laughlan, **II** 388
Macqueen, Thomas Potter, **II** 187
Mactier, J. Allan, **II** 493
Macy, Rowland H., **V** 168; **8** 442
Macy's, **I** 30
Macy's Atlanta, **V** 168
Macy's California, **V** 168–69
Macy's New Jersey, **V** 168
Macy's of New York, Inc., **V** 168–70; **8** 288
Madar, William P., **11** 357
Madden, John, **I** 270
Madden, Richard B., **8** 430
Maddingley Brown Coal Pty Ltd., **IV** 249
Maddox, John, **I** 355
Maddrey, Erwin, **8** 141
Maddux Air Lines, **I** 125
Madelung, Gero, **I** 75
Madison & Sullivan, Inc., **10** 215
Madison, Charles A., **IV** 636
Madison Gas & Electric Company, **6** 605–06
Madison, James, **II** 312
Madison Square Garden, **I** 452
Madonna, **II** 176–77
Maeda, Takeshiro, **II** 66
Maejima, Hisoka, **V** 477
Maes Group Breweries, **II** 475
Maeva Group, **6** 206
Magasins Armand Thiéry et Sigrand, **V** 11
Magazins Réal Stores, **II** 651
Magcobar, **III** 472
Magdeburg Insurance Group, **III** 377
Magdeburger Versicherungsgruppe, **III** 377
Magee, Frank, **IV** 15
Maggin, Daniel, **7** 145
Magic Chef, **8** 298
Magic Chef Co., **III** 573
Magic Pan, **II** 559–60
Magic Pantry Foods, **10** 382
MagicSoft Inc., **10** 557
Maginness, George, **I** 696
Magirus, **IV** 126
Maglificio di Ponzano Veneto dei Fratelli Benetton. *See* Benetton.
Magma Copper Company, 7 287–90, 385–87
Magma Electric Company; **11** 271
Magma Energy Company, **11** 270
Magma Power Company, 11 270–72
Magnaflux, **III** 519
Magne Corp., **IV** 160
Magnesium Metal Co., **IV** 118
Magness, Bob, **II** 160
Magnet Cove Barium Corp., **III** 472
Magnetic Controls Company, **10** 18
Magnolia Petroleum Co., **III** 497; **IV** 82, 464
Magnus Co., **I** 331
Magnus Eriksson, King (Sweden), **IV** 335
La Magona d'Italia, **IV** 228
Magoon, Robert, Jr., **9** 272
Magor Railcar Co., **I** 170
Magowan, Peter, **II** 655–56
Magowan, Robert, **II** 655
Magraw, Lester A., **6** 469–70
MAGroup Inc., **11** 123
Maguire, John J., **I** 312; **10** 154
Maguire, William G., **V** 691

Maharam Fabric, **8** 455. *See also* Design/ Craft Fabrics.
Maher, James R., **11** 334
Mahir, **I** 37
Mahone, William, **V** 484
Mahoney, Richard J., **I** 366; **9** 356
Mahoney, Terah, **I** 47
Mahou, **II** 474
MAI Basic Four, Inc., **10** 242
MAI Inc., **11** 486
Mai Nap Rt, **IV** 652; **7** 392
MAI Systems Corporation, 11 273–76
Maier, Cornell C., **IV** 123
Maier, Gerald, **V** 738
Maier, Russell W., **7** 446–47
Mailson Ferreira da Nobrega, **II** 200
MAIN. *See* Mid-American Interpool Network.
Main Event Management Corp., **III** 194
Main Street Advertising USA, **IV** 597
Mainline Travel, **I** 114
Mair, Alex, **7** 461–62
Mairs, Samuel, **I** 419; **11** 21–22
Maison Bouygues, **I** 563
Maizuru Heavy Industries, **III** 514
Majestic Contractors Ltd., **8** 419–20
Majestic Wine Warehouses Ltd., **II** 656
Major Video Concepts, **6** 410
Major Video, Inc., **9** 74
MaK Maschinenbau GmbH, **IV** 88
Mak van Waay, **11** 453
Makhteshim, **II** 47
Makita Electric Works, **III** 436
Makita, Jinichi, **I** 579–80
Makita, Shinichiro, **I** 580
Makiyama, **I** 363
Makkonen, Veikko, **II** 303
Mako, B.V., **8** 476
Malama Pacific Corporation, **9** 276
Malamud, Bernard, **IV** 622
Malapai Resources, **6** 546
Malayan Airways Limited, **6** 117
Malayan Breweries, **I** 256
Malayan Motor and General Underwriters, **III** 201
Malaysia LNG, **IV** 518–19
Malaysia-Singapore Airlines, **6** 117. *See also* Malaysian Airlines System BHD.
Malaysian Airlines System BHD, 6 71, **100–02**
Malaysian Airways Ltd., **6** 100, 117
Malaysian International Shipping Co., **IV** 518
Malaysian Sheet Glass, **III** 715
Malbak Ltd., **IV** 92–93
Malcolm's Diary & Time-Table, **III** 256
Malcolmson, Alexander, **I** 164; **11** 136
Malcus Industri, **III** 624
Malec, John, **10** 358
Malenick, Donald H., **7** 599
Maljers, Floris A., **7** 544
Malkin, Judd, **IV** 702–03
Malleable Iron Works, **II** 34
Mallinckrodt Inc., **III** 16; **IV** 146; **8** 85
Mallon, Henry Neil, **III** 471–72
Malmö Flygindustri, **I** 198
Malmsten & Bergvalls, **I** 664
Malnik, Alvin, **6** 200–01
Malone & Hyde, Inc., **II** 625, 670–71; **9** 52–53
Malone, John, **II** 160–61, 167
Malone, Thomas F., **III** 389
Malone, Wallace D., Jr., **11** 455
Maloney, George T., **9** 98

Maloney, Martin, **11** 387
Maloon, James, **9** 297
Malott, Robert H., **I** 443; **11** 134–35
Malozemoff, Plato, **7** 288, 386–87
Malrite Communications Group, **IV** 596
Malt-A-Milk Co., **II** 487
Maltby, Harold E., **9** 547
Maltby, John, **IV** 383
Malthus, Thomas, **7** 165
Mameco International, **8** 455
Mamlock, Max, **I** 64
Mamroth, Paul, **I** 410
Man Aktiengesellschaft, **III** 301, **561–63**
MAN B&W Diesel, **III** 563
MAN Gutehoffnungshütte, **III** 563
MAN Nutzfahrzeuge, **III** 563
MAN Roland, **III** 563
MAN Technologie, **III** 563
Management Decision Systems, Inc., **10** 358
Management Engineering and Development Co., **IV** 310
Management Recruiters International, **6** 140
Management Science America, Inc., **11** 77
Manbré and Garton, **II** 582
Manchester and Liverpool District Banking Co., **II** 307, 333
Manchester Commercial Buildings Co., **IV** 711
Mancuso, Frank, **II** 156
Mandabach & Simms, **6** 40
Mandai, Junshiro, **II** 325
Mandarin Oriental International Ltd., **I** 471; **IV** 700
Mandel Bros., **IV** 660
Mandel, Evan William, **III** 55
Mandel, Jack, **9** 419
Mandel, Joseph, **9** 419
Mandel, Morton, **9** 419–20
Mange, John I., **V** 629
Manhattan Co., **II** 217, 247
Manhattan Electrical Supply Co., **9** 517
Manhattan Fund, **I** 614
Manhattan Trust Co., **II** 229
Mani, Ravi, **6** 64
Maniatis, Thomas, **8** 215
Manifatture Cotoniere Meridionali, **I** 466
Manistique Pulp and Paper Co., **IV** 311
Manitoba Bridge and Engineering Works Ltd., **8** 544
Manitoba Paper Co., **IV** 245–46
Manitoba Rolling Mill Ltd., **8** 544
Manley, L.B., **III** 282
Manley, Marshall, **III** 263
Mann, Donald, **6** 360
Mann Egerton & Co., **III** 523
Mann, Ellery, **8** 511, 513
Mann, Horace, **III** 312
Mann, Jack, **8** 385
Mann Theatres Chain, **I** 245
Manne Tossbergs Eftr., **II** 639
Mannerheim, Carl Gustav Emil (Baron), **IV** 299, 348
Mannerheim, Carl Robert (Count), **IV** 299
Manners, Arthur, **I** 223
Mannesmann AG, **I** 411; **III 564–67**; **IV** 222, 469
Mannesmann Anlagenbau AG, **III** 565
Mannesmann Comercial S.A., **III** 566
Mannesmann, Max, **III** 564
Mannesmann Mobilfunk GmbH, **III** 566; **11** 11
Mannesmann, Reinhard, **III** 564

Mannesmann Tube Co., **III** 565
Mannesmannröhren-Werke, **III** 566
Mannheimer Bank, **IV** 558
Mannheimer, Theodor, **II** 351
Manning, Selvage & Lee, **6** 22
Mannstaedt, **IV** 128
Manoff, Tom, **7** 462
Manoogian, Alex, **III** 568–69
Manoogian, Charles, **III** 568
Manoogian, George, **III** 568
Manoogian, Richard, **III** 569–70
Manor Care, Inc., 6 187–90
Manor Healthcare Corporation, **6** 187–88
Manorfield Investments, **II** 158
Manpower, Inc., 6 10, 140; **9 326–27**
Manpower Southampton Ltd., **9** 326
Manship, Paul, **III** 275
Manufacturers & Merchants Indemnity Co., **III** 191
Manufacturers and Traders Trust Company, **11** 108–09
Manufacturers Hanover Consumer Credit Division, **11** 16
Manufacturers Hanover Corporation, **II** 254, **312–14**, 403; **III** 194; **9** 124
Manufacturers Hanover Investment Corp., **II** 446
Manufacturers Hanover Mortgage Corp., **III** 252
Manufacturers Hanover Trust, **I** 145, 402; **II** 312–13; **11** 54, 415
Manufacturers National Bank of Brooklyn, **II** 312
Manufacturers National Bank of Detroit, **I** 165; **11** 137
Manufacturers Railway, **I** 219
Manufacturers Trust Co., **II** 230, 312
Manus Nu-Pulse, **III** 420
Manutius, Aldus, **10** 34
Manville Building Materials Corp., **III** 708; **7** 293
Manville, Charles B., **III** 706; **7** 291
Manville Corporation, **III 706–09**, 721; **7 291–95 (upd.)**; **10** 43, 45; **11** 420, 422
Manville Covering Co., **III** 706; **7** 291
Manville Forest Products Corp., **III** 708; **7** 293
Manville, H.E., **III** 706–07; **7** 291
Manville, H.E., Jr., **III** 707; **7** 292
Manville International Corp., **III** 708; **7** 293
Manville Products Corp., **III** 708; **7** 293
Manville Sales Corp., **III** 707; **7** 292; **11** 421
Manville, T.F., Jr., **7** 291
Manville, Thomas F., **III** 706; **7** 291
Manville, Thomas F., Jr., **III** 706
Manzi, Jim P., **6** 254–56; **9** 344
Mao Zedong, **IV** 388
MAPCO Inc., IV 458–59
Maple Leaf Mills, **II** 513–14
Maples, Michael, **6** 260
Mapoma, Jameson, **IV** 240
MAPP. *See* Mid-Continent Area Power Planner.
Mar-O-Bar Company, **7** 299
A.B. Marabou, **II** 511
Marathon, **I** 612, 614
Marathon Oil Co., **IV** 365, 454, 487, 572, 574; **7** 549, 551
Maraven, **IV** 508
Marbeau, Henri, **IV** 107
Marboro Books, Inc., **10** 136
Marbro Lamp Co., **III** 571

Marceau Investments, **II** 356
Marceau, Richard E., **8** 72
Marcel, François, **III** 68
March, Fredric, **II** 155
Marchandise, Jacques, **IV** 618
Marchesano, Enrico, **III** 347
Marchland Holdings Ltd., **II** 649
Marconi Co., **II** 25, 88
Marconi, Guglielmo, **III** 534; **V** 284
Marconi Wireless Telegraph Co. of America, **II** 88
Marconiphone, **I** 531
Marcos, Ferdinand, **I** 494; **6** 107
Marcos, Imelda, **6** 107
Marcum, Joseph, **11** 370
Marcus, Bernard, **V** 75
Marcus Samuel & Co., **IV** 530
Marden, Bernard, **V** 172
Mardon Packaging International, **I** 426–27
Mardorf, Peach and Co., **II** 466
Maremont Corporation, **8** 39–40
de Mares, Roberto, **IV** 415
Margarine Unie N.V. *See* Unilever PLC (Unilever N.V.).
Margarine Union Limited. *See* Unilever PLC (Unilever N.V.).
Marge Carson, Inc., **III** 571
Marggraf, Andreas, **11** 13
Margo's La Mode, **10** 281–82
Margolis, David L., **I** 434
Marico Acquisition Corporation, **8** 448, 450
Marie-Claire Album, **III** 47
Marigold Foods Inc., **II** 528
Marinduque Mining & Industrial Corp., **IV** 146
Marine Bank and Trust Co., **11** 105
Marine Bank of Erie, **II** 342
Marine Computer Systems, **6** 242
Marine Diamond Corp., **IV** 66; **7** 123
Marine Group, **III** 444
Marine Midland Banks, **I** 548; **II** 298; **9** 475–76
Marine Midland Corp., **11** 108
Marine Office of America, **III** 220, 241–42
Marine Office of America Corp., **III** 242
Marine Office-Appleton Cox, **III** 242
Marine-Firminy, **IV** 227
Marineland Amusements Corp., **IV** 623
Mario, Ernest, **9** 264
Marion Freight Lines, **6** 370
Marion Laboratories Inc., **I** 648–49; **8** 149; **9** 328–29
Marion Manufacturing, **9** 72
Marion Merrell Dow, Inc., 9 328–29 (upd.)
Marionet Corp., **IV** 680–81
Mark Goldston, **8** 305
Mark IV Industries, Inc., 7 296–98
Mark, Mitchell, **II** 154
Mark, Reuben, **III** 24–25
Markborough Properties, **II** 222; **V** 81; **8** 525
Market Horizons, **6** 27
Marketime, **V** 55
Marketing Information Services, **6** 24
Markham & Co., **I** 573–74
Markham, George C., **III** 322
Markham, Richard J., **11** 291
Markkula, Mike, **III** 115, 116; **6** 218–19
Markley, Herbert, **8** 530
Marks and Spencer p.l.c., **I** 588; **II** 513, 678; **V 124–26**; **10** 442
Marks, Arthur H., **V** 231

Marks, Bernard, **6** 9
Marks, Harry, **8** 178
Marks, Michael, **V** 124
Marks, Randy, **11** 64
Marks, Simon, **V** 124–26
Marks-Baer Inc., **11** 64
Marland, Ernest Whitworth, **IV** 399–400
Marland Oil Co., **IV** 399
Marland Refining Co., **IV** 399–400
MarLennan Corp., **III** 283
Marley, James, **II** 8
Marley Tile, **III** 735
Marlin-Rockwell Corp., **I** 539
Marlio, Louis, **IV** 173–74
Marlow Foods, **II** 565
Marmon Group, **III** 97; **IV 135–38**
Marmon Holdings, **IV** 136
Marmon Motor Car Co., **IV** 136
Marmon-Herrington Co., **IV** 136
Marmon-Perry Light Company, **6** 508
Marmont (Marshall-Duke of), **IV** 227
Maroon, John F., **I** 694
Marples, Ernest, **V** 421–22
Marquard, William, **III** 664
Marquardt Aircraft, **I** 380
Marquette Paper Corp., **III** 766
Marquez, Thomas, **III** 136
Marriage Mailers, **6** 12
Marriott, Alice S., **III** 102–03
Marriott Corporation, **II** 173, 608; **III**
    92, 94, 99–100, **102–03**, 248; **7** 474–75;
    9 95, 426
Marriott, J. Willard (Bill), **III** 102
Marriott, J. Willard, Jr., **III** 102–03; **9** 368
Marriott, Oliver, **IV** 704
Marriott-Hot Shoppes, Inc., **III** 102
Marron, Donald, **II** 445
Mars Candies, **7** 299
Mars, Forrest E., **7** 299–300
Mars, Forrest E., Jr., **7** 300
Mars, Frank C., **7** 299
Mars, Inc., **II** 510–11; **III** 114; **7**
    299–301
Mars, John, **7** 300
Marschke Manufacturing Co., **III** 435
Marsene Corp., **III** 440
Marsh & McLennan Companies, Inc.,
    III 280, **282–84**; **10** 39
Marsh, Henry, **III** 282–83
Marsh, Leonard, **11** 449
Marsh, Miles, **7** 430–31
Marsh, Richard, **V** 423
Marsh, Ulmann and Co., **III** 282
Marshalk Co., **I** 16
Marshall, Alexander, **V** 492
Marshall, Colin, **I** 94
Marshall, Colin M. **6** 356
Marshall, Edwin H., **III** 224
Marshall Field & Co., **I** 13, 426; **III** 329;
    IV 660; **V** 43–44; **8** 33; **9** 213
Marshall, Gordon (Dr.), **III** 670
Marshall, Howard, **I** 415
Marshall, Jeremy, **10** 269
Marshall, Laurence, **II** 85–86; **11** 411–12
Marshall, Marvin, **9** 85
Marshall, Raymond Willett, **6** 65–66
Marshall, Sir Colin, **6** 132
Marshall, Thomas Elder, **10** 281
Marsin Medical Supply Co., **III** 9
The Mart, **9** 120
Martha, **IV** 486
Martin Aircraft Co., **II** 32, 67
Martin, Arminta, **I** 68
Martin Bros. Ltd., **III** 690

Martin, Cecil, **III** 751–52
Martin, Charles J., **III** 262
Martin, Christian, **I** 190
Martin Co., **I** 112
Martin Dennis Co., **IV** 409
Martin Electric Co., **III** 98
Martin, George A., **III** 744–45
Martin, Glenn, **I** 47, 67–68, 70, 529; **10**
    162; **11** 277
Martin, Ian A., **II** 557
Martin, James, **III** 286; **9** 309
Martin, John, **V** 685
Martin, John E., **7** 506
Martin, John G., **I** 259–60
Martin Marietta Corporation, **I** 47,
    67–69, 71, 102, 142–43, 184, 416; **III**
    671; **IV** 60, 163; **7** 356, 520; **8** 315; **9**
    310; **10** 162, 199, 484; **11** 166, 277–78,
    364
Martin Mathys, **8** 456
Martin, Milward, **I** 279
Martin, Reginald, **III** 690
Martin, Robin, **III** 752
Martin, Roger, **III** 677
Martin Rooks & Co., **I** 95
Martin Sorrell, **6** 54
Martin, William, **IV** 522–23
Martin, William McChesney, Jr., **9** 370
Martin's Bank of London, **II** 236
Martin-Brower Corp., **II** 500; **III** 21
Martin-Senour Co., **III** 744
Martindale, Joseph B., **II** 251
Martineau and Bland, **I** 293
Martini, Emil P., **V** 15
Martino, Joseph, **10** 435
Martins Bank, **II** 236, 308
Martosewojo, Soedarno, **IV** 492
Marubeni K.K., **I** 432, **492–95**, 510; **II**
    292, 391; **III** 760; **IV** 266, 525
Maruei & Co., **IV** 151
Marufuku Co., Ltd., **III** 586; **7** 394
Marui Advertising, **V** 127
Marui Co. Ltd., **V 127**
Marui Computer Centre, **V** 128
Marui Transport, **V** 127
Marukuni Kogyo Co., Ltd., **IV** 327
Marusi, Augustine R., **II** 471–73
Maruta, Yoshio, **III** 38
Marutaka Kinitsu Store Ltd., **V** 194
Maruzen Oil Co., Ltd., **II** 348; **IV** 403–04,
    476, 554
Marvel Entertainment Group, Inc., **10**
    400–02
Marvel Metal Products, **III** 570
Marvel-Schebler Carburetor Corp., **III** 438
Marvin, Selden E., **8** 12
Marvin Windows, **10** 95
Marwick, James, **10** 385
Marwick, Mitchell & Company, **10** 385
Marwitz & Hauser, **III** 446
Marx Bros., **II** 155
Marx, Groucho, **I** 20, 151, 247
Mary Ann Co. Ltd., **V** 89
Mary Ann Restivo, Inc., **8** 323
Mary Ellen's, Inc., **11** 211
Mary Kathleen Uranium, **IV** 59–60
Mary Kay Corporation, **9 330–32**
Mary Kay Cosmetics, **III** 16
Mary, Princess (of Teck), **II** 592
Maryland Casualty Co., **III** 193, 412
Maryland Cup Company, **8** 197
Maryland Distillers, **I** 285
Maryland National Corp., **11** 287

Maryland National Mortgage Corporation,
    11 121
Maryland Shipbuilding and Drydock Co., **I**
    170
Maryland Steel Co., **IV** 35; **7** 48
Mascall, A.J., **III** 360
Mascan Corp., **IV** 697
Maschinenbau AG Nürnberg, **III** 561
Maschinenbauanstalt Humboldt AG, **III**
    541
Maschinenfabrik Augsburg, **III** 561; **IV** 86
Maschinenfabrik Augsburg-Nürnberg. *See*
    M.A.N.
Maschinenfabrik Deutschland, **IV** 103
Maschinenfabrik für den Bergbau von
    Sievers & Co., **III** 541
Maschinenfabrik Gebr. Meer, **III** 565
Maschinenfabrik Sürth, **I** 581
Masco Corporation, **III 568–71**; **11** 385,
    534–35
Masco Industries, **III** 568, 570–71; **11** 534
Masco Screw Products Co., **III** 568–69
Mascon Toy Co., **III** 569
Mascotte, John P., **III** 243
Mase Westpac Limited, **11** 418
Masefield, Peter, **10** 121
Maserati S.p.A., **11** 104
Masi, Carl J., Jr., **6** 286
Masi, J. Carl, Jr., **III** 170
Masinfabriks A.B. Scania, **I** 197
Masius, Wynne-Williams, **6** 21
MASkargo Ltd., **6** 101
Maslak, Samuel, **10** 15
Mason & Hamlin, **III** 656
Mason, Austin B., **III** 645
Mason Best Co., **IV** 343
Mason, Charles, **II** 566
Mason, Dan, **II** 566
Mason, David, **I** 240
Mason, George, **I** 135
Mason, John, **I** 597; **II** 250; **10** 129
Mason, Roswell B., **11** 186
Mason, Sydney, **IV** 696–97
Masonite Corp., **III** 764
Masonite Holdings, **III** 687
Massachusetts Bank, **II** 207
Massachusetts Capital Resources Corp., **III**
    314
**Massachusetts Mutual Life Insurance
    Company**, **III** 110, **285–87**, 305
Massachusetts National Bank of Boston, **II**
    207
Massad, Alex, **IV** 492
Masse, Marcel, **IV** 495
Masselin, M., **III** 210
Massey Co., **III** 650
Massey Combines Corp., **III** 650
Massey Combines Ltd., **III** 652
Massey, Daniel, **III** 650
Massey family, **III** 651
Massey, Hart, **III** 650–51
Massey, Jack C., **III** 78–79
Massey, John (Jack), **7** 265–66
Massey Manufacturing Co., **III** 650
Massey-Ferguson, **II** 222, 245; **III** 439,
    650–52
Massey-Harris Co., Ltd., **III** 650–51
Massey-Harris-Ferguson, **III** 651
Massie, Edward L., **7** 93–94
Mast Industries, **V** 115–16
Master Boot Polish Co., **II** 566
Master Builders, **I** 673
Master Charge, **9** 334
Master Pneumatic Tool Co., **III** 436

Master Shield Inc., **7** 116
Master Tank and Welding Company, **7** 541
MasterCard International, Inc., 9 333–35
Mastercraft Homes, Inc., **11** 257
Mastercraft Industries Corp., **III** 654
Masuda, Katsunori, **III** 383
Masuda, Takashi, **I** 502–03, 506–07; **II** 325; **IV** 654–56
Masury, Alfred F., **I** 177
Matairco, **9** 27
Matazo, Kita, **IV** 150
Matco Tools, **7** 116
Materials Services Corp., **I** 58
Mather & Crother Advertising Agency, **I** 25
Mather Co., **I** 159
Mather Metals, **III** 582
Mather, Samuel H., **9** 474
Matheson & Co., **IV** 189
Matheson, Hugh, **IV** 189–90, 192
Matheson, James, **I** 468
Matheson, Jardine, **6** 78
Mathews, Harry V., **7** 322
Mathews, R.H.G., **II** 123
Mathewson, Charles W., **10** 375
Mathieson Alkali Works, **I** 379
Mathieson Chemical Corp., **I** 379–80, 695
Mathis, David B., **III** 271
Matra, **II** 38, 70; **IV** 617–19
Matra-Europe 1–Hachette, **IV** 617
Matricaria, Ronald, **11** 460
Matrix, **II** 8
Matson, Harold, **7** 304
Matson Navigation Company, Inc., **II** 490–91; **10** 40
Matson, William, **II** 490
Matsuda, Jugiro, **9** 340
Matsuda, Kohei, **9** 341
Matsuda, Tsuneji, **9** 340–41
Matsudata, Ko, **III** 296
Matsuhito, Emperor (Japan), **I** 505
Matsukata, Kojiro, **III** 538–39
Matsukata, Masanobu, **7** 220
Matsumoto, Chiyo, **III** 604
Matsumoto, Kanya, **III** 604–05
Matsumoto Medical Instruments, **11** 476
Matsumoto, Noboru, **III** 62–63
Matsumoto, Nozomu, **III** 604–05
Matsumoto, Seiya, **III** 604–05
Matsunaga, Yasuzaemon, **V** 727, 730
Matsuo, Shizuma, **I** 105
Matsuo, Taiichiro, **I** 493
Matsushita, **11** 487
Matsushita Denki Sangyo. *See* Matsushita Electric Industrial Co., Ltd.
Matsushita Electric Industrial Co., Ltd., **II** 5, **55–56**, 58, 61, 91–92, 102, 117–19, 361, 455; **III** 476, 710; **6** 36; **7** 163, 302; **10** 286, 389, 403, 432
Matsushita Electric Works, Ltd., III 710–11; 7 302–03 (upd.)
Matsushita Electric Works Netherlands, **III** 711; **7** 303
Matsushita Electronic Materials Inc., **7** 303
Matsushita, Konosuke, **II** 55–56, 91, 102, 118; **III** 710–11; **7** 302–03
Matsushita Kotobuki Electronics Industries, Ltd., **10** 458–59
Matsutani, Kenichiro, **V** 575
Matsuura Trading Co., Ltd., **IV** 327
Matsuzakaya Company, V 129–31
Matsuzawa, Takuji, **II** 293
Mattar, Ahmed, **6** 115

Mattei, Enrico, **IV** 419–21, 466
Mattel, **II** 136; **III** 506
Mattel, Inc., 7 304–07
Matthes & Weber, **III** 32
Matthew Bender & Company, Inc., **IV** 677; **7** 94
Matthews (Lord), **IV** 687
Matthews, Clark J., II, **7** 492
Matthews, Robert, **IV** 570
Matthews, Stewart, **9** 102
Matthews, William, **7** 408
Matthey, Edward, **IV** 117
Matthey, George, **IV** 117, 120
Matthiessen, C.H., **II** 496
Mattila, Olavi J., **III** 649; **IV** 276
Mattioli, Raffaele, **IV** 586
Mattoon, Bill, **11** 186
Maucher, Helmut, **II** 547–48; **7** 382–83
Mauchly, John W., **III** 165
Maud Foster Mill, **II** 566
Maui Electric Company, **9** 276
Mauna Kea Properties, **6** 129
Maurer, Pierre, **III** 293
Maurice, F.D., **7** 284
Maurice H. Needham Co., **I** 31
Mauritson, M.H., **II** 536
Mauroy, Pierre, **IV** 174
Maus-Nordmann, **V** 10
Max Factor, **6** 51
Max Factor & Co., **III** 54, 56
Max Klein, Inc., **II** 572
Maxcell Telecom Plus, **6** 323
Maxell, **I** 500
Maxi Vac, Inc., **9** 72
MAXI-Papier, **10** 498
Maxicare Health Plans, Inc., III 84–86
Maxoptix Corporation, **10** 404
Maxtor Corporation, 6 230; **10 403–05,** 459, 463–64
Maxus Energy Corporation, IV 410; **7 308–10; 10** 191
Maxwell Communication Corporation plc, IV 605, 611, **641–43; 7** 286, **311–13 (upd.),** 343; **10** 288
Maxwell, David O., **II** 411
Maxwell, Hamish, **II** 532; **V** 407
Maxwell House Coffee, **II** 531
Maxwell, Ian, **IV** 643
Maxwell, Kevin, **IV** 643
Maxwell Morton Corp, **I** 144, 414
Maxwell, Robert, **II** 319; **IV** 611, 623–24, 641–43, 650, 667, 684, 687; **7** 284, 286, 311–12, 341, 343, 389; **9** 505
Maxwell, Terence, **6** 241
MAXXAM Group Inc., **IV** 121, 123
MAXXAM Inc., 8 348–50
MAXXAM Property Company, **8** 348
May and Baker, **I** 388
The May Company, **I** 540; **8** 288
May, David, **V** 132
May Department Stores Company, II 414; **V 132–35; 11** 349
May, Francis H., Jr., **III** 707–08; **7** 292
May, George O., **9** 422
May, George S., **I** 173
May, Morton D., **V** 133
May, Morton J., **V** 132–33
May, Peter, **I** 602; **8** 537
May, William F., **I** 613; **III** 708; **7** 293
Maybach, Wilhelm, **I** 149; **III** 541
Maybelline, **I** 684
Mayer, Dick, **I** 260
Mayer, Harold, **II** 400; **10** 144
Mayer, John A., **II** 316

Mayer, Josef, **III** 68
Mayer, Louis B., **II** 148
Mayer, Richard, **7** 266–67
Mayfair Foods, **I** 438
Mayfield Dairy Farms, Inc., **7** 128
Mayflower Consumer Products Inc., **6** 410
Mayflower Contract Services, Inc., **6** 409–11
Mayflower Group Inc., 6 409–11
Mayflower Partners, **6** 410
Mayflower Transit, Inc., **6** 409–11
Maynard, Frederick, **IV** 696, 705
Maynard, James H., **10** 331
Mayne Nickless Ltd., **IV** 248
Mayo, Charles, **9** 337–38
Mayo, Ed, **IV** 344
Mayo Foundation, 9 336–39
Mayo, William, **9** 337–38
Mayo, William Worrall, **9** 336–37
Mayoux, Jacques, **II** 355
Mayrisch, Emile, **IV** 24–25
Mays, Milton, **III** 242
Maytag Co., **III** 572–73
Maytag Corporation, III 572–73
Maytag, E.H., **III** 572
Maytag, Fred, II, **III** 572
Maytag, Frederick Louis, **III** 572
Maytag, L.B., **III** 572
Mayville Metal Products Co., **I** 513
Mazankowski, Donald, **6** 61
Mazda Motor Corporation, I 520; **II** 4, 361; **III** 603; **9 340–42; 11** 86
Mazurek, Keith, **I** 182; **10** 430
Mazzanti, Giorgio, **IV** 422
MBNA Corporation, **11** 123
MBPXL Corp., **II** 494
MCA Artists, **II** 144
MCA Financial, **II** 144
MCA Inc., II 143–45; 6 162–63; **10** 286; **11** 557
MCA Recreation, **II** 144
MCA TV, **II** 144
McAdoo, William G., **III** 229
McAfee, Guy, **6** 209
McAndless, Alva (Mac), **III** 275–76
McArthur Glen Realty, **10** 122
McAuley, Brian D., **10** 431–32
McBee, Earl T., **I** 341
McBeth, A.J., **IV** 75
McBride, John, **I** 262
McCabe, Barkman C., **11** 270–71
McCabe, Thomas, **IV** 329–30
McCaffrey & McCall, **I** 33; **11** 496
McCaffrey, Robert H., **9** 98
McCain Feeds Ltd., **II** 484
McCain, Warren, **II** 602; **7** 20–21
McCall, John A., **III** 316
McCall, Joseph B., **11** 388
McCandless, John A., **9** 274
McCann, Dean, **10** 46
McCann, Harrison, **I** 16
McCann-Erickson Hakuhodo, Ltd., **I** 10, 14, 16–17, 234; **6** 30; **10** 227
McCardell, Archie R., **I** 182; **10** 430
McCarter, Thomas Nesbitt, **V** 701
McCarthy, Jack, **10** 208
McCarthy, Joseph, **II** 129, 133; **III** 267; **IV** 583; **6** 188; **7** 14; **10** 480
McCarthy, Leo, **II** 155
McCarthy, Mary, **IV** 672
McCarthy Milling, **II** 631
McCarthy, Walter J., **V** 593–94
McCaughan Dyson and Co., **II** 189
McCaughan, John F., **I** 313; **10** 154–55

McCausland, B.W., **III** 762
McCaw Cellular Communications, Inc.,
  II 331; **6** 274, **322–24**; **7** 15; **9** 320–21;
  10 433
McCaw, Craig O., **6** 322–23; **9** 321, 322
McCaw, John Elroy, **6** 322
McClanahan Oil Co., **I** 341
McClanahan, W.L., **I** 341
McClements, Robert, Jr., **IV** 550
McClintic-Marshall, **IV** 36; **7** 49
The McCloskey Corporation, **8** 553
McColl, Hugh L., Jr., **II** 336–37; **10**
  425–27
McColl-Frontenac Inc., **IV** 439
McCollum, Elmer V., **I** 639
McCollum, Leonard F., **IV** 400–01
McComb Manufacturing Co., **8** 287
McCone, John, **I** 558
McConnell, David H., **III** 15
McConnell, David H., Jr., **III** 15
McConnell, John H., **7** 598–99
McConnell, John P., **7** 599
McConnell, Tom, **9** 434
McConney, Edmund, **III** 329
McCord, William Charles, **V** 612
McCormack & Dodge, **IV** 605; **11** 77
McCormack, Buren, **IV** 602
McCormick & Company, Incorporated,
  7 314–16
McCormick, Annie, **IV** 582
McCormick, Brooks, **I** 182; **10** 429
McCormick, Charles P., **7** 314–15
McCormick, Charles P., Jr., **7** 316
McCormick, Cyrus Hall, **I** 180, 182; **10**
  377, 428
McCormick Harvesting Machine Co., **I**
  180; **II** 330
McCormick, James, **7** 415
McCormick, Katherine Medill, **IV** 682
McCormick, Medill, **IV** 682
McCormick, Peter H., **II** 214
McCormick, Richard D., **V** 343
McCormick, Robert R. (Col.), **IV** 682–83
McCormick, William M., **III** 251–52
McCormick, William T. Jr., **V** 579
McCormick, Willoughby M., **7** 314–15
McCoy, Charles B., **I** 329; **8** 152
McCoy, Chuck, **10** 132
McCoy, James, **10** 403–04
McCoy, John B., **10** 134
McCoy, John G., **10** 132–34
McCoy, John H., **10** 132–33
McCracken, Edward, **9** 471–72
McCraw, Carl, Sr., **10** 298
McCrory, John G., **9** 447
McCrory Stores, **II** 424; **9** 447–48
McCuiston, Tommy, **III** 603
McCulloch Corp., **III** 436; **8** 349
McCulloch Gas Transmission Co., **8** 348
McCulloch, George, **IV** 44
McCulloch, John, **7** 215
McCulloch Oil Corporation, **8** 348–49
McCulloch Oil Corporation of California, **8**
  348
McCulloch Properties Inc., **8** 349
McCulloch, Robert, **8** 348–49
McCulloch, Robert Jr., **8** 349
McCulloch-Hancock Oil & Gas Properties,
  Inc., **8** 348
McCullough, Alex, **10** 371
McCullough, Hugh, **10** 373
McCullough, J.F. "Grandpa," **10** 371–72
McCullough, Michael, **10** 175
McCune, Bill, **III** 609; **7** 438

McCurdy, Richard, **III** 305–06
McCurry, James B., **10** 124–25
McDermott Enterprises France, **III** 559
McDermott, Eugene, **II** 112; **11** 505
McDermott Fabricators, **III** 559
McDermott Far East, **III** 559
McDermott Inc., **III** 559
McDermott International, Inc., III
  558–60
McDermott, J. Ray, **II** 403; **III** 558
McDermott Overseas, **III** 559
McDermott, R. Thomas, **III** 558–59
McDermott, Robert F., **10** 542
McDonald, Alonzo, **I** 143; **9** 343
McDonald, Angus, **I** 517
McDonald brothers, **II** 613, 646–47
McDonald, David, **7** 106
McDonald, Eugene F., Jr., **II** 123–24
McDonald, F. James, **I** 172; **10** 326
McDonald Glass Grocery Co. Inc., **II** 669
McDonald, Malcolm S., **11** 447–48
McDonald, Marshall, **V** 624
McDonald, Maurice (Mac), **II** 646; **7** 317
McDonald, Richard, **II** 646; **7** 317
McDonald's Company (Japan) Ltd., **V** 205
McDonald's Corporation, I 23, 31, 129;
  II 500, 613–15 **646–48**; **III** 63, 94, 103;
  6 13.; **7** 128, 266–67, 316, **317–19**
  (upd.), 435, 505–06; **8** 261–62, 564; **9**
  74, 178, 290, 292, 305; **10** 122; **11** 82,
  308
McDonnell Aircraft, **I** 71
McDonnell Douglas Astronautics Co., **III**
  654
McDonnell Douglas Corporation, I
  41–43, 45, 48, 50–52, 54–56, 58–59,
  61–62, 67–68, **70–72**, 76–77, 82,
  84–85, 90, 105, 108, 111, 121–22, 321,
  364, 490, 511; **II** 442; **III** 512; **6** 68; **7**
  456, 504; **8** 49–51, 315; **9** 18, 183, 206,
  231, 233, 271–72, 418, 458, 460; **10**
  163–64, 317, 536; **11** 164–65, 267,
  277–80 (upd.), 285, 363–65
McDonnell, James, III, **I** 71–72; **11** 278
McDonnell, James Smith, **I** 71; **11** 278
McDonnell, John, **I** 71
McDonnell, John F., **11** 278–79
McDonnell, Sanford, **I** 71–72; **11** 278–79
McDonough Co., **II** 16; **III** 502
McDougal, Littell & Company, **10** 357
McDowell Energy Center, **6** 543
McDowell Furniture Company, **10** 183
McDuff, **10** 305
McElderry, Margaret, **IV** 622
McElroy, Neil, **III** 52; **8** 433
McElwain, J. Franklin, **V** 136
McElwee, John G., **III** 267–68
McEntyre, Peter, **III** 704
McFadden Industries, **III** 21
McFadden Publishing, **6** 13
McFadzean, Francis Scott, **I** 82–83
McFarland, James P., **II** 502; **10** 323
McFarlane, Robert, **II** 470
McGaughy, Marshall & McMillan, **6** 142
McGaw Inc., **11** 208
McGee, Alexander, **II** 312
McGee, Dean A., **IV** 445–46
McGee, Linious, **6** 65
McGee, Robert, **9** 92
McGee, W.J., **9** 367
McGill Manufacturing, **III** 625
McGillicuddy, John F., **II** 313
McGoldrick, Peter, **II** 663
McGovern, George, **IV** 596

McGovern, Patrick J., **7** 238–40
McGovern, R. Gordon, **II** 480–81; **7**
  67–68
McGowan, William, **V** 303
McGowen, Harry, **I** 351–52
McGowen, James, Jr., **II** 479
McGrath, Eugene R., **V** 588
McGraw Ryerson, **IV** 635
McGraw, Curtis, **IV** 636
McGraw, Donald C., **IV** 636
McGraw Electric Company, **6** 312. *See
  also* Centel Corporation.
McGraw family, **IV** 635–37
McGraw, Harold, Jr., **IV** 636–37
McGraw, James H., **IV** 634–36
McGraw, James H., Jr., **IV** 635–36
McGraw, Max, **6** 312, 314
McGraw Publishing Co., **IV** 634
McGraw-Edison Co., **II** 17, 87
McGraw-Hill Book Co., **IV** 634–35
McGraw-Hill Broadcasting Co., **IV** 637
McGraw-Hill Co. of Canada, Ltd., **IV** 635
McGraw-Hill, Inc., II 398; **IV** 584,
  634–37, 643, 656, 674; **10** 62
McGregor Cory, **6** 415
McGrew Color Graphics, **7** 430
McGuigan, John, **10** 127
McGuiness, Paul, **6** 109
McGuire, William, **9** 525
MCI Airsignal, Inc., **6** 300, 322
MCI Communications Corporation, II
  408; **III** 13, 149, 684; **V 302–04**; **6**
  51–52, 300; **7** 118–19; **8** 310; **9** 171,
  478–80; **10** 19, 80, 89, 97, 433, 500; **11**
  183, 185, 302, 409, 500
MCI International, **11** 59
McInnerney, Thomas, **II** 533; **7** 275
McKay, Robert, **7** 505–06
McKee Baking Company, **7** 320–21
McKee Corporation, Robert E., **6** 150
McKee, Ellsworth, **7** 320–21
McKee Foods Corporation, 7 320–21
McKee, Jack, **7** 320
McKee, James W., Jr., **II** 498
McKee, O.D., **7** 320
McKee, Paul B., **V** 688
McKee, Ruth, **7** 320
McKeen, John, **I** 661–63; **9** 402–04
McKenna, Reginald, **II** 318–19
McKenna, Regis, **III** 115; **6** 218
McKenzie, John, **10** 126
McKenzie, Kelvin, **IV** 651; **7** 391
McKesson & Robbins, **I** 496, 713
McKesson Corporation, I 413, **496–98**;
  II 652; **III** 10; **6** 279; **9** 532; **11** 91
McKesson Envirosystems, **8** 464
McKesson, John, **I** 496
McKinley, John K., **IV** 553
McKinley, William, **III** 302; **IV** 572, 604,
  625–26; **7** 549
McKinley, William B., **6** 504
McKinney, John A., **III** 707–09; **7** 292–94
McKinnon, Don, **9** 281–82
McKinnon, N.J., **II** 245
McKinsey & Company, Inc., I 108, 144,
  437, 497; **III** 47, 85, 670; **9 343–45; 10**
  175
McKinsey, James O., **9** 343
McKinstry, Bill, **10** 373
McKitterick, Leonard B., **V** 405
McKittrick, David, **IV** 290
McKnight, Roy, **I** 656–57
McKnight, William L., **I** 499–500; **8**
  369–70

McKone, Don T., **III** 641
McKone, Don T., Jr., **III** 642
McLachlan, Angus Henry, **7** 252
McLain Grocery, **II** 625
McLamore, James, **II** 613
McLane Company, Inc., **V** 217; **8** 556
McLane, Louis, **II** 381
McLaren, "Scotty", **7** 535
McLaren Consolidated Cone Corp., **II** 543; **7** 366
McLaren, Henry D. (Lord Aberconway), **III** 690
McLarty, Thomas F. III, **V** 551
McLaughlin, David, **7** 535
McLaughlin, Frank, **6** 566
McLaughlin Motor Company of Canada, **I** 171; **10** 325
McLaughlin, Peter, **IV** 346
McLaughlin, W. Earle, **II** 345
McLean Clinic, **11** 379
McLean, David, **IV** 209
McLean, Edward, **IV** 688
McLean, J.S., **II** 483
McLean, John G., **IV** 401
McLean, John R., **IV** 688
McLean, Malcolm, **I** 476
Mclean, St. John, **IV** 581
McLean, William, **II** 483
McLennan, Donald, **III** 282–83
McLeod, Henry C., **II** 220–21
McLeod, W. Norman, **IV** 645
McLintock, J. Dewar, **I** 191
McLucas, Walter S., **11** 339–40
MCM Electronics, **9** 420
McMahon, Kit, **II** 319
McMan Oil and Gas Co., **IV** 369
McManus, John & Adams, Inc., **6** 21
McMaster, Fergus, **6** 109–10
McMaster, John, **III** 331
McMaster, Ross, **IV** 208
McMaster, William, **II** 244; **IV** 208
McMillan, Dan, **11** 270
McMillan, John A., **V** 156, 158
McMillan, John D., **II** 616
McMillen, Charles, **IV** 345
McMillen, Dale, Jr., **7** 81
McMillen, Dale W., Sr., **7** 81
McMillen, Harold, **7** 81
McMoCo, **IV** 82–83; **7** 187
McMoRan, **IV** 83; **7** 187
McMoRan Exploration Co., **IV** 83; **V** 739; **7** 187
McMoRan Offshore Exploration Co., **IV** 83; **7** 187
McMoRan Oil & Gas Co., **IV** 81–82; **7** 185, 187
McMullin, Joseph S., **V** 222
McMurren, William H., **7** 356
McMurtrie, Adnah, **11** 515
McMurtry Manufacturing, **8** 553
MCN Corporation, 6 519–22
MCN Investment. *See* MCN Corporation.
McNabb, Joseph, **9** 61–62
McNaghten, Malcom, **V** 29
McNaghten, Stuart, **III** 360
McNair, Robert, **I** 372
McNamara, John F., **III** 10
McNamara, Robert, **9** 417
McNamara, Robert S., **I** 166–67, 484, 539; **11** 138–39, 263
McNamee, Frank L., **II** 147
McNealy, Scott, **7** 498, 500
McNeer, Charles S., **6** 603
McNeil, Fred, **II** 211

McNeil Laboratories, **III** 35–36; **8** 282
McNeil Pharmaceutical Company, **III** 36; **8** 282
McNeilab Inc., **8** 283
McNellan Resources Inc., **IV** 76
McNerney, Walter J., **10** 160
McNulty, James J., **6** 389
McNutt, Jack W., **7** 364
McNutt, Paul V., **II** 147
MCO Holdings Inc., **8** 349
MCO Properties Inc., **8** 348
MCO Resources, Inc., **8** 349
MCorp, **10** 134; **11** 122
McParland, James, **9** 407
McPhatter, Clyde, **II** 176
McPherson, Frank A., **IV** 446–47
McPherson, John D., **6** 345
McPherson, Rene C., **I** 152–53; **10** 264–65
McQuilkin, William, **7** 45
McRae, Milton, **7** 157
McRae, Milton A., **IV** 606
MCS, Inc., **10** 412
McSweeney, George, **7** 138
McSweeney, Howard, **6** 483
McSwiney, James W., **IV** 311
McVitie & Price, **II** 592–93
McVitie, Robert, **II** 592
McVitie, Robert, Jr., **II** 592
McVitie, William, **II** 592
McWhorter Inc., **8** 553
McWilliam, Michael, **II** 358
McWilliams, W.K., Jr., **IV** 82–83; **7** 187
MD Pharmaceuticals, **III** 10
MDI Co., Ltd., **IV** 327
MDS/Bankmark, **10** 247
MDU Resources Group, Inc., 7 322–25
Mead & Nixon Paper Co., **IV** 310
Mead and Weston, **IV** 310
Mead, Cecil, **6** 241
Mead, Charles, **IV** 310
Mead Corporation, IV 310–13, 327, 329, 342–43; **8** 267; **9** 261; **10** 406; **11** 421–22
Mead Cycle Co., **IV** 660
Mead, Dana G., **10** 528
Mead, Daniel (Col.), **IV** 310
Mead Data Central, Inc., IV 312; **7** 581; **10 406–08**
Mead, E.R., **IV** 75
Mead, Franklin B., **III** 274–75
Mead, Frederick, **I** 287
Mead, Gary L., **11** 243
Mead, George, **IV** 310–11; **8** 124–25; **9** 416
Mead, Harry, **IV** 310
Mead Johnson, **III** 17
Mead Paper Co., **IV** 310
Mead Paperboard Corp., **IV** 310
Mead Pulp & Paper Co., **IV** 310
Mead Sales Co., **IV** 310
Meade County Rural Electric Cooperative Corporation, **11** 37
Meadlock, James, **6** 246–48
Meadow Gold Dairies, Inc., **II** 473
Meadows, Thomas C., **8** 264
Means Services, Inc., **II** 607
Mears & Phillips, **II** 237
Measurex Corporation, **8** 243
Mebane, Benjamin Franklin, **9** 213
MEC Hawaii Corp., **IV** 714
MEC UK Ltd., **IV** 714
MEC USA, Inc., **IV** 714
Mecaslin, John H., **6** 446
Mecca Leisure, **I** 248

Mechanics Exchange Savings Bank, **9** 173
Mechanics Machine Co., **III** 438
Mechanics Universal Joint Co., **III** 438
Mecherle, G. Ermond, **III** 363
Mecherle, George, **III** 362–63
Mecherle, Ramond, **III** 363
Medal Distributing Co., **9** 542
Medallion Pictures Corp., **9** 320
Medco Containment Services Inc., 9 346–48; 11 291
Medco Foundation, **9** 348
Medcom Inc., **I** 628
Medd, C.R., **10** 372
Medeco Security Locks, Inc., **10** 350
Medfield Corp., **III** 87
Medi Mart Drug Store Co., **II** 667
Media General, Inc., III 214; **7 326–28**
Media Play, **9** 360–61
Medical Expense Fund, **III** 245
Medical Indemnity of America, **10** 160
Medical Marketing Group Inc., **9** 348
Medical Service Assoc. of Pennsylvania, **III** 325–26
Medical Tribune Group, **IV** 591
Medici, Giuseppi, **I** 369
Medicine Bow Coal Company, **7** 33–34
Medicus Intercon International, **6** 22
Medill, Joseph, **IV** 682
Medina, Harold R., **II** 431
Mediobanca Banca di Credito Finanziario SpA, **II** 191, 271; **III** 208–09; **11** 205
Mediplex Group, **III** 16
The Mediplex Group, Inc., **11** 282
Medis Health and Pharmaceuticals Services Inc., **II** 653
Meditrust, 11 281–83
Medlabs Inc., **III** 73
Medtronic, Inc., 8 351–54; 11 459
Medusa Corporation, **8** 135
Meeker, David A., **III** 611
Meeker, David B., **III** 611
Meeker, Richard H., **IV** 582, 584
Meeker, Samuel, **9** 221
Meelia, Richard J., **11** 220
Meenaghan, James J., **III** 263
Meer, Fritz ter, **I** 349
Mees & Hope, **II** 184
Mees, C.E. Kenneth (Dr.), **III** 474; **7** 161
Meese, William G., **V** 593
Meeus, Jacques, **IV** 498
Meeus, Laurent, **IV** 498
MEGA Natural Gas Company, **11** 28
Megargel, Roy C., **I** 276; **10** 450
Mehren, George L., **11** 25
Mei Foo Investments Ltd., **IV** 718
Meier, H. H., **6** 397
Meijer, Doug, **7** 331
Meijer, Frederick, **7** 329–31
Meijer, Gezina, **7** 329
Meijer, Hank, **7** 331
Meijer, Hendrik, **7** 329
Meijer Incorporated, 7 329–31
Meijer, Johanna, **7** 329
Meijer, Mark, **7** 331
Meiji Commerce Bank, **II** 291
Meiji, Emperor (Japan), **III** 532, 551; **IV** 147
Meiji Fire Insurance Co., **III** 384–85
Meiji Milk Products Company, Limited, II 538–39
Meiji Mutual Life Insurance Company, II 323; **III 288–89**
Meiji Seika (U.S.A.), **II** 540

Meiji Seika Kaisha, Ltd., I 676; II 540–41
Meiji Sugar Manufacturing Co., II 538
Meijiseimei Insurance Agency, III 289
Meijiseimei Insurance Services, III 289
Meijiseimei International, III 289
Meikle, Andrew, 10 377
Meikosha Co., II 72
Meinecke Muffler Company, 10 415
Meineke Discount Muffler Shops, III 495
Meis of Illiana, 10 282
Meisei Electric, III 742
Meissner, Ackermann & Co., IV 463; 7 351
Meiwa Co., III 758
Meiwa Manufacturing Co., III 758
N.V. Mekog, IV 531
Mel Klein and Partners, III 74
Melbur China Clay Co., III 690
Melco, II 58
Melick, Balthazar P., II 250
Melk, John, 9 73–74
Melkunie-Holland, II 575
Mellbank Security Co., II 316
de Mello, Fernando Collor, IV 501
Mellon, Andrew W., I 354, 584; II 315; IV 10
Mellon Bank (DE), II 316
Mellon Bank (East), II 316
Mellon Bank (MD), II 317
Mellon Bank Corporation, I 67–68, 584; II 315–17, 342; 9 470
Mellon, E.P., I 584
Mellon family, III 258
Mellon Indemnity Corp., III 258–59
Mellon, John, 7 246
Mellon National Bank, II 315–16; III 275
Mellon National Bank and Trust Co., II 316
Mellon National Corp., II 316
Mellon, Paul, 11 453
Mellon, Richard B., I 584; II 315–16; IV 14
Mellon, Richard K., II 316
Mellon Securities Ltd., II 317, 402
Mellon, Thomas, II 315
Mellon, Thomas A., I 584
Mellon-Stuart Co., I 584–85
Mellor, James, 10 318
Melone, Joseph, III 249, 340
Mélotte, III 418
Meloy Laboratories, Inc., 11 333
Melroe Company, 8 115–16
Melrose, Kendrick B., 7 534–35
Melrose, Kenrick B., 7 535
Meltzer, Edward A., 6 244
Melville Corporation, V 136–38; 9 192
Melville, Frank, V 136
Melville, Herman, IV 661
Melville, John Ward, V 136
Melvin Simon and Associates, Inc., 8 355–57
Melwire Group, III 673
Memorex, 6 282–83
Memorex Corp., III 110, 166
Menagh, Louis R., Jr., III 339
Menasco Manufacturing Co., I 435; III 415
Menasha Corporation, 8 358–61
Menasha Wooden Ware Company, 8 358
Menck, 8 544
Mendelssohn & Co., II 241
Mendozo Fleury, Lorenzo, I 230
Menem, Carlos, IV 578

Meneven, IV 508
Menge, Walter O., III 276
Menichella, Donato, I 465
de Menil, Jean, III 617
Menk, L. W., V 428
Menka Gesellschaft, IV 150
Mennen Company, 6 26
Mennen Toiletries, I 19
Menotti, Gian Carlo, IV 620
Mentholatum Co., IV 722
Mentor Graphics, 8 519
Mentor Graphics Corporation, III 143; 11 46–47, **284–86**, 490
Mény, Jules, IV 544, 558
Menzies, Robert, IV 45–46
Menzies, William C., II 220
MEPC Canada, IV 712
MEPC plc, IV **710–12**
Mer, Francis, IV 227–28
MeraBank, 6 546
Mercantile Agency, IV 604
Mercantile and General Reinsurance Co., III 335, 377
Mercantile Bank, II 298
Mercantile Bankshares Corp., 11 **287–88**
Mercantile Estate and Property Corp. Ltd., IV 710
Mercantile Fire Insurance, III 234
Mercantile Mutual, III 310
Mercantile Property Corp. Ltd., IV 710
Mercantile Security Life, III 136
Mercantile Stores Company, Inc., V 139
Mercantile Trust Co., II 229, 247
Mercedes Benz. *See* Daimler-Benz A.G.
Mercedes-Benz USA, I 27
Merchant Co., III 104
Merchants Bank, II 213
Merchants Bank of Canada, II 210
Merchants Bank of Halifax, II 344
Merchants Dispatch, II 395–96; 10 60
Merchants Fire Assurance Corp., III 396–97
Merchants Home Delivery Service, 6 414
Merchants Indemnity Corp., III 396–97
Merchants Life Insurance Co., III 275
Merchants National Bank, 9 228
Merchants National Bank of Boston, II 213
Merchants Union Express Co., II 396; 10 60
Merchants' Assoc., II 261
Merchants' Loan and Trust, II 261; III 518
Merchants' Savings, Loan and Trust Co., II 261
Mercier, I 272
Mercier, Ernest, IV 545, 557–58
Merck & Co., Inc., I 640, 646, **650–52**, 683–84, 708; II 414; III 42, 60, 66; 8 154, 548; 10 213; 11 9, 90, **289–91** (upd.)
Merck, Albert W., I 650; 11 290
Merck, E., 6 397
Merck, Finck & Co., III 299
Merck, Friedrich Jacob, I 650; 11 289–90
Merck, George, I 650; 11 289
Merck, George W., I 650; 11 289–90
Merck, Heinrich Emmanuel, I 650; 11 289
Mercury, 11 547–48
Mercury Communications, Ltd., V 280–82; 7 332–34; 10 456
Mercury, Inc., 8 311
Meredith and Drew, III 593
Meredith/Burda Cos., IV 661–62
Meredith Corporation, IV 661; 11 292–94

Meredith, E.T., III, 11 293
Meredith, Edwin Thomas (E.T.), 11 292
Meredith, William, II 593
Merensky, Hans (Dr.), IV 118
Meridian Bancorp, Inc., 11 295–97
Meridian Insurance Co., III 332
Meridian Oil Inc., 10 190–91
Merillat Industries, III 570
Merisel, 10 518–19
Merit Tank Testing, Inc., IV 411
Merivienti Oy, IV 276
Merkle, Hans, I 192
Merla Manufacturing, I 524
Merle, Henri, IV 173
Merlin Gerin, II 93–94
Merlin, Paul-Louis, II 93
Merlo, Harry A., IV 304–05
Merlotti, Frank, 7 494
Mermoz, Jean, V 471
Merpati Nusantara Airlines, 6 90–91
Merrell Drug, I 325
Merrell-Soule Co., II 471
Merriam and Morgan Paraffine Co., IV 548
Merriam, Otis, 8 552
Merriam-Webster, Inc., 7 165, 167
Merrick, David, II 170
Merrick, Samuel Vaughn, 10 71
Merrill, Charles, II 424, 654
Merrill, Fred H., III 251
Merrill Gas Company, 9 554
Merrill Lynch & Co., Inc., I 26, 339, 681, 683, 697; II 149, 257, 260, 268, 403, 407–08, 412, **424–26**, 441, 449, 451, 456, 654–55, 680; III 119, 340; 6 244; 7 130; 8 94; 9 125, 239, 301, 386
Merrill Lynch Capital Markets, III 263; 11 348
Merrill Lynch Capital Partners, III 440; 9 187
Merrill Lynch Capital Partners Inc., 11 122, 348, 557
Merrill Lynch, E.A. Pierce & Cassatt, II 424
Merrill Lynch International Bank, II 425
Merrill Lynch, Pierce, Fenner & Beane, II 424
Merrill Lynch, Pierce, Fenner & Smith, II 424–25, 445
Merrill Lynch Realty, III 340; 11 29
Merrill Lynch Relocation Management, III 340
Merrill, Pickard, Anderson & Eyre IV, 11 490
Merrill Publishing, IV 643; 7 312; 9 63
Merry Group, III 673
Merry Maids, 6 46
Merry-Go-Round Enterprises, Inc., 8 362–64
Merseles, T.F., III 706; 7 291
Merseles, Theodore, V 146
Mersey Paper Co., IV 258
Mersey White Lead Co., III 680
Merton, Alfred, IV 140
Merton, Henry R., IV 139–40
Merton, Ralph, IV 139
Merton, Richard, IV 140
Merton, Wilhelm, IV 139–40
Merton, William. *See* Merton, Wilhelm
Merv Griffin Enterprises, II 137
Mervyn's, V 43–44; 10 409–10
Merzagore, Cesare, III 208–09
Mesa Acquisition Corp., 11 300
Mesa Air Shuttle, Inc., 11 298

Mesa Airlines, Inc., 11 298–300
Mesa L.P., **IV** 410, 523
Mesa Limited Partnership, **11** 441
Mesa Petroleum, **IV** 392, 571
Mesaba Transportation Co., **I** 448
Messageries du Livre, **IV** 614
Messer, Walter L., **8** 395
Messerschmitt, Willy, **I** 73–75
Messerschmitt-Bölkow-Blohm GmbH., I
41–42, 46, 51–52, 55, **73–75,** 111, 121;
II 242; **III** 539; **11** 267
Messervy, Godfrey, **III** 556
Mestek, Inc., 10 411–13
Meston, Alexander W., **II** 18
Meston, Charles R., **II** 18
Meston, T.M., **II** 18
Metabio-Joullie, **III** 47
Metal Box & Printing Industries, **I** 604
Metal Box plc, I 604–06
Metal Closures, **I** 615
Metal Industries, **I** 531–32
Metal Manufactures, **III** 433–34
Metal Office Furniture Company, **7** 493
Metal Package Corporation, **I** 607
Metal-Cal, **IV** 253
Metaleurop, **IV** 108–09
Metall Mining Corp., **IV** 141
Metallbank, **IV** 229
Metallgesellschaft AG, IV 17, **139–42**
Metallgesellschaft Corp., **IV** 141
Metallgesellschaft of Australia (Pty) Ltd.,
IV 141
Metallurgische Gesellschaft
Aktiengesellschaft, **IV** 139–40, 229
MetalPro, Inc., **IV** 168
Metals and Controls Corp., **II** 113
Metals Exploration, **IV** 82
Metaphase Technology, Inc., **10** 257
Metcalf & Eddy Companies, Inc., **6** 143,
441
Metcalfe, Robert M., **11** 518–19
Methane Development Corporation, **6** 457
Metinox Steel Ltd., **IV** 203
MetLife Capital Corp., **III** 293
MetLife Capital Credit Corp., **III** 293
MetLife General Insurance Agency, **III**
293
MetLife HealthCare Management Corp.,
III 294
MetLife Marketing Corp., **III** 293
MetMor Financial, Inc., **III** 293
MetPath, Inc., **III** 684
Metro. *See* Metro Vermogensverwaltung
Gmbh & Co. of Dusseldorf.
Metro Drugs, **II** 649–50
Metro Glass, **II** 533
Metro Pictures, **II** 148
Metro Southwest Construction. *See* CRSS
Inc.
Metro Vermögensverwaltung GmbH & Co.
of Dusseldorf, **V** 104
Metro-Goldwyn-Mayer, **I** 286, 487; **II** 135,
146–47, 148–50, 155, 161, 167, 169,
174–75. *See also* MGM/UA
Communications Company.
Metro-Mark Integrated Systems Inc., **11**
469
Metro-Richelieu Inc., **II** 653
Metro-Verwegensverwaltung, **II** 257
Metromail Corp., **IV** 661
Metromedia Co., II 171; **6** 33, 168–69; **7**
91, **335–37**
Metromedia Communications Corp., **7** 336;
8 311

Metromedia Steakhouses, **7** 336
Metromedia Technologies, **7** 336
Metromont Materials, **III** 740
Metroplitan and Great Western Dairies, **II**
586
Metropolitan Accident Co., **III** 228
Metropolitan Bank, **II** 221, 318; **III** 239;
IV 644
Metropolitan Broadcasting Corporation, **7**
335
Metropolitan Distributors, **9** 283
Metropolitan District Railway Company, **6**
406
Metropolitan Estate and Property Corp.
(Rhodesia) Ltd., **IV** 711
Metropolitan Estate and Property Corp.
Ltd., **IV** 710–11
Metropolitan Gas Light Co., **6** 455
Metropolitan Housing Corp. Ltd., **IV** 710
Metropolitan Insurance and Annuity Co.,
III 293
Metropolitan Life and Affiliated Cos., **III**
293
Metropolitan Life Insurance Company,
II 679; **III** 265–66, 272, **290–94,** 313,
329, 337, 339–40, 706; **IV** 283; **6** 256;
8 326–27; **11** 482
Metropolitan National Bank, **II** 284
Metropolitan Petroleum Chemicals Co., **IV**
180
Metropolitan Petroleum Corp., **IV** 180–81
Metropolitan Property and Liability
Insurance, **III** 293
Metropolitan Railway, **6** 407
Metropolitan Railways Surplus Lands Co.,
IV 711
Metropolitan Reinsurance, **III** 293
Metropolitan Structures, **III** 293
Metropolitan Tower Life, **III** 293
Metropolitan Vickers, **III** 670
Oy Metsä-Botnia Ab, **IV** 315–16
Metsä-Sellu, **IV** 316
Metsä-Serla AB, **IV** 315
Metsä-Serla Oy, IV 314–16, 318, 350
Metsäliito Oy, **IV** 315
Metsäliiton Myyntikonttorit, **IV** 315
Oy Metsäliiton Paperi Ab, **IV** 315
Metsäliiton Selluloosa Oy, **IV** 315
Metsäliiton Teollisuus Oy, **IV** 314–15
Oy Metsäpohjanmaa-Skogsbotnia Ab., **IV**
315
Mettler, Ruben F., **I** 540–41; **11** 541–42
Mettler United States Inc., **9** 441
Metz, Auguste, **IV** 24
Metz, Charles, **IV** 24
Metz, Norbert, **IV** 24
de Metz, Victor, **IV** 545, 558–60
Metzenbaum, Howard, **III** 188
Metzger, Hutzel, **8** 489–90
Mexican Eagle Oil Co., **IV** 365, 531
Mexican Original Products, Inc., **II** 585
Mexofina, S.A. de C.V., **IV** 401
Meyenberg, John, **7** 428
Meyenberg, John B., **II** 486
Meyer, Alfred, **IV** 565
Meyer, Aloyse, **IV** 25
Meyer and Charlton, **IV** 90
Meyer, Andre, **IV** 79
Meyer, Carl, **I** 127
Meyer, Edward H., **6** 27–28
Meyer, Eugene, **I** 414–15; **IV** 688–89
Meyer, Fred G., **V** 54–56
Meyer, Fritz, **III** 411
Meyer, Georges, **V** 58–59

Meyer, Jerome J., **8** 519–20
Meyer, John R., **I** 118, 124
Meyer, Montague, **IV** 306
Meyer, Otto, **6** 133
Meyer, Raoul, **V** 57–58
Meyer, Russell, **8** 92
Meyer, Stephen, **I** 168
Meyer-Galow, Erhard, **8** 69
Meyercord, Wade, **10** 463
Meyers & Muldoon, **6** 40
Meyers and Co., **III** 9
Meyers, Gerald, **I** 136, 190
Meyers, Mike, **8** 553
Meyerson, Morton, H., **III** 137–38
Meyerson, Robert F., **10** 523–24
Meyo, Raymond, **10** 523–24
Meyrin, **I** 122
MFI, **II** 612
MFS Communications Company, Inc.,
11 301–03
MG Holdings. *See* Mayflower Group Inc.
MG Ltd., **IV** 141
MG&E. *See* Madison Gas & Electric.
MGM. *See* Metro-Goldwyn-Mayer.
MGM Grand Hotels, **III** 431; **6** 210
MGM/UA Classics, **II** 149
MGM/UA Communications Company, II
103, **146–50;** **IV** 676
MGM/UA Entertainment Co., **II** 146, 149,
161, 167, 408
MGM/UA Home Entertainment Group, **II**
149
MGM/UA Television Group, **II** 149
MGM-Loew's, **II** 148
MGM/UA Entertainment, **6** 172–73
mh Bausparkasse AG, **III** 377
MHT. *See* Manufacturers Hanover Trust
Co.
Miall, Stephen, **III** 680
Miami Power Corporation, **6** 466
Micamold Electronics Manufacturing
Corporation, **10** 319
MICHAEL Business Systems Plc, **10** 257
Michael, Gary, **7** 21
Michael Joseph, **IV** 659
Michael Reese Health Plan Inc., **III** 82
MichCon. *See* MCN Corporation.
Michelangelo, Buonarroti, **III** 251
Michelet, Jules, **IV** 617
Michelin, **III** 697; **7** 36–37; **8** 74; **11** 158,
473
Michelin, André, **V** 236
Michelin, Edouard, **V** 236, 238
Michelin et Compagnie, **V** 236
Michelin, François, **V** 238
Michiana Merchandising, **III** 10
Michie Co., **IV** 312
Michigan Automotive Compressor, Inc., **III**
593, 638–39
Michigan Carpet Sweeper Company, **9** 70
Michigan Consolidated Gas Company. *See*
MCN Corporation.
Michigan Fruit Canners, **II** 571
Michigan General, **II** 408
Michigan International Speedway, **V** 494
Michigan National Corporation, 11
304–06
Michigan Plating and Stamping Co., **I** 451
Michigan Radiator & Iron Co., **III** 663
Michigan State Life Insurance Co., **III** 274
Michigan Tag Company, **9** 72
Mick, Roger, **III** 80
Mickey Shorr Mobile Electronics, **10** 9–11
Micro D, Inc., **11** 194

Micro Decisionware, Inc., **10** 506
Micro-Circuit, Inc., **III** 645
Micro-Power Corp., **III** 643
MicroBilt Corporation, **11** 112
MicroComputer Accessories, **III** 614
Microcomputer Asset Management
    Services, **9** 168
Microdot Inc., **I** 440; **8 365–68**, 545
Microfal, **I** 341
Microform International Marketing Corp.,
    IV 642; **7** 312
Micron Technology, Inc., **III** 113; **11
    307–09**
Micropolis Corp., **10** 403, 458, 463
MicroPro International, **10** 556
Microseal Corp., **I** 341
Microsoft Corporation, **III** 116; **6**
    219–20, 224, 227, 231, 235, 254–56,
    257–60, 269–71; **9** 81, 140, 171, 195,
    472; **10** 22, 34, 57, 87, 119, 237–38,
    362–63, 408, 477, 484, 504, 557–58; **11**
    59, 77–78, 306, 519–20
Microtel Limited, **6** 309–10
Microware Surgical Instruments Corp., **IV**
    137
Microwave Communications, Inc., **V** 302
Mid America Tag & Label, **8** 360
Mid-America Capital Resources, Inc., **6**
    508
Mid-America Dairymen, Inc., **II** 536; **7
    338–40**
Mid-America Industries, **III** 495
Mid-America Interpool Network, **6** 602
Mid-America Packaging, Inc., **8** 203
Mid-American Dairymen, Inc., **11** 24
Mid-American Interpool Network, **6** 506
Mid-Central Fish and Frozen Foods Inc., **II**
    675
Mid-Continent Area Power Planner, **V** 672
Mid-Continent Computer Services, **11** 111
Mid-Continent Telephone Corporation. *See*
    Alltel Corporation.
Mid-Georgia Gas Company, **6** 448
Mid-Illinois Gas Co., **6** 529
Mid-Pacific Airlines, **9** 271
Mid-South Towing, **6** 583
Mid-Texas Communications Systems, **6**
    313
Mid-West Drive-In Theatres Inc., **I** 245
Mid-West Paper Ltd., **IV** 286
MidAmerican Communications
    Corporation, **8** 311
Midas International Corporation, **I**
    457–58; **10 414–15**, 554
MIDCO, **III** 340
Midcon, **IV** 481
Middle South Energy, Inc., **V** 619
Middle South Utilities, **V** 618–19
Middle West Corporation, **6** 469–70
Middle West Utilities Company, **V**
    583–84; **6** 555–56, 604–05
Middle Wisconsin Power, **6** 604
Middlebrook, John, **7** 462
Middleburg Steel and Alloys Group, **I** 423
Middlesex Bank, **II** 334
Middleton's Starch Works, **II** 566
Midhurst Corp., **IV** 658
Midial, **II** 478
Midland and International Bank, **II** 319
Midland, Archer Daniels, **7** 241
Midland Bank PLC, **II** 208, 236, 279,
    295, 298, **318–20**, 334, 383; **9** 505
Midland Cooperative, **II** 536
Midland Counties Dairies, **II** 587

Midland Electric Coal Co., **IV** 170
Midland Enterprises Inc., **6** 486–88
Midland Gravel Co., **III** 670
Midland Industrial Finishes Co., **I** 321
Midland Insurance, **I** 473
Midland International, **8** 56–57
Midland Investment Co., **II** 7
Midland Linseed Products Co., **I** 419
Midland Montagu, **II** 319
Midland National Bank, **11** 130
Midland Railway Co., **II** 306
Midland Southwest Corp., **8** 347
Midland United, **6** 556
Midland Utilities Company, **6** 532
Midlands Energy Co., **IV** 83; **7** 188
Midoro, Masuichi, **6** 70
Midrex Corp., **IV** 130
Midvale Steel and Ordnance Co., **IV** 35,
    114; **7** 48
Midway (Southwest) Airway Company, **6**
    120
Midway Airlines, **6** 105, 121
Midway Manufacturing, **III** 430
Midwest Agri-Commodities, **11** 15
Midwest Air Charter, **6** 345
Midwest Com of Indiana, Inc., **11** 112
Midwest Dairy Products, **II** 661
Midwest Energy Company, **6** 523–24
Midwest Express, **III** 40–41; **11** 299
Midwest Express Airlines, **11** 299
Midwest Federal Savings & Loan
    Association, **11** 162–63
Midwest Financial Group, Inc., **8** 188
Midwest Foundry Co., **IV** 137
Midwest Power Systems Inc., **6** 525
Midwest Refining Co., **IV** 368
Midwest Resources Inc., **6 523–25**
Midwest Synthetics, **8** 553
Miele & Cie., **III** 418
Mifflin, George Harrison, **10** 356
Mikko, **II** 70
Mikko Kaloinen Oy, **IV** 349
Milani, **II** 556
Milavsky, Harold, **10** 530–31
Milbank, Albert G., **II** 471
Milbank Insurance Co., **III** 350
Milbank, Isaac, **IV** 569
Milbank, Jeremiah, **II** 470–71
Milbank, Tweed, Hope & Webb, **II** 471
Milbourne, Robert J., **IV** 210
Milburn, Arthur W., **II** 471
Milcor Steel Co., **IV** 114
Miles Druce & Co., **III** 494
Miles, Franklin, **I** 653
Miles, J. Fred, **IV** 372
Miles Kimball Co., **9** 393
Miles Laboratories, **I** 310, **653–55**, 674,
    678; **6** 50
Miles, Michael, **7** 266–67
Miles, Michael A., **I** 260; **II** 534; **7** 276
Miles Redfern, **I** 429
Milgo Electronic Corp., **II** 83; **11** 408
Milgram Food Stores Inc., **II** 682
Milk Producers, Inc., **11** 24
Milken, Michael, **II** 407–09; **III** 253–54;
    IV 334; **6** 210–11; **8** 196, 389–90; **11**
    291
Millard, Killik, **II** 586
Millbrook Press Inc., **IV** 616
Miller, Alan B., **6** 191–93
Miller, Arjay, **I** 166–67; **11** 138–39, 263
Miller, Benjamin C., **III** 302

Miller Brewing Company, **I** 218–19,
    236–37, 254–55, 257–58, **269–70**, 283,
    290–91, 548; **10** 100; **11** 421
Miller, C. O. G., **V** 682
Miller, Charles, **6** 299
Miller, Charles D., **IV** 254
Miller, Charles Ransom, **IV** 647
Miller Chemical & Fertilizer Corp., **I** 412
Miller Container Corporation, **8** 102
Miller, Dane A., **10** 156–58
Miller, Darius, **V** 427
Miller, David, **V** 91–92
Miller, E. Kirdbride, **11** 494
Miller, Emil, **I** 269
Miller, Eric, **III** 698–99
Miller, Ernest, **I** 269
Miller, Eugene L., **II** 15–16
Miller, Fred A., **III** 470–71
Miller, Frederick, **I** 269
Miller, Frederick A., **I** 269
Miller, Frederick C., **I** 269
Miller Freeman, **IV** 687
Miller, G. William, **I** 529–30
Miller, George, **9** 553
Miller, Glen B., **I** 415
Miller, Henry J., **6** 465
Miller, Herman, **8** 255
Miller, J. Irwin, **I** 146–47
Miller, J.K. Cockburn, **I** 288
Miller, John R., **IV** 627
Miller, Malcolm, **III** 113
Miller, Mason and Dickenson, **III** 204–05
Miller, Monroe A., **11** 408
Miller, Paul, **IV** 612–13; **V** 683–84; **7**
    190–91
Miller, Richard W., **III** 170; **6** 286–87
Miller, Robert, **V** 683
Miller, Robert C., **8** 138
Miller, Ron, **II** 173; **6** 175
Miller, Thomas W., **IV** 17
Miller, W.O., **III** 380
Miller, Walter, **IV** 400
Miller, Whitney, **7** 534
Miller, William J., **10** 459
Millet's Leisure, **V** 177–78
Millicom, **11** 547
Milliken & Co., **V 366–68**; **8** 270–71
Milliken, Frank, **IV** 170; **7** 262–63
Milliken, Roger, **8** 13
Milliken, Tomlinson Co., **II** 682
Millipore, **9** 396
Mills, Hayley, **II** 173
Mills, Vic, **III** 52
Millsop, T.E., **IV** 236
Millstone Point Company, **V** 668–69
Millville Electric Light Company, **6** 449
Milne, Alasdair, **7** 54
Milner, **III** 98
Milstein, Henrietta, **10** 188
Milstein, Monroe G., **10** 188
Milton Bradley, **III** 504–06
Milton Roy Co., **8** 135
Milwaukee City Railroad Company, **6** 601
Milwaukee Electric Light, **6** 601
Milwaukee Electric Manufacturing Co., **III**
    534
Milwaukee Electric Railway & Transport
    Company, **6** 602
Milwaukee Electric Railway and Light
    Company, **6** 601–02, 604–05
Milwaukee Insurance Co., **III** 242
Milwaukee Light, Heat, and Traction
    Company, **6** 601–02

Milwaukee Mutual Fire Insurance Co., **III** 321
Milwaukee Street Railway Company, **6** 601
Minami, Kanji, **III** 405
Minato, Moriatsu, **II** 434; **9** 378
Minatome, **IV** 560
Minemet, **IV** 108
Minemet Recherche, **IV** 108
Miner, Robert N., **6** 272
Mineral Point Public Service Company, **6** 604
Minerals & Chemicals Philipp, **IV** 79–80
Minerals & Metals Trading Corporation of India Ltd., **IV** 143–44
Minerals and Resources Corp., **IV** 23
Minerals Technologies Inc., **11** 310–12
Minerec Corporation, **9** 363
Minerva, **III** 359
Minerve, **6** 208
Mines et Usines du Nord et de l'Est, **IV** 226
Minet Europe Holdings Ltd., **III** 357
Minet Holdings PLC, **III** 357
Minhinnik, John, **IV** 437
Mini Stop, **V** 97
Mining and Technical Services, **IV** 67
Mining Corp. of Canada Ltd., **IV** 164
Mining Development Corp., **IV** 239–40
Mining Trust Ltd., **IV** 32
MiniScribe, Inc., **6** 230; **10** 404
Minister of Finance Inc., **IV** 519
Minivator Ltd., **11** 486
Minneapolis General Electric of Minnesota, **V** 670
Minneapolis Heat Regulator Co., **II** 40–41
Minneapolis Millers Association, **10** 322
Minneapolis-Honeywell, **8** 21
Minneapolis-Honeywell Regulator Co., **II** 40–41, 86
Minnesota Cooperative Creameries Assoc., Inc., **II** 535
Minnesota Linseed Oil Co., **8** 552
Minnesota Mining & Manufacturing Company (3M), **I** 28, 387, 499–501; **II** 39; **III** 476, 487, 549; **IV** 251, 253–54; **6** 231; **7** 162; **8** 35, 369–71 (upd.); **11** 494
Minnesota Paints, **8** 552–53
Minnesota Power & Light Company, **11** 313–16
Minnesota Sugar Company, **11** 13
Minnesota Valley Canning Co., **I** 22
Minnetonka Corp., **II** 590; **III** 25
Minnig, Max, **I** 405
Minoli, Federico, **10** 151
Minolta Camera Co., Ltd., **III** 574–76, 583–84
Minolta Camera Handelsgesellschaft, **III** 575
Minolta Corp., **III** 575
Minomura, Rizaemon, **I** 505–06, **II** 325
Minorco, **III** 503; **IV** 67–68, 84, 97
Minstar Inc., **11** 397
Minute Maid Corp., **I** 234; **10** 227
Minute Tapioca, **II** 531
MIPS Computer Systems, **II** 45; **11** 491
Mirabito, Paul, **I** 142; **III** 166; **6** 282
Mirage Resorts, Inc., **6** 209–12
Miramar Hotel & Investment Co., **IV** 717
Mircali Asset Management, **III** 340
Mirkin, Morris, **9** 94
Miron, Robert, **IV** 583
Mirrlees Blackstone, **III** 509
Mirror Group Newspapers Ltd., **7** 312

Mirror Group Newspapers plc, **IV** 641; **7** 244, **341–43**
Mirror Printing and Binding House, **IV** 677
Misr Airwork. *See* AirEgypt.
Misrair. *See* AirEgypt.
Miss Clairol, **6** 28
Miss Selfridge, **V** 177–78
Missenden, Eustace, **V** 421
Misset Publishers, **IV** 611
Mission Energy Company, **V** 715
Mission First Financial, **V** 715
Mission Group, **V** 715, 717
Mission Insurance Co., **III** 192
Mission Land Company, **V** 715
Mississippi Chemical Corporation, **8** 183; **IV** 367
Mississippi Drug, **III** 10
Mississippi Gas Company, **6** 577
Mississippi Power & Light, **V** 619
Mississippi River Corporation, **10** 44
Missouri Book Co., **10** 136
Missouri Gas & Electric Service Company, **6** 593
Missouri Pacific Railroad, **10** 43–44
Missouri Public Service Company. *See* UtiliCorp United Inc.
Missouri Utilities Company, **6** 580
Missouri-Kansas-Texas Railroad, **I** 472; **IV** 458
Mistral Plastics Pty Ltd., **IV** 295
di Misurata, Giuseppe Volpi (Count), **III** 208
Mita, Katsushige, **I** 455
Mitarai, Takeshi, **III** 120–21, 575
Mitchell & Mitchell Gas & Oil, **7** 344–35
Mitchell, Billy, **I** 67
Mitchell, Charles, **IV** 392
Mitchell, Charles E., **I** 337; **II** 253–54; **9** 123
Mitchell Construction, **III** 753
Mitchell, David W., **III** 16
Mitchell, Dean H., **6** 532
Mitchell, Edward F., **6** 554
Mitchell Energy and Development Corporation, **7** 344–46
Mitchell, George P., **7** 344–46
Mitchell, Gerald B., **I** 153; **10** 265
Mitchell Hutchins, **II** 445
Mitchell International, **8** 526
Mitchell, Johnny, **7** 344
Mitchell, Rodger J., **11** 106
Mitchell, Roger, **10** 385
Mitchell, Sidney Z., **V** 546–47, 549, 564; **6** 565, 595
Mitchell, Tom, **8** 466–67
Mitchell, W., **IV** 19
Mitchell, William, **II** 655
Mitchells & Butler, **I** 223
Mitchum Co., **III** 55
Mitchum, Jones & Templeton, **II** 445
MiTek Industries Inc., **IV** 259
MiTek Wood Products, **IV** 305
MitNer Group, **7** 377
Mitsubishi, **V** 481–82; **7** 377
Mitsubishi Aircraft Co., **III** 578; **7** 348; **9** 349; **11** 164
Mitsubishi Atomic Power Industries, **III** 579; **7** 349
Mitsubishi Bank, Ltd., **II** 57, 273–74, 276, **321–22**, 323, 392, 459; **III** 289, 577–78; **7** 348
Mitsubishi Bank of California, **II** 322
Mitsubishi Cement Co., **III** 713

Mitsubishi Chemical Industries Ltd., **I** 319, **363–64**, 398; **II** 57; **III** 666, 760; **11** 207
Mitsubishi Corporation, **I** 261, 431–32, 492, **502–04**, 505–06, 510, 515, 519–20; **II** 57, 59, 101, 118, 224, 292, 321–25, 374; **III** 577–78; **IV** 285, 518, 713; **6** 499; **7** 82, 233, 590; **9** 294
Mitsubishi Development Corp., **IV** 713
Mitsubishi Electric Corporation, **II** 53, **57–59**, 68, 73, 94, 122; **III** 577, 586; **7** 347, 394
Mitsubishi Electric Manufacturing, **II** 58
Mitsubishi Estate Company, Limited, **IV** **713–14**
Mitsubishi Estate New York Inc., **IV** 714
Mitsubishi family, **III** 288
Mitsubishi Gas Chemical Company, **I** 330; **8** 153
Mitsubishi Goshi Kaisha, Ltd., **III** 538, 577–78, 713; **IV** 713; **7** 347
Mitsubishi Heavy Industries, **9** 349–50
Mitsubishi Heavy Industries, Ltd., **II** 57, 75, 323, 440; **III** 452–53, 487, 532, **577–79**, 685; **IV** 184; **7** 347–50 (upd.); **8** 51; **10** 33
Mitsubishi Internal Combustion Engine Co., Ltd., **9** 349
Mitsubishi Internal Combustion Engine Manufacturing Co., **III** 578; **7** 348
Mitsubishi Iron Works, **III** 577; **7** 348
Mitsubishi Kasei Corp., **III** 47–48, 477; **8** 343
Mitsubishi Kasei Industry Co. Ltd., **IV** 476
Mitsubishi Marine, **III** 385
Mitsubishi Materials Corporation, **III** **712–13**
Mitsubishi Metal Corp., **III** 712–13
Mitsubishi Mining & Cement, **III** 712–13
Mitsubishi Mining Co., **III** 713; **IV** 554
Mitsubishi Mining Corp., **III** 712–13
Mitsubishi Motor Sales of America, Inc., **8** 374
Mitsubishi Motors Australia Ltd., **9** 349
Mitsubishi Motors Corporation, **III** 516–17, 579; **7** 219, 349; **8** 72; **9** **349–51**
Mitsubishi Motors of America, **6** 28
Mitsubishi Oil Co., Ltd., **IV** **460–62**, 479, 492
Mitsubishi Paper Co., **III** 547
Mitsubishi Petrochemical Co., **I** 364; **III** 685
Mitsubishi Petroleum, **III** 760
Mitsubishi Pulp, **IV** 328
Mitsubishi Rayon Co. Ltd., **I** 330; **V** **369–71**
Mitsubishi Rayon Company, **8** 153
Mitsubishi Sha Holdings, **IV** 554
Mitsubishi Shipbuilding Co., **II** 57; **III** 513, 577–78; **7** 348
Mitsubishi Shipbuilding Co. Ltd., **9** 349
Mitsubishi Shoji Trading, **IV** 554
Mitsubishi Shokai, **III** 577; **IV** 713; **7** 347
Mitsubishi Trading Co., **IV** 460
Mitsubishi Trust, **II** 323
Mitsubishi Trust & Banking Corporation, **II** 323–24; **III** 289
Mitsubishi Yuka Pharmaceutical Co., **I** 364
Mitsui and Co., **I** 282; **IV** 18, 224, 432, 654–55; **V** 142; **6** 346; **7** 303
Mitsui Bank, Ltd., **II** 273–74, 291, **325–27**, 328, 372; **III** 295–97; **IV** 147, 320; **V** 142

Mitsui Bussan K.K., **I** 363, 431–32, 469, 492, 502–04, **505–08**, 510, 515, 519, 533; **II** 57, 66, 101, 224, 292, 323, 325–28, 392; **III** 295–96, 717–18; **IV** 147, 431; **9** 352–53
Mitsui Chemical, **IV** 145, 148
Mitsui family, **III** 288; **IV** 145, 715
Mitsui Gomei Kaisha, **IV** 715
Mitsui Group, **9** 352
Mitsui, Hachiroemon, **I** 505
Mitsui Harbour and Urban Construction Co., Ltd., **IV** 715
Mitsui Home Co., Ltd., **IV** 715–16
Mitsui House Code, **V** 142
Mitsui Light Metal Processing Co., **III** 758
Mitsui Line, **V** 473
Mitsui Marine and Fire Insurance Company, Limited, **III** 209, **295–96**, 297
Mitsui Mining & Smelting Co., Ltd., **IV** **145–46**, 147–48
Mitsui Mining Company, Limited, **IV** 145, **147–49**
Mitsui Mutual Life Insurance Company, **III** **297–98**
Mitsui O.S.K. Lines, Ltd., **I** 520; **IV** 383; **V** 473–76; **6** 398
Mitsui Petrochemical Industries, Ltd., **I** 390, 516; **9** **352–54**
Mitsui Real Estate Development Co., Ltd., **IV** **715–16**
Mitsui Real Estate Housing Service Co., Ltd., **IV** 716
Mitsui Real Estate Sales Co., Ltd., **IV** 715–16
Mitsui Sekka. *See* Mitsui Petrochemical Industries, Ltd.
Mitsui Shipbuilding and Engineering Co., **III** 295, 513
Mitsui, Sokubei, **I** 505; **III** 297
Mitsui Steamship Co., Ltd., **V** 473
Mitsui Taiyo Kobe Bank, **II** 372
Mitsui, Takatoshi, **I** 505; **III** 297
Mitsui Toatsu, **9** 353–54
Mitsui Trading, **III** 636
Mitsui Trust & Banking Company, Ltd., **II** 328; **III** 297
Mitsui Trust Co., **II** 328
Mitsui-no-Mori Co., Ltd., **IV** 716
Mitsukoshi Dry-Goods Store Company, **V** 143
Mitsukoshi Ltd., **I** 508; **V** **142–44**
Mitsuya Foods Co., **I** 221
Mitteldeutsche Creditbank, **II** 256
Mitteldeutsche Energieversorgung AG, **V** 747
Mitteldeutsche Privatbank, **II** 256
Mitteldeutsche Stickstoff-Werke Ag, **IV** 229–30
Mitteldeutsches Kraftwerk, **IV** 229
Mittelholzer, Walter, **I** 121, 138
Mitterand, François, **I** 46, 563; **II** 13, 93, 117, 259–60; **III** 123; **9** 148; **10** 195, 347, 472
Mitzotakis, Alexander, **I** 215
Mix, Tom, **II** 561
Mixconcrete (Holdings), **III** 729
Mixon, Malachi, **11** 200–02
Miyagawa, Chikuma, **V** 719
Miyamori, Yukio, **I** 184
Miyashita, Takeshiro, **IV** 298
Miyatake, Yasuo, **III** 406
Miyauchi, Koji, **V** 537
Miyoshi Electrical Manufacturing Co., **II** 6

Miyoshi, Takeo, **III** 406
Mizusawa, Kenzo, **III** 386
Mizushima Ethylene Co. Ltd., **IV** 476
MJB Coffee Co., **I** 28
MK-Ferguson Company, **7** 356
MLC Ltd., **IV** 709
MLH&P. *See* Montreal Light, Heat & Power Company.
MML Investors Services, **III** 286
MNC Financial Corp., **11** 447
MND Drilling, **7** 345
MNet, **11** 122
Mnookin, Nathan, **I** 370; **9** 500
Mo och Domsjö AB, **IV** 315, **317–19**, 340
Moa Bay Mining Co., **IV** 82; **7** 186
Mobay, **I** 310–11
Mobbs, Gerald, **IV** 723–24
Mobbs, Nigel (Sir), **IV** 724
Mobbs, Noel (Sir), **IV** 722–24
Mobil Chemical Company, **IV** 465; **7** 353; **9** 546
Mobil Communications, **6** 323
Mobil Corporation, **I** 34, 403, 478; **II** 379; **IV** 295, 363, 386, 401, 403, 406, 428, 454, **463–65**, 466, 472–74, 486, 492, 504–05, 531, 538–39, 545, 554, 564, 570–71; **V** 147–48; **7** 171, **351–54** (**upd.**); **8** 552–53
Mobil Oil Corp., **I** 30; **IV** 423, 465, 515, 517, 522, 555; **6** 530; **10** 440
Mobil Oil Indonesia, **IV** 492
Mobil Sekiyu K.K., **IV** 555
Mobil Southern Africa, **IV** 93
Mobil-Gelsenberg, **IV** 454
Mobile and Ohio Railroad, **I** 456
Mobile Communications Corp. of America, **V** 277–78
Mobira, **II** 69
Mobley Chemical, **I** 342
Mobu Company, **6** 431
Mobujidosha Bus Company, **6** 431
MOÇACOR, **IV** 505
Mocatta and Goldsmid Ltd., **II** 357
Mochida Pharaceutical Co. Ltd., **II** 553
Mockler, Colman M., Jr., **III** 28–29
Moctezuma Copper Co., **IV** 176–77
Modern Equipment Co., **I** 412
Modern Maid Food Products, **II** 500
Modern Patterns and Plastics, **III** 641
Modernistic Industries Inc., **7** 589
Modernistic Industries of Iowa, **7** 589
Modine, Arthur B., **8** 372–73
Modine Manufacturing Company, **8** **372–75**
MoDo. *See* Mo och Domsjö AB.
MoDo Consumer Products Ltd., **IV** 318
Moët, Claude, **I** 271
Moët, Claude-Louis, **I** 271
Moët et Chandon, **I** 271
Moët et Cie, **I** 271
Moët, Jean-Rémy, **I** 271
Moët, Victor, **I** 271
Moët-Hennessy, **I** **271–72**; **10** 398
Moët-Hennessy Louis Vuitton, **10** 397–98
Moffenbeier, David, **11** 284–85
Moffett, David, **11** 466
Moffett, George M, **II** 497
Moffett, James R. (Jim Bob), **IV** 82–84; **7** 187–88
Moffett, William, **9** 416
Moffitt, Donald E., **V** 434; **6** 390–91
Mogul Corp., **I** 321
Mogul Metal Co., **I** 158
Mohawk & Hudson Railroad, **9** 369

Mohawk Airlines, **I** 131; **6** 131
Mohawk Rubber Co. Ltd., **V** 256; **7** 116
Mohn family, **IV** 592
Mohn, Friederike Bertelsmann. *See* Bertelsmann, Friederike.
Mohn, Johannes, **IV** 592
Mohn, Reinhard, **IV** 592, 593–94
Mohn, Sigbert, **IV** 593
Mohr, Robert, **7** 531
Mohr-Value stores, **8** 555
Moilliet and Sons, **II** 306
Moist O'Matic, **7** 535
Mojo MDA Group Ltd., **11** 50–51
Mokta. *See* Compagnie de Mokta.
MOL. *See* Mitsui O.S.K. Lines, Ltd.
Molecular Biosystems, **III** 61
Molecular Genetics, **III** 61
Molex Incorporated, **II** 8; **11** **317–19**
Molinard, W. R., **6** 539
Moline National Bank, **III** 463
Molinos de Puerto Rico, **II** 493
Molinos Nacionales C.A., **7** 242–43
Molins Co., **IV** 326
Molkerie-Zentrak Sud GmbH, **II** 575
Moll, Hans, **III** 562–63
Molloy Manufacturing Co., **III** 569
Mölnlycke, **IV** 338–39
Moloney, Roy, **III** 430
Molotke, Joe, **7** 462
Molson Companies Ltd., **I** **273–75**, 333
Molson, John, **I** 273
Molson, John H.R., **I** 274
Molson, John, Jr., **I** 273–74
Molson, John Thomas, **I** 274
Molson Line, **I** 273
Molson, Thomas, **I** 273
Molson, William, **I** 273–74
Molson, William Markland, **I** 274
Molson's Bank, **I** 273; **II** 210
Molycorp, **IV** 571
Mon-Valley Transportation Company, **11** 194
MONACA. *See* Molinos Nacionales C.A.
Monaghan, Bernard A., **7** 573, 575
Monaghan, Jim, **7** 150
Monaghan, Tom, **7** 150–53
Monarch Food Ltd., **II** 571
Monarch Marking Systems, **III** 157
MonArk Boat, **III** 444
Mond, Alfred, **I** 351
Mond, Ludwig, **I** 351; **III** 680; **IV** 110
Mond Nickel Co., **IV** 110–11
Mondadori. *See* Arnoldo Monadori Editore S.p.A.
Mondadori, Alberto, **IV** 586
Mondadori, Andreina Monicelli, **IV** 585
Mondadori, Arnoldo, **IV** 585–87
Mondadori, Cristina, **IV** 586–87
Mondadori family, **IV** 585, 588
Mondadori, Giorgio, **IV** 586
Mondadori Informatica S.p.A., **IV** 588
Mondadori, Laura, **IV** 586–87
Mondadori, Leonardo Forneron, **IV** 587
Mondale, Walter, **I** 243
Mondi Paper Co., **IV** 22
Monet Jewelry, **II** 502–03; **9** 156–57; **10** 323–24
Money Access Service Corp., **11** 467
Monforte, Carmine, **III** 104–06; **IV** 420
Monforte, Pacifico, **III** 105
Mongtgomery, Robert H., **9** 137–38
Monheim Group, **II** 521
Monicelli, Tomaso, **IV** 585

Monier Roof Tile, **III** 687, 735
Monis Wineries, **I** 288
Monk, Alec, **II** 628–29
Monnerat, Jules, **II** 545; **7** 380
Monochem, **II** 472
Monod Jérome, **V** 657
Monogram Aerospace Fasteners, Inc., **11** 536
Monogramme Confections, **6** 392
Monolithic Memories, **6** 216
Monon Railroad, **I** 472
Monoprix, **V** 57–59
Monroe Auto Equipment, **I** 527
Monroe Calculating Machine Co., **I** 476, 484
Monroe Cheese Co., **II** 471
Monroe, Marilyn, **II** 143; **III** 46
Monroe Savings Bank, **11** 109
Monrovia Aviation Corp., **I** 544
Monsanto, **9** 466
Monsanto Chemical Co., **I** 365; **9** 318
Monsanto Company, **I** 310, 363, **365–67**, 402, 631, 666, 686, 688; **III** 741; **IV** 290, 379, 401; **8** 398; **9** 355–57 **(upd.)**, 466
Monsanto Oil Co., **IV** 367
Monsavon, **III** 46–47
Montagu (Lord), **I** 194
Montagu, Basil, **III** 272
Montagu, Samuel, **II** 319
Montague, Theodore G., **II** 471–72
Montale, Eugenio, **IV** 585
Montan Transport GmbH, **IV** 140
Montana Enterprises Inc., **I** 114
Montana Power Company, **6** 566; **7** 322; **11 320–22**
Montana Resources, Inc., **IV** 34
Montana-Dakota Utilities Co., **7** 322–23
Monte, Woodrow, **I** 688
Montecatini, **I** 368; **IV** 421, 470, 486
Montedison SpA, **I 368–69**; **IV** 413, 421–22, 454, 499
Montefibre, **I** 369
Montefina, **IV** 499
Montefiore, Moses (Sir), **III** 372
Montfort of Colorado, Inc., **II** 494
Montgomery, Bernard, **I** 178
Montgomery, Dan H., **11** 440
Montgomery, Dan T., **8** 113
Montgomery, James, **10** 339–40
Montgomery, Parker, **I** 667–68
Montgomery, Robert H., **9** 137
Montgomery Ward & Co., Incorporated, **III** 762; **IV** 465; **V 145–48**; **7** 353; **8** 509; **9** 210; **10** 10, 116, 172, 305, 391, 393, 490–91
Montgomery Ward Auto Club, **V** 147
Montgomery Ward Direct, **V** 148
Montreal Bank, **II** 210
Montreal Engineering Company, **6** 585
Montreal Gas Company, **6** 501
Montreal Island Power, **6** 502
Montreal Light, Heat & Power Company, **6** 501–02
Montreal Light, Heat & Power Consolidated, **6** 502
Montrose Chemical Company, **9** 118, 119
Montrose Chrome, **IV** 92
Monument Property Trust Ltd., **IV** 710
Monumental Corp., **III** 179
MONY Life of Canada, **III** 306
MONYCo., **III** 306
Moody family, **III** 91
Moody, Robert, **8** 28–29

Moody, Shearn, **8** 28
Moody, William Lewis, Jr., **8** 27–28
Moody's Investors Service, **IV** 605
Moon-Hopkins Billing Machine, **III** 165
Moore, B.C., **10** 154
Moore Business Forms de Centro America, **IV** 645
Moore Business Forms de Mexico, **IV** 645
Moore Business Forms de Puerto Rico, **IV** 645
Moore, Chistopher W., **11** 552–53
Moore, Clyde R., **11** 516
Moore Corporation Limited, **IV 644–46**, 679
Moore, Crawford, **11** 553–54
Moore, E. Allen, **III** 627
Moore, Everett, **8** 201
Moore, F. Rockwood, **6** 595
Moore Formularios Lda., **IV** 645
Moore, Francis C., **III** 240
Moore, Frank B., **V** 753
Moore, George, **II** 254; **9** 124
Moore, Gordon, **II** 44–46; **10** 365–67
Moore Group, **IV** 644
Moore, James, **11** 62
Moore, James L., **10** 223
Moore, John H., **I** 268
Moore, L.R., **6** 510
Moore, Philip, **11** 468
Moore, Robert, **III** 98
Moore, Samuel J., **IV** 644–45
Moore, Stephen D.R., **9** 140
Moore, William, **V** 224–25
Moore, William H., **II** 230–31; **10** 73
Moore, Willis, **9** 367
Moore-Handley Inc., **IV** 345–46
Moores, John, **V** 117–18
Moorhead, James T., **9** 516
Moorhouse, **II** 477
Mooty, John, **10** 374
Moran, Dan, **IV** 400
Moran Group Inc., **II** 682
MoRan Oil & Gas Co., **IV** 82–83
Morana, Inc., **9** 290
Morand, Paul, **IV** 618
Morcott, Southwood "Woody", **10** 265
More, Avery, **10** 232–33
Morehead May, James T., **I** 399
Moreland and Watson, **IV** 208
Moret, Marc, **I** 673
Moretti-Harrah Marble Co., **III** 691
Morey, Parker, **6** 548
Morgan & Cie International S.A., **II** 431
Morgan, Bill, **I** 568
Morgan, C. Powell, **7** 95
Morgan, Cary, **I** 61; **11** 164
Morgan Construction Company, **8** 448
Morgan Edwards, **II** 609
Morgan, Edwin B., **II** 380
Morgan Engineering Co., **8** 545
Morgan family, **III** 237
Morgan, Graham, J., **III** 763
Morgan Grampian Group, **IV** 687
Morgan Grenfell (Overseas) Ltd., **II** 428
Morgan Grenfell and Co., **II** 427
Morgan Grenfell and Co. Ltd., **II** 428
Morgan Grenfell Group PLC, **II** 280, 329, **427–29**; **IV** 21, 712
Morgan Grenfell Inc., **II** 429
Morgan Grenfell Laurie, **II** 427
Morgan Grenfell Securities, **II** 429
Morgan Guaranty International Banking Corp., **II** 331; **9** 124

Morgan Guaranty International Finance Corp., **II** 331
Morgan Guaranty Trust Co. of New York, **I** 26; **II** 208, 254, 262, 329–32, 339, 428, 431, 448; **III** 80; **10** 150
Morgan Guaranty Trust Company, **11** 421
Morgan, Harjes & Co., **II** 329
Morgan, Henry, **II** 430–31
Morgan, J.P. & Co. Inc. *See* J.P. Morgan & Co. Incorporated.
Morgan, James, **7** 13
Morgan, James C., **10** 108
Morgan, John Pierpont (J.P.), **I** 47, 61; **II** 229, 312, 329–32, 427, 430, 447; **III** 247; **IV** 110, 400, 572; **V** 146; **6** 605; **7** 261, 549; **9** 370; **10** 43, 72, 162; **11** 164
Morgan, John Pierpont, Jr. (Jack), **II** 227, 330, 427; **IV** 573; **7** 550
Morgan, Junius Spencer, **II** 329–30, 427–28
Morgan, Lewis, Githens & Ahn, Inc., **6** 410
Morgan Mitsubishi Development, **IV** 714
Morgan Stanley & Co., Inc., **II** 330, 408, 430–31
Morgan Stanley Group, Inc., **I** 34; **II** 211, 403, 406–07, 428, **430–32**, 441; **IV** 295, 447, 714; **9** 386
Morgan Stanley International, **II** 422
The Morgan Stanley Real Estate Fund, **11** 258
Morgan Yacht Corp., **II** 468
Morgan's Brewery, **I** 287
Morgens, Howard, **III** 52; **8** 433
Morgenthau, Hans, **II** 227
Morgridge, John, **11** 58–59
Mori Bank, **II** 291
Mori, Kaoru, **V** 455
Moria Informatique, **6** 229
Moriarity, Roy, **10** 287
Morino Associates, **10** 394
Morino, Mario M., **10** 394
Morison, William, **I** 497
Morita & Co., **II** 103
Morita, Akio, **II** 5, 56, 101–03; **7** 118
Morita family, **II** 103
Morita, Ko, **IV** 656
Morita, Kuzuaki, **II** 103
Moritz, Michael, **I** 145
Morley, Roger, **10** 62
Morley, Roger H., **II** 398; **IV** 637
Moro, Aldo, **IV** 586
Morohashi, Shinroku, **I** 504
Moroney, James, **10** 4
Moroz, Mykola, **9** 170–71
Morpurgo, Edgardo, **III** 207–08
Morpurgo, Giuseppe Lazzano, **III** 206
Morrill, Albert H., **II** 643–44
Morrill, Thomas C., **III** 364
Morris, Alan, **11** 51
Morris, Arthur J., **11** 446
Morris, Bert, **IV** 278
Morris, David H., **7** 534–35
Morris, Donald R., **IV** 311
Morris, Mervin, **10** 409–10
Morris Motors, **III** 256; **7** 459
Morris, Ray, **7** 430
Morris, Robert, **V** 712; **7** 430
Morrison, Garry, **III** 214
Morrison, Harley James, **III** 51
Morrison, Harry W., **7** 355–56; **11** 553
Morrison Industries Ltd., **IV** 278
Morrison, J.A., **11** 323

Morrison Knudsen Corporation, **IV** 55; **7** 355–58; **11** 401, 553
Morrison Restaurants Inc., **11** 323–25
Morrison-Knudsen Engineers, **7** 356
Morrison-Knudsen International Company, **7** 356
Morrison-Knudsen Services, **7** 356
Morrow, George, **II** 497
Morrow, Richard W., **IV** 371
Morrow, Winston V., Jr., **6** 356
Morse, Arthur, **II** 297
Morse Chain Co., **III** 439
Morse, Everett, **III** 439
Morse, Frank, **III** 439
Morse, Jeremy, **II** 309
Morse, Samuel, **6** 341
Morss and White, **III** 643
Morss, Charles A., **III** 643
Morstan Development Co., Inc., **II** 432
Mortgage & Trust Co., **II** 251
Mortgage Associates, **9** 229
Mortgage Insurance Co. of Canada, **II** 222
Mortgage Resources, Inc., **10** 91
Mortimer, James D., **6** 505, 601
Morton, David, **IV** 12
Morton, E. James, **III** 268
Morton Foods, Inc., **II** 502; **10** 323
Morton Industries, **I** 370; **9** 501
Morton International Inc., **9** 358–59 (upd.), 500
Morton, Joy, **I** 371; **9** 358
Morton, Nathan, **10** 235–36
Morton, Paul, **III** 247
Morton Salt, **I** 371
Morton Thiokol Inc., **I** 325, 370–72
MOS Technology, **7** 95
Mosby-Year Book, **IV** 678
Mosconi, Enrique (Gen.), **IV** 577
Moseley, Hallgarten, Estabrook, and Weeden, **III** 389
Moseley, Jack, **III** 397
Mosher, Gilbert E., **III** 171; **6** 288
Mosher Steel Company, **7** 540
Moskowitz, Louis, **11** 416–17
Mosler Safe, **III** 664–65
Mosler Safe Co., **7** 144, 146
Mosley, Leonard, **I** 330
Mosling, Bernhard A., **7** 416–17
Mosling, John, **7** 417
Mosling, Peter, **7** 418
Mosling, Stephen, **7** 418
Moss, B.S., **II** 169
Moss, Charles, **6** 51
Moss, Sanford, **9** 244
Mossgas, **IV** 93
Mostek, **I** 85; **II** 64; **11** 307–08
Moszkowski, George, **III** 195
Motel 6 G.P. Inc., **10** 13
Mother Karen's, **10** 216
Mother's Oats, **II** 558–59
Motion Designs, **11** 486
Motor Haulage Co., **IV** 181
Motor Parts Industries, Inc., **9** 363
Motor Transit Corp., **I** 448; **10** 72
Motoren-und-Turbinen-Union, **I** 151; **III** 563; **9** 418
Motoren-Werke Mannheim AG, **III** 544
Motorenfabrik Deutz AG, **III** 541
Motorenfabrik Oberursel, **III** 541
Motornetic Corp., **III** 590
Motorola, Inc., **I** 534; **II** 5, 34, 44–45, 56, **60–62**, 64; **III** 455; **6** 238; **7** 119, 494, 533; **8** 139; **9** 515; **10** 87, 365, 367,

431–33; **11** 45, 308, **326–29** (upd.), 381–82
Motorola Semiconductors Japan, **II** 61
Motown Records, **II** 145
Motoyama, Kazuo, **V** 256
Mott, Frank Luther, **9** 368
Mott, Tom, **10** 284
Moulin, Etienne, **V** 57–59
Moulton, William H., **III** 529
Mount Isa Mines, **IV** 61
Mount Vernon Group, **8** 14
Mountain, Denis, **I** 426
Mountain Fuel Resources, **6** 568–69
Mountain Fuel Supply Company, **6** 568–69
Mountain Pass Canning Co., **7** 429
Mountain State Telephone Company, **6** 300
Mountain States Telephone & Telegraph Co., **V** 341
Mountain States Wholesale, **II** 602
Mountbatten (Earl), **I** 469
Mounts Wire Industries, **III** 673
Mountsorrel Granite Co., **III** 734
Moussa, Pierre, **II** 259–60
Movado-Zenith-Mondia Holding, **II** 124
Movies To Go, Inc., **9** 74
Moving Co. Ltd., **V** 127
Moyers, Edward, **11** 188
MPB Corporation, **8** 529, 531
MPM, **III** 735
Mr. Gasket Company, **11** 84
Mr. How, **V** 191–92
Mr. M Food Stores, **7** 373
MRC Bearings, **III** 624
Mrozek, Donald J., **I** 80
Mrs. Paul's Kitchens, **II** 480
Mrs. Smith's Pie Co., **II** 525
MS-Relais, **III** 710
MS-Relais GmbH, **7** 302–03
MSAS Cargo International, **6** 415, 417
MSI Data, **10** 523
MSL Industries, **10** 44
MSU. See Middle South Utilities.
Mt. Carmel Public Utility Company, **6** 506
Mt. Goldsworthy Mining Associates, **IV** 47
Mt. Lyell Investments, **III** 672
Mt. Lyell Mining and Railway, **III** 673
Mt. Vernon Iron Works, **II** 14
MTC Pharmaceuticals, **II** 483
Mubarrak, Hosni, **6** 86
Muecke, Bertold, **8** 117
Muehsam, Philipp, **8** 68
Mueller Co., **III** 645
Mueller Furniture Company, **8** 252
Mueller, Hieronymous, **7** 359
Mueller Industries, Inc., **7** 359–61
Mueller, Louis, **I** 96
Mueller, Paul, **I** 633
Mueller, Richard, **7** 151–52
Mueller, Ronald, **9** 235
Muhammad Reza Shah Pahlevi (Shah of Iran), **I** 116, 195, 530, 563; **IV** 371
Muir, Malcolm, **IV** 635
Mujirushi Ryohin, **V** 188
Mukluk Freight Lines, **6** 383
Mulberger, Lorraine, **I** 269
Mule Battery Manufacturing Co., **III** 643
Mulford, Raymond, **I** 610
Mülheimer Bergwerksvereins, **I** 542
Mulholland, William, **II** 211
Mullane, Denis F., **III** 238
Mullane, Robert, **III** 431
Muller, Edouard, **II** 547; **7** 382
Müller, Heinrich, **III** 411
Mullins, Norman, **III** 671

Mullins, Tom, **IV** 170–71
Mulroney, Brian, **II** 211; **IV** 495
Multi Restaurants, **II** 664
Multibank Inc., **11** 281
Multicom Publishing Inc., **11** 294
MultiMed, **11** 379
Multimedia, Inc., **IV** 591; **11** 330–32
Multiple Access Systems Corp., **III** 109
Multiple Properties, **I** 588
MultiScope Inc., **10** 508
Mulvaney, William Thomas, **I** 542
Mulyono, Wage, **6** 91
Muma, Leslie, **11** 130, 132
Mumford, Lewis, **IV** 622
Mumford, Philip G., **9** 23
Mumford, Rufus, **6** 409
Münchener Rückversicherungs-Gesellschaft. See Munich Re.
Mundt, Ray, **I** 412–13; **III** 10
Mungana Mines, **I** 438
Munich Re, **II** 239; **III** 183–84, 202, **299–301**, 400, 747
Munich-American Reinsurance Co., **III** 401
Municipal Assistance Corp., **II** 448
Munising Paper Co., **III** 40
Munksund, **IV** 338
Munn, Stephen, **8** 80
Munoz, Jose, **7** 556
Munro, J. Richard, **IV** 675; **7** 528
Munroe, George B., **IV** 178–79
Munsell, Harry B., **6** 511
Munson, Donald W., **8** 322
Muntasir, Omar, **IV** 453
Munter, Herb, **I** 47
Murai, Tsutomu, **I** 221
Murakami, Kohei, **IV** 656
Muramoto, Shuzo, **II** 274
Murchison, Clint, **V** 737; **7** 145; **10** 43
Murchison, Clint, Jr., **10** 44
Murchison, John, **10** 44
Murdoch, Keith, **7** 389
Murdoch, Keith (Sir), **IV** 650, 652
Murdoch, Keith Rupert, **7** 252–53
Murdoch, Rupert, **II** 156, 169, 171, 176; **IV** 264, 611, 619, 630, 641, 650–53, 666, 684, 687, 703; **V** 524; **6** 16, 73; **7** 336, 389–92; **8** 527, 551; **9** 119, 429; **10** 288
Murdock, David, **II** 492; **9** 215–16
Murdock, David H., **8** 424; **9** 176
Murdock, Melvin Jack, **8** 517–18
Murfin Inc., **8** 360
Murless, Gordon, **9** 462
Murmic, Inc., **9** 120
Murphy, Charles H., Jr., **7** 362–63
Murphy, Charles H., Sr., **7** 362
Murphy Farms, **7** 477
Murphy, Henry C., **II** 312; **V** 428
Murphy, Jeremiah, **II** 388
Murphy, John, **I** 269–70
Murphy, John J., **III** 473
Murphy, Michael, **I** 98
Murphy Oil Corporation, **7** 362–64
Murphy, Ray, **III** 248
Murphy, Richard J., **III** 535
Murphy, Thomas, **10** 420
Murphy, Thomas S., **II** 131
Murphy, W.B., **II** 479–80
Murphy, W.H., **I** 473
Murray, Allen E., **IV** 465; **7** 353
Murray, Annie, **III** 20
Murray Bay Paper Co., **IV** 246
Murray Corp. of America, **III** 443

Murray Goulburn Snow, **II** 575
Murray, J. Terrence, **9** 229–30
Murray, John, **7** 548
Murray, Kenneth Sutherland, **I** 314–15
Murray, Pascall, **II** 476
Murray, Phillip, **IV** 114
Murray, T.G., **III** 672–73
Murray, William C.R., **III** 20
Murrayfield, **IV** 696
Murrow, Edward R., **II** 132; **6** 157
Murto, William H., **III** 124; **6** 221
Musashino Railway Company, **V** 510
Muscatine Journal, **11** 251
Muscocho Explorations Ltd., **IV** 76
Muse Air Corporation, **6** 120
Muse, M. Lamar, **6** 119–20
Music Corporation of America, **II** 143–44
Music Plus, **9** 75
Musica, Philip, **I** 496
Musicland Stores Corporation, **9**
    360–62; **11** 558
Muskegon Gas Company. *See* MCN
    Corporation.
Musotte & Girard, **I** 553
Mussadegh, Muhammad, **IV** 379, 440, 466,
    483, 559
Musser, Warren V., **10** 232, 473–74
Mussolini, Benito, **I** 161, 459, 465; **II** 271;
    III 208, 346; **IV** 632; **11** 102, 203
Mutoh Industries, Ltd., **6** 247
Mutual Benefit Financial Service Co., **III**
    304
Mutual Benefit Life Insurance Company,
    III 243, **302–04**
Mutual Gaslight Company. *See* MCN
    Corporation.
Mutual Life Insurance Co. of the State of
    Wisconsin, **III** 321
**Mutual Life Insurance Company of New
    York**, **II** 331; **III** 247, 290, **305–07**,
    316, 321, 380
Mutual Medical Aid and Accident
    Insurance Co., **III** 331
Mutual of Omaha, **III** 365
Mutual Oil Co., **IV** 399
Mutual Safety Insurance Co., **III** 305
Mutual Savings & Loan Assoc., **III** 215
Mutualité Générale, **III** 210
Mutualité Immobilière, **III** 210
Mutualité Mobilière, **III** 210
Mutuelle d'Orléans, **III** 210
Mutuelle de l'Quest, **III** 211
Mutuelle Vie, **III** 210
Mutuelles Unies, **III** 211
Muysken, J., **IV** 132
Muzak Corporation, **7** 90–91
Muzzy, J. Howard, **I** 158; **10** 292
Muzzy-Lyon Co., **I** 158–59
Mwinilunga Canneries Ltd., **IV** 241
MY Holdings, **IV** 92
Myanmar Oil and Gas Enterprise, **IV** 519
MYCAL Group, **V** 154
Myers, Burt, **10** 373
Myers, Charles F., **V** 354–55
Myers, Jerry, **7** 494
Myers, John Ripley, **III** 17; **9** 88
Myers, Malcolm, **8** 80
Myers, Mark B., **6** 290
Myers, William E., **7** 479
Mygind International, **8** 477
Myklebust, Egil, **10** 439
Mylan Laboratories, **I 656–57**
Myllykoski Träsliperi AB, **IV** 347–48
Mylod, Robert J., **11** 304–06

Myokenya, **III** 757
Myokenya Home Fixtures Wholesaling
    Co., Ltd., **III** 757
Myson Group PLC, **III** 671
Mysore State Iron Works, **IV** 205

N M Electronics, **II** 44
N.A. Otto & Cie., **III** 541
N.A. Woodworth, **III** 519
N.C. Cameron & Sons, Ltd., **11** 95
N.K. Fairbank Co., **II** 497
N.M. Rothschild & Sons, **IV** 64, 712
N.M.U. Transport Ltd., **II** 569
N.R.F. Gallimard, **IV** 618
N.W. Ayer & Son, **I** 36; **II** 542
Nabisco, **9** 318. *See also* RJR Nabisco *and*
    Nabisco Brands, Inc.
Nabisco Brands, Inc., **II** 475, 512,
    542–44; **7** 128, 365–67. *See also*
    Nabisco Foods Group *and* RJR Nabisco.
Nabisco Foods Group, **7 365–68 (upd.)**
Nabors Drilling Limited of Canada, **9** 363
Nabors Industries, Inc., **9 363–65**
Nabors Manufacturing, **9** 93
NACCO Industries, Inc., **7 369–71**
Nacional Financiera, **IV** 513
Nadeau, Bertin, **II** 653
Nader, Ralph, **I** 366, 393, 610, 633, 646,
    654; **9** 518; **11** 24, 90, 403
NAFI. *See* National Automotive Fibers,
    Inc.
Nagano Seiyu Ltd., **V** 188
Nagaoka, Takeshi, **V** 479
Nagaro, Takeshi, **III** 713
Nagasaki Shipyard, **I** 502
Nagasakiya Co., Ltd., **V 149–51**
Nagase & Company, Ltd., **8 376–78**
Nagase family, **III** 38
Nagase, Hideo, **8** 378
Nagase, Shozo, **8** 378
Nagase-Alfa, **III** 420
Nagel, Friedrich, **V** 466
Nagel Meat Markets and Packing House, **II**
    643
Nagoya Bank, **II** 373
Nagoya Electric Light Co., **IV** 62
Naguib, Mohammed, **6** 85
Naigai Tsushin, **6** 29
Naigai Tsushin Hakuhodo, **6** 29
Naikoku Tsu-un Kabushiki Kaisha, **V** 477
Naikoku Tsu-un Kaisha, **V** 477
Naito, Tashio, **I** 10
Nakabe, Ikujiro, **II** 578
Nakabe, Kaneichi, **II** 578
Nakada, Otakazu, **IV** 714
Nakagawa, Seibei, **I** 382
Nakagawi, Takeshi, **III** 540
Nakahara, Nobuhei, **IV** 554
Nakahashi, Tokugoro, **V** 473
Nakai Ltd., **IV** 292
Nakai, Reisaku, **IV** 157
Nakai, Saburobei, **IV** 292
Nakai Shoten Ltd., **IV** 292
Nakajima, Kumakichi, **III** 490
Nakajima, Michio, **III** 455
Nakajima, Shinji, **III** 454
Nakajima, Tatsuji, **III** 715
Nakajima, Yosaburo, **III** 454
Nakamigawa, Hikojiro, **I** 506–07; **II** 325;
    IV 320
Nakamura, Fumio, **III** 714
Nakamura, Kaneo, **II** 301
Nakasone, Yasuhiro, **I** 106; **IV** 728
Nakata, Kinkichi, **I** 519

Nakauchi, Isao, **V** 39–40
Nakayama, Hayao, **10** 482
Nakemura, Mitsugi, **III** 545
Nalco Chemical Corporation, **I 373–75**
Nalfloc, **I** 374
NAM. *See* Nederlandse Aardolie
    Maatschappij.
Namco, **III** 431
Namkwang Engineering & Construction
    Co. Ltd., **III** 749
Nampack, **I** 423
NANA Regional Corporation, **7** 558
Nance, Brent, **II** 620
Nankai Kogyo, **IV** 225
Nansei Sekiyu, **IV** 432
Nantucket Corporation, **6** 226
Nanyo Bussan, **I** 493
NAPC. *See* North American Philips Corp.
Napier, **I** 194
Napier, Macvey, **7** 166
Napier, Mark, **IV** 669
Napoleon I, Emperor (France). *See*
    Bonaparte, Napoleon.
Napoleon III, Emperor (France), **IV** 85,
    173, 227, 592
NAPP Systems, Inc., **11** 253
Nardin, William, **7** 428–29
Närger, Heribald, **II** 99
Narmco Industries, **I** 544
Narud, Odd, **10** 438
NASA. *See* National Aeronautics and
    Space Administration.
Nash DeCamp Company, **8** 379
Nash, Edgar, **8** 379
Nash Finch Company, **8 379–81**; **11** 43
Nash, Fred, **8** 379–80
Nash, Jeffrey, **6** 231
Nash Motors Co., **I** 135; **8** 75
Nash, Philip (Sir), **III** 670
Nash, Willis, **8** 379–80
Nash-Kelvinator Corp., **I** 135
Nashaming Valley Information Processing,
    III 204
Nashua Card, Gummed and Coated Paper
    Company, **8** 382. *See also* Nashua
    Corporation.
Nashua Corporation, **8 382–84**
The Nashville Network, **11** 153
Nason, Alex, **I** 360
Nason, Frank, **I** 360
Nassau Gas Light Co., **6** 455
Nasser, Gamal Abdel, **III** 392; **6** 85
Nast, Thomas, **III** 387
NASTECH, **III** 590
Nasu Aluminium Manufacturing Co., **IV**
    153
Natal Brewery Syndicate, **I** 287
Natco Corp., **I** 445
NaTec Ltd. *See* CRSS Inc.
Nathan, Alec, **I** 639; **9** 263–64
Nathan, Fernand, **IV** 614–15
Nathan, Joseph, **I** 639–40; **9** 263
Nathan, Louis, **I** 639; **9** 263
Nathan, Pierre, **IV** 614
Natio, Hisahiro, **IV** 478
National, **10** 419
National Advanced Systems, **II** 64–65
National Aeronautics and Space
    Administration, **II** 139; **6** 227–29, 327;
    11 201, 408
National Air Transport Co., **I** 128; **6** 128; **9**
    416; **11** 427
National Airlines, **I** 97, 116; **6** 388
National Aluminate Corp., **I** 373

National Aluminum Company, **11** 38
National American Life Insurance Co. of California, **II** 181
National American Title Insurance Co., **II** 181
National Aniline & Chemical Co., **I** 414
National Association of Securities Dealers, Inc., 10 416–18
National Australia Bank, **III** 673
National Automobile and Casualty Insurance Co., **III** 270
National Automotive Fibers, Inc., **9** 118
National Aviation, **I** 117
National Baby Shop, **V** 203
National Bancard Corporation, **11** 111–13
National Bank, **II** 312
National Bank for Cooperatives, **8** 489–90
National Bank für Deutschland, **II** 270
National Bank of Belgium, **II** 294
National Bank of Commerce, **II** 331; **9** 536; **11** 105–06
National Bank of Detroit, **I** 165
National Bank of Egypt, **II** 355
The National Bank of Jacksonville, **9** 58
National Bank of New Zealand, **II** 308
National Bank of North America, **II** 334
National Bank of South Africa Ltd., **II** 236
National Bank of the City of New York, **II** 312
National Bank of Turkey, **IV** 557
National BankAmericard Inc., **9** 536
National Bankers Express Co., **II** 396; **10** 60
National Bell Telephone Company, **V** 259
National Benefit and Casualty Co., **III** 228
National Benefit Co., **III** 228
National Binding Company, **8** 382
National Biscuit Co., **II** 542–43; **IV** 152; **7** 365
National Bridge Company of Canada, Ltd., **8** 544
National Broach & Machine Co., **I** 481–82
National Broadcasting Company, Inc., II 30, 88–90, 129–33, **151–53**, 170, 173, 487, 543; **III** 188, 329; **IV** 596, 608, 652; **6** 157–59, **164–66** (upd.); **10** 173
National Building Society, **10** 6–7
National Can Corp., I 601–02, **607–08**
National Can Overseas Corp., **IV** 154
National Car Rental System, Inc., I 489; **II** 419–20, 445; **6** 348–49; **10** 373, **419–20**
National Car Rental System International, Ltd., **10** 419
National Carbon, **I** 400
National Carbon Co., Inc., **9** 516; **11** 402
National Carriers, **6** 413–14
National Cash Register Company. *See* NCR Corporation.
National Chemsearch Corp., **8** 385. *See also* NCH Corporation.
National Child Care Centers, Inc., **II** 607
National City Bank, **9** 475
National City Bank of New York, **I** 337, 462; **II** 253–54; **III** 380; **IV** 81
National City Co., **II** 254; **9** 124
National City Corp., **9** 475
National Cleaning Contractors, **II** 176
National Coal Board, **IV** 38–40
National Coal Development Corp., **IV** 48
National Commercial, **11** 108
National Container Corp., **I** 609
National Convenience Stores Incorporated, 7 372–75

National Credit Office, **IV** 604
National CSS, **IV** 605
National Dairy Products Corp., **II** 533; **7** 275
National Demographics & Lifestyles Inc., **10** 461
National Development Bank, **IV** 56
National Disinfectant Company, **8** 385. *See also* NCH Corporation.
National Distillers and Chemical Corporation, I 226, **376–78**; **IV** 11; **8** 439–40; **9** 231; **10** 181
National Distillers Products Corporation, **I** 376; **8** 439–41
National Drive-In Grocery Corporation, **7** 372
National Drug Ltd., **II** 652
National Economic Research Associates, **III** 283
National Education Association, **9** 367
National Electric Company, **11** 388
National Electric Instruments Co., **IV** 78
National Electric Products Corp., **IV** 177
National Enquirer, **10** 287–88
National Express Laboratories, Inc., **10** 107
National Fidelity Life Insurance Co., **10** 246
National Fidelity Life Insurance Co. of Kansas, **III** 194; **IV** 343
National Finance Corp., **IV** 22–23
National Fire & Marine Insurance Co., **III** 213–14
National Fire Insurance Co., **III** 229–30
National Fuel Gas Company, 6 526–28
National Gateway Telecom, **6** 326–27
National General Corp., **III** 190–91
National Geographic Society, 9 366–68
National Greyhound Racing Club, **II** 142
National Grid Company, **11** 399–400
National Grocers of Ontario, **II** 631
National Gypsum Company, 8 43; **10 421–24**
National Health Enterprises, **III** 87
National Health Laboratories Incorporated, 11 333–35
National Hotel Co., **III** 91
National Hydrocarbon Corp., **IV** 543
National Import and Export Corp. Ltd., **IV** 240
National Indemnity Co., **III** 213–14
National Indemnity Co. of Florida, **III** 214
National Indemnity Co. of Minnesota, **III** 213–14
National India Rubber Company, **9** 228
National Industries, **I** 446
National Integrity Life Insurance, **III** 249
National Intergroup, Inc., IV 237, 574; **V 152–53**
National Iranian Oil Company, III 748; **IV** 370, 374, **466–68**, 484, 512, 535
National Iranian Oil Tanker Co., **IV** 467–68
National Kinney Corp., **IV** 720; **9** 391
National Lead Co., **III** 681; **IV** 32
National Liability and Fire Insurance Co., **III** 214
National Liberty Corp., **III** 218–19
National Life and Accident Insurance Co., **III** 194
National Life and Travelers' Insurance Co., **III** 290
National Life Insurance Co., **III** 290

National Life Insurance Co. of Canada, **III** 243
National Loss Control Service Corp., **III** 269
National Manufacturing Co., **III** 150; **6** 264
National Marine Service, **6** 530
National Market System, **9** 369
National Medical Enterprises, Inc., III 79, **87–88**; **6** 188; **10** 252
National Minerals Development Corp., **IV** 143–44
National Mortgage Agency of New Zealand Ltd., **IV** 278
National Mortgage Assoc. of Washington, **II** 410
National Motor Bearing Co., **I** 159
National Mutual Life Assurance of Australasia, **III** 249
National Oil Corp. *See* Libyan National Oil Corporation.
National Oil Distribution Co., **IV** 524
National Old Line Insurance Co., **III** 179
National Packaging, **IV** 333
National Paper Co., **8** 476
National Patent Development Corp., **7** 45
National Permanent Mutual Benefit Building Society, **10** 6
National Petrochemical Co., **IV** 467
National Petroleum Publishing Co., **IV** 636
National Pharmacies, **9** 346
National Potash Co., **IV** 82; **7** 186
National Power PLC, **11** 399–400
National Propane Corporation, **8** 535–37
National Provident Institution for Mutual Life Assurance, **IV** 711
National Provincial Bank, **II** 319–20, 333–34; **IV** 722
National Railways of Mexico, **IV** 512
National Regulator Co., **II** 41
National Reinsurance Co., **III** 276–77
National Rent-A-Car, **6** 392–93
National Research Corporation, **8** 397
National Rubber Machinery Corporation, **8** 298
National School Studios, **7** 255
National Science Foundation, **9** 266
National Seal, **I** 158
National Semiconductor Corporation, II 63–65; **III** 455, 618, 678; **6** 215, **261–63**; **9** 297; **11** 45–46, 308, 463
National Service Industries, Inc., 11 336–38
National Southwire, **11** 38
National Standard Corp., **IV** 137
National Star Brick & Tile Co., **III** 501; **7** 207
National Starch and Chemical Corp., **IV** 253
National Starch Manufacturing Co., **II** 496
National Steel and Shipbuilding Company, **7** 356
National Steel Car Corp., **IV** 73
National Steel Co., **7** 549; **8** 346; **11** 315
National Steel Corp., **I** 491; **IV** 74, 163, 236–37, 572; **V** 152–53; **8** 346, 479–80
National Student Marketing Corporation, **10** 385–86
National Supply Co., **IV** 29
National Surety Co. of New York, **III** 395
National System Company, **9** 41; **11** 469
National Tanker Fleet, **IV** 502
National Tea, **II** 631–32

National Telecommunications of Austin, **8** 311

National Telephone and Telegraph Corporation. *See* British Columbia Telephone Company.

National Telephone Co., **III** 162; **7** 332, 508

National Theatres, Inc., **III** 190

National Transcontinental, **6** 360

National Travelers' Insurance Co., **III** 290

National Trust Life Insurance Co., **III** 218

National Tube Co., **II** 330; **IV** 572; **7** 549

National Union Fire Insurance Co. of Pittsburgh, Pa., **III** 195–97

National Union Life and Limb Insurance Co., **III** 290

National Utilities & Industries Corporation, **9** 363

National Westminster Bank PLC, **II** 237, **333–35**; **IV** 642

National-Ben Franklin Insurance Co., **III** 242

Nationalbank, **I** 409

Nationale Bank Vereeniging, **II** 185

Nationale Levensverzekering-Bank. *See* Nationale Life Insurance Bank.

Nationale Life Insurance Bank, **III** 179, 308–10

Nationale-Nederlanden N.V., **III** 179, 200–01, **308–11**; **IV** 697

Nationar, **9** 174

NationsBank, **11** 126

NationsBank Corporation, **6** 357; **10** **425–27**

Nationwide Credit, **11** 112

Nationwide Income Tax Service, **9** 326

NATIOVIE, **II** 234

Native Plants, **III** 43

NATM Buying Corporation, **10** 9, 468

Natomas Co., **IV** 410; **6** 353–54; **7** 309; **11** 271

Natref, **IV** 535

Natronag, **IV** 325

Natronzellstoff-und Papierfabriken AG, **IV** 324

Natta, Giulio, **I** 368

Natudryl Manufacturing Company, **10** 271

Natural Gas Clearinghouse, **11** 355

Natural Gas Pipeline Company, **6** 530, 543; **7** 344–45

The Nature Company, **10** 215–16

Natus, Dietrich (Dr.), **IV** 141

NatWest. *See* National Westminster Bank PLC.

NatWest Investment Bank, **II** 334

NatWest USA, **II** 334

Nauclér, Olle **I** 386

Naugles, **7** 506

Nautilus Insurance Co., **III** 315

Nautilus Realty Corp., **III** 316

Nautor Ab, **IV** 302

Navale, **III** 209

de Navarro, Jose F., **III** 525

Naviera Vizcaina, **IV** 528

Navigation Mixte, **III** 348

Navistar International Corporation, **I** 152, 155, **180–82**, 186, 525, 527; **II** 330; **10** 280, **428–30 (upd.)**. *See also* International Harvester Co.

Nazeh, Hassan, **IV** 467

Nazer, Hisham, **IV** 538–39

NBC. *See* National Broadcasting Company, Inc.

NBC Radio, **II** 152; **6** 165

NBC-TV, **II** 152; **6** 165

NBD Bancorp, Inc., **9** 476; **11 339–41**, 466

NCA Corporation, **9** 36, 57, 171

NCB. *See* National City Bank of New York.

NCB Brickworks, **III** 501; **7** 207

NCH Corporation, **8 385–87**

Nchanga Consolidated Copper Mines, **IV** 239–40

NCNB Corporation, **II 336–37**

NCNB National Bank of Florida, **II** 336

NCR Corporation, **I** 540–41; **III** 147–52, **150–53**, 157, 165–66; **V** 263; **6** 250, **264–68 (upd.)**, 281–82; **9** 416; **11** 62, 151, 542

NCR Japan Ltd., **III** 152; **IV** 298

ND Marston, **III** 593

NDL. *See* Norddeutscher Lloyd.

NEA. *See* Newspaper Enterprise Association.

NEAC Inc., **I** 201–02

Neal, Eric J., **III** 673–74

Neal, Philip M., **IV** 254

Near, James W., **8** 564–65

Nebraska Consolidated Mills Company, **II** 493; **III** 52; **8** 433

Nebraska Furniture Mart, **III** 214–15

Nebraska Light & Power Company, **6** 580

NEC Corporation, **I** 455, 520; **II** 40, 42, 45, 56–57, **66–68**, 73, 82, 91, 104, 361; **III** 122–23, 130, 140, 715; **6** 101, 231, 244, 287; **9** 42, 115; **10** 257, 366, 463, 500; **11** 46, 308, 490

Neches Butane Products Co., **IV** 552

Neckermann Versand AG, **V** 100–02

Nedbank, **IV** 23

Nederland Line. *See* Stoomvaart Maatschappij Nederland.

Nederlandsche Heide Maatschappij, **III** 199

Nederlandsche Nieuw Guinea Petroleum Maatschappij, **IV** 491

Nederlandsche Stoomvart Maatschappij Oceaan, **6** 416

Nederlandse Aardolie Maatschappij **V** 658–61

Nederlandse Cement Industrie, **III** 701

Nederlandse Credietbank N.V., **II** 248

Nederlandse Dagbladunie NV, **IV** 610

N.V. Nederlandse Gasunie, **I** 326; **V** 627, **658–61**

Nederlandse Handel Maatschappij, **II** 183, 527; **IV** 132–33

Nederlandse Vliegtuigenfabriek, **I** 54

Nedsual, **IV** 23

Neeb, Louis P., **II** 614

Neeco, Inc., **9** 301

Needham and Harper, **I** 23, 30, 33

Needham, Harper & Steers, **I** 31

Needham Harper Worldwide, **I** 28, 31–32

Needham, Louis & Brorby Inc., **I** 31

Needham, Maurice, **I** 31

Needlecraft, **II** 560

Neenah Paper Co., **III** 40

Neenah Printing, **8** 360

NEES. *See* New England Electric System.

Neff, Grover, **6** 604–05

de Nehou, Richard Lucas, **III** 675

Neidhardt, Paul W., **8** 224

Neil, Andrew, **IV** 652; **7** 391

Neilson/Cadbury, **II** 631

Neiman Marcus, **I** 246; **II** 478; **V** 10, 31

Neimi, William F., Sr., **9** 189

Neisler Laboratories, **I** 400

Neisner Brothers, Inc., **9** 20

Nekoosa Edwards Paper Co., **IV** 282; **9** 261

NEL Equity Services Co., **III** 314

Nelio Chemicals, Inc., **IV** 345

Nelissen, Roelef, **II** 186

Nelson, Daniel R., **11** 554–55

Nelson, George, **8** 255

Nelson, Harold, **11** 24–25

Nelson, Kent C., **V** 534

Nelson, Michael, **IV** 669

Nelson, Sheffield, **V** 550

Nelson, Walter H., **I** 208

Nemuro Bank, **II** 291

Nenninger, John, **11** 466

Nenninger, Robin, **11** 466

Nenuco, **II** 567

Neodata, **11** 293

Neoterics Inc., **11** 65

Nepera Chemical, **I** 682

NERCO, Inc., **V** 689, **7 376–79**

Nerval, Gérard de, **IV** 617

Nesbitt, John M., **III** 223

Nesbitt Thomson, **II** 211

Nesher Cement, **II** 47

Nessler, Karl, **III** 68

Neste Battery Ltd., **IV** 471

Neste Oy, **IV** 435, **469–71**, 519

Nestlé, **6** 16; **11** 15

Nestlé Alimentana Co., **II** 547

Nestlé and Anglo-Swiss Holding Co. Ltd., **II** 547

Nestlé and Anglo-Swiss Milk Co., **II** 545–47

Nestlé Enterprises Inc., **8** 499

Nestlé, Henri, **II** 545; **7** 380

Nestlé S.A., **I** 15, 17, 251–52, 369, 605; **II** 379, 478, 486–89, 521, **545–49**, 568–70; **III** 47–48; **7 380–84 (upd.)**; **8** 131, 342–44; **10** 47, 324; **11** 205

Nestlé USA, Inc., **8** 498–500

Nestlé's Food Co. Inc., **II** 456

Nestlé's Milk Products Co., **II** 456

Netherland Bank for Russian Trade, **II** 183

Netherlands Fire Insurance Co. of Tiel, **III** 308, 310

Netherlands India Steam Navigation Co., **III** 521

Netherlands Insurance Co., **III** 179, 308–10

Netherlands Trading Co. *See* Nederlandse Handel Maatschappij.

Netron, **II** 390

Nettai Sangyo, **I** 507

Nettlefold, John Sutton, **III** 493

Nettlefolds Ltd., **III** 493

Netto, **11** 240

Netto, Curt, **IV** 139, 156

Network Communications Associates, Inc., **11** 409

Neubauer, Joseph, **II** 608

Neuber, Friedel, **II** 386

Neue Frankfurter Allgemeine Versicherungs-AG, **III** 184

Neue Holding AG, **III** 377

Neuenberger Versicherungs-Gruppe, **III** 404

Neuffert, Katherina, **III** 630, 632

Neuharth, Allen, **IV** 612–13; **7** 190–91

Neuhaus, Solomon. *See* Newhouse, Samuel I.

Neukirchen, Karl-Josef, **III** 544

Neumann, Billy, **III** 574

Neumann, Gerhard, **9** 245–46

Neuralgyline Co., **I** 698
Nevada Bell, **V** 318–20
Nevada Community Bank, **11** 119
Nevada National Bank, **II** 381
Nevada Power Company, 11 342–44
Neversink Dyeing Company, **9** 153
Nevett, T.R., **I** 35
Nevin, John, **II** 124
New, Alexander, **V** 139
New America Publishing Inc., **10** 288
New Asahi Co., **I** 221
New Broken Hill Consolidated, **IV** 58–61
New Consolidated Canadian Exploration Co., **IV** 96
New Consolidated Gold Fields, **IV** 21, 95
New Consolidated Gold Fields (Australasia), **IV** 96
New Daido Steel Co., Ltd., **IV** 62–63
New Departure, **9** 17
New Departure Hyatt, **III** 590
New England CRInc, **8** 562
New England Electric System, V 662–64
New England Glass Co., **III** 640
New England Life Insurance Co., **III** 261
New England Merchants Bank, **III** 313
New England Merchants Co., Inc., **II** 214
New England Merchants National Bank, **II** 213–14
New England Mutual Life Insurance Co., III 312–14
New England National Bank of Boston, **II** 213
New England Nuclear Corporation, **I** 329; **8** 152
New England Power Association, **V** 662
New England Trust Co., **II** 213
New Fire Office, **III** 371
New Found Industries, Inc., **9** 465
New Guinea Goldfields, **IV** 95
New Halwyn China Clays, **III** 690
New Hampshire Insurance Co., **III** 196–97
New Hampshire Oak, **III** 512
New Haven District Telephone Company. *See* Southern New England Telecommunications Corporation.
New Hokkai Hotel Co., Ltd., **IV** 327
New Ireland, **III** 393
New Jersey Bell, **9** 321
New Jersey Hot Water Heating Company, **6** 449
New Jersey Zinc, **I** 451
New London Ship & Engine, **I** 57
New Mather Metals, **III** 582
New Mitsui Bussan, **I** 507; **III** 296
New Nippon Electric Co., **II** 67
New Orleans Canal and Banking Company, **11** 105
New Orleans Refining Co., **IV** 540
New Plan Realty Trust, 11 345–47
New Process Cork Co., **I** 601
New, Robert, **II** 15
New Street Capital Inc., 8 388–90 (upd.). *See also* Drexel Burnham Lambert Incorporated.
New Sulzer Diesel, **III** 633
New United Motor Manufacturing Inc., **I** 205
New World Development Co., **8** 500
New World Development Company Ltd., IV 717–19
New World Hotels, **IV** 717
New York Air, **I** 90, 103, 118, 129; **6** 129
New York Airways, **I** 123–24

New York and Richmond Gas Company, **6** 456
New York and Suburban Savings and Loan Association, **10** 91
New York Biscuit Co., **II** 542
New York Central Railroad Company, **II** 329, 369; **IV** 181; **9** 228; **10** 43–44, 71–73
New York Chemical Manufacturing Co., **II** 250
New York City Transit Authority, **8** 75
New York Condensed Milk Co., **II** 470
New York Electric Corporation. *See* New York State Electric and Gas.
New York Evening Enquirer, **10** 287
New York Gas Light Company. *See* Consolidated Edison Company of New York.
New York Glucose Co., **II** 496
New York Guaranty and Indemnity Co., **II** 331
New York Harlem Railroad Co., **II** 250
New York Improved Patents Corp., **I** 601
New York, Lake Erie & Western Railroad, **II** 395; **10** 59
New York Life Insurance and Annuity Corp., **III** 316
New York Life Insurance and Trust Co., **II** 217–18
New York Life Insurance Company, **II** 330; **III** 305, **315–17**, 332; **10** 382
New York Magazine Co., **IV** 651; **7** 390
New York Manufacturing Co., **II** 312
New York Marine Underwriters, **III** 220
New York Quinine and Chemical Works, **I** 496
New York Quotation Company, **9** 370
New York, Rio and Buenos Aires Airlines, **I** 115
New York State Board of Tourism, **6** 51
New York State Electric and Gas Corporation, 6 534–36
New York State Gas and Electric. *See* New York State Electric and Gas Corporation.
New York Stock Exchange, Inc., 9 369–72; **10** 416–17
New York Telephone Co., **9** 321
New York Times, **6** 13
New York Times Company, **III** 40; **IV** **647–49**
New York Times Publishing Co., **IV** 647
New York Trust Co., **I** 378; **II** 251
New York, West Shore and Buffalo Railroad, **II** 329
New York-Newport Air Service Co., **I** 61
New Zealand Aluminum Smelters, **IV** 59
New Zealand Co., **II** 187
New Zealand Countrywide Banking Corporation, **10** 336
New Zealand Forest Products, **IV** 249–50
New Zealand Press Assoc., **IV** 669
New Zealand Sugar Co., **III** 686
New Zealand Wire Ltd., **IV** 279
New-York Life Insurance Co., **III** 291, 315–16
Newall, J.E. (Ted), **V** 675
Newark Electronics Co., **9** 420
Newbigging, David, **I** 469–70
Newbold, C.J., **I** 251
Newco Waste Systems, **V** 750
Newcombe, John, **III** 120
Newcrest Mining Ltd., **IV** 47
Newell, Albert, **9** 373
Newell, Allan, **9** 373–74

Newell and Harrison, **II** 668
Newell Co., 9 373–76
Newell, Edgar A., **9** 373
Newell Manufacturing Company, Inc. *See* Newell Co.
Newell Manufacturing Company Ltd. *See* Newell Co.
Newey and Eyre, **I** 429
Newgateway PLC, **II** 629
Newhouse Broadcasting, **6** 33
Newhouse, Donald E., **IV** 582–83
Newhouse family, **IV** 581, 583–84
Newhouse, John, **I** 43, 66
Newhouse, Mitzi Epstein, **IV** 582–83
Newhouse, Norman, **IV** 582–83
Newhouse, Samuel I., **8** 423
Newhouse, Samuel I. (S.I.), **IV** 581–83
Newhouse, Samuel I. (Si), Jr., **IV** 582–84
Newhouse, Theodore (Ted), **IV** 582–83
Newman, Floyd R., **IV** 373
Newman, J. Wilson, **IV** 605
Newman, Joseph, **II** 18
Newman, Morris B., **11** 345
Newman, Peter C., **I** 286
Newman, William, **11** 345–46
Newmarch, Michael, **III** 336
Newmont Corporation. *See* Newmont Mining Corporation.
Newmont Exploration Limited, **7** 385
Newmont Gold Company, **7** 385
Newmont Mining Corporation, **III** 248; **IV** 17, 20, 33, 171, 576; **7** 287–89, **385–88**
Newport News Shipbuilding & Drydock Co., **I** 58, 527
News and Westminster Ltd., **IV** 685
News Corp, **8** 551
News Corporation Limited, **II** 169; **IV** **650–53**; **7** 389–93 **(upd.)**; **9** 429
News International, **IV** 651–52
News Ltd., **IV** 650–53
News of the World Organization, **IV** 650–51; **7** 389
Newspaper Co-op Couponing, **8** 551
Newspaper Enterprise Association, **7** 157–58
Newspaper Proprietors' Assoc., **IV** 669
Newspaper Supply Co., **IV** 607
Newsweek, Inc., **IV** 688
Newton, Isaac, **11** 453
Newton, John T., **6** 515; **11** 238
Newton, Wesley Philips, **I** 100, 116
Newton, Wilfrid, **6** 408
Newtown Gas Co., **6** 455
Next Inc., **III** 116, 121; **6** 219
Next PLC, **6** 25
Nextel Communications, Inc., 10 431–33
Ney, Ed, **I** 37–38
Neyman, Percy, **III** 744
Neyveli Lignite Corp. Ltd., **IV** 49
Nezu, Kaichiro, **6** 430
NFC plc, 6 412–14
NHK, **9** 31. *See also* Japan Broadcasting Corporation.
NHK Gasket (Thailand) Co., **III** 580
NHK Gasket Singapore Co., **III** 580
NHK Inland Corp., **III** 581
NHK International Corp., **III** 580
NHK Spring Co., Ltd., III 580–82
NHK-Associated Spring Suspension Components, **III** 581
NHK-Cimebra Industria de Molas, **III** 580
NHK-Fastener do Brasil Industrial e Comercio, **III** 580

Niagara Fire Insurance Co., **III** 241–42
Niagara First Savings and Loan
    Association, **10** 91
Niagara Hudson Power Corporation, **V** 665
Niagara Insurance Co. (Bermuda) Ltd., **III**
    242
Niagara Mohawk Power Corporation, **V**
665–67; **6** 535
Niagara Silver Co., **IV** 644
Niagara Sprayer and Chemical Co., **I** 442
NIBRASCO, **IV** 55
Nicandros, Constantine S., **IV** 402
Nicaro Nickel Co., **IV** 82, 111; **7** 186
Nice Day, Inc., **II** 539
Nice Systems, **11** 520
NiceCom Ltd., **11** 520
Nichi-Doku Shashinki Shoten, **III** 574
Nichia Steel, **IV** 159
Nichibo, **V** 387
Nichii Co., Ltd., **V 154–55**
Nichimen Co., Ltd., **II** 442; **IV** 151–52,
    154
Nichimen Corporation, **II** 442; **IV**
150–52; **10** 439
Nichimen Jitsugyo, **IV** 151
Nichimo Sekiyu Co. Ltd., **IV** 555
Nicholas II, Czar (Russia), **III** 551
Nicholas Kiwi Ltd., **II** 572
Nicholas, Nicholas J., Jr., **IV** 675; **7** 528
Nicholas Ungar, **V** 156
Nicholls, Tom, **I** 379–80
Nichols & Company, **8** 561
Nichols, Bill J., **9** 452
Nichols, Charles, **I** 415
Nichols Copper Co., **IV** 164, 177
Nichols, John D., **III** 519
Nichols, Thomas S., **I** 695
Nichols, William H., **I** 414
Nicholson, Elmer L. (Nick), **III** 231
Nicholson File Co., **II** 16
Nicholson, Jack, **II** 136
Nicholson, Tom, **11** 308
Nicholson, William W., **III** 13
Le Nickel. *See* Société Le Nickel.
Nickerson, William, **III** 27
Nicolai Pavdinsky Co., **IV** 118
Nicolet Instrument Company, **11** 513
Nicoletti, Tom, **11** 245
Nicolin, Curt, **II** 2, 4
Nicoloff, Demetre, **11** 458
Nicolson, David, **I** 429
NICOR Inc., **6 529–31**
NICOR Oil and Gas, **6** 529
Niederbayerische Celluloserwerke, **IV** 324
Niederrheinische Hütte AG, **IV** 222
Niehler Maschinenfabrick, **III** 602
Nielsen, **10** 358
Nielsen & Petersen, **III** 417
Nielsen, Arthur C., Sr., **IV** 605
Nielsen, Claude, **IV** 615
Nielsen family, **IV** 605
Nielsen, L.C., **III** 417
Nielsen, Sven, **IV** 614
Niemann Chemie, **8** 464
Niemeier, Gustav, **7** 546
Niemeijer, J.W., **III** 309
Niemeyer, Oscar, **IV** 586
Niemier, Chuck, **10** 157
Niemöller, Martin, **IV** 593
Niese & Coast Products Co., **II** 681
Nieto, Augustine, Jr., **III** 431
Nieuwe Eerste Nederlandsche, **III** 177–79
Nieuwe HAV-Bank of Schiedam, **III** 200
Nigeria Airways, **I** 107

Nigerian Agip Oil Co., **IV** 472
Nigerian Gas Co. Ltd., **IV** 473
Nigerian Gas Development Co., **IV** 473
Nigerian National Oil Corp., **IV** 472–73
Nigerian National Petroleum
    Corporation, **IV 472–74**
Nigerian Petro Chemicals Co., **IV** 473
Nigerian Petroleum Development Co., **IV**
    473
Nigerian Petroleum Exploration and
    Exploitation Co., **IV** 473
Nigerian Petroleum Marine Transportation
    Co. Ltd., **IV** 473
Nigerian Petroleum Products Pipelines and
    Depots Co. Ltd., **IV** 473
Nigerian Petroleum Refining Co., Kadunda
    Ltd., **IV** 473
Nigerian Petroleum Refining Co., Port
    Harcourt Ltd., **IV** 473
Nigerian Petroleum Refining Co., Warri
    Ltd., **IV** 473
Nightingale, Florence, **II** 175
Nihol Repol Corp., **III** 757
Nihon Denko, **II** 118
Nihon Keizai Shimbun, Inc., **IV 654–56**
Nihon Kensetsu Sangyo Ltd., **I** 520
Nihon Lumber Land Co., **III** 758
Nihon Sangyo Co., **I** 183; **II** 118
Nihon Sugar, **I** 511
Nihon Synopsis, **11** 491
Nihon Teppan, **IV** 159
Nihon Timken K.K., **8** 530
Nihon Yusen Kaisha, **I** 503, 506; **III** 577,
    712
Nihron Yupro Corp., **III** 756
NII. *See* National Intergroup, Inc.
Niitsu Oil, **IV** 542
Nike, Inc., **V 372–74**, 376; **8** 303–04,
    391–94 (upd.); **9** 134–35, 437; **10** 525;
    11 50, 349
Nike-Japan Corp., **V** 373
Nikka Oil Co., **IV** 150
Nikka Whisky Distilling Co., **I** 220
Nikkei. *See* Nihon Keizai Shimbun, Inc.
Nikkei Aluminium Co., **IV** 153–54
Nikkei Aluminium Rolling Co., **IV** 154
Nikkei Aluminum Sales Co., **IV** 155
Nikkei Business Publications, Inc., **IV** 654,
    656
Nikkei Shimbun Toei, **9** 29
Nikkei Techno-Research Co., **IV** 154
Nikkei Thai Aluminium Co., Ltd., **IV** 155
Nikkei-McGraw Hill, **IV** 656
Nikken Stainless Fittings Co., Ltd., **IV** 160
Nikko Copper Electrolyzing Refinery, **III**
    490
Nikko International Hotels, **I** 106
Nikko Kasai Securities Co., **II** 434; **9** 378
Nikko Kido Company, **6** 431
Nikko Petrochemical Co. Ltd., **IV** 476
The Nikko Securities Company Limited,
    II 300, 323, 383, **433–35**; **9 377–79**
    (upd.)
Nikko Trading Co., **I** 106
Nikon Corporation, **III** 120–21, 575,
    583–85; **9** 251
Nile Faucet Corp., **III** 569
Nillmij, **III** 177–79
Nimas Corp., **III** 570
Nimitz, Chester, **9** 367
Nine West Group Inc., **11 348–49**
Nineteen Hundred Corp., **III** 653
Nineteen Hundred Washer Co., **III** 653

Nintendo Co., Ltd., **III 586–88**; **7 394–96**
    (upd.); **10** 124–25, 284–86, 483–84
Nintendo of America, Inc., **III** 587; **7** 395
Nintendo Playing Card Co., Ltd., **III**
    586–87; **7** 394
NIOC. *See* National Iranian Oil Company.
Nippon ARC Co., **III** 715
Nippon Beer Kosen Brewery, **I** 282
Nippon Breweries Ltd., **I** 220, 282
Nippon Broilers Co., **II** 550
Nippon Cargo Airlines, **6** 71
Nippon Chemical Industries, **I** 363
Nippon Credit Bank, **II** 310, **338–39**
Nippon Credit International, **II** 339
Nippon Educational Television (NET), **9**
    29. *See also* Asahi National
    Broadcasting Company, Ltd.
Nippon Electric Co., **II** 66–68
Nippon Express Co., Ltd., **II** 273; **V**
477–80
Nippon Fruehauf Co., **IV** 154
Nippon Fudosan Bank, **II** 338
Nippon Fukokin Kinyu Koku, **II** 300
Nippon Funtai Kogyo Co., **III** 714
Nippon Gakki Co., Ltd., **III** 656–58
Nippon Ginko, **III** 408
Nippon Glass Fiber Co., **III** 714
Nippon Gyomo Sengu Co. Ltd., **IV** 555
Nippon Hatsujo Kabushikikaisha. *See* NHK
    Spring Co., Ltd.
Nippon Helicopter & Aeroplane Transport
    Co., Ltd., **6** 70
Nippon Hoso Kyokai. *See* Japan
    Broadcasting Corporation.
Nippon Idou Tsushin, **7** 119–20
Nippon International Container Services, **8**
    278
Nippon Interrent, **10** 419–20
Nippon K.K. *See* Nippon Kokan K.K.
Nippon Kairiku Insurance Co., **III** 384
Nippon Kakoh Seishi, **IV** 293
Nippon Kangyo Bank, **II** 273–74
Nippon Kangyo Kakumara Securities, **II**
    274
Nippon Kogaku K.K., **III** 583–84
Nippon Kogyo Co. Ltd. *See* Nippon
    Mining Co. Ltd.
Nippon Kokan, **8** 449
Nippon Kokan K.K., **IV** 161–63, 184, 212
Nippon Life Insurance Company, **II** 374,
    451; **III** 273, 288, **318–20**; **IV** 727; **9**
    469
Nippon Life Lifesaving Society, **III** 318
Nippon Light Metal Company, Ltd., **IV**
153–55
Nippon Machinery Trading, **I** 507
Nippon Meat Packers, Inc., **II 550–51**
Nippon Menka Kaisha, **IV** 150–51
Nippon Merck-Banyu, **I** 651; **11** 290
Nippon Mining Co., Ltd., **III** 759; **IV**
475–77
Nippon Motorola Manufacturing Co., **II** 62
Nippon New Zealand Trading Co. Ltd., **IV**
    327
Nippon Oil Company, Limited, **IV** 434,
    475–76, **478–79**, 554
Nippon Onkyo, **II** 118
Nippon Paint Co., Ltd, **11** 252
Nippon Pelnox Corp., **III** 715
Nippon Petrochemicals Co., **IV** 479
Nippon Petroleum Gas Co., Ltd., **IV** 479
Nippon Petroleum Refining Co., Ltd., **IV**
    479

Nippon Polaroid Kabushiki Kaisha, **III** 608; **7** 437
Nippon Pulp Industries, **IV** 321
Nippon Rayon, **V** 387
Nippon Safety Glass, **III** 715
Nippon Sangyo Co., Ltd., **IV** 475
Nippon Sanso, **I** 359
Nippon Seiko Goshi Gaisha, **III** 589
Nippon Seiko K.K., **III 589–90**, 595
Nippon Sekiyu Co. *See* Nippon Oil Company, Limited.
Nippon Sheet Glass Company, Limited, **III 714–16**
Nippon Shinpan Company, Ltd., **II 436–37**, 442; **8** 118
Nippon Shinyo Hanbai Co., **II** 436
Nippon Silica Kogyo Co., **III** 715
Nippon Soda, **II** 301
Nippon Sogo Bank, **II** 371
Nippon Soken, **III** 592
Nippon Steel Chemical Co., **10** 439
Nippon Steel Corporation, **I** 466, 493–94, 509; **II** 300, 391; **IV** 116, 130, **156–58**, 184, 212, 228, 298; **6** 274
Nippon Suisan Kaisha, Limited, **II 552–53**
Nippon Tar, **I** 363
Nippon Telegraph and Telephone Corporation, **II** 51, 62; **III** 139–40; **V 305–07**; **7** 118–20; **10** 119
Nippon Telegraph and Telephone Public Corporation, **V** 305–06
Nippon Television, **7** 249; **9** 29
Nippon Tire Co., Ltd., **V** 234
Nippon Trust Bank, **II** 405
Nippon Typewriter, **II** 459
Nippon Victor (Europe) GmbH, **II** 119
Nippon Wiper Blade Co., Ltd., **III** 592
Nippon Yusen Kabushiki Kaisha, **V 481–83**
Nippon Yusen Kaisha, **IV** 713; **6** 398
Nippondenso (Deutschland) GmbH, **III** 593
Nippondenso (Europe) B.V., **III** 592
Nippondenso (Italia), **III** 594
Nippondenso (Malaysia) SDN./BHD., **III** 593
Nippondenso (U.K.) Ltd., **III** 593
Nippondenso Canada, **III** 592
Nippondenso Co., Ltd., **III 591–94**, 637–38
Nippondenso Finance (Holland) B.V., **III** 593
Nippondenso Manufacturing U.S.A., **III** 593
Nippondenso of Los Angeles, **III** 592
Nippondenso Sales, Inc., **III** 592
Nippondenso Taiwan Co., **III** 593
Nippondenso Tool and Die (Thailand) Co., Ltd., **III** 593
NIPSCO Development Company, **6** 533
NIPSCO Industries, Inc., **6 532–33**
Nirenberg, Charles, **7** 113–14
Nirenberg, Jan, **7** 114
Nishi, Itsuki, **IV** 297
Nishi Taiyo Gyogyo Tosei K.K., **II** 578
Nishikawa, Choju, **V** 209
Nishikawa, Toshio, **V** 209–10
Nishikawa, Yoshio, **V** 210
Nishikawaya Chain Co., Ltd., **V** 209
Nishikawaya Co., Ltd., **V** 209
Nishimbo Industries Inc., **IV** 442
Nishimura, Ryousuke, **III** 548
Nishio, Tetsuo, **8** 279
Nishiyama, Yataro, **IV** 124–25

Nishizono Ironworks, **III** 595
Nissan Construction, **V** 154
Nissan Diesel, **7** 219
Nissan Motor Acceptance Corp., **III** 485
Nissan Motor Company, Ltd., **I** 9, **183–84**, 207, 494; **II** 118, 292–93, 391; **III** 517, 536, 579, 591, 742, 750; **IV** 63; **7** 111, 120; **9** 243, 340–42; **10** 353; **11** 50–51, **350–52 (upd.)**
Nissan Motor Corp. USA, **I** 10, 183
Nisshin Badische Co., **II** 554
Nisshin Chemical Industries, **I** 397
Nisshin Chemicals Co., **II** 554
Nisshin Ferrite Co., Ltd., **IV** 160
Nisshin Flour Milling Company, Ltd., **II 554**
Nisshin Foods Co., **II** 554
Nisshin Pharaceutical Co., **II** 554
Nisshin Seifun do Brasil, **II** 554
Nisshin Steel Co., Ltd., **I** 432; **IV** 130, **159–60**
Nisshin Steel Corporation, **7** 588
Nisshin Stockfarming Center Co., **II** 554
Nissho Co., **I** 509–10
Nissho Iwai Corp., **8** 392
Nissho Iwai K.K., **I** 432, **509–11**; **IV** 160, 383; **V** 373; **6** 386
Nissho Kosan Co., **III** 715
Nissho-Iwai American Corporation, **8** 75
Nissui. *See* Nippon Suisan Kaisha.
Nitratos de Portugal, **IV** 505
Nitro Nobel, **9** 380
Nitroglycerin Ltd., **9** 380
Nittetsu Curtainwall Corp., **III** 758
Nittetsu Sash Sales Corp., **III** 758
Nitto Warehousing Co., **I** 507
Nittoku Metal Industries, Ltd., **III** 635
Nittsu. *See* Nippon Express Co., Ltd.
Niwa, Masaharu, **III** 710–11; **7** 302–03
Niwa, Yasujiro, **II** 66–67
Nixdorf Computer AG, **I** 193; **II** 279; **III** 109, **154–55**
Nixdorf, Heinz, **III** 154–55
Nixon, Richard M., **I** 20, 29, 76, 97, 136, 184, 277, 313, 420, 493, 500; **II** 152; **III** 137, 142, 505; **IV** 36, 366, 522, 596, 689; **10** 368
NKK Corporation, **IV** 74, **161–63**, 212–13; **V** 152
NL Industries, Inc., **III** 681; **10 434–36**
NLM City-Hopper, **I** 109
NLM Dutch Airlines, **I** 108
NLT Corp., **II** 122; **III** 194; **10** 66
NMH Stahlwerke GmbH, **IV** 128
NMT. *See* Nordic Mobile Telephone.
No-Leak-O Piston Ring Company, **10** 492
Nobel, Alfred Bernhard, **I** 351; **III** 693; **9** 380
Nobel Industries AB, **9 380–82**
Nobel Industries Ltd., **I** 351
Nobel-Bozel, **I** 669
Nobel-Hoechst Chimie, **I** 669
Nobili, Franco, **11** 205
Noble Affiliates, Inc., **11 353–55**
Noble, Allen, **11** 308
Noble, Daniel, **II** 60; **11** 326
Noble, Donald E., **III** 613–14
Noble, Ed, **11** 353
Noble, Edward, **II** 89, 129
Noble, Eva, **11** 353
Noble, Hattie, **11** 353
Noble, L.C., **II** 507
Noble, Lloyd, **11** 353
Noble, Sam, **11** 353

Noble, Sherb, **10** 371
Noblitt, Niles, **10** 156, 158
Noblitt, Quintin G., **8** 37–38
Noblitt-Sparks Industries, Inc., **8** 37–38
Noell, **IV** 201
Noels, Jacques, **10** 564
Nogano, Shigeo, **V** 158
Nogawa, Shoji, **III** 546
Noguchi, Isamu, **8** 255
Nogues, Maurice, **V** 471
Noha, Edward J., **III** 231–32
Nokia Consumer Electronics, **IV** 296
Nokia Corporation, **II 69–71**; **IV** 296
Nokia Data, **6** 242
Nokia Smurfit Ltd., **IV** 296
Nollen, Gerard, **III** 329
Noma family, **IV** 633
Noma, Hasashi, **IV** 632
Noma Industries, **11** 526
Noma, Koremichi, **IV** 633
Noma, Sae, **IV** 632
Noma, Sawako, **IV** 631, 633
Noma, Seiji, **IV** 631–33
Noma, Shoichi, **IV** 632–33
Nomura and Co., **II** 438
Nomura Bank, **II** 276
Nomura Europe GmbH, **II** 440
Nomura Europe N.V., **II** 440
Nomura International (Hong Kong), **II** 440
Nomura Investment Trust Management Co., **II** 440
Nomura Investment Trust Sales Co., **II** 440
Nomura Real Estate Development Co., Ltd., **II** 439
Nomura Securities Company, Limited, **II** 276, 326, 434, **438–41**; **9** 377, **383–86 (upd.)**
Nomura Securities Inc., **II** 440
Nomura Securities International, Inc., **II** 440–41
Nomura, Shinnosuke, **II** 438
Nomura Shoten, **II** 438
Nomura, Tokushichi, **II** 276, 438; **9** 383
Nomura, Tokushichi, II, **II** 438–39, 441; **9** 383–84, 386
Nomura Trust Co., **II** 276
Non-Stop Fashions, Inc., **8** 323
Nonpareil Refining Co., **IV** 488
Noorda, Raymond J., **6** 269–70; **10** 474, 559
Noordwinning Group, **IV** 134
Nopco Chemical Co., **IV** 409; **7** 308
Nopri, **V** 63–65
Nor-Am Agricultural Products, **I** 682
NORAND, **9** 411
Noranda Copper & Brass Ltd., **IV** 164
Noranda Copper Mills Ltd., **IV** 164
Noranda Energy, **IV** 164–65
Noranda Exploration Co., Ltd., **IV** 164
Noranda Forest Inc., **IV** 164–65; **7** 399
Noranda Inc., **IV 164–66**; **7 397–99 (upd.)**
Noranda Manufacturing Inc., **IV** 164–65
Noranda Manufacturing, Ltd., **IV** 165
Noranda Minerals Inc., **IV** 164–65
Noranda Mines Ltd., **IV** 164–65, 308; **7** 397–99; **9** 282
Noranda Power Co., Ltd., **IV** 164; **7** 397
Noranda Sales Corp. of Canada Ltd., **IV** 165
Norbye, Jan P., **I** 145
Norcast Manufacturing Ltd., **IV** 165
Norcen Energy Resources, Ltd., **8** 347
Norcliff Thayer, **III** 66

Norco Plastics, **8** 553
Norcon, Inc., **7** 558–59
Nord, Eric, **11** 356–57
Nord, Evan, **11** 356
Nord, Walter G., **11** 356
Nord-Aviation, **I** 45, 74, 82, 195; **7** 10
Nordarmatur, **I** 198
Nordbanken, **9** 382
Norddeutsche Affinerie, **IV** 141
Norddeutsche Bank A.G., **II** 279
Norddeutscher-Lloyd, **I** 542; **6** 397–98
Nordfinanzbank, **II** 366
Nordhoff, Heinz, **I** 206–08; **11** 549–50
Nordic American Banking Corp., **II** 366
Nordic Bank Ltd., **II** 366
Nordic Joint Stock Bank, **II** 302
Nordic Mobile Telephone, **II** 70
Nordica, **10** 151
NordicTrack, **10** 215–17
Nordland Papier GmbH, **IV** 300, 302
Nordli, Oddvar, **I** 210
Nordson Corporation, 11 356–58
Nordstahl AG, **IV** 201
Nordstjernan, **I** 553–54
Nordstrom Best, **V** 156
Nordstrom, Bruce, **V** 156, 158
Nordstrom, Inc., V 156–58; 11 349
Nordstrom, James, **V** 156, 158
Nordstrom, John, **V** 156, 158
Nordstrom Rack, **V** 157
Nordwestdeutsche Kraftwerke, **III** 466
Nordwestdeutsche Kraftwerke AG, **V** 698–700
Norell, **I** 696
Norex Laboratories, **I** 699
Norfolk and Western Railway Company, **V** 484–85; **6** 436, 487
Norfolk Carolina Telephone Company, **10** 202
Norfolk Southern Corporation, V 484–86
Norge Co., **III** 439–40
Norie-Miller, Francis, **III** 256–57
Norie-Miller, Stanley, **III** 257
Norinchukin Bank, II 340–41
Norinchukin Finanz (Schweiz), **II** 341
NORIS Bank GmbH, **V** 166
Norma Cie., **III** 622
Norman BV, **9** 93
Norman J. Hurll Group, **III** 673
Norman, Montagu, **II** 427
Normond/CMS, **7** 117
Noro, Kageyoshi, **IV** 156
Norrell Corporation, **6** 46
Norris, Alexander, **III** 50
Norris Cylinder Company, **11** 535
Norris, D.W., **8** 320–21
Norris, Ernest, **V** 485
Norris, John W., **8** 320
Norris, John W., Jr., **8** 320–21
Norris, Thomas C., **8** 414
Norris, William C., **III** 126–29; **10** 255–56
Norsk Hydro A.S., IV 405–06, 525; **10 437–40**
Norsk Olje AS, **IV** 406
Norstar Bancorp, **9** 229
Norstar Upstate Bank Group, **9** 229
Nortek Inc., **I** 482
Nortex Products, **7** 96
North & South Wales Bank, **II** 318
North Advertising, Inc., **6** 27
North African Petroleum Ltd., **IV** 455
North American Aviation, **I** 48, 71, 78, 81, 101; **7** 520; **9** 16; **10** 163; **11** 278, 427

North American Bancorp, **II** 192
North American Cellular Network, **9** 322
North American Coal Corporation, **7** 369–71
North American Company, **6** 443, 552–53, 601–02
North American Insurance Co., **II** 181
North American InTeleCom, Inc., **IV** 411
North American Life and Casualty Co., **III** 185, 306
North American Light & Power Company, **V** 609; **6** 504–05
North American Managers, Inc., **III** 196
North American Philips Corp., **II** 79–80
North American Printed Circuit Corp., **III** 643
North American Reassurance Co., **III** 377
North American Reinsurance Corp., **III** 377
North American Rockwell Corp., **10** 173
North American Van Lines, **I** 278
North British and Mercantile Insurance Co., **III** 234–35
North British Insurance Co., **III** 234
North Broken Hill Peko, **IV** 61
North Carolina National Bank Corporation, **II** 336; **10** 425–27
North Carolina Natural Gas Corporation, **6** 578
North Central Airlines, **I** 132
North Central Finance, **II** 333
North Central Financial Corp., **9** 475
North Cornwall China Clay Co., **III** 690
North Eastern Coalfields Ltd., **IV** 48
North Face, **8** 169
North Goonbarrow, **III** 690
North Holland Publishing Co., **IV** 610
North New York Savings Bank, **10** 91
North of Scotland Bank, **II** 318
North Pacific Paper Corp., **IV** 298
North Pacific Railroad, **II** 330
North, Philip, **II** 106–07
North Sea Oil and Gas, **10** 337
North Sea Sun Oil Co. Ltd., **IV** 550
North Shore Gas Company, **6** 543–44
North Shore Medical Centre Pty, Ltd., **IV** 708
North Star Marketing Cooperative, **7** 338
North West Water Group plc, 11 359–62
North, William A., **10** 422
North-West Telecommunications, **6** 327
Northamptonshire Union Bank, **II** 333
Northcliffe (Lord). *See* Harmsworth, Alfred (Lord Northcliffe).
Northcliffe, Lord. *See* Harmsworth, Alfred.
Northcliffe Newspapers, **IV** 685
Northcott, Bob, **III** 739
Northeast Airlines Inc., **I** 99–100; **6** 81
Northeast Petroleum Industries, Inc., **11** 194
Northeast Utilities, V 668–69
Northeastern Bancorp of Scranton, **II** 342
Northeastern New York Medical Service, Inc., **III** 246
Northen, Mary Moody, **8** 28
Northern Aluminum Co. Ltd., **IV** 9–10
Northern and Employers Assurance, **III** 235
Northern Arizona Light & Power Co., **6** 545
Northern Border Pipeline Co., **V** 609–10
Northern California Savings, **10** 340
Northern Crown Bank, **II** 344
Northern Dairies, **10** 441

Northern Development Co., **IV** 282
Northern Electric Company. *See* Northern Telecom Limited.
Northern Energy Resources Company. *See* NERCO, Inc.
Northern Fibre Products Co., **I** 202
Northern Foods, **I** 248; **II** 587
Northern Foods PLC, 10 441–43
Northern Illinois Gas Co., **6** 529–31
Northern Indiana Gas, **6** 532
Northern Indiana Power Company, **6** 556
Northern Indiana Public Service Company, **6** 532–33
Northern Joint Stock Bank, **II** 303
Northern Natural Gas Co., **V** 609–10
Northern Pacific Railroad, **II** 278, 329; **III** 228, 282
Northern Paper, **I** 614
Northern States Life Insurance Co., **III** 275
Northern States Power Company, V 670–72
Northern Sugar Company, **11** 13
Northern Telecom Canada Ltd., **6** 310
Northern Telecom Inc., **11** 69
Northern Telecom Limited, II 70; **III** 143, 164; **V** 271; **V 308–10**; **6** 242, 307; **9** 479; **10** 19, 432
Northern Trust Company, III 518; **9 387–89**
Northern Trust Corporation, **9** 389
Northern Trust International Banking Corporation, **9** 388
Northfield Metal Products, **11** 256
Northrop Corporation, I 47, 49, 55, 59, **76–77**, 80, 84, 197, 525; **III** 84; **9** 416, 418; **10** 162; **11** 164, 166, 266, 269, **363–65 (upd.)**
Northrop, Jack, **9** 12
Northrop, Jack Knudsen, **11** 266, 363
Northrop, John Knudson, **I** 64, 76–77
Northrup King Co., **I** 672
NorthStar Computers, **10** 313
Northwest Airlines Inc., I 42, 64, 91, 97, 100, 104, **112–14**, 125, 127; **6** 66, 74, 82 **103–05 (upd.)**; **9** 273; **11** 266, 315
Northwest Benefit Assoc., **III** 228
Northwest Engineering Co. *See* Terex Corporation.
Northwest Industries, **I** 342, 440; **II** 468 **8** 367. *See also* Chicago and North Western Holdings Corporation.
Northwest Instruments, **8** 519
Northwest Orient, **6** 123. *See also* Northwest Airlines, Inc.
Northwest Paper Company, **8** 430
Northwest Telecommunications Inc., **6** 598
Northwestern Bell Telephone Co., **V** 341
Northwestern Benevolent Society, **III** 228
Northwestern Expanded Metal Co., **III** 763
Northwestern Financial Corporation, **11** 29
Northwestern Industries, **III** 263
Northwestern Manufacturing Company, **8** 133
Northwestern Mutual Life Insurance Company, III 321–24, 352; **IV** 333
Northwestern National Insurance Co., **IV** 29
Northwestern Public Service Company, **6** 524
Northwestern States Portland Cement Co., **III** 702
Northwestern Telephone Systems, **6** 325, 328
Norton, Charles H., **8** 396

Norton Company, III 678; **8 395–97**
Norton Emery Wheel Company, **8** 395
Norton, Eugene, **IV** 81; **7** 185
Norton, Frank, **8** 395
Norton Healthcare Ltd., **11** 208
Norton Opax PLC, **IV** 259
Norton, Peter, **10** 508
Norton Simon Inc., **I** 446; **IV** 672; **6** 356
Norton Stone Ware, F.B., **8** 395
Norwales Confectionery Ltd., **11** 239
Norwales Development Ltd., **11** 239
Norwegian Assurance, **III** 258
Norwegian Globe, **III** 258
Norwegian Petroleum Consultants, **III** 499
Norwest Mortgage Inc., **11** 29
Norwest Publishing, **IV** 661
Norwich Pharmaceuticals, **I** 370–71; **9** 358
Norwich Union Fire Insurance Society,
   Ltd., **III** 242, 273, 404; **IV** 705
Norwich Winterthur Group, **III** 404
Norwich Winterthur Reinsurance Corp.
   Ltd., **III** 404
Norwich-Eaton Pharmaceuticals, **III** 53; **8**
   434
Nottingham Manufacturing Co., **V** 357
Nourse, Alexandra "Aagje," **10** 167
Nourse, Robert E.M., **10** 166–68
Nouvelles Galeries, **10** 205
Nouvelles Messageries de la Presse
   Parisienne, **IV** 618
Nova, an Alberta Corporation, **V** 674
Nova Corporation of Alberta, **V 673–75**
NovaCare, Inc., **11 366–68**
Novak, William, **I** 145
Novalta Resources Inc., **11** 441
Novell Data Systems. *See* Novell, Inc.
Novell, Inc., **6** 255–56, 260, **269–71**; **9**
   170–71; **10** 232, 363, 473–74, 558, 565;
   11 59, 519–20
Novello and Co., **II** 139
Novo Industri A/S, **I 658–60**, 697
Nowell Wholesale Grocery Co., **II** 681
Nox Ltd., **I** 588
Noxell Corporation, **III** 53; **8** 434
Noyce, Robert, **II** 44–46; **10** 365–66
Noyes, John Humphrey, **7** 406
Noyes, Pierrepont Burt, **7** 406–07
Nozaki, Hirota, **IV** 655
NRG Energy, Inc., **11** 401
NS. *See* Norfolk Southern Corporation.
NS Petites Inc., **8** 323
NSG America, Inc., **III** 715
NSG Foreign Trade, **III** 715
NSG Information System Co., **III** 715
NSG Materials Service Co., **III** 715
NSG-Taliq, **III** 715
NSK. *See* Nippon Seiko K.K.
NSK Bearings Europe, **III** 589
NSK Corp., **III** 589
NSK do Brasil Industria e Comercio de
   Rolamentos, **III** 589
NSK Kugellager, **III** 589
NSK-Torrington, **III** 589
NSMO. *See* Nederlandsche Stoomvart
   Maatschappij Oceaan.
NSP. *See* Northern States Power Company.
NSU Werke, **10** 261
NTCL. *See* Northern Telecom Canada Ltd.
NTN Bearing Corp. of America, **III** 595
NTN Bearing Corp. of Canada, **III** 595
NTN Bearing Manufacturing Corp., **III**
   595
NTN Bearings-GKN, **III** 595
NTN Bower Corp., **III** 596

NTN Corporation, **III 595–96**, 623
NTN de Mexico, **III** 596
NTN Driveshaft, **III** 596
NTN France, **III** 595
NTN Kugellagerfabrik, **III** 595–96
NTN Manufacturing Canada, **III** 595
NTN Manufacturing Co., Ltd., **III** 595
NTN Sales, **III** 595
NTN Suramericana, **III** 596
NTN Toyo Bearing Co., **III** 595–96
NTN Trading-Hong Kong, **III** 595
NTN Wälzlager Europa, **III** 595
NTRON, **11** 486
NTT. *See* Nippon Telegraph and Telephone
   Corp.
NTT International Corporation, **V** 305–06
NTTI. *See* NTT International Corporation.
NTTPC. *See* Nippon Telegraph and
   Telephone Public Corporation.
NU. *See* Northeast Utilities.
Nuclear Electric, **6** 453; **11** 399–401
Nucoa Butter Co., **II** 497
Nucor Corporation, **7 400–02**
Nucorp Energy, **II** 262, 620
NUG Optimus Lebensmittel-
   Einzelhandelgesellschaft mbH, **V** 74
Nugent, D. Eugene, **7** 420
Nugent, Frank, **III** 738
Nugget Polish Co. Ltd., **II** 566
Numerax, Inc., **IV** 637
Nunn, Sam, **10** 161
Nuovo Pignone, **IV** 420–22
NUR Touristic GmbH, **V** 100–02
Nurad, **III** 468
Nursefinders, **6** 10
Nusbaum, Aaron, **V** 180
NutraSweet Company, **II** 463, 582; **8**
   398–400
Nutrena, **II** 617
Nutri/System Inc., **10** 383
Nutrilite Co., **III** 11–12
Nutt, Roy, **6** 227
NVH L.P., **8** 401. *See also* NVR L.P.
NVHomes, Inc., **8** 401–02. *See also* NVR
   L.P.
NVR Finance, **8** 402–03
NVR L.P., **8 401–03**
NVRyan L.P., **8** 401. *See also* NVR L.P.
NWA Aircraft, **I** 114
NWK. *See* Nordwestdeutsche Kraftwerke
   AG.
NWL Control Systems, **III** 512
NWS BANK plc, **10** 336–37
Nya AB Atlas, **III** 425–26
Nybom, F.K., **II** 302
Nydqvist & Holm, **III** 426
Nye, David E., **I** 168
Nye, Gerald, **I** 57; **10** 315
Nyers, Howard, **IV** 673; **7** 527
Nyhamms Cellulosa, **IV** 338
NYK. *See* Nihon Yusen Kaisha.
NYK. *See* Nippon Yusen Kabushiki Kaisha
   and Nippon Yusen Kaisha.
Nylex Corp., **I** 429
Nyman & Schultz Affarsresbyraer A.B., **I**
   120
NYNEX Corporation, **V 311–13**; **6** 340;
   11 87
NYNEX Mobile Communications, **11** 19
Nyrop, **I** 113
Nyrop, Donald, **6** 104
Nysco Laboratories, **III** 55
NYSEG. *See* New York State Electric and
   Gas Corporation.

NZI Corp., **III** 257

O'Brien, Dan, **11** 51
O'Brien, John, **IV** 306; **11** 166
O'Brien, John J., **V** 711
O'Brien, Morgan, **III** 247; **10** 431–32
O'Brien, Raymond F., **V**, 433; **6** 390
O'Brien, Robert, **I** 185, 286
O'Brien, Thomas H., **II** 342
O'Brien, William, **II** 381
O'Connor, Flannery, **IV** 622
O'Connor, John, **III** 471
O'Donnell, William T., **III** 430–31
O'Donnell-Usen Fisheries, **II** 494
O'Gorman and Cozens-Hardy, **III** 725
O'Green, Fred, **I** 485; **11** 264
O'Hagan, Henry Osborne, **III** 669
O'Hagan, William D., **7** 361
O'Hara, J.B., **9** 177
O'Hara, John M., **10** 461
O'Hare, Dean R., **III** 221
O'Hare, Don R., **7** 504
O'Keefe, Bernard J., **8** 163–65
O'Kelley, Harold, **11** 68
O'Leary, Thomas, **10** 190
O'Malley, Shaun F., **9** 424
O'Malley, Thomas, **7** 538
O'Malley, William C., **11** 524
O'Neal, Edward, **I** 366; **9** 356
O'Neal, Jones & Feldman Inc., **11** 142
O'Neil, Jerry, **8** 207; **9** 248
O'Neil, John, **9** 248
O'Neil, John P., **9** 134
O'Neil, Thomas, **9** 248
O'Neil, William, **8** 206–07; **9** 247–48
O'Neil, William F., **8** 212–14
O'Neill, John, **III** 673
O'Neill, Paul, **IV** 16
O'Neill, Peter L., **II** 607
O'okiep Copper Compny, Ltd., **7** 385–86
O'Reilly, Anthony J.F., **II** 508; **11** 172–73
O'Shields, Richard, **10** 82
O'Toole, Robert J., **11** 6
O&Y. *See* Olympia & York Developments
   Ltd.
O.B. McClintock Co., **7** 144–45
Oahu Railway & Land Co., **I** 565–66
Oak Farms Dairies, **II** 660
Oak Hill Investment Partners, **11** 490
Oak Industries, **III** 512
Oakes, C. Gordon, **I** 714
Oakley, Annie, **11** 43
Oakley, Jonas, **III** 240
OakStone Financial Corporation, **11** 448
Oakville, **7** 518
OASIS, **IV** 454
Oasis Group P.L.C., **10** 506
Oates, James, Jr., **III** 248
Oates, Keith, **V** 126
Oats, Francis, **IV** 65
ÖBB. *See* Österreichische Bundesbahnen
   GmbH.
Obbola Linerboard, **IV** 339
Ober, Edgar B., **8** 369
Ober, John, **I** 499
Oberkotter, Harold, **V** 534
Oberrheinische Bank, **II** 278
Oberschlesische Stickstoff-Werge AG, **IV**
   229
Oberusel AG, **III** 541
Oberwinder, J. F., **6** 21
Obunsha, **9** 29
Occidental Chemical Corp., **IV** 481–82
Occidental Indemnity Co., **III** 251

Occidental Insurance Co., **III** 251
Occidental Libya, **IV** 454
Occidental Life Insurance, **I** 536–37
Occidental Minerals Corporation, **7** 376
Occidental Oil and Gas Corp., **IV** 481
Occidental Overseas Ltd., **11** 97
Occidental Petroleum, **8** 526
Occidental Petroleum Corporation, I
527; **II** 432, 516; **IV** 264, 312, 392, 410,
417, 453–54, 467, **480–82**, 486,
515–16; **7** 376
Occidental Petroleum of California, **IV** 481
Ocean, **III** 234
Ocean Combustion Services, **9** 109
Ocean Drilling and Exploration Company.
See ODECO.
Ocean Group plc, 6 415–17
Ocean Salvage and Towage Co., **I** 592
Ocean Spray Cranberries, Inc., 7
403–05; 10 525
Ocean Steam Ship Company, **6** 117, 415.
See also Malaysian Airlines System
BHD.
Ocean Systems Inc., **I** 400
Ocean Transport & Trading Ltd., **6** 417
Oceanic Contractors, **III** 559
Oceanic Properties, **II** 491–92
Ochoa, Francisco, **10** 302
Ochs, Adolph Simon, **IV** 647–48
Ochs, Iphigene. See Sulzberger, Iphigene
Ochs.
OCL. See Overseas Containers Ltd.
Ocoma Foods, **II** 584
Octel Communications, **III** 143
Octopus Publishing, **IV** 667
Oculinum, Inc., **10** 48
Oda, Kyuemon, **9** 30
Odaira, Namihei, **I** 454; **IV** 101
Odajama, Sadakichi, **IV** 656
Odakyu Electric Railway Company
Limited, V 487–89
Odam's and Plaistow Wharves, **II** 580–81
Odd Lot Trading Company, **V** 172–73
ODECO, **7** 362–64; **11** 522
Odell, Carl L., **10** 50
Odeon Cinema Holdings Ltd., **II** 158
Odeon Theatres Holdings Ltd., **II** 157
Odeon Theatres Ltd., **II** 157–59
Odhams Press Ltd., **IV** 259, 666–67; **7**
244, 342
Odlum, Floyd, **I** 512
Odom, Guy, **8** 542
Odyssey Partner L.P., **V** 135
Odyssey Partners, **II** 679
Oelman, Robert S., **III** 151–52; **6** 266
Oelwerken Julius Schindler GmbH, **7** 141
Oeri, Jakob, **I** 642
Oertel Brewing Co., **I** 226; **10** 180
Oësterreichischer Phönix in Wien, **III** 376
Oestrich, Hermann, **I** 139; **11** 32
Oetker Group, **I** 219
Off the Rax, **II** 667
Office Club, **8** 404–05; **10** 497
Office Depot Incorporated, 8 404–05; 10
235, 497
Office Mart Holdings Corporation, **10** 498
Office Max, **8** 404
Office National du Crédit Agricole, **II** 264
Official Airline Guides, Inc., **IV** 605, 643;
7 312, 343
Offset Gerhard Kaiser GmbH, **IV** 325
Offshore Co., **III** 558; **6** 577
Offshore Food Services Inc., **I** 514

Offshore Transportation Corporation, **11**
523
Ogden Corporation, I 512–14, 701; **6**
151–53, 600; **7** 39
Ogden Food Products, **7** 430
Ogden Gas Co., **6** 568
Ogden, Peter Skene, **V** 79–80
Ogden, William Butler, **6** 376
Ogilvie Flour Mills Co., **I** 268; **IV** 245
Ogilvie, Shirley, **IV** 245
Ogilvy & Mather, **I** 20, 31, 37; **6** 53; **9**
180. See also WPP Group PLC.
Ogilvy and Mather International, **I** 26
Ogilvy, David, **I** 12, 23, 25–26, 30, 36; **6**
53; **11** 52
Ogilvy Group Inc., I 25–27, 244; **6** 53.
See also WPP Group.
Oglethorpe Power Corporation, 6
537–38
Ogura, Masatune, **I** 519; **IV** 212; **11** 479
Ogura Oil, **IV** 479
Ohbayashi Corporation, **I** 586–87
Ohbayashi, Yoshigoro, **I** 586
Ohbayashi, Yoshio, **I** 586
Ohbayashi, Yoshiro, **I** 586
Ohga, Norio, **II** 101–02
Ohio Barge Lines, Inc., **11** 194
Ohio Brass Co., **II** 2
Ohio Casualty, **III** 190
Ohio Casualty Corp., 11 369–70
Ohio Edison Company, V 676–78
Ohio Electric Railway Co., **III** 388
Ohio Oil Co., **IV** 365, 400, 574; **6** 568; **7**
551
Ohio Pizza Enterprises, Inc., **7** 152
Ohio Pure Foods Group, **II** 528
Ohio River Company, **6** 487
Ohio Valley Electric Corporation, **6** 517
Ohkawa, Isao, **10** 482
Ohlmeyer Communications, **I** 275
Ohlsson's Cape Breweries, **I** 287–88
Ohmae, Kenici, **9** 343
Ohnishi, Masafumi, **V** 681
Ohnishi, Minoru, **III** 487–88
Ohno, Yoshio, **III** 63
Ohrbach's Department Store, **I** 30
Ohrstrom, George, Sr., **III** 467
Ohta Keibin Railway Company, **6** 430
Ohya, Shinzo, **V** 381–82
ÖIAG, **IV** 234
Oil Acquisition Corp., **I** 611
Oil and Natural Gas Commission, IV
440–41, **483–84**
Oil and Solvent Process Company, **9** 109
Oil City Oil and Grease Co., **IV** 489
Oil Co. of Australia, **III** 673
Oil Distribution Public Corp., **IV** 434
Oil Drilling, Incorporated, **7** 344
Oil India Ltd., **IV** 440, 483–84
Oil Shale Corp., **IV** 522; **7** 537
Oilfield Industrial Lines Inc., **I** 477
Oilfield Service Corp. of America, **I** 342
D'Oissel, Antoine-Pierre Hély, **III** 676
D'Oissel, Pierre Hély, **III** 677
Oita Co., **III** 718
Oji Paper Co., Ltd., I 506, 508; **II** 326;
IV 268, 284–85, 292–93, 297–98,
320–22, 326
Oji Paper Manufacturing Co., **IV** 320–21,
327
OK Bazaars, **I** 289
Okada, Shigeru, **V** 143
Okada, Takuya, **V** 96–98
Okadaya Co. Ltd., **V** 96

Okamoto, Norikazu, **III** 409
Okamoto, T., **9** 294
Okawa, Heizaburo, **IV** 320
Okazaki, Kaheito, **6** 70
Oki & Co., **II** 72
Oki America, Inc., **II** 73
Oki Electric Co., Ltd., **II** 72
Oki Electric Industry Company,
Limited, II 68, **72–74**
Oki, Kibataro, **II** 72–73
Oki Shokai, **II** 66
Oki Univac Kaisha, Ltd., **II** 73
Okidata, **9** 57
Okinoyama Coal Mine, **III** 759
Oklahoma Airmotive, **8** 349
Oklahoma Entertainment, Inc., **9** 74
Oklahoma Gas and Electric Company, 6
539–40
Oklahoma Natural Gas Company, **6** 530; **7**
409–10
Oklahoma Natural Gas Transmission
Company, **7** 409–11
Oklahoma Oil Co., **I** 31
Oklahoma Publishing Company, **11**
152–53
Okonite, **I** 489
Okoso, Yoshinori, **II** 550
Okubo, Shoji, **7** 219–20
Okuma, Shigenobu, **I** 502, 506; **V** 449
Okumura, Tsunao, **II** 439; **9** 385
Okura & Co. America, Inc., **IV** 168
Okura & Co., Ltd., IV 167–68
Okura, Kihachiro, **IV** 167
Okura Mining Co., **IV** 167
Okura Public Works Co., **IV** 167
Okura-gumi, **I** 282; **IV** 167–68
OLC. See Orient Leasing Co., Ltd.
Olcott & McKesson, **I** 496
Olcott, Charles, **II** 614
Old Colony Trust Co., **II** 207
Old Dominion Power Company, **6** 513,
515
Old El Paso, **I** 457
Old Kent Financial Corp., 11 371–72
Old Line Life Insurance Co., **III** 275
Old Mutual, **IV** 23, 535
Old Republic International Corp., 11
373–75
Oldham Estate, **IV** 712
Olds, Irving S., **IV** 573; **7** 550
Olds Motor Vehicle Co., **I** 171; **10** 325
Olds Oil Corp., **I** 341
Olds, Ransom Eli, **I** 171; **III** 438; **7** 400;
10 325
Oleochim, **IV** 498–99
Olesen, Douglas, **10** 140
OLEX. See Deutsche BP
Aktiengesellschaft.
Olex Cables Ltd., **10** 445
OLEX Deutsche Benzin und Petroleum
GmbH, **7** 141
OLEX Deutsche Petroleum-
Verkaufsgesellschaft mbH, **7** 140
OLEX-Petroleum-Gesellschaft mbH, **7** 140
D'Olier, Franklin, **III** 338
Olin Corporation, I 318, 330, **379–81**,
434; **III** 667; **IV** 482; **8** 23, 153
Olin, Franklin, **I** 379
Olin, John, **I** 379–80
Olin Mathieson Chemical Co., **I** 695
Olin Mathieson Chemical Corp., **11** 420
Olin, Spencer, **I** 379
Olinger, Glen S., **8** 299
Olinkraft, Inc., **II** 432; **III** 708–09; **11** 420

Olins Rent-a-Car, **6** 348
Olinvest, **IV** 454
Olive Garden Italian Restaurants, **10** 322, 324
de Oliveira, Eduardo Fernandes (Dr.), **IV** 504
Olivetti. *See* Ing. C. Olivetti & C., S.p.A.
Olivetti, **V** 339; **6** 233, 235; **11** 59
Olivetti, Adriano, **III** 144–45
Olivetti, Camillo, **III** 144
Olivetti Information Services, **III** 145
Olivetti Office, **III** 145
Olivetti Systems and Networks, **III** 145
Olivetti Technologies Group, **III** 145
Olivier, Laurence, **II** 157
Olivine Industries, Inc., **II** 508; **11** 172
Olmsted, George W., **V** 652
Olofsson, **I** 573
Olohana Corp., **I** 129; **6** 129
Olsen Dredging Co., **III** 558
Olsen, Fred, **7** 531–32
Olsen, Ken, **6** 233–36
Olsen, Kenneth, **III** 132–34
Olsen, Thomas, **7** 531
Olshan, Kenneth S., **6** 51–52
Olson & Wright, **I** 120
Olson, Arthur, **11** 353
Olson, Bruce F., **7** 503
Olson, Carl G., **III** 518
Olson, Frank A., **I** 130; **6** 130; **9** 283–84
Olson, Gene, **8** 462
Olson, H. Everett, **II** 488–89
Olson, Hugo, **7** 502–03
Olson, Robert A., **6** 510–11
Olsonite Corp., **I** 201
Olsson, Elis, **8** 102
Olsson, George C.P., **7** 404
Olsson, Sture, **8** 102
Olsten Corporation, **6 41–43**; **9** 327
Olsten, William, **6** 41–43
Olsten's Temporary Office Personnel. *See* Olsten Corporation.
Oltz, Harry M., **10** 371–73
Olveh, **III** 177–79
Olympia & York, **8** 327
Olympia & York Developments Ltd., **IV** 245, 247, 712, **720–21**; **6** 478; **9 390–92 (upd.)**
Olympia Arenas, Inc., **7** 278–79
Olympia Brewing, **I** 260; **11** 50
Olympia Floor & Tile Co., **IV** 720
Olympiaki, **III** 401
Olympic Airways, **II** 442
Olympic Fastening Systems, **III** 722
Olympus Sport, **V** 177–78
Omaha Cold Store Co., **II** 571
Oman Oil Refinery Co., **IV** 516
Omega Gas Company, **8** 349
Omega Gold Mines, **IV** 164
Omex Corporation, **6** 272
OMI International Corp., **IV** 34; **9** 111
OMI Investments Inc., **9** 111–12
Omlon, **II** 75
Ommium Française de Pétroles, **IV** 559
Omni Construction Company, Inc., **8** 112–13
Omni Hearing Aid Systems, **I** 667
Omni Products International, **II** 420
Omnibus Corporation, **9** 283
Omnicom Group, **I 28–32**, 33, 36
Omron Tateisi Electronics Company, **II 75–77**; **III** 549
Omura, Hikotaro, **V** 199

ÖMV Aktiengesellschaft, **IV** 234, 454, **485–87**
ÖMV Handels-Aktiengesellschaft, **IV** 486
On Cue, **9** 360
On-Line Software International Inc., **6** 225
Onan Corporation, **8** 72
Onbancorp Inc., **11** 110
Oncogen, **III** 18
Ondal GmbH, **III** 69
Ondetti, Miguel A., **I** 696
Ondulato Imolese, **IV** 296
One Hundredth Bank, **II** 321
One-Hundred Thirtieth National Bank, **II** 291
Oneida Bank & Trust Company, **9** 229
Oneida County Creameries Co., **7** 202
Oneida Gas Company, **9** 554
Oneida Ltd., **7 406–08**
ONEOK Inc., **7 409–12**
Ong, John D., **V** 233; **11** 158
Onitsuka Tiger Co., **V** 372; **8** 391
Online Distributed Processing Corporation, **6** 201
Online Financial Communication Systems, **11** 112
Ono family, **I** 506
Onoda Cement Co., Ltd., **I** 508; **III 717–19**
Onoda California, Inc., **III** 718
Onoda U.S.A., Inc., **III** 718
Ontario Hydro, **6 541–42**
Ontario Hydro-Electric Power Commission, **9** 461
Ontel Corporation, **6** 201
Oode Casting, **III** 551
Oode Casting Iron Works, **III** 551
Oode, Gonshiro, **III** 551–52
Oosterhoff, J., Jr., **III** 177
Opel, Fritz, **V** 241
Opel, Georg, **V** 241
Opel, John, **III** 149; **6** 252
Open Board of Brokers, **9** 369
Oppenheimer. *See* Ernest Oppenheimer and Sons.
Oppenheimer & Co., **I** 667; **II** 445
Oppenheimer, Ernest (Sir), **IV** 20–23, 64–66, 79, 191; **7** 121–23
Oppenheimer family, **IV** 20–21, 23
Oppenheimer, Harry, **IV** 22–23, 64, 66, 68, 79–80, 90; **7** 121, 123, 125
Oppenheimer, Nicky, **IV** 68; **7** 125
Oppenlander, Robert, **I** 100; **6** 82
Opperman, Dwight D., **7** 580
Opryland USA, **11** 152–53
OPTi Computer, **9** 116
Optimum Financial Services Ltd., **II** 457
Optronics, Inc., **6** 247
OPW, **III** 467–68
Oracle Corp., **11** 78
Oracle Data Publishing, **6** 273
Oracle Systems Corporation, **6 272–74**; **10** 361, 363, 505
Oracle USA, **6** 273
Orange Julius, **10** 371, 373
Orange Line Bus Company, **6** 604
Orcofi, **III** 48
Orcutt, Charles, **8** 83
Ordonez, Fernandez, **I** 460
Ordway, Lucius P., **I** 499
Ordway, Lucius Pond, **8** 369
Ordy, Greg M., **11** 491
Ore and Chemical Corp., **IV** 140
Ore-Ida Foods, Inc., **II** 508; **11** 172
L'Oréal, **II** 547; **III 46–49**, 62; **7** 382–83

Oreamuno, Walter R., **11** 273
Oreffice, P.F., **I** 325; **8** 149
Orford Copper Co., **IV** 110
Organon, **I** 665
Oriel Foods, **II** 609
Orient Glass, **III** 715
Orient Leasing (Asia), **II** 442
Orient Leasing (U.K.), **II** 442
Orient Leasing Co., Ltd., **II** 442–43, 259, 348. *See also* Orix Corporation.
Orient Leasing Interior Co., **II** 442
Orient Leasing Singapore, **II** 442
Orient Leasing USA Corp., **II** 442
Orient-U.S. Leasing Corp., **II** 442
Oriental Land Co., Ltd., **IV** 715
Origin Systems Inc., **10** 285
Original Wassertragers Hummel, **II** 163
Orinoco Oilfields, Ltd., **IV** 565
Orion, **III** 310
Orion Bank Ltd., **II** 271, 345, 385
Orion Healthcare Ltd., **11** 168
Orion Personal Insurances Ltd., **11** 168
Orion Pictures Corporation, **II** 147; **6 167–70**; **7** 336
Orit Corp., **8** 219–20
Orita, Shosuke, **III** 405
Orix Corporation, **II 442–43**. *See also* Orient Leasing Co., Ltd.
Orkem, **IV** 547, 560
Orkin Exterminating Company, **11** 431
Orkin Lawn Care, **11** 431–34
Orkin Pest Control, **11** 431–32, 434
Orlandini, Sergio, **I** 108
Orlean, M., **V** 658
Orm Bergold Chemie, **8** 464
Ornstein, Jonathan, **11** 299
ÖROP, **IV** 485–86
Orowheat Baking Company, **10** 250
Orr, Vernon, **I** 80; **11** 429
Orris, Donald C., **6** 354
Ortenberg, Arthur, **8** 329–30
Ortenzio, Robert A., **10** 253
Ortenzio, Rocco A., **10** 252–53
Ortho Diagnostic Systems, Inc., **10** 213
Ortho Pharmaceutical Corporation, **III** 35; **8** 281; **10** 79–80
Orthopedic Services, Inc., **11** 366
Orval Kent Food Company, Inc., **7** 430
Oryx Energy Company, **IV** 550; **7 413–15**
Osaka Aluminium Co., **IV** 153
Osaka Beer Brewing Co., **I** 220, 282
Osaka Electric Tramway, **V** 463
Osaka Gas Co., Ltd., **V 679–81**
Osaka Gas Engineering, **V** 681
Osaka General Bussan, **IV** 431
Osaka Iron Works, **III** 513
Osaka Marine and Fire Insurance Co., **III** 367
Osaka Nomura Bank, **II** 276, 438–39
Osaka North Harbor Co. Ltd., **I** 518
Osaka Shosen Kaisha, **I** 503; **V** 473–74, 481–82
Osaka Spinning Company, **V** 387
Osaka Sumitomo Marine and Fire Insurance Co., Ltd., **III** 367
Osaka Textile Co., **I** 506
Osakeyhtiö Gustaf Cederberg & Co., **IV** 301
Osakeyhtiö T. & J. Salvesen, **IV** 301
Osborn, A. T., **III** 744
Osborn, Alex, **I** 28
Osborn, E. B., **I** 331
Osborn, Fay, **I** 320

Osborn, Merrit J., **I** 331
Osborn, S. Bartlett, **I** 332
Osborne Books, **IV** 637
Osborne, Dean C., **10** 270
Osborne, John R., **10** 463
Osborne, Richard de J., **IV** 34
Osborne, Stan, **I** 380
Oscar Mayer, **II** 532; **7** 274, 276
Osco Drug, **II** 604–05
Osgood, Samuel, **II** 253; **9** 123
Oshawa Group Limited, II 649–50
Oshawa Wholesale Ltd., **II** 649
Oshima, Michitaro, **IV** 156
OshKosh B'Gosh, Inc., 9 393–95
Oshkosh Electric Power, **9** 553
Oshkosh Gas Light Company, **9** 553
Oshkosh Truck Corporation, 7 416–18
Osinsky, Meshe David. *See* Burton, Montague.
OSK. *See* Osaka Shosen Kaisha.
Oster. *See* Sunbeam-Oster.
Oster, Clinton V., **I** 118, 124
Oster, John, Sr., **9** 484
Ostern, Rolf, **10** 544
Österreichische Bundesbahnen GmbH, 6 418–20
Österreichische Creditanstalt-Wiener Bankverein, **IV** 230
Österreichische Elektrowerke, **IV** 230
Österreichische Industrieholding AG, **IV** 486–87
Österreichische Industriekredit AG, **IV** 230
Österreichische Länderbank, **II** 239
Österreichische Mineralölverwaltung AG, **IV** 485
Österreichische Post- und Telegraphenverwaltung, V 314–17
Österreichische Stickstoffswerke, **IV** 486
Ostrander, Patricia, **8** 196
Ostschweizer Zementwerke, **III** 701
Osuga, Jiro, **7** 111
Osuuskunta Metsäliito, **IV** 316
Oswald Tillotson Ltd., **III** 501; **7** 207
Otagiri Mercantile Co., **11** 95
Otake Paper Manufacturing Co., **IV** 327
OTC, **10** 492
Otis, Charles, **IV** 601
Otis Company, **6** 579
Otis Elevator, **I** 85, **III** 467, 663
Otis Engineering Corp., **III** 498
Otis, Harrison Gray (Gen.), **IV** 677
Otosan, **I** 167, 479–80
Otoshi, Yutaka, **II** 110
Otsego Falls Paper Company, **8** 358
Ottawa Fruit Supply Ltd., **II** 662
Otten, Frans, **II** 79
Otterson, John, **II** 155
Otto, Gustav, **I** 138
Otto, Michael, **V** 159–60
Otto, Nikolaus August, **I** 138; **III** 541
Otto Sumisho Inc., **V** 161
Otto, Werner, **V** 159
Otto-Versand (GmbH & Co.), V 159–61; 10 489–90
Ottolenghi family, **III** 347
Ottumwa Daily Courier, **11** 251
Oulliber, John A., **11** 106
Outboard Marine & Manufacturing Co., **III** 597–98
Outboard Marine Corporation, III 329, 597–600
Outboard Marine International S.A., **III** 598
Outboard Motors Corp., **III** 597; **8** 71

The Outdoorsman, Inc., **10** 216
Outlet, **6** 33
Outokumpu Oy, **IV** 276
Outwin, Edson L., **9** 96–97
Ouye, Takeshi, **III** 159–60
Ovako Oy, **III** 624
Ovako Steel, **III** 624
OVC, Inc., **6** 313
Overbey, John, **IV** 489
Overhill Farms, **10** 382
Overland Mail Co., **II** 380–81, 395; **10** 60
Overseas Air Travel Ltd., **I** 95
Overseas Containers Ltd., **6** 398, 415–16
Overseas Petroleum and Investment Corp., **IV** 389
Overseas Shipholding Group, Inc., 11 376–77
Overseas Telecommunications Commission, **6** 341–42
Overton, W.W., Jr., **II** 660
Ovitz, Mike, **11** 52
Owatonna Tool Co., **I** 200; **10** 493
Owen, Claude B., Jr., **7** 450
Owen, Evan Roger, **III** 234
Owen, Jim, **III** 738, 740
Owen, Lloyd, **II** 569
Owen, Nathan R., **9** 250–51
Owen-Jones, Lindsay, **III** 47–48; **8** 129, 31, 342–44
Owens & Minor Inc., **10** 143
Owens Bottle Machine Corp., **I** 609
Owens, Clifford Boyce, **9** 77
Owens, J. F., **6** 539
Owens, Jerry, **9** 77
Owens, Michael J., **III** 640
Owens Yacht Co., **III** 443
Owens-Corning Fiberglas Company, **8** 177
Owens-Corning Fiberglas Corporation, I 609; III 683, 720–23
Owens-Illinois Inc., I 609–11, 615; II 386; III 640, 720–21; IV 282, 343; 9 261
Owensboro Municipal Utilities, **11** 37
Oxdon Investments, **II** 664
Oxford Biscuit Fabrik, **II** 543
Oxford Chemical Corp., **II** 572
Oxford Industries, Inc., 8 406–08
Oxford Instruments, **III** 491
Oxford Manufacturing Company, **8** 406
Oxford of Atlanta, **8** 406
Oxford Paper Co., **I** 334–35; **10** 289
Oxirane Chemical Co., **IV** 456
Oxnard, Benjamin, **7** 465
Oxnard, Benjamin, Jr., **7** 465
Oxnard family, **11** 13
Oxnard, Henry, **11** 13
Oxnard, Robert, **11** 13
Oxnard, Thomas, **7** 465–66
Oxy Petrochemicals Inc., **IV** 481
Oxy Process Chemicals, **III** 33
OxyChem, **11** 160
Ozal, Korkut, **IV** 562
Ozal, Turgut, **I** 479–80
Ozalid Corp., **I** 337–38; **IV** 563
Ozark Airlines, **I** 127
Ozark Pipe Line Corp., **IV** 540
Ozark Utility Company, **6** 593
Ozkan, Selahattin, **IV** 563

P & M Manufacturing Company, **8** 386
P & O. *See* Peninsular & Oriental Steam Navigation Company.
P.A. Bergner and Co., **9** 142
P.A.J.W. Corporation, **9** 111–12

P.A. Rentrop-Hubbert & Wagner Fahrzeugausstattungen GmbH, **III** 582
P&C Foods Inc., 8 409–11
P&O, **6** 79
P.C. Hanford Oil Co., **IV** 368
P. D'Aoust Ltd., **II** 651
P.D. Magnetics, **8** 153
P.D. Kadi International, **I** 580
P.D. Magnetics, **I** 330
P.G. Realty, **III** 340
P.H. Glatfelter Company, 8 412–14
P.L. Porter Co., **III** 580
P.R. Mallory, **9** 179
P. Sharples, **III** 418
P.T. Dai Nippon Printing Indonesia, **IV** 599
P.T. Muaratewe Spring, **III** 581
P.T. Semen Nusantara, **III** 718
P.W. Huntington & Company, **11** 180
Paasikivi, J.K., **II** 302–03
Pabst Beer, **I** 217, 255; **10** 99
Pac-Am Food Concepts, **10** 178
Paccar Inc., I 155, 185–86; 10 280
Pace Companies, **6** 149
PACE Membership Warehouse, Inc., **V** 112; **10** 107
Pace, Stanley C., **I** 59; **10** 317
Pace-Arrow, Inc., **III** 484
Pacemaker Plastics, Inc., **7** 296
Pache, Bernard, **IV** 174
Pachena Industries Ltd., **6** 310
Pacific Aero Products Co., **I** 47; **10** 162
Pacific Air Freight, Incorporated, **6** 345
Pacific Air Transport, **I** 47, 128; **6** 128; **9** 416
Pacific Alaska Fuel Services, **6** 383
Pacific Alaska Line-West, **6** 383
Pacific Bell, **V** 318–20; **11** 59
Pacific Brick Proprietary, **III** 673
Pacific Car & Foundry Co., **I** 185
Pacific Cascade Land Co., **IV** 255
Pacific Coast Co., **IV** 165
Pacific Coast Condensed Milk Co., **II** 486
Pacific Coast Oil Co., **IV** 385
Pacific Communication Sciences, **11** 57
Pacific Dry Dock and Repair Co., **6** 382
Pacific Dunlop Holdings (China), **10** 446
Pacific Dunlop Limited, 10 444–46
Pacific Electric Heating Co., **II** 28
Pacific Electric Light Company, **6** 565
Pacific Enterprises, V 682–84
Pacific Express Co., **II** 381
Pacific Finance Company, **9** 536
Pacific Finance Corp., **I** 537
Pacific Gamble Robinson, **9** 39
Pacific Gas and Electric Company, I 96; V 685–87; 11 270
Pacific Guardian Life Insurance Co., **III** 289
Pacific Health Beverage Co., **I** 292
Pacific Indemnity Corp., **III** 220
Pacific Lighting Company, **V** 682–84
Pacific Lighting Corp., **IV** 492
Pacific Lighting Gas Development Company, **V** 683
Pacific Lumber Company, **III** 254; **8** 348–50
Pacific Magazines and Printing, **7** 392
Pacific Mail Steamship Company, **6** 353
Pacific Manifolding Book Co. Ltd., **IV** 644
Pacific Manifolding Box Co., **IV** 644
Pacific Metal Bearing Co., **I** 159
Pacific Monolothics Inc., **11** 520
Pacific National Bank, **II** 349

Pacific Natural Gas Corp., **9** 102
Pacific Northern, **6** 66
Pacific Northwest Bell Telephone Co., **V** 341
Pacific Northwest Laboratories, **10** 139
Pacific Northwest Pipeline Co., **9** 102–104, 540
Pacific Northwest Power Company, **6** 597
Pacific Pearl, **I** 417
Pacific Petroleum, **IV** 494
Pacific Petroleums Ltd., **9** 102
Pacific Platers Ltd., **IV** 100
Pacific Power & Light Company. *See* PacifiCorp.
Pacific Recycling Co. Inc., **IV** 296
Pacific Refining Co., **IV** 394–95
Pacific Resources Inc., **IV** 47
Pacific Silver Corp., **IV** 76
Pacific Southwest Airlines Inc., **I** 132; **6** 132
Pacific Steel Ltd., **IV** 279
Pacific Telecom, Inc., V 689; **6 325–28**
Pacific Telesis Group, V 318–20; **9** 321; **11** 10–11
Pacific Teletronics, Inc., **7** 15
Pacific Towboat. *See* Puget Sound Tug and Barge Company.
Pacific Trading Co., Ltd., **IV** 442
Pacific Western Oil Co., **IV** 537
Pacific-Burt Co., Ltd., **IV** 644
Pacific-Sierra Research, **I** 155
PacifiCare Behavioral Health, **11** 379
PacifiCare Health Systems, Inc., III 85; **11 378–80**
PacifiCare Life and Health, **11** 378
PacifiCare Military Health Systems, **11** 380
PacifiCare of Oregon, **11** 378
PacifiCare Wellness Company, **11** 379
PacifiCorp, V 688–90; 6 325–26, 328; **7** 376–78
Packaging Corp. of America, **I** 526
Packard, **9** 17
Packard, David, **I** 77; **III** 142–43; **6** 237–38; **11** 364
Packard, David Woodley, **III** 143; **6** 238
Packard, H. M., **III** 59
Packard Motor Co., **I** 81; **8** 74
Packard-Bell, **I** 524; **II** 86; **10** 521, 564; **11** 413
Packer, Kerry, **8** 551
Packer's Consolidated Press, **IV** 651
Packerland Packing Company, **7** 199, 201
PacTel. *See* Pacific Telesis Group.
PacTel Corporation, **6** 324; **11** 10
Paddington Corp., **I** 248
Paez, Luis, **II** 642
PAFS. *See* Pacific Alaska Fuel Services.
Page, Austin, **9** 513
Page, Bacon & Co., **II** 380
Page Boy Inc., **9** 320
Page, Charles, **II** 545; **7** 380
Page, George, **II** 545; **7** 380
Page, Howard, **IV** 537–38
Page, Robert, **IV** 178
Page, Thomas A., **V** 712–13
Pageland Coca-Cola Bottling Works, **10** 222
Pagezy, Bernard, **III** 209, 211
Paging Network Inc., 11 381–83
Pagoda Trading Co., **V** 351, 353
Paid Prescriptions, **9** 346
Paige, Clifford, **6** 456
Paine & Webber, **II** 444
Paine, Charles, **II** 444

Paine, Stephen, **II** 444
Paine, Webber & Co., **II** 444
Paine, Webber, Jackson & Curtis Inc., **II** 444–45
Paine, William A., **II** 444
PaineWebber Group Inc., I 245; **II 444–46**, 449; **III** 409
PaineWebber Incorporated, **II** 445
PaineWebber Mitchell Hutchins, **II** 445
Painter, John W., **8** 158
Painton Co., **II** 81
Paisley, David, **I** 697
La Paix, **III** 273
Pak Arab Fertilizers Ltd., **IV** 364
Pak-a-Sak, **II** 661
Pak-All Products, Inc., **IV** 345
Pak-Paino, **IV** 315
Pak-Well, **IV** 282; **9** 261
Pakhoed Holding, N.V., **9** 532
Pakkasakku Oy, **IV** 471
Paknet, **11** 548
Pakway Container Corporation, **8** 268
PAL. *See* Philippine Airlines, Inc.
Pal Plywood Co., Ltd., **IV** 327
Palatine Insurance Co., **III** 234
Paley, William, **6** 157–59
Paley, William S., **II** 132–34
Pall Corporation, 9 396–98
Pall, David, **9** 396
Palley, Stephen W., **9** 307
Palm Beach Holdings, **9** 157
Palmafina, **IV** 498–99
Palmer, Ben, **8** 462–63
Palmer, Chauncey, **III** 325
Palmer, Derek, **I** 224
Palmer, Dick, **II** 32
Palmer G. Lewis Co., **8** 135
Palmer, H. Bruce, **III** 303
Palmer, Henry L., **III** 321–22
Palmer, John, **V** 496
Palmer, Lowell M., **I** 695
Palmer, Potter, **III** 237
Palmer, Robert B., **6** 236
Palmer, Stanton, **7** 479
Palmer Tyre Ltd., **I** 428–29
Palmerston (Lord), **I** 468
Palmieri, Aldo, **10** 150, 152
Palmolive Co., **III** 23
Palo Alto Research Center, **10** 510
Pamour Porcupine Mines, Ltd., **IV** 164
Pamplin, Robert B., **IV** 281–82; **9** 259–260
Pan Am. *See* Pan American Airways Inc.
Pan Am Corp., **I** 116
Pan Am World Services, **III** 536
Pan American Airways Inc., **9** 231, 417
Pan American Banks, **II** 336
Pan American Grace Airways, **I** 547–48
Pan American International Oil Corp., **IV** 370
Pan American Petroleum & Transport Co., **IV** 368–70
Pan American Petroleum Corp., **IV** 370
Pan American World Airways Inc., I 20, 31, 44, 64, 67, 89–90, 92, 99, 103–04, 112–13, **115–16**, 121, 124, 126, 129, 132, 248, 452, 530, 547; **6** 51, 65–66, 71, 74–76, 81–82, 103–05, 110–11, 123, 129–30; **9** 231; **10** 561; **11** 266
Pan European Publishing Co., **IV** 611
Pan Ocean, **IV** 473
Panacon Corp., **III** 766
Panagra, **I** 547–48

Panama Refining and Petrochemical Co., **IV** 566
Panarctic Oils, **IV** 494
Panasonic, **9** 180; **10** 125
Panatech Research & Development Corp., **III** 160
Panavia Consortium, **I** 74–75
Pandel, Inc., **8** 271
Panhandle Eastern Corporation, IV 425; **V 691–92; 10** 82–84; **11** 28
Panhandle Eastern Pipe Co., **I** 377
Panhandle Eastern Pipeline Co., **I** 569
Panhandle Oil Corp., **IV** 498
Panhandle Power & Light Company, **6** 580
Panhard, **I** 194
Panhard-Levassor, **I** 149
AB Pankakoski, **IV** 274
Panmure Gordon, **II** 337
Panny, William, **I** 142
Panocean Storage & Transport, **6** 415, 417
Panola Pipeline Co., **7** 228
Pansophic Systems Inc., **6** 225
Pantepec Oil Co., **IV** 559, 570
Pantera Energy Corporation, **11** 27
Panther, **III** 750
Panther Express International Company, **6** 346
Pantry Pride, **I** 668; **II** 670, 674; **III** 56
Pants Corral, **II** 634
Pao, Yue-Kong (Sir), **I** 470; **III** 517
Pape and Co., Ltd., **10** 441
Papelera Navarra, **IV** 295
Papeleria Calparsoro S.A., **IV** 325
Paper Makers Chemical Corp., **I** 344
Paper Mate Co., **III** 28
Paper Recycling International, **V** 754
Paper Stock Dealers, Inc., **8** 476
Paperituote Oy, **IV** 347–48
Paperwork Data-Comm Services Inc., **11** 64
Papeterie de Pont Sainte Maxence, **IV** 318
Papeteries Aussedat, **III** 122
Papeteries Boucher S.A., **IV** 300
Les Papeteries Darblay, **IV** 258
Les Papeteries de la Chapelle, **IV** 258
Les Papeteries de la Chapelle-Darblay, **IV** 258–59, 302, 337
Papeteries Navarre, **III** 677
Papierfabrik Salach, **IV** 324
Papierwaren Fleischer, **IV** 325
Papierwerke Waldhof-Aschaffenburg AG, **IV** 323–24
Papyrus, **V** 336
Paquette, Joseph F., Jr., **11** 389
Para-Med Health Services, **6** 181–82
Parade Gasoline Co., **7** 228
Paragon, **IV** 552
Paramax, **6** 281–83
Paramount Communications, Inc., **II** 154–55; **IV** 671–72, 675; **7** 528; **9** 119, 429; **10** 175
Paramount Paper Products, **8** 383
Paramount Pictures Corporation, I 451–52; **II** 129, 135, 146–47, **154–56**, 171, 173, 175, 177; **IV** 672; **9** 428
Paramount-Publix, **II** 155
Paravision International, **III** 48; **8** 343
Parcelforce, **V** 498
PARCO, **V** 184–85
Parcor, **I** 676
Pardonner, William, **7** 465
Pare, Paul, **V** 401
Parente, Marco, **III** 206
Paresky, David, **9** 505

Paretti, Harold J., **I** 117
Parfet, Ray T., **I** 707; **8** 547
Parfums Christian Dior, **I** 272
Parfums Rochas, **I** 670; **III** 68; **8** 452
Parfums Stern, **III** 16
Pargas, **I** 378
Paribas. *See* Compagnie Financiere de Paribas.
Paribas/Parfinance, **III** 48
Paris, Alessio, **III** 206, 345
Park Chung Hee, **I** 516; **II** 54; **III** 747–48; **IV** 183
Park Consolidated Motels, Inc., **6** 187
Park Hall Leisure, **II** 140
Park Inn International, **11** 178
Park Ridge Corporation, **9** 284
Park Tae Chun (Maj. Gen.), **IV** 183–84
Park View Hospital, Inc., **III** 78
Parkdale Wines, **I** 268
Parke, Davis & Co., **I** 674, 711–12; **10** 550–51
Parke-Bernet, **11** 453
Parker, **III** 33
Parker Appliance Co., **III** 601–02
Parker, Art, **III** 601–02
Parker, Barry J.C., **9** 142–43
Parker, Bob, **11** 544
Parker Bros., **II** 502; **III** 505; **10** 323
Parker Drilling Company of Canada, **9** 363
Parker, Fernley, **9** 92
Parker, George B., **IV** 607
Parker, George S., **9** 326
Parker, Gordon, **7** 289
Parker Hannifin Corporation, **III** 601–03
Parker Hannifin NMF GmbH, **III** 602
Parker, Helen, **III** 601–02
Parker, Herbert L., **II** 18
Parker, Hugh, **9** 343
Parker, J. Harleston, **III** 267
Parker, Jack, **11** 5
Parker, John, **III** 751
Parker, Kenyon S., **III** 272
Parker, Lewis R., **8** 13
Parker, Morgan, **9** 96
Parker, Patrick, **III** 602–03
Parker Pen Corp., **III** 218; **9** 326
Parker Peter, **V** 423
Parker, Wayne A., **6** 539
Parkinson Cowan, **I** 531
Parkinson, J. David, **11** 516
Parkinson, Joseph L., **11** 307
Parkinson, Thomas, **III** 248
Parkinson, Ward, **11** 307
Parkmount Hospitality Corp., **II** 142
Parmalee, Harold J., **8** 538, 540
Parola, Olli, **IV** 350
Parr, David, **11** 24
Parr's Bank, **II** 334; **III** 724
Parretti, Giancarlo, **9** 149
Parry, Charles, **IV** 16
Parson and Hyman Co., Inc., **8** 112
Parson, Hubert T., **V** 225
Parson, James, Jr., **8** 112
The Parsons Corporation, **8** 415–17
Parsons Place Apparel Company, **8** 289
Parsons, Ralph M., **8** 415–16
Parsons, Richard D., **9** 173–74
Parsons, Wallace, **9** 304
Partek Corporation, **11** 312
Partex, **IV** 515
Parthenon Insurance Co., **III** 79
Participating Annuity Life Insurance Co., **III** 182

La Participation, **III** 210
Partlow Corporation, **7** 116
Partnership Pacific Ltd., **II** 389
Partridge, James F., **II** 200
Parts Industries Corp., **III** 494–95
Pasant, A.J. (Tony), **8** 276–77
Pasant, David A., **8** 277
Paschen Contractors Inc., **I** 585
Paskay, Alexander L., **III** 767
Pasman, James S., Jr., **V** 153
Pasminco, **IV** 61
El Paso & Southwestern Railroad, **IV** 177
Pasteur, Louis, **I** 256; **II** 175, 470
Pataling Rubber Estates Syndicate, **III** 697, 699
Patch, Lauren, **11** 370
Patchoque-Plymouth Co., **IV** 371
PATCO. *See* Philippine Aerial Taxi Company.
Patel, Vinodchandra Manubhai, **11** 169
Patent Nut & Bolt Co., **III** 493
Patent Slip and Dock Co., **I** 592
La Paternelle, **III** 210
Paternoster Stores plc, **V** 108
Paternot, Maurice, **II** 547; **7** 382
Paterson, John, **II** 357
Paterson Newark, **I** 592
Paterson, Simons & Co., **I** 592
Paterson, William, **I** 592
Path-Tek Laboratories, Inc., **6** 41
Pathé Cinéma, **6** 374
Pathe Communications Co., **IV** 676; **7** 529
Pathé Fréres, **IV** 626
Pathmark, **II** 672–74; **9** 173
Patience & Nicholson, **III** 674
Patient, William, **11** 160
Patil, Suhas, **11** 56
Patil Systems, **11** 56
Paton, Leonard (Sir), **III** 699
Patrick, J.C., **I** 370; **9** 500
Patrick, Jerry, **7** 33
Patriot Co., **IV** 582
Patriot Life Insurance Co., **III** 193
Pattberg, Emil J., **II** 402–03
Patterson, Clair, **I** 335
Patterson, Eleanor (Cissy), **IV** 683
Patterson, Elinor Medill, **IV** 682
Patterson, Ernest Minor, **IV** 635
Patterson, Frederick Beck, **III** 151; **6** 265
Patterson, Gordon, **I** 154; **10** 279
Patterson, James L., **10** 458
Patterson, John Henry, **III** 147, 150–51; **6** 250, 264–65
Patterson, Joseph (Capt.), **IV** 682–83
Patterson, Mary King, **IV** 683
Patterson, Pat, **10** 163
Patterson, Robert, **IV** 682
Patterson, Robert Livingston, **III** 302
Patterson, William, **I** 47, 96, 128–29; **10** 162
Patterson, William "Pat," **6** 128
Pattison & Bowns, Inc., **IV** 180
Patton, George, **I** 85
Patton Paint Co., **III** 731
Patton, William, **IV** 44
Patton, William B., **11** 274–75
Paul A. Brands, **11** 19
Paul C. Dodge Company, **6** 579
Paul, George, **III** 699
Paul, Jacques, **II** 476
Paul, Marcel, **V** 603
Paul Masson, **I** 285
Paul, Nicholas, **II** 476
Paul, Ron, **10** 139–40

Paul Wahl & Co., **IV** 277
Paul Williams Copier Corp., **IV** 252
Paul Wurth, **IV** 25
Paulhan, Louis, **I** 47
Pauls Plc, **III** 699
Paulson, Allen E., **7** 205–06
Paulucci, Jeno, **7** 469
Pavese, Cesare, **IV** 585
Pavia family, **III** 347
Pavitt, Ted, **IV** 91
Pavlis, Frank, **I** 297; **10** 31
Pavlovska, Irene, **III** 443
Pawling, Alonzo, **8** 241
Paxall, Inc., **8** 545
Paxson, Lowell W., **V** 77
Pay 'N Pak Stores, Inc., **9** 399–401
Pay Less, **II** 601, 604
Payless Cashways, Inc., **11** 384–86
Payless DIY, **V** 17, 19
Payless ShoeSource, Inc., **V** 132, 135
Payne, Samuel, **II** 432
Paz, Octavio, **IV** 624
PC Realty, Canada Ltd., **III** 340
PCI Acquisition, **11** 385
PCI/Mac-Pak Group, **IV** 261
PCL Industries Ltd., **IV** 296
PCO, **III** 685
PDO. *See* Petroleum Development Oman.
PDVSA. *See* Petróleos de Venezuela S.A.
Peabody & Co., **IV** 169; **10** 447
Peabody, Charles, **III** 306
Peabody Coal Company, **I** 559; **III** 248; **IV** 47, 169–71, 576; **7** 387–88; **10** 447–49
Peabody, Daniels & Co., **IV** 169
Peabody, Francis Stuyvesant, **IV** 169; **10** 447
Peabody, George, **II** 427
Peabody Holding Company, Inc., **IV** 19, 169–72; **6** 487; **7** 209
Peabody, Riggs & Co., **II** 427
Peabody, Stuyvesant (Jack), **IV** 169
Peabody, Stuyvesant, Jr., **IV** 170; **10** 447
Peace, Roger C., **11** 330
Peachtree Doors, **10** 95
Peachtree Federal Savings and Loan Association of Atlanta, **10** 92
Peacock, Kenneth (Sir), **III** 494
Peak Oilfield Service Company, **9** 364
Peake, Alonzo W., **IV** 369–70
Peake, Harald, **II** 308
Peakstone, **III** 740
Peale, Rembrandt, **V** 552
Pearce, Austin, **I** 52
Pearce, John, **I** 227
Pearl Health Services, **I** 249
Pearl Package Co., Ltd., **IV** 327
Pearle Vision Centres, **I** 688
Pearlman, Jerry, **II** 124–25
Pearson, Chester C., **I** 67–68
Pearson, Clive, **IV** 658
Pearson family, **IV** 512, 657–59
Pearson, George, **IV** 657
Pearson, George E., **I** 714
Pearson, Harold (second Viscount Cowdray), **IV** 658
Pearson Longman Ltd., **IV** 659
Pearson plc, **IV** 611, 652, 657–59
Pearson, Richard, **I** 127; **IV** 254
Pearson, Samuel, **IV** 657
Pearson, Weetman Dickinson (first Viscount Cowdray), **IV** 365, 531, 657–58
Peary, Robert E., **9** 367

Pease, J.W. Beaumont, **II** 307–08
Peat Marwick. *See* KPMG Peat Marwick.
Peat, Marwick, Mitchell & Company. *See* KPMG Peat Marwick.
Peat, Sir William B., **10** 385
Peaudouce, **IV** 339
Peavey Co., **II** 494
Pebble Beach Corp., **II** 170
Pébereau, George, **II** 356
PEC Plastics, **9** 92
Pechelbronn Oil Co., **III** 616
Pechiney, IV 12, 59, 108, **173–75**; **V** 605
Pechiney, A.R., **IV** 173
Pechiney Électrométallurgie, **IV** 174
Pechiney International, **IV** 175
Péchiney Metals Group, **I** 190
Pechiney Ugine Kuhlmann, **I** 341; **IV** 173, 174, 560
Péchiney-Saint-Gobain, **I** 389; **III** 677
Peck, Carson C., **V** 224–25
Peck, Gregory, **II** 143
PECO Energy Company, 11 387–90
Pecqueur, Michel, **I** 676–77; **IV** 547; **7** 484
Pedersen, E.E., **9** 160
Pedersen, Harald, **I** 658–59
Pedersen, Thorvald, **I** 658–59
Peebles, David, **II** 488
Peek, Burton F., **III** 462
Peek, Henry, **III** 233
Peel-Conner Telephone Works, **II** 24
Peerless, **III** 467; **8** 74; **11** 534
Peerless Gear & Machine Company, **8** 515
Peerless Industries, **III** 569
Peerless Paper Co., **IV** 310
Peerless Pump Co., **I** 442
Peet brothers, **III** 23
Pegulan, **I** 426–27
Pei, I.M., **II** 298
Peine, **IV** 201
Pekema Oy, **IV** 470–71
Pel-Tex Oil Co., **IV** 84; **7** 188
Pelican and British Empire Life Office, **III** 372
Pelican Homestead and Savings, **11** 107
Pelican Insurance Co., **III** 349
Pelican Life Assurance, **III** 371–72
Pelisson, Gérard, **10** 12–14
Pell, Alfred, **III** 305
Pella Corp., **10** 95
Pellegrino, Charles R., **I** 63
Pelli, Cesar, **10** 427
Pels, Donald A., **9** 320
Peltz, Nelson, **8** 537
Pelz, Nelson, **I** 602, 608
Pemberton, Brian, **6** 320
Pemberton, Francis R., **IV** 81; **7** 185
Pemberton, John Styth, **I** 232; **10** 225
Pemex. *See* Petróleos Mexicanos.
Peñarroya, **IV** 107–08
Pence, Harry, **III** 463
Pender, John, **V** 283; **6** 319
Pendexcare Ltd., **6** 181
Penguin Publishing Co. Ltd., **IV** 585, 659
Penhoet, Edward, **10** 213
Peninsular and Oriental Steam Navigation Company (Bovis Division), I 588–89
Peninsular and Oriental Steam Navigation Company, II 296; **III** 521–22, 712; **V 490–93**
Peninsular Portland Cement, **III** 704
Peninsular Power, **6** 602

Peninsular Steam Navigation Company, **V** 490
Penn Central Corp., **I** 435; **II** 255; **IV** 576; **10** 71, 73, 547
Penn Central Transportation Company, **10** 71
Penn Champ Co., **9** 72
Penn Controls, **III** 535–36
Penn Fuel Co., **IV** 548
Penn Health, **III** 85
Penn Square Bank, **II** 248, 262
Penn Texas Corp., **I** 434
Penn Traffic Co., **8** 409–10
Penn-American Refining Co., **IV** 489
Penn-Western Gas and Electric, **6** 524
Pennington Drug, **III** 10
Pennington, Fred V., **IV** 255
Pennington, William N., **6** 203–04
Pennington, William S., **9** 221
Pennock, Raymond (Sir), **III** 434
Pennroad Corp., **IV** 458
Pennsalt Chemical Corp., **I** 383
Pennsylvania Blue Shield, III 325–27
Pennsylvania Coal & Coke Corp., **I** 434
Pennsylvania Coal Co., **IV** 180
Pennsylvania Electric Company, **6** 535
Pennsylvania Farm Bureau Cooperative Association, **7** 17–18
Pennsylvania General Fire Insurance Assoc., **III** 257
Pennsylvania Glass Sand Co., **I** 464; **11** 198
Pennsylvania House, **10** 324
Pennsylvania International Raceway, **V** 494
Pennsylvania Power & Light Company, V 693–94; **11** 388
Pennsylvania Power Company, **V** 676
Pennsylvania Pump and Compressor Co., **II** 16
Pennsylvania Railroad, **I** 456, 472; **II** 329, 490; **6** 436; **10** 71–73
Pennsylvania Refining Co., **IV** 488–89
Pennsylvania Salt Manufacturing Co., **I** 383
Pennsylvania Steel Co., **IV** 35; **7** 48
Pennwalt Corporation, I 382–84; **IV** 547
Penny, James Cash, **V** 90–91
Pennzoil Co. (California), **IV** 489
Pennzoil Co. (New York), **IV** 489
Pennzoil Co. (Pennsylvania), **IV** 489
Pennzoil Company, IV 488–90, 551, 553; **10** 190
Pennzoil Louisiana and Texas Offshore, Inc., **IV** 490
Pennzoil of Australia, **III** 729
Pennzoil Offshore Gas Operators, **IV** 490
Pennzoil United, Inc., **IV** 488
Penray, **I** 373
Penrod Drilling Corporation, **7** 228, 558
Penser, Erik, **9** 381
Pension Benefit Guaranty Corp., **III** 255
Penske Corporation, V 494–95
Penske, Greg, **V** 495
Penske, Roger, **V** 494–95; **10** 273–75
Penske Transportation, **V** 495
Penske Truck Leasing Co., L.P., **V** 494–95
Pentair, Inc., III 715; **7 419–21**; **11** 315
Pental Insurance Company, Ltd., **11** 523
Pentane Partners, **7** 518
Pentaverken A.B., **I** 209
Pentland Industries, **V** 375
Penton, **9** 414
People Express Airlines Inc., I 90, 98, 103, **117–18**, 123–24, 129–30; **6** 129

People's Bank of Halifax, **II** 210
People's Bank of New Brunswick, **II** 210
People's Drug Store, **II** 604–05
People's Ice and Refrigeration Company, **9** 274
People's Insurance Co., **III** 368
People's Natural Gas, **6** 593
People's Trust Co. of Brooklyn, **II** 254; **9** 124
Peoples Bank of Youngstown, **9** 474
Peoples Energy Corporation, 6 543–44
Peoples Finance Co., **II** 418
Peoples Gas Light & Coke Co., **IV** 169; **6** 529, 543–44
Peoples Gas Light Co., **6** 455
Peoples Life Insurance Co., **III** 218
Peoples Natural Gas Co., **IV** 548
Peoples Natural Gas Company of South Carolina, **6** 576
Peoples Savings of Monroe, **9** 482
Peoples Security Insurance Co., **III** 219
PeopleSoft, Inc., **11** 78
Pep Auto Supply, **11** 391
The Pep Boys—Manny, Moe & Jack, 11 391–93
PEPCO. *See* Portland Electric Power Company *and* Potomac Electric Power Company.
Pepper, Dr. Charles, **9** 177
Pepperidge Farms, **I** 29; **II** 480–81; **7** 67–68
Pepsi-Cola, **11** 450
Pepsi-Cola General Bottlers, **I** 457; **10** 554
Pepsi-Cola South Africa, **II** 477
PepsiCo, Inc., I 234, 244–46, 257, 269, **276–79**, 281, 291; **II** 103, 448, 477, 608; **III** 106, 116, 588; **7** 265, 267, 396, 404, 434–35, 466, 505–06; **8** 399; **9** 177, 343; **10** 130, 199, 227, 324, **450–54 (upd.)**; **11** 421
Pepsodent Company, **I** 14; **9** 318
Perception Technology, **10** 500
Percival, Roger, **III** 726
Percy Bilton Investment Trust Ltd., **IV** 710
Percy, Charles, **9** 62–63
Percy Street Investments Ltd., **IV** 711
Perdriau, Henry, **10** 444
Perdue, Arthur W., **7** 422–23
Perdue Farms Inc., 7 422–24, 432
Perdue, Frank P., **7** 422–24
Perdue, James, **7** 423–24
Pereire, Jacob and Emile, **6** 379
Perelman, Ronald O., **II** 498, 679; **III** 29, 56; **9** 129
Perelman, S.J., **IV** 672
Pérez, Carlos Andrés, **IV** 507
Perfect Circle Corp., **I** 152
Perfect-Ventil GmbH, **9** 413
Performance Contracting, Inc., **III** 722
Performance Technologies, Inc., **10** 395
Pergamon Press Inc., **IV** 642; **7** 311–12
Pergamon Press Ltd., **IV** 641–43, 687
Pergamon Press plc, **IV** 611
Perignon, Dom, **I** 271
Perini, Bonfiglio, **8** 418
Perini Building Company, Inc., **8** 418–19
Perini Corporation, 8 418–21
Perini, David, **8** 418–20
Perini Land and Development Company, **8** 418–19
Perini, Louis, **8** 418–19
Perisem, **I** 281
Perkin, Richard, **7** 425–26
Perkin, William Henry, **I** 671

Perkin-Elmer Citizen, **III** 455
The Perkin-Elmer Corporation, **III** 455,
727; **7 425–27**; **9** 514
Perkins, **I** 147
Perkins Bacon & Co., **10** 267
Perkins Cake & Steak, **9** 425
Perkins, Charles, **V** 426
Perkins, D.T., **IV** 569
Perkins, Donald, **II** 605
Perkins Engines Ltd., **III** 545, 652; **10** 274;
11 472
Perkins, James H., **II** 254; **9** 124
Perkins, John, **IV** 605
Perkins Oil Well Cementing Co., **III** 497
Perkins, Philip T., **I** 332
Perkins Products Co., **II** 531
Perkins, Thomas J., **I** 637; **6** 278
Perkins, William, **I** 305
Perkinson, Peter, **7** 556
Perland Environmental Technologies Inc.,
8 420
Perlman, Alfred, **10** 72–73
Perlman, Clifford, **6** 199–201
Perlman, Lawrence, **III** 126, 128
Perlman, Stuart, **6** 199–200
Perlmutter, Isaac, **V** 172
Perlmutter, Milt, **II** 672–74
Perlstein, Maurice, **8** 287
Permaneer Corp., **IV** 281; **9** 259
Permanent General Companies, Inc., **11**
194
Permanente Cement Co., **I** 565
Permanente Metals Corp., **IV** 15, 121–22
Permian Corporation, **V** 152–53
PERMIGAN, **IV** 492
Permodalan, **III** 699
Pernod, M., **I** 280
Pernod Ricard S.A., **I** 248, **280–81**
Pernvo Inc., **I** 387
Péron, Juan Domingo (Col.), **IV** 577–78
Perot, H. Ross, **III** 136–38; **10** 124
Perret-Olivier, **III** 676
Perrin, **IV** 614
Perrin, George M., **11** 381
Perrin, Michael, **I** 714–15
Perrot Brake Co., **I** 141
Perrot, Henri, **I** 141
Perrow Motor Freight Lines, **6** 370
Perry, Bertrand, **III** 286
Perry, Lester, **III** 325
Perry, Matthew (Commodore), **I** 282, 431;
III 532
Perry, Norman A., **6** 508
Perry, Percival (Lord), **IV** 722
Perry, Richard W., **I** 195–96
Perry, Robert L., **I** 46
Perscombinatie, **IV** 611
Person, Robert T., **6** 559
Personal Performance Consultants, **9** 348
Personal Products Company, **III** 35; **8** 281,
511
Persons, Wallace R., **II** 19–20
Perstorp A.B., **I 385–87**
PERTAMINA, **IV** 383, 461, **491–93**, 517,
567
Perusahaan Minyak Republik Indonesia, **IV**
491
Perusahaan Tambang Minyak Negara
Republik Indonesia, **IV** 491
Perusahaan Tambang Minyak Republik
Indonesia, **IV** 491
Peruvian Corp., **I** 547
Pesatori, Enrico, **10** 563–64
Pesch, LeRoy, **III** 74

Pesenti, Carlo, **III** 347
Peskin, Kenneth, **II** 674
Pestalozzi, Martin O., **6** 9–11
Pestche, Albert, **V** 655–56
de Pesters, Jonkheer C.A., **I** 257
Pet Company, **10** 554
Pet Dairy Products Company, **7** 428
Pet Incorporated, **I** 457; **II** 486–87; **7**
428–31; **10** 554
Pet Milk Co. *See* Pet Incorporated.
Petain, Henri, **II** 12
Peter Bawden Drilling, **IV** 570
Peter, Cailler, Kohler, Chocolats Suisses
S.A., **II** 546; **7** 381
Peter Gast Shipping GmbH, **7** 40
Peter J. Schweitzer, Inc., **III** 40
Peter Jones, **V** 94
Peter Kiewit Sons' Inc., **I** 599–600; **III**
198; **8 422–24**
Peter Norton Computing Group, **10** 508–09
Peter Paul, **II** 477
Peter Paul/Cadbury, **II** 512
Peter, Thomas J., **6** 233
Peterbilt Motors Co., **I** 185–86
Peters, Bob, **I** 584–85
Peters, Donald C., **I** 584–85
Peters, J.F.M., **III** 179
Peters, Jon, **II** 137, 149
Peters Shoe Co., **III** 528
Peters, Thomas J., **I** 501; **III** 132
Petersen, Alfred, **IV** 140–41
Petersen, Donald, **I** 167
Petersen, George, **II** 504
Peterson, Duane, **V** 496
Peterson, Ethel, **II** 634
Peterson, Howell & Heather, **V** 496
Peterson, P.A., **III** 438
Peterson, Peter, **II** 451
Peterson, Peter G., **9** 63
Peterson, Rudy, **II** 228
Peterson Soybean Seed Co., **9** 411
Peterson, W.E. "Pete", **10** 556
Petite Sophisticate, **V** 207–08
Petitjean, Armand, **8** 129
Petito, Frank, **II** 432
Petrello, Anthony G., **9** 364
Petrie, Milton, **V** 203
Petrie, Milton J., **8** 425–27
Petrie Stores Corporation, **8 425–27**
Petrini's, **II** 653
Petro/Chem Environmental Services, Inc.,
IV 411
Petro-Canada, **IV** 367, 494–96, 499
Petro-Canada Inc., **IV** 496
Petro-Canada Limited, **IV 494–96**
Petro-Coke Co. Ltd., **IV** 476
Petro-Lewis Corp., **IV** 84; **7** 188
Petroamazonas, **IV** 511
Petrobel, **IV** 412
Petrobrás. *See* Petróleo Brasileiro S.A.
Petrobrás Distribuidora, **IV** 501–02
Petrobrás Fertilizantes S.A., **IV** 503
Petrobrás Mineracao, **IV** 503
Petrobrás Quimica S.A., **IV** 503
Petrocarbona GmbH, **IV** 197–98
Petrochemical Industries Co., **IV** 451
Petrochemie Danubia GmbH, **IV** 486–87
Petrochim, **IV** 498
Petrocomercial, **IV** 511
Petroecuador. *See* Petróleos del Ecuador.
Petrofertil, **IV** 501
Petrofina, **IV** 455, **497–500**, 576
Petrofina Canada Inc., **IV** 495, 499
Petrofina S.A., **IV** 497; **7** 179

Petrogal. *See* Petróleos de Portugal.
Petroindustria, **IV** 511
Petrol, **IV** 487
Petrol Ofisi Anonim Sirketi, **IV** 564
Petróleo Brasileiro S.A., **IV** 424, **501–03**
Petróleo Mecânica Alfa, **IV** 505
Petróleos de México S.A., **IV** 512
Petróleos de Portugal S.A., **IV 504–06**
Petróleos de Venezuela S.A., **II** 661; **IV**
391–93, **507–09**, 571
Petróleos del Ecuador, **IV 510–11**
Petróleos Mexicanos, **IV 512–14**, 528
Petróleos Mexicanos Internacional
Comercio Internacional, **IV** 514
Petroleum and Chemical Corp., **III** 672
Petroleum Authority of Thailand, **IV** 519
Petroleum Co. of New Zealand, **IV** 279
Petroleum Development (Oman and
Dhofar) Ltd., **IV** 515
Petroleum Development (Qatar) Ltd., **IV**
524
Petroleum Development (Trucial States)
Ltd., **IV** 363
Petroleum Development Corp. of the
Republic of Korea, **IV** 455
Petroleum Development Oman LLC, **IV**
515–16
Petroleum Projects Co., **IV** 414
Petroleum Research and Engineering Co.
Ltd., **IV** 473
Petrolgroup, Inc., **6** 441
Petroliam Nasional Bhd. *See* Petronas.
Petrolube, **IV** 538
Petromex. *See* Petróleos de Mexico S.A.
Petronas, **IV 517–20**
Petronas Carigali, **IV** 518–19
Petronas Carigali Overseas Sdn Bhd, **IV**
519
Petronas Dagangan, **IV** 518
Petronas Penapisan (Melaka) Sdn Bhd, **IV**
520
Petronor, **IV** 514, 528
Petropeninsula, **IV** 511
Petroproduccion, **IV** 511
Petroquímica de Venezuela SA, **IV** 508
Petroquimica Española, **I** 402
Petroquisa, **IV** 501
PETROSUL, **IV** 504, 506
Petrotransporte, **IV** 511
Petry, Thomas, **8** 158
Peugeot, Armand, **I** 187
Peugeot, Roland, **I** 187–88
Peugeot S.A., **I** 163, **187–88**; **II** 13; **III**
508; **11** 104
Pew, Arthur E., **IV** 549; **7** 413
Pew family, **I** 631
Pew, J. Howard, **IV** 548–49; **7** 413–14
Pew, James Edgar, **IV** 548; **7** 413
Pew, Joseph Newton, **IV** 548–49; **7** 413
Pew, Joseph Newton, Jr., **IV** 549; **7** 414
Pew, Robert Cunningham, **IV** 548; **7** 413,
494
Pew, Robert, III, **7** 494
Pew, Walter C., **7** 413
Peyrelevade, Jean, **III** 393–94
Pezim, Murray "The Pez," **9** 281–82
The Pfaltzgraff Co., **8** 508. *See also*
Susquehanna Pfaltzgraff Company.
Pfaltzgraff, George, **8** 508–09
Pfaltzgraff, Henry, **8** 508
Pfaltzgraff, Johann George, **8** 508
Pfaltzgraff, John B., **8** 508
Pfaudler Vacuum Co., **I** 287
PFCI. *See* Pulte Financial Companies, Inc.

Pfeiffer, Eckhard, **III** 125; **6** 222
Pfeiffer, Gustave A., **I** 710; **10** 549
Pfeiffer, Robert, **10** 42
Pfister, Robert K., **I** 700
Pfizer, Charles, **I** 661; **9** 402
Pfizer, Hoechst Celanese Corp., **8** 399
Pfizer Inc., **I** 301, 367, **661–63**, 668; **9** 356, **402–05 (upd.)**; **10** 53–54; **11** 207, 310–11, 459
Pflaumer, Robert, **III** 704
PGE. *See* Portland General Electric.
PGH Bricks and Pipes, **III** 735
Pharaon, Gaith, **6** 143
Pharma Plus Drugmarts, **II** 649–50
Pharmacia A.B., **I** 211, **664–65**
Pharmaco Dynamics Research, Inc., **10** 106–07
Pharmaco-LSR, **10** 107
Pharmacom Systems Ltd., **II** 652
PharmaKinetics Laboratories, Inc., **10** 106
Pharmaprix Ltd., **II** 663
Pharmazell GmbH, **IV** 324
Pharmedix, **11** 207
Pharos, **9** 381
Phelan & Collender, **III** 442
Phelan Faust Paint, **8** 553
Phelan, Michael, **III** 442
Phelps, Anson, **IV** 176
Phelps, Anson, Jr., **IV** 176
Phelps, Dodge & Co., **IV** 176–77
Phelps, Dodge & Co., Inc., **IV** 177
Phelps Dodge Aluminum Products Corp., **IV** 178
Phelps Dodge Copper Corp., **IV** 177
Phelps Dodge Copper Products Corp., **IV** 178
Phelps Dodge Corporation, **IV** 33, **176–79**, 216; **7** 261–63, 288
Phelps Dodge Industries, Inc., **IV** 176, 179
Phelps Dodge Mining Co., **IV** 176, 179
Phelps Dodge Products de Centro America S.A., **IV** 178
Phelps, Douglas, **III** 726
Phelps, Ed, **IV** 171
Phelps, Guy Rowland, **III** 225, 236–37
Phenix Bank, **II** 312
Phenix Cheese Corp., **II** 533
Phenix Flour Ltd., **II** 663
Phenix Insurance Co., **III** 240
Phenix Mills Ltd., **II** 662
PHF Life Insurance Co., **III** 263; **IV** 623
PHH Corporation, **V** 496–97
PHH Group, Incorporated, **6** 357
Phibro Corp., **II** 447–48; **IV** 80
Phibro Energy Inc., **II** 447
Phibro-Salomon Inc., **II** 447–48
Philadelphia and Reading Corp., **I** 440; **II** 329; **6** 377
Philadelphia Carpet Company, **9** 465
Philadelphia Coke Company, **6** 487
Philadelphia Company, **6** 484, 493
Philadelphia Drug Exchange, **I** 692
Philadelphia Electric Company, **V** **695–97**; **6** 450
Philadelphia Life, **I** 527
Philadelphia Smelting and Refining Co., **IV** 31
Philby, Harry St. John B., **IV** 536
Philco Corp., **I** 167, 531; **II** 86; **III** 604
Philip Morris Companies Inc., **V** 397, 404, **405–7**, 409, 417; **6** 52; **7** 272, 274, 276, 548; **8** 53; **9** 180
Philip Morris Inc., **I** 23, 269; **II** 530–34
Philipp Abm. Cohen, **IV** 139

Philipp Bros., Inc., **II** 447; **IV** 79–0
Philipp Holzmann, **II** 279, 386
Philippine Aerial Taxi Company, **6** 106
Philippine Airlines, Inc., **I** 107; **6 106–08**, 122–23
Philippine American Life Insurance Co., **III** 195
Philippine Sinter Corp., **IV** 125
Philips, **V** 339; **6** 101; **10** 269
Philips & Co., **II** 78
Philips, A. F., **IV** 132
Philips, Anton, **II** 78–79
Philips Electronics N.V., **9** 75; **10** 16
Philips, Frederik, **II** 78
Philips, Frits, **II** 79
Philips, Gerard, **II** 78–79
N.V. Philips Gloeilampenfabrieken, **I** 107, 330; **II** 25, 56, 58, **78–80**, 99, 102, 117, 119; **III** 479, 654–55; **IV** 680
Philips Incandescent Lamp Works, **II** 78–80
Philips, John N., **6** 486
Phillip Hawkins, **III** 169; **6** 285
Phillippe of California, **8** 16
N.V. Phillips, **8** 153
Phillips & Drew, **II** 379
Phillips Cables, **III** 433
Phillips Carbon Black, **IV** 421
Phillips, Charles L., **III** 396
Phillips Chemical Co., **IV** 522
Phillips, Donald J., **IV** 112
Phillips, Ellis, **V** 652–53
Phillips, Frank, **IV** 445, 521–22
Phillips, Harry, Sr., **V** 750
Phillips, John G., **7** 281–82
Phillips, John Spencer, **II** 307
Phillips, L. E., **IV** 521
Phillips Manufacturing Company, **8** 464
Phillips Petroleum, **11** 522
Phillips Petroleum Company, **I** 377; **II** 15, 408; **III** 752; **IV** 71, 290, 366, 405, 412, 414, 445, 453, 498, **521–23**, 567, 570–71, 575; **10** 84, 440
Phillips Sheet and Tin Plate Co., **IV** 236
Phillips, Ted, **III** 313–14
Phillips, Thomas L., **II** 86–87; **11** 412–13
Phillips, W. E., **III** 651
Phillips, Waite, **IV** 521
Phillips, Warren, **IV** 602–03
Phillips, Willard, **III** 312
Phillips, William G., **7** 242–43
Phinny, T.G., **7** 443
PHLCorp., **11** 261
PHM Corp., **8** 461
Phoenix Assurance Co., **III** 242, 257, 369, 370–74
Phoenix Continental S.A., **III** 242
Phoenix Financial Services, **11** 115
Phoenix Fire Office, **III** 234
Phoenix Insurance Co., **III** 389; **IV** 711
Phoenix Oil and Transport Co., **IV** 90
Phoenix State Bank and Trust Co., **II** 213
Phoenix-Rheinrohr AG, **IV** 222
Phone America of Carolina, **8** 311
Phuket Air Catering Company Ltd., **6** 123–24
Physician's Weight Loss Center, **10** 383
Physicians Formula Cosmetics, **8** 512
Piaton, Pierre, **IV** 173
Piaton, René, **IV** 174
PIC Realty Corp., **III** 339
Picard, Dennis J., **II** 87; **11** 413
Picasso, Paloma, **8** 129–30
Piccolo, Lance, **10** 199

Picher, Oliver S., **8** 155–56
Pick, **III** 98
Pick, Frank, **6** 407
Pick-N-Pay, **II** 642; **9** 452
Pickard, Samuel, **9** 393
Pickens, T. Boone, **7** 309
Pickens, T. Boone, Jr., **II** 408; **IV** 171, 410, 523, 571
Picker, Arnold, **II** 147
Picker, David, **II** 147
Picker International, **II** 25
Picker International Corporation, **8** 352
Pickett, Edwin G., **11** 16
Pickford, James, **6** 412
Pickford, Mary, **I** 537; **II** 146–47, 154
Pickfords Ltd., **6** 412–14
Pickfords Travel Service Ltd., **6** 414
Pickland Mather & Co., **IV** 409
PickOmatic Systems, **8** 135
Pickwick, **I** 613
Pickwick Dress Co., **III** 54
Pickwick International, **9** 360
Piclands Mather, **7** 308
Picture Classified Network, **IV** 597
PictureTel Corp., **10 455–57**
Piech, Ferdinand, **11** 551
Piedmont, **6** 132
Piedmont Coca-Cola Bottling Partnership, **10** 223
Piedmont Concrete, **III** 739
Piedmont Pulp and Paper Co., **IV** 351
Piehl, Harri, **IV** 302
Piepenstock, Hermann Diedrich, **IV** 103
Piepers, Ernst, **IV** 201
Pierburg GmbH, **9** 445–46
Pierce, **IV** 478
Pierce, A.E., **6** 447
Pierce, B.N., **III** 438
Pierce Brothers, **6** 295
Pierce, Edward Allen, **II** 424
Pierce, Frederick, **II** 131
Pierce Steam Heating Co., **III** 663
Piergallini, Alfred A., **7** 196–97
Pierpaili, Julio, **11** 153
Pierpont, Heldring, and Pierson, **II** 185
Pierson, Jean, **I** 42
Pietro's Pizza Parlors, **II** 480–81
Pietruski, John M., **I** 700
Pig Improvement Co., **II** 500
Piggly Wiggly, **II** 571, 624
Pignone, **IV** 420
Pigott, Charles, **I** 185
Pigott, Paul, **I** 185
Pigott, Thomas Digby, **7** 216
Pigott, William, **I** 185
Pike Adding Machine, **III** 165
Pike Corporation of America, **I** 570; **8** 191
Pikrose and Co. Ltd., **IV** 136
Pilgrim Curtain Co., **III** 213
Pilgrim, Lonnie A. (Bo), **7** 432–33
Pilgrim's Pride Corporation, **7 432–33**
Pilkington, Alastair, **III** 726–27
Pilkington, Antony (Sir), **III** 727
Pilkington, Arthur, **III** 726–27
Pilkington, Austin, **III** 725
Pilkington Bros. Ltd., **I** 429; **II** 475; **III** 641, 676–77, 714, 724–27. *See also* Pilkington Bros. plc *and* Pilkington plc.
Pilkington Bros. plc, **III** 642, 727. *See also* Pilkington Bros. Ltd. *and* Pilkington plc.
Pilkington, Cecil, **III** 725
Pilkington, David, **III** 726–27
Pilkington, Geoffrey Langton, **III** 726
Pilkington, Harry (Lord), **III** 726–27

Pilkington, Hope. *See* Cozens-Hardy, Hope.
Pilkington, Lawrence, **III** 726–27
Pilkington Optronics, **III** 727
Pilkington P.E., **III** 727
Pilkington plc, **III** 56, 715, **724–27**. *See also* Pilkington Bros. Ltd. *and* Pilkington Bros. plc.
Pilkington Reinforcements Ltd., **III** 726–27
Pilkington, Richard, **III** 724
Pilkington Visioncare, Inc., **III** 727
Pilkington, William, **III** 724
Pillar Holdings, **IV** 191
Pillay, J.Y., **6** 117
Pilliod, Charles J., **V** 247
Pillsbury, Charles A., **II** 42, 501, 555; **10** 322
Pillsbury, Charles S., **II** 555
Pillsbury Company, **II** 133, 414, 493–94, 511, **555–57**, 575, 613–15; **7** 106, 128, 277, 469, 547; **8** 53–54; **10** 147, 176; **11** 23
Pillsbury Flour Mills Co., **II** 555
Pillsbury, Fred C., **II** 556
Pillsbury, John E., **9** 367
Pillsbury Mills, **II** 555
Pillsbury, Philip W., **II** 555
Pillsbury-Washburn Flour Mills Co. Ltd., **II** 555
Pilot, **I** 531
Pilot Insurance Agency, **III** 204
Pinal-Dome Oil, **IV** 569
Pincus & Co., **7** 305
Pineau-Valencienne, Didier, **II** 94
Pinecliff Publishing Company, **10** 357
Pinelands, Inc., **9** 119
Pineville Kraft Corp., **IV** 276
Pinewood Studios, **II** 157
Pingree, G.E., **III** 162
Pingree, Hazen, **6** 519
Pininfarina, **I** 188
Pinkerton, Allan, **9** 406–07
Pinkerton, Allan, II, **9** 407–08
Pinkerton, Robert, **9** 407
Pinkerton, Robert, II, **9** 408
Pinkerton, William, **9** 407
Pinkerton's Inc., **9 406–09**
Pinnacle West Capital Corporation, **6 545–47**
Pinochet, Ugarte, **IV** 590
Pinola, Joseph J., **II** 228, 289–90
Pinsetter Corp., **III** 443
Pioneer Airlines, **I** 96
Pioneer Asphalt Co., **I** 404
Pioneer Asphalts Pty. Ltd., **III** 728
Pioneer Concrete Services Ltd., **III** 728–29
Pioneer Concrete U.K., **III** 729
Pioneer Electronic Corporation, **II** 103; **III 604–06**
Pioneer Federal Savings, **10** 340
Pioneer Federal Savings Bank, **11** 115
Pioneer Financial Corp., **11** 447
Pioneer Hi-Bred International, Inc., **9 410–12**
Pioneer International Limited, **III** 687, **728–30**
Pioneer Life Insurance Co., **III** 274
Pioneer Natural Gas Company, **10** 82
Pioneer Readymixed Concrete and Mortar Proprietary Ltd., **III** 728
Pioneer Saws Ltd., **III** 598
Pipe Line Service Company. *See* Plexco.

Pipeline and Products Marketing Co., **IV** 473
Piper Aircraft Corp., **I** 482; **II** 403; **8** 49–50
Piquet, Nelson, **I** 139; **11** 32
Pirandello, Luigi, **IV** 585
Pirelli, **IV** 174, 420
Pirelli & C., **V** 249
Pirelli Applicazione Elettroniche, S.p.A., **10** 319
Pirelli Cavi, **V** 250
Pirelli, Giovanni Battista, **V** 249
Pirelli Group, **10** 319
Pirelli Holdings S.A., **V** 249
Pirelli Prodotti Diversificati, **V** 250
Pirelli S.p.A., **V 249–51**
Pirelli Société Générale S.A., **V** 250
Pirelli Tire, **V** 250
Pischetsrieder, Bernd, **11** 33
Pispalan Werhoomo Oy, **I** 387
Pistner, Stephen, **V** 148; **10** 515
Piston Ring Co., **I** 199
The Piston Ring Company, **10** 492
Pitblado, John, **I** 500
Pitcairn Aviation, **I** 101
Pitcairn, Harold, **I** 101
Pitcairn, John, **III** 731–32
Pitkin, Walter B., **IV** 635
Pitner, Homer, **11** 554
Pitney, Arthur, **III** 156
Pitney Bowes Inc., **III 156–58**, 159
Pitney-Bowes Postage Meter Co., **III** 156–57
Pitt, William (Earl of Chatham), **II** 312
Pittman, Douglas, **11** 307
Pitts, Roy E., **V** 612
Pittsburgh & Lake Erie Railroad, **I** 472
Pittsburgh Brewing, **10** 169–70
Pittsburgh Chemical Co., **IV** 573; **7** 551
Pittsburgh Consolidation Coal Co., **8** 346
Pittsburgh Corning Corp., **III** 683
Pittsburgh Life, **III** 274
Pittsburgh National Bank, **II** 317, 342
Pittsburgh National Corp., **II** 342
Pittsburgh Paint & Glass. *See* PPG Industries, Inc.
Pittsburgh Plate Glass Co., **III** 641, 676, 725, 731–32
Pittsburgh Railway Company, **9** 413
Pittsburgh Reduction Co., **II** 315; **IV** 9, 14
Pittsburgh Steel Company, **7** 587
Pittsburgh Trust and Savings, **II** 342
Pittston Company, **IV 180–82**; **10** 44
Pittston Petroleum, **IV** 182, 566
Pittway Corporation, **9 413–15**
Pixel Semiconductor, **11** 57
Pizza Dispatch. *See* Dominos's Pizza, Inc.
Pizza Hut Inc., **I** 221, 278, 294; **II** 614; **7** 152–53, 267, **434–35**, 506; **10** 450; **11** 50
PizzaCo, Inc., **7** 152
PKbanken, **II** 353
Place Two, **V** 156
Placer Cego Petroleum Ltd., **IV** 367
Placer Development Ltd., **IV** 19
Placer Dome, **IV** 571
Placid Oil Co., **7** 228
Plaid Holdings Corp., **9** 157
Plain Jane Dress Company, **8** 169
Plainwell Paper Co., Inc., **8** 103
Plamondon, William N., **9** 94
Planet Insurance Co., **III** 343
Plank, Raymond, **10** 102–04
Plank Road Brewery, **I** 269

Plankinton Packing Co., **III** 534
Plankinton, William, **III** 534
Plant Genetics Inc., **I** 266
Planters Nut & Chocolate Co., **I** 219; **II** 544
Plastic Coating Corporation, **IV** 330; **8** 483
Plasticos Metalgrafica, **I** 231
Plastow, David, **I** 195
Plastrier, **III** 675
Platt & Co., **I** 506
Platt Bros., **III** 636
Platt, C.B., **11** 254
Platt, Charles, **III** 224
Platt, John O., **III** 224
Platt, Lewis E., **6** 239
Platt, Warren C., **IV** 636
Platt's Price Service, Inc., **IV** 636–37
Platten, Donald C., **II** 251–52
Platten, John W., **II** 251
Platts, John H., **III** 654
Playskool Mfg., **III** 504, 506
Playtex, **II** 448, 468
Playtex Family Products Corp., **8** 511
Plaza Coloso S.A. de C.V., **10** 189
Plaza Medical Group, **6** 184
Plaza Securities, **I** 170
Pleasurama, **I** 248
Pleshette, Suzanne, **II** 173
Pleskow, Eric, **II** 147
Plesman, Albert, **I** 107–08
Plessey, **6** 241
Plessey Co. Ltd., **II** 81
Plessey Company, PLC, **II** 25, 39, **81–82**; **IV** 100
Plessey Connectors, **II** 81–82
Plessey Controls, **II** 81–82
Plettner, Bernhard, **II** 99
Plews Manufacturing Co., **III** 602
Plexco, **7** 30–31
Plitt Theatres, **6** 162
Plon et Juillard, **IV** 614
Plough, Abe, **I** 683–84
Plough Inc., **I** 684
Plowden, Lord, **I** 51
Plumb Tool, **II** 16
Plummer, Henry, **9** 337
Plus Development Corporation, **10** 458–59
Plus Mark, Inc., **7** 24
Plus System Inc., **9** 537
Plus-Ultra, **II** 196
PMC Specialties Group, **III** 745
PMI Corporation, **6** 140
PMI Mortgage Insurance Company, **10** 50
PMS Consolidated, **8** 347
PN Pertambangan Minyak Dan Gas Bumi Negara, **IV** 492
PN PERTAMIN, **IV** 492
PNC Financial Corp of Pittsburgh, **9** 476
PNC Financial Corporation, **II** 317, **342–43**
Pneumo Abex Corp., **I** 456–58; **III** 512; **10** 553–54
Pneumo Corp., **I** 456; **10** 553
Pneumo Dynamics Corporation, **8** 409
PNL. *See* Pacific Northwest Laboratories.
PNM. *See* Public Service Company of New Mexico.
PNP. *See* Pacific Northwest Power Company.
POAS, **IV** 563
POB Polyolefine Burghausen GmbH, **IV** 487
Pochin family, **III** 690–91
Pocket Books, **10** 480

Poclain Company, **10** 380
Poe, Edgar Allan, **IV** 661
Pogo Producing, **I** 441
Pogue, Mack, **8** 326, 328
Pohang Iron and Steel Company Ltd.,
  IV 183–85
Pohjan Sellu Oy, **IV** 316
Pohjoismainen Osakepankki, **II** 302
Pohjola Voima Oy, **IV** 348
Pohjolan Osakepankki, **II** 303
Poincaré, Raymond, **IV** 544–45, 557–58
Polak & Schwarz Essencefabricken, **9** 290
Poland, Alan Blair, **I** 325
Polar Star Milling Company, **7** 241
Polaris, **I** 530
Polaroid Corporation, **I** 30–31; **II** 412;
  III 475–77, 549, 584, **607–09**; **IV** 330;
  7 161–62, **436–39 (upd.)**
Policy Management Systems
  Corporation, 11 394–95
Polillo, Sergio, **IV** 587
Poling, Harold, **I** 167; **11** 139
Polizzi, Michael, **7** 134
Polk, Ralph Lane, **10** 460
Polk, Ralph Lane, II, **10** 460–61
Polk, Ralph Lane, III, **10** 461
Polk, Ralph Lane, IV, **10** 461
Polk, Stephen R., **10** 462
Pollard, Charles, **10** 561–62
Pollard, William, **6** 45
El Pollo Loco, **II** 680
Pollock, Thomas, **II** 144
Pollock, William L., **9** 393
Polo by Ralph Lauren, **9** 157
Polo Food Corporation, **10** 250
Poly P, Inc., **IV** 458
Poly Version, Inc., **III** 645
Poly-Hi Corporation, **8** 359
Polyblend Corporation, **7** 4
Polycell Holdings, **IV** 666
Polydress Plastic GmbH, **7** 141
Polyken Technologies, **11** 220
Polysar Energy & Chemical Corporation of
  Toronto, **V** 674
Polysius AG, **IV** 89
Pomerantz, Fred, **8** 323–24
Pomerantz, John, **8** 323–25
Pomerantz, Laura, **8** 323, 325
Pomerantz, Marvin, **8** 203–05
Pommersche Papierfabrik Hohenkrug, **III**
  692
Pommery et Greno, **II** 475
Pompadour, Madame de, **I** 271
Pompey, **IV** 227
Pompidou, Georges, **I** 45; **IV** 107, 546
Pond, Theron, **8** 105
Ponderosa, **7** 336
Pont-à-Mousson, **III** 675, 677–78, 704
Pontiac, **III** 458; **10** 353
Pontificia, **III** 207
Pontikes, Ken, **9** 130–31
Ponto, Jürgen, **I** 411; **II** 283
Pontremoli, Mario, **III** 347
Pony Express, **II** 380–81, 395
Pool, George, **I** 297
Pool, Leonard Parker, **10** 31–32
Poor, Victor D., **11** 67
Pope, Alan M., **II** 402
Pope, Daniel, **I** 21
Pope, Generoso, Jr., **10** 287–88
Pope, Jack M., **I** 443; **11** 134
Pope Tin Plate Co., **IV** 236
Popeyes Famous Fried Chicken and
  Biscuits, Inc., **7** 26–28

Popoff, Frank, **8** 149–50
Popp, Franz Joseph, **I** 138; **11** 31–32
Poppa, Ryal R., **6** 275–76
Popsicle, **II** 573
Poranen, Timo, **IV** 316
Porath, Jerker, **I** 665
Pori, **IV** 350
Poron Diffusion, **9** 394
Porsche, Ferdinand, **I** 149, 206; **11** 549,
  551
Port Harcourt Refining Co., **IV** 473
Portal, Lord (Viscount of Hungerford), **IV**
  15
Portals Water Treatment, **11** 510
Porter, Cole, **IV** 671
Porter, Joseph F., **6** 510–11
Porter, Michael, **IV** 203
Porter, Robert, **6** 240
Porter, Seton, **I** 376–77; **8** 439
Portland Electric Power Company, **6** 549
Portland General Corporation, 6 548–51
Portland General Electric Co. *See* Portland
  General Corporation.
Portland General Holdings. *See* Portland
  General Corporation.
Portland Heavy Industries, **10** 369
Portland Railway Electric Light & Power
  Company, **6** 548–49
Portman, John, **III** 96
Portnet, **6** 435
Portways, **9** 92
Poseidon Exploration Ltd., **IV** 84; **7** 188
Poseidon Ltd., **IV** 84
Posey, Quest, Genova, **6** 48
Posner, Ronald, **10** 455
Posner, Victor, **I** 497, 608; **III** 263, 536; **7**
  360; **8** 235–37
Posnick, Ad, **8** 178
Post, Carroll, **II** 530
Post, Charles W., **II** 523, 530–31; **7**
  272–73
Post, Frank T., **6** 596–97
Post, George B., **9** 370
Post, Geradus, **II** 250
Post, Glen F., III, **9** 107
Post, Marjorie Merriwether, **II** 531; **7** 273
Post Office Counters, **V** 496
Post Office Group, V 498–501
Post, Troy, **I** 489
PostBank, **II** 189
La Poste, V 470–72
Posti- Ja Telelaitos, 6 329–31
Postma, Thijus, **I** 56
Postum Cereal Co., Ltd., **II** 523, 530–31; **7**
  272–73
Postum Co., **II** 497, 531
Poth, Edward, **I** 585
Potila, Antti, **6** 89
Potlatch Corporation, **IV** 282; **8 428–30**;
  9 260
Potlatch Forests, Inc., **8** 429–30
Potlatch Lumber Company, **8** 428–29
Potomac Electric Power Company, 6
  552–54
Potomac Insurance Co., **III** 257
Potomac Leasing, **III** 137
Potter & Brumfield Inc., 11 396–98
Potter, Elbert E., **11** 396
Potter, George Washington, **8** 156
Pottinger, Henry, **I** 468
Potts, **IV** 58
Poulenc, Etienne, **I** 388; **10** 470
Poullain, Ludwig, **II** 385–86
Poulsen Wireless, **II** 490

Pountain, Eric, **III** 753
de Pous, Jan Willem, **V** 658–59
Povey, Charles, **III** 369
Powell, Alan, **IV** 118
Powell Duffryn, **III** 502; **IV** 38
Powell, Elkan H. "Buck", **7** 166
Powell Energy Products, **8** 321
Powell, George E. III, **V** 539–41
Powell, George E. Jr., **V** 539–40
Powell, George E. Sr., **V** 539–40
Powell, J.C., **III** 371
Powell, James B., **11** 424
Powell, Jim, **11** 252
Powell, John, **11** 424
Powell, John Wesley, **9** 366
Powell River Co. Ltd., **IV** 306–07
Powell River Paper Co. Ltd., **IV** 306
Powell, Stanley, **10** 41
Powell, Thomas Edward, III, **11** 424
Powell, Thomas Edward, Jr., **11** 424
Powell, William, **II** 155
Powell, William A., **7** 339
Power Applications & Manufacturing
  Company, Inc., **6** 441
Power Corp., **III** 261
Power Financial Corp., **III** 260–61
Power, Frederick B., **I** 714
Power Jets Ltd., **I** 81
Power Parts Co., **7** 358
Power Products, **8** 515
Power Specialty Company, **6** 145
Power Team, **10** 492
PowerFone Holdings, **10** 433
PowerGen PLC, 11 399–401
Powers Accounting Machine Company, **6**
  240
Powers, Brian M., **I** 471
Powers, James, **6** 240
Powers, John A., **I** 261
Powers, John J., **I** 662–63; **9** 403–04
Powers, Joshua D. (Col.), **III** 216
Powers, Pat, **II** 172
Powers Regulator, **III** 535
Powers-Samas, **6** 240
Powersoft, **11** 77
Powis, Alfred, **IV** 165; **7** 398–99
Pownall, Thomas, G., **I** 68–69, 143
Pozzi-Renati Millwork Products, Inc., **8**
  135
PP&L. *See* Pennsylvania Power & Light
  Company.
PPG Industries, Inc., **I** 330, 341–42; **III**
  21, 641, 667, 722, **731–33**; **8** 153, 222,
  224
PR Newswire, **IV** 687
Prac, **I** 281
Prager, Arthur, **6** 561–62
Pragma Bio-Tech, Inc., **11** 424
Prairie Farmer Publishing Co., **II** 129
Prairie Holding Co., **IV** 571
Prairie Oil and Gas Co., **IV** 368
Prairielands Energy Marketing, Inc., **7** 322,
  325
Pratt & Whitney, **I** 47, 78, 82–85, 128; **II**
  48; **III** 482; **6** 128; **7** 456; **9** 14, 16–18,
  244–46, **416–18**; **10** 162; **11** 299, 427
Pratt & Whitney Canada, **9** 416
Pratt & Whitney Tools, **I** 434
Pratt, C. Dudley, Jr., **9** 276
Pratt, Dudley, **9** 276
Pratt, Edmund, Jr., **I** 663; **9** 404
Pratt, Elisha, **III** 236
Pratt, Enoch, **11** 287
Pratt, Francis, **9** 416

Pratt, Gregory A., **6** 244
Pratt Holding, Ltd., **IV** 312
Pratt, Lorne, **8** 349
Pratt Properties Inc., **8** 349
Pratt, Sereno, **IV** 601
Praxair, Inc., 11 402–04
Praxis Biologics, **8** 26
Pre-Fab Cushioning, **9** 93
Precious Metals Development, **IV** 79
Precision Optical Co., **III** 120, 575
Precor, **III** 610–11
Predica, **II** 266
Preferred Products, Inc., **II** 669
PREINCO Holdings, Inc., **11** 532
PREL&P. *See* Portland Railway Electric
    Light & Power Company.
Prelude Corp., **III** 643
Premark International, Inc., II 534; **III**
    610–12
Premex A.G., **II** 369
Premier (Transvaal) Diamond Mining Co.,
    IV 65–66
Premier & Potter Printing Press Co., Inc.,
    II 37
Premier Autoware Division, **9** 419
Premier Brands Foods, **II** 514
Premier Consolidated Oilfields PLC, **IV**
    383
Premier Cruise Lines, **6** 368
Premier Diamond Mining Company, **7** 122
Premier Fastener Co., **9** 419
Premier Health Alliance Inc., **10** 143
Premier Industrial Corporation, 9
    419–21
Premier Milling Co., **II** 465
Premiere Products, **I** 403
Preminger, Otto, **II** 147
Premisteres S.A., **II** 663
Prémontré, **III** 676
Prentice Hall Computer Publishing, **10** 24
Prentice, Thomas, **III** 699
Prentice-Hall Inc., **I** 453; **IV** 672
Prentis, Henning Webb, Jr., **III** 422–23
Presbrey, Frank, S., **I** 21
Prescott Ball & Turben, **III** 271
Prescription Learning Corporation, **7** 256
Présence, **III** 211
La Preservatrice, **III** 242
Preserves and Honey, Inc., **II** 497
Presidential Airlines, **I** 117
Presidio Oil Co., **III** 197; **IV** 123
Press Assoc., **IV** 669
Press Trust of India, **IV** 669
Presse Pocket, **IV** 614
Pressed Steel Car Co., **6** 395
Presses de la Cité, **IV** 614–15
Prest-O-Lite Co., Inc., **I** 399; **9** 16, 516; **11**
    402
Prestige et Collections, **III** 48
Presto, **II** 609–10
Presto Products, Inc., **IV** 187
Preston Corporation, 6 421–23
Preston, James E., **III** 16
Preston Trucking Company. *See* Preston
    Corporation.
Pretty Polly, **I** 429
Preussag AG, **I** 542–43; **II** 386; **IV** 109,
    201, 231
Preussenelektra Aktiengesellschaft, I
    542; **V 698–700**
Preussischen Bergwerks- und Hütten A.G.,
    I 542
Preussischen Elektrizitäts A.G., **I** 542
Priam Corporation, **10** 458

Price, A.B., **I** 196
Price, Charles, **II** 592
Price Club, **V** 162–64
Price Club Industries, **V** 163
Price Co. Ltd., **IV** 246–47
Price Company, II 664; **V 162–64**
Price, Frank, **II** 144
Price, Gwilym, **II** 121
Price, Julian, **11** 213–14
Price, Larry, **V** 162–63
Price, Martin, **I** 714
Price, Ralph Clay, **11** 214–15
Price, Robert, **III** 128; **V** 162, 164
Price, Rodney, **III** 729
Price, Samuel Lowell, **9** 422
Price, Sol, **V** 162, 164
Price, T. Rowe, **11** 493–96
Price Waterhouse, **III** 84, 420, 527; **9**
    422–24
Price, William, **IV** 246
Pricel, **6** 373
Prichard and Constance, **III** 65
Pricher, Lawrence, **10** 41
Pride & Clarke, **III** 523
Priesing, John, **I** 554
Priggen Steel Building Co., **8** 545
Primark Corporation, **10** 89–90
Prime Computer, Inc. *See* Computervision
    Corporation.
Prime Motor Inns, **III** 103; **IV** 718; **11** 177
Prime Telecommunications Corporation, **8**
    311
PrimeAmerica, **III** 340
Primerica Corporation, I 597, 599–602,
    604, 607–09, **612–14,** 615; **II** 422; **III**
    283 **8** 118; **9** 218–19, 360–61; **11** 29.
    See also American Can Co.
Primes Régal S.A., **II** 651
Primex Fibre Ltd., **IV** 328
Primo de Rivera, Miguel, **I** 459; **IV** 190,
    396, 527
Primo Foods Ltd., **I** 457; **7** 430
Prince, **II** 177
Prince Co., **II** 473
Prince Motor Co. Ltd., **I** 184
Prince Street Technologies, Ltd., **8** 271
Prince William Bank, **II** 337; **10** 425
Princess Cruises, **IV** 256
Princess Dorothy Coal Co., **IV** 29
Princeton Gas Service Company, **6** 529
Princeton Laboratories Products Company,
    8 84
Principal Casualty Insurance Co., **III** 330
Principal Financial Group, **III** 328, 330
Principal Health Care, Inc., **III** 330
Principal Management, **III** 329
**Principal Mutual Life Insurance
    Company, III 328–30**
Principal National Life Insurance Co., **III**
    330
Principles, **V** 21–22
Princor Financial Services Corp., **III** 329
Pringle, George H., **IV** 311
Printex Corporation, **9** 363
Prinz, Gerhard, **I** 151
Prinz, Günter, **IV** 590–91
Prior, Edward B., **11** 397
Prior, Frank, **IV** 369–70
Prior, Michael, **11** 30
Prism Systems Inc., **6** 310
Prismo Safety Corp., **III** 735
Prismo Universal, **III** 735
Prisunic SA, **V** 9–11
Pritchard, Richard E., **III** 627

Pritchett, Henry Smith, **III** 379–80
Pritzker & Pritzker, **III** 96–97
Pritzker, Abram Nicholas (A.N.), **III**
    96–97; **IV** 135
Pritzker, Donald, **III** 96–97; **IV** 135
Pritzker family, **IV** 135–37
Pritzker, Jay, **III** 96; **IV** 135–37; **11** 198
Pritzker, Nicholas, **IV** 135
Pritzker, Penny, **III** 97
Pritzker, Robert, **III** 96; **IV** 135–37
Pritzker, Thomas Jay, **III** 96
Privatbanken, **II** 352
Pro-Fac Cooperative Inc., **7** 104–06
Proal, A.B., **I** 399
Probst, Lawrence, **10** 285
Procino-Rossi Corp., **II** 511
Procordia, **II** 478
Procter & Gamble Company, I 34, 129,
    290, 331, 366; **II** 478, 493, 544, 590,
    684, 616; **III** 20–25, 36–38, 40–41, 44,
    50–53; **IV** 282, 290, 329–30; **6** 26–27,
    50–52, 129, 363; **7** 277, 300, 419; **8** 63,
    106–07, 253, 282, 344, 399, **431–35**
    (upd.), 477, 511–12; **9** 260, 291,
    317–19, 552; **10** 54, 288; **11** 41, 421
Procter & Gamble Defense Corp., **III** 52
Procter, Harley, **III** 51; **8** 432
Procter, William, **III** 50–51, 53; **8** 431–32
Procter, William Alexander, **III** 50–51; **8**
    431–32
Procter, William Cooper, **III** 51; **8** 432
Proctor & Collier, **I** 19
Prodi, Romano, **I** 466; **V** 326; **11** 204–06
Prodigy, **10** 237–38
Productos Ortiz, **II** 594
Produits Chimiques Ugine Kuhlmann, **I**
    303; **IV** 547
Proetz, Erma, **7** 429
Professional Care Service, **6** 42
Professional Computer Resources, Inc., **10**
    513
Professional Research, **III** 73
Profimatics, Inc., **11** 66
PROFITCo., **II** 231
Progil, **I** 389
Progress Development Organisation, **10**
    169
Progressive Corporation, 11 405–07
Progressive Grocery Stores, **7** 202
Progresso, **I** 514
Projiis, **II** 356
Prolabo, **I** 388
Prölss, Erich R., **III** 377
Promigas, **IV** 418
Promstroybank, **II** 242
Promus Companies, Inc., III 95; **9**
    425–27
Pronto Pacific, **II** 488
Prontophot Holding Limited, **6** 490
Prontor-Werk Alfred Gauthier GmbH, **III**
    446
Propernyn, B.V., **IV** 391–92, 508
Prophet Foods, **I** 449
Propst, Robert, **8** 256
Propwix, **IV** 605
Prosim, S.A., **IV** 409
Prospect Farms, Inc., **II** 584
The Prospect Group, Inc., **11** 188
Prospectors Airways, **IV** 165
Prosser, David, **III** 273
Prosser, Seward, **II** 229–30
Protective Closures, **7** 296–97
La Protectrice, **III** 346–47
Protek, **III** 633

Proto Industrial Tools, **III** 628
Proust, Marcel, **IV** 618
Proventus A.B., **II** 303
Provi-Soir, **II** 652
Provi-Viande, **II** 652
Provibec, **II** 652
Providence Bank, **9** 228
La Providence, **III** 210–11
Providence National Bank, **9** 228
Providencia, **III** 208
Provident Bank, **III** 190
Provident General Insurance Co., **III** 332
Provident Life and Accident Insurance Company of America, **III** 331–33, 404
Provident Life and Casualty Insurance Co., **III** 332
Provident National Assurance Co., **III** 332
Provident National Bank, **II** 342
Provident National Corp., **II** 342
Provident Services, Inc., **6** 295
Provident Travelers Mortgage Securities Corp., **III** 389
ProviFruit Inc., **II** 651
Provigo Inc., **II** 651–53
Provigo International, **II** 653
Provigo U.S.A., **II** 652
Les Provinces Réunies, **III** 235
Provincetown-Boston Airlines, **I** 118
Provincial Engineering Ltd, **8** 544
Provincial Gas Company, **6** 526
Provincial Insurance Co., **III** 373
Provincial Newspapers Ltd., **IV** 685–86
Provincial Traders Holding Ltd., **I** 437
Provinzial-Hülfskasse, **II** 385
Provo, Larry, **6** 377
Provost & Provost, **II** 651
Provost, Daniel, **7** 130
Provost, Ernest, **II** 651
Provost, René, **II** 651
Provost, Roland, **II** 651
Proxmire, William, **I** 59; **10** 317
Pru Capital Management, **III** 340
Pru Funding, **III** 340
Pru Service Participacos, **III** 340
Pru Supply, **III** 340
PRUCO, **III** 340
Prude, I.B., **8** 546
Prudential Assurance Co. Ltd., **III** 273, 290, 334–35, 337
Prudential Bache Securities, **9** 441
Prudential Corporation plc, **II** 319; **III** 334–36; **IV** 711; **8** 276–77
Prudential Friendly Society, **III** 337
Prudential General Insurance Co., **III** 340
Prudential Health Care Plan, **III** 340
Prudential Holborn, **III** 335–36
Prudential Insurance Company of America, **I** 19, 334, 402; **II** 103, 456; **III** 79, 92, 249, 259, 265–67, 291–93, 313, 329, 337–41; **IV** 410, 458; **10** 199; **11** 243
Prudential Investment, Loan, and Assurance Assoc., **III** 334
Prudential Lease, **III** 339
Prudential Life Insurance Co. Ltd., **III** 340
Prudential Life of Ireland, **III** 335
Prudential Ltd., **III** 340
Prudential Mortgage Capital Co., **III** 340
Prudential Mutual Assurance, Investment, and Loan Assoc., **III** 334
Prudential Oil & Gas, Inc., **6** 495–96
Prudential Portfolio Managers, **III** 335
Prudential Property and Casualty Insurance Co., **III** 339

Prudential Property Co., **III** 340
Prudential Property Services, **III** 335–36
Prudential Refining Co., **IV** 400
Prudential Reinsurance Co., **III** 339
Prudential Steel, **IV** 74
Prudential-Bache Trade Corp., **II** 51
Prulease, **III** 340
Pruyn, William J., **6** 487
PSA. *See* Pacific Southwest Airlines.
PSA Peugeot-Citroen Group, **7** 35
PSCCo. *See* Public Service Company of Colorado.
PSI Energy, **6** 555–57
PSI Holdings, Inc. *See* PSI Resources.
PSI Resources, **6** 555–57
Psychiatric Institutes of America, **III** 87–88
Psychological Corp., **IV** 623
PT PERMINA, **IV** 492, 517
Ptashne, Dr. Mark, **8** 215
PTI Communications, Inc. *See* Pacific Telecom, Inc.
PTT Post BV, **V** 299–301
PTT Telecom, **6** 303
PTT Telecom BV, **V** 299–301
PTV. *See* Österreichische Post- und Telegraphenverwaltung.
Public Home Trust Co., **III** 104
Public National Bank, **II** 230
Public Savings Insurance Co., **III** 219
Public Service Company of Colorado, **6** 558–60
Public Service Company of Indiana. *See* PSI Energy.
Public Service Company of New Mexico, **6** 561–64
Public Service Electric and Gas Company, **IV** 366; **V** 701–03; **11** 388
Public Service Enterprise Group, **V** 701–03
Publicker Industries Inc., **I** 226; **10** 180
Publishers Paper Co., **IV** 295, 677–78
Publishers Press Assoc., **IV** 607
Publix, **II** 627; **9** 186
Publix Super Markets Inc., **II** 155; **7** 440–42
Puckett, Allen, **II** 33
Puckett, B. Earl, **V** 25–26
Puéchal, Jacques, **I** 303
Puente Oil, **IV** 385
Puerto Rican Aqueduct and Sewer Authority, **6** 441
Puerto Rican-American Insurance Co., **III** 242
Puette, Robert, **III** 116; **6** 219
Puget Sound Alaska Van Lines. *See* Alaska Hydro-Train.
Puget Sound National Bank, **8** 469–70
Puget Sound Power And Light Company, **6** 565–67
Puget Sound Pulp and Timber Co., **IV** 281; **9** 259
Puget Sound Traction, Light & Power Company, **6** 565
Puget Sound Tug and Barge Company, **6** 382
Pugh, Lawrence, **V** 391
Puiseux, Robert, **V** 237–38
Puissant, Ferdinand, **IV** 52
Pulitzer, Joseph, **IV** 625, 671
Pullen, Charles, **III** 762
Pullen, William E., **III** 396
Pulliam, Eugene C., **10** 207
Pulliam, Eugene S., **10** 207
Pulliam, Naomi, **10** 207

Pullin, Charles R., **I** 355–56
Pullman Co., **II** 403; **III** 94, 744
Pullman Standard, **7** 540
Pulsifer, L. Valentine, **8** 552–53
Pulson, Swen, **8** 395
Pulte Corporation, **8** 436–38
Pulte Diversified Companies, Inc., **8** 436
Pulte Financial Companies, Inc., **8** 436
Pulte, William J., **8** 436
AB Pump-Separator, **III** 418–19
Punchcraft, Inc., **III** 569
Pundsack, Fred L., **III** 707–08; **7** 292–93
Purcell, Robert, **I** 142
Purdum, Robert L., **IV** 30
Pure Milk Products Cooperative, **11** 24
Pure Oil Co., **III** 497; **IV** 570
Pure Packed Foods, **II** 525
Purex Corp., **I** 450; **III** 21
Purex Pool Products, **I** 13, 342
Purfina, **IV** 497
Puritan Chemical Co., **I** 321
Purity Stores, **I** 146
Purity Supreme, Inc., **II** 674
Purle Bros., **III** 735
Purnell & Sons Ltd., **IV** 642; **7** 312
Purodenso Co., **III** 593
Purolator Courier Corporation, **6** 345–46, 390
Purolator Courier Limited of Canada, **6** 346
Purolator Products Co., **III** 593
Puskar, Milan, **I** 656
Puss 'n Boots, **II** 559
Putnam, Howard D., **6** 120
Putnam Management Co., **III** 283
Putnam Reinsurance Co., **III** 198
Putney, Mark W., **6** 524
Puttnam, David, **II** 136–37
Puttonen, Matti, **IV** 315
PWA Dekor GmbH, **IV** 325
PWA Grafische Papiere GmbH, **IV** 323, 325
PWA Group, **IV** 323–25
PWA Industriepapier GmbH, **IV** 323, 325
PWA Papierwerke Waldhof-Aschaffenburg AG, **IV** 324
PWA Waldhof GmbH, **IV** 323, 325
PWT Worldwide, **11** 510
PYA Monarch, **II** 675
Pyle, Ernie, **IV** 608
Pyle, Harry, **11** 67
Pyne, Percy R., **II** 253; **9** 123
Pyramid Communications, Inc., **IV** 623
Pyramid Electric Company, **10** 319
Pyramid Technology Corporation, **10** 504
Pytchley Autocar Co. Ltd., **IV** 722
Pyxis Resources Co., **IV** 182

Qaddafi, Muammar. *See* Khadafi, Moammar.
Qandil, Abul Hadi, **IV** 413
Qantair Limited, **6** 111
Qantas. *See* Queensland and Northern Territories Air Service.
Qantas Airways Limited, **6** 79, 91, 100, 105, **109–13**, 117
Qantas Empire Airways Limited. *See* Qantas Airways Limited.
Qatar Fertiliser Co., **IV** 525
Qatar General Petroleum Corporation, **IV** 524–26
Qatar LNG Co. Ltd., **IV** 525
Qatar Petrochemical Co., **IV** 525
Qatar Petroleum Co., **IV** 524

QGPC. *See* Qatar General Petroleum Corporation.
Qintex Australia Ltd., **II** 150
QSP, Inc., **IV** 664
Quaker Mill, **II** 558
Quaker Oats Company, **I** 30; **II** **558–60**, 575, 684
Quaker State Corporation, **7** **443–45**
Quale, J. G., **6** 602–03
Qualicare, Inc., **6** 192
QualiTROL Corporation, **7** 116–17
Quality Care Inc., **I** 249
Quality Importers, **I** 226; **10** 180
Quality Oil Co., **II** 624–25
Qualtec, Inc., **V** 623
Quandt family, **II** 283
Quantum, **6** 230–31
Quantum Chemical Corporation, **8** **439–41**; **11** 441
Quantum Computer Services, Inc., **10** 56
Quantum Corporation, **10** 403, **458–59**, 463
Quantum Overseas N.V., **7** 360
Quaritch, Bernard, **11** 452
Quasi-Arc Co., **I** 315
Quebec Bank, **II** 344
Quebéc Hydro-Electric Commission. *See* Hydro-Quebéc.
Queen Casuals, **III** 530
Queen Insurance Co., **III** 350
Queens Isetan Co., Ltd., **V** 87
Queensland Alumina, **IV** 59
Queensland and Northern Territories Air Service, **I** 92–93
Queensland Mines Ltd., **III** 729
Queensland Oil Refineries, **III** 672
Queeny, Edgar, **I** 365–66; **9** 355–56
Queeny, John Francisco, **I** 365; **9** 355
Queiroz Pereira, **IV** 504
Quelle Bank, **V** 166
Quelle Group, **V** **165–67**
Quennessen, **IV** 118
Quenon, Robert, **IV** 171; **10** 448
Quesnel River Pulp Co., **IV** 269
Questar Corporation, **6** **568–70**
Questar Pipeline Company, **6** 568–69
Questar Service Corporation, **6** 569
Questar Telecom, **10** 432
Questar Telecom Inc., **6** 568–69
Questor, **I** 332
Questrom, Allen, **9** 211
QUICK Corp., **IV** 656
Quick-Shop, **II** 619
Quickie Designs, **11** 202, 487–88
QuikWok Inc., **II** 556
Quilter Goodison, **II** 260
Quimica Industrial Huels Do Brasil Ltda., **I** 350
Quincy Compressor Co., **I** 434–35
Quincy Family Steak House, **II** 679
Quincy, Josiah, **III** 312
Quincy's, **10** 331
Quinlan, Michael R., **II** 647; **7** 319
Quinn, Brian, **V** 34
Quinn, C.K., **6** 473
Quinn, Patrick, **8** 481–82
Quinn, William J., **V** 428
Quintin, John, **II** 237
Quinton Hazell Automotive, **III** 495
Quinton Hazell Ltd., **IV** 382–83
Quintron, Inc., **11** 475
Quintus Computer Systems, **6** 248
Quirk, Des, **III** 729
Quixx Corporation, **6** 580

Quotron, **III** 119; **IV** 670; **9** 49, 125
Qureshey, Safi U., **9** 41–43
QVC Network Inc., **9** **428–29**; **10** 175

R & B Manufacturing Co., **III** 569
R.A. Waller & Co., **III** 282
R. Buckland & Son Ltd., **IV** 119
R-C Holding Inc. *See* Air & Water Technologies Corporation.
R. Cubed Composites Inc., **I** 387
R.E. Funsten Co., **7** 429
R.G. Dun & Co., **IV** 604
R.G. Dun Corp., **IV** 604–05
R.G. Dun-Bradstreet Corp., **IV** 604–05
R.H. Macy & Co., Inc., **V** 168–70; **8** **442–45 (upd.)**; **10** 282; **11** 349
R.H. Squire, **III** 283
R. Hoe & Co., **I** 602
R. Hornibrook (NSW), **I** 592
R.J. Brown Co., **IV** 373
R.J. Reynolds Industries Inc., **I** 259, 261, 363; **II** 542, 544; **III** 16; **IV** 523; **V** 396, 404–05, 407–10, 413, 415, 417–18; **7** 130, 132, 267, 365, 367; **9** 533
R.L. Manning Company, **9** 363–64
R.L. Polk & Co., **10** **460–62**
R.N. Coate, **I** 216
R.O. Hull Co., **I** 361
R.P. Scherer, **I** **678–80**
R.R. Donnelley & Sons Company, **IV** **660–62**, 673; **9** **430–32 (upd.)**; **11** 293
R. Scott Associates, **11** 57
R. Stock AG, **IV** 198
R.T. French USA, **II** 567
R.T. Securities, **II** 457
R.W. Sears Watch Company, **V** 180
R.W. Harmon & Sons, Inc., **6** 410
Raab, Kirk, **11** 9
Raab, Walter, **II** 8
Raade, Uolevi, **IV** 469–71
RABA PLC, **10** 274
RABA-Detroit Diesel Hungary, Kft., **10** 274
Rabb, Irving, **II** 666
Rabb, Norman S., **II** 666
Rabb, Sidney R., **II** 666–67
Rabbit Software Corp., **10** 474
Raber, W. F., **V** 711
Raboy, S. Caesar, **III** 238
Racal Electronics Ltd., **11** 408, 547
Racal Electronics PLC, **II** **83–84**
Racal Telecommunications Group Ltd., **11** 547
Racal-Datacom Inc., **11** **408–10**
Racal-Milgo, **11** 409
Racal-Milgo Ltd., **II** 83–84; **11** 408
Racal-Redac, **11** 490
Racal-Vadic, **II** 84
Racamier, Henry, **10** 398–99
Racine Hardware Co., **III** 58
Racine Threshing Machine Works, **10** 377
Rack Rite Distributors, **V** 174
Rada Corp., **IV** 250
Radavitz, Moe, **11** 391
Radiation Dynamics, **III** 634–35
Radiation, Inc., **II** 37–38
Radiation-Medical Products Corp., **I** 202
Radiator Specialty Co., **III** 570
Radio & Allied Industries, **II** 25
Radio Austria A.G., **V** 314–16
Radio Corporation of America, **6** 164–66, 240, 266, 281, 288, 334; **10** 173. *See also* RCA Corporation.
Radio Receptor Company, Inc., **10** 319

Radio Shack, **II** 106–08
Radio-Keith-Orpheum, **II** 32, 88, 135, 146–48, 175; **III** 428; **9** 247
Radiotelevision Española, **7** 511
Radium Pharmacy, **I** 704
Radnor Venture Partners, LP, **10** 474
Rae, John B., **I** 184
Raf. Haarla Oy, **IV** 349
Rafferty, James A., **I** 399
Raffineriegesellschaft Vohburg/Ingolstadt mbH, **7** 141
Ragazzi's, **10** 331
Ragland, S.E., **11** 120
Ragnar Benson Inc., **8** 43–43
RAI, **I** 466
Railway Express Agency, **I** 456; **II** 382; **6** 388–89
Railway Officials and Employees Accident Assoc., **III** 228
Railway Passengers Assurance Co., **III** 178, 410
Rainbird, George, **8** 526
Rainbow Crafts, **II** 502; **10** 323
Rainbow Home Shopping Ltd., **V** 160
Rainbow Production Corp., **I** 412
Rainbow Programming Holdings, **7** 63–64
Rainbow Resources, **IV** 576
Rainier, **I** 254
Rains, Claude, **II** 175
Rainwater, Richard, **III** 80
Raky-Danubia, **IV** 485
Rales, Mitchell, **III** 531; **7** 116
Rales, Steven M., **III** 531; **7** 116
Ralite, Jack, **I** 670
Ralli, Ambrogio, **III** 345
Ralli family, **III** 347
Ralli International, **III** 502; **IV** 259
The Ralph M. Parsons Company, **8** 415. *See also* The Parsons Corporations.
Ralph M. Parsons Group, **III** 749
Ralph Wilson Plastics, **III** 610–11
Ralston, (Dr.), **II** 561
Ralston Purina, **8** 180
Ralston Purina Company, **I** 608, **II** 544, 560, **561–63**, 617; **III** 588; **6** 50–52; **7** 209, 396, 547, 556; **9** 180
Ram dis Ticaret, **I** 479
Ram Golf Corp., **III** 24
Ram, Stephen, **III** 370
Ram's Insurance, **III** 370
Ramada International Hotels & Resorts, **II** 142; **III** 99; **IV** 718; **9** 426; **11** 177
Ramann, Christian, **6** 403
Ramazotti, **I** 281
Ramo, Simon, **I** 539; **II** 33; **11** 540
Ramo-Woolridge Corp., **I** 539
Ramón Areces Foundation, **V** 52
Ramos, Abraham Bennaton, **II** 596
Ramsay, John, **11** 494
Ramsay, Wolter, **IV** 275
Ramsden, Samuel, **IV** 248
Ramsey, Douglas K., **I** 118, 173, 176, 235
Rand, A. Barry, **6** 290
Rand, Addison Crittenden, **III** 525
Rand, Alfred T., **III** 525
Rand American Investments Ltd., **IV** 79
Rand Drill Co., **III** 525
Rand, Edgar E., **III** 529
Rand, Frank C., **III** 528–29
Rand Group, Inc., **6** 247
Rand, Henry H., **III** 529
Rand, Henry O., **III** 528
Rand Mines Ltd., **I** 422; **IV** 22, 79, 94
Rand Selection Corp. Ltd., **IV** 79

Randall, Clarence B., **IV** 115
Randall, James R., **11** 23
Randall, Jesse W., **III** 388
Randall, Walter D., **IV** 263; **9** 304
Randall, William S., **I** 393
Randolph, Jackson H., **6** 467
Random House, Inc., **II** 90; **IV** 583–84, 637, 648
Randone, Enrico, **III** 209
Randsworth Trust P.L.C., **IV** 703
Rangod, Alfred. *See* Pechiney, A.R.
Rank, Arthur, **II** 564–65
Rank, James, **II** 564
Rank, Joseph Arthur, **II** 157–58, 564–65
Rank Organisation PLC, **II** 139, 147, **157–59**; **III** 171; **IV** 698; **6** 288
Rank, Rowland, **II** 564
Rank Xerox, **II** 157, 159; **III** 171. *See also* Xerox Corporation.
Rankin, Alfred M., Jr., **7** 371
Rankin, B.M., Jr., **IV** 83; **7** 187
Rankin, George S., **IV** 255
Ranks Hovis McDougall PLC, **II** 157, **564–65**
Ranks Ltd., **II** 564–65
Ransom, A., **III** 239
Ransom and Randolph Company, **10** 271
Ransomes America Corp., **III** 600
Raphael, Sally Jessy, **11** 330
Rapicom, **III** 159
Rapid American, **I** 440
Rapides Bank & Trust Company, **11** 107
Rapier, Thomas G., **11** 106
Rapifax of Canada, **III** 160
Rapp, Karl, **I** 138; **11** 31
RAS. *See* Riunione Adriatica di Sicurtà SpA.
RASBANK, **III** 348
Rasche, Karl, **II** 282
Rasmussen, Arthur, **II** 419
Rasmussen, Wallace, **II** 468
Rasp, Charles, **IV** 44
Rassini Rheem, **III** 581
Rassweiler, C.F., **III** 707
Ratcliffe, George, **9** 287
Ratcliffe, Richard, **I** 222
Rathbone, Munroe, **IV** 537
Rathenau, Emil, **I** 409–10
Rathenau, Walter, **I** 410
Rathmann, George B., **10** 78
Ratican, Peter J., **III** 84–86
Rational Systems Inc., **6** 255
Ratjen, Karl Gustaf, **IV** 141
Rattigan, Thomas, **7** 97
Rau, Robert H., **9** 460
Rauland Corp., **II** 124
Rauma Oy, **IV** 350
Rauma-Repola Oy, **II** 302; **IV** 316, 340, 349–50
Rautalahti, Pentti O., **IV** 315
Rauth, J. Donald, **I** 68
Ravano family, **III** 347
Ravenseft Properties Ltd., **IV** 696, 704–05
Ravensfield Investment Trust Ltd., **IV** 705
Raw, George, **I** 287
Rawleigh Warner, Jr., **7** 353
Rawlings, Edwin W., **II** 502; **10** 323
Rawlings Sporting Goods, **7** 177
Rawlplug Co. Ltd., **IV** 382–83
Rawson, Holdsworth & Co., **I** 464
Ray C. Robbins, **8** 321–22
Ray, Charles, **IV** 682
Ray, E. Lansing, **IV** 582
Ray, Phil, **11** 67–68

Ray, Werner, **6** 11
Ray's Printing of Topeka, **II** 624
Rayan, Muhammed, **6** 86
Rayburn, William B., **7** 479–80
Raychem, **III** 492
Raychem Corporation, **8 446–47**
Raycom Sports, **6** 33
Rayden, Michael, **9** 190
Raymar Book Corporation, **11** 194
Raymer, Donald G., **6** 471
Raymond, Albert L., **I** 686–87
Raymond, Henry Jarvis, **IV** 647–48
Raymond, Jones & Co., **IV** 647
Raymond, Stanley, **V** 422
Raymund, Edward, **10** 518
Raymund, Steven, **10** 518
Rayner, Derek (Lord), **V** 126
Raynes, Burt, **9** 459
Raynet Corporation, **8** 447
Rayniak, Joseph G., **III** 598
Raytheon Company, **I** 463, 485, 544; **II** 41, 73, **85–87**; **III** 643; **8** 51, 157; **11** 197, **411–14 (upd.)**
Raytheon Inc., **II** 85–86
RCA Corporation, **I** 142, 454, 463; **II** 29–31, 34, 38, 56, 61, 85–86, **88–90**, 96, 102, 117–18, 120, 124, 129, 132–33, 151–52, 313, 645; **III** 118, 122, 132, 149, 152, 165, 171, 569, 653–54; **IV** 252, 583, 594; **7** 520; **8** 157; **9** 283; **11** 197, 318, 411. *See also* Radio Corporation of America.
RCA Inc., **II** 609
RCA Photophone, Inc., **II** 88
RCA Radiotron Co., **II** 88
RCA-Victor Co., **II** 88, 118
RCG International, Inc., **III** 344
REA. *See* Railway Express Agency.
Rea & Derick, **II** 605
Rea Magnet Wire Co., **IV** 15
React-Rite, Inc., **8** 271
Read, R.L., **II** 417
Read-Rite Corp., **10** 403–04, **463–64**
Reader, W.J., **I** 353, 606
Reader's Digest Association, Inc., **IV** **663–64**
Reading (Marquis of), **IV** 685
Reading and Bates, **III** 559
Reading Railroad, **9** 407
Ready Mix Kies, **III** 739
Ready Mixed Concrete, **III** 687, 737–40
Ready Mixed Concrete of Australia, **III** 737–39
Ready, Thomas J., **IV** 122–23
Readymix Asland, **III** 740
Readymix Zementwerke, **III** 738
Reagan, M. Allen, **11** 440
Reagan, Ronald, **I** 80, 332, 367, 482, 559–600, 694; **III** 149, 452, 463; **IV** 37, 367, 454, 624, 672; **7** 212–13, 559; **8** 164; **9** 14, 203, 246, 356; **11** 429
Reale Mutuale, **III** 273
Reall, J.H., **III** 418
Réassurances, **III** 392
Recamier, Henry, **I** 272
Recasens, Francisco, **IV** 396
Reckitt & Colman Holdings Ltd., **II** 566
Reckitt & Colman Ltd., **II** 566
Reckitt & Colman PLC, **II 566–67**
Reckitt & Sons Ltd., **II** 566
Reckitt, Isaac, **II** 566
Reconstruction Bank of Holland, **IV** 707
Reconstruction Finance Bank, **II** 292

Reconstruction Finance Corp., **I** 67, 203; **II** 261; **IV** 10, 333
Record Bar / Licorice Pizza, **9** 361
Record World Inc., **9** 361
Recoupe Recycling Technologies, **8** 104
Recovery Centers of America, **III** 88
Recticel S.A., **III** 581
Rectigraph Co., **III** 171
Rector, William G., **II** 16
Red & White, **II** 682
Red Arrow, **II** 138
Red Baron. *See* Von Richthofen, Manfred.
Red Kap, **V** 390–91
Red Lobster Restaurants, **II** 502–03; **6** 28; **10** 322–24
Red Owl Stores Inc., **II** 670
Red Rooster, **V** 35
Red Sea Insurance Co., **III** 251
Red Star Milling Co., **II** 501; **6** 397; **10** 322
Red Wing Shoe Company, Inc., **9** **433–35**
Redactron, **III** 166; **6** 282
Redd, William S. (Si), **10** 375
Redding, Robert, **I** 49
Reddy Elevator Co., **III** 467
Reddy Ice, **II** 661
Redentza, **IV** 504
Redfern, John, **III** 705
Redfield, Peter, **9** 296–97
Redhill Tile Co., **III** 734
Redi, **IV** 610
Rediffusion, **II** 139
Redken Laboratories, **8** 131
Redland Aggregates, **III** 734
Redland Holdings, **III** 734
Redland Pipes, **III** 734
Redland Plasterboard Ltd., **III** 688, 736
Redland plc, **III** 734–36
Redland Purle, **III** 495, 735
Redland Stone Products, **III** 735
Redland Tiles, **III** 734–35, 739
Redland Worth, **III** 735
Redland-Braas-Bredero Europa, **III** 735
Redmond & Co., **I** 376
Redmond, Albert G., **8** 37
Redmond, Paul A., **6** 597–98
La Redoute, S.A, **V** 11
Redpath Industries, **II** 581–82
Redstone, Sumner M., **6** 168–69; **7** 336
Redwood Design Automation, **11** 47
Redwood Fire & Casualty Insurance Co., **III** 214
Reebok, **8** 171
Reebok International Ltd., **V** 375–77; **8** 303–04, 393; **9** 134–35, **436–38 (upd.)**; **11** 50–51, 349
Reed, Albert, **IV** 665
Reed Corrugated Containers, **IV** 249
Reed Elsevier, **7** 244; **10** 407
Reed, Everett C., **8** 13
Reed, Henry M., **III** 664
Reed International P.L.C., **I** 423; **IV** 270, 642, **665–67**, 711; **7** 244–45, 343
Reed, John E., **10** 411–12
Reed, John S., **II** 255; **9** 125
Reed, Percy, **IV** 665
Reed, Ralph (Sir), **IV** 665–66
Reed, Ralph T., **II** 397; **10** 61
Reed Tool Co., **III** 429
Reeder, Charles, **I** 344
Reeder, Howard C., **III** 230–31
Reeder Light, Ice & Fuel Company, **6** 592
Reedpack, **IV** 339–40, 667

Reedy, Roy N., **V** 504
Reekie, Duncan W., **I** 641
Rees, LaVerne, **11** 458
Rees, William M., **III** 220
Rees-Mogg, William (Lord), **IV** 667
Reese Finer Foods, Inc., **7** 429
Reese Products, **III** 569; **11** 535
Reeves Banking and Trust Company, **11** 181
Reeves Pulley Company, **9** 440
Refco, Inc., **10** 251
Reference Software International, **10** 558
Refined Sugars, **II** 582
Reform Rt, **IV** 652; **7** 392
Regal Drugs, **V** 171
Regan, Donald T., **II** 425; **III** 611
Regan, John, **III** 283
Regency Electronics, **II** 101
Regency International, **10** 196
Regenerative Environmental Equipment Company, Inc., **6** 441
Regeneron Pharmaceuticals Inc., **10** 80
Regent Canal Co., **III** 272
Regent Insurance Co., **III** 343
Regent International Hotels Limited, **9** 238
Régie Autonome des Pétroles, **IV** 544–46
Régie des Mines de la Sarre, **IV** 196
Régie des Télégraphes et Téléphones. *See* Belgacom.
Régie Nationale des Usines Renault, I 136, 145, 148, 178–79, 183, **189–91,** 207, 210; **II** 13; **III** 392, 523; **7** 566–67; **11** 104
Regina Verwaltungsgesellschaft, **II** 257
Registered Vitamin Company, **V** 171
Regnecentralen AS, **III** 164
Rego, Anthony C., **9** 453
Rego Supermarkets, **9** 451
Rehab Hospital Services Corp., **III** 88; **10** 252
RehabClinics Inc., **11** 367
Rehm, Jack, **11** 293
Reich, Robert B., **I** 145
Reichardt, Carl, **II** 383
Reichenbach, Carl August, **III** 561
Reichert, Jack, **III** 444
Reichhold Chemicals, Inc., I 386, 524; **8** 554; **10 465–67**
Reichhold, Henry Helmuth, **10** 465–67
Reichmann, Albert, **IV** 720; **9** 390; **10** 530
Reichmann family, **I** 216, 264; **IV** 245, 247, 720–21; **9** 390–91
Reichmann, Paul, **IV** 720; **6** 478; **9** 390; **10** 530
Reichmann, Ralph, **IV** 720; **9** 390
Reichmann, Renee, **IV** 720
Reichmann, Samuel, **IV** 720; **9** 390
Reichs-Kredit-Gesellschaft mbH, **IV** 230
Reichs-Kredit- und Krontrollstelle GmbH, **IV** 230
Reichswerke AG für Berg- und Hüttenbetriebe Hermann Göring, **IV** 200
Reichswerke AG für Erzbergbau und Eisenhütten, **IV** 200
Reichswerke Hermann Göring, **IV** 233
Reid, **III** 673
Reid, Alex, **III** 360
Reid Bros. & Carr Proprietary, **III** 672–73
Reid, Bud, **IV** 480
Reid, Charles (Sir), **IV** 38
Reid Dominion Packaging Ltd., **IV** 645
Reid, Gene, **IV** 480
Reid, Harry, **6** 513; **11** 236–37
Reid Ice Cream Corp., **II** 471

Reid, Murdoch and Co., **II** 571
Reid Press Ltd., **IV** 645
Reid, Robert, **V** 423–24
Reid, Robert L., **10** 299
Reids Quarries, **III** 672
Reigel Products Corp., **IV** 289
Reilly, William F., **7** 286
Reimers, Ed, **10** 51
Reims Aviation, **8** 92
Rein Elektronik, **10** 459
Reinemund, Steven, **7** 435
Reiner, Ephraim, **II** 206
Reinhard, Keith, **I** 32
Reinicker, Bill, **6** 444
Reinicker, Lawrence T. (Bill), **6** 443
Reinsdorf, Jerry, **IV** 703
Reinsurance Agency, **III** 204–05
Reisebüro Bangemann, **II** 164
Reisebüro Dr. Degener, **II** 163
Reisebüro Luhrs, **II** 163
Reisebüro Scharnow, **II** 164
Reisholz AG, **III** 693
Reiss, John (Sir), **III** 670–71
Reith, John C., **7** 52
Reiue Nationale des Usines Renault, **7** 220
Relational Database Systems Inc., **10** 361–62
Relational Technology Inc., **10** 361
Release Technologies, **8** 484
Reliable Tool, **II** 488
Reliance Capital Group, L.P., **III** 344
Reliance Development Group, Inc., **III** 344
Reliance Electric Company, IV 429; **9 439–42**
Reliance Financial Services Corp., **III** 343
Reliance Group Holdings, Inc., II 173; **III 342–44; IV** 642
Reliance Group, Inc., **III** 343
Reliance Insurance Co., **III** 342–44
Reliance Insurance Co. of Illinois, **III** 343
Reliance Insurance Co. of New York, **III** 343
Reliance Insurance Cos. of Philadelphia, **III** 342–43
Reliance Life Distributors, **III** 344
Reliance Life Insurance Co., **III** 275–76
Reliance Life Insurance Co. of Rhode Island, **III** 343
Reliance Lloyds, **III** 343
Reliance Marketing Management, **III** 344
Reliance National Insurance Co., **III** 343
Reliance Reinsurance Corp., **III** 343–44
Relly, Gavin, **IV** 23
Rembrandt Group, **I** 289; **IV** 91, 93, 97; **V** 411–13
Remgro, **IV** 97
Remington Arms, **I** 329; **8** 152
Remington Cash Register Co., **III** 151; **6** 265
Remington Rand, **III** 122, 126, 148, 151, 165–66, 642; **6** 251, 265, 281–82; **10** 255
Renault. *See* Régie Nationale des Usines Renault.
Renault, Fernand, **I** 189
Renault Frères, **I** 189
Renault, Louis, **I** 189
Renault, Marcel, **I** 189
Rendeck International, **11** 66
René Garraud, **III** 68
Renfrew, Glen, **IV** 670
Rengo Co., Ltd., IV 326
Rengo Shiki, **IV** 326
Renier, James, **II** 42; **8** 21–22

Rénier, Léon, **10** 346–47
Rennies Consolidated Holdings, **I** 470
Reno, Moritz, **III** 290
Renoir, **IV** 269
Renschard, William S., **II** 251
Renschler, C. Arnold, **11** 366
Rentschler, Frederick, **I** 47, 84–85, 441; **II** 469; **6** 104, 128; **9** 416–17; **10** 162–63, 536–37
Rentschler, Gordon, **II** 254; **9** 124
REPESA, **IV** 528
Repola Oy, **IV** 316, 347, 350
Reppe, Julius Walter, **I** 338
Repsol Butano, **IV** 528–29
Repsol Exploracion, **IV** 528
Repsol Petroleo, **IV** 528
Repsol Quimica, **IV** 528
Repsol SA, IV 396–97, 506, 514, **527–29**
Repubblica, **IV** 587
Republic, **6** 104
Republic Aircraft Co., **I** 89
Republic Airlines, **I** 113, 132
Republic Aviation Corporation, **I** 55; **9** 205–07
Republic Corp., **I** 447
Republic Engineered Steels, Inc., 7 446–47
Republic Indemnity Co. of America, **III** 191
Republic Insurance, **III** 404
Republic Locomotive, **10** 274
Republic New York Corporation, 11 415–19
Republic Pictures, **9** 75
Republic Powdered Metals, Inc., **8** 454
Republic Realty Mortgage Corp., **II** 289
Republic Rubber, **III** 641
Republic Steel Corp., **I** 491; **IV** 114; **7** 446
Republic Supply Co. of California, **I** 570
Research Analysis Corporation, **7** 15
Research Cottrell, Inc., **6** 441
Research Polymers International, **I** 321
Research Publications, **8** 526
Resem SpA, **I** 387
Residence Inn Co., **III** 103
Residence Inns, **9** 426
Residential Funding Corporation, **10** 92–93
Resinous Products, **I** 392
Resolution Trust Corp., **10** 117, 134; **11** 371
Resor, Stanley, **I** 17, 19–20, 36
Resorts International Inc., **I** 452
Resource Associates of Alaska, Inc., **7** 376
Resource Electronics, **8** 385
Rest Assured, **I** 429
Restaurant Franchise Industries, **6** 200
Restaurants Les Pres Limitée, **II** 652
Resurgens Communications Group, **7** 336; **8** 311
Retail Credit Company. *See* Equifax.
Retailers Commercial Agency, Inc., **6** 24
Retirement Inns of America, **III** 16
Retirement Inns of America, Inc., **11** 282
Reuben H. Donnelley Corp., **IV** 605, 661
Reunion Properties, **I** 470
Reuter, Edvard, **I** 151
Reuter, Herbert de (Baron), **IV** 669
Reuter, Julius (Baron), **IV** 668–69
Reuter, Paul-Julius, **10** 345
Reuter Trust, **IV** 669–70
Reuter's Telegram Co. Ltd., **IV** 668–69
Reuters Founders Share Co., **IV** 670
Reuters Holdings PLC, IV 259, 652, 654, 656, **668–70; 10** 277, 407

Reuters Ltd., **IV** 668, 669–70
Revco D.S., Inc., II 449; **III** 10; **V** **171–73; 9** 67, 187
Revco Optical Center, **V** 172
Revere Copper and Brass Co., **IV** 32
Reviglio, Franco, **IV** 422
Revlon, **6** 27; **8** 131
Revlon Development Corp., **III** 55
Revlon Group, Inc., I 29, 449, 620, 633, 668, 677, 693, 696; **II** 498, 679; **III** 29, 46, **54–57**, 727; **8** 341; **9** 202–03, 291; **11** 8
Revlon, Inc., **III** 54, 55–56; **11** 333–34
Revlon Products Corp., **III** 54–55
Revson Bros., **III** 54
Revson, Charles, **III** 54–56; **9** 202–03
Revson, Joseph, **III** 54
Rex Pulp Products Company, **9** 304
REX Stores Corp., 10 468–69
Rexall Drug & Chemical Co., **II** 533–34; **III** 610
Rexene Products Co., **III** 760; **IV** 457
Rexham Corp., **IV** 259
Rexham Inc., **8** 483–84
Rexnord, **I** 524
Reymer & Bros., Inc., **II** 508; **11** 172
Reymersholm, **II** 366
Reynolds, A. D., **IV** 187
Reynolds, A. William, **8** 206–07
Reynolds, Bill, **9** 248
Reynolds, David P., **IV** 186–87
Reynolds family, **IV** 187
Reynolds International, Inc., **IV** 186
Reynolds, J. Louis, **IV** 186–87
Reynolds, John J., **9** 333
Reynolds Metals Company, II 421–22; **IV** 11–12, 15, 59, **186–88; IV** 122
Reynolds, Peter, **II** 565
Reynolds, Quentin, **II** 655
Reynolds, R.J., **IV** 186
Reynolds, R.S., **IV** 186
Reynolds, Richard Joshua, **V** 408
Reynolds, Richard S., Jr., **IV** 186
Reynolds, S.C., **I** 158; **10** 292
Reynolds Securities, **IV** 186
Reynolds, William G., **IV** 186–87
Reynolds, William G., Jr., **IV** 187
RF Communications, **II** 38
RHC Holding Corp., **10** 13
Rhea, Cleaves, **10** 310
Rhee, Syngman, **I** 516
Rhein, Timothy J., **6** 354
Rhein-Elbe Gelsenkirchener Bergwerks A.G., **IV** 25
Rheinelbe Union, **I** 542
Rheinisch Kalksteinwerke Wulfrath, **III** 738
Rheinisch Oelfinwerke, **I** 306
Rheinisch-Westfälische Bank A.G., **II** 279
Rheinisch-Westfälischer Sprengstoff AG, **III** 694
Rheinisch-Westfälisches Elektrizatätswerke AG, **I** 542–43; **III** 154; **IV** 231; **V** 744
Rheinische Aktiengesellschaft für Braunkohlenbergbau, **V** 708
Rheinische Creditbank, **II** 278
Rheinische Metallwaaren- und Maschinenfabrik AG, **9** 443–44
Rheinische Wasserglasfabrik, **III** 31
Rheinmetall Berlin AG, 9 443–46
Rheinmetall GmbH, **9** 445–46
Rheinmetall-Borsig AG, **9** 444–45
Rheinsche Girozentrale und Provinzialbank, Düsseldorf, **II** 385

Rheinstahl AG, **IV** 222
Rheinstahl Union Brueckenbau, **8** 242
Rheintalische Zementfabrik, **III** 701
Rhenus-Weichelt AG, **6** 424, 426
Rhines, Walden, **11** 286
RHM. *See* Ranks Hovis McDougall.
Rhoades, Donald, **IV** 122
Rhodes & Co., **8** 345
Rhodes, Allen F., **9** 363
Rhodes, Cecil, **IV** 20, 64–65, 94; **7** 121–22
Rhodes, Daniel P., **8** 345
Rhodes, Edward E., **III** 303
Rhodes, J.B., **9** 38
Rhodes, Stephen H., **III** 265–66
Rhodesian Anglo American Ltd., **IV** 21, 23
Rhodesian Development Corp., **I** 422
Rhodesian Selection Trust, Ltd., **IV** 17–18, 21
Rhodesian Sugar Refineries, **II** 581
Rhodiaceta, **I** 388–89
Rhodia Corp., **IV** 191
Rhone-Poulenc, **8** 153
Rhône-Poulenc S.A., I 303–04, 371, **388–90**, 670, 672, 692; **III** 677; **IV** 174, 487, 547; **8** 452; **9** 358; **10 470–72** **(upd.)**
Rhymey Breweries, **I** 294
Rhythm Watch, **III** 454
La Riassicuratrice, **III** 346
Ribaud, Antoine, **II** 474–75
Riboud, Jean, **III** 617–18
de la Rica, Jose Miguel, **I** 460
Ricard, **I** 280
Ricard, Patrick, **I** 280–81
Ricard, Paul, **I** 280
Ricardo, David, **7** 165
Riccardo, John J., **I** 145; **11** 54
Rice Broadcasting Co., Inc., **II** 166
Rice, Caleb, **III** 285
Rice, Charles E., **9** 58
Rice, Donald, **10** 522
Rice, Donald B., **11** 364
Rice, George W., **III** 285
Rice, Isaac Leopold, **I** 57; **10** 315
Rice, Victor A., **III** 650, 652
Rice-Stix Dry Goods, **II** 414
Rich, Dick, **6** 50
Rich, Lee, **II** 149
Rich, Marc, **II** 170–71
Rich Products Corporation, 7 448–49
Rich, Robert E., Sr., **7** 448
Rich, Robert, Jr., **7** 448
Rich's, **9** 209; **10** 515
Richard A. Shaw, Inc., **7** 128
Richard D. Irwin Inc., **IV** 602–03, 678
Richard Hellman Co., **II** 497
Richard Manufacturing Co., **I** 667
Richard P. Simmons, **8** 19
Richard Shops, **III** 502
Richard Thomas & Baldwins, **IV** 42
Richards Bay Minerals, **IV** 91
Richards, Benjamin Wood, **II** 315
Richards, Henry M., **6** 596
Richards, J. T., **IV** 408–09
Richards, James, **8** 479
Richards, Jr., Roy, **8** 479
Richards, Michael, **I** 592–93
Richards, R. C., **6** 376
Richards, Roy, **8** 478–80
Richardson, Frank H., **IV** 541
Richardson, J. Ernest, **IV** 308
Richardson, Kenneth, **I** 196
Richardson, Willard, **10** 3

Richardson-Vicks Company, **III** 53; **8** 434
Richdale, Gordon, **IV** 79
Richetti, Edmondo, **III** 207
Richey, J.B., **11** 201
Richfield Oil Corp., **IV** 375–76, 456
Richfood Holdings, Inc., 7 450–51
Richie, Lionel, **I** 278; **10** 452
Richie, R.J., **6** 110
Richland Co-op Creamery Company, **7** 592
Richland Gas Company, **8** 349
Richman, Herb, **8** 137
Richman, John M., **II** 533–34; **7** 275–76
Richman, Paul, **11** 462–63
Richmon Hill & Queens County Gas Light Companies, **6** 455
Richmond American Homes of Florida, Inc., **11** 258
Richmond Carousel Corporation, **9** 120
Richmond Corp., **I** 600
Richter, Hermann, **IV** 141
Richway, **10** 515
Ricils, **III** 47
Rickel Home Centers, **II** 673
Rickenbacker, Eddie, **I** 78, 99, 101–02, 475; **6** 81; **9** 18; **11** 427
Ricker, John B., Jr., **III** 243
Ricketts, Thomas R., **9** 481–83
Rickover, Admiral, **10** 317
Rickover, Hyman, **I** 59
Ricoh Company, **8** 278
Ricoh Company, Ltd., III 121, 157, **159–61**, 172, 454; **6** 289
Ricoh Corp. (Canada), **III** 160
Ricoh Electronics, **III** 159–60
Ricoh Espana, **III** 160
Ricoh Finance, **III** 160
Ricoh France, **III** 160
Ricoh Industrie France, **III** 160
Ricoh Industries USA, **III** 159
Ricoh Nederlands, **III** 160
Ricoh of America, **III** 159
Ricoh UK Products Ltd., **III** 160
Ridder, Bernard, **IV** 582, 629
Ridder, Bernard H., Jr., **IV** 612–13, 629–30; **7** 191
Ridder, Herman, **IV** 628–29
Ridder, Joseph, **IV** 582, 629
Ridder Publications, **IV** 612–13, 629; **7** 191
Ridder, Tony, **IV** 630
Ridder, Victor, **IV** 582, 629
Riddle, D. Raymond, **11** 338
Riddle, Michael, **10** 118
Ridge Tool Co., **II** 19
Ridgely, Henry, **II** 315
Rieck-McJunkin Dairy Co., **II** 533
Riedy, John K., **III** 530
Riegel Bag & Paper Co., **IV** 344
Riegel, John S., **IV** 344
Rieke Corp., **III** 569; **11** 535
Riemsdijk, Henk van, **II** 79
Riepl, Franz Xaver, **6** 418
Rieter, Heinrich (Col.), **III** 402
Rieter Machine Works, **III** 638
Rietveld, Adrian, **10** 557–58
Rig Tenders Company, **6** 383
Riggin, F.L., **7** 359
Riggio, Leonard, **10** 135–36
Riggio, Vincent, **I** 13
Riggs, Gus, **II** 34
Rihachi, Taguchi, **6** 427
Rijkens, Paul, **II** 589
Rike's, **10** 282
Riken Corp., **IV** 160; **10** 493

Riken Kankoshi Co. Ltd., **III** 159
Riken Optical Co., **III** 159
Riklis Family Corp., 9 447–50
Riklis, Meshulam, **6** 367; **9** 447–49
Riku-un Moto Kaisha, **V** 477
Riley, Jr., Victor J., **8** 295–97
Riley, Richard, **III** 440
Riley, W.P., **III** 261
Rinaldi, Michael, **8** 449
Rincliffe, R. George, **11** 389
Riney, Hal, **I** 26; **7** 463
Ringköpkedjan, **II** 640
Ringoen, Richard M., **I** 597–98; **10** 129–30
Rini, Charles A., Sr., **9** 453
Rini Supermarkets, **9** 451
Rinker Materials Corp., **III** 688
Rio Grande Oil Co., **IV** 375, 456
Rio Grande Valley Gas Co., **IV** 394
Rio Sul Airlines, **6** 133
Rio Tinto Co., **IV** 58, 189–91
Rio Tinto Mining Co. of Australia, **IV** 59
Rio Tinto-Zinc Corp., **II** 628; **IV** 56, 58–61, 380
Rioblanco, **II** 477
Riordan Holdings Ltd., **I** 457; **10** 554
Ris, Victor, **III** 697
Riser Foods, Inc., 9 451–54
Rising, Adolf, **I** 625
Rising Sun Petroleum Co., **IV** 431, 460, 542
Risk Planners, **II** 669
Risley, Janie, **11** 298
Risley, Larry L., **11** 298–300
Risse, Klaus H., **I** 654
Rit Dye Co., **II** 497
Ritchie, Cedric E., **II** 223
Ritchie, Martin, **IV** 259
Rite Aid Corporation, V 174–76; 9 187, 346
Rite-Way Department Store, **II** 649
Rittenhouse and Embree, **III** 269
Ritty, James, **III** 150; **6** 264
Ritty, John, **III** 150; **6** 264
Ritz, Cesar, **9** 455–57
Ritz, Charles, **9** 457
Ritz-Carlton Hotel Company, 9 455–57
Riunione Adriatica di Sicurtà SpA, III 185, 206, **345–48**
River Boat Casino, **9** 425–26
River Steam Navigation Co., **III** 522
River-Raisin Paper Co., **IV** 345
Riverside Iron Works, Ltd., **8** 544
Riverside National Bank of Buffalo, **11** 108
Riverside Press, **10** 355–56
Riverwood International Corporation, 7 294; **11 420–23**
Rivett, Rohan, **IV** 650; **7** 389
Riviana Foods, **III** 24, 25
Rizzoli Publishing, **IV** 586, 588
RJR Nabisco, **I** 249, 259, 261; **II** 370, 426, 477–78, 542–44; **7** 130, 132, 277, 596; **9** 469. *See also* Nabisco Brands, Inc.
RJR Nabisco Holdings Corp., V 408–10, 415
RKO. *See* Radio-Keith-Orpheum.
RKO Radio Sales, **6** 33
RKO-General, Inc., **8** 207
RLA Polymers, **9** 92
RM Marketing, **6** 14
RMC Group p.l.c., III 734, **737–40**
RMC-Australia, **III** 738
RMF Inc., **I** 412

RMP International, Limited, **8** 417
Roach, Hal, **II** 147–48
Roach, John, **II** 106–07
Roadline, **6** 413–14
Roadway Bodegas y Consolidación, **V** 503
Roadway Express, **V** 502–03
Roadway Package System, (RPS), **V** 503
Roadway Services, Inc., V 502–03
Roaman's, **V** 115
Roan Consolidated Mines Ltd., **IV** 239–40
Roan Selection Trust Ltd., **IV** 18, 239–40
Robarts, David, **II** 334
Robb Engineering Works, **8** 544
Robbers, Jacobus George, **IV** 610
Robbins Co., **III** 546
Robbins, Harold, **IV** 672
Robbins, Joseph, **II** 666
Robbins, Jr., John M., **8** 30–31
Robbins, Julius, **II** 666
Robeco Group, **IV** 193
Robens (Lord), **IV** 39
Roberk Co., **III** 603
Robert Allen Cos., **III** 571
Robert Benson & Co. Ltd., **II** 232, 421
Robert Benson, Lonsdale & Co. Ltd., **II** 421–22; **IV** 191
Robert Bosch GmbH., I 392–93, 411; **III** 554, 555, 591, 593
Robert, Christopher D., **9** 139–40
Robert Fleming & Co., **I** 471; **IV** 79
Robert Fleming Holdings Ltd., **11** 495
Robert Garrett & Sons, Inc., **9** 363
Robert Grace Contracting Co., **I** 584
Robert Johnson, **8** 281–82
Robert, Joseph C., **I** 336
Robert R. Mullen & Co., **I** 20
Robert W. Baird & Co., **III** 324; **7** 495
Robert Warschauer and Co., **II** 270
Robert Watson & Co. Ltd., **I** 568
Roberts, Brian, **7** 91
Roberts Express, **V** 503
Roberts, George A., **I** 523; **10** 520, 522
Roberts, George R., **9** 180
Roberts, John C., **III** 528
Roberts, John G., **I** 508
Roberts, Johnson & Rand Shoe Co., **III** 528–29
Roberts, Lawrence, **6** 385–86
Roberts, Leonard H., **7** 475–76
Roberts, Leslie, **II** 426
Roberts, Ralph, **9** 428; **10** 473
Roberts, Ralph J., **7** 90
Roberts, Roy, **IV** 480
Robertson, A.W., **II** 120–21
Robertson, Brian, **V** 421
Robertson Building Products, **8** 546
Robertson, Charles, **II** 644; **11** 169
Robertson, Cliff, **II** 136
Robertson, Hugh, **II** 123
Robertson, Mary Ella, **III** 267
Robertson, Miles E., **7** 407
Robertson, Nelson, **III** 257
Robertson, Norman T., **III** 241
Robertson, Oran W., **V** 55
Robertson, Reuben B., **IV** 263–64
Robertson, Reuben B., Jr., **IV** 264
Robertson, Robert M., **IV** 278
Robertson-Ceco Corporation, **8** 546
Robespierre, Maximilian, **III** 391
Robie, Richard S., **6** 356
Robin Hood Flour Mills, Ltd., **7** 241–43
Robinair, **10** 492, 494
Robinson, Charles H., **11** 43
Robinson Clubs, **II** 163–64

Robinson, Edward G., **II** 175
Robinson, Frederick, **10** 82
Robinson, Henry, **V** 569
Robinson, Henry S., **III** 238
Robinson, Homer, **6** 65
Robinson, James D., III, **II** 398; **IV** 637; **9** 470; **10** 62–63; **11** 417
Robinson, Kinsey M., **6** 596–97
Robinson, M. Richard, Jr., **10** 480–81
Robinson, Maurice R., **10** 479–80
Robinson, Morris, **III** 305
Robinson, Philip, **11** 285
Robinson, R.G., **IV** 708
Robinson Radio Rentals, **I** 531
Robinson, W.S., **IV** 95
Robinson's Japan Co. Ltd., **V** 89
Robinson-Danforth Commission Co., **II** 561
Robinson-Humphrey, **II** 398; **10** 62
Roc, **I** 272
Rocco, Fiammetta, **III** 335
Roche Biomedical Laboratories, Inc., 11 424–26
Roche, Gus, **11** 67–68
Roche Holding, Limited, **11** 424
Roche Holdings Ltd., **8** 209–10
Roche Insurance Laboratory, **11** 425
Roche, James M., **9** 18
Roche Products Ltd., **I** 643
Le Rocher, Compagnie de Reassurance, **III** 340
Rochereau, Denfert, **II** 232
Rochester American Insurance Co., **III** 191
Rochester Gas And Electric Corporation, 6 571–73
Rochester German Insurance Co., **III** 191
Rochester Tel Mobile Communications, **6** 334
Rochester Telephone Company. *See* Rochester Telephone Corporation.
Rochester Telephone Corporation, 6 332–34
Rochester Telephonic Exchange. *See* Rochester Telephone Corporation.
Röchling Industrie Verwaltung GmbH, **9** 443
Rock, Arthur, **II** 44; **10** 365
Rock, David, **IV** 577
Rock Island Oil & Refining Co., **IV** 448–49
Rock Island Plow Company, **10** 378
Rock-Tenn Co., **IV** 312
Rockcor Ltd., **I** 381
Rockcote Paint Company, **8** 552–53
Rockefeller & Andrews, **IV** 426; **7** 169
Rockefeller Center Properties, **IV** 714
Rockefeller, David, **II** 248
Rockefeller family, **I** 286; **III** 80, 347
Rockefeller Group, **IV** 714
Rockefeller, James, **II** 254; **9** 124
Rockefeller, John D., **II** 247, 397; **IV** 31, 368, 379, 426–29, 463, 488, 530, 714; **V** 590; **7** 169–71, 351; **9** 370
Rockefeller, William, **IV** 31, 426–27, 463–64; **6** 455; **7** 169, 351–52
Rockefeller, William A., **IV** 426
Rockford Drilling Co., **III** 439
Rockland Corp., **8** 271
Rockland React-Rite, Inc., **8** 270
Rockmoor Grocery, **II** 683
Rockne, Knute, **I** 54
Rockower of Canada Ltd., **II** 649
Rockport Company, **V** 376–77

Rockwell International Corporation, I
71, **78–80**, 154–55, 186; **II** 3, 94, 379;
6 263; **7** 420; **8** 165; **9** 10; **10** 279–80;
11 268, 278, **427–30 (upd.)**, 473
Rockwell, Willard, **I** 79–80; **11** 428
Rockwell, Willard, Jr., **I** 79–80; **11**
428–29
Rockwell-Standard, **I** 79; **11** 428
Rocky Mountain Pipe Line Co., **IV** 400
Rodamco, **IV** 698
Roddick, Anita, **11** 40–41
Roddick, Gordon, **11** 40–42
Rodenburg, Nico, **II** 79
Roderick, David M., **IV** 574; **7** 551
Rodeway Inns, **II** 142; **III** 94
Rodeway Inns of America, **11** 242
Rodgers, Richard, **IV** 671
Rodling, Ejnar, **IV** 336
Roe, John, **8** 55
Roebuck, Alvah, **V** 180
Roehr Products Co., **III** 443
Roels, Bernadette, **I** 45
Roentgen, Wilhelm Conrad, **II** 97
Roermond, **IV** 276
Roessel, Heinrich, **IV** 69
Roessler & Hasslacher Chemical Co., **IV**
69
Roessler family, **IV** 69
Roessler, Friedrich Ernst, **IV** 69
Roessler, Hector, **IV** 69
Roger Williams Foods, **II** 682
Rogers Bros., **I** 672
Rogers, Henry H., **IV** 31–32
Rogers, Jack, **V** 534
Rogers, James, **11** 443
Rogers, James E., **8** 483
Rogers, James, Jr., **6** 557
Rogers, Justin T., Jr., **V** 677
Rogers, Nat S., **9** 530–31
Rogers, Richard, **III** 280; **9** 330–31
Rogers, Theodore, **10** 435
Rogers, William J., **II** 471
Rohatyn, Felix, **III** 616
Rohde, Gilbert, **8** 255
Röhm and Haas, I 391–93
Röhm, Otto, **I** 391–92
Rohmer, Bruno, **IV** 615
Rohölgewinnungs AG, **IV** 485
Rohr, Frederick Hilmer, **9** 458–59
Rohr Incorporated, 9 458–60
Rohr Industries, **I** 62; **11** 165
Rohwedder, Detlev (Dr.), **IV** 105
Roja, **III** 47
Rojtman, Marc Bori, **10** 379
Rokuosha, **III** 547
Rol Oil, **IV** 451
Rola Group, **II** 81
Roland Morat SA. *See* Roland Murten AG.
Roland Murten A.G., 7 452–53
Rolex, **8** 477
Rollalong, **III** 502; **7** 208
Rolland, Ian M., **III** 276
Röller, Wolfgang, **II** 283; **IV** 141
Rollins Burdick Hunter Co., **III** 204
Rollins Communications, **II** 161
Rollins, Gary, **11** 433–34
Rollins, Inc., 11 431–34
Rollins, John, **11** 431
Rollins, O. Wayne, **11** 431–33
Rollins Protective Services, **11** 431–34
Rollins, R. Randall, **11** 432, 434
Rollins Specialty Group, **III** 204
Rolls, Charles Stewart, **I** 81, 194; **7**
454–55

Rolls-Royce Diesels International, **III** 652
Rolls-Royce Motors Ltd., I 25–26,
81–82, 166, **194–96**; **9** 16–18, 417–18;
11 138, 403
Rolls-Royce plc, I 41, 55, 65, **81–83**, 481;
III 507, 556; **7 454–57 (upd.)**; **9** 244;
11 268
Rollwagen, John, **III** 129–31
Rolm Systems, **II** 99; **III** 149
Rolshoven, Hubertus, **IV** 196–97
Rolston, C.M., **IV** 438
Roman, Kenneth, **I** 26
Romano, Phil, **10** 177–78
Rombas, **IV** 226
Rome, Benjamin T., **8** 112–13
Rome Cable and Wire Co., **IV** 15
Rommel, Erwin (Gen.), **IV** 593
Romney, George, **I** 135–36
Rompetrol, **IV** 454
Ron Nagle, **I** 247
Ronchetti, Joseph F., **8** 168
Rondel's, Inc., **8** 135
Ronningen-Petter, **III** 468
Rood, Henry F., **III** 276
Rooke, Denis, **V** 562
Rooney, Francis C., **V** 136
Rooney, Phillip, **6** 600
Rooney, Tom, **6** 345
Roos, Victor, **8** 90
Roosen-Runge, Ludwig August, **III** 541
Roosevelt, Franklin Delano, **I** 71, 126, 154,
165, 354, 365; **II** 85, 88, 151; **III** 148,
283, 292, 325, 423, 451, 601, 720; **IV**
32, 36, 252, 332, 358, 391, 392, 595,
607, 626, 674, 683, 688–89; **9** 367, 411,
417; **11** 37, 72, 128, 137, 278, 296, 314,
339
Roosevelt, Isaac, **II** 216
Roosevelt, Nicholas, **9** 162
Roosevelt, Theodore, **II** 531; **III** 247; **IV**
375, 573; **7** 550
Root, C.G., **III** 762
Roots-Connersville Blower Corp., **III** 472
Roper Corp., **III** 655
Rorem, C. Rufus, **10** 159
Rorer, Gerald F., **I** 666
Rorer Group, I 666–68
Rorer, William H., **I** 666
Rorer-Amchem, **I** 666
Rose, Abraham, **V** 67
Rose, Ernest, **I** 639
Rose Foundation, **9** 348
Rose, George, **V** 67
Rose, Jack, **V** 67
Rose, Joe, **7** 138
Rose, Michael, **III** 94–95
Rose, Michael D., **9** 425–26
Rose, Rowland, G., **I** 654
Rose, Stuart, **10** 468
Rosefield Packing Co., **II** 497
Rosemount, Inc., **II** 20
Rosen, Arnold P., **11** 257
Rosen, Ben, **III** 124–25; **6** 221–22, 254
Rosen, David, **10** 482–83
Rosen Enterprises, Ltd., **10** 482
Rosenberg, Anna, **I** 710; **10** 549
Rosenberg, Arthur J., **III** 643
Rosenberg, Henry A., Jr., **7** 101–02
Rosenberg, Morris, **6** 17–18
Rosenberg, Seymour, **7** 305
Rosenberg, Theodore, **6** 17–18
Rosenblads Patenter, **III** 419
Rosendahl, Bill, **10** 211
Rosenfeld, Emanuel, **11** 391–92

Rosenfeld, Murray, **11** 391
Rosenfelt, Frank, **II** 149
Rosenkranz, George, **I** 701, 703
Rosenshine, Alan, **I** 29
Rosenthal, **I** 347
Rosenthal, Lewis S., **V** 207
Rosenthal, Milton, **IV** 80
Rosenthal, Morton, **9** 139–140
Rosenthal, Richard, **7** 87
Rosenwald, Julius, **V** 180–81; **7** 166
Rosenwald, Lessing J., **10** 50
Rosevear, **III** 690
Rosholt, Aanon Michael, **I** 423–24
Rosier, Harry, **IV** 246
Rosmini, Giambattista, **III** 206
Ross, Adam A., **9** 137
Ross Carrier Company, **8** 115
Ross Gear & Tool Co., **I** 539
Ross Hall Corp., **I** 417
Ross, John, **6** 359
Ross, Joseph J., **10** 296–97
Ross, Steven, **II** 176; **IV** 675; **7** 529
Ross, T. Edward, **9** 137
Ross, William Henry, **I** 240, 285
Rossendale Combining Company, **9** 92
Rossi, Walter, **10** 410
Rössing Uranium Ltd., **IV** 191
Rössinger, Ludwig, **V** 467–68
Rosso, Jean-Pierre, **10** 381
Rossotti, Charles O., **11** 18–19
Rossville Union Distillery, **I** 285
Rostocker Brauerei VEB, **9** 87
Roswell Electric Light Company, **6** 579
Roswell Gas and Electric Company, **6** 579
Roswell Public Service Company, **6** 579
Rota Bolt Ltd., **III** 581
Rotan Mosle Financial Corp., **II** 445
Rotary Lift, **III** 467–68
Rotax, **III** 555–56
Rotelcom Business Systems, **6** 334
Rotelcom Consulting Services, **6** 334
Rotelcom Data, Inc., **6** 334
Rotex, **IV** 253
Roth, William J., **III** 20
Rothermere (Lord). *See* Harmsworth,
Harold (Lord Rothermere).
Rothlein, Bernard, **II** 63; **6** 261
Rothman's Inc., **I** 438
Rothmans, IV 93
Rothmans International p.l.c., V 411–13
Rothmeier, Steven G., **I** 113–14; **6** 104
Rothschild, Edmond de, **6** 206
Rothschild, Emma, **I** 173
Rothschild family, **II** 201; **III** 206; **IV** 21,
107, 110, 530; **11** 453
Rothschild Group, **6** 206
Rothschild, Guy de (Baron), **IV** 107–08;
11 453
Rothschild Investment Trust, **I** 248; **III** 699
Rothschild, Nathan Mayer (N.M.), **III** 347,
372; **IV** 118
Rothschild, Walter, **V** 26
Rotodiesel, **III** 556
Rotor Tool Co., **II** 16
Rotterdam Bank, **II** 183–85
Rotterdam Lloyd, **6** 403–04
Roubos, Gary L., **III** 468
Rouge et Or, **IV** 614
Rouge, Francis, **I** 188
Rouge Steel Company, 8 448–50
Roundup Wholesale Grocery Company, **V**
55
Rouse Real Estate Finance, **II** 445
Roush, Carroll, **V** 502

Roush, Galen, **V** 502
Roussel family, **8** 451–52
Roussel, Gaston, **I** 669
Roussel, Gaston, Dr., **8** 451
Roussel, Jean-Claude, **I** 669; **8** 451
Roussel Laboratories, **I** 670
Roussel Uclaf, I 669–70; 8 451–53 (upd.)
Rousselet, André, **10** 195–96, 347
Rousselot, **I** 677
Roussy, Emile-Louis, **II** 546; **7** 381
Routh, J.P., **IV** 180–81
Roux, Ambroise, **IV** 615
Roux, Charles, **6** 379
Roux, Henri, **IV** 173
The Rover Cycle Company Ltd., **7** 458
Rover Group Ltd., **11** 31, 33
Rover Group Plc, I 186; **7 458–60**
Rowan, Rena, **11** 216–17
Rowan, Robert, **I** 170
Rowe, Brian, **9** 246
Rowe Bros. & Co., **III** 680
Rowe, Jack, **11** 315
Rowe Price-Fleming International, Inc., **11** 495
Rowland, James A., **II** 656
Rowland, Raymond E., **II** 562
Rowland, Roland W., **V** 468
Rowlett, John, **6** 142
Rowntree and Co. Ltd., **II** 476, 521, 568–69
Rowntree, B. Seebohm, **II** 568–69
Rowntree, Henry Isaac, **II** 568
Rowntree, John, **II** 569
Rowntree, Joseph, **II** 568
Rowntree Mackintosh, II 548, **568–70**
Rowntree Mackintosh Ltd., **II** 511, 569
Rowntree Mackintosh PLC, **II** 568–70; **7** 383
Rowntree, Wilhelm John, **II** 568
Roxana Petroleum Co., **IV** 531, 540
Roxoil Drilling, **7** 344
Roy Farrell Import-Export Company, **6** 78
Roy Rogers, **III** 102
Royal Aluminium Ltd., **IV** 9
Royal Baking Powder Co., **II** 544
Royal Bank of Australia, **II** 188
Royal Bank of Canada, II 344–46
Royal Bank of Canada Trust Co., **II** 345
Royal Bank of Queensland, **II** 188
Royal Bank of Scotland, **10** 336–37
Royal Bank of Scotland Group, **II** 298, 358
Royal Brewing Co., **I** 269
Royal Business Machines, **I** 207, 485; **III** 549
Royal Canada, **III** 349
Royal Caribbean, **6** 368
Royal Copenhagen A/S, **9** 99
Royal Crown Cola, **II** 468; **6** 21, 50; **8** 536–37
Royal Doulton Ltd., **IV** 659
Royal Dutch Harbour Co., **IV** 707
Royal Dutch Paper Co., **IV** 307
Royal Dutch Petroleum Company, IV 530–32, 657. *See also* Royal Dutch/Shell *and* The "Shell" Transport and Trading Company p.l.c.
Royal Dutch/Shell, **I** 368, 504; **III** 616; **IV** 132–33, 378, 406, 413, 429, 434, 453–54, 460, 491–92, 512, 515, 517–18, 530–32, 540–45, 557–58, 569; **7** 56–57, 172–73, 481–82. *See also* Royal Dutch Petroleum Company *and*

The "Shell" Transport and Trading Company p.l.c.
Royal Electric Company, **6** 501
Royal Exchange Assurance Corp., **III** 233–34, 278, 349, 369–71, 373
Royal Food Distributors, **II** 625
Royal General Insurance Co., **III** 242
Royal Hawaiian Macadamia Nut Co., **II** 491
Royal Heritage Life, **III** 351
Royal Insurance (Int) Ltd., **III** 350
Royal Insurance (UK), **III** 349–50
Royal Insurance Co., **III** 349–50
Royal Insurance Holdings plc, III 349–51
Royal Insurance plc, **III** 349
Royal International, **II** 457; **III** 349
Royal Interocean Lines, **6** 404
Royal Jordanian, **6** 101
Royal Life Holdings, **III** 349
Royal Life Insurance Ltd., **III** 350
Royal London Mutual Insurance, **IV** 697
Royal Mail, **V** 498
Royal Mail Group, **6** 416
Royal Orchid Holidays, **6** 122
Royal Orchid K Hotel, **6** 123
Royal Packaging Industries Van Leer B.V., **9** 305
Royal Pakhoed N.V., **9** 532
Royal Re, **III** 349
Royal Sash Manufacturing Co., **III** 757
Royal Securities Company, **6** 585
Royal Securities Corp. of Canada, **II** 425
Royal Trust Co., **II** 456–57
Royal Trustco, **II** 456; **V** 25
Royal Union Life Insurance Co., **III** 275
Royal USA, **III** 349
Royal Wessanen, **II** 527
Royale Belge, **III** 177, 394
La Royale Belge, **III** 200
Royalite, **I** 285
Royce Electronics, **III** 569
Royce, Frederick Henry, **I** 81, 194; **7** 454–55
Royce Ltd., **I** 194
Royko, Mike, **IV** 684
Royster, Vermont, **IV** 602
Rozes, **I** 272
RPC Industries, **III** 635
RPI. *See* Research Polymers International.
RPM Inc., 8 454–57
RPM Manufacturing Co., **III** 598
RSI Corp., **8** 141–42
Rt. Hon. Lord Young of Graffham, **6** 320
RTE Corp., **II** 17
RTL-Véronique, **IV** 611
RTZ Corporation PLC, IV 189–92; 7 261, 263
Rubber Latex Limited, **9** 92
Rubbermaid Incorporated, III 613–15
Rubel, Albert C., **IV** 570
Ruben, James, **II** 669
Rubenstein, Helena, **8** 167
Ruberoid Corp., **I** 339
Rubicam, Raymond, **I** 25, 36–38
Rubin, Gerard, **11** 216–17
Rubloff Inc., **II** 442
Rubry Owen, **I** 154
Ruby, **III** 47
Ruckelshaus, William D., **V** 750
Ruckleshaus, William, **6** 556
Rudd, Charles, **IV** 64, 94; **7** 121
Ruder, David, **10** 127
Rudisill Printing Co., **IV** 661

Rudloff, Hans-Joerg, **II** 268
Rudolf Wolff & Co., **IV** 165
Rudolph Eberstadt, Jr., **8** 366
Rudolph Fluor & Brother, **I** 569
de la Rue, Paul, **10** 267
de la Rue, Stuart, **10** 268
de la Rue, Thomas Andros, **10** 267–68
de la Rue, Warren, **10** 267–68
de la Rue, William, **10** 268
Ruenheck, Jerry, **II** 614
Rueping, F.J., **10** 328
Ruggles, Henriette Erhart, **I** 96
Ruhnau, Heinz, **I** 111
Ruhr-Zink, **IV** 141
Ruhrgas AG, V 704–06; **7** 141
Ruhrkohle AG, III 566; **IV** 26, 89, 105, **193–95**
Ruinart Père et Fils, **I** 272
Rukeyser, Merryle Stanley, **IV** 671
Rule, Elton, **II** 130
Rumbelows, **I** 532
Rumsfeld, Donald, **10** 321
Rumsfeld, Donald H., **I** 687–88
Runcorn White Lead Co., **III** 680
Rundell, Reid, **7** 462
Runnymede Construction Co., **8** 544
Runo-Everth Treibstoff und Ol AG, **7** 141
Rupert, Anton, **I** 289; **IV** 93
Rupley, Ira, **8** 87
Rural Bank, **IV** 279
Rurhkohle AG, **V** 747
Rush, Benjamin, **III** 224
Rush Laboratories, Inc., **6** 41
Rushdie, Salman, **IV** 615
Russ, Carl, **II** 520
Russell & Co., **II** 296
Russell Athletic Division, **8** 458
Russell, Benjamin C., **8** 458
Russell, Charles T., **9** 537
Russell Corporation, 8 458–59
Russell, Edwin, **IV** 582
Russell Electric, **11** 412
Russell Electronics, **II** 85
Russell, F.A., **IV** 601
Russell, Frank A., **10** 207
Russell Kelly Office Services, Inc. *See* Kelly Services Inc.
Russell, Majors & Waddell, **II** 381
Russell, Richard L., **6** 410
Russell, Thomas Dameron, **8** 458
Russell, Thomas W., **III** 225
Russell, Tom, **I** 159; **10** 293
Russell-Walling, Edward, **IV** 383
Russwerke Dortmund GmbH, **IV** 70
Rust, Edward B., Jr., **III** 364
Rust, Henry B., **I** 354
Rust International, **V** 754; **6** 599–600
Rust International Inc., 11 435–36
Rustenburg Platinum Co., **IV** 96, 118, 120
Rutenberg, Arthur, **8** 541
Rutenberg, Charles, **8** 541
Rutenberg, Lueder, **9** 86
Rutgerswerke, **8** 81
Rütgerswerke AG, **IV** 193
Rutherford, Andrew, **6** 15
Rutherford, Ernest, **I** 395
Rutherford, Ira, **11** 25
Ruti Machinery Works, **III** 638
Rutland Plastics, **I** 321
Rutledge, William P., **10** 522
Rutman, Bernard, **I** 244
Rutter, William, **10** 213
Ruvane, Joseph J., Jr., **I** 640; **9** 264
Ruzicka, Rudolph, **IV** 661

RWE, **V** 698–700
RWE Group, V 707–10
Ryan Aeronautical, **I** 525; **10** 522; **11** 428
Ryan Aircraft Company, **9** 458
Ryan, Claude, **9** 458
Ryan Homes, Inc., **8** 401–02
Ryan Insurance Co., **III** 204
Ryan, James P., **8** 460
Ryan, John, **11** 484
Ryan, John D., **11** 320
Ryan Milk Company of Kentucky, **7** 128
Ryan, Patrick G., **III** 204
Ryan, Thomas, **III** 247; **IV** 180
Rybicki, Irv, **7** 462
Rycade Corp., **IV** 365, 658
Rydelle-Lion, **III** 45
Ryder, Don, **IV** 666–67
Ryder, James A., **V** 504–05
Ryder Systems, Inc., V 504–06
Ryder Truck Rental System, Inc., **V** 504
Rydin, Bo, **IV** 339
Ryerson, Martin, **8** 133
The Ryland Group, Inc., 8 460–61
Ryobi Ltd., **I** 202
Ryukyu Cement, **III** 760
Ryvita Co., **II** 466

S & H Diving Corporation, **6** 578
S Pearson & Son (Contracting Department) Ltd., **IV** 658
S Pearson & Son Inc., **IV** 657
S Pearson & Son Ltd., **IV** 657–59
S Pearson Publishers Ltd., **IV** 658
S. & W. Berisford, **II** 514, 528
S&A Restaurant Corp., **7** 336; **10** 176
S.B. Penick & Co., **8** 548
S.B. Irving Trust Bank Corp., **II** 218
S.B. Penick & Co., **I** 708
S.C. Johnson & Son, Inc., I 14; **III** 45, **58–59**; **10** 173
S.C. Johnson Co., **8** 130
S.C. Johnson Wax. *See* S.C. Johnson & Son, Inc.
S-C-S Box Company, **8** 173
S.D. Cohn & Company, **10** 455
S.D. Warren Co., **IV** 329–30
S-E Bank Group, **II** 351
S-E-Banken, **II** 352–53
S.E. Massengill, **III** 66
S.F. Braun, **IV** 451
S.G. Warburg and Co., **II** 232, 259–60, 422, 629
S.H. Benson Ltd., **I** 25–26
S.I.P., Co., **8** 416
S.M.A. Corp., **I** 622
S.R. Dresser and Co., **III** 470
S.R. Dresser Manufacturing Co., **III** 470–71
S.S. Kresge Company, **V** 110–12
S.S. White Dental Manufacturing Co., **I** 383
S. Smith & Sons, **III** 555
S.T. Dupont, **III** 28
SAA. *See* South African Airways.
SAAB. *See* Svenska Aeroplan Aktiebolaget.
Saab-Scania, **V** 339
Saab-Scania A.B., I 197–98, 210; **III** 556; **10** 86; **11 437–39 (upd.)**
Saar-Gummiwerk GmbH, **IV** 197
Saarberg Öl und Handel, **IV** 199
Saarberg-Konzern, IV 196–99
Saarbergwerke AG, **IV** 196–99
Saarinen, Eero, **III** 463

Saarkohlenwertsoffe GmbH, **IV** 197
Saarländische Fernwärme GmbH, **IV** 197
Saarstahl AG, **IV** 228
Saatchi & Saatchi plc, I 21, 28, **33–35**, 36; **6** 53
Saatchi & Saatchi's Cleveland Consulting Associates, **6** 229
Saatchi, Charles, **I** 33; **6** 53
Saatchi, Maurice, **I** 33; **6** 53
SAB. *See* South African Breweries Ltd.
Saba, Shoichi, **I** 535
Sabah Timber Co., **III** 699
Sabena, **6** 96
Saber Energy, Inc., **7** 553–54
Sabine Corporation, **7** 229
Sabine Investment Co. of Texas, Inc., **IV** 341
de Sabla, Eugene, Jr., **V** 685
Sacerdoti, Piero, **III** 347
Sacher, Paul, **I** 642
Sachs, Arthur, **II** 414
Sachs, Harry, **II** 414
Sachs, Henry E., **II** 414
Sachs, Howard J., **II** 414
Sachs, Jonathan, **6** 254
Sachs, Samuel, **II** 414
Sachsen-Weimar (Grand Duke of), **III** 445
Sachsgruppe, **IV** 201
Sacilor, **IV** 174, 226–27
Sackett, Augustine, **III** 762
Sackett Plasterboard Co., **III** 762
Sacks Industries, **8** 561
SACOR, **IV** 250, 504–06
SACOR MARITIMA, **IV** 505
Sacramento Savings & Loan Association, **10** 43, 45
Sadat, Anwar, **6** 86
Sadler, Carl L., **9** 460
Sadoine, Eugene, **IV** 51
Saeger Carbide Corp., **IV** 203
Saeki, Akira, **II** 96
Saemann, Sandy, **8** 304
Saes, **III** 347
SAFECARE Co., **III** 353
SAFECO Corporation, III 352–54
SAFECO Credit Co., **III** 353
SAFECO Insurance Co. of America, **III** 353
SAFECO Life Insurance Co., **III** 353
SAFECO Title Insurance Co., **10** 44
Safeguard Scientifics, Inc., 10 232–34, **473–75**
Safety Fund Bank, **II** 207
Safety Rehab, **11** 486
Safety Savings and Loan, **10** 339
Safety-Kleen Corp., 8 462–65
Safety-Kleen of Ireland, **8** 464
Safeway, **11** 239, 241
Safeway Stores Incorporated, II 424, 601, 604–05, 609–10, 628, 632, 637, **654–56**; **6** 364; **7** 61, 569; **9** 39; **10** 442
Safmarine, **IV** 22
Safra, Edmond, **11** 415–18
Safrap, **IV** 472
Saga, **IV** 406
Saga Corp., **II** 608; **III** 103
Sagan, Bruce, **III** 214
Sagittarius Productions Inc., **I** 286
Sahlberg, Karl-Erik, **I** 387
Sahlin, Gustaf, **III** 479
Saia Motor Freight Line, Inc., **6** 421–23
Saibu Gas, **IV** 518–19
Saiccor, **IV** 92
Said, Qaboos bin (Sultan), **IV** 515

Saihei, Hirose, **V** 473
Sain, Martin, **IV** 504
Sainer, Leonard, **V** 178
Sainrapt et Brice, **9** 9
Sainsbury, Alan, **II** 658
Sainsbury, Alfred, **II** 657
Sainsbury, Arthur, **II** 657–58
Sainsbury, David, **II** 658
Sainsbury, Frank, **II** 657
Sainsbury, George, **II** 657
Sainsbury, James, **II** 658
Sainsbury, John, **II** 658–59
Sainsbury, John Benjamin, **II** 657–58
Sainsbury, John James, **II** 657, 659
Sainsbury, Paul, **II** 657
Sainsbury, Robert, **II** 658
Sainsbury's. *See* J Sainsbury PLC.
St. Jude Medical, Inc., 11 458–61
Saint Paul Fire and Marine Insurance Co., **III** 355–56
St. Regis Corporation, **10** 265
Saint-Gobain. *See* Compagnie de Saint Gobain S.A.
Saint-Gobain Pont-à-Mousson, **IV** 227
Saint-Quirin, **III** 676
Sainte Anne Paper Co., **IV** 245–46
Saipem, **IV** 420–22, 453
Saison Group, **V** 184–85, 187–89
Saito Bros. Co., **IV** 268
Saito, Chiichiro, **IV** 268
Saito family, **IV** 268
Saito, Kenzo, **II** 109
Saito, Kikuzo, **IV** 269
Saito, Kiminori, **IV** 268–69
Saito Ltd., **IV** 268
Saito, Ryoei, **IV** 268–69
Saito, Shoichi, **I** 204; **11** 529
Saiwa, **II** 543
Sajak, Pat, **9** 306
Sakakura, Yoshiaki, **V** 143
Sakamaki, Hideo, **9** 386
Sakata, Koshiro, **III** 298
Sakiya, Tetuus, **I** 176
Saklatvala, Shapurji, **IV** 217
Sako, Seiji, **II** 292
Sakong, Il, **I** 517
Saks Fifth Avenue, **I** 426
Sakurai Co., **IV** 327
Salada Foods, **II** 525
Salazar, Antonio, **IV** 506
Salem Carpet Mills, Inc., **9** 467
Salem, Vita, **III** 345
Salen Energy A.B., **IV** 563
Saligman, Harvey, **III** 530–31
Salinger, Pierre, **I** 97
Salisbury (Marquis of), **III** 433
Salizzoni, Frank L., **II** 679–80
Sall, John, **10** 476
Sallie Mae. *See* Student Loan Marketing Association.
Sally Beauty Company, Inc., **8** 15–17
Salmi, Pentti, **IV** 276
Salmon Carriers, **6** 383
Salmon, John, **I** 34
Salomon, Arthur, **II** 447–49
Salomon Bros. & Hutzler, **II** 447
Salomon Bros. Asia, Ltd., **II** 449
Salomon Bros. Inc., **I** 630–31; **II** 268, 400, 403, 406, 426, 432, 434, 441, 447–49; **III** 221, 721; **IV** 137; **9** 378–79, 386. *See also* Salomon Inc.
Salomon Brothers Holding Co., **7** 114
Salomon Brothers Inc., **11** 35, 371
Salomon Commercial Finance AG, **II** 447

Salomon, Ferdinand, **II** 447
Salomon, Herbert, **II** 447–48
Salomon Inc., II 447–49; III 215; **IV** 80.
    See also Salomon Bros. Inc.
Salomon, Percy, **II** 447
Salomon, William, **II** 447–48
Salora, **II** 69
Salsåkers Ångsågs, **IV** 338
Salsbury, Stephen, **I** 330
Salt, Thomas, **II** 307
Salten, Felix, **IV** 671
Saltos del Sil, **II** 197
Salzgitter AG, IV 128, 198, **200–01**
Sam, Earl, **V** 90–91
Sam Goody, **I** 613; **9** 360–61
Sam's Clubs, **V** 216–17; **8** 555–57
Sam's Wholesale Clubs, **V** 216
Samancor Ltd., **IV** 92–93
Sambre-et-Moselle, **IV** 52
Samcor Glass, **III** 685
Samedan Oil Corporation, **11** 353
Samford, Frank P., Jr., **9** 507
Samford, Frank Park, **9** 506–07
Samim, **IV** 422
Samkong Fat Ltd. Co., **III** 747
Sammet, Jacque W., **III** 230
Sammis, Walter, **V** 676–77
Samna Corp., **6** 256
Samory, Luigi Vita, **IV** 588
Samples, R.E., **7** 33–34
Sampsell, Marshall, **6** 605
Sampson, Anthony, **I** 106, 122, 464
Sampson, Halbert G., **8** 99
Samsonite, **6** 50
Samsung Group, I 515–17; II 53–54; **III**
    143, 457–58, 517, 749; **IV** 519; **7** 233
The Samuel Austin & Son Company, **8** 41
Samuel, Harold, **IV** 696, 704–06
Samuel, Marcus, **IV** 530
Samuel, Marcus, Jr., **IV** 530
Samuel Meisel & Co., **11** 80–81
Samuel Montagu & Co., **II** 319
Samuel Moore & Co., **I** 155
Samuel, Samuel, **IV** 530
Samuel Samuel & Co., **IV** 530, 542
Samways, G.S., **I** 605
Samwha Paper Co., **III** 748
San Antonio Public Service Company, **6**
    473
San Diego Gas & Electric Company, V
    711–14; 6 590; **11** 272
San Giorgio Macaroni Inc., **II** 511
San Miguel Corp., **I** 221
SAN-MIC Trading Co., **IV** 327
Sanborn Co., **III** 142; **6** 237
Sanborn, Richard D., **V** 436
Sanchez, Joseph, **7** 462
Sand, George, **IV** 617
Sandberg, Michael, **II** 298; **IV** 717
Sandbulte, Arend "Sandy," **11** 315
Sandburg, Carl, **IV** 607
Sander, Ludwig, **III** 561
Sanders Associates, **9** 324
Sanders, Harland (Col.), **I** 260; **7** 265–67;
    8 563, 565
Sanders, Jerry, **6** 215–16
Sanderson & Porter, **I** 376
Sanderson Computers, **10** 500
Sandilands, Francis (Sir), **III** 234
Sandoz A.G., **7** 452
Sandoz Alimentation SA, **7** 452
Sandoz, Edouard, **I** 671
Sandoz Ltd., I 632–33, **671–73,** 675; **7**
    315; **8** 108–09, 215; **11** 173

Sandoz Pharmaceuticals Corporation, **10**
    48, 199
de Sandrinelli, Scipione, **III** 346
Sands, Comfort, **II** 216
Sandsund, A., **IV** 275
Sandvik AB, III 426–27; **IV 202–04**
Sandvik Coromant, **IV** 203
Sandvikens Jernwerks Aktiebolag, **IV**
    202–03
Sandwell, Inc., **6** 491
Sandys, Duncan, **I** 50
SANFLO Co., Ltd., **IV** 327
Sanford, Charles S., **II** 229, 231
Sanford I. Weill, **10** 62
Sanford, Richard D., **6** 243–45
Sanger, George P., **III** 265
Sangu Express Company, **V** 463
Sanitary Farm Dairies, Inc., **7** 372
Sanitas Food Co., **II** 523
Sanjushi Bank, **II** 347
Sanka Coffee Corp., **II** 531
Sankey, Joseph, **III** 493
Sankin Kai Group, **II** 274
Sanko K.K., **I** 432, 492
Sanko Steamship Co., **I** 494; **II** 311
Sankyo Company, 8 153
Sankyo Company Ltd., I 330, **674–75;**
    III 760
Sankyo Shoten, **I** 674
Sanlam, **IV** 91, 93, 535
Sano Railway Company, **6** 430
Sanofi. *See* Sanofi Winthrop.
Sanofi Elf Bio Industries, **I** 677
Sanofi Group, I 304, **676–77; III** 18; **IV**
    546
Sanofi Winthrop, **7** 484–85
Sanseisha Co., **IV** 326
Sant, Roger, **10** 25–27
Sant'Anna, Carlos, **II** 503
Santa Ana Savings and Loan, **10** 339
Santa Cruz Operation, **6** 244
Santa Cruz Portland Cement, **II** 490
Santa Fe Industries, **II** 448
Santa Fe International, **IV** 451–52
Santa Fe Pacific Corporation (SFP), V
    507–09
Santa Fe South Pacific Corporation, **6** 599
Santa Fe Southern Pacific Corp., **III** 512;
    IV 721; **6** 150; **9** 391
Santa Rosa Savings and Loan, **10** 339
Santiam Lumber Co., **IV** 358
Santo, Espirito (family), **IV** 506
Santos, Dante, **6** 107
Sanus Corp. Health Systems, **III** 317
Sanwa Bank, Ltd., II 276, 326, **347–48,**
    442, 511; **III** 188, 759; **IV** 150–51; **7**
    119
Sanwa Bank of California, **II** 348
Sanwa Business Credit Corp., **II** 348
Sanyo, **6** 101
Sanyo Chemical Manufacturing Co., **III**
    758
Sanyo Electric Company, Ltd., I 516; **II**
    55–56, **91–92; III** 569, 654
Sanyo Electric Works, **II** 91
Sanyo Ethylene Co. Ltd., **IV** 476
Sanyo Fisher (U.S.A.) Corp., **II** 92
Sanyo North America Corp., **II** 92
Sanyo Petrochemical Co. Ltd., **IV** 476
Sanyo Pulp Co., **IV** 327
Sanyo Railway Co., **I** 506; **II** 325
Sanyo-Kokusaku Industry Co., **IV** 327
Sanyo-Kokusaku Pulp Co., Ltd., IV 326,
    327–28

Sanyo-Scott, **IV** 327
SAP AG, **11** 78
Sapac, **I** 643
Sapirstein Greeting Card Company, **7** 23
Sapirstein, Harry, **7** 23
Sapirstein, Irving, **7** 23
Sapirstein, Jacob, **7** 23
Sapirstein, Morris, **7** 23
Sappi Ltd., **IV** 91–93
Sapporo Breweries Ltd., I 9, 220, 270,
    282–83, 508, 615; **II** 326
Sapporo Liquor, **I** 282
Sara Lee Corporation, I 15, 30; **II**
    571–73, 675; **7** 113 **8** 262; **10** 219–20;
    11 15, 486. *See also* Kitchens of Sara
    Lee.
Saraw, Arnold F., **III** 765
Sardanis, Andrew, **IV** 239
Sargeant, William H., **III** 286
Sargent & Lundy, **6** 556
Sargent, John A., **IV** 409
Sarget S.A., **IV** 71
SARMA, **III** 623–24
Sarni, Vincent A., **III** 732
Sarno, Jay, **6** 199–200, 203
Sarnoff, David, **II** 88–89, 120, 151; **6** 164
Sarnoff, Robert, **II** 90
Sarotti A.G., **II** 546
Sarpe, **IV** 591
Sartoretti, Luciano, **6** 69
Sartre, Jean-Paul, **IV** 586
SAS. *See* Scandinavian Airlines System.
SAS Institute Inc., 10 476–78
SAS International Hotels, **I** 120
Sasaki, Kunihiko, **II** 292
Sasaki, Sosuke, **V** 477–78
Saseba Heavy Industries, **II** 274
Sasol Limited, IV 533–35
Sason Corporation, **V** 187
Sassoon family, **IV** 699
Sasuga, Nobuo, **III** 715
SAT. *See* Stockholms Allmänna
    Telefonaktiebolag.
Satellite Business Systems, **III** 182
Satellite Information Services, **II** 141
Satellite Software International, **10** 556
Satellite Television PLC, **IV** 652; **7** 391
Satellite Transmission and Reception
    Specialist Company, **11** 184
Säteri Oy, **IV** 349
Sato, Eisaku, **III** 139
Sato, Kazuo, **I** 495, 535
Sato Yasusaburo, **I** 266
Satoh, Kiichiro, **II** 326
Satre, Wendell J., **6** 597
Saturday Evening Post Co., **II** 208; **9** 320
Saturn Corporation, III 593, 760; **7**
    461–64
SATV. *See* Satellite Television PLC.
Saucona Iron Co., **IV** 35; **7** 48
Saudi Arabian Airlines, 6 84, **114–16**
Saudi Arabian Basic Industries Corp., **IV**
    538
Saudi Arabian Oil Company, IV 536–39.
    See also Arabian American Oil Co.
Saudi Arabian Parsons Limited, **8** 416
Saudi Aramco. *See* Saudi Arabian Oil
    Company.
Saudi British Bank, **II** 298
Saudi Consolidated Electric Co., **IV** 538
Saudi Refining Inc., **IV** 539
Saudia. *See* Saudi Arabian Airlines.
Sauer Motor Co., **I** 177
Saul, Charlie, **7** 18

Saul Lerner & Co., **II** 450
Saul, Ralph, **II** 403; **III** 226
Saunders, Arnold C., **8** 345
Saunders, Charles, **III** 568
Saunders, Ernest, **I** 251–52
Saunders, Joe, **10** 419
Saunders, Stuart, **V** 484; **10** 73
Saunders, William Lawrence, **III** 525–26
Saunders-Roe Ltd., **IV** 658
Sautier, René, **I** 303, 676–77
Sauvageot, Jacques, **IV** 618
Sav-on Drug, **II** 605
Sav-X, **9** 186
Savacentre, **II** 658
Savage Shoes, Ltd., **III** 529
Savannah Foods & Industries, Inc., 7 465–67
Savannah Gas Company, **6** 448
Save & Prosper Group, **10** 277
Save-A-Lot, **II** 682; **11** 228
Saviem, **III** 543
Savin, **III** 159
Savings of America, **II** 182
Savio, **IV** 422
Oy Savo-Karjalan Tukkuliike, **8** 293
Savon Sellu Mills, **IV** 315
Savory Milln, **II** 369
Savoy Group, **I** 248; **IV** 705
Sawers, John, **II** 187–88
Sawyer, E.P., **9** 553
Sawyer Electrical Manufacturing Company, **11** 4
Saxe-Coburg-Gotha (Duke of), **IV** 669
Saxon and Norman Cement Co., **III** 670
Saxon Oil, **11** 97
Sayama Sekiyu, **IV** 554
Sayre, Grover, **9** 360
SBC. *See* Southwestern Bell Corporation.
SBC Portfolio Management International, Inc., **II** 369
Sberbank, **II** 242
SCA. *See* Svenska Cellulosa Aktiebolaget.
SCA Services, Inc., **V** 754; **9** 109
Scala, C. George, **10** 392
Scalfari, Eugenio, **IV** 586–87
Scali, McCabe and Sloves Co., **I** 27
Scalise, George M., **10** 403–04
Scan Screen, **IV** 600
Scana Corporation, 6 574–76
Scandinavian Airlines System, I 107, **119–20**, 121; **6** 96, 122
Scandinavian Bank, **II** 352
Scandinavian Banking Partners, **II** 352
Scandinavian Trading Co., **I** 210
ScanDust, **III** 625
Scania-Vabis, **I** 197–98. *See also* Saab-Scania AB.
Scanlon, Michael J., **IV** 306–07
Scanlon, Peter, **I** 438
Scarborough Public Utilities Commission, 9 461–62
Scarborough, William W., **6** 465
Scargill, Arthur, **IV** 40
Sceales, Ted, **I** 288
SCEcorp, V 713–14, **715–17**; **6** 590
Schacht, Henry, **I** 147–48
Schachte, Henry, **I** 21
Schaeberle, Robert, **II** 544; **7** 367
Schaefer, Alfred, **II** 378
Schaefer, George A., **III** 453
Schaefer, John F., **8** 126
Schaefer, John P., **6** 591
Schaeffer, Charles, **11** 493–94
Schaeffler, Johann, **I** 42

Schaffhausenschor Bankverein, **II** 281
Schaffner, Alfred, **III** 632; **8** 248
Schall, Richard, **7** 256
Schalon, Edward I., **10** 493
Schar, Dwight C., **8** 401
Scharff-Koken Manufacturing Co., **IV** 286
Scharffenberger, George T., **III** 263–64
Scharnow, **II** 163–64
Scharnow, Wilhelm, **II** 164
Scharnow-Reisen GmbH. K.G., **II** 164
Scharp, Anders, **III** 479–81
Schary, Dore, **II** 148
Schaum Publishing Co., **IV** 636
Schauman, Wilhelm, **IV** 301–02
Schauman Wood Oy, **IV** 277, 302
Scheinfeld, Aaron, **9** 326
Schenck, Joseph M., **II** 146, 148, 169
Schenck, Nicholas, **II** 148
Schenk, Boyd F., **7** 430
Schenker & Co. GmbH, **6** 424–26
Schenker, Eduard, **6** 425
Schenker Eurocargo AG, **6** 424
Schenker, Gottfried, **6** 424–25
Schenker International AG, **6** 424
Schenker Waggon- und Beteiligungs AG, **6** 424
Schenker-Angerer, August, **6** 425
Schenker-Rhenus Ag, 6 424–26
Schenley Industries Inc., **I** 226, 285; **9** 449; **10** 181
Scherer. *See* R.P. Scherer.
Scherer, Robert Pauli, **I** 678–79
Scherer, Robert Pauli, Jr., **I** 678–79
Schering & Glatz, **I** 681
Schering A.G., I 681–82, 684, 701; **10** 214
Schering Corp., **I** 681–83
Schering, Ernest, **I** 681
Schering USA, **I** 640
Schering-Plough, I 682, **683–85**; **II** 590; **III** 45, 61; **11** 142, 207
Schermer, Lloyd G., **11** 252
Schicht Co., **II** 588
Schicht, Georg, **II** 589
Schick Shaving, **I** 711; **III** 55
Schickendanz, Gustav, **V** 165–66
Schieffelin & Co., **I** 272
Schiemann, Ron, **9** 435
Schieren, Wolfgang, **III** 185, 348
Schierl, Paul J., **8** 197
Schiller, Karl, **IV** 194
Schimberni, Mario, **I** 369
Schimmelbusch, Heinz (Dr.), **IV** 141
Schinas, John, **9** 170–71
Schindler, Edwin C., **7** 479
Schindler Holdings, **II** 122
Schisgall, Oscar, **I** 450
Schlaet, Arnold, **IV** 551
Schlage Lock Co., **III** 526
Schlapp, Hermann, **IV** 44
Schlein, Dov C., **11** 417
Schleppschiffahrtsgesellschaft Unterweser, **IV** 140
Schlesinger, John, **6** 163
Schlesinger, Theodore, **V** 26
Schlesischer Bankverein, **II** 278
Schlitz Brewing Co., **I** 218, 255, 268, 270, 291, 600; **10** 100
Schloemer, Paul, **III** 603
Schlumberger, Conrad, **III** 616–17
Schlumberger, Dominique, **III** 617
Schlumberger Limited, III 429, 499, **616–18**
Schlumberger, Marcel, **III** 616–17

Schlumberger, Paul, **III** 616
Schlumberger, Pierre, **III** 617
Schlumberger Well Surveying Corp., **III** 616–17
Schmidheiny, Ernst, **III** 701
Schmidheiny, Max, **III** 701
Schmidheiny, Thomas, **III** 701
Schmidt, **I** 255
Schmidt, Adolph, **9** 547
Schmidt, Benno C., **IV** 83; **7** 187
Schmidt, Georg, **III** 376
Schmidt, Helmut, **II** 257, 279–80
Schmidt, Henry G., **7** 369–70
Schmidt, Josef, **II** 386
Schmidt, Peter, **9** 547
Schmidt, Ronald V., **10** 510, 512
Schmidt, Werner, **7** 428
Schmidt-Scheuber, Theodor, **II** 283
Schmidtmann, Waldemar, **8** 264–65
Schmiege, Robert, **6** 378
Schmitt, Kurt (Dr.), **III** 183–85, 300
Schmitt, Robert L., **V** 219
Schmitz, Paul A., **11** 39
Schmöle, Heinz, **III** 400
Schneider, Abe, **II** 136
Schneider, Charles, **II** 93
Schneider Co., **III** 113
Schneider et Cie, **IV** 25
Schneider, Eugene, **II** 354
Schneider, Joseph, **II** 354
Schneider S.A., II 93–94
Schneiderman, Howard, **I** 367
Schoeller, Alexander, **IV** 85
Schoeller, Hermann, **IV** 85
Schoellhorn, Robert, **11** 8–9
Schoellhorn, Robert A., **I** 619–20
Schoerghuber, Joseph, **II** 242
Schoffler, Heinz, **7** 453
Schoffler, Leopold, **7** 452–53
Schofield, Seth, **6** 131
Scholastic Corporation, 10 479–81
Scholey, Robert, **IV** 43
Scholl Inc., **I** 685
Scholz Homes Inc., **IV** 115
Schöndorff, Hermann, **V** 101
Schonrock, Keith, **6** 247
Schoonover, John A., **11** 554
Schorr, Daniel, **II** 133
Schott, Erich, **III** 446
Schott Glass Technologies Inc., **III** 446
Schott Glaswerke, **III** 445–47
Schott, Max, **IV** 17–18
Schott, Otto, **III** 445–46
Schott-Ruhrglas GmbH, **III** 446
Schott-Zwiesel-Glaswerke AG, **III** 446
Schrader Bellows, **III** 603
Schreiner, Carl, **III** 299
Schreyer, William A., **II** 425
Schriftgiesser, Karl, **III** 363
Schroder Darling & Co., **II** 389
Schroeder, John P., **III** 708; **7** 293
Schroeder, Kenneth L., **11** 232
Schroeder, Major R. W., **6** 128
Schroeder, R.W., **I** 128
Schroer, Edmund A., **6** 533
Schroeter, White and Johnson, **III** 204
Schroter, R. William, **7** 440
Schub, Craig, **11** 379
Schuchart, John A., **7** 324–25
Schueler, Jacob, **I** 236
Schueller, Eugène, **III** 46–47; **8** 341–43
Schuenke, Donald, **III** 324
Schuitema, **II** 642
Schuler, Jack W., **11** 9

Schuller International, Inc., **11** 421
Schulman, Alex, **8** 6–7
Schulman, Gerald, **III** 254
Schulte, Heinrich, **IV** 589
Schultz, Charles M., **IV** 608, 620
Schultz, Gerald, **9** 63
Schulze, Richard M., **9** 65–66
Schumacher Co., **II** 624
Schumacher, Ferdinand, **II** 558
Schuster, M. Lincoln, **IV** 671–72
Schwab, Charles, **8** 94
Schwab, Charles M., **III** 282; **IV** 35–36,
   110, 572; **7** 29, 48–49, 549
Schwabe-Verlag, **7** 42
Schwabel, William, **IV** 66
Schwalm, Luther, **11** 273
Schwan, Marvin, **7** 468–69
Schwan, Paul, **7** 468–69
**Schwan's Sales Enterprises, Inc., 7
   468–70**
Schwartz, Bernard, **8** 338–39; **9** 323–24
Schwartz, Fredric N., **III** 17; **9** 88
Schwartz, Robert, **III** 293–94
Schwarzkopf, Norman, **11** 166
Schweber, Seymour, **9** 55
Schwed, Peter, **IV** 672
Schweiz Allgemeine, **III** 377
Schweiz Allgemeine Direkt Versicherung
   AG, **III** 377
Schweiz Allgemeine Versicherungs-Aktien-
   Gesellschaft, **III** 377
Schweiz Transport-Vericherungs-
   Gesellschaft, **III** 410
Schweizer Rück Holding AG, **III** 377
Schweizer, Samuel, **II** 369
Schweizerische Bankgesellschaft AG, **II**
   379; **V** 104
Schweizerische Kreditanstalt, **III** 375, 410;
   6 489
Schweizerische Lebensversicherungs-und
   Rentenanstalt, **III** 375
Schweizerische Nordostbahn, **6** 424
**Schweizerische Post-, Telefon- und
   Telegrafen-Betriebe, V 321–24**
Schweizerische Ruckversicherungs-
   Gesellschaft. *See* Swiss Reinsurance
   Company.
Schweizerische Unfallversicherungs-
   Actiengesellschaft in Winterthur, **III** 402
Schweizerische Unionbank, **II** 368
Schweizerischer Bankverein, **II** 368
Schwemm, John B., **IV** 661
Schwenk, Otto G., **III** 467
Schweppe, Jacob, **II** 476
Schweppe, Paul & Gosse, **II** 476
Schweppes France, **II** 477
Schweppes Ltd., **I** 220, 288; **II** 476
Schweppes South Africa, **II** 477
Schweppes USA, **II** 477
Schwettmann, Fred, **10** 464
Schwitzer, **II** 420
SCI. *See* Service Corporation International.
SCI Manufacturing, Inc., **9** 464
SCI Systems, Inc., 9 463–64
SCI Technology, Inc., **9** 464
Scientific Communications, Inc., **10** 97
Scientific Data Systems, **II** 44; **III** 172; **6**
   289; **10** 365
Scientific Games, Inc., **III** 431
Scientific-Atlanta, Inc., 6 335–37
Scifres, Robert, **10** 422
SciMed Life Systems, **III** 18–19
Scioto Bank, **9** 475

SCM Corp., **I** 29; **III** 502; **IV** 330; **7** 208;
   8 223–24
Scobie, John C., **9** 423
Scohier, Pierre, **V** 65
Scor SA, **III** 394
Scot Bowyers, **II** 587
Scotia Securities, **II** 223
Scotiabank. *See* The Bank of Nova Scotia.
Scotsman Industries, **II** 420
Scott & Fetzer Co., **III** 214
Scott, Arthur Hoyt, **IV** 329
Scott, B.A., **III** 228
Scott, Bernard, **III** 556
Scott, C. Dennis, **10** 186–87
Scott, Clarence R., **IV** 329
Scott Communications, Inc., **10** 97
Scott, E. Irvin, **IV** 329
Scott, Foresman, **IV** 675
Scott, George E., **7** 30
Scott Graphics, **IV** 289; **8** 483
Scott, J.D., **7** 412
Scott, J.L., **7** 20
Scott, Joe, **I** 157; **11** 84
Scott, Jonathan L., **II** 602, 605–06, 637
Scott, Lary, **V** 434; **6** 390
Scott Lithgow, **III** 516; **7** 232
Scott, Mike, **III** 115; **6** 218
Scott Paper Company, III 749; **IV** 258,
   289–90, 311, 325, 327, **329–31**; **8** 483
Scott, Peter, **6** 15–16
Scott, Ridley, **11** 50
Scott, Terry L., **11** 381
Scott, W.C., **III** 599
Scott, Wallie, **6** 142
Scott, Walter, **7** 165
Scott, Walter Jr., **8** 424
Scott Worldwide, Inc., **IV** 331
Scott-McDuff, **II** 107
Scottish Aviation, **I** 50
Scottish Electric, **6** 453
Scottish General Fire Assurance Corp., **III**
   256
Scottish Land Development, **III** 501; **7** 207
Scottish Malt Distillers, **I** 240
Scottish Union Co., **III** 358
Scotts Stores, **I** 289
Scovill Mfg., **IV** 11
Scranton Corrugated Box Company, Inc., **8**
   102
Scranton Plastics Laminating Corporation,
   8 359
Screen Gems, **II** 135–36
SCREG, **I** 563
Scribbans-Kemp Ltd., **II** 594
Scriha & Deyhle, **10** 196
Scripps and Sweeney Co., **7** 157
Scripps, Charles E., **IV** 608
Scripps, E.W. *See* Scripps, Edward Willis.
Scripps, Edward Willis (E.W.), **IV** 606–09;
   7 157–58
Scripps, Ellen, **IV** 606
Scripps, George, **IV** 606
Scripps, George Henry, **7** 157
Scripps Howard Broadcasting Company, **7**
   158–59
Scripps Howard Inc., **7** 64
Scripps Howard League, **7** 158
Scripps Howard Productions, **IV** 609
Scripps, James, **IV** 606–07
Scripps, James Edmund, **7** 157
Scripps, James G., **7** 158
Scripps, John P., **IV** 609
Scripps News Assoc., **IV** 607
Scripps, Robert Paine, **IV** 607–08

Scripps, Robert Paine, Jr., **IV** 608
Scripps-Howard Broadcasting Co., **IV** 608
Scripps-Howard, Inc., **IV** 609, 628
Scripps-Howard Radio, Inc., **IV** 607
Scripps-McRae League, **7** 157
Scripps-McRae Press Assoc., **IV** 607
Scudder, Horace Elisha, **10** 355
Scudder, Stevens & Clark, **II** 448
Sculley, David W., **11** 173
Sculley, John, **III** 116; **6** 219–20
Scully, Vincent, **IV** 209
Scurlock Oil Co., **IV** 374
SDC Coatings, **III** 715
SDGE. *See* San Diego Gas & Electric
   Company.
SDK Parks, **IV** 724
Sea Diamonds Ltd., **IV** 66; **7** 123
Sea Far of Norway, **II** 484
Sea Insurance Co. Ltd., **III** 220
Sea Life Centre aquariums, **10** 439
Sea Ray, **III** 444
Sea World, Inc., **IV** 623–24
Sea-Alaska Products, **II** 494
Sea-Land Service Inc., **I** 476; **9** 510–11
Seaboard Fire and Marine Insurance Co.,
   III 242
Seaboard Life Insurance Co., **III** 193
Seaboard Lumber Sales, **IV** 307
Seaboard Oil Co., **IV** 552
Seaboard Surety Co., **III** 357
Seabourn Cruise Lines, **6** 368
Seabury & Smith, **III** 283
Seabury, Charles Ward, **III** 283
Seacoast Products, **III** 502
Seafirst. *See* Seattle First National Bank,
   Inc.
SeaFirst Corp., **II** 228
Seagal, Martin A., **7** 310
Seagate Technology, Inc., 6 230–31; **8**
   466–68; **9** 57; **10** 257, 403–04, 459; **11**
   56, 234
Seagram Company Ltd., I 26, 240, 244,
   284–86, 329, 403; **II** 456, 468; **IV** 401;
   7 155
Seagram, Joseph Emm, **I** 284
Seagrove, Gordon, **I** 711; **10** 550
Seagull Energy Corporation, 11 440–42
Sealand Petroleum Co., **IV** 400
Sealectro, **III** 434
Sealed Power Corporation, I 199–200;
   10 492–94
Sealed Power Technologies, **10** 492, 494
Seaman, Barrett, **I** 145
Seamless Rubber Co., **III** 613
Seaquist Manufacturing Corporation, **9**
   413–14
Searle & Co. *See* G.D. Searle & Co.
Searle, Daniel, **I** 686–88
Searle, Gideon D., **I** 686
Searle, John G., **I** 686
Searle, William L., **I** 686
Searls, Fred, **7** 385
Sears, John, **V** 177
Sears plc, V 177–79
Sears, Richard W., **V** 180
Sears, Roebuck & Co., I 26, 146, 516,
   556; **II** 18, 60, 134, 331, 411, 414; **III**
   259, 265, 340, 536, 598, 653–55; **V**
   180–83; **6** 12–13; **7** 166, 479; **8** 224,
   287–89; **9** 44, 65–66 156, 210, 213,
   219, 235–36, 430–31, 538; **10** 10,
   50–52, 199, 236–37, 288, 304–05,
   490–91; **11** 62, 349, 393, 498
Sears, William, **V** 177

Season-all Industries, **III** 735
SEAT. *See* Sociedad Española de
 Automoviles de Turismo.
Seaton, W. Bruce, **6** 354–55
Seattle Electric Company, **6** 565
Seattle Electric Light Company, **6** 565
Seattle First National Bank Inc., 8
 469–71
Seaview Oil Co., **IV** 393
Seaway Express, **9** 510
Seaway Food Town, Inc., **9** 452
Seawell, William, **I** 116
SEB-Fastigheter A.B., **II** 352
Sebart, Carl, **IV** 203
SECA, **IV** 401
de Secada, C. Alexander G., **I** 550
Secchia, Peter F., **10** 539–40
SECDO, **III** 618
SECO Industries, **III** 614
Second Bank of the United States, **II** 213;
 9 369
Second National Bank, **II** 254
Second National Bank of Bucyrus, **9** 474
Second National Bank of Ravenna, **9** 474
Secoroc, **III** 427
Le Secours, **III** 211
SecPac. *See* Security Pacific Corporation.
Secrétan, Hyacinthe, **IV** 190
Secure Horizons, **11** 378–79
Secure Horizons USA, **11** 379
Securicor, **11** 547
Securitas Esperia, **III** 208
Securities Industry Automation
 Corporation, **9** 370
Securities International, Inc., **II** 440–41
Security Connecticut Life Insurance Co.,
 III 276
Security Engineering, **III** 472
Security Express, **10** 269
Security First National Bank of Los
 Angeles, **II** 349
Security Life and Annuity Company, **11**
 213
Security Management Company, **8** 535–36
Security National Bank, **II** 251, 336
Security National Corp., **10** 246
Security National of Indiana Corp., **10** 246
Security Pacific Bank, **II** 349
Security Pacific Corporation, II 349–50,
 422; **III** 366; **8** 45, 48; **11** 447
Security Trust Company, **9** 229, 388
Security Union Title Insurance Co., **10**
 43–44
Sedgwick Group PLC, **I** 427; **III** 280, 366;
 10 38
See's Candies, **III** 213
Seeburg, **II** 22; **III** 430
Seed Solutions, Inc., **11** 491
Seefelder, Matthias, **I** 307
Seeger Refrigerator Co., **III** 653
Seeger-Orbis, **III** 624
Seekatz, Friedrich, **I** 55
Seelig, Sam, **II** 654
SEEQ Technology, Inc., **9** 114
SEG, **I** 463
Sega Enterprises, Ltd., **7** 396
Sega of America, Inc., 10 124–25,
 284–86, **482–85**
Segal, Carole, **9** 144
Segal, Gordon, **9** 144–45
Segawa, Minoru, **II** 439–40; **9** 385
Segel, Joseph M., **9** 428
Seger, Eberhardt, **III** 478
Segespar, **II** 265

Sego Milk Products Company, **7** 428
de Ségur (Comtesse), **IV** 617
Seguros El Corte Inglés, **V** 52
Seibels, Bruce & Co., **11** 394–95
Seiberling, Charles, **V** 244
Seiberling, Frank A., **V** 244
Seiberling Rubber Company, **V** 244
Seibert, Charles A., **III** 220
Seibert, Pete, **11** 543–44
Seibu Department Stores, **II** 273
Seibu Department Stores Kansai Co., Ltd.,
 V 184–85
Seibu Department Stores, Ltd., V
 184–86
Seibu Distribution Companies, **V** 187
Seibu Railway Co. Ltd., V 187, **510–11,**
 526
Seibu Railways Group, **V** 187
Seibu Saison, **6** 207
Seidemann, William A., **7** 479
Seidl, Alois, **III** 465
Seidl, John, **8** 350
Seiffert, Hans Albrecht, **II** 164
Seijo Green Plaza Co., **I** 283
Seikatsu-Soko, **V** 210
Seiko Corporation, I 488; **III 619–21**
Seiko Epson Corp., **III** 619, 621
Seiko Instruments & Electronics Co., **III**
 620
Seiko Instruments Inc., **III** 619, 621; **11** 46
Seiko Service Centre (Australia) Pty. Ltd.,
 III 620
Seiko Time (Panama) S.A., **III** 620
Seiko Time (U.K.) Ltd., **III** 620
Seiko Time AB, **III** 620
Seiko Time Corp., **III** 620
Seiko Time GmbH, **III** 620
Seiko Time Ltda., **III** 620
Seiko Time S.A., **III** 620
Seikosha Co. Ltd., **III** 619
Seine, **III** 391
Seino Transportation Company, Ltd., 6
 427–29
Seipp, Walter, **II** 257
Seismograph Service Corp., **II** 86; **11** 413
Seiwa Fudosan Co., **I** 283
Seiyu, **10** 389
Seiyu Group, **V** 187–88
Seiyu, Ltd., V 187–89
Seiyu Stores Kansai Ltd., **V** 188
Seiyu Stores Ltd., **V** 187–88
Seiyu Stores Nagano Ltd., **V** 188
Seki, Hiromasa, **6** 30
Seki, Hironao, **6** 29
Sekimoto, Tadahiro, **II** 68
Sekisui America Corp., **III** 742
Sekisui Chemical Co., Ltd., III 741–43
Sekisui Chemical GmbH, **III** 741
Sekisui House Industry, **III** 741–42
Sekisui International Finance, **III** 742
Sekisui Malaysia Co., **III** 741
Sekisui Products, Inc., **III** 741
Sekisui Sangyo, **III** 741
Sekisui Singapore (Private) Ltd., **III** 741
SEL, **I** 193, 463
Selby, Milton, **II** 655
Selby, Prideaux, **II** 187
Selden, **I** 164, 300
Selden, George B., **I** 164; **11** 136
Select-Line Industries, **9** 543
Selection Trust, **IV** 67, 380, 565
Selective Auto and Fire Insurance Co. of
 America, **III** 353
Selective Insurance Co., **III** 191

Selek, Y., **I** 478
Selenia, **I** 467; **II** 86
Self Service Restaurants, **II** 613
Selfridge, **V** 94
Selfridges, **V** 177–78
Selig, Lester, **6** 394
Selikoff, I.J. (Dr.), **III** 707; **7** 292
Sella, George, **I** 301–02; **8** 25–26
Sellars, Richard, **III** 36; **8** 282
Selleck Nicholls, **III** 691
Seller, Robert V., **IV** 392
Sellers, Rod, **9** 92
Sellon, John, **IV** 117–18
Sells, Boake, **V** 173
Sells, Harold, **V** 226
Seltel, **6** 33
Selznick, David O., **II** 147–48
Semarca, **11** 523
Sembler Company, **11** 346
Semenenko, Serge, **II** 208
Seminole Electric Cooperative, **6** 583
Seminole Fertilizer, **7** 537–38
Semmoto, Sachio, **7** 118, 120
Semrau and Sons, **II** 601
SEN AG, **IV** 128
Senelle-Maubeuge, **IV** 227
Senior Corp., **11** 261
Senior, John Lawson, **III** 704
Senn, George A., **8** 72
Senshusha, **I** 506
Sensormatic Electronics Corp., 11
 443–45
Sentinel Group, **6** 295
Sentinel Savings and Loan, **10** 339
Sentinel Technologies, **III** 38
Sentinel-Star Co., **IV** 683
Sentrust, **IV** 92
Sentry, **II** 624
Sentry Insurance Company, **10** 210
Senyo Kosakuki Kenkyujo, **III** 595
Seohan Development Co., **III** 516; **7** 232
Sepa, **II** 594
AB Separator, **III** 417–19
SEPIC, **I** 330
Sept, **IV** 325
Séquanaise, **III** 391
Séquanaise IARD, **III** 392
Séquanaise Vie, **III** 392
Sequent Computer Systems Inc., **10** 363
Sequoia Insurance, **III** 270
Sera-Tec, **V** 175–76
Sera-Tec Biologicals, **V** 174–75
Seraco Group, **V** 182
Serck Group, **I** 429
SEREB, **I** 45; **7** 10
Serewatt AG, **6** 491
Sergeant Drill Co., **III** 525
Sergeant, Henry Clark, **III** 525
Serlachius, Gösta, **IV** 299, 301
Serlachius, Gösta Michael, **IV** 314–15
Serlachius, Gustaf Adolf, **IV** 314
Serlachius, R. Erik, **IV** 314
Serling, Robert J., **I** 91, 98, 103, 127
Sero-Genics, Inc., **V** 174–75
Servam Corp., **7** 471–73
Servatius, Bernhard, **IV** 590–91
Servel, Inc., **III** 479
Service America Corp., 7 471–73
Service Bureau Corp., **III** 127
Service Corporation International, 6
 293–95
Service Games Company, **10** 482
Service Merchandise Company, Inc., V
 190–92; 6 287; **9** 400

Service Partner, I 120
Service Pipe Line Co., IV 370
Service Q. General Service Co., I 109
Service Systems, III 103
ServiceMaster Home Systems Service, 6 46
ServiceMaster Industries, Inc., 6 45
Servicemaster Limited Partnership, 6 44–46
Services Maritimes des Messageries Impériales. *See* Compagnie des Messageries Maritimes.
Servisco, II 608
ServoChem A.B., I 387
Servomation Corporation, 7 472–73
Servoplan, S.A., 8 272
Sespe Oil, IV 569
SET, I 466
Sette, Pietro, IV 422
Settsu Marine and Fire Insurance Co., III 367
Setzler, Bill, I 405
Seubert, Edward G., IV 369
Seven Arts Ltd., II 147
Seven Arts Productions, Ltd., II 176
7-Eleven. *See* The Southland Corporation.
7-Eleven Japan, V 88–89
Seven-Up Bottling Co. of Los Angeles, II 121
Seven-Up Co., I 245, 257; II 468, 477
Seversky Aircraft Corporation, 9 205
Seversky, Alexander P., 9 205–06
Sevin-Rosen Partners, III 124; 6 221
Sewell Coal Co., IV 181
Sewell Plastics, Inc., 10 222
Sexton, Lester, III 321
Seyama, Seigoro, IV 726
Seybold, 6 602
Seybold, L. F., 6 602
Seybold Machine Co., II 37
Seydoux, Jérôme, 6 373–75
Seydoux, René, III 617
Seymour, Dan, I 20
Seymour International Press Distributor Ltd., IV 619
Seymour, Lester, I 89; 6 75
Seymour Press, IV 619
SGC. *See* Supermarkets General Corporation.
SGS, II 117
SGS Corp., 11 46
Shabazian, Michael R., 6 243–44
Shad, John, II 409
Shafer, Thomas, 7 463
Shaffer Clarke, II 594
Shaffer, Richard A., 6 244
Shaftesbury (seventh Earl of), IV 118
Shagari, Alhaji Shehu, IV 473
Shah, Eddy, IV 652
Shah of Iran. *See* Muhammad Reza Shah Pahlevi (Shah of Iran).
Shakarian, David, 11 155–56
Shakespeare, William, III 15; IV 671
Shalit, Gene, I 344
Shamrock Advisors, Inc., 8 305
Shamrock Capital L.P., 7 81–82
Shamrock Holdings, III 609; 7 438; 9 75; 11 556
Shamrock Oil & Gas Co., I 403–04; IV 409; 7 308
Shanghai Hotels Co., IV 717
Shanks, Carroll M., III 338–39
Shannahan, John N., 6 532, 555
Shapiro, Irving, I 329–30; 8 152
Shapiro, Moses, 10 319–20

Sharbaugh, H. Robert, I 631; IV 550; 11 35
Sharbaugh, Robert, 7 414
Shared Financial Systems, Inc., 10 501
Shared Systems Corporation, 10 501
Shared Use Network Systems, Inc., 8 311
Sharer, Kevin W., 10 80
Sharon Steel Corp., I 497; 7 360–61; 8 536
Sharon Tank Car Corporation, 6 394
Sharp & Dohme, Incorporated, 11 289, 494
Sharp and Dohme Inc., I 650
Sharp, Bill, 7 217
Sharp Corporation, I 476; II 95–96; III 14, 428, 455, 480; 6 217, 231; 11 45
Sharp, Henry, I 314
Sharp, Isadore, 9 237–38
Sharp, Richard, 9 122
Sharp, Sir Eric, 6 320
Sharp-Hughes Tool Co., III 428
The Sharper Image Corporation, 10 486–88
Sharples Co., I 383
Sharples Separator Co., III 418–20
Shasta, II 571–73
Shattuck, Frank C., III 440
Shattuck, Robert, III 440
Shaub, Harold A., II 480; 7 67
Shaver, Clarence H., III 763
Shaw, Alexander, V 491
Shaw, Bud, 9 465
Shaw, George, II 37
Shaw, H.A., 8 241
Shaw, Harry A., III, 7 226
Shaw Industries, 9 465–67
Shaw, J.C., 9 465
Shaw, John S., 6 577
Shaw, Neil, II 582
Shaw, R. Nelson, V 140
Shaw, Robert, 9 465–66
Shaw's Supermarkets, II 658–59
Shawinigan Water and Power Company, 6 501–02
Shawmut National Bank, II 207
Shea, James, Jr., III 506
Shea, John, 10 491
Shea's Winnipeg Brewery Ltd., I 268
Shearson Hammill & Co., II 445, 450
Shearson Hayden Stone, II 450
Shearson Lehman Bros., I 202; II 478; III 319; 8 118
Shearson Lehman Brothers Holdings Inc., II 398–99, 450; 9 468–70 (upd.); 10 62–63; 11 418
Shearson Lehman Hutton, II 399, 451; III 119; 10 59, 63
Shearson Lehman Hutton Holdings Inc., II 450–52; 9 125
Shearson Loeb Rhoades Inc., II 398; 10 62
Shedd's Food Products Company, 9 318
Shedden, William Ian H., I 647; 11 91
Sheehy, Patrick, I 426–27
Sheepbridge Engineering, III 495
Sheets, Harold, IV 558
Sheffield Banking Co., II 333
Sheffield, Bill, 7 559
Sheffield Motor Co., I 158; 10 292
Sheffield Twist Drill & Steel Co., III 624
Sheib, Simon, 9 55–56
Sheinberg, Sidney, 6 162–63
Sheinberg, Sidney J., II 144
Shelby Insurance Company, 10 44–45
Shelby Steel Tube Co., IV 572; 7 550
Sheldon, Clifford, IV 666

Shell. *See* Shell Transport and Trading Company p.l.c. *and* Shell Oil Company.
Shell Australia Ltd., III 728
Shell BV, IV 518
Shell Chemical Co., IV 410, 481, 531–32, 540
Shell Chemical Corporation, 8 415
Shell Co.-Qatar, IV 524
Shell Co. of California, IV 540
Shell Co. of Portugal, IV 504
Shell Coal International, IV 532
Shell Development Co., IV 540
Shell Mining Co., IV 541
Shell Nederland BV, V 658–59
Shell of Colombia, IV 417
Shell Oil Company, I 20, 26, 569; III 559; IV 392, 400, 531, 540–41; 6 382, 457; 8 261–62; 11 522
Shell Petroleum Corp., IV 540
Shell Pipe Line Corp., IV 540
Shell Sekiyu, IV 542–43
Shell Transport and Trading Company p.l.c., I 605; II 436, 459; III 522, 735; IV 363, 378–79, 381–82, 403, 412, 423, 425, 429, 440, 454, 466, 470, 472, 474, 484–86, 491, 505, 508, 530–32, 564. *See also* Royal Dutch Petroleum Company *and* Royal Dutch/Shell.
Shell Union Oil Corp., IV 531, 540
Shell Western E & P, 7 323
Shell Winning, IV 413–14
Shell-BP Petroleum Development Co. of Nigeria Ltd., IV 472
Shell-Mex, IV 531
Sheller Manufacturing Corp., I 201
Sheller-Globe Corporation, I 201–02
Sheller-Ryobi Corp., I 202
Shelley, R. Gene, II 87; 11 413
Shelton, Lee, 11 29–30
Shenley Laboratories, I 699
Shenstone, Naomi Ann. *See* Donnelley, Naomi Shenstone.
Shepard, Alan, I 79; 11 428
Shepard, Horace, I 539–40; 11 540, 542
Shepard Warner Elevator Co., III 467
Shepard's Citations, Inc., IV 636–37
Shepherd, Mark, Jr., II 113–14; 11 506–07
Shepherd, William C., 10 47–48
Shepler Equipment Co., 9 512
Sheppard, Allen, I 249
Sheppard, Dick, IV 711
Sheppard, John R., 10 270
Shepperd, A.J., I 715
Shepperly, Chester E., III 707; 7 292
Sheraton Corp., 11 198
Sheraton Corp. of America, I 463–64, 487; III 98–99
Sheridan Bakery, II 633
Sheridan Catheter & Instrument Corp., III 443
Sherix Chemical, I 682
Sherman, Clifton W., IV 73
Sherman, Frank A., IV 73
Sherman, George M., 7 117
Sherman, Harry W., II 507
Sherman, Nate H., 10 414
Sherman, William Tecumseh, 6 446
Sherrill, Colonel, II 644
Sherritt Gordon Mines, 7 386–87
Sherwell, Chris, IV 250
Sherwin, E. D., V 712
Sherwin, Henry, III 744
Sherwin-Williams Company, III 744–46; 8 222, 224; 11 384

Sherwood, J. D., **6** 595
Sherwood Medical Group, **I** 624; **III** 443–44; **10** 70
Shetterly, Robert B., **III** 20–21
SHI Resort Development Co., **III** 635
ShianFu Optical Fiber, **III** 491
Shibaura Engineering Works, **I** 533
Shibusawa, Eiichi, **I** 265, 502–03, 506; **II** 273; **III** 383; **IV** 320
Shield, Lansing P., **7** 202
Shields & Co., **9** 118
Shields, Paul V., **9** 118–19
Shiely, Vincent R., **8** 71
Shiff, Richard, **9** 83–84
Shiflett, G. S. (Sam), **10** 448
Shijo, Takafusa, **III** 405
Shiki, Moriya, **II** 59
Shikoku Coca-Cola Bottling Co., **IV** 297
Shikoku Drinks Co., **IV** 297
Shikoku Electric Power Company, Inc., **V** 718–20
Shikoku Information & Telecommunications Network, **V** 719
Shikoku Machinery Co., **III** 634
Shimada family, **I** 506
Shimada, Mitsuhiro, **I** 63; **11** 166
Shimizu, Norihiku, **III** 552
Shimizu, Tsutomu, **V** 487
Shimkin, Leon, **IV** 671–72
Shimomura, Hikoemon, **V** 41
Shimomura, Shotaro, **V** 41
Shimotsuke Electric Railway Company, **6** 431
Shimura Kako, **IV** 63
Shin Nippon Machine Manufacturing, **III** 634
Shin-Nihon Glass Co., **I** 221
Shinano Bank, **II** 291
Shindo, Sadakazu, **II** 58–59
Shinji, Ichiro, **II** 119
Shinko Electric Co., Ltd., **IV** 129
Shinko Kinzoku Kogyo Ltd., **IV** 129
Shinko Koji K.K., **IV** 129
Shinko Pantec Co. Ltd., **IV** 129
Shinko Pfaudler Co., Ltd., **IV** 129
Shinko Rayon, **I** 363
Shinko Rayon Ltd., **V** 369–70
Shinko Wire Co., Ltd., **IV** 129
Shinn, Allen, **10** 369
Shinn, George L., **II** 403
Shinn, Richard R., **III** 293
Shinriken Kogyo, **IV** 63
Shintech, **11** 159–60
Shinwa Tsushinki Co., **III** 593
Shiomi Casting, **III** 551
Shiono, Gisaburo, **III** 60–61
Shiono, Kotaro, **III** 61
Shiono, Motozo, **III** 61
Shiono, Yoshihiko, **III** 61
Shionogi & Co., Ltd., **I** 646, 651; **III** **60–61**; **11** 90, 290
Ship 'n Shore, **II** 503; **9** 156–57; **10** 324
Shipley, Walter V., **II** 252
Shipowners and Merchants Tugboat Company, **6** 382
Shirai, Takaaki, **III** 592
Shiraishi, Ganjiro, **IV** 161
Shiraishi, Tashiro, **III** 545
Shirakawa, Hiroshi, **III** 756
Shirasu, Jiro, **V** 727
Shirasugi, Kanezo, **I** 586
Shirer, William L., **II** 132; **IV** 672
Shirley, Jon, **6** 258, 260; **11** 286
Shiro Co., Ltd., **V** 96

Shirokiya Co., Ltd., **V** 199
Shirokiya Drapery Shop Co., Ltd., **V** 199
Shiseido Company, Limited, **II** 273–74, 436; **III** 46, 48, **62–64**; **8** 341, 343
Shives, Robert, **I** 132
Shoda, Osamu, **II** 554
Shoda, Teiichiro, **II** 554
Shoe Corp., **I** 289
Shoen, Anna Mary, **6** 351
Shoen, Edward J. (Joe), **6** 352
Shoen, Leonard Samuel (L. S.), **6** 351–52
Shoen, Mark, **6** 352
Shoen, Mike, **6** 352
Shoen, Sam, **6** 352
Shoenbaum, Alex, **7** 474
Shohin Kaihatsu Kenkyusho, **III** 595
Shoman Milk Co., **II** 538
Shoney's, Inc., **7** **474–76**
Shop 'n Bag, **II** 624
Shop 'n Save, **II** 669, 682
Shop & Go, **II** 620
Shop & Save Ltd., **II** 649
Shop Rite Foods Inc., **7** 105
Shop-Rite, **II** 672–74
ShopKo Stores, Inc., **II** 669–70
Shopwell/Food Emporium, **II** 638
Shore, T. Spencer, **8** 157
Short Aircraft Co., **I** 50, 55, 92
Short, Bob, **6** 550
Shortess, Joanna, **8** 173
Shortess, William, **8** 173
Shoshi-Gaisha, **IV** 320
Shota, Heigoro, **III** 384
Shotton Paper Co. Ltd., **IV** 350
Showa Aircraft Industry Co., **I** 507–08
Showa Aluminum Corporation, **8** 374
Showa Bank, **II** 291–92
Showa Bearing Manufacturing Co., **III** 595
Showa Cotton Co., Ltd., **IV** 442
Showa Denko, **I** 493–94; **II** 292; **IV** 61
Showa Marutsutsu Co. Ltd., **8** 477
Showa Oil Co., Ltd., **II** 459; **IV** 542–43
Showa Paper Co., **IV** 268
Showa Photo Industry, **III** 548
Showa Products Company, **8** 476
Showa Shell Sekiyu K.K., **IV** **542–43**
Showering, Francis, **I** 215
Showerings, **I** 215
Showtime, **7** 222–23; **9** 74
Showtime Networks, Inc., **II** 173
Shredded Wheat Co., **II** 543; **7** 366
Shreve, Leven, **6** 516
Shrewsbury and Welshpool Old Bank, **II** 307
Shroeder, William J., **6** 230–31
Shrontz, Frank, **10** 164
Shu Uemura, **III** 43
Shubert, Lee, **II** 148
Shubrooks International Ltd., **11** 65
Shueisha, **IV** 598
Shugart, Alan, **8** 466–68
Shugart, Alan F., **6** 230
Shugart Associates, **6** 230; **8** 466
Shull Lumber & Shingle Co., **IV** 306
Shulman, Bernard, **V** 171
Shultz, George, **I** 559
Shultz, Robert J., **II** 35
Shun Fung Ironworks, **IV** 717
Shunan Shigyo Co., Ltd., **IV** 160
Shutt, Edwin H., Jr., **8** 512
SHV Holdings NV, **IV** 383
SI Holdings Inc., **10** 481
SIAS-MPA, **I** 281
Sibley, Frederic M., Sr., **I** 169

SIBV/MS Holdings, **IV** 295
Sicard Inc., **I** 185
Sickles, Daniel E. (Maj. Gen.), **III** 290
Siddeley Autocar Co., **III** 508
Siddeley, John Davenport, **III** 508
Siddeley-Deasy Motor Co., **III** 508
Siddell, Norman (Sir), **IV** 40
Sidélor, **IV** 226
Sidélor Mosellane, **IV** 227
Siderbrás, **IV** 125
Sidermex, **III** 581
Sidérurgie Maritime, **IV** 26
Sidewater, Arthur, **8** 97–98
Sidewater, Morris, **8** 97–98
SIDMAR NV, **IV** 128
Sieff, Israel, **V** 124–25
Sieff, Marcus, **V** 126
Siegas, **III** 480
Siegel, Benjamin "Bugsy," **6** 200, 209; **11** 343
Siegel, Herbert J., **II** 176; **9** 119
Siegel, Paul, **6** 12
Siegel, William M., **II** 608
Siegfried, Charles A., **III** 292
Siegler Heater Corp., **I** 481
Siemens, **7** 232
Siemens & Halske, **II** 97–98
Siemens & Halske Electric Co., **II** 97–98
Siemens A.G., **I** 74, 192, 409–11, 462, 478, 542; **II** 22, 25, 38, 80–82, **97–100**, 122, 257, 279; **III** 139, 154–55, 466, 482, 516, 724; **6** 215–16; **9** 11, 32; **10** 16, 363; **11** 59, 196, 235, 397–98, 460
Siemens, Arnold von, **II** 97–98
Siemens Bros., **II** 97–98
Siemens, Carl Friedrich von, **II** 98–99
Siemens, Carl Heinrich von, **II** 97–99
Siemens Corp., **9** 441
Siemens, Ernst von, **II** 98–99
Siemens family, **III** 564
Siemens, Georg von, **II** 98, 278
Siemens, Hermann von, **II** 98
Siemens, Inc., **II** 98
Siemens, Peter von, **II** 98–99
Siemens, Werner, **I** 409–10; **II** 97–99
Siemens, Wilhelm (William), **II** 97–98
Siemens-Allis Inc., **II** 99
Siemens-Rheinelbe-Schuckert-Union, **I** 542
Siemens-Schuckertwerke GmbH, **II** 97
Sier, H.E., **I** 714
Sierra Designs, Inc., **10** 215–16
Sierra Leone Selection Trust, **IV** 66
Sierrita Resources, Inc., **6** 590
Sigler, Andrew C., **IV** 264
Sigma Chemical Co., **I** 690
Sigma Coatings, **IV** 499
Sigma Network Systems, **11** 464
Sigma-Aldrich, I **690–91**
Sigmier, Charles, **III** 602
Sigmor Corp., **IV** 410
Signal Capital, **III** 512
Signal Companies, **I** 85, 414, 416; **III** 511; **6** 599; **11** 435
Signal Environmental Systems, **6** 599
Signal Landmark Holdings, **III** 512
Signal Oil & Gas Inc., **I** 71, 178; **IV** 382; **7** 537; **11** 278
Signalite, Inc., **10** 319
Signature Group, **V** 145
Signet Banking Corporation, 11 446–48
Signet Investment Banking Company, **11** 447
Signetics, **III** 684; **11** 56
Signode Industries, **III** 519

Sigoloff, Sanford C., **III** 721; **V** 223
Sigrist, Fred, **III** 507–08
Sihler, Helmut, **III** 33
Sihler, James, **9** 83
SIKEL NV, **IV** 128
Sikes Corporation, **III** 612
Sikorsky, **10** 162
Sikorsky Aerospace, **I** 47, 84, 115, 530; **III** 458, 602; **9** 416
SIL&P. *See* Southern Illinois Light & Power Company.
Silas, C.J. (Pete), **IV** 523
Silberfeld brothers, **IV** 118–19
Silberstein, Leopold, **I** 434
Silbert, Stephen, **II** 149
Silberzahn, Charles, **7** 269
Silenka, **III** 733
Silicon Beach Software, **10** 35
Silicon Compiler Systems, **11** 285
Silicon Graphics Inc., 9 471–73; 10 119, 257
Silicon Systems Inc., **II** 110
Silkin, John, **IV** 642
Silkwood, Karen, **IV** 446–47
Silliman, Benjamin, **IV** 569
Sillin, Lelan F., Jr., **V** 668
Silo Holdings, **9** 65
Silo Inc., **V** 50; **10** 306, 468
Silver & Co., **I** 428
Silver, Burdett & Ginn, **IV** 672
Silver Burdett Co., **IV** 672, 675; **7** 528
Silver City Casino, **6** 204
Silver King Mines, **IV** 76
Silver Screen Partners, **II** 174
Silver, Stephen W., **I** 428
Silver's India Rubber Works & Telegraph Cable Co., **I** 428
Silverado Banking, **9** 199
Silverman, Fred, **II** 130
Silverman, Harry B., **10** 88
Silverman, Henry, **11** 177–78
Silverman, Leon, **III** 709; **7** 294
Silverstar Ltd. S.p.A., **10** 113
Silverstein, Larry, **8** 356
Silvertown Rubber Co., **I** 428
Silvey Corp., **III** 350
Sim, Richard G., **9** 27
Simca, **I** 154, 162; **11** 103
Simkins Industries, Inc., **8** 174–75
Simmons, Harold, **8** 180; **11** 268
Simmons, Harold C., **10** 434–36
Simmons, Kenneth, **9** 524
Simmons, Richard P., **8** 19–20
Simms, **III** 556
Simms, Edward, **7** 280
Simon & Schuster Inc., II 155; **IV** **671–72**
Simon Adhesive Products, **IV** 253
Simon, Benjamin, **6** 199
Simon, Charles, **III** 376
Simon, David, **7** 58; **8** 357
Simon de Wit, **II** 641
Simon Engineering, **11** 510
Simon, Fred, **8** 355
Simon, Herb, **8** 355–56
Simon, Melvin, **8** 355–57
Simon, Paul, **II** 176
Simon, Pierre, **V** 603
Simon, Richard L., **IV** 671–72
Simon, William, **II** 448
Simonius'sche Cellulosefabriken AG, **IV** 324
Simonize, **I** 371
Simons, Arthur D. (Col.), **III** 137

Simons, Henry Minchin, **I** 592
Simons, Thomas C., **III** 218
AB Simpele, **IV** 347
Simpich, Frederick, Jr., **I** 418
Simplex Electrical Co., **III** 643–44
Simplex Wire and Cable Co., **III** 643–45
Simplicity Pattern, **I** 447
Simplicity Pattern Company, **8** 349
Simplot, John R., **11** 308
Simpson, Alexander H., **III** 358
Simpson, Dana, **10** 126
Simpson, George, **V** 79–80
Simpson, Howard E., **V** 439
Simpson, Jack W., **10** 407
Simpsons, **V** 80
Sims, Philip S., **9** 421
SimuFlite, **II** 10
Sincat, **IV** 453
Sinclair, Clive (Sir), **III** 113
Sinclair Coal Co., **IV** 170; **10** 447–48
Sinclair Crude Oil Purchasing Co., **IV** 369
Sinclair, Ian, **V** 430
Sinclair, Jeremy, **I** 33
Sinclair Oil & Refining Co., **IV** 456
Sinclair Oil Corp., **I** 355, 569; **IV** 376, 394, 456–57, 512, 575
Sinclair Petrochemicals Inc., **IV** 456
Sinclair Pipe Co., **IV** 368
Sinclair Pipe Line Co., **IV** 369
Sinclair Research Ltd., **III** 113
Sindeband, Maurice L., **I** 513
Sindo Ricoh Co., **III** 160
Sinegal, James D., **V** 36
Singapore Airlines Ltd., 6 100, **117–18**, 123
Singapore Airport Terminal Services Ltd., **6** 118
Singapore Cement, **III** 718
Singapore Petroleum Co., **IV** 452
Singapore Straits Steamship Company, **6** 117
Singapour, **II** 556
Singareni Collieries Ltd., **IV** 48–49
Singer and Friedlander, **I** 592
Singer Company, **I** 540; **II** 9–11; **6** 27, 241; **9** 232; **11** 150. *See also* Bicoastal Corp.
Singer Controls, **I** 155
Singer Hardware & Supply Co., **9** 542
Singer, Isaac Merritt, **II** 9
Singer Machine Combination, **II** 9
Singer Manufacturing Co., **II** 9
Singer, Mark, **II** 262
Singh, Arjun, **I** 400
Single Service Containers Inc., **IV** 286
Singleton, Henry A., **I** 523–25; **II** 33; **10** 520–22; **11** 263
Singleton Seafood, **II** 494
Singleton, William Dean, **IV** 678
Singular Software, **9** 80
Sioux City Electric Company. *See* Sioux City Gas and Electric Company.
Sioux City Gas and Electric Company, **6** 523–24
Sioux City Gas Light Company. *See* Sioux City Gas and Electric Company.
Sioux City Service Company, **6** 523
Sioux City Traction Company. *See* Sioux City Service Company.
SIP. *See* Società Italiana per L'Esercizio delle Telecommunicazioni p.A.
Sippl, Roger J., **10** 361–63
Sir Ernest. *See* Oppenheimer, Ernest.
SIRCOMA, **10** 375

Sirey, William, **I** 575
Sirloin Stockade, **10** 331
Sirrine. *See* CRSS Inc.
Sirrine Environmental Consultants, **9** 110
Sirte Oil Co., **IV** 454
Sise, C. F., **V** 308
Sise, Charles Fleetford, **6** 305
Sisters Chicken & Biscuits, **8** 564
SIT-Siemens. *See* Italtel.
Sitbon, Guy, **IV** 618
Sitzmann & Heinlein GmbH, **IV** 198–99
Siverd, Mr., **I** 301
Six Companies, Inc., **IV** 121; **7** 355
Six Flags Corp., **III** 431; **IV** 676
600 Fanuc Robotics, **III** 482–83
600 Group, **III** 482
Six, Robert Foreman, **I** 96–97
Sizes Unlimited, **V** 115
Skånes Enskilda Bank, **II** 351
Skånska Ättiksfabriken, **I** 385
Skadden, Arps, Slate, Meagher & Flom, **10** 126–27
Skaggs Cos., **II** 604–05
Skaggs Drugs Centers, **II** 602–04; **7** 20
Skaggs, L.L., **II** 604–05
Skaggs, L.S., **7** 19
Skaggs, Leonard S., **II** 604
Skaggs, Leonard S., Jr. (Sam), **II** 601, 604–06
Skaggs, M.B., **II** 654
Skaggs, Marion, **V** 120
Skaggs, O.P., **II** 605
Skaggs, S.M., **II** 654
Skaggs, Samuel, **II** 604
Skaggs-Albertson's Properties, **II** 604
Skagit Nuclear Power Plant, **6** 566
Skandinaviska Banken, **II** 351, 365–66
Skandinaviska Enskilda Banken, II **351–53; IV** 203
Skandinaviska Enskilda Banken (Luxembourg) S.A., **II** 352
Skandinaviska Enskilda Banken (South East Asia) Ltd., **II** 352
Skandinaviska Enskilda Banken Corp., **II** 352
Skandinaviska Enskilda Ltd., **II** 352
Skankinaviska Kredit-Aktiebolaget i Göteborg, **II** 351
Skanska AB, **IV** 204
Skates, Ronald, **8** 139
Skelly Oil Co., **IV** 575
Skelton, Red, **I** 14; **II** 133, 151; **III** 55
SKF Bearing Industries, **III** 624
SKF Bearing Services, **III** 624
SKF Española, **III** 624
SKF Industries, Inc., **III** 623–24
SKF Miniature Bearings, **III** 624
SKF Specialty Bearings, **III** 624
SKF Steel, **III** 624
Skillware, **9** 326
Skinner Macaroni Co., **II** 511
Skönvik, **IV** 338
Skouras, Spyros, **II** 147, 169
Skurrie, Alan, **IV** 250
SKW-Trostberg AG, **IV** 232
Sky Channel, **IV** 652
Sky Climber Inc., **11** 436
Sky Courier, **6** 345
Sky Merchant, Inc., **V** 78
Sky Television, **IV** 652–53; **7** 391–92
Skyband Inc., **IV** 652; **7** 391
Skyway Airlines, **11** 299
Skyways, **6** 78
Slater Co. Foods, **II** 607

Slater, Jim, **III** 502
Slater, Lee, **7** 580
Slater, Robert E., **III** 267
Slater Walker, **III** 501; **IV** 259; **7** 207
Slattery, Matthew, **I** 93
Slaughter, Lomis, Jr., **11** 225
Slavin, Roy H., **11** 397
Slayter, Games, **III** 720
Slichter, Donald, **III** 323
Slick Airways, **6** 388
Slip-X Safety Treads, **9** 72
SLN-Peñarroya, **IV** 108
Sloan, Albert, **I** 464
Sloan, Alfred, Jr., **10** 326
Sloan, Alfred P., **9** 16–17; **10** 273; **11** 339–40
Sloan, Alfred P., Jr., **I** 101, 171–73, 529
Sloan, Ronald, **I** 418
Sloan, Stuart, **9** 194–95
Slocum, George S., **V** 740
Sloneker, Howard, Jr., **11** 369–70
Sloneker, Howard L., Sr., **11** 369
Sloneker, John, **11** 369–70
Slosberg, Charles, **8** 502–03
Slosberg, Jacob A., **8** 502–03
Slosberg, Samuel, **8** 502–03
Slots-A-Fun, **6** 204
Slough Construction and Properties Ltd., **IV** 723
Slough Estates (Canada) Ltd., **IV** 723
Slough Estates Australia Pty. Ltd., **IV** 723–24
Slough Estates Ltd., **IV** 722–23
Slough Estates plc, IV, IV 722–25
Slough Trading Co. Ltd., **IV** 722
Smale, John G., **III** 53; **8** 434
Small, Frederick P., **II** 397; **10** 61
SMALLCO, **III** 340
Smalley Transportation Company, **6** 421–23
Smallman, Thomas, **IV** 437
Smallpeice, Basil, **I** 93
SMAN. *See* Societe Mecanique Automobile du Nord.
Smart, L. Edwin, **II** 679–80
Smart, S. Bruce, **I** 600
Smart Shirts Ltd., **8** 288–89
Smedley's, **II** 513
Smellie, William, **7** 165
Smelser, D. Paul, **III** 51
Smethwick Drop Forgings, **III** 494
Smirnoff, Vladimir, **I** 259
Smith & Hawken, **10** 215, 217
Smith, Alexander M., **11** 72
Smith, Alf, **III** 738
Smith, Anna, **V** 211
Smith, Archibald, **III** 522
Smith, Arthur O., **11** 3
Smith, Arvin, **11** 512
Smith Barney, Inc., **I** 614; **III** 569; **6** 410; **10** 63
Smith, Bill, **IV** 209
Smith, Bradford, Jr., **III** 225
Smith Bros., **I** 711
Smith, Bruce, **III** 518
Smith, Burnside, **6** 409
Smith, Byron L., **III** 518; **9** 387
Smith, C.B., **6** 585
Smith, Cecil, **7** 324
Smith, Charles G., **II** 85; **11** 411
Smith, Charles Jeremiah, **11** 3
Smith, Charles R., **8** 358
Smith, Christopher Columbus, **9** 118
Smith, Clement, **9** 553–54

Smith Corona, **III** 502
Smith Corona Corp., **7** 209
Smith, Cyrus Rowlett, **I** 89–90, 96; **6** 75–76
Smith, Daniel R., **8** 188
Smith, Darwin E., **III** 41
Smith, Dave, **6** 79
Smith, David, **II** 629; **V** 212
Smith, Dee, **8** 472–74
Smith, Donald, **II** 556, 614–15
Smith, Edward Byron, **9** 388
Smith, Elisha D., **8** 358
Smith, Elizabeth, **6** 348
Smith, Francis, **III** 23, 326
Smith, Frank, **8** 514
Smith, Frederick W., **V** 451–52
Smith, Geoffrey Maitland, **V** 178
Smith, George D., **V** 533
Smith, George F.B., **III** 238
Smith, George K., **I** 692
Smith, George W., **III** 313
Smith, Harold Byron, **III** 518–19
Smith, Harold Byron., Jr., **III** 519
Smith, Harold C., **III** 518
Smith, Harsen, **9** 118
Smith, Heber, **III** 321
Smith, Henry, **9** 118
Smith, Henry Edward, **V** 211
Smith, Henry Walton, **V** 211
Smith, Hermon, **III** 283
Smith, Hugh, **IV** 92
Smith, Hyrum W., **11** 147
Smith, Ian, **I** 423
Smith International, **III** 429
Smith, J. Henry, **III** 248
Smith, J. Lucian, **I** 234; **10** 227
Smith, J. Stanford, **IV** 287
Smith, Jack, **7** 463
Smith, Jack, Jr., **10** 327
Smith, James H., **IV** 272
Smith, Jerry, **9** 196
Smith, John Burnside, **6** 410
Smith, John Graham, **I** 304, 359, 390
Smith, John K., **I** 692
Smith, John L., **I** 661; **9** 402
Smith, John Sloan, **6** 409
Smith, Kelvin, **I** 360
Smith, Kent, **I** 360
Smith Kline & Co., **I** 692
Smith Kline & French Co., **I** 389, 692; **10** 471
Smith, L.B. "Ted," **11** 5
Smith, Leslie, **I** 315
Smith, Lloyd Raymond, **11** 3–4
Smith, Lorenzo, **8** 472
Smith Mackenzie & Co., **III** 522
Smith, Marianna, **7** 294
Smith, Marshall F., **7** 96
Smith Meter Co., **11** 4
Smith, Michael L., **6** 410
Smith, Neal, **II** 516
Smith, Olcott D., **III** 182
Smith, Owen, **9** 119
Smith Parts Co., **11** 3
Smith, Philip, **I** 245; **II** 532, 557; **7** 274
Smith, Raymond V., **IV** 308
Smith, Richard A., **I** 245–46
Smith, Robert A., **III** 355
Smith, Robert H., **V** 484
Smith, Rodney K., **III** 12
Smith, Roger, **7** 461–62; **9** 294; **10** 326
Smith, Roger B., **I** 172; **III** 137
Smith, Sherwood H. Jr., **V** 566
Smith, Solomon, **III** 518; **9** 387–88

Smith, Stuart, **III** 225–26
Smith, Theodore, **11** 274
Smith, Thomas, **III** 272
Smith, Tom, **II** 627
Smith, Vincent, **I** 360
Smith, Vivian Hugh, **II** 427–28
Smith, W.F., **8** 475
Smith, W.H., **IV** 617
Smith, Walter, **III** 518
Smith, Ward, **7** 370–71
Smith, William, **I** 482
Smith, William Henry, **V** 211
Smith, William Henry, II, **V** 211
Smith, Wilson, **II** 626
Smith, Winthrop, **II** 424
Smith's Food & Drug Centers, Inc., 8 472–74
Smith's Food King, **8** 474
Smith's Management Corporation, **8** 474
Smith's Stampings, **III** 494
Smith's Transfer Corp., **II** 607–08
Smith-Higgins, **III** 9–10
Smithburg, William D., **II** 559–60
Smither, B.C. **I** 288
Smithfield Foods, Inc., 7 477–78, 524–25
SmithKline Beckman Corporation, I 636, 640, 644, 646, 657, **692–94**, 696; **II** 331; **III** 65–66
SmithKline Beecham, **9** 347; **10** 47
SmithKline Beecham Clinical Laboratories, **11** 334
SmithKline Beecham PLC, III 65–67; 8 210; **11** 9, 90
Smiths Bank, **II** 333
Smiths Food Group, Ltd., **II** 502; **10** 323
Smiths Industries, **III** 555
Smitty's Super Valu Inc., **II** 663–64
SMS, **IV** 226; **7** 401
Smucker, Jerome Monroe, **11** 210
Smucker, Paul, **11** 210
Smucker, Timothy, **11** 211
Smucker, Willard, **11** 210–11
Smurfit, Alan, **IV** 294–95
Smurfit Carton de Colombia, **IV** 295
Smurfit Corrugated Ireland, **IV** 296
Smurfit de Venezuela, **IV** 295
Smurfit, Dermot, **IV** 294–95
Smurfit France, **IV** 296
Smurfit International B.V., **IV** 296
Smurfit, Jefferson, **IV** 294–95
Smurfit, Jefferson, Jr., **IV** 294–95
Smurfit, Michael, **IV** 294–95
Smurfit Natural Resources, **IV** 295
Smurfit Newsprint Corp., **IV** 295
Smurfit Newsprint Corp. of California, **IV** 296
Smurfit Paribas Bank Ltd., **IV** 295
Smurfit Print, **IV** 295
Smutny, Rudolf, **II** 448
Smuts, Jan Christiaan, **IV** 21, 95
SN Repal. *See* Société Nationale de Recherche de Pétrole en Algérie.
Snack Ventures Europe, **10** 324
Snam Montaggi, **IV** 420
Snam Progetti, **IV** 420, 422
Snap-on Tools Corporation, III 628; **7 479–80**
Snapper, **I** 447
Snapple Beverage Corporation, 11 449–51
Snappy Car Rentals, **6** 393
SNEA. *See* Société Nationale Elf Aquitaine.
Snead, Jack, **V** 432–33

Sneath, William, **8** 180
Sneath, William S., **9** 518
Sneider, Martin, **9** 192–93
Sneider, Mr., **I** 217
Snell, F. L., **6** 546
Snell, Richard, **6** 547
Snellman, Gustav, **6** 87
SNET. *See* Southern New England
    Telecommunications Corporation.
SNET Paging, Inc., **6** 340
SNMC Management Corporation, **11** 121
Snoqualmie Falls Plant, **6** 565
Snow Brand Belle Foret Winery, **II** 575
Snow Brand Milk Products Company,
    Limited, II 574–75
Snow Brand Pillsbury, Inc., **II** 575
Snow, John W., **V** 440
Snow King Frozen Foods, **II** 480
Snowy Mountains Hydro-Electric
    Authority, **IV** 707
SNPA, **IV** 453
Snyder, J. Luther, **10** 222
Snyder, Jack O., **IV** 623
Snyder, Richard E., **IV** 672
SnyderGeneral Corp., **8** 321
So, Callen, **III** 112, 114
Soap Opera Magazine, **10** 287
Sobel, Robert, **I** 184, 464, 491, 528; **II** 447
Sobell, Michael, **II** 25
Sobrom, **I** 341
Sobu Railway Company, **6** 431
Socal. *See* Standard Oil Company
    (California).
SOCAR, **IV** 505
Sochiku, **9** 30
Sociade Intercontinental de Compressores
    Hermeticos SICOM, S.A., **8** 515
La Sociale di A. Mondadori & C., **IV** 585
La Sociale, **IV** 585
Sociedad Alfa-Laval, **III** 419
Sociedad Bilbaina General de Credito, **II**
    194
Sociedad Española de Automobiles del
    Turismo S.A. (SEAT), **11** 550
Sociedad Española de Automoviles de
    Turismo, **I** 207, 459–60; **6** 47–48
Sociedade Anónima Concessionária de
    Refinacao em Portugal. *See* SACOR.
Sociedade de Lubrificantes e Combustiveis,
    IV 505
Sociedade Nacional de Petróleos, **IV** 504
Sociedade Portuguesa de Petroquimica, **IV**
    505
Sociedade Portuguesa e Navios-Tanques.
    See SOPONATA.
Società Anonima Fabbrica Italiana di
    Automobili, **I** 161
Società Azionaria Imprese Perforazioni, **IV**
    419–20
Società Concessioni e Costruzioni
    Autostrade, **I** 466
Società Edison, **II** 86
Società Finanziaria Idrocarburi, **IV** 421
Società Finanziaria Telefonica per
    Azioni, I 465–66; **V 325–27**
Società Generale di Credito Mobiliare, **II**
    191
Società Idrolettrica Piemonte, **I** 465–66
Societa Italiana Gestione Sistemi Multi
    Accesso, **6** 69
Società Italiana per L'Esercizio delle
    Telecommunicazioni p.A., **I** 466–67; **V**
    325–27

Società Italiana per la Infrastrutture e
    l'Assetto del Territoria, **I** 466
Società Italiana Pirelli, **V** 249
Società Italiana Vetro, **IV** 421
Società Nazionale Metanodotti, **IV** 419–21
Società Ravennate Metano, **IV** 420
Società Reale Mutua, **III** 207
Société Air France. *See* Groupe Air France.
Societe Anonyme Automobiles Citroen, **7**
    35–36
Société Anonyme de la Manufactures des
    Glaces et Produits Chimiques de Saint-
    Gobain, Chauny et Cirey, **III** 676
Société Anonyme des Ciments
    Luxembourgeois, **IV** 25
Société Anonyme des Hauts Fourneaux et
    Aciéries de Differdange-St. Ingbert-
    Rumelange, **IV** 26
Société Anonyme des Mines du
    Luxembourg et des Forges de
    Sarrebruck, **IV** 24
Societe Anonyme Francaise Timken, **8** 530
Société Anonyme Telecommunications, **III**
    164
Société Belge de Banque, **II** 294–95
Société Bic, **III** 29
Societe BIC, S.A., **8** 60–61
Société Calédonia, **IV** 107
Société Centrale Union des Assurances de
    Paris, **III** 391, 393
Société Chimiques des Usines du Rhône, **I**
    388
Societe Commerciale Citroen, **7** 36
Société d'Ougrée-Marihaye, **IV** 51
Societe de Construction des Batignolles, **II**
    93
Société de Crédit Agricole, **II** 264
Société de Développements et
    d'Innovations des Marchés Agricoles et
    Alimentaires, **II** 576
Société de Diffusion de Marques, **II** 576
Société de Diffusion Internationale Agro-
    Alimentaire, **II** 577
Societé de garantie des Crédits à court
    terme, **II** 233
Société de l'Oléoduc de la Sarre a.r.l., **IV**
    197
Société de Prospection Électrique, **III** 616
La Société de Traitement des Minerais de
    Nickel, Cobalt et Autres, **IV** 107
Societé des Eaux d'Evian, **II** 474
Société des Forges d'Eich–Metz et Cie, **IV**
    24
Société des Forges et Aciéries du Nord-Est,
    IV 226
Société des Forges et Fonderies de
    Montataire, **IV** 226
Société des Grandes Entreprises de
    Distribution, Inno-France, **V** 58
Société des Hauts Fourneaux et Forges de
    Denain-Anzin, **IV** 226
Société des Hauts Fourneaux et Laminoirs
    de la Sambre, **IV** 226
Société des Mines du Luxembourg et de
    Sarrebruck, **IV** 25
Société des Pétroles d'Afrique Equatoriale,
    IV 545; **7** 482
Société des Usines Chimiques des
    Laboratoires Français, **I** 669
Société des Vins de France, **I** 281
Société Électrométallurgique Francaise, **IV**
    173
Société European de Semi-Remorques, **7**
    513

Société Européenne de Brasseries, **II**
    474–75
Société Financiére Européenne, **II** 202–03,
    233
Société Française des Cables Electriques
    Bertrand-Borel, **9** 9
Société Française des Teintures
    Inoffensives pour Cheveux, **III** 46
Société Française pour l'Exploitation du
    Pétrole, **IV** 557
Société Gélis-Poudenx-Sans, **IV** 108
Société Générale, II 233, 266, 295,
    354–56; 9 148
Société Générale Alsacienne de Banque, **II**
    354
Société Générale Australia Ltd. Investment
    Bank, **II** 355
Société Générale de Banque, **II** 279, 295,
    319
Société Générale de Belgique, **II** 270,
    294–95; **IV** 26; **10** 13
Société Générale North America, **II** 355
Société Générale pour favoriser l'Industrie
    nationale, **II** 294
Société Générale pour favoriser le
    Développement du Commerce et de
    l'Industrie en France S.A., **II** 354–55
Société Industrielle Belge des Pétroles, **IV**
    498–99
Société Internationale Pirelli S.A., **V** 250
Société Irano-Italienne des Pétroles, **IV** 466
Société Le Nickel, **IV** 107–08, 110
Societe Mecanique Automobile de l'Est, **7**
    37
Societe Mecanique Automobile du Nord, **7**
    37
Société Métallurgique, **IV** 25
Société Métallurgique de Normandie, **IV**
    227
Société Métallurgique des Terres Rouges,
    IV 25–26
Société Minière de Bakwanga, **IV** 67
Société Minière des Terres Rouges, **IV**
    25–26
Société Nationale de Recherche de Pétrole
    en Algérie, **IV** 545, 559; **7** 482
Société Nationale de Transport et de
    Commercialisation des Hydrocarbures,
    IV 423
Société Nationale des Chemins de Fer
    Français, V 512–15
Société Nationale des Pétroles d'Aquitaine,
    I 303; **IV** 453, 544–46; **7** 481–84
Société Nationale Elf Aquitaine, I
    303–04, 670, 676–77; **II** 260; **IV** 174,
    397–98, 424, 451, 453–54, 472–74,
    499, 506, 515–16, 518, 525, 535,
    544–47, 559–60; **V** 628; **7 481–85**
    (upd.); 8 452; **11** 97
Société Nationale pour la Recherche, la
    Production, le Transport, la
    Transformation et la Commercialisation
    des Hydrocarbures, **IV** 423–24
Société Nord Africaine des Ciments
    Lafarge, **III** 703
Societe Parisienne pour l'Industrie
    Electrique, **II** 93
Société pour l'Eportation de Grandes
    Marques, **I** 281
Société pour l'Étude et la Realisation
    d'Engins Balistiques. *See* SEREB.
Société pour L'Exploitation de la
    Cinquième Chaîne, **6** 374
Societe Vendeenne des Embalages, **9** 305

Societe-Hydro-Air S.a.r.L., **9** 27
Society Corporation, 9 474–77
Society for Savings, **9** 474
Society National Bank, **9** 474
Society National Bank of Mid-Ohio, **9** 475
Society of Lloyd's, **III** 278–79
SOCO Chemical Inc., **8** 69
Socombel, **IV** 497
Socony. *See* Standard Oil Co. (New York).
Socony Mobil Oil Co., Inc., **IV** 465; **7** 353
Socony-Vacuum Corp., **IV** 463–64; **7** 172, 352
Socony-Vacuum Oil Co., Inc., **IV** 428–29, 464–65, 485, 504, 537; **7** 171, 352
Sodak Gaming, Inc., **9** 427
Sodastream Holdings, **II** 477
Soden, James, **10** 529–30
Söderlund, Gustaf, **IV** 203
SODIAAL, **II** 577
SODIMA, II 576–77
SODIMA CLB, **II** 576
SODIMA Frais, **II** 576
SODIMA International S.A., **II** 576
Sodyeco, **I** 673
Soeharto, **IV** 492
Soekor, **IV** 93
Soeparno, Moehamad, **6** 90
Sofia, Zuheir, **11** 182
Sofiran, **IV** 467
Sofrem, **IV** 174
SoftSolutions Technology Corporation, **10** 558
Software AG, **11** 18
Software Arts, **6** 254
Software Dimensions, Inc., **9** 35
Software International, **6** 224
Software Plus, Inc., **10** 514
Softwood Holdings Ltd., **III** 688
Soga, Chubei, **I** 518
Soga, Riemon, **I** 518; **III** 634; **IV** 214; **11** 477
Soga, Tomomochi, **I** 518; **11** 477
Soga, Tomonobu, **I** 518; **11** 478
Soga, Tomosada, **I** 518
Soga, Tomoyoshi, **I** 518
Sogebra S.A., **I** 257
Sogen International Corp., **II** 355
Sogexport, **II** 355
Soginnove, **II** 355–56
Sohken Kako Co., Ltd., **IV** 327
Sohl, Hans-Günther, **IV** 222
Soinlahti Sawmill and Brick Works, **IV** 300
Sokel, David, **9** 301
Sokolov, Richard S., **8** 161
Sola Holdings, **III** 727
La Solana Corp., **IV** 726
Solana, Luis, **V** 339
Solar, **IV** 614
Solberg, Carl, **I** 69
Solchaga, Carlos, **V** 608
Solel Boneh Construction, **II** 47
Soles, W. Roger, **11** 214–15
Soletanche Co., **I** 586
Solid Beheer B.V., **10** 514
Solid State Dielectrics, **I** 329; **8** 152
Solinsky, Robert, **I** 607–08
Sollac, **IV** 226–27
Solmer, **IV** 227
Solomon, Harry, **II** 513
Solomon, Howard, **11** 141–43
Solomon, James, **11** 45–46
Solomon, Martin, **10** 369–70
Solomon, Stephen D., **I** 393

Solomon Valley Milling Company, **6** 592
Solon Automated Services, **II** 607
Solvay & Cie S.A., I 303, **394–96,** 414–15; **III** 677; **IV** 300
Solvay, Alfred, **I** 394
Solvay, Ernest, **I** 394–95
Solvay, Jacques, **I** 395
Solvent Resource Recovery, Inc., **9** 109
Solvents Recovery Service of New Jersey, Inc., **8** 464
Somerfield, Stafford, **IV** 650; **7** 389
Somervell, Brehon Burke, **I** 354
Sommar, Ebbe, **IV** 315–16
Sommer, Charlie, **I** 366
Sommer, Julius, **IV** 140
Sommer, Steven, **I** 244
Sommers Drug Stores, **9** 186
Sommers, O. W., **6** 474
SONAP, **IV** 504–06
Sonat Coal Gas, Inc., **6** 578
Sonat Energy Services Company, **6** 578
Sonat Gas Gathering, Inc., **6** 578
Sonat Gas Supply, Inc., **6** 578
Sonat, Inc., 6 577–78
Sonat Marine, **6** 577
Sonat Marketing Company, **6** 578
Sonat Minerals, Inc., **6** 578
Sonat Minerals Leasing, Inc., **6** 578
Sonat Offshore Drilling, Inc., **6** 577
Sonat Subsea Services, **6** 578
Sonatrach, **V** 626
Sonatrach. *See* Entreprise Nationale Sonatrach.
Sondey, Edward, **6** 457
Sonecor Systems, **6** 340
Sonesson, **I** 211
Sonnabend, Abraham, **10** 44
Sonne, Karl-Heinz, **III** 543
Sonneborn Chemical and Refinery Co., **I** 405
Sonneborn, Henry, **I** 405–06
Sonnen Basserman, **II** 475
Sonoco Products Company, 8 475–77
Sonoma Mortgage Corp., **II** 382
Sonometrics Inc., **I** 667
Sony Chemicals, **II** 101
Sony Corp. of America, **II** 103
Sony Corporation, I 30, 534; **II** 56, 58, 91–92, **101–03,** 117–19, 124, 134, 137, 440; **III** 141, 143, 340, 658; **6** 30; **7** 118; **9** 385; **10** 86, 119, 403; **11** 46, 490–91, 557
Sony Kabushiki Kaisha. *See* Sony Corporation.
Sony Overseas, **II** 101–02
Sony USA Inc., **II** 135, 137
Sony-Prudential, **III** 340
Sonzogno, **IV** 585
Soo Line, **V** 429–30
Soo Line Mills, **II** 631
SOPEAL, **III** 738
Sophia Jocoba GmbH, **IV** 193
SOPI, **IV** 401
Sopwith Aviation Co., **III** 507–08
Sopwith, Thomas (Tommy) (Sir), **III** 507–09
Soravie, **II** 265
Sorbus, **6** 242
Sorcim, **6** 224
Soreal, **8** 344
Sorg, Paul J., **IV** 595
Soriano, Andres, **6** 106
Soros, George, **8** 519
Sorrell, Martin, **I** 21; **6** 53

Sorrells, John H., **IV** 607
SOS Co., **II** 531
Sosa, Bromley, Aguilar & Associates, **6** 22
Sosnoff, Martin, **6** 201
Sotheby, John, **11** 452
Sotheby Parke Bernet Group plc, **11** 454
Sotheby's Holdings, Inc., 11 452–54
Sotoumi, Tetsukiro, **I** 431
Souders, William F., **6** 390
Sound of Music Inc. *See* Best Buy Co., Inc.
Sound Warehouse, **9** 75
Source Perrier, **7** 383
Sousa, John Philip, **IV** 688
South African Airways Ltd., **6** 84, 433, 435
South African Breweries Ltd., I 287–89, 422
South African Coal, Oil and Gas Corp., **IV** 533
South African Railways, **6** 434–35
South African Railways and Harbours, **6** 433
South African Torbanite Mining and Refining Co., **IV** 534
South African Transport Services, **6** 433, 435
South African United Breweries, **I** 287
South American Cable Co., **I** 428
South Carolina Electric & Gas Company, **6** 574–76
South Carolina Industries, **IV** 333
South Carolina Power Company, **6** 575
South Central Bell Telephone Co. **V** 276–78
South China Morning Post (Holdings) Ltd., **II** 298; **IV** 652; **7** 392
South Coast Gas Compression Company, Inc., **11** 523
South Dakota Public Service Company, **6** 524
South Fulton Light & Power Company, **6** 514
South Improvement Co., **IV** 427
South Manchuria Railroad Co. Ltd., **IV** 434
South Penn Oil Co., **IV** 488–89
South Puerto Rico Sugar Co., **I** 452
South Puerto Rico Telephone Co., **I** 462
South Sea Textile, **III** 705
South Texas Stevedore Co., **IV** 81
South-Western Publishing Co., **8** 526–28
Southam, Frederick Neal, **7** 486–87
Southam, Harry, **7** 486
Southam Inc., 7 486–89
Southam, William, **7** 486–87
Southam, Wilson, **7** 486–87
Southco, **II** 602–03; **7** 20–21
Southeast Bank of Florida, **11** 112
Southeast Banking Corp., **II** 252
Southeast Public Service Company, **8** 536
Southeastern Power and Light Company, **6** 447
Southeastern Public Service Company, **8** 536
Southeastern Telephone Company, **6** 312
Southern Bank, **10** 426
Southern Bell, **10** 202
Southern Biscuit Co., **II** 631
Southern California Edison Co., **II** 402; **V** 711, 713–15, 717; **11** 272
Southern California Gas Co., **I** 569
Southern Casualty Insurance Co., **III** 214
Southern Clay Products, **III** 691

Southern Clays Inc., **IV** 82
Southern Colorado Power Company, **6** 312
Southern Comfort Corp., **I** 227
Southern Connecticut Newspapers Inc., **IV** 677
Southern Cotton Co., **IV** 224
Southern Cotton Oil Co., **I** 421; **11** 23
Southern Discount Company of Atlanta, **9** 229
Southern Extract Co., **IV** 310
Southern Forest Products, Inc., **6** 577
Southern Gage, **III** 519
Southern Guaranty Cos., **III** 404
Southern Illinois Light & Power Company, **6** 504
Southern Japan Trust Bank, **V** 114
Southern Kraft Corp., **IV** 286
Southern Lumber Company, **8** 430
Southern Manufacturing Company, **8** 458. *See also* Russell Athletic Division.
Southern National Bankshares of Atlanta, **II** 337; **10** 425
Southern Natural Gas Co., **III** 558; **6** 447–48, 577
Southern Natural Industries, Inc., **6** 577
Southern Natural Realty Corporation, **6** 577
Southern Natural Resources, Inc., **6** 577
Southern Nevada Power Company, **11** 343
Southern Nevada Telephone Company, **6** 313; **11** 343
Southern New England Telecommunications Corporation, 6 338–40
Southern New England Telephone Company, **6** 338
Southern Nitrogen Co., **IV** 123
Southern Oregon Broadcasting Co., **7** 15
Southern Pacific Communications Corporation, **9** 478–79
Southern Pacific Railroad, **I** 13; **II** 329, 381, 448; **IV** 625
Southern Pacific Transportation Company, V 516–18
Southern Peru Copper Corp., **IV** 33
Southern Pine Lumber Co., **IV** 341
Southern Railway Company, **V** 484–85
Southern States Trust Co., **II** 336
Southern Sun Hotel Corp., **I** 288
Southern Surety Co., **III** 332
Southern Television Corp., **II** 158; **IV** 650; **7** 389
Southern Utah Fuel Co., **IV** 394
Southern Video Partnership, **9** 74
The Southland Corporation, II 449, 620, **660–61; IV** 392, 508; **V** 89; **7** 114, 374, **490–92 (upd.); 9** 178
Southland Ice Co., **II** 660
Southland Royalty Co., **10** 190
Southlife Holding Co., **III** 218
Southmark, **11** 483
Southtrust Corporation, 11 455–57
Southview Pulp Co., **IV** 329
Southwest Airlines Co., I 106; **6** 72–74, **119–21**
Southwest Airmotive Co., **II** 16
Southwest Forest Industries, **IV** 287, 289, 334
Southwest Potash Corp., **IV** 18; **6** 148–49
Southwestern Bell Corporation, V 328–30; 6 324; **10** 431, 500
Southwestern Electric Service Company, **6** 580
Southwestern Gas Pipeline, **7** 344
Southwestern Illinois Coal Company, **7** 33

Southwestern Life Insurance, **I** 527; **III** 136
Southwestern Pipe, **III** 498
Southwestern Public Service Company, 6 579–81
Southwestern Refining Co., Inc., **IV** 446
Southwick, George, **10** 441
Southwire Company, Inc., 8 478–80
Souvall Brothers, **8** 473
Sovereign Corp., **III** 221
Sovey, William P., **11** 397
Sovran Financial, **10** 425–26
SovTransavto, **6** 410
Soye, C. Van, **II** 305
Soyland Power Cooperative, **6** 506
SP Reifenwerke, **V** 253
SP Tyres, **V** 253
Space Craft Inc., **9** 463
Space Systems/Loral, **9** 325
Spacek, Leonard, **10** 116
Spacemakers Inc., **IV** 287
Spackman, Walter S., **II** 479
Spang, Joseph P., Jr., **III** 28
Spanish International Communication, **IV** 621
Spanish River Pulp and Paper Mills, **IV** 246
SPARC International, **7** 499
Spare Change, **10** 282
Sparklets Ltd., **I** 315
Sparks Family Hospital, **6** 191
Sparks, Frank H., **8** 37–38
Sparks, Jack D., **III** 654; **8** 299
Sparling, F. H., **6** 565
Spartan Food Systems, Inc., **I** 127; **II** 679–80; **10** 302
Spartan Stores Inc., 8 481–82
Spartech Corporation, **9** 92
Spater, George A., **I** 90
Spaulding, Thomas, **10** 455
Spear, Arthur S., **7** 305
Spear, Lawrence, **I** 57; **10** 315–16
Spécia, **I** 388
Special Light Alloy Co., **IV** 153
Specialty Coatings Inc., 8 483–84
Specialty Papers Co., **IV** 290
Specialty Products Co., **8** 386
Spectra-Physics AB, **9** 380–81
Spectra-Physics Inc., **9** 381
Spectral Dynamics Corporation. *See* Scientific-Atlanta, Inc.
Spectrum Concepts, **10** 394–95
Spectrum Dyed Yarns of New York, **8** 559
Spectrum Technology, Inc., **7** 378
Speed-O-Lac Chemical, **8** 553
SpeeDee Marts, **II** 661
Speedy Muffler King, **10** 415
Speer, Edgar B., **IV** 574; **7** 551
Speer, Roy M., **V** 77
Speich, Rudolf, **II** 369
Speidel Newspaper Group, **IV** 612; **7** 191
Speigel Inc., **9** 190, 219
Spelling Entertainment, **9** 75
Spence, Richard C., **V** 435
Spencer Beef, **II** 536
Spencer Gifts, **II** 144
Spencer, Percy, **II** 85–86; **11** 412
Spencer, Tom, **V** 124
Spencer, Walter O., **III** 745
Spencer, William M., **III** 437
Spenco Medical Corp., **III** 41
Spenser, Mark, **II** 250
Spero, Joan E., **I** 464
Sperry Aerospace, **6** 283

Sperry Aerospace Group, **II** 40, 86
Sperry Corporation, **I** 101, 167; **III** 165, 642; **6** 281–82; **8** 92; **11** 139. *See also* Unisys Corporation.
Sperry Milling Co., **II** 501; **10** 322
Sperry Rand Corp., **II** 63, 73; **III** 126, 129, 149, 166, 329, 642; **6** 241, 261, 281–82
Spethmann, Dieter, **IV** 222
Sphere, **8** 526
Spicer, Clarence, **I** 152; **10** 264
Spicer Manufacturing Co., **I** 152; **III** 568
Spie-Batignolles, **I** 563; **II** 93–94
Spiegel, **III** 598; **V** 160
Spiegel, Arthur, **10** 489–90
Spiegel, Inc., 8 56–58; **10** 168, **489–91; 11** 498
Spiegel, Joseph, **10** 489
Spiegel, M.J., **10** 490
Spiegel, Modie, **10** 489
Spielberg, Steven, **II** 144
Spielvogel, Carl, **I** 18, 27
Spillers, **II** 500
Spin Physics, **III** 475–76; **7** 163
Spirella Company of Great Britain Ltd., **V** 356
Spitz, S.J., **9** 291–92
Spizzico, Giacinto, **IV** 588
Spock, Benjamin (Dr.), **IV** 671
Spoerle Electronic, **10** 113
Spokane Falls Electric Light and Power Company. *See* Edison Electric Illuminating Company.
Spokane Falls Water Power Company, **6** 595
Spokane Gas and Fuel, **IV** 391
Spokane Natural Gas Company, **6** 597
Spokane Street Railway Company, **6** 595
Spokane Traction Company, **6** 596
Spom Japan, **IV** 600
Spoor Behrins Campbell and Young, **II** 289
Spoor, William H., **II** 556–57
Spoornet, **6** 435
Sporck, Charles E., **6** 261–63
Sporck, Charles L., **II** 63–64
Sporloisirs S.A., **9** 157
Sporn, Philip, **V** 547–48
Sporting News Publishing Co., **IV** 677–78
Sports Experts Inc., **II** 652
Sportservice Corporation, **7** 133–35
Sportsystems Corporation, **7** 133, 135
Sprague, Benjamin, **7** 465–66
Sprague, Bill, **7** 466
Sprague Co., **I** 410
Sprague Devices, Inc., **11** 84
Sprague Electric Company, **6** 261
Sprague Electric Railway and Motor Co., **II** 27
Sprague, Frank Julian, **II** 27
Sprague, Peter, **II** 63
Sprague, Peter J., **6** 261, 263
Sprague, Richard, **7** 465
Sprague, Warner & Co., **II** 571
Sprague, William, Jr., **7** 466
Spray-Rite, **I** 366
Sprayon Products, **III** 745
Sprecher & Schub, **9** 10
Sprecher, Melvin, **7** 592
Spriggs, Frank S., **III** 508
Spring Forge Mill, **8** 412
Spring Grove Mill, **8** 412
Spring Industries, Inc., V 378–79
Spring Valley Brewery, **I** 265
Springbok Editions, **IV** 621

Springer, Axel Cäsar, **IV** 589–91
Springer family, **IV** 591
Springer, Ferdinand, **IV** 641; **7** 311
Springer, Friede, **IV** 590–91
Springer, Jerry, **11** 330
Springer, Julius, **I** 410
Springer Verlag GmbH & Co., **IV** 611, 641
Springer, William C., **11** 173
Springfield Bank, **9** 474
Springhouse Corp., **IV** 610
Springhouse Financial Corp., **III** 204
Springorum, Friedrich, **IV** 104
Springorum, Fritz, **IV** 104
Springs, Elliott White, **V** 378–79
Springs, Leroy, **V** 378
Springsteen, Bruce, **II** 134
Sprint. *See* US Sprint Communications.
Sprint Communications. *See* US Sprint Communications.
Sprint Communications Company, L.P., 9 478–80
Sprint Communications Corporation, L.P., **11** 500–01
Sprint Corp., **9** 478, 480; **10** 19, 57, 97, 201–03; **11** 183, 185
Sprint/Mid-Atlantic Telecom, **10** 203
Sprott, J.S., **I** 201
Spruce Falls Power and Paper Co., **III** 40; **IV** 648
Spruce, J. K., **6** 474
Spur Oil Co., **7** 362
SPX Corporation, 10 492–95
SQ Software, Inc., **10** 505
SQL Solutions, Inc., **10** 505
Squibb Beech-Nut, **I** 695–96
Squibb Corporation, I 380–81, 631, 651, 659, 675, **695–97**; **III** 17, 19, 67; **9** 6–7
Squibb, Edwin Robinson, **I** 695
Squibb Pharmaceutical Company, **8** 166
Squires, Charles P., **11** 342
Squires, John, **6** 230
SR Beteiligungen Aktiengesellschaft, **III** 377
SRI International, **10** 139
SRI Strategic Resources Inc., **6** 310
Ssangyong Cement (Singapore), **III** 748
Ssangyong Cement Industrial Co., Ltd., III 747–50
Ssangyong Computer Systems Corp., **III** 749
Ssangyong Construction Co. Ltd., **III** 749
Ssangyong Corp., **III** 748
Ssangyong Engineering Co. Ltd., **III** 749
Ssangyong Heavy Industries Co., **III** 748
Ssangyong Investment & Securities Co., **III** 749
Ssangyong Motor Co., **III** 750
Ssangyong Oil Refining Co. Ltd., **III** 748–49; **IV** 536–37, 539
Ssangyong Paper Co., **III** 748–49
Ssangyong Precision Industry Co., **III** 748
Ssangyong Shipping Co. Ltd., **III** 748
Ssangyong Software & Data Co., **III** 749
Ssangyong Trading Co. Ltd., **III** 748
SSC&B, **I** 17
SSC&B: Lintas Worldwide, **I** 16
SSI Medical Services, Inc., **10** 350
SSMC Inc., **II** 10
St. Alban's Sand and Gravel, **III** 739
St. Andrews Insurance, **III** 397
St. Charles Manufacturing Co., **III** 654
St. Clair Industries Inc., **I** 482
St. Clair Press, **IV** 570

St. Croix Paper Co., **IV** 281; **9** 259
St. Davids (Lord), **III** 669
St. George Reinsurance, **III** 397
St. Helens Crown Glass Co., **III** 724
St. Joe Minerals, **8** 192
St. Joe Minerals Corp., **I** 569, 571
St. Joe Paper Company, 8 485–88
St. John's Wood Railway Company, **6** 406
St. Joseph Co., **I** 286, 684
St. Jude Medical, Inc., **6** 345
St. Lawrence Cement, **III** 702
St. Lawrence Cement Inc., **8** 258–59
St. Lawrence Corp. Ltd., **IV** 272
St. Lawrence Steamboat Co., **I** 273
St. Louis and Illinois Belt Railway, **6** 504
St. Louis Refrigerator Car Co., **I** 219
St. Louis Troy and Eastern Railroad Company, **6** 504
St. Paul (U.K.) Ltd., **III** 357
St. Paul Bank for Cooperatives, 8 489–90
St. Paul Guardian Insurance Co., **III** 356
St. Paul Investment Management Co., **III** 356
St. Paul Life Insurance Co., **III** 356
St. Paul Mercury Indemnity Co., **III** 356
St. Paul Risk Services Inc., **III** 356
St. Paul Specialty Underwriting, **III** 357
St. Paul Surplus Lines, **III** 356
St. Regis Corp., **I** 153; **IV** 264, 282; **9** 260
St. Regis Paper Co., **IV** 289, 339
Stadelman, George M., **V** 244
Städtische Elecktricitäts-Werke A.G., **I** 410
de Staël, Madame, **I** 271
Staefa Control System Limited, **6** 490
Staelin, David, **10** 455
Stafford, John M., **II** 556
Stafford, John R., **I** 624; **10** 70
Stafford Old Bank, **II** 307
Stag Cañon Fuel Co., **IV** 177
Stahl-Urban Company, **8** 287–88
Ståhle, Gunnar, **6** 87–88
Stahle, Hans, **III** 420
Stahlwerke Peine-Salzgitter AG, **IV** 201
Stahlwerke Röchling AG, **III** 694–95
Stahlwerke Röchling-Buderus AG, **III** 695
Stahlwerke Südwestfalen AG, **IV** 89
STAL Refrigeration AB, **III** 420
Stal-Astra GmbH, **III** 420
Staley Continental, **II** 582
Stalin, Josef, **I** 166; **IV** 314, 348, 448
Stamford Drug Group, **9** 68
Stampleman, Samuel C., **III** 28
Stanadyne, **7** 336
Standard & Poor's Corp., **IV** 29, 482, 636–37
Standard Accident Co., **III** 332
Standard Aero, **III** 509
Standard Aircraft Equipment, **II** 16
Standard Alaska, **7** 559
Standard and Chartered Bank Ltd., **II** 358, 386
Standard and Chartered Banking Group Ltd., **II** 357–58
Standard and Chartered Leasing, **II** 357
Standard Bank, **II** 319, 357
Standard Bank of British South Africa, **II** 357
Standard Bank of Canada, **II** 244
Standard Brands, **I** 248; **II** 542, 544; **7** 365, 367
Standard Chartered Bank, **II** 357
Standard Chartered Bank of Britain, **10** 170

Standard Chartered PLC, II 298, 309, **357–59**
Standard Chemical Products, **III** 33
Standard Drug Co., **V** 171
Standard Electric Lorenz A.G., **II** 13, 70
Standard Electrica, **II** 13
Standard Equities Corp., **III** 98
Standard Federal Bank, 9 481–83
Standard Fire Insurance Co., **III** 181–82
Standard Fruit and Steamship Co. of New Orleans, **II** 491
Standard General Insurance, **III** 208
Standard Industrial Group Ltd., **IV** 658
Standard Insulation Co., **I** 321
Standard Insurance Co. of New York, **III** 385
Standard Investing Corp., **III** 98
Standard Life Assurance Company, III **358–61**; **IV** 696–98
Standard Life Insurance Company, **11** 481
Standard Magnesium & Chemical Co., **IV** 123
Standard Metals Corp., **IV** 76
Standard Microsystems Corporation, 11 **462–64**
Standard Milling Co., **II** 497
Standard Motor Co., **III** 651
Standard of America Life Insurance Co., **III** 324
Standard of Georgia Insurance Agency, Inc., **10** 92
Standard Oil Co., **III** 470, 513; **IV** 46, 372, 399, 426–29, 434, 463, 478, 488–89, 530–31, 540, 542, 551, 574, 577–78, 657; **V** 590, 601; **6** 455; **7** 169–72, 263, 351, 414, 551; **8** 415; **10** 110, 289
Standard Oil Co. (California), **II** 448; **IV** 18–19, 385–87, 403, 429, 464, 536–37, 545, 552, 560, 578; **7** 172, 352, 483
Standard Oil Co. (Illinois), **IV** 368
Standard Oil Co. (Indiana), **II** 262; **IV** 366, 368–71, 466–67; **7** 443; **10** 86
Standard Oil Co. (Minnesota), **IV** 368
Standard Oil Co. (New Jersey), **I** 334, 370; **IV** 368–70, 427–29, 488; **7** 170–72, 253, 351. *See also* Standard Oil Co. of New Jersey.
Standard Oil Co. (New York), **IV** 428, 431, 460, 463–64, 549, 558; **7** 351–52
Standard Oil Co. (Ohio), **IV** 373, 379, 427, 452, 463, 522, 571; **7** 57, 171, 263
Standard Oil Co. of Iowa, **IV** 385
Standard Oil Co. of Kentucky, **IV** 387
Standard Oil Co. of New Jersey, **I** 337; **II** 16, 496; **IV** 378–79, 385–86, 400, 415–16, 419, 426–27, 431–33, 438, 460, 463–64, 522, 531, 537–38, 544, 558, 565, 571; **V** 658–59. *See also* Standard Oil Co. (New Jersey).
Standard Oil Development Co., **IV** 554
Standard Oil of California, **6** 353
Standard Oil Trust, **IV** 31, 368, 375, 385–86, 427, 463
Standard Radio and Telefon, **II** 13
Standard Rate & Data Service, **IV** 639; **7** 286
Standard Sanitary, **III** 663–64
Standard Savings & Loan Association, **9** 481
Standard Shares, **9** 413–14
Standard Steel Prop, **10** 162
Standard Steel Prop and Hamilton Aero Manufacturing, **I** 47, 84
Standard Steel Propeller, **9** 416

Standard Telefon, **II** 13
Standard Telephone and Radio, **II** 13
Standard Telephones and Cables, Ltd., **III** 162–63; **6** 242
Standard-Vacuum Oil Co., **IV** 431–32, 440, 460, 464, 491–92, 554–55; **7** 352
Standertskjöld, Adi (Baron), **IV** 274
Standertskjöld, Hugo, **IV** 301
Standish, John C., **8** 13
Stanfill, Dennis C., **II** 170
Stangeland, Roger E., **7** 570
Stanhome Inc., **11** 94–96
STANIC, **IV** 419, 421
Stanko Fanuc Service, **III** 483
Stanko Service, **III** 483
Stanley, Albert, **6** 407
Stanley, David, **11** 384–86
Stanley Electric Manufacturing Co., **II** 28
Stanley, Frederick T., **III** 626–27
Stanley, Harold, **II** 430–32
Stanley, Henry M., **I** 713
Stanley Home Products, **9** 330; **11** 95
Stanley, Robert Crooks, **IV** 110–11
Stanley Rule & Level Co., **III** 627
Stanley, William, **II** 28; **III** 626
Stanley Works, III 626–29; **7** 480; **9** 543
Stanley's Bolt Manufactory, **III** 626
Stannard, E.T., **7** 261–62
Stanolind Crude Oil Purchasing Co., **IV** 369
Stanolind Oil & Gas Co., **III** 498; **IV** 365, 369–70
Stanolind Pipe Line Co., **IV** 365, 369–70
Stanton, Seabury, **III** 213
Staples, Inc., 8 404–05; **10 496–98**
Staples, Mary Ann, **II** 657–58
Star, **10** 287–88
Star Air Service. *See* Alaska Air Group, Inc.
Star Banc Corporation, 11 465–67
Star Bank, N.A., **11** 465
Star Enterprise, **IV** 536, 539, 553
Star Enterprises, Inc., **6** 457
Star Finishing Co., **9** 465
Star Paper Ltd., **IV** 300
Star Paper Mill Co. Ltd., **IV** 300
Star Video, Inc., **6** 313
Star-Kist Foods, **II** 508
Starcraft Power Boats, **III** 444
Stardent, **III** 553
Starke, Eric, **IV** 385
Starke, Herman (Dr.), **IV** 589
StarKist Foods, **11** 172
StarKist Seafood, **II** 508
Starlawerken, **I** 527
Starley, John Kemp, **7** 458
StarMed Staffing Corporation, **6** 10
Starpointe Savings Bank, **9** 173
Starr, Cornelius Vander, **III** 195–96
Stasior, William F., **10** 175
Stata, Ray, **10** 85–86
State Bank of Albany, **9** 228
State Farm Casualty Insurance Co., **III** 363
State Farm Fire and Casualty Co., **III** 363
State Farm Fire Insurance Co., **III** 363
State Farm General Insurance Co., **III** 363
State Farm Insurance Companies, **10** 50
State Farm Life and Accident Assurance Co., **III** 363
State Farm Life Insurance Co., **III** 363–64
State Farm Mutual Automobile Insurance Company, III 362–64
State Metal Works, **III** 647
State Savings Bank and Trust Co., **11** 180

State Street Boston Corporation, 8 491–93
State Trading Corp. of India Ltd., **IV** 143
State-Record Co., **IV** 630
Staten Island Advance Co., **IV** 581
Staten Island Advance Corp., **IV** 581–82
Statler Hilton Inns, **III** 92
Statler Hotel Co., **III** 92, 98
Statoil. *See* Den Norske Stats Oljeselskap AS.
Statoil Bamble, **IV** 406
Statoil Norge AS, **IV** 406
Statoil Petrokemi AB, **IV** 406
Statter, Inc., **6** 27
Staub, Walter, **9** 137
Staubli International, **II** 122
Staubli, Robert, **I** 122
Stauffacher, Werner, **I** 671
Stauffer Chemical Company, **8** 105–07
Stauffer, Grant, **10** 447
Stauffer-Meiji, **II** 540
STC PLC, III 141, **162–64**
Steag AG, **IV** 193
Steak & Ale, **II** 556–57; **7** 336
Steam and Gas Pipe Co., **III** 644
Stearman, **I** 47, 84; **9** 416; **10** 162
Stearman, Lloyd, **I** 64; **8** 49, 90; **11** 266
Stearns Catalytic World Corp., **II** 87; **11** 413
Stearns Coal & Lumber, **6** 514
Stearns, Robert, **II** 400; **10** 144
Steaua-Romana, **IV** 557
Stecklien, Al, **9** 243
Steel and Tube Co. of America, **IV** 114
Steel Authority of India Ltd., IV 205–07
Steel Ceilings and Aluminum Works, **IV** 22
Steel Co. of Canada Ltd., **IV** 208
Steel Corp. of Bengal, **IV** 205
Steel, Dawn, **II** 137
Steel Mills Ltd., **III** 673
Steel Products Engineering Co., **I** 169
Steel Stamping Co., **III** 569
Steelcase Inc., 7 493–95; **8** 251–52, 255, 405
Steele, Alfred N., **I** 277; **10** 451
Steele, Kenneth, **6** 79
Steell, John, **III** 359
Steelmade Inc., **I** 513
Steely, **IV** 109
Steenkolen Handelsvereniging, **IV** 132
Steenstrup, Christian, **II** 29
Steer, Edward, **III** 493
Steere, William C., Jr., **11** 311
Steering Aluminum, **I** 159
Stegemeier, Richard, **IV** 571
Stehn, John H., **7** 269
Steichen, Edward, **I** 20
Steil, Inc., **8** 271
Stein, Alfred J., **10** 113
Stein, Brennan, **II** 400; **10** 144
Stein, Cyril, **II** 141–42
Stein, Gilbert, **10** 373
Stein, Jules C., **II** 143
Stein, Louis, **8** 253
Steinbach and Co., **IV** 226
Steinberg, Arnold, **II** 662–63
Steinberg Corporation, **V** 163
Steinberg Distribution, **II** 664
Steinberg Foods Ltd., **II** 662
Steinberg, Ida, **II** 662, 664
Steinberg Incorporated, II 652–53, **662–65**
Steinberg, Joseph S., **11** 260–62

Steinberg, Sam, **II** 662–63
Steinberg, Saul, **II** 173, 408; **III** 342–43; **IV** 641; **6** 175; **7** 311
Steinberg's Service Stores Ltd., **II** 662
Steinberg's Shopping Centres, **II** 662
Steinbrenner, George III, **8** 160
Steiner, Arnold, **I** 671
Steinman & Grey, **6** 27
Steinmetz, Charles P., **II** 28–29
Steinmüller Verwaltungsgesellschaft, **V** 747
Stelco Inc., IV 208–10
Stella D'Oro Company, **7** 367
Stellar Computer, **III** 553
Stellenbosch Farmers Winery, **I** 288
Stemberg, Thomas G., **10** 496–97
Stempel, Robert, **7** 462, 464
Stenbeck, Hugo, **IV** 203
Stenner, Gustave H., **10** 411
Stenroth, Otto, **II** 302
Stensmölla Kemiska Tekniska Industri, **I** 385
Stentor Canadian Network Management, **6** 310
Stepanian, Ira, **II** 208
Stephen, A.G., **II** 297
Stephen F. Whitman & Son, Inc., **7** 429
Stephen, George, **V** 429
Stephens, **III** 76
Stephens, George, **II** 336
Stephens, Richard B., **IV** 83; **7** 187
Stephens, Robert, **10** 83
Stephens, W. Thomas, **III** 708–09; **7** 293–94
Stephens, Wilton R., **V** 550
Stephenson, John, **IV** 278
Stephenson, William L., **V** 106–07
Sterling Drug Inc., I 309–10, **698–700**; **III** 477; **7** 163
Sterling Engineered Products, **III** 640, 642
Sterling Forest Corp., **III** 264
Sterling Information Services, Ltd., **IV** 675; **7** 528
Sterling, Jeffrey, **V** 492
Sterling Manhattan, **7** 63
Sterling, Matthew, **9** 367
Sterling Oil, **I** 526
Sterling Oil & Development, **II** 490
Sterling Plastics, **III** 642
Sterling Products Inc., **I** 622; **10** 68
Sterling Remedy Co., **I** 698
Sterling, Robert, **10** 455
Sterling Software, Inc., 11 468–70
Sterling Winthrop, **7** 164
Stern & Stern Textiles, **11** 261
Stern Brothers, **V** 362–65
Stern, Howard, **11** 190–92
Stern, Jacques, **III** 123
Stern, Joseph S., Jr., **V** 207–08
Stern, Joseph S., Sr., **V** 207–08
Stern, Paul G., **III** 167; **V** 309–10; **6** 283
Stern's, **9** 209
Stern-Auer Shoe Company, **V** 207
Sternbach, Leo, **I** 643
Sternberg, Ernest R., **I** 179
Sternberg, Stanley, **10** 232
STET. *See* Società Finanziaria Telefonica per Azioni.
Stettinius, Edward R., Jr., **IV** 573; **7** 550
Steuben Glass, **III** 683
Steudel, Arthur W., **III** 745
Stevcoknit Fabrics Company, **8** 141–43
Stevens, Alfred, **III** 670
Stevens, Benjamin F., **III** 312

Stevens, David (Lord of Ludgate), **IV** 686–87
Stevens, John, **II** 428
Stevens Linen Associates, Inc., **8** 272
Stevens Park Osteopathic Hospital, **6** 192
Stevens Sound Proofing Co., **III** 706; **7** 291
Stevens, Thompson & Runyan, Inc. *See* CRSS Inc.
Stevenson, Frank, **8** 546
Stevenson, Joe R., **11** 471–72
Stevenson, John E., **11** 180
Stevenson, R.L., **7** 166
Steward Esplen and Greenhough, **II** 569
Steward, H. Leyton, **7** 282
Steward, Ida, **9** 202
Stewards Foundation, **6** 191
Stewart & Stevenson Services Inc., 11 471–73
Stewart Bolling Co., **IV** 130
Stewart, C. Jim, **11** 471–72
Stewart Cash Stores, **II** 465
Stewart, D., **V** 658
Stewart, Edward, **II** 60; **11** 326
Stewart, Jimmy, **II** 143
Stewart, John W., **IV** 306
Stewart, Lyman, **IV** 569–70
Stewart, Malcolm (Sir), **III** 670
Stewart P. Orr Associates, **6** 224
Stewart, Richard, **10** 482
Stewart, Robert, **I** 490
Stewart, Robert (Col.), **IV** 368
Stewart, Will, **IV** 569–70
Steyr Walzlager, **III** 625
Sticco, Elmer, **10** 369
Stichting Continuiteit AMEV, **III** 202
Stickens, Bob, **I** 593
Stillman, James, **II** 253; **9** 123
Stillman, James A., **II** 253
Stillman, W. Paul, **III** 303; **9** 222
Stillwagon, C.K., **11** 225
Stillwell, Bermar "Bib", **8** 315
Stilwell, Arthur Edward, **6** 400
Stimson & Valentine, **8** 552
Stimson, Augustine, **8** 552
Stinnes AG, 6 424, 426; 8 68–69, 494–97
Stinnes, Hugo, **I** 542–43; **III** 693; **V** 707–08, 744; **8** 494–95, 497
Stinnes, Hugo, Jr., **I** 543
Stinnes, Mathias, **I** 542; **8** 494–96
Stinson, William, **V** 430
Stiritz, William P., **II** 562–63
Stirling, David, **III** 670
Stirling, Duncan, **II** 334
Stirling Readymix Concrete, **III** 737–38
Stirling, Sam, **III** 737–39
Stix, Nathan, **V** 208
STM Systems Corp., **11** 485
Stock, **IV** 617–18
Stock Clearing Corporation, **9** 370
Stock, Valentine N., **II** 483–84
Stockdale, Noel, **II** 612
Stocker, T. Medland, **III** 690
Stockholder Systems Inc., **11** 485
Stockholm Southern Transportation Co., **I** 553
Stockholms Allmänna Telefonaktiebolag, **V** 334
Stockholms Enskilda Bank, **II** 1, 351, 365–66; **III** 419, 425–26
Stockholms Handelsbank, **II** 365
Stockholms Intecknings Garanti, **II** 366
Stockton and Hartlepool Railway, **III** 272
Stockton Wheel Co., **III** 450

Stockwell, T.E., **II** 677
Stoddard, George, **III** 419
Stoddard, Howard J., **11** 304
Stoddard, Ralph, **III** 419
Stoddard, Stanford "Bud," **11** 304
Stoelting Brothers Company, **10** 371
Stoff, Joshua, **I** 63
Stokely-Van Camp, **II** 560, 575
Stolk, William C., **III** 707
Stoll, Arthur, **I** 672
Stolwerk, D., **III** 199
Stolz, Otto, **9** 215
Stone, Alan, **IV** 333
Stone and Kimball, **IV** 660
Stone, Charles Augustus, **6** 565
Stone, Chester B., Jr., **7** 108–09
Stone, Clement, **III** 204
Stone Container Corporation, IV 332–34; 8 203–04
Stone Exploration Corp., **IV** 83; **7** 187
Stone family, **IV** 334
Stone Forest Industries, **IV** 334
Stone, Frank, **II** 536
Stone, Jerome H., **IV** 332–33
Stone, Joseph, **IV** 332
Stone, Joseph J., **11** 74
Stone, Malcolm B., **III** 645
Stone, Marvin, **IV** 332–33
Stone, Mildred F., **III** 303
Stone, Norman, **IV** 332–33
Stone, Oliver, **6** 163
Stone, Roger, **IV** 332–34
Stone, W. Clement, **III** 203–04
Stonecipher, Eldo H., **8** 38–39
Stonecipher, Harry, **7** 504
Stonega Coke & Coal Co., **7** 583–84. *See also* Westmoreland Coal Company.
Stonestreet, George Griffin, **III** 371
Stonewall Insurance Co., **III** 192
Stoomvaart Maatschappij Nederland, **6** 403–04
Stoop, Adrian, **IV** 491
Stop & Shop Companies, Inc., II 666–67
Stop & Shop Inc., **II** 666–67
Stop N Go, **7** 373
Stop-N-Shop, **9** 451, 453
Stora Kopparbergs Bergslags AB, III 693, 695; IV 335–37, 340
Storage Dimensions Inc., **10** 404
Storage Technology Corporation, III 110; 6 275–77
StorageTek. *See* Storage Technology Corporation.
Storebrand Insurance Co., **III** 122
Storer Communications, **II** 161; **IV** 596; **7** 91–92, 200–01
Storer Leasing, **6** 81
Storer Leasing Inc., **I** 99
Stork brothers, **IV** 132
Storz Instruments Co., **I** 678
Stouffer, Abraham, **8** 498
Stouffer Corp., I 485; II 489, 547; 7 382; 8 498–501
Stouffer, Mahala, **8** 498
Stouffer's, **6** 40
Stout Air Services, **I** 128; **6** 128
Stout Airlines, **I** 47, 84; **9** 416; **10** 162
Stout Metal Airplane Co., **I** 165
Stout, William, **I** 165; **11** 137
Stover, Jim, **I** 155; **10** 280
Stowe Woodward, **I** 428–29
STRAAM Engineers. *See* CRSS Inc.
Straetz, Bob, **I** 530

Straits Steamship Co. *See* Malaysian Airlines System.
Stran, **8** 546
Strang, Charles D., **III** 599
Strasser, Hans, **II** 369
Strata Energy, Inc., **IV** 29
StrataCom, **11** 59
Stratford, R.K., **IV** 438
Strathmore Consolidated Investments, **IV** 90
Stratos Boat Co., Ltd., **III** 600
Stratton, Frederick, Jr., **8** 72
Stratton, Frederick P., Jr., **8** 71
Stratton, Harold M., **8** 70–72
Stratton, Richard A., **9** 364
Stratus Computer, **6** 279
Stratus Computer, Inc., 10 499–501
Straubel, Rudolf, **III** 446
Straus family, **8** 442–44
Straus, Herbert, **V** 168–69
Straus, Isidor, **V** 168–69; **8** 442–43
Straus, Jack I., **V** 169; **8** 443
Straus, Jesse, **V** 168–69
Straus, Lazarus, **V** 168; **8** 442
Straus, Nathan, **V** 168–69; **8** 443
Straus, Oscar, **V** 168–69
Straus, Percy, **V** 168–69
Straus, Roger, **IV** 32–33, 624
Strauss, Benjamin, **11** 392
Strauss, Herbert, **6** 27
Strauss, Isaac, **11** 391
Strauss, Maurice, **11** 391
Strauss, Moe, **11** 392
Strauss Turnbull and Co., **II** 355
Strawbridge & Clothier's, **6** 243
Strawbridge, Peter, **6** 243
Street & Smith, **IV** 583
Street, Arthur (Sir), **IV** 38
Street, Daniel L., **I** 226; **10** 180
Street, Frank T., **11** 37
Strichman, George A., **I** 434–35
Strickland, Robert, **V** 122
Strickler, Ivan, **7** 339–40
Stride Rite Corporation, 8 502–04; 9 437
Stroehmann Bakeries, **II** 631
Stroh and Co., **IV** 486
Stroh, Bernhard, **I** 290
Stroh, Bernhard, Jr., **I** 290
Stroh Brewing Company, I 32, 255, 290–92
Stroh, Gari, **I** 290
Stroh, John, **I** 290
Stroh, Peter, **I** 290–91
Ströher, Franz, **III** 68
Ströher, Georg, **III** 68
Ströher, Karl, **III** 68
Strömberg, **IV** 300
Stromberg Carburetor Co., **I** 141
Stromberg-Carlson, **II** 82
Stromeyer GmbH, **7** 141
Strong, Benjamin, **II** 428
Strong, Benjamin, Jr., **II** 229
Strong Brewery, **I** 294
Strong, C.E., **IV** 399
Strong, George C., **11** 144
Strong, Henry A., **III** 474; **7** 160
Strong, Maurice, **IV** 494
Strother Drug, **III** 9–10
Strouse, Norman, **I** 20
Strowger, Almon B., **6** 341
Stroyan, John, **I** 287–88
Stroyan, John R.A., **I** 288
Struchen, J. Maurice, **9** 475

Structural Dynamics Research Corporation, 10 257
Strum, Donald, I 600
Stryker Corporation, 10 351; **11 474–76**
Stryker, Homer, 11 474–75
Stryker, L. Lee, 11 474
Stuart Co., I 584
Stuart, Dwight L., II 488–89
Stuart, Elbridge Amos, II 486–87
Stuart, Elbridge Hadley, II 487–88
Stuart, Harold, II 431
Stuart, J. M., 6 481
Stuart, James, 10 160
Stuart, James L., I 584
Stuart, John, II 559
Stuart Medical Inc., 10 143
Stuart Perlman, 6 200
Stuart, Robert Douglas, II 558–59
Stuart, Robert S., I 608
Stubberfield, Richard, 10 464
Stuckey's, Inc., 7 429
Stucki, Robert, 6 12
Studebaker, Clement, Jr., 6 504–05
Studebaker Co., I 141–42, 451; 8 74; 9 27
Studebaker Wagon Co., IV 660
Studebaker-Packard, 9 118; 10 261
Student Loan Marketing Association, II **453–55**
Studiengesellschaft, I 409
Stuffit Co., IV 597
Stultz, Bob, I 319
Stumpf, Bill, 8 256
Sturbridge Yankee Workshop, Inc., 10 216
Sturges, Preston, II 155
Sturm, Ernest, III 241
Stuttgart Gas Works, I 391
Stuttgarter Verein Versicherungs-AG, III 184
Stuyvesant Insurance Group, II 182
Stymer Oy, IV 470–71
Suanzes, Juan Antonio, I 459
Suard, Pierre, II 13; 9 10
Subaru, 6 28
Submarine Boat Co., I 57
Submarine Signal Co., II 85–86; 11 412
Subotnick, Stuart, 7 335
Suburban Cablevision, IV 640
Suburban Coastal Corporation, 10 92
Suburban Cos., IV 575–76
Suburban Propane, I 378
Suburban Savings and Loan Association, 10 92
Suchard Co., II 520
Suchard, Philippe, II 520
Sud-Aviation, I 44–45; 7 10; 8 313
Suddeutsche Bank A.G., II 279
Süddeutsche Donau-Dampfschiffahrts-Gesellschaft, 6 425
Süddeutsche Kalkstickstoffwerke AG, IV 229, 232
Sudikoff, Jeffrey P., 11 183–84
Sudler & Hennessey, I 37
Sudnik, Patricia E., I 330
Südpetrol, IV 421
Suematsu, Ken-ichi, II 326
Suenobu, Michinari, III 384–85
Suez Bank, IV 108
Suez Canal Co., IV 530
Suez Oil Co., IV 413–14
Sugar, Alan, III 112–14
Sugarman, Burt, II 149; 7 327
Sugasawa, Kiyoshi, III 461
Sugiura, Rokuemon, VI, III 547–48
Sugiura, Rokuemon, VIII, III 548

Sugiura, Rokusaburo, III 547
Suhr, Charles, IV 489
Suhr, Henry, IV 488
Suich, Maxwell Victor, 7 252–53
Suita Brewery, I 220
Suito Sangyo Co., Ltd. See Seino Transportation Company, Ltd.
Sukarno, II 183; III 309
Suke, Morino, I 578
Sulewski, Chester J., III 707; 7 292
Sulfina, Michele, III 208
Sullair Co., I 435
Sullivan, Barry F., II 286
Sullivan, Donald T., 9 295
Sullivan, Ed, II 143
Sullivan, Eugene C., III 683
Sullivan, Eugene J., II 472
Sullivan, Frank C., 8 454–55
Sullivan, Frank E., III 304
Sullivan, Fred, I 476–77
Sullivan, John, IV 480
Sullivan, Michael, 8 362–63
Sullivan, Mike, 10 374
Sullivan, Paul, 8 449–50
Sullivan Systems, III 420
Sullivan, Tom, 8 454–56
Sulphide Corp., IV 58
Sultan, Fouad, 6 86
Sulzbach, I 409
Sulzberger, Arthur Hays, IV 648
Sulzberger, Arthur Ochs, IV 648
Sulzberger, Iphigene Ochs, IV 648
Sulzer, Albert, III 631
Sulzer Brothers Limited, III 402, 516, **630–33**, 638
Sulzer, Carl, III 632
Sulzer, Edward, III 631–32
Sulzer, Georg, III 632–33
Sulzer, Hans, III 632
Sulzer, Heinrich, III 631
Sulzer, Henry, III 632
Sulzer, Johann Jakob, III 402, 630–31
Sulzer, Johann Jakob, Jr., III 630–31
Sulzer, Peter, III 633
Sulzer Rüti Group, III 633
Sulzer, Salomon, III 402, 630–31
Sulzer-Hirzel, Johann Jakob. See Sulzer, Johann Jakob, Jr.
Sulzer-Neuffert, Johann Jakob. See Sulzer, Johann Jakob.
Sulzer-Steiner, Heinrich, III 402
Sulzermedica, III 633
Sumas, Nicholas, 7 563–64
Sumas, Perry, 7 563–64
Sumas, Robert, 7 563
Suminoe Textile Co., 8 235
Sumisei Secpac Investment Advisors, III 366
Sumitomo, V 252
Sumitomo (S.H.I) Construction Machinery Co., Ltd., III 635
Sumitomo Bank, Ltd., I 587; II 104, 224, 273–74, 347, **360–62**, 363, 392, 415; IV 269, 726; 9 341–42
Sumitomo Bank of Hawaii, II 360
Sumitomo Chemical Company Ltd., I 363, **397–98**; II 361; III 715; IV 432
Sumitomo Coal Mining Co., Ltd., IV 215
Sumitomo Communication Industries, II 67
Sumitomo Copper Rolling Works, II 104
Sumitomo Corporation, I 431–32, 492, 502, 504–05, 510–11, 515, **518–20**; III 43, 365; V 161; 7 357; **11 477–80 (upd.)**, 490

Sumitomo Electric Industries, I 105; II **104–05**; III 490, 684; IV 179; V 252
Sumitomo Electric Wire and Cable Works, II 104
Sumitomo family, IV 215
Sumitomo Fertilizer Manufacturing Co., I 397; II 360
Sumitomo Fudosan Home Co., Ltd., IV 727
Sumitomo Goshi Co., IV 726
Sumitomo Heavy Industries Forging, III 635
Sumitomo Heavy Industries, Ltd., III 533, **634–35**; 10 381
Sumitomo Investment Co., (HK) Ltd., IV 726
Sumitomo Jukikai Environment, III 634
Sumitomo, Kichizaemon, III 367
Sumitomo Life Insurance Agency America, Inc., III 365
Sumitomo Life Insurance Co., II 104, 360, 422; III 288, **365–66**
Sumitomo Life Realty, III 366
Sumitomo Light Metal Industries, Ltd., IV 212
Sumitomo Light Metals, II 361
Sumitomo Machine Manufacturing Co., III 634
Sumitomo Machinery Co., II 360; III 634
Sumitomo Machinery Corp. of America, III 634
Sumitomo Maquinas Pesadas do Brasil, III 634
Sumitomo Marine and Fire Insurance Co. (Europe) Ltd., III 368
Sumitomo Marine and Fire Insurance Company, Limited, III **367–68**
Sumitomo, Masatomo, I 518–19; III 634; IV 214; 11 477
Sumitomo Metal Industries, Ltd., I 390; II 104, 361; IV 130, **211–13**, 216; 10 463–64; 11 246
Sumitomo Metal Mining Co., Ltd., IV **214–16**; 9 340
Sumitomo Mining Co., Ltd., II 360; IV 215
Sumitomo Property & Casualty Insurance Co., III 368
Sumitomo Real Estate Sales Co., Ltd., IV 726–27
Sumitomo Realty & Development CA., Inc., IV 726
Sumitomo Realty & Development Co., Ltd., IV **726–27**
Sumitomo Rubber Industries, Ltd., V **252–53**
Sumitomo Shoji Co., II 104; IV 476, 726
Sumitomo Steel, II 104
Sumitomo System Construction, IV 727
Sumitomo Trust & Banking Company, Ltd., II 104, **363–64**; IV 726
Sumitomo Trust Co., II 363
Sumitomo Warehouse Co., II 360
Sumitomo Wire Co., III 657
Summa Corporation, 9 266
Summer, James A., II 502; 10 323
Summer, Vergil C., 6 575
Summers, Lawrence H., 9 371
Summit Constructors. See CRSS Inc.
Summit Engineering Corp., I 153
Sun Alliance and London Insurance plc, III 369–74
Sun Alliance Group PLC, III 296, **369–74**, 400

Sun Alliance Insurance Ltd., **III** 373
Sun Co., **11** 484
Sun Company, Inc., I 286, 631; **IV** 449, **548–50**; **7** 114, 414
Sun Country Airlines, **I** 114
Sun Electronics, **9** 116
Sun Exploration and Production Co., **IV** 550; **7** 414
Sun Federal, **7** 498
Sun Federal Savings and Loan Association of Tallahassee, **10** 92
Sun Fire Coal Company, **7** 281
Sun Fire Office, **III** 349, 369–71
Sun Insurance Office, **III** 369–73
Sun Kyowa, **III** 43
Sun Life Assurance, **III** 369, 394
Sun Life Assurance Co. of Canada, **IV** 165
Sun Life Group of America, **11** 482
Sun Life Insurance Company of America, **11** 481
Sun Men's Shop Co., Ltd., **V** 150
Sun Microsystems, **II** 45, 62; **III** 125; **6** 222, 235, 238, 244
Sun Microsystems Computer Corporation, **7** 500
Sun Microsystems, Inc., 7 498–501; **9** 36, 471; **10** 118, 242, 257, 504; **11** 45–46, 490–91, 507
Sun Newspapers, **III** 213–14
Sun Oil Co., **III** 497; **IV** 371, 424, 548, 550; **7** 413–14; **11** 35
Sun Oil Co. (PA), **IV** 549–50; **7** 414
Sun Oil Line Co., **IV** 548
Sun Optical Co., Ltd., **V** 150
Sun Ship, **IV** 549
Sun Techno Services Co., Ltd., **V** 150
Sun Technology Enterprises, **7** 500
Sun Television & Appliances Inc., 10 502–03
Sun-Diamond Growers of California, 7 496–97
Sun-Maid Growers of California, **7** 496–97
Sun-Pat Products, **II** 569
SunAir, **11** 300
SunAmerica Inc., 11 481–83
Sunbeam. *See* Sunbeam-Oster Co., Inc.
Sunbeam-Oster Co., Inc., 9 484–86
Sunbelt Coca-Cola, **10** 223
Sunbird, **III** 600; **V** 150
Sunbird Finance Company, **V** 150
Sunciti Manufacturers, **III** 454
Sunclipse Inc., **IV** 250
Suncoast Motion Picture Company, **9** 360
SunCor Development Company, **6** 546–47
Sund, **IV** 338
Sundance Publishing, **IV** 609
Sunday Pictorial, **IV** 665–66
Sundblad, Erik, **IV** 336
Sundgren, Albert (Dr.), **IV** 469–70
Sundheim & Doetsch, **IV** 189
Sunds Defibrator AG, **IV** 339–40, 350
Sundstrand Corporation, 7 502–04
Sundstrand, David, **7** 502
Sundstrand, Oscar, **7** 502
SunGard Data Systems Inc., 11 484–85
Sunglee Electronics Co. Ltd., **III** 748–49
Sunglee Machinery Works Ltd., **III** 748
Sunila Oy, **IV** 348–49
Sunkist Growers, **7** 496
Sunkist Soft Drinks Inc., **I** 13
Sunkus Co. Ltd., **V** 150
Sunray DX Oil Co., **IV** 550, 575; **7** 414
Sunrise Medical Inc., 11 202, **486–88**
Sunrise Test Systems, **11** 491

SunSoft, **7** 500
Sunsweet Growers, **7** 496
Sunward Technologies, Inc., **10** 464
Supasnaps, **V** 50
Super D Drugs, **9** 52
Super 8 Motels, Inc., **11** 178
Super Quick, Inc., **7** 372
Super Rite, **V** 176
Super Valu International, **II** 670
Super Valu Stores, Inc., II 632, **668–71**; **6** 364; **7** 450; **8** 380
Super-Power Company, **6** 505
SuperAmerica Group, Inc., **IV** 374
Supercomputer Systems, Inc., **III** 130
Superdrug PLC, **V** 175
Superenvases Envalic, **I** 231
Superior Bearings Co., **I** 159
Superior Healthcare Group, Inc., **11** 221
Superior Industries International, Inc., 8 505–07
Superior Oil Co., **III** 558; **IV** 400, 465, 524; **7** 353
Supermarchés Montréal, **II** 662–63
Supermarkets General Corp., **II** 673–74
Supermarkets General Holdings Corporation, II 672–74
Supermarkets Operating Co., **II** 673
Supermart Books, **10** 136
Supersaver Wholesale Clubs, **8** 555
SuperStation WTBS, **6** 171
Supertest Petroleum Corporation, **9** 490
Supervised Investors Services, **III** 270
SupeRx, **II** 644
Suppiger, David, **7** 428
Supple, Barry, **III** 335
Supreme Sugar Co., **I** 421; **11** 23
Surdam, Robert M., **11** 340
Surety Life Insurance Company, **10** 51
Surgical Mechanical Research Inc., **I** 678
Surgikos, Inc., **III** 35
Surgitool, **I** 628
Surpass Software Systems, Inc., **9** 81
Survey Research Group, **10** 360
Susann, Jacqueline, **IV** 672
Susquehanna Cable Company, **8** 508. *See also* Susquehanna Pfaltzgraff Company.
Susquehanna Pfaltzgraff Company, 8 508–10
Susquehanna Radio Corporation, **8** 508. *See also* Susquehanna Pfaltzgraff Company.
Susser, Sam J., **IV** 392
Sussman, Stephen D., **III** 767
Sutherland, Thomas, **II** 296; **V** 491
Sutowo, Ibnu (Gen.), **IV** 492
Sutter, Theodore, **III** 429
Sutton, Louis V., **V** 565
Sutton, Thomas C., **III** 467
Sutton, William, **7** 458
Sutton, Willie, **9** 408
de Suvich, Fulvio, **III** 346
Suwa Seikosha, **III** 620
Suzaki Hajime, **V** 113–14
Suzaki, Sueko, **V** 113
Suzannah Farms, **7** 524
Suze, **I** 280
Suzuki & Co., **I** 509–10; **IV** 129; **9** 341–42
Suzuki, Chuji, **II** 463
Suzuki, Iwajiro, **I** 509
Suzuki Loom Manufacturing Company. *See* Suzuki Motor Corporation.
Suzuki, Masaya, **I** 519; **IV** 215; **11** 478
Suzuki, Michio, **9** 487

Suzuki Motor Company. *See* Suzuki Motor Corporation.
Suzuki Motor Corporation, III 581, 657; **7** 110; **8** 72; **9 487–89**
Suzuki, Saburosuke, **II** 463
Suzuki, Sakae, **III** 385
Suzuki Shoten Co., **V** 380, 457–58
Suzuki, Umetaro, **I** 674
Svartz, Nanna, **I** 664
Svea Choklad A.G., **II** 640
Svedberg, Tomas, **I** 664
Svedbern, Tomas, **I** 664
Svensk Fastighetskredit A.B., **II** 352
Svenska A.B. Humber & Co., **I** 197
Svenska Aeroplan A.B., **I** 119, 197
Svenska Aeroplan Aktiebolaget. *See* Saab-Scania AB.
Svenska Cellulosa Aktiebolaget, II 365–66; **IV** 295–96, 325, 336, **338–40**, 667
Svenska Centrifug AB, **III** 418
Svenska Elektron, **III** 478
A.B. Svenska Flaktfabriken, **II** 2
Svenska Flygmotor A.B., **I** 209
Svenska Handelsbanken, II 353, **365–67**; **IV** 338–39
Svenska Handelsbanken Asia Ltd., **II** 366
Svenska Handelsbanken S.A. Luxembourg, **II** 366
Svenska International, **II** 366
Svenska Järnvagsverkstäderna A.B., **I** 197
Svenska Kullagerfabriken, **7** 565
Svenska Kullagerfabriken A.B., **I** 209; **III** 622
Svenska Oljeslageri AB, **IV** 318
Svenska Varv, **6** 367
Svenskt Stål AB, **IV** 336
Svensson, Anton, **I** 197; **11** 437
Sverker Martin-Löf, **IV** 339
SVF. *See* Société des Vins de France.
Sviluppo Iniziative Stradali Italiene, **IV** 420
SVPW, **I** 215
Swallow Airplane Company, **8** 49
Swan, **10** 170
Swan Electric Light Co., **I** 410
Swan's Down Cake Flour, **II** 531
Swanljung, Kurt, **IV** 300
Swann Corp., **I** 366
Swanson, David H., **7** 82
Swanson, Earl, **10** 94
Swanson, Gloria, **II** 146; **9** 306
Swanson, Robert, **I** 637–38; **8** 209
Swarttouw, Frans, **I** 56
Swatch, **7** 532–33
Swayzee, Clare, **II** 34
Sweany, Gordon, **III** 353
Swearingen Aircraft Company, **9** 207
Swearingen, John, **II** 262; **IV** 370–71
Sweasy, J.R., **9** 433
Sweasy, William D., **9** 433–34
Sweasy, William J., Jr., **9** 433–34
Sweatt, Charles, **II** 40–41
Sweatt, Harold, **8** 21
Sweatt, Harold R., **II** 40–41
Sweatt, William, **II** 40–42
SwedeChrome, **III** 625
Swedish Furniture Research Institute, **V** 82
Swedish Intercontinental Airlines, **I** 119
Swedish Match, **IV** 336–37; **9** 381
Swedish Ordnance-FFV/Bofors AB, **9** 381–82
Swedish Telecom, V 331–33
Sweeney, James M., **10** 198
Sweeney, John, **7** 157

Sweeney, Robert J., **7** 363–64
Sweet & Maxwell, **8** 527
Sweetser, George, **10** 268
Swenson, Eric P., **IV** 81; **7** 185
Swenson, Hakon, **II** 639–40
Swett & Crawford Group, **III** 357
Swift & Co., **II** 447, 550
Swift Adhesives, **10** 467
Swift, Amasa E., **6** 523
Swift Independent Packing Co., **II** 494
Swift, John B., **8** 155–56
Swift-Armour S.A., **II** 480
Swift-Eckrich, **II** 467
Swikard, Ed, **10** 490
Swindells, George, **IV** 358
Swindells, William, **IV** 357–58
Swindells, William, Jr., **IV** 358
Swingline, Inc., **7** 3–5
Swinton, Ernest, **III** 451
Swirbul, Leon, **I** 61–62; **11** 164–65
Swire, Adrian, **I** 522; **6** 79
Swire Bottlers Ltd., **I** 522
Swire Group, **I** 521
Swire, John, **I** 521–22
Swire, John Kidston, **I** 521–22
Swire, John Kidston "Jock," **6** 78–79
Swire, John Samuel, **I** 521–22
Swire Pacific Ltd., **I** 470, **521–22**
Swire, William Hudson, **I** 521
Swirsky, Benjamin, **9** 83–85
Swiss Air Transport Company Ltd., **I** 107, 119, **121–22**; **9** 233
Swiss Banca della Svizzera Italiano, **II** 192
Swiss Bank and Trust Corp. Ltd., **II** 369
Swiss Bank Corporation, **II** 267, **368–70**, 378–79
Swiss Cement-Industrie-Gesellschaft, **III** 701
Swiss Colony Wines, **I** 377
Swiss Drilling Co., **IV** 372
Swiss Federal Railways (Schweizerische Bundesbahnen), **V** 519–22
Swiss General Chocolate Co., **II** 545–46; **7** 380–81
Swiss Locomotive and Machine Works, **III** 631–32
Swiss National Bank, **II** 267, 379
Swiss Oil Co., **IV** 372–73
Swiss Re. *See* Swiss Reinsurance Company.
Swiss Reinsurance Co. (UK) Ltd., **III** 377
Swiss Reinsurance Company, **III** 299, 301, 335, **375–78**
Swiss-American Corp., **II** 267
Swissair, **6** 60, 96, 117
Swissair Associated Co., **I** 122
Sybase, Inc., **6** 255, 279; **10** 361, **504–06**; **11** 77–78
SyberVision, **10** 216
Sydney Paper Mills Ltd., **IV** 248
Sydney Ross Co., **I** 698–99
Syfrets Trust Co., **IV** 23
Sykes, Charles, **I** 194
Sykes, William, **I** 215
Sylacauga Calcium Products, **III** 691
Sylvan Lake Telephone Company, **6** 334
Sylvania, **8** 157; **11** 197
Sylvania Companies, **I** 463; **II** 63; **III** 165, 475; **7** 161
Sylvania Electric Products, **V** 295
Sylvia Paperboard Co., **IV** 310
Symantec Corporation, **10** **507–09**
Symbiosis Corp., **10** 70
Symbol Technologies Inc., **10** 363, 523–24

Syme, Colin, **IV** 46
Symes, James, **10** 72
Symington, William Stuart, III, **II** 18–19
Symington-Wayne, **III** 472
Symonds, Henry Gardiner, **I** 526–27; **10** 526–27
Symons, John W., **III** 29
Syncrocom, Inc., **10** 513
Synergy Dataworks, Inc., **11** 285
Synopsis, Inc., **11** **489–92**
SynOptics Communications, Inc., **10** 194, **510–12**
SynOptics, Inc., **11** 475
Syntax Ophthalmic Inc., **III** 727
Syntex Corporation, **I** **701–03**; **III** 18, 53; **8** 216–17, 434, 548; **10** 53
Syntex S.A., **I** 512
Synthecolor S.A., **8** 347
Synthélabo, **III** 47–48
Syracuse China, **8** 510
Syrian Airways, **6** 85
Syrian Arab Airline, **6** 85
Sysco Corporation, **II** **675–76**
Sysco Food Services, **9** 453
Sysorex Information Systems, **11** 62
SysScan, **V** 339
System Development Co., **III** 166; **6** 282
System Fuels, Inc., **11** 194
System Integrators, Inc., **6** 279
System Software Associates, Inc., **10** **513–14**
Systematics, **6** 301
Systematics Inc., **11** 131
Systems and Services Co., **II** 675
Systems Center, Inc., **6** 279; **11** 469
Systems Construction Ltd., **II** 649
Systems Engineering and Manufacturing Company, **11** 225
Systems Engineering Laboratories, **11** 45
Systems Exploration Inc., **10** 547
Systems Magnetic Co., **IV** 101
Szabo, **II** 608
Szilagyi, Charles, **III** 360
Szirmai, Oskar, **7** 140

T/Maker, **9** 81
T.J. Falgout, **11** 523
T.J. Maxx, **V** 197–98
T. Kobayashi & Co., Ltd., **III** 44
T. Mellon & Sons, **II** 315
T. Rowe Price, **10** 89
T. Rowe Price Associates, Inc., **11** **493–96**
T.S. Farley, Limited, **10** 319
TA Associates, **10** 382
Tabacalera, S.A., **V** **414–16**
Table Supply Stores, **II** 683
Tabor, Rock Granite, **6** 447
Tabuchi, Setsuya, **II** 440; **9** 385–86
Tabuchi, Yoshihisa, **II** 440–41; **9** 385–86
Tabulating Machine Company, **III** 147; **6** 240. *See also* International Business Machines Corporation.
Tacke, David R., **9** 183
Taco Bell, **I** 278; **7** 267, **505–07**; **9** 178; **10** 450
El Taco, **7** 505
Taco Kid, **7** 506
Tadiran, **II** 47
Taehan Cement, **III** 748
Taft, William Howard, **III** 302; **IV** 375, 573; **7** 550
TAG. *See* Techniques d'Avant Garde Group SA.

Tagaki, Yasumoto, **I** 105–06
Taguchi Automobile. *See* Seino Transportation Company, Ltd.
Taguchi, Rihachi, **6** 427–28
Taguchi, Toshio, **6** 428–29
Taha Bakhsh, Abdullah, **8** 250
Taiba Corporation, **8** 250
Taikoo Dockyard Co., **I** 521
Taikoo Sugar Refinery, **I** 521
Taio Paper Mfg. Co., Ltd., **IV** 266, 269. *See also* Daio Paper Co., Ltd.
Taisho America, **III** 295
Taisho Marine and Fire Insurance Co., Ltd., **III** 209, 295–96
Taisho Pharmaceutical, **I** 676; **II** 361
Tait, Frank M., **6** 480–81
Taiwan Aerospace Corp., **11** 279
Taiwan Auto Glass, **III** 715
Taiway, **III** 596
Taiyo Bank, **II** 371
Taiyo Bussan, **IV** 225
Taiyo Fishery Company, Limited, **II** **578–79**
Taiyo Gyogyo K.K., **II** 578
Taiyo Kobe Bank, Ltd., **II** 326, **371–72**
Taiyo Metal Manufacturing Co., **III** 757
Taizo, Abe, **III** 288
Takada & Co., **IV** 151
Takada, Ryoichi, **7** 219–20
Takagi, Jotaro, **IV** 714
Takagi, Shinichiro, **IV** 727
Takagi, Shoichi. *See* Noma, Shoichi.
Takahashi, Kiyoshi, **IV** 543
Takahata, Seiichi, **I** 509
Takamine, Jokichi, **I** 674
Takanashi, Katsuya, **9** 386
Takaro Shuzo, **III** 42
Takasaki, Tatsunosuke, **I** 615
Takasaki, Yoshiro, **I** 615
Takashimaya Co., Limited, **V** **193–96**
Takashimaya Gofuku Store Co. Ltd., **V** 194
Takashimaya Iida Limited, **V** 193
Takashimaya Shoji Limited, **V** 195
Takatoshi, Suda, **III** 637
Takayama, Fujio, **II** 392
Takayanagi, Kenjiro, **II** 118–19
Takeda Abbott Products, **I** 705
Takeda Chemical Industries Ltd., **I** **704–06**; **III** 760
Takeda Food Industry, **I** 704
Takeda, Haruo, **III** 386
Takeda, Ohmiya Chobei, VI, **I** 704–05
Takeda Riken, **11** 504
Takei, Takeshi, **II** 109
Takeoka, Yoichi, **V** 719
Takeuchi, Keitaro, **I** 183
Takeuchi, Masahiko, **IV** 475
Takeuchi Mining Co., **III** 545
Takeuchi, Yasuoki, **IV** 479
Takimoto, Seihachiro, **III** 715
Takkyubin, **V** 537
Tako Oy, **IV** 314
Talbot, Harold, **I** 48
Talbot, J. Thomas, **9** 272
Talbot, Matthew, **7** 538
Talbot, Nancy, **11** 497
Talbot, Rudolf, **11** 497
Talbot's, **II** 503; **10** 324
Talbots Canada, Inc., **11** 498
The Talbots, Inc., **11** **497–99**
Talbot, H.E., **III** 151; **6** 265
Talbott, Harold, **II** 33
Talbott, W.H., **I** 265

Talcott National Corporation, **11** 260–61
Taliafero, Paul, **IV** 550
Taliaferro, W.C., **7** 450
Taliq Corp., **III** 715
Talisman Energy, 9 490–93
Talley Industries, Inc., **10** 386
Talmadge, Norma, **II** 146
TAM Ceramics, **III** 681
Tamar Bank, **II** 187
Tambrands Inc., 8 511–13
TAMET, **IV** 25
Tamm, Peter, **IV** 591
Tampa Electric Company, **6** 582–83
Tampax, **III** 40
Tampax Inc., **8** 511–12. *See also*
    Tambrands Inc.
Oy Tampella Ab, **II** 47; **III** 648; **IV** 276
Tampere Paper Board and Roofing Felt
    Mill, **IV** 314
Tampereen Osake-Pankki, **II** 303
Tampimex Oil, **11** 194
Tamuke, Jyuemon, **I** 518
Tamura Kisan Co., **II** 552
Tan, Thomas S., **9** 297
Tanabe, Masaru, **III** 742
Tanabe Seiyaku, **I** 648; **9** 328
Tanaka, **6** 71
Tanaka, Kakuei, **I** 66, 494; **IV** 728; **11** 268
Tanaka Kikinzoku Kogyo KK, **IV** 119
Tanaka, Kyubei, **II** 326
Tanaka Matthey KK, **IV** 119
Tanaka, Tadao, **II** 68
Tanaka, Taro, **III** 593
Tanaka, Tukujiro, **III** 385
Tandem Computers, Inc., 6 278–80; 10
    499; **11** 18
Tandem Telecommunications Systems,
    Inc., **6** 280
Tandy Brands, Inc., **10** 166
Tandy, Charles, **II** 106–08
Tandy Corporation, II 70, **106–08; 6**
    257–58; **9** 43, 115, 165; **10** 56–57,
    166–67, 236
Tandy Marketing Cos., **II** 107
Tang, Jack, **III** 705
Tang, Shiu-kin (Sir), **IV** 717
Tangent Systems, **6** 247–48
Tanii, Akio, **II** 56
Tanjong Pagar Dock Co., **I** 592
Tanks Oil and Gas, **11** 97
Tanner, Mikko, **IV** 469
Tanner, Nathan Eldon, **V** 738
TAP Air Portugal. *See* Transportes Aereos
    Portugueses.
Tapiola Insurance, **IV** 316
Taplin, Frank E., **7** 369
Tappan, Arthur, **IV** 604
Tappan, David S., Jr., **I** 571; **8** 192
Tappan, Lewis, **IV** 604
Tara Exploration and Development Ltd.,
    IV 165
Tara Foods, **II** 645
Tarbox, Richard C., **11** 485
Target Stores, V 35, 43–44; **10** 284,
    515–17
Tariki, Sayyid Abdullah H., **IV** 537
Tarkenton, Fran, **9** 309–10
Tarkington, Andrew W., **IV** 401
Tarmac America, **III** 753
Tarmac Civil Engineering, **III** 752
Tarmac Ltd., **III** 751–53
Tarmac PLC, III 734, **751–54**
Tarmac Roadstone, **III** 752
Tarmac Vinculum, **III** 752

TarMacadam (Purnell Hooley's Patent)
    Syndicate Ltd., **III** 751
Tarr, Robert J., **I** 245
Tarslag, **III** 752
Tartikoff, Brandon, **6** 165; **10** 288
Tasco, Frank J., **III** 283
Tashima, Hideo, **III** 575
Tashima, Kazuo, **III** 574–75
Tashima Shoten, **III** 574
Tashiro, Shigeki, **V** 384
Tasman Pulp and Paper (Sales) Ltd., **IV**
    279
Tasman Pulp and Paper Co. Ltd., **IV**
    278–79
Tasman U.E.B., **IV** 249
Tasmanian Fibre Containers, **IV** 249
Tata Airlines. *See* Air-India.
Tata, Dorabji (Sir), **IV** 217–18
Tata Electric Co., **IV** 219
Tata Engineering and Locomotive Co., **IV**
    218–19
Tata Enterprises, **III** 43
Tata family, **IV** 217–19
Tata Group, **IV** 218–19
Tata Hydro-Electric Power Supply Co., **IV**
    218
Tata Industries Ltd., **IV** 218–19
Tata Iron and Steel Company Ltd., IV
    48, 205–07, **217–19**
Tata, J.R.D., **6** 63
Tata, Jamsetji, **IV** 205, 218
Tata, Jamsetji Nusserwanji, **IV** 217–19
Tata, Jehangir Ratanji Dadabhoy, **IV** 219
Tata, Ratan Naval, **IV** 219
Tata, Ratanji, **IV** 217–19
Tata Services, **IV** 219
Tataka, Masao, **III** 546
Tate & Lyle PLC, II 514, **580–83; 7**
    466–67
Tate, Alfred, **II** 580
Tate, Caleb, **II** 580
Tate, Edwin, **II** 580
Tate, Ernest, **II** 580–81
Tate, Henry, **II** 580
Tate, Sidney B., **10** 299
Tate, Toyoo, **9** 350
Tate, Vernon, **II** 581
Tate, William, **II** 581
Tate, William Henry, **II** 580
Tatebayashi Flour Milling Co., **II** 554
Tateisi Electric Manufacturing, **II** 75
Tateisi, Kazuma, **II** 75–76
Tateisi Medical Electronics Manufacturing
    Co., **II** 75
Tateisi, Takao, **II** 76
Tatian, Marie, **III** 568
Tatò, Franco, **IV** 587
Tatsumi, Sotoo, **II** 361
Tatum, John, **11** 538
Tatung Co., **III** 482
Taub, Henry, **III** 117; **9** 48–49
Taub, Joe, **III** 117; **9** 48
Taubman, A. Alfred, **11** 454
Taurus Programming Services, **10** 196
Tavoulareas, William, **IV** 465; **7** 353
Taylor, Allan, **II** 345
Taylor, Andrew, **6** 393
Taylor, Arthur, **II** 133; **6** 158
Taylor, Bernard D., **9** 264
Taylor, Charles G., **III** 292
Taylor, Charles H., **7** 13–14; **9** 133
Taylor, Charles H., Jr., **7** 14
Taylor, Claude I., **6** 61
Taylor, David, **II** 262

Taylor Diving and Salvage Co., **III** 499
Taylor, Elizabeth, **II** 176
Taylor, Ernest, **II** 586
Taylor, Frank, **I** 590–91; **11** 61
Taylor, Frederick, **IV** 385
Taylor, Frederick W., **IV** 252
Taylor, George C., **II** 397; **10** 61
Taylor, Graham D., **I** 330
Taylor, Jack Crawford, **6** 392
Taylor, James, **II** 306
Taylor, James B., **8** 315
Taylor, James E., **11** 356–57
Taylor, James W., **10** 174
Taylor, John, **II** 306
Taylor, John, Jr., **II** 306
Taylor, John M., **III** 237–38
Taylor, John R., **III** 330
Taylor, Moses, **II** 253; **9** 123
Taylor, Myron C., **IV** 573; **7** 550
Taylor, Nathan A., **6** 161
Taylor, R.J., **III** 240
Taylor, Reese, **IV** 570
Taylor Rental Corp., **III** 628
Taylor, S. Blackwell, **III** 602
Taylor, S. Frederick, **II** 471
Taylor, William, **II** 306
Taylor, William Davis, **7** 15
Taylor, William H., **11** 388
Taylor, William O., **7** 14–15
Taylor Wines Co., **I** 234; **10** 227
Taylor Woodrow plc, I 590–91
Taylor Woodrow-Anglian, **III** 739
Taylor-Evans Seed Co., **IV** 409
Taylors and Lloyds, **II** 306
Tazuke & Co., **IV** 151
TBS. *See* Turner Broadcasting System, Inc.
TBWA Advertising, Inc., 6 47–49
TBWA Kerlick & Switzer, **6** 48
TBWA-NETHwork, **6** 48
TCBC. *See* Todays Computers Business
    Centers.
TCF Holdings, Inc., **II** 170–71
Tchuruk, Serge, **IV** 547, 560
TCI. *See* Tele-Communications, Inc.
TCPL. *See* TransCanada PipeLines Ltd.
TDK Corporation, I 500; **II** 109–11; **IV**
    680
TDS. *See* Telephone and Data Systems,
    Inc.
Teaberry Electronics Corp., **III** 569
Teachers Insurance and Annuity
    Association, III 379–82
Teachers Service Organization, Inc., **8**
    9–10
Teagle, Walter, **I** 337
Teagle, Walter C., Jr., **7** 179
Teague, Charles, **7** 496
Teal, Gordon, **II** 112; **11** 505
Team America, **9** 435
Team Penske, **V** 494
Tebbel, John, **IV** 636
Tebbets, Walter, **III** 313
Tebbit, Norman, **I** 83
Tebel Maschinefabrieken, **III** 420
Tebel Pneumatiek, **III** 420
Tech Data Corporation, 10 518–19
Techalloy Co., **IV** 228
Technical Publishing, **IV** 605
Technicare, **11** 200
Technicon Corp., **III** 56; **11** 333–34
Technifax, **8** 483
Techniques d'Avant Garde Group SA, **7**
    554
Techno-Success Company, **V** 719

AB Technology, **II** 466
Technology Venture Investors, **11** 490
Teck Corporation, **9** 282
Tecnamotor S.p.A., **8** 72, 515
Tecneco, **IV** 422
Tecnifax Corp., **IV** 330
TECO Coal, **6** 583
TECO Coalbed Methane, **6** 583
TECO Energy, Inc., 6 582–84
TECO Power Services, **6** 583
TECO Transport and Trade, **6** 583
Tecumseh Products Company, 8 72,
   514–16
Ted Bates & Co., **I** 33, 623; **10** 69
Tedelex, **IV** 91–92
Teerlink, Richard, **7** 213
Teets, John, **I** 450
Teets, John W., **8** 145
Teijin, **I** 511
Teijin Limited, V 380–82
Teikoku Bank, **I** 507; **II** 273, 325–26
Teikoku Hormone, **I** 704
Teikoku Jinken. *See* Teijin Limited.
Teikoku Sekiyu Co. Ltd., **IV** 475
Teikoku Shiki, **IV** 326
Teito Electric Railway, **V** 461
Teito Transport Co. Ltd., **V** 536
Teitsworth, Robert, **IV** 480
Tekrad, Inc., **8** 517. *See also* Tektronix,
   Inc.
Tekton Corp., **IV** 346
Tektronix, Inc., II 101; **8** 517–21; **10** 24;
   11 284–86
Tel-A-Data Limited, **11** 111
Tele-Communications, Inc., II 160–62,
   167; **10** 484, 506; **11** 479
TeleCheck Services, Inc., **11** 113
Teleclub, **IV** 590
Teleco Oilfield Services, Inc., **6** 578
TeleColumbus, **11** 184
Telecom Australia, 6 341–42
Telecom Australia (International), Ltd., **6**
   342
Telecom Canada. *See* Stentor Canadian
   Network Management.
Telecom Eireann, 7 508–10
Telecomputing Corp., **I** 544
Telecredit, Inc., **6** 25
Telectronic Pacing Systems, **10** 445
Teledyne Inc., I 486, **523–25**; **II** 33, 44;
   10 262–63, 365, **520–22 (upd.)**; **11** 265
Telefonaktiebolaget LM Ericsson, V
   331–32, **334–36**; **9** 381
Telefonbau und Normalzeit, **I** 193
Telefónica de España, S.A., V 337–40
Telefunken, **II** 117
Telefunken Fernseh & Rundfunk GmbH., **I**
   411
Telegraph Condenser Co., **II** 81
Telegraph Manufacturing Co., **III** 433
Telegraph Works, **III** 433
TeleMarketing Corporation of Louisiana, **8**
   311
Telemarketing Investments, Ltd., **8** 311
Telemecanique, **II** 94
Telemundo Group, Inc., **III** 344
Telenorma, **I** 193
Telenova, **III** 169; **6** 285
Telephone and Data Systems, Inc., 9
   494–96, 527–529
Telephone Company of Ireland, **7** 508
Telephone Management Corporation, **8** 310
Telephone Utilities, Inc. *See* Pacific
   Telecom, Inc.

Telephone Utilities of Washington, **6** 325,
   328
Telepictures, **II** 177
Teleprompter, **7** 222
Teleprompter Corp., **II** 122; **10** 210
Telerate, Inc., **IV** 603, 670
Telerate Systems Inc., **10** 276–78
Teleregister Corp., **I** 512
Telerent Europe, **II** 139
TeleRep, **IV** 596
Telesis Oil and Gas, **6** 478
Telesphere Network, Inc., **8** 310
Telesystems SLW Inc., **10** 524
Telettra, **V** 326
Telettra S.p.A., **9** 10; **11** 205
Television Española, S.A., 7 511–12
Television Sales and Marketing Services
   Ltd., **7** 79–80
Teleway Japan, **7** 118–19
Telex, **II** 87
Telfin, **V** 339
Telia Mobitel, **11** 19
Telihoras Corporation, **10** 319
Telinfo, **6** 303
Telinq Inc., **10** 19
Telios Pharmaceuticals, Inc., **11** 460
Tellabs, Inc., 11 500–01
Tellep, Daniel M., **11** 268
Telling, Edward, **V** 182
Telmer, Frederick H., **IV** 210
Telrad, **II** 48
Telxon Corporation, 10 523–25
Tembec, Inc., **IV** 296
Temco Electronics and Missile Co., **I** 489
Temenggong of Jahore, **I** 592
Temp World, Inc., **6** 10
Temple, Arthur, **IV** 341–42, 675; **7** 528
Temple Associates, Inc., **IV** 341
Temple, Barker & Sloan/Strategic Planning
   Associates, **III** 283
Temple, Edward A., **III** 328
Temple family, **IV** 341–42
Temple Industries, Inc., **IV** 341–42, 675; **7**
   528
Temple Lumber Co., **IV** 341
Temple Press Ltd., **IV** 294–95
Temple, Thomas Louis Latane, Sr., **IV**
   341–42
Temple-Eastex Inc., **IV** 341–43; **8** 267–68
Temple-Inland Financial Services, **8** 267
Temple-Inland Financial Services Inc., **IV**
   343
Temple-Inland Forest Products
   Corporation, **IV** 341–43; **8** 267
Temple-Inland Inc., IV 312, **341–43**, 675;
   8 267–69
Templeton, **II** 609
Templeton, John, **9** 240
Templier, Emile, **IV** 617
TEMPO Enterprises, **II** 162
10 Sen Kinitsu Markets, **V** 194
Tengelmann Group, **II** 636–38
Tengen Inc., **III** 587; **7** 395
Tengenmann, Wilhelm, **I** 349, 543
Tennant, Anthony, **I** 252
Tennant, Don, **I** 23
Tenneco Inc., I 182, **526–28**; **IV** 76, 152,
   283, 499; **6** 531; **10** 379–80, 430,
   526–28 (upd.); **11** 440
Tenneco Oil Co., **IV** 371
Tennenbaum, Michael, **7** 538
Tennessee Book Company, **11** 193
Tennessee Coal, Iron and Railroad Co., **IV**
   573; **7** 550

Tennessee Eastman, **III** 475; **7** 161
Tennessee Electric Power Co., **III** 332
Tennessee Gas Transmission Co., **I** 526
Tennessee Insurance Company, **11** 193–94
Tennessee Restaurant Company, **9** 426
Tennessee Valley Authority, **II** 2–3, 121;
   IV 181
Tenney, Edward Davies, **II** 490
Tenngasco, **I** 527
Teollisuusosuuskunta Metsä-Saimaa, **IV**
   315
TEP. *See* Tucson Electric Power Company.
ter Meer, Fritz, **I** 349
Teradata Corporation, **6** 267
Teradyne, Inc., 11 502–04
Terex Corporation, 7 513–15; **8** 116
Terman, Frederick, **III** 142; **6** 237
Terminal Transfer and Storage, Inc., **6** 371
Terminix International, **6** 45–46; **11** 433
Terracciano, Anthony P., **II** 317; **9** 223
Terrace Park Dairies, **II** 536
Terracor, **11** 260–61
Terre Haute Electric, **6** 555
Territorial Hotel Co., **II** 490
Territory Enterprises Ltd., **IV** 59
Terry Coach Industries, Inc., **III** 484
Terry Coach Manufacturing, Inc., **III** 484
Terry, Richard E., **6** 544
Terry's of York, **II** 594
Tervo, Penna, **IV** 469
Tesch, Emmanuel, **IV** 26
Tesch, Hjalmar Andersson, **I** 625
Tesch, Victor, **IV** 24, 26
Tesco, **10** 442; **11** 239, 241
Tesco PLC, II 513, **677–78**
Tesco Stores (Holdings) Ltd., **II** 677
Tesco Stores Ireland Ltd., **II** 678
Tesco Stores Ltd., **II** 677
Tesoro Petroleum Corporation, 7 516–19
Tesseract Corp., **11** 78
Testor Corporation, **8** 455
TETI, **I** 466
Tetley Inc., **I** 215
Tetley Tea, **I** 215
Tetra Plastics Inc., **V** 374; **8** 393
Teutonia National Bank, **IV** 310
Tevis, Lloyd, **I** 527; **II** 381; **10** 527
Tex-Star Oil & Gas Corp., **IV** 574; **7** 551
Texaco, **7** 172
Texaco Canada, **IV** 439
Texaco Chemical Co., **IV** 552–53
Texaco Inc., I 21, 360; **II** 31, 313, 448;
   III 760; **IV** 386, 403, 418, 425, 429,
   461, 464, 466, 472–73, 479–80, 484,
   488, 490, 510–11, 530–31, 536–39,
   545, **551–53**, 560, 565–66, 570, 575; **7**
   280, 483; **9** 232; **10** 190
Texada Mines, Ltd., **IV** 123
Texas Air Corporation, I 97, 100, 103,
   118, **123–24**, 127, 130; **6** 82, 129
Texas Almanac, **10** 3
Texas Butadiene and Chemical Corp., **IV**
   456
Texas Co., **III** 497; **IV** 386, 400, 464, 536,
   551; **7** 352
Texas Co. of California, **IV** 552
Texas Co. of Delaware, **IV** 551–52
Texas Commerce Bankshares, **II** 252
Texas Corp., **IV** 551–52
Texas Eastern Corp., **6** 487; **11** 97, 354
Texas Eastern Transmission Company, **11**
   28
Texas Eastman, **III** 475; **7** 161
Texas Electric Service Company, **V** 724

Texas Fuel Co., **IV** 551
Texas Gas Resources, **IV** 395
Texas Gypsum, **IV** 341
Texas Industries, Inc., 8 522–24
Texas Instruments, **8** 157
Texas Instruments Incorporated, I 315,
    482, 523, 620; **II** 64, **112–15**; **III** 120,
    124–25, 142, 499; **IV** 130, 365, 681; **6**
    216, 221–22, 237, 241, 257, 259; **7** 531;
    9 43, 116, 310; **10** 22, 87, 307; **11** 61,
    308, 490, 494, **505–08 (upd.)**
Texas International, **IV** 413
Texas International Airlines, **I** 117, 123; **II**
    408
Texas Life Insurance Co., **III** 293
Texas Metal Fabricating Company, **7** 540
Texas Oil & Gas Corp., **IV** 499, 572, 574;
    7 549, 551
Texas Overseas Petroleum Co., **IV** 552
Texas Pacific Coal and Oil Co., **I** 285–86
Texas Pacific Oil Co., **IV** 550
Texas Pipe Line Co., **IV** 552
Texas Power & Light Company, **V** 724
Texas Public Utilities, **II** 660
Texas Super Duper Markets, Inc., **7** 372
Texas Trust Savings Bank, **8** 88
Texas United Insurance Co., **III** 214
Texas Utilities Company, V 724–25
Texas Utilities Electric Company, **V**
    724–25
Texas Utilities Fuel Company, **V** 724–25
Texas Utilities Mining Company, **V** 725
Texas Utilities Services, Inc., **V** 725
Texas-New Mexico Power Co., **6** 580
Texas-New Mexico Utilities Company, **6**
    580
Texasgulf, **IV** 546–47
Texboard, **IV** 296
Texize, **I** 325, 371
Texkan Oil Co., **IV** 566
Texstar Petroleum Company, **7** 516
Texstyrene Corp., **IV** 331
Textile Paper Tube Company, Ltd., **8** 475
Textron, **11** 261
Textron Inc., I 186, **529–30**; **II** 420; **III**
    66, 628; **8** 93, 157, 315, 545; **9** 497, 499
Textron Lycoming Turbine Engine, 9
    497–99
TF-I, **I** 563
TFN Group Communications, Inc., **8** 311
TGEL&PCo. *See* Tucson Gas, Electric
    Light & Power Company.
TGI Friday's, **10** 331
Th. Pilter, **III** 417
TH:s Group, **10** 113
Thackeray, William Makepeace, **IV** 617
Thai Airways Company. *See* Thai Airways
    International Ltd.
Thai Airways International Ltd., I 119;
    II 442; **6 122–24**
Thai Aluminium Co. Ltd., **IV** 155
Thalassa International, **10** 14
Thalberg, Irving, **II** 148
Thalheimer, Richard, **10** 486–87
Thalhimer Brothers, **V** 31
Thames Board Ltd., **IV** 318
Thames Television Ltd., **I** 532
Thames Water International, **11** 510
Thames Water plc, 11 509–11
Tharsis Co., **IV** 189–90
Thatcher Glass, **I** 610
Thatcher, Margaret, **I** 34, 51, 83, 94, 556;
    III 336, 753; **IV** 38, 40, 380, 452,
    641–42; **7** 332, 532; **10** 121; **11** 204

Thayer, Charles J., **9** 485
Thayer Laboratories, **III** 55
Thayer, W. Paul, **I** 490–91
Theis, Fran, **6** 395
Theo H. Davies & Co., **I** 470
Theo Hamm Brewing Co., **I** 260
Theobald, Thomas, **II** 262
Théraplix, **I** 388
Therm-o-Disc, **II** 19
Therm-X Company, **8** 178
Thermacote Welco Company, **6** 146
Thermal Power Company, **11** 270
Thermo Electron Corporation, 7 520–22;
    11 512–13
Thermo Instrument Systems Inc., 11
    512–14
Thermodynamics Corp., **III** 645
Thermogas Co., **IV** 458–59
Thermoplast und Apparatebau GmbH, **IV**
    198
Thewes, Thomas, **10** 243
Thieme, Carl, **III** 183, 299–300
Thierry, Jacques, **II** 201–03
Thies, Wes, **9** 434
Thiess, **III** 687
Thiess Dampier Mitsui, **IV** 47
Thimont, Bernard, **7** 217
Think Entertainment, **II** 161
Think Technologies, **10** 508
Thiokol Chemical Corporation, **8** 472
Thiokol Corporation, 9 358–59, **500–02**
    (upd.)
Thiokol Inc., **I** 370
Third National Bank, **II** 291
Third National Bank of Dayton, **9** 475
Third National Bank of New York, **II** 253
Thistle Group, **9** 365
Thom McAn, **V**, 136–37; **11** 349
Thomas & Betts Corp., II 8; **11 515–17**
Thomas & Howard Co., **II** 682
Thomas and Hochwalt, **I** 365
Thomas, B.D., Dr., **10** 139
Thomas, Bailey, **7** 316
Thomas Barlow, **IV** 22
Thomas Barlow & Sons (South Africa)
    Ltd., **I** 422
Thomas Barlow & Sons Ltd., **I** 288, 422
Thomas, Bert L., **II** 683
Thomas, Charles, **I** 126, 366; **9** 355
Thomas Cook Travel Inc., 9 503–05
Thomas, Edward, **7** 234
Thomas, Edward D., **11** 62
Thomas, Edwin J., **V** 246
Thomas Firth & Sons, **I** 573
Thomas, George C., Jr., **11** 515
Thomas, Grant, **IV** 92
Thomas H. Lee Company, **11** 156, 450
Thomas Jefferson Life Insurance Co., **III**
    397
Thomas, John, **III** 720
Thomas, Joseph, **I** 484; **11** 263
Thomas, Ken W., **V** 523–25
Thomas Linnell & Co. Ltd., **II** 628
Thomas Nationwide Transport Limited, **V**
    523
Thomas Nelson & Sons, **8** 526
Thomas, O. Pendleton, **V** 233; **11** 158
Thomas, Patrick H., **11** 111
Thomas, Peter, **III** 114
Thomas, Philip E., **V** 438
Thomas, Philippe, **IV** 174
Thomas, R. David, **8** 563–65
Thomas, Robert E., **IV** 458–59
Thomas, Robert M., **11** 515

Thomas, Rubel, **6** 134
Thomas, S.B., **II** 498
Thomas, S.G., **IV** 24
Thomas Tilling plc, **I** 429
Thomas, Watson, **6** 250
Thomas Y. Crowell, **IV** 605
Thomasville Furniture Industries, **III** 423
Thomazin, George H., **II** 682
Thomopoulous, Anthony, **II** 149
Thompson, Adam, **I** 94
Thompson, Charles E., **11** 540
Thompson, David, **II** 513–14; **V** 80
Thompson, Edward K., **IV** 674; **7** 527
Thompson, Glenn W., **8** 38–39
Thompson, Harry, **6** 585
Thompson, J.J., **II** 24
Thompson, J. Walter, **I** 19–20
Thompson, Jack, **I** 400
Thompson, James S., **IV** 635–36
Thompson, Jere W., **II** 661; **7** 491
Thompson, Joe C. "Jodie", **7** 490
Thompson, John F., **IV** 111
Thompson, John P., **II** 660–61; **7** 490–91
Thompson, John S., **III** 303
Thompson, Joseph C., **II** 660; **7** 491
Thompson, Julian Ogilvie, **IV** 68; **7** 125
Thompson, Kay, **IV** 672
Thompson, M.B., **II** 505
Thompson, Peter, **6** 413–14
Thompson Products Co., **I** 539
Thompson, R. Duff, **10** 558
Thompson, Rupert, **I** 529
Thompson, W. Reid, **6** 553–54
Thompson, William, **I** 132
Thompson, William Boyce, **7** 287, 385
Thompson-Ramo-Woolridge, **I** 539
Thompson-Werke, **III** 32
Thomson, Alexander, **IV** 263
The Thomson Corporation, IV 651, 686;
    7 390; **8 525–28**
Thomson, Cy, **II** 505–05
Thomson, Elihu, **II** 27
Thomson family, **IV** 263–64
Thomson International, **10** 407
Thomson, J. Edgar, **10** 71
Thomson, Kenneth, **V** 80; **8** 525–67
Thomson, Logan, **IV** 263
Thomson, Peter, **IV** 263–64
Thomson, Richard Murray, **II** 376
Thomson, Roy, 8 525–27
Thomson, Roy (Lord of Fleet), **IV** 651
Thomson S.A., I 411; **II** 31, **116–17**; **7** 9
Thomson, S.C., **IV** 164
Thomson, Spencer, **III** 360
Thomson T-Line, **II** 142
Thomson, William Thomas, **III** 359–60
Thomson-Bennett, **III** 554
Thomson-Brandt, **I** 411; **II** 13, 116–17; **9**
    9
Thomson-CSF, **II** 116–17; **III** 556
Thomson-Houston Co., **II** 27
Thomson-Houston Electric Co., **II** 27, 116,
    330
Thomson-Lucas, **III** 556
Thomson-Ramo-Woolridge. *See* TRW Inc.
Thoreau, Henry David, **IV** 661
Thorley, Gerald (Sir), **IV** 712
Thorn Apple Valley, Inc., 7 523–25
Thorn Electrical Industries Ltd., **I** 531
Thorn EMI plc, I 52, 411, **531–32**; **II**
    117, 119; **III** 480
Thorn, Jules, **I** 531–32
Thorn/Radio Rentals, **I** 531
Thorne, George, **V** 145–46

Thorne, Oakleigh, **7** 93
Thornton, **III** 547
Thornton & Co., **II** 283
Thornton, Charles, **I** 166, 484–85; **II** 33; **11** 263–64
Thornton, Charles "Tex", **11** 138
Thornton, Clive, **10** 7
Thornton, George, **III** 265
Thornton, Henry, Sir, **6** 360
Thoroughgood, **II** 658
Thorpe, William, **11** 38
Thorssin, Fridolf, **I** 197
Thos. Cook, **6** 84
Thouron, George, **I** 344
3 Guys, **II** 678, **V** 35
Three-Diamond Company. *See* Mitsubishi Shokai.
3-in-One Oil Co., **I** 622
3COM, **III** 143
3Com Corp., **6** 238, 269; **10** 237; **11** **518–21**
3DO Inc., **10** 286
3M. *See* Minnesota Mining & Manufacturing Co.
3S Systems Support Services Ltd., **6** 310
Threlfall Breweries, **I** 294
Thresher, Stephen, **10** 377
Thrif D Discount Center, **V** 174
Thrift Drug, **V** 92
ThriftiCheck Service Corporation, **7** 145
Thriftway Foods, **II** 624
Thrifty Corporation, **V** 682, 684
Thrifty Rent-A-Car, **6** 349
Thrope, Joel M., **9** 320
Thruelsen, Richard, **I** 63
Thunström, Sölve, **IV** 275
Thurber, James, **IV** 672
Thuringia Insurance Co., **III** 299
Thurmond, Strom, **III** 188
Thurston, Severt W., **9** 547–48
Thy-Marcinelle, **IV** 52
Thy-Marcinelle et Monceau, **IV** 52
Thy-Marcinelle et Providence, **IV** 52
Thyssen & Co., **IV** 221
Thyssen AG, **II** 279; **III** 566; **IV** **221–23,** 228; **8** 75–76
Thyssen, August, **I** 542; **IV** 221
Thyssen family, **IV** 222
Thyssen, Fossoul & Co., **IV** 221
Thyssen, Fritz, **IV** 221
Thyssen Handelsunion AG, **IV** 222–23
Thyssen Industrie AG, **IV** 222
Thyssen Stahl AG, **IV** 195, 222
Thyssen-Hütte, **IV** 222
Thyssengas GmbH, **IV** 232
TI. *See* Texas Instruments.
TI Corporation, **10** 44
Tianjin Agricultural Industry and Commerce Corp., **II** 577
Tibbals Floring Co., **III** 611
Tibbitts, Samuel J., **11** 378
Tiburzi, Bonnie, **I** 91
Ticino Societa d'Assicurazioni Sulla Vita, **III** 197
Ticknor & Fields, **10** 356
Tickometer Co., **III** 157
Ticor Title Insurance Co., **10** 45
Tidel Systems, **II** 661
Tidén, Lorentz, **I** 553
Tidewater Associated Oil Co., **IV** 460
Tidewater Inc., **11** **522–24**
Tidewater Oil Co., **IV** 434, 460, 489, 522
Tidnam, F. H., **6** 539
Tidy House Products Co., **II** 556

Tiel Utrecht Fire Insurance Co., **III** 309–10
Tien Wah Press (Pte.) Ltd., **IV** 600
Le Tierce S.A., **II** 141
Tietgen, C.F., **II** 351
Tietz, Georg, **V** 72–73
Tietz, Hermann, **V** 72–73
Tietz, Leonhard, **V** 103–05
Tietz, Oskar, **V** 72–73
Tiffany & Co., **III** 16
Tiger Oats, **I** 424
Tigges, Hubert, **II** 163
Tigges, Maria, **II** 163
Tigges, Reinhold, **II** 163
Tigon Corporation, **V** 265–68
Tilcon, **I** 429
Tilden, Bill, **IV** 671
Tilden Interrent, **10** 419
Tilden, Samuel, **IV** 688
Tilford, Henry Morgan, **IV** 385, 399
Tilford, W.H., **IV** 385
Tilgate Pallets, **I** 592
Tillie Lewis Foods Inc., **I** 513–14
Tillinghast, Charles, **I** 97, 126–27
Tillman, Arthur B., **IV** 409
Tillman, Frederick, Jr., **7** 130
Tilney, A.A., **II** 229–30
Tim-Bar Corp., **IV** 312
Timber Realization Co., **IV** 305
Timberland Co., **11** 349
Time Inc., **II** 155 161, 168, 176–77, 252, 452; **III** 245; **IV** 341–42, 636, 673–75; **7** 63, 526–29; **8** 267–68, 527; **9** 469
Time Industries, **IV** 294
Time Insurance Co., **III** 200
Time Warner Cable, **7** 529–30
Time Warner Entertainment, **7** 529–30; **10** 168, 491
Time Warner Inc., **II** 155, 168, 175, 177; **IV** **673–76**; **6** 293; **7** 222–24, 396, **526–30 (upd.)**; **9** 119, 472; **10** 286, 484, 488. *See also* Warner Communications Inc.
Time Warner Publishing, **IV** 675; **7** 529
Time Warner Telecommunications, **7** 530
Time-Life Books, **IV** 675; **7** 528–29
Time-Life Broadcast, **IV** 674
Time-Life Films, **IV** 675
Time-O-Stat Controls Corp., **II** 41
Time-Sharing Information, **10** 357
Timely Brands, **I** 259
Timeplex, **III** 166; **6** 283; **9** 32
Times Media Ltd., **IV** 22
Times Mirror Broadcasting, **IV** 677
Times Mirror Company, **I** 90; **IV** 583, 630, **677–78**
Times Mirror Magazines, Inc., **IV** 677
Times Newspapers, **8** 527
Times-Picayune Publishing Co., **IV** 583
Timex, **III** 455; **10** 152
Timex Enterprises Inc., **7** **531–33**
Timken, **III** 596; **7** 447
The Timken Company, **8** **529–31**
Timken France, **8** 530
Timken, H.H., **8** 529–30
Timken, Henry, **7** 280; **8** 529
Timken, Jr., H.H., **8** 530
Timken, Jr., W. Robert, **8** 530
Timken Ordnance Company, **8** 530
The Timken Roller Bearing Company, **8** 529. *See also* The Timken Company.
Timken, W. Robert, **8** 530
Timken, William, **8** 529
Timken-Detroit Axle Company, **8** 529

Timm, Bernard, **I** 306
Timmis, Denis, **IV** 308
Timpte Industries, **II** 488
Tinker, Grant, **6** 165
Tioxide Group PLC, **III** 680
Tip Corp., **I** 278
TIPC Network, **10** 307. *See also* Gateway 2000.
Tippery, Miles, **8** 517
Tippett, Paul, Jr., **I** 190
Tippins, George W., **8** 19–20
Tipton Centers Inc., **V** 50
Tiroler Hauptbank, **II** 270
Tirpitz, Alfred von (Admiral), **IV** 86
Tisch, Al, **I** 487
Tisch, Bob, **I** 487–88
Tisch, James, **I** 488
Tisch, Larry, **6** 159
Tisch, Laurence A., **I** 487–88; **II** 134; **III** 231–32
Tisch, Robert, **V** 176
Tisch, Sadye, **I** 487
Tise, Jane, **8** 169
Tiselius, Arne, **I** 664
Tishman Realty and Construction, **III** 248
Tissue Papers Ltd., **IV** 260
Titanium Metals Corporation of America, **10** 434
Titianium Enterprises, **IV** 345
TITISA, **9** 109
Title Guarantee & Trust Co., **II** 230
Titmus Optical Inc., **III** 446
Tittman, Edward, **IV** 33
Tittman, O. H., **9** 367
TJX Companies, Inc., **V** **197–98**
TKD Electronics Corp., **II** 109
TKM Foods, **II** 513
TLC Associates, **11** 261
TLC Group, **II** 468
TML Information Services Inc., **9** 95
TMS, Inc., **7** 358
TMS Systems, Inc., **10** 18
TMT. *See* Trailer Marine Transport.
TNT, **IV** 651
TNT Limited, **V** **523–25**; **6** 346
Toa Airlines, **6** 427
Toa Domestic Airways, **I** 106
Toa Fire & Marine Reinsurance Co., **III** 385
Toa Kyoseki Co. Ltd., **IV** 476
Toa Nenryo Kogyo, **IV** 432
Toa Oil Co. Ltd., **IV** 476, 543
Toa Tanker Co. Ltd., **IV** 555
Toasted Corn Flake Co., **II** 523
Tobata Imaon Co., **I** 183
Tobey, Fred W., **7** 493
Tobias, Randall L., **11** 89, 91
Tobin, James, **10** 143
Tobin, Michael, **I** 400
Tobler, August Leonhard, **III** 411
Tobler Co., **II** 520–21
Tobler, Jean, **II** 520
Tobler, Johann Jakob, **II** 520
Tobler, Theodor, **II** 520
Tobu Group, **6** 431
Tobu Railway Co Ltd, **6** **430–32**
Tobu Store, **6** 432
Tocom, Inc., **10** 320
Tod, G. Robert, **10** 215
Toda, Benny, **6** 107
Toda, Kengo, **III** 593
Todays Computers Business Centers, **6** 243–44
Todays Temporary, **6** 140

Todd, Alan (Col.), **III** 350
Todd Company, **7** 138
Todd, Harry, **9** 460
Todd Shipbuilding Corp., **IV** 121
Todorovich Agency, **III** 204
Toei, **9** 29–30
Toeplitz, Giuseppe, **I** 368
Tofas, **I** 479–80
Toggenburger Bank, **II** 378
Togo, Yukiyasu, **I** 205
Toho Chemical Co., **I** 363
Toho Oil Co., **IV** 403
Tohoku Alps, **II** 5
Tohoku Pulp Co., **IV** 297
Tohuku Electric Power Company, Inc.,
    V 724, 732
Tojo Railway Company, **6** 430
Tojura, Sotaro, **III** 406
Tokai Aircraft Co., Ltd., **III** 415
Tokai Bank, Ltd., II 373–74
Tokai Bank of California, **II** 374
Tokai Bank of Canada, **II** 374
Tokai Paper Industries, **IV** 679
Tokai Trust Co. of New York, **II** 374
Tokan Kogyo, **I** 615
Tokio Marine and Fire Insurance Co.,
    Ltd., II 323; **III** 248, 289, 295, **383–86**
Tokio Marine Insurance Co., **III** 383–84
Tokiwa, Fumikatsu, **III** 38
Tokugawa family, **IV** 214
Tokugawa, Nariaki (Lord), **III** 532
Tokumasu, Sumao, **III** 368
Tokushima Ham Co., **II** 550
Tokushima Meat Processing Factory, **II**
    550
Tokushu Seiko, Ltd., **IV** 63
Tokuyama Soda, **I** 509
Tokuyama Teppan Kabushikigaisha, **IV**
    159
Tokyo Broadcasting, **7** 249; **9** 29
Tokyo Car Manufacturing Co., **I** 105
Tokyo Confectionery Co., **II** 538
Tokyo Corporation, **V** 199
Tokyo Dairy Industry, **II** 538
Tokyo Denki Kogaku Kogyo, **II** 109
Tokyo Dento Company, **6** 430
Tokyo Disneyland, **IV** 715; **6** 123, 176
Tokyo Electric Co., **I** 533
Tokyo Electric Express Railway Co., **IV**
    728
Tokyo Electric Light Co., **IV** 153
Tokyo Electric Power Company, **IV** 167,
    518; **V 729–33**
Tokyo Electronic Corp., **11** 232
Tokyo Express Highway Co., Ltd., **IV**
    713–14
Tokyo Express Railway Company, **V** 510,
    526
Tokyo Fire Insurance Co. Ltd., **III** 405–06,
    408
Tokyo Food Products, **I** 507
Tokyo Fuhansen Co., **I** 502, 506
Tokyo Gas and Electric Industrial
    Company, **9** 293
Tokyo Gas Co., Ltd., **IV** 518; **V 734–36**
Tokyo Ishikawajima Shipbuilding and
    Engineering Company, **9** 293
Tokyo Ishikawajima Shipyard Co., Ltd.,
    III 532
Tokyo Maritime Insurance Co., **III** 288
Tokyo Motors, **9** 293
Tokyo Sanyo Electric, **II** 91–92
Tokyo Shibaura Electric Co., **I** 507, 533
Tokyo Steel Works Co., Ltd., **IV** 63

Tokyo Tanker Co., Ltd., **IV** 479
Tokyo Telecommunications Engineering
    Corp. *See* Tokyo Tsushin Kogyo K.K.
Tokyo Trust & Banking Co., **II** 328
Tokyo Tsushin Kogyo K.K., **II** 101, 103
Tokyo Yokohama Electric Railways Co.,
    Ltd., **V** 199
Tokyu Companies, **V** 199
Tokyu Construction Industry, **IV** 728
Tokyu Corporation, **IV** 728; **V** 199,
    526–28
Tokyu Department Store Co., Ltd., V
    199–202
Tokyu Electric Power Company, **V** 736
Tokyu Gravel Co., **IV** 728
Tokyu Kyuko Elwctric Railway Coompany
    Ltd., **V** 526
Tokyu Land Corporation, IV 728–29
Tokyu Railway Company, **V** 461
Tokyu Real Estate Co., Ltd., **IV** 728
Toledo Edison Company. *See* Centerior
    Energy Corporation.
Toledo Scale Corp., **9** 441
Toledo Seed & Oil Co., **I** 419
Tolleson, John C., **11** 122
Tom Bowling Lamp Works, **III** 554
Tom Huston Peanut Co., **II** 502; **10** 323
Tom Piper Ltd., **I** 437
Tomakomai Paper Co., Ltd., **IV** 321
Tombs, Francis, **I** 82
Tombs, Lord, **7** 456
Tomei Fire and Marine Insurance Co., **III**
    384–85
Tomen Corporation, IV 224–25
Tomen Electronics Corp., **IV** 225
Tomen Information Systems Corp., **IV** 225
Tomen Transportgerate, **III** 638
Tomioka, Hiroshi, **III** 548–49
Tomkins plc, 11 525–27
Tomlee Tool Company, **7** 535
Tomlinson, Alexander, **III** 403
Tomlinson, Allan J., **IV** 410
Tomlinson, Roy E., **II** 543
Tomoe Trading Co., **III** 595
Tompkins, Doug, **8** 169–70
Tompkins, Susie, **8** 169–71
Tomyo, Kubo, **III** 578; **7** 348
Tonami Transportation Company, **6** 346
Tonen Corporation, IV 554–56
Tonen Energy International Corp., **IV** 555
Tonen Sekiyukagaku Co. Ltd., **IV** 555
Tonen System Plaza Inc., **IV** 556
Tonen Tanker Co. Ltd., **IV** 555
Tong Yang Group, **III** 304
Toni Co., **III** 28; **9** 413
Tonti, Lorenzo, **III** 291
Toohey, **10** 170
Tooker, Gary L., **11** 329
Tooker, Sterling, **III** 389
Toot, Jr., Joseph F., **8** 531
Tootal Group, **V** 356–57
Top End Wheelchair Sports, **11** 202
Top Man, **V** 21
Top Shop, **V** 21
Top Value Enterprises, **II** 645
Top Value Stamp Co., **II** 644; **6** 364
Topaloglu, Ihsan (Dr.), **IV** 562
Topol, Sidney, **6** 335–36
Toppan Containers, **IV** 679
Toppan Interamerica, **IV** 680
Toppan Moore Co., Ltd., **IV** 645, 679–80
Toppan Moore Learning, **IV** 680
Toppan Moore Systems, **IV** 680

Toppan Printing Co., Ltd., **IV** 598–99,
    679–81
Toppan Printronics U.S.A., **IV** 681
Toppan Shoji, **IV** 679
Toppan Technical Design Center, **IV** 680
Toppan West, **IV** 680
Topy Industries, Limited, **8** 506–07
Toray Industries, Inc., V 380, **383**
Torbensen Gear & Axle Co., **I** 154
Torchmark Corporation, **III** 194; **9**
    506–08; **10** 66; **11** 17
Torise Ham Co., **II** 550
Tormey, John L., **V** 502
Tornator Osakeyhtiö, **IV** 275–76
Törnudd, G., **IV** 275
Toro Assicurazioni, **III** 347
The Toro Company, **III** 600; **7 534–36**
Toro Manufacturing Company, **7** 534
Toronto and Scarborough Electric Railway,
    9 461
Toronto Electric Light Company, **9** 461
Toronto-Dominion Bank, **II** 319, **375–77**,
    456
Torpshammars, **IV** 338
Torres, Phillip, **9** 78
Torrey Canyon Oil, **IV** 569
Torrington Co., **III** 526, 589–90
Torstar Corp., **IV** 672; **7** 488–89
Tory, John A., **8** 525
Tosa Electric Railway Co., **II** 458
Tosaki, Shinobu, **IV** 125
Tosco Corporation, 7 537–39
Toshiba Corporation, **I** 221, 507–08,
    533–35; **II** 5, 56, 59, 62, 68, 73, 99,
    102, 118, 122, 326, 440; **III** 298, 461,
    533, 604; **6** 101, 231, 244, 287; **7** 529; **9**
    7, 181; **10** 518–19; **11** 328
Toshiba Ltd., **11** 46
Toshimitsu, Tsurumatasu, **V** 487
Toshin Kaihatsu Ltd., **V** 195
Toshin Paper Co., Ltd., **IV** 285
Tostem. *See* Toyo Sash Co., Ltd.
Tostem Cera Co., **III** 757
Tostem Thai Co., Ltd., **III** 758
Total. *See* Total Compagnie Française des
    Pétroles S.A.
Total CFD, **IV** 560
Total CFP. *See* Total Compagnie Française
    des Pétroles S.A.
Total Chimie, **IV** 560
Total Compagnie Française des Pétroles, **7**
    481, 483–84
Total Compagnie Française des Pétroles
    S.A., **I** 303; **III** 673; **IV** 425, 498, 515,
    525, 544, 547, **557–61**; **V** 628
Total Compagnie Minière, **IV** 560
Total Exploration S.A., **11** 537
Total Global Sourcing, Inc., **10** 498
Total-Austria, **IV** 486
TOTE, **9** 509–11
Totem Ocean Trailer Express, Inc. *See*
    TOTE.
Totem Resources Corporation, 9 509–11
Totino's Finer Foods, **II** 556
Toto Bank, **II** 326
Toto, Ltd., III 755–56
Totsu Co., **I** 493
Touborg, Jens, **8** 514
Toucey, Isaac, **III** 236
Touche Remnant Holdings Ltd., **II** 356
Touche Ross, **10** 529. *See also* Deloitte &
    Touche.
Touchstone Films, **II** 172–74; **6** 174–76
Tour d'Argent, **II** 518

Tourang Limited, **7** 253
Touristik Union International GmbH.
and Company K.G., II 163–65
Touron y Cia, **III** 419
Touropa, **II** 163–64
Toval Japon, **IV** 680
Tow, Andrew, **10** 210
Tow, Claire, **10** 210
Tow, Leonard, **7** 89; **10** 210–12
Towa Nenryo Kogyo Co. Ltd., **IV** 554–55
Towe, Kenneth, **I** 310; **8** 25
Tower Records, **9** 361; **10** 335; **11** 558
Towers, **II** 649
Towey, James, **I** 380
Town & City, **IV** 696
Town & Country, **7** 372
Town Investments, **IV** 711
Towne, Henry, **I** 154; **10** 279
Towne, James C., **6** 258
Townsend Hook, **IV** 296, 650, 652
Townsend, Ida, **I** 640; **9** 264
Townsend, Lynn, **I** 144–45; **11** 53–54
Townsend, Robert, **6** 356
Toy Biz, Inc., **10** 402
Toyad Corp., **7** 296
Toyama, Genichi, **II** 433; **9** 377
Toyo Bearing Manufacturing, **III** 595
Toyo Bearing Okayama Co., **III** 595
Toyo Building Sash Co., **III** 757
Toyo Cotton (Japan) Co., **IV** 225
Toyo Cotton Co., **IV** 224
Toyo Distribution Service Co., **III** 757
Toyo Glass, **I** 615
Toyo Juko Co., **III** 757
Toyo Kogyo, **I** 167; **II** 361; **11** 139
Toyo Kohan Co., **I** 615
Toyo Marine and Fire, **III** 385
Toyo Menka Kaisha Ltd., **I** 508; **IV**
224–25
Toyo Microsystems Corporation, **11** 464
Toyo Oil Co., **IV** 403
Toyo Pulp Co., **IV** 322
Toyo Rayon, **V** 381, 383
Toyo Sash Co., Ltd., III 757–58
Toyo Sash Housing Co., **III** 757
Toyo Sash Sales Co., **III** 757
Toyo Seikan Kaisha Ltd., I 615–16
Toyo Soda, **II** 301
Toyo Tire & Rubber Co., **9** 248
Toyo Toki Co., Ltd., **III** 755
Toyo Tozo Co., **I** 265
Toyo Trust and Banking Co., **II** 347, 371
Toyo Tyre and Rubber Co., **V** 255–56
Toyoda Automatic Loom Works, Ltd.,
III 591, 593, 632, **636–39**
Toyoda, Eiji, **I** 204–05; **III** 637; **11**
529–30
Toyoda Industrial Equipment
Manufacturing, Inc., **III** 638–39
Toyoda Industrial Trucks U.S.A., **III** 638
Toyoda, Kiichiro, **I** 203–04; **III** 591,
636–37; **11** 528–29
Toyoda Machine Works Ltd., **I** 203; **III**
637
Toyoda, Risaburo, **III** 636–38
Toyoda, Sakichi, **III** 636–38
Toyoda, Shoichiro, **11** 530
Toyoda Spinning and Weaving Works, **III**
636
Toyoda Steel Works, **III** 637
Toyoda Textile Machinery, **III** 638
Toyoda, Totsuro, **11** 531
Toyoda, Yoshitoshi, **III** 638
Toyoda-Sulzer Co., **III** 638

Toyokawa Works, **I** 579
Toyoko Co., Ltd., **V** 199
Toyoko Department Store Co., Ltd., **V** 199
Toyoko Kogyo, **V** 199
Toyomenka (America) Inc., **IV** 224
Toyomenka (Australia) Pty., Ltd., **IV** 224
Toyonaga, Kozo, **IV** 298
Toyota (GB) Ltd., **III** 521
Toyota Gossei, **I** 321
Toyota Motor Corporation, I 9–10, 174,
184, **203–05**, 507–08, 587; **II** 373; **III**
415, 495, 521, 523, 536, 579, 581,
591–93, 624, 636–38, 667, 715, 742; **IV**
702; **6** 514; **7** 111, 118, 212, 219–21; **8**
315; **9** 294, 340–42; **10** 353, 407; **11**
351, 377, 487, **528–31 (upd.)**
Toyota Motor Sales Co., **III** 638
Toys "R" Us, Inc., III 588; **V 203–06**; **7**
396; **10** 235, 284, 484
Tozer Kemsley & Milbourn, **II** 208
TPCR Corporation, **V** 163
Tracey Bros., **IV** 416
Tracey-Locke, **II** 660
Tracht, Doug "The Greaseman", **11** 191
Tracker Services, Inc., **9** 110
Traco International N.V., **8** 250
Tracor Inc., **10** 547
Tractor Supply Corp., **I** 446
Tracy, E.B., **7** 280
Tracy, Eugene A., **6** 544
Tradax, **II** 617
Trade Assoc. of Bilbao, **II** 194
Trade Development Bank, **11** 415–17
Trade Waste Incineration, Inc., **9** 109
Trade Winds Campers, **III** 599
TradeARBED, **IV** 25
Trader Publications, Inc., **IV** 597
Traders & General Insurance, **III** 248
Traders Bank of Canada, **II** 344
Traders Group Ltd., **II** 258
Tradesmens National Bank of Philadelphia,
II 342
The Trading Service, **10** 278
Traex Corporation, **8** 359
Trafalgar House, **I** 248–49, 572–74; **IV**
259, 711
Trafton, R.M., **III** 353
Tragos, William G., **6** 47–49
Trailer Marine Transport, **6** 383
Trailways, **I** 450; **9** 425
Tramiel, Jack, **7** 95–96; **9** 46
Trammell Crow, **IV** 343
Trammell Crow Company, 8 326–28,
532–34
Tran Telecommunications Corp., **III** 110
Trane Co., **III** 663, 665; **10** 525
Trans Air System, **6** 367
Trans Colorado, **11** 299
Trans International Airlines, **I** 537
Trans Ocean Products, **II** 578; **8** 510
Trans Rent-A-Car, **6** 348
Trans Union Corp., **IV** 137; **6** 25
Trans World Airlines Inc., I 58, 70, 90,
97, 99–100, 102, 113, 121, 123–24,
125–27, 132, 466; **II** 32–33, 425, 679;
III 92, 428; **6** 50, 68, 71, 74, 76–77,
81–82, 114, 130; **9** 17, 232; **10** 301,
316; **11** 277, 427
Trans World Corp., **II** 142, 679; **10**
301–03
Trans World Music, **9** 361
Trans-Arabian Pipe Line Co., **IV** 537, 552
Trans-Australia Airlines, **6** 110–12
Trans-Natal Coal Corp., **IV** 93

TransAlta Resources Corporation, **6** 585
TransAlta Utilities Corporation, 6
585–87
Transamerica, **8** 46
Transamerica Corporation, I 536–38; **II**
147–48, 227, 288–89, 422; **III** 344; **7**
236–37; **11** 273, 533
Transamerica Occidental, **III** 332
Transamerica Title Insurance Co., **III** 344
Transat. *See* Compagnie Générale
Transatlantique (Transat).
Transatlantic Holdings, Inc., III 198; **11**
532–33
Transatlantic Reinsurance Co., **III** 196–98
Transatlantische Dampfschiffahrts
Gesellschaft, **6** 397
Transatlantische Gruppe, **III** 404
Transbrasil, **6** 134
TransCanada PipeLines Limited, I 264;
V 270–71; **737–38**
Transco Energy Company, IV 367; **V**
739–40; **6** 143
Transco Exploration Company, **IV** 83; **V**
739
Transcontinental & Western Airways, **9**
416
Transcontinental Air Transport, **I** 125; **9**
17; **11** 427
Transcontinental Gas Pipe Line
Corporation, **V** 739; **6** 447
Transcontinental Pipeline Company, **6**
456–57
Transelco, Inc., **8** 178
TransEuropa, **II** 164
Transflash, **6** 404
Transfracht, **6** 426
Transinternational Life, **II** 422
Transit Mix Concrete and Materials
Company, **7** 541
Transkrit Corp., **IV** 640
Translite, **III** 495
Transnet Ltd., 6 433–35
TransOcean Oil, **III** 559
Transpac, **IV** 325
Transport Indemnity Co., **III** 192
Transport Management Co., **III** 192
Transport- und Unfall-Versicherungs-
Aktiengesellschaft Zürich, **III** 411
Transportation Insurance Co., **III** 229
Transportes Aereos Portugueses, S.A., 6
125–27
Transtar, **6** 120–21
Transvaal Silver and Base Metals, **IV** 90
Transway International Corp., **10** 369
Transworld Drilling Co. Ltd., **IV** 446
Tranzonic Companies, **8** 512
Traudes, F., **IV** 140
Trausch Baking Co., **I** 255
Trautlein, Donald, **IV** 37; **7** 50
Trautman, Gerald, **I** 450
Trautman, Gerald H., **8** 144–45
Trävaru Svartvik, **IV** 338
Travel Air Company, **8** 49
Travel Automation Services Ltd., **I** 95
Travelers Corporation, I 545; **III** 313,
329, **387–90**
Travelers Equities Fund, **III** 389
Travelers Indemnity Co., **III** 388–89
Travelers Insurance Co., **I** 37; **III** 387,
707–08; **6** 12
Travelers Keystone Fixed Income
Advisors, **III** 389
Travelers Lloyds Insurance Co., **III** 389
Travelers Plan Administrators, **III** 389

Traveller's Express, **I** 449
TraveLodge, **III** 94, 104–06
Travenol Laboratories, **I** 627–28; **10** 141–43
Travers, Oliver S., **9** 485
Travolta, John, **III** 306
Trayco, **III** 570
Traylor Engineering & Manufacturing Company, **6** 395
Treatment Centers of America, **11** 379
Trebek, Alex, **9** 306
Treble, J.H., **III** 359
Trechmann, Weekes and Co., **III** 669
Tredegar Industries, Inc., **10** 291
Tree of Life Inc., **II** 528
Trees, J.C., **IV** 415
Trees, Merle, **7** 76
TrefilARBED, **IV** 26
Tréfimétaux, **IV** 174
Trefoil Capital Investors, L.P., **8** 305
Trek, **IV** 90, 92
Trek Beleggings, **IV** 93
Trelleborg A.B., **III** 625; **IV** 166
Tremletts Ltd., **IV** 294
Trent Tube, **I** 435
Trenton Foods, **II** 488
Tresco, **8** 514
Tresnowski, Bernard, **10** 160
Trethowal China Clay Co., **III** 690
Treves, Emilio, **IV** 585
Trevor-Roper, Hugh (Lord Dacre), **IV** 651–52; **7** 391
de Trey, August, **10** 271
de Trey, Caesar, **10** 271
Treybig, James G., **6** 278–79
Tri-City Federal Savings and Loan Association, **10** 92
Tri-City Utilities Company, **6** 514
Tri-County National Bank, **9** 474
Tri-Miller Packing Company, **7** 524
Tri-Star Pictures, **I** 234; **II** 134, 136–37; **6** 158; **10** 227
Tri-State Improvement Company, **6** 465–66
Tri-State Refining Co., **IV** 372
Triangle Auto Springs Co., **IV** 136
Triangle Industries, **I** 602, 607–08, 614; **II** 480–81
Triangle Portfolio Associates, **II** 317
Triangle Publications, **IV** 652; **7** 391
Triangle Refineries, **IV** 446
Triarc Companies, Inc. (formerly DWG Corporation), 8 535–37
Triathlon Leasing, **II** 457
Tribune Company, III 329; **IV 682–84**; **10** 56; **11** 331
Tribune Entertainment Co., **IV** 684
Trical Resources, **IV** 84
Tricity Cookers, **I** 531–32
Trico Industries, **I** 186
Tridel Enterprises Inc., 9 512–13
Trident Seafoods, **II** 494
Trifari, Krussman & Fishel, Inc., **9** 157
Trigano, Gilbert, **6** 206–08
Trigen Energy Corp., **6** 512
Trilan Developments Ltd., **9** 512
Trilon Bancorp, **II** 456–57
Trilon Capital Markets, **II** 457
Trilon Financial Corporation, II 456–57; **IV** 721; **9** 391
TriMas Corp., III 571; **11 534–36**
Trinidad Oil Co., **IV** 95, 552

Trinidad-Tesoro Petroleum Company Limited, **7** 516, 518
Trinity Beverage Corporation, **11** 451
Trinity Industries, Incorporated, 7 540–41
Trinkaus und Burkhardt, **II** 319
TRINOVA Corporation, III 640–42, 731
Trintex, **6** 158
Triology Corp., **III** 110
Tripcovich, Diodato, **III** 208
Tripcovich, Mario, **III** 208
Triplex, **6** 279
Triplex (Northern) Ltd., **III** 725
Tripp, Frank, **IV** 612; **7** 190
Trippe, Juan, **I** 67, 89–90, 96, 99, 112, 115–16; **6** 81, 103; **9** 231, 417
Trippe Manufacturing Co., **10** 474
Triquet Paper Co., **IV** 282; **9** 261
Triton Bioscience, **III** 53
Triton Energy Corporation, 11 537–39
Triton Group Ltd., **I** 447
Triton Oil, **IV** 519
Tritton, John Henton, **II** 235
Triumph, Finlay, and Philips Petroleum, **11** 28
Triumph-Adler, **I** 485; **III** 145; **11** 265
Trivest Insurance Network, **II** 457
Trizec Corporation Ltd., 9 84–85; **10 529–32**
Trizzino, Victor F., **11** 463
Trojan, **III** 674
Trona Corp., **IV** 95
Tropical Oil Co., **IV** 415–16
Tropical Shipping & Construction Ltd., **6** 531
Tropical Shipping, Inc., **6** 529
Tropicana Products, **II** 468, 525
Tropsch, Hans, **IV** 534
Trotsky, Leon, **IV** 671
Trotter, Billy, **II** 613
Trotter, Jimmy, **II** 613
Trotter, Ronald (Sir), **IV** 278–79
Troughton, Charles, **V** 212
Troy Metal Products. *See* KitchenAid.
Troyfel Ltd., **III** 699
TRT Communications, Inc., **6** 327; **11** 185
Tru-Trac Therapy Products, **11** 486
Trudeau, Pierre Elliott, **IV** 494
True Form, **V** 177
True Value Hardware Stores, **V** 37–38
Trueller, Harry, **II** 543
Trugg-Hansa Holding AB, **III** 264
Truitt Bros., **10** 382
Trujillo, Bernardo, **10** 205
Truman Dunham Co., **III** 744
Truman Hanburg, **I** 247
Truman, Harry S, **I** 71, 90, 507; **IV** 114–15, 237, 522, 573, 621, 689; **7** 550; **8** 313; **11** 278
Trumball Asphalt, **III** 721
Trümmer-Verwertungs-Gesellschaft, **IV** 140
Trump, Donald, **III** 92, 431; **6** 201, 211; **9** 125, 426–27
Trunkline Gas Company, **6** 544
Trunkline LNG Co., **IV** 425
Trust House Forte, **I** 215
Trust Houses Group, **III** 104–05
Trustcorp, Inc., **9** 475–76
Trustees, Executors and Agency Co. Ltd., **II** 189
Trusthouse Forte PLC, III 104–06
TRW Inc., I 539–41; **II** 33; **6** 25; **8** 416; **9** 18, 359; **10** 293; **11** 68, **540–42 (upd.)**

Tryart Pty. Limited, **7** 253
Trygger, Ernst, **III** 419
Tsai, Gerald, **I** 614; **II** 412
Tsai, Gerald, Jr., **III** 231
Tsai, Gerry, **8** 194
Tsai Management & Research Corp., **III** 230–31
Tse, K.K., **III** 195
TSO. *See* Teacher's Service Organization, Inc.
TSO Financial Corp., **II** 420; **8** 10
Tsuang Hine Co., **III** 582
Tsuchida, Terumichi, **III** 289
Tsuganuma, Toshihiko, **III** 715
Tsuji, Gentaro, **III** 639
Tsuji, Haruo, **II** 96
Tsukumo Shokai, **I** 502; **III** 712
Tsumeb Corp., **IV** 17–18
Tsurumi Steelmaking and Shipbuilding Co., **IV** 162
Tsurumi, Yoshi, **I** 455
Tsurusaki Pulp Co., Ltd., **IV** 285
Tsutsumi, Seiji, **V** 184, 187–88
Tsutsumi, Yasujiro, **V** 184, 510–11
Tsutsumi, Yoshiaki, **V** 187, 511
Tsutsunaka Plastic, **8** 359
Tsutsunaka Plastic Industry Co., **III** 714
Tsuzuki, Mikihiko, **V** 537
TTK. *See* Tokyo Tsushin Kogyo K.K.
TTX Company, 6 436–37
Tu, Way, **11** 246
Tube Investments, **II** 422; **IV** 15
Tuborg, **9** 99
Tuborgs Fabrikker, **9** 99
Tuchbreiter, Roy, **III** 229–30
Tucher, Hans Christof Freiherr von, **II** 242
Tuck, Samuel, **8** 552
Tucker, Joe, **III** 651
Tuckey, James, **IV** 712
Tuckis, Robert, **7** 431
TUCO, Inc., **8** 78
Tucson Electric Power Company, V 713; **6 588–91**
Tucson Gas, Electric Light & Power Company. *See* Tuscon Electric Power Company.
Tucson Resources Inc., **6** 590
TUI. *See* Touristik Union International GmbH. and Company K.G.
Tuke, Anthony Favill, **II** 236; **IV** 192
Tuke, Anthony William, **II** 236
Tuke, Mary, **II** 568
Tuke, William, **II** 568
Tuke, William Favill, **II** 236
Tulagin, Vsevolod, **I** 338
Tullis, Richard, **II** 37–38
Tullis, Robert H., **III** 263
Tumpeer, David, **I** 404–05
Tumpeer, Julius, **I** 404–05
Tunhems Industri A.B., **I** 387
Tuohy, Walter J., **V** 439
Tupper, Earl, **III** 610
Tupperware, **I** 29; **II** 534; **III** 610–12
Tupperware Home Parties, **III** 610
Turbay, Julio Cesar, **IV** 417
Turbinbolaget, **III** 419
Turk, Seymour, **IV** 672
Turkish Engineering, Consultancy and Contracting Corp., **IV** 563
Turkish Petro Chemical Corp., **IV** 563
Turkish Petroleum Co. *See* Türkiye Petrolleri Anonim Ortaklığı.
Turkish-Petroleum International Co., **IV** 563–64

Türkiye Garanti Bankasi, **I** 479
Türkiye Petrolleri Anonim Ortakliği, IV
   464, 557–58, **562–64**; **7** 352
N.V. Turkse Shell, **IV** 563
Turley, K. L., **6** 546
Turley, Stewart, **9** 186–87
Turmel, Antoine, **II** 651–52
Turnbull, **III** 468
Turnbull, George, **7** 232
Turnbull, George (Sir), **III** 516, 523
Turner Advertising Co., **II** 166
Turner Broadcasting System, Inc., II
   134, 149, 161 **166–68**; **IV** 676; **6**
   171–73 (upd.); **7** 64, 99, 306, 529
Turner, Cedric, **6** 110
Turner Communications Corp., **II** 166
The Turner Corporation, 8 538–40
Turner, Frank, **7** 456
Turner, Fred, **II** 646–47; **7** 318–19
Turner, Henry C., **8** 538–39
Turner, Henry Gyles, **II** 388
Turner, Jim, **7** 494
Turner, Mark, **IV** 191–92
Turner, Michael, **II** 298
Turner Pictures, **II** 167
Turner Program Services, **II** 166
Turner Publishing, **II** 167
Turner, Robert Edward, III (Ted), **I** 488; **II**
   134, 149, 161, 166–67, 177, 408; **6**
   171–73
Turner, Ted. *See* Turner, Robert Edward
   III.
Turner, William J., **III** 118–19
Turner's Turkeys, **II** 587
Turnpaugh, Timothy E., **9** 195
TURPAS, **IV** 563
Turpin, Jack, **9** 55
Turrish, Henry, **8** 428
Tussauds Group Ltd., **IV** 659
Tuttle, Edwin E., **I** 383–84
Tuttle, Robert D., **I** 199–200; **10** 494
Tuttle, W. B., **6** 473
TV & Stereo Town, **10** 468
TV Asahi, **7** 249
TV Guide, **10** 287
TVE. *See* Television Española, S.A.
TVH Acquisition Corp., **III** 262, 264
TVW Enterprises, **7** 78
TVX, **II** 449
TW Kutter, **III** 420
TW Services, Inc., II 679–80; **10** 301–03
TWA. *See* Trans World Airlines *and*
   Transcontinental & Western Airways.
Tweed, William Marcy (Boss), **IV** 647
Twen-Tours International, **II** 164
Twentieth Century Co., **II** 169
Twentieth Century Fox Film
   Corporation, II 133, 135, 146, 155–56,
   169–71, 175; **IV** 652; **7** 391–92
Twentieth Century Fox Television, **II** 170
Twentieth Century Pictures, **II** 169
Twentsche Bank, **II** 183
Twenty-Second National Bank, **II** 291
Tweter, Clifford, **II** 289
Twining Crosfield Group, **II** 465
Twining, Thomas, **II** 465
Twinings Tea, **II** 465; **III** 696
Twinings' Foods International, **II** 466
Twinpak, **IV** 250
Twitchell, Herbert K., **II** 251
Twitchell, Karl, **IV** 386
2-in-1 Shinola Bixby Corp., **II** 497
Twomey, William P., **9** 297
TXL Oil Corp., **IV** 552

TXP Operation Co., **IV** 367
Ty-D-Bol, **III** 55
Tyco Laboratories, Inc., III 643–46
Tyler, Henry W., Captain, **6** 359
Tyler, Patrick, **I** 60
Tyndall Fund-Unit Assurance Co., **III** 273
Typhoo Tea, **II** 477
Typpi Oy, **IV** 469
Tyrolean Airways, **9** 233
Tyrrell, H. Victor, **IV** 638
Tyrvään Oy, **IV** 348
Tyson, Don, **II** 584–85
Tyson Feed & Hatchery, Inc., **II** 584
Tyson Foods, **7** 422–23
Tyson Foods, Incorporated, II 584–85
Tyson, John, **II** 584
Tyson's Foods, Inc., **II** 584; **7** 432
Tytler, James, **7** 165
Tytus, John Butler, **IV** 28

U S West Communications, **V** 342
U S West Financial Services, **V** 341–42
U S West, Inc., V 341–43; **11** 12
U S West New Vector Group Inc., **V** 341
U.C.L.A.F. *See* Roussel-Uclaf.
U-Haul International Inc. *See* Amerco.
U.K. Corrugated, **IV** 296
U.S. Bearings Co., **I** 159
U.S. Electrical Motors, **II** 19
U.S. Food Products Co., **I** 376
U.S.G. Co., **III** 762
U.S. Geological Survey, **9** 367
U.S. Guarantee Co., **III** 220
U.S. Healthcare, Inc., 6 194–96
U.S. Home Corporation, 8 541–43
U.S. Industrial Chemicals, **I** 377
U.S. Industries, **7** 208
U.S. International Reinsurance, **III** 264
U.S. Land Co., **IV** 255
U.S. Life Insurance, **III** 194
U.S. Lines, **I** 476; **III** 459; **11** 194
U.S. Lock, **9** 543
U.S. Marine Corp., **III** 444
U.S. Plywood Corp. *See* United States
   Plywood Corp.
U.S. Plywood-Champion Papers, Inc., **IV**
   264
U.S. Postal Service, **10** 60
U.S. Realty and Improvement Co., **III** 98
U.S. RingBinder Corp., **10** 313–14
U.S. Robotics Inc., 9 514–15
U.S. Rubber Company, **10** 388
U.S. Satellite Systems, **III** 169; **6** 285
U.S. Smelting Refining and Mining, **7** 360
U.S. Steel. *See* United States Steel Corp.
U.S. Steel Corp. *See* United States Steel
   Corp.
U.S. Telephone Communications, **9** 478
U.S. Tile Co., **III** 674
U.S. Trust Co. of New York, **II** 274
U.S. Vanadium Co., **9** 517
U.S. Vitamin & Pharmaceutical Corp., **III**
   55
U.S. West Information Systems Inc., **11** 59
U.S. Windpower, **11** 222–23
U-Tote'M, **7** 372
UAA. *See* AirEgypt.
UAL, Inc., **II** 680; **IV** 23; **9** 283. *See also*
   United Airlines.
UAP. *See* Union des Assurances de Paris.
UAP Assistance, **III** 393
UAP International, **III** 394
UAT. *See* UTA.
Ub Iwerks, **6** 174

Ube America, **III** 760
Ube Cement Co., **III** 759
Ube Dockyard, **III** 760
Ube Industries, Ltd., III 759–61
Ube Machinery Works, **III** 760
Ube Nitrogen Industrial Co., **III** 759
Ube Shinkawa Iron Works, **III** 759
Ube Wormser, **III** 760
UBE-EMS Yugen Kaisha, **III** 760
Uberseebank A.G., **III** 197
Übleis, Heinrich, **6** 420
UBS. *See* Union Bank of Switzerland.
UBS Australia Ltd., **II** 379
UBS Securities Inc., **II** 378
Ucabail, **II** 265
UCC-Communications Systems, Inc., **II** 38
Uccel, **6** 224
Uchiyama, **V** 727
UCI, **IV** 92
UCPMI, **IV** 226
Udall, Stewart L., **IV** 366
Uddeholm and Bohler, **IV** 234
Udet Flugzeugwerke, **I** 73
Udo Fischer Co., **8** 477
UE Automotive Manufacturing, **III** 580
Ueberroth, John, **9** 272–73
Ueberroth, Peter, **9** 272
Ueltschi, Albert, **9** 231–32
Ugarte, Pedro Toledo, **II** 195
UGI. *See* United Gas Improvement.
Ugine, **IV** 174
Ugine Steels, **IV** 227
Ugine-Kuhlmann, **IV** 108, 174
Uhl, Edward G., **9** 205
UI International, **6** 444
UIB. *See* United Independent Broadcasters,
   Inc.
Uinta Co., **6** 568
Uintah National Corp., **11** 260
Uitgeversmaatschappij Elsevier, **IV** 610
UK Paper, **IV** 279
UKF. *See* Unie van Kunstmestfabrieken.
Ukropina, James R., **V** 684
Ulbricht, Walter, **IV** 590
Ullrich Copper, Inc., **6** 146
Ullstein AV Produktions-und
   Vertriebsgesellschaft, **IV** 590
Ullstein Langen Müller, **IV** 591
Ullstein Tele Video, **IV** 590
Ulmann, Herbert J., **III** 282
Ulmer, Gordon I., **II** 214
ULPAC, **II** 576
Ulrich, Franz Heinrich, **II** 279
Ulrich, Gustavo Adolfo, **III** 345
Ulster Bank, **II** 334
Ultra Bancorp, **II** 334
Ultra High Pressure Units Ltd., **IV** 66; **7**
   123
Ultra Radio & Television, **I** 531
Ultramar American Ltd., **IV** 182
Ultramar Canada Ltd., **IV** 566
Ultramar Co. Ltd., **IV** 565–67
Ultramar Exploration Co. Ltd., **IV** 565
Ultramar Golden Eagle, **IV** 566–67
Ultramar PLC, IV 565–68
Ultronic Systems Corp., **IV** 669
UM Technopolymer, **III** 760
Umacs of Canada Inc., **9** 513
Umbreit, George M., **III** 572
Umm-al-Jawabi Oil Co., **IV** 454
Umstattd, William, **8** 530
Unadulterated Food Products, Inc., **11** 449
UNAT, **III** 197–98
Under Sea Industries, **III** 59

Underground Group, **6** 407
Underkofler, James, **6** 605–06
Underwood, **III** 145
Underwriters Adjusting Co., **III** 242
Underwriters Reinsurance Co., **10** 45
UNELCO. *See* Union Electrica de Canarias S.A.
Unfall, **III** 207
Ungermann-Bass, Inc., **6** 279
Uni Europe, **III** 211
Uni-Cardan AG, **III** 494
Uni-Charm, **III** 749
Uni-Sankyo, **I** 675
Unic, **V** 63
Unicare Health Facilities, **6** 182
Unicer, **9** 100
Unicoa, **I** 524
Unicomi, **II** 265
Unicon Producing Co., **10** 191
Unicorn Shipping Lines, **IV** 91
UniCorp, **8** 228
Unicorp Financial, **III** 248
Unicredit, **II** 265
UniDynamics Corporation, **8** 135
Unie van Kunstmestfabrieken, **I** 326
Uniface Holding B.V., **10** 245
Unified Management Corp., **III** 306
Unigate Ltd., **II** 586–87
Unigate PLC, **II** 586–87
Unigep Group, **III** 495
Unigesco Inc., **II** 653
UniHealth America, **11** 378–79
Unilac Inc., **II** 547
Unilever PLC / Unilever N.V., **I** 369, 590, 605; **II** 547, **588–91**; **III** 31–32, 46, 52, 495; **IV** 532; **7** 382, **542–45** (**upd.**), 577; **8** 105–07, 166, 168, 341, 344; **9** 449; **11** 205, 421
Unilife Assurance Group, **III** 273
Unilife Netherlands, **III** 273
UniMac Companies, **11** 413
Unimat, **II** 265
Unimation, **II** 122
Unimetal, **IV** 227
Uninsa, **I** 460
Union, **III** 391–93
Union & NHK Auto Parts, **III** 580
Union Acceptances Ltd., **IV** 23
Unión Aérea Española, **6** 95
Union Aéromaritime de Transport. *See* UTA.
Union Assurance, **III** 234
Union Bag & Paper Co., **IV** 344
Union Bag & Paper Corp., **IV** 344–45
Union Bag–Camp Paper Corp., **IV** 344–45
Union Bancorp of California, **II** 358
Union Bank, **II** 207; **8** 491. *See also* State Street Boston Corporation.
Union Bank, **8** 491–92
Union Bank of Australia, **II** 187–89
Union Bank of Birmingham, **II** 318
Union Bank of Canada, **II** 344
Union Bank of England, **II** 188
Union Bank of Finland, **II** 302, 352
Union Bank of Halifax, **II** 344
Union Bank of London, **II** 235
Union Bank of New London, **II** 213
Union Bank of New York, **9** 229
Union Bank of Prince Edward Island, **II** 220
Union Bank of Scotland, **10** 337
Union Bank of Switzerland, **II** 257, 267, 334, 369, 370, **378–79**

Union Bank of Switzerland Securities Ltd., **II** 378
Union Battery Co., **III** 536
Union Camp Corporation, **IV** 344–46; **8** 102
Union Carbide Chemicals & Plastics Co., **III** 742
Union Carbide Corporation, **I** 334, 339, 347, 374, 390, **399–401**, 582, 666; **II** 103, 313, 562; **III** 760; **IV** 92, 379, 521; **7** 376; **8** 180, 182, 376; **9** 16, **516–20** (**upd.**); **10** 289, 472; **11** 402–03
Union Carbide Petroleum Co., **IV** 374
Union Cervecera, **9** 100
Union Colliery Company, **V** 741
Union Commerce Corporation, **11** 181
Union Corp., **I** 423; **IV** 90–92, 95, 565
Union d'Etudes et d'Investissements, **II** 265
Union de Transports Aeriens, **I** 119, 121
Union des Assurances de Paris, **II** 234; **III** 201, **391–94**
Union des Transports Aériens. *See* UTA.
Union Electric Company, **V** 741–43; **6** 506
Union Electric Light and Power Company, **6** 505
Union Electrica de Canarias S.A., **V** 607
Union Equity Co-Operative Exchange, **7** 175
Union et Prévoyance, **III** 403
Union Fertilizer, **I** 412
Union Fidelity Corp., **III** 204
Union Gas & Electric Co., **6** 529
Union Générale de Savonnerie, **III** 33
l'Union Générale des Pétroles, **IV** 545–46, 560; **7** 482–83
Union Glass Co., **III** 683
Union Hardware, **III** 443
Union Hop Growers, **I** 287
l'Union Industrielle des Pétroles, **IV** 545; **7** 483
Union Levantina de Seguros, **III** 179
Union Light, Heat & Power Company, **6** 466
Union Marine, **III** 372
Union Mutual Life Insurance Co., **III** 236
Union National Bank, **II** 284; **10** 298
Union of Food Co-ops, **II** 622
Union of London, **II** 333
Union Oil Associates, **IV** 569
Union Oil Co., **9** 266
Union Oil Co. of California, **I** 13; **IV** 385, 400, 403, 434, 522, 531, 540, 569, 575; **11** 271
Union Pacific Corporation, **V** 529–32
Union Pacific Railroad, **I** 473; **II** 381; **III** 229
Union Pacific Tea Co., **7** 202
Union Paper Bag Machine Co., **IV** 344
Union Petroleum Corp., **IV** 394
L'Union pour le Developpement Régional, **II** 265
Union Rückversicherungs-Gesellschaft, **III** 377
Union Savings, **II** 316
Union Savings Bank, **9** 173
Union Steam Ship Co., **IV** 279
Union Steel Co., **IV** 22, 572; **7** 550
Union Sugar, **II** 573
Union Sulphur Co., **IV** 81; **7** 185
Union Supply Co., **IV** 573; **7** 550
Union Tank Car Co., **IV** 137
Union Texas Natural Gas, **I** 415

Union Texas Petroleum Holdings, Inc., **7** 379; **9** 521–23
Union Transfer and Trust Co., **II** 315
Union Trust Co., **II** 284, 313, 315–16, 382; **9** 228
Union Underwear, **I** 440–41
The Union Underwear Company, **8** 200–01
Union Wine, **I** 289
Union-Capitalisation, **III** 392
Union-Incendie, **III** 391–92
Union-Transport, **6** 404
Union-Vie, **III** 391–92
Union-Vol, **III** 392
Unionamerica Insurance Group, **III** 243
Uniroyal, **11** 159
Uniroyal Corp., **I** 30–31; **II** 472; **V** 242; **8** 503
Unisource, **I** 413
Unisys Corporation, **II** 42; **III** **165–67**; **6** **281–83** (**upd.**); **8** 92; **9** 32, 59
The Unit Companies, Inc., **6** 394, 396
Unit Group plc, **8** 477
United Acquisitions, **7** 114
United Agri Products, **II** 494
United Air Lines Transportation Company. *See* United Airlines.
United Aircraft and Transportation Co., **I** 76, 78, 441, 489; **9** 416, 418; **10** 162, 260
United Aircraft Co., **I** 48, 85–86, 96
United Airlines, **I** 23, 47, 71, 84, 90, 97, 113, 116, 118, 124, **128–30**; **II** 142, 419, 680; **III** 225; **6** 71, 75–77, 104, 121, 123, **128–30** (**upd.**), 131, 388–89; **9** 271–72, 283, 416, 549; **10** 162, 199, 561; **11** 299
United Alaska Drilling, Inc., **7** 558
United Alkalai Co., **I** 351
United American Insurance Company of Dallas, **9** 508
United American Lines, **6** 398
United Arab Airlines. *See* AirEgypt.
United Artists (UA), **6** 167
United Artists Communications, **II** 160
United Artists Corp., **I** 537; **II** 135, 146–48, 149, 157–58, 167, 169; **III** 721; **IV** 676. *See also* MGM/UA Communications Company.
United Artists Entertainment Co., **II** 160; **9** 74
United Bank of Arizona, **II** 358
United Biscuit Co., **II** 594
United Biscuits (Holdings) PLC, **II** 466, 540, **592–94**; **III** 503
United Biscuits Ltd., **II** 592–94
United Brands Company, **II 595–97**; **III** 28; **7** 84–85
United Breweries, **I** 221, 223, 288
United Breweries Ltd. *See* Carlsberg A/S.
United Cable Television Corporation, **II** 160; **9** 74
United California Bank, **II** 289
United Car, **I** 540
United Carbon Co., **IV** 373
United Central Oil Corporation, **7** 101
United Cigar Manufacturers, **II** 414
United City Property Trust, **IV** 705
United Co., **I** 70
United Communications Systems, Inc. **V** 346
United Computer Services, Inc., **11** 111
United Corp., **10** 44
United County Banks, **II** 235
United Dairies, **II** 586–87

United Dairy Farmers, **III** 190
United Dominion Corp., **III** 200
United Dominion Industries, **IV** 288
United Dominion Industries Limited, 8 544–46
United Drapery Stores, **III** 502; **7** 208
United Drug Co., **II** 533
United Engineering Steels, **III** 495
United Engineers & Constructors, **II** 86; **11** 413
United Express, **11** 299
United Features Syndicate, Inc., **IV** 607–08
United Federal Savings and Loan of Waycross, **10** 92
United Financial Group, Inc., **8** 349
United Fruit Co., **I** 529, 566; **II** 120, 595; **IV** 308; **7** 84–85
United Gas and Electric Company of New Albany, **6** 555
United Gas Corp., **IV** 488–90
United Gas Improvement Co., **IV** 549; **V** 696; **6** 446, 523; **11** 388
United Gas Industries, **III** 502; **7** 208
United Gas Pipe Line Co., **IV** 489–90
United Geophysical Corp., **I** 142
United Grocers, **II** 625
United Guaranty Corp., **III** 197
United Health, Inc., **6** 182
United Health Maintenance, Inc., **6** 181
United HealthCare Corporation, 9 524–26
United Independent Broadcasters, Inc., **II** 132
United Industrial Syndicate, **8** 545
United Information Systems, Inc., **V** 346
United Insurance Co., **I** 523
Oy United International, **IV** 349
United International Pictures, **II** 155
United Kent Fire, **III** 350
United Kingdom Atomic Energy Authority, **6** 451–52
United Liberty Life Insurance Co., **III** 190–92
United Life & Accident Insurance Co., **III** 220–21
United Light & Railway Co., **V** 609
United Light and Power, **6** 511
United Medical Service, Inc., **III** 245–46
United Meridian Corporation, **8** 350
United Metals Selling Co., **IV** 31
United Micronesia, **I** 97
United Molasses, **II** 582
United Natural Gas Company, **6** 526
United Netherlands Navigation Company. *See* Vereenigde Nederlandsche Scheepvaartmaatschappij.
United Newspapers Ltd., **IV** 685–87
United Newspapers plc, IV 685–87
United of Omaha, **III** 365
United Office Products, **11** 64
United Oil Co., **IV** 399
United Optical, **10** 151
United Pacific Financial Services, **III** 344
United Pacific Insurance Co., **III** 343
United Pacific Life Insurance Co., **III** 343–44
United Pacific Reliance Life Insurance Co. of New York, **III** 343
United Packages, **IV** 249
United Paper Mills Ltd., II 302; **IV** 316, **347–50**
United Paramount Theatres, **II** 129

United Parcel Service of America Inc. (UPS), V 533–35; **6** 345–46, 385–86, 390; **11** 11
United Pipeline Co., **IV** 394
United Power & Light, **6** 473
United Press Assoc., **IV** 607, 627, 669; **7** 158
United Press International, **IV** 670; **7** 158–59
United Retail Merchants Stores Inc., **9** 39
United Roasters, **III** 24
United Satellite Television, **10** 320
United Savings of Texas, **8** 349
United Servomation, **7** 471–72
United Skates of America, **8** 303
United Software Consultants Inc., **11** 65
United States Baking Co., **II** 542
United States Cellular Corporation, 9 494–96, **527–29**
United States Department of Defense, **6** 327
United States Distributing Corp., **IV** 180–82
United States Electric and Gas Company, **6** 447
The United States Electric Lighting Company, **11** 387
United States Export-Import Bank, **IV** 55
United States Express Co., **II** 381, 395–96; **10** 59–60
United States Fidelity and Guaranty Co., **III** 395
United States Filter Corp., **I** 429; **IV** 374
United States Foil Co., **IV** 186
United States Glucose Co., **II** 496
United States Graphite Company, **V** 221–22
United States Gypsum Co., **III** 762–64
United States Health Care Systems, Inc. *See* U.S. Healthcare, Inc.
United States Independent Telephone Company, **6** 332
United States Leasing Corp., **II** 442
United States Mortgage, **II** 251
United States National Bank of San Diego, **II** 355
United States Pipe and Foundry Co., **III** 766
United States Plywood Corp., **IV** 264, 282, 341; **9** 260
United States Realty-Sheraton Corp., **III** 98
United States Rubber, **I** 478
United States Shoe Corporation, V 207–08
United States Steel Corp., **I** 298, 491; **II** 129, 330; **III** 282, 326, 379; **IV** 35, 56, 110, 158, 572–74; **6** 514; **7** 48, 70–73, 401–02, 549–51; **10** 32; **11** 194. *See also* USX Corporation.
United States Sugar Refining Co., **II** 496
United States Surgical Corporation, 10 533–35
United States Tobacco Company, **9** 533
United States Trucking Corp., **IV** 180–81
United States Underseas Cable Corp., **IV** 178
United States Zinc Co., **IV** 32
United Steel, **III** 494
United Supers, **II** 624
United Technologies Corporation, I 68, **84–86**, 143, 411, 530, 559; **II** 64, 82; **III** 74; **9** 18, 418; **10 536–38 (upd.)**; **11** 308

United Telecom. *See* United Telecommunications, Inc.
United Telecommunications, Inc., V 344–47; **8** 310; **9** 478–80; **10** 202
United Telephone, **7** 508
United Telephone Company of the Carolinas, **10** 202
United Telephone System, Inc., **V** 346
United Telespectrum, **6** 314
United Television, Inc., **9** 119
United Television Programs, **II** 143
United Transportation Co., **6** 382
United Utilities, Inc., **V** 344; **10** 202
United Verde Copper Co., **IV** 178
United Vintners, **I** 243, 260–61
United Westphalia Electricity Co., **IV** 127
Unitek Corp., **III** 18
Unitel Communications, **6** 311
Unitika Ltd., V 387–89
Unity Joint-Stock Bank, **II** 334
UNIVAC, **III** 133, 152, 313; **6** 233, 240, 266
Univar, **8** 99
Univar Corporation, 9 530–32
Universal Adding Machine, **III** 165
Universal American, **I** 452
Universal Atlas Cement Co., **IV** 573–74; **7** 550–51
Universal Belo Productions, **10** 5
Universal Containers, **IV** 249
Universal Controls, Inc., **10** 319
Universal Cooler Corp., **8** 515
Universal Corporation, V 417–18
Universal Data Systems, **II** 61
Universal Foods Corporation, 7 546–48
Universal Forest Products Inc., 10 539–40
Universal Furniture, **III** 571
Universal Guaranty Life Insurance Company, **11** 482
Universal Health Services, Inc., 6 191–93
Universal Highways, **III** 735
Universal Industries, **10** 380
Universal Instruments Corp., **III** 468
Universal Leaf Tobacco Company. *See* Universal Corporation.
Universal Manufacturing, **I** 440–41
Universal Matthey Products Ltd., **IV** 119
Universal Paper Bag Co., **IV** 345
Universal Pictures, **II** 102, 135, 144, 154–55, 157; **10** 196
Universal Press Syndicate, **10** 4
Universal Resources Corporation, **6** 569
Universal Stamping Machine Co., **III** 156
Universal Studios, **II** 143–44
Universal Telephone, **9** 106
Universal Television, **II** 144
Universal Transfers Co. Ltd., **IV** 119
University Computing Co., **II** 38; **11** 468
University Microfilms, **III** 172; **6** 289
Univision Holdings Inc., **IV** 621
Unix, **6** 225
Unkefer, Ronald A., **10** 334–35
Uno-Ven, **IV** 571
Unocal Corporation, IV 508, **569–71**
Unruh, James A., **III** 167; **6** 283
Uny, **V** 154
Uny Co., Ltd., II 619; **V 209–10**
UPI. *See* United Press International.
Upjohn Company, I 675, 684, 686, 700, **707–09**; **III** 18, 53; **6** 42; **8 547–49 (upd.)**; **10** 79
Upjohn HealthCare Services, Inc., **6** 42
Upjohn, Henry, **I** 707; **8** 547

Upjohn, Lawrence, **8** 547
Upjohn, Lawrence N., **I** 707; **8** 547
Upjohn Pill and Granule Co., **I** 707
Upjohn, William, **I** 707; **8** 547
UPS. *See* United Parcel Service of America Inc.
Upton, Emory, **III** 653
Upton, Lou, **III** 653
Uraga Dock Co., **II** 361; **III** 634
Uraga Heavy Industries, **III** 634
Urann, Marcus L., **7** 403–04
Urbaine, **III** 391–92
Urbaine et la Seine, **III** 391–92
Urbaine-Accident, **III** 391
Urbaine-Incendie, **III** 391
Urbaine-Vie, **III** 391
Urban, Horst, **V** 242, 251
Urban Investment and Development Co., **IV** 703
Urban Systems Development Corp., **II** 121
Urenco, **6** 452
Urquhart, Lawrence, **IV** 383
Urwick Orr, **II** 609
US Air, **6** 121
US Industrial Alcohol Company, **8** 440
US Industrial Chemicals, Inc., **8** 440
US Order, Inc., **10** 560, 562
US Sprint Communications Company, **V** 295–96, 346–47; **6** 314; **8** 310; **9** 32; **10** 543; **11** 302. *See also* Sprint Communications Company, L.P.
US Telecom, **9** 478–79
US West, **11** 547
USAA, 10 541–43
USAir Group, Inc., I 55, **131–32; III** 215; **6 131–32 (upd.)**
USAir Inc., **11** 300
USCC. *See* United States Cellular Corporation.
USCP-WESCO Inc., **II** 682
USF&G Corporation, III 395–98; 11 494–95
USF&G Financial Services Corp., **III** 397
USG Corporation, III 762–64
Usines de l'Espérance, **IV** 226
Usines Métallurgiques de Hainaut, **IV** 52
Usinor, **IV** 226–27
Usinor Sacilor, IV 226–28
USLIFE, **III** 194
USM, **10** 44
USSC. *See* United States Surgical Corporation.
UST Inc., 9 533–35
USV Pharmaceutical Corporation, **11** 333
USX Corporation, I 466; **IV** 130, 228, **572–74; 7** 193–94, **549–52 (upd.)**
UTA, **6** 373–74, 93; **9** 233
Utag, **11** 510
Utah Construction & Mining Co., **I** 570; **IV** 146
Utah Gas and Coke Company, **6** 568
Utah Group Health Plan, **6** 184
Utah International, **II** 30
Utah Mines Ltd., **IV** 47
Utah Oil Refining Co., **IV** 370
Utah Power & Light Company, **9** 536
Utilicom, **6** 572
Utilicorp United Inc., 6 592–94
Utilities Power & Light Corporation, **I** 512; **6** 508
Utility Constructors Incorporated, **6** 527
Utility Engineering Corporation, **6** 580
Utility Fuels, **7** 377
UToteM, **II** 620

AB Utra Wood Co., **IV** 274
Utrecht Allerlei Risico's, **III** 200
Utter, Eero, **8** 294
UV Industries, Inc., **7** 360; **9** 440

V & V Cos., **I** 412
V.A.W. of America Inc., **IV** 231
V&S Variety Stores, **V** 37
V.L. Churchill Group, **10** 493
Vabis, **I** 197
Vabre, Jacques, **II** 520
Vacuum Metallurgical Company, **11** 234
Vacuum Oil Co., **IV** 463–64, 504, 549; **7** 351–52
Vadic Corp., **II** 83
Vadoise Vie, **III** 273
Vagelos, P.R., **I** 651; **11** 290–91
Vagnfabriks A.B., **I** 197
Vague, Richard, **11** 123
Vail Associates, Inc., 11 543–46
Vail, Charles D., **11** 543
Vail, Theodore, **III** 282
Vail, Theodore J., **V** 259–60
Vainio, Veikko, **IV** 315
Val Royal LaSalle, **II** 652
Valassis Communications, Inc., 8 550–51
Valassis, George, **8** 550–51
Valcambi S.A., **II** 268
Valdi Foods Inc., **II** 663–64
Valdiserri, Carl, **8** 450
Valdosta Drug Co., **III** 9–10
Valenstein, Larry, **6** 26–27
Valentin, Julius, **I** 409–10
Valentine & Company, **8** 552–53
Valentine, Donald T., **11** 58
Valentine, Henry, **8** 552
Valentine, Jack, **6** 12–13
Valentine, Lawson, **8** 552
Valentine, Robert M., **V** 168; **8** 442
Valenzuela, Pablo, **10** 213
Valeo, **III** 593
Valerio, Giorgio, **I** 368
Valero Energy Corporation, IV 394; **7 553–55**
Valhi, Inc., **10** 435–36
Valid Logic Systems Inc., **11** 46, 284
Valio-Finnish Co-operative Dairies' Assoc., **II** 575
Valke Oy, **IV** 348
Vallee, Rudy, **II** 151; **9** 306
Vallès, Jean-Paul, **11** 311
Valletta, Vittoria, **I** 161–62; **11** 102–03
Valley, Donald F., **11** 340
Valley East Medical Center, **6** 185
Valley Falls Co., **III** 213
Valley Federal of California, **11** 163
Valley Fig Growers, **7** 496–97
Valley Forge Insurance Co., **III** 230
Valley Forge Life Insurance Co., **III** 230
Valley National Bank, **II** 420
Valley Transport Co., **II** 569
Vallourec, **IV** 227
Valmac Industries, **II** 585
Valmet Aviation Industries, **III** 649
Valmet Corporation, I 198; **III 647–49; IV** 276, 471
Valmet Defence Equipment, **III** 649
Valmet do Brasil S.A., **III** 648–49
Valmet Instruments, **III** 649
Valmet Oy. *See* Valmet Corp.
Valmet Paper Machinery Inc., **III** 649; **IV** 350
Valmet Shipbuilding, **III** 649
Valmet Tractors, **III** 649

Valmet Transportation Equipment, **III** 649
The Valspar Corporation, 8 552–54
Valtec Industries, **III** 684
Valtur, **6** 207
Value Foods Ltd., **11** 239
Value House, **II** 673
Value Investors, **III** 330
Value Rent-A-Car, **9** 350
Valueland, **8** 482
Valvoline, Inc., **I** 291; **IV** 374
Valvtron, **11** 226
Van Ameringen, Arnold Louis, **9** 290–91
Van Ameringen-Haebler, Inc., **9** 290
Van Anda, Carr, **IV** 648
Van Andel, Jay, **III** 11–14
Van Arsdale, Elias, Jr., **9** 221
Van Brunt Manufacturing Co., **III** 462
Van Camp, Gilbert, **7** 556
Van Camp Seafood Company, Inc., II 562–63; **7 556–57**
van Cuylenburg, Peter, **7** 333
Van de Carr, Charles R., Jr., **IV** 311
Van de Kamp, **II** 556–57; **7** 430
Van de Kamp, John, **II** 605
Van de Maele, Albert, **9** 363
van den Berg, J. P., **V** 658
Van den Bergh Foods, **9** 319
Van den Berghs, **II** 588
van der Beugel, Ernst Hans, **I** 108
van der Heldt, Simon, **III** 309
Van der Horst Corp. of America, **III** 471
van der Post, C. P. M., **V** 658
van der Velden, J., **III** 309
Van Derzee, G. W., **6** 602
Van Dorn Electric Tool Co., **III** 435
Van Driel, Gerrit Hendrik, **II** 528
Van Dyke, John H., **III** 321
Van Dyke, John Wesley, **IV** 375
Van Dyke, William D., **III** 322–23
Van Fossan, Robert V., **III** 304
Van Gend and Loos, **6** 404
van Gogh, Vincent, **IV** 269
Van Halen, **II** 176–77
Van Horn, V.H., **7** 372–74
Van Houton, **II** 521
van Ishoven, Armand, **I** 75
van Kerchem, C.F.W. Wiggers, **III** 178
Van Kirk Chocolate, **7** 429
Van Kok-Ede, **II** 642
Van Leer, B., **IV** 133
Van Leer Holding, Inc., **9** 303, 305
van Marwijk, Kooy J.H., **I** 257
van Munching and Co., **I** 256
van Munching, Leo, **I** 256–57
Van Nortwick, John, **V** 425
Van Nostrand Reinhold, **8** 526
Van Orsdel, Ralph, **I** 418
van Reesema, William Siewertsz, **III** 309
van Rijn, Jaap, **III** 310
Van Ryn Gold Mines Estate, **IV** 90
Van Schaardenburg, **II** 528
Van Sickle, **IV** 485
van Steenwyk, E.A., **10** 159
Van Sweringen brothers, **IV** 180
Van Tuyle, Robert, **III** 76–77
van Vlissingen, F.H. Fentener, **IV** 132
Van Waters & Rogers, **8** 99
Van Waters, George, **9** 530
Van Westenbrugge, Isaac, **8** 225
Van Wyck, Allen, **6** 505–06
Vanant Packaging Corporation, **8** 359
Vance International Airways, **8** 349
Vancouver Pacific Paper Co., **IV** 286

Vander Pyl, John C., **9** 23
Vanderbilt, Cornelius, **10** 71–72
Vanderbilt, Gloria, **8** 130
Vanderbilt, William, **10** 72
Vanderlip, Frank A., **II** 253–54; **9** 123
Vanderlip, J., **III** 239
Vanderlip-Swenson-Tilghman Syndicate, **IV** 81; **7** 185
Vanderploeg, Watson H., **II** 524
Vandeveer, W.W., **IV** 373
VanDusen, Whitford Julien, **IV** 306–08
Vanessa and Biffi, **11** 226
Vanguard Group, **9** 239
Vanity Fair Mills, Inc., **V** 390–91
Vanity Fair Paper Mills, **IV** 281; **9** 259
Vannotti, Leonardo E., **9** 32–33
Vansickle Industries, **III** 603
Vantage Analysis Systems, Inc., **11** 490
Vantona Group Ltd., **V** 356
Vantress Pedigree, Inc., **II** 585
Vapor Corp., **III** 444
Varco-Pruden, Inc., **8** 544–46
Vare Corporation, **8** 366
Varga, George F., **11** 422
Vargas, Getúlio, **IV** 55
Variable Annuity Life Insurance Co., **III** 193–94
Varibus Corporation, **6** 495
VARIG Agropecuaria, **6** 133
VARIG, SA, 6 133–35
Varity Corporation, III 650–52; **7** 258, 260
Varner, Sterling, **IV** 449
Varney Air Lines, **I** 47, 128; **6** 128; **9** 416
Varney Speed Lines, **I** 96
Varney, Walter T., **I** 47
Varo, **7** 235, 237
Varta, **III** 536; **9** 180–81
Vartiainen, Väinö (Col.), **IV** 469
Vasco Metals Corp., **I** 523; **10** 520, 522
VASP, **6** 134
Vassar, James, **9** 96
Vassar-Smith, Richard, **II** 307
Vasseur, Benoit-Auguste, **IV** 226
Västerås (Bishop of), **IV** 335
de Vathaire, Hervé, **I** 45
Vaughan, Guy, **10** 260
Vaughan, John, **I** 412; **IV** 682
Vaughn, Jack, **11** 153
Vaughn, R.F., **III** 650
Vaughn, Richard, **IV** 480
Vauxelaire, François, **V** 63–65
VAW Leichtmetall GmbH, **IV** 231
VBB Viag-Bayernwerk-Beteiligungs-Gesellschaft mbH, **IV** 232
VDM Nickel-Technologie AG, **IV** 89
Veale, George, **I** 412
Veale, Tinkham, II, **I** 412–13; **III** 9
VEB Londa, **III** 69
VEBA A.G., I 349–50, **542–43**; **III** 695; **IV** 194–95, 455; **8** 69, 494–495
Veba Oel AG, **IV** 199, 508
Vecci, Raymond J., **6** 67
VECO Drilling, Inc., **7** 558–59
VECO Environmental and Professional Services, Inc., **7** 559
VECO International, Inc., 7 558–59
Vector Video, Inc., **9** 74
Veeder-Root Company, **7** 116–17
Velazquez, Cándido, **V** 339
Velazquez Gaztelu, Candido, **V** 415
Veliotis, Takis, **I** 59; **10** 317
Vellumoid Co., **I** 159
VeloBind, Inc., **10** 314

Velsicol, **I** 342, 440
Veltrie, William, **7** 558
Vemar, **7** 558
Venco, **IV** 402
Vendex, **10** 136–37
Vendors Supply of America, Inc., **7** 241–42
Venet, Zal, **II** 672
Vennootschap Nederland, **III** 177–78
Ventres, R.J., **II** 473
Venture, **V** 134
Venturi, Inc., **9** 72
Vepco. *See* Virginia Electric and Power Company.
Vera Cruz Electric Light, Power and Traction Co. Ltd., **IV** 658
Vera Imported Parts, **11** 84
Verbatim Corp., **III** 477; **7** 163
Verdoorn, Sid, **11** 43–44
Vereenigde Nederlandsche Scheepvaartmaatschappij, **6** 404
Vereeniging Refractories, **IV** 22
Vereeniging Tiles, **III** 734
Verein für Chemische Industrie, **IV** 70
Vereinigte Aluminium Werke AG, **IV** 229–30, 232
Vereinigte Deutsche Metallwerke AG, **IV** 140
Vereinigte Elektrizitäts und Bergwerke A.G., **I** 542
Vereinigte Elektrizitätswerke Westfalen AG, IV 195; **V** 744–47
Vereinigte Energiewerke AG, **V** 709
Vereinigte Flugtechnische Werke GmbH., **I** 42, 55, 74–75
Vereinigte Industrie-Unternehmungen Aktiengesellschaft, **IV** 229–30
Vereinigte Leichtmetall-Werke GmbH, **IV** 231
Vereinigte Papierwarenfabriken GmbH, **IV** 323
Vereinigte Stahlwerke AG, **III** 565; **IV** 87, 104–05, 132, 221
Vereinigte Versicherungsgruppe, **III** 377
Vereinigte Westdeutsche Waggonfabriken AG, **III** 542–43
Vereinsbank Wismar, **II** 256
Vereinte Versicherungen, **III** 377
N.V. Verenigde Fabrieken Wessanen and Laan, **II** 527
Verenigde Spaarbank Groep. *See* VSB Groep.
Verienigte Schweizerbahnen, **6** 424
Verity, C. William, Jr., **IV** 29
Verity, George M., **IV** 28–29
Verity, William, **III** 652
Verne, Jules, **IV** 610
Vernon and Nelson Telephone Company. *See* British Columbia Telephone Company.
Vernon Graphics, **III** 499
Vernon Paving, **III** 674
Vernon Savings & Loan, **9** 199
Vernons, **IV** 651
Vero, **III** 434
La Verrerie Souchon-Neuvesel, **II** 474
Verreries Champenoises, **II** 475
Verri, Carlo, **6** 69
Versicherungs-Verein, **III** 402, 410–11
Verspyck, T., **II** 528
Vesa, Yrjö, **III** 647–48
Vesce, Joe, **10** 410
Vesco, Robert, **10** 368–69
Vesuvius Crucible Co., **III** 681

Vesuvius USA Corporation, **8** 179
Veterinary Cos. of America, **III** 25
VEW, **IV** 234
VF Corporation, V 390–92
VFW-Fokker B.V., **I** 41, 55, 74–75
VIA/Rhin et Moselle, **III** 185
Viacao Aerea Rio Grandense of South America. *See* VARIG, SA.
Viacom Enterprises, **6** 33; **7** 336
Viacom International Inc., **7** 222–24, 530, **560–62; 9** 429; **10** 175
VIAG, IV 229–32, 323
VIASA, **I** 107; **6** 97
Viavant, James G., **7** 39
Vichy, **III** 46
Vickers, Harry F., **III** 642
Vickers Inc., **III** 640, 642
Vickers PLC, **I** 194–95; **II** 3; **III** 555, 652, 725
Vickers-Armstrong Ltd., **I** 50, 57, 82
Vicoreen Instrument Co., **I** 202
Vicra Sterile Products, **I** 628
Vicsodrive Japan, **III** 495
Victor Company, **10** 483
Victor Company of Japan, Ltd., I 411; **II** 55–56, 91, 102, **118–19; III** 605; **IV** 599
Victor Comptometer, **I** 676; **III** 154
Victor Emmanuel II, King (Sardinia), **III** 346
Victor, H.M., **10** 298
Victor Manufacturing and Gasket Co., **I** 152
Victor Musical Industries Inc., **II** 119; **10** 285
Victor Talking Machine Co., **II** 88, 118
Victor Value, **II** 678
Victoria, **III** 308
Victoria & Legal & General, **III** 359
VICTORIA am Rhein Allgemeine Versicherungs-Actien-Gesellschaft, **III** 400
VICTORIA am Rhein Feuer- und Transport-Versicherungs AG, **III** 400
Victoria Coach Station, **6** 406
VICTORIA Feuer-Versicherung AG, **III** 399
VICTORIA Health, **III** 400
VICTORIA Holding AG, III 399–401
VICTORIA Insurance, **III** 400
VICTORIA Life, **III** 400
Victoria Paper Co., **IV** 286
Victoria, Queen (England), **I** 271, 468; **II** 357, 470, 476, 592; **IV** 217, 669
Victoria Sugar Co., **III** 686
Victoria Wine Co., **I** 216
VICTORIA zu Berlin Allgemeine Versicherungs-Actien-Gesellschaft, **III** 399–400
Victoria's Secret, **V** 115–16; **11** 498
Victory Fire Insurance Co., **III** 343
Victory Insurance, **III** 273
Victory Oil Co., **IV** 550
Victory Savings and Loan, **10** 339
Video Concepts, **9** 186
Video Library, Inc., **9** 74
Video Superstores Master Limited Partnership, **9** 74
Videoconcepts, **II** 107
Videotex Network Japan, **IV** 680
Vieillard, Georges, **III** 122
Viele, Pete, **9** 180
Vienot, Marc, **II** 356
Viewdata Corp., **IV** 630

Viewlogic, **11** 490
Vigilance-Vie, **III** 393
Vigilant Insurance Co., **III** 220
Vigortone, **II** 582
Viiala Oy, **IV** 302
Viking, **II** 10; **IV** 659
Viking Brush, **III** 614
Viking Direct Limited, **10** 545
Viking Food Stores Inc., **8** 482
Viking Office Products, Inc., 10 544–46
Viking Penguin, **IV** 611
Viktor Achter, **9** 92
Villa, Pancho, **IV** 375
Villafana, Manuel A., **11** 458
Village Super Market, Inc., 7 563–64
Villager, Inc., **11** 216
Villalonga, Ignacio, **II** 197
Villanueva, Edward, **7** 450
Villard, Henry, **6** 601
de Villeméjane, Bernard, **IV** 107–09
Vincent, Francis T., **II** 136
Vincent, James L., **11** 9
Vincent, V.E., **I** 588
Vincke, Freiherr von, **II** 385
Vine Products Ltd., **I** 215
Vingaarden A/S, **9** 100
Vingresor A.B., **I** 120
Viniprix, **10** 205
Vinland Web-Print, **8** 360
Vinyl Maid, Inc., **IV** 401
Vipont Pharmaceutical, **III** 25
VIPS, **11** 113
Virden, John C., **I** 154; **10** 279
Virgin Retail, **9** 75, 361
Virginia Electric and Power Company
    (Vepco), **V** 596–98
Virginia Folding Box Co., **IV** 352
Virginia Laminating, **10** 313
Virginia National Bankshares, **10** 426
Virginia Railway and Power Company
    (VR&P), **V** 596
Virginia Trading Corp., **II** 422
Virkkunen, Matti, **II** 303
Visa International, II 200; **9** 333–35,
    536–38
Visco Products Co., **I** 373
Viscodrive GmbH, **III** 495
Viscount Industries Limited, **6** 310
Visentini, Bruno, **III** 145
Vishay Intertechnology, Inc., **11** 516
VisiCorp, **6** 254
Vision Centers, **I** 688
Visionworks, **9** 186
Visking Co., **I** 400
Visnews Ltd., **IV** 668, 670
VisQueen, **I** 334
Vista Chemical Company, I 402–03
Vista Chemicals, **V** 709
Vista Concepts, Inc., **11** 19
Visual Information Technologies, **11** 57
Visual Technology, **6** 201
Vita Lebensversicherungs-Gesellschaft, **III**
    412
Vita Liquid Polymers, **9** 92
Vita-Achter, **9** 92
Vitafoam Incorporated, **9** 93
Vitalink Communications Corp., **11** 520
Vitex Foods, **10** 382
Vitro Company, **8** 178
Vitro Corp., 10 547–48
de Vitry Raoul, **IV** 174
Vittoria, Joseph V., **6** 357
Viva Home Co., **III** 757
Vivesvata Iron and Steel Ltd., **IV** 207

Viviane Woodard Cosmetic Corp., **II** 531
Viyella, Carrington, **V** 356–57
VK Mason Construction Ltd., **II** 222
Vlasic Foods, **II** 480–81; **7** 67–68
Vlasic, Robert J., **II** 481; **7** 68
VLN Corp., **I** 201
VLSI Research Inc., **11** 246
VND, **III** 593
Vnesheconobank, **II** 242
VNS. *See* Vereenigde Nederlandsche
    Scheepvaartmaatschappij.
VNU/Claritas, **6** 14
Vodac, **11** 548
Vodafone, **II** 84
Vodafone Group plc, 11 547–48
Vodapage, **11** 548
Vodata, **11** 548
Voest. *See* Vereinigte Österreichische
    Eisen- und Stahlwerke AG.
Voest-Alpine Stahl AG, IV 233–35
Voest-Alpine Stahlhandel, **IV** 234
Vogel Peterson Furniture Company, **7** 4–5
Vogel, Walter, **II** 164
Vogelenzang, Onno, **II** 186
Vogels, Hanns Arnt, **I** 75
de Vogüé, Arnaud, **III** 677
de Vogüé, Melchior, **III** 676
de Vogüé, Robert-Jean (Count), **I** 272
Voice Response, Inc., **11** 253
Voisard, Otto, **III** 563
Voisin, Gabriel, **7** 9
Voith, **II** 22
Vokes, **I** 429
Volkart, Johann Georg, **III** 402
Volkart, Salomon, **III** 402
Volkert Stampings, **III** 628
Volkswagen A.G., I 30, 32, 186, 192,
    206–08, 460; **II** 279; **IV** 231; **7** 8; **10**
    14; **11** 104, **549–51 (upd.)**
Völling, Johannes, **II** 386
Vollum, Charles Howard, **8** 517–19
Volta Aluminium Co., Ltd., **IV** 122
Voluntary Hospitals of America, **6** 45
Volunteer State Life Insurance Co., **III** 221
AB Volvo, I 192, 198, **209–11; II** 5, 366;
    III 543, 591, 623, 648; **IV** 336; **7**
    565–68 (upd.); 9 284, 381
Volvo Car Corporation, **9** 350
Volvo North America Corporation, **9** 283-
    84
Volvo Penta, **10** 274
Volvo White, **I** 186
von Bechtolsheim, Clemens, **III** 418
von Bennigsen-Foerder, Rudolf, **I** 543
von Bismarck, Otto, **III** 299
von Bohlen und Halbach, Gustav. *See*
    Krupp von Bohlen und Halbach, Gustav.
von Dehn, Hyatt, **III** 96
Von der Ahe, Charles, **7** 569
von der Nahmer, Paul, **III** 183
von Euler, Hans, **I** 625
von Falkenhausen, Alex, **I** 139; **11** 32
von Gerstner, Franz Josef Ritter, **6** 418
von Gronau, Wolfgang, **I** 138
von Hemert, C.A., **6** 403
von Julin, Jacob, **IV** 301
von Kechel, Georg Carl Gottfried, **IV** 85
von Kechel, Wilhelm Georg Ludwig, **IV**
    85
von Krauss, Georg, **I** 582
von Kuenheim, Eberhard, **I** 139
von Linde, Carl, **I** 256, 314, 581
von Linde, Karl, **11** 402
von Miller, Oskar, **V** 555–56

von Neurath, Ludwig, **7** 140
von Opel, Wilhelm, **V** 241
von Reininghaus, Eberhard, **III** 300
Von Richthofen, Manfred (Red Baron), **III**
    507
von Rohr, Hans Christoph (Dr.), **IV** 128
von Roll, **6** 599
von Rosen (Count), **I** 97
von Rothschild, Salomon Freiherr, **6** 418
von Schack, Wesley W., **6** 484
von Siebold, Philipp Franz, **IV** 214
von Turnoy, Robert Freiherr Biedermann, **7**
    140
von Weise Gear Co., **III** 509
Von's Grocery Co., **II** 419; **8** 474
The Vons Companies, Incorporated, II
    655; **7 569–71**
Voorhees, Enders W., **IV** 573; **7** 550
VOP Acquisition Corporation, **10** 544
Voss, Ralph J., **II** 289
Voss, William, **7** 433
Vought Aircraft Co., **11** 364
Vought, Chance, **I** 84; **9** 416; **10** 536
Voxson, **I** 531
Voyage Conseil, **II** 265
Voyager Energy, **IV** 84
Voyager Petroleum Ltd., **IV** 83; **7** 188
VR&P. *See* Virginia Railway and Power
    Company.
Vranitzky, Franz, **IV** 487
Vrethem, Ake T., **II** 2
Vrumona B.V., **I** 257
VSA. *See* Vendors Supply of America, Inc.
VSB Groep, **III** 199, 201
VSM. *See* Village Super Market, Inc.
Vtel Corporation, **10** 456
Vucetich, Michele, **III** 206
Vuitton, Gaston, **10** 398
Vuitton, Georges, **10** 397–98
Vuitton, Louis, **I** 272; **10** 397
Vulcan Detinning Company, **7** 572–74
Vulcan Materials Company, 7 572–75
Vulcraft, **7** 400–02
Vuorilehto, Simo S., **II** 70
VVM, **III** 200
VW&R. *See* Van Waters & Rogers.
VWR Textiles & Supplies, Inc., **11** 256
VWR United Company, **9** 531

W H Smith & Son, **V** 211–12
W H Smith & Son (Holdings) Ltd., **V** 212
W H Smith Group PLC, V 211–13
W H Smith Television, **V** 212
W. & G. Turnbull & Co., **IV** 278
W. & M. Duncan, **II** 569
W.A. Bechtel Co., **I** 558
W.A. Harriman & Co., **III** 471
W. Atlee Burpee Co., **II** 532; **11** 198
W.B. Constructions, **III** 672
W.B. Doner & Company, **10** 420
W.B. Saunders Co., **IV** 623–24
W.C. Heraeus GmbH, **IV** 100
W.C. Norris, **III** 467
W.C. Platt Co., **IV** 636
W.C. Ritchie & Co., **IV** 333
W. Duke & Sons, **V** 395, 600
W.F. Linton Company, **9** 373
W. Gunson & Co., **IV** 278
AB W. Gutzeit & Co., **IV** 274–77
W. Gutzeit & Co., **IV** 274
W.H. McElwain Co., **III** 528
W.H. Morton & Co., **II** 398; **10** 62
W.J. Noble and Sons, **IV** 294
W.M. Ritter Lumber Co., **IV** 281; **9** 259

W.O. Daley & Company, **10** 387
W.R. Berkeley, **III** 248
W.R. Breen Company, **11** 486
W.R. Grace & Company, I 547–50; III
525, 695; **IV** 454; **11** 216
W. Rosenlew, **IV** 350
W.T. Young Foods, **III** 52; **8** 433
W. Ullberg & Co., **I** 553
W.V. Bowater & Sons, Ltd., **IV** 257–58
W. W. Grainger, Inc., V 214–15
W.W. Cargill and Brother, **II** 616
W.W. Cargill Co., **II** 616
Waage, John A., **11** 416
Waban Inc., **V** 198
Wabash Valley Power Association, **6** 556
Wabush Iron Co., **IV** 73
Wachovia Bank and Trust Company, **10**
425
Wachovia Corp., **II** 336
Wachs, David, **8** 97–98
Wachs, Ellis, **8** 97–98
Wachtel, David K., **7** 475
Wachtel, Joachim, **I** 111
Wachtmeister, Tom, **III** 427
Wacker Oil Inc., **11** 441
Wada, Yoshihiro, **9** 342
Waddell, John C., **10** 112–13
Waddell, Oliver, **11** 465–66
Wade, L. James, **III** 704
Wade, Marion E., **6** 44
Wadsworth Inc., **8** 526
Wadsworth, J.P., **II** 245
Waechter, Joseph, **6** 385
The Wagner & Brown Investment Group, **9**
248
Wagner, Cyril, Jr., **III** 763
Wagner, David J., **11** 372
Wagner, Georg, **I** 671
Wagner, Harold A., **10** 33
Wagner, Richard, **II** 241
Wagner, Robert, **IV** 236
Wah Chang Corp., **I** 523–24; **10** 520–21
Wahren, Axel Wilhelm, **IV** 299
Waialua Agricultural Co., **II** 491
Waidelich, Charles J., **IV** 392
Waite Amulet Mines Ltd., **IV** 164
Waite-Ackerman-Montgomery Mines, **IV**
164
Waitrose, **V** 94–95
Waitt, Norman, Jr.,, **10** 307
Waitt, Ted, **10** 307–08
Wakaki, Shigetoshi, **III** 42
Wakefern Cooperative, **II** 672
Wakefern Food Corp., **7** 563–64
Wakeman, Frederic, **I** 13
Wakodo Co., **I** 674
Wal-Mart Stores, Inc., II 108; **V 216–17;**
6 287; **7** 61, 331; **8** 33, 295, **555–57**
(upd.); 9 187, 361; **10** 236, 284,
515–16, 524; **11** 292
Walbridge, C. H., **6** 545
Waldbaum, **II** 638
Walden family, **IV** 349
Walden, Juuso, **IV** 348–49
Walden, Rudolf, **IV** 347–49
Waldenbooks, **V** 112; **10** 136–37
Waldes Truarc Inc., **III** 624
Oy Waldhof AB, **IV** 324
Waldron, Hicks B., **I** 260; **III** 16
Walgreen, C. R. (Cork), **III, V** 219
Walgreen, Charles, Jr., **V** 218–19
Walgreen, Charles R., **V** 218
Walgreen Co., V 218–20; 9 346
Walker & Lee, **10** 340

Walker, B.J., **10** 299
Walker Cain, **I** 215
Walker, Dan, **6** 530
Walker, E. Cardon "Card", **II** 173; **6** 175
Walker, E. Lee, **9** 165
Walker, Edward Chandler, **I** 262
Walker, Elisha, **I** 536; **II** 277
Walker family, **III** 679
Walker, Franklin Harrington, **I** 262
Walker, Franklin Hiram, **I** 262
Walker, H. Alan, **I** 223
Walker, Harrington, **I** 262
Walker, Henry A., Jr., **I** 417–18
Walker, Hiram, **I** 262
Walker Interactive Systems, **11** 78
Walker, James Harrington, **I** 262
Walker, John, **IV** 437; **10** 118
Walker Manufacturing, **I** 527
Walker, Martin, **8** 347
Walker McDonald Manufacturing Co., **III**
569
Walker, P.G., **IV** 666
Walker, Richard, **6** 560
Walker, Ronald F., **III** 192
Walker, William, **8** 519
Walker, Winston W., **III** 333
Walkers Parker and Co., **III** 679–80
Walki GmbH, **IV** 349
AB Walkiakoski, **IV** 347
Walkins Manufacturing Corp., **III** 571
Wall Paper Manufacturers, **IV** 666
Wall, Sir John, **6** 241
Wall Street Leasing, **III** 137
Wallace and Tiernan, **I** 383; **11** 361
Wallace, Blake, **9** 18
Wallace, David, **10** 44
Wallace, DeWitt, **IV** 663–64
Wallace, Dwane L., **8** 91–92
Wallace, Dwight, **8** 91
Wallace, Henry A., **9** 410–11
Wallace, Henry C., **9** 410
Wallace, Jim, **9** 411
Wallace, John H., **8** 83
Wallace, Lila Acheson, **IV** 663–64
Wallace, Mike, **II** 133
Wallace Murray Corp., **II** 420
Wallace, Robert F., **III** 599
Wallace Silversmith Inc., **I** 473
Wallace, W. Ray, **7** 540
Wallace, Wayne D., **10** 208
Wallace, William, **II** 315, 569; **III** 358
Wallbergs Fabriks A.B., **8** 14
Wallenberg, **III** 479
Wallenberg, André Oscar, **II** 351; **III** 425
Wallenberg family, **III** 425–27; **IV** 203,
336
Wallenberg, Jacob, **III** 419–20
Wallenberg, K.A., **II** 351
Wallenberg, Knut, **III** 425
Wallenberg, Marcus, **II** 351; **IV** 336; **9**
380–81
Wallenberg, Marcus, Jr., **III** 426
Wallenberg, Peter, **11** 437–38
Wallender, Jan, **II** 366
Wallens Dairy Co., **II** 586
Waller, Robert A., **III** 282
Wallin & Nordstrom, **V** 156
Wallin, Carl, **V** 156
Wallingford Bank and Trust Co., **II** 213
Wallis, **V** 177
Wallis, Stan, **IV** 249–50
Wallis Tin Stamping Co., **I** 605
Wallraff, Günter, **IV** 222
Walper, Marie, **11** 493

Walsh, Arthur, **III** 164
Walsh, Graham, **II** 429
Walsh, Matthew T., **III** 203–04
Walsh, Michael, **V** 531
Walsh, Michael H., **10** 528
Walston & Co., **II** 450; **III** 137
Walt Disney Company, II 102, 122, 129,
156, **172–74; III** 142, 504, 586; **IV** 585,
675, 703; **6** 15, **174–77 (upd.)**, 368; **7**
305; **8** 160; **10** 420
Walt Disney Productions, **II** 172
Walt Disney World, **6** 82, 175–76
Walter Baker's Chocolate, **II** 531
Walter Construction Co., **III** 765
Walter E. Heller & Co., **III** 765
Walter E. Heller International Corp., **II** 293
Walter, Henry, **9** 290–92
Walter Industries, Inc., III 765–67
Walter, James W., **III** 765–67
Walter, John R., **IV** 661
Walter, Joseph C., Jr., **11** 440
Walter Kidde & Co., **I** 475, 524
Walter Pierce Oil Co., **IV** 657
Walters, Barbara, **II** 130
Walton, Frederick, **III** 422
Walton, Howard, **I** 263
Walton, J.L. (Bud), **V** 216; **8** 555
Walton Manufacturing, **11** 486
Walton Monroe Mills, Inc., 8 558–60
Walton, Samuel, **V** 216–17; **8** 555–56
Waltrip, Robert L., **6** 293–95
Waltz, Russell J., **9** 160
Walz, Hans, **I** 192
Walz, Louis, **IV** 488
Walz, William C., **8** 232
Walz, William L., **8** 232
Wander Ltd., **I** 672
Wanderer Werke, **III** 154
Wang, **11** 68
Wang, An, **III** 168–70; **6** 284–86
Wang, Charles, **6** 224–25
Wang, Eugene, **10** 509
Wang, Fred, **III** 170; **6** 286
Wang Laboratories, Inc., II 208; **III**
168–70; 6 284–87 (upd.); 8 139; **9** 171;
10 34; **11** 274
Wang, Tony, **6** 224
Wanger, Walter, **II** 147
Wanishi, **IV** 157
Wankel, Felix, **9** 340–41
Wantland, Earl, **8** 518–19
Wanvig, Chester O., **III** 536
Waples-Platter Co., **II** 625
War Damage Corp., **III** 353, 356
War Emergency Tankers Inc., **IV** 552
War Production Board, **V** 676
Warburg, Paul, **I** 337
Warburg, Pincus & Company, **6** 13
Warburg, Pincus Capital Company L.P., **9**
524
Ward, Aaron Montgomery, **V** 145–46
Ward, J. A., **9** 370
Ward, John, **I** 252
Ward Manufacturing Inc., **IV** 101
Ward, Milton H., **IV** 83; **7** 109, 187
Ward, Ralph E., **8** 106–07
Warde, George, **I** 41
Warden, Matthias, **IV** 590
Wardley Ltd., **II** 298
Wards. *See* Circuit City Stores, Inc.
Ware, John H. III, **6** 444
Ware, John H., Jr., **6** 443
Waring, Bertram, **III** 555–56
Waring, W. George, **10** 138

Warmke, Hermann, **III** 738
Warnaco, Inc., **9** 156
Warne, Kate, **9** 406
Warner & Swasey Co., **III** 168; **6** 284
Warner, Albert, **II** 175–76
Warner Amex Cable, **II** 160–61, 176
Warner and Swasey Co., **8** 545
Warner, Benjamin, **II** 175
Warner Bros.-Seven Arts, **II** 176
Warner Bros. Pictures, **II** 88, 129, 135,
   146–47, 169–70, 175–77, 208; **III** 443;
   IV 675–76; **7** 529; **10** 196
Warner Cable, **II** 167; **7** 530
Warner Communications Inc., **II**
   154–55, **175–77**, 452; **III** 505; **IV** 623,
   673, 675; **7** 526, 528 **8** 527; **9** 44–45,
   119, 469; **11** 557. *See also* Time Warner
   Inc.
Warner Cosmetics, **III** 48; **8** 129
Warner Gear Co., **III** 438–39
Warner, Harry, **II** 175–76; **III** 438
Warner, Jack, **II** 175–76
Warner, Leslie H., **V** 295
Warner, Rawleigh, Jr., **IV** 465
Warner Records, **II** 177
Warner, Sam, **II** 175
Warner Sugar Refining Co., **II** 496
Warner, Tom, **III** 438
Warner, William, **I** 710
Warner-Hudnut, **I** 710–11
Warner-Lambert Co., **I** 643, 679, 696,
   710–12; **7** 596; **8** 62–63; **10 549–52**
   (upd.)
Warnock, John, **10** 22–24
Warnock, Maurice J., **III** 423
Warre, Felix, **11** 452
Warren, Al, **7** 462
Warren, Gorham & Lamont, **8** 526
Warren, Kenneth, **I** 353
Warren, Lingan, **II** 654–55
Warren, Louis A., **III** 275
Warren Oilfield Services, **9** 363
Warri Refining and Petrochemicals Co., **IV**
   473
Warringah Brick, **III** 673
Warrior River Coal Company, **7** 281
Warson, Toby G., **8** 22–23
Warters, Dennis, **III** 329
Wartsila, **III** 649
Wartsila Marine Industries Inc., **III** 649
Warwick Electronics, **III** 654
Wasa, **I** 672–73
Wasag-Chemie AG, **III** 694
Wasatch Gas Co., **6** 568
Washburn, Cadwallader, **II** 501; **10** 322
Washburn Crosby Co., **II** 501, 555; **10** 322
Washburn, Frank, **I** 300; **8** 24
Washburn, John H., **III** 263
Washington Energy Company, **9** 539, 541
Washington, George, **IV** 346
Washington Irrigation & Development
   Company, **6** 597
Washington National Corporation, **11** 482
Washington Natural Gas Company, **9**
   539–41
Washington Post Company, **III** 214; **IV**
   688–90; **6** 323; **11** 331
Washington Post Writers Group, **IV** 690
Washington Railway and Electric
   Company, **6** 552–53
Washington Water Power Company, **6**
   566, **595–98**
Washtenaw Gas Company. *See* MCN
   Corporation.

Wasik, Vincent A., **10** 419–20
Wassenaar, Andries (Dr.), **IV** 91
Wasserman, Bert, **II** 176
Wasserman, Fred W., **III** 84–85
Wasserman, Lew, **II** 143–45, 155; **6** 162
Wasserstein Perella & Co., **II** 629; **III** 512,
   530–31
Wasserstein, Perella Partners L.P., **V** 223
Waste Management, Inc., **V** 749–51,
   752–54; **6** 46, 600; **9** 73, 108–09; **11**
   435–36
Wästfelt, Axel, **III** 419–20
Watanabe, Fumio, **III** 386
Watanabe, Isuro, **III** 714
Watanabe, Masato, **IV** 162
Watanabe, Toshihide, **II** 67–68
Watanabe, Yusaku, **III** 759–60
Watari, Sugiichiro, **I** 535
Water Engineering, **11** 360
Water Pik, **I** 524–25
Water Products Company, **6** 487
Water Products Group, **6** 488
Water Street Corporate Recovery Fund, **10**
   423
Waterford, **IV** 296
Waterhouse, Edwin, **9** 422
Waterhouse, John, **10** 40–41
Waterloo Gasoline Engine Co., **III** 462
Waterlow and Sons, **10** 269
Waterman, Herman, **IV** 437
Waterman, Isaac, **IV** 437
Waterman, Lewis E., **8** 59
The Waterman Pen Company, **8** 59
Waterman, R. Lee, **III** 684
Waterman, Robert H., **III** 132; **6** 233
Waterman, Robert H., Jr., **I** 501
WaterPro Supplies Corporation, **6** 486, 488
Waters, George, **II** 397; **10** 61
Waters, Louis A., **V** 749–50
Watertown Insurance Co., **III** 370
Wathen, Thomas, **9** 408–09
Watkin, Edward, **6** 359
Watkins, Alan (Dr.), **III** 507, 509
Watkins, Hays T., **V** 439
Watkins Manufacturing Co., **I** 159
Watkins Rebabbitting Ltd., **I** 159
Watkinson, Harold, **IV** 477
Watmough and Son Ltd., **II** 594
Watney, **9** 99
Watney Mann and Truman Brewers, **I** 228,
   247
Watson, Burl, **IV** 392
Watson, Charles, **IV** 208
Watson, Dick, **III** 148; **6** 251
Watson, Elkanah, **9** 228
Watson, James, **6** 414
Watson, Robert I., **IV** 381
Watson, Stuart D., **I** 260
Watson, Thomas, **III** 147–48, 150–51; **6**
   250–51, 264–65
Watson, Thomas A., **III** 276
Watson, Thomas, Jr., **II** 113; **III** 148–49; **6**
   251–52
Watson-Wilson Transportation System, **V**
   540
Watt AG, **6** 491
Watt Electronic Products, Limited, **10** 319
Watt, Robert M., **6** 513
Watters, Pat, **I** 235
Wattie, James, **7** 576–77
Wattie Pict Ltd., **I** 437
Wattie's Ltd., **7 576–78**; **11** 173
Watts, Roy, **I** 94; **11** 509
Watts, Thomas, **III** 369

Watts, William E., **11** 156
Waugh, James, **9** 232
Waukesha Engine Servicenter, **6** 441
Waukesha Foundry Company, **11** 187
Waukesha Motor Co., **III** 472
Waverly Book Exchange, **10** 135
Waverly Oil Works, **I** 405
Waverly Pharmaceutical Limited, **11** 208
Waxman, Armond, **9** 542
Waxman Industries, Inc., **III** 570; **9**
   542–44
Waxman, Melvin, **9** 542
Waxman, Stanley, **9** 542
Way, Alva O., **III** 389
Way, S. B., **6** 602
Waycross-Douglas Coca-Cola Bottling, **10**
   222
Wayne, John, **II** 147, 176
Wayne Oakland Bank, **8** 188
WCI Holdings Corporation, **V** 223
WCRS Group plc, **6** 15
Weare, George, **6** 523
Wearly, William L., **III** 526–27
Wearn, Wilson C., **11** 331
Wearne Brothers, **6** 117
The Weather Department, Ltd., **10** 89
Weather Guard, **IV** 305
Weathers-Lowin, Leeam, **11** 408
Weaver, **III** 468
Weaver, Charles R., **III** 21–22
Weaver, Robert A., **8** 176–77
Webb & Knapp, **10** 43
Webb, Beatrice, **IV** 218
Webb, Dennis, **11** 147
Webb, Lynn, **11** 147
Webb, Sydney, **IV** 218
Webber, Wallace, **II** 444
Weber, Max O., **III** 722
Weber, Orlando F., **I** 414–15
Webers, **I** 409
Weblock, **I** 109
Webster, Charles, **V** 168; **8** 442
Webster, David, **II** 609
Webster, Edwin Sidney, **6** 565
Webster, Holt W., **6** 345
Webster Publishing Co., **IV** 636
Webster, Richard A., **I** 369
Webtron Corp., **10** 313
Wechsler, Albert, **9** 133
Wechsler, Raymond, **7** 361
Week's Dairy, **II** 528
Weekes, L.G., **IV** 46
Weeks, Edwin Ruthven, **6** 510
Weeks, Ronald (Gen. Sir), **III** 725
Wege, Peter, **7** 494
Wege, Peter M., **7** 493
Wegman, Danny, **9** 545
Wegman, Jack, **9** 545
Wegman, Robert, **9** 545
Wegman, Walter, **9** 545
Wegmans Food Markets, Inc., **9 545–46**
Wehtje, Walter, **III** 426
Weicker, Theodore, **I** 650, 695; **11** 289
Weidemann Brewing Co., **I** 254
Weight Watchers International, **II** 508; **10**
   383; **11** 172
Weil, Robert, **V** 169
Weill, Sanford I., **II** 398, 450–52; **III**
   251–52; **8** 118; **9** 468–69; **10** 62
Wein, Lawrence, **9** 279
Weinbach, Lawrence A., **10** 117
Weinberg, Harry, **I** 566; **10** 42
Weinberg, John L., **II** 415
Weinberg, Sidney J., **II** 415

Weinberg, Steve, **IV** 480
Weinberger, Caspar, **I** 559
Weiner, Walter H., **11** 416–17
Weingardner, Roy E., **9** 425–26
Weinglass, Leonard, **8** 362–63
Weinig, Robert W., **6** 487
Weinstein family, **11** 336
Weinstein, Milton N., **11** 336
Weinstock (Lord), **I** 52
Weinstock, Arnold, **II** 25
Weir, Don W., **V** 550
Weir, Ernest Tener, **IV** 236–37
Weir, Thomas C., **6** 591
Weirton Steel Co., **IV** 236
Weirton Steel Corporation, **I** 297; **IV** 236–38; **7** 447, 598; **8** 346, 450; **10** 31–32
Weisberger, Bernard A., **I** 173
Weisman, George, **I** 270
Weisman, Walter L., **III** 73–74
Weiss, Morry, **7** 24
Weiss, William Erhard, **I** 698–99
Weiss, William L., **V** 265–68
Weksel, William, **11** 275
Welbecson, **III** 501
Welch, Henry, **III** 697
Welch, Jerry, **7** 373
Welch, John F., Jr., **II** 30
Welch, Patrick, **IV** 306
Welcome Wagon, **III** 28
Weldless Steel Company, **8** 530
Weldon, James, **II** 654
Weldt, Charles, **III** 430
Welex Jet Services, **III** 498–99
Wella AG, **III** 68–70
Wella Group, **III** 68–70
Wella Hairdressing Requirements GmbH, **III** 69
Wellcome Chemical Works, **I** 713
Wellcome Foundation Ltd., **I** 638, **713–15**; **8** 210
Wellcome, Henry S., **I** 713–14
Wellcome plc, **I** 713; **8** 452; **9** 265; **10** 551
Wellcome Trust, **I** 713
Weller Electric Corp., **II** 16
Wellington, **II** 457
Wellington (Duke of), **I** 271; **II** 427
Wellman, Inc., **8 561–62**
Wellman International Limited, **8** 561–62
Wellmark, Inc., **10** 89
Wellness Co., Ltd., **IV** 716
Wells & Co., **II** 380, 395; **10** 59
Wells, Albert, **9** 272
Wells, Everett, **IV** 373
Wells Fargo, **III** 440
Wells Fargo & Co. Express, **II** 381
Wells Fargo & Company, **II 380–84**, 319, 395; **10** 59–60
Wells Fargo Bank & Union Trust Co., **II** 382
Wells Fargo Bank American Trust Co., **II** 382
Wells Fargo Nevada National Bank, **II** 381–82
Wells, Frank, **II** 173; **6** 175–76
Wells, Harry, **7** 315–16
Wells, Henry, **II** 380–81, 395–96; **10** 59–60
Wells, Hoyt M., **V** 247
Wells Lamont, **IV** 136
Wells, Mary, **6** 50–52
Wells Rich Greene BDDP, **6 50–52**
Welp, Theodore M., **6** 589–90
Welsbach Mantle, **6** 446

Welsh, John, **11** 443
Weltkunst Verlag GmbH, **IV** 590
Weltner, George, **II** 155
Weltzien, Robert, **7** 532
Wenckebach, H.J.E., **IV** 132
de Wendel, **IV** 227
Wendel, Fritz, **I** 73
de Wendel, Jean Martin, **IV** 226
de Wendel-Sidélor, **IV** 226–27
Wendell, E.W. "Bud", **11** 153
Wendt, Henry, **I** 692, 694; **III** 66–67; **10** 47
Wendt, Otto, **I** 386
Wendt, Wilhelm, **I** 385
Wendy's, **II** 614–15, 647; **7** 433
Wendy's International, Inc., **8 563–65**; **9** 178
Wenger, **III** 419
Wenlock Brewery Co., **I** 223
Wennberg, Harry, **III** 479
Wenner-Gren, Axel, **II** 365–66; **III** 478–79; **IV** 338–39
Wenstrom, Goran, **II** 1
Wenstrom, Jonas, **II** 1
Wenstroms & Granstoms Electriska Kraftbolag, **II** 1
Wentworth, Nathan H., **III** 242–43
Wenzel, Fred W., **8** 287–88
Weppler, George, **9** 287
Werner, Helmut, **V** 242
Werner International, **III** 344
Werner, Jesse, **I** 338–39
Wernicke Co., **I** 201
Werries, E. Dean, **II** 625
Wertheimer, Monroe, **8** 335
Werthen, Hans, **III** 479–80
Werzinger, Albert, **V** 442
Werzinger, Laurent, **V** 441
Wesco Financial Corp., **III** 213, 215
Wesco Food Co., **II** 644
Wesco-Financial Insurance Co., **III** 215
Wescoe, Clark, **I** 700
Wescot Decisison Systems, **6** 25
Weserflug, **I** 74
Wesray Corporation, **6** 357
Wessanen. *See* Koninklijke Wessanen N.V.
Wessanen, Adriaan, **II** 527
Wessanen and Laan, **II** 527
Wessanen Cacao, **II** 528
Wessanen USA, **II** 528
Wessanen's Koninklijke Fabrieken N.V., **II** 527
Wessman, Gunnar, **I** 386–87
Wessner, Kenneth T., **6** 44–45
West Australia Land Holdings, Limited, **10** 169
West Bend, **III** 610–11
West Coast Grocery Co., **II** 670
West Coast of America Telegraph, **I** 428
West Coast Savings and Loan, **10** 339
West Coast Telecom, **III** 38
West Fraser Timber Co. Ltd., **IV** 276
West Ham Gutta Percha Co., **I** 428
West Harrison Electric & Water Company, **6** 466
West Harrison Gas & Electric Company, **6** 466
West, Horatio, **7** 580
West India Oil Co., **IV** 416, 428
West Japan Heavy Industries, **III** 578–79; **7** 348
West Jersey Electric Company, **6** 449
West, John B., **7** 579–80
West, Mae, **II** 155; **III** 46

West Missouri Power Company. *See* UtiliCorp United Inc.
West of England, **III** 690
West of England Sack Holdings, **III** 501; **7** 207
West One Bancorp, **11 552–55**
West Penn Electric. *See* Allegheny Power System, Inc.
West Point-Pepperell, Inc., **8 566–69**; **9** 466
West Publishing Co., **IV** 312; **7 579–81**; **10** 407
West Rand Consolidated Mines, **IV** 90
West Rand Investment Trust, **IV** 21
West Richfield Telephone Company, **6** 299
West, Robert V., Jr., **7** 516–19
West Side Bank, **II** 312
West Surrey Central Dairy Co. Ltd., **II** 586
West Texas Utilities Company, **6** 580
West Virginia Paper, **IV** 351
West Virginia Pulp and Paper Co., **IV** 351–53
West Virginia Pulp Co., **IV** 351
West Witwatersrand Areas Ltd., **IV** 94–96
West Yorkshire Bank, **II** 307
West's Holderness Corn Mill, **II** 564
WestAir Holding Inc., **11** 300
Westall, Bernard, **10** 268
Westburne Group of Companies, **9** 364
Westby, Ben, **7** 419–20
Westchester County Savings & Loan, **9** 173
Westdeutsche Landesbank Girozentrale, **II** 257–58, **385–87**
Westerberg, Arne, **IV** 203–04
Westerberg, Sten, **II** 352
Westercamp, Bernard, **10** 12
Western Air Express, **I** 125; **III** 225; **9** 17
Western Air Lines, **I** 98, 100, 106; **6** 82
Western Alaska Fisheries, **II** 578
Western American Bank, **II** 383
Western Assurance Co., **III** 350
Western Atlas International, **III** 473
Western Auto Supply Co., **8** 56; **11** 392
Western Bancorp Venture Capital Co., **II** 289
Western Bancorporation, **I** 536; **II** 288–89
Western Bancorporation Data Processing Co., **II** 289
Western Bancorporation Mortgage Co., **II** 289
Western California Canners Inc., **I** 513
Western Canada Airways, **II** 376
Western Coalfields Ltd., **IV** 48–49
Western Condensing Co., **II** 488
Western Copper Mills Ltd., **IV** 164
Western Corrugated Box Co., **IV** 358
Western Crude, **11** 27
Western Dairy Products, **I** 248
Western Digital, **10** 403, 463; **11** 56, 463
Western Edison, **6** 601
Western Electric, **V** 259–64
Western Electric Co., **II** 57, 66, 88, 101, 112; **III** 162–63, 440; **IV** 181, 660; **7** 288; **11** 500–01
Western Electric Co. Ltd., **III** 162
Western Empire Construction. *See* CRSS Inc.
Western Federal Savings & Loan, **9** 199
Western Fire Equipment Co., **9** 420
Western Geophysical, **I** 485; **11** 265
Western Grocers, Inc., **II** 631, 670
Western Illinois Power Cooperative, **6** 506

Western Inland Lock Navigation Company, **9** 228
Western International Hotels, **I** 129; **6** 129
Western Kraft Corp., **IV** 358; **8** 476
Western Life Insurance Co., **III** 356
Western Light & Telephone Company. *See* Western Power & Gas Company.
Western Light and Power. *See* Public Service Company of Colorado.
Western Merchandise, Inc., **8** 556
Western Mining Corp., **IV** 61, 95
Western National Life Insurance, **10** 246
Western Natural Gas Company, **7** 362
Western New York State Lines, Inc., **6** 370
Western Newell Manufacturing Company. *See* Newell Co.
Western Nuclear, Inc., **IV** 179
Western Offset Publishing, **6** 13
Western Offshore Drilling and Exploration Co., **I** 570
Western Pacific Industries, **10** 357
Western Paper Box Co., **IV** 333
Western Piping and Engineering Co., **III** 535
Western Powder Co., **I** 379
Western Power & Gas Company, **6** 312–13. *See also* Centel Corporation.
Western Printing and Lithographing Co., **IV** 671
Western Public Service Corporation, **6** 568
Western Reserve Bank of Lake County, **9** 474
Western Reserve Telephone Company. *See* Alltel Corporation.
Western Rosin Company, **8** 99
Western Sizzlin', **10** 331
Western Slope Gas, **6** 559
Western Steer, **10** 331
Western Sugar Co., **II** 582
Western Union, **I** 512; **III** 644; **6** 227–28, 338, 386; **9** 536; **10** 263
Western Union Insurance Co., **III** 310
Western Veneer and Plywood Co., **IV** 358
Western-Mobile, **III** 735
Westerveldt, Conrad, **I** 47; **10** 162
Westfair Foods Ltd., **II** 649
Westfalenbank of Bochum, **II** 239
Westfalia AG, **III** 418–19
Westfalia Dinnendahl Gröppel AG, **III** 543
Westfälische Transport AG, **6** 426
Westfälische Verbands-Elektrizitätswerk, **V** 744
Westgate House Investments Ltd., **IV** 711
Westimex, **II** 594
Westin Hotel Co., **I** 129–30; **6** 129; **9** 283, **547–49**
Westinghouse, **6** 39, 164, 261, 452, 483, 556
Westinghouse Air Brake Co., **III** 664
Westinghouse Brake & Signal, **III** 509
Westinghouse Broadcasting, **II** 122
Westinghouse Electric and Manufacturing Company, **9** 162
Westinghouse Electric Corporation, **I** 4, 7, 19, 22, 28, 33, 82, 84–85, 524; **II** 57–58, 59, 80, 86, 88, 94, 98–99, **120–22**, 151; **III** 440, 467, 641; **IV** 59, 401; **9** 12, 17, 128, 245, 417, 439–40, 553; **10** 280, 536; **11** 318
Westinghouse, George, **II** 120; **III** 247; **6** 492–93
Westland Aircraft Ltd., **I** 50, 573; **IV** 658
WestLB. *See* Westdeutsche Landesbank Girozentrale.

Westmill Foods, **II** 466
Westminster Bank Ltd., **II** 257, 319, 320, 333–34
Westminster Press Ltd., **IV** 658
Westminster Trust Ltd., **IV** 706
Westmoreland Coal Company, **7 582–85**
Westmoreland Energy Inc., **7** 584
Westmoreland Inc., **7** 582
Westmoreland, William, **II** 133
Westmount Enterprises, **I** 286
Weston and Mead, **IV** 310
Weston Bakeries, **II** 631
Weston family, **II** 465
Weston Foods Ltd., **II** 631
Weston, Galen, **II** 465, 631–32
Weston, Garfield, **II** 465, 631
Weston, Garry, **II** 465
Weston, George, **II** 465, 631
Weston, Josh, **III** 117–18; **9** 49–51
Weston Pharmaceuticals, **V** 49
Weston Resources, **II** 631–32
Westpac Banking Corporation, **II 388–90**
Westphalian Provinzialbank-Hülfskasse, **II** 385
Westrick, Ludger, **IV** 231–32
Westvaco Chemical Corp., **I** 442
Westvaco Corporation, **IV 351–54**
Westwood Pharmaceuticals, **III** 19
Westwools Holdings, **I** 438
Wetmore, Charles W., **V** 592
Wetterau Food Services, **II** 682
Wetterau Foods Inc., **II** 681
Wetterau, George H., **II** 681
Wetterau, George, Jr., **II** 681
Wetterau Grocery Co., **II** 681
Wetterau Incorporated, **II** 645, **681–82**; **7** 450
Wetterau Industries, **II** 682
Wetterau, Oliver S., **II** 681
Wetterau, Otto, **II** 681
Wetterau, Ted, **II** 681–82
Wetterau, Theodore, **II** 681
Wetzel, Harry, **9** 14
Wetzel, Jay, **7** 462
Wexner, Bella, **V** 115
Wexner, Harry, **V** 115
Wexner, Leslie, **V** 115; **11** 41
Wexpro Company, **6** 568–69
Weyer, Deryk, **II** 236
Weyerhaeuser & Denkmann, **IV** 355
Weyerhaeuser, Charles, **8** 428
Weyerhaeuser Company, **I** 26; **IV** 266, 289, 298, 304, 308, **355–56**, 358; **8** 434; **9 550–52 (upd.)**
Weyerhaeuser family, **IV** 355–56
Weyerhaeuser, Frederick, **IV** 355; **8** 428–29; **9** 550
Weyerhaeuser, George, **IV** 355–56; **9** 550–51
Weyerhaeuser International S.A., **IV** 356
Weyerhaeuser, John P., **IV** 355; **9** 550
Weyerhaeuser, John P., Jr., **IV** 355
Weyerhaeuser, John Philip, Jr., **8** 429
Weyerhaeuser Real Estate Co., **IV** 356
Weyerhaeuser, Rudolph M., **8** 429
Weyerhaeuser Sales Co., **IV** 355–56
Weyerhaeuser Timber Co., **IV** 355–56; **8** 428
Weyman-Burton Co., **9** 533
Whalstrom & Co., **I** 14
Wharton, Clifton, Jr., **III** 381
Wharton, J. Bradford, Jr., **I** 67–68
Wheaton, Dr. T.C., **8** 570–71

Wheaton, Frank, Jr., **8** 571–72
Wheaton Industries, **8 570–73**
Wheaton, T. C., **8** 571
Wheel Horse, **7** 535
Wheelabrator Clean Air Company. *See* Wheelabrator Technologies, Inc.
Wheelabrator Frye, **6** 599
Wheelabrator Group, **6** 599
Wheelabrator Technologies, **11** 435
Wheelabrator Technologies Group, **III** 511–12
Wheelabrator Technologies, Inc., **V** 754; **6 599–600**
Wheelabrator-Frye, **I** 298; **II** 403; **III** 511
Wheelabrator-Frye Inc., **11** 435
Wheelbraton Fry Inc., **10** 32;
Wheeler Condenser & Engineering Company, **6** 145
Wheeler, Denis E., **I** 714–15
Wheeler, Fisher & Co., **IV** 344
Wheeler, G. E., **6** 539
Wheeler, John E., **IV** 682
Wheeler, Walter, II, **III** 156–57
Wheeling Corrugated Company, **7** 586
Wheeling Steel and Iron Company, **7** 586
Wheeling Steel Corporation, **7** 586
Wheeling-Pittsburgh Corp., **7 586–88**
Wheeling-Pittsburgh Steel Corp., **IV** 160
Wheelock Marden, **I** 470
Wheelon, Albert, **II** 34
Wheelwright, George, III, **III** 607; **7** 436
Wheelwright, Thomas S., **V** 596
Whelan, George J., **V** 405
Whemo Denko, **I** 359
Wherehouse Entertainment, **9** 361
Wherehouse Entertainment Incorporated, **11 556–58**
Whippet Motor Lines Corporation, **6** 370
Whirl-A-Way Motors, **11** 4
Whirlpool Corporation, **I** 30; **II** 80; **III** 572, 573, **653–55**; **8** 298–99; **11** 318
Whirlpool Finance Corp., **III** 654
Whirlpool International, **III** 654
Whirlpool Trading Co., **III** 654
Whirlpool-Seeger Corp., **III** 653
Whirlwind, **6** 233
Whirlwind, Inc., **7** 535
Whiskey Trust, **I** 376
Whitaker Health Services, **III** 389
Whitaker, John C., **V** 409
Whitaker, Uncas A., **II** 7–8
Whitaker-Glessner Company, **7** 586
Whitall Tatum, **III** 423
Whitbread & Company plc, **I** 288, **293–94**
Whitbread, Francis Pelham, **I** 294
Whitbread, Samuel, **I** 293–94
Whitbread, Samuel, II, **I** 293
Whitbread, Samuel Charles, **I** 293
Whitbread, Samuel Howard, **I** 294
Whitbread, William Henry, **I** 293–94
Whitby Pharmaceuticals, Inc., **10** 289
White Automotive, **10** 9, 11
White Brand, **V** 97
White Bus Line, **I** 448
White Consolidated Industries, **II** 122; **III** 480, 654, 573; **8** 298
White Eagle Oil & Refining Co., **IV** 464; **7** 352
White, Edward, II, **I** 79; **11** 428
White, Elton, **6** 267
White, Eugene R., **III** 110–11
White, Frederick, **III** 669
White Fuel Corp., **IV** 552

White, Gordon, **I** 477
White, Horace, **IV** 682
White Industrial Power, **II** 25
White, Jack, **IV** 59
White, James, **III** 258; **IV** 261–62
White, John Bazley, **III** 669
White, Lawrence J., **I** 137
White, Lord Vincent Gordon Lindsay, **7** 207–09
White Machine Tools, **III** 480
White, Maunsel, **11** 105
White Motor Co., **II** 16
White Oil Corporation, **7** 101
White, Peter, **11** 415–16
White, Phillip E., **10** 362–63
White, Robert, **II** 388–90
White Rock Corp., **I** 377
White, Roy B., **V** 438
White Stores, **II** 419–20
White Swan Foodservice, **II** 625
White, Vincent Gordon Lindsay (Sir), **III** 501–03
White Weld, **II** 268
White, William, **10** 72
White, William A., **6** 595–97
White, William G., **V** 433
White, William J., **9** 64
White-Rodgers, **II** 19
Whiteaway Laidlaw, **V** 68
Whiteford, William, **IV** 570
Whitehall Canadian Oils Ltd., **IV** 658
Whitehall Electric Investments Ltd., **IV** 658
Whitehall Labs, **8** 63
Whitehall Petroleum Corp. Ltd., **IV** 657–58
Whitehall Securities Corp., **IV** 658
Whitehall Securities Ltd., **IV** 658
Whitehall Trust Ltd., **IV** 658
Whitehead, Alfred North, **7** 166
Whitehead, Bill, **9** 13
Whitehead, Edward, **I** 25; **II** 477
Whitehead, John, **II** 415
Whitehouse, Arthur, **I** 69
Whiteley, George H., **10** 270
Whiteside, Arthur Dare, **IV** 604–05
Whitewater Group, **10** 508
Whiteway, Henry, **I** 215
Whitfield, Robert, **I** 42
Whitlam, Gough, **IV** 651; **7** 390
Whitman Chocolates, **I** 457
Whitman Corporation, **7** 430; **10** 414–15, **553–55 (upd.)**; **11** 188
Whitman, Reginald, **I** 473
Whitman, Walt, **III** 302
Whitman's Chocolates, **7** 431
Whitmore, Kay, **7** 163
Whitmore, Kay R., **III** 477
Whitmore, Olivia, **I** 250
Whitney, Amos, **9** 416
Whitney Communications Corp., **IV** 608
Whitney, Richard, **IV** 602
Whitney, Sonny, **I** 115
Whittaker Corporation, **I** 544–46; **III** 389, 444
Whittaker, Edmund, **III** 338
Whittaker, Howard E., **IV** 311
Whittaker, James W., **9** 189
Whittaker, William R., **I** 544
Whittar Steel Strip Co., **IV** 74
Whitteways, **I** 215
Whittle Communications, **IV** 675; **7** 528
Whittle, Frank, **I** 81; **II** 29; **9** 17, 244
Whitwam, David R., **III** 654; **8** 299

Whitworth, Ken, **IV** 686
The Wholesale Club, Inc., **8** 556
Whyte & Mackay Distillers Ltd., **V** 399
Wicat Systems, **7** 255–56
Wichita Industries, **11** 27
Wickes Boiler Company, **V** 221–22
Wickes Bros. Foundry, **V** 221–22
Wickes Bros. Iron Works, **V** 221
Wickes Co., **I** 453, 483; **II** 262
Wickes Companies, Inc., **III** 721; **V** 221–23; **10** 423
Wickes, Edward Noyes, **V** 221
Wickes, Henry Dunn, **V** 221
Wickes Lumber Company, **V** 222
Wickes Manufacturing Co., **III** 580
Wickman, Carl Eric, **I** 448
Wickman-Wimet, **IV** 203
Widengren, Ulf, **I** 626
Widmer-Kappeler, C., **III** 403
Widows and Orphans Friendly Society, **III** 337
Wiedemann, Joseph R., **III** 197
Wiedfeld, Otto, **IV** 87
Wiehn, Helmut, **III** 466
Wien Air Alaska, **II** 420
Wiener, Michael, **11** 190
Wiesendanger, Uli, **6** 47
Wifstavarfs, **IV** 325
Wiggin, Albert H., **II** 247–48, 397; **10** 61
Wiggins Teape Ltd., **I** 426; **IV** 290
Wight, Charles, **IV** 82; **7** 186
Wight, Robin, **6** 15
Wijkman, Oscar F., **II** 1
Wikner, Olof Johan, **IV** 317
Wilbourn, Hugh, **6** 299
Wilcox, Allen, **10** 41
Wilcox, Brodie McGhie, **V** 490–91
Wilcox, Charles Secord, **IV** 208
Wilcox, Stephen, **III** 465
Wilde, Frazar Bullard, **III** 225
Wilder, Billy, **II** 15
Wildi, John, **7** 428
Wiles, George, **III** 501; **7** 207
Wiles Group, **7** 207
Wiles Group Ltd., **III** 501
Wiley, L.R., **11** 537
Wiley Manufacturing Co., **8** 545
Oy Wilh. Schauman AB, **IV** 300–02
Wilhelm Fette GmbH, **IV** 198–99
Wilhelm II, Emperor (Germany), **IV** 86
Wilhelm Wilhelmsen Ltd., **7** 40
Wilhelmsen, Anders, **9** 111–12
Wilkie, John L., **6** 458
Wilkin, Alexander, **III** 355
Wilkins, Beriah, **IV** 688
Wilkins, Graham, **I** 532
Wilkins, Roger C., **III** 389
Wilkinson, Bernard, **III** 698
Wilkinson, Bruce, **6** 144
Wilkinson, John, **11** 452
Wilkinson Sword Co., **III** 23, 28–29
Will, Erwin, **V** 597
Willamette Falls Electric Company. See Portland General Corporation.
Willamette Industries, Inc., **IV** 357–59
Willamette Valley Lumber Co., **IV** 357–58
Willard, Daniel, **V** 438
Willers, Thomas, **IV** 264
William A. Rogers Ltd., **IV** 644
William B. Tanner Co., **7** 327
William Barnet and Son, Inc., **III** 246
William Barry Co., **II** 566
William Benton Foundation, **7** 165, 167
William Bonnel Co., **I** 334; **10** 289

William Burdon, **III** 626
William Colgate and Co., **III** 23
William Collins & Sons, **II** 138; **IV** 651–52; **7** 390–91
William Cory & Son Ltd., **6** 417
William Crawford and Sons, **II** 593
William, David R., **IV** 575
William Douglas McAdams Inc., **I** 662; **9** 403
William Duff & Sons, **I** 509
William E. Pollack Government Securities, **II** 390
William E. Wright Company, **9** 375
William Gaymer and Son Ltd., **I** 216
William H. Rorer Inc., **I** 666
William Hancock & Co., **I** 223
William I, King (Netherlands), **II** 183, 527
William III, King (Netherlands), **IV** 530
William J. Hough Co., **8** 99–100
William Johnson, **10** 553
William, King (Orange), **IV** 51
William Lyon Homes, **III** 664
William M. Mercer Inc., **III** 283
William Mackinnon & Co., **III** 522
William McDonald & Sons, **II** 593
William Morris, **III** 554
William Neilson, **II** 631
William Odhams Ltd., **7** 244
William Penn Cos., **III** 243, 273
William Press, **I** 568
William R. Warner & Co., **I** 710
William Southam and Sons, **7** 487
William T. Blackwell & Company, **V** 395
William Underwood Co., **7** 430
William Varcoe & Sons, **III** 690
William Zinsser & Co., **8** 456
Williams, Andy, **6** 199
Williams, Arthur, **6** 575
Williams, Beatty B., **II** 14–15
Williams Bros. Co., **IV** 575–76
Williams Bros. Corp., **IV** 575
Williams Brother Offshore Ltd., **I** 429
Williams, Carl, **9** 276
Williams, Carl H., **9** 276
Williams, Clarence, **10** 421
Williams, Clarke, **9** 105–07
Williams, Clarke, Jr., **9** 106–07
Williams, Claude, **V** 739
Williams, Clyde E., **10** 138
Williams Communications, **6** 340
Williams Companies, **III** 248; **IV** 84, 171, **575–76**
Williams Cos., **IV** 576
Williams, David, Jr., **IV** 575–76
Williams, David R., **11** 173
Williams, Don, **8** 533–34
Williams, Donnelley and Co., **IV** 660
Williams, Edward, **I** 711; **10** 550
Williams, Edward P., **III** 744
Williams Electronics, **III** 431
Williams Energy, **IV** 576
Williams, Ernest, **8** 303
Williams Exploration Co., **IV** 576
Williams, George J., **II** 251
Williams, Harrison, **6** 602
Williams International Group, **IV** 576
Williams, J.B., **II** 543
Williams, J.C., **IV** 236
Williams, John H., **IV** 575–76
Williams, Joseph, **IV** 576
Williams, Joseph D., **10** 551
Williams, Langbourne M., **IV** 82; **7** 186
Williams, Lawrence, **II** 15
Williams, Marie, **9** 105

Williams, Nicholas, **IV** 382
Williams, R. L., **6** 377
Williams, Ray, **III** 109
Williams, Raymond L., **8** 176–77
Williams, Robert C., **IV** 289–90
Williams, S. Miller, Jr., **IV** 575
Williams, Sterling, **11** 468
Williams Telecommunications Group, Inc.,
    IV 576
Williams, Tennessee, **II** 143
Williams, Walter F., **IV** 37; **7** 50–51
Williams, William, **II** 226
Williams, William Clarke, **9** 105
Williamsburg Gas Light Co., **6** 455
Williamson, Bert, **9** 303
Williamson, E.L., **7** 282
Williamson, Frederick E., **V** 427
Williamson, G.E., **I** 604
Williamson, George, **II** 97
Williamson, Gilbert P., **III** 152; **6** 267
Williamson, Harwood D., **9** 276
Williamson, John, **7** 123
Williamsons Ltd., **II** 677
Willima, Evans I.L., **IV** 240
Willis, Charles F., Jr., **6** 66
Willis Faber, **III** 280, 747
Williston Basin Interstate Pipeline
    Company, **7** 322, 324
Willits, Harris, **9** 96–98
Willits, John Frederick, **9** 96
Willkie, Wendell, **IV** 604, 671; **V** 578
Willor Manufacturing Corp., **9** 323
Willson, Thomas L., **I** 399
Willys-Overland, **I** 183; **8** 74
Wilmer, E. G., **V** 244
Wilmers, Robert G., **11** 109
Wilmington Coca-Cola Bottling Works,
    Inc., **10** 223
Wilmot, Robb, **6** 241–42
Wilson & Co., **I** 490
Wilson, Alan, **I** 640
Wilson, Alan, (Sir), **9** 264
Wilson Brothers, **8** 536
Wilson, Charles, **II** 29, 588
Wilson, Charles Rivers, Sir, **6** 359
Wilson, Dennis, **11** 307
Wilson, E.C., **II** 624
Wilson, Edward, **IV** 661
Wilson, Edward T., **IV** 399–400
Wilson, F. Perry, **8** 180; **9** 518
Wilson Foods Corp., **I** 489, 513; **II**
    584–85
Wilson, G. Larry, **11** 394–95
Wilson, Gary, **II** 173; **6** 104–05
Wilson, Harold, **III** 502; **IV** 381
Wilson, Ian, **II** 492
Wilson, Irving, **IV** 15
Wilson, Joe, **III** 171
Wilson Jones Company, **7** 4–5
Wilson, Joseph C., **6** 288
Wilson, Joseph R., **II** 159; **III** 171; **6** 288
Wilson, Kemmons, **III** 94; **9** 425
Wilson, Michael (Hon.), **IV** 496
Wilson, Peter, **11** 453–54
Wilson Pharmaceuticals & Chemical, **I** 489
Wilson, Robert E., **IV** 369
Wilson, Robert Lawrence, **I** 436
Wilson, Robert N., **III** 37; **8** 283
Wilson, Roland, **6** 110
Wilson, Sloan, **IV** 672
Wilson Sporting Goods, **I** 278, 489
Wilson, Thornton, **I** 48; **10** 163
Wilson, Woodrow, **III** 388; **IV** 557, 626; **7**
    14; **11** 292

Wilson's Motor Transit, **6** 370
Wilts and Dorset Banking Co., **II** 307
Wiltshire United Dairies, **II** 586
Wiman, Charles Deere, **III** 462
Wimpey's plc, **I** 315, 556
Wimpfeling, Jacob, **IV** 544
Win Schuler Foods, **II** 480
Win-Chance Foods, **II** 508
Wincanton Group, **II** 586–87
Winchell's Donut Shops, **II** 680
Winchester Arms, **I** 379–81, 434
Winckler, Nils, **I** 664
Windstar Sail Cruises, **6** 368
de Windt, E. Mandell, **I** 154–55; **10**
    279–80
Winfrey, Oprah, **9** 307
Wing, Daniel, **II** 207
Wingate, Harry S., **IV** 111
Wingquist, Sven, **III** 622
Wings Luggage, Inc., **10** 181
Winkel, Rudolf, **III** 446
Winkelman Stores, Inc., **8** 425–26
Winkhaus, Fritz, **IV** 104
Winkler, Clemens, **IV** 139
Winkler, L.E., **IV** 448
Winkler, M.J., **II** 172
Winkler-Grimm Wagon Co., **I** 141
Winmar Co., **III** 353
Winn & Lovett Grocery Co., **II** 683
Winn-Dixie Stores, Inc., **II** 626–27, 670,
    683–84; **7** 61; **11** 228
Winnebago Industries Inc., **7 589–91**
Winnerman, Robert H., **8** 541
Winners Apparel Ltd., **V** 197
Winschermann group, **IV** 198
Winship, Laurence, **7** 14–15
Winship, Thomas, **7** 15
Winston & Newell Co., **II** 668–69
Winston, Frederick, **III** 305
Winston Group, **10** 333
Winston, Harper, Fisher Co., **II** 668
Winston, Morton, **7** 537–38
Winter, Elmer L., **9** 326
Winter, J. Burgess, **7** 289
Winter, W. W., **6** 447
Winters, Robert C., **III** 340
Wintershall, **I** 306; **IV** 485
Winterthur Lebensversicherungs-
    Gesellschaft, **III** 403
Winterthur Rechtsschutz-versicherungs-
    Gesellschaft, **III** 403
**Winterthur Schweizerische
    Versicherungs-Gesellschaft**, **III** 343,
    402–04
Winterthur-Europe Assurance, **III** 404
Winterthur-Europe Vie, **III** 404
Winthrop Laboratories, **I** 698–99
Winton, Alexander, **V** 231; **10** 273
Winton Engines, **10** 273
Winton Motor Car Company, **V** 231
Winwood, Dick, **11** 147
Wipff, Dan R., **10** 524
Wire and Plastic Products PLC. *See* WPP
    Group PLC.
Wireless Hong Kong. *See* Hong Kong
    Telecommunications Ltd.
Wireless Management Company, **11** 12
Wireless Speciality Co., **II** 120
Wirth, Charles, Jr., **7** 547
Wirth, Leopold, **7** 546–47
Wirth, Russell, **7** 547–48
Wisaforest Oy AB, **IV** 302
Wisconsin Co-op Creamery Association, **7**
    592

Wisconsin Creamery Co-op, **7** 592
Wisconsin Dairies, **7 592–93**
Wisconsin Electric Power Company, **6**
    601–03, 605
Wisconsin Energy Corporation, **6**
    601–03
Wisconsin Gas and Electric, **6** 602
Wisconsin Knife Works, **III** 436
Wisconsin-Michigan Power Company, **6**
    602–03
Wisconsin Natural Gas, **6** 601–02
Wisconsin Power & Light, **6** 604–06
Wisconsin Power, Light & Heat Company,
    6 604
Wisconsin Public Service Corporation, **6**
    605; **9 553–54**
Wisconsin Steel, **10** 430
Wisconsin Tissue Mills Inc., **8** 103
Wisconsin Traction, Light, Heat and Power
    Company, **6** 601–02
Wisconsin Utilities Company, **6** 604
Wishnick, Robert I., **I** 404–05
Wishnick, William, **I** 405–06
Wishnick-Tumpeer Chemical Co., **I**
    403–05
Wisner, Edward, **7** 280
Wispark Corporation, **6** 601, 603
Wisvest Corporation, **6** 601, 603
Witco Corporation, **I** 403, **404–06**
Witech Corporation, **6** 601, 603
Withers, Bruce M., Jr., **7** 345
Witt, Wilhelm Berend, **III** 410–11
Witte, Merlin, **8** 349
Wm. Underwood Co., **I** 246, 457
Wm. Wrigley Jr. Company, **7 594–97**
WMS Industries, **III** 431
WMX Technologies, Inc., **11** 435–36
Wobst, Frank A., **11** 181–82
Wodehouse, P.G., **IV** 672
Woermann and German East African
    Lines, **I** 542
Woermann, Eduard, **I** 542
Wöhlk, **III** 446
Wohlstetter, Charles, **V** 296
Wolf, Bernhard, **10** 345
Wolf, Bob, **11** 50, 52
Wolf, H. Carl, **6** 447
Wolf, Stephen M., **6** 130
Wolfe, Harvey S., **II** 649
Wolfe, James R., **6** 377
Wolfe, Raphael, **II** 649
Wolfe, Ray D., **II** 649
Wolfe, William, **IV** 581
Wolfer, Herbert, **III** 632
Wolff, Bernard, **IV** 668–69
Wolff, David A., **11** 86
Wolff, Eugen, **IV** 275
Wolff family, **IV** 275
Wolff, Reguel, **IV** 275
Wolfson, Isaac, **V** 67–69
Wolfson, Leonard, **V** 69
Wolfson, Louis E., **V** 147
Wolle, Francis, **IV** 344
Wollenberg, H.L., **8** 335
Wolters Kluwer, **IV** 611
Wolters, Laurent, **IV** 497–98
Wolters Samson, **IV** 611
Wolvercote Paper Mill, **IV** 300
Wolverine Die Cast Group, **IV** 165
Womack Development Company, **11** 257
Womack, Jim, **11** 542
Wometco Coca-Cola Bottling Co., **10** 222
Wometco Coffee Time, **I** 514
Wometco Enterprises, **I** 246, 514

Wong, Albert C., **9** 41–42
Wood, Alan, **11** 101
Wood, Alexander, **IV** 208
Wood, C.V. Jr., **8** 348–49
Wood Fiberboard Co., **IV** 358
Wood Gundy, **II** 345
Wood, H. W., **V** 221
Wood Hall Trust plc, **I** 438, **592–93**
Wood, James, **II** 636–38; **7** 202
Wood, James P., **I** 32
Wood, Quentin, **7** 444
Wood, Richard, **I** 645–46; **11** 89–91
Wood River Oil and Refining Company, **11** 193
Wood, Robert, **V** 181–82
Wood, Robert (Gen.), **III** 536
Wood, Robert E., **7** 167; **10** 50
Wood, Roger, **IV** 383
Wood Shovel and Tool Company, **9** 71
Wood, Weldon, **6** 299
Wood, William, **8** 155
Wood, William Christie, **8** 155
Wood, Word H., **II** 336
Woodall Industries, **III** 641
Woodard-Walker Lumber Co., **IV** 358
Woodcock, Hess & Co., **9** 370
Woodfab, **IV** 295
Woodhaven Gas Light Co., **6** 455
Woodhill Chemical Sales Company, **8** 333
Woodlands, **7** 345–46
Woodlock, Thomas, **IV** 601
Woodrow, Jack, **I** 590
Woodruff, Robert Winship, **I** 233–34; **10** 226–27
Woods and Co., **II** 235
Woods, George D., **II** 402
Woods, James D., **III** 429
Woodside, William S., **I** 612–14
Woodson, Benjamin N., **III** 193–94; **10** 65–66
Woodville Appliances, Inc., **9** 121
Woodward, Bob, **IV** 672, 689
Woodward Corp., **IV** 311
Woodward, George C., **8** 472
Woodward, James T., **II** 313
Woolard, Edgar S., **IV** 402
Woolard, Edgar Smith, Jr., **8** 153
Woolco, **II** 634; **7** 444
Woolco Department Stores, **V** 107, 225–26
Wooldridge, Dean, **II** 33
Woolfe, Brian, **7** 289
Woolford, Cator, **6** 23
Woolford, Guy, **6** 23
Woolley, Clarence Mott, **III** 663–64
Woolman, Collet Everman, **I** 96, 99–100; **6** 81–82
Woolmer (Viscount), **III** 670
Woolridge, Dean, **I** 539; **11** 540
Woolverton Motors, **I** 183
Woolworth, Charles Sumner, **V** 224–25
Woolworth Corporation, **V** 106–09, **224–27**; **8** 509
Woolworth, Frank Winfield, **V** 224–25
Woolworth Holdings, **II** 139; **V** 108
Woolworth's Ltd., **II** 656
Wooster Preserving Company, **11** 211
Wooster Rubber Co., **III** 613
Wooten, James A., **6** 65–66
Worcester City and County Bank, **II** 307
Word Processors Personnel Service, **6** 10
WordPerfect Corporation, **6** 256; **10** 519, **556–59**
Work, Bertram G., **V** 240
Work Wear Corp., **II** 607

World Air Network, Ltd., **6** 71
World Airways, **10** 560–62
World Book Co., **IV** 622
World Communications, Inc., **11** 184
World Financial Network National Bank, **V** 116
World Flight Crew Services, **10** 560
World Gift Company, **9** 330
World Journal Tribune Inc., **IV** 608
World Publishing Co., **8** 423
World Trade Corporation. *See* International Business Machines Corporation.
World-Wide Shipping Group, **II** 298; **III** 517
WorldCorp, Inc., **10** 560–62
WorldGames, **10** 560
Worldwide Insurance Group, **III** 219
Worldwide Underwriters Insurance Co., **III** 218
Wormser, **III** 760
Wortham, Gus Sessions, **III** 193; **10** 65
Worthington & Co., **I** 223
Worthington Corp., **I** 142
Worthington Foods Co., **I** 653
Worthington Industries, Inc., **7** 598–600; **8** 450
Worthington Telephone Company, **6** 312
Wössner, Mark (Dr.), **IV** 594
Wouk, Herman, **IV** 672
Woven Belting Co., **8** 13
Wozniak, Steve, **III** 115; **6** 218
WPL Holdings, **6** 604–06
WPP Group plc, **I** 21; **6** 53–54
Wragge, George, **III** 669
Wray, Peter, **7** 420
Wrede, G.W. (Baron), **III** 648
Wrenn Furniture Company, **10** 184
WRG. *See* Wells Rich Greene BDDP.
WRG/BDDP. *See* Wells Rich Greene BDDP.
Wright Aeronautical, **9** 16
Wright Airplane Co., **III** 151; **6** 265
Wright and Son, **II** 593
Wright Company, **9** 416
Wright, Elizur, **III** 312
Wright Engine Company, **11** 427
Wright, Frank Lloyd, **III** 58; **IV** 673; **7** 494
Wright, George P., **6** 523
Wright, Henry, **II** 98
Wright, J. David, **I** 539; **11** 540–41
Wright, Jim, **6** 120
Wright, John, **II** 580
Wright, John T., **IV** 278
Wright Manufacturing Company, **8** 407
Wright, Michael W., **II** 670
Wright, Orville, **I** 44, 70; **III** 151; **IV** 9; **6** 265; **10** 260
Wright, Robert C., **6** 165–66
Wright, Robertson & Co., **IV** 278
Wright Stephenson & Co., **IV** 278
Wright, Wilbur, **I** 44, 70; **IV** 9; **10** 260
Wrigley, Fred, **I** 715
Wrigley, Philip K., **7** 595–96
Wrigley, William, **IV** 683; **7** 596
Wrigley, William, Jr., **7** 594–95
Wriston, Walter B., **II** 254–55; **9** 124
Write Right Manufacturing Co., **IV** 345
WSI Corporation, **10** 88–89
WSM Inc., **11** 152
WTC Airlines, Inc., **IV** 182
Wührer, **II** 474
Wunderlich Ltd., **III** 687
Wunderman, Ricotta & Kline, **I** 37

Wuoti, Mikko, **IV** 315
Wurtele, C. Angus, **8** 553
Württembergische Landes-Elektrizitäts AG, **IV** 230
Wurtzel, Alan, **9** 120–22
Wurtzel, Samuel S., **9** 120–21
Wussler, Robert J., **II** 166; **6** 171
Wyandotte Corp., **I** 306
Wyatt, Oscar, **IV** 394–95
Wyatt, Oscar S., Jr., **7** 553, 555
Wycherley, Bruce, **10** 7
Wyeth Chemical Co., **I** 623; **10** 69
Wyeth Laboratories, **I** 623; **10** 69
Wyeth, Stuart, **I** 523
Wygod, Martin, **9** 346–47; **11** 291
Wylie, W. Gill, **V** 600–01
Wyly, Charles, Jr., **11** 468
Wyly Corporation, **11** 468
Wyly, Sam, **11** 468–70
Wyman, Earl W., **9** 393
Wyman, Thomas H., **II** 133–34; **6** 158–59
Wyman, Thomas R., **9** 394
Wyman, Walter, **6** 461; **9** 304
Wyman, Winthrop A., **9** 112
Wymore Oil Co., **IV** 394
Wynant, Wilbur, **III** 274
Wynn, Ed, **II** 151; **IV** 552
Wynn, Steve, **III** 92
Wynn, Steven A., **6** 209–11
Wynncor Ltd., **IV** 693
Wyoming Mineral Corp., **IV** 401
Wyse, **10** 362
Wyzanski, Charles E., **III** 644

X-Chem Oil Field Chemicals, **8** 385
XA Systems Corporation, **10** 244
Xaos Tools, Inc., **10** 119
Xcelite, **II** 16
Xcor International, **III** 431
Xenia National Bank, **9** 474
Xerox Computer Services, **III** 172. *See also* Xerox Corporation.
Xerox Corporation, **I** 31–32, 338, 490, 693; **II** 10, 117, 157, 159, 412, 448; **III** 110, 116, 120–21, 157, 159, **171–73**, 475; **IV** 252, 703; **6** 244, **288–90 (upd.)**, 390; **7** 45, 161; **8** 164; **10** 22, 139, 430, 510–11; **11** 68, 494, 518
Xerox Financial Services, **III** 172–73. *See also* Xerox Corporation.
Xerox Palo Alto Research Center. *See* Xerox Corporation.
XRAL Storage and Terminaling Co., **IV** 411
Xynetics, **9** 251

Y & S Candies Inc., **II** 511
Yablans, Frank, **II** 149
Yacimientos Petrolíferos Fiscales Sociedad Anónima, **IV** 578
Yagi, Yasuhiro, **IV** 125
Yale & Towne Manufacturing Co., **I** 154–55; **10** 279
Yale, Linus, Jr., **I** 154; **10** 279
Yamabe, Takeo, **I** 506
Yamabun Oil Co., **IV** 403
Yamada, Eiinchi, **III** 454
Yamada, Minoru, **III** 461
Yamada, Mitsunari, **II** 436
Yamada, Shosaku, **V** 639
Yamaguchi Bank, **II** 347
Yamaguchi, Gonzaburo, **IV** 478
Yamaguchi, Takehiko, **III** 589
Yamaguchi, Yoshio, **II** 392

Yamaha Corporation, III 366, 599, **656–59**; **11** 50
Yamaha Motor Co. Ltd., III 657–58
Yamaha Organ Manufacturing Co., III 656
Yamaha, Torakusu, III 656
Yamaichi Bank (Switzerland), II 459
Yamaichi International (Deutschland), II 459
Yamaichi International (Nederland) N.V., II 459
Yamaichi Investment Trust Management Co. Ltd., II 458
Yamaichi Securities Company, Limited, II 300, 323, 434, **458–59**; **9** 377
Yamaji, Susumu, I 106
Yamamoto, Genzaemon, III 386
Yamamoto, Gonnohyoe, III 384
Yamamoto, Hiroma, IV 727
Yamamoto, Kenichi, **9** 342
Yamanaka, Hiroshi, III 289
Yamani (Sheikh), IV 538
Yamasaki, Yoshiki, **9** 341
Yamashiro, Yoshinari, IV 163
Yamashita, Toshihiko, II 56
Yamatame Securities, II 326
Yamato Computer Systems Development Co. Ltd., V 537
Yamato Transport Co. Ltd., V **536–38**
Yamauchi, Fusajiro, III 586; **7** 394
Yamauchi, Hiroshi, III 586–88; **7** 394–96
Yamazaki Baking Co., II 543; IV 152
Yamazaki, Rokuya, III 455
Yanagawa, Seisuke, III 405
Yanagi, Masuo, II 326
Yanagida, Seijiro, I 104–05
Yanke, Ron, **11** 307
Yankton Gas Company, **6** 524
Yansouni, Cyril J., **10** 463
Yao, Lily, **11** 116
Yara, Ron, **9** 115
Yaryan, I 343
Yashica Co., II 50–51
Yasuda Bank, II 391; III 408–09
Yasuda family, II 292
Yasuda Fire and Marine Insurance Company, Limited, II 292, 391; III **405–07**, 408
Yasuda, Hajime, III 408–09
Yasuda Life America Agency Inc., III 409
Yasuda Mutual Life Insurance Company, II 292, 391, 446; III 288, 405, **408–09**
Yasuda Shoten, II 291–92
Yasuda Trust and Banking Company, Ltd., II 273, 291, **391–92**
Yasuda, Zenjiro, II 291, 292; III 405–06, 408
Yasuda, Zennosuke, III 405, 408
Yasui, Seiichiro, IV 713
Yates, Alden P., I 559
Yates, Brock, I 137
Yates Circuit Foil, IV 26
Yatsui, Issaku, III 385
Yawata Iron & Steel Co., Ltd., I 493, 509; II 300; IV 130, 157, 212
Yawkey, Cyrus C., **7** 322
Yazijian, Harvey Z., I 235
Yeager, B. John, **6** 467
Year Book Medical Publishers, IV 677–78
Yeargin Construction Co., II 87; **11** 413
Yeiri, Akira, V 234
Yellow Cab Co., I 125; V 539; **10** 370
Yellow Freight System, Inc. of Deleware, V, 503, **539–41**

Yenne, Bill, I 49
Yeomans & Foote, I 13
Yeomans & Partners Ltd., I 588
Yerxa, Thomas E., II 486
YES!, **10** 306
Yeung Chi Shing Estates, IV 717
YGK Inc., **6** 465, 467
Yhtyneet Paperitehtaat Oy. *See* United Paper Mills Ltd.
Yili Food Co., II 544
YMOS A.G., IV 53
Yo, Woon-Hyong, III 747
Yocam, Delbert W., **8** 519–20
Yoh, Harold L., Jr. "Spike", **9** 163–64
Yokado Clothing Store, V 88
Yokogawa Electric Corp., III 142–43, 536
Yokogawa Electric Works, **6** 237
Yokohama Aeroquip, V 255
Yokohama Cooperative Wharf Co., IV 728
Yokohama Electric Cable Manufacturing Co., III 490
Yokohama Rubber Co., Ltd., V **254–56**
Yokohama Specie Bank, I 431; II 224
Yokota, Jiro V 528
Yonezawa, Yoshinobu, IV 285
Yoplait S.A., II 576
York & London, III 359
York Corp., III 440
York Developments, IV 720
York Safe & Lock Company, **7** 144–45
York, W. Thomas, **11** 397
York Wastewater Consultants, Inc., **6** 441
York-Benimaru, V 88
Yorkshire and Pacific Securities Ltd., IV 723
Yorkshire Insurance Co., III 241–42, 257
Yorkshire Paper Mills Ltd., IV 300
Yorkshire Post Newspapers, IV 686
Yorkshire Television Ltd., IV 659
Yorkville Group, IV 640
Yosemite Park & Curry Co., II 144
Yoshida, Hideo, I 9
Yoshikawa, Binyu, V 88
Yoshikazu Taguchi, **6** 428
Yoshimura, Jinbei, V 477
Yoshimura, Shiro, III 621
Yoshitomi Pharmaceutical, I 704
Young & Selden, **7** 145
Young & Son, II 334
Young, Alexander, I 433, 495, 511, 520
Young, Allan P., **10** 43
Young and Rubicam Inc., I 9–11, 25, **36–38**; II 129; **6** 14, 47; **9** 314
Young, Arthur, **9** 198
Young, Chi Wan, IV 717
Young, George W., **6** 455
Young, James Webb, I 20
Young, John, III 143; **6** 238–39
Young, John Orr, I 36–37
Young, Peter, III 739
Young, Robert, **10** 72
Young, Robert R., IV 180; **10** 43
Young, Scott, **11** 557
Young's Engineering Co., IV 717
Young-Herries, Michael, I 469
Younge, Robert, **10** 15
Younger, Ken, **6** 371
Youngs Drug Products Corporation, **8** 85
Youngs, Robert M., **7** 280–82
Youngstown, IV 114
Youngstown Pressed Steel Co., III 763
Youngstown Sheet & Tube, I 490–91
Yount-Lee Oil Co., IV 369
Yoyoteiki Cargo Co., Ltd., **6** 428

YPF Sociedad Anónima, IV **577–78**
Yuasa Battery Co., III 556
Yuba Heat Transfer Corp., I 514
Yuen, Thomas C. K., **9** 41–43
Yui, Taketsura, III 405
Yukawa, Kanchiki, I 519
Yuki, Toyotaro, II 291
Yule (Lady), II 157
Yule, David (Sir), IV 685
Yung An Hsiang, IV 389
Yung, Larry, **6** 80
Yunich, David L., V 169
Yurakucho Seibu Co., Ltd., V 185
Yutani Heavy Industries, Ltd., IV 130
Yves Rocher, IV 546
Yves Saint Laurent, I 697
Yves Soulié, II 266

Z.C. Mines, IV 61
Zaadunie B.V., I 672
Zaban, Erwin, **11** 336–38
Zacher, L. Edmund, III 388
Zaffaroni, Alejandro, **10** 53
Zahn, Joachim, I 150
Zahnfabrik Weinand Sohne & Co. G.m.b.H., **10** 271
Zahnradfabrik Friedrichshafen, III 415
de Zahony, Giovanni Cristoforo Ritter, III 206
Zaid, Abdullah Mat, **6** 100
Zalokar, Robert H., **11** 126
Zambezi Saw Mills (1968) Ltd., IV 241
Zambia Breweries, IV 240
Zambia Clay Industries Ltd., IV 241
Zambia Consolidated Copper Mines Ltd., IV 240
Zambia Copper Investments, IV 240
Zambia Industrial and Mining Corporation Ltd., IV **239–41**
Zander & Ingeström, III 419
Zanders Feinpapiere AG, IV 288
Zanni, Umberto, III 347–48
Zanuck, Darryl F., II 146, 169–70
Zanuck, Richard, II 169–70
Zanussi, III 480
Zapata Drilling Co., IV 489
Zapata Gulf Marine Corporation, **11** 524
Zapata Offshore Co., IV 489
Zapata Petroleum Corp., IV 489
Zarb, Frank G., **10** 38
Zax, Stanley R., III 191
Zayed (Shaikh), IV 364
Zayre Corp., V 197–98; **9** 20–21
Zecco, Inc., III 443; **6** 441
Zeckendorf, William, IV 720; **9** 390; **10** 529
Zeckendorf, William Jr., **8** 356
Zehrer, Hans, IV 589
Zehrmart, II 631
Zeiss, Carl, III 445; **7** 44
Zeiss Ikon AG, III 446
Zeiss, Roderich, III 445
Zekan, William, **8** 6–8
Zell, Samuel, **8** 228–30; **9** 297–98
Zellerbach, Harold, **8** 261
Zellers, V 80
Zellstoff AG, III 400
Zellstoffabrik Waldhof AG, IV 323–24
Zellweger Telecommunications AG, **9** 32
Zemke, E. Joseph, III 111
Zenith Data Corp., **6** 231
Zenith Data Systems, Inc., II 124–25; III 123; **10 563–65**

Zenith Electronics Corporation, II 102,
  123–25; 10 563; **11** 62, 318
Zenith Radio Corp., **II** 123–25
Zentec Corp., **I** 482
Zerbe, Harold U., **I** 451
Zerbe, Kenneth, **10** 284
Zerilli, Anthony, **7** 134
Zeus Components, Inc., **10** 113
Zewawell AG, **IV** 324
Ziebarth, Charles A., **9** 61–62
Ziegler, Henri, **I** 41
Ziegler, Ron, **I** 20
Ziegler, Vincent C., **III** 28
Ziff Communications Company, **7** 239–40
Zijlker, **IV** 491
Zimbabwe Sugar Refineries, **II** 581
Zimmer AG, **IV** 142
Zimmer Inc., **10** 156–57; **11** 475
Zimmer Manufacturing Co., **III** 18
Zimmer, William H., **6** 466
Zimmerman, Adam, **7** 398
Zimmerman, Adam H., **IV** 165, 308
Zimmerman, Balz, **I** 121
Zimmerman, Charles J., **III** 238
Zimmerman, Harry, **V** 190–91
Zimmerman, Mary, **V** 190–91
Zimmerman, Raymond, **V** 190–92
Zimmerman, Richard A., **II** 511
Zimmermann, John, **9** 162
Zinc Corp., **IV** 58–59, 61
Zingraff, René, **V** 238
Zippy Mart, **7** 102
Zircotube, **IV** 174
Zitting, R.T., **IV** 446
Zivnostenska, **II** 282
Zizinia, Stamaty, **III** 345
Zobel, Rya, **III** 609
Zody's Department Stores, **9** 120–22
Zoecon, **I** 673
Zombanakis, Minos, **II** 403
Zornow, Gerald B., **III** 476; **7** 162
Zortech Inc., **10** 508
Zotos International, **III** 63
ZS Sun Limited Partnership, **10** 502
Zucker, Theodore, **I** 639
Zuid Nederlandsche Handelsbank, **II** 185
Zukor, Adolph, **II** 154–55
Zürcher Bankverein, **II** 368
Zürich Allgemeine Unfall- und Haltpflicht-
  Versicherungs Aktiengesellschaft, **III**
  411
Zürich Versicherungs-Gesellschaft, **III** 194,
  402–03, **410–12**
Zviak, Charles, **III** 46–48; **8** 342–43
Zwick, Charles J., **III** 708; **7** 293
Zworykin, Vladimir, **II** 120
Zycad Corp., **11** 489–91
Zymaise, **II** 582
ZyMOS Corp., **III** 458

INDEX TO INDUSTRIES

Index to Industries

ACCOUNTING

Deloitte & Touche, 9
Ernst & Young, 9
Price Waterhouse, 9

ADVERTISING & OTHER BUSINESS SERVICES

Ackerley Communications, Inc., 9
Adia S.A., 6
Advo, Inc., 6
Aegis Group plc, 6
American Building Maintenance Industries, Inc., 6
Chiat/Day Inc. Advertising, 11
D'Arcy Masius Benton & Bowles, Inc., 6
Dentsu Inc., I
Equifax, Inc., 6
Foote, Cone & Belding Communications, Inc., I
Grey Advertising, Inc., 6
Hakuhodo, Inc., 6
Interpublic Group Inc., I
Japan Leasing Corporation, 8
JWT Group Inc., I
Katz Communications, Inc., 6
Kelly Services Inc., 6
Ketchum Communications Inc., 6
Leo Burnett Company Inc., I
The Ogilvy Group, Inc., I
Olsten Corporation, 6
Omnicom Group, I
Pinkerton's Inc., 9
Saatchi & Saatchi PLC, I
ServiceMaster Limited Partnership, 6
Sotheby's Holdings, Inc., 11
TBWA Advertising, Inc., 6
Wells Rich Greene BDDP, 6
WPP Group plc, 6
Young & Rubicam, Inc., I

AEROSPACE

Aerospatiale, 7
Avions Marcel Dassault-Breguet Aviation, I
Beech Aircraft Corporation, 8
The Boeing Company, I; 10 (upd.)
British Aerospace PLC, I
Cessna Aircraft Company, 8
Fairchild Aircraft, Inc., 9
G.I.E. Airbus Industrie, I
General Dynamics Corporation, I; 10 (upd.)
Grumman Corporation, I; 11 (upd.)
Gulfstream Aerospace Corp., 7
N.V. Koninklijke Nederlandse Vliegtuigenfabriek Fokker, I
Learjet Inc., 8
Lockheed Corporation, I; 11 (upd.)
Martin Marietta Corporation, I
McDonnell Douglas Corporation, I; 11 (upd.)
Messerschmitt-Bölkow-Blohm GmbH., I
Northrop Corporation, I; 11 (upd.)

Pratt & Whitney, 9
Rockwell International, I
Rockwell International Corporation, 11 (upd.)
Rolls-Royce plc, I; 7 (upd.)
Sundstrand Corporation, 7
Textron Lycoming Turbine Engine, 9
Thiokol Corporation, 9
United Technologies Corporation, I; 10 (upd.)

AIRLINES

Aeroflot Soviet Airlines, 6
Air Canada, 6
Air-India, 6
Alaska Air Group, Inc., 6
Alitalia—Linee Aeree Italiana, SPA, 6
All Nippon Airways Company Limited, 6
America West Airlines, 6
American Airlines, I; 6 (upd.)
British Airways PLC, I
Cathay Pacific Airways Limited, 6
Continental Airlines, I
Delta Air Lines, Inc., I; 6 (upd.)
Deutsche Lufthansa A.G., I
Eastern Airlines, I
EgyptAir, 6
Finnair Oy, I
Garuda Indonesia, 6
Groupe Air France, 6
HAL Inc., 9
Iberia Líneas Aéreas de España S.A., 6
Japan Air Lines Company Ltd., I
Koninklijke Luchtvaart Maatschappij, N.V., I
Korean Air Lines Co. Ltd., 6
Malaysian Airlines System BHD, 6
Mesa Airlines, Inc., 11
Northwest Airlines, Inc., I; 6 (upd.)
Pan American World Airways, Inc., I
People Express Airlines, Inc., I
Philippine Airlines, Inc., 6
Qantas Airways Limited, 6
Saudi Arabian Airlines, 6
Scandinavian Airlines System, I
Singapore Airlines Ltd., 6
Southwest Airlines Co., 6
Swiss Air Transport Company, Ltd., I
Texas Air Corporation, I
Thai Airways International Ltd., 6
Trans World Airlines, Inc., I
Transportes Aereos Portugueses, S.A., 6
United Airlines, I; 6 (upd.)
USAir Group, Inc., I; 6 (upd.)
VARIG, SA, 6

AUTOMOTIVE

Adam Opel AG, 7
American Motors Corporation, I
Arvin Industries, Inc., 8
Automobiles Citroen, 7
Bayerische Motoren Werke A.G., I; 11 (upd.)
Bendix Corporation, I

The Budd Company, 8
Chrysler Corporation, I; 11 (upd.)
Cummins Engine Corporation, I
Daihatsu Motor Company, Ltd., 7
Daimler-Benz A.G., I
Dana Corporation, I; 10 (upd.)
Eaton Corporation, I; 10 (upd.)
Echlin Inc., I; 11 (upd.)
Federal-Mogul Corporation, I; 10 (upd.)
Fiat Group, I
Fiat S.p.A, 11 (upd.)
Ford Motor Company, I; 11 (upd.)
Fruehauf Corporation, I
General Motors Corporation, I; 10 (upd.)
Genuine Parts Company, 9
Harley-Davidson Inc., 7
Hino Motors, Ltd., 7
Honda Motor Company Limited (Honda Giken Kogyo Kabushiki Kaisha), I; 10 (upd.)
Isuzu Motors, Ltd., 9
Kelsey-Hayes Group of Companies, 7
Mack Trucks, Inc., I
Mazda Motor Corporation, 9
Midas International Corporation, 10
Mitsubishi Motors Corporation, 9
Navistar International Corporation, I; 10 (upd.)
Nissan Motor Company Ltd., I; 11 (upd.)
Oshkosh Truck Corporation, 7
Paccar Inc., I
The Pep Boys—Manny, Moe & Jack, 11
Peugeot S.A., I
Regie Nationale des Usines Renault, I
Robert Bosch GmbH., I
Rolls-Royce Motors Ltd., I
Rover Group plc, 7
Saab-Scania A.B., I; 11 (upd.)
Saturn Corporation, 7
Sealed Power Corporation, I
Sheller-Globe Corporation, I
SPX Corporation, 10
Superior Industries International, Inc., 8
Suzuki Motor Corporation, 9
Toyota Motor Corporation, I; 11 (upd.)
Volkswagen A.G., I; 11 (upd.)
AB Volvo, I; 7 (upd.)
Winnebago Industries Inc., 7

BEVERAGES

Adolph Coors Company, I
Allied-Lyons PLC, I
Anheuser-Busch Companies, Inc., I; 10 (upd.)
Asahi Breweries, Ltd., I
Bass PLC, I
Brauerei Beck & Co., 9
Brown-Forman Corporation, I; 10 (upd.)
Carlsberg A/S, 9
Carlton and United Breweries Ltd., I
Cerveceria Polar, I
Coca Cola Bottling Co. Consolidated, 10
The Coca-Cola Company, I; 10 (upd.)
Distillers Company PLC, I

Dr Pepper/7Up Companies, Inc., 9
E & J Gallo Winery, I; 7 (upd.)
Foster's Brewing Group Ltd., 7
G. Heileman Brewing Company Inc., I
General Cinema Corporation, I
Grand Metropolitan PLC, I
Guinness PLC, I
Heineken N.V, I
Heublein, Inc., I
Hiram Walker Resources, Ltd., I
Kirin Brewery Company Ltd., I
Labatt Brewing Company Ltd., I
Miller Brewing Company, I
Moët-Hennessy, I
Molson Companies Ltd., I
Pepsico, Inc., I; 10 (upd.)
Pernod Ricard S.A., I
Sapporo Breweries, Ltd., I
The Seagram Company, Ltd., I
Snapple Beverage Corporation, 11
South African Breweries Ltd., I
The Stroh Brewing Company, I
Whitbread and Company PLC, I

CHEMICALS

A. Schulman, Inc., 8
Air Products and Chemicals, Inc., I; 10
    (upd.)
American Cyanamid, I; 8 (upd.)
ARCO Chemical Company, 10
Atochem S.A., I
BASF A.G., I
Bayer A.G., I
Betz Laboratories, Inc., I; 10 (upd.)
Boc Group PLC, I
Brenntag AG, 8
Cabot Corporation, 8
Celanese Corporation, I
Chemcentral Corporation, 8
Ciba-Geigy Ltd., I; 8 (upd.)
Crompton & Knowles, 9
Dexter Corporation, I
The Dow Chemical Company, I; 8 (upd.)
DSM, N.V, I
E.I. Du Pont de Nemours & Company, I; 8
    (upd.)
Ecolab, Inc., I
Ethyl Corporation, I; 10 (upd.)
Ferro Corporation, 8
First Mississippi Corporation, 8
G.A.F., I
Georgia Gulf Corporation, 9
Great Lakes Chemical Corporation, I
Hercules Inc., I
Hoechst A.G., I
Huls A.G., I
Huntsman Chemical Corporation, 8
IMC Fertilizer Group, Inc., 8
Imperial Chemical Industries PLC, I
International Flavors & Fragrances Inc., 9
Koppers Inc., I
L'air Liquide, I
Lubrizol Corporation, I
M.A. Hanna Company, 8
Mitsubishi Chemical Industries, Ltd., I
Mitsui Petrochemical Industries, Ltd., 9
Monsanto Company, I; 9 (upd.)
Montedison SpA, I
Morton International Inc., 9 (upd.)
Morton Thiokol, Inc., I
Nagase & Company, Ltd., 8
Nalco Chemical Corporation, I
National Distillers and Chemical
    Corporation, I
NCH Corporation, 8
NL Industries, Inc., 10
Nobel Industries AB, 9

NutraSweet Company, 8
Olin Corporation, I
Pennwalt Corporation, I
Perstorp A.B., I
Praxair, Inc., 11
Quantum Chemical Corporation, 8
Reichhold Chemicals, Inc., 10
Rhône-Poulenc S.A., I; 10 (upd.)
Rohm and Haas, I
Roussel Uclaf, I; 8 (upd.)
Solvay & Cie S.A., I
Sumitomo Chemical Company Ltd., I
Union Carbide Corporation, I; 9 (upd.)
Univar Corporation, 9
Vista Chemical Company, I
Witco Corporation, I

CONGLOMERATES

Accor SA, 10
AEG A.G., I
Alcatel Alsthom Compagnie Générale
    d'Electricité, 9
Alco Standard Corporation, I
Allied-Signal Inc., I
AMFAC Inc., I
Archer-Daniels-Midland Company, I; 11
    (upd.)
Barlow Rand Ltd., I
Bat Industries PLC, I
Bond Corporation Holdings Limited, 10
BTR PLC, I
C. Itoh & Company Ltd., I
CBI Industries, Inc., 7
Chesebrough-Pond's USA, Inc., 8
Colt Industries Inc., I
Delaware North Companies Incorporated, 7
The Dial Corp., 8
Elders IXL Ltd., I
Farley Northwest Industries, Inc., I
FMC Corporation, I; 11 (upd.)
Fuqua Industries, Inc., I
Gillett Holdings, Inc., 7
Great American Management and
    Investment, Inc., 8
Greyhound Corporation, I
Gulf & Western Inc., I
Hanson PLC, III; 7 (upd.)
Hitachi Ltd., I
IC Industries, Inc., I
Ingram Industries, Inc., 11
Instituto Nacional de Industria, I
International Controls Corporation, 10
International Telephone & Telegraph
    Corporation, I; 11 (upd.)
Istituto per la Ricostruzione Industriale, I
Jardine Matheson Holdings Ltd., I
Katy Industries, Inc., I
Kesko Ltd (Kesko Oy), 8
Kidde, Inc., I
KOC Holding A.S., I
Lancaster Colony Corporation, 8
Lear Siegler, Inc., I
Leucadia National Corporation, 11
Litton Industries, Inc., I; 11 (upd.)
Loews Corporation, I
Loral Corporation, 8
LTV Corporation, I
Marubeni K.K., I
MAXXAM Inc., 8
McKesson Corporation, I
Menasha Corporation, 8
Metromedia Co., 7
Minnesota Mining & Manufacturing
    Company, I; 8 (upd.)
Mitsubishi Corporation, I
Mitsui Bussan K.K., I
NACCO Industries, Inc., 7

National Service Industries, Inc., 11
Nissho Iwai K.K., I
Norsk Hydro A.S., 10
Ogden Corporation, I
Pentair, Inc., 7
Samsung Group, I
Sumitomo Corporation, I; 11 (upd.)
Swire Pacific Ltd., I
Teledyne, Inc., I; 10 (upd.)
Tenneco Inc., I; 10 (upd.)
Textron Inc., I
Thorn Emi PLC, I
Time Warner Inc., IV; 7 (upd.)
Tomkins plc, 11
Toshiba Corporation, I
Transamerica Corporation, I
Triarc Companies, Inc., 8
TRW Inc., I; 11 (upd.)
Unilever PLC, II; 7 (upd.)
Veba A.G., I
W.R. Grace & Company, I
Wheaton Industries, 8
Whitman Corporation, 10 (upd.)
Whittaker Corporation, I
WorldCorp, Inc., 10

CONSTRUCTION

A. Johnson & Company H.B., I
The Austin Company, 8
Baratt Developments PLC, I
Bechtel Group Inc., I
Bilfinger & Berger Bau A.G., I
Bouygues, I
Centex Corporation, 8
The Clark Construction Group, Inc., 8
Dillingham Corporation, I
Fairclough Construction Group PLC, I
Fluor Corporation, I; 8 (upd.)
John Brown PLC, I
John Laing PLC, I
Kajima Corporation, I
Kaufman and Broad Home Corporation, 8
The Koll Company, 8
Kumagai Gumi Company, Ltd., I
Lennar Corporation, 11
Lincoln Property Company, 8
Linde A.G., I
Mellon-Stuart Company, I
Morrison Knudsen Corporation, 7
NVR L.P., 8
Ohbayashi Corporation, I
The Peninsular & Oriental Steam
    Navigation Company (Bovis Division), I
Perini Corporation, 8
Peter Kiewit Sons' Inc., 8
Pulte Corporation, 8
The Ryland Group, Inc., 8
Taylor Woodrow PLC, I
Trammell Crow Company, 8
Tridel Enterprises Inc., 9
The Turner Corporation, 8
U.S. Home Corporation, 8
Wood Hall Trust PLC, I

CONTAINERS

Ball Corporation, I; 10 (upd.)
Continental Group Company, I
Crown, Cork & Seal Company, I
Gaylord Container Corporation, 8
Inland Container Corporation, 8
Keyes Fibre Company, 9
Longview Fibre Company, 8
Metal Box PLC, I
National Can Corporation, I
Owens-Illinois, Inc., I
Primerica Corporation, I
Sonoco Products Company, 8

Toyo Seikan Kaisha, Ltd., I

DRUGS

Abbott Laboratories, I; 11 (upd.)
ALZA Corporation, 10
American Home Products, I; 10 (upd.)
Amgen, Inc., 10
A.B. Astra, I
Baxter International Inc., I; 10 (upd.)
Becton, Dickinson & Company, I
Block Drug Company, Inc., 8
Carter-Wallace, Inc., 8
Chiron Corporation, 10
Ciba-Geigy Ltd., I; 8 (upd.)
Eli Lilly & Company, I; 11 (upd.)
F. Hoffmann-Laroche & Company A.G., I
Fisons plc, 9
Fujisawa Pharmaceutical Company Ltd., I
G.D. Searle & Company, I
Genentech, Inc., I; 8 (upd.)
Genetics Institute, Inc., 8
Glaxo Holdings PLC, I; 9 (upd.)
Johnson & Johnson, III; 8 (upd.)
Marion Merrell Dow, Inc., I; 9 (upd.)
Merck & Co., Inc., I; 11 (upd.)
Miles Laboratories, I
Mylan Laboratories, I
Novo Industri A/S, I
Pfizer Inc., I; 9 (upd.)
Pharmacia A.B., I
R.P. Scherer, I
Rorer Group, I
Roussel Uclaf, I; 8 (upd.)
Sandoz Ltd., I
Sankyo Company, Ltd., I
Sanofi Group, I
Schering A.G., I
Schering-Plough, I
Sigma-Aldrich, I
SmithKline Beckman Corporation, I
Squibb Corporation, I
Sterling Drug, Inc., I
Syntex Corporation, I
Takeda Chemical Industries, Ltd., I
The Upjohn Company, I; 8 (upd.)
Warner-Lambert Co., I; 10 (upd.)
The Wellcome Foundation Ltd., I

ELECTRICAL & ELECTRONICS

ABB ASEA Brown Boveri Ltd., II
Acuson Corporation, 10
Advanced Technology Laboratories, Inc., 9
Alps Electric Co., Ltd., II
AMP, Inc., II
Analog Devices, Inc., 10
Andrew Corporation, 10
Arrow Electronics, Inc., 10
Atari Corporation, 9
Autodesk, Inc., 10
Avnet Inc., 9
Bicoastal Corporation, II
Cabletron Systems, Inc., 10
Compagnie Générale d'Électricité, II
Cooper Industries, Inc., II
Digi International Inc., 9
E-Systems, Inc., 9
Emerson Electric Co., II
Fuji Electric Co., Ltd., II
General Electric Company, II
General Electric Company, PLC, II
General Instrument Corporation, 10
General Signal Corporation, 9
GM Hughes Electronics Corporation, II
Harris Corporation, II
Honeywell Inc., II
Hubbell Incorporated, 9
Intel Corporation, II; 10 (upd.)

Itel Corporation, 9
KitchenAid, 8
KnowledgeWare Inc., 9
Koor Industries Ltd., II
Kyocera Corporation, II
Loral Corporation, 9
Lucky-Goldstar, II
Matsushita Electric Industrial Co., Ltd., II
Mitsubishi Electric Corporation, II
Motorola, Inc., II; 11 (upd.)
National Semiconductor Corporation, II
NEC Corporation, II
Nokia Corporation, II
Oki Electric Industry Company, Limited, II
Omron Tateisi Electronics Company, II
N.V. Philips Gloeilampenfabrieken, II
Pittway Corporation, 9
The Plessey Company, PLC, II
Potter & Brumfield Inc., 11
Premier Industrial Corporation, 9
Racal Electronics PLC, II
Raychem Corporation, 8
Raytheon Company, II; 11 (upd.)
RCA Corporation, II
Read-Rite Corp., 10
Reliance Electric Company, 9
Sanyo Electric Company, Ltd., II
Schneider S.A., II
SCI Systems, Inc., 9
Sensormatic Electronics Corp., 11
Sharp Corporation, II
Siemens A.G., II
Silicon Graphics Incorporated, 9
Sony Corporation, II
Sumitomo Electric Industries, Ltd., II
Sunbeam-Oster Co., Inc., 9
Tandy Corporation, II
TDK Corporation, II
Tektronix, Inc., 8
Telxon Corporation, 10
Teradyne, Inc., 11
Texas Instruments Incorporated, II; 11
  (upd.)
Thomson S.A., II
Victor Company of Japan, Ltd., II
Vitro Corp., 10
Westinghouse Electric Corporation, II
Zenith Data Systems, Inc., 10
Zenith Electronics Corporation, II

ENGINEERING & MANAGEMENT SERVICES

Analytic Sciences Corporation, 10
The Austin Company, 8
CDI Corporation, 6
CRSS Inc., 6
Day & Zimmermann Inc., 9
EG&G Incorporated, 8
Foster Wheeler Corporation, 6
Jacobs Engineering Group Inc., 6
JWP Inc., 9
McKinsey & Company, Inc., 9
Ogden Corporation, 6
The Parsons Corporation, 8
Rust International Inc., 11
Susquehanna Pfaltzgraff Company, 8
United Dominion Industries Limited, 8
VECO International, Inc., 7

ENTERTAINMENT & LEISURE

Asahi National Broadcasting Company,
  Ltd., 9
Blockbuster Entertainment Corporation, 9
British Broadcasting Corporation, 7
Cablevision Systems Corporation, 7
Capital Cities/ABC Inc., II
CBS Inc., II; 6 (upd.)

Central Independent Television plc, 7
Cineplex Odeon Corporation, 6
Columbia Pictures Entertainment, Inc., II
Comcast Corporation, 7
Continental Cablevision, Inc., 7
Gaylord Entertainment Company, 11
Granada Group PLC, II
Home Box Office Inc., 7
Japan Broadcasting Corporation, 7
King World Productions, Inc., 9
Ladbroke Group PLC, II
MCA Inc., II
Media General, Inc., 7
MGM/UA Communications Company, II
National Broadcasting Company, Inc., II; 6
  (upd.)
Orion Pictures Corporation, 6
Paramount Pictures Corporation, II
Promus Companies, Inc., 9
Rank Organisation PLC, II
Sega of America, Inc., 10
Tele-Communications, Inc., II
Television Española, S.A., 7
Thomas Cook Travel Inc., 9
The Thomson Corporation, 8
Touristik Union International GmbH. and
  Company K.G., II
Turner Broadcasting System, Inc., II; 6
  (upd.)
Twentieth Century Fox Film Corporation,
  II
Vail Associates, Inc., 11
Viacom International Inc., 7
Walt Disney Company, II; 6 (upd.)
Warner Communications Inc., II

FINANCIAL SERVICES: BANKS

Abbey National PLC, 10
Algemene Bank Nederland N.V., II
American Residential Mortgage
  Corporation, 8
Amsterdam-Rotterdam Bank N.V., II
Anchor Bancorp, Inc., 10
Australia and New Zealand Banking Group
  Ltd., II
Banc One Corporation, 10
Banca Commerciale Italiana SpA, II
Banco Bilbao Vizcaya, S.A., II
Banco Central, II
Banco do Brasil S.A., II
Bank Brussels Lambert, II
Bank Hapoalim B.M., II
Bank of Boston Corporation, II
Bank of Montreal, II
Bank of New England Corporation, II
The Bank of New York Company, Inc., II
The Bank of Nova Scotia, II
Bank of Tokyo, Ltd., II
BankAmerica Corporation, II; 8 (upd.)
Bankers Trust New York Corporation, II
Banque Nationale de Paris S.A., II
Barclays PLC, II
BarclaysAmerican Mortgage Corporation,
  11
Barnett Banks, Inc., 9
Bayerische Hypotheken- und Wechsel-
  Bank AG, II
Bayerische Vereinsbank A.G., II
Beneficial Corporation, 8
Canadian Imperial Bank of Commerce, II
The Chase Manhattan Corporation, II
Chemical Banking Corporation, II
Citicorp, II; 9 (upd.)
Commercial Credit Company, 8
Commerzbank A.G., II
Compagnie Financiere de Paribas, II
Continental Bank Corporation, II

Crédit Agricole, II
Crédit Lyonnais, 9
Crédit National S.A., 9
Crédit Suisse, II
Credito Italiano, II
The Dai-Ichi Kangyo Bank Ltd., II
The Daiwa Bank, Ltd., II
Deutsche Bank A.G., II
Dime Savings Bank of New York, F.S.B., 9
Dresdner Bank A.G., II
First Chicago Corporation, II
First Commerce Corporation, 11
First Empire State Corporation, 11
First Fidelity Bank, N.A., New Jersey, 9
First Hawaiian, Inc., 11
First Interstate Bancorp, II
First of America Bank Corporation, 8
First Security Corporation, 11
First Tennessee National Corporation, 11
First Union Corporation, 10
First Virginia Banks, Inc., 11
Firstar Corporation, 11
Fleet Financial Group, Inc., 9
Fourth Financial Corporation, 11
The Fuji Bank, Ltd., II
Generale Bank, II
The Governor and Company of the Bank of Scotland, 10
Great Lakes Bancorp, 8
Great Western Financial Corporation, 10
H.F. Ahmanson & Company, II; 10 (upd.)
The Hongkong and Shanghai Banking Corporation Limited, II
Huntington Bancshares Inc., 11
The Industrial Bank of Japan, Ltd., II
J.P. Morgan & Co. Incorporated, II
Japan Leasing Corporation, 8
Kansallis-Osake-Pankki, II
KeyCorp, 8
Kredietbank N.V., II
Lloyds Bank PLC, II
Long-Term Credit Bank of Japan, Ltd., II
Manufacturers Hanover Corporation, II
Mellon Bank Corporation, II
Mercantile Bankshares Corp., 11
Meridian Bancorp, Inc., 11
Michigan National Corporation, 11
Midland Bank PLC, II
The Mitsubishi Bank, Ltd., II
The Mitsubishi Trust & Banking Corporation, II
The Mitsui Bank, Ltd., II
The Mitsui Trust & Banking Company, Ltd., II
National Westminster Bank PLC, II
NationsBank Corporation, 10
NBD Bancorp, Inc., 11
NCNB Corporation, II
Nippon Credit Bank, II
Norinchukin Bank, II
Northern Trust Company, 9
NVR L.P., 8
Old Kent Financial Corp., 11
PNC Financial Corporation, II
Pulte Corporation, 8
Republic New York Corporation, 11
The Royal Bank of Canada, II
The Ryland Group, Inc., 8
The Sanwa Bank, Ltd., II
Seattle First National Bank Inc., 8
Security Pacific Corporation, II
Signet Banking Corporation, 11
Skandinaviska Enskilda Banken, II
Société Générale, II
Society Corporation, 9
Southtrust Corporation, 11
St. Paul Bank for Cooperatives, 8

Standard Chartered PLC, II
Standard Federal Bank, 9
Star Banc Corporation, 11
State Street Boston Corporation, 8
The Sumitomo Bank, Ltd., II
The Sumitomo Trust & Banking Company, Ltd., II
Svenska Handelsbanken, II
Swiss Bank Corporation, II
The Taiyo Kobe Bank, Ltd., II
The Tokai Bank, Ltd., II
The Toronto-Dominion Bank, II
Union Bank of Switzerland, II
Wells Fargo & Company, II
West One Bancorp, 11
Westdeutsche Landesbank Girozentrale, II
Westpac Banking Corporation, II
The Yasuda Trust and Banking Company, Ltd., II

FINANCIAL SERVICES: NON-BANKS

A.G. Edwards, Inc., 8
ADVANTA Corp., 8
American Express Company, II; 10 (upd.)
American General Finance Corp., 11
Arthur Andersen & Company, Société Coopérative, 10
Bear Stearns Companies, Inc., II; 10 (upd.)
Charles Schwab Corp., 8
Coopers & Lybrand, 9
CS First Boston Inc., II
Daiwa Securities Company, Limited, II
Dow Jones Telerate, Inc., 10
Drexel Burnham Lambert Incorporated, II; updated under New Street Capital Inc., 8
Federal National Mortgage Association, II
Fidelity Investments, II
First USA, Inc., 11
FMR Corp., 8
Franklin Resources, Inc., 9
Goldman, Sachs & Co., II
Green Tree Financial Corporation, 11
H & R Block, Incorporated, 9
Household International, Inc., II
Istituto per la Ricostruzione Industriale S.p.A., 11
Kleinwort Benson Group PLC, II
KPMG Worldwide, 10
MasterCard International, Inc., 9
Merrill Lynch & Co. Inc., II
Morgan Grenfell Group PLC, II
Morgan Stanley Group Inc., II
National Association of Securities Dealers, Inc., 10
New York Stock Exchange, Inc., 9
The Nikko Securities Company Limited, II; 9 (upd.)
Nippon Shinpan Company, Ltd., II
Nomura Securities Company, Limited, II; 9 (upd.)
Orix Corporation, II
PaineWebber Group Inc., II
Safeguard Scientifics, Inc., 10
Salomon Inc., II
Shearson Lehman Brothers Holdings Inc., II; 9 (upd.)
State Street Boston Corporation, 8
Student Loan Marketing Association, II
T. Rowe Price Associates, Inc., 11
Trilon Financial Corporation, II
Visa International, 9
Yamaichi Securities Company, Limited, II

FOOD PRODUCTS

Agway, Inc., 7
Ajinomoto Co., Inc., II

Alberto-Culver Company, 8
American Crystal Sugar Company, 11
Associated British Foods PLC, II
Associated Milk Producers, Inc., 11
Beatrice Company, II
Ben & Jerry's Homemade, Inc., 10
Borden, Inc., II
BSN Groupe S.A., II
Cadbury Schweppes PLC, II
Campbell Soup Company, II; 7 (upd.)
Canada Packers Inc., II
Carnation Company, II
Castle & Cook, Inc., II
Central Soya Company, Inc., 7
Chiquita Brands International, Inc., 7
Conagra, Inc., II
Continental Grain Company, 10
CPC International Inc., II
Curtice-Burns Foods, Inc., 7
Dalgery, PLC, II
Darigold, Inc., 9
Dean Foods Company, 7
Del Monte Corporation, 7
Dole Food Company, Inc., 9
Emge Packing Co., Inc., 11
Farmland Foods, Inc., 7
General Mills, Inc., II; 10 (upd.)
George A. Hormel and Company, II
Gerber Products Company, 7
H. J. Heinz Company, II; 11 (upd.)
Hershey Foods Corporation, II
Hillsdown Holdings, PLC, II
IBP, Inc., II
International Multifoods Corporation, 7
Itoham Foods Inc., II
The J.M. Smucker Company, 11
Jacobs Suchard A.G., II
Kellogg Company, II
Koninklijke Wessanen N.V., II
Kraft General Foods Inc., II; 7 (upd.)
Land O'Lakes, Inc., II
Mars, Inc., 7
McCormick & Company, Incorporated, 7
McKee Foods Corporation, 7
Meiji Milk Products Company, Limited, II
Meiji Seika Kaisha, Ltd., II
Mid-America Dairymen, Inc., 7
Nabisco Foods Group, II; 7 (upd.)
Nestlé S.A., II; 7 (upd.)
Nippon Meat Packers, Inc., II
Nippon Suisan Kaisha, Limited, II
Nisshin Flour Milling Company, Ltd., II
Northern Foods PLC, 10
NutraSweet Company, 8
Ocean Spray Cranberries, Inc., 7
Perdue Farms Inc., 7
Pet Incorporated, 7
Pilgrim's Pride Corporation, 7
Pillsbury Company, II
Pioneer Hi-Bred International, Inc., 9
The Procter & Gamble Company, III; 8 (upd.)
Quaker Oats Company, II
Ralston Purina Company, II
Ranks Hovis McDougall PLC, II
Reckitt & Colman PLC, II
Rich Products Corporation, 7
Roland Murten A.G., 7
Rowntree Mackintosh, II
Sara Lee Corporation, II
Savannah Foods & Industries, Inc., 7
Schwan's Sales Enterprises, Inc., 7
Smithfield Foods, Inc., 7
Snow Brand Milk Products Company, Limited, II
SODIMA, II
Stouffer Corp., 8
Sun-Diamond Growers of California, 7

Taiyo Fishery Company, Limited, II
Tate & Lyle PLC, II
Thorn Apple Valley, Inc., 7
Tyson Foods, Incorporated, II
Unigate PLC, II
United Biscuits (Holdings) PLC, II
United Brands Company, II
Universal Foods Corporation, 7
Van Camp Seafood Company, Inc., 7
Wattie's Ltd., 7
Wisconsin Dairies, 7
Wm. Wrigley Jr. Company, 7

FOOD SERVICES & RETAILERS

Albertson's Inc., II; 7 (upd.)
America's Favorite Chicken Company,
   Inc., 7
American Stores Company, II
ARA Services, II
Argyll Group PLC, II
Asda Group PLC, II
Associated Grocers, Incorporated, 9
Bob Evans Farms, Inc., 9
Brinker International, Inc., 10
Bruno's Inc., 7
Buffets, Inc., 10
Burger King Corporation, II
C. H. Robinson, Inc., 11
Cargill, Inc., II
The Circle K Corporation, II
Cracker Barrel Old Country Store, Inc., 10
Dairy Mart Convenience Stores, Inc., 7
Domino's Pizza, Inc., 7
Edeka Zentrale A.G., II
Flagstar Companies, Inc., 10
Fleming Companies, Inc., II
Food Lion, Inc., II
The Gateway Corporation Ltd., II
George Weston Limited, II
Giant Food Inc., II
Golden Corral Corporation, 10
Gordon Food Service Inc., 8
Grand Union Company, 7
The Great Atlantic & Pacific Tea
   Company, Inc., II
ICA AB, II
International Dairy Queen, Inc., 10
J Sainsbury PLC, II
KFC Corporation, 7
Koninklijke Ahold N. V., II
The Kroger Company, II
Kwik Save Group plc, 11
Little Caesars International, Inc., 7
McDonald's Corporation, II; 7 (upd.)
Meijer Incorporated, 7
Morrison Restaurants Inc., 11
Nash Finch Company, 8
National Convenience Stores Incorporated,
   7
The Oshawa Group Limited, II
P&C Foods Inc., 8
Pizza Hut Inc., 7
Provigo Inc., II
Publix Supermarkets Inc., 7
Richfood Holdings, Inc., 7
Riser Foods, Inc., 9
Safeway Stores Incorporated, II
Service America Corp., 7
Shoney's, Inc., 7
Smith's Food & Drug Centers, Inc., 8
The Southland Corporation, II; 7 (upd.)
Spartan Stores Inc., 8
Steinberg Incorporated, II
The Stop & Shop Companies, Inc., II
Super Valu Stores, Inc., II
Supermarkets General Holdings
   Corporation, II

Sysco Corporation, II
Taco Bell, 7
Tesco PLC, II
TW Services, Inc., II
Village Super Market, Inc., 7
The Vons Companies, Incorporated, 7
Wegmans Food Markets, Inc., 9
Wendy's International, Inc., 8
Wetterau Incorporated, II
Winn-Dixie Stores, Inc., II

HEALTH & PERSONAL CARE PRODUCTS

Alberto-Culver Company, 8
Alco Health Services Corporation, III
Allergan, Inc., 10
Amway Corporation, III
Avon Products Inc., III
Bausch & Lomb Inc., 7
Becton, Dickinson & Company, 11 (upd.)
Bindley Western Industries, Inc., 9
Block Drug Company, Inc.
Bristol-Myers Squibb Company, III; 9
   (upd.)
C.R. Bard Inc., 9
Carter-Wallace, Inc., 8
Chesebrough-Pond's USA, Inc., 8
The Clorox Company, III
Colgate-Palmolive Company, III
Cosmair, Inc., 8
Dentsply International Inc., 10
Elizabeth Arden Co., 8
Estée Lauder Inc., 9
Forest Laboratories, Inc., 11
General Nutrition Companies, Inc., 11
The Gillette Company, III
Helene Curtis Industries, Inc., 8
Henkel KGaA, III
Invacare Corporation, 11
IVAX Corporation, 11
Johnson & Johnson, III; 8 (upd.)
Kao Corporation, III
Kendall International, Inc., 11
Kimberly-Clark Corporation, III
Kyowa Hakko Kogyo Co., Ltd., III
L'Oreal, III; 8 (upd.)
Lever Brothers Company, 9
Lion Corporation, III
Mary Kay Corporation, 9
Medco Containment Services Inc., 9
Medtronic, Inc., 8
The Procter & Gamble Company, III; 8
   (upd.)
Revlon Group Inc., III
Roche Biomedical Laboratories, Inc., 11
S. C. Johnson & Son, Inc., III
Shionogi & Co., Ltd., III
Shiseido Company, Limited, III
SmithKline Beecham PLC, III
Sunrise Medical Inc., 11
Tambrands Inc., 8
United States Surgical Corporation, 10
Wella Group, III

HEALTH CARE SERVICES

American Medical International, Inc., III
Applied Bioscience International, Inc., 10
Beverly Enterprises, Inc., III
Caremark International Inc., 10
Continental Medical Systems, Inc., 10
Extendicare Health Services, Inc., 6
FHP International Corporation, 6
Health Systems International, Inc., 11
Hospital Corporation of America, III
Humana Inc., III
Jenny Craig, Inc., 10
Manor Care, Inc., 6

Maxicare Health Plans, Inc., III
Mayo Foundation, 9
National Health Laboratories Incorporated,
   11
National Medical Enterprises, Inc., III
NovaCare, Inc., 11
PacifiCare Health Systems, Inc., 11
U.S. Healthcare, Inc., 6
United HealthCare Corporation, 9
Universal Health Services, Inc., 6

HOTELS

Caesars World, Inc., 6
Circus Circus Enterprises, Inc., 6
Club Méditerranée SA, 6
Four Seasons Hotels Inc., 9
Helmsley Enterprises, Inc., 9
Hilton Hotels Corporation, III
Holiday Inns, Inc., III
Hospitality Franchise Systems, Inc., 11
Hyatt Corporation, III
ITT Sheraton Corporation, III
La Quinta Inns, Inc., 11
Marriott Corporation, III
Mirage Resorts, Inc., 6
Promus Companies, Inc., 9
Ritz-Carlton Hotel Company, 9
Trusthouse Forte PLC, III
Westin Hotel Co., 9

INFORMATION TECHNOLOGY

Adobe Systems Incorporated, 10
Advanced Micro Devices, Inc., 6
Aldus Corporation, 10
Amdahl Corporation, III
America Online, Inc., 10
American Management Systems, Inc., 11
Amstrad PLC, III
Analytic Sciences Corporation, 10
Apple Computer, Inc., III; 6 (upd.)
ASK Group, Inc., 9
AST Research Inc., 9
Automatic Data Processing, Inc., III; 9
   (upd.)
Battelle Memorial Institute, Inc., 10
Bell and Howell Company, 9
Booz Allen & Hamilton Inc., 10
Borland International, Inc., 9
Cadence Design Systems, Inc., 11
Canon Inc., III
CHIPS and Technologies, Inc., 9
Cirrus Logic, Incorporated, 11
Cisco Systems, Inc., 11
Commodore International Ltd., 7
Compagnie des Machines Bull S. A., III
Compaq Computer Corporation, III; 6
   (upd.)
CompuAdd Computer Corporation, 11
CompuCom Systems, Inc., 10
CompuServe Incorporated, 10
Computer Associates International, Inc., 6
Computer Sciences Corporation, 6
Computervision Corporation, 10
Compuware Corporation, 10
Conner Peripherals, Inc., 6
Control Data Corporation, III
Control Data Systems, Inc., 10
Corporate Software Inc., 9
Cray Research, Inc., III
CTG, Inc., 11
Data General Corporation, 8
Datapoint Corporation, 11
Dell Computer Corp., 9
Digital Equipment Corporation, III; 6
   (upd.)
Dun & Bradstreet Software Services Inc.,
   11

Egghead Inc., 9
El Camino Resources International, Inc., 11
Electronic Arts Inc., 10
Electronic Data Systems Corporation, III
First Financial Management Corporation, 11
Fiserv Inc., 11
FlightSafety International, Inc., 9
Fujitsu Limited, III
Fujitsu-ICL Systems Inc., 11
Gateway 2000, Inc., 10
Hewlett-Packard Company, III; 6 (upd.)
ICL plc, 6
Information Resources, Inc., 10
Informix Corp., 10
Ing. C. Olivetti & C., S.p.a., III
Intelligent Electronics, Inc., 6
Intergraph Corporation, 6
International Business Machines Corporation, III; 6 (upd.)
KLA Instruments Corporation, 11
Komag, Inc., 11
Lam Research Corporation, 11
Legent Corporation, 10
Lotus Development Corporation, 6
MAI Systems Corporation, 11
Maxtor Corporation, 10
Mead Data Central, Inc., 10
Mentor Graphics Corporation, 11
Micron Technology, Inc., 11
Microsoft Corporation, 6
National Semiconductor Corporation, 6
NCR Corporation, III; 6 (upd.)
Nextel Communications, Inc., 10
Nixdorf Computer AG, III
Novell, Inc., 6
Oracle Systems Corporation, 6
Pitney Bowes Inc., III
Policy Management Systems Corporation, 11
Quantum Corporation, 10
Racal-Datacom Inc., 11
Ricoh Company, Ltd., III
SAS Institute Inc., 10
Seagate Technology, Inc., 8
Standard Microsystems Corporation, 11
STC PLC, III
Sterling Software, Inc., 11
Storage Technology Corporation, 6
Stratus Computer, Inc., 10
Sun Microsystems, Inc., 7
SunGard Data Systems Inc., 11
Sybase, Inc., 10
Symantec Corporation, 10
Synopsis, Inc., 11
System Software Associates, Inc., 10
Tandem Computers, Inc., 6
3Com Corp., 11
Unisys Corporation, III; 6 (upd.)
Wang Laboratories, Inc., III; 6 (upd.)
WordPerfect Corporation, 10
Xerox Corporation, III; 6 (upd.)

INSURANCE

AEGON N.V., III
Aetna Life and Casualty Company, III
AFLAC Inc., 10 (upd.)
Alexander & Alexander Services Inc., 10
Alleghany Corporation, 10
Allianz AG Holding, III
The Allstate Corporation, 10
American Family Corporation, III
American Financial Corporation, III
American General Corporation, III; 10 (upd.)
American International Group, Inc., III
American National Insurance Company, 8

American Premier Underwriters, Inc., 10
American Re Corporation, 10
N.V. AMEV, III
Aon Corporation, III
Assicurazioni Generali SpA, III
Axa, III
Berkshire Hathaway Inc., III
Blue Cross and Blue Shield Association, 10
Capital Holding Corporation, III
The Chubb Corporation, III
CIGNA Corporation, III
CNA Financial Corporation, III
Commercial Union PLC, III
Connecticut Mutual Life Insurance Company, III
Conseco Inc., 10
The Continental Corporation, III
Empire Blue Cross and Blue Shield, III
The Equitable Life Assurance Society of the United States Fireman's Fund Insurance Company, III
First Executive Corporation, III
GEICO Corporation, 10
General Accident PLC, III
General Re Corporation, III
Great-West Lifeco Inc., III
Guardian Royal Exchange Plc, 11
The Home Insurance Company, III
Jackson National Life Insurance Company, 8
Jefferson-Pilot Corporation, 11
John Hancock Mutual Life Insurance Company, III
Kemper Corporation, III
Legal & General Group PLC, III
Lincoln National Corporation, III
Lloyd's of London, III
Marsh & McLennan Companies, Inc., III
Massachusetts Mutual Life Insurance Company, III
The Meiji Mutual Life Insurance Company, III
Metropolitan Life Insurance Company, III
Mitsui Marine and Fire Insurance Company, Limited, III
Mitsui Mutual Life Insurance Company, III
Munich Re (Münchener Rückversicherungs-Gesellschaft), III
The Mutual Benefit Life Insurance Company, III
The Mutual Life Insurance Company of New York, III
Nationale-Nederlanden N.V., III
New England Mutual Life Insurance Company, III
New York Life Insurance Company, III
Nippon Life Insurance Company, III
Northwestern Mutual Life Insurance Company, III
Ohio Casualty Corp., 11
Old Republic International Corp., 11
Pennsylvania Blue Shield, III
Principal Mutual Life Insurance Company, III
Progressive Corporation, 11
Provident Life and Accident Insurance Company of America, III
Prudential Corporation PLC, III
The Prudential Insurance Company of America, III
Reliance Group Holdings, Inc., III
Riunione Adriatica di Sicurtà SpA, III
Royal Insurance Holdings PLC, III
SAFECO Corporaton, III
The St. Paul Companies, Inc., III
The Standard Life Assurance Company, III

State Farm Mutual Automobile Insurance Company, III
Sumitomo Life Insurance Company, III
The Sumitomo Marine and Fire Insurance Company, Limited, III
Sun Alliance Group PLC, III
SunAmerica Inc., 11
Swiss Reinsurance Company (Schweizerische Rückversicherungs-Gesellschaft), III
Teachers Insurance and Annuity Association, III
Texas Industries, Inc., 8
The Tokio Marine and Fire Insurance Co., Ltd., III
Torchmark Corporation, 9
Transatlantic Holdings, Inc., 11
The Travelers Corporation, III
Union des Assurances de Pans, III
USAA, 10
USF&G Corporation, III
VICTORIA Holding AG, III
"Winterthur" Schweizerische Versicherungs-Gesellschaft, III
The Yasuda Fire and Marine Insurance Company, Limited, III
The Yasuda Mutual Life Insurance Company, Limited, III
"Zürich" Versicherungs-Gesellschaft, III

LEGAL SERVICES

Baker & McKenzie, 10

MANUFACTURING

A. O. Smith Corporation, 11
ACCO World Corporation, 7
Aisin Seiki Co., Ltd., III
Aktiebolaget SKF, III
Alfa-Laval AB, III
Alliant Techsystems, Inc., 8
Allied Signal Engines, 9
Allison Gas Turbine Division, 9
AMETEK, Inc., 9
Andersen Corporation, 10
Applied Materials, Inc., 10
Applied Power, Inc., 9
Armstrong World Industries, Inc., III
Atlas Copco AB, III
Avondale Industries, Inc., 7
Baker Hughes Incorporated, III
Bally Manufacturing Corporation, III
BIC Corporation, 8
BICC PLC, III
Biomet, Inc., 10
BISSELL, Inc., 9
The Black & Decker Corporation, III
Borg-Warner Corporation, III
Briggs & Stratton Corporation, 8
Broyhill Furniture Industries, Inc., 10
Brunswick Corporation, III
Carl-Zeiss-Stiftung, III
Carrier Corporation, 7
Casio Computer Co., Ltd., III
Caterpillar Inc., III
Citizen Watch Co., Ltd., III
Clark Equipment Company, 8
Converse Inc., 9
Crane Co., 8
Curtiss-Wright Corporation, 10
Daewoo Group, III
Daikin Industries, Ltd., III
Danaher Corporation, 7
Deere & Company, III
Detroit Diesel Corporation, 10
Deutsche Babcock A.G., III
Diebold, Inc., 7
Dover Corporation, III

Dresser Industries, Inc., III
Duracell International Inc., 9
Eagle-Picher Industries, Inc., 8
Eastman Kodak Company, III; 7 (upd.)
Eddie Bauer Inc., 9
Electrolux Group, III
Enesco Corporation, 11
Fanuc Ltd., III
Federal Signal Corp., 10
Figgie International Inc., 7
First Brands Corporation, 8
Fisons plc, 9
Fleetwood Enterprises, Inc., III
Florsheim Shoe Company, 9
Fuji Photo Film Co., Ltd., III
The Furukawa Electric Co., Ltd., III
The Gates Corporation, 9
GE Aircraft Engines, 9
GenCorp Inc., 8; 9
Giddings & Lewis, Inc., 10
GKN plc, III
The Glidden Company, 8
H.B. Fuller Company, 8
Halliburton Company, III
Harnischfeger Industries, Inc., 8
Harsco Corporation, 8
Hasbro, Inc., III
Hawker Siddeley Group Public Limited
   Company, III
Haworth Inc., 8
The Henley Group, Inc., III
Herman Miller, Inc., 8
Hillenbrand Industries, Inc., 10
Hitachi Zosen Corporation, III
Holnam Inc., 8
Huffy Corporation, 7
Hyundai Group, III; 7 (upd.)
Illinois Tool Works Inc., III
IMI plc, 9
Imo Industries Inc., 7
Inchcape PLC, III
Ingersoll-Rand Company, III
Interco Incorporated, III
Interface, Inc., 8
The Interlake Corporation, 8
International Controls Corporation, 10
International Game Technology, 10
Ishikawajima-Harima Heavy Industries Co.,
   Ltd., III
J.I. Case Company, 10
Johnson Controls, Inc., III
Jones Apparel Group, Inc., 11
Jostens Inc., 7
Kawasaki Heavy Industries, Ltd., III
Keystone International, Inc., 11
KHD Konzern, III
Kohler Company, 7
Komatsu Ltd., III
Konica Corporation, III
Kubota Corporation, III
Leggett & Platt, Incorporated, 11
Lennox International Inc., 8
Loctite Corporation, 8
Louis Vuitton, 10
Lucas Industries PLC, III
MAN Aktiengesellschaft, III
Mannesmann A.G., III
Mark IV Industries, Inc., 7
Masco Corporation, III
Mattel, Inc., 7
Maytag Corporation, III
McDermott International, Inc., III
Mestek Inc., 10
Microdot Inc., 8
Minolta Camera Co., Ltd., III
Mitsubishi Heavy Industries, Ltd., III; 7
   (upd.)
Modine Manufacturing Company, 8

Molex Incorporated, 11
Mueller Industries, Inc., 7
Nashua Corporation, 8
National Gypsum Company, 10
Newell Co., 9
NHK Spring Co., Ltd., III
Nikon Corporation, III
Nintendo Co., Ltd., III; 7 (upd.)
Nippon Seiko K.K., III
Nippondenso Co., Ltd., III
Nordson Corporation, 11
Norton Company, 8
NTN Corporation, III
Oneida Ltd., 7
Outboard Marine Corporation, III
Pacific Dunlop Limited, 10
Pall Corporation, 9
Parker Hannifin Corporation, III
The Perkin-Elmer Corporation, 7
Pioneer Electronic Corporation, III
Polaroid Corporation, III; 7 (upd.)
Premark International, Inc., III
Raychem Corporation, 8
Red Wing Shoe Company, Inc., 9
Reichhold Chemicals, Inc., 10
Rheinmetall Berlin AG, 9
Rohr Incorporated, 9
RPM Inc., 8
Rubbermaid Incorporated, III
St. Jude Medical, Inc., 11
Schlumberger Limited, III
Seiko Corporation, III
Snap-on Tools Corporation, 7
The Stanley Works, III
Steelcase Inc., 7
Stewart & Stevenson Services Inc., 11
Stryker Corporation, 11
Sulzer Brothers Limited (Gebruder Sulzer
   Aktiengesellschaft), III
Sumitomo Heavy Industries, Ltd., III
Susquehanna Pfaltzgraff Company, 8
Tecumseh Products Company, 8
Tektronix, Inc., 8
Terex Corporation, 7
Thermo Electron Corporation, 7
Thermo Instrument Systems Inc., 11
Thomas & Betts Corp., 11
Timex Enterprises Inc., 7
The Timken Company, 8
The Toro Company, 7
Toyoda Automatic Loom Works, Ltd., III
TriMas Corp., 11
Trinity Industries, Incorporated, 7
TRINOVA Corporation, III
Tyco Laboratories, Inc., III
U.S. Robotics Inc., 9
United Dominion Industries Limited, 8
Valmet Corporation (Valmet Oy), III
The Valspar Corporation, 8
Varity Corporation, III
Wellman, Inc., 8
Whirlpool Corporation, III
Yamaha Corporation, III

84 Lumber Company, 9
Feldmuhle Nobel A.G., III
The Geon Company, 11
Harrisons & Crosfield plc, III
"Holderbank" Financière Glaris Ltd., III
Lafarge Coppée S.A., III
Manville Corporation, III; 7 (upd.)
Matsushita Electric Works, Ltd., III; 7
   (upd.)
Mitsubishi Materials Corporation, III
Nippon Sheet Glass Company, Limited, III
Onoda Cement Co., Ltd., III
Owens-Corning Fiberglass Corporation, III
Pilkington plc, III
Pioneer International Limited, III
PPG Industries, Inc., III
Redland plc, III
RMC Group p.l.c., III
Sekisui Chemical Co., Ltd., III
Shaw Industries, 9
The Sherwin-Williams Company, III
Ssangyong Cement Industrial Co., Ltd., III
Tarmac PLC, III
Toto, Ltd., III
Toyo Sash Co., Ltd., III
Ube Industries, Ltd., III
USG Corporation, III
Vulcan Materials Company, 7
Walter Industries, Inc., III
Waxman Industries, Inc., 9

MINING & METALS

Alcan Aluminium Limited, IV
Alleghany Corporation, 10
Allegheny Ludlum Corporation, 8
Aluminum Company of America, IV
AMAX Inc., IV
Amsted Industries Incorporated, 7
Anglo American Corporation of South
   Africa Limited, IV
ARBED S.A., IV
Arch Mineral Corporation, 7
Armco Inc., IV
ASARCO Incorporated, IV
Bethlehem Steel Corporation, IV; 7 (upd.)
British Coal Corporation, IV
British Steel plc, IV
Broken Hill Proprietary Company Ltd., IV
Coal India Limited, IV
Cockerill Sambre Group, IV
Companhia Vale do Rio Duce, IV
CRA Limited, IV
Cyprus Minerals Company, 7
Daido Steel Co., Ltd., IV
De Beers Consolidated Mines Limited/De
   Beers Centenary AG, IV; 7 (upd.)
Degussa Group, IV
Dofasco Inc., IV
Echo Bay Mines Ltd., IV
Engelhard Corporation, IV
Freeport-McMoRan Inc., IV; 7 (upd.)
Fried. Krupp GmbH, IV
Gencor Ltd., IV
Geneva Steel, 7
Gold Fields of South Africa Ltd., IV
Hemlo Gold Mines Inc., 9
Heraeus Holding GmbH, IV
Hitachi Metals, Ltd., IV
Hoesch AG, IV
Imetal S.A., IV
Inco Limited, IV
Inland Steel Industries, Inc., IV
Johnson Matthey PLC, IV
Kaiser Aluminum & Chemical Corporation,
   IV
Kawasaki Steel Corporation, IV
Kennecott Corporation, 7

Klockner-Werke AG, IV
Kobe Steel, Ltd., IV
Koninklijke Nederlandsche Hoogovens en
    Staalfabrieken NV, IV
Magma Copper Company, 7
The Marmon Group, IV
MAXXAM Inc., 8
Metallgesellschaft AG, IV
Minerals and Metals Trading Corporation
    of India Ltd., IV
Minerals Technologies Inc., 11
Mitsui Mining & Smelting Co., Ltd., IV
Mitsui Mining Company, Limited, IV
NERCO, Inc., 7
Newmont Mining Corporation, 7
Nichimen Corporation, IV
Nippon Light Metal Company, Ltd., IV
Nippon Steel Corporation, IV
Nisshin Steel Co., Ltd., IV
NKK Corporation, IV
Noranda Inc., IV; 7 (upd.)
Nucor Corporation, 7
Okura & Co., Ltd., IV
Peabody Coal Company, 10
Peabody Holding Company, Inc., IV
Pechiney, IV
Peter Kiewit Sons' Inc., 8
Phelps Dodge Corporation, IV
The Pittston Company, IV
Pohang Iron and Steel Company Ltd., IV
Republic Engineered Steels, Inc., 7
Reynolds Metals Company, IV
Rouge Steel Company, 8
The RTZ Corporation PLC, IV
Ruhrkohle AG, IV
Saarberg-Konzern, IV
Salzgitter AG, IV
Sandvik AB, IV
Southwire Company, Inc., 8
Steel Authority of India Ltd., IV
Stelco Inc., IV
Sumitomo Metal Industries, Ltd., IV
Sumitomo Metal Mining Co., Ltd., IV
Tata Iron and Steel Company Ltd., IV
Texas Industries, Inc., 8
Thyssen AG, IV
The Timken Company, 8
Tomen Corporation, IV
Usinor Sacilor, IV
VIAG Aktiengesellschaft, IV
Voest-Alpine Stahl AG, IV
Weirton Steel Corporation, IV
Westmoreland Coal Company, 7
Wheeling-Pittsburgh Corp., 7
Worthington Industries, Inc., 7
Zambia Industrial and Mining Corporation
    Ltd., IV

PAPER & FORESTRY

Abitibi-Price Inc., IV
Amcor Limited, IV
Avery Dennison Corporation, IV
Bemis Company, Inc., 8
Boise Cascade Corporation, IV; 8 (upd.)
Bowater PLC, IV
Bunzl plc, IV
Champion International Corporation, IV
Chesapeake Corporation, 8
Consolidated Papers, Inc., 8
Daio Paper Corporation, IV
Daishowa Paper Manufacturing Co., Ltd.,
    IV
Dillard Paper Company, 11
Domtar Inc., IV
Enso-Gutzeit Oy, IV
Esselte Pendaflex Corporation, 11
Federal Paper Board Company, Inc., 8

Fletcher Challenge Ltd., IV
Fort Howard Corporation, 8
Georgia-Pacific Corporation, IV; 9 (upd.)
Honshu Paper Co., Ltd., IV
International Paper Company, IV
James River Corporation of Virginia, IV
Japan Pulp and Paper Company Limited,
    IV
Jefferson Smurfit Group plc, IV
Jujo Paper Co., Ltd., IV
Kymmene Corporation, IV
Longview Fibre Company, 8
Louisiana-Pacific Corporation, IV
MacMillan Bloedel Limited, IV
The Mead Corporation, IV
Metsa-Serla Oy, IV
Mo och Domsjö AB, IV
Nashua Corporation, 8
NCH Corporation, 8
Oji Paper Co., Ltd., IV
P. H. Glatfelter Company, 8
Potlatch Corporation, 8
PWA Group, IV
Rengo Co., Ltd., IV
Riverwood International Corporation, 11
Sanyo-Kokusaku Pulp Co., Ltd., IV
Scott Paper Company, IV
Specialty Coatings Inc., 8
St. Joe Paper Company, 8
Stone Container Corporation, IV
Stora Kopparbergs Bergslags AB, IV
Svenska Cellulosa Aktiebolaget, IV
Temple-Inland Inc., IV
Union Camp Corporation, IV
United Paper Mills Ltd. (Yhtyneet
    Paperitehtaat Oy), IV
Universal Forest Products Inc., 10
Westvaco Corporation, IV
Weyerhaeuser Company, IV; 9 (upd.)
Willamette Industries, Inc., IV

PERSONAL SERVICES

The Davey Tree Expert Company, 11
Franklin Quest Co., 11
Manpower, Inc., 9
Rollins, Inc., 11
Service Corporation International, 6

PETROLEUM

Abu Dhabi National Oil Company, IV
Amerada Hess Corporation, IV
Amoco Corporation, IV
Anadarko Petroleum Corporation, 10
Apache Corp., 10
Ashland Oil, Inc., IV
Atlantic Richfield Company, IV
British Petroleum Company PLC, IV; 7
    (upd.)
Burlington Resources Inc., 10
Burmah Castrol plc, IV
Chevron Corporation, IV
Chiles Offshore Corporation, 9
Chinese Petroleum Corporation, IV
CITGO Petroleum Corporation, IV
The Coastal Corporation, IV
Compañia Española de Petróleos S.A., IV
Conoco Inc., IV
Cosmo Oil Co., Ltd., IV
Crown Central Petroleum Corporation, 7
Den Norse Stats Oljeselskap AS, IV
Deutsche BP Aktiengesellschaft, 7
Diamond Shamrock, Inc., IV
Egyptian General Petroluem Corporation,
    IV
Empresa Colombiana de Petróleos, IV
Ente Nazionale Idrocarburi, IV
Enterprise Oil plc, 11

Entreprise Nationale Sonatrach, IV
Exxon Corporation, IV; 7 (upd.)
FINA, Inc., 7
General Sekiyu K.K., IV
Global Marine Inc., 9
Hunt Oil Company, 7
Idemitsu Kosan K.K., IV
Imperial Oil Limited, IV
Indian Oil Corporation Ltd., IV
Kanematsu Corporation, IV
Kerr-McGee Corporation, IV
Koch Industries, Inc., IV
Kuwait Petroleum Corporation, IV
Libyan National Oil Corporation, IV
The Louisiana Land and Exploration
    Company, 7
Lyondell Petrochemical Company, IV
MAPCO Inc., IV
Maxus Energy Corporation, 7
Mitchell Energy and Development
    Corporation, 7
Mitsubishi Oil Co., Ltd., IV
Mobil Corporation, IV; 7 (upd.)
Murphy Oil Corporation, 7
Nabors Industries, Inc., 9
National Iranian Oil Company, IV
Neste Oy, IV
Nigerian National Petroleum Corporation,
    IV
Nippon Mining Co. Ltd., IV
Nippon Oil Company, Limited, IV
Noble Affiliates, Inc., 11
Occidental Petroleum Corporation, IV
Oil and Natural Gas Commission, IV
ÖMV Aktiengesellschaft, IV
Oryx Energy Company, 7
Pennzoil Company, IV
PERTAMINA, IV
Petro-Canada Limited, IV
Petrofina, IV
Petróleo Brasileiro S.A., IV
Petróleos de Portugal S.A., IV
Petróleos de Venezuela S.A., IV
Petróleos del Ecuador, IV
Petróleos Mexicanos, IV
Petroleum Development Oman LLC, IV
Petronas, IV
Phillips Petroleum Company, IV
Qatar General Petroleum Corporation, IV
Quaker State Corporation, 7
Repsol S.A., IV
Royal Dutch Petroleum Company/ The
    ''Shell'' Transport and Trading Company
    p.l.c., IV
Sasol Limited, IV
Saudi Arabian Oil Company, IV
Seagull Energy Corporation, 11
Shell Oil Company, IV
Showa Shell Sekiyu K.K., IV
Société Nationale Elf Aquitaine, IV; 7
    (upd.)
Sun Company, Inc., IV
Talisman Energy, 9
Tesoro Petroleum Corporation, 7
Texaco Inc., IV
Tonen Corporation, IV
Tosco Corporation, 7
Total Compagnie Française des Pétroles
    S.A., IV
Triton Energy Corporation, 11
Türkiye Petrolleri Anonim Ortakliği, IV
Ultramar PLC, IV
Union Texas Petroleum Holdings, Inc., 9
Unocal Corporation, IV
USX Corporation, IV; 7 (upd.)
Valero Energy Corporation, 7
The Williams Companies, Inc., IV
YPF Sociedad Anonima, IV

PUBLISHING & PRINTING

A.H. Belo Corporation, 10
Advance Publications Inc., IV
Affiliated Publications, Inc., 7
American Greetings Corporation, 7
Arnoldo Mondadori Editore S.p.A., IV
Axel Springer Verlag A.G., IV
Bauer Publishing Group, 7
Bertelsmann A.G., IV
Central Newspapers, Inc., 10
Commerce Clearing House, Inc., 7
Cox Enterprises, Inc., IV
Dai Nippon Printing Co., Ltd., IV
De La Rue PLC, 10
Deluxe Corporation, 7
Dow Jones & Company, Inc., IV
The Dun & Bradstreet Corporation, IV
The E.W. Scripps Company, IV; 7 (upd.)
Elsevier N.V., IV
Encyclopedia Britannica, Inc., 7
Enquirer/Star Group, Inc., 10
Gannett Co., Inc., IV; 7 (upd.)
Groupe de la Cite, IV
Hachette, IV
Hallmark Cards, Inc., IV
Harcourt Brace Jovanovich, Inc., IV
Havas, SA, 10
The Hearst Corporation, IV
Her Majesty's Stationery Office, 7
Houghton Mifflin Company, 10
International Data Group, 7
IPC Magazines Limited, 7
John Fairfax Holdings Limited, 7
Knight-Ridder, Inc., IV
Kodansha Ltd., IV
Lee Enterprises, Incorporated, 11
Maclean Hunter Limited, IV
Macmillan, Inc., 7
Marvel Entertainment Group, Inc., 10
Maxwell Communication Corporation plc,
   IV; 7 (upd.)
McGraw-Hill, Inc., IV
Meredith Corporation, 11
Mirror Group Newspapers plc, 7
Moore Corporation Limited, IV
Multimedia, Inc., 11
National Geographic Society, 9
The New York Times Company, IV
News Corporation Limited, IV; 7 (upd.)
Nihon Keizai Shimbun, Inc., IV
Pearson plc, IV
R.L. Polk & Co., 10
R.R. Donnelley & Sons Company, IV; 9
   (upd.)
The Reader's Digest Association, Inc., IV
Reed International P.L.C., IV
Reuters Holdings PLC, IV
Scholastic Corporation, 10
Simon & Schuster Inc., IV
Southam Inc., 7
The Thomson Corporation, 8
The Times Mirror Company, IV
Toppan Printing Co., Ltd., IV
Tribune Company, IV
United Newspapers plc, IV
Valassis Communications, Inc., 8
The Washington Post Company, IV
West Publishing Co., 7

REAL ESTATE

Bramalea Ltd., 9
Cheung Kong (Holdings) Limited, IV
The Edward J. DeBartolo Corporation, 8
The Haminerson Property Investment and
   Development Corporation plc, IV
Hongkong Land Holdings Limited, IV
JMB Realty Corporation, IV

Kaufman and Broad Home Corporation, 8
Kimco Realty Corporation, 11
The Koll Company, 8
Land Securities PLC, IV
Lend Lease Corporation Limited, IV
Lincoln Property Company, 8
Meditrust, 11
Melvin Simon and Associates, Inc., 8
MEPC plc, IV
Mitsubishi Estate Company, Limited, IV
Mitsui Real Estate Development Co., Ltd.,
   IV
New Plan Realty Trust, 11
New World Development Company Ltd.,
   IV
Olympia & York Developments Ltd., IV; 9
   (upd.)
Perini Corporation, 8
Slough Estates PLC, IV
Sumitomo Realty & Development Co.,
   Ltd., IV
Tokyu Land Corporation, IV
Trammell Crow Company, 8
Tridel Enterprises Inc., 9
Trizec Corporation Ltd., 10

RETAIL & WHOLESALE

ABC Appliance, Inc., 10
Ames Department Stores, Inc., 9
Au Printemps S.A., V
AutoZone, Inc., 9
Babbage's, Inc., 10
Barnes & Noble, Inc., 10
Belk Stores Services, Inc., V
Bergen Brunswig Corporation, V
Best Buy Co., Inc., 9
The Body Shop International PLC, 11
The Bombay Company, Inc., 10
The Boots Company PLC, V
Burlington Coat Factory Warehouse
   Corporation, 10
The Burton Group plc, V
C&A Brenninkmeyer KG, V
Campeau Corporation, V
Carrefour SA, 10
Carter Hawley Hale Stores, Inc., V
Circuit City Stores, Inc., 9
CML Group, Inc., 10
Coles Myer Ltd., V
Comdisco, Inc., 9
CompUSA, Inc., 10
Costco Wholesale Corporation, V
Cotter & Company, V
County Seat Stores Inc., 9
Crate and Barrel, 9
The Daiei, Inc., V
The Daimaru, Inc., V
Dayton Hudson Corporation, V
Dillard Department Stores, Inc., V
Dixons Group plc, V
Duty Free International, Inc., 11
Eckerd Corporation, 9
El Corte Inglés Group, V
Elder-Beerman Stores Corporation, 10
Federated Department Stores Inc., 9
Fingerhut Companies, Inc., 9
Florsheim Shoe Company, 9
Fred Meyer, Inc., V
Fretter, Inc., 10
Galeries Lafayette S.A., V
The Gap, Inc., V
General Binding Corporation, 10
GIB Group, V
The Good Guys!, Inc., 10
The Great Universal Stores P.L.C., V
Hankyu Department Stores, Inc., V
Hertie Waren- und Kaufhaus GmbH, V

The Home Depot, Inc., V
Home Shopping Network, Inc., V
Hudson's Bay Company, V
The IKEA Group, V
Isetan Company Limited, V
Ito-Yokado Co., Ltd., V
J.C. Penney Company, Inc., V
John Lewis Partnership PLC, V
JUSCO Co., Ltd., V
Karstadt Aktiengesellschaft, V
Kaufhof Holding AG, V
Kingfisher plc, V
Kmart Corporation, V
Kohl's Corporation, 9
Kotobukiya Co., Ltd., V
Lands' End, Inc., 9
Lechmere Inc., 10
Lechters, Inc., 11
The Limited, Inc., V
The Littlewoods Organisation PLC, V
Longs Drug Stores Corporation, V
Lowe's Companies, Inc., V
Marks and Spencer p.l.c., V
Marui Co., Ltd., V
Matsuzakaya Company Limited, V
The May Department Stores Company, V
Melville Corporation, V
Mercantile Stores Company, Inc., V
Merry-Go-Round Enterprises, Inc., 8
Mervyn's, 10
Mitsukoshi Ltd., V
Montgomery Ward & Co., Incorporated, V
Musicland Stores Corporation, 9
Nagasakiya Co., Ltd., V
National Intergroup, Inc., V
Nichii Co., Ltd., V
Nine West Group Inc., 11
Nordstrom, Inc., V
Office Depot Incorporated, 8
Otto-Versand (GmbH & Co.), V
Pay 'N Pak Stores, Inc., 9
Payless Cashways, Inc., 11
Petrie Stores Corporation, 8
The Price Company, V
Quelle Group, V
R.H. Macy & Co., Inc., V; 8 (upd.)
Revco D.S., Inc., V
REX Stores Corp., 10
Riklis Family Corp., 9
Rite Aid Corporation, V
Sears plc, V
Sears, Roebuck and Co., V
Seibu Department Stores, Ltd., V
The Seiyu, Ltd., V
Service Merchandise Company, Inc., V
The Sharper Image Corporation, 10
Spiegel, Inc., 10
Staples, Inc., 10
Stinnes AG, 8
Stride Rite Corporation, 8
Sun Television & Appliances Inc., 10
Takashimaya Co., Limited, V
The Talbots, Inc., 11
Target Stores, 10
Tech Data Corporation, 10
The TJX Companies, Inc., V
Tokyu Department Store Co., Ltd., V
Toys "R" Us, Inc., V
The United States Shoe Corporation, V
Uny Co., Ltd., V
Viking Office Products, Inc., 10
W H Smith Group PLC, V
W.W. Grainger, Inc., V
Wal-Mart Stores, Inc., V; 8 (upd.)
Walgreen Co., V
Wherehouse Entertainment Incorporated,
   11
Wickes Companies, Inc., V

Woolworth Corporation, V

RUBBER & TIRE

The BFGoodrich Company, V
Bridgestone Corporation, V
Carlisle Companies Incorporated, 8
Compagnie Générale des Établissements
   Michelin, V
Continental Aktiengesellschaft, V
Cooper Tire & Rubber Company, 8
General Tire, Inc., 8
The Goodyear Tire & Rubber Company, V
The Kelly-Springfield Tire Company, 8
Pirelli S.p.A., V
Sumitomo Rubber Industries, Ltd., V
The Yokohama Rubber Co., Ltd., V

TELECOMMUNICATIONS

ADC Telecommunications, Inc., 10
AirTouch Communications, 11
Alltel Corporation, 6
American Telephone and Telegraph
   Company, V
Ameritech, V
Ascom AG, 9
BCE Inc., V
Belgacom, 6
Bell Atlantic Corporation, V
Bell Canada, 6
BellSouth Corporation, V
British Columbia Telephone Company, 6
British Telecommunications plc, V
Cable and Wireless plc, V
Canal Plus, 10
Carolina Telephone and Telegraph
   Company, 10
Centel Corporation, 6
Century Communications Corp., 10
Century Telephone Enterprises, Inc., 9
Chris-Craft Industries, Inc., 9
Cincinnati Bell, Inc., 6
DDI Corporation, 7
Deutsche Bundespost TELEKOM, V
Directorate General of
   Telecommunications, 7
France Télécom Group, V
GTE Corporation, V
Havas, SA, 10
Hong Kong Telecommunications Ltd., 6
IDB Communications Group, Inc., 11
Infinity Broadcasting Corporation, 11
Koninklijke PTT Nederland NV, V
LDDS-Metro Communications, Inc., 8
LIN Broadcasting Corp., 9
McCaw Cellular Communications, Inc., 6
MCI Communications Corporation, V
Mercury Communications, Ltd., 7
MFS Communications Company, Inc., 11
Multimedia, Inc., 11
Nippon Telegraph and Telephone
   Corporation, V
Northern Telecom Limited, V
NYNEX Corporation, V
Österreichische Post- und
   Telegraphenverwaltung, V
Pacific Telecom, Inc., 6
Pacific Telesis Group, V
Paging Network Inc., 11
PictureTel Corp., 10
Posti- ja Telelaitos, 6
QVC Network Inc., 9
Rochester Telephone Corporation, 6
Schweizerische Post-, Telefon- und
   Telegrafen-Betriebe, V
Scientific-Atlanta, Inc., 6
Società Finanziaria Telefonica per Azioni,
   V

Southern New England
   Telecommunications Corporation, 6
Southwestern Bell Corporation, V
Sprint Communications Company, L.P., 9
Swedish Telecom, V
SynOptics Communications, Inc., 10
Telecom Australia, 6
Telecom Eireann, 7
Telefonaktiebolaget LM Ericsson, V
Telefónica de España, S.A., V
Telephone and Data Systems, Inc., 9
Tellabs, Inc., 11
U S West, Inc., V
United States Cellular Corporation, 9
United Telecommunications, Inc., V
Vodafone Group plc, 11

TEXTILES & APPAREL

Albany International Corp., 8
Amoskeag Company, 8
Benetton Group S.p.A., 10
Brown Group, Inc., V
Burlington Industries, Inc., V
Charming Shoppes, Inc., 8
Coach Leatherware, 10
Coats Viyella Plc, V
Cone Mills Corporation, 8
Courtaulds plc, V
Crystal Brands, Inc., 9
Delta Woodside Industries, Inc., 8
Edison Brothers Stores, Inc., 9
Esprit de Corp., 8
Fieldcrest Cannon, Inc., 9
Fruit of the Loom, Inc., 8
The Gitano Group, Inc. 8
Guilford Mills Inc., 8
Hartmarx Corporation, 8
Interface, Inc., 8
Kellwood Company, 8
L.A. Gear, Inc., 8
L.L. Bean, Inc., 10
Lee Apparel Company, Inc., 8
The Leslie Fay Companies, Inc., 8
Levi Strauss & Co., V
Liz Claiborne, Inc., 8
Milliken & Co., V
Mitsubishi Rayon Co., Ltd., V
Nike, Inc., V; 8 (upd.)
OshKosh B'Gosh, Inc., 9
Oxford Industries, Inc., 8
Reebok International Ltd., V; 9 (upd.)
Russell Corporation, 8
Springs Industries, Inc., V
Stride Rite Corporation, 8
Teijin Limited, V
Toray Industries, Inc., V
Unitika Ltd., V
VF Corporation, V
Walton Monroe Mills, Inc., 8
Wellman, Inc., 8
West Point-Pepperell, Inc., 8

TOBACCO

American Brands, Inc., V
Gallaher Limited, V
Imasco Limited, V
Japan Tobacco Incorporated, V
Philip Morris Companies Inc., V
RJR Nabisco Holdings Corp., V
Rothmans International p.l.c., V
Tabacalera, S.A., V
Universal Corporation, V
UST Inc., 9

TRANSPORT SERVICES

Airborne Freight Corp., 6

Alamo Rent A Car, Inc., 6
Alexander & Baldwin, Inc., 10
Amerco, 6
American President Companies Ltd., 6
Avis, Inc., 6
BAA plc, 10
British Railways Board, V
Budget Rent a Car Corporation, 9
Burlington Northern Inc., V
Canadian National Railway System, 6
Canadian Pacific Limited, V
Carlson Companies, Inc., 6
Carnival Cruise Lines, Inc., 6
Carolina Freight Corporation, 6
Chargeurs, 6
Chicago and North Western Holdings
   Corporation, 6
Compagnie Générale Maritime et
   Financière, 6
Consolidated Freightways, Inc., V
Consolidated Rail Corporation, V
Crowley Maritime Corporation, 6
CSX Corporation, V
Danzas Group, V
Deutsche Bundesbahn, V
DHL Worldwide Express, 6
East Japan Railway Company, V
Emery Air Freight Corporation, 6
Enterprise Rent-A-Car Company, 6
Federal Express Corporation, V
GATX, 6
Hankyu Corporation, V
Hapag-Lloyd AG, 6
The Hertz Corporation, 9
Illinois Central Corporation, 11
Kansas City Southern Industries, Inc., 6
Kawasaki Kisen Kaisha, Ltd., V
Keio Teito Electric Railway Company, V
Kinki Nippon Railway Company Ltd., V
Koninklijke Nedlloyd Groep N.V., 6
Kuhne & Nagel International A.G., V
La Poste, V
London Regional Transport, 6
Mayflower Group Inc., 6
Mitsui O.S.K. Lines, Ltd., V
National Car Rental System, Inc., 10
NFC plc, 6
Nippon Express Co., Ltd., V
Nippon Yusen Kabushiki Kaisha, V
Norfolk Southern Corporation, V
Ocean Group plc, 6
Odakyu Electric Railway Company
   Limited, V
Österreichische Bundesbahnen GmbH, 6
Overseas Shipholding Group, Inc., 11
The Peninsular and Oriental Steam
   Navigation Company, V
Penske Corporation, V
PHH Corporation, V
Post Office Group, V
Preston Corporation, 6
Roadway Services, Inc., V
Ryder System, Inc., V
Santa Fe Pacific Corporation, V
Schenker-Rhenus AG, 6
Seibu Railway Co. Ltd., V
Seino Transportation Company, Ltd., 6
Société Nationale des Chemins de Fer
   Français, V
Southern Pacific Transportation Company,
   V
Stinnes AG, 8
The Swiss Federal Railways
   (Schweizerische Bundesbahnen), V
Tidewater Inc., 11
TNT Limited, V
Tobu Railway Co Ltd, 6
Tokyu Corporation, V

Totem Resources Corporation, 9
Transnet Ltd., 6
TTX Company, 6
Union Pacific Corporation, V
United Parcel Service of America Inc., V
Yamato Transport Co. Ltd., V
Yellow Freight System, Inc. of Delaware,
  V

UTILITIES

The AES Corporation, 10
Air & Water Technologies Corporation, 6
Allegheny Power System, Inc., V
American Electric Power Company, Inc., V
American Water Works Company, 6
Arkla, Inc., V
Associated Natural Gas Corporation, 11
Atlanta Gas Light Company, 6
Atlantic Energy, Inc., 6
Baltimore Gas and Electric Company, V
Bayernwerk A.G., V
Big Rivers Electric Corporation, 11
British Gas plc, V
British Nuclear Fuels plc, 6
Brooklyn Union Gas, 6
Carolina Power & Light Company, V
Cascade Natural Gas Corporation, 9
Centerior Energy Corporation, V
Central and South West Corporation, V
Central Hudson Gas and Electricity
  Corporation, 6
Central Maine Power, 6
Chubu Electric Power Company,
  Incorporated, V
Chugoku Electric Power Company Inc., V
Cincinnati Gas & Electric Company, 6
CIPSCO Inc., 6
Citizens Utilities Company, 7
City Public Service, 6
CMS Energy Corporation, V
Cogentrix Energy, Inc., 10
The Coleman Company, Inc., 9
The Columbia Gas System, Inc., V
Commonwealth Edison Company, V
Consolidated Edison Company of New
  York, Inc., V
Consolidated Natural Gas Company, V
Consumers' Gas Company Ltd., 6
The Detroit Edison Company, V
Dominion Resources, Inc., V
DPL Inc., 6
DQE, Inc., 6
Duke Power Company, V
Eastern Enterprises, 6
Electricité de France, V
Elektrowatt AG, 6
ENDESA Group, V
Enron Corp., V
Enserch Corporation, V
Ente Nazionale per L'Energia Elettrica, V
Entergy Corporation, V
Equitable Resources, Inc., 6
Florida Progress Corporation, V
FPL Group, Inc., V
Gaz de France, V
General Public Utilities Corporation, V
Générale des Eaux Group, V
Gulf States Utilities Company, 6
Hawaiian Electric Industries, Inc., 9
Hokkaido Electric Power Company Inc., V
Hokuriku Electric Power Company, V
Hongkong Electric Company Ltd., 6
Houston Industries Incorporated, V
Hydro-Québec, 6
Illinois Power Company, 6
IPALCO Enterprises, Inc., 6
The Kansai Electric Power Co., Inc., V

Kansas City Power & Light Company, 6
Kenetech Corporation, 11
Kentucky Utilities Company, 6
KU Energy Corporation, 11
Kyushu Electric Power Company Inc., V
LG&E Energy Corporation, 6
Long Island Lighting Company, V
Lyonnaise des Eaux-Dumez, V
Magma Power Company, 11
MCN Corporation, 6
MDU Resources Group, Inc., 7
Midwest Resources Inc., 6
Minnesota Power & Light Company, 11
Montana Power Company, 11
National Fuel Gas Company, 6
N.V. Nederlandse Gasunie, V
Nevada Power Company, 11
New England Electric System, V
New York State Electric and Gas, 6
Niagara Mohawk Power Corporation, V
NICOR Inc., 6
NIPSCO Industries, Inc., 6
North West Water Group plc, 11
Northeast Utilities, V
Northern States Power Company, V
Nova Corporation of Alberta, V
Oglethorpe Power Corporation, 6
Ohio Edison Company, V
Oklahoma Gas and Electric Company, 6
ONEOK Inc., 7
Ontario Hydro, 6
Osaka Gas Co., Ltd., V
Pacific Enterprises, V
Pacific Gas and Electric Company, V
PacifiCorp, V
Panhandle Eastern Corporation, V
PECO Energy Company, 11
Pennsylvania Power & Light Company, V
Peoples Energy Corporation, 6
Philadelphia Electric Company, V
Pinnacle West Capital Corporation, 6
Portland General Corporation, 6
Potomac Electric Power Company, 6
PowerGen PLC, 11
PreussenElektra Aktiengesellschaft, V
PSI Resources, 6
Public Service Company of Colorado, 6
Public Service Company of New Mexico, 6
Public Service Enterprise Group
  Incorporated, V
Puget Sound Power and Light Company, 6
Questar Corporation, 6
Rochester Gas and Electric Corporation, 6
Ruhrgas A.G., V
RWE Group, V
San Diego Gas & Electric Company, V
SCANA Corporation, 6
Scarborough Public Utilities Commission,
  9
SCEcorp, V
Shikoku Electric Power Company, Inc., V
Sonat, Inc., 6
The Southern Company, V
Southwestern Public Service Company, 6
TECO Energy, Inc., 6
Texas Utilities Company, V
Thames Water plc, 11
Tohoku Electric Power Company, Inc., V
The Tokyo Electric Power Company,
  Incorporated, V
Tokyo Gas Co., Ltd., V
TransAlta Utilities Corporation, 6
TransCanada PipeLines Limited, V
Transco Energy Company, V
Tucson Electric Power Company, 6
Union Electric Company, V
UtiliCorp United Inc., 6

Vereinigte Elektrizitätswerke Westfalen
  AG, V
Washington Natural Gas Company, 9
Washington Water Power Company, 6
Wheelabrator Technologies, Inc., 6
Wisconsin Energy Corporation, 6
Wisconsin Public Service Corporation, 9
WPL Holdings, Inc., 6

WASTE SERVICES

Browning-Ferris Industries, Inc., V
Chemical Waste Management, Inc., 9
Safety-Kleen Corp., 8
Waste Management, Inc., V

NOTES ON CONTRIBUTORS

Notes on Contributors

BELLENIR, Karen. Free-lance writer whose essays and journalism have appeared in the *Detroit Free Press, Studies in American Fiction,* and other publications.

BENBOW-PFALZGRAFF, Taryn. Free-lance editor, writer, and consultant in the Chicago area.

BROWN, Susan Windisch. Free-lance writer and editor.

COHEN, Kerstan. Free-lance writer and French translator; editor for *Letter-Ex* poetry review.

COVELL, Jeffrey L. Free-lance writer and corporate history contractor.

DERDAK, Thomas. Free-lance writer, poet, and instructor in philosophy at Loyola University.

DUBLANC, Robin. Free-lance writer and copyeditor in Yorkshire, England.

FELDMAN, Heidi. Free-lance writer and arts consultant.

GASBARRE, April Dougal. Archivist and free-lance writer specializing in business and social history in Cleveland, Ohio.

GRANT, Tina. Free-lance writer and editor.

HEDDEN, Heather Behn. Business periodical abstractor and indexer, Information Access Company, Foster City, California. Senior staff writer, *Middle East Times* Cairo bureau, 1991–92.

JACOBSON, Robert R. Free-lance writer and musician.

MOTE, Dave. President of information retrieval company Performance Database.

PEDERSON, Jay P. Free-lance writer and editor.

PENDERGAST, Sara. Free-lance writer and copyeditor.

PENDERGAST, Tom. Free-lance writer and graduate student in American studies at Purdue University.

RIGGS, Thomas. Free-lance writer and editor.

ROULAND, Roger. Free-lance writer whose essays and journalism have appeared in the *International Fiction Review,* Chicago *Tribune,* and Chicago *Sun-Times.*

ROURKE, Elizabeth. Free-lance writer.

SUN, Douglas. Assistant professor of English at California State University at Los Angeles.

TROESTER, Maura. Free-lance writer based in Chicago.

WOODWARD, Angela. Free-lance writer.